THE EUROPEAN FOOTBALL YEARBOOK

2008-09

EDITION

uefa.com

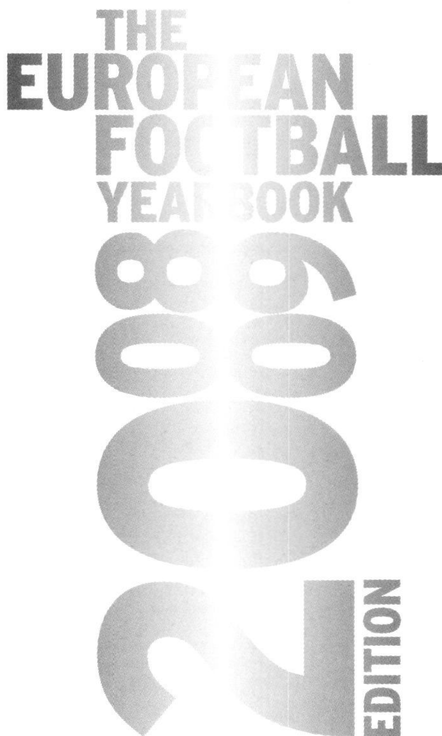

General Editor
Mike Hammond

The only authoritative annual on the European game

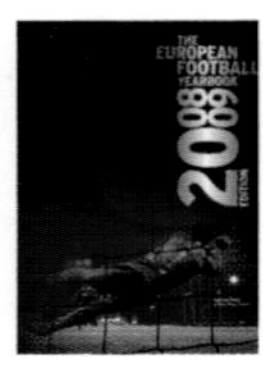

**Further copies of The European Football Yearbook 2008/09
are available from:
www.carltonbooks.co.uk
hotline number +44 (0) 141 306 3100**

The European Football Yearbook 2008/09

First Published in Great Britain
by m press (sales) ltd, England

ISBN 978-1-84732-220-3

UEFA - the Union of European Football Associations - is the governing body of football on the continent of Europe. UEFA's core mission is to promote, protect and develop European football at every level of the game, to promote the principles of unity and solidarity, and to deal with all questions relating to European football.

UEFA is an association of associations based on representative democracy, and is the governing body of European football.

UEFA
Route de Genève 46
Case postale
CH-1260 Nyon 2
Switzerland

Tel: +41 (0) 848 00 2727
Fax: +41 (0) 848 01 2727
Web: www.uefa.com
Email: info@uefa.com

Media Desk
Tel: +41 (0) 848 04 2727

UEFA Media Technologies, SA is the service company created by UEFA to provide all technology solutions, content solutions and assistance to ensure the development of European Football, explore and exploit all opportunities in the new media world and assist the football family in their technology developments.

It produces content around UEFA rights and properties, develops added value and assists in commercial opportunities in UEFA's right exploitation and develops technology solutions and services to assist UEFA in the organisation and development of European Football.

UEFA Media Technologies, SA
Route de St-Cergue 9
CH-1260 Nyon 1
Switzerland

Tel: +41 (0) 848 00 2525
Fax: +41 (0) 848 01 2525
Web: www.uefa.com
Email: info@uefa.com

All views expressed in the European Football Yearbook do not necessarily reflect those of UEFA. Every effort has been made to ensure the accuracy of the data in the European Football Yearbook, official and unofficial.

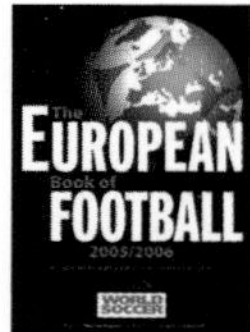

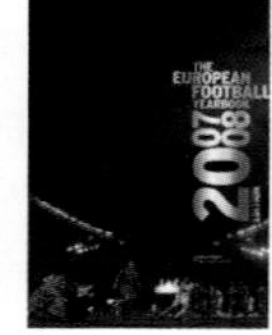

**Back issues of The European Book of Football 2005/06,
The European Book of Football 2006/07 and
The European Football Yearbook 2007/08
are available from:
www.calmproductions.com
orders@calmproductions.com
UK hotline 0845 408 2606**

THE EUROPEAN FOOTBALL YEARBOOK 2008/09 EDITION

General Editor
MIKE HAMMOND

Assistant Editor
Jesper Krogshede Sørensen

Nation-by-nation
Correspondents and Researchers
Mert Aydin (Turkey), Nikolai Belov (Russia), José Del Olmo (Spain), Sean DeLoughry (Republic of Ireland), Tamás Dénes (Hungary), Elred Faisst (Austria), Stoyan Georgiev (Bulgaria), Marshall Gillespie (Northern Ireland), Miron Goihman (Moldova), Michael Hansen (Denmark), Peter Hekkema (Netherlands), Romeo Ionescu (Romania), Michel Jambonet (France), Valery Karpushkin (Latvia), Mikael Kirakosyan (Armenia), Jean-Paul & Daniel Kolbusch (Luxembourg), Jesper Krogshede Sørensen (Faroe Islands, Italy), Fuad & Fedja Krvavac (Bosnia-Herzegovina), Zdeněk Kučera (Czech Republic), Tarmo Lehiste (Estonia), Dag Lindholm (Norway), Ewan Macdonald (Scotland), Erlan Manashev (Kazakhstan), Goran Mančevski (FYR Macedonia), Rasim Mövsümov (Azerbaijan), Giovanni Nappi (Albania), Kazimerz Oleszek (Poland), Olexandr Pauk (Belarus, Ukraine), Humberto Pereira Silva (Portugal), Aleksandar Radović (Montenegro), Ivan & Zdravko Reić (Croatia), Mike Ritter & Silvia Schäfer (Germany), Revaz Shengelia (Georgia), Vídir Sigurdsson (Iceland), Martin Sohlström (Sweden), Dušan Stamenković (Serbia), Andrej Stare (Slovenia), Algimantas Staskevičius (Lithuania), Edouard Stutz (Switzerland), Matej Széher (Slovakia), Mel Thomas & Tim Johnson (Wales), Vesa Tikander (Finland), Serge Van Hoof (Belgium), Victor Vassallo (Malta), Georgios J. Vassalos (Greece), Jacob Zelazo (Cyprus, Israel).

Top 100 Players statistical research
Daniel Fein

UEFA
Project management
David Farrelly, Rob Faulkner, Guillaume Sabran, Dan O'Toole, Grégory Lepesqueux, Mary-Laure Bollini

Editorial
James Wirth, Andrew Haslam, John Atkin, Paul Saffer, Michael Harrold, Sam Adams, Matt Spiro, Simon Hart, Chris Burke, Kevin Ashby, Patrick Hart, Frits Ahlstrøm, Graham Turner, Dominique Maurer

Production
Print
m press (sales) ltd, England, Cliff Moulder

Distribution
Carlton Books Ltd, Martin Corteel, Jim Greenhough

Design
The Works

Artwork/Layout
Keith Jackson, Chas Dickinson

Graphics
Mikhail Sipovich

Data Extraction
Delta3 Informatica, Paolo Calva, Paolo Lombardo, Luca Ferrero

Photography
Getty Images, Sportsfile, Getty Images/AFP, Getty Images/Bongarts

Foreword
Sir Alex Ferguson

Consultant
John Robinson

ISO CODES

There are many instances throughout the European Football Yearbook where country names are abbreviated using ISO three-letter codes. These codes are shown below, listed alphabetically by nation and divided into Europe and the Rest of the World.

Europe

ALB	Alb	Albania
AND	And	Andorra
ARM	Arm	Armenia
AUT	Aut	Austria
AZE	Aze	Azerbaijan
BLR	Blr	Belarus
BEL	Bel	Belgium
BIH	Bih	Bosnia-Herzegovina
BUL	Bul	Bulgaria
CRO	Cro	Croatia
CYP	Cyp	Cyprus
CZE	Cze	Czech Republic
DEN	Den	Denmark
ENG	Eng	England
EST	Est	Estonia
FRO	Fro	Faroe Islands
FIN	Fin	Finland
FRA	Fra	France
GEO	Geo	Georgia
GER	Ger	Germany
GRE	Gre	Greece
HUN	Hun	Hungary
ISL	Isl	Iceland
ISR	Isr	Israel
ITA	Ita	Italy
KAZ	Kaz	Kazakhstan
LVA	Lva	Latvia
LIE	Lie	Liechtenstein
LTU	Ltu	Lithuania
LUX	Lux	Luxembourg
MKD	Mkd	FYR Macedonia
MLT	Mlt	Malta
MDA	Mda	Moldova
MNE	Mne	Montenegro
NED	Ned	Netherlands
NIR	Nir	Northern Ireland
NOR	Nor	Norway
POL	Pol	Poland
POR	Por	Portugal
IRL	Irl	Republic of Ireland
ROU	Rou	Romania
RUS	Rus	Russia
SMR	Smr	San Marino
SCO	Sco	Scotland
SRB	Srb	Serbia
SVK	Svk	Slovakia
SVN	Svn	Slovenia
ESP	Esp	Spain
SWE	Swe	Sweden
SUI	Sui	Switzerland
TUR	Tur	Turkey
UKR	Ukr	Ukraine
WAL	Wal	Wales

Rest Of The World

ALG	Alg	Algeria
ANG	Ang	Angola
ARG	Arg	Argentina
AUS	Aus	Australia
BHR	Bhr	Bahrain
BAN	Ban	Bangladesh
BRB	Brb	Barbados
BEN	Ben	Benin
BER	Ber	Bermuda
BOL	Bol	Bolivia
BOT	Bot	Botswana
BRA	Bra	Brazil
BFA	Bfa	Burkina Faso
BDI	Bdi	Burundi
CMR	Cmr	Cameroon
CAN	Can	Canada
CPV	Cpv	Cape Verde Islands
CTA	Cta	Central African Republic
CHA	Cha	Chad
CHI	Chi	Chile
CHN	Chn	China PR
COL	Col	Colombia
CGO	Cgo	Congo
COD	Cod	Congo DR
CRC	Crc	Costa Rica
CUB	Cub	Cuba
DOM	Dom	Dominican Republic
ECU	Ecu	Ecuador
EGY	Egy	Egypt
SLV	Slv	El Salvador
ETH	Eth	Ethiopia
FIJ	Fij	Fiji
GAB	Gab	Gabon
GAM	Gam	Gambia
GHA	Gha	Ghana
GRN	Grn	Grenada
GUA	Gua	Guatemala
GUI	Gui	Guinea
GNB	Gnb	Guinea-Bissau
HAI	Hai	Haiti
HON	Hon	Honduras
HKG	Hkg	Hong Kong
IND	Ind	India
IRN	Irn	Iran
IRQ	Irq	Iraq
CIV	Civ	Ivory Coast
JAM	Jam	Jamaica
JPN	Jpn	Japan
JOR	Jor	Jordan
KEN	Ken	Kenya
PRK	Prk	Korea DPR
KOR	Kor	Korea Republic
KUW	Kuw	Kuwait
KGZ	Kgz	Kyrgyzstan
LIB	Lib	Lebanon
LBR	Lbr	Liberia
LBY	Lby	Libya
MAD	Mad	Madagascar
MWI	Mwi	Malawi
MLI	Mli	Mali
MTN	Mtn	Mauritania
MEX	Mex	Mexico
MAR	Mar	Morocco
MOZ	Moz	Mozambique
NAM	Nam	Namibia
ANT	Ant	Netherlands Antilles
NZL	Nzl	New Zealand
NGA	Nga	Nigeria
OMA	Oma	Oman
PAN	Pan	Panama
PAR	Par	Paraguay
PER	Per	Peru
QAT	Qat	Qatar
RWA	Rwa	Rwanda
KSA	Ksa	Saudi Arabia
SEN	Sen	Senegal
SLE	Sle	Sierra Leone
SIN	Sin	Singapore
SOL	Sol	Solomon Islands
SOM	Som	Somalia
RSA	Rsa	South Africa
SKN	Skn	St. Kitts & Nevis
SYR	Syr	Syria
TAH	Tah	Tahiti
TJK	Tjk	Tajikistan
THA	Tha	Thailand
TOG	Tog	Togo
TRI	Tri	Trinidad & Tobago
TUN	Tun	Tunisia
TKM	Tkm	Turkmenistan
UGA	Uga	Uganda
UAE	Uae	United Arab Emirates
USA	Usa	United States
URU	Uru	Uruguay
UZB	Uzb	Uzbekistan
VEN	Ven	Venezuela
VIE	Vie	Vietnam
ZAM	Zam	Zambia
ZIM	Zim	Zimbabwe

THE EUROPEAN FOOTBALL YEARBOOK 2008/09 EDITION

Contents

Welcome

Foreword

European Football and Manchester United FC. Or Manchester United FC and European Football. It doesn't matter which way round you put it – you're talking about a love affair that's been going on for the last half-century. Of course, it's a love affair that's had its ups and downs. Because a few months ago we were very solemnly commemorating the 50th anniversary of the club's saddest European adventure – a tragedy which left indelible marks on Manchester United's history. It's one of the reasons for feeling that our victory at the UEFA Champions League final in Moscow signified something special, not only for those of us who were on the pitch but also for the club and for its millions of supporters.

It's almost eerie to think that United's first European Cup came ten years after Munich and that our win in Barcelona in 1999 came on the day when Sir Matt Busby would have celebrated his 90th birthday. It's as if the club's history is still being measured against that fateful day in 1958.

But that's enough about sad memories because winning is all about feeling happy. And, in Europe, you have to work hard to earn that happiness. It's all too easy to think that being champions of Europe was all about beating Chelsea FC in a

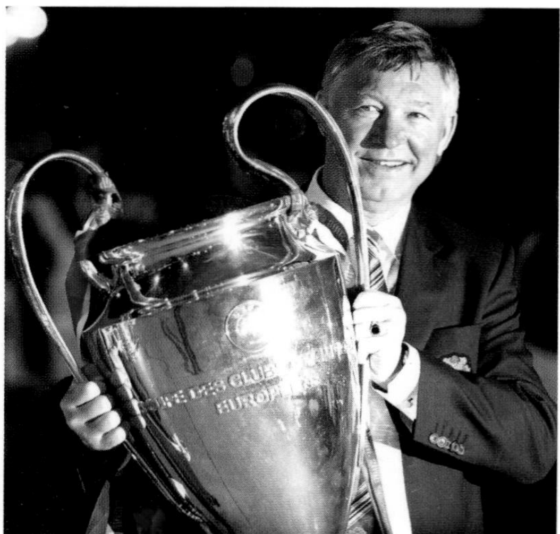

penalty shoot-out. It wasn't, of course. We had worked from September to May to earn ourselves the privilege of going to Moscow – and we had faced some top-class opposition on the way. Our objective was to reach the final. But you can't win a race just by thinking about the finishing line. You have to take it lap by lap, step by step. You don't get easy games in the UEFA Champions League and each match deserves to be taken very seriously indeed.

This was brought home to me when we travelled to Monaco to open the new European season against FC Zenit St. Petersburg in the UEFA Super Cup. I was looking through the match programme and noticed that the final in Moscow had been United's 193rd game in the competition. 193 matches for three titles! That paints a fair picture of the magnitude of the task.

That's why I like this book. Apart from it being a magnificent work of reference, it illustrates the magnitude of European football. Page by page, you can track how clubs and national teams have pursued their objectives and succeeded or failed to live up to expectations which vary a great deal. We were fortunate enough to win the domestic title and to be champions of Europe. The objectives at other clubs may focus on promotion, staying in the top division or qualifying for Europe – and this book helps to tell all those stories.

At United, expectations are high. They always are. And you know that as soon as you come to the club. We know that, as champions of Europe, we're the team that everybody wants to beat. We also know that nobody has ever managed to string together two wins in the UEFA Champions League. That's a challenge!

Sir Alex Ferguson
Manager
Manchester United FC
UEFA Champions League Winners 2007/08

From the General Editor

Welcome to the 2008/09 edition of The European Football Yearbook.

This is the second year that the publication has been produced in association with UEFA. I thank them, and in particular David Farrelly, for their support.

I am also very grateful to you, the reader, for parting with your hard-earned cash and contributing to the Yearbook's continued existence.

If this is the first time you have bought, or seen, the book, then welcome aboard. I hope it meets with your approval and satisfaction.

For those of you who are more familiar with the EFY, and have one or more previous editions in your collection, welcome back.

Reaction to the 2007/08 edition was very positive. The increased colour content, the new design and the official UEFA coverage appealed to many.

This year we have retained the same basic framework and design but, by popular demand, have changed a few things around, essentially to improve ease of reference but also, in some instances, to provide new or expanded information.

In the UEFA competitions section we have full coverage, of course, of the UEFA EURO 2008™ final tournament in Austria and Switzerland. I spent the month of June in Vienna and thoroughly enjoyed the event. The quality of the football was excellent, there was no shortage of drama, very little controversy, and the best team won. We have devoted 34 colourful pages to the finals, plus another 30 to the qualification round, both sections backed with official in-depth statistics.

The all-English UEFA Champions League final and everything that went before in that competition also gets a comprehensive review, as do the UEFA Cup and the UEFA Intertoto Cup.

This year we have moved all the detailed line-up information for these three club competitions into a special section (pages 160-235) and, to improve the visual impact, adorned it with colour logos and home and away team kits.

In the nation-by-nation section, the core club-by-club information remains, but we have made a few changes to the layout and also increased the photographic content. A new panel incorporating member association directory details as well as historical data related to the national team has also been added.

Major honours and years of formation have also been transported from the now-defunct Directory chapter and are shown above each club's results and appearances data.

The popular Top 100 Players of the Season section has been increased in size, with each player getting half a page to himself. As ever, considerable thought has been given to the final selection. Our criteria for inclusion have not changed, but interestingly most of the players have. Of the hundred who made it into last year's list, a mere 25 have re-appeared. That's quite a turnover, but, unlike many other contemporary polls, we base our selection on performance not reputation. So that means places for players like Cesc Fàbregas, Lionel Messi, Luka Modrić and Konstantin Zyryanov (some of my own particular favourites there) but no room – this year, at any rate – for underperforming superstars like Ronaldinho and Thierry Henry.

The Graphic Guide section has undergone a complete makeover. Although, for legal reasons, we are not permitted to include the logos of those clubs not participating in Europe, we have, this year, plotted every top-division and promoted club on the country map. Also included, for those who have them, are the official club websites. The designs of the home and away national team kits are also more defined and specific than before. And we've even thrown in the socks!

The book closes with various international dates for your diary in 2008/09, including all the major UEFA events as well as a complete listing of the European qualifying zone fixtures for the 2010 FIFA World Cup.

Although we have trimmed off 16 pages compared to last year, the colour content has risen significantly, from 368 pages to 432.

All in all, we think we have come up with a pretty comprehensive package – one that provides a broad and accurate reference of the 2007/08 season across Europe and also gives value for money.

For any comments you wish to make about the European Football Yearbook, please contact us at efy@uefa.ch. We will be delighted to hear from you.

Finally, as ever, a few thanks are in order....

...first of all to my patient and loving family – Sue, Rebecca and Charlie – who, with EURO and the Yearbook, have barely seen me this year. I'll make it up to you all, I promise!

...to the three people who did most to help me make this book happen – the inestimable David Farrelly of uefa.com (yes, I've already given him one mention but he deserves another); Jesper Krogshede Sørensen, my loyal and conscientious assistant, who liberated me from a lot of the statistical drudgery while I was in Austria; and Keith Jackson of m press, a man of considerable grace under pressure, who put these thousand-odd pages together.

...to all EFY correspondents and contributors, to my brother (and forgotten golfing partner) Phil, to Ian and all the guys I play football with (Mark, those match reports are brilliant, you're in the wrong line of business), to John Robinson, Cliff Moulder, Carlton Books, to cups of tea, my leather recliner, the internet, the doctor who sorted my dodgy back out with that big needle, whoever it was at UEFA who set up my laptop, and to Pavel Pogrebnyak, Andrei Arshavin, FC Zenit St. Petersburg and Russia for reminding me why I became so passionate about football in the first place.

MIKE HAMMOND
August, 2008

THE EUROPEAN FOOTBALL YEARBOOK

TOP 100 PLAYERS OF THE SEASON 2007/08

Turn to pages 961-1012, where you will find pictorial, narrative and statistical profiles of the European Football Yearbook's Top 100 Players of the Season.

Home
bwin
Fly
adidas
Benq
LFP

INTRO

Spain deservedly ended their 44-year wait to capture the UEFA European Football Championship, Luis Aragonés's side prevailing in an enthralling 16-team final tournament in Austria and Switzerland during June 2008, the showcase of UEFA's national team competitions. It proved a productive year for Spanish national teams as they also captured the UEFA European Futsal Championship in Portugal and the UEFA European Under-17 Championship in Turkey. Overall, the established football nations enjoyed a dominant year, with Germany winning U19 and WU17 crowns while Italy were victorious at WU19 level.

Next season will see Sweden host the eight-team UEFA European Under-21 Championship finals before the 2009/10 campaign kicks off with the UEFA European Women's Championship involving 12 teams in Finland.

At club level, honours went to Manchester United FC (UEFA Champions League), FC Zenit St. Petersburg (UEFA Cup), AC Milan (UEFA Super Cup), 1. FFC Frankfurt (UEFA Women's Cup) and MFK Viz-Sinara Ekaterinburg (UEFA Futsal Cup).

2007/08

CHAPTER

01

Final Tournament:

It did not end with the kind of drama that characterised the earlier stages of the tournament, but there was little doubt that, with Spain picking up the Henri Delaunay trophy for the first time since 1964, the best team won UEFA EURO 2008™. As striker David Villa, the tournament's top scorer, said: "We have had a great tournament and we have been the best team by a distance in all our games."

UEFA EURO 2008

While the free-flowing Netherlands, tenacious Turkey and a Russia side transformed by the arrival of Andrei Arshavin all stole Spain's thunder for a while, Luis Aragonés's side caught the eye from start to finish, only failing to score in one game. The only hat-trick scorer in Austria and Switzerland, four-goal Villa, missed the final itself, but Fernando Torres was on hand to score the only goal in the Ernst-Happel-Stadion dénouement against Germany. As Spanish paper AS concluded: "Spain triumphed but football was the winner."

UEFA
EURO2008
Austria-Switzerland
CAZORLA
UEFA EURO

GROUP A

It felt like UEFA EURO 2008™ had arrived when Group A favourites Portugal touched down at Geneva airport on 1 June to a rousing reception from thousands of their supporters. Switzerland were co- hosts, but with a 174,000-strong Portuguese community in the country, Luiz Felipe Scolari's side were far from second billing. The buzz that followed their every move in the build-up to the tournament set the mood for what would prove a thrilling section, thanks in large part to its dramatic finale involving the Czech Republic and Turkey.

Hope for hosts

If Portugal fans were in party mood, Switzerland supporters packed into St. Jakob-Park in Basel for the tournament's opening game against the Czech Republic more in hope than expectation. Their form since the 2006 FIFA World Cup had been disappointing, and although all-time leading scorer Alexander Frei was fit to start after a long-term injury, excitement was tempered by the news that coach Köbi Kuhn's wife had fallen seriously ill just days previously.

Finally, however, the waiting was over, and Switzerland kicked off their first competitive match in nearly two years with confidence, taking the game to the Czechs and enjoying the better of the chances. The crucial moment in the first half, though, came three minutes before the interval when Zdeněk Grygera caught Frei in a tackle that would end the striker's tournament. The image of Frei in tears, his left knee heavily strapped after partially tearing a ligament, hobbling down the touchline would ultimately sum up the co-hosts' campaign – no luck, little to cheer and over before it had really begun.

Commanding presence

Czech Republic substitute Václav Svěrkoš would add to Swiss pain with the only goal of the game 12 minutes after the restart. Karel Brückner's side had

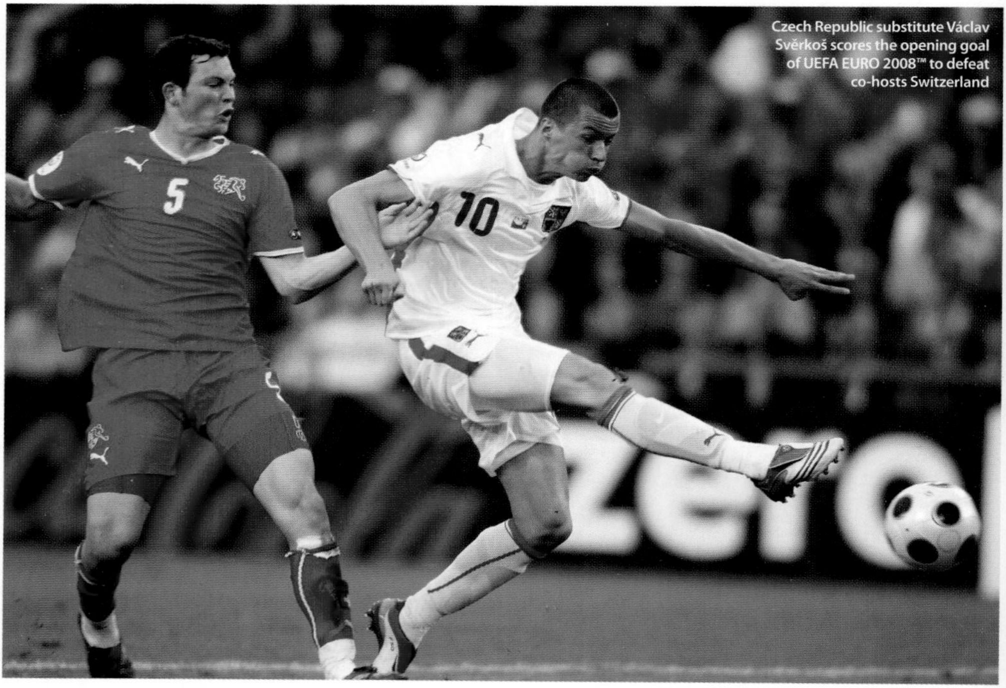

Czech Republic substitute Václav Svěrkoš scores the opening goal of UEFA EURO 2008™ to defeat co-hosts Switzerland

boasted the joint-toughest defence in qualifying, conceding just five times in 12 games, and they picked up where they left off thanks largely to the commanding presence of centre-back Tomáš Ujfaluši and some fine saves from Petr Čech, notably when he blocked Tranquillo Barnetta's shot with his legs before Johan Vonlanthen lifted the rebound against the crossbar with ten minutes to play. That was the closest Switzerland came as the Czech Republic, semi-finalists four years previously, held on for a 1-0 win.

If the Czech Republic's greatest strength was in defence, Portugal's lay in attack, and later that evening they got off to a positive start with an eye-catching 2-0 win against Turkey. Portugal looked composed and confident and had the chances to win by more than the two goals they scored through Pepe on the hour and Raul Meireles three minutes into added time. With Deco coming into form, Cristiano Ronaldo eager to impress and João Moutinho at ease in central midfield, it was easy to see why Portugal's array of attacking talent had earned them selection as many people's favourites. They lived up to that reputation, thrilling with their passing combinations and the pace of their attacking play.

Class shines through

Against the Czech Republic four days later, however, their limitations were also exposed as they struggled to come to terms with the opposition's physical approach and aerial power. Ultimately, though, class would tell in a 3-1 victory. Portugal went ahead on eight minutes. Nuno Gomes slid the ball through a crowd of players to send Ronaldo clear on goal and although Čech thwarted the striker, he pushed the ball into the path of Deco who prodded in scrappily from close range. Brückner's side, shorn of injured playmaker and captain Tomáš Rosický, had been short of creativity against Switzerland but not endeavour, and it was the same again here as they forced their way back into the game.

Libor Sionko's thumping header drew them level on 17 minutes and they rushed and harried Portugal off their stride for long spells thereafter. In Ronaldo, though, Portugal had the man capable of making the difference. His running duel with Čech – a legacy of the UEFA Champions League final in Moscow - had been a feature of the game, and after a succession of excellent saves Čech was eventually beaten again on 63 minutes. Deco squared the ball from the right and Ronaldo sidefooted home from the edge of the area. The 23-year-old then set up Ricardo Quaresma for the third in added time as Portugal purred into the quarter-finals.

Cristiano Ronaldo – a key figure in Portugal's 3-1 win over the Czech Republic

Rain-soaked drama

Their place as group winners was confirmed after a thrilling game in Basel where in pouring rain Turkey recovered from going a goal down to win 2-1 at the death. It was the first of four remarkable matches involving Fatih Terim's side. So heavy and destructive was the downpour that the St. Jakob-Park pitch would have to be replaced before the quarter-finals. By then it had at least given Kuhn's side their one spot of luck in the tournament. Eren Derdiyok's cross was stopped by a puddle in the goalmouth, allowing Hakan Yakin to complete the simplest of finishes. Turkey, though, would have the last laugh. Semih Şentürk headed them level on 57 minutes before Arda Turan stunned home hopes with a deflected shot two minutes into added time that revived their chances and ended the co-hosts' campaign at the earliest possible moment. It was a portent of things to come.

Switzerland would restore some pride with a 2-0 win against Portugal in a game that had nothing riding on it, Portugal already having been confirmed as group winners and Switzerland unable to advance. With one eye on the quarter-finals Portugal rested eight players, yet they still created a succession of chances, Nani coming closest when he struck the post early in the

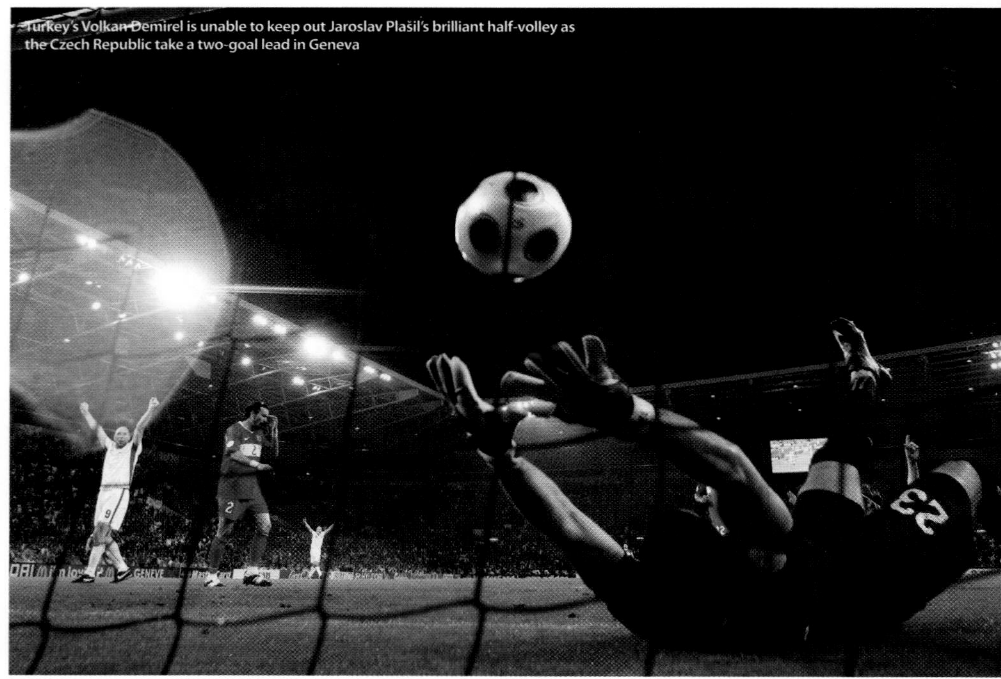
Turkey's Volkan Demirel is unable to keep out Jaroslav Plašil's brilliant half-volley as the Czech Republic take a two-goal lead in Geneva

second half. Quite what Eusébio, watching on from the stands, made of Portugal's profligacy did not bear thinking about, and they were made to pay by Hakin Yakin who struck on 71 and 83 minutes, the second from the penalty spot, to earn Switzerland their first victory in a UEFA European Championship. It also ended Kuhn's seven-year reign as Switzerland coach on a high.

High stakes in Geneva

The real drama, though, was in Geneva where Turkey met the Czech Republic with a quarter-final place at stake. The Czechs looked on course to advance when Jan Koller scored with a powerful header on 34 minutes, and that impression was confirmed 17 minutes into the second half when Jaroslav Plašil turned in Libor Sionko's cross. Jan Polák then hit the post, but Turkey too were making chances, and finally took one on 75 minutes when Hamit Altıntop crossed for Arda, the last-gasp hero against Switzerland, to score at the far post. Suddenly the complexion of the game changed. The Czech Republic retreated deeper and deeper into their own half as Turkey strode forward. They still looked like holding on until an uncharacteristic error from Čech gifted Nihat Kahveci the equaliser with three minutes to play. Čech dropped a straightforward cross from Hamit at the feet of the Villarreal CF striker, who simply knocked the ball into the unguarded net. Stunned into submission, the Czech Republic had no answer when two minutes later another Hamit pass split the Czech defence and put in Nihat, who, with great assurance and skill, curled a brilliant shot up and around Čech into the top corner to complete a remarkable and improbable comeback. More drama was to follow as Volkan Demirel was dismissed for a petulant shove on Koller. Tuncay Şanlı took over in goal, but Turkey had already done enough to set up a quarter-final meeting with Croatia, while Portugal would take on Germany. "We showed the world what we can do and we went on right to the very end," Terim said. "We believed in ourselves." As Turkey's attention turned to the Ernst-Happel-Stadion, the drama was only just beginning.

Group A Results

7/6/08, St. Jakob-Park, Basel
Switzerland 0-1 Czech Republic
Attendance: 39730
Switzerland: Benaglio, Magnin, Senderos, Lichtsteiner (Vonlanthen 75), Inler, Frei (Yakin 46), Streller, Fernandes, Barnetta, Behrami (Derdiyok 84), Müller. Coach: Jakob Kuhn (SUI)

Czech Republic: Čech, Grygera, Polák, Galásek, Jankulovski, Sionko (Vlček 83), Koller (Svěrkoš 56), Jarolím (Kováč 87), Plašil, Ujfaluši, Rozehnal. Coach: Karel Brückner (CZE)
Goal(s): 0-1 Svěrkoš 71
Yellow Card(s): Magnin 59 (Switzerland), Vonlanthen 76 (Switzerland), Barnetta 90+3 (Switzerland)
Referee: Rosetti (ITA)

7/6/08, Stade de Genève, Geneva
Portugal 2-0 Turkey
Attendance: 29106
Portugal: Ricardo, Paulo Ferreira, Bosingwa, Cristiano Ronaldo, Petit, João Moutinho, Simão (Raul Meireles 83), Pepe, Ricardo Carvalho, Deco (Fernando Meira 92), Nuno Gomes (Nani 69). Coach: Luiz Felipe Scolari (BRA)
Turkey: Volkan Demirel, Servet Çetin, Hakan Balta, Gökhan Zan (Emre Aşık 55), Emre Belözoğlu, Mehmet Aurélio, Nihat Kahveci, Tuncay Şanlı, Kazım Kazım, Mevlüt Erdinç (Sabri Sarıoğlu 46), Hamit Altıntop (Semih Şentürk 76). Coach: Fatih Terim (TUR)
Goal(s): 1-0 Pepe 61, 2-0 Raul Meireles 90+3
Yellow Card(s): Kazım Kazım 4 (Turkey), Gökhan Zan 51 (Turkey), Sabri Sarıoğlu 73 (Turkey)
Referee: Fandel (GER)

11/6/08, Stade de Genève, Geneva
Czech Republic 1-3 Portugal
Attendance: 29016
Czech Republic: Čech, Grygera, Polák, Galásek (Koller 73), Jankulovski, Sionko, Baroš, Matějovský (Vlček 68), Plašil (Jarolím 85), Ujfaluši, Rozehnal. Coach: Karel Brückner (CZE)
Portugal: Ricardo, Paulo Ferreira, Bosingwa, Cristiano Ronaldo, Petit, João Moutinho (Fernando Meira 75), Simão (Ricardo Quaresma 80), Pepe, Ricardo Carvalho, Deco, Nuno Gomes (Hugo Almeida 79). Coach: Luiz Felipe Scolari (BRA)
Goal(s): 0-1 Deco 8, 1-1 Sionko 17, 1-2 Cristiano Ronaldo 63, 1-3 Ricardo Quaresma 90+1
Yellow Card(s): Polák 22 (Czech Republic), Bosingwa 31 (Portugal)
Referee: Vassaras (GRE)

11/6/08, St. Jakob-Park, Basel
Switzerland 1-2 Turkey
Attendance: 39730
Switzerland: Benaglio, Magnin, Senderos, Lichtsteiner, Inler, Yakin (Gygax 85), Derdiyok, Fernandes (Cabanas 76), Barnetta (Vonlanthen 66), Behrami, Müller. Coach: Jakob Kuhn (SUI)
Turkey: Volkan Demirel, Servet Çetin, Hakan Balta, Mehmet Aurélio, Nihat Kahveci (Kazım Kazım 85), Gökdeniz Karadeniz (Semih Şentürk 46), Tümer Metin (Mehmet Topal 46), Arda Turan, Emre Aşık, Tuncay Şanlı, Hamit Altıntop. Coach: Fatih Terim (TUR)
Goal(s): 1-0 Yakin 32, 1-1 Semih Şentürk 57, 1-2 Arda Turan 90+2
Yellow Card(s): Tuncay Şanlı 31 (Turkey), Mehmet Aurélio 41 (Turkey), Hakan Balta 48 (Turkey), Derdiyok 55 (Switzerland)
Referee: Michel' (SVK)

15/6/08, St. Jakob-Park, Basel
Switzerland 2-0 Portugal
Attendance: 39730
Switzerland: Zuberbühler, Magnin, Senderos, Lichtsteiner (Grichting 83), Inler, Yakin (Cabanas 86), Derdiyok, Fernandes, Behrami, Müller, Vonlanthen (Barnetta 61). Coach: Jakob Kuhn (SUI)
Portugal: Ricardo, Paulo Ferreira (Jorge Ribeiro 41), Bruno Alves, Fernando Meira, Raul Meireles, Miguel, Pepe, Ricardo Quaresma, Miguel Veloso (João Moutinho 71), Nani, Hélder Postiga (Hugo Almeida 74). Coach: Luiz Felipe Scolari (BRA)
Goal(s): 1-0 Yakin 71, 2-0 Yakin 83(p)
Yellow Card(s): Yakin 27 (Switzerland), Paulo Ferreira 30 (Portugal), Vonlanthen 37 (Switzerland), Jorge Ribeiro 64 (Portugal), Fernando Meira 78 (Portugal), Miguel 81 (Portugal), Barnetta 81 (Switzerland), Fernandes 90+2 (Switzerland)
Referee: Plautz (AUT)

15/6/08, Stade de Genève, Geneva
Turkey 3-2 Czech Republic
Attendance: 29016
Turkey: Volkan Demirel, Servet Çetin, Hakan Balta, Mehmet Topal (Kazım Kazım 57), Mehmet Aurélio, Nihat Kahveci, Semih Şentürk (Sabri Sarıoğlu 46), Emre Güngör (Emre Aşık 63), Arda Turan, Tuncay Şanlı, Hamit Altıntop. Coach: Fatih Terim (TUR)
Czech Republic: Čech, Grygera, Polák, Galásek, Jankulovski, Sionko (Vlček 84), Koller, Matějovský (Jarolím 39), Plašil (Kadlec 80), Ujfaluši, Rozehnal. Coach: Karel Brückner (CZE)
Goal(s): 0-1 Koller 34, 0-2 Plašil 62, 1-2 Arda Turan 75, 2-2 Nihat Kahveci 87, 3-2 Nihat Kahveci 89
Red Card(s): Volkan Demirel 90+2 (Turkey)
Yellow Card(s): Mehmet Topal 6 (Turkey), Mehmet Aurélio 10 (Turkey), Arda Turan 62 (Turkey), Emre Aşık 73 (Turkey), Galásek 80 (Czech Republic), Ujfaluši 90+4 (Czech Republic), Baroš 90+5 (Czech Republic)
Referee: Fröjdfeldt (SWE)

Group A Table

		Pld	W	D	L	F	A	Pts
1	Portugal	3	2	0	1	5	3	6
2	Turkey	3	2	0	1	5	5	6
3	Czech Republic	3	1	0	2	4	6	3
4	Switzerland	3	1	0	2	3	3	3

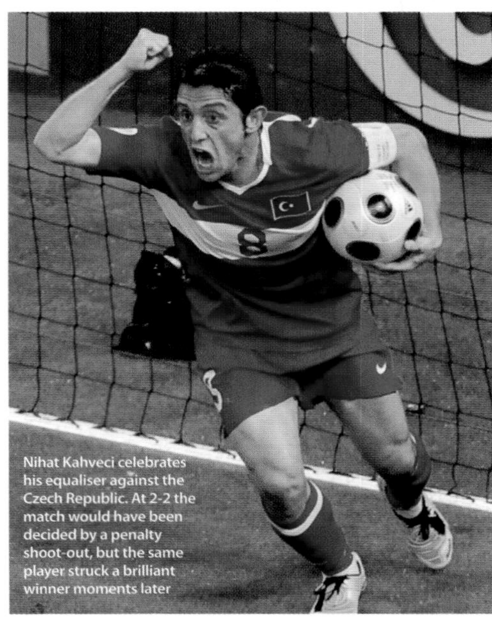

Nihat Kahveci celebrates his equaliser against the Czech Republic. At 2-2 the match would have been decided by a penalty shoot-out, but the same player struck a brilliant winner moments later

GROUP B

The prospect of Group C may have set pulses racing when the draw for the finals was made in Lucerne, yet Group B also created a fair amount of intrigue. It brought together three Central European neighbours – two of them debutants on the UEFA European Championship stage – and a young Croatia team bristling with confidence after twice overturning England in qualifying. They did not disappoint.

Luka Modrić gives Croatia victory from the penalty spot in the opening game against Austria

Record-making spot-kick

Slaven Bilić's team made a perfect start against co-hosts Austria in Vienna as Luka Modrić converted the fastest ever penalty in the history of the finals to set Croatia on their way. The mercurial playmaker scored in the fourth minute, firing in low and straight after Ivica Olić had been brought down by René Aufhauser. The home side took time to find their feet after that setback but mounted a stirring late charge, with substitute Roman Kienast heading narrowly past the post seconds before the whistle.

Germany's victory against Poland later that day was far more clear-cut on what proved to be an emotional night for Lukas Podolski in Klagenfurt. One of three Polish-born players in Joachim Löw's squad, the FC Bayern München striker did not celebrate after putting the three-time champions in front with a simple finish midway through the first half. His reaction was similarly understated after he doubled Germany's advantage with an emphatic volley 18 minutes from time and it was not until after the final whistle, when he ran to his family and Polish girlfriend in the stands, that he finally broke into a smile.

Croatia through

Podolski was on target again when Germany returned to the Wörthersee Stadion to take on Croatia four days later, but it was little more than a consolation as the Vatreni sealed their place in the quarter-finals with a well deserved 2-1 triumph. Bilić brought in midfielder Ivan Rakitić for Mladen Petrić and pushed Niko Kranjčar into a more advanced role following the opening game, but it was two wide players who combined to fashion the 24th-minute opener as Danijel Pranjić drove forward and delivered a superb deep cross which Darijo Srna, arriving ahead of Marcell Jansen at the far post, steered past Jens Lehmann. In so doing, the midfielder became his country's all-time second highest goalscorer.

The goal opened the game up after a cagey start, and although Germany came back into it, Croatia finished the opening period the stronger, with Kranjčar wasting another presentable chance as he volleyed Olić's pass straight at Lehmann. Joachim Löw replaced Jansen with winger David Odonkor at half-time, with Clemens Fritz and Philipp Lahm moving to right and left-back respectively as the coach tried to inject pace into his attack. The ploy resulted in more possession, but Germany still found it tough to carve out clear

Ivica Vastic celebrates the late equalising penalty against Poland that kept Austria in the tournament

opportunities and they fell further behind two minutes past the hour, albeit in unfortunate fashion.

Schweinsteiger dismissed

Lehmann reacted sharply to push Rakitić's deflected right-wing centre on to his near post, the ball having struck Podolski, but Olić was perfectly positioned to tap the rebound into an unguarded net. If that goal seemed to be the prelude to a comfortable last half-hour for Croatia, a Germany side apparently running out of ideas suddenly halved the deficit, with Podolski smartly volleying in Michael Ballack's knockdown from a Lahm cross. Yet the Nationalmannschaft failed to mount a late charge and a disappointing day was complete two minutes into added time when substitute Bastian Schweinsteiger was sent off for reacting to a challenge from Jerko Leko.

"For me, this victory is a bigger achievement than beating England at Wembley," said Bilić, referring to the 3-2 victory in their final qualifier. "I keep getting questions about similarities between this team and the team I played for in 1998. All I can say is that we are Croatians, we play for our fans. It was the same in 1998 and it's the same now. As for Luka Modrić [the Man of the Match against Germany], he was already a star before this tournament. I keep telling him that he is the best player in Europe but he's not the only great player in our team."

Poland penalised

Modrić would shine again, but first it was another Croatian-born playmaker, Austria's Ivica Vastic, who stole the limelight. With the co-hosts trailing fellow final debutants Poland 1-0 and set to follow Switzerland out of the tournament after just two outings, the LASK Linz veteran stepped up three minutes into added time after Marcin Wasilewski had pulled Sebastian Prödl's shirt. He sent the excellent Artur Boruc the wrong way to become the oldest player to score in a UEFA European Championship. More importantly, it cancelled out Roger Guerreiro's first-half goal, the Brazil-born midfielder turning in from close range after Marek Saganowski's shot had been deflected into his path. Roger had only been granted Polish citizenship five weeks before the finals.

That result left Austria needing to relive the glory of their famous 3-2 victory against West Germany at the 1978 FIFA World Cup in Cordoba, Argentina. Their coach Josef Hickersberger had been a member of that side but was apparently unable to convey belief to his charges as the home fans endured a tentative start in Vienna. Indeed, but for a remarkable Mario Gómez miss, the small Alpine mountain they needed to climb would have become Himalayan. Eventually, though, Austria found their feet, and with Ümit Korkmaz providing a spark they ended the first half strongly. There were sparks flying off the pitch too, where an ongoing dispute on the touchline between Hickersberger and Löw resulted in the pair being sent to the stands.

High for Löw

After shaking hands with German chancellor Angela Merkel, Löw took his seat next to Bastian Schweinsteiger, and four minutes after the restart he was embracing the FC Bayern München winger as Michael Ballack fired in a thunderous free-kick. There was no way back for Austria – whose coach quit soon after their elimination – as Germany sealed a last-eight meeting with Portugal. "Obviously we're happy to have made it to the quarter-finals, particularly after the difficult match against Croatia," said Ballack. "We had everything to lose when we were certainly favourites to win. I'm convinced this victory will give us the push to play even better against Portugal."

Croatia also ensured they reached the last eight in a positive frame of mind as a largely second-string side made it three wins out of three, beating Poland 1-0 in Klagenfurt. Poland's slim qualifying hopes rested on at least a two-goal victory plus a win for Austria over Germany, their plight potentially eased by a Croatia team showing nine changes from the XI that had sealed progress with a game to spare four days earlier. Ivan Klasnić scored the winner early in the second half to end another defiant show from Poland goalkeeper Boruc. Klasnić had only returned to international football in March after undergoing two kidney transplants in 2007 and admitted: "I'm happy just to be playing football again. I said before this game that I felt as though I have been given a new lease of footballing life, a second life, so what happened today feels like a dream to me." What they had achieved in Group B must have felt like a dream to Croatia as a whole.

Michael Ballack, the Germany captain, about to let fly with the free-kick that won the game against Austria

Group B Results

8/6/08, Ernst Happel, Vienna
Austria 0-1 Croatia
Attendance: 51428
Austria: Macho, Standfest, Stranzl, Pogatetz, Aufhauser, Linz (Kienast 73), Ivanschitz, Gercaliu (Korkmaz 69), Prödl, Säumel (Vastic 61), Harnik. Coach: Josef Hickersberger (AUT)
Croatia: Pletikosa, Šimunić, R. Kovač, Ćorluka, N. Kovač, Srna, Modrić, Olić (Vukojević 83), Kranjčar (Knežević 61), Petrić (Budan 72), Pranjić. Coach: Slaven Bilić (CRO)
Goal(s): 0-1 Modrić 4(p)
Yellow Card(s): Pogatetz 3 (Austria), Säumel 21 (Austria), R. Kovač 51 (Croatia), Prödl 68 (Austria)
Referee: Vink (NED)

8/6/08, Wörthersee, Klagenfurt
Germany 2-0 Poland
Attendance: 30000
Germany: Lehmann, Jansen, Fritz (Schweinsteiger 56), Frings, Gómez (Hitzlsperger 75), Klose (Kuranyi 91), Ballack, Lahm, Mertesacker, Podolski, Metzelder. Coach: Joachim Löw (GER)
Poland: Boruc, Golański (Saganowski 75), Dudka, Bąk, Smolarek, Krzynówek, Żurawski (Roger 46), Wasilewski, Żewłakow, Łobodziński (Piszczek 65), Lewandowski. Coach: Leo Beenhakker (NED)
Goal(s): 1-0 Podolski 20, 2-0 Podolski 72
Yellow Card(s): Smolarek 40 (Poland), Lewandowski 60 (Poland), Schweinsteiger 64 (Germany)
Referee: Øvrebø (NOR)

12/6/08, Wörthersee, Klagenfurt
Croatia 2-1 Germany
Attendance: 30461
Croatia: Pletikosa, Šimunić, R. Kovač, Ćorluka, Rakitić, N. Kovač, Srna (Leko 80), Modrić, Olić (Petrić 72), Kranjčar (Knežević 85), Pranjić. Coach: Slaven Bilić (CRO)
Germany: Lehmann, Jansen (Odonkor 46), Fritz (Kuranyi 82), Frings, Gómez (Schweinsteiger 66), Klose, Ballack, Lahm, Mertesacker, Podolski, Metzelder. Coach: Joachim Löw (GER)
Goal(s): 1-0 Srna 24, 2-0 Olić 62, 2-1 Podolski 79
Red Card(s): Schweinsteiger 90+2 (Germany)
Yellow Card(s): Srna 27 (Croatia), Šimunić 45+1 (Croatia), Ballack 75 (Germany), Lehmann 90+2 (Germany), Leko 90+2 (Croatia), Modrić 90+3 (Croatia)
Referee: De Bleeckere (BEL)

12/6/08, Ernst Happel, Vienna
Austria 1-1 Poland
Attendance: 51428
Austria: Macho, Stranzl, Pogatetz, Aufhauser (Säumel 74), Leitgeb, Linz (Kienast 64), Ivanschitz (Vastic 64), Korkmaz, Garics, Prödl, Harnik. Coach: Josef Hickersberger (AUT)
Poland: Boruc, Jop (Golański 46), Dudka, Bąk, Smolarek, Krzynówek, Saganowski (Łobodziński 83), Wasilewski, Żewłakow, Lewandowski, Roger (Murawski 85). Coach: Leo Beenhakker (NED)
Goal(s): 0-1 Roger 30, 1-1 Vastic 90+3(p)
Yellow Card(s): Korkmaz 56 (Austria), Wasilewski 58 (Poland), Krzynówek 61 (Poland), Prödl 72 (Austria), Bąk 90+3 (Poland)
Referee: Webb (ENG)

16/6/08, Ernst Happel, Vienna
Austria 0-1 Germany
Attendance: 51428

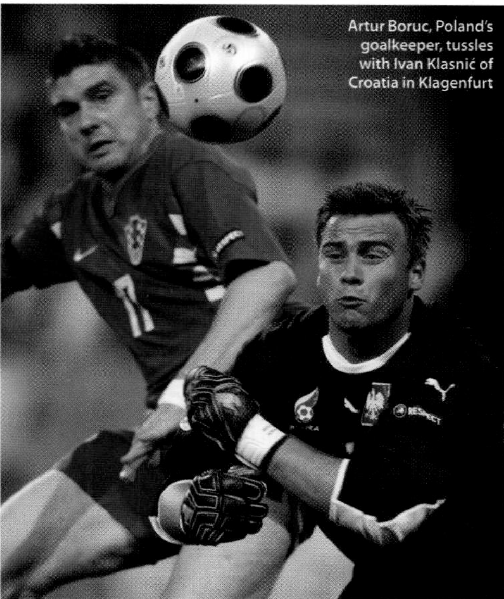
Artur Boruc, Poland's goalkeeper, tussles with Ivan Klasnić of Croatia in Klagenfurt

Austria: Macho, Stranzl, Pogatetz, Fuchs, Aufhauser (Säumel 63), Ivanschitz, Korkmaz, Garics, Hiden (Leitgeb 55), Harnik (Kienast 67), Hoffer. Coach: Josef Hickersberger (AUT)
Germany: Lehmann, Friedrich, Fritz (Borowski 93), Frings, Gómez (Hitzlsperger 60), Klose, Ballack, Lahm, Mertesacker, Podolski (Neuville 83), Metzelder. Coach: Joachim Löw (GER)
Goal(s): 0-1 Ballack 49
Yellow Card(s): Stranzl 13 (Austria), Hoffer 31 (Austria), Ivanschitz 48 (Austria)
Referee: Mejuto González (ESP)

16/6/08, Wörthersee, Klagenfurt
Poland 0-1 Croatia
Attendance: 30461
Poland: Boruc, Wawrzyniak, Dudka, Krzynówek, Saganowski (Zahorski 69), Wasilewski, Żewłakow, Łobodziński (Smolarek 55), Lewandowski (Kokoszka 46), Murawski, Roger. Coach: Leo Beenhakker (NED)
Croatia: Runje, Šimić, Vejić, Rakitić, Vukojević, Pokrivač, Knežević (Ćorluka 27), Leko, Klasnić (Kalinić 74), Petrić (Kranjčar 75), Pranjić. Coach: Slaven Bilić (CRO)
Goal(s): 0-1 Klasnić 53
Yellow Card(s): Lewandowski 38 (Poland), Vejić 45 (Croatia), Zahorski 84 (Poland), Vukojević 85 (Croatia)
Referee: Vassaras (GRE)

Group B Table

		Pld	W	D	L	F	A	Pts
1	Croatia	3	3	0	0	4	1	9
2	Germany	3	2	0	1	4	2	6
3	Austria	3	0	1	2	1	3	1
4	Poland	3	0	1	2	1	4	1

GROUP C

The Netherlands and Romania had already met in qualifying. The same was true of Italy and France, who had also contested the 2006 FIFA World Cup final, with the Azzurri prevailing 5-3 on penalties after a 1-1 draw in Berlin. Add to this the fact that Italy coach Roberto Donadoni and his Dutch counterpart Marco van Basten were also team-mates at AC Milan, and Group C always looked like being an intense affair. Romania coach Victor Piţurcă spelled out the prevailing mood after the draw, saying sardonically: "It is a very nice and easy group, with the world champions, the World Cup runners-up and Holland who we know very well."

A merciless draw was not the first UEFA European Championship disappointment of Piţurcă's career. Sacked on the eve of Romania's UEFA EURO 2000™ campaign following a row with senior players after leading his side through qualifying, Piţurcă was doubly determined to make his first taste of finals action last - despite the daunting opposition. Romania kicked off their campaign in Zurich against France, and held Raymond Domenech's side to a 0-0 draw. With Thierry Henry rested, a makeshift strike partnership of Nicolas Anelka and Karim Benzema rarely scrambled together anything other than half chances in what was to the only goalless game of the group stage. "France have good players but perhaps they have a couple of players who have got older," mused Piţurcă, while Domenech added testily: "I would have liked to have won this game 10-0 with a lot of very good chances, but that didn't happen."

Dutch rout

If France's start was disappointing, Italy's seemed nigh-on disastrous as the Netherlands beat them for the first time in 30 years, the 3-0 defeat in Berne representing the Azzurri's worst ever result at a UEFA European Championship. Ruud van Nistelrooy,

Romania's Daniel Niculae fires wide of the target as France goalkeeper Grégory Coupet looks on

somewhat controversially, and Wesley Sneijder, with a wonderful counterattacking goal, scored within five minutes of each other in a one-sided first half, and while Italy rallied after the break, Giovanni van Bronckhorst's headed effort at the end of another swift break ensured that the battle of the two Milan team-mates – and sometime golfing partners - ended in an emphatic win for Van Basten. "It started badly and ended up worse but this is already history and we need to think about the next game against Romania," said a rueful Donadoni.

But for a stunning penalty save from Gianluigi Buffon, that second game in Zurich would have marked the end of Italy's EURO dream. Adrian Mutu, boasting plenty of Serie A experience, led the line for Romania in a rousing tie, and his side had already seen one effort rebound of a post before he pounced on a weak Gianluca Zambrotta back-header to put Romania ahead after 55 minutes. Italy levelled with a close-range Christian Panucci header a minute later, but things looked desperate as Romania were awarded an 81st-minute penalty. Mutu struck it to Buffon's left but the goalkeeper produced a splendid save to usher the ball round the post. His and his team-mates' wild celebrations were indicative of the moment's importance.

Italy's Gianluigi Buffon gives Mauro Camoranesi the high fives after saving Adrian Mutu's penalty against Romania

Kuyt header

France, in the meantime, were pondering their own tournament mortality after a 4-1 defeat against the Netherlands in Berne in a game notable for more than just the 150,000 Dutch supporters who flocked to the Swiss federal capital to enjoy the flavour of UEFA EURO 2008™. Although Dirk Kuyt, carrying on his impressive form from the opening game, headed the Oranje into a ninth-minute lead, the Dutch were never as dominant as the scoreline suggested, and had Henry kept his lob down after being chipped through by Florent Malouda, Domenech's men could have restored parity early in the second half.

As it was, Arjen Robben set up fellow substitute Robin van Persie for the Netherlands' second, and even though Henry struck back on 71 minutes, Robben replied within a minute with a fierce shot from a tight angle before Sneijder's sublimely struck late fourth goal salted French wounds. The result sent the Dutch through and left both France and Italy on the brink of an early exit. "It all depends on the other match, Romania against the Netherlands," said Domenech, as he looked ahead nervously to the final round of games. "The Dutch have six points and I am convinced they won't play the same players. In the circumstances, we have to be very optimistic to imagine the Netherlands will beat Romania."

Romania unstuck

Sure enough, the Netherlands fielded just two of the players who had started their previous games in the match in Berne, but while Romania kept them firmly under wraps in the first 30 minutes, harrying for every ball, the anaesthetic soon wore off and the Dutch set about avenging the 1-0 qualifying defeat they suffered in Constanta in qualifying. With none of his team-mates able to match Mutu's drive and inspiration, it quickly became a matter of when – rather than whether – the Dutch would break through. Robben and Van Persie had both gone close before Klaas Jan Huntelaar opened his finals account from an Ibrahim Afellay cross. With Romania unable to conjure up much of a response, Van Persie underlined the class divide with a fiercely struck second on 87 minutes.

Franck Ribéry is consoled by Thierry Henry as he leaves the field with a serious injury during France's match against Italy

"Our great adventure is over," reflected Piţurcă, after news filtered through from the other game in Zurich. "It's a pity. We had a chance and could not take it, but that's football." The coach knew only too well how close Romania had come to eliminating both World Cup finalists, saying: "If we had scored that penalty against Italy we would have qualified." A delighted Van Basten added of his rampant side, now being lauded as potential European champions: "They are good players with good skills. The atmosphere is excellent, they laugh together and if we continue playing like this I don't know how it is going to end, but I hope it is going to last a long time."

France's Waterloo

Italy managed to make it through to the quarter-finals alongside Van Basten's men after a 2-0 win against a France side that, having hit rock bottom against the Dutch, started digging. Franck Ribéry – their most creative performer in the opening games - was carried off injured after just ten minutes, and Éric Abidal followed him to the dressing rooms on 24 minutes, dismissed for the reckless foul on Luca Toni that allowed Andrea Pirlo to open the scoring from the penalty spot. The ten men somehow rallied after the interval, but when De Rossi's 30-metre free-kick deflected off Henry's foot past Coupet for Italy's second, it was all over for France.

"This squad has always had a very special bond, win, lose or draw," said a relieved Donadoni. "It was there against France, against Romania, and also in the loss to the Netherlands. I'm not just saying that because we qualified, but because that's what our dressing room is like." Domenech, meanwhile, bowed out in bizarre style, publicly proposing marriage to his longtime partner Estelle Denis after the final whistle. "I don't have anything to say to the people who want me to resign," he said. "But I would like to ask Estelle for her hand [in marriage]. The only thing I'm thinking about from now is marrying Estelle, which is why I'm asking her for her hand today. I know it's difficult at this moment but it's during these difficult times that you need people – and personally I need her."

Group C Results

9/6/08, Letzigrund, Zurich
Romania 0-0 France
Attendance: 30585
Romania: Lobonț, Contra, Raț, Tamaș, Chivu, Rădoi (Dică 93), Mutu (M. Niculae 78), Cociș (Codrea 64), Goian, Nicoliță, D. Niculae. Coach: Victor Pițurcă (ROU)
France: Coupet, Abidal, Gallas, Makelele, Malouda, Anelka (Gomis 72), Benzema (Nasri 78), Thuram, Sagnol, Toulalan, Ribéry. Coach: Raymond Domenech (FRA)
Yellow Card(s): D. Niculae 27 (Romania), Contra 40 (Romania), Goian 43 (Romania), Sagnol 51 (France)
Referee: Mejuto González (ESP)

9/6/08, Stade de Suisse, Berne
Netherlands 3-0 Italy
Attendance: 30777
Netherlands: Van der Sar, Ooijer, Mathijsen, Van Bronckhorst, Engelaar, Van Nistelrooy (Van Persie 70), Sneijder, De Jong, Kuyt (Afellay 81), Boulahrouz (Heitinga 77), Van der Vaart. Coach: Marco van Basten (NED)
Italy: Buffon, Panucci, Barzagli, Gattuso, Toni, Di Natale (Del Piero 64), Ambrosini, Camoranesi (Cassano 75), Zambrotta, Pirlo, Materazzi (Grosso 54). Coach: Roberto Donadoni (ITA)
Goal(s): 1-0 Van Nistelrooy 26, 2-0 Sneijder 31, 3-0 Van Bronckhorst 79
Yellow Card(s): Toni 27 (Italy), Zambrotta 35 (Italy), Gattuso 51 (Italy), De Jong 58 (Netherlands)
Referee: Fröjdfeldt (SWE)

13/6/08, Letzigrund, Zurich
Italy 1-1 Romania
Attendance: 30585
Italy: Buffon, Panucci, Grosso, Chiellini, Del Piero (Quagliarella 77), Toni, De Rossi, Camoranesi (Ambrosini 85), Zambrotta, Perrotta (Cassano 57), Pirlo. Coach: Roberto Donadoni (ITA)
Romania: Lobonț, Contra, Raț, Tamaș, Chivu, Rădoi (Dică 25), Petre (Nicoliță 60), Codrea, Mutu (Cociș 88), Goian, D. Niculae. Coach: Victor Pițurcă (ROU)
Goal(s): 0-1 Mutu 55, 1-1 Panucci 56
Yellow Card(s): Mutu 43 (Romania), Chivu 58 (Romania), Pirlo 61 (Italy), Goian 73 (Romania), De Rossi 90+2 (Italy)
Referee: Øvrebø (NOR)

Giovanni van Bronckhorst – a goalscorer for the Netherlands against Italy

13/6/08, Stade de Suisse, Berne
Netherlands 4-1 France
Attendance: 30777
Netherlands: Van der Sar, Ooijer, Mathijsen, Van Bronckhorst, Engelaar (Robben 46), Van Nistelrooy, Sneijder, De Jong, Kuyt (Van Persie 55), Boulahrouz, Van der Vaart (Bouma 78). Coach: Marco van Basten (NED)
France: Coupet, Gallas, Makelele, Malouda (Gomis 60), Govou (Anelka 75), Henry, Evra, Thuram, Sagnol, Toulalan, Ribéry. Coach: Raymond Domenech (FRA)
Goal(s): 1-0 Kuyt 9, 2-0 Van Persie 59, 2-1 Henry 71, 3-1 Robben 72, 4-1 Sneijder 90+2
Yellow Card(s): Makelele 32 (France), Ooijer 51 (Netherlands), Toulalan 82 (France)
Referee: Fandel (GER)

17/6/08, Stade de Suisse, Berne
Netherlands 2-0 Romania
Attendance: 30777
Netherlands: Stekelenburg, Heitinga, De Zeeuw, Van Persie, Engelaar, Robben (Kuyt 61), Bouma, De Cler, Huntelaar (Vennegoor 83), Afellay, Boulahrouz (Melchiot 58). Coach: Marco van Basten (NED)
Romania: Lobonț, Contra, Raț, Tamaș, Chivu, Codrea (Dică 72), Mutu, Cociș, Ghionea, Nicoliță (Petre 82), M. Niculae (D. Niculae 59). Coach: Victor Pițurcă (ROU)
Goal(s): 1-0 Huntelaar 54, 2-0 Van Persie 87
Yellow Card(s): Chivu 78 (Romania)
Referee: Busacca (SUI)

17/6/08, Letzigrund, Zurich
France 0-2 Italy
Attendance: 30585
France: Coupet, Abidal, Gallas, Makelele, Benzema, Govou (Anelka 66), Henry, Evra, Clerc, Toulalan, Ribéry (Nasri 10; Boumsong 26). Coach: Raymond Domenech (FRA)
Italy: Buffon, Panucci, Grosso, Chiellini, Gattuso (Aquilani 82), Toni, De Rossi, Cassano, Zambrotta, Perrotta (Camoranesi 64), Pirlo (Ambrosini 55). Coach: Roberto Donadoni (ITA)
Goal(s): 0-1 Pirlo 25(p), 0-2 De Rossi 62
Red Card(s): Abidal 24 (France)
Yellow Card(s): Evra 18 (France), Pirlo 44 (Italy), Chiellini 45+4 (Italy), Govou 47 (France), Gattuso 54 (Italy), Boumsong 72 (France), Henry 85 (France)
Referee: Michel' (SVK)

Group C Table

		Pld	W	D	L	F	A	Pts
1	Netherlands	3	3	0	0	9	1	9
2	Italy	3	1	1	1	3	4	4
3	Romania	3	0	2	1	1	3	2
4	France	3	0	1	2	1	6	1

GROUP D

Group D offered the intriguing possibility of old versus new as holders Greece, looking to repeat their heroics of four years earlier, were drawn against perennial underachievers Spain, the old stagers of Sweden, and a Russia side under the guidance of the wily Guus Hiddink – who had never before failed to lead a team beyond the group stage of a major tournament.

Irresistible in Innsbruck

That impressive record looked to be under threat as Hiddink's charges were dismantled by a clinical Spain side in the section's opening game, David Villa scoring a brilliant hat-trick in Innsbruck. The Valencia CF striker broke the deadlock in the 20th minute, tapping into an empty net after Fernando Torres had raced clear of the Russia defence, and finished off a quick-fire team move to make it 2-0 a minute before half-time following clever combination play between Joan Capdevila, David Silva and Andrés Iniesta. Villa became only the seventh player to score three times in a match at the UEFA European Championship finals when, with 15 minutes left, he turned Roman Shirokov inside out before finding the net with a left-foot effort. There was still time for him to set up substitute Cesc Fàbregas for a first international goal after Roman Pavlyuchenko's 86th-minute header had reduced the deficit.

In Salzburg, meanwhile, came the first signs that Greece's reign would prove to be short-lived as Sweden ran out 2-0 winners. Otto Rehhagel's team won more points than any other in qualifying yet struggled to trouble the Swedish defence at the EM Stadion Wals-Siezenheim and never looked like getting back into the match once a moment of inspiration from Zlatan Ibrahimović had broken the deadlock midway through the second half. The Scandinavian side had the better of the play but were unable to unpick the Greece rearguard until the 67th minute, when Ibrahimović collected a throw-in and exchanged passes with Henrik Larsson – in the squad after again reversing his decision to retire from international football – before rifling in his first international goal since October 2005 from just outside the area. Five minutes later Petter Hansson bundled in a second to leave Greece facing a fight to hold on to their title.

Andrei Arshavin in customary celebration pose after putting Russia 2-0 up against Sweden

Holders out

Those slender hopes were extinguished altogether four days later, Russia bouncing back from their Spain setback to inflict a 1-0 defeat on the holders in Salzburg. Thus, the defence of the trophy won so memorably in 2004 had ended almost before it had begun. It was one of the heroes of Portugal whose error led to the only goal of the game. Goalkeeper Antonis Nikopolidis inexplicably chased a cross by Diniyar Bilyaletdinov almost all the way to the touchline, and he was made to pay in full for his 33rd-minute excursion. The Olympiacos CFP custodian was beaten to the ball by Russia captain Sergei Semak, who hooked it back over his head for Konstantin Zyryanov to guide casually into an unguarded net. "I can't criticise anyone, we lost to a very good team with

great forwards," said Rehhagel. "Anyone else who has to face Russia will have a rude awakening. Back in 2004 a miracle happened and that only happens once every 30 years or so. If it happened all the time we wouldn't call it a miracle, would we?"

That result also confirmed Spain's place in the quarter-finals following La Furia Roja's second successive group win, this time against Sweden in Salzburg. Luis Aragonés's side swiftly picked up where they had left off and took the lead in the 15th minute through Fernando Torres, who stretched to prod in David Silva's cross after a left-wing corner had been played short. An injury to Carles Puyol disrupted the Spanish defence, however, and Sweden struck back four minutes past the half-hour as Ibrahimović took advantage of some uncertain defending to hold off Sergio Ramos and shoot beyond Iker Casillas. The FC Internazionale Milano forward failed to reappear for the second half due to a knee injury, yet it still looked like Sweden would hold out for a point – until, two minutes into added time, Villa raced on to a long ball from left-back Capdevila and, as Hansson hesitated fatally, beat Andreas Isaksson with a low shot.

Arshavin impact

That meant Sweden needed a point from their final fixture, against Russia in Innsbruck, to secure progress beyond the group stage for the fourth successive major tournament. Instead, it was Andrei Arshavin who stole the show. Suspended for Russia's first two games after his red card in the final qualifying fixture in Andorra, the FC Zenit St. Petersburg playmaker was left to sweat on his place in the finals squad by Hiddink, who had suggested on the eve of the game that the 27-year-old was unlikely to play. The gamble to include him in both the squad and the starting lineup for the Sweden game brought immediate rewards, however, as Russia, needing a victory, took the lead in the 24th minute. Arshavin released Zyryanov down the right and the midfielder in turn found Aleksandr Anyukov's run inside the box. The right-back rolled a pass to Pavlyuchenko and the tall striker calmly finished for his second goal of the finals. Sweden almost levelled quickly but Larsson's clever header from a Mikael Nilsson cross bounced back off the bar while at the other end Pavlyuchenko's next effort struck an upright after another slick interchange involving Arshavin and Bilyaletdinov.

Konstantin Zyryanov turns to celebrate after scoring Russia's winning goal against Greece

The points and the quarter-final place were effectively settled five minutes after half-time, Yuriy Zhirkov racing away from the Sweden defence before he crossed for the returning hero Arshavin, who, on the run, skilfully directed the ball past Isaksson's right hand. Russia might have made the final margin of victory even more emphatic, Zyryanov's deflected attempt coming back off the post, but the two-goal margin was more than enough for Russia, leaving their coach purring. "I am especially proud of my team for their achievements and for the progress we have made in a few days," said Hiddink. "I told them to fight or go home. They chose to fight and play with their hearts and I am proud of them. The performance was incredible. Arshavin makes quick decisions and he can create danger. He lacked match fitness but the reason I brought him here was that he could make a difference and we were aiming for him to make that difference in this game."

Greece, meanwhile, were seeking to bow out with a win against a much-changed Spain side in Salzburg, yet it was their opponents who came closest to an early breakthrough, stand-in skipper Xabi Alonso nearly adding to his personal collection of goals from his own half. Greece's major threat throughout the tournament had come from set-pieces, and it was from such a route that their first goal of the finals came three minutes before half-time, Georgios Karagounis delivering the free-kick from which Angelos Charisteas headed in. Just as it looked as if Nikopolidis and defender Paraskevas Antzas, who had both announced that the game would be their last for Greece, might end with a win, Spain drew level in the 61st minute thanks to Rubén De la Red's first international goal, a missile of a right-foot shot. Greece were then denied even the consolation of a draw when the unmarked Daniel Güiza headed in his first goal for Spain from Sergio García's cross two minutes from time.

Group D Results

10/6/08, Tivoli Neu, Innsbruck
Spain 4-1 Russia
Attendance: 30772
Spain: Casillas, Marchena, Puyol, Iniesta (Santi Cazorla 63), David Villa, Xavi, Fernando Torres (Fàbregas 54), Capdevila, Sergio Ramos, Senna, Silva (Xabi Alonso 77). Coach: Luis Aragonés (ESP)
Russia: Akinfeev, Kolodin, Semak, Shirokov, Bilyaletdinov, Zyryanov, Zhirkov, Pavlyuchenko, Semshov (Torbinskiy 58), Sychev (Bystrov 46; Adamov 70), Anyukov. Coach: Guus Hiddink (NED)
Goal(s): 1-0 David Villa 20, 2-0 David Villa 44, 3-0 David Villa 75, 3-1 Pavlyuchenko 86, 4-1 Fàbregas 90+1
Referee: Plautz (AUT)

Daniel Güiza fires in a shot against Greece. The Spain striker won the game with a late header

10/6/08, EM Stadion Wals-Siezenheim, Salzburg
Greece 0-2 Sweden
Attendance: 31063
Greece: Nikopolidis, Seitaridis, Dellas (Amanatidis 70), Basinas, Charisteas, Karagounis, Torosidis, Kyrgiakos, Gekas (Samaras 46), Antzas, Katsouranis. Coach: Otto Rehhagel (GER)
Sweden: Isaksson, Nilsson, Mellberg, Hansson, Alexandersson (Stoor 74), Svensson, Ljungberg, Ibrahimović (Elmander 71), H. Larsson, Andersson, Wilhelmsson (Rosenberg 78). Coach: Lars Lagerbäck (SWE)
Goal(s): 0-1 Ibrahimović 67, 0-2 Hansson 72
Yellow Card(s): Charisteas 1 (Greece), Seitaridis 51 (Greece), Torosidis 61 (Greece)
Referee: Busacca (SUI)

14/6/08, Tivoli Neu, Innsbruck
Sweden 1-2 Spain
Attendance: 30772
Sweden: Isaksson, Nilsson, Mellberg, Hansson, Stoor, Svensson, Ljungberg, Ibrahimović (Rosenberg 46), Elmander (S. Larsson 79), H. Larsson (Källström 87), Andersson. Coach: Lars Lagerbäck (SWE)
Spain: Casillas, Marchena, Puyol (Albiol 24), Iniesta (Santi Cazorla 59), David Villa, Xavi (Fàbregas 59), Fernando Torres, Capdevila, Sergio Ramos, Senna, Silva. Coach: Luis Aragonés (ESP)
Goal(s): 0-1 Fernando Torres 15, 1-1 Ibrahimović 34, 1-2 David Villa 90+2
Yellow Card(s): Marchena 53 (Spain), Svensson 55 (Sweden)
Referee: Vink (NED)

14/6/08, EM Stadion Wals-Siezenheim, Salzburg
Greece 0-1 Russia
Attendance: 31063
Greece: Nikopolidis, Seitaridis (Karagounis 40), Patsatzoglou, Dellas, Basinas, Charisteas, Torosidis, Kyrgiakos, Amanatidis (Giannakopoulos 80), Katsouranis, Liberopoulos (Gekas 61). Coach: Otto Rehhagel (GER)
Russia: Akinfeev, Ignashevich, Torbinskiy, Kolodin, Semak, Bilyaletdinov (Saenko 70), Zyryanov, Zhirkov (V. Berezutskiy 87), Pavlyuchenko, Semshov, Anyukov. Coach: Guus Hiddink (NED)
Goal(s): 0-1 Zyryanov 33
Yellow Card(s): Karagounis 42 (Greece), Liberopoulos 58 (Greece), Saenko 77 (Russia), Torbinski 84 (Russia)
Referee: Rosetti (ITA)

18/6/08, EM Stadion Wals-Siezenheim, Salzburg
Greece 1-2 Spain
Attendance: 30883
Greece: Nikopolidis, Spiropoulos, Dellas, Basinas, Charisteas, Karagounis (Tziolis 74), Vintra, Salpingidis (Giannakopoulos 86), Kyrgiakos (Antzas 62), Amanatidis, Katsouranis. Coach: Otto Rehhagel (GER)
Spain: Reina, Albiol, Fernando Navarro, Iniesta (Santi Cazorla 58), Fàbregas, Xabi Alonso, Sergio García, Güiza, Arbeloa, Juanito, De la Red. Coach: Luis Aragonés (ESP)
Goal(s): 1-0 Charisteas 42, 1-1 De la Red 61, 1-2 Güiza 88
Yellow Card(s): Karagounis 34 (Greece), Güiza 41 (Spain), Arbeloa 45 (Spain), Basinas 72 (Greece), Vintra 90+1 (Greece)
Referee: Webb (ENG)

18/6/08, Tivoli Neu, Innsbruck
Russia 2-0 Sweden
Attendance: 30772
Russia: Akinfeev, Ignashevich, Kolodin, Arshavin, Semak, Bilyaletdinov (Saenko 66), Zyryanov, Zhirkov, Pavlyuchenko (Bystrov 90), Semshov, Anyukov. Coach: Guus Hiddink (NED)
Sweden: Isaksson, Nilsson (Allbäck 79), Mellberg, Hansson, Stoor, Svensson, Ljungberg, Ibrahimović, Elmander, H. Larsson, Andersson (Källström 56). Coach: Lars Lagerbäck (SWE)
Goal(s): 1-0 Pavlyuchenko 24, 2-0 Arshavin 50
Yellow Card(s): Isaksson 10 (Sweden), Elmander 49 (Sweden), Semak 57 (Russia), Arshavin 65 (Russia), Kolodin 76 (Russia)
Referee: De Bleeckere (BEL)

Sweden skipper Fredrik Ljungberg takes a tumble after a challenge from Russia's Denis Kolodin

Group D Table

		Pld	W	D	L	F	A	Pts
1	Spain	3	3	0	0	8	3	9
2	Russia	3	2	0	1	4	4	6
3	Sweden	3	1	0	2	3	4	3
4	Greece	3	0	0	3	1	5	0

QUARTER-FINALS

The winners of the 2000 and 2004 UEFA European Championships both triumphed after finishing second in their groups, and the adage that winners do not always come first rang true again at UEFA EURO 2008™. Of the four teams to top their group, three of them with a 100 per cent record, only Spain progressed to the last four as they threw out the history books to edge Italy on penalties. Indeed, tightness was the watchword in the last-eight ties, with only Germany's 3-2 victory against Portugal being decided in regulation time. Russia created a minor shock as they halted the Dutch juggernaut with an Andrei Arshavin-inspired extra-time victory, but the biggest drama was reserved for Turkey against Croatia.

Thrilling finale

Fatih Terim's Turkey had made a habit of last-gasp goals as they scraped into the quarter-finals, yet they eclipsed all that had gone before when they came up against Croatia in Vienna. The tie looked destined for penalties with the sides locked at 0-0 after 118 minutes of fairly stilted football – but the final 180 seconds made up for that with interest. With two minutes of extra time remaining the effervescent Luka Modrić, outstanding all evening, capitalised on an error by Rüştü Reçber, beating the goalkeeper to a loose ball on the byline and looping a cross over him for substitute Ivan Klasnić to head in at the near post.

Greece's Antonis Nikopolidis had made a similar error against Russia in the group stage and it sounded the death knell for the holders, but Rüştü – only in the side due to Volkan Demirel's suspension – would have his chance for redemption. Terim's team had struck decisive last-minute goals in each of their previous two matches and they completed a rare hat-trick at the Ernst-Happel-Stadion. Into the second minute of added time at the end of extra time, and with Slaven Bilić only just back in his technical area having joined in the manic celebrations following Klasnić's strike, Croatia broke forward through Ivan Rakitić.

Arda Turan (No14) leads the charge for Turkey after their dramatic penalty shoot-out victory over Croatia in Vienna

'Psychological advantage'

With the ground opening up, the midfielder opted to play in his strikers but the assistant referee's flag went up for offside. Rüştü pounced, launched the free-kick towards the edge of the penalty area where Niko Kovač and Josip Šimunić both jumped. The ball dropped for Semih Şentürk, who swung his left leg and drove the ball high into the net from just inside the area with the aid of a slight Robert Kovač deflection. "It seemed as though the match was over but to concede a goal certainly gave them a psychological advantage," said Bilić. "I can't say what was on the players' minds but I'm sure they weren't focused on the shoot-out."

So it proved. Until then Modrić had been an epitome of poise, carrying the burden of expectation unimpeded. Yet he put his effort wide. Rakitić would do likewise, and with Arda Turan, Semih and Hamit Altıntop all converting and only Darijo Srna doing likewise for Croatia, it left Mladen Petrić needing to score. He could not find a way past Rüştü, however, as Turkish celebrations began in earnest, even impending suspensions for Emre Aşık, Tuncay Şanlı and Arda failing to take the gloss off the victory. Terim's assessment that "you should never give up until the final whistle, that's what makes football interesting", was an understatement.

Germany through

That set Turkey up for a mouthwatering semi-final against Germany, who had booked their place in the last four the previous evening by seeing off Portugal in Basel. The St. Jakob-Park pitch had been re-laid since the group stage and Jens Lehmann spent much of the pre-match warm-up lifting up strips of turf before trampling them back down. Yet for much of the first half he need not have bothered as both sides began tentatively before, from nowhere, the Nationalmannschaft opened the scoring on 22 minutes with a wonderfully worked goal. Swift passing between Philipp Lahm, Michael Ballack and Lukas Podolski advanced the ball down the left, with Podolski bursting clear to drive in a low cross that Bastian Schweinsteiger converted on the slide.

Joachim Löw had told Schweinsteiger he had a "debt" to his team-mates after his red card against Croatia and here, in his first start of the finals, he resembled a man on a mission. The scorer of two goals against Portugal at the 2006 FIFA World Cup, he was the architect of their second, too, drifting a free-kick into the Portugal box that Miroslav Klose headed past

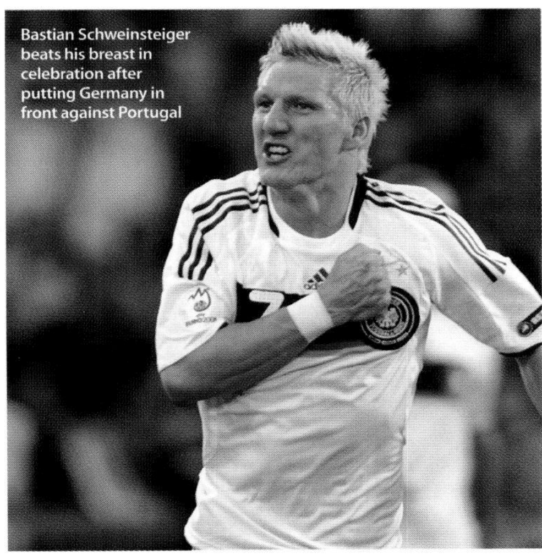
Bastian Schweinsteiger beats his breast in celebration after putting Germany in front against Portugal

Ricardo. Germany were on course to reach the UEFA European Championship semi-finals for the first time since they lifted the trophy in 1996.

Nuno Gomes lifeline

Having impressed in the group stage, Luiz Felipe Scolari – who was unveiled as the next Chelsea FC coach in the lead-up to the game – would have expected more of his side. There was a further setback when João Moutinho went off injured, but Portugal got their lifeline five minutes before the break through captain Nuno Gomes. Simão's crossfield ball sent Cristiano Ronaldo racing clear down the inside-left channel and although Jens Lehmann blocked his shot, the SL Benfica striker was first to the rebound, striking first time into the net via the foot of Christoph Metzelder. It was Nuno Gomes's sixth goal in three EURO final tournaments – a scoring span achieved only by Jürgen Klinsmann, Thierry Henry and Vladimír Šmicer before him.

Ronaldo was a whisker away from an equaliser moments before half-time and although Deco did find the net shortly after the interval he was in an offside position. The little midfielder then flicked on a Simão corner to set up Pepe, only for the defender to nod over. Ballack showed him how it should be done in the 61st minute when – to the displeasure of his future manager – he shrugged off club-mate Paulo Ferreira with a sly push and beat Ricardo to another Schweinsteiger free-kick to head home. "I had a bet and said today we would score from a set-piece," said assistant coach Hans-Dieter Flick, standing in for the suspended Löw. "There were two of them, so maybe I should double the stake."

Scolari bows out

Scolari sent on Nani and Hélder Postiga as Portugal chased the game, and the pair combined to ensure a nervy finale when the latter headed in. But it was too little, too late. "My feelings are of frustration," said Scolari. "I failed in my promise to be in the last four. That is my feeling right now. Maybe later – over dinner tonight or when I get home to Portugal – what I will feel is that I am leaving behind many friends. I am leaving a country where I was welcomed warmly. There will always be a part of me linked with Portugal."

Two days later, Marco van Basten was left with a similarly heavy heart at St. Jakob-Park as his ambition of becoming the first person to claim the UEFA European Championship as player and coach was ended in spectacular fashion by a resurgent Russia. From the off, Russia never allowed Van Basten's previously imperious side room for manoeuvre. Roman Pavlyuchenko's 56th-minute volley seemed to have won the game as Russia finally found a way past the heroic Edwin van der Sar, signing out in style as he made his Dutch-record 128th and last appearance.

Guus Hiddink (left) is overjoyed after leading Russia to victory over his native Netherlands

Late leveller

The 37-year-old had already denied Denis Kolodin and Yuriy Zhirkov, and after the goal he faced a renewed barrage. Aleksandr Anyukov, Pavlyuchenko and Dmitriy Torbinskiy were all left disappointed, and Russia looked like paying for their profligacy when, with four minutes left, Wesley Sneijder curled in a perfectly flighted free-kick for Ruud van Nistelrooy to head in at the far post and force an extra half-hour.

The late equaliser would have floored many teams but Russia, roused by their Dutch coach Guus Hiddink, merely stepped up a gear. If Hiddink really had wanted to "be the traitor of the year in Holland", as he suggested before the game, he was going the right way about it as he unleashed his wildcard, Arshavin. Suspended for the first two matches in Switzerland, the playmaker was a bundle of creative energy in extra time, setting up substitute Torbinskiy to restore the advantage and then adding another himself. "This is brilliant for me, for Russia, for my family," said Arshavin. "I don't know what to say – all I can say is that we won."

Van Basten departure

The mood in the Netherlands camp was much more sombre. "We tried everything and we got to 1-1 which gave us hope. But the players couldn't give any more and the Russians in the final moments were stronger. In the end we couldn't hold on any more and they scored two goals and deserved their victory," said Van Basten, for whom it was his last match before taking over at AFC Ajax. For Hiddink and Russia, it was on to a semi-final date with Spain, who held their collective nerve to claim victory against Italy.

Before the fourth quarter-final, in Vienna, Spain had lost three quarter-final penalty shoot-outs on the date of 22 June and had not beaten the Azzurri in a competitive fixture for 88 years. But they stopped the rot at the Ernst-Happel-Stadion, prevailing 4-2 on spot-kicks after 120 uneventful minutes had failed to produce a goal. Although Gianluigi Buffon saved from Daniel Güiza, Iker Casillas denied Daniele De Rossi and Antonio Di Natale, allowing Cesc Fàbregas to step up and send his side through.

Donadoni's last stand

Luis Aragonés's team had certainly enjoyed the better of the play on a humid night, Marcos Senna coming closest when he was denied by the post in the closing stages of normal time. Casillas's heroics saw them

Cesc Fàbregas drives his penalty past Gianluigi Buffon to put Spain into the semi-finals

through to a rematch with a Russia side they defeated 4-1 in the group stage, and if Spain coach Luis Aragonés's glass was "half-full" before the game it was rapidly getting closer to the brim. For Italy counterpart Roberto Donadoni, like Scolari and Van Basten, it was to prove his last game in charge as he was replaced by Marcello Lippi soon after the tournament.

Quarter-Final Results

19/6/08, St. Jakob-Park, Basel
Portugal 2-3 Germany
Attendance: 39374
Portugal: Ricardo, Paulo Ferreira, Bosingwa, Cristiano Ronaldo, Petit (Hélder Postiga 73), João Moutinho (Raul Meireles 31), Simão, Pepe, Ricardo Carvalho, Deco, Nuno Gomes (Nani 67). Coach: Luiz Felipe Scolari (BRA)
Germany: Lehmann, Friedrich, Rolfes, Schweinsteiger (Fritz 83), Klose (Jansen 89), Ballack, Hitzlsperger (Borowski 73), Lahm, Mertesacker, Podolski, Metzelder. Coach: Joachim Löw (GER)
Goal(s): 0-1 Schweinsteiger 22, 0-2 Klose 26, 1-2 Nuno Gomes 40, 1-3 Ballack 61, 2-3 Hélder Postiga 87
Yellow Card(s): Petit 26 (Portugal), Friedrich 48 (Germany), Lahm 49 (Germany), Pepe 60 (Portugal), Hélder Postiga 90 (Portugal)
Referee: Fröjdfeldt (SWE)

20/6/08, Ernst Happel, Vienna
Croatia 1-1 Turkey *(aet)*
Attendance: 51428
Croatia: Pletikosa, Šimunić, R. Kovač, Ćorluka, Rakitić, N. Kovač, Srna, Modrić, Olić (Klasnić 97), Kranjčar (Petrić 65), Pranjić. Coach: Slaven Bilić (CRO)
Turkey: Rüştü Reçber, Hakan Balta, Gökhan Zan, Mehmet Topal (Semih Şentürk 76), Nihat Kahveci (Gökdeniz Karadeniz 117), Arda Turan, Emre Aşık, Tuncay Şanlı, Kazım Kazım (Uğur Boral 61), Sabri Sarıoğlu, Hamit Altıntop. Coach: Fatih Terim (TUR)
Goal(s): 1-0 Klasnić 119, 1-1 Semih Şentürk 122
Yellow Card(s): Tuncay Şanlı 27 (Turkey), Arda Turan 49 (Turkey), Uğur Boral 89 (Turkey), Emre Aşık 107 (Turkey)
Referee: Rosetti (ITA)
Turkey win 3-1 on penalties.

21/6/08, St. Jakob-Park, Basel
Netherlands 1-3 Russia *(aet)*
Attendance: 38374
Netherlands: Van der Sar, Ooijer, Mathijsen, Van Bronckhorst, Engelaar (Afellay 62), Van Nistelrooy, Sneijder, De Jong, Kuyt (Van Persie 46), Boulahrouz (Heitinga 54), Van der Vaart. Coach: Marco van Basten (NED)
Russia: Akinfeev, Ignashevich, Kolodin, Saenko (Torbinskiy 81), Arshavin, Semak, Zyryanov, Zhirkov, Pavlyuchenko (Sychev 115), Semshov (Bilyaletdinov 69), Anyukov. Coach: Guus Hiddink (NED)
Goal(s): 0-1 Pavlyuchenko 56, 1-1 Van Nistelrooy 86, 1-2 Torbinskiy 112, 1-3 Arshavin 116
Yellow Card(s): Boulahrouz 50 (Netherlands), Van Persie 55 (Netherlands), Van der Vaart 60 (Netherlands), Kolodin 71 (Russia), Zhirkov 103 (Russia), Torbinskiy 111 (Russia)
Referee: Michel' (SVK)

22/6/08, Ernst Happel, Vienna
Spain 0-0 Italy *(aet)*
Attendance: 51178
Spain: Casillas, Marchena, Puyol, Iniesta (Santi Cazorla 59), David Villa, Xavi (Fàbregas 60), Fernando Torres (Güiza 85), Capdevila, Sergio Ramos, Senna, Silva. Coach: Luis Aragonés (ESP)
Italy: Buffon, Panucci, Grosso, Chiellini, Toni, De Rossi, Ambrosini, Cassano (Di Natale 75), Zambrotta, Perrotta (Camoranesi 58), Aquilani (Del Piero 108). Coach: Roberto Donadoni (ITA)
Yellow Card(s): Iniesta 11 (Spain), Ambrosini 31 (Italy), David Villa 72 (Spain), Santi Cazorla 112 (Spain)
Referee: Fandel (GER)
Spain win 4-2 on penalties.

SEMI-FINALS

The two semi-finals of UEFA EURO 2008™ were contrasting affairs, although no less dramatic for that. Whereas four years earlier in Portugal both ties had been even contests settled by a one-goal margin, in 2008 the two matches were open and entertaining, with all four teams keen to get on the front foot as quickly as possible.

Rapid start

The first semi-final brought together Germany and Turkey at St. Jakob-Park in Basel, and Christoph Metzelder's early slice from Uğur Boral's cross set the tone for an end-to-end encounter. Kazım Kazım broke confidently before Philipp Lahm's sloppiness allowed his FC Bayern München team-mate Hamit Altıntop – one of two German-born Turkey starters along with Hakan Balta – a half-chance he scuffed towards Jens Lehmann. Terim's team, severely depleted by injury and suspension, were playing as if they had nothing to lose. From Ayhan Akman's cutback, Kazım smashed against the crossbar; Semih nearly turned in a cross; then a telescopic leg from Per Mertesacker denied Ayhan.

After 17 minutes Germany woke up. Michael Ballack passed to Lahm, met the resulting cross with his head and sparked confusion in the opposition area. The Turkish thoroughbred had already bolted, though, and the first goal went their way after 22 minutes. Sabri Sarıoğlu threw the ball to Ayhan who chested it back, and from Sabri's cross Kazım's imperfect strike looped on to the crossbar. Happily for the Turkish fans an even untidier finish from Uğur burrowed under Lehmann's body to make it 1-0.

Schweinsteiger reply

Semih and Mehmet Aurélio might have doubled the advantage, only for Germany to equalise within four minutes against the run of play. Lukas Podolski delivered the centre which Bastian Schweinsteiger skilfully turned in from close range. It was a goal similar in construction, if not final execution, to his strike against Portugal. A Miroslav Klose chance at Turkey's end was then followed by Lehmann having to tip over a free-kick, although the taker, Hamit, then misplaced a pass that resulted in Podolski sprinting

Semih Şentürk squeezes the ball past goalkeeper Jens Lehmann at the near post to put Turkey level at 2-2

Philipp Lahm sends Rüştü Reçber the wrong way with a superb late winning strike in Basel

through but rifling over. Uğur's free-kick, won by the willing Kazım, elicited another Lehmann save. The forward runs of Kazım, Hamit, Ayhan and Uğur in support of Semih were causing Germany no end of trouble. Turkey's absentee list comprised four injured, four suspended and one half-fit substitute, yet those on parade were fresh, energetic and enthusiastic. Sabri's right-wing surge went unrewarded, then Uğur warmed Lehmann's hands as Turkey continued to attack through clever use of the flanks.

However, it was a long cross from a deeper position from Lahm that looked to have decided the match, goalkeeper Rüştü Reçber failing to reach a ball that Klose headed into the unguarded net. Turkey had redefined the term 'plucky underdog' with last-gasp goals against Switzerland, Czech Republic and Croatia, and duly came again. Sabri was the source, his cross being turned in at the near post by Semih Şentürk. Extra time loomed, but that was to discount the delightful one-two between Thomas Hitzlsperger and Lahm that provided the knockout punch, the left-back providing a cool finish to snatch a dramatic 90th-minute winner.

'Incredible feeling'

"We are absolutely delighted – an incredible feeling," said Joachim Löw. "It was a fantastic fight, a great drama, and with the late goals it had everything. After conceding their second goal, we were strong enough mentally to come back and then produced an excellent attack and a brilliant finish." Turkey's Fatih Terim, who announced his decision to step down immediately after the defeat but later opted to stay on until 2012, said: "It has always been important for me to have a team who enjoy what they are doing, who are creative and who score goals. Today we had it all. I told the players that I'm very proud of them. We are leaving as the most colourful team in the tournament."

Russia rematch

A day later the second semi-final in Vienna pitted an ever-improving Russia side, so impressive in dismantling Sweden and the Netherlands in their two previous fixtures, against a Spain team who had opened the tournament with a 4-1 defeat of Guus

Hiddink's side – although the key figure in that win, David Villa, was to experience vastly differing fortunes in the driving rain and spectacular lightning that greeted the start of this semi-final. Stung by criticism in some quarters of his performances thus far, Spain right-back Sergio Ramos started like a man possessed, just failing to get on the end of Xavi Hernández's fifth-minute cross.

Ramos's team-mates soon followed his lead, and as much as Aragonés had made plain his disdain for Spain's "mustard" – or yellow – away jerseys, he would have been glad his team were not the ones in red. Disjointed at the back and sluggish in midfield, Russia were struggling to find their feet. It took a well-timed tackle from Vasiliy Berezutskiy – in for the suspended Denis Kolodin – to deny Fernando Torres a run on goal though the striker soon tested Igor Akinfeev. The Russia goalkeeper was in action again to deny Villa as he fired in at the near post. Russia were looking for Andrei Arshavin to lift them out of the mire but refuge instead came from the right boot of Roman Pavlyuchenko in the shape of a blistering shot on the turn that Iker Casillas diverted away from the top corner. It soon got better for Russia as Villa limped off but almost immediately Pavlyuchenko poked wide with the goal at his mercy.

Second-half surge

His profligacy was underlined five minutes after half-time when Spain's midfield pivot Marcos Senna turned over possession and fed Xavi. A smart exchange of passes later and La Furia Roja were ahead, Xavi steering Andrés Iniesta's driven cross firmly past Akinfeev. Luis Aragonés's side were soon on the hunt for more. Having found his range with the goal, Iniesta released Villa's replacement Cesc Fàbregas, and though the substitute ran out of space, Aragonés's decision to switch to a five-man midfield was proving profitable, with the Arsenal FC youngster starting to demonstrate the full spectrum of his passing range. It took an excellent challenge from Yuriy Zhirkov to deny Torres before Fàbregas and Xabi Alonso had efforts tipped over. Alonso had been introduced moments earlier alongside Daniel Güiza, and the latter soon sealed

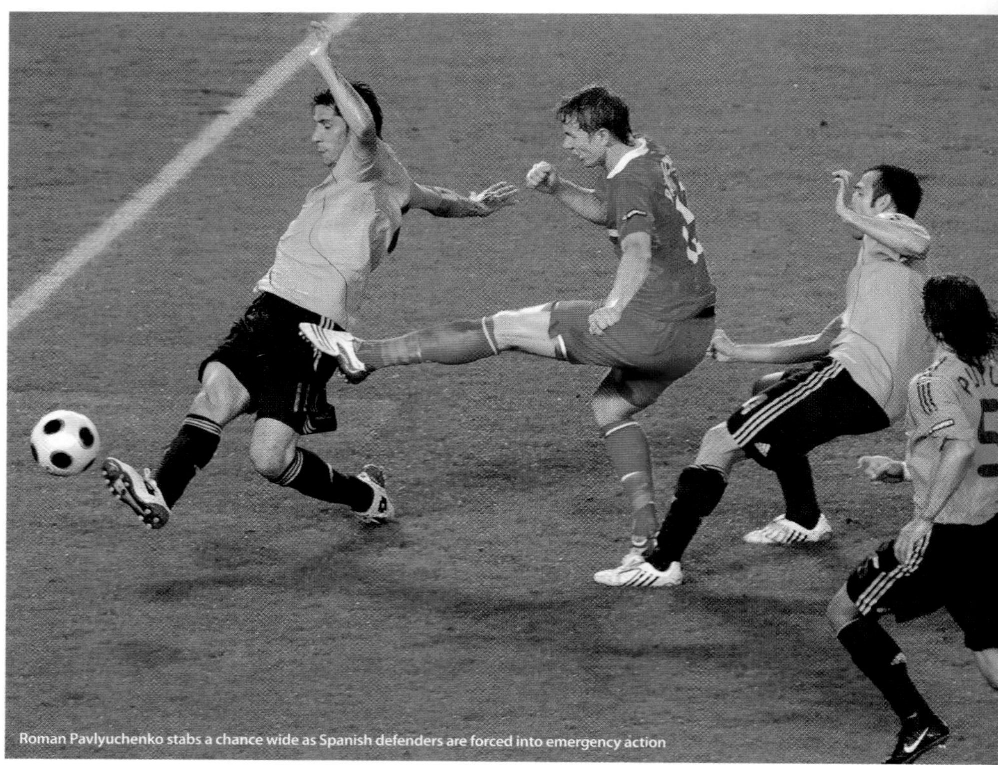
Roman Pavlyuchenko stabs a chance wide as Spanish defenders are forced into emergency action

Spain's place in the UEFA EURO 2008™ final is secure as David Silva finishes off Russia with a third goal

victory, lobbing Akinfeev after being put through by Fàbregas's perfectly-weighted dink over the defence. The No10 was the provider again moments later as his perfectly judged low cross was fired in by Silva to round off an impressive Spain display.

Russia coach Guus Hiddink, tasting semi-final defeat for the third time after last-four losses with the Netherlands (1998 FIFA World Cup) and South Korea (2002 World Cup), pinpointed the Spanish midfield as the difference, adding: " For an hour we could manage; after that against a team who can play such one-touch football it was very difficult. Their plan was to tire us with their very good positional game; that meant we ended up chasing our opponents. Then they had the power and the quality to strike. I'm always disappointed after a loss but we can be proud to reach this final stage; it's a tremendous success." Spain's Luis Aragonés concurred with that assessment, explaining: "We started playing the kind of football that Russia like – long passes and so on – but when we started touching the ball we were more complete, both attacking and defending. We scored three goals and in a semi-final that's very difficult indeed. We talked it over at half-time and said we had to quicken the pace because we knew if we scored we would hurt them badly, and that's what happened."

Semi-Final Results

25/6/08, St. Jakob-Park, Basel
Germany 3-2 Turkey
Attendance: 39374
Germany: Lehmann, Friedrich, Rolfes (Frings 46), Schweinsteiger, Klose (Jansen 90+2), Ballack, Hitzlsperger, Lahm, Mertesacker, Podolski, Metzelder. Coach: Joachim Löw (GER)
Turkey: Rüştü Reçber, Hakan Balta, Gökhan Zan, Mehmet Topal, Mehmet Aurélio, Semih Şentürk, Uğur Boral (Gökdeniz Karadeniz 84), Kazım Kazım (Tümer Metin 90+2), Ayhan Akman (Mevlüt Erdinç 81), Sabri Sarıoğlu, Hamit Altıntop. Coach: Fatih Terim (TUR)
Goal(s): 0-1 Uğur Boral 22, 1-1 Schweinsteiger 26, 2-1 Klose 79, 2-2 Semih Şentürk 86, 3-2 Lahm 90
Yellow Card(s): Semih Şentürk 53 (Turkey), Sabri Sarıoğlu 90+4 (Turkey)
Referee: Busacca (SUI)

26/6/08, Ernst Happel, Vienna
Russia 0-3 Spain
Attendance: 51428
Russia: Akinfeev, V. Berezutskiy, Ignashevich, Saenko (Sychev 57), Arshavin, Semak, Zyryanov, Zhirkov, Pavlyuchenko, Semshov (Bilyaletdinov 56), Anyukov. Coach: Guus Hiddink (NED)
Spain: Casillas, Marchena, Puyol, Iniesta, David Villa (Fàbregas 34), Xavi (Xabi Alonso 69), Fernando Torres (Güiza 69), Capdevila, Sergio Ramos, Senna, Silva. Coach: Luis Aragonés (ESP)
Goal(s): 0-1 Xavi 50, 0-2 Güiza 73, 0-3 Silva 82
Yellow Card(s): Zhirkov 56 (Russia), Bilyaletdinov 60 (Russia)
Referee: De Bleeckere (BEL)

FINAL

The final of UEFA EURO 2008™ brought together contrasting opponents – three-time winners Germany, in the showpiece for the sixth time, against a Spain side without a major international honour since triumphing in the 1964 UEFA European Championship on home soil. Furthermore, Spain had not progressed beyond the quarter-finals of any tournament in 24 years, when they lost 2-0 to a Michel Platini-inspired France side in the 1984 European final in Paris. Luis Aragonés's men chose to use that history as an inspiration rather than a burden, however, and were the more dangerous team throughout an entertaining contest at the Ernst-Happel-Stadion, although it took just one goal – in the 33rd minute, courtesy of Fernando Torres's pace, perseverance and unerring finish – to end their long wait.

Germany received a significant boost before kick-off, with captain Michael Ballack included in the starting line-up despite a much-publicised calf problem that had kept him out of training for the previous two days. Perhaps buoyed by that news, Joachim Löw's team settled quickly. Much had been made of the contrast in styles between the sides, yet in the opening exchanges it was Germany whose passing looked crisper, Miroslav Klose and Thomas Hitzlsperger failing to make the most of glimpses of goal for a Germany side showing just one change from the semi-final against Turkey, Torsten Frings replacing Simon Rolfes in the centre of midfield. Klose was eased off the ball by the excellent Carles Puyol after collecting a stray square pass from the otherwise faultless Sergio Ramos, while Hitzlsperger failed to connect properly with Lukas Podolski's cut-back, shooting straight at Iker Casillas. Meanwhile Spain, shorn of four-goal leading scorer David Villa due to a thigh injury picked up in the win against Russia three days before, struggled to find their feet in a new 4-5-1 formation in which Cesc Fàbregas was rewarded for an outstanding semi-final display with a starting place.

Germany's Michael Ballack and Spain's Marcos Senna in the heat of the midfield battle

Instinctive stop

As an indicator of the pattern of the match, however, Germany's bright beginning proved misleading. Spain soon worked their way into the contest. Germany goalkeeper Jens Lehmann, becoming, at 38 years 232 days, the oldest player to appear in a UEFA European Championship final, was called into action for the first time in the 14th minute. Although his instinctive save came when his own defender, Christoph Metzelder, inadvertently deflected Andrés Iniesta's cross towards his own goal, Xavi Hernández's fine through-pass had unpicked the Germany defence. The Spanish were finding their feet and, perhaps most worrying for Germany, this move was the first indication of the slick, sharp passing with which Spain had ultimately undone Russia in the last four.

Right-back Ramos, on one of his customary forays forward, was then allowed to cut inside and deliver a deep cross. Torres peeled away from his marker Per Mertesacker to create space for the header, only for the right-hand post to come to Lehmann's rescue. The warning signs were there for Germany, yet they failed to heed them and duly fell behind three minutes past the half-hour. Again Xavi was the architect, playing an angled pass in behind the Germany back line towards Torres, who outmuscled a hesitant Philipp Lahm and clipped the ball deftly over the diving Lehmann and just inside the far post. "Fernando is a great player, for Liverpool and for Spain," said Luis Aragonés in the aftermath of victory. "He can do anything. He has extraordinary speed and knows how to dribble at pace. He is so young and could learn how to do anything. He could be one of the best players in the world, no doubt."

Spain openings

Aragonés's side could and perhaps should have made the game safe before the interval as another swift interchange of passes caught out the Germany rearguard. Iniesta floated in a cross that found David Silva with time and space inside the penalty area, but, on his favoured left foot, the midfielder shot wildly over the crossbar. Spain had more openings in the early stages of the second half, Lehmann getting the merest of touches to Xavi's low shot before Sergio Ramos nearly guided in Silva's drive from the resulting corner. Yet a hint of the threat Germany still posed arrived on the hour, Marcell Jansen – a half-time replacement for the injured Lahm – and Bastian Schweinsteiger combining for Ballack to shoot fractionally wide from the edge of the area after Puyol had uncharacteristically given away possession. Klose

Spain full-back Sergio Ramos beats Germany substitute Mario Gómez to the ball

then deflected a Schweinsteiger effort past the post and, in response to these signs of Germany's renewed menace, Spain coach Aragonés promptly introduced Xabi Alonso and Santi Cazorla in place of Fàbregas and Silva. The switches reinvigorated Spain at a stroke, Lehmann making smart stops from Ramos - who could only head straight at the goalkeeper when left unmarked as Xavi's free-kick caught out Germany's offside trap - and Iniesta, while Torsten Frings blocked another Iniesta effort on the line following a corner.

As the final moved into the last 20 minutes, Spain had had seven shots on goal to Germany's one, but with Joachim Löw's efficient side having turned virtually one in two of their attempts on target into goals en route to the final, that statistic would have offered precious little comfort to Aragonés and his side. In the event, however, it was Spain who continued to carve out chances as the match reached its conclusion, with Marcos Senna, playing a crucial role once again in negating Germany's attacking threat from midfield, narrowly failing to apply the finishing touch to an unselfish header across goal from Daniel Güiza, the replacement for Torres. There was frustration that the second goal would not come, but after almost half a century, the celebrations would not be delayed much

Fernando Torres hurdles Jens Lehmann after clipping the ball over the Germany 'keeper and into the net for the only goal of the UEFA EURO 2008™ final

longer. Referee Roberto Rosetti's final whistle, when it came, was greeted by scenes of delirious joy from the Spanish players, coaching staff and massed ranks of supporters. There were quite a few neutrals present too who were extremely happy to see the tournament's most consistent performers come through to triumph.

Golden oldie

Spain were the only group winners to survive the quarter-finals and the first team since France 24 years earlier to win all three group games and go on to lift the trophy. Aragonés, aged 69 years and 338 days, became the oldest coach to guide a team to UEFA European Championship glory – although his players showed scant respect for his advancing years as they hoisted the veteran coach into the air to give him the celebratory "bumps".

"Many people will look at this Spain team because it's been a model for playing football," said Aragonés, for whom this was the last match in charge of the national team after four years. "All those that love football want people to make good combinations, get into the penalty area and score goals. At times we've been criticised but this has just led me to work even more. The moment will arrive when you are able to demonstrate who's right and who isn't. I don't get very emotional but there were details from some players that filled me with feeling. I don't show it but I'm so full of emotions. At the beginning I said that if we managed this squad well we would be champions. The team just thought I was trying to give them courage. I just hope Spain carry on in this way and have many more triumphs."

Final Result

29/6/08, Ernst Happel, Vienna
Germany 0-1 Spain
Attendance: 51428
Germany: Lehmann, Friedrich, Schweinsteiger, Frings, Klose (Gómez 79), Ballack, Hitzlsperger (Kuranyi 58), Lahm (Jansen 46), Mertesacker, Podolski, Metzelder. Coach: Joachim Löw (GER)
Spain: Casillas, Marchena, Puyol, Iniesta, Xavi, Fernando Torres (Güiza 78), Fàbregas (Xabi Alonso 63), Capdevila, Sergio Ramos, Senna, Silva (Santi Cazorla 66). Coach: Luis Aragonés (ESP)
Goal(s): 0-1 Fernando Torres 33
Yellow Card(s): Ballack 43 (Germany), Casillas 43 (Spain), Fernando Torres 74 (Spain), Kuranyi 88 (Germany)
Referee: Rosetti (ITA)

Champions of Europe! Jubilant Spain captain Iker Casillas holds aloft the Henri Delaunay trophy

GROUP A

SWITZERLAND

	DoB	Aps	(s)	Gls	Club
Goalkeepers					
1 Diego Benaglio	8/9/83	2			Wolfsburg (GER)
18 Pascal Zuberbühler	8/1/71	1			Xamax
21 Eldin Jakupovic	2/10/84				Lokomotiv Moskva (RUS)
Defenders					
2 Johan Djourou	18/1/87				Arsenal (ENG)
3 Ludovic Magnin	20/4/79	3			Stuttgart (GER)
4 Philippe Senderos	14/2/85	3			Arsenal (ENG)
5 Stephan Lichtsteiner	16/1/84	3			Lille (FRA)
13 Stéphane Grichting	30/3/79		(1)		Auxerre (FRA)
17 Christoph Spycher	30/3/78				Eintracht (GER)
20 Patrick Müller	17/12/76	3			Lyon (FRA)
23 Philipp Degen	15/2/83				Dortmund (GER)
Midfielders					
6 Benjamin Huggel	7/7/77				Basel
7 Ricardo Cabanas	17/1/79		(2)		Grasshoppers
8 Gökhan Inler	27/6/84	3			Udinese (ITA)
10 Hakan Yakin	22/2/77	2	(1)	3	Young Boys
14 Daniel Gygax	28/8/81		(1)		Metz (FRA)
15 Gelson Fernandes	2/9/86	3			Man. City (ENG)
16 Tranquillo Barnetta	22/5/85	2	(1)		Leverkusen (GER)
19 Valon Behrami	19/4/85	3			Lazio (ITA)
22 Johan Vonlanthen	1/2/86	1	(2)		Salzburg (AUT)
Attackers					
9 Alexander Frei	15/7/79	1			Dortmund (GER)
11 Marco Streller	18/6/81	1			Basel
12 Eren Derdiyok	12/6/88	2	(1)		Basel

CZECH REPUBLIC

	DoB	Aps	(s)	Gls	Club
Goalkeepers					
1 Petr Čech	20/5/82	3			Chelsea (ENG)
16 Jaromír Blažek	29/12/72				Nürnberg (GER)
23 Daniel Zítka	20/6/75				Anderlecht (BEL)
Defenders					
2 Zdeněk Grygera	14/5/80	3			Juventus (ITA)
6 Marek Jankulovski	9/5/77	3			Milan (ITA)
12 Zdeněk Pospěch	14/12/78				København (DEN)
13 Michal Kadlec	13/12/84		(1)		Sparta
21 Tomáš Ujfaluši	24/3/78	3			Fiorentina (ITA)
22 David Rozehnal	5/7/80	3			Lazio (ITA)
Midfielders					
3 Jan Polák	14/3/81	3			Anderlecht (BEL)
4 Tomáš Galásek	15/1/73	3			Nürnberg (GER)
5 Radoslav Kováč	27/11/79		(1)		Spartak Moskva (RUS)
14 David Jarolím	17/5/79	1	(2)		Hamburg (GER)
17 Marek Matějovský	20/12/81	2			Reading (ENG)
18 Tomáš Sivok	15/9/83				Sparta
19 Rudolf Skácel	17/7/79				Hertha (GER)
20 Jaroslav Plašil	5/1/82	3		1	Osasuna (ESP)
Attackers					
7 Libor Sionko	1/2/77	3		1	København (DEN)
8 Martin Fenin	16/4/87				Eintracht (GER)
9 Jan Koller	30/3/73	2	(1)	1	Nürnberg (GER)
10 Václav Svěrkoš	1/11/83		(1)	1	Baník
11 Stanislav Vlček	26/2/76		(3)		Anderlecht (BEL)
15 Milan Baroš	28/10/81	1			Portsmouth (ENG)

PORTUGAL

	DoB	Aps	(s)	Gls	Club
Goalkeepers					
1 Ricardo	11/2/76	4			Betis (ESP)
12 Nuno Espírito Santo	25/1/74				Porto
22 Rui Patrício	15/2/88				Sporting
Defenders					
2 Paulo Ferreira	18/1/79	4			Chelsea (ENG)
3 Bruno Alves	27/11/81	1			Porto
4 José Bosingwa	24/8/82	3			Porto
5 Fernando Meira	5/6/78	1	(2)		Stuttgart (GER)
13 Miguel	4/1/80	1			Valencia (ESP)
14 Jorge Ribeiro	9/11/81		(1)		Boavista
15 Pepe	26/2/83	4		1	Real Madrid (ESP)
16 Ricardo Carvalho	18/5/78	3			Chelsea (ENG)
Midfielders					
6 Raul Meireles	17/3/83	1	(2)	1	Porto
8 Petit	25/9/76	3			Benfica
10 João Moutinho	8/9/86	3	(1)		Sporting
11 Simão Sabrosa	31/10/79	3			Atlético (ESP)
17 Ricardo Quaresma	26/9/83	1	(1)	1	Porto
18 Miguel Veloso	11/5/86	1			Sporting
19 Nani	17/11/86	1	(2)		Man. United (ENG)
20 Deco	27/8/77	3		1	Barcelona (ESP)
Attackers					
7 Cristiano Ronaldo	5/2/85	3		1	Man. United (ENG)
9 Hugo Almeida	23/5/84		(2)		Bremen (GER)
21 Nuno Gomes	5/7/76	3		1	Benfica
23 Hélder Postiga	2/8/82	1	(1)	1	Panathinaikos (GRE)

TURKEY

	DoB	Aps	(s)	Gls	Club
Goalkeepers					
1 Rüştü Reçber	10/5/73	2			Beşiktaş
12 Tolga Zengin	10/10/83				Trabzonspor
23 Volkan Demirel	27/10/81	3			Fenerbahçe
Defenders					
2 Servet Çetin	17/3/81	3			Galatasaray
3 Hakan Balta	23/3/83	5			Galatasaray
4 Gökhan Zan	7/9/81	3			Beşiktaş
13 Emre Güngör	1/8/84	1			Galatasaray
15 Emre Aşık	13/12/73	2	(2)		Galatasaray
Midfielders					
5 Emre Belözoğlu	7/9/80	1			Newcastle (ENG)
6 Mehmet Topal	3/3/86	3	(1)		Galatasaray
7 Mehmet Aurélio	15/12/77	4			Fenerbahçe
10 Gökdeniz Karadeniz	11/1/80	1	(2)		Rubin (RUS)
11 Tümer Metin	14/10/74	1	(1)		Fenerbahçe
14 Arda Turan	30/1/87	3		2	Galatasaray
16 Uğur Boral	14/4/82	1	(1)	1	Fenerbahçe
19 Ayhan Akman	23/2/77	1			Galatasaray
20 Sabri Sarıoğlu	26/7/84	2	(2)		Galatasaray
22 Hamit Altıntop	8/12/82	5			Bayern (GER)
Attackers					
8 Nihat Kahveci	23/11/79	4		2	Villarreal (ESP)
9 Semih Şentürk	29/4/83	2	(3)	3	Fenerbahçe
17 Tuncay Şanlı	16/1/82	4			Middlesbrough (ENG)
18 Kazım Kazım	26/8/86	3	(2)		Fenerbahçe
21 Mevlüt Erdinç	25/2/87	1	(1)		Sochaux (FRA)

GROUP B

AUSTRIA

	DoB	Aps	(s)	Gls	Club
Goalkeepers					
1 Alexander Manninger	4/6/77				Siena (ITA)
21 Jürgen Macho	24/8/77	3			AEK (GRE)
23 Ramazan Özcan	28/6/84				Hoffenheim (GER)
Defenders					
2 Joachim Standfest	30/5/80	1			Austria Wien
3 Martin Stranzl	16/6/80	3			Spartak Moskva (RUS)
4 Emanuel Pogatetz	16/1/83	3			Middlesbrough (ENG)
12 Ronald Gercaliu	12/2/86	1			Austria Wien

		DoB	Aps	(s)	Gls	Club
13	Markus Katzer	11/12/79				Rapid Wien
15	Sebastian Prödl	21/6/87	2			Sturm
16	Jürgen Patocka	30/7/77				Rapid Wien
17	Martin Hiden	11/3/73	1			Austria Kärnten
Midfielders						
5	Christian Fuchs	7/4/86	1			Mattersburg
6	René Aufhauser	21/6/76	3			Salzburg
8	Christoph Leitgeb	14/4/85	1	(1)		Salzburg
10	Andreas Ivanschitz	15/10/83	3			Panathinaikos (GRE)
11	Ümit Korkmaz	17/9/85	2	(1)		Rapid Wien
14	György Garics	8/3/84	2			Napoli (ITA)
19	Jürgen Säumel	8/9/84	1	(2)		Sturm
Attackers						
7	Ivica Vastic	29/9/69		(2)	1	LASK
9	Roland Linz	9/8/81	2			Braga (POR)
18	Roman Kienast	29/3/84		(3)		Ham-Kam (NOR)
20	Martin Harnik	10/6/87	3			Bremen (GER)
22	Erwin Hoffer	14/4/87	1			Rapid Wien

CROATIA

		DoB	Aps	(s)	Gls	Club
Goalkeepers						
1	Stipe Pletikosa	8/1/79	3			Spartak Moskva (RUS)
12	Mario Galinović	15/11/76				Panathinaikos (GRE)
23	Vedran Runje	10/2/76	1			Lens (FRA)
Defenders						
2	Dario Šimić	12/11/75	1			Milan (ITA)
3	Josip Šimunić	18/2/78	3			Hertha (GER)
4	Robert Kovač	6/4/74	3			Dortmund (GER)
5	Vedran Ćorluka	5/2/86	3	(1)		Man. City (ENG)
6	Hrvoje Vejić	8/6/77	1			Tom (RUS)
15	Dario Knežević	20/4/82	1	(2)		Livorno (ITA)
Midfielders						
7	Ivan Rakitić	10/3/88	3			Schalke (GER)
8	Ognjen Vukojević	20/12/83	1	(1)		Dinamo Zagreb
10	Niko Kovač	15/10/71	3			Salzburg (AUT)
11	Darijo Srna	1/5/82	3		1	Shakhtar (UKR)
13	Nikola Pokrivač	26/11/85	1			Monaco (FRA)
14	Luka Modrić	9/9/85	3		1	Dinamo Zagreb
16	Jerko Leko	9/4/80	1	(1)		Monaco (FRA)
19	Niko Kranjčar	13/8/84	3	(1)		Portsmouth (ENG)
22	Danijel Pranjić	2/12/81	4			Heerenveen (NED)
Attackers						
9	Nikola Kalinić	5/1/88		(1)		Hajduk
17	Ivan Klasnić	29/1/80	1	(1)	2	Bremen (GER)
18	Ivica Olić	14/9/79	3		1	Hamburg (GER)
20	Igor Budan	22/4/80		(1)		Parma (ITA)
21	Mladen Petrić	1/1/81	2	(2)		Dortmund (GER)

GERMANY

		DoB	Aps	(s)	Gls	Club
Goalkeepers						
1	Jens Lehmann	10/11/69	6			Arsenal (ENG)
12	Robert Enke	24/8/77				Hannover
23	René Adler	15/1/85				Leverkusen
Defenders						
2	Marcell Jansen	4/11/85	2	(3)		Bayern
3	Arne Friedrich	29/5/79	4			Hertha
4	Clemens Fritz	7/12/80	3	(1)		Bremen
5	Heiko Westermann	14/8/83				Schalke
16	Philipp Lahm	11/11/83	6		1	Bayern
17	Per Mertesacker	29/9/84	6			Bremen
21	Christoph Metzelder	5/11/80	6			Real Madrid (ESP)
Midfielders						
6	Simon Rolfes	21/1/82	2			Leverkusen
7	Bastian Schweinsteiger	1/8/84	3	(2)	2	Bayern
8	Torsten Frings	22/11/76	4	(1)		Bremen
13	Michael Ballack	26/9/76	6		2	Chelsea (ENG)
14	Piotr Trochowski	22/3/84				Hamburg
15	Thomas Hitzlsperger	5/4/82	3	(2)		Stuttgart
18	Tim Borowski	2/5/80		(2)		Bremen
Attackers						
9	Mario Gómez	10/7/85	3	(1)		Stuttgart
10	Oliver Neuville	1/5/73		(1)		Mönchengladbach
11	Miroslav Klose	9/6/78	6		2	Bayern
19	David Odonkor	21/2/84		(1)		Betis (ESP)
20	Lukas Podolski	4/6/85	6		3	Bayern
22	Kevin Kuranyi	2/3/82		(3)		Schalke

POLAND

		DoB	Aps	(s)	Gls	Club
Goalkeepers						
1	Artur Boruc	20/2/80	3			Celtic (SCO)
12	Wojciech Kowalewski	11/5/77				Steaua (ROU)
22	Łukasz Fabiański	18/4/85				Arsenal (ENG)
Defenders						
2	Mariusz Jop	3/8/78	1			Moskva (RUS)
3	Jakub Wawrzyniak	7/7/83	1			Legia
4	Paweł Golański	12/10/82	1	(1)		Steaua (ROU)
5	Dariusz Dudka	9/12/83	3			Wisła Kraków
6	Jacek Bąk	24/3/73	2			Austria Wien (AUT)
13	Marcin Wasilewski	9/6/80	3			Anderlecht (BEL)
14	Michał Żewłakow	22/4/76	3			Olympiacos (GRE)
15	Michał Pazdan	21/9/87				Górnik Zabrze
23	Adam Kokoszka	6/10/86		(1)		Wisła Kraków
Midfielders						
7	Euzebiusz Smolarek	9/1/81	2	(1)		Racing (ESP)
8	Jacek Krzynówek	15/5/76	3			Wolfsburg (GER)
10	Łukasz Garguła	25/2/81				Bełchatów
17	Wojciech Łobodziński	20/10/82	2	(1)		Wisła Kraków
18	Mariusz Lewandowski	18/5/79	3			Shakhtar (UKR)
19	Rafał Murawski	9/10/81	1	(1)		Lech
20	Roger Guerreiro	25/5/82	2	(1)	1	Legia
Attackers						
9	Maciej Żurawski	12/9/76	1			Larissa (GRE)
11	Marek Saganowski	31/10/78	2	(1)		Southampton (ENG)
16	Łukasz Piszczek	3/6/85		(1)		Hertha (GER)
21	Tomasz Zahorski	22/11/84		(1)		Górnik Zabrze

GROUP C

NETHERLANDS

		DoB	Aps	(s)	Gls	Club
Goalkeepers						
1	Edwin van der Sar	29/10/70	3			Man. United (ENG)
13	Henk Timmer	3/12/71				Feyenoord
16	Maarten Stekelenburg	22/9/82	1			Ajax
Defenders						
2	André Ooijer	11/7/74	3			Blackburn (ENG)
3	John Heitinga	15/11/83	1	(2)		Ajax
4	Joris Mathijsen	5/4/80	3			Hamburg (GER)
5	Giovanni van Bronckhorst	5/2/75	3		1	Feyenoord
12	Mario Melchiot	4/11/76		(1)		Wigan (ENG)
14	Wilfred Bouma	15/6/78	1	(1)		Aston Villa (ENG)
15	Tim de Cler	8/11/78	1			Feyenoord
20	Ibrahim Afellay	2/4/86	1	(2)		PSV
21	Khalid Boulahrouz	28/12/81	4			Sevilla (ESP)
Midfielders						
6	Demy de Zeeuw	26/5/83	1			AZ
8	Orlando Engelaar	24/8/79	4			Twente
10	Wesley Sneijder	9/6/84	3		2	Real Madrid (ESP)
11	Arjen Robben	23/1/84	1	(1)	1	Real Madrid (ESP)
17	Nigel de Jong	30/11/84	3			Hamburg (GER)
23	Rafael van der Vaart	11/2/83	3			Hamburg (GER)

		DoB	Aps	(s)	Gls	Club
Attackers						
7	Robin van Persie	6/8/83	1	(3)	2	Arsenal (ENG)
9	Ruud van Nistelrooy	1/7/76	3		2	Real Madrid (ESP)
18	Dirk Kuyt	22/7/80	3	(1)	1	Liverpool (ENG)
19	Klaas Jan Huntelaar	12/8/83	1		1	Ajax
22	Jan Vennegoor of Hesselink	7/11/78		(1)		Celtic (SCO)

ITALY

		DoB	Aps	(s)	Gls	Club
Goalkeepers						
1	Gianluigi Buffon	28/1/78	4			Juventus
14	Marco Amelia	2/4/82				Livorno
17	Morgan De Sanctis	26/3/77				Sevilla (ESP)
Defenders						
2	Christian Panucci	12/4/73	4		1	Roma
3	Fabio Grosso	28/11/77	3	(1)		Lyon (FRA)
4	Giorgio Chiellini	14/8/84	3			Juventus
5	Alessandro Gamberini	27/8/81				Fiorentina
6	Andrea Barzagli	8/5/81	1			Palermo
19	Gianluca Zambrotta	19/2/77	4			Barcelona (ESP)
23	Marco Materazzi	19/8/73	1			Internazionale
Midfielders						
8	Gennaro Gattuso	9/1/78	2			Milan
10	Daniele De Rossi	24/7/83	3		1	Roma
13	Massimo Ambrosini	29/5/77	2	(2)		Milan
16	Mauro Camoranesi	4/10/76	2	(2)		Juventus
20	Simone Perrotta	17/9/77	3			Roma
21	Andrea Pirlo	19/5/79	3		1	Milan
22	Alberto Aquilani	7/7/84	1	(1)		Roma
Attackers						
7	Alessandro Del Piero	9/11/74	1	(2)		Juventus
9	Luca Toni	26/5/77	4			Bayern (GER)
11	Antonio Di Natale	13/10/77	1	(1)		Udinese
12	Marco Borriello	18/6/82				Genoa
15	Fabio Quagliarella	31/1/83		(1)		Sampdoria
18	Antonio Cassano	12/7/82	2	(2)		Sampdoria

ROMANIA

		DoB	Aps	(s)	Gls	Club
Goalkeepers						
1	Bogdan Lobonţ	18/1/78	3			Dinamo Bucureşti
12	Marius Popa	31/7/78				Naţional
23	Eduard Stăncioiu	3/3/81				CFR
Defenders						
2	Cosmin Contra	15/12/75	3			Getafe (ESP)
3	Răzvan Raţ	26/5/81	3			Shakhtar (UKR)
4	Gabriel Tamaş	9/11/83	3			Auxerre (FRA)
5	Cristian Chivu	26/10/80	3			Internazionale (ITA)
6	Mirel Rădoi	22/3/81	2			Steaua
13	Cristian Săpunaru	5/4/84				Rapid Bucureşti
14	Sorin Ghionea	11/5/79	1			Steaua
15	Dorin Goian	12/12/80	2			Steaua
17	Cosmin Moţi	3/12/84				Dinamo Bucureşti
22	Ştefan Radu	22/10/86				Lazio (ITA)
Midfielders						
7	Florentin Petre	15/1/76	1	(1)		CSKA Sofia (BUL)
8	Paul Codrea	4/4/81	2	(1)		Siena (ITA)
11	Răzvan Cociş	19/2/83	2	(1)		Lokomotiv Moskva (RUS)
16	Bănel Nicoliţă	7/1/85	2	(1)		Steaua
19	Adrian Cristea	30/11/83				Dinamo Bucureşti
Attackers						
9	Ciprian Marica	2/10/85				Stuttgart (GER)
10	Adrian Mutu	8/1/79	3		1	Fiorentina (ITA)
18	Marius Niculae	16/5/81	1	(1)		Inverness (SCO)
20	Nicolae Dică	9/5/80		(3)		Steaua
21	Daniel Niculae	6/10/82	2	(1)		Auxerre (FRA)

FRANCE

		DoB	Aps	(s)	Gls	Club
Goalkeepers						
1	Steve Mandanda	28/3/85				Marseille
16	Sébastien Frey	18/3/80				Fiorentina (ITA)
23	Grégory Coupet	31/12/72	3			Lyon
Defenders						
2	Jean-Alain Boumsong	14/12/79		(1)		Lyon
3	Éric Abidal	11/9/79	2			Barcelona (ESP)
5	William Gallas	17/8/77	3			Arsenal (ENG)
13	Patrice Evra	15/5/81	2			Man. United (ENG)
14	François Clerc	18/4/83	1			Lyon
15	Lilian Thuram	1/1/72	2			Barcelona (ESP)
17	Sébastien Squillaci	11/8/80				Lyon
19	Willy Sagnol	18/3/77	2			Bayern (GER)
Midfielders						
4	Patrick Vieira	23/6/76				Internazionale (ITA)
6	Claude Makelele	18/2/73	3			Chelsea (ENG)
7	Florent Malouda	13/6/80	2			Chelsea (ENG)
11	Samir Nasri	26/6/87		(2)		Marseille
20	Jérémy Toulalan	10/9/83	3			Lyon
21	Lassana Diarra	10/3/85				Portsmouth (ENG)
22	Franck Ribéry	7/4/83	3			Bayern (GER)
Attackers						
8	Nicolas Anelka	14/3/79	1	(2)		Chelsea (ENG)
9	Karim Benzema	19/12/87	2			Lyon
10	Sidney Govou	27/7/79	2			Lyon
12	Thierry Henry	17/8/77	2		1	Barcelona (ESP)
18	Bafetimbi Gomis	6/8/85		(2)		St-Étienne

GROUP D

GREECE

		DoB	Aps	(s)	Gls	Club
Goalkeepers						
1	Antonis Nikopolidis	14/1/71	3			Olympiacos
12	Kostas Chalkias	30/5/74				Aris
13	Alexandros Tzorvas	12/8/82				OFI
Defenders						
2	Giourkas Seitaridis	4/6/81	2			Atlético (ESP)
3	Christos Patsatzoglou	19/3/79	1			Olympiacos
4	Nikos Spiropoulos	10/10/83	1			Panathinaikos
5	Traianos Dellas	31/1/76	3			AEK
11	Loukas Vintra	5/2/81	1			Panathinaikos
15	Vassilis Torosidis	10/6/85	2			Olympiacos
16	Sotiris Kyrgiakos	23/7/79	3			Eintracht (GER)
18	Giannis Goumas	24/5/75				Panathinaikos
19	Paraskevas Antzas	18/8/76	1	(1)		Olympiacos
Midfielders						
6	Angelos Basinas	3/1/76	3			Mallorca (ESP)
8	Stelios Giannakopoulos	12/7/74		(2)		Bolton (ENG)
10	Georgios Karagounis	6/3/77	2	(1)		Panathinaikos
21	Kostas Katsouranis	21/6/79	3			Benfica (POR)
22	Alexandros Tziolis	13/2/85		(1)		Panathinaikos
Attackers						
7	Georgios Samaras	21/2/85		(1)		Celtic (SCO)
9	Angelos Charisteas	9/2/80	3		1	Nürnberg (GER)
14	Dimitris Salpingidis	18/8/81	1			Panathinaikos
17	Fanis Gekas	23/5/80	1	(1)		Leverkusen (GER)
20	Giannis Amanatidis	3/12/81	2	(1)		Eintracht (GER)
23	Nikos Liberopoulos	4/8/75	1			AEK

SWEDEN

		DoB	Aps	(s)	Gls	Club
Goalkeepers						
1	Andreas Isaksson	3/10/81	3			Man. City (ENG)
12	Rami Shaaban	30/6/75				Hammarby

13 Johan Wiland	24/1/81				Elfsborg
Defenders					
3 Olof Mellberg	3/9/77	3			Aston Villa (ENG)
4 Petter Hansson	14/12/76	3		1	Rennes (FRA)
5 Fredrik Stoor	28/2/84	2	(1)		Rosenborg (NOR)
14 Daniel Majstorovic	5/4/77				Basel (SUI)
15 Andreas Granqvist	16/4/85				Wigan (ENG)
23 Mikael Dorsin	6/10/81				CFR (ROU)
Midfielders					
2 Mikael Nilsson	24/6/78	3			Panathinaikos (GRE)
6 Tobias Linderoth	21/4/79				Galatasaray (TUR)
7 Niclas Alexandersson	29/12/71	1			Göteborg
8 Anders Svensson	17/7/76	3			Elfsborg
9 Fredrik Ljungberg	16/4/77	3			West Ham (ENG)
16 Kim Källström	24/8/82		(2)		Lyon (FRA)
18 Sebastian Larsson	6/6/85		(1)		Birmingham (ENG)
19 Daniel Andersson	28/8/77	3			Malmö
21 Christian Wilhelmsson	8/12/79	1			Deportivo (ESP)
Attackers					
10 Zlatan Ibrahimović	3/10/81	3		2	Internazionale (ITA)
11 Johan Elmander	27/5/81	2	(1)		Toulouse (FRA)
17 Henrik Larsson	20/9/71	3			Helsingborg
20 Marcus Allbäck	5/7/73		(1)		København (DEN)
22 Markus Rosenberg	27/9/82		(2)		Bremen (GER)

SPAIN

	DoB	Aps	(s)	Gls	Club
Goalkeepers					
1 Iker Casillas	20/5/81	5			Real Madrid
13 Andrés Palop	22/10/73				Sevilla
23 Pepe Reina	31/8/82	1			Liverpool (ENG)
Defenders					
2 Raúl Albiol	4/9/85	1	(1)		Valencia
3 Fernando Navarro	25/6/82	1			Mallorca
4 Carlos Marchena	31/7/79	5			Valencia
5 Carles Puyol	13/4/78	5			Barcelona
11 Joan Capdevila	3/2/78	5			Villarreal
15 Sergio Ramos	30/3/86	5			Real Madrid
18 Álvaro Arbeloa	17/1/83	1			Liverpool (ENG)
20 Juanito	23/7/76	1			Betis
Midfielders					
6 Andrés Iniesta	11/5/84	6			Barcelona
8 Xavi Hernández	25/1/80	5		1	Barcelona
10 Cesc Fàbregas	4/5/87	2	(4)	1	Arsenal (ENG)
12 Santi Cazorla	13/12/84		(5)		Villarreal
14 Xabi Alonso	25/11/81	1	(3)		Liverpool (ENG)
19 Marcos Senna	17/7/76	5			Villarreal
22 Rubén De la Red	5/6/85	1		1	Getafe
Attackers					
7 David Villa	3/12/81	4		4	Valencia
9 Fernando Torres	20/3/84	5		2	Liverpool (ENG)
16 Sergio García	9/6/83	1			Zaragoza
17 Daniel Güiza	17/8/80	1	(3)	2	Mallorca
21 David Silva	8/1/86	5		1	Valencia

RUSSIA

	DoB	Aps	(s)	Gls	Club
Goalkeepers					
1 Igor Akinfeev	8/4/86	5			CSKA Moskva
12 Vladimir Gabulov	19/10/83				Amkar
16 Vyacheslav Malafeyev	4/3/79				Zenit
Defenders					
2 Vasiliy Berezutskiy	20/6/82	1	(1)		CSKA Moskva
3 Renat Yanbayev	7/4/84				Lokomotiv Moskva
4 Sergei Ignashevich	14/7/79	4			CSKA Moskva
5 Aleksei Berezutskiy	20/6/82				CSKA Moskva
8 Denis Kolodin	11/1/82	4			Dinamo Moskva
14 Roman Shirokov	6/7/81	1			Zenit
22 Aleksandr Anyukov	28/9/82	5			Zenit
Midfielders					
7 Dmitriy Torbinskiy	28/4/84	1	(2)	1	Lokomotiv Moskva
11 Sergei Semak	27/2/76	5			Rubin
13 Oleg Ivanov	4/8/86				Krylya Sovetov
15 Diniyar Bilyaletdinov	27/2/85	3	(2)		Lokomotiv Moskva
17 Konstantin Zyryanov	5/10/77	5		1	Zenit
18 Yuriy Zhirkov	20/8/83	5			CSKA Moskva
20 Igor Semshov	6/4/78	5			Dinamo Moskva
23 Vladimir Bystrov	31/1/84		(2)		Spartak Moskva
Attackers					
6 Roman Adamov	21/6/82		(1)		Moskva
9 Ivan Saenko	17/10/83	2	(2)		Nürnberg (GER)
10 Andrei Arshavin	29/5/81	3		2	Zenit
19 Roman Pavlyuchenko	15/12/81	5		3	Spartak Moskva
21 Dmitriy Sychev	26/10/83	1	(2)		Lokomotiv Moskva

TOP GOALSCORERS

4 DAVID VILLA (Spain)

3 Hakan YAKIN (Switzerland)
SEMIH Şentürk (Turkey)
Roman PAVLYUCHENKO (Russia)
Lukas PODOLSKI (Germany)

2 Daniel GÜIZA (Spain)
Ivan KLASNIĆ (Croatia)
Zlatan IBRAHIMOVIĆ (Sweden)
Robin VAN PERSIE (Netherlands)
Ruud VAN NISTELROOY (Netherlands)
NIHAT Kahveci (Turkey)
Andrei ARSHAVIN (Russia)
Wesley SNEIJDER (Netherlands)
ARDA Turan (Turkey)
Bastian SCHWEINSTEIGER (Germany)
FERNANDO TORRES (Spain)
Miroslav KLOSE (Germany)
Michael BALLACK (Germany)

QUALIFYING TOURNAMENT

TOP GOALSCORERS

13	David HEALY (Northern Ireland)
10	EDUARDO da Silva (Croatia)
9	Euzebiusz SMOLAREK (Poland)
8	CRISTIANO RONALDO (Portugal) Lukas PODOLSKI (Germany)
7	DAVID VILLA (Spain) Steffen IVERSEN (Norway) Mladen PETRIĆ (Croatia) Jon Dahl TOMASSON (Denmark) Nikola ŽIGIĆ (Serbia)
6	Marcus ALLBÄCK (Sweden) Dimitar BERBATOV (Bulgaria) Roberto COLAUTTI (Israel) HAKAN Şükür (Turkey) Thierry HENRY (France) Jan KOLLER (Czech Republic) Marek MINTÁL (Slovakia) Adrian MUTU (Romania) Martin PETROV (Bulgaria)

GROUP A

Poland held their nerve in the latter part of their Group A qualifying campaign, but Portuguese nerves frayed as they eventually joined Leo Beenhakker's side in the finals.

Five-point lead

At the summer break Poland held a five-point lead over Serbia and Portugal at the top of the section, although both sides had two matches in hand. The Poles met Portugal in Lisbon in their first game after the restart and were within two minutes of a 2-1 defeat before Jacek Kryznówek's hopeful shot found its way into the net with a little help from the post and goalkeeper Ricardo's shoulder.

"I can't say we've had a perfect match because some of my boys did not handle the pressure well, but you must think positively when you get a draw in such emotional circumstances," said Beenhakker. Their next match was a less dramatic, but no less precious, 0-0 draw in Finland as Portugal's 2-2 draw with Serbia gave them breathing space.

Celebrations begin

Within two games, Poland had booked their place at the finals. Euzebiusz Smolarek hit a hat-trick to help his team come from behind to beat Kazakhstan 3-1 in Warsaw, then struck his eighth and ninth goals of the campaign to beat Belgium 2-0 in Chorzow on 17 November, thus igniting raucous celebrations for the UEFA EURO 2012™ co-hosts.

Smolarek remained calm amid the euphoria, saying: "It still does not feel like we have done anything historic." However, Dutchman Beenhakker – who won domestic titles in Spain and the Netherlands and led Trinidad & Tobago to the 2006 FIFA World Cup finals – conceded that qualifying was "one of the biggest successes of my career".

Doomsday scenario

A 2-2 draw against Poland in their final game was the end of the line for Javier Clemente's Serbia, as Portugal avoided a doomsday scenario, drawing 0-0 at home against Finland to earn second place in the section. Portugal lost only once in qualifying – 2-1 against Poland in Chorzow - but had their share of frustrating moments in the final stages.

After a 1-1 draw in Armenia in August, Portugal were denied victory against Poland by that late Kryznówek goal, then were held to a 1-1 draw at home to Serbia in their next game, with Branko Ivanković striking from close range two minutes from time to deny them another win. To make matters worse, coach Luiz Felipe Scolari was then involved in an altercation with Serbia's Ivica Dragutinović after the game.

Able deputy

UEFA eventually banned the Brazilian from the touchline for the next three games, although his assistant Flávio Teixeira proved to be an able deputy as Portugal won 2-0 in Azerbaijan and 2-1 in Kazakhstan before beating Armenia 1-0 at home. Scolari returned for the final home game against Finland and watched his team earn the point they needed to go through. Scolari conceded that his side "must improve for the finals" while Cristiano Ronaldo added of the Finland game: "We did not win, we just did what was needed" – a tidy enough assessment of their campaign.

While Portugal looked ahead, the final Group A fixtures meant the end of the line for Finland and Serbia. Serbia started the autumn badly, losing 3-2 away against a Belgium side revitalised by an influx of young talent, while a 0-0 draw at home against Finland in their next game represented a missed opportunity. The 1-1 draw in Portugal restored hope, but another goalless outcome in Armenia saw Serbia drop to fourth in the section.

Ian Porterfield, the Scottish coach of Armenia, who lost his battle with cancer in September 2007

Clemente dismissed

A 6-1 win in Azerbaijan just about kept the Serbian dream alive. "We wanted to be masters of our own destiny, but unfortunately we've lost that right," said striker Nikola Žigić. However, with their match against Kazakhstan postponed twice due to heavy snow in Belgrade, a 2-2 draw with Poland marked the death knell. They won 1-0 in the rescheduled game against Kazakhstan but it was too little too late and Clemente was dismissed before the end of the year.

Finland also ended the year without a coach, as Englishman Roy Hodgson resigned. A winning goal in Portugal in their final game would have secured an unlikely qualification but a goalless draw – their fourth of the autumn – proved to be the final word for a side blessed with considerable spirit but not enough attacking bite.

'A very good person'

Ian Porterfield imbued his Armenia side with spirit, but August's 1-1 draw against Portugal was his final game in charge, with his assistants taking over following his death on 11 September from cancer. "Of course we knew he was sick but we all hoped he would make it," said striker Armen Shahgeldyan. "He was a very good coach, but what is more important he was a very good person."

Group A Results

16/8/06
Belgium 0-0 Kazakhstan

2/9/06
Serbia 1-0 Azerbaijan
Goal(s): 1-0 Žigić 72
Poland 1-3 Finland
Goal(s): 0-1 Litmanen 54, 0-2 Litmanen 76(p), 0-3 Väyrynen 84, 1-3 Garguła 90

6/9/06
Azerbaijan 1-1 Kazakhstan
Goal(s): 1-0 Ladaga 16, 1-1 Byakov 36
Finland 1-1 Portugal
Goal(s): 1-0 Johansson 22, 1-1 Nuno Gomes 42
Poland 1-1 Serbia
Goal(s): 1-0 Matusiak 30, 1-1 Lazović 71
Armenia 0-1 Belgium
Goal(s): 0-1 Van Buyten 41

7/10/06
Serbia 1-0 Belgium
Goal(s): 1-0 Žigić 54
Armenia 0-0 Finland
Kazakhstan 0-1 Poland
Goal(s): 0-1 Smolarek 52

Portugal 3-0 Azerbaijan
Goal(s): 1-0 Cristiano Ronaldo 25, 2-0 Ricardo Carvalho 31, 3-0 Cristiano Ronaldo 63

11/10/06
Serbia 3-0 Armenia
Goal(s): 1-0 Stanković 54(p), 2-0 Lazović 62, 3-0 Žigić 90+2
Poland 2-1 Portugal
Goal(s): 1-0 Smolarek 9, 2-0 Smolarek 18, 2-1 Nuno Gomes 90+2
Belgium 3-0 Azerbaijan
Goal(s): 1-0 Simons 24(p), 2-0 Vandenbergh 47, 3-0 Dembélé 82
Kazakhstan 0-2 Finland
Goal(s): 0-1 Litmanen 27, 0-2 Hyypiä 65

15/11/06
Finland 1-0 Armenia
Goal(s): 1-0 Nurmela 10
Belgium 0-1 Poland
Goal(s): 0-1 Matusiak 19
Portugal 3-0 Kazakhstan
Goal(s): 1-0 Simão 8, 2-0 Cristiano Ronaldo 30, 3-0 Simão 86

24/3/07
Poland 5-0 Azerbaijan
Goal(s): 1-0 Bąk 3, 2-0 Dudka 6, 3-0 Łobodziński 34, 4-0 Krzynówek 58, 5-0 Kaźmierczak 84
Kazakhstan 2-1 Serbia
Goal(s): 1-0 Ashirbekov 47, 2-0 Zhumaskaliev 61, 2-1 Žigić 68
Portugal 4-0 Belgium
Goal(s): 1-0 Nuno Gomes 53, 2-0 Cristiano Ronaldo 55, 3-0 Ricardo Quaresma 69, 4-0 Cristiano Ronaldo 75

28/3/07
Azerbaijan 1-0 Finland
Goal(s): 1-0 Imamäliyev 82
Poland 1-0 Armenia
Goal(s): 1-0 Żurawski 26
Serbia 1-1 Portugal
Goal(s): 0-1 Tiago 5, 1-1 Janković 37

2/6/07
Kazakhstan 1-2 Armenia
Goal(s): 0-1 Arzumanyan 31, 0-2 Hovsepyan 39(p), 1-2 Baltiyev 88(p)
Finland 0-2 Serbia
Goal(s): 0-1 Janković 3, 0-2 Jovanović 86
Belgium 1-2 Portugal
Goal(s): 0-1 Nani 43, 1-1 Fellaini 55, 1-2 Hélder Postiga 64
Azerbaijan 1-3 Poland
Goal(s): 1-0 Subašić 6, 1-1 Smolarek 63, 1-2 Krzynówek 66, 1-3 Krzynówek 90

6/6/07
Kazakhstan 1-1 Azerbaijan
Goal(s): 0-1 Nadirov 30, 1-1 Baltiyev 53
Finland 2-0 Belgium
Goal(s): 1-0 Johansson 27, 2-0 A. Eremenko Jr 71
Armenia 1-0 Poland
Goal(s): 1-0 Mkhitaryan 66

22/8/07, Ratina, Tampere
Finland 2-1 Kazakhstan
Attendance: 13047
Finland: Jääskeläinen, Kallio, Hyypiä, Tihinen, Pasanen, R. Eremenko (Sjölund 46), Heikkinen, Kolkka (Nurmela 88), Tainio (Riihilahti 76), A. Eremenko Jr, Johansson. Coach: Roy Hodgson (ENG)
Kazakhstan: Loria, E. Azovski, Kuchma, Smakov, Irismetov, Skorykh (Chichulin 69), Larin (Ashirbekov 78), Baltiyev, Zhumaskaliev, Byakov, Ostapenko (Suyumagambetov 70). Coach: Arno Pijpers (NED)
Goal(s): 1-0 A. Eremenko Jr 13, 1-1 Byakov 23, 2-1 Tainio 61
Yellow Card(s): Baltiyev 32 (Kazakhstan), Skorykh 41 (Kazakhstan), Heikkinen 56 (Finland), Jääskeläinen 79 (Finland), Kallio 82 (Finland)
Referee: Kassai (HUN)

22/8/07, Roi Baudouin, Brussels
Belgium 3-2 Serbia
Attendance: 19202
Belgium: Stijnen, Simons, Hoefkens, Vermaelen, Kompany, Mudingayi, Goor, Geraerts, Mirallas (Vanden Borre 67), Dembélé (Lombaerts 90), Defour (M. Mpenza 86). Coach: René Vandereycken (BEL)
Serbia: Stojković, Rukavina, Vidić, Krstajić, Dragutinović, Kovačević, Kuzmanović, Janković, Koroman (Krasić 56), Lazović (Smiljanić 70), Pantelić (Jovanović 56). Coach: Javier Clemente (ESP)
Goal(s): 1-0 Dembélé 10, 2-0 Mirallas 30, 2-1 Kuzmanović 73, 3-1 Dembélé 88, 3-2 Kuzmanović 90+1
Yellow Card(s): Goor 32 (Belgium), Krstajić 78 (Serbia), Vidić 90+4 (Serbia)
Referee: Hauge (NOR)

22/8/07, Republican, Yerevan
Armenia 1-1 Portugal
Attendance: 14935
Armenia: Berezovski, Hovsepyan, Arzumanyan, Tadevosyan, A. Mkrtchyan, Pachajyan, Voskanyan, Arakelyan, Art. Karamyan (Melikyan 70), Mkhitaryan (Ghazaryan 59), Melkonyan (Khachatryan 90). Coach: Ian Porterfield (SCO)
Portugal: Ricardo, Miguel, Fernando Meira, Jorge Andrade (Bruno Alves 76), Paulo Ferreira, Raul Meireles, Tiago, Deco, Cristiano Ronaldo, Hélder Postiga (Nuno Gomes 61), Simão (Ricardo Quaresma 63). Coach: Luiz Felipe Scolari (BRA)
Goal(s): 1-0 Arzumanyan 11, 1-1 Cristiano Ronaldo 37
Yellow Card(s): Jorge Andrade 69 (Portugal)
Referee: Larsen (DEN)

8/9/07
Azerbaijan v Armenia cancelled

8/9/07, FK Crvena Zvezda, Belgrade
Serbia 0-0 Finland
Attendance: 10530
Serbia: Stojković, Rukavina, Ivanović, Dragutinović, D. Tošić (Z. Tošić 53), Kovačević, Kuzmanović, Stanković, Janković (Jovanović 54), Krasić, Lazović (Žigić 62). Coach: Javier Clemente (ESP)
Finland: Jääskeläinen, Pasanen, Hyypiä, Tihinen, Kuivasto, Nurmela, Tainio, Heikkinen, A. Eremenko Jr (Forssell 74), Sjölund, Johansson (Wiss 78). Coach: Roy Hodgson (ENG)
Yellow Card(s): Janković 20 (Serbia), Tainio 71 (Finland), Z. Tošić 77 (Serbia)
Referee: Braamhaar (NED)

8/9/07, Estádio do Sport Lisboa e Benfica, Lisbon
Portugal 2-2 Poland
Attendance: 48000
Portugal: Ricardo, Bosingwa, Fernando Meira, Bruno Alves, Marco Caneira (Miguel 12), Deco, Maniche, Petit, Cristiano Ronaldo, Nuno Gomes (Ricardo Quaresma 69), Simão (João Moutinho 81). Coach: Luiz Felipe Scolari (BRA)
Poland: Boruc, Jop, Bronowicki (Golański 55), Dudka, Smolarek (Łobodziński 73), Krzynówek, Żurawski (Matusiak 56), Wasilewski, Żewłakow, Błaszczykowski, Lewandowski. Coach: Leo Beenhakker (NED)
Goal(s): 0-1 Lewandowski 44, 1-1 Maniche 50, 2-1 Cristiano Ronaldo 73, 2-2 Krzynówek 88
Yellow Card(s): Boruc 20 (Poland), Wasilewski 29 (Poland), Bronowicki 37 (Poland)
Referee: Rosetti (ITA)

Euzebiusz Smolarek takes the applause after scoring one of the two goals against Belgium that secured Poland's first ever UEFA European Championship qualification

12/9/07
Armenia v Azerbaijan cancelled

12/9/07, Olympiastadion, Helsinki
Finland 0-0 Poland
Attendance: 34088
Finland: Jääskeläinen, Kuivasto, Hyypiä, Tihinen, Pasanen, Sjölund, Heikkinen (Wiss 90+1), Tainio, Kolkka, A. Eremenko Jr, Johansson (Forssell 72). Coach: Roy Hodgson (ENG)
Poland: Boruc, Golański, Jop, Żewłakow, Błaszczykowski, Dudka, Sobolewski, Lewandowski, Smolarek (Żurawski 80), Krzynówek, Rasiak (Saganowski 65). Coach: Leo Beenhakker (NED)
Yellow Card(s): A. Eremenko Jr 25 (Finland), Jop 33 (Poland), Błaszczykowski 89 (Poland)
Referee: Fandel (GER)

12/9/07, Tcentralny, Almaty
Kazakhstan 2-2 Belgium
Attendance: 18100
Kazakhstan: Loria, E. Azovski (Lyapkin 66), Smakov, Irismetov, Kuchma, Larin (Suyumagambetov 73), Skorykh, Karpovich, Zhumaskaliev, Ostapenko, Byakov. Coach: Arno Pijpers (NED)
Belgium: Stijnen, Simons, Kompany, Hoefkens, Vermaelen, Goor (M. Mpenza 84), Fellaini, Geraerts (Haroun 77), Defour, Mirallas (Vertonghen 63), Dembélé. Coach: René Vandereycken (BEL)
Goal(s): 0-1 Geraerts 13, 0-2 Mirallas 24, 1-2 Byakov 39, 2-2 Smakov 77(p)
Yellow Card(s): Irismetov 42 (Kazakhstan), Defour 51 (Belgium), Fellaini 75 (Belgium)
Referee: Tudor (ROU)

12/9/07, José Alvalade, Lisbon
Portugal 1-1 Serbia
Attendance: 48000
Portugal: Ricardo, Paulo Ferreira, Fernando Meira, Bruno Alves, Petit, Bosingwa, Deco (João Moutinho 77), Maniche (Raul Meireles 83), Cristiano Ronaldo, Nuno Gomes (Ricardo Quaresma 65), Simão. Coach: Luiz Felipe Scolari (BRA)
Serbia: Stojković, Rukavina, Dragutinović, Vidić, Ivanović, Z. Tošić (Žigić 61), Stanković, Kovačević, Krasić (Pantelić 61), Kuzmanović (Duljaj 71), Jovanović. Coach: Javier Clemente (ESP)
Goal(s): 1-0 Simão 11, 1-1 Ivanović 88
Red Card(s): Dragutinović 90+2 (Serbia)
Yellow Card(s): Stojković 36 (Serbia), Dragutinović 51 (Serbia), Vidić 59 (Serbia), Petit 86 (Portugal)
Referee: Merk (GER)

13/10/07, Republican, Yerevan
Armenia 0-0 Serbia
Attendance: 7150
Armenia: Berezovski, Hovsepyan, Arzumanyan, Dokhoyan, Tadevosyan, Pachajyan, Voskanyan (Khachatryan 70), Arakelyan, Art. Karamyan, Mkhitaryan (Ara Hakobyan 82), Melkonyan (Zebelyan 62). Coach: Vardan Minasyan (ARM)
Serbia: Stojković, Rukavina, Ivanović, Stepanov, D. Tošić, Kovačević, Kuzmanović (Z. Tošić 61), Stanković, Krasić (Janković 73), Pantelić (Lazović 62), Žigić. Coach: Javier Clemente (ESP)
Yellow Card(s): Mkhitaryan 23 (Armenia), Arakelyan 37 (Armenia), Stanković 51 (Serbia), Rukavina 60 (Serbia), Stepanov 90 (Serbia)
Referee: Johannesson (SWE)

13/10/07, Legia, Warsaw
Poland 3-1 Kazakhstan
Attendance: 11040
Poland: Boruc, Jop, Bronowicki, Dudka, Bąk, Smolarek, Krzynówek, Saganowski (Żurawski 46), Żewłakow (Wasilewski 46), Łobodziński (Kosowski 80), Lewandowski. Coach: Leo Beenhakker (NED)
Kazakhstan: Loria, Lyapkin, Kuchma, Smakov, Nurdauletov, Skorykh (Karpovich 81), Baltiyev, Zhumaskaliev, Larin (Suyumagambetov 73), Ostapenko, Byakov (Ashirbekov 85). Coach: Arno Pijpers (NED)
Goal(s): 0-1 Byakov 20, 1-1 Smolarek 56, 2-1 Smolarek 65, 3-1 Smolarek 66
Yellow Card(s): Lyapkin 40 (Kazakhstan)
Referee: Berntsen (NOR)

13/10/07, Roi Baudouin, Brussels
Belgium 0-0 Finland
Attendance: 21393
Belgium: Stijnen, Lombaerts, Van Buyten, Kompany, Gillet, Simons, Mudingayi, Haroun (Goor 67), Grégoire (Sonck 67), Mirallas (Sterchele 84), Dembélé. Coach: René Vandereycken (BEL)
Finland: Jääskeläinen, Hyypiä, Pasanen, Tihinen, Kallio, A. Eremenko Jr, R. Eremenko, Riihilahti, Johansson (Kuqi 90), Kolkka, Sjölund (Nurmela 90+2). Coach: Roy Hodgson (ENG)
Yellow Card(s): A. Eremenko Jr 43 (Finland), Mirallas 73 (Belgium)
Referee: Kapitanis (CYP)

13/10/07, Tofikh Bakhramov-Republic Stadium, Baku
Azerbaijan 0-2 Portugal
Attendance: 25000
Azerbaijan: Väliyev, E. Äliyev, S. Abbasov, A. Kärimov, Yunisoğlu, E. Quliyev, Chertoganov, Imamaliyev (Häşimov 7), I. Qurbanov (X. Mämmädov 56), Subašić, Äliyev (A. Qurbanov 73). Coach: Şahin Diniyev (AZE)
Portugal: Ricardo, Bruno Alves, Paulo Ferreira, Miguel (Jorge Ribeiro 75), Ricardo Carvalho, Maniche, Deco, Miguel Veloso, Cristiano Ronaldo, Ricardo Quaresma (Nani 70), Hugo Almeida. Coach: Flávio Teixeira (POR)
Goal(s): 0-1 Bruno Alves 12, 0-2 Hugo Almeida 45

Red Card(s): A. Kärimov 29 (Azerbaijan)
Yellow Card(s): Ricardo 28 (Portugal), Yunisoğlu 66 (Azerbaijan), Jorge Ribeiro 90+3 (Portugal)
Referee: Bebek (CRO)

17/10/07, Tcentralny, Almaty
Kazakhstan 1-2 Portugal
Attendance: 25057
Kazakhstan: Loria, Smakov, Zhalmagambetov, Irismetov, Kuchma, Larin (Lyapkin 37), Skorykh, Karpovich (Nurdauletov 89), Zhumaskaliev, Ostapenko, Byakov. Coach: Arno Pijpers (NED)
Portugal: Ricardo, Miguel, Ricardo Carvalho, Bruno Alves, Paulo Ferreira, Maniche (Nani 59), Deco, Miguel Veloso, Ricardo Quaresma (João Moutinho 85), Hugo Almeida (Makukula 63), Cristiano Ronaldo. Coach: Flávio Teixeira (POR)
Goal(s): 0-1 Makukula 84, 0-2 Cristiano Ronaldo 90+1, 1-2 Byakov 90+3
Yellow Card(s): Karpovich 6 (Kazakhstan), Maniche 33 (Portugal), Irismetov 36 (Kazakhstan), Smakov 40 (Kazakhstan)
Referee: Wegereef (NED)

17/10/07, Roi Baudouin, Brussels
Belgium 3-0 Armenia
Attendance: 14812
Belgium: Stijnen, Lombaerts (Vertonghen 83), Van Buyten (Kompany 60), Simons, Swerts, Defour, Fellaini, Goor, Geraerts, Dembélé, Mirallas (Sonck 46). Coach: René Vandereycken (BEL)
Armenia: Kasparov, Tadevosyan (A. Mkrtchyan 82), Hovsepyan, Arzumanyan, Dokhoyan, Arakelyan, Khachatryan (Aram Hakobyan 57), Pachajyan, Voskanyan, Melkonyan (Zebelyan 70), Art. Karamyan. Coach: Vardan Minasyan (ARM)
Goal(s): 1-0 Sonck 63, 2-0 Dembélé 69, 3-0 Geraerts 76
Yellow Card(s): Swerts 2 (Belgium)
Referee: Valgeirsson (ISL)

17/10/07, Tofikh Bakhramov-Republic Stadium, Baku
Azerbaijan 1-6 Serbia
Attendance: 3100
Azerbaijan: Väliyev (Häsänzadä 45), S. Abbasov, R. Quliyev, Häşimov (Baxşiyev 46), Sultanov (Ismayilov 69), E. Quliyev, A. Qurbanov, Chertoganov, R. Abbasov, Äliyev, Subašić. Coach: Şahin Diniyev (AZE)
Serbia: Stojković, Biševac, Ivanović, Rukavina, D. Tošić, Z. Tošić, Duljaj, Janković (Lazović 68), Kovačević (Smiljanić 65), Kuzmanović, Žigić (Pantelić 73). Coach: Javier Clemente (ESP)
Goal(s): 0-1 D. Tošić 4, 0-2 Žigić 17, 1-2 Äliyev 26, 1-3 Janković 41, 1-4 Žigić 42, 1-5 Smiljanić 75, 1-6 Lazović 81
Yellow Card(s): Sultanov 28 (Azerbaijan), Kuzmanović 37 (Serbia), Baxşiyev 69 (Azerbaijan)
Referee: Einwaller (AUT)

17/11/07, Olympiastadion, Helsinki
Finland 2-1 Azerbaijan
Attendance: 10325
Finland: Jääskeläinen, Pasanen, Hyypiä, Tihinen, Kallio (Väyrynen 66), Kolkka, R. Eremenko (Kuqi 80), Tainio, Sjölund, Forssell, Johansson (Litmanen 59). Coach: Roy Hodgson (ENG)
Azerbaijan: Väliyev, S. Abbasov, Nduka (E. Äliyev 46), Yunisoğlu, Räşad F. Sadiqov, Tağizadä, M. Qurbanov, Subašić, Ramazanov, R. Quliyev (Ladaga 61), Mähärrämov. Coach: Gjokica Hadžievski (MKD)
Goal(s): 0-1 M. Gurbonov 63, 1-1 Forssell 79, 2-1 Kuqi 86
Yellow Card(s): Nduka 23 (Azerbaijan), Yunisoğlu 33 (Azerbaijan), Pasanen 39 (Finland), M. Qurbanov 45 (Azerbaijan), E. Äliyev 54 (Azerbaijan), Subašić 85 (Azerbaijan)
Referee: Hamer (LUX)

17/11/07, Slaski, Chorzow
Poland 2-0 Belgium
Attendance: 41450
Poland: Boruc, Bronowicki, Bąk, Smolarek (Kosowski 85), Krzynówek, Żurawski (Murawski 82), Wasilewski, Żewłakow, Łobodziński (Błaszczykowski 46), Sobolewski, Lewandowski. Coach: Leo Beenhakker (NED)
Belgium: Stijnen, Vertonghen, Van Buyten, Kompany, Gillet, Goor, Haroun (Geraerts 84), Fellaini, Defour (Pieroni 61), Dembélé, Mirallas (Huysegems 76). Coach: René Vandereycken (BEL)
Goal(s): 1-0 Smolarek 45, 2-0 Smolarek 49
Yellow Card(s): Bąk 33 (Poland), Błaszczykowski 90+1 (Poland)
Referee: Larsen (DEN)

17/11/07, Dr. Magalhães Pessoa, Leiria
Portugal 1-0 Armenia
Attendance: 22048
Portugal: Ricardo, Bosingwa, Fernando Meira, Bruno Alves, Marco Caneira, Miguel Veloso, Maniche, Cristiano Ronaldo, Simão (Nani 77), Ricardo Quaresma (Manuel Fernandes 60), Hugo Almeida (Makukula 68). Coach: Flávio Teixeira (POR)
Armenia: Berezovski, Hovsepyan, Arzumanyan, Dokhoyan, Tadevosyan, Arakelyan, Voskanyan, Khachatryan (Mkhitaryan 59), Melkonyan (Manucharyan 63), Pachajyan, Art. Karamyan (A. Mkrtchyan 76). Coach: Vardan Minasyan (ARM)
Goal(s): 1-0 Hugo Almeida 42
Yellow Card(s): Pachajyan 45 (Armenia), Marco Caneira 64 (Portugal), Arzumanyan 70 (Armenia), Bosingwa 78 (Portugal)
Referee: Riley (ENG)

21/11/07, Republican, Yerevan
Armenia 0-1 Kazakhstan
Attendance: 3100
Armenia: Berezovski, Hovsepyan, Arzumanyan, Dokhoyan, Tadevosyan, Arakelyan (Khachatryan 56), Voskanyan (Ghazaryan 80), Art. Karamyan, Mkhitaryan, Pachajyan, Melkonyan (Manucharyan 59). Coach: Vardan Minasyan (ARM)
Kazakhstan: Loria, Nurdauletov, Kuchma, Zhalmagambetov, Irismetov, Baltiyev, Larin (Lyapkin 61), Skorykh, Zhumaskaliev, Ostapenko, Byakov. Coach: Arno Pijpers (NED)
Goal(s): 0-1 Ostapenko 64
Yellow Card(s): Zhalmagambetov 41 (Kazakhstan), Kuchma 63 (Kazakhstan), Ghazaryan 82 (Armenia)
Referee: Fautrel (FRA)

21/11/07, Estádio do Dragão, Porto
Portugal 0-0 Finland
Attendance: 49000
Portugal: Ricardo, Bosingwa, Pepe, Bruno Alves, Marco Caneira, Fernando Meira, Miguel Veloso, Maniche (Raul Meireles 73), Cristiano Ronaldo, Nuno Gomes (Makukula 77), Ricardo Quaresma (Nani 84). Coach: Luiz Felipe Scolari (BRA)
Finland: Jääskeläinen, Hyypiä, Kallio, Pasanen, Tihinen, Heikkinen, Kolkka (Johansson 75), Litmanen (Väyrynen 67), Sjölund, Tainio (R. Eremenko 69), Forssell. Coach: Roy Hodgson (ENG)
Yellow Card(s): Sjölund 39 (Finland), Hyypiä 47 (Finland), Forssell 62 (Finland), Marco Caneira 68 (Portugal), Pasanen 88 (Finland), Makukula 90 (Portugal)
Referee: Michel (SVK)

21/11/07, FK Crvena Zvezda, Belgrade
Serbia 2-2 Poland
Attendance: 3247
Serbia: Avramov, Rukavina, Ivanović, Krstajić (D. Tošić 64), Dragutinović, Kuzmanović, Kovačević, Duljaj (Lazović 46), Krasić (Janković 76), Jovanović, Žigić. Coach: Javier Clemente (ESP)
Poland: Fabiański, Wasilewski, Bąk (Żewłakow 77), Jop, Wawrzyniak, Łobodziński, Lewandowski, Bronowicki, Murawski, Kosowski

(Zahorski 19), Rasiak (Matusiak 46). Coach: Leo Beenhakker (NED)
Goal(s): 0-1 Murawski 28, 0-2 Matusiak 46, 1-2 Žigić 68, 2-2 Lazović 70
Yellow Card(s): Rukavina 30 (Serbia), Wawrzyniak 42 (Poland), Zahorski 43 (Poland), Bąk 72 (Poland), Lazović 88 (Serbia), Žigić 90 (Serbia)
Referee: Busacca (SUI)

21/11/07, Tofikh Bakhramov-Republic Stadium, Baku
Azerbaijan 0-1 Belgium
Attendance: 7000
Azerbaijan: Väliyev, Mälikov, S. Abbasov, Räşad F. Sadiqov, R. Quliyev, M. Qurbanov, A. Kärimov (X. Mämmädov 84), Mähärrämov (Ponomarev 77), Tağizadä (Gomes 70), Ramazanov, Subašić. Coach: Gjokica Hadžievski (MKD)
Belgium: Vandenbussche, Van Damme, Van Buyten, Gillet, Vertonghen, Fellaini, Grégoire (Goor 68), Swerts, Geraerts (Defour 46), Dembélé, Pieroni (Mirallas 81). Coach: René Vandereycken (BEL)
Goal(s): 0-1 Pieroni 52
Yellow Card(s): Tağizadä 27 (Azerbaijan), Geraerts 35 (Belgium), Pieroni 41 (Belgium), Fellaini 81 (Belgium)
Referee: Kenan (ISR)

24/11/07, FK Partizan, Belgrade
Serbia 1-0 Kazakhstan
Attendance: 500
Serbia: Avramov, Stevanović, Anđelković, Duljaj, Kačar, Ivanović, Despotovic, Tutorić, Jovanović (Babović 63), Krasić (Janković 24), Žigić (Fejsa 70). Coach: Javier Clemente (ESP)
Kazakhstan: Loria, Smakov, Skorykh, Zhalmagambetov, Nurdauletov, Lyapkin (Zhumaskaliev 73), Irismetov, Baltiyev (Ashirbekov 86), Karpovich, Byakov, Suyumagambetov (Ostapenko 73). Coach: Arno Pijpers (NED)
Goal(s): 1-0 Ostapenko 79(og)
Yellow Card(s): Krasić 19 (Serbia), Kačar 43 (Serbia), Byakov 68 (Kazakhstan), Baltiyev 86 (Kazakhstan), Zhalmagambetov 90+3 (Kazakhstan), Avramov 90+3 (Serbia)
Referee: Vassaras (GRE)

Group A Table

		Home					Away					Total					
	Pld	W	D	L	F	A	W	D	L	F	A	W	D	L	F	A	Pts
1 Poland	14	5	1	1	15	6	3	3	1	9	6	8	4	2	24	12	28
2 Portugal	14	4	3	0	14	3	3	3	1	10	7	7	6	1	24	10	27
3 Serbia	14	3	4	0	9	3	2	3	2	13	8	6	6	2	22	11	24
4 Finland	14	4	2	1	8	5	2	4	1	5	2	6	6	2	13	7	24
5 Belgium	14	3	2	2	10	5	1	2	4	4	11	5	3	6	14	16	18
6 Kazakhstan	14	1	2	4	7	11	1	3	3	4	10	2	4	8	11	21	10
7 Armenia	12	1	3	2	2	3	1	0	5	2	10	2	3	7	4	13	9
8 Azerbaijan	12	1	2	3	4	13	0	1	5	2	15	1	2	9	6	28	5

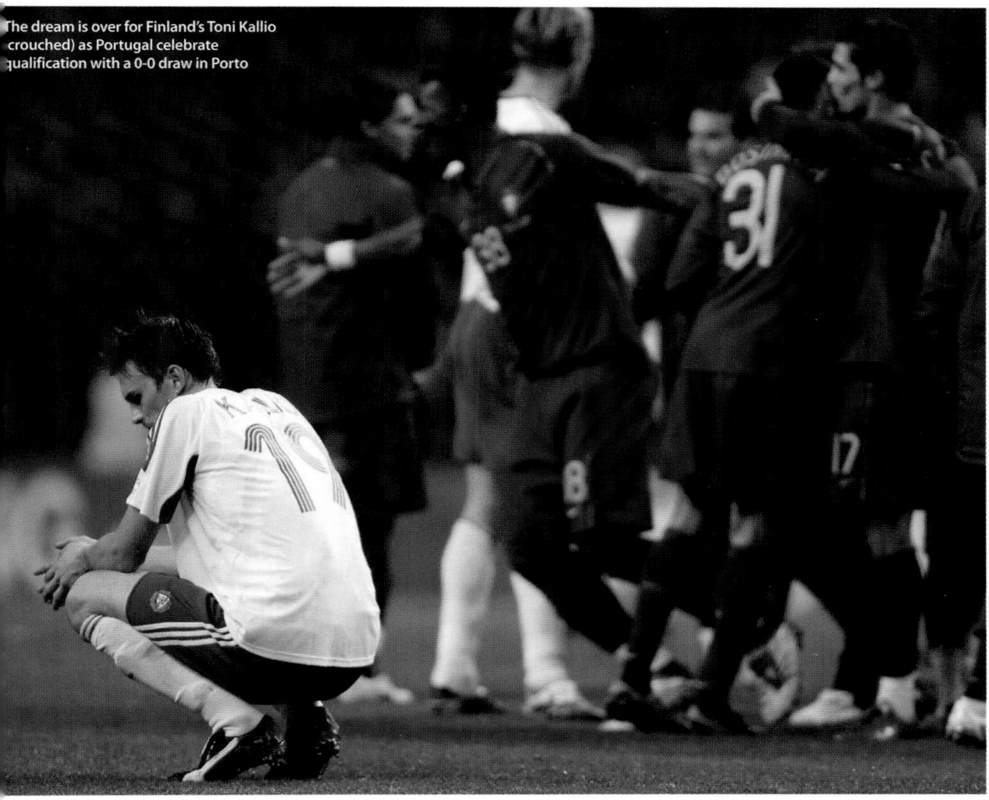

The dream is over for Finland's Toni Kallio (crouched) as Portugal celebrate qualification with a 0-0 draw in Porto

GROUP B

Italy and France's progress to UEFA EURO 2008™ as the top sides in Group B was no great shock, but while both qualified with a game to spare, neither had a straightforward journey through the qualifying maze.

France on top

France looked set to finish top of the section as the qualifying campaign entered its final straight. Having beaten Italy 3-1 at home, they drew 0-0 in Milan in their first game of the autumn to heap further pressure on Azzurri coach Roberto Donadoni, whose side had not dazzled in his first months since replacing Marcello Lippi.

Raymond Domenech's side had little time to rest on their laurels as they looked to avenge a 1-0 defeat against Scotland in their next game in Paris. "They are a team that closes you down all the time, runs for the whole 90 minutes and does not let you develop your game," said defender Claude Makelele ahead of the match.

'Hard to beat'

Sure enough, Scotland threw a spanner in the works for France again, with Alex McLeish earning the same result as his predecessor Walter Smith had against Les Bleus in Glasgow, James McFadden scoring the long-range 64th-minute goal that silenced the Parc des Princes. "To score a goal like that against a team like France is hard to beat," he acknowledged.

Defeat dropped France to third, and for all the clamour that greeted the arrivals of teenagers Samir Nasri and Karim Benzema into the squad, Domenech's side were left in a tricky position with three games left. "We have a gun to our heads," said the coach. "That's good. It's like playing cup matches – if we lose a game, we're out."

Italy recover

Italy, meanwhile, were busy making amends for their shaky start. Four days after their draw with France, a fortunate 2-1 win in Ukraine, with Antonio Di Natale scoring both goals, steadied the ship and a 2-0 win against Georgia returned Italy to second place in the section as they looked ahead to a decisive 17 November trip to Glasgow.

On 17 October, Thierry Henry scored his 42nd and 43rd goals for France in a 2-0 win against Lithuania, beating Michel Platini's record of 41, while the wheels came off Scotland's bandwagon in Tbilisi with a 2-0 defeat against an embryonic Georgia side featuring teenage goalkeeper Giorgi Makaridze and fellow youngsters David Mchelidze and Levan Kenia.

Christian Panucci's late header clinches Italy's qualification a
Scotland's expense in Glasgow

Scene set

The scene was set for the 17 November showdown at Hampden Park. Scotland, playing in their final game, knew a win would send them to the finals. Italy knew defeat could spell disaster, while France – at that point top of the section – knew an Italian triumph would put them through regardless of their result in Ukraine on 21 November.

Domenech imposed a media blackout, saying: "I know exactly where all the television sets are here at Clairefontaine [France's training base] and I will switch them off on Saturday." In doing so, he missed a thrilling finale, with Christian Panucci heading home in added time to give Italy a 2-1 win and send both the world champions and France to UEFA EURO 2008™ at a stroke.

McFadden miss

Panucci declared himself "as happy as a child" after the game as Italy took up their finishing place at the top of the section. However, the hero of Paris – McFadden – was anything but, having missed a great chance moments before the winner. McLeish said: "My life flashed before me and I thought: 'It's the winner'. I can't blame anybody. They've been brilliant for us, the whole bunch of players."

Group B Results

16/8/06
Faroe Islands 0-6 Georgia
Goal(s): 0-1 Mujiri 16, 0-2 Iashvili 18, 0-3 Arveladze 37, 0-4 Kobiashvili 51(p), 0-5 Arveladze 62, 0-6 Arveladze 82

2/9/06
Scotland 6-0 Faroe Islands
Goal(s): 1-0 Fletcher 7, 2-0 McFadden 10, 3-0 Boyd 24(p), 4-0 Miller 30(p), 5-0 Boyd 38, 6-0 O'Connor 85
Georgia 0-3 France
Goal(s): 0-1 Malouda 7, 0-2 Saha 16, 0-3 Asatiani 47(og)
Italy 1-1 Lithuania
Goal(s): 0-1 Danilevičius 21, 1-1 Inzaghi 30

6/9/06
Ukraine 3-2 Georgia
Goal(s): 1-0 Shevchenko 31, 1-1 Arveladze 38, 1-2 Demetradze 61, 2-2 Rotan 61, 3-2 Rusol 80
Lithuania 1-2 Scotland
Goal(s): 0-1 Dailly 46, 0-2 Miller 62, 1-2 Miceika 85
France 3-1 Italy
Goal(s): 1-0 Govou 2, 2-0 Henry 18, 2-1 Gilardino 20, 3-1 Govou 55

7/10/06
Faroe Islands 0-1 Lithuania
Goal(s): 0-1 Skerla 89
Scotland 1-0 France
Goal(s): 1-0 G. Caldwell 67
Italy 2-0 Ukraine
Goal(s): 1-0 Oddo 71(p), 2-0 Toni 79

11/10/06
Ukraine 2-0 Scotland
Goal(s): 1-0 Kucher 60, 2-0 Shevchenko 90(p)
France 5-0 Faroe Islands
Goal(s): 1-0 Saha 1, 2-0 Henry 22, 3-0 Anelka 77, 4-0 Trezeguet 78, 5-0 Trezeguet 84
Georgia 1-3 Italy
Goal(s): 0-1 De Rossi 18, 1-1 Shashiashvili 26, 1-2 Camoranesi 63, 1-3 Perrotta 71

24/3/07
Scotland 2-1 Georgia
Goal(s): 1-0 Boyd 11, 1-1 Arveladze 41, 2-1 Beattie 89
Faroe Islands 0-2 Ukraine
Goal(s): 0-1 Yezerskiy 20, 0-2 Gusev 57
Lithuania 0-1 France
Goal(s): 0-1 Anelka 73

28/3/07
Ukraine 1-0 Lithuania
Goal(s): 1-0 Gusev 47
Georgia 3-1 Faroe Islands
Goal(s): 1-0 Siradze 26, 2-0 Iashvili 45+1, 2-1 R. Jacobsen 56, 3-1 Iashvili 90+2(p)
Italy 2-0 Scotland
Goal(s): 1-0 Toni 12, 2-0 Toni 70

2/6/07
Faroe Islands 1-2 Italy
Goal(s): 0-1 Inzaghi 12, 0-2 Inzaghi 48, 1-2 R. Jacobsen 77
Lithuania 1-0 Georgia
Goal(s): 1-0 Mikoliūnas 78
France 2-0 Ukraine
Goal(s): 1-0 Ribéry 57, 2-0 Anelka 71

6/6/07
Faroe Islands 0-2 Scotland
Goal(s): 0-1 Maloney 31, 0-2 O'Connor 35
France 1-0 Georgia
Goal(s): 1-0 Nasri 33
Lithuania 0-2 Italy
Goal(s): 0-1 Quagliarella 31, 0-2 Quagliarella 45

8/9/07, Hampden Park, Glasgow
Scotland 3-1 Lithuania
Attendance: 52063
Scotland: Gordon, Hutton, Weir, McManus, McEveley, Teale (McFadden 69), Brown, Fletcher, McCulloch (Maloney 76), Boyd, O'Connor (Beattie 76). Coach: Alex McLeish (SCO)
Lithuania: Karčemarskas, M. Stankevičius (Jankauskas 56), Skerla, Žvirgždauskas, Klimavičius, Šemberas, Kalonas, D. Česnauskis, Morinas (Mikoliūnas 46), Danilevičius, Velička (Kšanavičius 46). Coach: Algimantas Liubinskas (LTU)
Goal(s): 1-0 Boyd 31, 1-1 Danilevičius 61(p), 2-1 McManus 77, 3-1 McFadden 85
Yellow Card(s): Velička 21 (Lithuania), M. Stankevičius 35 (Lithuania), Karčemarskas 40 (Lithuania), O'Connor 42 (Scotland), Žvirgždauskas 57 (Lithuania), Kšanavičius 64 (Lithuania), Hutton 77 (Scotland), Fletcher 87 (Scotland)
Referee: Skomina (SVN)

8/9/07, Boris Paichadze, Tbilisi
Georgia 1-1 Ukraine
Attendance: 24000
Georgia: Lomaia, Gvinianidze, Kaladze, Asatiani, Salukvadze, Tskitishvili, Menteshashvili (Tatanashvili 79), Jakobia (Siradze 62), Demetradze, Iashvili (Kenia 62), Martsvaladze. Coach: Klaus

Toppmöller (GER)
Ukraine: Shovkovskiy, Yezerskiy, Rusol, Kucher, Tymoshchuk, Rotan (Hai 80), Nazarenko, Gusev, Shelayev (Hladkiy 88), Shevchenko, Voronin (Kalynychenko 72). Coach: Oleh Blokhin (UKR)
Goal(s): 0-1 Shelayev 7, 1-1 Siradze 89
Yellow Card(s): Iashvili 51 (Georgia), Tskitishvili 63 (Georgia), Rotan 67 (Ukraine), Gvinianidze 89 (Georgia), Shevchenko 90 (Ukraine)
Referee: Hamer (LUX)

8/9/07, Stadio Giuseppe Meazza, Milan
Italy 0-0 France
Attendance: 81200
Italy: Buffon, Oddo, Cannavaro, Barzagli, Zambrotta, De Rossi, Gattuso, Pirlo, Camoranesi (Perrotta 58), Del Piero (Di Natale 83), Inzaghi (Lucarelli 65). Coach: Roberto Donadoni (ITA)
France: Landreau, Diarra, Thuram, Escudé, Abidal, Ribéry (Toulalan 86), Makelele, Vieira, Malouda, Henry, Anelka. Coach: Pierre Mankowski (FRA)
Yellow Card(s): Makelele 7 (France), Gattuso 31 (Italy), Henry 56 (France), De Rossi 86 (Italy)
Referee: Michěl (SVK)

12/9/07, S. Darius & S. Girenas, Kaunas
Lithuania 2-1 Faroe Islands
Attendance: 5500
Lithuania: Karčemarskas, Šemberas, Klimavičius, Skerla, Alunderis, Ivaškevičius, Mikoliūnas (Velička 32), D. Česnauskis (Kalonas 31), Kšanavičius, Jankauskas (Kučys 86), Danilevičius. Coach: Algimantas Liubinskas (LTU)
Faroe Islands: Mikkelsen, Benjaminsen, Danielsen, Holst (H.P. Samuelsen 74), J.R. Jacobsen, Thomassen, S. Samuelsen, C.H. Jacobsen (Fløtum 84), S. Olsen (P. Hansen 63), Borg, R. Jacobsen. Coach: Jógvan Martin Olsen (FRO)
Goal(s): 1-0 Jankauskas 8, 2-0 Danilevičius 53, 2-1 R. Jacobsen 90+3
Yellow Card(s): S. Olsen 35 (Faroe Islands), Danielsen 49 (Faroe Islands), Kučys 90+1 (Lithuania)
Referee: Georgiev (BUL)

12/9/07, Parc des Princes, Paris
France 0-1 Scotland
Attendance: 43342
France: Landreau, Diarra, Thuram, Escudé, Abidal (Benzema 77), Ribéry, Vieira (Nasri 69), Makelele, Malouda, Trezeguet, Anelka. Coach: Raymond Domenech (FRA)
Scotland: Gordon, Hutton, McManus, Weir, G. Alexander, McCulloch, Ferguson, Fletcher (Pearson 26), Brown, Hartley, McFadden (O'Connor 76). Coach: Alex McLeish (SCO)
Goal(s): 0-1 McFadden 64
Yellow Card(s): Vieira 22 (France), Fletcher 24 (Scotland), Hartley 58 (Scotland), Nasri 74 (France)
Referee: Plautz (AUT)

12/9/07, NSC Olympiyskiy Stadium, Kiev
Ukraine 1-2 Italy
Attendance: 41500
Ukraine: Shovkovskiy, Kucher, Yezerskiy, Rusol, Shelayev, Gusev (Milevskiy 88), Kalynychenko (Voronin 60), Tymoshchuk, Hai, Nazarenko (Hladkiy 69), Shevchenko. Coach: Oleh Blokhin (UKR)
Italy: Buffon, Panucci, Cannavaro, Barzagli, Zambrotta, Camoranesi (Oddo 78), Ambrosini, Pirlo, Perrotta (Aquilani 68), Iaquinta (Quagliarella 85), Di Natale. Coach: Roberto Donadoni (ITA)
Goal(s): 0-1 Di Natale 41, 1-1 Shevchenko 71, 1-2 Di Natale 77
Yellow Card(s): Cannavaro 28 (Italy), Perrotta 47 (Italy), Rusol 88 (Ukraine), Aquilani 90 (Italy)
Referee: Webb (ENG)

13/10/07, Hampden Park, Glasgow
Scotland 3-1 Ukraine

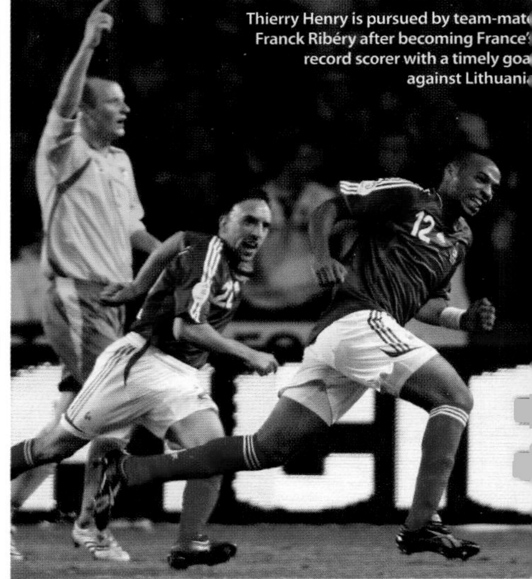
Thierry Henry is pursued by team-mate Franck Ribéry after becoming France's record scorer with a timely goal against Lithuania

Attendance: 52063
Scotland: Gordon, Hutton, Weir, McManus, Naysmith, Brown (Maloney 76), Ferguson, Pearson, McCulloch (Dailly 60), McFadden (O'Connor 80), Miller. Coach: Alex McLeish (SCO)
Ukraine: Shovkovskiy, Nesmachniy, Yezerskiy, Chyhrynskiy, Kucher, Gusev (Rotan 46), Tymoshchuk (Shelayev 73), Hladkiy, Vorobei (Nazarenko 62), Shevchenko, Voronin. Coach: Oleh Blokhin (UKR)
Goal(s): 1-0 Miller 4, 2-0 McCulloch 10, 2-1 Shevchenko 24, 3-1 McFadden 68
Yellow Card(s): Nesmachniy 3 (Ukraine), Shevchenko 15 (Ukraine), Vorobei 37 (Ukraine), McCulloch 45+4 (Scotland), Ferguson 45+4 (Scotland), Rotan 70 (Ukraine), Miller 72 (Scotland), O'Connor 89 (Scotland)
Referee: Vink (NED)

13/10/07, Tórsvøllur, Torshavn
Faroe Islands 0-6 France
Attendance: 1980
Faroe Islands: Mikkelsen, C.H. Jacobsen, J.R. Jacobsen, Benjaminsen, Hansen, S. Samuelsen (Fløtum 86), S. Olsen, Thomassen (Jespersen 78), Elttør (Midjord 46), R. Jacobsen, Holst. Coach: Jógvan Martin Olsen (FRO)
France: Landreau, Sagna, Abidal, Thuram, Evra, Rothen, Makelele (Diarra 73), Toulalan, Ribéry (Ben Arfa 64), Anelka (Benzema 46), Henry. Coach: Raymond Domenech (FRA)
Goal(s): 0-1 Anelka 6, 0-2 Henry 8, 0-3 Benzema 50, 0-4 Rothen 66, 0-5 Benzema 81, 0-6 Ben Arfa 90+4
Yellow Card(s): S. Olsen 57 (Faroe Islands)
Referee: Rossi (SMR)

13/10/07, Luigi Ferraris, Genoa
Italy 2-0 Georgia
Attendance: 23057
Italy: Buffon, Oddo, Panucci, Barzagli, Grosso, Pirlo, Gattuso, Ambrosini (Mauri 88), Quagliarella (Foggia 72), Di Natale, Toni. Coach: Roberto Donadoni (ITA)
Georgia: Lomaia, Shashiashvili (Siradze 60), Salukvadze, Asatiani, Khizanishvili, Kvirkvelia, Tskitishvili, Menteshashvili, Kankava, Mchedlidze (Kenia 60), Demetradze (Jakobia 85). Coach: Klaus

Toppmöller (GER)
Goal(s): 1-0 Pirlo 44, 2-0 Grosso 84
Yellow Card(s): Demetradze 41 (Georgia), Oddo 68 (Italy), Kvirkvelia 79 (Georgia)
Referee: Megía Dávila (ESP)

17/10/07, NSC Olympiyskiy Stadium, Kiev
Ukraine 5-0 Faroe Islands
Attendance: 5000
Ukraine: Pyatov, Nesmachniy, Rusol, Chyhrynskiy, Hai, Nazarenko, Tymoshchuk (Hrytsai 69), Gusev (Vorobei 62), Kalynychenko, Hladkiy (Milevskiy 46), Voronin. Coach: Oleh Blokhin (UKR)
Faroe Islands: Mikkelsen, Danielsen, Hansen, Ó. Hansen, J.R. Jacobsen, Davidsen, Thomassen (T. Hansen 8), Holst (Fløtum 75), C.H. Jacobsen (Thorleifsson 89), S. Samuelsen, R. Jacobsen. Coach: Jógvan Martin Olsen (FRO)
Goal(s): 1-0 Kalynychenko 40, 2-0 Gusev 43, 3-0 Gusev 45, 4-0 Kalynychenko 49, 5-0 Vorobei 64
Referee: Jakov (ISR)

17/10/07, Boris Paichadze, Tbilisi
Georgia 2-0 Scotland
Attendance: 29377
Georgia: Makaridze, Shashiashvili, Asatiani, Salukvadze, Khizanishvili, Kankava, Menteshashvili, Kenia (Kandelaki 79), Kvirkvelia, Siradze (Jakobia 89), Mchedlidze (Kvakhadze 85). Coach: Klaus Toppmöller (GER)
Scotland: Gordon, Murty, McManus, Weir, G. Alexander, Fletcher, Ferguson, Pearson (Boyd 66), Maloney, Miller (Beattie 66), McFadden. Coach: Alex McLeish (SCO)
Goal(s): 1-0 Mchedlidze 16, 2-0 Siradze 64
Yellow Card(s): McManus 61 (Scotland), Kankava 61 (Georgia), Beattie 72 (Scotland), Asatiani 90+5 (Georgia)
Referee: Kircher (GER)

17/10/07, La Beaujoire, Nantes
France 2-0 Lithuania
Attendance: 36650
France: Landreau, Diarra (Ben Arfa 69), Thuram, Gallas, Abidal, Toulalan, Makelele, Malouda, Ribéry, Henry, Benzema. Coach: Raymond Domenech (FRA)
Lithuania: Karčemarskas, Klimavičius, Dedura, Skerla, Žvirgždauskas, Kučys (Velička 84), Kšanavičius (Labukas 77), Kalonas (Savėnas 63), Morinas, Danilevičius, Jankauskas. Coach: Algimantas Liubinskas (LTU)
Goal(s): 1-0 Henry 80, 2-0 Henry 81
Yellow Card(s): Kšanavičius 34 (Lithuania), Kučys 53 (Lithuania), Dedura 80 (Lithuania)
Referee: Kassai (HUN)

17/11/07, Hampden Park, Glasgow
Scotland 1-2 Italy
Attendance: 51301
Scotland: Gordon, Hutton, Weir, McManus, Naysmith, Brown (Miller 74), Fletcher, Hartley, Ferguson, McCulloch (Boyd 90+2), McFadden. Coach: Alex McLeish (SCO)
Italy: Buffon, Panucci, Cannavaro, Barzagli, Zambrotta, Camoranesi (Chiellini 83), Gattuso (De Rossi 87), Pirlo, Ambrosini, Di Natale (Iaquinta 68), Toni. Coach: Roberto Donadoni (ITA)
Goal(s): 0-1 Toni 2, 1-1 Ferguson 65, 1-2 Panucci 90+1
Yellow Card(s): Naysmith 34 (Scotland), McCulloch 44 (Scotland), Toni 45 (Italy)
Referee: Mejuto González (ESP)

17/11/07, S. Darius & S. Girenas, Kaunas
Lithuania 2-0 Ukraine
Attendance: 3000
Lithuania: Karčemarskas, Paulauskas, Klimavičius, M. Stankevičius, Dedura, Skerla, Žvirgždauskas, Papečkys (Morinas 17), Savėnas, Danilevičius (Velička 82), Jankauskas (Kalonas 90). Coach: Algimantas Liubinskas (LTU)
Ukraine: Shovkovskiy (Pyatov 44), Chyhrynskiy, Vaschuk, Shelayev (Nazarenko 72), Yezerskiy, Hai, Tymoshchuk, Gusev, Rotan, Shevchenko, Voronin (Milevskiy 69). Coach: Oleh Blokhin (UKR)
Goal(s): 1-0 Savėnas 41, 2-0 Danilevičius 67
Yellow Card(s): Klimavičius 65 (Lithuania), Danilevičius 75 (Lithuania), Shevchenko 80 (Ukraine)
Referee: Malcolm (NIR)

21/11/07, Boris Paichadze, Tbilisi
Georgia 0-2 Lithuania
Attendance: 21300
Georgia: Makaridze, Salukvadze, Asatiani, Kaladze, Kvirkvelia, Kankava, Tskitishvili, Menteshashvili (Martsvaladze 31), Kenia, Mchedlidze, Siradze (Gelashvili 80). Coach: Klaus Toppmöller (GER)
Lithuania: Karčemarskas, M. Stankevičius, Žvirgždauskas, Skerla, Paulauskas, Dedura, Alunderis, Kšanavičius, Savėnas (Kalonas 67), Mikoliūnas (Morinas 76), Jankauskas (Velička 52). Coach: Algimantas Liubinskas (LTU)
Goal(s): 0-1 Kšanavičius 52, 0-2 Kšanavičius 90+6
Yellow Card(s): Jankauskas 35 (Lithuania), Mikoliūnas 76 (Lithuania), Karčemarskas 83 (Lithuania), Kšanavičius 90+3 (Lithuania)
Referee: Stavrev (MKD)

21/11/07, Alberto Braglia, Modena
Italy 3-1 Faroe Islands
Attendance: 16142
Italy: Amelia, Oddo, Cannavaro (Bonera 53), Chiellini, Grosso, De Rossi, Ambrosini (Quagliarella 58), Perrotta, Iaquinta, Palladino, Toni (Gilardino 74). Coach: Roberto Donadoni (ITA)
Faroe Islands: Mikkelsen, Davidsen, Benjaminsen, J.R. Jacobsen, Hansen, Danielsen, S. Olsen, R. Jacobsen, S. Samuelsen (Thorleifsson 75), C.H. Jacobsen, Holst (Fløtum 86). Coach: Jógvan Martin Olsen (FRO)
Goal(s): 1-0 Benjaminsen 11(og), 2-0 Toni 36, 3-0 Chiellini 41, 3-1 R. Jacobsen 83
Referee: Meyer (GER)

21/11/07, NSC Olympiyskiy Stadium, Kiev
Ukraine 2-2 France
Attendance: 7800
Ukraine: Pyatov, Vaschuk, Hrytsai, Romanchuk (Yezerskiy 81), Fedorov, Tymoshchuk, Gusev (Milevskiy 90+1), Rotan, Hai, Shevchenko, Voronin (Shelayev 85). Coach: Oleh Blokhin (UKR)
France: Frey, Clerc, Gallas, Thuram, Abidal, Ribéry (Ben Arfa 89), Makelele, Diarra, Govou, Henry, Benzema (Nasri 46). Coach: Raymond Domenech (FRA)
Goal(s): 1-0 Voronin 14, 1-1 Henry 20, 1-2 Govou 34, 2-2 Shevchenko 46
Yellow Card(s): Govou 53 (France), Hai 84 (Ukraine)
Referee: Øvrebø (NOR)

Group B Table

		Home					Away					Total					
	Pld	W	D	L	F	A	W	D	L	F	A	W	D	L	F	A	Pts
1 Italy	12	3	3	0	10	2	4	1	1	12	7	9	2	1	22	9	29
2 France	12	5	1	0	13	2	3	2	1	12	3	8	2	2	25	5	26
3 Scotland	12	5	0	1	16	5	2	1	3	5	7	8	0	4	21	12	24
4 Ukraine	12	4	2	0	14	6	1	1	4	4	10	5	2	5	18	16	17
5 Lithuania	12	3	0	3	6	6	2	1	3	5	7	5	1	6	11	13	16
6 Georgia	12	2	1	3	7	10	1	0	5	9	9	3	1	8	16	19	10
7 Faroe Islands	12	0	0	6	1	19	0	1	5	3	24	0	0	12	4	43	0

GROUP C

Greece went into the summer of 2007 with their lead at the top of Group C looking fragile, but they would end the campaign with the highest points total of any side in the competition, 31, while Turkey won a closely fought contest with Norway for second place.

Greek recovery

A 4-1 home defeat against Turkey early in the campaign seemed to suggest another disappointment was imminent for the heroes of UEFA EURO 2004™, with Otto Rehhagel's men still smarting from having missed out on the 2006 FIFA World Cup. However, they got their house in order, and a 2-2 draw against in-form Norway in their first autumn fixture set the tone.

Norway had gone into the summer level on points with both Turkey and Bosnia-Herzegovina, and with home games against both Greece and Turkey to come had reason for hope. Bosnia-Herzegovina – 2-1 winners in Oslo in the spring – also looked lively, but their challenge was to wilt grievously, with coach Fuad Muzurović being sacked after his side lost all five of their autumn fixtures.

Malta upset

Turkey looked set to have a miserable autumn too as their first match after the restart ended in a 2-2 draw against Malta. "I told my players that if we scored first we would not lose," Malta coach Dušan Fitzel said. "I firmly believe that we could have won the match had luck been on our side."

Greece, the reigning European champions, are through to the finals after victory in Turkey

Worse was to come for Turkey. After a 3-0 win against Hungary, they were held to a 1-1 draw against Moldova four days before hosting Greece in Istanbul. "Games we once called easy are not easy any more," said Turkey coach Fatih Terim. "In fact, the hard matches come easier to us. I have confidence in my players."

Rehhagel proud

That confidence proved to be misplaced. Ioannis Amanatidis scored the only goal of the game eleven minutes from time to send Greece to the finals. "Before the game I told my players they had a unique opportunity to take revenge for our defeat in Piraeus and to qualify for the finals," said Rehhagel. "We played a passionate and intelligent game. We went for the win and got it."

That result handed the initiative to Norway ahead of their final games, at home against Turkey and away to Malta. Two points behind Norway, Turkey remained defiant, although their coach admitted: "We had planned to be four points clear of Norway at this stage but some unwanted results have put us in a different situation."

Hareide devastated

The big game in Oslo on 17 November started badly for Turkey, with Erik Hagen giving Norway a 12th-minute lead, but goals from Emre Belözoglu and Nihat Kahveci settled the match in their favour. Norway coach Åge Hareide was devastated, saying: "I reached a new low after the game. Few words were exchanged in the dressing room; we all knew we had let everybody down."

Turkey, meanwhile, were celebrating a famous rescue mission. "I think we like to do it the hard way," joked Terim. His side needed a win in their final game against Bosnia-Herzegovina to put Norway out of their misery, but with fans answering Terim's call for "real passionate Turkish supporters" in Istanbul, Nihat's goal secured the necessary 1-0 win.

Terim's pledge

"Had we missed our chance, someone would have had to take responsibility and I would have done so," concluded Terim. "But now we are through, I will be with my team. I made a promise that we would qualify and make a significant contribution at the finals. The first part of that mission is accomplished – now it's time to focus on the second."

Nihat Kahveci scores the goal against Bosnia-Herzegovina that sends Turkey through to the finals

Group C Results

2/9/06

Malta 2-5 Bosnia-Herzegovina
Goal(s): 0-1 Barbarez 4, 1-1 Pace 6, 1-2 Hrgović 10, 1-3 Bartolović 45+1, 1-4 Muslimović 48, 1-5 Misimović 51, 2-5 M. Mifsud 85
Hungary 1-4 Norway
Goal(s): 0-1 Solskjær 15, 0-2 Strømstad 32, 0-3 Gamst Pedersen 41, 0-4 Solskjær 54, 1-4 Gera 90(p)
Moldova 0-1 Greece
Goal(s): 0-1 Liberopoulos 77

6/9/06

Norway 2-0 Moldova
Goal(s): 1-0 Strømstad 73, 2-0 Iversen 79
Turkey 2-0 Malta
Goal(s): 1-0 Nihat Kahveci 56, 2-0 Tümer Metin 77
Bosnia-Herzegovina 1-3 Hungary
Goal(s): 0-1 Huszti 36(p), 0-2 Gera 46, 0-3 Dárdai 49, 1-3 Misimović 64

7/10/06

Moldova 2-2 Bosnia-Herzegovina
Goal(s): 1-0 Rogaciov 13, 2-0 Rogaciov 32(p), 2-1 Misimović 62, 2-2 Grlić 68
Hungary 0-1 Turkey
Goal(s): 0-1 Tuncay Şanlı 41
Greece 1-0 Norway
Goal(s): 1-0 Katsouranis 33

11/10/06

Malta 2-1 Hungary
Goal(s): 1-0 Schembri 14, 1-1 Torghelle 19, 2-1 Schembri 53
Turkey 5-0 Moldova
Goal(s): 1-0 Hakan Şükür 35, 2-0 Hakan Şükür 37(p), 3-0 Hakan Şükür 43, 4-0 Tuncay Şanlı 68, 5-0 Hakan Şükür 73
Bosnia-Herzegovina 0-4 Greece
Goal(s): 0-1 Charisteas 8(p), 0-2 Patsatzoglou 82, 0-3 Samaras 85, 0-4 Katsouranis 90+4

24/3/07

Moldova 1-1 Malta
Goal(s): 0-1 Mallia 73, 1-1 Epureanu 85
Norway 1-2 Bosnia-Herzegovina
Goal(s): 0-1 Misimović 18, 0-2 Damjanović 33, 1-2 Carew 50(p)
Greece 1-4 Turkey
Goal(s): 1-0 Kyrgiakos 5, 1-1 Tuncay Şanlı 27, 1-2 Gökhan Ünal 55, 1-3 Tümer Metin 70, 1-4 Gökdeniz Karadeniz 81

28/3/07

Hungary 2-0 Moldova
Goal(s): 1-0 Priskin 9, 2-0 Gera 63
Malta 0-1 Greece
Goal(s): 0-1 Basinas 66(p)
Turkey 2-2 Norway
Goal(s): 0-1 Brenne 31, 0-2 Andresen 40, 1-2 Hamit Altıntop 72, 2-2 Hamit Altıntop 90

2/6/07

Bosnia-Herzegovina 3-2 Turkey
Goal(s): 0-1 Hakan Şükür 13, 1-1 Muslimović 27, 1-2 Sabri Sarıoğlu 39, 2-2 Džeko 45+2, 3-2 Čustović 90
Norway 4-0 Malta
Goal(s): 1-0 Hæstad 31, 2-0 Helstad 73, 3-0 Iversen 79, 4-0 Riise J.A. 90+1
Greece 2-0 Hungary
Goal(s): 1-0 Gekas 16, 2-0 Seitaridis 29

6/6/07

Norway 4-0 Hungary
Goal(s): 1-0 Iversen 22, 2-0 Braaten 57, 3-0 Carew 60, 4-0 Carew 78
Bosnia-Herzegovina 1-0 Malta
Goal(s): 1-0 Muslimović 6
Greece 2-1 Moldova
Goal(s): 1-0 Charisteas 30, 1-1 Frunza 80, 2-1 Liberopoulos 90+3

8/9/07, Sóstói, Szekesfehervar

Hungary 1-0 Bosnia-Herzegovina
Attendance: 10773
Hungary: Fülöp, Vanczák, Vaskó, Juhász, Szélesi, Vass, Tőzsér, Gera, Hajnal (Csizmadia 72), Dzsudzsák (Halmosi 90+3), Feczesin (Filkor 89). Coach: Peter Várhidi (HUN)
Bosnia-Herzegovina: Gušo, Berberović, Bajić, Radeljić, Maletić (Božić 79), Rahimić, Misimović, Hrgović (Čustović 84), Muslimović, Ibišević (Džeko 67), Blatnjak. Coach: Fuad Muzurović (BIH)
Goal(s): 1-0 Gera 39(p)
Yellow Card(s): Vaskó 16 (Hungary), Misimović 19 (Bosnia-Herzegovina), Rahimić 25 (Bosnia-Herzegovina), Bajić 38 (Bosnia-Herzegovina), Hrgović 45 (Bosnia-Herzegovina), Juhász 64 (Hungary)
Referee: Trefoloni (ITA)

8/9/07, Ta' Qali, Ta' Qali

Malta 2-2 Turkey
Attendance: 10500
Malta: Haber, Azzopardi, Said, Dimech, Agius, Briffa (Sammut 88), M. Mifsud, Woods (Mallia 83), Schembri (Scerri 90+1), Scicluna, Pace. Coach: Dušan Fitzel (CZE)
Turkey: Hakan Arıkan, Servet Çetin, İbrahim Toraman, Hamit Altıntop, İbrahim Üzülmez, Sabri Sarıoğlu (Gökdeniz Karadeniz 52), Emre Belözoğlu, Arda Turan (Ayhan Akman 30), Tuncay Şanlı (Deniz Barış 66), Halil Altıntop, Hakan Şükür. Coach: Fatih Terim (TUR)
Goal(s): 1-0 Said 41, 1-1 Halil Altıntop 45, 2-1 Schembri 76, 2-2 Servet Çetin 78
Yellow Card(s): Pace 33 (Malta), Schembri 37 (Malta), Said 51 (Malta), Ayhan Akman 63 (Turkey), Agius 82 (Malta), İbrahim Toraman 86 (Turkey)
Referee: Messner (AUT)

8/9/07, Zimbru, Chisinau

Moldova 0-1 Norway
Attendance: 10173

Moldova: Pascenco, Olexici (Rogaciov 78), Rebeja, Epureanu, Lascencov, Bordian, Gatcan, Zmeu (Suvorov 65), Comleonoc, Bugaiov, Frunza. Coach: Igor Dobrovolsky (MDA)
Norway: Opdal, Storbæk, Wæhler (Riseth 66), Hangeland, J.A. Riise, B.H. Riise, Andresen, Grindheim, Iversen (Helstad 68), Carew, Gamst Pedersen. Coach: Åge Hareide (NOR)
Goal(s): 0-1 Iversen 48
Yellow Card(s): Frunza 67 (Moldova)
Referee: Malek (POL)

12/9/07, Ullevaal, Oslo
Norway 2-2 Greece
Attendance: 24080
Norway: Opdal, Hagen, Hangeland, Andresen, Riise, Gamst Pedersen, B.H. Riise (Kippe 90+3), Solli (Helstad 70), Storbæk, Carew, Iversen (Riseth 80). Coach: Åge Hareide (NOR)
Greece: Chalkias, Seitaridis (Antzas 64), Patsatzoglou, Kyrgiakos, Dellas, Basinas (Samaras 76), Karagounis, Torosidis, Katsouranis, Salpingidis (Liberopoulos 46), Gekas. Coach: Otto Rehhagel (GER)
Goal(s): 0-1 Kyrgiakos 7, 1-1 Carew 15, 1-2 Kyrgiakos 30, 2-2 Riise 39
Yellow Card(s): Dellas 17 (Greece), Seitaridis 35 (Greece), Chalkias 52 (Greece), Carew 67 (Norway), Gekas 74 (Greece), Samaras 89 (Greece)
Referee: Busacca (SUI)

12/9/07, Koševo, Sarajevo
Bosnia-Herzegovina 0-1 Moldova
Attendance: 2000
Bosnia-Herzegovina: Gušo, Berberović, Bajić, Nadarević, Radeljić (Ibišević 46), Rahimić, Maletić (Ćustović 78), Zeba (Damjanović 47), Blatnjak, Muslimović, Džeko. Coach: Fuad Muzurović (BIH)
Moldova: Calancea, Epureanu, Lascencov, Golovatenco, Rebeja, Comleonoc (Se. Namasco 63), Corneencov, Gatcan (Josan 85), Bordian, Bugaiov, Doros (Rogaciov 73). Coach: Igor Dobrovolsky (MDA)
Goal(s): 0-1 Bugaev 22
Yellow Card(s): Gušo 10 (Bosnia-Herzegovina), Corneencov 17 (Moldova), Lascencov 78 (Moldova), Bugaiov 89 (Moldova)
Referee: Hyytiä (FIN)

12/9/07, Inönü, Istanbul
Turkey 3-0 Hungary
Attendance: 28020
Turkey: Hakan Arıkan, Emre Aşık, Hamit Altıntop, Servet Çetin, İbrahim Üzülmez, Mehmet Aurélio, Gökdeniz Karadeniz (Halil Altıntop 61), Ayhan Akman (Serdar Özkan 67), Tuncay Şanlı, Gökhan Ünal, Nihat Kahveci (Emre Belözoğlu 46). Coach: Fatih Terim (TUR)
Hungary: Fülöp (Balogh 71), Juhász, Szélesi, Vanczák, Csizmadia, Vaskó, Vass, Gera, Dzsudzsák (Halmosi 82), Hajnal, Priskin (Tóth 66). Coach: Peter Várhidi (HUN)
Goal(s): 1-0 Gökhan 68, 2-0 Aurelio 72, 3-0 Halil Altıntop 90+3
Red Card(s): Gera 63 (Hungary)
Yellow Card(s): Gera 19 (Hungary), Hamit Altıntop 23 (Turkey), Priskin 26 (Hungary), Vanczák 39 (Hungary), Gera 63 (Hungary), Hajnal 90 (Hungary)
Referee: Dougal (SCO)

13/10/07, Megyeri úti, Budapest
Hungary 2-0 Malta
Attendance: 7633
Hungary: Fülöp, Szélesi, Vaskó, Juhász, Balogh, Vass, Tőzsér, Gera, Filkor (Buzsáky 75), Feczesin (Rajczi 83), Dzsudzsák (Leandro 88). Coach: Peter Várhidi (HUN)
Malta: Haber, Azzopardi, Said, Scicluna, Dimech, Briffa, Sammut (Nwoko 66), Mallia, M. Mifsud, Woods (R. Bajada 90+1), Schembri (Scerri 83). Coach: Dušan Fitzel (CZE)
Goal(s): 1-0 Feczesin 34, 2-0 Tőzsér 78
Yellow Card(s): Woods 9 (Malta), Juhász 52 (Hungary)
Referee: Nalbandyan (ARM)

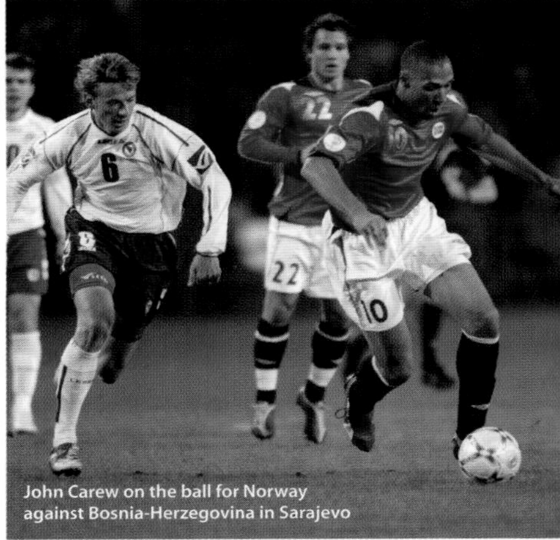
John Carew on the ball for Norway against Bosnia-Herzegovina in Sarajevo

13/10/07, Zimbru, Chisinau
Moldova 1-1 Turkey
Attendance: 9815
Moldova: Calancea, Golovatenco, Epureanu, Savinov, Corneencov, Bordian, Josan, Zmeu (Se. Namasco 67), Gatcan (Olexici 89), Comleonoc, Frunza (Calincov 86). Coach: Igor Dobrovolsky (MDA)
Turkey: Hakan Arıkan (Volkan Demirel 17), Servet Çetin, Gökhan Zan, İbrahim Üzülmez, Emre Belözoğlu, Mehmet Topuz, Mehmet Aurélio, Arda Turan (Tümer Metin 69), Selçuk İnan (Ümit Karan 46), Tuncay Şanlı, Gökhan Ünal. Coach: Fatih Terim (TUR)
Goal(s): 1-0 Frunza 11, 1-1 Ümit Karan 63
Yellow Card(s): Gökhan Zan 29 (Turkey), Epureanu 65 (Moldova)
Referee: Atkinson (ENG)

13/10/07, OACA Spyro Louis, Athens
Greece 3-2 Bosnia-Herzegovina
Attendance: 30250
Greece: Nikopolidis, Dellas, Kyrgiakos, Patsatzoglou, Torosidis, Basinas, Karagounis, Katsouranis, Amanatidis (Giannakopoulos 70), Gekas (Antzas 81), Charisteas (Liberopoulos 69). Coach: Otto Rehhagel (GER)
Bosnia-Herzegovina: Gušo, Berberović, Bajić, Nadarević, Krunić (Ibišević 46), Misimović (Salihović 82), Hrgović, Vladavić, Rahimić, Blatnjak (Merzić 62), Muslimović. Coach: Fuad Muzurović (BIH)
Goal(s): 1-0 Charisteas 10, 1-1 Hrgović 54, 2-1 Gekas 58, 3-1 Liberopoulos 73, 3-2 Ibišević 90+2
Red Card(s): Hrgović 56 (Bosnia-Herzegovina)
Yellow Card(s): Rahimić 29 (Bosnia-Herzegovina), Katsouranis 49 (Greece), Patsatzoglou 73 (Greece), Nadarević 80 (Bosnia-Herzegovina)
Referee: Gilewski (POL)

17/10/07, Ta' Qali, Ta' Qali
Malta 2-3 Moldova
Attendance: 7069
Malta: Haber, Scicluna (Scerri 46), Azzopardi (Nwoko 90+1), Said, Dimech, Briffa, Pace, Mallia, Woods, Schembri (Cohen 46), M. Mifsud. Coach: Dušan Fitzel (CZE)
Moldova: Pascenco, Golovatenco, Stroenco, Lascencov, Corneencov, Bordian, Josan, Gatcan (Zmeu 77), Comleonoc (Se. Namasco 69), Frunza (Doros 83), Bugaiov. Coach: Igor Dobrovolsky (MDA)
Goal(s): 0-1 Bugaiov 24(p), 0-2 Frunza 31, 0-3 Frunza 35, 1-3 Scerri 71, 2-3 M. Mifsud 84(p)
Red Card(s): Golovatenco 88 (Moldova)
Yellow Card(s): Gatcan 10 (Moldova), Stroenco 11 (Moldova), Dimech 13 (Malta), Scicluna 25 (Malta), Golovatenco 56 (Moldova), Pascenco 61

(Moldova), Woods 74 (Malta), Corneencov 86 (Moldova), Golovatenco 88 (Moldova)
Referee: Ishchenko (UKR)

17/10/07, Ali Sami Yen, Istanbul
Turkey 0-1 Greece
Attendance: 22818
Turkey: Volkan Demirel, Servet Çetin, Gökhan Zan, Hamit Altıntop, Emre Belözoğlu (Arda Turan 71), İbrahim Üzülmez, Mehmet Aurélio, Gökdeniz Karadeniz (Hakan Şükür 65), Ümit Karan (Tümer Metin 46), Gökhan Ünal, Tuncay Şanlı. Coach: Fatih Terim (TUR)
Greece: Chalkias, Dellas, Kyrgiakos, Antzas, Seitaridis, Torosidis, Karagounis, Basinas, Charisteas (Samaras 59), Amanatidis, Gekas (Liberopoulos 56). Coach: Otto Rehhagel (GER)
Goal(s): 0-1 Amanatidis 79
Yellow Card(s): Emre Belözoğlu 55 (Turkey), Torosidis 64 (Greece)
Referee: Mejuto González (ESP)

17/10/07, Koševo, Sarajevo
Bosnia-Herzegovina 0-2 Norway
Attendance: 1500
Bosnia-Herzegovina: Gušo, Berberović, Merzić, Bajić, Krunić, Blatnjak (Ibišević 46), Muslimović (Džeko 46), Misimović, Maletić (Muharemović 78), Nadarević, Salihović. Coach: Fuad Muzurović (BIH)
Norway: Opdal, Storbæk, Hangeland, Hagen, J.A. Riise, B.H. Riise (Bjørkøy 90+2), Andresen, Grindheim (Rushfeldt 58), Solli, Helstad (Braaten 76), Gamst Pedersen. Coach: Åge Hareide (NOR)
Goal(s): 0-1 Hagen 5, 0-2 B.H. Riise 74
Yellow Card(s): Salihović 37 (Bosnia-Herzegovina), Misimović 43 (Bosnia-Herzegovina), Hagen 67 (Norway), Rushfeldt 73 (Norway), Džeko 90+3 (Bosnia-Herzegovina)
Referee: Lannoy (FRA)

17/11/07, Zimbru, Chisinau
Moldova 3-0 Hungary
Attendance: 6483
Moldova: St. Namasco, Lascencov, Rebeja, Epureanu, Bordian, Se. Namasco, Cebotari (Bulgaru 50), Zmeu (Olexici 90+3), Josan, Bugaiov, Calincov (Alexeev 64). Coach: Igor Dobrovolsky (MDA)
Hungary: Fülöp, Szélesi, Vaskó, Csizmadia, Vanczák, Gera, Tőzsér (Buzsáky 38), Hajnal, Vadócz (Balogh 39), Dzsudzsák (Feczesin 71), Priskin. Coach: Peter Várhidi (HUN)
Goal(s): 1-0 Bugaiov 13, 2-0 Josan 23, 3-0 Alexeev 86
Yellow Card(s): Gera 30 (Hungary), Zmeu 75 (Moldova), Josan 80 (Moldova), Epureanu 84 (Moldova), Fülöp 84 (Hungary)
Referee: Královec (CZE)

17/11/07, Ullevaal, Oslo
Norway 1-2 Turkey
Attendance: 23783
Norway: Opdal, Storbæk (Rushfeldt 88), Hagen, Hangeland, J.A. Riise, B.H. Riise, Tettey, Hæstad (Skjelbred 68), Iversen (Helstad 84), Carew, Gamst Pedersen. Coach: Åge Hareide (NOR)
Turkey: Volkan Demirel, İbrahim Kas (Gökhan Gönül 15), Emre Aşık, Servet Çetin, Hakan Balta, Hamit Altıntop, Mehmet Aurélio, Emre Belözoğlu, Arda Turan (Tuncay Şanlı 87), Nihat Kahveci, Semih Şentürk (Yusuf Şimşek 67). Coach: Fatih Terim (TUR)
Goal(s): 1-0 Hagen 12, 1-1 Emre Belözoğlu 31, 1-2 Nihat Kahveci 59
Yellow Card(s): Hæstad 8 (Norway), Volkan Demirel 63 (Turkey), Yusuf 90+2 (Turkey)
Referee: Merk (GER)

17/11/07, OACA Spyro Louis, Athens
Greece 5-0 Malta
Attendance: 31332
Greece: Nikopolidis, Patsatzoglou, Dellas, Kyrgiakos, Torosidis (Spiropoulos 48), Basinas, Katsouranis, Karagounis (Tziolis 70), Giannakopoulos (Liberopoulos 46), Gekas, Amanatidis. Coach: Otto Rehhagel (GER)
Malta: Haber, J. Mifsud, Briffa, Said, Azzopardi, Pullicino, Pace, Sammut (Cohen 61), Nwoko, Schembri (Scerri 68), M. Mifsud (Sciberras 78). Coach: Dušan Fitzel (CZE)
Goal(s): 1-0 Gekas 32, 2-0 Basinas 54, 3-0 Amanatidis 61, 4-0 Gekas 72, 5-0 Gekas 74
Yellow Card(s): Nwoko 34 (Malta), Dellas 51 (Greece), Said 61 (Malta)
Referee: Kaldma (EST)

21/11/07, Ta' Qali, Ta' Qali
Malta 1-4 Norway
Attendance: 7000
Malta: Haber, Azzopardi, Dimech, Wellman, Briffa, Nwoko (Cohen 86), Pullicino, Woods (Barbara 83), Pace, Schembri, M. Mifsud (Scerri 87). Coach: Dušan Fitzel (CZE)
Norway: Opdal, Storbæk, Hagen, Hangeland, J.A. Riise, B.H. Riise (Hæstad 75), Riseth, Skjelbred, Iversen (Rushfeldt 84), Carew (Helstad 68), Gamst Pedersen. Coach: Åge Hareide (NOR)
Goal(s): 0-1 Iversen 25, 0-2 Iversen 27(p), 0-3 Iversen 45, 1-3 M. Mifsud 53, 1-4 Gamst Pedersen 75
Red Card(s): Schembri 68 (Malta)
Yellow Card(s): Hagen 12 (Norway), Riseth 37 (Norway), Wellman 40 (Malta), M. Mifsud 50 (Malta), Gamst Pedersen 52 (Norway), Schembri 56 (Malta), Schembri 68 (Malta), Woods 69 (Malta)
Referee: Baskakov (RUS)

21/11/07, Ferenc Puskás, Budapest
Hungary 1-2 Greece
Attendance: 32300
Hungary: Fülöp, Szélesi, Vaskó, Juhász, Vanczák, Vass, Tőzsér (Leandro 85), Buzsáky, Hajnal (Filkor 76), Halmosi (Feczesin 81), Priskin. Coach: Peter Várhidi (HUN)
Greece: Chalkias (Nikopolidis 46), Patsatzoglou, Kapsis, Vintra, Kyrgiakos, Basinas, Tziolis (Samaras 46), Karagounis, Katsouranis, Gekas (Amanatidis 82), Salpingidis. Coach: Otto Rehhagel (GER)
Goal(s): 1-0 Buzsáky 7, 1-1 Vanczák 22(og), 1-2 Basinas 59(p)
Yellow Card(s): Tőzsér 29 (Hungary), Kyrgiakos 62 (Greece), Patsatzoglou 70 (Greece), Vanczák 90+3 (Hungary)
Referee: Styles (ENG)

21/11/07, Ali Sami Yen, Istanbul
Turkey 1-0 Bosnia-Herzegovina
Attendance: 20106
Turkey: Rüştü Reçber, Gökhan Gönül, Emre Aşık, Servet Çetin, Hakan Balta, Hamit Altıntop, Mehmet Aurélio, Emre Belözoğlu, Arda Turan (Tuncay Şanlı 76), Nihat Kahveci (Gökdeniz Karadeniz 90), Semih Şentürk (Sabri Sarıoğlu 61). Coach: Fatih Terim (TUR)
Bosnia-Herzegovina: Gušo, Ibričić (Ibišević 75), Nadarević, Berberović, Merzić (Muharemović 89), Bajić, Krunić, Maletić, Misimović, Rahimić, Džeko (Salihović 83). Coach: Fuad Muzurović (BIH)
Goal(s): 1-0 Nihat Kahveci 43
Yellow Card(s): Berberović 39 (Bosnia-Herzegovina), Semih Şentürk 48 (Turkey), Nadarević 82 (Bosnia-Herzegovina)
Referee: Braamhaar (NED)

Group C Table

	Pld	Home W	D	L	F	A	Away W	D	L	F	A	Total W	D	L	F	A	Pts
1 Greece	12	4	1	1	14	7	5	1	0	11	3	10	1	1	25	10	31
2 Turkey	12	3	2	1	13	3	3	2	1	12	8	7	3	2	25	11	24
3 Norway	12	3	1	2	14	6	4	1	1	13	5	7	2	3	27	11	23
4 Bosnia-Herzegovina	12	2	0	4	5	12	2	2	2	11	10	4	1	7	16	22	13
5 Moldova	12	1	3	2	7	6	2	1	3	5	13	3	3	6	12	19	12
6 Hungary	12	3	0	3	7	7	1	0	5	4	15	4	0	8	11	22	12
7 Malta	12	1	1	4	9	16	0	1	5	1	15	1	2	9	10	31	5

GROUP D

Five points clear at the top of the section during the summer break, Germany were the first team to book a place at UEFA EURO 2008™ alongside hosts Austria and Switzerland. However, Group D was to have a sting in the tail for Joachim Löw's men.

Record time

Miroslav Klose scored twice as Germany resumed their campaign with a 2-0 win in Wales, and a 0-0 draw in Dublin on 13 October saw them confirm their place in the finals with a national-record 237 days to spare. Löw, who took over from Jürgen Klinsmann after the 2006 FIFA World Cup campaign, had accomplished his mission in clinical style.

"Now we can start making plans," said Löw after the stalemate against the Republic of Ireland. "It is good to have avoided any drama. It can be stressful if you have to wait to the end to qualify." However, if the coach was feeling relieved, he was not about to let his hair down. "Maybe we'll have a glass of wine in the hotel," Löw said. "But we mustn't overdo it."

Tirol training

His caution was perhaps sensible. Just four days after qualifying, Germany faced a rematch against the only side who had offered any serious resistance to their dominance of the section up to that point – Karel Brückner's Czech Republic. Beaten 2-1 in the corresponding fixture in Prague, the Czechs trained for the big game in the Tirol region with a view to returning to Austria and Switzerland for UEFA EURO 2008™.

Despite having Marek Jankulovski, Jan Polák and Milan Baroš suspended and playmaker Tomáš Rosický unavailable through injury, the Czechs went into the game confident of getting at least the point they needed to join Germany at the finals. "The Germans are very strong opponents – they are certainly no worse than they were at the [2006 FIFA] World Cup where they finished third," said goalkeeper Petr Čech. "They want to celebrate earning qualification in front of their own fans and will be motivated, so any newcomers in our side will have a great stage to perform on."

Shock defeat

That certainly proved to be the case, as first-half goals from Libor Sionko and Marek Matějovský, plus a third midway through the second period from Jaroslav Plašil,

Czech celebrations are intense as Germany are defeated 3-0 in Munich

condemned Germany to their first defeat in 24 UEFA European Championship qualifiers - a run stretching back nine years. "Qualifying is nice but the way we did it is even better," said centre-back David Rozehnal.

Despite the absence of Čech and Jankulovski for their final games, the Czechs piled on six more points and surprisingly stole top spot in the section. Going into their final fixture in Cyprus level on points with Löw's side, a 2-0 win in Nicosia proved decisive as Wales earned a 0-0 draw in Frankfurt to give their troubled campaign an upbeat ending.

Ominous prediction

However, the ending was not to be happy for the Republic of Ireland. A grim 5-2 defeat in Cyprus early in the campaign had undermined confidence in manager Stephen Staunton, with former international Mark Lawrenson predicting ominously "we won't qualify for UEFA EURO 2008™ and won't even go close". He was right.

In the autumn part of the campaign, the Irish drew four games and lost the other – 1-0 in the Czech Republic – and while they finished third in the section, they were a full ten points adrift of second-placed Germany. Staunton departed before the closing fixture – a 2-2 draw against Wales – with fans in Dublin having made it clear what they thought of his side during a 1-1 draw against Cyprus in his final game.

Group D Results

2/9/06
Czech Republic 2-1 Wales
Goal(s): 1-0 Lafata 76, 1-1 Jiránek 85(og), 2-1 Lafata 89
Slovakia 6-1 Cyprus
Goal(s): 1-0 Škrteľ 9, 2-0 Mintál 33, 3-0 Šebo 43, 4-0 Šebo 49, 5-0 Karhan 52, 6-0 Mintál 56, 6-1 Yiasoumi 90
Germany 1-0 Republic of Ireland
Goal(s): 1-0 Podolski 57

6/9/06
Slovakia 0-3 Czech Republic
Goal(s): 0-1 Sionko 10, 0-2 Sionko 21, 0-3 Koller 57
San Marino 0-13 Germany
Goal(s): 0-1 Podolski 11, 0-2 Schweinsteiger 28, 0-3 Klose 30, 0-4 Ballack 35, 0-5 Podolski 43, 0-6 Klose 45+1, 0-7 Schweinsteiger 47, 0-8 Podolski 64, 0-9 Hitzlsperger 66, 0-10 Podolski 72, 0-11 Hitzlsperger 73, 0-12 M. Friedrich 87, 0-13 Schneider 90(p)

7/10/06
Wales 1-5 Slovakia
Goal(s): 0-1 Švento 14, 0-2 Mintál 32, 1-2 Bale 37, 1-3 Mintál 38, 1-4 Karhan 51, 1-5 Vittek 59
Czech Republic 7-0 San Marino
Goal(s): 1-0 Kulič 15, 2-0 Polák 22, 3-0 Baroš 28, 4-0 Koller 43, 5-0 Jarolím 49, 6-0 Koller 52, 7-0 Baroš 68
Cyprus 5-2 Republic of Ireland
Goal(s): 0-1 Ireland 8, 1-1 M. Konstantinou 10, 2-1 Garpozis 16, 2-2 Dunne 44, 3-2 M. Konstantinou 50(p), 4-2 Charalambides 60, 5-2 Charalambides 75

11/10/06
Republic of Ireland 1-1 Czech Republic
Goal(s): 1-0 Kilbane 62, 1-1 Koller 64
Wales 3-1 Cyprus
Goal(s): 1-0 Koumas 33, 2-0 Earnshaw 39, 3-0 Bellamy 72, 3-1 Okkas 83
Slovakia 1-4 Germany
Goal(s): 0-1 Podolski 13, 0-2 Ballack 25, 0-3 Schweinsteiger 36, 1-3 Varga 58, 1-4 Podolski 72

15/11/06
Republic of Ireland 5-0 San Marino
Goal(s): 1-0 A. Reid 7, 2-0 Doyle 24, 3-0 Keane 31, 4-0 Keane 58(p), 5-0 Keane 85
Cyprus 1-1 Germany
Goal(s): 0-1 Ballack 16, 1-1 Okkas 43

7/2/07
San Marino 1-2 Republic of Ireland
Goal(s): 0-1 Kilbane 49, 1-1 Man. Marani 86, 1-2 Ireland 90+4

24/3/07
Republic of Ireland 1-0 Wales
Goal(s): 1-0 Ireland 39
Cyprus 1-3 Slovakia
Goal(s): 1-0 Aloneftis 45, 1-1 Vittek 54, 1-2 Škrteľ 67, 1-3 Jakubko 77
Czech Republic 1-2 Germany
Goal(s): 0-1 Kuranyi 42, 0-2 Kuranyi 62, 1-2 Baroš 77

28/3/07
Czech Republic 1-0 Cyprus
Goal(s): 1-0 Kováč 22
Republic of Ireland 1-0 Slovakia
Goal(s): 1-0 Doyle 12
Wales 3-0 San Marino
Goal(s): 1-0 Giggs 3, 2-0 Bale 20, 3-0 Koumas 63(p)

2/6/07
Wales 0-0 Czech Republic
Germany 6-0 San Marino
Goal(s): 1-0 Kuranyi 45, 2-0 Jansen 52, 3-0 Frings 56(p), 4-0 Gómez 63, 5-0 Gómez 65, 6-0 Fritz 67

6/6/07
Germany 2-1 Slovakia
Goal(s): 1-0 Ďurica 10(og), 1-1 Metzelder 20(og), 2-1 Hitzlsperger 43

22/8/07, Olimpico, Serravalle
San Marino 0-1 Cyprus
Attendance: 552
San Marino: A. Simoncini, C. Valentini, Vannucci, Albani, Della Valle, G. Bollini (Ciacci 77), Bonini (Nanni 84), Bugli, F. Bollini (Andreini 63), Man. Marani, Selva. Coach: Giampaolo Mazza (ITA)
Cyprus: Georgallides, Theodotou, Christou, Lambrou, Marangos (Nicolaou 24), Aloneftis, Michail, Garpozis (Charalambous 86), Yiasoumi (Charalambides 55), Okkas, M. Konstantinou. Coach: Angelos Anastasiadis (GRE)
Goal(s): 0-1 Okkas 54
Yellow Card(s): Bollini 14 (San Marino), Albani 30 (San Marino), Bugli 43 (San Marino), Della Valle 59 (San Marino), Ciacci 86 (San Marino)
Referee: Janku (ALB)

8/9/07, Millennium, Cardiff
Wales 0-2 Germany
Attendance: 27889
Wales: Hennessey, Ricketts, Gabbidon, Collins, Nyatanga, Ledley (Earnshaw 46), Bale, Koumas (Fletcher 67), Robinson, S. Davies (Crofts 79), Eastwood. Coach: John Toshack (WAL)
Germany: Lehmann, Friedrich, Mertesacker, Metzelder, Pander (Trochowski 46), Hilbert, Hitzlsperger, Schweinsteiger, Jansen, Kuranyi (Podolski 72), Klose (Helmes 87). Coach: Joachim Löw (GER)
Goal(s): 0-1 Klose 6, 0-2 Klose 60
Yellow Card(s): Gabbidon 38 (Wales), Collins 41 (Wales)
Referee: Mejuto González (ESP)

8/9/07, Olimpico, Serravalle
San Marino 0-3 Czech Republic
Attendance: 3412
San Marino: A. Simoncini, C. Valentini, Vannucci, D. Simoncini, Della Valle, G. Bollini (Mariotti 85), Bugli (Vitaioli 67), F. Bollini (Andreini 58), Man. Marani, Selva, Bonini. Coach: Giampaolo Mazza (ITA)
Czech Republic: Čech, Ujfaluši, Rozehnal, Kováč, Jankulovski, Galásek (Plašil 82), Rosický, Jarolím (Polák 69), Kulič (Vlček 56), Fenin, Koller. Coach: Karel Brückner (CZE)
Goal(s): 0-1 Rosický 33, 0-2 Jankulovski 75, 0-3 Koller 90+3
Red Card(s): Della Valle 65 (San Marino)
Yellow Card(s): Della Valle 31 (San Marino), D. Simoncini 52 (San Marino), Koller 61 (Czech Republic), Della Valle 65 (San Marino)
Referee: Filipović (SRB)

8/9/07, Tehelné Pole, Bratislava
Slovakia 2-2 Republic of Ireland
Attendance: 12360
Slovakia: Senecký, Greško, Čech, Ďurica, Klimpl, Krajčík, Hamšík, Sapara (Šebo 71), Mintál, Hološko, Šesták (Obžera 65). Coach: Ján Kocian (SVK)
Republic of Ireland: Given, O'Shea, Kelly, McShane, Dunne, Carsley, McGeady (Gibson 61), Ireland (Douglas 76), Kilbane, Doyle (D. Murphy 89), Keane. Coach: Stephen Staunton (IRL)
Goal(s): 0-1 Ireland 7, 1-1 Klimpl 37, 1-2 Doyle 57, 2-2 Čech 90+1
Yellow Card(s): Krajčík 69 (Slovakia), Ďurica 88 (Slovakia)
Referee: Farina (ITA)

12/9/07, Antona Malatinského, Trnava
Slovakia 2-5 Wales
Attendance: 5846
Slovakia: Senecký, Greško (Žofčák 64), Klimpl, Ďurica, Čech, Hamšík, P. Petráš, Sapara, Mintál, Šesták (Obžera 46), Hološko. Coach: Ján Kocian (SVK)
Wales: Hennessey, Ricketts, Gabbidon, Morgan, Collins, Bale, S. Davies, Robinson, Ledley (Vaughan 85), Bellamy, Eastwood (Fletcher 73). Coach: John Toshack (WAL)
Goal(s): 1-0 Mintál 12, 1-1 Eastwood 22, 1-2 Bellamy 34, 1-3 Bellamy 41, 2-3 Mintál 57, 2-4 Ďurica 78(og), 2-5 S. Davies 90
Yellow Card(s): Bellamy 24 (Wales), Obžera 89 (Slovakia)
Referee: Duhamel (FRA)

12/9/07, GSP, Nicosia
Cyprus 3-0 San Marino
Attendance: 1000
Cyprus: Georgallides, Charalambous (Garpozis 65), Okkarides, Christou, Michail, Elia (Theodotou 76), Makridis, Nicolaou, Okkas (Yiasoumi 46), M. Konstantinou, Aloneftis. Coach: Angelos Anastasiadis (GRE)
San Marino: F. Valentini, C. Valentini, Vannucci, Vitaioli, Albani (Benedettini 81), F. Bollini, Andreini, Bugli, Man. Marani (Nanni 87), Selva, Bonini (Mariotti 73). Coach: Giampaolo Mazza (ITA)
Goal(s): 1-0 Makridis 15, 2-0 Aloneftis 41, 3-0 Aloneftis 90+2
Yellow Card(s): Garpozis 78 (Cyprus), Selva 78 (San Marino), Nicolaou 88 (Cyprus)
Referee: Kulbakov (BLR)

12/9/07, Sparta Stadium, Prague
Czech Republic 1-0 Republic of Ireland
Attendance: 16648
Czech Republic: Čech, Ujfaluši, Rozehnal, Kováč, Jankulovski, Sionko (Vlček 74), Galásek (Sivok 46), Rosický, Polák, Plašil, Baroš (Jarolím 89). Coach: Karel Brückner (CZE)
Republic of Ireland: Given, Kelly, McShane, Dunne, O'Shea (Hunt 38), McGeady (Long 62), Carsley (Keogh 82), A. Reid, Kilbane, Doyle, Keane. Coach: Steve Staunton (IRL)
Goal(s): 1-0 Jankulovski 15
Red Card(s): Hunt 61 (Republic of Ireland)
Yellow Card(s): McShane 29 (Republic of Ireland), Kelly 36 (Republic of Ireland), Polák 45+3 (Czech Republic), Ujfaluši 45+3 (Czech Republic), Baroš 59 (Czech Republic), Sivok 84 (Czech Republic), Keane 89 (Republic of Ireland), Jankulovski 90 (Czech Republic), Long 90+2
Referee: Vassaras (GRE)

13/10/07, Športová hala Dubnica, Dubnica nad Vahom
Slovakia 7-0 San Marino
Attendance: 2576
Slovakia: Čontofalský, Škrteľ, Krajčík, Ďurica, Szabó, Sapara (Hesek 79), Čech, Hamšík, Kozák, Šesták (Vaščák 60), Hološko (Šebo 71). Coach: Ján Kocian (SVK)
San Marino: F. Valentini, Andreini, Vannucci, Vitaioli, Albani, Della Valle, G. Bollini (Benedettini 57), C. Valentini, Bugli (Bonifazi 68), Man. Marani (De Luigi 85), Nanni. Coach: Giampaolo Mazza (ITA)
Goal(s): 1-0 Hamšík 24, 2-0 Šesták 32, 3-0 Sapara 37, 4-0 Škrteľ 51, 5-0 Hološko 54, 6-0 Šesták 57, 7-0 Ďurica 76(p)
Yellow Card(s): Bollini 45 (San Marino), Sapara 64 (Slovakia), Man. Marani 77 (San Marino)
Referee: Wilmes (LUX)

13/10/07, GSP, Nicosia
Cyprus 3-1 Wales
Attendance: 2852
Cyprus: Georgallides, Okkarides, Satsias (Marangos 71), Elia (Charalambides 63), Michail (Yiasoumi 46), Christou, Garpozis, Makridis, Nicolaou, Aloneftis, Okkas. Coach: Angelos Anastasiadis (GRE)
Wales: Coyne, Ricketts (Easter 73), Collins (Morgan 44), Gabbidon, Bale, Nyatanga, Ledley, Robinson, S. Davies, Bellamy, Eastwood (Earnshaw 58). Coach: John Toshack (WAL)
Goal(s): 0-1 Collins 21, 1-1 Okkas 59, 2-1 Okkas 68, 3-1 Charalambides 79
Yellow Card(s): Eastwood 45 (Wales), Marangos 76 (Cyprus), Easter 77 (Wales), Aloneftis 90 (Cyprus)
Referee: Bertolini (SUI)

13/10/07, Croke Park, Dublin
Republic of Ireland 0-0 Germany
Attendance: 67495
Republic of Ireland: Given, Kelly, Dunne, J. O'Brien, Finnan, Carsley, A. Reid, Kilbane (D. Murphy 90+2), Keogh (McGeady 80), Doyle (Long 70), Keane. Coach: Stephen Staunton (IRL)
Germany: Lehmann, Friedrich, Fritz, Jansen, Mertesacker, Metzelder, Frings, Schweinsteiger (Rolfes 18), Trochowski (Castro 90), Gómez (Podolski 64), Kuranyi. Coach: Joachim Löw (GER)
Yellow Card(s): Carsley 36 (Republic of Ireland), Dunne 44 (Republic of Ireland), Lehmann 52 (Germany), Frings 55 (Germany), Friedrich 90 (Germany)
Referee: Hansson (SWE)

17/10/07, Croke Park, Dublin
Republic of Ireland 1-1 Cyprus
Attendance: 54861
Republic of Ireland: Given, Finnan, Kilbane, McShane, O'Shea, J. O'Brien (Miller 46), A. Reid, Keogh (McGeady 63), Doyle, Keane, Hunt (Douglas 74). Coach: Stephen Staunton (IRL)
Cyprus: Georgallides, Satsias (Marangos 69), Okkarides, Christou, Charalambides, Elia, Garpozis, Makridis (Theofilou 86), Nicolaou, Okkas, Yiasoumi (Michail 73). Coach: Angelos Anastasiadis (GRE)
Goal(s): 0-1 Okkarides 80, 1-1 Finnan 90+2
Red Card(s): Elia 90+4 (Cyprus)
Yellow Card(s): Miller 67 (Republic of Ireland), Satsias 68 (Cyprus)
Referee: Vuorela (FIN)

17/10/07, Olimpico, Serravalle
San Marino 1-2 Wales
Attendance: 1182
San Marino: A. Simoncini, C. Valentini, Vannucci (Bugli 76), Albani, Della Valle, Bonifazi (Bonini 62), D. Simoncini, Muccioli, Andreini, De Luigi (Vitaioli 80), Selva. Coach: Giampaolo Mazza (ITA)
Wales: Price, Bale, Eardley, Gabbidon, Nyatanga, Robinson, Vaughan (Ricketts 62), S. Davies, Ledley, Earnshaw, Bellamy. Coach: John Toshack (WAL)
Goal(s): 0-1 Earnshaw 13, 0-2 Ledley 36, 1-2 Selva 73
Red Card(s): Albani 85 (San Marino)
Yellow Card(s): C. Valentini 40 (San Marino), Bale 42 (Wales), Albani 55 (San Marino), Vannucci 68 (San Marino), Ledley 70 (Wales), Albani 85 (San Marino), Vitaioli 86 (San Marino), Ricketts 87 (Wales)
Referee: Zammit (MLT)

17/10/07, Allianz Arena, Munich
Germany 0-3 Czech Republic
Attendance: 66445
Germany: Hildebrand, Jansen, Friedrich, Mertesacker, Metzelder (Fritz 46), Schweinsteiger (Gómez 65), Frings, Trochowski (Rolfes 46), Odonkor, Kuranyi, Podolski. Coach: Joachim Löw (GER)
Czech Republic: Čech, Kováč, Rozehnal, Ujfaluši, Pospěch, Galásek, Pudil (Kulič 73), Matějovský, Sionko (Vlček 58), Plašil, Koller (Fenin 79). Coach: Karel Brückner (CZE)
Goal(s): 0-1 Sionko 2, 0-2 Matějovský 23, 0-3 Plašil 63
Yellow Card(s): Podolski 46 (Germany)
Referee: Webb (ENG)

17/11/07, Millennium, Cardiff
Wales 2-2 Republic of Ireland
Attendance: 24619
Wales: Hennessey, Eardley (Cotterill 81), Collins, Gabbidon, Gunter,

Gareth Bale of Wales (right) challenges with San Marino midfielder Luca Bonifazi

Ledley, Koumas, Robinson (Edwards 37), Fletcher, S. Davies, Eastwood (Easter 60). Coach: John Toshack (WAL)
Republic of Ireland: Given, Finnan, McShane, O'Shea, Kilbane, McGeady, Carsley, Miller (Hunt 60), A. Reid (Potter 87), Doyle, Keane. Coach: Don Givens (IRL)
Goal(s): 1-0 Koumas 23, 1-1 Keane 31, 1-2 Doyle 60, 2-2 Koumas 89(p)
Yellow Card(s): O'Shea 33 (Republic of Ireland), Koumas 57 (Wales)
Referee: Oriekhov (UKR)

17/11/07, AWD-Arena, Hannover
Germany 4-0 Cyprus
Attendance: 45016
Germany: Lehmann, Lahm, Metzelder, Mertesacker, Friedrich, Trochowski (Borowski 66), Hitzlsperger, Fritz (Hilbert 77), Podolski, Gómez (Hanke 73), Klose. Coach: Joachim Löw (GER)
Cyprus: Georgallides, Lambrou, Theodotou (Nicolaou 27), Christou, Garpozis, Okkas, Charalambides (Theofilou 46), Satsias, Aloneftis, Makridis, M. Konstantinou (Yiasoumi 68). Coach: Angelos Anastasiadis (GRE)
Goal(s): 1-0 Fritz 2, 2-0 Klose 20, 3-0 Podolski 53, 4-0 Hitzlsperger 82
Referee: Rasmussen (DEN)

17/11/07, Sparta Stadium, Prague
Czech Republic 3-1 Slovakia
Attendance: 15651
Czech Republic: Blažek, Pospěch, Kováč, Rozehnal, Grygera (Kadlec 45), Polák (Matějovský 86), Galásek, Rosický, Plašil, Koller, Baroš (Kulič 70). Coach: Karel Brückner (CZE)
Slovakia: Čontofalský, Krajčík, Škrteľ, Michalík, Čech, Štrba, Kisel (Halenár 88), Sapara, Kozák, Hamšík (Hološko 58), Mintál (Šesták 67). Coach: Ján Kocian (SVK)
Goal(s): 1-0 Grygera 13, 2-0 Kulič 76, 2-1 Kadlec 79(og), 3-1 Rosický 83
Yellow Card(s): Štrba 56 (Slovakia), Sapara 57 (Slovakia), Čech 69 (Slovakia), Škrteľ 78 (Slovakia)
Referee: Asumaa (FIN)

21/11/07, GSP, Nicosia
Cyprus 0-2 Czech Republic
Attendance: 5866
Cyprus: Georgallides, Christou, Lambrou, Nicolaou (Charalambous 56), Garpozis, Charalambides (Yiasoumi 62), Makridis (Michail 84), Satsias, Aloneftis, Okkas, M. Konstantinou. Coach: Angelos Anastasiadis (GRE)
Czech Republic: Zítka, Pospěch, Kováč, Rozehnal, Kadlec, Plašil (Kladrubský 87), Galásek, Matějovský, Pudil, Kulič (Baroš 57), Koller (Fenin 76). Coach: Karel Brückner (CZE)
Goal(s): 0-1 Pudil 11, 0-2 Koller 74
Yellow Card(s): Kadlec 65 (Czech Republic), Satsias 75 (Cyprus), Charalambous 88 (Cyprus)
Referee: Paniashvili (GEO)

21/11/07, Commerzbank Arena, Frankfurt am Main
Germany 0-0 Wales
Attendance: 49262
Germany: Lehmann, Castro (Hilbert 56), Mertesacker, Metzelder, Lahm, Fritz, Borowski, Hitzlsperger (Rolfes 46), Podolski, Gómez (Neuville 71), Klose. Coach: Joachim Löw (GER)
Wales: Hennessey, Ricketts, Gabbidon, Collins, Nyatanga, Gunter, Fletcher, S. Davies, Edwards (Crofts 90+1), Ledley, Earnshaw (Easter 56). Coach: John Toshack (WAL)
Yellow Card(s): Collins 82 (Wales), Gabbidon 83 (Wales), Hennessey 89 (Wales)
Referee: Balaj (ROU)

21/11/07, Olimpico, Serravalle
San Marino 0-5 Slovakia
Attendance: 538
San Marino: F. Valentini, C. Valentini, Mau. Marani (Andreini 84), D. Simoncini, Della Valle, Bollini (Berretti 61), Mic. Marani, Muccioli, Vannucci, Man. Marani, Selva (De Luigi 50). Coach: Giampaolo Mazza (ITA)
Slovakia: Senecký, Krajčík (P. Petráš 63), Michalík, Hubocan, Čech, Borbély, Hamšík, Kisel (Szabó 46), Kozák, Šesták (Halenár 75), Hološko. Coach: Ján Kocian (SVK)
Goal(s): 0-1 Michalík 42, 0-2 Hološko 51, 0-3 Hamšík 53, 0-4 Čech 57, 0-5 Čech 83
Yellow Card(s): Michalík 29 (Slovakia), Selva 44 (San Marino), Vannucci 52 (San Marino), Muccioli 59 (San Marino), Hubocan 73 (Slovakia), Mau. Marani 81 (San Marino), Halenár 81 (Slovakia), C. Valentini 89 (San Marino)
Referee: Sipailo (LVA)

Group D Table

	Pld	Home					Away					Total					Pts
		W	D	L	F	A	W	D	L	F	A	W	D	L	F	A	
1 Czech Republic	12	5	0	1	15	4	4	1	0	12	1	9	2	1	27	5	29
2 Germany	12	4	1	1	13	4	4	2	0	22	3	8	3	1	35	7	27
3 Republic of Ireland	12	3	2	0	9	2	1	2	3	8	12	4	5	3	17	14	17
4 Slovakia	12	2	1	3	18	15	2	1	3	15	8	5	1	6	33	23	16
5 Wales	12	2	2	2	9	10	2	1	3	9	9	4	3	5	18	19	15
6 Cyprus	12	3	1	2	13	9	0	2	4	4	15	4	2	6	17	24	14
7 San Marino	12	0	2	4	2	26	0	0	6	0	31	0	0	12	2	57	0

GROUP E

Unexpected results in Tel-Aviv and London defined the closing stages of Group E, with Croatia and Russia qualifying at the expense of a devastated England.

Massive achievement

All three sides, along with Dror Kashtan's Israel, harboured decent chances of qualifying as the campaign went into its summer break, but Croatia were the side that made the fewest false moves in the autumn, and ended up winning the section by a clear five points – a massive achievement for first-time coach Slaven Bilić.

Wins against Estonia, Andorra and Israel in their first three matches after the break saw them take control of their destiny, and their qualification was confirmed midway through their penultimate game against FYR Macedonia in Skopje on 17 November – which they lost 2-0. "The pitch was very, very bad, but everything ended well," said Bilić.

Israel undone

Croatia were able to take their foot off the pedal thanks to an entirely unexpected 2-1 home win for Israel against Russia in Tel-Aviv. Back-to-back defeats in England and Croatia had marked the end of Kashtan's side's hopes of qualifying, and with Russia needing a win to maintain their top-two place, Guus Hiddink's men were not expected to encounter much resistance.

Those predictions proved false, and Omer Golan's sensational late goal secured victory for Israel, and earned them the admiration of Bilić. "I want to say thank you to Israel," he said. "Not only because they helped us qualify, but because they showed what sporting integrity is."

England revived

At that stage it seemed that England would be the team to join Croatia in the finals. Steve McClaren's men had tested the patience of fans earlier in the campaign but successive 3-0 wins against Israel, Russia and Estonia in their first three competitive games at the reopened Wembley Stadium looked to have blown away the cobwebs.

However, the carpet was whipped out from under the Three Lions as they visited Moscow for their penultimate qualifier. With Wayne Rooney having spectacularly put them ahead after 29 minutes, England were cruising to victory until substitute Roman Pavlyuchenko struck twice within the space of four second-half minutes to leave Hiddink's Russia within two wins of guaranteed qualification.

'Cocky comments'

As they prepared to face Israel, the Dutchman was resolved. "I'm calm," he said. "A victory over Israel would practically secure our qualification. After all our hard work, a defeat in Israel is simply impossible." How wrong he was. Israel's Tal Ben Haim gloated afterwards, saying: "The Russians underestimated us before the match and made some cocky comments which acted in our favour."

Thus the stage was set for the last night. England hosted qualified Croatia and, thanks to Israel's last-gasp winner four days earlier, now needed only to avoid defeat to progress. Russia required a win in Andorra and a massive helping hand from Croatia. Bilić had no intention of letting Hiddink down. "Russia can be sure that we will give our best at Wembley," he said.

Wembley debacle

They did. Debutant goalkeeper Scott Carson allowed an early Niko Kranjčar shot to slip through his grasp

Croatia coach Slaven Bilić prepares to embrace match-winner Mladen Petrić after his team's momentous 3-2 victory over England at Wembley

before Ivica Olić silenced Wembley for a second time within the first 15 minutes to double Croatia's lead. David Beckham's arrival as a substitute prompted a revival, with a Frank Lampard penalty and a Peter Crouch strike levelling the scores, but a fearful, shambolic England had no answer to Mladen Petrić's perfectly struck 77th-minute winner.

Russia, meanwhile, won 1-0 in Andorra to progress. "I said we had to be realistic and I didn't believe it would end like that," Hiddink said. With England having missed out in disastrous circumstances, McClaren had little choice but to resign. "It is my responsibility," he said. "I live and die by results and the results have not gone my way. I said judge me on qualification and people have."

Group E Results

16/8/06
Estonia 0-1 FYR Macedonia
Goal(s): 0-1 Sedloski 73

2/9/06
England 5-0 Andorra
Goal(s): 1-0 Crouch 5, 2-0 Gerrard 13, 3-0 Defoe 38, 4-0 Defoe 47, 5-0 Crouch 66
Estonia 0-1 Israel
Goal(s): 0-1 Colautti 8

6/9/06
Russia 0-0 Croatia
Israel 4-1 Andorra
Goal(s): 1-0 Benayoun 9, 2-0 Ben Shushan 11, 3-0 Gershon 43(p), 4-0 Tamuz 69, 4-1 Fernández 84
FYR Macedonia 0-1 England
Goal(s): 0-1 Crouch 46

7/10/06
England 0-0 FYR Macedonia
Russia 1-1 Israel
Goal(s): 1-0 Arshavin 5, 1-1 Ben Shushan 84
Croatia 7-0 Andorra
Goal(s): 1-0 Petrić 12, 2-0 Petrić 37, 3-0 Petrić 48, 4-0 Petrić 50, 5-0 Klasnić 58, 6-0 Balaban 62, 7-0 Modrić 83

11/10/06
Andorra 0-3 FYR Macedonia
Goal(s): 0-1 Pandev 13, 0-2 Noveski 16, 0-3 Naumoski 31
Croatia 2-0 England
Goal(s): 1-0 Eduardo 61, 2-0 G. Neville 69(og)
Russia 2-0 Estonia
Goal(s): 1-0 Pogrebnyak 78, 2-0 Sychev 90+1

15/11/06
FYR Macedonia 0-2 Russia
Goal(s): 0-1 Bystrov 18, 0-2 Arshavin 32
Israel 3-4 Croatia
Goal(s): 1-0 Colautti 8, 1-1 Srna 35(p), 1-2 Eduardo 39, 1-3 Eduardo 54, 2-3 Benayoun 68, 2-4 Eduardo 72, 3-4 Colautti 89

24/3/07
Croatia 2-1 FYR Macedonia
Goal(s): 0-1 Sedloski 36, 1-1 Srna 58, 2-1 Eduardo 87
Israel 0-0 England
Estonia 0-2 Russia
Goal(s): 0-1 Bystrov 66, 0-2 Kerzhakov 78

28/3/07
Israel 4-0 Estonia
Goal(s): 1-0 Tal 19, 2-0 Colautti 29, 3-0 Sahar 77, 4-0 Sahar 80
Andorra 0-3 England
Goal(s): 0-1 Gerrard 54, 0-2 Gerrard 76, 0-3 Nugent 90+2

2/6/07
Russia 4-0 Andorra
Goal(s): 1-0 Kerzhakov 8, 2-0 Kerzhakov 16, 3-0 Kerzhakov 49, 4-0 Sychev 71
FYR Macedonia 1-2 Israel
Goal(s): 0-1 Itzhaki 11, 1-1 Stojkov 13, 1-2 Colautti 44
Estonia 0-1 Croatia
Goal(s): 0-1 Eduardo 32

6/6/07
Andorra 0-2 Israel
Goal(s): 0-1 Tamuz 37, 0-2 Colautti 53
Croatia 0-0 Russia
Estonia 0-3 England
Goal(s): 0-1 J. Cole 37, 0-2 Crouch 54, 0-3 Owen 62

22/8/07, A Le Coq Arena, Tallinn
Estonia 2-1 Andorra
Attendance: 7500
Estonia: Poom, Jääger, Stepanov, Piiroja, Kruglov, Reim, Dmitrijev, Klavan, Lindpere, Zelinski, Voskoboinikov (Kink 46). Coach: Viggo Jensen (DEN)
Andorra: Koldo, Txema, Sonejee, A. Lima, I. Lima, Escura, Ayala (Genís García 90), Pujol (Juli Sánchez 80), Sivera (Toscano 53), Vieira, Silva. Coach: David Rodrigo (ESP)
Goal(s): 1-0 Piiroja 34, 1-1 Silva 82, 2-1 Zelinski 90+2
Red Card(s): Klavan 45+1 (Estonia), Zelinski 90+2 (Estonia)
Yellow Card(s): Jääger 42 (Estonia), I. Lima 42 (Andorra), Escura 55 (Andorra), Zelinski 58 (Estonia), Silva 61 (Andorra), Toscano 69 (Andorra), A. Lima 73 (Andorra), Zelinski 90+2 (Estonia)
Referee: McCourt (NIR)

8/9/07, Wembley, London
England 3-0 Israel
Attendance: 85372
England: Robinson, Richards, Ferdinand, Terry, A. Cole, Wright-Phillips (Bentley 82), Gerrard (P. Neville 70), Barry, J. Cole, Heskey (Johnson 70), Owen. Coach: Steve McClaren (ENG)
Israel: Awat, Shpungin, Ben Haim, Gershon, Ziv, Benayoun, Badir, Benado (Golan 57), Tal, Katan (Zandberg 73), Itzhaki (Tamuz 46). Coach: Dror Kashtan (ISR)
Goal(s): 1-0 Wright-Phillips 20, 2-0 Owen 50, 3-0 Richards 66
Yellow Card(s): Gershon 15 (Israel), Benado 45+1 (Israel), Ziv 55 (Israel), Awat 66 (Israel), Terry 67 (England)
Referee: Vink (NED)

8/9/07, Lokomotiv Stadium, Moscow
Russia 3-0 FYR Macedonia
Attendance: 23000
Russia: Gabulov, V. Berezutskiy, Ignashevich, A. Berezutskiy, Bystrov

(Anyukov 89), Semshov, Zyryanov, Bilyaletdinov, Arshavin, Pavlyuchenko (Kerzhakov 66), Sychev (Malafeyev 70). Coach: Guus Hiddink (NED)
FYR Macedonia: Miloševski, G. Popov, Lazarevski, Sedloski, I. Mitreski, A. Mitreski (Trajanov 46), Šumulikoski, Tasevski, Vasoski (Toleski 88), Pandev, Stojkov (Maznov 46). Coach: Srečko Katanec (SVN)
Goal(s): 1-0 V. Berezutskiy 6, 2-0 Arshavin 83, 3-0 Kerzhakov 86
Red Card(s): Gabulov 70 (Russia)
Yellow Card(s): Pandev 46 (FYR Macedonia), I. Mitreski 82 (FYR Macedonia)
Referee: Øvrebø (NOR)

8/9/07, Maksimir, Zagreb
Croatia 2-0 Estonia
Attendance: 15102
Croatia: Pletikosa, Šimić, Šimunić, R. Kovač, Ćorluka, N. Kovač, Srna (Babić 82), Modrić, Kranjčar (Rakitić 61), Petrić (Olić 72), Eduardo. Coach: Slaven Bilić (CRO)
Estonia: Londak, Allas, Stepanov, Piiroja, Rooba (Anniste 85), Rähn, Dmitrijev, Kruglov, Lindpere (Reim 90+2), Kink (Saag 81), Oper. Coach: Viggo Jensen (DEN)
Goal(s): 1-0 Eduardo 39, 2-0 Eduardo 45+1
Yellow Card(s): Allas 19 (Estonia)
Referee: Laperrière (SUI)

12/9/07, Estadi Comunal, Andorra la Vella
Andorra 0-6 Croatia
Attendance: 925
Andorra: Koldo, A. Lima, Txema, Sonejee, Ayala, Sivera (Andorrà 59), Genís García, Ruíz (Somoza 82), Jiménez, Silva (Moreno 57), Vieira. Coach: David Rodrigo (ESP)
Croatia: Runje, Srna, R. Kovač, Ćorluka, Knežević, Kranjčar, Modrić (Balaban 46), Leko, Babić, Petrić (Pranjić 46), Eduardo (Rakitić 62). Coach: Slaven Bilić (CRO)
Goal(s): 0-1 Srna 34, 0-2 Petrić 38, 0-3 Petrić 44, 0-4 Kranjčar 49, 0-5 Eduardo 55, 0-6 Rakitić 64
Red Card(s): Genís García 77 (Andorra)
Yellow Card(s): Sivera 33 (Andorra), A. Lima 63 (Andorra)
Referee: Thual (FRA)

12/9/07, Wembley, London
England 3-0 Russia
Attendance: 86106
England: Robinson, Richards, Ferdinand, Terry, A. Cole, Wright-Phillips, Barry, Gerrard, J. Cole (P. Neville 88), Heskey (Crouch 80), Owen (Downing 90+1). Coach: Steve McClaren (ENG)
Russia: Malafeyev, V. Berezutskiy, Ignashevich, A. Berezutskiy, Anyukov (Kerzhakov 80), Bilyaletdinov, Zhirkov, Semshov (Bystrov 40), Sychev (Pavlyuchenko 63), Arshavin, Zyryanov. Coach: Guus Hiddink (NED)
Goal(s): 1-0 Owen 7, 2-0 Owen 31, 3-0 Ferdinand 84
Yellow Card(s): J. Cole 78 (England)
Referee: Hansson (SWE)

12/9/07, Gradski, Skopje
FYR Macedonia 1-1 Estonia
Attendance: 5000
FYR Macedonia: Miloševski, Lazarevski, Sedloski, Noveski, Vasoski, Grozdanoski, Trajanov (Položani 46), Šumulikoski, Maznov, Tasevski, Stojkov (Toleski 81). Coach: Srečko Katanec (SVN)
Estonia: Londak, Jääger, Stepanov, Piiroja, Kruglov, Rähn (Reim 62), Dmitrijev, Klavan, Lindpere, Oper (Anniste 90), Saag (Kink 79). Coach: Viggo Jensen (DEN)
Goal(s): 0-1 Piiroja 17, 1-1 Maznov 30
Yellow Card(s): Vasoski 42 (FYR Macedonia), Maznov 55 (FYR Macedonia), Kink 83 (Estonia)
Referee: Trattou (CYP)

13/10/07, Wembley, London
England 3-0 Estonia
Attendance: 86655
England: Robinson, Richards, Campbell, Ferdinand (Lescott 46), A. Cole (P. Neville 49), Wright-Phillips, Gerrard, Barry, J. Cole, Rooney, Owen (Lampard 70). Coach: Steve McClaren (ENG)
Estonia: Poom, Kruglov, Stepanov, Piiroja, Jääger, Rähn, Klavan, Dmitrijev, Lindpere, Kink (Viikmäe 62), Saag. Coach: Viggo Jensen (DEN)
Goal(s): 1-0 Wright-Phillips 11, 2-0 Rooney 32, 3-0 Rähn 33(og)
Yellow Card(s): Rähn 12 (Estonia), Lindpere 73 (Estonia)
Referee: Vollquartz (DEN)

13/10/07, Maksimir, Zagreb
Croatia 1-0 Israel
Attendance: 30084
Croatia: Pletikosa, Šimić, Šimunić, R. Kovač, Ćorluka, Srna, Modrić, Leko, Olić (Rakitić 81), Kranjčar (Pranjić 46), Eduardo. Coach: Slaven Bilić (CRO)
Israel: Davidovich, Meshumar, Gershon, Ben Haim, Antebi, Baruchyan (Golan 58), Alberman, Benayoun, Balili (Tamuz 67), Barda (Ohayon 76), Cohen. Coach: Dror Kashtan (ISR)
Goal(s): 1-0 Eduardo 52
Yellow Card(s): Leko 24 (Croatia), Eduardo 45 (Croatia), Balali 62 (Israel), Ben Haim 65 (Israel), Cohen 71 (Israel), Antebi 87 (Israel)
Referee: Stark (GER)

17/10/07, Luzhniki Stadium, Moscow
Russia 2-1 England
Attendance: 75000
Russia: Gabulov, A. Berezutskiy, Ignashevich, V. Berezutskiy (Torbinskiy 46), Anyukov, Zyryanov, Semshov, Bilyaletdinov, Zhirkov, Arshavin (Kolodin 90), Kerzhakov (Pavlyuchenko 58). Coach: Guus Hiddink (NED)
England: Robinson, Richards, Ferdinand, Campbell, Lescott (Lampard 79), Wright-Phillips (Downing 80), Gerrard, Barry, J. Cole (Crouch 80), Rooney, Owen. Coach: Steve McClaren (ENG)
Goal(s): 0-1 Rooney 29, 1-1 Pavlyuchenko 69(p), 2-1 Pavlyuchenko 73
Yellow Card(s): V. Berezutskiy 14 (Russia), Ferdinand 58 (England), Rooney 69 (England), Pavlyuchenko 74 (Russia)
Referee: Medina Cantalejo (ESP)

17/10/07, Gradski, Skopje
FYR Macedonia 3-0 Andorra
Attendance: 17500
FYR Macedonia: Pačovski, Lazarevski, Noveski, Sedloski, I. Mitreski, G. Popov, Šumulikoski, Tasevski (Trajanov 84), Maznov (Ristić 62), Naumoski (Položani 75), Pandev. Coach: Srečko Katanec (SVN)
Andorra: Koldo, Sonejee, Fernández, I. Lima, Ayala, Escura, Pujol, Ruíz (Andorrá 63), Jiménez (Somoza 78), Vieira, Toscano (Riera 82). Coach: David Rodrigo (ESP)
Goal(s): 1-0 Naumoski 30, 2-0 Sedloski 44, 3-0 Pandev 59
Yellow Card(s): I. Lima 26 (Andorra), Koldo 56 (Andorra), Sonejee 77 (Andorra)
Referee: Malžinskas (LTU)

17/11/07, Estadi Comunal, Andorra la Vella
Andorra 0-2 Estonia
Attendance: 700
Andorra: Koldo, Txema (Jiménez 46), Escura, Sonejee, A. Lima, I.

Lima (Ruíz 81), Vieira, Ayala, Moreno (Toscano 70), Pujol, Sivera. Coach: David Rodrigo (ESP)
Estonia: Londak, Jääger, Kruglov (Vassiljev 84), Piiroja, Stepanov, Dmitrijev, Klavan, Lindpere, Reim (Teniste 68), Saag, Oper (Kink 46). Coach: Viggo Jensen (DEN)
Goal(s): 0-1 Oper 31, 0-2 Lindpere 60
Yellow Card(s): Vieira 16 (Andorra), Kruglov 36 (Estonia), Reim 40 (Estonia), Pujol 45+4 (Andorra), Ayala 65 (Andorra), Toscano 84 (Andorra), Klavan 90+2 (Estonia)
Referee: Collum (SCO)

17/11/07, Gradski, Skopje
FYR Macedonia 2-0 Croatia
Attendance: 14500
FYR Macedonia: Miloševski, Noveski, I. Mitreski, G. Popov, Sedloski (Grnčarov 88), Lazarevski, Tasevski, Grozdanoski, Šumulikoski, Maznov, Naumoski (Položani 84). Coach: Srečko Katanec (SVN)
Croatia: Pletikosa, Šimić, Šimunić, R. Kovač, Ćorluka, N. Kovač, Srna, Modrić, Kranjčar (Vukojević 75), Petrić (Mandžukić 42), Eduardo (Olić 54). Coach: Slaven Bilić (CRO)
Goal(s): 1-0 Maznov 71, 2-0 Naumoski 83
Yellow Card(s): Tasevski 14 (FYR Macedonia), Naumoski 27 (FYR Macedonia)
Referee: De Bleeckere (BEL)

17/11/07, Ramat Gan, Tel-Aviv
Israel 2-1 Russia
Attendance: 29787
Israel: Awat, Shpungin, Keinan, Ben Haim, Ziv, Cohen, Alberman, Itzhaki (Ben Shushan 62), Buzaglo (Ohayon 64), Barda, Sahar (Golan 69). Coach: Dror Kashtan (ISR)

Roman Pavlyuchenko scores his second goal of the game as Russia come from behind to defeat England 2-1 in Moscow

Russia: Gabulov, A. Berezutskiy, Ignashevich, V. Berezutskiy (Pogrebnyak 68), Anyukov, Zyryanov, Semshov (Torbinskiy 30), Bilyaletdinov, Zhirkov, Arshavin, Pavlyuchenko (Sychev 52). Coach: Guus Hiddink (NED)
Goal(s): 1-0 Barda 10, 1-1 Bilyaletdinov 61, 2-1 Golan 90+2
Yellow Card(s): Alberman 45+1 (Israel), Sahar 53 (Israel), Anyukov 77 (Russia)
Referee: Farina (ITA)

21/11/07, Ramat Gan, Tel-Aviv
Israel 1-0 FYR Macedonia
Attendance: 2736
Israel: Awat, Shpungin, Keinan, Ben Haim, Ziv, Ohayon, Cohen, Buzaglo (Ben Shushan 46), Itzhaki (Baruchyan 72), Barda, Colautti (Sahar 55). Coach: Dror Kashtan (ISR)
FYR Macedonia: Miloševski, Noveski, G. Popov, Sedloski, I. Mitreski, Grozdanoski (Georgievski 66), Šumulikoski, Lazarevski, Maznov (Ristić 60), Tasevski (Položani 46), Stojkov. Coach: Srečko Katanec (SVN)
Goal(s): 1-0 Barda 35
Yellow Card(s): Barda 43 (Israel)
Referee: Mikulski (POL)

21/11/07, Wembley, London
England 2-3 Croatia
Attendance: 88017
England: Carson, Richards, Campbell, Lescott, Bridge, Wright-Phillips (Beckham 46), Gerrard, Barry (Defoe 46), Lampard, J. Cole (Bent 80), Crouch. Coach: Steve McClaren (ENG)
Croatia: Pletikosa, Ćorluka, Šimić, R. Kovač, Šimunić, Srna, Modrić, N. Kovač, Kranjčar (Pranjić 75), Olić (Rakitić 84), Eduardo (Petrić 69). Coach: Slaven Bilić (CRO)
Goal(s): 0-1 Kranjčar 8, 0-2 Olić 14, 1-2 Lampard 56(p), 2-2 Crouch 65, 2-3 Petrić 77
Yellow Card(s): R. Kovač 32 (Croatia), Eduardo 50 (Croatia)
Referee: Fröjdfeldt (SWE)

21/11/07, Estadi Comunal, Andorra la Vella
Andorra 0-1 Russia
Attendance: 780
Andorra: Koldo (Gómes 46), Escura, Bernaus, Sonejee (Riera 83), A. Lima, I. Lima, Vieira (Andorrà 50), Sivera, Jiménez, Ruíz, Moreno. Coach: David Rodrigo (ESP)
Russia: Gabulov, Anyukov, A. Berezutskiy, V. Berezutskiy (Torbinskiy 38), Kolodin, Bilyaletdinov, Zhirkov, Zyryanov, Arshavin, Kerzhakov, Sychev. Coach: Guus Hiddink (NED)
Goal(s): 0-1 Sychev 38
Red Card(s): Arshavin 84 (Russia)
Yellow Card(s): A. Berezutskiy 10 (Russia), Ruíz 24 (Andorra), Koldo 45 (Andorra), I. Lima 46 (Andorra), A. Lima 59 (Andorra), Escura 76 (Andorra)
Referee: Hauge (NOR)

Group E Table

		Home					Away					Total					
	Pld	W	D	L	F	A	W	D	L	F	A	W	D	L	F	A	Pts
1 Croatia	12	5	1	0	14	1	4	1	1	14	7	9	2	1	28	8	29
2 Russia	12	4	2	0	12	2	2	2	2	6	5	7	3	2	18	7	24
3 England	12	4	1	1	16	3	3	1	2	8	4	7	2	3	24	7	23
4 Israel	12	4	1	1	14	6	3	1	2	6	6	7	2	3	20	12	23
5 FYR Macedonia	12	2	1	3	7	6	2	1	3	5	6	4	2	6	12	12	14
6 Estonia	12	1	0	5	2	9	1	1	4	3	12	2	1	9	5	21	7
7 Andorra	12	0	1	5	0	17	0	0	6	2	25	0	0	12	2	42	0

GROUP F

Spain and Sweden took the top spots in Group F as the autumn fixtures lacked the dramas that had characterised the section's opening stages.

Opening tie

Successive defeats in Northern Ireland and Sweden had placed a large question mark over the future of Spain coach Luis Aragonés earlier in the campaign, but four straight wins before the summer recess had averted disaster. Spain's campaign resumed with a fixture against an Iceland side enduring one of their worst campaigns in recent memory, but Aragonés was wary. "You don't always do well at some venues and we don't play well in Iceland." he said.

Sure enough, following Xabi Alonso's early dismissal, it took a late goal from substitute Andrés Iniesta to earn a 1-1 draw. It was hardly an inspiring result, but midfielder Xavi Hernández felt his side could turn things around. "We're all in the same boat," he said. "We're committed, our work is good and we believe in what we're doing. We have to analyse what happened in the first half against Iceland but there's no need to be alarmist either. Our only focus is on reaching the final tournament."

'Doing our duty'

Spain were to do that in some comfort in the end, beating Latvia 2-0 before earning a creditable and crucial 3-1 win in Denmark and an authoritative 3-0 home win against Sweden to seal qualification before signing off with a 1-0 victory against Northern Ireland. However, Aragonés was in no mood for rejoicing. "Spain have been qualifying for tournaments for many years so this isn't a success – but simply doing our duty," he said.

Earlier clashes with the press had clearly got under Aragonés' skin. He said: "I accept criticism but I have felt insulted at times and I won't accept that." He would not entertain thoughts of extending his contract beyond its expiry after UEFA EURO 2008™, saying: "I'm like milk. Once it's gone past its expiry date, you can't drink it any more."

Lagerbäck glad

By contrast, Sweden coach Lars Lagerbäck was glad to extend his contract until the end of the 2010 FIFA World Cup after securing his side's place in the finals. He said: "It will be a delightful and big challenge to take Sweden to a sixth championship in a row, which it will be if we qualify for the World Cup in South Africa in 2010."

At the halfway stage Sweden, like Spain, had looked set for a testing duel with Northern Ireland to earn a qualifying place, but while it took until the final day of the campaign to be mathematically certain of their place in Austria and Switzerland, a series of measured performances were enough to get Lagerbäck's side where they wanted to go.

Important draws

They drew 0-0 at home against neighbours Denmark, won 3-0 in Liechtenstein and kept Northern Ireland at arm's length with a 1-1 home draw – which would have been a 1-0 win had Kyle Lafferty not scored a fine equaliser 18 minutes from time. A 3-0 defeat in Spain delayed their celebrations, but they knew a draw in their final game against Latvia would be enough. In the event, they won 2-1. "We did what we had to do and that's all that matters," said star striker Zlatan Ibrahimović.

Northern Ireland finished a distant third, with Nigel Worthington failing to lead his side on a run as

Spain coach Luis Aragonés urges his team on

inspiring as that of his predecessor Lawrie Sanchez, who quit to take charge at Premier League Fulham FC before the summer break. David Healy broke a UEFA European Championship record, finishing the qualifying campaign with 13 goals, the last of them a glorious winning strike against Denmark at Windsor Park, but damaging defeats in Latvia and Iceland in September left Northern Ireland with far too much to do in the closing stages.

Group F Results

2/9/06
Northern Ireland 0-3 Iceland
Goal(s): 0-1 Thorvaldsson 13, 0-2 Hreidarsson 20, 0-3 Gudjohnsen 37
Latvia 0-1 Sweden
Goal(s): 0-1 Källström 38
Spain 4-0 Liechtenstein
Goal(s): 1-0 Fernando Torres 20, 2-0 David Villa 45, 3-0 David Villa 62, 4-0 Luis García 66

6/9/06
Iceland 0-2 Denmark
Goal(s): 0-1 Rommedahl 5, 0-2 Tomasson 33
Sweden 3-1 Liechtenstein
Goal(s): 1-0 Allbäck 2, 1-1 M. Frick 27, 2-1 Allbäck 69, 3-1 Rosenberg 89
Northern Ireland 3-2 Spain
Goal(s): 0-1 Xavi 14, 1-1 Healy 20, 1-2 David Villa 52, 2-2 Healy 64, 3-2 Healy 80

7/10/06
Sweden 2-0 Spain
Goal(s): 1-0 Elmander 10, 2-0 Allbäck 82
Denmark 0-0 Northern Ireland
Latvia 4-0 Iceland
Goal(s): 1-0 Karlsons 14, 2-0 Verpakovskis 15, 3-0 Verpakovskis 25, 4-0 Višņakovs 52

11/10/06
Iceland 1-2 Sweden
Goal(s): 1-0 Vidarsson 6, 1-1 Källström 8, 1-2 Wilhelmsson 59
Northern Ireland 1-0 Latvia
Goal(s): 1-0 Healy 35
Liechtenstein 0-4 Denmark
Goal(s): 0-1 D. Jensen 29, 0-2 Gravgaard 32, 0-3 Tomasson 51, 0-4 Tomasson 64

24/3/07
Liechtenstein 1-4 Northern Ireland
Goal(s): 0-1 Healy 52, 0-2 Healy 74, 0-3 Healy 83, 1-3 Burgmeier 90+1, 1-4 McCann 90+2
Spain 2-1 Denmark
Goal(s): 1-0 Morientes 34, 2-0 David Villa 45+1, 2-1 Gravgaard 49

28/3/07
Liechtenstein 1-0 Latvia
Goal(s): 1-0 M. Frick 17
Northern Ireland 2-1 Sweden
Goal(s): 0-1 Elmander 26, 1-1 Healy 31, 2-1 Healy 58
Spain 1-0 Iceland
Goal(s): 1-0 Iniesta 80

2/6/07
Iceland 1-1 Liechtenstein
Goal(s): 1-0 B. Gunnarsson 27, 1-1 Rohrer 69
Denmark 3-3 Sweden (match abandoned; awarded as 0-3)
Goal(s): 0-1 Elmander 7, 0-2 Hansson 23, 0-3 Elmander 26, 1-3 Agger 34, 2-3 Tomasson 62, 3-3 Andreasen 75
Latvia 0-2 Spain
Goal(s): 0-1 David Villa 45, 0-2 Xavi 60

6/6/07
Sweden 5-0 Iceland
Goal(s): 1-0 Allbäck 11, 2-0 Svensson 42, 3-0 Mellberg 45, 4-0 Rosenberg 50, 5-0 Allbäck 51
Liechtenstein 0-2 Spain
Goal(s): 0-1 David Villa 8, 0-2 David Villa 14
Latvia 0-2 Denmark
Goal(s): 0-1 Rommedahl 15, 0-2 Rommedahl 17

22/8/07, Windsor Park, Belfast
Northern Ireland 3-1 Liechtenstein
Attendance: 13544
Northern Ireland: Taylor, Duff, McCartney, Baird, Craigan, Clingan, Gillespie (Jones 85), Davis, Lafferty (Feeney 75), Healy, Brunt (Elliott 62). Coach: Nigel Worthington (NIR)
Liechtenstein: Jehle, Mi. Stocklasa (Oehri 38), Ma. Stocklasa, Telser, D'Elia, Polverino, R. Büchel, D. Frick, Biedermann (Büchel 62), Rohrer (R. Beck 74), M. Frick. Coach: Hans-Peter Zaugg (SUI)
Goal(s): 1-0 Healy 5, 2-0 Healy 35, 3-0 Lafferty 56, 3-1 M. Frick 89
Yellow Card(s): Mi. Stocklasa 25 (Liechtenstein), Duff 44 (Northern Ireland), D'Elia 66 (Liechtenstein)
Referee: Matejek (CZE)

8/9/07, Skonto, Riga
Latvia 1-0 Northern Ireland
Attendance: 7500
Latvia: Vaņins, Zirnis, Gorkšs, Kļava, Ivanovs, Bleidelis, Laizāns, Astafjevs, Rubins, Verpakovskis (Blanks 90), Karlsons (Rimkus 71). Coach: Aleksandrs Starkovs (LVA)
Northern Ireland: Taylor, Baird, Duff, Evans, McCartney, Gillespie, Clingan, Davis, Elliott (Brunt 66), Healy, Lafferty (Feeney 71). Coach: Nigel Worthington (NIR)
Goal(s): 1-0 Baird 69(og)
Yellow Card(s): Baird 48 (Northern Ireland), Zirnis 64 (Latvia), Rimkus 74 (Latvia), Gillespie 90+2 (Northern Ireland)
Referee: Pedro Proença (POR)

8/9/07, Laugardalsvöllur, Reykjavik
Iceland 1-1 Spain
Attendance: 9483
Iceland: Arason, K. Sigurdsson, R. Sigurdsson, Ingimarsson, Hreidarsson, Steinsson, Vidarsson (Skúlason 69), Gudjónsson (Adalsteinsson 79), Hallfredsson, Árnason, Thorvaldsson (Björnsson 88). Coach: Eyjölfur Sverrisson (ISL)
Spain: Casillas, Sergio Ramos, Marchena, Juanito, Pernía (Albelda 26), Joaquín (Luis García Fernández 69), Xabi Alonso, Xavi, Silva, Fernando Torres (Iniesta 57), David Villa. Coach: Luis Aragonés (ESP)
Goal(s): 1-0 Hallfredsson 40, 1-1 Iniesta 86
Red Card(s): Xabi Alonso 21 (Spain)
Yellow Card(s): Pernía 8 (Spain), Gudjónsson 36 (Iceland), R. Sigurdsson 61 (Iceland)
Referee: Stark (GER)

8/9/07, Råsunda, Solna
Sweden 0-0 Denmark
Attendance: 33082
Sweden: Isaksson, Nilsson, Mellberg, Hansson, Edman, Alexandersson, Linderoth, Svensson (Källström 69), Wilhelmsson (Bakircioglü 57), Ibrahimović (Prica 89), Elmander. Coach: Lars Lagerbäck (SWE)
Denmark: T. Sørensen, Andreasen (Løvenkrands 81), M. Laursen, Agger, N. Jensen, Helveg, D. Jensen, Rommedahl, Kahlenberg

(Bendtner 54), Tomasson (Gravgaard 90+1), Grønkjær. Coach: Morten Olsen (DEN)
Yellow Card(s): D. Jensen 8 (Denmark), Agger 21 (Denmark), Mellberg 27 (Sweden), Elmander 56 (Sweden), Ibrahimović 80 (Sweden), Grønkjær 80 (Denmark)
Referee: De Bleeckere (BEL)

12/9/07, Laugardalsvöllur, Reykjavik
Iceland 2-1 Northern Ireland
Attendance: 7727
Iceland: Arason, K. Sigurdsson, Árnason (Ásgeirsson 88), R. Sigurdsson, Ingimarsson, Steinsson, Hreidarsson, Vidarsson, Thorvaldsson (Skúlason 79), Björnsson (Gudjohnsen 53), Hallfredsson. Coach: Eyjölfur Sverrisson (ISL)
Northern Ireland: Taylor, Baird, Duff, Evans, McCartney, Gillespie, Clingan, Davis (McCann 79), Brunt (Jones 83), Healy, Feeney. Coach: Nigel Worthington (NIR)
Goal(s): 1-0 Björnsson 6, 1-1 Healy 72(p), 2-1 Gillespie 90+1(og)
Yellow Card(s): Björnsson 19 (Iceland), Feeney 41 (Northern Ireland), Hreidarsson 65 (Iceland), Brunt 68 (Northern Ireland), Baird 86 (Northern Ireland)
Referee: Baskakov (RUS)

12/9/07, Atletion, Aarhus
Denmark 4-0 Liechtenstein
Attendance: 20005
Denmark: T. Sørensen, M. Laursen, Agger (Gravgaard 28), N. Jensen, Helveg, Andreasen, Grønkjær (Kahlenberg 46), Nordstrand, Tomasson (Løvenkrands 68), Rommedahl, Hansen. Coach: Morten Olsen (DEN)
Liechtenstein: Jehle, Telser, Ma. Stocklasa, Ritzberger (T. Beck 46), Oehri (D. Frick 46), R. Büchel, Burgmeier, D'Elia, Rohrer, Polverino, M. Frick (R. Beck 84). Coach: Hans-Peter Zaugg (SUI)
Goal(s): 1-0 Nordstrand 3, 2-0 M. Laursen 12, 3-0 Tomasson 18, 4-0 Nordstrand 36
Yellow Card(s): T. Beck 47 (Liechtenstein), D'Elia 62 (Liechtenstein), Ma. Stocklasa 87 (Liechtenstein)
Referee: Clattenburg (ENG)

12/9/07, Nuevo Carlos Tartiere, Oviedo
Spain 2-0 Latvia
Attendance: 22560
Spain: Casillas, Sergio Ramos, Marchena, Juanito, Pernía, Joaquín (Angulo 77), Albelda, Xavi, Silva (Fàbregas 69), Fernando Torres, David Villa (Iniesta 48). Coach: Luis Aragonés (ESP)
Latvia: Vaņins, Zirnis, Kļava, Gorkšs, Ivanovs, Bleidelis (Višņakovs 74), Astafjevs, Laizāns, Rubins, Karlsons (Pahars 63), Verpakovskis (Blanks 88). Coach: Aleksandrs Starkovs (LVA)
Goal(s): 1-0 Xavi 13, 2-0 Fernando Torres 85
Yellow Card(s): Astafjevs 51 (Latvia), Ivanovs 60 (Latvia)
Referee: Yefet (ISR)

13/10/07, Laugardalsvöllur, Reykjavik
Iceland 2-4 Latvia
Attendance: 5865
Iceland: Arason, K. Sigurdsson (Björnsson 88), H. Jónsson, R. Sigurdsson, Ingimarsson, Steinsson (Árnason 25), B. Gunnarsson, Gudjónsson, Hallfredsson, Thorvaldsson (H. Sigurdsson 65), Gudjohnsen. Coach: Eyjölfur Sverrisson (ISL)
Latvia: Vaņins, Kļava, Gorkšs, Ivanovs, Zirnis, Astafjevs, Laizāns, Soloņicins, Višņakovs (Žigajevs 90+2), Karlsons (Rimkus 59), Verpakovskis (Pahars 78). Coach: Aleksandrs Starkovs (LVA)
Goal(s): 1-0 Gudjohnsen 4, 1-1 Klava 27, 1-2 Laizans 31, 1-3 Verpakovskis 37, 1-4 Verpakovskis 46, 2-4 Gudjohnsen 52
Yellow Card(s): Verpakovskis 22 (Latvia), K. Sigurdsson 48 (Iceland), B. Gunnarsson 86 (Iceland)
Referee: Dean (ENG)

13/10/07, Rheinpark, Vaduz
Liechtenstein 0-3 Sweden
Attendance: 4131
Liechtenstein: Jehle, Telser, Oehri, Hasler, Burgmeier, R. Büchel, M. Büchel (Gerster 61), T. Beck, M. Frick (R. Beck 74), Rohrer, D. Frick (Fischer 60). Coach: Hans-Peter Zaugg (SUI)
Sweden: Isaksson, Concha, Hansson, Majstorovic, Edman, Wilhelmsson, Linderoth (Andersson 70), Svensson, Ljungberg (Källström 39), Allbäck, Elmander (Rosenberg 60). Coach: Lars Lagerbäck (SWE)
Goal(s): 0-1 Ljungberg 19, 0-2 Wilhelmsson 29, 0-3 Svensson 56
Yellow Card(s): Telser 67 (Liechtenstein), Andersson 88 (Sweden)
Referee: Dondarini (ITA)

13/10/07, Atletion, Aarhus
Denmark 1-3 Spain
Attendance: 19849
Denmark: T. Sørensen, Helveg, M. Laursen, U. Laursen, N. Jensen (Perez 79), C. Poulsen, D. Jensen, Andreasen (Bendtner 46), Rommedahl, Tomasson, Grønkjær (Kahlenberg 65). Coach: Morten Olsen (DEN)
Spain: Casillas, Marchena, Sergio Ramos, Capdevila, Albiol, Albelda (Pablo 64), Xavi, Iniesta, Joaquín (Riera 69), Fàbregas (Luis García Fernández 78), Tamudo. Coach: Luis Aragonés (ESP)
Goal(s): 0-1 Tamudo 14, 0-2 Sergio Ramos 40, 1-2 Tomasson 87, 1-3 Riera 89
Yellow Card(s): D. Jensen 2 (Denmark), Capdevila 18 (Spain), Bendtner 77 (Denmark)
Referee: Michel (SVK)

17/10/07, Rheinpark, Vaduz
Liechtenstein 3-0 Iceland
Attendance: 2589
Liechtenstein: Jehle, Telser, Hasler, Ma. Stocklasa, Oehri, R. Büchel, Gerster, Burgmeier, Fischer (T. Beck 62), Rohrer (R. Beck 68), M. Frick (D'Elia 90+1). Coach: Hans-Peter Zaugg (SUI)
Iceland: Arason, Hreidarsson, K. Sigurdsson, Ingimarsson, R. Sigurdsson, Gudjónsson (Björnsson 58), Hallfredsson, Vidarsson, B. Gunnarsson (Ásgeirsson 85), Thorvaldsson (H. Sigurdsson 71), Gudjohnsen. Coach: Eyjölfur Sverrisson (ISL)
Goal(s): 1-0 M. Frick 28, 2-0 T. Beck 80, 3-0 T. Beck 82
Yellow Card(s): Ma. Stocklasa 64 (Liechtenstein), Gudjohnsen 75 (Iceland), Telser 87 (Liechtenstein)
Referee: Zografos (GRE)

17/10/07, Parken, Copenhagen
Denmark 3-1 Latvia
Attendance: 19004
Denmark: T. Sørensen, M. Laursen, U. Laursen (Andreasen 32), C. Sørensen, Helveg, C. Poulsen (Grønkjær 71), D. Jensen, Kahlenberg, Rommedahl, Bendtner, Tomasson. Coach: Morten Olsen (DEN)
Latvia: Vaņins, Kļava, Ivanovs, Zirnis, Gorkšs, Astafjevs, Laizāns, Višņakovs (Žigajevs 78), Soloņicins, Rimkus (Butriks 63), Pahars (Kačanovs 90+1). Coach: Aleksandrs Starkovs (LVA)
Goal(s): 1-0 Tomasson 7(p), 2-0 U. Laursen 27, 2-1 Gorkšs 80, 3-1 Rommedahl 90
Yellow Card(s): D. Jensen 32 (Denmark)
Referee: Çakır (TUR)

17/10/07, Råsunda, Solna
Sweden 1-1 Northern Ireland
Attendance: 33112
Sweden: Isaksson, Concha, Mellberg, Hansson, Edman, Linderoth, Svensson, Wilhelmsson (Nilsson 45), Källström (Johansson 85), Ibrahimović, Elmander (Allbäck 73). Coach: Lars Lagerbäck (SWE)
Northern Ireland: Taylor, McAuley, Hughes, McCartney (Capaldi 87), Craigan, Davis, Clingan, Brunt, Healy, Sproule, Lafferty. Coach: Nigel Worthington (NIR)

Sweden's Zlatan Ibrahimović tangles with Jurijs Laizāns of Latvia

Goal(s): 1-0 Mellberg 15, 1-1 Lafferty 72
Yellow Card(s): Lafferty 19 (Northern Ireland), Concha 45+2 (Sweden), Hansson 82 (Sweden)
Referee: Layec (FRA)

17/11/07, Skonto, Riga
Latvia 4-1 Liechtenstein
Attendance: 4800
Latvia: Vaņins, Gorkšs, Kļava, Zirnis, Ivanovs, Bleidelis (Višņakovs 82), Laizāns, Astafjevs, Rubins, Karlsons (Pahars 71), Verpakovskis (Rimkus 77). Coach: Aleksandrs Starkovs (LVA)
Liechtenstein: Jehle, Ritzberger, Ma. Stocklasa, D'Elia, Hasler, R. Büchel (M. Büchel 80), Gerster, Burgmeier, Rohrer (D. Frick 72), M. Frick, Fischer (R. Beck 71). Coach: Hans-Peter Zaugg (SUI)
Goal(s): 0-1 Zirnis 13(og), 1-1 Karlsons 14, 2-1 Verpakovskis 30, 3-1 Laizāns 63, 4-1 Višņakovs 87
Yellow Card(s): Karlsons 40 (Latvia), R. Büchel 59 (Liechtenstein), Kļava 66 (Latvia), D. Frick 76 (Liechtenstein), Gerster 81 (Liechtenstein)
Referee: Moen (NOR)

17/11/07, Windsor Park, Belfast
Northern Ireland 2-1 Denmark
Attendance: 12997
Northern Ireland: Taylor, McAuley, Evans, Craigan, Clingan, Gillespie (Sproule 74), Davis, Healy, Feeney (Baird 85), Brunt, Hughes. Coach: Nigel Worthington (NIR)
Denmark: T. Sørensen, C. Poulsen, M. Laursen, Krøldrup, C. Sørensen, Priske (Würtz 72), Andreasen, Kahlenberg (Sørensen 46), Bendtner, Jørgensen (S.B. Poulsen 79), Rommedahl. Coach: Morten Olsen (DEN)
Goal(s): 0-1 Bendtner 51, 1-1 Feeney 62, 2-1 Healy 80
Yellow Card(s): Gillespie 21 (Northern Ireland), Andreasen 52 (Denmark), Evans 82 (Northern Ireland)
Referee: Vink (NED)

17/11/07, Santiago Bernabéu Stadium, Madrid
Spain 3-0 Sweden
Attendance: 67055
Spain: Casillas, Sergio Ramos, Puyol, Marchena, Capdevila, Iniesta (Joaquín 52), Fàbregas, Albelda, Xavi, Silva (Riera 66), David Villa (Tamudo 52). Coach: Luis Aragonés (ESP)
Sweden: Isaksson, Nilsson, Mellberg, Hansson, Edman, Wilhelmsson (Bakircioglü 79), Andersson (Källström 46), Svensson, Ljungberg, Ibrahimović, Rosenberg (Allbäck 60). Coach: Lars Lagerbäck (SWE)
Goal(s): 1-0 Capdevila 14, 2-0 Iniesta 39, 3-0 Sergio Ramos 65
Yellow Card(s): Hansson 76 (Sweden), Puyol 88 (Spain)
Referee: Rosetti (ITA)

21/11/07, Gran Canaria, Las Palmas de Gran Canaria
Spain 1-0 Northern Ireland
Attendance: 30339
Spain: Reina, Sergio Ramos, Albiol, Pablo, Pernía, Iniesta, Xavi (David Villa 67), Fàbregas (Joaquín 47), Senna, Silva, Güiza (Tamudo 57). Coach: Luis Aragonés (NIR)
Northern Ireland: Taylor, McAuley, Craigan, Hughes, Baird, Sproule (Robinson 46), Clingan, Davis, Brunt (Lafferty 59), Healy, Feeney (Paterson 72). Coach: Nigel Worthington (ENG)
Goal(s): 1-0 Xavi 52
Yellow Card(s): Healy 74 (Northern Ireland), Lafferty 76 (Northern Ireland)
Referee: Fandel (GER)

21/11/07, Parken, Copenhagen
Denmark 3-0 Iceland
Attendance: 15393
Denmark: T. Sørensen, Kvist, U. Laursen, Krøldrup, C. Sørensen, Rommedahl (S.B. Poulsen 73), D. Jensen, C. Poulsen, Jørgensen (Kahlenberg 53), Bendtner (Larsen 84), Tomasson. Coach: Morten Olsen (DEN)
Iceland: Arason, Steinsson, K. Sigurdsson (Gardarsson 7), Hreidarsson, R. Sigurdsson, T. Bjarnason, B. Gunnarsson, Gíslason, Hallfredsson (Jónsson 73), V. P. Gunnarsson (Ásgeirsson 84), Thorvaldsson. Coach: Ólafur Jóhannesson (ISL)
Goal(s): 1-0 Bendtner 34, 2-0 Tomasson 44, 3-0 Kahlenberg 59
Yellow Card(s): Steinsson 40 (Iceland), T. Bjarnason 68 (Iceland), Andreasen 68 (Denmark), Krøldrup 77 (Denmark), Gíslason 79 (Iceland)
Referee: Benquerença (POR)

21/11/07, Råsunda, Solna
Sweden 2-1 Latvia
Attendance: 26128
Sweden: Isaksson, Nilsson, Mellberg, Majstorovic, Edman, Wilhelmsson, Källström, Svensson, Ljungberg, Ibrahimović, Allbäck. Coach: Lars Lagerbäck (SWE)
Latvia: Koļinko, Gorkšs, Stepanovs, Ivanovs, Zirnis, Rubins, Laizāns, Astafjevs (Soloņicins 49), Bleidelis (Višņakovs 43), Karlsons (Pahars 62), Verpakovskis. Coach: Aleksandrs Starkovs (LVA)
Goal(s): 1-0 Allbäck 1, 1-1 Laizāns 26, 2-1 Källström 57
Yellow Card(s): Zirnis 58 (Latvia), Soloņicins 77 (Latvia)
Referee: Stark (GER)

Group F Table

		Home					Away					Total					
	Pld	W	D	L	F	A	W	D	L	F	A	W	D	L	F	A	Pts
1 Spain	12	6	0	0	13	1	3	1	2	10	7	9	1	2	23	8	28
2 Sweden	12	4	2	0	13	3	4	0	2	10	6	8	2	2	23	9	26
3 Northern Ireland	12	5	0	1	11	8	1	2	3	6	6	6	2	4	17	14	20
4 Denmark	12	3	1	2	11	7	3	1	2	10	4	6	2	4	21	11	20
5 Latvia	12	3	0	3	9	6	1	0	5	6	11	4	0	8	15	17	12
6 Iceland	12	1	2	3	7	11	1	0	5	3	16	2	2	8	10	27	8
7 Liechtenstein	12	2	0	4	5	13	0	1	5	4	19	2	1	9	9	32	7

GROUP G

Romania made it to their first major finals tournament since UEFA EURO 2000™ in some comfort, with a win against runners-up the Netherlands proving crucial.

Piţurcă vindicated

Marco van Basten's squad had grabbed the headlines in the first part of the qualifying campaign as a host of young players shone for the Netherlands, but it was Romania coach Victor Piţurcă who was to have the last word. Piţurcă had led Romania through qualifying for UEFA EURO 2000™ only to be dismissed before the final tournament after a dispute with senior players. However, there were no signs of unrest as Romania won 2-0 at the Josy Barthel stadium in Luxembourg to confirm their place in the finals with two games to spare.

"It has taken seven years' hard toil to achieve this qualification," said captain Cristian Chivu. "I dedicate this victory to all those who believed in us, who stuck with us and will stay with us. I am sorry for not having qualified for previous tournaments, but from now on we will reach all our goals."

Spousal premonition

While victory in Luxembourg was the final step, the battle was won in earnest four days previously on 13 October as Dorin Goian's close-range 71st-minute strike saw Romania beat the Netherlands for the very first time, 1-0 in rainy Constanta. The defender said afterwards: "It's the most important goal of my life. Before the match my wife told me several times that I would score against the Netherlands. I thank her for her support and I don't feel any pain from the knocks I received in this match because I am so happy."

Romania's run of six Group G wins in succession was to end in their penultimate tie as Velizar Dimitrov's early goal gave Bulgaria a 1-0 win in Sofia. However, it was to be a pyrrhic victory for Dimitar Penev's side as a nervy 1-0 win for the Netherlands in their home game against Luxembourg the same night put them through.

Koevermans thrilled

Danny Koevermans, the scorer of the only goal on his first start for the Oranje, said: "It could be worse. Making your debut in the Oranje first XI at the age of 29 is already great but I never imagined I would score the goal to take us to the finals." Van Basten, meanwhile, felt compelled to defend his side, saying: "We have a lot of players with good attacking qualities and that is a luxury, but most of them are young boys who need to mature. With more experience, we will have a chance to clinch a major title." Van Basten later announced that he would quit after UEFA EURO 2008™.

The Dutch autumn campaign had been more functional than thrilling, with a 2-0 home win against Bulgaria on 8 September the pick of their results. But

Celebration time for Romania as they qualify for UEFA EURO 2008™ – their first major tournament appearance in eight years

after displaying some of their frailties in the win over Luxembourg, they let their guard down in their final game, allowing Belarus to record a famous 2-1 win in Minsk – a huge relief for German coach Bernd Stange who had earlier seen his side become the first side to lose a competitive game to Luxembourg since 1995, going down 1-0 in Gomel.

Penev reappointed

Stange had replaced Yuriy Puntus during the summer recess, while Bulgaria had made their third appointment of the campaign in re-hiring Penev – the man who masterminded their fourth-placed finish at the 1994 FIFA World Cup finals. Hristo Stoichkov's decision to take charge at RC Celta de Vigo prompted PFC Levski Sofia coach Stanimir Stoilov to accept a temporary commission. Penev then took command, but despite the consistent marksmanship of Dimitar Berbatov, he could not drive a wedge between Romania and the Netherlands.

Group G Results

2/9/06
Belarus 2-2 Albania
Goal(s): 1-0 Kalachev 2, 1-1 Skela 7(p), 2-1 Romashchenko 24, 2-2 Hasi 86
Luxembourg 0-1 Netherlands
Goal(s): 0-1 Mathijsen 18
Romania 2-2 Bulgaria
Goal(s): 1-0 Roşu 40, 2-0 Marica 55, 2-1 M. Petrov 82, 2-2 M. Petrov 84

6/9/06
Albania 0-2 Romania
Goal(s): 0-1 Dică 65, 0-2 Mutu 75(p)
Bulgaria 3-0 Slovenia
Goal(s): 1-0 Bozhinov 58, 2-0 M. Petrov 72, 3-0 Telkiyski 81
Netherlands 3-0 Belarus
Goal(s): 1-0 Van Persie 33, 2-0 Van Persie 78, 3-0 Kuyt 90+2

7/10/06
Romania 3-1 Belarus
Goal(s): 1-0 Mutu 7, 2-0 Marica 10, 2-1 Kornilenko 20, 3-1 Goian 76
Slovenia 2-0 Luxembourg
Goal(s): 1-0 Novakovič 30, 2-0 Koren 44
Bulgaria 1-1 Netherlands
Goal(s): 1-0 M. Petrov 12, 1-1 Van Persie 62

11/10/06
Belarus 4-2 Slovenia
Goal(s): 1-0 Kovba 18, 1-1 Cesar 19, 1-2 Lavrič 43, 2-2 Kornilenko 52, 3-2 Kornilenko 60, 4-2 Korytko 85
Luxembourg 0-1 Bulgaria
Goal(s): 0-1 Tunchev 26
Netherlands 2-1 Albania
Goal(s): 1-0 Van Persie 15, 2-0 Beqaj 42(og), 2-1 Curri 67

24/3/07
Luxembourg 1-2 Belarus
Goal(s): 0-1 Kalachev 25, 0-2 Kutuzov 54, 1-2 Sagramola 68
Albania 0-0 Slovenia
Netherlands 0-0 Romania

28/3/07
Bulgaria 0-0 Albania
Romania 3-0 Luxembourg
Goal(s): 1-0 Mutu 26, 2-0 Contra 56, 3-0 Marica 90
Slovenia 0-1 Netherlands
Goal(s): 0-1 Van Bronckhorst 86

2/6/07
Albania 2-0 Luxembourg
Goal(s): 1-0 Kapllani 38, 2-0 Haxhi 57
Slovenia 1-2 Romania
Goal(s): 0-1 Tamaş 52, 0-2 Nicoliţă 69, 1-2 Vršič 90+4
Belarus 0-2 Bulgaria
Goal(s): 0-1 Berbatov 28, 0-2 Berbatov 46

6/6/07
Bulgaria 2-1 Belarus
Goal(s): 0-1 Vasilyuk 5(p), 1-1 M. Petrov 10, 2-1 Yankov 40
Luxembourg 0-3 Albania
Goal(s): 0-1 Skela 25, 0-2 Kapllani 36, 0-3 Kapllani 72
Romania 2-0 Slovenia
Goal(s): 1-0 Mutu 40, 2-0 Contra 70

8/9/07, Josy Barthel, Luxembourg
Luxembourg 0-3 Slovenia
Attendance: 2012
Luxembourg: Joubert, Bigard, Hoffmann, Peiffer (Da Mota 52), Peters, Strasser, Bettmer, Lombardelli (Payal 46), Ferreira, Mutsch, Huss (Kitenge 63). Coach: Guy Hellers (LUX)
Slovenia: Handanovič, Kokot, Mörec, Koren, Novakovič, Stevanovič, Vršič (Mihelič 78), Žlogar (Cipot 82), Lavrič, Kirm (Komac 64), Brečko. Coach: Matjaž Kek (SVN)
Goal(s): 0-1 Lavrič 7, 0-2 Novakovič 37, 0-3 Lavrič 47
Yellow Card(s): Mihelič 86 (Slovenia)
Referee: Berezka (UKR)

8/9/07, Dinamo, Minsk
Belarus 1-3 Romania
Attendance: 19320
Belarus: Khomutovskiy, Korytko, Radkov, Plaskonnyi, Tigorev, Kalachev (Skvernyuk 77), Romashchenko, A. Hleb, Stasevich, Kornilenko, Rodionov (Vasilyuk 61). Coach: Bernd Stange (GER)
Romania: Lobonţ, Raţ, Chivu, Goian, Marin, Codrea (Trică 90), O. Petre, Nicoliţă, Dică (Munteanu 67), Mutu, Se. Radu (F. Petre 56). Coach: Victor Piţurcă (ROU)
Goal(s): 0-1 Mutu 16, 1-1 Romashchenko 20, 1-2 Dică 42, 1-3 Mutu 77(p)
Yellow Card(s): Codrea 56 (Romania), Raţ 61 (Romania), Khomutovskiy 75 (Belarus), O. Petre 81 (Romania), Chivu 83 (Romania)
Referee: Fröjdfeldt (SWE)

8/9/07, Amsterdam ArenA, Amsterdam
Netherlands 2-0 Bulgaria
Attendance: 49500
Netherlands: Van der Sar, Melchiot (Boulahrouz 66), Mathijsen, Bouma, Van Bronckhorst, Heitinga, Sneijder (Seedorf 73), De Zeeuw (De Jong 81), Babel, Van Nistelrooy, Van Persie. Coach: Marco van Basten (NED)
Bulgaria: Ivankov, Wagner (Yankov 79), Kishishev, Tunchev, Tomašić, Angelov, Peev (Popov 59), M. Petrov, S. Petrov, Telkiyski (V. Dimitrov 68), Berbatov. Coach: Dimitar Penev (BUL)
Goal(s): 1-0 Sneijder 22, 2-0 Van Nistelrooy 58
Yellow Card(s): Melchiot 14 (Netherlands), Wagner 25 (Bulgaria)
Referee: Medina Cantalejo (ESP)

12/9/07, Arena Petrol, Celje
Slovenia 1-0 Belarus
Attendance: 3500
Slovenia: Handanovič, Ilič (Brečko 82), Jokič, Mörec, Cipot, Koren, Kirm, Stevanovič (Žinko 75), Birsa (Vršič 67), Novakovič, Lavrič. Coach: Matjaž Kek (SVN)
Belarus: Gayev, Tigorev, Radkov, Plaskonnyi, Kalachev, Stasevich, Romashchenko, A. Hleb, Kornilenko (Rodionov 46), Korytko (Kashevskiy 89), Bliznyuk (Filipenko 74). Coach: Bernd Stange (GER)
Goal(s): 1-0 Lavrič 3(p)
Red Card(s): Radkov 70 (Belarus)
Yellow Card(s): Radkov 69 (Belarus), Radkov 70 (Belarus), Mörec 72 (Slovenia), Vršič 87 (Slovenia), Lavrič 89 (Slovenia)
Referee: Banari (MDA)

12/9/07, Vassil Levski National Stadium, Sofia
Bulgaria 3-0 Luxembourg
Attendance: 4674
Bulgaria: Petkov, Tunchev, Tomašić, Zanev, Angelov, Popov (Kushev 74), Kishishev, S. Petrov (Yankov 60), V. Dimitrov, Berbatov, M. Petrov (Yovov 66). Coach: Dimitar Penev (BUL)
Luxembourg: Joubert, Bigard, Kinziger, Hoffmann, Peiffer (Collette 46), Strasser, Peters, Bettmer (Da Mota 83), Remy, Mutsch, Huss (Payal 46). Coach: Guy Hellers (LUX)
Goal(s): 1-0 Berbatov 27, 2-0 Berbatov 28, 3-0 M. Petrov 54(p)
Yellow Card(s): Remy 30 (Luxembourg), Zanev 39 (Bulgaria), Hoffmann 54 (Luxembourg), Angelov 82 (Bulgaria), Strasser 83 (Luxembourg)
Referee: Demirlek (TUR)

12/9/07, Qemal Stafa, Tirana
Albania 0-1 Netherlands
Attendance: 15000
Albania: Beqaj, Dallku, Dede, Curri, Vangjeli, Duro (Haxhi 69), Lala, Cana, Muka, Bogdani (Bulku 83), Kapllani (Bushi 46). Coach: Otto Barić (CRO)
Netherlands: Van der Sar, Melchiot, Mathijsen, Bouma (Emanuelson 63), Ooijer, De Zeeuw, Sneijder, Van Bronckhorst, Babel (Kuyt 75), Van Nistelrooy, Van Persie (Van der Vaart 46). Coach: Marco van Basten (NED)
Goal(s): 0-1 Van Nistelrooy 90+1
Red Card(s): Cana 87 (Albania)
Yellow Card(s): Kapllani 31 (Albania), Van Persie 37 (Netherlands), Dallku 45+1 (Albania), Duro 65 (Albania), Melchiot 71 (Netherlands), Sneijder 87 (Netherlands), Van Nistelrooy 87 (Netherlands)
Referee: Riley (ENG)

13/10/07, Tsentralny, Gomel
Belarus 0-1 Luxembourg
Attendance: 14000
Belarus: Zhevnov (Khomutovskiy 69), Omelyanchuk, Stasevich (Kalachev 62), Filipenko, Plaskonnyi, Korytko, Skvernyuk, Romashchenko, A. Hleb, Kornilenko, Voronkov (Rodionov 80). Coach: Bernd Stange (GER)
Luxembourg: Joubert, Lang, Kinziger, Wagner, Peters, Payal (Ferreira 79), Bettmer, Lombardelli (A. Leweck 47), Remy, Mutsch, Kitenge (Da Mota 61). Coach: Guy Hellers (LUX)
Goal(s): 0-1 A. Leweck 90+5
Yellow Card(s): Lombardelli 28 (Luxembourg), Peters 46 (Luxembourg), Lang 71 (Luxembourg), A. Leweck 78 (Luxembourg), Joubert 82 (Luxembourg), Da Mota 85 (Luxembourg)
Referee: Svendsen (DEN)

13/10/07, Farul, Constanta
Romania 1-0 Netherlands
Attendance: 12595
Romania: Lobonţ, Goian, Ogăraru, Raţ, Tamaş, Chivu, Nicoliţă, Codrea, Petre, Marica (D. Niculae 70), Mutu. Coach: Victor Piţurcă (ROU)
Netherlands: Stekelenburg, Van Bronckhorst, Heitinga (Jaliens 68), Ooijer (Koevermans 84), Mathijsen, Bouma, De Zeeuw, Van der Vaart, Seedorf, Van Nistelrooy, Robben (Babel 78). Coach: Marco van Basten (NED)
Goal(s): 1-0 Goian 71
Yellow Card(s): Van Nistelrooy 64 (Netherlands), Mathijsen 66 (Netherlands), Van Bronckhorst 75 (Netherlands), Ogăraru 76 (Romania), Tamaş 81 (Romania), Mutu 86 (Romania), Nicoliţă 90+1 (Romania), Codrea 90+2 (Romania)
Referee: Vassaras (GRE)

13/10/07, Arena Petrol, Celje
Slovenia 0-0 Albania
Attendance: 3700
Slovenia: Handanovič, Brečko, Jokič (Ilič 77), Mörec, Cipot, Žlogar, Kirm, Koren, Birsa (Mihelič 82), Novakovič (Rusič 61), Lavrič. Coach: Matjaž Kek (SVN)
Albania: Beqaj, Vangjeli, Curri, Dede, Rrustemi, Haxhi (Muka 60), Lala, Bulku, Duro (Bushi 77), Skela (Hyka 90+1), Bogdani. Coach: Otto Barić (CRO)
Yellow Card(s): Curri 22 (Albania), Rušič 74 (Slovenia), Kirm 75 (Slovenia), Brečko 90+4 (Slovenia)
Referee: Pereira Gomes (POR)

17/10/07, Josy Barthel, Luxembourg
Luxembourg 0-2 Romania
Attendance: 3584
Luxembourg: Joubert, Lang, Wagner, Kinziger, Hoffmann, Mutsch, Payal (A. Leweck 68), Peters, Bettmer (Ferreira 49), Remy, Kitenge (Da Mota 57). Coach: Guy Hellers (LUX)
Romania: Lobonţ, Ogăraru, Tamaş, Goian, Raţ, Petre, Mărgăritescu, Chivu (Petre 87), Marica, Dică (Cristea 68), D. Niculae (Bratu 76). Coach: Victor Piţurcă (ROU)
Goal(s): 0-1 Petre 42, 0-2 Marica 61
Yellow Card(s): Marica 61 (Romania), Petre 72 (Romania)
Referee: Brych (GER)

17/10/07, Philips Stadion, Eindhoven
Netherlands 2-0 Slovenia
Attendance: 32500
Netherlands: Stekelenburg, Jaliens, Heitinga, Bouma, Emanuelson, Sneijder, De Zeeuw, Seedorf, Van Persie (Ooijer 59), Huntelaar, Van der Vaart (Robben 29; Babel 62). Coach: Marco van Basten (NED)
Slovenia: Handanovič, Cesar, Koren, Mörec, Brečko, Žlogar, Kirm (Jokič 81), Lavrič, Birsa (Novakovič 67), Ilič, Komac (Ljubijankič 85). Coach: Matjaž Kek (SVN)
Goal(s): 1-0 Sneijder 14, 2-0 Huntelaar 86
Yellow Card(s): Bouma 75 (Netherlands), Cesar 89 (Slovenia)
Referee: Rizzoli (ITA)

17/10/07, Qemal Stafa, Tirana
Albania 1-1 Bulgaria
Attendance: 3000
Albania: Beqaj, Curri, Dallku, Dede, Vangjeli, Duro, Haxhi (Muka 46), Lala, Skela, Salihi (Bulku 73), Bogdani. Coach: Otto Barić (CRO)
Bulgaria: Petkov, Kishishev, Tomašić, V. Iliev, Wagner, Angelov, S. Petrov (Georgiev 46), Telkiyski (Yankov 46), Popov (Yovov 72), M. Petrov, Berbatov. Coach: Dimitar Penev (BUL)
Goal(s): 1-0 Kishishev 25(og), 1-1 Berbatov 87
Yellow Card(s): Angelov 28 (Bulgaria), Dallku 35 (Albania), Salihi 63 (Albania), Wagner 83 (Bulgaria), Beqaj 85 (Albania)
Referee: Stuchlik (AUT)

17/11/07, Vassil Levski National Stadium, Sofia
Bulgaria 1-0 Romania
Attendance: 6000
Bulgaria: Ivankov, Milanov, Tomašić, Tunchev, Zanev, Georgiev, S. Petrov, Yovov (Telkiyski 83), V. Dimitrov, M. Petrov (Lazarov 90), Berbatov. Coach: Dimitar Penev (BUL)
Romania: Lobonţ, Ogăraru, Tamaş (Cociş 58), Goian, Raţ, Codrea

(Trică 82), Petre, Chivu, Nicoliţă, Mazilu (Marica 65), D.Niculae. Coach: Victor Piţurcă (ROU)
Goal(s): 1-0 V. Dimitrov 6
Yellow Card(s): Codrea 49 (Romania), Trică 85 (Romania), Milanov 90 (Bulgaria)
Referee: Plautz (AUT)

17/11/07, Qemal Stafa, Tirana
Albania 2-4 Belarus
Attendance: 2064
Albania: Beqaj, Curri, Dede, Lala (Bushi 75), Rrustemi (Vangjeli 38), Skela, Cana, Dallku, Duro, Bogdani, Kapllani (Salihi 74). Coach: Slavko Kovačić (CRO)
Belarus: Zhevnov, Omelyanchuk, Filipenko, Plaskonnyi (Skvernyuk 65), Kirenkin, Kulchiy, Kalachev (Korytko 75), Romashchenko, A. Hleb, Bulyga, Kutuzov (Kornilenko 90). Coach: Bernd Stange (GER)
Goal(s): 0-1 Romashchenko 32, 1-1 Bogdani 43, 2-1 Kapllani 44, 2-2 Kutuzov 45+1, 2-3 Kutuzov 54, 2-4 Romashchenko 63(p)
Yellow Card(s): Plaskonnyi 3 (Belarus), Kirenkin 8 (Belarus), Kalachev 49 (Belarus), Skela 53 (Albania), Dallku 62 (Albania), Cana 86 (Albania), Filipenko 90 (Belarus)
Referee: Demirlek (TUR)

17/11/07, De Kuip, Rotterdam
Netherlands 1-0 Luxembourg
Attendance: 45000
Netherlands: Van der Sar, Melchiot, Mathijsen, Bouma, De Zeeuw, Van Bronckhorst, Van der Vaart, Sneijder, Seedorf (Emanuelson 77), Van Nistelrooy (Kuyt 46), Koevermans (Babel 84). Coach: Marco van Basten (NED)
Luxembourg: Joubert, Kinziger, Hoffmann, Wagner, Strasser, Mutsch, Peters, Payal, Bettmer (A. Leweck 66), Remy, Kitenge (Joachim 50; Da Mota 85). Coach: Guy Hellers (LUX)
Goal(s): 1-0 Koevermans 43
Yellow Card(s): Strasser 80 (Luxembourg)
Referee: Hansson (SWE)

Aleksei Skvernyuk of Belarus (foreground) eyes the ball with the Netherlands' Dirk Kuyt in misty Minsk

21/11/07, Lia Manoliu, Bucharest
Romania 6-1 Albania
Attendance: 23427
Romania: Lobonţ, Ogăraru, Tamaş (Constantin 78), Goian, Raţ, Petre (Bucur 65), Mărgăritescu, Cociş, D. Niculae, Marica (Mazilu 73), Dică. Coach: Victor Piţurcă (ROU)
Albania: Beqaj, Curri, Dede, Vangjeli (Kapllani 41), Lila, Haxhi, Lala, Bulku, Duro (Hyka 78), Skela, Bogdani (Bakaj 83). Coach: Slavko Kovačić (CRO)
Goal(s): 1-0 Dică 22, 2-0 Tamaş 53, 3-0 D. Niculae 62, 3-1 Kapllani 64, 4-1 D. Niculae 65, 5-1 Marica 69(p), 6-1 Dică 71(p)
Red Card(s): Curri 61 (Albania), Dede 70 (Albania)
Yellow Card(s): Curri 29 (Albania), Marica 30 (Romania), Vangjeli 37 (Albania), Dede 47 (Albania), Curri 61 (Albania), Dede 70 (Albania)
Referee: Trivković (CRO)

21/11/07, Arena Petrol, Celje
Slovenia 0-2 Bulgaria
Attendance: 3700
Slovenia: Handanovič, Jokič, Mörec, Cesar, Brečko, Žlogar, Koren, Stevanovič (Komac 56), Kirm, Birsa (Ilič 48), Lavrič (Novakovič 65). Coach: Matjaž Kek (SVN)
Bulgaria: Ivankov, Milanov (Todorov 46), Tomašić, Tunchev, Angelov, Georgiev, S. Petrov (Telkiyski 46), Yovov (Lazarov 75), V. Dimitrov, M. Petrov, Berbatov. Coach: Dimitar Penev (BUL)
Goal(s): 0-1 Georgiev 82, 0-2 Berbatov 84
Red Card(s): Jokič 45 (Slovenia)
Yellow Card(s): Žlogar 35 (Slovenia), S. Petrov 38 (Bulgaria), Ilič 53 (Slovenia), Komac 75 (Slovenia), Georgiev 82 (Bulgaria)
Referee: Webb (ENG)

21/11/07, Dinamo, Minsk
Belarus 2-1 Netherlands
Attendance: 11900
Belarus: Zhevnov, Omelyanchuk (Stasevich 90+1), Filipenko, Kirenkin, Skvernyuk, Korytko, A. Hleb (Kashevskiy 46), Kulchiy, Romashchenko, Kutuzov, Bulyga (Kornilenko 86). Coach: Bernd Stange (GER)
Netherlands: Stekelenburg, Melchiot, Mathijsen, Ooijer, Bouma, Sneijder (Kuyt 46), Van der Vaart, Van Bronckhorst (Engelaar 66), De Zeeuw (De Jong 69), Babel, Koevermans. Coach: Marco van Basten (NED)
Goal(s): 1-0 Bulyga 49, 2-0 Korytko 65, 2-1 Van der Vaart 89
Yellow Card(s): Omelyanchuk 9 (Belarus), Romashchenko 40 (Belarus), Babel 57 (Netherlands)
Referee: Layec (FRA)

Group G Table

		Home					Away					Total					
	Pld	W	D	L	F	A	W	D	L	F	A	W	D	L	F	A	Pts
1 Romania	12	5	1	0	17	4	4	1	1	9	3	9	2	1	26	7	29
2 Netherlands	12	5	1	0	10	1	3	1	2	5	4	8	2	2	15	5	26
3 Bulgaria	12	4	2	0	10	2	3	2	1	8	5	7	4	1	18	7	25
4 Belarus	12	2	1	3	9	11	2	0	4	8	12	4	1	7	17	23	13
5 Albania	12	1	2	3	5	8	1	3	2	7	10	2	5	5	12	18	11
6 Slovenia	12	2	1	3	4	5	1	1	4	5	11	3	2	7	9	16	11
7 Luxembourg	12	0	0	6	1	12	1	0	5	1	11	1	0	11	2	23	3

CHAPTER

02

Some 50 years after a great Manchester United FC side was decimated by the Munich air crash, another one claimed the English club's third European Champion Clubs' Cup in Moscow, prevailing 6-5 on penalties after a 1-1 draw with Premier League rivals Chelsea FC.

Crash survivor Sir Bobby Charlton, who went on to score twice in the 1968 European Cup final win against SL Benfica, led the United players up the stairs at the Luzhniki stadium to lift the trophy. "Fate played its hand," said manager Sir Alex Ferguson, who also led United to victory in 1999. "We had a cause which is important and people with causes become very difficult people to fight against." Edwin van der Sar denied Nicolas Anelka from the spot in what proved to be the final act of an enthralling tournament, but Chelsea fans know that, but for a slip from captain John Terry, it could have been a different story.

2007/08

UEFA
CHAMPIONS
LEAGUE

FIRST & SECOND QUALIFYING ROUNDS

The road to Moscow must have appeared long and daunting to the 28 clubs that entered the UEFA Champions League in the first qualifying round on 11 July - not least for the champions of San Marino, Andorra and Montenegro who were making their competition debuts.

Aldair return

S.S. Murata of San Marino may have been rank minnows yet they were able to boast a FIFA World Cup winner after former Brazil defender Aldair agreed to return to competitive action aged 41. "I haven't played on an eleven-a-side pitch for a while but you can trust me - I'm in very good physical condition," the former AS Roma stalwart said prior to Murata's tie with Tampere United. Aldair proved true to his word, impressing in a 2-1 first-leg defeat, but he missed the return as the Finnish title-holders secured their passage 4-1 on aggregate.

Andorran champions FC Rànger's also found the going tough, losing 5-0 to Moldova's FC Sheriff, but a 5-4 aggregate triumph for FK Zeta of Montenegro over Lithuania's FBK Kaunas ensured one of the new nations would be represented in the second round. Bosnia-Herzegovina's FK Sarajevo led the way on the scoring front, firing nine past Maltese champions Marsaxlokk FC, while MŠK Žilina of Slovakia withstood a spirited second-leg fightback from Luxembourg's F91 Dudelange to run out 7-5 victors.

The second qualifying round marked the arrival of two former winners, FC Steaua Bucureşti and FK Crvena Zvezda, as well as some big-name coaches. Steaua legend Gheorghe Hagi enjoyed a successful European debut in the dugout as the Romanian giants beat Zagłębie Lubin of Poland 3-1 on aggregate, and Crvena Zvezda edged past Estonia's FC Levadia Tallinn 2-1 to set up a mouthwatering clash with Rangers FC, who opened their campaign with a 3-0 win over FK Zeta.

Trapattoni lesson

For some the opportunity to rub shoulders with the best proved inspiring. FK Ventspils coach Roman Grigorchuk expressed his delight at drawing Giovanni Trapattoni's FC Salzburg, saying he looked forward to "a big lesson" from the Italian coach. So it proved, the

Brazilian World Cup winner Aldair came out of retirement to play for San Marino champions Murata

Austrians winning 7-0 on aggregate thanks to four René Aufhauser goals.

Finland's Tampere United clinched the result of the round, following up their first-ever victory in the competition with another, against PFC Levski Sofia. "It's a sensation for Finnish and European football," Tampere's proud coach Ari Hjelm said of the 2-0 aggregate triumph. Elsewhere, Belarus secured representation in the third qualifying round for the first time as FC BATE Borisov surprised FH Hafnarfjördur with a 3-1 first-leg success in Iceland. "I will play my best team in the second leg," vowed FH coach Gudmundur Sævarsson. "We'll go to Belarus with optimism." The damage had been done, however, and BATE progressed 4-2 on aggregate.

Notable scalp

FK Sarajevo also registered a notable scalp away from home, Veldin Muharemović's late strike sealing a 2-1 victory over Belgium's KRC Genk, who crashed out despite triumphing 1-0 in the return leg. Meanwhile, there were comfortable wins for FC Shakhtar Donetsk against Armenia's FC Pyunik, NK Dinamo Zagreb over Slovenia's NK Domžale, Beşiktaş JK over FC Sheriff, and for regular participants Rosenborg BK, who rattled in ten goals against FC Astana of Kazakhstan.

First Qualifying Round Results

17/7/07, Poladi, Rustavi
FC Olimpi Rustavi 0-0 FC Astana
Referee: Borski (POL)
24/7/07, Tcentralny, Kostanay
FC Astana 3-0 FC Olimpi Rustavi
Goal(s): 1-0 Kuchma 12, 2-0 Tlekhugov 55, 3-0 Zhalmagambetov 84
Referee: Banari (MDA)
Aggregate: 3-0; FC Astana qualify.

17/7/07, Tofikh Bakhramov-Republic Stadium, Baku
FK Khazar Länkäran 1-1 NK Dinamo Zagreb
Goal(s): 1-0 Ramazanov 58, 1-1 Etto 63
Referee: Levi (ISR)
24/7/07, Maksimir, Zagreb
NK Dinamo Zagreb 3-1 FK Khazar Länkäran
Goal(s): 0-1 Juninho 16, 1-1 Vugrinec 56, 2-1 Mandžukić 99, 3-1 Tadić 116
Referee: González Vázquez (ESP)
Aggregate: 4-2; NK Dinamo Zagreb qualify after extra time.

17/7/07, Windsor Park, Belfast
Linfield FC 0-0 IF Elfsborg
Referee: Tagliavento (ITA)
25/7/07, Borås Arena, Boras
IF Elfsborg 1-0 Linfield FC
Goal(s): 1-0 M. Svensson 32
Referee: Brych (GER)
Aggregate: 1-0; IF Elfsborg qualify.

17/7/07, GSP, Nicosia
APOEL FC 2-0 FC BATE Borisov
Goal(s): 1-0 Michail 42, 2-0 Machlas 61
Referee: Thual (FRA)
24/7/07, Gradski, Borisov
FC BATE Borisov 3-0 APOEL FC
Goal(s): 1-0 Stasevich 14, 2-0 Platonov 74, 3-0 Bliznyuk 104
Referee: Collum (SCO)
Aggregate: 3-2; FC BATE Borisov qualify after extra time.

17/7/07, Latham Park, Newtown
The New Saints FC 3-2 FK Ventspils
Goal(s): 1-0 Wilde 14, 1-1 Rimkus 26, 2-1 Baker 54, 2-2 Rimkus 89, 3-2 Hogan 90+4
Referee: Attard (MLT)
25/7/07, Ventspils Pilsetas, Ventspils
FK Ventspils 2-1 The New Saints FC
Goal(s): 1-0 Ndeki 17, 2-0 Kačanovs 53, 2-1 Naylor 90+2
Referee: Valgeirsson (ISL)
Aggregate: 4-4; FK Ventspils qualify on away goals.

17/7/07, Pod Goricom - Gradski, Podgorica
FK Zeta 3-1 FBK Kaunas
Goal(s): 1-0 Korać 34(p), 2-0 Tumbasević 36, 3-0 Stjepanović 59, 3-1 Kvaratskhelia 68
Referee: Kuipers (NED)
24/7/07, S. Darius & S. Girenas, Kaunas
FBK Kaunas 3-2 FK Zeta
Goal(s): 1-0 Beniušis 6, 2-0 Kvaratskhelia 16, 3-0 Ksanavicius 20, 3-1 Stjepanović 34, 3-2 Ćetković 89
Referee: Havrilla (SVK)
Aggregate: 4-5; FK Zeta qualify.

17/7/07, Olimpico, Serravalle
S.S. Murata 1-2 Tampere United
Goal(s): 1-0 Protti 43, 1-1 Niemi 68, 1-2 Niemi 88
Referee: Stavrev (MKD)
25/7/07, Ratina, Tampere
Tampere United 2-0 S.S. Murata
Goal(s): 1-0 Petrescu 7, 2-0 Niemi 21
Referee: Wilmes (LUX)
Aggregate: 4-1; Tampere United qualify.

18/7/07, Goce Delcev, Prilep
FK Pobeda 0-1 FC Levadia Tallinn
Goal(s): 0-1 Nahk 53
Referee: Nalbandyan (ARM)
25/7/07, Kadriorg, Tallinn
FC Levadia Tallinn 0-0 FK Pobeda
Referee: Fábian (HUN)
Aggregate: 1-0; FC Levadia Tallinn qualify.

18/7/07, Sheriff, Tiraspol
FC Sheriff 2-0 FC Rànger's
Goal(s): 1-0 Kuchuk 45+7, 2-0 Gorodetschi 79
Referee: Vad (HUN)
24/7/07, Estadi Comunal, Andorra la Vella
FC Rànger's 0-3 FC Sheriff
Goal(s): 0-1 Balima 68, 0-2 Kajkut 77, 0-3 Suvorov 89
Referee: Yusifov (AZE)
Aggregate: 0-5; FC Sheriff qualify.

18/7/07, Jos Nosbaum, Dudelange
F91 Dudelange 1-2 MŠK Žilina
Goal(s): 1-0 Di Gregorio 45(p), 1-1 Jež 48(p), 1-2 Lietava 73
Referee: Gonchar (RUS)
25/7/07, Pod Dubnon, Zilina
MŠK Žilina 5-4 F91 Dudelange
Goal(s): 1-0 Devátý 8, 2-0 Lietava 11, 3-0 Štyvar 29, 3-1 Di Gregorio 40, 3-2 Hammani 49, 4-2 Vomáčka 66, 4-3 Guthleber 71, 5-3 Štyvar 75, 5-4 Lukic 82
Referee: Paraty (POR)
Aggregate: 7-5; MŠK Žilina qualify.

18/7/07, Ta' Qali, Ta' Qali
Marsaxlokk FC 0-6 FK Sarajevo
Goal(s): 0-1 Raščić 5, 0-2 Raščić 9, 0-3 Obuća 20, 0-4 Maksimović 42, 0-5 Obuća 65, 0-6 Bučan 87
Referee: Vlk (SVK)
24/7/07, Koševo, Sarajevo
FK Sarajevo 3-1 Marsaxlokk FC
Goal(s): 1-0 Mešić 42, 2-0 Šaraba 60, 2-1 Frendo 65, 3-1 Turković 76
Referee: Todorov (BUL)
Aggregate: 9-1; FK Sarajevo qualify.

18/7/07, Športni park, Domzale
NK Domžale 1-0 KF Tirana
Goal(s): 1-0 Janković 44
Referee: Atkinson (ENG)
25/7/07, Qemal Stafa, Tirana
KF Tirana 1-2 NK Domžale
Goal(s): 0-1 Ljubijankič 30, 1-1 Duro 74, 1-2 Ljubijankič 77
Referee: Germanakos (GRE)
Aggregate: 1-3; NK Domžale qualify.

18/7/07, Brandywell, Derry
Derry City FC 0-0 FC Pyunik
Referee: Trifonos (CYP)
25/7/07, Republican, Yerevan
FC Pyunik 2-0 Derry City FC
Goal(s): 1-0 Avetisyan 28, 2-0 Ghazaryan 67
Referee: Krajnc (SVN)
Aggregate: 2-0; FC Pyunik qualify.

18/7/07, Kaplakrikavöllur, Hafnarfjordur
FH Hafnarfjördur 4-1 HB Tórshavn
Goal(s): 1-0 Bjarnason 14, 2-0 Vilhjálmsson 16, 2-1 Nielsen 44(og), 3-1 Ólafsson 52, 4-1 Vilhjálmsson 58
Referee: Black (NIR)
25/7/07, Tórsvøllur, Torshavn
HB Tórshavn 0-0 FH Hafnarfjördur
Referee: Kari (FIN)
Aggregate: 1-4; FH Hafnarfjördur qualify.

Second Qualifying Round Results

31/7/07, Ratina, Tampere
Tampere United 1-0 PFC Levski Sofia
Goal(s): 1-0 Petrescu 15
Referee: McDonald (SCO)
7/8/07, Vasil Levski National Stadium, Sofia
PFC Levski Sofia 0-1 Tampere United
Goal(s): 0-1 Niemi 40
Referee: Kinhöfer (GER)
Aggregate: 0-2; Tampere United qualify.

31/7/07, Republican, Yerevan
FC Pyunik 0-2 FC Shakhtar Donetsk
Goal(s): 0-1 Hladkiy 45, 0-2 Brandão 48
Referee: Messner (AUT)
8/8/07, RSC Olympiyskiy Stadium, Donetsk
FC Shakhtar Donetsk 2-1 FC Pyunik
Goal(s): 0-1 Ghazaryan 31, 1-1 Brandão 40, 2-1 Hladkiy 49
Referee: João Ferreira (POR)
Aggregate: 4-1; FC Shakhtar Donetsk qualify.

31/7/07, Ibrox, Glasgow
Rangers FC 2-0 FK Zeta
Goal(s): 1-0 Weir 55, 2-0 Novo 72
Referee: Kasnaferis (GRE)
7/8/07, Pod Goricom - Gradski, Podgorica
FK Zeta 0-1 Rangers FC
Goal(s): 0-1 Beasley 81
Referee: Dondarini (ITA)
Aggregate: 0-3; Rangers FC qualify.

31/7/07, Parken Stadium, Copenhagen
FC København 1-0 Beitar Jerusalem FC
Goal(s): 1-0 Allbäck 9
Referee: Iturralde González (ESP)
7/8/07, Teddy Maicha, Jerusalem
Beitar Jerusalem FC 1-1 FC København
Goal(s): 1-0 Itzhaki 60, 1-1 Allbäck 97
Referee: Rizzoli (ITA)
Aggregate: 1-2; FC København qualify after extra time.

31/7/07, Cristal Arena, Genk
KRC Genk 1-2 FK Sarajevo
Goal(s): 0-1 Raščić 15, 1-1 Cornelis 23, 1-2 Muharemović 86
Referee: Egorov (RUS)
8/8/07, Koševo, Sarajevo
FK Sarajevo 0-1 KRC Genk
Goal(s): 0-1 Mikulić 58
Referee: Tudor (ROU)
Aggregate: 2-2; FK Sarajevo qualify on away goals.

31/7/07, Oláh Gábor, Debrecen
Debreceni VSC 0-1 IF Elfsborg
Goal(s): 0-1 Mobaeck 65
Referee: Kaldma (EST)
8/8/07, Borås Arena, Boras
IF Elfsborg 0-0 Debreceni VSC
Referee: Circhetta (SUI)
Aggregate: 1-0; IF Elfsborg qualify.

31/7/07, Zagłębie, Lubin
Zagłębie Lubin 0-1 FC Steaua Bucureşti
Goal(s): 0-1 Goian 55
Referee: Dereli (TUR)
8/8/07, Steaua Stadium, Bucharest
FC Steaua Bucureşti 2-1 Zagłębie Lubin
Goal(s): 0-1 Stasiak 29, 1-1 Nicoliţă 37, 2-1 Zaharia 83
Referee: Clattenburg (ENG)
Aggregate: 3-1; FC Steaua Bucureşti qualify.

1/8/07, Skonto, Riga
FK Ventspils 0-3 FC Salzburg
Goal(s): 0-1 Aufhauser 20, 0-2 Aufhauser 27, 0-3 Aufhauser 83(p)
Referee: Bossen (NED)

Romanian great Gheorghe Hagi coached Steaua Bucureşti to victory over Polish champions Zagłębie Lubin in the second qualifying round

8/8/07, Salzburg, Wals-Siezenheim
FC Salzburg 4-0 FK Ventspils
Goal(s): 1-0 Aufhauser 9, 2-0 Dudić 48, 3-0 Ilić 77, 4-0 Leitgeb 90+2
Referee: Berntsen (NOR)
Aggregate: 7-0; FC Salzburg qualify.

1/8/07, Tcentralny, Kostanay
FC Astana 1-3 Rosenborg BK
Goal(s): 0-1 Koné 3, 1-1 Kuchma 26, 1-2 Iversen 56(p), 1-3 Koné 61
Referee: Gumienny (BEL)
8/8/07, Lerkendal, Trondheim
Rosenborg BK 7-1 FC Astana
Goal(s): 1-0 Koné 1, 2-0 Iversen 7, 3-0 Traoré 17, 3-1 Suchkov 22, 4-1 Koné 33, 5-1 Traoré 50, 6-1 Traoré 53, 7-1 Sapara 62
Referee: Courtney (NIR)
Aggregate: 10-2; Rosenborg BK qualify.

1/8/07, Kaplakrikavöllur, Hafnarfjordur
FH Hafnarfjördur 1-3 FC BATE Borisov
Goal(s): 1-0 Vilhjálmsson 18, 1-1 Likhtarovich 31, 1-2 Rodionov 50, 1-3 Bliznyuk 61
Referee: Granat (POL)
8/8/07, Gradski, Borisov
FC BATE Borisov 1-1 FH Hafnarfjördur
Goal(s): 0-1 T. Gudmundsson 33, 1-1 Platonov 90+3
Referee: Stuchlik (AUT)
Aggregate: 4-2; FC BATE Borisov qualify.

1/8/07, Pod Dubnon, Zilina
MŠK Žilina 0-0 SK Slavia Praha
Referee: Ingvarsson (SWE)
8/8/07, Evžena Rošického, Prague
SK Slavia Praha 0-0 MŠK Žilina
Referee: Pereira Gomes (POR)
Aggregate: 0-0; SK Slavia Praha qualify 4-3 on penalties.

1/8/07, FK Crvena Zvezda, Belgrade
FK Crvena Zvezda 1-0 FC Levadia Tallinn
Goal(s): 1-0 Koroman 35
Referee: Brugger (AUT)
8/8/07, Kadriorg, Tallinn
FC Levadia Tallinn 2-1 FK Crvena Zvezda
Goal(s): 1-0 Malov 33, 1-1 Burzanović 37, 2-1 Nahk 67
Referee: Megía Dávila (ESP)
Aggregate: 2-2; FK Crvena Zvezda qualify on away goal.

1/8/07, Športni park, Domzale
NK Domžale 1-2 NK Dinamo Zagreb
Goal(s): 0-1 Šokota 7, 0-2 Modrić 50(p), 1-2 Žeželj 87
Referee: Einwaller (AUT)
7/8/07, Maksimir, Zagreb
NK Dinamo Zagreb 3-1 NK Domžale
Goal(s): 1-0 Vukojević 18, 2-0 Šokota 22, 2-1 Zahora 27, 3-1 Sammir 60
Referee: Verbist (BEL)
Aggregate: 5-2; NK Dinamo Zagreb qualify.

1/8/07, Inönü, Istanbul
Beşiktaş JK 1-0 FC Sheriff
Goal(s): 1-0 İbrahim Toraman 73
Referee: Sippel (GER)
8/8/07, Sheriff, Tiraspol
FC Sheriff 0-3 Beşiktaş JK
Goal(s): 0-1 Bobô 58, 0-2 Bobô 69, 0-3 Koray Avcı 90
Referee: Brines (SCO)
Aggregate: 0-4; Beşiktaş JK qualify.

THIRD QUALIFYING ROUND

Sevilla FC's first tie on their UEFA Champions League debut was overshadowed by the death of Antonio Puerta who passed away aged 22 on 28 August, the day the Andalusian club were due to play AEK Athens FC in the second leg of their third qualifying round tie. A substitute in Sevilla's 2-0 first-leg victory on 15 August, the Spanish international defender died after suffering a heart attack during a Primera División match against Getafe CF. "This is one of the saddest days in the history of Sevilla," said club president José María del Nido.

Courageous win

The two-time UEFA Cup winners travelled to Greece for the rescheduled fixture the following week aiming to book their place in the group stage for the first time. "We need this win to get back to normality," said coach Juande Ramos. Puerta would have been proud of his former team-mates as two first-half goals by Luís Fabiano helped seal a courageous 4-1 win in Athens.

The third qualifying round produced few surprises but unfortunately for AFC Ajax their name featured once more at the top of the list of fallen giants. Eliminated by FC København at the same stage a year earlier, the five-time champions endured an equally ignominious exit as they lost both legs against SK Slavia Praha. Two Stanislav Vlček goals clinched a 3-1 aggregate success as Slavia reached the group stage for the first time. "This is the greatest moment of my career," enthused coach Karel Jarolím. "The whole side fought with great spirit."

British success

AC Sparta Praha failed to make it a Czech double, succumbing 5-0 to Arsenal FC, for whom Cesc Fàbregas was on target in both legs. England's other presence,

Sevilla players dedicate a goal to thei late team-mate Antonio Puert

Liverpool FC, were equally impressive, scoring five times without reply against Toulouse FC, while Rangers FC and Celtic FC battled through to ensure the presence of six British teams in the group stage.

FK Crvena Zvezda had beaten Rangers during their triumphant 1990/91 campaign, and Nacho Novo's late first-leg strike at Ibrox proved the only goal of the tie on this occasion. Perhaps the most gripping match-up involved Celtic and FC Spartak Moskva, who shared two 1-1 draws, with both sides squandering spot kicks at Parkhead before the hosts prevailed in a shoot-out. Celtic manager Gordon Strachan labelled goalkeeper Artur Boruc "a giant of a man" after the Pole's two penalty saves, adding: "I've had some great nights but this will be one of those I'll be sitting in 25 years time and thinking: 'What a game that was'."

Shakhtar joy

FC Shakhtar Donetsk were also celebrating after an amazing escape against FC Salzburg. Trailing 1-0 from the first leg, Mircea Lucescu's men conceded first at home before scoring three unanswered goals. "Fortune smiled on us tonight," Brazilian striker Brandão admitted after his 87th-minute winner. "It was very hard but we kept fighting and our prayers were answered." Shakhtar were joined by domestic arch-rivals FC Dynamo Kyiv, 4-0 victors over FK Sarajevo, while Turkey also boasted two qualifiers as champions Fenerbahçe SK defeated RSC Anderlecht 3-0 and Beşiktaş JK prevailed 3-1 against FC Zürich.

Third Qualifying Round Results

14/8/07, Ibrox, Glasgow
Rangers FC 1-0 FK Crvena Zvezda
Goal(s): 1-0 Novo 90
Referee: Hansson (SWE)
28/8/07, FK Crvena Zvezda, Belgrade
FK Crvena Zvezda 0-0 Rangers FC
Referee: Batista (POR)
Aggregate: 0-1; Rangers FC qualify.

14/8/07, Estádio do Sport Lisboa e Benfica, Lisbon
SL Benfica 2-1 FC København
Goal(s): 1-0 Rui Costa 25, 1-1 Hutchinson 35, 2-1 Rui Costa 85
Referee: Kassai (HUN)
29/8/07, Parken Stadium, Copenhagen
FC København 0-1 SL Benfica
Goal(s): 0-1 Katsouranis 17
Referee: Braamhaar (NED)
Aggregate: 1-3; SL Benfica qualify.

14/8/07, Stadio Olimpico, Rome
S.S. Lazio 1-1 FC Dinamo 1948 Bucureşti
Goal(s): 0-1 Dănciulescu 22, 1-1 Mutarelli 54
Referee: Øvrebø (NOR)
28/8/07, Lia Manoliu, Bucharest
FC Dinamo 1948 Bucureşti 1-3 S.S. Lazio
Goal(s): 1-0 Bratu 27, 1-1 Rocchi 47(p), 1-2 Pandev 53, 1-3 Rocchi 66
Referee: Mejuto González (ESP)
Aggregate: 2-4; S.S. Lazio qualify.

14/8/07, Mestalla, Valencia
Valencia CF 3-0 IF Elfsborg
Goal(s): 1-0 Vicente 14, 2-0 Silva 58, 3-0 Morientes 70
Referee: Malek (POL)
29/8/07, Borås Arena, Boras
IF Elfsborg 1-2 Valencia CF
Goal(s): 0-1 Iván Helguera 4, 1-1 Alexandersson 31, 1-2 David Villa 90
Referee: Baskakov (RUS)
Aggregate: 1-5; Valencia CF qualify.

15/8/07, Stadium, Toulouse
Toulouse FC 0-1 Liverpool FC
Goal(s): 0-1 Voronin 43
Referee: Vassaras (GRE)
28/8/07, Anfield, Liverpool
Liverpool FC 4-0 Toulouse FC
Goal(s): 1-0 Crouch 19, 2-0 Hyypiä 49, 3-0 Kuyt 87, 4-0 Kuyt 90+1
Referee: Stark (GER)
Aggregate: 5-0; Liverpool FC qualify.

15/8/07, Ratina, Tampere
Tampere United 0-3 Rosenborg BK
Goal(s): 0-1 Koppinen 19, 0-2 Koné 20, 0-3 Koné 81
Referee: Pedro Proença (POR)
29/8/07, Lerkendal, Trondheim
Rosenborg BK 2-0 Tampere United
Goal(s): 1-0 Sapara 45, 2-0 Ya 48
Referee: Hamer (LUX)
Aggregate: 5-0; Rosenborg BK qualify.

15/8/07, Gradski, Borisov
FC BATE Borisov 2-2 FC Steaua Bucureşti
Goal(s): 1-0 Radkov 39, 1-1 Goian 60, 1-2 Dică 85, 2-2 Bliznyuk 90+2
Referee: Trefoloni (ITA)
29/8/07, Steaua Stadium, Bucharest
FC Steaua Bucureşti 2-0 FC BATE Borisov
Goal(s): 1-0 Zaharia 12, 2-0 Neaga 54
Referee: Vink (NED)
Aggregate: 4-2; FC Steaua Bucureşti qualify.

15/8/07, Luzhniki Stadium, Moscow
FC Spartak Moskva 1-1 Celtic FC
Goal(s): 0-1 Hartley 21, 1-1 Pavlyuchenko 42
Referee: Fandel (GER)
29/8/07, Celtic Park, Glasgow
Celtic FC 1-1 FC Spartak Moskva
Goal(s): 1-0 McDonald 27, 1-1 Pavlyuchenko 45
Referee: Rosetti (ITA)
Aggregate: 2-2; Celtic FC qualify 4-3 on penalties.

15/8/07, Koševo, Sarajevo
FK Sarajevo 0-1 FC Dynamo Kyiv
Goal(s): 0-1 Shatskikh 13
Referee: Yefet (ISR)

Brandão's late goal put Shakhtar Donetsk through to t group stage at Salzburg's expen

29/8/07, Valeri Lobanovskiy, Kiev
FC Dynamo Kyiv 3-0 FK Sarajevo
Goal(s): 1-0 Bangoura 3, 2-0 Milošević 75(og), 3-0 Rebrov 90+2(p)
Referee: Dougal (SCO)
Aggregate: 4-0; FC Dynamo Kyiv qualify.

15/8/07, Hardturm, Zurich
FC Zürich 1-1 Beşiktaş JK
Goal(s): 0-1 Delgado 3, 1-1 Alphonse 90+7
Referee: Riley (ENG)
29/8/07, Inönü, Istanbul
Beşiktaş JK 2-0 FC Zürich
Goal(s): 1-0 Delgado 56, 2-0 Delgado 64
Referee: Fröjdfeldt (SWE)
Aggregate: 3-1; Beşiktaş JK qualify.

15/8/07, Weserstadion, Bremen
Werder Bremen 2-1 NK Dinamo Zagreb
Goal(s): 0-1 Balaban 45+1, 1-1 Hugo Almeida 46, 2-1 Jensen 85
Referee: Undiano (ESP)
29/8/07, Maksimir, Zagreb
NK Dinamo Zagreb 2-3 Werder Bremen
Goal(s): 0-1 Diego 13(p), 1-1 Vukojević 21, 1-2 Sanogo 38, 2-2 Modrić 40(p), 2-3 Diego 70(p)
Referee: Hauge (NOR)
Aggregate: 3-5; Werder Bremen qualify.

15/8/07, EM Stadion Wals-Siezenheim, Salzburg
FC Salzburg 1-0 FC Shakhtar Donetsk
Goal(s): 1-0 Zickler 10(p)
Referee: Skomina (SVN)
29/8/07, RSC Olympiyskiy Stadium, Donetsk
FC Shakhtar Donetsk 3-1 FC Salzburg
Goal(s): 0-1 Meyer 5, 1-1 Lucarelli 9, 2-1 Castillo 79(p), 3-1 Brandão 87
Referee: Duhamel (FRA)
Aggregate: 3-2; FC Shakhtar Donetsk qualify.

15/8/07, Amsterdam ArenA, Amsterdam
AFC Ajax 0-1 SK Slavia Praha
Goal(s): 0-1 Kalivoda 75(p)
Referee: Meyer (GER)

29/8/07, Evžena Rošického, Prague
SK Slavia Praha 2-1 AFC Ajax
Goal(s): 1-0 Vlček 23, 1-1 Luis Suárez 34, 2-1 Vlček 87
Referee: Larsen (DEN)
Aggregate: 3-1; SK Slavia Praha qualify.

15/8/07, Sparta Stadium, Prague
AC Sparta Praha 0-2 Arsenal FC
Goal(s): 0-1 Fàbregas 72, 0-2 Hleb 90+2
Referee: Medina Cantalejo (ESP)
29/8/07, Arsenal Stadium, London
Arsenal FC 3-0 AC Sparta Praha
Goal(s): 1-0 Rosický 7, 2-0 Fàbregas 88, 3-0 Eduardo 89
Referee: De Bleeckere (BEL)
Aggregate: 5-0; Arsenal FC qualify.

15/8/07, Ramón Sánchez-Pizjuán, Sevilla
Sevilla FC 2-0 AEK Athens FC
Goal(s): 1-0 Luís Fabiano 48, 2-0 Kanouté 68
Referee: Michel' (SVK)
3/9/07, OACA Spyro Louis, Athens
AEK Athens FC 1-4 Sevilla FC
Goal(s): 0-1 Luís Fabiano 31(p), 0-2 Keita 40, 0-3 Luís Fabiano 45, 0-4 Kerzhakov 53, 1-4 Rivaldo 82(p)
Referee: Allaerts (BEL)
Aggregate: 1-6; Sevilla FC qualify.

15/8/07, Sükrü Saraçoglu, Istanbul
Fenerbahçe SK 1-0 RSC Anderlecht
Goal(s): 1-0 Alex 32
Referee: Webb (ENG)
29/8/07, Constant Vanden Stock Stadium, Brussels
RSC Anderlecht 0-2 Fenerbahçe SK
Goal(s): 0-1 Kežman 4, 0-2 Alex 73
Referee: Busacca (SUI)
Aggregate: 0-3; Fenerbahçe SK qualify.

GROUP STAGE

GROUP A

Liverpool FC may have provided ample evidence of their ability to stage dramatic fightbacks in the Istanbul final of 2005, but even their most ardent supporters must have feared the worst after the Merseysiders took just one point from their first three Group A outings.

Successive defeats

The 2006/07 competition's beaten finalists began solidly enough away to FC Porto, earning a 1-1 draw as Dirk Kuyt cancelled out Lucho González's early penalty. However, successive defeats by Olympique de Marseille and Beşiktaş JK left Rafael Benítez's men on the brink of a premature exit. No French club had ever won at Anfield prior to Matchday 2 and few expected Marseille, who were struggling in Ligue 1 and had recently parted with their coach Albert Emon, to buck the trend.

Yet with Eric Gerets taking charge for the first time, Marseille displayed vigour and discipline in sealing a 1-0 win through Mathieu Valbuena's brilliant 77th-minute goal. "I thought I'd missed when I saw the ball hit the bar, but when it went in I was filled with joy," said the 23-year-old. With the pressure now on, Liverpool succumbed again in Istanbul, where Sami Hyypiä's own goal and a further strike from Brazilian striker Bobô set up victory for Beşiktaş before Steven Gerrard's late consolation.

Deserved point

Liverpool's stuttering start had left the door to qualification open and the section's top two teams, Marseille and Porto, knew the winner of their double confrontation on Matchdays 3 and 4 would have one foot in the last 16. Julien Rodriguez and Djibril Cissé had sealed victory in Marseille's opener against Beşiktaş but Porto proved tougher opponents at the Stade Vélodrome, and Lucho González's 79th-minute penalty earned a them a deserved point after Mamadou Niang had opened the scoring.

Niang was on target again in Porto, equalising Tarik Sektioui's superb individual effort, only for Lisandro López to head in the winner 12 minutes from time. The result put the Portuguese champions top with eight points, one more than Marseille, though events at Anfield that same evening suggested Liverpool might yet have their say.

Fernando Torres completes a snaking run through the Marseille defence with Liverpool's second goal in a 4-0 win at the Stade Vélodrome

Record victory

Knowing that anything less than a victory would spell the end, the English side destroyed Beşiktaş 8-0 in a mesmerising display, inspired by Yossi Benayoun's hat-trick. "In previous games we were creating chances but we couldn't score. Tonight we put that right," noted Benítez after the biggest-ever UEFA Champions League victory. "We still need to win the next two, and we'll go into the Porto game with confidence. Porto need to come to Anfield and they will be worried."

In reality, the 2004 winners equipped themselves far better than Beşiktaş. Lisandro drew the visitors level after Fernando Torres's early strike, and the Argentinian came agonisingly close to scoring again before the interval. Relief filled Anfield once Torres netted his second on 78 minutes, before Gerrard's penalty and a header from Crouch capped a dramatic night. "The 4-1 scoreline is not a fair reflection of the game," claimed Porto coach Jesualdo Ferreira. His side's first defeat would not prove costly, though, as a 2-0 home win over Beşiktaş on Matchday 6 ensured they finished top of the group.

'I always believed'

The second berth was decided in the south of France where a point would have sufficed for Marseille against the resurgent Reds. Such a scenario never looked likely, however, as the five-time winners roared into a two-goal lead through Gerrard and Torres inside eleven minutes. Kuyt and Ryan Babel then sealed an emphatic 4-0 triumph with goals after the break. "I always believed we could do it," insisted Benayoun, reflecting on another great Liverpool escape. "We knew every game would be like a final and we won all three."

Group A Results

18/9/07, Vélodrome, Marseille
Olympique de Marseille 2-0 Beşiktaş JK
Attendance: 35676
Goal(s): 1-0 Rodriguez 76, 2-0 Cissé 90+1
Referee: Trefoloni (ITA)

18/9/07, Estádio do Dragão, Porto
FC Porto 1-1 Liverpool FC
Attendance: 41208
Goal(s): 1-0 Lucho González 8(p), 1-1 Kuyt 17
Referee: Michel' (SVK)

3/10/07, Anfield, Liverpool
Liverpool FC 0-1 Olympique de Marseille
Attendance: 41355
Goal(s): 0-1 Valbuena 77
Referee: Plautz (AUT)

3/10/07, Inönü, Istanbul
Beşiktaş JK 0-1 FC Porto
Attendance: 19795
Goal(s): 0-1 Ricardo Quaresma 90+2
Referee: Vink (NED)

24/10/07, Inönü, Istanbul
Beşiktaş JK 2-1 Liverpool FC
Attendance: 25837
Goal(s): 1-0 Hyypiä 13(og), 2-0 Bobô 82, 2-1 Gerrard 85
Referee: Larsen (DEN)

24/10/07, Vélodrome, Marseille
Olympique de Marseille 1-1 FC Porto
Attendance: 46458
Goal(s): 1-0 Niang 69, 1-1 Lucho González 79(p)
Referee: Mejuto González (ESP)

6/11/07, Anfield, Liverpool
Liverpool FC 8-0 Beşiktaş JK
Attendance: 41143
Goal(s): 1-0 Crouch 19, 2-0 Benayoun 32, 3-0 Benayoun 53, 4-0 Benayoun 56, 5-0 Gerrard 69, 6-0 Babel 78, 7-0 Babel 81, 8-0 Crouch 89
Referee: Merk (GER)

6/11/07, Estádio do Dragão, Porto
FC Porto 2-1 Olympique de Marseille
Attendance: 42217
Goal(s): 1-0 Sektioui 27, 1-1 Niang 47, 2-1 Lisandro López 78
Referee: Stark (GER)

28/11/07, Inönü, Istanbul
Beşiktaş JK 2-1 Olympique de Marseille
Attendance: 19448
Goal(s): 1-0 Tello 27, 1-1 Taiwo 65, 2-1 Bobô 88
Referee: Medina Cantalejo (ESP)

28/11/07, Anfield, Liverpool
Liverpool FC 4-1 FC Porto
Attendance: 41095
Goal(s): 1-0 Fernando Torres 19, 1-1 Lisandro López 33, 2-1 Fernando Torres 78, 3-1 Gerrard 84(p), 4-1 Crouch 87
Referee: Rosetti (ITA)

11/12/07, Vélodrome, Marseille
Olympique de Marseille 0-4 Liverpool FC
Attendance: 53097
Goal(s): 0-1 Gerrard 4, 0-2 Fernando Torres 11, 0-3 Kuyt 48, 0-4 Babel 90+1
Referee: Hauge (NOR)

11/12/07, Estádio do Dragão, Porto
FC Porto 2-0 Beşiktaş JK
Attendance: 39608
Goal(s): 1-0 Lucho González 44, 2-0 Ricardo Quaresma 62
Referee: Fröjdfeldt (SWE)

Group A Table

		Home					Away					Total				
	Pld	W	D	L	F	A	W	D	L	F	A	W	D	L	F	A
1 FC Porto	6	2	1	0	5	2	1	1	1	3	5	3	2	1	8	7
2 Liverpool FC	6	2	0	1	12	2	1	1	1	6	3	3	1	2	18	5
3 Olympique de Marseille	6	1	1	1	3	5	1	0	2	3	4	2	1	3	6	9
4 Beşiktaş JK	6	2	0	1	4	3	0	0	3	0	12	2	0	4	4	15

GROUP B

Chelsea FC manager José Mourinho described Group B as "a very difficult and dangerous group" and he was to be proved right. The Portuguese boss left his post after just one disappointing result and was not the only coach to depart in a section where three of the four teams made managerial changes before the end of October.

Life after Mourinho

The combination of a low attendance and a poor Chelsea performance in their opening 1-1 draw against Rosenborg BK at Stamford Bridge seemed to convince the club's owner Roman Abramovich that a new man with new ideas was needed, and two days later Mourinho left by mutual consent to be replaced by Avram Grant. The Blues quickly proved there was life after the 'Special One' by winning their first two European games under the Israeli, beginning with a superb 2-1 success away against Valencia CF.

David Villa put the hosts ahead early on at the Mestalla, but goals from Joe Cole and Didier Drogba ensured a repeat of the 2-1 scoreline that eliminated the Spaniards in the previous season's quarter-final. Drogba was on the scoresheet again on Matchday 3, accompanied this time by Florent Malouda, as Chelsea surged to the top of the group by beating injury-ravaged FC Schalke 04 2-0 in west London. "We can play better but we played good football, positive football," Grant said. "Bit by bit we are on the way to achieving the style of play I want to see."

Flores sacked

While Chelsea were moving through the gears, Valencia remained stuck in neutral. The 2001 finalists may have enjoyed a perfect start by beating Schalke in Gelsenkirchen – Villa coolly slotting the game's only goal on 63 minutes – but the subsequent loss to Chelsea dented their confidence and, after a 2-0 reverse away to Rosenborg, their coach Quique Sánchez Flores was dismissed. "I lose a job, but get my life back," said the disappointed if relieved boss.

A more surprising development was Knut Tørum's departure from Rosenborg. The Trondheim side were languishing in sixth position in the Norwegian top flight, and despite Yssouf Koné and Vidar Riseth scoring to secure a surprise win over Valencia, Tørum left by mutual consent the next morning. As a result, there were two new faces in the dugouts when the sides met again on Matchday 4, and it proved a sobering evening for new Valencia boss Ronald Koeman who watched as Rosenborg – now coached by Trond Henriksen – secured another memorable 2-0 win thanks to two Steffen Iversen goals.

pensive José Mourinho (second right) watches Chelsea draw at home to Rosenborg hile Avram Grant (top left), his soon-to-be successor, looks on

Clinical away win

Valencia never recovered. Successive goalless draws against Schalke and Chelsea were not enough to lift them from the foot of the table. "We're getting better but with the injuries we've had, we haven't been able to score enough goals," Koeman mused. Rosenborg, meanwhile, were brought back to earth on Matchday 5 by Chelsea - and in particular Drogba. The Ivorian took his tally in the group stage to four by scoring twice in a clinical 4-0 away win that confirmed the English side's qualification as group winners with a game to spare.

Second place would be played out between Schalke and Rosenborg in Germany, with the visitors needing a point to reach the knockout phase for the first time since 1996/97. It proved to be Schalke's night, however, as first-half goals from Gerald Asamoah, Rafinha and Kevin Kuranyi set up a 3-1 triumph, qualifying the Bundesliga side for the last 16 for the first time. "I'm delighted with the result, the game and our progress," commented Schalke boss Mirko Slomka. As the only coach to keep his job throughout the Group B campaign, he had every right to feel satisfied.

Goalscorer Kevin Kuranyi (centre) leads the celebrations as Schalke go 3-1 up against Rosenborg

Group B Results

18/9/07, Stamford Bridge, London
Chelsea FC 1-1 Rosenborg BK
Attendance: 24973
Goal(s): 0-1 Koppinen 24, 1-1 Shevchenko 63
Referee: Duhamel (FRA)

18/9/07, Arena AufSchalke, Gelsenkirchen
FC Schalke 04 0-1 Valencia CF
Attendance: 53951
Goal(s): 0-1 David Villa 63
Referee: Wegereef (NED)

3/10/07, Mestalla, Valencia
Valencia CF 1-2 Chelsea FC
Attendance: 34935
Goal(s): 1-0 David Villa 9, 1-1 J. Cole 21, 1-2 Drogba 71
Referee: Rosetti (ITA)

3/10/07, Lerkendal, Trondheim
Rosenborg BK 0-2 FC Schalke 04
Attendance: 21361
Goal(s): 0-1 Jones 62, 0-2 Kuranyi 89
Referee: Gilewski (POL)

24/10/07, Lerkendal, Trondheim
Rosenborg BK 2-0 Valencia CF
Attendance: 21119
Goal(s): 1-0 Koné 53, 2-0 Riseth 61
Referee: Thomson (SCO)

24/10/07, Stamford Bridge, London
Chelsea FC 2-0 FC Schalke 04
Attendance: 40910
Goal(s): 1-0 Malouda 4, 2-0 Drogba 47
Referee: Fröjdfeldt (SWE)

6/11/07, Mestalla, Valencia
Valencia CF 0-2 Rosenborg BK
Attendance: 29725
Goal(s): 0-1 Iversen 31, 0-2 Iversen 58
Referee: Yefet (ISR)

6/11/07, Arena AufSchalke, Gelsenkirchen
FC Schalke 04 0-0 Chelsea FC
Attendance: 53951
Referee: Busacca (SUI)

28/11/07, Lerkendal, Trondheim
Rosenborg BK 0-4 Chelsea FC
Attendance: 21582
Goal(s): 0-1 Drogba 8, 0-2 Drogba 20, 0-3 Alex 40, 0-4 J. Cole 73
Referee: Benquerença (POR)

28/11/07, Mestalla, Valencia
Valencia CF 0-0 FC Schalke 04
Attendance: 29232
Referee: De Bleeckere (BEL)

11/12/07, Stamford Bridge, London
Chelsea FC 0-0 Valencia CF
Attendance: 41139
Referee: Gilewski (POL)

11/12/07, Arena AufSchalke, Gelsenkirchen
FC Schalke 04 3-1 Rosenborg BK
Attendance: 53951
Goal(s): 1-0 Asamoah 12, 2-0 Rafinha 19, 2-1 Koné 23, 3-1 Kuranyi 36
Referee: Riley (ENG)

Group B Table

		Home					Away					Total				
	Pld	W	D	L	F	A	W	D	L	F	A	W	D	L	F	A
1 Chelsea FC	6	1	2	0	3	1	2	1	0	6	1	3	3	0	9	2
2 FC Schalke 04	6	1	1	1	3	2	1	1	1	2	2	2	2	2	5	4
3 Rosenborg BK	6	1	0	2	2	6	1	1	1	4	4	2	1	3	6	10
4 Valencia CF	6	0	1	2	1	4	1	1	1	1	2	1	2	3	2	6

GROUP C

Few gave Olympiacos CFP much hope of qualifying from a group that included Real Madrid CF, Werder Bremen and S.S. Lazio, particularly after the Greek champions failed to beat the Italians at home in their opening match. Yet a historic away win on Matchday 2 gave Takis Lemonis's men just the lift they needed.

'A supreme effort'

The side from Piraeus had not won on the road in 31 attempts in the UEFA Champions League prior to their trip to Germany, and they would have been forgiven for fearing the worst when Hugo Almeida put Bremen ahead at the Weserstadion. However, they stepped up their efforts and completed a remarkable 3-1 triumph, with Ieroklis Stoltidis, Christos Patsatzoglou and Darko Kovačević all rattling in goals in the last 17 minutes. Lemonis hailed "a supreme effort", while one of the principal architects of the win, Lomana LuaLua, added: "We never let our heads drop and now we've made history."

Suddenly the 1-1 draw with Lazio, which was played behind closed doors, did not seem such a disaster, and Olympiacos travelled to Madrid with renewed optimism as section leaders. "There is no fear," insisted a bullish Lemonis before watching his side take a shock 2-1 lead at the Santiago Bernabéu through Júlio César just after the break, despite being reduced to ten men. This time, however, the visitors were the victims of a late rally as Robinho scored twice and newcomer Javier Ángel Balboa added another to seal a 4-2 success for Madrid.

Dogged start

The nine-time European Champion Clubs' Cup winners had made a dogged start under new coach Bernd Schuster, beating Bremen 2-1 at home with goals from Raúl González and Ruud van Nistelrooy, then drawing 2-2 at Lazio as two more Van Nistelrooy strikes matched Goran Pandev's brace. Schuster, though, remained concerned by Madrid's inability to kill games off. "Our opponents had too many chances," he said of the Olympiacos win. "We made it too hard for ourselves."

The return in Greece was a far tighter affair, finishing in a goalless stalemate after Madrid had twice struck the woodwork. Yet the Spanish club's defensive frailties resurfaced on Matchday 5 when they were run ragged by a Bremen side seemingly inspired by the threat of elimination. Robinho's brilliant effort restored parity following Markus Rosenberg's early goal, but the Swede then eclipsed his Brazilian counterpart with a stunning run and cross to set up Boubacar Sanogo on 40 minutes. Aaron Hunt and Van Nistelrooy were on target in the second half as Bremen edged it 3-2 to remain in contention.

'Fight like madmen'

With Olympiacos registering their second away win, 2-1 at Lazio, on the same evening, Thomas Schaaf's men needed to secure all three points in Athens to leapfrog their Matchday 6 opponents. The Greeks were in determined mood, however. Lemonis claimed his players would "fight like madmen" in order to reach the knockout phase for the first time in nine years, and they did not let him down, running out comfortable 3-0 victors. The hero of the hour, Stoltidis, was described as "a born winner" by his jubilant coach after scoring two goals and setting up the third for Kovacević.

Ieroklis Stoltidis and Lomana LuaLua celebrate a goal for Olympiacos in Bremen

Madrid ultimately pipped Olympiacos to top spot following their 3-1 home triumph over Lazio courtesy of a superior head-to-head record. Júlio Baptista, Raúl González and Robinho all scored in a one-sided first half, and though Pandev pulled one back with his fourth of the campaign, the visitors were soundly beaten, allowing Bremen to take the UEFA Cup berth. "We aren't a very experienced team," conceded Lazio coach Delio Rossi. "We worked hard last year to qualify for Europe and I feel bad because we're not going to play in the UEFA Cup."

Robinho is jubilant after putting Real Madrid 3-0 up against Lazio

Group C Results

18/9/07, Santiago Bernabéu, Madrid
Real Madrid CF 2-1 Werder Bremen
Attendance: 63500
Goal(s): 1-0 Raúl 16, 1-1 Sanogo 17, 2-1 Van Nistelrooy 74
Referee: Webb (ENG)

18/9/07, Georgios Karaiskakis, Piraeus
Olympiacos CFP 1-1 S.S. Lazio
Attendance: 171 (behind closed doors)
Goal(s): 1-0 Galletti 55, 1-1 Zauri 77
Referee: Braamhaar (NED)

3/10/07, Stadio Olimpico, Rome
S.S. Lazio 2-2 Real Madrid CF
Attendance: 52400
Goal(s): 0-1 Van Nistelrooy 8, 1-1 Pandev 32, 1-2 Van Nistelrooy 61, 2-2 Pandev 75
Referee: De Bleeckere (BEL)

3/10/07, Weserstadion, Bremen
Werder Bremen 1-3 Olympiacos CFP
Attendance: 37500
Goal(s): 1-0 Hugo Almeida 32, 1-1 Stoltidis 73, 1-2 Patsatzoglou 82, 1-3 Kovačević 87
Referee: Larsen (DEN)

24/10/07, Weserstadion, Bremen
Werder Bremen 2-1 S.S. Lazio
Attendance: 36587
Goal(s): 1-0 Sanogo 28, 2-0 Hugo Almeida 54, 2-1 Manfredini 82
Referee: Benquerença (POR)

24/10/07, Santiago Bernabéu, Madrid
Real Madrid CF 4-2 Olympiacos CFP
Attendance: 64477
Goal(s): 1-0 Raúl 2, 1-1 Galletti 7, 1-2 Júlio César 47, 2-2 Robinho 68, 3-2 Robinho 83, 4-2 Balboa 90+3
Referee: Øvrebø (NOR)

6/11/07, Stadio Olimpico, Rome
S.S. Lazio 2-1 Werder Bremen
Attendance: 28236
Goal(s): 1-0 Rocchi 57, 2-0 Rocchi 68, 2-1 Diego 88(p)
Referee: Bebek (CRO)

6/11/07, Georgios Karaiskakis, Piraeus
Olympiacos CFP 0-0 Real Madrid CF
Attendance: 30549
Referee: Micheľ (SVK)

28/11/07, Weserstadion, Bremen
Werder Bremen 3-2 Real Madrid CF
Attendance: 36350
Goal(s): 1-0 Rosenberg 5, 1-1 Robinho 14, 2-1 Sanogo 40, 3-1 Hunt 58, 3-2 Van Nistelrooy 71
Referee: Vink (NED)

28/11/07, Stadio Olimpico, Rome
S.S. Lazio 1-2 Olympiacos CFP
Attendance: 39996
Goal(s): 1-0 Pandev 30, 1-1 Galletti 35, 1-2 Kovačević 64
Referee: Webb (ENG)

11/12/07, Santiago Bernabéu, Madrid
Real Madrid CF 3-1 S.S. Lazio
Attendance: 70559
Goal(s): 1-0 Júlio Baptista 13, 2-0 Raúl 15, 3-0 Robinho 36, 3-1 Pandev 80
Referee: Busacca (SUI)

11/12/07, Georgios Karaiskakis, Piraeus
Olympiacos CFP 3-0 Werder Bremen
Attendance: 30297
Goal(s): 1-0 Stoltidis 12, 2-0 Kovačević 70, 3-0 Stoltidis 74
Referee: Duhamel (FRA)

Group C Table

		Home					Away					Total				
	Pld	W	D	L	F	A	W	D	L	F	A	W	D	L	F	A
1 Real Madrid CF	6	3	0	0	9	4	0	2	1	4	5	3	2	1	13	9
2 Olympiacos CFP	6	1	2	0	4	1	2	0	1	7	6	3	2	1	11	7
3 Werder Bremen	6	2	0	1	6	6	0	0	3	2	7	2	0	4	8	13
4 S.S. Lazio	6	1	1	1	5	5	0	1	2	3	6	1	2	3	8	11

GROUP D

AC Milan and Celtic FC were given the opportunity to renew hostilities after being drawn together in Group D alongside SL Benfica and FC Shakhtar Donetsk. While Milan's vice-president Adriano Galliani was quick to point out that "every time we face Celtic we end up playing in the final," the Scottish champions set their sights on avenging the extra-time defeat to the eventual winners in the previous season's first knockout round.

'Strong position'

Gordon Strachan's men were dealt an immediate blow, however, succumbing 2-0 in Donetsk to an impressive Shakhtar side for whom Brandão and new Italian recruit Cristiano Lucarelli were both on target inside eight minutes. Pooled alongside the holders and two other former European champions, the Ukrainians appeared anything but overawed and they duly registered their second win on Matchday 2, Brazilian midfielder Jádson scoring the only goal against Benfica in Lisbon. "It was a deserved result and we are now in a strong position," Shakhtar coach Mircea Lucescu said.

Unfortunately for Lucescu that was as good as it got. Their double confrontation with Milan served up two heavy defeats, including a 3-0 humbling at the RSC Olympiyskiy Stadium, and the slide continued with 2-1 losses against Celtic and Benfica. "Perhaps we are not good enough to be successful in the UEFA Champions League," concluded Lucescu after Benfica's win in Ukraine condemned Shakhtar to fourth spot. "It's hard to reach the next stage if you give away soft goals."

Tense night

Celtic, meanwhile, were under pressure to secure their first points when Milan visited Glasgow in October. On a tense night, it looked as though the hosts would be denied once more by their nemesis Kaká, who levelled from the penalty spot on 68 minutes after Stephen McManus had opened the scoring from a corner. Yet with seconds remaining, Scott McDonald bundled home a winner to spark euphoric scenes – and an ugly incident involving a Celtic fan and Milan goalkeeper Dida. "We showed great determination, kept on trying to win, and now we've beaten the European champions," Strachan enthused.

C Milan's Filippo Inzaghi ended roup D by setting a new uropean goalscoring record

Talk of falling standards at Milan was soon cut short as the Rossoneri dispatched Shakhtar 4-1 in their next outing. Alberto Gilardino and Clarence Seedorf scored two goals apiece, but coach Carlo Ancelotti singled out Kaká for special praise, saying: "His performance was extraordinary, especially from an athletic point of view. He was devastating." In the return match, two goals from Filipo Inzaghi and another from Kaká clinched a ruthless win that took Milan to the brink of qualification.

Dramatic finish

With Milan the only club showing real consistency, the battle for second moved towards a tantalising climax. Benfica stole a march on Celtic when Óscar Cardozo's 87th-minute strike sunk the Scottish visitors on Matchday 3, but that advantage evaporated after Aiden McGeady fired in the only goal between the sides in Glasgow. Celtic's home form was proving critical and, while Benfica shared a 1-1 draw with Milan on Matchday 5, more late drama was unfolding at Parkhead. The game against Shakhtar seemed destined to end in stalemate after Jiří Jarošík cancelled out an early goal from Brandão, yet with virtually the last kick Massimo Donati pounced to score Celtic's winner.

The former Milan player descibed his first-ever UEFA Champions League goal as "a fantastic finish to the game for me and my team". It ultimately clinched qualification for Celtic, who were left needing a draw in their final match at the San Siro to be certain of a place in the last 16. Although they failed to get it - Inzaghi scoring the only goal to become the highest scorer in the history of UEFA club competition with 63 strikes - Shakhtar's defeat at home to Benfica ensured that the nine points Celtic had claimed at home were good enough to see them through.

Group D Results

18/9/07, Stadio Giuseppe Meazza, Milan
AC Milan 2-1 SL Benfica
Attendance: 38358
Goal(s): 1-0 Pirlo 9, 2-0 Inzaghi 24, 2-1 Nuno Gomes 90+2
Referee: Riley (ENG)

18/9/07, RSC Olympiyskiy Stadium, Donetsk
FC Shakhtar Donetsk 2-0 Celtic FC
Attendance: 25700
Goal(s): 1-0 Brandão 6, 2-0 Lucarelli 8
Referee: Undiano (ESP)

3/10/07, Celtic Park, Glasgow
Celtic FC 2-1 AC Milan
Attendance: 58642
Goal(s): 1-0 McManus 61, 1-1 Kaká 68(p), 2-1 McDonald 89
Referee: Merk (GER)

3/10/07, Estádio do SL Benfica, Lisbon
SL Benfica 0-1 FC Shakhtar Donetsk
Attendance: 34647
Goal(s): 0-1 Jádson 42
Referee: Stark (GER)

24/10/07, Estádio do SL Benfica, Lisbon
SL Benfica 1-0 Celtic FC
Attendance: 38512
Goal(s): 1-0 Cardozo 87
Referee: Busacca (SUI)

24/10/07, Stadio Giuseppe Meazza, Milan
AC Milan 4-1 FC Shakhtar Donetsk
Attendance: 36850
Goal(s): 1-0 Gilardino 6, 2-0 Gilardino 14, 2-1 Lucarelli 51, 3-1 Seedorf 62, 4-1 Seedorf 69
Referee: Medina Cantalejo (ESP)

6/11/07, Celtic Park, Glasgow
Celtic FC 1-0 SL Benfica
Attendance: 58691
Goal(s): 1-0 McGeady 45
Referee: Hansson (SWE)

6/11/07, RSC Olympiyskiy Stadium, Donetsk
FC Shakhtar Donetsk 0-3 AC Milan
Attendance: 25700
Goal(s): 0-1 Inzaghi 66, 0-2 Kaká 72, 0-3 Inzaghi 90+3
Referee: Vink (NED)

28/11/07, Estádio do SL Benfica, Lisbon
SL Benfica 1-1 AC Milan
Attendance: 46034
Goal(s): 0-1 Pirlo 15, 1-1 Maxi Pereira 20
Referee: Fandel (GER)

28/11/07, Celtic Park, Glasgow
Celtic FC 2-1 FC Shakhtar Donetsk
Attendance: 59396
Goal(s): 0-1 Brandão 4, 1-1 Jarošík 45, 2-1 Donati 90+2
Referee: Layec (FRA)

4/12/07, Stadio Giuseppe Meazza, Milan
AC Milan 1-0 Celtic FC
Attendance: 38409
Goal(s): 1-0 Inzaghi 70
Referee: Øvrebø (NOR)

4/12/07, RSC Olympiyskiy Stadium, Donetsk
FC Shakhtar Donetsk 1-2 SL Benfica
Attendance: 24200
Goal(s): 0-1 Cardozo 6, 0-2 Cardozo 22, 1-2 Lucarelli 30(p)
Referee: Vassaras (GRE)

Group D Table

		Home					Away					Total				
	Pld	W	D	L	F	A	W	D	L	F	A	W	D	L	F	A
1 AC Milan	6	3	0	0	7	2	1	1	1	5	3	4	1	1	12	5
2 Celtic FC	6	3	0	0	5	2	0	0	3	0	4	3	0	3	5	6
3 SL Benfica	6	1	1	1	2	2	1	0	2	3	4	2	1	3	5	6
4 FC Shakhtar Donetsk	6	1	0	2	3	5	1	0	2	3	6	2	0	4	6	11

GROUP E

The challenge facing Rangers FC could hardly have been more daunting when they were pitted alongside FC Barcelona, French champions Olympique Lyonnais and German title-holders VfB Stuttgart in Group E, yet it was Walter Smith's men who seized the early initiative in a section that would throw up more than its share of upsets and drama.

'Extremely tough'

Stuttgart travelled to Glasgow confident of making a winning start despite their patchy form in the Bundesliga, and they duly went ahead early in the second half through Mario Gómez. The German international's goal merely stirred Rangers to life, however, and after Charlie Adam had equalised, Jean-Claude Darcheville slotted home from the penalty spot to clinch a 2-1 success. "We're in an extremely tough section but if we continue to get results like this it might make people sit up and take notice," Smith said.

If the home win over Stuttgart raised eyebrows, Rangers' next result sent shockwaves through Europe. Lyon had experienced an unsettling summer, with coach Gérard Houllier and leading players Éric Abidal, Florent Malouda and Tiago all departing. A record 3-0 defeat away to Barcelona was hardly an ideal start for their new boss Alain Perrin. Many expected a backlash when Rangers visited Lyon's Stade de Gerland fortress, but a superb counterattacking performance saw the Scottish club stun their hosts 3-0 with goals from Lee McCulloch, Daniel Cousin and DaMarcus Beasley.

Messi goals

"It's difficult to explain what happened," said a dumbfounded Perrin after overseeing Lyon's first home defeat in the group stage since 2002. For his part, Smith gleefully hailed "one of the biggest results Rangers have obtained in recent years." The only side matching Rangers' early form was Barcelona, who followed up their Lyon victory with a 2-0 win at Stuttgart, Lionel Messi adding to his opening-day goal with another in Germany.

There was a distinct split in the standings after two matchdays, with Barcelona and Rangers already six

Lyon crushed Rangers at Ibrox to atone for a home defeat by the same scoreline

points clear of their rivals. Even Lyon president Jean-Michel Aulas suggested his side focus on securing a UEFA Cup berth, and they took a giant step towards doing so by winning 2-0 at the Gottlieb-Daimler-Stadion. Fábio Santos scored the visitors' first goal of the campaign before Karim Benzema condemned Stuttgart to a third straight defeat. It got worse for Armin Veh's charges as they dropped out of contention entirely following a 4-2 loss in France. "Overall we've not been good enough at the back and we've made too many bad errors," Veh said.

Rangers stuttering

With Rangers picking up just a point from their two games against Barcelona, Lyon were suddenly breathing down their necks. A stubborn, backs-to-the-wall performance had kept the Catalan giants at bay during a scoreless contest at Ibrox, but first-half goals from Thierry Henry and Messi broke the visitors' resistance at the Camp Nou. Frank Rijkaard's team were making light work of qualification, and a 2-2 draw away to Lyon on Matchday 5 ensured they would finish as group winners. Rangers, by contrast, were stuttering, and a 3-2 defeat at already eliminated Stuttgart left them needing a point at home to Lyon to progress.

Rangers may have been unbeaten in their previous eleven European home games, but the momentum ahead of the make-or-break Ibrox showdown was with a Lyon side hungry for revenge. Sidney Govou capitalised on Lyon's early domination with a goal on 16 minutes, and after Darcheville missed a glorious chance to level, Benzema wrapped up a famous 3-0 triumph with two fine goals in the final five minutes. "We started the campaign in the worst possible way but tonight we got it all right," said a delighted Perrin as Lyon reached the last 16 for the fifth season in a row.

Group E Results

18/9/07, Ibrox, Glasgow
Rangers FC 2-1 VfB Stuttgart
Attendance: 49795
Goal(s): 0-1 Gómez 56, 1-1 Adam 62, 2-1 Darcheville 75(p)
Referee: Farina (ITA)

19/9/07, Camp Nou, Barcelona
FC Barcelona 3-0 Olympique Lyonnais
Attendance: 78689
Goal(s): 1-0 Clerc 21(og), 2-0 Messi 82, 3-0 Henry 90+1
Referee: Busacca (SUI)

2/10/07, Stade de Gerland, Lyon
Olympique Lyonnais 0-3 Rangers FC
Attendance: 38076
Goal(s): 0-1 McCulloch 23, 0-2 Cousin 48, 0-3 Beasley 53
Referee: Øvrebø (NOR)

2/10/07, Gottlieb-Daimler, Stuttgart
VfB Stuttgart 0-2 FC Barcelona
Attendance: 49725
Goal(s): 0-1 Puyol 53, 0-2 Messi 67
Referee: Hansson (SWE)

23/10/07, Gottlieb-Daimler, Stuttgart
VfB Stuttgart 0-2 Olympique Lyonnais
Attendance: 51000
Goal(s): 0-1 Fábio Santos 56, 0-2 Benzema 79
Referee: Batista (POR)

23/10/07, Ibrox, Glasgow
Rangers FC 0-0 FC Barcelona
Attendance: 49957
Referee: Plautz (AUT)

7/11/07, Stade de Gerland, Lyon
Olympique Lyonnais 4-2 VfB Stuttgart
Attendance: 38215
Goal(s): 1-0 Ben Arfa 6, 2-0 Källström 15, 2-1 Gómez 16, 3-1 Ben Arfa 37, 3-2 Gómez 56, 4-2 Juninho 90+3
Referee: Baskakov (RUS)

7/11/07, Camp Nou, Barcelona
FC Barcelona 2-0 Rangers FC
Attendance: 82887
Goal(s): 1-0 Henry 6, 2-0 Messi 43
Referee: Braamhaar (NED)

27/11/07, Gottlieb-Daimler, Stuttgart
VfB Stuttgart 3-2 Rangers FC
Attendance: 51000
Goal(s): 0-1 Adam 27, 1-1 Cacau 45+2, 2-1 Pardo 62, 2-2 Ferguson 70, 3-2 Marica 85
Referee: Ceferin (SVN)

27/11/07, Stade de Gerland, Lyon
Olympique Lyonnais 2-2 FC Barcelona
Attendance: 36500
Goal(s): 0-1 Iniesta 3, 1-1 Juninho 7, 1-2 Messi 58(p), 2-2 Juninho 80(p)
Referee: Farina (ITA)

12/12/07, Ibrox, Glasgow
Rangers FC 0-3 Olympique Lyonnais
Attendance: 50260
Goal(s): 0-1 Govou 16, 0-2 Benzema 85, 0-3 Benzema 88
Referee: Michel' (SVK)

12/12/07, Camp Nou, Barcelona
FC Barcelona 3-1 VfB Stuttgart
Attendance: 52761
Goal(s): 0-1 Da Silva 3, 1-1 Giovani 36, 2-1 Eto'o 57, 3-1 Ronaldinho 67
Referee: Lannoy (FRA)

Group E Table

		Home					Away					Total				
	Pld	W	D	L	F	A	W	D	L	F	A	W	D	L	F	A
1 FC Barcelona	6	3	0	0	8	1	1	2	0	4	2	4	2	0	12	3
2 Olympique Lyonnais	6	1	1	1	6	7	2	0	1	5	3	3	1	2	11	10
3 Rangers FC	6	1	1	1	2	4	1	0	2	5	5	2	1	3	7	9
4 VfB Stuttgart	6	1	0	2	3	6	0	0	3	4	9	1	0	5	7	15

GROUP F

The draw for Group F threw up a host of intruiging reunions as AS Roma were handed the opportunity to erase the painful memories of recent games against Manchester United FC and FC Dynamo Kyiv, while United pair Cristiano Ronaldo and Nani prepared to make emotional returns to their previous employers, Sporting Clube de Portugal.

Roma improvement

Before Luciano Spalletti's Roma could exorcise the ghost of their 7-1 drubbing at Old Trafford in the previous season's quarter-final, they hosted Dynamo in a repeat of the unsavoury 2004 encounter that was abandoned after referee Anders Frisk was struck by a missile. It proved an altogether happier evening for the Romans, who registered a 2-0 success thanks to goals from Simone Perrotta and Francesco Totti. Their trip to Manchester on Matchday 2 ended in another defeat, yet the performance and the slender 1-0 scoreline were sources of encouragement. "We were very, very good and should not have been beaten tonight," said Spalletti.

Four points from their next two meetings with Sporting took Roma to the brink of a second successive last-16 appearance, and they completed the job in style by beating Dynamo 4-1 in Kiev, Montenegrin striker Mirko Vučinić scoring twice to condemn the hosts to their fifth straight defeat.

Coaching changes

Nothing had gone right for the Ukrainian double winners who, after sacking their coach Anatoliy Demyanenko in the wake of the loss in Rome, soon lost the services of his replacement, the veteran József Szabó, due to health problems. Taking Szabó's place in the dugout for the final three games proved a harrowing experience for his assistant Oleh Luzhniy, and a dismal campaign ended with a 3-0 loss at Sporting. "We didn't show any character or spirit, so we can't compete at this level," Luzhniy complained. "Character is in a player's heart. When I pick him, I put my faith him. I cannot do any more, I cannot play for him."

nchester United match-winner stiano Ronaldo was humbled by the rm reception he received from orting fans on his return to Lisbon

United's fortunes contrasted vividly with those of Dynamo. From the moment Sir Alex Ferguson's side clinched a hard-fought 1-0 win away to Sporting in their opening game – with the goal coming almost inevitably from Cristiano Ronaldo - qualification seemed a formality. The winger's 62nd-minute header led to a poignant moment at the Estádio José Alvalade as the home fans applauded their former idol. "It was a strange feeling," the 22-year-old said. "I didn't celebrate [the goal]... and I want to praise the way that the Sporting fans reacted. It made me feel very proud."

Ferguson praise

The 2006/07 semi-finalists were in mercurial form and, perhaps most worryingly for their rivals, Ronaldo and Wayne Rooney were finding their European scoring boots at last after a lengthy drought. Rooney struck the only goal against Roma, and both he and his Portuguese colleague were on target in 4-2 and 4-0 routs of Dynamo. By the time Sporting came to town on Matchday 5, needing a win to keep in touch with second-placed Roma, United had already sealed qualification. Yet again Ronaldo proved the difference, lashing home a glorious free-kick in added time to seal a 2-1 win, United's fifth straight success, and eliminate his former club in the process.

Mancini's equaliser for Roma at the Stadio Olimpico denied United a perfect record as the Matchday 6 encounter finished 1-1 between the group's two qualifiers. Sporting, meanwhile, geared up for their UEFA Cup campaign with a resounding 3-0 win over Dynamo thanks to Anderson Polga's penalty and further strikes from João Moutinho and Liedson. "We paid for our poor results against Roma but at least we've finished the campaign in the best possible way," said their coach Paulo Bento after seeing Sporting accumulate seven points, their highest-ever tally in the group stage.

Group F Results

19/9/07, Stadio Olimpico, Rome
AS Roma 2-0 FC Dynamo Kyiv
Attendance: 35508
Goal(s): 1-0 Perrotta 9, 2-0 Totti 70
Referee: Hamer (LUX)

19/9/07, José Alvalade, Lisbon
Sporting Clube de Portugal 0-1 Manchester United FC
Attendance: 41510
Goal(s): 0-1 Cristiano Ronaldo 62
Referee: Fandel (GER)

2/10/07, Old Trafford, Manchester
Manchester United FC 1-0 AS Roma
Attendance: 73652
Goal(s): 1-0 Rooney 70
Referee: Mejuto González (ESP)

2/10/07, NSC Olympiyskiy Stadium, Kiev
FC Dynamo Kyiv 1-2 Sporting Clube de Portugal
Attendance: 37600
Goal(s): 0-1 Tonel 14, 1-1 Vashchuk 28, 1-2 Anderson Polga 38
Referee: Layec (FRA)

23/10/07, NSC Olympiyskiy Stadium, Kiev
FC Dynamo Kyiv 2-4 Manchester United FC
Attendance: 42000
Goal(s): 0-1 Ferdinand 10, 0-2 Rooney 18, 1-2 Diogo Rincón 34, 1-3 Cristiano Ronaldo 41, 1-4 Cristiano Ronaldo 68(p), 2-4 Bangoura 78
Referee: Kassai (HUN)

23/10/07, Stadio Olimpico, Rome
AS Roma 2-1 Sporting Clube de Portugal
Attendance: 26893
Goal(s): 1-0 Juan 15, 1-1 Liedson 18, 2-1 Vučinić 70
Referee: Hauge (NOR)

7/11/07, Old Trafford, Manchester
Manchester United FC 4-0 FC Dynamo Kyiv
Attendance: 75017
Goal(s): 1-0 Piqué 31, 2-0 Tévez 37, 3-0 Rooney 76, 4-0 Cristiano Ronaldo 88
Referee: Wegereef (NED)

7/11/07, José Alvalade, Lisbon
Sporting Clube de Portugal 2-2 AS Roma
Attendance: 32273
Goal(s): 0-1 Cassetti 4, 1-1 Liedson 22, 2-1 Liedson 64, 2-2 Anderson Polga 90(og)
Referee: De Bleeckere (BEL)

27/11/07, NSC Olympiyskiy Stadium, Kiev
FC Dynamo Kyiv 1-4 AS Roma
Attendance: 19700
Goal(s): 0-1 Panucci 4, 0-2 Giuly 32, 0-3 Vučinić 36, 1-3 Bangoura 63, 1-4 Vučinić 78
Referee: Stark (GER)

27/11/07, Old Trafford, Manchester
Manchester United FC 2-1 Sporting Clube de Portugal
Attendance: 74162
Goal(s): 0-1 Abel 21, 1-1 Tévez 61, 2-1 Cristiano Ronaldo 90+2
Referee: Larsen (DEN)

12/12/07, Stadio Olimpico, Rome
AS Roma 1-1 Manchester United FC
Attendance: 29490
Goal(s): 0-1 Piqué 34, 1-1 Mancini 71
Referee: Hansson (SWE)

12/12/07, José Alvalade, Lisbon
Sporting Clube de Portugal 3-0 FC Dynamo Kyiv
Attendance: 19402
Goal(s): 1-0 Polga 35(p), 2-0 João Moutinho 67, 3-0 Liedson 88
Referee: Dougal (SCO)

Group F Table

		Home					Away					Total				
	Pld	W	D	L	F	A	W	D	L	F	A	W	D	L	F	A
1 Manchester United FC	6	3	0	0	7	1	2	1	0	6	3	5	1	0	13	4
2 AS Roma	6	2	1	0	5	2	1	1	1	6	4	3	2	1	11	6
3 Sporting Clube de Portugal	6	1	1	1	5	3	1	0	2	4	5	2	1	3	9	8
4 FC Dynamo Kyiv	6	0	0	3	4	10	0	0	3	0	9	0	0	6	4	19

GROUP G

In a throwback to the early years of the European Champion Clubs' Cup, four domestic title-holders from different corners of the continent were drawn together in Group G. FC Internazionale Milano started as clear favourites in a section their coach Roberto Mancini described as "fascinating", though PSV Eindhoven, PFC CSKA Moskva and Fenerbahçe SK were all entitled to fancy their chances of progressing.

Quiet optimism

In their centenary year, Fenerbahçe seemed particularly determined to make some history. The Istanbul giants had never qualified from the group stage in four attempts, but with Brazilian coach Zico having guided them to the Turkish title in his first season, there was a feeling of quiet optimism when Inter visited in September. The Serie A champions were without nine first-team regulars and Fenerbahçe took full advantage, Deivid scoring the game's only goal with an acrobatic shot to spark wild celebrations. "We really deserved this win," said the Brazilian match-winner. "The whole team played well."

Inter were quickly back on track – thanks in no small measure to their Swedish striker Zlatan Ibrahimović, who scored five times in the next five games to fire the Italians through. "In my opinion he's the best player in the world," Mancini said after Ibrahimović's Matchday 2 double sank PSV Eindhoven 2-0. "He finishes well, he's quick and can beat defenders. He's yet to win the Ballon d'Or but I think he's going to win it once or twice." Argentine duo Hernán Crespo and Walter Samuel scored as Inter came from behind to win away to CSKA, and another Ibrahimović brace inspired a 4-2 triumph in the return at San Siro. Top spot was assured on Matchday 5 with a convincing 3-0 success over Fenerbahçe.

Brazilian spark

That was the first reverse of the campaign for Zico's men, who had taken confidence from their opening-day upset. Brazilians Deivid and Alex were providing plenty of attacking spark, and both hit the target in the

zilian striker Deivid was Fenerbahçe's
lscoring hero in the Turkish club's opening
against Internazionale

2-2 draw at CSKA. A solid defensive display then secured another point away to PSV in what proved to be Ronald Koeman's last European match in charge of the Dutch champions, as he left to take up a new challenge with Valencia CF.

PSV's caretaker boss Jan Wouters had little time to prepare for the Matchday 4 trip to Istanbul, and Fenerbahçe prevailed 2-0, with Kazım Kazım seeing his shot deflect in off Dirk Marcellis on 28 minutes before Semih Şentürk added another just moments later. "I've always wanted to be playing in the UEFA Champions League," said 21-year-old Kazım Kazım, who, in the previous season, had been involved in a relegation campaign in England with Sheffield United FC. "I always thought if I could show the best bits of my game someone might take a chance. This is a dream come true."

'We're a real team'

The Fenerbahçe fans were certainly in dreamland as their team homed in on a place in the last 16, although PSV's 1-0 win away to CSKA ensured the race for second place would go to the wire. PSV were just a point behind Fenerbahçe going in to Matchday 6 but ultimately nothing went their way. Inter seized the initiative in Eindhoven following the dismissal of Edison Méndez, and Julio Cruz netted the game's only goal on 64 minutes. Meanwhile, Fenerbahçe recovered from conceding first against CSKA and roared to a 3-1 win with a goal from Alex and two for UEFA Champions League novice Uğur Boral. "I want to thank all our supporters. Without them we couldn't have made it," said Zico. "I think Fenerbahçe are a real team. We have team spirit and I believe we'll be very successful in the next phase."

Group G Results

19/9/07, PSV-Stadion, Eindhoven
PSV Eindhoven 2-1 PFC CSKA Moskva
Attendance: 30000
Goal(s): 1-0 Lazović 59, 2-0 Perez 80, 2-1 Vágner Love 89
Referee: Pedro Proença (POR)

19/9/07, Sükrü Saraçoglu, Istanbul
Fenerbahçe SK 1-0 FC Internazionale Milano
Attendance: 44212
Goal(s): 1-0 Deivid 43
Referee: Medina Cantalejo (ESP)

2/10/07, Lokomotiv Stadium, Moscow
PFC CSKA Moskva 2-2 Fenerbahçe SK
Attendance: 25000
Goal(s): 0-1 Alex 9, 1-1 Krasić 50, 2-1 Vágner Love 53(p), 2-2 Deivid 85
Referee: Kircher (GER)

2/10/07, Stadio Giuseppe Meazza, Milan
FC Internazionale Milano 2-0 PSV Eindhoven
Attendance: 23882
Goal(s): 1-0 Ibrahimović 15(p), 2-0 Ibrahimović 31
Referee: Vassaras (GRE)

23/10/07, Lokomotiv Stadium, Moscow
PFC CSKA Moskva 1-2 FC Internazionale Milano
Attendance: 24000
Goal(s): 1-0 Jô 32, 1-1 Crespo 52, 1-2 Samuel 80
Referee: Riley (ENG)

23/10/07, PSV-Stadion, Eindhoven
PSV Eindhoven 0-0 Fenerbahçe SK
Attendance: 35000
Referee: Webb (ENG)

7/11/07, Stadio Giuseppe Meazza, Milan
FC Internazionale Milano 4-2 PFC CSKA Moskva
Attendance: 17495
Goal(s): 0-1 Jô 23, 0-2 Vágner Love 31, 1-2 Ibrahimović 32, 2-2 Cambiasso 34, 3-2 Cambiasso 67, 4-2 Ibrahimović 75
Referee: Allaerts (BEL)

7/11/07, Sükrü Saraçoglu, Istanbul
Fenerbahçe SK 2-0 PSV Eindhoven
Attendance: 46229
Goal(s): 1-0 Marcellis 28(og), 2-0 Semih Şentürk 30
Referee: Hamer (LUX)

27/11/07, Lokomotiv Stadium, Moscow
PFC CSKA Moskva 0-1 PSV Eindhoven
Attendance: 12418
Goal(s): 0-1 Farfán 39
Referee: Mejuto González (ESP)

27/11/07, Stadio Giuseppe Meazza, Milan
FC Internazionale Milano 3-0 Fenerbahçe SK
Attendance: 24736
Goal(s): 1-0 Cruz 55, 2-0 Ibrahimović 66, 3-0 Jiménez 90+2
Referee: Plautz (AUT)

12/12/07, PSV-Stadion, Eindhoven
PSV Eindhoven 0-1 FC Internazionale Milano
Attendance: 35000
Goal(s): 0-1 Cruz 64
Referee: Merk (GER)

12/12/07, Sükrü Saraçoglu, Istanbul
Fenerbahçe SK 3-1 PFC CSKA Moskva
Attendance: 45745
Goal(s): 0-1 Edu Dracena 30(og), 1-1 Alex 32, 2-1 Uğur Boral 45+1, 3-1 Uğur Boral 90
Referee: Trefoloni (ITA)

Group G Table

		Home					Away					Total				
	Pld	W	D	L	F	A	W	D	L	F	A	W	D	L	F	A
1 FC Internazionale Milano	6	3	0	0	9	2	2	0	1	3	2	5	0	1	12	4
2 Fenerbahçe SK	6	3	0	0	6	1	0	2	1	2	5	3	2	1	8	6
3 PSV Eindhoven	6	1	1	1	2	2	1	0	2	1	4	2	1	3	3	6
4 PFC CSKA Moskva	6	0	1	2	3	5	0	0	3	4	9	0	1	5	7	14

GROUP H

Kings of the UEFA Cup for the previous two seasons, Sevilla FC hoped to transfer their free-scoring and highly-successful brand of football to the toughest stage of all as they made their eagerly-anticipated debut in the UEFA Champions League group stage.

'World class'

A trip to Arsenal FC was a daunting introduction for Juande Ramos's team, not least because the 2006 finalists had made a flying start to their Premier League campaign. A 3-0 defeat in north London provided the men from Andalusia with a useful benchmark. "We lost because the team we were up against were superior," Ramos admitted. "We're now playing in a much more demanding competition." Cesc Fàbregas, Robin van Persie and Eduardo da Silva all scored, but striker Emmanuel Adebayor singled the Spaniard out as Arsenal's key man, saying: "Last season Cesc was already good but he's even better now. His all-round contribution makes him world class."

Sevilla possessed quality of their own, and they were soon scoring with typical regularity. Frédéric Kanouté and Luís Fabiano both struck in the 4-2 defeat of SK Slavia Praha, and the prolific pair repeated the trick three weeks later as FC Steaua Bucureşti became the Spanish club's second victims at the Ramón Sánchez-Pizjuán stadium. "Now we've steadied ourselves in the group it's 100 per cent my aim to try and win it," vowed Kanouté.

'Brilliant performance'

Such claims appeared fanciful when Arsenal followed up a 1-0 win in Bucharest with a record-equalling 7-0 romp at home to Slavia, the club's 12th successive win in all competitions. Fàbregas was again influential, scoring twice, while 18-year-old Theo Walcott registered his first two European goals. "It was a brilliant performance from the whole team," Walcott enthused. "We're playing well, we feel relaxed every time we go out and we're getting more and more confident."

Slavia had opened their debut campaign with a 2-1 win over Steaua – a result that hastened the

evilla full-back
ani Alves tussles
ith Arsenal
triker Eduardo

resignation of the Romanian team's illustrious coach Gheorghe Hagi - but eleven goals conceded in two games was a harsh dose of reality for their coach Karel Jarolím. They tightened up for the return fixture in Prague, earning a goalless draw against Arsenal, who nevertheless sealed their qualification with two matches to spare.

Ramos departure

Sevilla, meanwhile, were dealt a significant blow when Ramos joined Tottenham Hotspur FC in October having overseen a remarkable haul of five trophies in two years. New boss Manuel Jiménez may not have had much time to prepare for the Matchday 4 trip to Bucharest, but Sevilla's hosts appeared in even greater disarray. Indeed, following the departures of Hagi and Massimo Pedrazzini, Steaua had recently appointed their third coach of the season in Marius Lăcătuş, and the former Romania striker could do little to prevent Sevilla running out 2-0 victors thanks to Renato's double. The former European champions would secure their first point in a 1-1 draw with Slavia, yet still finished four points adrift of the Czech side.

If the identity of the two qualifiers had never really been in doubt, the race for top spot was proving more interesting. Arsenal led Sevilla by a solitary point prior to their second meeting and, while Gunners boss Arsène Wenger rested several key players, his Spanish counterpart looked to seize the opportunity. Eduardo put the visitors ahead before a superb strike from Seydou Keita and a Luís Fabiano header turned the game around. Kanouté made it 3-1 with a late penalty and Sevilla, who sealed their fifth straight win against Slavia in the final game, completed their debut campaign on top of the pile.

Group H Results

19/9/07, Arsenal Stadium, London
Arsenal FC 3-0 Sevilla FC
Attendance: 59992
Goal(s): 1-0 Fàbregas 27, 2-0 Van Persie 59, 3-0 Eduardo 90+2
Referee: Fröjdfeldt (SWE)

19/9/07, Evžena Rošického, Prague
SK Slavia Praha 2-1 FC Steaua Bucureşti
Attendance: 15723
Goal(s): 1-0 Šenkeřík 13, 1-1 Goian 33, 2-1 Belaid 63
Referee: Benquerença (POR)

2/10/07, Steaua Stadium, Bucharest
FC Steaua Bucureşti 0-1 Arsenal FC
Attendance: 12807
Goal(s): 0-1 Van Persie 76
Referee: Hauge (NOR)

2/10/07, Ramón Sánchez-Pizjuán, Sevilla
Sevilla FC 4-2 SK Slavia Praha
Attendance: 24202
Goal(s): 1-0 Kanouté 8, 1-1 Pudil 19, 2-1 Luís Fabiano 27, 3-1 Escudé 58, 4-1 Koné 68, 4-2 Kalivoda 90+2
Referee: Baskakov (RUS)

23/10/07, Ramón Sánchez-Pizjuán, Sevilla
Sevilla FC 2-1 FC Steaua Bucureşti
Attendance: 28945
Goal(s): 1-0 Kanouté 5, 2-0 Luís Fabiano 17, 2-1 Petre 63
Referee: Rosetti (ITA)

23/10/07, Arsenal Stadium, London
Arsenal FC 7-0 SK Slavia Praha
Attendance: 59621
Goal(s): 1-0 Fàbregas 5, 2-0 Hubáček 24(og), 3-0 Walcott 41, 4-0 Hleb 51, 5-0 Walcott 55, 6-0 Fàbregas 58, 7-0 Bendtner 89
Referee: Farina (ITA)

7/11/07, Steaua Stadium, Bucharest
FC Steaua Bucureşti 0-2 Sevilla FC
Attendance: 7984
Goal(s): 0-1 Renato 25, 0-2 Renato 65
Referee: Fandel (GER)

7/11/07, Evžena Rošického, Prague
SK Slavia Praha 0-0 Arsenal FC
Attendance: 18000
Referee: Layec (FRA)

27/11/07, Ramón Sánchez-Pizjuán, Sevilla
Sevilla FC 3-1 Arsenal FC
Attendance: 35529
Goal(s): 0-1 Eduardo 11, 1-1 Keita 24, 2-1 Luís Fabiano 34, 3-1 Kanouté 89(p)
Referee: Braamhaar (NED)

27/11/07, Steaua Stadium, Bucharest
FC Steaua Bucureşti 1-1 SK Slavia Praha
Attendance: 8287
Goal(s): 1-0 Badea 12, 1-1 Šenkeřík 78
Referee: Hamer (LUX)

12/12/07, Arsenal Stadium, London
Arsenal FC 2-1 FC Steaua Bucureşti
Attendance: 59786
Goal(s): 1-0 Diaby 8, 2-0 Bendtner 42, 2-1 Zaharia 68
Referee: Baskakov (RUS)

12/12/07, Evžena Rošického, Prague
SK Slavia Praha 0-3 Sevilla FC
Attendance: 11689
Goal(s): 0-1 Luís Fabiano 66, 0-2 Kanouté 69, 0-3 Dani Alves 87
Referee: Kassai (HUN)

Group H Table

		Home					Away					Total				
	Pld	W	D	L	F	A	W	D	L	F	A	W	D	L	F	A
1 Sevilla FC	6	3	0	0	9	4	2	0	1	5	3	5	0	1	14	7
2 Arsenal FC	6	3	0	0	12	1	1	1	1	2	3	4	1	1	14	4
3 SK Slavia Praha	6	1	1	1	2	4	0	1	2	3	12	1	2	3	5	16
4 FC Steaua Bucureşti	6	0	1	2	1	4	0	0	3	3	6	0	1	5	4	10

FIRST KNOCKOUT ROUND

A premature exit for holders AC Milan and the untimely demise of Real Madrid CF removed the two most successful clubs in the history of the European Champion Clubs' Cup from the 2007/08 UEFA Champions League equation in the first knockout round, leaving Liverpool FC as the most successful side left in the competition.

Holders and seven-time European Cup winners Milan came unstuck at the San Siro in the closing stages of their tie against Arsenal FC. Goalkeeper Željko Kalac emerged with plenty of credit as Milan earned a 0-0 draw in an enthralling first leg in London, but Arsenal manager Arsène Wenger was not too downhearted, saying: "I didn't dream of a 0-0, frankly, but overall not to concede is not a bad result."

Arsenal double

Milan prodigy Pato caught the eye again in the second leg, but it was not to be the holders' night. Having already hit the crossbar, Cesc Fàbregas opened the scoring in the tie with a marauding run and shot with six minutes of normal time remaining to leave the hosts with a mountain to climb. That mountain became an insurmountable cliff-face as Emmanuel Adebayor scored a second in added time to kill the Serie A side's dream of two straight European Cups stone dead. "Arsenal deserved to qualify," said Kaká, the hero of Milan's victory in 2006/07. "It is the first time that I have been eliminated from the Champions League so early, but it happens - that's football."

Kaká is down, and out, as holders AC Milan fall to Arsenal

Only Madrid have enjoyed more European triumphs than the Rossoneri, yet their recent downturn continued with a fourth consecutive exit at the last-16 stage. Raúl González gave the nine-time winners a perfect start against AS Roma with an away goal just eight minutes into the first leg, only for the hosts to battle back and finish with a slender 2-1 advantage.

Mancini steps up

With captain Francesco Totti struggling to assert himself on the night he surpassed Aldair's club record for appearances in Europe, Mancini stepped up to the plate, first setting up David Pizarro for the equaliser then scoring himself on 58 minutes. Delighted Roma coach Luciano Spalletti said: "It could have been a very difficult evening after conceding early, but we showed great maturity, continued to play our own game and were eventually rewarded."

If the Italians had shown enterprise and attacking verve at the Stadio Olimpico, their second-leg performance was all about resilience. Philippe Mexès patrolled the defence with authority, while Doni produced one fine save to deny Júlio Baptista before seeing the Brazilian's free-kick crash off the crossbar. The visitors did not merely defend, however, countering with menace and striking the woodwork twice themselves before deservedly going ahead through Taddei on 73 minutes, shortly after Madrid's Pepe had been dismissed.

Although Raúl then registered his 61st goal in the competition to extend his lead in the all-time scoring charts, Roma repeated the 2-1 winning scoreline thanks to Mirko Vučinić's last-gasp header, booking their place in the last eight for the second year running.

Last chance

Spalletti's team emerged as the only Italian representative in the quarter-finals after Serie A leaders FC Internazionale Milano succumbed to a resurgent Liverpool. The Reds, who were 19 points adrift of Manchester United FC in the Premier League and had been dumped unceremoniously out of the FA Cup by Barnsley FC five days earlier, knew the UEFA

Champions League represented their last chance of silverware. "We must win because we have to change what's happening," urged manager Rafael Benítez.

The Spaniard's wish was granted as late goals from Dirk Kuyt and Steven Gerrard sealed a 2-0 success at Anfield against an Inter side reduced to ten men for an hour following Marco Materazzi's red card.

Ill-discipline cost Roberto Mancini's men again in the return fixture when Nicolás Burdisso's 50th-minute sending off effectively sealed Inter's fate. Fernando Torres scored the game's only goal 14 minutes later, securing a second San Siro triumph in the space of a week for English clubs and earning the Spanish striker widespread acclaim. "Torres has been great all season," enthused team-mate Yossi Benayoun. "It's great to have such a big player on your side because in every game when we're struggling to score, he comes up with the goals."

With several prestigious clubs on their way out, Fenerbahçe SK and FC Schalke 04 seized their opportunities to reach the quarter-finals for the first time. There was a refreshing feel to the Turkish club's tie against Sevilla FC, as the two knockout-stage debutants attacked each other relentlessly over two matches, sharing ten goals in an exhilarating contest.

Fenerbahçe belief

Zico's charges took the lead no fewer than three times in the first leg, played at an electric Sükrü Saraçoglu stadium. Early strikes from Mateja Kežman and Diego Lugano were cancelled out by Edu Dracena's own goal and Julien Escudé's close-range effort, before substitute Semih Şentürk struck late on to give the Turkish title-holders a 3-2 victory.

Yet ten minutes into the second leg Fenerbahçe's narrow advantage had been obliterated by goals from Dani Alves and Seydou Keita. Deivid scored twice either side of Frédéric Kanouté's strike to ensure Sevilla's victory margin was cut to 3-2, resulting in extra time and a penalty shoot-out, in which Fenerbahçe goalkeeper Volkan Demirel, badly at fault earlier for two of Sevilla's goals, saved brilliantly from Escudé, Enzo Maresca and Alves. "We showed courage to take a step into the future," Zico said. "Demirel was fantastic - I have great confidence in him."

Penalties also settled Schalke's tie against FC Porto and again it was a special goalkeeping performance that separated the teams. Kevin Kuranyi's fourth-minute goal in Gelsenkirchen gave the Bundesliga outfit hope ahead of their trip to Portugal, but they were

Schalke goalkeep
Manuel Neuer mak
a save in the penal
shoot-out win ov
FC Port

outplayed for long periods of the second leg and only a series of sensational saves by Manuel Neuer preserved their advantage until the closing stages at the Estádio do Dragão.

The nervy visitors seemed to be edging towards victory when Jorge Fucile was sent off eight minutes from time, yet Lisandro López's ferocious strike brought the ten men of Porto level soon after. Neuer produced more heroics in the additional half hour, brilliantly denying Ricardo Quaresma, then saving from Bruno Alves and Lisandro to clinch to clinch victory in a nerve-jangling shoot-out.

Messi winner

Celtic FC came close to upsetting FC Barcelona in Glasgow but the class of Lionel Messi ultimately proved the difference in the first leg. The Argentine drew his side level following Jan Vennegoor of Hesselink's opener and after Thierry Henry's brilliant curler had cancelled out Barry Robson's goal, Messi struck again on 79 minutes to notch a valuable 3-2 away win and take his personal tally in the competition to six.

"They're another level up from us," conceded Celtic defender Gary Caldwell. "Now we need to win at the Camp Nou - it's going to be a big ask but we'll give it our best shot." Celtic's best was not enough. Xavi Hernández's early second-leg goal sealed Barcelona's

passage 4-2 on aggregate, although the gloss was taken off when the brilliant Messi sustained a thigh injury. "It's a very sad moment," lamented coach Frank Rijkaard.

Meanwhile, Manchester United and Chelsea FC secured an unprecedented quartet of English clubs in the quarter-finals following wins over Olympique Lyonnais and Olympiacos CFP respectively. The French champions had been targeting their fourth last-eight appearance in five years, and looked capable of achieving that feat when 20-year-old striker Karim Benzema handed them the lead at Stade de Gerland with a blistering low shot. An 87th-minute leveller from Carlos Tévez transformed the complexion of the tie, however, and Cristiano Ronaldo's solitary strike at Old Trafford sealed United's passage.

Chelsea had a smoother time against an Olympiacos side making their first appearance in the knockout stage since reaching the quarter-finals in 1998/99. After a goalless first leg, Michael Ballack, Frank Lampard and Salomon Kalou scored in the opening 48 minutes at Stamford Bridge to set up a highly impressive 3-0 win that underlined Chelsea's credentials - as well as silencing those claiming Ballack and Lampard are too similar to operate effectively in the same midfield. "I think that's three times we've played together this season and every time it's worked pretty well," the England international noted.

First Knockout Round Results

19/2/08, Arena AufSchalke, Gelsenkirchen
FC Schalke 04 1-0 FC Porto
Attendance: 53951
Goal(s): 1-0 Kuranyi 4
Referee: Duhamel (FRA)
5/3/08, Estádio do Dragão, Porto
FC Porto 1-0 FC Schalke 04
Attendance: 45316
Goal(s): 1-0 Lisandro López 86
Referee: Webb (ENG)
Aggregate: 1-1; FC Schalke 04 qualify 4-1 on penalties.

19/2/08, Anfield, Liverpool
Liverpool FC 2-0 FC Internazionale Milano
Attendance: 41999
Goal(s): 1-0 Kuyt 85, 2-0 Gerrard 90
Referee: De Bleeckere (BEL)
11/3/08, Stadio Giuseppe Meazza, Milan
FC Internazionale Milano 0-1 Liverpool FC
Attendance: 78923
Goal(s): 0-1 Fernando Torres 64
Referee: Øvrebø (NOR)
Aggregate: 0-3; Liverpool FC qualify.

19/2/08, Stadio Olimpico, Rome
AS Roma 2-1 Real Madrid CF
Attendance: 56231
Goal(s): 0-1 Raúl 8, 1-1 Pizarro 24, 2-1 Mancini 58
Referee: Fandel (GER)
5/3/08, Santiago Bernabéu, Madrid
Real Madrid CF 1-2 AS Roma
Attendance: 71569
Goal(s): 0-1 Taddei 73, 1-1 Raúl 75, 1-2 Vučinić 90+2
Referee: Vassaras (GRE)
Aggregate: 2-4; AS Roma qualify.

19/2/08, Georgios Karaiskakis, Piraeus
Olympiacos CFP 0-0 Chelsea FC
Attendance: 31302
Referee: Plautz (AUT)
5/3/08, Stamford Bridge, London
Chelsea FC 3-0 Olympiacos CFP
Attendance: 37721
Goal(s): 1-0 Ballack 5, 2-0 Lampard 25, 3-0 Kalou 48
Referee: Mejuto González (ESP)
Aggregate: 3-0; Chelsea FC qualify.

20/2/08, Celtic Park, Glasgow
Celtic FC 2-3 FC Barcelona
Attendance: 58426
Goal(s): 1-0 Vennegoor of Hesselink 16, 1-1 Messi 18, 2-1 Robson 38, 2-2 Henry 52, 2-3 Messi 79
Referee: Fröjdfeldt (SWE)
4/3/08, Camp Nou, Barcelona
FC Barcelona 1-0 Celtic FC
Attendance: 75326
Goal(s): 1-0 Xavi 3
Referee: Vink (NED)
Aggregate: 4-2; FC Barcelona qualify.

20/2/08, Stade de Gerland, Lyon
Olympique Lyonnais 1-1 Manchester United FC
Attendance: 39219
Goal(s): 1-0 Benzema 54, 1-1 Tévez 87
Referee: Medina Cantalejo (ESP)
4/3/08, Old Trafford, Manchester
Manchester United FC 1-0 Olympique Lyonnais
Attendance: 75520
Goal(s): 1-0 Cristiano Ronaldo 41
Referee: Rosetti (ITA)
Aggregate: 2-1; Manchester United FC qualify.

20/2/08, Arsenal Stadium, London
Arsenal FC 0-0 AC Milan
Attendance: 60082
Referee: Larsen (DEN)
4/3/08, Stadio Giuseppe Meazza, Milan
AC Milan 0-2 Arsenal FC
Attendance: 81879
Goal(s): 0-1 Fàbregas 84, 0-2 Adebayor 90+2
Referee: Plautz (AUT)
Aggregate: 0-2; Arsenal FC qualify.

20/2/08, Sükrü Saraçoglu, Istanbul
Fenerbahçe SK 3-2 Sevilla FC
Attendance: 46210
Goal(s): 1-0 Kežman 17, 1-1 Edu Dracena 23(og), 2-1 Lugano 57, 2-2 Escudé 66, 3-2 Semih Şentürk 87
Referee: Meyer (GER)
4/3/08, Ramón Sánchez-Pizjuán, Sevilla
Sevilla FC 3-2 Fenerbahçe SK
Attendance: 38626
Goal(s): 1-0 Dani Alves 5, 2-0 Keita 9, 2-1 Deivid 20, 3-1 Kanouté 41, 3-2 Deivid 79
Referee: Busacca (SUI)
Aggregate: 5-5; Fenerbahçe SK qualify 3-2 on penalties.

QUARTER-FINALS

As Chelsea FC, Liverpool FC and Manchester United FC booked their places in the last four for the second season running, AS Roma fans were not the only ones feeling a sense of déjà vu after seeing their side succumb once more to Sir Alex Ferguson's men. Yet the spirited displays of knockout-stage debutants FC Schalke 04 and Fenerbahçe SK against more illustrious opponents ensured there was no shortage of spice in the quarter-finals, with Anfield again providing the stage for one of the most dramatic European nights of recent times.

Thrilling battle

Having seen his emerging Arsenal FC side eliminate holders AC Milan, Arsène Wenger's quest for UEFA Champions League glory continued with a thrilling battle against 2006/07 runners-up Liverpool. "We were strong enough to knock the holders out so let's do it again against the finalists," urged the Frenchman. The Gunners had been eliminated by another English side, Chelsea, at the same stage in 2003/04 and this year would prove an equally agonising experience.

Emmanuel Adebayor's 23rd-minute goal gave them an ideal start in north London only for Rafael Benítez's charges to equalise three minutes later through Dirk Kuyt. Although they dominated for the remainder of the evening, Arsenal failed to score a second and their unwelcome habit of conceding shortly after scoring themselves would come back to haunt them in the second leg. "To finish a game like that at 1-1 is very disappointing," Wenger admitted. "We delivered the performance we wanted and we had chances to win."

Exquisite shot

Another assured start at Anfield saw Arsenal retake the lead in the tie through Abou Diaby, but again Liverpool responded, this time thanks to Sami Hyypiä's header. Benítez's deployment of Peter Crouch alongside Fernando Torres appeared increasingly shrewd as the hosts began to gain the upper hand in front of their fervent fans, and the partnership duly delivered on 69 minutes when the England striker flicked a header to his Spanish team-mate who turned brilliantly and rifled an exquisite shot into the top corner.

If the skilful and deadly nature of Torres's strike had the purists purring, Arsenal conjured an even more remarkable goal six minutes from time. Substitute Theo Walcott showed blistering pace to surge from one penalty area to the other, the teenager leaving four Liverpool players in his wake before setting up Adebayor to score. That breathtaking counterattack took the visitors to the brink of the last four, but no sooner had they finished celebrating than the referee was pointing to the spot at the other end following Kolo Touré's clumsy foul on Ryan Babel.

'Killer blow'

Steven Gerrard dispatched an immaculate penalty past Manuel Almunia, who, in added time, was beaten again by Babel on the break as the Reds progressed 4-2 on the night and 5-3 on aggregate. Few could argue

Cesc Fàbregas and Emmanuyel Adebayor show their feelings after Arsenal's agonising defeat at Anfield

with Benítez's assertion that it had been "a great night and a fantastic game", with the outcome remaining uncertain until the final seconds.

For the third time in four years, Liverpool's semi-final opponents would be Chelsea, but only after the Blues survived two nerve-jangling evenings against a Fenerbahçe side that won many admirers for their fearless, attacking approach throughout the campaign. Zico's men were up against it when Deivid put Florent Malouda's cross through his own net after just 13 minutes in Istanbul, yet they recovered brilliantly after the break, turning the game on its head with goals from London-born substitute Kazım Kazım and Brazilian forward Deivid, the latter atoning for his early mistake with a spectacular long-range strike nine minutes from time.

Rallying cry

The 2-1 victory represented one of the greatest in the club's history, but nobody was getting carried away in the home dressing room. "The first-half performance was not good and we had some hard discussions at half-time," Fenerbahçe playmaker Alex revealed. "If we want to get through we'll have to fight a lot harder in London." Despite the captain's rallying cry, the Turkish champions were caught cold again early on at Stamford Bridge, Michael Ballack levelling on aggregate by heading in Frank Lampard's free-kick.

After Joe Cole had been denied by a post, the visitors gradually found their footing and enjoyed a period of sustained pressure in the second half. Unfortuntely for them, Chelsea's third-choice goalkeeper Hilário - who replaced the injured Carlo Cudicini in the first half - was in vigilant mood, saving from Gökhan Gönül and Kazım Kazım, before Lampard's late goal secured Chelsea's passage 3-2 on aggregate.

Of the three English qualifiers, United emerged as the most comprehensive winners thanks to a fine 2-0 first-leg win away to Roma. The Italian club's hopes of avenging their 7-1 drubbing in England the previous year were dealt a significant blow before a ball had been kicked as captain Francesco Totti was ruled out with a thigh injury, and after a bright start at the Stadio Olimipico, the hosts were soon reliving a familiar nightmare.

Ferguson warning

Cristiano Ronaldo and Wayne Rooney, Roma's chief tormentors at Old Trafford 12 months earlier, both scored to leave United closing in on the last four again. "The result is fantastic, but we still have to prepare well for the return leg," warned Sir Alex Ferguson. "In football nothing is certain even if we have taken a big step towards the semi-finals." The United manager was right to be wary. Indeed, if Daniele De Rossi's 30th-minute penalty at Old Trafford had gone in, and not high over the crossbar, Luciano Spalletti's men might have clawed their way back into the contest.

Fenerbahçe's English-born Turkish international winger Kazım Kazım (formerly known as Colin Kazim-Richards) in action against Chelsea

Ultimately, however, the challenge proved too great and Carlos Tévez's perfectly placed second-half diving header sealed Roma's fate. "We must concede that over the two legs United were better than us and deserved their victory," said Roma boss Spalletti. "Of course we missed Francesco Totti very much. Anyone would like to have him in their team."

Bojan goal

FC Barcelona became the sole non-English representative in the semis after their 2-0 aggregate win over Schalke, yet the overriding view in Catalonia was that Frank Rijkaard's side would need to improve considerably on their unconvincing quarter-final displays if they were to emulate AC Milan's 2006/07 achievement. A first European goal from 17-year-old Bojan Krkić handed Barcelona the initiative in the first

Barcelona's Yaya Touré scores against Schalke at Camp No

leg in Gelsenkirchen but only poor finishing from the hosts preserved their advantage in the second half.

Gerald Asamoah, Halil Altıntop and Marcelo Bordon were all guilty of bad misses, leaving Schalke coach Mirko Slomka wondering how his side had lost. "We should have got more out of the second half," Slomka rued. "We decided to go for it and given the chances we created after half-time and our attacking play, we deserved a goal." It was a similar story at Camp Nou where, after more opportunities had been spurned by the Bundesliga outfit, Yaya Touré's 43rd-minute effort effectively finished the tie.

While Slomka paid a heavy price for the elimination, getting sacked four days later following a 5-1 defeat by Werder Bremen, Rijkaard turned his attentions to a semi-final with United. "We're happy to have won both quarter-final games and I imagine United are too. It'll be between two sides who play good football, but I don't want to talk about favourites."

Quarter-Final Results

1/4/08, Stadio Olimpico, Rome
AS Roma 0-2 Manchester United FC
Attendance: 60931
Goal(s): 0-1 Cristiano Ronaldo 39, 0-2 Rooney 66
Referee: De Bleeckere (BEL)
9/4/08, Old Trafford, Manchester
Manchester United FC 1-0 AS Roma
Attendance: 74423
Goal(s): 1-0 Tévez 70
Referee: Øvrebø (NOR)
Aggregate: 3-0; Manchester United FC qualify.

1/4/08, Arena AufSchalke, Gelsenkirchen
FC Schalke 04 0-1 FC Barcelona
Attendance: 53951
Goal(s): 0-1 Bojan 12
Referee: Vassaras (GRE)
9/4/08, Camp Nou, Barcelona
FC Barcelona 1-0 FC Schalke 04
Attendance: 72113
Goal(s): 1-0 Touré 43
Referee: Rosetti (ITA)
Aggregate: 2-0; FC Barcelona qualify.

2/4/08, Arsenal Stadium, London
Arsenal FC 1-1 Liverpool FC
Attendance: 60041
Goal(s): 1-0 Adebayor 23, 1-1 Kuyt 26
Referee: Vink (NED)
8/4/08, Anfield, Liverpool
Liverpool FC 4-2 Arsenal FC
Attendance: 41985
Goal(s): 0-1 Diaby 13, 1-1 Hyypiä 30, 2-1 Fernando Torres 69, 2-2 Adebayor 84, 3-2 Gerrard 85(p), 4-2 Babel 90+2
Referee: Fröjdfeldt (SWE)
Aggregate: 5-3; Liverpool FC qualify.

2/4/08, Sükrü Saraçoglu, Istanbul
Fenerbahçe SK 2-1 Chelsea FC
Attendance: 49055
Goal(s): 0-1 Deivid 13(og), 1-1 Kazım Kazım 65, 2-1 Deivid 81
Referee: Larsen (DEN)
8/4/08, Stamford Bridge, London
Chelsea FC 2-0 Fenerbahçe SK
Attendance: 38369
Goal(s): 1-0 Ballack 4, 2-0 Lampard 87
Referee: Fandel (GER)
Aggregate: 3-2; Chelsea FC qualify.

SEMI-FINALS

For the second year in succession, the UEFA Champions League semi-final line-up suggested the supremacy of English football at the highest echelons of the continental game. Once again, Manchester United FC, Chelsea FC and Liverpool FC stood at the gates of greatness, leaving FC Barcelona to take the baton from AC Milan as the one team capable of spoiling the party. But with Chelsea and Liverpool renewing their fierce rivalry at this stage of the competition, Moscow was sure to be decked in the colours of at least one Premier League side.

'Forget the past'

Previous form suggested it would be Liverpool. With tactics perfectly suited to knockout football, Rafael Benítez's men had ended Chelsea's dreams of gracing the showpiece in both 2004/05 and 2006/07, edging through thanks largely to nervy 1-0 second-leg wins at Anfield. This time, however, Merseyside was scheduled to host the opening encounter. "It's not so much putting the record straight; it's about what we can go on to achieve," commented Chelsea captain John Terry. "Forget what's happened in the past; it's about now and we need to take this opportunity."

Given that the six previous UEFA Champions League meetings between these two teams had yielded just three goals, no one was surprised by the cagey start at Liverpool's famous fortress. Neither team looked capable of imposing their will, but that did not stop the hosts from firing in their traditional goal in this fixture when Javier Mascherano's miscued shot looped over the Chelsea defence, allowing Dirk Kuyt to flash the loose ball beyond Petr Čech on 43 minutes.

Riise impact

Suddenly, the Anfield noise factor – so intimidating to the Londoners in the past – threatened to carry Liverpool home. Their passing became crisper and Čech saved smartly from Steven Gerrard and Fernando Torres before another player in red found the back of the net with practically the last touch of the game. Brought on as a 62nd-minute substitute, John Arne Riise had the misfortune of converting at the wrong end of the pitch, stooping low to head past Pepe Reina deep into added time. With that, the balance of the tie had shifted for good.

"The only thing we can do now is be positive and think about the next game," said Benítez. "We now need to go there and win." Liverpool's hopes of doing that took a blow when Didier Drogba pounced on a rebound to open the scoring at Stamford Bridge on 33 minutes, but the Reds stepped up their pressure after the restart and forced extra time when Yossi Benayoun evaded a series of tackles to release Fernando Torres in front of goal.

Emotional extra time

Unwilling to let their chance of a first final appearance slip away, and galvanised by the raucous backing of their own fans, Chelsea located a higher gear in the additional 30 minutes and seized back the lead when Sami Hyypiä felled Michael Ballack in the area. Returning to action less than a week after the death of his mother, Frank Lampard buried the resultant spot-kick and collapsed to the ground, his head filled with a potent mix of emotions. Drogba then doubled Chelsea's lead with his sixth of the campaign, rendering Ryan Babel's long-range effort redundant as the tie finished in frantic fashion.

Liverpool manager Rafa Benítez demands more from his players against Chelsea

"We have created history," said Chelsea coach Avram Grant, having taken the Blues a step further than his predecessor José Mourinho, and one game away from their first European title since the 1997/98 UEFA Cup Winners' Cup. "We did everything as I like to do it, in a positive way." Seven goals in two games certainly went against predictions of another dour tussle between the familiar foes, but perhaps that was not so surprising after all. Indeed, while the last two encounters between Manchester United and Barcelona had produced an incredible 12 goals, that mouth-watering statistic prepared absolutely no-one for their opener at the Camp Nou in the other semi-final.

Penalty miss

The scene of United's dramatic UEFA Champions League final victory in 1998/99, the Catalan venue still seemed to be smiling on Sir Alex Ferguson's men when they won a third-minute penalty for a Gabriel Milito handball. Cristiano Ronaldo stepped up to do the rest but despite his rich vein of scoring, the Portuguese skewed wide from the spot. That was as close as the visitors came too, and they spent the rest of the evening tidying up the dangers posed by Lionel Messi and Samuel Eto'o. "A victory is what we wanted obviously, but the semi-final is still open," commented Barça coach Frank Rijkaard after the game ended goalless. "The second leg won't be easy for them either."

Those words were about to prove prophetic – as was Sir Alex's promise to "attack more" – when chapter two kicked off at Old Trafford a week later. The tie had been billed from the start as a showdown between the sparkling talents of youngsters Ronaldo and Messi, but the night and the semi-final were to belong to one of the oldest players on the pitch. Having missed the 1999 final through suspension, Paul Scholes made his 100th UEFA Champions League appearance in the first leg and left his unique stamp on the second with a

Chelsea players and supporters celebrate their qualification for the UEFA Champions League fi
as Liverpool's Dirk Kuyt contemplates his team's eliminati

Paul Scholes' brilliant long-range strike at Old Trafford took Manchester United past Barcelona and into the UEFA Champions League final

blistering, unstoppable strike from distance that nestled in the top corner after Gianluca Zambrotta had failed to clear in the 14th minute.

Ferguson sentimental

Barça weaved some intricate patterns after that, sparking panic in the United rearguard on several occasions, but all too often the irrepressible Messi was left alone to conjure the magic. The Argentinian's best intentions were not enough to provide an equaliser and the disappointment of Barcelona's domestic campaign finally caught up with them on the European stage. For United, meanwhile, the first ever all-English UEFA Champions League final awaited, with Scholes guaranteed a starting berth in a rare display of sentimentality by his manager: "We can't expect him to score as many as when he was younger, but he certainly scored a good one tonight."

Semi-Final Results

22/4/08, Anfield, Liverpool
Liverpool FC 1-1 Chelsea FC
Attendance: 42180
Goal(s): 1-0 Kuyt 43, 1-1 Riise 90+4(og)
Referee: Plautz (AUT)
30/4/08, Stamford Bridge, London
Chelsea FC 3-2 Liverpool FC
Attendance: 38300
Goal(s): 1-0 Drogba 33, 1-1 Fernando Torres 64, 2-1 Lampard 98(p), 3-1 Drogba 105, 3-2 Babel 117
Referee: Rosetti (ITA)
Aggregate: 4-3; Chelsea FC qualify after extra time.

23/4/08, Camp Nou, Barcelona
FC Barcelona 0-0 Manchester United FC
Attendance: 95949
Referee: Busacca (SUI)
29/4/08, Old Trafford, Manchester
Manchester United FC 1-0 FC Barcelona
Attendance: 75061
Goal(s): 1-0 Scholes 14
Referee: Fandel (GER)
Aggregate: 1-0; Manchester United FC qualify.

FINAL

Having been unable to pip Manchester United FC to the Premier League title on the last day of the domestic season, Chelsea FC headed to Moscow aiming to capture club football's greatest prize at the Red Devils' expense. Following on from the all-Spanish final in 2000 and the 100 per cent Italian affair in 2003, the UEFA Champions League prepared for a midweek showpiece between familiar foes capable of mixing grit with flair.

Visa relaxation

Whoever prevailed, England was certain of moving level with Spain and Italy on eleven competition wins overall, while Chelsea were also vying to collect London's first. But the city dominating headlines in the run-up was the Russian capital itself. A week after FC Zenit St. Petersburg had tasted UEFA Cup glory, Moscow continued the Russian renaissance with an excellent level of organisation in and around the Luzhniki stadium. Above all, in what UEFA President Michel Platini called "an exceptional and unprecedented gesture", visa rules were relaxed to allow an estimated 40,000 fans with tickets to travel.

Moscow was also sure to prove an emotional venue for Roman Abramovich, Chelsea's billionaire Russian owner who swept into Stamford Bridge in 2003 with dreams of European glory. "We feel at home here, I must say," commented the Blues' manager Avram Grant. But while Abramovich's triumphant return was a story waiting to

Cristiano Ronaldo rises high to head home h 42nd goal of the season and put Manchest United 1-0 up in Mosco

be written, there was no shortage of significance in United's camp either, with Sir Alex Ferguson's side plotting to lay down a marker 40 years after their first continental title and 50 years after the Munich air disaster left eight of Sir Matt Busby's young team dead. "I'm proud that we're representing that history and we will not let them down," promised Ferguson.

Terry fit

Both teams kicked off at full strength, and that meant a starting berth for Blues captain John Terry, just ten days after dislocating his elbow. Determined to play his part, the England international could not have anticipated how his night was about to unfold, however, particularly after a cagey opening period. Eventually, United became the first side to settle, and no sooner had they established superiority than they took the lead, Wes Brown exchanging passes with Paul Scholes down the right touchline before sending a deep cross to the far post, where Cristiano Ronaldo shook off Michael Essien and headed a 26th-minute opener beyond Petr Čech.

The Portuguese winger's 42nd goal of the season was exceptionally well constructed, and United almost scored an even better one shortly afterwards when Wayne Rooney's laser-guided long crossfield ball brought Ronaldo into the game yet again. His swift control and cross deserved a better header than Carlos Tévez produced – instead, Čech pulled off a fantastic save before scrambling to keep out Michael Carrick's follow-up.

Lampard leveller

Edwin van der Sar had by that point made his own first intervention to prevent a Rio Ferdinand own goal, but it was increasingly United's game and Tévez came within mere centimetres of turning in Rooney's low centre with 43 minutes gone. This was scintillating stuff from the English champions, even if it left Ferguson aghast in the dugout. Perhaps United's veteran manager sensed what was coming next, as Chelsea restored parity on the stroke of half-time through Frank Lampard, who slotted past Van der Sar after Essien's long-range effort bobbled up invitingly following ricochets off both Nemanja Vidić and Ferdinand.

Having timed their blow to perfection, Chelsea built momentum after the break, with Ballack and Lampard planting a blue flag in midfield. Chances proved rare, but when they did come they fell to Grant's men, Didier Drogba almost registering with a fantastic curled shot from 25 metres that cannoned off a post. It was perhaps an untypical effort from a player

Frank Lampard salutes the Chelsea fans after his equalising goal

renowned for his physical presence, but this was no ordinary occasion, and Ryan Giggs added another layer of grandeur when he came on in the 87th minute to make a record-breaking 759th appearance for United.

Drogba dismissal

For the first time in three years, the final went to extra time, which began with Chelsea reacquainting themselves with the woodwork when Lampard unleashed an instinctive shot against the crossbar. United were by no means simply hanging on, though, and the game veered in their favour when Drogba saw red for lashing out at Vidić with four minutes remaining. With that, the Ivory Coast marksman disappeared from Chelsea's penalty shoot-out calculations, prompting Grant to send on Juliano Belletti, while Ferguson introduced Anderson.

It had not always been pretty up until that point, but it had been consistently engaging and both teams will have felt they deserved victory as Tévez, Ballack, Carrick and Belletti converted the first four spot-kicks with aplomb. Then Ronaldo stepped up, and having missed his penalty against FC Barcelona in the semi-final first leg, the 23-year-old's awkward stutter step failed to bamboozle Čech, who waited and picked off the listless shot that followed.

Terry turmoil

It looked as if the youngster's phenomenal season was about to end in despair, yet United fans familiar with the club's UEFA Champions League win in 1998/99 will have known not to give up prematurely – even as Terry placed the ball down in the knowledge he could win it for Chelsea. For Ferguson, this must have felt every bit as desperate as trailing FC Bayern München deep into added time at the Camp Nou, but Terry slipped on the wet grass and crashed his penalty against the post. Three efforts later, Giggs put United back into the lead before Van der Sar completed the win by diving to deny Nicolas Anelka.

Chelsea captain John Terry (right) trudges back to th halfway line after his penalty mi

"Fate played its hand today," said Ferguson, happy to have kept his promise to the Busby Babes. "Even John Terry slipping is a bit of fate. I just felt it was on our side this season. We had a cause which is important and people with causes become very difficult people to fight against. "Chelsea goalscorer Lampard, meanwhile, felt his side could be proud of the part they had played in a memorable match: "We didn't win but we gave everything and if you give everything you can't regret too much."

Edwin van der Sar saves Nicolas Anelka's penalty to win the UEFA Champions League for Manchester United

anchester United – Champions of Europe

Final Result

21/5/08, Luzhniki Stadium, Moscow
Manchester United FC 1-1 Chelsea FC
Attendance: 67310
Man. United: Van der Sar, Evra, Hargreaves, Ferdinand, Brown (Anderson 120+5), Cristiano Ronaldo, Rooney (Nani 101), Vidić, Carrick, Scholes (Giggs 87), Tévez. Coach: Sir Alex Ferguson (SCO)
Chelsea: Čech, A. Cole, Makelele (Belletti 120+4), Essien, Carvalho, Lampard, J. Cole (Anelka 99), Drogba, Ballack, Malouda (Kalou 92), Terry. Coach: Avram Grant (ISR)
Goal(s): 1-0 Cristiano Ronaldo 26, 1-1 Lampard 45
Red Card(s): Drogba 116 (Chelsea)
Yellow Card(s): Makelele 21 (Chelsea), Scholes 22 (Man. United), Ferdinand 43 (Man. United), Carvalho 45+2 (Chelsea), Vidić 111 (Man. United), Ballack 116 (Chelsea), Tévez 116 (Man. United), Essien 118 (Chelsea)
Referee: Michel' (SVK)
Manchester United FC win 6-5 on penalties.

TOP GOALSCORERS
(excluding qualifying rounds)

8 CRISTIANO RONALDO (Man. United)

6 Lionel MESSI (Barcelona)
FERNANDO TORRES (Liverpool)
Didier DROGBA (Chelsea)
Steven GERRARD (Liverpool)

5 Ryan BABEL (Liverpool)
Zlatan IBRAHIMOVIĆ (Internazionale)
Frédéric KANOUTÉ (Sevilla)
RAÚL González (Real Madrid)
DEIVID (Fenerbahçe)
Dirk KUYT (Liverpool)

UEFA CUP 2007/08

A new name was etched on the UEFA Cup trophy in 2007/08 as FC Zenit St. Petersburg became the second Russian team to claim the title in four years – announcing themselves on the European stage in style. Hardly dominant during the group stage, the side found their stride in the knockout rounds. They eliminated Villarreal CF, Olympique de Marseille and Bayer 04 Leverkusen before sending minor shockwaves reverberating throughout the continent by beating favourites FC Bayern München 4-0 in the second leg of their semi-final tie. The prize was a final against Rangers FC, a team their coach Dick Advocaat managed between 1998 and 2002, building up an association so strong that he repeatedly referred to them as "my team" in the lead up to the Manchester final. Yet by the end of the evening, as his ecstatic frame was hoisted high by jubilant Zenit players, his true allegiance was obvious.

CHAPTER
03

FIRST QUALIFYING ROUND

Just 63 days elapsed between Sevilla FC defending their UEFA Cup title on a murky May evening in Glasgow and 74 teams getting the 2007/08 campaign under way in the middle of sweltering July.

Big names

Minnows like JK Trans Narva, HŠK Zrinjski and FC Nistru Otaci rubbed shoulders with the stellar European footballing names of Henrik Larsson, FK Partizan and Budapest Honvéd FC respectively. Partizan and Larsson's Helsingborgs IF were barely troubled, claiming 11-1 and 9-0 aggregate victories respectively, but the Serbian club were nevertheless eliminated due to the misconduct of their supporters during the first leg in Mostar. Honvéd were given a huge scare by Nistru, needing the lottery of a penalty shoot-out to prevail after both legs had ended 1-1.

Maccabi Tel-Aviv FC also found qualification harder than expected as Andorra's FC Santa Coloma claimed a shock 1-0 first-leg win. A 4-0 triumph in the return put paid to any thoughts of an upset, but SV Mattersburg left it much later in an enthralling tie against Kazakhstan's FK Aktobe. German veteran Carsten Jancker was among the scorers as the home side scored three times to overturn a 1-0 first-leg deficit, but two late Aktobe goals, compounded by the dismissal of Adnan Mravac, left the Austrian side heading for elimination. An added-time Ákos Kovrig free-kick saved their blushes.

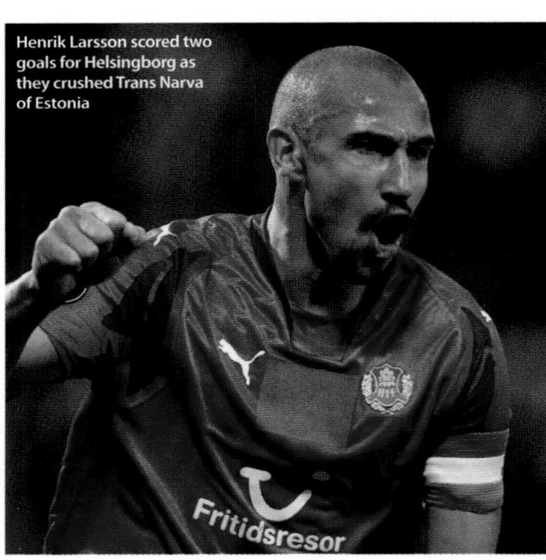

Henrik Larsson scored two goals for Helsingborg as they crushed Trans Narva of Estonia

First Qualifying Round Results

19/7/07, Estadi Comunal, Andorra la Vella
FC Santa Coloma 1-0 Maccabi Tel-Aviv FC
Goal(s): 1-0 Fernández 57
Referee: Tshagharyan (ARM)
2/8/07, Bloomfield, Tel-Aviv
Maccabi Tel-Aviv FC 4-0 FC Santa Coloma
Goal(s): 1-0 Mesika 12, 2-0 Mesika 25, 3-0 Shivhon 63, 4-0 Kamanan 71
Referee: Saliy (KAZ)
Aggregate: 4-1; Maccabi Tel-Aviv FC qualify.

19/7/07, FC ViOn, Zlate Moravce
FC ViOn Zlaté Moravce 3-1 FC Alma-Ata
Goal(s): 1-0 Gibala 51, 2-0 Greguška 71, 3-0 Gibala 78, 3-1 Larin 82
Referee: Kaasik (EST)
2/8/07, Tcentralny, Almaty
FC Alma-Ata 1-1 FC ViOn Zlaté Moravce
Goal(s): 1-0 Irismetov 58, 1-1 Černák 77
Referee: Stanković (SRB)
Aggregate: 2-4; FC ViOn Zlaté Moravce qualify.

19/7/07, Vojvodina, Novi Sad
FK Vojvodina 5-1 Hibernians FC
Goal(s): 1-0 Despotović 21, 2-0 Despotović 42, 3-0 Đurić 60, 4-0 Kačar 84, 4-1 Doffo 86(p), 5-1 Despotović 89(p)
Referee: Tsikinis (GRE)
2/8/07, Ta' Qali, Ta' Qali
Hibernians FC 0-2 FK Vojvodina
Goal(s): 0-1 Xuereb 30(og), 0-2 Despotović 62
Referee: Evans (WAL)
Aggregate: 1-7; FK Vojvodina qualify.

19/7/07, Gradski, Koprivnica
NK Slaven Koprivnica 6-2 KS Teuta
Goal(s): 0-1 D. Xhafaj 10, 1-1 Posavec 18(p), 2-1 Šehic 29, 3-1 Šehic 47, 4-1 Vručina 60, 4-2 Brahja 65, 5-2 Vručina 82, 6-2 Bošnjak 90
Referee: Toussaint (LUX)
2/8/07, Niko Dovana, Durres
KS Teuta 2-2 NK Slaven Koprivnica
Goal(s): 1-0 Kuli 45, 1-1 Kresinger 64, 1-2 Vručina 70, 2-2 Kuli 74
Referee: Kailis (CYP)
Aggregate: 4-8; NK Slaven Koprivnica qualify.

19/7/07, FK Partizan, Belgrade
FK Bežanija 2-2 KS Besa
Goal(s): 1-0 Đalovic 37, 1-1 Ishaka 49, 2-1 Đurovski 57(p), 2-2 Elokan 90
Referee: Müftüoglu (TUR)
2/8/07, Qemal Stafa, Tirana
KS Besa 0-0 FK Bežanija
Referee: Jorge Sousa (POR)
Aggregate: 2-2; KS Besa qualify on away goals.

19/7/07, Mikheil Meskhi, Tbilisi
FC Dinamo Tbilisi 2-0 FC Vaduz
Goal(s): 1-0 Merebashvili 66(p), 2-0 Akiremy 72
Referee: Sápi (HUN)
2/8/07, Rheinpark, Vaduz
FC Vaduz 0-0 FC Dinamo Tbilisi
Referee: Vučemilović-Šimunović, jr. (CRO)
Aggregate: 0-2; FC Dinamo Tbilisi qualify.

19/7/07, Tórsvøllur, Torshavn
B36 Tórshavn 1-3 FK Ekranas
Goal(s): 0-1 Lukšys 11, 1-1 Højsted 41, 1-2 Paulauskas 45, 1-3 Pogreban 67
Referee: Jug (SVN)
2/8/07, Aukštaitija, Panevezys
FK Ekranas 3-2 B36 Tórshavn
Goal(s): 1-0 Šidlauskas 51, 2-0 Lukšys 77, 2-1 Midjord 85, 2-2 Benjaminsen 86(p), 3-2 Lukšys 87
Referee: Rossi (SMR)
Aggregate: 6-3; FK Ekranas qualify.

9/7/07, A Le Coq Arena, Tallinn
'C Flora 0-1 Vålerenga Fotball
ioal(s): 0-1 Lange 31
teferee: Buttimer (IRL)
'/8/07, Ullevål, Oslo
'ålerenga Fotball 1-0 FC Flora
ioal(s): 1-0 Berre 90+2
teferee: Jech (CZE)
iggregate: 2-0; Vålerenga Fotball qualify.

9/7/07, Olympia, Helsingborg
lelsingborgs IF 6-0 JK Trans Narva
ioal(s): 1-0 Omotoyossi 28, 2-0 Dahl 30, 3-0 Larsson 59, 4-0 Larsson 4, 5-0 Karekezi 80, 6-0 C. Andersson 84
eferee: Zakharov (RUS)
/8/07, A Le Coq Arena, Tallinn
K Trans Narva 0-3 Helsingborgs IF
ioal(s): 0-1 Wahlstedt 18, 0-2 Svanbäck 32, 0-3 Unkuri 76
eferee: Van De Velde (BEL)
ggregate: 0-9; Helsingborgs IF qualify.

9/7/07, Finnair, Helsinki
IJK Helsinki 2-0 FC Etzella Ettelbrück
ioal(s): 1-0 Bah 24, 2-0 Sorsa 90+1
eferee: Žuta (LTU)
/8/07, Deich, Ettelbruck
C Etzella Ettelbrück 0-1 HJK Helsinki
oal(s): 0-1 Savolainen 26(p)
eferee: Ishchenko (UKR)
ggregate: 0-3; HJK Helsinki qualify.

9/7/07, Richmond Park, Carmarthen
armarthen Town AFC 0-8 SK Brann
oal(s): 0-1 Winters 8, 0-2 Helstad 17, 0-3 Helstad 28, 0-4 Winters 30, 5 Winters 45, 0-6 K. Sigurdsson 70, 0-7 Solli 83, 0-8 Björnsson 90+1
eferee: Godulyan (UKR)
'8/07, Brann, Bergen
K Brann 6-3 Carmarthen Town AFC
oal(s): 1-0 Vaagan Moen 9, 2-0 Björnsson 19, 3-0 Winters 27, 4-0 Vinters 32, 4-1 K. Thomas 36, 4-2 Hicks 47, 5-2 K. Sigurdsson 56, 6-2 anstveit 57, 6-3 Hicks 90
eferee: Schörgenhofer (AUT)
ggregate: 14-3; SK Brann qualify.

9/7/07, Anjalankosken Jalkapallokenttä, Anjalankoski
'yllykosken Pallo-47 1-0 EB/Streymur
oal(s): 1-0 Hyyrynen 11
eferee: Bede (HUN)
'8/07, Tórsvøllur, Torshavn
B/Streymur 1-1 Myllykosken Pallo-47
oal(s): 0-1 Kuparinen 70, 1-1 Potemkin 86
eferee: McKeon (IRL)
ggregate: 1-2; Myllykosken Pallo-47 qualify.

9/7/07, Åråsen, Lillestrom
illestrøm SK 2-1 UN Käerjéng 97
oal(s): 1-0 Occean 19, 2-0 Sundgot 45(p), 2-1 Andersen 45(og)
eferee: Whitby (WAL)
1/7/07, Josy Barthel, Luxembourg
N Käerjéng 97 1-0 Lillestrøm SK
oal(s): 1-0 Boulahfari 49
eferee: Guliyev (AZE)
ggregate: 2-2; UN Käerjéng 97 qualify on away goal.

9/7/07, Republican, Yerevan
C Banants 1-1 BSC Young Boys
oal(s): 0-1 Mangane 17, 1-1 Kakosyan 68
eferee: Svilokos (CRO)
'8/07, Stade de Suisse, Berne
SC Young Boys 4-0 FC Banants
oal(s): 1-0 João Paulo 11, 2-0 Tiago 21, 3-0 João Paulo 41, 4-0 M. chneuwly 58
eferee: Sidenko (MDA)
ggregate: 5-1; BSC Young Boys qualify.

9/7/07, Zimbru, Chisinau
C Nistru Otaci 1-1 Budapest Honvéd FC
oal(s): 1-0 Malitskiy 29, 1-1 Abraham 51
eferee: Demirlek (TUR)
2/8/07, József Bozsik, Budapest
Budapest Honvéd FC 1-1 FC Nistru Otaci
Goal(s): 1-0 Abraham 14, 1-1 Mekang 50
Referee: Svendsen (DEN)
Aggregate: 2-2; Budapest Honvéd FC qualify 5-4 on penalties.

19/7/07, Keflavíkurvöllur, Keflavik
Keflavík 3-2 FC Midtjylland
Goal(s): 0-1 Dadu 9, 0-2 Afriyie 20, 1-2 Steinarsson 27, 2-2 Troest 34(og), 3-2 Samuelsen 57
Referee: Bertolini (SUI)
2/8/07, Messecentret, Herning
FC Midtjylland 2-1 Keflavík
Goal(s): 0-1 Sigurdsson 11, 1-1 S. Poulsen 68, 2-1 Dadu 75
Referee: McCourt (NIR)
Aggregate: 4-4; FC Midtjylland qualify on away goals.

19/7/07, Ta' Qali, Ta' Qali
Sliema Wanderers FC 0-3 PFC Litex Lovech
Goal(s): 0-1 I. Popov 22, 0-2 Beto 53, 0-3 I. Popov 56
Referee: Mrković (BIH)
2/8/07, Gradski, Lovech
PFC Litex Lovech 4-0 Sliema Wanderers FC
Goal(s): 1-0 Boudarène 28, 2-0 Beto 48, 3-0 I. Popov 59, 4-0 Beto 60
Referee: Berezka (UKR)
Aggregate: 7-0; PFC Litex Lovech qualify.

19/7/07, Daugava, Liepaja
SK Liepājas Metalurgs 1-1 FC Dinamo Brest
Goal(s): 1-0 Ferreira 5, 1-1 Sokol 77
Referee: Wouters (BEL)
2/8/07, Brestsky, Brest
FC Dinamo Brest 1-2 SK Liepājas Metalurgs
Goal(s): 0-1 Kruglyak 40, 1-1 Sokol 47, 1-2 Karlsons 50
Referee: Spasić (SRB)
Aggregate: 2-3; SK Liepājas Metalurgs qualify.

19/7/07, Belle Vue, Rhyl
Rhyl FC 3-1 FC Haka
Goal(s): 0-1 Lehtinen 15, 1-1 Moran 26, 2-1 Hunt 36, 3-1 Garside 47
Referee: Vervecken (BEL)
2/8/07, Tehtaan Kenttä, Valkeakoski
FC Haka 2-0 Rhyl FC
Goal(s): 1-0 Innanen 62, 2-0 Popovich 64
Referee: Nikolaev (RUS)
Aggregate: 3-3; FC Haka qualify on away goal.

19/7/07, Skonto, Riga
Skonto FC 1-1 FC Dinamo Minsk
Goal(s): 0-1 Rák 11, 1-1 Pereplotkins 27
Referee: Zimmermann (SUI)
2/8/07, Dinamo, Minsk
FC Dinamo Minsk 2-0 Skonto FC
Goal(s): 1-0 Rák 57, 2-0 Rák 74
Referee: Stålhammar (SWE)
Aggregate: 3-1; FC Dinamo Minsk qualify.

19/7/07, Richmond Park, Dublin
Saint Patrick's Athletic FC 0-0 Odense BK
Referee: Fautrel (FRA)
2/8/07, Fionia Park, Odense
Odense BK 5-0 Saint Patrick's Athletic FC
Goal(s): 1-0 Andreasen 20, 2-0 K. Christensen 29, 3-0 Borring 45, 4-0 K. Christensen 73, 5-0 Mikkelsen 89
Referee: Blom (NED)
Aggregate: 5-0; Odense BK qualify.

19/7/07, The Oval, Belfast
Glentoran FC 0-5 AIK Solna
Goal(s): 0-1 Wilton 21, 0-2 Wilton 62, 0-3 Valdemarín 68, 0-4 Stephenson 73, 0-5 Johnson 84
Referee: Sipailo (LVA)
2/8/07, Råsunda, Solna
AIK Solna 4-0 Glentoran FC
Goal(s): 1-0 Özkan 7, 2-0 Karlsson 24, 3-0 Gerndt 88, 4-0 Johnson 89
Referee: Rogalla (SUI)
Aggregate: 9-0; AIK Solna qualify.

19/7/07, Windsor Park, Belfast
Dungannon Swifts FC 1-0 FK Sūduva
Goal(s): 1-0 McAllister 17
Referee: Vejlgaard (DEN)
2/8/07, Sūduva, Marijampole
FK Sūduva 4-0 Dungannon Swifts FC
Goal(s): 1-0 Grigas 29, 2-0 Urbšys 50, 3-0 Urbšys 55, 4-0 Urbšys 84
Referee: Edvartsen (NOR)
Aggregate: 4-1; FK Sūduva qualify.

19/7/07, Tofikh Bakhramov-Republic Stadium, Baku
FK MKT-Araz 0-0 Groclin Grodzisk Wielkopolski
Referee: Vialichka (BLR)
2/8/07, Groclin Dyskobolia, Grodzisk Wielkopolski
Groclin Grodzisk Wielkopolski 1-0 FK MKT-Araz
Goal(s): 1-0 Kłodawski 88
Referee: Moen (NOR)
Aggregate: 1-0; Groclin Grodzisk Wielkopolski qualify.

19/7/07, GSP, Nicosia
AC Omonia 2-0 FK Rudar Pljevlja
Goal(s): 1-0 Kaiafas 43, 2-0 Chailis 46
Referee: Deaconu (ROU)
2/8/07, Pod Goricom - Gradski, Podgorica
FK Rudar Pljevlja 0-2 AC Omonia
Goal(s): 0-1 Mguni 34, 0-2 Ricardo Sousa 75
Referee: Casha (MLT)
Aggregate: 0-4; AC Omonia qualify.

19/7/07, Ullevi, Gothenburg
BK Häcken 1-1 KR Reykjavík
Goal(s): 1-0 Hedén 12, 1-1 Pétursson 69
Referee: Malžinskas (LTU)
2/8/07, KR-Völlur, Reykjavik
KR Reykjavík 0-1 BK Häcken
Goal(s): 0-1 De Oliveira 83
Referee: Gvardis (RUS)
Aggregate: 1-2; BK Häcken qualify.

19/7/07, TJ Senec Montostroj, Senec
FC Artmedia Petržalka 1-1 FC Zimbru Chisinau
Goal(s): 1-0 M. Ďurica 21(p), 1-1 Zhdanov 70(p)
Referee: Strahonja (CRO)
2/8/07, Zimbru, Chisinau
FC Zimbru Chisinau 2-2 FC Artmedia Petržalka
Goal(s): 1-0 Kovalchuk 34, 2-0 Zhdanov 60(p), 2-1 Guédé 73, 2-2 Borbély 90+4
Referee: Pérez Burrull (ESP)
Aggregate: 3-3; FC Artmedia Petržalka qualify on away goals.

19/7/07, Športni Park, Nova Gorica
NK Gorica 1-2 FK Rabotnicki
Goal(s): 0-1 Šuler 79(og), 1-1 Matavž 83, 1-2 Velkoski 90+1
Referee: Jakov (ISR)
2/8/07, Gradski, Skopje
FK Rabotnicki 2-1 NK Gorica
Goal(s): 1-0 Velkoski 44, 2-0 Demiri 68, 2-1 Demirović 85(p)
Referee: Vadachkoria (GEO)
Aggregate: 4-2; FK Rabotnicki qualify.

19/7/07, Gradski, Skopje
FK Vardar 0-1 Anorthosis Famagusta FC
Goal(s): 0-1 Deyanov 88
Referee: Coltescu (ROU)
2/8/07, Antonis Papadopoulos, Larnaca
Anorthosis Famagusta FC 1-0 FK Vardar
Goal(s): 1-0 Žlogar 53
Referee: Mikołajewski (POL)
Aggregate: 2-0; Anorthosis Famagusta FC qualify.

19/7/07, NK Zrinjski, Mostar
HŠK Zrinjski 1-6 FK Partizan
Goal(s): 0-1 Diatta 32, 0-2 Maletić 40, 0-3 Jovetić 48, 0-4 Diatta 60, 0-5 Diatta 63, 1-5 Matko 68, 1-6 Lazetić 80
Referee: De Marco (ITA)
2/8/07, FK Partizan, Belgrade
FK Partizan 5-0 HŠK Zrinjski
Goal(s): 1-0 Maletić 4, 2-0 Moreira 32, 3-0 Jovetić 37, 4-0 Jovetić 51, 5-0 Jovetić 71
Referee: Jilek (CZE)
Aggregate: 11-1; FK Partizan disqualified; HŠK Zrinjski qualify.

19/7/07, Pod Goricom - Gradski, Podgorica
FK Budućnost Podgorica 1-1 HNK Hajduk Split
Goal(s): 0-1 Hrgović 28, 1-1 Šćepanović 59
Referee: Kenan (ISR)
2/8/07, Poljud, Split
HNK Hajduk Split 1-0 FK Budućnost Podgorica
Goal(s): 1-0 Damjanović 46
Referee: Zografos (GRE)
Aggregate: 2-1; HNK Hajduk Split qualify.

19/7/07, Fill Metallbau Stadion, Ried im Innkreis
SV Ried 3-1 PFK Neftçi
Goal(s): 1-0 Drechsel 2, 1-1 Äliyev 14, 2-1 Brenner 87, 3-1 Salihi 90+1
Referee: Rubinos Perez (ESP)
2/8/07, Tofikh Bakhramov-Republic Stadium, Baku
PFK Neftçi 2-1 SV Ried
Goal(s): 1-0 Subašić 14, 2-0 Räşad F. Sadiqov 21, 2-1 Salihi 85
Referee: Ristoskov (BUL)
Aggregate: 3-4; SV Ried qualify.

19/7/07, Megyeri úti, Budapest
MTK Budapest 2-1 FC MIKA
Goal(s): 1-0 Pintér 20, 1-1 Kléber Rodrigues 45, 2-1 Urbán 57
Referee: Hinriksson (ISL)
2/8/07, Ashtarak Kasakh, Yerevan
FC MIKA 1-0 MTK Budapest
Goal(s): 1-0 Adamyan 26
Referee: Constantin (ROU)
Aggregate: 2-2; FC MIKA qualify on away goal.

19/7/07, GKS, Belchatow
GKS Bełchatów 2-0 FC Ameri Tbilisi
Goal(s): 1-0 Pietrasiak 51, 2-0 Pietrasiak 82
Referee: Chapron (FRA)
2/8/07, Mikheil Meskhi, Tbilisi
FC Ameri Tbilisi 2-0 GKS Bełchatów
Goal(s): 1-0 Tatanashvili 12, 2-0 Davitashvili 46
Referee: Kister (KAZ)
Aggregate: 2-2; GKS Bełchatów qualify 4-2 on penalties.

19/7/07, Olimpico, Serravalle
SP Libertas 1-1 Drogheda United FC
Goal(s): 0-1 Zayed 44, 1-1 Pari 77
Referee: Janku (ALB)
2/8/07, Dalymount Park, Dublin
Drogheda United FC 3-0 SP Libertas
Goal(s): 1-0 Keegan 11, 2-0 Keegan 48, 3-0 Byrne 57
Referee: Wouters (BEL)
Aggregate: 4-1; Drogheda United FC qualify.

19/7/07, Pecara, Siroki Brijeg
NK Široki Brijeg 3-1 FC Koper
Goal(s): 0-1 Viler 8, 1-1 Célson 24, 2-1 Célson 33, 3-1 Ronielle 44
Referee: Kulbakov (BLR)
2/8/07, Arena Petrol, Celje
FC Koper 2-3 NK Široki Brijeg
Goal(s): 0-1 Karoglan 18, 0-2 R. Božič 25(og), 1-2 Volaš 34, 1-3 Ronielle 36, 2-3 Mejač 82
Referee: Hietala (FIN)
Aggregate: 3-6; NK Široki Brijeg qualify.

19/7/07, Tcentralny, Aktobe
FK Aktobe 1-0 SV Mattersburg
Goal(s): 1-0 Khayrullin 85
Referee: Aydınus (TUR)
2/8/07, Pappelstadion, Mattersburg
SV Mattersburg 4-2 FK Aktobe
Goal(s): 1-0 Jancker 22, 2-0 Wagner 62, 3-0 Csizmadia 67, 3-1 Bogomolov 71, 3-2 Kosolapov 77, 4-2 Kovrig 90+2
Referee: Hermansen (DEN)
Aggregate: 4-3; SV Mattersburg qualify.

SECOND QUALIFYING ROUND

The 37 sides that had progressed from the first qualifying round were joined by 16 new entrants and the eleven UEFA Intertoto Cup winners, and with 32 places in the UEFA Cup first round at stake competition was fierce.

Erciyesspor shock

The August fixtures saw an early introduction for 2000 winners Galatasaray AŞ, and although they fell behind to Croatia's NK Slaven Koprivnica early on in the first leg, they fought back to claim a 2-1 win, going through 4-2 on aggregate. Yet the Istanbul outfit's achievements were eclipsed by those of another Turkish side, second division Kayseri Erciyesspor, who caused an upset by knocking out Maccabi Tel-Aviv FC. Level at 1-1 after the first meeting in Israel, Erciyesspor raced into a 2-0 lead within 14 minutes of kick-off at home and there was no way back for Maccabi, who went on to lose 4-2 on aggregate.

With Maccabi Netanya FC also edged out, Israel's UEFA Cup aspirations were at least kept alive by Hapoel Tel-Aviv FC's 6-0 demolition of Bosnia-Herzegovina's NK Široki Brijeg. There was also a mixed return for Austria, FK Austria Wien and SK Rapid Wien progressing as SV Mattersburg and SV Ried fell to Swiss opposition. Swedish sides proved successful, however, with Hammarby, AIK Solna, Helsingborgs IF and second division BK Häcken all booking places in the first round.

w Galatasaray ch Karl Heinz dkamp had an ly introduction to UEFA Cup

Stronger sides

Hammarby and AIK required goals in the last five minutes to seal progress, and elsewhere PFC CSKA Sofia and FK Rabotnički struck in the last minute to ensure their names were in the Monaco draw. They were joined by R. Standard de Liège, FC Zenit St. Petersburg, RC Lens and Club Atlético de Madrid following easy wins, while Intertoto qualifiers Blackburn Rovers FC, UC Sampdoria and Hamburger SV also battled through.

Second Qualifying Round Results

16/8/07, FC ViOn, Zlate Moravce
FC ViOn Zlaté Moravce 0-2 FC Zenit St. Petersburg
Goal(s): 0-1 Hagen 38, 0-2 Ionov 90+2
Referee: Rasmussen (DEN)
30/8/07, Petrovsky, St Petersburg
FC Zenit St. Petersburg 3-0 FC ViOn Zlaté Moravce
Goal(s): 1-0 Pogrebnyak 10, 2-0 Maximov 61, 3-0 Kim 71
Referee: Bossen (NED)
Aggregate: 5-0; FC Zenit St. Petersburg qualify.

16/8/07, Niko Dovana, Durres
KS Besa 0-3 PFC Litex Lovech
Goal(s): 0-1 I. Popov 13, 0-2 I. Popov 20, 0-3 Beto 32
Referee: Dondarini (ITA)
30/8/07, Gradski, Lovech
PFC Litex Lovech 3-0 KS Besa
Goal(s): 1-0 Genchev 13, 2-0 Beto 69, 3-0 Tome 79
Referee: Kenan (ISR)
Aggregate: 6-0; PFC Litex Lovech qualify.

16/8/07, Anjalankosken Jalkapallokenttä, Anjalankoski
Myllykosken Pallo-47 0-1 Blackburn Rovers FC
Goal(s): 0-1 Santa Cruz 6
Referee: Thual (FRA)
30/8/07, Ewood Park, Blackburn
Blackburn Rovers FC 2-0 Myllykosken Pallo-47
Goal(s): 1-0 Bentley 48, 2-0 Roberts 90+1
Referee: Einwaller (AUT)
Aggregate: 3-0; Blackburn Rovers FC qualify.

16/8/07, Aukštaitija, Panevezys
FK Ekranas 1-1 Vålerenga Fotball
Goal(s): 1-0 Bička 45+1(p), 1-1 Dos Santos 76
Referee: Granat (POL)
30/8/07, Ullevål, Oslo
Vålerenga Fotball 6-0 FK Ekranas
Goal(s): 1-0 Grindheim 5, 2-0 Sørensen 42, 3-0 Grindheim 45+1, 4-0 Horn 67, 5-0 Storbæk 81, 6-0 Brix 90+1
Referee: Vad (HUN)
Aggregate: 7-1; Vålerenga Fotball qualify.

16/8/07, Mikheil Meskhi, Tbilisi
FC Dinamo Tbilisi 0-3 SK Rapid Wien
Goal(s): 0-1 Fabiano 24, 0-2 Hofmann 39, 0-3 Bazina 53
Referee: Mikulski (POL)
30/8/07, Gerhard Hanappi, Vienna
SK Rapid Wien 5-0 FC Dinamo Tbilisi
Goal(s): 1-0 Bazina 30, 2-0 Bilić 54, 3-0 Hofmann 59, 4-0 Kavlak 73, 5-0 Hofmann 75(p)
Referee: Kailis (CYP)
Aggregate: 8-0; SK Rapid Wien qualify.

16/8/07, Fill Metallbau Stadion, Ried im Innkreis
SV Ried 1-1 FC Sion
Goal(s): 1-0 Dospel 66, 1-1 Saborío 90+2
Referee: Brines (SCO)
30/8/07, Stade de Genève, Geneva
FC Sion 3-0 SV Ried
Goal(s): 1-0 Obradović 40, 2-0 Zakrzewski 44, 3-0 Domínguez 47
Referee: Asumaa (FIN)
Aggregate: 4-1; FC Sion qualify.

16/8/07, Gradski, Koprivnica
NK Slaven Koprivnica 1-2 Galatasaray AŞ
Goal(s): 1-0 Posavec 16, 1-1 Ayhan Akman 42, 1-2 Volkan Yaman 72
Referee: Lannoy (FRA)
30/8/07, Ali Sami Yen, Istanbul
Galatasaray AŞ 2-1 NK Slaven Koprivnica
Goal(s): 1-0 Ümit Karan 9, 1-1 Poljak 36, 2-1 Hakan Şükür 37
Referee: Rizzoli (ITA)
Aggregate: 4-2; Galatasaray AŞ qualify.

16/8/07, Finnair, Helsinki
HJK Helsinki 2-1 Aalborg BK
Goal(s): 1-0 Samura 15, 1-1 Risgård 37, 2-1 Samura 56
Referee: Matejek (CZE)
30/8/07, Aalborg, Aalborg
Aalborg BK 3-0 HJK Helsinki
Goal(s): 1-0 Enevoldsen 7, 2-0 Johansson 26, 3-0 Curth 43
Referee: Malcolm (NIR)
Aggregate: 4-2; Aalborg BK qualify.

16/8/07, Brann, Bergen
SK Brann 2-1 FK Sũduva
Goal(s): 1-0 Björnsson 24, 2-0 Winters 49, 2-1 Negreiros 56(p)
Referee: Wilmes (LUX)
30/8/07, Suduva, Marijampole
FK Sũduva 3-4 SK Brann
Goal(s): 0-1 Vaagan Moen 37, 0-2 Björnsson 45, 1-2 Urbšys 46, 1-3 Solli 57, 1-4 Huseklepp 63, 2-4 Maciulevičius 78, 3-4 Braga 84
Referee: Banari (MDA)
Aggregate: 4-6; SK Brann qualify.

16/8/07, Tehtaan Kenttä, Valkeakoski
FC Haka 1-2 FC Midtjylland
Goal(s): 0-1 Kristensen 13, 0-2 Kristensen 44, 1-2 Parviainen 53
Referee: Richmond (SCO)
30/8/07, Messecentret, Herning
FC Midtjylland 5-2 FC Haka
Goal(s): 1-0 Flinta 16, 2-0 Olsen 27, 2-1 Popovich 33, 3-1 Dadu 34, 4-1 Troest 67, 4-2 Kauppila 72, 5-2 Larsen 85
Referee: Stavrev (MKD)
Aggregate: 7-3; FC Midtjylland qualify.

16/8/07, Dinamo, Minsk
FC Dinamo Minsk 1-1 Odense BK
Goal(s): 1-0 Putilo 73, 1-1 Laursen 90+4
Referee: Courtney (NIR)
30/8/07, Fionia Park, Odense
Odense BK 4-0 FC Dinamo Minsk
Goal(s): 1-0 D. Nielsen 38, 2-0 D. Nielsen 55, 3-0 Absalonsen 77, 4-0 Absalonsen 79
Referee: Weiner (GER)
Aggregate: 5-1; Odense BK qualify.

16/8/07, Republican, Yerevan
FC MIKA 2-1 FC Artmedia Petržalka
Goal(s): 1-0 Shahgeldyan 8, 1-1 Fodrek 66, 2-1 Alex 80
Referee: Stanković (SRB)
30/8/07, TJ Senec Montostroj, Senec
FC Artmedia Petržalka 2-0 FC MIKA
Goal(s): 1-0 Obžera 5, 2-0 Obžera 72
Referee: Skjerven (NOR)
Aggregate: 3-2; FC Artmedia Petržalka qualify.

16/8/07, Megyeri úti, Budapest
Budapest Honvéd FC 0-0 Hamburger SV
Referee: Kuipers (NED)
30/8/07, Arena Hamburg, Hamburg
Hamburger SV 4-0 Budapest Honvéd FC
Goal(s): 1-0 Guerrero 9, 2-0 Guerrero 38, 3-0 Smiljanić 50(og), 4-0 Choupo-Moting 90
Referee: Rodríguez Santiago (ESP)
Aggregate: 4-0; Hamburger SV qualify.

16/8/07, Daugava, Liepaja
SK Liepājas Metalurgs 3-2 AIK Solna
Goal(s): 1-0 Karlsons 20, 2-0 Ivanovs 43, 2-1 Ivanovs 49(og), 2-2 Óbolo 61, 3-2 Tamošauskas 63
Referee: Georgiev (BUL)
30/8/07, Råsunda, Solna
AIK Solna 2-0 SK Liepājas Metalurgs
Goal(s): 1-0 Wilton 43, 2-0 Wilton 54
Referee: Richards (WAL)
Aggregate: 4-3; AIK Solna qualify.

16/8/07, Stade de Suisse, Berne
BSC Young Boys 1-1 RC Lens
Goal(s): 1-0 Tiago 71, 1-1 Monterrubio 75
Referee: Sandmoen (NOR)
30/8/07, Stade Félix-Bollaert, Lens
RC Lens 5-1 BSC Young Boys
Goal(s): 1-0 Dindane 13, 2-0 Akalé 16, 2-1 Varela 32, 3-1 Dindane 58, 4-1 Carrière 67, 5-1 Feindouno 89
Referee: Clattenburg (ENG)
Aggregate: 6-2; RC Lens qualify.

16/8/07, Tcentralny, Kostanay
FC Tobol Kostanay 0-1 Groclin Grodzisk Wielkopolski
Goal(s): 0-1 Muszalik 4
Referee: Sippel (GER)
30/8/07, Groclin Dyskobolia, Grodzisk Wielkopolski
Groclin Grodzisk Wielkopolski 2-0 FC Tobol Kostanay
Goal(s): 1-0 Sikora 5, 2-0 Sikora 19
Referee: Johannesson (SWE)
Aggregate: 3-0; Groclin Grodzisk Wielkopolski qualify.

16/8/07, Bloomfield, Tel-Aviv
Maccabi Tel-Aviv FC 1-1 Kayseri Erciyesspor
Goal(s): 0-1 Ilhan Özbay 5, 1-1 Kamanan 42
Referee: Egorov (RUS)
30/8/07, Kayseri Atatürk, Kayseri
Kayseri Erciyesspor 3-1 Maccabi Tel-Aviv FC
Goal(s): 1-0 Ilhan Özbay 7, 2-0 Köksal 14, 2-1 Haddad 40, 3-1 Öztekin 72
Referee: Tudor (ROU)
Aggregate: 4-2; Kayseri Erciyesspor qualify.

16/8/07, Dr. Magalhães Pessoa, Leiria
UD Leiria 0-0 Maccabi Netanya FC
Referee: Collum (SCO)
30/8/07, Kiryat Eliazer, Haifa
Maccabi Netanya FC 0-1 UD Leiria
Goal(s): 0-1 N'gal 84
Referee: Corpodean (ROU)
Aggregate: 0-1; UD Leiria qualify.

6/8/07, East End Park, Dunfermline
unfermline Athletic FC 1-1 BK Häcken
oal(s): 1-0 Hamilton 1, 1-1 Henriksson 57
eferee: Krajnc (SVN)
0/8/07, Ullevi, Gothenburg
K Häcken 1-0 Dunfermline Athletic FC
oal(s): 1-0 Skúlason 27
eferee: Havrilla (SVK)
ggregate: 2-1; BK Häcken qualify.

6/8/07, Dalymount Park, Dublin
rogheda United FC 1-1 Helsingborgs IF
oal(s): 0-1 Larsson 34, 1-1 Zayed 54
eferee: Kaldma (EST)
0/8/07, Olympia, Helsingborg
elsingborgs IF 3-0 Drogheda United FC
oal(s): 1-0 Jakobsson 52, 2-0 Omotoyossi 68, 3-0 Karekezi 90+1
eferee: Godulyan (UKR)
ggregate: 4-1; Helsingborgs IF qualify.

6/8/07, Gradski, Skopje
K Rabotnicki 0-0 NK Zrinjski
eferee: Olšiak (SVK)
0/8/07, Gradski, Mostar
IK Zrinjski 1-2 FK Rabotnicki
oal(s): 0-1 Milisavljević 33, 1-1 Ivanković 36, 1-2 Stanisic 90+2
eferee: Svendsen (DEN)
ggregate: 1-2; FK Rabotnicki qualify.

6/8/07, Josy Barthel, Luxembourg
N Käerjéng 97 0-3 R. Standard de Liège
oal(s): 0-1 Mbokani 59, 0-2 Witsel 81, 0-3 Witsel 86
eferee: Valgeirsson (ISL)
0/8/07, Maurice Dufrasne, Liege
. Standard de Liège 1-0 UN Käerjéng 97
oal(s): 1-0 De Camargo 89
eferee: Mihaljevic (MNE)
ggregate: 4-0; R. Standard de Liège qualify.

6/8/07, Råsunda, Solna
ammarby 2-1 Fredrikstad FK
oal(s): 1-0 Paulinho Guará 35, 2-0 Castro-Tello 49, 2-1 Kvisvik 74
eferee: Kelly (IRL)
0/8/07, Fredrikstad, Fredrikstad
redrikstad FK 1-1 Hammarby
oal(s): 1-0 Bjørkøy 85, 1-1 Eguren 90(p)
eferee: Sukhina (RUS)
ggregate: 2-3; Hammarby qualify.

6/8/07, Pecara, Siroki Brijeg
IK Široki Brijeg 0-3 Hapoel Tel-Aviv FC
oal(s): 0-1 Abedi 14, 0-2 Asulin 32, 0-3 Gabriel 74
eferee: Paniashvili (GEO)
0/8/07, Bloomfield, Tel-Aviv
apoel Tel-Aviv FC 3-0 NK Široki Brijeg
oal(s): 1-0 Asulin 41, 2-0 Badir 50, 3-0 Natcho 75
eferee: Szabo (HUN)
ggregate: 6-0; Hapoel Tel-Aviv FC qualify.

6/8/07, GSP, Nicosia
C Omonia 1-1 PFC CSKA Sofia
oal(s): 0-1 Nei 1, 1-1 Kaiafas 14
eferee: Atkinson (ENG)
0/8/07, Balgarska Armia, Sofia
FC CSKA Sofia 2-1 AC Omonia
oal(s): 0-1 Magno 8, 1-1 Nei 17, 2-1 Chilikov 88
eferee: Gumienny (BEL)
ggregate: 3-2; PFC CSKA Sofia qualify.

16/8/07, Meteor, Dnepropetrovsk
FC Dnipro Dnipropetrovsk 1-1 GKS Bełchatów
Goal(s): 0-1 Ujek 18, 1-1 Nazarenko 80
Referee: Çakır (TUR)
30/8/07, GKS, Belchatow
GKS Bełchatów 2-4 FC Dnipro Dnipropetrovsk
Goal(s): 0-1 Kravchenko 7, 1-1 Stolarczyk 10(p), 2-1 Nowak 21, 2-2 Shelayev 32, 2-3 Samodin 33, 2-4 Kornilenko 40
Referee: Messner (AUT)
Aggregate: 3-5; FC Dnipro Dnipropetrovsk qualify.

16/8/07, St. Jakob-Park, Basel
FC Basel 1893 2-1 SV Mattersburg
Goal(s): 0-1 Nakata 20(og), 1-1 Ergić 23, 2-1 Caicedo 53
Referee: Ingvarsson (SWE)
30/8/07, Pappelstadion, Mattersburg
SV Mattersburg 0-4 FC Basel 1893
Goal(s): 0-1 Caicedo 22, 0-2 Ergić 36, 0-3 Streller 41, 0-4 Carlitos 53
Referee: Dereli (TUR)
Aggregate: 1-6; FC Basel 1893 qualify.

16/8/07, Balgarska Armia, Sofia
PFC Lokomotiv Sofia 3-1 FC Oțelul Galați
Goal(s): 1-0 Dafchev 19, 2-0 Baldovaliev 62, 2-1 Semeghin 74, 3-1 Gilas 84
Referee: Hyytiä (FIN)
30/8/07, Otelul, Galati
FC Oțelul Galați 0-0 PFC Lokomotiv Sofia
Referee: Paulo Costa (POR)
Aggregate: 1-3; PFC Lokomotiv Sofia qualify.

16/8/07, CFR, Cluj-Napoca
CFR 1907 Cluj 1-3 Anorthosis Famagusta FC
Goal(s): 0-1 Žlogar 43, 0-2 William 48, 0-3 Sosin 58, 1-3 Trică 69(p)
Referee: Bertolini (SUI)
30/8/07, Antonis Papadopoulos, Larnaca
Anorthosis Famagusta FC 0-0 CFR 1907 Cluj
Referee: Dean (ENG)
Aggregate: 3-1; Anorthosis Famagusta FC qualify.

16/8/07, Franz Horr, Vienna
FK Austria Wien 4-3 FK Jablonec 97
Goal(s): 1-0 Ertl 8, 2-0 Kuljic 20, 2-1 Zelenka 28, 2-2 Zelenka 36, 3-2 Lasnik 47, 4-2 Kuljic 64, 4-3 Baránek 76
Referee: Megía Dávila (ESP)
30/8/07, Strelnice, Jablonec nad Nisou
FK Jablonec 97 1-1 FK Austria Wien
Goal(s): 0-1 Sariyar 39, 1-1 Rilke 83
Referee: Kasnaferis (GRE)
Aggregate: 4-5; FK Austria Wien qualify.

16/8/07, Poljud, Split
HNK Hajduk Split 0-1 UC Sampdoria
Goal(s): 0-1 Campagnaro 44
Referee: Paixão (POR)
30/8/07, Luigi Ferraris, Genoa
UC Sampdoria 1-1 HNK Hajduk Split
Goal(s): 1-0 Montella 34(p), 1-1 Hrgović 83
Referee: Královec (CZE)
Aggregate: 2-1; UC Sampdoria qualify.

16/8/07, Vicente Calderón, Madrid
Club Atlético de Madrid 3-0 FK Vojvodina
Goal(s): 1-0 Maxi 37, 2-0 Forlán 62, 3-0 Agüero 70
Referee: Circhetta (SUI)
30/8/07, Vojvodina, Novi Sad
FK Vojvodina 1-2 Club Atlético de Madrid
Goal(s): 1-0 Buač 39, 1-1 Luis García 54, 1-2 Seitaridis 75
Referee: Brych (GER)
Aggregate: 1-5; Club Atlético de Madrid qualify.

FIRST ROUND

Three former winners entered the fray for the first round draw, FC Bayern München, RSC Anderlecht and Tottenham Hotspur FC joining Galatasaray AŞ in an impressive list of 80 teams just one tie away from the competition's group stage.

Progressive steps

The Turkish press felt Galatasaray were on their way to the May showpiece in Manchester after a sterling comeback against FC Sion left them hearing "the footsteps of a team walking toward the UEFA Cup final". Trailing 3-2 after the first leg in Switzerland, Karl-Heinz Feldkamp's men were at risk of besmirching a superb start to the domestic season, but proved irresistible in the return. Ümit Karan helped himself to two first-half goals to set up an emphatic 5-1 victory.

While Galatasaray waltzed towards the group stage, the other Turkish representatives, minnows Kayseri Erciyesspor, were trampled by Club Atlético de Madrid, losing 9-0 on aggregate. It was a margin of victory bettered by nobody, though FC Basel 1893 and FC Spartak Moskva did claim 8-1 aggregate triumphs. Tottenham looked set for a similar win after a 6-1 first-leg victory against Anorthosis Famagusta FC left them in charge, yet the Cypriot side proved resilient in the return, and would have claimed a morale-boosting 1-0 triumph but for Robbie Keane's 78th-minute strike.

German might

Anderlecht saw off SK Rapid Wien, and Bayern ensured all four former winners progressed with a comfortable 3-0 aggregate triumph over CF Os Belenenses. It was Germany versus Portugal again when Bayer 04 Leverkusen met UD Leiria and although the Bundesliga outfit triumphed once more, it was a much closer affair, Michael Skibbe's side prevailing 5-4 on aggregate. It was even tighter in the eagerly-awaited meeting between AFC Ajax and NK Dinamo Zagreb, two of 16 clubs transferred from the UEFA Champions League third qualifying round.

Trailing 1-0 after the first leg in Croatia, captain Luka Modrić's penalty levelled matters for Dinamo in Amsterdam, eventually forcing extra time, during which two Marijo Mandžukić goals in three minutes set the visitors on course for victory. Klaas Jan Huntelaar replied in kind to level the aggregate scores but Dinamo prevailed on the away goals rule, leaving Modrić to reflect upon "the match of our generation". It was to prove a disappointing round for the Netherlands as five representatives were whittled down to one – group stage ever-presents AZ Alkmaar.

Dinamo Zagreb players celebrate taking the lead against Ajax in Amsterd

Heerenveen stunned

SC Heerenveen were among those exiting, although they played their part in the tie of the round against Helsingborgs IF. Seemingly cruising after a 5-3 first-leg victory, the Dutch side were stunned in Sweden, Henrik Larsson setting the home team on course for an incredible 8-6 aggregate triumph. It was also a memorable night for Georgios Donis, who said "heart and will prevailed" after his Larissa FC team joined four other Greek sides in the group stage by overcoming his ex-club Blackburn Rovers FC 3-2. Former European champions Hamburger SV and FK Crvena Zvezda were more predictable victors.

First Round Results

18/9/07, Gradski, Lovech
PFC Litex Lovech 0-1 Hamburger SV
Goal(s): 0-1 Castelen 75
Referee: Asumaa (FIN)
4/10/07, Arena Hamburg, Hamburg
Hamburger SV 3-1 PFC Litex Lovech
Goal(s): 0-1 R. Popov 38, 1-1 Guerrero 40, 2-1 Guerrero 52, 3-1 Van der Vaart 71
Referee: Allaerts (BEL)
Aggregate: 4-1; Hamburger SV qualify.

19/9/07, Stade Félix-Bollaert, Lens
RC Lens 1-1 FC København
Goal(s): 0-1 Allbäck 5, 1-1 Dindane 70
Referee: Skomina (SVN)
4/10/07, Parken Stadium, Copenhagen
FC København 2-1 RC Lens
Goal(s): 0-1 Carrière 13, 1-1 Allbäck 76, 2-1 Grønkjær 112
Referee: Pereira Gomes (POR)
Aggregate: 3-2; FC København qualify after extra time.

20/9/07, BayArena, Leverkusen
Bayer 04 Leverkusen 3-1 UD Leiria
Goal(s): 1-0 Kiessling 19, 1-1 João Paulo 29, 2-1 Rolfes 31, 3-1 Kiessling 77
Referee: Hriňák (SVK)
4/10/07, Dr. Magalhães Pessoa, Leiria
UD Leiria 3-2 Bayer 04 Leverkusen
Goal(s): 1-0 Cadu Silva 3, 1-1 Papadopulos 10, 2-1 João Paulo 21, 2-2 Kiessling 87, 3-2 Laranjeiro 90
Referee: Kapitanis (CYP)
Aggregate: 4-5; Bayer 04 Leverkusen qualify.

20/9/07, Groclin Dyskobolia, Grodzisk Wielkopolski
Groclin Grodzisk Wielkopolski 0-1 FK Crvena Zvezda
Goal(s): 0-1 Basta 19
Referee: Paniashvili (GEO)
4/10/07, FK Crvena Zvezda, Belgrade
FK Crvena Zvezda 1-0 Groclin Grodzisk Wielkopolski
Goal(s): 1-0 Castillo 43
Referee: Balaj (ROU)
Aggregate: 2-0; FK Crvena Zvezda qualify.

20/9/07, Panthessaliko, Volos
Larissa FC 2-0 Blackburn Rovers FC
Goal(s): 1-0 Bakayoko 33, 2-0 Cleiton 34
Referee: Sippel (GER)
4/10/07, Ewood Park, Blackburn
Blackburn Rovers FC 2-1 Larissa FC
Goal(s): 0-1 Cleiton 17, 1-1 Derbyshire 45+2(p), 2-1 Warnock 54
Referee: Circhetta (SUI)
Aggregate: 2-3; Larissa FC qualify.

20/9/07, Mestský, Mlada Boleslav
FK Mladá Boleslav 0-1 US Città di Palermo
Goal(s): 0-1 Janković 90+1
Referee: Kinhöfer (GER)
4/10/07, Renzo Barbera, Palermo
US Città di Palermo 0-1 FK Mladá Boleslav
Goal(s): 0-1 Sedláček 90+3
Referee: Iturralde González (ESP)
Aggregate: 1-1; FK Mladá Boleslav qualify on away goal.

20/9/07, Maksimir, Zagreb
NK Dinamo Zagreb 0-1 AFC Ajax
Goal(s): 0-1 Rommedahl 61
Referee: Lannoy (FRA)
4/10/07, Amsterdam ArenA, Amsterdam
AFC Ajax 2-3 NK Dinamo Zagreb
Goal(s): 0-1 Modrić 34(p), 0-2 Mandžukić 94, 0-3 Mandžukić 96, 1-3 Huntelaar 101, 2-3 Huntelaar 120
Referee: Clattenburg (ENG)
Aggregate: 3-3; NK Dinamo Zagreb qualify on away goals.

20/9/07, Auguste Bonal, Montbeliard
FC Sochaux-Montbéliard 0-2 Panionios GSS
Goal(s): 0-1 Djebbour 28, 0-2 Fernández 54
Referee: Corpodean (ROU)
4/10/07, Panionios, Athens
Panionios GSS 0-1 FC Sochaux-Montbéliard
Goal(s): 0-1 Yao Kumordzi 53(og)
Referee: Kelly (IRL)
Aggregate: 2-1; Panionios GSS qualify.

20/9/07, Luzhniki Stadium, Moscow
FC Spartak Moskva 5-0 BK Häcken
Goal(s): 1-0 Pavlyuchenko 6, 2-0 Pavlyuchenko 13, 3-0 Welliton 19, 4-0 Welliton 55, 5-0 Titov 56
Referee: Rogalla (SUI)
4/10/07, Ullevi, Gothenburg
BK Häcken 1-3 FC Spartak Moskva
Goal(s): 0-1 Titov 7, 0-2 Bazhenov 80, 1-2 Henriksson 84, 1-3 Dzyuba 90+1
Referee: Kaldma (EST)
Aggregate: 1-8; FC Spartak Moskva qualify.

20/9/07, OACA Spyro Louis, Athens
AEK Athens FC 3-0 FC Salzburg
Goal(s): 1-0 Geraldo Alves 2, 2-0 Rivaldo 57, 3-0 Kone 88
Referee: Dean (ENG)
4/10/07, EM Stadion Wals-Siezenheim, Salzburg
FC Salzburg 1-0 AEK Athens FC
Goal(s): 1-0 Lokvenc 20
Referee: Tagliavento (ITA)
Aggregate: 1-3; AEK Athens FC qualify.

20/9/07, Brann, Bergen
SK Brann 0-1 Club Brugge KV
Goal(s): 0-1 Sterchele 84
Referee: Jára (CZE)
4/10/07, Jan Breydel, Bruges
Club Brugge KV 1-2 SK Brann
Goal(s): 0-1 Helstad 14, 0-2 Winters 39, 1-2 Clement 76
Referee: Dereli (TUR)
Aggregate: 2-2; SK Brann qualify on away goals.

20/9/07, Allianz Arena, Munich
FC Bayern München 1-0 CF Os Belenenses
Goal(s): 1-0 Toni 34
Referee: Johannesson (SWE)
4/10/07, O Restelo, Lisbon
CF Os Belenenses 0-2 FC Bayern München
Goal(s): 0-1 Toni 59, 0-2 Hamit Altıntop 76
Referee: Granat (POL)
Aggregate: 0-3; FC Bayern München qualify.

20/9/07, Råsunda, Solna
Hammarby 2-1 SC Braga
Goal(s): 1-0 Andersson 50, 1-1 Linz 59, 2-1 Andersson 66
Referee: Oriekhov (UKR)

4/10/07, Municipal, Braga
SC Braga 4-0 Hammarby
Goal(s): 1-0 Wender 47, 2-0 Hussain 69, 3-0 Linz 81(p), 4-0 Hussain 90+2
Referee: Brines (SCO)
Aggregate: 5-2; SC Braga qualify.

20/9/07, Ratina, Tampere
Tampere United 2-3 FC Girondins de Bordeaux
Goal(s): 1-0 Wiss 8, 1-1 Cavenaghi 48, 2-1 Petrescu 69, 2-2 Micoud 90+2, 2-3 Cavenaghi 90+3
Referee: Richards (WAL)
4/10/07, Stade Chaban-Delmas, Bordeaux
FC Girondins de Bordeaux 1-1 Tampere United
Goal(s): 1-0 Chamakh 49, 1-1 Ojanperä 50
Referee: Ivanov (RUS)
Aggregate: 4-3; FC Girondins de Bordeaux qualify.

20/9/07, Messecentret, Herning
FC Midtjylland 1-3 FC Lokomotiv Moskva
Goal(s): 1-0 Babatunde 30, 1-1 Samedov 61, 1-2 Bilyaletdinov 69, 1-3 Sychev 90+1
Referee: Mikulski (POL)
4/10/07, Lokomotiv Stadium, Moscow
FC Lokomotiv Moskva 2-0 FC Midtjylland
Goal(s): 1-0 Bilyaletdinov 11, 2-0 Maminov 15
Referee: Kasnaferis (GRE)
Aggregate: 5-1; FC Lokomotiv Moskva qualify.

20/9/07, Gradski, Skopje
FK Rabotnicki 1-1 Bolton Wanderers FC
Goal(s): 1-0 Milisavljević 53, 1-1 Meïté 83
Referee: Szabo (HUN)
4/10/07, Reebok Stadium, Bolton
Bolton Wanderers FC 1-0 FK Rabotnicki
Goal(s): 1-0 Anelka 67
Referee: Skjerven (NOR)
Aggregate: 2-1; Bolton Wanderers FC qualify.

20/9/07, Goodison Park, Liverpool
Everton FC 1-1 FC Metalist Kharkiv
Goal(s): 1-0 Lescott 24, 1-1 Edmar 78
Referee: Stuchlik (AUT)
4/10/07, Metalist, Kharkov
FC Metalist Kharkiv 2-3 Everton FC
Goal(s): 1-0 Edmar 21, 1-1 Lescott 48, 2-1 Mahdoufi 52, 2-2 McFadden 72, 2-3 Anichebe 88
Referee: Hyytiä (FIN)
Aggregate: 3-4; Everton FC qualify.

20/9/07, White Hart Lane, London
Tottenham Hotspur FC 6-1 Anorthosis Famagusta FC
Goal(s): 1-0 Kaboul 5, 2-0 Dawson 39, 3-0 Keane 42, 4-0 Bent 43, 5-0 Defoe 65, 5-1 Žlogar 80, 6-1 Defoe 90+1
Referee: Dondarini (ITA)
4/10/07, Antonis Papadopoulos, Larnaca
Anorthosis Famagusta FC 1-1 Tottenham Hotspur FC
Goal(s): 1-0 Fabinho 54, 1-1 Keane 78
Referee: Královec (CZE)
Aggregate: 2-7; Tottenham Hotspur FC qualify.

20/9/07, Koševo, Sarajevo
FK Sarajevo 1-2 FC Basel 1893
Goal(s): 0-1 Carlitos 11, 0-2 Ergić 63, 1-2 Milošević 90+3
Referee: Lajuks (LVA)
4/10/07, St. Jakob-Park, Basel
FC Basel 1893 6-0 FK Sarajevo
Goal(s): 1-0 Carlitos 8, 2-0 Carlitos 9, 3-0 Streller 18, 4-0 Streller 29, 5-0 Huggel 75, 6-0 Caicedo 90
Referee: Paulo Costa (POR)
Aggregate: 8-1; FC Basel 1893 qualify.

20/9/07, Petrovsky, St Petersburg
FC Zenit St. Petersburg 3-0 R. Standard de Liège
Goal(s): 1-0 Arshavin 36, 2-0 Arshavin 65, 3-0 Kim 84
Referee: González Vázquez (ESP)
4/10/07, Maurice Dufrasne, Liege
R. Standard de Liège 1-1 FC Zenit St. Petersburg
Goal(s): 1-0 Onyewu 35, 1-1 Pogrebnyak 79
Referee: Thomson (SCO)
Aggregate: 1-4; FC Zenit St. Petersburg qualify.

20/9/07, Pittodrie, Aberdeen
Aberdeen FC 0-0 FC Dnipro Dnipropetrovsk
Referee: Berntsen (NOR)
4/10/07, Meteor, Dnepropetrovsk
FC Dnipro Dnipropetrovsk 1-1 Aberdeen FC
Goal(s): 0-1 Mackie 28, 1-1 Vorobei 76
Referee: Thual (FRA)
Aggregate: 1-1; Aberdeen FC qualify on away goal.

20/9/07, Tehelné Pole, Bratislava
FC Artmedia Petržalka 1-2 Panathinaikos FC
Goal(s): 1-0 Urbánek 46, 1-1 Papadopoulos 61(p), 1-2 N'Doye 90
Referee: Paixão (POR)
2/10/07, Apostolos Nikolaidis, Athens
Panathinaikos FC 3-0 FC Artmedia Petržalka
Goal(s): 1-0 Papadopoulos 45(p), 2-0 Papadopoulos 45+2, 3-0 Papadopoulos 74(p)
Referee: Gumienny (BEL)
Aggregate: 5-1; Panathinaikos FC qualify.

20/9/07, Sparta Stadium, Prague
AC Sparta Praha 0-0 Odense BK
Referee: Trivković (CRO)
4/10/07, Fionia Park, Odense
Odense BK 0-0 AC Sparta Praha
Referee: Egorov (RUS)
Aggregate: 0-0; AC Sparta Praha qualify 4-3 on penalties.

20/9/07, Stade de Genève, Geneva
FC Sion 3-2 Galatasaray AŞ
Goal(s): 1-0 Domínguez 6, 2-0 Vanczák 9, 3-0 Song 31(og), 3-1 Lincoln 38, 3-2 Linderoth 67
Referee: Megía Dávila (ESP)
4/10/07, Ali Sami Yen, Istanbul
Galatasaray AŞ 5-1 FC Sion
Goal(s): 1-0 Ümit Karan 22, 2-0 Ümit Karan 28, 3-0 Lincoln 36, 4-0 Arda Turan 68, 5-1 Nwaneri 90, 5-1 Bouzid 90
Referee: Weiner (GER)
Aggregate: 7-4; Galatasaray AŞ qualify.

20/9/07, Euroborg, Groningen
FC Groningen 1-1 ACF Fiorentina
Goal(s): 1-0 Lovre 25, 1-1 Semioli 65
Referee: Batista (POR)
4/10/07, Artemio Franchi, Florence
ACF Fiorentina 1-1 FC Groningen
Goal(s): 0-1 Nevland 55, 1-1 Mutu 59
Referee: Meyer (GER)
Aggregate: 2-2; ACF Fiorentina qualify 4-3 on penalties.

20/9/07, Dinamo, Bucharest
FC Dinamo 1948 Bucureşti 1-2 IF Elfsborg
Goal(s): 1-0 Niculescu 8, 1-1 Keene 10, 1-2 Keene 30
Referee: João Ferreira (POR)
4/10/07, Borås Arena, Boras
IF Elfsborg 0-1 FC Dinamo 1948 Bucureşti
Goal(s): 0-1 Dănciulescu 31
Referee: Courtney (NIR)
Aggregate: 2-2; IF Elfsborg qualify on away goals.

20/9/07, Balgarska Armia, Sofia
PFC Lokomotiv Sofia 1-3 Stade Rennais FC
Goal(s): 0-1 Hansson 39, 1-1 Dafchev 51, 1-2 Cheyrou 74, 1-3 Leroy 90
Referee: Malcolm (NIR)
4/10/07, Route de Lorient, Rennes
Stade Rennais FC 1-2 PFC Lokomotiv Sofia
Goal(s): 1-0 Marveaux 25, 1-1 Antunović 37, 1-2 Antunović 40
Referee: Jakobsson (ISL)
Aggregate: 4-3; Stade Rennais FC qualify.

20/9/07, Stadium, Toulouse
Toulouse FC 0-0 PFC CSKA Sofia
Referee: Vollquartz (DEN)
4/10/07, Balgarska Armia, Sofia
PFC CSKA Sofia 1-1 Toulouse FC
Goal(s): 1-0 Nei 65(p), 1-1 Gignac 90+5
Referee: Brugger (AUT)
Aggregate: 1-1; Toulouse FC qualify on away goal.

20/9/07, Frankenstadion, Nuremberg
1. FC Nürnberg 0-0 FC Rapid Bucureşti
Referee: Malek (POL)
4/10/07, Giuleşti, Bucharest
FC Rapid Bucureşti 2-2 1. FC Nürnberg
Goal(s): 1-0 Césinha 15, 1-1 Kluge 22, 1-2 Misimović 56, 2-2 Lazăr 90+3
Referee: Ingvarsson (SWE)
Aggregate: 2-2; 1. FC Nürnberg qualify on away goals.

20/9/07, Franz Horr, Vienna
FK Austria Wien 2-0 Vålerenga Fotball
Goal(s): 1-0 Kuljic 41, 2-0 Lasnik 62
Referee: McDonald (SCO)
4/10/07, Ullevål, Oslo
Vålerenga Fotball 2-2 FK Austria Wien
Goal(s): 0-1 Kuljic 22, 1-1 Dos Santos 51, 2-1 Holm 87, 2-2 Ačimovič 90+1
Referee: Matejek (CZE)
Aggregate: 2-4; FK Austria Wien qualify.

20/9/07, Abe Lenstra, Heerenveen
SC Heerenveen 5-3 Helsingborgs IF
Goal(s): 1-0 Bradley 20, 2-0 Sibon 30, 3-0 Sibon 35, 3-1 Larsson 53, 3-2 Omotoyossi 57, 4-2 Bak Nielsen 59, 5-2 Bradley 60, 5-3 Larsson 71(p)
Referee: Panić (BIH)
4/10/07, Olympia, Helsingborg
Helsingborgs IF 5-1 SC Heerenveen
Goal(s): 1-0 Larsson 18, 2-0 Dahl 37, 3-0 Omotoyossi 45+1, 4-0 Makondele 51, 5-0 Omotoyossi 80, 5-1 Sibon 89
Referee: Lehner (AUT)
Aggregate: 8-6; Helsingborgs IF qualify.

20/9/07, Luigi Ferraris, Genoa
UC Sampdoria 2-2 Aalborg BK
Goal(s): 1-0 Del Vecchio 18, 1-1 Prica 19, 1-2 Johansson 54, 2-2 Bellucci 59
Referee: Einwaller (AUT)
4/10/07, Aalborg, Aalborg
Aalborg BK 0-0 UC Sampdoria
Referee: Verbist (BEL)
Aggregate: 2-2; Aalborg BK qualify on away goals.

20/9/07, Constant Vanden Stock Stadium, Brussels
RSC Anderlecht 1-1 SK Rapid Wien
Goal(s): 1-0 Serhat 11, 1-1 Hofmann 82
Referee: Eriksson (SWE)

Helsingborg's René Makondele beats Heerenveen 'keeper Brian Vandenbussche to seal the Swedish team's passage to the group stage

4/10/07, Gerhard Hanappi, Vienna
SK Rapid Wien 0-1 RSC Anderlecht
Goal(s): 0-1 Hassan 22
Referee: Rizzoli (ITA)
Aggregate: 1-2; RSC Anderlecht qualify.

20/9/07, Vicente Calderón, Madrid
Club Atlético de Madrid 4-0 Kayseri Erciyesspor
Goal(s): 1-0 Mista 13, 2-0 Forlán 17, 3-0 Luis García 83, 4-0 Luis García 90+2
Referee: Bossen (NED)
4/10/07, Kayseri Atatürk, Kayseri
Kayseri Erciyesspor 0-5 Club Atlético de Madrid
Goal(s): 0-1 Agüero 6, 0-2 Jurado 14, 0-3 Agüero 44, 0-4 Maxi 53(p), 0-5 Forlán 79
Referee: Messner (AUT)
Aggregate: 0-9; Club Atlético de Madrid qualify.

20/9/07, Bloomfield, Tel-Aviv
Hapoel Tel-Aviv FC 0-0 AIK Solna
Referee: Sukhina (RUS)
4/10/07, Råsunda, Solna
AIK Solna 0-1 Hapoel Tel-Aviv FC
Goal(s): 0-1 Oved 64
Referee: Styles (ENG)
Aggregate: 0-1; Hapoel Tel-Aviv FC qualify.

20/9/07, Coliseum Alfonso Pérez, Getafe
Getafe CF 1-0 FC Twente
Goal(s): 1-0 Uche 90+1
Referee: Richmond (SCO)
4/10/07, Arke, Enschede
FC Twente 3-2 Getafe CF
Goal(s): 1-0 Wielaert 30, 1-1 Belenguer 101, 1-2 Granero 103, 2-2 Engelaar 117, 3-2 Zomer 120
Referee: Bebek (CRO)
Aggregate: 3-3; Getafe CF qualify on away goals.

20/9/07, Carlo Castellani, Empoli
Empoli FC 2-1 FC Zürich
Goal(s): 1-0 Piccolo 44, 2-0 Antonini 49(p), 2-1 Alphonse 74
Referee: Yefet (ISR)
4/10/07, Letzigrund, Zurich
FC Zürich 3-0 Empoli FC
Goal(s): 1-0 Kollar 37, 2-0 Abdi 78, 3-0 Alphonse 82
Referee: Ceferin (SVN)
Aggregate: 4-2; FC Zürich qualify.

20/9/07, Bessa XXI, Porto
FC Paços de Ferreira 0-1 AZ Alkmaar
Goal(s): 0-1 Pocognoli 89
Referee: Rasmussen (DEN)
4/10/07, DSB-Stadium, Alkmaar
AZ Alkmaar 0-0 FC Paços de Ferreira
Referee: Tudor (ROU)
Aggregate: 1-0; AZ Alkmaar qualify.

20/9/07, Kleanthis Vikelidis, Thessalonika
Aris Thessaloniki FC 1-0 Real Zaragoza
Goal(s): 1-0 Papadopoulos 6
Referee: Kassai (HUN)
4/10/07, La Romareda, Zaragoza
Real Zaragoza 2-1 Aris Thessaloniki FC
Goal(s): 1-0 Oliveira 19, 1-1 Javito 63, 2-1 Sergio García 72
Referee: Dougal (SCO)
Aggregate: 2-2; Aris Thessaloniki FC qualify on away goal.

20/9/07, El Madrigal, Villarreal
Villarreal CF 4-1 FC BATE Borisov
Goal(s): 1-0 Nihat 6, 2-0 Senna 18, 3-0 Nihat 50, 4-0 Tomasson 54, 4-1 Zhavnerchik 70
Referee: Piccirillo (FRA)
4/10/07, Dinamo, Minsk
FC BATE Borisov 0-2 Villarreal CF
Goal(s): 0-1 Cani 24, 0-2 Ángel 78
Referee: Sandmoen (NOR)
Aggregate: 1-6; Villarreal CF qualify.

GROUP STAGE

GROUP A

In only their third European campaign in 23 seasons, Everton FC blazed a trail in Group A, but it was congested behind them as 1. FC Nürnberg, FC Zenit St. Petersburg and AZ Alkmaar battled it out for the two remaining Round of 32 places.

Everton inspired

Everton breezed through with a 100 per cent record, but if games were only 80 minutes long rather than 90, things would have been very different. Five of their nine goals came in the last ten minutes, and promising striker Victor Anichebe scored three of them after coming off the bench.

The young Nigerian rounded off a 3-1 victory in the Merseyside outfit's opening game against Larissa FC – the first of four defeats for the Greek side – and then inspired a late win, scoring one and setting up another as Everton beat Nürnberg 2-0 on Matchday 2. "I would have brought Victor on earlier but he has not trained much recently," Everton manager David Moyes revealed. "But when he came on he had a massive impact once again."

AZ upset

It was Tim Cahill who grabbed a fortunate late winner against Zenit in the English side's third outing before another young Everton forward, 19-year-old James Vaughan, scored two minutes from time to earn the side a 3-2 victory at AZ and end the longest-standing unbeaten home record in UEFA club competition – a run stretching back 32 games.

The goal also ended AZ's UEFA Cup ambitions, as Nürnberg pipped them on the last day by adding a 3-1 win over Larissa to the 2-1 triumph against AZ in their previous outing. Zenit, who would have been eliminated had AZ won, went through in third. Inspired by playmaker Andrei Arshavin, their qualification completed an excellent year in which they also won the Russian Premier-Liga title for the first time.

Group A Results

25/10/07, Petrovsky, St Petersburg
FC Zenit St. Petersburg 1-1 AZ Alkmaar
Goal(s): 0-1 Ari 20, 1-1 Tymoshchuk 43(p)
Referee: Kapitanis (CYP)

Everton supersub Victor Anichebe (left) is congratulated by Ya... after another UEFA Cup g...

25/10/07, Goodison Park, Liverpool
Everton FC 3-1 Larissa FC
Goal(s): 1-0 Cahill 14, 2-0 Osman 50, 2-1 Cleiton 65, 3-1 Anichebe 85
Referee: Ingvarsson (SWE)

8/11/07, Panthessaliko, Volos
Larissa FC 2-3 FC Zenit St. Petersburg
Goal(s): 0-1 Pogrebnyak 39, 1-1 Alexandrou 58, 2-1 Fotakis 62, 2-2 Zyryanov 70, 2-3 Fatih Tekke 78
Referee: Vollquartz (DEN)

8/11/07, Frankenstadion, Nuremberg
1. FC Nürnberg 0-2 Everton FC
Goal(s): 0-1 Arteta 83(p), 0-2 Anichebe 88
Referee: Undiano (ESP)

29/11/07, Petrovsky, St Petersburg
FC Zenit St. Petersburg 2-2 1. FC Nürnberg
Goal(s): 0-1 Charisteas 25, 1-1 Pogrebnyak 76, 2-1 Ionov 79, 2-2 Benko 84
Referee: Královec (CZE)

29/11/07, DSB-Stadium, Alkmaar
AZ Alkmaar 1-0 Larissa FC
Goal(s): 1-0 Dembélé 77
Referee: Paniashvili (GEO)

5/12/07, Goodison Park, Liverpool
Everton FC 1-0 FC Zenit St. Petersburg
Goal(s): 1-0 Cahill 85
Referee: Jakobsson (ISL)

5/12/07, Frankenstadion, Nuremberg
1. FC Nürnberg 2-1 AZ Alkmaar
Goal(s): 0-1 De Zeeuw 29, 1-1 Mintál 83, 2-1 Mintál 85
Referee: Johannesson (SWE)

20/12/07, DSB-Stadium, Alkmaar
AZ Alkmaar 2-3 Everton FC
Goal(s): 0-1 Johnson 2, 1-1 Pellè 17, 1-2 Jagielka 44, 2-2 Jaliens 66, 2-3 Vaughan 80
Referee: Dereli (TUR)

20/12/07, Panthessaliko, Volos
Larissa FC 1-3 1. FC Nürnberg
Goal(s): 1-0 Kožlej 11, 1-1 Saenko 45, 1-2 Mintál 57, 1-3 Charisteas 73
Referee: Kaldma (EST)

oup A Table

		Home					Away					Total					
	Pld	W	D	L	F	A	W	D	L	F	A	W	D	L	F	A	Pts
rton FC	4	2	0	0	4	1	2	0	0	5	2	4	0	0	9	3	12
C Nürnberg	4	1	0	1	2	3	1	1	0	5	3	2	1	1	7	6	7
Zenit St. Petersburg	4	0	2	0	3	3	1	0	1	3	3	1	2	1	6	6	5
Alkmaar	4	1	0	1	3	3	0	1	1	2	3	1	1	2	5	6	4
issa FC	4	0	0	2	3	6	0	0	2	1	4	0	0	4	4	10	0

GROUP B

Confident predictions about which three teams would still be standing after ten Group B matches were hard to come by in early September as the fates colluded to select an evenly-matched section – and things predictably went down to a Matchday 5 winner-takes-all head-to-head.

Panathinaikos impress

The main focus of interest was largely over third place as Panathinaikos FC and Club Atlético de Madrid wasted no time planting themselves in the top two. Greek side Panathinaikos were particularly impressive early on, claiming successive victories against Aberdeen FC, FC København and FC Lokomotiv Moskva without conceding. They struck six themselves, with Dimitrios Salpingidis responsible for half of them, as José Peseiro's charges sealed progress with a match to spare.

Atlético's Sergio 'Kun' Agüero also scored three times in the group stage, including two in the opening-day draw with Lokomotiv as the sides shared six goals; a performance that left the Russian team's coach Anatoliy Byshovets - no mean forward himself - in wonderment. "He reminds me of Romário," said the former Soviet Union international of Agüero. "In fact I would go even further and say he's better than Romário. Seeing him play was as enjoyable as visiting the Prado Museum in Madrid."

Simão decider

The draw was a disappointment for Atlético, who had led 3-1 at one stage, but back-to-back victories over Aberdeen and København meant they went into the final game at home to Panathinaikos knowing a win

Atlético Madrid youngster Sergio Agüero takes on the FC Kobenhavn defence

would see them leapfrog their opponents into top spot. Simão's 96th-minute strike guaranteed just that, meaning Panathinaikos had to settle for second.

Lokomotiv had a grim campaign, picking up just two points, and leaving third place down to a December meeting between Aberdeen and København in Scotland, where four second-half goals brought the home side an emphatic victory – their best ever in the competition - to leap off the foot of the table and qualify with just four points.

Group B Results

25/10/07, Apostolos Nikolaidis, Athens
Panathinaikos FC 3-0 Aberdeen FC
Goal(s): 1-0 Goumas 11, 2-0 Papadopoulos 73, 3-0 Salpingidis 77
Referee: Einwaller (AUT)

25/10/07, Lokomotiv Stadium, Moscow
FC Lokomotiv Moskva 3-3 Club Atlético de Madrid
Goal(s): 0-1 Agüero 16, 1-1 Bilyaletdinov 27, 1-2 Forlán 47, 2-2 Odemwingie 61, 3-2 Odemwingie 64, 3-3 Agüero 85
Referee: Clattenburg (ENG)

8/11/07, Pittodrie, Aberdeen
Aberdeen FC 1-1 FC Lokomotiv Moskva
Goal(s): 1-0 Diamond 27, 1-1 Ivanović 45
Referee: Meyer (GER)

8/11/07, Parken Stadium, Copenhagen
FC København 0-1 Panathinaikos FC
Goal(s): 0-1 N'Doye 16
Referee: Hriňák (SVK)

29/11/07, Lokomotiv Stadium, Moscow
FC Lokomotiv Moskva 0-1 FC København
Goal(s): 0-1 Nordstrand 62(p)
Referee: Brugger (AUT)

29/11/07, Vicente Calderón, Madrid
Club Atlético de Madrid 2-0 Aberdeen FC
Goal(s): 1-0 Forlán 45(p), 2-0 Simão 61
Referee: Bebek (CRO)

5/12/07, Parken Stadium, Copenhagen
FC København 0-2 Club Atlético de Madrid
Goal(s): 0-1 Simão 21, 0-2 Agüero 62
Referee: Dondarini (ITA)

5/12/07, Apostolos Nikolaidis, Athens
Panathinaikos FC 2-0 FC Lokomotiv Moskva
Goal(s): 1-0 Salpingidis 70, 2-0 Salpingidis 74
Referee: Circhetta (SUI)

20/12/07, Pittodrie, Aberdeen
Aberdeen FC 4-0 FC København
Goal(s): 1-0 Ja. Smith 47, 2-0 Ja. Smith 55, 3-0 Antonsson 71(og), 4-0 Foster 83
Referee: Batista (POR)

20/12/07, Vicente Calderón, Madrid
Club Atlético de Madrid 2-1 Panathinaikos FC
Goal(s): 0-1 Salpingidis 34, 1-1 Luis García 74, 2-1 Simão 90+6
Referee: Kircher (GER)

Group B Table

		Home					Away					Total				
	Pld	W	D	L	F	A	W	D	L	F	A	W	D	L	F	A
1 Club Atlético de Madrid	4	2	0	0	4	1	1	1	0	5	3	3	1	0	9	4
2 Panathinaikos FC	4	2	0	0	5	0	1	0	1	2	2	3	0	1	7	2
3 Aberdeen FC	4	1	1	0	5	1	0	0	2	0	5	1	1	2	5	6
4 FC København	4	0	0	2	0	3	1	0	1	1	4	1	0	3	1	7
5 FC Lokomotiv Moskva	4	0	1	1	3	4	0	1	1	1	3	0	2	2	4	7

GROUP C

Such is the nature of the UEFA Cup group stage, with winter weather and tough away days, that a section which ends without a shock is almost a surprise in itself – yet Group C almost managed just that.

Elfsborg struggle

A 1-1 opening-day draw between Swedish champions IF Elfsborg and AEK Athens FC in Boras was perhaps as close as it got, Charilaos Pappas cancelling Daniel Mobaeck's early opener to earn the Greek visitors a point. That proved a rare boon for Elfsborg, who started their 2007/08 European quest in the first qualifying

Villarreal players congregat celebration after sco against Elfsb

ound of the UEFA Champions League and were to end t with the worst defensive record in the group stage, elped in significant part by an emphatic 6-1 loss at ACF iorentina in their second outing.

he Viola had begun with an impressive draw away to panish side Villarreal CF, a result that would have been ven better had Joan Capdevila not struck to earn the ome team a point two minutes from time. Two Martin ørgensen goals helped Fiorentina to that 6-1 triumph at ome to Elfsborg and although there was tragedy off he field when coach Cesare Prandelli's wife, Manuela, lied after a long illness, the Italian team progressed after ompleting an unbeaten campaign, drawing with AEK nd beating FK Mladá Boleslav.

trong finish

he Czech Republic outfit had still been in contention joing into that final-day fixture, despite defeats by illarreal and AEK earlier in their campaign, and victory t Fiorentina would have sent them through. Instead, EK held on to third place, with Fiorentina second, two oints behind section winners Villarreal. The Spanish ide had followed up the draw against the Viola with ack-to-back wins away to Mladá Boleslav and at home o Elfsborg before ending their campaign with a 2-1 ictory at AEK.

Group C Results

5/10/07, Borås Arena, Boras
F Elfsborg 1-1 AEK Athens FC
oal(s): 1-0 Mobaeck 15, 1-1 Pappas 49
eferee: Sippel (GER)

5/10/07, El Madrigal, Villarreal
illarreal CF 1-1 ACF Fiorentina
oal(s): 0-1 Vieri 48, 1-1 Capdevila 88
eferee: Lannoy (FRA)

/11/07, Mestský, Mlada Boleslav
K Mladá Boleslav 1-2 Villarreal CF
oal(s): 0-1 Nihat 33, 0-2 Santi Cazorla 56, 1-2 Mendy 90
eferee: Skomina (SVN)

/11/07, Artemio Franchi, Florence
CF Fiorentina 6-1 IF Elfsborg
oal(s): 1-0 Jørgensen 4, 2-0 Vieri 5, 2-1 Ishizaki 41, 3-1 Donadel 62, -1 Krøldrup 65, 5-1 Jørgensen 78, 6-1 Di Carmine 87
eferee: Dereli (TUR)

9/11/07, Borås Arena, Boras
F Elfsborg 1-3 FK Mladá Boleslav
oal(s): 1-0 M. Svensson 31, 1-1 Táborský 67, 1-2 Mendy 79, 1-3 oríšek 90+5
eferee: Kelly (IRL)

9/11/07, OACA Spyro Louis, Athens
EK Athens FC 1-1 ACF Fiorentina
oal(s): 0-1 Osvaldo 29, 1-1 Balzaretti 33(og)
eferee: Thomson (SCO)

5/12/07, Mestský, Mlada Boleslav
FK Mladá Boleslav 0-1 AEK Athens FC
Goal(s): 0-1 Nsaliwa 46
Referee: Verbist (BEL)

5/12/07, El Madrigal, Villarreal
Villarreal CF 2-0 IF Elfsborg
Goal(s): 1-0 Tomasson 2, 2-0 Tomasson 51
Referee: Tudor (ROU)

20/12/07, Artemio Franchi, Florence
ACF Fiorentina 2-1 FK Mladá Boleslav
Goal(s): 2-0 Mutu 44(p), 2-1 Rajnoch 60, 3-1 Vieri 67
Referee: João Ferreira (POR)

20/12/07, OACA Spyro Louis, Athens
AEK Athens FC 1-2 Villarreal CF
Goal(s): 0-1 Mavuba 40, 1-1 Rivaldo 68, 1-2 Tomasson 69
Referee: Lehner (AUT)

Group C Table

		Home					Away					Total					
	Pld	**W**	**D**	**L**	**F**	**A**	**W**	**D**	**L**	**F**	**A**	**W**	**D**	**L**	**F**	**A**	**Pts**
1 Villarreal CF	4	1	1	0	3	1	2	0	0	4	2	3	1	0	7	3	10
2 ACF Fiorentina	4	2	0	0	8	2	0	2	0	2	2	2	2	0	10	4	8
3 AEK Athens FC	4	0	1	1	2	3	1	1	0	2	1	1	2	1	4	4	5
4 FK Mladá Boleslav	4	0	0	2	1	3	1	0	1	4	3	1	0	3	5	6	3
5 IF Elfsborg	4	0	1	1	2	4	0	0	2	1	8	0	1	3	3	12	1

GROUP D

It is more than a decade since FC Schalke 04 last took the UEFA Cup to Germany, but Hamburger SV raised hopes of an end to an unusual drought as they set the pace in Group D.

Good Kompany

Marooned in the Bundesliga relegation zone as late as February 2007, Hamburg turned things around to finish in the top of half of the table and earn a UEFA Intertoto Cup berth. They arrived at the start of the UEFA Cup stage with six unbeaten European games already under their belt and hit the ground running by beating SK Brann 1-0 in Norway, Belgian defender Vincent Kompany scoring the only goal of the game just after the hour.

Hamburg followed up with a 3-0 victory at home to Stade Rennais FC, although two goals in the last six minutes made the scoreline a little flattering. They left it even later against NK Dinamo Zagreb. Goalless after 87 minutes, there was still time for a Nigel de Jong strike and Piotr Trochowski's penalty to seal three points that took the Bundesliga side through with a game to spare.

Basel impress

It was a result their coach Huub Stevens never doubted, saying: "We let Zagreb make the running and then when the time was right we struck. Three matches, nine points; we are already qualified and have to be pleased." Stevens' FC Basel 1893 counterpart Christian Gross had much to be content with too as his team finished second in the group thanks to two 1-0 home wins and two away draws, including against Hamburg in their final outing.

Third was expected to be a battle between Rennes and Dinamo Zagreb, the side that had dumped AFC Ajax in the previous round, but instead it was Brann who won through to the last 32. The newly-crowned Norwegian champions drew at Rennes before claiming a famous 2-1 win against ten-man Dinamo Zagreb on home soil to progress.

Group D Results

25/10/07, Brann, Bergen
SK Brann 0-1 Hamburger SV
Goal(s): 0-1 Kompany 62
Referee: Kasnaferis (GRE)

25/10/07, St. Jakob-Park, Basel
FC Basel 1893 1-0 Stade Rennais FC
Goal(s): 1-0 Streller 55
Referee: Rizzoli (ITA)

8/11/07, Route de Lorient, Rennes
Stade Rennais FC 1-1 SK Brann
Goal(s): 0-1 Karadas 24, 1-1 Cheyrou 88(p)
Referee: Lehner (AUT)

8/11/07, Maksimir, Zagreb
NK Dinamo Zagreb 0-0 FC Basel 1893
Referee: Gumienny (BEL)

29/11/07, Arena Hamburg, Hamburg
Hamburger SV 3-0 Stade Rennais FC
Goal(s): 1-0 Van der Vaart 30, 2-0 Choupo-Moting 84, 3-0 Zidan 90+1(p)
Referee: Clattenburg (ENG)

29/11/07, Brann, Bergen
SK Brann 2-1 NK Dinamo Zagreb
Goal(s): 1-0 Bjarnason 45+4(p), 1-1 Vukojević 49, 2-1 Bakke 72
Referee: Balaj (ROU)

5/12/07, Maksimir, Zagreb
NK Dinamo Zagreb 0-2 Hamburger SV
Goal(s): 0-1 De Jong 88, 0-2 Trochowski 90+3(p)
Referee: McDonald (SCO)

5/12/07, St. Jakob-Park, Basel
FC Basel 1893 1-0 SK Brann
Goal(s): 1-0 Carlitos 40
Referee: Egorov (RUS)

20/12/07, Arena Hamburg, Hamburg
Hamburger SV 1-1 FC Basel 1893
Goal(s): 0-1 Ergić 58, 1-1 Olić 73
Referee: Vollquartz (DEN)

20/12/07, Route de Lorient, Rennes
Stade Rennais FC 1-1 NK Dinamo Zagreb
Goal(s): 0-1 Vukojević 57, 1-1 M'Bia 88
Referee: Courtney (NIR)

Group D Table

		Home					Away					Total				
	Pld	W	D	L	F	A	W	D	L	F	A	W	D	L	F	A
1 Hamburger SV	4	1	1	0	4	1	2	0	0	3	0	3	1	0	7	1
2 FC Basel 1893	4	2	0	0	2	0	0	2	0	1	1	2	2	0	3	1
3 SK Brann	4	1	0	1	2	2	0	1	1	1	2	1	1	2	3	4
4 NK Dinamo Zagreb	4	0	1	1	0	2	0	1	1	2	3	0	2	2	2	5
5 Stade Rennais FC	4	0	2	0	2	2	0	0	2	0	4	0	2	2	2	6

Hamburg players celebrate the
of two late goals in Za

GROUP E

The ten Group E fixtures brought a record margin of victory, just one draw and, at the end of proceedings, progress for a side that had conceded six goals in their final two games. If nothing else, Group E offered plenty of excitement.

Zürich zest

At the halfway stage the surprise leaders were Swiss champions FC Zürich, who shocked AC Sparta Praha with an impressive 2-1 comeback victory in their opener. The triumph was slightly overshadowed by charges of gross unsporting conduct that led to coach Bernard Challandes and his striker Eric Hassli being suspended for one and three UEFA Cup matches, respectively, yet without them Zürich followed it up by beating Toulouse FC 2-0 at home.

It left them on the cusp on qualification, yet they did not have it all their own way thereafter. Their progress was confirmed despite a 1-0 loss at FC Spartak Moskva and they ended their campaign on a disappointing note as Bayer 04 Leverkusen swept them aside on Matchday 5, Switzerland international Tranquillo Barnetta among the scorers in a 5-0 triumph that left Zürich third.

'Perfect match'

That equalled the Bundesliga outfit's record margin of victory in UEFA club competition and left coach Michael Skibbe hailing a "perfect match" as his charges ensured that, like domestic rivals Hamburger SV and FC Bayern München, Leverkusen finished top of their section.

Spartak took second. They earned a 2-1 home win against Leverkusen courtesy of two second-half penalties but were unable to replicate their home form on their travels. Six points from six in Moscow and one more from away games against Sparta and Toulouse nonetheless proved to be more than enough. Toulouse finished bottom, although a 2-1 win against Spartak in their final game ended a dismal run of seven games without a win in Europe in 2007/08 since entering the UEFA Champions League third qualifying round.

Bayer Leverkusen striker Dmitriy Bulykin (left) is congratulated by team-mates after scoring against FC Zürich

Group E Results

25/10/07, Sparta Stadium, Prague
AC Sparta Praha 1-2 FC Zürich
Goal(s): 1-0 Slepička 24, 1-1 Kondé 38, 1-2 Alphonse 62
Referee: Dougal (SCO)

25/10/07, BayArena, Leverkusen
Bayer 04 Leverkusen 1-0 Toulouse FC
Goal(s): 1-0 Kiessling 35
Referee: Eriksson (SWE)

8/11/07, Luzhniki Stadium, Moscow
FC Spartak Moskva 2-1 Bayer 04 Leverkusen
Goal(s): 1-0 Pavlyuchenko 63(p), 2-0 Mozart 77(p), 2-1 Freier 90+1
Referee: Jakobsson (ISL)

8/11/07, Stadium, Toulouse
Toulouse FC 2-3 AC Sparta Praha
Goal(s): 1-0 Elmander 14, 1-1 Kisel 67, 1-2 Došek 68, 2-2 Mansaré 80, 2-3 Kisel 88
Referee: Iturralde González (ESP)

29/11/07, Sparta Stadium, Prague
AC Sparta Praha 0-0 FC Spartak Moskva
Referee: Richards (WAL)

29/11/07, Letzigrund, Zurich
FC Zürich 2-0 Toulouse FC
Goal(s): 1-0 Tihinen 42, 2-0 Raffael 64(p)
Referee: Kasnaferis (GRE)

6/12/07, BayArena, Leverkusen
Bayer 04 Leverkusen 1-0 AC Sparta Praha
Goal(s): 1-0 M. Friedrich 71
Referee: Atkinson (ENG)

6/12/07, Luzhniki Stadium, Moscow
FC Spartak Moskva 1-0 FC Zürich
Goal(s): 1-0 Titov 57
Referee: Trivković (CRO)

19/12/07, Letzigrund, Zurich
FC Zürich 0-5 Bayer 04 Leverkusen
Goal(s): 0-1 Greško 19, 0-2 Bulykin 23, 0-3 Barnetta 50, 0-4 Bulykin 57, 0-5 Kiessling 80
Referee: Rodríguez Santiago (ESP)

19/12/07, Stadium, Toulouse
Toulouse FC 2-1 FC Spartak Moskva
Goal(s): 1-0 Santos 41, 2-0 Santos 53, 2-1 Dzyuba 61(p)
Referee: Berntsen (NOR)

Group E Table

		Home					Away					Total					
	Pld	W	D	L	F	A	W	D	L	F	A	W	D	L	F	A	Pts
1 Bayer 04 Leverkusen	4	2	0	0	2	0	1	0	1	6	2	3	0	1	8	2	9
2 FC Spartak Moskva	4	2	0	0	3	1	0	1	1	1	2	2	1	1	4	3	7
3 FC Zürich	4	1	0	1	2	5	1	0	1	2	2	2	0	2	4	7	6
4 AC Sparta Praha	4	0	1	1	1	2	1	0	1	3	3	1	1	2	4	5	4
5 Toulouse FC	4	1	0	1	4	4	0	0	2	0	3	1	0	3	4	7	3

GROUP F

There were three former European Champion Clubs' Cup winners in the 2007/08 UEFA Cup group stage and Group F contained two of them. However, FC Bayern München and FK Crvena Zvezda were to have hugely contrasting campaigns.

Heavyweight meeting

The meeting between four-time winners Bayern and 1991 victors Crvena Zvezda was the most hotly anticipated of the opening round of fixtures and the two sides conjured up a memorable evening in Belgrade. Tied at 1-1 with 16 minutes remaining, Nenad Milijaš gave the home side the advantage only for Miroslav Klose to level ten minutes later with his second of the game.

It looked to have secured a 2-2 draw, but four minutes into added time 17-year-old Bayern substitute Toni Kroos swept in a dramatic winner – a sign of things to come for both teams. Disappointing back-to-back draws against Bolton Wanderers FC and SC Braga blunted Bayern's progress and left them needing a point from their final match against Aris Thessaloniki FC on Matchday 5.

Toni bags four

Having been held to successive goalless draws in the Bundesliga, they were not in the best of form but proved irresistible on the night, Luca Toni scoring four goals in a 6-0 triumph and leaving coach Ottmar Hitzfeld purring. "Luca just knows where the ball will come to, he is ice cold in front of the goal and is always keeping two or three opponents occupied," he said.

Crvena Zvezda, meanwhile, ended their campaign without a point as unfancied pair Braga and Bolton took the other two qualifying berths, finishing unbeaten, with the Portuguese outfit edging runners-up spot as they conceded one goal fewer. Aris, meanwhile, were left with the bitter taste of failure despite being the only team in the competition to claim five points and still be eliminated.

Bayern München scored two late goals to beat Crvena Zvezda in Belgrac

Group F Results

25/10/07, Reebok Stadium, Bolton
Bolton Wanderers FC 1-1 SC Braga
Goal(s): 1-0 Diouf 66, 1-1 Jailson 87
Referee: Ceferin (SVN)

25/10/07, FK Crvena Zvezda, Belgrade
FK Crvena Zvezda 2-3 FC Bayern München
Goal(s): 1-0 Koroman 16, 1-1 Klose 20, 2-1 Milijaš 74, 2-2 Klose 86, 2-3 Kroos 90+4
Referee: Trefoloni (ITA)

8/11/07, Allianz Arena, Munich
FC Bayern München 2-2 Bolton Wanderers FC
Goal(s): 0-1 Gardner 8, 1-1 Podolski 30, 2-1 Podolski 49, 2-2 Davies 82
Referee: Jára (CZE)

8/11/07, Kleanthis Vikelidis, Thessalonika
Aris Thessaloniki FC 3-0 FK Crvena Zvezda
Goal(s): 1-0 Papazoglou 76, 2-0 Papazoglou 89, 3-0 Koke 90+1
Referee: Ivanov (RUS)

29/11/07, Municipal, Braga
SC Braga 1-1 FC Bayern München
Goal(s): 0-1 Klose 47, 1-1 Linz 66
Referee: Eriksson (SWE)

29/11/07, Reebok Stadium, Bolton
Bolton Wanderers FC 1-1 Aris Thessaloniki FC
Goal(s): 0-1 Toni Calvo 44, 1-1 Giannakopoulos 90+2
Referee: Iturralde González (ESP)

6/12/07, FK Crvena Zvezda, Belgrade
FK Crvena Zvezda 0-1 Bolton Wanderers FC
Goal(s): 0-1 McCann 45
Referee: Allaerts (BEL)

6/12/07, Kleanthis Vikelidis, Thessalonika
Aris Thessaloniki FC 1-1 SC Braga
Goal(s): 0-1 Linz 6, 1-1 Ronaldo 26
Referee: Malek (POL)

19/12/07, Municipal, Braga
SC Braga 2-0 FK Crvena Zvezda
Goal(s): 1-0 Linz 11, 2-0 Wender 66
Referee: Hriňák (SVK)

19/12/07, Allianz Arena, Munich
FC Bayern München 6-0 Aris Thessaloniki FC
Goal(s): 1-0 Toni 25, 2-0 Toni 38, 3-0 Toni 64, 4-0 Toni 66, 5-0 Lell 78, 6-0 Lahm 81
Referee: Yefet (ISR)

oup F Table

		Home					Away					Total					
	Pld	W	D	L	F	A	W	D	L	F	A	W	D	L	F	A	Pts
C Bayern München	4	1	1	0	8	2	1	1	0	4	3	2	2	0	12	5	8
C Braga	4	1	1	0	3	1	0	2	0	2	2	1	3	0	5	3	6
olton Wanderers FC	4	0	2	0	2	2	1	1	0	3	2	1	3	0	5	4	6
ris Thessaloniki FC	4	1	1	0	4	1	0	1	1	1	7	1	2	1	5	8	5
K Crvena Zvezda	4	0	0	2	2	4	0	0	2	0	5	0	0	4	2	9	0

GROUP G

In two-time UEFA Cup winners Tottenham Hotspur FC and 1983 victors RSC Anderlecht, Group G contained some pedigree. Yet it was a team making their debut in Europe, Getafe CF, who made all the running as the rest battled for the other two qualifying spots.

Early marker

Getafe only made their Primera División debut in 2004/05 but have enjoyed a heady rise, and after edging past Dutch team FC Twente in the first round they laid down an early marker in the group stage. Trailing 1-0 to Tottenham Hotspur FC at White Hart Lane, Michael Laudrup's charges stormed back and goals from Esteban Granero and Braulio sealed an impressive 2-1 win.

A European Champion Clubs' Cup winner with FC Barcelona in 1992, Laudrup has a wealth of experience at the highest level and he needed to call on it after Getafe lost 2-1 at home to Hapoel Tel-Aviv FC in their second outing. Their late consolation came from Pablo Hernández, and the man on loan from Valencia CF subsequently set Getafe on course for 2-1 wins against Anderlecht and Aalborg BK.

Danish history

"Everything is possible" was the mantra that coach Erik Hamrén used to inspire his players at AaB, and while defeat at Getafe ended their hopes of progressing, the Danish side were to make a decisive contribution to the race for third place in the section.

Going into the final round of fixtures with Getafe and Tottenham already effectively through, focus fell on who would join them: Anderlecht or Hapoel. With Anderlecht losing their final match to Getafe, victory for Hapoel would have seen them progress but AaB had other ideas, Kasper Risgård scoring one and setting up another in a 2-1 triumph.

Group G Results

25/10/07, White Hart Lane, London
Tottenham Hotspur FC 1-2 Getafe CF
Goal(s): 1-0 Defoe 19, 1-1 Granero 21, 1-2 Braulio 70
Referee: Kircher (GER)

25/10/07, Constant Vanden Stock Stadium, Brussels
RSC Anderlecht 2-0 Hapoel Tel-Aviv FC
Goal(s): 1-0 Frutos 36, 2-0 Frutos 70
Referee: Tudor (ROU)

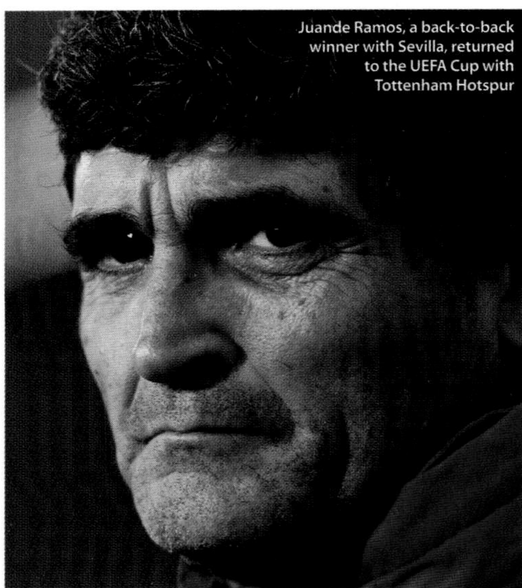
Juande Ramos, a back-to-back winner with Sevilla, returned to the UEFA Cup with Tottenham Hotspur

8/11/07, Bloomfield, Tel-Aviv
Hapoel Tel-Aviv FC 0-2 Tottenham Hotspur FC
Goal(s): 0-1 Keane 26, 0-2 Berbatov 31
Referee: Gilewski (POL)

8/11/07, Aalborg, Aalborg
Aalborg BK 1-1 RSC Anderlecht
Goal(s): 0-1 Jakobsen 59(og), 1-1 Lindström 86
Referee: Duhamel (FRA)

29/11/07, White Hart Lane, London
Tottenham Hotspur FC 3-2 Aalborg BK
Goal(s): 0-1 Enevoldsen 2, 0-2 Risgård 37, 1-2 Berbatov 46, 2-2 Malbranque 51, 3-2 Bent 66
Referee: Pedro Proença (POR)

29/11/07, Coliseum Alfonso Pérez, Getafe
Getafe CF 1-2 Hapoel Tel-Aviv FC
Goal(s): 0-1 Badir 5, 0-2 Dego 31, 1-2 Pablo Hernández 90+1(p)
Referee: Kapitanis (CYP)

6/12/07, Aalborg, Aalborg
Aalborg BK 1-2 Getafe CF
Goal(s): 0-1 Pablo Hernández 11, 0-2 Granero 78, 1-2 Prica 90+2
Referee: Rizzoli (ITA)

6/12/07, Constant Vanden Stock Stadium, Brussels
RSC Anderlecht 1-1 Tottenham Hotspur FC
Goal(s): 1-0 Goor 68, 1-1 Berbatov 71(p)
Referee: Skomina (SVN)

19/12/07, Coliseum Alfonso Pérez, Getafe
Getafe CF 2-1 RSC Anderlecht
Goal(s): 1-0 Pablo Hernández 6, 2-0 Celestini 50, 2-1 Théréau 90+1
Referee: Ivanov (RUS)

19/12/07, Bloomfield, Tel-Aviv
Hapoel Tel-Aviv FC 1-3 Aalborg BK
Goal(s): 0-1 Risgård 27, 1-1 Fábio Júnior 45+1, 1-2 Jakobsen 50(p), 1-3 Enevoldsen 66
Referee: Wegereef (NED)

Group G Table

		Home					Away					Total				
	Pld	W	D	L	F	A	W	D	L	F	A	W	D	L	F	A
1 Getafe CF	4	1	0	1	3	3	2	0	0	4	2	3	0	1	7	5
2 Tottenham Hotspur FC	4	1	0	1	4	4	1	1	0	3	1	2	1	1	7	5
3 RSC Anderlecht	4	1	1	0	3	1	0	1	1	2	3	1	2	1	5	4
4 Aalborg BK	4	0	1	1	2	3	1	0	1	5	4	1	1	2	7	7
5 Hapoel Tel-Aviv FC	4	0	0	2	1	5	1	0	1	2	3	1	0	3	3	8

GROUP H

FC Girondins de Bordeaux ended the group stage as one of only two teams – along with Everton FC – to hold a 100 per cent record. Theirs was very much a lesson in just doing enough. Led by a potent strike-force, Helsingborgs IF did enough too but the race for third went right to the wire.

Comeback kings

Bordeaux's campaign did not get off to the best of starts as they fell behind against Galatasaray AŞ, but Marouane Chamakh inspired a stirring second-half comeback, teeing up Fernando Cavenaghi for the equaliser before scoring the winner himself. "I gave my players a stern talking to at the break and I'm delighted with the way they reacted against a very experienced side," coach Laurent Blanc said. "It's a great start to the group phase."

It set the tone for Bordeaux. They fell behind against FK Austia Wien in their second outing before staging a comeback and made it three 2-1 wins in a row against Helsingborg. Already qualified, they went 2-0 down inside the first quarter away to Panionios GSS but triumphed after yet another fightback, culminating in Wilfried Moimbé's 87th-minute winner as the Greek side passed up what coach Ewald Lienen lamented as a "unique chance" to reach the UEFA Cup Round of 32.

Larsson joy

In the event, a draw would have sufficed for Panionios as Galatasaray ended up taking third place despite signing off with a goalless draw at home against an Austria Wien side who finally earned their first group stage point in two campaigns.

The Turkish side edged through on goal difference, three points behind surprise package Helsingborg who were indebted to a forward pairing at different ends of their career, Henrik Larsson and Razak Omotoyossi. The duo registered three goals apiece, both scoring in a memorable 3-2 triumph against Galatasaray on Matchday 2.

Group H Results

25/10/07, Olympia, Helsingborg
Helsingborgs IF 1-1 Panionios GSS
Goal(s): 0-1 Goundoulakis 45+1, 1-1 Larsson 83
Referee: Trivković (CRO)

25/10/07, Stade Chaban-Delmas, Bordeaux
FC Girondins de Bordeaux 2-1 Galatasaray AŞ
Goal(s): 0-1 Nonda 22(p), 1-1 Cavenaghi 53, 2-1 Chamakh 64
Referee: Malek (POL)

8/11/07, Ali Sami Yen, Istanbul
Galatasaray AŞ 2-3 Helsingborgs IF
Goal(s): 0-1 Larsson 30, 0-2 Omotoyossi 39, 1-2 Nonda 44, 1-3 C. Andersson 75, 2-3 Nonda 90+1
Referee: Dean (ENG)

8/11/07, Ernst Happel, Vienna
FK Austria Wien 1-2 FC Girondins de Bordeaux
Goal(s): 1-0 Kuljic 5, 1-1 Chamakh 45+1, 1-2 Wendel 88(p)
Referee: Pedro Proença (POR)

29/11/07, Olympia, Helsingborg
Helsingborgs IF 3-0 FK Austria Wien
Goal(s): 1-0 Skúlason 47, 2-0 Omotoyossi 66, 3-0 Omotoyossi 70
Referee: Genov (BUL)

29/11/07, Panionios, Athens
Panionios GSS 0-3 Galatasaray AŞ
Goal(s): 0-1 Serkan Çalık 50, 0-2 Song 63(p), 0-3 Hakan Şükür 82
Referee: Undiano (ESP)

6/12/07, Ernst Happel, Vienna
FK Austria Wien 0-1 Panionios GSS
Goal(s): 0-1 Majstorović 90+1
Referee: Granat (POL)

6/12/07, Stade Chaban-Delmas, Bordeaux
FC Girondins de Bordeaux 2-1 Helsingborgs IF
Goal(s): 1-0 Chamakh 12, 1-1 Larsson 17, 2-1 Jussiê 69
Referee: Meyer (GER)

19/12/07, Panionios, Athens
Panionios GSS 2-3 FC Girondins de Bordeaux
Goal(s): 1-0 Djebbour 6(p), 2-0 Makos 20, 2-1 Cavenaghi 39, 2-2 Trémoulinas 75, 2-3 Moimbe 87
Referee: Szabó (HUN)

19/12/07, Ali Sami Yen, Istanbul
Galatasaray AŞ 0-0 FK Austria Wien
Referee: Bossen (NED)

Group H Table

		Home					Away					Total					
	Pld	W	D	L	F	A	W	D	L	F	A	W	D	L	F	A	Pts
1 FC Girondins de Bordeaux	4	2	0	0	4	2	2	0	0	5	3	4	0	0	9	5	12
2 Helsingborgs IF	4	1	1	0	4	1	1	0	1	4	4	2	1	1	8	5	7
3 Galatasaray AŞ	4	0	1	1	2	3	1	0	1	4	2	1	1	2	6	5	4
4 Panionios GSS	4	0	0	2	2	6	1	1	0	2	1	1	1	2	4	7	4
5 FK Austria Wien	4	0	0	2	1	3	0	1	1	0	3	0	1	3	1	6	1

Bordeaux striker Marouane Chamakh (right) celebrates a goal against FK Austria Wien

ROUND OF 32

Germany may have been starved of a UEFA Cup winner since FC Schalke 04's triumph in 1997, but the Bundesliga clubs stamped their authority on the competition once again in the last 32. The formidable-looking quartet of FC Bayern München, Werder Bremen, Bayer 04 Leverkusen and Hamburger SV all progressed smoothly, with only 1. FC Nürnberg falling by the wayside after Angel de María's last-gasp strike at the Frankenstadion sealed a 3-2 aggregate win for SL Benfica.

Pulsating contest

Aberdeen FC were targeting a repeat of their 1972/73 heroics over Bayern in the UEFA Cup Winners' Cup quarter-finals, and a similar outcome seemed plausible when the Scottish club twice took the lead in a fluctuating first leg at Pittodrie. Ottmar Hitzfeld's men escaped with a 2-2 draw but then ran out emphatic 7-3 winners on aggregate thanks in part to Lukas Podolski's two goals in Bavaria.

Michael Skibbe's Leverkusen followed a similar route, drawing 0-0 away to 1999/2000 winners winners Galatasaray AŞ before romping to a 5-1 victory on home soil. Sergej Barbarez twice found the net at the BayArena, setting up a showdown with former club Hamburg in the next round. "He's an outstanding player, I'd rather he was on our team," commented playmaker Rafael van der Vaart after helping Huub Stevens' side to a 3-1 success over FC Zürich. David Jarolím, Ivica Olić and Piotr Trochowski all struck for Hamburg in an explosive 28-minute spell in the first leg in Switzerland to effectively end Zürich's challenge.

Leverkusen veteran Sergej Barbarez heads in the first of his team's five goals at home to Galatasaray

Everton romp

England also guaranteed strong representation in the last 16 as Bolton Wanderers FC, Tottenham Hotspur FC and Everton FC all prevailed. While the Goodison Park faithful were treated to a virtuoso display against SK Brann - David Moyes' charges following up their 2-0 success in Norway with a 6-1 romp that included a Yakubu Aiyegbeni hat-trick – Bolton and Spurs found the going far tougher. El Hadji Diouf's solitary goal in the first leg at home ultimately accounted for the much-fancied Club Atlético de Madrid, while two-time UEFA Cup winner Juande Ramos survived a scare as Tottenham edged past SK Slavia Praha 3-2 on aggregate.

There were mixed fortunes for Spanish clubs, with Villarreal CF following Atlético through the exit door after succumbing on away goals to Russian champions FC Zenit St. Petersburg, while debutants Getafe CF showed their more illustrious compatriots the way forward. Ismael Blanco's added-time goal may have denied Getafe victory in their first leg away to AEK Athens FC, but Michael Laudrup's emerging team proved too strong in front of their own fans, winning 3-0 thanks to Cosmin Contra's penalty and strikes from Esteban Granero and Braulio.

Nervy Marseille

Elsewhere, Nacho Novo's goal nine minutes from time clinched a 1-1 draw for Rangers FC at Panathinaikos FC, sending the Glasgow outfit through on the away-goals rule. They were joined by three more teams eyeing prolonged European runs having exited the UEFA Champions League – Olympique de Marseille, Sporting Clube de Portugal and PSV Eindhoven. Marseille appeared to be cruising past FC Spartak Moskva after a convincing 3-0 first-leg triumph, yet ended up clinging on in the dying moments of a 2-0 loss in the Russian capital.

PSV had no such troubles, defeating Helsingborgs IF 4-1 on aggregate with Danko Lazović on target in both games. Meanwhile, Simon Vukčević and Liedson registered twice to set up a 5-0 aggregate success for Sporting over FC Basel 1893, Belgian title-holders RSC Anderlecht claimed a notable scalp by pipping FC Girondins de Bordeaux 3-2 on aggregate, and ACF Fiorentina overcame Rosenborg BK 3-1.

Round of 32 Results

13/2/08, Ali Sami Yen, Istanbul
Galatasaray AŞ 0-0 Bayer 04 Leverkusen
Referee: Batista (POR)
21/2/08, BayArena, Leverkusen
Bayer 04 Leverkusen 5-1 Galatasaray AŞ
Goal(s): 1-0 Barbarez 12, 2-0 Kiessling 13, 3-0 Barbarez 22, 4-0 Haggui 55, 5-0 Schneider 61(p), 5-1 Barusso 87(p)
Referee: Skomina (SVN)
Aggregate: 5-1; Bayer 04 Leverkusen qualify.

13/2/08, OACA Spyro Louis, Athens
AEK Athens FC 1-1 Getafe CF
Goal(s): 0-1 De la Red 86, 1-1 Blanco 90+3
Referee: Layec (FRA)
21/2/08, Coliseum Alfonso Pérez, Getafe
Getafe CF 3-0 AEK Athens FC
Goal(s): 1-0 Granero 45+1, 2-0 Contra 82(p), 3-0 Braulio 84
Referee: Atkinson (ENG)
Aggregate: 4-1; Getafe CF qualify.

13/2/08, Petrovsky, St Petersburg
FC Zenit St. Petersburg 1-0 Villarreal CF
Goal(s): 1-0 Pogrebnyak 63
Referee: Weiner (GER)
21/2/08, El Madrigal, Villarreal
Villarreal CF 2-1 FC Zenit St. Petersburg
Goal(s): 0-1 Pogrebnyak 31, 1-1 Guille Franco 75, 2-1 Tomasson 90
Referee: Messner (AUT)
Aggregate: 2-2; FC Zenit St. Petersburg qualify on away goal.

13/2/08, Brann, Bergen
SK Brann 0-2 Everton FC
Goal(s): 0-1 Osman 59, 0-2 Anichebe 88
Referee: Genov (BUL)
21/2/08, Goodison Park, Liverpool
Everton FC 6-1 SK Brann
Goal(s): 1-0 Yakubu 36, 2-0 Johnson 41, 3-0 Yakubu 54, 3-1 Vaagan Moen 60, 4-1 Arteta 70, 5-1 Yakubu 72, 6-1 Johnson 90+2
Referee: Ivanov (RUS)
Aggregate: 8-1; Everton FC qualify.

13/2/08, Ibrox, Glasgow
Rangers FC 0-0 Panathinaikos FC
Referee: Rizzoli (ITA)
21/2/08, Apostolos Nikolaidis, Athens
Panathinaikos FC 1-1 Rangers FC
Goal(s): 1-0 Goumas 12, 1-1 Novo 81
Referee: Brych (GER)
Aggregate: 1-1; Rangers FC qualify on away goal.

13/2/08, Weserstadion, Bremen
Werder Bremen 3-0 SC Braga
Goal(s): 1-0 Naldo 5, 2-0 Jensen 27, 3-0 Hugo Almeida 90+5(p)
Referee: Kasnaferis (GRE)
21/2/08, Municipal, Braga
SC Braga 0-1 Werder Bremen
Goal(s): 0-1 Klasnić 78
Referee: Gumienny (BEL)
Aggregate: 0-4; Werder Bremen qualify.

13/2/08, Constant Vanden Stock Stadium, Brussels
RSC Anderlecht 2-1 FC Girondins de Bordeaux
Goal(s): 0-1 Jussiê 69(p), 1-1 Polák 79, 2-1 Mpenza 90+5
Referee: Tagliavento (ITA)
21/2/08, Stade Chaban-Delmas, Bordeaux
FC Girondins de Bordeaux 1-1 RSC Anderlecht
Goal(s): 0-1 Chatelle 34, 1-1 Cavenaghi 71
Referee: Dereli (TUR)
Aggregate: 2-3; RSC Anderlecht qualify.

13/2/08, José Alvalade, Lisbon
Sporting Clube de Portugal 2-0 FC Basel 1893
Goal(s): 1-0 Vukčević 8, 2-0 Vukčević 58
Referee: Blom (NED)
21/2/08, St. Jakob-Park, Basel
FC Basel 1893 0-3 Sporting Clube de Portugal
Goal(s): 0-1 Pereirinha 2, 0-2 Liedson 41, 0-3 Liedson 51
Referee: Skjerven (NOR)
Aggregate: 0-5; Sporting Clube de Portugal qualify.

13/2/08, Vélodrome, Marseille
Olympique de Marseille 3-0 FC Spartak Moskva
Goal(s): 1-0 Cheyrou 62, 2-0 Taiwo 68, 3-0 Niang 79
Referee: Pedro Proença (POR)
21/2/08, Luzhniki Stadium, Moscow
FC Spartak Moskva 2-0 Olympique de Marseille
Goal(s): 1-0 Pavlenko 39, 2-0 Pavlyuchenko 85
Referee: Einwaller (AUT)
Aggregate: 2-3; Olympique de Marseille qualify.

13/2/08, Philips Stadion, Eindhoven
PSV Eindhoven 2-0 Helsingborgs IF
Goal(s): 1-0 Simons 7(p), 2-0 Lazović 33
Referee: Kapitanis (CYP)
21/2/08, Olympia, Helsingborg
Helsingborgs IF 1-2 PSV Eindhoven
Goal(s): 0-1 Bakkal 47, 0-2 Lazović 65, 1-2 Leandro Castán 81
Referee: Szabó (HUN)
Aggregate: 1-4; PSV Eindhoven qualify.

14/2/08, Pittodrie, Aberdeen
Aberdeen FC 2-2 FC Bayern München
Goal(s): 1-0 Walker 24, 1-1 Klose 29, 2-1 Aluko 41, 2-2 Hamit Altıntop 55
Referee: Iturralde González (ESP)
21/2/08, Allianz Arena, Munich
FC Bayern München 5-1 Aberdeen FC
Goal(s): 1-0 Lúcio 12, 2-0 Van Buyten 36, 3-0 Podolski 71, 4-0 Podolski 77, 4-1 Lovell 83, 5-1 Van Bommel 85
Referee: Malek (POL)
Aggregate: 7-3; FC Bayern München qualify.

14/2/08, Reebok Stadium, Bolton
Bolton Wanderers FC 1-0 Club Atlético de Madrid
Goal(s): 1-0 Diouf 74
Referee: Rasmussen (DEN)
21/2/08, Vicente Calderón, Madrid
Club Atlético de Madrid 0-0 Bolton Wanderers FC
Referee: Granat (POL)
Aggregate: 0-1; Bolton Wanderers FC qualify.

14/2/08, Letzigrund, Zurich
FC Zürich 1-3 Hamburger SV
Goal(s): 0-1 Jarolím 49, 0-2 Olić 67, 0-3 Trochowski 77, 1-3 Rochat 88
Referee: Kelly (IRL)
21/2/08, Arena Hamburg, Hamburg
Hamburger SV 0-0 FC Zürich
Referee: Jakobsson (ISL)
Aggregate: 3-1; Hamburger SV qualify.

14/2/08, Estádio do SL Benfica, Lisbon
SL Benfica 1-0 1. FC Nürnberg
Goal(s): 1-0 Makukula 43
Referee: Tudor (ROU)
21/2/08, Frankenstadion, Nuremberg
1. FC Nürnberg 2-2 SL Benfica
Goal(s): 1-0 Charisteas 59, 2-0 Saenko 66, 2-1 Cardozo 89, 2-2 Di María 90+1
Referee: Bebek (CRO)
Aggregate: 2-3; SL Benfica qualify.

14/2/08, Lerkendal, Trondheim
Rosenborg BK 0-1 ACF Fiorentina
Goal(s): 0-1 Mutu 16
Referee: Clattenburg (ENG)
21/2/08, Artemio Franchi, Florence
ACF Fiorentina 2-1 Rosenborg BK
Goal(s): 1-0 Liverani 38, 2-0 Cacia 81, 2-1 Koné 88
Referee: Ceferin (SVN)
Aggregate: 3-1; ACF Fiorentina qualify.

14/2/08, Evžena Rošického, Prague
SK Slavia Praha 1-2 Tottenham Hotspur FC
Goal(s): 0-1 Berbatov 4, 0-2 Keane 30, 1-2 Střihavka 69
Referee: Circhetta (SUI)
21/2/08, White Hart Lane, London
Tottenham Hotspur FC 1-1 SK Slavia Praha
Goal(s): 1-0 O'Hara 7, 1-1 Krajčík 50
Referee: Eriksson (SWE)
Aggregate: 3-2; Tottenham Hotspur FC qualify.

ROUND OF 16

After putting seven goals past Aberdeen FC, FC Bayern München continued their intimidating march by scoring six more against a nerve-struck RSC Anderlecht. That was the only one-sided affair, however, in a thrilling Round of 16 that produced more than its share of spectacular turnarounds and penalty shoot-out drama.

Mesmerising display

Anderlecht had never previously lost at home in Europe by more than two goals, but that record was shattered by a rampant Bayern. Hamit Altıntop's wonderful long-range strike proved the prelude to a mesmerising display from the Bavarians, who notched up a 5-0 win with further goals from Luca Toni, Lukas Podolski, Miroslav Klose and Franck Ribéry. "We put in a great performance with attacking moves I haven't seen for a long time," said Mark van Bommel. A below-strength Bayern were beaten 2-1 in the return leg, yet Ottmar Hitzfeld's side had sounded another ominous warning to the rest.

Elsewhere, two-time finalists Olympique de Marseille appeared to be coasting after taking a three-goal lead against FC Zenit St. Petersburg at Stade Vélodrome. Djibril Cissé scored twice and Mamadou Niang once, with the latter twice striking the crossbar, before Andrei Arshavin reduced the deficit to 3-1. The Russian international's late intervention proved vital as Marseille succumbed 2-0 on Russian soil for the second time in three weeks, crashing out on away goals. "Arshavin's goal gave us confidence that everything would be all right," said Zenit's two-goal hero Pavel Pogrebnyak. "We always believed we could win."

Frey heroics

English clubs are renowned for their never-say-die attitude, and Everton FC and Tottenham Hotspur FC strengthened that image with stirring comebacks of their own. Goals from Zdravko Kuzmanović and Riccardo

Brazilian defender Breno, on a ra
outing for Bayern München, challeng
Anderlecht's Ahmed Hass

Montolivo gave ACF Fiorentina a distinct advantage ahead of their trip to Goodison Park, but Everton, roused by an electric atmosphere, forced extra time through Andrew Johnson and Mikel Arteta. Sébastien Frey ultimately won the day for the Italians, though, producing several fine saves before inspiring a 4-2 triumph in the shoot-out. "We were under pressure for the whole game," said the Fiorentina goalkeeper. "It felt like the final whistle would never come."

Tottenham suffered a similar fate against PSV Eindhoven. This time, however, the Premier League outfit recovered from a 1-0 home defeat - Jefferson Farfán netting the only goal of the first leg - to force penalties courtesy of Dimitar Berbatov's 81st-minute leveller at the Philips Stadion. Again the comeback proved fruitless as Heurelho Gomes saved Jermaine Jenas's potentially winning spot-kick before Pascal Chimbonda's wayward effort handed PSV victory. "We can have no regrets because we wanted to win on the night and we did that," reflected Spurs manager Juande Ramos, finally beaten in the competition he had won with Sevilla FC the previous two seasons.

Rangers triumph

With Bolton Wanderers FC also getting edged out by Sporting Clube de Portugal, Rangers FC were left to fly the British flag in the quarter-finals after securing a fine 2-1 aggregate victory over Werder Bremen, with Daniel Cousin and Steven Davis scoring the all-important first-leg goals at Ibrox before Diego pulled one back in Germany. Hamburger SV followed Bremen through the exit door despite recovering from a 1-0 first-leg defeat at Bayer 04 Leverkusen to level the all-Bundesliga tie at three apiece on aggregate. Ultimately, the away goals scored by Sergej Barbarez - on his old stomping ground - and Theofanis Gekas ensured Michael Skibbe's men prevailed. Spanish minnows Getafe CF, meanwhile, continued to confound expectations, beating two-time European champions SL Benfica home and away to reach the last eight on their competition debut.

Round of 16 Results

6/3/08, Constant Vanden Stock Stadium, Brussels
RSC Anderlecht 0-5 FC Bayern München
Goal(s): 0-1 Hamit Altıntop 9, 0-2 Toni 45+1, 0-3 Podolski 57, 0-4 Klose 67, 0-5 Ribéry 86
Referee: Benquerença (POR)
12/3/08, Allianz Arena, Munich
FC Bayern München 1-2 RSC Anderlecht
Goal(s): 1-0 Lúcio 9, 1-1 Serhat 20, 1-2 Yakovenko 35
Referee: Hauge (NOR)
Aggregate: 6-2; FC Bayern München qualify.

6/3/08, Ibrox, Glasgow
Rangers FC 2-0 Werder Bremen
Goal(s): 1-0 Cousin 45, 2-0 Davis 48
Referee: Hamer (LUX)
13/3/08, Weserstadion, Bremen
Werder Bremen 1-0 Rangers FC
Goal(s): 1-0 Diego 58
Referee: Hansson (SWE)
Aggregate: 1-2; Rangers FC qualify.

6/3/08, Reebok Stadium, Bolton
Bolton Wanderers FC 1-1 Sporting Clube de Portugal
Goal(s): 1-0 McCann 25, 1-1 Vukčević 69
Referee: Yefet (ISR)
13/3/08, José Alvalade, Lisbon
Sporting Clube de Portugal 1-0 Bolton Wanderers FC
Goal(s): 1-0 Pereirinha 85
Referee: Layec (FRA)
Aggregate: 2-1; Sporting Clube de Portugal qualify.

6/3/08, White Hart Lane, London
Tottenham Hotspur FC 0-1 PSV Eindhoven
Goal(s): 0-1 Farfán 34
Referee: Lannoy (FRA)
12/3/08, Philips Stadion, Eindhoven
PSV Eindhoven 0-1 Tottenham Hotspur FC
Goal(s): 0-1 Berbatov 81
Referee: Trefoloni (ITA)
Aggregate: 1-1; PSV Eindhoven qualify 6-5 on penalties.

6/3/08, Estádio do SL Benfica, Lisbon
SL Benfica 1-2 Getafe CF
Goal(s): 0-1 De la Red 25, 0-2 Pablo Hernández 67, 1-2 Mantorras 76
Referee: Gilewski (POL)
12/3/08, Coliseum Alfonso Pérez, Getafe
Getafe CF 1-0 SL Benfica
Goal(s): 1-0 Albín 77
Referee: Kassai (HUN)
Aggregate: 3-1; Getafe CF qualify.

6/3/08, Artemio Franchi, Florence
ACF Fiorentina 2-0 Everton FC
Goal(s): 1-0 Kuzmanović 70, 2-0 Montolivo 81
Referee: Allaerts (BEL)
12/3/08, Goodison Park, Liverpool
Everton FC 2-0 ACF Fiorentina
Goal(s): 1-0 Johnson 16, 2-0 Arteta 67
Referee: Braamhaar (NED)
Aggregate: 2-2; ACF Fiorentina qualify 4-2 on penalties.

6/3/08, Vélodrome, Marseille
Olympique de Marseille 3-1 FC Zenit St. Petersburg
Goal(s): 1-0 Cissé 37, 2-0 Niang 48, 3-0 Cissé 55, 3-1 Arshavin 82
Referee: Kircher (GER)
12/3/08, Petrovsky, St Petersburg
FC Zenit St. Petersburg 2-0 Olympique de Marseille
Goal(s): 1-0 Pogrebnyak 39, 2-0 Pogrebnyak 78
Referee: Riley (ENG)
Aggregate: 3-3; FC Zenit St. Petersburg qualify on away goal.

6/3/08, BayArena, Leverkusen
Bayer 04 Leverkusen 1-0 Hamburger SV
Goal(s): 1-0 Gekas 77
Referee: Thomson (SCO)
12/3/08, Arena Hamburg, Hamburg
Hamburger SV 3-2 Bayer 04 Leverkusen
Goal(s): 0-1 Barbarez 19, 1-1 Trochowski 53, 1-2 Gekas 55, 2-2 Guerrero 65, 3-2 Van der Vaart 81
Referee: Undiano (ESP)
Aggregate: 3-3; Bayer 04 Leverkusen qualify on away goals.

QUARTER-FINALS

Away victories were a recurring theme in the quarter-finals as FC Zenit St. Petersburg, Rangers FC and ACF Fiorentina all prevailed on the back of fine performances on their travels, while FC Bayern München pulled off a remarkable Houdini act in Spain to bring Getafe CF's campaign to a heartbreaking end.

'A historic moment'

Zenit's 4-1 success at Bayer 04 Leverkusen was perhaps the most eye-catching result of the round, yet it was the least the Russian title-holders deserved after giving the home side a lesson in counterattacking. Andrei Arshavin opened the scoring with a fine individual effort before setting up Pavel Pogrebnyak to register his eighth goal of the competition. Further strikes from Aleksandr Anyukov and Igor Denisov ensured that Zenit would reach their first European semi-final, despite losing the return 1-0 in Russia. "It's a historic moment for our club," enthused coach Dick Advocaat.

If Zenit's emergence added a certain freshness to the competition, Spanish outsiders Getafe were winning admirers for their fearless approach in the club's debut campaign. Having already defeated RSC Anderlecht, Tottenham Hotspur FC, AEK Athens FC and SL Benfica, Michael Laudrup's charges raised their game again in Munich, sealing a superb 1-1 draw as Cosmin Contra's last-gasp strike cancelled out a Luca Toni effort. "In the second half Getafe showed their quality - they really have fine football players," acknowledged Bayern boss Ottmar Hitzfeld.

Sending off

Seven days later, a full house packed into the tiny Coliseum Alfonso Pérez on the outskirts of Madrid for

Rangers players Jean-Claude Darcheville, Christian Dailly, Steven Davis and Brahim Hemdani (left to right) are all smiles after victory over Sporting in Lisbon

the biggest game in Getafe's history. The crowd's exuberance was tempered by the sixth-minute sending off of Rubén De la Red, yet the hosts made light of their numerical inferiority and deservedly opened the scoring through Contra just before the break. Franck Ribéry salvaged Bayern's dream of a second UEFA Cup title with a last-minute leveller, only for the ten men of Getafe to race 3-1 ahead within three minutes of the additional 30 thanks to Javier Casquero and Braulio.

With just five minutes remaining, goalkeeper Roberto Abbondanzieri spilled a harmless-looking free-kick into Toni's path to gift Bayern a lifeline, and the Italian striker duly punished Getafe by heading in his tenth European goal of the season in the dying seconds to send the Bavarians through on away goals. "We're desperately disappointed but we know in two or three days' time we will be very happy with the way we played," Laudrup said. "We were fantastic. We had ten men for 114 minutes, yet we attacked and created enough chances to win the tie."

Clinical Rangers

Elsewhere, Rangers manager Walter Smith appeared to have hit on a winning formula: keep a clean sheet at home and exploit the open spaces away. Having already shut out Panathinaikos FC and Werder Bremen at Ibrox, the Glasgow outfit secured a goalless draw against Sporting Clube de Portugal before punishing the 2004/05 finalists on the counterattack at the Estádio José Alvalade. Jean-Claude Darcheville and Steven Whittaker were on target in a 2-0 win that earned Rangers their first European semi-final in 36 years.

Fiorentina were to stand between Rangers and a place in the final after the Italian club confirmed their resurgence by triumphing over PSV Eindhoven. Cesare Prandelli's team could only draw 1-1 in the first leg at the Stadio Artemio Franchi - Danny Koevermans cancelling out Adrian Mutu's opener - but two more Mutu goals, including a sumptuous long-range free-kick, sealed a highly impressive victory in the Netherlands. "To perform as we did, in a match of this importance, was magnificent," Prandelli said.

Getafe striker Braulio shows his frustration after missing a chance against Bayern München

Quarter-Final Results

3/4/08, BayArena, Leverkusen
Bayer 04 Leverkusen 1-4 FC Zenit St. Petersburg
Goal(s): 0-1 Arshavin 20, 1-1 Kiessling 33, 1-2 Pogrebnyak 52, 1-3 Anyukov 61, 1-4 Denisov 64
Referee: Benquerença (POR)
10/4/08, Petrovsky, St Petersburg
FC Zenit St. Petersburg 0-1 Bayer 04 Leverkusen
Goal(s): 0-1 Bulykin 18
Referee: Mejuto González (ESP)
Aggregate: 4-2; FC Zenit St. Petersburg qualify.

3/4/08, Ibrox, Glasgow
Rangers FC 0-0 Sporting Clube de Portugal
Referee: Baskakov (RUS)
10/4/08, José Alvalade, Lisbon
Sporting Clube de Portugal 0-2 Rangers FC
Goal(s): 0-1 Darcheville 60, 0-2 Whittaker 90+2
Referee: Plautz (AUT)
Aggregate: 0-2; Rangers FC qualify.

3/4/08, Allianz Arena, Munich
FC Bayern München 1-1 Getafe CF
Goal(s): 1-0 Toni 26, 1-1 Contra 90
Referee: Webb (ENG)
10/4/08, Coliseum Alfonso Pérez, Getafe
Getafe CF 3-3 FC Bayern München
Goal(s): 1-0 Contra 44, 1-1 Ribéry 89, 2-1 Casquero 91, 3-1 Braulio 93, 3-2 Toni 115, 3-3 Toni 120
Referee: Busacca (SUI)
Aggregate: 4-4; FC Bayern München qualify on away goals.

3/4/08, Artemio Franchi, Florence
ACF Fiorentina 1-1 PSV Eindhoven
Goal(s): 1-0 Mutu 56, 1-1 Koevermans 63
Referee: Duhamel (FRA)
10/4/08, Philips Stadion, Eindhoven
PSV Eindhoven 0-2 ACF Fiorentina
Goal(s): 0-1 Mutu 38, 0-2 Mutu 53
Referee: Medina Cantalejo (ESP)
Aggregate: 1-3; ACF Fiorentina qualify.

SEMI-FINALS

If the elimination of seasoned campaigners Villarreal CF, Olympique de Marseille and Bayer 04 Leverkusen had not alerted those outside Russia to the talents of FC Zenit St. Petersburg, then the ruthless 4-0 semi-final second-leg defeat of FC Bayern München certainly made Europe sit up and take notice.

Fateful own goal

Franck Ribéry gave the Bundesliga side an 18th-minute lead at the Allianz Arena in the first leg, an advantage that was cancelled out on the hour when Bayern's Brazilian defender Lúcio inadvertently headed past Oliver Kahn to give Zenit some reward for an increasingly positive display. Despite the disappointment of being held at home - as they were in the quarter-finals against Getafe CF - Bayern will have harboured few fears as they travelled for the second instalment in St Petersburg. Yet the tournament favourites were left wondering just what had hit them at the Petrovsky stadium as the Russian title-holders combined resolute defending with lethal finishing to reach their maiden UEFA club competition final.

Though shorn of the creative talents of Andrei Arshavin (one of three players ruled out through suspension), Zenit were two goals up at the break thanks to Pavel Pogrebnyak and Konstantin Zyryanov, and were cruising nine minutes after the restart when Victor Fayzulin headed in a cross from Aleksandr Anyukov. Pogrebnyak added a brilliant fourth later on to draw level with Bayern's Luca Toni at the top of the goalscorers' chart on ten goals, though a harsh caution picked up moments later would rule the Russia striker out of the final. "At the moment, we still can't be compared with the top European teams, like Chelsea for example," Zenit's Dutch coach Dick Advocaat said. "But we are definitely moving in the right direction. We have great potential and hopefully a bright future. After winning against Villarreal, Marseille, and now Bayern, I think we deserve to win the final as well."

Rangers resilience

While Zenit rejoiced, ACF Fiorentina were crestfallen after a penalty shoot-out defeat by Rangers FC in the other semi-final. Following a goalless first leg in Glasgow, when prudence overcame attacking instinct, the Serie A outfit made all the running at the Stadio Artemio Franchi. Yet, for all the Viola's possession and slick passing, chances

Zenit striker Pavel Pogrebnyak slots home his second goal of the game to complete a brilliant 4-0 victory over Bayern München in St. Petersburg

rlos Cuéllar, a dominant figure in the Rangers defence, foils another Fiorentina attack

were at a premium, as Rangers - deploying Jean-Claude Darcheville up front on his own - were content to sit back and play on the break. Neither side could fashion a goal during regulation or extra time so it was left to spot-kicks to separate the teams after 210 goalless minutes across the two legs. Fabio Liverani had an effort saved by stand-in goalkeeper Neil Alexander and then Christian Vieri blasted over, allowing Rangers' Nacho Novo to seal an unlikely win and give the Scottish side their first European final appearance in 36 years.

Fiorentina were devastated, with coach Cesare Prandelli aptly summing up the feeling when he rued: "We dominated possession and the match, especially in the second half and in extra time, but did not manage to score the goal we deserved." His Rangers counterpart, Walter Smith, acknowledged the pressure his players had been put under in Florence, but was full of praise for the fortitude that brought a place in the Manchester final. "It was a great result tonight but I think we have done well during the whole campaign, showing great determination and spirit. Reaching a European final is a fantastic result for everybody connected to the club and for our fans. We knew Fiorentina would put us under pressure because they always do that when they play at home and tonight they played a good game."

Semi-Final Results

24/4/08, Ibrox, Glasgow
Rangers FC 0-0 ACF Fiorentina
Referee: Vassaras (GRE)
1/5/08, Artemio Franchi, Florence
ACF Fiorentina 0-0 Rangers FC
Referee: De Bleeckere (BEL)
Aggregate: 0-0; Rangers FC qualify 4-2 on penalties.

24/4/08, Allianz Arena, Munich
FC Bayern München 1-1 FC Zenit St. Petersburg
Goal(s): 1-0 Ribéry 18, 1-1 Lúcio 60(og)
Referee: Micheľ (SVK)
1/5/08, Petrovsky, St Petersburg
FC Zenit St. Petersburg 4-0 FC Bayern München
Goal(s): 1-0 Pogrebnyak 4, 2-0 Zyryanov 39, 3-0 Fayzulin 54, 4-0 Pogrebnyak 73
Referee: Øvrebø (NOR)
Aggregate: 5-1; FC Zenit St. Petersburg qualify.

FINAL

There may have been two teams participating in the UEFA Cup final, but with over 100,000 Rangers FC fans making the short journey to north-west England for the 2007/08 showpiece, the contest for biggest support was a walkover. Enough coaches were chartered in Glasgow to stretch 16km bumper to bumper along the M74 towards "Manchest-Ger", yet on the pitch they were pitted as underdogs. FC Zenit St. Petersburg's semi-final flaying of favourites FC Bayern München gave the Russian side, coached by former Rangers manager Dick Advocaat, a veneer of invincibility as they geared up for their first UEFA club competition final. The pre-match supposition was to prove accurate.

Defensive steel

Rangers had conceded only twice in eight outings after parachuting into the competition from the UEFA Champions League, and any hopes of a first European title since 1972 seemed based on these defensive foundations. They almost got off to the worst of starts when they allowed the talismanic Andrei Arshavin to break free in the fourth minute, but the playmaker fired into the side netting. It came from the sort of quick counterattack to which people watching Zenit had become accustomed, but much of their approach play was more considered, Anatoliy Tymoshchuk providing the pivot in midfield as Rangers chased shadows.

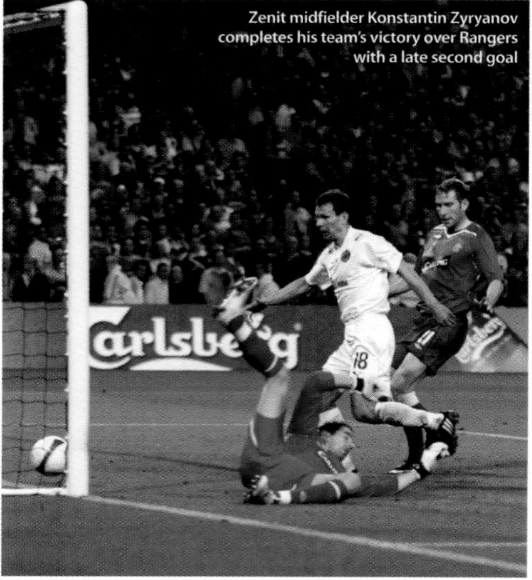

Zenit midfielder Konstantin Zyryanov completes his team's victory over Rangers with a late second goal

Arshavin proved particularly elusive and supplied a teasing cross that was meekly headed just over by Viktor Fayzulin. Advocaat would have wondered what suspended star striker Pavel Pogrebnyak might have done with the same opportunity, while for Rangers counterpart Walter Smith, it all looked very familiar. A fortnight before. his side had played a similar game, sitting back for much of the 120 minutes against ACF Fiorentina and inviting attack after attack, soaking it all up before delivering the knockout blow in the penalty shoot-out – footballing rope-a-dope.

Rangers' response

The tactic saw Rangers through to half-time, and they emerged for the second period with renewed vigour, as if heeding the message on the huge banner unfurled among their numerous supporters that read: "This is your chance. This is your time. Become legends." Vyacheslav Malafeyev denied Jean-Claude Darcheville, and it took a goalline clearance from Ivica Križanac to keep out Barry Ferguson, yet it only served to spur on Zenit. Twenty minutes from time they went ahead as Igor Denisov met the ball with a powerful midfield run, found Arshavin, then collected the return before coolly sliding it to Neil Alexander's left.

Rangers threw on Nacho Novo and Lee McCulloch, but to no avail, and as the vociferous Zenit supporters celebrated by defying the dropping temperature and removing their shirts en masse, Konstantin Zyryanov sealed victory in added time, converting Fatih Tekke's centre from point-blank range. It sparked even wilder Zenit celebrations, the club ensuring their name was etched on to the oldest trophy still up for grabs in UEFA club competition, three years after PFC CSKA Moskva had earned Russia's maiden European title.

'Special prize'

The sense of achievement was certainly not lost on Advocaat as he reflected on "good times for Russian football". The 60-year-old added: "Winning a prize like this doesn't happen very often in your life. I have won all sorts of championships in my career but never a European trophy, so it is a special prize. I'm very proud – the way we played in the tournament, we really deserved this. We knew Rangers could score a goal out

Zenit skipper Anatoliy Tymoshchuk holds aloft the UEFA Cup surrounded by team-mates and coach Dick Advocaat (bottom right)

of nothing, especially in the second half. But we scored two brilliant goals and over the 90 minutes we were the better side and deserved to win." That thought was echoed by Scottish counterpart Walter Smith, who was left to envy the special talent of Man of the Match Arshavin.

Final Result

14/5/08, City of Manchester, Manchester
FC Zenit St. Petersburg 2-0 Rangers FC
Attendance: 43878
Zenit: Malafeyev, Križanac, Fatih Tekke, Arshavin, Širl, Shirokov, Zyryanov, Fayzulin (Kim 90+3), Anyukov, Denisov, Tymoshchuk. Coach: Dick Advocaat (NED)
Rangers: Alexander, Weir, Papac (Novo 77), Ferguson, Hemdani (McCulloch 80), Thomson, Darcheville, Broadfoot, Cuéllar, Whittaker (Boyd 86), Davis. Coach: Walter Smith (SCO)
Goal(s): 1-0 Denisov 72, 2-0 Zyryanov 90+4
Yellow Card(s): Denisov 72 (Zenit), Malafeev 90+2 (Zenit), Broadfoot 90+4 (Rangers)
Referee: Fröjdfeldt (SWE)

TOP GOALSCORERS

(excluding qualifying rounds)

10 Pavel POGREBNYAK (Zenit)
Luca TONI (Bayern)

7 Stefan KIESSLING (Leverkusen)

6 Henrik LARSSON (Helsingborg)
Razak OMOTOYOSSI (Helsingborg)
Adrian MUTU (Fiorentina)

5 Dimitar BERBATOV (Tottenham)
Miroslav KLOSE (Bayern)
Lukas PODOLSKI (Bayern)
Dimitrios PAPADOPOULOS (Panathinaikos)
Sergio AGÜERO (Atlético)
Fernando CAVENAGHI (Bordeaux)
Roland LINZ (Braga)
Jon Dahl TOMASSON (Villarreal)

888.com
bwin
22
Joma

CHAPTER 04

UEFA SUPERCUP

2007

The UEFA Super Cup game in Monaco on 31 August raised the curtain on the 2007/08 European season, but the death of Sevilla FC's Antonio Puerta just three days before the big game cast a horrible shadow over what was supposed to be a celebration. UEFA Cup holders Sevilla had been challenging to become only the second club to win two successive Super Cups as they prepared to take on AC Milan, but Puerta's death, following a heart attack sustained during a Spanish League game, made such sporting concerns seem irrelevant. In the event, AC Milan won the match 3-1 with Andrea Pirlo performing brilliantly in midfield, but the occasion was not lost on him. "It was difficult to face up to the situation but we proved that we also played for [Puerta] and did it in the best possible spirit," he said.

Sevilla and Milan players join in silence to remember Antonio Pu

Antonio Puerta's death at the age of just 22 completely overshadowed Sevilla FC's preparations for the match at the Stade Louis II. Coach Juande Ramos admitted before the game that a "trance" of grief had descended upon his side, adding: "We don't want to forget him and we are not going to. Antonio Puerta will be with us throughout the season. He is not here physically but of course he will be present in our hearts and present in everything we do and we have to live with his memory."

Kaká honoured

While Sevilla girded themselves up to compete, UEFA Champions League winners AC Milan were to receive good news in the days leading up to the finals, with Kaká being named as the UEFA Club Footballer of the Year and best forward of 2007 at the UEFA Club Football Awards in Monaco. Team-mates Paolo Maldini and Clarence Seedorf were given the awards for the season's best defender and midfielder respectively, while Chelsea FC's Petr Čech broke the Milan monopoly as he was named best goalkeeper.

Kaká, who was the 2006/07 UEFA Champions League's top scorer with ten goals in 13 games, told uefa.com: "Winning trophies is what motivates me and I am looking forward to the next challenge. This UEFA Champions League, however, will always have a special place in my heart for the extra honour of ending up as the tournament's top scorer." Seedorf continued: "It's important to keep learning and improving, however long you've been around, and I'm enjoying my role a lot more now." Maldini added: "We've been the best team in Italy, Europe and the world over the past 20 years. And the cycle hasn't ended yet."

Milan revival

The final was to provide further evidence to back that conviction. Renato put Sevilla ahead after 13 minutes and they honoured their fallen colleague with a fine first-half performance. However, Milan emerged transformed after the interval, with Andrea Pirlo working wonders in midfield. Filippo Inzaghi headed them level from a Gennaro Gattuso cross after 54 minutes before Marek Jankulovski volleyed home with

Filippo Inzaghi heads Milan le

umptuous technique from a sweet Pirlo pass to make t 2-1 seven minutes later.

ndrés Palop denied Kaká from the penalty spot after 7 minutes, but the Brazilian was able to finish from he rebound. The Sevilla fans showed that their minds vere elsewhere, with chants of 'We love you, Puerta' choing down from the stands. Both teams, and ustrian referee Konrad Plautz, wore black armbands n memory of the player, and a minute's silence was bserved before kick-off.

Special circumstances'

The second half was too much for us," said Sevilla oach Ramos. "We wanted to win to dedicate the ame to Antonio but we at least played well. After osing a final, the team is not happy but we did our est." He continued: "We didn't have time to prepare ecause of the special circumstances. We had to try nd prepare on the board, not on the field. This has ot been a very typical week and people have worked ery hard to do what they could."

Milan coach Ancelotti said: "What has happened in the last few days with the death of Puerta created a unique atmosphere for this game. Obviously Sevilla were more affected by that than us but they played well particularly in the first half when we were a bit weary. But we recovered and did much better in the second half. We prepared really well, the team were compact and we kept calm when we were behind."

Final Result

31/8/07, Louis II, Monaco

AC Milan 3-1 Sevilla FC

Attendance: 17822

Milan: Dida, Kaladze, Gattuso (Emerson 72), Inzaghi (Gilardino 87), Seedorf (Brocchi 88), Nesta, Jankulovski, Pirlo, Kaká, Ambrosini, Oddo. Coach: Carlo Ancelotti (ITA)

Sevilla: Palop, Dragutinović, Dani Alves, Duda (Maresca 73), Jesús Navas, Poulsen, Renato, Kanouté, Escudé (Luis Fabiano 81), Martí (Kerzhakov 64), Keita. Coach: Juande Ramos (ESP)

Goal(s): 0-1 Renato 13, 1-1 Inzaghi 54, 2-1 Jankulovski 61, 3-1 Kaká 86

Yellow Card(s): Gattuso 6 (Milan), Duda 67 (Sevilla), Poulsen 69 (Sevilla)

Referee: Plautz (AUT)

AC Milan players and staff pose with the UEFA Super Cup after their 3-1 victory over Sevilla in Monaco

CHAPTER 05

UEFA INTERTOTO CUP 2007

In the second season since the UEFA Intertoto Cup expanded to offer eleven, rather than three, places in the UEFA Cup, new clubs and fresh nations again took their chance to gain kudos in the summer competition. FC Tobol Kostanay progressed all the way from the first of the three rounds to become the first side from Kazakhstan to win a European honour, while Sweden's Hammarby, who also entered at the initial stage, UD Leiria of Portugal and Romania's FC Oțelul Galați all became their countries' inaugural Intertoto victors. Of the other seven winners, only 2005 victors Hamburger SV and RC Lens had previously been on the roll of honour, which now also contains the names of Club Atlético de Madrid, UC Sampdoria and three clubs previously without European silverware, Aalborg BK, Blackburn Rovers FC and SK Rapid Wien.

FIRST ROUND

Among the 14 teams progressing from the first round were ŠK Slovan Bratislava, the 1968/69 UEFA Cup Winners' Cup winners and indeed one of the most successful teams in the pre-1995 Intertoto Cup.

They defeated Luxembourg's FC Differdange 03 5-0 on aggregate, but perhaps the tie of the round was that between Lithuania's FK Vėtra and Llanelli AFC of Wales. Vėtra won the first leg 3-1 but although Llanelli had to play the return at Carmarthen and trailed 6-3 overall at the break, Ryan Griffiths struck a second-half hat-trick to level the aggregate score – only for his team to exit on away goals.

First Round Results

23/6/07, Windsor Park, Belfast
Cliftonville FC 1-1 FC Dinaburg
Goal(s): 0-1 Sokolovs 20, 1-1 O'Connor 40
Referee: Stavrev (MKD)
1/7/07, Celtnieks, Daugavpils
FC Dinaburg 0-1 Cliftonville FC
Goal(s): 0-1 M. Holland 7
Referee: Wilmes (LUX)
Aggregate: 1-2; Cliftonville FC qualify.

23/6/07, Råsunda, Solna
Hammarby 1-0 KÍ Klaksvík
Goal(s): 1-0 Davies 3
Referee: Vialichka (BLR)
30/6/07, Toftir, Toftir
KÍ Klaksvík 1-2 Hammarby
Goal(s): 0-1 Jacobsen 34(og), 1-1 Ennigard 38, 1-2 Paulinho 58
Referee: Žuta (LTU)
Aggregate: 1-3; Hammarby qualify.

23/6/07, Estadi Comunal, Andorra La Vella
UE Sant Julià 2-3 FK Slavija Sarajevo
Goal(s): 0-1 Varela 23(og), 0-2 Jovanović 62, 1-2 Peppe 64, 2-2 Luis 67, 2-3 Spalević 87
Referee: Lautier (MLT)
30/6/07, Koševo, Sarajevo
FK Slavija Sarajevo 3-2 UE Sant Julià
Goal(s): 1-0 Jamina 22, 2-0 Fontan 65(og), 2-1 Varela 71, 2-2 Alejandro 88(p), 3-2 Vuksanović 90+4
Referee: Silagava (GEO)
Aggregate: 6-4; FK Slavija Sarajevo qualify.

23/6/07, NK Zagreb, Zagreb
NK Zagreb 2-1 KS Vllaznia
Goal(s): 0-1 Nora 3, 1-1 Nadarević 19, 2-1 Labudović 63
Referee: Müftüoglu (TUR)
30/6/07, Loro Boriçi, Shkoder
KS Vllaznia 1-0 NK Zagreb
Goal(s): 1-0 Nora 26
Referee: Attard (MLT)
Aggregate: 2-2; KS Vllaznia qualify on away goal.

23/6/07, Dasaki Achnas, Famagusta
Ethnikos Achnas FC 1-0 FK Makedonija Skopje
Goal(s): 1-0 Poyiatzis 6(p)
Referee: Whitby (WAL)

Slovan Bratislava fans give their team a ticker-tape welcome

/6/07, Gradski, Skopje
(Makedonija Skopje 2-0 Ethnikos Achnas FC
oal(s): 1-0 Stojanovski 13, 2-0 Stojanovski 65
eferee: Levi (ISR)
ggregate: 2-1; FK Makedonija Skopje qualify.

/6/07, Stroitel, Soligorsk
: Shakhtyor Soligorsk 4-1 FC Ararat Yerevan
oal(s): 1-0 Rios 22, 1-1 Marcos 41, 2-1 Gukailo 58, 3-1 Klimenko 69,
1 Nikiforenko 80
eferee: Kholmatov (KAZ)
'7/07, Republican, Yerevan
: Ararat Yerevan 2-0 FC Shakhtyor Soligorsk
oal(s): 1-0 N. Erzrumyan 32, 2-0 Marcos 54
eferee: Stanković (SRB)
ggregate: 3-4; FC Shakhtyor Soligorsk qualify.

/6/07, La Frontière, Esch-sur-Alzette
: Differdange 03 0-2 ŠK Slovan Bratislava
oal(s): 0-1 Poliaček 32, 0-2 Sedlák 86
eferee: Kovačić (CRO)
)/6/07, Tehelné Pole, Bratislava
(Slovan Bratislava 3-0 FC Differdange 03
oal(s): 1-0 Meszároš 4, 2-0 Masaryk 56, 3-0 Sylvestr 78
eferee: Amirkhanyan (ARM)
ggregate: 5-0; ŠK Slovan Bratislava qualify.

/6/07, Tofikh Bakhramov-Republic Stadium, Baku
(Bakı 1-1 FC Dacia Chişinău
oal(s): 0-1 Onila 45, 1-1 Andronic 80(og)
eferee: Bede (HUN)
)/6/07, Zimbru, Chisinau
C Dacia Chişinău 1-1 FK Bakı
oal(s): 1-0 Onila 7, 1-1 Mujiri 65
eferee: Trattou (CYP)
ggregate: 2-2; FC Dacia Chişinău qualify 3-1 on penalties.

/6/07, Tcentralny, Kostanay
C Tobol Kostanay 3-0 FC Zestafoni
oal(s): 1-0 Zhumaskaliev 61, 2-0 Baltiyev 63, 3-0 Bakaev 73
eferee: Jug (SVN)
)/6/07, Mikheil Meskhi, Tbilisi
C Zestafoni 2-0 FC Tobol Kostanay
oal(s): 1-0 Sajaia 3, 2-0 K. Chkhetiani 37
eferee: Svilokos (CRO)
ggregate: 2-3; FC Tobol Kostanay qualify.

/6/07, Laugardalsvöllur, Reykjavik
alur Reykjavík 0-2 Cork City FC
oal(s): 0-1 O'Brien 7, 0-2 Kearney 66
eferee: Gonchar (RUS)
)/6/07, Turner's Cross, Cork
ork City FC 0-1 Valur Reykjavík
oal(s): 0-1 Sigurdsson 22
eferee: Shandor (UKR)
ggregate: 2-1; Cork City FC qualify.

4/6/07, Hibernians Ground, Corradino
irkirkara FC 0-3 NK Maribor
oal(s): 0-1 Makriev 40, 0-2 Makriev 47, 0-3 Pekič 87
eferee: Borski (POL)
)/6/07, Ljudski vrt, Maribor
K Maribor 2-1 Birkirkara FC
oal(s): 1-0 Mezga 55, 1-1 M. Galea 57, 2-1 Vračko 78
eferee: Jareci (ALB)
ggregate: 5-1; NK Maribor qualify.

Maribor's Andrej Pečnik (left) takes on Jonathan Holland of Birkirkara

24/6/07, Gloria, Bistrita
CF Gloria 1922 Bistriţa 2-1 OFK Grbalj
Goal(s): 1-0 Zaharia 3, 1-1 Đalac 14, 2-1 Florea 88
Referee: Vejlgaard (DEN)
30/6/07, Pod Goricom - Gradski, Podgorica
OFK Grbalj 1-1 CF Gloria 1922 Bistriţa
Goal(s): 0-1 Coroian 42, 1-1 Đalac 44
Referee: Vervecken (BEL)
Aggregate: 2-3; CF Gloria 1922 Bistrita qualify.

24/6/07, Vetra, Vilnius
FK Vėtra 3-1 Llanelli AFC
Goal(s): 0-1 Mumford 53, 1-1 Šernas 57, 2-1 Stankevičius 72(p),
3-1 Milošeski 89
Referee: Reinert (FRO)
1/7/07, Richmond Park, Carmarthen
Llanelli AFC 5-3 FK Vėtra
Goal(s): 0-1 Severino 4, 1-1 Milošeski 17(og), 2-1 Thomas 38,
2-2 Stankevičius 43, 2-3 Juška 45+3, 3-3 Griffiths 54, 4-3 Griffiths 88,
5-3 Griffiths 90+3
Referee: Thorisson (ISL)
Aggregate: 6-6; FK Vėtra qualify on away goals.

24/6/07, Pohjola, Vantaa
FC Honka Espoo 0-0 FC TVMK Tallinn
Referee: Georgiev (BUL)
1/7/07, A Le Coq Arena, Tallinn
FC TVMK Tallinn 2-4 FC Honka Espoo
Goal(s): 0-1 Huuhtanen 6, 1-1 Terehhov 68, 1-2 Puustinen 69,
1-3 Hakanpää 74, 1-4 Puustinen 84, 2-4 Konsa 88
Referee: Mrković (BIH)
Aggregate: 2-4; FC Honka Espoo qualify.

SECOND ROUND

The 14 first-round victors were joined by as many new entrants, among them SK Rapid Wien. The famous Austrian club pipped ŠK Slovan Bratislava 3-2 on aggregate having held on in the second leg in Bratislava after going behind to an early goal. Trabzonspor saw off Albania's KS Vllaznia 10-0 over two legs. Five first-round survivors marched on, most dramatically Romania's CF Gloria 1922 Bistrița, who won 2-0 at Maccabi Haifa FC, lost by the same score at home, then prevailed 3-2 on penalties.

Legia ousted

Elsewhere, Moldova's FC Dacia Chişinău saw off Switzerland's FC St. Gallen on spot kicks, Hammarby defeated Cork City FC 2-1 on aggregate, FC Tobol Kostanay beat FC Slovan Liberec 3-1 thanks to a remarkable 2-0 second-leg win in the Czech Republic, while FK Vėtra were awarded their tie against Legia Warszawa by default due to trouble involving away supporters in the first leg in Lithuania.

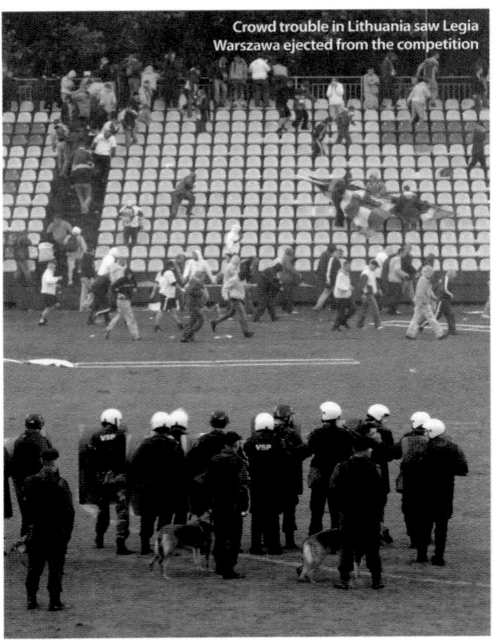
Crowd trouble in Lithuania saw Legia Warszawa ejected from the competition

Second Round Results

7/7/07, Ljudski vrt, Maribor
NK Maribor 2-0 FK Hajduk Kula
Goal(s): 1-0 Makriev 29, 2-0 Samardžič 51
Referee: Vad (HUN)
14/7/07, FK Crvena Zvezda, Belgrade
FK Hajduk Kula 5-0 NK Maribor
Goal(s): 1-0 Vasiljević 15, 2-0 Komazec 30, 3-0 Perić 38, 4-0 Radanović 45+1, 5-0 Komazec 67(p)
Referee: Malcolm (NIR)
Aggregate: 5-2; FK Hajduk Kula qualify.

7/7/07, Gradski, Skopje
FK Makedonija Skopje 0-4 PFC Cherno More Varna
Goal(s): 0-1 Bachev 53, 0-2 Da Silva 72, 0-3 Da Silva 73, 0-4 Stoyanov 8
Referee: Pérez Burrull (ESP)
14/7/07, Naftex, Burgas
PFC Cherno More Varna 3-0 FK Makedonija Skopje
Goal(s): 1-0 D. Georgiev 12, 2-0 Manolov 46, 3-0 Dimov 80
Referee: Van De Velde (BEL)
Aggregate: 7-0; PFC Cherno More Varna qualify.

7/7/07, Chornomorets, Odessa
FC Chornomorets Odesa 4-2 FC Shakhtyor Soligorsk
Goal(s): 1-0 Bugaiov 13, 1-1 Rios 14, 2-1 Venhlynskiy 18, 3-1 Bugaio 67, 3-2 Martinovich 79, 4-2 Bugaiov 88
Referee: Havrilla (SVK)
15/7/07, Stroitel, Soligorsk
FC Shakhtyor Soligorsk 0-2 FC Chornomorets Odesa
Goal(s): 0-1 Poltavets 27, 0-2 Hryshko 64
Referee: Laursen (DEN)
Aggregate: 2-6; FC Chornomorets Odesa qualify.

7/7/07, Jules Otten, Gent
KAA Gent 2-0 Cliftonville FC
Goal(s): 1-0 Foley 8, 2-0 Foley 63
Referee: Paraty (POR)
14/7/07, Windsor Park, Belfast
Cliftonville FC 0-4 KAA Gent
Goal(s): 0-1 Foley 12, 0-2 Olufade 44, 0-3 De Beule 45, 0-4 Olufade 8
Referee: Mikulski (POL)
Aggregate: 0-6; KAA Gent qualify.

7/7/07, Turner's Cross, Cork
Cork City FC 1-1 Hammarby
Goal(s): 1-0 O'Donovan 10, 1-1 Murray 57(og)
Referee: Lajuks (LVA)
14/7/07, Råsunda, Solna
Hammarby 1-0 Cork City FC
Goal(s): 1-0 Monteiro 53
Referee: Matejek (CZE)
Aggregate: 2-1; Hammarby qualify.

7/7/07, ZTE, Zalaegerszeg
Zalaegerszegi TE 0-3 FC Rubin Kazan
Goal(s): 0-1 Volkov 21, 0-2 Volkov 66, 0-3 Volkov 80(p)
Referee: Schörgenhofer (AUT)

Gent defender Aleksandar Mutavdžić and Cliftonville striker Chris Scannell dispute possession

14/7/07, Tsentralnyi, Kazan
FC Rubin Kazan 2-0 Zalaegerszegi TE
Goal(s): 1-0 Volkov 37(p), 2-0 Jean Narde 67
Referee: Constantin (ROU)
Aggregate: 5-0; FC Rubin Kazan qualify.

7/7/07, Gerhard Hanappi, Vienna
SK Rapid Wien 3-1 ŠK Slovan Bratislava
Goal(s): 1-0 Hofmann 31, 2-0 Bazina 38, 3-0 Hofmann 53, 3-1 Slovák 88
Referee: Banari (MDA)
14/7/07, Tehelné Pole, Bratislava
ŠK Slovan Bratislava 1-0 SK Rapid Wien
Goal(s): 1-0 Dobrotka 18
Referee: Todorov (BUL)
Aggregate: 2-3; SK Rapid Wien qualify.

7/7/07, Tcentralny, Kostanay
FC Tobol Kostanay 1-1 FC Slovan Liberec
Goal(s): 0-1 Nezmar 34, 1-1 Baltiyev 40
Referee: Brugger (AUT)
15/7/07, U Nisy, Liberec
FC Slovan Liberec 0-2 FC Tobol Kostanay
Goal(s): 0-1 Zhumaskaliev 16, 0-2 Ostapenko 35
Referee: Vuorela (FIN)
Aggregate: 1-3; FC Tobol Kostanay qualify.

7/7/07, Kiryat Eliazer, Haifa
Maccabi Haifa FC 0-2 CF Gloria 1922 Bistriţa
Goal(s): 0-1 Tilincă 12, 0-2 Zaharia 41
Referee: Oriekhov (UKR)
14/7/07, Gloria, Bistrita
CF Gloria 1922 Bistriţa 0-2 Maccabi Haifa FC
Goal(s): 0-1 Maimon 6, 0-2 Hemed 65
Referee: Panić (BIH)
Aggregate: 2-2; CF Gloria 1922 Bistriţa qualify 3-2 on penalties.

7/7/07, Zimbru, Chisinau
FC Dacia Chişinău 0-1 FC St. Gallen
Goal(s): 0-1 Garat 7
Referee: Jech (CZE)
14/7/07, Espenmoos, St Gallen
FC St. Gallen 0-1 FC Dacia Chişinău
Goal(s): 0-1 Lipa 56
Referee: Mikołajewski (POL)
Aggregate: 1-1; FC Dacia Chişinău qualify 3-0 on penalties.

7/7/07, Koševo II, Sarajevo
FK Slavija Sarajevo 0-0 FC Oţelul Galaţi
Referee: Kever (SUI)
14/7/07, Oţelul, Galati
FC Oţelul Galaţi 3-0 FK Slavija Sarajevo
Goal(s): 1-0 Jula 31, 2-0 Jula 42, 3-0 Paraschiv 70
Referee: Fábian (HUN)
Aggregate: 3-0; FC Oţelul Galaţi qualify.

8/7/07, Pohjola, Vantaa
FC Honka Espoo 2-2 Aalborg BK
Goal(s): 0-1 Lindström 1, 1-1 Porokara 8(p), 1-2 Prica 23, 2-2 Puustinen 30
Referee: Collum (SCO)
14/7/07, Aalborg, Aalborg
Aalborg BK 1-1 FC Honka Espoo
Goal(s): 0-1 Porokara 50, 1-1 Nomvethe 61
Referee: Filipović (SRB)
Aggregate: 3-3; Aalborg BK qualify on away goals.

8/7/07, Hüseyin Avni Aker, Trabzon
Trabzonspor 6-0 KS Vllaznia
Goal(s): 1-0 Ersen Martin 12, 2-0 Ceyhun Eriş 32, 3-0 Çağdaş Atan 39, 4-0 Ersen Martin 51, 5-0 Ersen Martin 58, 6-0 Ömer Riza 89
Referee: Nijhuis (NED)
14/7/07, Loro Boriçi, Shkoder
KS Vllaznia 0-4 Trabzonspor
Goal(s): 0-1 Umut Bulut 47, 0-2 Yattara 49, 0-3 Yusuf Kurtuluş 52, 0-4 Umut Bulut 89
Referee: Kelly (IRL)
Aggregate: 0-10; Trabzonspor qualify.

FK Vėtra w/o Legia Warszawa

THIRD ROUND

The eight top seeds entered the fray in the third round to join the battle for the eleven UEFA Cup second qualifying round berths on offer.

Forlán decider

Former European champions Hamburger SV were held 1-1 at FC Dacia Chişinău before a 4-0 home win, their aggregate score topped only by Blackburn Rovers FC, who totalled six goals without reply against FK Vėtra. Club Atlético de Madrid lost 2-1 at CF Gloria 1922 Bistriţa but Diego Forlán's early second-leg strike took them through on the away-goals rule.

Hammarby progressed in the same fashion after two draws with FC Utrecht, while UD Leiria lost 1-0 in Belgrade to FK Hajduk Kula before Éder's last-gasp goal forced extra-time in the return, after which the home side prevailed 4-2 on aggregate. While Gloria had fallen just short, compatriots FC Oţelul Galaţi moved on thanks to a pair of 2-1 victories against Trabzonspor.

Lens through

Ruslan Baltiyev's goal gave FC Tobol Kostanay a 1-0 first-leg win at home to OFI Crete FC, and they held on in the return before Andrei Kharabara put the result beyond doubt late on. RC Lens defeated FC Chernomorets Odesa 3-1 overall in the highlight of Guy Roux's brief reign as coach, while UC Sampdoria produced two 1-0 wins against PFC Cherno More Varna.

Third Round Results

21/7/07, Gloria, Bistrita
CF Gloria 1922 Bistriţa 2-1 Club Atlético de Madrid
Goal(s): 1-0 Zaharia 8, 2-0 Tilincă 39, 2-1 Seitaridis 55
Referee: Rizzoli (ITA)
28/7/07, Vicente Calderón, Madrid
Club Atlético de Madrid 1-0 CF Gloria 1922 Bistriţa
Goal(s): 1-0 Forlán 11
Referee: Richmond (SCO)
Aggregate: 2-2; Club Atlético de Madrid qualify on away goal.

21/7/07, Oţelul, Galati
FC Oţelul Galaţi 2-1 Trabzonspor
Goal(s): 1-0 Stan 27, 1-1 Ersen Martin 83, 2-1 Paraschiv 86
Referee: Muniz Fernandez (ESP)

Jason Roberts gets a hug from Robbie Savage as Blackburn Rovers cement their advantage over FK Vėtra at Ewood Park

8/7/07, Hüseyin Avni Aker, Trabzon
Trabzonspor 1-2 FC Oţelul Galaţi
Goal(s): 1-0 Ceyhun Eriş 8, 1-1 Szekely 12, 1-2 Jula 90+1(p)
Referee: Sukhina (RUS)
Aggregate: 2-4; FC Oţelul Galaţi qualify.

1/7/07, Naftex, Burgas
PFC Cherno More Varna 0-1 UC Sampdoria
Goal(s): 0-1 Lucchini 43
Referee: Sandmoen (NOR)
8/7/07, Luigi Ferraris, Genoa
UC Sampdoria 1-0 PFC Cherno More Varna
Goal(s): 1-0 Maggio 90+1
Referee: Kuipers (NED)
Aggregate: 2-0; UC Sampdoria qualify.

1/7/07, Chornomorets, Odessa
FC Chornomorets Odesa 0-0 RC Lens
Referee: Skjerven (NOR)
8/7/07, Stade Félix-Bollaert, Lens
RC Lens 3-1 FC Chornomorets Odesa
Goal(s): 0-1 Venhlynskiy 10, 1-1 Coulibaly 19, 2-1 Akalé 39, 3-1 Akalé 72
Referee: Graefe (GER)
Aggregate: 3-1; RC Lens qualify.

21/7/07, Jules Otten, Gent
KAA Gent 1-1 Aalborg BK
Goal(s): 1-0 Olufade 47(p), 1-1 Nomvethe 55
Referee: Laperrière (SUI)
29/7/07, Aalborg, Aalborg
Aalborg BK 2-1 KAA Gent
Goal(s): 0-1 Olufade 27, 1-1 Califf 31, 2-1 Johansson 78
Referee: Corpodean (ROU)
Aggregate: 3-2; Aalborg BK qualify.

21/7/07, Gerhard Hanappi, Vienna
SK Rapid Wien 3-1 FC Rubin Kazan
Goal(s): 0-1 Ryazantsev 29, 1-1 Hofmann 69, 2-1 Bilić 80(p), 3-1 Hofmann 90+3
Referee: McKeon (IRL)
29/7/07, Tsentralnyi, Kazan
FC Rubin Kazan 0-0 SK Rapid Wien
Referee: Johannesson (SWE)
Aggregate: 1-3; SK Rapid Wien qualify.

21/7/07, Zimbru, Chisinau
FC Dacia Chişinău 1-1 Hamburger SV
Goal(s): 1-0 Boicenco 7, 1-1 Van der Vaart 70
Referee: Paixão (POR)
29/7/07, Arena Hamburg, Hamburg
Hamburger SV 4-0 FC Dacia Chişinău
Goal(s): 1-0 Kompany 50, 2-0 Van der Vaart 71, 3-0 Benjamin 76, 4-0 Jarolím 89
Referee: Bebek (CRO)
Aggregate: 5-1; Hamburger SV qualify.

22/7/07, Råsunda, Solna
Hammarby 0-0 FC Utrecht
Referee: Kalt (FRA)
29/7/07, Galgenwaard, Utrecht
FC Utrecht 1-1 Hammarby
Goal(s): 1-0 Nelisse 64, 1-1 D. Johansson 66
Referee: Dean (ENG)
Aggregate: 1-1; Hammarby qualify on away goal.

Andreas Johansson turns away in delight after scoring AaB's winning goal against Gent

22/7/07, FK Crvena Zvezda, Belgrade
FK Hajduk Kula 1-0 UD Leiria
Goal(s): 1-0 Perić 42
Referee: Yıldırım (TUR)
29/7/07, Dr. Magalhães Pessoa, Leiria
UD Leiria 4-1 FK Hajduk Kula
Goal(s): 1-0 Éder 90+3, 2-0 Laranjeiro 97(p), 2-1 Bogić 107(p), 3-1 Sougou 112, 4-1 Laranjeiro 120(p)
Referee: Stuchlik (AUT)
Aggregate: 4-2; UD Leiria qualify after extra time.

22/7/07, Vetra, Vilnius
FK Vètra 0-2 Blackburn Rovers FC
Goal(s): 0-1 McCarthy 30, 0-2 Derbyshire 81
Referee: Asumaa (FIN)
28/7/07, Ewood Park, Blackburn
Blackburn Rovers FC 4-0 FK Vètra
Goal(s): 1-0 Gamst Pedersen 24, 2-0 Roberts 47, 3-0 McCarthy 53, 4-0 Gamst Pedersen 54
Referee: Weiner (GER)
Aggregate: 6-0; Blackburn Rovers FC qualify.

22/7/07, Tcentralny, Kostanay
FC Tobol Kostanay 1-0 OFI Crete FC
Goal(s): 1-0 Baltiyev 29
Referee: Ledentu (FRA)
29/7/07, Pankritio, Heraklion
OFI Crete FC 0-1 FC Tobol Kostanay
Goal(s): 0-1 Kharabara 86
Referee: Balaj (ROU)
Aggregate: 0-2; FC Tobol Kostanay qualify.

ALBANIA

KF TIRANA

UEFA CHAMPIONS LEAGUE

First Qualifying Round - NK Domžale (SVN)
A 0-1
Hidi, Abazaj, Çapja, Dede, Duro, Fortuzi (Merkoçi 69), Hajdari (Deliallisi 78), Muka, Sina, E. Xhafa, Sefa (Bakalli 69).
Yellow Card(s): E. Xhafa 83, Sina 90+2
H 1-2 *Duro (74)*
Hidi, Abazaj, Bakalli, Çapja, Dede, Deliallisi, Duro, Fortuzi (Merkoçi 61), Muka, Sina (Sefa 70), E. Xhafa.
Yellow Card(s): Duro 34

KS BESA

UEFA CUP

First Qualifying Round - FK Bežanija (SRB)
A 2-2 *Ishaka (49), Elokan (90)*
Zendeli, Belisha, Dragusha, Elokan (Kaja 90+3), Krasniqi, Veliaj (Alikaj 60), Xhihani, Ramadani, Fortunat (Nuhiji 72), Nana, Ishaka.
Yellow Card(s): Krasniqi 57
H 0-0
Zendeli, Belisha, Arapi, Alikaj (Fortunat 83), Krasniqi (Elokan 46), Veliaj (Kaja 90+2), Xhihani, Ramadani, Hoxha, Nana, Ishaka.
Red Card(s): Hoxha 65
Yellow Card(s): Nana 18, Alikaj 52, Hoxha 53, Hoxha 65

Second Qualifying Round - PFC Litex Lovech (BUL)
H 0-3
Zendeli, Alikaj, Elokan (Arapi 46), Ishaka, Krasniqi, Mërtiri, Nana, Veliaj (Nuhiji 46), Xhihani (Kaja 60), Ramadani, Duro.
A 0-3
Dura, Arapi, Hoxha, Kaja, Krasniqi, Lila, Nuhiji (Alikaj 90), Okshtuni, Veliaj, Xhihani, Ramadani.
Yellow Card(s): Arapi 16, Ramadani 44

KS TEUTA

UEFA CUP

First Qualifying Round - NK Slaven Koprivnica (CRO)
A 2-6 *D. Xhafaj (10), Brahja (65)*
Kapllani, Kapaj, Vrapi, Vila, Devolli, D. Xhafaj, Kuli (Fagu 46), Mado (Blloku 85), Mançaku, Pashaj (Brahja 50), Buna.
Red Card(s): Kapaj 22
Yellow Card(s): Vrapi 17, Kapaj 20, Kapaj 22, Pashaj 25
H 2-2 *Kuli (45, 74)*
Kapllani, Brahja (Stafa 90), Vrapi, Vila, Devolli, D. Xhafaj, Kuli, Mado, Bl (Likmeta 88), Sula (Hashani 27), Buna.
Yellow Card(s): Kuli 45

KS VLLAZNIA

UEFA INTERTOTO CUP

First Round - NK Zagreb (CRO)
A 1-2 *Nora (3)*
Grima, K. Dalipi (Cani 71), Kaçi (Hoti 75), Kotrri, Lici, Lika, Nora (Tafili 9 Teli, Osja, Tanko, Ahi.
Red Card(s): Ahi 73
Yellow Card(s): Lika 50, Ahi 70, Ahi 73
H 1-0 *Nora (26)*
Grima, Kaçi (Tafili 90+2), Kotrri, Lici, Lika, Nora (Beqiri 89), Sukaj (Sina 69), Teli, Osja, Hoti, Tanko.
Yellow Card(s): Kotrri 48, Tanko 66

Second Round - Trabzonspor (TUR)
A 0-6
Grima (Olsi 46), Sukaj, Kaçi, Kotrri (Ahi 46), Lici, Lika, Nora, Teli, Osja, T Hoti (Beqiri 70).
H 0-4
Olsi, Sinani (Ahi 58), Hoti (Tafili 69), Kaçi, Kotrri, Lici, Lika, Nora, Teli, O Dalipi 58), Tanko.
Yellow Card(s): Nora 58

ANDORRA

FC RÀNGER'S

UEFA CHAMPIONS LEAGUE

First Qualifying Round - FC Sheriff (MDA)
A 0-2
Rodríguez, Venturi, Moreira (Gómez Pérez 71), Porta, Caçador (N. Ma 90), Albanell, Cunha Gomes Da, Flavio, Walker (Serrano Contrer 16), M Somoza.
Red Card(s): Rodríguez 15, Albanell 86
Yellow Card(s): Somoza 26, Venturi 48, Mario 50, Albanell 67, Alban
H 0-3
Iñaki, Venturi, Moreira (Gonçalves Peire 66), Porta, Caçador (N. Martín 78), González, Flavio, Walker, Mario, Gómez Pérez, Somoza (Combarro
Yellow Card(s): González 80

FC SANTA COLOMA

UEFA CUP

Qualifying Round - Maccabi Tel-Aviv FC (ISR)
Fernández (57)
ndez Lizarte, Ayala, Fernández, Gil, M. Urbani (Aguirre Santinelli 74), bani (Toscano Beltrán 68), Rodriguez Soria, Dos Santos (Gabriel 87), so Da Cunha, Alvarez, Genís García.
w Card(s): Alvarez 19, Fernández Lizarte 83, Genís García 88, Ayala 90

ndez Lizarte, Ayala, Fernández, Gil, Alvarez, M. Urbani (Costa 88), García, N. Urbani, Rodriguez Soria, Dos Santos (Toscano Beltrán 46), so Da Cunha (Gabriel 54).
w Card(s): Rodriguez Soria 31, Alfonso Da Cunha 34, Genís García abriel 78, M. Urbani 85

UE SANT JULIÀ

UEFA INTERTOTO CUP

Round - FK Slavija Sarajevo (BIH)
Peppe (64), Luis (67)
onti, Luis, Fontan, Pacha (Goldschmidt 66), Peppe, Alejandro (Lobo arela, Wagner, Chino (Joval 85), Abdian, Spano.
w Card(s): Varela 25
Varela (71), Alejandro (88p)
onti, Luis, Fontan (Lucho 79), Peppe, Mauri (Rodríguez 89), Alejandro, , Wagner, Chino, Abdian (Lobo 69), Spano.
w Card(s): Alejandro 17, Varela 33, Fontan 42, Spano 63, Mauri 77

ARMENIA

FC PYUNIK

UEFA CHAMPIONS LEAGUE

Qualifying Round - Derry City FC (IRL)

rov, A. Mkrtchyan (Sahakyan 78), Nazaryan, Gevgozyan (Hzeyna 46), jyan, Arzumanyan, Dokhoyan, Yedigaryan, Ghazaryan (Mkhitaryan adevosyan, Hovsepyan.
w Card(s): Tadevosyan 44, Hzeyna 55
Avetisyan (28), Ghazaryan (67)
rov, Hovsepyan, Tadevosyan, A. Mkrtchyan, Nazaryan (Yedigaryan vetisyan (Mkhitaryan 70), Mkhitaryan, Pachajyan, Arzumanyan, aryan (Sahakyan 81), Dokhoyan.
w Card(s): Avetisyan 45, Tadevosyan 56, Mkhitaryan 87

nd Qualifying Round - FC Shakhtar Donetsk (UKR)

rov (López 44), Arzumanyan, Avetisyan (Sahakyan 46), Dokhoyan, epyan, Mkhitaryan, A. Mkrtchyan, Nazaryan (Mkhitaryan 46), jyan, Ghazaryan, Yedigaryan.
w Card(s): Mkhitaryan 20, Avetisyan 24, Hovsepyan 71
Ghazaryan (31)
, Arzumanyan, Dokhoyan, Hovsepyan, Hzeyna (Sahakyan 75), aryan, A. Mkrtchyan, Pachajyan (Gharabaghtsyan 88), Tadevosyan, aryan (Nazaryan 57), Yedigaryan.
ard(s): Yedigaryan 52

FC BANANTS

UEFA CUP

First Qualifying Round - BSC Young Boys (SUI)
H 1-1 *Kakosyan (68)*
Radača, Simonyan, Cherevko, Balabekyan, Melikyan, Ara Hakobyan, H. Grigoryan, Melkonyan (Muradyan 86), Jenebyan (Bareghamyan 55), Kakosyan, Khachatryan (Sargsyan 81).
A 0-4
Radača, Simonyan, Cherevko, Balabekyan (Muradyan 72), Ara Hakobyan, H. Grigoryan, Arakelyan, Melkonyan, Jenebyan (Karapetyan 36), Kakosyan, Khachatryan (Bareghamyan 43).
Yellow Card(s): H. Grigoryan 15, Ara Hakobyan 62

FC MIKA

UEFA CUP

First Qualifying Round - MTK Budapest (HUN)
A 1-2 *Kléber Rodrigues (45)*
F. Hakobyan, Antonyan (Acleisson 59), Alex, Thiago (Davtyan 69), Fursin, Mikaelyan, Kléber Nascimento (Campos Penteado 82), Petikyan, Ristich, Kléber Rodrigues, Shahgeldyan.
H 1-0 *Adamyan (26)*
F. Hakobyan, Adamyan (Meytikhanyan 83), Antonyan, Campos Penteado (Mikaelyan 52), Alex, Thiago, Fursin, Kléber Nascimento (Davtyan 69), Petikyan, Ristich, Kléber Rodrigues.
Yellow Card(s): Ristich 70

Second Qualifying Round - FC Artmedia Petržalka (SVK)
H 2-1 *Shahgeldyan (8), Alex (80)*
F. Hakobyan, Adamyan (Mikaelyan 39), Antonyan (Meloyan 78), Shahgeldyan (Davtyan 60), Alex, Thiago, Fursin, Kléber Nascimento, Petikyan, Ristich, Kléber Rodrigues.
Yellow Card(s): Antonyan 40
A 0-2
F. Hakobyan, Antonyan, Alex, Thiago (Davtyan 68), Fursin (Meloyan 45), Mikaelyan, Kléber Nascimento, Petikyan, Ristich, Kléber Rodrigues, Shahgeldyan (Campos Penteado 72).
Yellow Card(s): Kléber Rodrigues 14, Petikyan 18

FC ARARAT YEREVAN

UEFA INTERTOTO CUP

First Round - FC Shakhtyor Soligorsk (BLR)
A 1-4 *Marcos (41)*
Sargsyan, Harutyunyan, V. Minasyan, Mkoyan, Renato, Nranyan (H. Hovhannisyan 62), Petrosyan, Marcos, Simonyan (Movsisyan 77), Artur Voskanyan, A. Minasyan.

Yellow Card(s): Mkoyan 22
H 2-0 *N. Erzrumyan (32), Marcos (54)*
G. Hovhannisyan, N. Erzrumyan, Harutyunyan (Movsisyan 72), V. Minasyan, Mkoyan, Renato, Petrosyan (Grigoryan 85), Marcos, Simonyan, Artur Voskanyan, A. Minasyan.

AUSTRIA

FC SALZBURG

UEFA CHAMPIONS LEAGUE

Second Qualifying Round - FK Ventspils (LVA)
A 3-0 *Aufhauser (20, 27, 83p)*
Ochs, Aufhauser, Carboni, Dudić, N. Kovač (Leitgeb 74), Piták, Steinhöfer, Vargas, Vonlanthen (Ježek 85), Zickler (Lokvenc 74), Sekagya.
H 4-0 *Aufhauser (9), Dudić (48), Ilić (77), Leitgeb (90+2)*
Ochs, Aufhauser, Carboni, Dudić, Ježek (Ilić 71), Lokvenc, Steinhöfer (Alex 78), Vonlanthen (Janočko 56), Miyamoto, Sekagya, Leitgeb.

Third Qualifying Round - FC Shakhtar Donetsk (UKR)
H 1-0 *Zickler (10p)*
Ochs, Aufhauser, Carboni, Dudić, N. Kovač, Leitgeb, Miyamoto, Sekagya, Steinhöfer, Vonlanthen (Piták 89), Zickler (Lokvenc 85).
Yellow Card(s): Aufhauser 35, N. Kovač 49, Dudić 51, Zickler 65
A 1-3 *Meyer (5)*
Ochs, Aufhauser (Lokvenc 89), Carboni, N. Kovač, Leitgeb, Meyer, Miyamoto, Sekagya, Steinhöfer, Vonlanthen, Zickler.
Yellow Card(s): Aufhauser 36, Sekagya 77

UEFA CUP

First Round - AEK Athens FC (GRE)
A 0-3
Ochs, Carboni, Dudić, N. Kovač (Ježek 60), Leitgeb, Meyer (Vargas 46), Piták, Sekagya, Steinhöfer, Zickler, Rakić (Lokvenc 57).
Red Card(s): Vargas 72
Yellow Card(s): Carboni 38, Vargas 52, Lokvenc 69, Zickler 72, Vargas 72
H 1-0 *Lokvenc (20)*
Ochs, Aufhauser, Carboni, Dudić, Ježek, Leitgeb (Janočko 64), Lokvenc, Meyer, Steinhöfer, Vonlanthen (Rakić 60), Bodnár.
Yellow Card(s): Dudić 36

FK AUSTRIA WIEN

UEFA CUP

Second Qualifying Round - FK Jablonec 97 (CZE)
H 4-3 *Ertl (8), Kuljic (20, 64), Lasnik (47)*
Sáfár, Aigner (Lafata 74), Blanchard, Ertl, Schiemer, Majstorovic, Bąk, Sulimani (Okotie 79), Kuljic, Ačimovič (Sariyar 57), Lasnik.
Yellow Card(s): Blanchard 9, Sariyar 61
A 1-1 *Sariyar (39)*
Sáfár, Blanchard, Ertl, Schiemer, Majstorovic, Bąk, Sariyar, Kuljic (Aigner 68), Ačimovič (Gercaliu 88), Standfest, Lasnik (Lafata 65).
Yellow Card(s): Schiemer 27, Lasnik 60

First Round - Vålerenga Fotball (NOR)
H 2-0 *Kuljic (41), Lasnik (62)*
Sáfár, Blanchard, Gercaliu (Majstorovic 71), Schiemer, Aigner, Bąk, Sar Kuljic (Mair 84), Ačimovič, Standfest, Lasnik (Sulimani 81).
Yellow Card(s): Sariyar 83
A 2-2 *Kuljic (22), Ačimovič (90+1)*
Sáfár (Fornezzi 46), Bąk, Troyansky, Blanchard, Gercaliu (Majstorovic 8 Lafata (Metz 76), Schiemer, Sariyar, Kuljic, Ačimovič, Standfest.
Yellow Card(s): Blanchard 58, Sariyar 88

Group H
Match 1 - FC Girondins de Bordeaux (FRA)
H 1-2 *Kuljic (5)*
Sáfár, Troyansky, Bąk, Gercaliu, Metz, Schiemer, Sariyar, Ačimovič (Las 83), Standfest, Kuljic (Mair 75), Lafata (Sulimani 64).
Yellow Card(s): Metz 51, Bąk 88, Troyansky 90, Sariyar 90+3
Match 2 - Helsingborgs IF (SWE)
A 0-3
Fornezzi, Troyansky (Ertl 82), Bąk, Schiemer, Gercaliu, Metz (Sulimani Standfest, Ačimovič, Aigner, Okotie (Mair 72), Lafata.
Match 3 - Panionios GSS (GRE)
H 0-1
Fornezzi, Majstorovic, Bąk, Blanchard, Okotie (Lafata 80), Lasnik (Mair Ertl (Sulimani 64), Schiemer, Sariyar, Ačimovič, Standfest.
Yellow Card(s): Sariyar 28, Sulimani 90+1
Match 4 - Galatasaray AŞ (TUR)
A 0-0
Fornezzi, Troyansky (Schiemer 86), Ertl, Sariyar, Majstorovic, Mair (Aig 75), Blanchard, Metz, Lasnik, Ačimovič, Lafata (Okotie 79).

SV RIED

UEFA CUP

First Qualifying Round - PFK Neftçi (AZE)
H 3-1 *Drechsel (2), Brenner (87), Salihi (90+1)*
Berger, Brenner, Damjanović, Drechsel, Jank, Kujabi (Erbek 53), Rząsa Kovacevic (Toth 46), Đokić (Salihi 73), Dospel, Pichorner.
Yellow Card(s): Pichorner 29
A 1-2 *Salihi (85)*
Berger, Brenner, Drechsel, Glasner, Hackmair (Kovacevic 75), Jank, Rz Toth (Salihi 46), Đokić (Riegler 87), Erbek, Pichorner.
Yellow Card(s): Drechsel 35, Hans Peter Berger 56, Rząsa 86

Second Qualifying Round - FC Sion (SUI)
H 1-1 *Dospel (66)*
Berger, Brenner, Damjanović (Salihi 80), Drechsel, Erbek, Glasner, Hackmair, Jank, Pichorner (Kujabi 56), Rząsa, Toth (Dospel 56).
Yellow Card(s): Toth 24, Pichorner 35, Drechsel 62, Kujabi 76, Erbek Glasner 86
A 0-3
Berger, Jank, Glasner, Rząsa, Toth (Kujabi 56), Damjanović (Đokić 35), Erbek, Salihi (Muslic 73), Brenner, Hackmair, Dospel.
Yellow Card(s): Erbek 65, Dospel 67, Rząsa 75

SV MATTERSBURG

UEFA CUP

Qualifying Round - FK Aktobe (KAZ)

r, Atan, Csizmadia, Jancker, Kovrig, Kühbauer, Mravac, Pöllhuber
er 83), Schmidt, Sedloski, Wagner.
w Card(s): Schmidt 36, Kovrig 55
Jancker (22), Wagner (62), Csizmadia (67), Kovrig (90+2)
r, Atan, Csizmadia, Jancker, Kovrig, Kühbauer, Mörz, Mravac, Schmidt,
ski, Wagner.
Card(s): Mravac 76
w Card(s): Jancker 8, Kühbauer 78, Sedloski 81

nd Qualifying Round - FC Basel 1893 (SUI)
Nakata (20og)
r, Atan, Csizmadia, Jancker (Bürger 83), Kovrig, Kühbauer, Mörz,
noski (Pauschenwein 26), Schmidt, Sedloski, Wagner.
Card(s): Atan 17
w Card(s): Atan 8, Atan 17, Sedloski 36, Kovrig 77

r, Pöllhuber, Csizmadia, Jancker (Malić 66), Bürger, Kühbauer, Mörz
en 88), Naumoski (Lindner 83), Schmidt, Pauschenwein, Wagner.
w Card(s): Pauschenwein 12, Pöllhuber 64, Bürger 74, Naumoski 82

SK RAPID WIEN

UEFA INTERTOTO CUP

nd Round - ŠK Slovan Bratislava (SVK)
Hofmann (31, 53), Bazina (38)
r, Bazina, Bilić, Bošković, Hiden, Hofmann (Eder 79), Korkmaz (Harding
ara, Thonhofer, Patocka, Heikkinen (Kulovits 79).
w Card(s): Thonhofer 42, Heikkinen 50, Patocka 66, Hofmann 75,
ing 90

r, Bazina (Eder 76), Bilić, Bošković, Dober, Hofmann, Korkmaz,
vits, Sara, Patocka, Heikkinen.
Card(s): Kulovits 75
w Card(s): Kulovits 19, Patocka 54, Kulovits 75, Bošković 80, Payer 90+3

d Round - FC Rubin Kazan (RUS)
Hofmann (69, 90+3), Bilić (80p)
r, Bazina, Bilić, Bošković, Dober (Thonhofer 56), Heikkinen, Hiden,
nann, Korkmaz, Sara (Katzer 56), Tokić.

r, Bazina (Korkmaz 61), Bilić, Bošković, Dober, Hiden, Hofmann, Katzer,
ka, Tokić, Heikkinen.
w Card(s): Dober 27, Patocka 90+1

UEFA CUP

nd Qualifying Round - FC Dinamo Tbilisi (GEO)
Fabiano (24), Hofmann (39), Bazina (53)
r, Bazina, Bošković, Fabiano, Heikkinen (Sara 66), Hofmann (Bilić 66),
r, Kavlak (Dober 66), Tokić, Thonhofer, Patocka.
w Card(s): Thonhofer 57
Bazina (30), Bilić (54), Hofmann (59, 75p), Kavlak (73)
r, Bazina, Bilić, Bošković (Hoffer 56), Dober, Heikkinen (Kulovits 46),
nann, Katzer, Kavlak, Patocka (Eder 56), Hiden.

Round - RSC Anderlecht (BEL)
Hofmann (82)
r, Bazina (Hoffer 75), Bilić, Bošković, Heikkinen, Hiden, Hofmann (Eder
avlak (Korkmaz 61), Patocka, Thonhofer, Tokić.
w Card(s): Bilić 34

H 0-1
Payer, Bazina (Fabiano 58), Bilić, Bošković, Heikkinen, Hiden, Hofmann, Korkmaz (Kavlak 21), Patocka, Thonhofer, Tokić (Harding 73).
Yellow Card(s): Fabiano 75

AZERBAIJAN

FK XÄZÄR LÄNKÄRAN

UEFA CHAMPIONS LEAGUE

First Qualifying Round - NK Dinamo Zagreb (CRO)
H 1-1 *Ramazanov (58)*
Agäyev, Baxşiyev, Žutautas, Ämirquliyev, Sultanov (Bamba 84), Abdullayev (Mämmädov 79), Quliyev, Ramazanov (Qurbanov 88), Todorov, Dzhambazov, Juninho.
Red Card(s): Quliyev 73
Yellow Card(s): Dzhambazov 50
A 1-3 *Juninho (16) (aet)*
Agäyev, Baxşiyev, Žutautas, Ämirquliyev, N'tiamoah, Abdullayev (Bamba 85), Mämmädov (Qurbanov 49), Ramazanov, Todorov, Dzhambazov, Juninho.
Red Card(s): N'tiamoah 79
Yellow Card(s): Mämmädov 36, N'tiamoah 57, Ramazanov 60, Dzhambazov 61, Žutautas 72, N'tiamoah 79

PFK NEFTÇI

UEFA CUP

First Qualifying Round - SV Ried (AUT)
A 1-3 *Äliyev (14)*
Mičović, Adamia (Yusifov 89), Äliyev (Subašić 61), Allahverdiyev, Bairamov (Boret 73), R. Quliyev, Mälikov, Mämmädov, Räşad A. Sadiqov, Räşad F. Sadiqov, Tağizadä.
Yellow Card(s): Subašić 66, Allahverdiyev 82
H 2-1 *Subašić (14), Räşad F. Sadiqov (21)*
Mičović, Adamia,Äliyev (Boret 63), Bairamov, R. Quliyev, Mälikov, Mämmädov (Näbiyev 82), Räşad A. Sadiqov, Räşad F. Sadiqov, Subašić (Allahverdiyev 80), Tağizadä.
Red Card(s): Tağizadä 82
Yellow Card(s): Tağizadä 43, Subašić 72, Tağizadä 82

FK MKT-ARAZ

UEFA CUP

First Qualifying Round - Groclin Grodzisk Wielkopolski (POL)
H 0-0
Kovalyov, Barişev, Doroş, Vyshtalyuk, Poladov (Cabbarov 77), Yunisoğlu, C. Mämmädov (K. Quliyev 83), A. Abbasov, A. Mämmädov (İsmayilov 65), Häşimov, Danayev.

Yellow Card(s): A. Abbasov 12
A 0-1
Kovalyov, Barişev, Doroş, Vyshtalyuk, Poladov, Yunisoğlu, C. Mämmädov (K. Quliyev 84), A. Abbasov, A. Mämmädov (İsmayilov 74), Häşimov, Danayev.
Red Card(s): Doroş 81
Yellow Card(s): Yunisoğlu 6, Kovalyov 6, C. Mämmädov 9, Vyshtalyuk 85

FK BAKI

UEFA INTERTOTO CUP

First Round - FC Dacia Chişinau (MDA)
H 1-1 *Andronic (80og)*
Sissokho, A. Abbasov, Ämirbäyov, V. Quliyev, Xälilov (Mähärrämov 46), Äbdürähmanov, Mujiri, Hüseynov, Musayev (F. Quliyev 61), Tijani, Abdullayev (Ämiraslanov 89).
Yellow Card(s): Äbdürähmanov 10, Mujiri 77
A 1-1 *Mujiri (65) (aet; 1-3 on pens)*
Sissokho, Ämirbäyov, V. Quliyev, Xälilov (Nikolov 46), Ilić, Mujiri, Hüseynov, Tijani (Musayev 45), Abdullayev, F. Quliyev (Mähärrämov 74), A. Abbasov.
Yellow Card(s): V. Quliyev 10, Mähärrämov 83

BELARUS

FC BATE BORISOV

UEFA CHAMPIONS LEAGUE

First Qualifying Round - APOEL FC (CYP)
A 0-2
Fedorovich, Bliznyuk (Vishnyakov 77), P. Platonov (D. Platonov 57), Rodionov, Radkov, Stasevich (Zhavnerchik 68), Filipenko, Kazantsev, Likhtarovich, Sakharov, Yermakovich.
Red Card(s): Sakharov 71
Yellow Card(s): Sakharov 40, P. Platonov 42, Kazantsev 45, Sakharov 71
H 3-0 *Stasevich (14), Platonov (74), Bliznyuk (104) (aet)*
Fedorovich, Krivets, Rodionov, Zhavnerchik, Radkov, Stasevich (Sivakov 72), Filipenko, Kazantsev, Khagush (D. Platonov 64), Likhtarovich, Yermakovich (Bliznyuk 80).
Yellow Card(s): Likhtarovich 33, Zhavnerchik 34, Filipenko 73, Yermakovich 76, Bliznyuk 90+1, Sivakov 98, D. Platonov 112

Second Qualifying Round - FH Hafnarfjördur (ISL)
A 3-1 *Likhtarovich (31), Rodionov (50), Bliznyuk (61)*
Fedorovich, Bliznyuk (Zhavnerchik 65), Filipenko, Kazantsev, Khagush, Krivets, Likhtarovich (Sivakov 72), Rodionov (D. Platonov 73), Radkov, Stasevich, Yermakovich.
Yellow Card(s): Stasevich 81
H 1-1 *D. Platonov (90+3)*
Fedorovich, Bliznyuk (D. Platonov 82), Kazantsev, Khagush, Krivets (P. Platonov 63), Likhtarovich, Rodionov, Radkov, Stasevich (Zhavnerchik 88), Yermakovich, Filipenko.
Red Card(s): Rodionov 42
Yellow Card(s): Khagush 32, Radkov 49

Third Qualifying Round - FC Steaua Bucureşti (ROU)
H 2-2 *Radkov (39), Bliznyuk (90+2)*
Fedorovich, Bliznyuk, Filipenko, Kazantsev, Khagush, Likhtarovich (K 53), D. Platonov, P. Platonov (Sivakov 82), Radkov, Stasevich, Yermakc (Zhavnerchik 68).
Yellow Card(s): Khagush 7
A 0-2
Fedorovich, Bliznyuk, Filipenko, Kazantsev, Likhtarovich, D. Platonov, Platonov, Radkov, Sakharov (Krivets 56), Stasevich (Vishnyakov 84), Yermakovich (Radevich 77).
Yellow Card(s): Stasevich 24, Filipenko 58

UEFA CUP

First Round - Villarreal CF (ESP)
A 1-4 *Zhavnerchik (70)*
Fedorovich, Bliznyuk (Sivakov 73), Kazantsev, Khagush, Krivets, Likhtarovich (Zhavnerchik 62), D. Platonov, P. Platonov, Radkov, Sakh (Nekhaichik 68), Yermakovich.
H 0-2
Fedorovich, Bliznyuk (P. Platonov 86), Khagush, Krivets, Likhtarovich, Rodionov (D. Platonov 72), Radkov, Sakharov, Stasevich, Yermakovich (Zhavnerchik 85), Filipenko.
Yellow Card(s): Khagush 30

FC DINAMO BREST

UEFA CUP

First Qualifying Round - SK Liepājas Metalurgs (LVA)
A 1-1 *Sokol (77)*
Tsygalko, Chistyi (Goginashvili 69), Ishmakov, Kots, Kozak, Mozolevsk Panasyuk, Shchigolev, Sokol, Tsevan (Demidovich 85), Volodko.
Yellow Card(s): Tsevan 55, Goginashvili 87
H 1-2 *Sokol (47)*
Tsygalko, Chistyi, Kots, Kozak, Mozolevskiy (Trotsyuk 82), Shcherbo (Goginashvili 53), Shchigolev, Sokol, Tsevan (Zhersh 67), Volodko, Panasyuk.
Red Card(s): Kots 79, Shchigolev 88
Yellow Card(s): Sokol 25

FC DINAMO MINSK

UEFA CUP

First Qualifying Round - Skonto FC (LVA)
A 1-1 *Rák (11)*
Tumilovich, Khatskevich (Kislyak 68), Márcio, Pankov, Pavlyukovich, F Temryukov, Nudnii (Gigevich 75), Martynovich, Veretilo, Putilo (Yanushkevich 81).
Yellow Card(s): Putilo 45, Tumilovich 87, Pankov 90
H 2-0 *Rák (57, 74)*
Lesko, Khatskevich (Pavlyuchek 90), Mbanangoye, Pankov, Pavlyuko Rák, Temryukov, Nudnii (Gigevich 71), Martynovich, Veretilo, Putilo (Kislyak 87).
Yellow Card(s): Nudnii 19

d Qualifying Round - Odense BK (DEN)
Putilo (73)
Khatskevich (Kislyak 72), Mbanangoye, Nudnii, Pankov, Pavlyukovich, Yurchenko (Temryukov 79), Martinovich, Putilo (Pavlyuchek 86), Veretilo.
v Card(s): Putilo 35, Khatskevich 57

Khatskevich, Mbanangoye (Márcio 80), Edu, Nudnii (Rekish 84), v, Pavlyuchek, Rák, V. Yurchenko (Kislyak 60), Martynovich, Veretilo.
v Card(s): Pavlyuchek 27, Khatskevich 36

FC SHAKHTYOR SOLIGORSK

UEFA INTERTOTO CUP

ound - FC Ararat Yerevan (ARM)
Rios (22), Gukailo (58), Klimenko (69), Nikiforenko (80)
vskiy, Bychenok (Goncharik 56), Gukailo, Khrapkovskiy, Klimenko, kiy, Nikiforenko, Novik (Kovalchuk 72), Plaskonnyi, Rios novich 56), Yurevich.
Card(s): Klimenko 20

vskiy, Bychenok (Gukailo 57), Kovalchuk, Khrapkovskiy, Klimenko, kiy, Leonchik, Nikiforenko, Novik (Goncharik 50; Magomedov 88), nnyi, Yurevich.
ard(s): Klimenko 78
Card(s): Klimenko 61, Gukailo 75, Klimenko 78

d Round - FC Chornomorets Odesa (UKR)
Rios (14), Martinovich (79)
chik, Goncharik (Bychenok 62), Gukailo, Kovalchuk, Khrapkovskiy, kiy, Leonchik, Nikiforenko, Novik (Martinovich 64), Plaskonnyi, Rios kin 76).
Card(s): Makavchik 36

vskiy, Goncharik (Bukatkin 46), Gukailo, Kovalchuk, Klimenko, ik, Martinovich, Nikiforenko, Novik (Bychenok 60), Plaskonnyi, Rios.
Card(s): Novik 27, Baranovskiy 62

BELGIUM

RSC ANDERLECHT

UEFA CHAMPIONS LEAGUE

Qualifying Round - Fenerbahçe SK (TUR)

iglia, Boussoufa (Legear 83), De Man, Deschacht, Goor, Hassan, Tchité (Mpenza 77), Polák, Wasilewski.
Card(s): Wasilewski 72, Hassan 81

iglia, Boussoufa (Théréau 56), Deschacht, Hassan, Juhász, Pareja, Van Damme (Goor 76), Polák, Wasilewski (Legear 76).
Card(s): Biglia 43

UEFA CUP

First Round - SK Rapid Wien (AUT)
H 1-1 *Serhat (11)*
Zítka, Serhat, Biglia, Deschacht, Goor (Boussoufa 85), Hassan, Mpenza (Legear 66), Pareja, Polák, Van Damme, Wasilewski.
Yellow Card(s): Van Damme 71
A 1-0 *Hassan (22)*
Zítka, Serhat (Frutos 76), Biglia, De Man, Deschacht, Hassan, Juhász (Wasilewski 72), Pareja, Polák, Van Damme, Legear (Boussoufa 79).
Yellow Card(s): Serhat 75, Frutos 90+3

Group G
Match 1 - Hapoel Tel-Aviv FC (ISR)
H 2-0 *Frutos (36, 70)*
Zítka, Wasilewski, Pareja, Juhász, Deschacht, Legear (Théréau 83), Biglia, Polák, Goor (Van Damme 69), Hassan, Frutos (De Man 86).
Match 2 - Aalborg BK (DEN)
A 1-1 *Jakobsen (59og)*
Zítka, Deschacht, Pareja, Polák, Wasilewski, Biglia, Goor, Juhász, Frutos, Serhat (Van Damme 88), Hassan (Legear 82).
Yellow Card(s): Serhat 13, Pareja 36
Match 3 - Tottenham Hotspur FC (ENG)
H 1-1 *Goor (68)*
Zítka, Wasilewski, Juhász, Van Damme, Deschacht, Hassan, Biglia, Polák, Goor, Mpenza (Baseggio 72), Frutos (Théréau 55).
Yellow Card(s): Polák 62, Goor 62, Wasilewski 70, Hassan 72
Match 4 - Getafe CF (ESP)
A 1-2 *Théréau (90+1)*
Zítka, Deschacht, Biglia, Van Damme, Polák, Hassan, Goor, Théréau, Juhász, Wasilewski (Mpenza 53), Legear (De Man 75).
Yellow Card(s): Wasilewski 39, Polák 65, Goor 72

Round of 32 - FC Girondins de Bordeaux (FRA)
H 2-1 *Polák (79), Mpenza (90+5)*
Zítka, Wasilewski, Pareja, Juhász, Van Damme, Chatelle (Legear 84), Polák, Biglia, Goor (Mpenza 73), Boussoufa, Serhat.
Yellow Card(s): Juhász 6, Goor 70
A 1-1 *Chatelle (34)*
Zítka, Wasilewski, Juhász (De Man 89), Pareja, Van Damme, Chatelle (Mpenza 60), Biglia, Polák, Boussoufa, Gillet, Serhat (Hassan 69).
Yellow Card(s): Zítka 30, Juhász 30, Gillet 42, Hassan 85, Mpenza 90+1, Boussoufa 90+2

Round of 16 - FC Bayern München (GER)
H 0-5
Zítka, Wasilewski, Pareja, Juhász, Van Damme, Chatelle (Hassan 61), Gillet, Biglia, Polák, Boussoufa, Serhat (Goor 66).
Red Card(s): Wasilewski 43
Yellow Card(s): Wasilewski 42, Wasilewski 43, Gillet 65
A 2-1 *Serhat (20), Yakovenko (35)*
Zítka (Schollen 46), Gillet, Sare, Juhász, Deschacht, Yakovenko (Boussoufa 66), De Man, Biglia, Hassan, Goor, Serhat (Gillis 90).
Yellow Card(s): Juhász 7, Yakovenko 35, Deschacht 52, Boussoufa 90+3

KRC GENK

UEFA CHAMPIONS LEAGUE

Second Qualifying Round - FK Sarajevo (BIH)
H 1-2 *Cornelis (23)*
Bailly, Cornelis, Haroun, Matoukou (Ljubojević 74), Mikulić, Soetaers, Bošnjak, Caillet, Vrancken, Tiago (Dahmane 64), Tóth.
Yellow Card(s): Haroun 45, Bošnjak 61, Caillet 79, Mikulić 85
A 1-0 *Mikulić (58)*
Bailly, Cornelis, Matoukou, Mikulić, Soetaers (Vandooren 77), Bošnjak, Barda, Caillet (Ljubojević 70), Vrancken, De Decker (Tiago 38), Tóth.
Yellow Card(s): Mikulić 59, Cornelis 89

CLUB BRUGGE KV

UEFA CUP

First Round - SK Brann (NOR)
A 1-0 *Sterchele (84)*
Stijnen, Blondel, Clement, Englebert, Salou (Leko 82), Klukowski, Priske, Sonck (Sterchele 78), Simaeys, Kučera, Geraerts.
Yellow Card(s): Englebert 20, Simaeys 62, Salou 64
H 1-2 *Clement (76)*
Stijnen, Blondel, Clement, Englebert (Leko 46), Salou, Klukowski, Priske, Sonck, Simaeys, Kučera (Sterchele 46), Geraerts.
Red Card(s): Simaeys 81
Yellow Card(s): Priske 7, Salou 32, Simaeys 35, Clement 70, Simaeys 81, Blondel 90+2

R. STANDARD DE LIÈGE

UEFA CUP

Second Qualifying Round - UN Käerjéng 97 (LUX)
A 3-0 *Mbokani (59), Witsel (81, 86)*
Renard, De Camargo (Lukunku 71), Dupré, Fellaini, Sarr, Dembélé, Dante, Marcos (Mulemo 85), Mbokani, Toama (Jovanović 77), Witsel.
Yellow Card(s): Fellaini 79
H 1-0 *De Camargo (89)*
Aragon, De Camargo, Defour (Villano 62), Dupré, Sarr, Dembélé, Dante (Onyewu 46), Mulemo (Dachelet 90+3), Walasiak, Lukunku, Papassarantis.
Yellow Card(s): Dante 30

First Round - FC Zenit St. Petersburg (RUS)
A 0-3
Renard, De Camargo, Defour, Marcos, Dante, Onyewu, Fellaini, Mbokani (Lukunku 79), Sarr, Toama, Witsel (Dufer 82).
Yellow Card(s): Defour 36, Toama 39, Onyewu 59, Fellaini 67, Dante 89
H 1-1 *Onyewu (35)*
Aragon, De Camargo (Lukunku 78), Defour, Marcos, Dante, Onyewu, Xavier (Mbokani 46), Fellaini, Sarr, Toama (Dembélé 71), Witsel.
Red Card(s): Onyewu 39
Yellow Card(s): Onyewu 31, Onyewu 39, Defour 41, Marcos 68, Sarr 78, Fellaini 88

KAA GENT

UEFA INTERTOTO CUP

Second Round - Cliftonville FC (NIR)
H 2-0 *Foley (8, 63)*
Martinovic, De Beule, Foley, Gillet, Svetličić, Stoica (Haznadar 90), Olufade (Żewłakow 70), Grondin, Grégoire, Grncarov, Mutavdžić (Moia 79).
Red Card(s): Grégoire 90+1
Yellow Card(s): Gillet 90+2
A 4-0 *Foley (12), Olufade (44, 85), De Beule (45)*
Martinovic, De Beule, Foley, Gillet, Svetličić, Stoica (Rosales 70), Olufa Grondin (Pavlović 54), Moia, Grncarov, Żewłakow (Mirvić 80).
Red Card(s): Svetličić 77
Yellow Card(s): Moia 34, Olufade 67

Third Round - Aalborg BK (DEN)
H 1-1 *Olufade (47p)*
Martinovic, Azofeifa (Haznadar 86), De Beule, Foley, Gillet, Grncarov, Grondin, Moia (Vermuth 75), Mutavdžić, Olufade, Żewłakow.
Yellow Card(s): De Beule 88
A 1-2 *Olufade (27)*
Martinovic, De Beule, Foley, Gillet (Vermuth 83), Grncarov, Grondin, Olufade, Żewłakow, Stoica (Ruiz 83), Svetličić (Moia 21), Mutavdžić.
Yellow Card(s): Gillet 60, Żewłakow 75, Stoica 79

BOSNIA-HERZEGOVINA

FK SARAJEVO

UEFA CHAMPIONS LEAGUE

First Qualifying Round - Marsaxlokk FC (MLT)
A 6-0 *Raščić (5,9), Obuća (20, 65), Maksimović (42), Bučan (87)*
Alaim, Bučan, Hadžić, Ihtijarević, Muharemović, Obuća, Bašić, Miloše Grujić, Maksimović, Raščić.
Yellow Card(s): Bučan 88
H 3-1 *Mešić (42), Šaraba (60), Turković (76)*
Alaim, Bučan, Hadžić, Muharemović, Bašić, Milošević, Mesić, Grujić, K (Šaraba 46), Maksimović (Janjoš 79), Raščić (Turković 64).
Yellow Card(s): Grujić 66, Milošević 69

Second Qualifying Round - KRC Genk (BEL)
A 2-1 *Raščić (15), Muharemović (86)*
Alaim, Babić, Bašić, Bučan (Turković 68), Grujić, Hadžić (Džakmić 73), Maksimović, Milošević, Muharemović, Raščić (Mesić 77), Šaraba.
Yellow Card(s): Raščić 29, Hadžić 32, Maksimović 75, Alaim 90
H 0-1
Alaim, Bašić, Bučan (Turković 58), Džakmić, Grujić, Hadžić, Maksimov (Repuh 85), Milošević, Muharemović, Raščić (Babić 78), Šaraba.
Yellow Card(s): Muharemović 42, Šaraba 45+1

Third Qualifying Round - FC Dynamo Kyiv (UKR)
H 0-1
Alaim, Bašić, Bučan (Turković 57), Džakmić, Grujić, Hadžić (Repuh 46 Maksimović, Milošević, Muharemović, Raščić (Mesić 65), Šaraba.
Yellow Card(s): Muharemović 60, Maksimović 90
A 0-3
Alaim (Fejzić 60), Babić, Bašić, Džakmić, Grujić, Hadžić, Mesić (Handž Milošević, Raščić, Repuh (Janjoš 46), Šaraba.
Yellow Card(s): Janjoš 90

UEFA CUP

First Round - FC Basel 1893 (SUI)
H 1-2 *Milošević (90+3)*
Fejzić, Babić, Bašić, Džakmić (Turković 46), Grujić, Hadžić (Maksimov Milošević, Muharemović, Raščić, Repuh (Janjoš 72), Šaraba.
Yellow Card(s): Bašić 31, Repuh 61, Šaraba 88
A 0-6
Fejzić, Milošević, Zukić (Kurto 45), Muharemović, Bašić, Maksimović, Grujić, Mešić (Handžić 80), Bučan, Raščić, Janjoš (Škoro 78).
Yellow Card(s): Bučan 20, Kurto 66

NK ŠIROKI BRIJEG

UEFA CUP

Qualifying Round - FC Koper (SVN)
Célson (24, 33), Ronielle (44)
Célson (I. Bubalo 85), S. Bubalo, Ronielle, Hannich (Kožul 53), Jurić
: 72), Karoglan, Šilić, Topić, Vidić, Zelenika.
w Card(s): Célson 24, Šilić 42, Topić 64
Karoglan (18), R. Božič (25og), Ronielle (36)
S. Bubalo (Zovko 63), Ronielle (Bubalo 78), Hannich (Šakić 71), Jurić,
lan, Šilić, Topić, Vidić, Zelenika, Ricardo.

nd Qualifying Round - Hapoel Tel-Aviv FC (ISR)

ović, Célson, Bubalo, Ronielle (Hannich 46), Jurić (Kožul 46),
lan, Šilić, Topić, Vidić, Zelenika (Šakić 73), Marciano.
w Card(s): Zelenika 48, Šakić 76, Vidić 88

ović, Bubalo, Ronielle, Jurić (Marciano 59), Karoglan, Kožul (Božić 65),
er (Šakić 75), Šilić, Topić, Vidić, Zelenika.
w Card(s): Zelenika 77

HŠK ZRINJSKI

UEFA CUP

Qualifying Round - FK Partizan (SRB)
Matko (68)
Đurić (Karadža 24), I. Džidić (Landeka 24), D. Džidić (Matko 65),
, Žuržinov, Nikolić, Selimović, Smajić, Pezo, Rajović.
w Card(s): Nikolić 77

Branković, Jurić (Pezo 55), Karadža, Landeka, Bašić (Suton 65),
) (Selimović 72), Smajić, Rajović, Šunjić, Dragičević.
w Card(s): Šunjić 2, Matko 19
rtizan disqualified for crowd misbehaviour)

nd Qualifying Round - FK Rabotnički (MKD)

Nikolić, D. Džidić, Landeka, Selimović (Bašić 72), Smajić (Joldić 83),
Karadža, Rajović (Žižović 66), Ivanković, Suton.
ard(s): Jurić 65
w Card(s): Ivanković 18, Jurić 27, Selimović 50, Jurić 65
Ivanković (36)
, D. Džidić, Ivanković, Joldić, Karadža, Landeka, Nikolić, Rajović
ović 46), Smajić (Matko 54), Žižović (Đurić 74), Suton.
ard(s): Joldić 40, Landeka 75
w Card(s): Landeka 29, Ivanković 45, Landeka 75

FK SLAVIJA SARAJEVO

UEFA INTERTOTO CUP

First Round - UE Sant Julià (AND)
A 3-2 *Varela (23og), Jovanović (62), Spalević (87)*
Dujković, Belošević, Bjelica, Jovanović (Šešlija 78), Muminović, Regoje, Simić (Papaz 84), Spalević, Stanić (Jamina 66), Stanković, Vuksanović.
Yellow Card(s): Muminović 45+2, Šešlija 89
H 3-2 *Jamina (22), Fontan (65og), Vuksanović (90+4)*
Dujković, Damjanović (Padaz 84), Bjelica, Jamina (Stanić 88), Jovanović, Muminović, Regoje, Simić (Šešlija 94), Spalević, Stanković, Vuksanović.
Yellow Card(s): Spalević 36, Jamina 87

Second Round - FC Oţelul Galaţi (ROU)
H 0-0
Dujković, Benović, Bjelica, Jovanović, Muminović, Regoje, Simić (Lazić 81), Spalević, Jamina (Šešlija 86), Stanković, Vuksanović.
Yellow Card(s): Benović 46, Regoje 90+1
A 0-3
Dujković, Benović, Bjelica (Arsenijević 70), Jamina (Lazić 46), Jovanović, Muminović, Regoje, Simić (Šešlija 71), Spalević, Stanković, Vuksanović.
Red Card(s): Benović 73
Yellow Card(s): Benović 44, Benović 73

BULGARIA

PFC LEVSKI SOFIA

UEFA CHAMPIONS LEAGUE

Second Qualifying Round - Tampere United (FIN)
A 0-1
Petkov, Bardon (Jayeoba 80), Domovchiyski, Eromoigbe, Wagner, Milanov, Telkiyski, Tomašić, Yovov (Dimitrov 57), Tasevski (Ivanov 63), Benzoukane.
H 0-1
Petkov, Bardon (Koprivarov 75), Domovchiyski, Eromoigbe, Wagner, Hristov (Borimirov 42), Ivanov, Milanov (Jayeoba 46), Telkiyski, Yovov, Benzoukane.
Yellow Card(s): Bardon 75, Telkiyski 83, Koprivarov 83

PFC CSKA SOFIA

UEFA CUP

Second Qualifying Round - AC Omonia (CYP)
A 1-1 *Nei (1)*
Petrov, V. Dimitrov, Kabous, Petre (Lanzaat 68), Todorov, Tunchev, Yanchev, V. Iliev, Amuneke (Garcés 65), Nei (Udoji 82), Vujadinović.
Red Card(s): V. Iliev 66
Yellow Card(s): V. Iliev 49, Tunchev 53, V. Iliev 66, Petrov 85, Kabous 90+1
H 2-1 *Nei (17), Chilikov (88)*
Petrov, Udoji, V. Dimitrov (Chilikov 85), Lanzaat, Petre (Garcés 66), Todorov, Tunchev, Yanchev, Nei (Kabous 89), Marquinhos, Vujadinović.
Yellow Card(s): Marquinhos 35, Todorov 88

First Round - Toulouse FC (FRA)
A 0-0
Petrov, Udoji (Garcés 89), Nei, V. Dimitrov (Amuneke 76), V. Iliev, Kabous,

Marquinhos (G. Iliev 65), Todorov, Tunchev, Vujadinović, Yanchev.
Yellow Card(s): Yanchev 39, Udoji 61, Marquinhos 62
H 1-1 *Nei (65p)*
Petrov, Amuneke (Udoji 73), Nei, V. Dimitrov (Kotev 87), V. Iliev, Kabous, Lanzaat, Marquinhos (Garcés 59), Todorov, Vujadinović, Yanchev.
Red Card(s): Udoji 85
Yellow Card(s): V. Dimitrov 57, Nei 68, Udoji 78, Udoji 85, Petrov 90+3

PFC LOKOMOTIV SOFIA

UEFA CUP

Second Qualifying Round - FC Oțelul Galați (ROU)
H 3-1 *Dafchev (19), Baldovaliev (62), Gilas (84)*
Golubović, Antunović (Gilas 81), Dafchev (Zlatinski 89), Dobrev, Karadzhinov, Koilov (Ivanov 70), Markov, Orachev, Savić, Varbanov, Baldovaliev.
Yellow Card(s): Dobrev 21, Markov 78
A 0-0
Golubović, Antunović (Gilas 62), Dafchev, Dobrev, Ivanov, Karadzhinov (Koilov 83), Markov, Orachev, Savić, Varbanov, Baldovaliev (Paskov 72).
Yellow Card(s): Antunović 39, Dafchev 40, Ivanov 51, Golubović 54, Markov 55, Baldovaliev 67, Karadzhinov 75

First Round - Stade Rennais FC (FRA)
H 1-3 *Dafchev (51)*
Golubović, Antunović (Zlatinski 74), Dafchev, Dobrev, Paskov, Karadzhinov, Koilov (Atanasov 61), Orachev, Savić (Lopes 46), Varbanov, Baldovaliev.
Yellow Card(s): Paskov 74
A 2-1 *Antunović (37, 40)*
Golubović, Antunović (Gilas 80), Atanasov (Baldovaliev 71), Dafchev, Dobrev, D. Donchev, Karadzhinov, Koilov (Zlatinski 85), Markov, Orachev, Savić.
Yellow Card(s): Donchev 53

PFC LITEX LOVECH

UEFA CUP

First Qualifying Round - Sliema Wanderers FC (MLT)
A 3-0 *I. Popov (22, 56), Beto (53)*
Todorov, Boudarène, Sandrinho (Bibishkov 78), Wellington, Beto, Nikolov, R. Popov, I. Popov (Genchev 69), Venkov, Zlatinov (Manolev 60), Uras.
H 4-0 *Boudarène (28), Beto (48, 60), Popov (59)*
Todorov, Boudarène (Jelenković 46), Sandrinho, Wellington, Beto, Nikolov (Genchev 46), R. Popov, I. Popov, Tome (Bibishkov 46), Venkov, Uras.

Second Qualifying Round - KS Besa (ALB)
A 3-0 *I. Popov (13, 20), Beto (32)*
Todorov, Boudarène (Jelenković 46), Sandrinho, Wellington (Tome 46), Beto, Manolev, Nikolov, R. Popov, I. Popov (Bibishkov 46), Uras, Venkov.
Yellow Card(s): I. Popov 6
H 3-0 *Genchev (13), Beto (69), Tome (79)*
Todorov, Bibishkov (Hazurov 65), Cichero, Sandrinho, Wellington, Genchev, Nikolov (Cambon 78), I. Popov (Beto 60), Tome, Venkov, Bandlovski.
Yellow Card(s): Genchev 66

First Round - Hamburger SV (GER)
H 0-1
Todorov, Bibishkov, Boudarène, Cichero, Sandrinho, Wellington, Niko
R. Popov, I. Popov (Beto 80), Tome (Manolev 69), Venkov.
Yellow Card(s): Tome 62, Wellington 86
A 1-3 *R. Popov (38)*
Todorov, R. Popov, Cichero, Venkov, Wellington (Genchev 78), Sandrir
Boudarène (Bibishkov 78), Manolev (Tome 67), Nikolov, Beto, I. Popo

PFC CHERNO MORE VARNA

UEFA INTERTOTO CUP

Second Round - FK Makedonija GP Skopje (MKD)
A 4-0 *Bachev (53), Da Silva (72, 73), Stoyanov (82)*
Ilchev, Alexandrov, Bachev (Domakinov 87), Georgiev (Stoyanov 79), Tomash, Andonov, Da Silva (Manolov 77), Dzhorov, Kostadinov, Dimo
Ricardo André.
H 3-0 *Georgiev (12), Manolov (46), Dimov (80)*
Ilchev, Bachev, Georgiev (Setlinov 81), Manolov, Tomash, Da Silva (Stoyanov 69), Dzhorov, P. Kostadinov (V. Kostadinov 52), Dimov, Domakinov, Ricardo André.

Third Round - UC Sampdoria (ITA)
H 0-1
Ilchev, Bachev, Djalma, Dzhorov, Domakinov, Ferreira (Andonov 70), Geo
(Manolov 84), Fabiano, Ricardo André (Kostadinov 72), Tomash, Dimov.
Yellow Card(s): Ferreira 25, Dzhorov 55, Andonov 80
A 0-1
Ilchev, Andonov (Da Silva 86), Bachev, Djalma, Dzhorov, Domakinov, Ge
(Manolov 89), Fabiano, Ricardo André, Tomash, Dimov (Setlinov 89).
Yellow Card(s): Ricardo André 32, Fabiano 38, Bachev 71

CROATIA

NK DINAMO ZAGREB

UEFA CHAMPIONS LEAGUE

First Qualifying Round - FK Xäzär Länkäran (AZE)
A 1-1 *Etto (63)*
Koch, Pokrivač (Chago 85), Tadić (Mandžukić 46), Šokota, Ćale, Ćorluk
Sammir (Etto 58), Carlos, Drpić, Modrić, Vukojević.
Yellow Card(s): Carlos 68, Mandžukić 90
H 3-1 *Vugrinec (56), Mandžukić (99), Tadić (116) (aet)*
Koch, Tadić, Mandžukić, Chago (Vugrinec 46; Tomić 73), Sammir, Carl
Etto, Drpić (Ćale 46), Modrić, Schildenfeld, Vukojević.
Yellow Card(s): Mandžukić 28, Ćale 51, Etto 76, Tomić 113

Second Qualifying Round - NK Domžale (SVN)
A 2-1 *Šokota (7), Modrić (50p)*
Koch, Pokrivač (Chago 80), Etto, Šokota (Tadić 83), Ćale, Schildenfeld,
Sammir, Carlos, Guela (Mikić 75), Modrić, Vukojević.
H 3-1 *Vukojević (18), Šokota (22), Sammir (60)*
Koch, Ćale, Sammir (Mikić 82), Carlos, Etto, Guela (Chago 46), Mandžu
Modrić, Schildenfeld, Šokota (Drpić 63), Vukojević.
Yellow Card(s): Mandžukić 24

Qualifying Round - Werder Bremen (GER)
Balaban (45+1)
Balaban (Vrdoljak 80), Ćale, Sammir (Guela 88), Etto, Drpić, Modrić,
vač, Schildenfeld, Šokota (Mandžukić 37), Vukojević.
w Card(s): Balaban 38, Ćale 40, Pokrivač 87
Vukojević (21), Modrić (40p)
, Balaban, Sammir (Mikić 76), Carlos, Etto (Guela 78), Drpić,
žukić, Modrić, Pokrivač (Vugrinec 62), Schildenfeld, Vukojević.
w Card(s): Koch 13, Modrić 42, Vukojević 65, Carlos 67, Mandžukić 70

UEFA CUP

Round - AFC Ajax (NED)

, Balaban, Ćale, Sammir, Etto, Drpić, Modrić, Pokrivač, Schildenfeld,
nec (Šokota 46), Vukojević (Guela 69).
w Card(s): Vukojević 19, Čale 76
Modrić (34p), Mandžukić (94, 96) (aet)
, Ćale, Sammir (Guela 68), Etto, Drpić, Mandžukić, Modrić, Pokrivač,
denfeld (Carlos 106), Tadić (Mikić 78), Vukojević.
w Card(s): Tadić 39, Pokrivač 45, Mandžukić 61, Schildenfeld 63,
ić 76

p D
h 1 - FC Basel 1893 (SUI)

, Ćale (Carlos 70), Etto, Drpić, Schildenfeld, Vukojević, Pokrivač,
ić, Guela (Sammir 62), Mandžukić, Šokota (Tadić 74).
h 2 - SK Brann (NOR)
Vukojević (49)
, Ćale, Etto, Drpić, Pokrivač, Modrić, Sammir (Carlos 46), Vukojevic
la 79), Schildenfeld, Mandžukić, Balaban (Tadić 60).
Card(s): Schildenfeld 44
w Card(s): Carlos 56, Koch 90, Ćale 90
h 3 - Hamburger SV (GER)
2
, Ćale, Pokrivač (Šokota 90), Etto, Balaban (Tadić 58), Modrić, Carlos,
džukić, Sammir (Vrdoljak 76), Vukojević, Drpić.
w Card(s): Mandžukić 47, Sammir 58
h 4 - Stade Rennais FC (FRA)
1 *Vukojević (57)*
, Etto, Ćale (Šokota 88), Drpić, Sammir (Guela 65), Modrić, Vukojević,
ivač, Mandžukić, Tadić (Balaban 77), Carlos.
w Card(s): Carlos 34, Drpić 80, Vukojević 87

HNK HAJDUK SPLIT

UEFA CUP

Qualifying Round - FK Budućnost Podgorica (MNE)
1 *Hrgović (28)*
, Buljat, Živković, Pelaić, Cernat, Rukavina (Čubrilo 86), Gal, Andrić
njanović 74), Kalinić, Hrgović, Gabrić (Musa 86).
ow Card(s): Andrić 52, Čubrilo 90
0 *Damjanović (46)*
, Damjanović (Ljubičić 88), Živković, Pelaić, Cernat, Rukavina, Rubil,
dža, Andrić, Kalinić (Bartolović 79), Hrgović.
ow Card(s): Damjanović 67, Živković 84

ond Qualifying Round - UC Sampdoria (ITA)
1
, Andrić, Buljat, Cernat, Damjanović (Linić 79), Hrgović, Rubil
tolović 57), Rukavina, Živković, Kalinić, Sabljić (Pandža 48).
ow Card(s): Kalinić 30, Andrić 72

A 1-1 *Hrgović (83)*
Tomić, Pelaić, Buljat, Cernat, Linić, Hrgović, Rubil (Verpakovskis 46), Ljubičić, Živković, Kalinić (Rukavina 77), Bartolović (Peraić 46).
Yellow Card(s): Pelaić 35, Hrgović 53

NK SLAVEN KOPRIVNICA

UEFA CUP

First Qualifying Round - KS Teuta (ALB)
H 6-2 *Posavec (18p), Šehić (29 ,47), Vručina (60, 82), Bošnjak (90)*
Iveša, Čaval, Kristić, Božac, Poldrugač, Kresinger (Jurić 46), Posavec (Poljak 61), Sopić, Šehić (Bošnjak 74), Vručina, Radeljić.
Yellow Card(s): Čaval 26, Poljak 73, Kristić 74
A 2-2 *Kresinger (64), Vručina (70)*
Iveša (Rodić 46), Bošnjak, Kristić, Poldrugač, Kresinger, Posavec (Delić 75), Sopić, Poljak, Vručina, Radeljić, Jurić (Jajalo 40).
Yellow Card(s): Kresinger 51

Second Qualifying Round - Galatasaray AŞ (TUR)
H 1-2 *Posavec (16)*
Iveša, Bošnjak, Jajalo (Šomoci 46), Kristić, Poldrugač, Poljak (Delić 61), Posavec, Radeljić, Šehić, Sopić, Vručina (Kresinger 79).
Yellow Card(s): Sopić 72, Posavec 90+1
A 1-2 *Poljak (36)*
Ivesa, Bošnjak (Posavec 65), Božac, Jajalo, Kresinger (Tepurić 74), Poldrugač, Poljak, Radiček, Šehić (Vručina 52), Sopić, Radeljić.
Yellow Card(s): Radiček 22

NK ZAGREB

UEFA INTERTOTO CUP

First Round - KS Vllaznia (ALB)
H 2-1 *Nadarević (19), Labudović (63)*
Bašić, Labudović, Lovrek, Mujdža, Pejić, Čutura, Ibričić (Grgić 59), Lajtman (Jurendić 87), Mandžukić, Nadarević, Parlov.
Red Card(s): Lovrek 88
Yellow Card(s): Čutura 23, Lajtman 43, Parlov 48
A 0-1
Stojkić, Jurendić (Orsulić 85), Labudović (Mikulić 80), Mujdža, Pejić, Čutura, Ibričić (Grgić 59), Lajtman, Mandžukić, Nadarević, Parlov.

CYPRUS

APOEL FC

UEFA CHAMPIONS LEAGUE

First Qualifying Round - FC BATE Borisov (BLR)
H 2-0 *Michail (42), Machlas (61)*
Morfis, Nuno Morais, Florea, Kapsis, Kontis, Machlas (Barreto 90+1), Makridis, Michail, Tavares (Hélio Pinto 67), Ricardo Fernandes, Satsias (Sapanis 74).
Yellow Card(s): Satsias 39
A 0-3 *(aet)*
Morfis, Nuno Morais, Elia (Zé Carlos 81), Kapsis, Kontis, Machlas, Makridis, Michail, Tavares (Sapanis 25), Ricardo Fernandes, Hélio Pinto (Louka 68).
Yellow Card(s): Kontis 27, Sapanis 54, Ricardo Fernandes 66, Michail 82

ANORTHOSIS FAMAGUSTA FC

UEFA CUP

First Qualifying Round - FK Vardar (MKD)
A 1-0 *Deyanov (88)*
Beqaj, Poursaitidis, Katsavakis, Sosin (Belić 46), Panagi (Luís Loureiro 57), Fabinho, Ndikumana, Žlogar, Pahars (William 75), Lambrou, Deyanov.
Yellow Card(s): Lambrou 27
H 1-0 *Žlogar (53)*
Beqaj, Poursaitidis, Katsavakis, Sosin (Belić 62), Panagi, Fabinho, Ndikumana, Žlogar (Luís Loureiro 76), Pahars (Frousos 70), Lambrou, Deyanov.
Yellow Card(s): Lambrou 38, Ndikumana 63

Second Qualifying Round - CFR 1907 Cluj (ROU)
A 3-1 *Žlogar (43), William (48), Sosin (58)*
Beqaj, William, Konstantinou, Deyanov (Luís Loureiro 59), Katsavakis, Ndikumana (Loumpoutis 65), Panagi, Fabinho (Belić 77), Poursaitidis, Sosin, Žlogar.
Yellow Card(s): Poursaitidis 86, Beqaj 90+3
H 0-0
Beqaj, William, Deyanov (Loumpoutis 46), Katsavakis, Lambrou, Ndikumana, Panagi, Fabinho (Nicolaou 46), Poursaitidis, Sosin (Laban 79), Žlogar.
Yellow Card(s): Katsavakis 23, Ndikumana 46, Nicolaou 62, Lambrou 66

First Round - Tottenham Hotspur FC (ENG)
A 1-6 *Žlogar (80)*
Beqaj, Lambrou, Katsavakis, Žlogar (Deyanov 81), Poursaitidis, Fabinho (Pahars 64), Sosin, Nicolaou (Panagi 58), Loumpoutis, Skopelitis, William.
Yellow Card(s): Fabinho 32
H 1-1 Fabinho (54)
Nagy, William, Konstantinou, Frousos, Laban (Deyanov 82), Ndikumana, Nicolaou, Panagi, Fabinho (Pahars 62), Tripotseris, Žlogar (Skopelitis 46).

AC OMONIA

UEFA CUP

First Qualifying Round - FK Rudar Pljevlja (MNE)
H 2-0 *Kaiafas (43), Chailis (46)*
Georgallides, Torrão, Chailis, Ba (Grozdanovski 55), Georgiou, Kaiafas, Kakoyia Mguni, Magno (Vakouftsis 74), Nélson Veiga, Guilherme (Kaseke 64).
Yellow Card(s): Nelson Veiga 32
A 2-0 *Mguni (34), Ricardo Sousa (75)*
Georgallides, Torrão, Dobrasinović (Kaseke 70), Ba, Georgiou, Kaiafas, Kakoyia Mguni (Chailis 80), Magno, Nélson Veiga, Guilherme (Ricardo Sousa 59).
Yellow Card(s): Mguni 35

Second Qualifying Round - PFC CSKA Sofia (BUL)
H 1-1 *Kaiafas (14)*
Georgallides, Ba (Ricardo Sousa 77), Dobrasinović (Kaseke 40), Torrão (Theodotou 23), Georgiou, Kaiafas, Kakoyiannis, Mguni, Magno, Nélsc Veiga, Guilherme.
Yellow Card(s): Dobrasinović 31, Ba 35, Kaseke 70, Kaiafas 85
A 1-2 *Magno (8)*
Georgallides, Ba, Dobrasinović, Georgiou, Kaiafas, Kakoyiannis, Mguni Magno (Kaseke 82), Theodotou (Rui Pinto 73), Nélson Veiga, Guilherm (Ricardo Sousa 63).
Red Card(s): Ba 77, Nélson Veiga 88
Yellow Card(s): Nélson Veiga 13, Dobrasinović 27, Guilherme 29, Mag 32, Kaiafas 38, Ba 75, Ba 77, Nélson Veiga 88

ETHNIKOS ACHNAS FC

UEFA INTERTOTO CUP

First Round - FK Makedonija GP Skopje (MKD)
H 1-0 *Poyiatzis (6p)*
Adamović, Engomitis (Jovanović 75), Ipavec, Kotsonis, Pashialis, Poyiatz Schlichting, Siailis, Stjepanović (Cominelli 72), Grkinić, Suljanović (Gebrc
Yellow Card(s): Kotsonis 34, Siailis 62
A 0-2
Adamović, Blanco (Fernandes 63), Ipavec, Kotsonis, Pashialis, Poyiatzis Schlichting, Siailis, Stjepanović (Gebro 79), Grkinić, Suljanović.
Yellow Card(s): Schlichting 72

CZECH REPUBLIC

AC SPARTA PRAHA

UEFA CHAMPIONS LEAGUE

Third Qualifying Round - Arsenal FC (ENG)
H 0-2
Poštulka, Došek, Hušek, Kadlec, Pospěch, Řepka (Brezinský 36), Rezek

šovič 58), Horváth (Limberský 84), Kladrubský, Kulič, Abraham.
w Card(s): Hušek 9, Kulič 17

lka, Došek, Hušek, Kadlec, Pospěch, Řepka, Rezek (Kolář 73),
th, Kladrubský (Limberský 77), Abraham, Kulič (Žofčák 46).
w Card(s): Kulič 29, Řepka 51, Hušek 87

UEFA CUP

Round - Odense BK (DEN)

lka, Abraham, Došek (Rezek 67), Horváth, Kadlec, Kisel (Petržela 63),
ubský, Matušovič (Limberský 75), Pospěch, Řepka, Slepička.
w Card(s): Došek 52, Petržela 66
(aet; 4-3 on pens)
lka, Abraham (Horváth 91), Brezinský, Kadlec, Kisel, Kladrubský,
Pospěch, Řepka, Slepička (Došek 74), Sylvestre (Kolář 66).
w Card(s): Pospěch 67, Kisel 90, Řepka 98, Kladrubský 101

p E
h 1 - FC Zürich (SUI)
Slepička (24)
lka, Řepka, Brezinský, Kadlec, Limberský (Nádenícek 82), Kisel,
stre, Matušovič, Došek, Slepička, Rezek (Petržela 72).
w Card(s): Limberský 69, Rezek 72, Petržela 90+4
h 2 - Toulouse FC (FRA)
Kisel (67, 88), Došek (68)
r, Řepka, Kladrubský, Kadlec, Limberský, Kisel, Pospěch, Matušovič
an 84), Slepička (Došek 57), Rezek (Horváth 65), Kulič.
w Card(s): Pospěch 78, Došek 82
h 3 - FC Spartak Moskva (RUS)
)
r, Kladrubský, Řepka, Kadlec, Zabavník, Kisel, Horváth, Pospěch,
k (Limberský 80), Došek, Slepička.
h 4 - Bayer 04 Leverkusen (GER)

r, Řepka, Zabavník (Brezinský 89), Došek, Slepička, Rezek (Matušovič 72),
áth, Kladrubský, Kisel, Pospěch, Kadlec.
w Card(s): Kisel 39, Rezek 61

SK SLAVIA PRAHA

UEFA CHAMPIONS LEAGUE

nd Qualifying Round - MŠK Žilina (SVK)
0
ak, Aračić, Janda (Šmicer 63), Kalivoda (Suchý 85), Krajčík, Vlček,
ek, Tavares, Brabec, Šenkeřík (Švec 46), Dřížďal.
Card(s): Aračić 88
ow Card(s): Šenkeřík 40, Aračić 61, Aračić 88, Šmicer 90
0 *(aet; 4-3 on pens)*
ak, Janda, Kalivoda (Volešák 96), Krajčík, Vlček, Tavares, Brabec, Šmicer
c 78), Šenkeřík (Necid 69), Dřížďal, Suchý.
ow Card(s): Šmicer 40, Necid 81

d Qualifying Round - AFC Ajax (NED)
0 *Kalivoda (75p)*
iak, Janda (Belaid 86), Kalivoda (Volešák 80), Krajčík, Vlček (Gaúcho
Tavares, Brabec, Švec, Šenkeřík, Dřížďal, Suchý.
ow Card(s): Vlček 10, Tavares 61, Šenkeřík 90+4
1 *Vlček (23, 87)*
iak, Brabec, Dřížďal, Janda, Kalivoda (Volešák 76), Krajčík, Šmicer (Ivana
Necid 82), Tavares, Vlček, Suchý, Švec.
ow Card(s): Volešák 80

Group H
Match 1 - FC Steaua Bucureşti (ROU)
H 2-1 *Šenkeřík (13), Belaid (63)*
Vaniak, Tavares, Brabec (Janda 43), Latka (Hubáček 46), Vlček, Dřížďal, Šenkeřík, Pudil, Suchý, Krajčík, Belaid (Volešák 81).
Yellow Card(s): Volešák 90+1
Match 2 - Sevilla FC (ESP)
A 2-4 *Pudil (19), Kalivoda (90+2)*
Vaniak, Hubáček, Švec, Vlček, Janda (Kalivoda 63), Dřížďal (Ivana 46), Šourek, Pudil, Suchý, Krajčík, Belaid (Volešák 70).
Yellow Card(s): Šourek 39, Volešák 73
Match 3 - Arsenal FC (ENG)
A 0-7
Vaniak, Tavares (Belaid 63), Hubáček, Švec, Vlček, Šenkeřík, Pudil, Suchý, Krajčík, Ivana (Volešák 56), Kalivoda (Jablonský 46).
Yellow Card(s): Volešák 71
Match 4 - Arsenal FC (ENG)
H 0-0
Vorel, Tavares, Brabec, Hubáček, Švec, Šmicer (Kalivoda 64), Dřížďal, Šenkeřík (Ivana 77), Pudil (Jablonský 90), Suchý, Krajčík.
Yellow Card(s): Tavares 41, Švec 47, Krajčík 72, Pudil 84
Match 5 - FC Steaua Bucureşti (ROU)
A 1-1 *Šenkeřík (78)*
Vaniak, Tavares, Brabec, Hubáček, Švec (Belaid 29), Gaúcho (Necid 77), Šenkeřík, Pudil, Suchý, Krajčík, Volešák (Šourek 61).
Yellow Card(s): Hubáček 52, Krajčík 71, Šourek 73
Match 6 - Sevilla FC (ESP)
H 0-3
Vaniak, Tavares, Brabec, Hubáček, Šmicer (Jablonský 46), Pudil (Gaúcho 74), Suchý, Krajčík, Ivana, Belaid, Volešák (Necid 66).
Yellow Card(s): Krajčík 71

No	Player	Nat	DoB	Aps	(s)	Gls
Goalkeepers						
1	Michal Vorel		27/6/75	1		
28	Martin Vaniak		4/10/70	5		
Defenders						
3	Erich Brabec		24/2/77	4		
4	David Hubáček		23/2/77	5	(1)	
6	Martin Latka		28/9/84	1		
12	František Dřížďal		8/8/78	3		
13	Ondřej Šourek		26/4/83	1	(1)	
Midfielders						
2	Mickaël Tavares	FRA	25/10/82	5		
5	Michal Švec		19/3/87	4		
8	Petr Janda		5/1/87	1	(1)	
11	Vladimír Šmicer		24/5/73	2		
16	Daniel Pudil		27/9/85	6		1
17	Marek Suchý		29/3/88	6		
19	Matej Krajčík	SVK	19/3/78	6		
20	Milan Ivana	SVK	26/11/83	2	(2)	
21	Tijani Belaid	TUN	5/9/87	3	(2)	1
23	Ladislav Volešák		7/4/84	2	(3)	
25	David Kalivoda		25/8/82	1	(2)	1
26	Tomáš Jablonský		21/6/87		(3)	
Attackers						
7	Stanislav Vlček		26/2/76	3		
10	Gaúcho	BRA	28/9/79	1	(1)	
14	Zdeněk Šenkeřík		19/12/80	4		2
24	Tomáš Necid		13/8/89		(2)	

UEFA CUP

Round of 32 - Tottenham Hotspur FC (ENG)
H 1-2 *Střihavka (69)*
Vaniak, Dřížďal, Latka, Brabec, Hubáček, Suchý (Volešák 83), Tavares, Jarolím (Kalivoda 59), Černý, Pudil (Ivana 46), Střihavka.
Yellow Card(s): Hubáček 32, Ivana 63, Tavares 80
A 1-1 *Krajčík (50)*
Vorel, Brabec, Hubáček, Latka, Dřížďal (Volešák 80), Pudil, Suchý, Krajčík (Belaid 87), Kalivoda (Ivana 46), Střihavka, Černý.
Yellow Card(s): Krajčík 45, Pudil 72, Ivana 85

INTERTOTO CUP

FK MLADÁ BOLESLAV

UEFA CUP

First Round - US Città di Palermo (ITA)
H 0-1
Miller, Kopic, Kysela, Matějovský, Rajnoch, Rolko, Sedláček, Táborský (Řezníček 89), Voríšek, Hrdlička, Mendy (Kalina 67).
Yellow Card(s): Mendy 11, Sedláček 88
A 1-0 *Sedláček (90+3) (aet; 4-2 on pens)*
Miller, Kopic, Kysela (Holub 79), Matějovský, Poláček (Kalina 52), Rajnoch, Rolko, Sedláček, Táborský (Vaněček 72), Voríšek, Mendy.
Yellow Card(s): Táborský 46, Kalina 103, Matějovský 108, Sedláček 120

Group C
Match 1 - Villarreal CF (ESP)
H 1-2 *Mendy (90)*
Miller, Kalina (Vaněček 46), Hrdlička (Táborský 83), Procházka, Kopic, Mendy, Rajnoch, Voríšek, Sedláček (Řezníček 58), Matějovský, Kysela.
Yellow Card(s): Sedláček 31, Matějovský 57, Procházka 63, Vaněček 71
Match 2 - IF Elfsborg (SWE)
A 3-1 *Táborský (67), Mendy (79), Voríšek (90+5)*
Pižanowski, Voríšek, Procházka, Kopic, Hrdlička, Kysela (Poláček 93), Rajnoch, Matějovský, Vaněček (Kalina 45), Mendy, Řezníček (Táborský 47).
Yellow Card(s): Řezníček 27, Voríšek 44, Hrdlička 45+3, Procházka 72, Táborský 86
Match 3 - AEK Athens FC (GRE)
H 0-1
Pižanowski, Voríšek, Procházka, Kopic, Hrdlička, Sedláček (Holub 76), Řezníček (Táborský 53), Rajnoch, Matějovský, Kysela (Vaněček 63), Mendy.
Yellow Card(s): Kysela 38, Řezníček 41, Matějovský 73
Match 4 - ACF Fiorentina (ITA)
A 1-2 *Rajnoch (60)*
Pižanowski, Voríšek, Procházka, Kopic, Hrdlička (Vaněček 80), Sedláček, Rolko, Rajnoch, Kysela (Táborský 46), Mendy, Kalina (Holub 65).
Yellow Card(s): Kopic 45+1, Rajnoch 56, Procházka 85

FK JABLONEC 97

UEFA CUP

Second Qualifying Round - FK Austria Wien (AUT)
A 3-4 *Zelenka (28, 36), Baránek (76)*
Špit, Hamouz, Homola, Fukal, Vácha (Zábojník 88), Baránek, Rilke, Zelenka (Nulíček 79), Eliáš, Kordula (Valenta 70), Krejčí.
Yellow Card(s): Fukal 35
H 1-1 *Rilke (83)*
Špit, Zábojník, Flachbart (Rilke 46), Hamouz, Homola, Fukal, Vácha (Krejčí 88), Baránek, Zelenka, Svátek, Eliáš (Valenta 62).

FC SLOVAN LIBEREC

UEFA INTERTOTO CUP

Second Round - FC Tobol Kostanay (KAZ)
A 1-1 *Nezmar (34)*
Hauzr, Liška, Matula, Nezmar (Hochmeister 84), Papoušek (Hudson 6
Pudil, Polák, Bílek, Krátký, Jirouš (Radzinevičius 56), Hodúr.
Yellow Card(s): Liška 52
H 0-2
Bolek, Nezmar, Papoušek, Pudil (Liška 35), Hodúr, Koštál, Polák (Brezi
78), Bílek, Hudson, Krátký (Blažek 46), Dejmek.

DENMARK

FC KØBENHAVN

UEFA CHAMPIONS LEAGUE

Second Qualifying Round - Beitar Jerusalem FC (ISR)
H 1-0 *Allbäck (9)*
Christiansen, Allbäck (Antonsson 69), Gravgaard, Grønkjær, Hangelan
Kvist Jørgensen, Silberbauer, Nørregaard, Jensen, Nordstrand (Almeid
65), Hutchinson.
Yellow Card(s): Hangeland 57
A 1-1 *Allbäck (97) (aet)*
Christiansen, Allbäck (Almeida 100), Gravgaard, Grønkjær, Hangeland
Kvist Jørgensen, Silberbauer, Nørregaard, Jensen, Würtz (Antonsson 1
Hutchinson.
Yellow Card(s): Grønkjær 52, Allbäck 71, Kvist Jørgensen 75

Third Qualifying Round - SL Benfica (POR)
A 1-2 *Hutchinson (35)*
Christiansen, Allbäck (Nordstrand 78), Gravgaard, Grønkjær, Hangelar
Hutchinson, Jensen, Kvist Jørgensen, Nørregaard (Sionko 89), Silberba
Würtz.
Yellow Card(s): Grønkjær 45+1, Würtz 60
H 0-1
Christiansen, Allbäck, Gravgaard, Hangeland, Hutchinson, Jensen, Kvi
Jørgensen, Nordstrand (Almeida 74), Nørregaard, Silberbauer, Würtz (Sionko 58).
Yellow Card(s): Hutchinson 27

UEFA CUP

First Round - RC Lens (FRA)
A 1-1 *Allbäck (5)*
Christiansen, Allbäck (Nordstrand 71), Gravgaard, Grønkjær, Hangelan
Hutchinson (Sionko 71), Jensen, Kvist Jørgensen, Nørregaard, Silberba
Würtz.
Yellow Card(s): Würtz 63, Jensen 69, Kvist Jørgensen 81
H 2-1 *Allbäck (76), Grønkjær (112) (aet)*
Christiansen, Allbäck (Zanka Jørgensen 100), Gravgaard, Grønkjær, Hangeland, Hutchinson, Jensen, Kvist Jørgensen, Nørregaard (Nordstr
59), Silberbauer (Würtz 71), Sionko.
Red Card(s): Gravgaard 94
Yellow Card(s): Hangeland 80, Nordstrand 90+2

Group B
Match 1 - Panathinaikos FC (GRE)
H 0-1
Christiansen, Jensen, Hangeland, Antonsson, Kvist Jørgensen, Grønkjær, Hutchinson, Würtz (Nørregaard 56), Sionko (Silberbauer 56), Allbäck, Nordst
Yellow Card(s): Hangeland 43
Match 2 - FC Lokomotiv Moskva (RUS)
A 1-0 *Nordstrand (62p)*

stiansen, Nørregaard, Hangeland, Würtz (Sionko 32), Nordstrand eida 79), Allbäck, Hutchinson, Gravgaard, Antonsson, Wendt, Kvist ensen.
ow Card(s): Nørregaard 69
ch 3 - Club Atlético de Madrid (ESP)
2
stiansen, Jensen, Hangeland, Gravgaard, Kvist Jørgensen, Wendt, egaard, Würtz (Sionko 54), Hutchinson (Jørgensen 83), Nordstrand eida 53), Allbäck.
ow Card(s): Hangeland 70
ch 4 - Aberdeen FC (SCO)
4
stiansen, Kvist Jørgensen, Gravgaard, Antonsson, Wendt, Sionko, egaard (Silberbauer 50), Würtz (Almeida 58), Hutchinson, Allbäck, kjær (Nordstrand 70).
ow Card(s): Gravgaard 23, Würtz 39

ODENSE BK

UEFA CUP

Qualifying Round - Saint Patrick's Athletic FC (IRL)
0
szko, Borring, A. Christensen, Laursen, Oliveira (Andreasen 69), eg, Hansen, K. Christensen (Timm 80), S. Jensen, Bolaños, alonsen.
ow Card(s): Absalonsen 42
0 *Andreasen (20), K. Christensen (29, 73), Borring (45), Mikkelsen (89)*
szko, Borring, A. Christensen, Laursen, Sørensen, Timm, Andreasen kelsen 79), Helveg (Troest 46), Hansen, K. Christensen, Bolaños onjić 70).

nd Qualifying Round - FC Dinamo Minsk (BLR)
1 *Laursen (90+4)*
szko, Absalonsen (Radonjić 90), Bolaños (Mikkelsen 79), Borring, stensen, Hansen, Helveg, Laursen, Oliveira, Sørensen, D. Nielsen obsen 69).
0 *D. Nielsen (38, 55), Absalonsen (77, 79)*
szko, Absalonsen, Bolaños (Bisgaard 74), Borring, Christensen, sen, Helveg, Laursen, Oliveira (Andreasen 63), Sørensen, D. Nielsen obsen 83).

Round - AC Sparta Praha (CZE)
0
szko, Andreasen, Bisgaard (Mikkelsen 74), Borring, Christensen, Helveg, sen, D. Nielsen (Oliveira 88), Sørensen, Timm (Jacobsen 90+1), Troest.
ow Card(s): Onyszko 59
0 *(aet; 3-4 on pens)*
szko, Andreasen, Bisgaard, Borring, Christensen, Helveg, Laursen, D. sen (Oliveira 38), Sørensen, Timm (Jacobsen 46; Saeternes 101), Troest.
ow Card(s): Christensen 43, Oliveira 67, Troest 82, Borring 96

FC MIDTJYLLAND

UEFA CUP

First Qualifying Round - Keflavík (ISL)
A 2-3 *Dadu (9), Afriyie (20)*
Raška, Afriyie, Larsen, Dadu (Babatunde 75), C. Poulsen, D. Olsen, Oluwafemi, S. Poulsen (Madsen 61), Thygesen, Troest, Reid (Klimpl 70).
H 2-1 *S. Poulsen (68), Dadu (75)*
Raška, Afriyie (C. Olsen 41), Klimpl, Dadu, Oluwafemi (C. Poulsen 82), Jessen, Kristensen, Madsen (D. Olsen 57), S. Poulsen, Thygesen, Troest.
Yellow Card(s): S. Poulsen 88

Second Qualifying Round - FC Haka (FIN)
A 2-1 *Kristensen (13,44)*
Raška, Afriyie, Oluwafemi, Flinta, Jessen, Klimpl, Kristensen, S. Poulsen, Thygesen, Troest, Babatunde.
Yellow Card(s): Thygesen 50
H 5-2 *Flinta (16), Olsen (27), Dadu (34), Troest (67), Larsen (85)*
Raška, Afriyie, Dadu, Oluwafemi (Larsen 62), Flinta, Jessen, Klimpl, Kristensen (C. Olsen 60), D. Olsen (Madsen 64), Thygesen, Troest.

First Round - FC Lokomotiv Moskva (RUS)
H 1-3 *Babatunde (30)*
Raška, Afriyie, Oluwafemi, Klimpl, Kristensen (Larsen 77), Madsen (D. Olsen 66), C. Poulsen, S. Poulsen, Thygesen, Troest, Babatunde (C. Olsen 73).
Yellow Card(s): Oluwafemi 77
A 0-2
Raška, Afriyie, Dadu, Oluwafemi (Larsen 61), Klimpl, D. Olsen, C. Poulsen, S. Poulsen (Jessen 56), Thygesen, Troest, Babatunde (Kristensen 46).
Yellow Card(s): Afriyie 57, Poulsen 67

AALBORG BK

UEFA INTERTOTO CUP

Second Round - FC Honka Espoo (FIN)
A 2-2 *Lindström (1), Prica (23)*
Nielsen, Califf (Risgård 27), Lindström, Nomvethe, Olesen (Jacobsen 46), Olsen, Pedersen, Prica, Curth, Jakobsen, Sørensen (Enevoldsen 83).
Yellow Card(s): Jakobsen 32, Pedersen 66, Prica 74, Olsen 76, Lindström 77
H 1-1 *Nomvethe (61)*
Nielsen, Jacobsen (Mota 85), Lindström (Kristensen 65), Nomvethe, Olsen, Pedersen, Prica, Risgård, Caca (Enevoldsen 53), Curth, Jakobsen.
Yellow Card(s): Lindström 22, Jacobsen 62, Pedersen 69, Nomvethe 90+1

Third Round - KAA Gent (BEL)
A 1-1 *Nomvethe (55)*
Jensen, Califf, Curth, Jacobsen, Nomvethe, Olesen, Prica, Risgård, Johansson (Kristensen 66), Jakobsen, Enevoldsen (Olsen 81).
Red Card(s): Nomvethe 55
Yellow Card(s): Olesen 26, Nomvethe 31, Nomvethe 55
H 2-1 Califf (31), Johansson (78)
Jensen, Califf, Curth, Lindström, Olesen, Pedersen, Prica, Risgård, Johansson (Kristensen 91), Jakobsen, Enevoldsen.
Yellow Card(s): Prica 50, Pedersen 70

UEFA CUP

Second Qualifying Round - HJK Helsinki (FIN)
A 1-2 *Risgård (37)*
Jensen, Califf, Curth (Mota 68), Johansson, Lindström (Kristensen 76), Nomvethe, Olesen, Pedersen, Risgård, Enevoldsen (Caca 22), Jakobsen.
Yellow Card(s): Pedersen 88
H 3-0 *Enevoldsen (7), Johansson (26), Curth (43)*
Zaza, Califf, Curth (Lindström 59), Johansson (Caca 89), Nomvethe, Olesen, Prica, Risgård, Enevoldsen (Augustinussen 68), Jakobsen, Kristensen.
Yellow Card(s): Califf 44, Lindström 62, Nomvethe 79

First Round - UC Sampdoria (ITA)
A 2-2 *Prica (19), Johansson (54)*
Zaza, Augustinussen, Califf, Curth, Johansson, Olesen, Pedersen, Prica, Risgård, Enevoldsen, Jakobsen.
Yellow Card(s): Zaza 68, Olesen 85
H 0-0
Zaza, Jakobsen, Pedersen (Olfers 81), Califf, Johansson, Augustinussen, Prica, Nomvethe (Curth 70), Olesen, Risgård, Enevoldsen (Lindström 87).
Yellow Card(s): Zaza 68

Group G
Match 1 - RSC Anderlecht (BEL)
H 1-1 *Lindström (86)*
Zaza, Olesen, Califf, Jakobsen, Pedersen, Johansson (Enevoldsen 60), Augustinussen, Risgård, Nomvethe (Lindström 78), Curth, Prica.
Yellow Card(s): Pedersen 13, Prica 45+1, Risgård 90+2
Match 2 - Tottenham Hotspur FC (ENG)
A 2-3 *Enevoldsen (2), Risgård (37)*
Zaza, Olesen, Califf, Jakobsen, Pedersen, Risgård, Augustinussen, Nomvethe (Lindström 76), Johansson, Enevoldsen (Curth 76), Prica.
Yellow Card(s): Augustinussen 80
Match 3 - Getafe CF (ESP)
H 1-2 *Prica (90+2)*
Zaza, Jakobsen, Olesen, Califf, Johansson, Pedersen (Olfers 58), Augustinussen, Risgård (Nomvethe 58), Enevoldsen (Lindström 77), Prica, Curth.
Yellow Card(s): Curth 13, Enevoldsen 20, Jakobsen 23, Prica 90+4
Match 4 - Hapoel Tel-Aviv FC (ISR)
A 3-1 *Risgård (27), Jakobsen (50p), Enevoldsen (66)*
Zaza, Olesen, Califf, Jacobsen, Jakobsen, Olfers (Olsen 78), Risgård, Caca (Lindström 59), Johansson (Vilakazi 90), Enevoldsen, Curth.

ENGLAND

MANCHESTER UNITED FC

UEFA CHAMPIONS LEAGUE

Group F
Match 1 - Sporting Clube de Portugal (POR)
A 1-0 *Cristiano Ronaldo (62)*
Van der Sar, Evra, Ferdinand, Brown, Cristiano Ronaldo (Tévez 87), Rooney (Saha 72), Giggs (Anderson 76), Vidić, Carrick, Nani, Scholes.
Yellow Card(s): Nani 38, Van der Sar 82
Match 2 - AS Roma (ITA)
H 1-0 *Rooney (70)*
Kuszczak, Evra, Ferdinand, Cristiano Ronaldo, Saha (Tévez 66), Rooney (Anderson 85), Vidić, Carrick, Nani (Giggs 80), Scholes, O'Shea.
Match 3 - FC Dynamo Kyiv (UKR)
A 4-2 *Ferdinand (10), Rooney (18), Cristiano Ronaldo (41, 68p)*
Van der Sar (Kuszczak 80), Ferdinand, Brown, Cristiano Ronaldo, Anderson, Rooney, Giggs (Simpson 80), Vidić, O'Shea, Fletcher, Tévez (Nani 73).
Match 4 - FC Dynamo Kyiv (UKR)
H 4-0 *Piqué (31), Tévez (37), Rooney (76), Cristiano Ronaldo (88)*
Van der Sar (Kuszczak 46), Evra, Cristiano Ronaldo, Rooney, Vidić, Carrick, Nani, Piqué (Evans 73), Fletcher, Simpson, Tévez (Saha 68).
Yellow Card(s): Rooney 17
Match 5 - Sporting Clube de Portugal (POR)
H 2-1 *Tévez (61), Cristiano Ronaldo (90+2)*
Kuszczak, Evra, Ferdinand, Cristiano Ronaldo, Anderson, Saha (Hargreaves 79), Vidić, Carrick, Nani (Giggs 46), O'Shea, Fletcher (Tévez 46).
Yellow Card(s): Cristiano Ronaldo 80, Evra 83
Match 6 - AS Roma (ITA)
A 1-1 *Piqué (34)*
Kuszczak, Saha, Rooney (Dong 72), Carrick, Nani, Piqué, O'Shea (Brow 54), Evans, Fletcher, Simpson, Eagles.
Round of 16 - Olympique Lyonnais (FRA)
A 1-1 *Tévez (87)*
Van der Sar, Evra, Hargreaves (Carrick 78), Ferdinand, Brown, Cristiano Ronaldo, Anderson, Rooney, Giggs (Nani 65), Vidić, Scholes (Tévez 65).
Yellow Card(s): Hargreaves 39
H 1-0 *Cristiano Ronaldo (41)*
Van der Sar, Evra, Ferdinand, Brown, Cristiano Ronaldo (Hargreaves 92 Anderson (Tévez 70), Rooney, Vidić, Carrick, Nani, Fletcher.
Yellow Card(s): Evra 4, Nani 43, Fletcher 73

Quarter-Final - AS Roma (ITA)
A 2-0 *Cristiano Ronaldo (39), Rooney (66)*
Van der Sar, Evra, Ferdinand, Brown, Cristiano Ronaldo, Anderson (Hargreaves 55), Rooney (Tévez 84), Park, Vidić (O'Shea 33), Carrick, Scholes.
Yellow Card(s): Anderson 45+2
H 1-0 *Tévez (70)*
Van der Sar, Hargreaves, Ferdinand, Brown, Anderson (Neville 81), Gig (Rooney 74), Park, Carrick (O'Shea 74), Piqué, Silvestre, Tévez.

Semi-Final - FC Barcelona (ESP)
A 0-0
Van der Sar, Evra, Hargreaves, Ferdinand, Brown, Cristiano Ronaldo, Rooney (Nani 76), Park, Carrick, Scholes, Tévez (Giggs 85).
Yellow Card(s): Hargreaves 73
H 1-0 *Scholes (14)*
Van der Sar, Evra (Silvestre 90+3), Hargreaves, Ferdinand, Brown, Cristi Ronaldo, Park, Carrick, Nani (Giggs 77), Scholes (Fletcher 77), Tévez.
Yellow Card(s): Carrick 63, Cristiano Ronaldo 68

Final - Chelsea FC (ENG)
H 1-1 *Cristiano Ronaldo (26) (aet; 6-5 on pens)*
Van der Sar, Evra, Hargreaves, Ferdinand, Brown (Anderson 120+5), Cristi Ronaldo, Rooney (Nani 101), Vidić, Carrick, Scholes (Giggs 87), Tévez.
Yellow Card(s): Scholes 22, Ferdinand 43, Vidić 111, Tévez 116

No	Player	Nat	DoB	Aps	(s)	Gls
Goalkeepers						
1	Edwin van der Sar	NED	29/10/70	10		
29	Tomasz Kuszczak	POL	20/3/82	3	(2)	
Defenders						
2	Gary Neville		18/2/75		(1)	
3	Patrice Evra	FRA	15/5/81	10		
5	Rio Ferdinand		7/11/78	11		1
6	Wes Brown		13/10/79	9	(1)	
15	Nemanja Vidić	SRB	21/10/81	9		
19	Gerard Piqué	ESP	2/2/87	3		2
22	John O'Shea	IRL	30/4/81	4	(2)	
23	Jonny Evans	NIR	3/1/88	1	(1)	
25	Daniel Simpson		4/1/87	2	(1)	
27	Mikaël Silvestre	FRA	9/8/77	1	(1)	
Midfielders						
4	Owen Hargreaves		20/1/81	5	(3)	
8	Anderson	BRA	13/4/88	6	(3)	
11	Ryan Giggs	WAL	29/11/73	4	(5)	
13	Park Ji-sung	KOR	25/2/81	4		
16	Michael Carrick		28/7/81	11	(1)	
17	Nani	POR	17/11/86	7	(4)	
18	Paul Scholes		16/11/74	7		1
24	Darren Fletcher	SCO	1/2/84	5	(1)	
33	Chris Eagles		19/11/85	1		
Attackers						
7	Cristiano Ronaldo	POR	5/2/85	11		8
9	Louis Saha	FRA	8/8/78	3	(2)	
10	Wayne Rooney		24/10/85	10	(1)	4
21	Dong Fangzhuo	CHN	23/1/85		(1)	
32	Carlos Tévez	ARG	5/2/84	6	(6)	4

CHELSEA FC

UEFA CHAMPIONS LEAGUE

ıp B
ch 1 - Rosenborg BK (NOR)
1 *Shevchenko (63)*
, A. Cole (Ben Haim 74), Makelele, Essien, Shevchenko, J. Cole
ght-Phillips 74), Malouda, Kalou, Terry, Alex, Belletti.
ow Card(s): Essien 66
ch 2 - Valencia CF (ESP)
1 *J. Cole (21), Drogba (71)*
, A. Cole, Makelele, Essien (Sidwell 84), Ricardo Carvalho, J. Cole,
ba, Mikel (Alex 89), Malouda (Kalou 86), Paulo Ferreira, Terry.
ow Card(s): Mikel 89
ch 3 - FC Schalke 04 (GER)
0 *Malouda (4), Drogba (47)*
, Makelele, Essien (Mikel 70), Ricardo Carvalho, Lampard, J. Cole
vchenko 89), Drogba, Malouda (Kalou 84), Bridge, Paulo Ferreira, Alex.
ch 4 - FC Schalke 04 (GER)
0
(Cudicini 46), Makelele, Essien, Ricardo Carvalho, Lampard, J. Cole,
gba, Malouda (Wright-Phillips 78), Bridge, Alex, Belletti (Mikel 64).
ow Card(s): Essien 84
ch 5 - Rosenborg BK (NOR)
0 *Drogba (8, 20), Alex (40), J. Cole (73)*
icini, A. Cole, Makelele, Essien, Lampard (Pizarro 76), J. Cole, Drogba
vchenko 68), Wright-Phillips (Kalou 69), Terry, Alex, Belletti.
ch 6 - Valencia CF (ESP)
0
, Essien, Shevchenko (Makelele 46), Lampard (J. Cole 62), Pizarro,
ge, Paulo Ferreira (Belletti 72), Kalou, Ben Haim, Wright-Phillips, Terry.

nd of 16 - Olympiacos CFP (GRE)
0
, A. Cole, Makelele, Essien, Ricardo Carvalho, J. Cole (Anelka 75),
gba, Ballack (Lampard 86), Malouda (Kalou 75), Alex, Belletti.
ow Card(s): Alex 35, Belletti 56, Makelele 63, A. Cole 90+1
0 *Ballack (5), Lampard (25), Kalou (48)*
icini, A. Cole, Makelele, Ricardo Carvalho, Lampard (Essien 76), J. Cole
ght-Phillips 79), Drogba, Ballack, Paulo Ferreira, Kalou (Malouda 71),
y.
ow Card(s): Lampard 70, Paulo Ferreira 80, Terry 83

rter-Final - Fenerbahçe SK (TUR)
2 *Deivid (13og)*
icini, A. Cole, Makelele, Essien, Ricardo Carvalho, Lampard (Mikel 76),
ole (Anelka 86), Drogba, Ballack, Malouda, Terry.
0 *Ballack (4), Lampard (87)*
icini (Hilário 26), A. Cole, Makelele, Essien, Ricardo Carvalho, Lampard,
ole (Malouda 85), Drogba, Ballack, Kalou (Belletti 58), Terry.
ow Card(s): Essien 86, Ricardo Carvalho 90

ni-Final - Liverpool FC (ENG)
1 *Riise (90+4og)*
h, A. Cole, Makelele, Ricardo Carvalho, Lampard, J. Cole (Kalou 63),
gba, Ballack (Anelka 86), Malouda, Paulo Ferreira, Terry.
ow Card(s): Terry 90+3
2 *Drogba (33, 105), Lampard (98p) (aet)*
h, A. Cole, Makelele, Essien, Ricardo Carvalho, Lampard (Shevchenko
), J. Cole (Anelka 91), Drogba, Ballack, Kalou (Malouda 70), Terry.

al - Manchester United FC (ENG)
1 *Lampard (45) (aet; 5-6 on pens)*
h, A. Cole, Makelele (Belletti 120+4), Essien, Ricardo Carvalho,
npard, J. Cole (Anelka 99), Drogba, Ballack, Malouda (Kalou 92), Terry.
Red Card(s): Drogba 116
Yellow Card(s): Makelele 21, Ricardo Carvalho 45+2, Ballack 116, Essien 118

No	Player	Nat	DoB	Aps	(s)	Gls
Goalkeepers						
1	Petr Čech	CZE	20/5/82	9		
23	Carlo Cudicini	ITA	6/9/73	4	(1)	
40	Hilário	POR	21/10/75		(1)	
Defenders						
3	Ashley Cole		20/12/80	10		
6	Ricardo Carvalho	POR	18/5/78	10		
18	Wayne Bridge		5/8/80	3		
20	Paulo Ferreira	POR	18/1/79	5		
22	Tal Ben Haim	ISR	31/3/82	1	(1)	
26	John Terry		7/12/80	10		
33	Alex	BRA	17/6/82	5	(1)	1
35	Juliano Belletti	BRA	20/6/76	4	(3)	
Midfielders						
4	Claude Makelele	FRA	18/2/73	12	(1)	
5	Michael Essien	GHA	3/12/82	11	(1)	
8	Frank Lampard		20/6/78	10	(1)	4
9	Steve Sidwell		14/12/82		(1)	
10	Joe Cole		8/11/81	12	(1)	2
12	John Obi Mikel	NGA	22/4/87	1	(3)	
13	Michael Ballack	GER	26/9/76	7		2
15	Florent Malouda	FRA	13/6/80	8	(3)	1
24	Shaun Wright-Phillips		25/10/81	2	(3)	
Attackers						
7	Andriy Shevchenko	UKR	29/9/76	2	(3)	1
11	Didier Drogba	CIV	11/3/78	11		6
14	Claudio Pizarro	PER	3/10/78	1	(1)	
21	Salomon Kalou	CIV	5/8/85	5	(6)	1
39	Nicolas Anelka	FRA	14/3/79		(5)	

LIVERPOOL FC

UEFA CHAMPIONS LEAGUE

Third Qualifying Round - Toulouse FC (FRA)
A 1-0 *Voronin (43)*
Reina, Arbeloa, Carragher, Crouch, Finnan, Gerrard (Sissoko 64), Hyypiä, Mascherano, Voronin (Fernando Torres 78), Benayoun (Riise 58), Babel.
H 4-0 *Crouch (19), Hyypiä (49), Kuyt (87, 90+1)*
Reina, Agger (Finnan 81), Arbeloa, Crouch, Hyypiä, Kuyt, Mascherano, Riise, Sissoko (Lucas Leiva 68), Benayoun, Leto (Babel 75).

Group A
Match 1 - FC Porto (POR)
A 1-1 *Kuyt (17)*
Reina, Finnan, Hyypiä, Gerrard, Fernando Torres (Voronin 76), Pennant, Arbeloa, Kuyt, Babel (Fábio Aurélio 85), Mascherano, Carragher.
Red Card(s): Pennant 58
Yellow Card(s): Kuyt 18, Pennant 26, Pennant 58, Fernando Torres 73, Mascherano 90+2
Match 2 - Olympique de Marseille (FRA)
H 0-1
Reina, Finnan, Hyypiä, Gerrard, Fernando Torres, Benayoun, Fábio Aurélio, Crouch (Kuyt 75), Sissoko, Carragher, Leto (Riise 52).
Yellow Card(s): Gerrard 19, Sissoko 52, Carragher 63
Match 3 - Beşiktaş JK (TUR)
A 1-2 *Gerrard (85)*
Reina, Finnan, Hyypiä (Crouch 83), Riise, Gerrard, Voronin, Pennant (Benayoun 59), Kuyt, Babel, Mascherano (Lucas 76), Carragher.
Match 4 - Beşiktaş JK (TUR)
H 8-0 *Crouch (19, 89), Benayoun (32, 53, 56), Gerrard (69), Babel (78, 81)*

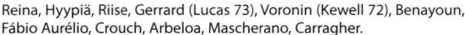

Reina, Hyypiä, Riise, Gerrard (Lucas 73), Voronin (Kewell 72), Benayoun, Fábio Aurélio, Crouch, Arbeloa, Mascherano, Carragher.
Match 5 - FC Porto (POR)
H 4-1 *Fernando Torres (19, 78), Gerrard (84p), Crouch (87)*
Reina, Finnan, Hyypiä, Gerrard, Fernando Torres, Voronin (Kewell 63), Benayoun (Crouch 71), Arbeloa, Babel (Kuyt 85), Mascherano, Carragher.
Yellow Card(s): Hyypiä 37
Match 6 - Olympique de Marseille (FRA)
A 4-0 *Gerrard (4), Fernando Torres (11), Kuyt (48), Babel (90+1)*
Reina, Hyypiä, Riise, Kewell (Fábio Aurélio 67), Gerrard, Fernando Torres (Babel 77), Benayoun, Arbeloa, Kuyt (Lucas 86), Mascherano, Carragher.
Yellow Card(s): Carragher 29, Fábio Aurélio 89

Round of 16 - FC Internazionale Milano (ITA)
H 2-0 *Kuyt (85), Gerrard (90)*
Reina, Finnan, Hyypiä, Gerrard, Fernando Torres, Fábio Aurélio, Kuyt, Babel (Pennant 72), Mascherano, Lucas (Crouch 64), Carragher.
A 1-0 *Fernando Torres (64)*
Reina, Hyypiä, Gerrard, Fernando Torres, Fábio Aurélio, Kuyt (Riise 81), Babel (Benayoun 61), Mascherano (Pennant 87), Lucas, Carragher, Škrteľ.
Yellow Card(s): Babel 12, Gerrard 47, Fábio Aurélio 56, Benayoun 74

Quarter-Final - Arsenal FC (ENG)
A 1-1 *Kuyt (26)*
Reina, Hyypiä, Gerrard, Fernando Torres (Voronin 86), Fábio Aurélio, Xabi Alonso (Lucas 77), Kuyt, Babel (Benayoun 58), Mascherano, Carragher, Škrteľ.
H 4-2 *Hyypiä (30), Fernando Torres (69), Gerrard (85p), Babel (90+2)*
Reina, Hyypiä, Gerrard, Fernando Torres (Riise 87), Fábio Aurélio, Xabi Alonso, Crouch (Babel 78), Kuyt (Arbeloa 93), Mascherano, Carragher, Škrteľ.

Semi-Final - Chelsea FC (ENG)
H 1-1 *Kuyt (43)*
Reina, Gerrard, Fernando Torres, Fábio Aurélio (Riise 62), Xabi Alonso, Arbeloa, Kuyt, Babel (Benayoun 76), Mascherano, Carragher, Škrteľ.
A 2-3 *Fernando Torres (64), Babel (117) (aet)*
Reina, Riise, Gerrard, Fernando Torres (Babel 98), Benayoun (Pennant 78), Xabi Alonso, Arbeloa, Kuyt, Mascherano, Carragher, Škrteľ (Hyypiä 22).
Yellow Card(s): Xabi Alonso 41, Arbeloa 99

No	Player	Nat	DoB	Aps	(s)	Gls
Goalkeepers						
25	Pepe Reina	ESP	31/8/82	12		
Defenders						
3	Steve Finnan	IRL	20/4/76	5		
4	Sami Hyypiä	FIN	7/10/73	10	(1)	1
6	John Arne Riise	NOR	24/9/80	4	(4)	
12	Fábio Aurélio	BRA	24/9/79	7	(2)	
17	Álvaro Arbeloa	ESP	17/1/83	6	(1)	
23	Jamie Carragher		28/1/78	12		
37	Martin Škrteľ	SVK	15/12/84	5		
Midfielders						
7	Harry Kewell	AUS	22/9/78	1	(2)	
8	Steven Gerrard		30/5/80	12		6
11	Yossi Benayoun	ISR	5/5/80	5	(4)	3
14	Xabi Alonso	ESP	25/11/81	4		
16	Jermaine Pennant		15/1/83	2	(3)	
20	Javier Mascherano	ARG	8/6/84	11		
21	Lucas Leiva	BRA	19/1/87	2	(4)	
22	Momo Sissoko	FRA	22/1/85	1		
33	Sebastián Leto	ARG	30/8/86	1		
Attackers						
9	Fernando Torres	ESP	20/3/84	10		6
10	Andriy Voronin	UKR	21/7/79	3	(3)	
15	Peter Crouch		30/1/81	3	(3)	3
18	Dirk Kuyt	NED	22/7/80	9	(2)	5
19	Ryan Babel	NED	19/12/86	7	(3)	5

ARSENAL FC

UEFA CHAMPIONS LEAGUE

Third Qualifying Round - AC Sparta Praha (CZE)
A 2-0 *Fàbregas (72), Hleb (90+2)*
Lehmann, Clichy, Eboué, Flamini, Gallas, Hleb, Rosický (Song 79), Tour
Van Persie, Sagna, Fàbregas.
Yellow Card(s): Fàbregas 25, Flamini 38, Van Persie 45+2
H 3-0 *Rosický (7), Fàbregas (88), Eduardo (89)*
Almunia, Clichy, Gilberto Silva, Diaby (Fàbregas 67), Hoyte, Rosický (Denilson 73), Senderos, Touré, Van Persie (Adebayor 67), Walcott, Eduardo.
Yellow Card(s): Walcott 84

Group H
Match 1 - Sevilla FC (ESP)
H 3-0 *Fàbregas (27), Van Persie (59), Eduardo (90+2)*
Almunia, Sagna, Fàbregas, Touré, Senderos, Rosický (Diaby 50), Van Pe
(Diarra 88), Hleb, Flamini, Clichy, Adebayor (Eduardo 83).
Yellow Card(s): Adebayor 49
Match 2 - FC Steaua Bucureşti (ROU)
A 1-0 *Van Persie (76)*
Almunia, Sagna, Fàbregas, Touré, Senderos, Van Persie, Hleb, Flamini, Clichy, Adebayor, Eboué (Gilberto Silva 73).
Yellow Card(s): Adebayor 15
Match 3 - SK Slavia Praha (CZE)
H 7-0 *Fàbregas (5, 58), Hubáček (24og), Walcott (41, 55), Hleb (51), Bendtner (89)*
Almunia, Sagna, Fàbregas, Touré, Gallas, Hleb (Rosický 63), Flamini (Gilberto Silva 63), Clichy, Adebayor (Bendtner 63), Eboué, Walcott.
Yellow Card(s): Flamini 11, Clichy 52, Hleb 59
Match 4 - SK Slavia Praha (CZE)
A 0-0
Almunia, Diaby, Diarra, Eduardo (Eboué 81), Gallas, Denilson, Song, Gilberto Silva, Clichy, Bendtner (Adebayor 77), Walcott.
Yellow Card(s): Diarra 52, Denilson 82
Match 5 - Sevilla FC (ESP)
A 1-3 *Eduardo (11)*
Almunia, Fàbregas (Rosický 56), Touré, Senderos, Eduardo, Denilson, Gilberto Silva, Bendtner, Eboué (Walcott 78), Traoré, Hoyte (Sagna 66).
Yellow Card(s): Hoyte 44, Denilson 50
Match 6 - FC Steaua Bucureşti (ROU)
H 2-1 *Diaby (8), Bendtner (42)*
Lehmann, Diaby (Eboué 71), Sagna (Diarra 71), Senderos, Gallas, Van Persie (Eduardo 65), Denilson, Song, Bendtner, Traoré, Walcott.
Yellow Card(s): Bendtner 39

Round of 16 - AC Milan (ITA)
H 0-0
Lehmann, Sagna, Fàbregas, Touré (Senderos 7), Eduardo (Bendtner 74), Gallas, Hleb, Flamini, Clichy, Adebayor, Eboué (Walcott 90).
Yellow Card(s): Senderos 70, Eboué 81
A 2-0 *Fàbregas (84), Adebayor (90+2)*
Almunia, Diaby, Sagna, Fàbregas, Senderos, Gallas, Hleb (Gilberto Silva 90), Flamini, Clichy, Adebayor, Eboué (Walcott 71).
Yellow Card(s): Hleb 33, Eboué 56, Clichy 72

Quarter-Final - Liverpool FC (ENG)
H 1-1 *Adebayor (23)*
Almunia, Fàbregas, Touré, Senderos, Gallas, Van Persie (Walcott 46), Hle
Flamini, Clichy, Adebayor, Eboué (Bendtner 67).
A 2-4 *Diaby (13), Adebayor (84)*
Almunia, Diaby (Van Persie 72), Fàbregas, Touré, Senderos, Gallas, Hleb, Flamini (Gilberto Silva 42), Clichy, Adebayor, Eboué (Walcott 72).
Yellow Card(s): Senderos 17, Touré 85

Player	Nat	DoB	Aps	(s)	Gls
keepers					
Jens Lehmann	GER	10/11/69	2		
Manuel Almunia	ESP	19/5/77	8		
nders					
Bacary Sagna	FRA	14/2/83	6	(1)	
Kolo Touré	CIV	19/3/81	7		
Philippe Senderos	SUI	14/2/85	7	(1)	
William Gallas	FRA	17/8/77	7		
Gaël Clichy	FRA	26/7/85	8		
Emmanuel Eboué	CIV	4/6/83	7	(2)	
Armand Traoré	FRA	8/10/89	2		
Justin Hoyte		20/11/84	1		
elders					
Abou Diaby	FRA	11/5/86	4	(1)	2
Cesc Fàbregas	ESP	4/5/87	8		4
Tomáš Rosický	CZE	4/10/80	1	(2)	
Lassana Diarra	FRA	10/3/85	1	(2)	
Aleksandr Hleb	BLR	1/5/81	7		1
Denilson	BRA	16/2/88	3		
Mathieu Flamini	FRA	7/3/84	7		
Alexandre Song	CMR	9/9/87	2		
Gilberto Silva	BRA	7/10/76	2	(4)	
kers					
Eduardo da Silva	CRO	25/2/83	3	(2)	2
Robin van Persie	NED	6/8/83	4	(1)	2
Emmanuel Adebayor	TGO	26/2/84	7	(1)	3
Nicklas Bendtner	DEN	16/1/88	3	(3)	2
Theo Walcott		16/3/89	3	(5)	2

TOTTENHAM HOTSPUR FC

UEFA CUP

Round - Anorthosis Famagusta FC (CYP)
1 *Kaboul (5), Dawson (39), Keane (42), Bent (43), Defoe (65, 90+1)*
ý, Assou-Ekotto (Bale 79), Chimbonda, Dawson, Huddlestone, Keane
›e 62), Malbranque (Taarabt 69), Zokora, Kaboul, Bent, Lennon.
1 *Keane (78)*
nson, Dawson, Defoe, Gardner, Huddlestone, Lee (Keane 75),
ranque, Stalteri, Zokora, Boateng (Bale 69), Bent (Taarabt 85).
ow Card(s): Robinson 54

up G
ch 1 - Getafe CF (ESP)
2 *Defoe (19)*
ý, Chimbonda, Kaboul, Gardner (Dawson 43), Lee, Lennon,
dlestone, Zokora (Tainio 73), Malbranque (Keane 71), Berbatov, Defoe.
ow Card(s): Defoe 87, Kaboul 90
ch 2 - Hapoel Tel-Aviv FC (ISR)
0 *Keane (26), Berbatov (31)*
nson, Chimbonda, Lee, Zokora, Stalteri, Jenas (Boateng 68), Berbatov,
e (Bent 68), Malbranque (Defoe 56), Dawson, Lennon.
ow Card(s): Berbatov 41, Defoe 62, Boateng 90+1
ch 3 - Aalborg BK (DEN)
2 *Berbatov (46), Malbranque (51), Bent (66)*
nson, Lee (Bent 46), Chimbonda, Dawson, Bale, Lennon, Jenas
dlestone 46), Zokora, Malbranque, Keane, Berbatov (Boateng 74).
ow Card(s): Boateng 82
ch 4 - RSC Anderlecht (BEL)
1 *Berbatov (71p)*
nson, Chimbonda, Dawson, Zokora, Lee (Stalteri 81), Lennon, Jenas,
dlestone, Malbranque, Keane (Berbatov 59), Bent (Defoe 72).
ow Card(s): Jenas 41, Zokora 75

Round of 32 - SK Slavia Praha (CZE)
A 2-1 *Berbatov (4), Keane (30)*
Černý, Tainio (O'Hara 59), Woodgate, Zokora, Chimbonda, Lennon, Huddlestone, Jenas, Malbranque, Berbatov, Keane (Bent 66).
Yellow Card(s): Tainio 35, Jenas 64, O'Hara 86
H 1-1 *O'Hara (7)*
Robinson, Chimbonda (Malbranque 60), Zokora, Tainio, Kaboul, Berbatov (Keane 46), O'Hara, Bent, Huddlestone, Lennon (Jenas 70), Woodgate.
Yellow Card(s): O'Hara 90+3

Round of 16 - PSV Eindhoven (NED)
H 0-1
Robinson, Chimbonda, Woodgate, King (Taarabt 73), Gilberto (O'Hara 46), Lennon, Jenas (Huddlestone 64), Zokora, Malbranque, Berbatov, Keane.
Yellow Card(s): Gilberto 26, Chimbonda 44, Berbatov 70
A 1-0 *Berbatov (81) (aet; 5-6 on pens)*
Robinson, Chimbonda, Woodgate, King (Lennon 61), Lee (Bent 46), Jenas, Zokora, Huddlestone, Malbranque, Berbatov, Keane (O'Hara 86).
Yellow Card(s): Jenas 38, King 44, Malbranque 90+2, Huddlestone 109, Zokora 118

EVERTON FC

UEFA CUP

First Round - FC Metalist Kharkiv (UKR)
H 1-1 *Lescott (24)*
Wessels, Baines, Johnson, Yakubu (Anichebe 66), Lescott, Carsley (Jagielka 78), Hibbert, McFadden, Neville, Osman, Yobo.
Yellow Card(s): Anichebe 82
A 3-2 *Lescott (48), McFadden (72), Anichebe (88)*
Howard, Stubbs, Pienaar, Yakubu (Baines 76), Jagielka (Anichebe 61), Lescott, Arteta, McFadden (Hibbert 89), Neville, Osman, Yobo.
Yellow Card(s): Neville 64, Osman 90+3

Group A
Match 1 - Larissa FC (GRE)
H 3-1 *Cahill (14), Osman (50), Anichebe (85)*
Howard, Hibbert, Yobo, Lescott, Baines, Pienaar (Stubbs 87), Osman, Carsley, Cahill (Gravesen 65), Arteta, McFadden (Anichebe 65).
Yellow Card(s): Lescott 30, Yobo 65, Gravesen 90
Match 2 - 1. FC Nürnberg (GER)
A 2-0 *Arteta (83p), Anichebe (88)*
Howard, Neville, Yobo, Lescott, Nuno Valente, Arteta, Carsley, Cahill (Jagielka 90+1), Osman, Pienaar (Hibbert 90+2), Yakubu (Anichebe 75).
Yellow Card(s): Nuno Valente 64, Yobo 87
Match 3 - FC Zenit St. Petersburg (RUS)
H 1-0 *Cahill (85)*
Howard, Neville, Jagielka, Lescott, Baines, Pienaar, Cahill, Carsley, Arteta, Johnson (Vaughan 81), McFadden (Anichebe 64).
Yellow Card(s): Johnson 39
Match 4 - AZ Alkmaar (NED)
A 3-2 *Johnson (2), Jagielka (44), Vaughan (80)*
Wessels, Hibbert, Jagielka, Lescott, Nuno Valente, Pienaar (Vidarsson 68), Gravesen (Rodwell 80), Carsley, McFadden, Anichebe, Johnson (Vaughan 68).
Yellow Card(s): Hibbert 78, Wessels 81

Round of 32 - SK Brann (NOR)
A 2-0 *Osman (59), Anichebe (88)*
Howard, Yobo, Lescott, Johnson (Anichebe 76), Jagielka, Cahill, Neville, Osman, Yakubu (Baines 93), Manuel Fernandes (Hibbert 89), Carsley.
Yellow Card(s): Manuel Fernandes 68
H 6-1 *Yakubu (36, 54, 72), Johnson (41, 90+2), Arteta (70)*
Howard, Neville, Jagielka, Lescott, Nuno Valente, Pienaar, Cahill (Manuel Fernandes 46), Carsley (Hibbert 46), Arteta, Johnson, Yakubu (Anichebe 73).

Yellow Card(s): Manuel Fernandes 67

Round of 16 - ACF Fiorentina (ITA)
A 0-2
Howard, Hibbert (Johnson 73), Yobo, Jagielka, Lescott, Osman (Arteta 56), Neville, Carsley, Pienaar, Cahill, Yakubu.
Yellow Card(s): Yakubu 36, Pienaar 40, Howard 60
H 2-0 *Johnson (16), Arteta (67) (aet; 2-4 on pens)*
Howard, Neville, Yobo, Jagielka, Lescott, Pienaar (Anichebe 106), Arteta, Carsley, Osman, Johnson (Gravesen 119), Yakubu.
Yellow Card(s): Yobo 74, Yakubu 80

BOLTON WANDERERS FC

UEFA CUP

First Round - FK Rabotnički (MKD)
A 1-1 *Meïté (83)*
Jääskeläinen, Davies, Diouf, Gardner, Hunt (J. O'Brien 75), Nolan, Speed, Anelka, Cid (Braaten 63), Meïté, McCann (A. O'Brien 63).
Yellow Card(s): McCann 25, Speed 26, Hunt 29, Diouf 60
H 1-0 *Anelka (67)*
Jääskeläinen, Davies (Anelka 67), Mikel Alonso (Giannakopoulos 46), Braaten (Diouf 75), Cid, Michalík, Wilhelmsson, Guthrie, McCann, A. O'Brien, J. O'Brien.

Group F
Match 1 - SC Braga (POR)
H 1-1 *Diouf (66)*
Jääskeläinen, Hunt, A. O'Brien, Meïté, Cid, Gardner (Teymourian 82), Guthrie (Diouf 61), McCann, Speed, Davies, Anelka.
Yellow Card(s): Cid 73
Match 2 - FC Bayern München (GER)
A 2-2 *Gardner (8), Davies (82)*
Al-Habsi, A. O'Brien, Cid, Michalík, Gardner, Mikel Alonso (Giannakopoulos 56), Nolan, Guthrie, McCann, Braaten (Teymourian 77), Davies.
Yellow Card(s): Davies 27, Braaten 45, Cid 62, An. O'Brien 78
Match 3 - Aris Thessaloniki FC (GRE)
H 1-1 *Giannakopoulos (90+2)*
Jääskeläinen, Hunt, A. O'Brien, Meïté, Cid, Giannakopoulos, Guthrie, Nolan, McCann (Mikel Alonso 12), Wilhelmsson (Diouf 64), Davies (Anelka 64).
Yellow Card(s): Meïté 67, Hunt 76, Giannakopoulos 80
Match 4 - FK Crvena Zvezda (SRB)
A 1-0 *McCann (45)*
Al-Habsi, Hunt, Meïté, Michalík, Samuel, Giannakopoulos, Speed, Teymourian, Wilhelmsson, McCann, Braaten (Sinclair 87).
Yellow Card(s): McCann 23

Round of 32 - Club Atlético de Madrid (ESP)
H 1-0 *Diouf (74)*
Jääskeläinen, Hunt, Cahill, A. O'Brien, Samuel, Iván Campo, Diouf, Guthrie (Giannakopoulos 59), Nolan, Taylor, Davies.
Yellow Card(s): Diouf 13
A 0-0
Jääskeläinen, Hunt, A. O'Brien, Cahill, Samuel, Giannakopoulos (Diouf 59), McCann (Iván Campo 58), Nolan, J. O'Brien (Meïté 85), Taylor, Davies.
Yellow Card(s): J. O'Brien 8, Nolan 23, Diouf 82, Davies 83

Round of 16 - Sporting Clube de Portugal (POR)
H 1-1 *McCann (25)*
Al-Habsi, Hunt, Iván Campo (Teymourian 84), Helguson (Giannakopoulos 55), Gardner, Davies, McCann, J. O'Brien (Guthrie 71), A. O'Brien, Taylor, Cahill.
Yellow Card(s): J. O'Brien 21, McCann 55
A 0-1
Al-Habsi, Hunt, Samuel, Meïté, Giannakopoulos, Helguson (Woolfe 76), Teymourian (Braaten 71), Guthrie, Vaz Té, J. O'Brien, Cahill.
Yellow Card(s): Teymourian 49, Guthrie 88

BLACKBURN ROVERS FC

UEFA INTERTOTO CUP

Third Round - FK Vėtra (LTU)
A 2-0 *McCarthy (30), Derbyshire (81)*
Friedel, Tugay (Mokoena 46), McCarthy (Rigters 65), Nelsen, Ooijer, Roberts, Savage, Warnock, Bentley (Derbyshire 65), Gamst Pedersen, Samba.
H 4-0 *Gamst Pedersen (24, 54), Roberts (47), McCarthy (53)*
Friedel, McCarthy (Rigters 56), Mokoena (Dunn 52), Nelsen, Ooijer, Rob (Derbyshire 56), Savage, Warnock, Bentley, Gamst Pedersen, Samba.
Yellow Card(s): McCarthy 33, Dunn 65

UEFA CUP

Second Qualifying Round - Myllykosken Pallo-47 (FIN)
A 1-0 *Santa Cruz (6)*
Friedel, Bentley, Dunn (Tugay 73), Nelsen, Ooijer, Gamst Pedersen (Eme 73), Roberts (Derbyshire 65), Samba, Savage, Warnock, Santa Cruz.
Yellow Card(s): Bentley 79
H 2-0 *Bentley (48), Roberts (90+1)*
Friedel, Bentley, Emerton, Tugay, Mokoena, Nelsen, Ooijer, Gamst Pedersen, Rigters (Derbyshire 76), Roberts, Warnock (Olsson 77).

First Round - Larissa FC (GRE)
A 0-2
Friedel, Bentley, Dunn, Emerton, McCarthy (Tugay 78), Nelsen (Khizanishvili 57), Ooijer, Gamst Pedersen (Derbyshire 62), Santa Cruz, Savage, Warnock.
Yellow Card(s): Warnock 37, Bentley 84
H 2-1 *Derbyshire (45+2p), Warnock (54)*
Friedel, Bentley, Derbyshire (McCarthy 68), Dunn (Savage 77), Emerton Tugay, Mokoena (Gamst Pedersen 65), Ooijer, Samba, Santa Cruz, Warn
Yellow Card(s): Tugay 66, Samba 87, Warnock 90+2

ESTONIA

FC LEVADIA TALLINN

UEFA CHAMPIONS LEAGUE

First Qualifying Round - FK Pobeda (MKD)
A 1-0 *Nahk (53)*
Kotenko, Dmitrijev, Kalimullin, Kink, Leitan, Lemsalu, Šišov, Smirnov, Vassiljev (Nahk 46), Zelinski (Čepauskas 64), Teniste (Malov 51).
Yellow Card(s): Smirnov 55
H 0-0
Kotenko, Andreev (Zelinski 46), Dmitrijev, Kalimullin, Kink, Leitan (Čepauskas 77), Lemsalu, Malov, Nahk, Šišov, Smirnov (Dovydenas 90).
Yellow Card(s): Zelinski 52, Šišov 60

nd Qualifying Round - FK Crvena Zvezda (SRB)

ko, Čepauskas, Dmitrijev, Kalimullin, Kink (Šadrin 85), Leitan
denas 89), Lemsalu, Malov, Šišov, Smirnov, Zelinski (Saag 63).
Malov (33), Nahk (67)
ko, Dmitrijev, Kalimullin, Kink (Saag 63), Leitan, Lemsalu, Malov,
Šišov, Smirnov (Teniste 56), Zelinski (Čepauskas 83).

JK TRANS NARVA

UEFA CUP

Qualifying Round - Helsingborgs IF (SWE)

tsev, Dobrovolski, Gorjatšov, Gorškov, Gruznov, Ivanov (Paitsev 70),
ov, Kulik, Lepik (Popov 80), Lipartov, Tarassenkov.
w Card(s): Dobrovolski 58

tsev, Dobrovolski, Gorjatšov, Paitsev (Dubõkin 69), Gruznov, Ivanov
nov 55), Kazakov, Kulik (Kitto 77), Lepik, Lipartov, Tarassenkov.

FC FLORA

UEFA CUP

Qualifying Round - Vålerenga Fotball (NOR)

, Allas, Bärengrub, Hurt (Ahjupera 65), Kams, Reim, Sidorenkov,
a (Taska 73), Vanna (Sirevičius 76), Vunk, Zahovaiko.
w Card(s): Vunk 30

, Allas, Bärengrub, Hakola, Kams (Ahjupera 73), Reim, Sidorenkov,
a (Hurt 58), Vanna, Vunk (Sirevičius 85), Zahovaiko.
w Card(s): Hurt 90+3

FC TVMK TALLINN

UEFA INTERTOTO CUP

Round - FC Honka Espoo (FIN)

Borissov, Dobrecovs (Zenjov 78), Kacanovs, Konsa (Gussev 82),
ov (Mašitšev 92), Rimas, Sarajev, Saviauk, Terehhov, Volodin.
Terehhov (68), Konsa (88)
Borissov, Jürgenson (Mašitšev 62), Kacanovs (Gabovs 75), Konsa,
ov, Rimas, Sarajev (Zenjov 46), Saviauk, Terehhov, Volodin.
w Card(s): Mašitšev 90+2

FAROE ISLANDS

HB TÓRSHAVN

UEFA CHAMPIONS LEAGUE

First Qualifying Round - FH Hafnarfjördur (ISL)
A 1-4 *Nielsen (44og)*
Vathnhamar, Akselsen, Borg, Hørg, C.H. Jacobsen, Lag, Nielsen, Nolsøe, Ólavsstovu (Joensen 71), Kuljic, Fløtum (Jespersen 60).
Yellow Card(s): Nielsen 63, Hørg 65
H 0-0
Vathnhamar, Akselsen, Hørg, R. Jacobsen, Jespersen (Dam 82), Lag, Nielsen, Nolsøe, Ólavsstovu (Leifsson 82), Kuljic, Fløtum (Joensen 76).
Yellow Card(s): Lag 28, Fløtum 72

B36 TÓRSHAVN

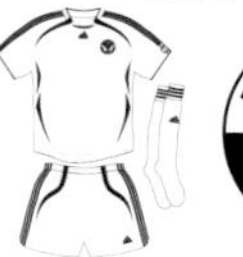

UEFA CUP

First Qualifying Round - FK Ekranas (LTU)
H 1-3 *Højsted (41)*
Mikkelsen, Benjaminsen, Alex, H. Jacobsen, K. Jacobsen, Matras, Midjord, Thomassen (Gunnarsson 89), Thorleifsson (Skorini 58), Sylla, Højsted (Rubeksen 83).
Yellow Card(s): Thomassen 25, Sylla 25, Matras 36, Alex 38
A 2-3 *Midjord (85), Benjaminsen (86p)*
Mikkelsen, Benjaminsen, Alex (Midjord 71), H. Jacobsen, K. Jacobsen, Matras, Gunnarsson, Thomassen, Skorini, Sylla, Højsted.
Yellow Card(s): Matras 6, H. Jacobsen 41, Højsted 62

EB/STREYMUR

UEFA CUP

First Qualifying Round - Myllykosken Pallo-47 (FIN)
A 0-1
Torgard, Bá. Olsen, Djurhuus (G. Hansen 84), Dam, H.P. Samuelsen, Bø, R. Samuelsen, S. Eliasen, Potemkin (Anghel 58), A.T. Hansen (H. Eliasen 68), Szekeres.
Yellow Card(s): Anghel 86
H 1-1 *Potemkin (86)*
Torgard, Bá. Olsen, Djurhuus, Dam, Anghel (H. Eliasen 79), H.Samuelsen, Bø, R. Samuelsen, S. Eliasen, Hansen (Potemkin 67), Szekeres (Kwieciński 65).
Yellow Card(s): Bø 90+4

KÍ KLAKSVÍK

UEFA INTERTOTO CUP

First Round - Hammarby (SWE)
A 0-1
M. Joensen, K. Lakjuni, Andreasen, Bertholdsen, Clapson, K. Jacobsen, S. Joensen, Kalsø (Ennigard 46), H. Lakjuni (Hammer 78), Madsen, Nielsen (Fles 83).
H 1-2 *Ennigard (38)*
M. Joensen, K. Lakjuni, Andreasen, Bertholdsen (Hammer 70), Clapson, Ennigard, K. Jacobsen (Bjartalid 78), S. Joensen, H. Lakjuni (Fles 70), Madsen, Nielsen.

FINLAND

TAMPERE UNITED

UEFA CHAMPIONS LEAGUE

First Qualifying Round - S.S. Murata (SMR)
A 2-1 *Niemi (68, 88)*
Kavén, Aho (Petrescu 52), Hynynen (Saarinen 89), Järvinen, Kujala, Lindström, Niemi, Ojanperä, Pohja, Juska Savolainen, Wiss.
Yellow Card(s): Wiss 90, Ojanperä 90+3
H 2-0 *Petrescu (7), Niemi (21)*
Kavén, Hynynen (Saarinen 46), Järvinen, Kujala, Lindström (Myntti 67), Niemi, Ojanperä, Pohja, Juska Savolainen, Wiss, Petrescu (Nwoke 80).
Yellow Card(s): Wiss 90+1

Second Qualifying Round - PFC Levski Sofia (BUL)
H 1-0 *Petrescu (15)*
Kavén, Hynynen (Aho 63), Järvinen, Kujala, Lindström, Niemi, Ojanperä (Nwoke 85), Pohja, Juska Savolainen, Saarinen, Petrescu (Hjelm 90+2).
Yellow Card(s): Hynynen 47
A 1-0 *Niemi (40)*
Kavén, Järvinen, Kujala, Lindström, Niemi (Nwoke 64), Ojanperä, Petrescu, Pohja, Saarinen (Hynynen 78), Juska Savolainen, Wiss.
Yellow Card(s): Juska Savolainen 21, Ojanperä 60

Third Qualifying Round - Rosenborg BK (NOR)
H 0-3
Kavén, Hynynen (Nwoke 71), Järvinen, Kujala, Lindström, Niemi, Petrescu (Hjelm 86), Pohja, Saarinen, Juska Savolainen, Wiss.
Yellow Card(s): Lindström 80
A 0-2
Kavén, Järvinen (Nwoke 74), Kujala, Lindström, Niemi, Ojanperä, Petrescu (Hjelm 85), Pohja, Saarinen (Aho 46), Juska Savolainen, Wiss.
Yellow Card(s): Ojanperä 26, Juska Savolainen 44

UEFA CUP

First Round - FC Girondins de Bordeaux (FRA)
H 2-3 *Wiss (8), Petrescu (69)*
Kavén, Aho (Hynynen 64), Järvinen, Kujala, Lindström, Myntti, Nwoke, Ojanperä, Petrescu, Pohja, Wiss.
Yellow Card(s): Myntti 47, Petrescu 76, Ojanperä 90
A 1-1 *Ojanperä (50)*
Kavén, Aho, Järvinen, Kujala, Lindström, Myntti, Niemi, Nwoke (Hjelm Ojanperä, Pohja, Juska Savolainen.
Yellow Card(s): Juska Savolainen 58, Myntti 66

HJK HELSINKI

UEFA CUP

First Qualifying Round - FC Etzella Ettelbrück (LUX)
H 2-0 *Bah (24), Sorsa (90+1)*
Wallén, Halsti, Savolainen, Vuorinen (Sorsa 63), Smith, Samura, Kamar (Äijälä 87), Bah, Raitala, Aalto, Zeneli (Parikka 51).
Yellow Card(s): Samura 32, Vuorinen 61, Smith 89
A 1-0 *Savolainen (26p)*
Wallén, Halsti, Nurmela (Äijälä 83), Savolainen (Aho 60), Vuorinen (Par 73), Smith, Samura, Kamara, Bah, Raitala, Aalto.
Yellow Card(s): Kamara 38, Vuorinen 46, Aalto 76

Second Qualifying Round - Aalborg BK (DEN)
H 2-1 *Samura (15, 56)*
Wallén, Aalto, Bah, Halsti, Kamara, Nurmela (Parikka 88), Raitala, Samu (Sorsa 78), Savolainen, Smith, Haapala.
Yellow Card(s): Halsti 9
A 0-3
Wallén, Aalto, Bah, Halsti, Kamara, Nurmela, Raitala, Savolainen, Smit (Vuorinen 55), Sorsa (Samura 69), Haapala (Parikka 90).
Yellow Card(s): Savolainen 67

FC HAKA

UEFA CUP

First Qualifying Round - Rhyl FC (WAL)
A 1-3 *Lehtinen (15)*
Dovbnya, Fowler, Holopainen, Innanen, Kangaskorpi, Kauppila, Lehtir Manninen (Mattila 72), Okkonen, Parviainen, Strandvall.
Red Card(s): Mattila 89
Yellow Card(s): Kangaskorpi 58, Parviainen 63
H 2-0 *Innanen (62), Popovich (64)*
Dovbnya, Fowler, Holopainen, Innanen, Kangaskorpi, Kauppila, Lehtir (Mahlakaarto 90), Manninen (Strandvall 64), Okkonen, Parviainen, Popovich.
Yellow Card(s): Fowler 56

Second Qualifying Round - FC Midtjylland (DEN)
H 1-2 *Parviainen (53)*
Dovbnya, Fowler, Holopainen, Innanen (Mattila 86), Kangaskorpi, Kauppila, Lehtinen (Mahlakaarto 86), Manninen (Strandvall 61), Okko Parviainen, Popovich.
Yellow Card(s): Parviainen 31
A 2-5 *Popovich (33), Kauppila (72)*
Dovbnya, Fowler, Holopainen, Innanen (Mahlakaarto 84), Kangaskorp Kauppila, Lehtinen (Mattila 64), Manninen (Strandvall 56), Okkonen, Popovich, Viljanen.
Yellow Card(s): Kauppila 47

MYLLYKOSKEN PALLO-47

UEFA CUP

t Qualifying Round - EB/Streymur (FRO)
0 *Hyyrynen (11)*
onen, Fofana (Kuparinen 75), Huttunen, Hyyrynen, Kansikas,
onen (Manso 62), Puhakainen, Pulkkinen, Tanska, Muinonen
gaskolkka 62), Agboh.
ow Card(s): Fofana 28, Manso 86
1 *Kuparinen (70)*
onen, Fofana (Puhakainen 63), Huttunen, Kansikas, Kuparinen
stafi 79), Miranda, Pellonen, Pulkkinen, Kangaskolkka, Muinonen
nso 63), Agboh.
ow Card(s): Fofana 52

ond Qualifying Round - Blackburn Rovers FC (ENG)
1
onen, Agboh, Huttunen, Hyyrynen, Kansikas, Kuparinen (Manso 65),
nda, Mustafi, Pellonen (Nykänen 79), Pulkkinen, Muinonen
akainen 53).
2
onen, Pulkkinen, Agboh, Kuparinen, Muinonen (Pellonen 73),
unen, Kangaskolkka (Helenius 60), Miranda, Kansikas, Gao
akainen 46), Mustafi.
ow Card(s): Agboh 90

FC HONKA ESPOO

UEFA INTERTOTO CUP

t Round - FC TVMK Tallinn (EST)
0
onen, Huuhtanen, Saarinen, Weckström (Otaru 71), Koskela,
stinen, Hakanpää (Perovuo 86), Patronen, Turunen, Porokara, Jalasto.
2 *Huuhtanen (6), Puustinen (69, 84), Hakanpää (74)*
onen, Huuhtanen (Kokko 82), Saarinen, Patronen, Weckström (Otaru
Koskela (Perovuo 73), Puustinen, Hakanpää, Turunen, Porokara,
sto.
ow Card(s): Hakanpää 16, Saarinen 35

ond Round - Aalborg BK (DEN)
2 *Porokara (8p), Puustinen (30)*
onen, Hakanpää, Huuhtanen, Koskela, Otaru, Patronen (Perovuo 46),
kara, Puustinen, Saarinen, Turunen, Jalasto.
ow Card(s): Koskela 43
1 *Porokara (50)*
onen, Hakanpää, Huuhtanen (Kokko 84), Jalasto, Koskela, Otaru
rala 76), Perovuo, Porokara, Puustinen, Saarinen, Turunen.
ow Card(s): Hakanpää 23, Turunen 55

FRANCE

OLYMPIQUE LYONNAIS

UEFA CHAMPIONS LEAGUE

Group E
Match 1 - FC Barcelona (ESP)
A 0-3
Vercoutre, Clerc, Bodmer, Källström (Keita 83), Juninho, Benzema (Ben Arfa 76), Govou, Réveillère, Belhadj (Baroš 62), Toulalan, Squillaci.
Match 2 - Rangers FC (SCO)
H 0-3
Vercoutre, Bodmer (Ben Arfa 60), Källström, Baroš (Keita 60), Juninho, Benzema, Grosso, Govou, Réveillère (Clerc 81), Anderson, Squillaci.
Yellow Card(s): Squillaci 44, Réveillère 77
Match 3 - VfB Stuttgart (GER)
A 2-0 *Fábio Santos (56), Benzema (79)*
Vercoutre, Källström, Juninho, Benzema (Bodmer 84), Grosso, Govou (Clerc 85), Ben Arfa (Keita 74), Réveillère, Anderson, Fábio Santos, Squillaci.
Yellow Card(s): Källström 30, Vercoutre 75
Match 4 - VfB Stuttgart (GER)
H 4-2 *Ben Arfa (6, 37), Källström (15), Juninho (90+3)*
Vercoutre, Källström, Juninho, Benzema (Belhadj 82), Grosso, Govou (Clerc 90+2), Ben Arfa (Keita 70), Réveillère, Anderson, Fábio Santos, Squillaci.
Yellow Card(s): Réveillère 58, Grosso 75, Govou 89, Keita 90+1
Match 5 - FC Barcelona (ESP)
H 2-2 *Juninho (7, 80p)*
Vercoutre, Juninho, Fred (Keita 60), Grosso, Govou, Ben Arfa (Rémy 82), Réveillère, Anderson, Fábio Santos (Källström 68), Toulalan, Squillaci.
Yellow Card(s): Fábio Santos 38, Juninho 58
Match 6 - Rangers FC (SCO)
A 3-0 *Govou (16), Benzema (85, 88)*
Vercoutre, Clerc, Källström, Juninho (Baroš 85), Benzema, Grosso, Govou (Réveillère 77), Ben Arfa (Bodmer 68), Anderson, Toulalan, Squillaci.
Yellow Card(s): Govou 48, Juninho 58

Round of 16 - Manchester United FC (ENG)
H 1-1 *Benzema (54)*
Coupet, Clerc (Ben Arfa 78), Källström, Juninho (Bodmer 74), Benzema (Fred 83), Grosso, Govou, Réveillère, Toulalan, Squillaci, Boumsong.
Yellow Card(s): Réveillère 34, Källström 36, Boumsong 39
A 0-1
Coupet, Clerc, Cris, Källström (Fred 79), Juninho, Benzema, Grosso, Govou (Keita 68), Ben Arfa, Toulalan, Squillaci.
Yellow Card(s): Grosso 23, Squillaci 55

No	Player	Nat	DoB	Aps	(s)	Gls
Goalkeepers						
1	Grégory Coupet		31/12/72	2		
30	Rémy Vercoutre		26/6/80	6		
Defenders						
2	François Clerc		18/4/83	4	(3)	
3	Cris	BRA	3/6/77	1		
11	Fabio Grosso	ITA	28/11/77	7		
20	Anthony Réveillère		10/11/79	6	(1)	
21	Nadir Belhadj	ALG	18/6/82	1	(1)	
22	Anderson	BRA	27/4/80	5		
29	Sébastien Squillaci		11/8/80	8		
32	Jean-Alain Boumsong		14/12/79	1		
Midfielders						
5	Mathieu Bodmer		22/11/82	2	(3)	
6	Kim Källström	SWE	24/8/82	7	(1)	1

No	Player	Nat	DoB	Aps	(s)	Gls
8	Juninho Pernambucano	BRA	30/1/75	8		3
18	Hatem Ben Arfa		7/3/87	5	(3)	2
26	Fábio Santos	BRA	9/10/80	3		1
28	Jérémy Toulalan		10/9/83	5		
Attackers						
7	Milan Baroš	CZE	28/10/81	1	(2)	
9	Fred	BRA	3/10/83	1	(2)	
10	Karim Benzema		19/12/87	7		4
12	Loïc Rémy		2/1/87		(1)	
14	Sidney Govou		27/7/79	8		1
23	Kader Keita	CIV	6/8/81		(6)	

OLYMPIQUE DE MARSEILLE

UEFA CHAMPIONS LEAGUE

Group A
Match 1 - Beşiktaş JK (TUR)
H 2-0 *Rodriguez (76), Cissé (90+1)*
Mandanda, Taiwo, Rodriguez, Faty, Ziani, Cissé, Zenden (Valbuena 76), Niang (Gragnic 86), Cana, Nasri (M'Bami 88), Bonnart.
Yellow Card(s): Faty 45+1, Rodriguez 47, Cissé 66, Valbuena 82, Nasri 88
Match 2 - Liverpool FC (ENG)
A 1-0 *Valbuena (77)*
Mandanda, Taiwo, Rodriguez, Ziani, Cheyrou, Zenden (Arrache 88), Niang (Cissé 70), Cana, Bonnart, Valbuena (Oruma 84), Givet.
Match 3 - FC Porto (POR)
H 1-1 *Niang (69)*
Mandanda, Faty, Cheyrou, Cissé (Ayew 88), Zenden (Arrache 55), Niang, Zubar, Cana, Bonnart, Valbuena, Givet (Taiwo 68).
Yellow Card(s): Niang 72, Mandanda 78
Match 4 - FC Porto (POR)
A 1-2 *Niang (47)*
Mandanda, Taiwo, Rodriguez, Niang (Cissé 63), M'Bami (Cheyrou 84), Cana, Nasri, Bonnart, Valbuena, Ayew (Arrache 77), Givet.
Match 5 - Beşiktaş JK (TUR)
A 1-2 *Taiwo (65)*
Mandanda, Rodriguez, Cheyrou, Zenden (Ayew 54), Niang, Zubar (Taiwo 46), Cana, Nasri (Cissé 26), Bonnart, Valbuena, Givet.
Yellow Card(s): Zenden 12, Cheyrou 44, Niang 63, Ayew 77, Cissé 90
Match 6 - Liverpool FC (ENG)
H 0-4
Mandanda, Taiwo, Rodriguez, Ziani, Cheyrou (Nasri 34), Zenden (Cissé 46), Niang, Cana, Bonnart, Valbuena, Givet (Faty 48).
Yellow Card(s): Cana 41

No	Player	Nat	DoB	Aps	(s)	Gls
Goalkeepers						
30	Steve Mandanda		28/3/85	6		
Defenders						
3	Taye Taiwo	NGA	16/4/85	4	(2)	1
4	Julien Rodriguez		11/6/78	5		1
5	Jacques Faty		25/2/84	2	(1)	
15	Ronald Zubar		20/9/85	2		
24	Laurent Bonnart		25/12/79	6		
32	Gaël Givet		9/10/81	5		
Midfielders						
6	Karim Ziani		17/8/82	3		
7	Benoît Cheyrou		3/5/81	4	(1)	
8	Wilson Oruma	NGA	30/12/76		(1)	
10	Boudewijn Zenden	NED	15/8/76	5		
17	Modeste M'Bami		9/10/82	1	(1)	
18	Vincent Gragnic		23/6/83		(1)	
19	Lorik Cana	ALB	27/7/83	6		
22	Samir Nasri		26/6/87	3	(1)	
28	Mathieu Valbuena		28/9/84	5	(1)	1
Attackers						
9	Djibril Cissé		12/8/81	2	(4)	1
11	Mamadou Niang	SEN	13/10/79	6		2
13	Salim Arrache		14/7/82		(3)	
29	André Ayew	GHA	17/12/89	1	(2)	

UEFA CUP

Round of 32 - FC Spartak Moskva (RUS)
H 3-0 *Cheyrou (62), Taiwo (68), Niang (79)*
Mandanda, Taiwo, Faty (Kaboré 46), Cheyrou, Cissé, Niang (Oruma 83), Cana, Nasri, Bonnart, Valbuena (Zenden 77), Givet.
Yellow Card(s): Cana 22, Nasri 42
A 0-2
Mandanda, Bonnart, Givet, Cana, Taiwo, Valbuena, M'Bami, Kaboré (Oruma 9), Nasri (Zenden 59), Cissé, Niang (Ziani 78).
Yellow Card(s): Givet 42, Cana 45+1, Mandanda 56

Round of 16 - FC Zenit St. Petersburg (RUS)
H 3-1 *Cissé (37, 55), Niang (48)*
Mandanda, Bonnart, Faty (Zubar 44), Givet, Taiwo, M'Bami, Cheyrou, Valbuena, Nasri (Kaboré 88), Niang (Zenden 62), Cissé.
Yellow Card(s): M'Bami 40, Zubar 54
A 0-2
Mandanda, Bonnart, Cana, Givet (Ayew 89), Taiwo, Cheyrou, M'Bami, Valbuena, Nasri, Niang, Cissé.
Yellow Card(s): M'Bami 33, Niang 38, Cissé 68

TOULOUSE FC

UEFA CHAMPIONS LEAGUE

Third Qualifying Round - Liverpool FC (ENG)
H 0-1
Douchez, Paulo César (Gignac 69), Bergougnoux (Mansaré 46), Dieuze, Ebondo (Sissoko 83), Elmander, Fofana, Mathieu, Sirieix, Emana, Cetto
Yellow Card(s): Elmander 59, Cetto 79, Sissoko 90+1
A 0-4
Douchez, Paulo César, Dieuze, Elmander, Fofana, Mathieu (Sissoko 82), Sirieix, Emana (Fabinho 76), Gignac (Bergougnoux 54), Cetto, Ilunga.

UEFA CUP

First Round - PFC CSKA Sofia (BUL)
H 0-0
Douchez, Batlles, Cetto, Congré, Dieuze, Elmander (Gignac 77), Emana, Fofana, Ilunga, Mansaré (Bergougnoux 58), Sirieix.
Yellow Card(s): Fofana 6
A 1-1 *Gignac (90+5)*
Douchez, Batlles (Bergougnoux 65), Cetto, Congré, Dieuze (Arribagé 90+3), Ebondo, Elmander, Emana, Ilunga, Mansaré, Sirieix (Gignac 78).
Yellow Card(s): Dieuze 43, Ebondo 48, Mansaré 68, Sirieix 76

Group E
Match 1 - Bayer 04 Leverkusen (GER)
A 0-1
Douchez, Ilunga, Congré, Cetto, Ebondo, Sirieix (Dieuze 87), Paulo Cés Fabinho (Bergougnoux 74), Emana, Gignac (Dupuis 90+2), Mansaré.
Yellow Card(s): Ebondo 19
Match 2 - AC Sparta Praha (CZE)
H 2-3 *Elmander (14), Mansaré (80)*
Douchez, Ebondo, Arribagé, Congré, Ilunga, Dieuze, Sirieix (Batlles 77) Paulo César (Bergougnoux 88), Emana, Mansaré, Elmander (Gignac 65
Yellow Card(s): Arribagé 53, Mansaré 70

h 3 - FC Zürich (SUI)
hez, Fofana, Arribagé, Mansaré (Bergougnoux 77), Elmander (Santos bondo, Fabinho (Sissoko 56), Emana, Gignac, Ilunga, Dieuze.
w Card(s): Dieuze 17, Ilunga 63, Mansaré 63, Bergougnoux 80
h 4 - FC Spartak Moskva (RUS)
Santos (41, 53)
Ilunga, Arribagé, M'Bengué, Fofana, Sirieix (Capoue 46), Emana, ze, Batlles (Sissoko 90+1), Bergougnoux, Santos (Dupuis 81).

FC SOCHAUX-MONTBÉLIARD

UEFA CUP

Round - Panionios GSS (GRE)
rt, Afolabi, Birsa (Quercia 46), Ndaw, Pichot, Pitau, Sène, Vargas ano 46), Dalmat, Pancrate, Perquis (Daf 82).
w Card(s): Pitau 33
Kumordzi (53og)
rt, Afolabi, Birsa, Dagano (Mevlüt 66), Isabey, Ndaw, Pichot, Pitau, (Pancrate 80), Dalmat (Quercia 35), Perquis.
w Card(s): Perquis 40, Isabey 44, N'daw 81

STADE RENNAIS FC

UEFA CUP

Round - PFC Lokomotiv Sofia (BUL)
Hansson (39), Cheyrou (74), Leroy (90)
lin, Fanni, Hansson, Leroy, Cheyrou, Edman, Jeunechamp (Marveaux M'Bia, Sorlin, Thomert (Emerson 78), Wiltord (Briand 64).
w Card(s): Jeunechamp 63
Marveaux (25)
Hansson, Borne, Cheyrou, Jeunechamp, Marveaux, M'Bia, Sorlin, (Briand 75), Badiane (Thomert 46), Ekoko (Leroy 46).
w Card(s): Luzi 90+1

p D
h 1 - FC Basel 1893 (SUI)
Fanni, Jeunechamp, Hansson, M'Bia (Borne 59), Sorlin, Didot (Wiltord Cheyrou, Marveaux, Briand, Pagis.
w Card(s): Briand 37, Jeunechamp 44
h 2 - SK Brann (NOR)
Cheyrou (88p)
Fanni, Hansson, Jeunechamp (Emerson 66), Mensah, Cheyrou, Leroy, eaux, Didot, Briand (Ekoko 81), Pagis.
w Card(s): Briand 57, Marcio 90+1
h 3 - Hamburger SV (GER)
lin, Edman (Thomert 46), Borne, Wiltord (Emerson 57), Leroy, Fanni ane 80), Hansson, Cheyrou, Briand, Sorlin, Marveaux.
w Card(s): Leroy 82
h 4 - NK Dinamo Zagreb (CRO)
M'Bia (88)
lin, Fanni, Hansson, Mensah, Sorlin, Leroy (Ekoko 65), Cheyrou, M'Bia, rd (Thomert 64), Pagis, Briand (Moreira 76).
w Card(s): Pagis 80

FC GIRONDINS DE BORDEAUX

UEFA CUP

First Round - Tampere United (FIN)
A 3-2 *Cavenaghi (48, 90+3), Micoud (90+2)*
Ramé, Chamakh, Jemmali, Fernando (Micoud 64), Trémoulinas (Wendel 65), Cavenaghi, Diawara, Brégerie, Ducasse, Marange, Obertan.
H 1-1 *Chamakh (49)*
Ramé, Chamakh, Jemmali, Planus (Diawara 46), Trémoulinas, Diarra (Micoud 66), Cavenaghi (Alonso 74), Brégerie, Ducasse, Marange, Obertan.

Group H
Match 1 - Galatasaray AŞ (TUR)
H 2-1 *Cavenaghi (53), Chamakh (64)*
Ramé, Marange, Trémoulinas (Wendel 75), Chalmé, Diawara, Jemmali (Planus 28), Fernando (Diarra 61), Micoud, Ducasse, Cavenaghi, Chamakh.
Yellow Card(s): Diarra 75
Match 2 - FK Austria Wien (AUT)
A 2-1 *Chamakh (45+1), Wendel (88p)*
Ramé, Trémoulinas, Planus, Chalmé, Diawara, Micoud, Wendel, Ducasse, Fernando, Obertan (Bellion 77), Chamakh.
Yellow Card(s): Chalmé 56
Match 3 - Helsingborgs IF (SWE)
H 2-1 *Chamakh (12), Jussiê (69)*
Ramé, Chalmé, Henrique, Planus, Marange, Obertan, Ducasse (Diarra 61), Fernando, Trémoulinas (Alonso 62), Chamakh (Cavenaghi 73), Jussiê.
Yellow Card(s): Jussiê 66, Diarra 78, Fernando 90+2
Match 4 - Panionios GSS (GRE)
A 3-2 *Cavenaghi (39), Trémoulinas (75), Moimbe (87)*
Valverde, Jemmali (Traoré 19), Brégerie, Manga, Trémoulinas (Moimbe 81), Jussiê (Perea 57), Ducasse, Lavie, Marange, Cavenaghi, Obertan.

Round of 32 - RSC Anderlecht (BEL)
A 1-2 *Jussiê (69p)*
Ramé, Chalmé, Henrique, Diawara, Jurietti, Diarra, Alonso (Wendel 61), Jussiê (Micoud 81), Ducasse, Obertan, Chamakh (Cavenaghi 61).
Yellow Card(s): Alonso 37, Diarra 53, Cavenaghi 76
H 1-1 *Cavenaghi (71)*
Ramé, Chalmé, Henrique, Diawara, Marange, Obertan (Wendel 77), Ducasse, Alonso (Micoud 52), Trémoulinas, Bellion (Cavenaghi 52), Chamakh.
Red Card(s): Trémoulinas 72, Chalmé 87
Yellow Card(s): Ramé 30, Micoud 61, Ducasse 64, Chalmé 82, Wendel 83, Chalmé 87

RC LENS

UEFA INTERTOTO CUP

Third Round - FC Chornomorets Odesa (UKR)
A 0-0
Runje, Coulibaly, Cousin, Demont, Monterrubio, Ramos (Aubey 46), Hilton, Carrière, Kovačević, Sablé, Akalé.
Yellow Card(s): Ramos 37
H 3-1 *Coulibaly (19), Akalé (39, 72)*
Runje, Coulibaly, Demont, Monterrubio, Hilton, Carrière (Keita 71), Kovačević, Akalé (Boukari 86), Aubey (Ramos 89), Sablé, Kalou
Yellow Card(s): Monterrubio 27, Runje 80, Kalou 88

UEFA CUP

Second Qualifying Round - BSC Young Boys (SUI)
A 1-1 *Monterrubio (75)*
Runje, Akalé, Aubey, Biševac, Coulibaly, Demont, Dindane (Carrière 75), Kalou (Boukari 90+2), Kovačević, Monterrubio, Sablé (Keita 87).
Yellow Card(s): Aubey 26, Kalou 41, Coulibaly 45, Sablé 85
H 5-1 *Dindane (13, 58), Akalé (16), Carrière (67), Feindouno (89)*
Runje, Akalé, Carrière (Keita 69), Biševac, Laurenti, Ramos, Dindane (Boukari 73), Hilton, Kovačević, Monterrubio, Sablé (Feindouno 75).
Yellow Card(s): Ramos 34

First Round - FC København (DEN)
H 1-1 *Dindane (70)*
Runje, Akalé (Monterrubio 56), Biševac, Carrière, Coulibaly, Demont, Kovačević, Laurenti, Sablé (Keita 45), Pieroni, Monnet-Paquet (Dindane 56).
Yellow Card(s): Keita 52, Kovačević 66, Laurenti 68, Dindane 80, Monterrubio 85
A 1-2 *Carrière (13) (aet)*
Runje, Akalé (Dindane 73), Aubey, Biševac, Carrière, Coulibaly, Demont, Keita (Kovačević 91), Sablé, Pieroni (Monterrubio 80), Lacourt.
Yellow Card(s): Runje 28, Keita 74, Biševac 111

GEORGIA

FC OLIMPI RUSTAVI

UEFA CHAMPIONS LEAGUE

First Qualifying Round - FC Astana (KAZ)
H 0-0
Merlani, Akouassaga, Chichveishvili, Dvali (Massouanga 56), Dvalishvili, Getsadze, Makhviladze, Navalovski, Orbeladze, Silagadze (Koshkadze 66), Zivković (Jikia 46).
Yellow Card(s): Dvali 25, Getsadze 79
A 0-3
Merlani, Akouassaga, Chichveishvili (Dvali 51), Getsadze, Kakhelishvili (Dvalishvili 70), Kebadze (Koshkadze 66), Navalovski, Orbeladze, Silagadze, Zivković, Jikia.
Red Card(s): Jikia 59
Yellow Card(s): Silagadze 86

FC AMERI TBILISI

UEFA CUP

First Qualifying Round - GKS Bełchatów (POL)
A 0-2
Kvachakhia, Didava, Bolkvadze, Chikviladze, Davitashvili (Tatanashvili 61), Davitnidze (Kobauri 90), Dobrovolski, Dolidze (Shalamberidze 75), Jeladze, Khvadagiani, Gotsiridze.
Yellow Card(s): Chikviladze 35, Davitnidze 85, Khvadagiani 90+4
H 2-0 *Tatanashvili (12), Davitashvili (46) (aet; 2-4 on pens)*
Kvachakhia, Didava, Bolkvadze (Kobauri 101), Davitashvili (Gotsiridze Davitnidze, Dekanosidze, Dobrovolski, Jeladze (Dolidze 70), Khvadagi Tatanashvili, Elbakidze.
Yellow Card(s): Jeladze 31

FC DINAMO TBILISI

UEFA CUP

First Qualifying Round - FC Vaduz (LIE)
H 2-0 *Merebashvili (66p), Akiremy (72)*
Ovono Ebang, Krško, S. Kashia, Zelic, Khmaladze, Merebashvili, Kobakhidze (Spasojević 81), Digmelashvili, Odikadze (Peikrishvili 55), Akiremy (Khutsishvili 86), Dobeš.
A 0-0
Ovono Ebang, G. Kashia, Krško, S. Kashia, Zelic, Khmaladze, Merebash Kobakhidze, Peikrishvili (Odikadze 76), Digmelashvili (Khutsishvili 89), Akiremy Owondo (Spasojevic 90+2).
Yellow Card(s): Digmelashvili 81

Second Qualifying Round - SK Rapid Wien (AUT)
H 0-3
Ovono Ebang (Loria 37), Akiremy, S. Kashia, Khmaladze, Kobakhidze (Spasojević 46), Krško, Merebashvili, Odikadze, Peikrishvili (Khutsishvi 76), Zelic, G. Kashia.
Yellow Card(s): Odikadze 24, Ovono Ebang 35, S. Kashia 52, Spasoje 71, Krško 82, Khutsishvili 85
A 0-5
Loria, Akiremy (Spasojević 61), Digmelashvili (Kobakhidze 56), Dobeš, Khmaladze, Khutsishvili (Pirtskhalava 86), Krško, Merebashvili, Peikris Zelic, G. Kashia.
Yellow Card(s): Khutsishvili 67, Zelic 77

FC ZESTAFONI

UEFA INTERTOTO CUP

First Round - FC Tobol Kostanay (KAZ)
A 0-3
Chanturia, Chelidze, K. Chkhetiani, Edson (G. Chkhetiani 35), Kessany, Oniani, Pipia, Sajaia, Todua, Jônatas (N. Kvaskhvadze 46), Vieira (Sanaia
Yellow Card(s): Sajaia 17, Oniani 66
H 2-0 *Sajaia (3), K. Chkhetiani (37)*
Chanturia, Benashvili (Torres 60), K. Chkhetiani, Edson, Kessany, N. Kvaskhvadze, Oniani, Pipia, Sajaia, Todua, Vieira (Gongadze 90).
Yellow Card(s): Sajaia 55, Pipia 80

GERMANY

VFB STUTTGART

UEFA CHAMPIONS LEAGUE

p E
:h 1 - Rangers FC (SCO)
Gómez (56)
'er, Osorio, Tasci, Fernando Meira, Pardo, Boka, Cacau, Hilbert, Da (Ewerthon 70), Khedira (Baştürk 78), Gómez.
w Card(s): Fernando Meira 74, Pardo 87
:h 2 - FC Barcelona (ESP)

'er, Osorio (Marica 63), Tasci, Fernando Meira, Farnerud (Magnin 76),), Boka, Cacau, Hilbert, Khedira (Meissner 76), Gómez.
h 3 - Olympique Lyonnais (FRA)

'er, Osorio, Tasci, Fernando Meira, Meissner (Khedira 62), Farnerud, ırk (Ewerthon 71), Pardo, Cacau, Hilbert, Gómez.
w Card(s): Hilbert 42, Khedira 64, Cacau 76
:h 4 - Olympique Lyonnais (FRA)
Gómez (16, 56)
'er, Beck (Osorio 77), Tasci, Fernando Meira, Baştürk, Hitzlsperger, erre, Cacau (Marica 58), Magnin (Farnerud 81), Khedira, Gómez.
w Card(s): Baştürk 51, Tasci 74
:h 5 - Rangers FC (SCO)
Cacau (45+2), Pardo (62), Marica (85)
'er, Beck, Fernando Meira, Hitzlsperger, Pardo, Delpierre, Cacau (Tasci Hilbert (Ewerthon 83), Marica, Magnin, Khedira (Da Silva 46).
w Card(s): Magnin 37
:h 6 - FC Barcelona (ESP)
Da Silva (3)
'er, Osorio, Tasci, Fernando Meira, Farnerud (Hilbert 58), Ewerthon, ay Baştürk (Meissner 72), Boka, Delpierre, Marica (Fischer 71), Da Silva.
w Card(s): Schäfer 36, Fernando Meira 49

Player	Nat	DoB	Aps	(s)	Gls
keepers					
Raphael Schäfer		30/1/79	6		
nders					
Andreas Beck		13/3/87	2		
Ricardo Osorio	MEX	30/3/80	4	(1)	
Serdar Tasci		24/4/87	5	(1)	
Fernando Meira	POR	5/6/78	6		
Arthur Boka	CIV	2/4/83	3		
Matthieu Delpierre	FRA	26/4/81	3		
Ludovic Magnin	SUI	20/4/79	2	(1)	
elders					
Silvio Meissner		19/1/73	1	(2)	
Alexander Farnerud	SWE	1/5/84	3	(1)	
Yıldıray Baştürk	TUR	24/12/78	3	(1)	
Thomas Hitzlsperger		5/4/82	2		
Pável Pardo	MEX	26/7/76	4		1
Roberto Hilbert		16/10/84	4	(1)	
António Da Silva	BRA	13/6/78	2	(1)	1
Sami Khedira		4/4/87	4	(1)	
:kers					
Ewerthon	BRA	10/6/81	1	(3)	
Cacau	BRA	27/3/81	5		1
Ciprian Marica	ROU	2/10/85	2	(2)	1
Manuel Fischer		19/9/89		(1)	
Mario Gómez		10/7/85	4		3

FC SCHALKE 04

UEFA CHAMPIONS LEAGUE

Group B
Match 1 - Valencia CF (ESP)
H 0-1
Neuer, Westermann, Bordon, Ernst, Rakitić, Jones, Asamoah (Özil 61), Rafinha (Grossmüller 73), Halil Altıntop (Løvenkrands 73), Kuranyi, Pander.
Yellow Card(s): Bordon 69, Grossmüller 76
Match 2 - Rosenborg BK (NOR)
A 2-0 *Jones (62), Kuranyi (89)*
Neuer, Westermann, Bordon, Ernst, Rakitić (Grossmüller 75), Løvenkrands (Asamoah 64), Jones (Varela 84), Rafinha, Kuranyi, Höwedes, Bajramović.
Yellow Card(s): Rafinha 17, Jones 69, Neuer 87
Match 3 - Chelsea FC (ENG)
A 0-2
Neuer, Westermann, Bordon, Ernst, Larsen, Løvenkrands, Jones, Asamoah (Rakitić 61), Rodríguez (Bajramović 81), Rafinha, Grossmüller (Azaouagh 77).
Yellow Card(s): Jones 24, Rodríguez 57
Match 4 - Chelsea FC (ENG)
H 0-0
Neuer, Westermann, Bordon, Larsen, Rakitić, Jones, Asamoah, Özil (Løvenkrands 60), Rafinha, Krstajić, Bajramović.
Yellow Card(s): Rakitić 85
Match 5 - Valencia CF (ESP)
A 0-0
Neuer, Westermann, Bordon, Ernst, Rakitić (Grossmüller 65), Jones (Bajramović 71), Özil, Rafinha, Halil Altıntop (Asamoah 80), Krstajić, Kuranyi.
Yellow Card(s): Rafinha 29, Jones 45+3, Özil 78
Match 6 - Rosenborg BK (NOR)
H 3-1 *Asamoah (12), Rafinha (19), Kuranyi (36)*
Neuer, Westermann, Bordon, Ernst, Asamoah (Höwedes 90+2), Rodríguez, Özil (Kobiashvili 86), Rafinha, Grossmüller, Kuranyi (Halil Altıntop 88), Bajramović.
Yellow Card(s): Kuranyi 37, Bordon 71

Round of 16 - FC Porto (POR)
H 1-0 *Kuranyi (4)*
Neuer, Westermann, Kobiashvili, Bordon, Ernst, Rakitić (Grossmüller 76), Jones, Asamoah (Halil Altıntop 80), Rafinha, Krstajić, Kuranyi (Vicente Sánchez 89).
Yellow Card(s): Jones 45+1, Ernst 67, Grossmüller 85
A 0-1 *(aet; 4-1 on pens)*
Neuer, Westermann, Kobiashvili, Bordon (Höwedes 114), Ernst, Jones, Rafinha, Halil Altıntop, Krstajić, Grossmüller (Rakitić 111), Kuranyi (Asamoah 79).
Yellow Card(s): Kuranyi 33, Jones 57, Westermann 65, Kobiashvili 116

Quarter-Final - FC Barcelona (ESP)
H 0-1
Neuer, Westermann, Kobiashvili, Bordon, Ernst, Asamoah (Larsen 73), Rafinha, Halil Altıntop (Løvenkrands 89), Krstajić, Kuranyi (Sánchez 60), Pander.
Yellow Card(s): Pander 83, Larsen 85, Ernst 87, Krstajić 90+3
A 0-1
Neuer, Westermann, Kobiashvili (Grossmüller 32), Bordon, Ernst, Jones, Asamoah (Sánchez 69), Rafinha (Larsen 77), Halil Altıntop, Krstajić, Kuranyi.
Yellow Card(s): Rafinha 10, Westermann 26

No	Player	Nat	DoB	Aps	(s)	Gls
	Goalkeepers					
1	Manuel Neuer		27/3/86	10		
	Defenders					
2	Heiko Westermann		14/8/83	10		

No	Player	Nat	DoB	Aps	(s)	Gls
5	Marcelo Bordon	BRA	7/1/76	10		
16	Darío Rodríguez	URU	17/9/74	2		
18	Rafinha	BRA	7/9/85	10		1
20	Mladen Krstajić	SRB	4/3/74	6		
23	Benedikt Höwedes		29/2/88	1	(2)	
24	Christian Pander		28/8/83	2		
Midfielders						
3	Levan Kobiashvili	GEO	10/7/77	4	(1)	
7	Gustavo Varela	URU	14/5/78		(1)	
8	Fabian Ernst		30/5/79	9		
10	Ivan Rakitić	CRO	10/3/88	5	(2)	
13	Jermaine Jones		3/11/81	8		1
17	Mesut Özil		15/10/88	3	(1)	
21	Carlos Grossmüller		4/5/83	3	(5)	
25	Zlatan Bajramović	BIH	12/8/79	3	(2)	
26	Mimoun Azaouagh		17/11/82		(1)	
Attackers						
9	Søren Larsen	DEN	6/9/81	2	(2)	
11	Peter Løvenkrands	DEN	29/1/80	2	(3)	
14	Gerald Asamoah		3/10/78	7	(3)	1
19	Halil Altıntop	TUR	8/12/82	5	(2)	
22	Kevin Kuranyi		2/3/82	8		3
27	Vicente Sánchez	URU	7/12/79		(3)	

WERDER BREMEN

UEFA CHAMPIONS LEAGUE

Third Qualifying Round - NK Dinamo Zagreb (CRO)
H 2-1 *Hugo Almeida (46), Jensen (85)*
Wiese, Andreasen (Jensen 46), Baumann, Mertesacker, Pasanen, Diego, Naldo, Schulz, Carlos Alberto (Harnik 74), Sanogo, Schindler (Hugo Almeida 46).
Yellow Card(s): Naldo 76
A 3-2 *Diego (13p, 70p), Sanogo (38)*
Wiese, Baumann, Jensen, Mertesacker, Pasanen, Hugo Almeida (Harnik 68), Diego, Naldo, Schulz (Tošić 81), Vranješ, Sanogo (Rosenberg 76).
Yellow Card(s): Schulz 57, Hugo Almeida 57

Group C
Match 1 - Real Madrid CF (ESP)
A 1-2 *Sanogo (17)*
Wiese, Pasanen, Naldo, Baumann, Vranješ, Rosenberg (Hugo Almeida 69), Diego, Tošić, Sanogo, Jensen, Mertesacker.
Yellow Card(s): Vranješ 72, Diego 90+2
Match 2 - Olympiacos CFP (GRE)
H 1-3 *Hugo Almeida (32)*
Vander, Pasanen, Naldo, Fritz (Borowski 63), Rosenberg (Sanogo 76), Diego, Tošić, Jensen, Frings, Hugo Almeida, Mertesacker.
Yellow Card(s): Sanogo 90
Match 3 - S.S. Lazio (ITA)
H 2-1 *Sanogo (28), Hugo Almeida (54)*
Wiese, Pasanen (Tošić 46), Naldo, Fritz, Diego, Sanogo (Rosenberg 64), Jensen, Frings, Hugo Almeida, Borowski (Andreasen 73), Mertesacker.
Yellow Card(s): Pasanen 30
Match 4 - S.S. Lazio (ITA)
A 1-2 *Diego (88p)*
Wiese, Pasanen, Naldo, Baumann (Jensen 31), Fritz (Harnik 76), Rosenberg, Diego, Andreasen, Hugo Almeida, Borowski, Mertesacker.
Red Card(s): Diego 90+5
Yellow Card(s): Diego 88, Andreasen 90, Diego 90+5
Match 5 - Real Madrid CF (ESP)
H 3-2 *Rosenberg (5), Sanogo (40), Hunt (58)*
Vander, Pasanen, Naldo, Baumann, Vranješ, Fritz (Tošić 6), Rosenberg, Hunt (Harnik 76), Sanogo (Carlos Alberto 87), Jensen, Mertesacker.
Yellow Card(s): Hunt 10

Match 6 - Olympiacos CFP (GRE)
A 0-3
Wiese, Pasanen, Naldo, Baumann (Tošić 82), Vranješ (Hunt 58), Fritz, Rosenberg, Diego, Sanogo (Hugo Almeida 67), Jensen, Borowski.
Yellow Card(s): Rosenberg 42, Jensen 71

No	Player	Nat	DoB	Aps	(s)	G
Goalkeepers						
1	Tim Wiese		17/12/81	4		
33	Christian Vander		24/10/80	2		
Defenders						
3	Petri Pasanen	FIN	24/9/80	6		
4	Naldo	BRA	10/9/82	6		
8	Clemens Fritz		7/12/80	5		
13	Duško Tošić	SRB	19/1/85	2	(3)	
16	Leon Andreasen	DEN	23/4/83	1	(1)	
29	Per Mertesacker		29/9/84	5		
Midfielders						
6	Frank Baumann		29/10/75	4		
7	Jurica Vranješ	CRO	31/1/80	3		
10	Diego	BRA	28/2/85	5		1
19	Carlos Alberto	BRA	11/12/84		(1)	
20	Daniel Jensen	DEN	25/6/79	5	(1)	
22	Torsten Frings		22/11/76	2		
24	Tim Borowski		2/5/80	3	(1)	
Attackers						
9	Markus Rosenberg	SWE	27/9/82	5	(1)	1
14	Aaron Hunt		4/9/86	1	(1)	1
18	Boubacar Sanogo	CIV	17/12/82	4	(1)	3
23	Hugo Almeida	POR	23/5/84	3	(2)	2
34	Martin Harnik	AUT	10/6/87		(2)	

UEFA CUP

Round of 32 - SC Braga (POR)
H 3-0 *Naldo (5), Jensen (27), Hugo Almeida (90+5p)*
Wiese, Owomoyela, Naldo, Mertesacker, Fritz, Jensen, Baumann, Dieg (Özil 73), Hunt (Borowski 59), Hugo Almeida, Rosenberg.
Yellow Card(s): Fritz 10, Wiese 35
A 1-0 *Klasnić (78)*
Wiese, Fritz, Mertesacker, Naldo, Owomoyela, Jensen, Özil (Vranješ 57 Baumann, Borowski (Boenisch 79), Hugo Almeida, Rosenberg (Klasnić
Yellow Card(s): Borowski 18, Fritz 48, Naldo 56

Round of 16 - Rangers FC (SCO)
A 0-2
Wiese, Pasanen (Boenisch 64), Naldo, Baumann, Vranješ (Hugo Almeic 60), Fritz, Rosenberg, Diego, Hunt, Jensen, Mertesacker.
Yellow Card(s): Naldo 67, Hugo Almeida 82
H 1-0 *Diego (58)*
Wiese, Owomoyela (Harnik 78), Mertesacker, Naldo, Boenisch, Jensen, Borowski, Hunt, Diego, Rosenberg, Hugo Almeida (Sanogo 66).

1. FC NÜRNBERG

  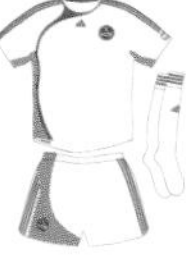

UEFA CUP

First Round - FC Rapid Bucureşti (ROU)
H 0-0
Blažek, Charisteas, Galásek, Kristiansen (Benko 84), Mnari (Kennedy 74 Mintál, Reinhardt, Wolf, Misimović, Kluge (Engelhardt 63), Pinola.
Yellow Card(s): Engelhardt 87
A 2-2 *Kluge (22), Misimović (56)*
Blažek, Galásek, Kristiansen, Mnari (Schmidt 68), Mintál (Charisteas 72 Reinhardt, Wolf, Misimović, Saenko, Kluge (Kennedy 85), Spiranovic.
Yellow Card(s): Wolf 47, Spiranovic 60

ıp A
ch 1 - Everton FC (ENG)
2
ɜk, Schmidt (Kennedy 76), Gláuber (Benko 86), Wolf, Reinhardt, sek, Kluge, Mnari, Mintál, Misimović, Saenko (Pagenburg 85).
ɔw Card(s): Gláuber 82, Blažek 85
ch 2 - FC Zenit St. Petersburg (RUS)
2 *Charisteas (25), Benko (84)*
ɜk, Reinhardt, Wolf, Beauchamp, Engelhardt (Benko 81), Galásek, e, Mintál (Kristiansen 74), Adler (Saenko 46), Misimović, Charisteas.
ɔw Card(s): Beauchamp 45
ch 3 - AZ Alkmaar (NED)
ɬ *Mintál (83, 85)*
ɜk, Reinhardt, Wolf, Beauchamp, Engelhardt, Galásek, Kluge, Benko tál 38), Misimović (Kristiansen 90), Adler (Saenko 61), Charisteas.
ɔw Card(s): Beauchamp 39, Misimović 50, Galásek 71
ch 4 - Larissa FC (GRE)
ɬ *Saenko (45), Mintál (57), Charisteas (73)*
ɜk, Reinhardt, Wolf, Beauchamp, Gláuber, Galásek, Misimović, Kluge, 'isteas, Saenko, Mintál.
ɔw Card(s): Beauchamp 61, Kluge 90+1

ɪnd of 32 - SL Benfica (POR)
1
ek, Reinhardt, Wolf, Gláuber, Pinola, Adler (Kristiansen 46), Kluge, sek, Engelhardt, Saenko, Koller.
ɔw Card(s): Wolf 66, Pinola 87
2 *Charisteas (59), Saenko (66)*
ek, Reinhardt, Wolf, Gláuber, Pinola, Galásek, Mnari (Abardonado 87), ɜlhardt, Charisteas, Koller, Saenko.
ɔw Card(s): Pinola 89

FC BAYERN MÜNCHEN

UEFA CUP

t Round - CF Os Belenenses (POR)
·0 *Toni (34)*
n, Lúcio, Demichelis, Jansen, Lell, Podolski, Ribéry (Schlaudraff 84), ʌeinsteiger (Hamit Altıntop 73), Toni (Wagner 63), Van Bommel, Zé erto.
·0 *Toni (59), Hamit Altıntop (76)*
sing, Hamit Altıntop, Lúcio, Demichelis, Jansen, Lell, Ribéry ılaudraff 68), Schweinsteiger (Kroos 80), Toni, Van Bommel, Zé Roberto ɪ 73).
ow Card(s): Toni 63

ıup F
tch 1 - FK Crvena Zvezda (SRB)
·2 *Klose (20, 86), Kroos (90+4)*
sing, Lahm, Lell, Lúcio, Jansen, Hamit Altıntop (Schlaudraff 71), Van ımel (Kroos 81), Zé Roberto, Schweinsteiger, Podolski, Klose.
ow Card(s): Lahm 58, Schweinsteiger 83
tch 2 - Bolton Wanderers FC (ENG)
-2 *Podolski (30, 49)*
ın, Jansen, Lúcio, Van Buyten, Lell, Ribéry (Kroos 60), Ottl, Van Bommel, weinsteiger (Hamit Altıntop 73), Podolski (Toni 57), Klose.
tch 3 - SC Braga (POR)
-1 *Klose (47)*
ın, Lell, Lúcio, Demichelis, Lahm, Hamit Altıntop (Sosa 81), Van ımel, Zé Roberto, Ribéry (Sagnol 90+1), Toni, Klose (Schlaudraff 67).
low Card(s): Kahn 45, Van Bommel 75, Toni 86
tch 4 - Aris Thessaloniki FC (GRE)
-0 *Toni (25, 38, 64, 66), Lell (78), Lahm (81)*
ın, Lell (Sagnol 79), Demichelis, Lúcio, Lahm, Ribéry, Van Bommel (Ottl 62), Schweinsteiger, Zé Roberto, Toni, Klose (Podolski 62).
Yellow Card(s): Van Bommel 15, Ribéry 83

Round of 32 - Aberdeen FC (SCO)
A 2-2 *Klose (29), Hamit Altıntop (55)*
Rensing, Lell (Lahm 46), Lúcio, Demichelis, Jansen, Hamit Altıntop, Ottl, Zé Roberto (Podolski 66), Schweinsteiger, Toni, Klose (Schlaudraff 80).
Yellow Card(s): Podolski 90
H 5-1 *Lúcio (12), Van Buyten (36), Podolski (71, 77), Van Bommel (85)*
Kahn, Sagnol, Lúcio, Van Buyten, Jansen, Hamit Altıntop (Schweinsteiger 75), Ottl, Van Bommel, Kroos (Sosa 69), Toni (Klose 65), Podolski.
Yellow Card(s): Kroos 65

Round of 16 - RSC Anderlecht (BEL)
A 5-0 *Hamit Altıntop (9), Toni (45+1), Podolski (57), Klose (67), Ribéry (86)*
Rensing, Sagnol, Van Buyten, Demichelis, Lahm, Schweinsteiger (Ribéry 46), Ottl, Hamit Altıntop (Sosa 57), Van Bommel, Podolski, Toni (Klose 46).
Yellow Card(s): Toni 43, Sosa 68
H 1-2 *Lúcio (9)*
Rensing, Sagnol, Lúcio, Breno, Lahm, Sosa, Ottl (Schlaudraff 72), Van Bommel, Kroos (Ribéry 46), Podolski, Klose (Hamit Altıntop 87).

Quarter-Final - Getafe CF (ESP)
H 1-1 *Toni (26)*
Kahn, Lúcio, Demichelis, Ribéry, Toni (Klose 80), Podolski, Zé Roberto, Van Bommel (Ottl 86), Lahm, Jansen (Lell 81), Schweinsteiger.
Yellow Card(s): Toni 5
A 3-3 *Ribéry (89), Toni (115, 120) (aet)*
Kahn, Lúcio, Demichelis, Ribéry, Toni, Zé Roberto (Podolski 75), Van Bommel, Klose, Lahm, Lell (Jansen 46), Schweinsteiger (Sosa 64).
Yellow Card(s): Lell 22, Lahm 37, Toni 104, Podolski 116

Semi-Final - FC Zenit St. Petersburg (RUS)
H 1-1 *Ribéry (18)*
Kahn (Rensing 67), Lúcio, Demichelis, Ribéry, Podolski, Zé Roberto, Van Bommel, Klose, Lahm (Kroos 80), Jansen, Schweinsteiger (Lell 66).
A 0-4
Kahn, Lúcio, Demichelis, Ribéry, Toni, Zé Roberto (Podolski 46), Van Bommel, Klose (Sosa 62), Lahm, Jansen (Lell 46), Schweinsteiger.
Yellow Card(s): Toni 67, Lell 81

BAYER 04 LEVERKUSEN

UEFA CUP

First Round - UD Leiria (POR)
H 3-1 *Kiessling (19, 77), Rolfes (31)*
Adler, Haggui, Kiessling, Rolfes, Schneider (Barbarez 57), Gekas (Papadopulos 81), Greško, Friedrich, Vidal, Barnetta, Castro.
Red Card(s): Greško 78
Yellow Card(s): Greško 48, Vidal 51, Greško 78
A 2-3 *Papadopulos (10), Kiessling (87)*
Adler, Barbarez, Barnetta (Dum 90), Haggui, Kiessling, Papadopulos (Schwegler 46), Rolfes, Friedrich, Sarpei, Vidal (Sinkiewicz 90), Castro.
Yellow Card(s): Haggui 43, Schwegler 58, Friedrich 76, Castro 90

Group E
Match 1 - Toulouse FC (FRA)
H 1-0 *Kiessling (35)*
Adler, Haggui, Friedrich, Rolfes, Barnetta, Sarpei, Castro, Barbarez (Sinkiewicz 78), Gekas (Freier 59; Papadopulos 90+2), Kiessling, Vidal.

Match 2 - FC Spartak Moskva (RUS)
A 1-2 *Freier (90+1)*
Adler, Rolfes, Haggui, Friedrich, Castro, Barbarez, Sarpei, Kiessling (Dum 80), Barnetta, Vidal (Bulykin 80), Gekas (Freier 69).
Yellow Card(s): Kiessling 62
Match 3 - AC Sparta Praha (CZE)
H 1-0 *Friedrich (71)*
Adler, Haggui, Friedrich, Rolfes, Barnetta, Freier (Schneider 66; Greško 83), Gekas (Sinkiewicz 78), Kiessling, Sarpei, Castro, Ramelow.
Red Card(s): Ramelow 60
Yellow Card(s): Castro 76, Barnetta 90+3
Match 4 - FC Zürich (SUI)
A 5-0 *Greško (19), Bulykin (23, 57), Barnetta (50), Kiessling (80)*
Fernandez, Sarpei, Friedrich (Callsen-Bracker 29), Haggui, Greško, Sinkiewicz (Faty 61), Rolfes, Kiessling, Barbarez, Barnetta, Bulykin (Gekas 78).

Round of 32 - Galatasaray AŞ (TUR)
A 0-0
Adler, Castro, Friedrich, Callsen-Bracker, Rolfes, Sarpei, Vidal (Schwegler 87), Schneider (Freier 61), Barbarez, Barnetta, Kiessling.
Yellow Card(s): Adler 69
H 5-1 *Barbarez (12, 22), Kiessling (13), Haggui (55), Schneider (61p)*
Fernandez, Castro, Friedrich, Haggui, Sarpei, Schneider (Dum 75), Vidal, Rolfes, Barbarez (Schwegler 65), Barnetta, Kiessling (Gekas 72).
Yellow Card(s): Kiessling 34, Schneider 54

Round of 16 - Hamburger SV (GER)
H 1-0 *Gekas (77)*
Adler, Castro, Friedrich, Haggui, Sarpei, Schneider (Vidal 75), Rolfes, Barbarez (Freier 67), Barnetta, Gekas (Callsen-Bracker 87), Kiessling.
Yellow Card(s): Haggui 49, Gekas 58
A 2-3 *Barbarez (19), Gekas (55)*
Adler, Haggui, Friedrich, Rolfes, Barnetta, Gekas (Callsen-Bracker 82), Kiessling, Sarpei, Vidal (Bulykin 87), Castro, Barbarez (Schwegler 72).
Yellow Card(s): Barbarez 59, Schwegler 82

Quarter-Final - FC Zenit St. Petersburg (RUS)
H 1-4 *Kiessling (33)*
Adler, Haggui, Friedrich, Rolfes, Barnetta, Gekas, Kiessling, Greško (Sarpei 66), Vidal (Sinkiewicz 74), Schneider (Barbarez 62), Castro.
Yellow Card(s): Barnetta 73, Friedrich 79
A 1-0 *Bulykin (18)*
Adler, Haggui, Freier (Kiessling 68), Bulykin, Dum (Gekas 75), Sarpei, Schwegler (Rolfes 59), Sinkiewicz, Schneider, Castro, Callsen-Bracker.
Yellow Card(s): Castro 29, Freier 29, Sinkiewicz 65

HAMBURGER SV

UEFA INTERTOTO CUP

Third Round - FC Dacia Chišinau (MDA)
A 1-1 *Van der Vaart (70)*
Rost, De Jong (Benjamin 65), Demel, Jarolím, Kompany, Mathijsen, Sanogo, Trochowski (Zidan 65), Van der Vaart, Laas, Olić.
Yellow Card(s): De Jong 22
H 4-0 *Kompany (50), Van der Vaart (71), Benjamin (76), Jarolím (89)*
Rost, Benjamin, De Jong, Demel (Brečko 77), Jarolím, Kompany, Mathijsen (Reinhardt 78), Trochowski, Van der Vaart, Olić, Zidan (Choupo-Moting 80).

UEFA CUP

Second Qualifying Round - Budapest Honvéd FC (HUN)
A 0-0
Rost, Atouba, De Jong, Demel, Jarolím, Kompany, Olić (Ben-Hatira 76), Reinhardt, Trochowski, Zidan (Guerrero 67), Castelen.
Yellow Card(s): De Jong 31, Jarolím 62, Trochowski 89
H 4-0 *Guerrero (9, 38), Smiljanic (50og), Choupo-Moting (90)*
Rost, Atouba, Demel, Guerrero (Choupo-Moting 59), Jarolím, Kompan Mathijsen, Olić (Trochowski 65), Reinhardt, Van der Vaart (Ben-Hatira 7 Castelen.

First Round - PFC Litex Lovech (BUL)
A 1-0 *Castelen (75)*
Rost, Atouba, Castelen (Ben-Hatira 86), De Jong, Demel, Guerrero (Olić 79), Jarolím, Mathijsen, Reinhardt, Trochowski, Van der Vaart (Zidan 89
Yellow Card(s): Guerrero 73
H 3-1 *Guerrero (40, 52), Van der Vaart (71)*
Rost, Atouba, Reinhardt, Mathijsen, De Jong, Guerrero (Choupo-Moting Olić (Ben-Hatira 79), Jarolím, Trochowski, Demel, Van der Vaart (Zidan 74
Yellow Card(s): Demel 84

Group D
Match 1 - SK Brann (NOR)
A 1-0 *Kompany (62)*
Rost, Demel, Boateng, Atouba, Reinhardt, Mathijsen, Kompany, Jarolín Trochowski (Benjamin 88), Olić, Zidan (Choupo-Moting 90).
Yellow Card(s): Zidan 14
Match 2 - Stade Rennais FC (FRA)
H 3-0 *Van der Vaart (30), Choupo-Moting (84), Zidan (90+1p)*
Rost, Reinhardt, Mathijsen, De Jong (Demel 68), Kompany, Olić (Chou Moting 79), Trochowski, Castelen, Boateng, Van der Vaart (Zidan 85), Benjamin.
Yellow Card(s): De Jong 45+1
Match 3 - NK Dinamo Zagreb (CRO)
A 2-0 *De Jong (88), Trochowski (90+3p)*
Rost, Atouba, Reinhardt, Mathijsen, De Jong, Kompany, Olić (Choupo-Moting 84), Jarolím, Castelen (Demel 76), Boateng, Van der Vaart (Trochowski 89).
Yellow Card(s): Atouba 34
Match 4 - FC Basel 1893 (SUI)
H 1-1 *Olić (73)*
Rost, Boateng, Reinhardt, Mathijsen, Atouba, Kompany (Castelen 71), Jong, Jarolím, Van der Vaart, Trochowski (Guerrero 62), Olić.
Yellow Card(s): Kompany 31

Round of 32 - FC Zürich (SUI)
A 3-1 *Jarolím (49), Olić (67), Trochowski (77)*
Rost, Demel, Reinhardt, Mathijsen, Benjamin, Trochowski, De Jong, Kompany, Van der Vaart (Guerrero 32), Jarolím (Brečko 86), Olić (Zidan
Yellow Card(s): Kompany 55, De Jong 64
H 0-0
Rost, Demel (Boateng 78), Reinhardt, Mathijsen, Benjamin, Kompany, D Jong, Jarolím, Trochowski (Fillinger 81), Olić, Guerrero (Choupo-Moting
Yellow Card(s): Jarolím 66, Benjamin 86

Round of 16 - Bayer 04 Leverkusen (GER)
A 0-1
Rost, Demel (Boateng 56), Reinhardt, Mathijsen, Benjamin, Jarolím, Va der Vaart, De Jong, Kompany, Olić (Trochowski 76), Guerrero (Zidan 79
Yellow Card(s): Kompany 36, Guerrero 43, De Jong 50
H 3-2 *Trochowski (53), Guerrero (65), Van der Vaart (81)*
Rost, Atouba (Boateng 61), Reinhardt, Mathijsen, Odjidja-Ofoe (Trocho 46), Guerrero, Olić (Sam 77), Jarolím, Demel, Van der Vaart, Brečko.
Yellow Card(s): Brečko 55, Guerrero 58, Van der Vaart 76

GREECE

OLYMPIACOS CFP

UEFA CHAMPIONS LEAGUE

C
1 - S.S. Lazio (ITA)
Galletti (55)
olidis, Patsatzoglou (Kovačević 80), Domi, Stoltidis, Galletti,
vić, Żewłakow, Antzas, Ledesma, LuaLua, Torosidis.
Card(s): Patsatzoglou 6
2 - Werder Bremen (GER)
Stoltidis (73), Patsatzoglou (82), Kovačević (87)
olidis, Patsatzoglou, Domi (Júlio César 19), Stoltidis, Galletti
ević 72), Đorđević, Raúl Bravo, Antzas, Ledesma, LuaLua, Torosidis
s 86).
Card(s): Ledesma 70
3 - Real Madrid CF (ESP)
Galletti (7), Júlio César (47)
olidis, Patsatzoglou, Júlio César, Stoltidis, Galletti, Đorđević, Raúl
(Żewłakow 75), Antzas, Ledesma (Núñez 86), LuaLua (Kovačević 72),
dis.
ard(s): Torosidis 13
Card(s): Đorđević 53, Patsatzoglou 70, Galletti 75, Antzas 90
4 - Real Madrid CF (ESP)

olidis, Patsatzoglou, Júlio César (Mendrinos 74), Stoltidis, Galletti,
ević (Konstantinou 80), Đorđević, Żewłakow, Raúl Bravo (Archubi
ntos, LuaLua.
Card(s): Đorđević 44, Stoltidis 49, Pantos 71
5 - S.S. Lazio (ITA)
Galletti (35), Kovačević (64)
olidis, Patsatzoglou (Mendrinos 75), Stoltidis, Galletti, Đorđević
glou 90+3), Żewłakow, Antzas, Ledesma, Pantos, LuaLua (Kovačević
rosidis.
Card(s): Đorđević 45+1, Ledesma 62, Kovačević 68, Torosidis 81
6 - Werder Bremen (GER)
Stoltidis (12, 74), Kovačević (70)
olidis, Patsatzoglou (Mendrinos 24), Stoltidis, Galletti (Núñez 85),
ević (Mitroglou 82), Żewłakow, Antzas, Ledesma, Pantos, LuaLua,
dis.
Card(s): Antzas 42, Mitroglou 89

d of 16 - Chelsea FC (ENG)

olidis, Júlio César, Stoltidis, Galletti (Leonardo 83), Kovačević (Núñez
rđević (Belluschi 76), Żewłakow, Antzas, Ledesma, Pantos, Torosidis.
Card(s): Belluschi 90+1

olidis, Patsatzoglou, Júlio César, Stoltidis, Kovačević, Đorđević
rdo 57), Żewłakow, Antzas, Ledesma (Belluschi 54), Pantos,
dis (Šišić 76).
Card(s): Pantos 7

No	Player	Nat	DoB	Aps	(s)	Gls
	epers					
	Antonis Nikopolidis		14/1/71	8		
	ders					
	Christos Patsatzoglou		19/3/79	7		1
	Didier Domi	FRA	2/5/78	2		
	Leonardo	BRA	4/8/85		(2)	
	Júlio César	BRA	18/11/78	4	(1)	1
	Michał Żewłakow	POL	22/4/76	6	(1)	
	Raúl Bravo	ESP	14/4/81	3		
18	Paraskevas Antzas		18/8/76	7		
30	Anastasios Pantos		5/5/76	5	(1)	
35	Vasilios Torosidis		10/6/85	7		
	Midfielders					
6	Ieroklis Stoltidis		2/2/75	8		3
8	Rodrigo Javier Archubi	ARG	6/6/85		(1)	
11	Predrag Đorđević	SRB	4/8/72	7		
19	Konstantinos Mendrinos		28/5/85		(3)	
22	Konstantinos Mitroglou		12/3/88		(2)	
25	Fernando Belluschi	ARG	10/9/83		(2)	
28	Cristián Raúl Ledesma	ARG	29/11/78	7		
77	Mirnes Šišić	SVN	8/8/81		(1)	
	Attackers					
7	Luciano Galletti	ARG	9/4/80	7		3
9	Darko Kovačević	SRB	18/11/73	4	(4)	3
10	Leonel Núñez	ARG	13/10/84		(3)	
23	Michalis Konstantinou	CYP	19/2/78		(1)	
32	Lomana LuaLua	COD	28/12/80	6		

AEK ATHENS FC

UEFA CHAMPIONS LEAGUE

Third Qualifying Round - Sevilla FC (ESP)
A 0-2
Moretto, Arruabarrena, Rivaldo (Kone 67), Júlio César, Dellas, Liberopoulos, Manduca, Nsaliwa, Geraldo Alves, Edson (Kafes 62), Zikos (Tőzsér 93).
Yellow Card(s): Arruabarrena 42, Zikos 90+1
H 1-4 *Rivaldo (82p)*
Moretto, Rivaldo, Bourbos, Júlio César (Tőzsér 46), Liberopoulos, Manduca, Nsaliwa (Pappas 46), Papastathopoulos, Geraldo Alves, Edson, Zikos (Pavlis 62).
Yellow Card(s): Zikos 19, Bourbos 43, Papastathopoulos 75

UEFA CUP

First Round - FC Salzburg (AUT)
H 3-0 *Geraldo Alves (2), Rivaldo (57), Kone (88)*
Macho, Arruabarrena, Rivaldo (Blanco 60), Júlio César (Tőzsér 29), Dellas, Kafes (Kone 51), Liberopoulos, Nsaliwa, Geraldo Alves, Edson, Manú.
Yellow Card(s): Edson 35, Geraldo Alves 40, Nsaliwa 76, Liberopoulos 88
A 0-1
Macho, Arruabarrena, Rivaldo (Papastathopoulos 67), Dellas, Kafes, Liberopoulos, Manduca (Blanco 50), Nsaliwa, Geraldo Alves, Edson, Tőzsér (Kone 88).
Yellow Card(s): Dellas 29, Liberopoulos 80

Group C
Match 1 - IF Elfsborg (SWE)
A 1-1 *Pappas (49)*
Moretto, Bourbos, Geraldo Alves, Papastathopoulos, Arruabarrena, Manú (Pappas 46), Tőzsér, Manduca, Nsaliwa (Kafes 63), Júlio César (Kone 76), Blanco.
Match 2 - ACF Fiorentina (ITA)
H 1-1 *Balzaretti (33og)*
Moretto, Edson, Dellas, Papastathopoulos, Arruabarrena, Nsaliwa (Kafes 71), Tőzsér, Kone (Manduca 54), Manú, Júlio César (Pappas 81), Blanco.
Yellow Card(s): Edson 12
Match 3 - FK Mladá Boleslav (CZE)
A 1-0 *Nsaliwa (46)*
Moretto, Edson, Dellas, Arruabarrena, Geraldo Alves, Nsaliwa, Tőzsér, Manú (Júlio César 75), Rivaldo (Papastathopoulos 89), Blanco (Manduca 46), Liberopoulos.
Yellow Card(s): Geraldo Alves 27, Arruabarrena 29, Tőzsér 65

Match 4 - Villarreal CF (ESP)
H 1-2 *Rivaldo (68)*
Macho, Edson, Geraldo Alves, Papastathopoulos, Arruabarrena, Tőzsér, Nsaliwa (Kafes 46), Kone (Manduca 60), Rivaldo (Pappas 82), Júlio César, Liberopoulos.
Yellow Card(s): Papastathopoulos 85, Kafes 90+4

Round of 32 - Getafe CF (ESP)
H 1-1 *Blanco (90+3)*
Moretto, Dellas, Papastathopoulos, Arruabarrena, Nsaliwa, Zikos, Kafes, Pappas (Blanco 82), Rivaldo, Manduca (Manú 66), Liberopoulos (Kallon 75).
Yellow Card(s): Zikos 72
A 0-3
Moretto, Nsaliwa, Dellas, Papastathopoulos, Arruabarrena, Kafes (Blanco 65), Zikos, Edson, Lagos (Manduca 57), Rivaldo, Kallon (Liberopoulos 72).
Yellow Card(s): Arruabarrena 14, Nsaliwa 38, Papastathopoulos 90+2

LARISSA FC

UEFA CUP

First Round - Blackburn Rovers FC (ENG)
H 2-0 *Bakayoko (33), Cleiton (34)*
Kotsolis, Alexandrou (Gikas 77), Bakayoko (Venetis 90+3), Förster, Fotakis, Katsiaros, Kiriakidis, Dabizas, Sarmiento, Cleiton (Kalantzis 85), Galitsios.
Yellow Card(s): Katsiaros 25, Bakayoko 90+2
A 1-2 *Cleiton (17)*
Kotsolis, Alexandrou (Kotsios 56), Bakayoko (Gikas 90), Förster, Katsiaros, Kiriakidis, Dabizas, Sarmiento, Cleiton, Galitsios (Kalantzis 77), Fotakis.
Yellow Card(s): Sarmiento 28, Kotsolis 45+1, Cleiton 66, Fotakis 82

Group A
Match 1 - Everton FC (ENG)
A 1-3 *Cleiton (65)*
Kotsolis, Galitsios, Förster (Venetis 79), Dabizas, Venetidis, Cleiton, Fotakis, Kiriakidis (Lambropoulos 75), Sarmiento, Parra (Kalantzis 58), Bakayoko.
Yellow Card(s): Dabizas 28
Match 2 - FC Zenit St. Petersburg (RUS)
H 2-3 *Alexandrou (58), Fotakis (62)*
Kotsolis, Kotsios, Venetidis (Katsiaros 46), Dabizas, Kiriakidis (Lambropoulos 83), Galitsios, Cleiton, Alexandrou (Kalantzis 74), Sarmiento, Fotakis, Bakayoko.
Yellow Card(s): Kotsios 84
Match 3 - AZ Alkmaar (NED)
A 0-1
Kotsolis, Dabizas, Katsiaros, Galitsios, Kotsios, Kiriakidis (Kožlej 82), Cleiton, Sarmiento, Fotakis, Alexandrou (Bahramis 82), Kalantzis (Parra 69).
Red Card(s): Kotsios 84
Yellow Card(s): Cleiton 48, Kotsios 74, Kotsios 84, Parra 87
Match 4 - 1. FC Nürnberg (GER)
H 1-3 *Kožlej (11)*
Kipouros, Venetis, Dabizas, Galitsios, Katsiaros, Kiriakidis, Gikas (Cleiton 61), Bahramis (Bakayoko 77), Parra (Alexandrou 71), Kalantzis, Kožlej.
Yellow Card(s): Parra 27, Dabizas 73, Katsiaros 80

PANATHINAIKOS FC

UEFA CUP

First Round - FC Artmedia Petržalka (SVK)
A 2-1 *Papadopoulos (61p), N'Doye (90)*
Malarz, Enakarhire, Goumas, Papadopoulos, Salpingidis (Romero 81), Dimoutsos (Mate Júnior 90+3), Karagounis (N'Doye 74), Nilsson, Tzio Vintra, Marcelo Mattos.
Yellow Card(s): Papadopoulos 85
H 3-0 *Papadopoulos (45p, 45+2, 74p)*
Malarz, Morris, Papadopoulos, Romero (Šerić 62), Sarriegui, Dimouts Karagounis (Ivanschitz 71), N'Doye (Mantzios 62), Nilsson, Tziolis, Vin
Yellow Card(s): Romero 19, Nilsson 69

Group B
Match 1 - Aberdeen FC (SCO)
H 3-0 *Goumas (11), Papadopoulos (73), Salpingidis (77)*
Malarz, Morris, Fyssas, Goumas, Marcelo Mattos, Tziolis, Ivanschitz (Šeri Nilsson, Dimoutsos, N'Doye (Papadopoulos 59), Salpingidis (Mantzios
Yellow Card(s): Dimoutsos 51
Match 2 - FC København (DEN)
A 1-0 *N'Doye (16)*
Galinović, Vintra, Enakarhire, Goumas, Fyssas, Marcelo Mattos, Karag (Šerić 87), Tziolis, Ivanschitz (Dimoutsos 67), Papadopoulos (Salpingi 76), N'Doye.
Yellow Card(s): Goumas 26
Match 3 - FC Lokomotiv Moskva (RUS)
H 2-0 *Salpingidis (70, 74)*
Galinović, Vintra, Morris, Sarriegui, Fyssas, Romero (Ninis 82), Tziolis, M Júnior, Dimoutsos (Karagounis 66), Papadopoulos, N'Doye (Salpingidi
Yellow Card(s): Mate Júnior 23
Match 4 - Club Atlético de Madrid (ESP)
A 1-2 *Salpingidis (34)*
Malarz, Vintra, Morris, Sarriegui, Fyssas, Mate Júnior (Dimoutsos 85), Tziolis, Marcelo Mattos, Romero (Ivanschitz 68), Salpingidis (Mantzios Papadopoulos.
Yellow Card(s): Tziolis 22, Romero 56, Ivanschitz 81

Round of 32 - Rangers FC (SCO)
A 0-0
Galinović, Nilsson, Morris, Goumas, Vintra, N'Doye, Tziolis, Marcelo M Mate Júnior, Karagounis, Salpingidis (Hélder Postiga 66).
Yellow Card(s): Mate Júnior 60, Nilsson 82
H 1-1 *Goumas (12)*
Galinović, Marcelo Mattos, Morris, Goumas, Hélder Postiga (N'Doye 6 Salpingidis, Karagounis, Tziolis (González 83), Vintra, Ivanschitz, Nilss (Papadopoulos 86).

ARIS THESSALONIKI FC

UEFA CUP

First Round - Real Zaragoza (ESP)
H 1-0 *Papadopoulos (6)*
Chalkias, Toni Calvo (Javito 59), Koke, Neto, Nacho García, Ronaldo, Felipe (Siston 49), Ivić (Koulouheris 81), Nebegleras, Papadopoulos, Marco Aurélio.
Yellow Card(s): Chalkias 87
A 1-2 *Javito (63)*
Chalkias, Toni Calvo (Javito 58), Koke (Koulouheris 81), Neto, Nacho García, Ronaldo, Siston (Vangjeli 88), Ivić, Nebegleras, Papadopoulos, Marco Aurélio.
Yellow Card(s): Marco Aurélio 51, Papadopoulos 55, Nebegleras 67

p F
h 1 - FK Crvena Zvezda (SRB)
Papazoglou (76, 89), Koke (90+1)
ias, Neto, Vangjeli, Papadopoulos, Ronaldo, Javito (Papazoglou 53),
gleras, Nacho García, Koke, Felipe (Siston 80), Ivić (Toni Calvo 66).
w Card(s): Papazoglou 90
h 2 - Bolton Wanderers FC (ENG)
Toni Calvo (44)
ias, Neto, Papadopoulos, Ronaldo, Karabelas, Prittas, Nacho García
oulias 82), Nebegleras, Toni Calvo (Javito 61), Koke (Kyriakos 86),
.
w Card(s): Papadopoulos 68, Gougoulias 88
h 3 - SC Braga (POR)
Ronaldo (26)
ias, Neto, Marco Aurélio, Papadopoulos, Ronaldo, Nebegleras, Nacho
, Siston (Toni Calvo 79), Ivić, Javito (Felipe 79), Koke.
w Card(s): Javito 62, Marco Aurélio 65
h 4 - FC Bayern München (GER)

ias, Vangjeli, Papadopoulos, Ronaldo, Marco Aurélio, Prittas,
gleras, Nacho García (Karabelas 86), Felipe, Koke (Siston 71), Ivić
o 46).
w Card(s): Vangjeli 33, Nebegleras 47, Chalkias 73, Papadopoulos 83

PANIONIOS GSS

UEFA CUP

Round - FC Sochaux-Montbéliard (FRA)
Djebbour (28), Fernández (54)
, Djebbour, Maniatis, Fernández (Gáspár 82), Kondi (Kapetanos 75),
umordzi, Majstorović, Pletsch, Goundoulakis (Wagner 90), Makos,
poulos.
w Card(s): Djebbour 42, Yao Kumordzi 75

, Djebbour, Maniatis, Fernández (Berthé 90), Kontoes (Nicolaou 46),
umordzi, Majstorović, Pletsch, Goundoulakis, Makos (Skoufalis 83),
poulos.
w Card(s): Makos 5, Yao Kumordzi 44, Fernández 71, Maniatis 75

p H
h 1 - Helsingborgs IF (SWE)
Goundoulakis (45+1)
, Maniatis, Berthé, Majstorović, Spiropoulos, Goundoulakis, Yao
ordzi, Makos (Skoufalis 88), Kapetanos (Pletsch 85), Nicolaou,
bour (Kondi 72).
w Card(s): Nicolaou 36, Goundoulakis 47, Pletsch 89
h 2 - Galatasaray AŞ (TUR)

asis, Maniatis, Pletsch, Spiropoulos, Fernández, Makos, Yao Kumordzi
sopoulos 63), Majstorović, Goundoulakis (Kondi 80), Djebbour,
dis (Skoufalis 63).
Card(s): Makos 63
w Card(s): Maniatis 50, Makos 62, Makos 63, Pletsch 72, Djebbour 85
h 3 - FK Austria Wien (AUT)
Majstorović (90+1)
, Maniatis, Berthé, Pletsch, Skoufalis (Koutsopoulos 85), Djebbour,
umordzi (Gáspár 87), Majstorović, Goundoulakis, Spiropoulos,
aou (Fernández 73).
w Card(s): Berthé 48, Fernández 83
h 4 - FC Girondins de Bordeaux (FRA)
Djebbour (6p), Makos (20)
, Maniatis (Aravidis 78), Berthé, Pletsch, Spiropoulos, Majstorović, Makos,
falis (Fernández 55), Goundoulakis, Yao Kumordzi (Gaspar 90), Djebbour.
w Card(s): Berthé 34, Pletsch 69

OFI CRETE FC

UEFA INTERTOTO CUP

Third Round - FC Tobol Kostanay (KAZ)
A 0-1
Peersman, Issa, Nwafor, Plousis (Pliagas 67), Šimić (Roumbakis 88), Pitsos, Bărcăuan, Popović, Gerber, Arvanitis, Taralidis.
Yellow Card(s): Bărcăuan 68
H 0-1
Peersman, Issa, Kounenakis, Nwafor, Šimić, Pitsos (Michelakakis 82), Bărcăuan, Roumbakis (Pliagas 56), Gerber, Arvanitis (Plousis 68), Taralidis.
Yellow Card(s): Taralidis 64, Bărcăuan 73, Michelakakis 85

HUNGARY

DEBRECENI VSC

UEFA CHAMPIONS LEAGUE

Second Qualifying Round - IF Elfsborg (SWE)
H 0-1
Balogh, Bernáth, Demjén (Czvitkovics 88), Dombi (Sándor 40), Komlósi, Leandro, Mészáros, Stojkov (Rudolf 74), Vukmir, Dzsudzsák, Kouemaha.
Yellow Card(s): Dzsudzsák 31
A 0-0
Balogh, Demjén (Kerekes 71), Komlósi, Leandro, Stojkov (Rudolf 55), Vukmir, Szűcs, Dzsudzsák, Kouemaha, Mészáros, Bernáth (Sándor 85).
Red Card(s): Kouemaha 88
Yellow Card(s): Komlósi 22, Kouemaha 67, Kerekes 85, Kouemaha 88, Sándor 90+2

BUDAPEST HONVÉD FC

UEFA CUP

First Qualifying Round - FC Nistru Otaci (MDA)
A 1-1 *Abraham (51)*
I. Tóth, Dobos, Hercegfalvi, Ivancsics (Koós 69), Pomper, Mogyorósi (Schindler 63), Smiljanić, B. Tóth, Bárányos, Benjamin (Genito 46), Abraham.
Yellow Card(s): B. Tóth 17, Pomper 75
H 1-1 *Abraham (14) (aet; 5-4 on pens)*
I. Tóth, Dobos (Benjamin 91), Hercegfalvi (Koós 46), Ivancsics, Z. Vincze, Pomper, Schindler, Smiljanić, Bárányos, Genito, Abraham (Diego 65).
Yellow Card(s): Genito 59

Second Qualifying Round - Hamburger SV (GER)
H 0-0
I. Tóth, Benjamin, Bárányos, Genito, Abraham (Koós 85), Hercegfalvi (Abass

78), Ivancsics, Mogyorósi, Smiljanić, Z. Vincze, Magasföldi (Diego 70).
Yellow Card(s): Genito 37, Hercegfalvi 40, Magasföldi 48, Z. Vincze 76
A 0-4
I. Tóth, Benjamin, Bárányos, Abraham (B. Tóth 78), Hercegfalvi, Mogyorósi, Diego, Smiljanić, Z. Vincze, G. Vincze (Abass 67), Magasföldi (Ivancsics 50).
Yellow Card(s): G. Vincze 27, Z. Vincze 47

MTK BUDAPEST

UEFA CUP

First Qualifying Round - FC MIKA (ARM)
H 2-1 *Pintér (20), Urbán (57)*
Végh, Bori, Horváth, Kanta (Szabó 84), Lambulić, Pál (Ladóczki 77), Pintér, Pollák, Urbán, Zsidai, Pátkai.
A 0-1
Végh, Horváth, Kanta, Lambulić, Pál, Pintér, Pollák, Urbán (Simon 83), Zsidai, Pátkai (Szabó 73), Ladóczki (Hrepka 46).

ZALAEGERSZEGI TE

UEFA INTERTOTO CUP

Second Round - FC Rubin Kazan (RUS)
H 0-3
Lipcák, Koplárovics, Botiş, Kádár, Molnár (N. Tóth 46), Simonfalvi, Z. Tóth (Balázs 69), Máté, Waltner, Diawara (Lukács 76), Polgár.
Red Card(s): Lipcák 78
Yellow Card(s): Botiş 21, Polgár 33, Molnár 45+1
A 0-2
Pogacsics, Koplárovics, Botiş, Kádár (Lukács 35), Simonfalvi, Z. Tóth, Máté, Waltner, Balázs (Diawara 63), Bozsik (Horváth 85), Polgár.
Yellow Card(s): Z. Tóth 28, Máté 51, Polgár 61

ICELAND

FH HAFNARFJÖRDUR

UEFA CHAMPIONS LEAGUE

First Qualifying Round - HB Tórshavn (FRO)
H 4-1 *Bjarnason (14), Vilhjálmsson (16, 58), Ólafsson (52)*
Lárusson, Bjarnason, Gardarsson, T. Gudmundsson, M. Gudmundsson, Nielsen, Ólafsson (Gudnason 74), Saevarsson, Siim (Ásgeirsson 77), Vidarsson, Vilhjálmsson.
Yellow Card(s): Gardarsson 34
A 0-0
Lárusson, Bjarnason, Gardarsson, T. Gudmundsson (Gudnason 79), M. Gudmundsson, Nielsen (Helgason 83), Ólafsson (Ásgeirsson 70), Saevarsson, Siim, Vidarsson, Vilhjálmsson.
Yellow Card(s): Siim 77

Second Qualifying Round - FC BATE Borisov (BLR)
H 1-3 *Vilhjálmsson (18)*
Lárusson, Bjarnason, Gardarsson, T. Gudmundsson, M. Gudmundsso (Snorrason 84), Nielsen, Ólafsson (A. Gunnlaugsson 70), Saevarsson, Vilhjálmsson, Vidarsson (Ásgeirsson 70).
Yellow Card(s): Siim 65
A 1-1 *T. Gudmundsson (33)*
Lárusson, Bjarnason, Gardarsson (Nielsen 78), T. Gudmundsson (Valgardsson 76), M. Gudmundsson, B. Gunnlaugsson, Helgason, Óla (Ásgeirsson 63), Saevarsson, Vidarsson, Vilhjálmsson.
Red Card(s): Helgason 42
Yellow Card(s): Helgason 21, Vidarsson 28, Saevarsson 34, Helgason M. Gudmundsson 52, Gardarsson 69

KEFLAVÍK

UEFA CUP

First Qualifying Round - FC Midtjylland (DEN)
H 3-2 *Steinarsson (27), Troest (34og), Samuelsen (57)*
Jóhannsson, Antoníusson, Jónasson (Einarsson 82), Kristjánsson (Gustafsson 82), Mete, Miličević, Samuelsen, Sigurdsson, Steinarsson (Saevarsson 68), Kotilainen, Jørgensen.
A 1-2 *Sigurdsson (11)*
B. Gudmundsson, Antoníusson, Jónasson (Gustafsson 77), Kristjánsso (Thorsteinsson 83), Mete, Miličević, Saevarsson, Samuelsen, Sigurdss Steinarsson, Jørgensen (Kotilainen 62).

KR REYKJAVÍK

UEFA CUP

First Qualifying Round - BK Häcken (SWE)
A 1-1 *Pétursson (69)*
S. Magnússon, Kristjánsson, K. Magnússon, G. Jónsson, Kristinsson, Marteinsson, Fridgeirsson, Pétursson, Einarsson, Gunnarsson, Ólafsso
Yellow Card(s): Kristjánsson 50
H 0-1
S. Magnússon, Kristjánsson, K. Magnússon, G. Jónsson, Lárusson (Hjartarson 68), Takefusa, Kristinsson, Marteinsson, Hauksson, Einars (Pétursson 88), Gunnarsson (Júlíusson 46).
Yellow Card(s): Lárusson 7, Kristjánsson 79, K. Magnússon 82

VALUR REYKJAVÍK

UEFA INTERTOTO CUP

First Round - Cork City FC (IRL)
H 0-2
Sturluson, Adalsteinsson, Pálmason (Benediktsson 76), Saevarsson, Sr Thórarinsson, Mortensen, Bett, Carlsen, Hjaltason (Einarsson 64),

ısson (Hreidarsson 76).
Sigurdsson (22)
son, Adalsteinsson (Hafsteinsson 85), Benediktsson (Hreidarsson
ılmason, Smith, Thórarinsson, Bett, Carlsen (Einarsson 46), H.
msson, Sigurdsson, Saevarsson.
ard(s): Hreidarsson 89
v Card(s): Saevarsson 13

ISRAEL

BEITAR JERUSALEM FC

UEFA CHAMPIONS LEAGUE

ıd Qualifying Round - FC København (DEN)

ılberman, Boateng, Gershon, Itzhaki, Tamuz (Mirosevic 60),
ıerg (Afek 84), Ziv, Benado, Tal, Álvarez.
ard(s): Boateng 53
v Card(s): Ziv 25, Itzhaki 33, Boateng 50, Boateng 53, Gershon 53
Itzhaki (60) (aet)
ılberman (Azriel 100), Gershon, Itzhaki, Zandberg, Ziv, Rômulo
ız 62), Benado, Tal, Álvarez, Mirosevic (Baruchyan 46).
v Card(s): Gershon 18, Ziv 79, Tal 110

HAPOEL TEL-AVIV FC

UEFA CUP

ıd Qualifying Round - NK Široki Brijeg (BIH)
Abedi (14), Asulin (32), Gabriel (74)
ma, Antebi, Badir, Dego (Oved 90+2), Gabriel, N'Sumbu, Abedi
ıo 85), Sabag (Fábio Júnior 69), Bondarev, Duani, Asulin.
v Card(s): Bondarev 49
Asulin (41), Badir (50), Natcho (75)
ma, Antebi, Badir (Chen 67), Dego (Oved 55), Gabriel, N'Sumbu,
, Bondarev, Duani, Fábio Júnior (Natcho 62), Asulin.
v Card(s): Dego 38, Badir 56, Chen 90

Round - AIK Solna (SWE)

ma, Antebi, Badir, Natcho (Oved 68), Gabriel, N'Sumbu, Abedi (Perez
ondarev, Duani, Fábio Júnior (Sabag 74), Asulin.
Oved (64)
ma, Antebi, Asulin (Dego 42), Badir, Gabriel, Mantzur (Chen 85),
ıbu, Oved (Natcho 88), Fábio Júnior, Abedi, Duani.
v Card(s): Oved 41, Badir 44, N'Sumbu 60

ɔ G
ı 1 - RSC Anderlecht (BEL)

ma, Mantzur, Duani, Antebi, Gabriel, Asulin (Sabag 62), Badir (Abedi
atcho, N'Sumbu, Oved (Sror 53), Fábio Júnior.

Match 2 - Tottenham Hotspur FC (ENG)
H 0-2
Enyeama, Bachshi (Mantzur 46), Chen, Gabriel, Shish, Natcho, N'Sumbu, Abutbul (Abedi 46), Dego (Antebi 58), Badir, Fábio Júnior.
Red Card(s): Shish 50
Yellow Card(s): Shish 41, Gabriel 42, Shish 50
Match 3 - Getafe CF (ESP)
A 2-1 *Badir (5), Dego (31)*
Enyeama, Antebi, Bondarev, Gabriel, Duani, Srur (Oved 82), Badir, Abutbul, Abedi (Natcho 75), Dego (Asulin 86), Fábio Júnior.
Yellow Card(s): Srur 17, Enyeama 28, Abutbul 90+3
Match 4 - Aalborg BK (DEN)
H 1-3 *Fábio Júnior (45+1)*
Enyeama, Bondarev, Duani, N'Sumbu, Antebi, Oved, Abutbul, Natcho, Dego (Srur 70), Asulin (Sabag 76), Fábio Júnior (Losky 87).

MACCABI NETANYA FC

UEFA CUP

Second Qualifying Round - UD Leiria (POR)
A 0-0
Shtrauber, Ben Dayan, Marín, Bundea (Rozental 76), Shechter, Saban, Tega (Yampolsky 87), Awudu, A. Cohen, Hermon, T. Cohen.
Yellow Card(s): Marín 62, A. Cohen 69, T. Cohen 84, Shechter 87
H 0-1
Shtrauber, Ben Dayan, Marín, Bundea (Rozental 77), Shechter, Saban, Tega, Awudu, A. Cohen (Yampolsky 67), Strul, T. Cohen.
Yellow Card(s): Ben Dayan 40, Tega 63

MACCABI TEL-AVIV FC

UEFA CUP

First Qualifying Round - FC Santa Coloma (AND)
A 0-1
Salomon, Kamanan, Martinović, Mesika, Mishaelof, Nimni, Peretz, Shitrit, Shpungin (Edri 85), Yeini, Biton (Ron 90+3).
Yellow Card(s): Mesika 43
H 4-0 *Mesika (12, 25), Shivhon (63), Kamanan (71)*
Salomon, Hadad, Kamanan, Martinović, Mesika, Nimni (Edri 75), Peretz (Gan 65), Shitrit, Shivhon (Biton 65), Shpungin, Yeini.
Red Card(s): Shitrit 28

Second Qualifying Round - Kayseri Erciyesspor (TUR)
H 1-1 *Kamanan (42)*
Jevrić, Kamanan (Malul 72), Martinović, Mesika, Nimni (Shivhon 58), Peretz, Shpungin, Yeini, Ifrah, Roman, Haddad (Azran 64).
Yellow Card(s): Peretz 36, Yeini 45, Nimni 45, Martinović 88
A 1-3 *Haddad (40)*
Jevrić, Azran (Peretz 64), Haddad, Kamanan (Biton 78), Mesika, Nimni, Shpungin, Yeini, Roman, Kapiloto, Haddad (Shivhon 71).

MACCABI HAIFA FC

UEFA INTERTOTO CUP

Second Round - CF Gloria 1922 Bistrița (ROU)
H 0-2
Al Madon, Bello, Keinan, Masudi, Shahbary, Suan (Hemed 65), Kiel, Maman, Refaelov, Buzaglo (Gita 53), Maimon (Hanuka 46).
Yellow Card(s): Kiel 46, Suan 50, Keinan 70, Shahbary 74
A 2-0 *Maimon (6), Hemed (65) (aet; 2-3 on pens)*
Davidovich, Bello (Hanuka 111), Gita, Keinan, Shahbary, Suan, Kiel (Hemed 62), Refaelov, Buzaglo, Maimon, Gafni.
Red Card(s): Suan 111
Yellow Card(s): Suan 21, Kiel 23, Shahbary 47, Suan 111

ITALY

AC MILAN

UEFA CHAMPIONS LEAGUE

Group D
Match 1 - SL Benfica (POR)
H 2-1 *Pirlo (9), Inzaghi (24)*
Dida, Kaladze, Gattuso, Inzaghi (Gilardino 84), Seedorf (Emerson 75), Nesta, Jankulovski, Pirlo, Kaká, Ambrosini, Oddo (Bonera 81).
Yellow Card(s): Inzaghi 67
Match 2 - Celtic FC (SCO)
A 1-2 *Kaká (68p)*
Dida (Kalac 94), Gattuso, Inzaghi (Gilardino 77), Seedorf (Gourcuff 55), Nesta, Jankulovski, Pirlo, Kaká, Ambrosini, Bonera, Oddo.
Yellow Card(s): Ambrosini 51, Nesta 72
Match 3 - FC Shakhtar Donetsk (UKR)
H 4-1 *Gilardino (6, 14), Seedorf (62, 69)*
Kalac, Kaladze, Gattuso, Seedorf, Gilardino (Serginho 75), Nesta, Favalli (Bonera 61), Pirlo, Kaká, Ambrosini (Emerson 83), Oddo.
Yellow Card(s): Gattuso 20, Ambrosini 45
Match 4 - FC Shakhtar Donetsk (UKR)
A 3-0 *Inzaghi (66, 90+3), Kaká (72)*
Dida, Kaladze, Gattuso, Seedorf (Maldini 79), Gilardino (Inzaghi 63), Nesta, Pirlo, Kaká, Ambrosini, Bonera, Serginho (Brocchi 85).
Yellow Card(s): Gattuso 19, Kaká 32, Ambrosini 71
Match 5 - SL Benfica (POR)
A 1-1 *Pirlo (15)*
Dida, Kaladze, Gattuso, Seedorf (Oddo 73), Gilardino, Nesta, Pirlo, Kaká, Bonera, Serginho (Maldini 46), Brocchi (Gourcuff 51).
Yellow Card(s): Kaladze 36, Serginho 41, Maldini 80
Match 6 - Celtic FC (SCO)
H 1-0 *Inzaghi (70)*
Kalac, Cafu, Gattuso, Inzaghi, Seedorf (Gourcuff 69), Šimić (Kaladze 30), Favalli, Pirlo (Brocchi 74), Kaká, Ambrosini, Bonera.

Round of 16 - Arsenal FC (ENG)
A 0-0
Kalac, Maldini, Kaladze, Pato (Gilardino 77), Gattuso, Seedorf (Emerson 86), Nesta (Jankulovski 50), Pirlo, Kaká, Ambrosini, Oddo.
Yellow Card(s): Pato 33
H 0-2
Kalac, Maldini, Kaladze, Pato, Gattuso, Inzaghi (Gilardino 69), Nesta, Kaká, Ambrosini, Oddo.
Yellow Card(s): Inzaghi 55, Kaká 80, Pirlo 85

No	Player	Nat	DoB	Aps	(s)
Goalkeepers					
1	Dida	BRA	7/10/73	4	
16	Željko Kalac	AUS	16/12/72	4	(1)
Defenders					
2	Cafu	BRA	7/6/70	1	
3	Paolo Maldini		26/6/68	2	(2)
4	Kakha Kaladze	GEO	27/2/78	6	(1)
13	Alessandro Nesta		19/3/76	7	
17	Dario Šimić	CRO	12/11/75	1	
18	Marek Jankulovski	CZE	9/5/77	2	(1)
19	Giuseppe Favalli		8/1/72	2	
25	Daniele Bonera		31/5/81	4	(2)
27	Serginho	BRA	27/6/71	2	(1)
44	Massimo Oddo		14/6/76	5	(1)
Midfielders					
5	Emerson	BRA	4/4/76		(3)
8	Gennaro Gattuso		9/1/78	8	
10	Clarence Seedorf	NED	1/4/76	7	
20	Yoann Gourcuff	FRA	11/7/86		(3)
21	Andrea Pirlo		19/5/79	8	
23	Massimo Ambrosini		29/5/77	7	
32	Cristian Brocchi		30/1/76	1	(2)
Attackers					
7	Pato	BRA	2/9/89	2	
9	Filippo Inzaghi		9/8/73	4	(1)
11	Alberto Gilardino		5/7/82	3	(4)
22	Kaká	BRA	22/4/82	8	

FC INTERNAZIONALE MILANO

UEFA CHAMPIONS LEAGUE

Group G
Match 1 - Fenerbahçe SK (TUR)
A 0-1
Júlio César, Zanetti, Stanković, Maxwell, Ibrahimović, Dacourt (Jimé 70), Cambiasso, Solari (Figo 57), Rivas, Samuel, Suazo (Crespo 72).
Yellow Card(s): Ibrahimović 15, Samuel 52, Jiménez 90+2
Match 2 - PSV Eindhoven (NED)
H 2-0 *Ibrahimović (15p, 31)*
Júlio César, Zanetti, Stanković, Maxwell, Figo, Ibrahimović, Crespo (S 61), Cambiasso, Solari (Bolzoni 70), Samuel, Chivu.
Red Card(s): Chivu 65, Suazo 90+3
Yellow Card(s): Chivu 29, Chivu 65, Samuel 80
Match 3 - PFC CSKA Moskva (RUS)
A 2-1 *Crespo (52), Samuel (80)*
Júlio César, Córdoba, Zanetti, Maxwell, Figo, Ibrahimović, Vieira (Sta 17), Dacourt (Solari 77), Crespo (Cruz 62), Cambiasso, Samuel.
Yellow Card(s): Figo 43, Ibrahimović 46, Solari 83
Match 4 - PFC CSKA Moskva (RUS)
H 4-2 *Ibrahimović (32, 75), Cambiasso (34,67)*
Júlio César, Córdoba, Zanetti, Maxwell (Solari 66), Ibrahimović (Suaz Maicon, Dacourt, Crespo (Cruz 63), Cambiasso, Samuel, Chivu.
Yellow Card(s): Dacourt 84
Match 5 - Fenerbahçe SK (TUR)
H 3-0 Cruz (55), Ibrahimović (66), Jiménez (90+2)
Júlio César, Córdoba, Zanetti, Stanković (Materazzi 89), Maxwell (Jir 72), Ibrahimović (Suazo 78), Cruz, Maicon, Cambiasso, Samuel, Chiv
Yellow Card(s): Ibrahimović 76, Samuel 87

h 6 - PSV Eindhoven (NED)
Cruz (64)
César, Córdoba, Maxwell (Zanetti 86), Cruz (Puccio 75), Crespo, Solari,
razzi, Rivas Lopez, Chivu (Cambiasso 68), Suazo, Bolzoni.

d of 16 - Liverpool FC (ENG)

César, Córdoba (Burdisso 76), Zanetti, Stanković, Maxwell,
imović, Cruz (Vieira 55), Maicon, Cambiasso, Materazzi, Chivu.
Card(s): Materazzi 30
w Card(s): Chivu 4, Materazzi 12, Materazzi 30

César, Zanetti, Stanković (Jiménez 84), Ibrahimović (Suazo 80), Cruz,
on, Vieira (Pelé 77), Burdisso, Cambiasso, Rivas, Chivu.
Card(s): Burdisso 50
w Card(s): Burdisso 34, Burdisso 50, Rivas 59, Stanković 73, Chivu 85

Player	Nat	DoB	Aps	(s)	Gls
eepers					
Júlio César	BRA	3/9/79	8		
nders					
Iván Córdoba	COL	11/8/76	5		
Javier Zanetti	ARG	10/8/73	7	(1)	
Maxwell	BRA	27/8/81	7		
Maicon	BRA	26/7/81	4		
Nicolás Burdisso	ARG	12/4/81	1	(1)	
Marco Materazzi		19/8/73	2	(1)	
Nélson Rivas	COL	25/3/83	3		
Walter Samuel	ARG	23/3/78	5		1
Cristian Chivu	ROU	26/10/80	6		
elders					
Dejan Stanković	SRB	11/9/78	5	(1)	
Luís Figo	POR	4/11/72	2	(1)	
Luis Antonio Jiménez	CHI	17/6/84		(3)	1
Patrick Vieira	FRA	23/6/76	2	(1)	
Olivier Dacourt	FRA	25/9/74	3		
Esteban Cambiasso	ARG	18/8/80	7	(1)	2
Santiago Solari	ARG	7/10/76	3	(2)	
Pelé	POR	14/9/87		(1)	
Francesco Bolzoni		7/5/89	1	(1)	
Gabriele Puccio		3/8/89		(1)	
kers					
Zlatan Ibrahimović	SWE	3/10/81	7		5
Julio Cruz	ARG	10/10/74	4	(2)	2
Hernán Crespo	ARG	5/7/75	4	(1)	1
David Suazo	HON	5/11/79	2	(4)	

AS ROMA

UEFA CHAMPIONS LEAGUE

up F
ch 1 - FC Dynamo Kyiv (UKR)
0 *Perrotta (9), Totti (70)*
, Juan (Ferrari 82), Mexès, Aquilani (Pizarro 83), Totti, Taddei, De Rossi,
otta, Tonetto, Mancini (Giuly 61), Cassetti.
ow Card(s): Tonetto 65
ch 2 - Manchester United FC (ENG)
1
, Cicinho, Juan, Mexès, Aquilani (Pizarro 62), Totti, Giuly (Esposito 80),
ossi, Perrotta, Tonetto, Mancini (Vučinić 74).
ow Card(s): Mexès 39

Match 3 - Sporting Clube de Portugal (POR)
H 2-1 *Juan (15), Vučinić (70)*
Doni, Panucci, Juan, Mexès, Pizarro, Totti (Vučinić 35), Giuly (Brighi 73), De Rossi, Tonetto, Mancini (Cicinho 87), Cassetti.
Yellow Card(s): Cassetti 44, Vučinić 70, Juan 90
Match 4 - Sporting Clube de Portugal (POR)
A 2-2 *Cassetti (4), Anderson Polga (90og)*
Doni, Cicinho, Juan, Mexès (Ferrari 46), Pizarro, Vučinić, Giuly (Brighi 90+1), De Rossi, Perrotta (Esposito 80), Mancini, Cassetti.
Yellow Card(s): Cicinho 29, Vučinić 44, Cassetti 52, Perrotta 67
Match 5 - FC Dynamo Kyiv (UKR)
A 4-1 *Panucci (4), Giuly (32), Vučinić (36, 78)*
Doni, Panucci, Juan, Pizarro, Vučinić (Cicinho 84), Taddei (Esposito 46), Giuly, De Rossi (Barusso 61), Ferrari, Tonetto, Cassetti.
Yellow Card(s): Cassetti 89
Match 6 - Manchester United FC (ENG)
H 1-1 *Mancini (71)*
Doni, Cicinho, Mexès, Pizarro, Totti, Taddei (De Rossi 46), Antunes, Esposito (Vučinić 62), Ferrari, Barusso (Giuly 62), Mancini.
Yellow Card(s): Barusso 49

Round of 16 - Real Madrid CF (ESP)
H 2-1 *Pizarro (24), Mancini (58)*
Doni, Panucci (Tonetto 67), Juan (Ferrari 77), Mexès, Pizarro (Aquilani 62), Totti, Giuly, De Rossi, Perrotta, Mancini, Cassetti.
Yellow Card(s): De Rossi 42, Perrotta 68, Cassetti 90+1
A 2-1 *Taddei (73), Vučinić (90+2)*
Doni, Cicinho (Panucci 87), Juan, Mexès, Aquilani, Totti, Taddei, De Rossi, Perrotta (Pizarro 76), Tonetto, Mancini (Vučinić 65).
Yellow Card(s): Taddei 20, De Rossi 35, Perrotta 55, Cicinho 67, Aquilani 83, Tonetto 84

Quarter-Final - Manchester United FC (ENG)
H 0-2
Doni, Panucci, Mexès, Pizarro, Aquilani (Esposito 77), Vučinić, Taddei (Giuly 59), De Rossi, Tonetto (Cicinho 68), Mancini, Cassetti.
Yellow Card(s): Pizarro 45+3, Mexès 53
A 0-1
Doni, Panucci, Juan, Mexès, Pizarro (Giuly 69), Vučinić, Taddei (Esposito 81), De Rossi, Perrotta, Mancini, Cassetti (Tonetto 57).
Yellow Card(s): Perrotta 73

No	Player	Nat	DoB	Aps	(s)	Gls
Goalkeepers						
1	Gianluca Curci		12/7/85	1		
32	Doni	BRA	22/10/79	9		
Defenders						
2	Christian Panucci		12/4/73	5	(1)	1
3	Cicinho	BRA	24/6/80	4	(3)	
4	Juan	BRA	1/2/79	8		1
5	Philippe Mexès	FRA	30/3/82	9		
21	Matteo Ferrari		5/12/79	2	(3)	
22	Max Tonetto		18/11/74	6	(2)	
77	Marco Cassetti		28/5/77	7		1
Midfielders						
7	David Pizarro	CHI	11/9/79	7	(3)	1
8	Alberto Aquilani		7/7/84	4	(1)	
11	Rodrigo Taddei	BRA	6/3/80	6		1
15	Vitorino Antunes	POR	1/4/87	1		
16	Daniele De Rossi		24/7/83	9	(1)	
20	Simone Perrotta		17/9/77	6		1
29	Ahmed Barusso	GHA	26/12/84	1	(1)	
33	Matteo Brighi		14/2/81		(2)	
Attackers						
9	Mirko Vučinić	MNE	1/10/83	4	(4)	4
10	Francesco Totti		27/9/76	6		1
14	Ludovic Giuly	FRA	10/7/76	5	(4)	1
18	Mauro Esposito		13/6/79	1	(5)	
30	Mancini	BRA	1/8/80	9		2

S.S. LAZIO

UEFA CHAMPIONS LEAGUE

Third Qualifying Round - FC Dinamo 1948 Bucureşti (ROU)
H 1-1 *Mutarelli (54)*
Ballotta, Behrami, Ledesma, Mauri (Del Nero 64), Mutarelli, Pandev, Rocchi, Cribari (Kolarov 23), Scaloni, Stendardo (De Silvestri 46), Zauri.
Red Card(s): Behrami 75, Mutarelli 87
Yellow Card(s): Pandev 38, Mutarelli 75, Kolarov 82, Mutarelli 87
A 3-1 *Rocchi (47p, 66), Pandev (53)*
Ballotta, De Silvestri, Del Nero (Belleri 85), Ledesma, Manfredini, Mudingayi, Pandev (Tare 89), Rocchi, Cribari, Stendardo (Scaloni 34), Zauri.
Yellow Card(s): Mudingayi 20

Group C
Match 1 - Olympiacos CFP (GRE)
A 1-1 *Zauri (77)*
Ballotta, Stendardo, Zauri, Mauri (Mutarelli 61), Rocchi, Pandev, Ledesma, Cribari, Mudingayi, De Silvestri (Scaloni 81), Manfredini (Del Nero 70).
Yellow Card(s): Stendardo 32, Mutarelli 73, Zauri 90
Match 2 - Real Madrid CF (ESP)
H 2-2 *Pandev (32, 75)*
Ballotta, Stendardo, Mutarelli, Zauri, Mauri (Del Nero 79), Rocchi (Makinwa 66), Pandev, Ledesma, Cribari, Mudingayi, Behrami (Scaloni 67).
Match 3 - Werder Bremen (GER)
A 1-2 *Manfredini (82)*
Ballotta, Stendardo, Kolarov, Mutarelli, Zauri, Rocchi (Tare 82), Pandev (Makinwa 69), Meghni (Del Nero 51), Mudingayi, Manfredini, Behrami.
Yellow Card(s): Pandev 21, Mutarelli 51, Zauri 55, Mudingayi 90+1
Match 4 - Werder Bremen (GER)
H 2-1 *Rocchi (57, 68)*
Ballotta, Stendardo, Mutarelli, Zauri (De Silvestri 18), Rocchi, Makinwa (Scaloni 87), Meghni (Manfredini 74), Ledesma, Cribari, Mudingayi, Behrami.
Red Card(s): Cribari 86
Yellow Card(s): Stendardo 45, De Silvestri 52, Cribari 54, Rocchi 69, Cribari 86
Match 5 - Olympiacos CFP (GRE)
H 1-2 *Pandev (30)*
Ballotta, Stendardo, Kolarov (De Silvestri 63), Mutarelli (Meghni 71), Mauri, Siviglia, Rocchi, Pandev, Ledesma, Mudingayi, Behrami (Scaloni 77).
Match 6 - Real Madrid CF (ESP)
A 1-3 *Pandev (80)*
Ballotta, Mutarelli, Scaloni, Siviglia, Rocchi, Pandev (Makinwa 82), Meghni (Manfredini 63), Ledesma (Baronio 46), Cribari, Mudingayi, De Silvestri.

No	Player	Nat	DoB	Aps	(s)	Gls
Goalkeepers						
32	Marco Ballotta		3/4/64	6		
Defenders						
2	Guglielmo Stendardo		6/5/81	5		
3	Aleksandar Kolarov	SRB	10/11/85	2		
6	Lionel Scaloni	ARG	16/5/78	1	(4)	
8	Luciano Zauri		20/1/78	4		1
13	Sebastiano Siviglia		29/3/73	2		
25	Cribari	BRA	6/3/80	4		
29	Lorenzo De Silvestri		23/5/88	2	(2)	
Midfielders						
5	Massimo Mutarelli		13/1/78	5	(1)	
10	Roberto Baronio		11/12/77		(1)	
11	Stefano Mauri		8/1/80	3		
23	Mourad Meghni	FRA	16/4/84	3	(1)	
24	Cristián Ledesma	ARG	24/9/82	5		
26	Gaby Mudingayi	BEL	1/10/81	6		
68	Christian Manfredini		1/5/75	2	(2)	
85	Valon Behrami	SUI	19/4/85	4		
Attackers						
17	Igli Tare	ALB	25/7/73		(1)	
18	Tommaso Rocchi		19/9/77	6		
19	Goran Pandev	MKD	27/7/83	5		
20	Stephen Makinwa	NGA	26/7/83	1	(3)	
81	Simone Del Nero		4/8/81		(3)	

US CITTÀ DI PALERMO

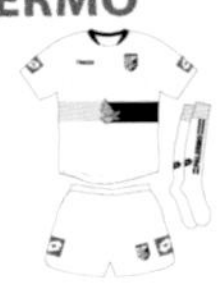

UEFA CUP

First Round - FK Mladá Boleslav (CZE)
A 1-0 *Janković (90+1)*
Agliardi, Barzagli, Bresciano (Amauri 69), Brienza (Caserta 58), Cavani Diana, Janković, Migliaccio, Rinaudo, Tedesco (Simplício 86), Zaccard
Yellow Card(s): Zaccardo 51, Amauri 72, Tedesco 76, Diana 83
H 0-1 *(aet; 2-4 on pens)*
Agliardi, Barzagli, Bresciano (Caserta 89), Capuano, Amauri (Janković Cassani, Cavani, Migliaccio, Rinaudo, Simplício, Tedesco (Diana 70).
Red Card(s): Guana 22
Yellow Card(s): Rinaudo 31, Capuano 83, Migliaccio 87, Janković 89, Diana 120

ACF FIORENTINA

UEFA CUP

First Round - FC Groningen (NED)
A 1-1 *Semioli (65)*
Frey, Gamberini, Krøldrup, Liverani, Mutu, Pasqual, Pazienza (Kuzmar 45), Semioli, Ujfaluši, Vieri (Pazzini 57), Montolivo.
Yellow Card(s): Mutu 78, Frey 86
H 1-1 *Mutu (59) (aet; 4-3 on pens)*
Frey, Donadel (Kuzmanović 97), Gamberini, Krøldrup, Liverani (Santa 58), Mutu, Pasqual, Semioli, Ujfaluši, Vieri (Pazzini 80), Montolivo.
Yellow Card(s): Donadel 64

Group C
Match 1 - Villarreal CF (ESP)
A 1-1 *Vieri (48)*
Frey, Ujfaluši, Dainelli, Krøldrup, Balzaretti, Pazienza, Liverani, Kuzmar (Donadel 74), Jørgensen (Vanden Borre 58), Mutu, Vieri (Osvaldo 65).
Yellow Card(s): Pazienza 19, Vanden Borre 85, Ujfaluši 89
Match 2 - IF Elfsborg (SWE)
H 6-1 *Jørgensen (4, 78), Vieri (5), Donadel (62), Krøldrup (65), Di Carmin*
Frey, Vanden Borre (Pasqual 69), Ujfaluši, Krøldrup, Balzaretti, Semioli, Dor Pazienza, Jørgensen, Osvaldo (Kuzmanović 63), Vieri (Di Carmine 82).
Yellow Card(s): Donadel 55
Match 3 - AEK Athens FC (GRE)
A 1-1 *Osvaldo (29)*
Frey, Krøldrup, Balzaretti, Dainelli, Pasqual, Liverani, Montolivo, Kuzmanović (Gobbi 81), Jørgensen, Osvaldo, Vieri (Pazzini 86).
Yellow Card(s): Krøldrup 66, Liverani 71
Match 4 - FK Mladá Boleslav (CZE)
H 2-1 *Mutu (44p), Vieri (67)*
Lupatelli, Ujfaluši, Dainelli, Krøldrup, Pasqual, Donadel (Pazienza 48),

i, Gobbi, Semioli, Pazzini (Vieri 62), Mutu (Osvaldo 76).
Card(s): Donadel 40

of 32 - Rosenborg BK (NOR)
Autu (16)
falusi, Krøldrup, Gamberini, Gobbi (Pasqual 47), Semioli,
ivo, Jørgensen, Kuzmanović (Santana 85), Mutu, Pazzini (Cacia 72).
Card(s): Montolivo 45
iverani (38), Cacia (81)
faluši, Krøldrup, Dainelli, Pasqual, Donadel, Liverani (Kuzmanović
ntolivo (Jørgensen 64), Semioli, Pazzini (Cacia 72), Mutu.

of 16 - Everton FC (ENG)
uzmanović (70), Montolivo (81)
faluši, Gamberini, Dainelli, Pasqual, Kuzmanović (Gobbi 76),
el, Montolivo, Jørgensen, Vieri (Pazzini 67), Osvaldo (Santana 74).
Card(s): Ujfaluši 40, Gobbi 90+3
aet; 4-2 on pens)
faluši, Dainelli, Gamberini, Pasqual, Kuzmanović (Gobbi 91),
el, Montolivo, Jørgensen (Santana 106), Osvaldo, Vieri (Pazzini 46).
Card(s): Dainelli 29, Montolivo 32, Pazzini 62, Gamberini 90, Jørgensen 100

r-Final - PSV Eindhoven (NED)
Autu (56)
amberini, Mutu, Liverani (Vieri 76), Montolivo, Gobbi, Jørgensen,
, Kuzmanović (Donadel 67), Santana (Osvaldo 90), Pazzini.
Card(s): Donadel 90
Autu (38, 53)
onadel, Gamberini, Mutu (Osvaldo 86), Liverani, Montolivo, Gobbi,
sen, Ujfaluši, Santana (Kuzmanović 78), Pazzini (Vieri 73).
Card(s): Mutu 19, Donadel 25

inal - Rangers FC (SCO)

amberini, Mutu, Liverani, Montolivo, Gobbi, Jørgensen, Ujfaluši,
nović, Santana, Pazzini (Vieri 81).
Card(s): Santana 22, Gamberini 78, Gobbi 83
aet; 2-4 on pens)
onadel (Kuzmanović 42), Gamberini, Mutu, Liverani, Montolivo,
Jørgensen, Ujfaluši, Santana (Semioli 94), Pazzini (Vieri 79).

EMPOLI FC

UEFA CUP

ound - FC Zürich (SUI)
Piccolo (44), Antonini (49p)
bate, Antonini (Vanigli 86), Marchisio, Marzoratti, Piccolo, Pozzi,
, Carlos Eduardo (Éder 84), Iacoponi (Raggi 84), Prevete.
Card(s): Piccolo 25, Prevete 69, Antonini 76, Iacoponi 84, Vanigli 90

bate, Ascoli (Antonini 61), Marchisio (Giovinco 46), Marianini,
atti, Piccolo, Vannucchi (Pozzi 46), Volpato, Giacomazzi, Carlos Eduardo.
rd(s): Carlos Eduardo 85
Card(s): Marchisio 36, Piccolo 89

UC SAMPDORIA

UEFA INTERTOTO CUP

Third Round - PFC Cherno More Varna (BUL)
A 1-0 *Lucchini (43)*
Castellazzi, Palombo, Sala, Volpi, Accardi, Pieri, Koman (Ziegler 60), Caracciolo (Foti 90), Bellucci, Maggio, Lucchini (Campagnaro 49).
Yellow Card(s): Koman 10, Accardi 41, Bellucci 45+1, Palombo 57, Ziegler 87
H 1-0 *Maggio (90+1)*
Castellazzi, Palombo, Sala, Volpi (Sammarco 86), Zenoni, Pieri, Koman (Maggio 61), Caracciolo (Montella 67), Campagnaro, Bellucci, Accardi.
Yellow Card(s): Palombo 49, Volpi 67

UEFA CUP

Second Qualifying Round - HNK Hajduk Split (CRO)
A 1-0 *Campagnaro (44)*
Castellazzi, Accardi (Campagnaro 42), Bellucci, Caracciolo (Montella 62), Del Vecchio, Lucchini, Pieri (Ziegler 76), Sala, Sammarco, Volpi, Zenoni.
Yellow Card(s): Sala 61, Lucchini 74, Montella 79, Ziegler 82
H 1-1 *Montella (34p)*
Mirante, Palombo, Bellucci (Del Vecchio 80), Campagnaro, Maggio, Lucchini, Pieri (Zenoni 89), Sala, Sammarco, Volpi, Montella (Caracciolo 72).
Yellow Card(s): Lucchini 36, Sala 40

First Round - Aalborg BK (DEN)
H 2-2 *Del Vecchio (18), Bellucci (59)*
Castellazzi, Bastrini (Pieri 82), Bellucci, Caracciolo, Del Vecchio (Montella 55), Franceschini, Palombo, Sammarco, Zenoni (Volpi 64), Ziegler, Gastaldello.
Yellow Card(s): Bellucci 81
A 0-0
Castellazzi, Ziegler (Pieri 84), Volpi, Lucchini, Bellucci, Sala (Del Vecchio 81), Campagnaro, Palombo, Sammarco, Caracciolo, Cassano (Montella 61).
Yellow Card(s): Cassano 19, Ziegler 74, Montella 90

KAZAKHSTAN

FC ASTANA

СКАЧАТЬ

UEFA CHAMPIONS LEAGUE

First Qualifying Round - FC Olimpi Rustavi (GEO)
A 0-0
Boychenko, Chichulin, Kuchma, Kumisbekov, Zhalmagambetov, Sergienko, Kochkaev (Tlekhugov 46), Suchkov, Kenzhesariev (Kukeev 73), Bulatov, Todorov (Aliyev 91).
Yellow Card(s): Todorov 36, Zhalmagambetov 68, Chichulin 74, Kuchma 78
H 3-0 *Kuchma (12), Tlekhugov (55), Zhalmagambetov (84)*
Boychenko, Chichulin (Aksyonov 84), Kuchma, Kumisbekov, Zhalmagambetov, Sergienko (Kukeev 90), Suyumagambetov (Tlekhugov 46), Suchkov, Kenzhesariev, Bulatov, Todorov.
Yellow Card(s): Todorov 70, Boychenko 79

Second Qualifying Round - Rosenborg BK (NOR)
H 1-3 *Kuchma (26)*
Boychenko, Aliyev (Tlekhugov 70), Bulatov, Chichulin, Kenzhesariev, Kochkaev (Suyumagambetov 50), Kuchma, Kumisbekov, Sergienko (Kukeev 61), Suchkov, Shishkin.
Yellow Card(s): Kochkaev 46, Boychenko 56
A 1-7 *Suchkov (22)*
Kuznetsov, Chichulin, Kenzhesariev, Kochkaev, Kuchma, Kumisbekov, Sergienko, Suchkov (Suyumagambetov 46), Bulatov, Todorov, Zhalmagambetov.
Yellow Card(s): Bulatov 61, Kenzhesariev 65

FC ALMA-ATA

UEFA CUP

First Qualifying Round - FC ViOn Zlaté Moravce (SVK)
A 1-3 *Larin (82)*
Bogdan, Kovalev, Kirov, Utabaev, Vorotnikov, Berco, Borovskoy (Rodionov 70), Byakov, Irismetov (Kenzhekhanov 79), Larin, Shakhmetov.
Yellow Card(s): Borovskoy 68, Utabaev 70, Rodionov 80
H 1-1 *Irismetov (58)*
Bogdan, Kovalev, Kirov, Utabaev (Rodionov 70), Vorotnikov, Berco, Borovskoy (Irismetov 46), Byakov, Kenzhekhanov, Larin, Shakhmetov (Klimov 75).
Red Card(s): Kovalev 82
Yellow Card(s): Shakhmetov 62

FK AKTOBE

UEFA CUP

First Qualifying Round - SV Mattersburg (AUT)
H 1-0 *Khayrullin (85)*
Dekhanov, Asanbaev, Badlo, Fokin (Logvinenko 75), Golovskoy, Khayrullin, Kosolapov, Mitrofanov, Shkurin, Smakov, Pushkarev (Bogomolov 46).
Yellow Card(s): Mitrofanov 23, Kosolapov 87, Golovskoy 88, Badlo 89
A 2-4 *Bogomolov (71), Kosolapov (77)*
Dekhanov, Asanbaev, Badlo, Fokin (Bogomolov 46), Golovskoy, Khayrullin, Kosolapov, Mitrofanov (Kiselev 87), Shkurin, Smakov, Logvinenko.
Yellow Card(s): Khayrullin 29, Logvinenko 45+1, Asanbaev 74, Kosolapov 83, Golovskoy 90+2

FC TOBOL KOSTANAY

UEFA INTERTOTO CUP

First Round - FC Zestafoni (GEO)
H 3-0 *Zhumaskaliev (61), Baltiyev (63), Bakaev (73)*
Pryadkin, Bakaev, Baltiyev, Dimitrov, Irismetov, Kharabara (Meshkov 82), Mukanov (Ostapenko 88), Nurdauletov, Skorykh, Yurin (Nurgaliev 53), Zhumaskaliev.
Yellow Card(s): Kharabara 65
A 0-2
Pryadkin (Petukhov 72), Baltiyev, Dimitrov, Irismetov, Kharabara, Mukanov, Nurdauletov, Nurgaliev (Yurin 46), Ostapenko (Lotov 90), Skorykh, Zhumaskaliev.
Yellow Card(s): Baltiyev 17, Ostapenko 55

Second Round - FC Slovan Liberec (CZE)
H 1-1 *Baltiyev (40)*
Petukhov, Baltiyev, Dimitrov (Lotov 88), Irismetov, Kharabara, Mukanov, Nurdauletov, Ostapenko (Urazov 70), Skorykh, Yurin (Nurgaliev 68), Zhumaskaliev.
Yellow Card(s): Baltiyev 28, Mukanov 46
A 2-0 *Zhumaskaliev (16), Ostapenko (35)*
Petukhov, Dimitrov, Irismetov, Lotov, Mukanov, Nurdauletov, Nurga (Sabalakov 79), Ostapenko (Garkusha 89), Skorykh, Yurin (Meshkov Zhumaskaliev.
Yellow Card(s): Irismetov 55, Yurin 57, Nurgaliev 67, Ostapenko 70

Third Round - OFI Crete FC (GRE)
H 1-0 *Baltiyev (29)*
Petukhov, Baltiyev, Dimitrov, Irismetov, Mukanov, Nurdauletov, Nur Skorykh, Urazov (Nurmagambetov 53), Yurin (Meshkov 65), Zhuma (Sabalakov 82).
A 1-0 *Kharabara (86)*
Petukhov, Baltiyev, Dimitrov, Irismetov, Mukanov, Nurdauletov, Nu (Meshkov 69), Ostapenko (Bakaev 42), Skorykh, Yurin (Kharabara 6 Nurmagambetov.
Yellow Card(s): Ostapenko 27, Nurdauletov 60, Kharabara 74, Nurmagambetov 75, Bakaev 83

UEFA CUP

Second Qualifying Round - Groclin Grodzisk Wielkopolski (PO
H 0-1
Pryadkin, Bakaev (Urazov 83), Baltiyev, Dimitrov, Irismetov, Mukan Nurdauletov, Nurgaliev (Ostapenko 70), Skorykh, Yurin (Meshkov 4 Zhumaskaliev.
Yellow Card(s): Baltiyev 53
A 0-2
Petukhov, Bakaev (Ostapenko 65), Baltiyev, Dimitrov, Irismetov, Me Mukanov, Nurdauletov, Nurgaliev (Yurin 72), Skorykh (Kharabara 4 Zhumaskaliev.
Yellow Card(s): Nurgaliev 23

LATVIA

FK VENTSPILS

UEFA CHAMPIONS LEAGUE

First Qualifying Round - The New Saints FC (WAL)
A 2-3 *Rimkus (26, 89)*
Davidovs, Dubenskiy, Kačanovs, Koļesničenko (Kosmačovs 65), Menteshashvili, Ndeki, Rimkus, Sernetskiy, Soleičuks, Tigirlas (Zang 69), Ziziļevs.
Yellow Card(s): Menteshashvili 69, Davidovs 78
H 2-1 *Ndeki (17), Kačanovs (53)*
Davidovs, Dubenskiy, Kačanovs, Koļesničenko (Kosmačovs 70), Menteshashvili (Mysikov 90), Ndeki, Rimkus, Sernetskiy (Sļesarčuks Tigirlas, Ziziļevs, Cilinšek.
Yellow Card(s): Tigirlas 3, Menteshashvili 51, Sernetskiy 57, Koļesr 69, Ndeki 83

Second Qualifying Round - FC Salzburg (AUT)
H 0-3
Davidovs, Dubenskiy, Kačanovs, Koļesničenko (Mysikov 76), Kosma Ndeki, Rimkus, Sļesarčuks (Sernetskiy 53; Grebis 85), Tigirlas, Cilinš Ziziļevs.
A 0-4
Vanins, Dubenskiy, Kačanovs, Koļesničenko (Kosmačovs 58), Menteshashvili, Ndeki, Rimkus (Butriks 75), Sļesarčuks (Grebis 46), Cilinšek, Ziziļevs.
Yellow Card(s): Dubenskiy 54, Menteshashvili 68

SK LIEPĀJAS METALURGS

UEFA CUP

Qualifying Round - FC Dinamo Brest (BLR)
Ferreira (5)
Ivanovs, Kalonas, Karlsons, Žuravļovs, Soloņicins, Surņins,
šauskas, Zirnis, Kruglyak (Kamešs 59; Kets 81), Ferreira.
v Card(s): Žuravļovs 47
Kruglyak (40), Karlsons (50)
Ivanovs, Kalonas (Kamešs 90+4), Karlsons, Kļava, Soloņicins,
ıs, Tamošauskas, Zirnis, Kruglyak (Žuravļovs 90+1), Ferreira.
v Card(s): Kļava 21, Karlsons 59

d Qualifying Round - AIK Solna (SWE)
Karlsons (20), Ivanovs (43), Tamošauskas (63)
Ferreira, Ivanovs, Karlsons, Kļava (Kruglyak 59), Soloņicins, Surņins,
šauskas, Zirnis, Bleidelis, Rubins.
v Card(s): Surnins 85

Kļava (Torres 80), Zirnis, Ferreira, Ivanovs, Rubins, Bleidelis,
šauskas, Surņins, Soloņicins (Kruglyak 64), Karlsons.
v Card(s): Kļava 31, Karlsons 69, Zirnis 75

SKONTO FC

UEFA CUP

Qualifying Round - FC Dinamo Minsk (BLR)
Perepļotkins (27)
s, Gamezardashvili, Dirnbach, Astafjevs (Semjonovs 68), Blanks (Kalniņš
auņa (Višņakovs 72), Kožans, Morozs, Perepļotkins, Piaček, Sluka.

s, Gamezardashvili (Gaiļus 46), Dirnbach, Astafjevs (Cauņa 78),
s, Višņakovs, Kožans, Morozs, Perepļotkins, Piaček, Sluka.

FC DINABURG

UEFA INTERTOTO CUP

Round - Cliftonville FC (NIR)
Sokolovs (20)
rovs, Čugunovs, Koļcovs, Kostenko, Krjauklis, Logins, Rodin
evsky 67), Sokolovs, Yashkin, Žuromskis (Vaļuškins 37), Kaziyev
v 81).
ard(s): Kostenko 60
v Card(s): Koļcovs 31, Fjodorovs 79, Popov 86

ıs, Čugunovs, Koļcovs, Krjauklis, Logins, Popov (Ryzhevsky 32), Rodin
alidze 46), Sokolovs, Vaļuškins (Kuleshov 60), Yashkin, Kaziyev.
ard(s): Yashkin 90+4

Yellow Card(s): Rodin 41, Logins 45+1, Koļcovs 57, Yashkin 73, Sokolovs 73, Kuleshov 75, Yashkin 90+4

LIECHTENSTEIN

FC VADUZ

UEFA CUP

First Qualifying Round - FC Dinamo Tbilisi (GEO)
A 0-2
Sommer, Alastra, Langlet (Rohrer 77), Maggetti, Reinmann (Akdemir 71), Ritzberger, Sturm, Polverino, Džombić, Cerrone, Grossklaus (Wieczorek 67).
Yellow Card(s): Cerrone 32
H 0-0
Sommer, Akdemir (Polverino 57), Gaspar (Rohrer 70), Maggetti, Reinmann, Ritzberger, Sturm, Sutter, Wieczorek, Cerrone, Grossklaus.

LITHUANIA

FBK KAUNAS

UEFA CHAMPIONS LEAGUE

First Qualifying Round - FK Zeta (MNE)
A 1-3 *Kvaratskhelia (68)*
Stonys, Bagužis (Grigalevičius 59), Beniušis (Činikas 76), Ksanavičius (Zubavičius 67), Kvaratskhelia, Rafael, Manchkhava, Mendy, Mrowiec, Radžius, Valkanov.
Red Card(s): Valkanov 26
Yellow Card(s): Bagužis 33, Mendy 65
H 3-2 *Beniušis (6), Kvaratskhelia (16), Ksanavičius (20)*
Kello, Bagužis, Beniušis, Ksanavičius (Klimek 46), Kvaratskhelia, Rafael, Manchkhava, Mendy, Mrowiec, Pehlić, Radžius (Screpis 69).
Yellow Card(s): Kvaratskhelia 15, Mendy 37, Manchkhava 72, Bagužis 76, Screpis 90

FK SŪDUVA

UEFA CUP

First Qualifying Round - Dungannon Swifts FC (NIR)
A 0-1
S. Klevinskas, Sobol, Skinderis, Braga (Juška 69), Maikel (Urbšys 46), G. Klevinskas, Maciulevičius, Miklinevičius, Mikuckis, Potapov, Willer.
Yellow Card(s): Skinderis 31, Willer 44, Sobol 66, Maciulevičius 89

H 4-0 *Grigas (29), Urbšys (50, 55, 84)*
S. Klevinskas, Sobol, Juška (Jasaitis 46), Braga, Urbšys (Potapov 84), G. Klevinskas, Maciulevičius (G. Slavickas 70), Miklinevičius, Mikuckis, Grigas, Willer.
Red Card(s): Willer 44
Yellow Card(s): Mikuckis 65, S. Klevinskas 75

Second Qualifying Round - SK Brann (NOR)
A 1-2 *Negreiros (56p)*
S. Klevinskas, Braga (V. Slavickas 46), Jasaitis (Potapov 80), G. Klevinskas, Maciulevičius (Negreiros 46), Miklinevičius, Mikuckis, Skinderis, Sobol, Urbšys, Klimavičius.
Yellow Card(s): Jasaitis 75
H 3-4 *Urbšys (46), Maciulevičius (78), Braga (84)*
S. Klevinskas, Jasaitis (Braga 74), Maciulevičius, Miklinevičius, Mikuckis, Negreiros, Skinderis, Sobol (G. Slavickas 46), V. Slavickas, Urbšys (Potapov 81), Klimavičius.
Red Card(s): Potapov 90+2
Yellow Card(s): Skinderis 60, Potapov 90, Potapov 90+2

FK EKRANAS

UEFA CUP

First Qualifying Round - B36 Tórshavn (FRO)
A 3-1 *Lukšys (11), Paulauskas (45), Pogreban (67)*
Stefanović, Gardžijauskas, Kavaliauskas, Lukšys (Varnas 87), Paulauskas, Pogreban, Skroblas, Tomkevičius (Galkevičius 75), Rähn, Šidlauskas, Bička (Saulėnas 85).
Yellow Card(s): Rähn 73
H 3-2 *Šidlauskas (51), Lukšys (77, 87)*
Skrupskis, Gardžijauskas, Kavaliauskas, Lukšys, Paulauskas, Pogreban, Skroblas (Rähn 46), Tomkevičius (Galkevičius 71), Rimavičius, Šidlauskas (Saulėnas 90), Bička.
Yellow Card(s): Skroblas 28, Šidlauskas 70

Second Qualifying Round - Vålerenga Fotball (NOR)
H 1-1 *Bička (45+1p)*
Skrupskis, Bička (Gardžijauskas 67), Kavaliauskas, Lukšys, Paulauskas, Pogreban, Rähn, Rimavičius, Skroblas, Tomkevičius (Saulėnas 82), Varnas.
Yellow Card(s): Kavaliauskas 49, Rimavičius 90+2
A 0-6
Stefanović, Bička, Gardžijauskas, Kavaliauskas, Lukšys, Paulauskas, Pogreban (Savėnas 54), Rähn, Rimavičius (Skroblas 54), Varnas (Saulėnas 70), Tomkevičius.
Yellow Card(s): Rähn 21, Rimavičius 22, Tomkevičius 34

FK VĖTRA

UEFA INTERTOTO CUP

First Round - Llanelli AFC (WAL)
H 3-1 *Šernas (57), Stankevičius (72p), Milošeski (89)*
Kozyrev, Božinovski, Budimir, Juška (Milošeski 58), Panka, Šernas, Skerla, Stankevičius (Tselyuk 84), Severino (Grigaitis 58), Usachov, Pedro Botelho.
Red Card(s): Šernas 90+6
Yellow Card(s): Šernas 76
A 3-5 *Severino (4), Stankevičius (43), Juška (45+3)*
Kozyrev, Božinovski, Budimir, Juška (Azizi 72), Milošeski (Karčemarskas 57), Panka (Butrimavičius 77), Skerla, Stankevičius, Severino, Usachov, Pe Botelho.
Yellow Card(s): Miloševski 41, Azizi 89, Kozyrev 90, Skerla 90+2
Second Round - Legia Warszawa (POL)
H 3-0 *(w/o) Severino (8), Miloševski (45)*
Kozyrev, Azizi, Pedro Botelho, Božinovski, Budimir, Juška, Milošeski, P Severino, Skerla, Usachov.
Yellow Card(s): Panka 34, Milošeski 45.

Third Round - Blackburn Rovers FC (ENG)
H 0-2
Žutautas, Pedro Botelho, Božinovski, Butrimavičius (Karčemarskas 63 Juška, Panka, Sasnauskas, Severino (Veževičius 74), Skerla, Stankevič (Azizi 63), Usachov.
Yellow Card(s): Usachov 50, Juška 90+2
A 0-4
Žutautas, Azizi (Karčemarskas 74), Pedro Botelho, Božinovski, Juška (Veževičius 57), Milošeski, Panka (Raliukonis 81), Sasnauskas, Severin Skerla, Usachov.
Red Card(s): Milošeski 39
Yellow Card(s): Milošeski 33, Milošeski 39, Sasnauskas 54, Veževičius Panka 76

LUXEMBOURG

F91 DUDELANGE

UEFA CHAMPIONS LEAGUE

First Qualifying Round - MŠK Žilina (SVK)
H 1-2 *Di Gregorio (45p)*
Joubert, Bellini, Borbiconi, Di Gregorio (Hug 79), Franceschi, Gruszcz (Coquelet 79), Guthleber, Hammani (Souto 67), Joly, Mouny, Remy.
Yellow Card(s): Hammani 27
A 4-5 *Di Gregorio (40), Hammani (49), Guthleber (71), Lukic (82)*
Joubert, Souto, Bellini (Coquelet 61), Bigard, Di Gregorio (Zeghdane Franceschi, Gruszczynski (Lukic 73), Guthleber, Hammani, Mouny, Re
Yellow Card(s): Souto 61

FC ETZELLA ETTELBRÜCK

UEFA CUP

First Qualifying Round - HJK Helsinki (FIN)
A 0-2
Diederich, Binsfeld (Engeldinger 88), Da Luz, Fernandes, Ferreira, Fév (Daniel Da Mota 9; Bombélé 84), Hoffmann, C. Leweck, Plein, Manno Rocha.
Yellow Card(s): C. Leweck 50
H 0-1
Flick, Daniel Da Mota (Bombélé 69), Binsfeld, Da Luz, Engeldinger, Fernandes, Ferreira, C. Leweck, Plein, Mannon, Lisboa (Reiter 46).
Yellow Card(s): C. Leweck 25, Mannon 54

UN KÄERJÉNG 97

UEFA CUP

Qualifying Round - Lillestrøm SK (NOR)
Andersen (45og)
Costa, Marinelli (Muslić 84), Matos, Pace (Mateos 35), Rolandi,
hfari (Thill 77), Da Costa, Facques, Kivunghe, Leite, Ramdedović.
Boulahfari (49)
Costa, Matos, Rolandi, Bianchini (Scholer 24), Boulahfari (Marinelli
a Costa (Martins 72), Facques, Kivunghe, Leite, Mateos, Ramdedović.
w Card(s): Da Costa 27, Boulahfari 48

nd Qualifying Round - R. Standard de Liège (BEL)

Costa, Boulahfari, Da Costa, Kivunghe, Leite, Mateos (Bianchini 83),
, Mukenge (Scholer 67), Ramdedović, Rolandi (Martins 75), Facques.

Costa (Dunkel 70), Da Costa, Facques, Kivunghe (Scholer 81), Leite,
elli, Matos, Mukenge (Boulahfari 64), Pace, Ramdedović, Rolandi.
w Card(s): Silva Costa 69

FC DIFFERDANGE 03

UEFA INTERTOTO CUP

Round - ŠK Slovan Bratislava (SVK)

ntz, Wagner, Groune (Kintziger 70), Peiffer, Soraire, Bukvic, Diop,
sne (P. Ribeiro 80), Piskor, Rodrigues, Amodio (B. Ribeiro 80).
w Card(s): Piskor 90+3

ntz, Kintziger, Wagner, Peiffer (Kettenmeyer 76), Soraire, Bukvic, Diop
mandrier 87), Lebresne, Piskor, B. Ribeiro (Albanese 72), Rodrigues.
w Card(s): Kintziger 4, Piskor 6

FYR MACEDONIA

FK POBEDA

UEFA CHAMPIONS LEAGUE

Qualifying Round - FC Levadia Tallinn (EST)
1
ski, Dameski, Georgiev (Obradović 58), Gešovski (Aceski 16), Itua,
nović (Nestorovski 70), Kapinkovski, Krsteski, Nacev, Savik, Stojković.
Card(s): Stojković 74
0
ski, Dameski, Georgiev (Nestorovski 84), Itua, Jovanović,
nkovski, Krsteski, Lončar (Šiškov 46), Nacev, Obradović, Aceski.
Red Card(s): Dameski 47
Yellow Card(s): Itua 15, Georgiev 21, Jovanović 84

FK VARDAR

UEFA CUP

First Qualifying Round - Anorthosis Famagusta FC (CYP)
H 0-1
Georgievski, Braga, Ristevski, Sekulovski, Perendija, Peev (José Carlos 59), Stjepanović, Kirovski (Kostovski 80), Bojović, Emurlai (Petrov 89), Mojsov.
Red Card(s): Perendija 88
Yellow Card(s): Emurlai 20, Perendija 24, Ristevski 88, Perendija 88
A 0-1
Georgievski, Braga, Ristevski (Petrov 79), Sekulovski, Tonev, Peev, Stjepanović, Kirovski (Kostovski 46), Bojović, Emurlai (Milosavljev 46), Mojsov.
Red Card(s): Sekulovski 57
Yellow Card(s): Kirovski 18, Sekulovski 34, Sekulovski 57

FK RABOTNIČKI

UEFA CUP

First Qualifying Round - NK Gorica (SVN)
A 2-1 *Šuler (79og), Velkovski (90+1)*
Madžovski, Božinovski, Demiri, Ignjatov (Velkovski 85), Kovačević, Lazarevski, Mihajlović, Osmani (Milisavljević 5), Pejčić, Stanišić, Tričkovski (Selim 80).
Yellow Card(s): Lazarevski 25, Božinovski 28, Milisavljević 75
H 2-1 *Velkovski (44), Demiri (68)*
Madžovski, Božinovski, Demiri (Lukmon 90+4), Ignjatov (Nedžipi 78), Kovačević, Lazarevski, Mihajlović, Milisavljević, Stanišić, Tričkovski (Selim 84), Velkovski.
Yellow Card(s): Ignjatov 17, Božinovski 27, Mihajlović 41, Kovačević 49, Madžovski 65

Second Qualifying Round - HŠK Zrinjski (BIH)
H 0-0
Madžovski, Pejčić (Velkovski 64), Demiri, Ignjatov (Ilijoski 76), Kovačević, Lazarevski (Gjoreski 73), Lukmon, Milisavljević, Stanišić, Tričkovski, Nedžipi.
Yellow Card(s): Ignjatov 68, Nedžipi 90
A 2-1 *Milisavljević (33), Stanišić (90+2)*
Madžovski, Lukmon, Demiri, Kovačević, Lazarevski, Mihajlović (Gligorov 12), Milisavljević (Ilijoski 65), Nedžipi (Stanišić 90), Tričkovski, Vajs, Velkovski.
Yellow Card(s): Kovačević 35, Vajs 40, Lazarevski 57, Ilijoski 67

First Round - Bolton Wanderers FC (ENG)
H 1-1 *Milisavljević (53)*
Madžovski, Demiri, Stanišić, Osmani (Pejčić 65), Tričkovski (Selim 89), Lukmon, Gligorov, Milisavljević (Velkovski 71), Božinovski, Vajs, Nedžipi.
Yellow Card(s): Milisavljević 6, Osmani 60, Vajs 61
A 0-1
Pačovski, Lukmon (Božinovski 75), Demiri, Gligorov, Kovačević, Milisavljević, Nedžipi, Osmani (Velkovski 46), Stanišić, Tričkovski (Pejčić 63), Vajs.
Yellow Card(s): Vajs 28, Stanišić 35, Gligorov 51, Kovačević 60, Božinovski 82

FK MAKEDONIJA GP SKOPJE

UEFA INTERTOTO CUP

First Round - Ethnikos Achnas FC (CYP)
A 0-1
Kolev, Brnjarčevski (Simovski 72), Despotovski, Jovanovski, Milosavljević, Milošević, Mitrev, Mojsov, Ristovski (Ljamčevski 32), Stojanovski (Jahović 83), Krivokapić.
Yellow Card(s): Milosavljević 26, Mitrev 39, Despotovski 66
H 2-0 *Stojanovski (13, 65)*
Kolev, Brnjarčevski, Despotovski, Jovanovski, Ljamčevski (Ismaili 60), Milosavljević, Milošević, Mitrev (Ristovski 60), Mojsov, Krivokapić, Stojanovski (Dimovski 82).
Yellow Card(s): Despotovski 68, Mojsov 80, Kolev 90

Second Round - PFC Cherno More Varna (BUL)
H 0-4
Kolev, Brnjarčevski (Iseni 65), Dimovski, Jovanovski, Ljamčevski (Ristovski 75), Milosavljević, Milošević, Mitrev (Ismaili 57), Mojsov, Krivokapić, Stojanovski.
Yellow Card(s): Ljamčevski 41, Stojanovski 83
A 0-3
Kolev, Brnjarčevski (Ljamčevski 85), Redžep, Jovanovski, Ristovski, Milosavljević, Milošević, Mitrev (Simovski 60), Despotovski, Krivokapić, Stojanovski (Jahović 66).
Yellow Card(s): Despotovski 7, Redžep 10, Brnjarčevski 37, Jahović 69

MALTA

MARSAXLOKK FC

UEFA CHAMPIONS LEAGUE

First Qualifying Round - FK Sarajevo (BIH)
H 0-6
Sauci, Pullicino, Bajada, Sammut, Sciberras, Tellus, Webb, Wellman, Licari, Magro, Pace.
Yellow Card(s): Pullicino 45, Licari 74
A 1-3 *Frendo (65)*
Debono, Bajada, Frendo, Sammut, Sciberras (Mizzi 81), Tellus, Wellman, Licari, Magro, Pace, Templeman.
Yellow Card(s): Wellman 36, Mizzi 86

HIBERNIANS FC

UEFA CUP

First Qualifying Round - FK Vojvodina (SRB)
A 1-5 *Doffo (86p)*
Muscat, Cohen (Fleri Soler 74), Failla, Mintoff, Nwoko, Pulis, Scerri, Xu
Doffo, Alcorsé, Agius.
Yellow Card(s): Failla 20, Nwoko 87, Muscat 88, Xuereb 88, Scerri 90-
H 0-2
Muscat, Cassar (Fleri Soler 87), Cohen, Failla, Mintoff, Pulis, Scerri, Xue
Doffo, Alcorsé (Vella 63), Agius.
Red Card(s): Doffo 50
Yellow Card(s): Pulis 23, Agius 35, Failla 41, Doffo 49, Doffo 50

SLIEMA WANDERERS FC

UEFA CUP

First Qualifying Round - PFC Litex Lovech (BUL)
H 0-3
Bonello, Anonam (Nwoko 79), Azzopardi, Bartolo, Chetcuti, I. Ciantar (
75), Madzar, Mattocks (Scerri 72), Pace, Said, Woods.
Yellow Card(s): I. Ciantar 32, Woods 35, Azzopardi 75
A 0-4
Bonello, Anonam, Azzopardi, Bartolo (Turner 74), Chetcuti, I. Ciantar, Mattocks (Muscat 6), Nwoko (Scerri 67), Pace, Said, Woods.
Yellow Card(s): Anonam 10

BIRKIRKARA FC

UEFA INTERTOTO CUP

First Round - NK Maribor (SVN)
H 0-3
B. Paris, Briffa, A. Galea, M. Galea, Holland, Mallia, T. Paris (Spiteri 82), Sammut (Anastasi 63), Scicluna, Tabone, Zerafa (Mifsud Triganza 71).
Yellow Card(s): Holland 31
A 1-2 *M. Galea (57)*
B. Paris, Anastasi, Briffa, A. Galea (Zerafa 86), M. Galea, Holland, Mallia, Paris, Sammut, Scicluna, Tabone (Mifsud Triganza 90).
Red Card(s): T. Paris 35
Yellow Card(s): Holland 32

MOLDOVA

FC SHERIFF

UEFA CHAMPIONS LEAGUE

First Qualifying Round - FC Rànger's (AND)
H 2-0 *Kuchuk (45+7), Gorodetschi (79)*
Pascenco, Tarkhnishvili (Suvorov 75), Wallace, Arbanaş (Gumenuk 60), Ferreira, Chinwo, Balima (Gorodetschi 69), Kuchuk, Constancia, Bulgar
Corneencov.
Yellow Card(s): Gumenuk 83

Balima (68), Kajkut (77), Suvorov (89)
...co, Wallace (Derme 80), Arbanaş, Ferreira, Chinwo, Balima,
...ba, Kuchuk (Kajkut 67), Constancia (Suvorov 72), Bulgaru,
...ncov.
...Card(s): Wallace 29, Balima 44, Chinwo 64

...d Qualifying Round - Beşiktaş JK (TUR)

...co, Arbanaş, Balima, Constancia (Kajkut 75), Corneencov (Demalde
...anou, Kuchuk, Mamah, Wallace, Rouamba, Tarkhnishvili.
...Card(s): Demalde 53, Wallace 58

...co, Arbanaş, Balima, Chinwo, Corneencov (Demalde 71), Gnanou,
...k, Rouamba (Gumenuk 30), Tarkhnishvili, Constancia (Suvorov 64),
...h.
...ard(s): Mamah 27
...Card(s): Kuchuk 88

FC ZIMBRU CHIŞINĂU

UEFA CUP

...Qualifying Round - FC Artmedia Petržalka (SVK)
Zhdanov (70p)
...cea, Gibaliuk, Kovalchuk (Nikulin 65), Savinov, Zhdanov (Kriuchikhin
...omidze, Berbinschi, Cojocari, Frantuz (Erhan 46), Andronic, Stan.
...ard(s): Lomidze 87
...Card(s): Calancea 20, Erhan 59, Zhdanov 66, Stan 90+1
Kovalchuk (34), Zhdanov (60p)
...cea, Gibaliuk, Kovalchuk, Savinov, Zhdanov, Kriuchikhin, Armas
...onic 68), Berbinschi, Cojocari, Frantuz (Levandovschi 62), Stan (Boiko 58).
...Card(s): Kriuchikhin 30, Zhdanov 53, Armas 68, Kovalchuk 89

FC NISTRU OTACI

UEFA CUP

...Qualifying Round - Budapest Honvéd FC (HUN)
Malitskiy (29)
..., Butelschi, Dolgov, Mekang, Matiura, Taranu (Studzinskiy 79), Al.
...uc, Sangare, Malitskiy (Ngaha 75), Groshev, Savchuk (Muhovikov 46).
...Card(s): Mekang 32, Taranu 72
Mekang (50) (aet; 4-5 on pens)
..., Dolgov, Mekang, Matiura, Lupascu, Al. Tcaciuc (Savchuk 73),
...are, Groshev, Ngaha (Butelschi 103), Studzinskiy (Taranu 78),
...vikov.
...Card(s): Lupascu 111
...Card(s): Lupascu 37, Muhovikov 94, Lupascu 111

FC DACIA CHIŞINĂU

UEFA INTERTOTO CUP

First Round - FK Bakı (AZE)
A 1-1 *Onila (45)*
Moraru, Andronic, Bolohan, Mardari, Mincev, Onica (Lipa 65), Onila, Orbu (Gusila 87), Pusca, Martin (Boicenco 73), Soimu.
H 1-1 *Onila (7) (aet; 3-1 on pens)*
Moraru, Andronic, Bolohan, Mardari, Mincev, Onica (Lipa 67), Onila (Gusila 66), Orbu, Pusca (Boicenco 81), Martin, Soimu.
Yellow Card(s): Pusca 42

Second Round - FC St Gallen (SUI)
H 0-1
Moraru, Andronic, Bolohan, Mardari, Martin (Boicenco 46), Mincev, Onica (Lipa 61), Onila, Orbu (Gusila 73), Pusca, Soimu.
Red Card(s): Onila 81
A 1-0 *Lipa (56) (aet; 3-0 on pens)*
Moraru, Andronic, Boicenco, Bolohan, Gusila, Mardari, Mincev, Onica, Orbu (Lipa 23), Pusca (Martin 100), Soimu.
Yellow Card(s): Bolohan 66, Gusila 90+19

Third Round - Hamburger SV (GER)
H 1-1 *Boicenco (7)*
Moraru, Andronic, Boicenco, Bolohan, Gusila (Pina 40), Lipa, Mardari (Belchev 80), Mincev, Onica (Martin 46), Pusca, Soimu.
Yellow Card(s): Pusca 44, Andronic 69, Boicenco 75
A 0-4
Moraru, Andronic, Bolohan, Gusila (Pina 63), Lipa (Calin 73), Mardari, Martin, Mincev, Onica, Soimu (Reshitsa 88), Orbu.
Yellow Card(s): Mincev 22, Onica 30

MONTENEGRO

FK ZETA

UEFA CHAMPIONS LEAGUE

First Qualifying Round - FBK Kaunas (LTU)
H 3-1 *Korać (34p), Tumbasević (36), Stjepanović (59)*
Ivanović, Igumanović, Ćetković, Ivanović, M. Kaluđerović, Korać (Z. Peličić 76), Marković (Boljević 89), Radulović, Stjepanović (Marinković 89), Tumbasević, Vučković.
Yellow Card(s): Korać 28
A 2-3 *Stjepanović (34), Ćetković (89)*
Ivanović (Muštur 76), Igumanović, Boljević (Vučković 46), Ćetković (Đurović 90), Ivanović, M. Kaluđerović, Korać, Marković, Radulović, Stjepanović, Tumbasević.
Yellow Card(s): Marković 39, Ćetković 77

Second Qualifying Round - Rangers FC (SCO)
A 0-2
Ivanović, Ćetković (Boljević 83), Ivanović, M. Kaluđerović, Korać, Marković, Radulović (Đurović 77), Stjepanović, Tumbasević, Vučković, Igumanović.
Yellow Card(s): Vučković 51, Tumbašević 71, Radulović 72

H 0-1
Ivanović, Ćetković, Đurović (Knežević 56), Ivanović (Boljević 71), M. Kaluđerović, Korać, Marković, Radulović, Stjepanović, Tumbasević (Vučković 84), Igumanović.
Yellow Card(s): Igumanović 23, Đurović 49, Stjepanović 75

FK RUDAR PLJEVLJA

UEFA CUP

First Qualifying Round - AC Omonia (CYP)
A 0-2
Mijatović, Vuković, Sekulić, Damjanović, Karadžić, Minić (Lujinović 79), Bojović, Lukovac (Đuraković 81), Vraneš, Reljić, Ramović (Bašić 61).
H 0-2
Mijatović, Vuković, Sekulić, Damjanović, Karadžić (Nestorović 61), Minić, Bojović, Lukovac (Brašanac 55), Vraneš, Reljić, Ramović (Lujinović 35).
Red Card(s): Vuković 88
Yellow Card(s): Karadžić 28, Lukovac 29

FK BUDUĆNOST PODGORICA

UEFA CUP

First Qualifying Round - HNK Hajduk Split (CRO)
H 1-1 *Šćepanovic (59)*
Vujadinović, N. Vukčević, Lakić, Perišić, Raičević (D. Božović 46), Vuković, Sekulić (Milić 77), Mugoša (Šćepanovic 46), Delić, Đurišić, Vlahović.
Yellow Card(s): N. Vukčević 42, Vuković 62
A 0-1
Vujadinović, N. Vukčević, Lakić, Perišić, Raičević (Tuzović 62), Vuković, Milić, Delić (D. Božović 8), Đurišić, Šćepanović (Mugoša 70), Vlahović.
Yellow Card(s): Vlahović 37, Đurišić 42, Lakić 57, D. Božović 84

OFK GRBALJ

UEFA INTERTOTO CUP

First Round - CF Gloria 1922 Bistrița (ROU)
A 1-2 *Đalac (14)*
Kljajević, Đalac, Grujić, Ivanišević (Vidakanić 85), M. Ivanović (Popović 80), Nedović, Pajović, Radenović, Rodić, Sadžakov, Tonković (Srečo 61).
Yellow Card(s): Radenović 22, Grujić 27, Ivanišević 31, Vidakanić 89
H 1-1 *Đalac (44)*
Kljajević, Đalac, Grujić, Ivanišević, M. Ivanović (Agbo 81), Nedović, Pajović, Radenović, Rodić (D. Ivanović 76), Sadžakov, Milic (Bošković 65).
Yellow Card(s): Nedović 62

NETHERLANDS

PSV EINDHOVEN

UEFA CHAMPIONS LEAGUE

Group G
Match 1 - PFC CSKA Moskva (RUS)
H 2-1 *Lazović (59), Perez (80)*
Gomes, Salcido, Da Costa, Simons, Méndez (Kromkamp 71), Lazović, Koevermans (Farfán 75), Alcides, Čulina, Addo, Afellay (Perez 28).
Match 2 - FC Internazionale Milano (ITA)
A 0-2
Gomes, Kromkamp (Bakkal 69), Salcido, Simons, Méndez (Koeverma 56), Lazović, Perez, Alcides, Čulina, Farfán (Aissati 75), Addo.
Yellow Card(s): Lazović 15, Čulina 85
Match 3 - Fenerbahçe SK (TUR)
H 0-0
Gomes, Kromkamp, Salcido, Simons, Méndez (Koevermans 58), Lazo Perez, Farfán, Addo (Zonneveld 58), Marcellis, Bakkal (Aissati 78).
Yellow Card(s): Marcellis 29, Lazović 45+5, Farfán 51
Match 4 - Fenerbahçe SK (TUR)
A 0-2
Gomes, Kromkamp (Zonneveld 46), Salcido, Simons, Méndez, Lazović, (Koevermans 63), Alcides, Farfán, Marcellis, Van der Leegte (Bakkal 80).
Yellow Card(s): Salcido 78
Match 5 - PFC CSKA Moskva (RUS)
A 1-0 *Farfán (39)*
Gomes, Salcido, Zonneveld, Méndez, Lazović (Perez 84), Alcides, Rajk Farfán (Koevermans 81), Afellay, Marcellis, Bakkal (Čulina 77).
Yellow Card(s): Méndez 30, Marcellis 57
Match 6 - FC Internazionale Milano (ITA)
H 0-1
Gomes, Salcido, Zonneveld, Simons, Méndez, Lazović (Jonathan 84), Alcides, Čulina, Farfán (Perez 62), Afellay (Aissati 65), Marcellis.
Red Card(s): Méndez 28

No	Player	Nat	DoB	Aps	(s)	G
Goalkeepers						
1	Heurelho Gomes	BRA	15/2/81	6		
Defenders						
2	Jan Kromkamp		17/8/80	3	(1)	
4	Manuel da Costa	POR	6/5/86	1		
13	Alcides	BRA	13/3/85	5		
14	Slobodan Rajković	SRB	3/2/89	1		
18	Addo	GHA	12/11/78	3		
20	Ibrahim Afellay		2/4/86	3		
24	Dirk Marcellis		13/4/88	4		
28	Otman Bakkal		27/2/85	2	(2)	
Midfielders						
3	Carlos Salcido	MEX	2/4/80	6		
5	Mike Zonneveld		27/10/80	2	(2)	
6	Timmy Simons	BEL	11/12/76	5		
8	Edison Méndez	ECU	16/3/79	6		
11	Kenneth Perez	DEN	29/8/74	3	(3)	1
16	Ismaïl Aissati		16/8/88		(3)	
26	Tommie van der Leegte		27/3/77	1		
Attackers						
9	Danko Lazović	SRB	17/5/83	6		1
10	Danny Koevermans		1/11/78	1	(4)	
15	Jason Čulina	AUS	5/8/80	3	(1)	
17	Jefferson Farfán	PER	26/10/84	5	(1)	1
19	Jonathan	BRA	6/6/89		(1)	

UEFA CUP

nd of 32 - Helsingborgs IF (SWE)
) *Simons (7p), Lazović (33)*
es, Kromkamp, Salcido, Marcellis, Zonneveld, Simons, Alcides
ović 65), Afellay, Bakkal, Dzsudzsák, Lazović (Koevermans 71).
w Card(s): Dzsudzsák 11
1 *Bakkal (47), Lazović (65)*
es, Salcido, Zonneveld, Simons, Méndez, Lazović (Koevermans 68),
les, Afellay (Aissati 72), Dzsudzsák (Rajković 78), Marcellis, Bakkal.
w Card(s): Gomes 34, Bakkal 53

nd of 16 - Tottenham Hotspur FC (ENG)
) *Farfán (34)*
es, Kromkamp, Marcellis, Salcido, Alcides, Čulina, Simons, Méndez,
n (Dzsudzsák 85), Koevermans (Lazović 77), Afellay (Bakkal 90+1).
w Card(s): Farfán 53
1 *(aet; 6-5 on pens)*
es, Kromkamp, Marcellis, Salcido, Alcides, Méndez (Bakkal 112),
ns, Čulina, Afellay (Dzsudzsák 82), Koevermans (Lazović 72), Farfán.
w Card(s): Simons 63

rter-Final - ACF Fiorentina (ITA)
1 *Koevermans (63)*
es (Roorda 59), Kromkamp, Salcido, Simons, Méndez, Koevermans
ović 64), Rajković, Čulina, Farfán (Väyrynen 96), Afellay, Marcellis.
w Card(s): Farfán 90+3
2
es, Kromkamp, Salcido, Simons, Méndez (Zonneveld 83),
ermans, Rajković, Čulina (Väyrynen 78), Dzsudzsák, Marcellis, Bakkal
ović 46).
w Card(s): Marcellis 69

AFC AJAX

UEFA CHAMPIONS LEAGUE

d Qualifying Round - SK Slavia Praha (CZE)
1
elenburg, Emanuelson, Gabri, Heitinga, Huntelaar, Stam, Vermaelen,
cioglü, Rommedahl (Sarpong 82), Colin, Suárez (Urzaiz 72).
w Card(s): Colin 24, Heitinga 25, Stekelenburg 74
2 *Suárez (34)*
elenburg, Emanuelson (Vertonghen 58), Gabri (Urzaiz 78), Heitinga,
telaar, Stam, Vermaelen, Bakircioglü (Rommedahl 65), Delorge, Colin,
ez.
w Card(s): Emanuelson 45, Stam 89

UEFA CUP

Round - NK Dinamo Zagreb (CRO)
0 *Rommedahl (61)*
elenburg, Emanuelson, Gabri, Heitinga, Huntelaar (Luque 83),
uro, Ogăraru, Rommedahl (Suárez 77), Stam, Vermaelen, Van der Wiel.
w Card(s): Maduro 57
3 *Huntelaar (101, 120) (aet)*
elenburg, Colin (Delorge 34), Emanuelson, Gabri, Heitinga, Huntelaar,
uro (Urzaiz 103), Rommedahl, Stam, Suárez, Van der Wiel (Ogăraru 61).
w Card(s): Heitinga 38, Suárez 44, Ogăraru 85

AZ ALKMAAR

UEFA CUP

First Round - FC Paços de Ferreira (POR)
A 1-0 *Pocognoli (89)*
Waterman, De Zeeuw, Dembélé (Pellè 58), Donk, Jaliens, Jenner (El Hamdaoui 80), Martens, Steinsson, Opdam (Pocognoli 73), Agustien, Ari.
H 0-0
Waterman, De Zeeuw, Dembélé (Cziommer 56), Donk, Jaliens, Jenner, Martens (Mendes da Silva 76), Steinsson, Opdam, Agustien, Ari.

Group A
Match 1 - FC Zenit St. Petersburg (RUS)
A 1-1 *Ari (20)*
Waterman, Koenders, Jaliens, Donk, Opdam, Mendes da Silva (El Hamdaoui 59), Cziommer (Međunjanin 92), Agustien, Martens (Pocognoli 49), Dembélé, Ari.
Red Card(s): Ari 39
Yellow Card(s): Mendes da Silva 26, Agustien 36, Martens 41, Opdam 42, Koenders 45+1, Jaliens 84
Match 2 - Larissa FC (GRE)
H 1-0 *Dembélé (77)*
Waterman (Romero 32), Jaliens, Opdam, Pocognoli, Steinsson, Mendes da Silva, Cziommer (Jenner 74), Agustien, De Zeeuw, Međunjanin (Pellè 65), Dembélé.
Yellow Card(s): Cziommer 24, Agustien 40, Pocognoli 90+1
Match 3 - 1. FC Nürnberg (GER)
A 1-2 *De Zeeuw (29)*
Waterman, Steinsson, Jaliens, Mendes da Silva, Opdam (Koenders 73), De Zeeuw, Agustien, Pocognoli, Cziommer (Jenner 79), Pellè, Dembélé.
Yellow Card(s): Cziommer 54, Pellè 75, Koenders 81
Match 4 - Everton FC (ENG)
H 2-3 *Pellè (17), Jaliens (66)*
Waterman, Jaliens, Opdam, Pocognoli (Agustien 77), Mendes da Silva, Cziommer (El Hamdaoui 64), Dembélé, De Zeeuw (Jenner 63), Steinsson, Vormer, Pellè.

FC TWENTE

UEFA CUP

First Round - Getafe CF (ESP)
A 0-1
Boschker, Braafheid, Denneboom (Brama 64), El Ahmadi, Engelaar, Heubach (Zomer 61), Huysegems (Elia 87), Nkufo, Wellenberg, Wielaert, Wilkshire.
Red Card(s): Braafheid 61
Yellow Card(s): Denneboom 9, Braafheid 28, Braafheid 61, Wellenberg 90+1
H 3-2 *Wielaert (30), Engelaar (117), Zomer (120) (aet)*
Boschker, Denneboom (Elia 105), El Ahmadi (Brama 105), Engelaar, Hersi (Arnautovic 111), Heubach, Nkufo, Wellenberg, Wielaert, Wilkshire, Zomer.
Red Card(s): Nkufo 72
Yellow Card(s): Wellenberg 31, El Ahmadi 60, Wielaert 77, Engelaar 93

SC HEERENVEEN

UEFA CUP

First Round - Helsingborgs IF (SWE)
H 5-3 *Bradley (20, 60), Sibon (30, 35), Bak Nielsen (59)*
Vandenbussche, Bradley (Prager 72), Breuer, Dingsdag, Pranjić, Bak Nielsen, Sulejmani, Sibon (Matusiak 66), Zuiverloon, Roorda (Poulsen 76), Beerens.
Yellow Card(s): Bradley 70, Prager 76
A 1-5 *Sibon (89)*
Vandenbussche, Afonso Alves (Prager 76), Bradley (Sibon 58), Breuer, Dingsdag, Pranjić, Bak Nielsen, Sulejmani (Matusiak 68), Zuiverloon, Roorda, Beerens.
Yellow Card(s): Roorda 62, Pranjić 90+3

FC GRONINGEN

UEFA CUP

First Round - ACF Fiorentina (ITA)
H 1-1 *Lovre (25)*
Van Loo, Kruiswijk, Levchenko, Lindgren, Lovre, Meerdink, Nevland (Kolder 90+1), Nÿland (Van de Laak 73), Sankoh, Silva, Stenman.
Yellow Card(s): Lindgren 60
A 1-1 *Nevland (55) (aet; 3-4 on pens)*
Van Loo, Berg (Van de Laak 46), Kruiswijk, Levchenko, Lindgren, Lovre, Meerdink, Nevland (Kolder 102), Sankoh, Silva, Stenman.
Yellow Card(s): Meerdink 73, Silva 115

FC UTRECHT

UEFA INTERTOTO CUP

Third Round - Hammarby (SWE)
A 0-0
Grandel, Cornelisse, Keller, Kruijs (George 84), Shew-Atjon (Pieters 88), Somers, Caluwé, Dickoh, Loval, Nelisse (Rossini 69), Van Dijk.
Yellow Card(s): Kruijs 41, Grandel 70, Rossini 86
H 1-1 *Nelisse (64)*
Grandel, Cornelisse, Keller, Kruijs (Van Buuren 84), Rossini, Shew-Atjon (Pieters 69), Somers (George 46), Caluwé, Dickoh, Nelisse, Van Dijk.
Red Card(s): Keller 61
Yellow Card(s): Rossini 42, Van Dijk 53, Caluwé 90+3

NORTHERN IRELAND

LINFIELD FC

UEFA CHAMPIONS LEAGUE

First Qualifying Round - IF Elfsborg (SWE)
H 0-0
Mannus, Curran, Dickson (Ferguson 87), Douglas, McAreavey (Mounce 77), Murphy, O'Kane, Bailie, Thompson (Stewart 80), Gault, Mulgrew.
A 0-1
Mannus, Curran (Ferguson 74), Dickson, Douglas (Mouncey 76), McArea O'Kane, Bailie, Thompson, Gault, Lindsay, Mulgrew (Stewart 64).
Yellow Card(s): Gault 7, Mouncey 79, McAreavey 90

GLENTORAN FC

UEFA CUP

First Qualifying Round - AIK Solna (SWE)
H 0-5
Dougherty, Fitzgerald, Hamill (Carson 69), Berry (Ward 80), Halliday, Hamilton, Hill (Morgan 69), Leeman, Nixon, Smyth, Ward.
Yellow Card(s): Carson 73
A 0-4
Dougherty, Fitzgerald, Ward (Hamill 84), Carson, Halliday (Morgan 83), Hamilton, Hill (McMenamin 72), Leeman, Neill, Nixon, Ward.
Yellow Card(s): Hill 56

DUNGANNON SWIFTS FC

UEFA CUP

First Qualifying Round - FK Sūduva (LTU)
H 1-0 *McAllister (17)*
Wells, Campbell (McGinn 74), Curran, Gallagher, Hegarty, McAllister (Baron 89), McCabe, McCluskey, McConkey, McMinn, Montgomery.
Yellow Card(s): Curran 90+3
A 0-4
Nelson, Campbell, Curran, Gallagher, Hegarty (McManus 64), McAllister McCabe, G. Fitzpatrick, McConkey (Baron 81), McMinn, T. Fitzpatrick (Magennis 64).
Yellow Card(s): McCabe 49, T. Fitzpatrick 66, Gallagher 72, G. Fitzpatrick

CLIFTONVILLE FC

UEFA INTERTOTO CUP

Round - FC Dinaburg (LVA)
1 *O'Connor (40)*
ıolly, Fleming, M. Holland, Johnston, McAlinden (Sweeney 87), ıullan (Kennedy 70), Murphy (Friars 82), O'Hara, C. Scannell, R. nell, O'Connor.
w Card(s): Johnston 28, R. Scannell 44, C. Scannell 47, McMullan 60, linden 72
) *M. Holland (7)*
ıolly, Fleming, Friars (B. Holland 71), M. Holland (Sweeney 83), ston, McAlinden, McMullan (Kennedy 66), O'Hara, C. Scannell, R. nell, O'Connor.
ow Card(s): Fleming 37, Johnston 57, Sweeney 90+1

nd Round - KAA Gent (BEL)
2
ıolly, Fleming, Friars (Kennedy 74), M. Holland, B. Holland, McAlinden, ıullan (Sweeney 74), O'Hara, C. Scannell, R. Scannell (Lyons 87), O'Connor.
Card(s): O'Hara 90+1
ow Card(s): R. Scannell 20, McMullan 57
4
ıolly, Fleming, M. Holland, Johnston, McAlinden (Smyth 50), B. Holland, ɔhy (Friars 54), O'Hara, Kennedy, Sweeney (McMullan 70), O'Connor.
ow Card(s): O'Hara 22, B. Holland 27

NORWAY

ROSENBORG BK

UEFA CHAMPIONS LEAGUE

ond Qualifying Round - FC Astana (KAZ)
-1 *Koné (3, 61), Iversen (56p)*
chfeld, Basma, Dorsin, Koné (Jamtfall 83), Koppinen, Strand (Stoor 75), ey, Ya (Storflor 36), Iversen, Sapara, Riseth.
ow Card(s): Koné 25
-1 *Koné (1, 33), Iversen (7), Traoré (17, 50, 53), Sapara (62)*
chfeld, Basma, Dorsin, Koné, Koppinen, Strand (Stoor 46), Tettey, sen, Traoré, Sapara (Jamtfall 64), Riseth (Skjelbred 46).

rd Qualifying Round - Tampere United (FIN)
-0 *Koppinen (19), Koné (20, 81)*
chfeld, Basma, Dorsin (Kvarme 84), Iversen (Storflor 25), Koné, ɔpinen, Riseth, Sapara, Stoor, Tettey, Traoré (Ya 90+1).
low Card(s): Tettey 88
-0 *Sapara (45), Ya (48)*
chfeld, Basma, Dorsin, Koné, Koppinen (Skjelbred 45), Riseth, Sapara rsen 76), Strand (Stoor 17), Tettey, Traoré, Ya.

oup B
tch 1 - Chelsea FC (ENG)
-1 *Koppinen (24)*
chfeld, Koppinen, Basma (Kvarme 46), Strand, Koné, Riseth, Skjelbred rsen 85), Tettey, Traoré, Sapara (Ya 69), Dorsin.
low Card(s): Dorsin 66, Koné 89

Match 2 - FC Schalke 04 (GER)
H 0-2
Hirschfeld, Koppinen, Basma, Strand, Riseth, Iversen, Skjelbred (Koné 68), Tettey, Traoré, Sapara, Dorsin (Ya 79).
Yellow Card(s): Sapara 41, Riseth 43
Match 3 - Valencia CF (ESP)
H 2-0 *Koné (53), Riseth (61)*
Hirschfeld, Strand (Stoor 86), Koné (Storflor 80), Riseth, Iversen, Skjelbred, Tettey, Traoré, Kvarme, Sapara, Dorsin.
Yellow Card(s): Traoré 33, Strand 51, Tettey 72
Match 4 - Valencia CF (ESP)
A 2-0 *Iversen (31, 58)*
Hirschfeld, Stoor, Koné, Riseth, Iversen, Skjelbred (Storflor 80), Tettey, Traoré, Kvarme, Sapara (Ya 84), Dorsin.
Match 5 - Chelsea FC (ENG)
H 0-4
Hirschfeld, Stoor, Koné (Ya 63), Riseth, Iversen, Skjelbred, Tettey, Traoré (Strand 56), Kvarme, Sapara, Dorsin (Basma 86).
Match 6 - FC Schalke 04 (GER)
A 1-3 *Koné (23)*
Hirschfeld, Stoor, Basma, Strand (Traoré 61), Koné (Ya 77), Riseth, Iversen, Skjelbred, Tettey, Kvarme, Sapara.
Yellow Card(s): Sapara 47

No	Player	Nat	DoB	Aps	(s)	Gls
Goalkeepers						
13	Lars Hirschfeld	CAN	17/10/78	6		
Defenders						
2	Miika Koppinen	FIN	5/7/78	2		1
4	Fredrik Stoor	SWE	28/2/84	3	(1)	
5	Christer Basma		1/8/72	3	(1)	
10	Vidar Riseth		21/4/72	6		1
26	Bjørn Tore Kvarme		17/6/72	4	(1)	
33	Mikael Dorsin	SWE	6/10/81	5		
Midfielders						
6	Roar Strand		2/2/70	4	(1)	
15	Per Ciljan Skjelbred		16/6/87	6		
19	Alexander Tettey		4/4/86	6		
27	Marek Sapara	SVK	31/7/82	6		
Attackers						
7	Yssouf Koné	CIV	19/2/82	5	(1)	2
8	Didier Konan Ya	CIV	25/2/84		(5)	
14	Steffen Iversen		10/11/76	5	(1)	2
17	Øyvind Storflor		18/12/79		(2)	
20	Abdou Razack Traoré	CIV	28/12/88	5	(1)	

UEFA CUP

Round of 32 - ACF Fiorentina (ITA)
H 0-1
Jarstein, Stoor, Kvarme, Demidov, Nordvik, Skjelbred, Strand (Storflor 81), Sapara, Traoré, Iversen (Ya 47), Koné.
A 1-2 *Koné (88)*
Jarstein, Basma (Lago 54), Nordvik, Kvarme, Demidov, Storflor, Tettey, Skjelbred, Ya (Iversen 71), Koné (Pelu 90), Sapara.
Yellow Card(s): Kvarme 53, Storflor 84

FREDRIKSTAD FK

UEFA CUP

Second Qualifying Round - Hammarby (SWE)
A 1-2 *Kvisvik (74)*
Shaaban, Bjørkøy, Czwartek, West (Ramberg 58), Sjöberg (Multaharju 46), Jóhannsson (Hoås 76), Gerrband, Kvisvik, Elyounoussi, Piiroja, Wehrman.

Yellow Card(s): Elyounoussi 38, Hoås 90
H 1-1 *Bjørkøy (85)*
Shaaban, Bjørkøy, Czwartek, Sjöberg (West 90+1), Jóhannsson (Hoås 72), Gerrband, Kvisvik, Elyounoussi, Piiroja, Wehrman, Ramberg (Kouadio 65).
Yellow Card(s): Sjöberg 83, Gerrband 90+3

SK BRANN

UEFA CUP

First Qualifying Round - Carmarthen Town AFC (WAL)
A 8-0 *Winters (8, 30, 45), Helstad (17, 28), Sigurdsson (70), Solli (83), Björnsson (90+1)*
Thorbjørnsen, Andresen (Jaiteh 46), Bjarnason, Dahl, Hanstveit, Helstad (Björnsson 58), Huseklepp (Gashi 74), Sigurdsson, Solli, Vaagan Moen, Winters.
Yellow Card(s): Vaagan Moen 88
H 6-3 *Vaagan Moen (9), Björnsson (19), Winters (27, 32), Sigurdsson (56), Hanstveit (57)*
Thorbjørnsen, Bakke, Bjarnason, Björnsson, Dahl, Hanstveit, Huseklepp, Jaiteh, Sigurdsson, Vaagan Moen (Guntveit 58), Winters.

Second Qualifying Round - FK Sūduva (LTU)
H 2-1 *Björnsson (24), Winters (49)*
Thorbjørnsen, Andresen, Bakke (El Fakiri 81), Bjarnason, Björnsson, Dahl, Hanstveit, Huseklepp (Sjöhage 86), Sigurdsson, Solli, Winters.
A 4-3 *Vaagan Moen (37), Björnsson (45), Solli (57), Huseklepp (63)*
Opdal, Bjarnason, Björnsson, Dahl, Hanstveit, Jaiteh, Sigurdsson, Solli (Guntveit 66), Vaagan Moen (Huseklepp 53), Winters (Sjöhage 79), El Fakiri.
Yellow Card(s): Björnsson 43

First Round - Club Brugge KV (BEL)
H 0-1
Opdal, Bjarnason, Björnsson, Walde, Hanstveit, Andresen (Karadas 56), Helstad (Bakke 56), Solli, Vaagan Moen, Guntveit (Huseklepp 68), El Fakiri.
Yellow Card(s): Bakke 58
A 2-1 *Helstad (14), Winters (39)*
Opdal, Andresen, Bakke, Bjarnason, Corrales, Dahl, Helstad, Huseklepp (Guntveit 81), Sigurdsson (Karadas 46), Solli, Winters (El Fakiri 56).
Yellow Card(s): Corrales 45, Helstad 61

Group D
Match 1 - Hamburger SV (GER)
H 0-1
Opdal, Dahl, Bjarnason, Sigurdsson, Hanstveit, Solli, El Fakiri, Jaiteh (Huseklepp 47), Vaagan Moen (Björnsson 85), Bakke (Karadas 47), Helstad.
Match 2 - Stade Rennais FC (FRA)
A 1-1 *Karadas (24)*
Opdal, Dahl, Bjarnason, Sigurdsson, Hanstveit, El Fakiri, Solli, Bakke, Huseklepp (Vaagan Moen 55), Karadas (Guntveit 55), Helstad.
Red Card(s): El Fakiri 90+2
Yellow Card(s): Dahl 31, Bakke 42, Helstad 70, Opdal 81
Match 3 - NK Dinamo Zagreb (CRO)
H 2-1 *Bjarnason (45+4p), Bakke (72)*
Opdal, Dahl, Hanstveit, Bjarnason, Corrales, Huseklepp (Björnsson 94), Solli, Bakke, Vaagan Moen, Karadas (Guntveit 85), Helstad.
Yellow Card(s): Bakke 36
Match 4 - FC Basel 1893 (SUI)
A 0-1
Opdal, Dahl, Hanstveit, Bjarnason, Corrales (Björnsson 46), Huseklepp, Guntveit (Sjöhage 51), Solli, Vaagan Moen, Helstad, Karadas.
Yellow Card(s): Bjarnason 20, Huseklepp 73, Vaagan Moen 76, Solli 77

Round of 32 - Everton FC (ENG)
H 0-2
Opdal, Dahl (Thwaite 89), Bjarnason, Sigurdsson, Hanstveit, Solli, Bakk Fakiri (Huseklepp 75), Vaagan Moen, Helstad, Karadas (Demba-Nyrén
A 1-6 *Vaagan Moen (60)*
Opdal, Dahl, Bjarnason (Karadas 65), Sigurdsson, Hanstveit, Vaagan M El Fakiri (Huseklepp 60), Bakke, Solli, Demba-Nyrén (Winters 72), Hels
Yellow Card(s): Bakke 33

VÅLERENGA FOTBALL

UEFA CUP

First Qualifying Round - FC Flora (EST)
A 1-0 *Lange (31)*
Arason, Berre, Førsund, Grindheim, Holm, Jalland (Mathisen 61), Jepse Johnsen, Lange, Sørensen (Roberts 79), Storbæk.
Yellow Card(s): Jalland 37
H 1-0 *Berre (90+2)*
Bolthof, Berre, Dos Santos, Fredheim Holm, Holm, Jalland, Jepsen, Johnsen (Horn 38), Storbæk, Wæhler, Fellah (Lange 50; Førsund 74).

Second Qualifying Round - FK Ekranas (LTU)
A 1-1 *Dos Santos (76)*
Arason, Berre, Dos Santos, Fredheim Holm (Roberts 74), Horn, Jepsen, Johnsen, Mila (Holm 46), Sørensen (Jalland 46), Storbæk, Thomassen.
Red Card(s): Thomassen 45
Yellow Card(s): Fredheim Holm 59
H 6-0 *Grindheim (5, 45+1), Sørensen (42), Horn (67), Storbæk (81), Brix (90+1)*
Arason, Fredheim Holm (Roberts 65), Grindheim (Brix 57), Horn, Jallan Jepsen, Johnsen (Mathisen 46), Mila, Sørensen, Storbæk, Wæhler.

First Round - FK Austria Wien (AUT)
A 0-2
Arason, Fredheim Holm, Grindheim, Horn, Dos Santos, Jepsen, Johnse Mila (Thorvaldsson 46), Berre, Storbæk, Thomassen.
Yellow Card(s): Mila 43, Grindheim 84, Horn 90
H 2-2 *Dos Santos (51), Holm (87)*
Arason, Jepsen, Dos Santos, Fredheim Holm, Jalland, Berre, Storbæk, Thomassen, Grindheim (Holm 66), Johnsen (Horn 60), Thorvaldsson (Mila
Yellow Card(s): Mila 58, Horn 70, Thomassen 90

LILLESTRØM SK

UEFA CUP

First Qualifying Round - UN Käerjéng 97 (LUX)
H 2-1 *Occean (19), Sundgot (45p)*
Fredrikson, Andersen, Brenne, Johansen, Mouelhi (Kiesenebner 63), Occean (Strand 77), Rambekk, Riise, Søgård (Myklebust 63), Stefanutto Sundgot.
Yellow Card(s): Mouelhi 30, Kiesenebner 73
A 0-1
Müller, Andersen, Brenne, Essediri (Rambekk 64), Kippe, Mouelhi, Occe Riise, Søgård, Stefanutto (Kiesenebner 77), Strand (Sundgot 64).
Yellow Card(s): Kippe 46, Occean 78, Sundgot 90+3

POLAND

ZAGŁĘBIE ŁUBIN

UEFA CHAMPIONS LEAGUE

nd Qualifying Round - FC Steaua Bucureşti (ROU)

vík, Arboleda, G. Bartczak, M. Bartczak, Tiago Gomes, Goliński
ndowicz 75), Iwański, Rui Miguel (Łobodziński 46), André Nunes,
ık, Włodarczyk (Chałbiński 57).
w Card(s): G. Bartczak 30, André Nunes 64
Stasiak (29)
vík, Arboleda, G. Bartczak, M. Bartczak, Chałbiński (Włodarczyk 57;
iguel 72), Tiago Gomes, Goliński, Iwański, Łobodziński, Stasiak,
ń (Kolendowicz 71).
w Card(s): Tiago Gomes 11, Iwański 74, Stasiak 88

ROCLIN GRODZISK WIELKOPOLSKI

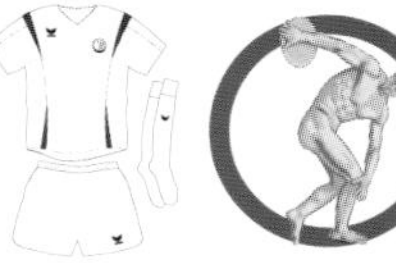

UEFA CUP

Qualifying Round – FK MKT-Araz (AZE)

owski, Sokołowski, Ivanovski (Kłodawski 68), Jodłowiec (Piechniak
oziol, Kumbev, Sikora, Lazarevski, Muszalik (Majewski 60), Lato,
owski.
w Card(s): Telichowski 83
Kłodawski (88)
owski, Jodłowiec, Ślusarski, Kozioł, Sikora (Sokołowski 90), Lazarevski
awski 81), Majewski, Mynář, Piechniak (Rocki 70), Lato, Telichowski.
w Card(s): Lazarevski 21, Piechniak 68, Kłodawski 88, Ślusarski 90

nd Qualifying Round - FC Tobol Kostanay (KAZ)
Muszalik (4)
owski, Jodłowiec, Ślusarski, Kozioł, Sokołowski, Lazarevski, Babnič
bev 69), Mynář, Piechniak (Rocki 90), Lato, Muszalik (Majewski 73).
w Card(s): Mynář 90+1
Sikora (5, 19)
owski, Ivanovski, Jodłowiec, Kozioł, Lato (Kłodawski 65), Lazarevski,
wski (Muszalik 77), Mynář (Piechniak 59), Sikora, Sokołowski,
owski.
w Card(s): Muszalik 80

Round - FK Crvena Zvezda (SRB)

owski, Ivanovski (Rocki 67), Jodłowiec, Kozioł, Lato (Babnič 78),
wski (Muszalik 64), Mynář, Piechniak, Sikora, Sokołowski, Telichowski.
w Card(s): Piechniak 45+1

owski, Jodłowiec, Kumbev, Lato, Lazarevski, Majewski (Babnič 64),
ř, Piechniak, Rocki (Ivanovski 54), Sikora, Telichowski (Leonardo 79).

GKS BEŁCHATÓW

UEFA CUP

First Qualifying Round - FC Ameri Tbilisi (GEO)
H 2-0 *Pietrasiak (51,82)*
Lech, Cecot, Costly (Ujek 82), Jarzębowski, Kowalczyk, Pietrasiak, Popek, Rachwał, Stolarczyk, Strąk, Wróbel (Marciniak 88).
Yellow Card(s): Jarzębowski 70
A 0-2 *(aet; 4-2 on pens)*
Lech, Cecot, Costly (Nowak 46), Grodzicki (Marciniak 103), Jarzębowski, Popek, Rachwał, Stolarczyk, Strąk, Ujek (Tosik 98), Wróbel.
Yellow Card(s): Ujek 43, Popek 50, Grodzicki 76, Rachwał 108

Second Qualifying Round - FC Dnipro Dnipropetrovsk (UKR)
A 1-1 *Ujek (18)*
Kozik, Cecot, Jarzębowski, Kowalczyk, Popek, Rachwał, Stolarczyk, Strąk, Ujek (Grodzicki 85), Herrera Zegarra (Wróbel 46), Dziedzic (Nowak 67).
Yellow Card(s): Jarzębowski 55
H 2-4 *Stolarczyk (10p), Nowak (21)*
Lech, Strąk, Stolarczyk, Garguła, Pietrasiak, Kowalczyk, Nowak (Sánchez Reyes 75), Herrera Zegarra (Wróbel 46), Rachwał, Ujek (Cecot 46), Dziedzic.
Yellow Card(s): Stolarczyk 30, Kowalczyk 85

LEGIA WARSZAWA

UEFA INTERTOTO CUP

Second Round - FK Vėtra (LTU)
A 0-3 *(w/o)*
Mucha, Bronowicki, Choto, Grzelak, Korzym, Radović, Smoliński, Vuković, Roger, Astiz, Wawrzyniak..

PORTUGAL

FC PORTO

UEFA CHAMPIONS LEAGUE

Group A
Match 1 - Liverpool FC (ENG)
H 1-1 *Lucho González (8p)*
Nuno, Bruno Alves, Paulo Assunção, Ricardo Quaresma, Lucho González, Lisandro López López, Bosingwa, Fucile, João Paulo, Raul Meireles (Mariano González 64), Sektioui (Farías 64).
Yellow Card(s): Bosingwa 9

Match 2 - Beşiktaş JK (TUR)
A 1-0 *Ricardo Quaresma (90+2)*
Helton, Bruno Alves, Stepanov, Paulo Assunção, Ricardo Quaresma, Lucho González, Lisandro López (Adriano 75), Bosingwa, Fucile, Raul Meireles (Leandro Lima 88), Sektioui (Čech 66).
Yellow Card(s): Lucho González 45, Bruno Alves 67
Match 3 - Olympique de Marseille (FRA)
A 1-1 *Lucho González (79p)*
Helton, Bruno Alves, Stepanov, Paulo Assunção, Ricardo Quaresma, Lucho González, Lisandro López, Mariano González (Hélder Postiga 46), Bosingwa, Fucile, Raul Meireles (Leandro Lima 72).
Yellow Card(s): Stepanov 74
Match 4 - Olympique de Marseille (FRA)
H 2-1 *Sektioui (27), Lisandro López (78)*
Helton, Bruno Alves, Stepanov, Čech (Hélder Postiga 59), Paulo Assunção, Ricardo Quaresma, Lisandro López, Bosingwa, Fucile, Raul Meireles (Bolatti 68), Sektioui (Mariano González 87).
Yellow Card(s): Helton 90+1, Fucile 90+2
Match 5 - Liverpool FC (ENG)
A 1-4 *Lisandro López (33)*
Helton, Bruno Alves, Stepanov, Čech, Paulo Assunção (Hélder Postiga 81), Ricardo Quaresma, Lucho González, Lisandro López, Mariano González (Sektioui 77), Bosingwa, Kaźmierczak (Raul Meireles 65).
Yellow Card(s): Paulo Assunção 48, Stepanov 82, Ricardo Quaresma 90+1
Match 6 - Beşiktaş JK (TUR)
H 2-0 *Lucho González (44), Ricardo Quaresma (62)*
Helton, Bruno Alves, Pedro Emanuel, Paulo Assunção, Ricardo Quaresma, Lucho González (Bolatti 81), Lisandro López, Bosingwa, Fucile (Čech 75), Raul Meireles, Sektioui (Hélder Postiga 74).
Yellow Card(s): Ricardo Quaresma 23

Round of 16 - FC Schalke 04 (GER)
A 0-1
Helton, Bruno Alves, Pedro Emanuel, Paulo Assunção, Ricardo Quaresma, Lucho González, Lisandro López, Fucile (Mariano González 85), João Paulo, Raul Meireles, Farías (Sektioui 56).
H 1-0 *Lisandro López (86) (aet; 1-4 on pens)*
Helton, Bruno Alves, Pedro Emanuel, Paulo Assunção, Ricardo Quaresma, Lucho González, Lisandro López, Bosingwa (Mariano González 54), Fucile, Raul Meireles (Čech 98), Sektioui (Farías 57).
Red Card(s): Fucile 82
Yellow Card(s): Lucho González 104

No	Player	Nat	DoB	Aps	(s)	Gls
Goalkeepers						
1	Helton	BRA	18/5/78	7		
33	Nuno Espírito Santo		25/1/74	1		
Defenders						
2	Bruno Alves		27/11/81	8		
3	Pedro Emanuel		11/2/75	3		
4	Milan Stepanov	SRB	2/4/83	4		
5	Marek Čech	SVK	26/1/83	2	(3)	
12	José Bosingwa		24/8/82	7		
13	Jorge Fucile	URU	19/11/84	7		
14	João Paulo		6/6/81	2		
Midfielders						
6	Paulo Assunção	BRA	25/1/80	8		
7	Ricardo Quaresma		26/9/83	8		2
8	Lucho González	ARG	19/1/81	7		3
11	Mariano González	ARG	5/5/81	2	(4)	
16	Raul Meireles		17/3/83	7	(1)	
17	Tarik Sektioui	MAR	13/5/77	5	(2)	1
18	Mario Bolatti	ARG	17/2/85		(2)	
20	Leandro Lima	BRA	19/12/87		(2)	
25	Przemysław Kaźmierczak	POL	5/5/82	1		
Attackers						
9	Lisandro López	ARG	2/3/83	8		3
19	Ernesto Farías	ARG	29/5/80	1	(2)	
23	Hélder Postiga		2/8/82		(4)	
28	Adriano	BRA	3/1/79		(1)	

SPORTING CLUBE DE PORTUGAL

UEFA CHAMPIONS LEAGUE

Group F
Match 1 - Manchester United FC (ENG)
H 0-1
Stojković, Anderson Polga, Izmailov (Vukčević 56), Ronny (Pereirinha
Tonel, Yannick Djaló, Miguel Veloso, João Moutinho, Romagnoli (Puro
68), Liedson, Abel.
Yellow Card(s): Romagnoli 16
Match 2 - FC Dynamo Kyiv (UKR)
A 2-1 *Tonel (14), Anderson Polga (38)*
Stojković, Anderson Polga, Ronny, Vukčević (Izmailov 68), Tonel, Yann
Djaló (Gladstone 90+2), Miguel Veloso, João Moutinho, Romagnoli (Paredes 77), Liedson, Abel.
Yellow Card(s): Anderson Polga 21, Vukčević 64
Match 3 - AS Roma (ITA)
A 1-2 *Liedson (18)*
Tiago, Izmailov (Celsinho 81), Ronny (Purović 77), Vukčević (Paredes 7
Tonel, Yannick Djaló, Miguel Veloso, João Moutinho, Romagnoli, Lied
Abel.
Yellow Card(s): Tonel 46, João Moutinho 87
Match 4 - AS Roma (ITA)
H 2-2 *Liedson (22, 64)*
Tiago, Anderson Polga, Izmailov (Pereirinha 89), Ronny, Tonel, Yannick
(Vukčević 63), Miguel Veloso, João Moutinho, Romagnoli, Liedson, Abe
Yellow Card(s): Abel 58, Miguel Veloso 81
Match 5 - Manchester United FC (ENG)
A 1-2 *Abel (21)*
Rui Patrício, Had, Anderson Polga, Izmailov (Pereirinha 82), Purović (Farnerud 82), Tonel, Miguel Veloso, João Moutinho, Romagnoli (Vuk
68), Liedson, Abel.
Yellow Card(s): Had 47, Anderson Polga 88
Match 6 - FC Dynamo Kyiv (UKR)
H 3-0 *Anderson Polga (35p), João Moutinho (67), Liedson (88)*
Rui Patrício, Anderson Polga, Adrien Silva, Izmailov, Ronny (Miguel V
61), Purović (Páez 86), Tonel, Farnerud (Vukčević 68), João Moutinho,
Liedson, Abel.

No	Player	Nat	DoB	Aps	(s)	G
Goalkeepers						
1	Rui Patrício		15/2/88	2		
16	Tiago		16/4/75	2		
34	Vladimir Stojković	SRB	28/7/83	2		
Defenders						
3	Marián Had	SVK	16/9/82	1		
4	Anderson Polga	BRA	9/2/79	5		
8	Ronny	BRA	11/5/86	5		
13	Tonel		13/4/80	6		
26	Gladstone	BRA	29/1/85		(1)	
78	Abel		22/12/78	6		
Midfielders						
5	Carlos Paredes	PAR	16/7/76		(2)	
6	Adrien Silva		15/3/89	1		
7	Marat Izmailov	RUS	21/9/82	5	(1)	
9	Milan Purović	MNE	7/5/85	2	(2)	
10	Simon Vukčević	MNE	29/1/86	2	(4)	
21	Pontus Farnerud	SWE	4/6/80	1	(1)	
24	Miguel Veloso		11/5/86	5	(1)	
25	Bruno Pereirinha		2/3/88		(3)	
28	João Moutinho		8/9/86	6		
30	Leandro Romagnoli	ARG	17/3/81	5		
88	Celsinho	BRA	25/8/88		(1)	
Attackers						
20	Yannick Djaló		5/5/86	4		

Liedson	BRA	17/12/77	6		4
Luis Páez	PAR	19/12/89		(1)	

UEFA CUP

d of 32 - FC Basel 1893 (SUI)
Vukčević (8, 58)
trício, Abel, Tonel, Anderson Polga, Grimi, Miguel Veloso, Izmailov
inha 72), Romagnoli, Vukčević (Rodrigo Tiuí 72), João Moutinho,
on.
Pereirinha (2), Liedson (41, 51)
trício, Anderson Polga (Gladstone 55), Tonel, Grimi (Ronny 68), Abel,
l Veloso, Pereirinha, João Moutinho, Romagnoli (Farnerud 60),
go Tiuí, Liedson.
v Card(s): Abel 79

d of 16 - Bolton Wanderers FC (ENG)
Vukčević (69)
trício, Anderson Polga, Izmailov (Gladstone 85), Vukčević, Tonel,
Rodrigo Tiuí (Adrien Silva 75), Miguel Veloso, Pereirinha, João
nho, Abel (Romagnoli 46).
v Card(s): Grimi 82
Pereirinha (85)
trício, Anderson Polga, Izmailov (Gladstone 87), Vukčević (Rodrigo
5), Tonel, Grimi, Pereirinha, João Moutinho, Romagnoli (Adrien Silva
edson, Abel.
v Card(s): João Moutinho 38

er-Final - Rangers FC (SCO)

trício, Anderson Polga, Izmailov (Pereirinha 70), Vukčević (Yannick
75), Tonel, Grimi, Miguel Veloso, João Moutinho, Romagnoli,
n, Abel.
v Card(s): Izmailov 20, Grimi 55, Liedson 59

trício, Izmailov (Yannick Djaló 62), Vukčević, Tonel, Grimi (Rodrigo
'), Miguel Veloso, Gladstone (Pereirinha 69), João Moutinho,
gnoli, Liedson, Abel.

SL BENFICA

UEFA CHAMPIONS LEAGUE

Qualifying Round - FC København (DEN)
Rui Costa (25, 85)
Nuno Assis (Nuno Gomes 74), Rui Costa, Luisão (Adu 37), Petit,
uranis, Léo, David Luiz, Luís Filipe, Cardozo, Bergessio (Fábio
rão 46).
v Card(s): Luís Filipe 53, Petit 58, David Luiz 67, Rui Costa 86
Katsouranis (17)
Rui Costa, Petit, Katsouranis, Léo, Nuno Gomes (Bergessio 90+3), Nélson
Assis 46), Luís Filipe, Di María (Romeu 74), Cardozo, Miguel Vítor.
v Card(s): Cardozo 57, Katsouranis 68, Miguel Vítor 87

p D
1 - AC Milan (ITA)
Nuno Gomes (90+2)
Luís Filipe, Edcarlos, Léo, Cardozo (Nuno Gomes 63), Katsouranis,
sta (Nuno Assis 87), Maxi Pereira, Di María, Cristián Rodríguez,
l Vítor (Binya 73).
v Card(s): Cardozo 61
1 2 - FC Shakhtar Donetsk (UKR)

Edcarlos, Luisão, Léo, Cardozo, Katsouranis, Rui Costa, Maxi Pereira,
ría (Binya 61), Nélson (Nuno Gomes 45), Rodríguez.

Yellow Card(s): Katsouranis 57, Cardozo 67, Rodríguez 79
Match 3 - Celtic FC (SCO)
H 1-0 *Cardozo (87)*
Quim, Luisão, Léo, Cardozo, Katsouranis, Rui Costa, Maxi Pereira, Binya, Bergessio (Adu 62), Nuno Assis (Di María 62), Rodríguez (Luís Filipe 84).
Yellow Card(s): Di María 90
Match 4 - Celtic FC (SCO)
A 0-1
Quim, Luís Filipe, Edcarlos, Luisão, Léo, Cardozo (Nuno Gomes 77), Katsouranis, Rui Costa (Bergessio 77), Maxi Pereira (Di María 61), Binya, Cristián Rodríguez.
Red Card(s): Binya 85
Yellow Card(s): Maxi Pereira 42
Match 5 - AC Milan (ITA)
H 1-1 *Maxi Pereira (20)*
Quim, Luís Filipe (Di María 74), Luisão, Léo, Petit, Katsouranis, Rui Costa, Maxi Pereira, Nuno Gomes (Cardozo 75), David Luiz (Adu 88), Cristián Rodríguez.
Yellow Card(s): Petit 68
Match 6 - FC Shakhtar Donetsk (UKR)
A 2-1 *Cardozo (6, 22)*
Quim, Luisão, Léo, Petit, Cardozo (Nuno Gomes 90), Katsouranis, Rui Costa, Maxi Pereira (Luís Filipe 83), Di María (Nuno Assis 67), Nélson, David Luiz.
Yellow Card(s): David Luiz 29, Luís Filipe 90+1

No	Player	Nat	DoB	Aps	(s)	Gls
Goalkeepers						
12	Quim		13/11/75	6		
Defenders						
2	Luís Filipe		14/6/79	3	(2)	
3	Edcarlos	BRA	10/5/85	3		
4	Luisão	BRA	13/2/81	5		
5	Léo	BRA	6/7/75	6		
22	Nélson		10/6/83	2		
23	David Luiz	BRA	22/4/87	2		
28	Miguel Vítor		30/6/89	1		
Midfielders						
6	Petit		25/9/76	2		
8	Kostas Katsouranis	GRE	21/6/79	6		
10	Rui Costa		29/3/72	6		
14	Maxi Pereira	URU	8/6/84	6		1
18	Gilles Binya	CMR	20/9/84	2	(2)	
25	Nuno Assis		25/11/77	1	(2)	
26	Cristián Rodríguez	URU	30/9/85	5		
Attackers						
7	Óscar Cardozo	PAR	20/5/83	5	(1)	3
19	Gonzalo Bergessio	ARG	20/7/84	1	(1)	
20	Ángel Di María	ARG	14/2/88	3	(3)	
21	Nuno Gomes		5/7/76	1	(4)	1
30	Freddy Adu	USA	2/6/89		(2)	

UEFA CUP

Round of 32 - 1. FC Nürnberg (GER)
H 1-0 *Makukula (43)*
Quim, Nélson, Luisão, Katsouranis, Léo, Petit, Nuno Assis (Adu 85), Rodríguez (David Luiz 85), Rui Costa, Makukula, Cardozo (Di María 59).
Yellow Card(s): Nélson 22, Petit 86
A 2-2 *Cardozo (89), Di María (90+1)*
Quim, Luís Filipe, Luisão, Edcarlos (Cardozo 70), Léo, Katsouranis, Petit, Maxi Pereira (Sepsi 70), Rui Costa, Nuno Assis (Di María 81), Makukula.
Yellow Card(s): Léo 10, Maxi Pereira 45+1, Luís Filipe 56, Makukula 67, Petit 77

Round of 16 - Getafe CF (ESP)
H 1-2 *Mantorras (76)*
Quim, Nélson, Luisão (Zoro 29), Edcarlos, Léo, Katsouranis, Rui Costa, Rodríguez, Di María (Mantorras 62), Sepsi, Cardozo.
Red Card(s): Cardozo 9
A 0-1
Quim, Nélson, Edcarlos (Sepsi 74), Petit, Léo, Katsouranis, Rui Costa, Maxi Pereira (Di María 59), Cristián Rodríguez, Nuno Gomes (Mantorras 66), Makukula.
Yellow Card(s): Katsouranis 14, Maxi Pereira 55, Edcarlos 68, Léo 88

SC BRAGA

UEFA CUP

First Round - Hammarby (SWE)
A 1-2 *Linz (59)*
Dani Mallo, Vandinho (Jailson 88), Carlos Fernandes, Frechaut, Paulo Jorge, Andrés Madrid, Wender (Hussain 83), João Pereira, Jorginho, Lenny Felisbino (João Pinto 61), Linz.
Yellow Card(s): Frechaut 20
H 4-0 *Wender (47), Hussain (69, 90+2), Linz (81p)*
Dani Mallo, Vandinho, Frechaut, Paulo Jorge, Andrés Madrid, Wender (Castanheira 85), João Pereira, César Peixoto, Jorginho (Jailson 76), Zé Manuel (Hussain 64), Linz.
Yellow Card(s): João Pereira 31, Wender 47

Group F
Match 1 - Bolton Wanderers FC (ENG)
A 1-1 *Jailson (87)*
Paulo Santos, João Pereira, Rodríguez, Paulo Jorge, César Peixoto, Vandinho, Castanheira (Stélvio 68), Andrés Madrid (Jailson 76), Jorginho, Wender (Nelsinho 67), Linz.
Yellow Card(s): Castanheira 61
Match 2 - FC Bayern München (GER)
H 1-1 *Linz (66)*
Paulo Santos, João Pereira, Paulo Jorge, Rodríguez, Frechaut, Roberto Brum, Stélvio (Jailson 58), Jorginho, Vandinho (João Pinto 52), Wender (Andrés Madrid 70), Linz.
Yellow Card(s): Roberto Brum 5, Linz 45, Stélvio 54, Andrés Madrid 72
Match 3 - Aris Thessaloniki FC (GRE)
A 1-1 *Linz (6)*
Paulo Santos, João Pereira, Anilton, Carlos Fernandes, Rodríguez, César Peixoto (João Pinto 53), Frechaut, Wender (Castanheira 82), Roberto Brum, Jorginho (Jailson 73), Linz.
Yellow Card(s): Wender 82
Match 4 - FK Crvena Zvezda (SRB)
H 2-0 *Linz (11), Wender (66)*
Paulo Santos, João Pereira, Paulo Jorge, Rodríguez, Carlos Fernandes, Roberto Brum (Andrés Madrid 89), Frechaut, Vandinho, Jorginho (Jailson 73), Linz, Wender (César Peixoto 71).
Yellow Card(s): Paulo Jorge 84

Round of 32 - Werder Bremen (GER)
A 0-3
Paulo Santos, Rodríguez, Paulo Jorge, Carlos Fernandes, Contreras (Stélvio 62), Frechaut, João Pereira, Jorginho (Jailson 78), Vandinho, Linz, Matheus (Wender 67).
Yellow Card(s): Contreras 42, Paulo Jorge 78, Stélvio 82, Carlos Fernandes 90+5
H 0-1
Kieszek, João Pereira, Paulo Jorge, Rodríguez, Carlos Fernandes, Stélvio (Vandinho 61), Roberto Brum, César Peixoto, Zé Manuel (João Tomás 47), Wender (Matheus 47), Linz.
Yellow Card(s): Roberto Brum 42, Stélvio 58, Paulo Jorge 82

CF OS BELENENSES

UEFA CUP

First Round - FC Bayern München (GER)
A 0-1
Costinha, Hugo Alcantara, Silas (João Paulo 63), José Pedro, Cândido Costa (Amaral 46), Rodrigo Alvim, Ruben Amorim, Rolando, Roncatto, Dević, Evandro Paulista (Fernando 55).
Yellow Card(s): Cândido Costa 32, José Pedro 68
H 0-2
Costinha, Hugo Alcantara, Silas, José Pedro, Cândido Costa (Amaral 1 Rodrigo Alvim, Weldon (João Paulo 78), Ruben Amorim, Rolando, Roncatto, Dević (Mendonça 73).
Yellow Card(s): Rodrigo Alvim 16, Dević 47

FC PAÇOS DE FERREIRA

UEFA CUP

First Round - AZ Alkmaar (NED)
H 0-1
Peçanha, Dedé, Luiz Carlos, Fernando Pilar (Pedrinha 71), Ricardinho (Renato Queirós 84), Rovérsio, Cristiano, Edson (Márcio Carioca 71), Mangualde, Filipe Anunciação, Valdir.
A 0-0
Peçanha, Dedé, Luiz Carlos, Fernando Pilar (Edson Di 80), Renato Que (Furtado 69), Ricardinho, Tiago Valente, Antonielton, Edson (Márcio Carioca 80), Mangualde, Filipe Anunciação.
Yellow Card(s): Tiago Valente 90+3

UD LEIRIA

UEFA INTERTOTO CUP

Third Round - FK Hajduk Kula (SRB)
A 0-1
Fernando, Alhandra (Sougou 68), Cadu Silva (Toñito 56), Renato Assunç Éder, Paulo César (Maciel 53), Laranjeiro, Faria, Éder Gaúcho, Tiago, João
Yellow Card(s): Alhandra 59, João Paulo 82, Faria 87
H 4-1 *Éder (90+3), Laranjeiro (97p, 120p), Sougou (112) (aet)*
Fernando, Cadu Silva (Paulo César 54), Renato Assunção, Éder, Laranjeiro, Sougou, Faria, Éder Gaúcho, Tiago, João Paulo (Jessui 66), Toñito (Alhand
Yellow Card(s): Renato Assunção 54, Éder 106, Sougou 118

UEFA CUP

Second Qualifying Round - Maccabi Netanya FC (ISR)
H 0-0
Fernando, Alhandra (N'Gal 58), Faria, Toñito (Cadu Silva 69), Éder, Rer Assunção, Éder Gaúcho, Paulo César, Marco, Sougou, Laranjeiro.
Yellow Card(s): Éder Gaúcho 63, Éder 66
A 1-0 *N'Gal (84)*
Fernando, Cadu Silva, Hugo Costa (Bruno Miguel 46), Faria, Renato Assunção (Alhandra 50), Tiago, Éder, João Paulo, Paulo César, Sougou (N'Gal 60), Laranjeiro.
Yellow Card(s): Laranjeiro 80

: Round - Bayer 04 Leverkusen (GER)
3 *João Paulo (29)*
ındo, Alhandra (Sougou 61), Cadu Silva (Toñito 65), Éder, Tiago, Éder
:ho, Paulo César, Laranjeiro, Łukasiewicz (Faria 49), Bruno Miguel, João Paulo.
Card(s): Faria 85
ɔw Card(s): Łukasiewicz 48, Faria 52, Éder Gaúcho 78, Faria 85
2 *Cadu Silva (3), João Paulo (21), Laranjeiro (90)*
ando, Alhandra (Marco 53), Cadu Silva, Hugo Costa, Toñito (Zongo
Éder Gaúcho, Maciel (N'Gal 62), Tiago, João Paulo, Laranjeiro, Sougou.
ɔw Card(s): Cadu Silva 35, João Paulo 42, Toñito 67, Marco 67, Tiago 78

REPUBLIC OF IRELAND

DERRY CITY FC

UEFA CHAMPIONS LEAGUE

Qualifying Round - FC Pyunik (ARM)

ngs, Farren (Hynes 85), Hargan, Hutton, Martyn, McCallion, McCourt,
ynn (Deery 57), Molloy, Morrow (McHugh 67), Oman.
w Card(s): Oman 90

ngs, Brennan, Deery (Higgins 82), Kelly, Martyn, McCallion, McCourt
n 65), McHugh, Molloy (O'Halloran 40), Morrow, Oman.
w Card(s): Jennings 17, Kelly 35, O'Halloran 56

DROGHEDA UNITED FC

UEFA CUP

Qualifying Round - SP Libertas (SMR)
Zayed (44)
ır, Gray (Webb 67), Tambouras, Shelley, Ristilä, Zayed (Grant 71),
O'Keefe (Baker 79), Gartland, Whelan, Robinson.
Keegan (11, 48), Byrne (57)
ır, Keegan, Tambouras, Shelley, Ristilä, Zayed, Byrne (Bradley 63),
Gartland, Keddy (O'Keefe 75), Robinson (Baker 60).

ıd Qualifying Round - Helsingborgs IF (SWE)
Zayed (54)
ır, Baker (Keegan 78), Byrne, Gartland, Keddy (Cahill 51), Ristilä
46), Robinson, Shelley, Webb, Zayed, Gavin.
ı Card(s): Baker 49, Robinson 86

ır, Byrne, Cahill, Gartland, Keddy (Bates 55), Keegan, Robinson
ın 79), Shelley, Webb, Zayed (O'Keefe 74), Gavin.
ı Card(s): Gartland 78

SAINT PATRICK'S ATHLETIC FC

UEFA CUP

First Qualifying Round - Odense BK (DEN)
H 0-0
Ryan, Brennan, Fahey, Keane (Mulcahy 63), Rogers, A. Murphy, Gibson (Foley-Sheridan 88), Guy (O'Connor 90), Paisley, Maguire, Quigley.
A 0-5
Ryan, Brennan, Kirby, Fahey, Keane (Paisley 16), Rogers, A. Murphy (O'Connor 59), Gibson, Guy, Maguire, Quigley (Foley-Sheridan 79).
Yellow Card(s): Gibson 11

CORK CITY FC

UEFA INTERTOTO CUP

First Round - Valur Reykjavík (ISL)
A 2-0 *O'Brien (7), Kearney (66)*
Devine, O'Brien, O'Donovan, O'Flynn (Softić 74), Woods, Gamble, Kelly (Behan 90+1), Murphy (Ci. Lordan 78), Murray, Horgan, Kearney.
Yellow Card(s): Gamble 56
H 0-1
Devine, O'Brien (Softić 90), O'Donovan, O'Flynn (Behan 73), Woods, Gamble, Kelly, Murphy (Ci. Lordan 82), Murray, Horgan, Kearney.
Yellow Card(s): Devine 66, Kelly 82, O'Donovan 87, Kearney 90+2

Second Round - Hammarby (SWE)
H 1-1 *O'Donovan (10)*
Devine, Healy, O'Donovan, O'Flynn (McSweeney 61), Woods, Gamble, Kelly (Ci. Lordan 79), Farrelly (Murphy 70), Murray, Horgan, Kearney.
Yellow Card(s): Healy 56, McSweeney 88
A 0-1
Devine, Farrelly, O'Donovan, O'Flynn, Woods, Gamble, Kelly, Healy, Murray, Horgan (Ci. Lordan 88), Kearney (Behan 83).
Yellow Card(s): O'Donovan 33, Murray 40, Gamble 47, Behan 90

ROMANIA

FC DINAMO 1948 BUCUREŞTI

UEFA CHAMPIONS LEAGUE

Third Qualifying Round - S.S. Lazio (ITA)
A 1-1 *Dănciulescu (22)*
Lobonţ, Blay, Cristea, Dănciulescu, Niculescu, Pulhac, Zicu (Opriţa 7; Chiacu 74), Izvoreanu, Năstase (Goian 32), Radu, Ropotan.
Red Card(s): Goian 90+1
Yellow Card(s): Ropotan 12, Cristea 31, Blay 57, Izvoreanu 61, Goian 88, Goian 90+1
H 1-3 *Bratu (27)*
Lobonţ, Blay, Cristea, Dănciulescu (Munteanu 71), Mărgăritescu (Niculescu 58), Pulhac, Bratu, Opriţa (Chiacu 58), Năstase, Radu, Ropotan.
Yellow Card(s): Pulhac 75

UEFA CUP

First Round - IF Elfsborg (SWE)
H 1-2 *Niculescu (8)*
Lobonţ, Cristea, Dănciulescu, Goian, Munteanu (Izvoreanu 69), Niculescu

(Bratu 46), Opriţa (Mărgăritescu 46), Pulhac, Galliquio, Radu, Ropotan.
Yellow Card(s): Ropotan 43
A 1-0 *Dănciulescu (31)*
Lobonţ, Pulhac, Moţi, Mărgăritescu (Ropotan 89), Munteanu, Dănciulescu, Bratu (Ganea 80), Cristea, Opriţa (Chiacu 65), Radu, Galliquio.
Yellow Card(s): Pulhac 20, Moţi 37, Dănciulescu 43, Mărgăritescu 45+2, Cristea 65

FC STEAUA BUCUREŞTI

UEFA CHAMPIONS LEAGUE

Second Qualifying Round - Zagłębie Łubin (POL)
A 1-0 *Goian (55)*
Cernea, Goian, Golański (Neşu 73), Rădoi, Marin, Rada, Neaga, Nicoliţă (Bădoi 77), Lovin, Croitoru (Petre 87), Dică.
Yellow Card(s): Golański 6, Nicoliţă 44, Lovin 77, Cernea 90
H 2-1 *Nicoliţă (37), Zaharia (83)*
Zapata, Golański, Rădoi, Marin, Rada, Petre, Neaga (Zaharia 80), Nicoliţă (Bicfalvi 92), Lovin, Croitoru (Bădoi 71), Dică.
Yellow Card(s): Marin 50, Croitoru 62, Bădoi 78

Third Qualifying Round - FC BATE Borisov (BLR)
A 2-2 *Goian (60), Dică (85)*
Zapata, Croitoru (Bicfalvi 53), Dică, Goian, Golański, Marin, Neaga, Nicoliţă (Zaharia 73), Rada (Lovin 59), Rădoi, Pleşan.
Yellow Card(s): Rădoi 29, Pleşan 56, Golański 86
H 2-0 *Zaharia (12), Neaga (54)*
Zapata, Dică, Goian, Lovin (Bicfalvi 56), Marin, Neaga (Croitoru 69), Neşu, Nicoliţă, Petre, Rada, Zaharia (Bădoi 53).
Yellow Card(s): Neşu 26, Dică 64

Group H
Match 1 - SK Slavia Praha (CZE)
A 1-2 *Goian (33)*
Zapata, Goian, Rada, Petre, Dică, Cristocea (Croitoru 53), Nicoliţă, Marin, Iacob (Badea 71), Lovin (Surdu 62), Bădoi.
Yellow Card(s): Goian 13, Lovin 27, Croitoru 88
Match 2 - Arsenal FC (ENG)
H 0-1
Zapata, Rada, Petre, Badea (Iacob 60), Dică, Emeghara, Nicoliţă, Baciu, Marin, Neaga (Zaharia 77), Surdu (Bădoi 84).
Yellow Card(s): Marin 18, Rada 32
Match 3 - Sevilla FC (ESP)
A 1-2 *Petre (63)*
Zapata, Goian, Rada, Petre, Dică (Badea 46), Emeghara, Nicoliţă, Marin, Iacob (Zaharia 71), Croitoru, Surdu (Neaga 46).
Yellow Card(s): Marin 6, Croitoru 75, Zaharia 84
Match 4 - Sevilla FC (ESP)
H 0-2
Zapata, Goian, Rada, Petre, Dică, Emeghara, Neşu, Nicoliţă, Iacob (Surdu 61), Lovin, Croitoru (Badea 46).
Yellow Card(s): Emeghara 20, Rada 56
Match 5 - SK Slavia Praha (CZE)
H 1-1 *Badea (12)*
Zapata, Goian, Rada, Petre, Badea (Cristocea 89), Dică, Emeghara, Neşu, Lovin (Bicfalvi 65), Neaga, Croitoru (Surdu 76).
Yellow Card(s): Croitoru 44
Match 6 - Arsenal FC (ENG)
A 1-2 *Zaharia (68)*
Zapata, Goian, Rada, Petre, Badea (Golański 81), Dică, Emeghara, Cristocea (Surdu 57), Neşu, Lovin, Neaga (Zaharia 64).
Yellow Card(s): Neaga 38

No	Player	Nat	DoB	Aps	(s)	Gl
Goalkeepers						
1	Róbinson Zapata	COL	30/9/78	6		
Defenders						
3	Dorin Goian		12/12/80	5		1
4	Paweł Golański	POL	12/10/82		(1)	
5	Ionuţ Rada		6/7/82	6		
13	Ifeanyi Emeghara	NGA	24/3/84	5		
15	Mihai Neşu		19/2/83	3		
17	Eugen Baciu		25/5/80	1		
18	Petre Marin		8/9/73	3		
29	Valentin Bădoi		16/12/75	1	(1)	
Midfielders						
7	Eric Bicfalvi		5/2/88		(1)	
8	Ovidiu Petre		22/3/82	6		1
14	Vasilică Cristocea		27/9/80	2	(1)	
16	Bănel Nicoliţă		7/1/85	4		
20	Florin Lovin		11/2/82	4		
26	Marius Croitoru		2/10/80	3	(1)	
Attackers						
9	Valentin Badea		23/10/82	3	(3)	1
10	Nicolae Dică		9/5/80	6		
19	Victoraş Iacob		14/10/80	3	(1)	
25	Adrian Neaga		4/6/79	3	(1)	
30	Dorel Zaharia		21/2/78		(3)	1
84	Romeo Surdu		12/1/84	2	(4)	

FC RAPID BUCUREŞTI

UEFA CUP

First Round - 1. FC Nürnberg (GER)
A 0-0
Andrade, Boya, Božović, Buga (Burdujan 46), Césinha (Mazilu 90+1), Grigore, Grigorie (Dică 63), Maftei, Măldărăşanu, Perja, Săpunaru.
Yellow Card(s): Grigorie 29, Boya 35, Božović 37
H 2-2 *Césinha (15), Lazăr (90+3)*
Andrade, Boya (Burdujan 63), Božović, Buga, Césinha, Constantin, Gri (Lazăr 46), Grigorie (Mazilu 58), Maftei, Măldărăşanu, Săpunaru.
Yellow Card(s): Lazăr 81

CFR 1907 CLUJ

UEFA CUP

Second Qualifying Round - Anorthosis Famagusta FC (CYP)
H 1-3 *Trică (69p)*
Stăncioiu, Panin (Fredy 46), Tony (Manuel José 70), Cadú, Sandberg, Mureşan, Trică, Semedo, Didy, Culio, Leão (Fabbiani 52).
Yellow Card(s): Leão 32, Trică 51, Fredy 89
A 0-0
Stăncioiu, Tony, Panin, Manuel José, Mureşan, Trică (Minteuan 69), De (Culio 58), Cadú, Fabbiani, Sousa, Didy (Semedo 46).
Yellow Card(s): Sousa 17, Fabbiani 22, Deac 55

FC OŢELUL GALAŢI

UEFA INTERTOTO CUP

nd Round - FK Slavija Sarajevo (BIH)

uskas, Gado (Cârjă 59), Giurgiu, Jula (Ilie 81), Labukas (Kim 55),
, Paraschiv, Semeghin, Sârghi, Stan, Szekely.
ard(s): Nogo 78
w Card(s): Nogo 41, Cârjă 72, Nogo 78
Jula (31, 42), Paraschiv (70)
uskas, Giurgiu, Ilie, Jula (Elek 83), Labukas (Boghiu 73), Paraschiv,
ghin, Sârghi, Stan (Cârjă 77), Szekely, Kim.
w Card(s): Szekely 44, Boghiu 90

Round - Trabzonspor (TUR)
Stan (27), Paraschiv (86)
uskas, Giurgiu, Jula (Ilie 88), Kim, Nogo, Paraschiv, Semeghin
kov 80), Sârghi, Stan (Labukas 69), Szekely, Zhelev.
w Card(s): Stan 62, Paraschiv 64, Zhelev 66, Giurgiu 88, Labukas 90+3
Szekely (12), Jula (90+1p)
uskas, Giurgiu, Jula, Kim (Ratnikov 70), Nogo, Paraschiv, Semeghin,
i, Stan (Labukas 14), Szekely (Ilie 90+1), Zhelev.
w Card(s): Szekely 53, Zhelev 64

UEFA CUP

nd Qualifying Round - PFC Lokomotiv Sofia (BUL)
Semeghin (74)
uskas, Gado, Giurgiu, Ilie (Ratnikov 55), Jula, Kim, Labukas (Cârjă 55),
, Paraschiv, Semeghin, Sârghi (Ngapounou 69).
w Card(s): Semeghin 30

Gado, Jula, Kim, Labukas (Ratnikov 60), Nogo (Cârjă 19), Paraschiv,
ghin, Szekely, Zhelev, Ngapounou (Ilie 83).
w Card(s): Nogo 14, Gado 87

CF GLORIA 1922 BISTRIŢA

UEFA INTERTOTO CUP

Round - OFK Grbalj (MNE)
Zaharia (3), Florea (88)
şanu, Astilean, Sepsi, Soare (Peres 46), Zaharia, Damian, Bucur (Băd
âju, Dumitra, Toma, Dobre (Florea 71).
v Card(s): Bucur 20
Coroian (42)
şanu, Abrudan, Nalaţi, Rus, Sepsi, Zaharia (Băd 90), Coroian,
ra, Tilincă (Damian 82), Toma, Dobre.
v Card(s): Dumitra 69, Toma 81

nd Round - Maccabi Haifa FC (ISR)
Tilincă (12), Zaharia (41)
Abrudan, Coroian (Câju 60), Costea (Bozeşan 74), Dobre, Nalaţi, Rus
escu 82), Sepsi, Tilincă, Toma, Zaharia.
v Card(s): Rus 16, Dobre 63, Nalaţi 88
(aet; 3-2 on pens)
Abrudan, Coroian, Costea (Damian 64), Dobre, Frăsinescu, Nalaţi
tra 62), Sepsi, Tilincă (Băd 96), Toma, Zaharia.
Yellow Card(s): Toma 7, Albuţ 58, Băd 90+8

Third Round - Club Atlético de Madrid (ESP)
H 2-1 *Zaharia (8), Tilincă (39)*
Albuţ, Abrudan, Coroian, Dobre, Frăsinescu, Nalaţi, Rus, Sepsi, Tilincă, Zaharia, Ragipović.
Yellow Card(s): Frăsinescu 29
A 0-1
Tătăruşanu, Abrudan, Coroian, Costea (Damian 78), Dobre, Frăsinescu, Nalaţi, Rus (Turcu 46), Sepsi (Dumitra 73), Tilincă, Toma.
Yellow Card(s): Sepsi 21, Costea 51, Tilincă 81

RUSSIA

PFC CSKA MOSKVA

UEFA CHAMPIONS LEAGUE

Group G
Match 1 - PSV Eindhoven (NED)
A 1-2 *Vágner Love (89)*
Mandrykin, Šemberas, Ignashevich, A. Berezutskiy, Vágner Love, Jô, Krasić, Zhirkov, Dudu Cearense, V. Berezutskiy, Rahimić (Eduardo Ratinho 78).
Yellow Card(s): Rahimić 73, Dudu Cearense 82
Match 2 - Fenerbahçe SK (TUR)
H 2-2 *Krasić (50), Vágner Love (53p)*
Mandrykin, Šemberas, Ignashevich, A. Berezutskiy, Vágner Love, Jô, Krasić, Zhirkov, Dudu Cearense (Aldonin 90), V. Berezutskiy, Rahimić.
Yellow Card(s): Krasić 66, Zhirkov 78
Match 3 - FC Internazionale Milano (ITA)
H 1-2 *Jô (32)*
Mandrykin, Ignashevich, A. Berezutskiy (Grigoryev 45), Daniel Carvalho, Jô, Krasić, Zhirkov, Dudu Cearense (Eduardo Ratinho 42; Janczyk 76), Aldonin, V. Berezutskiy, Rahimić.
Yellow Card(s): Dani Carvalho 61
Match 4 - FC Internazionale Milano (ITA)
A 2-4 *Jô (23), Vágner Love (31)*
Akinfeev, A. Berezutskiy, Dani Carvalho, Vágner Love, Jô (Aldonin 46), Krasić, Zhirkov, Dudu Cearense (Taranov 83), V. Berezutskiy (Eduardo Ratinho 69), Rahimić, Grigoryev.
Yellow Card(s): Rahimić 39, Dudu Cearense 45, V. Berezutskiy 65, Zhirkov 72
Match 5 - PSV Eindhoven (NED)
H 0-1
Akinfeev, Šemberas, Ignashevich, Ramón (Caner 61), A. Berezutskiy, Zhirkov, Janczyk, Dudu Cearense (Odiah 73), Aldonin, V. Berezutskiy, Rahimić (Grigoryev 86).
Yellow Card(s): A. Berezutskiy 13, Dudu Cearense 57, Rahimić 64
Match 6 - Fenerbahçe SK (TUR)
A 1-3 *Edu Dracena (30og)*
Akinfeev, Šemberas, Ignashevich, Ramón (Odiah 46), A. Berezutskiy, Zhirkov, Janczyk, Eduardo Ratinho (Taranov 77), Aldonin, Grigoryev, Caner (Mamayev 46).
Yellow Card(s): Caner 37, Šemberas 41, Zhirkov 90

No	Player	Nat	DoB	Aps	(s)	Gls
Goalkeepers						
1	Veniamin Mandrykin		30/8/81	3		
35	Igor Akinfeev		8/4/86	3		
Defenders						
2	Deividas Šemberas	LTU	2/8/78	4		
4	Sergei Ignashevich		14/7/79	5		
6	Aleksei Berezutskiy		20/6/82	6		
15	Chidi Odiah	NGA	17/12/83		(2)	
24	Vasiliy Berezutskiy		20/6/82	5		

50	Anton Grigoryev		13/12/85	2	(2)	
Midfielders						
5	Ramón	BRA	24/5/88	2		
7	Daniel Carvalho	BRA	1/3/83	2		
11	Pavel Mamayev		17/9/88		(1)	
17	Miloš Krasić	SRB	1/11/84	4		1
18	Yuriy Zhirkov		20/8/83	6		
20	Dudu Cearense	BRA	15/4/83	5		
21	Eduardo Ratinho	BRA	17/9/87	1	(3)	
22	Yevgeniy Aldonin		22/1/80	3	(2)	
25	Elvir Rahimić	BIH	4/4/76	5		
39	Ivan Taranov		22/6/86		(2)	
88	Caner Erkin	TUR	4/10/88	1	(1)	
Attackers						
9	Vágner Love	BRA	11/6/84	3		3
10	Jô	BRA	20/3/87	4		2
19	Dawid Janczyk	POL	6/7/89	2	(1)	

FC SPARTAK MOSKVA

UEFA CHAMPIONS LEAGUE

Third Qualifying Round - Celtic FC (SCO)
H 1-1 *Pavlyuchenko (42)*
Pletikosa, Bystrov (Kalynychenko 74), Kováč, Pavlyuchenko, Mozart, Şoava, Stranzl, Titov, Torbinskiy, Welliton, Shishkin.
Yellow Card(s): Stranzl 90+3
A 1-1 *Pavlyuchenko (45) (aet; 3-4 on pens)*
Pletikosa, Bystrov (Kalynychenko 95), Kováč, Pavlyuchenko, Mozart, Şoava, Stranzl, Titov, Torbinskiy (Boyarintsev 103), Welliton (Dedura 82), Shishkin.
Red Card(s): Stranzl 84
Yellow Card(s): Shishkin 83, Torbinskiy 101

UEFA CUP

First Round - BK Häcken (SWE)
H 5-0 *Pavlyuchenko (6, 13), Welliton (19, 55), Titov (56)*
Pletikosa, Bystrov (Boyarintsev 68), Dedura, Géder, Pavlyuchenko, Mozart (Sabitov 61), Welliton (Dzyuba 59), Şoava, Titov, Torbinskiy, Shishkin.
A 3-1 *Titov (7), Bazhenov (80), Dzyuba (90+1)*
Pletikosa, Boyarintsev, Dedura, Kalynychenko (Bazhenov 76), Kováč, Pavlyuchenko (Welliton 57), Mozart, Titov (Sabitov 61), Dzyuba, Kudryashov, Parshivlyuk.
Yellow Card(s): Kováč 58, Pletikosa 70

Group E
Match 1 - Bayer 04 Leverkusen (GER)
H 2-1 *Pavlyuchenko (63p), Mozart (77p)*
Pletikosa, Géder, Ivanov, Stranzl, Kováč, Torbinskiy (Boyarintsev 82), Mozart, Titov, Kalynychenko (Shishkin 87), Pavlyuchenko, Welliton (Dedura 89).
Yellow Card(s): Torbinskiy 53, Pavlyuchenko 54
Match 2 - AC Sparta Praha (CZE)
A 0-0
Pletikosa, Stranzl, Géder, Dedura, Ivanov, Şoava, Torbinskiy, Titov, Covalciuc, Welliton (Bazhenov 87), Dzyuba (Prudnikov 78).
Match 3 - FC Zürich (SUI)
H 1-0 *Titov (57)*
Pletikosa, Stranzl, Titov, Pavlyuchenko, Torbinskiy, Covalciuc, Bazhenov (Boyarintsev 71), Dzyuba (Welliton 58), Shishkin, Ivanov (Şoava 46), Dedura.
Yellow Card(s): Torbinskiy 29, Pavlyuchenko 86
Match 4 - Toulouse FC (FRA)
A 1-2 *Dzyuba (61p)*
Khomich, Stranzl, Kudryashov, Géder, Shishkin, Parshivlyuk, Covalciuc, Şoava, Dzyuba, Prudnikov (Bystrov 83), Welliton.
Yellow Card(s): Welliton 56, Dzyuba 90

Round of 32 - Olympique de Marseille (FRA)
A 0-3
Pletikosa, Stranzl, Mozart, Pavlenko (Prudnikov 83), Titov, Welliton, Ko Maidana (Dineyev 65), Bystrov (Pavlyuchenko 69), Parshivlyuk, Kudryashov.
Yellow Card(s): Kováč 16, Kudryashov 66
H 2-0 *Pavlenko (39), Pavlyuchenko (85)*
Pletikosa, Parshivlyuk (Dedura 88), Stranzl, Kováč, Kudryashov, Pavler Mozart, Titov (Bystrov 76), Maidana, Pavlyuchenko, Welliton (Dzyuba
Yellow Card(s): Maidana 30, Mozart 77

FC LOKOMOTIV MOSKVA

UEFA CUP

First Round - FC Midtjylland (DEN)
A 3-1 *Samedov (61), Bilyaletdinov (69), Sychev (90+1)*
Pelizzoli, Yefimov, Asatiani, Bilyaletdinov, Gurenko, Ivanović, Maminc Odemwingie, Sennikov, Sychev, Yanbayev (Samedov 51).
Yellow Card(s): Gurenko 52, Yefimov 55, Sychev 63, Maminov 86, Bilyaletdinov 90+3
H 2-0 *Bilyaletdinov (11), Maminov (15)*
Pelizzoli, Yefimov (Rodolfo 41), Asatiani, Bilyaletdinov, Gurenko, Ivanc Maminov (Samedov 59), Odemwingie, Sennikov (Yanbayev 46), Spa Sychev.

Group B
Match 1 - Club Atlético de Madrid (ESP)
H 3-3 *Bilyaletdinov (27), Odemwingie (61, 64)*
Pelizzoli, Ivanović, Yefimov (Yanbayev 60), Rodolfo, Sennikov, Spahić, Gu (Maminov 90), Bilyaletdinov, Samedov (Cociş 81), Odemwingie, Sychev.
Yellow Card(s): Ivanović 39
Match 2 - Aberdeen FC (SCO)
A 1-1 *Ivanović (45)*
Pelizzoli, Ivanović, Asatiani, Rodolfo, Sennikov, Spahić, Gurenko, Sam (Cociş 79), Bilyaletdinov, Sychev, Odemwingie.
Yellow Card(s): Spahić 57, Odemwingie 69, Asatiani 75
Match 3 - FC København (DEN)
H 0-1
Pelizzoli, Rodolfo, Spahić, Ivanović, Maminov, Odemwingie (Samedo Sychev (Cociş 85), Traoré, Asatiani, Gurenko, Bilyaletdinov.
Red Card(s): Spahić 88
Yellow Card(s): Spahić 29, Asatiani 60, Gurenko 80, Samedov 82, Spa
Match 4 - Panathinaikos FC (GRE)
A 0-2
Pelizzoli, Ivanović, Yanbayev, Asatiani, Sennikov, Gurenko, Samedov (Kuz 64), Maminov (Fomin 82), Bilyaletdinov, Traoré (Korchagin 86), Cociş.
Yellow Card(s): Traoré 17, Asatiani 21

FC ZENIT ST. PETERSBURG

UEFA CUP

Second Qualifying Round - FC ViOn Zlaté Moravce (SVK)
A 2-0 *Hagen (38), Ionov (90+2)*

'eyev (Čontofalský 59), Anyukov, Denisov (Maximov 75), Domínguez,
ι, Lombaerts, Pogrebnyak (Ionov 75), Širl, Tymoshchuk, Zyryanov, Kim.
w Card(s): Širl 90
Pogrebnyak (10), Maximov (61), Kim (71)
ɔfalský, Anyukov, Denisov, Hagen, Ionov, Lombaerts, Pogrebnyak, Širl
lo 68), Tymoshchuk (Radimov 46), Zyryanov (Maximov 46), Kim.
w Card(s): Tymoshchuk 44

Round - R. Standard de Liège (BEL)
Arshavin (36, 65), Kim (84)
ɔfalský, Anyukov, Arshavin, Domínguez, Hagen, Kim, Lombaerts,
ɛbnyak, Širl, Tymoshchuk, Zyryanov.
w Card(s): Hagen 24, Arshavin 59, Širl 81
Pogrebnyak (79)
ɔfalský, Anyukov, Arshavin, Denisov (Domínguez 71), Kim, Lombaerts,
ɛbnyak, Širl (Maximov 87), Škrteľ, Tymoshchuk, Zyryanov (Radimov 76).
Card(s): Pogrebnyak 79
w Card(s): Pogrebnyak 67, Pogrebnyak 79, Maximov 90

p A
h 1 - AZ Alkmaar (NED)
Tymoshchuk (43p)
ɔfalský, Kim, Lombaerts, Škrteľ, Anyukov, Širl, Tymoshchuk, Zyryanov,
nguez (Maximov 81), Arshavin, Fatih Tekke.
w Card(s): Fatih Tekke 85
h 2 - Larissa FC (GRE)
Pogrebnyak (39), Zyryanov (70), Fatih Tekke (78)
ɔfalský, Škrteľ, Kim, Lombaerts, Pogrebnyak (Radimov 72), Arshavin
ínguez 46), Širl, Zyryanov, Anyukov, Ricksen (Fatih Tekke 72),
ɔshchuk.
w Card(s): Ricksen 55
h 3 - 1. FC Nürnberg (GER)
Pogrebnyak (76), Ionov (79)
ɔfalský, Kim, Lombaerts (Ionov 72), Škrteľ, Anyukov, Širl, Tymoshchuk,
ɪnov, Domínguez (Radimov 80), Arshavin, Pogrebnyak.
w Card(s): Anyukov 24, Škrteľ 48
h 4 - Everton FC (ENG)

'eyev, Anyukov (Lee 78), Škrteľ, Lombaerts, Kim, Tymoshchuk,
ɪnov, Širl, Arshavin, Domínguez (Horshkov 47), Pogrebnyak (Hagen 61).
Card(s): Lombaerts 30
w Card(s): Pogrebnyak 22, Širl 34

ıd of 32 - Villarreal CF (ESP)
Pogrebnyak (63)
feyev, Kim, Anyukov, Križanac, Shirokov, Širl, Tymoshchuk, Zyryanov,
ılin, Arshavin, Pogrebnyak.
w Card(s): Anyukov 35, Pogrebnyak 73, Kim 78
Pogrebnyak (31)
feyev, Lombaerts (Križanac 34), Anyukov, Kim, Shirokov, Fayzulin (Lee
), Zyryanov, Tymoshchuk, Širl, Arshavin (Horshkov 86), Pogrebnyak.
Card(s): Shirokov 47, Širl 82
w Card(s): Shirokov 13, Širl 24, Kim 45, Shirokov 47, Malafeyev 65,
2, Zyryanov 88, Križanac 90+3

ıd of 16 - Olympique de Marseille (FRA)
Arshavin (82)
feyev, Anyukov, Gorshkov, Križanac, Kim, Ricksen (Denisov 70),
ɔshchuk, Zyryanov, Fayzulin (Radimov 81), Arshavin, Pogrebnyak.
w Card(s): Kim 27, Ricksen 32
Pogrebnyak (39, 78)
feyev, Anyukov, Shirokov, Križanac, Širl, Fayzulin (Fatih Tekke 75),
ɪnov, Denisov, Tymoshchuk, Arshavin, Pogrebnyak.
w Card(s): Denisov 10, Tymoshchuk 64, Arshavin 90+3

rter-Final - Bayer 04 Leverkusen (GER)
1 *Arshavin (20), Pogrebnyak (52), Anyukov (61), Denisov (64)*
feyev, Križanac, Pogrebnyak, Arshavin, Širl, Shirokov, Zyryanov,
ılin, Anyukov, Denisov, Tymoshchuk.
w Card(s): Križanac 23
1
feyev, Križanac, Pogrebnyak, Arshavin, Širl, Shirokov, Zyryanov,
ılin (Radimov 87), Anyukov, Denisov, Tymoshchuk.

Semi-Final - FC Bayern München (GER)
A 1-1 *Lúcio (60og)*
Malafeyev, Križanac, Pogrebnyak, Arshavin, Širl, Shirokov, Zyryanov, Fayzulin, Ricksen, Denisov, Tymoshchuk.
Yellow Card(s): Ricksen 17, Fayzulin 28, Širl 75, Arshavin 79
H 4-0 *Pogrebnyak (4, 73), Zyryanov (39), Fayzulin (54)*
Malafeyev, Križanac, Domínguez (Lee 89), Pogrebnyak, Shirokov, Zyryanov, Fayzulin, Anyukov, Denisov (Ionov 90+2), Tymoshchuk, Horshkov.
Yellow Card(s): Pogrebnyak 76

Final - Rangers FC (SCO)
H 2-0 *Denisov (72), Zyryanov (90+4)*
Malafeyev, Križanac, Fatih Tekke, Arshavin, Širl, Shirokov, Zyryanov, Fayzulin (Kim 90+3), Anyukov, Denisov, Tymoshchuk.
Yellow Card(s): Denisov 72, Malafeyev 90+2

FC RUBIN KAZAN

UEFA INTERTOTO CUP

Second Round - Zalaegerszegi TE (HUN)
A 3-0 *Volkov (21, 66, 80p)*
Koļinko, Gatcan (Noboa 52), Jean Narde, Ryazantsev, Salukvadze, Sinyov, Gabriel, Vasilyev, Volkov (Fábio 86), Bairamov (Gitselov 78), Sibaya.
H 2-0 *Volkov (37p), Jean Narde (67)*
Koļinko, Jean Narde, Noboa, Ryazantsev (Nesterenko 69), Sinyov, Gabriel, Vasilyev, Volkov, Bairamov (Yarkin 46), Fyodorov, Sibaya (Kireyev 46).
Yellow Card(s): Sibaya 45

Third Round - SK Rapid Wien (AUT)
A 1-3 *Ryazantsev (29)*
Koļinko, Bairamov, Budylin, Gabriel (Salukvadze 76), Jean Narde, Noboa, Ryazantsev, Sibaya (Fyodorov 87), Sinyov, Vasilyev (Ayupov 90+1), Volkov.
Red Card(s): Gabriel 73, Salukvadze 78
Yellow Card(s): Jean Narde 28, Bairamov 31, Vasilyev 53, Volkov 81
H 0-0
Koļinko, Bairamov (Kireyev 76), Budylin, Fyodorov, Gatcan (Ayupov 77), Jean Narde, Ryazantsev, Sibaya, Sinyov, Vasilyev (Yarkin 59), Volkov.
Red Card(s): Sibaya 66
Yellow Card(s): Gatcan 25

SAN MARINO

SS MURATA

UEFA CHAMPIONS LEAGUE

First Qualifying Round - Tampere United (FIN)
H 1-2 *Protti (43)*
Scalabrelli, Agostini, Albani, Bollini (Donati 72), D'Orsi, Aldair (B. Gasperoni 46), Protti, Teodorani, C. Valentini, Vannoni (Marani 84), Vitaioli.
Yellow Card(s): Protti 34, Agostini 82
A 0-2
Scalabrelli, Agostini, Albani, Bollini (Conti 72), D'Orsi, Gasperoni (Molinari 84), Teodorani, C. Valentini, Vannoni, Vitaioli, Zaboul (Bacciocchi 71).
Yellow Card(s): C. Valentini 26

SP LIBERTAS

UEFA CUP

First Qualifying Round - Drogheda United FC (IRL)
H 1-1 *Pari (77)*
Ceccoli, Sottili, Macerata, Fambri, Tarini, Gazzi, D. Simoncini (Pari 53), Cevoli, Santini, Semprini, Cavalli (Nanni 71).
Yellow Card(s): Semprini 55, Gazzi 69
A 0-3
Ceccoli, Sottili, Macerata, Fambri, Tarini, Gazzi, Valentini, Cevoli, Santini (Angelini 89), Semprini (Pari 58), Nanni (Toccaceli 79).
Yellow Card(s): Tarini 23, Cevoli 23, Santini 32

SCOTLAND

CELTIC FC

UEFA CHAMPIONS LEAGUE

Third Qualifying Round - FC Spartak Moskva (RUS)
A 1-1 *Hartley (21)*
Brown, Kennedy, McManus, Nakamura, Naylor, Vennegoor of Hesselink (McGeady 83), Wilson, Donati (Sno 75), S. Brown, Hartley, McDonald (Caldwell 80).
Yellow Card(s): Naylor 40, S. Brown 69
H 1-1 *McDonald (27) (aet; 4-3 on pens)*
Boruc, Caldwell, McManus, Nakamura, Naylor (O'Dea 110), Vennegoor of Hesselink, Wilson, Donati, S. Brown, McDonald (Żurawski 97), McGeady (Riordan 104).
Yellow Card(s): Caldwell 29, Riordan 118

Group D
Match 1 - FC Shakhtar Donetsk (UKR)
A 0-2
Boruc, Naylor, Caldwell, S. Brown, Vennegoor of Hesselink (Żurawski 85), Hartley, Wilson, Donati, Nakamura (McGeady 65), McDonald (Killen 68), McManus.
Yellow Card(s): S. Brown 17
Match 2 - AC Milan (ITA)
H 2-1 *McManus (61), McDonald (89)*
Boruc, Naylor, Caldwell, S. Brown, Hartley, Donati, Jarošík (Killen 84), Perrier-Doumbé (Kennedy 79), McDonald, McManus, McGeady (Nakamura 84).
Yellow Card(s): S. Brown 31, Donati 69, McDonald 71
Match 3 - SL Benfica (POR)
A 0-1
Boruc, Naylor, Caldwell, S. Brown, Hartley, Donati (Sno 63), Jarošík, Killen (McDonald 74), Kennedy, McManus, McGeady.
Yellow Card(s): McGeady 28, Killen 55, Hartley 72
Match 4 - SL Benfica (POR)
H 1-0 *McGeady (45)*
Boruc, Naylor, Caldwell, S. Brown (Sno 89), Vennegoor of Hesselink (Killen 66), Hartley, Jarošík (Donati 66), McDonald, Kennedy, McManus, McGeady.
Match 5 - FC Shakhtar Donetsk (UKR)
H 2-1 *Jarošík (45), Donati (90+2)*
Boruc, Naylor (Donati 16), Caldwell, S. Brown, Vennegoor of Hesselink (Killen 79), Hartley, Jarošík, McDonald, Kennedy (Pressley 42), McManus, McGeady.
Yellow Card(s): Jarošík 43, Vennegoor of Hesselink 56, Caldwell 80

Match 6 - AC Milan (ITA)
A 0-1
Boruc, Caldwell, S. Brown, Hartley, Pressley, Donati (Sno 71), Jarošík (Żurawski 78), McDonald (Vennegoor of Hesselink 65), McManus, McGeady, O'Dea.
Yellow Card(s): S. Brown 46

Round of 16 - FC Barcelona (ESP)
H 2-3 *Vennegoor of Hesselink (16), Robson (38)*
Boruc, Naylor, Caldwell, Vennegoor of Hesselink (Samaras 55), Hartley (D 65), Robson, Nakamura, McDonald, McManus, McGeady, Caddis (Wilson
Yellow Card(s): Robson 20, Hartley 61, Samaras 90+3
A 0-1
Boruc, Naylor, Caldwell, S. Brown, Vennegoor of Hesselink (Samaras 5 Hartley (McDonald 78), Wilson, Donati (Sno 46), Nakamura, McManus McGeady.
Yellow Card(s): S. Brown 89

No	Player	Nat	DoB	Aps	(s)	G
Goalkeepers						
1	Artur Boruc	POL	20/2/80	8		
Defenders						
3	Lee Naylor	ENG	19/3/80	7		
5	Gary Caldwell		12/4/82	8		
12	Mark Wilson		5/6/84	2	(1)	
17	Steven Pressley		11/10/73	1	(1)	
24	Jean-Joël Perrier-Doumbé	CMR	27/9/78	1		
41	John Kennedy		18/8/83	3	(1)	
44	Stephen McManus		10/9/82	8		
48	Darren O'Dea	IRL	4/2/87	1		
52	Paul Caddis		19/4/88	1		
Midfielders						
8	Scott Brown		25/6/85	7		
11	Paul Hartley		19/10/76	8		
15	Evander Sno	NED	9/4/87		(4)	
18	Massimo Donati	ITA	26/3/81	5	(3)	
20	Jiří Jarošík	CZE	27/10/77	5		
25	Shunsuke Nakamura	JPN	24/6/78	3	(1)	
46	Aiden McGeady	IRL	4/4/86	7	(1)	
Attackers						
7	Maciej Żurawski	POL	12/9/76		(2)	
9	Giorgos Samaras	GRE	21/2/85		(2)	
10	Jan Vennegoor of Hesselink	NED	7/11/78	5	(1)	
19	Barry Robson		7/11/78	1		
27	Scott McDonald	AUS	21/8/83	6	(2)	
33	Chris Killen	NZL	8/10/81	1	(4)	

RANGERS FC

UEFA CHAMPIONS LEAGUE

Second Qualifying Round - FK Zeta (MNE)
H 2-0 *Weir (55), Novo (72)*
McGregor, Boyd (Broadfoot 63), Adam (Novo 46), Ferguson, Hemdani Weir, Papac, Cuéllar, McCulloch, Hutton, Darcheville (Šebo 83).
Red Card(s): Hutton 59
Yellow Card(s): McCulloch 26, Hutton 58, Hutton 59, Novo 60, Cuélla
A 1-0 *Beasley (81)*
McGregor, Ferguson, Hemdani, Thomson (Adam 87), Weir, Broadfoot, Papac, Beasley, Cuéllar, McCulloch, Darcheville (Novo 61).
Yellow Card(s): Broadfoot 58

Third Qualifying Round - FK Crvena Zvezda (SRB)
H 1-0 *Novo (90)*
McGregor, Beasley (Novo 65), Broadfoot, Cuéllar, Darcheville (Cousin

uson, Hemdani, Hutton, McCulloch, Thomson, Weir.
0
regor, Cuéllar, Darcheville (Cousin 69), Ferguson, Hemdani, Hutton, ulloch, Papac, Thomson, Weir, Whittaker (Beasley 78).
ow Card(s): Hutton 82, McCulloch 84

up E
ch 1 - VfB Stuttgart (GER)
1 *Adam (62), Darcheville (75p)*
regor, Hutton, Weir, Papac, Ferguson, Hemdani, Thomson, Adam sley 67), Darcheville (Novo 83), Cuéllar, Whittaker (Faye 86).
ow Card(s): Hutton 75, Thomson 78, Faye 90
ch 2 - Olympique Lyonnais (FRA)
0 *McCulloch (23), Cousin (48), Beasley (53)*
regor, Hutton, Weir, Papac, Ferguson, Hemdani, Thomson, Beasley m 90), Cuéllar, McCulloch (Novo 81), Cousin (Whittaker 66).
ow Card(s): Weir 45, Ferguson 81, Thomson 87
ch 3 - FC Barcelona (ESP)
0
regor, Hutton, Weir, Papac, Ferguson, Thomson, Novo (Beasley 72), n, Cuéllar, McCulloch, Cousin.
ow Card(s): Thomson 36, Papac 50, Weir 71
ch 4 - FC Barcelona (ESP)
2
regor, Hutton, Weir, Papac, Ferguson, Hemdani, Adam (Darcheville Beasley (Novo 69), Cuéllar, McCulloch, Cousin (Naismith 78).
ch 5 - VfB Stuttgart (GER)
3 *Adam (27), Ferguson (70)*
regor, Hutton, Weir, Papac, Ferguson, Hemdani, Thomson, Darcheville sin 82), Beasley (Naismith 49), Cuéllar, McCulloch (Adam 26).
ow Card(s): McCulloch 24, Adam 87, Hutton 89
ch 6 - Olympique Lyonnais (FRA)
3
regor, Hutton, Weir, Papac (Darcheville 71), Ferguson, Hemdani (Boyd Thomson, Cuéllar, McCulloch, Whittaker, Cousin (Naismith 46).
Card(s): Darcheville 90+1
ow Card(s): Thomson 10, Hutton 23, Cuéllar 56

Player	Nat	DoB	Aps	(s)	Gls
keepers					
Allan McGregor		31/1/82	6		
nders					
Alan Hutton		30/11/84	6		
David Weir		10/5/70	6		
Saša Papac	BIH	7/2/80	6		
Carlos Cuéllar	ESP	23/8/81	6		
Steven Whittaker		16/6/84	2	(1)	
ielders					
Barry Ferguson		2/2/78	6		1
Brahim Hemdani	ALG	15/3/78	5		
Kevin Thomson		14/10/84	5		
Charles Adam		10/12/85	3	(2)	2
DaMarcus Beasley	USA	24/5/82	3	(2)	1
Lee McCulloch		14/5/78	5		1
Amdy Faye	SEN	12/3/77		(1)	
kers					
Kris Boyd		18/8/83		(1)	
Nacho Novo	ESP	26/3/79	1	(3)	
Jean-Claude Darcheville	FRA	25/7/75	2	(2)	1
Daniel Cousin	GAB	7/2/77	4	(1)	1
Steven Naismith		14/9/86		(3)	

UEFA CUP

nd of 32 - Panathinaikos FC (GRE)
0
regor, Broadfoot, Cuéllar, Weir, Papac, Novo (Burke 81), Ferguson, s, Hemdani, Adam (Cousin 67), McCulloch.
ow Card(s): Adam 45
1 *Novo (81)*
regor, Weir, Papac (Dailly 66), Ferguson, Hemdani (Burke 69), Boyd, o, Adam (Naismith 66), Broadfoot, Cuéllar, Davis.
ow Card(s): Burke 86

Round of 16 - Werder Bremen (GER)
H 2-0 *Cousin (45), Davis (48)*
McGregor, Weir, Papac, Ferguson, Hemdani, Adam, Broadfoot, Cuéllar, Cousin (McCulloch 75), Dailly, Davis.
Yellow Card(s): Hemdani 90
A 0-1
McGregor, Broadfoot, Weir, Cuéllar, Papac, Hemdani, Dailly, Ferguson, Davis, Adam (Whittaker 57), Novo (McCulloch 78).
Yellow Card(s): Adam 45

Quarter-Final - Sporting Clube de Portugal (POR)
H 0-0
McGregor, Weir, Papac, Ferguson, Hemdani, Thomson, Darcheville (Novo 72), Broadfoot, Cuéllar, McCulloch, Davis.
Yellow Card(s): Ferguson 13, Weir 88
A 2-0 *Darcheville (60), Whittaker (90+2)*
McGregor, Papac, Ferguson, Hemdani, Thomson, Darcheville (Cousin 72), Broadfoot, Cuéllar, McCulloch (Whittaker 78), Dailly, Davis.
Yellow Card(s): Thomson 49, Broadfoot 59, McCulloch 70, Ferguson 82, Papac 85

Semi-Final - ACF Fiorentina (ITA)
H 0-0
Alexander, Weir, Papac, Hemdani, Novo (Buffel 59), Darcheville (Cousin 60), Broadfoot, Cuéllar, Whittaker, Dailly, Davis.
A 0-0 *(aet; 4-2 on pens)*
Alexander, Weir, Papac, Ferguson, Hemdani, Thomson, Darcheville (Cousin 65), Broadfoot, Cuéllar, Whittaker, Davis (Novo 81).
Red Card(s): Cousin 109
Yellow Card(s): Thomson 28, Weir 70, Cousin 73, Cousin 109

Final - FC Zenit St. Petersburg (RUS)
A 0-2
Alexander, Weir, Papac (Novo 77), Ferguson, Hemdani (McCulloch 80), Thomson, Darcheville, Broadfoot, Cuéllar, Whittaker (Boyd 86), Davis.
Yellow Card(s): Broadfoot 90+4

ABERDEEN FC

UEFA CUP

First Round - FC Dnipro Dnipropetrovsk (UKR)
H 0-0
Langfield, Clark (Mair 90), McNamara (Foster 62), Severin, Ja. Smith, Nicholson, Miller, Hart, Diamond, Young (Lovell 71), Considine.
Yellow Card(s): Hart 90+2
A 1-1 *Mackie (28)*
Langfield, Clark, Mackie (Lovell 71), Severin, Ja. Smith (Mair 46), Nicholson, Hart, Diamond, Foster, Young, Considine.
Yellow Card(s): Considine 54, Foster 88

Group B
Match 1 - Panathinaikos FC (GRE)
A 0-3
Langfield, Hart, McNamara (De Visscher 75), Diamond, Foster, Considine (Mair 61), Severin (Aluko 86), Nicholson, Clark, Miller, Young.
Yellow Card(s): Severin 30
Match 2 - FC Lokomotiv Moskva (RUS)
H 1-1 *Diamond (27)*
Langfield, Hart, Diamond, Considine, Foster, Clark (Maguire 67), Nicholson, Severin, Aluko (De Visscher 81), Miller (Lovell 85), Young.
Match 3 - Club Atlético de Madrid (ESP)
A 0-2
Langfield, Hart, Byrne, McNamara (Clark 34), Diamond, Severin (Maguire 76), Ja. Smith (De Visscher 44), Foster, Touzani, Miller, Young.
Yellow Card(s): Hart 45, Langfield 56

Match 4 - FC København (DEN)
H 4-0 *Ja. Smith (47, 55), Antonsson (71og), Foster (83)*
Langfield, Hart, Byrne, Diamond, Considine, Nicholson, Severin, Clark, Aluko (Foster 59), Miller, Ja. Smith (Maguire 74).
Yellow Card(s): Nicholson 38

Round of 32 - FC Bayern München (GER)
H 2-2 *Walker (24), Aluko (41)*
Langfield, Maybury, Diamond, Considine, Mair, Nicholson, Walker (Touzani 87), Severin, Aluko, Mackie (Lovell 68), Miller.
Yellow Card(s): Mair 54
A 1-5 Lovell (83)
Langfield, Maybury, Diamond, Considine, Foster, Nicholson, Aluko (Lovell 79), Severin, Walker (Maguire 62), Mackie (De Visscher 72), Miller.
Yellow Card(s): Maybury 11, Walker 26, Aluko 35, Nicholson 42, Mackie 57

DUNFERMLINE ATHLETIC FC

UEFA CUP

Second Qualifying Round - BK Häcken (SWE)
H 1-1 *Hamilton (1)*
McKenzie (Murdoch 10), Bamba, Burchill, Glass, Hamilton, Harper, Shields, Simmons (Morrison 77), Wilson, Young, Thomson (Morrison 46).
Yellow Card(s): Shields 55, Burchill 62, Young 69
A 0-1
Gallacher, Bamba, Crawford, Glass, Hamilton, Harper, Morrison (Burchill 67), Morrison (McManus 53), Shields (Simmons 77), Wilson, Young.
Red Card(s): Hamilton 56
Yellow Card(s): Hamilton 27, Hamilton 56, Shields 74, Harper 79

SERBIA

FK CRVENA ZVEZDA

UEFA CHAMPIONS LEAGUE

Second Qualifying Round - FC Levadia Tallinn (EST)
H 1-0 *Koroman (35)*
Ranđelović, Milijaš, Koroman, Barcos (F. Đorđević 46), Lucas (Molina 64), Gueye, Castillo, Anđelković, Tutorić, Basta (Bronowicki 74), Milovanović.
Yellow Card(s): Basta 28
A 1-2 *Burzanović (37)*
Ranđelović, Koroman, Barcos (Milijaš 71), Burzanović (Trajković 54), Lucas, Gueye, Castillo, Anđelković, Tutorić, Basta (Bronowicki 61), Milovanović.
Yellow Card(s): Burzanović 20, Basta 59

Third Qualifying Round - Rangers FC (SCO)
A 0-1
Ranđelović, Anđelković, Bronowicki, Castillo, Lucas, Gueye, Koroman, Milijaš, Rašković (Molina 70), Tutorić, F. Đorđević (Milovanović 82).
Yellow Card(s): Tutorić 13, Anđelković 29, Koroman 36, Rašković 66, F. Đorđević 68, Molina 81, Castillo 90+2
H 0-0
Ranđelović, Anđelković, Basta, Burzanović (Barcos 69), Castillo, Lucas, Gueye, Koroman, Milijaš (Rašković 73), Tutorić, F. Đorđević.
Yellow Card(s): Gueye 44, Burzanović 65, Basta 75, Koroman 90+4

UEFA CUP

First Round - Groclin Grodzisk Wielkopolski (POL)
A 1-0 *Basta (19)*
Ranđelović, Anđelković (Bogdanović 90), Barcos (F. Đorđević 75), Bast
Bronowicki, Castillo, Lucas, Gueye, Milijaš, Salas (Bajalica 46), Tutorić.
Yellow Card(s): Lucas 45
H 1-0 *Castillo (43)*
Ranđelović, Anđelković, Basta, Castillo (Bogdanović 46), Lucas, Gueye, Koroman (Trišović 90+1), Milijaš, Molina, Tutorić, Ještrović (Barcos 66).

Group F
Match 1 - FC Bayern München (GER)
H 2-3 *Koroman (16), Milijaš (74)*
Ranđelović, Anđelković, Gueye, Basta (Bajalica 46), Milijaš, Koroman, Tutorić, Lucas, Molina (Bogdanović 90+2), Castillo, Barcos (Burzanović
Red Card(s): Bajalica 90+1
Yellow Card(s): Molina 64, Milijaš 75, Bajalica 76, Bajalica 90+1
Match 2 - Aris Thessaloniki FC (GRE)
A 0-3
Ranđelović, Gueye (Burzanović 83), Bronowicki, Anđelković, Basta, Mil
Koroman, Tutorić, Molina (Jestrović 79), Castillo, Lucas (Bogdanović 6
Yellow Card(s): Koroman 39
Match 3 - Bolton Wanderers FC (ENG)
H 0-1
Ranđelović, Bronowicki (Anđelković 80), Tutorić, Bajalica, Basta, Milijaš (Burzanović 73), Koroman, Lucas, Molina, Milovanović, Ještrović (F. Đorđevi
Yellow Card(s): Koroman 90
Match 4 - SC Braga (POR)
A 0-2
Banović, Basta (Lucas 18), V. Đorđević, Bajalica, Anđelković, Milovanov
Milijaš, Castillo, Salas (Molina 60), Koroman, Barcos (F. Đorđević 89).
Yellow Card(s): Koroman 84

FK PARTIZAN

UEFA CUP

First Qualifying Round - HŠK Zrinjski (BIH)
A 6-1 *Diatta (32, 60, 63), Maletić (40), Jovetić (48), Lazetić (80)*
D. Božovic, Juca, Moreira (Zajić 81), Jovetić (Neb. Marinković 76), Diatt (Lazetić 67), Lazarević, P. Lazić, Maletić, Mihajlov, Rukavina, Sikimić.
Yellow Card(s): Jovetić 71
H 5-0 *Maletić (4), Moreira (32), Jovetić (37, 51, 71)*
D. Božovic, Juca, Moreira, Jovetić (Neb. Marinković 75), Diatta (Veselin 56), Đ. Lazic (P. Lazić 68), Maletić, Mihajlov, Rnić, Rukavina, Obradović.
Yellow Card(s): Rnić 61
(disqualified for crowd misbehaviour)

FK VOJVODINA

UEFA CUP

First Qualifying Round - Hibernians FC (MLT)
H 5-1 *Despotović (21, 42, 89p), Đurić (60), Kačar (84)*
Kahriman, Popović, Stošić, Cotra (Kačar 56), Buač, Đurić, Marković, Leri (Šarac 79), Stojčev (Drakulić 60), Pekarić, Despotović.
Yellow Card(s): Marković 40, Buač 51, Kačar 85, Drakulić 90+2

Kuereb (30og), Despotović (62)
an (Brkić 81), Popović, Stošić (Milutinović 66), Buač (Smiljanić 85), Lerinc, Šarac, Kačar, Pekarić, Despotović, Tadić.
Card(s): Đurić 32, Popović 52, Tadić 70

d Qualifying Round - Club Atlético de Madrid (ESP)

an, Buač (Smiljanić 63), Despotović, Đurić, Kačar (Trivunović 66), vić, Milutinović, Pekarić, Popović (Milutinović 73), Stošić, Tadić.
rd(s): Milutinović 47
Card(s): Stošić 4, Milutinović 35, Milutinović 47, Marković 82
Buač (39)
an, Buač, Despotović, Đurić, Kačar, Pekarić, Popović, Stošić avljev 45), Trivunović (Milutinović 82), Tadić (Aleksić 59), Kizito.
Card(s): Stošić 41, Popović 88

FK BEŽANIJA

UEFA CUP

ualifying Round - KS Besa (ALB)
Dalović (37), Đurovski (57p)
ć, Baranin, Đalović, Đurovski (Milić 77), Osmanović, Pavlović, anin, Stančeski (Mihajlović 63), Vanić, Vukajlović (Nikolić 46), Ilić.
Card(s): Vukajlović 20, Stančeski 27, Baranin 41, Nikolić 77, Milić 82

ić, Baranin, Djalović, Đurovski (Pavlović 74), Osmanović (Milić 84), ć, Putinčanin, Stančeski, Vanić, Vukajlović, Mihajlović.
rd(s): Janković 73
Card(s): Pavlović 50, Stančeski 72

FK HAJDUK KULA

UEFA INTERTOTO CUP

d Round - NK Maribor (SVN)

Pavićević (Dojkić 85), Radanović, Radivojević, Bogić, Bulatović, v (Komazec 62), L. Fejsa, Vasiljević, Habenšus, Kozoš (Perić 68).
Card(s): Radivojević 36, Pavićević 72
asiljević (15), Komazec (30, 67p), Perić (38), Radanović (45+1)
Perić (Dojkić 53), Radanović, Radivojević, Bogić, Bulatović ović 84), D. Fejsa (Habenšus 19), L. Fejsa, Vasiljević, Komazec, KozoAs.
Card(s): Perić 7, Radanović 86

Round - UD Leiria (POR)
Perić (42)
Bogić, Bulatović, Dojkić, Habenšus, Kozoš, Perić (Jovanović 89), vić, Šodić, Vasiljević (Zelić 90+3), Komazec.
Card(s): Bogić 18, Habenšus 32, Bulatović 82, Đuričić 83
ogić (107p) (aet)
Bogić, Bulatović, D. Fejsa (Vasiljević 91), L. Fejsa, Habenšus (Dojkić ozoš, Pavićević, Perić (Zelić 90), Radivojević, Šodić.
rd(s): Šodić 120
Card(s): Šodić 94, Vasiljević 96

SLOVAKIA

MŠK ŽILINA

UEFA CHAMPIONS LEAGUE

First Qualifying Round - F91 Dudelange (LUX)
A 2-1 *Jež (48p), Lietava (73)*
Kuciak, Breška (Vladavić 69), Devátý, Hubočan, Jež, Leitner, Nemec (Lietava 59), Porázik (Štyvar 84), Štrba, Vomáčka, Pekarík.
Yellow Card(s): Devátý 30, Nemec 41, Vomáčka 41
H 5-4 *Devátý (8), Lietava (11), Štyvar (29, 75), Vomáčka (66)*
Kuciak, Breška (Vladavić 45), Devátý, Hubočan, Jež, Leitner, Štrba, Štyvar (Pečálka 89), Vomáčka, Pekarík, Lietava (Nemec 59).
Yellow Card(s): Vomácka 66

Second Qualifying Round - SK Slavia Praha (CZE)
H 0-0
Kuciak, Breška (Ančic 70), Devátý (Belák 90+3), Jež, Leitner, Pečálka, Porázik, Štrba, Štyvar (Lietava 59), Pekarík, Szórád.
Yellow Card(s): Pečálka 86
A 0-0 *(aet; 3-4 on pens)*
Kuciak, Breška (Vladavić 116), Devátý, Jež, Leitner, Lietava (Štyvar 54), Pečálka, Porázik (Belák 73), Štrba, Vomácka, Pekarík.

FC VION ZLATÉ MORAVCE

UEFA CUP

First Qualifying Round - FC Alma-Ata (KAZ)
H 3-1 *Gibala (51, 78), Greguška (71)*
Peškovič, Choma, Greguška, Juska, Kuračka, Číž, Černák, Pavlenda, Hözl (Gibala 46), Ondrejka (Farkaš 90+2), Chren (Pelegrini 86).
Yellow Card(s): Ondrejka 40
A 1-1 *Černák (77)*
Peškovič, Choma, Gibala (Chren 60), Greguška, Juska (Farkaš 70), Kuračka, Číž, Černák, Pavlenda, Hözl, Ondrejka (Balát 81).
Yellow Card(s): Černák 64, Gibala 78, Balát 88

Second Qualifying Round - FC Zenit St. Petersburg (RUS)
H 0-2
Peškovič, Choma, Číž, Gibala, Greguška, Hözl, Juska (Pelegrini 82), Kuračka, Ondrejka (Balát 46), Pavlenda, Klabal.
A 0-3
Peškovič, Černák, Choma, Číž (Žembera 75), Gibala, Greguška, Hözl (Farkaš 58), Juska (Chren 68), Kuračka, Ondrejka, Pavlenda.

FC ARTMEDIA PETRŽALKA

UEFA CUP

First Qualifying Round - FC Zimbru Chişinău (MDA)
H 1-1 *M. Ďurica (21p)*
Kamenár, Borbély, Burák (P. Ďurica 77), Čišovský, Dosoudil, M. Ďurica, Guédé (Gajdoš 71), Halenár, Kozák, Mráz (Obžera 55), Oravec.
Red Card(s): Dosoudil 87
Yellow Card(s): Guédé 22, Mráz 50, Borbély 66
A 2-2 *Guédé (73), Borbély (90+4)*
Kamenár, Borbély, Burák, Čišovský, M. Ďurica, Fodrek (Obžera 62), Gajdoš (Čvirik 87), Guédé, Halenár, Kozák, Mráz (P. Ďurica 67).
Red Card(s): P. Ďurica 90+4
Yellow Card(s): Čišovský 10, Fodrek 58, Obžera 90+1, Kozák 90+1, M. Ďurica 90+2

Second Qualifying Round - FC MIKA (ARM)
A 1-2 *Fodrek (66)*
Kamenár, T. Farkaš, Urbánek (Mráz 55), Čišovský, M. Ďurica (Čvirik 86), Fodrek, Gajdoš (Piroška 46), Guédé, Sninský, Kozák, Obžera.
Yellow Card(s): Čišovský 76
H 2-0 *Obžera (5, 72)*
Hýll, Borbély, Burák, Dosoudil, M. Ďurica (T. Farkaš 66), Fodrek, Guédé, Halenár (Piroška 75), Kozák, Obžera (Gajdoš 90), Urbánek.
Yellow Card(s): Piroška 65

First Round - Panathinaikos FC (GRE)
H 1-2 *Urbánek (46)*
Hýll, Borbély, Čišovský, Dosoudil, T. Farkaš (P. Ďurica 79), Fodrek, Guédé, Halenár (Mráz 87), Kozák, Obžera (Piroška 79), Urbánek.
Red Card(s): Borbély 89
Yellow Card(s): Dosoudil 60, Borbély 66, Obžera 67, Borbély 89
A 0-3
Hýll, Burák, Čišovský, Dosoudil, Fodrek (Gajdoš 77), Guédé, Halenár, Kozák, Obžera (Mráz 64), Piroška (T. Farkaš 46), Urbánek.
Red Card(s): Burák 43
Yellow Card(s): Čišovský 27, Obžera 28, Hýll 73, Kozák 73

ŠK SLOVAN BRATISLAVA

UEFA INTERTOTO CUP

First Round - FC Differdange 03 (LUX)
A 2-0 *Poliaček (32), Sedlák (86)*
Kiss, Chlebek, Hanek, Kosmeľ, Kubala, Masaryk (Meszároš 86), Poliaček (Sedlák 58), Slovák, Struhár, Szabó, Ibragimov.
Yellow Card(s): Chlebek 80
H 3-0 *Meszároš (4), Masaryk (56), Sylvestr (78)*
Kiss, Chlebek (Kubala 64), Hanek, Kosmeľ, Masaryk, Meszároš (Sylvestr 74), Poliaček (Breznaník 58), Sedlák, Slovák, Struhár, Szabó.
Yellow Card(s): Chlebek 17

Second Round - SK Rapid Wien (AUT)
A 1-3 *Slovák (88)*
Kiss, Dobrotka, Hanek, Kosmeľ, Kubala (Meszároš 85), Masaryk, Sedlák (Breznaník 46), Slovák, Struhár, Szabó, Iżvolt (Poliaček 73).
Yellow Card(s): Kosmeľ 22, Dobrotka 35, Hanek 45, Breznaník 70
H 1-0 *Dobrotka (18)*
Kiss, Breznaník (Poliaček 65), Dobrotka, Hanek, Iżvolt (Kosmeľ 65), Kubala, Masaryk (Meszároš 79), Slovák, Švestka, Sylvestr, Szabó.
Yellow Card(s): Szabó 15, Sylvestr 35, Švestka 60

SLOVENIA

NK DOMŽALE

UEFA CHAMPIONS LEAGUE

First Qualifying Round - KF Tirana (ALB)
H 1-0 *Janković (44)*
Nemec, Aljančič, Elsner, Varga, Grabič (Peškar 85), Juninho (Jusufi 67 Janković (Dvorančič 60), Žinko, Brezič, Ljubijankič, Kirm.
Yellow Card(s): Varga 24
A 2-1 *Ljubijankič (30, 77)*
Nemec, Aljančič, Elsner, Grabič, Juninho (Varga 13), Janković (Peška Žinko, Brezič, Zahora (Apatič 88), Ljubijankič, Kirm.
Yellow Card(s): Kirm 25

Second Qualifying Round - NK Dinamo Zagreb (CRO)
H 1-2 *Žeželj (87)*
Nemec, Aljančič, Brezič, Elsner, Grabič (Jusufi 79), Janković (Žeželj 6 Kirm, Ljubijankič, Varga, Zahora, Žinko.
Yellow Card(s): Janković 21, Žinko 40
A 1-3 *Zahora (27)*
Nemec, Aljančič, Apatič (Grabič 43), Brezič, Elsner, Janković (Knezov Kirm, Ljubijankič, Varga, Zahora (Žeželj 61), Žinko.
Yellow Card(s): Elsner 20, Aljančič 44, Brezič 70

FC KOPER

UEFA CUP

First Qualifying Round - NK Široki Brijeg (BIH)
A 1-3 *Viler (8)*
Hasič, Bordon (Sečič 64), M. Božič, Handanagič, Mejač, Rajčevič, Vile Božičič (R. Božič 90+1), Galun, Plut (Sučevič 88), Volaš.
Yellow Card(s): Plut 41, Volaš 49
H 2-3 *Volaš (34), Mejač (82)*
Hasič, Bordon (Plut 46), M. Božič, R. Božič (Mejač 28), Rajčevič, Sečič, Božičič, Galun (Klun 85), Ibeji, Volaš.
Yellow Card(s): Volaš 82

NK GORICA

UEFA CUP

First Qualifying Round - FK Rabotnički (MKD)
H 1-2 *Matavž (83)*
Simčič, Lerant, Osterc (Đukič 62), Dedič, Demirović, Jogan, N. Kovač Šuler, Živec, Matavž, Velikonja (Cvijanovič 74).
Yellow Card(s): Velikonja 46
A 1-2 *Demirović (85p)*

, Lerant, Đukič (Osterc 46), Dedič, Demirović, N. Kovačevič, Šuler, Kršić 82), Cvijanovič, Komel, Matavž (Velikonja 67).
v Card(s): Komel 13, Demirović 28, N. Kovačevič 76

NK MARIBOR

UEFA INTERTOTO CUP

ound - Birkirkara FC (MLT)
Makriev (40, 47), Pekič (87)
ar, Mihelič (Mujkanovič 58), Tomažič Šeruga, Pekič, Cipot, Pečnik, j (Mezga 41), Lungu, Popović, Makriev (Diarra 66), Samardžić.
v Card(s): Pregelj 0
Mezga (55), Vračko (78)
vič, Mihelič, Tomažič Šeruga, Pekič, Cipot (Medved 21), Pečnik, novič (Vračko 50), Lungu (Diarra 69), Mezga, Popović, Makriev.
v Card(s): Vuksanovič 29, Medved 65

d Round - FK Hajduk Kula (SRB)
Makriev (29), Samardžić (51)
ar, Mihelič (Bačinovič 76), Samardžić, Tomažič Šeruga, Brulc (Vračko ečnik, Vuksanovič, Lungu, Mezga (Medved 61), Popović, Makriev.
v Card(s): Pečnik 49, Tomažič Šeruga 56, Samardžić 88, Makriev 90+3

ar, Mihelič, Tomažič Šeruga, Mezga, Brulc, Pečnik, Vuksanovič (Zajc ıngu, Popović, Makriev, Samardžić.
v Card(s): Pečnik 35, Brulc 58, Mihelič 75

SPAIN

REAL MADRID CF

UEFA CHAMPIONS LEAGUE

p C
h 1 - Werder Bremen (GER)
Raúl (16), Van Nistelrooy (74)
as, Sergio Ramos, Cannavaro, Raúl (Robben 84), Gago, Marcelo, Guti the 77), Van Nistelrooy, Higuaín (Robinho 69), Metzelder, Sneijder.
w Card(s): Van Nistelrooy 88
h 2 - S.S. Lazio (ITA)
Van Nistelrooy (8, 61)
as, Sergio Ramos, Cannavaro, Diarra, Raúl (Saviola 83), Robben aín 79), Marcelo, Guti, Heinze, Van Nistelrooy, Sneijder (Drenthe 88).
w Card(s): Heinze 63
h 3 - Olympiacos CFP (GRE)
Raúl (2), Robinho (68, 83), Balboa (90+3)
as, Míchel Salgado (Higuaín 64), Sergio Ramos, Raúl (Torres 88), Gago, ho, Marcelo, Guti, Van Nistelrooy, Metzelder, Sneijder (Balboa 82).
w Card(s): Míchel Salgado 29, Robinho 65
h 4 - Olympiacos CFP (GRE)

as, Sergio Ramos, Cannavaro, Diarra, Raúl (Balboa 82), Gago, Robinho la 82), Marcelo, Heinze, Van Nistelrooy, Sneijder.
w Card(s): Casillas 10, Sergio Ramos 15
h 5 - Werder Bremen (GER)
Robinho (14), Van Nistelrooy (71)

Casillas, Pepe, Sergio Ramos, Diarra, Raúl, Gago (Higuaín 61), Robinho (Robben 75), Marcelo, Guti, Van Nistelrooy, Metzelder.
Yellow Card(s): Pepe 61, Sergio Ramos 80, Diarra 88
Match 6 - S.S. Lazio (ITA)
H 3-1 *Júlio Baptista (13), Raúl (15), Robinho (36)*
Casillas, Pepe, Sergio Ramos, Cannavaro, Diarra, Raúl, Robinho (Robben 46), Marcelo, Van Nistelrooy (Higuaín 73), Júlio Baptista, Sneijder (Guti 46).

Round of 16 - AS Roma (ITA)
A 1-2 *Raúl (8)*
Casillas, Sergio Ramos, Cannavaro, Diarra (Drenthe 79), Raúl, Gago, Robben (Júlio Baptista 79), Guti, Heinze, Van Nistelrooy, Torres.
Yellow Card(s): Diarra 23, Torres 64, Sergio Ramos 69
H 1-2 *Raúl (75)*
Casillas, Míchel Salgado (Torres 64), Pepe, Cannavaro, Diarra (Drenthe 61), Raúl, Gago, Robinho, Guti, Heinze, Júlio Baptista (Soldado 85).
Red Card(s): Pepe 71
Yellow Card(s): Heinze 14, Pepe 41, Pepe 71, Robinho 76, Guti 81

No	Player	Nat	DoB	Aps	(s)	Gls
Goalkeepers						
1	Iker Casillas		20/5/81	8		
Defenders						
2	Míchel Salgado		22/10/75	2		
3	Pepe	POR	26/2/83	3		
4	Sergio Ramos		30/3/86	7		
5	Fabio Cannavaro	ITA	13/9/73	6		
12	Marcelo	BRA	12/5/88	6		
15	Royston Drenthe	NED	8/4/87		(4)	
16	Gabriel Heinze	ARG	19/4/78	4		
21	Christoph Metzelder	GER	5/11/80	3		
22	Miguel Torres		28/1/86	1	(2)	
Midfielders						
6	Mahamadou Diarra	MLI	18/5/81	6		
8	Fernando Gago	ARG	10/4/86	6		
11	Arjen Robben	NED	23/1/84	2	(3)	
14	Guti		31/10/76	6	(1)	
19	Júlio Baptista	BRA	1/10/81	2	(1)	1
23	Wesley Sneijder	NED	9/6/84	5		
24	Javier Ángel Balboa		13/5/85		(2)	1
Attackers						
7	Raúl González		27/6/77	8		5
9	Roberto Soldado		27/5/85		(1)	
10	Robinho	BRA	25/1/84	5	(1)	4
17	Ruud van Nistelrooy	NED	1/7/76	7		4
18	Javier Saviola	ARG	11/12/81		(2)	
20	Gonzalo Higuaín	ARG	10/12/87	1	(4)	

FC BARCELONA

UEFA CHAMPIONS LEAGUE

Group E
Match 1 - Olympique Lyonnais (FRA)
H 3-0 *Clerc (21og), Messi (82), Henry (90+1)*
Víctor Valdés, Milito, Márquez, Xavi (Giovani 79), Ronaldinho (Iniesta 66), Zambrotta, Henry, Messi (Bojan 88), Deco, Abidal, Touré.
Yellow Card(s): Touré 33, Henry 71
Match 2 - VfB Stuttgart (GER)
A 2-0 *Puyol (53), Messi (67)*
Víctor Valdés, Márquez (Puyol 7; Sylvinho 64), Xavi, Iniesta, Ronaldinho (Bojan 82), Henry, Messi, Deco, Thuram, Abidal, Oleguer.
Yellow Card(s): Messi 41
Match 3 - Rangers FC (SCO)
A 0-0

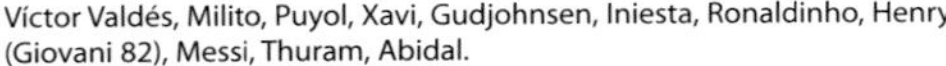

Víctor Valdés, Milito, Puyol, Xavi, Gudjohnsen, Iniesta, Ronaldinho, Henry (Giovani 82), Messi, Thuram, Abidal.
Yellow Card(s): Milito 48, Abidal 63
Match 4 - Rangers FC (SCO)
H 2-0 *Henry (6), Messi (43)*
Víctor Valdés, Milito, Puyol (Oleguer 85), Xavi, Iniesta (Gudjohnsen 71), Ronaldinho (Bojan 77), Henry, Messi, Thuram, Abidal, Touré.
Match 5 - Olympique Lyonnais (FRA)
A 2-2 *Iniesta (3), Messi (58p)*
Víctor Valdés, Milito, Puyol, Xavi, Gudjohnsen (Ronaldinho 71), Iniesta, Zambrotta (Márquez 82), Messi, Abidal, Touré, Bojan.
Yellow Card(s): Touré 44, Messi 59, Xavi 60, Puyol 61
Match 6 - VfB Stuttgart (GER)
H 3-1 *Giovani (36), Eto'o (57), Ronaldinho (67)*
Jorquera, Milito, Márquez, Puyol, Xavi (Marc Crosas 70), Gudjohnsen (Bojan 52), Eto'o (Iniesta 62), Ronaldinho, Sylvinho, Giovani, Thuram.
Yellow Card(s): Márquez 90+2

Round of 16 - Celtic FC (SCO)
A 3-2 *Messi (18, 79), Henry (52)*
Víctor Valdés, Milito, Márquez, Puyol, Iniesta, Ronaldinho (Eto'o 73), Henry (Gudjohnsen 88), Messi, Deco (Xavi 66), Abidal, Touré.
Yellow Card(s): Deco 30
H 1-0 *Xavi (3)*
Víctor Valdés, Puyol, Xavi (Gudjohnsen 82), Eto'o, Ronaldinho, Zambrotta, Sylvinho, Messi (Henry 38), Deco, Thuram, Touré (Edmílson 68).

Quarter-Final - FC Schalke 04 (GER)
A 1-0 *Bojan (12)*
Víctor Valdés, Milito, Puyol, Xavi, Iniesta, Eto'o (Giovani 82), Zambrotta, Henry, Abidal, Touré (Márquez 73), Bojan (Sylvinho 86).
Yellow Card(s): Milito 68, Giovani 90+2, Márquez 90+3, Puyol 90+5
H 1-0 *Touré (43)*
Víctor Valdés, Puyol, Xavi, Iniesta, Eto'o, Zambrotta, Henry (Gudjohnsen 90+1), Thuram, Abidal, Touré (Márquez 81), Bojan (Giovani 73).
Yellow Card(s): Puyol 63

Semi-Final - Manchester United FC (ENG)
H 0-0
Víctor Valdés, Milito, Márquez, Xavi, Iniesta, Eto'o, Zambrotta, Messi (Bojan 62), Deco (Henry 77), Abidal, Touré.
Yellow Card(s): Márquez 44
A 0-1
Víctor Valdés, Milito, Puyol, Xavi, Iniesta (Henry 61), Eto'o (Bojan 72), Zambrotta, Messi, Deco, Abidal, Touré (Gudjohnsen 88).
Yellow Card(s): Zambrotta 52, Deco 54, Touré 70

No	Player	Nat	DoB	Aps	(s)	Gls
Goalkeepers						
1	Víctor Valdés		14/1/82	11		
25	Albert Jorquera		3/3/79	1		
Defenders						
3	Gabriel Milito	ARG	7/9/80	9		
4	Rafael Márquez	MEX	13/2/79	5	(3)	
5	Carles Puyol		13/4/78	9	(1)	1
11	Gianluca Zambrotta	ITA	10/2/77	7		
15	Edmílson	BRA	10/7/76		(1)	
16	Sylvinho	BRA	12/4/74	2	(2)	
21	Lilian Thuram	FRA	1/1/72	6		
22	Éric Abidal	FRA	11/9/79	10		
23	Oleguer Presas		2/2/80	1	(1)	
Midfielders						
6	Xavi		25/1/80	11	(1)	1
8	Andrés Iniesta		11/5/84	9	(2)	1
20	Deco	POR	27/8/77	6		
24	Yaya Touré	CIV	13/5/83	9		1
26	Marc Crosas		9/1/88		(1)	
Attackers						
7	Eidur Gudjohnsen	ISL	15/9/78	3	(5)	
9	Samuel Eto'o	CMR	10/3/81	6	(1)	1
10	Ronaldinho	BRA	21/3/80	7	(1)	1
14	Thierry Henry	FRA	17/8/77	7	(3)	3
17	Giovani Dos Santos	MEX	11/5/89	1	(4)	1
19	Lionel Messi	ARG	24/6/87	9		
27	Bojan Krkić		28/8/90	3	(6)	

SEVILLA FC

UEFA CHAMPIONS LEAGUE

Third Qualifying Round - AEK Athens FC (GRE)
H 2-0 *Luís Fabiano (48), Kanouté (68)*
Palop, Luís Fabiano (Martí 71), Dragutinović, Fazio, Hinkel, Kanouté, M (Keita 46), Jesús Navas, Poulsen, Boulahrouz (Renato 46), Diego Capel.
Yellow Card(s): Maresca 42
A 4-1 *Luís Fabiano (31p, 45), Keita (40), Kerzhakov (53)*
Palop, Luís Fabiano (De Mul 46), Dragutinović, Escudé (Mosquera 60), F Kerzhakov, Jesús Navas, Poulsen (Maresca 62), Keita, Dani Alves, Diego

Group H
Match 1 - Arsenal FC (ENG)
A 0-3
Palop, Dragutinović, Dani Alves, Jesús Navas, Poulsen, Luís Fabiano (Kerz 46), Kanouté, Escudé, Diego Capel (Renato 67), Martí (Keita 66), Fazio.
Yellow Card(s): Dani Alves 74, Keita 85
Match 2 - SK Slavia Praha (CZE)
H 4-2 *Kanouté (8), Luís Fabiano (27), Escudé (58), Koné (68)*
Palop, Dragutinović, Dani Alves, Adriano (Hinkel 81), Jesús Navas (Du 75), Poulsen, Luís Fabiano (Koné 64), Kanouté, Escudé, Keita, Boulahr
Match 3 - FC Steaua Bucureşti (ROU)
H 2-1 *Kanouté (5), Luís Fabiano (17)*
Palop, Dragutinović, Dani Alves, Adriano, Jesús Navas, Poulsen, Luis Fabiano, Kanouté (Renato 71), Mosquera, Diego Capel (Martí 85), Kei
Yellow Card(s): Keita 32, Adriano 44
Match 4 - FC Steaua Bucureşti (ROU)
A 2-0 *Renato (25, 65)*
Palop, Dragutinović, Dani Alves, Adriano, Jesús Navas (Hinkel 89), Poulse Renato, Kanouté (Luís Fabiano 69), Mosquera, De Mul (Diego Capel 63),
Yellow Card(s): Kanouté 20, Adriano 54
Match 5 - Arsenal FC (ENG)
H 3-1 *Keita (24), Luís Fabiano (34), Kanouté (89p)*
Palop, Dragutinović, Dani Alves, Adriano (Martí 90), Jesús Navas, Pou Luís Fabiano (Kerzhakov 75), Kanouté, Keita, Crespo (Mosquera 64),
Yellow Card(s): Crespo 21, Adriano 44, Palop 50, Keita 90+1
Match 6 - SK Slavia Praha (CZE)
A 3-0 *Luís Fabiano (66), Kanouté (69), Dani Alves (87)*
De Sanctis, Dragutinović, Dani Alves, Jesús Navas, Renato (Maresca 64), Kanouté (Duda 70), Mosquera, Diego Capel, Martí, Koné (Luís Fabiano 59).
Yellow Card(s): Dragutinović 56

Round of 16 - Fenerbahçe SK (TUR)
A 2-3 *Edu Dracena (23og), Escudé (66)*
Palop, Dragutinović, Dani Alves, Duda (Diego Capel 63), Adriano, Jes Navas, Poulsen, Luis Fabiano, Kanouté, Escudé, Keita.
Yellow Card(s): Palop 69
H 3-2 *Dani Alves (5), Keita (9), Kanouté (41) (aet; 2-3 on pens)*
Palop, Dragutinović, Dani Alves, Adriano, Jesús Navas (Koné 105), Pou (Maresca 95), Luís Fabiano (Renato 78), Kanouté, Escudé, Diego Capel,
Yellow Card(s): Keita 67, Dani Alves 90

No	Player	Nat	DoB	Aps	(s)	G
Goalkeepers						
1	Andrés Palop		22/10/73	7		
13	Morgan De Sanctis	ITA	26/3/77	1		
Defenders						
3	Ivica Dragutinović	SRB	13/11/75	8		
4	Dani Alves	BRA	6/5/83	8		
14	Julien Escudé	FRA	17/8/79	4		

Player	Nat	DoB	Aps	(s)	Gls
Aquivaldo Mosquera	COL	22/6/81	3	(1)	
Khalid Boulahrouz	NED	28/12/81	1		
Andreas Hinkel	GER	26/3/82		(2)	
José Ángel Crespo		9/2/87	1		
Federico Fazio	ARG	17/3/87	2		
Lolo		22/8/84	1		
ders					
Duda	POR	27/6/80	1	(2)	
Adriano	BRA	26/10/84	6		
Christian Poulsen	DEN	28/2/80	7		
Renato	BRA	15/5/79	2	(3)	2
José Luis Martí		28/4/75	2	(2)	
Tom De Mul	BEL	4/3/86	1		
Seydou Keita	MLI	16/1/80	6	(1)	2
Enzo Maresca	ITA	10/2/80		(2)	
ers					
Jesús Navas		21/11/85	8		
Aleksandr Kerzhakov	RUS	27/11/82		(2)	
Luís Fabiano	BRA	8/11/80	6	(2)	4
Frédéric Kanouté	MLI	2/9/77	8		5
Diego Capel		16/2/88	4	(2)	
Arouna Koné	CIV	11/11/83	1	(2)	1

VALENCIA CF

UEFA CHAMPIONS LEAGUE

Qualifying Round - IF Elfsborg (SWE)
Vicente (14), Silva (58), Morientes (70)
res, Albelda, Albiol, Baraja, Silva, Marchena, Moretti, Vicente
ntes 59), Joaquín (Angulo 81), David Villa (Gavilán 78), Caneira.
ván Helguera (4), David Villa (90)
rand, Albiol, Gavilán, Silva (David Villa 61), Marchena, Moretti (Alexis
orientes (Arizmendi 56), Joaquín, Iván Iván Helguera, Sunday, Caneira.
Card(s): Iván Helguera 73

B
1 - FC Schalke 04 (GER)
David Villa (63)
res, Albiol, Marchena, Albelda, David Villa (Sunday 90), Morientes
endi 80), Angulo (Joaquín 75), Iván Helguera, Silva, Miguel, Moretti.
Card(s): Albelda 26, Marchena 52, Moretti 90+1
2 - Chelsea FC (ENG)
David Villa (9)
rand, Albiol, Marchena, Albelda (Baraja 75), David Villa, Morientes
59), Iván Helguera, Joaquín (Arizmendi 88), Silva, Miguel, Moretti.
Card(s): Marchena 79
3 - Rosenborg BK (NOR)

res, Albiol, Marchena (Baraja 67), Albelda, Morientes, Gavilán (Žigić
n Helguera, Joaquín, Silva, Miguel (Angulo 78), Moretti.
4 - Rosenborg BK (NOR)

rand, Manuel Fernandes, Albelda, David Villa, Morientes (Vicente
neira, Iván Helguera, Joaquín (Žigić 63), Silva, Miguel, Moretti
o 63).
Card(s): Angulo 72
5 - FC Schalke 04 (GER)

res, Marchena, Albelda, David Villa, Morientes (Manuel Fernandes 35),
(Albiol 43), Vicente (Silva 72), Iván Helguera, Joaquín, Edú, Miguel.
rd(s): Albelda 32
Card(s): David Villa 29, Morientes 29
6 - Chelsea FC (ENG)

Cañizares, Sunday, Albiol, Marchena, David Villa (Arizmendi 50), Morientes, Vicente (Mata 75), Iván Helguera, Silva, Miguel (Manuel Fernandes 65), Moretti.
Yellow Card(s): Cañizares 90+1

No	Player	Nat	DoB	Aps	(s)	Gls
Goalkeepers						
1	Santiago Cañizares		18/12/69	4		
13	Timo Hildebrand	GER	5/4/79	2		
Defenders						
4	Raúl Albiol		4/9/85	4	(1)	
5	Carlos Marchena		31/7/79	5		
12	Marco Caneira	POR	9/2/79	2		
15	Iván Helguera		28/3/75	6		
23	Miguel	POR	4/1/80	6		
24	Emiliano Moretti	ITA	11/6/81	5		
Midfielders						
2	Stephen Sunday	NGA	17/9/88	1	(1)	
3	Manuel Fernandes	POR	5/2/86	1	(2)	
6	David Albelda		1/9/77	5		
8	Rubén Baraja		11/7/75		(2)	
11	Jaime Gavilán		12/5/85	1		
14	Vicente Rodríguez		16/7/81	2	(1)	
16	Juan Manuel Mata		28/4/88		(1)	
17	Joaquín		21/7/81	4	(1)	
22	Edú	BRA	15/5/78	1		
Attackers						
7	David Villa		3/12/81	5		2
9	Fernando Morientes		5/4/76	6		
10	Miguel Ángel Angulo		23/6/77	1	(2)	
18	Nikola Žigić	SRB	25/9/80		(3)	
19	Javier Arizmendi		3/3/84		(3)	
21	David Silva		8/1/86	5	(1)	

VILLARREAL CF

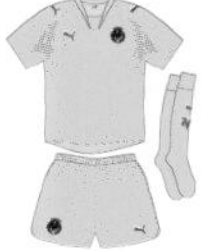

UEFA CUP

First Round - FC BATE Borisov (BLR)
H 4-1 *Nihat (6, 50), Senna (18), Tomasson (54)*
Diego López, Javi Venta, Senna (Mavuba 55), Nihat (Josico 79), Cani, Bruno, Ángel, Tomasson (Rossi 62), Matías Fernández, Fuentes, Godín.
A 2-0 *Cani (24), Ángel (78)*
Diego López, Javi Venta, Guille Franco (Santi Cazorla 73), Cani, Bruno, Capdevila (Ángel 70), Mavuba, Tomasson, Matías Fernández, Fuentes (Cygan 46), Godín.
Yellow Card(s): Fuentes 39

Group C
Match 1 - ACF Fiorentina (ITA)
H 1-1 *Capdevila (88)*
Diego López, Capdevila, Ángel, Godín, Fuentes, Cani (Nihat 64), Josico (Santi Cazorla 63), Senna, Matías Fernández, Tomasson (Pirès 79), Rossi.
Yellow Card(s): Capdevila 21
Match 2 - FK Mladá Boleslav (CZE)
A 2-1 *Nihat (33), Santi Cazorla (56)*
Diego López, Josemi, Cygan, Godín, Ángel (Capdevila 83), Matías Fernández, Mavuba, Josico, Santi Cazorla, Tomasson, Nihat (Guille Franco 73).
Yellow Card(s): Ángel 65, Guille Franco 82
Match 3 - IF Elfsborg (SWE)
H 2-0 *Tomasson (2,51)*
Diego López, Godín, Capdevila (Javi Venta 77), Santi Cazorla, Tomasson, Cygan, Matías Fernández, Nihat (Guille Franco 71), Ángel, Senna (Bruno 60), Mavuba.
Match 4 - AEK Athens FC (GRE)
A 2-1 *Mavuba (40), Tomasson (69)*

Diego López, Josemi, Fuentes, Cygan, Javi Venta, Santi Cazorla (Cani 46), Mavuba, Bruno, Matías Fernández, Rossi (Guille Franco 69), Tomasson (Ángel 89).
Yellow Card(s): Javi Venta 68, Josemi 90+1, Diego López 90+4

Round of 32 - FC Zenit St. Petersburg (RUS)
A 0-1
Diego López, Gonzalo, Josemi, Godín, Capdevila, Josico, Bruno (Cygan 82), Santi Cazorla (Tomasson 75), Cani, Guille Franco, Nihat (Rossi 66).
Yellow Card(s): Cani 36, Capdevila 82
H 2-1 *Guille Franco (75), Tomasson (90)*
Diego López, Godín, Gonzalo, Capdevila, Ángel, Santi Cazorla, Josico (Guille Franco 46), Senna (Bruno 63), Pirès, Tomasson, Rossi (Nihat 51).

REAL ZARAGOZA

UEFA CUP

First Round - Aris Thessaloniki FC (GRE)
A 0-1
López Vallejo, Zapater, Diogo (Gabi 71), Ayala, Luccin, Sergio García, D'Alessandro (Milito 71), Juanfran, Oliveira, Pavón, Matuzalem.
Yellow Card(s): Luccin 28
H 2-1 *Oliveira (19), Sergio García (72)*
César Sánchez, Cuartero (Gabi 65), Zapater, Ayala, Luccin, Aimar, D'Alessandro, Juanfran, Oliveira (Sergio García 61), Milito, Sergio.
Yellow Card(s): Luccin 5, Sergio García 65, Sergio 78

GETAFE CF

UEFA CUP

First Round - FC Twente (NED)
H 1-0 *Uche (90+1)*
Abbondanzieri, Cata Díaz, Belenguer, Celestini, Licht, Kepa (Albín 46), Uche, Cortés, Casquero (Sousa 81), Pablo Hernández, Granero (Braulio 70).
Yellow Card(s): Pablo Hernández 32, Casquero 55
A 2-3 *Belenguer (101), Granero (103) (aet)*
Abbondanzieri, Braulio (Uche 46), Belenguer, Del Moral, Celestini, De la Red, Nacho, Cata Díaz, Mario Cotelo (Sousa 82), Pablo Hernández (Granero 7), Licht.
Yellow Card(s): Braulio 19, Mario Cotelo 36, Licht 50, Cata Díaz 64, Granero 79

Group G
Match 1 - Tottenham Hotspur FC (ENG)
A 2-1 *Granero (21), Braulio (70)*
Ustari (Abbondanzieri 46), Cata Díaz, Belenguer, Signorino, Cortés, Granero (Mario Cotelo 76), Nacho, Albín, Casquero (Sousa 62), De la Red, Braulio.
Yellow Card(s): Albín 52, Abbondanzieri 87
Match 2 - Hapoel Tel-Aviv FC (ISR)
H 1-2 *Pablo Hernández (90+1p)*
Ustari, Contra, Cata Díaz, Belenguer (Sousa 67), Signorino, Pablo Hernández, Casquero (Del Moral 46), Albín, Granero, De la Red, Kepa (Braulio 46).
Yellow Card(s): Albín 45+1, Contra 79, Braulio 90+1
Match 3 - Aalborg BK (DEN)
A 2-1 *Pablo Hernández (11), Granero (78)*
Abbondanzieri, Contra, Cata Díaz, Belenguer (Mario 81), Licht, De la Red, Celestini (Cortés 60), Del Moral (Albín 76), Pablo Hernández, Granero, Braulio.
Yellow Card(s): Granero 34, Belenguer 41
Match 4 - RSC Anderlecht (BEL)
H 2-1 *Pablo Hernández (6), Celestini (50)*
Abbondanzieri, Contra, Cata Díaz, Belenguer, Celestini (Casquero 70 Pablo Hernández (Mario Cotelo 60), De la Red, Granero, Licht, Del M Braulio (Kepa 77).
Yellow Card(s): Granero 82

Round of 32 - AEK Athens FC (GRE)
A 1-1 *De la Red (86)*
Abbondanzieri, Contra, Cata Díaz, Belenguer, Signorino, Celestini, G (Cortés 61), Casquero (De la Red 68), Braulio, Uche (Del Moral 78), P Hernández.
Yellow Card(s): Signorino 42, Pablo Hernández 54
H 3-0 *Granero (45+1), Contra (82p), Braulio (84)*
Ustari, Contra, Belenguer, Mario, Celestini (Casquero 69), Licht, De la Albín (Uche 59), Braulio, Granero, Pablo Hernández (Cortés 78).
Yellow Card(s): Celestini 19

Round of 16 - SL Benfica (POR)
A 2-1 *De la Red (25), Pablo Hernández (67)*
Ustari, Contra, Belenguer, Cata Díaz, Licht, Albín, Casquero, Pablo Hern Granero (Mario Cotelo 46), De la Red (Celestini 73), Braulio (Del Moral 6
Yellow Card(s): Braulio 21, Granero 35, Licht 82, Casquero 85, Pablo Hernández 90+2
H 1-0 *Albín (77)*
Abbondanzieri, Contra, Tena, Licht, Mario Cotelo (Cortés 74), Celesti Casquero, Gavilán (Fuertes 79), Albín, Kepa (Signorino 69), De la Re
Yellow Card(s): Abbondanzieri 38, Mario Cotelo 60, Licht 73

Quarter-Final - FC Bayern München (GER)
A 1-1 *Contra (90)*
Ustari, Mario, De la Red, Albín, Uche (Del Moral 68), Signorino, Corté Casquero (Celestini 73), Tena, Pablo Hernández, Granero (Contra 78)
Yellow Card(s): Mario 4, Tena 5, Granero 34, De la Red 90+3
H 3-3 *Contra (44), Casquero (91), Braulio (93) (aet)*
Abbondanzieri, Contra (Mario Cotelo 66), Celestini, Gavilán, De la Re Licht, Del Moral (Braulio 62), Uche (Belenguer 21), Cortés, Casquero,
Red Card(s): De la Red 6
Yellow Card(s): Belenguer 121

CLUB ATLÉTICO DE MADRID

UEFA INTERTOTO CUP

Third Round - CF Gloria 1922 Bistrița (ROU)
A 1-2 *Seitaridis (55)*
Leo Franco, Antonio López, Perea, Maxi, Luccin (Costinha 76), Seitari Eller, Petrov (Jurado 57), Maniche, Mista (Braulio 70), Raúl García.
Yellow Card(s): Luccin 62
H 1-0 *Forlán (11)*
Leo Franco, Perea, Maxi, Luccin, Seitaridis (Eller 88), Pernía, Jurado, Maniche (Raúl García 77), Agüero (Braulio 89), Pablo, Forlán.
Yellow Card(s): Jurado 8

UEFA CUP

Second Qualifying Round - FK Vojvodina (SRB)
H 3-0 *Maxi (37), Forlán (62), Agüero (70)*
Leo Franco, Agüero (Luis García 76), Forlán, Raúl García, Pablo, Mani Perea, Pernía, Maxi (Jurado 82), Seitaridis, Simão (Reyes 64).
Yellow Card(s): Seitaridis 46, Raúl García 90, Reyes 90+3
A 2-1 *Luis García (54), Seitaridis (75)*
Abbiati, Eller (Seitaridis 62), Mista, Forlán (Jurado 68), Raúl García, L García, Antonio López, Perea, Zé Castro, Cléber Santana, Reyes (Sim
Yellow Card(s): Reyes 41, Abbiati 80

ound - Kayseri Erciyesspor (TUR)
Aista (13), Forlán (17), Luis García (83, 90+2)
, Eller, Mista (Agüero 69), Forlán, Luis García, Jurado (Simão 23),
› López, Perea, Zé Castro, Cléber Santana (Raúl García 80), Maniche.
Card(s): Zé Castro 64
güero (6, 44), Jurado (14), Maxi (53p), Forlán (79)
, Agüero (Forlán 46), Eller (Pablo 46), Raúl García (Reyes 61), Luis
Jurado, Antonio López, Pernía, Maxi, Zé Castro, Cléber Santana.
Card(s): Luis García 38, Antonio López 83

B
1 - FC Lokomotiv Moskva (RUS)
güero (16, 85), Forlán (47)
, Antonio López, Pablo, Eller, Pernía, Cléber Santana (Maxi 65), Raúl
Jurado (Maniche 75), Simão (Luis García 69), Forlán, Agüero.
Card(s): Antonio López 66, Raúl García 90+2
2 - Aberdeen FC (SCO)
orlán (45p), Simão (61)
, Antonio López, Pernía, Motta, Cléber Santana, Forlán (Mista 70),
rcía, Agüero (Simão 46), Maxi (Maniche 70), Eller, Pablo.
3 - FC København (DEN)
imão (21), Agüero (62)
Antonio López, Pablo, Eller, Pernía, Simão (Maxi 67), Motta, Cléber
a (Maniche 73), Luis García, Agüero, Forlán (Raúl García 72).
Card(s): Motta 72, Luis García 90+3
4 - Panathinaikos FC (GRE)
uis García (74), Simão (90+6)
Perea, Zé Castro (Reyes 61), Eller, Antonio López, Luis García, Raúl
Cléber Santana (Simão 46), Maxi, Forlán, Agüero (Pablo 90+6).
rd(s): Raúl García 81
Card(s): Zé Castro 45, Maxi 73, Luis García 83

of 32 - Bolton Wanderers FC (ENG)

Antonio López, Perea, Pablo, Pernía, Reyes (Agüero 59), Mista
88), Maxi, Cléber Santana, Simão (Jurado 72), Forlán.
rd(s): Agüero 73
Card(s): Reyes 13, Cléber Santana 45+2

Pernía, Pablo (Mista 67), Antonio López, Perea, Jurado, Cléber
, Maxi, Luis García (Miguel 54), Reyes, Forlán.
Card(s): Maxi 30

SWEDEN

UEFA CHAMPIONS LEAGUE

alifying Round - Linfield FC (NIR)

Mobaeck, Björck, Augustsson, Svensson, Ishizaki (Alexandersson 89),
son (Avdic 52), Berglund (Keene 68), Karlsson, Andersson, Holmén.
Card(s): Karlsson 35
. Svensson (32)
Mobaeck, Björck, Augustsson, Svensson (Avdic 60), Ishizaki, M.
n (Keene 49), Berglund (Alexandersson 83), Karlsson, Andersson,
.

Qualifying Round - Debreceni VSC (HUN)
obaeck (65)
Andersson, Augustsson, Berglund (Alexandersson 59), Björck,
Ishizaki (Bajrami 79), Karlsson, Keene, Mobaeck, Svensson (Avdic 19).
Card(s): Holmén 26, Andersson 55

H 0-0
Wiland, Andersson, Augustsson, Björck, Holmén, Ishizaki, Karlsson, Keene (Berglund 80), Mobaeck, Svensson (Avdic 66; Florén 86), M. Svensson.
Yellow Card(s): M. Svensson 29, Ishizaki 45+1, Wiland 74, Florén 90+3

Third Qualifying Round - Valencia CF (ESP)
A 0-3
Wiland, Augustsson, Björck, Holmén, Ilola (Avdic 76), Ishizaki, Karlsson, Keene (Berglund 63), Mobaeck, Svensson, M. Svensson (Alexandersson 70).
H 1-2 *Alexandersson (31)*
Wiland, Alexandersson, Augustsson, Avdic, Berglund, Björck, Ilola (M. Svensson 64), Karlsson (Andersson 75), Keene, Mobaeck (Florén 19), Svensson.
Yellow Card(s): M. Svensson 68, Berglund 73

UEFA CUP

First Round - FC Dinamo 1948 Bucureşti (ROU)
A 2-1 *Keene (10, 30)*
Wiland, Alexandersson (Avdic 83), Andersson, Augustsson, Björck, Ilola, Ishizaki (Bajrami 90), Karlsson, Keene (Berglund 80), Mobaeck, Svensson.
Yellow Card(s): Karlsson 68
H 0-1
Wiland, Karlsson, Andersson, Alexandersson (Ishizaki 73), Ilola, Svensson, M. Svensson, Mobaeck, Keene (Berglund 78), Björck (Bajrami 81), Augustsson.

Group C
Match 1 - AEK Athens FC (GRE)
H 1-1 *Mobaeck (15)*
Wiland, Andersson, Augustsson, Björck, Karlsson, Mobaeck, Ilola, Svensson, Ishizaki (Berglund 87), M. Svensson (Keene 78), Alexandersson.
Yellow Card(s): M. Svensson 60, Keene 90+2
Match 2 - ACF Fiorentina (ITA)
A 1-6 *Ishizaki (41)*
Wiland, Andersson, Augustsson, Björck, Karlsson, Mobaeck (Bajrami 81), Svensson, Ilola, Ishizaki, Alexandersson (Avdic 77), Keene (M. Svensson 21).
Yellow Card(s): Ishizaki 36
Match 3 - FK Mladá Boleslav (CZE)
H 1-3 *M. Svensson (31)*
Wiland, Andersson, Augustsson, Björck (Bajrami 84), Karlsson, Mobaeck, Svensson, Ilola (Avdic 70), Ishizaki, M. Svensson, Keene (Berglund 74).
Yellow Card(s): Andersson 17
Match 4 - Villarreal CF (ESP)
A 0-2
Wiland, Florén, Andersson, Svensson, M. Svensson (Falk-Olander 85), Mobaeck, Avdic, Keene (Berglund 82), Bajrami (Karlsson 82), Augustsson, Ishizaki.
Yellow Card(s): Avdic 73

HELSINGBORGS IF

UEFA CUP

First Qualifying Round - JK Trans Narva (EST)
H 6-0 *Omotoyossi (28), Dahl (30), Larsson (59, 64), Karakezi (80), C. Andersson (84)*
D. Andersson, C. Andersson, Dahl (Chansa 78), Tamboura, Beloufa, Jakobsson, Skúlason, Stefanidis (Unkuri 84), Omotoyossi (Karakezi 74), Larsson, Wahlstedt.
A 3-0 *Wahlstedt (18), Svanbäck (32), Unkuri (76)*
D. Andersson, C. Andersson, Dahl (Landgren 46), Mariga, Svanbäck, Jakobsson, Skúlason (Chansa 66), Rönningberg, Omotoyossi (Åström 62), Unkuri, Wahlstedt.

Second Qualifying Round - Drogheda United FC (IRL)
A 1-1 *Larsson (34)*
D. Andersson, C. Andersson, Dahl, Jakobsson, Larsson, Mariga, Omotoyossi, Rönningberg, Svanbäck, Tamboura, Wahlstedt.
H 3-0 *Jakobsson (52), Omotoyossi (68), Karakezi (90+1)*
D. Andersson, C. Andersson, Dahl (Mariga 86), Jakobsson, Larsson, Omotoyossi (Karakezi 86), Rönningberg, Skúlason, Svanbäck, Tamboura, Wahlstedt.
Yellow Card(s): Wahlstedt 87

First Round - SC Heerenveen (NED)
A 3-5 *Larsson (53, 71p), Omotoyossi (57)*
D. Andersson, C. Andersson, Beloufa (Leandro Castán 46), Dahl, Jakobsson, Larsson, Omotoyossi, Skúlason, Tamboura, Kolář (Unkuri 87), Lantz (Wahlstedt 46).
Yellow Card(s): Tamboura 28, Skúlason 64, Omotoyossi 76, C. Andersson 82
H 5-1 *Larsson (18), Dahl (37), Omotoyossi (45+1, 80), Makondele (51)*
D. Andersson, C. Andersson (Kolář 90), Leandro Castán, Dahl (Landgren 90), Jakobsson, Larsson, Omotoyossi (Unkuri 84), Skúlason, Tamboura, Wahlstedt, Makondele.
Yellow Card(s): Omotoyossi 68

Group H
Match 1 - Panionios GSS (GRE)
H 1-1 *Larsson (83)*
D. Andersson, Wahlstedt, Jakobsson, Rönningberg, Tamboura, Makondele, Dahl, Skúlason (Lantz 46), C. Andersson (Landgren 85), Larsson, Omotoyossi.
Yellow Card(s): C. Andersson 18
Match 2 - Galatasaray AŞ (TUR)
A 3-2 *Larsson (30), Omotoyossi (39), C. Andersson (75)*
D. Andersson, Wahlstedt, Jakobsson, Rönningberg, C. Andersson (Lantz 87), Tamboura, Skúlason, Dahl (Beloufa 90), Makondele (Svanbäck 66), Larsson, Omotoyossi.
Yellow Card(s): Wahlstedt 56, Dahl 80
Match 3 - FK Austria Wien (AUT)
H 3-0 *Skúlason (47), Omotoyossi (66, 70)*
D. Andersson, Wahlstedt, Jakobsson, Rönningberg, Tamboura, C. Andersson, Skúlason (Chansa 85), Dahl (Lantz 72), Makondele, Omotoyossi (Karakezi 89), Larsson.
Match 4 - FC Girondins de Bordeaux (FRA)
A 1-2 *Larsson (17)*
D. Andersson, Wahlstedt, Jakobsson, Rönningberg, Tamboura, Makondele (Unkuri 88), Lantz, Skúlason (Chansa 85), C. Andersson, Omotoyossi (Svanbäck 72), Larsson.
Red Card(s): Tamboura 64
Yellow Card(s): Skúlason 31, Tamboura 36, Tamboura 64, Lantz 66

Round of 32 - PSV Eindhoven (NED)
A 0-2
D. Andersson, Ekstrand, Jakobsson, C. Andersson, Landgren, Kolář (Unkuri 77), Lantz, Skúlason, Makondele, Larsson, Omotoyossi (Olsson 88).
Yellow Card(s): D. Andersson 6, Lantz 60
H 1-2 *Leandro Castán (81)*
D. Andersson, Tamboura (Landgren 46), Jakobsson, Lantz (Chansa 77), Omotoyossi, Skúlason, Makondele, Larsson, Kolář, C. Andersson, Ekstrand (Leandro Castán 46).
Yellow Card(s): Skúlason 1

AIK SOLNA

UEFA CUP

First Qualifying Round - Glentoran FC (NIR)
A 5-0 *Wilton (21, 62), Valdemarín (68), Stephenson (73), Johnson (84)*
Örlund, Tamandi, Tjernström (Bengtsson 82), N.E. Johansson, Óbolo (Daniel Mendes 76), Arnefjord, Wilton (Valdemarín 66), Johnson, Pavey, Stephenson, Karlsson.
Yellow Card(s): Wilton 48, Arnefjord 50
H 4-0 *Özkan (7), Karlsson (24), Gerndt (88), Johnson (89)*
Örlund, Tamandi, Özkan (Gerndt 67), N.E. Johansson, Arnefjord, Wil (Bengtsson 67), Johnson, Pavey, Stephenson, Valdemarín (Daniel M 67), Karlsson.

Second Qualifying Round - SK Liepājas Metalurgs (LVA)
A 2-3 *Ivanovs (49og), Óbolo (61)*
Örlund, Arnefjord, N.E. Johansson, Johnson, Jonsson, Karlsson, Óbo Özkan (Daniel Mendes 81), Stephenson (Pavey 62), Tjernström, Valdemarín (Wilton 62).
Yellow Card(s): Karlsson 17, Valdemarín 34, Arnefjord 42, Özkan 67, Ób
H 2-0 *Wilton (43, 54)*
Örlund, N.E. Johansson, Tjernström, Wilton (Daniel Mendes 86), Pav Tamandi, Jonsson, Stephenson (Karlsson 46), Óbolo (Bengtsson 89), Valdemarín, Johnson.

First Round - Hapoel Tel-Aviv FC (ISR)
A 0-0
Örlund, Monsalvo (Rubarth 71), Tjernström, Arnefjord, Pavey (Danie Mendes 90+2), Tamandi, Jonsson, Stephenson, Óbolo (Valdemarín 6 Carlsson, Johnson.
Yellow Card(s): Carlsson 74
H 0-1
Westberg-Andersson, Arnefjord, Óbolo, N.E. Johansson, Johnson, Jonsson, Tamandi (Stephenson 71), Tjernström, Valdemarín, Monsalvo (Bengtsson 8
Yellow Card(s): Pavey 45, Jonsson 75

BK HÄCKEN

UEFA CUP

First Qualifying Round - KR Reykjavík (ISL)
H 1-1 *Hedén (12)*
Hysén, Hedén, Henriksson, Jarlegren, Lind, Lucic (Forsell 50), Mumb Olofsson (Larsson 64), Rishoft (Holster 80), Skúlason, Williams.
A 1-0 *De Oliveira (83)*
Källkvist, De Oliveira, Forsell, Henriksson, Jarlegren, Lind, Ljung (Mu 46), Marek (Friberg 79), Pereira, Skúlason, Williams (Olofsson 76).
Yellow Card(s): Williams 28, Pereira 38, Friberg 90

Second Qualifying Round - Dunfermline Athletic FC (SCO)
A 1-1 *Henriksson (57)*
Källkvist, Forsell, Hedén, Henriksson, Larsson (Olofsson 86), Lind, Mu Marek, Pereira, Skúlason, Williams.
Yellow Card(s): Pereira 49, Williams 87
H 1-0 *Skúlason (27)*
Hysén, De Oliveira (Holster 90), Hedén, Henriksson, Larsson (Olofssc Lind, Ljung (Forsell 33), Lucic, Mumba, Marek, Skúlason.
Yellow Card(s): Marek 54

First Round - FC Spartak Moskva (RUS)
A 0-5
Hysén, De Oliveira, Forsell, Henriksson, Larsson (Ljung 65), Lind, Luc Mumba (Friberg 85), Marek, Pereira, Skúlason (Holster 72).
H 1-3 *Henriksson (84)*
Hysén, De Oliveira (Olofsson 68), Forsell, Henriksson, Jarlegren, Lars Ljung (Friberg 73), Lucic (Lind 68), Mumba, Marek, Skúlason.

HAMMARBY

UEFA INTERTOTO CUP

ound - KÍ Klaksvík (FRO)
Davies (3)
öm, D. Johansson, Chanko, Davies, Gunnarsson (E. Johansson 55), son (Zengin 57), Laitinen, Eguren, Monteiro, Nhleko (Paulinho 75), Traoré.
Jacobsen (34og), Paulinho Guará (58)
öm, Paulinho Guará (Sosseh 83), Dahlin, Gunnarsson, Jensen, son, Laitinen, Eguren (Nhleko 73), Malke, Monteiro, Traoré.

d Round - Cork City FC (IRL)
Murray (57og)
öm, D. Johansson, Chanko, Davies (Jensen 90+1), Paulinho Guará sson 85), E. Johansson, Laitinen, Eguren, Monteiro, Sleyman, Castro-Gunnarsson 73).
w Card(s): Sleyman 40, Dahlin 74, Gunnarsson 89
Monteiro (53)
öm, D. Johansson, Chanko, Sleyman, Zengin, Castro-Tello (Eguren aitinen (Jensen 78), Paulinho Guará (Júlíusson 90), Monteiro, sson, Traoré.

Round - FC Utrecht (NED)

öm, Andersson, Castro-Tello (Zengin 57), Paulinho Guará, Chanko, ansson, Laitinen (Davies 71), Eguren, Monteiro, Sleyman, Traoré.
w Card(s): Eguren 65, Sleyman 74, Paulinho Guará 86
D. Johansson (66)
öm, Andersson, Paulinho Guará (Davies 80), Chanko, Gunnarsson en 46), D. Johansson, Laitinen, Eguren, Monteiro, Traoré, Zengin o-Tello 87).
w Card(s): Laitinen 62, Davies 85, Chanko 89

UEFA CUP

d Qualifying Round - Fredrikstad FK (NOR)
Paulinho Guará (35), Castro-Tello (49)
öm, Andersson, Castro-Tello (Eguren 79), Paulinho Guará (Sosseh hanko, Jensen, D. Johansson, Laitinen, Monteiro, Traoré, Zengin es 87).
w Card(s): Laitinen 31, Chanko 65, Andersson 88
Eguren (90p)
öm, Andersson, Castro-Tello (Jensen 78), Paulinho Guará (Davies , Gunnarsson, D. Johansson, Júlíusson (Eguren 46), Monteiro, an, Traoré, Zengin.
w Card(s): Sleyman 28, Eguren 84, Jensen 86, Davies 90+3

Round - SC Braga (POR)
Andersson (50, 66)
röm, Andersson, Castro-Tello (Saarenpää 72), Paulinho Guará sson 88), Chanko, D. Johansson, Laitinen (Gunnarsson 90+3), eiro, Sleyman, Traoré, Zengin.
w Card(s): Zengin 90, Saarenpää 90

san, Andersson, Paulinho Guará (Davies 79), Chanko, ansson, Laitinen, Eguren, Sleyman, Traoré, Zengin (Castro-Tello 74), npää.
w Card(s): Laitinen 29, Moussan 45, D. Johansson 74, Eguren 80, é 90+2

SWITZERLAND

FC ZÜRICH

UEFA CHAMPIONS LEAGUE

Third Qualifying Round - Beşiktaş JK (TUR)
H 1-1 *Alphonse (90+7)*
Leoni, Alphonse, César (Hassli 83), Raffael, Stahel, Tihinen, Von Bergen, Aegerter (Tico 46), Rochat, Abdi, Chikhaoui.
Yellow Card(s): Stahel 31, Rochat 49, Von Bergen 55, Tico 90+3
A 0-2
Leoni, Barmettler, Raffael, Schneider (Kollar 67), Stahel (Scönbächler 83), Tihinen, Tico, Eudis (Hassli 67), Chikhaoui, Rochat, Abdi.
Yellow Card(s): Barmettler 66

UEFA CUP

First Round - Empoli FC (ITA)
A 1-2 *Alphonse (74)*
Leoni, Barmettler, Chikhaoui, Hassli (Alphonse 70), Tico, Rochat, Schneider, Stahel, Raffael, Abdi, Kondé.
Yellow Card(s): Stahel 47, Abdi 63
H 3-0 *Kollar (37), Abdi (78), Alphonse (82)*
Leoni, Alphonse (Hassli 83), Barmettler, Chikhaoui, Kollar, Tico, Rochat, Stahel (Lampi 27), Tihinen, Raffael (Kondé 76), Abdi.
Yellow Card(s): Chikhaoui 45+2, Tico 70, Raffael 74, Abdi 89

Group E
Match 1 - AC Sparta Praha (CZE)
A 2-1 *Kondé (38), Alphonse (62)*
Leoni, Schneider, Kollar, Stahel, Tihinen, Rochat, Abdi, Chikhaoui, Kondé, Raffael (Hassli 77), Alphonse (Lampi 87; Eudis 90+2).
Red Card(s): Hassli 80
Yellow Card(s): Rochat 28, Tihinen 74
Match 2 - Toulouse FC (FRA)
H 2-0 *Tihinen (42), Raffael (64p)*
Leoni, Lampi, Kondé, Tico, Alphonse (Eudis 62), Raffael (Schönbächler 89), Chikhaoui (Stahel 90+3), Rochat, Abdi, Schneider, Tihinen.
Yellow Card(s): Abdi 63, Eudis 72
Match 3 - FC Spartak Moskva (RUS)
A 0-1
Guatelli, Kondé, Aegerter (Gashi 81), Tico, Alphonse, Stahel, Raffael, Chikhaoui, Rochat, Schneider, Tihinen.
Yellow Card(s): Stahel 64, Raffael 69
Match 4 - Bayer 04 Leverkusen (GER)
H 0-5
Leoni, Kondé, Stahel, Rochat, Barmettler, Schneider, Aegerter (Tico 63), Abdi, Chikhaoui, Raffael (Schönbächler 85), Alphonse (Eudis 63).

Round of 32 - Hamburger SV (GER)
H 1-3 *Rochat (88)*
Leoni, Stahel, Barmettler (Lampi 69), Tihinen, Rochat, Tico, Aegerter, Abdi (Vasquez 86), Djuric, Chikhaoui (Tahirovi 75), Hassli.
Yellow Card(s): Rochat 17, Tico 45+2
A 0-0
Leoni, Lampi, Barmettler, Stahel, Rochat, Tico (Kondé 46), Aegerter, Abdi (Hassli 60), Chikhaoui, Djuric, Alphonse (Tahirovic 58).
Yellow Card(s): Tico 15, Kondé 87

FC BASEL 1893

UEFA CUP

Second Qualifying Round - SV Mattersburg (AUT)
H 2-1 *Ergić (23), Caicedo (53)*
Costanzo, Chipperfield, Eduardo (Derdiyok 68), Ergić, Majstorovic, Nakata, Zanni, Huggel, Carlitos (Frei 85), Caicedo, Marque.
Yellow Card(s): Carlitos 62
A 4-0 *Caicedo (22), Ergić (36), Streller (41), Carlitos (53)*

Costanzo, Chipperfield, Streller (Derdiyok 72), Ergić, Majstorovic, Nakata, Zanni, Huggel, Carlitos (Frei 83), Caicedo (Eduardo 58), Marque.
Yellow Card(s): Chipperfield 10, Huggel 17, Caicedo 28

First Round - FK Sarajevo (BIH)
A 2-1 *Carlitos (11), Ergić (63)*
Costanzo, Chipperfield (Frei 72), Streller (Eduardo 85), Ergić, Majstorovic, Nakata, Zanni, Huggel, Carlitos, Caicedo (Degen 65), Marque.
H 6-0 *Carlitos (8, 9), Streller (18, 29), Huggel (75), Caicedo (90)*
Costanzo, Carlitos (Degen 45), Caicedo, Eduardo (Burgmeier 72), Huggel, Majstorovic, Marque, Nakata, Streller (Derdiyok 61), Zanni, Frei.

Group D
Match 1 - Stade Rennais FC (FRA)
H 1-0 *Streller (55)*
Costanzo, Zanni, Majstorovic, Marque, Hodel, Carlitos (Frei 86), Chipperfield, Ergić, Huggel, Caicedo (Degen 60), Streller (Eduardo 88).
Match 2 - NK Dinamo Zagreb (CRO)
A 0-0
Costanzo, Zanni, Majstorovic, Marque, Hodel, Ergić, Degen, Chipperfield (Frei 73), Caicedo (Burgmeier 76), Eduardo, Streller.
Match 3 - SK Brann (NOR)
H 1-0 *Carlitos (40)*
Costanzo, Zanni, Majstorovic, Marque, Nakata, Carlitos, Huggel, Ergić, Caicedo (Degen 68), Eduardo, Derdiyok.
Yellow Card(s): Degen 76
Match 4 - Hamburger SV (GER)
A 1-1 *Ergić (58)*
Costanzo, Zanni, Majstorovic, Marque, Hodel, Huggel, Ba, Degen (Morganella 51), Ergić, Carlitos (Caicedo 81), Eduardo (Derdiyok 85).
Red Card(s): Zanni 49
Yellow Card(s): Zanni 20, Huggel 43, Zanni 49, Costanzo 88

Round of 32 - Sporting Clube de Portugal (POR)
A 0-2
Costanzo (Crayton 45), Ba, Marque, Majstorovic, Hodel, Huggel, Ergić, Carlitos, Degen (Cabral 64), Derdiyok, Eduardo.
Yellow Card(s): Carlitos 29
H 0-3
Crayton, Hodel, Majstorovic, Marque, Zanni, Huggel (Ba 46), Carlitos, Degen, Ergić (Perović 70), Eduardo (Frei 59), Derdiyok.

FC SION

UEFA CUP

Second Qualifying Round - SV Ried (AUT)
A 1-1 *Saborío (90+2)*
Vailati, Chedli, Obradović, Saborío, Nwaneri, Vanczák, Beto (Zakrzewski 68), Domínguez, Paíto, Geiger, Bühler.
Yellow Card(s): Chedli 21, Vanczák 47, Geiger 65
H 3-0 *Obradović (40), Zakrzewski (44), Domínguez (47)*
Vailati, Chedli (Reset 60), Obradović, Zakrzewski (Saborío 73), Nwaneri, Vanczák, Kali, Domínguez, Paíto, Ahouéya (Alioui 29), Bühler.

First Round - Galatasaray AŞ (TUR)
H 3-2 *Domínguez (6), Vanczák (9), Song (31og)*
Vailati, Alioui (Geiger 50), Bühler, Chedli, Domínguez, Kali (Mijadinoski 71), Paíto, Nwaneri, Obradović, Vanczák, Adeshina (Zakrzewski 62).
Yellow Card(s): Geiger 67, Nwaneri 89
A 1-5 *Nwaneri (90)*
Vailati, Alioui (Reset 63), Bühler, Domínguez, Beto (Geiger 63), Kali, Paíto, Nwaneri, Obradović, Vanczák, Adeshina (Saborío 73).
Yellow Card(s): Domínguez 19, Obradović 45

BSC YOUNG BOYS

UEFA CUP

First Qualifying Round - FC Banants (ARM)
A 1-1 *Mangane (17)*
Wölfli, Mangane, Regazzoni (Kallio 61), C. Schneuwly (Häberli 46), Ya
Yapo, Tiago, Portillo, Raimondi, Schwegler, Varela, João Paulo(Asamo
Frimpong 83).
H 4-0 *João Paulo (11, 41), Tiago (21), M. Schneuwly (58)*
Collaviti, Zayatte (Portillo 63), Regazzoni (M. Schneuwly 46), Yapi Yap
Asamoah Frimpong, Tiago, Raimondi, Schwegler, Varela, Yakin (C. Schneuwly 67), João Paulo.
Yellow Card(s): Schwegler 54, Tiago 62

Second Qualifying Round - RC Lens (FRA)
H 1-1 *Tiago (71)*
Wölfli, Tiago, João Paulo (Kallio 90+2), Mangane, Raimondi, Regazzor
Schneuwly 77), Schwegler, Varela, Yakin (Asamoah Frimpong 85), Yap
Yapo, Zayatte.
Red Card(s): Zayatte 89
Yellow Card(s): Zayatte 48, Varela 83, Zayatte 89
A 1-5 *Varela (32)*
Wölfli, Tiago, João Paulo, Hochstrasser (Asamoah Frimpong 60), Raim
Regazzoni, Portillo, Varela (Kavak 64), Yakin (C. Schneuwly 73), Kallio,
Schneuwly.
Yellow Card(s): Varela 33, Yakin 35, Raimondi 41, M. Schneuwly 59

FC ST GALLEN

UEFA INTERTOTO CUP

Second Round - FC Dacia Chişinău (MDA)
A 1-0 *Garat (7)*
Razzetti, Garat, Gelabert, Gjasula, Marazzi, Méndez (Ciccone 79), Tach
Mensah, Zellweger, Aguirre (Feutchine 63), Haas, Kül.
Yellow Card(s): Gelabert 81, Haas 88
H 0-1 *(aet; 0-3 on pens)*
Razzetti, Garat, Gelabert, Gjasula (Muntwiler 105), Marazzi, Méndez (Ciccone 81), Tachie-Mensah (Agouda 86), Zellweger, Aguirre, Haas, K
Yellow Card(s): Kül 62, Méndez 78, Tachie-Mensah 81

TURKEY

FENERBAHÇE SK

UEFA CHAMPIONS LEAGUE

Qualifying Round - RSC Anderlecht (BEL)
Alex (32)
Kulbilge, Edu Dracena, Mehmet Aurélio, Deniz Barış (Selçuk Şahin
eivid, Alex (Ali 83), Kežman, Lugano, Tümer Metin (Uğur Boral 68),
Turacı, Roberto Carlos.
Card(s): Mehmet Aurélio 63
Kežman (4), Alex (73)
Demirel, Edu Dracena, Mehmet Aurélio, Deniz Barış, Deivid
rson 82), Alex (Selçuk Şahin 76), Kežman, Lugano, Tümer Metin
Kazım 67), Önder Turacı, Roberto Carlos.
Card(s): Deniz Barış 31, Deivid 61, Önder Turacı 86

G
1 - FC Internazionale Milano (ITA)
Deivid (43)
Demirel, Lugano, Roberto Carlos, Wederson, Kežman (Semih
k 67), Mehmet Aurélio, Önder Turacı, Alex, Deniz Barış, Edu
na, Deivid.
Card(s): Önder Turacı 12, Lugano 31, Deivid 45+1
2 - PFC CSKA Moskva (RUS)
Alex (9), Deivid (85)
Demirel, Lugano (Gökhan Gönül 77), Roberto Carlos, Wederson,
n, Mehmet Aurélio, Önder Turacı, Alex, Deniz Barış (Kazım Kazım
u Dracena (Yasin Çakmak 72), Deivid.
Card(s): Edu Dracena 52, Lugano 65
3 - PSV Eindhoven (NED)

Demirel, Lugano, Roberto Carlos, Wederson, Mehmet Aurélio, Alex
, Semih Şentürk (Kazım Kazım 72), Deniz Barış, Edu Dracena,
n Gönül, Deivid.
ard(s): Deivid 64
Card(s): Mehmet Aurélio 32, Deniz Barış 45+2, Lugano 45+5
4 - PSV Eindhoven (NED)
Marcellis (28og), Semih Şentürk (30)
Demirel, Roberto Carlos, Yasin Çakmak, Wederson, Kazım Kazım
h 86), Mehmet Aurélio, Alex (Ali 71), Semih Şentürk, Deniz Barış,
acena, Gökhan Gönül (Önder Turacı 88).
5 - FC Internazionale Milano (ITA)

Demirel, Lugano, Roberto Carlos, Wederson, Mehmet Aurélio
h 62), Alex, Selçuk Şahin, Semih Şentürk (Kazım Kazım 66), Edu
a, Gökhan Gönül, Deivid (Tümer Metin 83).
Card(s): Lugano 50, Gökhan Gönül 78
6 - PFC CSKA Moskva (RUS)
Alex (32), Uğur Boral (45+1, 90)
Demirel, Lugano, Roberto Carlos (Wederson 90+1), Mehmet
, Alex, Selçuk Şahin, Semih Şentürk (Kazım Kazım 70), Uğur Boral
n 91), Edu Dracena, Gökhan Gönül, Deivid.
Card(s): Gökhan Gönül 39

of 16 - Sevilla FC (ESP)
Kežman (17), Lugano (57), Semih Şentürk (87)
Demirel, Lugano, Roberto Carlos (Wederson 68), Kežman (Semih
k 84), Mehmet Aurélio, Alex, Selçuk Şahin, Uğur Boral (Kazım Kazım
u Dracena, Gökhan Gönül, Deivid.
Card(s): Uğur Boral 26, Kežman 47, Roberto Carlos 65, Selçuk
90+1, Alex 90+3

A 2-3 *Deivid (20, 79) (aet; 3-2 on pens)*
Volkan Demirel, Lugano, Wederson, Kežman, Mehmet Aurélio, Alex (Ali 112), Selçuk Şahin (Semih Şentürk 63), Uğur Boral (Kazım Kazım 111), Edu Dracena, Gökhan Gönül, Deivid.
Yellow Card(s): Selçuk Şahin 5, Deivid 7, Gökhan Gönül 13, Wederson 73, Kežman 100

Quarter-Final - Chelsea FC (ENG)
H 2-1 *Kazım Kazım (65), Deivid (81)*
Volkan Demirel, Lugano, Wederson, Kežman (Semih Şentürk 72), Mehmet Aurélio, Önder Turacı, Alex, Uğur Boral (Kazım Kazım 54), Maldonado, Edu Dracena, Deivid.
A 0-2
Volkan Demirel, Lugano, Wederson (Ali 89), Kazım Kazım, Mehmet Aurélio, Alex, Semih Şentürk (Uğur Boral 75), Maldonado (Kežman 60), Edu Dracena, Gökhan Gönül, Deivid.

No	Player	Nat	DoB	Aps	(s)	Gls
Goalkeepers						
1	Volkan Demirel		27/10/81	10		
Defenders						
2	Diego Lugano	URU	2/11/80	9		1
3	Roberto Carlos	BRA	10/4/73	7		
5	Yasin Çakmak		6/1/85	1	(1)	
6	Wederson		22/7/81	8	(2)	
19	Önder Turacı		14/7/81	3	(1)	
24	Deniz Barış		2/7/77	4		
36	Edu Dracena	BRA	18/5/81	10		
77	Gökhan Gönül		4/1/85	7	(1)	
Midfielders						
4	Stephen Appiah	GHA	24/12/80		(2)	
11	Tümer Metin		14/10/74		(1)	
15	Mehmet Aurélio		15/12/77	10		
18	Ali Bilgin		17/12/81		(4)	
20	Alex	BRA	14/9/77	10		2
21	Selçuk Şahin		31/1/81	4		
25	Uğur Boral		14/4/82	4	(1)	2
33	Claudio Maldonado	CHI	3/1/80	2		
Attackers						
8	Kazım Kazım		26/8/86	2	(7)	1
9	Mateja Kežman	SRB	12/4/79	5	(2)	1
23	Semih Şentürk		29/4/83	5	(4)	2
99	Deivid	BRA	22/10/79	9		5

BEŞIKTAŞ JK

UEFA CHAMPIONS LEAGUE

Second Qualifying Round - FC Sheriff (MDA)
H 1-0 *İbrahim Toraman (73)*
Rüştü Reçber, Cissé (Koray Avcı 68), Bobô, Delgado (Batuhan Karadeniz 46), İbrahim Kas, Serdar Kurtuluş, Ricardinho (Mehmet Yozgatlı 86), Serdar Özkan, Tello, İbrahim Toraman, İbrahim Üzülmez.
Yellow Card(s): Tello 16, İbrahim Kas 83
A 3-0 *Bobô (58, 69), Koray Avcı (90)*
Hakan Arıkan, Koray Avcı, Cissé, Bobô (Márcio Nobre 75), Delgado (Ricardinho 67), İbrahim Kas (Baki Mercimek 46), Serdar Kurtuluş, Serdar Özkan, Tello, İbrahim Toraman, İbrahim Üzülmez.
Yellow Card(s): Tello 22, İbrahim Kas 40, Koray Avcı 67

Third Qualifying Round - FC Zürich (SUI)
A 1-1 *Delgado (3)*
Hakan Arıkan, Cissé, Bobô, Delgado (Burak Yılmaz 78), Serdar Kurtuluş, Ricardinho (Koray Avcı 62), Serdar Özkan, Ali Tandoğan (İbrahim Akın 46),

İbrahim Toraman, İbrahim Üzülmez, Gökhan Zan.
Yellow Card(s): Ali Tandoğan 34, Serdar Özkan 40, Hakan Arıkan 87, **Koray Avcı 90+6**
H 2-0 *Delgado (56, 64)*
Hakan Arıkan, Cissé, Bobô (Karadeniz 90+2), Delgado (Ali Tandoğan 74), Serdar Kurtuluş, Ricardinho (İbrahim Akın 78), Serdar Özkan, Tello, İbrahim Toraman, İbrahim Üzülmez, Gökhan Zan.
Yellow Card(s): Tello 41, Ali Tandoğan 77, Cissé 84

Group A
Match 1 - Olympique de Marseille (FRA)
A 0-2
Hakan Arıkan, Serdar Kurtuluş (İbrahim Kas 26), Delgado (Higuaín 75), Bobô, Tello, Diatta, Ricardinho (Koray Avcı 44), Cissé, İbrahim Üzülmez, Serdar Özkan, İbrahim Toraman.
Yellow Card(s): İbrahim Kas 50, Koray Avcı 63
Match 2 - FC Porto (POR)
H 0-1
Hakan Arıkan, Serdar Kurtuluş (Ali Tandoğan 71), Gökhan Zan, Delgado, Bobô (Márcio Nobre 27), Tello, Cissé, İbrahim Üzülmez, Serdar Özkan, İbrahim Akın (Higuaín 67), İbrahim Toraman.
Yellow Card(s): Márcio Nobre 57, Ali Tandoğan 86
Match 3 - Liverpool FC (ENG)
H 2-1 Hyypiä (13og), Bobô (82)
Hakan Arıkan, Serdar Kurtuluş (Koray Avcı 42), Gökhan Zan, Delgado (Higuaín 62), Bobô (Diatta 86), Tello, Cissé, İbrahim Üzülmez, Serdar Özkan, Ali Tandoğan, İbrahim Toraman.
Match 4 - Liverpool FC (ENG)
A 0-8
Hakan Arıkan, Serdar Kurtuluş (Higuaín 62), Mehmet Sedef (Ricardinho 78), Delgado, Bobô, Diatta, Cissé, İbrahim Üzülmez, Serdar Özkan (Ali Tandoğan 46), Koray Avcı, İbrahim Toraman.
Yellow Card(s): Serdar Özkan 11
Match 5 - Olympique de Marseille (FRA)
H 2-1 Tello (27), Bobô (88)
Rüştü Reçber, Baki Mercimek, Delgado, Bobô, Tello, Ricardinho (İbrahim Akın 66), Cissé (Koray Avcı 20), İbrahim Üzülmez, Serdar Özkan (Márcio Nobre 75), Ali Tandoğan, İbrahim Toraman.
Yellow Card(s): Baki Mercimek 75, İbrahim Akın 89
Match 6 - FC Porto (POR)
A 0-2
Rüştü Reçber, Burak Yılmaz (İbrahim Akın 45), Baki Mercimek, Delgado, Bobô, Tello (Higuaín 84), Cissé, İbrahim Üzülmez, Serdar Özkan, Ali Tandoğan, İbrahim Toraman.
Yellow Card(s): Rüştü Reçber 44, Bobô 64, İbrahim Akın 87

No	Player	Nat	DoB	Aps	(s)	Gls
Goalkeepers						
1	Rüştü Reçber		10/5/73	2		
84	Hakan Arıkan		17/8/82	4		
Defenders						
2	Serdar Kurtuluş		23/7/87	4		
3	Mehmet Sedef		5/8/87	1		
5	Gökhan Zan		7/9/81	2		
8	Baki Mercimek		17/9/82	2		
15	Lamine Diatta	SEN	2/7/75	2	(1)	
58	İbrahim Toraman		20/11/81	6		
78	İbrahim Kas		20/9/86		(1)	
Midfielders						
7	Burak Yılmaz		15/7/85	1		
10	Matías Delgado	ARG	15/12/82	6		
14	Rodrigo Tello	CHI	14/10/79	5		1
17	Ricardinho	BRA	23/5/76	2	(1)	
18	Edouard Cissé	FRA	30/3/78	6		
19	İbrahim Üzülmez		10/3/74	6		
21	Serdar Özkan		1/1/87	6		
22	Ali Tandoğan		25/12/77	3	(2)	
41	Koray Avcı		19/5/79	1	(3)	
55	İbrahim Akın		4/1/84	1	(2)	
Attackers						
9	Federico Higuaín	ARG	25/10/84		(5)	
11	Márcio Nobre	BRA	6/11/80		(2)	
13	Bobô	BRA	9/1/85	6		2

GALATASARAY AŞ

UEFA CUP

Second Qualifying Round - NK Slaven Koprivnica (CRO)
A 2-1 *Ayhan Akman (42), Volkan Yaman (72)*
Orkun Uşak, Ayhan Akman, Ümit Karan, Sabri Sarıoğlu (Okan Buruk 8 Hasan Şaş (Barış Özbek 52), Song, Hakan Şükür, Volkan Yaman, Serve Çetin, Mehmet Güven (Mehmet Topal 89), Uğur Uçar.
Yellow Card(s): Servet Çetin 16, Hasan Şaş 37
H 2-1 *Ümit Karan (9), Hakan Şükür (37)*
Orkun Uşak, Ayhan Akman, Ümit Karan (Okan Buruk 90+2), Sabri Sar Hasan Şaş, Song, Hakan Şükür (Serkan Çalık 88), Lincoln, Volkan Yam (Barış Özbek 46), Servet Çetin, Uğur Uçar.
Yellow Card(s): Orkun Uşak 35, Song 45+1

First Round - FC Sion (SUI)
A 2-3 *Lincoln (38), Linderoth (67)*
Orkun Uşak, Servet Çetin, Linderoth, Hasan Şaş, Song, Hakan Şükür (Bouzid 88), Volkan Yaman, Carrusca (Ayhan Akman 38), Nonda (Ümi Karan 61), Uğur Uçar, Lincoln.
Yellow Card(s): Uğur Uçar 55
H 5-1 *Ümit Karan (22, 28), Lincoln (36), Arda Turan (68), Bouzid (90)*
Orkun Uşak, Servet Çetin, Lincoln (Nonda 80), Ümit Karan, Linderoth (Bouzid 86), Barış Özbek, Song, Hakan Şükür, Arda Turan (Hasan Şaş 7 Uğur Uçar, Volkan Yaman.
Yellow Card(s): Uğur Uçar 80

Group H
Match 1 - FC Girondins de Bordeaux (FRA)
A 1-2 *Nonda (22p)*
Orkun Uşak, Song, Servet Çetin, Barış Özbek (Mehmet Topal 72), Volk Yaman, Linderoth (Serkan Çalık 86), Uğur Uçar (Carrusca 78), Arda Tu Hasan Şaş, Nonda, Ümit Karan.
Yellow Card(s): Hasan Şaş 73
Match 2 - Helsingborgs IF (SWE)
H 2-3 *Nonda (44, 90+1)*
Aykut Erçetin, Servet Çetin, Song, Volkan Yaman, Barış Özbek, Linder Lincoln, Sabri Sarıoğlu (Arda Turan 43), Hasan Şaş, Nonda, Hakan Şük (Ümit Karan 63).
Yellow Card(s): Song 63
Match 3 - Panionios GSS (GRE)
A 3-0 *Serkan Çalık (50), Song (63p), Hakan Şükür (82)*
Orkun Uşak, Song, Servet Çetin, Volkan Yaman, Linderoth (Hakan Şü 46), Mehmet Topal, Uğur Uçar, Arda Turan (Mehmet Güven 80), Linco Hasan Şaş, Serkan Çalık (Sabri Sarıoğlu 86).
Yellow Card(s): Mehmet Topal 67
Match 4 - FK Austria Wien (AUT)
H 0-0
Orkun Uşak, Uğur Uçar, Song, Servet Çetin, Volkan Yaman, Sabri Sarı (Serkan Çalık 82), Mehmet Topal, Barış Özbek (Ümit Karan 61), Arda T Hakan Şükür (Hasan Şaş 62), Nonda.

Round of 32 - Bayer 04 Leverkusen (GER)
H 0-0
Orkun Uşak, Servet Çetin, Emre Güngör, Volkan Yaman (Lincoln 83), Uçar, Ayhan Akman (Hakan Balta 65), Mehmet Topal, Barış Özbek, Ar Turan, Hakan Şükür (Nonda 78), Ümit Karan.
Yellow Card(s): Emre Güngör 4, Arda Turan 49
A 1-5 *Barusso (87p)*
Orkun Uşak, Emre Güngör, Ayhan Akman (Barusso 68), Servet Çetin, Volkan Yaman, Mehmet Topal (Sabri Sarıoğlu 46), Barış Özbek, Arda T Serkan Çalık (Lincoln 46), Ümit Karan, Hakan Şükür.
Yellow Card(s): Ümit Karan 10, Sabri Sarıoğlu 54, Emre Güngör 68

KAYSERI ERCIYESSPOR

UEFA CUP

nd Qualifying Round - Maccabi Tel-Aviv FC (ISR)
Ilhan Özbay (5)
l, Adem (Erbay 78), Dulda, Yildirim, Sener, Demir (Bozkurt 45), Ilhan
/, Köksal, Durdu, Coskun, Hüseyin Yogurtcu.
w Card(s): Yildirim 7, Hüseyin Yogurtcu 49, Coskun 81, Bozkurt 81
Ilhan Özbay (7), Köksal (14), Öztekin (72)
l, Erbay, Adem (Durdu 76), Dulda, Yildirim, Sener, Ilhan Özbay,
l, Coskun (Kozen 87), Bozkurt (Öztekin 58), Hüseyin Yogurtcu.
w Card(s): Yildirim 53, Sener 88, Durdu 90+1, Kozen 90+1

Round - Club Atlético de Madrid (ESP)

l, Coskun (Bozkurt 74), Dulda, Durdu, Erbay (Seker 84), Ilhan Özbay,
(Demir 69), Köksal, Hüseyin Yogurtcu, Kaya, Morgil.
w Card(s): Sener 18, Coskun 31, Morgil 52

Coskun, Adem, Kozen (Morgil 46), Ilhan Özbay, Öztekin, Seker (Erbay
ener, Köksal (Aliyev 86), Yildirim, Hüseyin Yogurtcu.
w Card(s): Yildirim 20, Öztekin 33, Hüseyin Yogurtcu 52

TRABZONSPOR

UEFA INTERTOTO CUP

nd Round - KS Vllaznia (ALB)
Ersen Martin (12, 51, 58), Ceyhun Eriş (32), Çağdaş Atan (39), Ömer Riza (89)
et Şahin, Ömer Riza, Çağdaş Atan, Hüseyin Çimşir (Yusuf Kurtuluş 59),
t Çökmüş Çökmüş, Celaleddin Koçak, Ersen Martin, Ceyhun Eriş
an Güngör 74), Tayfun Cora, Abdelaziz (Hasan Üçüncü 54), Serkan Balci.
Umut Bulut (47, 89), Yattara (49), Yusuf Kurtuluş (52)
et Şahin, Ömer Riza (Yusuf Kurtuluş 46), Çağdaş Atan, Yattara, Ferhat
nüş (Adnan Güngör 49), Celaleddin Koçak (Ataoglu 54), Umut Bulut,
n Üçüncü, Tayfun Cora, Abdelaziz, Serkan Balci.
w Card(s): Serkan Balci 69

d Round - FC Oţelul Galaţi (ROU)
Ersen Martin (83)
et Şahin, Abdelaziz, Çağdaş Atan, Serkan Balci (Adnan Güngör 82),
t Bulut, Hüseyin Çimşir, Ferhat Çökmüş, Gökdeniz Karadeniz (Ersen
n 82), Celaleddin Koçak, Hasan Üçüncü (Ceyhun Eriş 46), Yattara.
Card(s): Yattara 28, Çağdaş Atan 90+3
w Card(s): Çağdaş Atan 66, Çağdaş Atan 90+3
Ceyhun Eriş (8)
Zengin, Abdelaziz (Adnan Güngör 84), Serkan Balci, Umut Bulut
f Kurtuluş 75), Hüseyin Çimşir, Tayfun Cora, Ceyhun Eriş, Gökdeniz
deniz, Celaleddin Koçak, Ersen Martin, Erdinç Yavuz.
w Card(s): Ceyhun Eriş 56

UKRAINE

FC DYNAMO KYIV

UEFA CHAMPIONS LEAGUE

Third Qualifying Round - FK Sarajevo (BIH)
A 1-0 *Shatskikh (13)*
Shovkovskiy, Corrêa, Gavrančić, Marković, Mykhalyk, Nesmachniy, Rebrov (Bangoura 82), Shatskikh (Kléber 67), Diakhaté, Michael, Gusev (Ninković 63).
Yellow Card(s): Mykhalyk 46, Diakhaté 52
H 3-0 *Bangoura (3), Milošević (75og), Rebrov (90+2p)*
Shovkovskiy, Corrêa (Belkevich 78), El Kaddouri, Gavrančić, Marković, Shatskikh, Ghioane, Bangoura (Rebrov 84), Diakhaté, Michael (Rotan 82), Gusev.
Yellow Card(s): Ghioane 55, Gavrančić 81, Diakhaté 90+3

Group F
Match 1 - AS Roma (ITA)
A 0-2
Shovkovskiy, Fedorov, Bangoura (Diogo Rincón 46), Michael (Rebrov 56), Shatskikh, Mykhalyk, Gusev (Corrêa 71), El Kaddouri, Gavrančić, Yussuf, Marković.
Yellow Card(s): Yussuf 29
Match 2 - Sporting Clube de Portugal (POR)
H 1-2 *Vashchuk (28)*
Shovkovskiy, Ghioane (Gusev 56), Corrêa, Diogo Rincón, Shatskikh, Mykhalyk, Milevskiy (Kléber 58), Vashchuk, El Kaddouri, Gavrančić, Yussuf.
Yellow Card(s): Corrêa 55, Mykhalyk 62, Kléber 84
Match 3 - Manchester United FC (ENG)
H 2-4 *Diogo Rincón (34), Bangoura (78)*
Shovkovskiy, Diakhaté, Ghioane (Milevskiy 46), Corrêa (Rotan 83), Bangoura, Diogo Rincón, Shatskikh (Belkevich 46), Gusev, Nesmachniy, Gavrančić, Yussuf.
Yellow Card(s): Diakhaté 31
Match 4 - Manchester United FC (ENG)
A 0-4
Shovkovskiy, Fedorov, Diakhaté, Ghioane, Corrêa, Rotan (Rebrov 46), Gusev (Diogo Rincón 46), Milevskiy (Bangoura 76), Vashchuk, El Kaddouri, Marković.
Yellow Card(s): Diakhaté 31, Corrêa 37
Match 5 - AS Roma (ITA)
H 1-4 *Bangoura (63)*
Rybka, Ghioane, Bangoura, Rotan (Belkevich 46), Diogo Rincón (Milevskiy 69), Gusev, Nesmachniy, Vashchuk, Gavrančić, Ninković (Shatskikh 55), Dopilka.
Yellow Card(s): Vashchuk 72
Match 6 - Sporting Clube de Portugal (POR)
A 0-3
Lutsenko, Ghioane, Rebrov (Belkevich 80), Bangoura (Kravets 57), Shatskikh, Gusev, Nesmachniy, Gavrančić, Ninković, Marković, Dopilka.

No	Player	Nat	DoB	Aps	(s)	Gls
Goalkeepers						
1	Olexandr Shovkovskiy		2/1/75	4		
23	Taras Lutsenko		1/2/74	1		
55	Olexandr Rybka		10/4/87	1		
Defenders						
2	Serhiy Fedorov		18/2/75	2		
3	Pape Diakhaté	SEN	21/6/84	2		
7	Carlos Corrêa	BRA	29/12/80	3	(1)	
26	Andriy Nesmachniy		28/2/79	3		
27	Vladyslav Vashchuk		2/1/75	3		1
32	Goran Gavrančić	SRB	2/8/78	5		
81	Marjan Marković	SRB	28/9/81	3		
98	Oleh Dopilka		12/3/86	2		

Midfielders						
4	Tiberiu Ghioane	ROU	18/6/81	5		
8	Valentin Belkevich	BLR	27/1/73		(3)	
14	Ruslan Rotan		29/10/81	2	(1)	
15	Diogo Rincón	BRA	18/4/80	3	(2)	1
17	Taras Mykhalyk		28/10/83	2		
20	Oleh Gusev		25/4/83	5	(1)	
30	Badr El Kaddouri	MAR	31/1/81	3		
36	Miloš Ninković	SRB	25/12/84	2		
37	Yussuf Ayila	NGA	4/11/84	3		
Attackers						
5	Serhiy Rebrov		3/6/74	1	(2)	
9	Kléber	BRA	12/8/83		(1)	
10	Ismaël Bangoura	GNB	2/1/85	4	(1)	2
11	Michael	BRA	16/2/83	1		
16	Maksim Shatskikh	UZB	30/8/78	4	(1)	
19	Artem Kravets		3/6/89		(1)	
25	Artem Milevskiy		12/1/85	2	(2)	

FC SHAKHTAR DONETSK

UEFA CHAMPIONS LEAGUE

Second Qualifying Round - FC Pyunik (ARM)
A 2-0 *Hladkiy (45), Brandão (48)*
Pyatov, Duljaj (Priyomov 53), Hladkiy (Lucarelli 52), Kucher, Brandão (Fomin 70), Lewandowski, Fernandinho, Raţ, Jadson, Srna, Chyhrynskiy.
Yellow Card(s): Chyhrynskiy 90+4
H 2-1 *Brandão (40), Hladkiy (49)*
Pyatov, Duljaj, Fomin (Hladkiy 38), Hübschman, Brandão, Lewandowski, Luiz Adriano (Jadson 38), Priyomov, Raţ, Tkachenko (Srna 57), Yezerskiy.

Third Qualifying Round - FC Salzburg (AUT)
A 0-1
Pyatov, Duljaj, Hladkiy, Kucher, Brandão (Lucarelli 73), Fernandinho, Raţ, Jadson (Vukić 69), Srna, Chyhrynskiy, Ilsinho (Lewandowski 81).
Yellow Card(s): Srna 37, Ilsinho 52
H 3-1 *Lucarelli (9), Castillo (79p), Brandão (87)*
Pyatov, Hladkiy (Brandão 55), Kucher, Lewandowski (Castillo 57), Lucarelli, Fernandinho, Raţ, Jadson, Srna, Chyhrynskiy, Ilsinho (Duljaj 72).
Yellow Card(s): Lewandowski 35, Lucarelli 35, Chyhrynskiy 62, Brandão 88, Castillo 90+2

Group D
Match 1 - Celtic FC (SCO)
H 2-0 *Brandão (6), Lucarelli (8)*
Pyatov, Hübschman, Kucher, Fernandinho (Duljaj 86), Jadson (Castillo 65), Ilsinho, Lewandowski, Brandão, Raţ, Srna, Lucarelli (Hladkiy 70).
Yellow Card(s): Srna 30
Match 2 - SL Benfica (POR)
A 1-0 *Jadson (42)*
Pyatov, Kucher, Fernandinho, Jadson (Castillo 77), Ilsinho (Duljaj 79), Lewandowski (Hübschman 87), Brandão, Raţ, Chyhrynskiy, Srna, Lucarelli.
Yellow Card(s): Srna 79, Fernandinho 82, Castillo 83
Match 3 - AC Milan (ITA)
A 1-4 *Lucarelli (51)*
Pyatov, Kucher (Hübschman 17), Fernandinho, Jadson (Castillo 63), Ilsinho, Lewandowski, Brandão (Hladkiy 75), Raţ, Chyhrynskiy, Srna, Lucarelli.
Yellow Card(s): Brandão 20, Lucarelli 69, Fernandinho 74
Match 4 - AC Milan (ITA)
H 0-3
Pyatov, Hübschman, Fernandinho, Jadson, Ilsinho, Brandão (Hladkiy 84), Raţ (Willian 73), Chyhrynskiy, Srna, Yezerskiy, Lucarelli (Castillo 77).
Yellow Card(s): Fernandinho 45, Ilsinho 45+1

Match 5 - Celtic FC (SCO)
A 1-2 *Brandão (4)*
Pyatov, Hübschman, Kucher, Jadson, Ilsinho (Yezerskiy 83), Lewando
Brandão, Raţ, Chyhrynskiy, Srna, Lucarelli (Hladkiy 88).
Yellow Card(s): Brandão 37
Match 6 - SL Benfica (POR)
H 1-2 *Lucarelli (30p)*
Pyatov, Kucher, Fernandinho, Jadson, Ilsinho (Willian 67), Lewandows
(Hübschman 57), Brandão, Raţ, Chyhrynskiy, Srna, Lucarelli (Hladkiy 7
Yellow Card(s): Kucher 68, Brandão 90+4

No	Player	Nat	DoB	Aps	(s)	G
Goalkeepers						
30	Andriy Pyatov		28/6/84	6		
Defenders						
3	Tomáš Hübschman	CZE	4/9/81	3	(3)	
5	Olexandr Kucher		22/10/82	5		
11	Ilsinho	BRA	12/10/85	6		
26	Răzvan Raţ	ROU	26/5/81	6		
27	Dmytro Chyhrynskiy		7/11/86	5		
55	Volodymyr Yezerskiy		15/11/76	1	(1)	
Midfielders						
4	Igor Duljaj	SRB	29/10/79		(2)	
7	Fernandinho	BRA	4/5/85	5		
8	Jadson	BRA	5/10/83	6		
9	Nery Castillo	MEX	13/6/84		(4)	
18	Mariusz Lewandowski	POL	18/5/79	5		
22	Willian	BRA	9/8/88		(2)	
33	Darijo Srna	CRO	1/5/82	6		
Attackers						
21	Olexandr Hladkiy		24/8/87		(5)	
25	Brandão	BRA	16/6/80	6		
99	Cristiano Lucarelli	ITA	4/10/75	6		

FC METALIST KHARKIV

UEFA CUP

First Round - Everton FC (ENG)
A 1-1 *Edmar (78)*
Bordianu, Gancarczyk, Obradović, Rykun (Edmar 67), Valyayev, Slyusa
Goryainov, Babych, Dević, Gueye, Nwoga (Antonov 59; Mahdoufi 77).
Red Card(s): Gancarczyk 69, Babych 88
Yellow Card(s): Obradović 22, Bordianu 68, Babych 69, Gancarczyk 6
Babych 88
H 2-3 *Edmar (21), Mahdoufi (52)*
Bordianu (Nwoga 85), Jakobia (Danilov 75), Obradović, Rykun, Valyaye
Slyusar, Goryainov, Edmar, Dević (Zézé 89), Gueye, Mahdoufi.
Yellow Card(s): Danilov 83

FC DNIPRO DNIPROPETROVSK

UEFA CUP

Second Qualifying Round - GKS Bełchatów (POL)
H 1-1 *Nazarenko (80)*
Kernozenko, Andriyenko, Hrytsai (Liopa 60), Nazarenko, Rusol, Shelaye
Shershun, Denisov, Samodin (Kornilenko 65), Vorobei, Kravchenko.
Yellow Card(s): Rusol 16, Vorobei 66

Kravchenko (7), Shelayev (32), Samodin (33), Kornilenko (40)
›zenko, Shershun, Shelayev, Kornilenko, Samodin (Liopa 77), Rusol, ›ov, Kankava (Hrytsai 67), Andriyenko, Kravchenko, Nazarenko ılović 80).
w Card(s): Kernozenko 9, Shelayev 24, Kankava 45+1, Kornilenko 86

Round - Aberdeen FC (SCO)

ızenko, Andriyenko, Denisov, Hrytsai, Nazarenko, Rusol, Samodin (Kankava ıelayev, Shershun, Vorobei (Kornilenko 90), Kravchenko (Liopa 61).
w Card(s): Nazarenko 21, Kravchenko 59
Vorobei (76)
›zenko, Andriyenko, Denisov, Kankava (Kravchenko 58), Nazarenko, , Samodin (Kornilenko 73), Shelayev, Shershun, Vorobei, Liopa.
w Card(s): Shershun 73

FC CHORNOMORETS ODESA

UEFA INTERTOTO CUP

nd Round - FC Shakhtyor Soligorsk (BLR)
Bugaiov (13, 67, 88), Venhlynskiy (18)
nko, Bugaiov, Danylovskiy, Korytko (Yaroshenko 61), Kornev hko 90+3), Nizhegorodov, Poltavets, Venhlynskiy, Zotov, Shandruk, ıchenko (Valeyev 72).
w Card(s): Kornev 39, Shandruk 63
Poltavets (27), Hryshko (64)
nko, Bugaiov, Danylovskiy (Kyrlyk 79), Hryshko, Korytko, Kornev, ›gorodov, Poltavets (Valeyev 83), Shyshchenko (Yaroshenko 72), ›druk, Biletskiy.
w Card(s): Shyshchenko 30, Kornev 44, Bugaiov 60, Korytko 61

Round - RC Lens (FRA)

nko, Venhlynskiy, Danylovskiy, Hryshko, Korytko, Lozo, ›gorodov, Poltavets (Shyshchenko 65), Yaroshenko, Shandruk, kiy (Valeyev 87).
w Card(s): Nizhegorodov 80, Yaroshenko 90+2
Venhlynskiy (10)
nko, Danylovskiy, Hryshko, Korytko, Kirilchik (Poltavets 46), Kyrlyk ›kiy 46), Lozo, Nizhegorodov, Shandruk, Shyshchenko (Yaroshenko enhlynskiy.
w Card(s): Poltavets 49

WALES

THE NEW SAINTS FC

UEFA CHAMPIONS LEAGUE

Qualifying Round - FK Ventspils (LVA)
Wilde (14), Baker (54), Hogan (90+4)
›on, Baker, Beck, Courtney, Hogan, Holmes, King, Ruscoe (Leah 81), (Morgan 46), Wilde, Wood (Naylor 85).
Naylor (90+2)
›on, Baker, Beck, Courtney, Hogan (Naylor 72), Holmes, King, Lamb ›r 57), Ruscoe, Wilde (Morgan 64), Wood.
w Card(s): Hogan 74

CARMARTHEN TOWN AFC

UEFA CUP

First Qualifying Round - SK Brann (NOR)
H 0-8
N. Thomas, Cotterrall, Fowler, Hancock, Hicks, Palmer, Ramasut, Smothers, K. Thomas, Walters, Warton.
Red Card(s): Smothers 86
Yellow Card(s): Ramasut 64, Smothers 75, Smothers 86
A 3-6 *K. Thomas (36), Hicks (47, 90)*
N. Thomas, Cotterrall, Fowler, Hancock, Hughes, Palmer, Ramasut (Hicks 46), K. Thomas (Davies 74), Thomas, Walters, Warton (Brace 71).
Yellow Card(s): Thomas 31, Warton 53, Fowler 90+3

RHYL FC

UEFA CUP

First Qualifying Round - FC Haka (FIN)
H 3-1 *Moran (26), Hunt (36), Garside (47)*
Gann, Connelly, Garside, Horan, Hunt (Cameron 80), Moran, Ruffer, Kelly, M. Powell, Graves (Roberts 76), Brewerton (Desormeaux 90).
Yellow Card(s): Graves 51, Horan 59, Kelly 65
A 0-2
Gann, Connelly, Garside (Cameron 75), Horan, Hunt, Moran, Ruffer, Roberts (Jones 84), Kelly, M. Powell (Holt 90), Graves.
Yellow Card(s): Horan 56, Kelly 77, Connelly 90

LLANELLI AFC

UEFA INTERTOTO CUP

First Round - FK Vėtra (LTU)
A 1-3 *Mumford (53)*
Harrison, Corbisiero, R. Griffiths, Dale Griffiths, Lloyd, Small, Thomas, Thompson, C. Williams (Follows 65), Darren Griffiths (Clare 89), Mumford.
Yellow Card(s): Thomas 70, R. Griffiths 75
H 5-3 *Miloševski (17og), Thomas (38), R. Griffiths (54, 88, 90+3)*
Harrison, Corbisiero, R. Griffiths, Lloyd, Mumford, Small, Thomas, C. Williams, Jones, Blackman (Follows 75), Legg.
Yellow Card(s): Lloyd 90+3

ENGLAND
7
7

2009 U21 CHAMPIONSHIP

CHAPTER 07

Qualifying for the 2009 UEFA European Under-21 Championship threw up a number of surprises before the group stage had even concluded. Austria were the first side through to the play-offs, and Finland, Belarus and Wales all unexpectedly topped their groups going into the summer break. Elsewhere, though, the competition's traditional heavyweights were flexing their muscles, with champions the Netherlands, Italy, England and Spain in particular all well placed to claim a play-off berth. Fifty-one teams contested the qualifying round, split into nine groups of five and one of six. The ten group winners and the four best-placed runners-up meet in the play-offs, played over two legs on 11 and 15 October 2008, to determine which seven sides join hosts Sweden in the final tournament between 15 and 29 June 2009.

GROUP 1

Italy's play-off place looks assured with two games to go after winning seven and drawing one of their first eight matches.

With Croatia and Greece providing the Azzurrini's main threat in a section also including Albania, the Faroe Islands and Azerbaijan, Pierluigi Casiraghi's side quickly assumed control with four successive victories to open the campaign. Robert Acquafresca's double against Croatia in a 2-0 win on 12 October 2007 established Italy as the team to catch, and the only points they dropped in their first eight games came away to Greece four days after that, Konstantinos Mitroglou's 88th-minute penalty earning his side a 2-2 draw. The five-time champions conclude their campaign with games against Greece and Croatia, with the latter still hopeful of a play-off place thanks largely to a pair of high-scoring wins against Greece. Should Croatia fall short, they will rue their 1-0 loss to Albania in their third game on 8 September.

Group 1 Results

1/6/07, E. Mannucci, Pontedera
Italy 4-0 Albania
Goal(s): 1-0 Acquafresca 8, 2-0 Dessena 17, 3-0 Criscito 35, 4-0 Lupoli 81

2/6/07, NK Varteks, Varazdin
Croatia 2-0 Faroe Islands
Goal(s): 1-0 Rukavina 24, 2-0 Begović 90+2

2/6/07, Peristeri, Athens
Greece 4-1 Azerbaijan
Goal(s): 1-0 Hristodoulopoulos 4, 1-1 Abdullayev 56, 2-1 Yusifov 72(og), 3-1 Petropoulos 75, 4-1 Hristodoulopoulos 89

6/6/07, NK Inter Zaprešic, Zapresic
Croatia 3-2 Greece
Goal(s): 0-1 Aravidis 2, 1-1 Iličević 25, 2-1 Iličević 60, 3-1 Busić 84, 3-2 Petropoulos 90

6/6/07, Ruzhdi Bizhuta, Elbasan
Albania 1-0 Faroe Islands
Goal(s): 1-0 Bakaj 67(p)

7/9/07, Briamasco, Trento
Italy 2-1 Faroe Islands
Goal(s): 1-0 Russotto 27, 1-1 Hansen 31, 2-1 Cigarini 81

8/9/07, Ruzhdi Bizhuta, Elbasan
Albania 1-0 Croatia
Goal(s): 1-0 Cani 75

8/9/07, Tofikh Bakhramov-Republic Stadium, Baku
Azerbaijan 0-2 Greece
Goal(s): 0-1 Hristodoulopoulos 10, 0-2 Aravidis 53

11/9/07, Niko Dovana, Durres
Albania 0-1 Italy
Goal(s): 0-1 Acquafresca 64

11/9/07, NK Inter Zaprešic, Zapresic
Croatia 3-2 Azerbaijan
Goal(s): 1-0 Tadić 12, 2-0 Iličević 21, 2-1 Mämmädov 34, 3-1 Abushev 45(og), 3-2 Mämmädov 62

12/9/07, Toftir, Toftir
Faroe Islands 0-2 Greece
Goal(s): 0-1 Petropoulos 30, 0-2 Papastathopoulos 39

12/10/07, Guido Angelini, Chieti
Italy 2-0 Croatia
Goal(s): 1-0 Acquafresca 39, 2-0 Acquafresca 57

14/10/07, Toftir, Toftir
Faroe Islands 1-0 Azerbaijan
Goal(s): 1-0 Olsen 45

16/10/07, Apostolos Nikolaidis, Athens
Greece 2-2 Italy
Goal(s): 1-0 Petropoulos 19, 1-1 Rossi 62, 1-2 Dessena 81, 2-2 Mitroglou 88(p)

17/10/07, Ismet Qaibov, Baku
Azerbaijan 1-1 Albania
Goal(s): 1-0 Nadirov 74, 1-1 Shoshi 81

17/10/07, Tórsvøllur, Torshavn
Faroe Islands 1-2 Croatia
Goal(s): 1-0 Hansen 4, 1-1 Kalinić 14, 1-2 Busić 21

16/11/07, Bruno Recchioni, Fermo
Italy 5-0 Azerbaijan
Goal(s): 1-0 Ämirquliyev 41(og), 2-0 Acquafresca 45+2, 3-0 Cerci 77 4-0 Russotto 84, 5-0 Dessena 90+2

17/11/07, Toftir, Toftir
Faroe Islands 0-5 Albania
Goal(s): 0-1 Sukaj 25, 0-2 Sukaj 49, 0-3 Abilaliaj 51, 0-4 Sukaj 58, 0-5 Progmi 85

17/11/07, Panionios, Athens
Greece 3-4 Croatia
Goal(s): 0-1 Ljubičić 4, 1-1 Petropoulos 31, 1-2 Busić 42, 2-2 Tripotseris 47, 3-2 Dimoutsos 66, 3-3 Rukavina 81, 3-4 Rukavina

21/11/07, Tórsvøllur, Torshavn
Faroe Islands 0-1 Italy
Goal(s): 0-1 Pozzi 79

21/11/07, Ismet Qaibov, Baku
Azerbaijan 0-1 Croatia
Goal(s): 0-1 Busić 84

21/11/07, Apostolos Nikolaidis, Athens
Greece 2-1 Albania
Goal(s): 1-0 Hristodoulopoulos 28(p), 1-1 Sukaj 34, 2-1 Mitroglou 5

25/3/08, Tofikh Bakhramov-Republic Stadium, Baku
Azerbaijan 0-2 Italy
Goal(s): 0-1 Rossi 13, 0-2 Rossi 63(p)

Group 1 Table

		Home					Away					Total				
	Pld	W	D	L	F	A	W	D	L	F	A	W	D	L	F	A
1 Italy	8	4	0	0	13	1	3	1	0	6	2	7	1	0	19	3
2 Croatia	8	3	0	0	8	4	3	0	2	7	7	6	0	2	15	1
3 Greece	7	2	1	1	11	8	2	0	1	6	3	4	1	2	17	1
4 Albania	7	2	0	1	2	1	1	1	2	7	7	3	1	3	9	8
5 Faroe Islands	8	1	0	4	2	10	0	0	3	1	5	1	0	7	3	15
6 Azerbaijan	8	0	1	3	1	6	0	0	4	3	13	0	1	7	4	1

Italy striker Gius
Rossi conclude
season with a do
against Azerb
in

aining Fixtures
)8
ia v Greece
3
' Greece
3
aijan v Faroe Islands; Croatia v Albania
3
a v Italy; Greece v Faroe Islands
)8
ia v Azerbaijan

GROUP 2

alifying in this section began on 31 May 7, ten days before the 2007 final rnament had started.

enia defeated Liechtenstein 1-0 in Yerevan on that but the real tussle in Group 2 would begin later, with : champions the Czech Republic and Turkey vying for spot. The Czechs stumbled out of the blocks with a 1-aw against Armenia but hit their stride with a pair of vins against Liechtenstein before beating Armenia 3-0 e return fixture. Then came the first big test against ey, who battled back from a goal down to draw ks to İlhan Parlak's 73rd-minute strike. Turkey beat Ukraine and Liechtenstein twice and had the ces to defeat the Czech Republic as well, Serdar an notably missing a penalty in Jablonec. But with a e in hand on the Czech Republic, Turkey's fate ains in their hands and top spot is set to be decided n the sides meet again in Bursa on 6 September.

oup 2 Results

)7, Republican, Yerevan
nia 1-0 Liechtenstein
s): 1-0 Muradyan 84
7, Valeriy Lobanovskiy, Kiev
ne 1-2 Turkey
s): 1-0 Fomin 5, 1-1 Chyzhov 50(og), 1-2 Nuri 85
7, Metalist, Kharkov
ne 4-0 Armenia
s): 1-0 Kravchenko 12, 2-0 Oliynyk 61, 3-0 Hladkiy 67, iyomov 86
7, Republican, Yerevan
nia 1-1 Czech Republic
s): 1-0 V. Petrosyan 45+2, 1-1 Pekhart 46
7, Rheinpark, Vaduz
tenstein 2-3 Turkey
s): 1-0 Christen 6, 1-1 Ergin 14, 1-2 Bahtiyaroğlu 29, 2-2 Hasler 59, gin 90+5
)7, Horni Pocernice, Horni Pocernice
n Republic 8-0 Liechtenstein
s): 1-0 Fillo 4, 2-0 Pekhart 12, 3-0 Šmejkal 40, 4-0 Šmejkal 45, ekhart 49, 6-0 Dočkal 54, 7-0 Šmejkal 70, 8-0 Dočkal 85
)7, Republican, Yerevan
nia 0-2 Ukraine
s): 0-1 Yaroshenko 39, 0-2 Oliynyk 65(p)
/07, Sportpark Eschen-Mauren, Eschen
tenstein 0-4 Czech Republic
s): 0-1 Mazuch 35, 0-2 Dočkal 39, 0-3 Šmejkal 67, 0-4 Pekhart 77(p)
14/10/07, Sükrü Saraçoglu, Istanbul
Turkey 2-0 Ukraine
Goal(s): 1-0 Nuri 62, 2-0 Mevlüt Erdinç 65
17/10/07, Sportpark Eschen-Mauren, Eschen
Liechtenstein 1-3 Ukraine
Goal(s): 0-1 Antonov 45, 0-2 Antonov 65, 1-2 Hasler 75, 1-3 Priyomov 90+3
17/10/07, Frantiska Kloze, Kladno
Czech Republic 3-0 Armenia
Goal(s): 1-0 Střeštik 2, 2-0 Jeslínek 18, 3-0 Pekhart 29
17/11/07, Strelnice, Jablonec nad Nisou
Czech Republic 1-1 Turkey
Goal(s): 1-0 Střeštik 17, 1-1 İlhan Parlak 73
17/11/07, Metalurh, Zaporizhya
Ukraine 5-0 Liechtenstein
Goal(s): 1-0 Oliynyk 26, 2-0 Lopa 30, 3-0 Yaroshchenko 39, 4-0 Hladkiy 41, 5-0 Antonov 54
20/11/07, Sportpark Eschen-Mauren, Eschen
Liechtenstein 1-4 Armenia
Goal(s): 0-1 Nranyan 13, 0-2 Andrikyan 26, 0-3 Mkhitaryan 51, 0-4 Chilingaryan 59, 1-4 Martin Büchel 71
21/11/07, Metalurh, Zaporizhya
Ukraine 0-2 Czech Republic
Goal(s): 0-1 Jeslínek 73, 0-2 Rajtoral 83
26/3/08, 5 Ocak, Adana
Turkey 3-0 Liechtenstein
Goal(s): 1-0 İlhan Parlak 45, 2-0 Nuri 58, Yelen 85

Group 2 Table

		Home					Away					Total					
	Pld	W	D	L	F	A	W	D	L	F	A	W	D	L	F	A	Pts
1 Czech Republic	6	2	1	0	12	1	2	1	0	7	1	4	2	0	19	2	14
2 Turkey	5	2	0	0	5	0	2	1	0	6	4	4	1	0	11	4	13
3 Ukraine	7	2	0	2	10	4	2	0	1	5	3	4	0	3	15	7	12
4 Armenia	6	1	1	1	2	3	1	0	2	4	8	2	1	3	6	11	7
5 Liechtenstein	8	0	0	4	4	14	0	0	4	0	17	0	0	8	4	31	0

Remaining Fixtures
20/8/08
Armenia v Turkey
6/9/08
Turkey v Czech Republic
9/9/08
Czech Republic v Ukraine; Turkey v Armenia

GROUP 3

England were unfortunate to lose to the Netherlands 13-12 on penalties in the semi-finals in 2007, but Stuart Pearce's side soon put that defeat behind them in qualifying for the 2009 edition.

England, boasting a number of full internationals and a wealth of Premier League experience, beat Montenegro and Bulgaria twice each and the Republic of Ireland without conceding a goal in their first five matches, and a play-off place was almost assured when they drew 1-1 with main rivals Portugal on 20 November. Portugal have reached each of the past four Under-21 Championships, but a 1-0 defeat in Bulgaria on 12 October left their chances of prolonging that streak in the balance. A record attendance for an Under-21 qualifier is expected at Wembley on 5 September when England and Portugal meet again in a match Rui Caçador's side must win to keep their hopes alive.

Group 3 Results

5/6/07, Balgarska Armia, Sofia
Bulgaria 1-2 Montenegro
Goal(s): 0-1 Vukčević 50, 0-2 Jovetić 66, 1-2 Simović 90+1(og)
7/9/07, Turner's Cross, Cork
Republic of Ireland 0-2 Portugal
Goal(s): 0-1 Paulo Machado 7, 0-2 Miguel Veloso 54
7/9/07, Pod Goricom - Gradski, Podgorica
Montenegro 0-3 England
Goal(s): 0-1 Onuoha 6, 0-2 Agbonlahor 10, 0-3 Surnan 90
11/9/07, Balgarska Armia, Sofia
Bulgaria 0-2 England
Goal(s): 0-1 Huddlestone 25, 0-2 Noble 32
11/9/07, Dr. Jorge Sampaio, Vila Nova de Gaia (Porto)
Portugal 4-0 Montenegro
Goal(s): 1-0 Moreira 18, 2-0 Nuno Coelho 53, 3-0 Manuel Fernandes 66, 4-0 Manuel Fernandes 89
12/10/07, Vasil Levski National Stadium, Sofia
Bulgaria 1-0 Portugal
Goal(s): 1-0 Domovchiyski 43(p)
12/10/07, Denbigh, Milton Keynes
England 1-0 Montenegro
Goal(s): 1-0 Derbyshire 20
16/10/07, Pod Goricom - Gradski, Podgorica
Montenegro 1-2 Portugal
Goal(s): 1-0 Moreira 34(og), 1-1 Celestino Silva Soares 76, 1-2 Targino 81
16/10/07, Turner's Cross, Cork
Republic of Ireland 0-3 England
Goal(s): 0-1 Noble 10, 0-2 Noble 17, 0-3 Milner 26
16/11/07, Pod Goricom - Gradski, Podgorica
Montenegro 1-0 Republic of Ireland
Goal(s): 1-0 Vujović 18
16/11/07, Denbigh, Milton Keynes
England 2-0 Bulgaria
Goal(s): 1-0 Agbonlahor 41, 2-0 Milner 82(p)
20/11/07, Athlone Stadium, Athlone
Republic of Ireland 1-0 Bulgaria
Goal(s): 1-0 O'Toole 90+3
20/11/07, Municipal, Agueda
Portugal 1-1 England
Goal(s): 1-0 Vieirinha 3(p), 1-1 Johnson 49
5/2/08, St. Mary's, Southampton
England 3-0 Republic of Ireland
Goal(s): 1-0 Milner 59, 2-0 Milner 68, 3-0 Walcott 79
25/3/08, Terryland Park, Galway
Republic of Ireland 1-1 Montenegro
Goal(s): 0-1 Bojović 68, 1-1 Keogh 72
26/3/08, D. Afonso Henriques, Guimaraes
Portugal 2-0 Bulgaria
Goal(s): 1-0 Jõao Moreira 65, 2-0 Carlos Saleiro 68

Group 3 Table

		Home					Away					Total					
	Pld	W	D	L	F	A	W	D	L	F	A	W	D	L	F	A	Pts
1 England	7	3	0	0	6	0	3	1	0	9	1	6	1	0	15	1	19
2 Portugal	6	2	1	0	7	1	2	0	1	4	2	4	1	1	11	3	13
3 Montenegro	7	1	0	2	2	5	1	1	2	3	7	2	1	4	5	12	7
4 Republic of Ireland	6	1	1	2	2	6	0	0	2	0	4	1	1	4	2	10	4
5 Bulgaria	6	1	0	2	2	4	0	0	3	0	5	1	0	5	2	9	3

Remaining Fixtures
5/9/08
Bulgaria v Republic of Ireland; England v Portugal
9/9/08
Montenegro v Bulgaria; Portugal v Republic of Ireland

GROUP 4

Spain were the only side in the competition s boasting a 100 per cent record going into the summer recess, with five wins from five game 15 goals scored and none conceded.

Fresh from winning the 2007 UEFA European Under-17 Championship, FC Barcelona prodigy Bojan Krkić was quick to make a splash at Under-21 level, scoring aged 17 in the 2-0 win away to Poland on 12 October, then i subsequent victories against Poland, again, and Kazakhstan. Spain had opened their campaign with ba to-back wins against Georgia, and it was soon apparen that the only side capable of preventing them from winning the group would be Russia, who also started w maximum points from four games. A surprise 2-0 loss i Georgia on 20 November, however, has hurt Russia's chances and adds to the pressure as their crucial pair o games with Spain approach.

Group 4 Results

5/6/07, Boris Paichadze, Tbilisi
Georgia 0-1 Spain
Goal(s): 0-1 José 74
22/8/07, LKS Kmita, Zabierzow
Poland 3-1 Georgia
Goal(s): 1-0 Pawlowski 7, 2-0 Cwielong 57, 2-1 Ghvinianidze 67, 3-1 Majewski 83
22/8/07, Central Stadium, Karaganda
Kazakhstan 0-3 Russia
Goal(s): 0-1 Dzyuba 86
7/9/07, Poladi, Rustavi
Georgia 2-1 Kazakhstan
Goal(s): 1-0 Gotsiridze 17, 2-0 Merebashvili 43, 2-1 Noskov 90+1
7/9/07, Eduard Streltsov, Moscow
Russia 1-0 Poland
Goal(s): 1-0 Kozhanov 57
11/9/07, Miejski, Wodzislaw Slaski
Poland 1-0 Kazakhstan
Goal(s): 1-0 Pawlowski 59
11/9/07, Municipal de Deportes Francisco Bonet, Almuñecar
Spain 4-0 Georgia
Goal(s): 1-0 Jiménez Tejada 13, 2-0 Jurado 45+1(p), 3-0 Granero 68, 4-0 López 80
12/10/07, Osrodek Sportu i Rekreacji, Wloclawek
Poland 0-2 Spain
Goal(s): 0-1 Jurado 69, 0-2 Bojan 90+2
12/10/07, Eduard Streltsov, Moscow
Russia 4-0 Kazakhstan
Goal(s): 1-0 Kombarov 1, 2-0 Kombarov 43, 3-0 Fayzulin 48, 4-0 Kombarov 81
16/10/07, Public stadium, Torun
Poland 0-1 Russia
Goal(s): 0-1 Prudnikov 70
16/10/07, Tcentralny, Aktobe
Kazakhstan 4-1 Georgia
Goal(s): 1-0 Kenbaev 31, 2-0 Kenbaev 35, 3-0 Nurgaliyev 41(p), 3-1 Barabadze 86, 4-1 Nurgaliyev 88
16/11/07, El Toralin, Ponferrada
Spain 3-0 Poland
Goal(s): 1-0 Glik 41(og), 2-0 Bojan 90+3, 3-0 Diego Capel 90+4
20/11/07, Mikheil Meskhi, Tbilisi
Georgia 2-0 Russia
Goal(s): 1-0 Barabadze 36, 2-0 Gotsiridze 82

'08, Antequera, Antequera

n 5-0 Kazakhstan

(s): 1-0 Jurado 10, 2-0 Diego Capel 28, 3-0 Bojan 32, 4-0 Mata 39, osé Callejón 60

up 4 Table

	Pld	Home					Away					Total					Pts
		W	D	L	F	A	W	D	L	F	A	W	D	L	F	A	
n	5	3	0	0	12	0	2	0	0	3	0	5	0	0	15	0	15
sia	5	2	0	0	5	0	2	0	1	4	2	4	0	1	9	2	12
nd	6	2	0	2	4	4	0	0	2	0	4	2	0	4	4	8	6
rgia	6	2	0	1	4	2	0	0	3	2	11	2	0	4	6	13	6
akhstan	6	1	0	1	4	4	0	0	4	1	12	1	0	5	5	16	3

aining Fixtures

'08

khstan v Poland

'08

a v Spain

8

khstan v Spain; Russia v Georgia

8

n v Russia

'08

gia v Poland

GROUP 5

e restrictions meant Netherlands coach Foppe Haan had to rebuild his Jong Oranje side that d retained the title in June 2007, but although ne of the faces changed, the results by and ge stayed the same.

ston Drenthe, the star of the team that had won the title home soil, scored the only goal in their opening game nst FYR Macedonia, which preceded victories against way, Estonia (twice) and FYR Macedonia again. The herlands conceded their first goal and dropped their first nts in a surprise 1-0 defeat at home to Switzerland, udio Lustenberger hitting the winner. Although the Netherlands remain favourites to win the section, that result opened the door for both Switzerland and in particular Norway, who went into the summer break – like Switzerland - five points behind the leaders, but with a game in hand. The Netherlands' meetings with those two sides in early September will decide the outcome of the group.

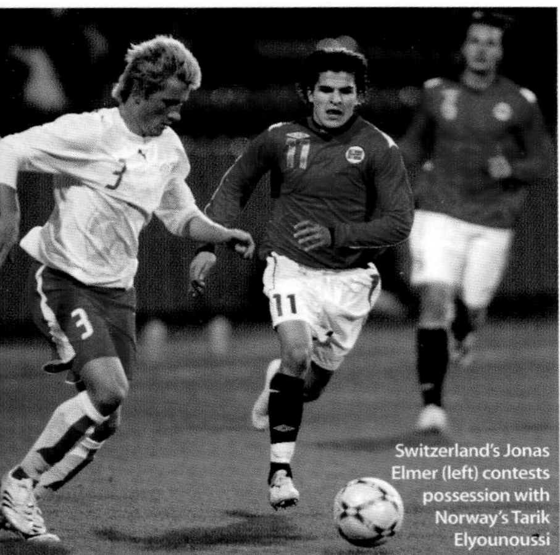

Switzerland's Jonas Elmer (left) contests possession with Norway's Tarik Elyounoussi

Group 5 Results

3/6/07, Kadriorg, Tallinn

Estonia 0-1 Norway

Goal(s): 0-1 Hanssen 90

22/8/07, Boris Trajkovski, Skopje

FYR Macedonia 0-1 Netherlands

Goal(s): 0-1 Drenthe 25

7/9/07, Fredrikstad, Fredrikstad

Norway 0-1 Netherlands

Goal(s): 0-1 Drenthe 71

8/9/07, Niedermatten, Wohlen

Switzerland 1-1 FYR Macedonia

Goal(s): 1-0 Derdiyok 36, 1-1 Zlatkovski 78

11/9/07, Boris Trajkovski, Skopje

FYR Macedonia 1-0 Estonia

Goal(s): 1-0 Alimi 75

12/10/07, Fredrikstad, Fredrikstad

Norway 2-1 Switzerland

Goal(s): 1-0 Elyounoussi 67, 1-1 Derdiyok 83, 2-1 Demidov 86

12/10/07, A Le Coq Arena, Tallinn

Estonia 0-3 Netherlands

Goal(s): 0-1 Sno 2, 0-2 Sno 44, 0-3 Beerens 53

16/10/07, Gorce Petrov, Skopje

FYR Macedonia 1-1 Norway

Goal(s): 0-1 Bjørdal 32, 1-1 Zlatkovski 47

16/10/07, A Le Coq Arena, Tallinn

Estonia 0-4 Switzerland

Goal(s): 0-1 Derdiyok 12, 0-2 Derdiyok 49, 0-3 Esteban 58, 0-4 Ural 74

16/11/07, De Goffert, Nijmegen

Netherlands 1-0 FYR Macedonia

Goal(s): 1-0 Sno 28

17/11/07, La Blancherie, Delemont

Switzerland 5-0 Estonia

Goal(s): 1-0 Derdiyok 2, 2-0 Feltscher 23, 3-0 Ziegler 30(p), 4-0 Derdiyok 45, 5-0 Lustenberger 50

20/11/07, Kristiansand, Kristiansand

Norway 2-0 Estonia

Goal(s): 1-0 Demidov 45+1, 2-0 Khalili 80

26/3/08, Gradski, Kumanovo

FYR Macedonia 2-1 Switzerland

Goal(s): 1-0 Tričkovski 12, 2-0 Zlatkovski 32, 2-1 Esteban 37

26/3/08, FC Emmen, Emmen

Netherlands 3-0 Estonia

Goal(s): 1-0 De Guzman 49, 2-0 Aissati 82, 3-0 De Guzman 90+2

23/5/08, Willem II, Tilburg

Netherlands 0-1 Switzerland

Goal(s): 0-1 Lustenberger 59

Group 5 Table

	Pld	Home					Away					Total					Pts
		W	D	L	F	A	W	D	L	F	A	W	D	L	F	A	
1 Netherlands	6	2	0	1	4	1	3	0	0	5	0	5	0	1	9	1	15
2 Norway	5	2	0	1	4	2	1	1	0	2	1	3	1	1	6	3	10
3 Switzerland	6	1	1	0	6	1	2	0	2	7	4	3	1	2	13	5	10
4 FYR Macedonia	6	2	1	1	4	3	0	1	1	1	2	2	2	2	5	5	8
5 Estonia	7	0	0	3	0	8	0	0	4	0	11	0	0	7	0	19	0

Remaining Fixtures

20/8/08

Estonia v FYR Macedonia; Switzerland v Norway

5/9/08

Netherlands v Norway

9/9/08

Norway v FYR Macedonia; Switzerland v Netherlands

GROUP 6

In one of the most open sections, Finland, Denmark and Scotland all harbour hopes of progressing as group winners as the contest builds to a dramatic climax.

Finland have never reached the final tournament of a UEFA European Under-21 Championship but they quickly looked on course to break that duck as Markku Kanerva's side seized the initiative with back-to-back wins against main rivals Denmark and Scotland in their first two games. They still boasted a perfect record after beating Slovenia then Lithuania twice to take command of the group, but Scotland threw qualification back in the balance by defeating the leaders 2-1 in March. Scotland, in third, trail Finland by five points but have a game in hand, while Denmark are second on 13 points from six games and will go top should they beat Finland in Turku on 5 September.

Group 6 Results

5/6/07, Športni park, Domzale
Slovenia 2-1 Lithuania
Goal(s): 1-0 Mihelič 57, 2-0 Matavž 60, 2-1 Galkevičius 74
6/6/07, Aalborg, Aalborg
Denmark 0-1 Finland
Goal(s): 0-1 Sparv 32
7/9/07, Aalborg, Aalborg
Denmark 4-0 Lithuania
Goal(s): 1-0 Storm 29, 2-0 Jakobsen 38, 3-0 Damborg 85, 4-0 Christensen 90+3
8/9/07, Hietalahti, Vaasa
Finland 3-2 Scotland
Goal(s): 1-0 Sadik 23, 1-1 Fletcher 45+2, 2-1 Petrescu 49, 2-2 Mulgrew 80, 3-2 Jalasto 89
11/9/07, Suduva, Marijampole
Lithuania 0-0 Slovenia
12/9/07, East End Park, Dunfermline
Scotland 0-0 Denmark
11/10/07, Easter Road, Edinburgh
Scotland 3-0 Lithuania
Goal(s): 1-0 McCormack 45, 2-0 Mulgrew 45+1, 3-0 Fletcher 58
13/10/07, Lahden, Lahti
Finland 1-0 Slovenia
Goal(s): 1-0 Sparv 8(p)
16/10/07, Športni park, Domzale
Slovenia 1-3 Denmark
Goal(s): 1-0 Lovrečič 5(p), 1-1 Troest 33, 1-2 Christensen 63, 1-3 Pedersen 66
17/10/07, S. Darius & S. Girenas, Kaunas
Lithuania 0-1 Finland
Goal(s): 0-1 Sparv 4
16/11/07, Vetra, Vilnius
Lithuania 0-3 Denmark
Goal(s): 0-1 Schöne 8, 0-2 Pedersen 83, 0-3 Christensen 90
17/11/07, Športni Park, Nova Gorica
Slovenia 0-4 Scotland
Goal(s): 0-1 Hamill 33, 0-2 McCormack 51, 0-3 Naismith 56(p), 0-4 Fletcher 61
20/11/07, Aalborg, Aalborg
Denmark 1-0 Slovenia
Goal(s): 1-0 Jakobsen 90+2(p)

Danish players celebrate after scoring against Slov

21/11/07, Finnair, Helsinki
Finland 2-1 Lithuania
Goal(s): 1-0 Hetemaj 20, 1-1 Grigaitis 26, 2-1 Parikka 33
26/3/08, Pittodrie, Aberdeen
Scotland 2-1 Finland
Goal(s): 1-0 Naismith 29, 1-1 Hämäläinen 40, 2-1 McDonald 82

Group 6 Table

		Home					Away					Total				
	Pld	W	D	L	F	A	W	D	L	F	A	W	D	L	F	A
1 Finland	6	3	0	0	6	3	2	0	1	3	2	5	0	1	9	5
2 Denmark	6	2	0	1	5	1	2	1	0	6	1	4	1	1	11	2
3 Scotland	5	2	1	0	5	1	1	0	1	6	3	3	1	1	11	4
4 Slovenia	6	1	0	2	3	8	0	1	2	0	2	1	1	4	3	10
5 Lithuania	7	0	1	2	0	4	0	0	4	2	11	0	1	6	2	15

Remaining Fixtures
20/8/08
Lithuania v Scotland
4/9/08
Scotland v Slovenia
5/9/08
Finland v Denmark
9/9/08
Slovenia v Finland; Denmark v Scotland

GROUP 7

Austria's UEFA EURO 2008™ campaign may have ended in disappointment but the Unde 21 side is proof that there is plenty of talent coming through.

Austria finished fourth at the 2007 FIFA U-20 World Cup and carried that momentum into qualifying for the 200 UEFA European Under-21 Championship, where they became the first team to reach the play-offs as group winners when Erwin Hoffer scored the only goal in victo against Slovakia on 26 March. Belgium had reached the semi-finals of the 2007 tournament but never looked lik repeating that feat after losing to Austria in their openin game then drawing with Iceland - results that allowed Manfred Zsak's side to seize control. With just two point

arating Slovakia, Belgium, Cyprus and Iceland, the ners-up spot is up for grabs, though the play-off places out of reach.

oup 7 Results

'07, Grindavíkurvöllur, Grindavik
nd 0-1 Cyprus
(s): 0-1 Dimitriou 70
7, National, Senec
akia 2-2 Iceland
(s): 1-0 Iżvolt 43(p), 1-1 Vidarsson 50(p), 2-1 Pilar 68,
Bjarnason 77
7, Achter de Kazerne, Mechelen
ium 0-1 Austria
(s): 0-1 Schiemer 74
'07, Akranesvöllur, Akranes
nd 0-0 Belgium
'07, National, Senec
akia 1-1 Austria
(s): 0-1 Dober 63, 1-1 J. Maslo 84
0/07, Sportzentrum Schwaz, Schwaz
ria 2-1 Cyprus
(s): 1-0 Hoheneder 38, 2-0 Klein 45, 2-1 Dimitriou 74
0/07, Charles Tondreau, Mons
ium 4-2 Slovakia
(s): 0-1 Opiela 21, 0-2 Jendrišek 55, 1-2 De Mul 66,
anden Borre 74, 3-2 Vanden Borre 86, 4-2 Rossini 89
0/07, Grindavíkurvöllur, Grindavik
nd 1-1 Austria
(s): 0-1 Dober 48, 1-1 Gíslason 64
0/07, TJ Senec Montostroj, Senec
akia 4-1 Cyprus
(s): 1-0 Jurco 59, 1-1 Aristidou 73, 2-1 Jurco 82, 3-1 Jurco 86(p),
iroška 89
1/07, Tasos Markou, Paralimni
us 1-2 Slovakia
(s): 0-1 Pekarík 30, 1-1 Avraam 45+1, 1-2 Piroška 72
1/07, Waldstadion, Pasching
ria 3-2 Belgium
(s): 0-1 Legear 12, 1-1 Erbek 32, 1-2 Yulu-Matondo 52, 2-2 Madl 81,
)kotie 90
1/07, Dasaki Achnas, Famagusta
us 1-2 Austria
(s): 0-1 Hoffer 9, 1-1 Shelis 19, 1-2 Stankovic 56
1/07, Edmond Machtens, Brussels
ium 1-2 Iceland
(s): 0-1 Bjarnason 15, 0-2 Smarason 25, 1-2 De Mul 81
)8, Paphiako, Paphos
us 2-0 Iceland
(s): 1-0 Panagi 54(p), 2-0 Shelis 56
'08, Paphiako, Paphos
us 0-2 Belgium
(s): 0-1 Vanden Borre 65, 0-2 De Mul 82
'08, Waldstadion, Pasching
ria 1-0 Slovakia
(s): 1-0 Hoffer 7

up 7 Table

	Pld	Home W	D	L	F	A	Away W	D	L	F	A	Total W	D	L	F	A	Pts
tria	7	3	0	0	6	3	2	2	0	5	3	5	2	0	11	6	17
vakia	6	1	2	0	7	4	1	0	2	4	6	2	2	2	11	10	8
gium	6	1	0	2	5	5	1	1	1	4	3	2	1	3	9	8	7
rus	7	1	0	3	4	6	1	0	2	3	6	2	0	5	7	12	6
and	6	0	2	1	1	2	1	1	1	4	5	1	3	2	5	7	6

aining Fixtures
)8
ria v Iceland; Slovakia v Belgium
)8
nd v Slovakia; Belgium v Cyprus

GROUP 8

Belarus travel to Latvia on 10 September needing victory to win the section and confirm their place in the play-offs.

It is a mark of their quality that they have been able to hold off the challenge of a Serbia side that reached the final of the 2007 UEFA European Under-21 Championship in their first tournament as an independent nation. Yuriy Kurnenin's team have also shown their resolve, bouncing back from a 3-1 defeat to Serbia in September to move top of a section also featuring Hungary, Latvia and San Marino. The 1-1 draw in the reverse fixture against Serbia in Vitebsk in November keeps Belarus in control of their destiny and leaves Slobodan Krčmarević's Serbia team hoping for a second chance after dropping crucial points against Latvia and Hungary earlier in the campaign. Should Belarus slip up, victory at home to Hungary will take Serbia through.

Group 8 Results

2/6/07, Vojvodina, Novi Sad
Serbia 1-1 Latvia
Goal(s): 0-1 Fertovs 63, 1-1 Neb. Marinković 69
2/6/07, Gradski, Borisov
Belarus 1-0 Hungary
Goal(s): 1-0 Kovel 15
6/6/07, Ferenc Puskás, Budapest
Hungary 1-0 Latvia
Goal(s): 1-0 Feczesin 21
6/6/07, Olimpico, Serravalle
San Marino 0-3 Belarus
Goal(s): 0-1 Kovel 25, 0-2 Kislyak 42(p), 0-3 Putilo 90
22/8/07, Gradski, Borisov
Belarus 2-1 Latvia
Goal(s): 1-0 Kryvets 48, 2-0 Komarovski 78, 2-1 Malasenoks 85
7/9/07, Olimpico, Serravalle
San Marino 1-6 Hungary
Goal(s): 0-1 Szalai 10, 1-1 Cibelli 26, 1-2 Farkas 45, 1-3 Iváncsics 59,
1-4 Szalai 70, 1-5 Szalai 74, 1-6 Szabó 88
8/9/07, Omladinski, Belgrade
Serbia 3-1 Belarus
Goal(s): 1-0 Petković 21, 2-0 Fejsa 61, 3-0 Đurđić 87, 3-1 Kryvets 90
11/9/07, Skonto, Riga
Latvia 2-0 San Marino
Goal(s): 1-0 Lukjanovs 29, 2-0 Kozlovs 55
12/9/07, Megyeri úti, Budapest
Hungary 2-1 Serbia
Goal(s): 1-0 Petković 23(og), 2-0 Hrepka 33, 2-1 Sulejmani 50
13/10/07, Omladinski, Belgrade
Serbia 3-0 San Marino
Goal(s): 1-0 Babović 10, 2-0 Neb. Marinković 30, 3-0 Pavlović 62
16/10/07, Üllöi úti, Budapest
Hungary 0-1 Belarus
Goal(s): 0-1 Komarovski 42
17/10/07, Skonto, Riga
Latvia 0-2 Serbia
Goal(s): 0-1 F. Đorđević 57, 0-2 F. Đorđević 69
16/11/07, Central, Vitebsk
Belarus 6-0 San Marino
Goal(s): 1-0 Komarovski 14, 2-0 Afanasiev 18, 3-0 Kovel 42,
4-0 Komarovski 45, 5-0 Kuchuk 79, 6-0 Verkhautsou 82

18/11/07, Skonto, Riga
Latvia 1-0 Hungary
Goal(s): 1-0 Gauracs 65
20/11/07, Central, Vitebsk
Belarus 1-1 Serbia
Goal(s): 1-0 Kryvets 48, 1-1 Z. Tošić 58
26/3/08, Olimpico, Serravalle
San Marino 0-5 Serbia
Goal(s): 0-1 F. Đorđević 13, 0-2 Petković 27, 0-3 Kačar 28, 0-4 Babović 50, 0-5 F. Đorđević 90+3

Group 8 Table

		Home					Away					Total					
	Pld	W	D	L	F	A	W	D	L	F	A	W	D	L	F	A	Pts
1 Belarus	7	3	1	0	10	2	2	0	1	5	3	5	1	1	15	5	16
2 Serbia	7	2	1	0	7	2	2	1	1	9	3	4	2	1	16	5	14
3 Hungary	6	2	0	1	3	2	1	0	2	6	3	3	0	3	9	5	9
4 Latvia	6	2	0	1	3	2	0	1	2	2	4	2	1	3	5	6	7
5 San Marino	6	0	0	3	1	14	0	0	3	0	11	0	0	6	1	25	0

Remaining Fixtures
20/8/08
Hungary v San Marino
5/9/08
San Marino v Latvia
6/9/08
Serbia v Hungary
9/9/08
Latvia v Belarus

GROUP 9

Germany hold pole position going into the final rounds and look to be stepping up a gear after successive 7-0 and 6-0 victories against Luxembourg.

With key games against Israel and Northern Ireland to come, though, Dieter Eilts's side know the job is far from done. Israel, who reached their first UEFA European Under-21 Championship in 2007, are level on points with Germany but have played a game more, while Northern Ireland are a further point back but with just one game to play. The likes of Jan Rosenthal, Marc Kruska, Sami Khedira and Manuel Neuer bring Germany plenty of Bundesliga experience - and, in seven-goal Rouwen Hennings, a real cutting edge up front. By the summer break their tally of 21 goals was the most scored by any team in the competition.

Group 9 Results

1/6/07, Sheriff, Tiraspol
Moldova 0-1 Northern Ireland
Goal(s): 0-1 Turner 2
7/9/07, Ramat Gan, Tel-Aviv
Israel 3-0 Luxembourg
Goal(s): 1-0 Buzaglo 19, 2-0 Shechter 25(p), 3-0 Gabbay 80
7/9/07, Mourneview Park, Lurgan
Northern Ireland 0-3 Germany
Goal(s): 0-1 Ebert 78, 0-2 Özil 90, 0-3 Hennings 90+2
11/9/07, Sheriff, Tiraspol
Moldova 1-0 Israel
Goal(s): 1-0 Stinga 89

Rouwen Hennings (right) - Germany's leading scorer with seven goals

12/9/07, Henri Dunant, Beggen
Luxembourg 1-2 Northern Ireland
Goal(s): 1-0 Sagramola 10, 1-1 Fordyce 53, 1-2 Waterworth 74
12/10/07, Ramat Gan, Tel-Aviv
Israel 2-2 Germany
Goal(s): 0-1 Hennings 18, 1-1 Buzaglo 43, 2-1 Azriel 70, 2-2 Hennings 78
13/10/07, Op Flor, Grevenmacher
Luxembourg 0-2 Moldova
Goal(s): 0-1 Frantuz 76(p), 0-2 Stinga 83
16/10/07, Husterhöhe, Pirmasens
Germany 3-0 Moldova
Goal(s): 1-0 Özil 36, 2-0 Özil 69, 3-0 Hennings 90+3
17/10/07, Mourneview Park, Lurgan
Northern Ireland 1-3 Israel
Goal(s): 0-1 Buzaglo 1, 0-2 Shechter 51, 1-2 Turner 57, 1-3 Azriel 81
16/11/07, Mourneview Park, Lurgan
Northern Ireland 5-0 Luxembourg
Goal(s): 1-0 Buchanan 2, 2-0 Waterworth 5, 3-0 Turner 8, 4-0 Ward 27
5-0 Turner 56
20/11/07, Mourneview Park, Lurgan
Northern Ireland 3-0 Moldova
Goal(s): 1-0 O'Connor 4, 2-0 Ward 10, 3-0 Buchanan 11
20/11/07, Josy Barthel, Luxembourg
Luxembourg 0-7 Germany
Goal(s): 0-1 Hennings 8, 0-2 Kruska 12(p), 0-3 Rosenthal 19, 0-4 Rosenthal 23, 0-5 Barış Özbek 30, 0-6 Hennings 44, 0-7 Dejagah 9
6/2/08, Ramat Gan, Tel-Aviv
Israel 2-1 Northern Ireland
Goal(s): 1-0 Sahar 66, 1-1 Stewart 81, 2-1 Srur 86
25/3/08, BRITA-Arena, Wiesbaden
Germany 6-0 Luxembourg
Goal(s): 1-0 Khedira 28, 2-0 Khedira 47, 3-0 Özil 50, 4-0 Hennings 54, 5-0 Khedira 58, 6-0 Barış Özbek 85
26/3/08, Ramat Gan, Tel-Aviv
Israel 1-0 Moldova
Goal(s): 1-0 Sahar 7

Group 9 Table

		Home					Away					Total				
	Pld	W	D	L	F	A	W	D	L	F	A	W	D	L	F	A
1 Germany	5	2	0	0	9	0	2	1	0	12	2	4	1	0	21	2
2 Israel	6	3	1	0	8	3	1	0	1	3	2	4	1	1	11	5
3 Northern Ireland	7	2	0	2	9	6	2	0	1	4	3	4	0	3	13	9
4 Moldova	6	1	0	1	1	1	1	0	3	2	7	2	0	4	3	8
5 Luxembourg	6	0	0	3	1	11	0	0	3	0	14	0	0	6	1	25

ining Fixtures
)8
›va v Germany
'
ıbourg v Israel; Germany v Northern Ireland
3
›va v Luxembourg; Germany v Israel

GROUP 10

es have been one of the biggest surprises of lifying and led a section France and nania were expected to dominate going the summer break.

e was little to suggest what was to follow when Wales ed off their campaign with a 1-0 defeat to France, but that Brian Flynn's side did not drop a point in five hes and were set to win the group with victory over ania on 20 August. Ched Evans has been their star, ng seven times already including a hat-trick in a 4-2 against France on 20 November that seriously aged Les Bleuets' chances of making the play-offs. The ear-old followed that with goals in victories against Malta and Bosnia-Herzegovina before hitting the er on his full international debut against Iceland in Romania, who conceded no goals in four games after ing with a 1-1 draw against France, went into the mer break four points behind Wales, level with France, with a game in hand on both sides.

oup 10 Results

', Francis-Le-Blé, Brest
e 1-1 Romania
s): 0-1 Marange 19(og), 1-1 Samassa 49
', Hibernians Ground, Corradino
0-1 Romania
s): 0-1 Palimaru 90+4
', Lesdiguières, Grenoble
e 1-0 Wales
s): 1-0 Eardley 50(og)
', Bilino Polje, Zenica
a-Herzegovina 4-0 Malta
s): 1-0 Aganović 3, 2-0 Adilović 27, 3-0 Adilović 60, 4-0 Perić 86
)7, 1 Mai, Râmnicu Vâlcea
nia 3-0 Bosnia-Herzegovina
s): 1-0 Torje 6, 2-0 Torje 36, 3-0 Keseru 76
'7, Ta' Qali, Ta' Qali
0-2 France
s): 0-1 Gouffran 15, 0-2 Bellaid 74
/07, Municipal Stadium, Albi
e 4-0 Bosnia-Herzegovina
s): 1-0 Gouffran 29, 2-0 Gakpé 64, 3-0 Marveaux 69, 4-0 Marveaux 78
'07, Emil Alexandrescu, Iasi
nia 0-0 France
/07, The Racecourse, Wrexham
3-1 Malta
s): 1-0 Williams 15, 2-0 Church 41, 3-0 Vokes 73, 3-1 Zammit 80
/07, Ceahlaul, Piatra Neamt
nia 4-0 Malta
s): 1-0 Sirghi 21, 2-0 Stancu 45+1, 3-0 Scutaru 50, 4-0 Diviu Ganea 53
17/11/07, The Racecourse, Wrexham
Wales 4-0 Bosnia-Herzegovina
Goal(s): 1-0 McDonald 30, 2-0 Vokes 56, 3-0 Evans 75, 4-0 Collison 89
20/11/07, Hibernians Ground, Corradino
Malta 2-1 Bosnia-Herzegovina
Goal(s): 0-1 Adilović 8, 1-1 Fenech 15, 2-1 Bartolo 61
20/11/07, Ninian Park, Cardiff
Wales 4-2 France
Goal(s): 1-0 Evans 45, 1-1 Gourcuff 72(p), 1-2 Payet 77, 2-2 Evans 79(p), 3-2 Bradley 81, 4-2 Evans 90+1(p)
5/2/08, Hibernians Ground, Corradino
Malta 0-4 Wales
Goal(s): 0-1 Evans 60, 0-2 Church 79, 0-3 Collison 87, 0-4 Evans 90+1(p)
26/3/08, Koševo, Sarajevo
Bosnia-Herzegovina 1-2 Wales
Goal(s): 1-0 Boubacar Daliba 59, 1-1 Church 87, 1-2 Evans 88

Group 10 Table

		Home					Away					Total					
	Pld	W	D	L	F	A	W	D	L	F	A	W	D	L	F	A	Pts
1 Wales	6	3	0	0	11	3	2	0	1	6	2	5	0	1	17	5	15
2 Romania	5	2	1	0	7	0	1	1	0	2	1	3	2	0	9	1	11
3 France	6	2	1	0	6	1	1	1	1	4	4	3	2	1	10	5	11
4 Bosnia-Herzegovina	6	1	0	1	5	2	0	0	4	1	13	1	0	5	6	15	3
5 Malta	7	1	0	3	2	8	0	0	3	1	11	1	0	6	3	19	3

Remaining Fixtures
20/8/08
Wales v Romania
5/9/08
France v Malta
6/9/08
Bosnia-Herzegovina v Romania
9/9/08
Bosnia-Herzegovina v France; Romania v Wales

France's Didier Digard (left) and Aaron Ramsey of Wales stage an aerial battle

CHAPTER
08

The seventh UEFA European Under-19 Championship started in unusual fashion as Spain – winners of the competition in four of the previous six seasons, including 2006 and 2007 – suffered a rare defeat against a powerful Germany side. The result proved to be decisive for both teams, Germany going on to lift the trophy for the first time – the country's first European youth title since 1992 – by winning all five games in the Czech Republic, defeating the hosts 2-1 in the semi-finals and saving the best till last with an inspired display against Italy in the final despite playing more than half the match with ten men. For Spain and England, however, there was a disappointingly early exit, while the hosts were unfortunate to lose in the last four and Hungary enjoyed a finals debut to remember, going down narrowly to Italy in the last four but departing with the scalp of the holders.

2007/08

QUALIFYING ROUND

Group 1 Results

1/11/07, Varzim, Povoa do Varzim
Republic of Ireland 0-2 Belarus
1/11/07, CD Trofense, Trofa
Portugal 1-0 Andorra
3/11/07, Rio Ave, Vila do Conde
Republic of Ireland 3-0 Andorra
3/11/07, Dr. José Vieira Carvalho, Maia
Belarus 1-2 Portugal
6/11/07, Varzim, Povoa do Varzim
Portugal 2-1 Republic of Ireland
6/11/07, Padroense FC, Padrao Legua
Andorra 1-5 Belarus

Group 1 Table

	Pld	W	D	L	F	A	Pts
1 Portugal	3	3	0	0	5	2	9
2 Belarus	3	2	0	1	8	3	6
3 Republic of Ireland	3	1	0	2	4	4	3
4 Andorra	3	0	0	3	1	9	0

Group 2 Results

8/10/07, Tatabánya Városi, Tatabanya
Switzerland 1-1 Wales
8/10/07, Sóstói, Szekesfehervar
Hungary 6-0 Kazakhstan
10/10/07, Tatabánya Városi, Tatabanya
Switzerland 6-1 Kazakhstan
10/10/07, Sóstói, Szekesfehervar
Wales 1-3 Hungary
13/10/07, Tatabánya Városi, Tatabanya
Hungary 2-1 Switzerland
13/10/07, Sóstói, Szekesfehervar
Kazakhstan 2-1 Wales

Group 2 Table

	Pld	W	D	L	F	A	Pts
1 Hungary	3	3	0	0	11	2	9
2 Switzerland	3	1	1	1	8	4	4
3 Kazakhstan	3	1	0	2	3	13	3
4 Wales	3	0	1	2	3	6	1

Group 3 Results

12/10/07, Bootham Crescent, York
Belgium 4-0 Romania
12/10/07, Keepmoat, Doncaster
England 5-1 Iceland
14/10/07, Glanford Park, Scunthorpe
Romania 0-6 England
14/10/07, Spotland, Rochdale
Belgium 1-3 Iceland
17/10/07, Oakwell, Barnsley
England 3-1 Belgium
17/10/07, Keepmoat, Doncaster
Iceland 2-0 Romania

Group 3 Table

	Pld	W	D	L	F	A	Pts
1 England	3	3	0	0	14	2	9
2 Iceland	3	2	0	1	6	6	6
3 Belgium	3	1	0	2	6	6	3
4 Romania	3	0	0	3	0	12	0

Group 4 Results

26/10/07, Henri Dunant, Beggen
Slovenia 3-0 Luxembourg
26/10/07, John Grün, Mondorf les Bains
France 2-2 Greece
28/10/07, Henri Dunant, Beggen
Slovenia 0-1 Greece
28/10/07, La Frontière, Esch-sur-Alzette
Luxembourg 0-5 France
31/10/07, La Frontière, Esch-sur-Alzette
France 2-0 Slovenia
31/10/07, John Grün, Mondorf les Bains
Greece 5-1 Luxembourg

Group 4 Table

	Pld	W	D	L	F	A	Pts
1 France	3	2	1	0	9	2	7
2 Greece	3	2	1	0	8	3	7
3 Slovenia	3	1	0	2	3	3	3
4 Luxembourg	3	0	0	3	1	13	0

Group 5 Results

18/10/07, La Forana, Alginet
Serbia 3-0 Liechtenstein
18/10/07, La Forana, Alginet
Spain 2-0 Albania
20/10/07, Luis Suner, Alzira
Albania 2-1 Serbia
20/10/07, Luis Suner, Alzira
Spain 0-0 Liechtenstein
23/10/07, El Collao, Alcoy
Serbia 1-1 Spain
23/10/07, La Forana, Alginet
Liechtenstein 0-0 Albania

Group 5 Table

	Pld	W	D	L	F	A	Pts
1 Spain	3	1	2	0	3	1	5
2 Albania	3	1	1	1	2	3	4
3 Serbia	3	1	1	1	5	3	4
4 Liechtenstein	3	0	2	1	0	3	2

Group 6 Results

12/10/07, Svartavallen, Boxholm
Israel 3-0 FYR Macedonia
12/10/07, Motala Idrottspark, Motala
Sweden 2-0 Finland
14/10/07, Svartavallen, Boxholm
Sweden 3-1 FYR Macedonia
14/10/07, Vifolkavallen, Mjölby
Finland 0-1 Israel
17/10/07, Vifolkavallen, Mjölby
Israel 1-0 Sweden
17/10/07, Motala Idrottspark, Motala
FYR Macedonia 0-3 Finland

Group 6 Table

	Pld	W	D	L	F
1 Israel	3	3	0	0	5
2 Sweden	3	2	0	1	5
3 Finland	3	1	0	2	3
4 FYR Macedonia	3	0	0	3	1

Group 7 Results

20/10/07, Sūduva, Marijampole
Poland 5-0 San Marino
20/10/07, S. Darius & S. Girenas, Kaunas
Armenia 2-2 Lithuania
22/10/07, Sūduva, Marijampole
Armenia 1-0 San Marino
22/10/07, S. Darius & S. Girenas, Kaunas
Lithuania 1-1 Poland
25/10/07, Sūduva, Marijampole
Poland 0-0 Armenia
25/10/07, S. Darius & S. Girenas, Kaunas
San Marino 0-4 Lithuania

Group 7 Table

	Pld	W	D	L	F	A
1 Lithuania	3	1	2	0	7	[illegible]
2 Armenia	3	1	2	0	3	2
3 Poland	3	1	2	0	6	[illegible]
4 San Marino	3	0	0	3	0	1

Group 8 Results

18/10/07, Poladi, Rustavi
Norway 2-0 Latvia
18/10/07, Mikheil Meskhi, Tbilisi
Netherlands 2-1 Georgia
20/10/07, Temur Stepania, Bolnisi
Netherlands 2-0 Latvia
20/10/07, Mikheil Meskhi, Tbilisi
Georgia 0-1 Norway
23/10/07, Poladi, Rustavi
Norway 3-1 Netherlands
23/10/07, Mikheil Meskhi, Tbilisi
Latvia 2-0 Georgia

Group 8 Table

	Pld	W	D	L	F	A
1 Norway	3	3	0	0	6	1
2 Netherlands	3	2	0	1	5	4
3 Latvia	3	1	0	2	2	4
4 Georgia	3	0	0	3	1	5

oup 9 Results

'07, Gradski, Nessebar
y 3-1 Faroe Islands
'07, Naftex, Bourgas
ark 0-1 Bulgaria
'07, Gradski, Nessebar
Islands 0-2 Denmark
'07, Naftex, Bourgas
y 2-0 Bulgaria
'07, Gradski, Nessebar
ark 0-0 Turkey
'07, Naftex, Bourgas
ria 0-0 Faroe Islands

p 9 Table

	Pld	W	D	L	F	A	Pts
key	3	2	1	0	5	1	7
garia	3	1	1	1	1	2	4
nmark	3	1	1	1	2	1	4
oe Islands	3	0	1	2	1	5	1

oup 10 Results

'07, Paphiako, Paphos
ia 1-0 Northern Ireland
'07, Municipal, Geroskipou
kia 5-1 Cyprus
7, Paphiako, Paphos
ia 1-2 Cyprus
7, Peyia Municipal, Paphos
ern Ireland 1-2 Slovakia
7, Municipal, Geroskipou
kia 2-0 Austria
7, Peyia Municipal, Paphos
s 1-1 Northern Ireland

Group 10 Table

	Pld	W	D	L	F	A	Pts
1 Slovakia	3	3	0	0	9	2	9
2 Cyprus	3	1	1	1	4	7	4
3 Austria	3	1	0	2	2	4	3
4 Northern Ireland	3	0	1	2	2	4	1

Group 11 Results

26/10/07, Zimbru, Chisinau
Scotland 0-1 Moldova
26/10/07, District Sport Complex, Orhei
Ukraine 3-0 Azerbaijan
28/10/07, Zimbru, Chisinau
Ukraine 2-1 Moldova
28/10/07, District Sport Complex, Orhei
Azerbaijan 2-0 Scotland
31/10/07, District Sport Complex, Orhei
Scotland 0-1 Ukraine
31/10/07, Zimbru, Chisinau
Moldova 0-0 Azerbaijan

Group 11 Table

	Pld	W	D	L	F	A	Pts
1 Ukraine	3	3	0	0	6	1	9
2 Moldova	3	1	1	1	2	2	4
3 Azerbaijan	3	1	1	1	2	3	4
4 Scotland	3	0	0	3	0	4	0

Group 12 Results

24/9/07, Krylya Sovetov, Moscow
Germany 8-1 Bosnia-Herzegovina
24/9/07, Spartak, Schelkovo
Russia 7-0 Estonia
26/9/07, Spartak, Schelkovo
Germany 5-1 Estonia
26/9/07, Moskvich, Moscow
Bosnia-Herzegovina 0-1 Russia
29/9/07, Krylya Sovetov, Moscow
Russia 3-2 Germany
29/9/07, Moskvich, Moscow
Estonia 2-2 Bosnia-Herzegovina

Group 12 Table

	Pld	W	D	L	F	A	Pts
1 Russia	3	3	0	0	11	2	9
2 Germany	3	2	0	1	15	5	6
3 Bosnia-Herzegovina	3	0	1	2	3	11	1
4 Estonia	3	0	1	2	3	14	1

Group 13 Results

10/11/07, Comunale, Iesi
Croatia 3-0 Malta
10/11/07, Comunale, Castelfidardo
Italy 3-1 Montenegro
12/11/07, Comunale, Castelfidardo
Croatia 2-1 Montenegro
12/11/07, Comunale, Iesi
Malta 0-2 Italy
15/11/07, Comunale, Castelfidardo
Italy 3-1 Croatia
15/11/07, Comunale, Iesi
Montenegro 3-0 Malta

Group 13 Table

	Pld	W	D	L	F	A	Pts
1 Italy	3	3	0	0	8	2	9
2 Croatia	3	2	0	1	6	4	6
3 Montenegro	3	1	0	2	5	5	3
4 Malta	3	0	0	3	0	8	0

nany's Mario Vrancic (right) competes for the ball with Russia's Sergei Morozov

ELITE ROUND

Group 1 Results

26/5/08, Gradski, Borisov
England 2-0 Poland
Goal(s): 1-0 Sears 28, 2-0 Sears 87(p)

26/5/08, Traktor, Minsk
Belarus 0-4 Serbia
Goal(s): 0-1 Vuković 1, 0-2 Vuković 41, 0-3 Milojevic 57, 0-4 Gulan 75

28/5/08, Gradski, Borisov
England 1-0 Serbia
Goal(s): 1-0 Henry 56

28/5/08, Traktor, Minsk
Poland 0-1 Belarus
Goal(s): 0-1 Talkanitsa 77

31/5/08, Traktor, Minsk
Belarus 0-0 England

31/5/08, Gradski, Borisov
Serbia 0-1 Poland
Goal(s): 0-1 Lukasz 66

Group 1 Table

	Pld	W	D	L	F	A	Pts
1 England	3	2	1	0	3	0	7
2 Belarus	3	1	1	1	1	4	4
3 Poland	3	1	0	2	1	3	3
4 Serbia	3	1	0	2	4	2	3

Group 2 Results

19/5/08, Tatabánya Városi, Tatabanya
Portugal 5-0 Cyprus
Goal(s): 1-0 Romeu Ribeiro 5, 2-0 Castro Oliveira 7, 3-0 Miguel Vítor 15, 4-0 Carvalhas 33, 5-0 Kyriakou 90(og)

19/5/08, Sóstói, Szekesfehervar
Hungary 2-2 Lithuania
Goal(s): 1-0 Gosztonyi 33, 2-0 Présinger 52, 2-1 Papsys 66, 2-2 Papsys 72

21/5/08, Tatabánya Városi, Tatabanya
Lithuania 1-3 Portugal
Goal(s): 0-1 Miguel Vítor 34, 1-1 Papsys 73, 1-2 Ruben Lima 85, 1-3 Castro Oliveira 90+4

21/5/08, Sóstói, Szekesfehervar
Hungary 2-1 Cyprus
Goal(s): 1-0 Németh 37(p), 2-0 Németh 57, 2-1 Efrem 78

24/5/08, Sóstói, Szekesfehervar
Portugal 0-1 Hungary
Goal(s): 0-1 Németh 62

24/5/08, Tatabánya Városi, Tatabanya
Cyprus 1-0 Lithuania
Goal(s): 1-0 Efrem 70(p)

Group 2 Table

	Pld	W	D	L	F
1 Hungary	3	2	1	0	5
2 Portugal	3	2	0	1	8
3 Cyprus	3	1	0	2	2
4 Lithuania	3	0	1	2	3

Group 3 Results

27/4/08, Lisleby, Fredrikstad
Israel 0-1 Bulgaria
Goal(s): 0-1 Tsvetanov 11

27/4/08, Melløs, Moss
Norway 2-3 Iceland
Goal(s): 0-1 Sigurdsson 23, 1-1 Khalili 43, 1-2 Gunnarsson 45, 1-3 Gunnarsson 64, 2-3 Gulsvik 69

29/4/08, Lisleby, Fredrikstad
Norway 0-2 Bulgaria
Goal(s): 0-1 Aleksandrov 28(p), 0-2 Musta

29/4/08, Sarpsborg, Sarpsborg
Iceland 1-0 Israel
Goal(s): 1-0 Sigurdsson 7

2/5/08, Sarpsborg, Sarpsborg
Israel 0-2 Norway
Goal(s): 0-1 Orry Larsen 8, 0-2 Orry Larsen

2/5/08, Råde Idrettspark, Rade
Bulgaria 2-1 Iceland
Goal(s): 1-0 Tsvetanov 30, 2-0 Zehirov 90+ 2-1 Sigurdsson 90+4(p)

Group 3 Table

	Pld	W	D	L	F
1 Bulgaria	3	3	0	0	5
2 Iceland	3	2	0	1	5
3 Norway	3	1	0	2	4
4 Israel	3	0	0	3	0

Group 4 Results

22/5/08, SFM Senec, Velky Biel
Slovakia 1-1 Croatia
Goal(s): 1-0 Stoch 12, 1-1 Poljak 41

22/5/08, National, Senec
Germany 2-0 Albania
Goal(s): 1-0 Aydilek 6, 2-0 Diekmeier 36

24/5/08, National, Senec
Slovakia 2-2 Albania
Goal(s): 0-1 Metani 8, 0-2 Mustafaj 14, 1-2 Jakubjak 27, 2-2 Sylvestr 41

24/5/08, FC Nitra, Nitra
Croatia 2-2 Germany
Goal(s): 1-0 Prijić 51(p), 2-0 Smrekar 59, 2-1 Gebhart 64, 2-2 Gebhart 86(p)

Dennis Naki of Germany evades the tackle of Albania's Klodian Samina

8, FC Nitra, Nitra
any 5-2 Slovakia
s): 0-1 Diekmeier 4(og), 1-1 Naki 8,
bhart 16(p), 3-1 Fischer 43, 3-2 Supak 55,
se 71(p), 5-2 Sven Bender 84

8, National, Senec
ia 0-2 Croatia
s): 0-1 Prijić 10, 0-2 Maloca 64

p 4 Table

	Pld	W	D	L	F	A	Pts
many	3	2	1	0	9	4	7
atia	3	1	2	0	5	3	5
vakia	3	0	2	1	5	8	2
ania	3	0	1	2	2	6	1

oup 5 Results

8, Argos Orestiko, Argos Orestiko
a 2-2 Netherlands
s): 1-0 Maguire 5(og), 1-1 Wijnaldum 18,
ochalin 46, 2-2 Fer 71

8, Kastoria, Kastoria
e 1-2 Moldova
s): 0-1 Catan 29, 1-1 Matsoukas 62,
dronic 80

8, Argos Orestiko, Argos Orestiko
a 2-1 Moldova
): 1-0 Ryzhov 21, 1-1 Catan 34, 2-1 Pesegov 50

8, Kastoria, Kastoria
rlands 1-2 Greece
s): 0-1 Matsoukas 71, 1-1 Zeefuik 87,
nis 90+1(p)

8, Kastoria, Kastoria
e 3-1 Russia
s): 1-0 Pavlis 17, 1-1 Gorbatenko 21,
padopoulos 54, 3-1 Pavlis 63

8, Argos Orestiko, Argos Orestiko
ova 0-0 Netherlands

p 5 Table

	Pld	W	D	L	F	A	Pts
eece	3	2	0	1	6	4	6
ssia	3	1	1	1	5	6	4
ldova	3	1	1	1	3	3	4
therlands	3	0	2	1	3	4	2

oup 6 Results

8, Octodure, Martigny
2-0 Sweden
s): 1-0 Paloschi 42, 2-0 Forestieri 76

08, Saint-Germain, Savièse
e 3-2 Switzerland
s): 1-0 Malonga 31, 1-1 Frei 61,
alonga 63, 3-1 Robert 80, 3-2 Frei 90(p)

Igor Prijić puts Croatia ahead against Germany from the penalty spot

28/5/08, Tourbillon, Sion
Italy 2-0 Switzerland
Goal(s): 1-0 Paloschi 53, 2-0 Okaka Chuka 78

28/5/08, Saint-Germain, Saviese
Sweden 1-2 France
Goal(s): 0-1 Robert 3, 0-2 Obertan 32,
1-2 Faceberg 82

31/5/08, Tourbillon, Sion
France 0-2 Italy
Goal(s): 0-1 Mazzarani 65, 0-2 Mazzarani 90+3

31/5/08, Octodure, Martigny
Switzerland 4-1 Sweden
Goal(s): 0-1 Ekdal 55, 1-1 Frei 64, 2-1
Gavranovic 68, 3-1 Stocker 73, 4-1 Frei 90+3

Group 6 Table

	Pld	W	D	L	F	A	Pts
1 Italy	3	3	0	0	6	0	9
2 France	3	2	0	1	5	5	6
3 Switzerland	3	1	0	2	6	6	3
4 Sweden	3	0	0	3	2	8	0

Group 7 Results

22/5/08, Kotayk, Abovyan
Turkey 2-1 Armenia
Goal(s): 1-0 Yildrim 10, 1-1 Voskanyan 43,
2-1 Sentürk 61

22/5/08, Ashtarak Kasakh, Yerevan
Ukraine 1-3 Spain
Goal(s): 1-0 Iarmolenko 18(p), 1-1 Emilio 22,
1-2 Aarón 65, 1-3 Emilio 90+1

24/5/08, Kotayk, Abovyan
Ukraine 1-0 Armenia
Goal(s): 1-0 Antonyan 23(og)

24/5/08, Ashtarak Kasakh, Yerevan
Spain 3-0 Turkey
Goal(s): 1-0 Camacho 47, 2-0 Bolado 62,
3-0 Camacho 83

27/5/08, Ashtarak Kasakh, Yerevan
Turkey 0-3 Ukraine
Goal(s): 0-1 Kravets 17, 0-2 Dovgiy 41,
0-3 Kravets 76

27/5/08, Kotayk, Abovyan
Armenia 2-4 Spain
Goal(s): 1-0 Voskanyan 21, 2-0 Gyozalyan 45+1,
2-1 Bolado 45+2, 2-2 Antonyan 50(og),
2-3 Mérida 84, 2-4 Mérida 87

Group 7 Table

	Pld	W	D	L	F	A	Pts
1 Spain	3	3	0	0	10	3	9
2 Ukraine	3	2	0	1	5	3	6
3 Turkey	3	1	0	2	2	7	3
4 Armenia	3	0	0	3	3	7	0

FINAL TOURNAMENT

GROUP A

When the draw put Spain, the holders, and Germany, semi-finalists in 2005 and 2007, alongside finals debutants Hungary and Bulgaria in Group A, the established powerhouses of youth football seemed clear favourites to progress again. Hungary coach Tibor Sisa was in confident mood, however, describing his squad as "a good generation" – and his charges were to vindicate that faith in impressive fashion.

Spain shock

The section's opening game pitted Sisa's side against Bulgaria in Zizkov, and Krisztián Németh scored what proved to be the only goal in the tenth minute, racing on to Vlagyimir Komán's long pass to shoot low into the net. Bulgaria had their chances, Todor Georgiev striking the crossbar with a thunderous long-range effort, but the equaliser would not come. Spain went into their fixture against Germany in Plzen unbeaten in 22 competitive U19 fixtures, but they fell behind to Richard Sukuta-Pasu's seventh-minute strike. Eleven minutes into the second period, Ömer Toprak headed in from a corner with goalkeeper David de Gea out of position, and although Jordi Alba pulled one back, Spain slipped to their first defeat since April 2005.

That left Ginés Meléndez's side with little room for manoeuvre when they met Hungary in Pribram three days later, but another De Gea mistake 19 minutes from time proved costly, the goalkeeper dropping a cross for Oliver Nagy to prod in. Spain might still have taken at least a point, but Daniel Parejo and Emilio Nsue twice spurned golden chances in a frantic finale. Spain's elimination, and Hungary's place in the semi-finals, was confirmed as Germany also booked their berth in the last four with a 3-0 dismantling of Bulgaria, Dennis Diekmeier and Savio Nsereko striking in the first half and Lars Bender adding a third early in the second.

Germany momentum

Germany won the section with a third successive win against a Hungary side who made seven changes for the match in Pribram and fell behind to Stefan Reinartz's powerful header in the 36th minute. András Simon levelled with 16 minutes left, but Marcel Risse's crashing drive two minutes later settled the game. Spain claimed the consolation prize of the group's final place in the 2009 FIFA U-20 World Cup with a 4-0 win against Bulgaria in Zizkov, Aarón Ñíguez scoring from the halfway line in the 14th minute before Emilio (two) and Fran Mérida rounded off a convincing win - although th deposed holders did lose Álvaro Domínguez Soto late o for a second bookable offence.

Group A Results

14/7/08, FK Viktoria Žižkov, Prague
Bulgaria 0-1 Hungary
Bulgaria: Karadjov, Panov, Uzunov, Makendzhiev (Tsachev 52), Georgiev, Tsvetanov, Dimov, Gadzhalov, Aleksandrov (Zlatkov 85), Zehirov, Kirov (Kostadinov 74). Coach: Mihail Nikolov Madanski (BUL
Hungary: Gulácsi, Nagy, Korcsmár, Debreceni, Présinger, Busai, Gál (Iszlai 69), Gosztonyi, Komán, Szabó (Nikházi 85), Németh (András Simon 88). Coach: Tibor Sisa (HUN)
Goal(s): 0-1 Németh 10
Yellow Card(s): Tsvetanov 3 (Bulgaria), Korcsmár 45+1 (Hungary), Dimov 59 (Bulgaria), Gál 66 (Hungary), Gadzhalov 77 (Bulgaria)
Referee: Toussaint (LUX)

14/7/08, Štruncovy sady, Plzen
Germany 2-1 Spain
Germany: Zieler, Diekmeier, Reinartz, Toprak (Kopplin 79), Jungwirth, Sven Bender, Risse, Latza, Gebhart, Sukuta-Pasu (Soyudogru 88), Nsereko. Coach: Horst Hrubesch (GER)
Spain: De Gea, Azpilicueta, Antón, Ortiz, Sanjosé, Camacho (Luque 63), Daniel Parejo, Aarón (Castellano 77), Alba, Aquino (Bolado 54), Emilio. Coach: Ginés Meléndez (ESP)
Goal(s): 1-0 Sukuta-Pasu 7, 2-0 Toprak 56, 2-1 Alba 66
Yellow Card(s): Sukuta-Pasu 45+3 (Germany), Aarón 48 (Spain), Camacho 60 (Spain)
Referee: Collum (SCO)

17/7/08, Na Litavce, Pribram
Spain 0-1 Hungary
Spain: De Gea, Azpilicueta, Castellano, Domínguez Soto, Antón (Luque 72), Camacho, Daniel Parejo, Emilio, Mérida (Aquino 65), Aarón, Bolado (Alba 46). Coach: Ginés Meléndez (ESP)
Hungary: Gulácsi, Nagy, Korcsmár, Debreceni, Présinger, Busai, Iszla Gosztonyi (András Simon 88), Komán, Nikházi (Szabó 57), Németh (Bajner 90). Coach: Tibor Sisa (HUN)
Goal(s): 0-1 Nagy 71
Yellow Card(s): Castellano 28 (Spain), Németh 47 (Hungary), Daniel Parejo 51 (Spain), Korcsmár 74 (Hungary), András Simon 89 (Hungary)
Referee: Stavrev (MKD)

17/7/08, Štruncovy sady, Plzen
Germany 3-0 Bulgaria
Germany: Zieler, Kopplin, Reinartz, Jungwirth, Diekmeier, Lars Bender (Vrancic 83), Gebhart, Latza (Sven Bender 46), Nsereko, Naki,

ı Mérida scores Spain's final goal in their 4-0 romp against Bulgaria

ukuta-Pasu (Soyudogru 39). Coach: Horst Hrubesch (GER)
ulgaria: Karadjov, Panov (Aleksandrov 21), Zlatkov, Uzunov, adzhalov, Georgiev, Dimov, Zehirov, Mustafa (Kirov 47), Vasilev /elev 66), Tsvetanov. Coach: Mihail Nikolov Madanski (BUL)
ioal(s): 1-0 Diekmeier 16, 2-0 Nsereko 43, 3-0 Lars Bender 56
'ellow Card(s): Zlatkov 41 (Bulgaria), Nsereko 41 (Germany), ıleksandrov 71 (Bulgaria), Gadzhalov 90+1 (Bulgaria)
teferee: Moen (NOR)

0/7/08, Na Litavce, Pribram
Hungary 1-2 Germany
Hungary: Pokorni, Szekeres, Lengyel, Debreceni, Présinger, Szabó, iál, Nikházi, Iszlai (Busai 71), András Simon, Bajner (Nagy 61) Gosztonyi 78). Coach: Tibor Sisa (HUN)
iermany: Zieler, Kopplin, Reinartz (Toprak 46), Jungwirth,)iekmeier, Sven Bender, Lars Bender (Latza 46), Risse, Naki, Nsereko Oczipka 90), Gebhart. Coach: Horst Hrubesch (GER)
ioal(s): 0-1 Reinartz 36, 1-1 András Simon 74, 1-2 Risse 76
'ellow Card(s): András Simon 21 (Hungary), Iszlai 23 (Hungary), einartz 26 (Germany), Jungwirth 69 (Germany), Debreceni 82 Hungary)
teferee: Filipović (SRB)

20/7/08, FK Viktoria Žižkov, Prague
Spain 4-0 Bulgaria
Spain: De Gea (Mejías 75), Azpilicueta, Castellano, Domínguez Soto, Morgado (Ruiz 70), Camacho, Daniel Parejo, Aarón (Aquino 23), Mérida, Emilio, Alba. Coach: Ginés Meléndez (ESP)
Bulgaria: Karadjov, Panov, Uzunov (Zlatkov 72), Georgiev, Tsvetkov, Aleksandrov, Velev, Dimov (Tsachev 46), Zehirov, Vasilev (Kostadinov 58), Tsvetanov. Coach: Mihail Nikolov Madanski (BUL)
Goal(s): 1-0 Aarón 14, 2-0 Emilio 17, 3-0 Emilio 52, 4-0 Mérida 64
Red Card(s): Domínguez Soto 75 (Spain)
Yellow Card(s): Panov 33 (Bulgaria), Dimov 41 (Bulgaria), Daniel Parejo 45+2 (Spain), Domínguez Soto 60 (Spain), Domínguez Soto 75 (Spain)
Referee: Thual (FRA)

Group A Table

		Pld	W	D	L	F	A	Pts
1	Germany	3	3	0	0	7	2	9
2	Hungary	3	2	0	1	3	2	6
3	Spain	3	1	0	2	5	3	3
4	Bulgaria	3	0	0	3	0	8	0

GROUP B

Group B was a mixture of sides who had recently impressed in this competition and two of Europe's big names who had endured several years' struggle. Hosts the Czech Republic – semi-finalists in 2006 – were joined by 2007 runners-up Greece, England and Italy, the latter two countries appearing in the finals for the first time since 2005 and 2004 respectively.

Early toils

Both England and Italy struggled in the opening round of matches, the former going down to the hosts in front of more than 6,000 spectators in Jablonec. Tomáš Necid did the damage, scoring in the 54th minute after confusion in the England defence and adding a second four minutes later. The only black marks for the Czechs were late red cards for Jakub Heidenreich and Roman Brunclík, both for second bookable offences. In Mlada Boleslav it looked as if Greece would also make a winning start as Michail Pavlis gave them a 23rd-minute lead, but with a minute left Italy's Andrea Poli went down under Kyriakos Papadopoulos's challenge and Alberto Paloschi smashed in the penalty.

There was no shortage of drama in the second round of matches. What was lacking were goals as a Greece side reduced to ten men by the 63rd-minute dismissal of Sotiris Ninis held out to frustrate the Czechs in Liberec. It was a similar story in Jablonec, England and Italy both having opportunities to record their first win yet neither able to make the crucial breakthrough.

Final-day drama

That meant all four sides could still qualify, and England gave themselves a fighting chance as Ben Mee, Freddie Sears, with a penalty, and Daniel Sturridge secured a 3-0 win against Greece in Liberec. Progress depended on Italy failing to beat the Czechs, however, and those hopes looked bleak when Poli gave the Azurrini a 21st-minute lead in Mlada Boleslav. Necid swiftly equalised, only for Giacomo Bonaventura to restore the Italian advantage eleven minutes into the second half.

Again the Czech response came within two minutes, this time from Jan Morávek, but Paloschi's penalty put Italy back in front with 19 minutes left. Andrea Mazzarani was then sent off for a second yellow card, but it mattered

Tomáš Necid scores his second goa four minutes against England to g hosts the Czech Republic a winning s

:tle as Poli made it 4-2 in the 79th minute, and the ten ıen held on despite Morávek's 86th-minute strike. The ːsult left Italy top of the section, one point above the zech runners-up, with England having to settle for a lace in the 2009 FIFA U-20 World Cup.

iroup B Results

1/7/08, Strelnice, Jablonec nad Nisou
zech Republic 2-0 England
zech Republic: Vaclík, Polák, Heidenreich, Brunclík, Řezník, Vošahlík ecjaks 75), Zeman (Štěpánek 85), Hable (Mareček 46), Morávek, einberk, Necid. Coach: Jakub Dovalil (CZE)
ngland: Button, Cork, Tomkins, Pearce, Bertrand, Sinclair (Obadeyi 4), Gosling (Chandler 78), Gibbs, Rose, Sturridge, Sears. Coach: Brian astick (ENG)
oal(s): 1-0 Necid 54, 2-0 Necid 58
ed Card(s): Heidenreich 72 (Czech Republic), Brunclík 82 (Czech epublic)
ellow Card(s): Brunclík 28 (Czech Republic), Heidenreich 40 (Czech epublic), Heidenreich 72 (Czech Republic), Brunclík 82 (Czech epublic), Obadeyi 89 (England)
eferee: Stavrev (MKD)

1/7/08, Mestský, Mlada Boleslav
reece 1-1 Italy
reece: Babaniotis, Barboudis, Papadopoulos, Argyropoulos, alanis, Gentzoglou, Kyrgias (Stratacis 68), Papadopoulos, Ninis, atsoukas (Psianos 59), Pavlis (Giannou 82). Coach: Alexandros exiou (GRE)
aly: Fiorillo, Darmian, Bruscagin, Tagliani, Gentili, Mazzarani, Poli, onaventura, Forestieri, Paloschi, Zamblera (Eusepi 73). Coach: esualdo Piacenti (ITA)
oal(s): 1-0 Pavlis 23, 1-1 Paloschi 89(p)
ellow Card(s): Galanis 24 (Greece), Argyropoulos 45+1 (Greece), apadopoulos 47 (Greece), Babaniotis 63 (Greece), Bruscagin 80 :aly), Gentili 84 (Italy)
eferee: Filipović (SRB)

7/7/08, U Nisy, Liberec
zech Republic 0-0 Greece
zech Republic: Vaclík, Štěpánek, Polák, Zeman, Vošahlík (Kozák 85), orávek, Necid, Lecjaks (Reinberk 46), Řezník, Wojnar (Nuc 77), areček. Coach: Jakub Dovalil (CZE)
reece: Babaniotis, Barboudis, Lampropoulos, Papadopoulos, outzikos (Argyropoulos 56), Gentzoglou, Ninis, Matsoukas (Psianos 7), Pavlis (Kyrgias 88), Galanis, Papadopoulos. Coach: Alexandros lexiou (GRE)
ed Card(s): Ninis 63 (Greece)
ellow Card(s): Barboudis 4 (Greece), Lecjaks 32 (Czech Republic), avlis 59 (Greece), Ninis 63 (Greece), Ninis 63 (Greece)
eferee: Toussaint (LUX)

7/7/08, Strelnice, Jablonec nad Nisou
ngland 0-0 Italy
ngland: Button, Cork, Tomkins, Pearce, Bertrand, Gibbs, Rose)elph 77), Moses, Mee, Sturridge, Sears (Sinclair 86). Coach: Brian astick (ENG)
aly: Fiorillo, Darmian, Bruscagin (Albertazzi 65), Tagliani, Gentili, azzarani (Raggio Garibaldi 46), Forestieri, Poli, Bonaventura, aloschi (Zamblera 84), Okaka Chuka. Coach: Francesco Rocca (ITA)
ellow Card(s): Gentili 32 (Italy), Bertrand 68 (England)
eferee: Thual (FRA)

20/7/08, Mestský, Mlada Boleslav
Italy 4-3 Czech Republic
Italy: Fiorillo, Darmian, Formiconi (Tagliani 89), Albertazzi, Bruscagin, Raggio Garibaldi, Mazzarani, Poli, Forestieri (Bonaventura 46), Paloschi (Marchetti 77), Okaka Chuka. Coach: Francesco Rocca (ITA)
Czech Republic: Vaclík, Řezník, Štěpánek, Polák, Lecjaks, Reinberk (Wojnar 73), Mareček, Morávek, Zeman, Vošahlík (Kozák 77), Necid. Coach: Jakub Dovalil (CZE)
Goal(s): 1-0 Poli 21, 1-1 Necid 23, 2-1 Bonaventura 56, 2-2 Morávek 58, 3-2 Paloschi 71(p), 4-2 Poli 79, 4-3 Morávek 86
Red Card(s): Mazzarani 74 (Italy)
Yellow Card(s): Morávek 20 (Czech Republic), Mazzarani 20 (Italy), Poli 52 (Italy), Mazzarani 74 (Italy)
Referee: Collum (SCO)

20/7/08, U Nisy, Liberec
England 3-0 Greece
England: Button, Cork, Pearce, Mattock, Mee, Bertrand (Gosling 87), Moses (Delph 73), Gibbs, Rose, Sturridge, Sears (Sinclair 83). Coach: Brian Eastick (ENG)
Greece: Babaniotis, Barboudis, Galanis, Argyropoulos (Karapetsas 59), Lampropoulos, Boutzikos (Psianos 12; Pavlis 50), Papadopoulos, Gentzoglou, Papadopoulos, Giannou, Matsoukas. Coach: Alexandros Alexiou (GRE)
Goal(s): 1-0 Mee 47, 2-0 Sears 67(p), 3-0 Sturridge 84
Yellow Card(s): Lampropoulos 67 (Greece)
Referee: Moen (NOR)

Group B Table

		Pld	W	D	L	F	A	Pts
1	Italy	3	1	2	0	5	4	5
2	Czech Republic	3	1	1	1	5	4	4
3	England	3	1	1	1	3	2	4
4	Greece	3	0	2	1	1	4	2

SEMI-FINALS

The semi-finals brought together Group B winners Italy and finals debutants Hungary, the runners-up in Group A, while Germany took on hosts the Czech Republic. Of the four, only Italy had previously claimed the trophy – in 2003 – whereas Germany had been beaten by Spain in the 2002 showpiece, the first U19 final since the switch from a U18 event.

Italy hold on

That mattered little in the first tie in Plzen, however, as Hungary pressed Italy back from the outset, Vlagyimir Komán and Krisztián Németh drawing saves from Vincenzo Fiorillo before the latter shot into the side-netting as half-time approached. In the main, however, Hungary struggled to penetrate a disciplined Italian rearguard and paid the price five minutes past the hour, Silvano Raggio's perfectly-weighted pass allowing substitute Fernando Forestieri to slide in the only goal. Fiorillo had previously denied Attila Busai and then kept out Németh's shot from distance, but he was beaten by András Gosztonyi deep into stoppage time – only for the post to rescue the goalkeeper, and Italy.

Germany seized the early initiative in the second semi-final in Mlada Boleslav. Savio Nsereko had already gone close by the time Marcel Risse opened the scoring in the 17th minute, goalkeeper Tomáš Vaclík managing only to help his low diagonal shot into the net at the near post. If Germany thought they were in control, however, the Czechs quickly changed their minds as they drew level seven minutes later, Tomáš Necid looping a header beyond goalkeeper Ron-Robert Zieler from Lukáš Mareček's right-sided free-kick for his fourth finals goal. In front of 5,000 spectators the hosts began to look the more threatening, but Necid passed up three presentable chances, and in the final minute of extra time that profligacy cost the Czechs dear as Richard Sukuta-Pasu raced clear to smash in the winning goal and take Germany into the final.

Fernando Forestieri scored Italy's semi-final winner against Hungary

Semi-Final Results

23/7/08, Štruncovy sady, Plzen
Italy 1-0 Hungary
Italy: Fiorillo, Darmian, Tagliani, Gentili, Formiconi (Forestieri 46), Albertazzi, Raggio Garibaldi, Poli, Bonaventura, Paloschi (Eusepi 85) Okaka Chuka. Coach: Francesco Rocca (ITA)
Hungary: Gulácsi, Debreceni, Szekeres, Présinger, Busai (Bajner 77), Korcsmár, Gál, Komán, Szabó, Gosztonyi, Németh. Coach: Tibor Sisa (HUN
Goal(s): 1-0 Forestieri 65
Yellow Card(s): Albertazzi 15 (Italy), Darmian 29 (Italy), Korcsmár 47 (Hungary), Forestieri 88 (Italy), Szabó 90+3 (Hungary)
Referee: Moen (NOR)

23/7/08, Mestský, Mlada Boleslav
Germany 2-1 Czech Republic
Germany: Zieler, Kopplin, Reinartz, Jungwirth, Diekmeier, Sven Bender (Latza 97), Lars Bender, Risse, Naki (Sukuta-Pasu 65), Gebhar (Vrancic 108), Nsereko. Coach: Horst Hrubesch (GER)
Czech Republic: Vaclík, Řezník, Polák, Brunclík, Heidenreich, Hable (Reinberk 98), Morávek (Zeman 65), Mareček, Lecjaks (Wojnar 104), Vošahlík, Necid. Coach: Jakub Dovalil (CZE)
Goal(s): 1-0 Risse 17, 1-1 Necid 24, 2-1 Sukuta-Pasu 119
Yellow Card(s): Vošahlík 43 (Czech Republic), Lars Bender 76 (Germany), Hable 85 (Czech Republic), Gebhart 101 (Germany), Kopplin 109 (Germany), Nsereko 120 (Germany)
Referee: Thual (FRA)

FINAL

In contrast to much of the previous two weeks in the Czech Republic, the final was played on a baking hot day in Jablonec, with Germany many people's favourites to take the title for the first time despite the absence of Savio Nsereko through suspension following his late yellow card in the semi-final. Richard Sukuta-Pasu was fit to lead the attack having finally shaken off an ankle injury, although it was Timo Gebhart who provided much of the early threat, volleying Sven Bender's flick-on just too high after 20 minutes.

Eventful final

Gebhart played a crucial role in the opening goal four minutes later, combining with Lars Bender to create confusion in the Italy defence. When the ball broke to the latter on the edge of the area, he lashed a left-foot shot into the net. The favourites were on their way, although the balance of the match looked to have shifted seven minutes before half-time when captain Florian Jungwirth collected his second yellow card in three minutes for tripping Stefano Okaka Chuka.

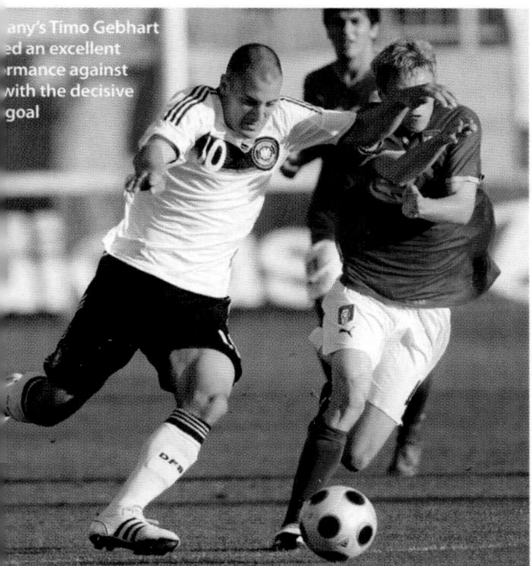

any's Timo Gebhart ed an excellent rmance against with the decisive goal

ermany weathered the resulting spell of Italian 'essure, however, and continued to threaten on the ounterattack, duly doubling their lead a minute past e hour as Gebhart and Deniz Naki combined to work ace for Sukuta-Pasu, the forward unerringly finding e bottom corner with a low shot.

Italy's hopes looked to have finally ended when Matteo Gentili joined Jungwirth in collecting a second yellow card on 69 minutes, but instead Silvano Raggio Garibaldi halved the deficit nine minutes later. Dreams of a comeback were unceremoniously dashed within two minutes, however, when the outstanding Gebhart headed in Naki's free-kick to secure the title. "We were the best team in the tournament," said the victorious coach Horst Hrubesch. "We've won all five games in the finals, so we deserve to be European champions."

Final Result

26/7/08, Strelnice, Jablonec nad Nisou
Germany 3-1 Italy
Attendance: 4100
Germany: Zieler, Diekmeier, Jungwirth, Reinartz, Kopplin, Risse (Latza 39), Lars Bender (Toprak 66), Sven Bender, Naki (Oczipka 89), Gebhart, Sukuta-Pasu. Coach: Horst Hrubesch (GER)
Italy: Fiorillo, Darmian, Gentili, Tagliani, Bruscagin, Poli (Bonaventura 46), Mazzarani, Forestieri (Eusepi 78), Raggio Garibaldi, Paloschi (Zamblera 59), Okaka Chuka. Coach: Francesco Rocca (ITA)
Goal(s): 1-0 Lars Bender 24, 2-0 Sukuta-Pasu 61, 2-1 Raggio Garibaldi 78, 3-1 Gebhart 80
Red Card(s): Jungwirth 36 (Germany), Gentili 69 (Italy)
Yellow Card(s): Gentili 11 (Italy), Jungwirth 34 (Germany), Jungwirth 36 (Germany), Bonaventura 47 (Italy), Gentili 69 (Italy), Gebhart 80 (Germany), Fiorillo 80 (Italy), Tagliani 82 (Italy), Kopplin 90+1 (Germany)
Referee: Collum (SCO)

iany celebrate their first UEFA European Under-19 Championship title

CHAPTER
09

UEFA U17 2007/08

In a season that marked Juan Santisteban's 20th in charge of Spain's junior squad – and, if reports were to be believed, his last as head coach – it was appropriate that he became the first trainer to win two consecutive UEFA European Under-17 Championship titles. Before the finals in the southern Turkish city of Antalya, there had been suggestions that Spain did not have the talent of the previous year's Bojan Krkić-inspired champions, but they eased through the group stage, which featured a memorable 3-3 draw with France, and showed resolve to edge past the Netherlands in the semi-finals. But they saved their best for last in the final against France, in which Keko, Thiago and Sergi led a stunning attacking performance that produced a 4-0 victory. "I am an old man and have watched a lot of football, and this is the best performance I have seen from any of our youth teams," purred Santisteban.

QUALIFYING ROUND

Group 1 Results

19/10/07, Campo Al Ram, Bodio
Greece 1-1 Luxembourg
19/10/07, Cornaredo, Lugano
Switzerland 4-0 Kazakhstan
21/10/07, Cornaredo, Lugano
Greece 3-1 Kazakhstan
21/10/07, Comunale, Ascona
Luxembourg 0-4 Switzerland
24/10/07, Campo Al Ram, Bodio
Switzerland 2-1 Greece
24/10/07, Comunale, Ascona
Kazakhstan 2-3 Luxembourg

Group 1 Table

	Pld	W	D	L	F	A	Pts
1 Switzerland	3	3	0	0	10	1	9
2 Greece	3	1	1	1	5	4	4
3 Luxembourg	3	1	1	1	4	7	4
4 Kazakhstan	3	0	0	3	3	10	0

Group 2 Results

1/10/07, Sports and Recreational Facility Complex, Niechorze
Austria 4-2 Norway
1/10/07, City Stadium, Trzebiatow
Poland 4-1 FYR Macedonia
3/10/07, Sports and Recreational Facility Complex, Niechorze
Norway 0-0 Poland
3/10/07, City Stadium, Trzebiatow
Austria 2-3 FYR Macedonia
6/10/07, Sports and Recreational Facility Complex, Niechorze
Poland 0-1 Austria
6/10/07, City Stadium, Trzebiatow
FYR Macedonia 0-4 Norway

Group 2 Table

	Pld	W	D	L	F	A	Pts
1 Austria	3	2	0	1	7	5	6
2 Norway	3	1	1	1	6	4	4
3 Poland	3	1	1	1	4	2	4
4 FYR Macedonia	3	1	0	2	4	10	3

Group 3 Results

19/9/07, Bayview, Methil
Belarus 5-1 Liechtenstein
19/9/07, Stark's Park, Kircaldy
Scotland 0-4 Slovakia
21/9/07, Bayview, Methil
Belarus 0-2 Slovakia
21/9/07, Almondvale Park, Livingston
Liechtenstein 0-8 Scotland
24/9/07, Broadwood, Cumbernauld
Scotland 5-1 Belarus
24/9/07, Stark's Park, Kircaldy
Slovakia 5-0 Liechtenstein

Group 3 Table

	Pld	W	D	L	F	A	Pts
1 Slovakia	3	3	0	0	11	0	9
2 Scotland	3	2	0	1	13	5	6
3 Belarus	3	1	0	2	6	8	3
4 Liechtenstein	3	0	0	3	1	18	0

Group 4 Results

1/10/07, Estadi Comunal, Andorra la Vella
Spain 6-0 San Marino
1/10/07, Estadi Comunal, Andorra la Vella
Wales 1-0 Andorra
3/10/07, Estadi Comunal, Andorra la Vella
Spain 3-0 Andorra
3/10/07, Estadi Comunal, Andorra la Vella
San Marino 1-4 Wales
6/10/07, Estadi Comunal, Andorra la Vella
Wales 2-2 Spain
6/10/07, Estadi Comunal, Andorra la Vella
Andorra 3-0 San Marino

Group 4 Table

	Pld	W	D	L	F
1 Spain	3	2	1	0	11
2 Wales	3	2	1	0	7
3 Andorra	3	1	0	2	3
4 San Marino	3	0	0	3	1

Group 5 Results

14/9/07, Athlone Stadium, Athlone
Denmark 1-1 Slovenia
14/9/07, Terryland Park, Galway
Ukraine 1-3 Republic of Ireland
16/9/07, Flancare Park, Longford
Slovenia 1-1 Ukraine
16/9/07, Athlone Stadium, Athlone
Denmark 0-2 Republic of Ireland
19/9/07, Terryland Park, Galway
Ukraine 0-2 Denmark

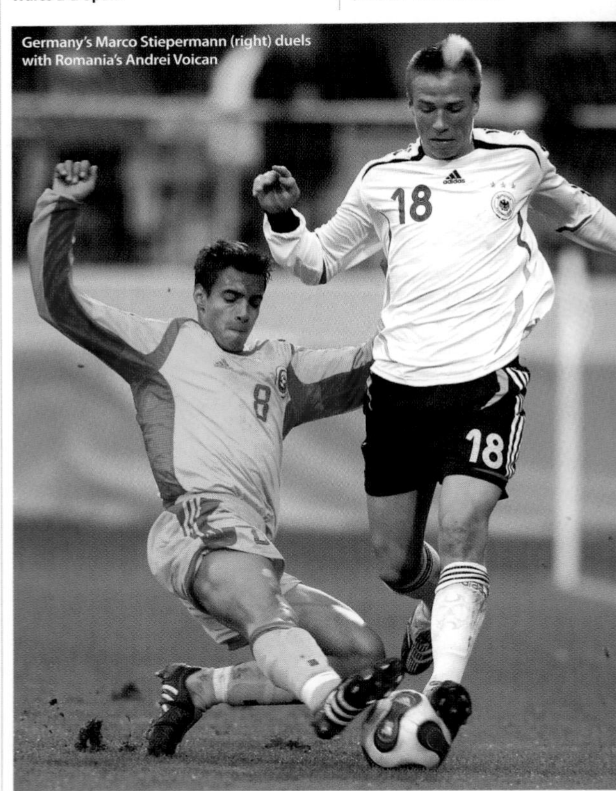

Germany's Marco Stiepermann (right) duels with Romania's Andrei Voican

7, Flancare Park, Longford
lic of Ireland 1-0 Slovenia

p 5 Table

	Pld	W	D	L	F	A	Pts
ublic of Ireland	3	3	0	0	6	1	9
mark	3	1	1	1	3	3	4
enia	3	0	2	1	2	3	2
aine	3	0	1	2	2	6	1

up 6 Results

07, Albstadion, Heidenheim
ny 8-0 Faroe Islands
07, Stadion im Stauferpark, Donauworth
nia 1-0 Sweden
07, Stadion am Schlüsselhäuser Kreuz,
g
Islands 0-0 Romania
07, Rieser Sportpark, Nordlingen
ny 1-1 Sweden
07, Wald Stadion, Aalen
nia 1-1 Germany
07, Rieser Sportpark, Nordlingen
n 5-2 Faroe Islands

p 6 Table

	Pld	W	D	L	F	A	Pts
many	3	1	2	0	10	2	5
nania	3	1	2	0	2	1	5
den	3	1	1	1	6	4	4
e Islands	3	0	1	2	2	13	1

up 7 Results

7, Cika Daca, Kragujevac
1-0 Iceland
7, Gradski, Jagodina
0-0 Lithuania
7, Gradski, Jagodina
2-0 Lithuania
7, Cika Daca, Kragujevac
d 0-3 Israel
7, Cika Daca, Kragujevac
2-1 Serbia
7, Gradski, Jagodina
nia 0-1 Iceland

p 7 Table

	Pld	W	D	L	F	A	Pts
el	3	2	1	0	5	1	7
bia	3	2	0	1	4	2	6
and	3	1	0	2	1	4	3
uania	3	0	1	2	0	3	1

up 8 Results

7, Albena 1, Albena
a 4-0 Georgia
7, Kaliakra, Kavarna
ry 3-0 Bulgaria
7, Albena 1, Albena
ia 0-1 Hungary

26/9/07, Kaliakra, Kavarna
Croatia 2-0 Bulgaria
29/9/07, Albena 1, Albena
Hungary 0-0 Croatia
29/9/07, Kaliakra, Kavarna
Bulgaria 2-5 Georgia

Group 8 Table

	Pld	W	D	L	F	A	Pts
1 Croatia	3	2	1	0	6	0	7
2 Hungary	3	2	1	0	4	0	7
3 Georgia	3	1	0	2	5	7	3
4 Bulgaria	3	0	0	3	2	10	0

Group 9 Results

1/10/07, Grbavica, Sarajevo
Finland 0-1 Bosnia-Herzegovina
1/10/07, Koševo, Sarajevo
Russia 1-1 Azerbaijan
3/10/07, Kreševo, Kresevo
Finland 2-2 Azerbaijan
3/10/07, Koševo, Sarajevo
Bosnia-Herzegovina 0-2 Russia
6/10/07, Kreševo, Kresevo
Russia 1-1 Finland
6/10/07, Koševo, Sarajevo
Azerbaijan 0-1 Bosnia-Herzegovina

Group 9 Table

	Pld	W	D	L	F	A	Pts
1 Bosnia-Herzegovina	3	2	0	1	2	2	6
2 Russia	3	1	2	0	4	2	5
3 Finland	3	0	2	1	3	4	2
3 Azerbaijan	3	0	2	1	3	4	2

Group 10 Results

23/10/07, Niko Dovana, Durres
France 1-0 Latvia
23/10/07, Selman Stermazi, Tirana
Netherlands 3-0 Albania
25/10/07, Selman Stermazi, Tirana
France 6-0 Albania
25/10/07, Niko Dovana, Durres
Latvia 1-3 Netherlands
28/10/07, Niko Dovana, Durres
Netherlands 1-0 France
28/10/07, Selman Stermazi, Tirana
Albania 1-1 Latvia

Group 10 Table

	Pld	W	D	L	F	A	Pts
1 Netherlands	3	3	0	0	7	1	9
2 France	3	2	0	1	7	1	6
3 Latvia	3	0	1	2	2	5	1
4 Albania	3	0	1	2	1	10	1

Group 11 Results

21/10/07, Kadriorg, Tallinn
England 6-0 Malta
21/10/07, A Le Coq Arena, Tallinn
Portugal 2-0 Estonia
23/10/07, Kadriorg, Tallinn
Malta 0-6 Portugal
23/10/07, A Le Coq Arena, Tallinn
England 6-0 Estonia
26/10/07, Kadriorg, Tallinn
Portugal 0-0 England
26/10/07, A Le Coq Arena, Tallinn
Estonia 0-0 Malta

Group 11 Table

	Pld	W	D	L	F	A	Pts
1 England	3	2	1	0	12	0	7
2 Portugal	3	2	1	0	8	0	7
3 Estonia	3	0	1	2	0	8	1
4 Malta	3	0	1	2	0	12	1

Group 12 Results

22/10/07, Maurits De Waelestadion, Maldegem
Northern Ireland 3-0 Moldova
22/10/07, KFC Eeklo, Eeklo
Belgium 2-0 Montenegro
24/10/07, Gemeentelijke, Aalter
Montenegro 0-1 Northern Ireland
24/10/07, Gemeentelijke, Aalter
Belgium 3-0 Moldova
27/10/07, Maurits De Waelestadion, Maldegem
Northern Ireland 1-0 Belgium
27/10/07, KFC Eeklo, Eeklo
Moldova 3-1 Montenegro

Group 12 Table

	Pld	W	D	L	F	A	Pts
1 Northern Ireland	3	3	0	0	5	0	9
2 Belgium	3	2	0	1	5	1	6
3 Moldova	3	1	0	2	3	7	3
4 Montenegro	3	0	0	3	1	6	0

Group 13 Results

2/10/07, Podještedský FC, Cesky Dub
Italy 2-1 Armenia
2/10/07, Benátky, Benatky nad Jizerou
Czech Republic 8-0 Cyprus
4/10/07, Benátky, Benatky nad Jizerou
Italy 7-1 Cyprus
4/10/07, Hrádek, Hradek nad Nisou
Armenia 1-5 Czech Republic
7/10/07, Podještedský FC, Cesky Dub
Czech Republic 1-2 Italy
7/10/07, Hrádek, Hradek nad Nisou
Cyprus 3-0 Armenia

Group 13 Table

	Pld	W	D	L	F	A	Pts
1 Italy	3	3	0	0	11	3	9
2 Czech Republic	3	2	0	1	14	3	6
3 Cyprus	3	1	0	2	4	15	3
4 Armenia	3	0	0	3	2	10	0

ELITE ROUND

Group 1 Results

13/3/08, Athlone Stadium, Athlone
Portugal 1-1 Greece
Goal(s): 1-0 Castro Oliveira 18, 1-1 Papadopoulos 80+1

13/3/08, Terryland Park, Galway
Republic of Ireland 1-1 Germany
Goal(s): 0-1 Kroos 8, 1-1 Cunningham 67

15/3/08, Terryland Park, Galway
Germany 0-2 Portugal
Goal(s): 0-1 Pereira Reis 68, 0-2 Teixeira Caetan 74

15/3/08, Athlone Stadium, Athlone
Republic of Ireland 1-2 Greece
Goal(s): 0-1 Dunleavy 39(og), 1-1 Gunning 52, 1-2 Belios 76

18/3/08, Terryland Park, Galway
Portugal 0-2 Republic of Ireland
Goal(s): 0-1 Sullivan 46, 0-2 Gunning 55

18/3/08, Athlone Stadium, Athlone
Greece 0-2 Germany
Goal(s): 0-1 Gulde 37(p), 0-2 Cincotta 69

Group 1 Table

	Pld	W	D	L	F	A	Pts
1 Republic of Ireland	3	1	1	1	4	3	4
2 Portugal	3	1	1	1	3	3	4
2 Germany	3	1	1	1	3	3	4
4 Greece	3	1	1	1	3	4	4

Group 2 Results

19/3/08, Town Sports Center, Makarska
Switzerland 1-1 Belgium
Goal(s): 0-1 Bruno 48, 1-1 Ben Khalifa 73

19/3/08, Metković, Metkovic
Croatia 3-0 Denmark
Goal(s): 1-0 Kramarić 11, 2-0 Kramarić 17, 3-0 Adrijasević 54

21/3/08, Ploce, Ploce
Switzerland 1-0 Denmark
Goal(s): 1-0 Mehmedi 5

21/3/08, Gospin Dolac, Imotski
Belgium 0-4 Croatia
Goal(s): 0-1 Ivanović 29(p), 0-2 Vrsaljko 35, 0-3 Kramarić 56(p), 0-4 Maričić 80

24/3/08, Gospin Dolac, Imotski
Denmark 2-5 Belgium
Goal(s): 0-1 David 1, 1-1 Lund Lindsten 13, 2-1 Saric 15, 2-2 Pottiez 33, 2-3 Cosemans 37, 2-4 Pottiez 74, 2-5 Bruno 80

25/3/08, Town Sports Center, Makarska
Croatia 0-1 Switzerland
Goal(s): 0-1 Borkovic 80+3

Group 2 Table

	Pld	W	D	L	F	A	Pts
1 Switzerland	3	2	1	0	3	1	7
2 Croatia	3	2	0	1	7	1	6
3 Belgium	3	1	1	1	6	7	4
4 Denmark	3	0	0	3	2	9	0

Group 3 Results

25/3/08, Municipal, Rishon Le-Zion
England 1-1 France
Goal(s): 1-0 Rodwell 58, 1-1 Nego 78

25/3/08, Nes-Ziona, Nes-Ziona
Israel 3-1 Russia
Goal(s): 1-0 Golsa 22, 2-0 Ghadir 25, 3-0 Hakim 43, 3-1 Logua 61(p)

27/3/08, Municipal, Rishon Le-Zion
England 2-3 Russia
Goal(s): 0-1 Kokorin 36, 0-2 Stolyarenko 39, 1-2 James 45, 1-3 Pugachev 67, 2-3 Delfouneso 73

27/3/08, Nes-Ziona, Nes-Ziona
France 3-2 Israel
Goal(s): 0-1 Golsa 8, 1-1 Grenier 17, 2-1 Tafer 39, 2-2 Ghadir 47, 3-2 Tafer 69

30/3/08, Nes-Ziona, Nes-Ziona
Israel 2-2 England
Goal(s): 1-1 Ghadir 38, 2-1 Hakim 63, 2-2 Delfouneso 80+2

30/3/08, Municipal, Rishon Le-Zion
Russia 1-3 France
Goal(s): 0-1 Kakuta 13, 1-1 Zabolotniy 39 1-2 Kakuta 49, 1-3 Damour 80+2

Group 3 Table

	Pld	W	D	L	F
1 France	3	2	1	0	7
2 Israel	3	1	1	1	7
3 Russia	3	1	0	2	5
4 England	3	0	2	1	5

Group 4 Results

26/3/08, Cika Daca, Kragujevac
Slovakia 1-3 Serbia
Goal(s): 0-1 Aleksić 5, 1-1 Bagi 17, 1-2 Lja 1-3 Aleksić 46

26/3/08, FK Badnjevac, Badnjevac
Czech Republic 6-0 Sweden
Goal(s): 1-0 Stourac 34, 2-0 Vydra 56, 3-0 Stourac 61, 4-0 Kadlec 63, 5-0 Putz 65 6-0 Dolezel 80+1

Conor Clifford helpe Republic of Ir qualify for the

FC Barcelona's Rubén Rochina – one of Spain's hottest young prospects

, FK Badnjevac, Badnjevac
ia 1-2 Sweden
: 1-0 Mak 9, 1-1 Söder 27, 1-2 Lundberg 62(p)

, Cika Daca, Kragujevac
2-1 Czech Republic
): 1-0 Aleksić 35(p), 2-0 Aleksić 55,
llec 58

, FK Badnjevac, Badnjevac
Republic 1-2 Slovakia
: 0-1 Bagi 38, 1-1 Folprecht 76, 1-2 Mak 80+2

, Cika Daca, Kragujevac
n 1-1 Serbia
): 1-0 Kacaniklić 40, 1-1 Aleksić 57(p)

4 Table

	Pld	W	D	L	F	A	Pts
ia	3	2	1	0	6	3	7
den	3	1	1	1	3	8	4
akia	3	1	0	2	4	6	3
h Republic	3	1	0	2	8	4	3

up 5 Results

, Mourneview Park, Lurgan
1-1 Slovenia
: 0-1 Besič 51, 1-1 Stephens 67

, The Oval, Belfast
rn Ireland 1-3 Scotland
: 0-1 Fleck 5(p), 0-2 McHugh 9,
k 18, 1-3 Curran 68

19/3/08, The Showgrounds, Newry
Scotland 1-0 Wales
Goal(s): 1-0 Campbell 70

19/3/08, The Showgrounds, Newry
Northern Ireland 0-2 Slovenia
Goal(s): 0-1 Bracko 3, 0-2 Vučkič 10

22/3/08, Mourneview Park, Lurgan
Wales 3-1 Northern Ireland
Goal(s): 1-0 Edwards 5, 2-0 Dawkin 13,
2-1 McLaughlin 43, 3-1 Williams 49

22/3/08, The Showgrounds, Newry
Slovenia 0-1 Scotland
Goal(s): 0-1 Fleck 75

Group 5 Table

	Pld	W	D	L	F	A	Pts
1 Scotland	3	3	0	0	5	1	9
2 Wales	3	1	1	1	4	3	4
3 Slovenia	3	1	1	1	3	2	4
4 Northern Ireland	3	0	0	3	2	8	0

Group 6 Results

26/3/08, Mogosoaia, Mogosoaia
Spain 2-2 Romania
Goal(s): 0-1 Alibec 7, 0-2 Pop 42,
1-2 Rochina 45, 2-2 Gaztañaga 63

26/3/08, Concordia, Chiajna
Italy 1-1 Austria
Goal(s): 0-1 Dragovic 9, 1-1 Destro 33(p)

28/3/08, Concordia, Chiajna
Austria 0-1 Spain
Goal(s): 0-1 Canales 80+2

28/3/08, Mogosoaia, Mogosoaia
Italy 1-1 Romania
Goal(s): 1-0 Borini 40, 1-1 Alibec 79

31/3/08, Concordia, Chiajna
Spain 1-0 Italy
Goal(s): 1-0 Gavilán 60

31/3/08, Mogosoaia, Mogosoaia
Romania 1-0 Austria
Goal(s): 1-0 Albu 8

Group 6 Table

	Pld	W	D	L	F	A	Pts
1 Spain	3	2	1	0	4	2	7
2 Romania	3	1	2	0	4	3	5
3 Italy	3	0	2	1	2	3	2
4 Austria	3	0	1	2	1	3	1

Group 7 Results

13/3/08, De Winkewijert, Apeldoorn
Netherlands 0-1 Bosnia-Herzegovina
Goal(s): 0-1 Fazlić 64

13/3/08, CSV Apeldoorn, Apeldoorn
Hungary 1-1 Norway
Goal(s): 0-1 Ibrahim 63,
1-1 Andersen Aase 80+3(og)

15/3/08, Sportpark Muldersingel, Wezep
Netherlands 2-0 Norway
Goal(s): 1-0 Castillion 19, 2-0 Cabral 38

15/3/08, De Winkewijert, Apeldoorn
Bosnia-Herzegovina 2-2 Hungary
Goal(s): 1-0 Durak 9, 1-1 Csorba 27,
1-2 Tischler 36, 2-2 Fazlić 61

18/3/08, CSV Apeldoorn, Apeldoorn
Hungary 0-2 Netherlands
Goal(s): 0-1 Castillion 36, 0-2 Sneijder 45

18/3/08, Sportpark Muldersingel, Wezep
Norway 2-0 Bosnia-Herzegovina
Goal(s): 1-0 Eggen Hedenstad 62, 2-0
Johansen 69

Group 7 Table

	Pld	W	D	L	F	A	Pts
1 Netherlands	3	2	0	1	4	1	6
2 Norway	3	1	1	1	3	3	4
3 Bosnia-Herzegovina	3	1	1	1	3	4	4
4 Hungary	3	0	2	1	3	5	2

FINAL TOURNAMENT

GROUP A

One opening game immediately caught the eye when the draw was made a month before the finals – hosts Turkey against the Netherlands, a rematch of the 2005 final. Serbia and Scotland, who had both qualified convincingly, were also involved.

In the final three years earlier Turkey had won 2-0. Now, with a team said to be equally talented, they went one better at the Mardan Sport Complex, a 7,500-seater arena constructed especially for the finals and that would stage a record eight televised games. Öztürk Karataş struck early, but the Netherlands then started to match their opponents, and it was only in the last nine minutes that the hosts sealed the game with goals from substitutes Eren Albayrak and Muhammet Demir, both back from injury, the latter having recovered from a groin problem that had kept him out for six months. Over at the World of Wonders Football Centre two goals from Danijel Aleksić, the first an acrobatic volley on the stroke of half-time, gave Serbia a 2-0 win against Scotland.

Tight affair

Three days later Turkey were up against Scotland and again pleased the Mardan Sport Complex crowd, though Emrah Yollu's 13th-minute goal was all that separated the teams in a tight affair. Serbia could now seal both their and Turkey's progress with a defeat of the Netherlands, but seven minutes before half-time Dutch striker Geoffrey Castillion poked the ball in from a seemingly impossible angle, and after the break goalkeeper Jeroen Zoet performed heroics to keep out Aleksić and co. and preserve his team's lead.

Still mattters were not completely in the Netherlands' hands. Even if they defeated Scotland – who themselves retained mathematical hopes – they had to hope that Serbia did not beat Turkey as that result would have taken both teams through at the expense of the Netherlands provided the hosts did not lose by six goals or more. The Netherlands did the job they needed to against Scotland, Castillion scoring on 34 minutes and Ricardo van Rhijn adding a second just after the break, but they faced a nervous wait before confirmation that Turkey had held Serbia 0-0 to top th group and ensure Dutch progress in second place. "W didn't know what was happening so we were quakin in those three minutes until we knew we were in the semi-finals," said Netherlands player Jerson Cabral. Defiant Serbia coach Dejan Đurđević claimed his players "proved that they could play for our senior national team".

Group A Results

4/5/08, World of Wonders Football Centre, Antalya
Scotland 0-2 Serbia
Scotland: Adam, Forbes, Deland, Durie, Cooper, Ness, Slane (Coop 67), Smith (Thomson 35), Campbell, Fleck, McHugh (Keatings 52). Coach: Ross Mathie (SCO)
Serbia: Čaković, Liščević, Rodić, Gavrilović, Milanović, Brkić (Rajić 8 Ignjovski, Stevanović, Mitošević, Ljajić (Milivojević 70), Aleksić (Obradović 78). Coach: Dejan Đurđevic (SRB)
Goal(s): 0-1 Aleksić 40+1, 0-2 Aleksić 42
Referee: Hermansen (DEN)

4/5/08, Mardan Sport Complex, Antalya
Turkey 3-0 Netherlands
Turkey: Uçar, Karayer, Yollu, Eren, Çek, Töre, Aydoğdu, Kayalı, Sever (Albayrak 53), Karataş (Çolak 72), Karadeniz (Demir 81). Coach: Şen Ustaömer (TUR)
Netherlands: Zoet, Eekman, Van Rhijn, Gouweleeuw, Burnet, Bonevacia (Özyakup 77), Sneijder, Clasie, Van La Parra (Mokthar 52) Cabral, Castillion. Coach: Albert Stuivenberg (NED)
Goal(s): 1-0 Karataş 11, 2-0 Albayrak 71, 3-0 Demir 80+1
Yellow Card(s): Mokthar 76 (Netherlands)
Referee: Kovařík (CZE)

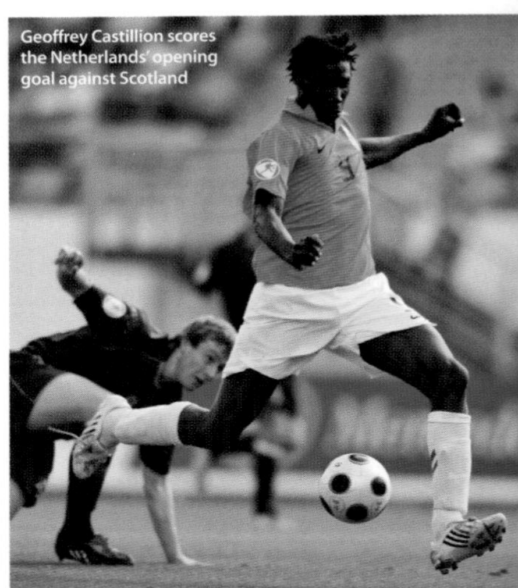
Geoffrey Castillion scores the Netherlands' opening goal against Scotland

Turkey's youngsters acknowledge their fans after beating Scotland 1-0

/5/08, Mardan Sport Complex, Antalya
urkey 1-0 Scotland
urkey: Uçar, Karayer, Eren, Yollu, Çek, Sever (Çolak 57), Kayalı Yardımcı 72), Aydoğdu, Töre, Karataş (Albayrak 41), Karadeniz. oach: Şenol Ustaömer (TUR)
cotland: Adam, Forbes, Durie, Cooper, Cooper, Ness, Campbell, mith, Fleck, Slane (Deland 41), Keatings (Robinson 64). Coach: Ross 1athie (SCO)
ioal(s): 1-0 Yollu 13
ellow Card(s): Fleck 46 (Scotland), Karayer 47 (Turkey), Kayalı 51 Turkey), Çolak 71 (Turkey)
eferee: Nieminen (FIN)

/5/08, World of Wonders Football Centre, Antalya
letherlands 1-0 Serbia
letherlands: Zoet, Eekman, Najah, Van Rhijn, Burnet, Van La Parra Mokthar 56), Clasie, Castillion, Sneijder, Cabral (Ebecilio 72), onevacia (Van Haaren 69). Coach: Albert Stuivenberg (NED)
erbia: Čaković, Liščević, Gavrilović, Milanović, Brkić (Obradović 57), gnjovski, Stevanović, Mitošević, Ljajić (Rajić 75), Aleksić, mederevac. Coach: Dejan Đurđevic (SRB)
ioal(s): 1-0 Castillion 33
eferee: Siejewicz (POL)

0/5/08, World of Wonders Football Centre, Antalya
erbia 0-0 Turkey
erbia: Čaković, Liščević, Gavrilović, Milanović, Brkić, Ignjovski, Mitošević (Obradović 74), Ljajić, Aleksić, Milivojević (Stevanović 64), mederevac. Coach: Dejan Đurđevic (SRB)
Turkey: Uçar, Eren, Kayalı, Karataş (Karadeniz 41), Töre, Dikmen, Neziroğluları, Sever (Aydoğdu 68), Yardımcı, Demir (Albayrak 49), Çolak. Coach: Şenol Ustaömer (TUR)
Yellow Card(s): Aleksić 47 (Serbia), Neziroğluları 63 (Turkey), Töre 80+2 (Turkey)
Referee: Mazeika (LTU)

10/5/08, Mardan Sport Complex, Antalya
Netherlands 2-0 Scotland
Netherlands: Zoet, Eekman, Najah, Van Rhijn, Burnet, Cabral, Sneijder (Van Haaren 54), Clasie (Özyakup 76), Bonevacia, Castillion, Mokthar (Ebecilio 28). Coach: Albert Stuivenberg (NED)
Scotland: Adam, Forbes, Deland, Durie, Ness, Smith (Thomson 71), Campbell, Fleck, Robinson (Slane 41), Keatings (McHugh 54), McAuliffe. Coach: Ross Mathie (SCO)
Goal(s): 1-0 Castillion 34, 2-0 van Rhijn 46
Yellow Card(s): Clasie 8 (Netherlands), Forbes 38 (Scotland), Campbell 70 (Scotland)
Referee: Angelov (BUL)

Group A Table

		Pld	W	D	L	F	A	Pts
1	Turkey	3	2	1	0	4	0	7
2	Netherlands	3	2	0	1	3	3	6
3	Serbia	3	1	1	1	2	1	4
4	Scotland	3	0	0	3	0	5	0

GROUP B

Holders Spain, former champions France and Switzerland, plus debutant qualifiers – albeit Under-16 winners in 1998 – the Republic of Ireland were matched in Group B, and some high quality football was the result.

France and Spain were the pre-group favourites, and the holders were comfortable enough in opening with a 2-0 win against Switzerland, both goals coming on 52 and 61 minutes from Sergi García, who had not played an U17 international before but was given his chance with the suspension of Rubén Rochina and injuries to other key men. By contrast, France fell behind on 32 minutes to Ireland through Paul Murphy, and only when Sean McCaffrey's side visibly tired late on did Yannis Tafer equalise with 15 minutes left and substitute Alexandre Lacazette give Les Mini-Bleus a 2-1 win deep into injury time.

Six-goal thriller

Ireland and Switzerland now had a do-or-die fixture at the World of Wonders Football Centre, and in a close affair Gavin Gunning's 49th-minute own goal earned Yves Debonnaire's side the points. Goals were not in short supply at the Mardan Sport Complex, where France took on Spain. There were two before the break as Tafer's opener was cancelled out by Thiago Alcántara's free-kick. Within eight minutes of the interva France were 3-2 up as Clément Grenier and William Remy scored either side of a Pulido effort, but with 13 minutes left Thiago produced another superb dead-bal effort to ensure a draw in a game some suggested reached UEFA Champions League standard.

That meant Ireland, hit by injury and illness throughout their stay, were out, but they still showed spirit against Spain to lead on 15 minutes through Conor Hourihane's well-worked goal. Only when Rubén was brought on for Sergi at the interval did

France go 3-2 up against Sp

pain hit their stride, the FC Barcelona player scoring n 47 and 56 minutes before setting up Keko to make 3-1 with seven minutes left. That was enough to give pain first place on goal difference as France beat witzerland 2-0, both goals coming from Tafer – lthough until Keko's clincher the top two were lestined to be split on Fair Play ranking. Looking back n Switzerland's exit, Debonnaire admitted: "I think here are many, many differences between Switzerland and France]: technical, physical and in the se of space." McCaffrey reflected: "It's hugely lisappointing to come here and lose the three natches - for me, the staff and most of all for the layers who put in unbelievable effort."

Group B Results

/5/08, Mardan Sport Complex, Antalya
rance 2-1 Republic of Ireland
rance: Mfa Mezui, Auras (Remy 65), Fauré, Kakuta, Fofana, Reale, unu (Lacazette 59), Nego, Kolodziecziak, Grenier (Salibur 54), Tafer. Coach: Francis Smerecki (FRA)
Republic of Ireland: Hanley, Ormsby, Gunning, Connolly, Morrissey, Doran (Timmins 73), Clifford, Cunningham, Murphy (Sullivan 41), Brady (Satelle 49), Joyce. Coach: Seán McCaffrey (IRL)
Goal(s): 0-1 Murphy 32, 1-1 Tafer 65, 2-1 Lacazette 80+3
Yellow Card(s): Reale 32 (France), Ormsby 54 (Republic of Ireland), Salibur 70 (France)
Referee: Mazeika (LTU)

4/5/08, World of Wonders Football Centre, Antalya
Spain 2-0 Switzerland
Spain: Álex, Montoya, Carles, Pulido, Sielva, López, Gontán (Martínez 76), Alcántara (Canales 67), Carmona (Gavilán 51), Oriol, García. Coach: Juan Santisteban (ESP)
Switzerland: Borkovic, Rochat, Daprelà, Koch, Lang, Ukoh, Xhaka, Pasche (Frey 54), Dürig (Shaqiri 41), Mehmedi (Rebronja 69), Ben Khalifa. Coach: Yves Debonnaire (SUI)
Goal(s): 1-0 García 52, 2-0 García 61
Yellow Card(s): Daprelà 45 (Switzerland), Koch 76 (Switzerland)
Referee: Siejewicz (POL)

7/5/08, World of Wonders Football Centre, Antalya
Republic of Ireland 0-1 Switzerland
Republic of Ireland: Hanley, Ormsby, Gunning, Connolly, Morrissey (Murphy 9), Doran, Clifford, Cunningham (Satelle 78), Hourihane (Brady 61), Joyce, Towell. Coach: Seán McCaffrey (IRL)
Switzerland: Borkovic, Rochat, Daprelà, Koch, Lang, Ukoh, Frey, Xhaka, Mehmedi, Pasche (Shaqiri 80), Rebronja (Dürig 78). Coach: Yves Debonnaire (SUI)
Goal(s): 0-1 Gunning 49(og)
Yellow Card(s): Mehmedi 25 (Switzerland), Doran 26 (Republic of Ireland)
Referee: Kovařík (CZE)

7/5/08, Mardan Sport Complex, Antalya
France 3-3 Spain
France: Mfa Mezui, Nego, Fauré, Remy, Kolodziecziak, Fofana, Damour, Lacazette (Sunu 62), Grenier (Reale 73), Kakuta, Tafer. Coach: Francis Smerecki (FRA)
Spain: Álex, Montoya, Martínez, Oriol, López (Gerardo 64), Gontán (Canales 57), Alcántara, Rochina, Pulido, Sielva, Carmona (Gavilán 53). Coach: Juan Santisteban (ESP)
Goal(s): 1-0 Tafer 11, 1-1 Alcántara 31, 2-1 Grenier 43, 2-2 Pulido 45, 3-2 Remy 48, 3-3 Alcántara 67
Yellow Card(s): Remy 37 (France), Rochina 38 (Spain), Fofana 77 (France), Kakuta 80+3 (France)
Referee: Angelov (BUL)

10/5/08, World of Wonders Football Centre, Antalya
Switzerland 0-2 France
Switzerland: Borkovic, Rochat, Daprelà, Koch, Lang, Ukoh, Xhaka, Mehmedi (Shaqiri 63), Pasche (Ben Khalifa 47), Dürig, Rebronja (Lehmann 69). Coach: Yves Debonnaire (SUI)
France: Mfa Mezui, Remy, Fauré, Kakuta, Fofana, Reale, Sunu, Nego (Adegoroye 76), Kolodziecziak, Grenier (Salibur 53), Tafer (Lacazette 65). Coach: Francis Smerecki (FRA)
Goal(s): 0-1 Tafer 33, 0-2 Tafer 51
Yellow Card(s): Nego 31 (France), Daprelà 32 (Switzerland)
Referee: Hermansen (DEN)

10/5/08, Mardan Sport Complex, Antalya
Republic of Ireland 1-3 Spain
Republic of Ireland: Hanley, Ormsby, Towell, Connolly, Gunning (Brady 57), Clifford, Dunleavy, Doran, Hourihane, Murphy, Cunningham (Joyce 83). Coach: Seán McCaffrey (IRL)
Spain: Ángel Díez, Montoya, Martínez, Gaztañaga, López (Canales 41), Gontán, Alcántara (Gavilán 61), Pulido, García (Rochina 41), Sielva, Carmona. Coach: Juan Santisteban (ESP)
Goal(s): 1-0 Hourihane 15, 1-1 Rochina 47, 1-2 Rochina 56, 1-3 Gontán 73
Yellow Card(s): Hourihane 8 (Republic of Ireland), Gunning 55 (Republic of Ireland)
Referee: Nieminen (FIN)

Group B Table

		Pld	W	D	L	F	A	Pts
1	Spain	3	2	1	0	8	4	7
2	France	3	2	1	0	7	4	7
3	Switzerland	3	1	0	2	1	4	3
4	Republic of Ireland	3	0	0	3	2	6	0

SEMI-FINALS

Prior to their semi-final against France at the Mardan Sport Complex, Turkey coach Şenol Ustaömer mused: "We have achieved the results we were hoping to achieve but are not reaching the standards we wanted because we have many players carrying injuries."

One of them, Eren Albayrak, started for the first time in the finals and had a superb first half on the left wing, sparking the attack that led to Turkey captain

Abdülkadir Kayalı's long-range opening goal on 31 minutes. But Eren was to limp off on the hour mark, and nine minutes later Thimothée Kolodziecziak equalised. A penalty shoot-out was the consequence and, just like Belgium the previous year, the hosts went out on spot-kicks; Abdülkadir and Yannis Tafer had initial efforts saved but crucially France goalkeeper Anthony Mfa Mezui also stopped Turkey's fourth shot by Batuhan Karadeniz and Kolodziecziak and substitute Alexandre Lacazette converted to give Les Mini-Bleus a 4-3 win, though they did have William Remy suspended for the final.

Extra-time win

Spain were expected to set up a rematch with France after meeting the Netherlands at the Antalya Atatürk Stadium and indeed they did, but only just. In fact, the Netherlands were the better team in the first half as they adopted a pressing game that bore fruit when Rodney Sniejder, younger brother of Wesley, headed in Jerson Cabral's cross. So there was some relief when Pulido equalised for Spain early in the second half after a corner was only partially cleared to Thiago, who hooked the ball back into the box. Now it was anyone's game, but it turned out to be Spain's with eight extra-time minutes left when Ángel Martínez, brought on at left-back after the regulation 80 were up, produced a stunning volley from outside the area to win the game.

Semi-Final Results

13/5/08, Mardan Sport Complex, Antalya
Turkey 1-1 France
Turkey: Uçar, Karayer, Eren, Yollu, Çek, Albayrak (Yardımcı 60), Aydoğdu (Karataş 71), Kayalı, Çolak, Töre (Sever 41), Karadeniz. Coach: Şenol Ustaömer (TUR)
France: Mfa Mezui, Kolodziecziak, Fauré, Remy, Nego (Adegoroye 64), Fofana, Reale, Sunu (Lacazette 41), Grenier (Salibur 52), Kakuta, Tafer. Coach: Francis Smerecki (FRA)
Goal(s): 1-0 Kayalı 31, 1-1 Kolodziecziak 69
Yellow Card(s): Remy 40+3 (France), Çek 41 (Turkey), Yollu 51 (Turkey)
Referee: Mazeika (LTU)
France win 4-3 on penalties.

13/5/08, Atatürk, Antalya
Spain 2-1 Netherlands
Spain: Álex, Montoya, Oriol, Gontán, Alcántara, Rochina, Canales (López 85), Pulido, Carles (Martínez 81), Sielva, Carmona (Gavilán 51). Coach: Juan Santisteban (ESP)
Netherlands: Zoet, Eekman, Najah, Van Rhijn, Burnet, Clasie, Castillion, Sneijder, Cabral (Ebecilio 74), Bonevacia (Van Haaren 94), Mokthar (Van La Parra 63). Coach: Albert Stuivenberg (NED)
Goal(s): 0-1 Sneijder 34, 1-1 Pulido 46, 2-1 Martínez 102
Yellow Card(s): Carles 19 (Spain), Cabral 57 (Netherlands)
Referee: Hermansen (DEN)

France are through to the final after beating hosts Turkey on penal

Spain's jubilant players surround the UEFA European Under-17 Championship trophy

FINAL

A close match was predicted in the final, a rematch of the 2004 decider - when hosts France had beaten Spain 2-1 with a late Samir Nasri winner - as well as of the Group B game nine days earlier, also at the Mardan Sport Complex, in which the holders had come from behind three times to draw. Instead it turned out to be the most one-sided final in the competition's history and as stunning a display from Spain as any team have ever produced at this level.

Inspired display

It was obvious from the outset that Spain were inspired by the occasion. Having begun the tournament slowly, Spain were now rampant and set up camp in the France half from the opening minutes, eventually breaking the deadlock just after the half-hour when the peerless Keko turned in Thiago's pass across the face of goal. Six minutes into the second half, Keko, aka Club Atlético de Madrid winger Sergio Gontán, won the ball in midfield and advanced before setting up Sergi to double the lead. Thiago, probably the tournament's most consistent player, now got in on the act when he converted a penalty after Sielva was felled in the box, and substitute Manu Gavilán rounded off the scoring by heading in with eleven minutes left after a superb turn and cross by Keko.

There was little tournament top scorer Yannis Tafer or his team-mates could do about it. In an emotional post-game press conference, Spain coach Juan Santisteban exclaimed: "Twenty years in this job and I can say I have never seen a final played in such a magnificent fashion. I think for a youth team to play like that is something really exceptional. I think they have produced a performance that nobody will forget, probably the best I have seen at this level, really sensational."

Final Result

16/5/08, Mardan Sport Complex, Antalya
France 0-4 Spain
Attendance: 600
France: Mfa Mezui, Adegoroye (Nego 41), Fauré, Damour (Auras 48), Kakuta, Fofana, Reale, Sunu, Kolodziecziak, Grenier (Boly 50), Tafer. Coach: Francis Smerecki (FRA)
Spain: Álex, Montoya, Gaztañaga, López, Gontán, Alcántara (Canales 68), Pulido, Carles, García (Rochina 74), Sielva, Carmona (Gavilán 55). Coach: Juan Santisteban (ESP)
Goal(s): 0-1 Gontán 31, 0-2 García 46, 0-3 Alcántara 63(p), 0-4 Gavilán 69
Yellow Card(s): Sunu 3 (France), Gaztañaga 27 (Spain), Carmona 35 (Spain), Nego 45 (France), Auras 53 (France), Fauré 61 (France), Reale 68 (France), Fofana 68 (France), Pulido 80+1 (Spain)
Referee: Kovařík (CZE)

CHAPTER 10

WOMEN'S EURO

UEFA WOMEN'S EURO 2009™ qualifying is set to go to the wire. Although two of the groups were settled as the competition entered its summer break, in the other four the second-placed team faced crunch fixtures at home against the leaders in a decisive week starting 27 September. In May, world champions Germany, aiming for a fifth straight European title, became the first team to join hosts Finland in the finals, and the following month Sweden emulated them. Norway are also in a strong position but elsewhere Iceland and Ukraine have the edge over more established rivals France and Denmark, while England face a tough examination from Spain. The six group winners qualify for the expanded 12-team finals from 23 August to 10 September 2009 alongside Finland. They will be joined by the winners of five two-legged play-offs involving the six group runners-up and the four third-placed teams with the best record against the top quartet in their pool.

FINLAND • 2009

GROUP 1

England were top seeds for this group but are being pushed all the way by Spain and the Czech Republic.

Hope Powell's side began strongly enough with 4-0 wins against Northern Ireland and Belarus, and after their FIFA Women's World Cup quarter-final run in September, Karen Carney's goal proved enough to defeat Spain in Shrewsbury. But although they gained further victories against the two group minnows, they were held 0-0 by the Czech Republic in March. However, while the Czech Republic have also picked up maximum points against Belarus and Northern Ireland, their results against Spain have proved costly as they conceded an added-time Vanessa Gimber goal in October for a 2-2 home draw and then lost 4-1 in Madrid in May. England go to the Czech Republic on 28 September and Spain four days later aware that two draws would take them to the finals. Spain would qualify with a win, and a draw would be enough if the Czech Republic defeat England by fewer than five goals. That is the margin of victory the Czechs need for automatic qualification, and they would still require the other game to be drawn, but, like Spain and England, they are already guaranteed a play-off place.

Group 1 Results

13/5/07
England 4-0 Northern Ireland
26/5/07
Northern Ireland 1-3 Czech Republic
30/5/07
Belarus 0-3 Spain

1/8/07, Spartak, Bobruisk
Belarus 5-0 Northern Ireland
Goal(s): 1-0 Kazeeva 26, 2-0 Tatarynova 49, 3-0 Davydovich 57, 4-0 Kuzniatsova 80, 5-0 Tatarynova 90

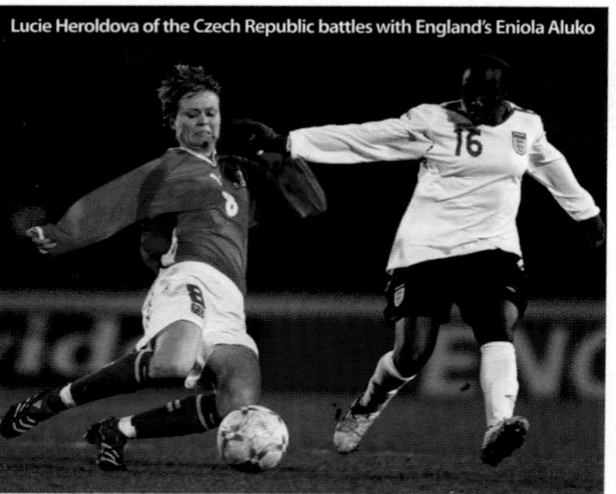
Lucie Heroldova of the Czech Republic battles with England's Eniola Aluko

26/8/07, Spartak, Bobruisk
Belarus 1-4 Czech Republic
Goal(s): 1-0 Kuzniatsova 4, 1-1 Heroldova 8, 1-2 Scasna 33, 1-3 Scasna 57(p), 1-4 Scasna 61

27/10/07, Bescot, Walsall
England 4-0 Belarus
Goal(s): 1-0 Scott 10, 2-0 Smith 32, 3-0 Aluko 48, 4-0 Scott 64

27/10/07, Štruncovy sady, Plzen
Czech Republic 2-2 Spain
Goal(s): 1-0 Martinkova 18, 1-1 Martín 35, 2-1 Knavova 78, 2-2 Vilanova Tous 90+4

25/11/07, The New Stadium, Shrewsbury
England 1-0 Spain
Goal(s): 1-0 Carney 64

16/2/08, El Montecillo, Aranda de Duero
Spain 4-0 Northern Ireland
Goal(s): 1-0 Del Rio Garcia 17, 2-0 Bermudez Tribano 27, 3-0 María Paz 59, 4-0 Garcia 74

6/3/08, Mourneview Park, Lurgan
Northern Ireland 0-2 England
Goal(s): 0-1 Williams 18, 0-2 White 84

20/3/08, Keepmoat, Doncaster
England 0-0 Czech Republic

26/4/08, SK Roudnice nad Labem, Roudnice
Czech Republic 4-0 Northern Ireland
Goal(s): 1-0 Knavova 21, 2-0 Martinkova 43, 3-0 Martinkova 79(p), 4-0 Doskova 90+3

3/5/08, Pabellón de la Ciudad del Fútbol, Madrid
Spain 6-1 Belarus
Goal(s): 1-0 Vazquez Morales 11, 2-0 Romero 28, 2-1 Shpak 36, 3-1 Vazquez Morales 40, 4-1 Cuesta 68, 5-1 Perez Gonzalez 88, 6-1 Romero 90

8/5/08, Darida, Minsk
Belarus 1-6 England
Goal(s): 0-1 Scott 1, 0-2 Williams 7, 0-3 Williams 25, 1-3 Ryzhevich 30, 1-4 Sanderson 44, 1-5 Williams 87, 1-6 White 90

8/5/08, Pabellón de la Ciudad del Fútbol, Madrid
Spain 4-1 Czech Republic
Goal(s): 0-1 Heroldova 33, 1-1 Gimber 46(p), 2-1 Boquete Giadans 57, 3-1 Marta Torrejón 84, 4-1 Boquete Giadans 90+2(p)

28/5/08, The Showgrounds, Newry
Northern Ireland 0-3 Spain
Goal(s): 0-1 Vazquez Morales 9, 0-2 Vazquez Morales 11, 0-3 Boquete Giadans 72

26/6/08, TJ Ludgerovice, Ludgerovice
Czech Republic 3-1 Belarus
Goal(s): 1-0 Ringelova 19, 2-0 Martinkova 51, 2-1 Kiose 62, 3-1 Martinkova 81

Group 1 Table

		Pld	W	D	L	F	A	Pts
1	England	6	5	1	0	17	1	16
2	Spain	7	5	1	1	22	5	16
3	Czech Republic	7	4	2	1	17	9	14
4	Belarus	7	1	0	6	9	26	3
5	Northern Ireland	7	0	0	7	1	25	0

Remaining Fixtures
25/7/08
Northern Ireland v Belarus
28/9/08
Czech Republic v England
2/10/08
Spain v England

GROUP 2

Sweden's 5-0 win in the Republic of Ireland in June ensured the 1984 champions another berth in the European finals.

t had seldom been in doubt as it was their sixth victory and 28th goal without reply. The foundations were laid in Лay 2007 with a 2-0 win in Italy, who would prove their :losest challengers, followed by 7-0 triumphs against Romania and Hungary the next month. Sweden disappointed at the World Cup in China, but they bounced back the following spring as substitute Jessica .andström struck an injury-time winner to see off Italy -0 four days after Hungary had been dispatched 6-0. The comfortable victory in Dublin sealed first place, with Karolin Westberg scoring twice and Victoria Svensson, osephine Öqvist and Lotta Schelin also finding the net. taly, whose only points dropped were against Sweden, are the only nation who can say with certainty that they will be in October's play-offs, the keys being a 2-1 win in reland in May 2007 and a 4-1 home triumph in February's return. Ireland's perfect record against Romania and Hungary has secured them third place with a play-off chance; a point in Sweden on 1 October would make that a near certainty.

Group 2 Results

/4/07
Republic of Ireland 2-1 Hungary
/5/07
:aly 0-2 Sweden
/5/07
Hungary 3-3 Romania
0/5/07
Republic of Ireland 1-2 Italy
6/6/07
Romania 0-7 Sweden
0/6/07
weden 7-0 Hungary

5/8/07, Football center Mogosoaia, Mogosoaia
Romania 0-2 Republic of Ireland
ioal(s): 0-1 Curtis 12, 0-2 Curtis 14

7/10/07, Buk, Buk
Hungary 1-3 Italy
ioal(s): 0-1 Dadda 58, 1-1 Padár 70(p), 1-2 Panico 76, 1-3 Tuttino 87

7/10/07, Richmond Park, Dublin
epublic of Ireland 2-1 Romania
ioal(s): 1-0 O'Brien 18, 2-0 Curtis 31, 2-1 Pufulete 40

1/10/07, Il Noce, Parma
:aly 5-0 Romania
ioal(s): 1-0 Boni 27, 2-0 Panico 41, 3-0 Paliotti 60, 4-0 Paliotti 66, -0 Gabbiadini 68

6/2/08, Communale, Villacidro
:aly 4-1 Republic of Ireland
ioal(s): 0-1 Taylor 13, 1-1 Fuselli 83, 2-1 Gabbiadini 85, -1 Panico 86, 4-1 Conti 90+1

Sweden's Jessica Landström (hidden) is mobbed by team-mates after her last-minute winning goal against Italy

23/4/08, Diósgyöri, Miskolc
Hungary 0-2 Republic of Ireland
Goal(s): 0-1 O'Brien 1, 0-2 Curtis 63

3/5/08, Sóstói, Szekesfehervar
Hungary 0-6 Sweden
Goal(s): 0-1 Karlsson 12, 0-2 Larsson 23, 0-3 Lundin 34, 0-4 Fischer 37, 0-5 Lundin 69, 0-6 Edlund 79

7/5/08, Behrn, Orebro
Sweden 1-0 Italy
Goal(s): 1-0 Landström 90

24/5/08, Town Stadium, Buftea
Romania 1-6 Italy
Goal(s): 0-1 Gabbiadini 13, 0-2 Panico 26, 1-2 Spanu 29, 1-3 Zorri 41(p), 1-4 Conti 48, 1-5 Gabbiadini 67, 1-6 Fuselli 85

28/5/08, Municipal, Oradea
Romania 3-1 Hungary
Goal(s): 1-0 Amza 9, 1-1 Padár 16, 2-1 Spanu 31, 3-1 Sarghie 82

25/6/08, Carlisle, Dublin
Republic of Ireland 0-5 Sweden
Goal(s): 0-1 Westberg 18, 0-2 Svensson 23, 0-3 Öqvist 28, 0-4 Westberg 73, 0-5 Schelin 86

Group 2 Table

		Pld	W	D	L	F	A	Pts
1	Sweden	6	6	0	0	28	0	18
2	Italy	7	5	0	2	20	7	15
3	Republic of Ireland	7	4	0	3	10	13	12
4	Romania	7	1	1	5	8	26	4
5	Hungary	7	0	1	6	6	26	1

Remaining Fixtures
27/9/08
Sweden v Romania
1/10/08
Sweden v Republic of Ireland
2/10/08
Italy v Hungary

GROUP 3

When Iceland produced a surprise 1-0 home win against France in June 2007 it looked likely that this group would be decided in the return fixture on 27 September 2008 – and with the two teams level on points, that is precisely how it will be.

Iceland followed up their win against France with a 5-0 defeat of Serbia in front of nearly 6,000 fans, but two months later they slipped to a shock 2-1 loss in Slovenia. However, in 2008 a 4-0 victory in Serbia was followed by a 5-0 defeat of Slovenia and 7-0 win against Greece, Margrét Lára Vidarsdóttir scoring a total of seven goals in those games to take her tally to a tournament-leading eleven. France recovered from their loss in Iceland with two useful October away wins, 8-0 in Serbia and 2-0 in Slovenia, and a 5-0 victory in Greece and 2-0 success against Serbia in the spring have kept their hopes alive, but they still need to beat Iceland to avoid the play-offs. Slovenia may have lost to Iceland in June but the month before they won 3-0 in Serbia and 3-1 against Greece and look likely to finish third. A point in Greece on 2 October should ensure a play-off spot.

Group 3 Results

11/4/07
France 6-0 Greece
5/5/07
Slovenia 0-5 Serbia
30/5/07
France 6-0 Slovenia
31/5/07
Greece 0-3 Iceland
16/6/07
Iceland 1-0 France
21/6/07
Iceland 5-0 Serbia

25/8/07, FK Rad, Belgrade
Serbia 1-2 Greece
Goal(s): 0-1 Panteleiadou 23, 1-1 Dimitridević 71, 1-2 Tsoukala 73

26/8/07, Športni Center, Dravograd
Slovenia 2-1 Iceland
Goal(s): 0-1 Vidarsdóttir 5, 1-1 Benak 13, 2-1 Milenkovič 14(p)

27/10/07, FK Rad, Belgrade
Serbia 0-8 France
Goal(s): 0-1 Traikia 12, 0-2 Abily 25, 0-3 Necib 56, 0-4 Bretigny 62, 0-5 Thomis 64, 0-6 Thomis 68, 0-7 Thiney 72, 0-8 Bussaglia 73

31/10/07, Športni Center, Dravograd
Slovenia 0-2 France
Goal(s): 0-1 Bussaglia 67, 0-2 Thomis 81

23/4/08, Akratitos, Athens
Greece 0-5 France
Goal(s): 0-1 Soubeyrand 39, 0-2 Herbert 49, 0-3 Bompastor 70, 0-4 Petit 85, 0-5 Thomis 90

France coach Bruno Bi reflective m

3/5/08, Gradski Zemun, Belgrade
Serbia 0-3 Slovenia
Goal(s): 0-1 Zver 58, 0-2 Zver 85, 0-3 Zver 88

8/5/08, Fred-Aubert, Saint-Brieuc
France 2-0 Serbia
Goal(s): 1-0 Bretigny 53, 2-0 Bretigny 71

28/5/08, Cika Daca, Kragujevac
Serbia 0-4 Iceland
Goal(s): 0-1 Vidarsdóttir 3, 0-2 S. Gunnarsdóttir 47, 0-3 Vidarsdóttir 68, 0-4 Omarsdóttir 70

28/5/08, Športni Center, Dravograd
Slovenia 3-1 Greece
Goal(s): 0-1 Arvanitaki 31, 1-1 Benak 36, 2-1 Zver 38, 3-1 Petrovič 90+1

21/6/08, Laugardalsvöllur, Reykjavik
Iceland 5-0 Slovenia
Goal(s): 1-0 Vidarsdóttir 11(p), 2-0 Vidarsdóttir 25, 3-0 Vidarsdóttir 50, 4-0 Jonsdóttir 62, 5-0 Omarsdóttir 88

26/6/08, Laugardalsvöllur, Reykjavik
Iceland 7-0 Greece
Goal(s): 1-0 S. Gunnarsdóttir 4, 2-0 Magnusdóttir 13, 3-0 Vidarsdóttir 30, 4-0 Magnusdóttir 53, 5-0 Magnusdóttir 56, 6-0 Omarsdóttir 66, 7-0 Vidarsdóttir 68

Group 3 Table

		Pld	W	D	L	F	A	Pt
1	Iceland	7	6	0	1	26	2	18
2	France	7	6	0	1	29	1	18
3	Slovenia	7	3	0	4	8	20	9
4	Greece	6	1	0	5	3	25	3
5	Serbia	7	1	0	6	6	24	3

Remaining Fixtures
27/9/08
France v Iceland
Greece v Serbia
2/10/08
Greece v Slovenia

GROUP 4

Germany are unbeaten in UEFA European Women's Championship qualifying since 1996 and it was no surprise that the holders were the first team to book their place in Finland.

Even before their successful World Cup defence that looked a certainty, with comfortable wins against the Netherlands, Wales and Switzerland in the bag. The global title again secured, Germany beat Belgium 3-0 on 28 October and won 1-0 in the Netherlands four days later, Annike Krahn settling an unusually close game. With their rivals taking points off each other, a 5-0 win in Belgium on 7 May gave Germany an unassailable lead; a 4-0 defeat of Wales put them eleven points clear. Although Wales are without a point, the others are in a tight race for second, Belgium having lost 1-0 in Switzerland but beaten them 3-1 in April just after being held 2-2 by a late equaliser from the Netherlands, who drew earlier in Switzerland by the same score. The Netherlands are at home to Switzerland on 30 August and Belgium on 27 September looking for four points. A Belgium win should do for them unless Switzerland shock Germany - whose stalwarts Silke Rottenberg, Renate Lingor and Steffi Jones have now retired from international football - on 2 October.

Group 4 Results

2/4/07
Germany 5-1 Netherlands
/5/07
Switzerland 1-0 Belgium
/5/07
Switzerland 2-2 Netherlands
0/5/07
Wales 0-6 Germany

Germany's Ariane Hingst (right) and Birgit Prinz embrace after going 1-0 up against Wales

22/8/07, Oberwerth, Koblenz
Germany 7-0 Switzerland
Goal(s): 1-0 Smisek 14, 2-0 Behringer 16, 3-0 Prinz 33, 4-0 Behringer 35, 5-0 Garefrekes 52, 6-0 Garefrekes 64, 7-0 Garefrekes 90

26/8/07, Veronica, Volendam
Netherlands 2-1 Wales
Goal(s): 1-0 Melis 47, 2-0 Smit 64, 2-1 Jones 75

28/10/07, Lohmühle, Lubeck
Germany 3-0 Belgium
Goal(s): 1-0 Garefrekes 8, 2-0 Minnert 11, 3-0 Prinz 74

28/10/07, Belle Vue, Rhyl
Wales 0-2 Switzerland
Goal(s): 0-1 Graf 41, 0-2 Moser 83

31/10/07, KFC Dessel, Dessel
Belgium 1-0 Wales
Goal(s): 1-0 Zeler 75

1/11/07, Veronica, Volendam
Netherlands 0-1 Germany
Goal(s): 0-1 Krahn 36

17/2/08, Jenner Park, Barry
Wales 0-1 Belgium
Goal(s): 0-1 Maes 69

20/2/08, Newport, Newport
Wales 0-1 Netherlands
Goal(s): 0-1 Melis 47

23/4/08, Patro, Maasmechelen
Belgium 2-2 Netherlands
Goal(s): 1-0 Verelst 41, 1-1 Hoogendijk 45+1, 2-1 Verelst 56, 2-2 Melis 89

27/4/08, Des Géants, Ath
Belgium 3-1 Switzerland
Goal(s): 1-0 Maes 25, 1-1 Bürki 38, 2-1 Maes 88, 3-1 Cayman 90+1

7/5/08, Kehrweg, Eupen
Belgium 0-5 Germany
Goal(s): 0-1 Pohlers 20, 0-2 Garefrekes 52, 0-3 Pohlers 58, 0-4 Garefrekes 59, 0-5 Bresonik 78

8/5/08, FC Oberdorf, Oberdorf
Switzerland 2-0 Wales
Goal(s): 1-0 Dickenmann 44, 2-0 Dickenmann 76(p)

29/5/08, Auestadion, Kassel
Germany 4-0 Wales
Goal(s): 1-0 Hingst 9, 2-0 Pohlers 12, 3-0 Krahn 30, 4-0 Behringer 77

Group 4 Table

		Pld	W	D	L	F	A	Pts
1	Germany	7	7	0	0	31	1	21
2	Belgium	7	3	1	3	7	12	10
3	Switzerland	6	3	1	2	8	12	10
4	Netherlands	6	2	2	2	8	11	8
5	Wales	8	0	0	8	1	19	0

Remaining Fixtures
30/8/08
Netherlands v Switzerland
27/9/08
Netherlands v Belgium
2/10/08
Switzerland v Germany

GROUP 5

Ukraine have never qualified for a women's final tournament, but that could all change after Darina Apanaschenko's goal gave them a 1-0 win against Denmark in June. Neither side had dropped a point up to that stage.

Denmark started qualifying late but in October beat Portugal 5-1 and won 1-0 in Scotland, opponents they then came from behind to beat 2-1 in April shortly after a 4-1 triumph in Slovakia. In May, Denmark won 4-0 in Portugal and 6-1 against Slovakia, Merete Pedersen's hat-trick taking her goal tally to nine. However, although Ukraine's success a month later was a surprise, the signs had been there ever since a 2-1 win against Scotland in May 2007; a year on Apanaschenko's injury-time goal in Perth ensured a 1-0 victory in the return. Ukraine even have something to play for when they face bottom side Portugal on 27 September as a five-goal win would ensure Denmark having to beat the leaders by a two-goal margin in Viborg four days later to win the group; otherwise Denmark could qualify with a 1-0 success. Scotland are third but although they only need to draw with Slovakia on 28 September to confirm that position, a victory could be vital if they want a play-off berth.

Group 5 Results

14/4/07
Slovakia 2-1 Portugal
6/5/07
Scotland 0-0 Portugal
9/5/07
Slovakia 0-4 Ukraine
30/5/07
Ukraine 2-1 Scotland
20/6/07
Ukraine 5-0 Slovakia

27/10/07, National, Senec
Slovakia 0-3 Scotland
Goal(s): 0-1 Kerr 2, 0-2 Hamill 16, 0-3 Fleeting 71

27/10/07, Viborg, Viborg
Denmark 5-1 Portugal
Goal(s): 1-0 M. Pedersen 40, 1-1 Fernandes 41, 2-1 Pape 51, 3-1 Andersen 60, 4-1 Pape 71, 5-1 M. Pedersen 82

31/10/07, McDiarmid Park, Perth
Scotland 0-1 Denmark
Goal(s): 0-1 M. Pedersen 62

16/2/08, Municipal, Rio Maior
Portugal 0-1 Slovakia
Goal(s): 0-1 Budosova 11

21/2/08, Municipal de Abrantes, Abrantes
Portugal 0-1 Ukraine
Goal(s): 0-1 Zinchenko 70

23/4/08, National, Senec
Slovakia 1-4 Denmark
Goal(s): 0-1 Pape 6, 0-2 Rasmussen 16, 0-3 Rasmussen 47, 0-4 Pape 55, 1-4 Zubková 70

27/4/08, Viborg, Viborg
Denmark 2-1 Scotland
Goal(s): 0-1 Sneddon 28, 1-1 Andersen 50, 2-1 M. Pedersen 67

3/5/08, Varzim, Povoa do Varzim
Portugal 1-4 Scotland
Goal(s): 0-1 Beattie 12, 0-2 Fleeting 20, 0-3 Fleeting 25, 0-4 Fleeting 38(p), 1-4 Fernandes 44

8/5/08, Sports Center CF Fão, Fão
Portugal 0-4 Denmark
Goal(s): 0-1 Rasmussen 18, 0-2 Pape 53, 0-3 M. Pedersen 71, 0-4 M. Pedersen 78

28/5/08, McDiarmid Park, Perth
Scotland 0-1 Ukraine
Goal(s): 0-1 Apanaschenko 9

28/5/08, Viborg, Viborg
Denmark 6-1 Slovakia
Goal(s): 1-0 Andersen 25, 2-0 M. Pedersen 35, 2-1 Lukacsova 44, 3-1 Pape 61, 4-1 M. Pedersen 62, 5-1 Pape 81, 6-1 M. Pedersen 90+1

22/6/08, Y. Gagarin, Chernigov
Ukraine 1-0 Denmark
Goal(s): 1-0 Apanaschenko 28

Group 5 Table

		Pld	W	D	L	F	A	Pts
1	Ukraine	6	6	0	0	14	1	18
2	Denmark	7	6	0	1	22	5	18
3	Scotland	7	2	1	4	9	7	7
4	Slovakia	7	2	0	5	5	23	6
5	Portugal	7	0	1	6	3	17	1

Remaining Fixtures
27/9/08
Ukraine v Portugal
28/9/08
Scotland v Slovakia
1/10/08
Denmark v Ukraine

Denmark midfiel
Kathrine Søren

GROUP 6

Norway are not officially confirmed in the inals, but with seven wins and 26 inanswered goals they are as good as there.

ustria, Poland and Israel have all been beaten twice and a -0 win against Russia in October, with goals from Melissa Viik, Solveig Gulbrandsen and Leni Larsen Kaurin, ensured ontrol of the group for the 2005 runners-up despite the ost-World Cup semi-final retirements of Ragnhild iulbrandsen, Lise Klaveness and Camilla Huse. Russia had egun the group with a 6-0 win against Israel, 3-1 defeat f Poland and 5-1 victory in Austria, and they bounced ack in May to beat Israel 5-0. But to qualify outright, ussia must win against Austria on 27 August and in oland a month later before defeating Norway by four oals on 2 October. Those are the only remaining fixtures r Austria and Poland, separated by two points, and it oks likely that either would need victory to have any ope of reaching the play-offs. Poland seemed to have the pper hand in that race when they began qualifying with 1-0 win in Austria but the tables were turned in Kutno in lay, the visitors prevailing 4-2.

Group 6 Results

'5/07
ustria 0-1 Poland
)/5/07
rael 2-2 Poland
)/5/07
rael 0-6 Russia
5/6/07
ussia 3-1 Poland
7/6/07
rael 0-3 Norway
/6/07
bland 4-1 Israel
/6/07
orway 3-0 Austria

3/8/07, Anger, Anger
ustria 1-5 Russia
oal(s): 1-0 Fuhrmann 6, 1-1 Kurochkina 36, 1-2 Mokshanova 48, 3 Barbashina 62, 1-4 Mokshanova 65, 1-5 Barbashina 90+3

5/8/07, Sparkassenstadion Gleisdorf, Gleisdorf
ustria 5-0 Israel
oal(s): 1-0 Wenninger 2, 2-0 Burger 48, 3-0 Burger 72, 0 Celouch 74, 5-0 Burger 90

7/10/07, Viking, Stavanger
orway 3-0 Russia
oal(s): 1-0 Wiik 23, 2-0 Gulbrandsen 62, 3-0 Kaurin 88

5/08, Sør Arena, Kristiansand
orway 7-0 Israel
oal(s): 1-0 Wiik 12, 2-0 Gulbrandsen 19, 3-0 Wiik 45, 4-0 Mykjaland 52, 0 Christensen 54, 6-0 S. Nordby 75(p), 7-0 Gulbrandsen 82

5/08, Viking, Stavanger
orway 3-0 Poland
oal(s): 1-0 Storlokken 19, 2-0 Gulbrandsen 39, 3-0 Wiik 46

Norway's prolific striker Melissa Wiik – bound for Finland in 2009

28/5/08, City Stadium, Kutno
Poland 2-4 Austria
Goal(s): 0-1 Gröbner 7, 0-2 Aigner 27, 0-3 Burger 40, 1-3 Winczo 58, 1-4 Burger 71, 2-4 Stobba 89

29/5/08, Krasnoarmeysk, Krasnoarmeysk
Russia 4-0 Israel
Goal(s): 1-0 Letyushova 9, 2-0 Letyushova 22, 3-0 Mokshanova 59(p), 4-0 Barbashina 67

21/6/08, Ertl Glas (SKU), Amstetten
Austria 0-4 Norway
Goal(s): 0-1 Mykjaland 7, 0-2 Gulbrandsen 19, 0-3 Mykjaland 58, 0-4 Mykjaland 74

25/6/08, City Stadium, Kutno
Poland 0-3 Norway
Goal(s): 0-1 Gulbrandsen 38, 0-2 Mykjaland 50, 0-3 Herlovsen 88

25/6/08, Beit She'an Municipal, Beit She'an
Israel 0-2 Austria
Goal(s): 0-1 Tieber 9, 0-2 Burger 43

Group 6 Table

		Pld	W	D	L	F	A	Pts
1	Norway	7	7	0	0	26	0	21
2	Russia	5	4	0	1	18	5	12
3	Austria	7	3	0	4	12	15	9
4	Poland	7	2	1	4	10	16	7
5	Israel	8	0	1	7	3	33	1

Remaining Fixtures
27/8/08
Russia v Austria
27/9/08
Poland v Russia
2/10/08
Russia v Norway

2007/08

The seventh UEFA Women's Cup season had the feel of a milestone campaign, not least because the competition's only multiple winners, 1. FFC Frankfurt and Umeå IK, met in the final, with the second leg in the German city's main stadium attracting 27,640 fans, more than double the previous record attendance for the tournament. Frankfurt won 3-2 to complete a 4-3 aggregate win and become the first three-time champions. Birgit Prinz and Tina Wunderlich were participants in each triumph, as would Steffi Jones have been had she not retired in mid-season. Final goalscorers Conny Pohlers and Tina Wunderlich also became the first players to win the trophy with different clubs, having aided 1. FFC Turbine Potsdam's 2005 success, while Umeå, beaten finalists for the second successive season, had the consolation of reaching a record fifth final.

CHAPTER 11

UEFA WOMEN'S CUP

QUALIFYING ROUNDS

First Qualifying Round

Group A1 Results

9/8/07, City Stadium, Siauliai
FFC Zuchwil 05 5-1 Glentoran Belfast United

9/8/07, City Stadium, Siauliai
Everton LFC 4-0 Gintra Universitetas

11/8/07, City Stadium, Siauliai
Everton LFC 11-0 Glentoran Belfast United

11/8/07, City Stadium, Siauliai
Gintra Universitetas 0-6 FFC Zuchwil 05

14/8/07, City Stadium, Siauliai
FFC Zuchwil 05 0-5 Everton LFC

14/8/07, Pakruojo, Pakruojis
Glentoran Belfast United 1-2 Gintra Universitetas

Group A1 Table

		Pld	W	D	L	F	A	Pts
1	Everton LFC	3	3	0	0	20	0	9
2	FFC Zuchwil 05	3	2	0	1	11	6	6
3	Gintra Universitetas	3	1	0	2	2	11	3
4	Glentoran Belfast United	3	0	0	3	2	18	0

Group A2 Results

9/8/07, Svangaskard, Toftir
Valur Reykjavik 2-1 FC Honka Espoo

9/8/07, Svangaskard, Toftir
ADO Den Haag 1-1 KÍ Klaksvík

11/8/07, Svangaskard, Toftir
FC Honka Espoo 1-0 ADO Den Haag

11/8/07, Svangaskard, Toftir
Valur Reykjavik 6-0 KÍ Klaksvík

14/8/07, Svangaskard, Toftir
ADO Den Haag 1-5 Valur Reykjavik

14/8/07, Tórsvøllur, Torshavn
KÍ Klaksvík 1-4 FC Honka Espoo

Group A2 Table

		Pld	W	D	L	F	A	Pts
1	Valur Reykjavik	3	3	0	0	13	2	9
2	FC Honka Espoo	3	2	0	1	6	3	6
3	ADO Den Haag	3	0	1	2	2	7	1
4	KÍ Klaksvík	3	0	1	2	2	11	1

Group A3 Results

9/8/07, Wienerwaldstadion, Neulengbach
Uczniowski KS GOL 4-1 Mayo FC

9/8/07, Wienerwaldstadion, Neulengbach
SV Neulengbach 4-3 Hibernian LFC

11/8/07, Wienerwaldstadion, Neulengbach
Hibernian LFC 4-1 Uczniowski KS GOL

11/8/07, Wienerwaldstadion, Neulengbach
SV Neulengbach 3-0 Mayo FC

14/8/07, Wienerwaldstadion, Neulengbach
Uczniowski KS GOL 1-8 SV Neulengbach

14/8/07, Stadt Sportanlage, St Polten
Mayo FC 0-8 Hibernian LFC

Group A3 Table

		Pld	W	D	L	F	A	Pts
1	SV Neulengbach	3	3	0	0	15	4	9
2	Hibernian LFC	3	2	0	1	15	5	6
3	Uczniowski KS GOL	3	1	0	2	6	13	3
4	Mayo FC	3	0	0	3	1	15	0

Julie Fleeting of Arsenal Ladies FC

Group A4 Results

9/8/07, Olimpija, Osijek
FCL Rapide Wezemaal 2-0 Cardiff City L

9/8/07, Gradski vrt, Osijek
SU 1° Dezembro 7-0 WFC Osijek

11/8/07, Gradski vrt, Osijek
Cardiff City LFC 0-2 SU 1° Dezembro

11/8/07, Gradski vrt, Osijek
FCL Rapide Wezemaal 2-0 WFC Osijek

14/8/07, Olimpija, Osijek
SU 1° Dezembro 0-1 FCL Rapide Wezem

14/8/07, Gradski vrt, Osijek
WFC Osijek 2-1 Cardiff City LFC

Group A4 Table

		Pld	W	D	L	F
1	FCL Rapide Wezemaal	3	3	0	0	5
2	SU 1° Dezembro	3	2	0	1	9
3	WFC Osijek	3	1	0	2	2
4	Cardiff City LFC	3	0	0	3	1

Group A5 Results

9/8/07, ŽŠD, Ljubljana
Athletic Club BFKEB 4-0 ŽNK KRKA Novo

9/8/07, Športni park, Domzale
ASD CF Bardolino Verona 16-0 Birkirka

11/8/07, ŽŠD, Ljubljana
Athletic Club BFKEB 16-0 Birkirkara FC

11/8/07, Športni park, Domzale
ŽNK KRKA Novo Mesto 0-5 ASD CF Bardolino Verona

14/8/07, ŽŠD, Ljubljana
ASD CF Bardolino Verona 1-0 Athletic BFKEB

14/8/07, Športni park, Domzale
Birkirkara FC 1-5 ŽNK KRKA Novo Mes

Group A5 Table

		Pld	W	D	L	F
1	ASD CF Bardolino Verona	3	3	0	0	22
2	Athletic Club BFKEB	3	2	0	1	20
3	ŽNK KRKA Novo Mesto	3	1	0	2	5
4	Birkirkara FC	3	0	0	3	1

Mami Yamaguchi of Umeå IK

oup A6 Results

7, Mladost, Strumica
pique Lyonnais 12-0 FK Slovan Duslo

7, FC Turnovo, Strumica
SFK 2000 Sarajevo 2-1 ZFK Skiponjat

'07, Mladost, Strumica
pique Lyonnais 10-0 ZFK Skiponjat

'07, FC Turnovo, Strumica
ovan Duslo Sala 0-2 ZNK SFK 2000 Sarajevo

'07, Mladost, Strumica
SFK 2000 Sarajevo 0-7 Olympique Lyonnais

'07, FC Turnovo, Strumica
Skiponjat 3-1 FK Slovan Duslo Sala

up A6 Table

	Pld	W	D	L	F	A	Pts
ympique Lyonnais	3	3	0	0	29	0	9
NK SFK 2000 rajevo	3	2	0	1	4	8	6
K Skiponjat	3	1	0	2	4	13	3
Slovan Duslo Sala	3	0	0	3	1	17	0

Group A7 Results

9/8/07, Krasnoarmeysk, Krasnoarmeysk
Zhilstroy-1 Kharkov 14-0 FC Iveria

9/8/07, Krasnoarmeysk, Krasnoarmeysk
WFC Rossiyanka 7-0 FK Napredak Kruševac

11/8/07, Krasnoarmeysk, Krasnoarmeysk
FK Napredak Kruševac 2-4 Zhilstroy-1 Kharkov

11/8/07, Krasnoarmeysk, Krasnoarmeysk
WFC Rossiyanka 18-0 FC Iveria

14/8/07, Krasnoarmeysk, Krasnoarmeysk
Zhilstroy-1 Kharkov 0-3 WFC Rossiyanka

14/8/07, Spartak, Schelkovo
FC Iveria 2-6 FK Napredak Kruševac

Group A7 Table

	Pld	W	D	L	F	A	Pts
1 WFC Rossiyanka	3	3	0	0	28	0	9
2 Zhilstroy-1 Kharkov	3	2	0	1	18	5	6
3 FK Napredak Kruševac	3	1	0	2	8	13	3
4 FC Iveria	3	0	0	3	2	38	0

Group A8 Results

9/8/07, FAK Stavroupolis, Thessalonika
FC NSA Sofia 3-1 Pärnu FC

9/8/07, Toumba, Thessalonika
WFC Universitet Vitebsk 4-0 FC PAOK

11/8/07, FAK Stavroupolis, Thessalonika
WFC Universitet Vitebsk 6-0 Pärnu FC

11/8/07, Toumba, Thessalonika
FC PAOK 2-2 FC NSA Sofia

14/8/07, FAK Stavroupolis, Thessalonika
FC NSA Sofia 0-2 WFC Universitet Vitebsk

14/8/07, Toumba, Thessalonika
Pärnu FC 2-3 FC PAOK

Group A8 Table

	Pld	W	D	L	F	A	Pts
1 WFC Universitet Vitebsk	3	3	0	0	12	0	9
2 FC NSA Sofia	3	1	1	1	5	5	4
3 FC PAOK	3	1	1	1	5	8	4
4 Pärnu FC	3	0	0	3	3	12	0

Group A9 Results

9/8/07, Zimbru, Chisinau
1. FC Femina Budapest 6-0 Ruslan 93

9/8/07, District Sport Complex, Orhei
Alma KTZH 5-0 FC Narta Chisinau

11/8/07, Zimbru, Chisinau
Alma KTZH 5-0 Ruslan 93

11/8/07, District Sport Complex, Orhei
FC Narta Chisinau 0-2 1. FC Femina Budapest

14/8/07, Zimbru, Chisinau
1. FC Femina Budapest 1-3 Alma KTZH

14/8/07, District Sport Complex, Orhei
Ruslan 93 1-3 FC Narta Chisinau

Group A9 Table

	Pld	W	D	L	F	A	Pts
1 Alma KTZH	3	3	0	0	13	1	9
2 1. FC Femina Budapest	3	2	0	1	9	3	6
3 FC Narta Chisinau	3	1	0	2	3	8	3
4 Ruslan 93	3	0	0	3	1	14	0

Group A10 Results

9/8/07, Municipal, Rishon Le-Zion
AC Sparta Praha 1-1 CFF Clujana

9/8/07, Holon Municipal, Holon
Maccabi Holon FC 5-1 AEK Kokkinochovion

11/8/07, Holon Municipal, Holon
AC Sparta Praha 19-0 AEK Kokkinochovion

11/8/07, Teddy Maicha, Jerusalem
CFF Clujana 3-0 Maccabi Holon FC

14/8/07, Teddy Maicha, Jerusalem
Maccabi Holon FC 3-4 AC Sparta Praha

14/8/07, Municipal, Rishon Le-Zion
AEK Kokkinochovion 0-11 CFF Clujana

Group A10 Table

		Pld	W	D	L	F	A	Pts
1	AC Sparta Praha	3	2	1	0	24	4	7
2	CFF Clujana	3	2	1	0	15	1	7
3	Maccabi Holon FC	3	1	0	2	8	8	3
4	AEK Kokkinochovion	3	0	0	3	1	35	0

Second Qualifying Round

Group B1 Results

11/10/07, Meadow Park, Borehamwood
ASD CF Bardolino Verona 3-2 SV Neulengbach
Goal(s): 0-1 Celouch 30, 1-1 Panico 50, 1-2 Gstöttner 55, 2-2 Tuttino 61, 3-2 Boni 76(p)

11/10/07, Meadow Park, Borehamwood
Arsenal Ladies FC 4-0 Alma KTZH
Goal(s): 1-0 Carney 21, 2-0 Carney 26, 3-0 Chapman 33, 4-0 Sanderson 44

13/10/07, St Albans Clarence Park, St Albans
Arsenal Ladies FC 7-0 SV Neulengbach
Goal(s): 1-0 Ludlow 9, 2-0 Fleeting 28, 3-0 Ludlow 31, 4-0 Carney 32, 5-0 Fleeting 36, 6-0 Chapman 72, 7-0 Grant 78

13/10/07, St Albans Clarence Park, St Albans
Alma KTZH 1-5 ASD CF Bardolino Verona
Goal(s): 0-1 Panico 10, 0-2 Gabbiadini 33, 0-3 Panico 52, 0-4 Boni 68, 1-4 Kirgizbaeva 70, 1-5 Manieri 87

16/10/07, Meadow Park, Borehamwood
ASD CF Bardolino Verona 3-3 Arsenal Ladies FC
Goal(s): 0-1 Fleeting 27, 0-2 Sanderson 48, 1-2 Gabbiadini 49, 2-2 Manieri 59, 2-3 Smith 85, 3-3 Panico 90+2

16/10/07, St Albans Clarence Park, St Albans
SV Neulengbach 3-0 Alma KTZH
Goal(s): 1-0 Burger 28, 2-0 Burger 45+2, 3-0 Santos Augusto 90+2

Group B1 Table

		Pld	W	D	L	F	A	Pts
1	Arsenal Ladies FC	3	2	1	0	14	3	7
2	ASD CF Bardolino Verona	3	2	1	0	11	6	7
3	SV Neulengbach	3	1	0	2	5	10	3
4	Alma KTZH	3	0	0	3	1	12	0

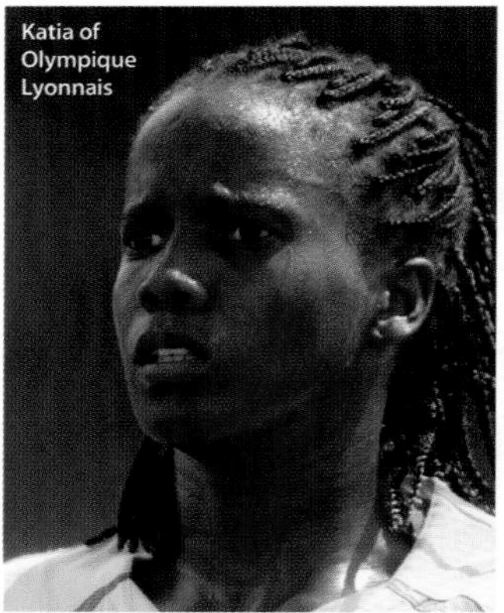
Katia of Olympique Lyonnais

Group B2 Results

11/10/07, Gammliavallen, Umea
WFC Rossiyanka 3-1 WFC Universitet Vitebsk
Goal(s): 1-0 Petrova 5, 2-0 Tsybutovich 36, 2-1 Malinouskaya 46, 3-1 Morozova 87

11/10/07, Gammliavallen, Umea
Umeå IK 3-1 CFF Clujana
Goal(s): 1-0 Klaveness 14, 2-0 Klaveness 29(p), 2-1 Ilinca 61, 3-1 Edlund 83

14/10/07, Gammliavallen, Umea
CFF Clujana 1-2 WFC Rossiyanka
Goal(s): 0-1 Mokshanova 30, 1-1 Ilinca 73, 1-2 Petrova 78

14/10/07, Gammliavallen, Umea
Umeå IK 2-0 WFC Universitet Vitebsk
Goal(s): 1-0 Pedersen 51, 2-0 Pedersen 70

16/10/07, Gammliavallen, Umea
WFC Universitet Vitebsk 1-0 CFF Clujana
Goal(s): 1-0 Ziuzkova 18

16/10/07, Gammliavallen, Umea
WFC Rossiyanka 2-2 Umeå IK
Goal(s): 0-1 Marta26(p), 0-2 Marta40, 1-2 Barbashina 52, 2-2 Barbashina 56

Group B2 Table

		Pld	W	D	L	F	A	Pts
1	Umeå IK	3	2	1	0	7	3	7
2	WFC Rossiyanka	3	2	1	0	7	4	7
3	WFC Universitet Vitebsk	3	1	0	2	2	5	3
4	CFF Clujana	3	0	0	3	2	6	0

Group B3 Results

11/10/07, KHO Bierbeek 1, Bierbeek
1. FFC Frankfurt 3-1 Valur Reykjavik
Goal(s): 0-1 Vidarsdóttir 43, 1-1 Prinz 81, 2-1 Wimbersky 89, 3-1 Wimbersky 90+2

11/10/07, KHO Bierbeek 1, Bierbeek
FCL Rapide Wezemaal 2-1 Everton LFC
Goal(s): 0-1 Evans 48, 1-1 Verelst 72, 2-1 Verelst 90+1

13/10/07, KHO Bierbeek 1, Bierbeek
1. FFC Frankfurt 2-1 Everton LFC
Goal(s): 0-1 Williams 3, 1-1 Prinz 28, 2-1 Pohlers 90+2

13/10/07, KHO Bierbeek 1, Bierbeek
Valur Reykjavik 4-0 FCL Rapide Wezema
Goal(s): 1-0 Jónsdóttir 56, 2-0 Vidarsdóttir
3-0 Vidarsdóttir 75, 4-0 Vidarsdóttir 80

16/10/07, KHO Bierbeek 1, Bierbeek
Everton LFC 3-1 Valur Reykjavik
Goal(s): 1-0 Handley 40, 2-0 Dowie 53, 3-0 Handley 55, 3-1 Jónsdóttir 60

16/10/07, KHO Bierbeek 1, Bierbeek
FCL Rapide Wezemaal 1-1 1. FFC Frankfu
Goal(s): 1-0 Torreele 23, 1-1 Pohlers 34

Group B3 Table

		Pld	W	D	L	F	A
1	1. FFC Frankfurt	3	2	1	0	6	3
2	FCL Rapide Wezemaal	3	1	1	1	3	6
3	Everton LFC	3	1	0	2	5	5
4	Valur Reykjavik	3	1	0	2	6	6

Group B4 Results

11/10/07, Stade de Gerland, Lyon
Brøndby IF 0-0 Olympique Lyonnais

11/10/07, Pierre Duboeuf, Bron
Kolbotn IL 3-1 AC Sparta Praha
Goal(s): 1-0 Angus 3, 1-1 Kladrubská 62, 2-1 Gulbrandsen 70, 3-1 Gulbrandsen 73

13/10/07, Pierre Duboeuf, Bron
Brøndby IF 2-1 AC Sparta Praha
Goal(s): 0-1 Mouchova 21, 1-1 Matysova 49(og), 2-1 L Jensen 82

13/10/07, Stade de Gerland, Lyon
Olympique Lyonnais 1-0 Kolbotn IL
Goal(s): 1-0 Abily 10

16/10/07, Pierre Duboeuf, Bron
Kolbotn IL 0-1 Brøndby IF
Goal(s): 0-1 Olsen 90+1

16/10/07, Stade de Gerland, Lyon
AC Sparta Praha 1-2 Olympique Lyonnais
Goal(s): 0-1 Abily 50, 0-2 Renard 55, 1-2 Bertholdova 80

Group B4 Table

		Pld	W	D	L	F	A
1	Brøndby IF	3	2	1	0	3	1
1	Olympique Lyonnais	3	2	1	0	3	1
3	Kolbotn IL	3	1	0	2	3	3
4	AC Sparta Praha	3	0	0	3	3	7

QUARTER-FINALS

:ven before the knockout stage there was excitement aplenty as in a desperately :ight second qualifying round group debutants Everton LFC and Valur Reykjavík were both eliminated on a thrilling last day as Belgium's FCL Rapide Wezemaal held able-toppers 1. FFC Frankfurt to a 1-1 draw. Meanwhile, newcomers Olympique .yonnais eliminated Kolbotn IL but were denied first place by the other 2006/07 semi-finalists, Brøndby IF, after the drawing of lots.

Holders ousted

Therefore Lyon faced holders Arsenal Ladies FC, whose orm had been mixed since England's FIFA Women's World Cup campaign, and while Arsenal drew 0-0 at the Stade de Gerland, Lyon triumphed 3-2 at Borehamwood with goals from Katia, Camille Abily and Elodie Thomis. That set up a meeting with Umeå IK, who defeated Wezemaal 10-0 on aggregate.

Umeå's fellow two-time winners Frankfurt were held 0-0 at WFC Rossiyanka in Moscow, but first-half goals from Petra Wimbersky and Birgit Prinz in Germany took them through 2-1. Italy's ASD CF Bardolino Verona surprisingly won through to face Frankfurt. Having earned a dramatic 3-3 draw with Arsenal in the previous round they bettered that by overcoming a 1-0 home defeat against Brøndby to win by the same scoreline in Denmark and take the tie 3-2 on penalties.

Quarter-Final Results

14/11/07, Stade de Gerland, Lyon
Olympique Lyonnais 0-0 Arsenal Ladies FC
Lyon: Mainguy, Dusang, Renard, Georges, Gomes Jatoba, Bompastor, Katia, Thomis (Abily 63), Necib, Cruz Trana, Lattaf.
Coach: Farid Benstiti (FRA)

Lisa Dahlqvist of Umeå IK is hurdled by Rapide Wezemaal's Kristian Elsen

Arsenal LFC: Byrne, Scott, Ludlow, White, Smith, Sanderson, Carney (Fleeting 61), Yankey, Chapman, Asante, Phillip. Coach: Vic Akers (ENG)
Yellow Card(s): Renard 54 (Olympique Lyonnais), Carney 55 (Arsenal Ladies FC), Bompastor 68 (Olympique Lyonnais), Georges 69 (Olympique Lyonnais), Smith 80 (Arsenal Ladies FC)
Referee: Steinhaus (GER)
21/11/07, Meadow Park, Borehamwood
Arsenal Ladies FC 2-3 Olympique Lyonnais
Arsenal LFC: Byrne, Scott, Ludlow, White, Smith, Sanderson, Yankey, Fleeting, Chapman (Carney 77), Asante, Phillip. Coach: Vic Akers (ENG)
Lyon: Mainguy, Dusang, Abily, Georges, Gomes Jatoba, Bompastor, Katia, Cruz Trana, Lepailleur, Necib, Lattaf (Thomis 66). Coach: Farid Benstiti (FRA)
Goal(s): 0-1 Katia 16, 1-1 Smith 24, 2-1 Yankey 33, 2-2 Abily 38, 2-3 Thomis 85
Yellow Card(s): Abily 61 (Olympique Lyonnais), Ludlow 69 (Arsenal Ladies FC), Bompastor 70 (Olympique Lyonnais), Smith 81 (Arsenal Ladies FC), Gomes Jatoba 89 (Olympique Lyonnais)
Referee: Palmqvist (SWE)
Aggregate: 2-3; Olympique Lyonnais qualify.

14/11/07, Staaien, Sint-Truiden
FCL Rapide Wezemaal 0-4 Umeå IK
Rapide Wezemaal: Vandenhouwe, Meeus (Wuyts 89), Elsen, Heiremans, Hemelsoet, Meykens, Timmermans, Van de Goor (Torreele 46), Vanderauwera, Verelst, Van Malenstein. Coach: Andrée Jeglertz (SWE)
Umeå IK: Rönnlund, Westberg, Bergqvist, Paulsson, Edlund (Pedersen 81), Dahlqvist, Karlsson, Berglund, Bachmann, Marta, Ljungberg (Konradsson 65). Coach: Victor Crabbe (BEL)
Goal(s): 0-1 Marta 9, 0-2 Westberg 35, 0-3 Bachmann 75, 0-4 Marta 90
Yellow Card(s): Westberg 72 (Umeå IK)
Referee: Avdonchenko (RUS)
22/11/07, Gammliavallen, Umea
Umeå IK 6-0 FCL Rapide Wezemaal
Umeå IK: Rönnlund, Moura, Klaveness, Ljungberg (Dahlqvist 61), Westberg, Bergqvist, Paulsson, Edlund (Karlsson 68), Berglund, Bachmann (Pedersen 61), Marta. Coach: Andrée Jeglertz (SWE)
Rapide Wezemaal: Vandenhouwe, Timmermans, Hemelsoet, Heiremans, Verelst, Van de Goor, Vanderauwera, Meeus, Elsen, Meykens (Torreele 55), Van Malenstein. Coach: Victor Crabbe (BEL)
Goal(s): 1-0 Van Malenstein 6(og), 2-0 Edlund 18, 3-0 Edlund 28, 4-0 Marta 44, 5-0 Ljungberg 60, 6-0 Marta67
Referee: Gaal (HUN)
Aggregate: 10-0; Umeå IK qualify.

14/11/07, Marc'Antonio Bentegodi, Verona
ASD CF Bardolino Verona 0-1 Brøndby IF
Bardolino: Brunozzi, Panico, Stefanelli, Sorvillo, Boni, Tuttino, Motta, Barbierato (Magrini 66), Gabbiadini, Lonardi (Perobello 83), Mencaccini (Vicchiarello 46). Coach: Renato Longega (ITA)
Brøndby: Cederkvist, A. Nielsen, L. Jensen (Pedersen 85), Falk, Rydahl Bukh (Christiansen 66), Sørensen, Andersen, Olsen, Kjær Jensen, L. Hansen, Pape (Christensen 52). Coach: Henrik Jensen (DEN)
Goal(s): 0-1 Christensen 65
Yellow Card(s): Kjær Jensen 26 (Brøndby), Gabbiadini 36 (Bardolino), Vicchiarello 66 (Bardolino), Sorvillo 71 (Bardolino), Falk 72 (Brøndby)
Referee: Beck (GER)

Umeå IK's Madelaine Edlund scored twice in the 6-0 home win over Rapide Wezemaal

21/11/07, Brøndby, Brondby
Brøndby IF 0-1 ASD CF Bardolino Verona
Brøndby: Cederkvist, A. Nielsen, L. Jensen (Pedersen 99), Falk, Rydah Bukh (Christiansen 66), Sørensen, Andersen, Olsen, Kjær Jensen, L. Hansen, Pape (Christensen 79). Coach: Henrik Jensen (DEN)
Bardolino: Brunozzi, Barbierato (Lonardi 114), Boni, Gabbiadini, Magrini, Motta, Panico, Vicchiarello (Mencaccini 68), Stefanelli, Sorvillo, Tuttino. Coach: Renato Longega (ITA)
Goal(s): 0-1 Tuttino 37
Yellow Card(s): L. Hansen 22 (Brøndby), L Jensen 43 (Brøndby), Vicchiarello 56 (Bardolino), Boni 120 (Bardolino)
Referee: Petignat (SUI)
Aggregate: 1-1; ASD CF Bardolino Verona qualify 3-2 on penalties.

15/11/07, Rodina, Moscow
WFC Rossiyanka 0-0 1. FFC Frankfurt
Rossiyanka: Zvarich, Pekur, Barbashina, Poriadina, Skotnikova (Kremleva 72), Petrova, Morozova, Tsybutovich, Mokshanova, Ekpo, George. Coach: Vladimir Gerasimov (RUS)
Frankfurt: Rottenberg, Wunderlich, Prinz, Kliehm, Wimbersky, Pohlers, Bartusiak, Garefrekes, Thomas (Lewandowski 76), Weber, Krieger. Coach: Hans-Jürgen Tritschoks (GER)
Yellow Card(s): Pekur 53 (Rossiyanka), Wimbersky 63 (Frankfurt)
Referee: Dorcioman (ROU)
21/11/07, Am Brentano Bad, Frankfurt am Main
1. FFC Frankfurt 2-1 WFC Rossiyanka
Frankfurt: Rottenberg, Wunderlich, Prinz (Jones 89), Kliehm, Wimbersky, Pohlers (Thomas 77), Bartusiak, Garefrekes, Weber (Lingor 66), Lewandowski, Krieger. Coach: Hans-Jürgen Tritschoks (GER)
Rossiyanka: Zvarich, Pekur, Barbashina, Dyatchkova, Skotnikova, Morozova, Tsybutovich, Kozhnikova, Mokshanova, Ekpo (Kremleva 61), George (Petrova 41). Coach: Vladimir Gerasimov (RUS)
Goal(s): 1-0 Wimbersky 23, 2-0 Prinz 44, 2-1 Morozova 90+1
Yellow Card(s): Tsybutovich 12 (Rossiyanka), Pekur 62 (Rossiyanka)
Referee: Toms (ENG)
Aggregate: 2-1; 1. FFC Frankfurt qualify.

SEMI-FINALS

.yon and Bardolino's rewards for reaching heir first semi-finals were ties against eams appearing for the fifth time at this tage, Umeå and Frankfurt. Travelling to ;ermany for the first leg in late March, ;ardolino were 2-0 down in 19 minutes hrough Conny Pohlers and Birgit Prinz. Aaria Sorvillo pulled one back just before he break, and although Prinz and Pohlers cored again, a late Melania Gabbiadini oal gave the Italian champions hope. More than 12,000 fans were in attendance week later in Verona, but Frankfurt howed their class in the last 22 minutes is goals from Karolin Thomas, Kerstin ;arefrekes and Pohlers sealed a omprehensive 7-2 aggregate win.

/ital away goal

around 12,000 spectators were also present at the ;tade de Gerland for the first leg of Lyon's tie with Jmeå, but most were left disappointed as Madelaine :dlund struck what eventually proved to be a vital joal for the visitors in the 57th minute. Louisa Necib equalised 15 minutes later, meaning that Lyon were till firmly in contention when they travelled to ;weden, and they so nearly turned the tie when Camille Abily hit the crossbar early on and Sonia ;ompastor struck the post in injury time, but Umeå ıltimately prevailed on away goals. Umeå coach Andrée Jeglertz said. "I've never faced a better team vith this club."

Semi-Final Results

'9/3/08, Am Brentano Bad, Frankfurt am Main
. FFC Frankfurt 4-2 ASD CF Bardolino Verona
rankfurt: Rottenberg, Krieger, Lewandowski, Weber, Pohlers, ;ünther, Wimbersky, Smisek (Garefrekes 46), Prinz, Wunderlich Thomas 27), Wunderlich. Coach: Hans-Jürgen Tritschoks (GER)
;ardolino: Brunozzi, Girelli (Manieri 46) (Toselli 82), Gabbiadini, Aagrini, Barbierato (Ledri 68), Motta, Tuttino, Boni, Sorvillo, ;tefanelli, Panico. Coach: Renato Longega (ITA)
;oal(s): 1-0 Pohlers 5, 2-0 Prinz 19, 2-1 Sorvillo 48, 3-1 Prinz 79, -1 Pohlers 82, 4-2 Gabbiadini 84
'ellow Card(s): Girelli 26 (Bardolino)
;eferee: Brohet (BEL)
;/4/08, Marc'Antonio Bentegodi, Verona
\SD CF Bardolino Verona 0-3 1. FFC Frankfurt
;ardolino: Brunozzi, Sorvillo (Toselli 71), Ledri (Magrini 64), ;abbiadini, Panico, Boni, Barbierato, Vicchiarello (Girelli 57), Tuttino, ;tefanelli, Motta. Coach: Renato Longega (ITA)
Frankfurt: Rottenberg, Lewandowski, Pohlers, Wunderlich, Prinz, Lingor, Kliehm, Weber (Garefrekes 46), Günther (Krieger 66), Wimbersky, Thomas. Coach: Hans-Jürgen Tritschoks (GER)
Goal(s): 0-1 Thomas 68, 0-2 Garefrekes 80, 0-3 Pohlers 81
Yellow Card(s): Lingor 26 (Frankfurt), Gabbiadini 34 (Bardolino), Tuttino 43 (Bardolino), Kliehm 47 (Frankfurt)
Referee: Olander (EST)
Aggregate: 2-7; 1. FFC Frankfurt qualify.

30/3/08, Stade de Gerland, Lyon
Olympique Lyonnais 1-1 Umeå IK
Olympique Lyonnais: B. Nordby, Dusang, Renard (Thomis 61), Georges, Gomes Jatoba, Katia, Abily, Cruz Trana, Necib, Lattaf (Bretigny 87), Dalum Jensen. Coach: Farid Benstiti (FRA)
Umeå IK: Rönnlund, Paulsson, Frisk, Westberg, Dahlqvist, Edlund, Pedersen (Berglund 81), Rasmussen, Yamaguchi (Bachmann 70), Marta, Östberg. Coach: Andrée Jeglertz (SWE)
Goal(s): 0-1 Edlund 57, 1-1 Necib 72
Yellow Card(s): Östberg 54 (Umeå IK)
Referee: Schett (AUT)
6/4/08, Gammliavallen, Umea
Umeå IK 0-0 Olympique Lyonnais
Umeå IK: Rönnlund, Marta, Bachmann, Berglund, Dahlqvist, Frisk, Edlund (Jakobsson 90+1), Paulsson, Rasmussen, Östberg, Yamaguchi. Coach: Andrée Jeglertz (SWE)
Olympique Lyonnais: B. Nordby, Cruz Trana, Katia (Lepailleur 89), Gomes Jatoba, Necib, Abily, Dusang, Georges, Lattaf (Thomis 57), Bompastor, Dalum Jensen (Bretigny 90+1). Coach: Farid Benstiti (FRA)
Yellow Card(s): Georges 55 (Olympique Lyonnais), Bretigny 90+5 (Olympique Lyonnais)
Referee: Ihringova (ENG)
Aggregate: 1-1; Umeå IK qualify on away goal.

1. FFC Frankfurt star Birgit Prinz

FINAL

For the third time in the seven UEFA Women's Cup finals, Umeå and Frankfurt came face to face, the German side having prevailed 2-0 at the old Waldstadion in 2002 and their Swedish rivals gaining an 8-0 aggregate revenge two years later. That was Umeå's second straight triumph but they suffered another final defeat by Arsenal LFC in 2007 after a frustrating 1-0 home first-leg loss. They toiled fruitlessly that day; this time they took only 12 seconds to break the deadlock through Brazilian superstar Marta, though after Pohlers' swift equaliser Umeå again saw chances go begging as the game ended 1-1.

Petra Wimbersky is a… with joy after putt… Frankfurt 3-1 up in… second leg of the f… with a superb free-…

Record attendance

Frankfurt had chosen to hold the second leg at the former Waldstadion, which since the 2002 fixture had been transformed for the 2006 FIFA World Cup. That year Frankfurt had won their second European title against Potsdam in front of a competition record 13,200 fans at the Bornheimer Hang Stadium in the city, but long before this match enough tickets had been sold to smash that mark and in the end the 27,640 attendance was over 5,000 more than had ever previously watched a women's match in Germany - and indeed was the highest for a European female club match anywhere in the modern era.

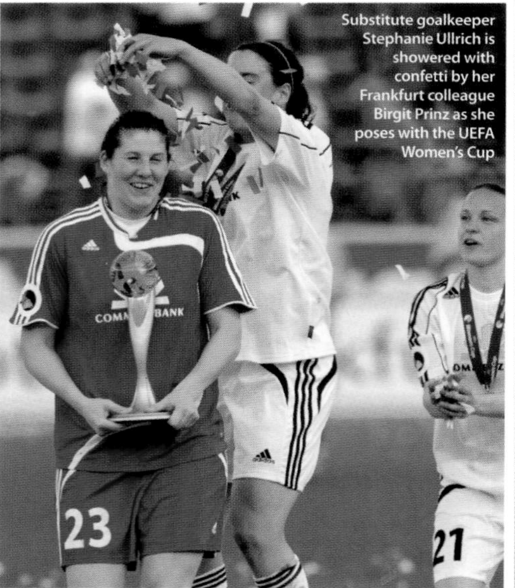
Substitute goalkeeper Stephanie Ullrich is showered with confetti by her Frankfurt colleague Birgit Prinz as she poses with the UEFA Women's Cup

Within seven minutes the stadium had erupted as Pohlers turned in Garefrekes' cross. Frankfurt held that lead at the break, when a foot injury forced off goalkeeper Silke Rottenberg and gave a chance to Stephanie Ullrich, who had sat on the bench for Potsdam in their runs to the 2005 and 2006 finals and repeated the role for Frankfurt this time around, only now making her competition debut. However, that did not unsettle the home side as Pohlers doubled the lead in the 55th minute, the eighth UEFA Women's Cup final goal of her career.

Frankfurt hold on

On 68 minutes Marta was felled in the box by Gina Lewandowski and Lisa Dahlqvist converted Umeå's penalty. But three minutes later a brilliant Wimbersky free-kick restored Frankfurt's cushion, and although Umeå captain Frida Östberg reduced arrears again with seven minutes left and Marta and substitute Ramona Bachmann grazed the woodwork, the German side's 4-3 aggregate lead proved sufficient. In his swansong season Frankfurt chief Hans-Jürgen Tritschoks was now the first coach to win this trophy twice. He said: "I want

› congratulate my team on an amazing performance. ›e have reached a new dimension in women's football ›day. The attendance says it all."

›inal Result

›7/5/08, Gammliavallen, Umea

›meå IK 1-1 1. FFC Frankfurt

›meå IK: Rönnlund, Paulsson, Frisk, Westberg, Östberg, Dahlqvist, ›maguchi, Bachmann (Konradsson 68), Marta, Edlund, Rasmussen. ›ach: Andrée Jeglertz (SWE)

›ankfurt: Rottenberg, Kliehm (Günther 56), Lewandowski, ›underlich, Bartusiak, Garefrekes, Krieger, Weber, Wimbersky, ›hlers (Smisek 83), Prinz. Coach: Hans-Jürgen Tritschoks (GER)

›oal(s): 1-0 Marta 1, 1-1 Pohlers 5

Yellow Card(s): Garefrekes 37 (Frankfurt), Weber 87 (Frankfurt), Prinz 90 (Frankfurt), Frisk 90+2 (Umeå IK)

Referee: Gaal (HUN)

24/5/08, Commerzbank Arena, Frankfurt am Main

1. FFC Frankfurt 3-2 Umeå IK

Frankfurt: Rottenberg (Ullrich 46), Kliehm (Günther 47), Wunderlich, Lewandowski, Bartusiak, Garefrekes, Weber, Krieger, Wimbersky (Thomas 90), Prinz, Pohlers. Coach: Hans-Jürgen Tritschoks (GER)

Umeå IK: Rönnlund, Paulsson, Frisk, Westberg, Östberg, Dahlqvist, Rasmussen, Yamaguchi, Berglund (Bachmann 46), Edlund (Jakobsson 63), Marta. Coach: Andrée Jeglertz (SWE)

Goal(s): 1-0 Pohlers 7, 2-0 Pohlers 55, 2-1 Dahlqvist 68(p), 3-1 Wimbersky 71, 3-2 Östberg 83

Yellow Card(s): Kliehm 15 (Frankfurt)

Referee: Ihringova (ENG)

Aggregate: 4-3; 1. FFC Frankfurt win.

The triumphant Frankfurt players raise their arms in celebration

15
17

HAPTER
12

WU19 2007/08

Iolders Germany arrived in the Loire Valley with the favourites' tag once again dangling from heir neck after a typically impressive qualification. An 8-3 thrashing of well-fancied Russia aught the eye in particular, and a sixth title in eleven seasons was, for some, a formality. Yet heir coach Maren Meinert admitted she thought differently, and so it panned out.

Germany's route to the semi-finals looked easier as they were paired in Group B alongside Sweden and Scotland, returning from an absence of two and three years respectively. England provided their first opponents, however, in a rematch of the 2007 final, and in the French hosts' Group A, Norway and Spain both contained maturing squads full of experience from the previous event in Iceland. Then there was Italy, an improving force but only in France after finishing as best runners-up in qualifying. Surely they would not mount a serious challenge...

QUALIFYING ROUNDS

First Qualifying Round

Group 1 Results

27/9/07, De Anadia, Anadia
Portugal 4-0 Greece

27/9/07, Training Center, Luso
Iceland 4-0 Romania

29/9/07, Municipal, Agueda
Portugal 0-2 Romania

29/9/07, Municipal Stadium, Oliveira do Bairro
Greece 1-4 Iceland

2/10/07, Training Center, Luso
Iceland 3-2 Portugal

2/10/07, De Anadia, Anadia
Romania 0-1 Greece

Group 1 Table

	Pld	W	D	L	F	A	Pts
1 Iceland	3	3	0	0	11	3	9
2 Portugal	3	1	0	2	6	5	3
3 Romania	3	1	0	2	2	5	3
4 Greece	3	1	0	2	2	8	3

Group 2 Results

27/9/07, KS Proszowianka, Proszowice
Poland 7-1 Turkey

27/9/07, LKS Przeboj, Wolbrom
Austria 4-0 Bulgaria

29/9/07, KS Proszowianka, Proszowice
Poland 2-3 Bulgaria

29/9/07, LKS Przeboj, Wolbrom
Turkey 2-3 Austria

2/10/07, LKS Przeboj, Wolbrom
Austria 1-1 Poland

2/10/07, KS Proszowianka, Proszowice
Bulgaria 0-4 Turkey

Group 2 Table

	Pld	W	D	L	F	A	Pts
1 Austria	3	2	1	0	8	3	7
2 Poland	3	1	1	1	10	5	4
3 Turkey	3	1	0	2	7	10	3
4 Bulgaria	3	1	0	2	3	10	3

Group 3 Results

26/9/07
Sweden 3-0 Georgia (w/o)

26/9/07, Södermalms IP, Skovde
Hungary 13-0 Kazakhstan

28/9/07
Georgia 0-3 Hungary (w/o)

28/9/07, Ulvesborg, Tidaholm
Sweden 12-0 Kazakhstan

1/10/07, Södermalms IP, Skovde
Hungary 1-1 Sweden

1/10/07
Kazakhstan 3-0 Georgia (w/o)

Group 3 Table

	Pld	W	D	L	F	A	Pts
1 Hungary	3	2	1	0	17	1	7
2 Sweden	3	2	1	0	16	1	7
3 Kazakhstan	3	1	0	2	3	25	3
4 Georgia	3	0	0	3	0	9	0

Group 4 Results

27/9/07, Krasnoarmeysk, Krasnoarmeysk
Italy 7-0 Northern Ireland

27/9/07, Krasnoarmeysk, Krasnoarmeysk
Russia 7-0 Israel

29/9/07, Krasnoarmeysk, Krasnoarmeysk
Israel 1-5 Italy

29/9/07, Krasnoarmeysk, Krasnoarmeysk
Russia 2-0 Northern Ireland

2/10/07, Krasnoarmeysk, Krasnoarmeysk
Italy 1-1 Russia

2/10/07, Spartak, Schelkovo
Northern Ireland 3-4 Israel

Group 4 Table

	Pld	W	D	L	F	A	Pts
1 Italy	3	2	1	0	13	2	7
2 Russia	3	2	1	0	10	1	7
3 Israel	3	1	0	2	5	15	3
4 Northern Ireland	3	0	0	3	3	13	0

Group 5 Results

27/9/07, Torpedo, Minsk
Serbia 0-0 Belarus

27/9/07, Darida, Minsk
Finland 8-0 Estonia

29/9/07, Torpedo, Minsk
Belarus 0-3 Finland

29/9/07, Darida, Minsk
Serbia 5-1 Estonia

2/10/07, Traktor, Minsk
Finland 1-0 Serbia

2/10/07, Torpedo, Minsk
Estonia 0-3 Belarus

Group 5 Table

	Pld	W	D	L	F
1 Finland	3	3	0	0	12
2 Serbia	3	1	1	1	5
3 Belarus	3	1	1	1	3
4 Estonia	3	0	0	3	1

Group 6 Results

27/9/07, Grbavica, Sarajevo
Denmark 2-0 Bosnia-Herzegovina

27/9/07, Kreševo, Kresevo
Belgium 2-0 Latvia

29/9/07, Kreševo, Kresevo
Denmark 10-0 Latvia

29/9/07, Grbavica, Sarajevo
Bosnia-Herzegovina 0-6 Belgium

2/10/07, Grbavica, Sarajevo
Belgium 1-2 Denmark

2/10/07, Kreševo, Kresevo
Latvia 1-2 Bosnia-Herzegovina

Group 6 Table

	Pld	W	D	L	F
1 Denmark	3	3	0	0	14
2 Belgium	3	2	0	1	9
3 Bosnia-Herzegovina	3	1	0	2	2
4 Latvia	3	0	0	3	1

Group 7 Results

27/9/07, Ldau, Dublyany
Ukraine 3-0 Azerbaijan

27/9/07, SCA, Lvov
Scotland 13-0 Armenia

29/9/07, Ldau, Dublyany
Ukraine 2-0 Armenia

, SCA, Lvov
ijan 0-3 Scotland

, Ldau, Dublyany
d 2-2 Ukraine

SCA, Lvov
a 2-2 Azerbaijan

7 Table

	Pld	W	D	L	F	A	Pts
and	3	2	1	0	18	2	7
ine	3	2	1	0	7	2	7
baijan	3	0	1	2	2	8	1
enia	3	0	1	2	2	17	1

up 8 Results

NTS Nemšová, Nemsova
land 3-0 Slovakia

, FK AFC, Novo Mesto
ic of Ireland 5-1 Croatia

, FK Druzstevnik Trencianske Sta,
nkse Stankovce
land 6-2 Croatia

NTS Nemšová, Nemsova
a 0-5 Republic of Ireland

FK AFC, Novo Mesto
ic of Ireland 3-2 Switzerland

, FK Druzstevnik Trencianske Sta,
kse Stankovce
2-1 Slovakia

8 Table

	Pld	W	D	L	F	A	Pts
blic of Ireland	3	3	0	0	13	3	9
erland	3	2	0	1	11	5	6
tia	3	1	0	2	5	12	3
kia	3	0	0	3	1	10	0

up 9 Results

, Mladost, Strumica
-0 FYR Macedonia

FC Turnovo, Strumica
ny 6-0 Czech Republic

Mladost, Strumica
-3 Czech Republic

FC Turnovo, Strumica
cedonia 0-12 Germany

Mladost, Strumica
ny 7-0 Wales

2/10/07, FC Turnovo, Strumica
Czech Republic 4-1 FYR Macedonia

Group 9 Table

	Pld	W	D	L	F	A	Pts
1 Germany	3	3	0	0	25	0	9
2 Czech Republic	3	2	0	1	7	9	6
3 Wales	3	1	0	2	4	10	3
4 FYR Macedonia	3	0	0	3	1	18	0

Group 10 Results

27/9/07, Mestni Stadion Ptuj, Ptuj
Netherlands 7-0 Slovenia

27/9/07, Sportni Park, Lendava
Norway 14-0 Moldova

29/9/07, Fazanerija, Murska Sobota
Netherlands 11-0 Moldova

29/9/07, Sportni Park, Lendava
Slovenia 0-3 Norway

2/10/07, Mestni Stadion Ptuj, Ptuj
Norway 2-0 Netherlands

2/10/07, Fazanerija, Murska Sobota
Moldova 0-5 Slovenia

Group 10 Table

	Pld	W	D	L	F	A	Pts
1 Norway	3	3	0	0	19	0	9
2 Netherlands	3	2	0	1	18	2	6
3 Slovenia	3	1	0	2	5	10	3
4 Moldova	3	0	0	3	0	30	0

Toni Duggan of England

Group 11 Results

27/9/07, S. Darius & S. Girenas, Kaunas
England 7-1 Faroe Islands

27/9/07, Sūduva, Marijampole
Spain 14-0 Lithuania

29/9/07, S. Darius & S. Girenas, Kaunas
Spain 12-0 Faroe Islands

29/9/07, Sūduva, Marijampole
Lithuania 0-10 England

2/10/07, S. Darius & S. Girenas, Kaunas
England 0-0 Spain

2/10/07, Sūduva, Marijampole
Faroe Islands 2-2 Lithuania

Group 11 Table

	Pld	W	D	L	F	A	Pts
1 Spain	3	2	1	0	26	0	7
2 England	3	2	1	0	17	1	7
3 Faroe Islands	3	0	1	2	3	21	1
4 Lithuania	3	0	1	2	2	26	1

Second Qualifying Round

Group 1 Results

24/4/08, Sportzentrum, Trumau
Sweden 3-0 Czech Republic
Goal(s): 1-0 Florková 49(og), 2-0 Lundh 73, 3-0 Asllani 85

24/4/08, Sportzentrum, Trumau
Finland 0-3 Austria
Goal(s): 0-1 Tieber 6, 0-2 Makas 54, 0-3 Makas 82

26/4/08, Stadt Sportanlage, St Polten
Finland 1-2 Czech Republic
Goal(s): 1-0 Ruutu 10, 1-1 Pincová 58, 1-2 Kruzová 61

26/4/08, Stadt Sportanlage, St Polten
Austria 0-2 Sweden
Goal(s): 0-1 Lyckberg 35(p), 0-2 Hammarbäck 90+2

29/4/08, Stadt Sportanlage, St Polten
Sweden 1-1 Finland
Goal(s): 0-1 Tikkanen 31, 1-1 Lyckberg 48(p)

29/4/08, Sportzentrum, Trumau
Czech Republic 1-0 Austria
Goal(s): 1-0 Vyštejnová 44

Group 1 Table

	Pld	W	D	L	F	A	Pts
1 Sweden	3	2	1	0	6	1	7
2 Czech Republic	3	2	0	1	3	4	6
3 Austria	3	1	0	2	3	3	3
4 Finland	3	0	1	2	2	6	1

Group 2 Results

24/4/08, Honsfeld SV, Bullingen
Iceland 0-1 Belgium
Goal(s): 0-1 Stevens 65

24/4/08, Kehrweg, Eupen
England 7-0 Poland
Goal(s): 1-0 White 18, 2-0 White 20, 3-0 Rafferty 47, 4-0 Bradley 52, 5-0 White 62, 6-0 Walton 76, 7-0 Walton 90(p)

26/4/08, FC Rocherat, Rocherat
Iceland 2-2 Poland
Goal(s): 1-0 Thorvaldsdóttir 3, 1-1 Gunnlaugsdóttir 12(og), 1-2 Zdunczyk 24, 2-2 S. Gunnarsdóttir 55

26/4/08, Kehrweg, Eupen
Belgium 0-4 England
Goal(s): 0-1 Allen 2, 0-2 White 63, 0-3 Duggan 83, 0-4 Clarke 87

29/4/08, Honsfeld SV, Bullingen
England 1-0 Iceland
Goal(s): 1-0 Walton 87

29/4/08, FC Rocherat, Rocherat
Poland 0-1 Belgium
Goal(s): 0-1 Philtjens 89(p)

Group 2 Table

	Pld	W	D	L	F	A	Pts
1 England	3	3	0	0	12	0	9
2 Belgium	3	2	0	1	2	4	6
3 Iceland	3	0	1	2	2	4	1
4 Poland	3	0	1	2	2	10	1

Group 3 Results

24/4/08, Mogosoaia, Mogosoaia
Germany 8-3 Russia
Goal(s): 1-0 Pollmann 9(p), 2-0 Pollmann 16, 3-0 Pollmann 17, 4-0 Kulig 28, 5-0 Kulig 40, 6-0 Kulig 43, 6-1 Ploskonenko 45+1, 7-1 Schwab 50, 7-2 Bakulina 54, 8-2 Kulig 60, 8-3 Gokhman-Lazareva 64

24/4/08, Town Stadium, Buftea
Hungary 2-3 Romania
Goal(s): 0-1 Birtoiu 14, 1-1 Rapp 30, 1-2 Ilinca 35, 2-2 Jakabi 48, 2-3 Birtoiu 88

26/4/08, Mogosoaia, Mogosoaia
Germany 4-0 Romania
Goal(s): 1-0 Kulig 45, 2-0 Wich 71, 3-0 Mirlach 73, 4-0 Schwab 85

26/4/08, Town Stadium, Buftea
Russia 0-1 Hungary
Goal(s): 0-1 Jakabi 50

29/4/08, Mogosoaia, Mogosoaia
Hungary 0-2 Germany
Goal(s): 0-1 Schwab 9, 0-2 Chandraratne 12

29/4/08, Town Stadium, Buftea
Romania 0-4 Russia
Goal(s): 0-1 Zapotichnaya 22, 0-2 Korovkina 64, 0-3 Korovkina 90, 0-4 Korovkina 90+2

Group 3 Table

	Pld	W	D	L	F	A	Pts
1 Germany	3	3	0	0	14	3	9
2 Russia	3	1	0	2	7	9	3
3 Hungary	3	1	0	2	3	5	3
4 Romania	3	1	0	2	3	10	3

Group 4 Results

24/4/08, Censuy, Renens
Denmark 2-0 Switzerland
Goal(s): 1-0 Veje 52, 2-0 Overgaard Munk 90

24/4/08, Municipal, Yverdon
Scotland 3-1 Belarus
Goal(s): 0-1 Kiose 4, 1-1 Littlejohn 12, 2-1 Littlejohn 53, 3-1 Littlejohn 60

26/4/08, Bois Gentils, Lausanne
Switzerland 2-2 Scotland
Goal(s): 1-0 Crnogorcevic 31, 1-1 Corsie 81, 2-1 Mehmeti 86(p), 2-2 Littlejohn 90+4

26/4/08, Censuy, Renens
Denmark 2-0 Belarus
Goal(s): 1-0 Kragh 34, 2-0 Shaiko 51(og)

29/4/08, Bois Gentils, Lausanne
Scotland 2-1 Denmark
Goal(s): 0-1 Overgaard Munk 6, 1-1 Ross 14, 2-1 Murray 85

29/4/08, Municipal, Yverdon
Belarus 1-4 Switzerland
Goal(s): 0-1 Crnogorcevic 1, 1-1 Kiose 2, 1-2 Crnogorcevic 43, 1-3 Crnogorcevic 60, 1-4 Remund 65

Group 4 Table

	Pld	W	D	L	F	A	Pts
1 Scotland	3	2	1	0	7	4	7
2 Denmark	3	2	0	1	5	2	6
3 Switzerland	3	1	1	1	6	5	4
4 Belarus	3	0	0	3	2	9	0

Group 5 Results

24/4/08, Dr. José Vieira Carvalho, Maia
Norway 6-1 Ukraine
Goal(s): 1-0 Tarnes 13, 2-0 Isaksen 15, 2-1 Boychenko 47, 3-1 Mjelde 51, 4-1 Mjelde 60, 5-1 Vasylets 79(og), 6-1 Tarnes 82

24/4/08, Varzim, Povoa do Varzim
Italy 4-0 Portugal
Goal(s): 1-0 Parisi 21, 2-0 Girelli 31, 3-0 Bonetti 66, 4-0 Marchese 83

26/4/08, CD Trofense, Trofa
Norway 5-1 Portugal
Goal(s): 1-0 Andresen 36, 1-1 Meira Ventura 74, 2-1 Eide 75, 3-1 Isaksen 80, 4-1 Mjelde 8
5-1 Hansen 90+2

26/4/08, Sports Center CF Fão, Fao
Ukraine 0-4 Italy
Goal(s): 0-1 Bonometti 13, 0-2 Marchese
0-3 Bonometti 31, 0-4 Gueli 89

29/4/08, Varzim, Povoa do Varzim
Italy 1-2 Norway
Goal(s): 0-1 Herregården 33, 0-2 Enget
1-2 Parisi 59

29/4/08, Sports Center CF Fão, Fao
Portugal 2-2 Ukraine
Goal(s): 0-1 Romanenko 16, 0-2 Sorokin
1-2 Ferreira Mendes 50, 2-2 Branco Cruz

Group 5 Table

	Pld	W	D	L	F
1 Norway	3	3	0	0	13
2 Italy	3	2	0	1	9
3 Portugal	3	0	1	2	3
4 Ukraine	3	0	1	2	3

Group 6 Results

24/4/08, Pabellón de la Ciudad del Fútbol,
Republic of Ireland 0-2 Netherlands
Goal(s): 0-1 De Ridder 42, 0-2 De Ridder

24/4/08, Pabellón de la Ciudad del Fútbol,
Spain 7-0 Serbia
Goal(s): 1-0 Casas Llopis 27, 2-0 Casas L
53, 3-0 Cristina Martínez 57, 4-0 Correde
5-0 Marta Torrejón 67, 6-0 Liria 81,
7-0 Ana Servia 82

26/4/08, Pabellón de la Ciudad del Fútbol,
Republic of Ireland 7-0 Serbia
Goal(s): 1-0 McDonall 4, 2-0 Parkes 14,
3-0 Russell 31, 4-0 Roche 41, 5-0 Madde
6-0 Murray 78, 7-0 Murray 90

26/4/08, Pabellón de la Ciudad del Fútbol,
Netherlands 0-1 Spain
Goal(s): 0-1 Ana Servia 37

29/4/08, Pabellón de la Ciudad del Fútbol,
Spain 3-1 Republic of Ireland
Goal(s): 1-0 Cristina Martínez 17, 1-1 Gr
2-1 Marta Torrejón 70, 3-1 Patri 89

29/4/08, Pabellón de la Ciudad del Fútbol,
Serbia 1-7 Netherlands
Goal(s): 0-1 Hulshof 12, 0-2 Hulshof 25,
0-3 Beekhuis 27, 0-4 Slegers 34, 0-5 De
0-6 Lewerissa 70, 0-7 De Ridder 77,
1-7 Stankovic 88

Group 6 Table

	Pld	W	D	L	F
1 Spain	3	3	0	0	11
2 Netherlands	3	2	0	1	9
3 Republic of Ireland	3	1	0	2	8
4 Serbia	3	0	0	3	1

FINAL TOURNAMENT

GROUP A

The question for many as Group A got under way was which, from three "very strong and evenly-matched" teams according to Norway coach Jarl Torske, would join France in the last four. Yet after opening their account with a crowd-pleasing victory against Spain, it was not to go the hosts' way. Julie Machart's exceptional goal set up a richly-deserved 1-0 win against Spain in Blois, finally ending the resistance of goalkeeper Laura Rafols, but it was events 40km away in Romorantin that were to have a bigger bearing on the outcome of the section.

Dramatic win

Locked at 0-0 going into added time, a moment of inspiration from substitute Tatiana Bonetti earned Italy a dramatic win against Norway. Making their first appearance in the finals for four years, Corrado Corradini's team gave a good account of themselves against a much-fancied Norway side, soaking up some intense second-half pressure before striking the winner on 90 minutes. Bonetti had only been on the pitch for 24 minutes when she collected possession on the left, cut inside and unleashed a superb curling shot into the top corner of the net.

na Bonetti scored
-minute winner
nst Norway in
's opening match

Corradini labelled Bonetti his "Maradona", but when the Azzurrine followed up that victory by beating France 3-1 three days later, it was clear he had a few more tricks up his sleeve. Once again, Italy soaked up long periods of pressure and proved more efficient in the final third. After Alessandra Barecca's first-half goal had been cancelled out by Eugénie Le Sommer, strikes from Pamela Gueli and Cristina Bonometti sealed the win. It took the side through to the last four with a game to spare, allowing Corradini to make what would prove to be vital, wholesale changes for the last group game, a 3-0 loss to already eliminated Spain.

Winner-takes-all

Spain's aspirations had been ended by a 2-1 defeat to Norway, a result that set up a winner-takes-all meeting between Torske's team and France in the final round of games. A point would see Norway through on goal difference, and so it proved as they withstood a barrage of late pressure from France to clinch a hard-fought 1-1 draw after Les Bleuettes' captain Le Sommer had cancelled out Maren Mjelde's first-half strike on 73 minutes. It left France coach Stéphane Pilard ruing "a cruel failure", but for Norway and Italy it was onwards and upwards.

Group A Results

7/7/08, Jules Ladoumègue, Romorantin
Italy 1-0 Norway
Italy: Penzo, Crespi, Gama, Pisano, Sampietro, Bonometti (Bonetti 66), Barreca (Lotto 62), Parisi, Gueli, Rodella, Bartoli (Rosucci 82). Coach: Corrado Corradini (ITA)
Norway: Thorbjørnsen, Ree, Walde, Herregården, Mjelde, Wold, Isaksen, Enget (Dyngvold 83), Tarnes, Hansen, Andresen (Eide 76). Coach: Jarl Torske (NOR)
Goal(s): 1-0 Bonetti 90
Yellow Card(s): Isaksen 47 (Norway)
Referee: Damjanovic (CRO)

7/7/08, Les Allées, Blois
France 1-0 Spain
France: Benameur, Hamidouche, Chazal (Brocheray 33), Renard, Agard, Pervier (Mazaloubeaud 67), Bilbault, Butel, Le Sommer, Machart, Bultel (Cugat 78). Coach: Stéphane Pilard (FRA)
Spain: Laura Rafols, Ioana Falviano (Rocío Ruiz 45), Melanie Serrano,

Alexandra López, Marta Torrejón, Silvia Meseguer, María Casado, Casas Llopis (Liria 66), Cristina Martínez, Georgina Carreras, del Río (Corredera 61). Coach: Ignacio Quereda (ESP)
Goal(s): 1-0 Machart 59
Yellow Card(s): Ioana Falviano 42 (Spain), Mazaloubeaud 85 (France)
Referee: Dorcioman (ROU)

10/7/08, Georges Boulogne, Amboise
Spain 1-2 Norway
Spain: Laura Rafols, Ioana Falviano, Alexandra López, Marta Torrejón, Silvia Meseguer, María Casado, Cristina Martínez, Georgina Carreras (Nabaskues 71), Rocío Ruiz, Corredera, Liria (González 73). Coach: Ignacio Quereda (ESP)
Norway: Thorbjørnsen, Ree, Walde, Herregården, Mjelde, Wold, Isaksen, Enget (Hansen 69), Tarnes, Andresen (Dyngvold 89), Ryland (Fugelsnes 90+2). Coach: Jarl Torske (NOR)
Goal(s): 0-1 Herregården 58, 0-2 Hansen 75, 1-2 Ioana Falviano 90+1
Yellow Card(s): Ree 41 (Norway)
Referee: Subotic (SVN)

10/7/08, Les Allées, Blois
France 1-3 Italy
France: Benameur (Gérard 55), Hamidouche, Renard, Agard, Mazaloubeaud (Hamraoui 79), Pervier (Bultel 85), Bilbault, Butel, Le Sommer, Machart, Cugat. Coach: Stéphane Pilard (FRA)
Italy: Penzo, Crespi (Rodella 46), Gama, Pisano, Sampietro, Bonometti, Barreca, Marchese (Bonetti 87), Parisi (Fusetti 80), Gueli, Bussu. Coach: Corrado Corradini (ITA)
Goal(s): 0-1 Barreca 34, 1-1 Le Sommer 62, 1-2 Gueli 69, 1-3 Bonometti 89
Yellow Card(s): Bonometti 34 (Italy)
Referee: Monzul (UKR)

13/7/08, Jules Ladoumègue, Romorantin
Norway 1-1 France
Norway: Thorbjørnsen, Ree, Walde, Mjelde, Herregården, Wold, Andresen, Tarnes, Isaksen, Enget, Ryland (Hansen 72). Coach: Jarl Torske (NOR)
France: Benameur, Hamidouche (Peslerbe 87), Renard, Agard, Cugat, Butel, Pervier (Machart 46), Bilbault, Hamraoui, Bultel (Berger 75), Le Sommer. Coach: Stéphane Pilard (FRA)
Goal(s): 1-0 Mjelde 35, 1-1 Le Sommer 73
Referee: Tosun Ayer (TUR)

13/7/08, Municipal, Vineuil
Spain 3-0 Italy
Spain: Sarasola, Rocío Ruiz, Marta Torrejón, Sandra García (Alexandra López 77), Ioana Falviano, Nabaskues, González, Silvia Meseguer, Casas Llopis, Liria (del Río 46), María Casado. Coach: Ignacio Quereda (ESP)
Italy: Buiatti, Bartoli, Bussu, Gama (Sampietro 46), Crespi, Rosucci, Fusetti, Lotto, Rodella, Bonetti, Marchese. Coach: Corrado Corradini (ITA)
Goal(s): 1-0 Rocío Ruiz 25, 2-0 Silvia Meseguer 61, 3-0 González 88
Yellow Card(s): Crespi 45 (Italy), Ioana Falviano 52 (Spain), Bussu 70 (Italy)
Referee: Adamkova (CZE)

Group A Table

		Pld	W	D	L	F	A	Pts
1	Italy	3	2	0	1	4	4	6
2	Norway	3	1	1	1	3	3	4
3	France	3	1	1	1	3	4	4
4	Spain	3	1	0	2	4	3	3

GROUP B

Germany coach Maren Meinert admitted she was "taking nothing for granted" in the eve-of-finals press conference in Tours, but it looked like business as usual as the holders swept England aside in Avoine. Twelve months previously Mo Marley's team had pushed Germany into extra time in the 2007 final, but Marie Pollmann ensured there would be no repeat as she scored twice without reply to give holders Germany the perfect start to their defence. It was an impressive showing by the HSV Borussia Friedenstal forward, eclipsing the highly regarded Kim Kulig in the Germany attack.

Top scorer

Pollmann would go on to finish top scorer in the Loire Valley, adding another against Sweden three days later, though Sofia Jakobsson restricted Germany to a 1-1 draw to leave the sides level on four points. They were both nonetheless well placed to progress to the last four before their final group games, Sweden thanks to a stroke of fortune having required a 94th-minute goal against the run of play to see off Scotland in their opening fixture. Scotland appeared to have salvaged a point when Christie Murray cancelled out Emmelie Konradsson's 69th-minute opener with eight minutes remaining, but there was still time for substitute Sara Sjöstedt to break Scottish hearts.

Scotland came from behind again three days later against England under the shadow of the nuclear power station that dominates the skyline at Avoine's Stade Péteseilles, but once more it proved insufficient. The 15-year-old Jordan Nobbs and Ruesha Littlejohn traded early goals before Toni Duggan came to the fore, putting England ahead against the run of play in first-half added time before sealing victory. It put England "back on track" according to Marley, and three days later, when Everton LFC striker Duggan opened the scoring in a must-win meeting with Sweden, England had a tentative foot in the semi-finals.

Comeback queens

Sweden are past masters at the comeback, however, and after holding off earnest England pressure they were level just after the hour, Louise Fors converting from the penalty spot after Kosovare Asllani had been upended by Gilly Flaherty. Fors undid her good work soon afterwards when she was sent off. Thereafter England

Germany's Marie Pollmann (left), the tournament's top scorer with four goals, takes on Lauren MacMillan of Scotland

ırew everything forward but to no avail, Nobbs coming losest when she hit the frame of the goal in the dying ıinutes. It meant a trip home for England and the last ›ur for Sweden, alongside Germany, whose progress ever looked in doubt as they overwhelmed Scotland -0 in Amboise, six different players finding the net.

Group B Results

'7/08, Georges Boulogne, Amboise

weden 2-1 Scotland

weden: Fellbrandt, Lindblom, Ekroth, Ölander, Fröjdfeldt (Agné 80), sllani (Sjöstedt 77), Fors, Appelquist, Jakobsson (Ekebom 59), ›nradsson, Lyckberg. Coach: Calle Barrling (SWE)

cotland: Harrison, Small, MacMillan, Daiziel, Beattie, Corsie, Ross, ttle, Littlejohn, Ross (Lauder 71), Murray (McCulloch 83). Coach: chard Wilson (SCO)

oal(s): 1-0 Konradsson 69, 1-1 Murray 82, 2-1 Sjöstedt 90+4

ellow Card(s): Ölander 78 (Sweden)

eferee: Tosun Ayer (TUR)

'7/08, Péteseilles, Avoine

ermany 2-0 England

ermany: Burmeister, Brosius (Martini 67), Bunte, Mirlach, Henning, egering, Chandraratne (Schwab 56), Kulig, Pollmann, Weber, Simic Vagner 71). Coach: Maren Meinert (GER)

England: Spencer, Weston, Rafferty, Allen, Bradley, Flaherty, Moore (Holbrook 85), Edwards (Nobbs 75), Duggan, Chaplen, Clarke. Coach: Maureen Marley (ENG)

Goal(s): 1-0 Pollmann 35, 2-0 Pollmann 59

Yellow Card(s): Chandraratne 43 (Germany), Rafferty 49 (England), Allen 62 (England)

Referee: Monzul (UKR)

10/7/08, Guy Drut, Saint-Cyr-sur-Loire

Sweden 1-1 Germany

Sweden: Fellbrandt, Lindblom, Hellenberg (Hammarbäck 83), Ölander, Agné, Fröjdfeldt, Fors (Heimersson 77), Appelquist, Jakobsson (Sjöstedt 69), Konradsson, Lyckberg. Coach: Calle Barrling (SWE)

Germany: Schumann, Bunte, Mirlach, Henning, Hegering, Chandraratne (Martini 46), Kulig (Wagner 80), Pollmann, Weber, Wich (Schwab 54), Simic. Coach: Maren Meinert (GER)

Goal(s): 0-1 Pollmann 25, 1-1 Jakobsson 31

Referee: Adamkova (CZE)

10/7/08, Péteseilles, Avoine

Scotland 1-3 England

Scotland: Harrison, Small, MacMillan, Beattie, Corsie, Ross (McKean 77), Little, Littlejohn, Ross (Lauder 54), Murray (McCulloch 69), Williamson. Coach: Richard Wilson (SCO)

England: Spencer, Weston, Rafferty, Allen, Bradley, Flaherty, Moore (Christiansen 58), Duggan, Chaplen, Clarke, Nobbs. Coach: Maureen Marley (ENG)

Goal(s): 0-1 Nobbs 4, 1-1 Littlejohn 6, 1-2 Duggan 45+4, 1-3 Duggan 74

Referee: Damjanovic (CRO)

13/7/08, Guy Drut, Saint-Cyr-sur-Loire

England 1-1 Sweden

England: Spencer, Weston, Bradley, Flaherty, Rafferty (Hinnigan 84), Allen, Chaplen, Nobbs, Christiansen (Giddings 73), Duggan, Clarke. Coach: Maureen Marley (ENG)

Sweden: Fellbrandt, Agné, Ekroth, Ölander, Lindblom, Appelquist, Fröjdfeldt (Heimersson 57), Fors, Jakobsson (Lyckberg 68), Konradsson, Asllani. Coach: Calle Barrling (SWE)

Goal(s): 1-0 Duggan 10, 1-1 Fors 63(p)

Red Card(s): Fors 64 (Sweden)

Yellow Card(s): Fors 45 (Sweden), Allen 45+1 (England), Flaherty 62 (England), Fors 64 (Sweden), Rafferty 78 (England), Duggan 89 (England)

Referee: Dorcioman (ROU)

13/7/08, Georges Boulogne, Amboise

Scotland 0-7 Germany

Scotland: Ramsay, Small, MacMillan (Lauder 46), Daiziel (King 46), Beattie, Corsie, Ross, Little, Littlejohn, Murray, Williamson (Calder 75). Coach: Richard Wilson (SCO)

Germany: Schumann, Bunte (Ewers 46), Mirlach, Henning, Hegering, Kulig (Wich 46), Pollmann (Wagner 53), Weber, Schwab, Faisst, Simic. Coach: Maren Meinert (GER)

Goal(s): 0-1 Schwab 10, 0-2 Kulig 18, 0-3 Pollmann 32, 0-4 Mirlach 37, 0-5 Schwab 45+1, 0-6 Hegering 47, 0-7 Wagner 64

Yellow Card(s): MacMillan 35 (Scotland)

Referee: Subotic (SVN)

Group B Table

		Pld	W	D	L	F	A	Pts
1	Germany	3	2	1	0	10	1	7
2	Sweden	3	1	2	0	4	3	5
3	England	3	1	1	1	4	4	4
4	Scotland	3	0	0	3	2	12	0

SEMI-FINALS

Sweden coach Calle Barrling admitted he thought "this could be our year as we are in a flow" after booking progress to the last four, but his side were overwhelmed by an Azzurrine surge in Blois. Goals either side of half-time from Pamela Gueli and Cristina Bonometti set Italy on their way, and the excellent Alice Parisi made it 3-0 midway through the second period. It was to get worse for Sweden, their day summed up as the otherwise faultless Nina Fellbrant failed to deal with Elisa Bartoli's looping right-wing cross and Gueli completed the rout from point-blank range to set up a final against Norway, who ousted Germany later in the evening.

Cruel end

The holders' bid to win a third consecutive UEFA European Women's Under-19 Championship came to a cruel end as they lost 4-2 on penalties after a pulsating semi-final had finished one apiece after extra time. Centre-back Stefanie Mirlach gave Germany an early advantage before the Scandinavian side hit back through Ida Elise Enget to force an additional 30 minutes and, ultimately, penalties. Marina Hegering struck Germany's first spot-kick against the post, and after Selina Wagner's effort had been saved by Ingrid Thorbjørnsen, Enget made no mistake to fire Norway into the final for a third time.

It was especially harsh on Wagner. The substitute had earlier been denied by Thorbjørnsen following Marie Pollmann's cutback and seen a header cleared off the line by Kathrine Andresen, According to coach Maren Meinert it summed up Germany's day. "I'm really proud of my players," she said. "I don't think we did much wrong. We were fantastic in defence and I thought we weren't lacking much in attack either. But in a knockout game anything game happen. A penalty shoot-out is always a lottery and unfortunately it didn't go our way."

Semi-Final Results

16/7/08, Les Allées, Blois
Italy 4-0 Sweden
Italy: Penzo, Bartoli, Sampietro, Gama, Rodella (Bussu 77), Bonometti (Bonetti 84), Pisano, Parisi, Barreca, Gueli, Marchese (Fusetti 64). Coach: Corrado Corradini (ITA)
Sweden: Fellbrandt, Agné, Ölander, Ekroth, Lindblom (Ekebom 56), Appelquist (Sjöstedt 62), Fröjdfeldt, Heimersson, Konradsson, Asllani (Hammarbäck 75), Jakobsson. Coach: Calle Barrling (SWE)
Goal(s): 1-0 Gueli 37, 2-0 Bonometti 54, 3-0 Parisi 72(p), 4-0 Gueli 7
Yellow Card(s): Gueli 62 (Italy), Rodella 73 (Italy)
Referee: Monzul (UKR)

Alice Parisi celebrates after putting Italy 3-0 up against Sweden in the semi-final

16/7/08, Vallée du Cher, Tours
Germany 1-1 Norway
Germany: Schumann, Faisst, Ewers (Martini 113), Mirlach, Henning, Simic, Weber, Hegering, Kulig (Wich 103), Pollmann, Schwab (Wagner 73). Coach: Maren Meinert (GER)
Norway: Thorbjørnsen, Walde, Herregården, Mjelde, Wold, Andresen, Tarnes (Fugelsnes 68), Ree, Isaksen, Enget, Ryland (Hansen 46). Coach: Jarl Torske (NOR)
Goal(s): 1-0 Mirlach 2, 1-1 Enget 49
Yellow Card(s): Enget 119 (Norway)
Referee: Tosun Ayer (TUR)
Norway win 4-2 on penalties.

FINAL

Alice Parisi struck a second-half penalty as Italy claimed the UEFA European Women's Under-19 Championship trophy in their maiden final appearance as the showpiece proved a game too far for Norway. Parisi had just seen a free-kick deflected on to the post when she was presented with another dead-ball opportunity on 71 minutes - after Pamela Gueli had been checked by Gunhild

Herregården as she powered into the penalty area. The Italy No10 had converted from the spot in the semi-final win against Sweden and repeated the feat, firing into the top corner. Norway just did not have the legs to conjure a reply.

Friendly embrace

The match ended with coaches Corrado Corradini and Jarl Torske embracing on the halfway line, as they had just before kick-off. That spirit of generosity continued as the game got under way, both teams guilty of some wayward passing. The nerves were perhaps understandable, with Norway's 2003 loss to France the only previous time either side had graced the final. Gradually the butterflies settled, and it was the Azzurrine making much of the running, Silvia Pisano a waspish presence in midfield, biting into tackles, putting her body on the line and constantly looking for the incisive pass.

Gradually her team-mates followed suit, and once Italy were ahead the title was theirs, leaving coach Corradini struggling to "comprehend what is happening" as his side became the seventh different nation to etch their name on to the trophy. He lauded his players, who had qualified for the finals only as best runners-up to the team they beat in the final. It was, therefore, their third meeting in as many months, and while Corradini joked that he and Norway coach Jarl Torkse were now "almost engaged", his Norwegian counterpart cast himself in the role of Mr Silver after ending a final on the losing side yet again. His side, he honestly acknowledged, deserved nothing more in Tours.

Final Result

19/7/08, Vallée du Cher, Tours
Italy 1-0 Norway
Attendance: 1810
Italy: Penzo, Bussu, Gama, Sampietro, Crespi (Rodella 65), Barreca, Parisi, Pisano, Gueli (Bonetti 72), Marchese (Fusetti 46), Bonometti. Coach: Corrado Corradini (ITA)
Norway: Thorbjørnsen, Herregården, Mjelde, Walde, Ree (Dyngvold 82), Tarnes (Ryland 58), Andresen (Eide 76), Wold, Isaksen, Enget, Hansen. Coach: Jarl Torske (NOR)
Goal(s): 1-0 Parisi 71(p)
Yellow Card(s): Gueli 43 (Italy), Marchese 44 (Italy), Fusetti 74 (Italy)
Referee: Dorcioman (ROU)

Italy's match-winner Alice Parisi holds aloft the UEFA Women's European Under-19 Championship trophy with team-mate Sara Gama

CHAPTER
13

WU17 2007/08

The first UEFA European Women's Under-17 Championship was played in 2007/08, but while the competition was new the winners were very familiar. Germany added the title to their continental female crowns at senior and Under-19 level, and a grand slam was completed the day after the 3-0 triumph against France in Nyon as 1. FFC Frankfurt lifted the UEFA Women's Cup. On 22 May 2006 the UEFA Executive Committee approved the new tournament, which would also supply four teams to the inaugural 2008 FIFA U-17 Women's World Cup in New Zealand. By February 2007 an impressive 40 nations were in the draw, and in September fixtures kicked off with Norway defeating Bulgaria 11-0 and Germany overcoming Bulgaria 8-0. Germany and Norway were among 16 teams to reach the second qualifying round, with only four finals places on offer. Germany secured theirs with a match to spare, by which time France, England and Denmark had also qualified.

QUALIFYING ROUNDS

First Qualifying Round

Group 1 Results

11/10/07, Kleine Allmend, Frauenfeld
Wales 10-0 Cyprus

11/10/07, Bergholz, Wil
Switzerland 5-0 Lithuania

13/10/07, Kleine Allmend, Frauenfeld
Switzerland 4-0 Cyprus

13/10/07, Güttingersreuti, Weinfelden
Lithuania 2-2 Wales

16/10/07, Güttingersreuti, Weinfelden
Wales 2-2 Switzerland

16/10/07, Bergholz, Wil
Cyprus 0-2 Lithuania

Group 1 Table

	Pld	W	D	L	F	A	Pts
1 Switzerland	3	2	1	0	11	2	7
2 Wales	3	1	2	0	14	4	5
3 Lithuania	3	1	1	1	4	7	4
4 Cyprus	3	0	0	3	0	16	0

Group 2 Results

8/10/07, OSiR, Zawiercie
Netherlands 2-0 Azerbaijan

8/10/07, Miejski, Jaworzno
Poland 4-0 Greece

10/10/07, OSiR, Zawiercie
Poland 4-0 Azerbaijan

10/10/07, Miejski, Jaworzno
Greece 0-3 Netherlands

13/10/07, OSiR, Zawiercie
Netherlands 2-0 Poland

13/10/07, Miejski, Jaworzno
Azerbaijan 2-1 Greece

Group 2 Table

	Pld	W	D	L	F	A	Pts
1 Netherlands	3	3	0	0	7	0	9
2 Poland	3	2	0	1	8	2	6
3 Azerbaijan	3	1	0	2	2	7	3
4 Greece	3	0	0	3	1	9	0

Group 3 Results

11/9/07, Kadriorg, Tallinn
Belgium 5-1 Faroe Islands

11/9/07, A Le Coq Arena, Tallinn
Finland 12-1 Estonia

13/9/07, Kadriorg, Tallinn
Finland 9-0 Faroe Islands

13/9/07, A Le Coq Arena, Tallinn
Estonia 0-4 Belgium

16/9/07, Kadriorg, Tallinn
Belgium 1-3 Finland

16/9/07, A Le Coq Arena, Tallinn
Faroe Islands 1-0 Estonia

Group 3 Table

	Pld	W	D	L	F	A	Pts
1 Finland	3	3	0	0	24	2	9
2 Belgium	3	2	0	1	10	4	6
3 Faroe Islands	3	1	0	2	2	14	3
4 Estonia	3	0	0	3	1	17	0

Group 4 Results

17/9/07, Sportni Park, Lendava
Ukraine 2-2 Slovenia

Dzsenifer Marozsan of Germany

17/9/07, Mestni Stadion Ptuj, Ptuj
Iceland 7-1 Latvia

19/9/07, Sportni Park, Lendava
Ukraine 2-1 Latvia

19/9/07, Fazanerija, Murska Sobota
Slovenia 0-5 Iceland

22/9/07, Fazanerija, Murska Sobota
Iceland 3-0 Ukraine

22/9/07, Mestni Stadion Ptuj, Ptuj
Latvia 0-3 Slovenia

Group 4 Table

	Pld	W	D	L	F	A
1 Iceland	3	3	0	0	15	1
2 Slovenia	3	1	1	1	5	7
3 Ukraine	3	1	1	1	4	6
4 Latvia	3	0	0	3	2	12

Group 5 Results

16/10/07, Mladost, Strumica
France 11-0 FYR Macedonia

16/10/07, FC Turnovo, Strumica
Denmark 24-0 Armenia

18/10/07, Mladost, Strumica
France 16-0 Armenia

18/10/07, FC Turnovo, Strumica
FYR Macedonia 0-6 Denmark

21/10/07, Mladost, Strumica
Denmark 0-4 France

21/10/07, FC Turnovo, Strumica
Armenia 1-3 FYR Macedonia

Group 5 Table

	Pld	W	D	L	F	A
1 France	3	3	0	0	31	0
2 Denmark	3	2	0	1	30	4
3 FYR Macedonia	3	1	0	2	3	18
4 Armenia	3	0	0	3	1	43

Group 6 Results

19/10/07, World Wonder Football Centre 2, Antalya
Sweden 12-0 Moldova

19/10/07, World of Wonders Football Centre, Antc
Republic of Ireland 5-0 Turkey

)7, World Wonder Football Centre 2,

lic of Ireland 5-0 Moldova

7, World of Wonders Football Centre, Antalya
1-3 Sweden

7, World Wonder Football Centre 2, Antalya
n 2-1 Republic of Ireland

7, World of Wonders Football Centre, Antalya
va 0-7 Turkey

o 6 Table

	Pld	W	D	L	F	A	Pts
den	3	3	0	0	17	2	9
ublic of Ireland	3	2	0	1	11	2	6
key	3	1	0	2	8	8	3
dova	3	0	0	3	0	24	0

up 7 Results

7, Pabellón de la Ciudad del Fútbol, Madrid
-2 Belarus

7, Pabellón de la Ciudad del Fútbol, Madrid
1-1 Czech Republic

7, Pabellón de la Ciudad del Fútbol, Madrid
-3 Czech Republic

7, Pabellón de la Ciudad del Fútbol, Madrid
is 0-12 Spain

'07, Pabellón de la Ciudad del Fútbol,
d
1-1 Italy

'07, Pabellón de la Ciudad del Fútbol,
d
Republic 8-0 Belarus

p 7 Table

	Pld	W	D	L	F	A	Pts
ch Republic	3	2	1	0	12	3	7
in	3	1	2	0	14	2	5
/	3	1	1	1	9	6	4
arus	3	0	0	3	2	26	0

oup 8 Results

/07, Laco, Novigrad
and 6-0 Northern Ireland

/07, Gradski, Umag
ary 6-0 Croatia

/07, Veli Jozc, Porec
and 4-0 Croatia

/07, Laco, Novigrad
hern Ireland 0-2 Hungary

Anne Thirup Rudmose (left) and Linette Andreasen of Denmark

25/10/07, Gradski, Umag
Hungary 1-3 Scotland

25/10/07, Zminj, Zminj
Croatia 0-0 Northern Ireland

Group 8 Table

	Pld	W	D	L	F	A	Pts
1 Scotland	3	3	0	0	13	1	9
2 Hungary	3	2	0	1	9	3	6
3 Northern Ireland	3	0	1	2	0	8	1
4 Croatia	3	0	1	2	0	10	1

Group 9 Results

5/9/07, Overlands, Stjordals
Norway 11-0 Bulgaria

5/9/07, Moan Idrettspark, Levanger
Germany 8-0 Israel

7/9/07, Moan Idrettspark, Levanger
Germany 10-0 Bulgaria

7/9/07, Overlands, Stjordals
Israel 0-10 Norway

10/9/07, Moan Idrettspark, Levanger
Norway 1-6 Germany

10/9/07, Overlands, Stjordals
Bulgaria 0-1 Israel

Group 9 Table

	Pld	W	D	L	F	A	Pts
1 Germany	3	3	0	0	24	1	9
2 Norway	3	2	0	1	22	6	6
3 Israel	3	1	0	2	1	18	3
4 Bulgaria	3	0	0	3	0	22	0

Group 10 Results

27/10/07, Poladi, Rustavi
Russia 3-1 Slovakia

27/10/07, Mikheil Meskhi, Tbilisi
England 13-0 Georgia

29/10/07, Poladi, Rustavi
Georgia 0-3 Russia

29/10/07, Mikheil Meskhi, Tbilisi
England 3-1 Slovakia

1/11/07, Poladi, Rustavi
Russia 0-1 England

1/11/07, Mikheil Meskhi, Tbilisi
Slovakia 6-0 Georgia

Group 10 Table

	Pld	W	D	L	F	A	Pts
1 England	3	3	0	0	17	1	9
2 Russia	3	2	0	1	6	2	6
3 Slovakia	3	1	0	2	8	6	3
4 Georgia	3	0	0	3	0	22	0

Second Qualifying Round

Group 1 Results

25/3/08, Slavoj Vysehrad, Prague
England 4-0 Czech Republic
Goal(s): 1-0 Jane 3, 2-0 Carter 49, 3-0 Carter 61, 4-0 Holbrook 80+1

25/3/08, Horni Pocernice, Horni Pocernice
Netherlands 1-1 Belgium
Goal(s): 1-0 Oudejans 32(p), 1-1 Daniels 47

27/3/08, AFK Libčice, Libcice nad Vlatvou
England 3-1 Belgium
Goal(s): 1-0 Flaherty 20, 2-0 Daly 40, 2-1 Vanhaevermaet 59, 3-1 Carter 80+3

27/3/08, Slavoj Vysehrad, Prague
Czech Republic 0-2 Netherlands
Goal(s): 0-1 Oudejans 4, 0-2 van de Sanden 10

30/3/08, SK Lhota, Lhota
Netherlands 0-0 England

30/3/08, Slavoj Vysehrad, Prague
Belgium 1-3 Czech Republic
Goal(s): 1-0 Daniels 19, 1-1 Pivonková 38, 1-2 Culová 50, 1-3 Pospisilová 64

Group 1 Table

	Pld	W	D	L	F	A	Pts
1 England	3	2	1	0	7	1	7
2 Netherlands	3	1	2	0	3	1	5
3 Czech Republic	3	1	0	2	3	7	3
4 Belgium	3	0	1	2	3	7	1

Group 2 Results

18/3/08, Jean Laffon, Perpignan
Scotland 1-0 Republic of Ireland
Goal(s): 1-0 Thomson 26

18/3/08, Canet-en-Roussillon, Canet en Roussillon
France 2-0 Norway
Goal(s): 1-0 Perdrizet 60, 2-0 Augis 80

20/3/08, Jean Laffon, Perpignan
France 2-0 Republic of Ireland
Goal(s): 1-0 Crammer 53, 2-0 Barbance 80

20/3/08, Canet-en-Roussillon, Canet en Roussillon
Norway 0-1 Scotland
Goal(s): 0-1 Thomson 80+1

23/3/08, Canet-en-Roussillon, Canet en Roussillon
Scotland 0-1 France
Goal(s): 0-1 Crammer 61

23/3/08, Jean Laffon, Perpignan
Republic of Ireland 1-0 Norway
Goal(s): 1-0 Ryan 35

Group 2 Table

	Pld	W	D	L	F	A	Pts
1 France	3	3	0	0	5	0	9
2 Scotland	3	2	0	1	2	1	6
3 Republic of Ireland	3	1	0	2	1	3	3
4 Norway	3	0	0	3	0	4	0

Group 3 Results

10/4/08, Am Hallo, Essen
Sweden 1-1 Poland
Goal(s): 0-1 Sikora 23, 1-1 Klinga 34

Germany's Marie-L
Bagedorn (ric
challenged by C
Borgeström of Sw

10/4/08, Am Hallo, Essen
Germany 4-0 Switzerland
Goal(s): 1-0 Zumbült 23, 2-0 Rudelic 65, 3-0 Rudelic 69, 4-0 Popp 77

12/4/08, Jahnstadion, Bottrop
Switzerland 1-1 Sweden
Goal(s): 1-0 Kiwic 13, 1-1 Wegerman 39

12/4/08, Jahnstadion, Bottrop
Germany 3-0 Poland
Goal(s): 1-0 Knaak 4, 2-0 Knaak 19, 3-0 Popp 35

15/4/08, Am Hallo, Essen
Sweden 1-4 Germany
Goal(s): 1-0 Schough 18, 1-1 Mester 34, 1-2 Popp 38, 1-3 Popp 58(p), 1-4 Popp 68

15/4/08, Jahnstadion, Bottrop
Poland 2-0 Switzerland
Goal(s): 1-0 Sikora 16, 2-0 Lesińka 27

Group 3 Table

	Pld	W	D	L	F	A	Pts
1 Germany	3	3	0	0	11	1	9
2 Poland	3	1	1	1	3	4	4
3 Sweden	3	0	2	1	3	6	2
4 Switzerland	3	0	1	2	1	7	1

Group 4 Results

24/3/08, Vildbjerg, Vildbjerg
Iceland 3-4 Russia
Goal(s): 0-1 Zinovyeva 11, 1-1 Thorvaldsdóttir 17, 2-1 Valmundsdóttir 22, 3-1 Omarsdóttir 3 Akimova 43, 3-3 Ananyeva 48(p), 3-4 Zinovyeva 73

24/3/08, Vildbjerg, Vildbjerg
Finland 0-0 Denmark

27/3/08, Spjald, Spjald
Finland 1-0 Russia
Goal(s): 1-0 Ojanperä 25

27/3/08, Spjald, Spjald
Denmark 4-2 Iceland
Goal(s): 1-0 Andreasen 12, 1-1 Valdimarsd 25, 2-1 Junge Pedersen 54, 3-1 Veje 70, 3-2 Thorvaldsdóttir 72, 4-2 Boye Sørensen

29/3/08, Spjald, Spjald
Iceland 2-4 Finland
Goal(s): 0-1 Alanen 11, 0-2 Ojanperä 49, 1-2 Antonsdóttir 53, 1-3 Räihälä 58, 2-3 Alanen 61(og), 2-4 Meller 64

29/3/08, Vildbjerg, Vildbjerg
Russia 0-2 Denmark
Goal(s): 0-1 Hohol 62, 0-2 Olsen 80

Group 4 Table

	Pld	W	D	L	F	A
1 Denmark	3	2	1	0	6	2
2 Finland	3	2	1	0	5	2
3 Russia	3	1	0	2	4	6
4 Iceland	3	0	0	3	7	1

FINAL TOURNAMENT

SEMI-FINALS

EFA decided to act as tournament hosts hemselves for the first two seasons of the ew competition, staging the games at the olovray Stadium directly across the road rom its headquarters in Nyon, witzerland. Germany and Denmark icked off the competition, and four ninutes into the second half Dzsenifer Marozsan struck what was to prove the nly goal with a strong finish.

ight encounter

ater that day Germany's final opponents were decided fter a tight encounter between England and France. ngland withstood plenty of pressure before taking the ead themselves through Stephanie Marsh in the 46th ninute, but France swiftly replied with a penalty when Marina Makanza was felled in the box and Pauline rammer converted. England goalkeeper Lauren Davey ept her team in the game until the last six minutes of xtra time when substitute Marine Augis found the target. In the final minute Makanza won another penalty, which this time she scored herself.

Semi-Final Results

20/5/08, Colovray, Nyon
Germany 1-0 Denmark
Germany: Sarholz, Bujna, Wesely, Kleiner, Simon, Bagehorn, Knaak, Zumbült (Mester 56), Marozsan, Huth, Popp (Linden 62). Coach: Ralf Peter (GER)
Denmark: Gissel Rasmussen, Østergaard, Jensen, Olsen, Black, Madsen, Veje, Hohol (Kappel Bendtsen 70), Harder, Mikkelsen (Thirup Rudmose 54), Andreasen (Boye Sørensen 67). Coach: Bent Eriksen (DEN)
Goal(s): 1-0 Marozsan 44
Yellow Card(s): Hohol 10 (Denmark), Mester 80+3 (Germany)
Referee: Daly (IRL)

20/5/08, Colovray, Nyon
England 1-3 France
England: Davey, Bronze (Rose 84), Marsh, Holbrook, Jacobs, Bonner, Wiltshire (Staniforth 64), Nobbs, Carter, Jane (Daly 62), Christiansen. Coach: Lois Fidler (ENG)
France: Philippe, Hellio, La Villa, Butel, Rousseau, Poulain (Olivier 102), Jaurena (Lavaud 87), Barbance (Augis 51), Crammer, Rubio, Makanza. Coach: Gérard Sergent (FRA)
Goal(s): 1-0 Marsh 46, 1-1 Crammer 49(p), 1-2 Augis 104, 1-3 Makanza 109(p)
Yellow Card(s): Bonner 28 (England)
Referee: Zeien (LUX)

ne Augis (left) puts France ad in extra time against and

FINAL

Between them Germany and France had featured in all ten of the previous UEFA European Women's Under-18 and Under-19 Championship finals, so it was appropriate that they would meet for the inaugural Under-17 crown. Germany got the better of France in the 2002 and 2006 U19 deciders, giving them four titles to their rivals' one, and would repeat the 3-0 scoreline that decided the outcome of the older age-group final.

Popp on top

Watched by UEFA President Michel Platini, Dzsenifer Marozsan again opened the scoring with an opportunist finish in the 33rd minute. Alexandra Popp, the joint-top scorer across all teams in qualifying, with ten goals, ensured that she ended the competition on top overall when she doubled Germany's lead nine minutes into the second half with a low finish. France were seldom in the game, and all doubt was removed with eight minutes left

Alexandra Popp of Germany, the tournament's top scorer overall with eleven goals

Dzsenifer Marozsan opens the scoring in the final against France

Champions Germany celebrate with the trophy

when Marozsan found space on the right and crossed for substitute Ivana Rudelic to seal victory, after which the frustrated Caroline La Villa was sent off.

Germany coach Ralf Peter said: "The opening goal was important for us, as this allowed us to be a bit more relaxed. We know France are a very good side as we lost to them at last year's Nordic Cup, so we're very pleased to come through this very difficult match. In the second half we justified the score with a solid performance." France's Gérard Sergent added: "I don't have any regrets today as Germany were simply stronger than us." Third place went to Denmark as they recovered from conceding a second-minute goal to England by completing a 4-1 victory. But England, like Denmark, France and Germany, have the chance of global glory as they represent Europe in the 16-team World Cup from 28 October to 5 November.

Third Place Play-off Result

23/5/08, Colovray, Nyon

England 1-4 Denmark

England: Davey, Marsh, Jacobs, Bonner (Daly 74), Rose, Holbrook, Nobbs, Christiansen, Carter, Jane (Wiltshire 42), Chadwick. Coach: Lois Fidler (ENG)

Denmark: Gissel Rasmussen, Jensen, Ramlov, Black (Boye Sørensen 26), Olsen, Østergaard, Veje, Hohol, Madsen (Nyhegn 53), Harder (Andreasen 73), Thirup Rudmose. Coach: Bent Eriksen (DEN)

Goal(s): 1-0 Jane 2, 1-1 Boye Sørensen 28, 1-2 Hohol 66, 1-3 Thirup Rudmose 75, 1-4 Andreasen 80+3

Yellow Card(s): Bonner 73 (England)

Referee: Zeien (LUX)

Final Result

23/5/08, Colovray, Nyon

France 0-3 Germany

Attendance: 1500

France: Philippe, Hellio, La Villa, Butel, Rousseau, Poulain, Jaurena (Barbance 54), Makanza, Rubio (Lavaud 41), Crammer (Thomas 75), Augis. Coach: Gérard Sergent (FRA)

Germany: Sarholz, Bujna, Wesely, Kleiner, Simon, Bagehorn, Knaak (Kemme 76), Zumbült (Mester 64), Huth (Rudelic 60), Marozsan, Popp. Coach: Ralf Peter (GER)

Goal(s): 0-1 Marozsan 33, 0-2 Popp 49, 0-3 Rudelic 72

Red Card(s): La Villa 78 (France)

Yellow Card(s): Bujna 40+1 (Germany)

Referee: Daly (IRL)

FUTSAL CHAMPIONSHIP 2007

CHAPTER
14

Spain retained the UEFA European Futsal Championship title with victory against old rivals Italy to continue their dominance of the international game. The holders lost long-standing coach Javier Lozano to Real Madrid CF's football staff just two months before the finals in Porto, but José Venancio stepped in and Spain barely missed a beat - at least not until the semi-final when Portugal led 2-0 late in the game only to concede twice and lose on penalties. Russia then pipped the hosts for bronze, but the locals embraced the tournament, turning out even on days when Portugal were not playing while SIC's live TV coverage topped the ratings in its time slot. Meanwhile, the performances of surprise qualifiers Romania and Serbia suggested that when the finals expand to 12 teams for the 2009 edition in Hungary, the extra contenders ought to be able to hold their own with the established forces.

GROUP A

There had not been a goalless draw in the competition since Portugal's opener against Belgium in 1999, but that all changed in the very first match of the 2007 finals in Gondomar. Portugal were again involved and had to hold firm to shut out Italy. However, there were goals aplenty immediately afterwards as newcomers Romania, who had only discovered they had qualified in a tie-break while driving back from their mini-tournament in Slovenia, defeated the Czech Republic 8-4. Three times the Czechs fought back to equalise, but Florin Matei completed a hat-trick late on as Romania gained the best result by any debutant nation in Futsal EURO finals history.

Two days later, though, Romania – who only entered international futsal in 2003 - found life tougher as 2003 winners Italy equalled the finals record margin of victory with a 7-1 triumph that included three goals from Carlos Morgado. Roman Mareš, who had postponed his international retirement to join the Czech squad, put his team 1-0 and 3-1 up against Portugal, but four unanswered goals from the hosts ended the hopes of the former semi-finalists.

Now Portugal needed to take a point off Romania to reach the first semi-final, and goals early in each half - from 21-year-old starlet Ricardinho and an opportunist Leitão header - sealed a 3-0 win for the hosts. However, it was Italy who progressed in first place thanks to an impressive 4-0 defeat of the Czech Republic in Santo Tirso as Sandro Zanetti's opener and an acrobatic Adriano Foglia strike were followed by a Fabiano Assad double. Czech coach Tomáš Neumann admitted: "We had a big problem because we cannot score goals." Romania had plenty to be proud of, with Matei declaring: "I think we were the sixth best team and that is simply amazing because this was our debut."

Group A Results

16/11/07, Multiusos Gondomar, Porto
Portugal 0-0 Italy
Attendance: 3300
Portugal: João Benedito, Cristiano, Ricardinho, Zé Maria, Pedro Costa, Ivan, Leitão, Israel, Gonçalo, Arnaldo, Formiga. Coach: Orlando Duarte (POR)
Italy: Caio, Feller, Grana, Pellegrini, Montovanelli, Jubanski, Bertoni, Assis, Fabiano, Foglia, Morgado. Coach: Alessandro Nuccorini (ITA)
Yellow Card(s): Pellegrini 21 (Italy), Forte 28 (Italy), Israel 37 (Portugal)

Romania exceed expectations on th finals det

16/11/07, Multiusos Gondomar, Porto
Czech Republic 4-8 Romania
Attendance: 1800
Czech Republic: Gerčák, Meller, Blažej, Sluka, R. Mareš, Dlouhý, Kopecký, Frič, Rešetár, M. Mareš, Sláma. Coach: Tomás Neumann (CZE)
Romania: Klein, Rizan, Matei, Lo. Szöcs, Mihaly, Dobre, Molomfalean, Şotîrcă, Lupu, Gherman, Tomescu. Coach: Zoltán Jakab (ROU)
Goal(s): 0-1 Matei 11, 1-1 Frič 14, 1-2 Gherman 16, 2-2 Sluka 17, 2-3 Lupu 22, 2-4 Molomfalean 23, 3-4 Rešetár 26, 4-4 M. Mareš 29, 4-5 Lo. Szöcs 31, 4-6 Lupu 34, 4-7 Matei 36, 4-8 Matei 39(pen)
Yellow Card(s): Sláma 4 (Czech Republic), Frič 18 (Czech Republic), Matei 27 (Romania), R. Mareš 35 (Czech Republic)

18/11/07, Multiusos Gondomar, Porto
Italy 7-1 Romania
Attendance: 1988
Italy: Feller, Caio, Pellegrini, Bertoni, Morgado, Forte, Grana, Bacaro, Assis, Fabiano, Foglia. Coach: Alessandro Nuccorini (ITA)
Romania: Klein, Rizan, Matei, Molomfalean, Lupu, Gherman, Lo. Szöcs, Mihaly, Dobre, Şotîrcă, Tomescu. Coach: Zoltán Jakab (ROU)
Goal(s): 1-0 Morgado 1, 2-0 Assis 5, 3-0 Foglia 9, 3-1 Gherman 13, 4-1 Foglia 18, 5-1 Morgado 20, 6-1 Morgado 22, 7-1 Grana 25
Yellow Card(s): Dobre 31 (Romania)

18/11/07, Multiusos Gondomar, Porto
Portugal 5-3 Czech Republic
Attendance: 3648
Portugal: João Benedito, Cristiano, Ricardinho, Pedro Costa, Ivan, Arnaldo, Joel Queirós, Leitão, Israel, Gonçalo, Formiga. Coach: Orlando Duarte (POR)
Czech Republic: Krayzel, Meller, Novotný, R. Mareš, Frič, M. Mareš, Blažej, Sluka, Dlouhý, Rešetár, Sláma. Coach: Tomás Neumann (CZE)
Goal(s): 0-1 R. Mareš 1, 1-1 Ricardinho 6, 1-2 Frič 8, 1-3 R. Mareš 11, 2-3 Gonçalo 14, 3-3 Arnaldo 19, 4-3 Marcelinho 27, 5-3 Formiga 35
Yellow Card(s): Novotný 25 (Czech Republic)

21/11/07, Multiusos Gondomar, Porto
Romania 0-3 Portugal
Attendance: 3450
Romania: Klein, Rizan, Matei, Molomfalean, Lupu, Gherman, Lo. Szöcs, Mihaly, Dobre, Stoica, La. Szöcs. Coach: Zoltán Jakab (ROU)
Portugal: João Benedito, Cristiano, Ricardinho, Pedro Costa, Arnaldo, Marcelinho, Zé Maria, Ivan, Joel Queirós, Leitão, Israel. Coach: Orlando Duarte (POR)
Goal(s): 0-1 Ricardinho 1, 0-2 Ricardinho 24, 0-3 Leitão 33
Yellow Card(s): Gherman 17 (Romania)

/11/07, Pavilhão Municipal Santo Tirso, Porto
aly 4-0 Czech Republic
ttendance: 900
aly: Feller, Caio, Montovanelli, Jubanski, Bacaro, Zanetti, Grana, rtoni, Assis, Fabiano, Foglia. Coach: Alessandro Nuccorini (ITA)
ech Republic: Krayzel, Meller, Novotný, R. Mareš, Frič, M. Mareš, ažej, Sluka, Dlouhý, Rešetár, Sláma. Coach: Tomás Neumann (CZE)
oal(s): 1-0 Zanetti 10, 2-0 Foglia 22, 3-0 Fabiano 31, 4-0 Fabiano 35

roup A Table

	Pld	W	D	L	F	A	Pts
Italy	3	2	1	0	11	1	7
Portugal	3	2	1	0	8	3	7
Romania	3	1	0	2	9	14	3
Czech Republic	3	0	0	3	7	17	0

ROUP B

pain had a new coach but a familiar lineup of ars, and against a Ukraine team much hanged since reaching the 2001 and 2003 nals the holders cruised to a 6-2 opening win despite seeing an early two-goal lead ancelled out. Russia took the lead after just 6 seconds against Serbia through Brazilian-orn Cirilo, who, like MFK Dinamo Moskva ub-mate Pelé Júnior, had been naturalised arlier in the year. The same player doubled e lead, but with ten minutes to go Serbia – their first finals since Yugoslavia qualified in 999 – had fought back to 3-3. That was short-ved, though, as Cirilo completed a hat-trick nd Vladislav Shayakhmetov made it 5-3.

ıssia had a more comfortable time on Matchday 2 ainst Ukraine, winning 4-1 after Olexandr Khursov's vn goal on half-time had given them the lead. Andreu t Spain ahead 18 minutes in against Serbia but the derdogs were not disheartened and deservedly ined a tremendous 1-1 draw when Predrag Rajić ualised in the dying seconds. It was some result for a am that had played only one international in the three ars from January 2004.

ose results meant Russia were through and Ukraine ıt regardless of the final-day outcomes. Serbia knew ey could still pip Spain if they beat Ukraine and the lders lost to Russia. The latter outcome became a ssibility when Konstantin Maevski gave Russia an rly lead, but Andreu and Daniel struck just before lf-time to put Spain in control and they went on to n 4-1. Still, Serbia ended on a high with a 3-2 defeat Ukraine in Santo Tirso, with two more Rajić goals tting him top of the scorers' table with a tally of five. e and brilliant young playmaker Marko Perić would rn lucrative moves after the tournament to MFK namo Moskva.

Group B Results

17/11/07, Multiusos Gondomar, Porto
Spain 6-2 Ukraine
Attendance: 1000
Spain: Luis Amado, Juanjo, Álvaro, Kike, Marcelo, Daniel, Ortiz, Javi Eseverri, Jordi Torras, Werner, Rodríguez. Coach: José Venancio (ESP)
Ukraine: Sukhomlinov, Ivanyak, Cheporniuk, Vakhula, Khursov, Zamyatin, Ivanov, Rogachov, Silchenko, Sytin, Taranchuk. Coach: Gennadiy Lysenchuk (UKR)
Goal(s): 1-0 Marcelo 14, 2-0 Kike 16, 2-1 Cheporniuk 16, 2-2 Cheporniuk 26, 3-2 Álvaro 26, 4-2 Jordi Torras 32, 5-2 Daniel 34, 6-2 Marcelo 37
Red Card(s): Javi Eseverri 19 (Spain)
Yellow Card(s): Javi Eseverri 19 (Spain), Javi Eseverri 19 (Spain)

17/11/07, Multiusos Gondomar, Porto
Serbia 3-5 Russia
Attendance: 1000
Serbia: Brzakovic, Ranisavljević, Perić, Šoša, Pavićević, Rajić, Cvetanović, Bogdanović, Rakić, Borojević, Bojović. Coach: Aca Kovačević (SRB)
Russia: Stepanov, Zuev, Fukin, Kobzar, Pelé Júnior, Cirilo, Shayakhmetov, Dushkevich, Maevski, Chistopolov, Khamadiev. Coach: Oleg Ivanov (RUS)
Goal(s): 0-1 Cirilo 1, 0-2 Cirilo 14, 1-2 Rajić 23, 1-3 Khamadiev 23, 2-3 Perić 25, 3-3 Rajić 30, 3-4 Cirilo 33, 3-5 Shayakhmetov 36
Yellow Card(s): Šoša 31 (Serbia)

19/11/07, Multiusos Gondomar, Porto
Ukraine 1-4 Russia
Attendance: 748
Ukraine: Sukhomlinov, Ivanyak, Silchenko, Sytin, Taranchuk, Iakunin, Cheporniuk, Vakhula, Ivanov, Ovsyanykov, Khursov. Coach: Gennadiy Lysenchuk (UKR)
Russia: Stepanov, Zuev, Kobzar, Pelé Júnior, Cirilo, Khamadiev, Shayakhmetov, Fukin, Sergeev, Dushkevich, Maevski. Coach: Oleg Ivanov (RUS)
Goal(s): 0-1 Khursov 19(og), 0-2 Cirilo 25(pen), 0-3 Shayakhmetov 26, 1-3 Khamadiev 34(og), 1-4 Zuev 35
Yellow Card(s): Silchenko 12 (Ukraine), Vakhula 15 (Ukraine), Iakunin 34 (Ukraine)

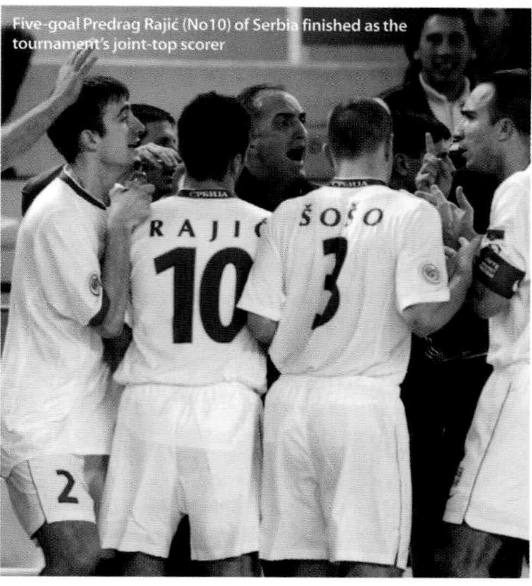

Five-goal Predrag Rajić (No10) of Serbia finished as the tournament's joint-top scorer

19/11/07, Multiusos Gondomar, Porto
Spain 1-1 Serbia
Attendance: 1100
Spain: Luis Amado, Cristian, Jordi Torras, Rodríguez, Kike, Daniel, Ortiz, Werner, Álvaro, Andreu, Borja. Coach: José Venancio (ESP)
Serbia: Brzakovic, Ranisavljević, Perić, Šoša, Pavićević, Rajić, Cvetanović, Bogdanović, Dimić, Borojević, Bojović. Coach: Aca Kovačević (SRB)
Goal(s): 1-0 Andreu 17, 1-1 Rajić 39
Yellow Card(s): Kike 37 (Spain)

21/11/07, Multiusos Gondomar, Porto
Russia 1-4 Spain
Attendance: 1313
Russia: Stepanov, Zuev, Kobzar, Pelé Júnior, Cirilo, Khamadiev, Fukin, Azizov, Sergeev, Dushkevich, Maevski. Coach: Oleg Ivanov (RUS)
Spain: Luis Amado, Juanjo, Álvaro, Kike, Andreu, Marcelo, Javi Eseverri, Jordi Torras, Ortiz, Rodríguez, Borja. Coach: José Venancio (ESP)
Goal(s): 1-0 Maevski 5, 1-1 Andreu 16, 1-2 Daniel 19, 1-3 Marcelo 22, 1-4 Daniel 37

21/11/07, Pavilhão Municipal Santo Tirso, Porto
Ukraine 2-3 Serbia
Attendance: 850
Ukraine: Sukhomlinov, Ivanyak, Cheporniuk, Vakhula, Ivanov, Zamyatin, Rogachov, Khursov, Sytin, Taranchuk, Iakunin. Coach: Gennadiy Lysenchuk (UKR)
Serbia: Brzakovic, Ranisavljević, Šoša, Cvetanović, Pavićević, Rajić, Perić, Zivić, Bogdanović, Dimić, Borojević. Coach: Aca Kovačević (SRB)
Goal(s): 0-1 Rajić 4, 0-2 Cvetanović 13, 1-2 Cheporniuk 20, 1-3 Rajić 22, 2-3 Sytin 23

Group B Table

		Pld	W	D	L	F	A	Pts
1	Spain	3	2	1	0	11	4	7
2	Russia	3	2	0	1	10	8	6
3	Serbia	3	1	1	1	7	8	4
4	Ukraine	3	0	0	3	5	13	0

SEMI-FINALS

Having been pipped to first place in Group B by Spain, Russia were charged with repeating their 2005 semi-final victory against Italy. But just three minutes in, the leading scorer from that tournament, Nando Grana, scored with a free-kick that deflected in off Cirilo, and from that moment the Azzurri allowed Russia little space. Cirilo had a shot that hit the crossbar and the line and Pelé Júnior struck the post, but Fabiano Assad doubled the lead with ten minutes left. Alexander Feller, for so long the understudy to Italy goalkeeper Gianfranco Angelini - who missed the tournament for personal reasons - was in brilliant form and completed his finals-record third clean sheet.

The second semi-final between Portugal and Spain was a less tactical contest, and a shock seemed to be on the cards when Gonçalo chipped a superb opener on the half-hour and Ricardinho acrobatically put the hosts 2-0 up with five minutes left. However, amid the hubbub of a delirious crowd, Daniel and Andreu kept their head to level. There was no extra time, and Luis Amado saved Portugal's second penalty from Joel Queirós before Leitão hit the post with his final effort, ensuring Spain won 4-3.

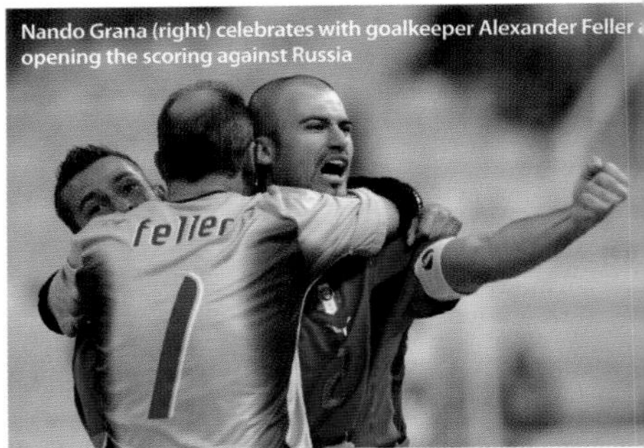

Nando Grana (right) celebrates with goalkeeper Alexander Feller a opening the scoring against Russia

Semi-Final Results

23/11/07, Multiusos Gondomar, Porto
Italy 2-0 Russia
Attendance: 1882
Italy: Feller, Caio, Pellegrini, Bertoni, Morgado, Forte, Grana, Bacaro Assis, Fabiano, Foglia. Coach: Alessandro Nuccorini (ITA)
Russia: Stepanov, Zuev, Kobzar, Pelé Júnior, Cirilo, Malyshev, Shayakhmetov, Fukin, Dushkevich, Maevski, Chistopolov. Coach: Oleg Ivanov (RUS)
Goal(s): 1-0 Grana 2, 2-0 Fabiano 30

23/11/07, Multiusos Gondomar, Porto
Spain 2-2 Portugal
Attendance: 3900
Spain: Luis Amado, Cristian, Álvaro, Kike, Andreu, Marcelo, Ortiz, Ja Eseverri, Jordi Torras, Rodríguez, Borja. Coach: José Venancio (ESP)
Portugal: João Benedito, Cristiano, Ricardinho, Pedro Costa, Arnaldo, Marcelinho, Zé Maria, Ivan, Joel Queirós, Leitão, Gonçalo. Coach: Orlando Duarte (POR)
Goal(s): 0-1 Gonçalo 30, 0-2 Ricardinho 34, 1-2 Daniel 35, 2-2 Andreu 38
Yellow Card(s): Marcelo 33 (Spain), Borja 33 (Spain), Marcelinho 39 (Portugal)
Spain win 4-3 on penalties.

FINAL

The curtain was raised on final day by Russia's exciting 3-2 victory against Portuga for third place, Vladislav Shayakhmetov striking the winner with four minutes left just seconds after Leitão had equalised. Then, just as in the 2004 FIFA Futsal World Cup final, Spain needed to beat Italy to hold on to their crown.

pain had won the world final 2-1 in Chinese Taipei but
his time they did not have to wait until the second half
efore taking the lead. On nine minutes the energetic
lvaro crossed for Marcelo to head in at the far post. It
as a reward for a positive start by Spain, and although
aly now upped their game, they conceded again early
the second half as Daniel pounced on a rebound to
ke his tournament goal-tally to five, which left him
int-leading scorer with Serbia's Predrag Rajić and
ussia's Cirilo, who had struck earlier in the third-place
atch. Spain captain Javi Rodríguez, the last-gasp two-
oal hero of the 2000 World Cup final, then scored for the
rst time in a European decider to further turn the screw.

aly goalkeeper Alexander Feller had now conceded
ree times as many goals in one game than in the rest
f the finals, but with ten minutes left he got his team
ack in the game with a superb strike from long range.
owever, despite Nando Grana taking over from Feller
a 'flying goalkeeper', Italy could not score again and
pain became the first team to make a successful
efence of the European futsal title. Rodríguez, who
ow has a third European Championship crown to add
his two World Cups, said: "We never tire of winning.
e always want to be in the final, and we have to carry
n working for that."

Third Place Play-off Result

25/11/07, Multiusos Gondomar, Porto
Russia 3-2 Portugal
Attendance: 3100
Russia: Stepanov, Zuev, Shayakhmetov, Fukin, Maevski, Khamadiev, Kobzar, Pelé Júnior, Dushkevich, Cirilo, Chistopolov. Coach: Oleg Ivanov (RUS)
Portugal: João Benedito, Cristiano, Ricardinho, Pedro Costa, Arnaldo, Marcelinho, Zé Maria, Ivan, Joel Queirós, Leitão, Israel. Coach: Orlando Duarte (POR)
Goal(s): 0-1 Gonçalo 14, 1-1 Cirilo 16, 2-1 Fukin 17, 2-2 Leitão 35, 3-2 Shayakhmetov 35
Yellow Card(s): Maevski 20+3 (Russia), Cirilo 20+10 (Russia), Dushkevich 20+12 (Russia)

Final Result

25/11/07, Multiusos Gondomar, Porto
Italy 1-3 Spain
Attendance: 3600
Italy: Feller, Caio, Pellegrini, Bertoni, Morgado, Forte, Grana, Bacaro, Assis, Fabiano, Foglia. Coach: Alessandro Nuccorini (ITA)
Spain: Luis Amado, Juanjo, Álvaro, Kike, Andreu, Marcelo, Ortiz, Javi Eseverri, Jordi Torras, Rodríguez, Borja. Coach: José Venancio (ESP)
Goal(s): 0-1 Marcelo 8, 0-2 Daniel 21, 0-3 Rodríguez 26, 1-3 Feller 29
Yellow Card(s): Foglia 5 (Italy), Andreu 21 (Spain), Daniel 37 (Spain), Grana 38 (Italy), Álvaro 39 (Spain)

, the European Futsal champions of 2007

lotto
TMK
3
ELPOZO
ELPOZO

As predicted, the UEFA Futsal Cup Final Four in Moscow was won by a Russian team - except the European champions are no longer MFK Dinamo Moskva but a side accustomed to life below them in the Russian Super League, MFK Viz-Sinara Ekaterinburg. While Dinamo were exiting the competition on penalties to ElPozo Murcia FS in the semi-finals, Ekaterinburg were easing past Kairat Almaty. Then, against a Murcia side aiming to provide Spain's fifth success in seven seasons of this competition, Ekaterinburg produced three second-half equalisers to draw 4-4 and prevail against the renowned spot-kick specialists on penalties to lift the trophy. It was a notable achievement for a club who resisted the usual importation of Brazilians and instead relied on their own local talent for their European debut. It was also a rare example of a team winning a continental title before their first domestic league crown, with Ekaterinburg yet to take the title in Russia.

2007/08

FUTSALCUP

CHAPTER
15

PRELIMINARY ROUND

Group A Results

13/8/07, Neot Ashelim Sports Hall, Rishon Le-Zion
FCK De Hommel 4-2 Uni Futsal Team Bulle

13/8/07, Neot Ashelim Sports Hall, Rishon Le-Zion
Hapoel Ironi Rishon Lezion 7-2 FK Nafta Mazeikiai

14/8/07, Neot Ashelim Sports Hall, Rishon Le-Zion
FK Nafta Mazeikiai 4-3 FCK De Hommel

14/8/07, Neot Ashelim Sports Hall, Rishon Le-Zion
Hapoel Ironi Rishon Lezion 7-2 Uni Futsal Team Bulle

16/8/07, Neot Ashelim Sports Hall, Rishon Le-Zion
Uni Futsal Team Bulle 6-4 FK Nafta Mazeikiai

16/8/07, Neot Ashelim Sports Hall, Rishon Le-Zion
FCK De Hommel 0-4 Hapoel Ironi Rishon Lezion

Group A Table

	Pld	W	D	L	F	A	Pts
1 Hapoel Ironi Rishon Lezion	3	3	0	0	18	4	9
2 FCK De Hommel	3	1	0	2	7	10	3
3 Uni Futsal Team Bulle	3	1	0	2	10	15	3
4 FK Nafta Mazeikiai	3	1	0	2	10	16	3

Group B Results

16/8/07, Palais des Sports Robert Charpentier, Issy-les-Moulineaux
AGBU Ararat Nicosia FC 3-5 KMF Municipium Casino Pljevlja

16/8/07
Issy Futsal 3-0 KS ALI DEMI (w/o)

18/8/07, Palais des Sports Robert Charpentier, Issy-les-Moulineaux
AGBU Ararat Nicosia FC 6-3 KS ALI DEMI

18/8/07, Palais des Sports Robert Charpentier, Issy-les-Moulineaux
Issy Futsal 2-3 KMF Municipium Casino Pljevlja

19/8/07, Palais des Sports Robert Charpentier, Issy-les-Moulineaux
KS ALI DEMI 0-3 KMF Municipium Casino Pljevlja

19/8/07, Palais des Sports Robert Charpentier, Issy-les-Moulineaux
Issy Futsal 4-0 AGBU Ararat Nicosia FC

Group B Table

	Pld	W	D	L	F	A	Pts
1 KMF Municipium Casino Pljevlja	3	3	0	0	11	5	9
2 Issy Futsal	3	2	0	1	9	3	6
3 AGBU Ararat Nicosia FC	3	1	0	2	9	12	3
4 KS ALI DEMI	3	0	0	3	3	12	0

Group C Results

11/8/07, Olimpiskais Sporta Centrs, Riga
FC Camelot Chisinau 6-0 FC Anzhi Tallinn

11/8/07, Olimpiskais Sporta Centrs, Riga
FK Kauguri 10-1 FV Eppelborn

12/8/07, Olimpiskais Sporta Centrs, Riga
FV Eppelborn 3-9 FC Camelot Chisinau

12/8/07, Olimpiskais Sporta Centrs, Riga
FK Kauguri 9-1 FC Anzhi Tallinn

14/8/07, Olimpiskais Sporta Centrs, Riga
FC Anzhi Tallinn 6-0 FV Eppelborn

14/8/07, Olimpiskais Sporta Centrs, Riga
FC Camelot Chisinau 3-0 FK Kauguri

Group C Table

	Pld	W	D	L	F	A	P
1 FC Camelot Chisinau	3	3	0	0	18	3	9
2 FK Kauguri	3	2	0	1	19	5	6
3 FC Anzhi Tallinn	3	1	0	2	7	15	3
4 FV Eppelborn	3	0	0	3	4	25	0

Group D Results

12/8/07, Hollgasse Hall, Vienna
Stela Rossa Vienna 6-1 Fair City Santos

12/8/07, Hollgasse Hall, Vienna
Politekhnik Yerevan 3-2 Shamrock Rovers FUT

13/8/07, Hollgasse Hall, Vienna
Fair City Santos 2-8 Politekhnik Yerevan

13/8/07, Hollgasse Hall, Vienna
Stela Rossa Vienna 5-1 Shamrock Rovers FUT

15/8/07, Hollgasse Hall, Vienna
Fair City Santos 3-6 Shamrock Rovers FUT

15/8/07, Hollgasse Hall, Vienna
Stela Rossa Vienna 2-4 Politekhnik Yerevan

Group D Table

	Pld	W	D	L	F	A	P
1 Politekhnik Yerevan	3	3	0	0	15	6	9
2 Stela Rossa Vienna	3	2	0	1	13	6	6
3 Shamrock Rovers FUT	3	1	0	2	9	11	3
4 Fair City Santos	3	0	0	3	6	20	0

Group E Results

117/8/07, Skövde Arena, Skovde
Skövde AIK 8-2 Jeepers

18/8/07, Skövde Arena, Skovde
Jeepers 3-18 MNK Kaskada Gracanica

19/8/07, Skövde Arena, Skovde
MNK Kaskada Gracanica 1-2 Skövde AIK

Group E Table

	Pld	W	D	L	F	A	P
1 Skövde AIK	2	2	0	0	10	3	6
2 MNK Kaskada Gracanica	2	1	0	1	19	5	3
3 Jeepers	2	0	0	2	5	26	0

Group F Results

16/8/07, Solski Center, Tolmin
KMN Puntar 5-3 London White Bear FC

17/8/07, Solski Center, Tolmin
London White Bear FC 7-3 Granvalira FC Encamp

18/8/07, Solski Center, Tolmin
Granvalira FC Encamp 3-7 KMN Puntar

Group A Table

	Pld	W	D	L	F	A	Pt
1 KMN Puntar	2	2	0	0	12	6	6
2 London White Bear FC	2	1	0	1	10	8	3
3 Granvalira FC Encamp	2	0	0	2	6	14	0

MAIN ROUND

roup 1 Results

/9/07
earex Chorzów 3-0 KMF Alfa Parf Skopje (w/o)

/9/07, Hala MORIS, Chorzow
Mapid Minsk 3-7 Hapoel Ironi Rishon Lezion

/9/07
MF Alfa Parf Skopje 0-3 FC Mapid Minsk (w/o)

/9/07, Hala MORIS, Chorzow
earex Chorzów 3-1 Hapoel Ironi Rishon Lezion

/9/07
apoel Ironi Rishon Lezion 3-0 KMF Alfa Parf Skopje (w/o)

/9/07, Hala MORIS, Chorzow
Mapid Minsk 4-3 Clearex Chorzów

roup 1 Table

	Pld	W	D	L	F	A	Pts
Hapoel Ironi Rishon Lezion	3	2	0	1	11	6	6
Clearex Chorzów	3	2	0	1	9	5	6
FC Mapid Minsk	3	2	0	1	10	10	6
KMF Alfa Parf Skopje	3	0	0	3	0	9	0

Kobzar of Dinamo Moskva

Group 2 Results

13/9/07, Palace of Culture and Sports, Varna
MFC Varna 1-10 SK Energia

13/9/07, Palace of Culture and Sports, Varna
SL Benfica 17-2 Politekhnik Yerevan

14/9/07, Palace of Culture and Sports, Varna
SK Energia 11-2 Politekhnik Yerevan

14/9/07, Palace of Culture and Sports, Varna
SL Benfica 4-1 MFC Varna

16/9/07, Palace of Culture and Sports, Varna
MFC Varna 6-2 Politekhnik Yerevan

16/9/07, Palace of Culture and Sports, Varna
SK Energia 2-6 SL Benfica

Group 2 Table

	Pld	W	D	L	F	A	Pts
1 SL Benfica	3	3	0	0	27	5	9
2 SK Energia	3	2	0	1	23	9	6
3 MFC Varna	3	1	0	2	8	16	3
4 Politekhnik Yerevan	3	0	0	3	6	34	0

Group 3 Results

10/9/07, Palace of Sport, Baku
Slov-Matic Fofo Bratislava 6-2 FC Camelot Chisinau

10/9/07, Palace of Sport, Baku
Araz Naxçivan 0-3 Luparense Calcio A5

11/9/07, Palace of Sport, Baku
Luparense Calcio A5 1-0 Slov-Matic Fofo Bratislava

11/9/07, Palace of Sport, Baku
Araz Naxçivan 4-1 FC Camelot Chisinau

13/9/07, Palace of Sport, Baku
FC Camelot Chisinau 0-8 Luparense Calcio A5

13/9/07, Palace of Sport, Baku
Slov-Matic Fofo Bratislava 4-3 Araz Naxçivan

Group 3 Table

	Pld	W	D	L	F	A	Pts
1 Luparense Calcio A5	3	3	0	0	12	0	9
2 Slov-Matic Fofo Bratislava	3	2	0	1	10	6	6
3 Araz Naxçivan	3	1	0	2	7	8	3
4 FC Camelot Chisinau	3	0	0	3	3	18	0

Kike of ElPozo Murcia

Group 4 Results

8/9/07, Váci Sportcsarnok, Vac
Futsal Topsport Antwerpen 2-2 KMF Municipium Casino Pljevlja

8/9/07, Váci Sportcsarnok, Vac
Futsal Club Gödöllö 6-2 Athina '90 Athens

9/9/07, Váci Sportcsarnok, Vac
Athina '90 Athens 1-9 Futsal Topsport Antwerpen

9/9/07, Váci Sportcsarnok, Vac
Futsal Club Gödöllö 1-5 KMF Municipium Casino Pljevlja

11/9/07, Váci Sportcsarnok, Vac
KMF Municipium Casino Pljevlja 5-0 Athina '90 Athens

11/9/07, Váci Sportcsarnok, Vac
Futsal Topsport Antwerpen 6-0 Futsal Club Gödöllö

Group 4 Table

	Pld	W	D	L	F	A	Pts
1 Futsal Topsport Antwerpen	3	2	1	0	17	3	7
2 KMF Municipium Casino Pljevlja	3	2	1	0	12	3	7
3 Futsal Club Gödöllö	3	1	0	2	7	13	3
4 Athina '90 Athens	3	0	0	3	3	20	0

Group 5 Results

112/9/07, Sports Hall, Gospic
HMNK Gospić 2-2 Iberia 2003 Tbilisi

12/9/07, Sports Hall, Gospic
CIP Deva 2-2 KMN Puntar

13/9/07, Sports Hall, Gospic
Iberia 2003 Tbilisi 3-4 CIP Deva

13/9/07, Sports Hall, Gospic
HMNK Gospić 3-3 KMN Puntar

15/9/07, Sports Hall, Gospic
KMN Puntar 2-2 Iberia 2003 Tbilisi

15/9/07, Sports Hall, Gospic
CIP Deva 2-5 HMNK Gospić

Group 5 Table

	Pld	W	D	L	F	A	Pts
1 HMNK Gospić	3	1	2	0	10	7	5
2 CIP Deva	3	1	1	1	8	10	4
3 KMN Puntar	3	0	3	0	7	7	3
4 Iberia 2003 Tbilisi	3	0	2	1	7	8	2

Group 6 Results

10/9/07, Zimní Stadión, Chrudim
KMF Marbo Beograd 5-2 Skövde AIK

10/9/07, Zimní Stadión, Chrudim
FK Era-Pack Chrudim 6-3 Ilves FS Tampere

11/9/07, Zimní Stadión, Chrudim
Ilves FS Tampere 2-3 KMF Marbo Beograd

11/9/07, Zimní Stadión, Chrudim
FK Era-Pack Chrudim 7-3 Skövde AIK

13/9/07, Zimní Stadión, Chrudim
Skövde AIK 6-3 Ilves FS Tampere

13/9/07, Zimní Stadión, Chrudim
KMF Marbo Beograd 1-4 FK Era-Pack Chrudim

Group 6 Table

	Pld	W	D	L	F	A	Pts
1 FK Era-Pack Chrudim	3	3	0	0	17	7	9
2 KMF Marbo Beograd	3	2	0	1	9	8	6
3 Skövde AIK	3	1	0	2	11	15	3
4 Ilves FS Tampere	3	0	0	3	8	15	0

ELITE ROUND

Group A Results

15/10/07, Hala MORIS, Chorzow
ElPozo Murcia FS 5-1 KMF Marbo Beograd

15/10/07, Hala MORIS, Chorzow
Clearex Chorzów 3-3 HMNK Gospić

16/10/07, Hala MORIS, Chorzow
HMNK Gospić 2-4 ElPozo Murcia FS

16/10/07, Hala MORIS, Chorzow
Clearex Chorzów 1-2 KMF Marbo Beograd

18/10/07, Hala MORIS, Chorzow
KMF Marbo Beograd 0-3 HMNK Gospić

18/10/07, Hala MORIS, Chorzow
ElPozo Murcia FS 3-2 Clearex Chorzów

Group A Table

		Pld	W	D	L	F	A	Pts
1	ElPozo Murcia FS	3	3	0	0	12	5	9
2	HMNK Gospić	3	1	1	1	8	7	4
3	KMF Marbo Beograd	3	1	0	2	3	9	3
4	Clearex Chorzów	3	0	1	2	6	8	1

Group B Results

18/10/07, PalaNec, Padova
MFK Dinamo Moskva 10-1 KMF Municipium Casino Pljevlja

18/10/07, PalaNec, Padova
Luparense Calcio A5 2-2 SL Benfica

19/10/07, PalaNec, Padova
MFK Dinamo Moskva 8-4 SL Benfica

19/10/07, PalaNec, Padova
Luparense Calcio A5 5-1 KMF Municipium Casino Pljevlja

21/10/07, PalaNec, Padova
SL Benfica 7-2 KMF Municipium Casino Pljevlja

21/10/07, PalaNec, Padova
Luparense Calcio A5 2-2 MFK Dinamo Moskva

Group B Table

		Pld	W	D	L	F	A	Pts
1	MFK Dinamo Moskva	3	2	1	0	20	7	7
2	Luparense Calcio A5	3	1	2	0	9	5	5
3	SL Benfica	3	1	1	1	13	12	4
4	KMF Municipium Casino Pljevlja	3	0	0	3	4	22	0

Group C Results

15/10/07, Zimní Stadión, Chrudim
Kairat Almaty 4-3 Slov-Matic Fofo Bratislava

15/10/07, Zimní Stadión, Chrudim
FK Era-Pack Chrudim 3-1 Futsal Topsport Antwerpen

16/10/07, Zimní Stadión, Chrudim
Futsal Topsport Antwerpen 1-5 Kairat Almaty

16/10/07, Zimní Stadión, Chrudim
FK Era-Pack Chrudim 5-1 Slov-Matic Fofo Bratislava

18/10/07, Zimní Stadión, Chrudim
Slov-Matic Fofo Bratislava 5-5 Futsal Topsport Antwerpen

18/10/07, Zimní Stadión, Chrudim
Kairat Almaty 5-4 FK Era-Pack Chrudim

Group C Table

		Pld	W	D	L	F	A	Pts
1	Kairat Almaty	3	3	0	0	14	8	9
2	FK Era-Pack Chrudim	3	2	0	1	12	7	6
3	Slov-Matic Fofo Bratislava	3	0	1	2	9	14	1
4	Futsal Topsport Antwerpen	3	0	1	2	7	13	1

Group D Results

14/10/07, Palace of Sports, Ekaterinburg
MFK Viz-Sinara Ekaterinburg 2-1 SK Energia

14/10/07, Palace of Sports, Ekaterinburg
Hapoel Ironi Rishon Lezion 3-5 CIP Deva

15/10/07, Palace of Sports, Ekaterinburg
MFK Viz-Sinara Ekaterinburg 10-3 CIP Deva

15/10/07, Palace of Sports, Ekaterinburg
SK Energia 4-3 Hapoel Ironi Rishon Lezion

17/10/07, Palace of Sports, Ekaterinburg
CIP Deva 4-3 SK Energia

17/10/07, Palace of Sports, Ekaterinburg
Hapoel Ironi Rishon Lezion 1-3 MFK Viz-Sinara Ekaterinburg

Group D Table

		Pld	W	D	L	F	A	Pts
1	MFK Viz-Sinara Ekaterinburg	3	3	0	0	15	5	9
2	CIP Deva	3	2	0	1	12	16	6
3	SK Energia	3	1	0	2	8	9	3
4	Hapoel Ironi Rishon Lezion	3	0	0	3	7	12	0

FINAL FOUR

A record entry of 44 clubs began the 2007/08 UEFA Futsal Cup, which for the second year running was to end with a one-venue Final Four tournament staged over three days in April. 2006/07 winners MFK Dinamo Moskva and ElPozo Murcia FS both reached the final four for the second year running, along with fellow elite-round seeds MFK Viz-Sinara Ekaterinburg and Kairat Almaty.

Tatu (right) is acknowledged by Dinamo Moskva team-mates Cirilo (l and Edu after scoring a penalty against Kairat Alm

European debut

Unlike their fellow contenders, who all had semi-final experience, Ekaterinburg had never played in European competition before, qualifying as Russian runners-up to UEFA Futsal Cup holders Dinamo, who were also selected as Final Four hosts. Ekaterinburg may have been worried when they fell behind in the first semi-final against Kairat at the impressive Krylatskoe Sport Palace as Aleksei Mokhov put through his own goal, but after the break the counterattacking Russian side equalised through Dmitriy Prudnikov, and with six minutes left Vladislav Shayakhmetov's penalty put Ekaterinburg ahead - after hitting both the crossbar and goalkeeper Marcinho - before Ilydar Makayev and Konstantin Agapov sealed a 4-1 victory with late breakaway strikes.

The other semi-final between Dinamo and 2007 bronze-medallists Murcia, the two pre-tournament favourites, lived up to the billing. Rodrigues de Brito, aka Ciço, took just four minutes to put Murcia in front but Pula, whose last-gasp strike had settled the previous season's final against Interviú Boomerang, equalised late in the first half. Dinamo were forced to defend in depth just to get to a penalty shoot-out. But Murcia are famously proficient when it comes to spot kicks, and goalkeeper Juanjo's saves from Tatu and Cirilo ensured Dinamo's reign was ended by a 4-2 reverse.

Ekaterinburg goalkeeper Sergei Zuev saves a penalty

Ekaterinburg win on penalties

Consolation for Dinamo came with a 5-0 third-place play-off defeat of Kairat, with Sergei Ivanov and Tatu striking before the break and Aleksandr Rakhimov, Joan and Cirilo adding late goals. Dinamo would go on to complete the Russian double, but by then Ekaterinburg were European champions. They scored first in the final through Makayev. Kike equalised before the break, and in the second half Ciço, Vinicius Elías and Mauricio all put Murcia ahead only for Shayakhmetov, Prudnikov and Pavel Chistopolov to equalise each time. Another penalty shoot-out was thus required, and this time Dinamo goalkeeper Sergei Zuev emerged as the hero, eclipsing his opposite number Juanjo by denying Vinicius, Álvaro and Kike as Ekaterinburg took the title 3-2. Coach Sergei Skorovich said: "Few expected this from us or thought we would battle for the top places, but we kept faith and kept working to do so."

Semi-Final Results

25/4/08, Krylatskoe Sport Palace, Moscow
Kairat Almaty 1-4 MFK Viz-Sinara Ekaterinburg
Kairat: Khayavin, Marcinho, Dertinho, Butrin, Pica Pau, Rafael, Terentyev, Garcez, Samohvalov, Dantas, Etienne. Coach: José Alésio da Silva (BRA)

katerinburg: Zuev, Shayakhmetov, Prudnikov, Timoshchenkov, gapov, Mokhov, Afanasev, Makayev, Shabanov, Gromilin, histopolov. Coach: Sergei Skorovich (RUS)
oal(s): 1-0 Mokhov 9(og), 1-1 Prudnikov 25, -2 Shayakhmetov 34(p), 1-3 Makayev 36, 1-4 Agapov 39
ellow Card(s): Shayakhmetov 25 (Ekaterinburg)

5/4/08, Krylatskoe Sport Palace, Moscow
lPozo Murcia FS 1-1 MFK Dinamo Moskva
lPozo Murcia: Juanjo, Caio, Mauricio, Rodrigues de Brito, Álvaro, ike, Raúl, Bacaro, Serrejón, Vinicius, Gomes da Silva. Coach: Eduardo ad Thiago (ESP)
inamo Moskva: Popov, Stepanov, Tatu, Caetano, Cirilo, Joan, Pula, akhimov, Kobzar, Kelson, Ivanov. Coach: Yuriy Rudnev (RUS)
oal(s): 1-0 Rodrigues de Brito 4, 1-1 Pula 16
ellow Card(s): Caetano 93 (Dinamo Moskva)
lPozo Murcia FS win 4-2 on penalties.

hird Place Play-off Result

7/4/08, Krylatskoe Sport Palace, Moscow
airat Almaty 0-5 MFK Dinamo Moskva
airat: Khayavin, Gustavo, Samohvalov, Dantas, Cacau, Rafael, Terentyev, Bondarev, Dertinho, Garcez, Butrin. Coach: José Alésio da Silva (BRA)
Dinamo Moskva: Popov, Stepanov, Tatu, Caetano, Cirilo, Joan, Pula, Rakhimov, Kobzar, Kelson, Ivanov. Coach: Yuriy Rudnev (RUS)
Goal(s): 0-1 Ivanov 6, 0-2 Tatu 17(p), 0-3 Rakhimov 36, 0-4 Joan 39, 0-5 Cirilo 39
Yellow Card(s): Pica Pau 18 (Kairat), Rafael 37 (Kairat)

Final Result

27/4/08, Krylatskoe Sport Palace, Moscow
MFK Viz-Sinara Ekaterinburg 4-4 ElPozo Murcia FS
Ekaterinburg: Zuev, Garagulya, Shayakhmetov, Mokhov, Prudnikov, Agapov, Afanasev, Makayev, Shabanov, Bondar, Chistopolov. Coach: Sergei Skorovich (RUS)
ElPozo Murcia: Juanjo, Caio, Mauricio, Rodrigues de Brito, Álvaro, Kike, Raúl, Bacaro, Serrejón, Vinicius, Gomes da Silva. Coach: Eduardo Sad Thiago (ESP)
Goal(s): 1-0 Makayev 6, 1-1 Kike 18, 1-2 Rodrigues de Brito 24, 2-2 Shayakhmetov 27, 2-3 Vinicius 30, 3-3 Prudnikov 35, 3-4 Mauricio 36, 4-4 Chistopolov 36
Yellow Card(s): Timoshchenkov 5 (Ekaterinburg), Kike 40 (ElPozo Murcia), Shayakhmetov 91 (Ekaterinburg)
MFK Viz-Sinara Ekaterinburg win 3-2 on penalties.

Viz-Sinara Ekaterinburg's Sergei Zuev (left) and Vladislav Shayakhmetov prepare to lift the UEFA Futsal Cup

DIFFERENT LANGUAGES,ONE GOA

NO TO RACISM

Nation-by-nation

Welcome to the Nation-by-nation section of the European Football Yearbook.

Here you will find separate chapters, alphabetically arranged, on each of the 53 UEFA member associations.

Nation-by-nation explained

Included for each UEFA member association is a narrative and pictorial review of the season accompanied by the following statistics:

ASSOCIATION DIRECTORY

Address, contact details and senior officials followed by international honours, major international tournament appearances and the member association's top five international cap-holders and goalscorers.

NATIONAL TEAM RESULTS

Details on all international matches played between July 2007 and June 2008 with date, opponent, venue, result and scorer details.

Key: H = home, A = away, N = Neutral, og = own-goal, (p) = penalty, (aet) = after extra time, (ECF) = UEFA EURO 2008™ final tournament match, (ECQ) = UEFA EURO 2008™ qualification round match.

NATIONAL TEAM APPEARANCES

Details on all participants in the aforementioned matches (coaches and players), including name, date of birth and, for each player, club, match-by-match appearances, minutes played and all-time international caps and goals scored.

Opponents are ranged across the top and abbreviated with the appropriate ISO three-letter code – capital letters identify a UEFA EURO 2008™ final tournament or qualification round match.

Changes of national team coach are indicated with the appropriate date; temporary coaches are indicated in brackets.

Non-native clubs are indicated with the appropriate ISO three-letter country code.

Key: G = goalkeeper, D = defender, M = midfielder, A = attacker, s = substitute.

The number appearing after the letter indicates the time a substitution took place.

DOMESTIC LEAGUE

FINAL TABLE

The final standings of the member association's top division including home, away and total records.

Key: Pld = matches played, W = matches won, D = matches drawn, L = matches lost, F = goals for (scored), A = goals against (conceded), Pts = points.

·············· = *play-off line*
\- - - - - - - - = *relegation line*

Any peculiarities, such as the deduction of points or clubs withdrawn, are indicated as N.B. at the foot of the table.

TOP GOALSCORERS

A list of the top ten goalscorers (with clubs) in the member association's top division (league goals only).

CLUB-BY-CLUB

Information on each top-division club is provided in four parts:

1) Club name followed by the coach(es)/manager(s) used during the season and, in the case of new appointments, the dates on which they took place.
2) The year the club was founded, followed, where applicable, by major honours, including European, international and domestic competitions. National 'super cups', secondary leagues and minor or age-restricted knockout competitions are not included.
3) League fixtures, including dates, opponents, results and scorers.

Key: h = home, a = away, og = own-goal, (p) = penalty, (w/o) = walkover/forfeit

4) A list of all players used in the league campaign, including name, nationality, playing position, appearances and goals. Where applicable, and known, squad numbers are also included.

Key: No = squad (jersey) number, Name = full name (listed alphabetically with family name or football nickname in capitals), Nat = nationality (native unless listed with ISO three-letter code), Pos = playing position, Aps =number of appearances in the starting lineup, (s) =number of appearances as a substitute, Gls = number of goals scored, G = goalkeeper, D = defender, M = midfielder; A = attacker.

PROMOTED CLUB(S)

nformation on each promoted club is provided in two parts:

) Club name followed by the coach(es)/manager(s) used during the season and, in the case of new appointments, the dates on which they took place.

) The year the club was founded, followed, where applicable, by major honours, including European, international and domestic competitions. National 'super cups', secondary leagues and minor or age-restricted knockout competitions are not included.

SECOND LEVEL FINAL TABLE

he final classification of the member association's second evel (i.e. feeder league to the top division) table(s). Play-ff details, where applicable, are also indicated.

ey: Pld = matches played, W = matches won, D = matches rawn, L = matches lost, F = goals for (scored), A = goals gainst (conceded), Pts = points.

- - - - - - - = *promotion line (at the top)*
.... = *play-off line*
- - - - - - - = *relegation line (at the bottom)*

ny peculiarities, such as the deduction of points or clubs ithdrawn, are indicated as N.B. at the foot of the final ague table.

DOMESTIC CUP(S)

esults from the member association's main domestic nockout competition, beginning at the round in which ne top-division clubs (or some of them) enter. oalscorers and times of goals are indicated from the uarter-final stage with complete lineups for the final.

etails of the latter stages of significant secondary nockout competitions are also included for some nember associations.

ey; (aet) = after extra time

.B. A complete key to all ISO three-letter codes can be ound on page 6.

NATION-BY-NATION

INDEX

Domestic rol

Country	Champions	Top league goalscorer(s)	Cup winners
ALB	KS Dinamo Tirana	Vioresin Sinani (Vllaznia) 20	KS Vllaznia
AND	FC Santa Coloma		UE Sant Julià
ARM**	FC Pyunik	Marcos Pizelli Pineiro (Ararat) 20	FC Ararat Yerevan
AUT	SK Rapid Wien	Alexander Zickler (Salzburg) 16	–
AZE	PİK İnter Bakı	Xaqani Mämmädov (İnter Bakı)	FK Xäzär Länkäran
BLR**	FC BATE Borisov	Roman Vasilyuk (Gomel) 24	FC MTZ-RIPO Minsk
BEL	R. Standard de Liège	Joseph Akpala (Charleroi) 18	RSC Anderlecht
BIH	FK Modriča	Darko Spalević (Slavija) 18	HŠK Zrinjski
BUL	PFC CSKA Sofia	Georgi Hristov (Botev) 19	PFC Litex Lovech
CRO	NK Dinamo Zagreb	Želimir Terkeš (Zadar) 21	NK Dinamo Zagreb
CYP	Anorthosis Famagusta FC	Łukasz Sosin (Anorthosis) & David Pereira (Doxa) 16	APOEL FC
CZE	SK Slavia Praha	Václav Svěrkoš (Baník) 15	AC Sparta Praha
DEN	Aalborg BK	Jeppe Curth (AaB) 17	Brøndby IF
ENG	Manchester United FC	Cristiano Ronaldo (Man. United) 31	Portsmouth FC
EST**	FC Levadia Tallinn	Dmitri Lipartov (Trans) 30	FC Flora
FRO***	NSÍ Runavík	Ahmed Davy Sylla (B36) 18	EB/Streymur (2007) EB/Streymur (2008)
FIN*	Tampere United	Rafael (Lahti) 14	Tampere United
FRA	Olympique Lyonnais	Karim Benzema (Lyon) 20	Olympique Lyonnais
GEO	FC Dinamo Tbilisi	Mikheil Khutsishvili (Dinamo Tbilisi) 16	FC Zestafoni
GER	FC Bayern München	Luca Toni (Bayern) 24	FC Bayern München
GRE	Olympiacos CFP	Ismael Blanco (AEK Athens) 19	Olympiacos CFP
HUN	MTK Budapest	Róbert Waltner (ZTE) 18	Debreceni VSC
ISL*	Valur Reykjavík	Jónas Grani Gardarsson (Fram) 14	FH Hafnarfjördur
ISR	Beitar Jerusalem FC	Samuel Yeboah (H. Kfar-Saba) 15	Beitar Jerusalem FC
ITA	FC Internazionale Milano	Alessandro Del Piero (Juventus) 21	AS Roma
KAZ*	FK Aktobe	Zhafar Irismetov (Alma-Ata) 17	FC Tobol Kostanay
LVA***	FK Ventspils	Vīts Rimkus (Ventspils) 20	FK Ventspils (2007) FC Daugava (2008)
LIE	–	–	FC Vaduz
LTU**	FBK Kaunas	Povilas Lukšys (Ekranas) 26	FBK Kaunas

07/08

f honour

ry	Champions	Top league goalscorer(s)	Cup winners
	F91 Dudelange	Emmanuel Coquelet (Dudelange) 20	CS Grevenmacher
	FK Rabotnički	Ivica Gligorovski (Milano) 15	FK Rabotnički
	Valletta FC	Sebastián Monesterolo (Valletta) 19	Birkirkara FC
	FC Sheriff	Igor Picusciac (Tiraspol/Sheriff) 14	FC Sheriff
	FK Budućnost Podgorica	Miloš Đalac (Grbalj/Zeta) 13	FK Mogren
	PSV Eindhoven	Klaas Jan Huntelaar (Ajax) 33	Feyenoord
	Linfield FC	Peter Thompson (Linfield) 29	Linfield FC
*	SK Brann	Thorstein Helstad (Brann) 22	Lillestrøm SK
	Wisła Kraków	Paweł Brożek (Wisła Kraków) 23	Legia Warszawa
	FC Porto	Lisandro López (Porto) 24	Sporting Clube de Portugal
	Drogheda United FC	David Mooney (Longford) 19	Cork City FC
	CFR 1907 Cluj	Ionel Dănciulescu (Dinamo Bucureşti) 21	CFR 1907 Cluj
*	FC Zenit St. Petersburg	Roman Adamov (Moskva) & Roman Pavlyuchenko (Spartak Moskva) 14	PFC CSKA Moskva
	S.S. Murata	Marco Fantini (Juvenes/Dogana) 16	S.S. Murata
	Celtic FC	Scott McDonald (Celtic) 25	Rangers FC
	FK Partizan	Nenad Jestrović (Crvena Zvezda) 13	FK Partizan
	FC Artmedia Petržalka	Ján Novak (Košice) 17	FC Artmedia Petržalka
	NK Domžale	Dario Zahora (Domžale) 22	NK IB Ljubljana
	Real Madrid CF	Daniel Güiza (Mallorca) 27	Valencia CF
*	IFK Göteborg	Razak Omotoyossi (Helsingborg) & Marcus Berg (Göteborg) 14	Kalmar FF
	FC Basel 1893	Hakan Yakin (Young Boys) 24	FC Basel 1893
	Galatasaray AŞ	Semih Şentürk (Fenerbahçe) 17	Kayserispor
	FC Shakhtar Donetsk	Marko Dević (Metalist) 19	FC Shakhtar Donetsk
	Llanelli AFC	Rhys Griffiths (Llanelli) 40	Bangor City FC

= League and Cup in 2007

= League in 2007, Cup in 2008

= League in 2007, Cups in 2007 and 2008

Relegated/pr

Country	Relegated clubs	Promoted clubs
ALB	(3) KS Skënderbeu, KS Besëlidhja, KS Kastrioti	(3) KS Bylis, KS Apolonia, KS Lushnja
AND	(1) SE Casa del Benfica	(1) UE Santa Coloma
ARM	(0)	(0)
AUT	(1) FC Wacker Innsbruck	(1) Kapfenberger SV
AZE	(2) FK ABN Bärdä, PFK Gänclärbirliyi	(2) PFK Bakılı Bakı, PFK MOİK Bakı
BLR	(1) FC Minsk	(3) FC Savit Mogilev, FC Granit Mikashevichi, FC Lokomotiv Minsk
BEL	(2) FC Brussels, K. Sint-Truidense VV	(2) KV Kortrijk, AFC Tubize
BIH	(2) NK Žepče, NK Jedinstvo	(2) NK Zvijezda, FK Borac
BUL	(3) PFC Marek Dupnitza, PFC Vidima Rakovski, PFC Beroe Stara Zagora	(3) PFC Sliven 2000, PFC Lokomotiv Mezdra, PFC Minyor Pernik
CRO	(1) NK Međimurje	(1) NK Croatia Sesvete
CYP	(3) Olympiakos Nicosia FC, Nea Salamis FC, Aris Limassol FC	(3) AEP Paphos FC, APEP FC, Atromitos Yereskipou F
CZE	(2) FK SIAD Most, Bohemians 1905	(2) Bohemians Praha, FK Marila Příbram
DEN	(2) Lyngby BK, Viborg FF	(2) Vejle BK, SønderjyskE
ENG	(3) Derby County FC, Birmingham City FC, Reading FC	(3) West Bromwich Albion FC, Stoke City FC, Hull City
EST	(2) FC Ajax Lasnamäe, FC Kuressaare	(2) JK Kalev Sillamäe, JK Kalju Nömme
FRO	(2) VB/Sumba Vágur, AB Argir	(2) B68 Toftir, ÍF Fuglafjørdur
FIN	(2) AC Oulu, FC Viikingit	(2) KuPS Kuopio, RoPS Rovaniemi
FRA	(3) FC Metz, RC Strasbourg, RC Lens	(3) Le Havre AC, FC Nantes, Grenoble Foot 38
GEO	(4) FC Dila Gori, FC Dinamo Batumi, FC Merani Tbilisi, FC Ameri Tbilisi	(1) FC Gagra
GER	(3) MSV Duisburg, FC Hansa Rostock, 1. FC Nürnberg	(3) VfL Borussia Mönchengladbach, TSG 1899 Hoffenheim, 1. FC Köln
GRE	(3) Apollon Kalamarias FC, GAS Veria, Atromitos FC	(3) Panserraikos FC, Thrasivoulos Filis FC, Panthrakikos FC
HUN	(2) FC Sopron, FC Tatabánya	(2) Szombathelyi Haladás FC, Kecskeméti TE
ISL	(1) Víkingur Reykjavík	(3) Grindavík, Thróttur Reykjavík, Fjölnir Reykjavík
ISR	(2) Maccabi Herzliya FC, Hapoel Kfar-Saba FC	(2) Hakoah Amidar Ramat Gan FC, Hapoel Petach-Tikva FC

07/08

...noted clubs

...try	Relegated clubs	Promoted clubs
	(3) AS Livorno Calcio, Parma FC, Empoli FC	(3) AC Chievo Verona, Bologna FC, US Lecce
	(2) FC Taraz, FC Ekibastuzets	(2) FC MegaSport Almaty, FC Energetik Pavlodar
	(0)	(2) FC Vindava Ventspils, SK Blāzma Rēzekne
	(2) FK Interas, FC Vilnius	(0)
	(3) CS Pétange, FC Victoria Rosport, FC Wiltz 71	(3) US Rumelange, CS Fola Esch, FC Sporting Steinfort
	(2) FK Cementarnica 55, FK Shkendija 79	(2) FK Turnovo, FK Metalurg Skopje
	(2) Pietà Hotspurs FC, Mqabba FC	(2) Tarxien Rainbows FC, Qormi FC
	(2) FC Rapid Ghidighici, FC Politehnica Timişoara	(1) FC Academia UTM Chişinău
	(2) FK Mladost Podgorica, FK Bokelj	(2) FK Jezero, FK Jedinstvo Bijelo Polje
	(2) SC Excelsior, VVV-Venlo	(2) FC Volendam, ADO Den Haag
	(5) Armagh City FC, Limavady United FC, Larne FC, Donegal Celtic FC, Portadown FC	(1) Bangor FC
	(3) Sandefjord Fotball, IK Start, Odd Grenland	(3) Molde FK, HamKam Fotball, FK Bodø/Glimt
	(4) GKS Zagłębie Sosnowiec, RTS Widzew Łódź, Zagłębie Lubin, Korona Kielce	(4) KS Lechia Gdańsk, WSK Śląsk Wrocław, KS Piast Gliwice, Arka Gdynia
	(2) UD Leiria, Boavista FC	(2) CD Trofense, Rio Ave FC
	(2) Longford Town FC, Waterford United FC	(2) Cobh Ramblers FC, Finn Harps FC
	(4) FC Universitatea Craiova, FCM UTA Arad, CS Dacia Mioveni, FC Ceahlăul Piatra Neamţ	(4) FC Braşov, CS Otopeni, FC Argeş Piteşti, CS Gaz Metan Mediaş
	(2) FC Rostov, FC Kuban Krasnodar	(2) FC Shinnik Yaroslavl, FC Terek Grozny
	(1) Gretna FC	(1) Hamilton Academical FC
	(3) FK Bežanija, FK Banat, FK Smederevo	(3) FK Javor, FK Jagodina, FK Rad
	(1) AS Trenčín	(1) 1. FC Tatran Presov
	(1) NK Livar	(1) NK Rudar Velenje
	(3) Levante UD, Real Murcia CF, Real Zaragoza	(3) CD Numancia de Soria, Málaga CF, Real Sporting de Gijón
	(1) IF Brommapojkarna	(3) IFK Norrköping, Ljungskile SK, GIF Sundsvall
	(2) FC Thun, FC St Gallen	(2) FC Vaduz, AC Bellinzona
	(3) Kasımpaşa SK, Rizespor, Vestel Manisaspor	(3) Kocaelispor, Antalyaspor, Eskişehirspor
	(2) FC Zakarpattya Uzhgorod, FC Naftovyk-Ukrnafta Okhtyrka	(2) FC Illychivets Mariupil, FC Lviv
	(1) Llangefni Town FC	(1) Prestatyn Town FC

Dinamo hold on in title thriller

KS Dinamo Tirana returned to the summit of Albanian football for the first time in six years after a tense last-day encounter against city rivals and closest challengers FK Partizani.

Having led the Kategoria Superiore from day one, and by six points at the winter break, Dinamo almost surrendered the title at the last. Doggedly pursued to the finishing line by Partizani, who had matched the leaders' results in each of the previous seven rounds, Dinamo still held a two-point advantage as they went into the championship decider.

Partizani's hopes of earning the victory they required to claim their first national title for 15 years soared when, at 1-1, Dinamo had two players sent off in a crazy three-minute spell just after half-time. An Italian referee, Paul Tagliavento, had been imported to ensure fair play, and he became the game's central figure when he ordered off Artim Položani and Dinamo's early goalscorer Bekim Kuli in quick succession. However, this open invitation to Partizani was not accepted, and Dinamo not only resisted gallantly with nine men but also ended their season in style with a dramatic 93rd-minute winner from substitute Nertil Ferraj.

Foreign assistance

Unlike Partizani, whose squad was all-Albanian, Dinamo owed much to a sizeable foreign contingent, four of them from Croatia, including leading scorer Pero Perić (18 goals). Nigerian defender Abraham Alechenwu, who started 31 of the team's 33 matches – only ever-present goalkeeper Elvis Kotorri was more assiduous – achieved a remarkable Albanian title hat-trick, having been victorious with KS Elbasani in 2005/06 and KF Tirana in 2006/07.

Arie Haan (left) – the new head coach of Albania

Ilir Daja, the man who led Dinamo across the finish line, was also able to savour a second title, having been Elbasan's coach two years previously. He was appointed only in late February in succession to Agim Canaj, who lost his job after a 1-0 defeat at Partizani. With six wins and a draw in his eight games, Daja, a former Dinamo player, confirmed his reputation as one of Albania's pre-eminent young coaches.

Partizani were led from start to finish by Hasan Lika, one of only four top-flight coaches to go the full distance. Tirana, the defending champions, went through three. The return of ulejman Starova, who had steered the club to the 004/05 title, proved ill fated as he resigned after just our matches. His replacement, ex-national team boss strit Hafizi, lasted until February before he, too, made vay, handing over to Sulejman Mema.

lthough a successful title defence was never on for irana after a poor start, Mema did lead the club into he Albanian Cup final. But at the Ruzhdi Bizhuta tadium, where Tirana had defeated local club Elbasan -0 in the first leg of the semi-final, they were beaten -0 by KS Vllaznia, the club from Shkodar thus taking he trophy for the first time in 21 years. Two first-half oals from midfielder Gilman Lika and striker Xhevair ukaj put Vllaznia in charge; indeed so irate was Tirana resident Refik Halili at the interval that he instructed oach Mema to withdraw three players (among them xperienced Albanian international Klodian Duro, who ad recently scored a hat-trick against Vllaznia in the eague), claiming that they weren't trying.

op scorer Sinani

'llaznia maintained their 2-0 advantage, rewarding he club's 1999/2000 league title-winning coach)ervis Hadziosmanovic, who had been re-appointed wo months earlier in place of Mirel Josa. Vllaznia's Cup inal win was achieved without their injured star triker Vioresin Sinani. Re-recruited from Tirana, the rolific 30-year-old retained his league top scorer rown with a tally of 20 goals.

Vhile Vllaznia joined Partizani in the 2008/09 UEFA Cup, Tirana, who finished a disappointing sixth in the eague, missed out on European competition for the irst time in eleven years. The UEFA Intertoto Cup erth went to 2007 Cup winners KS Besa, who finished creditable third, but two other clubs that had elebrated success a year earlier, newly promoted KS Skënderbeu and KS Besëlidhja, both went straight back down. KS Kastrioti, who had played home games on neutral turf all season due to stadium reconstruction, unluckily joined them in relegation after a penalty shoot-out defeat to KS Lushnja, but KS Teuta saved themselves in the other play-off with a 114th-minute penalty to beat KS Burreli 2-1. The two automatic promotion places were taken by FK Bylis Ballsh and KS Apolonia, the latter returning after just a year away.

Disastrous double-header

Albania's calamitous end to the UEFA EURO 2008™ qualifying campaign, in which they lost their last two matches 4-2 at home to Belarus and 6-1 away to Romania (their heaviest defeat since 1990) resulted in the departure of the team's veteran Croatian coach Otto Barić. Things had been going reasonably well until that disastrous November double-header, with Barić set for a contract extension. But for a stoppage-time goal conceded to the Netherlands (0-1) and a late penalty missed by Ervin Skela against Bulgaria (1-1), Albania might even have aspired to third place. But after watching from afar (due to a touchline ban) as his team conceded ten goals in their final two qualifiers – after shipping just eight in the previous ten – Barić offered his resignation.

In January, Dutchman Arie Haan was appointed as his replacement. However, his preparations for the 2010 FIFA World Cup qualifying campaign were hit by a two-month ban imposed jointly by FIFA and UEFA after government interference in the affairs of the Albanian FA. With a tough World Cup group to negotiate – including Portugal, Sweden and Denmark – and several stalwarts such as Skela, Duro, Erjon Bogdani and skipper Altin Lala now well into their thirties, the former Netherlands midfield star will have his work cut out simply to keep the team on an even keel.

Federata Shqiptarë e Futbollit (FShF)

Rruga Labinoti
Pallati perballe Shkolles
Gjuhet e Huaja
AL-TIRANË
tel - +355 4346605
fax - +355 4346609
website – www.fshf.org
email – fshf@fshf.org.al
Year of Formation - 1930
President – Armando Duka

General Secretary – Arben Bici
Press Officer - Tritan Kokona
Stadium - Qemal Stafa, Tirana (16,200)

TOP FIVE ALL-TIME CAPS:
Foto Strakosha (73); Igli Tare (68); Alban Bushi (67); Altin Haxhi (66); Altin Rraklli (63)

TOP FIVE ALL-TIME GOALS:
Alban Bushi (14); Altin Rraklli (11); Igli Tare & Sokol Kushta (10); Ervin Skela (9)

ALBANIA

NATIONAL TEAM RESULTS 2007/08

22/8/07	Malta	H	Tirana	3-0	*Salihi (38), Berisha (47), Duro (60)*
12/9/07	Netherlands (ECQ)	H	Tirana	0-1	
13/10/07	Slovenia (ECQ)	A	Celje	0-0	
17/10/07	Bulgaria (ECQ)	H	Tirana	1-1	*Kishishev (25og)*
17/11/07	Belarus (ECQ)	H	Tirana	2-4	*Bogdani (43), Kapllani (44)*
21/11/07	Romania (ECQ)	A	Bucharest	1-6	*Kapllani (64)*
27/5/08	Poland	N	Reutlingen (GER)	0-1	

NATIONAL TEAM APPEARANCES 2007/08

Coach – Otto BARIĆ (CRO) (Slavko KOVAČIĆ (CRO)) /(4/1/08) Arie HAAN (NED)	**12/6/32 14/5/50 16/11/48**		**Mlt**	**NED**	**SVN**	**BUL**	**BLR**	**ROU**	**Pol**	**Cps**	**Goa**
Arjan BEQAJ	25/8/75	Anorthosis (CYP)	G46	G	G	G	G	G		31	-
Armend DALLKU	16/6/83	Vorskla (UKR)	D	D		D	D		D	23	-
Nevil DEDE	10/1/75	Tirana	D	D	D	D	D	D		31	-
Kristi VANGJELI	5/9/85	Aris (GRE)	D	D	D	D	s38	D41	D	8	-
Altin HAXHI	17/6/75	Ergotelis (GRE)	D46	s69	M60	M46		M		66	3
Altin LALA	18/11/75	Hannover (GER)	M46	M	M	M	M75	M	M71	63	3
Ervin SKELA	17/11/76	Energie (GER)	M46		M90	M	M	M	M	50	9
Devi MUKA	21/12/76	Tirana	M46	M	s60	s46				40	-
Erjon BOGDANI	14/4/77	Chievo (ITA) /Livorno (ITA)	A22	A83	A	A	A	A83	A46	45	8
Besart BERISHA	29/7/85	Burnley (ENG)	A64							7	1
Edmond KAPLLANI	31/7/82	Karlsruhe (GER)	A46	A46			A74	s41	s46	21	5
Hamdi SALIHI	19/1/84	Ried (AUT)	s22			A73	s74		A80	7	1
Isli HIDI	15/10/80	Tirana /Kryvbas (UKR)	s46						G	5	-
Klodian DURO	21/12/77	Tirana	s46	M69	M77	M	M	M78	M46	47	2
Ervin BULKU	3/3/81	Kryvbas (UKR)	s46	s83	M	s73		M	s71	11	-
Jahmir HYKA	8/3/88	Tirana	s46		s90			s78	s46	5	-
Alban BUSHI	20/8/73	Kalamarias (GRE)	s46	s46	s77		s75			67	14
Blerim RRUSTEMI	4/2/83	Horsens (DEN)	s46		D		D38			3	-
Erjon XHAFA	31/5/82	Tirana	s64							3	-
Debatik CURRI	28/12/83	Vorskla (UKR)		D	D	D	D	D	D	14	1
Lorik CANA	27/7/83	Marseille (FRA)		M			M		M	30	1
Andi LILA	12/2/86	Besa						D	D46	2	-
Elis BAKAJ	25/6/87	Partizani						s83		1	-
Endrit VRAPI	23/5/82	Tirana							s46	3	-
Dorian BYLYKBASHI	8/8/80	Kryvbas (UKR)							s80	2	-

DOMESTIC LEAGUE 2007/08

ATEGORIA SUPERIORE FINAL TABLE

	Pld	Home W	D	L	F	A	Away W	D	L	F	A	Total W	D	L	F	A	Pts
KS Dinamo Tirana	33	12	3	2	38	8	9	4	3	18	6	21	7	5	56	14	70
FK Partizani	33	12	5	0	30	6	6	6	4	17	16	18	11	4	47	22	65
KS Besa	33	14	0	3	26	8	3	5	8	19	28	17	5	11	45	36	56
KS Elbasani	33	9	7	1	28	8	4	6	6	12	16	13	13	7	40	24	52
KS Shkumbini	33	11	4	1	24	7	3	4	10	11	21	14	8	11	35	28	50
KF Tirana	33	9	4	4	28	16	5	3	8	18	20	14	7	12	46	36	49
KS Vllaznia	33	9	4	4	29	17	3	5	8	17	29	12	9	12	46	46	45
KS Flamurtari	33	7	7	2	20	12	3	7	7	15	25	10	14	9	35	37	44
KS Teuta	33	4	5	7	17	21	5	3	9	15	24	9	8	16	32	45	35
KS Kastrioti	33	8	2	6	14	14	2	3	12	10	29	10	5	18	24	43	35
KS Besëlidhja	33	5	5	6	21	23	4	2	11	10	29	9	7	17	31	52	34
KS Skënderbeu	33	2	2	12	16	32	1	0	16	10	48	3	2	28	26	80	11

TOP GOALSCORERS

20 Vioresin SINANI (Vllaznia)

18 Pero PEJIĆ (Dinamo Tirana)

15 Klodian DURO (Tirana)

13 Parid XHIHANI (Besa)
Skerdi BEJZADE (Elbasan)

12 Mario NGJELA (Skënderbeu/Besëlidhja)
Elis BAKAJ (Partizani)

10 Bledar MANÇAKU (Besa)
Devis MEMA (Flamurtari)
Erjon RIZVANOLLI (Kastrioti)
Gjergji MUZAKA (Partizani)
Xhevair SUKAJ (Vllaznia)

CLUB-BY-CLUB

KS BESA

Coach - Silviu Dumitrescu (ROU); (29/11/07) Iljaz Haxhiaj; (3/12/07) Sulejman Starova; (6/4/08) Iljaz Haxhiaj

Founded – 1922

MAJOR HONOURS: Albanian Cup – (1) 2007.

007				
5/8	Kastrioti	h	3-1	*Elokan, Xhihani 2*
/9	Teuta	a	1-0	*Xhihani*
5/9	Flamurtari	h	2-0	*Mançaku, Elokan*
1/9	Skënderbeu	a	1-1	*Elokan*
0/9	Tirana	h	3-1	*Elokan, Veliaj 2 (1p)*
/10	Elbasan	h	1-0	*Nana Bikoula*
0/10	Dinamo Tirana	a	0-0	
1/10	Partizani	h	2-1	*Alikaj, Xhihani*
/11	Shkumbini	a	0-2	
/11	Besëlidhja	h	2-0	*Veliaj (p), Arapi*
0/11	Vllaznia	a	1-1	*Elokan*
5/11	Kastrioti	a	1-2	*Xhihani*
/12	Teuta	h	0-1	
/12	Flamurtari	a	0-1	
5/12	Skënderbeu	h	2-0	*Xhihani, Hamzaj*
2/12	Tirana	a	0-2	
9/12	Elbasan	a	0-2	
008				
/2	Dinamo Tirana	h	0-2	
/2	Partizani	a	3-3	*Xhihani 2, Leçi*
7/2	Shkumbini	h	1-0	*Xhihani*
3/2	Besëlidhja	a	2-2	*Alikaj, Shaqiri*
/3	Vllaznia	h	1-0	*Mançaku*
/3	Kastrioti	h	1-0	*Salihu*
3/3	Flamurtari	a	1-2	*Mançaku*
9/3	Shkumbini	h	3-0	*Xhihani 2, Alikaj*
/4	Elbasan	a	1-3	*og (Ahmataj)*
2/4	Tirana	h	2-1	*Mançaku 2 (2p)*
9/4	Skënderbeu	h	1-0	*Mançaku (p)*
26/4	Vllaznia	a	3-2	*Mançaku 2 (1p), Progri*
/5	Partizani	h	0-1	
0/5	Dinamo Tirana	a	0-2	
4/5	Besëlidhja	h	2-0	*Xhihani 2*
17/5	Teuta	a	5-3	*Roshi, Okshtuni, Mançaku 2, Alikaj*

No	Name	Nat	Pos	Aps	(s)	Gls
20	Enkeleid ALIKAJ		M	25	(4)	4
3	Renato ARAPI		D	13	(2)	1
8	Amarildo BELISHA		D	31		
7	Emanuel Nana BIKOULA	CMR	M	13	(2)	1
	Saimir ÇELHAKA		D		(1)	
	Sokol ÇIKALLESHI		M		(1)	
	Eglajd DEDEJ		D		(1)	
5	Alban DRAGUSHA		D	3	(1)	
1	Bledar DURA		G	11		
26	Albert DURO		D	2	(2)	
99	François Herbert ELOKAN	CMR	A	11	(1)	5
14	Herby FORTUNAT	FRA	A	7	(4)	
18	Romeo HAMZAJ		A	2	(7)	1
15	Erand HOXHA		D	11	(6)	
29	Elvis KAJA		D	2	(2)	
22	Dritan KRASNIQI		M	20	(3)	
3	Liridon LEÇI		D	10	(1)	1
6	Andi LILA		D	29		
21	Bledar MANÇAKU		M	29	(2)	10
2	Ilirjan MËRTIRI		D	4	(2)	
23	Meglid MIHANI		M	9	(14)	
10	Arben NUHIJI	MKD	A	1	(8)	
13	Bruno OKSHTUNI		A	1	(1)	1
19	Gerard PROGRI		M	15	(1)	1
78	Zekrija RAMADANI	MKD	D	23		
	Daniel ROSHI		A	2	(3)	1
11	Abdullah Isshaka SALIHU	CMR	M	10	(8)	1
10	Artim SHAQIRI	MKD	M	7	(1)	1
	Bledar TAFXHAFA		M		(1)	
16	Bazjon TRAGA		D	3	(1)	
28	Emiljano VELIAJ		M	18	(7)	3
9	Parid XHIHANI		A	29	(3)	13
12	Suad ZENDELI	MKD	G	22		

KS BESËLIDHJA

Coach - Stavri Nica; (11/9/07) Ritvan Kulli; (1/12/07) Neptun Bajko; (22/2/08) Ilir Gjyla

Founded – 1930

2007				
25/8	Dinamo Tirana	a	0-4	
1/9	Partizani	h	1-2	*Roshi*
15/9	Shkumbini	a	1-2	*Petrevski*
22/9	Tirana	a	1-0	*Lika*
28/9	Vllaznia	h	2-2	*Roshi (p), Smajli*
5/10	Kastrioti	a	1-2	*Grizha*
21/10	Teuta	h	0-0	
31/10	Flamurtari	a	1-1	*Petrevski*
3/11	Skënderbeu	h	4-2	*Petrevski, Lika, Roshi, Gruda*
7/11	Besa	a	0-2	
10/11	Elbasan	h	0-1	
25/11	Dinamo Tirana	h	0-2	
1/12	Partizani	a	0-4	
8/12	Shkumbini	h	2-1	*Petrevski, Mićić*
15/12	Tirana	h	0-2	
22/12	Vllaznia	a	0-3	
29/12	Kastrioti	h	1-2	*Përlleshi*
2008				
2/2	Teuta	a	0-2	
9/2	Flamurtari	h	2-2	*Gilson, Përlleshi*
20/2	Skënderbeu	a	2-0	*Petrevski, Gilson*
23/2	Besa	h	2-2	*Toma, Petrevski*
1/3	Elbasan	a	2-1	*Balić, Ngjela*
8/3	Partizani	a	0-1	
22/3	Dinamo Tirana	h	1-0	*Ivanaj*
29/3	Skënderbeu	a	2-0	*Ngjela (p), Gilson*
5/4	Teuta	a	0-2	
12/4	Kastrioti	h	1-1	*Smajli*
19/4	Flamurtari	a	0-0	
26/4	Shkumbini	h	0-2	
3/5	Elbasan	a	0-3	
10/5	Tirana	h	1-0	*Hashani*
14/5	Besa	a	0-2	
17/5	Vllaznia	h	4-2	*Gruda, Gilson 2, Mićić*

No	Name	Nat	Pos	Aps	(s)	Gls
	Alert ALCANI		D	8	(2)	
	Emin BALIĆ		D	4	(2)	1
	Klaudio BARAKU		D		(2)	
	Alban BRUKA		D	1	(3)	
16	Sadush DANAJ		D	5	(5)	
	Aleksander DIMITROVSKI	MKD	D	1	(1)	
21	Paulinho FERNANDO	BRA	M	11		
20	GILSON Jesus da Silva	BRA	A	15		5
12	Erildo GJOKA		G	2	(1)	
6	Robert GRIZHA		D	17		1
18	Mirsad GRUDA		M	12	(11)	2
15	Erdin HASHANI		D	28	(2)	1
	Kreshnik IVANAJ		A	7	(2)	1
12	Armend JUSUFI		G	1		
1	Arvis KOÇI		G	15		
23	Dejan KOSTEVSKI	MKD	M	3	(5)	
13	Alket KRUJA		M	9	(8)	
5	Edvin LIKA		D	27		2
	Romario LINI		A	1	(1)	
	Dorjan MAÇORRI		D	1		
	Ergys MALLOTA		M	6	(10)	
	Renato MALLOTA		M		(1)	
10	Dragan MIĆIĆ	SRB	A	25	(4)	2
1	Eduart MIÇO		G	11		
22	Mario NGJELA		A	15		2
	Vladimir NIKOLLI		M	1	(2)	
17	Theodhori PËRLLESHI		A	6	(17)	2
19	Goce PETREVSKI	MKD	A	28		6
	Arben PRELA		D	12		
10	Klevis ROSHI		A	16		3
	Aldi SHYTI		D		(1)	
2	Dritan SMAJLI		D	26	(1)	2
	Ralf SOKOLI		A	1	(7)	
	Ilja STOJČEVSKI	MKD	M	2		
21	Iljo TASEV	MKD	M	12	(3)	
	Aleksandar TOLEVSKI	MKD	M	2		
	Bernard TOMA		M	3	(1)	
4	Sokol TOMA		D	25		1
12	Dejan UGRENOVIÅ	SRB	G	4		

KS DINAMO TIRANA

Coach - Agim Canaj; (24/2/08) Ilir Daja

Founded – 1950

MAJOR HONOURS: Albanian League – (17) 1950, 1951, 1952, 1953, 1955, 1956, 1960, 1967, 1973, 1975, 1976, 1977, 1980, 1986, 1990, 2002, 2008; Albanian Cup – (13) 1950, 1951, 1952, 1953, 1954, 1960, 1971, 1974, 1978, 1982, 1989, 1990, 2003.

2007				
25/8	Besëlidhja	h	4-0	*Kuli, Allmuça, Vinčetić, Plaku (p)*
1/9	Vllaznia	a	1-0	*Diop*
15/9	Kastrioti	h	4-0	*Pejić 3, Poçi*
22/9	Teuta	a	1-0	*Plaku*
28/9	Flamurtari	h	0-1	
6/10	Skënderbeu	a	2-1	*Plaku, Pejić*
20/10	Besa	h	0-0	
31/10	Elbasan	a	0-0	
3/11	Tirana	h	0-2	
7/11	Partizani	h	2-0	*Plaku, Pejić*
10/11	Shkumbini	a	0-0	
25/11	Besëlidhja	a	2-0	*Pisha, Pejić*
1/12	Vllaznia	h	0-0	
8/12	Kastrioti	a	3-0	*Pejić, Plaku 2*
15/12	Teuta	h	2-1	*Ferraj, Pejić*
21/12	Flamurtari	a	2-1	*Kuli, Pejić*
28/12	Skënderbeu	h	7-0	*Plaku 2 (1p), Pejić 4, Mile*
2008				
2/2	Besa	a	2-0	*Allmuça 2*
9/2	Elbasan	h	0-0	
16/2	Tirana	a	0-0	
23/2	Partizani	a	0-1	
1/3	Shkumbini	h	1-0	*Poçi*
8/3	Skënderbeu	h	3-1	*Pema, Pejić 2 (1p)*
22/3	Besëlidhja	a	0-1	
30/3	Teuta	h	2-1	*Ishka, Kuli (p)*
5/4	Kastrioti	a	0-1	
12/4	Flamurtari	h	6-0	*Položani 2, Kuli (p), Pejić, Pema 2*
19/4	Shkumbini	a	0-0	
26/4	Elbasan	h	3-1	*Poçi, Pejić, Allmuça*
3/5	Tirana	a	2-1	*Pejić, Kuli (p)*
10/5	Besa	h	2-0	*Kuli (p), Položani*
14/5	Vllaznia	a	3-0	*Ishka, Pema, Daja*
17/5	Partizani	h	2-1	*Kuli (p), Ferraj*

No	Name	Nat	Pos	Aps	(s)	Gls
3	Abraham ALECHENWU	NGA	D	31		
14	Igli ALLMUÇA		M	28		4
	Klevis BEJTJA		D		(1)	
22	Dario BODRUSIĆ	CRO	M	24	(2)	
14	Ilirjan ÇAUSHAJ		M	3	(5)	
	Sokol ÇELA		M		(2)	
11	Asjon DAJA		A		(2)	1
23	Ablade Papa DIOP	SEN	D	15	(10)	1
7	Nertil FERRAJ		M	3	(19)	2
22	Goran GRANIĆ	CRO	D	26	(3)	

No	Name	Nat	Pos	Aps	(s)	Gls
1	Mauricio Fabio HANUCH	ARG	M	1	(3)	
2	Alban HOXHA		G		(2)	
8	Sokol ISHKA		M	24	(5)	2
4	Oerd KOTJA		M		(3)	
	Elvis KOTORRI		G	33		
0	Bekim KULI		M	27	(1)	7
0	Vangjëll MILE		A		(10)	1
5	Pero PEJIĆ	CRO	A	29	(2)	18
	Eleandro PEMA		A	8	(10)	4
	Roland PEQINI		D		(1)	
	Arjan PISHA		D	29	(1)	1
1	Sebino PLAKU		A	14	(2)	8
3	Artion POÇI		M	27	(1)	3
1	Artim POLOŽANI	MKD	M	14	(1)	3
	Goran VINČETIĆ	CRO	D	27	(3)	1

KS ELBASANI

Coach - Krenar Alimehmeti

Founded – 1923

MAJOR HONOURS: Albanian League – (2) 1984, 2006; Albanian Cup – (2) 1975, 1992.

007				
5/8	Vllaznia	h	0-0	
/9	Kastrioti	a	0-2	
5/9	Teuta	h	1-0	*Bejzade*
1/9	Flamurtari	a	1-0	*Xhafa*
9/9	Skënderbeu	h	3-0	*Bejzade 3 (1p)*
/10	Besa	a	0-1	
0/10	Tirana	h	1-1	*Xhafa*
1/10	Dinamo Tirana	h	0-0	
/11	Partizani	a	0-0	
/11	Shkumbini	h	0-0	
0/11	Besëlidhja	a	1-0	*Bejzade (p)*
5/11	Vllaznia	a	1-2	*Karcěv*
/12	Kastrioti	h	2-0	*og (Brahja), Nallbani*
/12	Teuta	a	1-0	*Bejzade*
5/12	Flamurtari	h	2-2	*Bejzade (p), Xhafa*
3/12	Skënderbeu	a	1-0	*Karcěv*
9/12	Besa	h	2-0	*Sheta, Nuhiji Ard.*
008				
/2	Tirana	a	2-2	*Ahmataj, Bejzade*
/2	Dinamo Tirana	a	0-0	
6/2	Partizani	h	0-0	
2/2	Shkumbini	a	0-1	
/3	Besëlidhja	h	1-2	*Bejzade (p)*
/3	Shkumbini	h	1-0	*Nuhiji Arb.*
3/3	Skënderbeu	h	4-0	*Bejzade, Dalipi, Nuhiji Ard., Karcěv*
8/3	Tirana	a	1-2	*Bejzade*
/4	Besa	h	3-1	*Nuhiji Ard., Ahmataj (p), Dalipi*
2/4	Vllaznia	a	0-0	
9/4	Partizani	h	0-0	
6/4	Dinamo Tirana	a	1-3	*Ahmataj (p)*
/5	Besëlidhja	h	3-0	*Bejzade, Xhafa, Karcěv*
0/5	Teuta	a	1-1	*Xhafa*
4/5	Kastrioti	h	5-2	*og (Gallo), Nenaj, Dalipi, Nuhiji Arb., Bejzade*
7/5	Flamurtari	a	2-2	*Nenaj, og (Bega)*

No	Name	Nat	Pos	Aps	(s)	Gls
7	Julian AHMATAJ		M	23		3
11	Shpëtim BABAJ		M	12	(2)	
13	Nertil BAKO		M	1	(6)	
9	Skerdi BEJZADE		A	28		13
	Aldo BELLO		D		(3)	
10	Richard BOKATOLA		M	4	(3)	
9	Sokol BULKU		M	9	(6)	
8	Endri DALIPI		M	21	(2)	3
27	Julian GERXHO		M	4	(2)	
	Endri HALILI		M		(1)	
	Renato HYSHMERI		M	1	(7)	
	Ganjol KAÇULI		M	1		
51	Nikola KARČEV	MKD	D	29		4
26	Stavrion LAKO		D	16	(3)	
1	Ilion LIKA		G	17		
17	Toni MEGLENSKI	MKD	M	13	(1)	
6	Armando MEHMETAJ		D	27		
	Erjol MERXHA		M	5	(7)	
20	Ilir NALLBANI		M	12	(5)	1
2	Roland NENAJ		M	5	(6)	2
18	Arben NUHIJI	MKD	M	10	(5)	2
11	Ardian NUHIJI	MKD	M	21	(9)	3
	Fisnik PAPUÇI		D	2		
	Eder PETI		A		(1)	
19	Arsim PLEPOLLI		D	5	(6)	
20	Artan SAKAJ		D	12		
5	Arjan SHETA		D	28	(1)	1
	Gentian STOJKU		A		(1)	
	Alsid TAFILI		A		(3)	
14	Erind TETOVA		M	15	(4)	
12	Irakli TOÇI		G	12		
1	Dragan VRANIĆ	SRB	G	4		
30	Fjodor XHAFA		A	26	(2)	5

KS FLAMURTARI

Coach - Eqerem Memushi; (9/3/08) Slavko Kovačić (CRO)

Founded – 1923

MAJOR HONOURS: Albanian League – (1) 1991; Albanian Cup – (2) 1985, 1988.

2007				
25/8	Tirana	h	1-0	*Veliu*
1/9	Skënderbeu	h	3-1	*Deco Júnior, Veliu, Strati*
15/9	Besa	a	0-2	
21/9	Elbasan	h	0-1	
28/9	Dinamo Tirana	a	1-0	*Rustemi*
6/10	Partizani	h	0-0	
20/10	Shkumbini	a	0-0	
31/10	Besëlidhja	h	1-1	*Sakaj*
3/11	Vllaznia	a	1-1	*Deco Júnior*
7/11	Kastrioti	h	1-0	*Mema (p)*
10/11	Teuta	a	2-3	*Guga, Mema*
25/11	Tirana	a	0-2	
1/12	Skënderbeu	a	1-1	*Mema (p)*
8/12	Besa	h	1-0	*Guga*
15/12	Elbasan	a	2-2	*Cani, Rustemi*
21/12	Dinamo Tirana	h	1-2	*Mema*
29/12	Partizani	a	0-0	
2008				
2/2	Shkumbini	h	0-0	
9/2	Besëlidhja	a	2-2	*Mema, Zeqiri*
17/2	Vllaznia	h	2-2	*Brajković 2*
23/2	Kastrioti	a	1-0	*Mema*
1/3	Teuta	h	2-2	*og (Stafa), Bega*
8/3	Tirana	a	0-1	
23/3	Besa	h	2-1	*Dedaj, Brajković*
29/3	Vllaznia	a	0-2	
5/4	Partizani	h	3-0	*Cani, Mema, Guga*
12/4	Dinamo Tirana	a	0-6	
19/4	Besëlidhja	h	0-0	
26/4	Teuta	a	1-1	*Mema*
3/5	Kastrioti	h	1-0	*Mema*
10/5	Skënderbeu	a	4-1	*Brajković 2, Mema, Arifaj*
14/5	Shkumbini	a	0-1	
17/5	Elbasan	h	2-2	*Alves (p), Shabani*

No	Name	Nat	Pos	Aps	(s)	Gls
8	Daniel ALVES	CRO	M	13		1
5	Besmir ARIFAJ		A	5	(4)	1
	Darling BANUSHI		D	1	(1)	
10	Flávio DECO JÚNIOR	BRA	A	16	(4)	2
21	Renaldo BEDINI		D	7	(2)	
6	Halim BEGA		D	25	(3)	1
33	Orjand BEQIRI		D	20	(2)	
13	Parid BERDUFI		G	7	(1)	
25	Mate BRAJKOVIĆ	CRO	A	14	(1)	5
18	Nevian CANI		A	8	(12)	2
	Albano ÇAUSHI		M		(2)	
22	Anton DEDAJ		M	9	(1)	1
12	Abada Narcise FISH	SEN	M	10	(4)	
4	Bledion GUGA		D	25		3
	Aldo GUNA		M		(5)	
	Edom IDRIZI		D	1		
20	Taulant KUQI		D	13	(8)	
1	Flamur KYÇYKU		G	3		
3	Liridon LEÇI		D	12	(1)	
	Faiket LIÇAJ		M		(1)	
18	Arber MALAJ		D	5	(1)	
9	Devis MEMA		A	30		10
24	Shpëtim MOÇKA		G	23		
	Eduart MUÇO		M		(1)	
	Armando MYRTAJ		M		(1)	
	Paulo Robert OLIVEIRA	BRA	M	1		
	Jorge Arturo OROPEZA TORRES	MEX	A		(1)	
13	Branko PANIĆ	CRO	D	29		
7	Arlindo RUSTEMI		M	13	(5)	2
	Artan SAKAJ		D	14		1
	Andi SHABANI		A	1	(1)	1
	Ardit SHEHAJ		A	8	(4)	
14	Ermir STRATI		M	13	(14)	1
11	Franc VELIU		A	15	(9)	2
	Klodian XHELILI		G		(1)	
19	Hajr ZEQIRI		D	22	(4)	1

KS KASTRIOTI

Coach - Ramazan Ndreu; (10/10/07) Vasil Bici; (3/2/08) Ramazan Ndreu

Founded – 1926

2007				
25/8	Besa	a	1-3	*og (Belisha)*
1/9	Elbasan	h	2-0	*Turdiu, Rizvanolli*
15/9	Dinamo Tirana	a	0-4	
23/9	Partizani	h	0-1	
29/9	Shkumbini	a	0-1	*Turdiu (p), Arifaj*
5/10	Besëlidhja	h	2-1	
20/10	Vllaznia	a	1-3	*Ziambo*
31/10	Tirana	a	0-0	
3/11	Teuta	h	1-0	*Shameti*
7/11	Flamurtari	a	0-1	
10/11	Skënderbeu	h	1-0	*Shameti*
25/11	Besa	h	2-1	*Kalari, Rizvanolli*
1/12	Elbasan	a	0-2	
8/12	Dinamo Tirana	h	0-3	
14/12	Partizani	a	1-2	*Rizvanolli*
22/12	Shkumbini	h	0-0	
29/12	Besëlidhja	a	2-1	*Kalari 2*
2008				
2/2	Vllaznia	h	3-1	*Abazaj, Rizvanolli 2*
9/2	Tirana	h	0-3	
16/2	Teuta	a	0-2	
23/2	Flamurtari	h	0-1	
1/3	Skënderbeu	a	0-2	
8/3	Besa	a	0-1	
23/3	Vllaznia	h	0-1	
29/3	Partizani	a	0-0	
5/4	Dinamo Tirana	h	1-0	*Rizvanolli*
12/4	Besëlidhja	a	1-1	*Rizvanolli*
19/4	Teuta	h	0-0	
26/4	Skënderbeu	a	2-0	*Turdiu (p), Rizvanolli*
3/5	Flamurtari	a	0-1	
10/5	Shkumbini	h	1-0	*Rizvanolli*
14/5	Elbasan	a	2-5	*Rizvanolli, Shameti*
17/5	Tirana	h	1-2	*Tali*

No	Name	Nat	Pos	Aps	(s)	Gls
14	Orjand ABAZAJ		A	7		1
21	Besmir ARIFAJ		A	8	(3)	1
	Oltion BALLUKU		D		(1)	
40	Malek Piko BINOGOL	CMR	M	10	(3)	
20	Richard BOKATOLA	CMR	M	12		
6	Julian BRAHJA		D	25	(2)	
77	Florjan BRAHO		M	16	(13)	
21	Sokol BULKU		D	10	(4)	
4	Fatmir CACA		M	15	(8)	
3	Alpin GALLO		D	30		
2	Elton GRAMI		D	30		
	Arjan HASA		D		(1)	
5	Rigers HOXHA		D	10	(4)	
16	Alban HYKA		A	10	(3)	
9	Renaldo KALARI		M	17	(5)	3
12	Arvis KOÇI		G	2		
22	Erind LLESHI		M	1	(8)	
8	Erjol MERXHA		M	13		
1	Arjon MUSTAFA		G	28		
30	James Ogandima OSUSI	CMR	M	18	(9)	
15	Erjon RIZVANOLLI		A	26	(4)	10
7	Shkelzen RUSTAMI		M	23	(2)	
13	Ylli SHAMETI		D	23	(1)	3
30	Helton SHKURTI		A		(1)	
	Olgert STAFA		A	1	(6)	
	Erkan SULEJMANI	MKD	M	1	(2)	
32	Gledis TAFAJ		G	3		
	Sokol TALI		D	1	(2)	1
11	Erald TURDIU		A	20	(3)	3
	Charles UDEKE	CMR	A	1		
	Indrit YMERAJ		D		(2)	
	January ZIAMBO	ZAM	A	2	(4)	1

FK PARTIZANI

Coach - Hasan Lika

Founded – 1945

MAJOR HONOURS: Albanian League – (15) 1947, 1948, 1949, 1954, 1957, 1958, 1959, 1961, 1963, 1964, 1971, 1979, 1981, 1987, 1993; Albanian Cup – (15) 1948, 1949, 1957, 1958, 1961, 1964, 1966, 1968, 1970, 1973, 1980, 1991, 1993, 1997, 2004.

2007				
26/9	Shkumbini	h	2-1	*Abilaliaj, Muzaka (p)*
1/9	Besëlidhja	a	2-1	*og (Alcani), Gjyla*
15/9	Vllaznia	h	1-0	*Bakaj*
23/9	Kastrioti	a	1-0	*Muzaka*
29/9	Teuta	h	4-0	*Muzaka (p), Shkëmbi, Bakaj, Osmani*
6/10	Flamurtari	a	0-0	
20/10	Skënderbeu	h	4-0	*Muzaka, Abilaliaj, Gjyla, Bakaj*
31/10	Besa	a	1-2	*Gjyla*
3/11	Elbasan	h	0-0	
7/11	Dinamo Tirana	a	0-2	
10/11	Tirana	h	0-0	
25/11	Shkumbini	a	1-1	*Bakaj*
1/12	Besëlidhja	h	4-0	*Muzaka 2, Dhëmbi, Abilaliaj*
8/12	Vllaznia	a	1-1	*Bakaj*
14/12	Kastrioti	h	2-1	*Bakaj, Muzaka (p)*

3/12	Teuta	a	1-1	*Beqiri*
9/12	Flamurtari	h	0-0	
2008				
/2	Skënderbeu	a	2-1	*Dhëmbi, Bakaj*
/2	Besa	h	3-3	*Shkëmbi, Dhëmbi, Bakaj*
6/2	Elbasan	a	0-0	
3/2	Dinamo Tirana	h	1-0	*Muzaka*
/3	Tirana	a	4-1	*Osmani, Devolli, Shkëmbi, Abilaliaj*
/3	Besëlidhja	h	1-0	*Muzaka*
3/3	Teuta	a	2-1	*Abilaliaj 2*
9/3	Kastrioti	h	0-0	
/4	Flamurtari	a	0-3	
2/4	Shkumbini	h	2-0	*Dhëmbi, Bakaj*
9/4	Elbasan	a	0-0	
6/4	Tirana	h	2-1	*Dhëmbi, Bakaj*
/5	Besa	a	1-0	*Hallaçi*
0/5	Vllaznia	h	2-0	*Dhëmbi, Bakaj*
4/5	Skënderbeu	h	2-0	*Muzaka, Bakaj*
7/5	Dinamo Tirana	a	1-2	*Osmani*

No	Name	Nat	Pos	Aps	(s)	Gls
1	Arber ABILALIAJ		A	18	(1)	6
	Dritan BABAMUSTA		M	11	(8)	
9	Elis BAKAJ		A	29		12
	Ardit BEQIRI		D	25		1
	Arbër CAPO		D		(2)	
	Alban DASHI		A		(4)	
2	Bledar DEVOLLI		M	21		1
0	Pavlin DHËMBI		M	30	(1)	6
1	Viktor GJYLA		D	24	(8)	3
3	Rahman HALLAÇI		D	31	(2)	1
	Gerard HASMETA		M		(1)	
	Erindo KARABECI		D		(4)	
3	Artan KARAPICI		M	3	(16)	
	Enco MALINDI		A	6	(10)	
7	Gjergji MUZAKA		M	31	(1)	10
	Tefik OSMANI		D	31		3
	Luan PINARI		D	25	(1)	
4	Gerard PROGRI		M	6	(6)	
	Orges SHEHI		G	33		
0	Bledi SHKËMBI		M	22	(3)	3
	Fatjon TAFAJ		M	17	(6)	

KS SHKUMBINI

Coach - Gugash Magani

Founded – 1924

2007				
26/9	Partizani	a	1-2	*Dalipi*
/9	Tirana	a	0-2	
15/9	Besëlidhja	h	2-1	*Stojku 2*
22/9	Vllaznia	a	1-3	*Stojku*
29/9	Kastrioti	h	1-0	*Dalipi*
5/10	Teuta	a	1-1	*Qorri*
20/10	Flamurtari	h	0-0	
31/10	Skënderbeu	a	2-1	*Qorri (p), Dalipi*
3/11	Besa	h	2-0	*Byzhyti (p), Mustafaj*
7/11	Elbasan	a	0-0	
10/11	Dinamo Tirana	h	0-0	
25/11	Partizani	h	1-1	*Qorri (p)*
1/12	Tirana	h	0-2	
8/12	Besëlidhja	a	1-2	*Stojku*
16/12	Vllaznia	h	4-0	*Qorri (p), Stojku 2, Dervishi*
22/12	Kastrioti	a	0-0	
29/12	Teuta	h	2-0	*Xhyra 2*
2008				
2/2	Flamurtari	a	0-0	
9/2	Skënderbeu	h	3-1	*Qorri (p), Nora, Dervishi*
17/2	Besa	a	0-1	
22/2	Elbasan	h	1-0	*Dabulla*
1/3	Dinamo Tirana	a	0-1	
8/3	Elbasan	a	0-1	
23/3	Tirana	h	1-0	*Dalipi*
29/3	Besa	a	0-3	
5/4	Vllaznia	h	3-2	*Dalipi 2, Nora*
12/4	Partizani	a	0-2	
19/4	Dinamo Tirana	h	0-0	
26/4	Besëlidhja	a	2-0	*Mustafaj 2*
3/5	Teuta	h	3-0	*Dalipi, Qorri, Nora*
10/5	Kastrioti	a	0-1	
14/5	Flamurtari	h	1-0	*Dalipi*
17/5	Skënderbeu	a	3-1	*Mustafaj 2, Dalipi*

No	Name	Nat	Pos	Aps	(s)	Gls
12	Kadri BIRJA		G	2		
8	Albano BYZHYTI		M	29	(1)	1
3	Rezart DABULLA		D	25	(1)	1
9	Klevis DALIPI		A	27		9
18	Roland DERVISHI		A	20	(1)	2
	Eljo ELEZI		M	1		
	Arvis GJATA		M	3	(14)	
	Ergys ISMAILI		M		(2)	
	Aleksandar JAKIMOVSKI	MKD	D	6	(9)	
17	Merdian KACOLLJA		D	17	(4)	
	Elidon KAFAZI		D		(1)	
16	Egert KUÇI		M	10	(10)	
1	Ervin LLANI		G	31		
	Emiljan LLUCA		D		(1)	
	Ligor MAÇOLLI		M	1	(3)	
11	Erjon MUSTAFAJ		A	3	(19)	5
4	Laert NDONI		D	26	(7)	
	Astrit NEXHA		M		(7)	
21	Arlind NORA		A	14		3
22	Emeiuru OKWURDILI	NGA	A	5	(1)	
7	Lorenc PASHA		D	32		
21	Saimir PATUSHI		M	6	(3)	
14	Ilir QORRI		A	26		6
2	Alfred SALLIU		D	4	(7)	
5	Fejzo SHENAJ		D	30		
10	Gentian STOJKU		D	16		6
	Ervin SULEJMANI		M		(1)	
15	Klement XHYRA		M	29	(2)	2

KS SKËNDERBEU

Coach - Faruk Sejdini; (10/11/07) Renato Rrapo; (30/11/07) (Shkëlqim Velo); (4/12/07) Renato Rrapo

Founded – 1923

MAJOR HONOURS: Albanian League - (1) 1933.

2007				
25/8	Teuta	h	1-3	*Ngjela*
2/9	Flamurtari	a	1-3	*Tiko (p)*
15/9	Tirana	h	4-2	*Ngjela 3, Tiko*
21/9	Besa	h	1-1	*Ngjela*
29/9	Elbasan	a	0-3	
6/10	Dinamo Tirana	h	1-2	*Tiko (p)*
20/10	Partizani	a	0-4	
31/10	Shkumbini	h	1-2	*Tiko*
3/11	Besëlidhja	a	2-4	*Ngjela, Tiko*
7/11	Vllaznia	h	2-3	*Ngjela, Tiko*
10/11	Kastrioti	a	0-1	
25/11	Teuta	a	2-0	*Ngjela 2*
1/12	Flamurtari	h	1-1	*Larti*
8/12	Tirana	a	2-3	*Çajku, Ngjela*
15/12	Besa	a	0-2	
23/12	Elbasan	h	0-1	
28/12	Dinamo Tirana	a	0-7	

2008				
2/2	Partizani	h	1-2	*Shtupina*
9/2	Shkumbini	a	1-3	*Shtupina (p)*
20/2	Besëlidhja	h	0-2	
23/2	Vllaznia	a	0-2	
1/3	Kastrioti	h	2-0	*Thana 2*
8/3	Dinamo Tirana	a	1-3	*Çajku*
23/3	Elbasan	a	0-4	
29/3	Besëlidhja	h	0-2	
5/4	Tirana	a	0-4	
12/4	Teuta	h	0-2	
19/4	Besa	a	0-1	
26/4	Kastrioti	h	0-2	
3/5	Vllaznia	a	1-2	*Thana*
10/5	Flamurtari	h	1-4	*Shtupina (p)*
14/5	Partizani	a	0-2	
17/5	Shkumbini	h	1-3	*Kokona (p)*

No	Name	Nat	Pos	Aps	(s)	Gls
22	Olgert AMETLLI		G	3	(1)	
9	Vasian BALLÇO		M	6	(1)	
1	Efstrat BILLA		G	8		
11	Endri ÇAJKU		D	19	(1)	2
	Andi CENOLLI		D	1	(2)	
7	Jorgo ÇIPI		D	19	(4)	
17	Elidon DEMIRI		D	14		
14	Daniel DRABAJ		D	17		
	Elsner GEGA		D		(1)	
	El Hadji GOUDJABI	SEN	A	2		
4	Saidi GURI		D	16		
	Rezart HYSO		M	6	(9)	
8	Shpëtim IMERAJ		M	13		
22	Ismaila JAGNE	GAM	A	6	(4)	
	Devis JANI		M	2	(4)	
18	Bruno KEPI		D	13	(1)	
	Denis KITA		D	1	(4)	
	Igli KOKONA		M	1	(4)	1
15	Gentian KOTE		M	13		
16	Ervin KOTOMELO		D	3	(3)	
	Fidel KREKA		D		(3)	
14	Klajdi LARTI		D	15		1
12	Erjon LLAPANJI		G	21		
	Robert MAPOSA	BOT	D	2		
2	Ilirjan MËRTIRI		M	14		
14	Lulëzim META		M	12		
	Eugest NELI		M	1		
10	Mario NGJELA		A	15	(1)	10
3	Andrelis PASHAJ		D	26	(2)	
12	Edi PELLESHI		G	1		
	Fernando Semedo PINHA	POR	M	9		
21	Frensis RRAPO		D	7	(15)	
	Mathens SHOLLA		D		(1)	
21	Ndriçim SHTUPINA		A	15		3
7	Bledar TAFXHAFA		M	8	(1)	
5	Jozef THANA		M	17	(7)	3
20	Ligoraq TIKO		A	20	(1)	6
22	Erjon VUKAJ		M	7	(5)	
	Arlind XAKA		M	7	(2)	
	Endri XHANARI		M	1	(5)	
	Jurgen XHEKA		M	2	(2)	
	Kostika XHOGA		D		(2)	

KS TEUTA

Coach - Hysen Dedja; (1/10/07) Gentian Begeja; (27/11/07) Kristaq Mile

Founded – 1922

MAJOR HONOURS: Albanian League – (1) 1994; Albanian Cup – (3) 1995, 2000, 2005.

2007				
25/8	Skënderbeu	a	3-1	*Hysa 2, Dragusha (p)*
1/9	Besa	h	0-1	
15/9	Elbasan	a	0-1	
22/9	Dinamo Tirana	h	0-1	
29/9	Partizani	a	0-4	
5/10	Shkumbini	h	1-1	*Çota*
21/10	Besëlidhja	a	0-0	
31/10	Vllaznia	h	0-3	
3/11	Kastrioti	a	0-1	
7/11	Tirana	a	1-2	*Haliti*
10/11	Flamurtari	h	3-2	*Haliti, Likmeta, Hysa*
25/11	Skënderbeu	h	0-2	
1/12	Besa	a	1-0	*Gega*
8/12	Elbasan	h	0-1	
15/12	Dinamo Tirana	a	1-2	*Gega*
23/12	Partizani	h	1-1	*Dushku*
29/12	Shkumbini	a	0-2	
2008				
2/2	Besëlidhja	h	2-0	*Mile, Haliti*
9/2	Vllaznia	a	0-2	
16/2	Kastrioti	h	2-0	*Hodo, Gega*
22/2	Tirana	h	0-0	
1/3	Flamurtari	a	2-2	*Hysa, Gega*
8/3	Vllaznia	a	2-1	*Çaushaj, Hodo (p)*
23/3	Partizani	h	1-2	*Mile*
30/3	Dinamo Tirana	a	1-2	*Hysa*
5/4	Besëlidhja	h	2-0	*Pashaj, Mile*
12/4	Skënderbeu	a	2-0	*Mile, Hysa*
19/4	Kastrioti	a	0-0	
26/4	Flamurtari	h	1-1	*Mile (p)*
3/5	Shkumbini	a	0-3	
10/5	Elbasan	h	1-1	*Hodo (p)*
14/5	Tirana	a	2-1	*Çota, Dushku*
17/5	Besa	h	3-5	*Mile 2, Gashi*

No	Name	Nat	Pos	Aps	(s)	Gls
19	Liridon AHMETI		D	22	(1)	
24	Alert ALCANI		M	1	(1)	
20	Edar BËRZEZI		A	8	(5)	
	Albion BLLOKU		A		(3)	
5	Qazim BUNA		M	20	(4)	
29	Ilirjan ÇAUSHAJ		M	14		1
7	Mirel ÇOTA		M	12	(8)	2
1	Henri DAFA		G	1		
	Albi DOSTI		M	1		
11	Muhamet DRAGUSHA		M	5	(4)	1
16	Erjon DUSHKU		D	27	(1)	2
	Enid FURRXHI		D	1		
	Gazmend GASHI		M		(1)	1
28	Ermal GEGA		A	10	(10)	4
55	Genti GJONDEDA		M	15	(2)	
10	Labinot HALITI		M	17	(3)	3
18	Romeo HAMZAJ		A	1	(3)	
7	Burim HASHANI		D	5	(3)	
13	Bledar HODO		D	28		3
	Orjan HOXHA		D	1		
9	Vilfor HYSA		A	22	(8)	6
29	Ismaila JAGNE	GAM	A	4	(4)	
1	Xhevair KAPLLANI		G	22		
8	Oerd KOTJA		M	1	(2)	
14	Vasiljevsk LAMAJ		D	10	(1)	
25	Arben LIKMETA		M	25	(3)	1
	Qazim LUSHAKU		D	1		
23	Vangjell MILE		A	15		7
	Eni NAÇO		G		(1)	
6	Entonio PASHAJ		D	13	(1)	1
15	Gentian SHKOZA		M	1	(4)	
11	Kreshnik SINANI		D		(1)	
28	Shaqir STAFA		A	25	(1)	

No	Name	Nat	Pos	Aps	(s)	Gls
	Renato SULA		M		(1)	
2	Bledar VASHAKU		G	10		
	Erstel VIEROS		D	4	(4)	
7	Emiljano VILA		M	21	(3)	
	Orjand XHEMALI		M		(1)	

KF TIRANA

Coach - Sulejman Starova; (23/9/07) Astrit Hafizi; (3/2/08) Sulejman Mema

Founded – 1920

MAJOR HONOURS: Albanian League – (23) 1930, 1931, 1932, 1934, 936, 1937, 1965, 1966, 1968, 1970, 1982, 1985, 1988, 1989, 1995, 1996, 1997, 1999, 2000, 2003, 2004, 2005, 2007; Albanian Cup – (13) 1939, 963, 1976, 1977, 1983, 1984, 1986, 1994, 1996, 1999, 2001, 2002, 2006.

007				
5/8	Flamurtari	a	0-1	
9	Shkumbini	h	2-0	*Fortuzi (p), Sefa*
5/9	Skënderbeu	a	2-4	*Sefa, Duro*
2/9	Besëlidhja	h	0-1	
0/9	Besa	a	1-3	*Duro*
10	Vllaznia	h	0-0	
0/10	Elbasan	a	1-1	*Duro*
1/10	Kastrioti	h	0-0	
11	Dinamo Tirana	a	2-0	*Sefa, Dede*
11	Teuta	h	2-1	*Xhafa D., Fortuzi*
0/11	Partizani	a	0-0	
5/11	Flamurtari	h	2-0	*Fortuzi, Duro (p)*
12	Shkumbini	a	2-0	*Arapi, Çapja*
12	Skënderbeu	h	3-2	*Arapi, Fortuzi, Xhafa D.*
5/12	Besëlidhja	a	2-0	*Duro, Arapi*
2/12	Besa	h	2-0	*Xhafa D., Duro*
3/12	Vllaznia	a	1-4	*Duro*
008				
2	Elbasan	h	2-2	*Duro 2 (1p)*
2	Kastrioti	a	3-0	*Duro, Fortuzi, Hyka*
5/2	Dinamo Tirana	h	0-0	
2/2	Teuta	a	0-0	
3	Partizani	h	1-4	*Fortuzi*
3	Flamurtari	h	1-0	*Fortuzi*
3/3	Shkumbini	a	0-1	
3/3	Elbasan	h	2-1	*Xhafa D., Hyka*
4	Skënderbeu	h	4-0	*Fagu, Kćira, Duro 2*
2/4	Besa	a	1-2	*Deliallisi*
9/4	Vllaznia	h	5-1	*Xhafa D., Duro 3, Arapi*
5/4	Partizani	a	1-2	*Xhafa D.*
5	Dinamo Tirana	h	1-2	*Xhafa D. (p)*
0/5	Besëlidhja	a	0-1	
4/5	Teuta	h	1-2	*Xhafa D.*
7/5	Kastrioti	a	2-1	*Çapja, Mohellebi*

o	Name	Nat	Pos	Aps	(s)	Gls
4	Orjand ABAZAJ		A	4	(4)	
7	Florenc ARAPI		M	20	(7)	4
9	Egert BAKALLI		D	2	(9)	
3	Hetlen ÇAPJA		M	19	(9)	2
	Nevil DEDE		D	15		1
0	Erald DELIALLISI		M	11	(8)	1
1	Klodian DURO		M	27	(1)	15
5	Erbim FAGU		M	24	(5)	1
1	Indrit FORTUZI		A	17	(1)	7
	Sašo GJOREVSKI	MKD	M	9	(2)	
	Blerti HAJDARI		D		(1)	
6	Gentian HAJDARI		D	14	(4)	
	Jahmir HYKA		M	27	(6)	2
	Berat HYSENI		A	2	(7)	
	Kipjon KAZAZI		M		(1)	
	Lek KĆIRA	CRO	D	13		1
	Klajdi KUKA		G		(1)	
	Eldorado MERKOÇI		M	1	(6)	
14	Laurent MOHELLEBI	FRA	M	12		1
	Fatjon MUHAMETI		A	1		
10	Devi MUKA		M	3		
1	Blendi NALLBANI		G	21		
12	Alfred OSMANI		G	12		
8	Jetmir SEFA		M	13		3
2	Elvis SINA		D	24		
	Ergys SORRA		D		(1)	
24	Endrit VRAPI		D	27		
22	Daniel XHAFA		A	30	(2)	8
5	Erjon XHAFA		D	15	(6)	

KS VLLAZNIA

Coach - Mirel Josa; (8/3/08) Dervis Hadziosmanovic

Founded – 1919

MAJOR HONOURS: Albanian League – (9) 1945, 1946, 1972, 1974, 1978, 1983, 1992, 1998, 2002; Albanian Cup – (6) 1965, 1972, 1979, 1981, 1987, 2008.

2007				
25/8	Elbasan	a	0-0	
1/9	Dinamo Tirana	h	0-1	
15/9	Partizani	a	0-1	
22/9	Shkumbini	h	3-1	*Nora, Lici (p), og (Ndoni)*
28/9	Besëlidhja	a	2-2	*Lici (p), Sukaj*
6/10	Tirana	a	0-0	
20/10	Kastrioti	h	3-1	*Sinani 2, Kaçi*
31/10	Teuta	a	3-0	*Sinani 3*
3/11	Flamurtari	h	1-1	*Lika*
7/11	Skënderbeu	a	3-2	*Sinani, Kaçi, Lika*
10/11	Besa	h	1-1	*Sinani*
25/11	Elbasan	h	2-1	*Sukaj, Sinani*
1/12	Dinamo Tirana	a	0-0	
8/12	Partizani	h	1-1	*Osja*
16/12	Shkumbini	a	0-4	
22/12	Besëlidhja	h	3-0	*Sukaj 2, Sinani (p)*
28/12	Tirana	h	4-1	*Sinani 3, Sukaj*
2008				
2/2	Kastrioti	a	1-3	*Sinani (p)*
9/2	Teuta	h	2-0	*Sukaj, Kaçi*
17/2	Flamurtari	a	2-2	*Sinani, Lika*
23/2	Skënderbeu	h	2-0	*Delain, Jusufi*
1/3	Besa	a	0-1	
8/3	Teuta	h	1-2	*Sukaj*
23/3	Kastrioti	a	1-0	*Sinani*
29/3	Flamurtari	h	2-0	*Sinani 2*
5/4	Shkumbini	a	2-3	*Sinani 2*
12/4	Elbasan	h	0-0	
19/4	Tirana	a	1-5	*Sukaj*
26/4	Besa	h	2-3	*Sinani, Rraboshta*
3/5	Skënderbeu	h	2-1	*Sukaj, Rraboshta*
10/5	Partizani	a	0-2	
14/5	Dinamo Tirana	h	0-3	
17/5	Besëlidhja	a	2-4	*Sukaj (p), Rraboshta*

No	Name	Nat	Pos	Aps	(s)	Gls
8	Franc AHI		D	4	(4)	
	Bekim BALLA		A		(1)	
	Arsen BEQIRI		D	3	(7)	
29	Elvin BEQIRI		D	3	(2)	
12	Olti BISHANI		G	7	(1)	
6	Sasa DELAIN	COD	D	23	(3)	1
	Ilir DIBRA		M		(2)	
	Edmond DOÇI		M	2	(5)	
	Olsi GOÇAJ		M	1		
1	Armir GRIMA		G	26		
	Edom HASANI		M	1	(3)	
13	Arjon HOTI		D	20	(1)	
18	Alban JUSUFI	SWE	A	2	(6)	1

No	Name	Nat	Pos	Aps	(s)	Gls
10	Albert KAÇI		A	30	(1)	3
27	Marenglen KAPAJ		D	27	(2)	
25	Uliks KOTRRI		M	22	(1)	
2	Ervis KRAJA		M	3	(3)	
14	LEANDRO Gil da Silva	BRA	M	3	(8)	
3	Suad LICI		M	23	(3)	2
21	Gilman LIKA		M	28	(2)	3
	Bledar MURATI		M		(1)	
28	Ilir NALLBANI		M	14	(1)	
28	Arlind NORA		A	8	(8)	1
5	Safet OSJA		D	27	(2)	1
	Arlind PIRANAJ		M		(1)	
	Jasmin RRABOSHTA		A	2	(2)	3
9	Vioresin SINANI		A	30		20
11	Xhevair SUKAJ		A	21	(7)	10
29	Simo TANKO	CMR	M	4	(4)	
4	Admir TELI		D	29		
	Erjon VUÇAJ		D		(1)	

PROMOTED CLUBS

KS BYLIS

Coach – Faruk Sejdini

Founded – 1972

KS APOLONIA

Coach – Gjert Haxhiu

Founded – 1925

MAJOR HONOURS: Albanian Cup – (1) 1998.

KS LUSHNJA

Coach – Artan Bano

Founded – 1927

SECOND LEVEL FINAL TABLE 2007/08

		Pld	W	D	L	F	A	Pts
1	KS Bylis	34	23	5	6	70	20	74
2	KS Apolonia	34	23	4	7	70	23	73
3	KS Lushnja	34	22	7	5	57	26	73
4	KS Burreli	34	21	4	9	51	26	67
5	KF Laçi	34	19	9	6	57	29	66
6	KS Ada	34	17	6	11	50	37	57
7	KS Luftëtari	34	14	6	14	48	43	48
8	KF Skrapari	34	15	3	16	39	39	48
9	KS Pogradeci	34	13	6	15	34	32	45
10	KS Dajti	34	12	8	14	37	29	44
11	KS Turbina	34	14	2	18	34	48	44
12	KF Bilisht-Sport	34	13	4	17	37	48	43
13	KS Sopoti	34	13	4	17	30	42	43
14	KF Naftëtari	34	12	4	18	36	51	40
15	KF Erzeni	34	11	6	17	29	42	39
16	KS Tomori	34	8	7	19	29	56	31
17	KF Gramshi	34	9	2	23	28	58	29
18	SK Tepelena	34	2	3	29	22	109	9

PROMOTION/RELEGATION PLAY-OFFS

(24/5/08)
Teuta 2, Burrel 1 (aet)
(25/5/08)
Kastrioti 0, Lushnja 0 *(aet; 2-4 on pens)*

DOMESTIC CUP 2007/0

KUPA E SHQIPËRISË

FIRST ROUND

(27/11/07 & 4/12/07)
Butrinti v Tirana 2-2; 2-4 *(4-6)*
(28/11/07 & 2/12/07)
Tepelena v Skënderbeu 3-2; 0-1 *(3-3; Skënderbeu on away goals)*
(28/11/07 & 4/12/07)
Skrapar v Partizani 0-2; 1-2 *(1-4)*
Bylis v Besa 2-3; 0-3 *(2-6)*
(28/11/07 & 5/12/07)
Iliria v Teuta 1-1; 1-3 *(2-4)*
Naftëtari v Vllaznia 2-3; 1-6 *(3-9)*
Dajti v Dinamo Tirana 0-2; 1-3 *(1-5)*
Tomori v Elbasan 0-0; 2-7 *(2-7)*
Burrel v Kastrioti 3-2; 0-2 *(3-4)*
Ada v Flamurtari 2-0; 1-4 *(3-4)*
Bilisht-Sport v Shkumbini 4-5; 1-3 *(5-8)*
Gramsh v Luftëtari 2-0; 0-6 *(2-6)*
Sopoti v Apolonia 2-1; 0-3 *(2-4)*
Pogradec v Besëlidhja 2-0; 0-8 *(2-8)*
Erzeni v Turbina 1-1; 0-2 *(1-3)*
Laç v Lushnja 3-1; 1-1 *(4-2)*

SECOND ROUND

(13/2/08 & 27/2/08)
Laç v Tirana 1-1; 1-3 *(2-4)*
Turbina v Teuta 0-0; 0-4 *(0-4)*
Besëlidhja v Vllaznia 0-1, 0-0 *(0-1)*
Skënderbeu v Partizani 1-0; 0-5 *(1-5)*
Apolonia v Dinamo Tirana 0-1; 3-3 *(3-4)*
Luftëtari v Besa 1-1; 0-2 *(1-3)*
Shkumbini v Elbasan 2-0; 0-3 *aet (2-3)*
Flamurtari v Kastrioti 1-1; 0-1 *(1-2)*

QUARTER-FINALS

(5/3/08 & 19/3/08)
Kastrioti 0, Tirana 3 *(Duro 45, Xhafa D. 67, Arapi 75)*
Tirana 1 *(Hyka 13)*, Kastrioti 1 *(Rizvanolli 75)*
(Tirana 4-1)

Elbasan 1 *(Nenaj 35)*, Teuta 1 *(Gega 75)*
Teuta 2 *(Hysa 12, Gega 15)*, Elbasan 2 *(Ahmataj 33, Nuhiji Ard. 82)*
(3-3; Elbasani on away goals)

Besa 2 *(Xhihani 33, Lila 75)*, Vllaznia 2 *(Sinani 55, Ramadani 90og)*
Vllaznia 5 *(Delain 23, Kaçi 51, 90+1, Sukaj 63, Jusufi 90+3)*, Besa 1 *(Sha 55p)*
(Vllaznia 7-3)

Dinamo Tirana 3 *(Allmuça 6, Pejić 45, Ishka 72)*, Partizani 1 *(Devolli 89)*
Partizani 0, Dinamo Tirana 0
(Dinamo Tirana 3-1)

SEMI-FINALS

(9/4/08 & 23/4/08)
Vllaznia 4 *(Sinani 3p, Kaçi 7, 21, Sukaj 43)*, Dinamo Tirana 0
Dinamo Tirana 0, Vllaznia 3 *(Bejtja 8og, Bodrusić 83og, Jusufi 90)*
(Vllaznia 7-0)

Elbasan 0, Tirana 3 *(Xhafa D. 71, Duro 73p, 85)*
Tirana 1 *(Duro 48p)*, Elbasan 3 *(Xhafa 44, 89, Nuhiji Ard. 68)*
(Tirana 4-3)

FINAL

(7/5/08)
Ruzhdi Bizhuta stadium, Elbasan
KS VLLAZNIA 2 *(Lika 2, Sukaj 38)*
KF TIRANA 0
Referee – *Rafati*
VLLAZNIA – *Grima, Teli, Lici, Delain, Kapaj, Osja, Kotrri, Kaçi, Nallbani (I 81), Lika, Sukaj.*
TIRANA – *Osmani, Sina (Arapi 46), Kçira, Vrapi (Hajdari G. 46), Deliallisi, hellebi, Duro (Gjorevski 46), Hyka, Fagu, Fortuzi, Xhafa D.*

Cup specialists win the league

C Santa Coloma were Andorra's team of the season in 2007/08. Although their long winning run in the national cup competition, the Copa Constitució, ame to an end, they made up for that disappointment y winning the Primera Divisió title and thus booking iemselves in for the qualifying phase of the UEFA hampions League for the first time.

ı July 2007 Santa Coloma caused a minor sensation /hen they became the first Andorran club to win a ıatch in European club competition, defeating ʻlaccabi Tel-Aviv FC 1-0 in the home leg of the UEFA up first qualifying round. Although they went own 4-0 in Israel, veteran Andorran international uli Fernández's 57th-minute winner created a iece of history for the tiny mountain nation and lso allowed his team to steal much of the ıunder from local rivals FC Rànger's, who were etting their own milestone by becoming the first lub from Andorra to compete in the UEFA hampions League (they lost 5-0 on aggregate to ʻloldovan champions FC Sheriff).

anta Coloma triumphant

laving sampled UEFA's flagship competition once, ànger's were keen to do so again, but Santa oloma led them by three points at the 14-match cut-off point with an unbeaten record, and although the situation remained tight throughout the play-off phase, with UE Sant Julià also involved, it was the 2007/08 runners-up who triumphed this time, clinching their first title in four years with a match to spare.

It was a stoppage-time equaliser from Xavier Gil in Santa Coloma's penultimate fixture, at home to Rànger's, that brought his team a 2-2 draw and the point they needed – with Sant Julià simultaneously losing 4-2 at home to FC Lusitans – to take the title for the fourth time. The triumph tasted particularly sweet

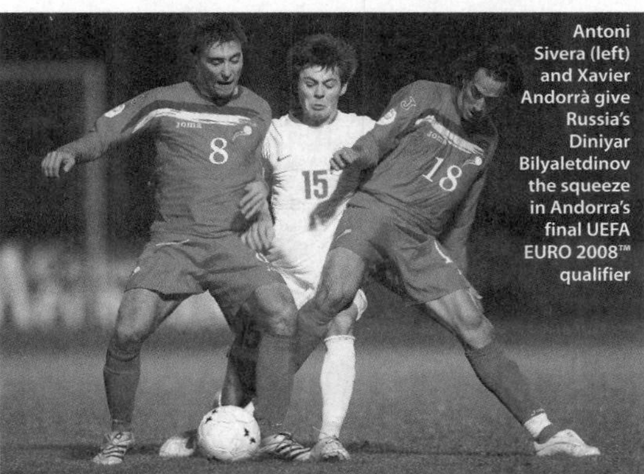
Antoni Sivera (left) and Xavier Andorrà give Russia's Diniyar Bilyaletdinov the squeeze in Andorra's final UEFA EURO 2008™ qualifier

Federació Andorrana de Futbol (FAF)

Avinguda Carlemany, 67 3° pis
Apartado postal 65
AD-Escaldes-Engordany
tel – +376 805830
fax – +376 862006
website – www.fedandfut.com
email – info@fedandfut.com
Year of Formation – 1994
President – Francesc Amat Escobar
Secretary – Tomás Gea

Stadium - Comunal, Andorra la Vella (1,604)

TOP FIVE ALL-TIME CAPS
Oscar Sonejee (74); Jesús Álvarez "Koldo" (71); José Manuel García Txema (68); Justo Ruíz (67); Juli Sánchez (60)

TOP FIVE ALL-TIME GOALS
Ildefons Lima (5); Jesús Julián Lucendo (3); Juli Sánchez, Justo Ruiz, Fernando Silva & Emiliano González (2)

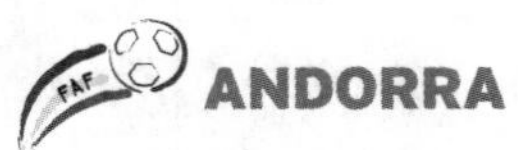

ANDORRA

NATIONAL TEAM RESULTS 2007/08

22/8/07	Estonia (ECQ)	A	Tallinn	1-2	*Silva (82)*
12/9/07	Croatia (ECQ)	H	Andorra la Vella	0-6	
17/10/07	FYR Macedonia (ECQ)	A	Skopje	0-3	
17/11/07	Estonia (ECQ)	H	Andorra la Vella	0-2	
21/11/07	Russia (ECQ)	H	Andorra la Vella	0-1	
26/3/08	Latvia	H	Andorra la Vella	0-3	
4/6/08	Azerbaijan	H	Andorra la Vella	1-2	*Lima I. (51)*

NATIONAL TEAM APPEARANCES 2007/08

Coach – David RODRIGO (ESP) 8/5/68			**EST**	**CRO**	**MKD**	**EST**	**RUS**	**Lva**	**Aze**	**Caps**	**Go**
Jesús Álvarez "KOLDO"	4/9/70	FC Andorra (ESP)	G	G	G	G	G46	G46	s46	71	-
José Manuel García TXEMA	4/12/74	FC Andorra (ESP)	D	D		D46		s46	s46	68	-
Oscar SONEJEE	26/3/76	FC Andorra (ESP)	D	D	D	M	D83	D85	D	74	1
Antoni LIMA	22/9/70	Eivissa (ESP)	D	D		D	D	D	D	57	-
Ildefons LIMA	10/12/79	Triestina (ITA)	D		D	D81	D	D	D83	52	5
Jordi ESCURA	19/4/80	Benavent (ESP)	M		M	D	D	D46	D46	52	-
José Manuel AYALA	8/4/80	FC Santa Coloma	M90	D	D	M		M89	M	36	-
Marc PUJOL	21/8/82	Manresa (ESP)	M80		M	M			s62	35	1
Antoni SIVERA	13/4/78	Campello (ESP)	M53	M59		M	M			23	-
Marcio VIEIRA	10/10/80	Teruel (ESP)	M	M	M	M	M50	M	M	17	-
Fernando SILVA	16/5/77	Imperio Mérida (ESP)	A	A57						20	2
Juan Carlos TOSCANO	14/8/84	FC Santa Coloma /Gimnástico Alcázar (ESP)	s53		A82	s70		A52	A68	11	-
Juli SÁNCHEZ	20/6/78	FC Andorra (ESP)	s80							60	2
Genís GARCÍA	18/5/78	FC Santa Coloma	s90	M				M46		34	-
Justo RUÍZ	31/8/69	Rànger's		M82	M63	s81	M	M52		67	2
Manolo JIMÉNEZ	12/8/76	FC Andorra (ESP)		M	M78	s46	M	M70	M	57	1
Sergi MORENO	25/11/87	Gimnástico Alcázar (ESP)		s57		A70	A	s52	A62	17	-
Xavier ANDORRÀ	7/6/85	Gimnástico Alcázar (ESP)		s59	s63		s50	s46	M77	8	-
Álex SOMOZA	7/7/86	Rànger's		s82	s78			s85		5	-
Juli FERNÁNDEZ	19/11/74	FC Santa Coloma			D					34	1
Gabriel RIERA	5/6/85	Gimnástico Alcázar (ESP)			s82		s83	s52	s68	13	1
Marc BERNAUS	2/2/77	Ejido (ESP)					D			15	1
José Antonio GÓMES	3/12/86	Eivissa (ESP)					s46	s46	G46	4	-
Víctor HUGO Moreira	5/10/82	Rànger's						s70		1	-
Marc VALES	4/4/90	Sabadell (ESP)						s89	s77	2	-
Emili GARCÍA	11/1/89	FC Andorra (ESP)							s83	1	-

DOMESTIC LEAGUE 2007/08

MERA DIVISIÓ FINAL TABLES

-OFFS

npionship Group	Pld	W	D	L	F	A	Pts
FC Santa Coloma	20	14	5	1	69	10	44
UE Sant Julià	20	12	5	3	59	19	41
FC Rànger's	20	12	4	4	47	30	40
FC Lusitans	20	10	1	9	44	29	31

gation Group	Pld	W	D	L	F	A	Pts
CE Principat	20	9	3	8	33	37	30
Inter Club d'Escaldes	20	6	2	12	23	37	20
UE Engordany	20	4	1	15	21	79	13
SE Casa del Benfica	20	2	1	17	13	68	7

T PHASE

	Pld	W	D	L	F	A	Pts
FC Santa Coloma	14	11	3	0	58	4	36
FC Rànger's	14	10	3	1	37	16	33
UE Sant Julià	14	9	3	2	46	11	30
FC Lusitans	14	9	0	5	34	13	27
CE Principat	14	5	2	7	20	33	17
UE Engordany	14	3	1	10	17	61	10
Inter Club d'Escaldes	14	2	1	11	11	32	7
SE Casa del Benfica	14	0	1	13	4	57	1

League splits into two groups of four after 14 matches.

or Santa Coloma coach Vicenç Marguès, Rànger's' hampionship-winning coach two years previously.

anta Coloma were still on for the double at that stage, ut the team that had won the Copa Constitució five ears running had their stranglehold on the ompetition released in dramatic fashion. An 86th-ninute goal from Juli Fernández appeared to have iven Santa Coloma a semi-final win, but opponents usitans struck a late equaliser and went on to win the natch 4-3 on penalties. As Santa Coloma's two previous up final victories had been achieved via shoot-out uccesses, they could hardly complain. Nevertheless, heir sense of regret was magnified six days later when usitans were thrashed 6-1 in the final by Sant Julià.

lo goals at home

s expected, Andorra concluded their UEFA EURO 008™ campaign with five straight defeats, thus naintaining their unwanted record of never having laimed a point in UEFA European Championship ualification. The team's failure to score a single goal in ix home games was particularly hard to swallow.

SECOND LEVEL FINAL TABLE

		Pld	W	D	L	F	A	Pts
1	UE Santa Coloma	16	14	2	0	66	11	44
2	UE Extremenya	16	14	0	2	42	13	42
3	FC Encamp	16	9	3	4	38	14	30
4	FC Lusitans B	16	7	2	7	39	30	23
5	CE Principat B	16	6	0	10	35	39	18
6	Atlètic Club d'Escaldes	16	5	2	9	30	33	17
7	FC Rànger's B	16	4	3	9	24	48	15
8	Sporting Club d'Escaldes	16	4	0	12	33	66	12
9	Inter Club d'Escaldes B	16	2	2	12	17	70	8

PROMOTION/RELEGATION PLAY-OFFS

(18/5/08)
Engordany 2, Extremenya 3
(25/5/08)
Extremenya 0, Engordany 3
(Engordany 5-3)

DOMESTIC CUP 2007/08

COPA CONSTITUCIÓ

SECOND ROUND

(27/1/08)
Rànger's B 1, Principat 5
Extremenya 7, Casa Benfica 1
Atlètic Escaldes 0, Inter Escaldes 3
UE Santa Coloma 1, Engordany 2
Byes – FC Santa Coloma, Rànger's, Sant Julià, Lusitans

QUARTER-FINALS

(6/2/08)
Principat 1, FC Santa Coloma 2

(10/2/08)
Inter Escaldes 1, Rànger's 2
Extremenya 0, Sant Julià 6
Engordany 0, Lusitans 1

SEMI-FINALS

(18/5/08)
Sant Julià 6 *(Alejandro Romero 19p, Fabrizio 23, 40, 90, Xinos 55, Yael 73)*, Rànger's 1 *(Justo Ruiz 88p)*
Lusitans 1 *(Riera 90)*, Santa Coloma 1 *(Juli Fernàndez 86) (aet; 4-3 on pens)*

FINAL

(24/5/08)
Aixovall stadium, Andorra la Vella
UE SANT JULIÀ 6 *(Xinos 23, Alejandro Romero 36, 53, 60, 86, Juan 90)*
FC LUSITANS 1 *(Franklin 5)*
Referee – *Chato*
SANT JULIÀ – *Tremonti, Walter, Diego (Luis 77), Yael, Xinos, Alejandro Romero (Pablo 88), Edu (Juan 86), Maxi, Valentin, Fabrizio, Varela.*
LUSITANS – *Perlanes, Leonel, Hugo Freitas (Joel 64), Ricardo, Pardal, Franklin, Baixinho, Pinto (Maurício 79), Filipe (Nuno 67), Riera, Luís.*

Pyunik pressed all the way

FC Pyunik were duly crowned champions of Armenia for the seventh successive year, but, unlike many of their previous triumphs, it was no easy romp to the 2007 Premier League title for the Yerevan-based club.

Pyunik collected 16 points fewer than they had managed in 2006 – 57 to 73 – and were challenged strongly by three other teams – FC Banants, FC MIKA and the country's most prominent club in Soviet times, FC Ararat Yerevan. Indeed, Ararat were firm favourites to lift their first national title for 14 years until they disintegrated in the run-in, losing to each of their title rivals in successive matches. The third of them, a 4-1 defeat at Pyunik, enabled the defending champions to retain their title with a game to spare, while Ararat ended up a disappointing fourth behinc runners-up Banants and third-placed MIKA.

Levon Pachajyan (left), the 2007 Armenian Footballer of the Year, in UEFA EURO 2008™ qualifying action against Serbia

Pyunik prevailed despite losing a quarter of their Premier League matches. Coach Samvel Petrosyan, the man who had overseen their procession to the 2006 title, resigned after only four games, apparently in disagreement with the club's policy of promoting youngsters from their academy in place of more established players. He was replaced by his assistant and national Under-19 boss – Armen Gyulbudaghyants who, despite the odd hiccup including a potentially disastrous 3-0 home defeat b Banants in early October, managed to keep Pyunik o a steady course. Thoroughbred skipper Sargis Hovsepyan, Armenia's most capped international, proved a calming influence on the colts around him, while 24-year-old midfielder Levon Pachajyan enjoye a splendid season, embellished with ten league goal and, ultimately, the title of 2007 Armenian Footballer of the Year.

Exodus abroad

Pachajyan was one of several Pyunik stalwarts to par company with the club after that seventh straight titl had been secured. While he left for Swedish Allsvenskan club GAIS of Gothenburg, his fellow Armenian internationals Alexander Tadevosyan and Robert Arzumanyan departed, respectively, for Belarus and Denmark.

The thinning of resources at Pyunik offered hope for others to end the club's hegemony in 2008, and a firs indication of the sea change came in the Armenian Cup where Pyunik, having struggled to overcome FC Gandzasar Kapan on penalties in the quarter-finals, were routed 5-1 on aggregate in the semis by Ararat. The latter went on to win the final, beating holders Banants 2-1 after extra time in Idjevan and thus securing themselves a UEFA Cup berth in 2008/09. Banants, as league runners-up, were already guaranteed a UEFA Cup spot, but Ararat's win

emoted MIKA, third in the league, to the UEFA ıtertoto Cup.

rarat's Cup final match-winner was none other than ıeir imported Brazilian playmaker/striker Marcos Pizelli, ıe top scorer in the 2007 Premier League with 22 goals seven of them against bottom club FC Kilikia, who ırvived relegation only because there was no club om the second level ready to take their place. Marcos, 3, was to take out Armenian citizenship and make a oalscoring debut for the Armenian national team, gainst Moldova, a few weeks after his Cup final heroics.

ıe man who gave Marcos his debut in that 2-2 draw in hisinau was Jan B. Poulsen, the Dane newly appointed ; Armenia's national team coach. An assistant to chard Møller-Nielsen when Denmark won Euro '92, the 2-year-old was handed the job despite his confession ıat he knew very little about Armenian football having atched them play on only a couple of occasions.

Porterfield passes away

Poulsen was the permanent replacement for Ian Porterfield, who sadly died from cancer the previous September while Armenia were still engaged in UEFA EURO 2008™ qualifying. The Scotsman's final game in charge was a highly creditable 1-1 draw at home to Portugal, which came on the back of two memorable wins against Kazakhstan and Poland. The team were clearly shocked and disrupted by Porterfield's untimely death and ended the campaign poorly under the temporary stewardship of his erstwhile assistants Tom Jones and Vardan Minasyan, failing to score in each of their last four matches and losing 1-0 at home to Kazakhstan in their final fixture to end up seventh in the eight-team Group A, ahead only of neighbours Azerbaijan – against whom they had not competed, home or away, due to the inability of the two associations to reach a compromise over political and security issues.

Hayastani Futboli Federacia (HFF)

Khanjyan Street 27
AM-0010 Yerevan
tel - +374 10 568883
fax - +374 10 547173
website – www.ffa.am
email - media@ffa.am
Year of Formation – 1992
President – Ruben Hayrapetyan
General Secretary - Armen Minasyan
Press Officer – George Matevosyan
Stadium - Republican, Yerevan (14,935)

TOP FIVE ALL-TIME CAPS
Sargis Hovsepyan (97); Artur Petrosyan (69); Harutyun Vardanyan (63); Hamlet Mkhitaryan (55); Armen Shahgeldyan & Romik Khachatryan (53)

TOP FIVE ALL-TIME GOALS
Artur Petrosyan (11); Armen Shahgeldyan (6); Ara Hakobyan & Arman Karamyan (5); Tigran Yesayan (4)

ATIONAL TEAM RESULTS 2007/08

/07	Portugal (ECQ)	H	Yerevan	1-1	*Arzumanyan (11)*
/07	Cyprus	A	Akhnas	1-3	*Arzumanyan (35)*
/07	Malta	A	Ta' Qali	1-0	*Voskanyan (29)*
0/07	Serbia (ECQ)	H	Yerevan	0-0	
0/07	Belgium (ECQ)	A	Brussels	0-3	
1/07	Portugal (ECQ)	A	Leiria	0-1	
1/07	Kazakhstan (ECQ)	H	Yerevan	0-1	
/08	Kazakhstan	N	Rotterdam (NED)	1-0	*Manucharyan (65)*
/08	Moldova	A	Tiraspol	2-2	*Marcos (25), Pachajyan (74)*
)8	Greece	N	Offenbach (GER)	0-0	

ARMENIA

NATIONAL TEAM APPEARANCES 2007/08

			POR	Cyp	Mlt	SRB	BEL	POR	KAZ	Kaz	Mda	Gre	Caps
Coach – Ian PORTERFIELD (SCO)		**11/2/46**											
/(30/9/07) Tom JONES (ENG)		**7/10/64**											
/(15/11/07) Vardan MINASYAN		**5/1/74**											
/(24/1/08) Jan B. POULSEN (DEN)		**23/3/46**											
Roman BEREZOVSKI	15/8/74	Khimki (RUS)	G			G		G	G				51
Alexander TADEVOSYAN	9/8/80	Pyunik	D	D	D	D	D82	D	D				
		/Vitebsk (BLR)								D	D	D	31
Sargis HOVSEPYAN	2/11/72	Pyunik	D	D	D	D	D	D	D	D	D	D	97
Robert ARZUMANYAN	24/7/85	Pyunik	D	D	D	D	D	D	D				
		/Randers (DEN)								D	D	D	27
Aghvan MKRTCHYAN	27/2/81	Pyunik	D	D65	s68		s82	s76		M	D	D	28
Ararat ARAKELYAN	1/2/84	Banants	M	M67	M	M	M	M	M56				
		/Metalurh Donetsk (UKR)								s46	M	M	13
Levon PACHAJYAN	20/9/83	Pyunik	M	M	M75	M	M	M	M				
		/GAIS (SWE)								M	M	M	22
Artur VOSKANYAN	13/8/76	Ararat	M	M	M	M70	M	M	M80				
		/Vitebsk (BLR)								M46	M	M	42
Hamlet MKHITARYAN	24/11/73	Rah-Ahan (IRN)	M59			M82		s59	M	M67	M74	M65	55
Artavazd KARAMYAN	14/11/79	Poli Timişoara (ROU)	M70	M		M	M	M76	M				40
Samvel MELKONYAN	15/3/84	Banants	A90	A82	A70	A62	A70	A63	A59				
		/Metalurh Donetsk (UKR)									A46	s60	19
Gevorg GHAZARYAN	5/4/88	Pyunik	s59							s46	s46	A60	5
		/Banants							s80				
Yeghishe MELIKYAN	13/8/79	Banants	s70	s65	M68								30
Romik KHACHATRYAN	23/8/78	Unirea (ROU)	s90										
		/Univ Cluj (ROU)		s67		s70	M57	M59	s56				
		/APOP (CYP)								M70			53
Mayis AZIZYAN	1/5/78	Ulis		G									1
Arman KARAMYAN	14/11/79	Poli Timişoara (ROU)		A77									37
Ara HAKOBYAN	4/11/80	Zimbru (MDA)		s77	A82	s82				s66	s63	s54	38
Arsen AVETISYAN	8/10/73	Pyunik		s82	s70								25
Felix HAKOBYAN	11/3/81	MIKA			G								1
Karen DOKHOYAN	6/11/76	Pyunik			D	D	D	D	D				45
Vahagn MINASYAN	25/4/85	Ararat			s75								3
Artur H. MINASYAN	4/6/77	Ararat			s82						s74	s65	9
Robert ZEBELYAN	31/3/84	Khimki (RUS)				s62	s70						4
Gevorg KASPAROV	25/7/80	Rah-Ahan (IRN)					G			G	G	G	12
Aram HAKOBYAN	15/8/79	Banants					s57						16
Edgar MANUCHARYAN	19/1/87	Ajax (NED)						s63	s59	A66			15
Karlen MKRTCHYAN	25/11/88	Pyunik								D46			1
Henrik MKHITARYAN	21/1/89	Pyunik								s67			3
Karen ALEKSANYAN	17/9/80	Banants								s70			20
MARCOS Pizelli	3/10/84	Ararat									A63	A54	2

DOMESTIC LEAGUE 2007

EMIER LEAGUE FINAL TABLE

	Pld	Home W	D	L	F	A	Away W	D	L	F	A	Total W	D	L	F	A	Pts
C Pyunik	28	9	1	4	29	13	9	2	3	29	9	18	3	7	58	22	57
C Banants	28	9	1	4	25	10	7	3	4	31	16	16	4	8	56	26	52
C MIKA	28	8	4	2	30	15	6	4	4	12	9	14	8	6	42	24	50
C Ararat Yerevan	28	9	2	3	25	20	6	2	6	24	22	15	4	9	49	42	49
C Gandzasar Kapan	28	6	4	4	18	12	5	2	7	17	19	11	6	11	35	31	39
C Shirak	28	5	4	5	12	14	4	3	7	15	23	9	7	12	27	37	34
C Ulisses Yerevan	28	4	2	8	12	20	4	4	6	9	26	8	6	14	21	46	30
C Kilikia	28	0	2	12	5	38	1	0	13	5	32	1	2	25	10	70	5

lo relegation.

TOP GOALSCORERS

22 MARCOS Pizelli Pinheiro (Ararat)
15 Arsen BALABEKYAN (Banants)
12 Henrikh MKHITARYAN (Pyunik)
Gevorg GHAZARYAN (Pyunik/Banants)
10 Samvel MELKONYAN (Banants)
Levon PACHAJYAN (Pyunik)
8 Artur KOCHARYAN (Gandzasar)
ALEX Henrique da Silva (MIKA)
7 Ivan RISTICH (MIKA)
Artyom BERNETSYAN (Shirak)

CLUB-BY-CLUB

FC ARARAT YEREVAN

Coach – Varuzhan Sukiasyan; (20/4/07) Dušan Mijić (SRB)

Founded – 1935

MAJOR HONOURS: USSR League – (1) 1973; Armenian League – (1) 993; USSR Cup - (2) 1973, 1975; Armenian Cup – (5) 1993, 1994, 1995, 1997, 2008.

07

'4	Gandzasar	a	0-1	
'4	Kilikia	h	5-0	*Renato, Marcos 3, Movsisyan*
/4	Shirak	a	1-0	*Marcos (p)*
5	Pyunik	h	0-0	
'5	Banants	a	0-1	
'5	MIKA	h	2-0	*Minasyan A., Mehrabyan*
/5	Ulisses	h	2-0	*Marcos 2*
5	Gandzasar	h	1-0	*Marcos (p)*
'6	Kilikia	a	4-0	*Marcos 2 (1p), Movsisyan 2*
'6	Shirak	h	1-0	*Erzrumyan N.*
'	Pyunik	a	4-3	*Marcos 2, Hovhannisyan H., Mehrabyan*
'	MIKA	a	2-2	*Simonyan, Marcos*
'7	Ulisses	a	3-0	*Marcos, Minasyan V., Erzrumyan N.*
'7	Banants	h	2-1	*Marcos 2 (1p)*
3	Gandzasar	a	1-2	*Emílio*
'8	Kilikia	h	2-1	*Renato 2*
'8	Shirak	a	2-0	*Erzrumyan N., Marcos*
/8	Pyunik	h	0-6	
)	Banants	h	0-6	
'9	MIKA	a	1-4	*Marcos*
'9	Ulisses	h	0-0	
'9	Gandzasar	h	5-4	*Erzrumyan N. 2, Minasyan V., Nranyan 2*
0	Kilikia	a	3-1	*Erzrumyan N., Marcos 2 (1p)*
0	Shirak	h	4-0	*Marcos 2 (1p), Erzrumyan S., Sargsyan (p)*
'10	Banants	a	0-2	
1	MIKA	h	1-2	*Petrosyan A.*
1	Pyunik	a	1-4	*Minasyan V.*
'11	Ulisses	a	2-2	*Nranyan, Marcos*

No	Name	Nat	Pos	Aps	(s)	Gls
17	Petar ASTERIĆ	SRB	A	1	(6)	
24	Armen BABAYAN		M	1	(5)	
19	BAIANO	BRA	M	1	(2)	
12	EMÍLIO Palucci Calcani	BRA	M	7	(4)	1
10	Nshan ERZRUMYAN		A	14	(1)	6
9	Sergei ERZRUMYAN		M	11	(4)	1
21	Grigor GRIGORYAN		D	2	(5)	
22	Mkhitar GRIGORYAN		M	2	(2)	
4	Hovhannes HARUTYUNYAN		D	15		
1	Garnik HOVHANNISYAN		G	12		
14	Harutyun HOVHANNISYAN		A	3	(8)	1
6	LUÍS Ricardo Bernardes	BRA	D	2	(1)	
15	MARCOS Pizelli Pinheiro		M	26		22
20	Vahe MEHRABYAN		D	20	(5)	2
7	Artur H. MINASYAN		M	26	(1)	1
19	Vahagn MINASYAN		D	25	(1)	3
5	Hrayr MKOYAN		D	24		
2	Sargis MOVSISYAN		A	3	(10)	3
17	Gevorg NRANYAN		A	5	(10)	3
18	Artur PETROSYAN		M	19	(1)	1
16	Gevorg PRAZYAN		G		(1)	
3	RENATO de Morães	BRA	A	25	(1)	3
16	Nikolay SARGSYAN		G	16		1
11	Gagik SIMONYAN		M	14	(2)	1
12	Andranik TADEVOSYAN		M		(6)	
22	Ara VOSKANYAN		D	9	(1)	
8	Artur VOSKANYAN		M	24		
21	Slavko VUČKOVIĆ	SRB	A	1	(1)	

FC BANANTS

Coach – Jan Poštulka (CZE); (25/8/07) Nikolai Kostov (BUL)

Founded – 1992

MAJOR HONOURS: Armenian Cup – (2) 1992, 2007.

2007

14/4	Shirak	a	0-0	
22/4	Pyunik	h	1-2	*Grigoryan A.*
26/4	Ulisses	h	2-0	*Butenko, Melkonyan*
5/5	MIKA	a	1-1	*Muradyan*
14/5	Ararat	h	1-0	*Simonyan*
19/5	Gandzasar	a	1-0	*Muradyan*
24/5	Kilikia	h	3-0	*Melikyan, Balabekyan, Muradyan*
9/6	Shirak	h	3-0	*Balabekyan 2, Bareghamyan*

14/6	Pyunik	a	1-5	*Melikyan*
18/6	Ulisses	a	3-2	*Grigoryan H., Melkonyan 2*
23/6	MIKA	h	1-1	*Hakobyan Ara (p)*
8/7	Gandzasar	h	2-3	*Jenebyan 2*
14/7	Kilikia	a	3-0	*Hakobyan Ara 2, Balabekyan*
26/7	Ararat	a	1-2	*Balabekyan*
6/8	Shirak	a	1-1	*Hakobyan Ara (p)*
12/8	Pyunik	h	2-1	*Hakobyan Aram 2*
17/8	Ulisses	h	1-2	*Melikyan (p)*
1/9	Ararat	a	6-0	*Ghazaryan G. 3, Balabekyan 2, Jenebyan*
18/9	Gandzasar	h	3-0	*Arakelyan, Balabekyan, Ghazaryan G.*
23/9	Kilikia	h	2-0	*Ghazaryan G. (p), Balabekyan*
26/9	MIKA	a	2-0	*Melkonyan, Balabekyan*
29/9	Shirak	h	2-0	*Balabekyan, Hakobyan Aram (p)*
3/10	Pyunik	a	3-0	*Melkonyan 2, Balabekyan*
7/10	Ulisses	a	1-2	*Hakobyan Aram (p)*
26/10	Ararat	h	2-0	*Melkonyan 2*
4/11	Gandzasar	a	2-3	*Melkonyan, Muradyan*
7/11	MIKA	h	0-1	
10/11	Kilikia	a	6-0	*Balabekyan 3, Ghazaryan G., Khachatryan, Melkonyan*

No	Name	Nat	Pos	Aps	(s)	Gls
17	Ararat ARAKELYAN		D	26		1
11	Arsen BALABEKYAN		A	21	(7)	15
19	Aram BAREGHAMYAN		M	7	(15)	1
6	Andriy BURDIAN	UKR	D	11		
12	Roman BUTENKO	UKR	M	4	(3)	1
15	Andriy CHEREVKO	UKR	D	23		
19	Gagik DAGHBASHYAN		M		(1)	
19	Artak DASHYAN		M		(2)	
14	Gevorg GHAZARYAN		A	18	(5)	6
16	Stepan GHAZARYAN		G		(2)	
19	Ashot GRIGORYAN		M	3		1
20	Hovhannes GRIGORYAN		D	23	(1)	1
18	Norayr GYOZALYAN		A		(3)	
23	Ara HAKOBYAN		A	4	(1)	4
25	Aram Kh. HAKOBYAN		A	7	(3)	4
4	Aghvan HAYRAPETYAN		M		(12)	
3	Jan JELÍNEK	CZE	D	10		
7	Romeo JENEBYAN		M	25		3
8	Edvard KAKOSYAN		M	4	(5)	
24	Sargis KARAPETYAN		M	1	(15)	
12	Noa KASULE	UGA	M	12	(1)	
12	Ara E. KHACHATRYAN		M	5	(3)	1
10	Yeghishe MELIKYAN		M	22		3
21	Samvel MELKONYAN		M	23	(1)	10
14	Semyon MURADYAN		M	10	(11)	4
16	Dmitri PYVAVORENKO	RUS	G	7		
1	Nenad RADAČA	SRB	G	21		
25	Suren SARGSYAN		M	1	(3)	
5	Karen SIMONYAN		D	20	(4)	1

FC GANDZASAR KAPAN

Coach – Suren Barseghyan; (1/5/07) Abraham Khashmanyan; (13/6/07) Samvel Petrosyan

Founded - 2004

2007

14/4	Ararat	h	1-0	*Kocharyan*
21/4	Ulisses	a	2-0	*Khachatryan K., Davtyan*
27/4	Kilikia	a	0-0	
5/5	Shirak	h	0-0	
13/5	Pyunik	a	0-1	
19/5	Banants	h	0-1	
23/5	MIKA	a	2-3	*Davtyan, Kocharyan*
9/6	Ararat	a	0-1	
14/6	Ulisses	h	0-0	
18/6	Kilikia	h	2-0	*Safaryan E. 2*
24/6	Shirak	a	0-0	
1/7	Pyunik	h	0-1	
8/7	Banants	a	3-2	*Tbilashvili, Petrosyan Manucharyan E.*
14/7	MIKA	h	0-2	
5/8	Ararat	h	2-1	*Davtyan, Manuchrya B.*
12/8	Ulisses	a	1-0	*Manucharyan B.*
15/8	Kilikia	a	2-0	*Kocharyan, Manucharyan B.*
26/8	Shirak	h	4-2	*Kocharyan 3 (1p), Davtyan*
1/9	Pyunik	a	2-1	*Kocharyan, Tbilashvil*
18/9	Banants	a	0-3	
23/9	MIKA	h	1-1	*Kocharyan*
29/9	Ararat	a	4-5	*Manucharyan B., Paunescu, Safaryan E Alexanyan*
3/10	Ulisses	h	1-2	*Marşavela*
7/10	Kilikia	h	4-0	*Petrosyan A. 2, Stepanyan, Davtyan*
21/10	Shirak	a	1-2	*Tbilashvili*
26/10	Pyunik	h	0-0	
4/11	Banants	h	3-2	*Safaryan E., Stepanya Alexanyan*
10/11	MIKA	a	0-1	

No	Name	Nat	Pos	Aps	(s)	Gls
6	Valeri ALEXANYAN		D	20	(1)	2
14	Hayrapet AVAGYAN		M		(2)	
12	Garik BOYAKHCHYAN		G	4	(1)	
1	Levan BUBETEISHVILI	GEO	G	2		
6	Vahe DAVTYAN		M	13	(12)	5
16	Mihai DOBRE	ROU	D		(1)	
19	Alexandru GAVRILOAE	ROU	M	1	(1)	
17	Arman GRIGORYAN		M		(2)	
3	Vakhtang HAKOBYAN	GEO	D	4		
15	Ara R. KHACHATRYAN		D	12	(2)	
25	Karen N. KHACHATRYAN		M	6	(1)	1
10	Artur KOCHARYAN		A	24		8
9	Beniamin MANUCHARYAN		M	17	(4)	4
5	Edik MANUCHARYAN		A	1	(8)	1
8	Virgil MARŞAVELA	ROU	M	9	(1)	1
22	Gurgen MELIKSETYAN	RUS	A	8	(3)	
16	David OHANYAN		M		(1)	
9	Artak OSEYAN		M	13	(4)	
10	Constantin PAUNESCU	ROU	A	6	(1)	1
2	Armen PETROSYAN		D	25	(1)	3
17	Vardan K. PETROSYAN		M	2	(6)	
20	Edgar SAFARYAN		A	11	(13)	4
3	Rafayel SAFARYAN		D	7	(3)	
7	Andranik SARGSYAN		A	1	(4)	
19	Edward SHAHNAZARYAN		M		(2)	
24	Vladimir STEPANYAN		D	17	(4)	2
13	Armen TATINTSYAN		D	26	(1)	
8	Gaga TBILASHVILI	GEO	A	25	(2)	3
7	Armen TIGRANYAN		M	5	(3)	
5	Hakob TUMBARYAN		M	1	(1)	
11	Karen YEGHIAZARYAN		D		(2)	
1	Edik YERITSYAN		G	22		
4	Karen ZAKARYAN		D	26	(1)	

FC KILIKIA

Coach – Sergey Aghababyan; (1/6/07) Rafael Galstyan

Founded - 1992

2007

14/4	MIKA	h	1-2	*Mkrtchyan R.*

/4	Ararat	a	0-5	
/4	Gandzasar	h	0-0	
;	Ulisses	a	0-2	
/5	Shirak	a	1-0	*Mkrtchyan A.*
/5	Pyunik	h	0-5	
/5	Banants	a	0-3	
;	MIKA	a	1-2	*Torosyan*
/6	Ararat	h	0-4	
/6	Gandzasar	a	0-2	
/6	Ulisses	h	0-0	
/6	Shirak	h	1-4	*Mkrtchyan R.*
/7	Pyunik	a	0-2	
/7	Banants	h	0-3	
;	MIKA	h	0-2	
/8	Ararat	a	1-2	*Mkrtchyan R.*
/8	Gandzasar	h	0-2	
/8	Ulisses	a	0-1	
	Shirak	a	1-2	*Mkrtchyan R.*
/9	Pyunik	h	0-2	
/9	Banants	a	0-2	
/9	MIKA	a	1-3	*Hovhannisyan*
0	Ararat	h	1-3	*Mkrtchyan H.*
0	Gandzasar	a	0-4	
/10	Ulisses	h	1-2	*Badoyan*
/10	Shirak	h	1-3	*Hovhannisyan*
1	Pyunik	a	0-2	
/11	Banants	h	0-6	

Name	Nat	Pos	Aps	(s)	Gls
Vahagn ARABYAN		M	5	(5)	
Artashes ARAKELYAN		M	22	(1)	
Artur ARAKELYAN		A	2	(5)	
Artyom ARAKELYAN		D	15	(5)	
Areg AVAGYAN		A	1	(4)	
Aghvan AYVAZYAN		M	24		
Zaven BADOYAN		M	10	(15)	1
Artashes BAGHDASARYAN		D	8		
David GEVORGYAN		D	21	(3)	
Levon GHASABOGHLYAN		M	11	(1)	
Gagik GHASABYAN		A	5		
Garnik GHASABYAN		A	7	(1)	
Gor GHAZARYAN		A		(1)	
Sergey GHAZARYAN		M	1	(5)	
Vitali HAKOBYAN		D	14		
Aghvan HAYRAPETYAN		M		(1)	
Harutyun HOVHANNISYAN		M	6		2
Vachagan HOVSEPYAN		D	1	(3)	
Armen KHACHATRYAN		G	10		
Edgar KHACHATRYAN		M	9	(7)	
Karen KHACHATRYAN		A	8	(1)	
Armen KIRAKOSYAN		G	2		
Gegham KOCHARYAN		M	18		
Artavazd MKRTCHYAN		D	28		1
Hayk MKRTCHYAN		A	12	(13)	1
Rafayel MKRTCHYAN		A	24	(1)	4
Martik MKRTUMYAN		G	16		
Mher NAZARETYAN		M		(3)	
Shiraz POGHASYAN		A		(4)	
Edgar TOROSYAN		A	12	(7)	1
Suren VOSKANYAN		A	1	(2)	
Hrachya YEGHIAZARYAN		D	15	(5)	

FC MIKA

Coach – Armen Adamyan; (25/5/07) Arkadi Andreasyan

Founded – 1997

AJOR HONOURS: Armenian Cup – (5) 2000, 2001, 2003, 2005, 2006.

7

4	Kilikia	a	2-1	*Acleisson 2*
4	Shirak	h	3-1	*Kléber L.3*
4	Pyunik	a	0-1	
	Banants	h	1-1	*Shahgeldyan*
5	Ulisses	h	7-0	*Adamyan, Kléber L., Alex, Ristich 2, Acleisson, Shahgeldyan (p)*
19/5	Ararat	a	0-2	
23/5	Gandzasar	h	3-2	*Tales, Shahgeldyan, Alex*
9/6	Kilikia	h	2-1	*Petikyan, Adamyan*
14/6	Shirak	a	0-1	
18/6	Pyunik	h	1-2	*Shahgeldyan*
23/6	Banants	a	1-1	*Adamyan (p)*
2/7	Ulisses	a	1-0	*Alex*
9/7	Ararat	h	2-2	*Kléber S., Davtyan*
14/7	Gandzasar	a	2-0	*Fursin, og (Zakaryan)*
6/8	Kilikia	a	2-0	*Ristich, Petikyan*
11/8	Shirak	h	1-1	*Alex*
3/9	Ulisses	h	1-1	*Adamyan*
18/9	Ararat	h	4-1	*Alex, Ristich 3*
23/9	Gandzasar	a	1-1	*Ristich*
26/9	Banants	h	0-2	
29/9	Kilikia	h	3-1	*Beglaryan, Alex, Davtyan*
3/10	Shirak	a	0-0	
7/10	Pyunik	h	1-0	*Kléber L.*
26/10	Ulisses	a	0-0	
30/10	Pyunik	a	0-1	
4/11	Ararat	a	2-1	*Alex, Adamyan*
7/11	Banants	a	1-0	*Beglaryan*
10/11	Gandzasar	h	1-0	*Alex*

No	Name	Nat	Pos	Aps	(s)	Gls
17	Artyom ADAMYAN		A	24	(3)	5
15	ACLEISSON Scaion	BRA	M	10	(2)	3
22	ALEX Henrique da Silva	BRA	D	27		8
6	Artashes ANTONYAN		M	10	(7)	
1	Yervand ARAKELYAN		G	1		
17	Karen AVOYAN		A	2	(4)	
1	Mayis AZIZYAN		G	6		
25	Narek BEGLARYAN		D	7	(8)	2
8	Arkadi CHILINGARYAN		M	13		
8	Tigran DAVTYAN		M	20	(7)	2
23	Nikita FURSIN	RUS	M	20	(2)	1
81	Felix HAKOBYAN		G	15		
14	Stepan HAKOBYAN		A	5	(3)	
19	KLÉBER Luis Rodrigues	BRA	M	26	(1)	5
21	KLÉBER Silva Nascimento	BRA	A	12	(6)	1
1	Alexander LAPIN	RUS	G	6		
4	Arsen MELOYAN		D	14	(6)	
18	Virab MEYTIKHANYAN		M	2	(7)	
11	Hrachya MIKAYELYAN		M	19	(5)	
10	Karen MURADYAN		M	5	(3)	
3	Armen PETIKYAN		D	11		2
19	Gevorg POGHOSYAN		M	4	(2)	
15	Mikael POGHOSYAN		M		(2)	
14	Ivan RISTICH	RUS	M	11	(1)	7
23	Marat SAFARYAN		A	1	(1)	
15	Andranik SARGSYAN		M		(1)	
5	Armen SHAHGELDYAN		A	12	(4)	4
25	Fernando TALES	BRA	A	10	(3)	1
9	THIAGO Manoel de Souza	BRA	D	15	(1)	

FC PYUNIK

Coach – Samvel Petrosyan; (10/5/07) Armen Gyulbudaghyants

Founded – 1992

MAJOR HONOURS: Armenian League – (10) 1992, 1996, 1997, 2001, 2002, 2003, 2004, 2005, 2006, 2007; Armenian Cup – (3) 1996, 2002, 2004.

2007

14/4	Ulisses	h	5-0	*Avetisyan, Petrosyan A. 2, Pachajyan 2*
22/4	Banants	a	2-1	*Nazaryan, Ghazaryan*
27/4	MIKA	h	1-0	*Pachajyan*
5/5	Ararat	a	0-0	
13/5	Gandzasar	h	1-0	*Arzumanyan*
18/5	Kilikia	a	5-0	*Avetisyan, Dokhoyan,*

				Hovsepyan, Petrosyan V., Ghazaryan
23/5	Shirak	h	1-2	*Ghazaryan*
10/6	Ulisses	a	2-1	*Ghazaryan, Hovsepyan*
14/6	Banants	h	5-1	*Mkhitaryan He., Nazaryan, Ghazaryan, Pachajyan, Hovsepyan (p)*
18/6	MIKA	a	2-1	*Avetisyan, Pachajyan*
1/7	Gandzasar	a	1-0	*Mkhitaryan Ham.*
5/7	Ararat	h	3-4	*Hovsepyan (p), Avetisyan 2*
10/7	Kilikia	h	2-0	*Mkhitaryan He. 2*
4/8	Ulisses	h	3-0	*Hzeyna 2, og (Mkrtchyan M.)*
12/8	Banants	a	1-2	*Ghazaryan*
26/8	Ararat	a	6-0	*Yedigaryan Artur, Mkrtchyan, Pachajyan 3, Arzumanyan*
1/9	Gandzasar	h	1-2	*Mkhitaryan He.*
18/9	Kilikia	a	2-0	*Petrosyan V., Mkhitaryan He.*
23/9	Shirak	a	5-1	*Mkhitaryan He. 3, Yedigaryan Artur 2*
26/9	Shirak	h	0-0	
29/9	Ulisses	a	3-0	*Pachajyan, Hzeyna, Petrosyan V.*
3/10	Banants	h	0-3	
7/10	MIKA	a	0-1	
26/10	Gandzasar	a	0-0	
30/10	MIKA	h	1-0	*Mkhitaryan He.*
4/11	Kilikia	h	2-0	*Mkhitaryan He. 2*
7/11	Ararat	h	4-1	*Pachajyan, Avetisyan, Mkrtchyan A., Mkhitaryan He.*
10/11	Shirak	a	0-2	

No	Name	Nat	Pos	Aps	(s)	Gls
12	Zlatan ADROVIĆ	BIH	G	5		
24	Artak ANDRIKYAN		D	5	(4)	
16	Robert ARZUMANYAN		D	24		2
9	Arsen AVETISYAN		A	18	(4)	6
23	Hamik BEGLARYAN		M		(1)	
15	Hayk CHILINGARYAN		D	1	(1)	
7	Narek DAVTYAN		M	12	(5)	
14	Karen DOKHOYAN		D	24		1
10	Gevorg GHAZARYAN		A	11		6
23	Tigran GHARABAGHTSYAN		A	6	(2)	
4	Sargis HOVSEPYAN		D	26		4
18	Felix HZEYNA	CMR	M	10	(6)	3
3	Artak KHACHATRYAN		A	3	(16)	
21	Vyacheslav KHORKIN	RUS	G	2		
30	Ignacio Javier Bordad LÓPEZ	URU	G	14		
22	Edgar MALAKYAN		D		(1)	
18	Mihran MANASYAN		M		(1)	
21	Grigor MELIKSETYAN		G	5	(1)	
1	Jeofak MILLER	CMR	G	2		
15	Hamlet MKHITARYAN		M	2	(2)	1
35	Henrikh MKHITARYAN		M	23	(2)	12
7	Aghvan MKRTCHYAN		D	12	(1)	2
13	Karlen MKRTCHYAN		M	7	(4)	
15	Grigor MOVSISYAN		M		(1)	
20	Rafayel NAZARYAN		M	12	(8)	2
19	Levon PACHAJYAN		M	25		10
10	Alexander PETROSYAN		A	5	(1)	2
17	Vardan A. PETROSYAN		A	8	(11)	3
11	Norayr SAHAKYAN		M	8	(9)	
10	Albert TADEVOSYAN		M		(1)	
3	Alexander TADEVOSYAN		D	17		
19	Tigran VOSKANYAN		M	1	(2)	
24	Artak YEDIGARYAN		M		(1)	
5	Artur YEDIGARYAN		D	20	(5)	3
13	Artur YUZBASHYAN		A		(1)	

FC SHIRAK

Coach – Zhora Barseghyan

Founded – 1955

MAJOR HONOURS: Armenian League – (3) 1992, 1994, 1999.

2007				
14/4	Banants	h	0-0	
22/4	MIKA	a	1-3	*Bernetsyan*
27/4	Ararat	h	0-1	
5/5	Gandzasar	a	0-0	
13/5	Kilikia	h	0-1	
19/5	Ulisses	a	2-0	*Bernetsyan, Bichakhchyan*
23/5	Pyunik	a	2-1	*Harutyunyan, Bichakhchyan*
9/6	Banants	a	0-3	
14/6	MIKA	h	1-0	*Hovhannisyan T.*
18/6	Ararat	a	0-1	
24/6	Gandzasar	h	0-0	
30/6	Kilikia	a	4-1	*Bernetsyan, Hovhannisyan G., Hakobyan, Gasparya*
8/7	Ulisses	h	3-1	*Bernetsyan 2, Bichakhchyan*
6/8	Banants	h	1-1	*Bernetsyan*
11/8	MIKA	a	1-1	*Hakobyan*
15/8	Ararat	h	0-2	
26/8	Gandzasar	a	2-4	*Harutyunyan, Mkrtchyan*
1/9	Kilikia	h	2-1	*Mkrtchyan, Bernetsy (p)*
19/9	Ulisses	a	0-2	
23/9	Pyunik	h	1-5	*Khachatryan*
26/9	Pyunik	a	0-0	
29/9	Banants	a	0-2	
3/10	MIKA	h	0-0	
7/10	Ararat	a	0-4	
21/10	Gandzasar	h	2-1	*Harutyunyan, Hakobyan*
26/10	Kilikia	a	3-1	*Mkrtchyan, Sargsyar Bichakhchyan*
4/11	Ulisses	h	0-1	
10/11	Pyunik	h	2-0	*Khachatryan 2*

No	Name	Nat	Pos	Aps	(s)	Gl
19	Henrik BADIKYAN		M	5		
12	Andranik BARIKYAN		A	9	(10)	
5	Artyom BERNETSYAN		A	20	(3)	7
11	Vardan BICHAKHCHYAN		A	18	(7)	4
4	Hovhannes DEMIRCHYAN		D	26		
8	Vladimir GASPARYAN		A	3	(12)	1
14	Armen GHAZARYAN		M		(1)	
9	Yervand HAKOBYAN		M	15	(5)	3
15	Ararat HARUTYUNYAN		M	21	(2)	3
21	Gevorg HOVHANNISYAN		D	16	(1)	1
13	Hovhannes HOVHANNISYAN		G	1	(1)	
3	Tigran S. HOVHANNISYAN		M	24	(1)	1
17	Karen KARAPETYAN		M		(1)	
7	Karen G. KHACHATRYAN		A	21		3
2	Felix KHOJOYAN		D	21	(1)	
18	Ara MKRTCHYAN		D	12	(6)	3
10	Hrachya MNATSAKANYAN		M	11	(10)	
2	Mkrtich NALBANDYAN		D		(4)	
20	Rafayel PALTAJYAN		A		(6)	
17	Garnik SARGSYAN		A	16	(4)	1
7	Hovhannes TAHMAZYAN		D	10	(3)	
6	Arman TONOYAN		D	15	(5)	
17	Eduard VARDANYAN		D	17	(3)	
1	Raymond ZADURYAN		G	27		

FC ULISSES YEREVAN

Coach – Arsen Chilingaryan; (2/5/07) Suren Barseghyan

Founded - 2006

07				
'4	Pyunik	a	0-5	
'4	Gandzasar	h	0-2	
'4	Banants	a	0-2	
;	Kilikia	h	2-0	*Urazov, Hakobyan H.*
'5	MIKA	a	0-7	
'5	Shirak	h	0-2	
'5	Ararat	a	0-2	
'6	Pyunik	h	1-2	*Urazov*
'6	Gandzasar	a	0-0	
'6	Banants	h	2-3	*Navoyan, Urazov*
'6	Kilikia	a	0-0	
'	MIKA	h	0-1	
'	Shirak	a	1-3	*Kocharyan G.*
'7	Ararat	h	0-3	
;	Pyunik	a	0-3	
'8	Gandzasar	h	0-1	
'8	Banants	a	2-1	*Khachatryan, Hovhannisyan T.*
'8	Kilikia	h	1-0	*Khachatryan*
'	MIKA	a	1-1	*Showboy*
'9	Shirak	h	2-0	*Grigoryan, Atabekyan*
'9	Ararat	a	0-0	
'9	Pyunik	h	0-3	
0	Gandzasar	a	2-1	*Showboy, Harutyunyan*
0	Banants	h	2-1	*Navoyan, Stepanyan*
'10	Kilikia	a	2-1	*Navoyan 2 (1p)*
'10	MIKA	h	0-0	
1	Shirak	a	1-0	*Grigoryan*
'11	Ararat	h	2-2	*Simonyan, Azizyan (p)*

Name	Nat	Pos	Aps	(s)	Gls
Albert ACHEMYAN		A	12		
Manvel AFRIKYAN		G	6		
Hovhannes ANTONYAN		A		(1)	
Gor ATABEKYAN		A	20	(2)	1
Mayis AZIZYAN		G	16	(1)	1
Shota CHOMAKHIDZE	GEO	M	4		
Artur GALSTYAN		A		(1)	
Hrant GHUKASYAN		D	1	(1)	
Ashot GRIGORYAN		D	7	(1)	2
Aram H. HAKOBYAN		M	5	(2)	
Hayk HAKOBYAN		A	11	(8)	1
Hovhannes HARUTYUNYAN		M	5	(1)	1
Sergey HOVHANNISYAN		M	8	(8)	
Tigran L. HOVHANNISYAN		M	7	(1)	1
Vardan HOVHANNISYAN		D	16	(6)	
Khalid Radjab IBRAHIM	EGY	A	6		
Vadims JAVOIŠS	LVA	D	6		
Vachagan KARAPETYAN		D	8	(4)	
Gorik KHACHATRYAN		M	15	(4)	2
Gegham KOCHARYAN		A		(2)	1
Vahram LOBYAN		M	12		
Vahe MARTIROSYAN		A	2	(1)	
Gor MIRZAKHANYAN		M	11	(5)	
Marat MKRTCHYAN		M	13	(2)	
Sergey MKRTCHYAN		M	2	(4)	
Karen NAVOYAN		M	13	(4)	4
Tigran PETROSYAN		A	7	(1)	
Tigran PETROSYANTS		M	1	(3)	
Rusaldo RAMÍREZ	MEX	G	6	(1)	
Adoeffe Efe SHOWBOY	NGA	A	10	(3)	2
Gagik SIMONYAN		A	15	(2)	1
Karen STEPANYAN		D	21	(1)	1
Georgi SULABERIDZE	GEO	M	2		
Dragan TATAREVIĆ	BIH	M		(5)	
Tengiz UGREKELIDZE	GEO	D	13	(10)	
Dayanchgylych URAZOV	TKM	A	7	(3)	3
Hrachya VARDAZARYAN		M	5	(6)	
Arkadi YEPREMYAN		D	15		

SECOND LEVEL FINAL TABLE 2007

		Pld	W	D	L	F	A	Pts
1	FC Pyunik-2	21	14	2	5	54	19	44
2	FC MIKA-2	21	10	9	2	42	23	39
3	FC Ararat-2 Yerevan	21	9	7	5	43	26	34
4	FC Dinamo Yerevan	21	10	3	8	47	38	33
5	FC Banants-2	21	8	4	9	35	38	28
6	FC Gandzasar-2 Kapan	21	8	4	9	26	37	28
7	FC Shirak-2	21	3	10	8	23	44	19
8	FC Patani	21	2	1	18	19	64	7

N.B. No promotion as only eligible team, FC Dinamo Yerevan, were dissolved; FC Bentonit Ijevan withdrew after three matches.

DOMESTIC CUP 2008

ARMENIAN INDEPENDENCE CUP

FIRST ROUND

(21/3/08 & 28/3/08)
Kilikia v MIKA-2 2-0; 3-2 *(5-2)*
MIKA v Ararat-2 7-0; 4-0 *(11-0)*
Shirak v Shengavit 3-1; 0-1 *(3-2)*

(22/3/08 & 28/3/08)
Ulisses v Banants-2 4-1; 2-1 *(6-2)*

(22/3/08 & 29/3/08)
Pyunik v Patani 11-2; 4-0 *(15-2)*
Gandzasar v Pyunik–2 3-0; 5-0 *(8-0)*

QUARTER-FINALS

(3/4/08 & 10/4/08)
Shirak 0, Banants 1 *(Karapetyan S. 89)*
Banants 0, Shirak Gyumri 1 *(Kasule 8og)*
(1-1; Banants 6-5 on pens)
MIKA 1 *(Beglaryan 23)*, Kilikia 0
Kilikia 1 *(Ghasaboghlyan 48p)*, MIKA 2 *(Alex 32, Avoyan 45)*
(MIKA 3-1)
Ararat 0, Ulis 1 *(Atabekyan 25)*
Ulisses 0 Ararat 2 *(Nranyan 20, Minasyan A.H. 42)*
(Ararat 2-1)
Pyunik 0, Gandzasar 0
Gandzasar 0, Pyunik 0
(0-0; Pyunik 4-1 on pens)

SEMI-FINALS

(14/4/08 & 23/4/08)
Banants 3 *(Gyozalyan 61, 72p, Zlatyev 86)*, MIKA 1 *(Alex 43)*
MIKA 0, Banants 2 *(Khachatryan 1, Krumov 25)*
(Banants 5-1)
Pyunik 1 *(Manasyan 85)*, Ararat 2 *(Movsisyan 47, Marcos 78)*
Ararat 3 *(Movsisyan 2, Erzrumyan S. 56, Marcos 71)*, Pyunik 0
(Ararat 5-1)

FINAL

(9/5/08)
Arnar stadium, Idjevan
FC ARARAT YEREVAN 2 *(Minasyan V. 75, Marcos 115)*
FC BANANTS 1 *(Ganchev 36)*
(aet)
Referee – *Chagharyan*
ARARAT – *Sargsyan, Minasyan V., Mehrabyan (Safaryan 60), Mkoyan, Petrosyan (Kalsami 116), Minasyan A., Renato, Navoyan, Marcos, Erzrumyan S. (Tadevosyan 95), Movsisyan.*
BANANTS – *Matyugin, Krumov, Cherevko, Burdian, Daghbashyan (Hayrapetyan 77), Khachatryan R. (Grigoryan 46), Kasule, Alexanyan, Ganchev, Melikyan, Zlatyev (Balabekyan 72).*

EURO challenge exposes limitations

Austria cleared the decks for UEFA EURO 2008™. The Bundesliga finished early, the national Cup competition was put on hold for a year. Preparations were meticulous. No stone, it seemed, was left unturned in the desire to get Team Österreich ready for the biggest sporting event the country had ever staged.

Unfortunately, however, when it came to the real thing, Josef Hickersberger and his players were unable to rise to the occasion, and Austria, like co-hosts Switzerland, slumped out in the group stage. Not that the majority of Austrians, in their heart of hearts, had expected anything different. In fact, so low was the local expectation for the team going into the championship that disappointment was impossible. In the end it was simply a case of accepting that Austria, though game and willing, were just not quite good enough.

The lowest ranked of the 16 participants, and competing in their first UEFA European Championship, Austria may have had the sizeable benefit of home advantage, but poor results in the lead-up to the tournament meant that any optimism was founded essentially on hope. Unfortunately, at no stage were Hickersberger's team ever able to get the spectators a the Ernst-Happel-Stadion roaring excitedly in suppor They fell behind in all three of their Group B matches against Croatia, Poland and Germany, and although they never conceded more than one goal in any gam they found the net just once themselves – and that from the penalty spot with virtually the last kick of th game against Poland.

Shot-shy attack

While defensively sound – two of the goals they conceded were from set-pieces and the other was suspiciously offside – it was Austria's blunt strike forc that proved their undoing. Between them central strikers Roland Linz (who played against Croatia and Poland) and Erwin Hoffer (brought in against Germany) failed to muster a single shot on target. Martin Harnik, nominally a forward but generally deployed on the right wing, managed only two – bot

Ivica Vastic, the oldest participant at UEFA EURO 2008™, scores Austria's late equalising penalty against Pol

ear-cut openings early in the game against Poland ring Austria's best period of play in the tournament.

ere was also a strong finish to the opening game ainst Croatia when Austria, assisted by substitutes ca Vastic, Ümit Korkmaz and Roman Kienast, forced e play and, by common consent, deserved an ualiser. While veteran Vastic, 38, was the only strian player to score, youngster Korkmaz, 22, was obably the one member of his team to emerge from e tournament with his reputation considerably hanced, the tricky left-winger demonstrating a peated eagerness to take on the full-back and lift e spectators from their seats.

contrast, Andreas Ivanschitz, Austria's captain and aymaker, never lived up to his lofty reputation. At 24, is still young enough to come again – as are many hers in the team, like Korkmaz, Hoffer, Harnik, ristoph Leitgeb and Sebastian Prödl, all of whom ve already proved successful for Austria with youth d Under-21 selections and can only have gained m the experience of competing at the highest vel. Their senior education, however, will have to ntinue without the guidance of father-figure ckersberger, whose response to criticism of his ections and methods after Austria's elimination was backtrack on an initial desire to stay on, and nounce his resignation.

time, the 60-year-old's groundwork with the young uad may well be fully appreciated. The overall pression, acknowledged by many Austrian fans, was at, despite all the best laid plans, UEFA EURO 2008™ nply came two years, maybe four, too early for this neration of players. A 2010 FIFA World Cup alifying programme in which they take on France, mania and Serbia will pose a severe examination of stria's rate of development, but, with the perienced Karel Brückner now in charge, it is not yond the bounds of possibility that they could be mpeting in South Africa in two years' time.

apid's title

mestic football in Austria may have taken a back at in 2007/08, but for the supporters of SK Rapid en, the country's record champions, it was a season treasure. Unheralded at the start of the campaign, e Green and Whites confounded expectations to ock favourites and defending champions FC lzburg off their lofty perch and take the league title the 32nd time in their illustrious history.

Rapid Wien captain and Bundesliga Player of the Year Steffen Hofmann

The transferral of power was achieved in the most remarkable fashion, with Rapid sensationally destroying their rivals 7-0 in their own Wals-Siezenheim stadium a month before the end of the season. Salzburg coach Giovanni Trapattoni called it the most embarrassing defeat of his long career, and it was not difficult to understand why. His team were actually topping the table going into the match and would have built up a seemingly unassailable five-point lead with five games to go had they achieved a third win of the season over their closest pursuers. But Rapid, coached by former striker Peter Pacult, produced a performance that was universally acknowledged as one of the greatest in the club's history. Young strikers Hoffer (three goals) and Stefan Maierhofer (two) did most of the damage, the other goals going to Korkmaz and the Bundesliga's Player of the Year, club captain Steffen Hofmann.

After that result, Rapid's confidence was so high that there was simply no stopping them as they accelerated away from the pack towards the finishing line, collecting maximum points from their last five matches and securing the title with a round to spare after a 3-0 home win over SCR Altach.

Österreichischer Fussball-Bund (ÖFB

Ernst-Happel-Stadion
Sektor A/F
Meiereistrasse 7
AT-1020 Wien
tel - +43 1 727180
fax - +43 1 7281632
website - www.oefb.at
email – office@oefb.at
Year of Formation - 1904
President - Friedrich Stickler
General Secretary – Alfred Ludwig
Press Officer – Peter Klinglmüller
Stadium - Ernst-Happel-Stadion, Vienna (50,000)

INTERNATIONAL TOURNAMENT APPEARANCES
FIFA World Cup Finals - (7) 1934 (4th), 1954 (3rd), 1958, 1978 (2nd phase), 1982 (2nd phase), 1990, 1998; UEFA European Championship – (1) 2008.

TOP FIVE ALL-TIME CAPS
Andreas Herzog (103); Anton Polster (95); Gerhard Hanappi (93); Karl Koller (86); Friedl Koncilia & Bruno Pezzey (84)

TOP FIVE ALL-TIME GOALS
Anton Polster (44); Hans Krankl (34); Johann Horvath (29); Erich Hof (28); Anto Schall (27)

NATIONAL TEAM RESULTS 2007/08

22/8/07	Czech Republic	H	Vienna	1-1	*Harnik (78)*
7/9/07	Japan	H	Klagenfurt	0-0	*(4-3 on pens)*
11/9/07	Chile	H	Vienna	0-2	
13/10/07	Switzerland	A	Zurich	1-3	*Aufhauser (11)*
17/10/07	Ivory Coast	H	Innsbruck	3-2	*Kuljic (30p), Ivanschitz (64p), Standfest (74)*
16/11/07	England	H	Vienna	0-1	
21/11/07	Tunisia	H	Vienna	0-0	
6/2/08	Germany	H	Vienna	0-3	
26/3/08	Netherlands	H	Vienna	3-4	*Ivanschitz (6), Prödl (18, 35)*
27/5/08	Nigeria	H	Graz	1-1	*Kienast (12)*
30/5/08	Malta	H	Graz	5-1	*Aufhauser (8), Linz (11, 67p), Vastic (77), Harnik (90)*
8/6/08	Croatia (ECF)	H	Vienna	0-1	
12/6/08	Poland (ECF)	H	Vienna	1-1	*Vastic (90+3p)*
16/6/08	Germany (ECF)	H	Vienna	0-1	

Austrian core

Although the contributions of German schemer Hofmann and fellow foreigners Branko Bošković, Markus Heikkinen and Mario Bazina to the title triumph were considerable, Rapid had an Austrian core, as demonstrated by the inclusion of four of their players – Korkmaz, Hoffer and defenders Markus Katzer and Jürgen Patocha – in the UEFA EURO 2008™ squad. The figure would have been six but for an illness sustained on the eve of the tournament by Austria's No1 goalkeeper, Helge Payer, and the mid-season departure of veteran defender Martin Hiden to SK Austria Kärnten. Maierfhofer and another young gun, Veli Kavlak, were also close to Hickersberger's final selection.

Salzburg, on the other hand, were overloaded with legionnaires, with only three Austrians – René Aufhauser, Marc Janko and Leitgeb – starting a leagu

ATIONAL TEAM APPEARANCES 2007/08

h - Josef HICKERSBERGER	27/8/48		Cze	Jpn	Chi	Sui	Civ	Eng	Tun	Ger	Ned	Nga	Mlt	CRO	POL	GER	Caps	Goals
nder MANNINGER	4/6/77	Siena (ITA)	G			G		s26	G	G			G				27	-
us KATZER	11/12/79	Rapid Wien	D										s76				11	-
eas IBERTSBERGER	27/7/82	Freiburg (GER)	D49						s63								12	1
tian PRÖDL	21/6/87	Sturm	D	D	D81	D40				D	D	D	s84	D	D		12	2
n STRANZL	16/6/80	Spartak Moskva (RUS)	D					D86	D	D		D	D84	D	D	D	48	2
AUFHAUSER	21/6/76	Salzburg	M	M	M71	M	M81	M	M	M69		M	M76	M	M74	M63	54	11
oph LEITGEB	14/4/85	Salzburg	M72	M	M79			s46	M65		M	s81	M		M	s55	21	-
el MÖRZ	2/4/80	Mattersburg	M82	M59	s62	s65	s86										12	-
im STANDFEST	30/5/80	Austria Wien	M	M	M	M65	M	M78		M	s64	M		M			31	2
as PRAGER	13/9/85	Heerenveen (NED)	M46	s84	M62					s69							13	1
KULJIC	10/10/77	Austria Wien	A	A75	A	A65	A46	A46	A46								20	3
n SÄUMEL	8/9/84	Sturm	s46	M85	s71					M	M	M	s76	M61	s74	s63	14	-
d LINZ	9/8/81	Braga (POR)	s49	s59	A74					A81	A64	A81	A	A73	A64		34	7
n HARNIK	10/6/87	Bremen (GER)	s72	s75 /84		s82		s65	s46	A73	M64		s46	A	A	A67	11	2
SALMUTTER	3/1/84	Sturm	s82	s85	s79												4	-
PAYER	9/8/79	Rapid Wien		G			G				G						15	-
ian FUCHS	7/4/86	Mattersburg		D	D74	D	s81		s65	M	M74	M61				M	18	-
y GARICS	8/3/84	Napoli (ITA)		D	D	D	D	D	D63		D		D		D	D	14	1
n HIDEN	11/3/73	Rapid Wien /Austria Kärnten		D	D	D	D	s86	s77				s84			D55	50	1
n MACHO	24/8/77	AEK (GRE)			G			G26				G		G	G	G	17	-
d GERCALIU	12/2/86	Austria Wien			s74		D	D	D		D		D76	M69			12	-
HOFFER	14/4/87	Rapid Wien			s74							s46	A58			A	5	-
n PATOCKA	30/7/77	Rapid Wien			s81												2	-
l SARIYAR	1/8/79	Austria Wien				M	M	M65	s74								13	1
us WEISSENBERGER	8/3/75	Eintracht (GER)				M65	M81	M46			s74						29	1
eas IVANSCHITZ	15/10/83	Panathinaikos (GRE)				M82	M86	M	M	M	M	M70	M	M	M64	M	42	6
SCHIEMER	21/3/86	Austria Wien				s40	D	D	D77								4	-
nnes ERTL	13/11/82	Austria Wien				s65	s81										7	-
an KIENAST	29/3/84	HamKam (NOR)				s65	s46	s46	A	s73		A46		s73	s64	s67	9	1
AVLAK	3/11/88	Rapid Wien						s78	M74	s81							4	-
uel POGATETZ	16/1/83	Middlesbrough (ENG)								D	D	D	D84	D	D	D	30	1
JANKO	25/6/83	Salzburg									s64						3	-
KORKMAZ	17/9/85	Rapid Wien										s61	M46	s69	M	M	5	-
VASTIC	29/9/69	LASK										s70	s58	s61	s64		50	14

game for the club. Runaway champions under Trapattoni the previous season, the team bankrolled by energy drink tycoon Dietrich Mateschitz never managed to find the same rhythm. While their home form was generally excellent – that outrageous blip against Rapid aside – they struggled badly on their travels, winning just three matches (as opposed to 15 at home). For the second season in a row Salzburg's captain, German striker Alexander Zickler, was the Bundesliga's top scorer, but his winning total fell from 22 to 16, all but one of them coming before the end of February. Salzburg's most consistent performer in the spring was Serbian playmaker Saša Ilić, who had been widely labelled a flop in the early weeks following his summer 2007 arrival from Galatasaray AŞ.

European woes

Even harder to bear for Salzburg than the loss of their title was their narrow failure to qualify for the group phase of the UEFA Champions League – a prize snatched from them by the Ukrainians of FC Shakhtar Donetsk with three minutes of the third qualifying round tie remaining after they had at one stage led 2-0 on aggregate. A second successive first-round exit in the UEFA Cup – by AEK Athens FC – simply added to the club's European woes under Trapattoni, whose departure to take charge of the Republic of Ireland led to the appointment of another high-profile foreign coach, Dutchman Co Adriaanse.

With only one domestic trophy to play for due to the temporary removal from the professional clubs' agenda of the Austrian Cup, the incentive to finish in the top four of the Bundesliga was strong, with third place guaranteeing a UEFA Cup place and fourth earning a spot in the UEFA Intertoto Cup.

FK Austria Wien recovered from a poor run of results in March that cost coach Georg Zellhofer his job to take that third spot under his replacement Didi Constantini. The Violetten had been the most successful of five Austrian participants in the 2007/08 UEFA Cup (including UEFA Champions League drop-outs Salzburg and UEFA Intertoto Cup refugees Rapid), reaching the group stage, where, for the second year running, they failed to win a game.

The UEFA Intertoto Cup berth went to SK Sturm Graz. The debt-ridden club reinvented themselves under German coach Franco Foda, with former Austrian international striker Mario Haas scoring 14 goals to spearhead an astonishing revival. Two more veteran forwards, Ivica Vastic (13 goals) and Christian Mayrleb (eleven), had a similar effect on newly promoted LASK Linz who were denied a European place only by a po[or] finish (just one point from their last five games). LASK, like Sturm, had at one stage led the league.

Wacker down

Down at the foot of the table FC Wacker Innsbruck (formerly Tirol) bit the dust, their tally of 29 points leaving them four short of the safety mark. One place above them were SK Austria Kärnten, the franchise club that had competed as FCS Pasching – and finished fifth – a year earlier. The biggest fall was that of SV Ried. Runners-up to Salzburg the previous season, they ended up a disappointing seventh – a consequence of the mid-autumn departure of coach Helmut Kraft to Wacker, where he almost worked a miracle after his predecessor Lars Søndergaard's disastrous start. Replacing the Innsbruck club in the Bundesliga for 2008/09 were Kapfenberger SV, runaway winners of the Erste Liga (second level) und[er] ex-Grazer AK coach Werner Gregoritsch and back in the top flight for the first time in 41 years.

Salzburg's German st[riker] Alexander Zickler wa[s the] Bundesliga's top marks[man] for the second year in a

DOMESTIC LEAGUE 2007/08

BUNDESLIGA FINAL TABLE

		Pld	Home W	D	L	F	A	Away W	D	L	F	A	Total W	D	L	F	A	Pts
1	SK Rapid Wien	36	13	2	3	41	19	8	4	6	28	17	21	6	9	69	36	69
2	FC Salzburg	36	15	1	2	44	15	3	8	7	19	27	18	9	9	63	42	63
3	FK Austria Wien	36	8	8	2	27	15	7	5	6	19	18	15	13	8	46	33	58
4	SK Sturm Graz	36	10	4	4	37	16	5	7	6	23	25	15	11	10	60	41	56
5	SV Mattersburg	36	10	7	1	37	20	3	7	8	18	23	13	14	9	55	43	53
6	LASK Linz	36	11	4	3	36	16	3	7	8	18	31	14	11	11	54	47	53
7	SV Ried	36	7	6	5	26	16	3	2	13	12	37	10	8	18	38	53	38
8	SCR Altach	36	6	7	5	22	21	2	5	11	15	43	8	12	16	37	64	36
9	SK Austria Kärnten	36	5	6	7	13	21	3	3	12	13	37	8	9	19	26	58	33
10	FC Wacker Innsbruck	36	5	7	6	18	20	1	4	13	14	43	6	11	19	32	63	29

TOP GOALSCORERS

16 Alexander ZICKLER (Salzburg)
14 Mario HAAS (Sturm)
13 Ivica VASTIC (LASK)
12 Carsten JANCKER (Mattersburg)
Hamdi SALIHI (Ried)
11 Sanel KULJIC (Austria Wien)
Christian MAYRLEB (LASK)
Samir MURATOVIĆ (Sturm)
10 Erwin HOFFER (Rapid Wien)
Steffen HOFMANN (Rapid Wien)

CLUB-BY-CLUB

SCR ALTACH

Coach – Manfred Bender (GER); (22/1/08) Heinz Fuchsbichler

Founded – 1929

07

/7	Salzburg	a	1-4	*Hutwelker*
/7	Ried	h	2-3	*Mattle, Kirchler*
/7	Wacker	h	2-1	*Hutwelker 2*
8	Rapid Wien	h	0-1	
8	Mattersburg	a	1-4	*Karatay*
/8	Sturm	a	1-3	*Chinchilla*
/8	Austria Kärnten	h	4-1	*Schoppitsch, Mattle, Schmid, Kirchler*
/8	Austria Wien	a	0-1	
/8	LASK	h	2-2	*Schoppitsch 2*
/9	LASK	a	0-2	
/9	Salzburg	h	1-1	*Gramann*
/9	Ried	a	0-3	
/9	Rapid Wien	a	2-0	*Carreño 2*
/10	Mattersburg	h	0-0	
/10	Wacker	a	1-0	*Schoppitsch*
/10	Sturm	h	0-0	
/10	Austria Kärnten	a	1-1	*Schoppitsch*
11	Austria Wien	h	1-0	*og (Schiemer)*
/11	Wacker	h	1-1	*Carreño*
/11	Sturm	a	1-6	*Schmid*
12	LASK	h	0-0	
12	Mattersburg	a	3-3	*Kirchler, Schmid, Kling*
/12	Austria Kärnten	h	0-1	

08

/2	Austria Wien	a	1-1	*Jaqua*
/2	Rapid Wien	h	2-1	*Kirchler (p), Jaqua*
/2	Salzburg	a	0-4	
3	Ried	a	1-3	*Orman*
3	Ried	h	3-2	*Kirchler 2, Mattle*
/3	Wacker	a	1-1	*Kirchler*
/3	Sturm	h	1-2	*Jaqua*
/3	LASK	a	0-3	
/3	Mattersburg	h	2-0	*Kirchler (p), Jaqua*
4	Austria Kärnten	a	1-1	*Kirchler*
/4	Austria Wien	h	0-4	
/4	Rapid Wien	a	0-3	
/4	Salzburg	h	1-1	*Jaqua*

No	Name	Nat	Pos	Aps	(s)	Gls
22	Müslüm ATAV		A		(1)	
6	Dario BALDAUF		D	4		
2	Tiago BERNARDI	BRA	M	10	(5)	
16	Mario BOLTER		D	9	(5)	
12	Fernando CARREÑO	URU	D	23	(1)	3
15	Pablo CHINCHILLA	CRC	D	26	(3)	1
25	Daniel GRAMANN		D	20	(7)	1
17	Alexander GUEM		M	33		
7	Karsten HUTWELKER	GER	M	28	(6)	3
11	Modou JAGNE	GAM	A	9	(5)	
5	Jonathan JAQUA	USA	A	13		5
19	Dursun KARATAY		M	2	(9)	1
8	Roland KIRCHLER		M	26	(4)	9
13	Stephan KLING	GER	D	27	(2)	1
1	Mario KRASSNITZER		G	22	(1)	
14	LEONARDO Ferreira da Silva	BRA	A	9	(7)	
18	Oliver MATTLE		A	14	(13)	3
9	Patrick MAYER		M	15	(13)	
24	Andreas MICHL		G	14	(1)	
27	Alen ORMAN		D	18		1
28	Manfred PAMMINGER		M	12		
4	Enrico PFISTER		D	15	(3)	
3	Manuel SCHMID		M	19	(4)	3
23	Kai Walter SCHOPPITSCH		M	20		5
20	Bernd WINKLER		M	5	(6)	
5	Ulrich WINKLER		M	3	(6)	

SK AUSTRIA KÄRNTEN

Coach – Walter Schachner; (5/12/07) (Klaus Schmidt); (23/2/08) Frenk Schinkels (NED)

Founded – 2007

2007

10/7	LASK	a	0-1	
15/7	Salzburg	h	1-0	*Fidjeu-Tazemeta*
22/7	Ried	h	0-3	
3/8	Wacker	a	1-1	*Mössner*
8/8	Rapid Wien	a	0-4	
11/8	Mattersburg	h	1-1	*Kollmann*
17/8	Altach	a	1-4	*Hauser*
26/8	Sturm	a	3-1	*Hauser, Kollmann 2*

2/9	Austria Wien	a	0-1	
16/9	Austria Wien	h	2-1	*Kollmann, Ortlechner*
22/9	LASK	h	1-4	*Kabát (p)*
26/9	Salzburg	a	0-3	
29/9	Ried	a	1-3	*Krajic*
7/10	Rapid Wien	h	1-2	*og (Thonhofer)*
20/10	Wacker	h	2-0	*Krajic, Junuzovic*
27/10	Mattersburg	a	2-5	*Krajic, Wolf*
31/10	Altach	h	1-1	*og (Orman)*
3/11	Sturm	h	0-0	
11/11	Austria Wien	h	0-1	
24/11	Salzburg	a	1-1	*og (Vargas)*
30/11	Wacker	h	0-2	
8/12	LASK	a	0-4	
15/12	Altach	a	1-0	*Kabát*
2008				
16/2	Rapid Wien	h	0-2	
23/2	Ried	a	0-3	
26/2	Sturm	h	0-2	
1/3	Mattersburg	a	0-1	
8/3	Mattersburg	h	1-0	*Chiquinho*
15/3	Austria Wien	a	1-0	*Kollmann*
19/3	Salzburg	h	0-0	
22/3	Wacker	a	0-0	
29/3	LASK	h	2-1	*Weber, Mössner*
4/4	Altach	h	1-1	*Junuzovic*
11/4	Rapid Wien	a	1-2	*Wolf*
20/4	Ried	h	0-0	
26/4	Sturm Graz	a	1-3	*Bukva*

No	Name	Nat	Pos	Aps	(s)	Gls
12	Wolfgang BUBENIK		D	28	(6)	
20	Stephan BÜRGLER		D		(2)	
24	Haris BUKVA		M	1	(1)	1
2	Carlos CHAILE	ARG	D	24	(1)	
8	Alexandre da Silva "CHIQUINHO"	BRA	M	10	(4)	1
11	Thierry FIDJEU-TAZEMETA	CMR	A	14	(3)	1
17	Alexander HAUSER		M	11	(5)	2
4	Martin HIDEN		D	10		
18	Thomas HINUM		M		(2)	
16	Zlatko JUNUZOVIC		M	24	(4)	2
22	Péter KABÁT	HUN	M	5	(6)	2
7	Marcel KETELAER	GER	M	6		
28	Roland KOLLMANN		A	18	(8)	5
13	Gerald KRAJIC		A	13	(10)	3
5	Adam LEDWOŃ	POL	M	30		
9	Lukas MÖSSNER		A	10	(17)	2
10	Joseph Mpumelelo NGWENYA	ZIM	A	1		
14	Manuel ORTLECHNER		D	34	(1)	1
3	Thomas PIRKER		D	6	(3)	
26	Gernot PLASSNEGGER		D	14	(4)	
15	Christian PRAWDA		D	19	(3)	
6	Thomas RIEDL	GER	D	8	(13)	
1	Andreas SCHRANZ		G	36		
25	Stephan STÜCKLER		D		(1)	
19	Manuel WEBER		M	29	(2)	1
33	Patrick WOLF		M	33		2
23	Sandro ZAKANY		M	12	(9)	

FK AUSTRIA WIEN

Coach – Georg Zellhofer; (19/3/08) Dietmar Constantini

Founded – 1911

MAJOR HONOURS: Austrian League - (23) 1924, 1926, 1949, 1950, 1953, 1961, 1962, 1963, 1969, 1970, 1976, 1978, 1979, 1980, 1981, 1984, 1985, 1986, 1991, 1992, 1993, 2003, 2006; Austrian Cup - (26) 1921, 1924, 1925, 1926, 1933, 1935, 1936, 1948, 1949, 1960, 1962, 1963, 1967, 1971, 1974, 1977, 1980, 1982, 1986, 1990, 1992, 1994, 2003, 2005, 2006, 2007.

2007				
11/7	Sturm	a	2-2	*Ačimovič, Aigner*
14/7	LASK	h	1-1	*Schiemer*
22/7	Salzburg	h	2-2	*Kuljic 2*
27/7	Ried	a	1-0	*Kuljic*
5/8	Rapid Wien	a	0-0	
10/8	Wacker	h	6-1	*Sulimani, Blanchard 2, Ertl, Kuljic, Troyansky*
19/8	Mattersburg	a	1-0	*Lasnik*
25/8	Altach	h	1-0	*Ačimovič*
2/9	Austria Kärnten	h	1-0	*Kuljic*
16/9	Austria Kärnten	a	1-2	*Kuljic*
23/9	Sturm	h	1-0	*Bąk*
26/9	LASK	a	1-1	*Bąk*
30/9	Salzburg	a	1-0	*Sulimani*
7/10	Ried	h	2-1	*Mair, Gercaliu*
21/10	Rapid Wien	h	2-2	*Sariyar, Aigner*
28/10	Wacker	a	0-2	
31/10	Mattersburg	h	2-2	*Standfest, Kuljic (p)*
3/11	Altach	a	0-1	
11/11	Austria Kärnten	a	1-0	*Schiemer*
25/11	Rapid Wien	h	0-0	
2/12	Ried	a	1-1	*Ertl*
9/12	Sturm	h	1-2	*Lafata*
14/12	Mattersburg	a	1-1	*Lafata*
2008				
16/2	Altach	h	1-1	*Aigner*
23/2	Salzburg	h	3-1	*Okotie, Kuljic, Ačimov*
27/2	Wacker	a	2-1	*Okotie, Bąk*
5/3	LASK	h	0-0	
8/3	LASK	a	1-2	*Kuljic*
15/3	Austria Kärnten	h	0-1	
18/3	Rapid Wien	a	0-2	
22/3	Ried	h	2-0	*Lafata 2*
29/3	Sturm	a	2-1	*Okotie, Kuljic*
5/4	Mattersburg	h	0-0	
13/4	Altach	a	4-0	*Aigner, Schiemer, Lafata, Kuljic*
20/4	Salzburg	a	0-2	
26/4	Wacker	h	2-1	*Sariyar, Sulimani*

No	Name	Nat	Pos	Aps	(s)	Gls
30	Milenko AČIMOVIČ	SVN	A	29	(1)	3
11	Johannes AIGNER		A	12	(17)	4
6	Jacek BĄK	POL	D	26		3
15	Jocelyn BLANCHARD	FRA	M	31		2
22	Johannes ERTL		D	22	(4)	2
32	Sašo FORNEZZI	SVN	G	13		
16	Ronald GERCALIU		D	23	(5)	1
2	Alexander GRÜNWALD		M		(1)	
27	Sanel KULJIC		A	32	(2)	11
14	David LAFATA	CZE	A	11	(11)	5
20	Andreas LASNIK		M	12	(13)	1
9	Wolfgang MAIR		A	12	(10)	1
5	Mario MAJSTOROVIC		M	18	(1)	
18	Florian METZ		M	19	(3)	
19	Rafael Rubin OKOTIE		A	10	(9)	3
17	Thomas PICHLMANN		A		(1)	
8	Arek RADOMSKI	POL	D	6		
26	Yüksel SARIYAR		M	15	(10)	2
24	Franz SCHIEMER		D	25	(1)	3
31	Joachim STANDFEST		M	32	(2)	1
23	Emin SULIMANI		M	18	(11)	3
1	Szabolcs SÁFÁR	HUN	G	23		
3	Ariel Fernando TROYANSKY	ARG	D	4	(2)	1
10	Štěpán VACHOUŠEK	CZE	D	3	(2)	

LASK LINZ

Coach – Karl Daxbacher
Founded – 1908
MAJOR HONOURS: Austrian League – (1) 1965; Austrian Cup – (1) 1965.

2007				
0/7	Austria Kärnten	h	1-0	*Klein*
4/7	Austria Wien	a	1-1	*Panis*
20/7	Sturm	a	0-4	
28/7	Salzburg	a	1-2	*Vastic (p)*
5/8	Ried	h	1-0	*Saurer*
12/8	Rapid Wien	h	2-0	*Mayrleb, Vastic*
18/8	Wacker	a	2-1	*Mayrleb, Vastic*
25/8	Mattersburg	h	0-2	
31/8	Altach	a	2-2	*Mayrleb, Vastic*
15/9	Altach	h	2-0	*Saurer, Mijatović*
22/9	Austria Kärnten	a	4-1	*Vastic, Mijatović, og (Bubenik), Wendel*
26/9	Austria Wien	h	1-1	*Mijatović*
29/9	Sturm	h	2-2	*Saurer, Vastic*
7/10	Salzburg	h	4-1	*Mijatović 2, Panis, Dollinger*
20/10	Ried	a	0-3	
26/10	Rapid Wien	a	4-4	*Mayrleb 2 (1p), Wisio, Baur*
31/10	Wacker	h	5-0	*Vastic 2, Hoheneder, Mayrleb (p), Mijatović*
4/11	Mattersburg	a	0-0	
9/11	Salzburg	h	1-1	*Mayrleb*
24/11	Wacker	a	0-2	
1/12	Altach	a	0-0	
3/12	Austria Kärnten	h	4-0	*Wendel, Adi, Mayrleb, Pichler*
16/12	Rapid Wien	a	0-2	
2008				
17/2	Ried	h	1-0	*Wendel*
22/2	Sturm	a	2-1	*Mayrleb 2*
27/2	Mattersburg	h	2-1	*Vastic (p), Mayrleb (p)*
5/3	Austria Wien	a	0-0	
8/3	Austria Wien	h	2-1	*Saurer, Adi*
16/3	Salzburg	a	0-4	
19/3	Wacker	h	3-3	*Vastic 2, Saurer*
22/3	Altach	h	3-0	*Baur, Saurer, Mijatović*
29/3	Austria Kärnten	a	1-2	*Vastic*
5/4	Rapid Wien	h	1-2	*Wendel*
12/4	Ried	a	1-1	*Vastic*
20/4	Sturm Graz	h	1-2	*Mijatović*
26/4	Mattersburg	a	0-1	

No	Name	Nat	Pos	Aps	(s)	Gls
11	ADI Rocha Sobrinho Filho	BRA	A	9	(9)	2
28	Michael BAUR		D	35		2
1	Silvije ČAVLINA	CRO	G	36		
7	Matthias DOLLINGER		M	13	(6)	1
5	Gerald GANSTERER		M	16		
27	Ali HAMDEMIR		M		(3)	
3	Niklas HOHENEDER		D	36		1
10	Almedin HOTA	BIH	M	24	(5)	
13	Wolfgang KLAPF		D	23	(4)	
19	Florian KLEIN		M	34		1
4	Georg MARGREITTER		D	4	(4)	
17	Christian MAYRLEB		A	23	(2)	11
18	Mario MIJATOVIĆ	CRO	A	9	(21)	8
8	Jürgen PANIS		M	32		2
2	Sascha PICHLER		M		(5)	1
31	Matías Nicolás RODRÍGUEZ	ARG	M	1		
22	Harald RUCKENDORFER		A		(2)	
20	Christoph SAURER		M	21	(12)	6
26	Ralph SPIRK		D		(3)	
29	Marino Néstor TORRES	ARG	A	4	(4)	
9	Ivica VASTIC		A	32		13
30	Richard WEMMER		M	3	(1)	
15	WENDEL Raul Gonçalves Gomes	BRA	M	23	(1)	4
6	Tomasz WISIO	POL	D	18	(5)	1

SV MATTERSBURG

Coach – Franz Lederer
Founded – 1922

2007				
11/7	Ried	a	2-1	*Mörz (p), Jancker*
22/7	Wacker	a	2-2	*Fuchs, Schmidt*
25/7	Rapid Wien	h	3-2	*Jancker, Schmidt, Wagner*
28/7	Sturm	h	2-2	*Csizmadia, Fuchs*
5/8	Altach	h	4-1	*Jancker, Mörz 2 (1p), Wagner*
11/8	Austria Kärnten	a	1-1	*Wagner*
19/8	Austria Wien	h	0-1	
25/8	LASK	a	2-0	*og (Vastic), Naumoski*
2/9	Salzburg	h	1-1	*Csizmadia*
15/9	Salzburg	a	1-2	*Sedloski (p)*
21/9	Ried	h	5-1	*Mörz 3 (1p), Schmidt, Jancker*
26/9	Rapid Wien	a	0-1	
29/9	Wacker	h	3-1	*Jancker 2, Naumoski*
5/10	Sturm	a	0-0	
20/10	Altach	a	0-0	
27/10	Austria Kärnten	h	5-2	*Sedloski, Jancker, Naumoski, Schmidt, og (Bubenik)*
31/10	Austria Wien	a	2-2	*Naumoski, Jancker*
4/11	LASK	h	0-0	
10/11	Rapid Wien	a	1-3	*Atan*
24/11	Ried	h	1-1	*Naumoski*
1/12	Sturm	a	1-2	*Wagner*
8/12	Altach	h	3-3	*Mörz 2, Pöllhuber*
14/12	Austria Wien	h	1-1	*Jancker*
2008				
15/2	Salzburg	a	0-4	
23/2	Wacker	h	2-1	*Mörz, Jancker*
27/2	LASK	a	1-2	*Jancker*
1/3	Austria Kärnten	h	1-0	*Fuchs*
8/3	Austria Kärnten	a	0-1	
14/3	Rapid Wien	h	1-0	*Jancker*
19/3	Ried	a	0-0	
22/3	Sturm	h	1-1	*Sedloski*
29/3	Altach	a	0-2	
5/4	Austria Wien	a	0-0	
12/4	Salzburg	h	3-2	*Pöllhuber, Sedloski, Atan*
20/4	Wacker	a	5-0	*Lindner 2, Kühbauer 2, Kovrig*
26/4	LASK	h	1-0	*Kovrig*

No	Name	Nat	Pos	Aps	(s)	Gls
21	Robert ALMER		G	11		
27	Cem ATAN		M	30	(3)	2
1	Thomas BORENITSCH		G	25		
12	Patrick BÜRGER		D	1	(8)	
26	Csaba CSIZMADIA	HUN	D	29	(3)	2
14	Dominik DOLESCHAL		M	3	(1)	
25	Christian FUCHS		M	33		3
8	Carsten JANCKER	GER	A	32	(1)	12
17	Ákos KOVRIG	HUN	M	13	(7)	2
10	Dietmar KÜHBAUER		M	29		2
11	Matthias LINDNER		A	2	(5)	2
4	Nedejko MALIĆ	BIH	D		(3)	
15	Jürgen MANSBERGER		D	1	(8)	
5	Michael MÖRZ		M	34	(1)	9

7	Adnan MRAVAC		D	28	(1)	
24	Ilco NAUMOSKI	MKD	A	21	(8)	5
6	Anton PAUSCHENWEIN		M	4	(6)	
2	Alexander PÖLLHUBER		D	22	(2)	2
19	Markus SCHMIDT		M	26	(4)	4
3	Goce SEDLOSKI	MKD	D	35		4
9	Thomas WAGNER		A	17	(17)	4

SK RAPID WIEN

Coach – Peter Pacult

Founded – 1899

MAJOR HONOURS: Austrian League - (32) 1912, 1913, 1916, 1917, 1919, 1920, 1921, 1923, 1929, 1930, 1935, 1938, 1940, 1941, 1946, 1948, 1951, 1952, 1954, 1956, 1957, 1960, 1964, 1967, 1968, 1982, 1983, 1987, 1988, 1996, 2005, 2008; Austrian Cup - (14) 1919, 1920, 1927, 1946, 1961, 1968, 1969, 1972, 1976, 1983, 1984, 1985, 1987, 1995.

2007				
11/7	Wacker	h	3-1	*Patocka, Bošković, Hofmann*
25/7	Mattersburg	a	2-3	*Bilić, Katzer*
1/8	Altach	a	1-0	*Bazina (p)*
5/8	Austria Wien	h	0-0	
8/8	Austria Kärnten	h	4-0	*Bazina, Katzer, Bilić, Bošković*
12/8	LASK	a	0-2	
19/8	Salzburg	h	1-0	*Katzer*
25/8	Ried	a	3-0	*Bošković, Hofmann, Bilić*
2/9	Sturm	a	0-1	
15/9	Sturm	h	1-5	*Bazina*
23/9	Wacker	a	1-1	*Hiden*
26/9	Mattersburg	h	1-0	*Bilić*
29/9	Altach	h	0-2	
7/10	Austria Kärnten	a	2-1	*Kavlak, Bazina*
21/10	Austria Wien	a	2-2	*Kulovits, Bilić*
26/10	LASK	h	4-4	*Hiden, Dober, Kavlak, Patocka*
30/10	Salzburg	a	1-2	*Bošković*
3/11	Ried	h	4-0	*Bazina, Hofmann (p), Dober, Hoffer*
10/11	Mattersburg	h	3-1	*Dober, Bazina, Hofmann (p)*
25/11	Austria Wien	a	0-0	
1/12	Salzburg	h	1-3	*Tokić*
8/12	Wacker	a	1-1	*Heikkinen*
16/12	LASK	h	2-0	*Bazina, Hofmann*
2008				
16/2	Austria Kärnten	a	2-0	*Hoffer 2*
24/2	Altach	a	1-2	*Bošković*
27/2	Ried	h	4-0	*Hoffer, Bošković, Dober, Eder*
2/3	Sturm	a	2-0	*Maierhofer, Bazina*
7/3	Sturm	h	2-1	*Bazina, Hofmann (p)*
14/3	Mattersburg	a	0-1	
18/3	Austria Wien	h	2-0	*Maierhofer 2*
23/3	Salzburg	a	7-0	*Hoffer 3, Maierhofer 2, Korkmaz, Hofmann*
29/3	Wacker	h	4-1	*Maierhofer, Hofmann (p), Eder, Bošković*
5/4	LASK	a	2-1	*Hofmann (p), Korkmaz*
11/4	Austria Kärnten	h	2-1	*Hofmann, Hoffer*
20/4	Altach	h	3-0	*Bošković, Maierhofer, Hoffer*
26/4	Ried	a	1-0	*Hoffer*

No	Name	Nat	Pos	Aps	(s)	Gls
10	Mario BAZINA	CRO	A	30	(4)	9
9	Mate BILIĆ	CRO	M	11	(8)	5
25	Branko BOŠKOVIĆ	MNE	M	28	(6)	8
23	Andreas DOBER		D	23	(1)	4
18	Hannes EDER		D	11	(3)	2
20	FABIANO de Lima Campos	BRA	M	3	(14)	
22	Georg HARDING		D	3	(7)	
1	Raimund HEDL		G		(1)	
8	Markus HEIKKINEN	FIN	M	28		1
4	Martin HIDEN		D	11	(6)	2
11	Steffen HOFMANN	GER	M	36		10
21	Erwin HOFFER		A	16	(13)	10
13	Markus KATZER		D	15	(2)	3
17	Veli KAVLAK		M	20	(7)	2
14	Ümit KORKMAZ		M	22	(9)	2
7	Stefan KULOVITS		M	14	(9)	1
9	Stefan MAIERHOFER		A	6	(5)	7
32	Stefan PALLA		A		(1)	
3	Jürgen PATOCKA		D	35		2
24	Helge PAYER		G	36		
16	Mario SARA		D	3	(1)	
6	Christian THONHOFER		D	24	(2)	
2	Mario TOKIĆ	CRO	D	21	(1)	1

SV RIED

Coach – Helmut Kraft; (22/10/07) Thomas Weissenböck

Founded – 1912

2007				
11/7	Mattersburg	h	1-2	*Damjanović*
14/7	Altach	a	3-2	*Kujabi, Damjanović 2*
22/7	Austria Kärnten	a	3-0	*Drechsel 2, Pichorner*
27/7	Austria Wien	h	0-1	
5/8	LASK	a	0-1	
11/8	Salzburg	a	0-2	
19/8	Sturm	h	5-3	*Salihi, Pichorner, Erbek, Drechsel, Damjanović*
25/8	Rapid Wien	h	0-3	
2/9	Wacker	a	1-0	*Salihi*
15/9	Wacker	h	0-0	
21/9	Mattersburg	a	1-5	*Salihi*
26/9	Altach	h	3-0	*Salihi 2, Tóth*
29/9	Austria Kärnten	h	3-1	*Drechsel 2 (2p), Salihi*
7/10	Austria Wien	a	1-2	*Drechsel (p)*
20/10	LASK	h	3-0	*Dospel, Brenner, Akagündüz*
27/10	Salzburg	h	2-0	*Salihi, Drechsel*
31/10	Sturm	a	0-5	
3/11	Rapid Wien	a	0-4	
10/11	Sturm	h	0-0	
24/11	Mattersburg	a	1-1	*Salihi*
2/12	Austria Wien	h	1-1	*Đokić*
7/12	Salzburg	a	0-2	
15/12	Wacker	h	0-0	
2008				
17/2	LASK	a	0-1	
23/2	Austria Kärnten	h	3-0	*Drechsel, Salihi 2*
27/2	Rapid Wien	a	0-4	
1/3	Altach	h	3-1	*Akagündüz, Drechsel, Salihi*
8/3	Altach	a	2-3	*Akagündüz, Dospel*
15/3	Sturm	a	0-2	
19/3	Mattersburg	h	0-0	
22/3	Austria Wien	a	0-2	
30/3	Salzburg	h	1-2	*Salihi*
5/4	Wacker	a	0-1	
12/4	LASK	h	1-1	*Akagündüz*
20/4	Austria Kärnten	a	0-0	
26/4	Rapid Wien	h	0-1	

No	Name	Nat	Pos	Aps	(s)	Gls
15	Muhammet AKAGÜNDÜZ		A	25	(2)	4
1	Hans-Peter BERGER		G	26		
18	Ewald BRENNER		D	25	(5)	1
9	Jovan DAMJANOVIĆ	SRB	A	7	(1)	4
11	Rade ĐOKIĆ	BIH	A	6	(19)	1

No	Name	Nat	Pos	Aps	(s)	Gls
7	Ernst DOSPEL		D	30		2
6	Herwig DRECHSEL		M	30		9
3	Harun ERBEK		M	22	(11)	1
4	Thomas GEBAUER		G	10	(1)	
	Oliver GLASNER		D	28		
9	Peter HACKMAIR		M	28	(1)	
0	Anel HADŽIĆ	BIH	D	2	(12)	
1	Mario ILLIBAUER		M	1	(1)	
	Christoph JANK		D	36		
	Bozo KOVACEVIC		M	7	(3)	
	Pa Saikou KUJABI	GAM	D	13	(10)	1
	Thomas LECHNER		D		(2)	
0	Sebastian MARTINEZ		M	7	(7)	
3	Miron MUSLIC		A		(4)	
8	Jürgen PICHORNER		D	20	(5)	2
	Tomasz RZASA	POL	D	27	(1)	
4	Hamdi SALIHI	ALB	A	31	(2)	12
5	Manuel SCHMIDL		M		(5)	
	Daniel TOTH		M	15	(13)	1

FC SALZBURG

Coach – Giovanni Trapattoni (ITA)

Founded – 1933

MAJOR HONOURS: Austrian League - (4) 1994, 1995, 1997, 2007.

007				
1/7	Altach	h	4-1	*Ježek, Leitgeb, Zickler 2*
5/7	Austria Kärnten	a	0-1	
2/7	Austria Wien	a	2-2	*Vonlanthen, Sekagya*
8/7	LASK	h	2-1	*Zickler 2*
/8	Sturm	a	0-0	
1/8	Ried	h	2-0	*Piták, Alex*
9/8	Rapid Wien	a	0-1	
5/8	Wacker	h	3-1	*Lokvenc, Kovač, Carboni*
/9	Mattersburg	a	1-1	*Zickler*
5/9	Mattersburg	h	2-1	*Zickler, Meyer*
3/9	Altach	a	1-1	*Vonlanthen*
6/9	Austria Kärnten	h	3-0	*Ježek, Leitgeb, Lokvenz*
9/9	Austria Wien	h	0-1	
/10	LASK	a	1-4	*Ježek*
0/10	Sturm	h	4-1	*Leitgeb, Lokvenc, Zickler, Aufhauser (p)*
7/10	Ried	a	0-2	
0/10	Rapid Wien	h	2-1	*Steinhöfer, Zickler*
/11	Wacker	a	1-3	*Sekagya*
0/11	LASK	a	1-1	*Ilić*
4/11	Austria Kärnten	h	1-1	*Zickler*
/12	Rapid Wien	a	3-1	*Leitgeb, Steinhöfer, Zickler*
/12	Ried	h	2-0	*Zickler, Piták*
6/12	Sturm	a	1-1	*Rakić*
008				
5/2	Mattersburg	h	4-0	*Janko, Zickler, Kovač (p), Ilić*
4/2	Austria Wien	a	1-3	*Zickler*
7/2	Altach	h	4-0	*Zickler 2, Janko, Sekagya*
/3	Wacker	h	2-0	*Ilić, Janko (p)*
/3	Wacker	a	2-1	*Janko, Ilić*
6/3	LASK	h	4-0	*Rakic, Ilić (p), og (Klapf), Dudić*
9/3	Austria Kärnten	a	0-0	
23/3	Rapid Wien	h	0-7	
30/3	Ried	a	2-1	*Ježek, Kovač*
/4	Sturm	h	3-0	*Ngwat-Mahop, Ježek, Ilić*
12/4	Mattersburg	a	2-3	*Janko, Ilić*
20/4	Austria Wien	h	2-0	*Ilić, Zickler*
26/4	Altach	a	1-1	*Vonlanthen*

No	Name	Nat	Pos	Aps	(s)	Gls
8	Alessandro Santos ALEX	JPN	D	11		1
28	René AUFHAUSER		M	12	(10)	1
2	Laszló BODNÁR	HUN	D	7	(2)	
5	Ezequiel Alejo CARBONI	ARG	M	31	(1)	1
3	Milan DUDIĆ	SRB	D	17	(3)	1
22	Saša ILIĆ	SRB	M	24	(6)	8
21	Mark JANKO		A	10	(4)	5
27	Vladimír JANOČKO	SVK	M	2	(1)	
11	Patrik JEŽEK	CZE	M	26	(2)	5
15	Aleksander KNAVS	SVN	D		(2)	
6	Niko KOVAČ	CRO	M	24	(1)	3
24	Christoph LEITGEB		M	24	(7)	4
9	Vratislav LOKVENC	CZE	A	6	(11)	3
18	Remo MEYER	SUI	M	7	(4)	1
17	Tsuneyasu MIYAMOTO	JPN	D	10	(2)	
29	Louis Clement NGWAT-MAHOP	CMR	A	5	(7)	1
1	Timo OCHS	GER	G	36		
14	Sonko Pa OUSMAN	GAM	D		(1)	
8	Manuel PAMIĆ	CRO	M	6		
16	Karel PITÁK	CZE	M	11	(9)	2
4	Norman PRENN		M		(1)	
19	Đorđe RAKIĆ	SRB	M	5	(11)	2
23	Ibrahim SEKAGYA	UGA	D	34		3
20	Markus STEINHÖFER	GER	M	30	(2)	2
31	Jorge VARGAS	CHI	D	23		
10	Johan VONLANTHEN	SUI	M	7	(13)	3
7	Alexander ZICKLER	GER	A	28	(1)	16

SK STURM GRAZ

Coach – Franco Foda (GER)

Founded – 1909

MAJOR HONOURS: Austrian League - (2) 1998, 1999; Austrian Cup - (3) 1996, 1997, 1999.

2007				
11/7	Austria Wien	h	2-2	*Haas, Krammer*
14/7	Wacker	a	0-0	
20/7	LASK	h	4-0	*Stanković 3, Salmutter*
28/7	Mattersburg	a	2-2	*Muratović, Salmutter*
4/8	Salzburg	h	0-0	
11/8	Altach	h	3-1	*Haas, Rabihou 2*
19/8	Ried	a	3-5	*Rabihou, Muratović, Haas*
26/8	Austria Kärnten	h	1-3	*Stanković*
2/9	Rapid Wien	h	1-0	*Krammer*
15/9	Rapid Wien	a	5-1	*Haas, Salmutter 2, Säumel, Muratović*
23/9	Austria Wien	a	0-1	
26/9	Wacker	h	3-0	*Säumel, Haas 2*
29/9	LASK	a	2-2	*Muratović, Haas*
5/10	Mattersburg	h	0-0	
20/10	Salzburg	a	1-4	*Kienzl*
27/10	Altach	a	0-0	
31/10	Ried	h	5-0	*Haas, Muratović 2, Säumel, Salmutter*
3/11	Austria Kärnten	a	0-0	
10/11	Ried	a	0-0	
24/11	Altach	h	6-1	*Haas, Jantscher, Muratović, Stanković, Säumel, Beichler*
1/12	Mattersburg	h	2-1	*Haas, Prettenthaler*
9/12	Austria Wien	a	2-1	*Haas, Salmutter*
15/12	Salzburg	h	1-1	*Prödl*
2008				
16/2	Wacker	a	0-1	
22/2	LASK	h	1-2	*Muratović*
26/2	Austria Kärnten	a	2-0	*Säumel, Muratović*
2/3	Rapid Wien	h	0-2	
7/3	Rapid Wien	a	1-2	*Krammer*
15/3	Ried	h	2-0	*Prettenthaler, Stanković*

19/3	Altach	a	2-1	*Stanković, Prettenthaler*
22/3	Mattersburg	a	1-1	*Muratović*
29/3	Austria Wien	h	1-2	*og (Bqk)*
5/4	Salzburg	a	0-3	
12/4	Wacker	h	2-0	*Haas, Muratović*
20/4	LASK	a	2-1	*Haas, Jantscher*
26/4	Austria Kärnten	h	3-1	*Prödl, Haas, Kienzl*

No	Name	Nat	Pos	Aps	(s)	Gls
28	Daniel BEICHLER		D	3	(3)	1
29	Sandro FODA	GER	D		(1)	
18	Thomas FRIESS		D	1	(2)	
1	Christian GRATZEI		G	31	(1)	
11	Mario HAAS		A	35		14
13	Jakob JANTSCHER		M	4	(8)	2
31	Leonhard KAUFMANN		D		(2)	
19	Mario KIENZL		M	28	(2)	2
14	Thomas KRAMMER		M	33	(1)	3
16	Mario KREIMER		M		(7)	
26	Christoph KRÖPFL		A	1	(2)	
2	Fabian LAMOTTE	GER	D	36		
20	Sandro LINDSCHINGER		D	1	(7)	
10	Samir MURATOVIĆ	BIH	M	34		11
7	Ozren PERIĆ	BIH	M	1	(14)	
5	Mark PRETTENTHALER		D	30		2
15	Sebastian PRÖDL		D	26	(1)	3
33	Jürgen PRUTSCH		M		(1)	
17	Amadou RABIHOU	CMR	A	1	(6)	3
8	Herbert RAUTER		M		(1)	
21	Klaus SALMUTTER		M	25	(5)	6
24	Jürgen SÄUMEL		M	30		5
22	Josef SCHICKLGRUBER		G	5		
6	Giorgi SHASHIASHVILI	GEO	D	32		
4	Mario SONNLEITNER		D	18	(2)	
9	Marko STANKOVIC		A	18	(17)	7
23	Gernot SUPPAN		D	3	(10)	

FC WACKER INNSBRUCK

Coach – Lars Søndergaard (DEN); (22/10/07) Helmut Kraft

Founded - 1913

MAJOR HONOURS: Austrian League – (10) 1971, 1972, 1973, 1975, 1977, 1989, 1990, 2000, 2001, 2002; Austrian Cup – (7) 1970, 1973, 1975, 1978, 1979, 1989, 1993.

2007				
11/7	Rapid Wien	a	1-3	*Aganun*
14/7	Sturm	h	0-0	
22/7	Mattersburg	h	2-2	*Orosz, Mimm*
29/7	Altach	a	1-2	*Orosz*
3/8	Austria Kärnten	h	1-1	*Orosz*
10/8	Austria Wien	a	1-6	*Schreter*
18/8	LASK	h	1-2	*Eder*
25/8	Salzburg	a	1-3	*Eder*
2/9	Ried	h	0-1	
15/9	Ried	a	0-0	
23/9	Rapid Wien	h	1-1	*Madl*
26/9	Sturm	a	0-3	
29/9	Mattersburg	a	1-3	*Dollinger*
20/10	Austria Kärnten	a	0-2	
24/10	Altach	h	0-1	
28/10	Austria Wien	h	2-0	*Orosz 2 (1p)*
31/10	LASK	a	0-5	
3/11	Salzburg	h	3-1	*Hattenberger 2, Mader*
10/11	Altach	a	1-1	*Orosz*
24/11	LASK	h	2-0	*Orosz, Hattenberger*
30/11	Austria Kärnten	a	2-0	*Feldhofer, Hölzl*
8/12	Rapid Wien	h	1-1	*Mimm*
15/12	Ried	a	0-0	
2008				
16/2	Sturm	h	1-0	*Knabel*
23/2	Mattersburg	a	1-2	*Hölzl*
27/2	Austria Wien	h	1-2	*Schreter (p)*
5/3	Salzburg	a	0-2	
9/3	Salzburg	h	1-2	*Orosz*
15/3	Altach	h	1-1	*Hölzl*
19/3	LASK	a	3-3	*Kloušek, Orosz, Madl*
22/3	Austria Kärnten	h	0-0	
29/3	Rapid Wien	a	1-4	*Schrott*
5/4	Ried	h	1-0	*Aganun*
12/4	Sturm Graz	a	0-2	
20/4	Mattersburg	h	0-5	
26/4	Austria Wien	a	1-2	*Koloušek*

No	Name	Nat	Pos	Aps	(s)	Gls
30	Olushola Olumuyiwa AGANUN	NGA	A	8	(13)	2
21	Emmanuel CLOTTEY	GHA	A	3	(2)	
35	Dario DARKOVIC		D	1		
24	Martin DOLLINGER		M	7	(14)	1
6	Amer DURMIC		D	4		
21	Thomas EDER		M	10	(8)	2
3	Ferdinand FELDHOFER		D	20		1
1	Pascal GRÜNWALD		G	10		
25	Theo GRÜNER		M	5		
5	Matthias HATTENBERGER		M	19		3
11	Andras HÖLZL		M	25		3
23	Besian IDRIZAJ		M	1	(1)	
2	Giullermo Sergio IMHOFF	ARG	M	4		
28	Thorsten KNABEL		D	22	(4)	1
8	Václav KOLOUŠEK	CZE	M	31	(1)	2
27	Mattias LINDSTRÖM	SWE	M	13		
10	Florian MADER		M	22		1
15	Michael MADL		M	21		2
7	Dennis MIMM		D	32	(1)	2
9	Péter OROSZ	HUN	A	29	(5)	9
19	Željko PAVLOVIĆ	CRO	G	26		
22	Julius PERSTALLER		M		(1)	
26	Benjamin PRANTNER		D		(1)	
32	Martin SALTUARI		A		(7)	
18	Sandro SAMWALD		M	11	(14)	
13	Marcel SCHRETER		M	13	(11)	2
14	Andreas SCHROTT		D	27	(1)	1
16	Markus SEELAUS		M	6	(10)	
17	Bernd WINDISCH		D	26	(7)	

PROMOTED CLUB

KAPFENBERGER SV

Coach – Werner Gregoritsch

Founded - 1919

SECOND LEVEL FINAL TABLE 2007/08

		Pld	W	D	L	F	A	P
1	Kapfenberger SV	33	19	9	5	79	45	6
2	FC Gratkorn	33	15	10	8	51	35	5
3	SC Austria Lustenau	33	15	9	9	59	45	5
4	FC Lustenau 07	33	15	8	10	50	39	5
5	FK Austria Wien Amateure	33	14	8	11	45	44	5
6	FC Salzburg Amateure	33	13	7	13	51	52	4
7	SC Schwanenstadt	33	13	6	14	48	51	4
8	DSV Leoben	33	11	8	14	44	46	4
9	SK Schwadorf	33	12	5	16	48	53	4
10	FC Kärnten	33	11	7	15	37	51	4
11	SC/ESV Parndorf 1919	33	10	7	16	45	61	3
12	SV Bad Aussee	33	4	8	21	35	70	2

Vogts comes to the rescue

Rock bottom of UEFA EURO 2008™ Qualifying Group A with five points from 12 matches – the two fixtures against Armenia were cancelled – and ccupying their lowest position in the FIFA world ankings – 137th – for a decade, Azerbaijan's new ederation president Rovnaq Abdullayev decided to nake his mark by appointing a prestigious foreign oach, German Berti Vogts, in advance of the 2010 FIFA Vorld Cup qualifying campaign.

'ogts, who led Nigeria into the 2008 African Cup of lations in January was appointed as the new Azerbaijan ead coach in April. His first two matches, in early June, rought mixed fortunes – a 1-0 defeat by Bosnia-lerzegovina followed by a 2-1 win four days later in ndorra. The two goalscorers, curiously, were both aturalised foreigners – Brazilian-born midfielder Fábio nd Serbian striker Branimir Subašić.

mong the teams Vogts will be facing on the road to outh Africa are Germany, his country of birth and the eam he steered to UEFA European Championship glory 1 1996. He should be well settled into the job before the rst of those two fixtures – in Baku on 19 August 2009.

oreign trend

'ogts was preceded as Azerbaijan oach by Gjokica Hadžievski, lthough the former FYR Macedonia oss was in charge for just three natches, including the final two JEFA EURO 2008™ qualifiers. This rend for hiring foreign coaches is not mited to the national team. ladžievski doubled as the coach of K Bakı in 2007/08, while several ther leading Premyer Liqa clubs vere commanded by well known nports, such as Rasim Kara (Turkey, K Qarabağ), Kakhaber Tskhadadze Georgia, FK Standard Bakı), Vlastimil etržela (Czech Republic, PFC Neftçi) and Anatoliy Demyanenko (Ukraine, also Neftçi).

The most successful foreign coach was Ukrainian Valentyn Khodukhin who, in his second full season in charge of PİK İnter Bakı, brought the club their first national title. Sponsored by the Azerbaijan International Bank, İnter stormed to the summit with six successive victories in the closing weeks, enabling them to pursue, catch and overtake city rivals FK Olimpiki Bakı and Neftçi right at the death.

Olimpik, coached by ex-national team boss Äsgär Abdullayev and also seeking a maiden league triumph, were firm favourites to take the championship going into the final day – thanks chiefly to their remarkable record of having conceded just six goals in their 25 matches. Leading by three points and needing just one more to be champions, they were moving comfortably towards their seventh goalless draw of the campaign, at home to Qarabağ, when, with ten minutes remaining, the visitors scored through defender Zaur Häşimov. Olimpik were unable to recover and thus İnter, simultaneous 4-0 winners at PFK Qäbälä, took the title. Although the two teams were level on 58 points, the local rule that rewards the team with the most victories favoured İnter, 18 to 17.

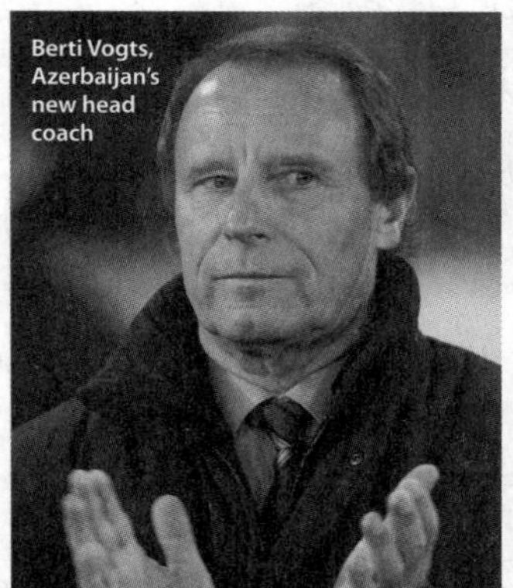
Berti Vogts, Azerbaijan's new head coach

Goals galore

That İnter also massively outscored Olimpik, 55 goals to 29, suggested the more deserving team had triumphed. Seventeen of those goals came in the six-game winning run at the end, with five of that total going to Xaqani Mämmädov, who thus consolidated his position as the Premyer Liqa's top scorer (with 19 in total), and another four to Uruguayan forward Walter Guglielmone (11 in all), a former French league player with AC Ajaccio.

AZERBAIJAN

Azärbaycan Futbol Federasiyalar Assosiasiyasi (AFFA)

2208 Nobel Prospekt
AZ-1025 Bakı
tel - +944 12 4908308
fax - +994 12 4908722
website – www.affa.az
President – Rövnaq Abdullayev
General Secretary – Elkhan Mämmädov
Press Officer – Mikayıl Quliyev

TOP FIVE ALL-TIME CAPS
Aslan Kärimov (79); Tärlan Ähmädov (73); Mahmud Qurbanov (70); Qurban Qurbanov (65); Emin Ağayev (64)

TOP FIVE ALL-TIME GOALS
Qurban Qurbanov (12); Zaur Tağızadä (6); Färrux İsmayılov, Vyaçeslav Lıçkin, Vidadi Rzayev, Branimir Subašić & Nazim Süleymanov (5)

NATIONAL TEAM RESULTS 2007/08

22/8/07	Tajikistan	A	Dushanbe	3-2	*Äliyev S. (25, 43), Subašić (26)*
12/9/07	Georgia	H	Baku	1-1	*Subašić (44)*
13/10/07	Portugal (ECQ)	H	Baku	0-2	
17/10/07	Serbia (ECQ)	H	Baku	1-6	*Äliyev S. (26)*
17/11/07	Finland (ECQ)	A	Helsinki	1-2	*Qurbanov M. (63)*
21/11/07	Belgium (ECQ)	H	Baku	0-1	
3/2/08	Kazakhstan	N	Antalya (TUR)	0-0	
26/3/08	Lithuania	A	Vilnius	0-1	
1/6/08	Bosnia-Herzegovina	A	Zenica	0-1	
4/6/08	Andorra	A	Andorra la Vella	2-1	*Fábio (17), Subašić (43)*

Outgoing champions FK Xäzär Länkäran finished a disappointing fourth in the league but rescued their season by retaining the domestic Cup. Two late extra-time goals from Brazilian midfielder Juninho enabled coach Agasälim Mircavadov to add to his copious trophy collection as Xäzär overcame İnter 2-0. The match took place four days before the final league game of the season, so at the final whistle it appeared that İnter were destined to finish second in both domestic competitions … until Olimpik's final-day slip-up against Qarabağ.

CIS Cup success

Although Xäzär, like Azerbaijan's other European representatives, could not pass the first hurdle of the UEFA Champions League qualifying phase in summer 2007 – they were eliminated 4-2 on aggregate by NK Dinamo Zagreb – they did the nation proud by winning the prestigious CIS Cup, an annual indoor tournament fo the champions of former Soviet republics. They took the trophy in St. Petersburg after a thrilling 4-3 victory over holders FC Pakhtakor Tashkent in the final, with UEFA president Michel Platini among the interested spectators. Coach Mircavadov had also won the trophy two years earlier with Neftçi.

FK ABN Bärdä, who had only competed in the 2007/08 Premyer Liqa due to UEFA Cup participants FK MKT-Araz Imişli's withdrawal for financial reasons, lasted just one season among the elite. After five successive defeats they failed to fulfil their final fixture against Neftçi and were relegated along with PFK Gänclärbirliyi. The two promotion places were filled by FK Bakılı Bakı and FK MOİK Bakı, raising the number of top-flight clubs from the capital in 2008/09 to seven – 50 per cent of the total.

ATIONAL TEAM APPEARANCES 2007/08

ch – Şahin DİNİYEV 12/8/66
/10/07) Gjokica HADŽIEVSKI (MKD) 31/3/55
/3/08) Nazim SÜLEYMANOV 17/2/65
4/08) Berti VOGTS (GER) 30/12/46

			Tjk	Geo	POR	SRB	FIN	BEL	Kaz	Ltu	Bih	And	Caps	Goals
ad VÄLİYEV	1/11/80	Qarabağ	G46	G	G	G46	G	G	G	G		G	21	-
ir ABBASOV	1/2/78	Inter Bakı	D	D	D	D	D	D	D		D	D	22	-
in QULİYEV	22/6/81	Neftçi	D	s87		D	D61	D	D85				18	-
n KÄRİMOV	1/1/73	Qarabağ	D	D87	D			D84	D26				79	-
ksandr CHERTOGANOV	8/2/80	Neftçi	M62	M	M	M			s26	M	M54		18	-
azan ABBASOV	22/9/83	Neftçi	M54	s63		M							9	-
n İMAMÄLİYEV	7/8/80	Inter Bakı	M58	M63	M7								44	1
n QULİYEV	12/4/77	Xäzär Länkäran	M		M	M			M	M16			50	3
hun SULTANOV	12/6/79	Xäzär Länkäran	M53	M66		M69							15	1
ir ÄLİYEV	14/4/79	Neftçi	A65	A78	A73	A							34	4
imir SUBAŠIĆ	7/4/82	Neftçi	A60	A84	A	A	A	A	A	A	A	A46	17	5
angir HÄSÄNZADÄ	4/8/79	Inter Bakı	s46			s46							34	-
ar BAXŞIYEV	3/8/80	Xäzär Länkäran	s53	M		s46				s16	M80	s80	21	-
ad AĞAKİŞİYEV	13/6/85	Qarabağ	s54										3	-
r HAŞİMOV	24/10/81	Xäzär Länkäran	s58	D	s7	D46							19	-
ani MÄMMÄDOV	29/9/76	Inter Bakı	s60	s78	s56			s84	A74		A	s46	20	1
QURBANOV	5/12/77	Xäzär Länkäran	s62	M74	s73	M							10	1
ÄLİYEV	21/8/84	Olimpik	s65		D		s46				D	s58	5	-
ux İSMAYILOV	30/8/78	Olimpik		s66		s69							33	5
ad KÄRİMOV	2/4/86	Xäzär Länkäran		s74									1	-
ir ŞÜKÜROV	12/12/82	Inter Bakı /Länkäran		s84							D78	D58	23	-
YUNİSOĞLU	18/12/85	Groclin (POL)			D		D		D46			s20	7	-
QURBANOV	25/4/86	Sivasspor (TUR)			M56				s85	s56		s58	29	1
n NDUKA	23/3/85	Olimpik					D46			D	D	D20	6	-
ad F. SADIQOV	16/6/82	Neftçi					D	D		D	D	D	43	3
r TAĞIZADÄ	21/2/79	Neftçi					M	M70		M			40	6
mud QURBANOV	10/5/73	Inter Bakı					M	M	M	M		M80	70	1
şid MÄHÄRRÄMOV	3/10/83	Bakı					M	M77					2	-
r RAMAZANOV	27/7/76	Xäzär Länkäran					A	A	A	A56	s80	A90	14	-
RÉ Luiz LADAGA	19/2/75	Bakı					s61						11	1
MÄLİKOV	18/12/85	Neftçi						D	D	D		D	11	-
NDRO Melino GOMES	24/8/76	Bakı						s70					9	-
toli PONOMAREV	12/6/82	GAIS (SWE) /Bakı						s77	s74				14	1
el ÄMİRBÄYOV	23/2/76	Bakı							s46				18	-
r ALLAHVERDİYEV	2/11/83	Neftçi								D			1	-
f MEHDİYEV	17/10/76	Olimpik									G		4	-
O Luís Ramim	10/4/81	Olimpik									M	M	2	1
nal ZEYNALOV	6/12/79	Karvan									s54	M58	4	-
an ÄMİRCANOV	1/2/85	Standard									s78		1	-
d HÜSEYNOV	9/3/88	Inter Bakı										s90	1	-

AZERBAIJAN

DOMESTIC LEAGUE 2007/08

PREMYER LIQA FINAL TABLE

			Home					Away					Total					
		Pld	W	D	L	F	A	W	D	L	F	A	W	D	L	F	A	Pts
1	PİK İnter Bakı	26	10	3	0	29	5	8	1	4	26	13	18	4	4	55	18	58
2	FK Olimpik Bakı	26	10	2	1	18	2	7	5	1	11	5	17	7	2	29	7	58
3	PFK Neftçi	26	9	2	2	24	8	7	5	1	18	10	16	7	3	42	18	55
4	FK Xäzär Länkäran	26	7	5	1	22	7	7	5	1	22	9	14	10	2	44	16	52
5	FK Qarabağ	26	5	5	3	15	10	6	3	4	10	6	11	8	7	25	16	41
6	PFK Qäbälä	26	7	3	3	18	12	4	0	9	15	24	11	3	12	33	36	36
7	PFK Simurq	26	7	4	2	18	7	2	5	6	13	18	9	9	8	31	25	36
8	FK Bakı	26	4	7	2	21	13	4	4	5	14	13	8	11	7	35	26	35
9	FK Standard Bakı	26	4	4	5	21	13	4	4	5	15	13	8	8	10	36	26	32
10	FK Masallı	26	6	3	4	21	15	2	3	8	9	25	8	6	12	30	40	30
11	İK Karvan	26	2	3	8	7	14	4	2	7	16	22	6	5	15	23	36	23
12	PFK Turan	26	3	1	9	12	27	1	5	7	9	22	4	6	16	21	49	18
13	PFK Gänclärbirliyi	26	3	1	9	13	32	1	1	11	8	36	4	2	20	21	68	14
14	FK ABN Bärdä	26	2	3	8	9	24	0	3	10	3	32	2	6	18	12	56	12

TOP GOALSCORERS

19 Xaqani MÄMMÄDOV (İnter Bakı)
14 Branimir SUBAŠIĆ (Neftçi)
11 Walter Fernando GUGLIELMONE (İnter Bakı)
JUNIVAN Soares de Melo (Olimpi
Zaur RAMAZANOV (Xäzär Länkä
10 Volodymyr MAZYAR (Simurq)
9 Giorgi ADAMIA (Neftçi)
Roman AKHALKATSI (Karvan)
8 Vitaliy BALAMESTNY (Qäbälä)
Fernando Néstor PÉREZ (Bakı)
"LÉO" Leonardo da Silva ROCHA (Standard)

CLUB-BY-CLUB

FK ABN BÄRDÄ

Coach - Faiq Cabbarov; (9/10/07) Äli Quliyev

Founded - 2005

2007

19/8	Simurq	h	1-1	*Paşayev*
25/8	Karvan	a	0-2	
2/9	Xäzär Länkäran	h	0-4	
9/9	Olimpik	a	0-1	
16/9	Qarabağ	a	1-3	*Muradov*
22/9	Masallı	a	1-1	*Muradov*
29/9	Turan	h	0-0	
7/10	Gänclärbirliyi	a	0-4	
27/10	Qäbälä	h	1-2	*Äläkbärov*
3/11	İnter Bakı	a	0-4	
11/11	Standard	h	0-1	
24/11	Bakı	a	0-0	
1/12	Neftçi	h	0-2	

2008

16/2	Olimpik	h	1-1	*Qurbanov*
23/2	Simurq	a	1-3	*Babayev*
1/3	Karvan	h	2-0	*Babayev, Paşayev*
16/3	Xäzär Länkäran	a	0-0	
29/3	Masallı	h	1-2	*Rüstämov*
5/4	Turan	a	0-3	
12/4	Gänclärbirliyi	h	2-0	*Salahov, Cälalov*
19/4	Qäbälä	a	0-2	
26/4	Qarabağ	h	0-3	
3/5	İnter Bakı	h	1-4	*Orucov*
9/5	Standard	a	0-6	
17/5	Bakı	h	0-4	
28/5	Neftçi	a	0-3	*(w/o)*

No	Name	Nat	Pos	Aps	(s)	Gls
12, 9	Xaliq ÄLÄKBÄROV		A	12	(2)	1
24	Samir BABAYEV		M	12		2
6	Azär BAĞIROV		D	10		
18, 9	Bähruz CÄLALOV		M	1	(5)	1
1, 22	Bäxtiyar GÖZÄLOV		G	6	(2)	
20, 12	İlqar HÜSEYNOV		M	19	(2)	
15	Ruslan HÜSEYNOV		M	19		
17	Qädir İLYASOV		A		(7)	
14	Pärvin MÄDÄTOV		M	16	(4)	
5	Nail MÄMMÄDOV		M	10		
17	Ramin MÄMMÄDOV		M	7	(1)	
16	Säbuhi MÄMMÄDOV		M		(3)	
3, 18	Ramil MEHDİYEV		D	17		
24	Xalid MURADOV		A	6	(2)	2
23	Samir MÜTÄLLİMOV		M	14	(1)	
6	Rahib NÄCÄFOV		M	1	(2)	
9, 10	Ramil NÄSİBOV		M	9	(2)	
8	Eldäniz ORUCOV		M	22	(2)	1
7	Samir PAŞAYEV		M	14	(6)	2
27	Anar QASIMOV		A	16	(6)	
12	Marat QULİYEV		M	1		
10	Sänan QURBANOV		A	10		1
11	Ruslan RÜSTÄMOV		A	8	(12)	1
2	Ruslan SADIQOV		D	5		
4	Aqşin SALAHOV		D	4	(4)	1
4	Vasif VÄLİYEV		D	12		
18	Elmar XEYİROV		M	5	(2)	
1, 22	Xäyal ZEYNALOV		G	19		

FK BAKI

Coach - Böyükağa Hacıyev; (3/9/07) Gjokica Hadžievski (MKD); (24/5/08) (Asif Äliyev)

Founded - 1997

MAJOR HONOURS: Azerbaijan League - (1) 2006; Azerbaijan Cup - (1) 2005.

2007

12/8	Gänclärbirliyi	h	3-1	*Xälilov, Mujiri, Pérez*
19/8	Qäbälä	a	0-2	
25/8	İnter Bakı	h	0-0	
1/9	Standard	a	1-1	*Rodríguez*
15/9	Masallı	h	2-1	*Quliyev V., Gogoberishvili*
30/9	Olimpik	a	0-3	
7/10	Simurq	h	1-1	*Pérez*

/10	Neftçi	h	5-1	*Tijani 3, Leandro Gomes, Mujiri*
/10	Karvan	a	1-0	*Pérez*
11	Xäzär Länkäran	h	2-2	*Leandro Gomes (p), Pérez*
/11	Qarabağ	a	1-1	*Tijani*
/11	ABN	h	0-0	
12	Turan	a	2-0	*Pérez, Tijani*
08				
/2	Gänclärbirliyi	a	3-0	*Mujiri, Mähärrämov, Pérez*
/2	Qäbälä	h	3-0	*Tijani, Cissé, Ponomarev*
3	İnter Bakı	a	0-1	
/3	Standard	h	0-1	
/3	Neftçi	a	2-3	*Leandro Gomes, og (Sadıqov R. F.)*
4	Olimpik	h	0-1	
/4	Simurq	a	0-0	
/4	Karvan	h	3-3	*Cissé, Tijani, Branković*
/4	Masallı	a	0-2	
5	Xäzär Länkäran	a	0-0	
/5	Qarabağ	h	0-0	
/5	ABN	a	4-0	*Bachev, Cissé, Mujiri, Abdullayev*
/5	Turan	h	2-2	*Pérez 2*

	Name	Nat	Pos	Aps	(s)	Gls
	Asif ABBASOV		D	11		
	Elnur ABBASOV		D	8	(1)	
	Elnur ABDULLAYEV		M	9	(10)	1
	İlqar ÄBDÜRÄHMANOV		D	5	(3)	
	Hafiz ÄLİYEV		A		(1)	
	Vasif ÄLİYEV		M	1		
	Emin ÄMİRASLANOV		A	1		
	Rafael ÄMİRBÄYOV		D	23		
	ANDRÉ Luiz LADAGA		M	9	(4)	
	Stanislav BACHEV	BUL	D	11		1
	Dejan BRANKOVIĆ	SRB	D	11	(1)	1
, 9	Ely CISSÉ	SEN	A	7	(2)	3
	Cvetan CURLINOV	MKD	M		(1)	
	Aleksandre GOGOBERISHVILI	GEO	M	18	(1)	1
, 22	Säbuhi HÄSÄNOV		D	11	(1)	
	Ramal HÜSEYNOV		M	11		
	Bojan ILIĆ	SRB	D	2	(1)	
	LEANDRO Melino GOMES		A	14	(5)	3
	Cämşid MÄHÄRRÄMOV		M	20	(1)	1
	Aqil MÄMMÄDOV		G	3		
	Orxan MİRZÄYEV		G	6		
	Amiran MUJIRI	GEO	M	12	(7)	4
	Asen NIKOLOV	BUL	M	1	(3)	
	Fernando Néstor PÉREZ	ARG	A	21	(3)	8
11	Anatoli PONOMAREV		M	6	(2)	1
	Färid QULİYEV		A	1	(5)	
	Vüqar QULİYEV		D	7	(2)	1
	Israel Rodrigo RODRÍGUEZ	PAR	A	4	(4)	1
	Khalidou SISSOKHO	SEN	G	17		
	Ernad SKULIĆ	CRO	M	10		
	Bäxtiyar SOLTANOV		A	3	(3)	
	Ahmed TIJANI	NGA	A	16	(1)	7
, 11	Tärlan XÄLİLOV		M	5	(7)	1
	Elnur YUSİFOV		M	2		

PFK GÄNCLÄRBİRLİYİ

Coach – Sabir Äliyev; (25/1/08) İsmail Batur (TUR); (15/2/08) Sabir Äliyev

Founded - 2003

07				
/8	Bakı	a	1-3	*Tağıyev*
/8	Neftçi	h	2-6	*Paşayev, Stanić (p)*
/8	Olimpik	a	0-1	
9	Simurq	h	0-3	
/9	Karvan	a	2-1	*Mehdiyev, Sadiqov*
/9	Xäzär Länkäran	h	1-2	*Nuriyev*
/9	Qarabağ	a	1-3	*Stanić (p)*
7/10	ABN	h	4-0	*Musayev 2, Mehdiyev, Tağıyev*
27/10	Turan	a	0-2	
3/11	Masallı	a	0-6	
11/11	Qäbälä	h	0-6	
25/11	İnter Bakı	a	0-3	
1/12	Standard	h	1-5	*Sadiqov*
2008				
16/2	Bakı	h	0-3	
23/2	Neftçi	a	0-2	
1/3	Olimpik	h	0-1	
16/3	Simurq	a	0-3	
29/3	Xäzär Länkäran	a	0-5	
6/4	Qarabağ	h	0-1	
12/4	ABN	a	0-2	
19/4	Turan	h	1-1	*Mämmädov İ.*
26/4	Karvan	h	3-1	*Sadiqov, Mämmädov İ., Mämmädov Z.*
3/5	Masallı	h	1-0	*Äsädov*
12/5	Qäbälä	a	2-2	*Mämmädov Z., Ämiraslanov*
18/5	İnter Bakı	h	0-3	
27/5	Standard	a	2-3	*Mämmädov İ., Stanić*

No	Name	Nat	Pos	Aps	(s)	Gls
	İlqar ABDULLAYEV		M	1	(10)	
20, 2	Orxan AĞAYARZADÄ		D	6	(1)	
24, 6	Ramil AĞAYEV		M	10		
22	Mätläb ÄLÄSOV		M		(1)	
14	Rüstäm ÄLİYEV		D	7		
	Emin ÄMİRASLANOV		A	7	(2)	1
6, 24	Zaur ÄSÄDOV		M	7	(2)	1
1	İlkin BAĞIYEV		G	1	(1)	
19	Karim BANGOURA	GUI	D	2		
25, 20	Seidou Ba CAMARA	GUI	M	6	(1)	
	Tural CÄLİLOV		M	5	(5)	
	ÇETİN Güner	TUR	A	4		
22, 6	ERMAN Güraçar	TUR	D	2		
21, 5	Zaur HİDAYÄTOV		D	10		
6	Ramin HÜSEYNOV		D	6	(1)	
	Zeynalabdin HÜSEYNOV		M	12	(3)	
1, 16	Davud KÄRİMİ		G	13	(2)	
16	Vladimir KRAMARENKO		G	3		
1, 12	Ruslan MÄCİDOV		G	9		
17	Elçin MÄMMÄDOV		M	1	(4)	
7, 15	İsmayıl MÄMMÄDOV		M	9		3
2, 5	Orxan MÄMMÄDOV		D	3	(4)	
	Räşad MÄMMÄDOV		D	8	(2)	
14	Zaur MÄMMÄDOV		M	6	(3)	2
21	Azär MEHDİYEV		M	11		2
	Räşad MURADOV		D	3	(2)	
10	Ruslan MUSAYEV		M	21	(1)	2
22	Äfqan NAĞIYEV		M	4		
4	Ädahim NİFTÄLİYEV		D	11	(1)	
13	Kamil NURÄHMÄDOV		M		(1)	
15	Elvin NURİYEV		M	12		1
8	Emil PAŞAYEV		M	17	(2)	1
	Säbuhi SADİQOV		M	18	(3)	3
19	Azär SÄFÄRLİ		M		(3)	
	Tomislav STANIĆ	BIH	A	16	(2)	3
18	Fäqan ŞAHBAZOV		A	7	(1)	
	Nicat TAĞIYEV		A	3	(7)	2
3	Ramin TANRIVERDİYEV		D	10		
3	Abdul Sittu TAURED	NGA	D	10		
19, 17	Elçin XÄLİLOV		M	5	(2)	

PİK İNTER BAKI

Coach - Valentyn Khodukin (UKR)

Founded – 2004

MAJOR HONOURS: Azerbaijan League - (1) 2008.

2007				
11/8	Masallı	h	3-0	*Mämmädov X., İmamäliyev, Hacıyev*

18/8	Standard	h	1-1	*Hacıyev*
25/8	Bakı	a	0-0	
2/9	Neftçi	h	0-0	
16/9	Olimpik	a	0-1	
29/9	Karvan	a	3-0	*Qurbanov 2, Mämmädov X.*
6/10	Xäzär Länkäran	h	2-2	*İmamäliyev, Zagorac*
20/10	Simurq	h	2-0	*Gedgaudas, Hacıyev (p)*
28/10	Qarabağ	a	1-0	*Mämmädov X.*
3/11	ABN	h	4-0	*Mämmädov X. 2, Guglielmone 2*
10/11	Turan	a	4-0	*Guglielmone, Mämmädov X. 3 (1p)*
25/11	Gänclärbirliyi	h	3-0	*Guglielmone 2, Ražanauskas*
2/12	Qäbälä	a	1-2	*Hacıyev*
2008				
16/2	Masallı	a	3-0	*Mämmädov X., Mämmädov E., İmamäliyev (p)*
24/2	Standard	a	2-1	*Mämmädov X. 2 (1p)*
1/3	Bakı	h	1-0	*Zlatinov*
15/3	Neftçi	a	0-2	
29/3	Simurq	a	4-3	*İmamäliyev, Cuello, Mämmädov X., Georgiev*
6/4	Karvan	h	3-1	*Mämmädov X. 2 (1p), Guglielmone*
13/4	Xäzär Länkäran	a	1-3	*Guglielmone*
19/4	Qarabağ	h	1-0	*Qurbanov*
28/4	Olimpik	h	2-0	*Mämmädov X., Zlatinov*
3/5	ABN	a	4-1	*Guglielmone 2, Zlatinov, Mämmädov X.*
11/5	Turan	h	3-1	*Mämmädov X., Guglielmone, Hüseynov*
18/5	Gänclärbirliyi	a	3-0	*Guglielmone, Mämmädov X. (p), Georgiev*
28/5	Qäbälä	h	4-0	*Cuello, Mämmädov X., Qurbanov, Zlatinov*

No	Name	Nat	Pos	Aps	(s)	Gls
19	Ruslan ABBASOV		D	15	(1)	
9	Samir ABBASOV		D	21		
14	Ramil AĞAYEV		M		(2)	
21	Daniel AXTYAMOV		A		(3)	
18, 11	Goran ARNAUT	SRB	A	22		
22, 13	Branislav ČERVENKA	CZE	M	12	(5)	
4	Román Marcelo CUELLO	URU	A	3	(6)	2
11	Andrius GEDGAUDAS	LTU	A	5	(3)	1
23	Georgi Vladimirov GEORGIEV	BUL	A	2	(9)	2
24, 22	Walter Fernando GUGLIELMONE	URU	A	16	(4)	11
8	Nizami HACIYEV		M	8	(6)	4
42	Elxan HÄSÄNOV		G	2		
1, 12	Cahangir HÄSÄNZADÄ		G	6		
25	Cavid HÜSEYNOV		A	1	(5)	1
10	Emin İMAMÄLİYEV		M	18	(1)	4
6	Aliyar ISMAILOV	RUS	M	23		
4	Nikola JOLOVIĆ	SRB	D	1		
3	Mixail KİTELMAN		M	1	(6)	
15	Vladimir LEVIN		D	11	(1)	
17	Elvin MÄMMÄDOV		M	7	(2)	1
20	Xaqani MÄMMÄDOV		A	22	(1)	19
12	Xäyal MUSTAFAYEV		D	5	(3)	
7, 77	Ramin NÄSİBOV		A	4	(1)	
	Mahmud QURBANOV		M	21	(2)	4
16	Tomas RAŽANAUSKAS	LTU	M	10	(4)	1
2	Şähriyar RÄHİMOV		D		(1)	
77, 88	Svilen SIMEONOV	BUL	G	18		
	Mahir ŞÜKÜROV		D	12		
5	Milan ZAGORAC	SRB	D	16	(1)	1
	Petar ZLATINOV	BUL	M	4	(6)	4

İK KARVAN

Coach – Täbriz Häsänov; (29/12/07) Yunis Hüseynov

Founded - 2004

2007				
12/8	Xäzär Länkäran	h	0-1	
18/8	Qarabağ	a	1-0	*Akhalkatsi*
25/8	ABN	h	2-0	*Marcos (p), Camara*
1/9	Turan	a	5-1	*Camara 2, Akhalkatsi Marcos (p)*
15/9	Gänclärbirliyi	h	1-2	*Camara (p)*
23/9	Qäbälä	a	0-1	
29/9	İnter Bakı	h	0-3	
7/10	Standard	a	2-1	*Quliyev, Akhalkatsi*
28/10	Bakı	h	0-1	
3/11	Neftçi	a	1-2	*Karadanov*
10/11	Olimpik	h	0-1	
24/11	Simurq	a	1-0	*Akhalkatsi*
1/12	Masallı	h	0-1	
2008				
17/2	Xäzär Länkäran	a	0-0	
24/2	Qarabağ	h	0-0	
1/3	ABN	a	0-2	
15/3	Turan	h	1-0	*Mogaâdi*
30/3	Qäbälä	h	1-2	*Camara*
6/4	İnter Bakı	a	1-3	*Akhalkatsi*
12/4	Standard	h	1-1	*Camara*
20/4	Bakı	a	3-3	*Camara, Akhalkatsi, Zeynalov*
26/4	Gänclärbirliyi	a	1-3	*Hüseynov El.*
4/5	Neftçi	h	0-1	
12/5	Olimpik	a	0-2	
18/5	Simurq	h	1-1	*Akhalkatsi*
27/5	Masallı	a	1-4	*Akhalkatsi*

No	Name	Nat	Pos	Aps	(s)	Gls
9	Samir ABDULOV		A	9	(9)	
35	Roman AKHALKATSI	GEO	M	19	(2)	9
11	Souleymane CAMARA	CIV	A	21		7
1	Elçin CÄFÄROV		G	5	(1)	
5	ERNANI Pereira		D	13		
17	Eldar HÜSEYNOV		M	6	(6)	1
6	Emil HÜSEYNOV		D	9	(8)	
10, 88	Elnur İMANQULİYEV		A	5	(2)	
24	Aleksandre INTSKIRVELI	GEO	D	24		
88, 20	Mamedali KARADANOV	TKM	A	5	(5)	1
77, 12	Sahil KÄRİMOV		G	21	(1)	
13	Elnur MÄMMÄDOV		M	2	(1)	
19	Mätläb MÄMMÄDOV		M	16	(5)	
55	Orxan MÄMMÄDOV		M		(2)	
20	Zaur MÄMMÄDOV		M		(1)	
22	MARCOS Ferreira Javier	BRA	M	12		2
34	Cavad MİRZÄYEV		M	17	(4)	
10	Béchir MOGAÂDI	TUN	M	11		1
27	Räşad MURADOV		D	1	(1)	
14	Mekan NASYROV	TKM	M	18	(1)	
88, 4	Adekunle NIYI Julius	NGA	D	2		
14	Francis Uchenna OKONKWO	NGA	D	1		
8	Mübariz ORUCOV		M	3	(4)	
28	Äziz QULİYEV		M	18	(3)	1
15	Cavid RÄHİMOV		A		(10)	
5	Ramin TANRIVERDİYEV		D	6		
7, 27	Gocha TRAPAIDZE	GEO	M	15	(4)	
3	İlham YADULLAYEV		D	17	(1)	
22	Zeynal ZEYNALOV		M	10		1

FK MASALLI

Coach – Qähräman Äliyev; (29/10/07) Fazil Äsädov

Founded - 2006

2007				
11/8	İnter Bakı	a	0-3	
18/8	Xäzär Länkäran	h	0-3	
25/8	Standard	a	1-4	*Äliyev*

'9	Qarabağ	h	1-0	*Fabinho*
5/9	Bakı	a	1-2	*Osmar*
2/9	ABN	h	1-1	*Mehräliyev*
9/9	Neftçi	a	0-4	
'10	Turan	h	3-1	*Celsinho, Osmar, Daşdämirov*
7/10	Olimpik	a	1-3	*Osmar*
'11	Gänclärbirliyi	h	6-0	*Celsinho 2, Osmar 2, Häşimov A, Äsädov*
1/11	Simurq	a	0-1	
4/11	Qäbälä	h	1-0	*Osmar*
'12	Karvan	a	1-0	*Fabinho*
008				
5/2	İnter Bakı	h	0-3	
3/2	Xäzär Länkäran	a	1-4	*Häşimov A.*
'3	Standard	h	1-1	*Hüseynov V.*
5/3	Qarabağ	a	1-1	*Ämiraslanov*
9/3	ABN	a	2-1	*Goncharov, Lomashvili*
'4	Neftçi	h	0-2	
2/4	Turan	a	0-0	
9/4	Olimpik	h	1-2	*Goncharov*
5/4	Bakı	h	2-0	*Nadirov, Dadaşov*
'5	Gänclärbirliyi	a	0-1	
1/5	Simurq	h	1-1	*Mehdiyev*
8/5	Qäbälä	a	1-1	*Hugo*
7/5	Karvan	h	4-1	*Hugo, Dadaşov, Nadirov 2*

o	Name	Nat	Pos	Aps	(s)	Gls
5	Amil AĞACANOV		G	6		
	Fuad ÄLİYEV		A	5	(4)	1
9	Rövşän ÄMİRASLANOV		M	9	(10)	1
7	Zaur ÄSÄDOV		M	7	(4)	1
3	Azär BAĞIROV		D	4		
4, 33	Celso Ferreira de Carvalho "CELSINHO"	BRA	A	18	(3)	3
	Teymur DADAŞOV		M	19	(3)	2
4	Arif DAŞDÄMİROV		M	17	(3)	1
0	Fábio Ricardo Catanhede "FABINHO"	BRA	A	10	(3)	2
3	Boris GONCHAROV	GEO	A	10	(1)	2
1, 28	Namiq HÄSÄNOV		M	1	(3)	
0	Aqşin HÄŞİMOV		A	7	(6)	2
	Elçin HÄŞİMOV		D	1	(5)	
7	HUGO Saldanha dos Santos	BRA	D	8	(2)	2
0	Amid HÜSEYNOV		A	1	(4)	
	Vüsal HÜSEYNOV		M	11		1
	Deviko KHINJAZOV	GEO	D	21		
3	Emil KİTELMAN		M	3	(2)	
	Vaja LOMASHVILI	GEO	D	12		1
2	Elnur MÄMMÄDOV		A		(2)	
3	Ramin MÄMMÄDOV		M	9	(1)	
7	Azär MEHDİYEV		M	6	(5)	1
	Bäxtiyar MEHRÄLİYEV		D	10	(3)	1
7	Vüqar NADİROV		A	11		3
	Mikayıl NAMAZOV		D	22	(1)	
8	Ramil NÄSİBOV		M	2	(1)	
5	Anar NİFTÄLİYEV		G	11		
1	Ädahim NİFTÄLİYEV		D	3		
9, 27	OSMAR Sigueira Rodrigues	BRA	A	10	(5)	6
3	Miroslav SAVIĆ	SRB	D	1		
	Elşad TAHİROV		G	9	(1)	
	Anar VÄLİYEV		D	8		
7	Vüqar YUSİFLİ		A	1	(1)	
	Bähruz ZEYNALOV		M	13	(1)	

PFK NEFTÇİ

Coach – Qurban Qurbanov; (29/8/07) Vlastimil Petržela (CZE); (4/1/08) Anatoliy Demyanenko (UKR)

Founded - 1937

MAJOR HONOURS: Azerbaijan League - (5) 1992, 1996, 1997, 2004, 2005; Azerbaijan Cup - (5) 1995, 1996, 1999, 2002, 2004,

2007.				
11/8	Turan	h	1-2	*Subašić*
18/8	Gänclärbirliyi	a	6-2	*Tağızadä, Subašić 3, Allahverdiyev, Adamia*
26/8	Qäbälä	h	2-0	*Mämmädov, Subašić*
2/9	İnter Bakı	a	0-0	
16/9	Standard	h	3-1	*Sadıqov R.F. 2 (2p), Subašić*
29/9	Masallı	h	4-0	*Sadıqov R.F. (p), Äliyev 2, Adamia*
6/10	Olimpik	h	0-0	
20/10	Bakı	a	1-5	*Subašić*
28/10	Simurq	h	2-1	*Sadıqov R.F. 2 (2p)*
3/11	Karvan	h	2-1	*Tağızadä, Subašić*
10/11	Xäzär Länkäran	a	1-0	*Adamia*
25/11	Qarabağ	h	0-0	
1/12	ABN	a	2-0	*Subašić 2 (1p)*
2008				
17/2	Turan	a	1-0	*Allahverdiyev*
23/2	Gänclärbirliyi	h	2-0	*Tağızadä, Subašić*
2/3	Qäbälä	a	3-2	*Subašić, Kruglov, Adamia (p)*
15/3	İnter Bakı	h	2-0	*Kruglov, Subašić*
30/3	Bakı	h	3-2	*Subašić, Adamia, og (Ämirbäyov)*
5/4	Masallı	a	2-0	*Adamia 2*
13/4	Olimpik	a	0-0	
19/4	Simurq	a	0-0	
27/4	Standard	a	1-1	*Adamia*
4/5	Karvan	a	1-0	*Adamia (p)*
11/5	Xäzär Länkäran	h	0-1	
17/5	Qarabağ	a	0-0	
28/5	ABN	h	3-0	*(w/o)*

No	Name	Nat	Pos	Aps	(s)	Gls
11, 19	Ramazan ABBASOV		M	5	(7)	
15	Ruslan ABIŞOV		D	11	(1)	
10	Giorgi ADAMIA	GEO	A	21	(4)	9
5	Elnur ALLAHVERDİYEV		D	19	(2)	2
9	Samir ÄLİYEV		A	7	(4)	2
32, 3	Nazar BAIRAMOV	TKM	M	7	(7)	
7	Vadim BORET	MDA	M	14	(6)	
8	Aleksandr CHERTOGANOV		M	22		
67	Ramal HÜSEYNOV		M	1	(2)	
21	JOSÉ dos Reis CARLOS	BRA	A	1	(9)	
4	Dmitri KRUGLOV	EST	D	10		2
9, 25	MARCOS Ferreira Javier	BRA	M	2	(2)	
55	Ruslan MÄCİDOV		G	1		
12	Hüseyn MÄHÄMMÄDOV		G	2		
2	Rail MÄLİKOV		D	21		
17	Aqil MÄMMÄDOV		M	11	(11)	1
1	Vladimir MIČOVIĆ	SRB	G	22		
21	Nadir NÄBİYEV		A	1	(4)	
14, 44	Svetoslav Petrov STEFANOV	BUL	M	8		
23	Eşqin QULİYEV		M		(1)	
77	Ramin QULİYEV		D	11	(3)	
14	Räşad F. SADIQOV		D	19		5
6	Räşad Ä. SADİQOV		M	13	(6)	
20	Branimir SUBAŠIĆ		A	25		14
22	Zaur TAĞIZADÄ		M	19		3
4	Namiq YUSİFOV		M	2	(1)	
25	Zeynal ZEYNALOV		M		(1)	

FK OLİMPİK BAKI

Coach – Äsgär Abdullayev

Founded - 1996

2007				
19/8	Turan	a	3-1	*Nduka, Bangoura, Drobnjak*
26/8	Gänclärbirliyi	h	1-0	*Bangoura*
2/9	Qäbälä	a	1-0	*İsmayılov*
9/9	ABN	h	1-0	*Mandić*
16/9	İnter Bakı	h	1-0	*Junivan*

22/9	Standard	a	0-0	
30/9	Bakı	h	3-0	*Junivan 2, Abuzärov*
6/10	Neftçi	a	0-0	
27/10	Masallı	h	3-1	*Junivan, Mandić, og (Väliyev)*
4/11	Simurq	h	1-0	*Junivan*
10/11	Karvan	a	1-0	*Junivan*
25/11	Xäzär Länkäran	h	0-0	
1/12	Qarabağ	a	1-0	*Junivan*
2008				
16/2	ABN	a	1-1	*Fábio*
23/2	Turan	h	3-0	*Junivan 2, Musayev*
1/3	Gänclärbirliyi	a	1-0	*Junivan*
15/3	Qäbälä	h	2-0	*Junivan, Fábio*
30/3	Standard	h	1-0	*İsmayılov*
6/4	Bakı	a	1-0	*Musayev*
13/4	Neftçi	h	0-0	
19/4	Masallı	a	2-1	*Velija, Musayev*
28/4	İnter Bakı	a	0-2	
4/5	Simurq	a	0-0	
12/5	Karvan	h	2-0	*Fábio, Musayev*
17/5	Xäzär Länkäran	a	0-0	
28/5	Qarabağ	h	0-1	

No	Name	Nat	Pos	Aps	(s)	Gls
77	Yaşar ABUZÄROV		M	18	(3)	1
17	ALEXANDRE de Paula Campos Pereira	BRA	M	1	(1)	
4	Tärlan ÄHMÄDOV		D	26		
14	Elvin ÄLİYEV		D	23		
11	Namiq ÄLİYEV		M	21	(3)	
22	Pathé BANGOURA	GUI	A	5	(3)	2
9	Jovan DROBNJAK	SRB	A	1	(14)	1
10	FÁBIO Luís Ramim	BRA	M	22	(1)	3
22	Serhiy GRIBANOV	UKR	A	1	(6)	
21, 18	Ilami HALIMI	MKD	A	4	(1)	
21	Cavid HÜSEYNOV		A	1	(2)	
16	Färrux İSMAYILOV		A	15	(6)	2
8	JUNIVAN Soares de Melo	BRA	M	17	(4)	11
5	Dragan MANDIĆ	SRB	D	20	(3)	2
44	Rauf MEHDİYEV		G	23		
20	Samir MUSAYEV		A	5	(5)	4
21	Yuriy MUZYKA		M	4	(2)	
7	Aqil NÄBİYEV		D	24	(2)	
3	Usim NDUKA		D	26		1
19	Dmitriy PARKHACHEV	BLR	A	18	(7)	
96	Elşän POLADOV		G	3	(1)	
2	İlyas QURBANOV		D		(7)	
17	Orxan RÄCÄBOV		M		(1)	
18	Narvik SIRKHAEV		M	1		
18	Fäqan ŞAHBAZOV		A		(3)	

FK QARABAĞ

Coach – Rasim Kara (TUR)

Founded - 1987

MAJOR HONOURS: Azerbaijan League - (1) 1993; Azerbaijan Cup - (2) 1993, 2006.

2007				
11/8	Simurq	a	0-1	
18/8	Karvan	h	0-1	
26/8	Xäzär Länkäran	a	0-2	
1/9	Masallı	a	0-1	
16/9	ABN	h	3-1	*Cavadov 2, Igbekoyi*
22/9	Turan	a	2-0	*Igbekoyi 2*
30/9	Gänclärbirliyi	h	3-1	*Cavadov, Igbekoyi, Abbasov*
6/10	Qäbälä	a	2-1	*Kärimov A., Beraia G.*
28/10	İnter Bakı	h	0-1	
4/11	Standard	a	1-0	*Cavadov*
10/11	Bakı	h	1-1	*Hacıyev (p)*
25/11	Neftçi	a	0-0	
1/12	Olimpik	h	0-1	
2008				
16/2	Simurq	h	2-2	*Cavadov, Pupo*
24/2	Karvan	a	0-0	
2/3	Xäzär Länkäran	h	2-0	*Cavadov, Häşimov*
15/3	Masallı	h	1-1	*Äliyev*
30/3	Turan	h	0-0	
6/4	Gänclärbirliyi	a	1-0	*Mämmädov E.*
13/4	Qäbälä	h	2-1	*Kärimov K., Kärimov A*
19/4	İnter Bakı	a	0-1	
26/4	ABN	a	3-0	*Ağakişiyev, Igbekoyi, Kärimov K.*
4/5	Standard	h	1-0	*Abbasov*
12/5	Bakı	a	0-0	
17/5	Neftçi	h	0-0	
28/5	Olimpik	a	1-0	*Häşimov*

No	Name	Nat	Pos	Aps	(s)	Gls
15	Ayxan ABBASOV		D	18	(3)	2
10, 9	Murad AĞAKİŞİYEV		M	15	(8)	1
11	Rauf ÄLİYEV		A	1	(6)	1
7	Goga BERAIA	GEO	M	12	(4)	1
9	Irakli BERAIA	GEO	A	1	(3)	
20	Vaqif CAVADOV		A	19	(6)	6
3	Aftandil HACIYEV		D	17	(1)	1
26, 21	Zaur HÄŞİMOV		D	10	(2)	2
14	Victor Kayode IGBEKOYI	NGA	A	17	(5)	5
2	Hüseyn İSGÄNDÄROV		D	16		
23, 16	Äfran İSMAYILOV		M	4	(2)	
22	Timur İSRAFİLOV		M	4		
8	Aslan KÄRİMOV		D	20		2
18	Bayram KÄRİMOV		D		(1)	
	Känan KÄRİMOV		A	19	(1)	2
4	Azär MÄMMÄDOV		D	18		
19	Elşän MÄMMÄDOV		A	1	(7)	1
13, 30	Nodar MÄMMÄDOV		D	14	(4)	
5	Maksim MEDVEDYEV		D	11	(7)	
16, 26	Taqim NOVRUZOV		M	2	(2)	
25	Isaac PUPO Tuko	LBR	M	16	(7)	1
6	Mamadouba SOUMAH Lansana	GHA	D	24	(1)	
99	Osman UMAROV		G	2		
1	Färhad VÄLİYEV		G	24		
21, 17	Şähriyar XÄLİLOV		M	1	(3)	
2	Bilal VELIJA	MKD	D	7	(2)	1

PFK QÄBÄLÄ

Coach – Ramiz Mämmädov

Founded - 2005

2007				
11/8	Standard	a	1-0	*Aptisauri*
19/8	Bakı	h	2-0	*Balamestnyi, Aptisaur*
26/8	Neftçi	a	0-2	
2/9	Olimpik	h	0-1	
15/9	Simurq	a	0-2	
23/9	Karvan	h	1-0	*Fiston*
30/9	Xäzär Länkäran	a	1-2	*Aptsiauri*
6/10	Qarabağ	h	1-2	*Fiston*
27/10	ABN	a	2-1	*Fiston 2*
3/11	Turan	h	2-1	*Zärgärov (p), Adışirinc*
11/11	Gänclärbirliyi	a	6-0	*Balamestnyi 4, Cabbarov, Zärgärov*
24/11	Masallı	a	0-1	
2/12	İnter Bakı	h	2-1	*Balamestnyi 2*
2008				
17/2	Standard	h	1-0	*Taranu*
24/2	Bakı	a	0-3	
2/3	Neftçi	h	2-3	*Cabbarov, Vashakidze*
15/3	Olimpik	a	0-2	
30/3	Karvan	a	2-1	*Zärgärov (p), Cabbarc*
5/4	Xäzär Länkäran	h	1-1	*Mämmädov C.*
13/4	Qarabağ	a	1-2	*Taranu*
19/4	ABN	h	2-0	*Taranu, Balamestnyi*
27/4	Simurq	h	1-0	*Mustafayev*
3/5	Turan	a	2-4	*Aptisauri, Taranu*
12/5	Gänclärbirliyi	h	2-2	*Hüseynov, İsmayılov*

3/5	Masallı	h	1-1	*Cabbarov*
3/5	İnter Bakı	a	0-4	

o	Name	Nat	Pos	Aps	(s)	Gls
3	ABDULKADİR Öz	TUR	M	5	(3)	
4	Äli ABIŞOV		M		(1)	
0, 15	Ceyhun ADIŞİRİNOV		D	7	(3)	1
0	Tornike APTISAURI	GEO	M	22	(2)	4
7, 18	Rähman ÄZİZOV		M	2	(2)	
	Vitaliy BALAMESTNY	RUS	A	17	(1)	8
0, 28	Azär CABBAROV		M	14	(4)	4
8, 6	Abdoul Kader CAMARA	GUI	M	14	(4)	
1	ERIVELTO Alixandrino da Silva	BRA	A		(2)	
5, 11	Bokungu Ndjoli FISTON	CGO	A	5	(6)	4
7	Giorgi GABIDAURI	GEO	M	13	(6)	
9	Vüqar HÄSÄNOV		D	22	(1)	
1	Azär HÄŞİMOV		M	14	(1)	
	İbrahim HÜSEYNOV		M	5	(2)	1
	Äli İSMAYILOV		D	20	(1)	1
	Elnar KÄRİMOV		G	5		
, 12	Zurab MAMALADZE	GEO	G	21		
, 29	Camal MÄMMÄDOV		M	18	(1)	1
1, 20	Samir MÄMMÄDOV		M	11	(4)	
6	Säbuhi MÄMMÄDOV		M		(1)	
	Şähruz MUSTAFAYEV		M	16	(2)	1
1, 22	Pärvin PAŞAYEV		M	2	(3)	
	Aqşin SALAHOV		D		(2)	
	Eldäniz SÜLEYMANOV		D	1	(4)	
4	Vladimir TARANU	MDA	A	7	(5)	4
	Anatoliy TEBLOEV	RUS	M	13		
4, 4	Irakli VASHAKIDZE	GEO	D	22	(2)	1
5	Samir ZÄRGÄROV		A	10	(14)	3

PFK SİMURQ

Coach – Roman Pokora (UKR)

Founded - 2005

2007				
11/8	Qarabağ	h	1-0	*Mazyar*
19/8	ABN	a	1-1	*Sayadov*
25/8	Turan	h	3-0	*Ömärov, Mazyar 2*
1/9	Gänclärbirliyi	a	3-0	*Mazyar, Hüseynov 2*
15/9	Qäbälä	h	2-0	*Sayadov, Danayev*
29/9	Standard	h	1-0	*Musayev*
7/10	Bakı	a	1-1	*Danayev*
20/10	İnter Bakı	a	0-2	
28/10	Neftçi	a	1-2	*Mazyar*
4/11	Olimpik	a	0-1	
11/11	Masallı	h	1-0	*Qämbärov*
24/11	Karvan	h	0-1	
2/12	Xäzär Länkäran	a	1-2	*Danayev (p)*
2008				
16/2	Qarabağ	a	2-2	*Näsibov, Sayadov*
23/2	ABN	h	3-1	*Mazyar 2, Bolkvadze (p)*
2/3	Turan	a	2-1	*Mazyar, Bolkvadze*
16/3	Gänclärbirliyi	h	3-0	*Bolkvadze (p), Mazyar, Mämmädov E.*
29/3	İnter Bakı	h	3-4	*Kachur, İsayev, Chkhetiani*
5/4	Standard	a	0-3	
13/4	Bakı	h	0-0	
19/4	Neftçi	h	0-0	
27/4	Qäbälä	a	0-1	
4/5	Olimpik	h	0-0	
11/5	Masallı	a	1-1	*Mazyar*
18/5	Karvan	a	1-1	*Ömärov (p)*
28/5	Xäzär Länkäran	h	1-1	*Bolkvadze*

No	Name	Nat	Pos	Aps	(s)	Gls
18	Renat ABDAŞEV		D	8		
18	David BOLKVADZE	GEO	M	13		4
8	Miryusif CAVADOV		M		(2)	
15	Tural CÄLİLOV		M	6	(4)	
23	Kakhaber CHKHETIANI	GEO	M	10	(1)	1
1	Taras CHOPIK	UKR	G	12		
23, 8	Andriy DANAYEV	UKR	M	18	(4)	3
5	Ramin HACIYEV		D	12	(5)	
21	Ramiz HÜSEYNOV		D	12	(3)	2
19	Arif İSAYEV		A	4	(8)	1
11	Ruslan KACHUR	UKR	A	4	(3)	1
3	Mykola LAPKO	UKR	D	9	(3)	
27	Vyaçeslav LIÇKİN		M	7	(2)	
4	Aleksandr MALYGIN	RUS	D	23		
13	Volodymyr MAZYAR	UKR	A	19	(2)	10
20	Elnur MÄMMÄDOV		M	11		1
17	Rüstäm MÄMMÄDOV		M	11	(3)	
9	Samir MUSAYEV		A	10		1
7	Ramin NÄSİBOV		A	9	(3)	1
12	Andriy NIKITIN	UKR	G	11		
10	Aqşin ÖMÄROV		M	14	(4)	2
20	Olexandr POKLONSKIY	UKR	M	2		
11, 7	Elşän QÄMBÄROV		M		(9)	1
7	Orxan RÄCÄBOV		M	3	(1)	
14	Ravi RÄHMANOV		M	3	(8)	
25	Ramil SAYADOV		M	22		3
2	Mykhailo STAROSTYAK	UKR	D	25		
22	Rinat SULTANOV		A	1	(6)	
3	Oleh TYMCHYSHYN	UKR	D	4	(5)	
12	Nikolai ZBARAKH	UKR	G	3		

FK STANDARD BAKI

Coach – Yunis Hüseynov; (4/1/08) Kakhaber Tskhadadze (GEO)

Founded – 2006

2007				
11/8	Qäbälä	h	0-1	
18/8	İnter Bakı	a	1-1	*Martínez*
25/8	Masallı	h	4-1	*Martínez, Mämmädov İ., Doros, Mämmädov A.*
1/9	Bakı	h	1-1	*Närimanov*
16/9	Neftçi	a	1-3	*Léo Rocha*
22/9	Olimpik	h	0-0	
29/9	Simurq	a	0-1	
7/10	Karvan	h	1-2	*Martínez*
28/10	Xäzär Länkäran	a	2-2	*Léo Rocha (p), Vintilă*
4/11	Qarabağ	h	0-1	
11/11	ABN	a	1-0	*Léo Rocha*
24/11	Turan	h	1-1	*Mämmädov E.*
1/12	Gänclärbirliyi	a	5-1	*og (Hidayätov), Närimanov, Doros 3*
2008				
17/2	Qäbälä	a	0-1	
24/2	İnter Bakı	h	1-2	*Léo Rocha*
1/3	Masallı	a	1-1	*Mämmädov A.*
16/3	Bakı	a	1-0	*Gutiérrez*
30/3	Olimpik	a	0-1	
5/4	Simurq	h	3-0	*Gutiérrez, Léo Rocha, Pisla*
12/4	Karvan	a	1-1	*Pisla*
20/4	Xäzär Länkäran	h	0-1	
27/4	Neftçi	h	1-1	*Martínez*
4/5	Qarabağ	a	0-1	
9/5	ABN	h	6-0	*Léo Rocha 2, Gutiérrez, Martínez 2, Vintilă*
18/5	Turan	a	2-0	*Gutiérrez, Léo Rocha*
27/5	Gänclärbirliyi	h	3-2	*Gutiérrez, Pisla, Paripović*

No	Name	Nat	Pos	Aps	(s)	Gls
18	Ruslan ÄMİRCANOV		D	16	(1)	
9, 11	Dejan DJENIĆ	SRB	A	3	(3)	
21	Anatoly DOROS	MDA	A	6	(5)	4
25, 7	Räcäb FÄRÄCZADÄ		M	9	(9)	
11	Ángel Gustavo GUTIÉRREZ	URU	A	13		5
4	Vasif HAQVERDİYEV		M	4	(1)	
55, 24	Anar HÄSÄNOV		M	2	(2)	
20	Vüsal HÜSEYNOV		M	2		
	Zaur İSMAYILOV		M	1	(10)	
1	Vitali KOVALYOV		G	24		
4, 10	"LÉO" Leonardo da Silva ROCHA	BRA	M	15	(4)	8
2	Osvaldo LUCAS Vázquez	MEX	D	10	(2)	

No	Name	Nat	Pos	Aps	(s)	Gls
3	Edvinas LUKOSEVICIUS	LTU	D	13		
	Daniel Sebastián MARTÍNEZ	URU	A	17	(7)	6
	Asif MÄMMÄDOV		A	9	(9)	2
88, 9	Elşän MÄMMÄDOV		A	8		1
7	İsmayıl MÄMMÄDOV		M	11		1
4	Tural MÄMMÄDOV		D		(1)	
	Tural NÄRİMANOV		D	12	(2)	2
17	Ognjen PARIPOVIĆ	SRB	D	24		1
	Daniel Petru PISLA	MDA	A	8	(2)	3
77, 18	Ruslan POLADOV		M	11		
12	Väli QAFAROV		G	2	(1)	
5	Ruslan QAFİTULLİN		D	22	(1)	
6, 14	Kamal QULİYEV		D	22		
21	Israel Rodrigo RODRÍGUEZ	PAR	A	1	(6)	
	Vladimer UGREKHELIDZE	GEO	M	7	(5)	
2, 8	Marius Constantin VINTILĂ	ROU	M	14	(3)	2

PFK TURAN

Coach – Sakit Alıyev; (29/2/08) (Nizami Ocaqverdiyev); (6/3/08) Selahattin Dervent (TUR)

Founded - 1992

MAJOR HONOURS: Azerbaijan League - (1) 1994.

Date	Opponent		Score	Scorers
2007				
11/8	Neftçi	a	2-1	*Mämmädov, Qädiri*
19/8	Olimpik	h	1-3	*Qarayev V.*
25/8	Simurq	a	0-3	
1/9	Karvan	h	1-5	*Qarayev V.*
16/9	Xäzär Länkäran	a	0-2	
22/9	Qarabağ	h	0-2	
29/9	ABN	a	0-0	
6/10	Masallı	a	1-3	*Qarayev V.*
27/10	Gänclärbirliyi	h	2-0	*Abbasov C., Qarayev V.*
3/11	Qäbälä	a	1-2	*Färhadov*
10/11	İnter Bakı	h	0-4	
24/11	Standard	a	1-1	*Hüseynpur*
2/12	Bakı	h	0-2	
2008				
17/2	Neftçi	h	0-1	
23/2	Olimpik	a	0-3	
2/3	Simurq	h	1-2	*Novruzov*
15/3	Karvan	a	0-1	
30/3	Qarabağ	a	0-0	
5/4	ABN	h	3-0	*Carabulea, Qädiri, Äläkbärov*
12/4	Masallı	h	0-0	
19/4	Gänclärbirliyi	a	1-1	*Qarayev V.*
27/4	Xäzär Länkäran	h	0-4	
3/5	Qäbälä	h	4-2	*Qädiri, Hüseynov, Qarayev V., Äläkbärov (p)*
11/5	İnter Bakı	a	1-3	*Abbasov Y.*
18/5	Standard	h	0-2	
27/5	Bakı	a	2-2	*Beraia 2*

No	Name	Nat	Pos	Aps	(s)	Gls
18, 15	Cavid ABBASOV		M	13	(5)	1
	Yasin ABBASOV		A	3	(11)	1
20	Paul Monday AKPAN	NGA	A	7	(5)	
77, 2	Kamal ÄLÄKBÄROV		D	11		2
20	Färmayıl ÄLİYEV		A		(3)	
18	Hafiz ÄLİYEV		M	10		
15	Ramil ÄLİYEV		M	5	(2)	
16	Ramin ÄLİYEV		M	10	(3)	
5	Eltay ASLANOV		D	19	(3)	
7	Irakli BERAIA	GEO	A	8	(3)	2
19	Evgheny CARABULEA	MDA	M	6	(1)	1
4	Elxan CÄBRAYILOV		D	5	(4)	
11	Zoran CVETKOVIĆ	SRB	M	10		
7	Vüqar FÄRHADOV		M	9	(3)	1
3	Vurğun HÜSEYNOV		D	23	(2)	1
8	Äliağa HÜSEYNPUR		M	11	(3)	1
6	Elvin MÄMMÄDOV		M	13		1
2	Ruslan NAMAZOV		D	4		
	Anar NÄZİROV		G	26		
6	Taqim NOVRUZOV		M	9	(3)	1
17	Eric OBIDIKE	NGA	D	23		
14	Räşad ORUCOV		M		(9)	
10	Xäyal QARAYEV		M	16	(6)	
9	Vüsal QARAYEV		A	20	(3)	6
21	Asäf QÄDİRİ		M	14	(1)	3
4	Anar VÄLİYEV		D	11		

FK XÄZÄR LÄNKÄRAN

Coach - Ağasälim Mircavadov

Founded – 2004

MAJOR HONOURS: Azerbaijan League - (1) 2007; Azerbaijan Cup - (2) 2007, 2008.

Date	Opponent		Score	Scorers
2007				
12/8	Karvan	a	1-0	*Bamba*
18/8	Masallı	a	3-0	*Bamba 2, Ramazanov*
26/8	Qarabağ	h	2-0	*Baxşıyev, Juninho*
2/9	ABN	a	4-0	*Ramazanov (p), Juninho, N'Tiamoah, Bamba*
16/9	Turan	h	2-0	*Quliyev 2*
23/9	Gänclärbirliyi	a	2-1	*N'Tiamoah 2*
30/9	Qäbälä	h	2-1	*Ramazanov, Quliyev*
6/10	İnter Bakı	a	2-2	*Abdullayev, N'Tiamoah*
28/10	Standard	h	2-2	*N'Tiamoah, Todorov*
4/11	Bakı	a	2-2	*Juninho, Ramazanov*
10/11	Neftçi	h	0-1	
25/11	Olimpik	a	0-0	
2/12	Simurq	h	2-1	*Abdullayev, Ramazanov*
2008				
17/2	Karvan	h	0-0	
23/2	Masallı	h	4-1	*Souza, Ramazanov 2, og (Lomashvili)*
2/3	Qarabağ	a	0-2	
16/3	ABN	h	0-0	
29/3	Gänclärbirliyi	h	5-0	*Ramazanov, Diego Souza, Näbiyev 3*
5/4	Qäbälä	a	1-1	*Ramazanov*
13/4	İnter Bakı	h	3-1	*Ämirquliyev, Souza, Abdullayev*
20/4	Standard	a	1-0	*Souza*
27/4	Turan	a	4-0	*Souza, Bamba (p), Baxşıyev, Ramazanov*
4/5	Bakı	h	0-0	
11/5	Neftçi	a	1-0	*Abdullayev*
17/5	Olimpik	h	0-0	
28/5	Simurq	a	1-1	*Ramazanov*

No	Name	Nat	Pos	Aps	(s)	Gls
27	Räşad ABDULLAYEV		M	21	(3)	4
25	Kamran AĞAYEV		G	17		
14	Rahid ÄMİRQULİYEV		M	12	(4)	1
50	Yacouba BAMBA	CIV	A	9	(5)	5
8	Elmar BAXŞIYEV		M	24	(1)	2
3	DÊNIS Silva Cruz	BRA	D	10	(1)	
33	DIEGO SOUZA Gusmão	BRA	M	9	(1)	1
19	Kostadin DZHAMBAZOV	BUL	D	22		
3	Zaur HAŞİMOV		D	9	(2)	
55	Osvaldo Júnior "JUNINHO"	BRA	M	10	(1)	3
11	Räşad KÄRİMOV		M	1	(4)	
1	Dmitri KRAMARENKO		G	9		
6	Füzuli MÄMMÄDOV		D	8	(3)	
17	Vüqar NADİROV		A	1	(8)	
17	Nadir NÄBİYEV		A	3	(3)	3
20	Edmond N'TIAMOAH	GHA	A	8	(4)	5
7	Ruslan POLADOV		M	6	(2)	
5	Emin QULİYEV		M	14		3
18	Alim QURBANOV		M	12	(6)	
10	Zaur RAMAZANOV		A	25		11
28	ROBERTO dos SANTOS Silva	BRA	A	2	(3)	
30	Mário Sérgio "SOUZA" Aumarante Santana"	BRA	M	10		4
9	Ceyhun SULTANOV		M	10	(7)	
4	Mahir ŞÜKÜROV		D	10	(1)	
21	Radomir TODOROV	BUL	D	24		1

PROMOTED CLUBS

PFK BAKILI BAKI

Coach – Mämmädäli Qäniyev; (20/11/07) Asäf Namazov
Founded – 1995

PFK MOİK BAKI

Coach – Ramil Äliyev
Founded – 1961 .

ECOND LEVEL FINAL TABLES 2007/08

UP A	Pld	W	D	L	F	A	Pts
FK NBC Salyan	16	10	4	2	26	8	34
PFK Abşeron Bakı	16	10	2	4	31	18	32
PFK Bakılı Bakı	16	8	6	2	32	13	30
FK ANŞAD-Petrol Neftçala	16	6	7	3	33	22	25
FK Qarabağ-2 Ağdam	16	6	6	4	27	14	24
PİK İnter-2 Bakı	16	6	4	6	17	24	22
FK Bakı-2	16	4	6	6	15	19	18
PFK Spartak Quba	16	3	2	11	15	37	11
FK Ädliyyä Bakı	16	0	1	15	5	46	1

FK Samux withdrew after round 8; PFK Abşeron Bakı withdrew after
d 16 and did not enter promotion play-offs.

UP B	Pld	W	D	L	F	A	Pts
FK MKT-Araz İmişli	16	11	2	3	29	11	35
PFK MOİK Bakı	16	10	4	2	26	15	34
FK Şahdağ QusarN	16	10	3	3	23	9	33
FK Göyäzän Qazax	16	8	3	5	35	19	27
PFK Neftçi-2 Bakı	16	7	5	4	20	16	26
PFK Energetik Mingäçevir	16	4	4	8	19	25	16
FK Xäzär Länkäran-2	16	2	4	10	13	26	10
PFK Turan-2 Tovuz	16	2	4	10	13	33	10
FK Standard-2 Bakı	16	1	5	10	10	34	8

GEN Bakı withdrew after round 9.

MOTION PLAY-OFFS	Pld	W	D	L	F	A	Pts
PFK Bakılı Bakı	10	5	4	1	8	4	19
PFK MOİK Bakı	10	4	5	1	10	6	17
FK NBC Salyan	10	4	4	2	11	9	16
FK MKT-Araz İmişli	10	4	1	5	12	10	13
FK ANŞAD-Petrol Neftçala	10	3	2	5	10	15	11
FK Şahdağ Qusar	10	1	2	7	5	12	5

OMESTIC CUP 2007/08

AZERBAYCAN KUBOKU

FINALS

/07 & 3/10/07)
i-2 v Karvan 0-3; 0-2 *(0-5)*
Salyan v Xäzär Länkäran 1-3; 2-7 *(3-10)*
ağ Qusar v Neftçi 0-7; 0-1 *(0-8)*
yä v Gänclärbirliyi 1-6; 0-6 *(1-12)*
v Olimpik 0-3; 1-1 *(1-4)*
v Qäbälä 0-2; 0-2 *(0-4)*
ıx v ABN Bärdä 2-3; 1-3 *(3-6)*
bağ-2 v Standard 0-1; 0-4 *(0-5)*
2 v Turan 0-2; 0-3 *(0-5)*
-Araz v Qarabağ 0-1; 0-4 *(0-5)*
Xäzär Länkäran-2 v Masallı 0-2; 1-2 *(1-4)*
GEN Bakı v İnter Bakı 1-3; 0-5 *(1-8)*

(26/9/07 & 4/10/07)
Simurq v ANŞAD-Petrol 1-0; 2-0 *(3-0)*
Abşeron v Energetik 3-1; 1-2 *(4-3)*

(26/9/07 & 10/10/07)
Standard-2 v Bakı 1-5; 0-2 *(1-7)*
İnter Bakı -2 v Göyäzän *(w/o; Göyäzän withdrew)*

1/8 FINALS

(24/10/07 & 31/10/07)
Turan v Qarabağ 0-2; 1-2 *(1-4)*
Masallı v İnter Bakı 0-2; 2-3 *(2-5)*
Gänclärbirliyi v Xäzär Länkäran 1-4; 0-5 *(1-9)*
Qäbälä v Simurq 1-0; 1-2 *(2-2; Qäbälä on away goal)*
ABN Bärdä v Olimpik 1-1; 1-3 *(2-4)*
Neftçi v Abşeron 3-0; 1-0 *(4-0)*

(25/10/07 & 31/10/07)
Bakı v İnter Bakı -2 3-0; 2-0 *(5-0)*

(31/10/07 & 7/11/07)
Standard v Karvan 2-0; 2-0 *(4-0)*

QUARTER-FINALS

(6/3/08 & 19/3/08)
Qarabağ 2 *(Äliyev 61, 85)*, İnter Bakı 2 *(Cuello 45+1, 71)*
İnter Bakı 1 *(Cuello 82)*, Qarabağ 0
(İnter Bakı 3-2)

(6/3/08 & 20/3/08)
Bakı 1 *(Tijani 28)*, Qäbälä 1 *(Zärgärov 22)*
Qäbälä 1 *(Balamestnyi 44)*, Bakı 1 *(Mujiri 35) (aet)*
(2-2; Qäbälä 4-3 on pens)

Olimpik 1 *(Dzhambazov 13og)*, Xäzär Länkäran 0
Xäzär Länkäran 2 *(Ramazanov 39, Diego Souza 47)*, Olimpik 0
(Xäzär Länkäran 2-1)

(7/3/08 & 20/3/08)
Neftçi 4 *(Stefanov 21, Adamia 57, 70, 90+2)*, Standard 1 *(Martínez 75)*
Standard 0, Neftçi 1 *(José Carlos 64)*
(Neftçi 5-1)

SEMI-FINALS

(9/4/08 & 23/4/08)
Qäbälä 1 *(Hüseynov 75)*, Xäzär Länkäran 3 *(Ramazanov 12, 56, Vashakidze 15og)*
Xäzär Länkäran 1 *(Ämirquliyev 79)*, Qäbälä 1 *(Mustafayev 64)*
(Xäzär Länkäran 4-2)

Neftçi 2 *(Subašić 2, José Carlos 6)*, İnter Bakı 2 *(Guglielmone 37, 79)*
İnter Bakı 1 *(Hüseynov 57)*, Neftçi 0
(İnter 3-2)

FINAL

(24/5/08)
Tofiq Bähramov stadium, Baku
FK XÄZÄR LÄNKÄRAN 2 *(Juninho 115, 119) (aet)*
PİK İNTER BAKI 0
Referee – *Graefe*
XÄZÄR LÄNKÄRAN – *Kramarenko, Dênis, Şükürov, Dzhambazov, Todorov, Baxşıyev, Ämirquliyev, Abdullayev (Bamba 70), Diego Souza (Qurbanov 82), Juninho (Mämmädov 120), Ramazanov.*
İNTER BAKI – *Simeonov, Zagorac (Mustafayev 68), Abbasov S., Levin, Ismailov, Qurbanov, Cervenka, Zlatinov, Arnaut, Mämmädov X. (Hüseynov 63), Guglielmone (Mämmädov E. 77).*

BATE retain title with ease

Taken right to the wire the previous season, FC BATE Borisov had an easier ride to the Vysshaya Liga title in 2007. No team had made a successful defence of the Belarussian championship since FC Dinamo Minsk in 1995, but BATE, skilfully commanded once again by coach Igor Kriushenko, ensured their second successive title – and fourth in all – with four of their 26 matches still to play.

BATE were fully into their stride right from the off. They won eight of their opening nine matches, the only blip being a shock 2-1 defeat at FC Dinamo Brest, the very team that two weeks later would defeat BATE on penalties in the Cup final. With star striker Gennadiy Bliznyuk and his up-and-coming partner Vitaliy Rodionov finding the net in almost every game, it was evident at the halfway point of the season that only a sudden and dramatic collapse in BATE's form could reintroduce a competitive element to the title race.

But Kriushenko and his players were relentless, even allowing themselves the luxury of an extended stay in Europe. With APOEL FC of Cyprus and FH Hafnarfjördu of Iceland as their victims, BATE succeeded in reaching the third qualifying round of the UEFA Champions League for the first time. Access to the group phase was denied by FC Steaua Bucureşti but only after Belarus's finest had put up a brave fight, earning a 2-2 draw in the home leg thanks to a late Bliznyuk equaliser and coming close to taking the lead in the Romanian capital before Steaua stamped their authority and won 2-0. BATE's bonus adventure in the UEFA Cup lasted just one round as they were humbled 6-1 on aggregate by Villarreal CF of Spain.

Twelve-point cushion

The consistent accumulation of league points in the spring and summer enabled BATE to take it easy in the autumn, and the championship was duly sewn up on 21 October when they drew 0-0 at closest challengers FC MTZ-RIPO Minsk - the very team that had handed them their heaviest defeat of the season, 3-0 on their own turf, four months earlier. BATE were able to lose two of their remaining four matches, including a 2-1 home defeat on the final day to bottom club FC Minsk (the only team relegated as the Vysshaya Liga increased to 16 in 2008), and still end up with a 12-point advantage in the final table.

Vitaliy Bulyga (left) celebrates his late equaliser for Belarus in a friendly international away to Germany

Title celebrations were dampened somewhat when coach Kriushenko announced that he was leaving to join Dinamo Minsk on a three-year contract. BATE also lost their two talented young defenders, Artem Radkov and Yegor Filipenko, who, like many Belarussian internationals before them, crossed the border to pursue their careers in the Russian Premier-Liga, the former joining

Khimki, the latter trying his luck at FC Spartak ɔskva. The good news was that Bliznyuk (who ished up with 18 league goals) and Rodionov (15) th stayed on for the title hat-trick bid in 2008, where ey would be coached by Kriushenko's former cond-in-command, Viktor Goncharenko.

th BATE so dominant at the top, the major point of erest in the closing weeks was which team could ish second and secure qualification for the 2008/09 FA Cup. With Dinamo Minsk, the previous season's nners-up, having a season to forget under ex-FC namo Kyiv and Belarus midfielder Aleksandr atskevich, especially away from home where they on only once, the battle for silver became a four-way ntest between MTZ-RIPO, FC Shakhtyor Soligorsk, FC omel and surprise package FC Torpedo Zhodino.

omel's goal kings

TZ-RIPO's last-day 1-0 defeat at Torpedo enabled oth Gomel and Shakhtyor, who were level on points, leapfrog them with 1-0 wins of their own. It was omel's superior goal difference (with the head-to-ad records equal) that gave them the runners-up ot, a fitting reward for the evergreen goalscoring ills of Roman Vasilyuk and Valeriy Stripeikis, the sshaya Liga's all-time leading marksmen, who each ded significantly to their cumulative tallies, the rmer topping the charts with 24 goals, the latter oring 14.

akhtyor, the 2005 champions, thus finished third for e second season running and, as in 2006, their UEFA ɹp place would be taken away from them several onths later by the winners of the Belarussian Cup, aving them in the UEFA Intertoto Cup instead.

Shakhtyor's pain was intensified by the fact that they were the beaten finalists. A late equaliser by new signing Stripeikis appeared to have earned them a reprieve after they had been behind for most of the game to Vyacheslav Hleb's early strike for MTZ-RIPO, but midfielder Oleg Strakhanovich's immediate response brought victory for the team from Minsk, now under the command of Yuriy Puntus, the coach who had also led them to Cup glory three years earlier.

Stange stunned

Puntus had left MTZ-RIPO at the end of the 2006 season to devote himself full-time to the Belarus national team, but in June 2007 he announced his resignation after a disappointing run in the UEFA EURO 2008™ qualifiers. His replacement was the well travelled German, Bernd Stange, who must have wondered what he had let himself in for when his first three qualifying matches all ended in defeat, the last of them, stunningly, at home to little Luxembourg, who had not won a competitive international for a generation.

However, there was clearly no residual damage from that débâcle as Belarus closed their campaign with two morale-boosting victories – 4-2 in Albania and 2-1 in the Minsk fog against the Netherlands. The latter had already qualified for the finals, but two beautifully constructed goals, the first scored by Vitaliy Bulyga from a Vladimir Korytko pass, the second vice-versa, revealed new possibilities for the team, and there was further evidence of brighter times ahead the following May when Stange's men held Germany to a 2-2 draw in Kaiserslautern, with Bulyga scoring both goals, the second two minutes from time, as the visitors successfully retrieved a two-goal deficit.

Belorusskaja Federacija Futbola (BFF)

Prospekt Pobeditelei 20/3
220020 Minsk
tel - +375 172 545600
fax - +375 172 544483
website – www.bff.by
email – info@bff.by
Year of Formation – 1989
President - Gennadiy Nevyglas
General Secretary – Vadim Zhuk
CEO - Leonid Dmitranitsa
Press Officer – Sergei Novysh

Stadium - Dinamo, Minsk (41,040)

TOP FIVE ALL-TIME CAPS
Sergei Gurenko (80); Sergei Shtanyuk (71); Aleksandr Kulchiy (68); Maxim Romashchenko (64); Valentin Belkevich (56)

TOP FIVE ALL-TIME GOALS
Maxim Romashchenko (20); Vitaliy Kutuzov (13); Valentin Belkevich & Roman Vasilyuk (10); Vitaliy Bulyga (8)

BELARUS

NATIONAL TEAM RESULTS 2007/08

22/8/07	Israel	H	Minsk	2-1	*Vasilyuk (3), Romashchenko (90p)*
8/9/07	Romania (ECQ)	H	Minsk	1-3	*Romashchenko (20)*
12/9/07	Slovenia (ECQ)	A	Celje	0-1	
13/10/07	Luxembourg (ECQ)	H	Gomel	0-1	
17/10/07	Israel	A	Tel-Aviv	1-2	*Romashchenko (65)*
17/11/07	Albania (ECQ)	A	Tirana	4-2	*Romashchenko (32, 63p), Kutuzov (45+1, 54)*
21/11/07	Netherlands (ECQ)	H	Minsk	2-1	*Bulyga (49), Korytko (65)*
2/2/08	Iceland	N	Ta'Qali (MLT)	2-0	*Vasilyuk (33), Plaskonnyi (47)*
4/2/08	Armenia	N	Ta'Qali (MLT)	1-2	*Hleb V. (5)*
6/2/08	Malta	A	Ta'Qali	1-0	*Romashchenko (89)*
26/3/08	Turkey	H	Minsk	2-2	*Kutuzov (34), Hleb V. (64)*
27/5/08	Germany	A	Kaiserslautern	2-2	*Bulyga (61, 88)*
2/6/08	Finland	A	Turku	1-1	*Shitov (90+2)*

NATIONAL TEAM APPEARANCES 2007/08

Coach - Bernd STANGE (GER)	14/3/48		Isr	ROU	SVN	LUX	Isr	ALB	NED	Isl	Arm	Mlt	Tur	Ger	Fin	Caps	G
Vasiliy KHOMUTOVSKIY	30/8/78	Tom (RUS) /Carl Zeiss Jena (GER)	G46	G		s69							s46	G	G	26	
Sergei OMELYANCHUK	8/8/80	Rostov (RUS)	D			M	M	D	D90	D80	D	D		D		45	
Yan TIGOREV	10/3/84	Metalurh Zaporizhya (UKR)	D46	D	D											9	
Artem RADKOV	26/8/85	BATE /Khimki (RUS)	D	D	D		D53					D66				8	
Pavel PLASKONNYI	29/1/85	Shakhtyor /Panionios (GRE)	D75	D	D	D	s53	D65		D	D46		s23		s89	12	
Timofei KALACHEV	1/5/81	Rostov (RUS) /Krylya Sovetov (RUS)	M	M77	M	s62	M84	M75				M				30	
Igor STASEVICH	21/10/85	BATE	M46	D	D	M62	M		s90							6	
Maxim ROMASHCHENKO	31/7/76	Torpedo Moskva (RUS) /Bursaspor (TUR)	M	M	M	M	M	M	M	M85	M	s60	M	M46		64	2
Aleksandr HLEB	1/5/81	Arsenal (ENG)	M83	M	M	M	M69	M	M46			M	M	M		41	
Roman VASILYUK	23/11/78	Gomel	A46	s61						A	A67					24	1
Sergei KORNILENKO	14/6/83	Dnipro (UKR)	A	A	A46	A	A69	s90	s86	A54	s67			s90	s68	29	
Anton AMELCHENKO	27/3/80	Moskva (RUS)	s46													1	
Vladimir KORYTKO	6/7/79	Chornomorets (UKR)	s46	M	M89	D	D	s75	M				D	D		35	
Nikolai KASHEVSKIY	5/10/80	Metalurh Zaporizhya (UKR)	s46		s89				s46			M60	M	s55	D89	10	
Vitaliy RODIONOV	11/12/83	BATE	s46	A61	s46	s80	s69								A68	6	
Gennadiy BLIZNYUK	30/7/80	BATE	s75		A74					A54	A46					8	
Dmitriy MOZOLEVSKIY	30/4/85	Brest	s83				s84									2	
Aleksei SKVERNYUK	13/10/85	Krylya Sovetov (RUS)		s77		D	s69	s65	D			D	D23			7	
Vladimir GAYEV	28/10/77	Chornomorets (UKR)			G											4	
Yegor FILIPENKO	10/4/88	BATE /Spartak Moskva (RUS)			s74	D	D	D	D	D	D	D	D	D		10	

TIONAL TEAM APPEARANCES 2007/08 (contd.)

			Isr	ROU	SVN	LUX	Isr	ALB	NED	Isl	Arm	Mlt	Tur	Ger	Fin	Caps	Goals
ZHEVNOV	17/4/81	Moskva (RUS)				G69	G	G	G			G	G46			22	-
i VORONKOV	8/2/89	Dynamo Kyiv (UKR)				A80										1	-
iy MOLOSH	10/12/81	Nosta Novotroitsk (RUS)					D									2	-
n KIRENKIN	20/2/81	Zhodino						D	D	D46			D		s46	5	-
andr KULCHIY	1/11/73	Tom (RUS) /Rostov (RUS)						M	M	M	M	M		M		69	5
BULYGA	12/1/80	Tom (RUS) /unattached /Luch-Energia (RUS)						A	A86	M	M	A60	A	A90	A	32	8
KUTUZOV	20/3/80	Pisa (ITA)						A90	A			A	A46			39	13
i VEREMKO	16/10/82	BATE								G						1	-
AVLYUCHEK	27/6 /84	Dinamo Minsk								s46	D	s66				3	-
andr PAVLOV	18/8/84	Dnepr								s54				s74	M	3	-
eslav HLEB	12/2/83	MTZ-RIPO								s54	M	s60	s46	A55	s46	23	7
HITOV	24/10/86	Zhodino								s80			s88		s83	3	1
i KRIVETS	8/6/86	BATE								s85						1	-
andr LENTSEVICH	2/5/79	Gomel									G					1	-
n PUTILO	23/6/87	Hamburg (GER)									s46		M88	M74	M46	4	-
ai OSIPOVICH	29/5/86	MTZ-RIPO									s46					1	-
iy LENTSEVICH	20/6/83	Bohemians Praha (CZE)												D	D46	8	-
SITKO	17/12/85	Vitebsk												s46	M	2	-
iy VERKHOVTSEV	10/10/86	Naftan													D	1	-
i CHUKHLEI	2/10/87	Dinamo Minsk													D	1	-
n KONTSEVOI	20/5/83	MTZ-RIPO													M83	10	-

DOMESTIC LEAGUE 2007

SSHAYA LIGA FINAL TABLE

		Home					Away					Total					
	Pld	W	D	L	F	A	W	D	L	F	A	W	D	L	F	A	Pts
C BATE Borisov	26	11	0	2	32	13	7	2	4	18	12	18	2	6	50	25	56
C Gomel	26	8	4	1	30	14	4	4	5	19	14	12	8	6	49	28	44
C Shakhtyor Soligorsk	26	5	5	3	23	17	7	3	3	18	10	12	8	6	41	27	44
C Torpedo Zhodino	26	8	3	2	19	10	3	7	3	9	11	11	10	5	28	21	43
C MTZ-RIPO Minsk	26	6	4	3	16	13	5	5	3	16	12	11	9	6	32	25	42
C Neman Grodno	26	7	2	4	15	12	2	7	4	8	10	9	9	8	23	22	36
C Naftan Novopolotsk	26	5	6	2	13	9	4	3	6	15	21	9	9	8	28	30	36
C Dinamo Minsk	26	7	3	3	11	7	1	8	4	16	21	8	11	7	27	28	35
C Vitebsk	26	4	5	4	11	11	5	3	5	14	17	9	8	9	25	28	35
C Smorgon	26	4	6	3	9	9	2	2	9	6	20	6	8	12	15	29	26
C Darida Zhdanovichi	26	4	2	7	12	22	3	2	8	15	24	7	4	15	27	46	25
C Dinamo Brest	26	4	5	4	12	10	2	2	9	11	21	6	7	13	23	31	25
C Dnepr Mogilev	26	3	5	5	14	15	2	3	8	7	18	5	8	13	21	33	23
C Minsk	26	3	5	5	11	17	1	4	8	7	17	4	9	13	18	34	21

TOP GOALSCORERS

24 Roman VASILYUK (Gomel)
18 Gennadiy BLIZNYUK (BATE)
15 Vitaliy RODIONOV (BATE)
14 Valeriy STRIPEIKIS (Gomel)
10 Andrei SHERYAKOV (Zhodino)
9 Sergei NIKIFORENKO (Shakhtyor)
Aleksandr ALUMONA (Neman)
Viktor SOKOL (Brest)
8 Ruslan USOV (Vitebsk)
Aleksandr KLIMENKO (Shakhtyor)

CLUB-BY-CLUB

FC BATE BORISOV

Coach - Igor Kriushenko

Founded - 1996

MAJOR HONOURS: Belarus League – (4) 1999, 2002, 2006, 2007; Belarus Cup – (1) 2006.

2007				
15/4	Neman	h	2-1	*Bliznyuk 2 (1p)*
21/4	Smorgon	h	4-2	*Bliznyuk, Filipenko, Krivets, Rodionov*
27/4	Vitebsk	a	1-0	*Bliznyuk*
6/5	Zhodino	h	3-0	*Platonov D., Bliznyuk, Rodionov*
12/5	Brest	a	1-2	*Zhavnerchik*
18/5	Darida	h	4-1	*Rodionov 3, Bliznyuk*
22/5	Gomel	a	3-1	*Bliznyuk 2 (1p), Rodionov*
10/6	Naftan	h	4-2	*Rodionov, Stasevich, Sivakov, Bliznyuk*
15/6	Shakhtyor	a	4-3	*Likhtarovich, Rodionov, Bliznyuk 2*
20/6	MTZ-RIPO	h	0-3	
28/6	Dinamo Minsk	a	3-0	*Krivets, Bliznyuk, Zhavnerchik*
4/7	Dnepr	h	2-0	*Bliznyuk 2 (1p)*
10/7	Minsk	a	1-0	*Vishnyakov*
5/8	Smorgon	a	0-1	
11/8	Vitebsk	h	4-1	*Rodionov 2, Bliznyuk, Krivets*
24/8	Zhodino	a	1-0	*Bliznyuk*
2/9	Brest	h	2-1	*Rodionov, Bliznyuk*
16/9	Darida	a	0-1	
24/9	Gomel	h	2-0	*Rodionov 2*
30/9	Naftan	a	2-2	*Yermakovich, Krivets*
7/10	Shakhtyor	h	1-0	*Filipenko*
21/10	MTZ-RIPO	a	0-0	
27/10	Dinamo Minsk	h	3-0	*(w/o; original result 2-1 Rodionov, Krivets)*
31/10	Neman	a	0-1	
4/11	Dnepr	a	2-1	*Khagush, Bliznyuk*
9/11	Minsk	h	1-2	*Rodionov*

No	Name	Nat	Pos	Aps	(s)	Gls
9	Gennadiy BLIZNYUK		A	23	(1)	18
1	Aleksandr FEDOROVICH		G	18		
21	Yegor FILIPENKO		D	17	(3)	2
24	Vitaliy KAZANTSEV	RUS	D	22	(3)	
14	Anri KHAGUSH	RUS	D	22		1
18	Aleksandr KOLOTSEI		A		(1)	
10	Sergei KRIVETS		M	20	(5)	5
2	Dmitriy LIKHTAROVICH		M	23		1
13	Pavel NEKHAICHIK		M		(3)	
3	Yuriy OSTROUKH		D	6	(2)	
35	Boris PANKRATOV		G	8		
8	Dmitriy PLATONOV		M	8	(11)	1
5	Pavel PLATONOV		M	4	(19)	
6	Valentin RADEVICH		M	1	(2)	
4	Artem RADKOV		D	20		
20	Vitaliy RODIONOV		A	23	(1)	15
16	Anton SAKHAROV	RUS	D	12		
17	Mikhail SIVAKOV		M	4	(6)	1
	Maxim SKAVISH		A		(1)	
22	Igor STASEVICH		M	18	(3)	1
11	Aleksandr VISHNYAKOV		A	1	(3)	1
7	Aleksandr YERMAKOVICH		M	24	(1)	1
15	Maxim ZHAVNERCHIK		M	12	(11)	2

FC DARIDA ZHDANOVICHI

Coach - Anatoliy Baidachnyi; (14/6/07) Vadim Brazovskiy

Founded - 2000

2007				
15/4	Shakhtyor	h	0-3	
21/4	MTZ-RIPO	a	0-1	
28/4	Dinamo Minsk	h	1-0	*og (Kontsevoi)*
6/5	Dnepr	a	1-0	*Misyuk*
12/5	Minsk	h	0-0	
18/5	BATE	a	1-4	*Misyuk*
26/5	Smorgon	a	1-1	*Razin*
10/6	Vitebsk	a	1-2	*Gorbach*
15/6	Zhodino	h	1-2	*Akopyants*
20/6	Brest	a	1-2	*Razin*
27/6	Neman	h	0-1	
4/7	Gomel	h	2-7	*Misyuk, Akopyants*
11/7	Naftan	a	1-1	*Makovskiy V.*
29/7	Shakhtyor	a	1-3	*Shepetovskiy*
5/8	MTZ-RIPO	h	1-1	*Gorbach*
11/8	Dinamo Minsk	a	1-2	*Loshankov*
25/8	Dnepr	h	2-1	*Misyuk, Zenkovich*
1/9	Minsk	a	2-0	*Voledenkov, Zenkovic*
16/9	BATE	h	1-0	*Misyuk*
22/9	Smorgon	h	1-0	*Voledenkov*
1/10	Vitebsk	h	2-3	*Voledenkov, Gorbach*
6/10	Zhodino	a	2-4	*og (Kirenkin), Makovskiy V.*
21/10	Brest	h	1-2	*Makovskiy V.*
27/10	Neman	a	3-0	*Gorbach, Makovskiy Tarlovskiy*
4/11	Gomel	a	0-4	
10/11	Naftan	h	0-2	

No	Name	Nat	Pos	Aps	(s)	Gls
21	Andrei AKOPYANTS	RUS	M	13		2
16	Roman ASTAPENKO		G	6		
9	Sergei AVRAMCHIKOV		A	4	(7)	
22	Yuriy DUBROVIN	RUS	M	2	(2)	
8	Dmitriy GINTOV		D	8	(3)	
3	Maxim GORBACH		D	24	(1)	4
22	Aleksei GURKO		M	1	(6)	
34	Sergei KABELSKIY		D	7	(1)	
2	Dmitriy KALACHEV		D	8	(2)	
5	Serhiy KOLESNYCHENKO	UKR	M	9	(8)	
21	Yevgeniy LOSHANKOV		M	11	(1)	1
23	Mikhail MAKOVSKIY		M		(4)	
11	Vladimir MAKOVSKIY		A	25		4
7	Andrei MISYUK		M	26		5
10	Andrei MOROZOV		M	11	(1)	
10	Karen MURADYAN	ARM	M	3	(4)	
17	NICOLAS Ceolin	BRA	A		(1)	
1	Aleksandr PLOTNIKOV	RUS	G	20		
30	Andrei RAZIN		M	11		2
4	Anton RYABTSEV		D	19	(1)	
27	Vitaliy SHEPETOVSKIY		M	16	(8)	1
	Denis SHINGIREI		A		(3)	
2	Roman STEFANOV	RUS	D	10		
	Aleksandr TARLIKOVSKIY		M		(1)	
33	Igor TARLOVSKIY		D	21	(3)	1
20	VÁGNER Pereira Costa	BRA	M	4	(6)	
	Vitaliy VOLODENKOV		A	9		3
12	Idris ZAINULABIDOV	RUS	M	3	(3)	
6	Sergei ZENEVICH		D	5	(1)	
12	Igor ZENKOVICH		A	10	(3)	2

FC DINAMO BREST

Coach – Vladimir Gevorkyan

Founded - 1960

MAJOR HONOURS: Belarus Cup – (1) 2007.

7				
4	MTZ-RIPO	h	0-1	
4	Dinamo Minsk	a	2-0	*Mozolevskiy, Kozak*
4	Dnepr	h	1-1	*Kozak*
	Minsk	a	0-0	
5	BATE	h	2-1	*Sokol 2 (1p)*
5	Smorgon	a	0-1	
5	Vitebsk	h	0-1	
6	Zhodino	a	0-1	
6	Neman	h	0-0	
6	Darida	h	2-1	*Mozolevskiy, Chistyi*
6	Gomel	a	1-4	*Sokol (p)*
	Naftan	h	0-0	
7	Shakhtyor	a	2-3	*Sokol, Goginashvili*
7	MTZ-RIPO	a	1-2	*Sokol (p)*
	Dinamo Minsk	h	2-2	*Todua, Mozolevskiy*
8	Dnepr	a	1-3	*Sokol (p)*
8	Minsk	h	0-0	
	BATE	a	1-2	*Volodko*
9	Smorgon	h	4-0	*Mozolevskiy 3, Demeshko*
9	Vitebsk	a	1-3	*Sokol (p)*
9	Zhodino	h	1-0	*Todua*
0	Neman	a	0-1	
10	Darida	a	2-1	*Sokol 2 (1p)*
10	Gomel	h	0-2	
1	Naftan	a	0-0	
11	Shakhtyor	h	0-1	

Name	Nat	Pos	Aps	(s)	Gls
Andrei CHISTYI		M	13	(3)	1
Aleksandr DEMESHKO		M	8	(9)	1
Vadim DEMIDOVICH		M	9	(6)	
Pavel DOVGULEVETS		D	2	(2)	
Dmytro DUNETS	UKR	M		(1)	
Vitaliy GAIDUCHIK		D	1	(1)	
Roman GOGINASHVILI	GEO	A	5	(12)	1
Vadym ISHMAKOV	UKR	D	12		
Roman KHOVAVKO		M	1	(2)	
Roman KOTS	UKR	D	15		
Sergei KOZAK		M	19	(1)	2
Dmitriy MOZOLEVSKIY		A	20	(5)	6
Edgar OLEKHNOVICH		M	2	(2)	
Vitaliy PANASYUK		D	23		
Sergei SAKHARUK		G	3	(1)	
Vladimir SHCHERBO		D	19		
Aleksei SHCHIGOLEV		D	26		
Viktor SOKOL		M	20	(4)	9
Roman STEPANOV	UKR	A	2	(4)	
Gia TODUA	GEO	A	9	(4)	2
Viktor TROTSYUK		A	10	(4)	
Andrei TSEVAN		A	16	(6)	
Yuriy TSYGALKO		G	7	(1)	
Aleksandr VOLODKO		M	25		1
Dmitriy YEKIMOV	RUS	G	16		
Roman ZHERSH	UKR	M	3	(8)	

FC DINAMO MINSK

Coach - Aleksandr Khatskevich

Founded - 1927

JOR HONOURS: USSR League – (1) 1982; Belarus League – (7) 1992, 93, 1994, 1995 (spring), 1995 (autumn), 1997, 2004; Belarus Cup – (3) 1992, 1994, 2003.

07				
4	Zhodino	a	2-2	*Kislyak, Putilo*
4	Brest	h	0-2	
4	Darida	a	0-1	
7/5	Gomel	h	1-0	*Márcio*
12/5	Naftan	a	0-1	
19/5	Shakhtyor	h	1-0	*Kislyak*
26/5	MTZ-RIPO	a	0-1	
10/6	Neman	a	1-1	*Márcio*
16/6	Dnepr	h	1-0	*Gigevich*
20/6	Minsk	a	2-2	*Márcio, Chukhlei*
28/6	BATE	h	0-3	
4/7	Smorgon	a	1-0	*Mbanangoye*
10/7	Vitebsk	h	0-0	
28/7	Zhodino	h	0-0	
6/8	Brest	a	2-2	*Yurchenko V., Mbanangoye*
11/8	Darida	h	2-1	*Mbanangoye, Rák*
25/8	Gomel	a	4-4	*Mbanangoye 2, Khatskevich 2*
16/9	Shakhtyor	a	2-2	*Yurchenko V., Rák*
22/9	MTZ-RIPO	h	0-1	
26/9	Naftan	h	3-0	*Mbanangoye, Rák, Gigevich*
30/9	Neman	h	0-0	
6/10	Dnepr	a	1-1	*Rák*
21/10	Minsk	h	1-0	*Kislyak*
27/10	BATE	a	0-3	*(w/o; original result 1-2 Rák)*
4/11	Smorgon	h	2-0	*Rák, Mbanangoye*
10/11	Vitebsk	a	1-1	*Yurchenko V.*

No	Name	Nat	Pos	Aps	(s)	Gls
	ADRIANO Alves de Melo	BRA	M		(2)	
	Andrei CHUKHLEI		M	10	(6)	1
13	Eduardo Moreira "EDU"	BRA	A	17	(5)	
18	Sergei GIGEVICH		M	4	(13)	2
5	Eric KAMDEM	CMR	D	10		
7	Aleksandr KHATSKEVICH		M	7	(1)	2
10	Sergei KISLYAK		M	19	(2)	3
3	Sergei KONTSEVOI		D	10	(2)	
1	Artur LESKO		G	11		
11	José da Silva MÁRCIO	BRA	A	16	(6)	3
23	Aleksandr MARTYNOVICH		D	24		
17	Bruno Zito MBANANGOYE	GAB	M	15	(2)	7
5	Aleksandr MRINSKIY		M		(3)	
	Sergiu NUDNII	MDA	M		(1)	
6	Yevgeniy PANKOV	RUS	D	12		
16	Kirill PAVLYUCHEK		D	16	(1)	
22	Sergei PAVLYUKOVICH		M	11		
14	Anton PUTILO		M	19	(2)	1
21	Róbert RÁK	SVK	A	14		6
15	Dmitriy REKISH		A	5	(7)	
24	Sergei TEMRYUKOV	RUS	D	6		
12	Gennadiy TUMILOVICH		G	4		
20	Oleg VERETILO		D	24		
	Vitaliy VOLODENKOV		A	6	(2)	
4	Aleksei YANUSHKEVICH		D	5	(7)	
6	Igor YASINSKIY		M		(1)	
35	David YURCHENKO	RUS	G	11		
9	Vladimir YURCHENKO		M	10	(6)	3

FC DNEPR MOGILEV

Coach - Vladimir Kostyukov; (23/6/07) Vladimir Brezhezinskiy

Founded - 1960

MAJOR HONOURS: Belarus League – (1) 1998.

2007				
15/4	Vitebsk	a	2-0	*Gavryushko, Shubladze*
21/4	Zhodino	h	1-1	*Kapov*
27/4	Brest	a	1-1	*Gavryushko*
6/5	Darida	h	0-1	
12/5	Gomel	a	0-4	
19/5	Naftan	h	0-0	
26/5	Shakhtyor	a	0-2	
10/6	MTZ-RIPO	h	2-1	*Bondarev, Tupchiy*
16/6	Dinamo Minsk	a	0-1	

BELARUS

20/6	Neman	h	1-3	*Rybak (p)*
27/6	Minsk	h	0-0	
4/7	BATE	a	0-2	
11/7	Smorgon	h	0-0	
29/7	Vitebsk	h	1-2	*Lyasyuk*
5/8	Zhodino	a	0-2	
11/8	Brest	h	3-1	*Matveyenko, Gavryushko, Shubladze (p)*
25/8	Darida	a	1-2	*Gavryushko*
1/9	Gomel	h	2-0	*Lyasyuk, Pavlov*
16/9	Naftan	a	0-1	
22/9	Shakhtyor	h	2-3	*Berdnyk, Matveyenko*
30/9	MTZ-RIPO	a	3-2	*Gavryushko 2, Matveyenko*
6/10	Dinamo Minsk	h	1-1	*Berdnyk*
23/10	Neman	a	0-0	
27/10	Minsk	a	0-0	
4/11	BATE	h	1-2	*Pavlov*
10/11	Smorgon	a	0-1	

No	Name	Nat	Pos	Aps	(s)	Gls
7	Oleksiy BAHNYUK	UKR	D	17	(1)	
18	Maxim BERDNYK	RUS	M	5	(2)	2
26	Vitaliy BONDAREV	UKR	A	2	(7)	1
3	Aleksandr CHAIKA		M	1	(2)	
8	Danylo CHUPRYNA	UKR	M	21	(1)	
23	Aleksandr GAVRYUSHKO		M	24	(1)	6
16	Andrei GORBUNOV		G	25		
32	Dmitriy IGNATENKO		M	1	(7)	
92	Dmitriy KALACHEV		D	11		
2	Yevgeniy KAPOV		D	26		1
1	Ruslan KOPANTSOV		G	1		
12	Andrei KORZYUK		D	5		
19	Yuriy LUKASHOV		M	5	(2)	
	Andrei LYASYUK		A	5		2
10	Anton MATVEYENKO		M	24		3
28	Aleksandr MAXIMENKO		D	2	(2)	
15	Valeriy NOVOSELOV		M		(1)	
17	Aleksandr PAVLOV		M	24	(1)	2
9	Aleksandr RAYEVSKIY		M	3	(5)	
87	Denys RYBAK	UKR	A	1	(1)	1
30	Aleksandr SAZANKOV		M	2	(9)	
	Anton SHEPELEV		D	1		
29	Denis SHEVELEV	RUS	D	23		
5	Aleksandre SHUBLADZE	GEO	A	12	(1)	2
6	Vladimir SHUNEIKO		D	20	(1)	
11	Dmytro TERESHCHENKO	UKR	M	13	(6)	
21	Olexiy TUPCHIY	UKR	M	12	(6)	1
13	Ruslan YUDENKOV		A		(8)	

FC GOMEL

Coach – Anatoliy Yurevich

Founded - 1995

MAJOR HONOURS: Belarus League – (1) 2003; Belarus Cup – (1) 2002.

2007				
14/4	Naftan	h	3-1	*Stripeikis, Vasilyuk 2 (1p)*
21/4	Shakhtyor	a	0-0	
28/4	MTZ-RIPO	h	2-2	*Vasilyuk, Stripeikis*
7/5	Dinamo Minsk	a	0-1	
12/5	Dnepr	h	4-0	*Vasilyuk 3 (1p), Stripeikis*
18/5	Minsk	a	6-2	*Vasilyuk 2, Stripeikis, Gatiyev, Dashuk, Kobets*
22/5	BATE	h	1-3	*Vasilyuk*
10/6	Smorgon	a	1-1	*Stripeikis*
15/6	Vitebsk	h	2-1	*Stripeikis 2*
20/6	Zhodino	a	1-2	*Vasilyuk*
27/6	Brest	h	4-1	*Vasilyuk 3, Stripeikis*
4/7	Darida	a	7-2	*Kobets 2, Vasilyuk 2, Stripeikis 2, Rybak*
10/7	Neman	h	2-0	*Vasilyuk 2*
29/7	Naftan	a	0-1	
5/8	Shakhtyor	h	1-1	*Stripeikis*
12/8	MTZ-RIPO	a	1-1	*Stripeikis*
25/8	Dinamo Minsk	h	4-4	*Kobets, Vasilyuk 2 (1 Stripeikis*
1/9	Dnepr	a	0-2	
16/9	Minsk	h	1-0	*Kobets*
24/9	BATE	a	0-2	
30/9	Smorgon	h	1-0	*Kobets*
6/10	Vitebsk	a	0-0	
21/10	Zhodino	h	1-1	*Vasilyuk*
27/10	Brest	a	2-0	*Bressan, Vasilyuk*
4/11	Darida	h	4-0	*Vasilyuk 3, Kondrash*
10/11	Neman	a	1-0	*Stripeikis*

No	Name	Nat	Pos	Aps	(s)	Gl
21	Viktor BOREL		A		(2)	
19	Nikolai BRANFILOV		D	9	(3)	
8	Renan BRESSAN	BRA	M	18	(7)	1
13	Andrei DASHUK		A	2	(9)	1
14	Stanislav DRAGUN		M	11	(13)	
6	Eduard GATIYEV	RUS	D	19	(3)	1
3	Eric KAMDEM	CMR	D	2		
17	Aleksandr KOBETS		M	25		6
7	Ruslan KONDRASHUK		M	24		1
22	Sergei KONTSEVOI		D	4	(2)	
15	Andrei KUKHARENOK		M		(12)	
1	Vasiliy KUZNETSOV	RUS	G	19		
77	Igor LOGVINOV		G	7		
	Sergei MATVEICHIK		D		(1)	
4	Vitaliy NADIYEVSKIY		M	21	(1)	
20	Sergei NIKITENKO		M		(3)	
18	Pavel RYBAK		D	18	(3)	1
2	Aleksandr SHAGOIKO		D	25		
11	Valeriy STRIPEIKIS		A	25		1
	Ivan SULIM		M		(2)	
9	Vitaliy TARASHCHIK		M	23	(1)	
10	Roman VASILYUK		A	25		2
5	Miloš ZIVKOVIĆ	SRB	D	9	(4)	

FC MINSK

Coach - Sergei Yaromko

Founded - 2005

2007				
15/4	Smorgon	a	1-2	*Khachaturyan*
22/4	Vitebsk	h	2-1	*Pyatrauskas, Osipen*
28/4	Zhodino	a	1-2	*Martynets*
6/5	Brest	h	0-0	
12/5	Darida	a	0-0	
18/5	Gomel	h	2-6	*Lyasyuk 2*
26/5	Naftan	a	0-3	
10/6	Shakhtyor	h	0-0	
15/6	MTZ-RIPO	a	1-2	*Pyatrauskas*
20/6	Dinamo Minsk	h	2-2	*Martynets, Mikhnov*
27/6	Dnepr	a	0-0	
4/7	Neman	a	1-3	*Litvinchuk (p)*
10/7	BATE	h	0-1	
29/7	Smorgon	h	1-0	*Makar*
5/8	Vitebsk	a	0-1	
11/8	Zhodino	h	0-0	
25/8	Brest	a	0-0	
1/9	Darida	h	0-2	
16/9	Gomel	a	0-1	
22/9	Naftan	h	1-2	*Makar*
30/9	Shakhtyor	a	1-1	*Makarov*
6/10	MTZ-RIPO	h	1-2	*Makar*
22/10	Dinamo Minsk	a	0-1	
27/10	Dnepr	h	0-0	
4/11	Neman	h	2-1	*Makar (p), Makarov*
9/11	BATE	a	2-1	*Litvinchuk, Branovit*

Name	Nat	Pos	Aps	(s)	Gls
Yevgeniy BRANOVITSKIY		D	11		1
Aleksei DOBROVOLSKIY		D	4	(6)	
Aleksandr FEDOSEYEV		D		(2)	
Andrei KHACHATURYAN		M	11	(8)	1
Mikhail KOLYADKO		M		(5)	
Aleksei KOZLOV		M		(5)	
Dmitriy LABETSKIY		D	15	(2)	
Aleksandr LENTSEVICH		G	13		
Mikhail LITVINCHUK		A	8	(10)	2
Andrei LYASYUK		A		(6)	2
Dmitriy MAKAR		M	13		4
Igor MAKAROV		M	25	(1)	2
Aleksei MARTYNETS		M	19		2
Aleksandr MIKHNOVETS		M	20	(5)	1
Andrei MILEVSKIY		D	13		
Dmitriy OSIPENKO		A	25	(1)	1
Denis PARECHIN		G	5		
Oleg PIKTA		D	17	(1)	
Jonas PYATRAUSKAS	LTU	D	26		2
Artur SAAKYAN		D	22	(2)	
Aleksandr SACHIVKO		M	19	(1)	
Denis VERKHOV		M	1	(1)	
Pavel YEVSEYENKO		M	10	(8)	
Vladimir YURKEVICH		G	8	(1)	
Nikolai ZENKO		A	1	(1)	

FC MTZ-RIPO MINSK

Coach - Andrei Zygmantovich

Founded - 1947

MAJOR HONOURS: Belarus Cup – (2) 2005, 2008.

7				
4	Brest	a	1-0	*Soro*
4	Darida	h	1-0	*Valkanov*
4	Gomel	a	2-2	*Valkanov, Hleb*
	Naftan	h	1-0	*Zubovich*
	Shakhtyor	a	1-1	*Shchegrikovich*
	Neman	a	1-2	*Hleb*
	Dinamo Minsk	h	1-0	*Zubovich*
	Dnepr	a	1-2	*Valkanov*
	Minsk	h	2-1	*Kontsevoi 2*
	BATE	a	3-0	*Afanasiev, Hleb, Mamiж*
	Smorgon	h	2-2	*Hleb 2*
	Vitebsk	a	0-0	
	Zhodino	h	2-0	*Kontsevoi 2*
	Brest	h	2-1	*Kontsevoi, Afanasiev*
	Darida	a	1-1	*Strakhanovich*
8	Gomel	h	1-1	*Afanasiev*
8	Naftan	a	2-2	*Hleb (p), Bubnov*
	Shakhtyor	h	1-3	*Afanasiev*
	Neman	h	1-1	*Afanasiev (p)*
	Dinamo Minsk	a	1-0	*Sashcheko*
	Dnepr	h	2-3	*Tarasenko 2*
	Minsk	a	2-1	*Soro, Bordachev*
0	BATE	h	0-0	
0	Smorgon	a	1-0	*Hleb*
	Vitebsk	h	0-1	
1	Zhodino	a	0-1	

No	Name	Nat	Pos	Aps	(s)	Gls
	Mikhail AFANASIEV		M	22	(3)	5
	Tomasz BALUL	POL	D	1	(1)	
	Maxim BORDACHEV		M	11	(4)	1
	Anton BUBNOV		M	3	(6)	1
	Aleksandr BYLINA		D	3	(1)	
30	Aboubakar CAMARA	GUI	M	10	(2)	
	Ilgiz FATTAKHOV	RUS	A		(2)	
	Artem FEDORCHENKO	UKR	D	8		
	Vyacheslav HLEB		A	19		7
	Sergiu JAPALAU	MDA	M	2	(4)	
	Artem KONTSEVOI		A	15	(1)	5
	Igor MALTSEV		M	24	(1)	
6	Bojan MAMIĆ	SRB	A	7	(7)	1
16	Nikolai OSIPOVICH		D	16	(3)	
14	Oleg POPEL		D	5	(6)	
10	Denis SASHCHEKO		A	15	(8)	1
8	Dmitriy SHCHEGRIKOVICH		M	13	(10)	1
15	Taina Adama SORO	CIV	M	24		2
88	Oleg STRAKHANOVICH		M	12		1
1	Aleksandr SULIMA		G	26		
3	Valeriy TARASENKO		D	19		2
23	Aleksandr TOLKANITSA		M		(1)	
5	Yanko VALKANOV	BUL	D	12		3
9	Mikhail YEREMCHUK		A	17	(6)	
22	Yegor ZUBOVICH		A	2	(10)	2

FC NAFTAN NOVOPOLOTSK

Coach – Igor Gasyuto; (24/7/07) Igor Kovalevich

Founded - 1995

2007				
14/4	Gomel	a	1-3	*Verkhovtsev*
21/4	Neman	a	2-3	*Chumachenko, Tsygalko*
28/4	Shakhtyor	h	0-2	
6/5	MTZ-RIPO	a	0-1	
12/5	Dinamo Minsk	h	1-0	*Belousov*
19/5	Dnepr	a	0-0	
26/5	Minsk	h	3-0	*Pakulin, Politevich, Karolik*
10/6	BATE	a	2-4	*Degterev (p), Karolik*
15/6	Smorgon	h	0-1	
20/6	Vitebsk	a	2-1	*Aleshchenko 2*
27/6	Zhodino	h	1-1	*Trukhov*
4/7	Brest	a	0-0	
11/7	Darida	h	1-1	*Degterev (p)*
29/7	Gomel	h	1-0	*Chumachenko*
5/8	Neman	h	1-0	*Komarovskiy*
11/8	Shakhtyor	a	1-3	*Rudik (p)*
26/8	MTZ-RIPO	h	2-2	*Verkhovtsev, Degterev*
16/9	Dnepr	h	1-0	*Verkhovtsev*
22/9	Minsk	a	2-1	*Rudik (p), Aleshchenko*
26/9	Dinamo Minsk	a	0-3	
30/9	BATE	h	2-2	*Trukhov, Bordok*
6/10	Smorgon	a	1-1	*Trukhov*
21/10	Vitebsk	h	0-0	
27/10	Zhodino	a	2-1	*Belousov, Rudik*
4/11	Brest	h	0-0	
10/11	Darida	a	2-0	*Komarovskiy, Rudik (p)*

No	Name	Nat	Pos	Aps	(s)	Gls
3	Yuriy ALESHCHENKO		A	1	(14)	3
11	Igor ANTSYPOV		D	7	(1)	
15	Aleksei BELOUSOV		D	25		2
	Anton BORDOK		A		(4)	1
7	Ihor CHUMACHENKO	UKR	M	17	(1)	2
12	Aleksandr DEGTEREV		M	23		3
8	Vitaliy DEIKALO		A	1	(16)	
4	Mikhail GORBACHEV		D	18	(2)	
12	Denis KAROLIK		M	6	(8)	2
14	Maxim KARPOVICH		M	23	(3)	
17	Dmitriy KOMAROVSKIY		A	13		2
71	Anton KOVALEVSKIY		G	20		
9	Artem PAKULIN		M	4	(2)	1
6	Sergei POLITEVICH		D	6	(5)	1
2	Dmitriy RADKOV		D	3		
10	Maxim RAZUMOV		M	15	(3)	
5	Vitaliy ROGOZHKIN		D	16		
22	Vadim ROMANOV	RUS	D	13		
19	Filipp RUDIK	RUS	M	11	(6)	4
1,72	Vladimir SELKIN		G	6		
21	Igor TRUKHOV		M	19	(3)	3
10	Maxim TSYGALKO		A	2	(3)	1
23	Andrei URUPIN		M		(1)	
18	Dmitriy VERKHOVTSEV		D	17	(2)	3
20	Roman VOLKOV		A	6	(2)	
6	Konstantin YAKUBOVSKIY		M	14	(2)	

BELARUS

FC NEMAN GRODNO

Coach - Ludas Rumbutis

Founded - 1964

MAJOR HONOURS: Belarus Cup – (1) 1993.

2007				
15/4	BATE	a	1-2	*Alumona*
25/4	Naftan	h	3-2	*Kirenya (p), Kryvobok, Kovalyuk*
27/4	Smorgon	a	0-0	
6/5	Shakhtyor	h	2-0	*Alumona, Makar*
12/5	Vitebsk	a	0-0	
19/5	MTZ-RIPO	h	2-1	*Kovalyuk, Kovalenok*
26/5	Zhodino	a	0-0	
10/6	Dinamo Minsk	h	1-1	*Alumona*
15/6	Brest	a	0-0	
20/6	Dnepr	a	3-1	*Kovalenok, Yezerskiy, Alumona*
27/6	Darida	a	1-0	*Alumona*
4/7	Minsk	h	3-1	*Juvenal, Alumona, Denisevich*
10/7	Gomel	a	0-2	
5/8	Naftan	a	0-1	
11/8	Smorgon	h	0-1	
25/8	Shakhtyor	a	1-1	*Kovalyuk*
1/9	Vitebsk	h	2-1	*Ichim, Juvenal*
16/9	MTZ-RIPO	a	1-1	*Alumona*
22/9	Zhodino	h	0-1	
30/9	Dinamo Minsk	a	0-0	
6/10	Brest	h	1-0	*Juvenal*
21/10	Dnepr	h	0-0	
27/10	Darida	h	0-3	
31/10	BATE	h	1-0	*Alumona*
4/11	Minsk	a	1-2	*Alumona (p)*
10/11	Gomel	h	0-1	

No	Name	Nat	Pos	Aps	(s)	Gls
11	Aleksandr ALUMONA	RUS	A	21	(3)	9
20	Ivan DENISEVICH		M	10	(7)	1
24	Andrei GORBACH		A	8	(2)	
5	Oleg ICHIM	MDA	D	26		1
15	JUVENAL Gomes da Silva	BRA	D	21		3
2	Sergei KHALETSKIY		D	22		
7	Oleg KIRENYA		M	19	(3)	1
21	Mikhail KOTIN		D	3	(4)	
10	Dmitriy KOVALENOK		A	7	(7)	2
8	Sergei KOVALYUK		M	21	(5)	3
6	Ihor KRYVOBOK	UKR	A	20	(3)	1
22	Igor LISITSA		M	1	(5)	
9	Dmitriy MAKAR		M	2	(9)	1
13	Dmitriy ROVNEIKO		D	13	(4)	
19	Yevgeniy SAVOSTYANOV		M	5	(4)	
9	Ruslan SHEKULOVICH		A	2	(4)	
3	Sergei SOSNOVSKIY		D	26		
18	Aleksei TISHCHENKO		M	10	(5)	
16	Sergei VEREMKO		G	26		
12	Vyacheslav YAROSLAVSKIY		M	6	(4)	
4	Nikolai YEZERSKIY		D	17	(8)	1

FC SHAKHTYOR SOLIGORSK

Coach – Yuriy Vergeichik

Founded - 1963

MAJOR HONOURS: Belarus League – (1) 2005; Belarus Cup – (1) 2004.

2007				
15/4	Darida	a	3-0	*Gukailo, Goncharik, Nikiforenko*
21/4	Gomel	h	0-0	
28/4	Naftan	a	2-0	*Klimenko 2*
6/5	Neman	a	0-2	
12/5	MTZ-RIPO	h	1-1	*Klimenko*
19/5	Dinamo Minsk	a	0-1	
26/5	Dnepr	h	2-0	*Novik, Klimenko (p)*
10/6	Minsk	a	0-0	
15/6	BATE	h	3-4	*Leonchik 2, Klimenk*
19/6	Smorgon	a	2-0	*Novik, Klimenko*
27/6	Vitebsk	h	1-2	*Goncharik (p)*
11/7	Brest	h	3-2	*Rios, Klimenko (p), Leonchik*
29/7	Darida	h	3-1	*Nikiforenko, Leonch Klimenko*
5/8	Gomel	a	1-1	*Nikiforenko*
11/8	Naftan	h	3-1	*Nikiforenko, Gonchc Leonchik*
15/8	Zhodino	a	1-1	*Krot*
25/8	Neman	h	1-1	*Krot*
11/9	MTZ-RIPO	a	3-1	*Nikiforenko, Zyulev, Zhukovskiy*
16/9	Dinamo Minsk	h	2-2	*Nikiforenko, Timofe*
22/9	Dnepr	a	3-2	*Kovalchuk 2, Gonch*
30/9	Minsk	h	1-1	*Leonchik*
7/10	BATE	a	0-1	
21/10	Smorgon	h	3-0	*Zyulev 2, Nikiforenk*
27/10	Vitebsk	a	2-1	*Nikiforenko 2*
4/11	Zhodino	h	0-2	
10/11	Brest	a	1-0	*Zhukovskiy*

No	Name	Nat	Pos	Aps	(s)	G
16	Mikhail BARANOVSKIY		G	26		
24	Pavel BEGANSKIY		A	1	(5)	
3	Nikolai BRANFILOV		D	13		
8	Nikita BUKATKIN		M	5	(4)	
22	Aleksandr BYCHENOK		M	10	(13)	
2	Aleksandr BYLINA		D	9	(3)	
6	Dmitriy CHALEI		D	2		
4	Artem GONCHARIK		A	15	(10)	4
12	Maxim GUKAILO		M	21	(3)	1
19	Aleksandr KHRAPKOVSKIY		D	8	(1)	
9	Aleksandr KLIMENKO		A	11	(2)	8
20	Sergei Vlad. KOVALCHUK		M	17	(2)	2
27	Sergei KROT		M	1	(3)	2
18	Vadim LASOVSKIY		D	6	(1)	
7	Andrei Ivanovich LEONCHIK		M	21		6
14	Ishref MAGOMEDOV	RUS	A		(6)	
11	Mikhail MARTINOVICH		M	13	(9)	
10	Sergei NIKIFORENKO		M	24		9
13	Aleksandr NOVIK		M	12	(1)	2
2	Paulius PAKNIS	LTU	D		(1)	
21	Pavel PLASKONNYI		D	21		
17	Aleksei RIOS		M	17	(3)	1
23	Vitaliy TIMOFEYEV	RUS	M	11	(1)	1
5	Aleksandr YUREVICH		D	11		
5	Valeriy ZHUKOVSKIY		M	2	(9)	2
18	Igor ZYULEV		A	9	(1)	3

FC SMORGON

Coach - Georgiy Kondratyev

Founded - 1987

2007				
15/4	Minsk	h	2-1	*Dorokhevich, Bobov*
21/4	BATE	a	2-4	*Mardas, Zyulev*
27/4	Neman	h	0-0	
6/5	Vitebsk	h	1-1	*Lebedev*
12/5	Zhodino	a	0-1	
19/5	Brest	h	1-0	*Zyulev*
26/5	Darida	h	1-1	*Mardas (p)*
10/6	Gomel	h	1-1	*Lebedev*
15/6	Naftan	a	1-0	*Trindyuk*
19/6	Shakhtyor	h	0-2	
27/6	MTZ-RIPO	a	2-2	*Zyulev, og (Tarasenk*
4/7	Dinamo Minsk	h	0-1	
11/7	Dnepr	a	0-0	
29/7	Minsk	a	0-1	

3	BATE	h	1-0	*Parfenov*
/8	Neman	a	1-0	*og (Yaroslavskiy)*
/8	Vitebsk	a	0-1	
)	Zhodino	h	0-0	
/9	Brest	a	0-4	
/9	Darida	a	0-1	
/9	Gomel	a	0-1	
0	Naftan	h	1-1	*Margulets*
/10	Shakhtyor	a	0-3	
/10	MTZ-RIPO	h	0-1	
1	Dinamo Minsk	a	0-2	
/11	Dnepr	h	1-0	*Belmokhtar (p)*

	Name	Nat	Pos	Aps	(s)	Gls
	Aleksandr BARANOV		M	24	(2)	
	Vasyl BARANOV	UKR	M	9		
	Said BELMOKHTAR	UKR	A	4	(3)	1
	Ihor BOBOVYCH	UKR	A	2	(4)	1
	Aleksandr DAVIDOVICH		D	18	(3)	
	Sergei DOROKHEVICH		M	20	(1)	1
	Vladislav DUKSO		D	18	(1)	
	Aleksei DVORETSKIY		M	15	(6)	
	Suliko KAKABADZE	GEO	A	8	(2)	
	Aleksandr KHRAPKOVSKIY		D	11		
	Andrei KORDUN	RUS	A	3	(4)	
	Dmitriy LEBEDEV		A	2	(18)	2
	Gennadiy MARDAS		D	20		2
	Vladimir MARGULETS		M	7	(10)	1
	Dmitriy PARFENOV		A	3	(8)	1
	Aleksei POGE		G	15		
	Serhiy PONOMARENKO	UKR	D	21		
	Andrei SHILO		M	15	(3)	
	Roman SMISHKO	UKR	G	9	(1)	
	Serhiy STARENKYI	UKR	M	14	(3)	
	Dmitriy TRINDYUK		D	20	(3)	1
	Sergei TSVETINSKIY		D	13	(5)	
	Rodion ZHUK		G	2		
	Igor ZUYLEV		A	13		3

FC TORPEDO ZHODINO

Coach - Oleg Kubarev

Founded - 1961

07				
'4	Dinamo Minsk	h	2-2	*Zalevskiy, Sheryakov*
'4	Dnepr	a	1-1	*Sheryakov*
'4	Minsk	h	2-1	*Sheryakov, Voronkov*
;	BATE	a	0-3	
'5	Smorgon	h	1-0	*Kryklyvyi*
'5	Vitebsk	a	1-1	*Klimovich*
'5	Neman	h	0-0	
'6	Brest	h	1-0	*Horbarnenko*
'6	Darida	a	2-1	*Terentiev, Sheryakov*
'6	Gomel	h	2-1	*Voronkov, Horbarnenko*
'6	Naftan	a	1-1	*Sheryakov (p)*
'7	MTZ-RIPO	a	0-2	
'7	Dinamo Minsk	a	0-0	
;	Dnepr	h	2-0	*Sheryakov 2*
'8	Minsk	a	0-0	
'8	Shakhtyor	h	1-1	*Terentiev*
'8	BATE	h	0-1	
	Smorgon	a	0-0	
'9	Vitebsk	h	2-0	*Sheryakov, Radchenko*
'9	Neman	a	1-0	*Sheryakov*
'9	Brest	a	0-1	
0	Darida	h	4-2	*Klimovich, Zalevskiy, Zanemonets, Radchenko*
'10	Gomel	a	1-1	*Terentiev*
'10	Naftan	h	1-2	*Terentiev*
1	Shakhtyor	a	2-0	*og (Gukailo), Sheryakov*
'11	MTZ-RIPO	h	1-0	*Zalevskiy*

No	Name	Nat	Pos	Aps	(s)	Gls
17	ADRIANO Alves de Melo	BRA	M	9	(3)	
1	Vladimir BUSHMA		G	24		
28	Pavel DOVGULEVETS		D	12		
19	Stanislav GNEDKO		M	10	(4)	
33	Artem GOMELKO		G	2		
8	Aleksandr GRENKOV		M	22	(2)	
9	Vyacheslav HORBARNENKO	UKR	M	11	(12)	2
20	Roman KIRENKIN		D	25		
13	Dmitriy KLIMOVICH		D	23		2
12	Dmitriy KOVALENKO	RUS	D	3	(1)	
14	Olexandr KRYKLYVYI	UKR	A	5	(5)	1
22	Sergei KUZMINICH		M	9	(1)	
7	Pavel LYUTKO		M	1	(1)	
29	Roman RADCHENKO	MDA	A	3	(6)	2
3	Igor SARASEK		M	1	(5)	
18	Aleksandr SAVINOV		M	5	(4)	
6	Andrei SHERYAKOV		A	22	(2)	10
4	Igor SHITOV		D	24		
21	Aleksandr TERENTIEV		M	18	(3)	4
2	Ihor VORONKOV	UKR	M	26		2
25	Yakiv ZALEVSKIY	UKR	D	24	(1)	3
15	Igor ZANEMONETS		A	7	(10)	1

FC VITEBSK

Coach - Andrei Chernyshov (RUS)

Founded - 1960

MAJOR HONOURS: Belarus Cup – (1) 1998.

2007				
15/4	Dnepr	h	0-2	
22/4	Minsk	a	1-2	*Bogdanov*
27/4	BATE	h	0-1	
6/5	Smorgon	a	1-1	*Zuyev*
12/5	Neman	h	0-0	
18/5	Zhodino	h	1-1	*Usov*
23/5	Brest	a	1-0	*Irkha*
10/6	Darida	h	2-1	*Usov, Zuyev*
15/6	Gomel	a	1-2	*Zuyev*
20/6	Naftan	h	1-2	*Baranok*
27/6	Shakhtyor	a	2-1	*Rubnenko, Zuyev*
4/7	MTZ-RIPO	h	0-0	
10/7	Dinamo Minsk	a	0-0	
29/7	Dnepr	a	2-1	*Rubnenko, Usov*
5/8	Minsk	h	1-0	*Rubnenko*
11/8	BATE	a	1-4	*Usov*
25/8	Smorgon	h	1-0	*Usov*
1/9	Neman	a	1-2	*Usov*
16/9	Zhodino	a	0-2	
22/9	Brest	h	3-1	*Zuyev, Usov, Svizhuk*
1/10	Darida	a	3-2	*Usov, Zuyev, Buloichik*
6/10	Gomel	h	0-0	
21/10	Naftan	a	0-0	
27/10	Shakhtyor	h	1-2	*og (Branfilov)*
4/11	MTZ-RIPO	a	1-0	*Svizhuk*
10/11	Dinamo Minsk	h	1-1	*Svizhuk*

No	Name	Nat	Pos	Aps	(s)	Gls
5	Sergei ANDROSOV	RUS	M	2		
10	Andrei BARANOK		M	23		1
8	Sergei BOGDANOV	RUS	D	1	(8)	1
24	Aleksandr BULOICHIK		M	15	(3)	1
30	Pavel CHESNOVSKIY		G	16		
	Rostislav DENISOV	RUS	M		(3)	
15	Andrei DIVAKOV		M	24		
2	Duško ĐUKIĆ	SRB	D	3	(1)	
20	Andrei GOROVTSOV		D	23		
69	Darlington IHEJENE	NGA	A	3	(1)	
27	Sergei IRKHA		M	16	(6)	1
3	Anton IVANOV	RUS	D	3		
15	Aleksandr KOLOTSEI		A	1	(8)	
12	Artem KOSAK		D	22		
32	Pavel KOSINETS		M		(2)	
17	Sergei KUZMINICH		M	13		

BELARUS

9	Leonid LAGUN		M		(1)	
33	Pavel LYUTKO		M	2		
	Kirill PAKULIN		M	1	(2)	
18	Dmitriy RUBNENKO		M	14	(3)	3
6	Pavel SITKO		M	13	(5)	
14	Vladimir SVIZHUK	RUS	M	14	(11)	3
4	Aleksandr TISHKEVICH		M	5	(2)	
7	Roman TREPACHKIN		M	22	2	
11	Ruslan USOV		A	18	(6)	8
1	Vitaliy VARIVONCHIK		G	2		
16	Yuriy VASYUTIN		G	8		
	Marat VORONOV		M		(1)	
29	Denis ZHUKOV		M	2	(4)	
23	Yevgeniy ZUYEV		A	20	(2)	6

PROMOTED CLUBS

FC SAVIT MOGILEV
Coach – Aleksandr Sednev
Founded - 2005

FC GRANIT MIKASHEVICHI
Coach – Valery Bohno
Founded - 1978

FC LOKOMOTIV MINSK
Coach – Serghey Yasinsky
Founded - 2000

SECOND LEVEL FINAL TABLE 2007

		Pld	W	D	L	F	A	Pts
1	FC Savit Mogilev	26	16	5	5	50	21	53
2	FC Granit Mikashevichi	26	16	4	6	39	22	52
3	FC Lokomotiv Minsk	26	16	4	6	49	21	52
4	FC Belshina Bobruisk	26	15	7	4	46	26	49
5	FC Khimik Svetlogorsk	26	12	8	6	46	31	44
6	FC Veras Nesvizh	26	12	4	10	28	25	40
7	FC Volna Pinsk	26	11	6	9	34	38	39
8	FC Dinamo-BelCard Grodno	26	11	3	12	33	37	36
9	FC Baranovichi	26	10	5	11	23	28	35
10	FC Vedrich-97 Rechitsa	26	9	6	11	29	26	33
11	FC Polotsk	26	6	5	15	26	49	23
12	FC Kommunalnik Slonim	26	5	5	16	22	48	20
13	FC Mozyr	26	4	6	16	26	44	18
14	FC Zvezda-BGU Minsk	26	2	4	20	17	58	10

N.B. FC Belshina Bobruisk 3 points deducted.

DOMESTIC CUP 2007/08

KUBOK BELAROSI

SECOND ROUND

(16/8/07)
PMK-7 Gantsevichi 2, MTZ-RIPO 3
Khimik Svetlogorsk 1, Naftan 0
Kommunalnik Zhlobin 1, FC Smorhon 1 *(aet, 2:1 on pens)*
Kommunalnik Slonim 0, FC Gomel 5
Volna Pinsk 0, Dinamo Brest 1
Vedrich-97 Rechitsa 0, FC Minsk 1
Vertikal Kalinkovichi 0, Darida 3
FC Baranovichi 0, Neman 3
Dinamo-Belkard Grodno 1, FC Vitebsk 2
Lida 1, Dnepr 2
Zvezda-BGU Minsk 1, Lokomotiv Minsk 2 *(aet)*
Veras Nesvizh 2, Belshina 0

(19/8/07)
Spartak Shklov 0, BATE 2

(5/9/07)
Savit Mogilev 0, Shakhtyor 2

(6/9/07)
Myasokombinat Vitebsk 2, Zhodino 0

(11/9/07)
FC Mozyr 1, Dinamo Minsk 4

THIRD ROUND

(15/3/08 & 21/3/08)
Lokomotiv Minsk v Dinamo Minsk 0-2; 1-0 *(1-2)*
Kommunalnik Zhlobin v MTZ-RIPO *(MTZ-RIPO w/o)*

(15/3/08 & 22/3/08)
Dinamo Brest v FC Gomel 0-2; 2-1 *(2-3)*
FC Minsk v Shakhtyor 0-1; 2-3 *(2-4)*

(16/3/08 & 21/3/08)
BATE v Veras Nesvizh 1-0; 1-0 *(2-0)*
Dnepr v FC Vitebsk 1-0; 1-0 *(2-0)*

(16/3/08 & 22/3/08)
Khimik Svetlogorsk v Myasokombinat Vitebsk 1-0; 1-0 *(2-0)*
Darida v Neman Grodno 1-0; 1-0 *(2-0)*

QUARTER-FINALS

(29/3/08 & 2/4/08)
Khimik Svetlogorsk 1 *(Gavrilovich 60)*, BATE 3 *(Bliznyuk 4, 64, Platonov*
BATE 0, Khimik Svetlogorsk 0
(BATE 3-1)

MTZ-RIPO 4 *(Hleb 32p, Sashcheko 53, Nicolas 67p, Strakhanovich 89)*, G
Gomel 2 *(Dragun 40, Bressan 85)*, MTZ-RIPO 0
(MTZ-RIPO 4-2)

Darida 1 *(Shepetovskiy 59)*, Shakhtyor 2 *(Stripeikis 46, 79)*
Shakhtyor 1 (Bychenok 80), Darida 0
(Shakhtyor 3-1)

Dnepr 0, Dinamo Minsk 0
Dinamo Minsk 1 *(Lebedev 103)*, Dnepr 0 *(aet)*
(Dinamo Minsk 1-0)

SEMI-FINALS

(16/4/08 & 30/4/08)
Shakhtyor 1 *(Leonchik 38)*, Dinamo Minsk 0
Dinamo Minsk 2 *(Shkabara 56, Rák 65p)*, Shakhtyor 3 *(Zhukovskiy 38*
Bychenok 48, Gukailo 54)
(Shakhtyor 4-2)

BATE 2 *(Nekhaichik 11, Likhtarovich 31)*, MTZ-RIPO 4 *(Yeremchuk 24, Kontsevoi 37, Hleb 69)*
MTZ-RIPO 2 *(Camara 29, Hleb 44)*, BATE 1 *(Bliznyuk 81)*
(MTZ-RIPO 6-3)

FINAL

(18/5/08)
Dinamo stadium, Minsk
FC MTZ-RIPO MINSK 2 *(Hleb 5, Strakhanovich 84)*
FC SHAKHTYOR SOLIGORSK 1 *(Stripeikis 82)*
Referee – *Kulbakov*
MTZ-RIPO – *Sulima, Stashchenyuk, Zrnanović, Osipovich, Yeremchuk, Camara (Nicolas 59), Shchegrikovich (Bubnov 68), Strakhanovich, Sashcheko (Tolkanitsa 78), Hleb, Kontsevoi.*
Sent off: *Strakhanovich (84).*
SHAKHTYOR – *Gayev, Bylina, Kovalchuk, Branfilov, Gukailo, Leonchik, Bukatkin (Bychenok 46), Martinovich (Zyulev 52), Balanovich (Stripeik Zhukovskiy, Nikiforenko.*

Long wait over for Standard

ook them a quarter of a century, but R. Standard de ge finally returned to the pinnacle of Belgian tball in 2007/08, winning the Eerste Klasse ampionship in irrepressible style under the mmand of their former goalkeeper turned coach, chel Preud'homme.

e myriad disappointments and near misses of the evious 25 years were forgotten as Les Rouches nched the title in style, beating in-form reigning ampions RSC Anderlecht 2-0 at home on Sunday 20 ril to move into an unassailable lead with three mes remaining. DR Congo striker Dieumerci okani, recently recruited from Anderlecht, was ndard's hero, scoring twice in the second half to e his team the win that, with Club Brugge KV wing 0-0 at KAA Gent, ensured the club's sixth gian title.

litary defeat

ndard's triumph brooked no argument. Out of the ps with five successive wins, the first four of them h bringing four goals, Standard fought neck and k with Club Brugge for most of the campaign. o factors gave them the edge – a refusal to submit defeat that lasted right through until the title was ure (their only loss came a week later, 2-1 at R. arleroi SC), and home and away victories over their ect rivals. The 2-1 victory in Bruges in mid-February, led by a double from top-scoring Serbian striker an Jovanović, was especially crucial as defeat uld have left Standard six points in arrears. Instead ir win effectively broke Club Brugge's resolve, gering a spate of defeats for the Blue and Blacks t bottomed out when they lost 6-2 at home to C Genk.

osing 2-0 to Anderlecht on the penultimate ekend Club Brugge missed out on second place - d a shot at the 2008/09 UEFA Champions League – t much more devastating was the tragic death of ir top-scoring Belgian international striker François Sterchele. The 26-year-old lost his life in the early hours of Thursday 8 May when his Porsche crashed at high speed into a tree near the town of Bredene as he was returning home after visiting friends.

Sterchele's final goal had come a few weeks earlier, giving his team a priceless 1-0 win over local rivals Cercle Brugge KSV, who proved to be the surprise package of the season, finishing fourth. Skilfully led by

François Sterchele, the Club Brugge and Belgium striker, died tragically in a road accident in May

Steven Defour, the Standard Liège captain, poses with the prestigious Golden Shoe

rookie coach Glen de Boeck, Cercle scored more goa (62) than any other team in the division. That figure would surely have been even greater but for the serious knee ligament damage sustained in February by leading scorer Tom De Sutter while playing for Belgium's Olympic team.

Standard scoop awards

De Sutter, one of Belgian football's brightest hopes, might have been in line for the 2007/08 Players' Play of the Year award had he not missed the final three months of the campaign. He had finished third behir Standard's young captain Steven Defour and runner-up Ahmed Hassan of Anderlecht in the prestigious Golden Shoe award in January (for the Best Player of 2007). The end-of-season prize went to another Standard player, Jovanović, and the newly crowned champions were recognised in several other categories besides – midfielder Marouane Fellaini picked up the Ebony Shoe for best player of African origin while Axel Witsel took the Best Young Player award and, not surprisingly, Preud'homme was name best coach.

There was a bitter postscript to Standard's triumph when Preud'homme announced that he was leaving to join Gent, citing Standard's 'lack of ambition' – a euphemism for the unsatisfactory short-term contra

Union Royale des Sociétés de Footbal Association (URBSFA), Koninklijke Belgische Voetbalbond (KBVB)

Houba de Strooperlaan 145
BE-1020 Bruxelles
tel - +32 2 4771211
fax - +32 2 4782391
website - www.footbel.com
email - urbsfa.kbvb@footbel.com
Year of Formation – 1895
President – François De Keersmaecker
General Secretary – Jean-Paul Houben
Press Officer – Nicolas Cornu
Stadium – Stade Roi Baudouin, Brussels (50,024)

INTERNATIONAL TOURNAMENT APPEARANCES
FIFA World Cup - (11) 1930, 1934, 1938, 1954, 1970, 1982 (2nd phase). 1986 (4th), 1990 (2nd round), 1994 (2nd round), 1998, 2002 (2nd roun
UEFA European Championship - (3) 1972 (3r 1980 (runners-up), 2000.

TOP FIVE ALL-TIME CAPS
Jan Ceulemans (96); Eric Gerets & Franky Van D Elst (86); Vincenzo Scifo (84); Paul Van Himst (8

TOP FIVE ALL-TIME GOALS
Paul Van Himst & Bernard Voorhoof (30); Ma Wilmots (28); Joseph Mermans (27); Raymor Braine & Robert De Veen (26)

TIONAL TEAM RESULTS 2007/08

7	Serbia (ECQ)	H	Brussels	3-2	*Dembélé (10, 88), Mirallas (30)*
7	Kazakhstan (ECQ)	A	Almaty	2-2	*Geraerts (13), Mirallas (24)*
07	Finland (ECQ)	A	Brussels	0-0	
07	Armenia (ECQ)	H	Brussels	3-0	*Sonck (63), Dembélé (69), Geraerts (76)*
07	Poland (ECQ)	A	Chorzow	0-2	
07	Azerbaijan (ECQ)	A	Baku	1-0	*Pieroni (52)*
8	Morocco	H	Brussels	1-4	*Witsel (51)*
8	Italy	A	Florence	1-3	*Sonck (90+2)*

TIONAL TEAM APPEARANCES 2007/08

– René VANDEREYCKEN	22/7/53		SRB	KAZ	FIN	ARM	POL	AZE	Mar	Ita	Caps	Goals
TJNEN	7/4/81	Club Brugge	G	G	G	G	G		G	G	19	-
DEFKENS	6/10/78	West Brom (ENG)	D	D						D46	21	1
SIMONS	11/12/76	PSV (NED)	D	D	M	D			M	M	60	3
s VERMAELEN	14/11/85	Ajax (NED)	D	D					D		12	-
t KOMPANY	10/4/86	Hamburg (GER)	D	D	D	s60	D		M85	D	23	-
UDINGAYI	1/10/81	Lazio (ITA)	M		M				M	M84	11	-
DOR	9/4/73	Anderlecht	M	M84	s67	M	M	s68			77	13
ERAERTS	5/1/82	Club Brugge	M	M77		M	s84	M46	s85		18	4
DEFOUR	15/4/88	Standard	M86	M		M	M61	s46		M57	13	-
MIRALLAS	5/10/87	Lille (FRA)	A67	A63	A84	A46	A76	s81	A63	s57	8	2
a DEMBÉLÉ	16/7/87	AZ (NED)	A90	A	A	A	A	A	A81	A57	15	4
ıy VANDEN BORRE	24/10/87	Fiorentina (ITA)	s67								17	1
PENZA	4/12/76	Anderlecht	s86	s84							56	3
LOMBAERTS	20/3/85	Zenit (RUS)	s90		D	D83					4	-
ane FELLAINI	22/11/87	Standard		M		M	M	M	s46	M	10	1
RTONGHEN	24/4/87	Ajax (NED)		s63		s83	D	D	D	D	8	-
AROUN	22/9/85	Genk		s77	M67		M84				4	-
VAN BUYTEN	7/2/78	Bayern (GER)			D	D60	D	D	D46		43	4
me GILLET	9/3/84	AA Gent /Anderlecht			D		D	D	D46	s70	5	-
phe GRÉGOIRE	20/4/80	AA Gent			M67			M68			2	-
is STERCHELE	14/3/82	Club Brugge			s84						4	-
SONCK	9/8/78	Club Brugge			s67	s46			s63	s57	41	17
ERTS	23/9/82	Vitesse (NED)				D		M	s46	s46	7	-
IERONI	8/9/80	Lens (FRA) /Anderlecht					s61	A81	s81		25	2
UYSEGEMS	16/6/82	Twente (NED)					s76			s84	10	-
'ANDENBUSSCHE	24/9/81	Heerenveen (NED)						G			3	-
AN DAMME	10/10/83	Anderlecht						D			17	-
E SMET	27/3/85	Cercle Brugge							A46		1	-
'ITSEL	12/1/89	Standard							s46	M70	2	1
ien POCOGNOLI	1/8/87	AZ (NED)								D	1	-

they had offered him. So, rather than lead Les Rouches into UEFA Champions League qualifying, he chose to help Gent in the UEFA Cup, for which they qualified as runners-up to Anderlecht in the Belgian Cup. Gent reached the final – their first since 1984 – by thrashing Standard 4-0 in the second leg of the semi-final (staged five days before the crunch league game against Anderlecht), but in an exciting Brussels final they lost 3-2 to a winning goal scored by Guillaume Gillet, a player who had left Gent only in January.

Vanden Stock mourned

Anderlecht's Cup win, mastermined by man-of-the-match midfielder Mbark Boussoufa, gave them something to celebrate in their Centenary year and was a fulsome reward for an outstanding second half of the season under caretaker coach Ariël Jacobs, who had stepped up from assistant coach in November following the dismissal of Frank Vercauteren. It was the Mauves' first win in the domestic knockout competition for 14 years and was dedicated to the memory of former president Constant Vanden Stock, who had died, aged 93, the previous month. The man who put the club on the European map, and his name on the club's stadium, is widely considered to be the greatest figure in Anderlecht's 100-year history.

Although there was no Belgian representative in the UEFA Champions League group phase – for the first time since 1999 – Anderlecht, who missed out after a qualifying defeat by Fenerbahçe SK, gave the country something to cheer in Europe by knocking out Ligue 1 high fliers FC Girondins de Bordeaux to reach the UEFA Cup Round of 16. A 5-0 home defeat by FC Bayern München put an abrupt end to that particular adventure, but Anderlecht did at least save some face by winning the second leg 2-1.

New contract

The Belgian national side ended their doomed UEFA EURO 2008™ qualifying bid by winning three and drawing two of their last six matches, but although that was considered sufficient to earn head coach René Vandereycken a new two-year contract, a couple of heavy friendly defeats by Morocco and Italy reminded everybody how difficult the task will be to qualify for the 2010 FIFA World Cup, not least because Belgium's qualifying group contains UEFA EURO 2008™ semi-finalists Turkey and the new champions of Europe, Spain.

DOMESTIC LEAGUE 2007/08

EERSTE KLASSE FINAL TABLE

			Home					Away					Total					
		Pld	W	D	L	F	A	W	D	L	F	A	W	D	L	F	A	Pts
1	R Standard de Liège	34	14	3	0	39	11	8	8	1	22	8	22	11	1	61	19	77
2	RSC Anderlecht	34	14	2	1	35	10	7	5	5	24	21	21	7	6	59	31	70
3	Club Brugge KV	34	12	2	3	26	14	8	5	4	19	16	20	7	7	45	30	67
4	Cercle Brugge KSV	34	10	6	1	33	9	7	3	7	29	24	17	9	8	62	33	60
5	KFC Germinal Beerschot Antwerpen	34	10	3	4	28	14	6	4	7	18	20	16	7	11	46	34	55
6	KAA Gent	34	9	5	3	35	21	5	5	7	22	25	14	10	10	57	46	52
7	SV Zulte Waregem	34	10	3	4	28	24	3	5	9	19	30	13	8	13	47	54	47
8	R. Charleroi SC	34	7	5	5	21	20	6	2	9	20	25	13	7	14	41	45	46
9	KVC Westerlo	34	6	6	5	26	17	6	3	8	17	20	12	9	13	43	37	45
10	KRC Genk	34	8	3	6	28	23	4	6	7	26	32	12	9	13	54	55	45
11	R. Excelsior Mouscron	34	7	4	6	20	19	5	2	10	18	24	12	6	16	38	43	42
12	KSC Lokeren OV	34	5	9	3	15	10	4	6	7	17	23	9	15	10	32	33	42
13	KV Mechelen	34	7	5	5	26	23	3	5	9	19	29	10	10	14	45	52	40
14	KSV Roeselare	34	7	4	6	24	25	2	7	8	12	30	9	11	14	36	55	38
15	FCV Dender EH	34	6	3	8	18	28	3	3	11	15	31	9	6	19	33	59	33
16	RAEC Mons	34	4	8	5	19	16	3	4	10	18	29	7	12	15	37	45	33
17	K. Sint-Truidense VV	34	3	6	8	15	25	3	3	11	17	33	6	9	19	32	58	27
18	FC Molenbeek Brussels	34	3	3	11	18	32	1	4	12	9	34	4	7	23	27	66	19

TOP GOALSCORER

18 Joseph AKPALA (Charleroi)

16 Sanharib MALKI (Germinal Beerschot)
Elyaniv BARDA (Genk)
Milan JOVANOVIĆ (Standard)
Mbaye LEYE (Zulte Waregem)

15 Dieumerci MBOKANI (Standa

14 Mahamadou DISSA (Roeselar

13 Aloys NONG (Mechelen)

11 François STERCHELE (Club Br
Dominic FOLEY (AA Gent)
Bertin TOMOU (Mouscron)
Bryan RUIZ Gonzales (AA Ger

CLUB-BY-CLUB

RSC ANDERLECHT

Coach - Frank Vercauteren; (12/11/07) Ariël Jacobs

Founded – 1908

MAJOR HONOURS: UEFA Cup Winners' Cup - (2) 1976, 1978; ‑A Cup - (1) 1983; UEFA Super Cup - (2) 1976, 1978; Belgian League -) 1947, 1949, 1950, 1951, 1954, 1955, 1956, 1959, 1962, 1964, 1965, 6, 1967, 1968, 1972, 1974, 1981, 1985, 1986, 1987, 1991, 1993, 1994, '5, 2000, 2001, 2004, 2006, 2007; Belgian Cup - (9) 1965, 1972, 1973, 1975, 1976, 1988, 1989, 1994, 2008.

7

	Mechelen	*a*	*1-0*	*Wasilewski*
3	Lokeren	h	1-0	*Tchité*
3	Dender	a	2-2	*Hassan, Boussoufa*
3	Brussels	h	3-0	*Théréau, Wasilewski, Legear*
	Mouscron	a	2-1	*Von Schlebrügge, Van Damme*
9	Zulte Waregem	h	2-2	*Hassan 2*
9	Genk	a	1-1	*Serhat*
9	Charleroi	h	0-1	
)	Roeselare	a	2-2	*Polák, Frutos (p)*
10	AA Gent	h	2-1	*Legear, Frutos*
10	Cercle Brugge	a	0-0	
1	Westerlo	h	3-1	*Goor, Serhat 2*
11	Germinal Beerschot	a	0-2	
11	Standard	h	0-0	
2	Sint-Truiden	a	3-4	*Hassan 2 (1p), Van Damme*
12	Club Brugge	a	0-1	
12	Mons	h	3-2	*Vadis, Hassan, og (Nibombé)*

08

1	Mechelen	h	1-0	*og (Vleminckx)*
1	Lokeren	a	0-0	
	Dender	h	1-0	*Chatelle (p)*
	Brussels	a	4-2	*Van Damme, Gillet 2, Wasilewski*
2	Mouscron	h	2-1	*Polák, Pieroni*
2	Zulte Waregem	a	0-1	
	Genk	h	1-0	*Vlček*
	Charleroi	a	2-0	*Hassan, Boussoufa*
3	Roeselare	h	5-0	*Hassan, Boussoufa, Biglia, Pieroni 2*
3	AA Gent	a	3-2	*Vlček 2, Frutos (p)*
3	Cercle Brugge	h	3-1	*Van Damme 2, Boussoufa*
	Westerlo	a	2-0	*Gillet, Frutos*
4	Germinal Beerschot	h	2-0	*Vlček, Frutos*
4	Standard	a	0-2	
4	Sint-Truiden	h	4-1	*Frutos 3, Boussoufa*
	Club Brugge	h	2-0	*Vlček, Van Damme*
'5	Mons	a	2-1	*Vlček, Van Damme*

	Name	Nat	Pos	Aps	(s)	Gls
	Walter BASEGGIO		M	1	(2)	
	Lucas BIGLIA	ARG	M	30		1
	Mbark BOUSSOUFA	MAR	M	21	(1)	5
	Thomas CHATELLE		M	5	(3)	1
	Mark DE MAN		D	14	(7)	
	Olivier DESCHACHT		D	26	(1)	
	Nicolás FRUTOS	ARG	A	11	(3)	8
	Guillaume GILLET		D	17		3
	Bart GOOR		M	20	(10)	1
	Ahmed HASSAN	EGY	M	18	(8)	8
	Roland JUHÁSZ	HUN	D	29	(2)	
	Jonathan LEGEAR		A	9	(10)	2
	Mbo MPENZA		A	6	(7)	
	Nicolás PAREJA	ARG	D	18		
	Luigi PIERONI		A	6	(6)	3
8	Jan POLÁK	CZE	M	28	(1)	2
19	Bakary SARE	CIV	D		(1)	
22	Davy SCHOLLEN		G	6		
24	SERHAT Akın	TUR	A	7	(8)	3
7	Mohammed TCHITÉ		A	3	(1)	1
15	Cyril THÉRÉAU	FRA	A	4	(7)	1
39	Vadis ODJIDJA-OFOE		D	1	(2)	1
6	Jelle VAN DAMME		D	24	(5)	7
7	Stanislav VLČEK	CZE	A	15	(1)	6
4	Max VON SCHLEBRÜGGE	SWE	D	2		1
27	Marcin WASILEWSKI	POL	D	25	(1)	3
20	Olexandr YAKOVENKO	UKR	A		(3)	
1	Daniel ZÍTKA	CZE	G	28		

CERCLE BRUGGE KSV

Coach – Glen De Boeck

Founded – 1899

MAJOR HONOURS: Belgian League - (3) 1911, 1927, 1930; Belgian Cup - (2) 1927, 1985.

2007

4/8	Genk	a	1-3	*De Smet*
11/8	Zulte Waregem	h	2-0	*Gombami, Serebrennikov (p)*
19/8	Standard	a	1-4	*Yashchuk*
25/8	Dender	h	3-0	*Snelders, De Sutter, Yashchuk*
1/9	AA Gent	h	4-1	*Gombami, Yashchuk 2, De Smet*
15/9	Roeselare	a	2-0	*Gombami 2*
22/9	Germinal Beerschot	h	1-1	*Portier*
29/9	Westerlo	a	1-1	*De Sutter*
6/10	Sint-Truiden	h	5-1	*Gombami, De Smet 2, Serebrennikov 2 (2p)*
20/10	Mechelen	a	4-0	*De Sutter 2, Yashchuk, Portier*
28/10	Anderlecht	h	0-0	
3/11	Mons	a	2-0	*Gombami, Snelders*
9/11	Club Brugge	h	1-2	*De Sutter*
1/12	Lokeren	a	1-1	*Serebrennikov (p)*
8/12	Mouscron	h	3-0	*Gombami, Yashchuk, De Sutter*
15/12	Brussels	a	4-1	*De Sutter, Yashchuk, Boi, Snelders*
23/12	Charleroi	h	3-1	*Yashchuk, De Sutter, Gombami*

2008

20/1	Genk	h	5-1	*De Sutter 2, Yashchuk, De Smet 2*
25/1	Zulte Waregem	a	3-0	*Portier, Yashchuk, Serebrennikov*
3/2	Standard	h	0-0	
9/2	Dender	a	4-2	*Nyoni, Snelders, Serebrennikov (p), De Smet*
15/2	AA Gent	a	2-3	*De Smet, Snelders*
23/2	Roeselare	h	0-0	
2/3	Germinal Beerschot	a	0-3	
8/3	Westerlo	h	1-0	*Sergeant*
15/3	Sint-Truiden	a	0-0	
22/3	Mechelen	h	2-0	*Sergeant, Gombami*
30/3	Anderlecht	a	1-3	*Sergeant*
5/4	Mons	h	0-0	
13/4	Club Brugge	a	0-1	
18/4	Lokeren	h	3-2	*De Smet, Sergeant, Boi*
26/4	Mouscron	a	0-1	
3/5	Brussels	h	0-0	
10/5	Charleroi	a	3-1	*De Smet, Vandenbussche, Snelders*

BELGIUM

No	Name	Nat	Pos	Aps	(s)	Gls
23	Wouter ARTZ	NED	D	1		
12	Frederik BOI		M	31	(2)	2
1	Rubin DANTSCHOTTER		G	7	(1)	
19	Stijn DE SMET		A	32	(1)	10
10	Tom DE SUTTER		A	18	(2)	10
16	Jimmy DE WULF		D	6	(9)	
15	Osahon EBOIGBE	NGA	A		(3)	
20	Igor GJUZELOV	MKD	D	1		
5	Honour GOMBAMI	ZIM	M	32	(1)	9
4	Besnik HASI	ALB	M	31		
11	Armand MAHAN	CIV	D	1	(5)	
22	Vusumuzi Prince NYONI	ZIM	M	14	15	1
3	Anthony PORTIER		D	33		3
14	Serhiy SEREBRENNIKOV	UKR	M	33		6
17	Tony SERGEANT		M	12	(1)	4
8	Slobodan SLOVIĆ	SRB	M		(1)	
18	Kristof SNELDERS		A	13	(18)	6
8	Obidiah TARUNBWA	ZIM	M	1	(3)	
6	Tom VAN MOL		D	22	(4)	
21	Bram VANDENBUSSCHE		D	3	(14)	1
25	Bram VERBIST		G	27		
7	Denis VIANE		D	32		
9	Oleh YASHCHUK	UKR	A	24	(3)	10

CLUB BRUGGE KV

Coach – Jacky Mathijssen

Founded – 1891

MAJOR HONOURS: Belgian League - (13) 1920, 1973, 1976, 1977, 1978, 1980, 1988, 1990, 1992, 1996, 1998, 2003, 2005; Belgian Cup - (10) 1968, 1970, 1977, 1986, 1991, 1995, 1996, 2002, 2004, 2007.

2007				
4/8	Mons	h	2-1	*Sterchele 2*
12/8	Germinal Beerschot	a	1-0	*Leko (p)*
17/8	Sint-Truiden	h	3-2	*Alcaraz, Geraerts, Leko (p)*
27/8	Mechelen	a	1-1	*Clement*
2/9	Standard	a	1-2	*Vermant*
15/9	Lokeren	h	1-1	*Blondel*
23/9	Charleroi	a	1-1	*Sterchele (p)*
29/9	Mouscron	h	1-0	*Sonck*
7/10	Brussels	a	3-1	*Sonck, Simaeys, Đokić*
20/10	Dender	h	2-0	*Sonck, Geraerts*
28/10	Genk	a	2-1	*Leko (p), Đokić*
3/11	Zulte Waregem	h	1-0	*Đokić*
9/11	Cercle Brugge	a	2-1	*Blondel, Sterchele*
2/12	AA Gent	h	0-0	
9/12	Roeselare	a	2-1	*Geraerts, Clement*
16/12	Anderlecht	h	1-0	*Sterchele*
2008				
18/1	Mons	a	1-0	*Simaeys*
22/1	Westerlo	a	0-0	
26/1	Germinal Beerschot	h	3-0	*Geraerts, Leko, Simaeys*
3/2	Sint-Truiden	a	1-1	*Blondel*
9/2	Mechelen	h	2-0	*Sterchele 2*
17/2	Standard	h	1-2	*Sonck*
24/2	Lokeren	a	1-0	*Sterchele (p)*
29/2	Charleroi	h	0-2	
8/3	Mouscron	a	0-2	
15/3	Brussels	h	1-0	*Đokić*
22/3	Dender	a	0-1	
30/3	Genk	h	2-6	*Sterchele 2*
5/4	Zulte Waregem	a	3-2	*Leko, Salou, Geraerts*
13/4	Cercle Brugge	h	1-0	*Sterchele*
20/4	AA Gent	a	0-0	
27/4	Roeselare	h	1-0	*Salou*
3/5	Anderlecht	a	0-2	
10/5	Westerlo	h	4-0	*Leko, Sonck 2, Capon*

No	Name	Nat	Pos	Aps	(s)	Gls
30	Antolin ALCARAZ	PAR	D	9	(1)	1
11	Jonathan BLONDEL		M	25	(1)	3
28	Brecht CAPON		A	7	(11)	1
19	Daniel CHÁVEZ	PER	A	4	(3)	
6	Philippe CLEMENT		M	19	(1)	2
29	Gertjan DE METS		M	1		
9	Dušan ĐOKIĆ	SRB	A	20	(6)	
8	Gaëtan ENGLEBERT		M	12	(9)	
22	Karel GERAERTS		M	31		5
32	Alexandre JANSEN DA SILVA	BRA	D	1		
5	Michael KLUKOWSKI	CAN	D	31		
15	Stépan KUCERA	CZE	D	3	(2)	
18	Ivan LEKO	CRO	M	32		
26	Birger MAERTENS		D	7	(5)	
27	Roy MEEUS		A		(1)	
24	Brian PRISKE	DEN	D	32		
25	Ibrahim SALOU	GHA	A	5	(16)	2
14	Jeroen SIMAEYS		M	28	(1)	3
10	Wesley SONCK		A	13	(8)	6
23	François STERCHELE		A	31		1
1	Stijn STIJNEN		G	31		
4	Joos VALGAEREN		D	15	(2)	
16	Elrio VAN HEERDEN	RSA	M	5	(3)	
13	Glenn VERBAUWHEDE		G	3		
3	Sven VERMANT		M	5	8	1
21	Jorn VERMEULEN		D	4	(6)	

FC MOLENBEEK BRUSSELS

Coach – Albert Cartier; (24/1/08) Franky Van der Elst

Founded – 2003

2007				
4/8	Westerlo	h	0-1	
11/8	Standard	a	1-4	*Čulek*
18/8	AA Gent	h	0-2	
25/8	Anderlecht	a	0-3	
1/9	Roeselare	h	0-0	
15/9	Mons	a	1-2	*Lutula*
22/9	Sint-Truiden	h	2-0	*Fort, Gorius*
29/9	Lokeren	a	1-0	*Mokulu*
7/10	Club Brugge	h	1-3	*Matumona*
20/10	Germinal Beerschot	a	0-3	
27/10	Charleroi	h	1-2	*Fort*
4/11	Mechelen	a	0-4	
10/11	Dender	h	4-1	*og (Oumouri), Hayd Gorius, Bruno*
1/12	Mouscron	a	1-1	*Matumona*
8/12	Genk	h	0-5	*(w/o)*
15/12	Cercle Brugge	h	1-4	*Gorius*
22/12	Zulte Waregem	a	0-1	
2008				
19/1	Westerlo	a	2-7	*Gorius 2*
27/1	Standard	h	0-1	
2/2	AA Gent	a	0-1	
9/2	Anderlecht	h	2-4	*Guterstam, Landu-Tu*
16/2	Roeselare	a	0-2	
23/2	Mons	h	1-1	*Gorius*
1/3	Sint-Truiden	a	1-1	*Guterstam*
8/3	Lokeren	h	2-0	*Sorokin, Guterstam*
15/3	Club Brugge	a	0-1	
22/3	Germinal Beerschot	h	1-2	*Gueye*
29/3	Charleroi	a	0-1	
5/4	Mechelen	h	2-2	*Gorius (p), Guterstam*
12/4	Dender	a	1-1	*Neziri*
19/4	Mouscron	h	0-2	
26/4	Genk	a	1-2	*Sutchuin*
3/5	Cercle Brugge	a	0-0	
9/5	Zulte Waregem	h	1-2	*Gueye*

No	Name	Nat	Pos	Aps	(s)	Gl
9	Jean-Louis AKPA AKPRO	FRA	A		(3)	
50	ALEX da Silva	BRA	M	5	(6)	
77	Marko ANDIĆ	SRB	D	11	(1)	
	Cédric BAES		A		(1)	
7	Christ BRUNO		D	23		1
	Geoffroy CABEKE		D		(1)	
23	Aurélien COPPIN		A		(11)	
27	Michaël CORDIER		G	10	(1)	
5	Richard ČULEK	CZE	M	7	(3)	1
15	Michael DE GREEF		M		(3)	
2	Eric DEFLANDRE		D	14		

No	Name	Nat	Pos	Aps	(s)	Gls
3	Quentin DURIEUX		D	4	(3)	
8	Pavel FOŘT	CZE	A	12		2
4	Julien GORIUS	FRA	M	28	(2)	7
9	Moussa GUEYE	SEN	A	3	(6)	2
	Olof GUTERSTAM	SWE	A	14		4
	Alan HAYDOCK		M	30	(1)	1
	Sydney KARGBO	SLE	D	11	(1)	
1	Cheiko KOUYATÉ	SEN	M	10		
3	Christian LANDU-TUBI	COD	A	4	(9)	1
	Flavien LE POSTOLLEC	FRA	M	23	(2)	
4	Jean-Pierre LUTULA	COD	A	20	(3)	1
0	Zola MATUMONA	COD	A	21	(8)	2
	Benjamin MOKULU Tembe		M	3	(9)	1
	Bojan NEZIRI	SRB	D	14		1
	Patrick NYS		G	12		
1	Dieudonné OWONA	FRA	D	15	(2)	
7	Zoltán PETÖ	HUN	D	17		
	Sébastien PHIRRI		M		(1)	
5	Valeriy SOROKIN	RUS	M	15		1
8	Arnaud Djum SUTCHUIN	CMR	M	6	(2)	1
	Sven VERDONCK		D	6	(2)	
2	Olivier WERNER		G	11		
6	Atte-Oudeyi Mohama ZANZAN	TOG	D	4	(2)	
	Stéphane ZUBAR	FRA	D	10	(1)	

R. CHARLEROI SC

Coach – Philippe Vande Walle; (10/12/07) Thierry Siquet

Founded – 1904

007				
/8	Roeselare	h	1-1	*Smolders*
0/8	Westerlo	a	0-1	
8/8	Mechelen	h	1-0	*Akpala*
6/8	Sint-Truiden	a	3-1	*Akpala 3*
1/8	Mons	h	3-1	*Oulmers, Smolders, Habibou*
5/9	Germinal Beerschot	a	0-1	
3/9	Club Brugge	h	1-1	*Akpala*
9/9	Anderlecht	a	1-0	*Smolders*
/10	Mouscron	h	1-3	*Akpala*
0/10	Lokeren	a	0-1	
7/10	Brussels	a	2-1	*Camus, Akpala*
/11	Dender	h	1-0	*Orlando*
0/11	Genk	a	0-1	
/12	Zulte Waregem	h	2-3	*Jovial, Orlando*
/12	Standard	a	1-5	*Mujangi*
6/12	AA Gent	h	1-2	*Habibou*
3/12	Cercle Brugge	a	1-3	*Mujangi*
008				
9/1	Roeselare	a	2-1	Camus, Akpala
6/1	Westerlo	h	1-1	*Théréau*
/2	Mechelen	a	0-1	
/2	Sint-Truiden	h	1-1	*Smolders*
6/2	Mons	a	0-0	
3/2	Germinal Beerschot	h	0-0	
9/2	Club Brugge	a	2-0	*Smolders, Théréau*
/3	Anderlecht	h	0-2	
5/3	Mouscron	a	1-3	*Akpala*
2/3	Lokeren	h	1-0	*Akpala*
9/3	Brussels	h	1-0	*Théréau*
/4	Dender	a	4-2	*Mujangi, Akpala 2, Théréau*
2/4	Genk	h	3-1	*Akpala 3*
9/4	Zulte Waregem	a	2-2	*Akpala, Théréau*
7/4	Standard	h	2-1	*Chakouri, og (Mbokani)*
/5	AA Gent	a	1-2	*Akpala*
0/5	Cercle Brugge	h	1-3	*Akpala*

No	Name	Nat	Pos	Aps	(s)	Gls
	Joseph AKPALA	NGA	A	28	(3)	18
	Michaël BLANC	FRA	D		(1)	
5	Fabien CAMUS	FRA	M	22		2
	Mohamed CHAKOURI		D	15		1
	Grégory CHRIST	FRA	M	23	(9)	
6	Laurent CIMAN		D	22	(2)	
	Frank DEFAYS		D	13		
	Ibrahima DIALLO	GUI	D	18		
18	Mahamadou HABIBOU	FRA	A	2	(8)	2
24	Brice JOVIAL	FRA	A	4	(6)	1
16	Mahamadou KÉRÉ	BFA	D	31		
28	Bertrand LAQUAIT	FRA	G	34		
18	Cristian LEIVA	ARG	M	21		
14	Damien MICELI		M	3	(16)	
10	Geoffrey MUJANGI Bia	COD	M	14	(3)	3
25	Michaël N'DRI	FRA	A	1	(22)	
22	ORLANDO dos Santos Costa	BRA	A	16	(8)	2
21	Abdeljamid OULMERS	FRA	M	24		1
29	Juan Pablo PINO	COL	A	2	(2)	
4	Filippo PORCO		M	1	(2)	
3	Salaheddine SBAI	MAR	D	24	(2)	
30	Rémi SERGIO	FRA	M	5	(7)	
7	Tim SMOLDERS		M	34		5
19	Cyril THÉRÉAU		A	14	(1)	5
27	Sébastien VAN AERSCHOT		D	3	(1)	

FCV DENDER EH

Coach – Jean-Pierre Vande Velde; (27/11/07) Johan Boskamp (NED)

Founded – 2005

2007				
4/8	Germinal Beerschot	h	1-2	*Destorme*
11/8	Roeselare	a	1-3	*Stuckens*
18/8	Anderlecht	h	2-2	*Destorme, Munyaneza*
25/8	Cercle Brugge	a	0-3	
1/9	Sint-Truiden	h	1-0	*Destorme*
15/9	Westerlo	a	0-0	
22/9	Mons	h	0-3	
30/9	Mechelen	a	2-2	*Munyaneza 2*
6/10	Lokeren	h	0-1	
20/10	Club Brugge	a	0-2	
27/10	Mouscron	h	0-3	
3/11	Charleroi	a	0-1	
10/11	Brussels	a	1-4	*Munyaneza*
2/12	Genk	h	2-0	*Iribarren, De Pever*
8/12	Zulte Waregem	a	2-1	*Munyaneza, Sylla*
15/12	Standard	h	0-0	
22/12	AA Gent	a	4-2	*De Pever, Munyaneza, Sylla 2*
2008				
19/1	Germinal Beerschot	a	0-1	
26/1	Roeselare	h	2-1	*De Petter, og (Oliseh)*
2/2	Anderlecht	a	0-1	
9/2	Cercle Brugge	h	2-4	*Barbé, Munyaneza*
16/2	Sint-Truiden	a	2-1	*Degroote, Sylla*
23/2	Westerlo	h	2-0	*og (Van Den Eede), Sylla*
1/3	Mons	a	2-2	*Sylla, Munyaneza*
8/3	Mechelen	h	0-3	
15/3	Lokeren	a	0-1	
22/3	Club Brugge	h	1-0	*Sanchez D'Avolio*
29/3	Mouscron	a	1-2	*De Petter*
5/4	Charleroi	h	2-4	*Derijck, Munyaneza*
12/4	Brussels	h	1-1	*Żewłakow*
19/4	Genk	a	0-2	
26/4	Zulte Waregem	h	2-1	*Sylla 2*
3/5	Standard	a	0-3	
10/5	AA Gent	h	0-3	

No	Name	Nat	Pos	Aps	(s)	Gls
8	Steve BARBÉ		M	16	(7)	1
30	Cédric BERTHELIN	FRA	G	14		
9	Anthony CABEKE		D	1	(3)	
5	Steven DE PETTER		D	31		2
21	Daan DE PEVER		A	11	(6)	2
6	Eric DEFLANDRE		D	11		
19	Wouter DEGROOTE		M	21	(5)	1
4	Timothy DERIJCK		M	30		1
14	David DESTORME		M	15		3
10	Sébastien DUFOOR		A	13	(15)	
17	Predrag FILIPOVIĆ	MNE	M	25	(2)	
9	David GEEROMS		M		(1)	
3	Johan GERETS		D	13	(8)	
18	Gabriel IRIBARREN	ARG	M	5	(2)	1

No	Name	Nat	Pos	Aps	(s)	Gls
	Juan Manuel JUANMA	ESP	D	9	(1)	
1	Erwin LEMMENS		G	14		
20	Dieter MALFAIT		G	3		
11	Henri MUNYANEZA	RWA	A	31		9
4	Fabrice MVEMBA		D	1	(1)	
12	Grégoire NEELS		D	7	(6)	
15	Samuel NÉVA	FRA	D	10	(1)	
2	Younous OUMOURI	FRA	D	17	(4)	
7	Tom PEETERS		M	12	(5)	
25	Dieter REYNAERT		G		(1)	
27	Francisco SANCHEZ D'AVOLIO		M	10	(3)	1
24	Gil SERVAES		D	4	(5)	
15	Kevin STUCKENS		A		(2)	1
16	Norman SYLLA	FRA	A	17	(15)	8
20	Jan VAN STEENBERGHE		G	3		
6	Sven VANDEPUT		D	7		
13	Frederik VANDERBIEST		M	11	(3)	
31	Marcin ŻEWŁAKOW	POL	A	12		1

KRC GENK

Coach – Hugo Broos; (23/2/08) Ronny Vangeneugden

Founded – 2005

MAJOR HONOURS: Belgian League - (2) 1999, 2002; Belgian Cup - (2) 1998, 2000.

Date	Opponent		Score	Scorers
2007				
4/8	Cercle Brugge	h	3-1	*Bošnjak, Soetaers, Caillet*
11/8	AA Gent	a	0-5	
18/8	Roeselare	h	0-0	
25/8	Germinal Beerschot	a	2-1	*Alex, Barda*
1/9	Westerlo	h	1-0	*Bošnjak*
16/9	Sint-Truiden	a	2-1	*Vrancken, Barda*
23/9	Anderlecht	h	1-1	*Barda*
28/9	Mons	a	1-1	*Vandooren*
6/10	Mechelen	h	2-1	*Ljubojević, Alex*
20/10	Mouscron	a	1-1	*Vrancken*
28/10	Club Brugge	h	1-2	*Barda*
4/11	Lokeren	a	1-1	*Barda*
10/11	Charleroi	h	1-0	*Dahmane*
2/12	Dender	a	0-2	
8/12	Brussels	h	5-0	*(w/o)*
14/12	Zulte Waregem	h	5-2	*Barda 3, Vossen, Vrancken*
23/12	Standard	a	1-3	*Vossen*
2008				
20/1	Cercle Brugge	a	1-5	*Haroun*
26/1	AA Gent	h	3-3	*Barda 2 (1p), Tóth*
2/2	Roeselare	a	0-0	
10/2	Germinal Beerschot	h	1-3	*Soetaers*
16/2	Westerlo	a	1-2	*Barda*
22/2	Sint-Truiden	h	0-1	
2/3	Anderlecht	a	0-1	
8/3	Mons	h	1-2	*Itzhaki*
16/3	Mechelen	a	2-2	*Bošnjak, Itzhaki*
21/3	Mouscron	h	3-1	*Barda, Tóth, Haroun*
30/3	Club Brugge	a	6-2	*Itzhaki, Haroun, Barda 2, Vrancken, De Decker*
5/4	Lokeren	h	2-3	*Barda, Vossen*
12/4	Charleroi	a	1-3	*Tóth*
19/4	Dender	h	2-0	*og (Vanderbiest), Soetaers*
26/4	Brussels	h	2-1	*Dugary, Barda*
2/5	Zulte Waregem	a	2-2	*Haroun, Matoukou*
10/5	Standard	h	0-2	

No	Name	Nat	Pos	Aps	(s)	Gls
30	ALEX da Silva	BRA	M	9	(2)	2
16	Ngonca ANELE	RSA	M	2	(1)	
26	Logan BAILLY		G	31		
18	Elyaniv BARDA	ISR	A	30	(2)	16
17	Christian BENTEKE		A	3	(4)	
27	Sinan BOLAT		G	2	(2)	
9	Ivan BOŠNJAK	CRO	A	19	(8)	3
22	Jean-Philippe CAILLET	FRA	D	22		1
12	Thomas CHATELLE		M	2	(1)	
23	Hans CORNELIS		D	24		
12	Dimitri DAESELAIRE		D	3	(1)	
21	Mohamed DAHMANE	FRA	A	5	(6)	1
6	Wim DE DECKER		M	21	(2)	1
8	Ndabashinze DUGARY	RSA	A	1	(3)	1
7	Faris HAROUN		M	20	(8)	4
3	David HUBERT		M	5	(3)	
99	Barak ITZHAKI	ISR	A	14	(1)	3
29	Goran LJUBOJEVIĆ	CRO	A	1	(3)	1
28	Igor LOLO	CIV	D	26	(1)	
5	Eric MATOUKOU	CMR	D	22	(3)	1
4	Tomislav MIKULIĆ	CRO	D	4	(1)	
10	Tom SOETAERS		M	18	(5)	3
15	TIAGO da Silva dos Santos	BRA	D	15		
20	Balász TÓTH	HUN	M	23		3
30	Nemanja TUBIĆ	SRB	D	6		
11	Gonzague VANDOOREN		D	8	(4)	1
4	Sven VERDONCK		D	1	(2)	
1	Davino VERHULST		G		(1)	
19	Jelle VOSSEN		A	7	(10)	3
2	Wouter VRANCKEN		M	19	(4)	4
14	Olexandr YAKOVENKO	UKR	A		(4)	

KAA GENT

Coach – Trond Sollied (NOR)

Founded – 1898

MAJOR HONOURS: Belgian Cup - (2) 1964, 1984.

Date	Opponent		Score	Scorers
2007				
5/8	Mouscron	a	4-1	*Grégoire 2, Żewłakow, Vermouth*
11/8	Genk	h	5-0	*Grncarov, Żewłakow, Grégoire, Olufade, Azofeifa*
18/8	Brussels	a	2-0	*Grégoire, Moia*
25/8	Zulte Waregem	h	1-1	*Grégoire*
1/9	Cercle Brugge	a	1-4	*Azofeifa*
16/9	Standard	h	1-1	*Thijs*
22/9	Roeselare	h	1-1	*Olufade*
29/9	Germinal Beerschot	a	2-2	*Ruiz, Marić*
6/10	Westerlo	h	1-1	*Gillet*
21/10	Anderlecht	a	1-2	*Ruiz*
26/10	Mons	h	2-0	*Azofeifa, Foley*
3/11	Sint-Truiden	a	1-2	*Foley*
11/11	Mechelen	h	4-1	*Olufade 2 (1p), Ruiz, Fole*
2/12	Club Brugge	a	0-0	
8/12	Lokeren	h	4-2	*Ruiz 3, Foley*
16/12	Charleroi	a	2-1	*Foley, Grncarov*
22/12	Dender	h	2-4	*Foley, Marić*
2008				
20/1	Mouscron	h	2-0	*Ruiz, Żewłakow*
26/1	Genk	a	3-3	*Ruiz, Foley 2*
2/2	Brussels	h	1-0	*Ruiz*
10/2	Zulte Waregem	a	1-2	*Suler*
15/2	Cercle Brugge	h	3-2	*Olufade 2, Marić*
23/2	Standard	a	0-0	
1/3	Roeselare	a	1-0	*Ruiz*
9/3	Germinal Beerschot	h	2-1	*Ruiz, Foley*
15/3	Westerlo	a	0-2	
23/3	Anderlecht	h	2-3	*Foley, Haznadar*
29/3	Mons	a	0-4	
4/4	Sint-Truiden	h	2-3	*Olufade 2 (1p)*
12/4	Mechelen	a	0-1	
20/4	Club Brugge	h	0-0	
25/4	Lokeren	a	1-1	*Olufade*
3/5	Charleroi	h	2-1	*Foley, Azofeifa*
10/5	Dender	a	3-0	*Marić, Grncarov, Azofeif*

No	Name	Nat	Pos	Aps	(s)	Gls
10	Randall AZOFEIFA	CRC	M	8	(10)	5
	Mehmedalija ČOVIĆ	BIH	D	1	(1)	
21	Davy DE BEULE		M	6	(3)	
27	Jonas DE ROECK		D	15	(3)	
99	Khalilou FADIGA	SEN	A	14	(3)	
18	Dominic FOLEY	IRL	A	25	(7)	11
12	Guillaume GILLET		M	16		1
14	Christophe GRÉGOIRE		M	15	(1)	5
5	Boban GRNCAROV	MKD	D	20		3
7	Christophe GRONDIN	FRA	M	13	(7)	

5	Admir HAZNADAR	BIH	A	2	(5)	1
9	Bojan JORGACEVIĆ	SRB	G	33		
0	Zlatan LJUBIJANKIČ	SVN	A	1	(6)	
3	Laurens MALDRIE		D		(1)	
8	Miloš MARIĆ	SRB	M	28	(1)	4
	Alexandre MARTINOVIC	FRA	G	1		
2	Massimo MOIA		M	20	(4)	1
4	Aleksandar MUTAVDŽIĆ	SRB	D	19	(2)	
5	Adekanmi OLUFADE	TOG	A	20	(5)	9
	Nebojša PAVLOVIĆ	SRB	M	1	(1)	
7	Roberto ROSALES	VEN	D	10	(5)	
0	Bryan RUIZ Gonzales	CRC	A	26	(5)	11
	Dario SMOJE	CRO	D	5		
6	Alin STOICA	ROU	M	8		
	Marko ŠULER	SVN	D	13		1
	Đorđe SVETLIČIĆ	SRB	D	14	(4)	
	Bernd THIJS		M	21	(1)	1
1	Gil VERMUTH	ISR	A	5	(16)	1
9	Dieter WITTESAELE		A		(1)	
	Marcin ŻEWŁAKOW	POL	A	14	(2)	3

KFC GERMINAL BEERSCHOT ANTWERPEN

Coach – Harm Van Veldhoven

Founded – 1999

MAJOR HONOURS: Belgian Cup - (2) 1997, 2005.

007				
/8	Dender	a	2-1	*og (Gerets), Malki*
2/8	Club Brugge	h	0-1	
8/8	Lokeren	a	0-0	
5/8	Genk	h	1-2	*Losada (p)*
/9	Zulte Waregem	a	1-2	*Ederson*
5/9	Charleroi	h	1-0	*Ederson*
2/9	Cercle Brugge	a	1-1	*Dosunmu*
9/9	AA Gent	h	2-2	*Losada (p), Ederson*
/10	Standard	a	1-3	*Dosunmu*
0/10	Brussels	h	3-0	*Malki 2, Verhoeven*
7/10	Westerlo	a	2-1	*Ederson, Losada (p)*
/11	Roeselare	h	2-0	*Monteyne, Dosunmu*
1/11	Anderlecht	h	2-0	*Malki, Losada*
/12	Sint-Truiden	a	3-0	*Malki 2, Losada*
'12	Mons	h	2-0	*Dosunmu, Malki*
5/12	Mechelen	a	2-1	*Dosunmu, Losada*
2/12	Mouscron	h	3-0	*Malki 2, Losada*
008				
9/1	Dender	h	1-0	*Malki*
6/1	Club Brugge	a	0-3	
'2	Lokeren	h	1-1	*Dheedene (p)*
0/2	Genk	a	3-1	*Ederson, Malki, Losada*
6/2	Zulte Waregem	h	0-0	
3/2	Charleroi	a	0-0	
/3	Cercle Brugge	h	3-0	*Dheedene (p), Malki, Dosunmu*
/3	AA Gent	a	1-2	*Dheedene (p)*
4/3	Standard	h	1-2	*Losada*
2/3	Brussels	a	2-1	*Malki, Dheedene (p)*
9/3	Westerlo	h	0-2	
/4	Roeselare	a	0-1	
3/4	Anderlecht	a	0-2	
9/4	Sint-Truiden	h	2-1	*Malki, og (Collen)*
6/4	Mons	a	0-0	
/5	Mechelen	h	4-3	*Dosunmu, Gyan, Malki 2*
0/5	Mouscron	a	0-1	

lo	Name	Nat	Pos	Aps	(s)	Gls
	Aristide BANCE	BFA	A	2	(8)	
	Jurgen CAVENS		A	2	(6)	
	Sébastien CHABAUD	FRA	M	4	(1)	
6	Gustavo COLMAN	ARG	M	17	(1)	
0	Daniel CRUZ	COL	M	19	(5)	
	Kris DE WREE		M	7	(15)	
'2	Didier DHEEDENE		D	23		4
2	Serigne Mor DIOP	SEN	M		(1)	
1	Abdoulaye DJIRE "JUNIOR"	CIV	M		(2)	
15	Tosin DOSUNMU	NGA	A	27	(3)	7
6	EDERSON Tormena	BRA	D	29	(2)	5
14	King GYAN Osei	GHA	M	16	(9)	1
21	Nzelo LEMBI	COD	D	13	(1)	
17	Hernán LOSADA	ARG	M	22	(2)	9
24	Sanharib MALKI	SYR	A	30	(3)	16
22	Martijn MONTEYNE		D	29	(2)	1
5	Pieter-Jan MONTEYNE		D	33		
1	Jan MOONS		G	5		
23	Emmanuel OKODUWA	NGA	A	3	(1)	
28	Daniel OWUSU	GHA	M	3	(5)	
33	Mike SMET		M		(1)	
30	Kenny STEPPE		G	29		
4	Kurt VAN DOOREN		D	32		
3	Jasper VANMEERBERGEN		D		(1)	
13	Vicenzo VERHOEVEN		A	1	(19)	1
29	Justice WAMFOR	CMR	M	28		
19	Toufik ZERARA	FRA	M		(7)	

KSC LOKEREN OV

Coach – Georges Leekens

Founded – 1970

2007				
4/8	Sint-Truiden	h	2-1	*Tambwe, João Carlos (p)*
11/8	Anderlecht	a	0-1	
18/8	Germinal Beerschot	h	0-0	
25/8	Mons	a	1-0	*Tambwe*
1/9	Mechelen	h	3-1	*El Mouataz, Vukomanović, Tambwe*
15/9	Club Brugge	a	1-1	*Vukomanović*
22/9	Mouscron	a	0-2	
29/9	Brussels	h	0-1	
6/10	Dender	a	1-0	*Mbayo*
20/10	Charleroi	h	1-0	*Camara*
27/10	Zulte Waregem	a	1-1	*El Mouataz (p)*
4/11	Genk	h	1-1	*Carevic*
10/11	Standard	a	0-1	
1/12	Cercle Brugge	h	1-1	*Tambwe*
08/12	AA Gent	a	2-4	*Tambwe 2*
15/12	Westerlo	h	1-1	*Camara*
2008				
19/1	Sint-Truiden	a	1-1	*Tambwe*
22/1	Roeselare	a	1-1	*Armoumen*
27/1	Anderlecht	h	0-0	
3/2	Germinal Beerschot	a	1-1	*Golan*
9/2	Mons	h	1-2	*Carević*
16/2	Mechelen	a	1-1	*Golan*
24/2	Club Brugge	h	0-1	
1/3	Mouscron	h	0-0	
8/3	Brussels	a	0-2	
15/3	Dender	h	1-0	*Carević*
22/3	Charleroi	a	0-1	
29/3	Zulte Waregem	h	0-0	
5/4	Genk	a	3-2	*Carević, João Carlos (p), Mbayo*
11/4	Standard	h	0-0	
18/4	Cercle Brugge	a	2-3	*Mbayo, Maazou*
25/4	AA Gent	h	1-1	*Golan*
3/5	Westerlo	a	2-1	*João Carlos (p), Golan*
10/5	Roeselare	h	3-0	*Golan, Camara, Mbayo*

No	Name	Nat	Pos	Aps	(s)	Gls
13	Marko ANDIĆ	SRB	D	1	(2)	
28	Mohamed ARMOUMEN	MAR	A	2	(15)	1
30	Boubacar Copa BARRY	CIV	G	23		
14	Ali BOUABÉ	MAR	D	8	(3)	
15	Aboubacar M`Baye CAMARA	GUI	M	9	(16)	3
18	Mario CAREVIĆ	CRO	M	24	(1)	4
3	JOÃO CARLOS Chaves Pinto	BRA	D	32		3
31	Stijn DE WILDE		M		(7)	
32	Benjamin DE WILDE		D		(1)	
20	Frederik DE WINNE		D		(4)	
4	Olivier DOLL		D	28		
33	Frédéric DUPRE		D	14		

No	Name	Nat	Pos	Aps	(s)	Gls
2	Hassan EL MOUATAZ	MAR	D	22	(1)	2
31	Omer GOLAN	ISR	A	14	(1)	5
9	Boban JANČEVSKI	MKD	A	3	(4)	
12	Jugoslav LAZIĆ	SRB	G	11		
20	Ouwo Moussa MAAZOU	BFA	M	4	(4)	1
26	Saidou MADY	BFA	D	25	(3)	
10	Marcel MBAYO	COD	M	30		4
5	Veldin MUHAREMOVIĆ	BIH	D	7	(7)	
7	Killian OVERMEIRE		M	32		
8	Nebojša PAVLOVIĆ	SRB	M	23		
22	Ibrahim SOME	COD	A		(3)	
27	Patiyo TAMBWE	COD	A	27	(3)	7
6	Tsholola TIKO	COD	M	24	(4)	
24	Michaël VAN HOEY		D	1	(3)	
5	Ivan VUKOMANOVIĆ	SRB	M	10	(6)	2

KV MECHELEN

Coach – Peter Maes

Founded – 1904

MAJOR HONOURS: UEFA Cup Winners' Cup - (1) 1988; UEFA Super Cup - (1) 1989; Belgian League - (4) 1943, 1946, 1948, 1989; Belgian Cup - (1) 1987.

Date	Opponent		Score	Scorers
2007				
3/8	Anderlecht	h	0-1	
11/8	Mons	a	1-1	*Dunković*
18/8	Charleroi	a	0-1	
27/8	Club Brugge	h	1-1	*Bajevski*
1/9	Lokeren	a	1-3	*Nong*
15/9	Mouscron	h	2-2	*Bajevski, Ivens (p)*
22/9	Zulte Waregem	a	0-2	
30/9	Dender	h	2-2	*Ivens 2 (2p)*
6/10	Genk	a	1-2	*Imschoot*
20/10	Cercle Brugge	h	0-4	
27/10	Standard	a	2-2	*Persoons 2*
4/11	Brussels	h	4-0	*Ivens (p), Geudens, Nong 2*
11/11	AA Gent	a	1-4	*Nong*
1/12	Roeselare	h	4-3	*Nong 2, Van Goethem, Asare*
8/12	Westerlo	a	1-1	*Vleminckx*
15/12	Germinal Beerschot	h	1-2	*Nong*
22/12	Sint-Truiden	a	1-0	*Geudens*
2008				
19/1	Anderlecht	a	0-1	
26/1	Mons	h	2-0	*Vleminckx 2*
2/2	Charleroi	h	1-0	*Imschoot*
9/2	Club Brugge	a	0-2	
16/2	Lokeren	h	1-1	*Vleminckx*
23/2	Mouscron	a	1-0	*Dunković*
1/3	Zulte Waregem	h	2-1	*Vleminckx, Dunković*
8/3	Dender	a	3-0	*Vleminckx, Mellemans, Nong*
16/3	Genk	h	2-2	*Van Hoevelen, Nong*
22/3	Cercle Brugge	a	0-2	
29/3	Standard	h	0-1	
5/4	Brussels	a	2-2	*Geudens, Nong*
12/4	AA Gent	h	1-0	*Vleminckx*
19/4	Roeselare	a	2-2	*Nong 2*
26/4	Westerlo	h	1-0	*Charaï*
3/5	Germinal Beerschot	a	3-4	*Vleminckx 2, Dunković*
10/5	Sint-Truiden	h	2-3	*Boussaidi, Nong*

No	Name	Nat	Pos	Aps	(s)	Gls
1	Miloš ADAMOVIĆ	SRB	G	13	(1)	
17	Nana ASARE	GHA	M	21	(1)	1
99	Aleksandar BAJEVSKI	MKD	A	4	(4)	2
19	Maxime BISET		M	9	(8)	
	Anis BOUSSAIDI	TUN	D	6	(4)	1
11	Issame CHARAI		A	6	(11)	1
8	Xavier CHEN		D	8	(1)	
	Jerome COLINET		M	1	(3)	
9	Pieter CRABEELS		D	3	(3)	
13	Antun DUNKOVIĆ	CRO	M	23	7	4
16	Kevin GEUDENS		M	30	(1)	3
	Ruben GÓMEZ GARCÍA	ARG	M	1	(2)	
10	Abdul-Yakinu IDDI	GHA	M	3	(13)	
	Kristof IMSCHOOT		M	27		2
3	Jonas IVENS		D	34		4
20	Kevin KEMPENEER		G	4		
12	Jean-Paul KIELO-LEZI	COD	A	4	(10)	
22	Pieter MBEMBA	COD	D	2	(2)	
4	Jeroen MELLEMANS		M	25	(3)	1
14	Aloys NONG	CMR	A	27	(3)	13
	Patrice NOUKEU	CMR	M	1	(4)	
6	Koen PERSOONS		M	30		2
	Olivier RENARD		G	17		
7	Kenneth VAN GOETHEM		M	20	(5)	1
5	Kenny VAN HOEVELEN		D	29		1
15	Wesley VANBELLE		D	1	(6)	
18	Björn VLEMINCKX		A	25	(6)	9

RAEC MONS

Coach – José Riga; (29/1/08) Albert Cartier (FRA)

Founded – 1910

Date	Opponent		Score	Scorers
2007				
4/8	Club Brugge	a	1-2	*Zoko*
11/8	Mechelen	h	1-1	*Brahami*
18/8	Mouscron	a	1-3	*Dalmat (p)*
25/8	Lokeren	h	0-1	
31/8	Charleroi	a	1-3	*Mirri*
15/9	Brussels	h	2-1	*Landu Tubi, Cordaro*
22/9	Dender	a	3-0	*Dalmat, Landu-Tubi, Roussel (p)*
28/9	Genk	h	1-1	*Dalmat*
6/10	Zulte Waregem	a	1-2	*Adriano*
21/10	Standard	h	1-1	*Zoko*
26/10	AA Gent	a	0-2	
3/11	Cercle Brugge	h	0-2	
12/11	Roeselare	a	3-4	*Zoko, og (Smits), Cordar*
1/12	Westerlo	h	1-3	*Stolica*
8/12	Germinal Beerschot	a	0-2	
15/12	Sint-Truiden	h	0-0	
22/12	Anderlecht	a	2-3	*Zoko 2*
2008				
18/1	Club Brugge	h	0-1	
26/1	Mechelen	a	0-2	
2/2	Mouscron	h	2-0	*Stolica, Dalmat*
9/2	Lokeren	a	2-1	*Brahami, Adriano*
16/2	Charleroi	h	0-0	
23/2	Brussels	a	1-1	*Dahmane*
1/3	Dender	h	2-2	*Dahmane, Zoko*
8/3	Genk	a	2-1	*Brahami, Nicaise*
15/3	Zulte Waregem	h	3-0	*Dahmane (p), Nicaise, Seka*
23/3	Standard	a	0-2	
29/3	AA Gent	h	4-0	*Zoko 2, Dahmane (p), Stolica*
5/4	Cercle Brugge	a	0-0	
12/4	Roeselare	h	1-1	*Okkonen*
19/4	Westerlo	a	0-0	
26/4	Germinal Beerschot	h	0-0	
3/5	Sint-Truiden	a	1-1	*Dahmane*
10/5	Anderlecht	h	1-2	*Dalmat*

No	Name	Nat	Pos	Aps	(s)	Gls
5	ADRIANO Duarte Mansur da Silva	BRA	D	27		2
25	Mohamed AMROUNE	ALG	A		(1)	
1	Cédric BERTHELIN	FRA	G	11		
17	Mohamed Fadel BRAHAMI	ALG	D	20	(11)	3
3	Johan CAVALLI	FRA	M	3	(6)	
11	Alessandro CORDARO		M	29	(1)	2
92	Mohamed DAHMANE	FRA	A	12		5
7	Wilfried DALMAT	FRA	M	32	(1)	5
29	Mohammed Aliyu DATTI	NGA	A	3	(10)	
24	Kevin HATCHI	FRA	M	2	(1)	
23	Fréderic HERPOEL		G	20		
15	Frédéric JAY	FRA	D	30	(1)	
12	Charly KONSTANTIDINIS		G	3	(1)	
6	Danijel KRIVIĆ	BIH	D	11	(4)	
	Christian LANDU-TUBI	COD	A	3	(9)	2

0	Ali LUKUNKU	COD	A	2	(5)	
	Roberto MIRRI	ITA	D	30	(1)	1
1	Daré NIBOMBÉ	TOG	D	18	(7)	
3	Benjamin NICAISE	FRA	M	17	(3)	2
9	Antti OKKONEN	FIN	M	12	(1)	1
	Alessandro PISTONE	ITA	D	7		
	Hocine RAGUED	FRA	M	31		
0	Cédric ROUSSEL		A	9	(4)	1
7	Roméo Affessi SEKA	CIV			(7)	1
3	Ilija STOLICA	BIH	A	13	(12)	3
4	Michaël WIGGERS		D	5	(5)	
3	François Bernard ZOKO	CIV	A	24	(8)	8

R. EXCELSIOR MOUSCRON

Coach – Marc Brys; (27/12/07) Enzo Scifo

Founded – 1964

007				
8	AA Gent	h	1-4	*Čustović (p)*
1/8	Sint-Truiden	a	2-0	*Tomou, Oussalah*
3/8	Mons	h	3-1	*Čustović (p), Tomou, Coto*
5/8	Westerlo	a	2-0	*Coto, Tomou*
9	Anderlecht	h	1-2	*Čustović*
5/9	Mechelen	a	2-2	*Niçoise, Čustović*
2/9	Lokeren	h	2-0	*Sapina, Čustović (p)*
9/9	Club Brugge	a	0-1	
10	Charleroi	a	3-1	*Tomou, Grondin, Fellahi*
0/10	Genk	h	1-1	*Čustović (p)*
7/10	Dender	a	3-0	*Tomou 3*
11	Standard	h	0-0	
0/11	Zulte Waregem	a	1-2	*Tomou*
12	Brussels	h	1-1	*Čustović*
12	Cercle Brugge	a	0-3	
5/12	Roeselare	h	1-3	*Tomou*
2/12	Germinal Beerschot	a	0-3	
008				
0/1	AA Gent	a	0-2	
5/1	Sint-Truiden	h	0-0	
2	Mons	a	0-2	
2	Westerlo	h	1-2	*Deranja*
7/2	Anderlecht	a	1-2	*Tomou*
3/2	Mechelen	h	0-1	
3	Lokeren	a	0-0	
3	Club Brugge	h	2-0	*Ouali, Chantry*
5/3	Charleroi	h	3-1	*Baseggio, Čustović, Ouali*
1/3	Genk	a	1-3	*Baseggio*
9/3	Dender	h	2-1	*Ouali, Tomou*
4	Standard	a	0-1	
2/4	Zulte Waregem	h	0-2	
9/4	Brussels	a	2-0	*Ouali 2*
5/4	Cercle Brugge	h	1-0	*Walasiak*
5	Roeselare	a	1-2	*Baseggio*
0/5	Germinal Beerschot	h	1-0	*Čustović*

o	Name	Nat	Pos	Aps	(s)	Gls
7	Alexis ALLART	FRA	A	1	(1)	
	Mathieu ASSOU-EKOTTO	FRA	M	16	(4)	
	Demba BA	FRA	A	1	(1)	
3	Walter BASEGGIO		M	13		3
	Marco BERNA Ballester	ESP	D		(2)	
9	Bastien CHANTRY		M	18	(5)	1
	Jean-Philippe CHARLET		D	12		
7	Carles COTO	ESP	M	6	(15)	2
	Adnan ČUSTOVIĆ	BIH	A	29	(1)	9
	Zvonimir DERANJA	CRO	A	4	(1)	1
3	Michael DESCAMPS		G		(1)	
	Steve DUGARDEIN		M	25	(1)	
6	Karim FELLAHI	ALG	M	4	(12)	1
2	Dražen GOVIĆ	CRO	M		(3)	
0	David GRONDIN	FRA	D	19		1
1	Hamdi HARBAOUI	TUN	A	1	(5)	
4	Jérémy HUYGHEBAERT		D	2	(2)	
1	Alioune KEBE	SEN	A		(1)	
1	Christophe MARTIN		G	1		
9	Mickaël NIÇOISE	FRA	A	13	(4)	1
6	Idir OUALI	FRA	M	8	(1)	5
14	Mustapha OUSSALAH		M	29	(3)	1
	Miguel PALENCIA	ESP	D		(1)	
10	Francisco SANCHEZ D'AVOLIO		M	8	(1)	
25	Jérémy SAPINA	FRA	D	28		1
	Asanda SISHUBA	RSA	A	6	(4)	
	Alin STOICA	ROU	M		(5)	
22	Alexandre TEKLAK		D	13	(8)	
6	Adolph TOHOUA	CIV	M	1	(3)	
14	Bertin TOMOU	CMR	A	19	(6)	11
18	Geoffray TOYES	FRA	D	19	(3)	
15	Daan VAN GIJSEGHEM		D	23		
	Gonzague VANDOOREN		D	11		
1	Mark VOLDERS		G	33		
	Jonathan WALASIAK		M	11	(2)	1

KSV ROESELARE

Coach – Dirk Geeraerd

Founded – 1999

2007				
4/8	Charleroi	a	1-1	*Akgül*
11/8	Dender	h	3-1	*Tanghe 2, Kpaka*
18/8	Genk	a	0-0	
25/8	Standard	h	0-4	
1/9	Brussels	a	0-0	
15/9	Cercle Brugge	h	0-2	
22/9	AA Gent	a	1-1	*Dissa*
29/9	Zulte Waregem	h	3-2	Dissa 2, Mirvić
7/10	Anderlecht	h	2-2	*Dissa 2*
20/10	Westerlo	a	0-6	
27/10	Sint-Truiden	h	2-0	*Kpaka, Akgül*
3/11	Germinal Beerschot	a	0-2	
12/11	Mons	h	4-3	*Tanghe, Joseph-Augustin, Dissa, Akgül*
1/12	Mechelen	a	3-4	*Dissa, Kpaka, De Vleeschauwer*
9/12	Club Brugge	h	1-2	*Dissa*
15/12	Mouscron	a	3-1	*Kpaka, Dissa 2*
2008				
19/1	Charleroi	h	1-2	*Thompson*
22/1	Lokeren	h	1-1	*Tanghe*
26/1	Dender	a	1-2	*Akgul*
2/2	Genk	h	0-0	
9/2	Standard	a	0-0	
16/2	Brussels	h	2-0	*Tanghe, Thompson*
23/2	Cercle Brugge	a	0-0	
1/3	AA Gent	h	0-1	
8/3	Zulte Waregem	a	1-3	*Dissa*
15/3	Anderlecht	a	0-5	
22/3	Westerlo	h	0-2	
29/3	Sint-Truiden	a	1-0	*Thompson*
5/4	Germinal Beerschot	h	1-0	*Thompson*
12/4	Mons	a	1-1	*Dissa*
19/4	Mechelen	h	2-2	*Thompson, Dissa*
27/4	Club Brugge	a	0-1	
3/5	Mouscron	h	2-1	*Dissa, Vaesen*
10/5	Lokeren	a	0-3	

No	Name	Nat	Pos	Aps	(s)	Gls
9	Izzet AKGÜL	TUR	A	10	(8)	4
12	Wouter BIEBAUW		G	12	(1)	
19	Mehmedahlija ČOVIĆ	BIH	D	5	(3)	
6	Koen DE VLEESCHAUWER		M	25		1
29	Joeri DEQUEVY		D	3	(4)	
23	Mahamadou "Mama" DISSA	MLI	A	24	(4)	14
17	Chemcedine EL ARAICHI		D	26		
21	FELIPE Soares	BRA	D	9	(6)	
10	Adil HERMACH	MAR	D	9	(2)	
13	Jonathan JOSEPH-AUGUSTIN	CIV	D	12	(2)	1
14	Gabriel Ngalula Mbuyi JUNIOR		M	1	(4)	
25	Dieudonné KALULIKA	COD	A	2	(3)	
11	Serhiy KOVALENKO	UKR	A	1	(7)	
18	Paul KPAKA	SLE	A	24	(6)	4
27	Benjamin LUTUN		D	10	(15)	
3	Damir MIRVIĆ	BIH	M	30	(1)	1
2	Azubuike OLISEH	NGA	M	9	(1)	

No	Name	Nat	Pos	Aps	(s)	Gls
22	Davy OYEN		D	2	(3)	
	Tom RAES		D		(1)	
1	Jurgen SIERENS		G	22		
7	Björn SMITS		D	16	(5)	
8	Stefaan TANGHE		M	30		5
	Michel TERNEST		A		(3)	
5	Kenny THOMPSON		D	27	(3)	5
4	Daan VAESEN		D	22	(3)	1
2	David VAN HOYWEGHEN		D		(4)	
20	Anthony VAN LOO		D	18	(4)	
10	Frederik VANDERBIEST		M	16		
44	Yves VANDERHAEGHE		M	9	(2)	
	Jeroen VANTOURNHOUT		A		(1)	

K. SINT-TRUIDENSE VV

Coach – Valére Billen; (18/9/07) Peter Voets; (10/12/07) Dennis van Wijk (NED)

Founded – 1924

Date	Opponent		Score	Scorers
2007				
4/8	Lokeren	a	1-2	*Coulibaly*
11/8	Mouscron	h	0-2	
17/8	Club Brugge	a	2-3	*Chimedza, Coulibaly*
26/8	Charleroi	h	1-3	*Dreesen*
1/9	Dender	a	0-1	
16/9	Genk	h	1-2	*Hartog*
22/9	Brussels	a	0-2	
29/9	Standard	h	0-0	
6/10	Cercle Brugge	a	1-5	*Coulibaly*
20/10	Zulte Waregem	h	2-1	*Milenković, Hendrikx*
27/10	Roeselare	a	0-2	
3/11	AA Gent	h	2-1	*Chimedza 2 (2p)*
10/11	Westerlo	a	0-2	
1/12	Germinal Beerschot	h	0-3	
9/12	Anderlecht	h	4-3	*Peeters, Van Houdt, Sishuba, Coulibaly*
15/12	Mons	a	0-0	
22/12	Mechelen	h	0-1	
2008				
19/1	Lokeren	h	1-1	*Debroux*
26/1	Mouscron	a	0-0	
3/2	Club Brugge	h	1-1	*Cantaluppi*
9/2	Charleroi	a	1-1	*Delorge*
16/2	Dender	h	1-2	*Gobec*
22/2	Genk	a	1-0	*Coulibaly*
1/3	Brussels	h	1-1	*Hendrikx*
7/3	Standard	a	1-2	*Peeters*
15/3	Cercle Brugge	h	0-0	
22/3	Zulte Waregem	a	2-3	*Peeters, Cantaluppi*
29/3	Roeselare	h	0-1	
4/4	AA Gent	a	3-2	*Buvens, og (Thijs), Peeters*
12/4	Westerlo	h	0-2	
19/4	Germinal Beerschot	a	1-2	*Coulibaly*
26/4	Anderlecht	a	1-4	*Coulibaly*
3/5	Mons	h	1-1	*Cantaluppi (p)*
10/5	Mechelen	a	3-2	*Wilmet, Pospisil 2*

No	Name	Nat	Pos	Aps	(s)	Gls
27	Mirsad BEŠLIJA	BIH	M	4	(7)	
20	Frank BOECKX		G	9	(1)	
11	Kris BUVENS		M	12	(6)	1
5	Mario CANTALUPPI	SUI	D	15		3
10	Francesco CARRATTA		M		(1)	
13	Cephas CHIMEDZA	ZIM	M	26	(2)	3
18	Pieter COLLEN		D	15	(1)	
12	Adamo COULIBALY	FRA	A	15	(13)	7
2	Sander DEBROUX		M	19	(1)	1
26	Giel DEFERM		M	3	(3)	
17	Peter DELORGE		M	32		1
21	Timothy DREESEN		D	12	(9)	1
25	Sebastjan GOBEC	SVN	D	12		1
23	Michiel GOVAERTS		A		(2)	
25	Ashley HARTOG	RSA	A	3	(2)	1
3	Nicky HAYEN		D	32		
6	Marc HENDRIKX		M	18	(1)	2
18	Dieudonné KALULIKA	COD	A	1	(6)	
22	Simon MIGNOLET		G	25		
89	Ninoslav MILENKOVIĆ	BIH	D	9		1
7	Rocky PEETERS		M	28	(1)	4
28	Michal POSPÍŠIL	CZE	A	14	(2)	2
19	Ibrahim SIDIBE	SEN	M	7	(7)	
24	Asanda SISHUBA	RSA	M	12	(5)	1
19	Matthias TRENSON		D	5	(1)	
	Christian VALENTIN		M		(1)	
8	Kevin VAN DESSEL		M	14	(7)	
9	Peter VAN HOUDT		A	9	(3)	1
14	Pieter-Jan VAN OUDENHOVE		D	3		
4	Stijn VREVEN		D	11		
29	Jonathan WILMET		A	4	(5)	1
15	Egon WISNIOWSKI		D	5	(5)	

R. STANDARD DE LIÈGE

Coach – Michel Preud'homme

Founded – 1898

MAJOR HONOURS: Belgian League - (9) 1958, 1961, 1963, 1969, 1970, 1971, 1982, 1983, 2008; Belgian Cup - (5) 1954, 1966, 1967, 1981, 1993

Date	Opponent		Score	Scorers
2007				
5/8	Zulte Waregem	a	4-1	*Fellaini, Onyewu, De Camargo, Witsel*
11/8	Brussels	h	4-1	*Jovanović 3 (2p), Fellaini*
19/8	Cercle Brugge	h	4-1	*Mbokani 2, Fellaini, Witsel*
25/8	Roeselare	a	4-0	*Jovanović 3, Mbokani*
2/9	Club Brugge	h	2-1	*Jovanović, Mbokani*
16/9	AA Gent	a	1-1	*De Camargo*
24/9	Westerlo	h	2-1	*Toama 2*
29/9	Sint-Truiden	a	0-0	
7/10	Germinal Beerschot	h	3-1	*Fellaini, De Camargo, Witsel*
20/10	Mons	a	1-1	*De Camargo*
27/10	Mechelen	h	2-2	*Defour, Mbokani*
2/11	Mouscron	a	0-0	
10/11	Lokeren	h	1-0	*De Camargo*
30/11	Anderlecht	a	0-0	
7/12	Charleroi	h	5-1	*Witsel (p), De Camargo 2, Marcos, Jovanović*
15/12	Dender	a	0-0	
23/12	Genk	h	3-1	*Dufer, Witsel, Jovanović*
2008				
19/1	Zulte Waregem	h	3-1	*Dante (p), Witsel (p), Mbokani*
26/1	Brussels	a	1-0	*Mbokani*
3/2	Cercle Brugge	a	0-0	
9/2	Roeselare	h	0-0	
17/2	Club Brugge	a	2-1	*Jovanović 2*
23/2	AA Gent	h	0-0	
1/3	Westerlo	a	3-1	*Fellaini, Mbokani, Witsel*
7/3	Sint-Truiden	h	2-1	*Mbokani, De Camargo*
14/3	Germinal Beerschot	a	2-1	*Jovanović, Fellaini*
23/3	Mons	h	2-0	*Mbokani, Goreux*
29/3	Mechelen	a	1-0	*Jovanović*
6/4	Mouscron	h	1-0	*Onyewu*
11/4	Lokeren	a	0-0	
20/4	Anderlecht	h	2-0	*Mbokani 2*
27/4	Charleroi	a	1-2	*Jovanović (p)*
3/5	Dender	h	3-0	*Mbokani 2, Jovanović*
10/5	Genk	a	2-0	*Mbokani, Jovanović*

No	Name	Nat	Pos	Aps	(s)	Gls
1	Rorys ARAGON Espinoza	ECU	G	25		
4	DANTE Bonfim Costa	BRA	D	33		1
10	Igor DE CAMARGO	BRA	A	19	(13)	8
18	Jérémy DE VRIENDT		G	2	(1)	
8	Steven DEFOUR		M	24		1
30	Siramana DEMBÉLÉ	FRA	M	5	(12)	
7	Grégory DUFER		A	16	(6)	1
6	Frédéric DUPRÉ		D		(3)	
27	Marouane FELLAINI		M	31		6
2	Réginal GOREUX		D	9	(2)	1
29	Marco INGRAO		M	2	(6)	
23	Milan JOVANOVIĆ	SRB	A	28	(3)	16

5	Ali LUKUNKU	COD	A		(5)	
7	MARCOS Camozzato	BRA	D	32		1
	Dieumerci MBOKANI	COD	A	24	(8)	15
4	Landry MULEMO		D	9	(9)	
	Oguchi ONYEWU	USA	D	33		2
2	Yanis PAPASSARANTIS		M		(1)	
4	Thomas PHIBEL	FRA	D		(1)	
6	Olivier RENARD		G	7		
9	Mohamed Adama SARR	SEN	D	24		
1	Salim TOAMA	ISR	M	14	(7)	2
3	Vittorio VILLANO		M		(1)	
8	Axel WITSEL		M	33		7
6	Frederi Burgel XAVIER	BRA	D	4	(4)	

KVC WESTERLO

Coach – Jan Ceulemans

Founded – 1933

MAJOR HONOURS: Belgian Cup - (1) 2001.

007				
/8	Brussels	a	1-0	*Van Imschoot*
0/8	Charleroi	h	1-0	*Evens*
8/8	Zulte Waregem	a	0-1	
5/8	Mouscron	h	0-2	
/9	Genk	a	0-1	
5/9	Dender	h	0-0	
4/9	Standard	a	1-2	*Dirar*
9/9	Cercle Brugge	h	1-1	*Van den Eede*
/10	AA Gent	a	1-1	*Sarki*
0/10	Roeselare	h	6-0	*Farssi 2, Van Hout, Coelho 2, Van den Eede*
7/10	Germinal Beerschot	h	1-2	*og (Gyan)*
/11	Anderlecht	a	1-3	*Wils*
0/11	Sint-Truiden	h	2-0	*Van den Eede, Delen*
/12	Mons	a	3-1	*Wagemakers, Coelho 2*
/12	Mechelen	h	1-1	*Dekelver*
5/12	Lokeren	a	1-1	*Mennes*
008				
9/1	Brussels	h	7-2	*Van den Eede 3, Evens, Dirar, Mennes, Dekelver*
2/1	Club Brugge	h	0-0	
6/1	Charleroi	a	1-1	*Mennes*
/2	Zulte Waregem	h	1-1	*Mennes*
/2	Mouscron	a	2-1	*Wils, Delen*
6/2	Genk	h	2-1	*Corstjens, Dekelver*
3/2	Dender	a	0-2	
/3	Standard	h	1-3	*Van den Eede*
/3	Cercle Brugge	a	0-1	
5/3	AA Gent	h	2-0	*Dekelver, Van Imschoot (p)*
2/3	Roeselare	a	2-0	*Van Hout, Zelenka*
9/3	Germinal Beerschot	a	2-0	*Van den Eede, Imschoot (p)*
/4	Anderlecht	h	0-2	
2/4	Sint-Truiden	a	2-0	*Odita, Dekelver*
9/4	Mons	h	0-0	
6/4	Mechelen	a	0-1	
/5	Lokeren	h	1-2	*Odita*
0/5	Club Brugge	a	0-4	

o	Name	Nat	Pos	Aps	(s)	Gls
0	Moses ADAMS	NGA	M		(4)	
	Jackson Avelino COELHO Jaja	BRA	M	8	(1)	4
	Wouter CORSTJENS		D	24	(2)	1
9	Yves DE WINTER		G	34		
	Dieter DEKELVER		A	12	(9)	5
8	Jef DELEN		M	32		2
3	Nabil DIRAR	MAR	M	20	(4)	2
	Bernt EVENS		D	24	(1)	2
1	Rachid FARSSI		D	20	(6)	2
	Wim MENNES		M	21	(4)	4
4	Michael MODUBI	RSA	M	4		
7	Obiora Emmanuel ODITA	NGA	A	5	(4)	2
	Patrick OGUNSOTO	NGA	A	8	(2)	
0	Emmanuel SARKI	NGA	M	21	(7)	1
	Wouter SCHEELEN		M		(5)	
2	Bart VAN DEN EEDE		A	15	(6)	8
8	Joris VAN HOUT		A	14	(14)	2
15	Tom VAN IMSCHOOT		M	20	(2)	3
11	Nico VAN KERCKHOVEN		D	23	(1)	
32	Gunther VANAUDENAERDE		D	23	(1)	
2	Marc WAGEMAKERS		D	16	(7)	1
6	Stef WILS		D	23	(3)	2
8	Lukáš ZELENKA	CZE	M	7	(8)	1

SV ZULTE WAREGEM

Coach – Francky Dury

Founded – 2001

MAJOR HONOURS: Belgian Cup - (1) 2006.

2007				
5/8	Standard	h	1-4	*Jelavić*
11/8	Cercle Brugge	a	0-2	
18/8	Westerlo	h	1-0	*Matthys*
25/8	AA Gent	a	1-1	*Leye*
1/9	Germinal Beerschot	h	2-1	*Leye, Meert*
15/9	Anderlecht	a	2-2	*Jelavić 2*
22/9	Mechelen	h	2-0	*D'Haemers, Roelandts*
29/9	Roeselare	a	2-3	*Leye 2*
6/10	Mons	h	2-1	*Leandro 2*
20/10	Sint-Truiden	a	1-2	*Matthys*
27/10	Lokeren	h	1-1	*Leye*
3/11	Club Brugge	a	0-1	
10/11	Mouscron	h	2-1	*Sankaré, Van Nieuwenhuyze*
1/12	Charleroi	a	3-2	*Leye 2, Van Nieuwenhuyze*
8/12	Dender	h	1-2	*Matthys*
14/12	Genk	a	2-5	*Sankaré, Matthys*
22/12	Brussels	h	1-0	*Roelandts*
2008				
19/1	Standard	a	1-3	*Leye*
25/1	Cercle Brugge	h	0-3	
2/2	Westerlo	a	1-1	*Roelandts*
10/2	AA Gent	h	2-1	*Roelandts, Leandro*
16/2	Germinal Beerschot	a	0-0	
24/2	Anderlecht	h	1-0	*Leye*
1/3	Mechelen	a	1-2	*Van Zundert*
8/3	Roeselare	h	3-1	*Roelandts 2, Leye*
15/3	Mons	a	0-3	
22/3	Sint-Truiden	h	3-2	*Van Zundert, Meert, Leye*
29/3	Lokeren	a	0-0	
5/4	Club Brugge	h	2-3	*Roelandts, Leye*
12/4	Mouscron	a	2-0	*Matthys (p), Leye*
19/4	Charleroi	h	2-2	*Van Nieuwenhuyze, Buysse*
26/4	Dender	a	1-2	*Leye*
2/5	Genk	h	2-2	*Coppin, Leye (p)*
9/5	Brussels	a	2-1	*Coppin, Leye*

No	Name	Nat	Pos	Aps	(s)	Gls
16	LEANDRO Barrios	BRA	A	2	(8)	3
21	Sammy BOSSUT		G	11		
23	Bart BUYSSE		D	8	(3)	1
20	Janis COPPIN		A	1	(8)	2
1	Geert DE VLIEGER		G	23		
15	Nathan D'HAEMERS		M	12	(8)	1
24	Karel D'HAENE		D	29		
22	Frédéric DINDELEUX	FRA	D	23	(1)	
9	Nikica JELAVIĆ	CRO	A	20	(3)	3
14	Mbaye LEYE	SEN	A	30	(1)	16
7	Tim MATTHYS		A	22	(5)	5
11	Stijn MEERT		M	25	(5)	2
2	Stijn MINNE		D	13	(1)	
5	Loris REINA	FRA	D	31		
8	Kevin ROELANDTS		M	22	(9)	7
12	RUDISON Ferreira	BRA	M		(4)	
17	Khalifa Papa SANKARÉ	SEN	D	8	(1)	2
3	David TRIANTAFILIDIS		D	3		
6	Ludwin VAN NIEUWENHUYZE		M	31		3
4	Bart VAN ZUNDERT		D	21	(3)	2
19	Jonas VANDERMALIERE		M		(3)	
18	Lander VANSTEENBRUGGHE		M	15	(5)	
10	Matthieu VERSCHUÈRE	FRA	M	24	(3)	

BELGIUM

PROMOTED CLUBS

KV KORTRIJK
Coach – Hein Vanhaezebrouck
Founded - 1971

AFC TUBIZE
Coach – Philippe Saint-Jean
Founded - 1990

SECOND LEVEL FINAL TABLE 2007/08

		Pld	W	D	L	F	A	Pts
1	KV Kortrijk	36	23	7	6	73	35	76
2	AFC Tubize	36	19	9	8	49	29	66
3	Oud-Heverlee Leuven	36	18	7	11	61	42	61
4	KVSK United Overpelt-Lommel	36	16	12	8	51	36	60
5	R. Antwerp FC	36	16	11	9	64	38	59
6	R. Excelsior Virton	36	15	11	10	56	44	56
7	K. Lierse SK	36	15	8	13	47	36	53
8	KFC VW Hamme	36	14	7	15	54	45	49
9	KSK Beveren	36	14	6	16	48	56	48
10	KVK Tienen	36	13	9	14	49	51	48
11	R. Olympic Charleroi	36	13	7	16	40	53	46
12	RFC Tournai	36	12	10	14	34	37	46
13	K. AS Eupen	36	11	12	13	45	49	45
14	KV Red Star Waasland	36	10	13	13	46	47	43
15	KSK Deinze	36	10	13	13	44	58	43
16	KV Oostende	36	11	9	16	44	59	42
17	UR Namur	36	10	12	14	51	63	42
18	R. Union Saint-Gilloise	36	11	7	18	48	61	40
19	KFC Verbroedering Geel	36	4	4	28	33	98	16

PROMOTION PLAY-OFF FINAL TABLE

		Pld	W	D	L	F	A	Pts
1	AFC Tubize	6	6	0	0	9	1	18
2	R. Antwerp FC	6	4	0	2	10	5	12
3	KVSK United Overpelt-Lommel	6	2	0	4	6	12	6
4	Oud-Heverlee Leuven	6	0	0	6	2	9	0

DOMESTIC CUP 2007/08

COUPE DE BELGIQUE / BEKER VAN BELGIË

FIRST ROUND

(23/11/07)
Brussels 2, Oud-Heverlee Leuven 3 *(aet)*

(24/11/07)
Lokeren 0, Red Star Waasland 5 *(w/o)*
Oostende 0, Zulte Waregem 3
Club Brugge 4, Francs Borains 2
Kortrijk 2, Mouscron 0
Mons 2, Standaard Wetteren 2 *(aet; 3-2 on pens)*
Sint-Truiden 1, Eendracht Aalst 2
Genk 4, Charleroi-Marchienne 2
Charleroi 3, Deinze 0
Anderlecht 2, Hamme 1
Standard 3, KVSK United 0
Roeselare 4, Eupen 1 (aet)
AA Gent 2, Tienen 0

(25/11/07)
Dender EH 4, Westerlo 1
Germinal Beerschot 1, Union Saint-Gilloise 0

(26/11/07)
Mechelen 2, Cercle Brugge 4

SECOND ROUND

(12/1/08)
Anderlecht 2, Red Star Waasland 0
Mons 0, AA Gent 1 *(aet)*
Germinal Beerschot 2, Oud-Heverlee Leuven 2 *(aet; 3-1 on pens)*
Kortrijk 2, Zulte Waregem 1 *(aet)*

(13/1/2008)
Dender 2, Eendracht Aalst 1
Roeselare 2, Charleroi-Marchienne 2 *(aet ; 5-4 on pens)*

(14/1/2008)
Standard 2, Genk 0
Cercle Brugge 1, Club Brugge 0

QUARTER-FINALS

(30/1/08 & 27/2/08)
Germinal Beerschot 5 *(Monteyne P.J. 13, 66, Losada 26, Malki 80, Cruz 84*
Roeselare 1 *(Akgül 32)*
Roeselare 1 *(Čović 34)*, Germinal Beerschot 1 *(Cruz 88)*
(Germinal Beerschot 6-2)

Cercle Brugge 4 *(Nyoni 26, Xavier 45og, Snelders 66, De Sutter 74)*, Standard 1 *(Witsel 17)*
Standard 4 *(Fellaini 52, Defour 58, Goreux 88, Jovanović 90+2)*, Cercle Brugge 0
(Standard 5-4)

Anderlecht 3 *(Vlček 2, 48, Mpenza 88)*, Dender 0
Dender 1 *(Żewłakow 89)*, Anderlecht 1 *(Goor 17)*
(Anderlecht 4-1)

Kortrijk 5 *(Bakx 12, 43, 63, Nfor 55, Bétrémieux 89p)*, AA Gent 1 *(Ruiz 7*
AA Gent 4 *(Marić 12, 20, Mutavdžić 81, Ljubijankič 90+2)*, Kortrijk 0
(5-5; AA Gent on away goal)

SEMI-FINALS

(18/3/08 & 15/4/08)
Standard 2 *(De Camargo 18, Mbokani 35)*, AA Gent 2 *(Azofeifa 70, Ruiz 9*
AA Gent 4 *(Foley 45, Ruiz 67, Moia 70, Vermuth 81)*, Standard 0
(AA Gent 6-2)

(19/3/08 & 16/4/08)
Anderlecht 1 *(Dheedene 86og)*, Germinal Beerschot 0
Germinal Beerschot 1 *(Colman 45)*, RSC Anderlecht 1 *(Vlček 52)*
(RSC Anderlecht 2-1)

FINAL

(18/5/08)
Stade Roi Baudouin, Brussels
RSC ANDERLECHT 3 *(Polák 7, Boussoufa 71, Gillet 73)*
KAA GENT 2 *(Foley 6, Olufade 33)*
Referee - *Gumienny*
ANDERLECHT – *Proto, Wasilewski (Hassan 64), Pareja, Van Damme, Deschacht, Gillet, Biglia, Polák, Vlček (Chatelle 46), Frutos (Goor 90), Boussoufa.*
AA GENT – *Jorgacević, Rosales, Šuler, De Roeck (Azofeifa 86), Mutavdžić, Marić, Thijs, Fadiga (Vermuth 75), Olufade (Ljubijankič 75), Foley, Ruiz.*

Modriča hold on for maiden title

closely contested battle for the Bosnia-Herzegovina Premijer Liga title was won, narrowly and nervously, by FK Modriča. A modest club from a town of just)00 inhabitants in the north-east of the country, they ntually prevailed by a point from NK Široki Brijeg pite losing more matches than they won in the ond half of the season.

ır points in front at the winter break, Modriča were ebted to the similarly fluctuating spring form of their ef rivals Široki Brijeg and NK Čelik. There is no other gue in Europe that consistently produces such a huge erential in home and away outcomes, and in 2007/08 trend was maintained, with the home team winning of the 240 fixtures and the visiting side just 25. With ay wins so hard to come by, it was virtually ossible for any team to string a run of three-pointers ether. Thus, Modriča were able to withstand the body w of four successive defeats on their return to action 1arch before top-scoring striker Stevo Nikolić scovered his form and the team edged across the shing line with a 3-0 home win over NK Jedinstvo, ɔ were consequently relegated.

driča's rookie coach, Slaviša Božičić, the replacement ong-serving Mitar Lukić, confessed that it had been a ggle but nonetheless took pride in becoming the first 1 to lead the club to the championship title – four rs after Lukić had brought Cup success.

njski's Cup

r days after the conclusion of the Premijer Liga ıpaign, HŠK Zrinjski, the 2005 league champions, won two-legged final of the Bosnia-Herzegovina Cup, ting FK Sloboda Tuzla 4-1 on penalties after each n had prevailed 2-1 at home. The Mostar team thus ed Modriča in an elite group of six clubs to have won h domestic trophies, the others being Čelik, Široki eg, FK Sarajevo and FK Željezničar.

two big clubs from the capital both had a season to get. Defending champions Sarejevo made good progress in Europe, reaching the third qualifying round of the UEFA Champions League at the expense of KRC Genk, but made a poor start at home and never recovered, eventually finishing fifth. Željezničar ended up two places below, also missing out on 2008/09 UEFA competition, but did possess the league's most exciting young talent in 21-year-old playmaker-striker Semir Štilić. He scored ten goals – eight fewer than Premijer Liga top gun Darko Spalević of FK Slavija Sarajevo – but moved abroad at the season's end, signing a four-year contract with Polish club Lech Poznań.

National team turmoil

Štilić was one of 53 players who represented the Bosnia-Herzegovina national side in 2007/08. It was a season of turmoil and upheaval for the team. The UEFA EURO 2008™ qualifying campaign ended ignominiously with five successive defeats (after three straight victories), the inevitable consequence of this being the dismissal of coach Fuad Muzurović. He was replaced by the inexperienced former international Meho Kodro, who managed to persuade some players such as Kenan Hasagić and Emir Spahić to end their self-imposed international boycott but was then sacked himself after a disagreement with the national federation over friendly international arrangements, notably in refusing to lead the side in a planned fixture against Iran in Tehran.

Semir Štilić of FK Željezničar – the Premijer Liga's leading attraction in 2007/08

BOSNIA-HERZEGOVINA

Nogometni/Fudbalski Savez Bosne i Hercegovine (NFSBiH)

Ulica Ferhadija 30
BA-71000 Sarajevo
tel - +387 33 276676
fax - +387 33 444332
website – www.nfsbih.ba
email - nsbih@bih.net.ba

Year of Formation – 1992
President – Iljo Dominković
General Secretary - Munib Ušanović
Press Officer – Slavica Pecikoza

Stadium – Olympic Asim Ferhatović Hase Kosevo, Sarajevo (35,630)

TOP FIVE ALL-TIME CAPS
Elvir Bolić (51); Sergej Barbarez (47); Ve Musić (45); Hasan Salihamidžić (42); Muhamed Konjić (39)

TOP FIVE ALL-TIME GOALS
Elvir Bolić (22); Sergej Barbarez (17); Elv Baljić (14); Zvjezdan Misimović (9); Zlat Muslimović (7)

NATIONAL TEAM RESULTS 2007/08

22/8/07	Croatia	H	Sarajevo	3-5	*Muslimović (40, 70, 77)*
8/9/07	Hungary (ECQ)	A	Szekesfehervar	0-1	
12/9/07	Moldova (ECQ)	H	Sarajevo	0-1	
13/10/07	Greece (ECQ)	A	Athens	2-3	*Hrgović (54), Ibišević (90+2)*
17/10/07	Norway (ECQ)	H	Sarajevo	0-2	
21/11/07	Turkey (ECQ)	A	Istanbul	0-1	
30/1/08	Japan	A	Tokyo	0-3	
26/3/08	FYR Macedonia	H	Zenica	2-2	*Damjanović (17, 21)*
1/6/08	Azerbaijan	H	Zenica	1-0	*Nikolić Ste. (72)*

NATIONAL TEAM APPEARANCES 2007/08

Coach – Fuad MUZUROVIĆ /(5/1/08) Meho KODRO /(16/5/08) Denijal PIRIĆ	**3/11/45 12/1/67 27/9/46**		**Cro**	**HUN**	**MDA**	**GRE**	**NOR**	**TUR**	**Jpn**	**Mkd**	**Aze**	**Caps**
Adnan GUŠO	30/11/75	Pandurii (ROU)	G46	G	G	G	G	G				22
Džemo BERBEROVIĆ	5/11/81	Litex (BUL) /Kuban (RUS)	D	D	D	D	D	D				21
Branimir BAJIĆ	19/10/79	Koblenz (GER)	D	D	D	D	D	D				20
Ivan RADELJIĆ	14/9/80	Slaven (CRO)	D46	D	D46							6
Mirko HRGOVIĆ	5/2/79	Hajduk (CRO)	D82	D84		D			M83			28
Dario DAMJANOVIĆ	23/7/81	Hajduk (CRO) /Luch-Energia (RUS)	M46		s47				D	D66		10
Elvir RAHIMIĆ	4/4/76	CSKA Moskva (RUS)	M	M	M	M		M		M		8
Zajko ZEBA	22/5/83	KamAZ (RUS)	M85		M47							5
Zvjezdan MISIMOVIĆ	5/6/82	Nürnberg (GER)	M	M		M82	M	M		M87		32
Zlatan MUSLIMOVIĆ	6/3/81	Atalanta (ITA)	A	A	A	A	A46					11
Adnan ČUSTOVIĆ	14/4/78	Mouscron (BEL)	A46	s84	s78							5
Safet NADAREVIĆ	30/8/80	Zagreb (CRO)	s46		D	D	D	D		D		12

TIONAL TEAM APPEARANCES 2007/08 (contd.)

			Cro	HUN	MDA	GRE	NOR	TUR	Jpn	Mkd	Aze	Caps	Goals
ŽEKO	17/3/86	Wolfsburg (GER)	s46	s67	A		s46	A83		A		8	1
IBRIČIĆ	26/9/86	Zagreb (CRO)	s46					M75		M		8	-
ned ALAIM	10/2/81	Sarajevo	s46									1	-
n BARTOLOVIĆ	10/4/77	Hajduk (CRO)	s82									16	1
IBIŠEVIĆ	6/8/84	Hoffenheim (GER)	s85	A67	s46	s46	s46	s75				7	1
MALETIĆ	20/10/80	Partizan (SRB)		M79	M78		M78	M		s13		8	-
n BLATNJAK	1/8/81	Khimki (RUS)		M	M	M62	M46					12	-
BOŽIĆ	25/5/83	Fehérvár (HUN)		s79								1	-
VLADAVIĆ	29/6/82	Žilina (SVK)				M			M61	M		7	-
av KRUNIĆ	28/1/79	Moskva (RUS)				M46	M	M				5	-
MERZIĆ	29/6/84	Teplice (CZE)				s62	D	D89	D			4	-
SALIHOVIĆ	8/10/84	Hoffenheim (GER)				s82	A	s83		A13		4	-
MUHAREMOVIĆ	6/12/84	Sarajevo					s78	s89				3	-
HASAGIĆ	1/2/80	İstanbul BB (TUR)							G	G		24	-
PAHIĆ	18/8/80	Lokomotiv Moskva (RUS)							D	D		23	1
VIDIĆ	12/4/79	Široki Brijeg							D			10	-
NIKOLIĆ	28/11/80	Zrinjski							D53		D90	2	-
nir JOVANOVIĆ	3/4/85	Slavija							M46		M	2	-
n ŽIŽOVIĆ	27/12/80	Zrinjski							M83		M61	2	-
RAŠČIĆ	16/9/81	Sarajevo							A46			2	-
UGO	5/12/82	Velež							s46			1	-
NIKOLIĆ	4/12/84	Modriča							s46		s71	2	1
REGOJE	2/12/81	Slavija							s53		D75	2	-
KORO	30/3/81	Rijeka (CRO)							s61			3	-
SALČINOVIĆ	26/6/87	Čelik							s83			1	-
ŠTILIĆ	8/10/87	Željezničar							s83			1	-
AHIĆ	10/12/81	Aris (GRE)								D		1	-
USEJNOVIĆ	18/5/88	Sloboda								s66		1	-
PEJIĆ	18/3/88	Orašje								s87		1	-
BURIĆ	18/2/87	Čelik									G	1	-
edalija ČOVIĆ	16/3/86	AA Gent (BEL)									D	1	-
ANDŽA	15/12/86	Hajduk (CRO)									D	3	-
USIĆ	10/11/85	Cibalia (CRO)									M	2	-
DAJIĆ	21/8/84	Fehérvár (HUN)									A56	1	-
TERKEŠ	8/1/81	Zadar (CRO)									A71	1	-
AGANOVIĆ	25/8/86	Ćukarički (SRB)									A46	1	-
ANDŽIĆ	20/6/90	Sarajevo									s46	1	-
LULIĆ	18/1/86	Bellinzona (SUI)									s56	1	-
UKAČEVIĆ	3/11/83	Čelik									s61	1	-
OPIĆ	22/10/82	Široki Brijeg									s75	1	-
ČEJVANOVIĆ	9/8/86	Sloboda									s90	1	-

BOSNIA-HERZEGOVINA

DOMESTIC LEAGUE 2007/08

PREMIJER LIGA FINAL TABLE

		Pld	Home W	Home D	Home L	Home F	Home A	Away W	Away D	Away L	Away F	Away A	Total W	Total D	Total L	Total F	Total A	Pts
1	FK Modriča	30	14	0	1	40	12	4	1	10	17	33	18	1	11	57	45	55
2	NK Široki Brijeg	30	13	1	1	24	6	4	2	9	20	23	17	3	10	44	29	54
3	NK Čelik	30	14	1	0	29	4	2	3	10	9	28	16	4	10	38	32	52
4	HŠK Zrinjski	30	12	3	0	32	7	3	1	11	14	20	15	4	11	46	27	49
5	FK Sarajevo	30	11	3	1	32	10	3	3	9	10	19	14	6	10	42	29	48
6	FK Sloboda Tuzla	30	14	0	1	33	6	1	2	12	11	32	15	2	13	44	38	47
7	FK Željezničar	30	14	1	0	41	8	0	2	13	6	27	14	3	13	47	35	45
8	FK Velež	30	13	2	0	30	9	1	0	14	9	37	14	2	14	39	46	44
9	FK Slavija Sarajevo	30	12	1	2	29	11	2	1	12	10	33	14	2	14	39	44	44
10	FK Laktaši	30	13	1	1	39	15	0	3	12	3	25	13	4	13	42	40	43
11	NK Posušje	30	11	3	1	26	9	2	1	12	16	37	13	4	13	42	46	43
12	HNK Orašje	30	13	2	0	37	7	0	1	14	13	38	13	3	14	50	45	42
13	NK Travnik	30	12	1	2	28	11	1	2	12	7	28	13	3	14	35	39	42
14	FK Leotar	30	12	0	3	29	11	1	2	12	9	34	13	2	15	38	45	41
15	NK Jedinstvo	30	11	4	0	21	7	1	0	14	7	36	12	4	14	28	43	40
16	NK Žepče	30	2	1	12	18	35	0	0	15	7	38	2	1	27	25	73	7

TOP GOALSCORER

18 Darko SPALEVIĆ (Slavija)

14 Senad MUJIĆ (Orašje)
Ivan KRSTANOVIĆ (Posušje)
Stevo NIKOLIĆ (Modriča)

13 Feđa DUDIĆ (Travnik)

12 Sanel JAHIĆ (Željezničar)

11 Krešimir KORDIĆ (Posušje)
Emir HADŽIĆ (Čelik)

10 Semir ŠTILIĆ (Željezničar) Jovi
VICO (Leotar)
Mislav KAROGLAN (Široki Brij
Stanko BUBALO (Široki Brijeg)

CLUB-BY-CLUB

NK ČELIK

Coach - Ivo Ištuk

Founded - 1945

MAJOR HONOURS: Bosnia-Herzegovina League - (3) 1994, 1996, 1997; Bosnia-Herzegovina Cup - (2) 1995, 1996.

Date	Opponent		Score	Scorers
2007				
4/8	Modriča	a	0-2	
11/8	Velež	h	2-0	*Lukačević, Novaković*
19/8	Slavija	a	1-0	*Hadžić*
25/8	Travnik	h	0-0	
15/9	Posušje	h	3-0	*Pupčević, Novaković 2*
19/9	Široki Brijeg	a	0-0	
23/9	Žepče	a	2-0	*Hadžić, Lukačević*
29/9	Željezničar	h	3-0	*Lukačević (p), Hadžić 2*
7/10	Leotar	a	0-2	
20/10	Zrinjski	h	1-0	*Novaković*
27/10	Sloboda	a	0-2	
3/11	Laktaši	h	1-0	*Lukačević*
10/11	Jedinstvo	a	1-1	*Hadžić*
14/11	Orašje	a	0-3	
24/11	Sarajevo	h	1-0	*Hadžić*
2008				
1/3	Modriča	h	3-1	*Lukačević (p), Novaković, Hadžić*
9/3	Velež	a	0-2	
15/3	Slavija	h	2-0	*Lukačević (p), Mašić*
22/3	Travnik	a	0-0	
29/3	Široki Brijeg	h	3-2	*Šabić, Hadžić, Hasanović*
2/4	Posušje	a	2-3	*Lukačević (p), Hećo*
5/4	Žepče	h	4-1	*Hadžić (p), og (Krajišnik), Lukačević, Mašić*
13/4	Željezničar	a	2-3	*Pupčević, Šabić*
19/4	Leotar	h	2-0	*Hadžić, Hasanović*
26/4	Zrinjski	a	1-3	*Novaković*
3/5	Sloboda	h	1-0	*Hadžić*
10/5	Laktaši	a	0-4	
17/5	Jedinstvo	h	1-0	*Novaković*
24/5	Orašje	h	2-0	*Lukačević, Novakov*
31/5	Sarajevo	a	0-3	

Name	Nat	Pos	Aps	(s)	G
Jasmin BURIĆ		G	28		
Amir DUVNJAK		D	1		
Adin DŽAFIĆ		D	2	(5)	
Zlatan GAFUROVIĆ		D	1	(5)	
Emir HADŽIĆ		M	27	(2)	
Almir HASANOVIĆ		D	22		
Šerif HASIĆ		M	3	(15)	
Haris HEĆO		D	1	(8)	
Armin IMAMOVIĆ		D	19	(2)	
Mladen JURČEVIĆ		D	21		
Emir JUSIĆ		D	3	(3)	
Mahir KARIĆ		D	8	(17)	
Josip LUKAČEVIĆ		M	27		
Bojan MARKOVIĆ		M	23	(2)	
Adnan MAŠIĆ		M	10	(8)	
Jasmin MORANJKIĆ		A	22	(3)	
Zoran NOVAKOVIĆ		M	24	(3)	
Amel PJANIĆ		G	1		
Ismar POJSKIĆ		G	1		
Bojan PUPČEVIĆ		M	24		
Hernán RAVANIERA	ARG	M	3	(9)	
Nermin ŠABIĆ		M	24		
Fenan SALČINOVIĆ		M	25		
Mirnes SMAJLOVIĆ		M	1	(4)	
Haris ZATAGIĆ		M	9	(5)	

NK JEDINSTVO

Coach - Ahmet Kečalović; (31/12/07) Mehmed Janjoš

Founded - 1919

2007				
4/8	Velež	a	1-2	*Kapetan*
11/8	Slavija	h	3-1	*Mirvić, Vranešević, Mehadžić*
18/8	Travnik	a	0-2	
25/8	Široki Brijeg	h	1-0	*Mirvić*
2/9	Posušje	a	0-1	
15/9	Žepče	h	2-0	*Mirvić, Dedić*
22/9	Željezničar	a	0-6	
29/9	Leotar	h	0-0	
7/10	Zrinjski	a	1-4	*Mirvić*
20/10	Sloboda	h	2-1	*Vranešević, Seferović*
27/10	Laktaši	a	0-2	
3/11	Orašje	a	1-2	*Basara*
10/11	Čelik	h	1-1	*Kapetan*
14/11	Sarajevo	a	0-4	
24/11	Modriča	h	1-1	*Mirvić*
2008				
1/3	Velež	h	1-0	*Mehadžić*
9/3	Slavija	a	1-2	*Sejdić*
15/3	Travnik	h	1-0	*Dujmović*
22/3	Široki Brijeg	a	1-2	*Vranešević*
29/3	Posušje	h	3-2	*Vranešević, Kapetan 2*
2/4	Žepče	a	1-0	*Hodžić*
5/4	Željezničar	h	1-0	*Seferović*
12/4	Leotar	a	1-4	*Selimović*
19/4	Zrinjski	h	2-1	*Kapetan, Dujmović (p)*
26/4	Sloboda	a	0-1	
3/5	Laktaši	h	2-0	*Čahtarević, Mirvić*
10/5	Orašje	h	0-0	
17/5	Čelik	a	0-1	
24/5	Sarajevo	h	1-0	*Dujmović*
31/5	Modriča	a	0-3	

Name	Nat	Pos	Aps	(s)	Gls
Igor ABDIHODŽIĆ		M	1	(2)	
Frane ANUŠIĆ		A	9	(5)	
Admir ARNAUTOVIĆ		M	2	(3)	
Marko BASARA	SRB	M	11	(1)	1
Vahidin ČAHTAREVIĆ		M	8	(2)	1
Alen DEDIĆ		A	26		1
Miroslav DUJMOVIĆ		A	15		3
Adis DŽAFEROVIĆ		M	24	(1)	
Ekrem HODŽIĆ		D	13		
Haris HRKIĆ		M		(2)	1
Aldin KAHRIMANOVIĆ		M		(2)	
Armin KAPETAN		A	27		5
Elvis MEHADŽIĆ		M	20	(1)	2
Admir MIRVIĆ		M	19	(5)	6
Denis MUJKIĆ		G	28		
Elmedin MUJNOVIĆ		D	3	(8)	
Emir MULIĆ		D	19	(5)	
Zoran POPOVIĆ		M		(5)	
Nihad PORČIĆ		M		(2)	
Albert RAČIČ		M		(1)	
Damir ŠAHINOVIĆ		M	4	(4)	
Almir SEFEROVIĆ		D	25		2
Edin SEJDIĆ		D	18	(7)	1
Dino SELIMOVIĆ		M	17	(9)	1
Mehmed SELMANOVIĆ		M		(4)	
Ervin SMAJLAGIĆ		D	17	(2)	
Edin ŠUŠNJAR		G	2	(1)	
Ahmet TREJIĆ		M		(1)	
Semir VELADŽIĆ		M		(1)	
Duško VRANEŠEVIĆ		A	22	(5)	4

FK LAKTAŠI

Coach - Zoran Jagodić; (31/12/07) Zoran Ćurguz

Founded - 1974

2007				
5/8	Slavija	a	0-0	
11/8	Travnik	h	3-1	*Mučalović, Ljubojević, Studen*
19/8	Široki Brijeg	a	0-1	
25/8	Posušje	h	1-1	*Ljubojević*
2/9	Žepče	a	1-1	*Ćirković*
15/9	Željezničar	h	3-2	*Đurić, Mučalović, Inđić (p)*
22/9	Leotar	a	0-4	
29/9	Zrinjski	h	3-2	*Gošić 3*
7/10	Sloboda	a	0-1	
20/10	Orašje	a	0-1	
27/10	Jedinstvo	h	2-0	*Gošić 2 (1p)*
3/11	Čelik	a	0-1	
10/11	Sarajevo	h	1-3	*Đorić*
14/11	Modriča	a	0-1	
24/11	Velež	h	3-2	*Đorić, Gošić 2*
2008				
1/3	Slavija	h	2-1	*Mitić 2*
9/3	Travnik	a	1-5	*Mikić*
15/3	Široki Brijeg	h	2-0	*Rađenović, Studen*
22/3	Posušje	a	1-1	*Benić*
29/3	Žepče	h	2-0	*Ujić 2*
2/4	Željezničar	a	0-1	
5/4	Leotar	h	4-0	*Studen, Mitić 2, Đorić (p)*
13/4	Zrinjski	a	0-2	
19/4	Sloboda	h	2-0	*Đorić, Ljubojević*
24/4	Orašje	h	5-2	*Marinović, Mitić, Rađenović, Mikić 2*
3/5	Jedinstvo	a	0-2	
10/5	Čelik	h	4-0	*Rađenović 3, Đorić*
17/5	Sarajevo	a	0-2	
24/5	Modriča	h	2-1	*Rađenović, Mikić*
31/5	Velež	a	0-2	

Name	Nat	Pos	Aps	(s)	Gls
Miloš BABIĆ		D	5		
Miljan BAJIĆ		D	24		
Božidar BAŠA		G	10		
Dragan BENIĆ		A	1	(4)	1
Marko BLAGOJEVIĆ		D		(10)	
Leonid ĆORIĆ		D	21	(2)	
Dušan ĆIRKOVIĆ		M	7	(4)	1
Zlatko ĐORIĆ		M	22	(6)	5
Siniša ĐURIĆ		D	12	(5)	1
Đorđe GOŠIĆ		A	9		7
Nikola ILIĆ		M	3	(3)	
Đorđe INĐIĆ		A	6	(5)	1
Darko LJUBOJEVIĆ		D	20		3
Vinko MARINOVIĆ		D	25		1
Miroslav MILOŠEVIĆ		M	12		
Borislav MIKIĆ		M	6	(2)	4
Igor MIRKOVIĆ		M	14	(4)	
Saša MITIĆ		A	11	(1)	5
Siniša MRKOBRADA		G	8		
Milutin MUČALOVIĆ		D	10	(5)	2
Aleksandar RADULOVIĆ		M	5	(7)	
Dragan OLUJIĆ		M	1	(3)	
Dejan RAĐENOVIĆ		D	8	(1)	6
Milan RISTIĆ		M		(4)	
Željko SEKULIĆ		M	24		
Dragan STARČEVIĆ		G	12		
Nenad STUDEN		M	16		3
Aleksandar ŠOLAK		D		(2)	
Marko TEŠIĆ		D	10		

		Pos	Aps	(s)	Gls
Jovica TOLJAGIĆ		M	1	(1)	
Željko TRIVIĆ		M	10	(7)	
Vladimir VUKOVIĆ		D		(5)	
Slaviša UJIĆ		M	17	(6)	2

FK LEOTAR

Coach - Srđan Bajić

Founded - 1925

MAJOR HONOURS: Bosnia-Herzegovina League - (1) 2003.

2007				
5/8	Posušje	a	0-0	
11/8	Žepče	h	2-0	*Zečević, Mulina (p)*
18/8	Željezničar	a	0-3	
25/8	Orašje	a	0-3	
4/9	Zrinjski	h	0-2	
15/9	Sloboda	a	0-2	
22/9	Laktaši	h	4-0	*Komnenić, Šešlija, Vico 2*
29/9	Jedinstvo	a	0-0	
7/10	Čelik	h	2-0	*Vico 2*
20/10	Sarajevo	a	0-3	
27/10	Modriča	h	1-2	*Golubović*
3/11	Velež	a	2-3	*Samardžić, Golubović (p)*
10/11	Slavija	h	4-3	*Šešlija 3, Prelo*
14/11	Travnik	a	1-4	*Ramić*
24/11	Široki Brijeg	h	1-2	*Šešlija*
2008				
1/3	Posušje	h	1-0	*Dreč*
9/3	Žepče	a	2-0	*Vico, Dinčić*
15/3	Željezničar	h	1-0	*Šešlija*
22/3	Orašje	h	2-0	*Šešlija 2*
29/3	Zrinjski	a	1-2	*Dreč*
2/4	Sloboda	h	2-0	*Dinčić, Ramić*
5/4	Laktaši	a	0-4	
12/4	Jedinstvo	h	4-1	*Čorlija, Vico 3*
19/4	Čelik	a	0-2	
26/4	Sarajevo	h	2-0	*Zečević 2*
3/5	Modriča	a	1-2	*Vučinić*
10/5	Velež	h	2-1	*Šešlija, Vico*
17/5	Slavija	a	2-4	*Mulina, Vico*
24/5	Travnik	h	1-0	*Zečević*
31/5	Široki Brijeg	a	0-2	

Name	Nat	Pos	Aps	(s)	Gls
Miloš ATELJEVIĆ		M		(1)	
Dušan BERAK		G	2	(1)	
Gavrilo ČORLIJA		M	14	(2)	1
Oleg ĆURIĆ		D	25		
Slobodan DINČIĆ		A	9	(5)	2
Darko DREČ		M	19	(1)	2
Bojan GOLUBOVIĆ	SRB	A	9	(3)	2
Pajo JANKOVIĆ		M	4	(14)	
Srđan KARANOVIĆ		G	13	(1)	
Rajko KOMNENIĆ		M	25	(1)	1
Bojan KULJANIN		G		(1)	
Marko LAZIĆ		M	3	(9)	
Rajko MIČETA		D	13		
Vukmir MILJANOVIĆ		G	15		
Siniša MULINA		M	25	(1)	2
Marko PALAVESTRIĆ		M	11	(2)	
Miroslav PRELO		M	3	(8)	1
Zoran POPOVIĆ		M		(1)	
Željko RADOVIĆ		M	18	(4)	
Anel RAMIĆ		M	20	(4)	2
Milan SAMARDŽIĆ	SRB	M	12		1
Branko ŠEŠLIJA		A	21	(6)	9
Vladimir TODOROVIĆ		M	29		
Jovica VICO		A	18	(1)	10
Bojan VUČINIĆ		D	5	(10)	1
Predrag VUKIČEVIĆ		D	1		
Nenad ZEČEVIĆ	SRB	M	16		4

FK MODRIČA

Coach - Slaviša Božičić

Founded - 1974

MAJOR HONOURS: Bosnia-Herzegovina League - (1) 2008; Bosnia-Herzegovina Cup - (1) 2004.

2007				
4/8	Čelik	h	2-0	*Belošević, Nikolić*
11/8	Orašje	h	4-1	*Savić (p), Pereira, Bojić, Živković*
25/8	Velež	h	3-1	*Nikolić, Stjepanović, Purić*
2/9	Slavija	a	0-1	
15/9	Travnik	h	6-1	*Arsić, Bojić, Savić 2 (1p), Nikolić 2*
22/9	Široki Brijeg	a	1-4	*Vasić*
26/9	Sarajevo	a	4-2	*Pereira 2, Arsić, Nikolić*
29/9	Posušje	h	4-1	*Pereira 2, Savić 2 (1p)*
9/10	Žepče	a	3-1	*Stokić, Živković, Bogičević*
20/10	Željezničar	h	1-0	*Nikolić*
27/10	Leotar	a	2-1	*Tripić, Savić*
3/11	Zrinjski	h	2-1	*Savić, Pereira*
10/11	Sloboda	a	0-3	
14/11	Laktaši	h	1-0	*Pereira*
24/11	Jedinstvo	a	1-1	*Pereira*
2008				
1/3	Čelik	a	1-3	*Stokić*
9/3	Sarajevo	h	0-1	
15/3	Orašje	a	0-4	
22/3	Velež	a	0-1	
29/3	Slavija	h	1-0	*Dugić*
2/4	Travnik	a	0-1	
5/4	Široki Brijeg	h	2-1	*Purić, Nikolić*
13/4	Posušje	a	3-1	*Živković, Nikolić, Purić*
19/4	Žepče	h	6-2	*Ćosić 2, Nikolić 2, Dugić 2*
26/4	Željezničar	a	1-4	*Dugić*
3/5	Leotar	h	2-1	*Vasić (p), Nikolić*
10/5	Zrinjski	a	0-4	
17/5	Sloboda	h	3-2	*Stokić, Nikolić 2*
24/5	Laktaši	a	1-2	*Nikolić*
31/5	Jedinstvo	h	3-0	*Vasić, Dugić, Zafirović*

Name	Nat	Pos	Aps	(s)	Gls
Nemanja ARSIĆ		M	7	(8)	2
Marko BAJIĆ	SRB	D	10		
Zoran BELOŠEVIĆ	SRB	A	15		1
Jadranko BOGIČEVIĆ		D	24		1
Mladen BOJIĆ		A	4	(9)	2
Božidar ĆOSIĆ		D	14		2
Slaviša DUGIĆ		A	5	(5)	5
Željko GAVRILOVIĆ		D	1	(3)	
Anto JANJIŠ		M		(7)	
Dragan JOLOVIĆ	SRB	D	25		
Željko KLJALJEVIĆ		M	11	(3)	
Dražen LUKIĆ		M		(2)	
Petar MATOVIĆ		M	1	(1)	
Bojan MAKSIMOVIĆ		D		(1)	
Vladimir MILJKOVIĆ		D	5	(8)	
Stevo NIKOLIĆ		A	28		14
Godoi Rafael PEREIRA	BRA	A	13		8
Nemanja PAVLOVIĆ		M	4	(2)	
Milan PETROVIĆ		G	2	(2)	
Dario PURIĆ		M	15	(3)	3

Đorđe SAVIĆ		A	15	(9)	7
Nemanja STJEPANOVIĆ		D	27		1
Joco STOKIĆ		M	20	(2)	3
Bojan TRIPIĆ		G	28		1
Sreten VASIĆ	SRB	M	26	(1)	3
Nikola VASILJEVIĆ		D	3	(1)	
Dragan VUKOVIĆ		M	1	(3)	
Đorđe ZAFIROVIĆ		A	8	(6)	1
Marko ŽIVKOVIĆ	SRB	M	18	(4)	3

HNK ORAŠJE

Coach - Pavao Strugačevac; (15/10/07) Željko Baotić

Founded - 1996

MAJOR HONOURS: Bosnia-Herzegovina Cup – (1) 2006.

2007				
4/8	Sarajevo	a	1-4	*Živković P.*
11/8	Željezničar	h	1-0	*Vidović A.*
18/8	Modriča	a	1-4	*Ristanić*
25/8	Leotar	h	3-0	*Pejić I., Vidović A., Đurić*
1/9	Velež	a	1-3	*Pejić I.*
15/9	Zrinjski	h	0-0	
23/9	Slavija	a	2-3	*Đurić, Draganović*
29/9	Sloboda	h	2-2	*Đurić, Sarajlić*
7/10	Travnik	a	0-1	
20/10	Laktaši	h	1-0	*Pejić I.*
28/10	Široki Brijeg	a	0-1	
3/11	Jedinstvo	h	2-1	*Pejić I., Mujić*
11/11	Posušje	a	1-3	*Đurić*
14/11	Čelik	h	3-0	*Pejić I. 2 (2p), Mujić*
25/11	Žepče	a	4-5	*Mujić 2, Vidović A., Sarajlić*
2008				
1/3	Sarajevo	h	3-1	*Pejić I., Mujić, Živković A.*
9/3	Željezničar	a	1-2	*Joldić (p)*
15/3	Modriča	h	4-0	*Joldić, Živković A. 2, Mujić*
22/3	Leotar	a	0-2	
29/3	Velež	h	6-0	*Pejić M., Joldić 2, Mujić 3*
2/4	Zrinjski	a	0-2	
5/4	Slavija	h	2-1	*Mujić, Živković A.*
13/4	Sloboda	a	0-1	
19/4	Travnik	h	2-0	*Halilović, Joldić*
26/4	Laktaši	a	2-5	*Halilović, Joldić*
3/5	Široki Brijeg	h	2-0	*Halilović, Mujić*
10/5	Jedinstvo	a	0-0	
17/5	Posušje	h	4-2	*Jurić, Mujić 2 (1p), Mikić*
24/5	Čelik	a	0-2	
31/5	Žepče	h	2-0	*Joldić, Mujić*

Name	Nat	Pos	Aps	(s)	Gls
Darko ALEKSIĆ	SRB	M	25		
Marin ANDRIJEVIĆ		M		(3)	
Luka BRAŠNIĆ		D	6		
Velimir BRAŠNIĆ		A	2	(2)	
Mario BILEN		M	7	(3)	
Slaven DAMJANOVIĆ		A	9	(1)	
Adnan DŽAKIĆ		M		(1)	
Dejan DRAGANOVIĆ	CRO	M	3	(5)	1
Miron DUBRAVAC		D	2		
Marko ĐURIĆ		A	10	(3)	4
Almir HALILOVIĆ		M	13		3
Mato IBIĆ		M		(3)	
Admir JOLDIĆ		A	13	(1)	7
Goran JURIĆ		M	9	(1)	1
Miro KLAIĆ		D	13	(1)	
Luka KOBAŠ		G	28		
Slavko KOBAŠ		D	24	(1)	
Dženan KRAJIŠNIK		D	4		
Amir KURTALIĆ		D	1	(2)	
Ivan ORKIĆ		M		(2)	
Zlatko MIKIĆ		M	5	(11)	1
Drago MIŠKOVIĆ		M	23		
Senad MUJIĆ		A	10	(10)	14
Ivo PEJIĆ		M	26		7
Matijas PEJIĆ		M	15	(3)	1
Ilija RISTANIĆ		M	12		1
Adnan SARAJLIĆ		M	13		2
Raif SMAJIĆ		G	2		
Antonio VIDOVIĆ		M	6		3
Mario VIDOVIĆ		M	13	(4)	
Anto ŽIVKOVIĆ		A	12	(5)	4
Goran ŽIVKOVIĆ		D	20	(1)	
Pavo ŽIVKOVIĆ		A	4	(11)	1

NK POSUŠJE

Coach - Dragan Jović; (20/10/07) Vinko Jurišić; (14/4/08) Ivan Katalinić

Founded - 1950

2007				
5/8	Leotar	h	0-0	
12/8	Zrinjski	a	0-1	
19/8	Sloboda	h	4-1	*Ivanković, Vranjković, Sedarušić, Mešanović*
25/8	Laktaši	a	1-1	*Krstanović*
2/9	Jedinstvo	h	1-0	*Lima*
15/9	Čelik	a	0-3	
23/9	Sarajevo	h	0-0	
29/9	Modriča	a	1-4	*Krstanović (p)*
7/10	Velež	h	1-0	*Ivanković*
21/10	Slavija	a	0-2	
27/10	Travnik	h	1-0	*Krstanović (p)*
4/11	Široki Brijeg	a	2-1	*Daničić, Kordić*
11/11	Orašje	h	3-1	*Krstanović 2 (1p), Kordić*
14/11	Žepče	h	3-1	*Kordić, Krstanović, Daničić*
24/11	Željezničar	a	2-4	*Kordić, Krstanović*
2008				
1/3	Leotar	a	0-1	
9/3	Zrinjski	h	1-0	*Krstanović*
15/3	Sloboda	a	2-4	*Ljubić, Kordić*
22/3	Laktaši	h	1-1	*Vranjković*
29/3	Jedinstvo	a	2-3	*Kordić, Ljubić*
2/4	Čelik	h	3-2	*Krstanović 3 (1p)*
5/4	Sarajevo	a	1-3	*Daničić*
13/4	Modriča	h	1-3	*Kordić*
19/4	Velež	a	0-2	
26/4	Slavija	h	3-0	*Krstanović, Kordić, Vranjković*
3/5	Travnik	a	0-2	
11/5	Široki Brijeg	h	1-0	*Krstanović*
17/5	Orašje	a	2-4	*Rogulj, Ljubić*
24/5	Žepče	a	3-2	*Serdarušić, Kordić, Krstanović*
31/5	Željezničar	h	3-0	*Stojanović, Kordić 2*

Name	Nat	Pos	Aps	(s)	Gls
Boris BAČAK		G	5	(1)	
Marin BAGO		M		(2)	
Josip BARIŠIĆ		M	13	(1)	
Mateo BEŠLIĆ		M		(1)	
Mirko BUDIMIR		D	3	(8)	
Robert ĆESIĆ		M		(1)	
Antonio ĆORIĆ		A	1	(5)	
Ante DANIČIĆ	CRO	M	13	(6)	3
Franjo FILIPOVIĆ		M	3	(5)	

Name	Nat	Pos	Aps	(s)	Gls
Vlado HRKAČ		D	6	(2)	
Jure IVANKOVIĆ		M	26	(2)	2
Stanko KARAČIĆ		M	2	(8)	
Krešimir KORDIĆ		A	21	(2)	11
Dražen KOŠTRO		D		(1)	
Ivan KRSTANOVIĆ		A	26	(1)	14
Mate KUKIĆ		M		(1)	
Fabrício LIMA	BRA	A	4	(3)	1
Mario LJUBIĆ		M	16	(7)	3
Vladimir MARKOTIĆ		G	25		
Alen MEŠANOVIĆ		M	3	(3)	1
Didier PAASS	TOG	M	2	(1)	
Bruno PRLIĆ		M	24	(3)	
Boris RADOVANOVIĆ		M	5	(2)	
Stipe REŽIĆ	CRO	M	27		
Kaja ROGULJ	CRO	D	25		1
Duško SAKAN		M	11	(10)	
Ante SERDARUŠIĆ		M	27	(1)	2
Danijel STOJANOVIĆ		A	25	(1)	1
Ante VOLAREVIĆ	CRO	D	2		
Mladen VRANJKOVIĆ		M	15		3

FK SARAJEVO

Coach - Husref Musemić

Founded - 1946

MAJOR HONOURS: Yugoslav League - (2) 1967, 1985; Bosnia-Herzegovina League – (1) 2007; Bosnia-Herzegovina Cup - (4) 1997, 1998, 2002, 2005.

2007

4/8	Orašje	h	4-1	*Muharemović, Raščić, Turković, Kurto*
11/8	Velež	a	2-2	*Raščić, Milošević*
25/8	Slavija	h	1-1	*Grujić*
2/9	Travnik	a	0-1	
15/9	Široki Brijeg	h	2-2	*Hadžić, Milošević*
23/9	Posušje	a	0-0	
26/9	Modriča	h	2-4	*Mešić, Grujić*
29/9	Žepče	h	3-0	*Turković, Kurto 2*
7/10	Željezničar	a	0-0	
20/10	Leotar	h	3-0	*Mešić, Bučan (p), Grujić*
28/10	Zrinjski	a	0-4	
3/11	Sloboda	h	2-1	*Raščić, Muharemović (p)*
10/11	Laktaši	a	3-1	*Turković, Raščić, Hadžić*
14/11	Jedinstvo	h	4-0	*Milošević, Handžić 2, Hadžić*
24/11	Čelik	a	0-1	

2008

1/3	Orašje	a	1-3	*Handžić*
9/3	Modriča	a	1-0	*Hadžić*
15/3	Velež	h	1-0	*Bućan*
22/3	Slavija	a	0-1	
29/3	Travnik	h	1-0	*Kurto*
2/4	Široki Brijeg	a	0-1	
5/4	Posušje	h	3-1	*Raščić, Handžić, Duro*
13/4	Žepče	a	3-1	*Handžić, Bućan (p), Duro*
19/4	Željezničar	h	0-0	
26/4	Leotar	a	0-2	
4/5	Zrinjski	h	1-0	*Bućan*
10/5	Sloboda	a	0-1	
17/5	Laktaši	h	2-0	*Raščić 2*
24/5	Jedinstvo	a	0-1	
31/5	Čelik	h	3-0	*Raščić, Handžić, Maksimović*

Name	Nat	Pos	Aps	(s)	Gls
Muhamed ALAIM		G	19		
Miloš BABIĆ		D	5	(2)	
Alen BAŠIČ		M	22	(2)	
Sead BUĆAN		A	18	(4)	4
Samir DURO		M	11	(1)	2
Muhamed DŽAKMIC		M	16	(1)	
Vladan GRUJIĆ		M	14		3
Irfan FEJZIĆ		G	6		
Damir HADŽIC		M	26	(1)	4
Haris HANDŽIĆ		A	14	(9)	6
Dino HAMZIĆ		G	5	(2)	
Emir JANJOŠ		M	5	(2)	
Muamer KURTO		A	9	(6)	4
Bojan MAGAZIN		M	4	(6)	
Marko MAKSIMOVIĆ		M	16	(5)	1
Mirza MEŠIĆ		A	5	(6)	2
Semjon MILOŠEVIĆ		D	26		3
Ninoslav MILENKOVIĆ		D	13		
Muhamed MIRVIĆ		M	1	(1)	
Veldin MUHAREMOVIĆ		M	12		2
Almir PLISKA		A	2	(8)	
Admir RAŠČIĆ		A	24	(3)	8
Senad REPUH		M	3	(4)	
Elvis SADIKOVIĆ		D	4	(4)	
Duško STAJIĆ		A	6	(6)	
Nihad SULJEVIĆ		D	5	(1)	
Zdravko ŠARABA		D	5	(2)	
Anel ŠKORO		A		(2)	
Almir TURKOVIĆ		A	23	(4)	3
Muhidin ZUKIĆ		D	11	(3)	

NK ŠIROKI BRIJEG

Coach - Ivica Barbarić; (26/8/07) Mario Ćutuk

Founded - 1948

MAJOR HONOURS: Bosnia-Herzegovina League - (2) 2004, 2006; Bosnia-Herzegovina Cup – (1) 2007.

2007

5/8	Zrinjski	h	1-0	*Ronielle*
11/8	Sloboda	a	0-3	
19/8	Laktaši	h	1-0	*Wagner*
25/8	Jedinstvo	a	0-1	
15/9	Sarajevo	a	2-2	*Bubalo S., Zovko*
19/9	Čelik	h	0-0	
23/9	Modriča	h	4-1	*Šilić, Ronniele, Topić, Karoglan*
29/9	Velež	a	1-1	*Šakić*
7/10	Slavija	h	3-1	*Bubalo S. 2, Šilić*
21/10	Travnik	a	5-1	*Bubalo S. 2, Karoglan, Ronielle, Célson*
28/10	Orašje	h	1-0	*Karoglan*
4/11	Posušje	h	1-2	*Wagner*
10/11	Žepče	a	3-0	*Bubalo S., Karoglan, Zelenika*
14/11	Željezničar	h	2-1	*Zelenika, Karoglan*
24/11	Leotar	a	2-1	*Karoglan, Wagner*

2008

2/3	Zrinjski	a	1-2	*Bubalo S.*
9/3	Sloboda	h	2-0	*Bubalo S., Wagner*
15/3	Laktaši	a	0-2	
22/3	Jedinstvo	h	2-1	Bubalo S., Karoglan (p)
29/3	Čelik	a	2-3	Wagner, Šilić
2/4	Sarajevo	h	1-0	Šilić
5/4	Modriča	a	1-2	Božić
13/4	Velež	h	2-0	Karoglan (p), Šilić
20/4	Slavija	a	2-0	Karoglan, Bubalo S.
26/4	Travnik	h	1-0	Wagner
3/5	Orašje	a	0-2	
11/5	Posušje	a	0-1	
17/5	Žepče	h	1-0	Karoglan
24/5	Željezničar	a	1-2	Wagner
31/5	Leotar	h	2-0	Ricardo, Célson

me	Nat	Pos	Aps	(s)	Gls
ip BARIŠIĆ		M	11		
an BANDOVIĆ		G	6	(1)	
nislav BOŽIĆ	CRO	M	13	(5)	1
vko BREKALO		M		(1)	
n BUBALO		D		(2)	
nko BUBALO		A	26	(3)	10
.SON Borges Jesus	BRA	A	9	(12)	2
rko HANNICH	CRO	M	10	(6)	
rko JURIĆ	CRO	M	27	(1)	
slav KAROGLAN	CRO	A	29		10
ibor KOŽUL		M	4	(2)	
nijel KOŽUL		M	1	(6)	
m KVESIĆ		M	3	(2)	
e Nasimento MARCIANO		M	23	(2)	
nijel NJITRAJ	CRO	M	1	(4)	
ter da Costa RICARDO		D	23	(2)	1
NIELLE Faria Gomes	BRA	M	27	(1)	3
njo ŠAKIĆ		M	5	(6)	1
ibor ŠILIĆ		M	27		5
tonio SOLDO		G		(1)	
ip TOPIĆ		M	20	(1)	1
dimir VASILJ		G	24		
n ZOVKO		M		(11)	1
dimir VIDIĆ		D	14		
rko ZELENIKA	CRO	A	8		2
GNER Santos Lago	BRA	M	19	(3)	7

FK SLAVIJA SARAJEVO

ach - Milomir Odović; (20/8/07) Zoran Erbez; (10/9/07) Dušan Jevrić; (3/4/08) Zoran Erbez

Founded - 1908

07				
	Laktaši	h	0-0	
'8	Jedinstvo	a	1-3	*Lazić*
'8	Čelik	h	0-1	
'8	Sarajevo	a	1-1	*Spalević*
	Modriča	h	1-0	*Vuksanović (p)*
'9	Velež	a	0-4	
'9	Orašje	h	3-2	*Vuksanović, Spalević 2*
'9	Travnik	h	4-0	*Vuksanović (p), Lazić, Muminović, Spalević*
0	Široki Brijeg	a	1-3	*Radovanović*
'10	Posušje	h	2-0	*Spalević 2*
'10	Žepče	a	1-0	*Vuksanović*
1	Željezničar	h	3-0	*Vuksanović (p), Spalević (p), Muminović*
'11	Leotar	a	3-4	*Spalević 2, Vitković*
'11	Zrinjski	h	2-0	*Vuksanović, Regoje*
'11	Sloboda	a	0-2	
08				
	Laktaši	a	1-2	*Spalević (p)*
	Jedinstvo	h	2-1	*Kokot, Ščepanović*
/3	Čelik	a	0-2	
/3	Sarajevo	h	1-0	*Spalević*
'3	Modriča	a	0-1	
	Velež	h	2-1	*Kokot 2*
	Orašje	a	1-2	*Spalević*
/4	Travnik	a	1-0	*Kokot*
/4	Široki Brijeg	h	0-2	
/4	Posušje	a	0-3	
	Žepče	h	2-1	*Gavarić, Spalević (p)*
/4	Željezničar	a	0-4	
/4	Leotar	h	4-2	*Kokot, Vuksanović, Spalević 2 (1p)*
/5	Zrinjski	a	0-2	
/5	Sloboda	h	3-1	*Spalević 3 (1p)*

Name	Nat	Pos	Aps	(s)	Gls
Branislav ARSENIJEVIĆ	SRB	D	28		
Vukašin BENOVIĆ		M	14	(4)	
Dragan BJELICA		D	16		
Ognjen DAMJANOVIČ		D		(3)	
Ratko DUJKOVIĆ		G	22		
Stefan GAVARIĆ		A	12	(2)	1
Bojan JAMINA		M	8	(12)	
Ivan JEŠIĆ		A	3	(1)	
Vlastimir JOVANOVIĆ		D	18	(4)	
Zoran KOKOT		A	13		5
Aleksandar KOSORIĆ		A	13	(5)	
Nemanja KNEŽEVIĆ		M		(4)	
Levan KUTALIA	GEO	M		(4)	
Dragiša LAZIĆ		M	11	(8)	2
Mladen LUČIĆ		G	2		
Vladimir MARIĆ		G	5		
Vladimir MIĆEVIĆ		D	1	(4)	
Dejan MILJKOVIĆ	SRB	M	2	(3)	
Milan MUMINOVIĆ		M	21	(1)	2
Predrag PAPAZ		M	9	(5)	
Igor RADOVANOVIĆ		A	3	(4)	1
Bojan REGOJE		D	27		1
Vučina ŠĆEPANOVIĆ		A	3	(6)	1
Nemanja ŠEŠLIJA		M	3	(9)	
Goran SIMIĆ		M	25	(3)	
Darko SPALEVIĆ	SRB	A	27		18
Ivan STANKOVIĆ	SRB	M	16	(1)	
Srdjan VITKOVIĆ		M	1	(2)	1
Stefan TOMOVIĆ		G	1	(1)	
Sretko VUKSANOVIĆ		M	26	(1)	7

FK SLOBODA TUZLA

Coach - Sakib Malkočević

Founded - 1919

2007				
4/8	Travnik	a	1-2	*Divković*
11/8	Široki Brijeg	h	3-0	*Tosunović, Kuduzović, Zoletić*
19/8	Posušje	a	1-4	*Tosunović*
25/8	Žepče	h	3-0	*Okanović, Tosunović, Kasapović*
1/9	Željezničar	a	0-4	
15/9	Leotar	h	2-0	*Zoletić, Huseinović*
23/9	Zrinjski	a	0-0	
29/9	Orašje	a	2-2	*Tosunović, Okanović*
7/10	Laktaši	h	1-0	*Mikelini*
20/10	Jedinstvo	a	1-2	*Ahmetović*
27/10	Čelik	h	2-0	*Prodanović, Tosunović*
3/11	Sarajevo	a	1-2	*Prodanović*
10/11	Modriča	h	3-0	*Kuduzović, Kasapović, Huseinović*
14/11	Velež	a	0-2	
24/11	Slavija	h	2-0	*Okanović (p), Tosunović*
2008				
1/3	Travnik	h	2-0	*Huseinović (p), Babić*
9/3	Široki Brijeg	a	0-2	
15/3	Posušje	h	4-2	*Čejvanović K., Kuduzović, Osmanhodžić 2*
22/3	Žepče	a	2-1	*Huseinović, Kuduzović*
29/3	Željezničar	h	2-1	*Babić, Osmanhodžić (p)*
2/4	Leotar	a	0-2	
5/4	Zrinjski	h	1-2	*Osmanhodžić (p)*
13/4	Orašje	h	1-0	*Huseinović*
19/4	Laktaši	a	0-2	
26/4	Jedinstvo	h	1-0	*Mešić*
3/5	Čelik	a	0-1	
10/5	Sarajevo	h	1-0	*Tosunović*

17/5	Modriča	a	2-3	*Sarajlić, Okanović*
24/5	Velež	h	5-1	*Mešić 2, Tosunović, Omić, Zoletić*
31/5	Slavija	a	1-3	*Kasapović*

Name	Nat	Pos	Aps	(s)	Gls
Mersudin AHMETOVIĆ		D	4	(7)	1
Asmir AVDUKIĆ		G	4		
Ivica BABIĆ		M	23		2
Almir BEKIĆ		A	1	(3)	
Semir BOROGOVAC		M		(1)	
Admir BRĐANOVIĆ		A	2	(1)	
Musa CAKIĆ		M		(2)	
Mirza ČEJVANOVIĆ		D	2	(2)	
Kenan ČEJVANOVIĆ		D	25		1
Gradimir CRNOGORAC		D	1		
Denis DIVKOVIĆ		M	7	(8)	1
Alimir HALILOVIĆ		M		(3)	
Said HUSEINOVIĆ		A	25		5
Besim IBRIČIĆ		M		(5)	
Adnan JAHIĆ		M	25	(2)	
Bojan JOVIĆ		G	23		
Emir KASAPOVIĆ		M	15	(10)	3
Samir KUDUZOVIĆ		D	14	(4)	4
Mario LAMEŠIĆ		M	11	(2)	
Tarik OKANOVIĆ		A	7	(13)	4
Muhamed OMIĆ		M	13	(6)	1
Adnan OSMANHODŽIĆ		M	10	(3)	4
Benjamin RAHMANOVIĆ		M		(1)	
Almir MEDIĆ		G	3		
Mirza MEŠIĆ		A	7	(7)	3
Nikola MIKELINI		D	23		1
Ilija PRODANOVIĆ		D	21		2
Adnan SARAJLIĆ		M	11	(2)	1
Damir TOSUNOVIĆ		A	23	(4)	8
Darko VOJVODIĆ		M	4	(3)	
Muamer ZOLETIĆ		D	26	(1)	3

NK TRAVNIK

Coach - Kemal Hafizović; (23/10/07) Mirza Golubica; (20/4/08) Nedžad Selimović

Founded - 1922

2007

4/8	Sloboda	h	2-1	*Dudić, Derviši*
11/8	Laktaši	a	1-3	*Derviši*
18/8	Jedinstvo	h	2-0	*Dudić, Terzić*
25/8	Čelik	a	0-0	
2/9	Sarajevo	h	1-0	*Pranjković*
15/9	Modriča	a	1-6	*Pranjković*
22/9	Velež	h	2-0	*Dudić, Stupac*
30/9	Slavija	a	0-4	
7/10	Orašje	h	1-0	*Bučinski*
21/10	Široki Brijeg	h	1-5	*Dudić*
28/10	Posušje	a	0-1	
3/11	Žepče	h	4-1	*Varupa E., Dudić 2, Hrustanović*
10/11	Željezničar	a	0-1	
14/11	Leotar	h	4-1	*Varupa E. 2 (1p), Hrustanović, Nemeljaković*
24/11	Zrinjski	a	1-1	*Nemeljaković*

2008

1/3	Sloboda	a	0-2	
9/3	Laktaši	h	5-1	*Dudić 2, Pranjković, Hrustanović, Varupa E. (p)*
15/3	Jedinstvo	a	0-1	
22/3	Čelik	h	0-0	
29/3	Sarajevo	a	0-1	
2/4	Modriča	h	1-0	*Varupa E. (p)*
5/4	Velež	a	1-2	*Ćurić*
12/4	Slavija	h	0-1	
19/4	Orašje	a	0-2	
26/4	Široki Brijeg	a	0-1	
3/5	Posušje	h	2-0	*Dudić 2*
11/5	Žepče	a	3-2	*Dudić 2, Pranjković*
17/5	Željezničar	h	1-0	*Šiljak*
24/5	Leotar	a	0-1	
31/5	Zrinjski	h	2-1	*Dudić, Varupa E.*

Name	Nat	Pos	Aps	(s)	Gls
Stjepan BADROV		M	9	(3)	
Nedžad BEGIĆ		M		(1)	
Luka BILOBRK		G	6		
Ekrem BRADARIĆ		D	28		
Mihajlo BUČINSKI		D	7	(4)	1
Anel ĆURIĆ		M	2	(12)	1
Alen DELIĆ		G	1		
Alen DERVIŠI		A	5	(5)	2
Velimir DOLIĆ		A	1	(2)	
Feđa DUDIĆ		A	28		13
Almir HELVIDA		M	6	(5)	
Aldin HODŽIĆ		M	7	(9)	
Rusmir HRUSTANOVIĆ		M	14	(12)	3
Kenan NEMELJAKOVIĆ		M	20	(6)	2
Adis NURKOVIĆ		G	23		
Sanid MUJAKIĆ		M	2	(9)	
Dario PRANJKOVIĆ		M	26	(1)	4
Nihad RIBIĆ		M	22		
Midhat SARAJČIĆ		D	25		
Jeton SEFERI		M	1	(5)	
Ekrem ŠILJAK		D	24		1
Aldin SIVAC		M		(1)	
Arnel STUPAC		M	10	(5)	1
Simbad TERZIĆ		D	27	(1)	1
Boris VAREŠKOVIČ		M		(3)	
Elvedin VARUPA		D	27		6
Nermin VARUPA		M		(1)	
Zdravko VUKOJA		D		(1)	
Ivan ZEKO		M	9		

FK VELEŽ

Coach - Anel Karabeg

Founded - 1922

MAJOR HONOURS: Yugoslav Cup – (2) 1981, 1986.

2007

4/8	Jedinstvo	h	2-1	*Bajić, Džafić*
11/8	Čelik	a	0-2	
18/8	Sarajevo	h	2-2	*Obad, Jugo*
25/8	Modriča	a	1-3	*Kajtaz (p)*
1/9	Orašje	h	3-1	*Kajtaz (p), Serdarević, Jugo*
15/9	Slavija	h	4-0	*Obad, Serdarević, Gubeljić, Delalić*
22/9	Travnik	a	0-2	
29/9	Široki Brijeg	h	1-1	*Serdarević*
7/10	Posušje	a	0-1	
20/10	Žepče	h	1-0	*og (Mirčeta)*
27/10	Željezničar	a	0-4	
3/11	Leotar	h	3-2	*Čolić, Delalić, Serdarević,*
11/11	Zrinjski	a	0-2	
14/11	Sloboda	h	2-0	*Čolić, Jugo*
24/11	Laktaši	a	2-3	*Čolić,Velagić*

2008

1/3	Jedinstvo	a	0-1	
9/3	Čelik	h	2-0	*Kajtaz (p), Obad*
15/3	Sarajevo	a	0-1	
23/3	Modriča	h	1-0	*Zaimović*

'3	Orašje	a	0-6	
	Slavija	a	1-2	*Ljeljak*
	Travnik	h	2-1	*Zaimović, Kajtaz (p)*
4	Široki Brijeg	a	0-2	
4	Posušje	h	2-0	*Conrad, Obad*
4	Žepče	a	3-1	*Drakul, Kodro, Obad*
	Željezničar	h	2-1	*Obad, Kajtaz (p)*
5	Leotar	a	1-2	*Ljeljak*
5	Zrinjski	h	1-0	*Škaljić Ar.*
5	Sloboda	a	1-5	*Obad*
5	Laktaši	h	2-0	*Ljeljak 2*

me	Nat	Pos	Aps	(s)	Gls
gan BABIĆ		G	2		
imir BAJIĆ		D	22	(1)	1
an BOBIĆ		G	1		
in ČAJDIN		M		(3)	
r ĆOLIĆ		D	24	(1)	3
sell Mark CONRAD	USA	A	1	(2)	1
el DELALIĆ		M	4	(12)	2
d DEMIĆ		M	2	(3)	
el DEMIĆ		M		(2)	
an DRAKUL		M	10	(5)	1
nan DURAKOVIĆ		D	1	(6)	
nir DŽAFIĆ		M	2	(10)	1
ko GUBELJIĆ		M	22		1
ir HADŽIĐULBIĆ		G	2		
ram HAMZIĆ		M	1	(1)	
em HODŽIĆ		D	11		
an KADRIĆ		D	7	(1)	
er JUGO		M	17		3
KAJAN		D		(6)	
nir KAJTAZ		M	21		5
stafa KODRO		M	28		1
n KOZICA		D		(2)	
s KURTANOVIĆ		G	25		
er LJELJAK		A	4	(3)	4
ijel MAJKIĆ		M	10		
MUSLI		D	7	(3)	
s OBAD		A	27		7
n PAJIĆ		M	1	(4)	
ir RAŠČIĆ		M	13	(6)	
r REMETIĆ		M	2	(2)	
džad SERDAREVIĆ		M	14		4
el ŠKALJIĆ		D	9	(2)	1
m ŠKALJIĆ		M	13		
mir VELAGIĆ		M	10	(4)	1
enan ZAIMOVIĆ		M	17	(1)	2
nir ZOLJ		M		(3)	

FK ŽELJEZNIČAR

Coach - Enver Hadžiabdić; (7/1/08) Simo Krunić

Founded - 1921

MAJOR HONOURS: Yugoslav League - (1) 1972; Bosnia-Herzegovina League - (3) 1998, 2001, 2002; Bosnia-Herzegovina Cup - (3) 2000, 2001, 2003.

07				
	Žepče	a	0-3	*(w/o; original result 0-1)*
'8	Orašje	a	0-1	
'8	Leotar	h	3-0	*Jahić 2, Vugdalić*
'8	Zrinjski	a	1-1	*Štilić*
	Sloboda	h	4-0	*Jahić, Dialiba, Dudo, Štilić*
'9	Laktaši	a	2-3	*Dialiba, Bešlija*
'9	Jedinstvo	h	6-0	*Bekrić, Jahić 3, Dialiba 2*
'9	Čelik	a	0-3	
0	Sarajevo	h	0-0	
'10	Modriča	a	0-1	
'10	Velež	h	4-0	*Jahić 2, Dialiba 2*
4/11	Slavija	a	0-3	
10/11	Travnik	h	1-0	*Jahić*
14/11	Široki Brijeg	a	1-2	*Jahić*
24/11	Posušje	h	4-2	*Jahić 2 (1p), Dudo, Kamber*
2008				
1/3	Žepče	h	1-0	*Štilić*
9/3	Orašje	h	2-1	*Rovčanin, Kuduzović*
15/3	Leotar	a	0-1	
22/3	Zrinjski	h	2-1	*Pelak 2 (2p)*
29/3	Sloboda	a	1-2	*Cocalić*
2/4	Laktaši	h	1-0	*Rovčanin*
5/4	Jedinstvo	a	0-1	
13/4	Čelik	h	3-2	*Cocalić, Dialiba, Pelak*
19/4	Sarajevo	a	0-0	
26/4	Modriča	h	4-1	*Štilić 2, Rovčanin, Dialiba*
3/5	Velež	a	1-2	*Štilić*
10/5	Slavija	h	4-0	*Štilić 3, Dialiba*
17/5	Travnik	a	0-1	
24/5	Široki Brijeg	h	2-1	*Vugdalić, Štilić*
31/5	Posušje	a	0-3	

Name	Nat	Pos	Aps	(s)	Gls
Admir AVDIĆ		A	1		
Zdenko BAOTIĆ		G	10		
Samir BEKRIĆ		M	16	(9)	1
Haris BEŠLIJA		A	2	(7)	1
Elmedin BRANKOVIĆ		M	1	(2)	
Edin COCALIĆ		M	23		2
Boubacar DIALIBA	SEN	A	28		9
Edin DUDO		M	12	(3)	2
Romeo FILIPOVIĆ	GER	M	3	(1)	
Jure GUVO	CRO	A	2	(1)	
Sanel JAHIĆ		M	14		12
Adis JAHOVIĆ		M	2		
Nermin JAMAK		M	9	(5)	
Omer JOLDIĆ		D	18	(6)	
Marjan JUGOVIĆ	SRB	A	1	(1)	
Kerim KADRIĆ		M	2		
Đorđe KAMBER	SRB	D	13	(2)	1
Semir KERLA		D	8		
Elmir KUDUZOVIĆ		M	15	(1)	1
Dino MUHAREMOVIĆ		D	15	(3)	
Edis MULALIĆ		D	17	(1)	
Esmir OMEROVIĆ		M		(3)	
Albin PELAK		M	11		3
Haris REDŽEPI		A	3	(7)	
Rasim REIZ		A	2	(2)	
Damir ROVČANIN	SRB	A	10	(1)	3
Džemal SADIKOVIĆ		M	5	(3)	
Salem SALKIĆ		M	3		
Ibrahim ŠEHIĆ		G	20		
Amir SPAHIĆ		D	7	(2)	
Srđan STANIĆ		A	2	(11)	
Semir ŠTILIĆ		A	24	(1)	10
Muamer SVRAKA		M		(6)	
Muamer VUGDALIĆ	SVN	D	24		2
Neal WOOD	ENG	M	7	(2)	

NK ŽEPČE

Coach - Omer Kopić; (5/9/07) Milan Jovin; (5/11/07) Pavle Skočibušić; (31/12/07) Ilija Šainović

Founded - 1919

2007				
5/8	Željezničar	h	3-0	*(w/o; original result 1-0 Imamović)*
11/8	Leotar	a	0-2	
21/8	Zrinjski	h	1-4	*Rizvanović*
25/8	Sloboda	a	0-3	

2/9	Laktaši	h	1-1	*Imamović*
15/9	Jedinstvo	a	0-2	
23/9	Čelik	h	0-2	
29/9	Sarajevo	a	0-3	
9/10	Modriča	h	1-3	*Imamović*
20/10	Velež	a	0-1	
28/10	Slavija	h	0-1	
3/11	Travnik	a	1-4	*Mirčeta*
10/11	Široki Brijeg	h	0-3	
14/11	Posušje	a	1-3	*Duspara P.*
25/11	Orašje	h	5-4	*Duspara P. 3, Idrizović, Lučić*
2008				
1/3	Željezničar	a	0-1	
9/3	Leotar	h	0-2	
15/3	Zrinjski	a	1-2	*Rizvanović*
22/3	Sloboda	h	1-2	*Dizdarević*
29/3	Laktaši	a	0-2	
2/4	Jedinstvo	h	0-1	
5/4	Čelik	a	1-4	*Dizdarević*
13/4	Sarajevo	h	1-3	*Đananović*
19/4	Modriča	a	2-6	*Duspara P., Lučić*
26/4	Velež	h	1-3	*Lučić*
4/5	Slavija	a	1-2	*Dizdarević*
11/5	Travnik	h	2-3	*Tomić, Rizvanović*
17/5	Široki Brijeg	a	0-1	
24/5	Posušje	h	2-3	*Tomić, Rizvanović*
31/5	Orašje	a	0-2	

Name	Nat	Pos	Aps	(s)	Gls
Elmedin BRANKOVIĆ		M	5	(7)	
Dino DIZDAREVIĆ		M	4	(10)	3
Eldar ĐANANOVIĆ		M	7	(6)	1
Josip DUSPARA		M	7	(3)	
Petar DUSPARA		A	14	(8)	5
Anel FAKIĆ		D		(2)	
Mirza HASANOVIĆ		M	3	(5)	
Ferid IDRIZOVIĆ		D	11		1
Vahidin IMAMOVIĆ		A	14		3
Aladin ISAKOVIĆ		M	19	(1)	
Marko JEFTIĆ		D	15		
Josip JURIĆ		G		(1)	
Dženan KRAJIŠNIK		D	12		
Besim KRDŽALIĆ		D	27		
Senid KULAŠ		D	11		
Aner LJELJAK		A	5		
Alen LJEVAKOVIĆ		M	6	(2)	
Vlado LUČIĆ		M	9	(1)	3
Zumbul MAHALBAŠIĆ		M	13	(1)	
Josip MARKOVIĆ		A		(1)	
Eldin MAŠIĆ		M	17	(1)	
Boris MILEKIĆ		D	13	(1)	
Igor MIRČETA		D	8		1
Ermin ORUČ		D	7	(2)	
Adnan PAŠIĆ		G	3	(2)	
Vladimir RAKIĆ		M	1	(4)	
Igor RAŠIĆ		D		(1)	
Mirza RIZVANOVIĆ		A	28	(1)	4
Amar ŠABANOVIĆ		M	1	(3)	
Džemal SADIKOVIĆ		M	7	(2)	
Danijel SAVIĆ		M	10	(3)	
Zoran VUKOVIĆ		D	10		
Dejan TOMIĆ		M	9	(2)	2
Nikola TROGRLIĆ		G	27		
Elvis ŽIGONJA		D	7	(2)	

HŠK ZRINJSKI

Coach - Blaž Slišković; (20/10/07) Dragan Jović

Founded - 1912

MAJOR HONOURS: Bosnia-Herzegovina League – (1) 2005; Bosnia-Herzegovina Cup - (1) 2008.

2007				
5/8	Široki Brijeg	a	0-1	
12/8	Posušje	h	1-0	*Suton*
21/8	Žepče	a	4-1	*Selimović, Joldić (p), Zadro, Matko*
26/8	Željezničar	h	1-1	*Karadža*
4/9	Leotar	a	2-0	*Rajović, Ivanković*
15/9	Orašje	a	0-0	
23/9	Sloboda	h	0-0	
29/9	Laktaši	a	2-3	*Ivanković, Joldić*
7/10	Jedinstvo	h	4-1	*Nikolić 2, Ivanković, Đ*
20/10	Čelik	a	0-1	
28/10	Sarajevo	h	4-0	*Nikolić, Rajović, Selimović, Žižović*
3/11	Modriča	a	1-2	*Džidić D.*
11/11	Velež	h	2-0	*Žižović, Matko*
14/11	Slavija	a	0-2	
24/11	Travnik	h	1-1	*Matko*
2008				
2/3	Široki Brijeg	h	2-1	*Ivanković, Peraica*
9/3	Posušje	a	0-1	
15/3	Žepče	h	2-1	*Matko, Nikolić*
22/3	Željezničar	a	1-2	*Đurić*
29/3	Leotar	h	2-1	*Ivanković 2 (1p)*
2/4	Orašje	h	2-0	*Aničić, Matko*
5/4	Sloboda	a	2-1	*Selimović, Matko*
13/4	Laktaši	h	2-0	*Ivanković, Žižović (p)*
19/4	Jedinstvo	a	1-2	*Ivanković*
26/4	Čelik	h	3-1	*Karadža, Peraica, Đu*
4/5	Sarajevo	a	0-1	
10/5	Modriča	h	4-0	*Selimović, Žižović, Matk*
17/5	Velež	a	0-1	
24/5	Slavija	h	2-0	*Žižović, Matko*
31/5	Travnik	a	1-2	*Zadro*

Name	Nat	Pos	Aps	(s)	Gls
Marin ANIČIĆ		M	3	(1)	1
Marko BAŠIĆ		M	1		
Ivan BUBALO		A	2	(1)	
Semir ĆILIĆ		M	1		
Mateo ĆUBELA		M	1		
Danijel ĆULUM		M	1		
Saša DRAGIČEVIĆ		M		(1)	
Velibor ĐURIĆ		M	17	(4)	3
Damir DŽIDIĆ		M	12		1
Ivica DŽIDIĆ		D	16		
Toni GAGRO		D	1		
Mario IVANKOVIĆ		M	21	(3)	8
Admir JOLDIĆ		A	3	(5)	2
Goran JURIĆ		M	4	(2)	
Alvin KARADŽA		M	25		2
Sandro KREZIĆ		D	1	(1)	
Davor LANDEKA		D	24		
Nikola MARIĆ		G	8		
Matija MATKO	CRO	A	18	(5)	9
Romeo MITROVIĆ		G	22	(1)	
Staniša NIKOLIĆ		D	29		4
Boško PERAICA		M	6	(5)	2
Toni PEZO	CRO	M	13	(5)	
Zoran RAJOVIĆ	CRO	A	12	(5)	2
Oliver ŠAKOTA		M		(1)	
Vernes SELIMOVIĆ		M	18	(7)	4
Toni SLIŠKOVIĆ		A		(1)	
Sulejman SMAJIĆ		M	10	(6)	
Toni ŠUNJIĆ		M	4	(3)	
Josip SUTON		M	7	(8)	1
Vlado ZADRO		A	8	(10)	2
Kasim ZAHIROVIĆ		D		(1)	
Mladen ŽIŽOVIĆ		M	24	(3)	5
Igor ŽURŽINOV	SRB	A	17	(4)	
Deni VLAHO		M	1		

PROMOTED CLUBS

NK ZVIJEZDA GRADAČAC

Coach - Ratko Ninković

Founded – 1922

FK BORAC BANJA LUKA

Coach - Stanislav Karasi; (1/9/07) Josip Pelc; (16/9/07) Milomir Odović

Founded - 1926

MAJOR HONOURS: Yugoslav Cup - (1) 1988.

:OND LEVEL FINAL TABLES 2007/08

iga FBiH	Pld	W	D	L	F	A	Pts
K Zvijezda Gradačac	30	21	6	3	56	11	69
ƆŠK Gabela	30	16	1	13	44	35	49
< Rudar Kakanj	30	14	4	12	44	39	46
K Bratstvo Gračanica	30	13	6	11	38	32	45
< Budućnost Banovići	30	13	5	12	40	30	44
< Iskra Bugojno	30	13	5	12	40	33	44
< Troglav Livno	30	13	5	12	36	31	44
< SAŠK Napredak Sarajevo	30	13	5	12	36	31	44
< Ozren Semizovac	30	13	5	12	38	37	44
< Bosna Visoko	30	13	4	13	41	39	43
< Drinovci	30	13	4	13	30	38	43
< Radnički Lukavac	30	13	4	13	34	43	43
< Igman Konjic	30	11	8	11	39	42	41
< Gradina Srebrenik	30	8	5	17	27	50	29
< Kreševo	30	7	7	16	28	49	28
< Brotnjo Čitluk	30	8	2	20	31	62	26

iga RS	Pld	W	D	L	F	A	Pts
< Borac Banja Luka	30	21	4	5	62	31	67
< Sloga Doboj	30	16	5	9	60	40	53
< Kozara Bos. Gradiška	30	14	10	6	43	25	52
< Sloboda Bos. Novi	30	15	5	10	43	29	50
< Famos Vojkovići	30	14	6	10	48	38	48
< Ljubić Prnjavor	30	14	4	12	43	35	46
< Sutjeska Foča	30	13	7	10	39	32	46
< Drina Zvornik	30	12	9	9	43	32	45
< Proleter Teslić	30	13	3	14	48	42	42
< Drina Višegrad	30	13	2	15	38	48	41
< Mladost Gacko	30	11	7	12	23	36	40
;K Banja Luka	30	10	8	12	42	47	38
< Radnik Bijeljina	30	10	7	13	39	36	37
< Borac Bos. Šamac	30	8	8	14	30	44	32
< Rudar Ugljevik	30	5	9	16	22	47	24
< Jedinstvo Crknice	30	1	6	23	14	75	7

dinstvo Crkvine - 2 pts deducted

OMESTIC CUP 2007/8

KUP BOSNE I HERCEGOVINE

ALS

7)

Gračanica 2, Rudar Kakanj 2 *(4-3 on pens)*

, Podgmeč Sanski Most 0

onjic 1, Velež Mostar 2

Tuzla 1, Budućnost Banovići 0

Brotnjo Čitluk 6, Sloga Doboj 0

Željezničar 5, Kolina Ustikolina 0

Modriča 5, Troglav Livno 0

Drina HE Višegrad 0, Zrinjski 3

Radnik Hadžići 1, Sarajevo 5

Široki Brijeg 1, Žepče 0

Posušje 5, Radnik Bijeljina 0

Travnik 2, Ljubić Prnjavor 1

Borac Bosanski Šamac 0, Slavija 1

Leotar 4, Drinovci 1

Čelik 3, Jedinstvo Bihać 0

(30/10/07)

Borac Banja Luka 0, Lakataši 2

1/8 FINALS

(7/11/07 & 27/11/07)

Travnik v Leotar 0-0; 1-2 *(1-2)*

(7/11/07 & 28/11/07)

Bratstvo v Široki Brijeg 0-1; 1-3 *(1-4)*

Posušje v Čelik 2-0; 2-0 (4-0)

Sarajevo v Velež 1-1; 2-2 *(3-3; Sarajevo on away goals)*

Modriča Maxima v Željezničar 3-3; 2-3 *(5-6)*

Brotnjo v Laktaši 2-2; 1-4 *(3-6)*

Orašje v Sloboda 0-0; 1-5 *(1-5)*

Slavija v Zrinjski 2-3; 0-1 *(2-4)*

QUARTER-FINALS

(5/3/08 & 19/3/08)

Posušje 1 *(Krstanović 35)*, Laktaši 0

Laktaši 1 *(Studen 68)*, Posušje 3 *(Kordić 47, Krstanović 70, Ivanković 74)*

(Posušje 4-1)

Sloboda 6 *(Čejvanović K. 45, 45+2, Kasapović 57, Kuduzović 74, Osmanhodžić 86, Tosunović 89)*, Leotar 1 *(Dreč 32)*

Leotar 1 *(Dinčić 30)*, Sloboda 0

(Sloboda 6-2)

Zrinjski 1 *(Peraica 26)*, Široki Brijeg 0

Široki Brijeg 1 *(Bubalo S. 52)*, Zrinjski 0

(1-1; Zrinjski 3-2 on pens)

(12/3/08 & 19/3/08)

Željezničar 3 *(Pelak 21, Cocalić 45, Muharemović 71)*, Sarajevo 1 *(Turković 8)*

Sarajevo 4 *(Turković 18, 81, Hadžić 33, Handžić 70)*, Željezničar 2 *(Dialiba 16, Rovčanin 50)*

(5-5; Željezničar on away goals)

SEMI-FINALS

(9/4/08 & 23/4/08)

Željezničar 1 *(Pelak 75)*, Sloboda 1 *(Huseinović 55)*

Sloboda 1 *(Tosunović 38)*, Željezničar 0

(Sloboda 2-1)

Zrinjski 4 *(Nikolić 30, 40, 74, Matko 74)*, Posušje 0

Posušje 0, Zrinjski 2 *(Rajović 61, Peraica 84)*,

(Zrinjski 6-0)

FINALS

(14/5/08)

Tušanj stadium, Tuzla

FK SLOBODA TUZLA 2 *(Huseinović 13, Kasapović 90p)*

HŠK ZRINJSKI 1 *(Prodanović 66og)*

Referee – *Skakić*

SLOBODA – *Jović, Čejvanović K., Omić, Mikelini, Prodanović, Jahić, Lamešić (Kuduzović 85), Tosunović, Huseinović, Okanović (Brđanović 65), Osmanhodžić (Kasapović 50).*

ZRINJSKI – *Mitrović, Džidić I., Nikolić, Landeka, Matko (Peraica 90), Selimović (Smajić 54), Ivanković, Pezo, Žižović, Karadža, Đurić.*

(4/6/08)

Bijeli Brijeg stadium, Mostar

HŠK ZRINJSKI 2 *(Dzidic I. 3, Landeka 67)*

FK SLOBODA TUZLA 1 *(Tosunović 48)*

Referee – *Mrković*

ZRINJSKI – *Mitrović, Džidić I. (Šunjić 84), Nikolić, Landeka, Matko, Selimović (Smajić 53), Ivanković, Pezo (Peraica 54), Žižović, Karadža, Đurić.*

SLOBODA – *Jurić, Prodanović, Mikelini, Čejvanović K., Babić (Brđanović 90), Okanović (Osmanhodžić 81), Zoletić, Jahić, Kasapović (Lamešić 57), Tosunović, Huseinović.*

(3-3; ZRINJSKI 4-1 on pens)

Painful postscript for champions CSKA

The 2007/08 season in Bulgaria was dominated by financial problems for the country's top two clubs, PFC CSKA Sofia and PFC Levski Sofia.

It should have been one of the most memorable campaigns in CSKA's history. Bulgaria's most successful club won the league for a record-extending 31st time and did so in some style, becoming the first team to go through a 30-match campaign undefeated. Under the guidance of club legend Stoicho Mladenov, the Sofia Reds stormed to the summit of the A PFG table after five matches and never looked back. With a run of eleven straight wins in the autumn, CSKA created a gap that was never going to be breached. They gradually extended their lead and by the end of the season had built up a 16-point cushion over runners-up Levski.

Out of Europe

But the title celebrations, which took place on the club's 60th anniversary, were to have a painful sting in the tail when it emerged that CSKA were unable to fulfil the licensing criteria required for them to compete both domestically and in Europe in 2008/09. Although

CSKA Sofia's top scorer Nei (right) celebrates a goal for the Bulgarian champions

a domestic licence was subsequently obtained, there was no way back into Europe, which meant that the prized possession of a place in the second qualifying round of the UEFA Champions League had not only been lost but, worse still, passed over to bitter rivals Levski. Just to add to the woe, the European exclusio led to the exodus of several of CSKA's most prominen players, among them Bugarian internationals Velizar Dimitrov and Alexander Tunchev, goalkeeper Ivailo Petrov and Romanian UEFA EURO 2008™ participant Florentin Petre.

Petre, the former FC Dinamo 1948 Bucureşti right-winger, scored eleven goals in the title win, just three fewer than CSKA's leading marksman Nei. Two of the Brazilian striker's goals, plus one from Petre, came in t 3-1 win at PFC Botev Plovdiv that sealed CSKA's trium on the last day of April with three games to spare.

There was heavy irony in the fact that Levski should b the beneficiaries of CSKA's agony because they had major cashflow problems of their own. The Blues, so unstoppable in 2006/07, when they won the Bulgaria double and reached the group phase of the UEFA Champions League, were forced to dispense with several of their star players as early as the winter brea with influential Frenchman Cédric Bardon leaving for Bnei Yehuda Tel-Aviv FC and being followed through the exit door by the Bulgarian international trio of Elin Topuzakov, Dimitar Telkiyski and 2006/07 Player of the Year Hristo Yovov. Levski's dreams of another season rubbing shoulders with Europe's elite lasted only as long as the second qualifying round when they were humiliatingly knocked out by Finnish champions Tampere United, losing both legs 1-0. All hopes of a successful title defence disappeared when they failed win any of their last four matches going into the winte shutdown, particularly as one of them was a 1-0 hom defeat by CSKA. Furthermore, they surrendered their hold on the Bulgarian Cup when they lost on penaltie in the quarter-final to PFC Litex Lovech, the team they had defeated with an extra-time penalty from Bardon the previous season's final.

oilov pays price

'ski coach Stanimir Stoilov did not see out the son, paying the price for the club's fall from grace t before the capital derby against CSKA on 10 May. was replaced by Velislav Vutov, who, as events uld unfold, had the honour of taking Levski into UEFA Champions League qualifiers after only two mes in charge. The knock-on effect of CSKA's opean exclusion also benefited the two Black Sea bs, fifth-placed PFC Cherno More Varna earning omotion' to the UEFA Cup while sixth-placed PFC ernomorets Burgas took their place in the UEFA ertoto Cup.

th no Sofia club reaching the last four of the garian Cup for the first time since 1962, the way s clear for Litex, the country's leading provincial b, to take the trophy for the third time in eight rs. The competition brought particular redemption Litex defender Stanislav Manolev. The man who d fatally conceded the extra-time penalty to Levski he 2007 showdown not only got his team to the al again with two late goals against PFC Botev vdiv but also proved to be his team's match-winner he Vassil Levski stadium, scoring the only goal of game with a 56th-minute header from Brazilian nger Wellington's free-kick. Litex had begun the son under the familiar figure of Ferario Spasov but oor start led to his replacement by Serbian tician Miodrag Ješić, who duly steered the club to glory and fourth place – a point behind PFC comotiv Sofia – before leaving for a new post in nania.

legation drama

ere was excitement a-plenty at the bottom of the A table. Although it became obvious early on that of the relegation places would be filled by PFC rek Dupnitza and PFC Vidima Rakovski, the battle avoid 14th place was intense and dramatic. PFC asitsa Petrich looked doomed after a 1-1 draw at rek in their penultimate game, but it transpired t their hosts had fielded an ineligible player and asitsa, after a successful appeal, were awarded a 3-vin. This left them three points behind PFC Beroe ra Zagora with a game to go. The only way for the m from Petrich to survive was to beat PFC Botev vdiv at home and hope that Beroe lost at comotiv Sofia. Sure enough, both results went their , and with Belasitsa having the superior head-to-ad record, it was Beroe who went down.

Dimitar Berbatov – more goals for Bulgaria than Hristo Stoichkov

Botev would surely have been in the thick of the relegation battle had it not been for the prolific goalscoring of their 23-year-old striker Georgi Hristov, who became the first Botev player to top the Bulgarian goal charts in 22 years (after Atanas Pashev in 1986) with his tally of 19 goals. His exploits did not go unnoticed, earning him a summer transfer to Levski.

Markov returns

Bulgaria's outside hopes of qualifying for UEFA EURO 2008™ were finally extinguished by a 2-0 defeat in the Netherlands and a 1-1 draw in Albania. Dimitar Penev, the veteran coach who had led the team to the semi-finals of the 1994 FIFA World Cup, predictably vacated the position after his short-term contract ended, with another former incumbent, Plamen Markov, being re-appointed for the 2010 World Cup campaign. Captain Dimitar Berbatov, who enjoyed another fine season in England with Tottenham Hotspur FC, scored four goals in Bulgaria's last four UEFA EURO 2008™ qualifiers to lift his cumulative tally to 39 and overtake the great Hristo Stoichkov as his country's second highest scorer. The classy centre-forward's next target is the all-time record of 48 set by Hristo Bonev.

BULGARIA

Bulgarski Futbolen Soyuz (BFS)

26 Tzar Ivan Assen II Street
BG-1124 Sofia
tel - +359 2 9426202
fax - +359 2 9426200
website - www.bfunion.bg
email - bfu@bfunion.bg
Year of Formation – 1923
President – Borislav Mihaylov
General Secretary – Borislav Popov
Press Officer – Borislav Konstantinov
Stadium - Vasil Levski National Stadium, Sofia (43,230)

INTERNATIONAL TOURNAMENT APPEARANCES
FIFA World Cup - (7) 1962, 1966, 1970, 19 1986 (2nd round), 1994 (4th), 1998. UEFA European Championship - (2) 1996, 200

TOP FIVE ALL-TIME CAPS
Borislav Mihailov (102); Hristo Bonev (9 Krasimir Balakov (92); Dimitar Penev (9 Hristo Stoichkov (83)

TOP FIVE ALL-TIME GOALS
Hristo Bonev (48); Dimitar Berbatov (39 Hristo Stoichkov (37); Emil Kostadinov (26); Ivan Kolev, Lyubomir Angelov & Petar Zhekov (25)

NATIONAL TEAM RESULTS 2007/08

22/8/07	Wales	H	Burgas	0-1	
8/9/07	Netherlands (ECQ)	A	Amsterdam	0-2	
12/9/07	Luxembourg (ECQ)	H	Sofia	3-0	Berbatov (27, 28), Petrov M. (54p)
17/10/07	Albania (ECQ)	A	Tirana	1-1	Berbatov (87)
17/11/07	Romania (ECQ)	H	Sofia	1-0	Dimitrov V. (6)
21/11/07	Slovenia (ECQ)	A	Celje	2-0	Georgiev (82), Berbatov (84)
6/2/08	Northern Ireland	A	Belfast	1-0	Evans (38og)
26/3/08	Finland	H	Sofia	2-1	Lazarov (49), Genchev (90)

NATIONAL TEAM APPEARANCES 2007/08

Coach – Dimitar PENEV /(12/1/08) Plamen MARKOV	12/7/45 11/9/57		Wal	NED	LUX	ALB	ROU	SVN	Nir	Fin	Caps
Dimitar IVANKOV	30/10/75	Kayserispor (TUR)	G46	G			G	G	s46	G46	52
Radostin KISHISHEV	30/7/74	Leicester (ENG)	D51	D	D	D					78
Alexander TUNCHEV	10/7/81	CSKA Sofia	D	D	D		D	D	D66	D	20
Igor TOMAŠIĆ	14/12/76	Levski	D	D	D	D	D	D	D	D	13
Lúcio WAGNER	15/6/76	Levski	D53	D79		D					13
Stilian PETROV	5/7/79	Aston Villa (ENG)	M	M	M60	M46	M	M46		M	78
Stanislav ANGELOV	12/4/78	Energie (GER)	M	M	M	M		D	M	M	17
Dimitar TELKIYSKI	5/5/77	Levski	M46	M68		M46	s83	s46			17
Hristo YOVOV	4/11/77	Levski	M66		s66	s72	M83	M75			29
Martin PETROV	15/1/79	Man. City (ENG)	M	M	M66	M	M90	M	M	M75	73
Georgi CHILIKOV	23/8/78	CSKA Sofia	A46								6
Georgi PETKOV	14/3/76	Levski	s46		G	G			G46	s46	11
Ivelin POPOV	26/10/87	Litex	s46	s59	M74	M72			s66		5
Velizar DIMITROV	13/4/79	CSKA Sofia	s46	s68	M		M	M		M	21

ATIONAL TEAM APPEARANCES 2007/08 (contd.)

			Wal	NED	LUX	ALB	ROU	SVN	Nir	Fin	Caps	Goals
‹dar YANKOV	29/3/84	Hannover (GER)	s51	s79	s60	s46					31	5
r ZANEV	18/10/85	Celta (ESP)	s53		D		D		s74		7	-
tan GENKOV	8//2/84	Dinamo Moskva (RUS)	s66								10	-
·gi PEEV	11/3/79	Amkar (RUS)		M59							47	-
itar BERBATOV	30/1/81	Tottenham (ENG)		A	A	A	A	A	A82	A85	64	39
:in KUSHEV	25/8/73	Amkar (RUS)			s74						1	-
ntin ILIEV	11/7/80	CSKA Sofia /Terek (RUS)				D				s56	13	-
oi GEORGIEV	21/12/81	Duisburg (GER)				s46	M	M	M	M65	25	2
ko MILANOV	15/7/84	Levski					D	D46	D	D46	5	-
vko LAZAROV	20/2/76	Slavia /Shinnik (RUS)					s90	s75	A66	s46	28	3
an TODOROV	27/7/81	CSKA Sofia						s46			5	1
il VENKOV	28/7/83	Litex							D74	D56	6	-
r YANCHEV	19/5/76	CSKA Sofia							M46		17	-
lai DIMITROV	15/10/87	Levski							s46		1	-
KARASLAVOV	8/6/80	Greuther Fürth (GER)							s66		10	-
i DOMOVCHIYSKI	5/10/86	Hertha (GER)							s82		4	-
islav GENCHEV	20/3/81	Litex								s65	1	1
·gi KAKALOV	18/7/84	Botev								s75	1	-
·gi SARMOV	7/9/85	Levski								s85	1	-

DOMESTIC LEAGUE 2007/08

FG FINAL TABLE

		Home					Away					Total					
	Pld	W	D	L	F	A	W	D	L	F	A	W	D	L	F	A	Pts
FC CSKA Sofia	30	13	2	0	31	5	11	4	0	22	6	24	6	0	53	11	78
FC Levski Sofia	30	12	0	3	37	10	7	5	3	19	9	19	5	6	56	19	62
FC Lokomotiv Sofia	30	9	3	3	26	15	7	6	2	21	13	16	9	5	47	28	57
FC Litex Lovech	30	10	5	0	32	9	6	3	6	19	17	16	8	6	51	26	56
FC Cherno More arna	30	9	4	2	21	8	4	5	6	18	20	13	9	8	39	28	48
FC Chernomorets urgas	30	10	3	2	19	9	3	5	7	20	23	13	8	9	39	32	47
FC Slavia Sofia	30	10	4	1	25	7	3	4	8	13	21	13	8	9	38	28	47
FC Pirin 1922	30	8	3	4	19	13	5	4	6	14	16	13	7	10	33	29	46
FC Lokomotiv lovdiv 1936	30	9	4	2	23	8	3	3	9	14	20	12	7	11	37	28	43
FC Vihren Sandanski	30	6	4	5	18	14	3	2	10	8	15	9	6	15	26	29	33
FC Spartak Varna	30	6	4	5	14	12	2	3	10	7	22	8	7	15	21	34	31
FC Botev Plovdiv	30	7	4	4	24	13	1	2	12	12	41	8	6	16	36	54	30
FC Belasitsa Petrich	30	6	3	6	16	19	1	2	12	7	24	7	5	18	23	43	26
FC Beroe Stara agora	30	5	7	3	19	15	1	1	13	4	24	6	8	16	23	39	26
FC Vidima Rakovski	30	4	4	7	11	19	0	2	13	6	42	4	6	20	17	61	18
FC Marek Dupnitza	30	5	0	10	11	33	0	3	12	5	33	5	3	22	16	66	18

TOP GOALSCORERS

19	Georgi HRISTOV (Botev)
14	NEI (CSKA Sofia)
13	Marcho DAFCHEV (Lokomotiv Sofia)
12	Zoran BALDOVALIEV (Lokomotiv Sofia)
11	Plamen KRUMOV (Chernomorets Burgas) Florentin PETRE (CSKA Sofia) Ivelin POPOV (Litex)
10	German PIETROBON (Pirin 1922) Ivan NAIDENOV (Spartak Varna) Alexander Yordanov ALEXANDROV (Cherno More)

BULGARIA

CLUB-BY-CLUB

PFC BELASITSA PETRICH

Coach – Miroslav Mitev; (2/11/07) Aliosha Andonov; (13/4/08) Stjepan Deverić (CRO)

Founded - 1923

Date	Opponent		Score	Scorers
2007				
12/8	Chernomorets Burgas	h	1-6	*Santos Du Bala*
19/8	CSKA Sofia	a	0-2	
25/8	Vihren	h	1-0	*Santos Du Bala*
2/9	Litex	a	0-2	
16/9	Levski	h	0-0	
22/9	Spartak Varna	h	2-1	*Orlovski, Santos Du Bala*
29/9	Vidima	a	0-1	
7/10	Pirin 1922	h	0-1	
20/10	Lokomotiv Sofia	a	0-1	
27/10	Slavia	h	1-2	*Nikolov*
3/11	Beroe	a	1-2	*Santos Du Bala*
11/11	Lokomotiv Plovdiv	h	0-0	
24/11	Cherno More	a	1-1	*Kiki*
30/11	Marek	h	1-0	*Santos Du Bala*
8/12	Botev	a	0-2	
2008				
2/3	Chernomorets Burgas	a	0-0	
8/3	CSKA Sofia	h	1-3	*Trifonov*
15/3	Vihren	a	0-2	
19/3	Litex	h	1-2	*Kabranov*
22/3	Levski	a	0-4	
30/3	Spartak Varna	a	0-1	
5/4	Vidima	h	1-0	*Marques (p)*
9/4	Pirin 1922	a	1-2	*og (Georgiev)*
12/4	Lokomotiv Sofia	h	0-1	
19/4	Slavia	a	1-3	*Semina*
25/4	Beroe	h	3-1	*Vavá, Gospodinov, Marques (p)*
29/4	Lokomotiv Plovdiv	a	0-1	
4/5	Cherno More	h	1-1	*Kabranov*
10/5	Marek	a	3-0	*(w/o; original result 1-1 Vavá)*
17/5	Botev	h	3-1	*Beto, Villa, Gospodinov*

No	Name	Nat	Pos	Aps	(s)	Gls
21	Hristo BAHTARLIEV		G	24		
10	BETO da Silva	BRA	M	17	(3)	1
16	Marin DAMYANOV		M		(2)	
2	Cláudio DIANU dos Santos	BRA	D	25		
7	Kiril DIMITROV		M		(4)	
16	Daniel DYULGEROV		M	11	(10)	
3	Daniel GADZHEV		D		(3)	
23	Hristo GOSPODINOV		M	28		2
33	Nikolai HRISTOV		M		(2)	
9	Vladimir KABRANOV		A	10	(10)	2
12	Petar KARACHOROV		A	1	(8)	
22	Kostadin KATSIMERSKI		M		(2)	
16	Joel KIKI	BRA	D	9	(2)	1
4	Anton LICHKOV		D	15		
1	Angel MANOLOV		G	6		
8	Eli MARQUES	BRA	D	29		2
11	Alexander MITUSHEV		M		(1)	
3	Plamen NENOV		D	2	(2)	
14	Georgi NIKOLOV		D	19	(6)	1
17	Dobri ORLOVSKI		M	20	(1)	1
6	Georgi PETROV		M	7		
10	Goran PROJKOV	MKD	M	6	(2)	
11	Eduardo dos SANTOS DU BALA	BRA	A	15		5
24	Krasen SAVOV		M	6	(1)	
25	Klodian SEMINA	ALB	D	10	(2)	1
15	Aleksandar STOJANOVSKI	MKD	M	7	(6)	
3	Petar TRIFONOV		A	25	(2)	1
40	Marcelo VAVÁ	BRA	A	8	(1)	2
20	Ivailo VELINOV		D	15	(10)	
29	Roberto da Costa VILLA	BRA	M	15		1

PFC BEROE STARA ZAGORA

Coach – Radoslav Zdravkov; (16/10/07) Nikolai Demirev; (5/2/08) Ilian Iliev

Founded – 1916

MAJOR HONOURS: Bulgarian League - (1) 1986.

Date	Opponent		Score	Scorers
2007				
12/8	Slavia	a	0-2	
18/8	Levski	a	0-1	
25/8	Lokomotiv Plovdiv	h	0-0	
1/9	Cherno More	a	0-1	
15/9	Marek	h	1-1	*Mitev*
22/9	Botev	a	0-1	
29/9	Chernomorets Burgas	h	2-1	*Tanev, Mitev*
7/10	CSKA Sofia	a	0-1	
20/10	Vihren	h	2-0	*Džaferović 2*
27/10	Litex	a	1-1	*Mitev*
3/11	Belasitsa	h	2-1	*Ivanov I. 2*
10/11	Spartak Varna	a	0-1	
24/11	Vidima	h	2-0	*Zakov, Atanasov*
1/12	Pirin 1922	a	0-1	
8/12	Lokomotiv Sofia	h	1-3	*Mitev (p)*
2008				
1/3	Slavia	h	2-2	*Apostolov, Zlatinov*
8/3	Levski	h	0-1	
15/3	Lokomotiv Plovdiv	a	0-2	
19/3	Cherno More	h	0-0	
23/3	Marek	a	1-0	*Apostolov*
29/3	Botev	h	3-1	*Tanev 2, Bukleev*
5/4	Chernomorets Burgas	a	0-2	
9/4	CSKA Sofia	h	0-1	
13/4	Vihren	a	0-2	
20/4	Litex	h	2-2	*Vidolov (p), Atanasov*
25/4	Belasitsa	a	1-3	*Kolev Pe.*
30/4	Spartak Varna	h	0-0	
4/5	Vidima	a	1-3	*Atanasov*
10/5	Pirin 1922	h	2-2	*Atanasov, Zlatinov*
17/5	Lokomotiv Sofia	a	0-3	

No	Name	Nat	Pos	Aps	(s)	Gls
27	Atanas APOSTOLOV		A	8	(8)	2
25	Doncho ATANASOV		A	15	(7)	4
22	Daniele BEKONO	CMR	G	15		
16	Aleksandr BUKLEEV	RUS	A	11	(3)	1
17	Nikolai CHIPEV		M	1	(3)	
5	Peicho DELIMINKOV		D	15		
5	Vanja DŽAFEROVIĆ	CRO	D	13		2
20	Marcel Jason ELAME	CMR	D	12	(1)	
21	Dian GENCHEV		M	9	(2)	
13	Genadi GRUDEV		M		(1)	
23	Nikolai HARIZANOV		D	12		
4	Milen HRISTOV		D	12	(2)	
17	Marko ILIĆ	SRB	M	2	(5)	
29	Galin IVANOV		M	6	(3)	
15	Ivo IVANOV		D	14		2
6	Ivan KARAMANOV		M	5	(1)	
3	Petar KOLEV		D	2	(3)	1
1	Plamen KOLEV		G	14	(1)	
28	Yanko KOSTURKOV		D	10	(2)	
26	Igor LAMBULIĆ	MNE	A		(2)	
19	Nedko MILENOV		M	3	(5)	
18	Vladan MILOSAVLJEVIĆ	SRB	D	11		
28	Simeon MINCHEV		M	8	(3)	
10	Danail MITEV		A	10	(4)	4
16	Anton OGNYANOV		M	8	(1)	

No	Name	Nat	Pos	Aps	(s)	Gls
3	Vladimir PEKIN		M	6	(8)	
2	Plamen PETROV		G	1		
	Yanko SANDANSKI		M	11	(1)	
	Milcho TANEV		M	21	(1)	3
	Todor TODOROV		D	11		
4	Zdravko TODOROV		A	1	(7)	
3	Anton VERGILOV		D	7		
	Kostadin VIDOLOV		M	13		1
	Gerasim ZAKOV		A	11	(4)	1
	Slavi ZHEKOV		M	10		
	Zhelio ZHELEV		A	7	(11)	
	Vladislav ZLATINOV		A	15		2

PFC BOTEV PLOVDIV

Coach – Svetoslav Garkov; (3/10/07) Tencho Tenev

Founded – 1912

MAJOR HONOURS: Bulgarian League – (2) 1929, 1967; Bulgarian Cup - (1) 1929, 1962 (as Soviet Army Cup).

2007

/8	Spartak Varna	a	2-2	*Krustev 2*
/8	Vidima	h	5-0	*Hristov 3, Bozhkov (p), Saidhodzha*
/8	Pirin 1922	a	0-1	
9	Lokomotiv Sofia	h	2-2	*Hristov, Velichkov*
/9	Slavia	a	2-4	*Garkov, Hristov (p)*
/9	Beroe	h	1-0	*Avramov*
/9	Lokomotiv Plovdiv	a	0-4	
10	Cherno More	h	1-1	*Hristov*
/10	Marek	a	0-1	
/20	Levski	a	2-6	*Hristov, Minev*
11	Chernomorets Burgas	h	0-0	
/11	CSKA Sofia	a	0-2	
/11	Vihren	h	1-0	*Manchev*
12	Litex	a	0-6	
12	Belasitsa	h	2-0	*Hristov 2*

2008

3	Spartak Varna	h	2-0	*Hristov, Saidhodzha*
3	Vidima	a	1-0	*Velichkov*
/3	Pirin 1922	h	0-0	
/3	Lokomotiv Sofia	a	2-2	*Kakalov 2*
/3	Slavia	h	3-0	*Hristov 2 (1p), Saidhodzha*
/3	Beroe	a	1-3	*Hristov (p)*
4	Lokomotiv Plovdiv	h	1-2	*Hristov*
4	Cherno More	a	0-2	
/4	Marek	h	4-0	*Saidhodzha, Hristov 2 (1p), Avramov*
/4	Levski	h	0-3	
/4	Chernomorets Burgas	a	1-3	*Hristov*
/4	CSKA Sofia	h	1-3	*Hristov (p)*
5	Vihren	a	0-2	
/5	Litex	h	1-2	*Saidhodzha*
/5	Belasitsa	a	1-3	*Hristov (p)*

No	Name	Nat	Pos	Aps	(s)	Gls
	Mauro ALEGRE	ARG	M	13	(4)	
	Lilcho ARSOV		G	24		
	Georgi AVRAMOV		A	27		2
	Danail BOZHKOV		D	30		1
	Atanas CHIPILOV		A		(4)	
	Nikolai DIMITROV		M	1	(2)	
	Yordan ETOV		D	2	(8)	
	Kostadin GADZHALOV		D	1	(8)	
	Vasil GARKOV		M	7	(3)	1
	Iliyan GAROV		D	30		
	Nikolai HARIZANOV		D	12	(1)	
	Georgi HRISTOV		A	30		19
	Georgi KAKALOV		A	14	(3)	2
	Borislav KARAMATEV		M	8	(6)	
	Georgi KORUDZHIEV		M		(1)	
	Krasimir KRUSTEV		M	12	(9)	2
	Nikolai MANCHEV		A	18	(9)	1
	Yordan MINEV		D	25		1
15	Apostol POPOV		M	15		
99	Dormushali SAIDHODZHA		A	24	(2)	5
28	Mohamed SELYAM		M		(3)	
22	Pavel STANEV		G		(2)	
8	Todor TIMONOV		M	4	(5)	
30	Slavcho TOSHEV		G	6		
21	Emil URUMOV		A		(3)	
2	Vasil VASILEV		D	6	(5)	
5	Velichko VELICHKOV		D	21		2
26	Dimitar VITANOV		D		(1)	
16	Iliyan YORDANOV		M		(1)	

PFC CHERNO MORE VARNA

Coach – Nikola Spasov

Founded – 1945 (following merger of Vladislav Varna and Ticha Varna)

MAJOR HONOURS: Bulgarian League – (4) 1925, 1926, 1934 (as Vladislav Varna), 1939 (as Ticha Varna).

2007

11/8	Pirin 1922	a	0-1	
19/8	Lokomotiv Sofia	h	1-1	*Moke*
26/8	Slavia	a	1-3	*Ricardo André*
1/9	Beroe	h	1-0	*Aleksandrov A.Y.*
15/9	Lokomotiv Plovdiv	a	1-2	*Moke*
22/9	Levski Sofia	a	0-4	
30/9	Marek	h	0-0	
6/10	Botev	a	1-1	*Fabiano*
20/10	Chernomorets Burgas	h	2-1	*Aleksandrov A., Aleksandrov A.Y.*
27/10	CSKA Sofia	a	0-1	
3/11	Vihren	h	1-0	*Georgiev*
11/11	Litex	a	1-1	*Ricardo André*
24/11	Belasitsa	h	1-1	*Stoyanov*
1/12	Spartak Varna	a	1-0	*Manolov*
8/12	Vidima	h	7-0	*Manolov, Georgiev 2, Aleksandrov A.Y. 2 (1p), Kolev, Domakinov*

2008

1/3	Pirin 1922	h	1-0	*Manolov*
8/3	Lokomotiv Sofia	a	3-4	*Ricardo André, Aleksandrov A.Y. 2*
15/3	Slavia	h	1-0	*Kolev*
19/3	Beroe	a	0-0	
23/3	Lokomotiv Plovdiv	h	2-1	*Moke, Manolov*
30/3	Levski	h	0-1	
5/3	Marek	a	4-1	*Stoyanov, Manolov 3*
9/4	Botev	h	2-0	*Aleksandrov A.Y. 2 (1p)*
12/4	Chernomorets Burgas	a	1-0	*Manolov*
20/4	CSKA Sofia	h	0-2	
25/4	Vihren	a	1-1	*Lazarov*
30/4	Litex	h	2-1	*Andonov, Aleksandrov A.Y.*
4/5	Belasitsa	a	1-1	*Georgiev*
10/5	Spartak Varna	h	0-0	
17/5	Vidima	a	3-0	*Andonov, Manolov, Aleksandrov A.Y.*

No	Name	Nat	Pos	Aps	(s)	Gls
15	Alexander ALEXANDROV		D	25	(2)	1
30	Alexander Yordanov ALEXANDROV		M	27	(1)	10
11	Georgi ANDONOV		A	12	(8)	2
24	Radoslav BACHEV		D	14	(4)	
28	Marcos DA SILVA	BRA	A	5	(7)	
2	Daniel DIMOV		D	4	(2)	
21	DJALMA Enrique da Silva	BRA	M	8	(2)	
5	Nikolai DOMAKINOV		D	21	(2)	1
6	Kiril DZHOROV		D	13	(3)	
22	FABIANO Aguiar Laurentino	BRA	A	5	(8)	1
23	Daniel GEORGIEV		M	26	(1)	4
14	Tigran GHARABAGHTSYAN	ARM	M	5	(3)	
1	Karamfil ILCHEV		G	25	(1)	
3	JOVALDIR Peres	BRA	D	21	(1)	
33	Krasimir KOLEV		G	5		

13	Todor KOLEV		A	2	(8)	2
18	Petar KOSTADINOV		D	8	(1)	
19	Vladimir KOSTADINOV		M	2	(2)	
32	Mihail LAZAROV		D	5	(5)	1
31	Miroslav MANOLOV		A	20	(3)	9
10	Konstantin MIRCHEV		M	4	(3)	
9	Masena MOKE	COD	A	6	(8)	3
8	RICARDO ANDRÉ Pires	BRA	M	27	(1)	3
6	Kristian SPREĆAKOVIĆ	SRB	D	1	(1)	
7	Stanislav STOYANOV		M	17	(8)	2
26	Alexander TOMASH		D	22		

PFC CHERNOMORETS BURGAS

Coach – Dimitar Dimitrov

Founded – 2005

2007				
12/8	Belasitsa	a	6-1	*Karakanov 3 (1p), Márcio, Krumov 2*
18/8	Spartak Varna	h	1-0	*Remzi*
25/8	Vidima	a	1-1	*Yanev*
1/9	Pirin 1922	h	1-4	*Krumov*
14/9	Lokomotiv Sofia	a	0-4	
22/9	Slavia	h	2-0	*Dyakov, Krumov*
29/9	Beroe	a	1-2	*Krumov*
6/10	Lokomotiv Plovdiv	h	1-0	*Bozhilov*
20/10	Cherno More	a	1-2	*Krumov*
26/10	Marek	h	1-0	*Trajanov*
4/11	Botev	a	0-0	
24/11	CSKA Sofia	h	1-1	*Todorov*
2/12	Vihren	a	2-1	*Krustev, Todorov*
9/12	Litex	h	2-0	*Dyakov, Krumov*
2008				
24/2	Levski	a	1-2	*Márcio*
2/3	Belasitsa	h	0-0	
8/3	Spartak Varna	a	1-1	*Karakanov*
15/3	Vidima	h	1-0	*Krumov*
20/3	Pirin 1922	a	0-1	
23/3	Lokomotiv Sofia	h	1-1	*Krumov*
30/3	Slavia	a	1-1	*Remzi*
5/4	Beroe	h	2-0	*Karakanov, Krumov*
9/4	Lokomotiv Plovdiv	a	1-1	*Krumov*
12/4	Cherno More	h	0-1	
20/4	Marek	a	4-1	*Karakanov, Bozhilov 2, og (Sokolov)*
25/4	Botev	h	3-1	*Nikolov, Bozhilov, Márcio*
30/4	Levski	h	2-1	*Bozhilov, Krustev*
4/5	CSKA Sofia	a	0-3	
10/5	Vihren	h	1-0	*Nikolov*
17/5	Litex	a	1-2	*og (Cambon)*

No	Name	Nat	Pos	Aps	(s)	Gls
14	Georgi BOZHILOV		M	17	(8)	5
18	Atanas CHIPILOV		A	4	(3)	
1	Ivan ĆVOROVIĆ	SRB	G	1		
29	Todorin DIMITROV		M		(2)	
10	Kostadin DYAKOV		M	18	(3)	2
2	Trayan DYANKOV		D	28	(1)	
21	Atanas FIDANIN		M	19		
18	Ventsislav IVANOV		A	1	(1)	
6	Georgi KARAKANOV		M	19	(7)	6
3	Slavi KOSTENSKI		D	2	(4)	
11	Nikita KOŠUTIĆ	SRB	M	3	(4)	
25	Plamen KRUMOV		A	19	(4)	11
5	Nikolai KRUSTEV		D	25	(1)	2
17	Lyubomir LYUBENOV		A	13	(4)	
26	MÁRCIO Abreu	POR	A	19	(3)	3
13	Nikolai NIKOLOV		D	21	(2)	2
19	Veselin PENEV		D	5	(2)	
1	Todor POPOV		G	1		
24	Shener REMZI		M	23	(3)	2
33	Vladislav STOYANOV		G	28		
28	Emil TODOROV		A	2	(14)	2
7	Stefan TRAIKOV		M	23	(5)	

15	Vančo TRAJANOV	MKD	M	25	(2)	1
30	Ivan TSANKOV		M	8	(5)	
22	Tsvetomir TSONKOV		M	1	(2)	
23	Kosta YANEV		D	5	(5)	1

PFC CSKA SOFIA

Coach – Stoicho Mladenov

Founded – 1948

MAJOR HONOURS: Bulgarian League – (31) 1948, 1951, 1952, 1954, 1955, 1956, 1957, 1958, 1959, 1960, 1961, 1962, 1966, 1969, 1971, 197 1973, 1975, 1976, 1980, 1981, 1982, 1983, 1987, 1989, 1990, 1992, 199 2003, 2005, 2008; Bulgarian Cup – (19) 1951, 1954, 1955, 1961, 1965, 1969, 1972, 1973, 1974 (as Soviet Army Cup), 1981, 1983, 1985, 1987, 1988, 1989, 1993, 1997, 1999, 2006.

2007				
11/8	Litex	a	1-1	*Chilikov*
19/8	Belasitsa	h	2-0	*Garcés, Chilikov*
25/8	Spartak Varna	a	2-0	*Vujadinović, Petre (p)*
2/9	Vidima	h	3-1	*Nei 2, Chilikov*
15/9	Pirin 1922	a	1-0	*Garcés*
23/9	Lokomotiv Sofia	h	3-1	*Nei 3 (1p)*
29/9	Slavia	a	1-0	*Amuneke*
7/10	Beroe	h	1-0	*Iliev G.*
20/10	Lokomotiv Plovdiv	a	1-0	*Nei (p)*
27/10	Cherno More	h	1-0	*Amuneke*
3/11	Marek	a	3-1	*Tunchev, Yanchev, Machado*
11/11	Botev	h	2-0	*Dimitrov, Yanchev*
24/11	Chernomorets Burgas	a	1-1	*Dimitrov*
2/12	Levski	a	1-0	*Machado*
9/12	Vihren	h	1-0	*Iliev V.*
2008				
1/3	Litex	h	0-0	
8/3	Belasitsa	a	3-1	*Petre 2, Marquinhos (*
14/3	Spartak Varna	h	3-2	*og (Marinov), Dimitro (p), Yordanov*
19/3	Vidima	a	0-0	
23/3	Pirin 1922	h	3-0	*Petre, Tunchev, Nei (p)*
29/3	Lokomotiv Sofia	a	0-0	
5/4	Slavia	h	2-0	*Petre (p), Tunchev*
9/4	Beroe	a	1-0	*Petre*
12/4	Lokomotiv Plovdiv	h	2-0	*Udoji, Todorov*
20/4	Cherno More	a	2-0	*Nei 2*
25/4	Marek	h	4-0	*Petre, Nei 2, Yurukov*
30/4	Botev	a	3-1	*Nei 2 (1p), Petre*
4/5	Chernomorets Burgas	h	3-0	*Petre 3*
10/5	Levski	h	1-1	*Dimitrov (p)*
17/5	Vihren	a	2-1	*Nei, Garcés*

No	Name	Nat	Pos	Aps	(s)	Gls
11	Kevin AMUNEKE	NGA	M	5	(5)	2
19	Georgi CHILIKOV		A	4	(8)	3
7	Ivailo DIMITROV		A		(1)	
8	Velizar DIMITROV		M	21	(3)	4
9	José Luis GARCÉS	PAN	A	5	(9)	3
11	Emil GARGOROV		M	11	(2)	
10	Georgi ILIEV		M	7	(9)	1
14	Valentin ILIEV		D	14		1
17	JOSÉ RUI Tavares De Veiga	POR	M	7	(6)	
23	Abderrahmane KABOUS	MAR	M	5	(3)	
6	Kiril KOTEV		D	16	(2)	
27	Quido LANZAAT	NED	D	7	(2)	
84	Felipe MACHADO	BRA	D	13	(2)	2
28	MARQUINHOS Junior	BRA	M	19	(6)	1
12	Nenad NASTIĆ	SRB	D	4	(3)	
99	Claudinei 'NEI' Aparecido	BRA	A	23	(5)	14
18	Florentin PETRE	ROU	M	24		11
12	Ivailo PETROV		G	28		
22	Ilko PIRGOV		G	2		
30	Yordan TODOROV		D	24	(2)	1
24	Alexander TONEV		A		(2)	
3	Alexander TUNCHEV		D	26		3
21	Shikoze UDOJI	NGA	M	17	(6)	1

Nikola VUJADINOVIĆ	MNE	D	16	(1)	1
Todor YANCHEV		M	26	(2)	2
Evgeni YODANOV		A	3	(5)	1
Yordan YURUKOV		M	3	(5)	1

PFC LEVSKI SOFIA

Coach – Stanimir Stoilov; (7/5/07) Velislav Vutsov

Founded – 1914

MAJOR HONOURS: Bulgarian League – (25) 1933, 1937, 1942, 1946, 57, 1949, 1950, 1953, 1965, 1968, 1970, 1974, 1977, 1979, 1984, 1985, 988, 1993, 1994, 1995, 2000, 2001, 2002, 2006, 2007; Bulgarian Cup – (26) 1942 (as Tsar's Cup), 1946, 1947, 1949, 1950, 1956, 1957, 1959, 967, 1970, 1971, 1976, 1977, 1979 (as Soviet Army Cup), 1982, 1984, 1986, 1991, 1992, 1994, 1998, 2000, 2002, 2003, 2005, 2007.

07

'8	Vihren	a	1-0	*Milanov*
'8	Beroe	h	1-0	*Eromoigbe*
'8	Litex	a	1-2	*Tasevski*
	Lokomotiv Plovdiv	h	3-1	*Domovchiyski (p), Dimitrov, Tasevski*
'9	Belasitsa	a	0-0	
'9	Cherno More	h	4-0	*Dimitrov, Telkiyski, Domovchiyski 2 (1p)*
'9	Spartak Varna	a	2-1	*Dimitrov, Telkiyski*
0	Marek	h	4-2	*Domovchiyski 3, Telkiyski*
'10	Vidima	a	3-1	*Bardon 2, Tasevski*
'10	Botev	h	6-2	*Telkiyski, Yovov, Borimirov, Dimitrov, Bardon, Milanov*
1	Pirin 1922	a	1-1	*Domovchiyski (p)*
'11	Lokomotiv Sofia	a	0-0	
2	CSKA Sofia	h	0-1	
2	Slavia	a	0-0	
8				
'2	Chernomorets Burgas	h	2-1	*Jean Carlos, Borimirov*
	Vihren	h	1-0	*Krastovchev*
	Beroe	a	1-0	*Sarmov*
'3	Litex	h	0-1	
'3	Lokomotiv Plovdiv	a	0-1	
'3	Belasitsa	h	4-0	*Dimitrov, Jean Carlos, Zé Soares, Joãozinho*
3	Cherno More	a	1-0	*Ivanov*
	Spartak Varna	h	3-0	*Ivanov, Jean Carlos 2*
	Marek	a	4-0	*Krastovchev 4*
'4	Vidima	h	3-0	*Dimitrov (p), Jean Carlos, og (Zelenkov)*
4	Botev	a	3-0	*Ivanov, Milanov, Joãozinho (p)*
'4	Pirin 1922	h	4-0	*Jean Carlos, Dimitrov (p), Zé Soares, Borimirov*
3	Chernomorets Burgas	a	1-2	*Dimitrov*
	Lokomotiv Sofia	h	0-1	
5	CSKA Sofia	a	1-1	*Krastovchev*
5	Slavia	h	2-1	*Tasevski, Krastovchev*

No	Name	Nat	Pos	Aps	(s)	Gls
	Lachezar BALTANOV		M	1	(8)	
	Cédric BARDON	FRA	M	12	(1)	3
	Chakib BENZOUKANE	MAR	D	5	(1)	
	Daniel BORIMIROV		M	17	(5)	3
	Nikolai DIMITROV		M	24	(5)	8
	Valeri DOMOVCHIYSKI		A	10	(3)	7
	Richard EROMOIGBE	NGA	M	7	(1)	1
	Viktor GENEV		D	1		
	Ismail ISA		A		(3)	
	Mirolsav IVANOV		M	14	(4)	3
	Ekundayo JAYEOBA	NGA	A		(4)	
	JEAN CARLOS Sales Bemvindo	BRA	A	11		6
	Joao 'JOÃOZINHO' Dos Santos	BRA	M	5	(7)	2
	Alexander KIROV		A		(1)	
	Enyo KRASTOVCHEV		A	8	(6)	7
	Zhivko MILANOV		D	24	(1)	3
14	Veselin MINEV		D	18		
12	Bozhidar MITREV		G	2		
16	Mariyan OGNYANOV		A	5	(6)	
1	Georgi PETKOV		G	28		
5	Youssef RABEH	MAR	D	26		
8	Georgi SARMOV		M	13	(9)	1
19	Boyan TABAKOV		A		(1)	
22	Darko TASEVSKI	MKD	M	23	(4)	4
21	Dimitar TELKIYSKI		M	13	(1)	4
4	Igor TOMAŠIĆ		D	28	(1)	
11	Elin TOPUZAKOV		D	5	(1)	
25	Lucio WAGNER		D	10	(4)	
10	Hristo YOVOV		A	6	(5)	1
11	José ZÉ SOARES da Silva Filho	BRA	M	14	(5)	2
13	Eli ZIZOV	ISR	M		(1)	

PFC LITEX LOVECH

Coach – Ferario Spasov; (5/11/07) Miodrag Ješić (SRB)

Founded – 1925

MAJOR HONOURS: Bulgarian League – (2) 1998, 1999; Bulgarian Cup – (3) 2001, 2004, 2008.

2007

11/8	CSKA Sofia	h	1-1	*Wellington*
19/8	Vihren	a	1-2	*Beto*
25/8	Levski	h	2-1	*Popov I., Boudarène*
2/9	Belasitsa	h	2-0	*Wellington, Popov I.*
14/9	Spartak Varna	a	0-0	
23/9	Vidima	h	4-1	*Beto 2, Popov I. (p), Wellington*
28/9	Pirin 1922	a	3-1	*Popov I., Genchev, Beto*
7/10	Lokomotiv Sofia	h	1-1	*Popov I.*
20/10	Slavia	a	0-1	
27/10	Beroe	h	1-1	*Wellington*
3/11	Lokomotiv Plovdiv	a	0-1	
11/11	Cherno More	h	1-1	*Popov I.*
24/11	Marek	a	3-0	*Tome, Beto*
1/12	Botev	h	6-0	*Popov I. 2 (2p), Beto, Sandrinho, Jankovic, Bibishkov*
9/12	Chernomorets Burgas	a	0-2	

2008

1/3	CSKA Sofia	a	0-0	
8/3	Vihren	h	2-0	*Niflore, Popov I.*
15/3	Levski	a	1-0	*Santos Du Bala*
19/3	Belasitsa	a	2-1	*Uras, Niflore*
22/3	Spartak Varna	h	1-0	*Niflore*
29/3	Vidima	a	2-3	*Niflore, Popov I. (p)*
5/4	Pirin 1922	h	1-0	*Sandrinho*
9/4	Lokomotiv Sofia	a	2-1	*Manolev, Niflore*
12/4	Slavia	h	1-1	*Jelenković*
20/4	Beroe	a	2-2	*Wellington, Bibishkov*
25/4	Lokomotiv Plovdiv	h	3-1	*Manolev, Niflore, Bibishkov*
30/4	Cherno More	a	1-2	*Sandrinho*
4/5	Marek	h	4-0	*Popov I. (p), Manolev, Bibishkov, Angelov*
10/5	Botev	a	2-1	*Bibishkov, Genchev (p)*
17/5	Chernomorets Burgas	h	2-1	*Cambon, Nikolov*

No	Name	Nat	Pos	Aps	(s)	Gls
28	Emil ANGELOV		A	4	(7)	2
20	Ivan BANDLOVSKI		D	1	(1)	
14	Ventsislav BENGYUZOV		M		(2)	
33	Džemal BERBEROVIĆ	BIH	D	7	(5)	
11	André Roberto "BETO"	BRA	A	14	(1)	7
18	Krum BIBISHKOV		A	11	(12)	5
17	Fabien BOUDARÈNE	FRA	M	11		1
21	Cédric CAMBON	FRA	D	13	(1)	
4	Alejandro CICHERO	VEN	D	6		
7	Stanislav GENCHEV		M	16	(9)	2
4	Emil GROZEV		D		(1)	
9	Kostadin HAZUROV		A		(7)	
21	Zoran JANKOVIĆ		A	5	(4)	1

BULGARIA

23	Noebojša JELENKOVIĆ	SRB	M	14	(2)	1
16	Stanislav MANOLEV		D	21	(4)	3
19	Wilfred NIFLORE	FRA	A	8	(2)	6
1	Iliyan NIKOLOV		G	1	(1)	
22	Plamen NIKOLOV		D	22		1
32	Ivelin POPOV		M	24	(3)	11
2	Robert POPOV	MKD	D	13		
10	Alessandro Corea "SANDRINHO"	BRA	M	27		3
9	Eduardo dos SANTOS DU BALA	BRA	A	4	(5)	1
7	Ivan SKERLEV		D	2		
12	Todor TODOROV		G	29		
26	Carlos TOME	BRA	A	8	(5)	1
27	Momchil TSVETANOV		M	2	(5)	
6	Cédric URAS	FRA	D	14	(3)	1
5	Mihail VENKOV		D	27		
8	WELLINGTON Brito da Silva	BRA	M	25	(3)	5
24	Petar ZLATINOV		M	1	(4)	

PFC LOKOMOTIV PLOVDIV 1936

Coach – Ivan Marinov; (24/9/07) Yassen Petrov; (15/3/08) (Ayan Sadakov); (19/3/08) Dragan Kanatlarovski (MKD)

Founded – 1936

MAJOR HONOURS: Bulgarian League – (1) 2004.

2007				
11/8	Lokomotiv Sofia	a	1-2	*Zlatkovski*
18/8	Slavia	h	1-1	*Vandev*
25/8	Beroe	a	0-0	
1/9	Levski	a	1-3	*Goranov*
15/9	Cherno More	h	2-1	*Kamburov, Dakson*
22//9	Marek	a	1-2	*Zlatkovski*
29/9	Botev	h	4-0	*og (Velichkov), Kamburov, Vandev, Zlatinov*
6/10	Chernomorets Burgas	a	0-1	
20/10	CSKA Sofia	h	0-1	
27/10	Vihren	a	2-0	*Sakaliev, Dakson*
3/11	Litex	h	1-0	*Dakson*
11/11	Belasitsa	a	0-0	
25/11	Spartak Varna	h	1-0	*Miliev*
1/12	Vidima	a	3-0	*Kamburov 3 (1p)*
9/12	Pirin 1922	h	0-0	
2008				
2/3	Lokomotiv Soifa	h	1-2	*Goranov*
8/3	Slavia	a	0-1	
15/3	Beroe	h	2-0	*Sechkov, Iliev*
19/3	Levski	h	1-0	*Miliev*
23/3	Cherno More	a	1-2	*Kiki*
29/3	Marek	h	0-0	
5/4	Botev	a	2-1	*Vandev, Goranov (p)*
9/4	Chernomorets Burgas	h	1-1	*Dakson*
12/4	CSKA Sofia	a	0-2	
19/4	Vihren	h	2-1	*Vandev, Goranov (p)*
25/4	Litex	a	1-3	*Ewerton*
29/4	Belasitsa	h	1-0	*Velli*
4/5	Spartak Varna	a	1-2	*Vandev*
10/5	Vidima	h	6-1	*Sechkov 2, Zakov 2, Vandev, Dakson (p)*
17/5	Pirin 1922	a	1-1	*Goranov*

No	Name	Nat	Pos	Aps	(s)	Gls
12	Kiril AKALSKI		G	3		
20	Radoslav ANEV		D	10	(2)	
25	Teodor BANEV		M		(1)	
2	Alexander BRANEKOV		D	5	(2)	
11	DAKSON Soares da Silva	BRA	M	29		5
19	Krasimir DIMITROV		M	21	(4)	
7	Rumen GORANOV		M	22	(6)	5
10	Ilami HALIMI	MKD	M	3	(3)	
26	Berthran HAYTAM	GHA	M	2	(4)	
14	Dimitar ILIEV		A	6	(3)	1
22	Ivan IVANOV		D	24		
7	Martin KAMBUROV		M	11	(1)	5
27	Dani KIKI		M	19	(5)	1
12	Stoyan KOLEV		G	6		
15	Petar KYUMYURDZHIEV		D	14		
23	Georgi MECHECHIEV		D	15		
5	Yordan MILIEV		D	26	(1)	2
4	Daniel MORALES	BRA	M	17		
26	Hristian POPOV		M		(1)	
29	Stoiko SAKALIEV		A	12	(1)	1
24	Martin SECHKOV		D	7	(2)	3
1	Stoyan STAVREV		G	21		
6	Stanko STOICHEV		M		(7)	
17	Anatoli TODOROV		A	2	(7)	
20	Giglio Fernando Evertom TOM	BRA	A	5	(3)	1
26	Lyubomir TSEKOV		A		(1)	
18	Yavor VANDEV		A	17	(3)	6
10	Gyursel VELI		A	7	(6)	1
25	Angel YOSHEV		D	17	(3)	
21	Gerasim ZAKOV		A	7	(5)	2
11	Vladislav ZLATINOV		A	1	(10)	1
16	Zoran ZLATKOVSKI		A	1	(7)	2

PFC LOKOMOTIV SOFIA

Coach – Stefan Grozdanov; (10/4/08) Dimitar Vasev

Founded – 1929

MAJOR HONOURS: Bulgarian League – (4) 1940, 1945, 1964, 1978; Bulgartian Cup – (3) 1948, 1953 (as Soviet Army Cup), 1995.

2007				
11/8	Lokomotiv Plovdiv	h	2-1	*Antunović, Dafchev (*
19/8	Cherno More	a	1-1	*Baldovaliev*
25/8	Marek	h	2-0	*Koilov, Zlatinski*
2/9	Botev	a	2-2	*Baldovaliev, Dafchev*
14/9	Chernomorets Burgas	h	4-0	*Karadzhinov 4*
23/9	CSKA Sofia	a	1-3	*Atanasov*
28/9	Vihren	h	3-2	*Antunović, Krumov, Dafchev*
7/10	Litex	a	1-1	*Dafchev (p)*
20/10	Belasitsa	h	1-0	*Dafchev*
27/10	Spartak Varna	a	1-0	*Baldovaliev*
3/11	Vidima	h	2-0	*Dafchev 2 (1p)*
11/11	Pirin 1922	a	3-1	*Baldovaliev, Dafchev (1p)*
24/11	Levski	h	0-0	
2/12	Slavia	h	1-2	*Gilas*
8/12	Beroe	a	3-1	*Dafchev, Gilas, Ivanc*
2008				
2/3	Lokomotiv Plovdiv	a	2-1	*Atanasov, Baldovalie*
8/3	Cherno More	h	4-3	*Baldovaliev 2, Dafch 2 (1p)*
15/3	Marek	a	4-1	*Baldovaliev, Dafchev Gilas, Mitev*
19/3	Botev	h	2-2	*Baldovaliev 2*
23/3	Chernomorets Burgas	a	1-1	*Ivanov*
29/3	CSKA Sofia	h	0-0	
5/4	Vihren	a	0-1	
9/4	Litex	h	1-2	*Dobrev*
12/4	Belasitsa	a	1-0	*Baldovaliev*
20/4	Spartak Varna	h	1-0	*Dobrev*
25/4	Vidima	a	0-0	
30/4	Pirin 1922	h	0-3	
4/5	Levski	a	1-0	*Zlatinski*
10/5	Slavia	a	0-0	
17/5	Beroe	h	3-0	*Baldovaliev, og (Kostrukov), Orachev*

No	Name	Nat	Pos	Aps	(s)	Gls
14	Saša ANTUNOVIĆ	SRB	A	10	(7)	2
30	Dimo ATANASOV		M	14	(6)	2
28	Zoran BALDOVALIEV	MKD	A	23	(3)	1[illegible]
20	Ivan BANDOLOVSKI		D	5	(2)	
10	Marcho DAFCHEV		M	26		13
27	Ivailo DIMITROV		M	1	(1)	
11	Kristiyan DOBREV		M	20	(2)	2
3	Deyan DONCHEV		D	16		
28	Stefan DONCHEV		D	2	(1)	

No	Name	Nat	Pos	Aps	(s)	Gls
	Vanja DžAFEROVIć	CRO	D	5		
2	Valentin GALEV		G	2		
	Vladimir GILAS	SRB	A	15	(9)	3
	Uroš GOLUBOVIĆ	SRB	G	28		
3	Ivailo IVANOV		M	21	(3)	2
3	Kaloyan KARADZHINOV		M	13	(1)	4
5	Hristo KOILOV		M	16	(10)	1
	Plamen KRUMOV		A		(1)	1
)	Adelino LOPES		D	10		
	Georgi MARKOV		D	22	(1)	
5	Danail MITEV		A	4	(6)	1
7	Malin ORACHEV		M	23	(4)	1
4	Ivan PASKOV		M	11	(7)	
2	Rumen RANGELOV		M		(1)	
9	Darko SAVIĆ	SRB	D	25	(1)	
	Viktor ŠPISIĆ	CRO	M	2	(6)	
	Yordan VARBANOV		D	5	(2)	
	Hristo ZLATINSKI		M	11	(12)	2

PFC MAREK DUPNITZA

oach – Stoyan Kotsev; (30/8/07) (Vassil Pavlov); (20/9/07) Yuri Vasev; (10/11/07) (Vasil Pavlov); (22/11/07) Georgi Dimitrov; (18/3/08) Stoyan Kotsev; (24/4/08) Aliosha Andonov

Founded – 1947

MAJOR HONOURS: Bulgarian Cup – (1) 1978 (as Soviet Army Cup).

007

/8	Vidima	a	0-1	
3/8	Pirin 1922	h	0-2	
5/8	Lokomotiv Sofia	a	0-2	
'9	Slavia	h	1-0	*Mladenov*
5/9	Beroe	a	1-1	*Krastovchev*
2/9	Lokomotiv Plovdiv	h	2-1	*Mladenov 2*
0/9	Cherno More	a	0-0	
'10	Levski	a	2-4	*Yordanov, Pavlović*
0/10	Botev	h	1-0	*Taskovic*
5/10	Chernomorets Burgas	a	0-1	
'11	CSKA Sofia	h	1-3	*Krastovchev*
0/11	Vihren	a	1-3	*Mladenov*
4/11	Litex	h	0-3	
0/11	Belasitsa	a	0-1	
'12	Spartak Varna	h	1-0	*Redovski*

008

3	Vidima	h	2-1	*Pargov 2 (1p)*
3	Pirin 1922	a	0-4	
5/3	Lokomotiv Sofia	h	1-4	*Pargov (p)*
0/3	Slavia	a	1-2	*Ez-Zahid*
3/3	Beroe	h	0-1	
9/3	Lokomotiv Plovdiv	a	0-0	
4	Cherno More	h	1-4	*Tasković*
4	Levski	h	0-4	
2/4	Botev	a	0-4	
9/4	Chernomorets Burgas	h	1-4	*Pargov*
5/4	CSKA Sofia	a	0-4	
0/4	Vihren	h	0-3	
5	Litex	a	0-4	
0/5	Belasitsa	h	0-3	*(w/o; original result 1-1 Mladenov)*
7/5	Spartak Varna	a	0-2	

o	Name	Nat	Pos	Aps	(s)	Gls
)	Georgi ANDREEV		M	1	(6)	
2	Daniel BELCHEV		G	26		
5	Slavcho BOICHEV		D	24	(3)	
	Kostadin BOSHIKYOV		D	5	(1)	
	Lyubomir BOZHANKOV		A		(1)	
	Mario DANAILOV		M	2	(1)	
4	Noureddine EZ ZAHID	MAR	M	6		1
7	Dimitar GEORGIEV		M	16	(8)	
	Svetoslav GEORGIEV		D	25	(1)	
	Alexander GORANOV		D	11	(4)	
	Radoslav IVANOV		M	20	(7)	
3	Mario KARACHORSKI		M	1		
9	Borsilav KRALEV		M		(1)	
8	Angel KRUMOV		M	3	(5)	
14	Kiril KRUSTEV		D	11	(1)	
11	Enyo KRASTOVCHEV		A	11	(2)	2
10	Angelo KYUCHUKOV		M	15		
3	Yanek KYUCHUKOV		D	17		
6	Atanas LAZAROV		M	1		
14	Daniel MLADENOV		A	15	(13)	5
9	Ivailo PARGOV		A	17	(1)	4
15	Milan PAVLOVIĆ	SRB	M	16	(7)	1
2	Nikola PESHEV		D	1	(1)	
8	Karou RADOUN	MAR	M	1		
8	Ivan REDOVSKI		M	18	(6)	1
18	Ivailo SIMEONOV		M		(2)	
5	Ivailo SOKOLOV		D	26		
6	Nenad STAMENKOVIĆ	SRB	M	1	(1)	
19	Igor TASKOVIĆ	SRB	M	26		2
17	Nikola TAVOLICHKI		M	1		
1	Emil VARADINOV		G	4	(2)	
16	Emil VIYACHKI		M		(1)	
20	Evgeni YORDANOV		A	9	(1)	1

PFC PIRIN 1922

Coaches – Petar Tsvetkov & Petar Mihtarski

Founded – 1931

2007

11/8	Cherno More	h	1-0	*Dyakov*
18/8	Marek	a	2-0	*Vitanov, Dyakov (p)*
25/8	Botev	h	1-0	*Peitrobon*
1/9	Chernomorets Burgas	a	4-1	*Metushev 2, Pietrobon, Vitanov*
15/9	CSKA Sofia	h	0-1	
23/9	Vihren	a	1-1	*og (Paulo Teixeira)*
28/9	Litex	h	1-3	*Pietrobon*
7/10	Belasitsa	a	1-0	*Metushev*
20/10	Spartak Varna	h	1-2	*Pietrobon*
27/10	Vidima	a	1-0	*Bodurov*
3/11	Levski	h	1-1	*Metushev*
11/11	Lokomotiv Sofia	h	1-3	*Pietrobon*
25/11	Slavia	a	0-1	
1/12	Beroe	h	1-0	*Pietrobon*
9/12	Lokomotiv Plovdiv	a	0-0	

2008

1/3	Cherno More	a	0-1	
8/3	Marek	h	4-0	*Pietrobon 3, Hazurov*
16/3	Botev	a	0-0	
20/3	Chernomorerts Burgas	h	1-0	*Palankov*
23/3	CSKA Sofia	a	0-3	
29/3	Vihren	h	0-0	
5/4	Litex	a	0-1	
9/4	Belasitsa	h	2-1	*Pietrobon, Dyakov*
12/4	Spartak Varna	a	0-2	
20/4	Vidima	h	3-1	*Hazurov, Stoyanov, Kostadinov*
25/4	Levski	a	0-4	
30/4	Lokomotiv Sofia	a	3-0	*Vitanov 2, Metushev*
4/5	Slavia	h	1-0	*Nikolov*
10/5	Beroe	a	2-2	*Kostadinov, Palankov*
17/5	Lokomotiv Plovdiv	h	1-1	*Nikolov*

No	Name	Nat	Pos	Aps	(s)	Gls
3	Nikolai BODUROV		D	27		1
12	Nikolai CHAVDAROV		G	19	(1)	
2	Lachezar DAFKOV		D	10	(12)	
8	Svetoslav DYAKOV		M	27		3
6	Georgi GEORGIEV		M	12	(2)	
18	Borislav HAZUROV		A	11	(12)	2
17	Velik IRMIEV		D		(1)	
1	Ivailo IVANIKOV		G	11		
5	Dimitar KOEMDZHIEV		D	29		
7	Stefan KOSTADINOV		M	12	(11)	2
15	Rumen LAPANTOV		M	2	(3)	
18	Emmanuel MARTÍNEZ	ARG	M		(4)	
11	Mario METUSHEV		A	22	(3)	5

No	Name	Nat	Pos	Aps	(s)	Gls
23	Dimitar NAKOV		D	12	(1)	
15	Kiril NIKOLOV		M	11	(3)	2
10	Todor PALANKOV		M	28	(1)	2
21	Germán PIETROBON	ARG	A	27	(2)	10
4	Yulian POPEV		D	8	(3)	
13	Andrei STOEV		D	20	(3)	
16	Ivan STOICHEV		M	2	(1)	
9	Veselin STOIKOV		A	3	(7)	
19	Kaloyan STOYANOV		M		(11)	1
14	Lyubomir VITANOV		M	17	(4)	4
17	Daniel ZLATKOV		M	1		
28	Miroslav RIZOV		D	19	(3)	

PFC SLAVIA SOFIA

Coach – Stevica Kuzmanovski (MKD)

Founded – 1913

MAJOR HONOURS: Bulgartian League – (7) 1928, 1930, 1936, 1939, 1941, 1943, 1996; Bulgarian Cup – (7) 1952, 1963, 1964, 1966, 1975, 1980 (as Soviet Army Cup), 1996.

2007				
12/8	Beroe	h	2-0	*Simonović, Elton*
18/8	Lokomotiv Plovdiv	a	1-1	*Elton*
26/8	Cherno More	h	3-1	*Simonović, Ortega 2*
1/9	Marek	a	0-1	
16/9	Botev	h	4-2	*Georgievski, Ortega 2, Vodenicharov*
22/9	Chernomorets Burgas	a	0-2	
29/9	CSKA Sofia	h	0-1	
6/10	Vihren	a	1-1	*Orlinov*
20/10	Litex	h	1-0	*Lazarov*
27/10	Belasitsa	a	2-1	*Ortega 2*
4/11	Spartak Varna	h	5-0	*Lazarov 2 (1p), Iliev, Kerchev, Orlinov*
10/11	Vidima	a	2-0	*Kerchev, Iliev*
25/11	Pirin 1922	h	1-0	*Lazarov (p)*
2/12	Lokomotiv Sofia	a	2-1	*Kerchev, Simonović*
8/12	Levski	h	0-0	
2008				
1/3	Beroe	a	2-2	*Iliev, Koprivarov*
8/3	Lokomotiv Plovdiv	h	1-0	*Simonović*
15/3	Cherno More	a	0-1	
20/3	Marek	h	2-1	*Petrov (p), Simonović*
23/3	Botev	a	0-3	
30/3	Chernomorets Burgas	h	1-1	*Kavdanski*
5/4	CSKA Sofia	a	0-2	
9/4	Vihren	h	0-0	
12/4	Litex	a	1-1	*Elton*
19/4	Belasitsa	h	3-1	*Petkov, Kerchev, Simonović*
25/4	Spartak Varna	a	1-2	*Malindi*
29/4	Vidima	h	2-0	*Malindi, Simonović*
4/5	Pirin 1922	a	0-1	
10/5	Lokomotiv Sofia	h	0-0	
17/5	Levski	a	1-2	*og (Tomasic)*

No	Name	Nat	Pos	Aps	(s)	Gls
18	Radoslav ANEV		D	7	(2)	
3	Zoran BELOŠEVIĆ	SRB	D	12	(1)	
13	Viktor DENIRAN	NGA	D	1		
21	Bogomil DYAKOV		D	15		
16	Nikolai DYULGEROV		M		(6)	
22	ELTON de Souza	BRA	A	11	(6)	3
4	Slavčo GEORGIEVSKI	MKD	M	14	(1)	1
23	Yordan GOSPODINOV		G	23		
15	Martin HRISTOV		A		(4)	
7	Iliya ILIEV		M	23	(5)	3
14	Galin IVANOV		M	4	(2)	
2	Vladimir IVANOV		D	22	(3)	
5	Martin KAVDANSKI		D	23		1
17	Martin KERCHEV		M	28	(2)	4
12	Mario KIREV		G	1	(2)	
77	Milan KOPRIVAROV		A	5	(1)	1
3	Petar KYUMYURDZHIEV		D	5		
77	Zdravko LAZAROV		A	7		4
99	Enco MALINDI	ALB	M	9	(1)	2
25	Georgi MECHECHIEV		D	7	(3)	
19	Srđan NOVIKOVIĆ	SRB	M	9	(4)	
20	Orlin ORLINOV		M	2	(13)	2
11	Deniran ORTEGA	NGA	A	14	(2)	6
24	Borislav PAVLOV		M	12	(4)	
16	Dimitar PETKOV		M		(2)	
35	Yordan PETKOV		D	23		1
12	Emil PETROV		G	6	(1)	
30	Nikolai PETROV		M	16	(4)	1
8	Radoslav RANGELOV		M	2		
6	Georgi SAMOKISHEV		D	1	(1)	
10	Saša SIMONOVIĆ	SRB	M	23		7
19	Dimitar VODENICHAROV		A	1	(6)	1
9	Zoran ZLATKOVSKI	MKD	A	4	(7)	

PFC SPARTAK VARNA

Coach – Georgi Ivanov; (29/8/07) Atanas Atanasov; (10/3/08) Radoslav Zdravkov

Founded – 1945

MAJOR HONOURS: Bulgartian League – (1) 1932 (as Shipchenski Soko

2007				
11/8	Botev	h	2-2	*Naidenov, Mirchev*
18/8	Chernomorets Burgas	a	0-1	
25/8	CSKA Sofia	h	0-2	
1/9	Vihren	a	1-0	*Zhekov*
14/9	Litex	h	0-0	
22/9	Belasitsa	a	1-2	*Naidenov*
29/9	Levski	h	1-2	*Stoev*
6/10	Vidima	h	0-0	
20/10	Pirin 1922	a	2-1	*Naidenov, Hikmet*
27/10	Lokomotiv Sofia	h	0-1	
4/11	Slavia	a	0-5	
10/11	Beroe	h	1-0	*Georgiev*
25/11	Lokomotiv Plovdiv	a	0-1	
1/12	Cherno More	h	0-1	
8/12	Marek	a	0-1	
2008				
1/3	Botev	a	0-2	
8/3	Chernomorets Burgas	h	1-1	*Vodenicharov*
14/3	CSKA Sofia	a	2-3	*Naidenov, Ivanović*
19/3	Vihren	h	0-1	
22/3	Litex	a	0-1	
30/3	Belasitsa	h	1-0	*Naidenov (p)*
5/4	Levski	a	0-3	
9/4	Vidima	a	1-1	*Marinov*
12/4	Pirin 1922	h	2-0	*Naidenov, Ivanović*
20/4	Lokomotiv Sofia	a	0-1	
25/4	Slavia	h	2-1	*Naidenov, Ivanović*
30/4	Beroe	a	0-0	
4/5	Lokomotiv Plovdiv	h	2-1	*Naidenov 2 (1p)*
10/5	Cherno More	a	0-0	
17/5	Marek	h	2-0	*Georgiev, Naidenov*

No	Name	Nat	Pos	Aps	(s)	Gls
12	Georgi ARNAUDOV		G	2		
13	Vasil BOEV		M	7	(12)	
16	Martin DIMOV		D	13		
17	Budimir ĐUKIĆ	SRB	M	17	(5)	
3	Stoyan GEORGIEV		D	24	(2)	2
8	Ahmet HIKMET		M	14	(1)	1
15	Boyan ILIEV		M	28		
23	Velimir IVANOVIĆ	SRB	M	24	(1)	3
8	Kuncho KUNCHEV		M	23	(2)	
5	Ventsislav MARINOV		D	17	(6)	1
24	Ivo MIHAILOV		M	2	(6)	
11	Vladislav MIRCHEV		A	22	(5)	1
20	Ivan NAIDENOV		M	28		10
16	Marko PALAVESTRIĆ	SRB	D	5	(2)	
18	Yordan PENEV		D		(1)	
19	Stanislav PETROV		D	27		
7	Marko SAVIĆ	SRB	D		(4)	
12	Genko SLAVOV		G	1	(1)	

Name	Nat	Pos	Aps	(s)	Gls
Radostin STANEV		G	11		
Dimitar STEFANOV		M	2	(7)	
Mladen STOEV		M	4	(5)	1
Darin TODOROV		A	5	(8)	
Tsvetomir TSANKOV		G	16	(2)	
Kaloyan TSVETKOV		M		(1)	
Boiko VELICHKOV		M	8	(6)	
Federico VILLAR	ARG	D		(1)	
Dimitar VODENICHAROV		A	10	(4)	1
Stanislav ZHEKOV		M	20		1

PFC VIDIMA RAKOVSKI

Coach – Kostadin Angelov; (12/3/08) Manol Georgiev

Founded – 1997

Opponent		Score	Scorers
Marek	h	1-0	*Lahchev (p)*
Botev	a	0-5	
Chernomorets Burgas	h	1-1	*Chalakov*
CSKA Sofia	a	1-3	*Chalakov*
Vihren	h	0-1	
Litex	a	1-4	*Chalakov*
Belasitsa	h	1-0	*Ivanov D.*
Spartak Varna	a	0-0	
Levski	h	1-3	*Ivanov D.*
Pirin 1922	h	0-1	
Lokomotiv Sofia	a	0-2	
Slavia	h	0-2	
Beroe	a	0-2	
Lokomotiv Plovdiv	h	0-3	
Cherno More	a	0-7	
Marek	a	1-2	*Pisarov*
Botev	h	0-1	
Chernomorets Burgas	a	0-1	
CSKA Sofia	h	0-0	
Vihren	a	1-1	*Hazurov*
Litex	h	3-2	*Hazurov 3*
Belasitsa	a	0-1	
Spartak Varna	h	1-1	*Hristov*
Levski	a	0-3	
Pirin 1922	a	1-3	*Hazurov*
Lokomotiv Sofia	h	0-0	
Slavia	a	0-2	
Beroe	h	3-1	*Pisarov, Zelenkov, Hazurov (p)*
Lokomotiv Plovdiv	a	1-6	*Chalakov*
Cherno More	h	0-3	

Name	Nat	Pos	Aps	(s)	Gls
Abdi ABDIKOV		G	11		
Mariyan BLAZHEV		M	6		
Mario BLIZNAKOV		M	3	(2)	
Boris BORISOV		D	10	(7)	
Asen CHALAKOV		M	21	(1)	4
Borislav DICHEV		A	10	(4)	
Mariyan DRAGNEV		M	5	(2)	
Georgi GAIDAROV		D	6	(3)	
Manol GEORGIEV		M	8	(1)	
Kostadin HAZUROV		A	15		6
Martin HRISTOV		A	6	(7)	1
Dragomir IVANOV		M	6	(5)	2
Georgi IVANOV		D	5	(1)	
Hristo IVANOV		G	19	(2)	
Iliyan IVANOV		M		(1)	
Lyubomir IVANOV		M	2	(1)	
Vladislav KALAIDZHIEV		M		(1)	
Mileb LAHCHEV		D	23		1
Hristo MARKOV		M	2	(4)	
Iliyan MEKIKOV		M	21	(6)	
Deyan PETROV		M	3	(3)	
Iskren PISAROV		A	19	(6)	2
Bogomil SPASOV		M	1	(1)	
Todor STOEV		D	10	(6)	

No	Name	Nat	Pos	Aps	(s)	Gls
24	Borislav STOICHEV		D	21		
5	Georgi STOICHEV		D	10	(4)	
9	Georgi STOYANOV		A	11	(6)	
8	Iliya TASEV		M	1		
3	Ivan TODOROV		D	24	(2)	
17	Iliyan TRIFONOV		M	13	(1)	
20	Toni TSONEV		A		(1)	
15	Ivailo TSVETKOV		M	9	(3)	
21	Petar VANKOV		D	5	(1)	
7	Kostadin ZELENKOV		M	24	(6)	1

PFC VIHREN SANDANSKI

Coach – Rui Dias (POR); (11/9/07) Eduard Eranosyan; (30/10/07) Filip Filipov

Founded – 1957

Date	Opponent		Score	Scorers
2007				
11/8	Levski	h	0-1	
19/8	Litex	h	2-1	*Miranda, Hristozov*
25/8	Belasitsa	a	0-1	
1/9	Spartak Varna	h	0-1	
15/9	Vidima	a	1-0	*Dyakov*
23/9	Pirin 1922	h	1-1	*Eriwerton*
28/9	Lokomotiv Sofia	a	2-3	*Hugo Santos, Miranda*
6/10	Slavia	h	1-1	*Eriwerton*
20/10	Beroe	a	0-2	
27/10	Lokomotiv Plovdiv	h	0-2	
3/11	Cherno More	a	0-1	
10/11	Marek	h	3-1	*Dyakov, Simoes, Velichkov*
24/11	Botev	a	0-1	
2/12	Chernomorets Burgas	h	1-2	*Velichkov*
9/12	CSKA Sofia	a	0-1	
2008				
2/3	Levski	a	0-1	
8/3	Litex	a	0-2	
15/3	Belasitsa	h	2-0	*Hugo Santos, Fehér*
19/3	Spartak Varna	a	1-0	*Fehér*
22/3	Vidima	h	1-1	*Hugo Santos*
29/3	Pirin 1922	a	0-0	
5/4	Lokomotiv Sofia	h	1-0	*Lukács*
9/4	Slavia	a	0-0	
13/4	Beroe	h	2-0	*Eriwerton, Simovic*
19/4	Lokomotiv Plovdiv	a	1-2	*Dyakov*
25/4	Cherno More	h	1-1	*Eskerdinha*
30/4	Marek	a	3-0	*Eriwerton, Karademitros, Simovic*
4/5	Botev	h	2-0	*Simovic, Lukács*
10/5	Chernomorets Burgas	a	0-1	
17/5	CSKA Sofia	h	1-2	*Lukács*

No	Name	Nat	Pos	Aps	(s)	Gls
21	Xavier ADEMAR	BRA	A	2	(6)	
23	Diogo ANDRADE	BRA	M		(2)	
27	Sibi CANONIN	FRA	M	6	(3)	
24	Radoslav DAVIDOV		M		(1)	
29	Luis Filipe Viegas DIAS	POR	M	2		
7	Petar DIMITROV		M	12	(5)	
5	Tanko DYAKOV		D	24		3
17	ERIWERTON Santos Lima	BRA	A	23	(5)	4
11	ESQUERDINHA	BRA	A	19		1
6	Zoltán FEHÉR	HUN	M	14		2
3	Valeri GEORGIEV		D	16	(5)	
1	Georgi HRISTOV Ivanov		G	1		
4	Nikolai HRISTOZOV		D	29		1
20	HUGO Felipe Dos SANTOS	POR	M	24	(2)	3
10	Ruslan IVANOV		M	3	(5)	
10	Dimitris KARADEMITROS	GRE	M	7	(6)	1
30	Rodolfo LIMA	POR	M	3	(3)	
9	Tihamér LUKÁCS	HUN	M	14	(1)	3
13	MIRANDA Richard Garcia	BRA	A	10	(3)	2
9	Stoicho MLADENOV		A		(3)	
21	Bruno PAES	BRA	M	4	(2)	
26	Paulo TEIXEIRA	POR	M	10		

22	Svetoslav PETROV		D	6	(11)	
14	Svetoslav SAVATOV		M		(1)	
15	Georgi SHEITANOV		G	29		
28	Bruno ŠIKLIĆ	CRO	D	2	(3)	
6	Eduardo SIMÕES	BRA	M	16		1
19	Edgardo SIMOVIC	URU	M	9	(2)	3
6	TIAGO COSTA	POR	M	4	(2)	
18	Emil TRENKOV		M	25		
29	Lyubomir VELICHKOV		M	2	(8)	2
2	Pavel VIDANOV		D	14		

PROMOTED CLUBS

PFC SLIVEN 2000

Coach – Dragoljub Simonović (SRB)
Founded - 2000
MAJOR HONOURS: Bulgarian Cup – (1) 1990.

PFC LOKOMOTIV MEZDRA

Coach – Anatoli Kirilov; (10/2/09) Stamen Belchev
Founded - 1929

PFC MINYOR PERNIK

Coach – Dimitar Aleksiev
Founded - 1952

SECOND LEVEL FINAL TABLES 2007/08

EASTERN B PFG		Pld	W	D	L	F	A	Pts
1	PFC Sliven 2000	26	19	3	4	63	23	60
2	PFC Kaliakra Kavarna	26	16	6	4	49	17	54
3	PFC Rodopa Smolyan	26	17	2	7	44	18	53
4	PFC Nesebar	26	16	2	8	43	29	50
5	PFC Dunav Ruse	26	12	6	8	35	28	42
6	FC Spartak Plovdiv	26	10	5	11	28	34	35
7	FC Maritsa 1921 Plovdiv	26	10	5	11	34	41	35
8	PFC Naftex Burgas	26	9	7	10	40	35	34
9	FC Panayot Volov	26	9	4	13	23	35	31
10	PFC Svetkavitsa Targovishte	26	8	4	14	26	46	28
11	PFC Minyor Radnevo	26	7	5	14	32	50	26
12	FC Svilengrad 1921	26	7	4	15	30	43	25
13	FC Benkovski Bjala	26	6	4	16	26	41	22
14	PFC Haskovo	26	6	3	17	24	57	21

WESTERN B PFG		Pld	W	D	L	F	A	Pts
1	PFC Lokomotiv Mezdra	26	20	3	3	56	12	63
2	PFC Minyor Pernik	26	14	5	7	45	31	47
3	PFC Chavdar Etropole	26	14	4	8	39	23	46
4	PFC Rilski Sportist Samokov	26	13	6	7	44	33	45
5	PFC Belite orli Pleven	26	11	5	10	33	31	38
6	PFC Sportist Svoge	26	10	6	10	35	30	36
7	PFC Montana	26	9	7	10	29	29	34
8	PFC Etar 1924 Veliko Tarnovo	26	8	10	8	33	39	34
9	PFC Akademik 1947 Sofia	26	9	5	12	41	43	32
10	PFC Spartak Pleven	26	8	8	10	29	40	32
11	PFC Pirin Gotse Delchev	26	8	7	11	28	33	31
12	PFC Chavdar Byala Slatina	26	6	7	13	19	34	25
13	FC Yantra Gabrovo	26	6	6	14	31	48	24
14	PFC Velbazhd Kyustendil	26	5	3	18	20	56	18

PROMOTION PLAY-OFF

(24/5/08)
Kaliakra Kavarna 1, Minyor Pernik 1 *(aet; 4-5 on pens)*

DOMESTIC CUP 2007/(

KUPA NA BULGARIYA

SECOND ROUND

(31/10/07)
Lyubimets 2007 Lyubimets 0, Chernomorets Burgas 2
Lokomotiv Plovdiv 1, CSKA Sofia 0
Bansko 1951 Bansko 0, Yantra Gabrovo 0 *(aet; 4-3 on pens)*
Svetkavitsa Targovishte 0, Cherno More 1 *(aet)*
Sliven 2000 Sliven 2, Spartak Varna 2 *(aet; 6-7 on pens)*
Velbazhd Kyustendil 0, Litex Lovech 2
Kaliakra Kavarna 4, Etar 1924 Veliko Turnovo 1
Minyor Pernik 2, Belasitsa Petrich 1
Chavdar Etropole 0, Marek 0 *(aet; 5-3 on pens)*
Sportist Svoge 1, Dunav Ruse 0
Lokomotiv Mezdra 1, Levski Sofia 2 *(aet)*
Pirin 1922 Blagoevgrad 0, Vidima-Rakovski 0 *(aet; 5-4 on pens)*
Benkovski Byala 0, Slavia Sofia 2
Beroe Stara Zagora 0, Vihren Sandanski 3
Minyor Radnevo 0, Lokokotiv Sofia 1
Naftex Burgas 0, Botev Plovdiv 1

THIRD ROUND

(5/12/07)
Litex Lovech 3, Vihren Sandanski 0

(12/12/07)
Chavdar Etropole 0, Kaliakra Kavarna 2
Sportist Svoge 1, Lokomotiv Plovdiv 4
Lokomotiv Sofia 1, Spartak Varna 0
Bansko 1951 Bansko 2, Cherno More Varna 6
Minyor Pernik 0, Pirin 1922 Blagoevgrad 1
Botev Plovdiv 4, Slavia Sofia 2
Chernomorets Burgas 0, Levski Sofia 2

QUARTER-FINALS

(12/3/08)
Lokomotiv Sofia 0, Botev Plovdiv 2 *(Garov 33, Hristov 89p)*
Kaliakra Kavarna 3 *(Raichev 42, Karadzhov 63, Stanchev 85)*, Lokomotiv Plovdiv 1 *(Dakson 71)*

Cherno More Varna 1 *(Stoyanov 68)*, Pirin 1922 Blagoevgrad 0
Litex Lovech 0, Levski 0 *(aet; 4-3 on pens)*

SEMI-FINALS

(16/4/08)
Kaliakra Kavarna 1 *(Kiskinov 49)*, Cherno More Varna 3 *(Dimitrov 6 Da Silva 66, Georgiev 69)*

Litex Lovech 4 *(Popov I. 45, Wellington 78, Manolev 85, 90)*, Botev Plovdiv 2 *(Hristov 53, 63p)*

FINAL

(14/5/08)
Vasil Levski National Stadium, Sofia
PFC LITEX LOVECH 1 *(Manolev 56)*
PFC CHERNO MORE VARNA 0
Referee *–Yordanov*
LITEX *– Todorov, Manolev, Cambon, Nikolov, Venkov, Genchev, Pop (Angelov 90), Jelenković, Wellington (Tome 89), Sandrinho, Bibishkc (Berberović 61).*
CHERNO MORE *– Ilchev, Tomash, Domakinov, Aleksandrov A., Jovc Ricardo André, Georgiev (Dzhorov 60), Lazarov, Stoyanov (Gharabaghtsyan 61), Aleksandrov A.Y., Manolov.*

CROATIA

Traumatic exit for Bilić's braves

roatia coach Slaven Bilić was the first to admit that his team's cruel elimination from UEFA EURO 2008™ would be the source of deep pain and anguish for a ıg time to come.

lose on penalties is one thing; to be defeated in a oot-out after conceding an equaliser with the last :k of the game – and after taking the lead moments rlier – is about as tough as it gets. In Croatia's case, e sense of heartbreak from their defeat by Turkey was en more agonising because they had proved beyond ubt, in taking maximum points from their three oup games, that UEFA EURO 2008™ was a urnament they were well capable of winning. After , awaiting them in the semi-final were Germany, an ponent they had already conquered, 2-1, in the oup stage. Furthermore, with none of their players ured or suspended, they, unlike their Turkish nquerors, would have been at full strength.

ositive experience

t it was not to be. Although they left the tournament deeply frustrated beaten quarter-finalists, Croatia's ne in Austria had to be viewed overall as a positive perience. They had played good football and reached e knockout stage of a major finals for the first time in a cade, winning three of their four games and drawing e other. It was only penalties – and perhaps a touch of experience, not least from their coach, after Ivan asnić's late goal against Turkey - that condemned them.

veral players distinguished themselves. Goalkeeper ipe Pletikosa, official Man of the Match in the opening 0 win against Austria, conceded only two goals. teran central defenders Robert Kovač and Josip munić also performed with diligence and thority...until that last fateful moment against Turkey. nd while Darijo Srna confirmed himself as a fine set-ece specialist and young gun Ivan Rakitić dovetailed ell in a promising left-sided partnership with Danijel anjić, it was up front, if anywhere, that the team sappointed – an inevitable consequence perhaps of the absence of Brazilian-born striker Eduardo da Silva, the team's top scorer in qualifying with ten goals, who suffered a horrific double leg-break while playing for Arsenal FC in a Premier League game at Birmingham City FC in February.

Ivica Olić began the tournament alongside Mladen Petrić, but when Bilić's tactic of using him alone up front against Germany paid off, that was repeated against Turkey. Although Olić had his chances in the quarter-final, including one seemingly unmissable opportunity that he smacked against the crossbar in the first half, he was often isolated, and with Niko Kranjčar failing to live up to expectations as an advanced midfielder, Croatia became heavily reliant on the inventive promptings of schemer Luka Modrić to pierce the opposition defence.

Magical Modrić

Notwithstanding his penalty miss against Turkey, Modrić was Croatia's outstanding performer, making an impact on all three of his appearances – with the winning goal against Croatia, a Man of the Match display against

Slaven Bilić consoles Darijo Srna after Croatia's cruel elimination from UEFA EURO 2008™

Hrvatski Nogometni Savez (HNS

Rusanova 13
HR-10000 Zagreb
tel - +385 1 2361555
fax - +385 1 2441500
website - www.hns-cff.hr
email – info@hns-cff.hr
Year of Formation – 1912
President - Vlatko Marković
General Secretary - Zorislav Srebrić
Press Officer – Davor Gavran
Stadium - Maksimir, Zagreb (38,079)

INTERNATIONAL TOURNAMENT APPEARANCES
FIFA World Cup - (3) 1998 (3rd), 2002, 20
UEFA European Championship - (3) 1996 (qtr-finals), 2004, 2008 (qtr-finals).

TOP FIVE ALL-TIME CAPS
Dario Šimić (99); Robert Jarni (81); Niko Kovač (80); Robert Kovač (77); Stipe Pletikosa (72)

TOP FIVE ALL-TIME GOALS
Davor Šuker (45); Darijo Srna (16); Goran Vlaović (15); Eduardo da Silva & Niko Kovač (13)

NATIONAL TEAM RESULTS 2007/08

22/8/07	Bosnia-Herzegovina	A	Sarajevo	5-3	*Eduardo (18), Srna (35, 74), Kovač N. (72, 81)*
8/9/07	Estonia (ECQ)	H	Zagreb	2-0	*Eduardo (39, 45+1)*
12/9/07	Andorra (ECQ)	A	Andorra la Vella	6-0	*Srna (34), Petrić (38, 44), Kranjčar (49), Eduardo (55), Rakitić (64)*
13/10/07	Israel (ECQ)	H	Zagreb	1-0	*Eduardo (52)*
16/10/07	Slovakia	H	Rijeka	3-0	*Olić (45, 69), Vukojević (48)*
17/11/07	FYR Macedonia (ECQ)	A	Skopje	0-2	
21/11/07	England (ECQ)	A	Wembley	3-2	*Kranjčar (8), Olić (14), Petrić (77)*
6/2/08	Netherlands	H	Split	0-3	
26/3/08	Scotland	A	Glasgow	1-1	*Kranjčar (10)*
24/5/08	Moldova	H	Rijeka	1-0	*Kovač N. (30)*
31/5/08	Hungary	A	Budapest	1-1	*Kovač N. (24)*
8/6/08	Austria (ECF)	A	Vienna	1-0	*Modrić (4p)*
12/6/08	Germany (ECF)	N	Klagenfurt (AUT)	2-1	*Srna (24), Olić (62)*
16/6/08	Poland (ECF)	N	Klagenfurt (AUT)	1-0	*Klasnić (53)*
20/6/08	Turkey (ECF)	N	Vienna (AUT)	1-1	*Klasnić (119) (aet; 1-3 on pens)*

Germany and a delightful assist and exquisite all-round performance of skill and invention against Turkey. At 22, his future looks extremely bright, especially as he has now left his homeland for the English Premier League.

Modrić's move to Tottenham Hotspur FC was signed and sealed before UEFA EURO 2008™, leaving many bigger-budget clubs in England and elsewhere looking on in envy. The young playmaker had publicised his talent during Croatia's excellent qualifying campaign, not least with a stirring display in the famous 3-2 win over England at Wembley, but his performances in Austria raised his profile to a whole new level.

The youngster signed off from Croatia's domestic scene in style, helping NK Dinamo Zagreb to a League and Cu double that set the club far apart from the rest of the teams in the country. There was even a big scalp for Dinamo in Europe as they atoned for a disappointing – i expected - elimination by Werder Bremen in the third qualifying round of the UEFA Champions League by knocking AFC Ajax out of the UEFA Cup with a majestic

TIONAL TEAM APPEARANCES 2007/08

– Slaven BILIĆ 11/9/68			Bih	EST	AND	ISR	Svk	MKD	ENG	Ned	Sco	Mda	Hun	AUT	GER	POL	TUR	Caps	Goals
ı RUNJE	10/2/76	Lens (FRA)	G		G		G46									G		5	-
ĆORLUKA	5/2/86	Man. City (ENG)	D	D	D	D	D	D	D	D	D85	D	D	D	D	s27	D	24	-
ŠIMIĆ	12/11/75	Milan (ITA)	D	D		D	D57	D	D	D46	s85	s46				D		99	3
KOVAČ	6/4/74	Dortmund (GER)	D	D	D	D		D	D	D70	D73	D46	D63	D	D		D	77	-
ŠIMUNIĆ	18/2/78	Hertha (GER)	D	D		D	s57	D	D	D	D	D46	D	D	D		D	65	3
SRNA	1/5/82	Shakhtar (UKR)	M82	M82	M	M	s70	M	M	M86	M64		M	M	M80		M	58	16
OVAČ	15/10/71	Salzburg (AUT)	M	M				M	M	M70	M46	M59	M	M	M		M	80	13
VRANJEŠ	31/1/80	Bremen (GER)	M				M											26	-
ı PETRIĆ	1/1/81	Dortmund (GER)	A71	A72	A46			A42	s69	A	A58		A63	A72	s72	A75	s65	27	9
DO da Silva	25/2/83	Arsenal (ENG)	A61	A	A62	A	A	A54	A69	A70								22	13
DAN	22/4/80	Parma (ITA)	A82								s58	A62		s72				6	-
BABIĆ	28/1/81	Betis (ESP)	s61	s82	D		D70			s86								49	3
LIĆ	14/9/79	Hamburg (GER)	s71	s72		A81	A70	s54	A84	s46	A58	A46	A46	A83	A72		A97	57	10
BALABAN	15/10/78	Dinamo Zagreb	s82		s46													35	10
PRANJIĆ	2/12/81	Heerenveen (NED)	s82		s46	s46			s75	s46	D	D	D	D	D	D	D	15	-
LETIKOSA	8/1/79	Spartak Moskva (RUS)		G		G		G	G	G	G	G	G	G	G		G	72	-
ODRIĆ	9/9/85	Dinamo Zagreb		M	M46	M	s70	M	M	M	M	M	M	M	M		M	29	4
RANJČAR	13/8/84	Portsmouth (ENG)		M61	M	M46		M75	M75	M46	M		M78	M61	M85	s75	M65	45	7
AKITIĆ	10/3/88	Schalke (GER)		s61	s62	s81	M		s84	s70		M	s46		M	M	M	11	1
NEŽEVIĆ	20/4/82	Livorno (ITA)			D		D			s70	s73		s63	s61	s85	D27		10	1
EKO	9/4/80	Monaco (FRA)			M	M	M46			s70	s64	s73			s80	M		54	2
RPIĆ	26/5/81	Dinamo Zagreb					D											1	-
ı VUKOJEVIĆ	20/12/83	Dinamo Zagreb					s46	s75			s46	M73	s78	s83		M		7	1
GALINOVIĆ	15/11/76	Panathinaikos (GRE)					s46											2	-
MANĐUKIĆ	21/5/86	Dinamo Zagreb						s42										1	-
LASNIĆ	29/1/80	Bremen (GER)									s58	s46	s63			A74	s97	30	10
VEJIĆ	8/6/77	Tom (RUS)										s46				D		3	-
POKRIVAČ	26/11/85	Monaco (FRA)										s59				M		2	-
KALINIĆ	5/1/88	Hajduk										s62				s74		2	-

3-2 extra-time victory in Amsterdam. Alas, there would be no further victories in a group phase that pitted Dinamo against FC Basel 1893, SK Brann, Hamburger SV and Stade Rennais FC – a disappointing sequence that would ultimately cost coach Branko Ivanković his job, even if the axe did not officially fall until mid-January when he resigned in the face of a volley of criticism from the club's all-powerful vice-president Zdravko Mamić.

Dominant Dinamo

On the home front Dinamo were a class apart. Despite the summer sale of Eduardo and Vedran Ćorluka to England, the title race quickly became a non-event as the defending champions scorched into action with eight successive victories, scoring 29 goals in the process. By mid-November, with almost half the season complete, they had dropped only three points. With kingpin Modrić leading the way, ably supported in the goalscoring department by ex-Aston Villa FC striker Boško Balaban, fellow Croatian international midfielder Ognjen Vukojević and Amsterdam ArenA hero Mario Mandžukić, the only issue of interest at the top of the table was how many points Dinamo could accrue. In the end, with new coach Zvonimir Soldo, the former Croatian international midfielder, overseeing the spring campaign, they raised

Boško Balaban scored eleven goals in NK Dinamo Zagreb's runaway Croatian championship triumph

their tally to 82. It was ten points fewer than their 2006/07 haul but it still earned them a massive 28-poir winning margin over the team that headed a tight race for second place, NK Slaven Koprivnica.

With the 1.HNL title in the bag, Dinamo focused their attention on the Croatian Cup. Having seen off Slaven in the quarter-finals and city rivals NK Zagreb in the semis, they came face to face with arch-foes HNK Hajduk Split in the two-legged final. Not in the habit living on their nerves, Dinamo effectively rendered th second match redundant after winning the home leg 3-0, Mandžukić again making his mark with a brace o goals after his in-form strike-partner Josip Tadić had provided an early lead. The return ended 0-0 and Dinamo had a ninth Croatian Cup to add to their ten Croatian championship title.

There was an unusual postscript to the season, however, when Soldo resigned as Dinamo coach, to b replaced for the 2008/09 campaign by his predecesso Ivanković, who agreed to return after the volatile Mamić apologised for his mid-season rant.

Hard times at Hajduk

Hajduk's appearance in the Cup final ensured their qualification, alongside surprise package Slaven, for the UEFA Cup, giving Croatia the same trio of Europe qualifiers as in the previous season, but their defeat Dinamo compounded a miserable league campaign which, despite a major recruitment drive, they never managed to string more than two wins together and could finish only fifth. Coach Robert Jarni, the former Croatia left-back, made little impression and left at th season's end. With Hajduk suffering hard times financially, the only genuine source of pleasure for th club's fans was the thrilling form of 20-year-old strike Nikola Kalinić, whose 17 goals earned him a place – i preference to Dinamo's Mandžukić - in Croatia's UEFA EURO 2008™ squad.

NK Osijek and NK Rijeka both finished above Hajduk, the latter taking the UEFA Intertoto Cup spot, and the was a reprieve for newly promoted strugglers NK Inte Zaprešić, who escaped an immediate return to the second division by winning the end-of-season play-of NK Međimurje's automatic relegation was almost as clear-cut as Dinamo's title triumph as the club from Cakovec managed just three wins in their 33 matches NK Croatia Sesvete, from the Zagreb suburbs, won th second division to reach the top flight for the first tim

DOMESTIC LEAGUE 2007/08

NL FINAL TABLE

		Home					Away					Total					
	Pld	W	D	L	F	A	W	D	L	F	A	W	D	L	F	A	Pts
Dinamo Zagreb	33	16	0	1	54	12	10	4	2	37	22	26	4	3	91	34	82
Slaven Koprivnica	33	14	3	0	40	10	2	3	11	5	19	16	6	11	45	29	54
Osijek	33	11	3	3	28	13	5	3	8	15	21	16	6	11	43	34	54
Rijeka	33	11	5	1	39	18	3	6	7	14	23	14	11	8	53	41	53
Hajduk Split	33	10	4	3	42	20	4	6	6	15	21	14	10	9	57	41	52
Zagreb	33	8	5	3	33	17	3	6	8	18	23	11	11	11	51	40	44
Varteks	33	8	3	5	32	21	3	4	10	14	32	11	7	15	46	53	40
Cibalia	33	9	4	3	27	12	2	3	12	13	36	11	7	15	40	48	40
Zadar	33	8	5	4	28	18	3	2	11	21	43	11	7	15	49	61	40
Šibenik	33	7	6	3	17	14	2	6	9	17	38	9	12	12	34	52	39
Inter Zaprešić	33	6	6	4	15	14	2	3	12	12	45	8	9	16	27	59	33
Međimurje	33	3	4	9	23	26	0	2	15	14	55	3	6	24	37	81	15

TOP GOALSCORERS

21 Želimir TERKEŠ (Zadar)

18 Radomir ĐALOVIĆ (Rijeka)

17 Nikola KALINIĆ (Hajduk)

14 Krunoslav LOVREK (Zagreb)

13 Luka MODRIĆ (Dinamo Zagreb)

12 Željko MALČIĆ (Cibalia)
Senijad IBRIČIĆ (Zagreb)
Mario MANDŽUKIĆ (Dinamo Zagreb)

11 Anas SHARBINI (Rijeka)
Ognjen VUKOJEVIĆ (Dinamo Zagreb)
Josip TADIĆ (Dinamo Zagreb)
Boško BALABAN (Dinamo Zagreb)

CLUB-BY-CLUB

HNK CIBALIA

Coach – Srećko Lušić

Founded - 1919

7

	Varteks	h	1-0	*Bagarić (p)*
	Rijeka	a	0-3	
	Hajduk	h	0-0	
3	Dinamo Zagreb	a	1-2	*Studenović*
3	Zadar	h	0-2	
3	Inter Zaprešić	a	0-1	
	Šibenik	h	3-3	*Kerić, Husić, Medvid*
	Osijek	h	2-0	*Dodik 2*
	Međimurje	a	1-0	*Kerić*
	Zagreb	h	3-1	*Malčić 2, Maroslavac*
	Slaven	a	2-2	*Kerić, Dodik*
10	Varteks	a	1-2	*Bagarić (p)*
10	Rijeka	h	2-0	*Bagarić 2 (1p)*
10	Hajduk	a	2-2	*Malčić 2*
	Dinamo Zagreb	h	1-2	*Malčić*
11	Zadar	a	1-1	*Bagarić (p)*
11	Inter Zaprešić	h	2-0	*Bagarić (p), Malčić*
2	Šibenik	a	0-2	
2	Osijek	a	1-5	*Husić*

8

2	Međimurje	h	2-0	*Malčić, Kujundžija*
	Zagreb	a	1-4	*Zore*
	Slaven	h	3-0	*Malčić 2, Baraban*
3	Dinamo Zagreb	a	0-4	
3	Osijek	a	1-2	*Malčić*
3	Zagreb	h	2-2	*Dodik 2*
3	Zadar	a	0-1	
4	Šibenik	h	2-0	*Jurić, Bagarić*
4	Slaven	a	0-2	
4	Varteks	h	0-1	
4	Hajduk	a	2-1	*Husić, Bagarić*
4	Inter Zaprešić	h	1-1	*Malčić*
	Rijeka	a	0-2	
5	Međimurje	h	3-0	*Husić, Malčić, Džafić*

No	Name	Nat	Pos	Aps	(s)	Gls
14	Mario ANDRIČEVIĆ		D	2	(10)	
1	Marijan ANTOLOVIĆ		G	2		
10	Dalibor BAGARIĆ		M	31		8
25	Ivan BARABAN		A	3	(10)	1
21	Marko BLAŠKOVIĆ		A		(1)	
18	Krešimir BRKIĆ		M		(3)	
12	Davor BURCSA		G	31		
3	Tomislav ČULJAK		M	5	(6)	
11	Marijo DODIK		A	26	(2)	5
15	Adin DŽAFIĆ	BIH	A	3	(8)	1
20	Ivan GRGIĆ		M	4	(11)	
28	Edin HUSIĆ	BIH	M	22	(5)	4
21	Tomislav JURIĆ		M	6	(1)	1
15	Andrej KERIĆ		A	16	(1)	3
22	Luka KUJUNDŽIJA		M	1	(6)	1
5	Boris LEUTAR		D	26	(1)	
9	Željko MALČIĆ		A	24		12
7	Ivan MAROSLAVAC		M	27	(1)	1
26	Marijan MATIĆ		D	1	(2)	
19	Ivan MEDVID		D	24		1
6	Elvis MEŠIĆ		D	29	(2)	
4	Marko RADAS		D	28	(1)	
16	Tomislav RADOTIĆ		D	25	(3)	
17	Vlatko ŠIMUNAC		A		(1)	
17	Mijo STUDENOVIĆ	BIH	D	11	(2)	1
9	Marijan VUKA		A	5	(2)	
21	Ivan ŽGELA		A	2	(2)	
2	Ante ZORE		D	9	(8)	1

NK DINAMO ZAGREB

Coach – Brako Ivanković; (15/1/08) Zvonimir Soldo

Founded – 1945

MAJOR HONOURS: Inter Cities Fairs Cup – (1) 1967; Yugoslav League – (4) 1948, 1954, 1958, 1982; Croatian League - (10) 1993, 1996, 1997, 1998, 1999, 2000, 2003, 2006, 2007, 2008; Yugoslav Cup – (7) 1951, 1960, 1963, 1965, 1969, 1980, 1983; Croatian Cup – (9) 1994, 1996, 1997, 1998, 2001, 2002, 2004, 2007, 2008.

CROATIA

2007				
21/7	Šibenik	h	5-0	*Modrić 2 (1p), Mandžukić, Sammir, Vukojević*
28/7	Zadar	h	5-1	*Schildenfeld, Šokota, Sammir, Mandžukić, Vukojević*
7/8	Inter Zaprešić	a	4-0	*Mandžukić, Modrić, Jertec, og (Skulić)*
10/8	Cibalia	h	2-1	*Modrić, Balaban*
19/8	Osijek	a	3-1	*Balaban, Modrić 2 (1p)*
24/8	Međimurje	h	3-1	*Mandžukić, Pokrivač, Vukojević*
1/9	Zagreb	a	3-1	*Mandžukić 2, Pokrivač*
15/9	Slaven	h	4-0	*Balaban 2, Modrić (p), Pokrivač*
23/9	Varteks	a	3-4	*Balaban, Pokrivač, Modrić*
29/9	Rijeka	h	1-0	*Vukojević*
7/10	Hajduk	a	2-1	*Modrić, Mandžukić*
20/10	Šibenik	a	2-0	*Vukojević, Šokota (p)*
27/10	Zadar	a	2-1	*Šokota 2*
31/10	Inter Zaprešić	h	5-0	*Sammir, Guela, Mandžukić, Šokota, Pokrivač*
3/11	Cibalia	a	2-1	*Vukojević, Guela*
11/11	Osijek	h	1-0	*Vukojević*
24/11	Međimurje	a	1-1	*Vugrinec*
2/12	Zagreb	h	6-3	*Mandžukić, Balaban, Modrić, Vrdoljak, Tadić 2*
8/12	Slaven	a	2-5	*Carlos, Buljat*
2008				
23/2	Varteks	h	1-2	*Tadić*
1/3	Rijeka	a	4-2	*Modrić, Vrdoljak, Mikić, Vukojević*
8/3	Hajduk	h	1-0	*Vrdoljak*
15/3	Cibalia	h	4-0	*Tadić, Čale, Balaban 2*
19/3	Zagreb	a	0-0	
22/3	Šibenik	h	5-1	*Balaban, Modrić 2 (1p), Tadić, Drpić*
29/3	Varteks	a	1-1	*Balaban*
29/4	Inter Zaprešić	h	1-0	*Mandžukić*
12/4	Međimurje	a	2-1	*Vugrinec, Sammir*
16/4	Osijek	h	3-2	*Manđukić, Tadić, Vukojević*
19/4	Zadar	a	5-2	*Tadić 2, Vugrinec 2, Buljat*
26/4	Slaven	h	1-0	*Balaban*
3/5	Hajduk	a	1-1	*Etto*
10/5	Rijeka	h	6-1	*Tadić 3, Mandžukić, Vukojević 2*

No	Name	Nat	Pos	Aps	(s)	Gls
16	Domagoj ANTOLIĆ		M		(5)	
9	Boško BALABAN		A	17	(1)	11
6	Tomislav BARBARIĆ		D	3	(2)	
22	Igor BIŠĆAN		D	9		
2	Marijan BULJAT		M	9	(7)	2
15	CARLOS Santos de Jesús	BRA	D	12	(3)	1
13	Matthias CHAGO	CMR	M	4	(6)	
3	Hrvoje ČALE		D	26		1
26	Dino DRPIĆ		D	21	(1)	1
7	ETTO Oélilton Araújo dos Santos	BRA	D	20	(3)	1
19	Franck Manga GUELA	CIV	A	15	(6)	2
16	Dario JERTEC		M		(2)	1
12	Ivan KELAVA		G	6	(1)	
1	Georg KOCH	GER	G	25		
12	Filip LONČARIĆ		G	2		
17	Mario MANDŽUKIĆ		A	24	(5)	12
14	Mihael MIKIĆ		A	15	(6)	1
5	Tomislav MIKULIĆ		D	10		
10	Luka MODRIĆ		M	25		1
27	Ivan PEKO		A		(1)	
6	Nikola POKRIVAČ		M	16	(1)	5
18	Jorge Cruz Campos SAMMIR	BRA	M	17	(6)	4
23	Gordon SCHILDENFELD		D	17		1
25	Tomo ŠOKOTA		A	7	(6)	5
11	Josip TADIĆ		A	14	(13)	1
7	Ante TOMIĆ		M		(2)	
21	Ivica VRDOLJAK		D	15	(9)	3
30	Davor VUGRINEC		M	5	(8)	4
20	Ognjen VUKOJEVIĆ		M	29		1

HNK HAJDUK SPLIT

Coach – Ivan Pudar; (22/8/07) (Mario Ćutuk); (25/8/07) Sergi Krešić; (26/10/07) Robert Jarni

Founded – 1911

MAJOR HONOURS: Yugoslav League – (11) 1927, 1929, 1941, 194 1950, 1952, 1955, 1971, 1974, 1975, 1979; Croatian League – (6) 19 1994, 1995, 2001, 2004, 2005; Yugoslav Cup – (9) 1967, 1972 ,197 1974, 1976, 1977, 1984, 1987, 1991; Croatian Cup – (4) 1993, 199 2000, 2003.

2007				
22/7	Zadar	a	0-0	
28/7	Inter Zaprešić	h	7-1	*Kalinić 2, Rukavina (1p), Cernat 2*
5/8	Cibalia	a	0-0	
11/8	Osijek	h	1-0	*Kalinić*
19/8	Međimurje	a	1-1	*Rubil*
25/8	Zagreb	h	2-0	*Bartolović, Kalinić*
2/9	Slaven	a	2-2	*Rukavina, Oremuš*
15/9	Varteks	h	3-1	*Kalinić 2 (1p), Cerna*
22/9	Rijeka	a	0-4	
29/9	Šibenik	a	0-1	
7/10	Dinamo Zagreb	h	1-2	*Kalinić*
20/10	Zadar	h	4-1	*Kalinić 3, Linić*
27/10	Inter Zaprešić	a	1-0	*Kalinić*
31/10	Cibalia	h	2-2	*Rubil, Verpakovskis*
3/11	Osijek	a	1-0	*Tudor*
10/11	Međimurje	h	3-3	*Cernat, Kalinić, Verpakovskis*
24/11	Zagreb	a	0-1	
1/12	Slaven	h	1-0	*Kalinić (p)*
8/12	Varteks	a	3-1	*Linić, Hrgović 2 (1p)*
2008				
23/2	Rijeka	h	1-1	*Verpakovskis*
1/3	Šibenik	h	2-0	*Živković, Verpakovsk*
8/3	Dinamo Zagreb	a	0-1	
15/3	Šibenik	h	4-1	*Kalinić 2 (1p), Verpakovskis, Andrić*
19/3	Varteks	a	0-4	
22/3	Inter Zaprešić	h	7-2	*Cernat 2, Rukavina, Rubil, Andrić, Živkov Gabrić*
29/3	Međimurje	a	2-2	*Kalinić, Cernat*
29/4	Osijek	h	0-2	
12/4	Zadar	a	3-1	*Rukavina 2, Cernat*
16/4	Slaven	h	2-0	*Rukavina, Gabrić*
19/4	Cibalia	h	1-2	*Kalinić*
26/4	Rijeka	a	1-1	*Čop*
3/5	Dinamo Zagreb	h	1-1	*Rukavina*
10/5	Zagreb	a	1-2	*Linić*

No	Name	Nat	Pos	Aps	(s)	Gl
12	Vladimir BALIĆ		G	12		
11	Srđan ANDRIĆ		M	22	(1)	2
16	Mladen BARTOLOVIĆ	BIH	A	12	(6)	1
5	Jurica BULJAT		D	18	(2)	
10	Florin CERNAT	ROU	M	27	(1)	8

1	Duje ČOP		M	5	(9)	1
0	Ivan ĆURJURIĆ		M		(1)	
7	Branko ČUBRILO		D	1	(1)	
	Dario DAMJANOVIĆ	BIH	M	9	(2)	
5	Drago GABRIĆ		M	15	(8)	2
2	Igor GAL		D	2	(1)	
8	Mirko HRGOVIĆ	BIH	M	19		2
	Goran JOZINOVIĆ	BIH	D	7	(4)	
	Nikola KALINIĆ		A	23	(2)	17
	Siniša LINIĆ		M	18	(7)	3
4	Marin LJUBIČIĆ		M	12	(8)	
1	Krešimir MAKARIN		A	1	(2)	
2	Mario MALOČA		D	11	(1)	
7	Hrvoje MILIĆ		M		(2)	
	Igor MUSA		M		(1)	
9	Mirko OREMUŠ		M		(1)	1
8	Boris PANDŽA	BIH	D	7	(3)	
9	Mladen PELAIĆ		D	16	(1)	
	Niko PERAIĆ		M	4		
6	Goran RUBIL		M	22	(5)	3
3	Ante RUKAVINA		A	22	(4)	9
0	Goran SABLIĆ		D	16		
4	Mate SELAK		M		(1)	
2	Vjekoslav TOMIĆ		G	10		
3	Igor TUDOR		D	7	(1)	1
	Miro VARVODIĆ		G	11		
9	Maris VERPAKOVSKIS	LVA	A	15	(3)	5
	Boris ŽIVKOVIĆ		D	19	(1)	2

NK INTER ZAPREŠIĆ

Coach – Ante Čačić; (18/8/07) Milivoj Bračun

Founded – 1929

MAJOR HONOURS: Croatian Cup – (1) 1992.

007				
0/7	Rijeka	h	0-1	
8/7	Hajduk	a	1-7	*Kukec*
/8	Dinamo Zagreb	h	0-4	
1/8	Zadar	a	0-3	
7/8	Šibenik	h	2-2	*Šarić 2*
5/8	Cibalia	h	1-0	*Šarić*
/9	Osijek	a	0-1	
4/9	Međimurje	h	3-0	*Gulić (p), Sivonjić 2*
2/9	Zagreb	a	0-3	
9/9	Slaven	h	1-0	*Starčević*
/10	Varteks	a	2-1	*Biskup, Sivonjić*
0/10	Rijeka	a	1-2	*Grgurović (p)*
7/10	Hajduk	h	0-1	
1/10	Dinamo Zagreb	a	0-5	
/11	Zadar	h	2-1	*Gulić, Sivonjić*
0/11	Šibenik	a	1-1	*Gulić*
4/11	Cibalia	a	0-2	
/12	Osijek	h	1-1	*Verhas*
/12	Međimurje	a	3-2	*Grgurević, Gulić (p), og (Štefulj)*
008				
2/2	Zagreb	h	1-1	*Vidović*
/3	Slaven	a	0-2	
/3	Varteks	h	0-0	
5/3	Zadar	a	1-3	*Rašić*
9/3	Slaven	h	0-0	
2/3	Hajduk	a	2-7	*Kukec 2*
9/3	Rijeka	h	2-1	*Kukec, Gulić (p)*
9/4	Dinamo Zagreb	a	0-1	
2/4	Zagreb	a	0-0	
6/4	Šibenik	a	0-0	
9/4	Varteks	h	1-0	*Kukec (p)*
6/4	Cibalia	a	1-1	*Kukec*
/5	Međimurje	a	0-4	
0/5	Osijek	h	1-2	*Lovren*

No	Name	Nat	Pos	Aps	(s)	Gls
7	Luko BISKUP		M	2	(2)	1
19	Kristijan BRČIĆ		M	2	(5)	
17	Silvijo CAVRIĆ		D	22	(2)	
2	Tomislav CERAJ		M	3	(2)	
24	Godfroid Emmanuel Mahi EBEM	CMR	D	2	(2)	
11	GLAUVER Aranha Pinheiro	BRA	A		(1)	
13	Mario GRGUROVIĆ		M	16	(7)	2
9	Bernard GULIĆ		A	22	(2)	5
3	Mahir IFTIĆ	BIH	D	27		
26	Tomislav IVANKOVIĆ		A		(1)	
10	Tomislav JONJIĆ		M	12	(7)	
8	JUNIOR Osmar Ferreira	BRA	A	3	(3)	
3	Mario JURIN		M	1	(2)	
27	Dario KRIŠTO		M	8	(4)	
6	Damir KRZNAR		D	30		
14	Davor KUKEC		M	26	(3)	6
2	Patrice KWEDI	CMR	M	6	(3)	
20	Marko LONČAR		A		(1)	
16	Dejan LOVREN		D	29		1
21	Mijo NAĐ		D	9	(5)	
3	Jaroslav NESVADBA	CZE	M	6		
11	Marijan NIKOLIĆ		A	2	(3)	
21	Saško PANDEV	MKD	A	6	(7)	
20	Mario RAŠIĆ		A	5	(13)	1
16	RENATO Alves Gomides	BRA	M	3		
15	Miroslav ŠARIĆ		M	6	(2)	3
1	Marko ŠARLIJA		G	10		
18	Ante ŠIMUNAC		M		(3)	
8	Ilija SIVONJIĆ		A	21		4
7	Ernard SKULIĆ		M	11	(2)	
4	Dalibor STARČEVIĆ		D	23		1
18	Mladen STIPKOVIĆ		M	6		
15	Petar TOMIĆ		D	1	(2)	
15	Domagoj VERHAS		D	11	(9)	1
11	Rajko VIDOVIĆ		A	9	(2)	1
12	Tomislav VRANJIĆ		G	23	(1)	

NK MEĐIMURJE

Coach – Boško Anić; (29/8/07) Ivan Bedi; (24/9/07) Miljenko Dovečer

Founded – 2003

2007				
21/7	Zagreb	h	0-3	
28/7	Slaven	a	0-2	
4/8	Varteks	h	4-1	*Šaranović 3, Piškor*
11/8	Rijeka	a	1-3	*Štefulj*
19/8	Hajduk	h	1-1	*Šaranović*
24/8	Dinamo Zagreb	a	1-3	*Šaranović*
1/9	Zadar	h	2-4	*Milardović, Šaranović*
14/9	Inter Zaprešić	a	0-3	
22/9	Cibalia	h	0-1	
29/9	Osijek	a	0-4	
6/10	Šibenik	h	2-2	*Piškor 2*
20/10	Zagreb	a	1-1	*Bratković*
27/10	Slaven	h	2-0	*Šaranović, Perajica*
31/10	Varteks	a	0-2	
3/11	Rijeka	h	0-1	
10/11	Hajduk	a	3-3	*Darmopil, Piškor, Perajica*
24/11	Dinamo Zagreb	h	1-1	*Milardović*
1/12	Zadar	a	0-4	
8/12	Inter Zaprešić	h	2-3	*Piškor, Eliomar*
2008				
23/2	Cibalia	a	0-2	
1/3	Osijek	h	0-1	
8/3	Šibenik	a	2-4	*Babić, Eliomar*
15/3	Osijek	a	1-3	*Eliomar*
19/3	Zadar	h	2-3	*Milardović (p), Babić*

22/3	Slaven	a	0-4	
29/3	Hajduk	h	2-2	*Eliomar, Darmopil*
29/4	Rijeka	a	2-5	*Jarić, Milardović*
12/4	Dinamo Zagreb	h	1-2	*Darmopil*
16/4	Zagreb	a	1-6	*Milardović*
19/4	Šibenik	h	0-1	
26/4	Varteks	a	2-3	*Krišto 2*
3/5	Inter Zaprešić	h	4-0	*Eliomar 2, Pintarić, Ratković*
10/5	Cibalia	a	0-3	

No	Name	Nat	Pos	Aps	(s)	Gls
16	Roberto ALVIŽ		D	2	(5)	
19	ANDRE Silva Batista	BRA	D	8		
19	Ivan BABIĆ		A	10	(1)	2
12	Ivan BANOVIĆ		G	19		
22	Tomislav BAŠIĆ		G	7		
15	Krunoslav BRATKOVIĆ		D	29		1
23	Vedran CELIŠĆAK		A	18		
7	CICERO LIMA Pereira Paulo	BRA	M	5	(11)	
1	Davor ČONKAŠ		G	7	(1)	
17	Mario DARMOPIL		D	29	(1)	3
18	Samir DURO	BIH	M	5	(4)	
27	ELIOMAR dos Santos Silva	BRA	A	23	(6)	6
4	Danijel GEORGIEVSKI	MKD	D	8	(9)	
10	Antun GRIZELJ		M	1	(2)	
13	Ivan HABUŠ		D	10	(5)	
10	Marko JANJETOVIĆ		M	12	(1)	
5	Ivan JARIĆ		D	3		1
13	Saša KOLIĆ		D	7	(2)	
26	Matej KRIŠTO		D	17		2
8	Josip MILARDOVIĆ		D	29	(1)	5
20	Igor MOSTARLIĆ		A	1		
28	Saško PANDEV	MKD	A	3	(1)	
24	Boško PERAICA		A	7	(10)	2
3	Franjo PINTARIĆ		M	13	(5)	1
25	Davor PIŠKOR		A	17	(2)	5
24	Dejan PRIJIĆ		M	5	(2)	
6	RADAELLI Fernando Chemin	BRA	D	4		
21	Zoran RATKOVIĆ		A	9	(4)	1
25	Renato ŠAKA		M	4	(1)	
9	Edin ŠARANOVIĆ	BIH	A	14	(1)	7
18	Dario ŠOLTIĆ		M	2	(9)	
2	Danijel ŠTEFULJ		D	15		1
14	Martin TISAJ		A	1	(3)	
7	Igor TKALČEVIĆ		D	1		
5	Tvrtko TOPIĆ		D	2		
6	Damir VITAS		D	6	(1)	
11	Andrej VUK		A		(3)	
6	Ante ZURAK		D	10	(2)	

NK OSIJEK

Coach – Ilija Lončarević

Founded – 1945

MAJOR HONOURS: Croatian Cup – (1) 1999.

2007

22/7	Slaven	h	1-0	*Babić (p)*
28/7	Varteks	a	2-1	*Babić (p), Primorac*
4/8	Rijeka	h	2-2	*Jukić, Babić*
11/8	Hajduk	a	0-1	
19/8	Dinamo Zagreb	h	1-3	*Jukić*
25/8	Zadar	a	1-5	*Jukić*
1/9	Inter Zaprešić	h	1-0	*og (Starčević)*
15/9	Cibalia	a	0-2	
22/9	Šibenik	h	1-1	*Nikšić*
29/9	Međimurje	h	4-0	*Nikšić 3, Pavličić*
6/10	Zagreb	a	2-0	*Smoje, Nikšić*
210	Slaven	a	0-2	
27/10	Varteks	h	0-1	
31/10	Rijeka	a	1-1	*Hrnčević*
3/11	Hajduk	h	0-1	
11/11	Dinamo Zagreb	a	0-1	
24/11	Zadar	h	1-0	*Jukić (p)*
1/12	Inter Zaprešić	a	1-1	*Nikšić*
8/12	Cibalia	h	5-1	*Jukić 2, Nikšić 2, Hrnčević*

2008

23/2	Šibenik	a	0-1	
1/3	Međimurje	a	1-0	*Pavličić*
8/3	Zagreb	h	1-1	*Pavličić*
15/3	Međimurje	h	3-1	*Hrnčević 2, Šolić*
19/3	Cibalia	h	2-1	*Smoje, og (Radas)*
22/3	Zadar	a	1-1	*Višević*
29/3	Slaven	h	1-0	*Primorac*
29/4	Hajduk	a	2-0	*Primorac 2*
12/4	Rijeka	h	1-0	*Smoje*
16/4	Dinamo Zagreb	a	2-3	*Vitaić 2*
19/4	Zagreb	h	2-1	*Vidaković, Babić (p)*
26/4	Šibenik	a	0-1	
3/5	Varteks	h	2-0	*Todorčev, Šolić*
10/5	Inter Zaprešić	a	2-1	*Babić, Primorac*

No	Name	Nat	Pos	Aps	(s)	Gls
22	Valentin BABIĆ		D	28		5
23	Marko DINJAR		M	8	(5)	
2	Dino GAVRIĆ		M	2	(2)	
11	Antonio HRNČEVIĆ		A	16	(7)	4
21	Stjepan JUKIĆ		A	11	(2)	6
13	Josip KNEŽEVIĆ		M	5	(8)	
14	Ivica LONČAREVIĆ		M	12	(8)	
2	David Júnior LOPES	BRA	D	17		
17	Vedran NIKŠIĆ		M	12	(6)	8
19	Milan PAVLIČIĆ		A	25	(1)	3
3	Jurica PRANJIĆ		D	16	(2)	
21	Igor PRIJIĆ		A	1	(2)	
9	Karlo PRIMORAC		A	16	(5)	5
15	Marko PRSKALO		M		(5)	
1	Marin SKENDER		G	33		
18	Mile ŠKORIĆ		A		(1)	
24	Ivo SMOJE		D	27		3
8	Aleksandar ŠOLIĆ		A	25	(7)	2
18	Tomislav ŠORŠA		D	1	(4)	
13	Slobodan STRANATIĆ		D	21	(2)	
16	Goran TODORČEV	MKD	D	24	(4)	1
19	Domagoj VIDA		M	19	(2)	
25	Srđan VIDAKOVIĆ		M	2	(7)	1
6	Tomislav VIŠEVIĆ		D	21		1
17	Ante VITAIĆ		M	15	(7)	2
5	Matej VLAOVIĆ		M	2	(1)	
4	Damir VUICA		D	4	(3)	

HNK RIJEKA

Coach – Zlatko Dalić

Founded – 1946

MAJOR HONOURS: Yugoslav Cup – (2) 1978, 1979; Croatian Cup – (2) 2005, 2006.

2007

20/7	Inter Zaprešić	a	1-0	*Sharbini*
28/7	Cibalia	h	3-0	*Ivanov (p), Đalović, Bule*
4/8	Osijek	a	2-2	*Đalović, Bule*
11/8	Međimurje	h	3-1	*Sharbini 2, Đalović (p)*
18/8	Zagreb	a	2-2	*Škoro 2*
25/8	Slaven	h	1-0	*Đalović*
1/9	Varteks	a	2-1	*Škoro, Bule*
15/9	Šibenik	a	2-3	*Đalović 2*
22/9	Hajduk	h	4-0	*Škoro, Sharbini, Ivanov (p), Đalović*

/9	Dinamo Zagreb	a	0-1	
/10	Zadar	h	2-0	*Škoro, Pamić*
/10	Inter Zaprešić	h	2-1	*Budicin, Đalović*
/10	Cibalia	a	0-2	
/10	Osijek	h	1-1	*Đalović*
/11	Međimurje	a	1-0	*Đalović*
/11	Zagreb	h	2-1	*Đalović 2(1p)*
/11	Slaven	a	0-1	
/12	Varteks	h	1-1	*Štrok*
/12	Šibenik	h	2-0	*Đalović, Štrok*
008				
/2	Hajduk	a	1-1	*Sharbini*
/3	Dinamo Zagreb	h	2-4	*Škoro, Šafarić*
/3	Zadar	a	0-0	
/3	Zagreb	h	1-1	*Štrok*
/3	Šibenik	h	0-0	
/3	Varteks	h	2-2	*Sharbini 2*
/3	Inter Zaprešić	a	1-2	*Šafarić*
/4	Međimurje	h	5-2	*Sharbini, Božić 2, Škoro, Đalović*
/4	Osijek	a	0-1	
/4	Zadar	h	5-3	*Vučko, Đalović 3, Sharbini*
/4	Slaven	a	1-1	*Božić*
/4	Hajduk	h	1-1	*Sharbini*
/5	Cibalia	h	2-0	*Sharbini, Đalović*
/5	Dinamo Zagreb	a	1-6	*Tadejević*

No	Name	Nat	Pos	Aps	(s)	Gls
	ANDRÉ LUIZ Ferreira Cardoso	BRA	M	1	1	
	Duje BAKOVIĆ		D	1	(6)	
	Ivan BOŽIĆ		A	5	(13)	3
	Mate BRAJKOVIĆ		A	4	(6)	
	Fausto BUDICIN		D	32		1
	Nino BULE		A	22	(4)	3
	Igor ČAGALJ		D	15	(3)	
	Radomir ĐALOVIĆ	MNE	A	22	(2)	18
	Georgi IVANOV	BUL	A	20	(1)	2
	Sergej JAKIROVIĆ		M	7	(15)	
	Dario JERTEC		M	19	(4)	
	Damir KREILACH		M		(4)	
	Filip MARČIĆ		M	28	(1)	
	Manuel PAMIĆ		M	18		1
	Mario PRIŠĆ		M	8	(4)	
	Velimir RADMAN		G	10		
	Zedi RAMADANI		M		(2)	
	Anas SHARBINI		M	27	(1)	11
	Nikola ŠAFARIĆ		M	22	(5)	2
	Alen ŠKORO	BIH	A	21	(6)	7
	Hrvoje ŠTROK		M	24	(15)	3
	Mario TADEJEVIĆ		D	2	(2)	1
	Vedran TURKALJ		D		(1)	
	Luka VUČKO		D	32		1
	Dragan ŽILIĆ	SRB	G	23		

HNK ŠIBENIK

Coach – Ivica Kalinić

Founded – 1932

007				
1/7	Dinamo Zagreb	a	0-5	
3/7	Zagreb	h	0-0	
/8	Zadar	a	2-2	*Zec 2*
1/8	Slaven	h	0-2	
7/8	Inter Zaprešić	a	2-2	*Batur 2*
5/8	Varteks	h	4-3	*Zec, Vitaić, Gabriel, Jambrušić*
/9	Cibalia	a	3-3	*Zec 2, Vitaić*
5/9	Rijeka	h	3-2	*Vitaić 3 (1p)*
2/9	Osijek	a	1-1	*og (Lopes)*
29/9	Hajduk	h	1-0	*Vitaić*
6/10	Međimurje	a	2-2	*Roglić, Lapić*
20/10	Dinamo Zagreb	h	0-2	
27/10	Zagreb	a	1-3	*Jambrušić*
31/10	Zadar	h	0-0	
3/11	Slaven	a	0-1	
10/11	Inter Zaprešić	h	1-1	*Vitaić*
28/11	Varteks	a	0-3	
1/12	Cibalia	h	2-0	*Roglić, Zec*
8/12	Rijeka	a	0-2	
2008				
23/2	Osijek	h	1-0	*Makarin*
1/3	Hajduk	a	0-2	
8/3	Međimurje	h	4-2	*Bulat A. 2 (1p), Makarin, Zec*
15/3	Hajduk	a	1-4	*Gabriel*
19/3	Rijeka	a	0-0	
22/3	Dinamo Zagreb	a	1-5	*Vitaić*
29/3	Zagreb	h	0-2	
30/4	Cibalia	a	0-2	
12/4	Varteks	a	1-1	*Jambrušić*
16/4	Inter Zaprešić	h	0-0	
19/4	Međimurje	a	1-0	*Bonacin*
26/4	Osijek	h	1-0	*Jambrušić*
3/5	Zadar	a	2-0	*Zec (p), Jambrušić*
10/5	Slaven	h	0-0	

No	Name	Nat	Pos	Aps	(s)	Gls
25	Arijan ADEMI		A		(1)	
23	Marin BATUR		A	2	(3)	2
3	Josip BONACIN		D	26		1
19	Dario BRGLES		M	5	(4)	
15	Ante BULAT		D	18	(7)	2
7	Ivan BULAT		M	7	(2)	
20	Ivan CRLJEN		M		(1)	
13	Nikola ĐIRA		M	6	(7)	
16	João GABRIEL da Silva	BRA	A	21	(6)	2
27	Dražen GOVIĆ		M	4		
29	Ivo GRGAS – GRANDO		A	1	(6)	
8	Juraj GRIZELJ		M	5	(17)	
5	Goran GRUICA		D	7	(7)	
17	Krunoslav JAMBRUŠIĆ		M	10	(7)	5
26	Joško KOVAČ		M		(5)	
20	Mario KRALJ		M	3	(1)	
24	Ante KULUŠIĆ		D	30		
6	Patrice KWEDI	CMR	M	2	(1)	
18	Stipe LAPIĆ		D	25	(1)	1
14	Marko LOZO		A		(3)	
14	Krešimir MAKARIN		A	4		2
1	Ivica MATAS		G	5		
2	Damir MILANOVIĆ		M	26	(2)	
25	Boris RAIČ		D	25		
6	Zoran ROGLIĆ		M	26	(1)	2
22	Zlatko RUNJE		G	13		
12	Hrvoje SLAVICA		G	15		
28	Alen ŠUBIĆ		M	3	(8)	
18	William Etchu TABI	CMR	M	19	(2)	
21	Frane VITAIĆ		M	28	(1)	8
19	Ermin ZEC		A	27	(3)	8

NK SLAVEN KOPRIVNICA

Coach – Krunoslav Jurčić

Founded – 1907

2007				
22/7	Osijek	a	0-1	
28/7	Međimurje	h	2-0	*Vručina, Poljak*
5/8	Zagreb	a	2-0	*Jajalo, Šehić*
11/8	Šibenik	a	2-0	*Sopić, Šehić*
19/8	Varteks	h	6-0	*Kristić, Poljak, Posavec 2 (1p), Sopić, Vručina*

25/8	Rijeka	a	0-1	
2/9	Hajduk	h	2-2	*Kristić, Vručina*
15/9	Dinamo Zagreb	a	0-4	
22/9	Zadar	h	4-2	*Radeljić, Poljak (p), Poldrugač, Čaval*
29/9	Inter Zaprešić	a	0-1	
6/10	Cibalia	h	2-2	*Jurić, Poljak (p)*
20/10	Osijek	h	2-2	*Posavec 2 (2p)*
27/10	Međimurje	a	0-2	
31/10	Zagreb	h	1-0	*Jajalo*
3/11	Šibenik	h	1-0	*Poljak*
10/11	Varteks	a	1-1	*Vručina*
24/11	Rijeka	h	1-0	*Šehić*
2/12	Hajduk	a	0-1	
8/12	Dinamo Zagreb	h	5-2	*Delić, Jajalo 2, Vručina 2*
2008				
23/2	Zadar	a	0-1	
1/3	Inter Zaprešić	h	2-0	*Poljak, Posavec*
8/3	Cibalia	a	0-3	
15/3	Varteks	h	2-1	*Šiklić, Čaval*
19/3	Inter Zaprešić	a	0-0	
22/3	Međimurje	h	4-0	*Šehić 2, Delić, Poljak*
29/3	Osijek	a	0-1	
29/4	Zadar	h	2-0	*Čaval, Šehić*
12/4	Cibalia	h	2-0	*Čaval, Poljak*
16/4	Hajduk	a	0-2	
19/4	Rijeka	h	1-1	*Čaval*
26/4	Dinamo Zagreb	a	0-1	
3/5	Zagreb	h	1-0	*Posavec*
10/5	Šibenik	a	0-0	

No	Name	Nat	Pos	Aps	(s)	Gls
2	Petar BOŠNJAK		D	20	(6)	
6	Dalibor BOŽAC		D	12		
3	Kristijan ČAVAL		D	23	(2)	5
14	Mateas DELIĆ		M	7	(19)	2
20	Mario GREGURINA		M		(3)	
1	Vanja IVEŠA		G	29		
19	Mato JAJALO		M	25	(6)	4
21	Mario JURIĆ		M	14	(5)	1
4	Elvis KOKALOVIĆ		D	10	(5)	
9	Dino KRESINGER		A	15	(11)	
5	Matija KRISTIĆ		D	28		2
7	Dalibor POLDRUGAČ		D	16	(1)	1
15	Stjepan POLJAK		M	28	(3)	8
10	Srebrenko POSAVEC		M	14	(12)	6
16	Vedran PURIĆ		M	8		
21	Ivan RADELJIĆ	BIH	D	17		1
22	Danijel RADIČEK		M	5	(6)	
12	Silvio RODIĆ		G	4	(2)	
13	Željko SOPIĆ		M	32		2
11	Asim ŠEHIĆ	BIH	A	18	(5)	6
18	Ronald ŠIKLIĆ		M	21	(1)	1
8	Dejan ŠOMOCI		A		(7)	
24	Franjo TEPURIĆ		A	1	(1)	
17	Bojan VRUČINA		A	16	(1)	6

NK VARTEKS

Coach – Josip Kuže; (15/8/07) Dražen Besek

Founded – 1932

2007				
21/7	Cibalia	a	0-1	
28/7	Osijek	h	1-2	*Mumlek*
4/8	Međimurje	a	1-4	*Semler*
11/8	Zagreb	h	0-1	
19/8	Slaven	a	0-6	
25/8	Šibenik	a	3-4	*Semler, Prahić, Novinić*
1/9	Rijeka	h	1-2	*Brezovec*
15/9	Hajduk	a	1-3	*Conjar*
23/9	Dinamo Zagreb	h	4-3	*Fábio, og (Etto), Prahić, Mumlek*
29/9	Zadar	a	0-2	
6/10	Inter Zaprešić	h	1-2	*Mumlek*
20/10	Cibalia	h	2-1	*Mumlek, Prahić*
27/10	Osijek	a	1-0	*Smrekar*
21/10	Međimurje	h	2-0	*Mujanović, Papa*
3/11	Zagreb	a	0-0	
10/11	Slaven	h	1-1	*Mumlek (p)*
24/11	Šibenik	h	3-0	*Fábio, Mujanović, Semler*
1/12	Rijeka	a	1-1	*Smrekar*
8/12	Hajduk	h	1-3	*Lučić (p)*
2008				
23/2	Dinamo Zagreb	a	2-1	*Mumlek, Mujanović*
1/3	Zadar	h	2-0	*Mumlek, Mujanović*
7/3	Inter Zaprešić	a	0-0	
15/3	Slaven	a	1-2	*Mumlek*
19/3	Hajduk	h	4-0	*Smrekar 2, Mujanović,*
22/3	Rijeka	a	2-2	*Mumlek, Mujanović*
29/3	Dinamo Zagreb	h	1-1	*Novinić*
29/4	Zagreb	a	1-3	*Ivančić*
12/4	Šibenik	h	1-1	*Lučić (p)*
16/4	Cibalia	a	1-0	*Lučić*
19/4	Inter Zaprešić	a	0-1	
26/4	Međimurje	h	3-2	*Novinić, Vuk 2*
3/5	Osijek	a	0-2	
10/5	Zadar	h	5-2	*Brezovec, Vuk 2, Balajić, Melnjak*

No	Name	Nat	Pos	Aps	(s)	Gls
18	Andrija BALAJIĆ		M	8	(4)	1
17	Ivan BEGOVIĆ		M		(2)	
12	Luka BEŠENIĆ		G	1	(1)	
4	Josip BREZOVEC		M	20	(6)	2
25	Mario BRLEČIĆ		M		(2)	
16	Ivan CONJAR		M	19		1
12	Antonio CVANČIĆ		G	1		
27	FÁBIO Gilvan Silva	BRA	A	7	(3)	2
25	Nikola FRLJUŽEC		A		(1)	
6	Gordan GOLIK		M	20	(7)	
5	Danijel HRMAN		M	1	(10)	
2	Zoran IVANČIĆ		D	17	(4)	1
13	Lek KĆIRA		D	1	(1)	
23	LESJAK ZORAN		M	1	(8)	
25	Tomislav LIBER		D	2		
3	Mario LUČIĆ		D	30		3
1	Danijel MAĐARIĆ		G	26		
10	Nikola MELNJAK		M	25	(1)	1
7	Goran MUJANOVIĆ		M	24		7
10	Miljenko MUMLEK		M	25		9
9	Enes NOVINIĆ		A	16	(7)	3
17	Asmir ORAŠČANIN		D	3		
8	Drago PAPA		M	30	(1)	1
5	Igor PRAHIĆ		D	32		3
15	Grgur RADOŠ		M		(1)	
1	Zlatko RUNJE		G	5		
13	Borut SEMLER	SVN	A	12	(4)	3
16	Matija SMREKAR		A	12	(7)	4
27	Martin ŠABAN		A		(1)	
14	Karlo ŠIMEK		M	12	(4)	
24	Dino ŠKVORC		D		(1)	
11	Gordan VUK		A	9	(9)	4
18	Vladimir VLADIMIR		D	4		

NK ZADAR

Coach – Dalibor Zebić

Founded – 1945

07				
'7	Hajduk	h	0-0	
'7	Dinamo Zagreb	a	1-5	*Ćustić*
3	Šibenik	h	2-2	*Terkeš 2*
/8	Inter Zaprešić	h	3-0	*Župan, Terkeš 2*
/8	Cibalia	a	2-0	*Terkeš, Župan (p)*
'8	Osijek	h	5-1	*Tomasov, Puljić, Parmaković 2, Župan*
)	Međimurje	a	4-2	*Tomasov, Župan, Surać, Štefančić*
/9	Zagreb	h	1-0	*Surać*
/9	Slaven	a	2-4	*Župan, Terkeš (p)*
/9	Varteks	h	2-0	*Župan, Elez*
0	Rijeka	a	0-2	
/10	Hajduk	a	1-4	*Terkeš*
/10	Dinamo Zagreb	h	1-2	*Terkeš*
/10	Šibenik	a	0-0	
1	Inter Zaprešić	a	1-2	*Mitrović*
/11	Cibalia	h	1-1	*Tomasov*
'11	Osijek	a	0-1	
2	Međimurje	h	4-0	*Terkeš 3, Župan*
12	Zagreb	a	2-7	*Tomasov, Parmaković*
08				
'2	Slaven	h	1-0	*Surać*
3	Varteks	a	0-2	
3	Rijeka	h	0-0	
/3	Inter Zaprešić	h	3-1	*Terkeš 2, Mišlov*
/3	Međimurje	a	3-2	*Terkeš 2, Tomasov*
/3	Osijek	h	1-1	*Terkeš*
/3	Cibalia	h	1-0	*Mitrović*
/4	Slaven	a	0-2	
/4	Hajduk	h	1-3	*Mitrović (p)*
/4	Rijeka	a	3-5	*Terkeš 3*
'4	Dinamo Zagreb	h	2-5	*Terkeš 2 (1p)*
/4	Zagreb	a	0-0	
5	Šibenik	h	0-2	
/5	Varteks	a	2-5	*Surać, Rašo*

Name	Nat	Pos	Aps	(s)	Gls
Valerio BALAŠKOVIĆ		M	18	(4)	
Naum BATKOSKI	MKD	D	32		
Mate BATURINA		A	3	(10)	
Josip BILAVER		M	13	(6)	
Hrvoje ĆUSTIĆ		A	10	(10)	1
Ivan ELEZ		D	22	(3)	1
Šime GREGOV		D	5	(6)	
Jure JERBIĆ		M	1	(4)	
Antonio JEŽINA		G	3	(1)	
Mario KRUNEŠ		M		(1)	
Šime MARUNA		M	2	(1)	
Ante MILETIĆ		M		(1)	
Ferdo MILIN		D	24	(1)	
Roko MIŠLOV		M	5	(8)	1
Ante MITROVIĆ		A	14	(13)	3
Josip MODRIĆ		D	9	(4)	
Ninoslav PARMAKOVIĆ		D	26	(1)	3
Jerko PRTENJAČA		D		(1)	
Ante PULJIĆ		M	28	(1)	1
Marko RAŠO		M	1	(5)	1
Ante ROŽIĆ	AUS	D	5		
Danijel SUBAŠIĆ		G	28		
Jakov SURAĆ		M	25	(1)	4
Matija ŠTEFANČIĆ		A	1	(4)	1
Dragan TADIĆ		M	2		
Želimir TERKEŠ	BIH	A	29		21
Antonio TIČAK		M		(2)	
Marin TOMASOV		M	30	(1)	5
Andrija VUKOVIĆ		G	2		
Dragan ŽUPAN		M	25	(2)	7

NK ZAGREB

Coach – Miroslav Blažević

Founded – 1904

MAJOR HONOURS: Croatian League – (1) 2002.

2007				
21/7	Međimurje	a	3-0	*og (Topić), Lovrek 2*
28/7	Šibenik	a	0-0	
5/8	Slaven	h	0-2	
11/8	Varteks	a	1-0	*Lovrek*
18/8	Rijeka	h	2-2	*Lovrek, Parlov*
25/8	Hajduk	a	1-2	*Lovrek*
1/9	Dinamo Zagreb	h	1-3	*Lajtman*
15/9	Zadar	a	0-1	
22/9	Inter Zaprešić	h	3-0	*Brkljača, Lovrek, Mujdža*
29/9	Cibalia	a	1-3	*Lovrek*
6/10	Osijek	h	0-2	
20/10	Međimurje	h	1-1	*Lovrek*
27/10	Šibenik	h	3-1	*Lovrek, Ibričić 2*
31/10	Slaven	a	0-1	
3/11	Varteks	h	0-0	
10/11	Rijeka	a	1-2	*Brkljača*
24/11	Hajduk	h	1-0	*Ibričić*
2/12	Dinamo Zagreb	a	3-6	*Lovrek 2, Mujdža*
8/12	Zadar	h	7-2	*Brkljača, Čutura, Pejić, Lovrek 3, Kartelo*
2008				
22/2	Inter Zaprešić	a	1-1	*Grgić*
1/3	Cibalia	h	4-1	*Ibričić 2 (1p), Piškor 2*
8/3	Osijek	a	1-1	*Mujdža*
15/3	Rijeka	a	1-1	*Ibričić*
19/3	Dinamo Zagreb	h	0-0	
22/3	Cibalia	a	2-2	*Parlov, Kartelo*
29/3	Šibenik	a	2-0	*Kartelo, Oršulić*
29/4	Varteks	h	3-1	*Grgić, Ibričić, Nadarević*
12/4	Inter Zaprešić	a	0-0	
16/4	Međimurje	h	6-1	*Ibričić 4 (1p), Pejić 2*
19/4	Osijek	a	1-2	*Grgić*
26/4	Zadar	h	0-0	
3/5	Slaven	a	0-1	
10/5	Hajduk	h	2-1	*Jurendić, Ibričić*

No	Name	Nat	Pos	Aps	(s)	Gls
18	Ivan BJELOBRADIĆ		M		(1)	
6	Mario BRKLJAČA		M	29		3
3	Mario ČUTURA		D	30		1
5	Damir DŽIDIĆ		D		(5)	
25	Marko GRGIĆ		M	18	(11)	3
10	Senijad IBRIČIĆ	BIH	M	29	(1)	12
20	Vedran IVANKOVIĆ		D	21		
17	Igor JUGOVIĆ		M		(3)	
7	Josip JURENDIĆ		A	20	(8)	1
18	Marko KARTELO		M	31	(3)	3
4	Tomislav LABUDOVIĆ		D	22	(1)	
13	Ivan LAJTMAN		M	2	(7)	1
19	Krunoslav LOVREK		A	15	(1)	14
26	Haris MEHMEDAGIĆ	BIH	D	7	(4)	
23	Josip MIKULIĆ		D	15	(2)	
24	Mensur MUJDŽA	BIH	M	29		3
13	Safet NADAREVIĆ	BIH	D	27		1
29	NIKOLIĆ		A		(1)	
2	Marin ORŠULIĆ		M	2	(13)	1
22	Ivan PARLOV		M	18	(9)	2
9	Miroslav PEJIĆ	BIH	M	11	(11)	3
8	Davor PIŠKOR		A	4	(1)	2
1	Dragan STOJKIĆ	BIH	G	29		
12	Josip ŠKORIĆ		G	4		
27	Josip ŠOLJIĆ		A		(1)	
14	Matija ŠPIĆIĆ		M		(3)	

PROMOTED CLUB

NK CROATIA SESVETE

Coach – Zlatko Kranjčar

Founded - 1957

SECOND LEVEL FINAL TABLE 2007/08

		Pld	W	D	L	F	A	Pts
1	NK Croatia Sesvete	30	20	6	4	67	25	66
2	NK Hrvatski dragovoljac Zagreb	30	19	7	4	60	28	64
3	NK Istra 1861 Pula	30	17	7	6	42	14	58
4	NK Pomorac Kostrena	30	14	7	9	42	28	49
5	NK Vinogradar Jastrebarsko	30	12	8	10	42	43	44
6	NK Slavonac Stari Perkovsi	30	14	2	14	44	51	44
7	NK Segesta Sisak	30	11	10	9	39	37	43
8	HNK Trogir	30	12	6	12	40	37	42
9	HNŠK Moslavina Kutina	30	11	8	11	51	42	41
10	NK Imotski	30	11	7	12	49	53	40
11	NK Mosor Žrnovnica	30	10	8	12	27	42	38
12	NK Solin	30	10	7	13	46	48	37
13	NK Marsonia Slavonski Brod	30	8	7	15	34	58	31
14	NK Kamen Ingrad Velika	30	7	7	16	26	49	28
15	NK Vukovar '91	30	6	6	18	29	53	24
16	NK Belišće	30	3	7	20	23	53	16

PROMOTION/RELEGATION PLAY-OFFS

(17/5/08)
NK Inter Zaprešić 2, NK Hrvatski Dragovoljac 0

(21/5/08)
NK Hrvatski Dragovoljac 0, NK Inter Zaprešić 0

(Inter Zaprešić 2-0)

DOMESTIC CUP 2007/08

HRVATSKI NOGOMETNI KUP

FIRST ROUND

(26/9/07)
Bjelovar 3, Belišće 3 *(aet; 7-6 on pens)*
Croatia Sesvete 2, HAŠK 0
Đakovo 2, Kamen Ingrad 1
Graničar 1, Zagreb 3
Međimurje 2, Šibenik 2 *(aet; 6-7 on pens)*
Mladost Molve 1, Hajduk 9
Ogulin 2, Osijek 3
Oriolik 1, Cibalia 4
Podravina 2, Istra 0
Primorac 0, Inter Zaprešić 5
Segesta 1, Zadar 0
Slavonac 0, Slaven 1
Slavonija 1, Pomorac 4
Trogir 1, Varteks 2
Virovitica 1, Dinamo Zagreb 3
Zelina 0, Rijeka 4

SECOND ROUND

(24/10/07)
Bjelovar 1, Varteks 1 *(aet; 4-6 on pens)*
Cibalia 2, Osijek 1
Đakovo 0, Zagreb 7
Hajduk 2, Croatia Sesvete 0
Inter Zaprešić 1, Podravina 0
Segesta 3, Rijeka 0
Slaven 1, Pomorac 0
Šibenik 2, Dinamo Zagreb 3

QUARTER-FINALS

(7/11/07 & 28/11/07)
Segesta 0, Zagreb 0
Zagreb 3 *(Parlov 19, Čutura 44, Grgić 82)*, Segesta 2 *(Božić 10, Oštrić*
(Zagreb 3-2)

Varteks 4 *(Mumlek 5, Prahić 19, Mujanović 37, Semler 67)*, Cibalia 0
Cibalia 0, Varteks 2 *(Semler 7, Fábio 25)*
(Varteks 6-0)

Hajduk 2 *(Kalinić 3p, Pelaić 42)*, Inter Zaprešić 1 *(Sivonjić 71)*
Inter Zaprešić 0, Hajduk 4 *(Kalinić 14p, 29, Cernat 20, Hrgović 86)*
(Hajduk 6-1)

(27/2/08 & 12/3/08)
Slaven 0, Dinamo Zagreb 1 *(Bišćan 45)*
Dinamo Zagreb 2 *(Modrić 39, Tadić 67)*, Slaven 1 *(Šomoci 82)*
(Dinamo Zagreb 3-1)

SEMI-FINALS

(9/4/08 & 23/4/08)
Dinamo Zagreb 3 *(Mandžukić 30, Tadić 42, Vugrinec 90)*, Zagreb 1 *(Ibri*
Zagreb 2 *(Parlov 16, Pejić 37)*, Dinamo Zagreb 3 *(Mikulić 35og, Ivanko*
43og, Mikić 88)
(Dinamo Zagreb 6-3)

Varteks 1 *(Novinić 26)*, Hajduk 1 *(Maloča 65)*
Hajduk 4 *(Cernat 15, Rukavina 32, 60, Kalinić 45p)*, Varteks 0
(Hajduk 5-1)

FINALS

(7/5/08)
Maksimir stadium, Zagreb
NK DINAMO ZAGREB 3 *(Tadić 8, Mandžukić 20,88)*
HNK HAJDUK SPLIT 0
Referee – *Ljubičić*
DINAMO ZAGREB – *Koch, Ćale, Mikulić, Etto, Modrić, Tadić (Šokota 83,*
Mikić, Mandžukić, Vukojević, Vrdoljak, Drpić.
HAJDUK – *Balić, Jozinović, Živković, Linić, Kalinić, Rukavina, Ljubičić, G*
Sablić (Buljat 46), Čop, Maloča.

(14/5/08)
Poljud stadium, Split
HNK HAJDUK SPLIT 0
NK DINAMO ZAGREB 0
Referee – *Kovačić*
HAJDUK – *Balić, Živković, Maloča, Pandža, Ljubičić, Linić, Gabrić, Barto*
(Tičinović 63), Cernat (Ćurjurić 46), Rukavina, Kalinić (Varvodić 21).
Sent off: *Balić (19)*
DINAMO ZAGREB – *Koch, Bišćan, Mikulić, Vrdoljak, Etto, Ćale, Vukojevi*
Mikić (Buljat 46), Modrić (Sammir 89), Mandžukić, Tadić (Balaban 82).
Sent off: *Ćale (19); Mandžukić (69)*

(DINAMO ZAGREB 3-0)

nvincible Anorthosis eturn to power

here would be no record-breaking 20th Cypriot championship win for either of the big Nicosia clubs, APOEL FC or AC Omonia, in 2007/08. Instead e title returned to the south coast, where Anorthosis magusta FC, coached by former Georgian ernational Temuri Ketsbaia, made history by going ough the entire league campaign undefeated.

ollon Limassol FC had been unbeaten champions in 05/06 but over 26 matches. Anorthosis's feat was hieved over 32 games – the 26 standard league tures plus another six tacked on at the end. A new ay-off system had been introduced to spice up the osing weeks of the campaign, but the split at the p, which brought the top four teams together into a -game mini-league, ultimately served little purpose Anorthosis, having built up an eleven-point lead er the regular season, were already practically aranteed to finish first.

enalty scare

the event, Anorthosis would have their title nfirmed without kicking a ball - when APOEL lost 0 to AEK Larnaca FC on 12 April. They still had four of eir six play-off fixtures to negotiate, and in the first them, the following evening at home to Omonia, ey almost let their unbeaten record slip, surviving a oppage-time penalty that struck e frame of the goal. Anorthosis ded up drawing five of their six ay-off games, winning only the st of them, at home to runners- APOEL, when Polish striker ukasz Sosin, a summer signing om Apollon, scored all the goals a 3-0 victory to become the A atigoria's joint-top scorer ongside Doxa Katokopia FC's azilian import David da Costa.

/ith Cyprus's membership of the uropean Union lifting the barrier to quotas on foreign players, the A Katigoria was awash with imports from all over the world. Anorthosis barely had room for any Cypriots, and it was a similar story elsewhere. Locally-born coaches were also in the minority, and it was a Serb, Ivan Jovanović, who led APOEL to victory in the Cypriot Cup. The club's 2003/04 championship-winning coach returned at the start of the year to replace Marinos Ouzounidis, who had led APOEL to the title in 2006/07, and he ensured there would be no double for Anorthosis as goals from Nuno Morais – a Portuguese - and Nenad Mirosavljević – another Serb – defeated the newly crowned champions 2-0 in the GSP stadium.

If APOEL's season finished on a high, there was no consoling Omonia. A third successive season without a trophy was bad enough, but they were lucky to finish third and claim the other UEFA Cup spot ahead of AEK after failing to win any of their play-off games under caretaker coach Nedim Tutić.

Cyprus, not unexpectedly, lost their final two UEFA EURO 2008™ qualifying matches, away to Germany and at home to the Czech Republic, but despite the disappointment of failing to finish outside the bottom two in a qualifying group for the first time, the islanders could reflect on the campaign with considerable pride. They accumulated more points – 14 – and scored more goals – 17 - than in any previous qualifying series. They held Germany at home, beat Wales and were within seconds of doing the double over the Republic of Ireland. For his efforts – and they were considerable given the diminishing of his resources in the A Katigoria – head coach Angelos Anastasiadis was rewarded with a new two-year contract.

Angelos Anastasiadis led Cyprus through an impressive UEFA EURO 2008™ qualifying campaign

Kypriaki Omospondia Podosfairon (KOP) / Cyprus Football Association (CFA

10 Achaion Street
2413 Engomi
PO Box 25071
CY-1306 Nicosia
tel - +357 22 352341
fax - +357 22 590544
email – info@cfa.com.cy
Year of Formation – 1934
President - Costakis Koutsokoumnis
General Secretary – George Economides
Press Officer – Kyriakos Georgallis
Stadium – GSP, Nicosia (22,859)

TOP FIVE ALL-TIME CAPS
Pambos Pittas & Yiannis Okkas (82); Nik Panayiotou (75); Giorgos Theodotou (70 Yiannakis Yiangoudakis (68)

TOP FIVE ALL-TIME GOALS
Michalis Konstantinou (25); Yiannis Okk (21); Marios Agathocleus (10); Kostas Charalambides, Siniša Gogić, Andros Sotiriou, Milenko Spoljarić & Phivos Vrahimis (8)

NATIONAL TEAM RESULTS 2007/08

22/8/07	San Marino (ECQ)	A	Serravalle	1-0	*Okkas (54)*
8/9/07	Armenia	H	Achnas	3-1	*Michail (31), Okkas (42), Konstantinou (52)*
12/9/07	San Marino (ECQ)	H	Nicosia	3-0	*Makrides (15), Aloneftis (41, 90+2)*
13/10/07	Wales (ECQ)	H	Nicosia	3-1	*Okkas (59, 68), Charalambides (79)*
17/10/07	Republic of Ireland (ECQ)	A	Dublin	1-1	*Okkarides (80)*
17/11/07	Germany (ECQ)	A	Hannover	0-4	
21/11/07	Czech Republic (ECQ)	H	Nicosia	0-2	
6/2/08	Ukraine	H	Nicosia	1-1	*Aloneftis (19p)*
19/5/08	Greece	A	Patras	0-2	

NATIONAL TEAM APPEARANCES 2007/08

Coach – Angelos ANASTASIADIS (GRE) 3/10/53			SMR	Arm	SMR	WAL	IRL	GER	CZE	Ukr	Gre	Caps	Gc
Antonis GEORGALLIDES	30/1/82	Omonia	G	G46	G	G	G	G	G	G	G46	19	
Giorgos THEODOTOU	1/1/74	Omonia	D	s55	s76			D27		s59		70	
Paraskevas CHRISTOU	2/2/84	AEK	D		D	D	D	D	D	D	D	10	
Lambros LAMBROU	9/9/77	Anorthosis	D	D74				D	D	s46	s62	33	
Christos MARANGOS	9/5/83	Apollon	D24			s71	s69			s67		10	
Stathis ALONEFTIS	29/3/83	Energie (GER)	M	M55	M	M		M	M	M79		24	5
Chrysis MICHAIL	26/5/77	APOEL	M	M72	M	M46	s73		s84	M46	M	47	5
Alexandros GARPOZIS	5/9/80	Apollon	M86		s65	M	M	M	M	s46	M	25	1
Yiasemakis YIASOUMI	31/5/75	Aris	A55	s72	s46	s46	A73	s68	s62	A60	A81	56	7
Yiannis OKKAS	11/2/77	unattached /Celta (ESP)	A	A74	A46	A	A	A	A			82	2
Michalis KONSTANTINOU	19/2/78	Olympiacos (GRE)	A	A85	A			A68	A		A68	62	2

ATIONAL TEAM APPEARANCES 2007/08 (contd.)

			SMR	Arm	SMR	WAL	IRL	GER	CZE	Ukr	Gre	Caps	Goals
ios NICOLAOU	4/10/83	Panionios (GRE)	s24	M	M	M	M	s27	M56	M	M	18	-
tas CHARALAMBIDES	25/7/81	unattached	s55										
		/Carl Zeiss Jena (GER)				s63	M	M46	M62				
		/APOEL								M	M46	41	8
CHARALAMBOUS	25/9/80	PAOK (GRE)	s86	D55	D65				s56	D		31	-
ios OKKARIDIS	15/11/77	Apollon		D	D	D	D			D46	D62	31	1
ios ELIA	14/4/79	APOEL		D	D76	D63	D						
		/Ethnikos Achnas									D	30	1
stantinos MAKRIDES	13/1/82	APOEL		M	M	M	M86	M	M84	M59	M72	36	1
onis AVGOUSTI	9/3/77	AEK		s46							s46	4	-
ktarios ALEXANDROU	19/12/83	Larissa (GRE)		s55								4	-
istis THEOFILOU	30/4/80	Apollon		s74			s86	s46				10	-
rgos PANAGI	3/11/86	Anorthosis		s74							s68	2	-
os SOLOMOU	30/11/85	Apollon		s85								2	-
inos SATSIAS	24/5/78	APOEL				D71	D69	D	D	D67		42	-
nstantinos GEORGIADIS	5/2/85	Ethnikos Achnas								s60		1	-
kos ALEKOU	13/12/83	Aris								s79		3	-
akos PAVLOU	4/9/86	Omonia									s46	1	-
nitris CHRISTOFI	28/9/88	Paralimni									s72	1	-
nitris DASKALAKIS	18/11/77	APOEL									s81	12	-

DOMESTIC LEAGUE 2007/08

KATIGORIA FINAL TABLE

		Home					Away					Total					
	Pld	W	D	L	F	A	W	D	L	F	A	W	D	L	F	A	Pts
Anorthosis Famagusta FC	32	13	3	0	37	9	7	9	0	21	10	20	12	0	58	19	72
APOEL FC	32	12	2	2	33	10	6	5	5	25	18	18	7	7	58	28	61
AC Omonia	32	9	5	2	22	10	5	5	6	20	21	14	10	8	42	31	52
AEK Larnaca FC	32	7	5	4	23	22	7	3	6	23	20	14	8	10	46	42	50
Apollon Limassol FC	32	10	4	2	36	22	2	7	7	13	19	12	11	9	49	41	47
Enosis Neon Paralimni FC	32	6	3	7	16	20	7	4	5	26	25	13	7	12	42	45	46
Ethnikos Achnas FC	32	8	3	5	27	20	5	1	10	17	23	13	4	15	44	43	43
APOP/Kinyras Peyias FC	32	8	3	5	26	20	3	6	7	21	29	11	9	12	47	49	42
Alki Larnaca FC	32	9	3	4	27	17	2	4	10	14	27	11	7	14	41	44	40
AEL Limassol FC	32	6	5	5	19	20	5	2	9	20	25	11	7	14	39	45	40
Doxa Katokopia FC	32	8	6	2	26	18	2	3	11	17	30	10	9	13	43	48	39
Aris Limassol FC	32	7	2	7	24	22	1	4	11	7	26	8	6	18	31	48	30
Nea Salamis FC	26	4	5	4	14	17	2	1	10	14	37	6	6	14	28	54	24
Olympiakos Nicosia FC	26	2	5	6	14	20	1	0	12	9	34	3	5	18	23	54	14

B. 1-4 Championship Group; 5-8 Intertoto Group; 9-12 Relegation Group

TOP GOALSCORERS

16 Łukasz SOSIN (Anorthosis)
DAVID da Costa (Doxa)

13 Constantinos MAKRIDES (APOEL)

12 Bernardo VASCONCELOS (APOP/Omonia)
FREDDY (Doxa/Paralimni)
Adrian MIHALCEA (Aris)
Rista NAUMOV (Ethnikos Achnas)

11 Ignacio RISSO (Apollon)
Sunni KINGSLEY (AEK)

10 Elpídio SILVA (Alki)
Nikos MACHLAS (APOEL)
Gaston SANGOY (Apollon)
Levan KEBADZE (Ethnikos Achnas)

CLUB-BY-CLUB

AEK LARNACA FC

Coach – Marios Konstantinou; (5/10/07) Nir Klinger (ISR)

Founded – 1994

MAJOR HONOURS: Cypriot Cup - (1) 2004.

Date	Opponent		Score	Scorers
2007				
1/9	Aris	h	1-0	*Neophytou*
16/9	Omonia	a	2-3	*og (Kaseke), Rey (p)*
23/9	AEL	h	2-2	*Christou, Kingsley*
30/9	Doxa	a	3-3	*Kaondera, Kingsley, Neophytou*
8/10	Anorthosis	h	1-1	*Rey*
21/10	APOP	a	1-0	*Razić*
28/10	Paralimni	h	1-3	*og (Kissi)*
4/11	APOEL	a	0-1	
10/11	Apollon	h	0-2	
26/11	Olympiakos	a	2-0	*González (p), Wooter*
2/12	Nea Salamis	h	2-2	*Adorno, Jankauskas*
9/12	Alki	h	2-0	*Razić 2*
17/12	Ethnikos Achnas	a	2-0	*Kingsley 2*
23/12	Aris	a	3-2	*Kingsley 2, Wooter*
2008				
5/1	Omonia	h	1-0	*Jankauskas*
13/1	AEL	a	2-0	*Kingsley, Jankauskas*
19/1	Doxa	h	1-2	*Jankauskas*
27/1	Anorthosis	a	1-2	*Kingsley*
3/2	APOP	h	1-1	*Razić*
10/2	Paralimni	a	1-0	*Rey (p)*
13/2	APOEL	h	0-3	
26/2	Apollon	a	0-2	
1/3	Olympiakos	h	2-1	*González, Neophytou*
9/3	Nea Salamis	a	0-2	
15/3	Alki	a	2-0	*Kingsley, João Paiva*
23/3	Ethnikos Achnas	h	1-0	*Razić*
29/3	Anorthosis	h	2-2	*Adorno 2*
5/4	Omonia	a	0-0	
12/4	APOEL	h	1-0	*João Paiva*
20/4	APOEL	a	1-2	*Adorno*
3/5	Anorthosis	a	3-3	*Kingsley, González (p), Christou*
10/5	Omonia	h	5-3	*Rhanem 2, Kingsley, Tininho, Neophytou*

No	Name	Nat	Pos	Aps	(s)	Gls
2	Stelios ACHILLEOS		M	1	(1)	
12	Aldo ADORNO	PAR	A	16	(9)	4
33	Sofronis AVGOUSTI		G	31		
22	CÁSSIO Fernandes	BRA	D	20	(2)	
21	Paraskevas CHRISTOU		D	24	(1)	2
24	Ivica FRANCISKOVIĆ	SRB	M	6	(3)	
20	Héctor GONZÁLEZ	VEN	M	28	(1)	3
15	Peter HODULIK	SVK	G	1		
88	Dejan ILIĆ	SRB	M	4	(3)	
99	Joshua IZUCHUKWU	NGA	M	2	(2)	
9	Edgaras JANKAUSKAS	LTU	A	7	(8)	4
89	JOÃO Pedro PAIVA	POR	A	5	(7)	2
11	Shingayi KAONDERA	ZIM	M	7	(3)	1
32	Antonis KATSIS		M	10	(3)	
39	Sunny KINGSLEY	NGA	A	30	(1)	11
29	Kyriakos KYRIAKOU		D	8		
5	Dimitris MARIS	GRE	M	2	(1)	
40	Michalis MICHAIL		D	3	(2)	
23	Konstantinos MINA		D	18	(2)	
10	Marios NEOPHYTOU		A	5	(10)	4
8	Charis NICOLAOU		M	14	(9)	
4	Azubuike OLISEH	NGA	D	10		
6	Emmanuel PAPPOE	GHA	D	25		
27	Pavel PERGL	CZE	D	15	(2)	
16	Esad RAZIC	SWE	M	11	(10)	5
3	José REY	VEN	D	20		3
13	Hamid RHANEM	MAR	M	10	(2)	2
19	Ronildo Pereira "TININHO"	BRA	D	12	(7)	1
6	Klimenti TSITAISHVILI	GEO	A		(1)	
14	Nordin WOOTER	NED	M	7	(4)	2

AEL LIMASSOL FC

Coach – Eli Gutman (ISR); (6/12/07) Mariano Barreto (POR); (6/12/08) Andreas Michaelides

Founded - 1930

MAJOR HONOURS: Cypriot League - (5) 1941, 1953, 1955, 1956, 1968; Cypriot Cup - (6) 1939, 1940, 1948, 1985, 1987, 1989.

Date	Opponent		Score	Scorers
2007				
1/9	Apollon	a	3-4	*Krassas, Tiquinho, Louka*
16/9	Olympiakos	h	3-1	*Castillo 2, Tiquinho*
23/9	AEK	a	2-2	*Castillo 2*
30/9	Alki	h	2-0	*Louka, De Bruno (p)*
6/10	Ethnikos Achnas	a	1-2	*De Bruno*
21/10	Aris	h	0-0	
27/10	Omonia	a	0-1	
3/11	Nea Salamis	a	2-0	*Hélio Roque, De Bruno*
11/11	Doxa	h	2-1	*Louka, Krassas*
25/11	Anorthosis	a	1-3	*N'Diaye*
1/12	APOP	h	0-2	
8/12	Paralimni	a	1-1	*De Bruno*
15/12	APOEL	h	1-1	*Tiquinho*
22/12	Apollon	h	0-0	
2008				
6/1	Olympiakos	a	2-1	*N'Diaye, Tiquinho*
13/1	AEK	h	0-2	
19/1	Alki	a	0-2	
28/1	Ethnikos Achnas	h	1-2	*Fassotte*
3/2	Aris	a	1-2	*Filaniotis*
10/2	Omonia	h	1-1	*Kerkez*
13/2	Nea Salamis	h	1-0	*Kerkez*
27/2	Doxa	a	1-2	*Hélio Roque*
2/3	Anorthosis	h	1-2	*Fassotte*
8/3	APOP	a	1-0	*Hélio Roque*
16/3	Paralimni	h	1-4	*Tiquinho*
23/3	APOEL	a	0-2	
29/3	Doxa	h	2-2	*Filaniotis, Tiquinho*
5/4	Aris	a	2-0	*og (Seper), N'Diaye*
12/4	Alki	h	1-0	*Joca (p)*
19/4	Alki	a	1-2	*Filaniotis*
3/5	Doxa	a	2-1	*Krassas, Joca (p)*
10/5	Aris	h	3-2	*Theofanous, Chatzigeorgiou, Musa (p)*

No	Name	Nat	Pos	Aps	(s)	Gls
3	Daniel CARRICO	POR	D	13	(1)	
19	Jairo CASTILLO	COL	A	5		4
31	Nikos CHATZIGEORGIOU		M	2	(1)	1
10	Luciano DE BRUNO	ARG	M	14		4
4	Laurent FASSOTTE	BEL	D	29		2
33	Petros FILANIOTIS		A	15	(9)	3
99	FILIPE Vazde AZEVEDO	POR	A	6	(4)	
34	Kleopas GIANNOU	GRE	G	12		
28	HÉLIO José ROQUE	POR	M	13	(14)	3
23	Ricardo Pereira "JOCA"	POR	M	14	(7)	2
5	Moises KANDÉ	MTN	D	14	(1)	
13	Dušan KERKEZ	BIH	M	27	(2)	2
70	Panos KONSTANTINOU		G	13		
40	Simos KRASSAS		M	23	(5)	3
12	Xenios KYRIAKOU		M	14	(3)	
20	Liasos LOUKA		M	10	(1)	3
8	Igor MUSA	CRO	M	9	(9)	1
14	Seyni N'DIAYE	SEN	A	15	(11)	3
18	Gonzala N'TUMPA N'SAFU	COD	A	2	(3)	

No	Name	Nat	Pos	Aps	(s)	Gls
	Predrag OCOKOLJIĆ	SRB	D	24		
7	Rafael PANAYIOTOU		D	2	(1)	
5	Kyriakos PELEDRITIS		D	3		
1	Moses SAKYI	GHA	A	3	(3)	
2	Yiannis SAMPSON		D	17	(2)	
2	Dimitris THEOFANOUS		A	2	(1)	1
	Fábio Ferraz "TIQUINHO"	POR	M	20	(11)	6
6	Aleksandar TODOROVSKI	SRB	D	12	(2)	
	Géza VLASZÁK	HUN	G	1		
5	Giorgis XENIS		M		(1)	
4	Tasos YIALLOURIS		G	6		
	José Gonçalves "ZÉ NANDO"	POR	D	12	(3)	

ALKI LARNACA FC

Coach – Christos Kassianos

Founded - 1948

007				
/9	Ethnikos Achnas	h	1-3	*Silva*
5/9	Aris	a	5-2	*Clayton 2, Mário Carlos, Soares, Silva*
2/9	Omonia	h	2-1	*Silva, Clayton*
0/9	AEL	a	0-2	
/10	Doxa	h	1-1	*Clayton*
1/10	Anorthosis	a	0-1	
7/10	APOP	h	3-1	*Cabarcos, Soares, Hernâni*
/11	Paralimni	a	1-2	*Cabarcos*
1/11	APOEL	h	0-4	
5/11	Apollon	a	0-1	
/12	Olympiakos	h	5-0	*Soares 2, Clayton, Rouga, Chainho*
/12	AEK	a	0-2	
5/12	Nea Salamis	h	4-1	*Jocivalter, Clayton, Rouga, Soares*
2/12	Ethnikos Achnas	a	1-1	*Silva*
008				
/1	Aris	h	1-1	*Clayton (p)*
4/1	Omonia	a	0-3	
9/1	AEL	h	2-0	*Rivarola, Clayton*
27/1	Doxa	a	0-1	
2/2	Anorthosis	h	0-0	
9/2	APOP	a	3-5	*Rouga, Chainho, Iordache*
19/2	Paralimni	h	0-1	
26/2	APOEL	a	0-3	
1/3	Apollon	h	1-0	*Silva*
9/3	Olympiakos	a	1-1	*Silva*
15/3	AEK	h	0-2	
22/3	Nea Salamis	a	1-1	*Silva*
30/3	Aris	a	2-1	*Soares, Silva*
5/4	Doxa	h	1-0	*Soares*
12/4	AEL	a	0-1	
19/4	AEL	h	2-1	*Gadiaga, Silva*
3/5	Aris	h	4-1	*Clayton, Soares, Silva, Rouga*
10/5	Doxa	a	0-0	

No	Name	Nat	Pos	Aps	(s)	Gls
30	Athos ANGELI		A	2	(11)	
6	"ARCELINO" Souza Santos	BRA	D	22	(4)	
27	Daniel BALĂN	ROU	D	22	(3)	
9	David CABARCOS	ESP	A	2	(1)	2
22	Carlos Narciso CHAINHO	POR	M	22	(8)	2
18	Athos CHRYSOSTOMOU		G	21		
10	CLAYTON Ferreira da Cruz	BRA	M	19	(2)	9
14	Charis DRAKOS		M	4	(3)	
26	Cheikh GADIAGA	SEN	M	17	(6)	1
5	Carlos GARCÍA	URU	D	4	(4)	
25	José Borges "HERNÂNI"	CPV	A	5	(7)	1
20	Adrian IORDACHE	ROU	D	25		1
29	Dragan ISAILOVIĆ	SRB	A	4	(4)	
12	Liberato JOCIVALTER	BRA	M	10	(3)	1
28	Nikos KOUVARAKIS	GRE	G		(1)	
24	MÁRIO CARLOS	POR	M	17	(8)	1
19	Michalis MARKOU		D	9	(5)	
5	Miroslav MILOŠEVIĆ	SRB	D	2		
3	Fernando Rodrigues "NANDINHO"	POR	D	22	(4)	
16	Antonis PANAGI		M		(6)	
9	Diego RIVAROLA	ARG	A	9	(3)	1
14	Julio RODRÍGUEZ	URU	A	1	(3)	
21	Enrique ROUGA	VEN	D	29		4
11	Elpídio SILVA	BRA	A	24	(2)	10
7	Alexander SOARES	BRA	A	26	(3)	8
1	Ádám VEZÉR	HUN	G	11	(1)	
4	Alex VON SCHWEDLER Vasquas	CHI	D	23		

ANORTHOSIS FAMAGUSTA FC

Coach – Temuri Ketsbaia (GEO)

Founded - 1911

MAJOR HONOURS: Cypriot League - (13) 1950, 1957, 1958, 1960, 1962, 1963, 1965, 1997, 1998, 1999, 2000, 2005, 2008; Cypriot Cup - (9) 1949, 1962, 1964, 1971, 1975, 1998, 2002, 2003, 2007.

2007				
3/9	Paralimni	a	2-1	*Sosin, Žlogar*
15/9	APOEL	h	1-0	*Nicolaou*
24/9	Apollon	a	2-2	*Deyanov, Žlogar*
29/9	Olympiakos	h	1-0	*Sosin*
8/10	AEK	a	1-1	*Sosin (p)*
21/10	Alki	h	1-0	*Belić*
27/10	Ethnikos Achnas	a	1-0	*Frousos*
4/11	Aris	h	4-0	*Nicolaou 2, Sosin, Žlogar*
10/11	Omonia	a	1-1	*Belić*
25/11	AEL	h	3-1	*Sosin (p), Nicolaou, William*
2/12	Doxa	a	1-1	*Sosin*
9/12	Nea Salamis	a	4-0	*Frousos, Sosin (p), Nicolaou, Žlogar*
16/12	APOP	h	3-1	*Katsavakis 2, Laban*
23/12	Paralimni	h	1-0	*Frousos*
2008				
5/1	APOEL	a	1-0	*Skopelitis*
12/1	Apollon	h	1-1	*Sosin*
19/1	Olympiakos	a	1-0	*Laban*
27/1	AEK	h	2-1	*Sosin, Tsitaishvili*
2/2	Alki	a	0-0	
9/2	Ethnikos Achnas	h	5-1	*Sosin 2, Žlogar, Paolo Costa, Deyanov*
14/2	Aris	a	0-0	
27/2	Omonia	h	2-0	*Tsitaishvili, Katsavakis*
2/3	AEL	a	2-1	*Tsitaishvili, Frousos*
8/3	Doxa	h	2-1	*Paolo Costa, Konstantinou*
15/3	Nea Salamis	h	5-0	*Katsavakis, Sosin 2, Paolo Costa, Deyanov*
22/3	APOP	a	2-0	*Žlogar, Laban*
29/3	AEK	a	2-2	*Frousos, Žlogar*
6/4	APOEL	a	1-1	*Nicolaou*
13/4	Omonia	h	0-0	
19/4	Omonia	a	0-0	
3/5	AEK	h	3-3	*Frousos 3 (1p)*
10/5	APOEL	h	3-0	*Sosin 3*

No	Name	Nat	Pos	Aps	(s)	Gls
18	Milan BELIĆ	SRB	A	9	(12)	2
75	Arian BEQAJ	ALB	G	27		
22	Metodi DEYANOV	BUL	M	5	(11)	3
8	FABINHO dos Santos Pereira	BRA	M	3	(10)	
20	Nikos FROUSOS	GRE	A	10	(13)	8
4	Nikos KATSAVAKIS	GRE	M	28	(1)	4
24	Andreas KONSTANTINOU	GRE	D	29		1
20	Vincent LABAN	FRA	M	23	(2)	3
3	Lambros LAMBROU		D	13		
15	Konstantinos LOUMPOUTIS	GRE	D	2	(1)	
33	LUÍS de Graça LOUREIRO	POR	M		(2)	
77	Amir MEGAHED	EGY	D	11	(1)	

No	Name	Nat	Pos	Aps	(s)	Gls
30	Zoltán NAGY	HUN	G	5		
31	Hamed NDIKUMANA	RWA	D	15	(1)	
5	Nikos NICOLAOU		D	10	(4)	6
7	Marians PAHARS	LVA	A	1	(1)	
21	Giorgos PANAGI		M	10	(11)	
10	PAOLO Sérgio COSTA	POR	M	15	(2)	3
7	Savvas POURSAITIDIS	GRE	M	19	(2)	
23	Konstantinos SAMARAS		D	5		
6	Giannis SKOPELITIS	GRE	M	14	(1)	1
9	Łukasz SOSIN	POL	A	28	(3)	16
2	Theodoros TRIPOTSERIS	GRE	D	16	(5)	
16	Klimenti TSITAISHVILI	GEO	A	12	(5)	3
88	WILLIAM Boaventure	BRA	A	16	(3)	1
36	Anton ŽLOGAR	SVN	A	26	(3)	7

APOEL FC

Coach – Marinos Ouzounidis (GRE);
(8/1/08) Ivan Jovanović (SRB)

Founded - 1926

MAJOR HONOURS: Cypriot League - (19) 1936, 1937, 1938, 1939, 1940, 1947, 1948, 1949, 1952, 1965, 1973, 1980, 1986, 1990, 1992, 1996, 2002, 2004, 2007; Cypriot Cup - (19) 1937, 1941, 1947, 1951, 1963, 1968, 1969, 1973, 1976, 1978, 1979, 1984, 1993, 1995, 1996, 1997, 1999, 2006, 2008.

2007				
2/9	Doxa	h	3-2	*Machlas 2, Michail (p)*
15/9	Anorthosis	a	0-1	
22/9	APOP	h	4-0	*Michail 2 (1p), Makrides, Machlas*
29/9	Paralimni	a	0-1	
7/10	Nea Salamis	h	3-1	*Satsias, Machlas, Ricardo Fernandes*
21/10	Apollon	h	2-0	*Hélio Pinto, Machlas*
28/10	Olympiakos	a	2-2	*Machlas, Makrides*
4/11	AEK	h	1-0	*Makrides (p)*
11/11	Alki	a	4-0	*Machlas 2, Makrides, Ricardo Fernandes*
25/11	Ethnikos Achnas	h	2-1	*Kontis, Michail*
2/12	Aris	a	2-2	*Makrides, Michail (p)*
8/12	Omonia	h	1-0	*Makrides (p)*
15/12	AEL	a	1-1	*Hélio Pinto*
23/12	Doxa	a	2-2	*Daskalakis, Makrides (p)*
2008				
5/1	Anorthosis	h	0-1	
12/1	APOP	a	1-1	*Čorović*
20/1	Paralimni	h	0-1	
26/1	Nea Salamis	a	3-1	*Zé Carlos 3*
2/2	Apollon	a	2-0	*Zé Carlos, Michail (p)*
10/2	Olympiakos	h	4-0	*Čorović, Makrides, Broerse, Charalambides*
13/2	AEK	a	3-0	*Zé Carlos 2, Makrides*
26/2	Alki	h	3-0	*Machlas, Broerse, Satsias*
1/3	Ethnikos Achnas	a	2-0	*Machlas, Makrides*
8/3	Aris	h	3-0	*Charalambides 2, Louka*
15/3	Omonia	a	1-2	*Mirosavljević*
23/3	AEL	h	2-0	*Makrides 2 (1p)*
29/3	Omonia	a	2-1	*Michail (p), Charalambides*
6/4	Anorthosis	h	1-1	*Zé Carlos*
12/4	AEK	a	0-1	
20/4	AEK	h	2-1	*Michail (p), Mirosavljević*
3/5	Omonia	h	2-2	*Makrides, Kontis*
10/5	Anorthosis	a	0-3	

No	Name	Nat	Pos	Aps	(s)	Gls
15	Marios ANTONIADIS		D	2		
14	Joost BROERSE	NED	M	16		2
7	Kostas CHARALAMBIDES		M	7	(3)	4
69	Nemanja ČOROVIĆ	SRB	A	3	(11)	2
18	Dimitris DASKALAKIS		D	14	(3)	1
19	Marios ELIA		D		(1)	
6	EMERSON Moises	BRA	M	10	(3)	
3	Daniel FLOREA	ROU	D	25		
32	Altin HAXHI	ALB	D	14	(1)	
23	HÉLIO PINTO	POR	M	21	(7)	2
4	Michalis KAPSIS	GRE	D	6	(1)	
88	Tasos KISSAS		G	1		
24	Christos KONTIS	GRE	M	25	(2)	2
11	Marios LOUKA		M	7	(11)	1
32	Nikos MACHLAS	GRE	A	26	(4)	10
20	Constantinos MAKRIDES		M	29		13
33	Chrisis MICHAIL		M	21	(7)	8
30	Nenad MIROSAVLJEVIĆ	SRB	A	4	(10)	2
1	Michalis MORFIS		G	8		
12	Jane NIKOLOSKI	MKD	G	23		
26	NUNO Miguel MORAIS	POR	M	11	(2)	
40	Giorgos OIKONOMIDIS		M	1	(1)	
77	Panayiotis PANAYIOTOU		D	2	(4)	
10	RICARDO FERNANDES	POR	M	17	(2)	2
7	RUBENS Veira	BRA	M	1	(4)	
22	Miltos SAPANIS	GRE	M		(4)	
26	Marinos SATSIAS		M	25	(1)	2
8	Bark SEGHIRI	FRA	D	18	(1)	
21	Marcos TAVARES	BRA	A		(4)	
6	Marios THEODOOU		M		(1)	
31	José Silva "ZÉ CARLOS"	BRA	A	15	(4)	7

APOLLON LIMASSOL FC

Coach – Siniša Gogić; (7/11/07) Yossi Mizrahi (ISR)

Founded - 1954

MAJOR HONOURS: Cypriot League (3) 1991, 1994, 2006; Cypriot Cup - (5) 1966, 1967, 1986, 1992, 2001.

2007				
1/9	AEL	h	4-3	*Sangoy 2, Babangida 2*
16/9	Doxa	a	0-1	
24/9	Anorthosis	h	2-2	*Sangoy, Garpozis*
29/9	APOP	a	0-1	
7/10	Paralimni	h	3-0	*Sangoy, Risso, Solomou*
21/10	APOEL	a	0-2	
27/10	Nea Salamis	h	4-1	*Babangida, Merkis 2, Risso*
4/11	Olympiakos	h	3-2	*Babangida, Risso, Korolovszky*
10/11	AEK	a	2-0	*Risso, Babangida*
25/11	Alki	h	1-0	*Babangida*
1/12	Ethnikos Achnas	a	1-2	*Garpozis*
8/12	Aris	h	2-1	*Risso (p), Solomou*
16/12	Omonia	a	1-1	*Sangoy*
22/12	AEL	a	0-0	
2008				
5/1	Doxa	h	2-2	*Sangoy, Okkarides*
12/1	Anorthosis	a	1-1	*Risso*
20/1	APOP	h	2-0	*Iencsi, Torresi*
26/1	Paralimni	a	2-2	*Sangoy, Asulin*
2/2	APOEL	h	0-2	
10/2	Nea Salamis	a	0-0	
13/2	Olympiakos	a	2-2	*Sangoy, Risso (p)*
26/2	AEK	h	2-0	*Risso, Torresi*
1/3	Alki	a	0-1	
8/3	Ethnikos Achnas	h	2-1	*Sangoy, Moustakas*
15/3	Aris	a	1-3	*Marangos*
23/3	Omonia	h	3-3	*Risso, Babangida, Solomou*
29/3	Ethnikos Achnas	a	1-1	*Sangoy*
5/4	APOP	a	2-1	*Risso 2 (1p)*
13/4	Paralimni	h	4-1	*Babangida 2, Iencsi, Marangos*
19/4	Paralimni	a	0-1	
3/5	Ethnikos Achnas	h	0-2	
11/5	APOP	h	2-2	*Pantos, Avraam*

No	Name	Nat	Pos	Aps	(s)	Gls
6	Bogdan ANDONE	ROU	M	21	(4)	

Name	Nat	Pos	Aps	(s)	Gls
Lior ASULIN	ISR	A	7	(1)	1
Andreas AVRAAM		M	3	(9)	1
Haruna BABANGIDA	NGA	A	19	(4)	9
Marko BARUN	SVN	D	15	(5)	
Christoforos CHRISTOFI		A		(1)	
Aleš CHVALOVSKÝ	CZE	G	32		
Michalis DIMITRIOU		M	3	(5)	
Alexis GARPOZIS		M	28	(1)	2
Mihai IENCSI	ROU	D	21		2
JOÃO Pedro PAIVA	POR	A	2	(8)	
Gábor KOROLOVSZKY	HUN	D	17	(6)	1
Levan MAGHRADZE	GEO	D	12	(6)	
Christos MARANGOS		M	20	(4)	2
Giorgos MERKIS		M	8	(3)	2
Pericles MOUSTAKAS		D	7	(1)	1
Christos NIKOLAOU		M		(1)	
Stelios OKKARIDIS		D	26		1
Waheed OSENI	NGA	M	5	(4)	
Stamatis PANTOS		A	2		1
Ignacio RISSO	URU	A	25	(6)	11
Gaston SANGOY	ARG	A	24	(1)	10
Athos SOLOMOU		M	15	(7)	3
Christis THEOFILOU		D	23	(3)	
Luis TORRESI	ARG	M	17	(12)	2

APOP/KINYRAS PEYIAS FC

Coach – Dušan Mitosević (SRB);
(5/11/07) Eduard Eranosyan (BUL)
Founded - 2003

07				
9	Nea Salamis	h	4-2	*Olisadebe 2, Vasconcelos, Vargas*
/9	Paralimni	h	1-1	*Vargas (p)*
/9	APOEL	a	0-4	
/9	Apollon	h	1-0	*Vasconcelos*
10	Olympiakos	a	1-1	*Vasconcelos*
/10	AEK	h	0-1	
/10	Alki	a	1-3	*Vargas*
11	Ethnikos Achnas	h	2-1	*Vasconcelos 2*
/11	Aris	a	2-1	*Paulo Sousa, Vasconcelos*
/11	Omonia	h	0-0	
12	AEL	a	2-0	*Vasconcelos, Vargas*
12	Doxa	h	3-1	*Vasconcelos, Sfakianakis, Chatzis*
/12	Anorthosis	a	1-3	*Vasconcelos*
/12	Nea Salamis	a	1-1	*Calado (p)*
08				
1	Paralimni	a	2-0	*Sfakianakis, Efthymiou*
/1	APOEL	h	1-1	*Efthymiou*
/1	Apollon	a	0-2	
/1	Olympiakos	h	3-1	*Olisadebe 2, Efthymiou*
2	AEK	a	1-1	*Efthimiou*
2	Alki	h	5-3	*Calado, og (Rouga), Marques, Mykhailenko, Efthymiou*
/2	Ethnikos Achnas	a	1-2	*Olisadebe*
/2	Aris	h	1-0	*Olisadebe*
3	Omonia	a	0-1	
3	AEL	h	0-1	
/3	Doxa	a	2-2	*Vargas 2 (1p)*
/3	Anorthosis	h	0-2	
/3	Paralimni	a	3-4	*Pikramenos, Vargas (p), Lima*
4	Apollon	h	1-2	*Tiago*
/4	Ethnikos Achnas	a	2-2	*Palates, Chatzis (p)*
/4	Ethnikos Achnas	h	1-0	*Calado (p)*
5	Paralimni	h	3-4	*Pikramenos, Sfakianakis, Marques*
/5	Apollon	a	2-2	*Vargas, Lima*

No	Name	Nat	Pos	Aps	(s)	Gls
44	Michalis AGATHANGELOU		M	3	(1)	
99	ALEXANDRE NEGRI	BRA	G	8		
1	Gábor BARDI	HUN	G	24		
22	Jose CALADO	POR	M	25	(1)	3
13	CARLOS Manuel MARQUES	POR	D	24	(1)	
25	Nikos CHATZIS		M	13	(11)	2
11	Marios CHRISTODOULOU		M	7		
18	Angelos EFTHYMIOU		M	12	(9)	5
2	Filippos FILIPPOU		D	7	(3)	
6	Theodoros GALANIS	GRE	D	22	(2)	
4	Kyriakos IGNATIOU		D		(3)	
10	Romik KHACHATRYAN	ARM	M	8		
9	Rosen KIRILOV	BUL	D	20	(2)	
50	Gabriel LIMA	BRA	A	7	(7)	2
3	MÁRCIO FERREIRA	BRA	D	19	(2)	
11	Eduardo MARQUES	BRA	M	10	(3)	2
17	Joel MOGOROSI	BOT	M		(2)	
19	Dmytro MYKHAILENKO	UKR	M	20	(5)	1
23	Emmanuel OLISADEBE	POL	A	12	(5)	6
12	Cristos PALATES		A	2		1
66	José PAULO SOUSA	POR	M	13		1
87	Savvas PIKRAMENOS		M	7	(3)	2
5	Giannis SFAKIANAKIS	GRE	D	24	(1)	3
2	TIAGO Viera	POR	M	5	(7)	1
8	Paolo TINGA	BRA	D	12	(5)	
10	Adorcelinho TUTA	BRA	D	8	(6)	
55	Miguel VARGAS	POR	M	25	(5)	8
10	Bernardo VASCONCELOS	POR	A	15	(2)	9

ARIS LIMASSOL FC

Coach – Andreas Michaelides; (18/9/07) Henk Houwaart (NED);
(7/11/07) Mihai Stoichiţă (ROU)
Founded - 1930

2007				
1/9	AEK	a	0-1	
15/9	Alki	h	2-5	*Mihalcea 2 (1p)*
22/9	Ethnikos Achnas	a	0-2	
29/9	Nea Salamis	a	0-0	
6/10	Omonia	h	1-2	*Mihalcea*
21/10	AEL	a	0-0	
28/10	Doxa	h	1-0	*Paulo Costa (p)*
4/11	Anorthosis	a	0-4	
10/11	APOP	h	1-2	*Mihalcea (p)*
25/11	Paralimni	a	0-1	
2/12	APOEL	h	2-2	*Mihalcea, Seper*
8/12	Apollon	a	1-2	*Mihalcea*
16/12	Olympiakos	h	3-0	*Yiasemakis 2, Paolo Costa*
23/12	AEK	h	2-3	*Parpas, Mihalcea*
2008				
6/1	Alki	a	1-1	*Yiasemakis*
12/1	Ethnikos Achnas	h	0-1	
19/1	Nea Salamis	h	1-0	*Alekou*
26/1	Omonia	a	0-0	
3/2	AEL	h	2-1	*Mihalcea (p), Diniţă*
10/2	Doxa	a	1-2	*Mihalcea (p)*
14/2	Anorthosis	h	0-0	
26/2	APOP	a	0-1	
1/3	Paralimni	h	2-1	*Yovov, Vasiliou*
8/3	APOEL	a	0-3	
15/3	Apollon	h	3-1	*Mozacu, Mihalcea 2*
22/3	Olympiakos	a	1-0	*Mihalcea*
30/3	Alki	h	1-2	*Vasiliou*
5/4	AEL	h	0-2	
12/4	Doxa	a	0-2	
19/4	Doxa	h	3-0	*Diniţă, Vasiliou 2*
3/5	Alki	a	1-4	*Diniţă*
10/5	AEL	a	2-3	*Markou, Elia*

CYPRUS

No	Name	Nat	Pos	Aps	(s)	Gls
33	Alekos ALEKOU		A	1	(18)	1
4	Marios ANTONIOU		D	10	(3)	
25	Menelaos ARISTIDOU		M	3	(9)	
1	Gilbert BAYIHA N'DJEMA	FRA	G	9		
8	Antas BORNOSUZOV	BUL	M	14		
28	Giorgos CHARALAMBOUS		G	4	(2)	
11	Laurențiu DINIȚĂ	ROU	A	20	(4)	3
18	Elias ELIA		D	2	(1)	1
2	Miha GOLOB	SVN	D	21		
14	Leopoldo JIMÉNEZ	VEN	M		(1)	
6	Nikolas KISSONERGIS		M	2	(1)	
35	Tomáš KUCHÁR	CZE	M	12		
69	Carl LOMBE	ARM	D	9	(4)	
30	Kostas MARKOU		M	9	4)	1
9	Adrian MIHALCEA	ROU	A	23	(2)	12
42	Costel Ciprian MOZACU	ROU	D	23	(2)	1
29	Edwin OUON	FRA	D	20	(2)	
24	Stelios PARPAS		D	16	(3)	1
99	PAULO COSTA	POR	M	12	(1)	2
20	Giorgos PEGLIS	GRE	M	13	(4)	
6	Manuel Sanchez "PUMA"	POR	A	7	(2)	
3	Ákos SEPER	HUN	D	20	(1)	1
12	Radostin STANEV	BUL	G	2		
10	Mihai STERE	ROU	M	8	(6)	
61	Ivan TRABALÍK	SVK	G	17		
19	Giorgos VASILIOU		M	26	(4)	4
5	Jan VOREL	CZE	D	26	(1)	
31	Yiasemis YIASEMAKIS		A	11	(13)	3
7	Hristo YOVOV	BUL	A	12	(2)	1

DOXA KATOKOPIA FC

Coach – Charalambos Christodoulou

Founded - 1954

Date	Opponent		Score	Scorers
2007				
2/9	APOEL	a	2-3	*David 2*
16/9	Apollon	h	1-0	*Edmar Silva*
23/9	Olympiakos	a	1-2	*Buyse*
30/9	AEK	h	3-3	*David, Buyse, Alabi*
7/10	Alki	a	1-1	*Edmar Silva*
20/10	Ethnikos Achnas	h	2-1	*Edmar Silva, Aniweta*
28/10	Aris	a	0-1	
3/11	Omonia	h	1-0	*Freddy*
11/11	AEL	a	1-2	*Ndaw*
24/11	Nea Salamis	a	1-2	*Freddy*
2/12	Anorthosis	h	1-1	*Freddy*
8/12	APOP	a	1-3	*Kostis (p)*
15/12	Paralimni	h	2-2	*David, Edmar Silva*
23/12	APOEL	h	2-2	*Ndaw, David*
2008				
5/1	Apollon	a	2-2	*Buyse, David*
13/1	Olympiakos	h	2-0	*Kostis (p), David*
19/1	AEK	a	2-1	*David 2*
27/1	Alki	h	1-0	*David*
2/2	Ethnikos Achnas	a	1-3	*Kostis (p)*
10/2	Aris	h	2-1	*Vourkou, Buyse*
14/2	Omonia	a	1-2	*Júnior*
27/2	AEL	h	2-1	*David, Vourkou*
2/3	Nea Salamis	h	2-3	*Alabi, David*
8/3	Anorthosis	a	1-2	*Hélder Neto*
15/3	APOP	h	2-2	*David, Buyse*
23/3	Paralimni	a	1-0	*Kostis (p)*
29/3	AEL	a	2-2	*Alabi, Buyse*
5/4	Alki	a	0-1	
12/4	Aris	h	2-0	*David 2*
19/4	Aris	a	0-3	
3/5	AEL	h	1-2	*David*
10/5	Alki	h	0-0	

No	Name	Nat	Pos	Aps	(s)	Gls
18	Rasheed ALABI	NGA	D	29	(1)	3
1	Armen AMBARTSUMYAN	ARM	G	6		
30	Louis ANIWETA	NGA	D	20	(3)	1
28	Panagiotis ARGYROU		M		(2)	
2	Fagio BUYSE	BEL	M	29	(1)	6
9	DAVID da Costa	BRA	A	27	(3)	16
19	EDMAR da SILVA	BRA	M	14	(2)	4
15	Frederico Santos "FREDDY"	ANG	M	7		3
7	Raúl GONZÁLEZ	VEN	D	28		
19	HÉLDER NETO	ANG	A	7	(1)	1
44	Dimitris IGNATIADIS	GRE	D	8	(7)	
27	Giorgos IOANNIDIS	GRE	D	4	(14)	
23	JOÃO PAULO	POR	M	15		
3	Rui JÚNIOR	POR	D	29		1
13	Giorgos KAMARLINGOS		M	2	(6)	
10	Giorgos KOSTIS		M	24	(4)	4
70	Loizos LOUVARIS		M	2	(10)	
35	Andreas MAVRIS		G	7		
6	Dimitris MORALES	GRE	D	25	(2)	
99	Mustapha Kamal NDAW	GAM	A	6	(5)	2
17	NUNO RODRIGUES	POR	D	4		
78	PEDRO PEREIRA	POR	D	9	(5)	
8	Kyriakos POLYKARPOU		M	9	(5)	
33	Dimitris RIZOS	GRE	G	19	(1)	
77	RUI ANDRADE	POR	M	17	(1)	
20	Efdokimos SERDARIS		D	1		
43	Sofoklis SOFOKLEOUS		M		(2)	
11	Christos VASILOU		M		(1)	
14	Sotiris VOURKOU		A	4	(11)	2

ENOSIS NEON PARALIMNI FC

Coach – Nir Klinger (ISR); (17/9/07) Nikos Andronikou; (26/10/07) Marios Konstantinou

Founded - 1936

Date	Opponent		Score	Scorers
2007				
3/9	Anorthosis	h	1-2	*Neri*
15/9	APOP	a	1-1	*Rhanem*
22/9	Nea Salamis	h	1-0	*Eleftheriou*
29/9	APOEL	h	1-0	*Eleftheriou*
7/10	Apollon	a	0-3	
20/10	Olympiakos	h	0-1	
28/10	AEK	a	3-1	*Elia 2, Eleftheriou*
3/11	Alki	h	2-1	*Neri, Goumenos*
10/11	Ethnikos Achnas	a	1-0	*og (Blanco)*
25/11	Aris	h	1-0	*Christofi*
1/12	Omonia	a	1-0	*Kissi*
8/12	AEL	h	1-1	*Christofi*
15/12	Doxa	a	2-2	*Paquito, Popara*
23/12	Anorthosis	a	0-1	
2008				
6/1	APOP	h	0-2	
13/1	Nea Salamis	a	1-1	*Tutuana*
20/1	APOEL	a	1-0	*Freddy*
26/1	Apollon	h	2-2	*Freddy, Ejiofor*
3/2	Olympiakos	a	2-2	*Freddy (p), Christofi*
10/2	AEK	h	0-1	
19/2	Alki	a	1-0	*Kissi*
27/2	Ethnikos Achnas	h	0-2	
1/3	Aris	a	1-2	*Spyrou*
8/3	Omonia	h	1-3	*Kolanis*
16/3	AEL	a	4-1	*Karas, Christofi, Freddy, Edmar Silva*
23/3	Doxa	h	0-1	
29/3	APOP	h	4-3	*Freddy, Goumenos, Christofi, Edmar Silva*
5/4	Ethnikos Achnas	h	1-1	*Christofi*
13/4	Apollon	a	1-4	*Karas*
19/4	Apollon	h	1-0	*Christofi*
3/5	APOP	a	4-3	*Freddy 3 (1p), Christofi*
10/5	Ethnikos Achnas	a	3-4	*Freddy, Edmar Silva, Christofi*

No	Name	Nat	Pos	Aps	(s)	Gls
12	Dimitris CHRISTOFI		M	21	(6)	9

No	Name	Nat	Pos	Aps	(s)	Gls
1	EDMAR da SILVA	BRA	M	12		3
1	Adamos EFSTATHIOU		M	3	(4)	
5	Eric EJIOFOR	NGA	D	21	(1)	1
9	Lefteris ELEFTHERIOU		M	16	(5)	3
	Kostas ELIA		A	8	(5)	2
	Michael FELGATE		D		(1)	
	Fredrico Santos "FREDDY"	ANG	M	17		9
7	Dimos GOUMENOS		M	23	(2)	2
	Igor JANČEVSKI	MKD	M		(4)	
	Bekim KAPIČ	SVN	D	26		
	Mrios KARAS		M	10	(8)	2
9	Abdekarim KISSI	MAR	M	23		2
1	Giorgos KOLANIS		M	21	(5)	1
7	Spyros MACHATOS		M		(4)	
0	Lefteris MERTAKAS		D	8	(5)	
	Petar MILOSEVSKI	MKD	G	27		
8	Vassilis MYTILINEOS	GRE	G	5	(1)	
4	Junas NACIRI	NED	M	1	(1)	
2	Adriano Miranda "NENE"	POR	M	6	(4)	
1	NERI Valmerino	BRA	A	9	(1)	2
0	Pinheiro "PAQUITO"	BRA	M	4	(3)	1
8	Christos PIERETTIS		M		(4)	
0	Pavle POPARA	SRB	M	7	(10)	1
	Manuel Sánchez "PUMA"	CPV	A	14		
3	Hamid RHANEM	MAR	M	5	(3)	1
0	Henri SIQUEIRA-BARRAS	SUI	D	8	(4)	
3	Panikos SPYROU		D	27	(1)	1
	Almir TANJIČ	SVN	M	16	(4)	
3	Jeff TUTUANA	COD	A	14	(5)	1

ETHNIKOS ACHNAS FC

Coach – Svetozar Šapurić (SRB)

Founded - 1968

007				
/9	Alki	a	3-1	*Poyiatzis 2 (2p), Kebadze*
6/9	Nea Salamis	a	0-2	
2/9	Aris	h	2-0	*Sialis, Stjepanović*
9/9	Omonia	a	1-2	*Kebadze*
/10	AEL	h	2-1	*Stjepanović 2*
0/10	Doxa	a	1-2	*Poyiatzis*
7/10	Anorthosis	h	0-1	
/11	APOP	a	1-2	*Engomitis*
0/11	Paralimni	h	0-1	
5/11	APOEL	a	1-2	*Georgiadis*
/12	Apollon	h	2-1	*Georgiadis, Stjepanović*
/12	Olympiakos	a	0-1	
7/12	AEK	h	0-2	
2/12	Alki	h	1-1	*Kebadze*
008				
/1	Nea Salamis	h	5-0	*Poyiatzis (p), Kebadze 2, Stjepanović, Naumov*
2/1	Aris	a	1-0	*Naumov*
9/1	Omonia	h	1-2	*Kebadze*
8/1	AEL	a	2-1	*Grkinić, Naumov*
/2	Doxa	h	3-1	*Stjepanović, Sialis, Kebadze*
/2	Anorthosis	a	1-5	*Naumov*
3/2	APOP	h	2-1	*Kebadze, Naumov*
7/2	Paralimni	a	2-0	*Stjepanović, Kebadze*
/3	APOEL	h	0-2	
/3	Apollon	a	1-2	*Guilherme*
5/3	Olympiakos	h	2-1	*Naumov, Kebadze*
3/3	AEK	a	0-1	
9/3	Apollon	h	1-1	*Naumov*
/4	Paralimni	a	1-1	*Naumov*
2/4	APOP	h	2-2	*Poyiatzis 2 (1p)*
9/4	APOP	a	0-1	
/5	Apollon	a	2-0	*Naumov 2*
0/5	Paralimni	h	4-3	*Naumov 2, Stjepanović, Engomitis*

No	Name	Nat	Pos	Aps	(s)	Gls
1	Guillermo ÁLVAREZ	ARG	G	14		
3	Daniel BLANCO	ARG	M	12	(2)	
19	Nemanja ĐUROVIĆ	BIH	M	3	(6)	
16	Elpidoporos ELIA		D	2	(4)	
9	Marios ELIA		D	11		
30	Yiotis ENGOMITIS		M	9	(11)	2
11	George GEBRO	LBR	M	1	(2)	
24	Constantinos GEORGIADIS		A	8	(7)	2
5	Goran GRKINIĆ	SRB	D	23	(2)	1
25	GUILHERME Weisheimer	BRA	A	3	(12)	1
13	Patrik IPAVEC	SVN	A	10	(9)	
18	Branislav JOVANOVIĆ	SRB	D	12	(6)	
29	Levan KEBADZE	GEO	A	27	(2)	10
33	Szabolcs KEMENES	HUN	G	18		
6	Christos KOTSONIS		M	28	(2)	
23	Charis LOIZOU		M	1	(1)	
11	Riste NAUMOV	MKD	A	18		12
25	NÍLTON Rogério	POR	M	5	(4)	
17	Christos PASHIALIS		D	9	(1)	
20	Ivan PETROVIĆ	SRB	M	16	(1)	
10	Christos POYIATZIS		A	29		6
26	Aleš PUS	SVN	D	7		
8	Lars SCHLICHTING	GER	M	18	(5)	
4	Christos SIALIS		D	21	(1)	2
15	Dimitris SIMOV		D	11	(5)	
7	Zoran STJEPANOVIĆ	BIH	M	32		8
6	Damir SULJANOVIĆ	SRB	M		(3)	
2	António Lopes "TONI"	POR	D	3		
9	Ljubiša VUKELJA	SRB	A	1	(2)	

NEA SALAMIS FC

Coach – Georgios Kostikos; (29/10/07) Panikos Orfanidis

Founded - 1948

2007				
1/9	APOP	a	2-4	*Domoraud, Bangura*
16/9	Ethnikos Achnas	h	2-0	*Bilibani, Dário (p)*
22/9	Paralimni	a	0-1	
29/9	Aris	h	0-0	
7/10	APOEL	a	1-3	*Rui Dolores*
20/10	Omonia	h	0-2	
27/10	Apollon	a	1-4	*Domoraud*
3/11	AEL	h	0-2	
11/11	Olympiakos	a	4-2	*Bangura 3, Nicolaou*
24/11	Doxa	h	2-1	*Nicolaou, Tchipev*
2/12	AEK	a	2-2	*Bangura 2*
9/12	Anorthosis	h	0-4	
15/12	Alki	a	1-4	*Nicolaou*
22/12	APOP	h	1-1	*Eleftheriou*
2008				
5/1	Ethnikos Achnas	a	0-5	
13/1	Paralimni	h	1-1	*Rui Lima*
19/1	Aris	a	0-1	
26/1	APOEL	h	1-3	*Louka (p)*
2/2	Omonia	a	0-3	
10/2	Apollon	h	0-0	
13/2	AEL	a	0-1	
26/2	Olympiakos	h	4-2	*Louka 2 (1p), Torrão, Bangura*
2/3	Doxa	a	3-2	*Dário, Bangura, Eleftheriou*
9/3	AEK	h	2-0	*Bangura, Kyprianou*
15/3	Anorthosis	a	0-5	
22/3	Alki	h	1-1	*Rui Lima*

No	Name	Nat	Pos	Aps	(s)	Gls
7	Panagiotis ASSIOTIS		D	3	(8)	
10	Mustapha BANGURA	SLE	A	20	(3)	9
26	Admir BILIBANI	SUI	D	10		1
11	DÁRIO Alberto Monteiro	MOZ	A	20	(4)	2
23	Gilles DOMORAUD	CIV	M	18		2
27	Giorgos ELEFTHERIOU		M	7	(8)	2

12	Aleksandr FILIMONOV	RUS	G	8		
30	Andreas IOANNIDES		D	4	(3)	
24	Orthodoxos IOANNOU		D	15	(3)	
5	Tamás JUHÁR	HUN	D	15		
88	Charalambos KAIRINOS		G	18		
16	Shingayi KAONDERA	ZIM	M	6		
25	Theodoros KATSIARIS		M		(1)	
18	Miloš KOLAKOVIĆ	SRB	A		(6)	
2	Kostas KONSTANTINIDIS	GRE	M	6		
19	Panikos KOSMA		M	1	(4)	
21	Andreas KYPRIANOU		A	4	(4)	1
8	Liasos LOUKA		M	11		3
29	MARCO ALMEIDA	POR	D	3		
9	Giorgos NICOLAOU		A	8	(9)	3
17	RUI DOLORES	POR	M	14	(9)	1
26	RUI LIMA	POR	M	10	(1)	2
25	Nordine SAM	ALG	D	7		
28	José de SOUSA	BRA	M	8	(1)	
14	Angel STOYKOV	BUL	M	12	(5)	
4	Tamás SZAMOSI	HUN	D	14		
19	Tzvetomir TCHIPEV	BUL	M	8	(1)	1
20	TIAGO LEMOS	POR	M	3	(6)	
12	Pedro Miguel TORRÃO	POR	M	9		1
3	Jose VALLENILLA	VEN	D	24	(1)	

OLYMPIAKOS NICOSIA FC

Coach – Juan Ramón Rocha (ARG); (11/10/07) Jorge Walter Barrios (URU); (18/12/07) Nikos Andronikou

Founded – 1907

MAJOR HONOURS: Cypriot League – (3) 1967, 1969, 1971; Cypriot Cup – (1) 1977.

2007				
3/9	Omonia	h	0-1	
16/9	AEL	a	1-3	*De Porras*
23/9	Doxa	h	2-1	*Hugo Machado (p), González*
29/9	Anorthosis	a	0-1	
6/10	APOP	h	1-1	*Đenić*
20/10	Paralimni	a	1-0	*González*
28/10	APOEL	h	2-2	*González, Panigutti*
4/11	Apollon	a	2-3	*González, Hugo Machado*
11/11	Nea Salamis	h	2-4	*Đenić, Hugo Machado*
26/11	AEK	h	0-2	
3/12	Alki	a	0-5	
9/12	Ethnikos Achnas	h	1-0	*Panigutti*
16/12	Aris	a	0-3	
22/12	Omonia	a	0-2	
2008				
6/1	AEL	h	1-2	*Leonardo Oliveira*
13/1	Doxa	a	0-2	
19/1	Anorthosis	h	0-1	
26/1	APOP	a	1-3	*Grzybowski*
3/2	Paralimni	h	2-2	*Zandi 2*
10/2	APOEL	a	0-4	
13/2	Apollon	h	2-2	*Leonardo Oliveira, Hugo Machado*
26/2	Nea Salamis	a	2-4	*Hugo Machado, Futi*
1/3	AEK	a	1-2	*Zandi*
9/3	Alki	h	1-1	*Zandi*
15/3	Ethnikos Achnas	a	1-2	*Deugoué*
22/3	Aris	h	0-1	

No	Name	Nat	Pos	Aps	(s)	Gls
33	Iiro AALTO	FIN	D	6		
13	Andreas ALKIBIADIS		A		(1)	
99	Mamadi BERTHE	MLI	A	1	(4)	
16	Braima INIAL	GUB	M	13		
32	Mariano CORSICO	ARG	D	7	(2)	
5	Agustín DE LA CANAL	ARG	M	2	(3)	
18	Gonzalo DE PORRAS	ARG	A	3	(2)	1
4	Boris DEUGOUÉ	FRA	M	6	(8)	1
45	Petar ĐENIĆ	SRB	D	22	(2)	2
22	Christos EFTHYMIOU		D	8	(3)	
84	Adam FUTI	AUS	M	6	(2)	1
9	Silvio GONZÁLEZ	ARG	A	10	(3)	4
11	Zbigniew GRZYBOWSKI	POL	A	17	(3)	1
30	Adnan GUŠO	BIH	G	4		
27	HUGO COELHO	POR	D	12	(1)	
37	HUGO MACHADO	POR	M	23	(2)	5
29	Giorgos KOSTA		M		(2)	
38	LEONARDO OLIVEIRA	BRA	M	9		2
12	Marios NICOLAOU		D	3	(3)	
21	Nikos NICOLAOU		D	19		
24	Nikos NICOLAOU		M	18	(2)	
1	Paco BAZAN	PER	G	1		
32	Feidias PANAYIOTOU		M	1	(5)	
19	Emerson PANIGUTTI	ARG	M	16	(7)	2
6	Makis PAPAIOANNOU		D	16		
8	Alexis PITTAS		M	7	(12)	
7	Alexander POLKING	GER	M	4	(7)	
14	Rodríguez PAGANO	ARG	D	20		
36	José SOUSA	POR	D	2	(1)	
20	Dimitris STYLIANOU		G	18		
17	Simos TSIAKKAS		G	3		
77	Ferydoon ZANDI	IRN	M	9	(1)	4

AC OMONIA

Coach – Dragomir Okuka (SRB); (29/10/07) Giorgos Savvides; (3/3/08) (Nedim Tutić (SRB))

Founded - 1920

MAJOR HONOURS: Cypriot Championship - (19) 1961, 1966, 1972, 1974, 1975, 1976, 1977, 1978, 1979, 1981, 1982, 1983, 1984, 1985, 1987, 1989, 1993, 2001, 2003; Cypriot Cup - (12) 1965, 1972, 1974, 1980, 1981, 1982, 1983, 1988, 1991, 1994, 2000, 2005.

2007				
3/9	Olympiakos	a	1-0	*Magno*
16/9	AEK	h	3-2	*Chailis (p), Rui Lima, Kaiafas*
22/9	Alki	a	1-2	*Kaiafas*
29/9	Ethnikos Achnas	h	2-1	*Chailis, Mguni*
6/10	Aris	a	2-1	*Kaiafas, Mguni*
20/10	Nea Salamis	a	2-0	*Dobrasinović, Vakouftsis*
27/10	AEL	h	1-0	*Chailis*
3/11	Doxa	a	0-1	
10/11	Anorthosis	h	1-1	*Vakouftsis*
24/11	APOP	a	0-0	
1/12	Paralimni	h	0-1	
8/12	APOEL	a	0-1	
16/12	Apollon	h	1-1	*Magno*
22/12	Olympiakos	h	2-0	*Chailis, Magno*
2008				
5/1	AEK	a	0-1	
14/1	Alki	h	3-0	*Nélson Veiga, Magno, Mguni*
19/1	Ethnikos Achnas	a	2-1	*Pavlou, Mguni*
26/1	Aris	h	0-0	
2/2	Nea Salamis	h	3-0	*Cafú, Mguni, Dobrasinović*
10/2	AEL	a	1-1	*Vasconcelos*
14/2	Doxa	h	2-1	*Vasconcelos, Chailis*
27/2	Anorthosis	a	0-2	
1/3	APOP	h	1-0	*Cafu*
8/3	Paralimni	a	3-1	*Kaiafas, Vasconcelos, Magno*
15/3	APOEL	h	2-1	*Cafu, Maris*
22/3	Apollon	a	3-3	*Kakoyiannis, Vattis, Kaiafas*
29/3	APOEL	h	1-2	*Kaiafas (p)*
5/4	AEK	h	0-0	
13/4	Anorthosis	a	0-0	
19/4	Anorthosis	h	0-0	
3/5	APOEL	a	2-2	*Kaseke, Chailis*
10/5	AEK	a	3-5	*Pavlou, Ioakim, Mguni*

Name	Nat	Pos	Aps	(s)	Gls
Ismaila BA	SEN	M	14	(13)	
Arlindo Semedo "CAFU"	POR	A	11	(3)	3
Kyriakos CHAILIS		A	14	(9)	6
Sinisa DOBRASINOVIĆ	SRB	M	25	(4)	2
EDGAR MARCELINHO	POR	M	6	(9)	
Antonis GEORGALLIDES		G	30		
Nikolas GEORGIOU		M	24		
Vlatko GROZDANOVSKI	MKD	M	2	(8)	
GUILHERME Weisheimer	BRA	A	2	(5)	
Akis IOAKIM		D	3		1
Kostas KAIAFAS		M	26		6
Loizos KAKOYIANNIS		D	22	(1)	1
Noel KASEKE	ZIM	D	26		1
Dimitris LEONIS		G	2		
MAGNO Mocelin	BRA	M	23	(5)	5
Dimitris MARIS	GRE	M	12	(2)	1
Musawenkosi MGUNI	ZIM	A	14	(3)	6
Riste NAUMOV	MKD	A		(1)	
NÉLSON VEIGA	POR	D	27		1
Kyriakos PAVLOU		A	10	(3)	2
Marcelo PLETSCH	BRA	D	12	(1)	
RICARDO SOUSA	POR	M		(4)	
RUI LIMA	POR	M	4	(2)	1
Giorgos THEODOTOU		D	7	(7)	
Pedro Miguel TORRÃO	POR	M	4	(3)	
Giorgos TSIKKOS		M	2		
Stavros TZIORTZIOPOULOS	GRE	D	4	(1)	
Giorgos VAKOUFTSIS	GRE	A	10	(3)	2
Bernardo VASCONCELOS	POR	A	9		3
Elias VATTIS		M	7	(3)	1

PROMOTED CLUBS

AEP PAPHOS FC
Coach – Savvas Constantinou
Founded - 2000

APEP PITSILIA FC
Coach – Tasos Kyriako
Founded - 1979

ATROMITOS YEROSKIPOU FC
Coach – Sofoklis Sofokleou
Founded - 1956

SECOND LEVEL FINAL TABLE 2007/08

		Pld	W	D	L	F	A	Pts
1	AEP Paphos FC	26	17	3	6	46	22	54
2	APEP Pitsilia FC	26	15	6	5	44	25	51
3	Atromitos Yeroskipou FC	26	13	7	6	41	23	46
4	Digenis Akritas Morphou FC	26	14	4	8	44	26	46
5	Ermis Aradippou FC	26	11	5	10	51	43	38
6	Onisilos Sotira FC	26	9	11	6	32	23	38
7	Ayia Napa FC	26	9	7	10	32	32	34
8	Omonia Aradippou	26	8	9	9	24	24	33
9	ASIL FC	26	8	8	10	21	24	32
10	ENTHOI Lakatamias FC	26	8	7	11	28	41	31
11	MEAP Nisou FC	26	9	4	13	33	50	31
12	Anagennisi Derynias FC	26	8	6	12	21	35	30
13	Akritas Chloraka FC	26	5	7	14	22	38	22
14	Olympos Xylofagou FC	26	4	8	18	23	56	16

DOMESTIC CUP 2007/08

KYPELLO KYPROY

RTH ROUND
10/07 & 31/10/07)
nia v Olympiakos 1-0; 4-2 *(5-2)*
10/07 & 31/10/07)
v Ayia Napa 0-2; 1-1 *(1-3)*
v Ethnikos Achnas 1-1; 0-1 *(1-2)*
is Aradippou v Aris 1-2; 1-1 *(2-3)*
EL v Olympos Xylofagou 6-0; 3-0 *(9-0)*
P v Anorthosis 0-2; 0-2 *(0-4)*
Salamis v Paralimni 1-0; 2-3 *(3-3; Nea*
mis on away goals)
10/07 & 1/11/07)
llon v Dighenis 3-1; 2-0 *(5-1)*

RTER-FINALS
UP A
11/07)
Salamis 2, Ethnikos Achnas 0
nia 2, Apollon 2
12/07)
llon 2, Nea Salamis 0
ikos Achnas 0, Omonia 2
/08)
llon 5, Ethnikos Achnas 1
nia 2, Nea Salamis 0
1/08)
ikos Achnas 1, Apollon 1
Salamis 2, Omonia 1
(19/3/08)
Apollon 1, Omonia 1
Ethnikos Achnas 1, Nea Salamis 3
(9/4/08)
Omonia 1, Ethnikos Achnas 1
Nea Salamis 1, Apollon 2

FINAL STANDINGS:
1. Apollon 12pts; 2. Omonia 9pts; 3. Nea Salamis 9pts; 4. Ethnikos Achnas 2pts

GROUP B
(5/12/07)
Ayia Napa 0, Aris 3
Anorthosis 1, APOEL 1
(19/12/07)
APOEL 3, Ayia Napa 1
Aris 2, Anorthosis 3
(16/1/08)
Aris 0, APOEL 2
Anorthosis 3, Ayia Napa 0
(30/1/08)
APOEL 3, Aris 1
Ayia Napa 0, Anorthosis 1
(2/4/08)
Aris 2, Ayia Napa 4
APOEL 0, Anorthosis 0
(16/4/08)
Ayia Napa 1, APOEL 0
Anorthosis 2, Aris 1

FINAL STANDINGS:
1. Anorthosis 14pts; 2. APOEL 11pts; 3. Ayia Napa 6pts; 4. ARIS 3pts

SEMI-FINALS
(23/4/08 & 7/5/08)
Apollon 1 *(Risso 81)*, Anorthosis 0
Anorthosis 4 *(Frousos 6, 20, 64, Katsavakis 66)*, Apollon 1 *(Garpozis 45)*
(Anorthosis 4-2)
(30/4/08 & 7/5/08)
Omonia 2 *(Mguni 8, Pletsch 33)*, APOEL 1 *(Makrides 83)*
APOEL 2 *(Michail 40, Mirosavljević 72)*, Omonia 0
(APOEL 3-2)

FINAL
(17/5/08)
GSP stadium, Nicosia
APOEL FC 2 *(Nuno Morais 53, Mirosavljević 75)*
ANORTHOSIS FAMAGUSTA FC 0
Referee – *Kasnaferis*
APOEL – *Nikoloski, Florea, Kontis, Seghiri, Broerse, Nuno Morais, Charalambidis (Daskalakis 88), Makridis, Hélio Pinto, Mirosavljević (Machlas 90), Zé Carlos (Haxhi 82).*
ANORTHOSIS – *Beqai, Tripotseris, Lambrou, Konstantinou, Katsavakis, Panagi (Deyanov 60), Žlogar, Laban (Tsitaishvili 73), Paulo Costa, Frousos, Sosin.*

Shattering end to Brückner's reign

The Czech Republic reached the end of an era at UEFA EURO 2008™, with veteran coach Karel Brückner stepping down after six and a half years at the helm. It looked as if he would bow out on a high, but the team's remarkable surrender to Turkey in their final group game, losing 3-2 after being two goals to the good with just 15 minutes remaining, left the silver-haired 68-year-old in a state of dismay and disbelief.

That defeat, the Czech Republic's first to Turkey, spelt elimination from a tournament in which Brückner's team had played well in patches but on the whole proved too disjointed and erratic, especially in defence, to prolong their involvement into the knockout stages. It was practically a carbon copy of the 2006 FIFA World Cup, in which the Czechs had also won their opening game before losing the next two and exiting in the first round.

If the opening 1-0 win against co-hosts Switzerland was blessed by good fortune, substitute Václav Svěrkoš's mishit winning goal coming against the run of play in the face of a Swiss onslaught and captain Tomáš Ujfaluši's handball in the penalty area going unpunished by the referee, the Czechs showed an improvement in their next game against Portugal, with goalscoring winger Libor Sionko very much to the fore, only to be denied a share of the spoils by the sharper finishing of Cristiano Ronaldo and co in a 3-1 defeat.

Karel Brückner's long reign as Czech Republic coach ended with a dramatic 3-2 defeat by Turkey at UEFA EURO 2008™

Everything appeared to be going to plan against Turk when, after a dominant first half adorned by Jan Koll 55th international goal, the Czechs doubled their lea with a sweet finish from Jaroslav Plašil. With Jan Polák hitting the post soon afterwards, there was no hint o the horror show to come. But ultimately it was a who uncharacteristic handling error from goalkeeper Petr Čech that proved the turning point and allowed the Turks to record one of the greatest comeback victorie the UEFA European Championship has ever witnesse It was also, remarkably, the first time the Czech Repu had ever lost a competitive international in which Ko had scored. And with the giant striker subsequently announcing his international retirement – along with midfield pivot Tomáš Galásek and reserve 'keeper Jaromír Blažek – it was also the last.

Rosický missed

After the initial shock of defeat, and elimination, the Czechs were left to reflect on what might have been had their captain and most creative player, Arsenal F midfielder Tomáš Rosický, been available for selectior Unfortunately, injury ruled him out and there was nobody of his vision and invention to fill the breach. attempt to bring former skipper Pavel Nedvěd out of international retirement for a second time proved fruitless, and although Plašil and Sionko performed w in wide roles, the service to the front players from the centre of the pitch was too pedestrian and predictab

Members of the Czech Republic squad affiliated to domestic clubs were few and far between, with only Svěrkoš, of FC Baník Ostrava, and Michal Kadlec, of A Sparta Praha, getting on to the field – and, in each ca only once as a substitute. There was no place in the 2 man party for any players from 2007/08 Czech 1. Liga champions SK Slavia Praha, although left-winger Dan Pudil was in the original squad before he had to withdraw with a broken bone in his hand, and striker Stanislav Vlček had starred for Slavia in the first half o the season before moving to Belgian giants RSC Anderlecht.

Praha striker Milan
in action against
nham in the UEFA Cup

avia, coached by Karel Jarolím, father of UEFA EURO
08™ participant David, won their first national
ampionship for 12 years. They also made 2007/08 a
ason to remember by reaching the UEFA Champions
eague group phase for the first time in six attempts
/hile arch-rivals Sparta fell at the qualifying stage) and
nding the season back in their beautifully
constructed Eden stadium after an eight-year exile.

avia required penalties, after two goalless draws, to
e off MŠK Žilina from neighbouring Slovakia in the
cond qualifying round of the UEFA Champions
eague, but there was no luck involved in the next
und as they beat AFC Ajax 1-0 in Amsterdam and 2-1
Prague, with two-goal Vlček and acrobatic
oalkeeper Martin Vaniak proving to be the star turns
s the Dutch heavyweights were sent packing in
npressive style. A 7-0 annihilation by Arsenal FC apart,
arolím's men did not disgrace themselves in the group
ames and even pipped Romania's FC Steaua Bucureşti
finish third and earn themselves post-Christmas
uropean football in the UEFA Cup, where they were slightly unfortunate to be eliminated, for the second successive season, by Arsenal's north London rivals Tottenham Hotspur FC after an excellent second-half performance in the second leg at White Hart Lane (1-1).

At the time of their UEFA Cup exit, Slavia were leading the way in the 1. Liga. Five points to the good at the winter break, and with a rare 2-0 win over Sparta at the Letná (their first for 14 years) to boot, they made a stuttering start to the spring campaign – despite a raft of new signings brought in to compensate for the departure of talisman Vlček – and were soon caught up by defending champions Sparta, who strung together a ten-match unbeaten run. It looked as if history would repeat itself once again, with Slavia having to accept the bridesmaid's role, when they lost successive games against FK Teplice (1-3 away) and FK Viktoria Žižkov (0-3 at home) to fall four points behind Sparta with three games to go, but this time, extraordinarily, it was Sparta whose wheels came off with the finishing line in sight.

Bílek sacked

As Slavia, with the pressure effectively off, pulled themselves together and won their next two matches, Sparta, incredibly, lost back-to-back home games against 1. FC Brno (0-2) and Baník (1-2), and suddenly found themselves two points behind their rivals with one match remaining. It was too much to bear for the Sparta board, who sacked Michal Bílek, the previous season's double-winning coach – even though there was still a chance that he could emulate his 2006/07 achievement in the days to come, with a Cup final against FC Slovan Liberec and, four days later, a final league fixture against the same opposition.

Instead it was Bílek's former team-mate in the Czechoslovakian national team, Jozef Chovanec, who returned after an eleven-year gap to oversee Sparta's season dénouement. The Cup was duly won – for an unprecedented record third year in a row – after a penalty shoot-out victory in a near-empty Strahov stadium in which defender Kadlec converted the decisive kick, but the big prize, the league, was to escape Sparta – as, curiously, it had done in every even-numbered year since 2000 – when they lost 4-3 to Liberec on the final day while Slavia, in front of a capacity crowd of 21,000, took the title with a 2-2 draw against FK Jablonec 97.

While the two major team trophies were shared between the big Prague rivals, the prize of the 1. Liga's top goalscorer went to Svěrkoš, whose 15 goals

CZECH REPUBLIC

Českomoravský fotbalový svaz (CMFS)

Diskarská 100
CZ-160 17 Praha 6
tel - +420 2 330 29111
fax - +420 2 333 53107
website - www.fotbal.cz
email - cmfs@fotbal.cz
Year of Formation - 1901
President – Pavel Mokrý
General Secretary – Rudolf Řepka
Press Officer – Václav Tichý

*INTERNATIONAL HONOURS**
UEFA European Championship - (1) 1976.

*INTERNATIONAL TOURNAMENT APPEARANCES**
FIFA World Cup - (8) 1934 (runners-up), 1938 (qtr-finals), 1954, 1958, 1962 (runners-up), 1970, 1982, 1990 (qtr-finals), 2006.
UEFA European Championship - (7) 1960 (3rd), 1976 (Winners), 1980 (3rd), 1996 (runners-up), 2000, 2004 (semi-finals), 20

TOP FIVE ALL-TIME CAPS (including Czechoslovakia)
Karel Poborský (118); Pavel Nedvěd (91); Zdeněk Nehoda & Jan Koller (90); Pavel Kuka (87)

TOP FIVE ALL-TIME GOALS (including Czechoslovakia)
Jan Koller (55); Antonín Puč (35); Zdeněk Nehoda & Milan Baroš (31); Oldřich Nejedlý & Pavel Kuka (29)

(before 1996 as Czechoslovakia)*

NATIONAL TEAM RESULTS 2007/08

Date	Opponent		Venue	Score	Scorers
22/8/07	Austria	A	Vienna	1-1	*Koller (32)*
8/9/07	San Marino (ECQ)	A	Serravalle	3-0	*Rosický (33), Jankulovski (75), Koller (90+3)*
12/9/07	Republic of Ireland (ECQ)	H	Prague	1-0	*Jankulovski (15)*
17/10/07	Germany (ECQ)	A	Munich	3-0	*Sionko (2), Matějovský (23), Plašil (63)*
17/11/07	Slovakia (ECQ)	H	Prague	3-1	*Grygera (13), Kulič (76), Rosický (83)*
21/11/07	Cyprus (ECQ)	A	Nicosia	2-0	*Pudil (11), Koller (74)*
6/2/08	Poland	N	Larnaca (CYP)	0-2	
26/3/08	Denmark	A	Herning	1-1	*Koller (42)*
27/5/08	Lithuania	H	Prague	2-0	*Koller (39, 62)*
30/5/08	Scotland	H	Prague	3-1	*Sionko (60, 90), Kadlec (84)*
7/6/08	Switzerland (ECF)	N	Basel (SUI)	1-0	*Svěrkoš (71)*
11/6/08	Portugal (ECF)	N	Geneva (SUI)	1-3	*Sionko (17)*
15/6/08	Turkey (ECF)	N	Geneva (SUI)	2-3	*Koller (34), Plašil (62)*

helped Baník to an impressive third place, just five points off the pace, ensuring a UEFA Cup spot for Karel Večeřa's team alongside defeated Cup finalists Liberec. Although Brno finished fourth, on the same number of points as Baník, they declined to take the UEFA Intertoto Cup place on offer and relinquished it to fifth-placed Teplice.

The issue of relegation and promotion produced an element of confusion, with Bohemians 1905 dropping down and being replaced by the similarly branded, but independent and newly formed, Bohemians Praha. FK SIAD Most also surrendered their top-flight place, which was taken by second division runners-up FK Marila Příbram, who once traded under the famous name of FC Dukla Praha.

ATIONAL TEAM APPEARANCES 2007/08

h – Karel BRÜCKNER	13/11/39		Aut	SMR	IRL	GER	SVK	CYP	Pol	Den	Ltu	Sco	SUI	POR	TUR	Caps	Goals
ČECH	20/5/82	Chelsea (ENG)	G	G	G	G			G		G	G	G	G	G	62	-
ěk GRYGERA	14/5/80	Juventus (ITA)	D41				D46		D		D		D	D	D	56	2
ROZEHNAL	5/7/80	Newcastle (ENG)	D	D	D	D	D	D									
		/Lazio (ITA)							D	D	D	s46	D	D	D	48	-
slav KOVÁČ	27/11/79	Spartak Moskva (RUS)	D46	D	D	D	D	D			s75	D	s87			24	1
š UJFALUŠI	24/3/78	Fiorentina (ITA)	D	D	D	D			D46	D	D75	D46	D	D	D	71	2
OLÁK	14/3/81	Anderlecht (BEL)	M57	s69	M		M86		M	M	M46	M	M	M	M	41	6
š GALÁSEK	15/1/73	Nürnberg (GER)	M	M82	M46	M	M	M		M46	s46	M	M	M73	M	69	1
JAROLÍM	17/5/79	Hamburg (GER)	M46	M69	s89					M73	M83	s46	M87	s85	s39	19	1
PITÁK	28/1/80	Salzburg (AUT)	M17													3	-
OLLER	30/3/73	Monaco (FRA)	A46	A		A79	A	A76									
		/Nürnberg (GER)							A	A	A	A46	A56	s73	A	90	55
BAROŠ	28/10/81	Lyon (FRA)	A		A89		A70	s57									
		/Portsmouth (ENG)							A	A63	M46			A		65	31
av PLAŠIL	5/1/82	Monaco (FRA)	s17														
		/Osasuna (ESP)		s82	M	M	M	M87	M85	s46	M79	s46	M	M85	M80	40	3
š ZÁPOTOČNÝ	13/9/80	Udinese (ITA)	s41													4	-
š SIVOK	15/9/83	Udinese (ITA)	s46		s46												
		/Sparta										s74				6	-
KULIČ	11/10/75	Sparta	s46	A56		s73	s70	A57	s85							12	3
n FENIN	16/4/87	Teplice	s46	A		s79		s76									
		/Eintracht (GER)								s63						5	-
MATĚJOVSKÝ	20/12/81	Mladá Boleslav	s57			M	s86	M									
		/Reading (ENG)							M	s46	s83	M46		M68	M39	12	1
JANKULOVSKI	9/5/77	Milan (ITA)		D	D						D65	D46	D	D	D	67	10
š ROSICKÝ	4/10/80	Arsenal (ENG)		M	M		M									68	19
slav VLČEK	26/2/76	Slavia		s56	s74	s58											
		/Anderlecht (BEL)							s76		M		s83	s68	s84	13	-
SIONKO	1/2/77	København (DEN)			M74	M58			M76	M46		M	M83	M	M84	33	7
ěk POSPĚCH	14/12/78	Sparta				D	D	D									
		/København (DEN)							D	D		D74				8	-
PUDIL	27/9/85	Slavia				M73		M								3	1
ír BLAŽEK	29/12/72	Nürnberg (GER)					G			G						14	-
l KADLEC	13/12/84	Sparta					s46	D	s46	D	s65	s46			s80	7	1
l ZÍTKA	20/6/75	Anderlecht (BEL)						G								1	-
ADRUBSKÝ	19/11/85	Sparta						s87								1	-
STŘEŠTÍK	1/2/87	Brno								s73						1	-
v SVĚRKOŠ	1/11/83	Baník									s46	s46	s56			3	1
lf SKÁCEL	17/7/79	Hertha (GER)									s79	M46				5	1

CZECH REPUBLIC

DOMESTIC LEAGUE 2007/08

1. LIGA FINAL TABLE

			Home					Away					Total					
		Pld	W	D	L	F	A	W	D	L	F	A	W	D	L	F	A	Pts
1	SK Slavia Praha	30	9	5	1	24	9	8	4	3	21	15	17	9	4	45	24	60
2	AC Sparta Praha	30	11	0	4	27	12	6	6	3	26	14	17	6	7	53	26	57
3	FC Baník Ostrava	30	10	4	1	33	12	5	6	4	18	16	15	10	5	51	28	55
4	1. FC Brno	30	9	4	2	22	13	7	3	5	21	19	16	7	7	43	32	55
5	FK Teplice	30	11	2	2	26	11	5	3	7	14	16	16	5	9	40	27	53
6	FC Slovan Liberec	30	6	7	2	23	15	6	1	8	12	16	12	8	10	35	31	44
7	FK Mladá Boleslav	30	5	4	6	18	20	6	5	4	19	16	11	9	10	37	36	42
8	FC Zlín	30	4	5	6	12	11	6	3	6	16	20	10	8	12	28	31	38
9	FC Viktoria Plzeň	30	7	4	4	22	14	3	4	8	10	23	10	8	12	32	37	38
10	FK Viktoria Žižkov	30	8	3	4	20	15	2	4	9	15	33	10	7	13	35	48	37
11	SK Sigma Olomouc	30	7	6	2	15	10	1	6	8	5	16	8	12	10	20	26	36
12	FK Jablonec 97	30	7	3	5	14	11	1	6	8	10	21	8	9	13	24	32	33
13	Dynamo České Budějovice	30	7	6	2	18	9	1	2	12	9	26	8	8	14	27	35	32
14	SK Kladno	30	5	3	7	21	20	1	6	8	10	25	6	9	15	31	45	27
15	Bohemians 1905	30	4	7	4	15	16	1	4	10	9	24	5	11	14	24	40	26
16	FK SIAD Most	30	4	4	7	20	28	0	4	11	11	30	4	8	18	31	58	20

TOP GOALSCORERS

15 Václav SVĚRKOŠ (Baník)
12 Miroslav SLEPIČKA (Sparta)
11 Jan RAJNOCH (Mladá Boleslav)
10 Goce TOLESKI (Most/Slavia)
9 Lukáš MAGERA (Baník)
8 Lukáš DOŠEK (Sparta)
Libor ŽŮREK (Zlín)
Robert ZEHER (Baník)
7 Stanislav VLČEK (Slavia)
Martin FENIN (Teplice)
Aleš BESTA (Brno)
Adam VARADI (Baník/Plzeň)

CLUB-BY-CLUB

FC BANÍK OSTRAVA

Coach – Karel Večeřa

Founded - 1922

MAJOR HONOURS: Czechoslovakian/Czech League - (4) 1976, 1980, 1981, 2004; Czechoslovakian /Czech Cup - (4) 1973, 1978, 1991, 2005.

Date	Opponent		Score	Scorers
2007				
5/8	Bohemians 1905	a	2-0	*Svěrkoš, Magera*
11/8	Most	h	5-2	*Zeher 2, Metelka, Svěrkoš (p), Bystroň*
18/8	Liberec	h	3-1	*Magera (p), Zeher, Metelka*
27/8	Zlín	a	2-2	*Magera, Marek*
1/9	Plzeň	h	2-0	*Zeher 2*
15/9	Slavia	a	0-0	
23/9	Sigma	h	0-1	
1/10	Žižkov	a	2-0	*Bystroň, Svěrkoš*
7/10	Teplice	h	0-0	
21/10	Jablonec	a	1-1	*Rajtoral*
28/10	Mladá Boleslav	h	3-3	*Mičola 2, Svěrkoš*
4/11	České Budějovice	a	0-3	
10/11	Brno	h	2-1	*Bystroň, Magera*
26/11	Kladno	a	0-3	
2/12	Sparta	h	0-0	
9/12	Most	a	2-0	*Tchuř, Varadi*
2008				
18/2	Liberec	a	1-1	*Svěrkoš*
23/2	Zlín	h	2-1	*Bystroň, Svěrkoš*
2/3	Plzeň	a	4-0	*Magera 2, og (Malcharek), Svěrkoš*
9/3	Slavia	h	2-2	*Magera 2*
15/3	Sigma	a	0-1	
22/3	Žižkov	h	3-0	*Svěrkoš 2, Rajtoral*
30/3	Teplice	a	1-1	*Bolf*
5/4	Jablonec	h	3-0	*Svěrkoš 2, Neuwirth*
13/4	Mladá Boleslav	a	1-3	*Svěrkoš (p)*
19/4	České Budějovice	h	2-0	*Svěrkoš, Zeher*
28/4	Brno	a	0-0	
3/5	Kladno	h	4-1	*Mičola, Svěrkoš, Zeher, Rajtoral*
10/5	Sparta	a	2-1	*Otepka, Svěrkoš*
17/5	Bohemians 1905	h	2-0	*Magera, Zeher*

No	Name	Nat	Pos	Aps	(s)	Gls
5	René BOLF		D	12		1
6	David BYSTROŇ		D	27	(1)	4
12	Petr CIGÁNEK		D	13		
15	Petr ČOUPEK		D	17	(2)	
21	Ondřej FICEK		M		(4)	
4	Martin LUKEŠ		M	5	(5)	
17	Lukáš MAGERA		A	25	(2)	9
18	Tomáš MAREK		M	28		1
24	František METELKA		M	11	(8)	2
9	Tomáš MIČOLA		M	18	(5)	3
7	Vladimír MIŠINSKÝ		M	2	(6)	
23	Aleš NEUWIRTH		D	14		1
8	Rudolf OTEPKA		M	25	(1)	1
19	Petr PAVLÍK		D	3		
11	František RAJTORAL		M	21	(4)	3
27	Pavel RICKA		D	1		
3	Radim ŘEZNÍK		D	25		
25	Václav SVĚRKOŠ		A	20	(4)	15
13	Dušan TESAŘÍK		M	2	(4)	
20	Petr TOMAŠÁK		M		(1)	
22	Daniel TCHUŘ		D	19	(2)	1
14	Adam VARADI		A	1	(10)	1
30	Petr VAŠEK		G	30		

Name	Nat	Pos	Aps	(s)	Gls
Tomáš VRŤO		A		(3)	
Robert ZEHER	SVK	A	11	(15)	8

BOHEMIANS 1905

Coach – Václav Hradecký; (4/12/07) Zbyněk Busta; (7/4/08) Michal Zach

Founded - 1905

MAJOR HONOURS: Czechoslovakian League - (1) 1983.

7				
	Baník	h	0-2	
3	Liberec	a	0-0	
3	Sigma	h	0-0	
3	Plzeň	a	0-2	
	Žižkov	h	2-2	*Turtenwald, Slezák*
9	Jablonec	a	0-0	
9	Slavia	h	2-0	*Škoda, Kunášek*
9	Mladá Boleslav	a	0-2	
0	České Budějovice	h	0-2	
10	Kladno	a	1-2	*Matúš*
10	Most	h	1-0	*Lukáš*
1	Brno	a	0-2	
11	Sparta	a	1-3	*Ordoš*
11	Zlín	h	1-2	*Sňozík (p)*
2	Teplice	a	0-2	
2	Liberec	h	1-0	*Škoda*
8				
2	Sigma	a	1-1	*Ordoš*
2	Plzeň	h	2-2	*Morávek, Rezek*
	Žižkov	a	1-2	*Morávek*
	Jablonec	h	1-1	*Morávek*
3	Slavia	a	1-2	*Škoda*
3	Mladá Boleslav	h	1-1	*Škoda*
3	České Budějovice	a	0-2	
	Kladno	h	1-1	*Rezek*
4	Most	a	4-2	*og (Webster), og (Švenger), Slezák, Ordoš*
4	Brno	h	3-1	*Kotyza 2, Bartek*
4	Sparta	h	0-0	
	Zlín	a	0-0	
5	Teplice	h	0-2	
5	Baník	a	0-2	

No	Name	Nat	Pos	Aps	(s)	Gls
	Lukáš ADAM		M	6	(6)	
	Vladimír BÁLEK		A	3	(5)	
	David BARTEK		A	17	(10)	1
	Ivan HAŠEK		M	16	(2)	
	Pavel HAŠEK		M	4	(1)	
	Vlastimil KARAL		M	5		
	Martin KNAKAL		D	5	(1)	
	Martin KOTYZA		M	7	(8)	2
	Tomáš KUCHAŘ		M		(1)	
	Petr KUNÁŠEK		M	11	(4)	1
	Pavel LUKÁŠ		D	18	(1)	1
	Lukáš MAREK		D	22	(1)	
	Lukáš MATÚŠ		A	3	(3)	1
	Jan MORAVEC		M	14	(3)	
	Jan MORÁVEK		M	15	(1)	3
	Marek NIKL		D	19		
	Michal ORDOŠ		A	15	(9)	3
	Michal PÁVEK		D	5		
	Michal POLODNA		A	4	(2)	
	Karel RADA		D	27		
	Jan REZEK		A	9	(1)	2
	Jan RŮŽIČKA		D	5		
	Jiří RYCHLÍK		M	4	(6)	
	Milan ŠKODA		D	15	(9)	4
	Dalibor SLEZÁK		M	18	(8)	2
	Michal ŠMARDA		D	27		
1	Radek SŇOZÍK		G	26		1
12	Vít TURTENWALD		D	2		1
7	Jiří VÁGNER		M	4	(2)	
29	Lukáš ZICH		G	4	(1)	

1. FC BRNO

Coach – Petr Uličný

Founded - 1913

MAJOR HONOURS: Czechoslovakian League - (1) 1978.

2007				
5/8	Zlín	h	0-0	
12/8	Žižkov	a	4-3	*Došek 2, Holek, Pacanda*
19/8	Plzeň	h	0-1	
25/8	Slavia	a	0-1	
15/9	Sigma	a	1-1	*Trousil*
19/9	Teplice	h	2-2	*Došek, Besta*
23/9	Jablonec	h	2-1	*Pacanda 2*
30/9	Kladno	a	2-1	*Trousil, Wagner*
8/10	Mladá Boleslav	h	0-3	
21/10	Most	a	2-2	*Trousil, Došek*
28/10	České Budějovice	h	2-1	*Besta, Kalouda*
4/11	Bohemians 1905	h	2-0	*Polách, Kalouda*
10/11	Baník	a	1-2´	*Besta*
25/11	Sparta	h	4-2	*Kalouda 2, Došek, Polách*
3/12	Liberec	a	1-1	*Střeštík*
9/12	Žižkov	h	3-1	*Střeštík, Besta, Kalouda*
2008				
17/2	Plzeň	a	0-2	
25/2	Slavia	h	2-1	*Besta, Střeštík*
2/3	Teplice	a	1-0	*Lira*
9/3	Sigma	h	1-0	*Trousil*
16/3	Jablonec	a	0-2	
23/3	Kladno	h	0-0	
30/3	Mladá Boleslav	a	3-1	*Střeštík, Besta, Polách*
6/4	Most	h	2-1	*Besta, Wagner*
13/4	České Budějovice	a	2-0	*Pavlík (p), Wagner*
20/4	Bohemians 1905	a	1-3	*Švejnoha*
28/4	Baník	h	0-0	
4/5	Sparta	a	2-0	*Střeštík, Došek*
10/5	Liberec	h	2-0	*Pavlík (p), Baláž*
17/5	Zlín	a	1-0	*og (Kroča)*

No	Name	Nat	Pos	Aps	(s)	Gls
2	Libor BALÁŽ		M	1	(8)	1
14	Aleš BESTA		M	21	(4)	7
17	Tomáš BUREŠ		G	5		
26	Tomáš DOŠEK		A	20	(5)	6
29	Josef DVORNÍK		D	10	(1)	
6	Marin HANÁK		M		(4)	
5	Mario HOLEK		M	14		1
19	Luboš KALOUDA		M	17	(2)	5
3	Lukáš KUBÁŇ		D	14	(7)	
18	Martin KUNCL		D	14	(1)	
1	Martin LEJSAL		G	25		
4	Elton Santiago dos Santos "LIRA"	BRA	D	3	(2)	1
5	Lukáš MAREČEK		M	8		
4	Radek MEZLÍK		D	1		
9	Tomáš OKLEŠTĚK		M		(8)	
11	Milan PACANDA		A	6	(4)	3
24	Petr PAVLÍK		D	26	(3)	2
21	Tomáš POLÁCH		M	26		3
10	Patrik SIEGL		D	29		
29	Pavel SIMR		A	1	(5)	
15	Marek STŘEŠTÍK		A	29		5
30	Martin ŠVEJNOHA		D	16	(4)	1
22	Jan TROUSIL		D	27		4

No	Name	Nat	Pos	Aps	(s)	Gls
12	Karel VEČEŘA		M	12	(4)	
13	Pavel VRÁNA		A		(1)	
17	René WAGNER		A	4	(15)	3
13	Martin ŽIVNÝ		D	1	(6)	
16	Jan SVÁTEK		A	10	(3)	2
27	Vlastimil ŠVEHLA		D		(1)	
20	Martin VOZÁBAL		M	25	(1)	3
25	Karel ZELINKA		A	1		
11	Michael ŽIŽKA		D	21	(2)	

SK DYNAMO ČESKÉ BUDĚJOVICE

Coach – František Cipro; (1/9/07) František Straka

Founded - 1905

2007				
5/8	Sigma	h	2-0	*Radzinevičius, Vozábal*
11/8	Zlín	a	0-1	
19/8	Slavia	h	1-2	*Vozábal*
26/8	Jablonec	a	0-1	
2/9	Mladá Boleslav	h	2-2	*og (Voříšek), Hořejš*
16/9	Kladno	a	1-5	*Radzinevičius*
23/9	Žižkov	h	1-1	*Plocek*
30/9	Most	h	1-0	*Homoláč*
7/10	Bohemians 1905	a	2-0	*Mrkvička, Plocek*
21/10	Sparta	h	1-1	*Černý*
28/10	Brno	a	1-2	*Černý*
4/11	Baník	h	3-0	*Mrkvička, Radzinevičius, Hořejš*
11/11	Teplice	a	2-4	*Černý, Mrkvička*
25/11	Liberec	h	2-0	*Černý, Stráský*
2/12	Plzeň	a	1-1	*Peroutka*
9/12	Zlín	h	1-0	*Radzinevičius (p)*
2008				
17/2	Slavia	a	0-1	
24/2	Jablonec	h	0-0	
2/3	Mladá Boleslav	a	1-2	*Mrkvička*
9/3	Kladno	h	0-0	
16/3	Žižkov	a	0-2	
23/3	Most	a	1-3	*Hořejš*
30/3	Bohemians 1905	h	2-0	*Svátek, Vozábal*
5/4	Sparta	a	0-1	
13/4	Brno	h	0-2	
19/4	Baník	a	0-2	
27/4	Teplice	h	1-0	*Svátek*
4/5	Liberec	a	0-0	
10/5	Plzeň	h	1-1	*Hořejš*
17/5	Sigma	a	0-1	

No	Name	Nat	Pos	Aps	(s)	Gls
7	Jiří ADAMEC		A	2	(2)	
14	Ondřej BÍRO		A	1	(2)	
26	Jaroslav ČERNÝ		M	16		4
17	Petr DOLEJŠ		M	4	(5)	
9	Jaroslav HÍLEK	SVK	M	27		
4	David HOMOLÁČ		D	17	(5)	1
3	David HOŘEJŠ		D	27		4
2	Tomáš HUNAL		D	23		
15	Martin JASANSKÝ		M		(1)	
19	Marek JUNGR		M	3	(3)	
30	Zdeněk KŘÍŽEK		G	4		
1	Pavel KUČERA		G	26		
19	Martin LEŠTINA		D	7	(2)	
7	Michal MAŠÁT		M	2	(6)	
10	Pavel MEZLÍK		M	7	(5)	
12	Václav MRKVIČKA		A	15	(8)	4
22	Zdeněk ONDRÁŠEK		A	4	(2)	
24	Jiří PEROUTKA		D	17	(8)	1
5	Roman PIVOŇKA		D		(1)	
18	Marek PLICHTA	SVK	M	3	(6)	
13	Jaromír PLOCEK		M	26	(2)	2
15	Tomas RADZINEVIČIUS	LTU	A	15		4
21	Agostino RENAN	BRA	A		(3)	
6	Petr ŠÍMA		M	12		
23	Michal ŠMÍD		D	8	(3)	
14	Tomáš STRÁSKÝ		A	7	(9)	1

FK JABLONEC 97

Coach – Luboš Kozel; (13/10/07) František Komňacký

Founded - 1945

MAJOR HONOURS: Czech Cup - (1) 1998.

2007				
5/8	Slavia	h	0-1	
12/8	Teplice	a	0-1	
19/8	Mladá Boleslav	h	1-1	*Hamouz*
26/8	České Budějovice	h	1-0	*Fukal*
2/9	Kladno	a	1-1	*Zábojník*
16/9	Bohemians 1905	h	0-0	
23/9	Brno	a	1-2	*Svátek*
30/9	Sparta	h	0-2	
7/10	Most	a	1-2	*Svátek (p)*
21/10	Baník	h	1-1	*Baranek*
27/10	Zlín	a	1-0	*Homola*
5/11	Liberec	h	1-2	*Svátek*
10/11	Sigma	a	1-1	*Nulíček*
25/11	Plzeň	h	0-1	
2/12	Žižkov	a	0-2	
9/12	Teplice	h	1-0	*Baranek*
2008				
17/2	Mladá Boleslav	a	1-1	*Necid*
24/2	České Budějovice	a	0-0	
2/3	Kladno	h	1-0	*Straka*
9/3	Bohemians 1905	a	1-1	*Necid*
16/3	Brno	h	2-0	*Straka 2*
22/3	Sparta	a	0-1	
30/3	Most	h	1-0	*Michálek*
5/4	Baník	a	0-3	
13/4	Zlín	h	0-4	
20/4	Liberec	a	1-2	*Fujerik*
27/4	Sigma	h	2-0	*Valenta, Necid*
4/5	Plzeň	a	0-2	
10/5	Žižkov	h	3-0	*Necid 2, Krejčí*
17/5	Slavia	a	2-2	*Žofčák, Krejčí*

No	Name	Nat	Pos	Aps	(s)	Gls
11	Miroslav BARÁNEK		M	19	(5)	2
13	Pavel ELIÁŠ		D	16	(6)	
8	Jan FLACHBART		D	8	(1)	
8	Lukáš FUJERIK		A	3	(5)	1
27	Milan FUKAL		D	17	(3)	1
9	Josef HAMOUZ		M	25	(1)	1
3	Anes HAURDIĆ	BIH	M		(2)	
10	Adam HLOUŠEK		A	17	(1)	
22	Jiří HOMOLA		D	29		1
25	Tomáš HUBER		D	14		
12	Filip KLAPKA		M	19	(5)	
24	Michal KORDULA		M	3	(1)	
18	Jiří KREJČÍ		D	10	(4)	2
26	Jaroslav LACIGA		D	1	(1)	
15	Luboš LOUČKA		D	13		
23	Tomáš MICHÁLEK		M	9	(3)	1
2	Jakub MIČKAL		A		(1)	
21	Tomáš NECID		A	7	(6)	5
19	Dušan NULÍČEK		A	3	(4)	1
16	Emil RILKE		A	5	(5)	
1	Michal ŠPIT		G	30		
4	Vojtěch ŠTĚPÁN		M	2	(1)	
14	Vlastimil STOŽICKÝ		M	1	(4)	
14	Pavol STRAKA	SVK	A	11	(3)	3
23	Jan SVÁTEK		A	8	(6)	3

No	Name	Nat	Pos	Aps	(s)	Gls
	Lukáš VÁCHA		M	8	(2)	
	Jiří VALENTA		M	13	(10)	1
	Petr ZÁBOJNÍK		D	20	(1)	1
1	Luděk ZELENKA		A	9	(2)	
6	Igor ŽOFČÁK	SVK	M	10		1

SK KLADNO

Coach – Jaroslav Šilhavý

Founded - 1903

Date	Opponent		Result	Scorers
007				
/8	Teplice	h	0-2	
2/8	Slavia	a	0-2	
9/8	Žižkov	h	3-2	*Jeslínek 2, Cigánek*
7/8	Mladá Boleslav	a	1-2	*Cigánek*
/9	Jablonec	h	1-1	*Dočkal*
6/9	České Budějovice	h	5-1	*Jeslínek 2, Gecov, Zachariáš, Vršajevič*
3/9	Most	a	2-2	*Zachariáš, Szabo*
0/9	Brno	h	1-2	*Szabo (p)*
/10	Liberec	a	1-1	*Kúdela*
1/10	Bohemians 1905	h	2-1	*Čáp, Jeslínek*
8/10	Sparta	a	1-4	*Bartoš*
/11	Plzeň	h	1-2	*Dočkal*
0/11	Zlín	a	0-4	
6/11	Baník	h	3-0	*Szabo 2 (1p), Semerák*
/12	Sigma	a	1-1	*Bartoš*
/12	Slavia	h	0-1	
008				
7/2	Žižkov	a	0-1	
4/2	Mladá Boleslav	h	0-1	
/3	Jablonec	a	0-1	
/3	České Budějovice	a	0-0	
6/3	Most	h	1-1	*Krob (p)*
3/3	Brno	a	0-0	
0/3	Liberec	h	1-3	*Bartoš*
/4	Bohemians 1905	a	1-1	*Kroupa*
3/4	Sparta	h	0-1	
0/4	Plzeň	a	2-1	*Killar, Cigánek*
7/4	Zlín	h	2-2	*Klinka, Bartoš*
/5	Baník	a	1-4	*Klinka*
0/5	Sigma	h	1-0	*Bartoš*
7/5	Teplice	a	0-1	

o	Name	Nat	Pos	Aps	(s)	Gls
	Pavel BARTOŠ		D	22		5
4	Vít BENEŠ		D	5	(4)	
	David BRUNCLÍK		M	7	(4)	
4	Tomáš ČÁP		M	13	(7)	1
0	Tomáš CIGÁNEK		M	24	(5)	3
1	Bořek DOČKAL		M	12	(2)	2
8	Martin FARBÁK	SVK	D	13	(1)	
8	Marcel GECOV		M	9		1
6	Patrik GROSS		D	19	(1)	
	David HLAVA		M	1		
	Radek HOCHMEISTER		D	14		
9	Josef HOFFMANN		D	5	(3)	
3	Antonín HOLUB		M	2	(1)	
1	Tomáš JABLONSKÝ		M	12	(2)	
	Jiří JESLÍNEK		M	15		5
7	Lukáš KILLAR		D	27	(1)	1
9	Tomáš KLINKA		A	6		2
	Peter KOSTOLANSKÝ	SVK	G	3		
	Miloslav KOUSAL		A	1	(6)	
1	Jan KROB		D	11		1
0	Karel KROUPA		A	8	(5)	1
	Ondřej KUDELA		M	9	(1)	1
0	Roman PAVLÍK		G	27		
	Jakub RADA		M	1		
0	Radek ŠELICHA		M	2		

No	Name	Nat	Pos	Aps	(s)	Gls
26	Josef SEMERÁK		A	5	(7)	1
11	Jaromír ŠILHAN		A	3	(4)	
6	Ondřej SZABÓ		M	26		4
27	Avdija VRŠAJEVIĆ	BIH	M	4	(14)	1
12	Michal ZACHARIÁŠ		A	14	(8)	2
15	Lukáš ZOUBELE		M	10	(12)	

FK MLADÁ BOLESLAV

Coach – Luděk Zajíc; (3/9/07) Zdeněk Ščasný; (18/3/08) Karel Stanner

Founded - 1902

Date	Opponent		Result	Scorers
2007				
5/8	Žižkov	h	0-1	
11/8	Sigma	a	0-1	
19/8	Jablonec	a	1-1	*Kysela*
28/8	Kladno	h	2-1	*Holub, Rolko*
2/9	České Budějovice	a	2-2	*Kysela, Rajnoch*
16/9	Most	h	1-1	*Rajnoch*
24/9	Sparta	a	1-0	*Holub*
30/9	Bohemians 1905	h	2-0	*Táborský 2*
8/10	Brno	a	3-0	*Sedláček T., Mendy, Rajnoch*
22/10	Liberec	h	0-2	
28/10	Baník	a	3-3	*Matějovský, Kysela, Vaněček*
4/11	Zlín	h	0-1	
11/11	Plzeň	a	0-2	
24/11	Teplice	h	1-1	*Rajnoch (p)*
2/12	Slavia	a	1-1	*Rajnoch*
9/12	Sigma	h	1-1	*Holub*
2008				
17/02	Jablonec	h	1-1	*Rajnoch (p)*
24/2	Kladno	a	1-0	*Rajnoch*
2/3	České Budějovice	h	2-1	*Řezníček 2*
9/3	Most	a	1-2	*Holub*
17/3	Sparta	h	1-4	*Holub*
23/3	Bohemians 1905	a	1-1	*Holub*
30/3	Brno	h	1-3	*Kopic*
5/4	Liberec	a	2-1	*Řezníček, Táborský*
13/4	Baník	h	3-1	*Rajnoch 2 (1p), Rolko*
19/4	Zlín	a	1-0	*Táborský*
27/4	Plzeň	h	3-0	*Rajnoch, Hrdlička, Sedláček T.*
4/5	Teplice	a	2-1	*Rajnoch, Řezníček*
10/5	Slavia	h	0-2	
17/5	Žižkov	a	0-1	

No	Name	Nat	Pos	Aps	(s)	Gls
22	David BRUNCLÍK		M	5	(2)	
24	Jaroslav DITTRICH		M		(1)	
15	Giorgi GANUGRAVA	GEO	M	1	(1)	
37	Ivan HODÚR	SVK	M	8	(1)	
7	Radim HOLUB		A	9	(12)	6
23	Tomáš HRDLIČKA		M	13	(7)	1
6	Václav KALINA		M	20	(6)	
9	Milan KOPIC		D	22	(1)	1
20	Jan KYSELA		A	29		3
25	Jiří MAŠEK		A	2	(3)	
8	Marek MATĚJOVSKÝ		M	15		1
18	Alexandre MENDY	FRA	A	21	(3)	1
27	Miroslav MILLER		G	23		
33	Lukáš OPIELA	SVK	M	1	(2)	
1	Petr PIŽANOWSKI		G	5	(1)	
13	Tomáš POLÁČEK		M	16	(8)	
26	Václav PROCHÁZKA		D	13		
17	Jan RAJNOCH		D	29		11
4	Adrian ROLKO		D	24		2
16	Jakub ŘEZNÍČEK		A	13	(6)	4
25	Jiří SCHUBERT		A		(1)	

No	Name	Nat	Pos	Aps	(s)	Gls
12	Jan ŠEDA		G	2		
19	Michal SEDLÁČEK		M	1	(1)	
11	Tomáš SEDLÁČEK		A	13	(14)	2
3	František ŠEVÍNSKÝ		D	14		
10	Ivo TÁBORSKÝ		A	14	(13)	4
28	David VANĚČEK		A	3	(6)	1
15	Petr VOŘÍŠEK		M	14		

FK SIAD MOST

Coach – Robert Žák

Founded - 1909

2007				
5/8	Plzeň	h	1-1	*Toleski*
11/8	Baník	a	2-5	*Pilař, Toleski*
19/8	Teplice	h	2-3	*Procházka, Prášil*
25/8	Sigma	a	2-2	*Toleski 2*
2/9	Slavia	h	2-3	*Toleski, Webster*
16/9	Mladá Boleslav	a	1-1	*Pilař*
23/9	Kladno	h	2-2	*Škoda, Da Silva*
30/9	České Budějovice	a	0-1	
7/10	Jablonec	h	2-1	*Toleski, Oboya*
21/10	Brno	h	2-2	*Pilař 2*
28/10	Bohemians 1905	a	0-1	
4/11	Sparta	h	0-5	
10/11	Liberec	a	1-2	*Toleski (p)*
25/11	Žižkov	h	1-0	*og (Labant)*
1/12	Zlín	a	1-1	*Loos*
9/12	Baník	h	0-2	
2008				
17/2	Teplice	a	0-1	
24/2	Sigma	h	1-1	*Studík*
2/3	Slavia	a	0-2	
9/3	Mladá Boleslav	h	2-1	*Webster, Pešír*
16/3	Kladno	a	1-1	*Oboya*
23/3	České Budějovice	h	3-1	*Webster, Stožický, Procházka*
30/3	Jablonec	a	0-1	
6/4	Brno	a	1-2	*og (Pavlík)*
14/4	Bohemians 1905	h	2-4	*Webster, Trubila*
20/4	Sparta	a	0-3	
27/4	Liberec	h	0-1	
4/5	Žižkov	a	0-1	
10/5	Zlín	h	0-1	
17/5	Plzeň	a	2-6	*Schut, Bogdanov*

No	Name	Nat	Pos	Aps	(s)	Gls
1	Lupce ACEVSKI	AUS	G	7		
21	Lubomir BOGDANOV	BUL	M	9	(18)	1
26	Pavel ČERMÁK		D	5	(2)	
2	Andrei Camargo DA SILVA	BRA	M	15	(1)	1
7	Patrik GEDEON		M	13		
4	André HAINAULT	CAN	D	13		
31	Stanislav HOFMANN		M		(1)	
23	Jan HOLENDA		A	8		
24	Jaroslav HORSKÝ		D		(1)	
15	Pavel HRESCHISKA	BLR	D	1	(1)	
18	Ladislav JAMRICH		D	11	(3)	
6	Jiří JEDINÁK		M	2	(2)	
29	Petr JOHANA		D	9	(1)	
3	Kevin LAFRANCE	FRA	D		(1)	
11	Petr LOOS		D	10	(9)	1
13	Brandon MABIALA	FRA	A	2	(1)	
13	Alexandre Noël MENDY	FRA	A	4		
22	Vincent MENDY	FRA	M	4	(8)	
16	Patrick OBOYA	KEN	A	17	(10)	2
23	Tomáš PEŠÍR		A	10	(1)	1
10	Peter PHILIPAKOS	GRE	A		(1)	
8	Tomáš PILAŘ		M	25		4
25	Ondřej PRÁŠIL		D	18	(2)	1
14	Jan PROCHÁZKA		D	11		2
9	Emil RILKE		A	11		
28	Ezequiel ROSENDO	ARG	M		(1)	
17	Lukáš SCHUT		M	12	(5)	1
10	Dave SIMPSON	CAN	A	1	(3)	
4	Jiří ŠISLER		M	2	(2)	
19	Jaroslav ŠKODA		M	19	(2)	1
7	Václav ŠTÍPEK		A		(5)	
6	Vlastimil STOŽICKÝ		M	11		1
28	Jiří STUDÍK		D	4	(1)	1
1	Milan ŠVENGER		G	9		
30	Martin SVOBODA		G	14		
20	Goce TOLESKI	MKD	A	13		7
5	Vitaliy TRUBILA	BLR	M	21	(1)	1
27	Byron WEBSTER	ENG	D	19	(4)	4

SK SIGMA OLOMOUC

Coach – Martin Pulpit; (29/4/08) Jiří Fryš

Founded - 1919

2007				
5/8	České Budějovice	a	0-2	
11/8	Mladá Boleslav	h	1-0	*Kazár*
20/8	Bohemians 1905	a	0-0	
25/8	Most	h	2-2	*Rossi, Bajer (p)*
2/9	Sparta	a	0-1	
15/9	Brno	h	1-1	*Hartig*
23/9	Baník	a	1-0	*Hartig*
29/9	Liberec	h	1-0	*Hartig*
6/10	Zlín	a	0-0	
20/10	Teplice	h	1-0	*Melinho*
28/10	Plzeň	a	0-2	
4/11	Žižkov	a	0-2	
10/11	Jablonec	h	1-1	*Randa*
23/11	Slavia	a	0-0	
1/12	Kladno	h	1-1	*Hubník*
9/12	Mladá Boleslav	a	1-1	*Kazár*
2008				
16/2	Bohemians 1905	h	1-1	*Hubník*
24/2	Most	a	1-1	*Hudec*
3/3	Sparta	h	0-0	
9/3	Brno	a	0-1	
15/3	Baník	h	1-0	*Hudec*
22/3	Liberec	a	1-2	*Bajer*
29/3	Zlín	h	0-1	
6/4	Teplice	a	1-1	*Bajer*
12/4	Plzeň	h	1-0	*Onofrej (p)*
19/4	Žižkov	h	2-0	*Bajer, Bueno*
27/4	Jablonec	a	0-2	
5/5	Slavia	h	1-3	*Heidenreich*
10/5	Kladno	a	0-1	
17/5	České Budějovice	h	1-0	*Schulmeister*

No	Name	Nat	Pos	Aps	(s)	Gls
14	Lukáš BAJER		M	22	(4)	4
3	David BANACZEK	POL	A	1	(3)	
15	Daniel Mariano BUENO	BRA	A	4	(6)	1
7	Martin ČUPR		D	1		
20	Petr DROBISZ		G	30		
29	Lukáš HARTIG		A	7	(2)	3
3	Jakub HEIDENREICH		D	11	(10)	1
26	Tomáš HOŘAVA		M	6	(2)	
10	Michal HUBNÍK		A	24		2
25	Martin HUDEC		D	20	(3)	2
23	Tomáš JANOTKA		A	14	(5)	
17	Josef JINDŘÍŠEK		D	19	(5)	
21	Dejan JURKIČ	SVN	D	10		
5	Marek KAŠČÁK	SVK	M	20	(3)	
9	Tomáš KAZÁR		A	10	(11)	2
13	Zdeněk KLESNIL		A		(1)	

No	Name	Nat	Pos	Aps	(s)	Gls
5	Martin KNAKAL		M	3	(3)	
	Martin KOMÁREK		D	2	(4)	
7	Filip LUKŠÍK	SVK	M	2	(5)	
	Tarciso Rogério Pereira "MELINHO"	BRA	M	13	(2)	1
	Ladislav ONOFREJ	SVK	M	17	(1)	1
2	Jakub PETR		A	2	(3)	
3	Martin PULKERT		A	1	(4)	
	Tomáš RANDA		D	18	(2)	1
	Daniel Silva ROSSI	BRA	M	24		1
4	Filip RÝDEL		M		(4)	
5	Vojtěch SCHULMEISTER		A	6	(12)	1
2	Aleš ŠKERLE		D	24		
	Vojtěch ŠTĚPÁN		M		(2)	
	Darko ŠUŠKAVČEVIĆ	MNE	D	19	(1)	

SK SLAVIA PRAHA

Coach – Karel Jarolím

Founded - 1893

MAJOR HONOURS: Czechoslovakian/Czech League - (11) 1925, 1929, 1930, 1931, 1933, 1934, 1935, 1937, 1947, 1996, 2008; Czech Cup - (3) 1997, 1999, 2002.

007				
8	Jablonec	a	1-0	*Vlček*
/8	Kladno	h	2-0	*Volešák, Šmicer (p)*
/8	České Budějovice	a	2-1	*Kalivoda, Šenkeřík*
/8	Brno	h	1-0	*Vlček*
9	Most	a	3-2	*Vlček 2, Gaúcho*
/9	Baník	h	0-0	
/9	Bohemians 1905	a	0-2	
/9	Zlín	h	7-1	*Belaid 2, Vlček, Ivana, Pudil, Volešák, Šourek*
10	Sparta	a	2-0	*Pudil, Šenkeřík*
/10	Plzeň	h	3-0	*Vlček 2, Suchý*
/10	Liberec	a	1-1	*Dřížďal*
11	Teplice	h	1-0	*Volešák*
/11	Žižkov	a	1-1	*Pudil*
/11	Sigma	h	0-0	
12	Mladá Boleslav	h	1-1	*Pudil*
12	Kladno	a	1-0	*Šmicer*
008				
/2	České Budějovice	h	1-0	*Černý*
/2	Brno	a	1-2	*Pudil*
3	Most	h	2-0	*Blažek, Tavares*
3	Baník	a	2-2	*Střihavka, Abraham*
/3	Bohemians 1905	h	2-1	*og (Hašek), Tavares*
/3	Zlín	a	1-0	*Toleski*
/3	Sparta	h	1-1	*Kalivoda*
4	Plzeň	a	0-0	
/4	Liberec	h	1-0	*Šenkeřík*
/4	Teplice	a	1-3	*Brabec (p)*
/4	Žižkov	h	0-3	
5	Sigma	a	3-1	*Toleski, Jarolím, Abraham*
/5	Mladá Boleslav	a	2-0	*Toleski, Belaid*
/5	Jablonec	h	2-2	*Belaid, Pudil*

o	Name	Nat	Pos	Aps	(s)	Gls
	Martin ABRAHAM		M	7	(5)	2
	Tijani BELAID	TUN	M	8	(7)	4
	Jan BLAŽEK		A	5	(2)	1
	Erich BRABEC		D	24		1
5	Jaroslav ČERNÝ		M	10	(2)	1
2	František DŘÍŽĎAL		D	17		1
	Rogério Botelho GAÚCHO	BRA	A	1	(3)	1
2	Theodor GEBRE SELASSIE		M	9		
	David HUBÁČEK		D	23	(2)	
	Milan IVANA	SVK	A	11	(2)	1
5	Tomáš JABLONSKÝ		M	2	(6)	

No	Name	Nat	Pos	Aps	(s)	Gls
8	Petr JANDA		M	5		
10	Marek JAROLÍM		M	6	(2)	1
25	David KALIVODA		M	10	(8)	2
19	Matej KRAJČÍK	SVK	M	22	(3)	
6	Martin LATKA		D	10	(2)	
24	Tomáš NECID		A		(3)	
16	Daniel PUDIL		M	17	(4)	6
14	Zdeněk ŠENKEŘÍK		A	13	(9)	3
11	Vladimír ŠMICER		M	11	(1)	2
13	Ondřej ŠOUREK		D	2		1
27	David STŘIHAVKA		A	5	(2)	1
17	Marek SUCHÝ		M	24	(1)	1
5	Michal ŠVEC		M	7	(1)	
18	Dušan ŠVENTO	SVK	M	3	(3)	
2	Mickaël TAVARES	FRA	M	18	(3)	2
9	Goce TOLESKI	MKD	A	8	(4)	3
28	Martin VANIAK		G	24	(1)	
7	Stanislav VLČEK		A	13		7
23	Ladislav VOLEŠÁK		M	9	(8)	3
1	Michal VOREL		G	6		

FC SLOVAN LIBEREC

Coach – Michal Zach; (1/10/07) Ladislav Škorpil

Founded - 1921

MAJOR HONOURS: Czech League - (2) 2002, 2006; Czech Cup - (1) 2000.

2007				
6/8	Sparta	a	0-1	
13/8	Bohemians 1905	h	0-0	
18/8	Baník	a	1-3	*Nezmar*
27/8	Teplice	a	0-2	
1/9	Zlín	h	0-1	
16/9	Žižkov	a	1-1	*Bílek*
22/9	Plzeň	h	2-0	*Blažek, Nezmar*
29/9	Sigma	a	0-1	
6/10	Kladno	h	1-1	*Hodúr*
22/10	Mladá Boleslav	a	2-0	*Bílek, Nezmar*
28/10	Slavia	h	1-1	*Papoušek*
5/11	Jablonec	a	2-1	*Blažek, Nezmar*
10/11	Most	h	2-1	*Dort, Blažek*
25/11	České Budějovice	a	0-2	
3/12	Brno	h	1-1	*Dohnálek*
9/12	Bohemians 1905	a	0-1	
2008				
17/2	Baník	h	1-1	*Papoušek*
23/2	Teplice	h	4-0	*Papoušek 2, Dort, Kerić*
1/3	Zlín	a	1-0	*Kerić*
8/3	Žižkov	h	2-2	*Dort (p), Kerić*
16/3	Plzeň	a	1-0	*Kerić*
22/3	Sigma	h	2-1	*Kerić, Nezmar*
30/3	Kladno	a	3-1	*Dort, Holeňák, Dočkal*
5/4	Mladá Boleslav	h	1-2	*Kerić*
13/4	Slavia	a	0-1	
20/4	Jablonec	h	2-1	*Dort (p), Smetana*
27/4	Most	a	1-0	*Radzinevičius*
4/5	České Budějovice	h	0-0	
10/5	Brno	a	0-2	
17/5	Sparta	h	4-3	*Smetana 2, Nezmar, Papoušek*

No	Name	Nat	Pos	Aps	(s)	Gls
22	Radek BEJBL		M	3	(5)	
7	Jiří BÍLEK		M	27		2
28	Jan BLAŽEK		A	6		3
6	Vítězslav BROŽÍK		A	1	(2)	
31	Robin DEJMEK		A	1	(4)	
18	Bořek DOČKAL		M	12	(2)	1
25	Jakub DOHNÁLEK		M	6	(9)	1
29	Filip DORT		A	17	(5)	5
20	Tomáš FREJLACH		M	12	(4)	

No	Name	Nat	Pos	Aps	(s)	Gls
10	Marcel GECOV		M	3	(1)	
1	Zbyněk HAUZR		G	6	(1)	
12	Radek HOCHMEISTER		M	3	(4)	
10	Ivan HODÚR	SVK	M	15		1
11	Miroslav HOLEŇÁK		D	11	(4)	1
5	Fernando HUDSON	BRA	M	7	(7)	
17	Tomáš JANŮ		D	16	(1)	
4	Martin JIROUŠ		A	1	(4)	
24	Michal JONÁŠ	SVK	D	1	(2)	
15	Andrej KERIĆ	CRO	A	10	(2)	6
14	Pavel KOŠŤÁL		D	23	(2)	
6	Petr KRÁTKÝ		D	1	(3)	
16	Diego LATTMANN	SUI	M	1	(2)	
8	Jiří LIŠKA		D	10	(3)	
2	Milan MATULA		D	4		
27	Jan NEZMAR		A	21	(4)	6
23	Petr PAPOUŠEK		M	23		5
15	Adam PETROUŠ		D	13		
13	Jan POLÁK		D	17	(3)	
26	Daniel PUDIL		M	3		
26	Tomas RADZINEVIČIUS	LTU	A	5	(4)	1
19	Peter ŠINGLÁR	SVK	D	23		
21	Ondřej SMETANA		A	4	(7)	3
30	Maxim UVARENKO	LVA	G	1		
9	Ján VLASKO	SVK	M		(1)	
31	Zdeněk ZLÁMAL		G	23		

AC SPARTA PRAHA

Coach – Michal Bílek; (12/5/08) Jozef Chovanec

Founded - 1893

MAJOR HONOURS: Czechoslovakian/Czech League - (29) 1926, 1927, 1932, 1936, 1938, 1946, 1948, 1952, 1954, 1965, 1967, 1984, 1985, 1987, 1988, 1989, 1990, 1991, 1993, 1994, 1995, 1997, 1998, 1999, 2000, 2001, 2003, 2005, 2007; Czechoslovakian /Czech Cup - (13) 1964, 1972, 1976, 1980, 1984, 1988, 1989, 1992, 1996, 2004, 2006, 2007, 2008.

2007				
6/8	Liberec	h	1-0	*Došek*
11/8	Plzeň	a	0-0	
18/8	Zlín	h	2-1	*Došek, Matušovič*
25/8	Žižkov	a	4-1	*Kisel, Horváth (p), Abraham, Došek (p)*
2/9	Sigma	h	1-0	*Došek*
16/9	Teplice	a	1-2	*Slepička*
24/9	Mladá Boleslav	h	0-1	
30/9	Jablonec	a	2-0	*Kisel 2*
8/10	Slavia	h	0-2	
21/10	České Budějovice	a	1-1	*Slepička*
28/10	Kladno	h	4-1	*Kisel, Pospěch, Došek, Slepička*
4/11	Most	a	5-0	*Kulič 2, Rezek, Kolář, Došek*
12/11	Bohemians 1905	h	3-1	*Zeman, Horváth, Došek*
25/11	Brno	a	2-4	*Kisel, Slepička*
2/12	Baník	a	0-0	
10/12	Plzeň	h	3-1	*Došek, Slepička, Kadlec*
2008				
16/2	Zlín	a	2-0	*Slepička, Vacek*
24/2	Žižkov	h	6-1	*Slepička 2, Matušovič, Vacek, Kolář, Kladrubský*
3/3	Sigma	a	0-0	
10/3	Teplice	h	1-0	*Kadlec*
17/3	Mladá Boleslav	a	4-1	*Slepička, Voříšek, Kladrubský, Jeslínek*
22/3	Jablonec	h	1-0	*Slepička*
31/3	Slavia	a	1-1	*Kadlec*
5/4	České Budějovice	h	1-0	*Horváth*
13/4	Kladno	a	1-0	*Kolář*
20/4	Most	h	3-0	*Řepka, Sivok, Holenda*
27/4	Bohemians 1905	a	0-0	
4/5	Brno	h	0-2	
10/5	Baník	h	1-2	*Horváth (p)*
17/5	Liberec	a	3-4	*Slepička 2, Holenda*

No	Name	Nat	Pos	Aps	(s)	Gls
26	Martin ABRAHAM		M	4	(1)	1
19	Miloš BREZINSKÝ	SVK	D	9	(1)	
9	Libor DOŠEK		A	13	(7)	8
31	Tomáš GRIGAR		G	19		
8	Andrew HAINAUT	CAN	D	1	(1)	
16	Jan HOLENDA		A	2	(5)	2
14	Pavel HORVÁTH		M	24		4
27	Luboš HUŠEK		M	16		
31	Jiří JESLÍNEK		A	2	(5)	1
23	Michal KADLEC		D	29		3
18	Karol KISEL	SVK	M	18	(5)	5
15	Jiří KLADRUBSKÝ		D	20	(6)	2
11	Daniel KOLÁŘ		A	7	(10)	3
30	Marek KULIČ		A	24	(2)	2
6	David LIMBERSKÝ		M	8	(4)	
28	Miroslav MATUŠOVIČ		M	18	(10)	2
4	Milan PETRŽELA		M		(1)	
20	Zdeněk POSPĚCH		D	16		1
22	Tomáš POŠTULKA		G	11		
2	Tomáš ŘEPKA		D	20		1
12	Jan REZEK		A	5	(6)	1
3	Jan ŠIMŮNEK		D	1		
16	Tomáš SIVOK		D	14		1
10	Miroslav SLEPIČKA		A	18	(6)	12
17	Ludovic SYLVESTRE	FRA	M	3	(3)	
25	Kamil VACEK		M	8	(3)	2
19	Petr VOŘÍŠEK		M	14		1
8	Radoslav ZABAVNÍK	SVK	D	4		
22	Martin ZEMAN		M	1	(7)	1
21	Igor ŽOFČÁK	SVK	M	1	(4)	

FK TEPLICE

Coach – Petr Rada

Founded - 1945

MAJOR HONOURS: Czech Cup - (1) 2003.

2007				
5/8	Kladno	a	2-0	*Fenin 2*
12/8	Jablonec	h	1-0	*Fenin*
19/8	Most	a	3-2	*Smíšek 2, Doležal*
27/8	Liberec	h	2-0	*Sabou, Fenin*
16/9	Sparta	h	2-1	*Lukáš, Fenin*
19/9	Brno	a	2-2	*Smíšek, Doležal*
22/9	Zlín	a	0-1	
30/9	Plzeň	h	1-0	*Klein*
7/10	Baník	a	0-0	
20/10	Sigma	a	0-1	
28/10	Žižkov	h	4-1	*Doležal 2 (1p), Fenin, Kroupa*
3/11	Slavia	a	0-1	
11/11	České Budějovice	h	4-2	*Verbíř 3, Fenin*
24/11	Mladá Boleslav	a	1-1	*Doležal (p)*
2/12	Bohemians 1905	h	2-0	*Štohanzl, Mareš*
9/12	Jablonec	a	0-1	
2008				
17/2	Most	h	1-0	*Jun*
23/2	Liberec	a	0-4	
2/3	Brno	h	0-1	
10/3	Sparta	a	0-1	
16/3	Zlín	h	2-1	*Klein, Smíšek*
23/3	Plzeň	a	2-0	*Lukáš, Rosa*
30/3	Baník	h	1-1	*Jun*
6/4	Sigma	h	1-1	*Smejkal*
13/4	Žižkov	a	2-1	*Doležal, Smejkal*

/4	Slavia	h	3-1	*Smejkal, Klein, Sabou*
'/4	České Budějovice	a	0-1	
5	Mladá Boleslav	h	1-2	*Jun*
)/5	Bohemians 1905	a	2-0	*Benát, Jun*
'/5	Kladno	h	1-0	*Verbíř*

o	Name	Nat	Pos	Aps	(s)	Gls
)	Petr BENÁT		M	2	(8)	1
!	Michal DOLEŽAL		M	30		6
5	Martin FENIN		A	15		7
	Michal GAŠPARÍK	SVK	M	11	(3)	
	Pavel HAŠEK		M		(1)	
)	Andrej HESEK	SVK	A	2	(9)	
5	Tomáš JUN		A	14		4
	Josef KAUFMAN		D	17	(4)	
	Martin KLEIN		D	28		3
5	Zdeněk KOUKAL		M	3	(3)	
	Pavel KRMAŠ		D	1		
)	Karel KROUPA		A		(9)	1
3	Admir LJEVAKOVIĆ	BIH	M	9	(11)	
5	Petr LUKÁŠ		D	29		2
	Jakub MAREŠ		M	12	(12)	1
4	Samir MERZIĆ	BIH	D	22	(2)	
!	Antonín ROSA		D	16	(6)	1
	Jiří SABOU		M	21	(1)	2
	Martin SLAVÍK		G	30		
3	Michal SMEJKAL		A	8	(2)	3
3	Petr SMÍŠEK		A	13	(7)	4
4	Jan ŠTOHANZL		M	11	(10)	1
	Vlastimil VIDLIČKA		D	8	(2)	
	Leandro VIEIRA	BRA	M		(3)	
	Pavel VERBÍŘ		M	28	(1)	4

FC VIKTORIA PLZEŇ

Coach – Stanislav Levý; (22/4/08) Karel Krejčí

Founded - 1911

)07				
8	Most	a	1-1	*Psohlavec*
/8	Sparta	h	0-0	
)/8	Brno	a	1-0	*Procházka*
5/8	Bohemians 1905	h	2-0	*Jarolím, Fillo (p)*
9	Baník	a	0-2	
'/9	Zlín	h	1-1	*Fillo (p)*
!/9	Liberec	a	0-2	
)/9	Teplice	a	0-1	
'10	Žižkov	h	3-1	*Fillo 2, Halama*
)/10	Slavia	a	0-3	
3/10	Sigma	h	2-0	*og (Randa), Jarolím*
'11	Kladno	a	2-1	*Psohlavec, Šmejkal*
/11	Mladá Boleslav	h	2-0	*Jarolím, Fillo*
5/11	Jablonec	a	1-0	*Jarolím*
'12	České Budějovice	h	1-1	Jarolím (p)
/12	Sparta	a	1-3	Psohlavec
)08				
'/2	Brno	h	2-0	*Varadi, Sylvestre (p)*
4/2	Bohemians 1905	a	2-2	*Róth, Varadi*
'3	Baník	h	0-4	
'3	Zlín	a	1-3	*Trapp*
5/3	Liberec	h	0-1	
3/3	Teplice	h	0-2	
)/3	Žižkov	a	0-0	
'4	Slavia	h	0-0	
2/4	Sigma	a	0-1	
)/4	Kladno	h	1-2	*Petržela*
'/4	Mladá Boleslav	a	0-3	
'5	Jablonec	h	2-0	*Varadi, Borek*
)/5	České Budějovice	a	1-1	*Varadi*
7/5	Most	h	6-2	*Varadi 2, Sylvestre 2 (1p), Navrátil, Petržela*

No	Name	Nat	Pos	Aps	(s)	Gls
23	Tomáš BOREK		M	6	(12)	1
17	Vítězslav BROŽÍK		A	2	(7)	
25	Michal DANĚK		G	15		
11	Martin FILLO		M	15		5
12	Jan HALAMA		D	16	(1)	1
1	Luboš ILIZI	SVK	G	6		
13	Marek JAROLÍM		M	16		5
3	Petr KNAKAL		D	8	(3)	
19	Lukáš KRBEČEK		G	6	(1)	
9	Tomáš KRBEČEK		A	19	(5)	
8	Jan LECJAKS		D	16	(2)	
16	Vladimír MALÁR		A	1	(1)	
26	Pavel MALCHAREK		A	20	(7)	
5	Martin MÜLLER		D	7		
21	Jakub NAVRÁTIL		D	8	(4)	1
11	Milan PETRŽELA		M	10		2
6	Václav PROCHÁZKA		D	3		1
14	Martin PSOHLAVEC		A	10	(13)	3
4	Tomáš RADA		D	24	(2)	
10	Paulo RODRIGUES	BRA	M	2	(1)	
20	Ferenc RÓTH	HUN	M	10	(2)	1
15	Petr ŠÍMA		M	10		
15	Ondřej ŠIML		M	1	(1)	
10	Jaromír ŠIMR		M		(1)	
21	Michal SMEJKAL		D	5	(9)	
29	Zdeněk ŠMEJKAL		D	11		1
22	Marek SMOLA		D	20	(2)	
2	Jakub SÜSSER		D		(1)	
18	Ludovic SYLVESTRE	FRA	M	14		3
30	Martin TICHÁČEK		G	3		
7	Petr TRAPP		M	25	(1)	1
17	Adam VARADI		A	11		6
28	Ondřej VRZAL		A	2	(8)	
18	Jan ZAKOPAL		D	8		

FK VIKTORIA ŽIŽKOV

Coach – Stanislav Griga

Founded - 1903

MAJOR HONOURS: Czechoslovakian League - (1) 1928; Czech Cup - (2) 1994, 2001.

2007				
5/8	Mladá Boleslav	a	1-0	*Moughfire*
12/8	Brno	h	3-4	*Kušnír, Švancara, Kalod*
19/8	Kladno	a	2-3	*Bukač, Kučera*
25/8	Sparta	h	1-4	*Novotný*
3/9	Bohemians 1905	a	2-2	*Švancara, Bukač*
16/9	Liberec	h	1-1	*Stracený*
23/9	České Budějovice	a	1-1	*Procházka T.*
1/10	Baník	h	0-2	
8/10	Plzeň	a	1-3	*Stracený*
21/10	Zlín	h	2-0	*Procházka T., Kušnír*
28/10	Teplice	a	1-4	*Stracený*
4/11	Sigma	h	2-0	*Novotný, Kušnír*
11/11	Slavia	h	1-1	*Kalod*
25/11	Most	a	0-1	
2/12	Jablonec	h	2-0	*Moughfire, Kalod*
9/12	Brno	a	1-3	*Švancara (p)*
2008				
17/2	Kladno	h	1-0	*Švancara (p)*
24/2	Sparta	a	1-6	*Bukač*
2/3	Bohemians 1905	h	2-1	*Tinga, Švancara*
8/3	Liberec	a	2-2	*Kušnír, Demjan*
16/3	České Budějovice	h	2-0	*Kalod, Tinga*
22/3	Baník	a	0-3	
30/3	Plzeň	h	0-0	
5/4	Zlín	a	0-0	
13/4	Teplice	h	1-2	*Procházka T.*
19/4	Sigma	a	0-2	

26/4	Slavia	a	3-0	*Koukal, Šťastný (p), Švancara*
4/5	Most	h	1-0	*Labant*
10/5	Jablonec	a	0-3	
17/5	Mladá Boleslav	h	1-0	*Kalod*

No	Name	Nat	Pos	Aps	(s)	Gls
27	Peter BARTALSKÝ	SVK	G	27		
12	Marek BAŽÍK	SVK	M		(6)	
8	Pavel BESTA		D	22		
21	Lubomír BLAHA		A		(8)	
24	Radek BUKAČ		A	9	(9)	3
15	Róbert DEMJAN	SVK	A	7	(2)	1
10	Milan JAMBOR	SVK	D		(3)	
10	Richard KALOD		A	14	(10)	5
20	Zdeněk KOUKAL		M	8	(3)	1
3	Tomáš KROPÍK		D	16		
14	Tomáš KUČERA		D	17		1
13	Ondřej KUŠNÝR		M	26		4
5	Branislav LABANT	SVK	D	21	(1)	1
2	Aldo Andres MORES	ARG	D	2		
7	Youssef MOUGHFIRE	FRA	M	14	(9)	2
4	Jan NOVOTNÝ		M	11	(6)	2
1	Oldřich PAŘÍZEK		G	3		
22	Radek PILAŘ		M	7		
6	Jaroslav PROCHÁZKA		D	1	(1)	
11	Tomáš PROCHÁZKA		M	28		3
19	Luděk STRACENÝ		M	24		3
18	Marcel ŠŤASTNÝ		D	22	(2)	1
9	Petr ŠVANCARA		A	22	(6)	6
16	Roberto da Silva TINGA	BRA	M	15	(8)	2
25	Xavier Hervé ZENGUE	CMR	D	14	(1)	

FC ZLÍN

Coach – Pavel Hoftych

Founded - 1919

MAJOR HONOURS: Czechoslovakian Cup - (1) 1970.

2007				
5/8	Brno	a	0-0	
11/8	České Budějovice	h	1-0	*Žůrek*
18/8	Sparta	a	1-2	*Žůrek*
27/8	Baník	h	2-2	*Zbožínek 2*
1/9	Liberec	a	1-0	*Opiela*
17/9	Plzeň	a	1-1	*Žůrek*
22/9	Teplice	h	1-0	*Zúbek*
28/9	Slavia	a	1-7	*Zbožínek*
6/10	Sigma	h	0-0	
21/10	Žižkov	a	0-2	
27/10	Jablonec	h	0-1	
4/11	Mladá Boleslav	a	1-0	*Žůrek*
10/11	Kladno	h	4-0	*Zbožínek, Vidlička, Žůrek, Malár*
25/11	Bohemians 1905	a	2-1	*Vyskočil 2*
1/12	Most	h	1-1	*Bača*
9/12	České Budějovice	a	0-1	
2008				
16/2	Sparta	h	0-2	
23/2	Baník	a	1-2	*Malár*
1/3	Liberec	h	0-1	
8/3	Plzeň	h	3-1	*Šmahaj, Zúbek, Kroča*
16/3	Teplice	a	1-2	*Zbožínek*
24/3	Slavia	h	0-1	
29/3	Sigma	a	1-0	*Šmahaj*
5/4	Žižkov	h	0-0	
13/4	Jablonec	a	3-0	*Šmahaj 2, Vyskočil (p)*
19/4	Mladá Boleslav	h	0-1	
27/4	Kladno	a	2-2	*Žůrek 2*
3/5	Bohemians 1905	h	0-0	
10/5	Most	a	1-0	*Žůrek*
17/5	Brno	h	0-1	

No	Name	Nat	Pos	Aps	(s)	Gls
27	Martin BAČA		A	5		1
24	Martin BAČÍK		A		(2)	
1	Vít BARÁNEK		G	27		
20	Gejza BARANYAI	SVK	A	2	(6)	
25	Ondřej ČELŮSTKA		D	2		
2	Tomáš DUJKA		D	3	(3)	
12	Pavel ELŠÍK		M	5	(4)	
27	Tomáš GAVLÁK	SVK	D		(1)	
18	Zdeněk KONEČNÍK		M	1	(8)	
30	Aleš KOŘÍNEK		G	3		
26	Jan KRAUS		A	11	(8)	
5	Zdeněk KROČA		D	29		1
9	Vladimír MALÁR		A	21	(4)	2
6	James McQUILKIN	NIR	M		(4)	
18	Petr MUSIL		M	11	(3)	
23	Lukáš OPIELA	SVK	M	12		1
18	Bronislav OTRUBA		M		(1)	
14	Milan PACANDA		A	5	(3)	
9	Lukáš PAZDERA		D	14	(3)	
19	Miloslav PENNER		D	22		
20	David ŠMAHAJ		M	27	(1)	4
24	Vlastimil VIDLIČKA		D	13		1
8	Vít VRTĚLKA		M	11	(6)	
10	Martin VYSKOČIL		A	21	(6)	3
2	Václav ZAPLETAL		M	7	(7)	
15	Ivo ZBOŽÍNEK		D	30		5
4	Marek ZÚBEK		M	24	(3)	2
7	Libor ŽŮREK		A	24	(5)	8

PROMOTED CLUBS

BOHEMIANS PRAHA

Coach – Luboš Urban

Founded - 2005

FK MARILA PŘÍBRAM

Coach – Frantisek Barát; (1/4/08) Ivan Pahávek; (30/4/08) Massimo Morales (ITA)

Founded - 1948

MAJOR HONOURS: Czechoslovakian League - (11) 1953, 1956, 195 1961, 1962, 1963, 1964, 1966, 1977, 1979, 1982; Czechoslovakian Cup - (8) 1961, 1965, 1966, 1969, 1981, 1983, 1985, 19

SECOND LEVEL FINAL TABLE 2007/0

		Pld	W	D	L	F	A
1	Bohemians Praha	30	15	8	7	46	38
2	FK Marila Příbram	30	14	10	6	33	18
3	Slezský FC Opava	30	15	5	10	46	31
4	FC Hradec Králové	30	13	11	6	34	24
5	1.FC Slovácko Uherské Hradiště	30	13	9	8	40	27
6	Fotbal Fulnek	30	12	11	7	36	36
7	FC Vysočina Jihlava	30	11	10	9	42	35
8	1.HFK Olomouc	30	11	8	11	33	38
9	FK Baník Sokolov	30	9	13	8	26	24
10	FK Fotbal Třinec	30	10	6	14	26	39
11	FC Vítkovice	30	10	6	14	35	41
12	FK Ústí nad Labem	30	9	7	14	35	44
13	FC Zenit Čáslav	30	8	9	13	37	44
14	FK Dukla Praha	30	9	6	15	36	44
15	FC Hlučín	30	7	9	14	26	35
16	SK Sparta Krč	30	4	12	14	27	40

DOMESTIC CUP 2007/08

POHÁR ČMFS

ECOND ROUND

5/9/07)

aník Sokolov 1, Sparta Praha 5
řeclav 1, Dosta Bystrc-Kníničky 0
homutov 4, Slavia Vejprnice 0
obrovice 1, Kolín 2
vůr Králové 1, Bohemians 1905 4
rýdek-Místek 2, Baník Ostrava 0
ulnek 5, Vítkovice 3
lanácká Kroměříž 0, 1.Hanácký Olomouc 1
loražďovice 0, České Budějovice 1
skra Nový Bor 0, Cheb 2001 2
skra Rýmařov 3, SFC Opava 2
skra Třeboň 3, Písek 0
latovy 0, Plzeň 3
íšeň 2, Znojmo 1
lutěnice 3, Brno 4
láchod-Deštné 0, Letohrad 0 *(5-4 on pens)*
ový Bydžov 0, Jablonec 7
lavia Orlová-Lutyně 0, Karviná 3
lavoj Vyšehrad 0, Dukla Praha 3
lovan Varnsdorf 0, Most 3
okol Konice 0, Sigma 0 *(5-4 on pens)*
okol Libiš 1, Mladá Boleslav 5
okol Vilémov 0, Teplice 4
okol Živanice 1, Hradec Králové 3
ničov 0, Slovácko 3
elké Karlovice+Karolinka 0, Slavia 4
lašin 0, Žižkov 1
dár nad Sázavou 2, Vysočina Jihlava 3
enit Čáslav 0, Liberec 2

12/9/07)

řinec 1, Zlín 1 *(5-4 on pens)*
parta Krč 1, Marila Příbram 3

19/9/07)

ohemians Praha 1, Kladno 1 *(4-2 on pens)*

HIRD ROUND

26/9/07)

ohemians Praha 1, Hradec Králové 0
řeclav 0, Bohemians 1905 1
heb 2001 0, České Budějovice 1
homutov 0, Most 0 *(5-4 on pens)*
ukla Praha 1, Sparta 3
rýdek-Místek 2, Karviná 1
lanácký Olomouc 2, Teplice 1
skra Rýmařov 0, Liberec 4
skra Třeboň 0, Jablonec 2
olín 0, Mladá Boleslav 4
larila Příbram 0, Plzeň 1
láchod-Deštné 1, Žižkov 4
okol Konice 1, Fulnek 3
řinec 0, Slovácko 0 *(5-4 on pens)*
ysočina Jihlava 0, Brno 2

11/10/07)

íšeň 4, Slavia 3

FOURTH ROUND

(10/10/07)

Chomutov 0, 1.Hanácký Olomouc 3
Frýdek-Místek 1, Jablonec 2
Fulnek 1, Liberec 1 *(3-4 on pens)*
Líšeň 0, Žižkov 1

(16/10/07)

Třinec 2, Mladá Boleslav 1

(31/10/07)

Bohemians Praha 2, Plzeň 0
České Budějovice 0, Brno 2
Sparta 2, Bohemians 1905 0

QUARTER-FINALS

(9/4/08 & 16/4/08)

Hanácky Olomouc 1 *(Lukášek 19)*, Sparta 2 *(Slepička 65, 69)*
Sparta 3 *(Kulič 22, Holenda 47, Kolář 80)*, Hanácky Olomouc 1 *(Korčián 48)*
(Sparta 5-2)

Jablonec 0, Brno 3 (Polách 31, Besta 36, Večeřa 82)
Brno 2 (Baláž 45, Trousil 74), Jablonec 1 (Michálek 85p)
(Brno 5-1)

Třinec 0, Liberec 3 (Papoušek 7, Frejlach 80, Dočkal 86)
Liberec 2 (Radzinevičius 42, Frejlach 83), Třinec 2 (Cieslar 50, Lukšík 90)
(Liberec 5-2)

Žižkov 1 (Koukal 6), Bohemians Praha 1 (Ibe 66)
Bohemians Praha 0, Žižkov 0
(1-1; Bohemians Praha on away goal)

SEMI-FINALS

(30/4/08 & 7/5/08)

Bohemians Praha 0, Sparta 1 *(Jeslínek 43)*
Sparta 1 *(Jeslínek 73)*, Bohemians Praha 0
(Sparta 2-0)

Brno 2 *(Došek 21, Pavlík 79p)*, Liberec 2 *(Dočkal 1, Dort 9p)*
Liberec 2 *(Nezmar 78, Smetana 90+3)*, Brno 1 *(Došek 64)*
(Liberec 4-3)

FINAL

(13/5/08)

Evžena Rošického stadium, Prague
AC SPARTA PRAHA 0
FC SLOVAN LIBEREC 0
(4-3 on pens)
Referee – *Příhoda*
SPARTA – *Poštulka, Voříšek, Sivok (Kladrubský 35), Řepka, Kadlec, Vacek (Kolář 78), Hušek, Horváth, Matušovič, Jeslínek, Holenda (Slepička 84).*
LIBEREC – *Hauzr, Matula, Holeňák, Košťál, Janů, Dočkal, Bílek, Dort (Frejlach 73), Papoušek (Radzinevičius 89), Kerič, Nezmar (Smetana 79).*

AaB break Copenhagen cycle

There was a refreshing look to the Danish Superliga in 2008/09. After several years of total domination by the two clubs from the capital, FC København and Brøndby IF, the championship title went west, to Aalborg BK.

With long-serving Swedish coach Erik Hamrén at the helm, the Red and Whites from Jutland defied expert opinion to become champions of Denmark for only the third time in their 123-year history. While other clubs, defending champions København included, had spells at the top of the table, it was AaB's consistency of performance throughout the ten-month campaign that earned them the top prize.

Top of the table

A stuttering start, which included a 5-0 roasting by early pace-setters FC Randers, was quickly forgotten as Hamrén's men rattled off six successive wins in the early autumn and also took time out to create a big shock in Europe by eliminating UC Sampdoria from the UEFA Cup. By the winter break they were at the summit of the Superliga table, their place sealed by a dramatic 5-3 win at home to strugglers Lyngby BK. There was no let-up in the spring – despite the sale of nine-goal Swedish international Rade Prica – and with unsung 24-year-old striker Jeppe Curth continuing to find the net (his final 17-goal tally was the best in the division), AaB not only maintained their position at the top but strengthened it considerably.

Jeppe Curth of AaB – the Danish Superliga's top goalscorer in 2007/08

They had the opportunity to clinch the title at outgoing champions København, but that opportunity went begging as the home side, still seeking a runners-up berth, shot them down in flames, winning 4-0. Not that AaB were too disheartened because three days later they had a second opportunity at home to Brøndby, and with a season's best crowd of 13,647 to cheer them on, they did not disappoint, scoring twice in the first half and cruising to the 2-0 win that made them mathematically uncatchable on top of the Superliga table. With Hamrén having announced in mid-season that he would be joining Rosenborg BK at the conclusion of the campaign, he could not have wished for a better send-off. He, the players and the AaB fans duly celebrated their achievement long into the night.

København, the richest team in Denmark by some distance, were pipped to second place by another Jutland outfit, FC Midtjylland, the only Superliga team to avoid defeat at home. Despite heavy investment, with local talents such as Rasmus Würth and Morten Nordstrand being joined in the recruitment drive by Czech internationals Libor Sionko and Zdeněk Pospěch, 'FCK' finished in their lowest position for eight years.

Cup consolation for Brøndby

The fortunes for Brøndby were even worse as their final placing of eighth was their lowest in Superliga history. They continued to be plagued by ruinous away form. Without a win on their travels during the whole of the previous season, they could only manage two this time around. Paradoxically, they found away wins much easier to come by in the Danish Cup, claiming four of them en route to the final at Parken, where they overcame Esbjerg fB in an exciting final, midfielder Martin Retov's 85th-minute strike securing a 3-2 win that brought Brøndby the trophy for the sixth time.

ɜB's hopes of a double were extinguished in a urth-round penalty shoot-out defeat by Vejle BK, ho went on to win the second division by the ·overbial street, winning 25 of their 30 matches. ıey were accompanied into the Superliga by ɔnderjyskE, with long-condemned Lyngby and borg FF moving in the opposite direction.

ıere was no Danish presence at the UEFA European ıampionship finals for the first time since 1980 as orten Olsen's team eventually finished well off the ɜce in Qualifying Group F, even ceding third place Northern Ireland after a shock 2-1 defeat in Belfast. espite that failed campaign, at the heart of which as the infamous abandoned home game against weden (awarded 3-0 to the visitors), Olsen has been kept on for the 2010 FIFA World Cup qualifying series, which, if he is successful and leads the team to South Africa, will see him complete a decade in charge.

Tomasson poised

Jon Dahl Tomasson ended the 2007/08 season poised, on 99 caps, to join the four-strong elite group of Danish centurions headed by 129-cap Peter Schmeichel. He also scored five goals to lift his all-time tally to 51 – one short of the 83-year-old national record held by Poul "Tist" Nielsen. Encouragement for the future was provided by Tomasson's 20-year-old strike partner, Arsenal FC's Nicklas Bendtner, who found the net in four successive internationals.

Dansk Boldspil-Union

House of Football
DBU Allé 1
DK-2605 Brøndby
tel - +45 43 262222
fax - +45 43 262245
website - www.dbu.dk
email - dbu@dbu.dk
Year of Formation - 1889
President - Allan Hansen
General Secretary - Jim Stjerne Hansen
Press Officer – Lars Berendt
Stadium - Parken, Copenhagen (41,652)

INTERNATIONAL HONOURS
UEFA European Championship - (1) 1992.

INTERNATIONAL TOURNAMENT APPEARANCES
FIFA World Cup - (3) 1986 (2nd round), 1998 (qtr-finals), 2002 (2nd round).
UEFA European Championship - (7) 1964 (4th), 1984 (semi-finals), 1988, 1992 (Winners), 1996, 2000, 2004 (qtr-finals).

Top Five All-time Caps
Peter Schmeichel (129); Thomas Helveg (108); Michael Laudrup (104); Morten Olsen (102);
Jon Dahl Tomasson (99)

Top Five All-time Goals
Poul "Tist" Nielsen (52); Jon Dahl Tomasson (51); Pauli Jørgensen (44); Ole Madsen (42); Preben Elkjær (38)

ɅTIONAL TEAM RESULTS 2007/08

·/07	Republic of Ireland	H	Aarhus	0-4	
07	Sweden (ECQ)	A	Solna	0-0	
/07	Liechtenstein (ECQ)	H	Aarhus	4-0	*Nordstrand (3, 36), Laursen M. (12), Tomasson (18)*
0/07	Spain (ECQ)	H	Aarhus	1-3	*Tomasson (87)*
0/07	Latvia (ECQ)	H	Copenhagen	3-1	*Tomasson (7p), Laursen U. (27), Rommedahl (90)*
1/07	Northern Ireland (ECQ)	A	Belfast	1-2	*Bendtner (51)*
1/07	Iceland (ECQ)	H	Copenhagen	3-0	*Bendtner (34), Tomasson (44), Kahlenberg (59)*
08	Slovenia	A	Nova Gorica	2-1	*Tomasson (30), Bendtner (62)*
/08	Czech Republic	H	Herning	1-1	*Bendtner (25)*
/08	Netherlands	A	Eindhoven	1-1	*Poulsen C. (55)*
08	Poland	A	Chorzow	1-1	*Vingaard (27)*

DENMARK

NATIONAL TEAM APPEARANCES 2007/08

Coach – Morten OLSEN	14/8/49		Irl	SWE	LIE	ESP	LVA	NIR	ISL	Svn	Cze	Ned	Pol	Caps
Jesper CHRISTIANSEN	24/4/78	København	G									G		9
Kasper BØGELUND	8/10/80	Mönchengladbach (GER)	D46											15
Michael GRAVGAARD	3/4/78	København	D46	s91	s28									18
Daniel AGGER	12/12/84	Liverpool (GER)	D	D	D28									18
Niclas JENSEN	17/8/74	København	D46	D	D	D79					s59			62
Rasmus WÜRTZ	18/9/83	København	M68					s72						9
Daniel JENSEN	25/6/79	Bremen (GER)	M46	M		M	M		M	M65				36
Dennis ROMMEDAHL	22/7/78	Ajax (NED)	M	A	A	A	A	A	A73	A	M	A	M	78
Jon Dahl TOMASSON	29/8/76	Villarreal (ESP)	M59	A91	M68	A	M		M	M46	A73	s46		99
Jesper GRØNKJÆR	12/8/77	København	M	A	A46	A65	s71							70
Nicklas BENDTNER	16/1/88	Arsenal (ENG)	A	s54		s46	A	A	A84	A	A	A	A88	18
William Kvist JØRGENSEN	24/2/85	København	s46						D	D	D	D82	s66	6
Martin LAURSEN	26/7/77	Aston Villa (ENG)	s46	D	D	D	D	D			D46			49
Jan KRISTIANSEN	4/8/81	Nürnberg (GER)	s46											11
Thomas KAHLENBERG	20/3/83	Auxerre (FRA)	s46	M54	s46	s65	A	A46	s53			M46		24
Morten NORDSTRAND	8/6/83	København	s59		A								A46	4
Peter LØVENKRANDS	29/1/80	Schalke (GER)	s68	s81	s68									20
Thomas SØRENSEN	12/6/76	Aston Villa (ENG)		G	G	G	G	G	G	G	G		G	73
Thomas HELVEG	24/6/71	OB		D	D	D	D							108
Leon ANDREASEN	23/4/83	Bremen (GER) /Fulham (ENG)		M81	M	M46	s32	M		s46		D77		10
Esben HANSEN	10/8/81	Kaiserslautern (GER)			M									1
Ulrik LAURSEN	28/2/76	OB /København				D	D32		D	D	D			5
Christian Bager POULSEN	28/2/80	Sevilla (ESP)				M	M71	M	M	M46	M	M	M77	56
Kenneth PEREZ	29/8/74	PSV (NED) /Ajax (NED)				s79				s46	s46	A77	s46	24
Chris SØRENSEN	27/7/77	OB					D	D	D	D46				4
Brian PRISKE	14/5/77	Club Brugge (BEL)						D72						24
Per KRØLDRUP	31/7/79	Fiorentina (ITA)						D	D	D	s46	D	D	22
Martin JØRGENSEN	6/10/75	Fiorentina (ITA)						M79	A53	A71		M62	D46	85
Simon Busk POULSEN	7/10/84	Midtjylland						s79	s73					3
Dennis SØRENSEN	24/5/81	Energie (GER)						s46					s88	5
Søren LARSEN	6/9/81	Schalke (GER)							s84					10
Thomas RASMUSSEN	16/4/77	Brøndby								s46	D59	s82	s46	6
Niki ZIMLING	19/4/85	EfB								s65				1
Mikkel BECKMANN	24/10/83	Lyngby								s71	M46			2
Thomas KRISTENSEN	17/4/83	Nordsjælland									M65		s63	2
Anders RANDRUP	16/7/88	Brøndby									s65			1
Mikkel THYGESEN	22/10/84	Midtjylland									s73			2
Lars JACOBSEN	20/9/79	Nürnberg (GER)										D	D	15
Martin RETOV	5/5/80	Brøndby										s62	M63	3
Anders Møller CHRISTENSEN	26/7/77	OB										s77	D	2
Martin VINGAARD	20/3/85	EfB										s77	M66	2
Thomas AUGUSTINUSSEN	20/3/81	AaB											s77	1

DOMESTIC LEAGUE 2007/08

PERLIGA FINAL TABLE

		Home					Away					Total					
	Pld	W	D	L	F	A	W	D	L	F	A	W	D	L	F	A	Pts
alborg BK	33	14	2	1	37	12	8	3	5	23	26	22	5	6	60	38	71
C Midtjylland	33	13	4	0	36	16	5	4	7	17	20	18	8	7	53	36	62
C København	33	11	4	2	30	12	6	5	5	21	17	17	9	7	51	29	60
dense BK	33	5	11	1	21	10	7	5	4	25	17	12	16	5	46	27	52
C Horsens	33	9	5	2	29	20	5	5	7	18	23	14	10	9	47	43	52
anders FC	33	9	4	3	25	12	4	4	9	16	21	13	8	12	41	33	47
sbjerg fB	33	8	3	5	25	23	5	3	9	34	31	13	6	14	59	54	45
røndby IF	33	9	4	4	28	15	2	6	8	16	29	11	10	12	44	44	43
C Nordsjælland	33	8	4	5	29	23	3	6	7	18	28	11	10	12	47	51	43
GF	33	2	5	9	15	24	5	3	9	18	27	7	8	18	33	51	29
borg FF	33	4	2	10	17	32	1	3	13	12	36	5	5	23	29	68	20
ngby BK	33	2	4	10	17	35	1	5	11	16	34	3	9	21	33	69	18

TOP GOALSCORERS

17 Jeppe CURTH (AaB)

14 Martin BERNBURG (Nordsjælland)

13 Peter GRAULUND (AGF)
Henrik HANSEN (Horsens)

12 Frank KRISTENSEN (Midtjylland)

9 Christian HOLST (Lyngby)
Gilberto MACENA (Horsens)
Morten NORDSTRAND (København)
Rade PRICA (AaB)

8 Marcus ALLBÄCK (København)
Hans Henrik ANDREASEN (OB)
Mikkel BECKMANN (Lyngby)
Atiba HUTCHINSON (København)
Rawez LAWAN (Horsens)

CLUB-BY-CLUB

AALBORG BK

Coach – Erik Hamrén (SWE)
Founded – 1885
MAJOR HONOURS: Danish League - (3) 1995, 1999, 2008; Danish Cup - (2) 1966, 1970.

007

/7	København	h	1-1	*Nomvethe*
8	Randers	a	0-5	
8	Horsens	a	1-1	*Prica*
8	Midtjylland	a	1-2	*Nomvethe*
/8	AGF	h	2-0	*Johansson, Prica*
/8	OB	h	2-3	*Jakobsen (p), Johansson*
/8	EfB	a	2-1	*og (Jørgensen), Prica*
9	Nordsjælland	h	2-1	*Curth, Prica*
/9	Brøndby	h	3-0	*Curth, Nomvethe 2*
/9	Lyngby	a	4-3	*Jakobsen (p), Prica 2, Johansson*
/9	Viborg	h	3-2	*Nomvethe, Curth, Risgård*
10	AGF	a	5-3	*Curth 3, Johansson, Prica*
/10	København	h	0-0	
/10	EfB	h	2-0	*Curth 2*
11	Randers	a	0-1	
/11	Nordsjælland	a	2-1	*Prica, Augustinussen*
/11	Midtjylland	h	1-0	*Nomvethe*
12	Lyngby	h	5-3	*Johansson, Enevoldsen, Curth 2, Prica*

008

/3	OB	a	1-1	*Nilsson*
/3	Horsens	a	2-1	*Risgård, Nilsson*
/3	Viborg	h	2-0	*Risgård, Enevoldsen*
/3	Brøndby	a	1-0	*Augustinussen*
4	Nordsjælland	h	3-1	*Johansson, Risgård, Curth*
/4	Midtjylland	a	0-2	
/4	EfB	a	1-1	*Curth*
/4	Randers	h	3-0	*Jakobsen (p), Curth, Bræmer*
28/4	Horsens	h	1-0	*Bræmer*
4/5	Viborg	a	1-0	*Johansson*
8/5	AGF	h	3-1	*Curth 2, Enevoldsen*
12/5	København	a	0-4	
15/5	Brøndby	h	2-0	*og (Von Schlebrügge), Risgård*
18/5	Lyngby	a	2-0	*Curth, Bræmer*
24/5	OB	h	2-0	*Olfers, Curth*

No	Name	Nat	Pos	Aps	(s)	Gls
9	Thomas AUGUSTINUSSEN		M	21	(5)	2
20	Simon BRÆMER		A	1	(7)	3
18	Lucas CACA de Deus Santos	BRA	M		(2)	
4	Danny CALIFF	USA	D	30		
25	Chrystiano CHRYS Gomes Ferraz	BRA	A		(1)	
14	Jeppe CURTH		A	30	(3)	17
7	Anders DUE		M	4	(1)	
23	Thomas ENEVOLDSEN		M	22	(9)	3
5	Jón Rói JACOBSEN	FRO	D	3	(4)	
2	Michael JAKOBSEN		D	32		3
29	Martin S. JENSEN		G	7		
8	Andreas JOHANSSON	SWE	M	28	(3)	7
27	Patrick KRISTENSEN		A	2	(10)	
7	Mattias LINDSTRÖM	SWE	M	9	(9)	
11	José Roberto Rodrigues MOTA	BRA	A	4	(2)	
30	Kenneth Stenild NIELSEN		G	7		
10	Lars NILSSON	SWE	A	12		2
15	Siyabonga NOMVETHE	RSA	M	18	(8)	6
16	Allan OLESEN		D	30		
6	Steve OLFERS	NED	D	18	(3)	1
19	Suni OLSEN	FRO	M	1	(2)	
3	Martin PEDERSEN		D	19	(9)	
10	Rade PRICA	SWE	A	15	(1)	9
21	Kasper RISGÅRD		D	30	(2)	5
32	Ronnie SCHWARTZ		A		(3)	
24	Jens-Kristian SØRENSEN		M		(3)	
17	Benedict VILAKAZI	RSA	M	1	(4)	
1	Karim ZAZA	MAR	G	19		

DENMARK

AGF

Coach – Ove Pedersen

Founded – 1880

MAJOR HONOURS: Danish League - (5) 1955, 1956, 1957, 1960, 1986; Danish Cup - (9) 1955, 1957, 1960, 1961, 1965, 1987, 1988, 1992, 1996.

2007				
18/7	Horsens	h	1-2	*Graulund*
22/7	OB	h	0-2	
30/7	EfB	a	2-2	*Lucena, Graulund*
4/8	København	h	0-1	
12/8	AaB	a	0-2	
18/8	Brøndby	a	1-0	*Tullberg*
27/8	Lyngby	h	0-0	
1/9	Viborg	a	0-2	
16/9	Randers	a	1-0	*Williams*
22/9	Nordsjælland	h	1-2	*Valencia*
30/9	Midtjylland	a	0-2	
8/10	AaB	h	3-5	*Graulund 2, Williams*
21/10	Brøndby	a	1-2	*Graulund*
27/10	Lyngby	a	3-1	*Graulund 2, Pleidrup*
3/11	København	h	0-2	
12/11	Viborg	a	2-0	*Krabbe, Graulund*
29/11	Nordsjælland	h	3-3	*Graulund 3 (1p)*
2/12	Midtjylland	h	2-0	*Graulund, og (Kjær)*
2008				
16/3	Horsens	a	0-0	
20/3	Randers	h	0-0	
23/3	OB	a	0-2	
30/3	EfB	h	0-1	
7/4	Viborg	h	0-0	
13/4	Nordsjælland	a	2-3	*Blicher, White*
20/4	Lyngby	h	3-1	*Lucena, Williams, White*
24/4	København	a	1-1	*Graulund*
27/4	Randers	a	1-4	*Valencia*
3/5	OB	h	0-2	
8/5	AaB	a	1-3	*White*
11/5	Brøndby	h	1-1	*Kure*
15/5	EfB	a	1-0	*Williams*
18/5	Midtjylland	a	2-3	*Kure, Williams*
24/5	Horsens	h	1-2	*Blicher*

No	Name	Nat	Pos	Aps	(s)	Gls
34	Morten Beck ANDERSEN		A		(1)	
8	Kári ÁRNASON	ISL	M	25		
36	Jesper BLICHER		M	10	(6)	2
5	Ole BUDTZ		D	29	(1)	
18	Garra DEMBÉLÉ	FRA	A		(3)	
13	Peter FOLDGAST		A	8	(6)	
19	Jens GJESING		M	10	(13)	
11	Peter GRAULUND		A	28		13
35	Dennis HØEGH		A	1	(8)	
10	Mads JØRGENSEN		M	1	(1)	
2	Frederik KRABBE		D	18	(3)	1
20	Niels KRISTENSEN		M		(6)	
27	Anders KURE		D	12	(6)	2
6	Ulrik LINDKVIST		D	15	(5)	
21	Jerry LUCENA		M	33		2
28	Michael LUMB		D	33		
4	Kim MADSEN		D	24	(2)	
26	Martin MIKKELSEN		M		(2)	
7	Lars PLEIDRUP		M	18	(2)	1
25	Kasper POVLSEN		M	2	(1)	
1	Steffen RASMUSSEN		G	33		
24	Razak SALIFU	GHA	M		(4)	
17	Peter SAND		A		(1)	
22	Cheikh SARR		D	3	(1)	
18	Mike TULLBERG		A	5	(1)	1
30	Alex VALENCIA	NOR	M	13	(10)	2
15	Jeremiah WHITE	USA	M	23	(6)	3
9	Dioh WILLIAMS	LBR	A	19	(1)	5

BRØNDBY IF

Coach –Tom Køhlert

Founded – 1964

MAJOR HONOURS: Danish League - (10) 1985, 1987, 1988, 1990, 199 1996, 1997, 1998, 2002, 2005; Danish Cup - (6) 1989, 1994, 1998, 200 2005, 2008; Royal League – (1) 2007.

2007				
18/7	EfB	a	0-1	
21/7	Nordsjælland	h	2-2	*Mikkelsen, Ericsson*
29/7	Midtjylland	a	0-5	
5/8	Lyngby	h	3-0	*Ericsson, Rasmussen M "Duncan", Daugaard*
13/8	Viborg	a	1-1	*Rasmussen M. "Duncan"*
18/8	AGF	h	0-1	
26/8	Horsens	a	2-4	*Lorentzen, Gíslason*
2/9	OB	h	1-1	*Madsen*
16/9	AaB	a	0-3	
23/9	København	h	0-1	
30/9	Randers	h	1-1	*Rasmussen M. "Duncan"*
6/10	Viborg	a	2-1	*Retov 2*
21/10	AGF	h	2-1	*Rasmussen M. "Duncan", Williams*
28/10	OB	a	0-0	
4/11	Lyngby	h	3-0	*Ericsson, Rasmussen M "Duncan" 2*
10/11	Horsens	h	3-0	*Mikkelsen, Williams 2*
25/11	EfB	a	2-3	*Katongo, Gíslason*
2/12	København	a	1-1	*Howard*
2008				
16/3	Randers	h	3-1	*Rasmussen T. 2, Rasmussen M. "Duncan"*
20/3	Midtjylland	h	2-1	*Retov, Gíslason*
23/3	Nordsjælland	a	0-1	
30/3	AaB	h	0-1	
5/4	Horsens	a	3-1	*Retov, Ericsson, Katongo*
12/4	EfB	h	2-1	*Gíslason, Katongo*
20/4	OB	h	0-2	
23/4	Lyngby	a	2-2	*Holmén, Von Schlebrügge*
26/4	Midtjylland	a	1-1	*Lorentzen*
4/5	Nordsjælland	h	3-0	*Gíslason, Holmén, Ericsson (p)*
7/5	Viborg	h	1-1	*Katongo*
11/5	AGF	a	1-1	*Ericsson*
15/5	AaB	a	0-2	
18/5	København	h	2-1	*Holmén, Katongo*
24/5	Randers	a	1-2	*Ericsson*

No	Name	Nat	Pos	Aps	(s)	Gls
16	Stephan ANDERSEN		G	33		
15	Ruben BAGGER		A		(1)	
33	Jacob BERTHELSEN		D	6	(4)	
24	Mikkel BISCHOFF		D	2		
8	Kim DAUGAARD		M	9	(6)	1
10	Martin ERICSSON	SWE	M	24	(6)	7
20	Stefán GÍSLASON	ISL	M	26	(3)	5
6	Samuel HOLMÉN	SWE	M	23		3
5	Mark HOWARD	ENG	D	23	(1)	1
26	Mike JENSEN		M	4	(9)	
11	Mads JØRGENSEN		M		(3)	
34	Pierre KANSTRUP		D		(3)	
28	Chris KATONGO	ZAM	A	18	(9)	5
6	Marcus LANTZ	SWE	M	3		
7	Kasper LORENTZEN		A	18	(6)	2
13	Peter MADSEN		A	9	(4)	1
25	Tobias MIKKELSEN		M	14	(5)	2

No	Name	Nat	Pos	Aps	(s)	Gls
	Patrick MORTENSEN		A	1	(2)	
	Per NIELSEN		D	16	(4)	
	Anders RANDRUP		D	20	(5)	
	Morten RASMUSSEN		D	5	(3)	
	Morten "Duncan" RASMUSSEN		A	17	(2)	7
	Thomas RASMUSSEN		D	27	(1)	2
	Martin RETOV		M	23	(3)	4
	Thomas RYTTER		D	11		
	Martin SPELMANN		M	5	(6)	
	Max VON SCHLEBRÜGGE	SWE	D	14		1
	Daniel WASS		D	7	(6)	
	David WILLIAMS	AUS	A	5	(5)	3

ESBJERG FB

Coach – Troels Bech

Founded – 1924

MAJOR HONOURS: Danish League - (5) 1961, 1962, 1963, 1965, 1979; Danish Cup - (2) 1964, 1976.

07

/7	Brøndby	h	1-0	*Jørgensen (p)*
/7	Viborg	a	5-0	*Lekic 3, Nøhr 2*
/7	AGF	h	2-2	*Vingaard, Murcy*
8	Randers	h	1-3	*Høgh*
/8	København	a	2-5	*Zimling, Demba-Nyrén*
/8	Lyngby	a	6-1	*Rieks 2, Lange, Vingaard, Høgh, Lekic*
/8	AaB	h	1-2	*Demba-Nyrén*
9	Horsens	a	3-4	*Mikkelsen (p), Demba-Nyrén 2*
/9	Nordsjælland	a	1-3	*Lange*
/9	Midtjylland	h	2-0	*Murcy, Rieks*
/9	OB	a	1-1	*Bech*
10	OB	h	0-0	
/10	Midtjylland	a	2-2	*Bech, Zimling*
/10	AaB	a	0-2	
11	Nordsjælland	h	1-2	*Bech*
/11	Lyngby	a	3-1	*Zimling, Demba-Nyrén, Lange*
/11	Brøndby	h	3-2	*Demba-Nyrén 2, Mikkelsen*
12	Horsens	h	1-3	*Lange*

08

/3	Viborg	a	4-0	*Vingaard 2, Murcy, Lekic*
/3	København	h	2-1	*Rieks, Jørgensen (p)*
/3	Randers	a	0-1	
/3	AGF	a	1-0	*Bech*
/4	Lyngby	h	2-1	*Lekic, Murcy*
2/4	Brøndby	a	1-2	*Murcy*
/4	AaB	h	1-1	*Rieks*
4/4	Nordsjælland	a	2-3	*Rieks, Lange*
7/4	København	a	1-2	*Borges*
/5	Randers	h	3-2	*Björck, Vingaard, Lange*
/5	OB	a	1-1	*Bech*
2/5	Midtjylland	h	3-2	*Vingaard 2, Rieks*
5/5	AGF	h	0-1	
8/5	Horsens	a	1-3	*Ornoch*
4/5	Viborg	h	2-1	*Murcy, Høgh*

No	Name	Nat	Pos	Aps	(s)	Gls
1	Jesper BECH		A	18	(3)	5
	Jonas BJURSTRÖM	SWE	M	1	(2)	
1	Fredrik BJÖRCK	SWE	D	12		1
0	Thiago Pinto BORGES	BRA	M	3	(8)	1
3	Kevin CONBOY		D	2	(3)	
	Njogu DEMBA-NYRÉN	SWE	A	16	(1)	7
	Fernando DERVELD	NED	D	9	(2)	
	Frank HANSEN		D	31	(1)	
4	Nicolai HØGH		D	22	(1)	3
19	Jesper JØRGENSEN		M	27		2
15	Andreas KLARSTRÖM	SWE	M	25		
22	Jesper LANGE		A	17	(13)	6
8	Rajko LEKIC		A	11	(12)	6
18	Jeppe MEHL		M		(2)	
12	Jesper MIKKELSEN		M	14	(1)	2
25	Michaël MURCY	FRA	A	16	(9)	6
17	Lars Christian NIELSEN		D	2	(1)	
5	Anders NØHR		M		(4)	2
20	Kristian Flittie ONSTAD	NOR	D	23	(2)	
5	Andrew ORNOCH	CAN	M	5	(2)	1
31	Søren RIEKS		M	18	(9)	7
4	Igors N. STEPANOVS	LVA	D	3		
12	Emmanuel UKPAI	NGA	A	2	(6)	
26	Mikkel VENDELBO		M	10	(3)	
14	Martin VINGAARD		M	28	(4)	7
16	Lars WINDE		G	33		
6	Niki ZIMLING		M	15	(1)	3

AC HORSENS

Coach – Kent Nielsen

Founded – 1994

2007

18/7	AGF	a	2-1	*Macena, Lodberg*
23/7	Midtjylland	h	2-1	*Hansen 2 (1p)*
29/7	OB	a	3-3	*Hansen, Lawan, Rieper*
5/8	AaB	h	1-1	*Hansen (p)*
12/8	Lyngby	a	0-0	
19/8	Viborg	a	1-2	*Petersen*
26/8	Brøndby	h	4-2	*Petersen, Macena 2, Lawan*
2/9	EfB	h	4-3	*og (Jørgensen), Lawan, Avci, Rieper*
15/9	København	a	0-1	
23/9	Randers	h	1-0	*Hansen*
1/10	Nordsjælland	a	0-0	
7/10	Lyngby	h	2-1	*Lawan, Friis*
21/10	OB	a	0-2	
28/10	Nordsjælland	a	2-1	*Macena, Johansen*
4/11	Midtjylland	h	1-1	*Hansen*
10/11	Brøndby	a	0-3	
25/11	Viborg	h	1-1	*Friis*
3/12	EfB	a	3-1	*Nøhr, Hansen (p), Algreen*

2008

16/3	AGF	h	0-0	
19/3	AaB	h	1-2	*Macena*
22/3	København	a	0-1	
30/3	Randers	h	1-0	*Hansen (p)*
5/4	Brøndby	h	1-3	*Hansen (p)*
14/4	Viborg	a	3-1	*Friis, Lawan 2*
20/4	Nordsjælland	h	2-0	*Macena, Johansen*
23/4	Midtjylland	a	1-1	*Hansen*
28/4	AaB	a	0-1	
5/5	København	h	3-2	*Macena, Lawan, Lauser*
8/5	Lyngby	a	1-4	*Christensen*
11/5	OB	h	2-2	*Hansen 2 (1p)*
15/5	Randers	a	0-0	
18/5	EfB	h	3-1	*Macena, Lawan, Lodberg (p)*
24/5	AGF	a	2-1	*Macena, Hansen*

No	Name	Nat	Pos	Aps	(s)	Gls
5	Steffen ALGREEN		D	9	(1)	1
25	Yasin AVCI		M	10	(13)	1
18	Bosun AYENI	NGA	M	1	(2)	
28	Ibrahim BABATUNDE	NGA	A		(6)	
19	Nick CHRISTENSEN		A		(12)	1
20	Janus DRACHMANN		M	10	(9)	

18	Joseph ELANGA	CMR	D	15		
14	Søren FRIIS		M	17	(14)	3
2	Per GADE		D	30		
3	Martin HALLE		D	16		
8	Henrik HANSEN		M	31		13
1	Søren JOCHUMSEN		G	32		
17	Casper JOHANSEN		A	5	(10)	2
13	Thomas KORTEGAARD		M	30		
23	Steffen LAUSER	GER	M		(5)	1
12	Rawez LAWAN	SWE	A	29	(2)	8
11	Niels LODBERG		M	21	(10)	2
9	Gilberto MACENA	BRA	A	32		9
27	Anders NØHR		M	16	(1)	1
22	Kenneth Emil PETERSEN		D	28	(1)	2
4	Mads RIEPER		D	29		2
26	Blerim RRUSTEMI	ALB	D		(1)	
7	Magne STURØD	NOR	M		(1)	
10	Allan SØGAARD		M	1	(4)	
16	Kenneth SØRENSEN		M		(1)	
21	Lasse SØRENSEN		G	1		

FC KØBENHAVN

Coach – Ståle Solbakken (NOR)

Founded – 1992

MAJOR HONOURS: Danish League - (6) 1993, 2001, 2003, 2004, 2006, 2007; Danish Cup - (3) 1995, 1997, 2004; Royal League - (2) 2005, 2006.

2007

18/7	Nordsjælland	a	0-1	
25/7	AaB	a	1-1	*Hangeland*
28/7	Viborg	h	3-1	*Hutchinson, Nordstrand 2*
4/8	AGF	a	1-0	*Hutchinson*
11/8	EfB	h	5-2	*Nørregaard, Gravgaard, Sionko, Nordstrand 2*
19/8	Midtjylland	h	0-0	
25/8	OB	a	0-0	
2/9	Randers	h	1-0	*Grønkjær*
15/9	Horsens	h	1-0	*Nordstrand*
23/9	Brøndby	a	1-0	*Nørregaard*
29/9	Lyngby	h	2-0	*Sionko, Nørregaard (p)*
7/10	Nordsjælland	h	1-1	*Allbäck*
20/10	AaB	a	0-0	
28/10	Randers	h	0-1	
3/11	AGF	a	2-0	*Hutchinson, Sionko*
11/11	Midtjylland	a	2-2	*Allbäck, Antonsson*
24/11	OB	h	2-1	*Allbäck, Hangeland*
2/12	Brøndby	h	1-1	*Allbäck*

2008

16/3	Lyngby	a	4-1	*Sionko, Pospech, Jørgensen M., Júnior*
19/3	EfB	a	1-2	*Grønkjær*
22/3	Horsens	h	1-0	*Sionko (p)*
31/3	Viborg	a	3-2	*Nordstrand, Júnior, Grønkjær*
6/4	Midtjylland	h	0-2	
13/4	OB	a	0-0	
19/4	Randers	a	1-2	*Nordstrand*
24/4	AGF	h	1-1	*Hutchinson*
27/4	EfB	h	2-1	*Gravgaard. Pospech*
5/5	Horsens	a	2-3	*Nordstrand, Allbäck*
8/5	Nordsjælland	a	2-1	*Hutchinson, Allbäck*
12/5	AaB	h	4-0	*Silberbauer, Hutchinson, Nordstrand (p), Almeida*
15/5	Viborg	h	3-0	*Júnior, Almeida 2*
18/5	Brøndby	a	1-2	*Allbäck*
24/5	Lyngby	h	3-1	*Hutchinson 2, Allbäck*

No	Name	Nat	Pos	Aps	(s)	Gls
11	Marcus ALLBÄCK	SWE	A	23	(6)	8
7	Aílton ALMEIDA	BRA	A	6	(20)	3
15	Mikael ANTONSSON	SWE	D	10	(3)	1
1	Jesper CHRISTIANSEN		G	32		
41	Nathan COE	AUS	G	1		
14	Michael GRAVGAARD		D	23		2
10	Jesper GRØNKJÆR		M	21	(4)	3
5	Brede HANGELAND	NOR	D	18		2
13	Atiba HUTCHINSON	CAN	M	26	(5)	8
3	Niclas JENSEN		D	16	(2)	
18	José Luiz Guimarães JÚNIOR	BRA	A	3	(5)	3
25	Mathias "Zanka" JØRGENSEN		D	5	(7)	1
23	William Kvist JØRGENSEN		M	29	(3)	
5	Ulrik LAURSEN		D	10	(1)	
27	Jacob NEESTRUP		D		(1)	
9	Morten NORDSTRAND		A	25	(4)	9
4	Hjalte Bo NØRREGAARD		M	21	(9)	3
2	Zdeněk POSPĚCH	CZE	D	13	(2)	2
8	Michael SILBERBAUER		M	22	(5)	1
24	Libor SIONKO	CZE	M	22	(5)	5
17	Oscar WENDT	SWE	D	21	(3)	
6	Rasmus WÜRTZ		M	16	(1)	

LYNGBY BK

Coach – Kasper Hjulmand

Founded – 1921

MAJOR HONOURS: Danish League - (2) 1983, 1992; Danish Cup - (3) 1984, 1985, 1990.

2007

22/7	Randers	h	0-3	
25/7	OB	a	1-1	*Holst*
29/7	Nordsjælland	a	1-0	*Aabech*
5/8	Brøndby	a	0-3	
12/8	Horsens	h	0-0	
20/8	EfB	h	1-6	*Holst*
27/8	AGF	a	0-0	
2/9	Midtjylland	h	1-2	*Holst*
16/9	Viborg	a	1-2	*Christiansen M.*
23/9	AaB	h	3-4	*Holst 2, Håkansson*
29/9	København	a	0-2	
7/10	Horsens	a	1-2	*Beckmann*
21/10	Viborg	h	2-0	*Holst, Thomsen*
27/10	AGF	h	1-3	*Beckmann*
4/11	Brøndby	a	0-3	
11/11	EfB	h	1-3	*Thomsen*
25/11	Randers	a	2-2	*Beckmann, Aabech*
2/12	AaB	a	3-5	*Christiansen M., Aabech, Beckmann (p)*

2008

16/3	København	h	1-4	*Beckmann*
23/3	Midtjylland	a	1-2	*Hansen R.*
30/3	Nordsjælland	h	0-0	
2/4	OB	h	0-3	
6/4	EfB	a	1-2	*Holst*
13/4	Randers	h	0-0	
20/4	AGF	a	1-3	*Holst*
23/4	Brøndby	h	2-2	*Melchiorsen, Hansen T.*
27/4	OB	a	1-1	*Christiansen M.*
4/5	Midtjylland	h	1-2	*Beckmann*
8/5	Horsens	h	4-1	*Beckmann 2, Hansen T., Håkansson*
12/5	Viborg	a	2-3	*Christiansen M., Holst*
15/5	Nordsjælland	a	0-0	
18/5	AaB	h	0-2	
24/5	København	a	1-3	*Håkansson*

Name	Nat	Pos	Aps	(s)	Gls
Kim AABECH		A	25	(6)	3
Danny ANDERSEN		A	7	(9)	
Martin ANDERSEN		M	1	(4)	
Mikkel BECHMANN		M	26		8
Andreas BJELLAND		M	9	(2)	
Jakob BRESEMANN		D	33		
Morten CHRISTIANSEN		M	31		4
Rasmus S. CHRISTIANSEN		D	9	(1)	
Rasmus DAUGAARD		D	15	(2)	
Emil DYRE		M	4	(5)	
Alexander FISCHER		D	19	(1)	
Brian HAMALEINEN		D	9	(3)	
Ronni HANSEN		M	7	(7)	1
Tem HANSEN	FRO	M	6	(6)	2
Christian HOLST	FRO	A	28	(3)	9
Jesper HÅKANSSON		A	22	(1)	3
Anders JOCHUMSEN		A		(4)	
Jesper Mølgaard KRISTENSEN		M	4	(9)	
Rasmus MARVITS		D	14	(12)	
Nicolai MELCHIORSEN		M	21	(3)	1
Marc MØLLER		D	7	(2)	
Allan NIELSEN		M	7	(4)	
Martin NIELSEN		M		(1)	
Rune PEDERSEN		G	27	(1)	
Morten PETERSEN		D	16		
Lasse RISE		A	4	(1)	
Kevin SCHMIDT		M		(3)	
Thomas SEIDELIN		G	4		
Rang SHAWKAT		D	1	(2)	
Mads THOMSEN		A	5	(5)	2
Josh WAGENAAR	CAN	G	2		

FC MIDTJYLLAND

Coach – Erik Rasmussen

Founded – 1999

2007

3/7	Horsens	a	1-2	*Kristensen*
9/7	Brøndby	h	5-0	*Madsen, Babatunde, Poulsen S., Kristensen, Olsen C.*
/8	Viborg	h	1-0	*Olsen C.*
/8	AaB	h	2-1	*Kristensen, Babatunde*
2/8	Nordsjælland	a	1-1	*Babatunde*
9/8	København	a	0-0	
5/8	Randers	h	3-2	*Poulsen S., Thygesen, Kristensen*
/9	Lyngby	a	2-1	*Dadu (p), Kristensen*
6/9	OB	h	2-1	*Dadu, Troest*
3/9	EfB	a	0-2	
0/9	AGF	h	2-0	*Dadu, Poulsen S.*
/10	Randers	a	0-3	
2/10	EfB	h	2-2	*Oluwafemi, Dadu (p)*
8/10	Viborg	h	2-1	*Kristensen, Klimpl*
/11	Horsens	a	1-1	*Kristensen*
1/11	København	h	2-2	*Thygesen, Kristensen*
5/11	AaB	a	0-1	
/12	AGF	a	0-2	

2008

7/3	Nordsjælland	h	1-0	*Kristensen*
0/3	Brøndby	a	1-2	*Kristensen*
3/3	Lyngby	h	2-1	*Kristensen 2*
9/3	OB	a	1-0	*Olsen P.*
/4	København	a	2-0	*Olsen P., Thygesen*
3/4	AaB	h	2-0	*Thygesen, Olsen D.*
0/4	Viborg	a	1-1	*Fagerberg*
3/4	Horsens	h	1-1	*Afriyie*
6/4	Brøndby	h	1-1	*Fagerberg*
/5	Lyngby	a	2-1	*Thygesen, Salami*
7/5	Randers	h	2-1	*Poulsen C., Jessen*
12/5	EfB	a	2-3	*Troest, Florescu*
15/5	OB	h	3-1	*Olsen D. 2, Fagerberg*
18/5	AGF	h	3-2	*Troest, Florescu (p), Nworuh*
24/5	Nordsjælland	a	3-0	*Afriyie, Olsen D., Nworuh*

No	Name	Nat	Pos	Aps	(s)	Gls
3	Kolja AFRIYIE	GER	D	29		2
30	Babajide Collins BABATUNDE	NGA	A	11	(7)	3
9	Serghei DADU	MDA	A	10	(5)	4
24	Ken FAGERBERG	SWE	A	9	(4)	3
28	Dennis FLINTA		M	7	(10)	
9	George FLORESCU	ROU	M	15		2
22	Ibrahim GNANOU	BFA	D	1		
25	Lasse HEINZE		G	11	(1)	
19	Leon JESSEN		D	5	(7)	1
4	Simon KJÆR		D	17	(2)	
5	Maroš KLIMPL	SVK	D	13	(1)	1
23	Frank KRISTENSEN		A	24	(5)	12
8	Thomas Røll LARSEN		M	3	(4)	
13	Ayinde Jamiu LAWAL	NGA	M		(1)	
7	Claus MADSEN		A	9	(15)	1
39	Jude Ikechukwu NWORUH	NGA	A		(5)	2
20	Christian OLSEN		A	1	(8)	2
21	Danny OLSEN		M	23	(6)	4
11	Petter Furuseth OLSEN	NOR	M	13		2
26	Ajilore OLUWAFEMI	NGA	M	18		1
15	Christopher POULSEN		D	29	(2)	1
11	Simon POULSEN		M	16	(2)	3
16	Martin RAŠKA	CZE	G	22		
29	Winston REID		D	7	(2)	
41	Adeola Lanre RUNSEWE	NGA	M	1	(4)	
27	Adigun Taofeek SALAMI	NGA	M	16	(2)	1
10	Mikkel THYGESEN		M	24	(1)	5
2	Magnus TROEST		D	29		3

FC NORDSJÆLLAND

Coach – Morten Wieghorst

Founded – 2003

2007

18/7	København	h	1-0	*Nakajima-Farran*
21/7	Brøndby	a	2-2	*Bernburg, Kildentoft*
29/7	Lyngby	h	0-1	
6/8	OB	a	0-3	
12/8	Midtjylland	h	1-1	*Pode*
19/8	Randers	a	1-1	*Fetai*
26/8	Viborg	h	4-0	*Kristensen 2 (1p), Nakajima-Farran, Storm*
3/9	AaB	a	1-2	*Bernburg*
17/9	EfB	h	3-1	*Jensen, Pedersen, Bernburg*
22/9	AGF	a	2-1	*Bernburg 2*
1/10	Horsens	h	0-0	
7/10	København	a	1-1	*Cagara*
21/10	Randers	h	2-1	*Bødker, Nakajima-Farran*
28/10	Horsens	h	1-2	*Fetai*
4/11	EfB	a	2-1	*Fetai, Bernburg*
11/11	AaB	h	1-2	*Fetai*
29/11	AGF	a	3-3	*Bernburg, Nakajima-Farran, Pedersen*
2/12	OB	h	3-3	*Nakjima-Farran, Lundberg, Kildentoft*

2008

17/3	Midtjylland	a	0-1	

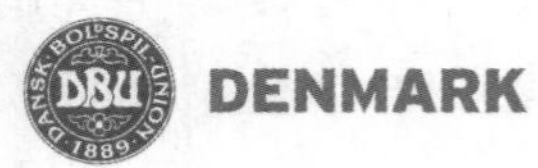

20/3	Viborg	a	3-2	*Nakajima-Farran, Pedersen, Kildentoft*
23/3	Brøndby	h	1-0	*Bernburg*
30/3	Lyngby	a	0-0	
6/4	AaB	a	1-3	*Bernburg*
13/4	AGF	h	3-2	*Bernburg, Kristensen (p), Nakajima-Farran*
20/4	Horsens	a	0-2	
24/4	EfB	h	3-2	*Fetai 2, Kristensen (p)*
27/4	Viborg	h	5-3	*Bernburg 2, Kristensen 2 (1p), Richter J.*
4/5	Brøndby	a	0-3	
8/5	København	h	1-2	*Bernburg*
12/5	Randers	a	1-2	*Bernburg*
15/5	Lyngby	h	0-0	
18/5	OB	a	1-1	*Dahl*
24/5	Midtjylland	h	0-3	

No	Name	Nat	Pos	Aps	(s)	Gls
9	Martin BERNBURG		A	30	(2)	14
25	Henrik BØDKER		M	11	(8)	1
3	Dennis CAGARA		D	18		1
1	Kim CHRISTENSEN		G	18		
17	Søren CHRISTENSEN		M	25	(4)	
24	Andreas DAHL	SWE	M	14		1
15	Bajram FETAI		A	12	(10)	6
22	Jesper HANSEN		G	15		
23	Daniel JENSEN		D	17	(8)	1
6	Morten KARLSEN		M	16	(3)	
4	Henrik KILDENTOFT		D	18	(3)	3
16	Thomas KRISTENSEN		M	25	(2)	6
7	Søren KROGH		M	1		
24	Thomas LINDRUP		M		(1)	
5	Johnny LUNDBERG	SWE	D	26		1
11	Issey Morgan NAKAJIMA-FARRAN	CAN	A	26	(4)	7
14	Christian NIELSEN		D	8	(7)	
8	Allan OLESEN		D	29	(1)	
18	Kenni OLSEN		M	4	(13)	
28	Nicklas PEDERSEN		A	9	(3)	3
20	Stephan PETERSEN		M	6	(5)	
10	Marcus PODE	SWE	A	8	(5)	1
2	Michael RIBERS		D	2		
26	Jonathan RICHTER		M	10	(3)	1
21	Simon RICHTER		D	4		
13	Kris STADSGAARD		D	6		
12	Bo STORM		M	4	(8)	1
13	Mads THOMSEN		A	1	(8)	

ODENSE BK

Coach – Lars Olsen

Founded – 1887

MAJOR HONOURS: Danish League - (3) 1977, 1982, 1989; Danish Cup - (5) 1983, 1991, 1993, 2002, 2007.

2007

22/7	AGF	a	2-0	*Absalonsen, Timm*
25/7	Lyngby	h	1-1	*Timm*
29/7	Horsens	h	3-3	*Sørensen (p), Nielsen, Christensen K.*
6/8	Nordsjælland	h	3-0	*Bolaños 2, Timm*
12/8	Randers	a	0-0	
19/8	AaB	a	3-2	*Absalonsen 2, Borring*
25/8	København	h	0-0	
2/9	Brøndby	a	1-1	*Andreasen*
16/9	Midtjylland	a	1-2	*Christensen A.*
24/9	Viborg	h	4-0	*Borring 2, Andreasen, Mikkelsen*
30/9	EfB	h	1-1	*Timm*
7/10	EfB	a	0-0	
21/10	Horsens	h	2-0	*Sæternes, Andreasen*
28/10	Brøndby	h	0-0	
5/11	Viborg	a	2-0	*Absalonsen, Andrease[n]*
11/11	Randers	h	0-0	
24/11	København	a	1-2	*Nielsen*
2/12	Nordsjælland	a	3-3	*Nielsen, Laursen, Mikkelsen*

2008

15/3	AaB	h	1-1	*og (Olfers)*
23/3	AGF	h	2-0	*Borring 2*
29/3	Midtjylland	h	0-1	
2/4	Lyngby	a	3-0	*Fall 3*
6/4	Randers	a	2-0	*Andreasen 2*
13/4	København	h	0-0	
20/4	Brøndby	a	2-0	*Andreasen, Fall*
23/4	Viborg	h	1-0	*Fall*
27/4	Lyngby	h	1-1	*Bolaños*
3/5	AGF	a	2-0	*Borring, Absalonsen*
7/5	EfB	h	1-1	*Bisgaard*
11/5	Horsens	a	2-2	*Fall, Andreasen*
15/5	Midtjylland	a	1-3	*Fall*
18/5	Nordsjælland	h	1-1	*Borring*
24/5	AaB	a	0-2	

No	Name	Nat	Pos	Aps	(s)	Gls
11	Johan ABSALONSEN		A	23	(2)	5
4	Hans Henrik ANDREASEN		M	26	(4)	8
17	Morten BISGAARD		M	10	(10)	1
22	Christian BOLAÑOS	CRC	M	14	(8)	3
29	Jonas BORRING		M	31	(1)	7
5	Anders Møller CHRISTENSEN		D	30		1
20	Kim CHRISTENSEN		A	2	(1)	1
9	Baye Djiby FALL	SEN	A	13		7
14	Esben HANSEN		M	20		
6	Thomas HELVEG		D	16	(1)	
3	Atle Roar HÅLAND	NOR	D	13		
28	Anders K. JACOBSEN		A		(10)	
16	Søren JENSEN		D	8	(2)	
3	Ulrik LAURSEN		D	15		1
27	Anders LINDEGAARD		G	1		
21	Peter Nymann MIKKELSEN		M	21	(6)	2
10	David NIELSEN		A	9	(5)	3
26	Matti Lund NIELSEN		M	1	(7)	
8	Bechara Jalkh Leonardo OLIVEIRA	BRA	M	10	(4)	
1	Arkadiusz ONYSZKO	POL	G	32		
2	Jan Tore OPHAUG	NOR	D	1	(1)	
24	Srđan RADONJIĆ	MNE	A		(5)	
9	Bengt SÆTERNES	NOR	A	5	(4)	1
15	Chris SØRENSEN		D	32		1
7	Mads TIMM		A	8	(7)	4
18	Jonas TROEST		D	22	(4)	

RANDERS FC

Coach – Colin Todd (ENG)

Founded – 1898

MAJOR HONOURS: Danish Cup - (4) 1967, 1968, 1973, 2006.

2007

18/7	Viborg	h	2-0	*Dalgaard 2*
22/7	Lyngby	a	3-0	*Dalgaard, Frederiksen, Buval*
1/8	AaB	h	5-0	*Dalgaard 3, Pedersen K. (p), Fabinho*
5/8	EfB	a	3-1	*Sane, Dalgaard, Da Silva*
12/8	OB	h	0-0	
19/8	Nordsjælland	h	1-1	*Sane*
26/8	Midtjylland	a	2-3	*Sane 2*

	København	a	0-1	
9	AGF	h	0-1	
9	Horsens	a	0-1	
9	Brøndby	a	1-1	*Fredgaard*
0	Midtjylland	h	3-0	*Da Silva 2, Sane*
10	Nordsjælland	a	1-2	*Brandrup*
10	København	a	1-0	*Pedersen K. (p)*
1	AaB	h	1-0	*Buval*
11	OB	a	0-0	
11	Lyngby	h	2-2	*Buval 2*
2	Viborg	h	0-2	
08				
3	Brøndby	a	1-3	*Fabinho*
3	AGF	a	0-0	
3	EfB	h	1-0	*Pedersen R.*
3	Horsens	a	0-1	
	OB	h	0-2	
4	Lyngby	a	0-0	
4	København	h	2-1	*Berg, Fabinho*
4	AaB	a	0-3	
4	AGF	h	4-1	*Buval 2, Nygaard 2*
	EfB	a	2-3	*Nygaard 2*
	Midtjylland	a	1-2	*Nygaard*
5	Nordsjælland	h	2-1	*Buval, Andreasen*
5	Horsens	h	0-0	
5	Viborg	a	1-0	*Sane*
5	Brøndby	h	2-1	*Nygaard (p), Berg*

Name	Nat	Pos	Aps	(s)	Gls
Issah AHMED	GHA	D	21		
Christian ANDREASEN		A		(5)	1
Robert ARZUMANYAN	ARM	D	8	(1)	
Alain BEHI	FRA	M	3	(4)	
Søren BERG		M	14	(1)	2
Jeppe BRANDRUP		M	12	(8)	1
Bédi BUVAL	FRA	A	23	(4)	7
Kian CHRISTENSEN		D	1		
Alex DA SILVA	BRA	M	5	(3)	3
Thomas DALGAARD		A	8	(7)	7
Jonas DAMBORG		M	11	(5)	
Kevin Stuhr ELLEGAARD		G	33		
Fabio FABINHO Trindade da Silveira	BRA	A	9	(13)	3
Carsten FREDGAARD		M	28	(2)	1
Jan FREDERIKSEN		D	33		1
Rasmus HANSEN		M	3	(2)	
Søren HOLDGAARD		D	10	(4)	
Will JOHN	USA	M		(1)	
Lee NGUYEN	USA	M	9	(4)	
Marc NYGAARD		A	8	(1)	6
Kenneth Møller PEDERSEN		M	29	(3)	2
Ralf PEDERSEN		D	27		1
Søren PEDERSEN		D	32		
Tidiane SANE	SEN	M	28		6
Stig TØFTING		M	1		
Søren Ulrik VESTERGAARD		A	7	(7)	

VIBORG FF

oach – Anders Linderoth (SWE); (9/11/07) (Stephen Lowe (ENG) & Jan Østergaard); (1/1/08) Hans Eklund (SWE)

Founded – 1896

MAJOR HONOURS: Danish Cup - (1) 2000.

007				
3/7	Randers	a	0-2	
2/7	EfB	h	0-5	
3/7	København	a	1-3	*Muomaife*
'8	Midtjylland	a	0-1	
3/8	Brøndby	h	1-1	*Olsen P.*
19/8	Horsens	h	2-1	*Frandsen (p), Nielsen*
26/8	Nordsjælland	a	0-4	
1/9	AGF	h	2-0	*Muomaife, Radonjić*
16/9	Lyngby	h	2-1	*Højer, Olsen P.*
24/9	OB	a	0-4	
30/9	AaB	a	2-3	*Carlos (p), Muomaife*
6/10	Brøndby	h	1-2	*Carlos*
21/10	Lyngby	a	0-2	
28/10	Midtjylland	a	1-2	*Olesen*
5/11	OB	h	0-2	
12/11	AGF	h	0-2	
25/11	Horsens	a	1-1	*Nagel*
1/12	Randers	a	2-0	*Rask, Nagel*
2008				
16/3	EfB	h	0-4	
20/3	Nordsjælland	h	2-3	*Bertolt, Vestergaard*
23/3	AaB	a	0-2	
31/3	København	h	2-3	*Vestergaard, Olsen C.*
7/4	AGF	a	0-0	
14/4	Horsens	h	1-3	*Olsen S.*
20/4	Midtjylland	h	1-1	*Muomaife*
23/4	OB	a	0-1	
27/4	Nordsjælland	a	3-5	*Vestergaard, Sennels, Muomaife*
4/5	AaB	h	0-1	
7/5	Brøndby	a	1-1	*Gíslason*
12/5	Lyngby	h	3-2	*Gíslason, Olsen C., Johansen (p)*
15/5	København	a	0-3	
18/5	Randers	h	0-1	
24/5	EfB	a	1-2	*Olesen*

No	Name	Nat	Pos	Aps	(s)	Gls
1	John ALVBÅGE	SWE	G	21		
30	Alexander Juel ANDERSEN		D		(2)	
2	Jesper ANDERSEN		D	1	(1)	
3	Thomas ANDIE		D	5		
78	Zoltán BALOG	HUN	D	15		
9	Morten BERTOLT		M	9	(1)	1
3	Simeon BULGARU	MDA	D	7		
18	Luiz CARLOS	BRA	A	3	(2)	2
10	Alex DA SILVA	BRA	M	4	(3)	
15	Thomas FRANDSEN		M	17	(2)	1
17	Rurik GÍSLASON	ISL	A	12	(14)	2
24	Steffen HØJER		A	14	(3)	1
32	Dan Anton JOHANSEN		D	11		1
12	Kristian KIRK		G	1		
8	Lasse KRYGER		M	6	(11)	
21	Christian MUOMAIFE	NGA	A	9	(16)	5
7	Simon NAGEL		M	29		2
14	Jakob Glerup NIELSEN		M	23		1
19	Jacob OLESEN		A	6	(13)	2
11	Christian OLSEN		A	12	(3)	2
9	Petter Furuseth OLSEN	NOR	M	17		2
18	Suni OLSEN	FRO	M	4	(2)	1
27	Giorgi POPKHADZE	GEO	D	13	(1)	
10	Srđan RADONJIĆ	MNE	A	3	(2)	1
4	Mikkel RASK		D	19	(1)	1
23	Anders RASMUSSEN		G	3		
16	Robbie RUSSELL	USA	D	3	(1)	
28	Asbjørn SENNELS		D	32		1
5	Thomas TENGSTEDT		D	15		
20	Niclas TÜCHSEN		M	1	(1)	
26	Søren Ulrik VESTERGAARD		A	14	(1)	3
23	Robert VESELOVSKÝ	SVK	G	8		
6	Robert ÅHMAN-PERSSON	SWE	M	22	(5)	
11	Martin ÅSLUND	SWE	M	4	(4)	

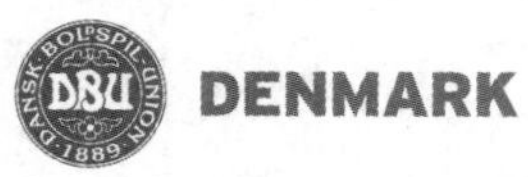

DENMARK

PROMOTED CLUBS

VEJLE BK

Coach – Ove Christensen

Founded - 1891

MAJOR HONOURS: Danish Championship – (5) 1958, 1971, 1972, 1978, 1984; Danish Cup - (6) 1958, 1959, 1972, 1975, 1977, 1981.

SØNDERJYSKE

Coach – Carsten Broe

Founded – 2004

SECOND LEVEL FINAL TABLE 2007/08

		Pld	W	D	L	F	A	Pts
1	Vejle BK	30	25	3	2	80	24	78
2	SønderjyskE	30	17	10	3	55	32	61
3	Silkeborg IF	30	16	9	5	60	33	57
4	Herfølge BK	30	15	6	9	55	43	51
5	FC Fredericia	30	12	8	10	49	36	44
6	Akademisk Bøldklub	30	11	8	11	38	36	41
7	Kolding FC	30	11	7	12	53	47	40
8	Næstved BK	30	11	7	12	36	39	40
9	Hvidovre IF	30	10	7	13	31	33	37
10	Skive IK	30	10	4	16	36	52	34
11	BK Frem	30	12	3	15	46	54	33
12	Lolland-Falster Alliancen	30	8	9	13	28	41	33
13	Køge BK	30	8	9	13	36	51	33
14	Hellerup IK	30	8	7	15	36	56	31
15	Aarhus Fremad	30	7	7	16	22	43	28
16	Ølstykke FC	30	4	6	20	20	61	18

N.B. BK Frem- 6 pts deducted.

DOMESTIC CUP 2007/08

LANDSPOKALTURNERINGEN

SECOND ROUND

(28/8/07)
BPI 0, Skive 6
Holbæk B&I 6, HIK 2
Raklev GI 0, Skjold 3
Søhus 1, FC Hjørring 3
(29/8/07)
Allerød 1, Brøndby 4
Brabrand 1, Fredericia 4
Brønshøj 2, Lolland-Falster Alliancen 5 *(aet)*
Dragør 0, Næstved 5
Fremad Amager 1, Herfølge 4
Glostrup 0, Lyngby 2
Greve Fodbold 1, Roskilde 0
Herlev 0, Randers 1
Hjørring AIK Frem 0, Kolding 3
Hobro 3, Holstebro 1
Jægersborg 0, Hvidovre 1
Jetsmark 1, Viborg 1-1 *(aet; 5-4 on pens.)*
Lejre 1, Nordsjælland 6
Marstal/Rise 0, Thisted 2
Odder IGF Fodbold 0, SønderjyskE 2
RIK/Knudsker 2, Værløse 3
Skovbakken 2, Vejle 6
Struer 0, Fyn 5
Sydvest 05 0, Horsens 10
Søllerød-Vedbæk 2, Ølstykke 6
Tåsinge 0, AGF 1
Vanløse 0, EfB 2
Varde 1, Aarhus Fremad 0
(5/9/07)
Svendborg 0, Silkeborg 2
Byes – AaB, FCK, Midtjylland, OB

THIRD ROUND

(25/9/07)
Jetsmark 2, Skive 3 (aet)
(26/9/07)
Fredericia 1, FCK 3
Fyn 0, AaB 2
FC Hjørring 0, Midtjylland 3
Greve Fodbold 4, Hobro 0
Herfølge 4, Lyngby 2
Holbæk B&I 0, SønderjyskE 1
Næstved 3, Horsens 2
Silkeborg 1, Brøndby 2
Skjold 1, Kolding 4
Thisted 0, AGF 2
Varde 7, Lolland-Falster Alliancen 3
Vejle 2, Nordsjælland 1
Værløse 1, EfB 4
Ølstykke 0, Randers 3
(27/9/07)
Hvidovre 0, OB 2

FOURTH ROUND

(31/10/07)
AGF 0, Midtjylland 1
Greve Fodbold 0, Skive 2
Næstved 5, Kolding 2
OB 0, Brøndby 1 *(aet)*
SønderjyskE 0, Randers 2 *(aet)*
Varde 0, FCK 4
Vejle 0, AaB 0 *(aet; 5-4 on pens.)*
(1/11/07)
Herfølge 0, EfB 1 *(aet)*

QUARTER-FINALS

(8/3/08)
Næstved 0, FCK 2 *(Almeida 56, Júnior 80)*
(9/3/08)
Brøndby 2 *(Gíslason 51, Rasmussen M. "Duncan" 59)*, Randers 1 *(Fabi*
Skive 0, EfB 4 *(Lange 14, 89, Bech 45, Murcy 61)*
Vejle 1 *(Larsen 26)*, Midtjylland 2 *(Oluwafemi 83p, 89p)*

SEMI-FINALS

(9/4/08 & 16/4/08)
FCK 0, EfB 1 *(Murcy 67)*
EfB 2 *(Bech 104, Lange 120)*, FCK 2 *(Jørgensen M. 67, Grønkjær 114) (*
(EfB 3-2)
(9/4/08 & 17/4/08)
Brøndby 3 *(Katongo 34, 73, Holmén 64)*, Midtjylland 0
Midtjylland 0, Brøndby 2 *(Katongo 10, Von Schlebrügge 81)*
(Brøndby 5-0)

FINAL

(1/5/08)
Parken, Copenhagen
BRØNDBY IF 3 *(Holmén 15, Schlebrügge 69, Retov 85)*
ESBJERG FB 2 *(Rieks 62, 79)*
Referee – *Larsen*
BRØNDBY – *Andersen, Randrup, Howard, Von Schlebrügge, Rasmusse Lorentzen (Mikkelsen 73), Gíslason, Holmén, Retov, Ericsson, Katongo (Daugaard 88).*
EFB – *Winde, Hansen, Onstad, Björck, Klarström, Rieks (Conboy 90), Jørgensen, Vingaard, Borges (Lange 46), Bech (Zimling 46), Murcy.*

Leading clubs lift ation's spirits

he failure of the national team to qualify for UEFA EURO 2008™ was a major bombshell for English football. It was the first time England had been sent from the UEFA European Championship finals 24 years. The pride of a nation was severely unded by the trials and tribulations of Steve Claren's underperforming side. But while nothing uld quite make up for the country's non-rticipation in the biggest football event of the year, ere was plenty of solace to be found in the llective performance of English teams in the UEFA ampions League.

a unit, the Premier League's four-strong presentation could not have performed any better. anchester United FC won the trophy, Chelsea FC ished runners-up, Liverpool FC went out in the mi-finals (to Chelsea), and Arsenal FC were minated in the quarter-finals (by Liverpool). Not one the four clubs fell to foreign opposition.

nited rule

ere could only, of course, be one winner, and anchester United, led by the indefatigable Sir Alex rguson, took the trophy for the third time, ercoming Chelsea on penalties after a 1-1 draw in a nse and thrilling final in Moscow. It would all have ded in tears for the Reds had John Terry, the Chelsea ptain, not slipped on the wet turf and fired his cisive spot-kick against the post. But in the year that arked the 50th anniversary of the Munich air saster, fate was on United's side, and Edwin van der r's subsequent save from Nicolas Anelka ensured at the most glamorous and popular club in England, rhaps the world, flew home with the trophy.

had been a close call, but United deserved their ctory. They went through the13-match campaign defeated and won every match at home. They ored 20 goals and conceded only six, and in istiano Ronaldo they boasted not only the mpetition's outstanding individual but also its top goalscorer, the Portuguese flier finding the net eight times and completing his tally with the opening goal in Moscow.

United breezed through their group, winning their first five matches. Olympique Lyonnais proved doughty opponents in the first knockout round, but a late equaliser by Carlos Tévez in France proved crucial, and Ronaldo's goal at Old Trafford saw United safely through. Next up was a re-match with AS Roma, the team United had crushed in the quarter-finals a year earlier and also re-encountered twice in the group stage. A 2-0 win in the Stadio Olimpico put Ferguson's men in command, and although United survived a missed Roma penalty in the return, another Tévez strike sealed their progress.

UEFA Champions League winner Wayne Rooney savours the moment in Moscow

It was United's turn to miss a penalty in the first leg of the semi-final, away to FC Barcelona, when Ronaldo blazed his kick wide in the opening minutes. Although Ferguson's team came away from Camp Nou with a 0-0 draw, the nagging feeling remained that Ronaldo's faux pas could prove crucial. Indeed, the Catalans raised their game considerably at Old Trafford, dominating possession and offering real attacking menace through Lionel Messi. But a thunderous long-range goal from Paul Scholes ultimately proved enough as United's defence, superbly marshalled by Rio Ferdinand and backed by a wall of noise from the crowd, held firm.

Manchester United's Cri
Ronaldo (foreground) cele
scoring the opening goal
UEFA Champions League fina
eighth of the compe

In Moscow, United got the goal, through Ronaldo's 26th-minute header, that their first-half dominance deserved, but the concession of an unfortunate equaliser just before the interval rocked them, and Chelsea were on top for long periods of the game thereafter. Ryan Giggs came off the bench to break Sir Bobby Charlton's club appearance record, and although he wasted a glorious opportunity in extra time, it was ultimately his coolly converted penalty – the 13th of the shoot-out – that proved conclusive. While Terry's miss negated an earlier one from Ronaldo, Tévez, Michael Carrick, Owen Hargreaves, Nani and Anderson all held their nerve before Van der Sar's save transported United to paradise.

Unforgettable season

Victory in Europe crowned an unforgettable season. Ten days before Moscow, United retained the Premier League title with a 2-0 win at Wigan Athletic FC. As in the UEFA Champions League, they were taken to the limit by Chelsea. The two rivals went into the final day separated only by United's vastly superior goal difference. Although they had led the race for several weeks, a 2-1 defeat at Stamford Bridge had left the defending champions vulnerable. The feeling was that anything less than victory at Wigan would let in Chelsea, who, unbeaten at home in the league for the fourth successive season, looked sure to beat lowly Bolton Wanderers FC – a team with nothing left to play for.

It was a nail-biting afternoon. United appeared in control when Ronaldo scored his 31st Premier League goal of the season, from the penalty spot, after 33 minutes, but a goal for Chelsea, just after the hour mark, ensured a fraught finale. It was only when Giggs slotted home Wayne Rooney's measured pass to make it 2-0 that United were home and dry. An extra cherry was even placed on top of their Premier League celebration cake when Bolton scored a stoppage-tim equaliser, enabling United to win the title on points rather than goal difference.

Chelsea's challenge was gallant and sustained, but, as in Europe, United were worthy winners. They had recovered from a stuttering start by registering eight successive victories, which enabled them to claw bac the deficit on autumnal pace-setters Arsenal FC. It wa after Christmas that United found their best form. Wit the exception of a second defeat by Manchester City FC – at Old Trafford on the day of the Munich commemoration – their form was rampant. The remarkable Ronaldo led the charge with an endless succession of riveting performances and incredible goals. One free-kick against Portsmouth FC was simpl sensational, while a back-heeled 'nutmeg' against Aston Villa FC was improvised impudence at his very best. A 2-1 home win over Arsenal effectively ended the Gunners' faltering challenge, and although Chelse clung on to their coat-tails to the finish, United came through to record their 17th domestic championship title – just one behind Liverpool.

naldo, with 42 goals in all competitions, enjoyed a ison beyond belief, but the Player and Footballer of : Year was no one-man show. Ferdinand was mendous in defence and a good stand-in skipper the permanently injured Gary Neville. Wes Brown, manja Vidić and Patrice Evra also performed nsistently well, giving United the best defensive ures in the league. Unusually, United's midfield was settled. Carrick was the only constant, but new ning Anderson, technical and powerful, looked a eful buy, as did the hard-working Hargreaves when Ronaldo worked his magic on both wings as well as front of goal, but with Louis Saha forever injured ere was no specialist centre-forward, which placed a avy burden on Rooney and Tévez. The former, uffled from position to position, showed his true m only sporadically, but the latter, another wcomer, was more consistent and scored several cial goals.

helsea choked

elsea, twice so close to glory, ended up with thing. It was the first season since 2003/04 – the one fore José Mourinho's arrival – that they ended a mpaign empty-handed. Mourinho, sensationally, t his job in mid-September after a home draw ainst Rosenborg BK. Club owner Roman ramovich appointed unassuming 'technical director' ram Grant, the former national coach of Israel, to place him. It was a surprising choice, and inevitably l to fears that the team would self-destruct. But thing of the sort happened. Grant's record turned t to be exceptional. He steered the Blues to the final the UEFA Champions League – a feat beyond his edecessor - and was within one miscued penalty of nning the trophy. He also led the team on an beaten 21-match run in the league that came within whisker of snatching the domestic title.

t Grant would not be permitted a second chance. In e immediate aftermath of the UEFA Champions ague final he was sacked. It was a harsh, ruthless cision, but it was also no surprise. Many journalists peared to have it in for the Israeli from the start, and hough Grant kept confounding their prejudices with results, the press got their wish in the end. Unlike counterpart at United, the Chelsea manager did t have a permanently in-form megastar to rely on. though Chelsea had a huge squad, with adequate ver for every position, no individuals consistently one. Joe Cole came back well from injury to provide ir and creativity, and Petr Čech and Frank Lampard continued to do what was expected of them, but Didier Drogba, though an explosive presence when he played, missed a lot of matches, and there were extended spells on the sidelines also for Terry, Ricardo Carvalho and Michael Essien. Michael Ballack finally came into imperious form in the second half of the season but he was absent for the whole of the first half. Given the disruption, Grant's achievements bordered on the miraculous.

Chelsea's ability to grind out results was in stark contrast to Arsenal, who played much the better, more entertaining football but failed to stand the test of time and dropped out of contention for silverware long before the season's dénouement. Arsène Wenger's team made a terrific start to life after Thierry Henry. As their all-time top scorer struggled at FC Barcelona, the team he left behind took the Premier League by storm. With young Cesc Fàbregas pulling the strings in midfield and Emmanuel Adebayor and Robin van Persie banging in the goals, they soared to the summit of the table and, even after the Dutchman was lost (again) to injury, remained there until well into the New Year.

Arsenal falter

In the early spring, however, Arsenal went five games without a win. The start of their malaise was an infamous game at Birmingham City FC, in which new signing Eduardo suffered a horrendous injury. With his team-mates in shock at the damage done to his

Cesc Fàbregas (right) is consoled by fellow Spaniard Xabi Alonso as Arsenal go out of the UEFA Champions League to Liverpool

The Football Association (FA)

25 Soho Square
GB-London W1D 4FA
tel - +44 207 7454545
fax - +44 207 7454546
website - www.thefa.com
email - info@thefa.com
Year of Formation – 1863
Chairman – Lord David Triesman
Chief Executive – Brian Barwick
Press Officer – Adrian Bevington
Stadium – Wembley, London (90,000)

INTERNATIONAL HONOURS
FIFA World Cup - (1) 1966.

INTERNATIONAL TOURNAMENT APPEARANCES
FIFA World Cup - (11) 1950, 1954 (qtr-finals), 1958, 1962 (qtr-finals), 1966 (Winners), 19 (qtr-finals), 1982 (2nd phase), 1986 (qtr-finals), 1990 (4th), 1998 (2nd round), 2002 (qtr-finals), 2006 (qtr-finals).
UEFA European Championship - (7) 1968 (3rd), 1980, 1988, 1992, 1996 (semi-finals), 2000, 2004 (qtr-finals).

TOP FIVE ALL-TIME CAPS
Peter Shilton (125); Bobby Moore (108); Bobby Charlton (106); Billy Wright (105); David Beckham (102)

TOP FIVE ALL-TIME GOALS
Bobby Charlton (49); Gary Lineker (48); Jimmy Greaves (44); Michael Owen (40); Alan Shearer, Nat Lofthouse & Tom Finney (30)

NATIONAL TEAM RESULTS 2007/08

22/8/07	Germany	H	Wembley	1-2	*Lampard (9)*
8/9/07	Israel (ECQ)	H	Wembley	3-0	*Wright-Phillips (20), Owen (50), Richards (66)*
12/9/07	Russia (ECQ)	H	Wembley	3-0	*Owen (7, 31), Ferdinand (84)*
13/10/07	Estonia (ECQ)	H	Wembley	3-0	*Wright-Phillips (11), Rooney (32), Rähn (33og)*
17/10/07	Russia (ECQ)	A	Moscow	1-2	*Rooney (29)*
16/11/07	Austria	A	Vienna	1-0	*Crouch (44)*
21/11/07	Croatia (ECQ)	H	Wembley	2-3	*Lampard (56p), Crouch (65)*
6/2/08	Switzerland	H	Wembley	2-1	*Jenas (40), Wright-Phillips (62)*
26/3/08	France	A	Saint-Denis	0-1	
28/5/08	United States	H	Wembley	2-0	*Terry (38), Gerrard (59)*
1/6/08	Trinidad & Tobago	A	Port of Spain	3-0	*Barry (12), Defoe (15, 49)*

NATIONAL TEAM APPEARANCES 2007/08

Coach – Steve McCLAREN 3/5/61 /(14/12/07) Fabio CAPELLO (ITA) 18/6/46			**Ger**	**ISR**	**RUS**	**EST**	**RUS**	**Aut**	**CRO**	**Sui**	**Fra**	**Usa**	**Tri**	**Caps**
Paul ROBINSON	15/10/79	Tottenham	G46	G	G	G	G							41
Micah RICHARDS	24/6/88	Man. City	D	D	D	D	D	D	D					11
Rio FERDINAND	7/11/78	Man. United	D46	D	D	D46	D			D	D	D	D46	68
John TERRY	7/12/80	Chelsea	D	D	D						D46	D		44
Nicky SHOREY	19/2/81	Reading	D											2
David BECKHAM	2/5/75	LA Galaxy (USA)	M					M62	s46		M63	M46	M46	102

TIONAL TEAM APPEARANCES 2007/08 (contd.)

			Ger	ISR	RUS	EST	RUS	Aut	CRO	Sui	Fra	Usa	Tri	Caps	Goals
AMPARD	20/6/78	Chelsea	M			s70	s79	M	M			M57		61	14
CARRICK	28/7/81	Man. United	M55											14	-
E	8/11/81	Chelsea	M70	M	M88	M	M80	M46	M80	M57	M46	s78		50	7
ITH	28/10/80	Newcastle	A57					s73						19	1
OWEN	14/12/79	Newcastle	A57	A	A91	A70	A	A34			s46			89	40
AMES	1/8/70	Portsmouth	s46							G	G	G	G46	39	-
OWN	13/10/79	Man. United	s46					s46		D	D63	D57		17	-
BARRY	23/2/81	Aston Villa	s55	M	M	M	M	s46	M46	M74	M	s57	M	20	1
ROUCH	30/1/81	Liverpool	s57		s80		s80	A73	A	s57	s46	s69	s46	28	14
OYER	29/12/78	West Ham	s57											33	-
VRIGHT-PHILLIPS	25/10/81	Chelsea	s70	M82	M	M	M80		M46	s57				19	4
COLE	20/12/80	Chelsea		D	D	D49				D74	D	D82		64	-
GERRARD	30/5/80	Liverpool		M70	M	M	M	M46	M	M	M46	M	M	67	13
ESKEY	11/1/78	Wigan		A70	A80									45	5
VILLE	21/1/77	Everton		s70	s88	s49								59	-
JOHNSON	10/2/81	Everton		s70										8	-
ENTLEY	27/8/84	Blackburn		s82				s62		M	s63	s46	s46	6	-
DOWNING	22/7/84	Middlesbrough			s91		s80				s46		M58	18	-
MPBELL	18/9/74	Portsmouth				D	D	D46	D					73	1
ROONEY	24/10/85	Man. United				A	A			A87	A46	A78		43	14
ESCOTT	16/8/82	Everton				s46	D79	D	D		s46			5	-
ARSON	3/9/85	Aston Villa						G	G					2	-
BRIDGE	5/8/80	Chelsea						D	D	s74		s82	D84	30	1
DEFOE	7/10/82	Tottenham /Portsmouth						s34	s46			A69	A69	28	5
OUNG	9/7/85	Aston Villa						s46		s87			s58	3	-
BENT	6/2/84	Tottenham							s80					3	-
v UPSON	18/4/79	West Ham								D				8	-
e JENAS	18/2/83	Tottenham								M57				18	1
ARGREAVES	20/1/81	Man. United								s74	M	M		42	-
HNSON	23/8/84	Portsmouth									s63	s57	D	8	-
n WOODGATE	22/1/80	Tottenham											D	7	-
SHTON	24/11/83	West Ham											A46	1	-
RT	19/4/87	Man. City											s46	1	-
IELKA	17/8/82	Everton											s46	1	-
ALCOTT	16/3/89	Arsenal											s69	2	-
n WARNOCK	12/12/81	Blackburn											s84	1	-

Manager Harry Redknapp and captain Sol Campbell pose with the FA Cup after Portsmouth's victory over Cardiff at We

shattered left ankle and lower leg, there was a surreal atmosphere to the contest, but victory appeared to be Arsenal's until a controversial late penalty, which, with captain William Gallas having stomped off to the halfway line in protest, the home side converted to draw 2-2. Arsenal would show their mettle with a brilliant Fàbregas-inspired display in the San Siro to eliminate AC Milan from the UEFA Champions League, but domestically their form deserted them, and a pair of 2-1 defeats at Chelsea and Manchester United – after they had led in both games – finished off their challenge.

Taken apart by Tottenham in the semi-finals of the League Cup and destroyed by United in the fifth round of the FA Cup, Arsenal's bid for European glory was shattered by Liverpool, who scored two late goals at Anfield to win the tie 5-3 on aggregate. Once again, Liverpool's best form was reserved for the UEFA Champions League, where they recovered from a terrible start to crush Beşiktaş JK 8-0, hammer Olympique de Marseille 4-0, and comprehensively beat Italian league leaders FC Internazionale Milano before seeing off Arsenal. They would probably have overcome Chelsea, too, but for an own-goal conceded in the last seconds of the home leg. Their hopes of reaching a third final in four years ended in extra time at Stamford Bridge.

The Merseysiders' anticipated challenge for the Prem League title petered out at a relatively early stage. Despite the magnificence of new record signing Fernando Torres, who scored 24 goals in the league, and the continuing excellence of skipper Steven Gerrard, Liverpool could not win the games that rea mattered. They drew twice against both Chelsea anc Arsenal and were beaten home and away by Manchester United. A proliferation of drawn matche against some of the lesser clubs put paid to any lingering hopes of a first national title in 18 years, w a humiliating home defeat to Barnsley FC skewered their FA Cup ambitions.

Pompey's Cup

Barnsley would also kill another giant in the quarter-finals, beating Chelsea 1-0 at home. With Mancheste United also exiting the competition, after a 1-0 defe at Old Trafford against Portsmouth, and another cou of Championship (second level) clubs, Cardiff City FC and West Bromwich Albion FC, winning the other tw ties, the FA Cup was left with an unusual semi-final cast. Both semi-finals were staged at Wembley and both finished 1-0, with Portsmouth beating West Brc and Cardiff bringing Barnsley's heroic run to an end. The final, too, ended 1-0, Pompey's Nigerian striker vankwo Kanu scoring the winner – as he had in the mi-final – to give the south coast club their first ophy for 58 years and enable them to qualify for rope for the first time. It was a sweet victory, too, for e club's manager, Harry Redknapp, who thus llected the first major honour of his career.

ttenham qualified for the UEFA Cup as League Cup nners. They lost manager Martin Jol after a bad start d gained Juande Ramos, the highly regarded aniard who had won successive UEFA Cups with villa FC. Spurs threw everything into the knockout mpetitions. Manchester United ended their interest the FA Cup, and the new manager's bid for a hat-ck of UEFA Cup wins ended with a penalty shoot-out feat at PSV Eindhoven, but they came good in the ague Cup, coming from behind to beat Chelsea in e Wembley final with a strange headed winner from d-season signing Jonathan Woodgate. Almost better an that, though, was the 5-1 annihilation of arch-als Arsenal (albeit not their first XI) in the second leg the semi-final.

erton FC took the only UEFA Cup place available rough the Premier League, David Moyes' team ishing clear in fifth place – five points above Martin Neill's Aston Villa , who, winless in their last three mes, had to make do with a UEFA Intertoto Cup ace. Both clubs enjoyed progressive seasons, hough Everton shared Tottenham's anguish in exiting e UEFA Cup on penalties at the round-of-16 stage, aten by ACF Fiorentina after a rousing second-leg splay at Goodison Park. With Bolton also departing in e same round, there was no English representation in e UEFA Cup quarter-finals – quite a contrast to the ccess of the 'Big Four' in the UEFA Champions League d a particular disappointment given that the final as to take place at the City of Manchester Stadium. e residents of that impressive arena, Manchester City, d a season of two halves – splendid in the autumn, etched in the spring. Had it been the other way und, former England manager Sven Göran Eriksson ght have survived, but despite the club's ninth-place ish, he was sacked, his job going to another former ternational manager, Mark Hughes, who had just ken Blackburn Rovers FC to seventh.

ewly promoted Derby County FC officially became e Premier League's worst ever team as they toiled eir way to a measly eleven points. The scrap to avoid e other two relegation places remained intense to e end, with Fulham FC staging a great escape under oy Hodgson to send Reading FC and Birmingham down on the final day. West Brom won the Championship but there was a big surprise as fellow Midlanders Stoke City FC went up with them and a shock of seismic proportions as Hull City AFC, alien to England's top flight hitherto, won the play-offs, beating Bristol City FC 1-0 in the final at Wembley with a brilliant goal from veteran hometown hero Dean Windass.

England out

There was no fairytale finish at Wembley to England's UEFA EURO 2008™ qualifying campaign. It ended in utter disaster, and elimination, as they lost 3-2 to already qualified Croatia. What made the defeat harder to swallow was that, with Israel having done them a favour four days earlier by beating rivals Russia 2-1, England needed only a draw to qualify. Short of key players and confidence, they made a terrible, nerve-ridden start but rallied well to draw level at 2-2 with a brilliant goal by Peter Crouch, only to fall apart again at the end and concede a third, fatal goal.

McClaren was summarily dismissed the following day, his 18-month reign entering the archives as the least

Steve McClaren – a figure of dejection as England lose in the rain to Croatia

distinguished of any England manager. The FA decided that, as the experiment with an Englishman had gone so badly wrong, they would swing the pendulum back in the other direction and hire a renowned, top-of-the-range foreigner. Enter Fabio Capello, an Italian of impeccable club pedigree but with no previous experience of English football or – David Beckham apart – English footballers. He began his reign with three wins and a defeat, and he also started to speak English. His big test, though, would come in the autumn with the start of the 2010 FIFA World Cup qualifiers. Perish the thought that England, with such an illustrious figurehead, should fail again, but with Croatia again in their group (along with Ukraine, Belarus, Kazakhstan and Andorra), and big decisions to be made with regard to the goalkeeping position and who to play up front (areas in which resources are decidedly thin), qualification is far from guaranteed.

England's clubs rule the continent, but the national team is in disarray. If the FA's stated target for the team – to reach the semi-finals in South Africa - is to come even close to being realised, it will take more than just a quick fix. Signor Capello is going to have to earn his money.

DOMESTIC LEAGUE 2007/08

PREMIER LEAGUE FINAL TABLE

		Home					Away					Total					
	Pld	W	D	L	F	A	W	D	L	F	A	W	D	L	F	A	Pts
1 Manchester United FC	38	17	1	1	47	7	10	5	4	33	15	27	6	5	80	22	87
2 Chelsea FC	38	12	7	0	36	13	13	3	3	29	13	25	10	3	65	26	85
3 Arsenal FC	38	14	5	0	37	11	10	6	3	37	20	24	11	3	74	31	83
4 Liverpool FC	38	12	6	1	43	13	9	7	3	24	15	21	13	4	67	28	76
5 Everton FC	38	11	4	4	34	17	8	4	7	21	16	19	8	11	55	33	65
6 Aston Villa FC	38	10	3	6	34	22	6	9	4	37	29	16	12	10	71	51	60
7 Blackburn Rovers FC	38	8	7	4	26	19	7	6	6	24	29	15	13	10	50	48	58
8 Portsmouth FC	38	7	8	4	24	14	9	1	9	24	26	16	9	13	48	40	57
9 Manchester City FC	38	11	4	4	28	20	4	6	9	17	33	15	10	13	45	53	55
10 West Ham United FC	38	7	7	5	24	24	6	3	10	18	26	13	10	15	42	50	49
11 Tottenham Hotspur FC	38	8	5	6	46	34	3	8	8	20	27	11	13	14	66	61	46
12 Newcastle United FC	38	8	5	6	25	26	3	5	11	20	39	11	10	17	45	65	43
13 Middlesbrough FC	38	7	5	7	27	23	3	7	9	16	30	10	12	16	43	53	42
14 Wigan Athletic FC	38	8	5	6	21	17	2	5	12	13	34	10	10	18	34	51	40
15 Sunderland AFC	38	9	3	7	23	21	2	3	14	13	38	11	6	21	36	59	39
16 Bolton Wanderers FC	38	7	5	7	23	18	2	5	12	13	36	9	10	19	36	54	37
17 Fulham FC	38	5	5	9	22	31	3	7	9	16	29	8	12	18	38	60	36
18 Reading FC	38	8	2	9	19	25	2	4	13	22	41	10	6	22	41	66	36
19 Birmingham City FC	38	6	8	5	30	23	2	3	14	16	39	8	11	19	46	62	35
20 Derby County FC	38	1	5	13	12	43	0	3	16	8	46	1	8	29	20	89	11

TOP GOALSCORERS

31 CRISTIANO RONALDO (Man. United)

24 Emmanuel ADEBAYOR (Arsenal)
FERNANDO TORRES (Liverpool)

19 Roque SANTA CRUZ (Blackburn)

15 Dimitar BERBATOV (Tottenham)
Robbie KEANE (Tottenham)
BENJANI Mwaruwari (Portsmouth/Man. City)
YAKUBU Aiyegbeni (Everton)

14 Carlos TÉVEZ (Man. United)

13 John CAREW (Aston Villa)

CLUB-BY-CLUB

ARSENAL FC

Manager – Arsène Wenger (FRA)

Founded - 1886

MAJOR HONOURS: UEFA Cup Winners' Cup - (1) 1994; Inter Cities Fairs Cup - (1) 1970; English League - (13) 1931, 1933, 1934, 1935, 1938, 1948, 1953, 1971, 1989, 1991, 1998, 2002, 2004; FA Cup - (10) 1930, 1936, 1950, 1971, 1979, 1993, 1998, 2002, 2003, 2005; League Cup - (2) 1987, 1993.

2007

12/8	Fulham	h	2-1	*Van Persie (p), Hleb*
19/8	Blackburn	a	1-1	*Van Persie*
25/8	Man. City	h	1-0	*Fàbregas*
2/9	Portsmouth	h	3-1	*Adebayor (p), Fàbregas, Rosický*
15/9	Tottenham	a	3-1	*Adebayor 2, Fàbregas*
22/9	Derby	h	5-0	*Diaby, Adebayor 3 (1p), Fàbregas*
29/9	West Ham	a	1-0	*Van Persie*
7/10	Sunderland	h	3-2	*Van Persie 2, Senderos*
20/10	Bolton	h	2-0	*Touré, Rosický*
28/10	Liverpool	a	1-1	*Fàbregas*
3/11	Man. United	h	2-2	*Fàbregas, Gallas*
12/11	Reading	a	3-1	*Flamini, Adebayor, Hleb*
24/11	Wigan	h	2-0	*Gallas, Rosický*
1/12	Aston Villa	a	2-1	*Flamini, Adebayor*

2	Newcastle	a	1-1	*Adebayor*
2	Middlesbrough	a	1-2	*Rosický*
12	Chelsea	h	1-0	*Gallas*
12	Tottenham	h	2-1	*Adebayor, Bendtner*
12	Portsmouth	a	0-0	
12	Everton	a	4-1	*Eduardo 2, Adebayor, Rosický*
8				
	West Ham	h	2-0	*Eduardo, Adebayor*
	Birmingham	h	1-1	*Adebayor (p)*
	Fulham	a	3-0	*Adebayor 2, Rosický*
	Newcastle	h	3-0	*Adebayor, Flamini, Fàbregas*
	Man. City	a	3-1	*Adebayor 2, Eduardo*
2	Blackburn	h	2-0	*Senderos, Adebayor*
2	Birmingham	a	2-2	*Walcott 2*
	Aston Villa	h	1-1	*Bendtner*
	Wigan	a	0-0	
3	Middlesbrough	h	1-1	*Touré*
3	Chelsea	a	1-2	*Sagna*
3	Bolton	a	3-2	*Gallas, Van Persie (p), og (Samuel)*
	Liverpool	h	1-1	*Bendtner*
4	Man. United	a	1-2	*Adebayor*
4	Reading	h	2-0	*Adebayor, Gilberto Silva*
4	Derby	a	6-2	*Bendtner, Van Persie, Adebayor 3, Walcott*
	Everton	h	1-0	*Bendtner*
5	Sunderland	a	1-0	*Walcott*

Name	Nat	Pos	Aps	(s)	Gls
Emmanuel ADEBAYOR	TOG	A	32	(4)	24
Manuel ALMUNIA	ESP	G	29		
Nicklas BENDTNER	DEN	A	7	(20)	5
Gaël CLICHY	FRA	D	37	(1)	
DENILSON Pereira Neves	BRA	M	4	(9)	
Abou DIABY	FRA	M	9	(6)	1
Lassana DIARRA	FRA	M	4	(3)	
Johan DJOUROU	SUI	D	1	(1)	
Emmanuel EBOUÉ	CIV	M	20	(3)	
EDUARDO da Silva	CRO	A	13	(4)	4
Łukasz FABIAŃSKI	POL	G	3		
Cesc FÀBREGAS	ESP	M	32		7
Mathieu FLAMINI	FRA	M	30		3
William GALLAS	FRA	D	31		4
GILBERTO Aparecido da SILVA	BRA	M	12	(11)	1
Aleksandr HLEB	BLR	M	29	(2)	2
Justin HOYTE		D	2	(3)	
Jens LEHMANN	GER	G	6	(1)	
Mark RANDALL		M		(1)	
Tomáš ROSICKÝ	CZE	M	15	(3)	6
Bacary SAGNA	FRA	D	29		1
Philippe SENDEROS	SUI	D	14	(3)	2
Alexandre SONG BILLONG	CMR	M	5	(4)	
Kolo TOURÉ	CIV	D	29	(1)	2
Armand TRAORÉ	FRA	D	1	(2)	
Robin VAN PERSIE	NED	A	13	(2)	7
Theo WALCOTT		A	11	(14)	4

ASTON VILLA FC

Manager – Martin O'Neill (NIR)

Founded - 1874

AJOR HONOURS: European Champion Clubs' Cup - (1) 1982; UEFA er Cup - (1) 1982; English League - (7) 1894, 1896, 1897, 1899, 1900, 910, 1981; FA Cup - (7) 1887, 1895, 1897, 1905, 1913, 1920, 1957; League Cup - (5) 1961, 1975, 1977, 1994, 1996.

3	Liverpool	h	1-2	*Barry (p)*
3	Newcastle	a	0-0	
3	Fulham	h	2-1	*Young, Maloney*
2/9	Chelsea	h	2-0	*Knight, Agbonlahor*
16/9	Man. City	a	0-1	
23/9	Everton	h	2-0	*Carew, Agbonlahor*
1/10	Tottenham	a	4-4	*Laursen 2, Agbonlahor, Gardner*
6/10	West Ham	h	1-0	*Gardner*
20/10	Man. United	h	1-4	*Agbonlahor*
28/10	Bolton	a	1-1	*Moore*
3/11	Derby	h	2-0	*Laursen, Young*
11/11	Birmingham	a	2-1	*og (Ridgewell), Agbonlahor*
24/11	Middlesbrough	a	3-0	*Carew, Mellberg, Agbonlahor*
28/11	Blackburn	a	4-0	*Carew, Barry (p), Young, Harewood*
1/12	Arsenal	h	1-2	*Gardner*
8/12	Portsmouth	h	1-3	*Barry (p)*
15/12	Sunderland	a	1-1	*Maloney*
22/12	Man. City	h	1-1	*Carew*
26/12	Chelsea	a	4-4	*Maloney 2, Laursen, Barry (p)*
29/12	Wigan	a	2-1	*Davies, Agbonlahor*
2008				
1/1	Tottenham	h	2-1	*Mellberg, Laursen*
12/1	Reading	h	3-1	*Carew 2, Laursen*
21/1	Liverpool	a	2-2	*Harewood, og (Fábio Aurélio)*
26/1	Blackburn	h	1-1	*Young*
3/2	Fulham	a	1-2	*og (Hughes)*
9/2	Newcastle	h	4-1	*Bouma, Carew 3 (1p)*
24/2	Reading	a	2-1	*Young, Harewood*
1/3	Arsenal	a	1-1	*og (Senderos)*
12/3	Middlesbrough	h	1-1	*Barry (p)*
15/3	Portsmouth	a	0-2	
22/3	Sunderland	h	0-1	
29/3	Man. United	a	0-4	
5/4	Bolton	h	4-0	*Barry 2, Agbonlahor, Harewood*
12/4	Derby	a	6-0	*Young, Carew, Petrov, Barry, Agbonlahor, Harewood*
20/4	Birmingham	h	5-1	*Young 2, Carew 2, Agbonlahor*
27/4	Everton	a	2-2	*Agbonlahor, Carew*
3/5	Wigan	h	0-2	
11/5	West Ham	a	2-2	*Young, Barry*

No	Name	Nat	Pos	Aps	(s)	Gls
11	Gabriel AGBONLAHOR		A	37		11
6	Gareth BARRY		M	37		9
23	Patrik BERGER	CZE	M		(8)	
3	Wilfred BOUMA	NED	D	38		1
21	Gary CAHILL		D		(1)	
10	John CAREW	NOR	A	32		13
22	Scott CARSON		G	35		
15	Curtis DAVIES		D	9	(3)	1
26	Craig GARDNER		M	15	(8)	3
9	Marlon HAREWOOD		A	1	(22)	5
16	Zat KNIGHT		D	25	(2)	1
5	Martin LAURSEN	DEN	D	38		6
28	Shaun MALONEY	SCO	A	11	(11)	4
4	Olof MELLBERG	SWE	D	33	(1)	2
8	Luke MOORE		A	8	(7)	1
27	Isaiah OSBOURNE		M	1	(7)	
19	Stilian PETROV	BUL	M	22	(6)	1
20	Nigel REO-COKER		M	36		
18	Wayne ROUTLEDGE		M		(1)	
17	Moustapha SALIFOU	TOG	A		(4)	
13	Stuart TAYLOR		G	3	(1)	
7	Ashley YOUNG		M	37		9

ENGLAND

BIRMINGHAM CITY FC

Manager – Steve Bruce; (19/11/07) (Eric Black (SCO)); (28/11/07) Alex McLeish (SCO)

Founded - 1875

MAJOR HONOURS: League Cup – (1) 1963.

Date	Opponent		Score	Scorers
2007				
12/8	Chelsea	a	2-3	*Forssell, Kapo*
15/8	Sunderland	h	2-2	*og (McShane), O'Connor*
18/8	West Ham	h	0-1	
25/8	Derby	a	2-1	*Jerome 2*
1/9	Middlesbrough	a	0-2	
15/9	Bolton	h	1-0	*Kapo*
22/9	Liverpool	a	0-0	
29/9	Man. United	h	0-1	
7/10	Blackburn	a	1-2	*Jerome*
20/10	Man. City	a	0-1	
27/10	Wigan	h	3-2	*Kapo 2 (1p), Ridgewell*
3/11	Everton	a	1-3	*Kapo*
11/11	Aston Villa	h	1-2	*Forssell*
24/11	Portsmouth	h	0-2	
2/12	Tottenham	a	3-2	*McSheffrey (p), Jerome, Larsson*
8/12	Newcastle	a	1-2	*Jerome*
15/12	Reading	h	1-1	*Forssell*
22/12	Bolton	a	0-3	
26/12	Middlesbrough	h	3-0	*og (Downing), Forssell, McSheffrey (p)*
29/12	Fulham	h	1-1	*Larsson*
2008				
1/1	Man. United	a	0-1	
12/1	Arsenal	a	1-1	*O'Connor*
19/1	Chelsea	h	0-1	
29/1	Sunderland	a	0-2	
2/2	Derby	h	1-1	*Larsson*
9/2	West Ham	a	1-1	*McFadden (p)*
23/2	Arsenal	h	2-2	*McFadden 2 (1p)*
1/3	Tottenham	h	4-1	*Forssell 3, Larsson*
12/3	Portsmouth	a	2-4	*Muamba, Larsson*
17/3	Newcastle	h	1-1	*McFadden*
22/3	Reading	a	1-2	*Zárate*
29/3	Man. City	h	3-1	*Zárate 2, McSheffrey (p)*
5/4	Wigan	a	0-2	
12/4	Everton	h	1-1	*Zárate*
20/4	Aston Villa	a	1-5	*Forssell*
26/4	Liverpool	h	2-2	*Forssell, Larsson*
3/5	Fulham	a	0-2	
11/5	Blackburn	h	4-1	*Murphy, Jerome 2, Muamba*

No	Name	Nat	Pos	Aps	(s)	Gls
17	Neil DANNS		M		(2)	
20	Daniël DE RIDDER	NED	M	6	(4)	
16	Johan DJOUROU	SUI	D	13		
13	Colin DOYLE	IRL	G	3		
9	Mikael FORSSELL	FIN	A	21	(9)	9
24	Radhi JAIDI	TUN	D	18		
10	Cameron JEROME		A	21	(12)	7
22	Damien JOHNSON	NIR	M	17		
23	Olivier KAPO	FRA	M	22	(4)	5
2	Stephen KELLY	IRL	D	38		
18	Richard KINGSON	GHA	G	1		
7	Sebastian LARSSON	SWE	M	32	(3)	6
16	James McFADDEN	SCO	A	10	(2)	4
11	Gary McSHEFFREY		A	24	(8)	3
26	Fabrice MUAMBA		M	37		2
14	David MURPHY		D	14		1
12	Mehdi NAFTI	TUN	M	19	(7)	
8	Garry O'CONNOR	SCO	A	5	(18)	2
29	Borja OUBIÑA Meléndez	ESP	D	1	(1)	
28	Wilson PALACIOS	HON	M	4	(3)	
21	Stuart PARNABY		D	4	(9)	
15	Franck QUEUDRUE	FRA	D	14	(2)	
6	Liam RIDGEWELL		D	35		1
3	Mathew SADLER		D	3	(2)	
5	Rafael SCHMITZ	BRA	D	12	(3)	
1	Maik TAYLOR	NIR	G	34		
4	Martin TAYLOR		D	4		
19	Mauro ZÁRATE	ARG	A	6	(8)	4

BLACKBURN ROVERS FC

Manager – Mark Hughes (WAL)

Founded - 1875

MAJOR HONOURS: English League - (3) 1912, 1914, 1995; FA Cup - 1884, 1885, 1886, 1890, 1891, 1928; League Cup - (1) 2002.

Date	Opponent		Score	Scorers
2007				
11/8	Middlesbrough	a	2-1	*Santa Cruz, Derbysh*
19/8	Arsenal	h	1-1	*Dunn*
25/8	Everton	a	1-1	*Santa Cruz*
2/9	Man. City	h	1-0	*McCarthy*
15/9	Chelsea	a	0-0	
23/9	Portsmouth	h	0-1	
29/9	Sunderland	a	2-1	*Bentley, Santa Cruz*
7/10	Birmingham	h	2-1	*Bentley, McCarthy (p*
20/10	Reading	h	4-2	*McCarthy 2 (1p), Sar Cruz, Tugay*
28/10	Tottenham	a	2-1	*McCarthy, Samba*
3/11	Liverpool	h	0-0	
11/11	Man. United	a	0-2	
25/11	Fulham	a	2-2	*Emerton, Warnock*
28/11	Aston Villa	h	0-4	
1/12	Newcastle	h	3-1	*Bentley 2, Tugay*
9/12	West Ham	h	0-1	
15/12	Wigan	a	3-5	*Santa Cruz 3*
23/12	Chelsea	h	0-1	
27/12	Man. City	a	2-2	*Santa Cruz 2*
30/12	Derby	a	2-1	*Santa Cruz, Bentley*
2008				
2/1	Sunderland	h	1-0	*McCarthy (p)*
13/1	Bolton	a	2-1	*Samba, Roberts*
19/1	Middlesbrough	h	1-1	*Derbyshire*
26/1	Aston Villa	a	1-1	*Santa Cruz*
2/2	Everton	h	0-0	
11/2	Arsenal	a	0-2	
24/2	Bolton	h	4-1	*McCarthy 2 (2p), Bentley, Gamst Pedersen*
1/3	Newcastle	a	1-0	*Derbyshire*
8/3	Fulham	h	1-1	*Gamst Pedersen*
15/3	West Ham	a	1-2	*Santa Cruz*
22/3	Wigan	h	3-1	*Santa Cruz 2, Robert*
29/3	Reading	a	0-0	
5/4	Tottenham	h	1-1	*Gamst Pedersen*
13/4	Liverpool	a	1-3	*Santa Cruz*
19/4	Man. United	h	1-1	*Santa Cruz*
27/4	Portsmouth	a	1-0	*Santa Cruz*
3/5	Derby	h	3-1	*Santa Cruz 2, Roberts*
11/5	Birmingham	a	1-4	*Gamst Pedersen*

No	Name	Nat	Pos	Aps	(s)	Gl
11	David BENTLEY		M	37		6
20	Bruno BERNER	SUI	D	2		
27	Matt DERBYSHIRE		A	4	(19)	3
19	David DUNN		M	25	(6)	1
7	Brett EMERTON	AUS	M	31	(2)	1
1	Brad FRIEDEL	USA	G	38		
12	Morten GAMST PEDERSEN	NOR	M	32	(5)	4
13	Zurab KHIZANISHVILI	GEO	D	10	(3)	
10	Benni McCARTHY	RSA	A	21	(10)	8

Aaron MOKOENA	RSA	D	8	(10)	
Ryan NELSEN	NZL	D	22		
Martin OLSSON	SWE	D		(2)	
André OOIJER	NED	D	23	(4)	
Steven REID	IRL	M	20	(4)	
Maceo RIGTERS	NED	A		(2)	
Jason ROBERTS	GRN	A	11	(15)	3
Christopher SAMBA	CGO	D	33		2
Roque SANTA CRUZ	PAR	A	36	(1)	19
Robbie SAVAGE	WAL	M	10	(2)	
TUGAY Kerimoğlu	TUR	M	12	(8)	2
Johann VOGEL	SUI	M	6		
Stephen WARNOCK		D	37		1

BOLTON WANDERERS FC

Manager – Sammy Lee; (18/10/07) (Archie Knox (SCO)); (25/10/07) Gary Megson

Founded - 1874

MAJOR HONOURS: FA Cup - (4) 1923, 1926, 1929, 1958.

7				
	Newcastle	h	1-3	*Anelka*
	Fulham	a	1-2	*Helguson*
	Portsmouth	a	1-3	*Anelka*
	Reading	h	3-0	*Speed, Anelka, Braaten*
	Everton	h	1-2	*Anelka*
	Birmingham	a	0-1	
	Tottenham	h	1-1	*Iván Campo*
	Derby	a	1-1	*Anelka*
	Chelsea	h	0-1	
0	Arsenal	a	0-2	
0	Aston Villa	h	1-1	*Anelka*
	West Ham	a	1-1	*Nolan*
1	Middlesbrough	h	0-0	
1	Man. United	h	1-0	*Anelka*
	Liverpool	a	0-4	
	Wigan	h	4-1	*og (Scharner), Nolan, Davies, Anelka*
2	Man. City	a	2-4	*Diouf, Nolan*
2	Birmingham	h	3-0	*Diouf, Anelka 2*
2	Everton	a	0-2	
2	Sunderland	a	1-3	*Diouf*
8				
	Derby	h	1-0	*Giannakopoulos*
	Blackburn	h	1-2	*Nolan*
	Newcastle	a	0-0	
	Fulham	h	0-0	
	Reading	a	2-0	*Nolan, Helguson*
	Portsmouth	h	0-1	
	Blackburn	a	1-4	*Davies*
	Liverpool	h	1-3	*Cohen*
	Wigan	a	0-1	
	Man. United	a	0-2	
	Man. City	h	0-0	
	Arsenal	h	2-3	*Taylor 2*
	Aston Villa	a	0-4	
	West Ham	h	1-0	*Davies*
	Middlesbrough	a	1-0	*McCann*
	Tottenham	a	1-1	*Giannakopoulos*
	Sunderland	h	2-0	*Diouf, og (Murphy)*
	Chelsea	a	1-1	*Taylor*

No	Name	Nat	Pos	Aps	(s)	Gls
	Ali AL-HABSI	OMA	G	10		
	Nicolas ANELKA	FRA	A	18		10
	Daniel Omoya BRAATEN	NOR	A		(6)	1
	Gary CAHILL		D	13		
	Gérald CID	FRA	D	6	(1)	
	Tamir COHEN	ISR	M	3	(7)	1
	Kevin DAVIES		A	31	(1)	3
25	Abdoulaye DIAGNE-FAYE	SEN	D	1		
21	El-Hadji DIOUF	SEN	A	30	(4)	4
11	Ricardo GARDNER	JAM	M	25	(1)	
7	Stelios GIANNAKOPOULOS	GRE	M	1	(14)	2
17	Danny GUTHRIE		M	21	(4)	
9	Heidar HELGUSON	ISL	A	3	(3)	2
2	Nicky HUNT		D	12	(2)	
8	IVÁN CAMPO	ESP	M	25	(2)	1
22	Jussi JÄÄSKELÄINEN	FIN	G	28		
19	Gavin McCANN		M	21	(10)	1
5	Abdoulaye MEÏTÉ	CIV	D	21		
28	Ľubomír MICHALÍK	SVK	D	5	(2)	
18	MIKEL ALONSO	ESP	M	4	(3)	
4	Kevin NOLAN		M	33		5
31	Andy O'BRIEN	IRL	D	31	(1)	
24	Joey O'BRIEN	IRL	D	15	(4)	
47	Grzegorz RASIAK	POL	A	2	(5)	
3	JLloyd SAMUEL		D	14	(6)	
6	Gary SPEED	WAL	M	11	(3)	1
15	Grétar Rafn STEINSSON	ISL	M	16		
32	Matthew TAYLOR		M	16		3
16	Andranik TEYMOURIAN	IRN	M	1	(2)	
20	Ricardo VAZ TÉ	POR	A	1		
10	Christian WILHELMSSON	SWE	M		(8)	

CHELSEA FC

Manager – José Mourinho (POR); (20/9/07) Avram Grant (ISR)

Founded - 1905

MAJOR HONOURS: UEFA Cup Winners' Cup - (2) 1971, 1998; UEFA Super Cup - (1) 1998; English League - (3) 1955, 2005, 2006; FA Cup - (4) 1970, 1997, 2000, 2007; League Cup - (4) 1965, 1998, 2005, 2007.

2007				
12/8	Birmingham	h	3-2	*Pizarro, Malouda, Essien*
15/8	Reading	a	2-1	*Lampard, Drogba*
19/8	Liverpool	a	1-1	*Lampard (p)*
25/8	Portsmouth	h	1-0	*Lampard*
2/9	Aston Villa	a	0-2	
15/9	Blackburn	h	0-0	
23/9	Man. United	a	0-2	
29/9	Fulham	h	0-0	
7/10	Bolton	a	1-0	*Kalou*
20/10	Middlesbrough	a	2-0	*Drogba, Alex*
27/10	Man. City	h	6-0	*Essien, Drogba 2, Cole J., Kalou, Shevchenko*
3/11	Wigan	a	2-0	*Lampard, Belletti*
11/11	Everton	h	1-1	*Drogba*
24/11	Derby	a	2-0	*Kalou, Wright-Phillips*
1/12	West Ham	h	1-0	*Cole J.*
8/12	Sunderland	h	2-0	*Shevchenko, Lampard (p)*
16/12	Arsenal	a	0-1	
23/12	Blackburn	a	1-0	*Cole J.*
26/12	Aston Villa	h	4-4	*Shevchenko 2 (1p), Alex, Ballack*
29/12	Newcastle	h	2-1	*Essien, Kalou*
2008				
1/1	Fulham	a	2-1	*Kalou, Ballack (p)*
12/1	Tottenham	h	2-0	*Belletti, Wright-Phillips*
19/1	Birmingham	a	1-0	*Pizarro*
30/1	Reading	h	1-0	*Ballack*
2/2	Portsmouth	a	1-1	*Anelka*
10/2	Liverpool	h	0-0	
1/3	West Ham	a	4-0	*Lampard (p), Cole J., Ballack, Cole A.*
12/3	Derby	h	6-1	*Lampard 4 (1p), Kalou, Cole J.*
15/3	Sunderland	a	1-0	*Terry*
19/3	Tottenham	a	4-4	*Drogba, Essien, Cole J. 2*

23/3	Arsenal	h	2-1	*Drogba 2*
30/3	Middlesbrough	h	1-0	*Ricardo Carvalho*
5/4	Man. City	a	2-0	*og (Dunne), Kalou*
14/4	Wigan	h	1-1	*Essien*
17/4	Everton	a	1-0	*Essien*
26/4	Man. United	h	2-1	*Ballack 2 (1p)*
5/5	Newcastle	a	2-0	*Ballack, Malouda*
11/5	Bolton	h	1-1	*Shevchenko*

No	Name	Nat	Pos	Aps	(s)	Gls
33	ALEX Rodrigo Dias da Costa	BRA	D	22	(6)	2
39	Nicolas ANELKA	FRA	A	10	(4)	1
13	Michael BALLACK	GER	M	16	(2)	7
35	Juliano Haus BELLETTI	BRA	D	20	(3)	2
22	Tal BEN HAIM	ISR	D	10	(3)	
18	Wayne BRIDGE		D	9	(2)	
1	Petr ČECH	CZE	G	26		
3	Ashley COLE		D	27		1
10	Joe COLE		M	28	(5)	7
23	Carlo CUDICINI	ITA	G	10		
11	Didier DROGBA	CIV	A	17	(2)	8
5	Michael ESSIEN	GHA	M	23	(4)	6
40	Henrique HILÁRIO	POR	G	2	(1)	
2	Glen JOHNSON		D	1	(1)	
21	Salomon KALOU	CIV	A	24	(6)	7
8	Frank LAMPARD		M	23	(1)	10
4	Claude MAKELELE	FRA	M	15	(3)	
15	Florent MALOUDA	FRA	M	16	(5)	2
12	John Obi MIKEL	NGA	M	21	(8)	
20	PAULO FERREIRA	POR	D	15	(3)	
14	Claudio PIZARRO	PER	A	4	(17)	2
6	RICARDO CARVALHO	POR	D	21		1
7	Andriy SHEVCHENKO	UKR	A	8	(9)	5
9	Steve SIDWELL		M	7	(8)	
17	Scott SINCLAIR		M		(1)	
26	John TERRY		D	23		1
24	Shaun WRIGHT-PHILLIPS		M	20	(7)	2

DERBY COUNTY FC

Manager – Billy Davies (SCO); (28/11/07) Paul Jewell

Founded - 1884

MAJOR HONOURS: English League – (2) 1972, 1975; FA Cup – (1) 1946.

2007				
11/8	Portsmouth	h	2-2	*Oakley, Todd*
15/8	Man. City	a	0-1	
18/8	Tottenham	a	0-4	
25/8	Birmingham	h	1-2	*Oakley*
1/9	Liverpool	a	0-6	
17/9	Newcastle	h	1-0	*Miller*
22/9	Arsenal	a	0-5	
29/9	Bolton	h	1-1	*Miller*
7/10	Reading	a	0-1	
20/10	Fulham	a	0-0	
28/10	Everton	h	0-2	
3/11	Aston Villa	a	0-2	
10/11	West Ham	h	0-5	
24/11	Chelsea	h	0-2	
1/12	Sunderland	a	0-1	
8/12	Man. United	a	1-4	*Howard*
15/12	Middlesbrough	h	0-1	
23/12	Newcastle	a	2-2	*Barnes, Miller*
26/12	Liverpool	h	1-2	*McEveley*
30/12	Blackburn	h	1-2	*Oakley*
2008				
2/1	Bolton	a	0-1	
12/1	Wigan	h	0-1	
19/1	Portsmouth	a	1-3	*Nyatanga*
30/1	Man. City	h	1-1	*og (Sun)*
2/2	Birmingham	a	1-1	*Villa*
9/2	Tottenham	h	0-3	
23/2	Wigan	a	0-2	
1/3	Sunderland	h	0-0	
12/3	Chelsea	a	1-6	*Jones*
15/3	Man. United	h	0-1	
22/3	Middlesbrough	a	0-1	
29/3	Fulham	h	2-2	*Villa 2*
6/4	Everton	a	0-1	
12/4	Aston Villa	h	0-6	
19/4	West Ham	a	1-2	*Mears*
28/4	Arsenal	h	2-6	*McEveley, Earnsha*
3/5	Blackburn	a	1-3	*Miller*
11/5	Reading	h	0-4	

No	Name	Nat	Pos	Aps	(s)	G
32	Miles ADDISON		D	1		
28	Giles BARNES		M	14	(7)	
43	Stephen BYWATER		G	18		
3	Mohammed CAMARA	GUI	D	1		
31	Roy CARROLL	NIR	G	14		
19	Claude DAVIS	JAM	D	19		
10	Robert EARNSHAW	WAL	A	7	(15)	
2	Marc EDWORTHY		D	7	(2)	
11	Craig FAGAN		A	17	(5)	
22	Benny FEILHABER	USA	M	1	(9)	
40	Hossam GHALY	EGY	M	13	(2)	
15	Andy GRIFFIN		D	13	(2)	
9	Steve HOWARD		A	14	(6)	
6	Michael JOHNSON	JAM	M	1	(2)	
7	David JONES		M	11	(3)	
5	Darren LEACOCK		D	22	(4)	
15	Eddie LEWIS	USA	M	22	(2)	
12	Jon MACKEN	IRL	A		(3)	
21	Bob MALCOLM	SCO	D	1		
4	Jay McEVELEY	SCO	D	21	(8)	
24	Tyrone MEARS		D	22	(3)	
14	Kenny MILLER		A	30		
27	Danny MILLS		D	2		
23	Darren MOORE	JAM	D	29	(2)	
30	Lewin NYATANGA	WAL	D	2		
8	Matt OAKLEY		M	19		
25	Stephen PEARSON	SCO	M	23	(1)	
1	Lewis PRICE	WAL	G	6		
26	Laurent ROBERT	FRA	M	3	(1)	
44	Robbie SAVAGE	WAL	M	16		
41	Paris SIMMONS		A		(1)	
21	Mile STERJOVSKI	AUS	M	9	(3)	
8	Alan STUBBS		D	8		
16	Gary TEALE		M	9	(9)	
17	Andy TODD		D	14	(5)	
9	Emanuel VILLA	ARG	A	9	(7)	

EVERTON FC

Manager – David Moyes (SCO)

Founded - 1878

MAJOR HONOURS: UEFA Cup Winners' Cup - (1) 1985; English Leag (9) 1891, 1915, 1928, 1932, 1939, 1963, 1970, 1985, 1987; FA Cup - 1906, 1933, 1966, 1984, 1995.

2007				
11/8	Wigan	h	2-1	*Osman, Anichebe*
14/8	Tottenham	a	3-1	*Lescott, Osman, Stu*
18/8	Reading	a	0-1	
25/8	Blackburn	h	1-1	*McFadden*
1/9	Bolton	a	2-1	*Yakubu, Lescott*
15/9	Man. United	h	0-1	
23/9	Aston Villa	a	0-2	
30/9	Middlesbrough	h	2-0	*Lescott, Pienaar*
7/10	Newcastle	a	2-3	*Johnson, og (Given*
20/10	Liverpool	h	1-2	*og (Hyypiä)*

0	Derby	a	2-0	*Arteta, Yakubu*
	Birmingham	h	3-1	*Yakubu, Carsley, Vaughan*
1	Chelsea	a	1-1	*Cahill*
1	Sunderland	h	7-1	*Yakubu 2, Cahill 2, Pienaar, Johnson, Osman*
	Portsmouth	a	0-0	
	Fulham	h	3-0	*Yakubu 3*
2	West Ham	a	2-0	*Yakubu, Johnson*
2	Man. United	a	1-2	*Cahill*
2	Bolton	h	2-0	*Neville, Cahill*
2	Arsenal	h	1-4	*Cahill*
8				
	Middlesbrough	a	2-0	*Johnson, McFadden*
	Man. City	h	1-0	*Lescott*
	Wigan	a	2-1	*Johnson, Lescott*
	Tottenham	h	0-0	
	Blackburn	a	0-0	
	Reading	h	1-0	*Jagielka*
	Man. City	a	2-0	*Yakubu, Lescott*
	Portsmouth	h	3-1	*Yakubu 2, Cahill*
	Sunderland	a	1-0	*Johnson*
	Fulham	a	0-1	
	West Ham	h	1-1	*Yakubu*
	Liverpool	a	0-1	
	Derby	h	1-0	*Osman*
	Birmingham	a	1-1	*Lescott*
	Chelsea	h	0-1	
	Aston Villa	h	2-2	*Neville, Yobo*
	Arsenal	a	0-1	
	Newcastle	h	3-1	*Yakubu 2 (1p), Lescott*

Name	Nat	Pos	Aps	(s)	Gls
Victor ANICHEBE	NGA	A	10	(17)	1
Mikel ARTETA	ESP	M	27	(1)	1
Leighton BAINES		D	13	(9)	
Tim CAHILL	AUS	M	18		7
Lee CARSLEY	IRL	M	33	(1)	1
Thomas GRAVESEN	DEN	M	1	(7)	
Tony HIBBERT		D	22	(2)	
Tim HOWARD	USA	G	36		
Phil JAGIELKA		M	27	(7)	1
Andrew JOHNSON		A	20	(9)	6
Joleon LESCOTT		D	37	(1)	8
MANUEL FERNANDES	POR	M	9	(3)	
James McFADDEN	SCO	A	5	(7)	2
Phil NEVILLE		M	37		2
NUNO VALENTE	POR	D	8	(1)	
Leon OSMAN		M	26	(2)	4
Steven PIENAAR	RSA	M	25	(3)	2
Jack RODWELL		D		(2)	
Alan STUBBS		D	7	(1)	1
James VAUGHAN		A		(8)	1
Stefan WESSELS	GER	G	2		
YAKUBU Aiyegbeni	NGA	A	26	(3)	15
Joseph YOBO	NGA	D	29	(1)	1

FULHAM FC

nager – Lawrie Sanchez (NIR); (21/12/07) (Ray Lewington); (30/12/07) Roy Hodgson

Founded - 1879

7				
	Arsenal	a	1-2	*Healy*
	Bolton	h	2-1	*Healy, Smertin*
	Middlesbrough	h	1-2	*McBride*
	Aston Villa	a	1-2	*Dempsey*
	Tottenham	h	3-3	*Dempsey, Smertin, Kamara*
15/9	Wigan	a	1-1	*Dempsey*
22/9	Man. City	h	3-3	*Davies, Bouazza, Murphy*
29/9	Chelsea	a	0-0	
7/10	Portsmouth	h	0-2	
20/10	Derby	h	0-0	
27/10	Sunderland	a	1-1	*Davies*
3/11	Reading	h	3-1	*Davies, Dempsey, Healy*
10/11	Liverpool	a	0-2	
25/11	Blackburn	h	2-2	*Murphy (p), Kamara*
3/12	Man. United	a	0-2	
8/12	Everton	a	0-3	
15/12	Newcastle	h	0-1	
22/12	Wigan	h	1-1	*Dempsey*
26/12	Tottenham	a	1-5	*Dempsey*
29/12	Birmingham	a	1-1	*Bocanegra*
2008				
1/1	Chelsea	h	1-2	*Murphy (p)*
12/1	West Ham	a	1-2	*Davies*
19/1	Arsenal	h	0-3	
29/1	Bolton	a	0-0	
3/2	Aston Villa	h	2-1	*Davies, Bullard*
9/2	Middlesbrough	a	0-1	
23/2	West Ham	h	0-1	
1/3	Man. United	h	0-3	
8/3	Blackburn	a	1-1	*Bullard*
16/3	Everton	h	1-0	*McBride*
22/3	Newcastle	a	0-2	
29/3	Derby	a	2-2	*Kamara, og (Leacock)*
5/4	Sunderland	h	1-3	*Healy*
12/4	Reading	a	2-0	*McBride, Nevland*
19/4	Liverpool	h	0-2	
26/4	Man. City	a	3-2	*Kamara 2, Murphy*
3/5	Birmingham	h	2-0	*McBride, Nevland*
11/5	Portsmouth	a	1-0	*Murphy*

No	Name	Nat	Pos	Aps	(s)	Gls
26	Leon ANDREASEN	DEN	M	9	(4)	
38	Nathan ASHTON		D	1		
34	Chris BAIRD	NIR	D	17	(1)	
3	Carlos BOCANEGRA	USA	D	18	(4)	1
24	Hameur BOUAZZA	ALG	M	15	(5)	1
21	Jimmy BULLARD		M	15	(2)	2
5	Philippe CHRISTANVAL	FRA	D		(1)	
25	Simon DAVIES	WAL	M	36	(1)	5
10	Steven DAVIS	NIR	M	22		
23	Clint DEMPSEY	USA	M	29	(7)	6
14	Papa Bouba DIOP	SEN	M		(2)	
32	Brede HANGELAND	NOR	D	15		
9	David HEALY	NIR	A	15	(15)	4
18	Aaron HUGHES	NIR	D	29	(1)	
15	Collins JOHN	NED	A		(2)	
14	Eddie JOHNSON	USA	A	4	(2)	
11	Diomansy KAMARA	SEN	A	17	(11)	5
1	Kasey KELLER	USA	G	13		
6	Zat KNIGHT		D	4		
4	Paul KONCHESKY		D	33		
14	Shefki KUQI	FIN	A	3	(7)	
20	Brian McBRIDE	USA	A	14	(13)	4
27	Danny MURPHY		M	28	(5)	5
15	Erik NEVLAND	NOR	A	2	(6)	2
29	Antti NIEMI	FIN	G	22		
22	Elliot OMOZUSI		D	8		
19	Ian PEARCE		D		(1)	
7	SEOL Ki-hyeon	KOR	M	4	(8)	
8	Aleksei SMERTIN	RUS	M	11	(4)	2
17	Paul STALTERI	CAN	D	13		
6	Dejan STEFANOVIĆ	SRB	D	13		
2	Moritz VOLZ	GER	D	5	(4)	
12	Tony WARNER		G	3		

ENGLAND

LIVERPOOL FC

Manager – Rafael Benítez (ESP)

Founded - 1892

MAJOR HONOURS: European Champion Clubs' Cup/UEFA Champions League - (5) 1977, 1978, 1981, 1984, 2005; UEFA Cup - (3) 1973, 1976, 2001; UEFA Super Cup - (3) 1977, 2001, 2006; English League - (18) 1901, 1906, 1922, 1923, 1947, 1964, 1966, 1973, 1976, 1977, 1979, 1980, 1982, 1983, 1984, 1986, 1988, 1990; FA Cup - (7) 1965, 1974, 1986, 1989, 1992, 2001, 2006; League Cup - (7) 1981, 1982, 1983, 1984, 1995, 2001, 2003.

2007				
11/8	Aston Villa	a	2-1	*og (Laursen), Gerrard*
19/8	Chelsea	h	1-1	*Fernando Torres*
25/8	Sunderland	a	2-0	*Sissoko, Voronin*
1/9	Derby	h	6-0	*Xabi Alonso 2, Babel, Fernando Torres 2, Voronin*
15/9	Portsmouth	a	0-0	
22/9	Birmingham	h	0-0	
29/9	Wigan	a	1-0	*Benayoun*
7/10	Tottenham	h	2-2	*Voronin, Fernando Torres*
20/10	Everton	a	2-1	*Kuyt 2 (2p)*
28/10	Arsenal	h	1-1	*Gerrard*
3/11	Blackburn	a	0-0	
10/11	Fulham	h	2-0	*Fernando Torres, Gerrard (p)*
24/11	Newcastle	a	3-0	*Gerrard, Kuyt, Babel*
2/12	Bolton	h	4-0	*Hyypiä, Fernando Torres, Gerrard (p), Babel*
8/12	Reading	a	1-3	*Gerrard*
16/12	Man. United	h	0-1	
22/12	Portsmouth	h	4-1	Benayoun, og (Distin), Fernando Torres 2
26/12	Derby	a	2-1	Fernando Torres, Gerrard
30/12	Man. City	a	0-0	
2008				
2/1	Wigan	h	1-1	*Fernando Torres*
12/1	Middlesbrough	a	1-1	*Fernando Torres*
21/1	Aston Villa	h	2-2	*Benayoun, Crouch*
30/1	West Ham	a	0-1	
2/2	Sunderland	h	3-0	*Crouch, Fernando Torres, Gerrard (p)*
10/2	Chelsea	a	0-0	
23/2	Middlesbrough	h	3-2	*Fernando Torres 3*
2/3	Bolton	a	3-1	*og (Jääskeläinen), Babel, Fábio Aurélio*
5/3	West Ham	h	4-0	*Fernando Torres 3, Gerrard*
8/3	Newcastle	h	3-0	*Pennant, Fernando Torres, Gerrard*
15/3	Reading	h	2-1	*Mascherano, Fernando Torres*
23/3	Man. United	a	0-3	
30/3	Everton	h	1-0	*Fernando Torres*
5/4	Arsenal	a	1-1	*Crouch*
13/4	Blackburn	h	3-1	*Gerrard, Fernando Torres, Voronin*
19/4	Fulham	a	2-0	*Pennant, Crouch*
26/4	Birmingham	a	2-2	*Crouch, Benayoun*
4/5	Man. City	h	1-0	*Fernando Torres*
11/5	Tottenham	a	2-0	*Voronin, Fernando Torres*

No	Name	Nat	Pos	Aps	(s)	Gls
5	Daniel AGGER	DEN	D	4	(1)	
17	Álvaro ARBELOA	ESP	D	26	(2)	
19	Ryan BABEL	NED	M	15	(15)	4
11	Yossi BENAYOUN	ISR	M	15	(15)	4
23	Jamie CARRAGHER		D	34	(1)	
15	Peter CROUCH		A	9	(12)	
12	FÁBIO AURÉLIO	BRA	D	13	(3)	
9	FERNANDO TORRES	ESP	A	29	(4)	2
3	Steve FINNAN	IRL	D	21	(3)	
8	Steven GERRARD		M	32	(2)	1
46	Jack HOBBS		D	1	(1)	
4	Sami HYYPIÄ	FIN	D	24	(3)	
48	Emiliano INSÚA	ARG	D	2	(1)	
7	Harry KEWELL	AUS	M	8	(2)	
18	Dirk KUYT	NED	A	24	(8)	
21	LUCAS Leiva	BRA	M	12	(6)	
20	Javier MASCHERANO	ARG	M	25		
16	Jermaine PENNANT		M	14	(4)	
47	Damien PLESSIS	FRA	M	2		
25	José Manuel 'Pepe' REINA	ESP	G	38		
6	John Arne RIISE	NOR	D	22	(7)	
22	Momo SISSOKO	MLI	M	6	(3)	
37	Martin ŠKRTEĽ	SVK	D	13	(1)	
10	Andriy VORONIN	UKR	A	13	(6)	
14	XABI ALONSO	ESP	M	16	(3)	

MANCHESTER CITY FC

Manager – Sven Göran Eriksson (SWE)

Founded - 1887

MAJOR HONOURS: UEFA Cup Winners' Cup - (1) 1970; English Leag (2) 1937, 1968; FA Cup - (4) 1904, 1934, 1956, 1969; League Cup - 1970, 1976.

2007				
11/8	West Ham	a	2-0	*Bianchi, Geovanni*
15/8	Derby	h	1-0	*Johnson*
19/8	Man. United	h	1-0	*Geovanni*
25/8	Arsenal	a	0-1	
2/9	Blackburn	a	0-1	
16/9	Aston Villa	h	1-0	*Johnson*
22/9	Fulham	a	3-3	*Petrov 2, Mpenza*
29/9	Newcastle	h	3-1	*Petrov, Mpenza, Ela*
7/10	Middlesbrough	h	3-1	*og (Riggott), Elano*
20/10	Birmingham	h	1-0	*Elano*
27/10	Chelsea	a	0-6	
5/11	Sunderland	h	1-0	*Ireland*
11/11	Portsmouth	a	0-0	
24/11	Reading	h	2-1	*Petrov, Ireland*
1/12	Wigan	a	1-1	*Geovanni*
9/12	Tottenham	a	1-2	*Bianchi*
15/12	Bolton	h	4-2	*Bianchi, og (Michal Vassell, Etuhu*
22/12	Aston Villa	a	1-1	*Bianchi*
27/12	Blackburn	h	2-2	*Vassell, og (Nelsen)*
30/12	Liverpool	h	0-0	
2008				
2/1	Newcastle	a	2-0	*Elano, Fernandes*
12/1	Everton	a	0-1	
20/1	West Ham	h	1-1	*Vassell*
30/1	Derby	a	1-1	*Sturridge*
2/2	Arsenal	h	1-3	*Fernandes*
10/2	Man. United	a	2-1	*Vassell, Benjani*
25/2	Everton	h	0-2	
1/3	Wigan	h	0-0	
8/3	Reading	a	0-2	
16/3	Tottenham	h	2-1	*Ireland, Onuoha*
22/3	Bolton	a	0-0	
29/3	Birmingham	a	1-3	*Elano (p)*
5/4	Chelsea	h	0-2	
12/4	Sunderland	a	2-1	*Elano (p), Vassell*
20/4	Portsmouth	h	3-1	*Vassell, Petrov, Ben*
26/4	Fulham	h	2-3	*Ireland, Benjani*
4/5	Liverpool	a	0-1	
11/5	Middlesbrough	a	1-8	*Elano*

	Name	Nat	Pos	Aps	(s)	Gls
	Michael BALL		D	19	(9)	
	BENJANI Mwaruwari	ZIM	A	13		3
	Rolando BIANCHI	ITA	A	7	(12)	4
	Valeri BOZHINOV	BUL	A	1	(2)	
	Felipe CAICEDO	ECU	A		(10)	
	Nery Alberto CASTILLO	MEX	M	2	(5)	
	Vedran ĆORLUKA	CRO	D	34	(1)	
	Richard DUNNE	IRL	D	36		
	ELANO Blumer	BRA	M	29	(5)	8
	Kelvin ETUHU		M	2	(4)	1
	Gelson FERNANDES	SUI	M	21	(5)	2
	Javier GARRIDO	ESP	D	21	(6)	
	GEOVANNI Deiberson	BRA	M	2	(17)	3
	Dietmar HAMANN	GER	M	26	(3)	
	Joe HART		G	26		
	Stephen IRELAND	IRL	M	32	(1)	4
	Andreas ISAKSSON	SWE	G	5		
	Michael JOHNSON		M	23		2
	Émile MPENZA	BEL	A	8	(7)	2
	Nedum ONUOHA		D	13	(3)	1
	Martin PETROV	BUL	M	34		5
	Micah RICHARDS		D	25		
	Georgios SAMARAS	GRE	A	2	(3)	
	Kasper SCHMEICHEL	DEN	G	7		
	Daniel STURRIDGE		A	2	(1)	1
	SUN Jihai	CHN	D	7	(7)	
	Darius VASSELL		A	21	(6)	6
	Sam WILLIAMSON		D		(1)	

MANCHESTER UNITED FC

Manager – Sir Alex Ferguson (SCO)

Founded - 1878

MAJOR HONOURS: European Champion Clubs' Cup/UEFA Champions League - (3) 1968, 1999, 2008; UEFA Cup Winners' Cup - (1) 1991; UEFA Super Cup - (1) 1991; World Club Cup - (1) 1999; English League - (17) 1908, 1911, 1952, 1956, 1957, 1965, 1967, 1993, 1994, 1996, 1997, 1999, 2000, 2001, 2003, 2007, 2008; FA Cup - (11) 1909, 1948, 1963, 1977, 1983, 1985, 1990, 1994, 1996, 1999, 2004; League Cup - (2) 1992, 2006.

2007

/8	Reading	h	0-0	
/8	Portsmouth	a	1-1	*Scholes*
/8	Man. City	a	0-1	
/8	Tottenham	h	1-0	*Nani*
9	Sunderland	h	1-0	*Saha*
/9	Everton	a	1-0	*Vidić*
/9	Chelsea	h	2-0	*Tévez, Saha (p)*
/9	Birmingham	a	1-0	*Cristiano Ronaldo*
10	Wigan	h	4-0	*Tévez, Cristiano Ronaldo 2, Rooney*
/10	Aston Villa	a	4-1	*Rooney 2, Ferdinand, Giggs*
/10	Middlesbrough	h	4-1	*Nani, Rooney, Tévez 2*
11	Arsenal	a	2-2	*og (Gallas), Cristiano Ronaldo*
/11	Blackburn	h	2-0	*Cristiano Ronaldo 2*
/11	Bolton	a	0-1	
12	Fulham	h	2-0	*Cristiano Ronaldo 2*
12	Derby	h	4-1	*Giggs, Tévez 2, Cristiano Ronaldo (p)*
/12	Liverpool	a	1-0	*Tévez*
/12	Everton	h	2-1	*Cristiano Ronaldo 2 (1p)*
/12	Sunderland	a	4-0	*Rooney, Saha 2 (1p), Cristiano Ronaldo*
/12	West Ham	a	1-2	*Cristiano Ronaldo*

2008

1	Birmingham	h	1-0	*Tévez*
2/1	Newcastle	h	6-0	*Cristiano Ronaldo 3, Tévez 2, Ferdinand*
/1	Reading	a	2-0	*Rooney, Cristiano Ronaldo*
30/1	Portsmouth	h	2-0	*Cristiano Ronaldo 2*
2/2	Tottenham	a	1-1	*Tévez*
10/2	Man. City	h	1-2	*Carrick*
23/2	Newcastle	a	5-1	*Rooney 2, Cristiano Ronaldo 2, Saha*
1/3	Fulham	a	3-0	*Hargreaves, Park, og (Davies)*
15/3	Derby	a	1-0	*Cristiano Ronaldo*
19/3	Bolton	h	2-0	*Cristiano Ronaldo 2*
23/3	Liverpool	h	3-0	*Brown, Cristiano Ronaldo, Nani*
29/3	Aston Villa	h	4-0	*Cristiano Ronaldo, Tévez, Rooney 2*
6/4	Middlesbrough	a	2-2	*Cristiano Ronaldo, Rooney*
13/4	Arsenal	h	2-1	*Cristiano Ronaldo (p), Hargreaves*
19/4	Blackburn	a	1-1	*Tévez*
26/4	Chelsea	a	1-2	*Rooney*
3/5	West Ham	h	4-1	*Cristiano Ronaldo 2, Tévez, Carrick*
11/5	Wigan	a	2-0	*Cristiano Ronaldo (p), Giggs*

No	Name	Nat	Pos	Aps	(s)	Gls
8	ANDERSON Oliveira	BRA	M	16	(8)	
6	Wes BROWN		D	34	(2)	1
39	Fraizer CAMPBELL		A		(1)	
16	Michael CARRICK		M	24	(7)	2
7	CRISTIANO RONALDO	POR	M	31	(3)	31
33	Chris EAGLES		M	1	(3)	
3	Patrice EVRA	FRA	D	33		
5	Rio FERDINAND		D	35		2
24	Darren FLETCHER	SCO	M	5	(11)	
12	Ben FOSTER		G	1		
11	Ryan GIGGS	WAL	M	26	(5)	3
4	Owen HARGREAVES		M	16	(7)	2
24	Tomasz KUSZCZAK	POL	G	8	(1)	
17	Luís Cunha "NANI"	POR	M	16	(10)	3
22	John O'SHEA	IRL	D	10	(18)	
13	PARK Ji-sung	KOR	M	8	(4)	1
19	Gerard PIQUÉ Bernabeu	ESP	D	5	(4)	
10	Wayne ROONEY		A	25	(2)	12
9	Louis SAHA	FRA	A	6	(11)	5
18	Paul SCHOLES		M	22	(2)	1
27	Mikaël SILVESTRE	FRA	D	3		
25	Danny SIMPSON		D	1	(2)	
32	Carlos TÉVEZ	ARG	A	31	(3)	14
1	Edwin VAN DER SAR	NED	G	29		
15	Nemanja VIDIĆ	SRB	D	32		1

MIDDLESBROUGH FC

Manager – Gareth Southgate

Founded - 1876

MAJOR HONOURS: League Cup - (1) 2004.

2007

11/8	Blackburn	h	1-2	*Downing*
15/8	Wigan	a	0-1	
18/8	Fulham	a	2-1	*Mido, Cattermole*
26/8	Newcastle	h	2-2	*Mido, Arca*
1/9	Birmingham	h	2-0	*Wheater, Downing*
15/9	West Ham	a	0-3	
22/9	Sunderland	h	2-2	*Arca, Downing*
30/9	Everton	a	0-2	
7/10	Man. City	a	1-3	*Hutchinson*
20/10	Chelsea	h	0-2	
27/10	Man. United	a	1-4	*Aliadière*
3/11	Tottenham	h	1-1	*Young*
11/11	Bolton	a	0-0	

24/11	Aston Villa	h 0-3	
1/12	Reading	a 1-1	*Tuncay*
9/12	Arsenal	h 2-1	*Downing (p), Tuncay*
15/12	Derby	a 1-0	*Tuncay*
22/12	West Ham	h 1-2	*Wheater*
26/12	Birmingham	a 0-3	
29/12	Portsmouth	a 1-0	*Tuncay*
2008			
1/1	Everton	h 0-2	
12/1	Liverpool	h 1-1	*Boateng*
19/1	Blackburn	a 1-1	*Wheater*
29/1	Wigan	h 1-0	*Aliadière*
3/2	Newcastle	a 1-1	*Huth*
9/2	Fulham	h 1-0	*Aliadière*
23/2	Liverpool	a 2-3	*Tuncay, Downing*
1/3	Reading	h 0-1	
12/3	Aston Villa	a 1-1	*Downing*
15/3	Arsenal	a 1-1	*Aliadière*
22/3	Derby	h 1-0	*Tuncay*
30/3	Chelsea	a 0-1	
6/4	Man. United	h 2-2	*Afonso Alves 2*
12/4	Tottenham	a 1-1	*Downing*
19/4	Bolton	h 0-1	
26/4	Sunderland	a 2-3	*Tuncay, Afonso Alves*
3/5	Portsmouth	h 2-0	*Riggott, Tuncay*
11/5	Man. City	h 8-1	*Downing 2 (1p), Afonso Alves 3, Johnson, Rochemback, Aliadière*

No	Name	Nat	Pos	Aps	(s)	Gls
12	AFONSO ALVES	BRA	A	7	(4)	6
11	Jérémie ALIADIÈRE	FRA	A	26	(3)	5
3	Julio ARCA	ARG	M	23	(1)	2
7	George BOATENG	NED	M	29	(4)	1
27	Lee CATTERMOLE		M	10	(14)	1
42	Tom CRADDOCK		A	1	(2)	
24	Andrew DAVIES		D	3	(1)	
19	Stewart DOWNING		M	38		9
40	Jonathan GROUNDS		D	5		
38	Seb HINES		D		(1)	
36	Ben HUTCHINSON		A		(8)	1
14	Robert HUTH	GER	D	9	(4)	1
28	Adam JOHNSON		M	3	(16)	1
22	Brad JONES	AUS	G	1		
18	LEE Dong-gook	KOR	A	5	(9)	
29	Anthony McMAHON		D		(1)	
9	Ahmed Hossam "MIDO"	EGY	A	8	(4)	2
4	Gary O'NEIL		M	25	(1)	
6	Emanuel POGATETZ	AUT	D	23	(1)	
5	Chris RIGGOTT		D	9	(1)	1
10	Fábio ROCHEMBACK	BRA	M	21	(5)	1
1	Mark SCHWARZER		G	34		
15	Mohamed SHAWKY	EGY	M	3	(2)	
33	Andrew TAYLOR		D	18	(1)	
17	TUNCAY Şanlı		A	27	(7)	8
21	Ross TURNBULL		G	3		
31	David WHEATER		D	34		3
8	Jonathan WOODGATE		D	16		
20	YAKUBU Aiyegbeni	NGA	A	2		
2	Luke YOUNG		D	35		1

NEWCASTLE UNITED FC

Manager – Sam Allardyce; (9/1/08) (Nigel Pearson); (16/1/08) Kevin Keegan

Founded - 1881

MAJOR HONOURS: Inter Cities Fairs Cup - (1) 1969; English League - (4) 1905, 1907, 1909, 1927; FA Cup - (6) 1910, 1924, 1932, 1951, 1952, 1955.

2007			
11/8	Bolton	a 3-1	*N'Zogbia, Martins 2*
18/8	Aston Villa	h 0-0	
26/8	Middlesbrough	a 2-2	*N'Zogbia, Viduka*
1/9	Wigan	h 1-0	*Owen*
17/9	Derby	a 0-1	
23/9	West Ham	h 3-1	*Viduka 2, N'Zogbia*
29/9	Man. City	a 1-3	*Martins*
7/10	Everton	h 3-2	*Butt, Emre, Owen*
22/10	Tottenham	h 3-1	*Martins, Caçapa, Milr*
27/10	Reading	a 1-2	*og (Duberry)*
3/11	Portsmouth	h 1-4	*og (Campbell)*
10/11	Sunderland	a 1-1	*Milner*
24/11	Liverpool	h 0-3	
1/12	Blackburn	a 1-3	*Martins*
5/12	Arsenal	h 1-1	*Taylor*
8/12	Birmingham	h 2-1	*Martins (p), Beye*
15/12	Fulham	a 1-0	*Barton (p)*
23/12	Derby	h 2-2	*Viduka 2*
26/12	Wigan	a 0-1	
29/12	Chelsea	a 1-2	*Butt*
2008			
2/1	Man. City	h 0-2	
12/1	Man. United	a 0-6	
19/1	Bolton	h 0-0	
29/1	Arsenal	a 0-3	
3/2	Middlesbrough	h 1-1	*Owen*
9/2	Aston Villa	a 1-4	*Owen*
23/2	Man. United	h 1-5	*Diagne-Faye*
1/3	Blackburn	h 0-1	
8/3	Liverpool	a 0-3	
17/3	Birmingham	a 1-1	*Owen*
22/3	Fulham	h 2-0	*Viduka, Owen*
30/3	Tottenham	a 4-1	*Butt, Geremi, Owen, Martins*
5/4	Reading	h 3-0	*Martins, Owen, Viduk*
12/4	Portsmouth	a 0-0	
20/4	Sunderland	h 2-0	*Owen 2 (1p)*
26/4	West Ham	a 2-2	*Martins, og (McCartne*
5/5	Chelsea	h 0-2	
11/5	Everton	a 1-3	*Owen (p)*

No	Name	Nat	Pos	Aps	(s)	Gls
23	Shola AMEOBI		A	2	(4)	
7	Joey BARTON		M	20	(3)	1
21	Habib BEYE	SEN	D	27	(2)	1
22	Nicky BUTT		M	35		3
6	Cláudio CAÇAPA	BRA	D	16	(3)	1
2	Stephen CARR	IRL	D	8	(2)	
39	Andy CARROLL		A	1	(3)	
25	Abdoulaye DIAGNE-FAYE	SEN	D	20	(2)	1
15	Lamine DIATTA	SEN	D		(2)	
11	Damien DUFF	IRL	M	12	(4)	
30	David EDGAR		D	2	(3)	
5	EMRE Belözoğlu	TUR	M	6	(8)	1
20	GEREMI Njitap	CMR	M	24	(3)	1
1	Shay GIVEN		G	19		
13	Steve HARPER		G	19	(2)	
3	JOSÉ ENRIQUE Sánchez	ESP	D	18	(5)	
38	Kazenga LUALUA	COD	M		(2)	
9	Obafemi MARTINS	NGA	A	23	(8)	9
16	James MILNER		M	25	(4)	2
14	Charles N'ZOGBIA	FRA	M	27	(5)	3
10	Michael OWEN		A	24	(5)	11
26	Peter RAMAGE		D		(3)	
4	David ROZEHNAL	CZE	D	16	(5)	
17	Alan SMITH		M	26	(7)	
15	Nolberto SOLANO	PER	M		(1)	
27	Steven TAYLOR		D	29	(2)	1
36	Mark VIDUKA	AUS	A	19	(7)	7

PORTSMOUTH FC

Manager – Harry Redknapp

Founded - 1898

AJOR HONOURS: English League - (2) 1949, 1950; FA Cup - (2) 1939, 2008.

07

/8	Derby	a	2-2	*Benjani, Utaka*
/8	Man. United	h	1-1	*Benjani*
/8	Bolton	h	3-1	*Kanu, Utaka, Taylor (p)*
/8	Chelsea	a	0-1	
	Arsenal	a	1-3	*Kanu*
/9	Liverpool	h	0-0	
/9	Blackburn	a	1-0	*Kanu*
/9	Reading	h	7-4	*Benjani 3, Hreidarsson, Kranjčar, og (Ingimarsson), Muntari (p)*
10	Fulham	a	2-0	*Benjani, Hreidarsson*
/10	Wigan	a	2-0	*Benjani, Johnson*
/10	West Ham	h	0-0	
1	Newcastle	a	4-1	*Pamarot, Benjani, Utaka, Kranjčar*
/11	Man. City	h	0-0	
/11	Birmingham	a	2-0	*Muntari, Kranjčar*
2	Everton	h	0-0	
2	Aston Villa	a	3-1	*og (Gardner), Muntari 2*
/12	Tottenham	h	0-1	
/12	Liverpool	a	1-4	*Benjani*
/12	Arsenal	h	0-0	
/12	Middlesbrough	h	0-1	

08

	Reading	a	2-0	*Campbell, Utaka*
/1	Sunderland	a	0-2	
/1	Derby	h	3-1	*Benjani 3*
/1	Man. United	a	0-2	
2	Chelsea	h	1-1	*Defoe*
2	Bolton	a	1-0	*Diarra*
/2	Sunderland	h	1-0	*Defoe (p)*
3	Everton	a	1-3	*Defoe*
/3	Birmingham	h	4-2	*Defoe 2 (1p), Hreidarsson, Kanu*
/3	Aston Villa	h	2-0	*Defoe, og (Reo-Coker)*
/3	Tottenham	a	0-2	
/3	Wigan	h	2-0	*Defoe 2*
4	West Ham	a	1-0	*Kranjčar*
/4	Newcastle	h	0-0	
/4	Man. City	a	1-3	*Utaka*
/4	Blackburn	h	0-1	
5	Middlesbrough	a	0-2	
/5	Fulham	h	0-1	

	Name	Nat	Pos	Aps	(s)	Gls
	Jamie ASHDOWN		G	3		
	Lucien AUBEY		D	1	(2)	
	Milan BAROŠ	CZE	A	8	(4)	
	BENJANI Mwaruwari	ZIM	A	21	(2)	12
	Sol CAMPBELL		D	31		1
	Martin CRANIE		D	1	(1)	
	Sean DAVIS		M	18	(4)	
	Jermain DEFOE		A	12		8
	Lassana DIARRA	FRA	M	11	(1)	1
	Papa Bouba DIOP	SEN	M	25		
	Sylvain DISTIN	FRA	D	36		
	Hermann HREIDARSSON	ISL	D	30	(2)	3
	Richard HUGHES	SCO	M	8	(5)	
	David JAMES		G	35		
	Glen JOHNSON		D	29		1
	Nwankwo KANU	NGA	A	13	(12)	4
	Niko KRANJČAR	CRO	M	31	(3)	4
4	LAUREN Etame Mayer	CMR	D	11	(4)	
11	Sulley MUNTARI	GHA	M	27	(2)	4
18	Arnold MVUEMBA	FRA	M	3	(5)	
10	David NUGENT		A	5	(10)	
26	Gary O'NEIL		M	2		
16	Noé PAMAROT	FRA	D	14	(3)	1
30	PEDRO MENDES	POR	M	14	(4)	
34	Franck SONGO'O	FRA	A		(1)	
14	Matthew TAYLOR		M	3	(10)	1
6	Djimi TRAORÉ	MLI	D	1	(2)	
17	John UTAKA	NGA	M	25	(4)	5

READING FC

Manager – Steve Coppell

Founded - 1871

2007

12/8	Man. United	a	0-0	
15/8	Chelsea	h	1-2	*Bikey*
18/8	Everton	h	1-0	*Hunt*
25/8	Bolton	a	0-3	
1/9	West Ham	h	0-3	
15/9	Sunderland	a	1-2	*Kitson*
22/9	Wigan	h	2-1	*Kitson, Harper*
29/9	Portsmouth	a	4-7	*Hunt, Kitson, Long, og (Campbell)*
7/10	Derby	h	1-0	*Doyle*
20/10	Blackburn	a	2-4	*Doyle 2*
27/10	Newcastle	h	2-1	*Kitson, Long*
3/11	Fulham	a	1-3	*Doyle*
12/11	Arsenal	h	1-3	*Shorey*
24/11	Man. City	a	1-2	*Harper*
1/12	Middlesbrough	h	1-1	*Kitson*
8/12	Liverpool	h	3-1	*Hunt (p), Doyle, Harper*
15/12	Birmingham	a	1-1	*Hunt (p)*
22/12	Sunderland	h	2-1	*Ingimarsson, Hunt*
26/12	West Ham	a	1-1	*Kitson*
29/12	Tottenham	a	4-6	*Cissé, Ingimarsson, Kitson 2*

2008

1/1	Portsmouth	h	0-2	
12/1	Aston Villa	a	1-3	*Harper*
19/1	Man. United	h	0-2	
30/1	Chelsea	a	0-1	
2/2	Bolton	h	0-2	
9/2	Everton	a	0-1	
24/2	Aston Villa	h	1-2	*Shorey*
1/3	Middlesbrough	a	1-0	*Harper*
8/3	Man. City	h	2-0	*Long, Kitson*
15/3	Liverpool	a	1-2	*Matějovský*
22/3	Birmingham	h	2-1	*Bikey 2*
29/3	Blackburn	h	0-0	
5/4	Newcastle	a	0-3	
12/4	Fulham	h	0-2	
19/4	Arsenal	a	0-2	
26/4	Wigan	a	0-0	
3/5	Tottenham	h	0-1	
11/5	Derby	a	4-0	*Harper, Kitson, Doyle, Lita*

No	Name	Nat	Pos	Aps	(s)	Gls
22	André BIKEY	CMR	D	14	(8)	3
4	Kalifa CISSÉ	FRA	M	11	(11)	1
17	Bobby CONVEY	USA	M	12	(8)	
23	Ulises DE LA CRUZ	ECU	D	3	(3)	
9	Kevin DOYLE	IRL	A	34	(2)	6
29	Michael DUBERRY		D	12	(1)	
20	Emerse FAÉ	CIV	M	3	(5)	
33	Scott GOLBOURNE		D	1		
6	Brynjar GUNNARSSON	ISL	M	18	(2)	

1	Marcus HAHNEMANN		G	38		
14	John HALLS		D		(1)	
15	James HARPER		M	38		6
10	Stephen HUNT	IRL	M	37		5
16	Ívar INGIMARSSON	ISL	D	33	(1)	2
30	Jimmy KÉBÉ	MLI	M	1	(4)	
12	Dave KITSON		A	28	(6)	10
8	Leroy LITA		A	10	(4)	1
7	Glen LITTLE		M		(2)	
24	Shane LONG	IRL	A	7	(22)	3
28	Marek MATĚJOVSKÝ	CZE	M	10	(4)	1
2	Graeme MURTY		D	28		
11	John OSTER	WAL	M	12	(6)	
19	Leroy ROSENIOR		D	15	(2)	
19	SEOL Ki-hyeon	KOR	M	2	(1)	
3	Nicky SHOREY		D	36		2
5	Ibrahima SONKO	SEN	D	15	(1)	

SUNDERLAND AFC

Manager – Roy Keane (IRL)

Founded - 1879

MAJOR HONOURS: English League – (6) 1892, 1893, 1895, 1902, 1913, 1936; FA Cup – (2) 1937, 1973.

2007

11/8	Tottenham	h	1-0	*Chopra*
15/8	Birmingham	a	2-2	*Chopra, John*
18/8	Wigan	a	0-3	
25/8	Liverpool	h	0-2	
1/9	Man. United	a	0-1	
15/9	Reading	h	2-1	*Jones, Wallace*
22/9	Middlesbrough	a	2-2	*Leadbitter, Miller*
29/9	Blackburn	h	1-2	*Leadbitter*
7/10	Arsenal	a	2-3	*Wallace, Jones*
21/10	West Ham	a	1-3	*Jones*
27/10	Fulham	h	1-1	*Jones*
5/11	Man. City	a	0-1	
10/11	Newcastle	h	1-1	*Higginbotham*
24/11	Everton	a	1-7	*Yorke*
1/12	Derby	h	1-0	*Stokes*
8/12	Chelsea	a	0-2	
15/12	Aston Villa	h	1-1	*Higginbotham*
22/12	Reading	a	1-2	*Chopra (p)*
26/12	Man. United	h	0-4	
29/12	Bolton	h	3-1	*Richardson, Jones, Murphy*

2008

2/1	Blackburn	a	0-1	
13/1	Portsmouth	h	2-0	*Richardson 2*
19/1	Tottenham	a	0-2	
29/1	Birmingham	h	2-0	*Murphy, Prica*
2/2	Liverpool	a	0-3	
9/2	Wigan	h	2-0	*Etuhu, Murphy*
23/2	Portsmouth	a	0-1	
1/3	Derby	a	0-0	
9/3	Everton	h	0-1	
15/3	Chelsea	h	0-1	
22/3	Aston Villa	a	1-0	*Chopra*
29/3	West Ham	h	2-1	*Jones, Reid*
5/4	Fulham	a	3-1	*Collins, Chopra, Jones*
12/4	Man. City	h	1-2	*Whitehead*
20/4	Newcastle	a	0-2	
26/4	Middlesbrough	h	3-2	*Higginbotham, Chopra, og (Pogatetz)*
3/5	Bolton	a	0-2	
11/5	Arsenal	h	0-1	

No	Name	Nat	Pos	Aps	(s)	Gls
21	Russell ANDERSON	SCO	D		(1)	
26	Phil BARDLEY		D	11		
16	Michael CHOPRA		A	21	(12)	6
20	Andrew COLE		A	3	(4)	
15	Danny COLLINS	WAL	D	32	(4)	1
31	David CONNOLLY	IRL	A	1	(2)	
7	Carlos EDWARDS	TRI	M	11	(2)	
4	Dickson ETUHU	NGA	M	18	(2)	1
44	Jonny EVANS	NIR	D	15		
32	Márton FÜLÖP	HUN	G	1		
1	Craig GORDON	SCO	G	34		
2	Greg HALFORD		D	8		
3	Ian HARTE	IRL	D	3	(5)	
14	Danny HIGGINBOTHAM		D	21		3
14	Stern JOHN	TRI	A		(1)	1
17	Kenwyne JONES	TRI	A	33		7
18	Grant LEADBITTER		M	17	(14)	2
6	Paul McSHANE	IRL	D	20	(1)	
12	Liam MILLER	IRL	M	16	(8)	1
11	Daryl MURPHY		A	20	(8)	3
5	Nyron NOSWORTHY		D	29		
23	Roy O'DONOVAN	IRL	A	4	(13)	
45	Rade PRICA	SWE	A		(6)	1
20	Andy REID	IRL	M	11	(2)	1
10	Kieran RICHARDSON		M	15	(2)	3
9	Anthony STOKES	IRL	A	8	(12)	1
39	Martyn WAGHORN		A	1	(2)	
33	Ross WALLACE	SCO	M	18	(3)	2
13	Darren WARD	WAL	G	3		
8	Dean WHITEHEAD		M	27		1
19	Dwight YORKE	TRI	M	17	(3)	1

TOTTENHAM HOTSPUR FC

Manager – Martin Jol (NED); (29/10/07) Juande Ramos (ESP)

Founded - 1882

MAJOR HONOURS: UEFA Cup Winners' Cup - (1) 1963; UEFA Cup - (2) 1972, 1984; English League - (2) 1951, 1961; FA Cup - (8) 1901, 1921, 1961, 1962, 1967, 1981, 1982, 1991; League Cup - (4) 1971, 1973, 1999, 2008.

2007

11/8	Sunderland	a	0-1	
14/8	Everton	h	1-3	*Gardner*
18/8	Derby	h	4-0	*Malbranque 2, Jenas, Bent*
26/8	Man. United	a	0-1	
1/9	Fulham	a	3-3	*Kaboul, Berbatov, Bale*
15/9	Arsenal	h	1-3	*Bale*
23/9	Bolton	a	1-1	*Keane*
1/10	Aston Villa	h	4-4	*Berbatov, Chimbonda, Keane (p), Kaboul*
7/10	Liverpool	a	2-2	*Keane 2*
22/10	Newcastle	a	1-3	*Keane*
28/10	Blackburn	h	1-2	*Keane (p)*
3/11	Middlesbrough	a	1-1	*Bent*
11/11	Wigan	h	4-0	*Jenas 2, Lennon, Bent*
25/11	West Ham	a	1-1	*Dawson*
2/12	Birmingham	h	2-3	*Keane 2 (1p)*
9/12	Man. City	h	2-1	*Chimbonda, Defoe*
15/12	Portsmouth	a	1-0	*Berbatov*
22/12	Arsenal	a	1-2	*Berbatov*
26/12	Fulham	h	5-1	*Keane 2, Huddlestone Defoe*
29/12	Reading	h	6-4	*Berbatov 4, Malbranque, Defoe*

2008

1/1	Aston Villa	a	1-2	*Defoe*
12/1	Chelsea	a	0-2	
19/1	Sunderland	h	2-0	*Lennon, Keane*

/1	Everton	a	0-0	
2	Man. United	h	1-1	*Berbatov*
2	Derby	a	3-0	*Keane, Kaboul, Berbatov (p)*
3	Birmingham	a	1-4	*Jenas*
3	West Ham	h	4-0	*Berbatov 2, Gilberto, Bent*
/3	Man. City	a	1-2	*Keane*
/3	Chelsea	h	4-4	*Woodgate, Berbatov, Huddlestone, Keane*
/3	Portsmouth	h	2-0	*Bent, O'Hara*
/3	Newcastle	h	1-4	*Bent*
4	Blackburn	a	1-1	*Berbatov*
/4	Middlesbrough	h	1-1	*og (Grounds)*
/4	Wigan	a	1-1	*Berbatov*
/4	Bolton	h	1-1	*Malbranque*
5	Reading	a	1-0	*Keane*
/5	Liverpool	h	0-2	

	Name	Nat	Pos	Aps	(s)	Gls
	Benoît ASSOU-EKOTTO	CMR	D	1		
	Gareth BALE	WAL	D	8		2
	Darren BENT		A	11	(16)	6
	Dimitar BERBATOV	BUL	A	33	(3)	15
	Kevin-Prince BOATENG	GER	M	7	(6)	
	Radek ČERNÝ	CZE	G	13		
	Pascal CHIMBONDA	FRA	D	31	(1)	2
	Michael DAWSON		D	26	(1)	1
	Jermain DEFOE		A	3	(16)	4
	Anthony GARDNER		D	4		1
	GILBERTO da Silva Melo	BRA	D	3	(3)	1
	Chris GUNTER	WAL	D	1	(1)	
	Tom HUDDLESTONE		M	18	(10)	3
	Alan HUTTON	SCO	D	14		
	Jermaine JENAS		M	28	(1)	4
	Younes KABOUL	FRA	D	19	(2)	3
	Robbie KEANE	IRL	A	32	(4)	15
	Ledley KING		D	4		
	LEE Young-pyo	KOR	D	17	(1)	
	Aaron LENNON		M	25	(4)	2
	Steed MALBRANQUE	FRA	M	35	(2)	4
	Jamie O'HARA		M	9	(8)	1
	RICARDO ROCHA	POR	D	4	(1)	
	Paul ROBINSON		G	25		
	Wayne ROUTLEDGE		M	1	(1)	
	Paul STALTERI	CAN	D	3		
	Adel TAARABT	FRA	M		(6)	
	Teemu TAINIO	FIN	M	6	(10)	
	Jonathan WOODGATE		D	12		1
	Didier ZOKORA	CIV	M	25	(3)	

WEST HAM UNITED FC

Manager – Alan Curbishley

Founded - 1900

MAJOR HONOURS: UEFA Cup Winners' Cup – (1) 1965; FA Cup – (3) 1964, 1975, 1980.

07				
/8	Man. City	h	0-2	
/8	Birmingham	a	1-0	*Noble (p)*
/8	Wigan	h	1-1	*Bowyer*
9	Reading	a	3-0	*Bellamy, Etherington 2*
/9	Middlesbrough	h	3-0	*Bowyer, og (Young), Ashton*
/9	Newcastle	a	1-3	*Ashton*
/9	Arsenal	h	0-1	
10	Aston Villa	a	0-1	
/10	Sunderland	h	3-1	*Cole, og (Gordon), Bellamy*
/10	Portsmouth	a	0-0	
4/11	Bolton	h	1-1	*McCartney*
10/11	Derby	a	5-0	*Bowyer 2, Etherington, Spector, Solano*
25/11	Tottenham	h	1-1	*Cole*
1/12	Chelsea	a	0-1	
9/12	Blackburn	a	1-0	*Ashton*
15/12	Everton	h	0-2	
22/12	Middlesbrough	a	2-1	*Ashton, Parker*
26/12	Reading	h	1-1	*Solano*
29/12	Man. United	h	2-1	*Ferdinand, Upson*
2008				
1/1	Arsenal	a	0-2	
12/1	Fulham	h	2-1	*Ashton, Ferdinand*
20/1	Man. City	a	1-1	*Cole*
30/1	Liverpool	h	1-0	*Noble (p)*
2/2	Wigan	a	0-1	
9/2	Birmingham	h	1-1	*Ljungberg*
23/2	Fulham	a	1-0	*Solano*
1/3	Chelsea	h	0-4	
5/3	Liverpool	a	0-4	
9/3	Tottenham	a	0-4	
15/3	Blackburn	h	2-1	*Ashton, Sears*
22/3	Everton	a	1-1	*Ashton*
29/3	Sunderland	a	1-2	*Ljungberg*
8/4	Portsmouth	h	0-1	
12/4	Bolton	a	0-1	
19/4	Derby	h	2-1	*Zamora, Cole*
26/4	Newcastle	h	2-2	*Noble, Ashton*
3/5	Man. United	a	1-4	*Ashton*
11/5	Aston Villa	h	2-2	*Solano, Ashton*

No	Name	Nat	Pos	Aps	(s)	Gls
9	Dean ASHTON		A	20	(11)	10
10	Craig BELLAMY	WAL	A	7	(1)	2
34	Luís BOA MORTE	POR	M	18	(9)	
29	Lee BOWYER		M	12	(3)	4
33	Henri CAMARA	SEN	A	3	(7)	
12	Carlton COLE		A	21	(10)	4
20	James COLLINS	WAL	D	2	(1)	
39	Jack COLLISON		M	1	(1)	
32	Kieron DYER		M	2		
11	Matthew ETHERINGTON		M	15	(3)	3
20	Julien FAUBERT	FRA	M	4	(3)	
5	Anton FERDINAND		D	22	(3)	2
4	Danny GABBIDON	WAL	D	8	(2)	
1	Robert GREEN		G	38		
7	Fredrik LJUNGBERG	SWE	M	22	(3)	2
3	George McCARTNEY	NIR	D	38		1
17	Hayden MULLINS		M	32	(2)	
2	Lucas NEILL	AUS	D	34		
16	Mark NOBLE		M	25	(6)	3
14	John PAINTSIL	GHA	D	4	(10)	
8	Scott PARKER		M	17	(1)	1
28	Kyel REID		M		(1)	
12	Freddie SEARS		A	1	(6)	1
15	Nolberto SOLANO	PER	M	14	(9)	4
18	Jonathan SPECTOR	USA	D	13	(13)	1
30	James TOMKINS		D	5	(1)	
6	Matthew UPSON		D	29		1
25	Bobby ZAMORA		A	11	(2)	1

WIGAN ATHLETIC FC

Manager – Chris Hutchings; (5/11/07) (Frank Barlow); (19/11/07) Steve Bruce

Founded - 1932

2007				
11/8	Everton	a	1-2	*Sibierski*
15/8	Middlesbrough	h	1-0	*Sibierski*

18/8	Sunderland	h	3-0	*Heskey, Landzaat (p), Sibierski (p)*
25/8	West Ham	a	1-1	*Scharner*
1/9	Newcastle	a	0-1	
15/9	Fulham	h	1-1	*Koumas (p)*
22/9	Reading	a	1-2	*Bent*
29/9	Liverpool	h	0-1	
6/10	Man. United	a	0-4	
20/10	Portsmouth	h	0-2	
27/10	Birmingham	a	2-3	*Bent 2*
3/11	Chelsea	h	0-2	
11/11	Tottenham	a	0-4	
24/11	Arsenal	a	0-2	
1/12	Man. City	h	1-1	*Scharner*
9/12	Bolton	a	1-4	*Landzaat*
15/12	Blackburn	h	5-3	*Landzaat, Bent 3, Scharner*
22/12	Fulham	a	1-1	*Bent*
26/12	Newcastle	h	1-0	*Taylor*
29/12	Aston Villa	h	1-2	*Bramble*
2008				
2/1	Liverpool	a	1-1	*Bramble*
12/1	Derby	a	1-0	*Sibierski*
20/1	Everton	h	1-2	*og (Jagielka)*
29/1	Middlesbrough	a	0-1	
2/2	West Ham	h	1-0	*Kilbane*
9/2	Sunderland	a	0-2	
23/2	Derby	h	2-0	*Scharner, Valencia*
1/3	Man. City	a	0-0	
9/3	Arsenal	h	0-0	
16/3	Bolton	h	1-0	*Heskey*
22/3	Blackburn	a	1-3	*King (p)*
29/3	Portsmouth	a	0-2	
5/4	Birmingham	h	2-0	*Taylor 2*
14/4	Chelsea	a	1-1	*Heskey*
19/4	Tottenham	h	1-1	*Heskey*
26/4	Reading	h	0-0	
3/5	Aston Villa	a	2-0	*Valencia 2*
11/5	Man. United	h	0-2	

No	Name	Nat	Pos	Aps	(s)	Gls
15	Julius AGHAHOWA	NGA	A	2	(12)	
23	Marcus BENT		A	25	(6)	7
17	Emmerson BOYCE		D	24	(1)	
19	Titus BRAMBLE		D	26		2
11	Michael BROWN		M	27	(4)	
22	David COTTERILL	WAL	M	2		
3	Erik EDMAN	SWE	D	5		
31	Maynor FIGUEROA	HON	D	1	(1)	
20	Caleb FOLAN	IRL	A	1	(1)	
4	Andreas GRANQVIST	SWE	D	13	(1)	
32	Erik HAGEN	NOR	D	1		
5	Fitz HALL		D		(1)	
9	Emile HESKEY		A	27	(1)	4
8	Kevin KILBANE	IRL	D	33	(2)	1
14	Marlon KING		A	8	(7)	1
1	Chris KIRKLAND		G	37		
10	Jason KOUMAS	WAL	M	21	(9)	1
14	Denny LANDZAAT	NED	M	19		3
25	Mario MELCHIOT	NED	D	31		
20	Salomon OLEMBÉ	CMR	M	2	(6)	
5	Wilson PALACIOS	HON	M	16		
12	Mike POLLITT		G	1		
18	Paul SCHARNER	AUT	D	37		4
6	Antoine SIBIERSKI	FRA	A	10	(20)	4
24	Josip SKOKO	AUS	M	7	(5)	
2	Ryan TAYLOR		M	12	(5)	3
16	Luis Antonio VALENCIA	ECU	M	30	(1)	3

PROMOTION CLUBS

WEST BROMWICH ALBION FC

Manager – Tony Mowbray

Founded – 1878

MAJOR HONOURS: English League – (1) 1920; FA Cup – (5) 1888, 1
1931, 1954, 1968; League Cup – (1) 1966.

STOKE CITY FC

Manager – Tony Pulis

Founded – 1868

MAJOR HONOURS: League Cup – (1) 1972.

HULL CITY AFC

Manager – Phil Brown

Founded – 1904

SECOND LEVEL FINAL TABLE 2007/0

		Pld	W	D	L	F	A
1	West Bromwich Albion FC	46	23	12	11	88	55
2	Stoke City FC	46	21	16	9	69	55
3	Hull City FC	46	21	12	13	65	47
4	Bristol City FC	46	20	14	12	54	53
5	Crystal Palace FC	46	18	17	11	58	42
6	Watford FC	46	18	16	12	62	56
7	Wolverhampton Wanderers FC	46	18	16	12	53	48
8	Ipswich Town FC	46	18	15	13	65	56
9	Sheffield United FC	46	17	15	14	56	51
10	Plymouth Argyle FC	46	17	13	16	60	50
11	Charlton Athletic FC	46	17	13	16	63	58
12	Cardiff City FC	46	16	16	14	59	55
13	Burnley FC	46	16	14	16	60	67
14	Queens Park Rangers FC	46	14	16	16	60	66
15	Preston North End FC	46	15	11	20	50	56
16	Sheffield Wednesday FC	46	14	13	19	54	55
17	Norwich City FC	46	15	10	21	49	59
18	Barnsley FC	46	14	13	19	52	65
19	Blackpool FC	46	12	18	16	59	64
20	Southampton FC	46	13	15	18	56	72
21	Coventry City FC	46	14	11	21	52	64
22	Leicester City FC	46	12	16	18	42	45
23	Scunthorpe United FC	46	11	13	22	46	69
24	Colchester United FC	46	7	17	22	62	86

PROMOTION PLAY-OFFS

(10/5/08 & 13/5/08)
Crystal Palace 1, Bristol City 2
Bristol City 2, Crystal Palace 1 *(aet)*
(Bristol City 4-2)

(11/5/08 & 14/5/08)
Watford 0, Hull 2
Hull 4, Watford 1
(Hull 6-1)

(24/5/08)
Hull City 1 Bristol City 0

DOMESTIC CUPS 2007/08

FA CUP

HIRD ROUND

'/1/08)
ston Villa 0, Manchester United 2
arnsley 2, Blackpool 1
ackburn 1, Coventry 4
olton 0, Sheffield United 1
ighton 1, Mansfield 2
istol City 1, Middlesbrough 2
harlton 1, West Brom 1
hasetown 1, Cardiff 3
helsea 1, QPR 0
olchester 1, Peterborough 3
'erton 0, Oldham 1
uddersfield 2, Birmingham 1
swich 0, Portsmouth 1
orwich 1, Bury 1
ymouth 3, Hull 2
eston 1, Scunthorpe 0
outhampton 2, Leicester 0
outhend 5, Dagenham & Redbridge 2
inderland 0, Wigan 3
vansea 1, Havant & Waterlooville 1
vindon 1, Barnet 1
ttenham 2, Reading 2
anmere 2, Hereford 2
'alsall 0, Millwall 0
atford 2, Crystal Palace 0
est Ham 0, Manchester City 0
'olves 2, Cambridge 1

/1/08)
urnley 0, Arsenal 2
erby 2, Sheffield Wednesday 2
ilham 2, Bristol Rovers 2
uton 1, Liverpool 1
oke 0, Newcastle 0

eplays

5/1/08)
ury 2, Norwich 1
verpool 5, Luton 0
illwall 2, Walsall 1
eading 0, Tottenham 1
'est Brom 2, Charlton 2 *(aet; 4-3 on pens)*

(16/1/08)
Havant & Waterlooville 4, Swansea 2
Hereford 1, Tranmere 0
Manchester City 1, West Ham 0
Newcastle 4, Stoke 1

(22/1/08)
Barnet 1, Swindon 1 *(aet; 2-0 on pens)*
Bristol Rovers 0, Fulham 0 *(aet; 5-3 on pens)*
Sheffield Wednesday 1, Derby 1 *(aet; 2-4 on pens)*

FOURTH ROUND

(25/1/07)
Southend 0, Barnsley 1

(26/1/07)
Arsenal 3, Newcastle 0
Barnet 0, Bristol Rovers 1
Coventry 2, Millwall 1
Derby 1, Preston 4
Liverpool 5, Havant & Waterlooville 2
Mansfield 0, Middlesbrough 2
Oldham 0, Huddersfield 1
Peterborough 0, West Brom 3
Portsmouth 2, Plymouth 1
Southampton 2, Bury 0
Watford 1, Wolves 4
Wigan 1, Chelsea 2

(27/1/08)
Hereford 1, Cardiff 2
Manchester United 3, Tottenham 1
Sheffield United 2, Manchester City 1

FIFTH ROUND

(16/2/08)
Bristol Rovers 1, Southampton 0
Cardiff 2, Wolves 0
Chelsea 3, Huddersfield 1
Coventry 0, West Brom 5
Liverpool 1, Barnsley 2
Manchester United 4, Arsenal 0

(17/2/08)
Preston 0, Portsmouth 1
Sheffield United 0, Middlesbrough 0

Replay

(27/2/08)
Middlesbrough 1, Sheffield United 0 (aet)

QUARTER-FINALS

(8/3/07)
Barnsley 1 *(Odejayi 66)*, Chelsea 0
Manchester United 0, Portsmouth 1 *(Muntari 78p)*

(9/3/07)
Bristol Rovers 1 *(Coles 31)*, West Brom 5 *(Morrison 16, Miller 30, 69, 85, Phillips 73)*
Middlesbrough 0, Cardiff 2 *(Whittingham 9, Johnson 23)*

SEMI-FINALS

(5/4/08)
Portsmouth 1 *(Kanu 54)*, West Brom 0

(6/4/08)
Cardiff 1 *(Ledley 9)*, Barnsley 0

FINAL

(17/5/08)
Wembley Stadium, London
PORTSMOUTH FC 1 *(Kanu 37)*
CARDIFF CITY FC 0
Referee – *Dean*
PORTSMOUTH – *James, Johnson, Campbell, Distin, Hreidarsson, Utaka (Nugent 69), Pedro Mendes (Diop 78), Diarra, Muntari, Kranjčar, Kanu (Baroš 87).*
CARDIFF – *Enckelman, McNaughton, Johnson, Loovens, Capaldi, Whittingham (Ramsey 61), Rae (Sinclair 87), McPhail, Ledley, Parry, Hasselbaink (Thompson 71).*

LEAGUE CUP

UARTER-FINALS

2/12/07)
'est Ham 1 *(Cole 12)*, Everton 2 *(Osman 40, akubu 88)*

8/12/07)
lackburn 2 *(Santa Cruz 42, 60)*, Arsenal 3 *Diaby 6, Eduardo 29, 104) (aet)*
lanchester City 0, Tottenham 2 *(Defoe 5, 'albranque 82)*

'9/12/07)
helsea 2 *(Lampard 59, Shevchenko 90)*, iverpool 0

SEMI-FINALS

(8/1/08 & 23/1/08)
Chelsea 2 *(Wright-Phillips 26, Lescott 90og)*, Everton 1 *(Yakubu 64)*
Everton 0, Chelsea 1 *(Cole J. 69)*
(Chelsea 3-1)

(9/1/08 & 22/1/08)
Arsenal 1 *(Walcott 79)*, Tottenham 1 *(Jenas 37)*
Tottenham 5 *(Jenas 3, Bendtner 27og, Keane 48, Lennon 60, Malbranque 90)*, Arsenal 1 *(Adebayor 70)*
(Tottenham 6-2)

FINAL

(24/2/08)
Wembley Stadium, London
TOTTENHAM HOTSPUR FC 2 *(Berbatov 70p, Woodgate 94)*
CHELSEA FC 1 *(Drogba 39)*
(aet)
Referee – *Halsey*
TOTTENHAM – *Robinson, Hutton, Woodgate, King, Chimbonda (Huddlestone 61), Lennon, Jenas, Zokora, Malbranque (Tainio 75), Berbatov, Keane (Kaboul 102).*
CHELSEA – *Čech, Belletti, Ricardo Carvalho, Terry, Bridge, Wright-Phillips (Kalou 72), Essien (Ballack 88), Lampard, Mikel (Cole J. 98), Anelka, Drogba.*

ESTONIA

Free-scoring Levadia retain title

The Estonian Meistriliiga was won for the second year in succession by FC Levadia Tallinn. The club does not boast many fans but those who came to support them were regularly treated to a flurry of goals, with Levadia chalking up 126 in their 36 matches – a healthy average of 3.5 per game.

It took Levadia until their penultimate fixture – a 3-0 win at new merger club JK Maag Tammeka Tartu – to clinch the title, but at no stage during the previous eight months had it ever looked like escaping the defending champions. Apart from a shock early defeat at newcomers JK Kalev Tallinn, Levadia claimed victories as a matter of course. From mid-April to late August they racked up 16 wins and two draws from 18 games, defeating all of their prospective challengers in the process.

23-goal Zelinski

Veteran Estonian international striker Indrek Zelinski accounted for 23 of Levadia's massive goal tally and was the team's top scorer, finishing second only in the overall league listings to JK Trans Narva's 30-goal Dmitri Lipartov. No fewer than 17 Levadia players got their name on the scoresheet at least once, with young Estonian international Tarmo Kink the next best on 16, closely followed by Russian teenage supersub Nikita Andreev on 13.

Raio Piiroja retained his title of Estonian Player of the Year

Tarmo Rüütli, Levadia's coach since 2003, oversaw his third title triumph, but although he was handed the reins of the Estonian national team – for the second time – in December 2007 as the replacement for short-term incumbent Viggo Jensen, it was agreed that Rüütli would initially fulfil both roles, allowing him the opportunity to complete a Meistriliiga hat-trick. But after the opening game of the 2008 domestic season, in which Levadia were trounced 4-1 in the Super Cup by Trans, he decided to quit and devote himself exclusively to Estonia.

Jensen, a former FC Bayern München and Denmark player, was always likely to step down after his six-month contract ended. He led the team to a couple of wins against Andorra and a draw away to FYR Macedonia, which gave Estonia their only points of a disastrous UEFA EURO 2008™ campaign. The first Estonian player to register a goal in the competition – in the 2-1 home win over Andorra – was defender Raio Piiroja. The 28-year-old from Norwegian club Fredrikstad FK was also on target in Skopje and closed 2007 by retaining his Estonian Footballer of the Year award.

Piiroja's former club, Flora, ended their long wait for a domestic trophy by winning the 2008 Estonian Cup. It had been ten years since their previous Cup win, and there was one survivor from that 1998 triumph, veteran midfielder Martin Reim, who, having returned to the national side for the end of the UEFA EURO 2008™ campaign, set a new European international record of 156 caps, bypassing the previous mark of 150 set by (West) Germany's Lothar Matthäus. Flora took the trophy after defeating holders Levadia on penalties in the semi-final and overcoming Maag Tammeka 3-1 in the final, their opening goal, from defender-turned-striker Sander Post, coming after just 28 seconds.

Having finished second in the 2007 Meistriliiga, following a closing 19-match unbeaten run, Flora were already assured of their place in the 2008/09

FA Cup prior to the Cup final. However, their victory s cheered by third-placed FC TVMK Tallinn, who is claimed the second UEFA Cup spot, while fourth-ced Trans earned admittance to the UEFA Intertoto p. Thus the same four Estonian teams that had alified for Europe the previous season returned.

Levadia, who had made history by reaching the first round of the UEFA Cup in 2006, came close to another European exploit when they were defeated only on away goals by former champions FK Crvena Zvezda in the second qualifying round of the UEFA Champions League.

Eesti Jalgpalli Liit (EJL)

A. Le Coq Arena
Asula 4c
EE-11312 Tallinn
tel - +372 6279960
fax - +372 6279969
website - www.jalgpall.ee
email - efa@jalgpall.ee
Year of Formation – 1921
President – Aivar Pohlak
General Secretary - Tõnu Sirel
Press Officer – Mihkel Uiboleht

Stadium - A. Le Coq Arena, Tallinn (9,692)

TOP FIVE ALL-TIME CAPS
Martin Reim (156); Marko Kristal (143); Mart Poom (118); Andres Oper (108); Kristen Viikmäe (106)

TOP FIVE ALL-TIME GOALS
Andres Oper (33); Indrek Zelinski (27); Eduard Ellmen-Eelma (21); Arnold Pihlak (17); Richard Kuremaa (16)

TIONAL TEAM RESULTS 2007/08

7	Andorra (ECQ)	H	Tallinn	2-1	*Piiroja (34), Zelinski (90+2)*
	Croatia (ECQ)	A	Zagreb	0-2	
7	FYR Macedonia (ECQ)	A	Skopje	1-1	*Piiroja (17)*
'07	England (ECQ)	A	Wembley	0-3	
'07	Montenegro	H	Tallinn	0-1	
7	Saudi Arabia	A	Jeddah	0-2	
'07	Andorra (ECQ)	A	Andorra la Vella	2-0	*Oper (31), Lindpere (60)*
'07	Uzbekistan	A	Tashkent	0-0	
8	Poland	A	Wronki	0-2	
08	Canada	H	Tallinn	2-0	*Stalteri (59og), Zahovaiko (90)*
08	Georgia	H	Tallinn	1-1	*Kink (64p)*
08	Latvia	A	Riga	0-1	
08	Lithuania	N	Jurmala (LVA)	0-1	
	Faroe Islands	H	Tallinn	4-3	*Zahovaiko (9, 14), Kink (28), Novikov (75)*

TIONAL TEAM APPEARANCES 2007/08

– Viggo JENSEN (DEN) /07) Tarmo RÜÜTLI		15/9/47 11/8/54	AND	CRO	MKD	ENG	Mne	Ksa	AND	Uzb	Pol	Can	Geo	Lva	Ltu	Fro	Caps	Goals
OOM	3/2/72	Watford (ENG)	G			G								G		G46	118	-
ÄÄGER	18/11/84	Aalesund (NOR)	D		D	D	D	D	D	D	s84	D90				D	53	-
KRUGLOV	24/5/84	Torpedo Moskva (RUS) /Neftçi (AZE)	D	M	D	D			D84	s56		D					33	1
IIROJA	11/7/79	Fredrikstad (NOR)	D	D	D	D		D	D	D			D				75	6

ESTONIA

NATIONAL TEAM APPEARANCES 2007/08 (contd.)

Coach – Viggo JENSEN (DEN) /(1/12/07) Tarmo RÜÜTLI		15/9/47 11/8/54	AND	CRO	MKD	ENG	Mne	Ksa	AND	Uzb	Pol	Can	Geo	Lva	Ltu	Fro	Caps
Andrei STEPANOV	16/3/79	Khimki (RUS)	D	D	D	D	D		D	D				D	D	D	78
Aleksandr DMITRIJEV	18/2/82	Levadia	M	M	M	M	M88	M	M	M	M	M74					
		/Hønefoss (NOR)											M	s60	M	M46	34
Ragnar KLAVAN	30/10/85	Heracles (NED)	M		M	M	M		M	M66		M56	D	D	D		46
Joel LINDPERE	5/10/81	Tromsø (NOR)	M	M92	M	M	M	M57	M	M			s58	M			59
Martin REIM	14/5/71	Flora	M	s92	s62		M78	M85	M68								156
Vladimir VOSKOBOINIKOV	2/2/83	Torpedo Moskva (RUS)	A46								s58			s60	A	s60	7
Indrek ZELINSKI	13/11/74	Levadia	A														102
Tarmo KINK	6/10/85	Levadia	s46	A81	s79	A62	s81	s57	s46	A75	M73	A85	M	A	s66	A61	23
Pavel LONDAK	14/5/80	Bodø/Glimt (NOR)		G	G				G	G	G	G	G				10
Urmas ROOBA	8/7/78	TPS (FIN)		D85			D	D70				s85	s71			D	70
Teet ALLAS	2/6/77	Flora		D				s85									73
Taavi RÄHN	16/5/81	Ekranas (LTU)		M	M62	M	s78			M	D	D					38
Andres OPER	7/1/77	Roda (NED)		A	A90				A46								108
Kaimar SAAG	5/8/88	Levadia		s81	A79	A	A81	A	A	A46							
		/Silkeborg (DEN)									s89	A	A46				10
Aivar ANNISTE	18/2/80	TVMK		s85	s90			M85		s75	M67		M57	M60	M69	s72	43
Kristen VIIKMÄE	10/2/79	Flora				s62	s66										
		/Jönköping (SWE)											A71				106
Mihkel AKSALU	7/11/84	Flora					G46	G							G		3
Alo BÄRENGRUB	12/2/84	Flora					D	D									
		/Bodø/Glimt (NOR)									D	D	D				13
Tarmo NEEMELO	10/2/82	Sundsvall (SWE)					A66										20
Sergei PAREIKO	31/1/77	Tom (RUS)					s46										5
Sergei TEREHHOV	18/4/75	TVMK					s88										94
Vjatšeslav ZAHOVAIKO	29/12/81	Flora						A70			A58	s69	s46	A60	A66	A60	37
Taijo TENISTE	31/1/88	Levadia						s70	s68	D56							3
Jarmo AHJUPERA	13/4/84	Flora						s70		s46							5
Gert KAMS	25/5/85	Flora						s85									5
Konstantin VASSILJEV	16/8/84	Levadia							s84	s66							
		/Lendava (SVN)									M89	M				M72	9
Andrei SIDORENKOV	12/2/84	Flora									D			D	s88	s61	11
Tihhon ŠIŠOV	11/2/83	Levadia									D84	s90	D	D	D		11
Ats PURJE	3/8/85	Inter Turku (FIN)									M	M69	M58	M60	M88	M	8
Martin VUNK	21/8/84	Flora									s67	s74	s57	M	s69	s72	6
Oliver KONSA	4/03/85	TVMK									s73	s56					7
Sander PURI	7/5/88	Levadia												s60	M	M72	3
Igor MOROZOV	27/5/89	Levadia													D	D	2
Artur KOTENKO	20/8/81	Sandnes Ulf (NOR)														s46	15
Jevgeni NOVIKOV	28/6/80	Rīga (LVA)														s46	13

DOMESTIC LEAGUE 2007

STRILIIGA FINAL TABLE

		Home					Away					Total					
	Pld	W	D	L	F	A	W	D	L	F	A	W	D	L	F	A	Pts
Levadia Tallinn	36	15	2	1	65	10	14	2	2	61	10	29	4	3	126	20	91
Flora	36	14	2	2	77	14	12	3	3	31	16	26	5	5	108	30	83
TVMK Tallinn	36	14	2	2	79	18	11	2	5	37	18	25	4	7	116	36	79
Trans Narva	36	12	1	5	46	17	13	2	3	43	11	25	3	8	89	28	78
Maag Tammeka tu	36	9	4	5	30	19	9	4	5	24	21	18	8	10	54	40	62
Kalev Tallinn	36	7	2	9	22	31	6	2	10	22	46	13	4	19	44	77	43
Tulevik Viljandi	36	5	2	11	19	33	6	2	10	24	47	11	4	21	43	80	37
Vaprus Pärnu	36	3	1	14	9	38	5	0	13	26	58	8	1	27	35	96	25
Kuressaare	36	2	2	14	10	43	3	1	14	15	51	5	3	28	25	94	18
Ajax Lasnamäe	36	0	1	17	6	68	1	1	16	8	85	1	2	33	14	153	5

TOP GOALSCORERS

30 Dmitri LIPARTOV (Trans)
23 Indrek ZELINSKI (Levadia)
20 Tiit TIKENBERG (Kalev)
18 Maksim GRUZNOV (Trans)
17 Jarmo AHJUPERA (Flora)
16 Tarmo KINK (Levadia)
14 Juha Pekka HAKOLA (Flora)
Vjatšeslav ZAHOVAIKO (Flora)
Sergei ZENJOV (TVMK)
Aleksandr DUBÕKIN (Trans)

CLUB-BY-CLUB

FC AJAX LASNAMÄE

Coach – Boris Dugan

Founded – 1993

7

3	Levadia	a	0-5	
3	Maag Tammeka	h	0-2	
3	Vaprus	a	0-1	
	Tulevik	a	0-2	
	Flora	h	0-2	
4	TVMK	a	1-7	*O'Konnel-Bronin*
4	Trans	h	0-4	
4	Kuressaare	a	2-2	*Jõgiste, O'Konnel-Bronin*
4	Kalev	h	1-4	*Kirpu A.*
	Kalev	a	0-5	
5	Kuressaare	h	1-4	*Teivan*
5	Trans	a	0-2	
5	TVMK	h	0-6	
	Kuressaare	a	1-0	*Abdullajev*
	Flora	a	0-11	
6	Tulevik	h	0-5	
6	Vaprus	h	0-5	
6	Maag Tammeka	a	0-2	
	Levadia	h	0-10	
7	Kalev	h	1-1	*Papichyts*
7	Trans	h	0-3	
	TVMK	a	0-13	
8	Flora	h	0-4	
8	Tulevik	a	1-4	*Televinov*
8	Vaprus	a	0-2	
	Maag Tammeka	h	0-2	
9	Levadia	a	1-7	*O'Konnel-Bronin*
9	Levadia	h	1-2	*Teivan (p)*
9	Vaprus	h	1-7	*Abdullajev*
9	Maag Tammeka	a	1-5	*Rõtškov*
0	Tulevik	h	0-3	
0	Flora	a	0-10	
10	TVMK	h	0-2	
10	Trans	a	1-6	*O'Konnel-Bronin*
1	Kuressaare	h	1-2	*Papichyts*
11	Kalev	a	0-1	

me	Nat	Pos	Aps	(s)	Gls
rijar ABDULLAJEV		M	26	(4)	2
ksandr ALTOSAR		D	11	(3)	
Ilya AVDEYENKO	RUS	D	7	(2)	
Aleksandr BORODINOV		M		(5)	
Valentin FUKSOV	RUS	D	11	(3)	
Vladimir GERASIMOV		D	22	(4)	
Sergei IVANOV		D	14		
Deniss JÕGISTE		A	24	(8)	1
Ilja KASSJATŠUK		G	21		
Aleksandr KIRPU		D	19	(6)	1
Jevgeni KIRPU		M		(1)	
Sergei KONONOV		D	7	(6)	
Igor KOROLJOV		M	15	(3)	
Aleksandr KOVTUN		M	22	(5)	
Deniss KOVTUN		D		(1)	
Aleksandr LAMONOV		A	10	(6)	
Sergei LEVOTŠSKI		M	3		
Vladimir LJAHHOVETSKI		M		(1)	
Dmitri MAKAREVITŠ		A	15		
Maksim MAMUTOV		G	10	(1)	
Maksim MAMUTOV (same player)		M	1	(1)	
Šamil MUSSAJEV		D	1	(3)	
Ivan O'KONNEL-BRONIN		A	32		4
Dzmitry PAPICHYTS	BLR	M	13		2
Konstantin PETROV		G	1		
Pavel POGODAJEV		G	4	(8)	
Robert RAUDSAAR		M	1	(7)	
Maksim RÕTSKOV		M	18		1
Gevorg SARGSYAN	ARM	M		(3)	
Anton SEREDA		M	6	(4)	
Deniss SKOBELEV		M	7	(1)	
Aleksandr STARODUB		M	1	(4)	
Dmitri TARASSENKO		D	9	(4)	
Roman TEIVAN		A	25	(1)	2
Konstantin TELEVINOV		A	33		1
Austris UNGURS		M	7	(1)	

FC FLORA

Coach - Pasi Rautiainen (FIN)

Founded - 1990

MAJOR HONOURS: Estonian League - (7) 1994, 1995, 1998, 1998, 2001, 2002, 2003; Estonian Cup - (3) 1995, 1998, 2008.

2007

10/3	Kalev	a	1-0	*Mošnikov*
17/3	Levadia	h	1-2	*Jääger*
31/3	Maag Tammeka	a	0-0	

ESTONIA

Date	Opponent		Score	Scorers
3/4	Vaprus	h	7-0	*Hakola 2 (1p), Bärengrub, Taska, Mošnikov, Kalda, Viikmäe*
7/4	Ajax Lasnamäe	a	2-0	*Sirevičius, Hakola (p)*
14/4	Tulevik	a	2-1	*Post, Jääger*
21/4	TVMK	h	2-2	*Hakola, Viikmäe*
24/4	Trans	a	1-3	*Viikmäe*
28/4	Kuressaare	h	5-0	*Viikmäe 2, Jääger, Hakola (p), Kalda*
5/5	Kuressaare	a	1-0	*Jääger*
12/5	Trans	h	0-2	
19/5	TVMK	a	0-6	
26/5	Tulevik	h	4-0	*Jääger 2, Viikmäe, Taska*
9/6	Ajax Lasnamäe	h	11-0	*Hakola 3 (1p), Ahjupera 2, Post, Taska, Hurt, Reim, Jääger, Mošnikov*
16/6	Vaprus	a	3-0	*Bärengrub 2, Taska*
19/6	Maag Tammeka	h	3-0	*Jääger, Mošnikov, Hakola*
30/6	Levadia	a	1-2	*Mošnikov*
7/7	Kalev	h	4-2	*Ahjupera 3, Mošnikov*
14/7	Kuressaare	h	5-1	*Zahovaiko 3, Vanna, Bärengrub*
24/7	Trans	a	3-0	*Kams 2, Reim*
28/7	TVMK	h	2-0	*Vunk, Ahjupera*
7/8	Tulevik	a	3-0	*Ahjupera 3*
11/8	Ajax Lasnamäe	a	4-0	*Vunk 2, Bärengrub, Kalda*
18/8	Vaprus	h	8-1	*Zahovaiko 4 (1p), Hakola 2, Ahjupera, Kalda*
25/8	Maag Tammeka	a	0-0	
1/9	Levadia	h	3-2	*Bärengrub, Ahjupera, Zahovaiko (p)*
15/9	Kalev	a	3-1	*Viikmäe 2, Zahovaiko*
18/9	Kalev	h	4-1	*Viikmäe, Ahjupera, Reim, Zahovaiko*
22/9	Levadia	a	1-1	*Zahovaiko*
29/9	Maag Tammeka	h	3-1	*Zahovaiko, Sirevičius, Ahjupera*
2/10	Vaprus	a	1-0	*Reim*
6/10	Ajax Lasnamäe	h	10-0	*Sirevičius 3, Ahjupera 2, Sidorenkov, Hakola, Post, Bärengrub, og (Mamutov)*
20/10	Tulevik	h	5-0	*Ahjupera 2, Sirevičius, Hakola, Mošnikov*
27/10	TVMK	a	2-1	*Zahovaiko, Kams*
3/11	Trans	h	0-0	
10/11	Kuressaare	a	3-1	*Zahovaiko, Bärengrub, Hakola*

Name	Nat	Pos	Aps	(s)	Gls
Jarmo AHJUPERA		A	9	(16)	17
Mihkel AKSALU		G	30		
Teet ALLAS		D	25		
Alo BÄRENGRUB		D	31		8
Alo DUPIKOV		D		(2)	
Juha Pekka HAKOLA	FIN	A	30	(1)	14
Martin HURT		M	13	(2)	1
Enver JÄÄGER		A	18		8
Janek KALDA		A	2	(20)	4
Gert KAMS		M	17	(11)	3
Tõnis KAUKVERE		M		(1)	
Andres KOOGAS		D	2		
Jürgen KURESOO		A	1	(12)	
Andrei MAZURKEVITŠ		D	9	(3)	
Sergei MOŠNIKOV		M	22	(7)	7
Aiko ORGLA		G	5		
Stanislav PEDÕK		G	1		
Sander POST		D	10	(10)	3
Martin REIM		M	35		4
Siim ROOPS		D	6	(4)	
Andrei SIDORENKOV		M	29		1
Tomas SIREVIČIUS	LTU	M	19	(2)	6
Heikki TALIMAA		A	11	(2)	
Martin TASKA		D	13	(5)	4
Janar TÜKK		M		(1)	
Tõnis VANNA		D	19	(2)	1
Kristen VIIKMÄE		A	15	(3)	9
Martin VUNK		M	7	(1)	3
Vjatšeslav ZAHOVAIKO		A	17		14

JK KALEV TALLINN

Coach - Aavo Sarap

Founded – 1911

2007				
10/3	Flora	h	0-1	
17/3	TVMK	a	0-5	
31/3	Trans	h	0-2	
3/4	Kuressaare	a	3-1	*Vahtramäe, Timofeje Tiismann*
7/4	Tulevik	h	2-1	*Saag, Tikenberg*
14/4	Levadia	h	1-0	*Mõistlik*
21/4	Maag Tammeka	a	1-1	*Tikenberg*
24/4	Vaprus	h	0-2	
28/4	Ajax Lasnamäe	a	4-1	*Tikenberg 3, Kõrtsmi*
5/5	Ajax Lasnamäe	h	5-0	*Timofejev 2, Afanaso Tikenberg, Kiis*
12/5	Vaprus	a	1-0	*Tikenberg*
19/5	Maag Tammeka	h	0-2	
26/5	Levadia	a	2-4	*Kirilov 2*
9/6	Tulevik	a	1-2	*Demutski*
16/6	Kuressaare	h	2-1	*Tikenberg 2*
19/6	Trans	a	1-0	*Kiis*
7/7	Flora	a	2-4	*Tikenberg 2 (1p)*
14/7	Ajax Lasnamäe	a	1-1	*Kiis*
17/7	TVMK	h	1-2	*Kõrtsmik*
21/7	Vaprus	h	2-1	*Kärson, Timofejev*
28/7	Maag Tammeka	a	1-4	*Tikenberg*
11/8	Tulevik	h	1-1	*Kirilov*
14/8	Levadia	h	0-4	
18/8	Kuressaare	a	0-2	
25/8	Trans	h	1-5	*Kirilov (p)*
1/9	TVMK	a	0-5	
15/9	Flora	h	1-3	*Tikenberg (p)*
18/9	Flora	a	1-4	*Afanasov*
22/9	TVMK	h	1-3	*Tikenberg (p)*
29/9	Trans	a	0-2	
2/10	Kuressaare	h	2-1	*Tikenberg 2 (1p)*
6/10	Tulevik	a	2-1	*Tikenberg (p), Kiis*
20/10	Levadia	a	0-8	
27/10	Maag Tammeka	h	2-2	*Tikenberg 2 (1p)*
3/11	Vaprus	a	2-1	*Kiis, Tikenberg*
10/11	Ajax Lasnamäe	h	1-0	*Afanasov*

Name	Nat	Pos	Aps	(s)	Gls
Andrei AFANASOV		A	19	(8)	3
Pavel APALINSKI		A	2	(3)	
Anton ARISTOV		D	19		
Aleksei DEMUTSKI		M	22		1
Paul GROSS		G	1		
Janno HERMANSON		G	32		
Marek KAHR		D	19	(2)	
Aleksandr KARPÕTŠEV		D	25	(2)	
Paul KASK		M		(1)	
Vahur KIIS		A	19	(6)	5
Marto KIISK		D		(2)	
Dmitri KIRILOV		M	11	(6)	4
Sergei KOBJAKOV		D	5	(3)	
Christian KÕRTSMIK		A	5	(7)	2
Vladimir KOZÕRKOV		G	2		
Reino KRANBERG		M	3	(3)	
Aleksandr KUSLAP		M	12	(5)	

Name	Nat	Pos	Aps	(s)	Gls
iim KÄRSON		A	24	(1)	1
iivo LEETMA		M	12	(1)	
'ameš MAMEDOV		M		(2)	
1ario MÕISTLIK		M	13	(7)	1
riit MURUMETS		A	23	(2)	
/lait NÕMME		D	11	(2)	
irigori OŠOMKOV		G	1		
/lagnus ROSEN		M		(1)	
aimar SAAG		A	13	(1)	1
'adim SAMULIN		D	1	(6)	
ndrek SISKA		A		(1)	
ene TEINO		M	4	(4)	
uri TIISMANN		M	20	(3)	1
'iit TIKENBERG		M	32	(2)	20
ndrei TIMOFEJEV		M	23	(2)	4
'ahur VAHTRAMÄE		M	22	(2)	1
/larek VIIKLAID		M	1		

FC KURESSAARE

Coach - Jan Vazinski

Founded – 1997

007				
0/3	TVMK	h	0-2	
7/3	Trans	a	1-3	*Pukk*
1/3	Tulevik	h	0-1	
/4	Kalev	h	1-3	*Meet*
'/4	Levadia	a	0-4	
4/4	Maag Tammeka	h	0-2	
4/4	Ajax Lasnamäe	h	2-2	*Kulikov, Kaljuste*
8/4	Flora	a	0-5	
/5	Vaprus	a	0-0	
/5	Flora	h	0-1	
2/5	Ajax Lasnamäe	a	4-1	*Veskimäe, Aljas, Kulikov, Pukk*
9/5	Vaprus	h	3-0	*Veskimäe, Pukk, og (Pedõk)*
6/5	Maag Tammeka	a	1-4	*Kulikov*
9/5	Trans	h	0-5	
/6	Ajax Lasnamäe	h	0-1	
/6	Levadia	h	0-5	
6/6	Kalev	a	1-2	*Kulikov*
9/6	Tulevik	a	1-0	*Koplimäe*
4/7	Flora	a	1-5	*Veskimäe*
4/7	TVMK	a	0-4	
8/7	Vaprus	a	0-2	
/8	Maag Tammeka	h	1-1	*Kluge (p)*
1/8	Levadia	a	0-4	
8/8	Kalev	h	2-0	*Veskimäe, Kulikov*
5/8	Tulevik	h	0-2	
/9	Trans	a	0-5	
5/9	TVMK	h	0-6	
8/9	TVMK	a	1-5	*Kriska*
22/9	Trans	h	0-3	
29/9	Tulevik	a	2-3	*Kluge (p), Pukk*
2/10	Kalev	a	1-2	*Kriska*
6/10	Levadia	h	0-3	
20/10	Maag Tammeka	a	0-1	
27/10	Vaprus	h	0-3	
3/11	Ajax Lasnamäe	a	2-1	*Mihkelson, Kluge*
13/11	Flora	h	1-3	*Alt*

Name	Nat	Pos	Aps	(s)	Gls
Rene ALJAS		A	5	(8)	1
Viktor ALONEN		M	29		
Reio ALT		A	11	(9)	1
Taavi AZAROV		M	25	(2)	
Janek HEPNER		D	19	(2)	
Hans HIIUVÄIN		A		(3)	
Vitali IŠTŠUK		A	4	(2)	
Rene KAAS		G	22		
Kuldar KALJUSTE		M	18	(5)	1
Märt KLUGE		D	27	(1)	3
Andrus KOPLIMÄE		M	22	(6)	1
Jaanis KRISKA		D	19	(4)	2
Dmitri KULIKOV		D	26	(3)	5
Roland KÜTT		G	10		
Aivo LAUL		M	2	(1)	
Kristjan LEEDO		D	6	(1)	
Janek MEET		D	18	(1)	1
Janek MEET		G	1		
Lauri MIHKELSON		A	30	(2)	1
Maikko MÖLDER		A		(2)	
Ken MÜÜR		G	3		
Pelle POHLAK		M	8	(8)	
Martti PUKK		A	14	(10)	4
Kaarel RAAMAT		M	20	(9)	
Margus RAJAVER		M	3	(2)	
Mikk RAJAVER		A		(4)	
Urmas RAJAVER		D	3	(7)	
Kevin RAND		A	3	(2)	
Martin SALONG		A	4	(4)	
Kristo SALUMAA		M	1	(1)	
Ludvig TASANE		A	1	(2)	
Elari VALMAS		D		(2)	
Rainer VESKIMÄE		M	30	(2)	4
Sander VIIRA		D	12	(2)	

FC LEVADIA TALLINN

Coach - Tarmo Rüütli

Founded - 1998

MAJOR HONOURS: Estonian League - (5) 1999, 2000, 2004, 2006, 2007; Estonian Cup - (5) 1999, 2000, 2004, 2005, 2007.

2007				
3/3	Maag Tammeka	h	4-0	*Zelinski, Nahk (p), Leitan, Kalimullin*
10/3	Ajax Lasnamäe	h	5-0	*Purje 2, Zelinski 2, Šadrin*
17/3	Flora	a	2-1	*Nahk 2 (1p)*
31/3	TVMK	h	2-0	*Vassiljev, Zelinski*
3/4	Trans	a	0-0	
7/4	Kuressaare	h	4-0	*Kalimullin 2, Purje 2*
14/4	Kalev	a	0-1	
21/4	Tulevik	h	4-0	*Zelinski, Vassiljev, Purje, Čepauskas*
24/4	Maag Tammeka	h	2-2	*Zelinski 2*
28/4	Vaprus	a	5-0	*Kink 4, Purje*
5/5	Vaprus	h	4-1	*Vassiljev, Zelinski, Kink, Dovydenas*
12/5	Maag Tammeka	a	3-1	*Vassiljev, Zelinski, Lemsalu*
19/5	Tulevik	a	4-0	*Šadrin 2, Purje, Smirnov*
26/5	Kalev	h	4-2	*Šadrin, Smirnov, Dovydenas, Vassiljev*
9/6	Kuressaare	a	5-0	*Zelinski 2, Smirnov, Šadrin, Dovydenas*
16/6	Trans	h	2-0	*Vassiljev, Leitan*
19/6	TVMK	a	1-1	*Leitan*
30/6	Flora	h	2-1	*Kink, Leitan*
7/7	Ajax Lasnamäe	a	10-0	*Zelinski 3 (1p), Leitan 2, Čepauskas, Dovydenas, Šadrin, Smirnov, og (Mamutov)*
14/7	Vaprus	a	2-0	*Zelinski 2 (2p)*
28/7	Tulevik	h	5-0	*Andreev 2, Šišov, Saag, Dovydenas*
11/8	Kuressaare	h	4-0	*Kink 2, Malov, Teniste*
14/8	Kalev	a	4-0	*Kink 2, Saag, Malov*
18/8	Trans	a	3-0	*Zelinski, Leitan, Kink*
25/8	TVMK	h	1-0	*Leitan*
1/9	Flora	a	2-3	*Nahk (p), Malov*
15/9	Ajax Lasnamäe	h	7-1	*Andreev 2, Leitan 2, Lemsalu 2, Smirnov*
18/9	Ajax Lasnamäe	a	2-1	*Kink, Čepauskas*
22/9	Flora	h	1-1	*Zelinski*
29/9	TVMK	a	6-2	*Kink 2, Lemsalu, Leitan,*

ESTONIA

				Zelinski, Andreev
2/10	Trans	h	1-2	Nahk (p)
6/10	Kuressaare	a	3-0	Saag, Zelinski, Andreev
20/10	Kalev	h	8-0	Andreev 3, Nahk (p), Lemsalu, Zelinski (p), Čepauskas, Kink
27/10	Tulevik	a	6-0	Andreev, Zelinski, Leitan, Lemsalu, Smirnov, Malov
3/11	Maag Tammeka	a	3-0	Andreev, Nahk, Kink
10/11	Vaprus	h	5-0	Andreev 2, Zelinski (p), Nahk, Smirnov

Name	Nat	Pos	Aps	(s)	Gls
Nikita ANDREEV	RUS	A	9	(10)	13
Anton ARISTOV		D		(1)	
Vitoldas ČEPAUSKAS	LTU	D	24	(5)	4
Aleksandr DMITRIJEV		M	26	(2)	
Marius DOVYDENAS	LTU	M	7	(9)	5
Martin KAALMA		G	22	(2)	
Andrei KALIMULLIN		D	28	(3)	3
Tarmo KINK		A	26	(5)	16
Artur KOTENKO		G	13		
Vitali LEITAN		M	27	(5)	12
Marek LEMSALU		D	30		6
Sergei LEPMETS		G	1	(1)	
Deniss MALOV		M	22	(1)	4
Igor MOROZOV		D	1		
Konstantin NAHK		M	30	(2)	8
Eino PURI		M		(2)	
Sander PURI		M	1		
Ats PURJE		A	9	(7)	7
Miroslav RÕŠKEVITŠ		M	5	(10)	
Kaimar SAAG		A	5	(8)	3
Andrei ŠADRIN		A	9	(12)	6
Tihhon ŠIŠOV		D	23	(0)	1
Maksim SMIRNOV		M	20	(11)	7
Taijo TENISTE		D	17	(2)	1
Konstantin VASSILJEV		M	12	(4)	6
Indrek ZELINSKI		A	29	(2)	23

JK MAAG TAMMEKA TARTU

Coach - Sergei Ratnikov

Founded - 1989

2007				
3/3	Levadia	a	0-4	
10/3	Vaprus	h	2-0	Kasimir, Bazyukin
17/3	Ajax Lasnamäe	a	2-0	Tiirik, Kask
31/3	Flora	h	0-0	
3/4	TVMK	a	0-2	
7/4	Trans	h	0-2	
14/4	Kuressaare	a	2-0	Marozas, Lõsanov
21/4	Kalev	h	1-1	Ratnikov E. (p)
24/4	Levadia	a	2-2	Ratnikov E. (p), Lõsanov
28/4	Tulevik	h	1-1	Lõsanov
5/5	Tulevik	a	1-0	Tiirik
12/5	Levadia	h	1-3	Sirel
19/5	Kalev	a	2-0	Tiirik 2
26/5	Kuressaare	h	4-1	Starovoitov, Ratnikov E. (p), Marozas, Kasimir
9/6	Trans	a	1-0	Kasimir
16/6	TVMK	h	1-3	Lõsanov
19/6	Flora	a	0-3	
30/6	Ajax Lasnamäe	h	2-0	Lõsanov, Bazyukin
7/7	Vaprus	a	1-0	Kasimir
14/7	Tulevik	h	3-1	Lõsanov 3
28/7	Kalev	h	4-1	Kasimir, Sirel, Tiirik, Lõsanov
4/8	Kuressaare	a	1-1	Kasimir
11/8	Trans	h	2-1	Tiirik, Starovoitov
18/8	TVMK	a	0-2	
25/8	Flora	h	0-0	
1/9	Ajax Lasnamäe	a	2-0	Tomson, Ratnikov D.
15/9	Vaprus	h	3-0	Tomson, Tiirik, Bazyukin
18/9	Vaprus	a	4-0	Kasimir 2 (1p), Meerits, Ratnikov D.
22/9	Ajax Lasnamäe	h	5-1	Kasimir, Vaino, Tomson, Tamm, og (Kovtun A.)
29/9	Flora	a	1-3	Tomson
2/10	TVMK	h	0-1	
6/10	Trans	a	3-2	Tiirik 2, Kasimir
20/10	Kuressaare	h	1-0	Tomson
27/10	Kalev	a	2-2	Lõsanov, Meerits
3/11	Levadia	h	0-3	
10/11	Tulevik	a	0-0	

Name	Nat	Pos	Aps	(s)	Gls
Maksim BAZYUKIN	RUS	M	34		3
Aleksandr DJATŠENKO		G	5		
Mario HANSI		M	1	(3)	
Ando HAUSENBERG		D	23	(7)	
Siksten KASIMIR		M	32		10
Taivo KASK		M	9	(16)	1
Mihkel KURESOO		D		(1)	
Kert KÜTT		G	31		
Nikolai LÕSANOV		A	29	(3)	10
Eimantas MAROZAS	LTU	A	6	(8)	2
Ott MEERITS		M	29	(4)	2
Mihkel MIKHEIM		M		(11)	
Sergei OTTŠIK		D	5	(3)	
Marti PÄHN		D		(6)	
Daniil RATNIKOV		M	20	(9)	2
Eduard RATNIKOV		M	15		3
Stanislav RUSSAKOV		D		(6)	
Jaanus SIREL		D	15	(8)	2
Marko SONN		D		(2)	
Sergei STAROVOITOV		D	27	(1)	2
Heiko TAMM		M	3	(10)	1
Timo TENISTE		D	36		
Kristjan TIIRIK		A	33	(1)	9
Rasmus TOMSON		M	12	(2)	5
Kait-Kaarel VAINO		D	31	(1)	1

JK TRANS NARVA

Coach - Valeri Bondarenko

Founded - 1979

MAJOR HONOURS: Estonian Cup - (1) 2001.

2007				
10/3	Tulevik	h	5-1	Lipartov 2, Gorjatšov, Dubõkin, Kulik
17/3	Kuressaare	h	3-1	Lipartov 2, Dubõkin
31/3	Kalev	a	2-0	Ivanov, Kitto (p)
3/4	Levadia	h	0-0	
7/4	Maag Tammeka	a	2-0	Dubõkin (p), Lipartov
14/4	Vaprus	h	2-0	Lipartov, Gruznov
21/4	Ajax Lasnamäe	a	4-0	Lipartov 2, Gruznov 2
24/4	Flora	h	3-1	Gruznov 2, Lipartov
28/4	TVMK	a	2-2	Gruznov, Dubõkin
5/5	TVMK	h	3-1	Dubõkin 2 (1p), Lipartov
12/5	Flora	a	2-0	Lipartov, Gruznov
19/5	Ajax Lasnamäe	h	2-0	Kazakov, og (Rõtškov)
26/5	Vaprus	a	3-0	Tarassenkov 2, Gruznov
29/5	Kuressaare	a	5-0	Gruznov 3, Lipartov, Kulik
9/6	Maag Tammeka	h	0-1	
16/6	Levadia	a	0-2	
19/6	Kalev	h	0-1	
7/7	Tulevik	a	2-0	Dubõkin, Ivanov
14/7	TVMK	a	0-1	
24/7	Flora	h	0-3	
28/7	Ajax Lasnamäe	a	3-0	Gorjatšov (p), Lipartov,

 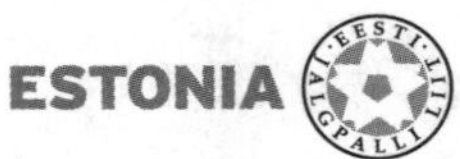

				Gruznov
7/8	Vaprus	h	2-1	Dubõkin, Tarassenkov
11/8	Maag Tammeka	a	1-2	Lipartov
18/8	Levadia	h	0-3	
25/8	Kalev	a	5-1	Lipartov 2, Gruznov, Ivanov, Dubõkin
1/9	Kuressaare	h	5-0	Lipartov 2, Dubõkin, Gruznov, Ivanov
15/9	Tulevik	h	7-0	Lipartov 3, Ivanov 3, og (Koppel)
18/9	Tulevik	a	4-1	Gruznov 2, Lipartov 2
22/9	Kuressaare	a	3-0	Gorjatšov, Lipartov, Gruznov
29/9	Kalev	h	2-0	Ivanov, Lipartov
2/10	Levadia	a	2-1	Gruznov, Lipartov
6/10	Maag Tammeka	h	2-3	Lipartov 2
20/10	Vaprus	a	3-1	Dubõkin (p), Tarassenkov, Ivanov
27/10	Ajax Lasnamäe	h	6-1	Dubõkin 2, Ivanov 2, Lipartov, Losev
3/11	Flora	a	0-0	
13/11	TVMK	h	4-0	Ivanov 2, Dubõkin, Lipartov

Name	Nat	Pos	Aps	(s)	Gls
Dmytro DOBROVOLSKI	UKR	D	33	(2)	
Aleksandr DUBÕKIN		M	32		14
Oleg GORJATŠOV		M	26	(7)	3
Aleksei GORŠKOV		D	35		
Maksim GRUZNOV		A	24	(6)	18
Vladislav IVANOV		M	24	(7)	13
Sergei KAZAKOV		M	19	(11)	1
Stanislav KITTO		M	20	(4)	1
Aleksandr KULIK		D	33		2
Oleg LEPIK		D	27	(2)	
Dmitriy LIPARTOV	RUS	A	36		30
Igor LOSEV	RUS	M	1	(4)	1
Anatoliy MARTYNOVCHENKO	RUS	M	1		
Kirill NESTEROV	RUS	A		(1)	
Anton PAITSEV		M	5	(18)	
Sergei POPOV		M	11	(14)	
Dmitri ŠELEHHOV		D	2	(5)	
Valeri SMELKOV		G	2	(1)	
Dmitri SMIRNOV		M		(5)	
Aleksandr TARASSENKOV		M	31	(1)	4
Sergei USSOLTSEV		G	34		

JK TULEVIK VILJANDI

Coach - Marko Lelov

Founded - 1912

2007				
10/3	Trans	a	1-5	Saharov (p)
17/3	Vaprus	h	0-1	
31/3	Kuressaare	a	1-0	Naris
3/4	Ajax Lasnamäe	h	2-0	Henn, Saharov
7/4	Kalev	a	1-2	Savitski
14/4	Flora	h	1-2	Saharov (p)
21/4	Levadia	a	0-4	
24/4	TVMK	h	1-1	Saharov
28/4	Maag Tammeka	a	1-1	Rüütli
5/5	Maag Tammeka	h	0-1	
12/5	TVMK	a	1-3	Ištšuk
19/5	Levadia	h	0-4	
26/5	Flora	a	0-4	
9/6	Kalev	h	2-1	Saharov, Ištšuk
16/6	Ajax Lasnamäe	a	5-0	Saharov 2, Kudu 2, Ištšuk (p)
19/6	Kuressaare	h	0-1	
30/6	Vaprus	a	3-2	Ištšuk 2, Kudu
7/7	Trans	h	0-2	
14/7	Maag Tammeka	a	1-3	Saharov (p)
21/7	TVMK	h	0-1	
28/7	Levadia	a	0-5	
7/8	Flora	h	0-3	
11/8	Kalev	a	1-1	Kudu
18/8	Ajax Lasnamäe	h	4-1	Ištšuk 2, Kudu, Savotškin
25/8	Kuressaare	a	2-0	Oja, Savitski
1/9	Vaprus	h	4-1	Puri S. 2, Puri E., Oja
15/9	Trans	a	0-7	
18/9	Trans	h	1-4	Oja
22/9	Vaprus	a	3-0	Puri S. 2, Kudu
29/9	Kuressaare	h	3-2	Ištšuk (p), Savitski, Oja
2/10	Ajax Lasnamäe	a	3-0	Lember 2, Martinson
6/10	Kalev	h	1-2	Savitski
20/10	Flora	a	0-5	
27/10	Levadia	h	0-6	
3/11	TVMK	a	1-5	Kosemets
10/11	Maag Tammeka	h	0-0	

Name	Nat	Pos	Aps	(s)	Gls
Mait ANTON		D	2		
Marko ARGE		M	24	(4)	
Jürgen HENN		M	28		1
Mihhail IŠTŠUK		M	25	(7)	8
Rivo KALJU		D	1		
Rait KASTERPALU		M	4	(5)	
Sander KOOSER		D	2		
Kaido KOPPEL		G	4		
Märt KOSEMETS		M	20	(7)	1
Markko KUDU		A	30	(3)	6
Arko KUNINGAS		D		(1)	
Joonas LAASBERG		M		(5)	
Mati LEMBER		M	29	(2)	2
Dmitri LIPETSKI		G	1		
Magnus MARTINSON		A	23	(9)	1
Raiko MUTLE		D	14		
Armand NARIS		D	24	(3)	1
Reimo OJA		A	3	(24)	4
Eino PURI		M	12		1
Sander PURI		M	14		4
Henri RÜÜTLI		M	20	(2)	1
Mihkel SAAR		M	3	(17)	
Aleksander SAHAROV		A	18	(1)	8
Aleksei SAVITSKI		D	33		4
Andrei SAVOTŠKIN		A	12	(8)	1
Kauri SIIM		D	13	(1)	
Theimo TARVIS		A	6	(4)	
Toomas TOHVER		G	31		
Rauno TUTK		D		(2)	
Vladimir VASSILJEV		A		(1)	

FC TVMK TALLINN

Coach - Vjatšeslav Smirnov

Founded - 1951

MAJOR HONOURS: Estonian League – (1) 2005; Estonian Cup - (3) 1993, 2003, 2006.

2007				
10/3	Kuressaare	a	2-0	Konsa 2
17/3	Kalev	h	5-0	Kulatšenko 2, Konsa, Terehhov, Ossipov (p)
31/3	Levadia	a	0-2	
3/4	Maag Tammeka	h	2-0	Konsa, Ossipov (p)
7/4	Vaprus	a	2-0	Zenjov, og (Põldme)
14/4	Ajax Lasnamäe	h	7-1	Zenjov 2, Ossipov (p), Haavistu M., Haavistu K., Kulatšenko, og (O'Konnel-Bronin)
21/4	Flora	a	2-2	Terehhov, Konsa
24/4	Tulevik	a	1-1	Dobrecovs
28/4	Trans	h	2-2	Ossipov, Kacanovs
5/5	Trans	a	1-3	Kulatšenko
12/5	Tulevik	h	3-1	Konsa, Mašitšev, Kulatšenko

ESTONIA

19/5	Flora	h	6-0	*Dobrecovs 2, Ossipov, Mašitšev, Konsa, Leetma*
26/5	Ajax Lasnamäe	a	6-0	*Mašitšev 2, Konsa, Jürgenson, Gussev, Dobrecovs*
9/6	Vaprus	h	9-0	*Zenjov 2, Dobrecovs 2, Konsa, Mašitšev, Terehhov, Kulatšenko, Ossipov*
16/6	Maag Tammeka	a	3-1	*Terehhov 3*
19/6	Levadia	h	1-1	*Dobrecovs*
14/7	Trans	h	1-0	*Terehhov*
17/7	Kalev	a	2-1	*Zenjov, og (Murumets)*
21/7	Tulevik	a	1-0	*Rimas*
24/7	Kuressaare	h	4-0	*Zenjov, Ossipov, Kuvšinovs, Borissov*
28/7	Flora	a	0-2	
4/8	Ajax Lasnamäe	h	13-0	*Kulatšenko 4, Anniste 4, Konsa 2 (1p), Gussev 2, Zenjov*
11/8	Vaprus	a	5-0	*Saviauk, Terehhov, Kulatšenko, Gussev, Zenjov*
18/8	Maag Tammeka	h	2-0	*Konsa, Gussev*
25/8	Levadia	a	0-1	
1/9	Kalev	h	5-0	*Ossipov 2 (1p), Anniste, Gussev, Dmitrijev*
15/9	Kuressaare	a	6-0	*Gussev 3, Zenjov, Anniste, Dmitrijev*
18/9	Kuressaare	h	5-1	*Zenjov 4, Kulatšenko*
22/9	Kalev	a	3-1	*Terehhov 2, Sarajev*
29/9	Levadia	h	2-6	*Saviauk, og (Nahk)*
2/10	Maag Tammeka	a	1-0	*Gussev*
6/10	Vaprus	h	6-3	*Gussev 2, Anniste 2, Jürgenson, Terehhov*
20/10	Ajax Lasnamäe	a	2-0	*Rimas, Ossipov (p)*
27/10	Flora	h	1-2	*Anniste (p)*
3/11	Tulevik	h	5-1	*Ossipov 2, Jürgenson, Kulatšenko, Anniste (p)*
13/11	Trans	a	0-4	

Name	Nat	Pos	Aps	(s)	Gls
Aivar ANNISTE		M	14		10
Andrei ANTONOV		A		(4)	
Andrei BORISSOV		M	34	1	1
Artjom DMITRIJEV		M	2	(4)	2
Viktors DOBRECOVS	LVA	A	8	(4)	7
Vladislavs GABOVS	LVA	D	19	(4)	
Vladislav GUSSEV		M	11	(12)	12
Kert HAAVISTU		M	3	(3)	1
Mikk HAAVISTU		D	6	(9)	1
Sergei JEGOROV		A		(1)	
Markus JÜRGENSON		A	10	(10)	3
Jevgenijs KACANOVS	LVA	D	29	(1)	1
Oliver KONSA		A	28	(2)	12
Aleksandr KULATŠENKO		A	13	(15)	13
Jevgeni KURJANOV		D	1		
Andris KUVŠINOVS	LVA	M	5	(3)	1
Liivo LEETMA		M	10	(1)	1
Nikolai MAŠITŠEV		A	11	(10)	5
Artur OSSIPOV		M	25	(3)	12
Tomas RIMAS	LTU	D	27	1	2
Eduard SARAJEV		D	17	(2)	1
Erko SAVIAUK		D	23	(2)	2
Vitali TELEŠ		G	32	(1)	
Sergei TEREHHOV		M	25		11
Antons TRIFONOVS	LVA	G	4	(2)	
Aleksandr VOLODIN		D	22	(3)	
Sergei ZENJOV		A	17	(5)	14

JK VAPRUS PÄRNU

Coach - Kalev Pajula

Founded – 1922

2007

10/3	Maag Tammeka	a	0-2	
17/3	Tulevik	a	1-0	*Velikopolje*
31/3	Ajax Lasnamäe	h	1-0	*Lepik (p)*
3/4	Flora	a	0-7	
7/4	TVMK	h	0-2	
14/4	Trans	a	0-2	
24/4	Kalev	a	2-0	*Uibo, Lepik*
28/4	Levadia	h	0-5	
1/5	Kuressaare	h	0-0	
5/5	Levadia	a	1-4	*Joost*
12/5	Kalev	h	0-1	
19/5	Kuressaare	a	0-3	
26/5	Trans	h	0-3	
9/6	TVMK	a	0-9	
16/6	Flora	h	0-3	
19/6	Ajax Lasnamäe	a	5-0	*Lepik 2, Kazak, Joost, Uib*
30/6	Tulevik	h	2-3	*Senješ, Novikov*
7/7	Maag Tammeka	h	0-1	
14/7	Levadia	h	0-2	
21/7	Kalev	a	1-2	*Rand*
28/7	Kuressaare	h	2-0	*Velikopolje, Joost*
7/8	Trans	a	1-2	*Kazak*
11/8	TVMK	h	0-5	
18/8	Flora	a	1-8	*Sõrmus*
25/8	Ajax Lasnamäe	h	2-0	*Senješ, Novikov*
1/9	Tulevik	a	1-4	*Senješ*
15/9	Maag Tammeka	a	0-3	
18/9	Maag Tammeka	h	0-4	
22/9	Tulevik	h	0-3	
29/9	Ajax Lasnamäe	a	7-1	*Kazak 4, Novikov, Lepik (p), Joost*
2/10	Flora	h	0-1	
6/10	TVMK	a	3-6	*Kazak, Velikopolje, Vebe*
20/10	Trans	h	1-3	*Rand*
27/10	Kuressaare	a	3-0	*Joost, Velikopolje, Rand*
3/11	Kalev	h	1-2	*og (Aristov)*
10/11	Levadia	a	0-5	

Name	Nat	Pos	Aps	(s)	Gls
Aleksei GALKIN		A	32		
Ott JOALA		G	1		
Indrek JOOST		M	29	(1)	5
Ott KANGUR		M		(4)	
Kristo KASEMETS		M	23	(5)	
Mihhail KAZAK		A	22	(7)	7
Ivo KIVISELG		D	3		
Ranet LEPIK		M	31		5
Tanel MELTS		M	1	(9)	
Taavi MIDENBRITT		M	7		
Jevgeni NOVIKOV		D	15	(6)	3
Gert OLESK		D	8		
Martin PARTSIOJA		M	15	(4)	
Stanislav PEDÕK		G	12		
Priit PIKKER		G	1	(2)	
Veiko PÕLDEMAA		G	22	(1)	
Rain PÕLDME		D	23	(2)	
Rando RAND		D	30		3
Raido RAUDNAGEL		M	4	(5)	
Lauri SENJEŠ		A	15	(6)	3
Kauri SIIM		D	5		
Kajar SOOSAAR		D	21	(6)	
Rait SÕRMUS		M	4	(14)	1
Ilja ŠUSTROV		M	1	(7)	
Viljar TAMMELEHT		M	2	(4)	
Verner UIBO		M	26	(2)	2
Jesper VEBER		D	12	(1)	1
Ivan VELIKOPOLJE		M	29	(5)	4
Konstantin VOZNJUK		M	2	(2)	

PROMOTED CLUBS

JK KALEV SILLAMÄE
Coach – Vadim Dobiza (UKR)
Founded - 1951

JK KALJU NÕMME
Coach – Fredo GETÚLIO Aurélio (BRA)
Founded - 1923

SECOND LEVEL FINAL TABLE 2007

	Pld	W	D	L	F	A	Pts
C Levadia II Tallinn	36	27	5	4	95	20	86
C Flora II	36	24	6	6	97	33	78
K Kalev Sillamäe	36	20	9	7	67	40	69
C TVMK II Tallinn	36	15	8	13	81	68	53
K Maag Tammeka II Tartu	36	14	11	11	51	39	53
K Kalju Nõmme	36	13	9	14	69	69	48
C Warrior Valga	36	13	5	18	72	73	44
K Tulevik II Viljandi	36	9	7	20	37	84	34
älk 494 Tartu	36	7	8	21	49	93	29
C Elva	36	3	2	31	17	116	11

Levadia II Tallinn, FC Flora II Tallinn, FC TVMK II Tallinn and JK Maag eka II Tartu ineligible for promotion.

ev Sillamäe promoted directly and JK Kalju Nõmme enter play offs.

PROMOTION/RELEGATION PLAY-OFFS
(18/11/07)
JK Kalju Nõmme 0, FC Kuressaare 1
(24/11/07)
FC Kuressaare 1, JK Kalju Nõmme 2
(2-2; JK Kalju Nõmme on away goals)

OMESTIC CUP 2007/08

EESTI KARIKAS

ROUND

Kuressaare 4
õmme II 4, Tallinna Soccernet 2
a 4, Eston Villa 1
, Tapa 1
II 1, Ganvix Türi 2
snamäe 9, WC Guwalda 1
tli 1, Kaitseliit Kalev 0
Põlva Lootos 7
ea 0, Kohila Püsivus 5
)
2, Ararat 1
)
e 0, Elva 3
9, Trummi 0
United 0, Haiba 6
6, Rakvere 1
4 7, Jalgpallihaigla 1
u Rada 3, Tulevik II 5 *(aet)*
õmme 3, Kalev 2 *(aet)*
iv 0, Kiviõli Tamme Auto 5
7)
omed 0, Flora 8
1, Maag Tammeka III 2
4, Ühinenud Depood 0
Flora Linnameeskond 2, Vaprus 4
1, Tulevik 6
EBS Team 2, Kehra Tempori 1
(15/8/07)
Maardu Esteve 8, Tallinn United 0
Tabasalu 7, Reaal 1
Operi 0, Maag Tammeka 3
Lelle 1, Warrior 3
(23/8/07)
Twister 0, Sport 5
Klooga 1, Maag Tammeka II 17
(28/8/07)
Levadia 11, Anzi 0
(29/8/07)
Rock&Roll 0, Kalev 6

SECOND ROUND

(4/9/07)
EBS Team 0, Tabasalu 4
(5/9/07)
Levadia 6, Warrior 0
Rapla Atli 0, Maag Tammeka II 1
Hiiumaa 2, Maardu Esteve 3 *(aet)*
(6/9/07)
Kiviõli Tamme Auto 0, TVMK 2
Kohila Püsivus 1, Tulevik II 4
Kuressaare 0, Trans 5
Välk 494 8, Põlva Lootos 1
(11/9/07)
Trans II 1, Ajax Lasnamäe 1 *(aet; 5-4 on pens)*
Kalju Nõmme II 2, Elva 3
(13/9/07)
Ganvix Türi 3, Enter 1
Maag Tammeka III 7, Haiba 0
(25/9/07)
Tulevik 1, Kalev 2
Sport 0, Flora 10
(26/9/07)
Maag Tammeka 2, Kalju Nõmme 2 *(aet; 3-2 on pens)*
(24/10/07)
Vaprus 1, Flora II 3

THIRD ROUND

(30/10/07)
Flora 6, Tabasalu 0
Levadia 4, Maag Tammeka III 1
Kalev 1, Trans II 0
TVMK 1, Maag Tammeka 3
(31/10/07)
Trans 9, Maardu Esteve 1
Välk 494 3, Tulevik II 1
Maag Tammeka II 4, Ganvix Türi 0
Elva 1, Flora II 8

QUARTER-FINALS

(15/4/08)
Levadia 3 *(Zelinski 2, Andreev 44, 57)*, Trans 1 *(Lõsanov 74)*
(16/4/08)
Maag Tammeka II 1 *(Perlin 58)*, Flora 4 *(Post 7, Anier 8, 71, Hurt 57)*
Kalev 1 *(Tikenberg 37)*, Flora II 3 *(Reinsoo 58p, Toomet 76, Kallaste 85)*
Santos 0, Maag Tammeka 3 *(Ossipov 23, Starovoitov 52, Prosa 82)*

SEMI-FINALS

(29/4/08)
Flora 1 *(Kasimir 13)*, Levadia 1 *(Malov 85) (aet; 4-1 on pens)*
(30/4/08)
Flora II 0, Maag Tammeka 3 *(Starovoitov 4, 15, 17)*

FINAL

(13/5/08)
Kadriorg stadium, Tallinn
FC FLORA 3 *(Post 1, Hakola 47p, 64)*
JK MAAG TAMMEKA TARTU 1 *(Ossipov 72p)*
Referee – *Kaasik*
FLORA – *Aksalu, Zahovaiko (Pedõk 69), Allas, Vunk, Hurt, Reim, Kams (Kasimir 61), Hakola (Mošnikov 87), Post, Vanna, Sidorenkov.*
Sent off: *Aksalu (69).*
MAAG TAMMEKA – *Djatšenko, Hausenberg, Valtna, Teniste, Ossipov, Sonn, Sirel, Tiirik, Tomson (Mikheim 70), Komarov (Tamm 81), Starovoitov (Prosa 75).*
Sent off: *Ossipov (90+1)*

Knudsen bows out on a high

Jens Martin Knudsen, the bobble-hatted goalkeeper who earned immortal fame for his contribution towards the Faroe Islands' sensational defeat of Austria in their first competitive international, retired from football in 2007 at the age of 40. He bowed out in style, keeping goal in all 27 matches of his final Formuladeildin campaign and helping NSÍ Runavík, the club of his formative years, to win their first ever national title.

For the second year running EB/Streymur had to settle for second place, but mercifully there was no repeat of the previous season's hard-luck story. This time they finished the season with a bang rather than a whimper, winning their last five games and scoring 20 goals in the process to overtake the two faltering favourites from the capital, B36 Tórshavn and HB Tórshavn, and finish seven points adrift of NSÍ, who sewed the title up in their penultimate fixture.

Two Cups for EB/Streymur

Better still, EB/Streymur claimed their first major honour by winning the Faroe Islands Cup. They defeated HB 4-3 in a classic final in August 2007 then made a successful defence of the trophy the following June, with B36 their victims after another epic contest in the Gundadalur stadium, which they won 3-2 with two goals from ace marksman Arnbjørn T. Hansen and one from midfielder Hans Pauli Samuelsen. Both youngsters had also scored in the previous year's final.

The Faroe Islands national team, for whom both Hansen and Samuelsen played in 2007/08, disappointingly ended their UEFA EURO 2008™ qualifying campaign without a point. In fact, the balance sheet was worse than that as a couple of friendly losses in Finland and Estonia extended the team's consecutive number of defeats in all competitions to 22 – a run stretching back to October 2004. The main positive note was Rógvi Jacobsen's goal against Italy in Modena (1-3), his second in UEFA EURO 2008™ qualifying against the world champions, which enabled the carpenter from Klasksvik to become the first Faroe Islands footballer to score ten international goals.

Rógvi Jacobsen scores against Italy in Modena – his tenth international goal

Fóltbóltssamband Føroya

Gundadalur
PO Box 3028
FO-110 Tórshavn
tel - +298 316707
fax - +298 319079
website - www.football.fo
email - fsf@football.fo
Year of Formation – 1979
President - Høgni í Stórustovu
General Secretary - Ísak Mikladal
Press Officer – Ísak Mikladal
Stadium - Svangaskard, Toftir (4,000)

TOP FIVE ALL-TIME CAPS
Óli Johannesen (83); Jens Martin Knudsen (65); Julian Johnsson (62); John Petersen (57); Jákup Mikkelsen (56)

TOP FIVE ALL-TIME GOALS
Rógvi Jacobsen (10); Todi Jónsson (9); Uni Arge (8); John Petersen (6); Julian Johnsson & Jan Allan Müller (4)

‹TIONAL TEAM RESULTS 2007/08

)7	Lithuania (ECQ)	A	Kaunas	1-2	*Jacobsen R. (90+3)*
/07	France (ECQ)	H	Torshavn	0-6	
/07	Ukraine (ECQ)	A	Kiev	0-5	
/07	Italy (ECQ)	A	Modena	1-3	*Jacobsen R. (83)*
)8	Iceland	A	Kopavogur	0-3	
3	Estonia	A	Tallinn	3-4	*Holst (63, 66), Olsen (70)*

TIONAL TEAM APPEARANCES 2007/08

– Jógvan Martin OLSEN	30/7/61		LTU	FRA	UKR	ITA	Isl	Est	Caps	Goals
MIKKELSEN	14/8/70	B36 /KÍ	G	G	G	G	G	G	56	-
ANIELSEN	15/8/83	Frem (DEN)	D		M	M	M80		25	-
BENJAMINSEN	14/12/77	B36 /HB	D	D		D	D	D	48	2
5i JACOBSEN	7/4/83	AaB (DEN)	D	D	D	D			31	-
á BORG	26/10/79	HB	D					M44	53	2
SAMUELSEN	21/5/85	Notodden (NOR) /Keflavík (ISL)	M	M86	M	M75	M68	M	17	1
al THOMASSEN	12/1/76	B36	M	M78	M8				9	-
)LSEN	7/3/81	AaB (DEN) /Viborg (DEN)	M63	M		M		M84	32	2
ian Høgni JACOBSEN	12/5/80	NSÍ /HB	M84	D	M89	M	M73	s44	41	2
JACOBSEN	5/3/79	HB /Hødd (NOR)	A	A	A	A	A	A	50	10
ian Lamhauge HOLST	25/12/81	Lyngby (DEN)	A74	A	A75	A86		A85	11	2
HANSEN	9/4/80	Skála	s63						6	-
Pauli SAMUELSEN	18/10/84	EB/Streymur	s74						3	-
w av FLØTUM	13/6/79	HB	s84	s86	s75	s86			29	1
HANSEN	2/4/88	NSÍ		D	D	D	D80	D	5	-
ím ELLTØR	21/9/80	NSÍ		M46			s73		15	-
r MIDJORD	20/4/85	B36		s46			s68		2	-
av Fløtum JESPERSEN	16/3/85	HB /Fremad Amager (DEN)		s78			s73		2	-
Troest DAVIDSEN	31/1/88	NSÍ			D	D	D	D	4	-
NSEN	26/11/77	NSÍ			D		D		3	-
HANSEN	18/1/84	Lyngby (DEN)			s8			M63	3	-
THORLEIFSSON	19/12/85	B36			s89	s75			3	-
ØJSTED	12/11/85	B36					M80		5	-
ørn Theodor HANSEN	27/2/86	EB/Streymur					A73	s85	3	-
int MATRAS	20/5/81	B36					s80		2	-
ffur JACOBSEN	7/11/88	KÍ					s80		1	-
n úr HØRG	21/9/80	HB					s80		6	-
Tór NÆS	27/12/86	Køge (DEN)						D	1	-
MADSEN	4/2/85	ÍF						s63	1	-
IELSEN	3/3/81	HB						s84	7	-

FAROE ISLANDS

DOMESTIC LEAGUE 2007

FORMULADEILDIN FINAL LEAGUE TABLE

		Pld	Home					Away					Total					Pts
			W	D	L	F	A	W	D	L	F	A	W	D	L	F	A	
1	NSÍ Runavík	27	11	2	1	33	13	8	2	3	19	11	19	4	4	52	24	61
2	EB/Streymur	27	8	2	4	31	17	9	1	3	27	16	17	3	7	58	33	54
3	B36 Tórshavn	27	8	5	1	27	10	7	2	4	20	13	15	7	5	47	23	52
4	HB Tórshavn	27	9	1	4	36	18	6	3	4	23	16	15	4	8	59	34	49
5	GÍ Gøta	27	3	2	8	16	27	8	3	3	30	26	11	5	11	46	53	38
6	Skála Ítróttarfelag	27	4	2	7	11	17	6	2	6	16	23	10	4	13	27	40	34
7	KÍ Klaksvík	27	6	3	5	29	26	3	3	7	15	21	9	6	12	44	47	33
8	B71 Sandur	27	3	3	7	15	23	6	2	6	24	26	9	5	13	39	49	32
9	AB Argir	27	2	3	8	19	27	2	2	10	11	28	4	5	18	30	55	17
10	VB/Sumba Vágur	27	2	1	10	10	24	0	4	10	17	47	2	5	20	27	71	11

N.B. GÍ Gøta and LÍF Leirvik merged into Víkingur Gøta for 2008 season.

TOP GOALSCORERS

18 Ahmed Davy SYLLA (B36)

14 Arnbjørn T. HANSEN (EB/Streymur)
Paul CLAPSON (KÍ)

13 Christian LUNDBERG (GÍ)

11 CLAYTON Soares (B71)
Sorin ANGHEL (EB/Streymur)
Rógvi JACOBSEN (HB)

10 ANDERSON Castilho Cardena (B36)

9 Andrew av FLØTUM (HB)

8 Hans Pauli SAMUELSEN (EB/Streymur)
Fródi BENJAMINSEN (B36)

CLUB-BY-CLUB

AB ARGÍR

Coach – Oddbjørn Joensen; (30/5/07) Sigfridur Clementsen

Founded - 1973

2007

1/4	VB/Sumba	a	0-1	
5/4	GÍ	h	4-4	*Overgaard, Barbá, Rubeksen H., Rubeksen T.*
9/4	EB/Streymur	a	0-3	
15/4	Skála	a	2-0	*Joensen J., Rubeksen T.*
22/4	B71	h	1-2	*Christensen*
28/4	B36	a	1-4	*Clementsen*
2/5	KÍ	h	1-3	*Barbá*
6/5	HB	h	2-2	*Barbá 2*
13/5	NSÍ	a	1-2	*Barbá (p)*
20/5	EB/Streymur	h	1-2	*Rubeksen H.*
28/5	VB/Sumba	h	2-2	*Clementsen, Barbá*
10/6	GÍ	a	1-1	*Jørgensen B.*
17/6	B36	h	2-1	*Poulsen Ró., Clementsen (p)*
24/6	B71	a	0-1	
4/7	KÍ	a	0-1	
8/7	Skála	h	1-2	*Mørkøre*
7/8	HB	a	0-4	
12/8	NSÍ	h	0-2	
19/8	EB/Streymur	a	2-2	*Poulsen Ró., Blé*
26/8	VB/Sumba	a	2-1	*Ellingsgaard 2*
2/9	GÍ	h	1-3	*Clementsen*
16/9	KÍ	h	3-1	*Mørkøre (p), Poulsen Ró., Nielsen*
23/9	NSÍ	a	1-2	*Mørkøre*
30/9	B36	a	1-4	*og (Jacobsen H.)*
7/10	HB	h	1-2	*Ellingsgaard*
21/10	B71	h	0-1	
27/10	Skála	a	0-2	

No	Name	Nat	Pos	Aps	(s)	Gls
9	Súni Fridi BARBÁ		A	12		6
7	Evrard BLÉ	CIV	M	8		1
11	Jón BREKKU		D	3		
15	Peter B. CHRISTENSEN		M	10	(4)	1
5	Rani D. CHRISTIANSEN		D	18	(3)	
6	Fródi CLEMENTSEN		D	23	(1)	4
10	Johan ELLINGSGAARD		M	8		3
20	Bogi HERMANSEN		M	3	(2)	
22	Rogvi HOLM		M	8	(1)	
10	Rúni HVANNASTEIN		M	2	(2)	
18	Dion B. JACOBSEN		D	5	(5)	
3	Hanus JACOBSEN		D	17	(5)	
14	Høgni M. JOENSEN		M	11	(2)	
8	Jákup Martin JOENSEN		M	12	(3)	1
21	Bjarni JØRGENSEN		A	22	(3)	1
17	Pætur T. JØRGENSEN		M	9	(2)	
10	Vagnur Mohr MORTENSEN		D		(1)	
9	Allan MØRKØRE		A	12	(1)	3
19	Jón NIELSEN		A	8	(5)	1
11	Jónas Tór NÆS		M	10	(1)	
13	Morten OVERGAARD	DEN	D	20		1
20	Christos PATSAMANIS	DEN	M	3	(4)	
2	Bernhard PETERSEN		D	10	(7)	
1	Magnus Emil POULSEN		G	22		
15	Ragnar POULSEN		M	2		
22	Rógvi POULSEN		M	24	(1)	3
16	Danny RASMUSSEN		G	2		
17	Hendrik RUBEKSEN		A	8	(4)	2
7	Tummas Hans RUBEKSEN		A	2	(10)	2
16	Hedin STENBERG		G	2		
12	Jónas STENBERG		M		(4)	
14	Hans Jacob THOMSEN		M		(1)	
1	Tórdur THOMSEN		G	1		

B36 TÓRSHAVN

Coach – Kurt Mørkøre

Founded – 1936

MAJOR HONOURS: Faroe Islands League - (8) 1946, 1948, 1950, 1959, 196 1997, 2001, 2005; Faroe Islands Cup - (5) 1965, 1991, 2001, 2003, 200

2007

1/4	KÍ	h	1-0	*Sylla*
5/4	NSÍ	a	0-3	
9/4	VB/Sumba	a	4-0	*Alex, Benjaminsen 2, Mørkøre*
15/4	HB	h	1-1	*Nysted*
22/4	EB/Streymur	a	1-0	*Benjaminsen*
28/4	AB	h	4-1	*Sylla 3, Benjaminsen (*
2/5	GÍ	a	3-0	*Midjord 2, Benjaminse*
6/5	B71	a	2-1	*Sylla 2*
13/5	Skála	h	1-1	*Thomassen*

5	VB/Sumba	h	2-0	*Sylla 2*
5	KÍ	a	1-1	*Alex*
6	NSÍ	h	1-1	*Thomassen (p)*
6	AB	a	1-2	*Sylla*
6	EB/Streymur	h	1-0	*Alex*
6	HB	a	2-0	*Sylla, Benjaminsen*
	GÍ	h	4-0	*Sylla, Thomassen 2, Thorleifsson*
	B71	h	3-0	*Matras, Sylla 2*
8	Skála	a	2-0	*Matras, Sylla*
8	VB/Sumba	h	2-0	*Sylla 2*
8	KÍ	h	2-2	*Thomassen, Benjaminsen*
	NSÍ	a	1-1	*Benjaminsen*
9	GÍ	a	1-0	*Skorini*
9	Skála	h	1-1	*Alex*
9	AB	h	4-1	*Alex 2, Sylla, Anderson*
0	B71	a	0-1	
10	EB/Streymur	a	2-4	*Gunnarsson, Sylla*
10	HB	h	0-2	

Name	Nat	Pos	Aps	(s)	Gls
ALEX dos Santos	BRA	D	24		6
ANDERSON Castilho Cardena	BRA	A	3	(5)	1
Fródi BENJAMINSEN		M	27		8
Johan ELLINGSGAARD		M		(2)	
Odmar FÆRØ		M	6	(5)	
Christian i GARDI		M		(1)	
Jóhan V. GUNNARSSON		D	17	(7)	1
Ingi HØJSTED		M	8	(4)	
Herbert i Lon JACOBSEN		D	25	(1)	
Jóan Pauli JACOBSEN		G	1	(2)	
Kenneth JACOBSEN		D	15	(6)	
Bardur H. JOENSEN		D	1	(2)	
Klæmint MATRAS		D	25	(1)	2
Bergur MIDJORD		M	21	(4)	2
Jakup MIKKELSEN		G	26		
Allan MØRKØRE		A	4	(3)	1
Ovi NYSTED		D	10	(2)	1
Tummas Hans RUBEKSEN		A		(1)	
Heini i SKORINI		M	19	(6)	1
Ahmed Davy SYLLA	CIV	A	26		18
Mikkjal THOMASSEN		M	17	(4)	5
Hanus THORLEIFSSON		M	22	(5)	1

B71 SANDUR

Coach – Dušan Mokan (SRB); (1/6/07) Eli Hentze

Founded – 1971

MAJOR HONOURS: Faroe Islands League - (1) 1989; Faroe Islands Cup - (1) 1993.

07				
	NSÍ	h	0-1	
	HB	a	3-0	*Olsen 3*
	KÍ	a	3-3	*Clayton 2, Wellington*
4	EB/Streymur	h	2-3	*Poulsen, Hentze E. (p)*
4	AB	a	2-1	*Clayton, Hansen S.*
4	GÍ	h	1-1	*Olsen*
	Skála	a	0-2	
	B36	h	1-2	*Olsen*
5	VB/Sumba	a	4-1	*Jensen, Clayton 3*
5	KÍ	h	3-3	*Flávio, Hansen S. 2*
5	NSÍ	a	0-3	
6	HB	h	2-1	*Wellington, Hentze E.*
6	GÍ	a	2-3	*Hansen S., Clayton*
6	AB	h	1-0	*Clayton*
	Skála	h	0-2	
	EB/Streymur	a	4-2	*Thomsen 2, Clayton, Clementsen R.*
	B36	a	0-3	
8	VB/Sumba	h	0-0	
8	KÍ	a	1-3	*Hansen S.*
8	NSÍ	h	1-3	*Nielsen G.*
2/9	HB	a	1-3	*Clayton (p)*
16/9	Skála	a	0-0	
23/9	VB/Sumba	a	3-2	*Olsen, Nielsen R., Clayton (p)*
30/9	GÍ	h	2-3	*Nielsen R. 2*
7/10	B36	h	1-0	*Nielsen G.*
21/10	AB	a	1-0	*Hansen S.*
27/10	EB/Streymur	h	1-4	*Olsen*

No	Name	Nat	Pos	Aps	(s)	Gls
10	CLAYTON Soares	BRA	A	24		11
29	Hanus CLEMENTSEN		D	13		
9	Rene CLEMENTSEN		A		(5)	1
29	Tummas CLEMENTSEN		M		(1)	
4	FÁBIO Vieira	BRA	D	25		
16	FLÁVIO Lúcio Silva de Santana	BRA	M	22	(3)	1
1	Simin Rógvi HANSEN		G	27		
7	Simin HANSEN		A	23	(1)	6
14	Eli HENTZE		M	19	(2)	2
25	Mikkjal T. HENTZE		M	2	(7)	
21	Jóhannis JENSEN		M	22	(2)	1
23	Áslakkur KJÆRBO		D	2	(2)	
18	Høgni MIDJORD		A	1	(6)	
17	Gudmund NIELSEN		M	9	(5)	2
20	Rasmus NIELSEN		A	12	(11)	3
19	Magnus OLSEN		M	26		7
15	Jón Koytu PETERSEN		M		(2)	
8	Eirikur POULSEN		D	23		1
3	Anders RASMUSSEN	DEN	D	22		
5	Jónsvein THOMSEN		A	1	(15)	2
11	WELLINGTON Soares	BRA	M	24		2

EB/STREYMUR

Coach – Piotr Krakowski (POL)

Founded – 1993

MAJOR HONOURS: Faroe Islands Cup - (2) 2007, 2008.

2007				
1/4	GÍ	a	2-0	*Djurhuus, Niclasen*
5/4	Skála	h	3-0	*Anghel, Eliasen H., og (Berg)*
9/4	AB	h	3-0	*Samuelsen H.P., Anghel, Bø*
15/4	B71	a	3-2	*Bø, Samuelsen R. (p), Samuelsen H.P.*
22/4	B36	h	0-1	
29/4	KÍ	a	2-1	*Anghel, og (Andreasen)*
2/5	NSÍ	h	1-0	*Dam*
6/5	VB/Sumba	h	4-2	*Olsen Bá. 2, Samuelsen H.P. 2*
14/5	HB	a	0-3	
20/5	AB	a	2-1	*Dam, Olsen Bá.*
28/5	GÍ	h	1-1	*Olsen Br.*
10/6	Skála	a	1-2	*Hansen A.*
16/6	KÍ	h	2-1	*Hansen A., Dam*
24/6	B36	a	0-1	
1/7	NSÍ	a	1-1	*Hansen A.*
8/7	B71	h	2-4	*Hansen A., Samuelsen R. (p)*
5/8	VB/Sumba	a	2-1	*Eliasen S., Hansen A.*
12/8	HB	h	1-2	*Anghel*
19/8	AB	h	2-2	*Hansen A., Potemkin*
26/8	GÍ	a	4-1	*Anghel 2 (1p), Hansen A., Samuelsen H.P.*
2/9	Skála	h	2-0	*Anghel, Samuelsen H.P.*
16/9	NSÍ	h	0-1	
23/9	HB	a	1-0	*Anghel*
30/9	KÍ	a	5-2	*Hansen A. 3, Eliasen H., Anghel*
7/10	VB/Sumba	h	6-1	*Hansen A. 2, Samuelsen H.P. 2, Anghel, Olsen Bá.*
21/10	B36	h	4-2	*Eliasen H. 2, Hansen A., Potemkin*

27/10	B71	a	4-1	*Hansen A., Bø 2 (1p), Anghel*

No	Name	Nat	Pos	Aps	(s)	Gls
10	Sorin ANGHEL	ROU	A	18	(1)	11
8	Egil a BØ		D	26		4
6	John Heri DAM		D	19	(6)	3
12	Marni DJURHUUS		D	27		1
3	Esmar EIDISGARD		D		(5)	
14	Hanus ELIASEN		A	23	(4)	4
20	Simun ELIASEN		D	27		1
22	Arnbjørn T. HANSEN		A	14	(2)	14
4	Gert HANSEN		D	16	(4)	
25	Jákup Martin JOENSEN		M		(4)	
17	Teitur JOENSEN		M		(4)	
9	Rafać KWIECIĆSKI	POL	M	13	(10)	
23	Leif NICLASEN		A	2	(9)	1
15	Bárdur OLSEN		M	27		4
18	Brian OLSEN		M	6	(9)	1
30	Károly POTEMKIN	HUN	A	2	(7)	2
11	Hans Pauli SAMUELSEN		M	24	(1)	8
7	Ronnie SAMUELSEN		M	24	(1)	2
13	Zsolt SZEKERES	HUN	M	2	(1)	
1	Rene TORGARD		G	27		
5	Knút VESTURTÚN		D		(1)	

GÍ GØTA

Coach – Petur Mohr

Founded – 1926

MAJOR HONOURS: Faroe Islands League - (6) 1983, 1986, 1993, 1994, 1995, 1996; Faroe Islands Cup - (6) 1983, 1985, 1996, 1997, 2000, 2005.

2007				
1/4	EB/Streymur	h	0-2	
5/4	AB	a	4-4	*Ennigard 2, Justinussen P., Jacobsen Sv.*
9/4	HB	a	3-2	*Højgaard, og (Lag), Petersen H.*
15/4	VB/Sumba	a	1-0	*Jacobsen E.*
22/4	Skála	h	0-3	
29/4	B71	a	1-1	*Dalheim*
2/5	B36	h	0-3	
6/5	NSÍ	h	1-2	*Justinussen P.*
13/5	KÍ	a	3-2	*Justinussen P., Ennigard, Jacobsen E.*
20/5	HB	h	3-2	*Jacobsen Sv., Ennigard, Justinussen P.*
28/5	EB/Streymur	a	1-1	*Justinussen P.*
10/6	AB	h	1-1	*Justinussen P.*
17/6	B71	h	3-2	*Jacobsen Sí. 2, Jacobsen Sa.*
24/6	Skála	a	1-0	*Niclasen*
1/7	B36	a	0-4	
7/7	VB/Sumba	h	2-2	*Jacobsen Sa., Sajdak*
5/8	NSÍ	a	1-3	*Lundberg*
12/8	KÍ	h	0-1	
20/8	HB	a	1-4	*Lundberg*
26/8	EB/Streymur	h	1-4	*Lundberg*
2/9	AB	a	3-1	*Lundberg 3*
16/9	B36	h	0-1	
23/9	KÍ	a	4-0	*Rubeksen 2, Lundberg, Jacobsen Sv.*
30/9	B71	a	3-2	*Lundberg 2 (1p), Petersen H.*
7/10	NSÍ	h	0-4	
21/10	Skála	h	5-0	*Djurhuus, Lundberg 2, Jacobsen Sa., Rubeksen*
27/10	VB/Sumba	a	4-2	*og (Hørg), Lundberg 2, og (Djurhuus)*

No	Name	Nat	Pos	Aps	(s)	Gls
2	Jónreid DALHEIM		M	7	(16)	1
15	Hans Jørgin DJURHUUS		D	7	(2)	1
5	Poul ENNIGARD		D	19	(1)	4
4	Atli GREGERSEN		D	23		
15	Per GREGERSEN		M		(1)	
13	Jóhan Dávur HØJGAARD		M	4	(5)	1
20	Erling JACOBSEN		M	6	(7)	2
18	Poul Andrias JACOBSEN		M		(4)	
14	Sam JACOBSEN		M	26		3
11	Símun Louis JACOBSEN		M	18		2
12	Sverri JACOBSEN		A	19	(4)	3
10	Magni JARNSKOR		M		(3)	
16	Mortan JOENSEN		G	1		
8	Samal JOENSEN		M	15	(1)	
19	Finnur JUSTINUSSEN		M		(7)	
3	Pól Jóhannus JUSTINUSSEN		D	23	(3)	6
9	Christian LUNDBERG	DEN	A	11		13
17	Niclas NICLASEN		D	24	(1)	1
6	Áslakkur R. PETERSEN		D	20	(2)	
7	Hans Pauli PETERSEN		D	18	(4)	2
18	Jan POULSEN		M		(2)	
20	Hendrik RUBEKSEN		A	10	(1)	3
10	Tomasz SAJDAK	POL	A	11	(9)	1
13	Magnus SKORDALID		M	9	(4)	
1	Géza TURI	HUN	G	26		

HB TÓRSHAVN

Coach – Krzysztof Popczynski (POL); (9/7/07) Albert Ellefsen

Founded – 1904

MAJOR HONOURS: Faroe Islands League - (19) 1955, 1960, 1963, 19 1965, 1971, 1973, 1974, 1975, 1978, 1981, 1982, 1988, 1990, 1998, 20 2003, 2004, 2006; Faroe Islands Cup - (26) 1955, 1957, 1959, 1962, 19 1964, 1968, 1969, 1971, 1972, 1973, 1975, 1976, 1978, 1979, 1980, 19 1982, 1984, 1987, 1988, 1989, 1992, 1995, 1998, 2004.

2007				
1/4	Skála	a	5-2	*Jacobsen R. 2, Nolsøe Jacobsen C.H., Joens*
5/4	B71	h	0-3	
9/4	GÍ	h	2-3	*Hørg, Lag*
15/4	B36	a	1-1	*Jacobsen R.*
22/4	KÍ	h	3-1	*Jespersen, Jacobsen C.H., Borg (p)*
29/4	NSÍ	h	2-0	*Hørg, Jacobsen R.*
2/5	VB/Sumba	h	3-1	*Kuljić, Joensen, Jacobse*
6/5	AB	a	2-2	*Borg 2*
14/5	EB/Streymur	h	3-0	*Jacobsen R., Borg, og (Samuelsen R.)*
20/5	GÍ	a	2-3	*Jacobsen C.H., Lag*
28/5	Skála	h	5-2	*Jacobsen R., Nolsøe Borg 2*
10/6	B71	a	1-2	*Lag*
16/6	NSÍ	a	0-1	
20/6	KÍ	a	2-0	*Jacobsen R., Akselsen*
27/6	B36	h	0-2	
1/7	VB/Sumba	a	0-0	
7/8	AB	h	4-0	*Fløtum 3, Kuljić*
12/8	EB/Streymur	a	2-1	*Kuljić, Joensen*
20/8	GÍ	h	4-1	*Fløtum 2, Jespersen*
26/8	Skála	a	3-1	*Fløtum, Jacobsen R., Kuljić*
2/9	B71	h	3-1	*Lag, Borg, Joensen*
16/9	VB/Sumba	h	6-2	*Nielsen, Kuljić 3(1p), Jespersen 2*
23/9	EB/Streymur	h	0-1	
30/9	NSÍ	a	1-2	*Jacobsen R.*
7/10	AB	a	2-1	*Fløtum 2*
21/10	KÍ	h	1-1	*Fløtum*
27/10	B36	a	2-0	*Nolsøe, Jacobsen R.*

No	Name	Nat	Pos	Aps	(s)	Gls
6	Tór-Ingar AKSELSEN		M	20	(5)	1
9	Jákup á BORG		A	16	(3)	7
17	Poul Thomas DAM		D	12	(7)	

Name	Nat	Pos	Aps	(s)	Gls
Marcin DAWID	POL	G	14		
Sjúrdur ELLEFSEN		M		(1)	
Andrew av FLØTUM		A	11		9
Mortan úr HØRG		D	23	(4)	2
Christian Høgni JACOBSEN		A	13	(1)	3
Rógvi JACOBSEN		M	25	(1)	11
Svenn JACOBSEN		M	1	(5)	
Rókur av Fløtum JESPERSEN		M	24	(3)	5
Páll Mohr JOENSEN		A	17	(5)	4
Pætur T. JØRGENSEN		M	1	(8)	
Torkil KOLLSKER		D		(1)	
Klæmint MATRAS		D	20	(4)	7
Hans á LAG		D	17	(3)	4
Emil Nolsøe LEIFSSON		M	13	(8)	
Vagnur Mohr MORTENSEN		D	10		
Kári NIELSEN		M	23	(2)	1
Rasmus NOLSØE		D	21	(3)	4
Ólavur i ÓLAVSSTOVU		M	3	(13)	
Tróndur VATHHAMAR		G	13		

KÍ KLAKSVÍK

Coach – Tony Paris (ENG); (15/5/07) (Trygvi Mortensen); (22/5/07) Eydun Klakstein

Founded – 1904

JOR HONOURS: Faroe Islands League - (17) 1942, 1945, 1952, 1953, 4, 1956, 1957, 1958, 1961, 1966, 1967, 1968, 1969, 1970, 1972, 1991, 1999; Faroe Islands Cup - (5) 1966, 1967, 1990, 1994, 1999.

7

	B36	a	0-1	
	VB/Sumba	h	5-0	*Ceroni, Nielsen, Clapson, Joensen S., Fles*
	B71	h	3-3	*Fles, Nielsen, Clapson*
4	NSÍ	h	2-0	*Clapson 2*
4	HB	a	1-3	*Ennigard*
4	EB/Streymur	h	1-2	*Clapson*
	AB	a	3-1	*Nielsen 2, Clapson*
	Skála	a	0-1	
5	GÍ	h	2-3	*Clapson 2*
5	B71	a	3-3	*Clapson, Lakjuni H., Fles*
5	B36	h	1-1	*Nielsen*
5	VB/Sumba	a	0-1	
5	EB/Streymur	a	1-2	*Bjartalid*
5	HB	h	0-2	
	AB	h	1-0	*Lakjuni H.*
	NSÍ	a	1-3	*Clapson*
	Skála	h	1-0	*Bertholdsen*
8	GÍ	a	1-0	*Conteh*
8	B71	h	3-1	*Jacobsen K., Clapson, Kalsø*
8	B36	a	2-2	*Nysted, Clapson*
	VB/Sumba	h	6-3	*Clapson 2 (1p), Nielsen, Joensen S., Nysted, Jacobsen K.*
9	AB	a	1-3	*Jacobsen K.*
9	GÍ	h	0-4	
9	EB/Streymur	h	2-5	*Lakjuni H., Conteh*
)	Skála	a	1-0	*Lakjuni K.*
10	HB	a	1-1	*Joensen S.*
10	NSÍ	h	2-2	*Joensen M. (p), Conteh (p)*

Name	Nat	Pos	Aps	(s)	Gls
Jan ANDREASEN		D	26		
Harley BERTHOLDSEN		D	23	(3)	1
Leon BJARTALID		D	11	(11)	1
Chris CERONI	USA	A	3	(1)	1
Alvur CHRISTIANSEN		D	1	(1)	
Paul CLAPSON	ENG	A	24	(1)	14
Denni CONTEH	DEN	A	5	(3)	3
Atli DANIELSEN		D	1		
Kaj ENNIGARD		D	15	(1)	1

No	Name	Nat	Pos	Aps	(s)	Gls
11	Erling FLES		A	8	(4)	3
6	John HAMMER		M	6	(5)	
20	Kristoffur JACOBSEN		D	20	(6)	3
3	Sigmund JACOBSEN		D	8	(1)	
16	Meinhardt JOENSEN		G	27		1
8	Símin JOENSEN		M	22		3
17	Steffan KALSØ		D	3	(11)	1
12	Páll KLETTSKARD		M		(2)	
18	Hedin á LAKJUNI		A	26		3
11	Kristian á LAKJUNI		M	12	(2)	1
6	Oddmar á LAKJUNI		M	4	(4)	
7	Høgni MADSEN		M	18	(4)	
10	Gunnar NIELSEN	ARG	A	26	(1)	6
17	Ovi NYSTED		D	6	(3)	2
2	Julian SAMUELSEN		D	1	(2)	
1	Mathias SAMUELSEN		G		(2)	
9	Eli SIMONSEN		A		(2)	
17	Kereem SMITH	TRI	D	1	(1)	
14	Marek WIERZBICKI	POL	D		(1)	

NSÍ RUNAVÍK

Coach – Jóhan Nielsen

Founded – 1957

MAJOR HONOURS: Faroe Islands League - (1) 2007; Faroe Islands Cup - (2) 1986, 2002.

2007

1/4	B71	a	1-0	*Hansen Ó.*
5/4	B36	h	3-0	*Anderson 3*
9/4	Skála	h	3-1	*Frederiksberg, og (Berg), Danielsen*
15/4	KÍ	a	0-2	
22/4	VB/Sumba	h	5-2	*Anderson 4, Dalbud*
29/4	HB	a	0-2	
2/5	EB/Streymur	a	0-1	
6/5	GÍ	a	2-1	*Hansen E., Stanković*
13/5	AB	h	2-1	*Løkin, Hansen Ó.*
20/5	Skála	a	1-0	*Elttør*
28/5	B71	h	3-0	*Olsen A., Anderson (p), Dalbud*
10/6	B36	a	1-1	*Hansen Ó.*
16/6	HB	h	1-0	*Mortensen*
23/6	VB/Sumba	a	2-1	*Hansen E., Dalbud*
1/7	EB/Streymur	h	1-1	*Elttør*
8/7	KÍ	h	3-1	*Frederiksberg, Anderson, Olsen A.*
5/8	GÍ	h	3-1	*Hansen Ó. 2 (2p), Jacobsen C.H.*
12/8	AB	a	2-0	*Elttør, Løkin*
19/8	Skála	h	1-2	*Hansen Ó.*
26/8	B71	a	3-1	*Frederiksberg, Jacobsen C.H., Elttør*
2/9	B36	h	1-1	*Løkin*
16/9	EB/Streymur	a	1-0	*Stanković*
23/9	AB	h	2-1	*Jacobsen S., Frederiksberg*
30/9	HB	h	2-1	*Frederiksberg, Hansen E.*
7/10	GÍ	a	4-0	*Jacobsen C.H. 2, Løkin, Hansen Ó. (p)*
21/10	VB/Sumba	h	3-1	*Frederiksberg, og (Janković), Jacobsen C.H.*
27/10	KÍ	a	2-2	*Olsen A., Elttør (p)*

No	Name	Nat	Pos	Aps	(s)	Gls
9	ANDERSON Castilho Cardena	BRA	A	14		9
16	Øssur DALBUD		D	2	(20)	3
19	Debes DANIELSEN		M	1	(6)	1
8	Jóhan Troest DAVIDSEN		D	27		
10	Hjalgrim ELTTØR		A	26		5
17	Jónhard FREDERIKSBERG		A	26	(1)	6
12	Einar HANSEN		D	25	(2)	3
6	Jústinus R. HANSEN		M	18	(5)	

No	Name	Nat	Pos	Aps	(s)	Gls
3	Óli HANSEN		D	26		7
9	Christian Høgni JACOBSEN		A	9		5
18	Sjúrdur JACOBSEN		D	20	(6)	1
1	Jens Martin KNUDSEN		G	27		
14	Bogi LØKIN		M	22	(2)	4
5	Jann Martin MORTENSEN		M		(12)	1
19	Brynjólvur NIELSEN		D		(2)	
11	Andy OLSEN		M	17	(8)	3
13	Klæmint OLSEN		M		(5)	
7	Nenad STANKOVIĆ	SRB	M	23		2
20	Tórdur THOMSEN		G		(2)	
4	Pól THORSTEINSSON		D	14	(2)	

SKÁLA ÍTRÓTTARFELAG

Coach – Dragan Kovačević (SRB); (19/4/07) John Petersen

Founded – 1965

2007				
1/4	HB	h	2-5	*Gregersen 2*
5/4	EB/Streymur	a	0-3	
9/4	NSÍ	a	1-3	*Johansen*
15/4	AB	h	0-2	
22/4	GÍ	a	3-0	*Jacobsen P., Hanssen, Johansen*
29/4	VB/Sumba	a	1-0	*Kaplanović*
2/5	B71	h	2-0	*Berg A., Johansen (p)*
6/5	KÍ	h	1-0	*Hansen*
13/5	B36	a	1-1	*Gregersen*
20/5	NSÍ	h	0-1	
28/5	HB	a	2-5	*Onyebuchi 2*
10/6	EB/Streymur	h	2-1	*Johansen (p), Gregersen*
17/6	VB/Sumba	h	1-1	*Kaplanović*
24/6	GÍ	h	0-1	
1/7	B71	a	2-0	*Johansen, Kaplanović*
8/7	AB	a	2-1	*Kaplanović, Poulsen*
4/8	KÍ	a	0-1	
12/8	B36	h	0-2	
19/8	NSÍ	a	2-1	*Gregersen, Johansen*
26/8	HB	h	1-3	*Hansen (p)*
2/9	EB/Streymur	a	0-2	
16/9	B71	h	0-0	
24/9	B36	a	1-1	*Kaplanović*
30/9	VB/Sumba	a	1-0	*Jacobsen P.*
7/10	KÍ	h	0-1	
21/10	GÍ	a	0-5	
27/10	AB	h	2-0	*Hanssen, Danielsen D.*

No	Name	Nat	Pos	Aps	(s)	Gls
22	Arnhold BERG		D	19		1
18	Jógvan BERG		A		(1)	
11	Milić CURČIĆ	SRB	D	26		
2	Bárdur DANIELSEN		D	12	(2)	
18	Debes DANIELSEN		M	12	(1)	1
7	Erland Berg DANIELSEN		M	3	(1)	
17	Bogi GREGERSEN		A	21	(4)	5
16	Pauli G. HANSEN		M	15	(4)	2
8	Levi HANSSEN		M	26		2
6	Pætur Dam JACOBSEN		M	26		2
19	Rói JACOBSEN		D		(6)	
14	Jógvan G. JOENSEN		M	1	(5)	
4	Teitur R. JOENSEN		D	19	(4)	
10	Alexandur JOHANSEN		M	18	(3)	6
12	Hans JØRGENSEN		G	9		
15	Slaviča KAPLANOVIČ	SRB	M	15	(11)	5
1	Predrag MARKOVIČ	SRB	G	18		
3	Petur Pauli MIKKELSEN		D	3	(2)	
20	Okeke Obele ONYEBUCHI	NGA	A	21	(4)	2
10	Elieser OLSEN		M		(1)	
19	John PETERSEN		M		(2)	
9	Poul N. POULSEN		M	6	(11)	1
5	Rúni RASMUSSEN		D	26		
7	Tony RASMUSSEN		A	1	(2)	
12	Eugen VODA	ROU	G		(1)	

VB /SUMBA VÁGUR

Coach – Predrag Pršić (SRB)

Founded – 2006

MAJOR HONOURS (as VB): Faroe Islands League - (1) 2000; Faroe Islands Cup - (1) 1974.

2007				
1/4	AB	h	1-0	*Olsen*
5/4	KÍ	a	0-5	
9/4	B36	h	0-4	
15/4	GÍ	h	0-1	
22/4	NSÍ	a	2-5	*Pandurević, Tausen M*
29/4	Skála	h	0-1	
2/5	HB	a	1-3	*Jørgensen (p)*
6/5	EB/Streymur	a	2-4	*Jørgensen, Pandurev (p)*
13/5	B71	h	1-4	*Joensen H.D.*
20/5	B36	a	0-2	
28/5	AB	a	2-2	*Jørgensen, Hørg*
10/6	KÍ	h	1-0	*Poulsen J.K.*
17/6	Skála	a	1-1	*Tausen T.*
23/6	NSÍ	h	1-2	*Jørgensen*
1/7	HB	h	0-0	
7/7	GÍ	a	2-2	*Joensen D.J., Jørgens*
5/8	EB/Streymur	h	1-2	*Poulsen J.K.*
12/8	B71	a	0-0	
19/8	B36	a	0-2	
26/8	AB	h	1-2	*Djurhuus (p)*
2/9	KÍ	a	3-6	*Djurhuus 2, Pandure (p)*
16/9	HB	a	2-6	*Djurhuus, Moravčić*
23/9	B71	h	2-3	*Hørg, Moravčić*
30/9	Skála	h	0-1	
7/10	EB/Streymur	a	1-6	*Janković*
21/10	NSÍ	a	1-3	*Moravčić*
27/10	GÍ	h	2-4	*Djurhuus, Janković*

No	Name	Nat	Pos	Aps	(s)	Gl
11	Palli AUGUSTINUSSEN		M		(3)	
5	Heini BECH		D	3	(5)	
7	Evrard BLÉ	CIV	M	10	(1)	
9	Jonar Borg DAHL		M	18	(4)	
14	Dan DJURHUUS		A	23		5
1	Vlada FILIPOVIĆ	SRB	G	27		
13	Suni úr HØRG		D	24		2
6	Dimitrije JANKOVIĆ	SRB	D	26		2
12	Dánjal Jóhan JOENSEN		M	14	(4)	1
14	Hallur Dam JOENSEN		M	1	(2)	1
7	Henning JOENSEN		M	7	(1)	
18	Julian JOENSEN		D		(2)	
21	Finn JOHANNESEN		D		(1)	
3	Rani JOHANNESSEN		G		(1)	
19	Birgir JØRGENSEN		A	13	(2)	5
3	Janus KJÆRBO		D		(1)	
12	Kenneth KJÆRBO		A	3	(1)	
5	Birni KÆRBECH		D	13	(6)	
2	Eydstein í LÁGABØ		D	4	(2)	
29	Kári í LÁGABØ		D		(2)	
12	Eydfinn LUDVIG		M		(2)	
19	Marco MORAVČIĆ	SRB	M	11		3
4	Jákup F. OLSEN		D	17	(2)	1
11	Aco PANDUREVIĆ	SRB	M	21		3
10	John POULSEN		A	5	(2)	
10	Jón Krosslá POULSEN		A	22		2
3	Jón SAMUELSEN		D	12	(2)	
10	Jacob SKAANING		A	1	(1)	
18	Arthur TAUSEN		A	1	(4)	
8	Martin TAUSEN		M	18	(4)	1
13	Teitur TAUSEN		M	3	(5)	1

PROMOTED CLUBS

B68 TOFTIR

Coach – Rúni Nolsøe
Founded – 1962
MAJOR HONOURS: Faroe Islands League - (3) 1984, 1985, 1992.

ÍF FUGLAFJØRDUR

Coach – Jón Simonsen
Founded – 1946
MAJOR HONOURS: Faroe Islands League - (1) 1979.

SECOND LEVEL FINAL TABLE 2007

	Pld	W	D	L	F	A	Pts
B68 Toftir	27	23	3	1	79	20	72
ÍF Fuglafjørdur	27	19	4	4	84	22	61
FS Vágar	27	16	3	8	47	40	51
TB Tvøroyri	27	14	4	9	56	30	46
LÍF Leirvík	27	14	1	12	68	45	43
NSÍ Runavik II	27	9	4	14	49	68	31
HB Tórshavn II	27	9	2	16	38	61	29
SÍ Sørvágur	27	8	4	15	40	66	28
KÍ Klaksvík II	27	5	2	20	28	70	17
B36 Tórshavn II	27	3	3	21	22	89	12

DOMESTIC CUP 2007

LØGMANSSTEYPID

ND ROUND

07)
1, Vágar 0
ÍÍ 0
AB 3
HB 2 (aet)
Undri 1

07)
eymur 4, B71 1
07)
VB/Sumba 3
07)
Í 4

TER-FINALS

07)
eymur 4 *(Samuelsen R. 7, 38, 115p, Eliasen H. 42)*, ÍF 4 *(Taser 22, 67, 79, Zachariasen 108) (aet; 5-4 on pens)*
Akselsen 2, 44, Kuljić 37, Jespersen 83), AB 0
kála 0 *(aet; 5-6 on pens)*
mba 3 *(Pandurević 54, Jørgensen 90, Poulsen J.K. 90)*, TB 1 *nnesen 83)*

FINALS

07 & 11/7/07)
Kuljić 64, Jacobsen C.H. 67, Ólavsstovu 73), VB/Sumba 1 *(Jørgensen 30)*
mba 0, HB 1 *(Ólavsstovu 90)*
(HB Tórshavn 4-1)
Skála 0, EB/Streymur 2 *(Samuelsen R. 52, Eliasen H. 74)*
EB/Streymur 1 *(Olsen Bá. 83)*, Skála 0
(EB/Streymur 3-0)

FINAL

(15/8/07)
Gundadalur stadium, Torshavn
EB/STREYMUR 4 *(Anghel 3, Samuelsen H.P. 6, Hansen A. 21, Potemkin 80)*
HB TÓRSHAVN 3 *(Joensen 77, Jacobsen R. 81, Mortensen 85)*
Referee – *Rasmussen*
EB/STREYMUR – *Torgard, Olsen Bá., Djurhuus, Bø, Dam, Samuelsen H.P., Eliasen S., Samuelsen R. (Hansen G. 71), Eliasen H., Hansen A. (Potemkin 25), Anghel (Kwiecinski 86).*
HB – *Vatnhamar, Hørg (Joensen 30), Nolsøe (Mortensen 30), Lag, Dam, Jespersen, Nielsen, Kuljić (Ólavsstovu 65), Borg, Fløtum, Jacobsen R.*

DOMESTIC CUP 2008

LØGMANSSTEYPID

SECOND ROUND

(20/3/08)
EB/Streymur 1, NSÍ 0
VB/Sumba 1, AB 2 (aet)
TB 6, MB 1 (aet)
07 Vestur 1, Víkingur 1 (aet; 4-2 on pens)
B71 2, B68 1 (aet)

(22/3/08)
ÍF 2, HB 3
Fram 1, KÍ 4
B36 1, Skála 0

QUARTER-FINALS

(2/4/08)
07 Vestur 2 *(Rasmussen 69, 72)*, B36 2 *(Højsted 51, Potemkin 74) (aet; 3-5 on pens)*
HB 5 *(Jacobsen C.H. 21, 35, Fløtum 57p, Rubeksen 70, 87)*, TB 1 *(Moutitsen 81p)*
EB/Streymur 2 *(Niclasen 3, Samuelsen H.P. 85)*, KÍ 0
B71 4 *(Nielsen R. 45, 78, 82, Clayton 88)*, AB 0

SEMI-FINALS

(16/4/08 & 12/5/08)
B36 0, HB 0
HB 1 *(Fløtum 68p)*, B36 2 *(Potemkin 53, Nagy 60)*
(B36 2-1)

B71 1 *(Olsen 84)*, EB/Streymur 1 *(Thomasen 21)*
EB/Streymur 2 *(Hansen A. 34, Eliasen H. 86)*, B71 1 *(Fábio 20)*
(EB/Streymur 3-2)

FINAL

(15/6/08)
Gundadalur stadium, Torshavn
EB/STREYMUR 3 *(Hansen A. 9, 76, Samuelsen H.P. 19)*
B36 TÓRSHAVN 2 *(Potemkin 38, 79)*
Referee – *Reinert*
EB/STREYMUR – *Torgard, Hanssen, Bø, Niclasen, Djurhuus, Olsen Bá., Samuelsen H.P., Olsen Br. (Clementsen 84), Eliasen H. (Balog 87), Anghel, Hansen A.*
B36 – *Joensen, Alex, Janković, Jacobsen H., Gunnarsson (Jacobsen R. 80), Olsen, Matras, Nagy, Midjord, Potemkin, Ellingsgaard.*

Easy does it for defending champions

The race for the 2007 Finnish title did not reach the excitement levels of many previous editions. Tampere United were firm favourites to retain their title and they duly delivered, setting the pace in the Veikkausliiga from the sixth round onwards.

The decisive match took place on 27 September when the Blues hosted closest pursuers FC Haka at the Ratina stadium. Antti Pohja's spectacular stoppage-time goal gave the home side a 2–1 victory that extended their lead to seven points with five rounds remaining. United could even afford a mini-slump at the end of the season as Haka failed to win any of their next four matches.

Tampere strength in depth

Ari Hjelm's title-winning team showed strength in every department. Mikko Kavén enhanced his reputation as the league's outstanding goalkeeper while Mathias Lindström and Jussi Kujala worked assuredly in central defence. Midfield general Jarkko Wiss was flanked by the revelation of the season, Juska Savolainen, while up front veterans Jari Niemi and Antti Pohja were assisted by young Tomi Petrescu in the league's most productive strike force. United also gave the best Finnish performance in Europe for nine years, eliminating PFC Levski Sofia in the UEFA Champions League qualifiers before succumbing to the Norwegians of Rosenborg BK, their self-stated role models. They rounded up their European tour by giving FC Girondins de Bordeaux a run for their money in the UEFA Cup.

Jarkko Wiss, Tampere United's experienced midfield general

Haka may have faltered late on but second place was better than had been expected of Olli Huttunen's small squad whose lynchpin, yet again, was evergreen Russian playmaker Valeriy Popovich. The league's most entertaining, and best-supported, team was FC TPS Turku, guided to third place with infectious enthusiasm by coach Mixu Paatelainen. Almost inevitably, he left in the close season for Scotland to take over at his old club Hibernian FC.

HJK Helsinki, founded in 1907 as Finland's first football club, had entertained high hopes for their centenary year, but their season turned sour early on - when star striker Farid Ghazi returned homesick to Algeria - and never improved. Coach Keith Armstrong was fired in early September, to be followed a month later by his successor Aki Hyryläinen, who was replaced by former national team coach Antti Muurinen, poached from FC Lahti. HJK finished a dismal seventh, their last chance to salvage a place in Europe ending in a Cup semi-final defeat to local rivals FC Honka Espoo.

Myllykosken-Pallo 47 finished the season brightly despite losing their coach Ilkka Mäkelä, who resigned after a string of defeats in mid-season. Mäkelä later joined FC Lahti, whose only reward was the top scorer crown claimed by 14-goal Brazilian striker Rafael. IFK Mariehamn produced the turnaround of the season. After winning only one of their first 14 matches, the islanders hauled themselves to safety with eight wins and three draws in the next eleven.

Promoted clubs down

The battle against relegation ultimately claimed both promoted sides - FC Viikingit, a small club from east Helsinki staffed with mainly local players, and AC Oulu, who employed no fewer than 16 foreigners. Oulu ended up with the wooden spoon, with Viikingit losing to RoPS Rovaniemi in the promotion/relegation play-offs. The Laplanders thus returned to the Veikkausliiga after a two-year break while KuPS from Kuopio bounced back up after one season.

ıe 2007 Finnish Cup Final drew a paltry 1,457 to the ınnair stadium for the season-ending finale between ımpere United and Honka. Ironically, those spectators ho did show up were treated to the most entertaining ıatch of the season. Miki Sipiläinen equalised for the ıampions in the final minute. They then scored twice ıore in extra time, only to see Honka draw level at 3–3 ıd force a penalty shoot-out. Goalkeeper Kavén then ıved two penalties to earn Tampere United their first ouble.

lthough entertainment was not readily forthcoming om the Finland national team in the closing stretch of ıeir UEFA EURO 2008™ qualifying series, Roy Hodgson's ıuad came agonisingly close to qualifying for the final ırnament. The Englishman's defensive tactics worked near-perfection as Finland conceded just seven goals 14 matches. Unfortunately, there was no-one to ciprocate up front. Goalless draws in Serbia, at home Poland and in Belgium were followed by a fourth in the Finnish FA Centenary Match against Spain. A tortuous home win over Azerbaijan kept Finland in contention before the last qualifying match away to Portugal, where only a victory would do. Goalkeeper Jussi Jääskeläinen, the 2007 Finnish Footballer of the Year, bravely kept another clean sheet but, not untypically, the player who came closest to scoring for Finland was a Portuguese defender, Bruno Alves, four minutes from time.

Baxter in for Hodgson

Hodgson left and was succeeded by Stuart Baxter, another Briton who had made his name in Swedish football. Baxter set out to rejuvenate the squad, but the first indications were that the team still appeared alarmingly dependent on its thirtysomethings and would find the going extremely tough in a 2010 FIFA World Cup qualifying group containing two top UEFA EURO 2008™ performers, Germany and Russia.

Suomen Palloliitto - Finlands Bollförbund (SPF-FBF)

Urheilukatu 1
PO Box 191
FI-00251 Helsinki
tel - +358 9 742151
fax - +358 9 74215201
website - www.palloliitto.fi
email – firstname.lastname@palloliitto.fi
Year of Formation – 1907
President - Pekka Hämäläinen
General Secretary - Kimmo J. Lipponen
Press Officer – Sami Terävä
Stadium - Olympic, Helsinki (37,500)

TOP FIVE ALL-TIME CAPS
Jari Litmanen (114); Ari Hjelm (100); Sami Hyypiä (90); Jonatan Johansson (89); Joonas Kolkka (86)

TOP FIVE ALL-TIME GOALS
Jari Litmanen (30); Ari Hjelm (20); Mika-Matti Paatelainen (18); Verner Eklöf & Mikael Forssell (17)

ATIONAL TEAM RESULTS 2007/08

'07	Kazakhstan (ECQ)	H	Tampere	2-1	*Eremenko A. (13), Tainio (61)*
7	Serbia (ECQ)	A	Belgrade	0-0	
'07	Poland (ECQ)	H	Helsinki	0-0	
0/07	Belgium (ECQ)	A	Brussels	0-0	
0/07	Spain	H	Helsinki	0-0	
1/07	Azerbaijan (ECQ)	H	Helsinki	2-1	*Forssell (79), Kuqi (86)*
1/07	Portugal (ECQ)	A	Porto	0-0	
)8	Greece	N	Nicosia (CYP)	1-2	*Litmanen (66)*
/08	Bulgaria	A	Sofia	1-2	*Litmanen (22p)*
/08	Turkey	N	Duisburg (GER)	0-2	
)8	Belarus	H	Turku	1-1	*Kallio (90+4)*

FINLAND

NATIONAL TEAM APPEARANCES 2007/08

Coach – Roy HODGSON (ENG) /(1/2/08) Stuart BAXTER (ENG)	9/8/47 16/8/53		KAZ	SRB	POL	BEL	Esp	AZE	POR	Gre	Bul	Tur	Blr	Caps
Jussi JÄÄSKELÄINEN	19/4/75	Bolton (ENG)	G	G	G	G		G	G					42
Petri PASANEN	24/9/80	Bremen (GER)	D	D	D	D	D	D	D					45
Hannu TIHINEN	1/7/76	Zürich (SUI)	D	D	D	D	s46	D	D					64
Sami HYYPIÄ	7/10/73	Liverpool (ENG)	D	D	D	D	D46	D	D					90
Toni KALLIO	9/8/78	Young Boys (SUI) /Fulham (ENG)	D			D	D	D66	D	D	D	D82	D	39
Roman EREMENKO	19/3/87	Udinese (ITA)	M46			M	M	M80	s69		M84	M	M	9
Markus HEIKKINEN	13/10/78	Rapid Wien (AUT)	M	M	M91				M	M		M61	s81	36
Joonas KOLKKA	28/9/74	NAC (NED)	M88		M	M	M76	M	M75		M	M	M	86
Teemu TAINIO	27/11/79	Tottenham (ENG)	M76	M	M			M	M69		M73		M81	43
Alexei EREMENKO Jr.	24/3/83	Saturn (RUS)	A	A74	A	A	s66			M		A61		35
Jonatan JOHANSSON	16/8/75	Malmö (SWE)	A	A78	A72	A90	A	A59	s75	A76	A	s61	A	89
Daniel SJÖLUND	22/4/83	Djurgården (SWE)	s46	M	M	M92		M	M					15
Aki RIIHILAHTI	9/9/76	Djurgården (SWE)	s76			M	M46							69
Mika NURMELA	26/12/71	HJK	s88	M		s92	s46							71
Toni KUIVASTO	31/12/75	Djurgården (SWE)		D	D		D				D	D	D	72
Mikael FORSSELL	15/3/81	Birmingham (ENG)		s74	s72			A	A	A	A61	A78	A81	55
Jarkko WISS	17/4/72	Tampere United		s78	s91									45
Shefki KUQI	10/11/76	Fulham (ENG)				s90	A66	s80						52
Antti NIEMI	31/5/72	Fulham (ENG)					G							67
Mika VÄYRYNEN	28/12/81	PSV (NED)					M84	s66	s67	M	s73	M	s55	36
Veli LAMPI	18/7/84	Zürich (SUI)					s76			s78	D79	s53	D	8
Jari ILOLA	24/11/78	Elfsborg (SWE)					s84							30
Jari LITMANEN	20/2/71	unattached /Fulham (ENG) /unattached						s59	A67	A70	A46	s61	A55	114
Peter ENCKELMAN	10/3/77	Cardiff (ENG)								G	G	G46	s69	11
Ari NYMAN	7/2/84	Thun (SUI)								D78	s79	D	D	18
Markus HALSTI	19/3/84	GAIS (SWE)								D				1
Juha PASOJA	16/11/76	HamKam (NOR)								D	D	D53		15
Roni POROKARA	12/12/83	Honka								s70				2
Kari ARKIVUO	23/6/83	Sandefjord (NOR)								s76				6
Antti POHJA	11/1/77	Tampere United									s46			20
Fredrik SVANBÄCK	12/5/79	Helsingborg (SWE)									s61			2
Janne SAARINEN	28/2/77	Häcken (SWE)									s84			42
Otto FREDRIKSON	30/11/81	Lillestrøm (NOR)										s46		1
Berat SADIK	14/9/86	Lahti										s78	s81	2
Niklas MOISANDER	29/9/85	Zwolle (NED)										s82		1
Niki MÄENPÄÄ	23/1/85	Den Bosch (NED)											G69	1

DOMESTIC LEAGUE 2007

'EIKKAUSLIIGA FINAL LEAGUE TABLE

	Pld	Home W	D	L	F	A	Away W	D	L	F	A	Total W	D	L	F	A	Pts
Tampere United	26	10	2	1	24	12	6	4	3	21	15	16	6	4	45	27	54
FC Haka	26	7	4	2	21	10	6	3	4	18	13	13	7	6	39	23	46
FC TPS Turku	26	8	2	3	27	13	5	2	6	16	20	13	4	9	43	33	43
FC Honka Espoo	26	5	5	3	14	10	5	6	2	20	15	10	11	5	34	25	41
Myllykosken Pallo-47	26	6	3	4	14	13	5	4	4	15	13	11	7	8	29	26	40
IFK Mariehamn	26	4	5	4	12	14	5	5	3	19	16	9	10	7	31	30	37
HJK Helsinki	26	4	6	3	18	12	3	7	3	13	13	7	13	6	31	25	34
FC Lahti	26	5	3	5	25	20	4	3	6	13	14	9	6	11	38	34	33
FC International Turku	26	5	4	4	20	13	4	2	7	12	15	9	6	11	32	28	33
0 VPS Vaasa	26	4	7	2	14	9	3	4	6	12	26	7	11	8	26	35	32
1 FF Jaro	26	4	3	6	11	12	3	4	6	19	29	7	7	12	30	41	28
2 FC KooTeePee	26	5	2	6	18	20	2	3	8	9	18	7	5	14	27	38	26
3 FC Viikingit	26	3	3	7	15	25	2	5	6	10	19	5	8	13	25	44	23
4 AC Oulu	26	4	5	4	22	20	1	2	10	6	29	5	7	14	28	49	22

TOP GOALSCORERS

14 RAFAEL (Lahti)

11 Toni LEHTINEN (Haka)

9 Berat SADIK (Lahti)
Mikko PAATELAINEN (TPS)

8 Jami PUUSTINEN (Honka)
Mika ÄÄRITALO (TPS)

7 Vili SAVOLAINEN (HJK)
Kim LILJEQVIST (KooTeePee)
Jari NIEMI (Tampere United)

6 Mikko INNANEN (Haka)
Dominic CHATTO (Inter Turku)
Jonas EMET (Jaro)
Toni JUNNILA (Jaro)
Tomi PETRESCU (Tampere United)
Antti POHJA (Tampere United)
Armand ONÉ (TPS)
Tero TAIPALE (VPS)

CLUB-BY-CLUB

FC HAKA

Coach – Olli Huttunen

Founded - 1934

MAJOR HONOURS: Finnish League - (9) 1960, 1962, 1965, 1977, 1995, 1998, 1999, 2000, 2004; Finnish Cup - (12) 1955, 1959, 1960, 1963, 1969, 1977, 1982, 1985, 1988, 1997, 2002, 2005.

2007				
23/4	Inter Turku	h	1-0	*Popovich*
26/4	Jaro	a	2-1	*og (Portin Jo.), Lehtinen*
3/5	Lahti	h	1-2	*Popovich*
10/5	Mariehamn	a	1-0	*Parviainen*
16/5	VPS	h	1-0	*Manninen*
24/5	MyPa	h	0-0	
27/5	KooTeePee	a	2-1	*Innanen 2*
14/6	Tampere United	h	1-1	*Mattila*
17/6	HJK	a	1-2	*Lehtinen (p)*
28/6	Oulu	h	2-0	*Lehtinen, Innanen*
1/7	Inter Turku	a	1-3	*Lehtinen*
9/7	HJK	h	3-3	*Fowler, Lehtinen 2 (1p)*
25/7	Honka	a	2-0	*Lehtinen, Popovich*
5/8	Jaro	h	4-0	*Mahlakaarto, Fowler, Innanen 2*
9/8	MyPa	a	3-0	*Popovich, og (Pulkkinen), Strandvall*
25/8	TPS	h	2-1	*Lehtinen (p), Holopainen*
3/9	VPS	a	0-0	
13/9	TPS	a	1-2	*Strandvall*
16/9	Viikingit	h	1-0	*Lehtinen*
21/9	KooTeePee	h	3-0	*Fowler, Innanen, Lehtinen*
27/9	Tampere United	a	1-2	*Mattila*
30/9	Oulu	a	1-1	*Kauppila*
7/10	Honka	h	1-1	*Lehtinen*
20/10	Lahti	a	1-1	*Popovich*
24/10	Mariehamn	h	1-2	*Strandvall (p)*
27/10	Viikingit	a	2-0	*Manninen, Mahlakaarto*

No	Name	Nat	Pos	Aps	(s)	Gls
1	Aleksandr DOVBNYA	RUS	G	26		
20	Cheyne FOWLER	RSA	M	25		3
21	Pietari HOLOPAINEN		D	22	(3)	1
7	Mikko INNANEN		M	24	(2)	6
2	Juuso KANGASKORPI		D	22		
8	Jani KAUPPILA		M	25		1
11	Toni LEHTINEN		A	25		11
15	Janne MAHLAKAARTO		M	7	(14)	2
9	Mikko MANNINEN		M	24	(2)	2
22	Jarno MATTILA		A	2	(16)	2
4	Jarkko OKKONEN		D	21	(1)	
5	Ville PAJULA		D		(3)	
10	Kalle PARVIAINEN		A	18		1
14	Valeriy POPOVICH	RUS	A	21		5
13	Erno ROSENBERG		M	2	(7)	
6	Sebastian STRANDVALL		M	16	(8)	3
16	Joel SUNABACKA		M		(4)	
3	Petri VILJANEN		D	6	(4)	

HJK HELSINKI

Coach – Keith Armstrong (ENG); (6/9/07) Aki Hyryläinen; (10/10/07) Antti Muurinen

Founded - 1907

MAJOR HONOURS: Finnish League - (21) 1911, 1912, 1917, 1918, 1919, 1923, 1925, 1936, 1938, 1964, 1973, 1978, 1981, 1985, 1987, 1988, 1990, 1992, 1997, 2002, 2003; Finnish Cup - (9) 1966, 1981, 1984, 1993, 1996, 1998, 2000, 2003, 2006.

2007				
21/4	KooTeePee	a	3-1	*Ghazi, Hetemaj, Parikka*
26/4	Oulu	h	0-0	
7/5	TPS	a	1-0	*Savolainen (p)*
11/5	Lahti	a	1-3	*Savolainen*
17/5	Mariehamn	h	2-2	*Smith, Parikka*
20/5	Viikingit	a	1-1	*Ghazi*
23/5	Tampere United	h	0-2	

FINLAND

27/5	Honka	a	0-0	
10/6	Jaro	h	2-2	*Savolainen, Samura*
17/6	Haka	h	2-1	*Nurmela, Savolainen*
28/6	Inter Turku	a	1-1	*og (Hooiveld)*
1/7	VPS	h	0-0	
9/7	Haka	a	3-3	*Samura, Savolainen (p), Vuorinen*
26/7	MyPa	h	5-0	*Samura, Vuorinen 3, Bah*
6/8	Viikingit	h	1-1	*Parikka*
9/8	Jaro	a	0-0	
25/8	KooTeePee	h	1-1	*Sorsa*
3/9	Honka	h	0-1	
16/9	MyPa	a	0-0	
19/9	VPS	a	1-2	*Bah*
24/9	Inter Turku	h	2-0	*Bah, Kamara*
1/10	Tampere United	a	1-2	*Savolainen*
7/10	Lahti	h	0-2	
20/10	Mariehamn	a	0-0	
24/10	Oulu	a	1-0	*Nurmela*
27/10	TPS	h	3-0	*Kamara, Aalto (p), Savolainen*

No	Name	Nat	Pos	Aps	(s)	Gls
6	Iiro AALTO		D	23	(2)	1
18	Tuomas AHO		D	17	(1)	
2	Ilari ÄIJÄLÄ		D	9	(5)	
17	Dawda BAH	GAM	A	10	(2)	3
9	Farid GHAZI	ALG	A	7		2
21	Tuomas HAAPALA		M	8	(1)	
22	Markus HALSTI		D	19	(1)	
28	Mehmet HETEMAJ		M	5	(3)	1
12	Mika JOHANSSON		G	2	(1)	
4	Mohamed "Medo" KAMARA	SLE	M	23	(3)	2
30	John KEISTER	SLE	A		(1)	
10	Mohamed MEDJOUDJ	ALG	M	3	(1)	
14	Mika NURMELA		M	24	(1)	2
16	Jarno PARIKKA		A	7	(17)	3
31	Akseli PELVAS		A		(2)	
20	Jukka RAITALA		D	20	(3)	
8	Kabba SAMURA	SLE	A	15	(6)	3
7	Vili SAVOLAINEN		M	21	(1)	7
15	Grant SMITH	SCO	M	15	(6)	1
27	Sebastian SORSA		A	17	(6)	1
11	Hermanni VUORINEN		A	8	(6)	4
1	Ville WALLÉN		G	24		
24	Erfan ZENELI		M	9	(3)	

FC HONKA ESPOO

Coach – Mika Lehkosuo

Founded - 1957

2007

22/4	MyPa	h	2-1	*Puustinen, Weckström*
27/4	Viikingit	a	2-3	*Puustinen, Saarinen*
4/5	Tampere United	h	1-2	*Patronen*
11/5	VPS	a	1-1	*Patronen*
17/5	Inter Turku	a	1-1	*Vasara V.*
20/5	Mariehamn	h	2-0	*Huuhtanen, Puustinen*
23/5	Jaro	a	2-1	*Huuhtanen, Porokara*
27/5	HJK	h	0-0	
14/6	TPS	a	3-1	*Puustinen 2, Weckström*
18/6	Lahti	h	0-0	
4/7	TPS	h	2-0	*Koskela, Otaru*
22/7	Oulu	a	3-3	*Porokara 2, Hakanpää*
25/7	Haka	h	0-2	
5/8	Lahti	a	2-2	*Otaru, Puustinen*
9/8	Viikingit	h	1-1	*Hakanpää*
13/8	KooTeePee	a	2-1	*Weckström, Huuhtar*
16/8	Mariehamn	a	0-0	
30/8	VPS	h	1-0	*Puustinen*
3/9	HJK	a	1-0	*Koskela*
19/9	Oulu	h	2-0	*Huuhtanen, Puustine*
24/9	MyPa	a	0-1	
1/10	Jaro	h	2-2	*og (Matrone), Perovu*
7/10	Haka	a	1-1	*Saarinen (p)*
20/10	KooTeePee	h	0-0	
24/10	Inter Turku	h	1-2	*Weckström*
27/10	Tampere United	a	2-0	*Saarinen, Perovuo*

No	Name	Nat	Pos	Aps	(s)	Gl
11	Hannu HAARALA		D	4	(11)	
18	Rami HAKANPÄÄ		M	15	(1)	2
3	Roope HEILALA		D	10		
19	Mika HELIN		D	11		
7	Peke HUUHTANEN		A	15	(8)	4
4	Ville JALASTO		D	26		
15	Aleksandr KOKKO		A	1	(5)	
16	Tero KOSKELA		M	20	(2)	2
22	Niko KUKKA		D	5	(1)	
5	Lasse LAGERBLOM		D	1	(2)	
26	Jaakko LEPOLA		M	1	(1)	
12	Tomi MAANOJA		G	14		
20	Nicholas OTARU		M	12	(7)	2
8	Hannu PATRONEN		D	14	(2)	2
1	Tuomas PELTONEN		G	11	(1)	
21	Joel PEROVUO		M	5	(10)	2
33	Roni POROKARA		A	26		3
17	Jami PUUSTINEN		A	21	(3)	8
10	Janne SAARINEN		M	21	(1)	3
27	Tuomo TURUNEN		D	25	(1)	
14	Jussi VASARA		A	1	(3)	
9	Vesa VASARA		M	3	(11)	1
6	Ilpo VERNO		M	3		
30	Jan VESTERINEN		G	1	(1)	
13	John WECKSTRÖM		M	20	(4)	4

FC INTERNATIONAL TURKU

Coach – Job Dragtsma (NED)

Founded - 1990

2007

23/4	Haka	a	0-1	
26/4	VPS	h	5-0	*Mutumba, Gustafsso, Chatto 2, Turunen*
3/5	Oulu	a	0-2	
10/5	TPS	h	1-1	*Chatto*
17/5	Honka	h	1-1	*Laaksonen*
20/5	Tampere United	a	1-2	*Lehtonen*
24/5	Viikingit	h	0-1	
27/5	Mariehamn	a	0-2	
17/6	MyPa	a	3-1	*Lehtonen, Laaksonen, Mäkitalo*
28/6	HJK	h	1-1	*Ojala*
1/7	Haka	h	3-1	*Ojala, Turunen, Chatt*
8/7	VPS	a	0-0	
18/7	Jaro	a	0-1	
29/7	Lahti	h	0-1	
5/8	Oulu	h	1-0	*Turunen (p)*
8/8	KooTeePee	a	2-0	*Ojala 2*
12/8	Lahti	a	2-2	*Paajanen, Hooiveld*
16/8	Jaro	h	5-2	*Mutumba 3, Chatto, Turunen*
30/8	TPS	a	0-1	
3/9	Tampere United	h	1-1	*Aho*
20/9	Mariehamn	h	0-2	

9	HJK	a	0-2	
0	MyPa	h	1-2	*Furuholm*
10	Viikingit	a	2-0	*Laaksonen, Chatto*
10	Honka	a	2-1	*Laaksonen 2*
10	KooTeePee	h	1-0	*Furuholm*

Name	Nat	Pos	Aps	(s)	Gls
Joni AHO		D	26		1
Patrick BANTAMOI	SLE	G	25		
Dominic CHATTO	NGA	M	23		6
Diego CORPACHE	ARG	D	13		
Oskari FORSMAN		G	1		
Timo FURUHOLM		A	2	(12)	2
Jermu GUSTAFSSON		D	9		1
Jussi HENRIKSSON		D	1		
Jos HOOIVELD	NED	D	26		1
Miikka ILO		A	5	(8)	
Valtter LAAKSONEN		A	14	(6)	5
LAÉRCIO Ramos Júnior	BRA	A	2	(3)	
Henri LEHTONEN		D	24		2
Mika MÄKITALO		M	21	(4)	1
Martin MUTUMBA	SWE	A	24	(1)	4
Ville NIKKARI		D	6	(7)	
Mika OJALA		A	22	(2)	4
Prince OTOO		A		(1)	
Severi PAAJANEN		M	7	(11)	1
Sami SANEVUORI		M	13	(3)	
Teemu TURUNEN		M	22	(2)	4

FF JARO

Coach – Mika Laurikainen

Founded - 1965

7

4	Lahti	a	4-1	*Koivisto, Junnila, Piracaía, Aalto*
4	Haka	h	1-2	*Matrone*
4	Mariehamn	h	1-1	*Emet*
5	MyPa	a	0-2	
5	KooTeePee	h	0-0	
5	VPS	a	2-1	*Junnila, Aalto*
5	Honka	h	1-2	*og (Turunen)*
5	HJK	a	2-2	*Emet 2*
5	Viikingit	h	2-0	*Emet 2*
5	Tampere United	a	1-2	*og (Savolainen Juska)*
	Viikingit	a	2-1	*Aalto, Matrone*
7	Inter Turku	h	1-0	*Roiko*
7	VPS	h	0-1	
7	KooTeePee	a	1-2	*Koivisto*
	Haka	a	0-4	
	HJK	h	0-0	
3	Inter Turku	a	2-5	*Portin Jo., Junnila*
	Oulu	a	1-5	*Aalto*
9	Tampere United	h	0-2	
9	TPS	h	2-0	*Junnila 2*
9	MyPa	h	0-3	
9	Mariehamn	a	1-1	*Aalto (p)*
0	Honka	a	2-2	*Emet, Storbacka*
10	Oulu	h	0-1	
10	TPS	a	1-1	*Junnila*
10	Lahti	h	3-0	*Roiko 2, Koivisto*

No	Name	Nat	Pos	Aps	(s)	Gls
	Jussi AALTO		A	15	(10)	5
	Chad BOTHA	RSA	M	14	(5)	
	Jonas EMET		M	22	(4)	6
	Vesa HEIKINHEIMO		D	15	(3)	
	Toni JUNNILA		A	24	(2)	6
12	Antti-Jussi KARNIO		G	6		
11	Jani KOIVISTO		A	5	(15)	3
1	Markus KOLJANDER		G	20		
3	Mathias KULLSTRÖM		D	21		
7	Marco MATRONE		M	20	(5)	2
17	Tom MELARTI		A		(5)	
19	PIRACAÍA	BRA	M	18	(5)	1
22	Jens PORTIN		D	19		
20	Jonas PORTIN		D	25		1
13	Jussi ROIKO		A	14	(8)	3
25	Jari SARA		M	3	(2)	
2	Niklas STORBACKA		M	25		1
5	Jesper TÖRNQVIST		D	10	(2)	
9	Jimmy WARGH		M	10	(8)	
24	Ruslan ZANEVSKIY	UKR	A		(1)	

FC KOOTEEPEE

Coach – Vesa Tauriainen

Founded - 1999

2007

21/4	HJK	h	1-3	*og (Savolainen)*
26/4	Tampere United	a	1-2	*Kinnaslampi*
3/5	Viikingit	a	1-0	*Pukki*
9/5	Oulu	h	3-0	*Ikävalko, Pukki 2*
16/5	Jaro	a	0-0	
21/5	MyPa	a	0-1	
27/5	Haka	h	1-2	*Inutile*
14/6	VPS	h	1-1	*Liljeqvist*
17/6	Oulu	a	2-1	*Äijälä, Liljeqvist*
28/6	VPS	a	0-1	
8/7	TPS	h	4-2	*Hänninen, Kinnaslampi, Eronen, Liljeqvist*
15/7	TPS	a	2-3	*Liljeqvist, Inutile*
23/7	Viikingit	h	1-0	*Majava*
29/7	Jaro	h	2-1	*Liljeqvist, Hänninen*
4/8	Mariehamn	a	2-3	*Liljeqvist 2*
8/8	Inter Turku	h	0-2	
13/8	Honka	h	1-2	*Eronen*
25/8	HJK	a	1-1	*Inutile*
30/8	Lahti	a	0-2	
3/9	MyPa	h	1-0	*Hänninen*
17/9	Lahti	h	2-2	*Tuunainen, Inutile*
21/9	Haka	a	0-3	
30/9	Mariehamn	h	1-2	*Hänninen*
20/10	Honka	a	0-0	
24/10	Tampere United	h	0-3	
27/10	Inter Turku	a	0-1	

No	Name	Nat	Pos	Aps	(s)	Gls
11	Ilari ÄIJÄLÄ		M	6		1
2	David DAVIDSON	GHA	D	14	(4)	
26	Immo ERONEN		M	22	(1)	2
8	Mika HÄNNINEN		M	25		4
23	Vesa HELENIUS		A	19	(5)	
1	Janne HENRIKSSON		G	26		
10	Niko IKÄVALKO		A	18	(5)	1
9	Antonio INUTILE		A	6	(12)	4
11	Tero KARHU		M	6		
4	Jussi KINNASLAMPI		D	23		2
28	Jani LÄHDE		D	14	(1)	
15	Jani LAURETSALO		M	2	(11)	
18	Kim LILJEQVIST		A	15	(3)	7
21	Juha MAJAVA		D	19	(6)	1
16	Teemu PUKKI		A	10	(14)	3
14	Julius RIKBERG		M		(2)	
20	Joni RUUSKANEN		A		(2)	
5	Jarno TUUNAINEN		D	26		1

17	Marko TYYSKÄ	M	11	(9)
7	Anssi VIREN	D	24	

FC LAHTI

Coach – Antti Muurinen; (10/10/07) Luciano Martins (BRA)

Founded - 1996

2007

22/4	Jaro	h	1-4	*Sadik*
26/4	Mariehamn	a	0-0	
3/5	Haka	a	2-1	*Sadik, Hauhia*
11/5	HJK	h	3-1	*Rafael 2, Taulo*
16/5	TPS	a	1-3	*Rafael*
20/5	Oulu	h	2-1	*Rafael, Sadik*
28/5	Tampere United	a	0-1	
8/6	VPS	h	6-0	*Kainu 2, Hietanen, Rafael, Korte, og (Taipale)*
18/6	Honka	a	0-0	
29/6	Viikingit	h	0-2	
2/7	MyPa	a	0-1	
15/7	VPS	a	0-1	
23/7	Mariehamn	h	4-1	*Sadik, Moilanen, Taulo, Rafael*
29/7	Inter Turku	a	1-0	*Rafael*
5/8	Honka	h	2-2	*Rafael, Kainu*
12/8	Inter Turku	h	2-2	*Rafael, Sadik*
16/8	Oulu	a	1-2	*Sadik*
30/8	KooTeePee	h	2-0	*Kärkkäinen, Rafael (p)*
17/9	KooTeePee	a	2-2	*Kärkkäinen, Taulo*
20/9	Viikingit	a	4-0	*Sadik (p), Rafael 2, Kärkkäinen*
24/9	Tampere United	h	0-2	
1/10	TPS	h	2-3	*Sadik 2*
7/10	HJK	a	2-0	*Kainu, Rafael*
20/10	Haka	h	1-1	*Rafael*
24/10	MyPa	h	0-1	
27/10	Jaro	a	0-3	

No	Name	Nat	Pos	Aps	(s)	Gls
6	Kalle EEROLA		D	26		
2	Heikki HAARA		D	17		
23	Jere HALME		M		(1)	
3	Mikko HAUHIA		D	26		1
14	Konsta HIETANEN		M	16	(10)	1
11	Pekka KAINU		A	22	(4)	4
7	Pyry KÄRKKÄINEN		D	26		3
19	Ville KARLSSON		D	1	(1)	
20	Jonne KEMPPINEN		A		(5)	
17	Eero KORTE		M	11	(11)	1
15	Niko LEPPÄNEN		D	4	(4)	
13	Joachim LINDHOLM		M	3	(12)	
4	Janne MOILANEN		D	22		1
12	Saku PESONEN		G	2		
9	RAFAEL Pires Vieira	BRA	A	26		14
25	Kaarlo RANTANEN		M		(4)	
21	Olli RIIKONEN		M		(4)	
8	Berat SADIK		A	20	(3)	9
22	Ville-Veikko SAVOLAINEN		A		(1)	
16	Drilon SHALA		A		(3)	
30	Michał SŁAWUTA	POL	G	24		
10	Christian SUND		M	18	(5)	
18	Ville TAULO		M	21	(1)	3
24	Tommi VARTIAINEN		D	1	(6)	

IFK MARIEHAMN

Coach – Pekka Lyyski

Founded - 1919

2007

22/4	TPS	a	0-0	
26/4	Lahti	h	0-0	
30/4	Jaro	a	1-1	*Björk*
10/5	Haka	h	0-1	
17/5	HJK	a	2-2	*Niskala, Weckström*
20/5	Honka	a	0-2	
27/5	Inter Turku	h	2-0	*Björk, Niskala*
13/6	MyPa	a	0-0	
17/6	TPS	h	0-3	
25/6	MyPa	h	0-2	
2/7	Tampere United	a	1-2	*Blomberg*
15/7	Oulu	h	0-0	
23/7	Lahti	a	1-4	*Lyyski*
29/7	Viikingit	a	2-2	*Carlsson D., Vajanne*
4/8	KooTeePee	h	3-2	*Vajanne, Hachilensa, Gustafsson*
12/8	VPS	a	3-1	*Hansell, Björk, Wirta*
16/8	Honka	h	0-0	
2/9	Viikingit	h	4-2	*Carlsson D. 3, Vajann*
16/9	Oulu	a	3-0	*Gustafsson, Vajanne, Weckström K.*
20/9	Inter Turku	a	2-0	*Gustafsson, Björk*
23/9	Jaro	h	1-1	*Vajanne*
30/9	KooTeePee	a	2-1	*Johansson, Lyyski*
7/10	Tampere United	h	1-0	*Gustafsson*
20/10	HJK	h	0-0	
24/10	Haka	a	2-1	*Johansson 2*
27/10	VPS	h	1-3	*Ahnström*

No	Name	Nat	Pos	Aps	(s)	Gl
6	Daniel AHNSTRÖM	SWE	M	7	(9)	1
16	Andreas BJÖRK		M	20	(4)	4
5	Peter BLOMBERG		M	22		1
9	David CARLSSON	SWE	A	13	(1)	4
4	Johan CARLSSON	SWE	M	9	(2)	
15	Amos EKHALIE	KEN	M		(2)	
21	Mats GUSTAFSSON		D	21		4
26	Clive HACHILENSA	ZAM	M	6	(2)	1
17	André HANSELL		D	21		1
13	Daniel JOHANSSON	SWE	A	4	(3)	3
14	Kenneth KNUDSEN	DEN	A	2		
30	Antti KUISMALA		G	17		
10	Peter LUNDBERG		A		(1)	
8	Jani LYYSKI		D	26		2
11	Mika NISKALA		M	22		2
1	Willis OCHIENG	KEN	G	8		
12	Anders ÖVERSTRÖM		G	1		
3	Patrik RIKAMA		D	9	(5)	
23	Erik SANDVÄRN	SWE	D	10	(3)	
22	Peter SJÖLUND		A	8	(7)	
7	Saša STEVIĆ	SRB	M	11	(3)	
2	Mikael SUNDSTRÖM		M		(1)	
24	Justus VAJANNE		A	11	(9)	5
20	Alexander WECKSTRÖM		A	1	(3)	
19	Kristoffer WECKSTRÖM		M	25		2
18	Tommy WIRTANEN		M	12	(8)	1

MYLLYKOSKEN PALLO-47

Coach – Ilkka Mäkelä; (10/8/07) Janne Hyppönen

Founded - 1947

MAJOR HONOURS: Finnish League - (1) 2005; Finnish Cup - (3) 1992, 1995, 2004.

07				
/4	Honka	a	1-2	*Huttunen (p)*
/4	TPS	h	0-2	
	VPS	a	0-0	
/5	Jaro	h	2-0	*Kuparinen, Muinonen*
/5	Viikingit	a	4-1	*Kuparinen (p), Puhakainen, Gao 2*
/5	KooTeePee	h	1-0	*Hyyrynen*
/5	Haka	a	0-0	
/5	Oulu	a	1-1	*Helenius*
/6	Mariehamn	h	0-0	
/6	Inter Turku	h	1-3	*Hyyrynen*
/6	Mariehamn	a	2-0	*Fofana, Hyyrynen*
	Lahti	h	1-0	*Puhakainen*
	Tampere United	h	4-1	*Muinonen, Peltonen 2, Marchis (p)*
/7	HJK	a	0-5	
	TPS	a	0-1	
	Haka	h	0-3	
/8	VPS	h	0-1	
	KooTeePee	a	0-1	
/9	HJK	h	0-0	
/9	Jaro	a	3-0	*Nykänen, Manso (p), Kangaskolkka*
/9	Honka	h	1-0	*Helenius*
0	Inter Turku	a	2-1	*Puhakainen, Kansikas*
0	Viikingit	h	1-1	*Kangaskolkka*
/10	Tampere United	a	1-1	*Puhakainen*
/10	Lahti	a	1-0	*Kangaskolkka*
/10	Oulu	h	3-2	*Nykänen, Manso, Hyyrynen*

	Name	Nat	Pos	Aps	(s)	Gls
	Kuami AGBOH	TOG	M	18	(1)	
	Mohamed FOFANA	GUI	M	13	(11)	1
	GAO Leilei	CHN	M	6	(1)	2
	Niki HELENIUS		A	11	(6)	2
	Toni HUTTUNEN		D	25		1
	Mikko HYYRYNEN		A	16	(6)	4
	Aleksei KANGASKOLKKA		A	10	(6)	3
	Tuomas KANSIKAS		D	24		1
	Tero KARHU		M	1	(2)	
	Koffi KONAN	CIV	A	1	(4)	
	Janne KORHONEN		G	24		
	Tuomas KUPARINEN		A	13		2
	Jani LUUKKONEN		G	2		
	Marco MANSO	BRA	M	2	(8)	2
	Vasile MARCHIS	ROU	D	6	(3)	1
	Hugo MIRANDA	PAR	D	22		
	Eetu MUINONEN		M	17	(2)	2
	Nebi MUSTAFI	MKD	M	12	(5)	
	Juho NYKÄNEN		M	12	(5)	2
	Eero PELTONEN		A	8	(7)	2
	Saku PUHAKAINEN		A	17	(8)	4
	Heikki PULKKINEN		D	26		
	Jani TANSKA		D		(1)	

AC OULU

Coach – Harri Kampman

Founded - 2002

07				
/4	Viikingit	h	1-1	*Banduliev*
/4	HJK	a	0-0	
	Inter Turku	h	2-0	*Stafsula 2*
	KooTeePee	a	0-3	
/5	Tampere United	h	2-0	*Konaté 2*
/5	Lahti	a	1-2	*Rafinha*
23/5	TPS	h	1-3	*og (Heinikangas)*
27/5	MyPa	h	1-1	*Siekkinen*
11/6	VPS	a	0-5	
17/6	KooTeePee	h	1-2	*Brovkin*
28/6	Haka	a	0-2	
15/7	Mariehamn	a	0-0	
22/7	Honka	h	3-3	*Hietanen 2 (1p), Essomba*
5/8	Inter Turku	a	0-1	
12/8	Viikingit	a	1-3	*Konaté*
16/8	Lahti	h	2-1	*Essomba, Koivuranta*
25/8	Tampere United	a	1-4	*Hietanen*
2/9	Jaro	h	5-1	*Edereho, Lehtinen, Konaté, Yobe, Hietanen*
16/9	Mariehamn	h	0-3	
19/9	Honka	a	0-2	
23/9	VPS	h	3-3	*og (Saranpää), Edereho, Hietanen (p)*
30/9	Haka	h	1-1	*Edereho*
7/10	TPS	a	0-4	
21/10	Jaro	a	1-0	*Järvitalo*
24/10	HJK	h	0-1	
27/10	MyPa	a	2-3	*Järvitalo 2*

No	Name	Nat	Pos	Aps	(s)	Gls
18	Olavi ARVOLA		M	3	(4)	
9	Toni BANDULIEV	MKD	M	5		1
10	Dmytro BROVKIN	UKR	A	7		1
3	Anatoliy BULGAKOV	RUS	D	7	(1)	
28	Raphael EDEREHO	NGA	A	9		3
16	Titi ESSOMBA	CMR	A	16	(6)	2
4	Ilya FOMICHEV	KAZ	D	21	(1)	
20	Iyam FRIDAY	NGA	M	6	(2)	
25	Petri HEINÄNEN		D	5		
2	Janne HIETANEN		D	25		5
28	Modou JALLOW	SWE	A	1		
7	Vesa JÄRVITALO		M	10	(2)	3
5	Kim KAIJALAINEN		D	13	(1)	
8	Tarmo KOIVURANTA		M	15	(5)	1
19	Saša KOLIĆ	CRO	M	12	(2)	
21	Mamadou KONATÉ	CIV	A	7	(18)	4
78	Ville LEHTINEN		A	10	(1)	1
23	Valeri MINKENEN		M	8	(2)	
6	Antti PEHKONEN		D	22	(3)	
11	RAFINHA	BRA	A	21	(1)	1
17	Tommi SIEKKINEN		A	1	(4)	1
25	Miki SIPILÄINEN		A	4		
29	Yacine SLATNI	ALG	D	2		
22	Dritan STAFSULA	ALB	M	10	(10)	2
14	Jarno TENKULA		M	2	(10)	
13	Irakliy TSYKOLIYA	UKR	D	1		
1	Jani VIANDER		G	26		
15	Ymer XHAFERI	SRB	M	3	(1)	
24	Dominic YOBE	ZAM	M	14		1

TAMPERE UNITED

Coach – Ari Hjelm

Founded - 1998

MAJOR HONOURS: Finnish League - (3) 2001, 2006, 2007; Finnish Cup - (1) 2007.

2007				
21/4	VPS	a	1-1	*Hynynen*
26/4	KooTeePee	h	2-1	*Kujala, Järvinen*
4/5	Honka	a	2-1	*Saarinen, Pohja*
10/5	Viikingit	h	1-0	*Niemi*
16/5	Oulu	a	0-2	
20/5	Inter Turku	h	2-1	*Järvinen 2*

23/5	HJK	a	2-0	*Petrescu, Hynynen*
28/5	Lahti	h	1-0	*Hynynen*
14/6	Haka	a	1-1	*Lindström*
17/6	Jaro	h	2-1	*Niemi, Wiss*
29/6	TPS	a	3-1	*Petrescu, Niemi, Hynynen*
2/7	Mariehamn	h	2-1	*Wiss, Nwoke*
8/7	MyPa	a	1-4	*og (Huttunen)*
4/8	VPS	h	2-2	*Saarinen, Niemi*
19/8	TPS	h	3-0	*Niemi, Petrescu, Savolainen Juska*
25/8	Oulu	h	4-1	*Pohja 3, Nwoke*
3/9	Inter Turku	a	1-1	*Myntti*
10/9	Jaro	a	2-0	*og (Heikinheimo), Hjelm*
13/9	Viikingit	a	3-3	*Ojanperä, Myntti, Pohja*
24/9	Lahti	a	2-0	*Petrescu 2 (1p)*
27/9	Haka	h	2-1	*Niemi, Pohja*
1/10	HJK	h	2-1	*Niemi, Petrescu*
7/10	Mariehamn	a	0-1	
20/10	MyPa	h	1-1	*Nwoke*
24/10	KooTeePee	a	3-0	*Sipiläinen, Nwoke, Hjelm*
27/10	Honka	h	0-2	

No	Name	Nat	Pos	Aps	(s)	Gls
19	Heikki AHO		D	20	(1)	
21	Jonne HJELM		A	1	(8)	2
9	Antti HYNYNEN		A	8	(14)	4
2	Toni JÄRVINEN		M	22	(4)	3
1	Mikko KAVÉN		G	26		
7	Jussi KUJALA		M	23	(2)	1
6	Jussi KUOPPALA		D	1		
3	Mathias LINDSTRÖM		D	20	(1)	1
15	Henri MYNTTI		D	14	(4)	2
30	Jari NIEMI		A	19	(2)	7
16	Daniel NWOKE	NGA	A	4	(14)	4
5	Antti OJANPERÄ		D	25		1
10	Tomi PETRESCU		A	22	(2)	6
8	Antti POHJA		A	23	(1)	6
13	Sakari SAARINEN		M	10	(4)	2
20	Juska SAVOLAINEN		M	26		1
11	Jussi-Pekka SAVOLAINEN		M	1		
17	Miki SIPILÄINEN		A	2	(3)	1
14	Jarkko WISS		M	19		2

FC TPS TURKU

Coach – Mixu Paatelainen

Founded - 1922

MAJOR HONOURS: Finnish League - (8) 1928, 1939, 1941, 1949, 1968, 1971, 1972, 1975; Finnish Cup - (2) 1991, 1994.

2007				
21/4	Mariehamn	h	0-0	
26/4	MyPa	a	2-0	*Oné, Vellamo*
7/5	HJK	h	0-1	
10/5	Inter Turku	a	1-1	*Heinikangas*
16/5	Lahti	h	3-1	*Paatelainen, Ääritalo, Nuorela*
23/5	Oulu	a	3-1	*Oné (p), Ääritalo 2*
27/5	VPS	h	5-1	*Cleaver, Paatelainen, Oné 2, Ady*
10/6	Viikingit	a	1-0	*Oné*
14/6	Honka	h	1-3	*Heinikangas*
17/6	Mariehamn	a	3-0	*Ääritalo, Paatelainen, Cleaver*
29/6	Tampere United	h	1-3	*og (Kujala)*
4/7	Honka	a	0-2	
8/7	KooTeePee	a	2-4	*Paatelainen, Hakala*
16/7	KooTeePee	h	3-2	*Ääritalo 2, Heinikang*
6/8	MyPa	h	1-0	*Hämäläinen*
19/8	Tampere United	a	0-3	
25/8	Haka	a	1-2	*Hakala*
30/8	Inter Turku	h	1-0	*Ääritalo*
13/9	Haka	h	2-1	*Paatelainen 2*
16/9	Jaro	a	0-2	
24/9	Viikingit	h	5-0	*Hämäläinen 2, Paatelainen, Lomski 2*
1/10	Lahti	a	3-2	*Ady 2 (1p), Paatelaine*
7/10	Oulu	h	4-0	*Paatelainen, Ääritalo, Hämäläinen, Oné*
20/10	VPS	a	0-0	
24/10	Jaro	h	1-1	*Ady (p)*
27/10	HJK	a	0-3	

No	Name	Nat	Pos	Aps	(s)	Gls
11	Mika ÄÄRITALO		A	23	(3)	8
10	ADY Pereira dos Santos	BRA	M	12	(8)	4
18	Chris CLEAVER	ENG	A	21		2
21	Jussi HAIJANEN		M	2	(8)	
9	Antti HAKALA		A	5	(10)	2
14	Kasper HÄMÄLÄINEN		M	19	(5)	4
8	Jarno HEINIKANGAS		M	24		3
1	Ville IISKOLA		G	2	(1)	
4	Ville LEHTONEN		D	8		
12	Jukka LEHTOVAARA		G	24		
19	Patrik LOMSKI		A		(5)	2
2	Jussi NUORELA		D	14		1
16	Armand ONÉ	FRA	A	18	(4)	6
28	Mikko PAATELAINEN		A	25		9
20	Owen PRICE	ENG	M		(2)	
7	Sami RÄHMÖNEN		D	13		
17	Riku RISKI		M		(6)	
24	Urmas ROOBA	EST	D	8		
13	Jani SARAJÄRVI		D	13		
6	Jukka-Pekka TUOMANEN		M	6	(8)	
15	Joonas TURSAS		D	7	(2)	
5	Simo VALAKARI		M	25		
3	Janne VELLAMO		M	13	(1)	1
26	Kheireddine ZARABI	ALG	D	4		

FC VIIKINGIT

Coach – Jari Europaeus

Founded - 1998

2007				
21/4	Oulu	a	1-1	*Jalava*
27/4	Honka	h	3-2	*Heikelä, Hirvonen 2 (1*
3/5	KooTeePee	h	0-1	
10/5	Tampere United	a	0-1	
14/5	MyPa	h	1-4	*Ojanen*
20/5	HJK	h	1-1	*Malakeyev*
24/5	Inter Turku	a	1-0	*Sarelius*
10/6	TPS	h	0-1	
14/6	Jaro	a	0-2	
29/6	Lahti	a	2-0	*Ojanen, Mollberg*
2/7	Jaro	h	1-2	*Solehmainen*
23/7	KooTeePee	a	0-1	
29/7	Mariehamn	h	2-2	*Mollberg, Sarelius*
6/8	HJK	a	1-1	*Ojanen*
9/8	Honka	a	1-1	*Peteri*
12/8	Oulu	h	3-1	*Peteri, Sarelius, Lundberg*
2/9	Mariehamn	a	2-4	*Malakeyev 2*
13/9	Tampere United	h	3-3	*Ojanen, Peteri 2*
16/9	Haka	a	0-1	

/9	Lahti	h	0-4	
/9	TPS	a	0-5	
/9	VPS	h	1-0	*Jäntti (p)*
0	MyPa	a	1-1	*Vasse*
/10	Inter Turku	h	0-2	
/10	VPS	a	1-1	*Vasse*
/10	Haka	h	0-2	

Name	Nat	Pos	Aps	(s)	Gls
Jussi HEIKELÄ		D	13		1
Mehmet HETEMAJ		M	8	(1)	
Jukka HIRVONEN		M	12	(10)	2
Petri JALAVA		D	21		1
Ilkka JÄNTTI		D	16	(1)	1
Jarno KALLIJÄRVI		D	6		
Osmo KLEEMOLA		D	15	(1)	
Kristian KUNNAS		M	6	(6)	
Panu KUUSELA		D	11	(4)	
Lasse LIND		M	14	(4)	
LUÍS FERNANDO	BRA	G	26		
Max LUNDBERG		M	12	(10)	1
Lassi LUOTO		M	3	(2)	
Vyacheslav MALAKEYEV	RUS	A	16	(6)	3
Janne MOLLBERG		A	6	(4)	2
Risto OJANEN		A	12	(7)	4
Jussi PETERI		A	17	(5)	4
Kim RAIMI		D	4	(3)	
Joonas SARELIUS		A	25		3
Pasi SOLEHMAINEN		M	22	(1)	1
Kalle SORJA		D	16		
Kalle VASSE		A	5	(12)	2

VPS VAASA

Coach – Jari Pyykölä; (9/6/07) (Mika Koivumäki); (18/6/07) Janne Lindberg

Founded - 1924

MAJOR HONOURS: Finnish League - (2) 1945, 1948.

07				
/4	Tampere United	h	1-1	*Taipale (p)*
/4	Inter Turku	a	0-5	
	MyPa	h	0-0	
/5	Honka	h	1-1	*Taipale*
/5	Haka	a	0-1	
/5	Jaro	h	1-2	*Taipale*
/5	TPS	a	1-5	*Taipale (p)*
	Lahti	a	0-6	
/6	Oulu	h	5-0	*Hietaharju 2, Louke, Ylinen, Hahto*
/6	KooTeePee	a	1-1	*Louke*
/6	KooTeePee	h	1-0	*Nygård J.*
	HJK	a	0-0	
	Inter Turku	h	0-0	
/7	Lahti	h	1-0	*Hietaharju*
/7	Jaro	a	1-0	*Scheweleff*
	Tampere United	a	2-2	*Uotinen, Ylinen*
/8	Mariehamn	h	1-3	*Hietaharju*
/8	MyPa	a	1-0	*Taipale*
/8	Honka	a	0-1	
	Haka	h	0-0	
/9	HJK	h	2-1	*Scheweleff, Nygård T.*
/9	Oulu	a	3-3	*Scheweleff, Nygård T., Paija*
/9	Viikingit	a	0-1	
/10	TPS	h	0-0	
/10	Viikingit	h	1-1	*Nygård T.*
/10	Mariehamn	a	3-1	*Uotinen, Taipale (p), Itälä*

No	Name	Nat	Pos	Aps	(s)	Gls
21	Ansi AGOLLI	ALB	D	16	(2)	
12	Janne AHOLA		G	1	(1)	
20	Jussi EKSTRÖM		D		(1)	
17	Miika EKSTRÖM		A		(12)	
11	Toni HAHTO		M	9	(11)	1
23	Jyri HIETAHARJU		M	19	(2)	4
2	Mikko-Ville HYYHÖNEN		D	5		
8	Joonas IKÄLÄINEN		D	15	(1)	
6	Olli-Pekka ITÄLÄ		D	11	(6)	1
3	Ville KOSKIMAA		D	24		
10	Rami LOUKE		A	4	(6)	2
14	Jens NYGÅRD		M	24		1
26	Tomas NYGÅRD		A	6	(1)	3
15	Patrice OLLO Ndoumba	CMR	M	15	(3)	
18	Markus PAIJA		D	13	(3)	1
16	Jyrki SARANPÄÄ		A	23	(2)	
22	Henri SCHEWELEFF		A	20		3
1	Henri SILLANPÄÄ		G	25		
4	Tero TAIPALE		M	26		6
26	Maciej TATAJ	POL	A		(1)	
7	Jani UOTINEN		M	14	(6)	2
25	Solomon "VICTOR" Raymond	NGA	A	4	(1)	
19	Ville YLINEN		M	12	(6)	2

PROMOTED CLUBS

KUOPION PALLOSEURA (KUPS)

Coach – Kai Nyyssönen

Founded - 1923

MAJOR HONOURS: Finnish League - (5) 1956, 1958, 1966, 1974, 1976; Finnish Cup - (2) 1968, 1989.

ROVANIEMEN PALLOSEURA (ROPS)

Coach – Matti Helin

Founded - 1950

MAJOR HONOURS: Finnish Cup - (1) 1986

SECOND LEVEL FINAL TABLE 2007

		Pld	W	D	L	F	A	Pts
1	KuPS Kuopio	26	16	8	2	44	17	56
2	RoPS Rovaniemi	26	16	7	3	44	23	55
3	JJK Jyväskylä	26	11	8	7	45	30	41
4	FC Hämeenlinna	26	11	8	7	37	27	41
5	TP-47 Tornio	26	10	7	9	36	29	37
6	VIFK Vaasa	26	9	9	8	31	35	36
7	Atlantis FC	26	9	7	10	33	32	34
8	PK-35 Helsinki	26	8	9	9	36	33	33
9	JIPPO Joensuu	26	8	8	10	32	37	32
10	KPV Kokkola	26	8	7	11	27	46	31
11	TPV Tampere	26	8	6	12	24	37	30
12	GBK Kokkola	26	7	6	13	28	38	27
13	PP-70 Tampere	26	6	7	13	31	44	25
14	Klubi-04 Helsinki	26	2	9	15	25	45	15

PROMOTION/RELEGATION PLAY-OFFS

(3/11/07)

RoPS 1, Viikingit 0

(7/11/07)

Viikingit 1, RoPS 1

(RoPS 2-1)

FINLAND

DOMESTIC CUP 2007

SUOMEN CUP

FOURTH ROUND

BET 0, JIPPO 3
BK-46 1, JyTy 2
EBK 0, PK-35 5
GBK/2 1, KPV 11
Gnistan/2 0, Lahti 4
HIFK 2, Gnistan 0
HIFK/2 0, PoPa/2 2
HJK/U20 0, Inter Turku 5
Honka/2 2, TKT 1
HP-47 1, JJK 6
HPS 1, LoPa 3
Ilves/U20 1, PP-70 6
JäPS 4, FC Espoo 1
JIlves 0, MyPa 3
KaaPo/A 0, SoVo 5
AC Kajaani 0, Norrvalla FF 0 *(aet; 2-4 on pens)*
KäPa/U20 2, P-Iirot 3
Karhu 2, Oulu 5
Kasiysi 3, FJK 3 *(aet; 6-4 on pens)*
Kiffen 1, City Stars 2
FC K-Jazz 2, VPS 9
KTP 0, KuPS 7
Kultsu FC 3, JoPS 0
FC Kurenpojat 2, FC Kipparit 1
Lieto 3, Stars 2
MaKu 1, TPS 7
IK Myran 0, TP-47 4
Naseva 1, TuTo 5
NIK 2, KajHa 0
NouLa 1, Viikingit 3
FC OPA 2, VIFK 1
OuJK 0, FC YPA 5
OuTa 0, RoPS 4
Pato 3, TOVE 1
PH-99 2, uSa 0
PIF 0, PK Keski-Uusimaa 3
P-Iirot/2 0, FC POHU 1
PK-35/U20 0, PoPa 3
Ponteva 1, Pöxyt 2
Riverball/JKKI 2, PK-37 1
Salon Vilpas 2, Haka/U20 1
SAPA 0, FC Hämeenlinna 3
SawU 2, SC Riverball 10
SCR 2, HyPS 2 *(aet; 4-5 on pens)*
SiPS 0, KooTeePee 4
Sporting 0, Jaro 4
TiPS 0, Atlantis 3
ToiP-49 1, KooVee 3
TP-47/2 3, PS Kemi 2
AC Vantaa 2, TPV 1
ViiPV 1, Honka/U20 3
Virkiä 0, GBK 4
VKajo 2, KoPa 1
VPS/U20 3, JBK 1
WIFK/JKKI 0, FC Kuusankoski 7
Zyklon 0, GrIFK 5

FIFTH ROUND

(29/5/07)
Salon Vilpas 1, Viikingit 4
TP-47 2, Jaro 4

(31/5/07)
PH-99 1, SoVo 6

(1/6/07)
VPS 2, Oulu 3 (aet)

(3/6/07)
VKajo 0, FC Kuusankoski 7

(6/6/07)
FC OPA 1, KPV 3

(7/6/07)
Honka/U20 0, Atlantis 1
JJK 3, TPS 2 *(aet)*
TuTo 0, PoPa 6

(8/6/07)
Kasiysi 0, PK Keski-Uusimaa 13
Riverball/JKKI 1, NIK 2

(9/6/07)
JyTy 3, FC POHU 2
Kultsu FC 5, AC Vantaa 4

(10/6/07)
GrIFK 1, KooTeePee 0
HIFK 1, PK-35 0
HyPS 0, PP-70 1
JäPS 1, FC Hämeenlinna 4 (aet)
KooVee 1, MyPa 3
FC Kurenpojat 0, GBK 8
Lieto 1, Honka/2 3
Pato 1, Inter Turku 5
PoPa/2 0, LoPa 4
Pöxyt 1, City Stars 2
SC Riverball 1, KuPS 6
RoPS 1, JIPPO 2
TP-47/2 0, FC YPA 3
VPS/U20 2, Norrvalla FF 1

(12/6/07)
P-Iirot 0, Lahti 3

SIXTH ROUND

(20/6/07)
KPV 0, Tampere United 2

(21/6/07)
GBK 1, KuPS 1 *(aet; 10-9 on pens)*
Haka 5, NIK 0
FC Hämeenlinna 0, MyPa 2
HIFK 1, PoPa 0
HJK 2, Jaro 1
Honka/2 0, JJK 4
JIPPO 2, Viikingit 1
Kultsu FC 0, Inter Turku 4
FC Kuusankoski 2, PK Keski-Uusimaa 1
Lahti 2, LoPa 0
Oulu 8, GrIFK 1
SoVo 9, JyTy 3
VPS/U20 1, City Stars 2
FC YPA 1, PP-70 3

(26/8/07)
Honka 2, Atlantis 1 *(aet)*

SEVENTH ROUND

(12/7/07)
GBK 1, City Stars 0
HJK 8, SoVo 1
Inter Turku 2, HIFK 0
JIPPO 1, Tampere United 4
JJK 2, MyPa 0 *(aet)*
Oulu 2, Haka 0
PP-70 1, Lahti 3

(13/9/07)
Honka 4, FC Kuusankoski 0

QUARTER-FINALS

(27/9/07)
GBK 0, Lahti 0 *(aet; 5-3 on pens)*
Honka 2 *(Saarinen 34, 112p)*, Inter Turku 2 *(Chatto 85, Laaksonen 119) (aet; 4-2 on pens)*
JJK 0, HJK 4 *(Parikka 28, Sorsa 69,71, Äijälä 80)*

(31/10/07)
Tampere United 0, Oulu 0 *(aet; 4-3 on pens)*

SEMI-FINALS

(3/11/07)
HJK 0, Honka 1 *(Weckström 31)*
Tampere United 2 *(Sipiläinen 18, Järvinen 39)*, GBK 0

FINAL

(11/11/07)
Finnair stadium, Helsinki
TAMPERE UNITED 3 *(Sipiläinen 90, Hynynen 95, Myntti 101)*
FC HONKA ESPOO 3 *(Puustinen 60, Jalasto 114, Saarinen 116)*
(aet; 3-1 on pens)
Referee - *Hätilä*
TAMPERE UNITED – *Kavén, Järvinen, Lindström, Ojanperä, Kujala, Pohja, Myntti, Nwoke (Sipiläinen 82), Aho (Kuoppala 68), Savolainen Juska, Hjelm (Hynynen 46).*
Sent off: *Savolainen Juska (30).*
HONKA – *Maanoja, Heilala, Jalasto, Huuhtanen (Puustinen 29), Saarinen, Weckström, Helin, Otaru, Perovuo (Hakanpää 70), Turunen, Porokara (Koskela 77).*
Sent off: *Weckström (49).*

Domenech survives EURO débâcle

rance were the big losers of UEFA EURO 2008™. It was always going to be tough for them in the so-called Group of Death, and they did not enjoy the ›st of luck during their fortnight in Switzerland. But e standard of football they produced was desperately sappointing, so it was a surprise to many when coach ıymond Domenech was confirmed in his position ter the tournament by the French Football Federation FF), who preferred to retain the same leadership hile developing a new, younger team.

ance went home with just one point from their ree matches – and that from the only goalless draw the entire group phase, a laborious affair against omania in Zurich. Their only goal was scored in the cond match - by Thierry Henry, an absentee from e first game – but as their Dutch opponents scored ur, it was not much of a consolation. In fairness, omenech's team were the Netherlands' equals for ng periods, but their defending was not up to ratch, with 35-year-old midfield pivot Claude akelele and 36-year-old Lilian Thuram, a stand-in ipper for the injured Patrick Vieira, both clearly owing their age.

arly exit

uram, France's record cap-holder, was dropped for e decisive group game against Italy – a 2006 FIFA orld Cup final re-match that France were obliged to in to stand any chance of making it through to the uarter-finals. They never looked likely to after losing eir only source of midfield creativity, Franck Ribéry, a serious injury early on and being reduced to ten en, and consequently going a goal down, midway rough the first half when Éric Abidal clumsily onceded a penalty. The final score was 2-0 to the zzurri, leaving France at the bottom of the group and ontemplating their first ever first-round elimination om a 16-team UEFA European Championship.

espite his achievements in Germany in 2006, omenech would have been forgiven for believing that, with public opinion turning against him, his four-year reign was about to end – just as Roger Lemerre had been jettisoned after Les Bleus' 2002 World Cup failure. But the FFF, showing leniency and a desire for continuity, decided to keep him on. The team's performances in the 2010 World Cup qualifying campaign will ascertain whether or not that is the right move, but the pressure on Domenech will doubtless be considerable. He suggested that UEFA EURO 2008™ would help the younger players in the squad to prepare for the World Cup, but Karim Benzema and Samir Nasri, the two men expected to lead the next generation, were under-utilised in Switzerland and unable to show their true colours.

Thuram and Makelele have now retired from international football – for good, surely, this time –

Raymond Domenech pleads for more from his team

but while it should not be too difficult to find viable alternatives to those old soldiers, there remains a gaping void in the centre of the France midfield that has not been filled since the great Zinedine Zidane hung up his boots. UEFA EURO 2008™ was the first tournament France had gone into without 'Zizou' since Euro '92, when they also exited after the first round. For years the brilliant playmaker pulled the strings for France, with almost every attack of substance being channelled through his dancing feet. If anyone doubted whether he was irreplaceable, they got their answer in Switzerland.

But Zidane is long gone, and the France team of the future must rely on someone else to make the play. The obvious candidate is Ribéry. The 25-year-old raised his profile enormously during a brilliant first season with FC Bayern München in 2007/08 and, while not in the class of Zidane, he was easily France's most inventive and unpredictable player in Switzerland. Benzema, just 20, also looks capable of leading the French attack for many years, while much hope will also be placed on the shoulders of Nasri, now under Arsène Wenger's wing at Arsenal FC, and another exciting youngster, Hatem Ben Arfa, who in the summer left Benzema and Olympique Lyonnais for Nasri's former club Olympique de Marseille.

Despite this crop of promising youngsters, France cannot expect an easy ride to South Africa, with fellow UEFA EURO 2008™ participants Romania and Austria, as well as Serbia, in their qualifying group. After all, Domenech's team made hard work of their previous qualifying campaign, with Scotland beating them 1-0 home and away. It was only thanks to a couple of late goals against Lithuania from Henry – which took him past Michel Platini as Les Bleus' all-time top scorer – plus a helping hand from Italy at Hampden Park, that saw them safely through. Indeed, of the 15 matches France played in 2007/08, none could be said to have brought total satisfaction – with the possible exception of a 6-0 win in the Faroe Islands. It was that kind of year for Les Bleus.

Show-stopper Benzema

There was not much joy to be had, either, from France's collective performance in the European club competitions. Perennial standard-bearers Lyon managed to force their way through to the knockout phase of the UEFA Champions League for the fifth year in a row, but it required a major salvage operation after they were beaten 3-0 in their first two

Lyon striker Karim Benzema – Ligue 1's top scorer and Player of the Season

group games. Fortunately, Benzema put on a show i[n] their Matchday Six decider against Rangers FC in Glasgow, and Lyon won 3-0 to progress. Despite another Benzema special in the home leg of the first knockout-round tie against Manchester United FC, a late goal conceded in the Stade Gerland proved costly, and a 1-0 defeat at Old Trafford shattered the club's dreams of that big European breakthrough for another year.

Another club from the north-west of England, Liverpool FC, were responsible for ending the UEFA Champions League adventures of Toulouse FC – in th[e] third qualifying round – and Marseille, whose humbling 4-0 home defeat to the Reds was their thir[d] defeat on the trot following a wonderful start that included a momentous 1-0 win at Anfield. Marseille moved over to the UEFA Cup, where they outlasted France's other five participants (including Toulouse) b[y] reaching the round of 16. Seemingly coasting throug[h] to the quarter-finals after two Djibril Cissé goals and one from Mamadou Niang had put them into a 3-0 lead at home to FC Zenit St. Petersburg, they

ɔmmitted the cardinal sin of conceding a late away ɔal, and the Russians made them pay by winning the turn 2-0 and taking the tie.

though Marseille's defeat to the eventual UEFA Cup inners closed the book on Europe, there was plenty get excited about on the domestic front, with serial ampions Lyon, for once, not having things all their wn way in Ligue 1. The challenge to their hegemony ame not from Marseille, the previous season's inners-up, but from FC Girondins de Bordeaux. Led / former French international defender Laurent anc, who had replaced AS Monaco FC-bound cardo at the start of the season, Bordeaux took a hile to find their best form, but in the second half of e season, with Brazilian left-winger Wendel and rgentine striker Fernando Cavenaghi leading the ay, they stealthily applied the pressure with a equence of positive results that maintained the trigue and kept the title race open until the very nd.

on, however, would not be denied their record eventh successive national title. Requiring a draw vay to AJ Auxerre on the final day, they took the ad after only a few seconds, fittingly with Benzema's)th league goal of the season, and made it 2-0, rough Brazilian striker Fred, ten minutes later. A ird goal early in the second half, from Swedish idfielder Kim Källström, finished off any lingering oubts.

yon's double

was Lyon's seventh title but the first for coach Alain errin, who had arrived, as Gérard Houllier's placement, from FC Sochaux-Montbéliard the revious summer. He had won the final of the Coupe e France – against ex-club Marseille - with Sochaux e previous season, and he was to recapture the ophy with Lyon a week after the league triumph as aris Saint-Germain FC were beaten 1-0 in the Stade e France thanks to an extra-time goal from Sidney ovou, one of three players – together with oalkeeper Grégory Coupet and midfield maestro uninho Pernambucano – to participate in all seven gue 1 successes.

ut although Perrin had steered Lyon to the first eague and Cup double in their history, he was nable to celebrate the achievement as he would ave wanted. One week later, somewhat stupefyingly, e was out of a job, his contract having been terminated by mutual consent. Despite his success Perrin had never looked completely at ease, and rumours of his impending departure had been circulating for many weeks in advance of the season's successful climax. His job was handed to Claude Puel, the long-serving coach of LOSC Lille Métropole, whose team had hired the Stade de France for their home game against Lyon on 1 March, drawing a record league attendance of 77,840. The message from club president Jean-Michel Aulas to Puel was that, in addition to keeping Lyon at the top domestically, he must also take the club that extra mile in Europe.

Perrin was entitled to feel hard done by. While Lyon had not been the omnipotent force of old, they finished up with only two points fewer than in 2006/07, when they won the title by a landslide, and also scored ten goals more. If their goal difference of plus-37 was identical, that was partly explained by the absence for the first four months of the season of Coupet and for the first six months of captain and defensive linchpin Cris. Another defender, Swiss international Patrick Müller, missed practically the entire campaign. On the plus side, Jérémy Toulalan was consistently diligent and effective in midfield while Mathieu Bodmer, recruited from Lille, was the best of the new signings. Juninho, though absent for a spell with a broken toe, was as inspirational as ever,

Lyon's double-winning coach Alain Perrin with the Coupe de France – he left the club a few days later

FRANCE

Fédération Française de Football (FFF

87 boulevard de Grenelle
FR-75783 Paris Cedex
tel - +33 1 44 317300
fax - +33 1 44317373
website – www.fff.fr
email - webmaster@fff.fr
Year of formation – 1919
President – Jean-Pierre Escalettes
General Secretary – Jacques Lambert
Press Officer – Yann Le Guillard
Stadium - Stade de France, Saint-Denis (80,000)

INTERNATIONAL HONOURS
FIFA World Cup - (1) 1998.
UEFA European Championship - (2) 1984, 2000.

INTERNATIONAL TOURNAMENT APPEARANCES
FIFA World Cup - (11) 1930, 1938 (2nd round 1954, 1958 (3rd), 1966, 1978, 1982 (4th), 1986 (3rd), 1998 (Winners), 2002, 2006 (runners-up).
UEFA European Championship - (7) 1960 (4th), 1984 (Winners), 1992, 1996 (semi-finals), 2000 (Winners), 2004 (qtr-finals), 200

TOP FIVE ALL-TIME CAPS
Lilian Thuram (142); Marcel Desailly (116); Zinedine Zidane (108); Patrick Vieira (105); Didier Deschamps (103)

TOP FIVE ALL-TIME GOALS
Thierry Henry (45); Michel Platini (41); David Trezeguet (34); Zinedine Zidane (31); Just Fontaine & Jean-Pierre Papin (30)

NATIONAL TEAM RESULTS 2007/08

22/8/07	Slovakia	A	Trnava	1-0	*Henry (39)*
8/9/07	Italy (ECQ)	A	Milan	0-0	
12/9/07	Scotland (ECQ)	H	Paris	0-1	
13/10/07	Faroe Islands (ECQ)	A	Torshavn	6-0	*Anelka (6), Henry (8), Benzema (50, 81), Rothen (66), Ben Arfa (90-*
17/10/07	Lithuania (ECQ)	H	Nantes	2-0	*Henry (80, 81)*
16/11/07	Morocco	H	Saint-Denis	2-2	*Govou (15), Nasri (75)*
21/11/07	Ukraine (ECQ)	A	Kiev	2-2	*Henry (20), Govou (34)*
6/2/08	Spain	A	Malaga	0-1	
26/3/08	England	H	Saint-Denis	1-0	*Ribéry (32p)*
27/5/08	Ecuador	H	Grenoble	2-0	*Gomis (59, 86)*
31/5/08	Paraguay	H	Toulouse	0-0	
3/6/08	Colombia	H	Saint-Denis	1-0	*Ribéry (23)*
9/6/08	Romania (ECF)	N	Zurich (SUI)	0-0	
13/6/08	Netherlands (ECF)	N	Berne (SUI)	1-4	*Henry (71)*
17/6/08	Italy (ECF)	N	Zurich (SUI)	0-2	

but it was Benzema, in his first season as a 'titulaire', who took most of the plaudits. He was not only the leading marksman in Ligue 1 but also scooped the Player of the Season prize.

Although Lyon won the double, Bordeaux were, in many people's eyes, the team of the season. A mere sixth in 2006/07, the Girondins increased their points tally from 57 to 75. Blanc proved to be a master motivator, drawing the best from a low-profile squad,

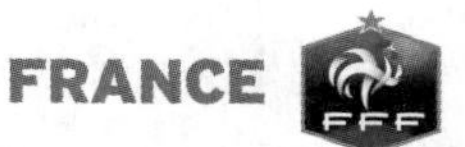

TIONAL TEAM APPEARANCES 2007/08

– Raymond DOMENECH 24/1/52			Svk	ITA	SCO	FRO	LTU	Mar	UKR	Esp	Eng	Ecu	Par	Col	ROU	NED	ITA	Caps	Goals
ël LANDREAU	14/5/79	PSG	G	G	G	G	G	G										11	-
ɔis CLERC	18/4/83	Lyon	D63					D	D		D	s74	D				D	13	-
pe MEXÈS	30/3/82	Roma (ITA)	D88															8	-
BIDAL	11/7/79	Barcelona (ESP)	D	D	D77	D	D	s46	D	D	D	D		D	D		D	37	-
e EVRA	15/5/81	Man. United (ENG)	D			D		D				s46	D			D	D	13	-
k VIEIRA	23/6/76	Internazionale (ITA)	M58	M	M69					M82								105	6
e MAKELELE	18/2/73	Chelsea (ENG)	M	M	M	M73	M	M46	M		M		M46	M	M	M	M	71	-
t MALOUDA	13/6/80	Chelsea (ENG)	M	M	M		M			M	M	s78	M	M	M	M60		41	3
k RIBÉRY	1/4/83	Bayern (GER)	M73	M86	M	M64	M		M89		M		M46	M75	M	M	M10	30	4
s ANELKA	14/3/79	Bolton (ENG)	A	A	A	A46		s64											
		/Chelsea (ENG)								A60	A80	A	s63	s76	A72	s75	s66	51	11
y HENRY	17/8/77	Barcelona (ESP)	A85	A		A	A		A	A			A46	A76		A	A	102	45
y TOULALAN	10/9/83	Lyon	s58	s86		M	M	s46		M	M		M71	M	M	M	M	16	-
y SAGNA	14/2/83	Arsenal (ENG)	s63			D												2	-
NASRI	20/6/87	Marseille	s73		s69			M	s46			M	s71	s75	s78		s10 /26	12	2
BENZEMA	17/12/87	Lyon	s85		s77	s46	A	A64	A46	s60			A63	A65	A78		A	13	3
Alain BOUMSONG	14/12/79	Juventus (ITA)	s88																
		/Lyon											D				s26	24	1
na DIARRA	10/3/85	Arsenal (ENG)		D	D	s73	D69	M	M										
		/Portsmouth (ENG)								M		M	s46	s65				13	-
THURAM	1/1/72	Barcelona (ESP)		D	D	D	D	D64	D	D46	D	D		D	D	D		142	2
ESCUDÉ	17/8/79	Sevilla (ESP)		D	D					s46		D46						7	-
TREZEGUET	15/10/77	Juventus (ITA)			A						A64							71	34
e ROTHEN	31/3/78	PSG				M		M81										13	1
n BEN ARFA	7/3/87	Lyon				s64	s69	s74	s89	s82		M78						6	1
m GALLAS	17/8/77	Arsenal (ENG)					D	D46	D	D	D			D	D	D	D	65	2
y GOVOU	27/7/79	Lyon						A74	M		s64		s46			M75	M66	34	7
tien SQUILLACI	11/8/80	Lyon						s64					D					13	-
eu FLAMINI	7/3/84	Arsenal (ENG)						s81				s46						2	-
tien FREY	18/3/80	Fiorentina (ITA)							G			G46						2	-
ry COUPET	31/12/72	Lyon								G	G		G	G	G	G	G	34	-
SAGNOL	18/3/77	Bayern (GER)								D		D74		D	D	D		58	-
CISSÉ	12/8/81	Marseille									s80	A46						37	9
DIARRA	15/7/81	Bordeaux										M46						13	-
MANDANDA	28/3/85	Marseille										s46						1	-
mbi GOMIS	6/8/85	St-Étienne										s46	s46		s72	s60		4	2

in which even striker David Bellion, who had failed to make the grade in England, came alive, scoring a dozen goals. Bordeaux might have taken the title had it not been for the results of their two head-to-head encounters with Lyon. They were outclassed in both matches, losing 3-1 at home in October and 4-2 away in March. Even so, their ability to pick up points consistently elsewhere secured UEFA Champions League qualification at an early stage.

Conversely, the battle for the UEFA Champions League qualifying place raged until the final weekend. AS Nancy-Lorraine, the outsiders from north-east France, occupied a top-three position for almost the whole campaign but blew their chances in gut-wrenching fashion on the last day when they were beaten 3-2 at home by Stade Rennais FC. It was the club's first home defeat in over a year, and with Marseille simultaneously beating relegated RC Strasbourg 4-3 in a thrilling, see-saw match at the Stade Vélodrome, it left them with only a UEFA Cup spot for their season's exertions. Although the campaign ended on a low, it had been a remarkable effort by Pablo Correa and his group of unsung players, who had climbed up nine places from the previous season.

Eric Gerets restored order at Marseille and led the club to third place in Ligue 1

Marseille owed their return to Europe's top table to t steely, disciplined coaching of Eric Gerets, who had arrived in the early autumn to replace Albert Emon with the club toiling away at the wrong end of the table. The departure of Ribéry to Bayern appeared to have destabilised the team, but Gerets, the former Belgian international who had won titles as a coach i three different countries – Belgium, the Netherlands and Turkey – restored order, and with Cissé and Nian doing the business up front (16 goals for the former, 18 for the latter), and youngster Steve Mandanda proving a revelation in goal, 'OM' eventually got their reward, coming through to beat Strasbourg when it mattered most and thus making up for five earlier defeats in front of their large, passionate crowds in the Vélodrome.

Erratic PSG

Former Marseille hero Jean-Pierre Papin had led Strasbourg up into Ligue 1 in 2006/07, but while the Alsace club went straight back down, he accompanie them into Ligue 2 as the coach of RC Lens, who lost their place after 17 years among the elite. A 2-2 draw on at home to Bordeaux on the final day, combined with wins for fellow relegation candidates Toulouse and PSG, sealed their fate.

Paul Le Guen's PSG had a dreadful time in the league winning only ten games and escaping relegation by the skin of their teeth, but in the knockout competitions they were a very different beast. Although they lost the final of the Coupe de France t Lyon – and in the process bade a tearful farewell to their retiring skipper and goalscorer extraordinaire, Pauleta – they were triumphant at the Stade de Franc a couple of months earlier when they overcame Lens 2-1 in the final of the League Cup, their winning goal coming deep into stoppage time from a controversia penalty converted by defender Bernard Mendy.

FC Metz slid straight back down to the second divisio after being stranded at the foot of the Ligue 1 table a season. Thanks to the formidable scoring of their gia centre-forward from Reunion, 28-goal Guillaume Hoarau, Le Havre AC won Ligue 2. In second place, ar making an immediate return to the big time, were FC Nantes, the last club to win the French title before Lyon went on their winning spree, while third place went to Grenoble Foot 38, who celebrated promotio in the same year that they unveiled a splendid new stadium - the state-of-the-art, solar-panelled Stade des Alpes.

DOMESTIC LEAGUE 2007/08

›UE 1 FINAL TABLE

	Pld	Home W	D	L	F	A	Away W	D	L	F	A	Total W	D	L	F	A	Pts
ympique Lyonnais	38	14	4	1	44	16	10	3	6	30	21	24	7	7	74	37	79
: Girondins de ›rdeaux	38	13	4	2	38	17	9	5	5	27	21	22	9	7	65	38	75
'ympique de arseille	38	11	3	5	34	21	6	8	5	24	24	17	11	10	58	45	62
; Nancy-Lorraine	38	13	5	1	31	11	2	10	7	13	19	15	15	8	44	30	60
; Saint-Étienne	38	12	6	1	30	4	4	4	11	17	30	16	10	12	47	34	58
ade Rennais FC	38	10	2	7	27	19	6	8	5	20	25	16	10	12	47	44	58
)SC Lille Métropole	38	8	7	4	29	18	5	11	3	16	14	13	18	7	45	32	57
GC Nice	38	8	7	4	20	14	5	9	5	15	16	13	16	9	35	30	55
Mans UC 72	38	9	6	4	23	16	5	5	9	23	33	14	11	13	46	49	53
: Lorient	38	9	7	3	18	12	3	9	7	14	23	12	16	10	32	35	52
/I Caen	38	10	5	4	31	19	3	7	9	17	34	13	12	13	48	53	51
; Monaco FC	38	7	5	7	22	24	6	3	10	18	24	13	8	17	40	48	47
ılenciennes FC	38	11	4	4	33	13	1	5	13	9	27	12	9	17	42	40	45
: Sochaux-ontbéliard	38	3	9	7	13	21	7	5	7	21	22	10	14	14	34	43	44
Auxerre	38	8	4	7	20	17	4	4	11	13	35	12	8	18	33	52	44
ıris Saint-Germain FC	38	4	8	7	22	23	6	5	8	15	22	10	13	15	37	45	43
ulouse FC	38	4	11	4	14	15	5	4	10	22	27	9	15	14	36	42	42
: Lens	38	5	11	3	26	22	4	2	13	17	30	9	13	16	43	52	40
: Strasbourg	38	5	5	9	19	20	4	3	12	15	35	9	8	21	34	55	35
: Metz	38	3	3	13	18	34	2	6	11	10	30	5	9	24	28	64	24

TOP GOALSCORERS

20 Karim BENZEMA (Lyon)

18 Mamadou NIANG (Marseille)

16 Djibril CISSÉ (Marseille)
Bafétimbi GOMIS (St-Étienne)

15 Fernando CAVENAGHI (Bordeaux)

14 Rafik SAÏFI (Lorient)
Bakary KONÉ (Nice)

13 Túlio DE MELO (Le Mans)
Steve SAVIDAN (Valenciennes)

12 David BELLION (Bordeaux)
Geraldo WENDEL (Bordeaux)
Mickaël PAGIS (Rennes)

CLUB-BY-CLUB

AJ AUXERRE

Coach – Jean Fernandez

Founded - 1905

MAJOR HONOURS: French League - (1) 1996; French Cup - (4) 1994, 1996, 2003, 2005.

07

3	Lyon	a	0-2	
/8	Bordeaux	h	0-2	
'8	Strasbourg	a	0-3	
'8	Caen	h	1-0	*Maoulida*
/8	Nancy	a	1-4	*Lejeune*
/8	Rennes	h	0-2	
)	Toulouse	a	0-2	
/9	Nice	h	2-0	*Lejeune, Niculae*
'9	Marseille	h	2-0	*Niculae 2*
10	Lens	a	0-2	
/10	Lorient	h	5-3	*Niculae 2, Jeleń 3*
'10	St-Étienne	a	0-0	
11	Lille	h	0-1	
/11	Sochaux	a	1-1	*Kahlenberg (p)*
/11	Le Mans	h	3-0	*Chafni, Niculae, Jeleń*
12	Metz	a	1-0	*Kahlenberg*
12	PSG	h	0-1	
/12	Valenciennes	a	0-3	
/12	Monaco	h	1-0	*Traoré*

08

/1	Bordeaux	a	1-4	*Niculae*
19/1	Strasbourg	h	1-1	*Niculae*
23/1	Caen	a	0-0	
26/1	Nancy	h	0-0	
9/2	Rennes	a	2-1	*Oliech 2*
16/2	Toulouse	h	1-0	*Niculae*
23/2	Nice	a	2-1	*Niculae, Chafni*
1/3	Marseille	a	1-2	*Pedretti*
8/3	Lens	h	0-0	
15/3	Lorient	a	1-1	*Jaurès (p)*
22/3	St-Étienne	h	1-3	*og (Benalouane)*
30/3	Lille	a	2-0	*Oliech, Niculae*
5/4	Sochaux	h	0-1	
12/4	Le Mans	a	0-3	
19/4	Metz	h	0-0	
26/4	PSG	a	1-3	*Mignot*
3/5	Valenciennes	h	2-0	*Lejeune, Jeleń*
10/5	Monaco	a	0-3	
17/5	Lyon	h	1-3	*Thomas*

No	Name	Nat	Pos	Aps	(s)	Gls
8	Issa BA	SEN	M		(3)	
7	Kamel CHAFNI	MAR	M	28	(3)	2
20	Ludovic GENEST		A	1	(1)	
4	Stéphane GRICHTING	SUI	D	26	(3)	
26	Maxime JASSE		D		(2)	
3	Jean-Sébastien JAURÈS		D	33	(1)	1
22	Ireneusz JELEŃ	POL	A	16	(16)	5

10	Thomas KEHLENBERG	DEN	M	24	(5)	2
13	Kévin LEJEUNE		A	35	(3)	3
11	Jean-Michel LESAGE		A	2	(9)	
9	Toifilou MAOULIDA		A	10	(5)	1
6	MARCOS ANTÓNIO Elias Santos	BRA	D	7	(3)	
15	Baptiste MARTIN		D	4	(2)	
12	Jean-Pascal MIGNOT		D	24	(3)	1
9	Vlad MUNTEANU	ROU	M	2	(7)	
21	Daniel NICULAE	ROU	A	30	(5)	11
14	Dennis OLIECH	KEN	A	20	(6)	3
17	Benoît PEDRETTI		M	37		1
28	Robert POPOV	MKD	D	4	(2)	
11	Julien QUERCIA		A	5	(8)	
16	Rémy RIOU		G	19		
30	Arnaud SAUVAGE		G		(1)	
1	Olivier SORIN		G	19		
18	Gabriel TAMAŞ	ROU	D	25	(2)	
5	Frédéric THOMAS		M	22	(4)	1
27	Alain TRAORÉ	BFA	M		(1)	
29	Sammy TRAORÉ	MLI	D	25		1

FC GIRONDINS DE BORDEAUX

Coach – Laurent Blanc

Founded - 1881

MAJOR HONOURS: French League - (5) 1950, 1984, 1985, 1987, 1999; French Cup - (3) 1941, 1986, 1987; League Cup - (2) 2002, 2007.

2007

4/8	Lens	h	1-0	*Bellion*
11/8	Auxerre	a	2-0	*Wendel 2*
15/8	Le Mans	h	1-2	*Bellion*
18/8	St-Étienne	a	0-0	
25/8	Lorient	h	2-2	*Bellion 2*
29/8	Metz	a	1-0	*Diarra*
1/9	Monaco	h	2-1	*Chamakh, Wendel*
15/9	Lille	a	1-1	*Bellion*
23/9	PSG	a	2-0	*Micoud, Bellion*
7/10	Lyon	h	1-3	*Jussiê*
20/10	Strasbourg	a	1-1	*Bellion*
27/10	Valenciennes	h	2-1	*Jussiê (p), Bellion*
3/11	Nancy	a	0-1	
11/11	Rennes	h	3-0	*Bellion 2 (1p), Obertan*
24/11	Caen	a	0-5	
2/12	Toulouse	h	4-3	*Wendel 3, Diarra*
9/12	Nice	a	1-1	*Micoud*
16/12	Marseille	h	2-2	*Chamakh, Jussiê*
22/12	Sochaux	a	1-0	*Jussiê*

2008

12/1	Auxerre	h	4-1	*Cavenaghi 2, Planus, Bellion*
19/1	Le Mans	a	2-1	*Cavenaghi, Fernando*
24/1	St-Étienne	h	1-0	*Cavenaghi*
27/1	Lorient	a	0-1	
9/2	Metz	h	3-0	*Cavenaghi 2, Diarra*
17/2	Monaco	a	6-0	*Cavenaghi 2, Micoud 2, Chamakh, Obertan*
24/2	Lille	h	0-0	
2/3	PSG	h	3-0	*Wendel 3*
9/3	Lyon	a	2-4	*Wendel, Cavenaghi (p)*
16/3	Strasbourg	h	3-0	*Henrique 2, Cavenaghi*
22/3	Valenciennes	a	1-3	*Wendel*
29/3	Nancy	h	2-1	*Cavenaghi 2*
5/4	Rennes	a	2-0	*Diarra, Fernando*
13/4	Caen	h	2-1	*Cavenaghi 2 (1p)*
20/4	Toulouse	a	1-0	*Micoud*
26/4	Nice	h	0-0	
4/5	Marseille	a	2-1	*Wendel, Ducasse*
10/5	Sochaux	h	2-0	*Fernando, Chamakh*
17/5	Lens	a	2-2	*Cavenaghi, Bellion*

No	Name	Nat	Pos	Aps	(s)	Gls
8	Alejandro ALONSO	ARG	M	26	(6)	
11	David BELLION		A	31	(6)	12
9	Fernando CAVENAGHI	ARG	A	15	(8)	15
21	Mathieu CHALMÉ		D	33	(1)	
29	Marouane CHAMAKH	MAR	A	17	(15)	4
4	Alou DIARRA		M	36		4
14	Souleymane DIAWARA	SEN	D	28		
19	Pierre DUCASSE		M	2	(13)	1
5	FERNANDO Menegazzo	BRA	M	27	(5)	3
3	Carlos HENRIQUE dos Santos	BRA	D	17		2
13	David JEMMALI	TUN	D	6	(2)	
6	Franck JURIETTI		D	30	(2)	
15	JUSSIÊ Ferreira Vieira	BRA	A	14	(8)	4
23	Florian MARANGE		D	5	(2)	
7	Johan MICOUD		M	23	(6)	5
26	Gabriel OBERTAN		A	6	(20)	2
27	Marc PLANUS		D	24		1
16	Ulrich RAMÉ		G	36		
25	Henri SAIVET		A		(1)	
28	Benoît TRÉMOULINAS		D	6	(3)	
30	Mathieu VALVERDE		G	2	(3)	
17	WENDEL Geraldo Maurício da Silva	BRA	M	34	(2)	12

SM CAEN

Coach – Franck Dumas & Patrick Parizon

Founded - 1913

2007

4/8	Nice	h	1-0	*Compan*
11/8	Nancy	a	0-1	
18/8	Auxerre	a	0-1	
25/8	Marseille	h	1-2	*Samson*
1/9	Sochaux	h	2-2	*Eluchans, Proment*
15/9	St-Étienne	a	0-3	
22/9	Metz	h	1-2	*Gouffran*
30/9	Toulouse	h	2-1	*Compan, Nivet*
6/10	Lorient	a	0-0	
20/10	Lille	h	1-0	*og (Tafforeau)*
27/10	Monaco	a	0-0	
4/11	Le Mans	h	3-2	*Gouffran 2, Eluchans*
10/11	Valenciennes	a	0-3	
24/11	Bordeaux	h	5-0	*Gouffran, Sorbon, Grand (p), Eluchans, Gomis*
28/11	Lens	a	1-1	*Sorbon*
1/12	PSG	a	1-0	*Florentin*
8/12	Lyon	h	1-0	*Gouffran*
15/12	Rennes	a	2-1	*Deroin (p), Eluchans*
22/12	Strasbourg	h	2-0	*Eluchans, Hengbart (p*

2008

12/1	Nancy	h	0-0	
19/1	Toulouse	a	1-1	*Deroin*
23/1	Auxerre	h	0-0	
26/1	Marseille	a	1-6	*Toudic*
10/2	Lens	h	1-4	*Lemaître*
16/2	Sochaux	a	1-1	*Gouffran*
23/2	St-Étienne	h	1-3	*Compan*
1/3	Metz	a	1-2	*Jemaa (p)*
8/3	Lorient	h	0-0	
15/3	Lille	a	0-5	
22/3	Monaco	h	4-1	*Hengbart (p), Sorbon, Gouffran (p), Jemaa*
30/3	Le Mans	a	1-1	*Gouffran*
5/4	Valenciennes	h	1-0	*Jemaa*
13/4	Bordeaux	a	1-2	*Sorbon*
19/4	PSG	h	3-0	*Deroin, Lemaître, Gouffra*
26/4	Lyon	a	2-2	*Eluchans, Compan*
3/5	Rennes	h	2-2	*Compan, Nivet*
10/5	Strasbourg	a	4-1	*Toudic 2, og (Dos Santos), Gouffran*
17/5	Nice	a	1-3	*Toudic*

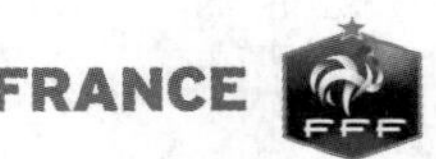

No	Name	Nat	Pos	Aps	(s)	Gls
3	Florian BOUCANSAUD		D	1	(2)	
5	Lilian COMPAN		A	15	(13)	5
	Benoît COSTIL		G	5		
	Anthony DEROIN		M	24	(5)	3
8	Juan ELUCHANS	ARG	M	32	(4)	6
7	Nicolas FLORENTIN		A	14	(19)	1
9	Rémi GOMIS		M	20	(4)	1
0	Yoan GOUFFRAN		A	34	(2)	10
1	Elliot GRANDIN		A	2	(10)	1
2	Cédric HENGBART		D	32	(1)	2
1	Issam JEMAA	TUN	A	9	(12)	3
4	Grégory LECA		M	15	(3)	
0	Reynald LEMAÎTRE		M	15	(3)	2
	Sébastien MAZURE		A	4	(6)	
0	Oumar N'DIAYE		D	2	(3)	
7	Benjamin NIVET		M	33	(2)	2
6	Vincent PLANTÉ		G	31		
2	Grégory PROMENT		M	32	(1)	1
8	Guillaume QUELLIER		M		(3)	
	Alexandre RAINEAU		M		(1)	
	Stéphane SAMSON		A	2	(6)	1
	Nicolas SEUBE		D	28		
9	Jérémy SORBON		D	38		4
	Karl SVENSSON	SWE	D	6		
0	Alexis THÉBAUX		G	2		
	Ibrahim THIAM	MLI	D	15	(1)	
4	Julien TOUDIC		A	7	(11)	4

LE MANS UC 72

Coach – Rudi Garcia

Founded - 1985

2007				
/8	Metz	h	1-0	*Baša*
1/8	Sochaux	a	3-1	*De Melo 3 (1p)*
5/8	Bordeaux	a	2-1	*De Melo, Grafite*
8/8	Lille	h	1-1	*Grafite*
5/8	Monaco	a	1-3	*Matsui*
9/8	PSG	h	0-2	
/9	Lyon	a	2-3	*Sessegnon 2*
5/9	Valenciennes	h	2-0	*Sessegnon, De Melo*
2/9	Strasbourg	a	1-0	*Romaric*
/10	Nice	h	2-0	*De Melo, Matsui*
0/10	Rennes	a	0-3	
8/10	Toulouse	h	1-1	*Sessegnon*
/11	Caen	a	2-3	*Baša, De Melo*
0/11	St-Étienne	h	3-2	*De Melo 2 (2p), Romaric*
5/11	Auxerre	a	0-3	
/12	Nancy	h	2-1	*Yebda, Gervinho*
/12	Lens	a	3-1	*De Melo, Gervinho, Le Tallec*
15/12	Lorient	h	0-0	
22/12	Marseille	a	0-1	
2008				
12/1	Sochaux	h	0-2	
19/1	Bordeaux	h	1-2	*Douillard*
23/1	Lille	a	1-3	*Yebda*
26/1	Monaco	h	1-0	*Matsui*
9/2	PSG	a	0-0	
16/2	Lyon	h	1-0	*De Melo*
23/2	Valenciennes	a	2-1	*Baša, Le Tallec*
1/3	Strasbourg	h	0-1	
8/3	Nice	a	0-0	
15/3	Rennes	h	1-1	*De Melo*
22/3	Toulouse	a	1-1	*Yebda*
30/3	Caen	h	1-1	*Baša*
5/4	St-Étienne	a	1-4	*Le Tallec*
12/4	Auxerre	h	3-0	*Samassa, Le Tallec, Sessegnon*
19/4	Nancy	a	1-1	*Le Tallec*
26/4	Lens	h	3-2	*Matsui 2, Baša*
3/5	Lorient	a	0-0	
10/5	Marseille	h	0-0	
17/5	Metz	a	3-4	*De Melo, Coutadeur, Baal*

No	Name	Nat	Pos	Aps	(s)	Gls
24	Ludovic BAAL		M	7	(5)	1
25	Marko BAŠA	SRB	D	28		5
3	Saber BEN FREJ	TUN	D	4	(1)	
18	Samuel BOUHOURS		D	15		
23	Jean CALVÉ		D	32	(2)	
29	Ibrahima CAMARA	GUI	D	22	(3)	
5	Grégory CERDAN		D	22	(1)	
20	Mathieu COUTADEUR		M	29	(4)	1
7	Túlio DE MELO	BRA	A	29	(2)	13
26	Martin DOUILLARD		M	6	(11)	1
6	Brahim EL-BAHIRI	MAR	M	1	(2)	
2	Camilo António GÉDER	BRA	D	15		
27	Gervais Yao Kouassi "GERVINHO"	CIV	A	19	(7)	2
10	Batista Libânio Edinaldo "GRAFITE"	BRA	A	5	(1)	2
15	Alphousseyni KEITA	MLI	M	1	(1)	
21	Anthony LE TALLEC		A	15	(11)	5
8	Guillaume LORIOT		M	2	(11)	
13	Cyriaque LOUVION		D	8	(9)	
9	Modibo MAÏGA	MLI	A	4	(15)	
22	Daisuke MATSUI	JPN	M	31	(3)	5
30	Yohann PELÉ		G	31		
14	Clément PINAULT		D	1	(4)	
16	Rodolphe ROCHE		G	7	(2)	
11	ROMARIC N'Dri	CIV	M	32	(1)	2
19	Mamadou SAMASSA		A	5	(10)	1
28	Stéphane SESSEGNON	BEN	M	30		5
17	Hassan YEBDA		M	17	(6)	3

RC LENS

Coach – Guy Roux; (25/8/07) Jean-Pierre Papin

Founded – 1906

MAJOR HONOURS: French League - (1) 1998; League Cup - (1) 1999.

2007				
4/8	Bordeaux	a	0-1	
12/8	PSG	h	0-0	
19/8	Valenciennes	h	0-0	
25/8	Strasbourg	a	1-2	*Keita*
2/9	Nice	a	0-1	
15/9	Nancy	h	1-0	*Dindane (p)*
22/9	Toulouse	a	1-1	*Monterrubio*
29/9	Lyon	a	0-3	
6/10	Auxerre	h	2-0	*Pieroni (p), Mangane*
21/10	Marseille	a	0-1	
28/10	Rennes	h	1-2	*Monterrubio*
4/11	St-Étienne	h	3-2	*Coulibaly, Demont, Dindane*
10/11	Metz	a	2-1	*Monterrubio, Khiter*
24/11	Lorient	h	1-1	*Pieroni*
28/11	Caen	h	1-1	*Dindane*
1/12	Sochaux	a	2-0	*Dindane, Monterrubio*
8/12	Le Mans	h	1-3	*Dindane*
15/12	Monaco	a	0-2	
2008				
13/1	PSG	a	0-3	
20/1	Lyon	h	3-0	*Maoulida, Biševac, Mangane*
23/1	Valenciennes	a	2-1	*Hilton, Monnet-Paquet*
26/1	Strasbourg	h	2-2	*Monterrubio 2 (1p)*
10/2	Caen	a	4-1	*Maoulida, Mangane, Rémy, og (Seube)*
16/2	Nice	h	0-0	
23/2	Nancy	a	1-2	*Mangane*
1/3	Toulouse	h	1-1	*Rémy*

8/3	Auxerre	a	0-0	
11/3	Lille	h	1-2	*Hilton*
16/3	Marseille	h	3-3	*Maoulida, Mangane, Rémy*
23/3	Rennes	a	1-3	*Maoulida*
5/4	Metz	h	1-1	*Monterrubio (p)*
9/4	St-Étienne	a	0-2	
12/4	Lorient	a	0-1	
19/4	Sochaux	h	3-2	*Coulibaly, Dindane 2*
26/4	Le Mans	a	2-3	*Dindane, Monnet-Paquet*
3/5	Monaco	h	0-0	
10/5	Lille	a	1-2	*Monterrubio (p)*
17/5	Bordeaux	h	2-2	*Monterrubio, Maoulida*

No	Name	Nat	Pos	Aps	(s)	Gls
11	Kanga AKALÉ	CIV	M	7	(2)	
19	Lucien AUBEY		D	10	(2)	
11	Nadir BELHADJ	ALG	D	18	(1)	
25	Milan BIŠEVAC	SRB	D	26		1
7	Abdoulrazak BOUKARI		M	10	(9)	
10	Éric CARRIÈRE		M	11	(11)	
4	Adama COULIBALY	MLI	D	29	(1)	2
9	Daniel COUSIN	GAB	A		(1)	
26	Yohan DEMONT		D	27	(4)	1
5	Mounir DIANE	MAR	M	2	(1)	
27	Aruna DINDANE	CIV	A	24	(4)	8
38	Simon FEINDOUNO		A		(1)	
3	Vitorino HILTON	BRA	D	23		2
8	Bonaventure KALOU	CIV	M	4		
21	Sidi Yaya KEITA	MLI	M	12	(7)	1
29	Seïd KHITER		M	1	(8)	1
23	Nenad KOVAČEVIĆ	SRB	M	33	(1)	
22	Jonathan LACOURT		M	11	(6)	
15	Fabien LAURENTI		D	26	(3)	
6	Abdou Kader MANGANE	SEN	M	17	(5)	5
8	Toifilou MAOULIDA		A	12	(4)	5
14	Kévin MONNET-PAQUET		A	7	(11)	2
18	Olivier MONTERRUBIO		M	30	(4)	9
9	Luigi PIERONI	BEL	A	6	(5)	2
41	David POLLET	BEL	A		(1)	
2	Marco RAMOS		D	12	(1)	
9	Loïc RÉMY		A	9	(1)	3
1	Vedran RUNJE	CRO	G	38		
28	Julien SABLÉ		M	13	(3)	

LOSC LILLE MÉTROPOLE

Coach – Claude Puel

Founded - 1944

MAJOR HONOURS: French League - (2) 1946, 1954; French Cup - (5) 1946, 1947, 1948, 1953, 1955.

2007

4/8	Lorient	h	0-0	
12/8	Metz	a	2-1	*Michel Bastos, Marić*
15/8	Sochaux	h	1-1	*Dumont*
18/8	Le Mans	a	1-1	*Fauvergue*
26/8	PSG	a	1-1	*Makoun*
29/8	Monaco	h	0-1	
1/9	Rennes	a	2-2	*Franquart, Michel Bastos*
15/9	Bordeaux	h	1-1	*Cabaye*
23/9	Lyon	a	1-1	*Michel Bastos*
6/10	Valenciennes	h	3-0	*Kluivert (p), Lichtsteiner, Plestan*
20/10	Caen	a	0-1	
27/10	Strasbourg	h	0-3	
3/11	Auxerre	a	1-0	*og (Grichting)*
10/11	Nice	h	1-1	*Fauvergue*
24/11	Nancy	a	0-2	
1/12	Marseille	h	1-1	*Kluivert*
8/12	Toulouse	a	0-1	
15/12	St-Étienne	h	3-0	*Lichtsteiner, Plestan, Cabaye (p)*

2008

12/1	Metz	h	1-1	*Cabaye*
19/1	Sochaux	a	1-1	*Obraniak*
23/1	Le Mans	h	3-1	*Mirallas, Obraniak, Cabaye*
26/1	PSG	h	0-0	
9/2	Monaco	a	0-0	
16/2	Rennes	h	3-1	*Kluivert 2 (1p), Michel Bastos*
24/2	Bordeaux	a	0-0	
1/3	Lyon	h	0-1	
8/3	Valenciennes	a	0-0	
11/3	Lens	a	2-1	*Michel Bastos, Béria*
15/3	Caen	h	5-0	*Lichtsteiner 2, Cabaye (1p), Frau*
22/3	Strasbourg	a	1-0	*Mavuba*
30/3	Auxerre	h	0-2	
5/4	Nice	a	0-0	
12/4	Nancy	h	2-1	*Michel Bastos (p), Mirallas*
20/4	Marseille	a	3-1	*Mirallas 2, Makoun*
26/4	Toulouse	h	3-2	*Mirallas 2, Michel Bastos (p)*
4/5	St-Étienne	a	0-0	
10/5	Lens	h	2-1	*Cabaye, Frau*
17/5	Lorient	a	1-1	*Michel Bastos*

No	Name	Nat	Pos	Aps	(s)	Gls
18	Franck BÉRIA		D	38		1
7	Yohan CABAYE		M	34	(2)	7
22	Aurélien CHEDJOU	CMR	M	1	(1)	
2	Mathieu DEBUCHY		M	11	(5)	
29	Stéphane DUMONT		M	15	(6)	1
15	EMERSON da Conceição	BRA	D	6	(2)	
28	Henri EWANE ELONG	CMR	M		(1)	
13	Nicolas FAUVERGUE		A	9	(12)	2
19	Peter FRANQUART		D	17	(2)	1
6	Pierre-Alain FRAU		A	6	(6)	2
36	Eden HAZARD		M		(4)	
9	Patrick KLUIVERT	NED	A	8	(5)	4
34	Badis LEBBIHI		M		(1)	
26	Stephan LICHTSTEINER	SUI	D	30	(4)	4
12	Cris MAKIESE		A		(2)	
17	Jean MAKOUN	CMR	M	25	(1)	2
16	Grégory MALICKI		G	8		
21	Marko MARIĆ	CRO	M		(4)	1
24	Rio Antonio MAVUBA		M	17		1
8	Fernandes MICHEL BASTOS	BRA	M	27	(8)	8
27	Kevin MIRALLAS	BEL	A	19	(16)	6
10	Ludovic OBRANIAK		M	30	(5)	2
25	Nicolas PLESTAN		D	23		2
23	Adil RAMI		D	24		
3	Samuel ROBAIL		M		(1)	
1	Tony SYLVA	SEN	G	30		
20	Grégory TAFFOREAU		D	31		
6	Emra TAHIROVIC	SWE	A	1	(1)	
5	Larsen TOURÉ	GUI	A	3	(6)	
33	Jerry VANDAM		D		(1)	
14	Luis Alfredo YÁÑEZ	COL	A	1	(1)	
11	Souleymane YOULA	GUI	A	4	(11)	

FC LORIENT

Coach – Christian Gourcuff

Founded - 1926

MAJOR HONOURS: French Cup – (1) 2002.

2007

4/8	Lille	a	0-0	
11/8	Monaco	h	2-1	*Saïfi 2*

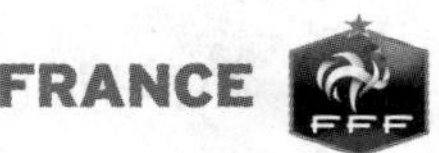

5/8	PSG	a	3-1	*Vahirua 2, Saïfi (p)*
3/8	Lyon	h	2-1	*Vahirua 2*
5/8	Bordeaux	a	2-2	*Saïfi, Namouchi*
3/8	Valenciennes	h	1-3	*Marchal*
/9	Strasbourg	a	0-0	
6/9	Rennes	h	0-1	
2/9	Nancy	a	0-2	
/10	Caen	h	0-0	
0/10	Auxerre	a	3-5	*Saïfi 2, Bourhani*
7/10	Nice	h	0-0	
/11	Marseille	a	0-0	
1/11	Toulouse	h	1-0	*Abriel*
4/11	Lens	a	1-1	*Vahirua*
/12	St-Étienne	h	1-1	*Saïfi*
/12	Sochaux	h	2-1	*Vahirua, Le Pen*
5/12	Le Mans	a	0-0	
2/12	Metz	h	2-0	*Saïfi, Marin*
008				
2/1	Monaco	a	0-1	
9/1	PSG	h	1-0	*og (Bourillon)*
3/1	Lyon	a	0-2	
7/1	Bordeaux	h	1-0	*Jallet (p)*
/2	Valenciennes	a	0-3	
6/2	Strasbourg	h	1-0	*Le Pen*
3/2	Rennes	a	0-2	
/3	Nancy	h	0-0	
/3	Caen	a	0-0	
5/3	Auxerre	h	1-1	*Saïfi*
2/3	Nice	a	2-1	*Vahirua, Saïfi*
0/3	Marseille	h	1-2	*Saïfi (p)*
/4	Toulouse	a	0-0	
24	Lens	h	1-0	*Saïfi*
9/4	St-Étienne	a	0-1	
6/4	Sochaux	a	1-1	*Jouffre*
/5	Le Mans	h	0-0	
0/5	Metz	a	2-1	*Saïfi, Abriel*
7/5	Lille	h	1-1	*Saïfi*

lo	Name	Nat	Pos	Aps	(s)	Gls
	Fabrice ABRIEL		M	38		2
6	Fabien AUDARD		G	38		
	Kemal BOURHANI		A	1	(10)	1
	Marc BOUTRUCHE		D	4	(5)	
	Alain CANTAREIL		D	9	(10)	
	Michael CIANI		D	36		
	Oscar EWOLO	CGO	M	28	(6)	
	Benjamin GENTON		D	9	(1)	
8	Yohan HAUTCOEUR		M	25	(8)	
4	Christophe JALLET		M	37		1
6	Yann JOUFFRE		M	11	(7)	1
1	Ulrich LE PEN		M	22		2
3	Yazid MANSOURI	ALG	M	14	(16)	
9	Sylvain MARCHAL		D	28		1
0	Nicolas MARIN		A	14	(16)	1
9	David M'BODJI		A		(1)	
5	Jérémy MOREL		D	29		
20	Rafael MOURA	BRA	A		(2)	
27	Hamed NAMOUCHI	TUN	M	11	(2)	1
21	Frédéric NIMANI		A		(2)	
12	Bertrand ROBERT		M		(5)	
28	Fabien ROBERT		A	2	(9)	
13	Rafik SAÏFI	ALG	A	37		14
14	Marama VAHIRUA		A	25	(1)	7

OLYMPIQUE LYONNAIS

Coach – Alain Perrin

Founded - 1950

MAJOR HONOURS: French League - (7) 2002, 2003, 2004, 2005, 2006, 2007, 2008; French Cup - (4) 1964, 1967, 1973, 2008; League Cup - (1) 2001.

2007				
5/8	Auxerre	h	2-0	*Baroš, Benzema*
11/8	Toulouse	a	0-1	
18/8	Lorient	a	1-2	*Benzema*
26/8	St-Étienne	h	1-0	*Benzema*
29/8	Sochaux	a	2-1	*Benzema, Bodmer*
1/9	Le Mans	h	3-2	*Govou, Benzema, Baroš*
15/9	Metz	a	5-1	*Benzema 3, Ben Arfa, Juninho*
23/9	Lille	h	1-1	*Govou*
29/9	Lens	h	3-0	*Fábio Santos, Källström, Benzema*
7/10	Bordeaux	a	3-1	*Anderson, Benzema, Källström*
20/10	Monaco	h	3-1	*Juninho (p), Reveillère, Benzema*
28/10	PSG	a	3-2	*Ben Arfa 2, Govou*
3/11	Valenciennes	h	2-0	*Juninho, Govou*
11/11	Marseille	h	1-2	*Juninho*
24/11	Rennes	a	2-0	*Juninho (p), Ben Arfa*
2/12	Strasbourg	h	5-0	*Källström 2 (1p), Juninho, Benzema, Clerc*
8/12	Caen	a	0-1	
15/12	Nice	h	0-0	
22/12	Nancy	a	1-1	*Baroš*
2008				
12/1	Toulouse	h	3-2	*Ben Arfa, Juninho, Benzema*
20/1	Lens	a	0-3	
23/1	Lorient	h	2-0	*Ben Arfa, Benzema*
27/1	St-Étienne	a	1-1	*Benzema*
9/2	Sochaux	h	4-1	*Bodmer 2, Govou, Benzema*
16/2	Le Mans	a	0-1	
23/2	Metz	h	2-0	*Fred 2*
1/3	Lille	a	1-0	*Fred*
9/3	Bordeaux	h	4-2	*Bodmer 2, Benzema, Keita*
15/3	Monaco	a	3-0	*Keita 2, Fred*
23/3	PSG	h	4-2	*Fred 2, Govou, Juninho*
30/3	Valenciennes	a	2-1	*Keita, Govou*
6/4	Marseille	a	1-3	*og (Cana)*
12/4	Rennes	h	1-1	*Cris*
19/4	Strasbourg	a	2-1	*Bodmer, Grosso*
26/4	Caen	h	2-2	*Benzema 2*
3/5	Nice	a	0-0	
10/5	Nancy	h	1-0	*og (André Luiz)*
17/5	Auxerre	a	3-1	*Benzema, Fred, Källström*

No	Name	Nat	Pos	Aps	(s)	Gls
22	ANDERSON Cléber Beraldo	BRA	D	11	(1)	1
7	Milan BAROŠ	CZE	A	6	(6)	3
21	Nadir BELHADJ	ALG	D	3	(6)	
18	Hatem BEN ARFA		M	17	(13)	6
10	Karim BENZEMA		A	32	(4)	20
5	Mathieu BODMER		M	29	(8)	6
32	Jean-Alain BOUMSONG		D	8		
2	François CLERC		D	20	(7)	1
1	Grégory COUPET		G	19		
3	Cristiano Marques Gomes "CRIS"	BRA	D	13		1
21	Marc CROSAS	ESP	M	3	(5)	
19	César DELGADO	ARG	A	2	(5)	
26	FÁBIO dos SANTOS Barbosa	BRA	M	6	(2)	1
9	Frederico Chaves Guedes "FRED"	BRA	A	13	(8)	7
14	Sidney GOVOU		A	26	(6)	7
11	Fabio GROSSO	ITA	D	30		1
8	JUNINHO Pernambucano	BRA	M	29	(3)	8
6	Kim KÄLLSTRÖM	SWE	M	28	(9)	5
23	Kader KEITA	CIV	M	19	(11)	4

No	Name	Nat	Pos	Aps	(s)	Gls
27	Anthony MOUNIER		A		(1)	
4	Patrick MÜLLER	SUI	D	1		
15	Sandy PAILLOT		D		(1)	
12	Loïc RÉMY		A		(6)	
20	Anthony RÉVEILLÈRE		D	22	(6)	1
29	Sébastien SQUILLACI		D	33	(1)	
28	Jérémy TOULALAN		M	29	(1)	
30	Rémy VERCOUTRE		G	19		

OLYMPIQUE DE MARSEILLE

Coach – Albert Emon; (25/9/07) Eric Gerets (BEL)

Founded - 1899

MAJOR HONOURS: UEFA Champions League - (1) 1993 ; French League - (8) 1937, 1948, 1971, 1972, 1989, 1990, 1991, 1992; French Cup - (10) 1924, 1926, 1927, 1935, 1938, 1943, 1969, 1972, 1976, 1989.

2007

4/8	Strasbourg	a	0-0	
11/8	Rennes	h	0-0	
15/8	Valenciennes	a	1-2	*Ziani*
19/8	Nancy	h	2-2	*Niang, Cissé*
25/8	Caen	a	2-1	*Rodriguez, Niang*
29/8	Nice	h	0-2	
2/9	PSG	a	1-1	*Cissé*
15/9	Toulouse	h	1-2	*Zubar*
22/9	Auxerre	a	0-2	
6/10	St-Étienne	a	0-1	
21/10	Lens	h	1-0	*Zenden*
27/10	Sochaux	a	1-2	*Niang*
3/11	Lorient	h	0-0	
11/11	Lyon	a	2-1	*Niang 2 (1p)*
24/11	Metz	h	3-1	*Zenden, Niang 2*
1/12	Lille	a	1-1	*Niang*
8/12	Monaco	h	2-0	*Rodriguez, Cana*
16/12	Bordeaux	a	2-2	*Niang, Cheyrou*
22/12	Le Mans	h	1-0	*Niang*

2008

13/1	Rennes	a	1-3	*Cissé*
19/1	Valenciennes	h	3-1	*Cissé 2, Rodriguez*
23/1	Nancy	a	1-1	*Nasri*
26/1	Caen	h	6-1	*Cissé 3, Valbuena 2, Nasri*
10/2	Nice	a	2-0	*Niang, Cissé*
17/2	PSG	h	2-1	*Taiwo, Niang*
24/2	Toulouse	a	0-0	
1/3	Auxerre	h	2-1	*Cana, Cissé*
9/3	St-Étienne	h	2-0	*Valbuena, Taiwo*
16/3	Lens	a	3-3	*Nasri, Cheyrou, Cissé*
22/3	Sochaux	h	0-1	
30/3	Lorient	a	2-1	*Akalé, Niang*
6/4	Lyon	h	3-1	*Cissé, Niang 2*
12/4	Metz	a	2-1	*Cissé, Nasri*
20/4	Lille	h	1-3	*Niang*
27/4	Monaco	a	3-2	*Nasri, Taiwo, Cissé*
4/5	Bordeaux	h	1-2	*Niang*
10/5	Le Mans	a	0-0	
17/5	Strasbourg	h	4-3	*Niang, Cissé 2 (1p), Nasri*

No	Name	Nat	Pos	Aps	(s)	Gls
2	Kanga AKALÉ	CIV	M	11	(8)	1
13	Salim ARRACHE	ALG	A	1	(6)	
29	André AYEW	GHA	A	3	(6)	
23	Habib BEYE	SEN	D	4		
24	Laurent BONNART		D	34	(1)	
19	Lorik CANA	ALB	M	34		2
1	Cédric CARRASSO		G	4		
7	Benoît CHEYROU		M	32	(3)	2
9	Djibril CISSÉ		A	29	(6)	16
5	Jacques FATY		D	7	(2)	
32	Gaël GIVET		D	28	(1)	
33	Guy GNABOUYOU		A		(1)	
18	Vincent GRAGNIC		M	1	(2)	
18	Elliot GRANDIN		A	2	(6)	
12	Charles KABORÉ	BFA	M	6	(6)	
23	Juan KRUPOVIESA	ARG	M	5	(1)	
30	Steve MANDANDA		G	34		
17	Modeste M'BAMI	CMR	M	19	(5)	
27	Pape M'BOW		D		(1)	
21	Matt MOUSSILOU		A		(4)	
22	Samir NASRI		M	30		6
14	Leyti N'DIAYE	SEN	D	2		
11	Mamadou NIANG	SEN	A	27	(2)	18
8	Wilson ORUMA	NGA	M	2	(5)	
4	Julien RODRIGUEZ		D	20	(1)	3
26	Jean-Philippe SABO		D		(1)	
3	Taye Ismaila TAIWO	NGA	D	26	(2)	3
28	Mathieu VALBUENA		M	18	(11)	3
10	Boudewijn ZENDEN	NED	M	11	(16)	2
6	Karim ZIANI	ALG	M	14	(7)	1
15	Ronald ZUBAR		D	14	(7)	1

FC METZ

Coach – Francis De Taddeo; (24/12/07) Yvon Pouliquen

Founded - 1932

MAJOR HONOURS: French Cup – (2) 1984, 1988; League Cup – (1) 1996

2007

5/8	Le Mans	a	0-1	
12/8	Lille	h	1-2	*N'Diaye*
15/8	Monaco	a	0-2	
18/8	PSG	h	0-0	
25/8	Rennes	a	0-2	
29/8	Bordeaux	h	0-1	
1/9	Valenciennes	a	0-0	
15/9	Lyon	h	1-5	*Gueye B.*
22/9	Caen	a	2-1	*N'Diaye, Gygax*
6/10	Strasbourg	h	1-2	*François*
20/10	Nice	a	1-3	*Barbosa*
27/10	Nancy	h	0-0	
4/11	Toulouse	a	0-0	
10/11	Lens	h	1-2	*Aguirre*
24/11	Marseille	a	1-3	*Gueye C.*
1/12	Auxerre	h	0-1	
8/12	St-Étienne	a	0-2	
15/12	Sochaux	h	1-2	*Pjanić (p)*
22/12	Lorient	a	0-2	

2008

12/1	Lille	a	1-1	*Gygax*
19/1	Monaco	h	1-4	*Aguirre*
23/1	PSG	a	0-3	
26/1	Rennes	h	1-1	*N'Diaye*
9/2	Bordeaux	a	0-3	
16/2	Valenciennes	h	2-1	*Gueye B., og (Martínez)*
23/2	Lyon	a	0-2	
1/3	Caen	h	2-1	*Diop, Gueye B. (p)*
8/3	Strasbourg	a	3-2	*Gueye B., Barbosa, N'Diaye*
15/3	Nice	h	1-2	*Pjanić (p)*
22/3	Nancy	a	1-2	*Bessat*
30/3	Toulouse	h	0-2	
5/4	Lens	a	1-1	*Pjanić*
12/4	Marseille	h	1-2	*Barbosa*
19/4	Auxerre	a	0-0	
26/4	St-Étienne	h	0-1	
3/5	Sochaux	a	0-0	
10/5	Lorient	h	1-2	*Gueye B.*
17/5	Le Mans	h	4-3	*Barbosa, Pjanić, Gueye B., Bessat*

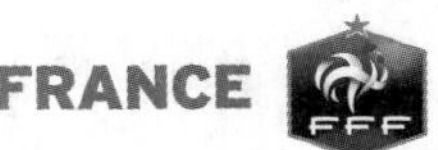

No	Name	Nat	Pos	Aps	(s)	Gls
	Laurent AGOUAZI		M	28	(4)	
	Wilmer AGUIRRE	PER	A	13	(4)	2
	Arnaud ANASTASSOWA		D	1		
	Cédric ANTON		D	1		
	Abdoulaye BALDÉ		A	1	(2)	
	Cédric BARBOSA		M	19	(1)	4
	Sébastien BASSONG		D	19		
	Flavien BELSON		M	3	(3)	
	Vincent BESSAT		M	9	(9)	2
	Gaëtan BONG	CMR	D	5	(6)	
	Julien CARDY		M	1		
	Cyril CHAPUIS		A	3	(4)	
	Papiss Demba CISSÉ	SEN	A	5	(4)	
	Manuel CORRALES	PER	D	3	(1)	
	Éric CUBILIER		D	22		
	Luís DELGADO	ANG	D	3		
	Pascal DELHOMMEAU		D	20	(5)	
	Pape Malick DIOP	SEN	D	27	(1)	1
3	Dino DJIBA	SEN	M	2	(4)	
	Pierre EBEDE OWONO	CMR	G		(1)	
3	Jean-Emmanuel EFFA OWONA	CMR	A	3	(2)	
	Julien FRANÇOIS		M	33		1
4	Emmanuel FRANÇOISE		A		(1)	
4	Rudy GESTEDE		A	6	(6)	
	Babacar GUEYE	SEN	A	17	(9)	6
2	Cheikh GUEYE	SEN	D	28	(3)	1
4	Daniel GYGAX	SUI	M	21	(4)	2
3	Stéphane LONI		D	10	(1)	
	Christophe MARICHEZ		G	36		
5	Momar N'DIAYE	SEN	A	9	(19)	4
3	OU Kyoung-jun	KOR	A		(1)	
5	Miralem PJANIĆ	LUX	M	27	(5)	4
5	Oumar POUYE	SEN	M	1	(3)	
6	Sébastien RENOUARD		M	13	(4)	
4	Jeff STRASSER	LUX	D	16	(1)	
	Milan THOMAS		M	1		
6	Richard TRIVINO		G	2		
2	Mathéus VIVIAN	BRA	D	10	(1)	

AS MONACO FC

Coach – Ricardo Gomes (BRA)

Founded - 1924

MAJOR HONOURS: French League - (7) 1961, 1963, 1978, 1982, 1988, 1997, 2000; French Cup - (5) 1960, 1963, 1980, 1985, 1991; League Cup - (1) 2003.

007				
/8	St-Étienne	h	1-1	*Piquionne*
1/8	Lorient	a	1-2	*Gakpé*
5/8	Metz	h	2-0	*Modesto, Piquionne*
8/8	Sochaux	a	3-0	*Koller 2, Ménez*
5/8	Le Mans	h	3-1	*Cufré (p), Ménez, Piquionne*
9/8	Lille	a	1-0	*Piquionne*
/9	Bordeaux	a	1-2	*Nenê*
6/9	PSG	h	1-2	*Ménez*
2/9	Valenciennes	a	0-1	
/10	Nancy	h	1-3	*Koller*
0/10	Lyon	a	1-3	*Monsoreau*
7/10	Caen	h	0-0	
/11	Rennes	a	1-0	*Piquionne*
0/11	Strasbourg	h	3-0	*Gakpé, Nenê 2*
24/11	Toulouse	a	0-0	
/12	Nice	h	1-1	*Koller*
3/12	Marseille	a	0-2	
15/12	Lens	h	2-0	*Ménez 2*
22/12	Auxerre	a	0-1	
2008				
12/1	Lorient	h	1-0	*Lô Sambou*
19/1	Metz	a	4-1	*Ménez 2, Piquionne, Gakpé*
23/1	Sochaux	h	1-0	*Piquionne*
26/1	Le Mans	a	0-1	
9/2	Lille	h	0-0	
17/2	Bordeaux	h	0-6	
23/2	PSG	a	1-1	*Almirón*
1/3	Valenciennes	h	0-0	
8/3	Nancy	a	0-2	
15/3	Lyon	h	0-3	
22/3	Caen	a	1-4	*Lô Sambou*
31/3	Rennes	h	1-2	*Lô Sambou*
5/4	Strasbourg	a	2-0	*Nenê, Fábio Santos*
12/4	Toulouse	h	0-2	
19/4	Nice	a	2-0	*Meriem, Almirón*
27/4	Marseille	h	2-3	*González, Leko*
3/5	Lens	a	0-0	
10/5	Auxerre	h	3-0	*Bakar, Nenê, Meriem*
17/5	St-Étienne	a	0-4	

No	Name	Nat	Pos	Aps	(s)	Gls
12	ADRIANO Pereira da Silva	BRA	D	23	(1)	
8	Sergio ALMIRÓN	ARG	M	9	(2)	2
28	Djamel BAKAR		M	8	(9)	1
7	Lucas Ademar BERNARDI	ARG	M	18	(1)	
3	Jérémy BERTHOD		D	9	(3)	
22	Fabian Guedes "BOLÍVAR"	BRA	D	21	(1)	
25	Leandro CUFRÉ	ARG	D	22	(3)	1
19	FÁBIO SANTOS Romeu	BRA	D	3	(2)	1
17	Serge GAKPÉ		A	12	(18)	3
20	Ignacio GONZÁLEZ	URU	M	2	(3)	1
8	Mohamed KALLON	SLE	A	2		
9	Jan KOLLER	CZE	A	11	(7)	4
23	Jerko LEKO	CRO	M	22	(7)	1
26	Massamba LÔ SAMBOU	SEN	D	12		3
14	Malaury MARTIN		M	4	(3)	
10	Jérémy MÉNEZ		A	21	(4)	7
21	Camel MERIEM		M	24	(3)	2
4	François MODESTO		D	24	(3)	1
24	Cédric MONGONGU	COD	D	2	(3)	
2	Sylvain MONSOREAU		D	23	(3)	1
13	Vincent MURATORI		D	22		
11	Anderson Luís de Carvalho "NENÊ"	BRA	M	24	(4)	5
5	Diego PÉREZ	URU	M	23	(2)	
33	Steve PINAU		D		(2)	
20	Juan Pablo PINO	COL	M	5	(11)	
18	Frédéric PIQUIONNE		A	26	(6)	7
6	Jaroslav PLAŠIL	CZE	M	3	(1)	
6	Nikola POKRIVAČ	CRO	M	5	(4)	
30	Flavio ROMA	ITA	G	29		
16	Stéphane RUFFIER		G	9	(1)	

AS NANCY-LORRAINE

Coach – Pablo Correa (URU)

Founded - 1966

MAJOR HONOURS: French Cup – (1) 1978; League Cup – (1) 2006.

2007				
4/8	Rennes	a	2-0	*Fortuné, Hadji*
11/8	Caen	h	1-0	*Kim*
16/8	Nice	h	2-1	*Puygrenier, Berenguer*
19/8	Marseille	a	2-2	*Gavanon (p), Hadji*
25/8	Auxerre	h	4-1	*Malonga, Kim, Biancalani, Fortuné*
1/9	St-Étienne	h	2-0	*Kim, Fortuné*
15/9	Lens	a	0-1	
22/9	Lorient	h	2-0	*Hadji 2*
5/10	Monaco	a	3-1	*Kim 2, Dia*
21/10	Sochaux	h	1-1	*Kim*
27/10	Metz	a	0-0	
3/11	Bordeaux	h	1-0	*Malonga*
10/11	PSG	a	0-0	

24/11	Lille	h	2-0	*Puygrenier, Brison*
1/12	Le Mans	a	1-2	*Gavanon (p)*
5/12	Toulouse	a	1-1	*Malonga*
8/12	Valenciennes	h	0-0	
16/12	Strasbourg	a	0-0	
22/12	Lyon	h	1-1	*Malonga*
2008				
12/1	Caen	a	0-0	
20/1	Nice	a	0-1	
23/1	Marseille	h	1-1	*Brison*
26/1	Auxerre	a	0-0	
9/2	Toulouse	h	1-0	*Puygrenier*
16/2	St-Étienne	a	0-4	
23/2	Lens	h	2-1	*Berenguer, Hadji*
1/3	Lorient	a	0-0	
8/3	Monaco	h	2-0	*og (Modesto), Hadji*
15/3	Sochaux	a	1-1	*Zerka*
22/3	Metz	h	2-1	*Hadji, Zerka*
29/3	Bordeaux	a	1-2	*Zerka*
6/4	PSG	h	1-0	*Fortuné*
12/4	Lille	a	1-2	*André Luiz*
19/4	Le Mans	h	1-1	*Fortuné*
27/4	Valenciennes	a	1-1	*Berenguer*
3/5	Strasbourg	h	3-0	*Berenguer, Fortuné, Zerka*
10/5	Lyon	a	0-1	
17/5	Rennes	h	2-3	*Malonga, André Luiz*

No	Name	Nat	Pos	Aps	(s)	Gls
5	ANDRÉ LUIZ Silva	BRA	D	35		2
6	Pascal BÉRENGUER		M	33	(2)	4
8	Frédéric BIANCALANI		D	23	(2)	1
1	Gennaro BRACIGLIANO		G	38		
22	Jonathan BRISON		M	15	(11)	2
19	Basile CAMERLING		A		(1)	
20	Michaël CHRÉTIEN	MAR	D	30		
17	Gaston CURBELO		A	8	(24)	
10	Issiar DIA		A	25	(6)	1
2	Marc-Antoine FORTUNÉ		A	34	(3)	6
24	Benjamin GAVANON		M	31	(5)	2
2	Ludovic GUERREIRO		M	2	(5)	
15	Youssouf HADJI	MAR	M	24	(1)	7
9	Carlos Henrique Dias "KIM"	BRA	A	19	(5)	6
13	Damian MACALUSO	URU	D	5	(5)	
4	Francis Chris MALONGA		M	18	(14)	5
26	Landry N'GUEMO	CMR	M	17	(8)	
28	Sébastien PUYGRENIER		D	33		3
18	Adrián SARKISSIAN	URU	M		(2)	
27	David SAUGET		D	20	(2)	
11	Moncef ZERKA	MAR	M	8	(7)	4

OGC NICE

Coach – Frédéric Antonetti

Founded - 1904

MAJOR HONOURS: French League - (4) 1951, 1952, 1956, 1959; French Cup - (3) 1952, 1954, 1997.

2007				
4/8	Caen	a	0-1	
11/8	Strasbourg	h	1-0	*Hognon*
16/8	Nancy	a	1-2	*Bamogo (p)*
19/8	Rennes	h	1-1	*Koné*
25/8	Toulouse	h	1-1	*Ederson*
29/8	Marseille	a	2-0	*Hognon, Hellebuyck*
2/9	Lens	h	1-0	*Koné*
15/9	Auxerre	a	0-2	
22/9	St-Étienne	h	3-0	*Koné 2, Hellebuyck*
6/10	Le Mans	a	0-2	
20/10	Metz	h	3-1	*Koné 2 (1p), Kanté*
27/10	Lorient	a	0-0	
3/11	Sochaux	h	0-0	
10/11	Lille	a	1-1	*og (Plestan)*
25/11	PSG	h	2-1	*Laslandes, Koné*
1/12	Monaco	a	1-1	*Laslandes*
9/12	Bordeaux	h	1-1	*Koné*
15/12	Lyon	a	0-0	
22/12	Valenciennes	h	1-0	*Hellebuyck*
2008				
12/1	Strasbourg	a	1-0	*Ederson*
20/1	Nancy	h	1-0	*Hellebuyck*
23/1	Rennes	a	1-1	*Modeste*
26/1	Toulouse	a	1-1	*Ederson*
10/2	Marseille	h	0-2	
16/2	Lens	a	0-0	
23/2	Auxerre	h	1-2	*Koné*
2/3	St-Étienne	a	0-0	
8/3	Le Mans	h	0-0	
15/3	Metz	a	2-1	*Bamogo, Ederson (p)*
22/3	Lorient	h	1-2	*Koné*
30/3	Sochaux	a	0-1	
5/4	Lille	h	0-0	
13/4	PSG	a	3-2	*Koné 2, Ederson*
19/4	Monaco	h	0-2	
26/4	Bordeaux	a	0-0	
3/5	Lyon	h	0-0	
10/5	Valenciennes	a	2-1	*Ederson, Koné*
17/5	Caen	h	3-1	*Hellebuyck, Ederson (p* *Koné*

No	Name	Nat	Pos	Aps	(s)	Gls
13	Jacques ABARDONADO		D	4	(6)	
25	Onyekachi APAM	NGA	D	30		
14	Florent BALMONT		M	35	(1)	
22	Habib BAMOGO		A	18	(17)	2
2	Patrick BARUL		D	4	(4)	
24	Gérald CID		D	6	(3)	
23	Drissa DIAKITÉ	MLI	M	11	(11)	
6	Olivier ECHOUAFNI		M	32	(4)	
10	EDERSON Honorato Campos	BRA	M	36		7
18	Ismaël GACÉ		D	3	(2)	
8	David HELLEBUYCK		M	34	(2)	5
4	Vincent HOGNON		D	16	(1)	2
27	Cyril JEUNECHAMP		D	19	(3)	
11	Joseph-Désiré JOB	CMR	A	3	(6)	
5	Cédric KANTÉ	MLI	D	32		1
12	Bakary KONÉ	CIV	A	29	(1)	14
20	Kamel LARBI		M		(1)	
9	Lilian LASLANDES		A	21	(3)	2
16	Lionel LETIZI		G	8	(2)	
1	Hugo LLORIS		G	30		
15	Anthony MODESTE		A	11	(9)	1
26	Cyril ROOL		M	32		
28	Anthony SCARAMOZZINO		D		(1)	
17	Mahmane El Hadji TRAORÉ	MLI	M		(10)	
3	Alaeddine YAHIA	MAR	D	4	(3)	

PARIS SAINT-GERMAIN FC

Coach – Paul Le Guen

Founded - 1970

MAJOR HONOURS: UEFA Cup Winners' Cup - (1) 1996; French League - (2) 1986, 1994; French Cup - (7) 1982, 1983, 1993, 199 1998, 2004, 2006; League Cup - (3) 1995, 1998, 2008.

2007				
4/8	Sochaux	h	0-0	
12/8	Lens	a	0-0	
15/8	Lorient	h	1-3	*Pauleta*
18/8	Metz	a	0-0	
26/8	Lille	h	1-1	*Frau*
29/8	Le Mans	a	2-0	*Armand, Diané*
2/9	Marseille	h	1-1	*Luyindula*
16/9	Monaco	a	2-1	*Armand, Diané*
23/9	Bordeaux	h	0-2	

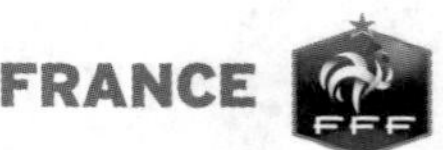

0	Rennes	h	1-3	*Cearà*
/10	Valenciennes	a	0-0	
/10	Lyon	h	2-3	*Pauleta 2*
1	Strasbourg	a	2-1	*og (Rodrigo), Arnaud*
/11	Nancy	h	0-0	
/11	Nice	a	1-2	*N'Gog*
2	Caen	h	0-1	
2	Auxerre	a	1-0	*Luyindula*
/12	Toulouse	h	1-2	*Pauleta (p)*
/12	St-Étienne	a	1-0	*Luyindula*
08				
/1	Lens	h	3-0	*Pauleta, Diané 2*
/1	Lorient	a	0-1	
/1	Metz	h	3-0	*Luyindula, Rothen, Diané*
/1	Lille	a	0-0	
	Le Mans	h	0-0	
/2	Marseille	a	1-2	*Rothen (p)*
/2	Monaco	h	1-1	*Diané*
	Bordeaux	a	0-3	
	Rennes	a	0-2	
/3	Valenciennes	h	1-1	*Pauleta*
/3	Lyon	a	2-4	*Camara, Rothen (p)*
	Strasbourg	h	1-0	*Diané*
	Nancy	a	0-1	
/4	Nice	h	2-3	*Luyindula, Pauleta*
/4	Caen	a	0-3	
/4	Auxerre	h	3-1	*Pauleta, Diané 2*
	Toulouse	a	1-1	*Mendy*
/5	St-Étienne	h	1-1	*Clément*
/5	Sochaux	a	2-1	*Diané 2*

	Name	Nat	Pos	Aps	(s)	Gls
	Sylvain ARMAND		D	35		2
	Loris ARNAUD		A	9	(9)	1
	Yannick BOLI		A		(1)	
	Grégory BOURILLON		D	20	(2)	
	Zoumana CAMARA		D	38		1
	Marcos Venâncio de Albuquerque"CEARÁ"	BRA	D	28	(2)	1
	Clément CHANTÔME		M	21	(7)	
	Jérémy CLÉMENT		M	38		1
	Amara DIANÉ	CIV	A	25	(13)	11
	Didier DIGARD		M	13	(3)	
	EVERTON Leandro dos SANTOS Pinto	BRA	A		(1)	
	Pierre-Alain FRAU		A	7	(4)	1
	Marcelo GALLARDO	ARG	M	1	(8)	
	Mickaël LANDREAU		G	38		
	Péguy LUYINDULA		A	24	(7)	5
	Larrys MABIALA	COD	D		(1)	
	Bernard MENDY		D	16	(7)	1
	Youssouf MULUMBU	COD	M	1		
	David N'GOG		A	8	(6)	1
	Granddi NGOYI		M	5	(2)	
	Pedro Miguel Resendes "PAULETA"	POR	A	18	(9)	8
	Jérôme ROTHEN		M	32		3
	Mamadou SAKHO		D	8	(4)	
	Younousse SANKHARÉ		M	2	(7)	
	Williamis de SOUZA Silva	BRA	A	5	(7)	
	Sammy TRAORÉ	MLI	D	1		
	Mario YEPES	COL	D	25	(2)	

STADE RENNAIS FC

Coach – Pierre Dréossi; (17/12/07) Guy Lacombe

Founded - 1901

MAJOR HONOURS: French Cup - (2) 1965, 1971.

2007				
4/8	Nancy	h	0-2	
11/8	Marseille	a	0-0	
15/8	St-Étienne	h	1-0	*Hansson*
19/8	Nice	a	1-1	*Briand*
25/8	Metz	h	2-0	*Thomert 2*
29/8	Auxerre	a	2-0	*M'Bia, Briand*
1/9	Lille	h	2-2	*Leroy, Didot*
16/9	Lorient	a	1-0	*Didot*
23/9	Sochaux	h	0-2	
6/10	PSG	a	3-1	*Leroy, Briand, Wiltord*
20/10	Le Mans	h	3-0	*Pagis, Wiltord, Esteban*
28/10	Lens	a	2-1	*Wiltord, Leroy*
3/11	Monaco	h	0-1	
11/11	Bordeaux	a	0-3	
24/11	Lyon	h	0-2	
2/12	Valenciennes	a	0-3	
8/12	Strasbourg	a	0-3	
15/12	Caen	h	1-2	*Pagis*
23/12	Toulouse	a	0-0	
2008				
13/1	Marseille	h	3-1	*Pagis, Wiltord 2*
19/1	St-Étienne	a	0-2	
23/1	Nice	h	1-1	*Briand*
26/1	Metz	a	1-1	*Thomert*
9/2	Auxerre	h	1-2	*Pagis*
16/2	Lille	a	1-3	*Pagis*
23/2	Lorient	h	2-0	*Briand, Leroy*
1/3	Sochaux	a	0-0	
8/3	PSG	h	2-0	*og (Sakho), Briand*
15/3	Le Mans	a	1-1	*Thomert*
23/3	Lens	h	3-1	*Leroy, Pagis, Thomert*
31/3	Monaco	a	2-1	*Hansson, Pagis*
5/4	Bordeaux	h	0-2	
12/4	Lyon	a	1-1	*M'Bia*
19/4	Valenciennes	h	1-0	*Wiltord*
26/4	Strasbourg	h	3-0	*Pagis 2, Lemoine*
3/5	Caen	a	2-2	*Leroy, Briand*
10/5	Toulouse	h	2-1	*Pagis, Mensah*
17/5	Nancy	a	3-2	*M'Bia, Pagis 2*

No	Name	Nat	Pos	Aps	(s)	Gls
23	Lhadji BADIANE		A		(5)	
4	Guillaume BORNE		D	3	(2)	
19	Jimmy BRIAND		A	36	(1)	7
14	Bruno CHEYROU		M	23	(4)	
29	Romain DANZÉ		M	7	(2)	
27	Bira DEMBÉLÉ		D	3	(4)	
22	Étienne DIDOT		M	15	(9)	2
2	Uwa ECHIEJILE	NGA	D	4		
3	Erik EDMAN	SWE	D	12		
20	Jirès Kembo EKOKO	COD	A		(7)	
25	Márcio EMERSON Passos	BRA	A		(3)	
21	Juan ESTEBAN	SUI	A		(3)	1
12	Rod FANNI		D	28		
13	Petter HANSSON	SWE	D	34	(1)	2
27	Cyril JEUNECHAMP		D	3	(2)	
18	Fabien LEMOINE		M	18		1
7	Jérôme LEROY		M	30	(1)	6
16	Patrice LUZI		G	19		
26	Sylvain MARVEAUX		M	11	(13)	
17	Stéphane M'BIA	CMR	M	25		3
5	John MENSAH	GHA	D	25		1
10	Daniel MOREIRA		A	2	(8)	
9	Mickaël PAGIS		A	24	(7)	12
30	Simon POUPLIN		G	19		
24	Olivier SORLIN		M	26	(8)	
15	Moussa SOW		A		(2)	
11	Olivier THOMERT		A	21	(4)	5
3	Djimi TRAORÉ	MLI	D	15		
6	Sylvain WILTORD		A	15	(10)	6

AS SAINT-ÉTIENNE

Coach – Laurent Roussey

Founded - 1920

MAJOR HONOURS: French League - (10) 1957, 1964, 1967, 1968, 1969, 1970, 1974, 1975, 1976, 1981; French Cup - (6) 1962, 1968, 1970, 1974, 1975, 1977.

2007				
4/8	Monaco	a	1-1	*Feindouno (p)*
11/8	Valenciennes	h	3-1	*Gomis, Feindouno 2*
15/8	Rennes	a	0-1	
18/8	Bordeaux	h	0-0	
26/8	Lyon	a	0-1	
29/8	Strasbourg	h	2-0	*Ilan (p), og (Abdessadki)*
1/9	Nancy	a	0-2	
15/9	Caen	h	3-0	*Ilan 2, Gomis*
22/9	Nice	a	0-3	
6/10	Marseille	h	1-0	*Dernis*
20/10	Toulouse	a	2-0	*Gomis 2*
27/10	Auxerre	h	0-0	
4/11	Lens	a	2-3	*Gigliotti, Landrin*
10/11	Le Mans	a	2-3	*Varrault, Gigliotti (p)*
24/11	Sochaux	h	1-0	*Ilan*
1/12	Lorient	a	1-1	*Gomis*
8/12	Metz	h	2-0	*Landrin, Feindouno*
15/12	Lille	a	0-3	
23/12	PSG	h	0-1	
2008				
12/1	Valenciennes	a	0-2	
19/1	Rennes	h	2-0	*Dernis, Gomis*
24/1	Bordeaux	a	0-1	
27/1	Lyon	h	1-1	*Gomis*
9/2	Strasbourg	a	0-3	
16/2	Nancy	h	4-0	*Perrin, Gomis 2, Feindouno (p)*
23/2	Caen	a	3-1	*Dernis 2, Gomis*
2/3	Nice	h	0-0	
9/3	Marseille	a	0-2	
15/3	Toulouse	h	0-0	
22/3	Auxerre	a	3-1	*Landrin, Ilan, Feinsouno*
5/4	Le Mans	h	4-1	*Dernis 2, Gomis, Feindouno*
9/4	Lens	h	2-0	*Gomis 2*
12/4	Sochaux	a	1-1	*Ilan*
19/4	Lorient	h	1-0	*og (Jallet)*
26/4	Metz	a	1-0	*Gomis*
4/5	Lille	h	0-0	
10/5	PSG	a	1-1	*Perrin*
17/5	Monaco	h	4-0	*Gomis 2, Dernis, Feindouno*

No	Name	Nat	Pos	Aps	(s)	Gls
26	Moustapha BAYAL SALL	SEN	M	29	(2)	
28	Yohan BENALOUANE		D	5	(1)	
21	Mouhamadou DABO		D	31	(1)	
11	Geoffrey DERNIS		M	23	(6)	7
22	Fousseni DIAWARA	MLI	D	1	(3)	
17	Rudolphe DOUALA	CMR	A	2	(10)	
29	Maodomalick FAYE	SEN	A		(3)	
14	Pascal FEINDOUNO	GUI	A	29	(4)	8
9	David GILGIOTTI		A	7	(10)	2
18	Bafétimbi GOMIS		A	27	(8)	16
10	Freddy GUARIN	COL	M	5	(13)	
9	ILAN Araújo Dall'Igna	BRA	A	22	(9)	6
16	Jérémie JANOT		G	21	(1)	
19	Christophe LANDRIN		M	33	(2)	3
12	Blaise MATUIDI		M	32	(3)	
25	Lasse NILSSON	SWE	A	1	(4)	
3	NIVALDO Batista Santana	BRA	D	13	(1)	
7	Dmitri PAYET		M	26	(5)	
24	Loïc PERRIN		M	32	(3)	2
4	Efstathios TAVLARIDIS	GRE	D	34		
15	Siake TIÉNÉ	CIV	M	9	(10)	
2	Cédric VARRAULT		D	19	(5)	1
1	Jody VIVIANI		G	17		

FC SOCHAUX-MONTBÉLIARD

Coach – Frédéric Hantz; (12/12/07) (Jean-Luc Ruty); (31/12/07) Francis Gillot

Founded - 1930

MAJOR HONOURS: French League - (2) 1935, 1938; French Cup - (2) 1937, 2007; League Cup - (1) 2004.

2007				
4/8	PSG	a	0-0	
11/8	Le Mans	h	1-3	*Birsa*
15/8	Lille	a	1-1	*Dalmat*
18/8	Monaco	h	0-3	
25/8	Valenciennes	a	1-3	*Quercia*
29/8	Lyon	h	1-2	*Birsa (p)*
1/9	Caen	a	2-2	*Ndaw, Birsa*
15/9	Strasbourg	h	0-0	
23/9	Rennes	a	2-0	*Dalmat, Isabey*
7/10	Toulouse	h	0-1	
21/10	Nancy	a	1-1	*Mevlüt*
27/10	Marseille	h	2-1	*og (Zubar), og (Bonnart)*
3/11	Nice	a	0-0	
10/11	Auxerre	h	1-1	*Pitau*
24/11	St-Étienne	a	0-1	
1/12	Lens	h	0-2	
8/12	Lorient	a	1-2	*Mevlüt*
15/12	Metz	a	2-1	*Mevlüt, Dalmat (p)*
22/12	Bordeaux	h	0-1	
2008				
12/1	Le Mans	a	2-0	*Mevlüt, Isabey*
19/1	Lille	h	1-1	*Mevlüt*
23/1	Monaco	a	0-1	
26/1	Valenciennes	h	1-0	*Bréchet*
9/2	Lyon	a	1-4	*Pancrate*
16/2	Caen	h	1-1	*Maurice-Belay*
23/2	Strasbourg	a	2-0	*Isabey, Mevlüt*
1/3	Rennes	h	0-0	
8/3	Toulouse	a	2-1	*Mevlüt 2*
15/3	Nancy	h	1-1	*Mevlüt*
22/3	Marseille	a	1-0	*Ndaw*
30/3	Nice	h	1-0	*Pitau*
5/4	Auxerre	a	1-0	*Perquis*
12/4	St-Étienne	h	1-1	*Grax*
19/4	Lens	a	2-3	*Mevlüt, Bréchet*
26/4	Lorient	h	1-1	*Mevlüt*
3/5	Metz	h	0-0	
10/5	Bordeaux	a	0-2	
17/5	PSG	h	1-2	*Ndaw*

No	Name	Nat	Pos	Aps	(s)	Gls
2	Rabiu AFOLABI	NGA	D	27		
10	ÁLVARO Márcio SANTOS	BRA	A		(3)	
20	Valter BIRSA	SVN	A	13	(9)	3
13	Jérémie BRÉCHET		D	21		2
27	Omar DAF	SEN	D	6	(2)	
9	Moumouni DAGANO	BFA	A	11	(10)	
6	Stéphane DALMAT		M	32	(3)	3
5	Boukary DRAMÉ	SEN	D	9	(1)	
4	Sébastien GRAX		A	6	(6)	1
12	Mickaël ISABEY		M	31	(6)	3
14	Bojan JOKIČ	SVN	D	15	(2)	
17	Maxime JOSSE		D	10	(2)	
18	Lionel MATHIS		M	8	(8)	
21	Nicolas MAURICE-BELAY		M	16	(9)	1
26	MEVLÜT Erdinç	TUR	A	24	(5)	11
8	Guirane NDAW	SEN	M	29	(1)	3

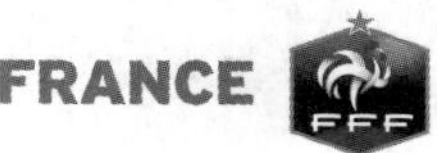

Name	Nat	Pos	Aps	(s)	Gls
Vincent NOGUEIRA		M	1	(2)	
Fabrice PANCRATE		A	11	(7)	1
Damien PERQUIS		D	23		1
Stéphane PICHOT		D	32	(2)	
Romain PITAU		M	29	(3)	2
Sloan PRIVAT		A		(1)	
Julien QUERCIA		A	9	(9)	1
Teddy RICHERT		G	38		
Badara SÈNE	SEN	M	11	(2)	
Kandia TRAORÉ	CIV	A	6	(7)	
Gonzalo VARGAS	URU	A		(4)	

RC STRASBOURG

Coach – Jean-Marc Furlan

Founded - 1906

MAJOR HONOURS: French League – (1) 1979; French Cup – (3) 1951, 1966, 2001; League Cup – (2) 1997, 2005.

07				
	Marseille	h	0-0	
'8	Nice	a	0-1	
'8	Auxerre	h	3-0	*Renteria 2, Gameiro*
'8	Toulouse	a	3-1	*Mouloungui, Fanchone, Gameiro*
'8	Lens	h	2-1	*Renteria, Cohade*
'8	St-Étienne	a	0-2	
	Lorient	h	0-0	
'9	Sochaux	a	0-0	
'9	Le Mans	h	0-1	
0	Metz	a	2-1	*Mouloungui, Renteria*
'10	Bordeaux	h	1-1	*Gameiro*
'10	Lille	a	3-0	*Mouloungui, Rodrigo, Johansen*
1	PSG	h	1-2	*Renteria*
'11	Monaco	a	0-3	
'11	Valenciennes	h	0-0	
2	Lyon	a	0-5	
2	Rennes	h	3-0	*Álvaro Santos 2, Renteria*
'12	Nancy	h	0-0	
'12	Caen	a	0-2	
08				
'1	Nice	h	0-1	
'1	Auxerre	a	1-1	*Fanchone*
'1	Toulouse	h	2-0	*Gameiro, Cohade*
'1	Lens	a	2-2	*Renteria, Álvaro Santos*
	St-Étienne	h	3-0	*Cohade, Álvaro Santos, Mulenga*
'2	Lorient	a	0-1	
'2	Sochaux	h	0-2	
	Le Mans	a	1-0	*Renteria*
	Metz	h	2-3	*og (Diop), Álvaro Santos (p)*
'3	Bordeaux	a	0-3	
'3	Lille	h	0-1	
	PSG	a	0-1	
	Monaco	h	0-2	
'4	Valenciennes	a	0-2	
'4	Lyon	h	1-2	*Renteria*
'4	Rennes	a	0-3	
	Nancy	a	0-3	
'5	Caen	h	1-4	*Gameiro*
'5	Marseille	a	3-4	*Fanchone, Gameiro, Zenke*

	Name	Nat	Pos	Aps	(s)	Gls
	Yacine ABDESSADKI	MAR	M	17	(6)	
	Ahmed ABOU MOSLEM	EGY	D	1	(1)	
	ÁLVARO Márcio SANTOS	BRA	A	9	(19)	5
	Mamadou BAH	GUI	M	4	(1)	
	Habib BELLAÏD		D	32		
29	Pascal CAMADINI		M		(3)	
16	Stéphane CASSARD		G	38		
8	Renaud COHADE		M	26		3
3	Manuel DOS SANTOS		D	37		
4	Pierre DUCROCQ		D	15	(1)	
17	James FANCHONE		A	21	(8)	3
9	Kevin GAMEIRO		A	22	(12)	6
28	Emil GARGOROV	BUL	M		(2)	
14	Romain GASMI		M		(1)	
18	Pascal JOHANSEN		M	16	(5)	1
19	Guillaume LACOUR		M	26		
7	Ali-Azouz MATHIOUTHI		A		(3)	
11	Eric MOULOUNGUI	GAB	A	28	(5)	3
7	Jacob MULENGA	ZAM	A	8	(14)	1
27	Quentin OTHON		M	4		
22	Grégory PAISLEY		D	36		
1	Nicolas PUYDEBOIS		G		(1)	
21	Wason RENTERIA	COL	A	21	(7)	9
6	Lacerda Ramos "RODRIGO"		M	34		1
13	Morgan SCHNEIDERLIN		M	2	(1)	
15	Zoltán SZÉLESI	HUN	D	21	(1)	
33	Simon ZENKE	NGA	A		(2)	1

TOULOUSE FC

Coach – Élie Baup

Founded - 1937

MAJOR HONOURS: French Cup – (1) 1957.

2007				
4/8	Valenciennes	a	1-3	*Dieuze*
11/8	Lyon	h	1-0	*Elmander*
18/8	Strasbourg	h	1-3	*Gignac*
25/8	Nice	a	1-1	*Gignac*
1/9	Auxerre	h	2-0	*Elmander, Sissoko*
15/9	Marseille	a	2-1	*Emana, Elmander*
22/9	Lens	h	1-1	*Bergougnoux*
30/9	Caen	a	1-2	*Emana*
7/10	Sochaux	a	1-0	*Emana*
20/10	St-Étienne	h	0-2	
28/10	Le Mans	a	1-1	*Dieuze*
4/11	Metz	h	0-0	
11/11	Lorient	a	0-1	
24/11	Monaco	h	0-0	
2/12	Bordeaux	a	3-4	*Elmander 3 (1p)*
5/12	Nancy	h	1-1	*Elmander*
8/12	Lille	h	1-0	*Elmander*
15/12	PSG	a	2-1	*Elmander 2*
23/12	Rennes	h	0-0	
2008				
12/1	Lyon	a	2-3	*og (Réveillère), Fabinho*
19/1	Caen	h	1-1	*Dieuze*
23/1	Strasbourg	a	0-2	
26/1	Nice	h	1-1	*Arribagé*
9/2	Nancy	a	0-1	
16/2	Auxerre	a	0-1	
24/2	Marseille	h	0-0	
1/3	Lens	a	1-1	*Emana*
8/3	Sochaux	h	1-2	*Emana*
15/3	St-Étienne	a	0-0	
22/3	Le Mans	h	1-1	*og (Géder)*
30/3	Metz	a	2-0	*Emana 2*
5/4	Lorient	h	0-0	
12/4	Monaco	a	2-0	*Batlles, Elmander*
20/4	Bordeaux	h	0-1	
26/4	Lille	a	2-3	*Dieuze, Mansaré*
3/5	PSG	h	1-1	*Fofana*
10/5	Rennes	a	1-2	*Sirieix*
17/5	Valenciennes	h	2-1	*Mathieu, Sirieix*

FRANCE

No	Name	Nat	Pos	Aps	(s)	Gls
19	Salim ARRACHE	ALG	A	11	(5)	
4	Dominique ARRIBAGÉ		D	25	(2)	1
8	Laurent BATLLES		M	14	(8)	1
10	Bryan BERGOUGNOUX		M	6	(12)	1
29	Étienne CAPOUE		M	1	(4)	
28	Mauro CETTO	ARG	D	24		
3	Daniel CONGRÉ		D	8	(1)	
23	Kévin CONSTANT	GUI	M		(2)	
25	Nicolas DIEUZE		M	33		4
16	Nicolas DOUCHEZ		G	35		
13	Albin EBONDO		D	33	(1)	
9	Johan ELMANDER	SWE	A	32		11
20	Achille EMANA	CMR	M	31		7
17	Fábio Alves "FABINHO"	BRA	M	6	(3)	1
2	Mohamed FOFANA		D	18	(2)	1
21	André-Pierre GIGNAC		A	13	(15)	2
24	Herita N'Kongolo ILUNGA	COD	D	32	(3)	
6	Jon JÖNSSON	SWE	D	1		
7	Fodé MANSARÉ	GUI	A	23	(6)	1
5	Jérémy MATHIEU		D	11	(3)	1
12	Cheikh M'BENGUÉ		D	1	(2)	
15	PAULO CÉSAR Arruda Parente	BRA	D	12	(7)	
1	Rudy RIOU		G	3	(1)	
11	Francileudo dos SANTOS	TUN	A	1	(2)	
14	François SIRIEIX		M	22	(6)	2
22	Moussa SISSOKO		M	22	(8)	1

VALENCIENNES FC

Coach – Antoine Kombouaré

Founded - 1913

2007				
4/8	Toulouse	h	3-1	*Audel 3*
11/8	St-Étienne	a	1-3	*Audel*
15/8	Marseille	h	2-1	*Savidan 2*
19/8	Lens	a	0-0	
25/8	Sochaux	h	3-1	*Bezzaz, Chelle, Savidan*
28/8	Lorient	a	3-1	*Pujol 2, Roudet*
1/9	Metz	h	0-0	
15/9	Le Mans	a	0-2	
22/9	Monaco	h	1-0	*Audel*
6/10	Lille	a	0-3	
20/10	PSG	h	0-0	
27/10	Bordeaux	a	1-2	*og (Diawara)*
3/11	Lyon	a	0-2	
10/11	Caen	h	3-0	*Šebo 2, Savidan*
24/11	Strasbourg	a	0-0	
2/12	Rennes	h	3-0	*Savidan, Pujol 2*
8/12	Nancy	a	0-0	
15/12	Auxerre	h	3-0	*Savidan (p), Chelle, Audel*
22/12	Nice	a	0-1	
2008				
12/1	St-Étienne	h	2-0	*Doumeng, Pujol*
19/1	Marseille	a	1-3	*Audel*
23/1	Lens	h	1-2	*Savidan*
26/1	Sochaux	a	0-1	
9/2	Lorient	h	3-0	*Savidan, Roudet, Šebo*
16/2	Metz	a	1-2	*Belmadi*
23/2	Le Mans	h	1-2	*Savidan*
1/3	Monaco	a	0-0	
8/3	Lille	h	0-0	
15/3	PSG	a	1-1	*og (Cearà)*
22/3	Bordeaux	h	3-1	*Roudet, Šebo, Savidan*
30/3	Lyon	h	1-2	*Chelle*
5/4	Caen	a	0-1	
12/4	Strasbourg	h	2-0	*Savidan 2*
19/4	Rennes	a	0-1	
27/4	Nancy	h	1-1	*Audel*
3/5	Auxerre	a	0-2	
10/5	Nice	h	1-2	*Savidan (p)*
17/5	Toulouse	a	1-2	*Audel*

No	Name	Nat	Pos	Aps	(s)	Gls
7	Johan AUDEL		A	17	(6)	9
10	Djamel BELMADI	ALG	M	21	(5)	1
19	Yassine BEZZAZ	ALG	M	10	(10)	1
12	Éric CHELLE		D	21		3
8	Geoffrey DOUMENG		M	23	(4)	1
2	David DUCOURTIOUX		D	27	(4)	
16	Willy GRONDIN		G	1		
4	JEOVÂNIO Rocha do Nascimento	BRA	M	9	(4)	
5	Khaled KHARROUBI		M		(3)	
21	Williams MARTÍNEZ	URU	D	5	(2)	
25	Rudy MATER		D	28	(3)	
6	Abdeslam OUADDOU	MAR	D	32		
1	Nicolas PENNETEAU		G	37		
28	Grégory PUJOL		A	18	(11)	5
3	Guillaume RIPPERT		D	13	(5)	
18	Sébastien ROUDET		M	24	(6)	3
23	José SAEZ		M	26	(2)	
17	Carlos SÁNCHEZ	COL	M	30	(4)	
9	Steve SAVIDAN		A	31	(7)	13
29	Filip ŠEBO	SVK	A	13	(19)	4
4	David SOMMEIL		D	17	(2)	
13	Mody TRAORÉ		D	15	(10)	

PROMOTED CLUBS

LE HAVRE AC

Coach – Jean-Marc Nobilo

Founded – 1872

MAJOR HONOURS: French Cup – (1) 1959.

FC NANTES

Coach – Michel Der Zakarian

Founded – 1943

MAJOR HONOURS: French League – (8) 1965, 1966, 1973, 1977, 1 1983, 1995, 2001; French Cup – (3) 1979, 1999, 2000.

GRENOBLE FOOT 38

Coach – Mehmed Baždarević (BIH)

Founded – 1892

SECOND LEVEL FINAL TABLE 2007/0

		Pld	W	D	L	F	A
1	Le Havre AC	38	22	12	4	66	30
2	FC Nantes	38	19	13	6	58	34
3	Grenoble Foot 38	38	17	12	9	44	30
4	CS Sedan Ardennes	38	15	13	10	46	40
5	Clermont Foot Auvergne	38	14	15	9	50	41
6	ES Troyes Aube Champagne	38	15	12	11	46	44
7	Stade Brestois 29	38	15	12	11	38	38
8	Montpellier Hérault SC	38	14	12	12	43	32
9	AC Ajaccio	38	14	12	12	37	41
10	Angers SCO	38	13	14	11	39	35
11	SC Bastia	38	14	9	15	45	46
12	En Avant Guingamp	38	11	15	12	41	37
13	Stade de Reims	38	12	10	16	44	52
14	Amiens SCF	38	11	12	15	49	51
15	La Berrichonne de Châteauroux	38	11	12	15	34	42
16	US Boulogne CO	38	12	7	19	37	54
17	Dijon FCO	38	9	15	14	32	51
18	Chamois Niortais FC	38	11	8	19	38	48
19	FC Libourne-Saint-Seurin	38	7	11	20	41	62
20	FC Gueugnon	38	5	12	21	39	59

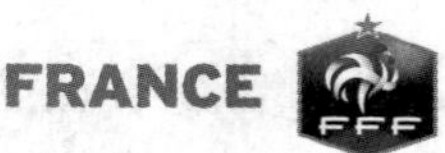

DOMESTIC CUPS 2007/08

COUPE DE FRANCE

2 FINALS

1/08)
ıs 0, Niort 1

1/08)
CO Ajaccio 1, Fréjus 0
ıiens 2, Guingamp 1
gers 2, Vannes 0
ĸerre 3, St-Étienne 2 *(aet)*
ranches 0, Dijon 2
ıuvais 0, Marseille 2
rquefou 1, Gueugnon 0
ıix de Savoie 1, Raon l'Étape 1 *(aet; 4-3 on pens)*
nal 0, PSG 2
Poiré-sur-Vie 4, Coulaines 1
ient 2, Valenciennes 1
ɔn-Duchère 3, Luzenac 2
rignane 1, Arles 1 *(aet; 2-3 on pens)*
ıntluçon 0, Nantes 3
ıntpellier 1, Troyes 0
ncy 2, Reims 1
:e 2, Le Havre 1 *(aet)*
evilly 1, Bordeaux 3
morantin 1, Boulogne 2
ıen 0, Strasbourg 0 *(aet; 4-5 on pens)*
nt-Omer 0, Tours 3
dan 3, Caen 2
ongey 2, Le Mans 3 *(aet)*
soul 1, Metz 6
y-Châtillon 2, Bastia 5

1/08)
ion 0, Lille 3
ıst 1, Monaco 3 *(aet)*
éteil 0, Lyon 4
rtigues 0, Rennes 3
ubeuge 0, Sochaux 2
ılouse 1, Paris FC 2

6 FINALS

2/08)
ılogne 1, Tours 2 *(aet)*
asbourg 0, Metz 3

2/08)
ıiens 1, GFCO Ajaccio 0
gers 3, Nice 1
es 0, Niort 0 *(aet; 8-7 on pens)*
stia 3, Auxerre 0
rdeaux 1, Le Mans 0
Poiré-sur-Vie 1, PSG 3
ient 0, Rennes 0 *(aet; 3-1 on pens)*
ɔn-Duchère 0, Lille 1
is FC 0, Dijon 0 *(aet; 5-6 on pens)*
dan 0, Nantes 0 *(aet; 4-2 on pens)*
chaux 1, Montpellier 1 *(aet; 4-3 on pens)*

2/08)
rquefou 2, Nancy 1 *(aet)*
ɔix-de-Savoie 0, Lyon 1
ırseille 3, Monaco 1

3 FINALS

/3/08)
on 3, Tours 1
ɔn 2, Sochaux 1
G 2, Bastia 1
dan 2, Angers 0

(19/3/08)
Amiens 1, Arles 1 *(aet; 4-2 on pens)*
Bordeaux 2, Lille 0
Carquefou 1, Marseille 0
Lorient 0, Metz 1

QUARTER-FINALS

(15/4/08)
Amiens 1 *(Contout 88)*, Dijon 0
Lyon 1 *(Benzema 38)*, Metz 0
(16/4/08)
Bordeaux 0, Sedan 0 *(aet; 3-4 on pens)*
Carquefou 0, PSG 1 *(Pauleta 77)*

SEMI-FINALS

(6/5/08)
Amiens 0, PSG 1 *(Boli 71)*

(7/5/08)
Lyon 1 *(Juninho 88)*, Sedan 0

FINAL

(24/5/08)
Stade de France, Saint-Denis
OLYMPIQUE LYONNAIS 1 *(Govou 102)*
PARIS SAINT-GERMAIN FC 0
(aet)
Referee – *Kalt*
LYON – *Coupet, Réveillère, Squillaci, Boumsong, Grosso, Toulalan, Juninho (Clerc 117), Källström (Bodmer 68), Govou, Fred (Keita 73), Benzema.*
PSG – *Alonzo, Ceará, Camara, Yepes, Arnaud, Clément, Bourillon (Souza 105), Rothen, Chantôme (Mendy 83), Pauleta (Luyindula 80), Diané.*

COUPE DE LA LIGUE

QUARTER-FINALS

(16/1/08)
Auxerre 1 *(Pedretti 90)*, Marseille 0
Le Mans 1 *(Matsui 26)*, Lyon 0
Lens 3 *(Demont 15, Maoulida 44, Monterrubio 58p)*, Nancy 0
PSG 4 *(Pauleta 2p, Diané 56, 61, Rothen 70)*, Valenciennes 0

SEMI-FINALS

(26/2/08)
PSG 3 *(Yepes 31, Pauleta 43, Mendy 79)*, Auxerre 2 *(Landreau 9og, Quercia 90+3)*

(27/2/08)
Le Mans 4 *(Gervinho 22, Yebda 45, Matsui 66, De Melo 67)*, Lens 5 *(De Melo 35og, Rémy 46, Dindane 53, Pelé 64og, Keita 119) (aet)*

FINAL

(29/3/08)
Stade de France, Saint-Denis
PARIS SAINT-GERMAIN FC 2 *(Pauleta 19, Mendy 90+4p)*
RC LENS 1 *(Carrière 53)*
Referee – *Duhamel*
PSG – *Landreau, Ceará, Camara, Sakho, Armand, Chantôme (Mendy 64), Bourillon, Clément, Rothen, Pauleta (Luyindula 66), Diané.*
LENS – *Le Crom, Laurenti, Coulibaly, Hilton, Belhadj, Rémy (Monterrubio 14), Mangane, Carrière, Kovačević, Monnet-Paquet (Dindane 69), Maoulida (Demont 84).*

GEORGIA

Toppmöller takes his leave

German coach Klaus Toppmöller's spell in charge of the Georgian national team ended in March 2008 when he was dismissed from office following an embarrassing 4-1 defeat by Northern Ireland in a friendly international in Belfast.

The 56-year-old former West German international and Bayer 04 Leverkusen boss lasted a little over two years in the job. That period incorporated the whole of the team's UEFA EURO 2008™ qualifying campaign, which, as expected given the quality of the Group B opposition – Italy, France, Scotland, Ukraine – ended in disappointment, with Georgia managing to scrape together only ten points, all but four of them having come at the expense of the Faroe Islands.

Klaus Toppmöller lost his job as Georgia national team coach in the spring

Teenage rampage

The undoubted high point of Toppmöller's reign was th 2-0 home win over Scotland – a team on a serious mission to qualify for Austria/Switzerland – in Georgia's penultimate EURO qualifier. A young, experimental side severely weakened by injuries (Kakha Kaladze, Levan Kobiashvili) and suspension (Giorgi Demetradze), not to mention the premature international retirement a few months earlier of record marksman Shota Arveladze, produced a stirring display to win 2-0 with eye-catching performances from two 17-year-olds – goalkeeper Gior Makaridze and striker Levan Mchedlidze – plus another youngster, Levan Kenia, who was not due to turn 17 un the next day. All three young guns were retained by Toppmöller the following month for the final qualifier a home to Lithuania, but this time Georgia were on the receiving end of a 2-0 scoreline and therefore finished u six points behind their conquerors, in fifth place, in the final table.

With Toppmöller discarded, the job was taken on temporarily by Croat Petar Segrt, the Georgian Under-2 coach, for a couple of friendlies against Estonia and Portugal in May pending the appointment of a permanent successor ahead of a 2010 FIFA World Cup qualifying programme that pitted Georgia with Italy, Bulgaria, the Republic of Ireland, Cyprus and Montenegro. In early August, Héctor Cúper was appointed, but one name previously touted had been Arveladze, who decided to hang up his boots once and for all after an ill-starred final season in Spain at UD Levante. He arranged a gala farewell match in Tbilisi in early June, to which many of his former team-mates an colleagues were invited. As a tribute to his contribution to the national team over a 15-year period, Georgia hav permanently withdrawn the No11 shirt.

Dinamo power

On the domestic scene, one of Arveladze's former clubs, FC Dinamo Tbilisi, returned to their familiar perch as the champions of Georgia. Led by Dušan Uhrin, the veteran

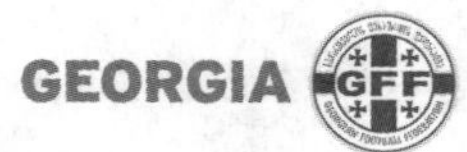

ach who steered the Czech Republic to the final of Euro 5™, the country's most famous footballing institution oved too powerful for the opposition and grabbed their th Georgian title. It was an impressive show of strength, th Dinamo winning 23 of their 26 matches to finish ten oints ahead of runners-up FC WIT Georgia.

namo began as they meant to go on, defeating efending champions FC Olimpi Rustavi 2-0 away in their ening game. That was the first of eight successive ins, their charge being halted only by a home defeat to IT (0-1) in mid-October. There would be only one more efeat – in the reverse fixture against Olimpi that started e spring campaign – as Uhrin's happy crew, starring naglesi Liga top scorer Mikheil Khutsishvili (16 goals), ontenegrin striker Ilija Spasović and two impressive ports from Gabon, goalkeeper Didier Ovono Ebang d forward Georges Akiremy, raced untroubled towards e finish line.

estafoni revenge

namo's championship was sealed with two games to are on May 3 when they won 1-0 away to FC Zestafoni. ur days later, on the same ground, against the same ponents, the champions' hopes of a double were attered when Zestafoni reversed that scoreline to win e two-legged Georgian Cup semi-final 2-1 on gregate and qualify for their fourth final in as many ars. Remarkably, the team awaiting them in the owpiece at the Boris Paichadze stadium for the third ar running were FC Ameri Tbilisi.

neri were bidding for a Cup hat-trick, but 2008 was to Zestafoni's year at last. After three successive final efeats they finally took home the spoils. Two goals early the second half from midfielder Roin Oniani and striker Beta Gotsiridze – also the semi-final marksmen against Dinamo Tbilisi - put Zestafoni in command, and although substitute Dimitri Tatanashvili, Ameri's match-winner in the 2007 final, provided a few jitters by making it 2-1 in the last minute, Zestafoni were not to be denied their first major trophy – or a cherished UEFA Cup spot.

One up, three down

With the Umaglesi Liga returning to a 12-club entity in 2008/09 – its complement from 2000-04 - three teams were relegated automatically, with a fourth seeking salvation in a relegation/promotion play-off. FC Spartaki Tskhinvali duly retained their status at the expense of FC Gagra, who had earlier lost another play-off (on penalties) to the other second division regional winners FC Magaroeli Chiatura. Magaroeli's promotion was countered by the direct descent of FC Dila Gori, FC Dinamo Batumi and FC Merani Tbilisi.

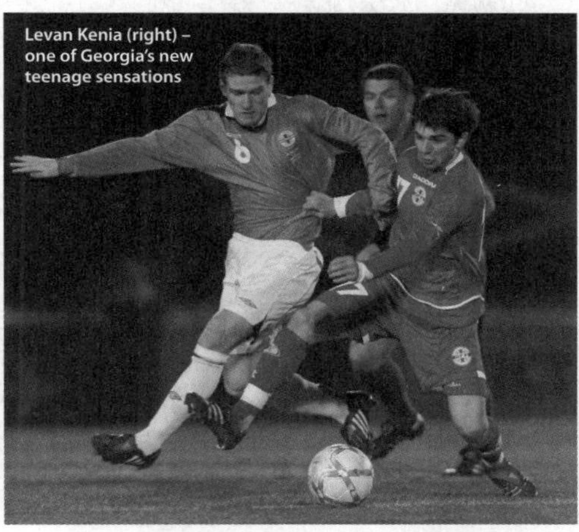

Levan Kenia (right) – one of Georgia's new teenage sensations

Georgian Football Federation (GFF)

76a Chavchavadze Avenue
GE-0162 Tbilisi
tel - +995 32 912680
fax - +995 32 915 995
website - www.gff.ge
email - gff@gff.ge
Year of Formation – 1990
President – Nodar Akhalkatsi
General Secretary – Ucha Ugulava
Press Officer – Aleksandre Tsnobiladze
Stadium - Boris Paichadze, Tbilisi (54,549)

TOP FIVE ALL-TIME CAPS
Levan Kobiashvili (72); Giorgi Nemsadze (69); Gocha Jamarauli & Kakha Kaladze (62); Shota Arveladze (61)

TOP FIVE ALL-TIME GOALS
Shota Arveladze (26); Temur Ketsbaia (17); Aleksandre Iashvili & Giorgi Demetradze (12); Mikheil Kavelashvili (9)

GEORGIA

NATIONAL TEAM RESULTS 2007/08

22/8/07	Luxembourg	A	Luxembourg	0-0	
8/9/07	Ukraine (ECQ)	H	Tbilisi	1-1	*Siradze (89)*
12/9/07	Azerbaijan	A	Baku	1-1	*Tatanashvili (47)*
13/10/07	Italy (ECQ)	A	Genoa	0-2	
17/10/07	Scotland (ECQ)	H	Tbilisi	2-0	*Mchedlidze (16), Siradze (64)*
16/11/07	Qatar	A	Doha	2-1	*Kankava (46), Salukvadze (74)*
21/11/07	Lithuania (ECQ)	H	Tbilisi	0-2	
6/2/08	Latvia	H	Tbilisi	1-3	*Kaladze (46)*
26/3/08	Northern Ireland	A	Belfast	1-4	*Healy (54og)*
27/5/08	Estonia	A	Tallinn	1-1	*Kenia (83)*
31/5/08	Portugal	A	Viseu	0-2	

NATIONAL TEAM APPEARANCES 2007/08

Coach – Klaus TOPPMÖLLER (GER) 12/8/51 /(27/5/08) Petar SEGRT (CRO) 8/5/66			Lux	UKR	Aze	ITA	SCO	Qat	LTU	Lva	Nir	Est	Por	Caps	Go
Giorgi LOMAIA	8/8/79	Karpaty (UKR)	G												
		/unattached		G		G								33	-
Otar KHIZANEISHVILI	26/9/81	Freiburg (GER)	D		D									20	-
Zurab KHIZANISHVILI	6/10/81	Blackburn (ENG)	D			D	D	D61				D	D	53	-
Kakha KALADZE	27/2/78	Milan (ITA)	D	D				D	D	D	D			62	1
David KVIRKVELIA	27/6/80	Metalurh Zaporozhya (UKR)	M			M	M	M86	M						
		/Rubin (RUS)									M	M76		33	-
Levan TSKITISHVILI	10/10/76	unattached	M76	M	M79	M		M	M						
		/Lokomotivi Tbilisi									M90	M	M46	55	1
Levan KOBIASHVILI	10/7/77	Schalke (GER)	M31									M	M46	72	7
Vladimer BURDULI	26/10/80	Zarya (UKR)	M46											21	2
Malkhaz ASATIANI	4/8/81	Lokomotiv Moskva (RUS)	M46	D	D	D	D	D	D	D		D	D	33	4
Aleksandre IASHVILI	23/10/77	Karlsruhe (GER)	A	M62							A	A90	A46	41	1
David SIRADZE	21/10/81	Paderborn (GER)	A46	s62		s60	A89		A80	A				12	4
Aleksandre AMISULASHVILI	20/8/82	Spartak Nalchik (RUS)	s31											10	1
Otar MARTSVALADZE	14/7/84	Zakarpattya (UKR)	s46	M	s62				s31					10	1
David MUJIRI	2/1/78	Krylya Sovetov (RUS)	s46												
		/Lokomotiv Moskva (RUS)										s90	s38	24	1
Vasil GIGIADZE	3/6/77	Naftovyk-Ukrnafta (UKR)	s46											6	-
Zurab MENTESHASHVILI	30/1/80	Ventspils (LVA)	s76	M79		M	M		M31				M68	32	1
Mate GVINIANIDZE	10/12/86	1860 München (GER)		D										5	-
Lasha SALUKVADZE	21/12/81	Rubin (RUS)		D	s76	D	D	s61	D	D	D			23	1
Lasha JAKOBIA	20/8/80	Metalist (UKR)		A62	A62	s85	s89	s46			s80			13	1
Giorgi DEMETRADZE	26/9/76	Arsenal (UKR)		A		A85								56	1
Levan KENIA	18/10/90	Lokomotivi Tbilisi		s62	M60	s60	M79	M69	M						
		/Schalke (GER)								M	M81	s61	M68	10	1
Dimitri TATANASHVILI	19/10/83	Ameri		s79	A									2	1
Giorgi MAKARIDZE	31/3/90	Dinamo Tbilisi			G		G	G	G		G			5	-
Aleksandre KVAKHADZE	17/8/84	WIT			D75		s85	s81			D			4	-
Ilia KANDELAKI	26/12/81	Carl Zeiss Jena (GER)			D		s79							12	-
Jaba KANKAVA	18/3/86	Dnipro (UKR)			M	M	M	M81	M	M	M			24	2
Grigol DOLIDZE	25/10/82	Ameri			M76									1	-

...TIONAL TEAM APPEARANCES 2007/08 (contd.)

			Lux	UKR	Aze	ITA	SCO	Qat	LTU	Lva	Nir	Est	Por	Caps	Goals
DEKANOSIDZE	2/1/81	Ameri			s60			s86						2	-
LOMAIA	18/5/85	WIT			s75									1	-
BOLKVADZE	5/6/80	Ameri			s79									1	-
SHASHIASHVILI	1/9/79	Sturm (AUT)				D60	D	s61			D80			24	1
MCHEDLIDZE	24/3/90	Empoli (ITA)				A60	A85	A46	A	A41				5	1
...n SANAIA	3/9/89	Le Mans (FRA)						D61					s68	2	-
GRIGALASHVILI	21/6/86	Borjomi /Dinamo Tbilisi						M		s74				3	-
...oz GELASHVILI	5/8/85	WIT						s69	s80					2	-
REVISHVILI	2/3/87	Rubin (RUS)								G				8	-
LIAVA	3/1/85	Skonto (LVA)								D	s90			7	-
KHIDESHELI	23/1/88	Zestafoni								M83	s81			2	-
...a GOGUA	4/10/83	Spartak Nalchik (RUS)								M74				19	1
...andre KOBAKHIDZE	12/2/87	Dnipro (UKR)								s41	M			3	-
GOTSIRIDZE	21/2/88	Zestafoni								s83		s68	s46	4	-
LORIA	27/1/86	Dinamo Tbilisi										G	G	2	-
LOBJANIDZE	23/2/87	Zestafoni										D	D	2	-
NAVALOVSKI	28/6/86	Anzhi (RUS)										D	D81	2	-
ODIKADZE	14/4/81	Dinamo Tbilisi										M68		5	-
LEKSIDZE	3/8/78	Lokomotivi Tbilisi										A61	A38	21	2
KLIMIASHVILI	30/5/88	WIT										s76	s46	2	-
DEVDARIANI	28/10/87	Olimpi											s46	1	-
BARABADZE	4/10/88	Anzhi (RUS)											s68	1	-
MEREBASHVILI	15/8/86	Dinamo Tbilisi											s81	1	-

DOMESTIC LEAGUE 2007/08

...AGLESI LIGA FINAL TABLE

		Home					Away					Total					
	Pld	W	D	L	F	A	W	D	L	F	A	W	D	L	F	A	Pts
Dinamo Tbilisi	26	11	0	2	41	13	12	1	0	26	5	23	1	2	67	18	70
WIT Georgia	26	10	1	2	25	7	9	2	2	20	7	19	3	4	45	14	60
Zestafoni	26	11	1	1	38	7	7	4	2	18	9	18	5	3	56	16	59
Olimpi Rustavi	26	9	1	3	11	7	7	3	3	15	9	16	4	6	26	16	52
Ameri Tbilisi	26	8	2	3	30	14	7	1	5	18	13	15	3	8	48	27	48
Meskheti ...khaltsikhe	26	6	4	3	15	11	5	2	6	14	19	11	6	9	29	30	39
Mglebi Zugdidi	26	7	2	4	16	10	3	1	9	11	23	10	3	13	27	33	33
Sioni Bolnisi	26	6	2	5	21	14	3	3	7	13	21	9	5	12	34	35	32
Borjomi	26	7	1	5	22	20	2	3	8	10	19	9	4	13	32	39	31
Lokomotivi Tbilisi	26	5	2	6	15	15	2	4	7	12	20	7	6	13	27	35	27
Spartaki Tskhinvali	26	3	4	6	8	13	2	4	7	7	15	5	8	13	15	28	23
Merani Tbilisi	26	3	1	9	6	21	3	0	10	9	33	6	1	19	15	54	19
Dinamo Batumi	26	2	4	7	7	18	2	0	11	9	33	4	4	18	16	51	16
Dila Gori	26	1	4	8	7	17	0	1	12	5	36	1	5	20	12	53	8

...C Ameri Tbilisi withdrew before 2008/09 season.

TOP GOALSCORERS

16 Mikheil KHUTSISHVILI (Dinamo Tbilisi)

13 Dimitri TATANASHVILI (Ameri)

12 Gilvan Gomes VIEIRA (Zestafoni)

11 Giorgi MEREBASHVILI (Dinamo Tbilisi)

10 Georges Edouard AKIREMY Owondo (Dinamo Tbilisi)
Nikoloz GELASHVILI (WIT/Zestafoni)
Revaz GOTSIRIDZE (Ameri)

9 Rati ALEKSIDZE (Lokomotivi Tbilisi)
Zurab IONANIDZE (Zestafoni)
David INASARIDZE (Meskheti)
Shota JIKIA (Borjomi/Sioni)
Ilija SPASOJEVIĆ (Dinamo Tbilisi)
Mate VATSADZE (Dinamo Tbilisi)

GEORGIA

CLUB-BY-CLUB

FC AMERI TBILISI

Coach - Giorgi Chikhradze
Founded - 2002
MAJOR HONOURS: Georgian Cup - (2) 2006, 2007.

2007

10/8	Lokomotivi Tbilisi	a	1-2	*Tatanashvili (p)*
17/8	Dila	h	3-2	*Tatanashvili, Chikviladze, Davitashvili*
25/8	Olimpi	a	0-1	
2/9	Sioni	h	2-0	*Dolidze, Alavidze*
15/9	Borjomi	a	0-3	
23/9	Merani	h	7-0	*Davitashvili, Dobrovolski, Gotsiridze 2, Dolidze, Tatanashvili, Jeladze*
29/9	Spartaki Tskhinvali	a	1-0	*Tatanashvili (p)*
6/10	Dinamo Tbilisi	h	0-2	
19/10	Batumi	a	3-0	*Gotsiridze, Dolidze, Tatanashvili*
27/10	Mglebi	a	1-0	*Davitnidze*
24/11	Meskheti	a	2-1	*Bolkvadze, Davitnidze*
1/12	Zestafoni	h	1-2	*Davitnidze*
5/12	WIT	h	0-3	*(w/o; match abandoned after 55 minutes at 0-1)*

2008

24/2	Lokomotivi Tbilisi	h	1-1	*Dekanosidze (p)*
2/3	Dila	a	2-0	*Kakashvili, Tatanashvili (p)*
8/3	Olimpi	h	2-1	*Shalamberidze, Tatanashvili*
16/3	Sioni	a	0-0	
21/3	Borjomi	h	3-2	*Gotsiridze, og (Karkuzashvili), Chimakadze*
29/3	Merani	a	5-1	*Didava, Dekanosidze, Gotsiridze, Tatanashvili 2*
4/4	Spartaki Tskhinvali	h	2-0	*Gotsiridze, Dobrovolski*
13/4	Dinamo Tbilisi	a	1-2	*Didava*
19/4	Batumi	h	4-1	*Gotsiridze 2, Kakashvili (p), Tatanashvili*
25/4	Mglebi	h	5-0	*Gotsiridze, Elbakidze, Dobrovolski, Tatanashvili 2*
3/5	WIT	a	1-0	*Tatanashvili (p)*
11/5	Meskheti	h	0-0	
20/5	Zestafoni	a	1-3	*Gotsiridze*

Name	Nat	Pos	Aps	(s)	Gls
Archil ALAVIDZE		M	1	(12)	1
David BOLKVADZE		M	10		1
Tengiz CHIKVILADZE		D	17	(2)	1
Besik CHIMAKADZE		A		(5)	1
Suliko DAVITASHVILI		A	19	(2)	2
Giorgi DAVITNIDZE		D	22		3
Giorgi DEKANOSIDZE		M	24	(1)	2
Givi DIDAVA		D	23		2
Denis DOBROVOLSKI		M	23	(1)	3
Grigol DOLIDZE		M	19	(4)	3
Giorgi ELBAKIDZE		D	22	(1)	1
Revaz GOTSIRIDZE		A	20	(5)	10
Gizo JELADZE		M	6	(4)	1
Vladimer KAKASHVILI		D	14	(1)	2
Vakhtang KHVADAGIANI		D	3		
Mikheil KOBAURI		D	3	(2)	
Zurab KVACHAKHIA		G	12		
David MCHEDLISHVILI		M	2	(1)	
Giorgi MEMARNISHVILI		D	7	(4)	
Mikheil MESKHI		M	5	(6)	
Lado NADIRASHVILI		G	14	(1)	
Koba SHALAMBERIDZE		M	8	(5)	1
Giorgi SILAGAVA		M	1	(3)	
Dimitri TATANASHVILI		A	11	(12)	13
Bachana TSKHADADZE		A		(3)	

FC BORJOMI

Coach - Vladimer Khachidze
Founded - 1936

2007

12/8	Merani	h	1-0	*Jikia*
17/8	Spartaki Tskhinvali	a	0-0	
25/8	Dinamo Tbilisi	h	1-2	*Memarnishvili*
1/9	Batumi	a	1-1	*Jikia*
15/9	Ameri	h	3-0	*Jikia, Khanishvili, Grigalashvili*
23/9	WIT	a	2-1	*Jikia, Grigalashvili*
28/9	Meskheti	h	2-0	*Kvelashvili, Grigalashvili*
7/10	Zestafoni	a	0-1	
19/10	Lokomotivi Tbilisi	h	2-1	*Grigalashvili, Jikia*
27/10	Dila	a	0-0	
24/11	Sioni	a	1-0	*Nergadze*
2/12	Mglebi	h	4-3	*Jikia, Kvelashvili, Karkuzashvili, Tediashvili*
5/12	Olimpi	h	0-0	

2008

24/2	Merani	a	0-1	
1/3	Spartaki Tskhinvali	h	2-1	*Megreladze 2 (1p)*
7/3	Dinamo Tbilisi	a	2-4	*Megreladze, Lomidze*
15/3	Batumi	h	1-2	*Tediashvili*
21/3	Ameri	a	2-3	*Chirikashvili, Megreladze*
29/3	WIT	h	1-2	*Megreladze*
5/4	Meskheti	a	0-2	
13/4	Zestafoni	h	0-2	
19/4	Lokomotivi Tbilisi	a	0-1	
26/4	Dila	h	3-2	*Chirikashvili 2, Karkuzashvili*
3/5	Olimpi	a	0-1	
11/5	Sioni	h	2-5	*Rokhvadze, Lomidze*
20/5	Mglebi	a	2-4	*Rokhvadze, Gachechiladze*

Name	Nat	Pos	Aps	(s)	Gls
Levan AKOBIA		D	10		
Shota BABUNASHVILI		M	11		
Bakar BAKRADZE		M	2	(2)	
Irakli BARAMIA		M	1		
Valeri BOLKVADZE		M	9		
Lasha CHELIDZE		D	13		
Irakli CHIRIKASHVILI		M	6		3
Givi CHKHETIANI		M	5		
Gocha DATUASHVILI		G	2		
Djousse Donald DERING	CMR	A	8	(1)	
Nodar DEVIDZE		A	2	(5)	
Levan GACHECHILADZE		A	2	(1)	1
Kakha GLUNCHADZE		G	1		
David GOGICHAISHVILI		M	9	(10)	
Ucha GOGOLADZE		M		(1)	

rab GOGOLADZE	D	2	(2)	
muraz GONGADZE	D	10		
ota GRIGALASHVILI	M	12	(1)	4
so GRISHIKASHVILI	G	3		
rgi GUGAVA	A	6	(1)	
rgi GURULI	D	6		
eksi IOBASHVILI	M		(1)	
ota JIKIA	A	10	(2)	6
van JIKIDZE	A	1		
van KAKUBAVA	D	9		
i KARKUZASHVILI	D	15	(4)	2
rgi KAVTARADZE	M	10		
za KENCHOSHVILI	D	1		
a KHACHIDZE	M	2	(2)	
ba KHANISHVILI	M	11	(1)	1
vid KHELISUFALI	M		(1)	
muka KHITARISHVILI	D	2		
khtang KHUTSISHVILI	A	1		
khaber KIRTADZE	D	8		
iran KVELASHVILI	M	7	(5)	2
a LOMIDZE	D	7	(6)	2
rgi MEGRELADZE	A	5	(1)	5
rgi MEMARNISHVILI	D	12		1
van MEREBASHVILI	D	13		
naz NASKIDASHVILI	A	3	(10)	
rgi NERGADZE	M	12		1
kheil NOZADZE	M	1		
rgi PEIKRISHVILI	M	2		
vid PIRTSKHALAVA	M		(1)	
vid ROKHVADZE	A	2		2
nstantine SEPIASHVILI	G	8		
ka SHEKRILADZE	G	12		
van TEDIASHVILI	A	12	(7)	2
edo TSIKARISHVILI	G		(1)	

FC DILA GORI

ach - Mamuka Vardosanidze; (27/10/07) Zurab Khorguashvili

Founded - 1949

07

/8	Batumi	h	1-0	*Chitaia*
/8	Ameri	a	2-3	*Sadagashvili, Chitaia*
/8	WIT	h	0-1	
	Meskheti	a	0-2	
/9	Zestafoni	h	1-2	*Sadagashvili*
/9	Lokomotivi Tbilisi	a	0-1	
/9	Mglebi	h	1-3	*Nozadze*
0	Olimpi	h	1-1	*Tlashadze*
/10	Sioni	a	1-5	*Chitaia*
/10	Borjomi	h	0-0	
/11	Spartaki Tskhinvali	h	0-0	
2	Dinamo Tbilisi	a	0-5	
2	Merani	a	0-1	

08

/2	Batumi	a	0-0	
	Ameri	h	0-2	
	WIT	a	0-2	
/3	Meskheti	h	0-1	
/3	Zestafoni	a	0-5	
/3	Lokomotivi Tbilisi	h	1-1	*Shatakishvili*
	Mglebi	a	0-5	
/4	Olimpi	a	0-1	
/4	Sioni	h	0-1	
/4	Borjomi	a	2-3	*Shatakishvili, Gvetadze*
	Merani	h	2-3	*Mikadze 2*
/5	Spartaki Tskhinvali	a	0-3	*(w/o; match abandoned after 45 minutes at 0-1)*
/5	Dinamo Tbilisi	h	0-2	

Name	Nat	Pos	Aps	(s)	Gls
Giorgi ABRAMISHVILI		M	4	(1)	
Giorgi BALASHVILI		D	21		
Lasha BALIASHVILI		D	22	(1)	
Jaba BERIANIDZE		D	7		
David CHERKEZISHVILI		A		(3)	
Beka CHITAIA		A	12	(3)	3
Mikheil GAGNIDZE		M	2	(1)	
Giorgi GIORGOBIANI		A	1	(1)	
Giorgi GOBEJISHVILI		D	1		
Irakli GVETADZE		D	11	(1)	1
Giorgi ICHKITI		A	4	(7)	
Tamaz ILURIDZE		G	10	(1)	
Besik KECHKHUASHVILI		G	10	(1)	
David KHANISHVILI		D	13		
Mikheil KIRKITADZE		M		(1)	
Irakli KOBAKHIDZE		D	1		
Ioseb KURTANIDZE		M	1	(3)	
Giorgi KVITAISHVILI		M		(1)	
Zaza LATSABIDZE		D	21		
Ilia LOMIDZE		M	7	(6)	
Aleksandre MARIAMIDZE		M		(1)	
Giorgi MASURASHVILI		D	4		
Giorgi MIKADZE		A	7		2
Nodar NOZADZE		M	19	(3)	1
Lasha RATIANI		D	7		
Lasha REKHVIASHVILI		M	1	(3)	
Nikoloz SADAGASHVILI		M	18	(2)	2
Albert SAKVARELIDZE		M	1	(3)	
Guram SAMADASHVILI		M	12	(1)	
Kristefore SHATAKISHVILI		A	15	(4)	2
Zurab SHERMADINI		M	1	(4)	
Saba SULTANISHVILI		M	18	(2)	
David TLASHADZE		M	17	(5)	1
Avtandil TSERTSVADZE		G	6		
Giorgi TSINAMDZGVRISHVILI		M	5	(2)	
Lasha TURMANIDZE		M		(5)	
Dickson Chukwu UWADIEGWU	NGA	A	2	(1)	
Giorgi VARDOSANIDZE		M	5	(4)	

FC DINAMO BATUMI

Coach - Amiran Gogitidze; (22/9/07) (Soso Nasuashvili); (19/10/07) Avtandil Kunchulia

Founded - 1923

MAJOR HONOURS: Georgian Cup - (1) 1998.

2007

11/8	Dila	a	0-1	
18/8	Olimpi	h	0-1	
24/8	Sioni	a	0-1	
1/9	Borjomi	h	1-1	*Modebadze*
15/9	Merani	a	1-2	*Galogre*
22/9	Spartaki Tskhinvali	h	0-1	
29/9	Dinamo Tbilisi	a	0-7	
6/10	Mglebi	a	0-1	
19/10	Ameri	h	0-3	
28/10	WIT	a	1-4	*Darchidze*
24/11	Zestafoni	a	0-4	
1/12	Lokomotivi Tbilisi	h	1-0	*Batsikadze*
5/12	Meskheti	h	1-2	*Makharadze K.*

2008

23/2	Dila	h	0-0	
2/3	Olimpi	a	0-1	
7/3	Sioni	h	1-1	*Kebadze (p)*
15/3	Borjomi	a	2-1	*Chkhetiani 2*
21/3	Merani	h	0-2	
30/3	Spartaki Tskhinvali	a	1-0	*Okruashvili*
4/4	Dinamo Tbilisi	h	1-4	*Kakaladze*
12/4	Mglebi	h	2-0	*Kebadze 2 (2p)*
19/4	Ameri	a	1-4	*Tsanava*
25/4	WIT	h	0-3	

2/5	Meskheti	a	2-3	*Kebadze (p), Chkhetiani*
11/5	Zestafoni	h	0-0	
20/5	Lokomotivi Tbilisi	a	1-4	*Kebadze*

Name	Nat	Pos	Aps	(s)	Gls
Shota BABUNASHVILI		M	8		
Archil BAJELIDZE		D	2	(4)	
Aleksandre BATSIKADZE		M	3	(3)	1
Geno BEJANIDZE		A	19	(3)	
Demur CHAZMAVA		M		(1)	
Giorgi CHELEBADZE		A		(1)	
Giorgi CHELIDZE		A	7		
Zaza CHELIDZE		M	8		
Gaga CHKHETIANI		A	9	(1)	3
Vitali DARCHIDZE		M	12	(1)	1
Besik DEMURADZE		M	11	(5)	
David GALOGRE		D	15	(2)	1
Giorgi KAKABADZE		M		(1)	
Mikhel KAKALADZE		A	12	(2)	1
Lasha KEBADZE		A	13		5
Vasil KUNCHULIA		M	20	(1)	
Zviad KUTATELADZE		M	4	(4)	
Karen MAKARIAN		M	20	(1)	
Boris MAKHARADZE		M	2	(2)	
Kakha MAKHARADZE		D	20		1
Levan MAKHARADZE		M	6	(3)	
Shota MAMINASHVILI		G	5	(1)	
Giorgi MODEBADZE		A	8		1
Irakli NACHKEBIA		D	1		
Giorgi OKRUASHVILI		M	10	(11)	1
Archil PARTENADZE		A	2	(4)	
Zviad STURUA		G	8		
Beglar TEDORADZE		D	25		
Irakli TOTLADZE		G	13	(2)	
Irakli TSANAVA		D	16	(4)	1
Irakli TUGUSHI		M	1	(12)	
Giorgi TURMANIDZE		D	6		
Giorgi ZAKAREISHVILI		M		(1)	

FC DINAMO TBILISI

Coach - Dušan Uhrin (CZE)

Founded - 1925

MAJOR HONOURS: UEFA Cup Winners' Cup - (1) 1981; USSR League - (2) 1964, 1978; USSR Cup - (2) 1976, 1979; Georgian League - (13) 1990, 1991, 1992, 1993, 1994, 1995, 1996, 1997, 1998, 1999, 2003, 2005, 2008; Georgian Cup - (8) 1992, 1993, 1994, 1995, 1996, 1997, 2003, 2004.

2007				
11/8	Olimpi	a	2-0	*Akiremy, Khutsishvili*
18/8	Sioni	h	3-0	*Khutsishvili, Merebashvili, Akiremy*
25/8	Borjomi	a	2-1	*Merebashvili, Spasojević*
3/9	Merani	h	3-0	*Merebashvili, Spasojević, Khutsishvili*
15/9	Spartaki Tskhinvali	a	3-0	*Spasojević, og (Khachiperidze), Akiremy*
22/9	Mglebi	a	2-1	*og (Kakabadze), Khutsishvili*
29/9	Batumi	h	7-0	*Khutsishvili, Khmaladze, Spasojević, Kobakhidze 2, Akiremy 2*
6/10	Ameri	a	2-0	*Spasojević, Khutsishvili*
19/10	WIT	h	0-1	
27/10	Meskheti	a	2-0	*Spasojević, Akiremy*
24/11	Lokomotivi Tbilisi	a	2-1	*Merebashvili 2*
2/12	Dila	h	5-0	*Merebashvili 2, Khutsishvili 3*
6/12	Zestafoni	h	2-0	*Digmelashvili, Khutsishvili*
2008				
23/2	Olimpi	h	1-2	*Merebashvili*
1/3	Sioni	a	2-1	*Merebashvili, Vatsad*
7/3	Borjomi	h	4-2	*Vatsadze 2, Spasojev Khutsishvili*
15/3	Merani	a	2-0	*Odikadze, Merebashv*
22/3	Spartaki Tskhinvali	h	2-1	*Vatsadze 2*
30/3	Mglebi	h	1-0	*Merebashvili*
4/4	Batumi	a	4-1	*Khutsishvili 2, Spasojević, Khmalad*
13/4	Ameri	h	2-1	*Khutsishvili (p), Odikadze*
18/4	WIT	a	0-0	
23/4	Meskheti	h	5-1	*Akiremy 3, Spasojevi Vatsadze*
3/5	Zestafoni	a	1-0	*Vatsadze*
11/5	Lokomotivi Tbilisi	h	6-5	*Vatsadze 2, Akiremy, Khutsishvili 2, Khmaladze*
20/5	Dila	a	2-0	*Kashia G., Odikadze*

Name	Nat	Pos	Aps	(s)	Gl
Georges Edouard AKIREMY Owondo	GAB	A	20	(2)	10
David DIGMELASHVILI		M	26		1
Roman DOBEŠ	SVK	D	15	(1)	
Shota GRIGALASHVILI		M	1		
Oleg GVELESIANI		D	8	(1)	
Nikoloz JISHKARIANI		A		(1)	
Zviad KANTARIA		A	1	(1)	
Guram KASHIA		D	9	(6)	1
Shota KASHIA		D	24		
Levan KHMALADZE		M	25		3
Mikheil KHUTSISHVILI		A	23	(2)	16
Aleksandre KOBAKHIDZE		M	3	(8)	2
Miloš KRŠKO	SVK	D	22		
Giorgi LORIA		G	4		
Giorgi MEREBASHVILI		M	20	(1)	11
Giorgi NERGADZE		M	2	(3)	
David ODIKADZE		M	15	(9)	3
Didier Janvier OVONO EBANG	GAB	G	22		
Giorgi PEIKRISHVILI		M	4	(4)	
Nikoloz PIRTSKHALAVA		D	1	(9)	
Ilija SPASOJEVIĆ	MNE	A	9	(14)	9
Gulverd TOMASHVILI		D	1	(5)	
Mate VATSADZE		A	8	(5)	9
Ned ZELIC	AUS	D	23		

FC LOKOMOTIVI TBILISI

Coach - Giorgi Kiknadze

Founded - 1936

MAJOR HONOURS: Georgian Cup - (3) 2000, 2002, 2005.

2007				
10/8	Ameri	h	2-1	*Samkharadze (p), Gusharashvili*
18/8	WIT	a	0-1	
24/8	Meskheti	h	2-3	*Mikadze, Kenia*
31/8	Zestafoni	a	0-5	
14/9	Mglebi	h	0-1	
22/9	Dila	h	1-0	*Barbakadze*
29/9	Olimpi	a	0-1	
7/10	Sioni	h	1-0	*Imedadze (p)*
19/10	Borjomi	a	1-2	*Gusharashvili*
28/10	Merani	h	0-2	
24/11	Dinamo Tbilisi	h	1-2	*Gusharashvili*
1/12	Batumi	a	0-1	
5/12	Spartaki Tskhinvali	a	0-2	
2008				
24/2	Ameri	a	1-1	*Kutsurua*
1/3	WIT	h	0-1	

'	Meskheti	a	0-0	
'3	Zestafoni	h	1-1	*Aleksidze*
'3	Mglebi	a	0-0	
'3	Dila	a	1-1	*Aleksidze*
'	Olimpi	h	0-1	
'4	Sioni	a	3-0	*Aleksidze, Tskitishvili, Daraselia*
'4	Borjomi	h	1-0	*Parulava*
'4	Merani	a	1-0	*Daraselia*
'	Spartaki Tskhinvali	h	2-2	*Aleksidze 2 (1p)*
'5	Dinamo Tbilisi	a	5-6	*Samkharadze 2, Daraselia, Aleksidze 2*
'5	Batumi	h	4-1	*Aleksidze 2, Parulava, Kvakhadze*

me	Nat	Pos	Aps	(s)	Gls
rgi ALAVERDASHVILI		A	5	(7)	
kheil ALAVIDZE		G	12		
i ALEKSIDZE		A	7	(4)	9
re BAKHTADZE		A		(2)	
ga BARBAKADZE		M	12	(4)	1
nike BERIDZE		M	1		
kheil BOBOKHIDZE		A	2	(3)	
rgi BUDAGASHVILI		M	1	(5)	
vid CHAGELISHVILI		A	6	(10)	
an CHAGELISHVILI		D	5	(3)	
ad CHKHETIANI		M	10		
ali DARASELIA		M	10		3
eb GILAURI		M	4	(8)	
rgi GULORDAVA		M	19		
a GUSHARASHVILI		D	20		3
vid GVARAMADZE		G	12		
gol IMEDADZE		A	6	(4)	1
kheil JGENTI		M	3	(3)	
kle KACHAKHIDZE		M	2	(2)	
an KENIA		M	4		1
i KHOKHONISHVILI		D	8	(1)	
ga KIRKITADZE		M		(2)	
hil KOBIASHVILI		D	3		
aki KUKHILAVA		D	20		
rgi KUTSURUA		M	6	(2)	1
rgi KVAKHADZE		D	10	(4)	1
ksandre LAGADZE		M	10		
kli MALICHAVA		M	10		
nar MIGINEISHVILI		G	2		
rgi MIKADZE		A	9	(2)	1
rgi NIKOLAISHVILI		D	1		
muraz PARULAVA		D	10	(1)	2
chi POPKHADZE		D	26		
kli SAMKHARADZE		M	15	(1)	3
rgi TIKURISHVILI		M	2	(5)	
an TSKITISHVILI		M	7		1
vaz TSULADZE		M	6	(2)	

FC MERANI TBILISI

Coach - Tamaz Kostava; (5/10/07) David Ejibishvili

Founded - 2003

07				
'8	Borjomi	a	0-1	
'8	Mglebi	a	0-1	
'8	Spartaki Tskhinvali	h	0-1	
'	Dinamo Tbilisi	a	0-3	
'9	Batumi	h	2-1	*Gochashvili, Khuchua*
'9	Ameri	a	0-7	
'9	WIT	h	0-3	
0	Meskheti	a	1-2	*Kobalia*
'10	Zestafoni	h	0-1	
'10	Lokomotivi Tbilisi	a	2-0	*Tkeshelashvili, Gochashvili*
'11	Olimpi	a	0-2	
2/12	Sioni	h	1-1	*og (Okropiridze)*
6/12	Dila	h	1-0	*Gochashvili*
2008				
24/2	Borjomi	h	1-0	*Shengelia*
2/3	Mglebi	h	0-1	
7/3	Spartaki Tskhinvali	a	0-1	
15/3	Dinamo Tbilisi	h	0-2	
21/3	Batumi	a	2-0	*Shengelia (p), Tielidze*
29/3	Ameri	h	1-5	*Jangidze*
5/4	WIT	a	0-3	
12/4	Meskheti	h	0-4	
18/4	Zestafoni	a	1-6	*Tielidze*
26/4	Lokomotivi Tbilisi	h	0-1	
2/5	Dila	a	3-2	*Gochashvili 2, Saralidze*
11/5	Olimpi	h	0-1	
20/5	Sioni	a	0-5	

Name	Nat	Pos	Aps	(s)	Gls
David ABSHILAVA		D	4	(1)	
Irakli AKHALAIA		M	1		
Konstantine AVALIANI		M	1	(1)	
Zurab AVALIANI		M	4	(4)	
Giorgi ARAKISHVILI		D	2		
Irakli ARVELADZE		A	2		
Levan BAKURADZE		M	9		
Mikheil BESARASHVILI		M	9	(5)	
Irakli BURCHULADZE		A		(2)	
Giga BURJANADZE		M	2	(1)	
Lasha CHIKAIDZE		M	1		
Iago DEISADZE		M	7	(5)	
Iakob DEISADZE		A	4	(2)	
Irakli DGEBUADZE		G	2		
David GIGAURI		D	21		
Vladimer GOCHASHVILI		A	17		5
Levan GRIGALASHVILI		D	6		
Lasha JANGIDZE		D	18	(1)	1
Beka JGENTI		M	7	(3)	
Mikheil JGENTI		M	2		
David KAKULIA		M		(1)	
Anzor KALADZE		D	4	(4)	
Mindia KAVTARADZE		D	1		
Ilia KEMASHVILI		D	7	(6)	
Shalva KHUCHUA		A		(3)	1
Roman KIKALISHVILI		D	2		
Giorgi KILASONIA		M	1	(1)	
Zaza KOBAKHIDZE		M		(1)	
Akaki KOBALIA		M		(2)	1
Irakli KOBALIA		M	1		
Mikheil KOBERIDZE		M	12	(3)	
Tengiz KOBIASHVILI		D	11		
David KOKIASHVILI		M	2	(4)	
Giorgi KORIDZE		A	1		
Giorgi LOLADZE		D	19		
Vaja LOMASHVILI		D	9	(1)	
Giorgi MAKHARASHVILI		M		(1)	
Nika MAKHVILADZE		A	1		
Levan NAKASHIDZE		A	2		
Beka NOZADZE		M	7		
Giorgi PATARKALISHVILI		M	1	(1)	
Irakli PIRANISHVILI		M	2	(4)	
Teimuraz PURTUKHIA		M	6	(4)	
Kakha SAGIRASHVILI		M		(1)	
Levan SARALIDZE		D	22		1
Irakli SHENGELIA		A	8	(1)	2
Konstantine SEPIASHVILI		G	4		
David SEVASTOPULO		A	2	(1)	
Irakli SIRBILADZE		A		(1)	
Giorgi TAVBERIDZE		D	5	(1)	
Revaz TEVDORADZE		G	20		
Zurab TIELIDZE		A	4	(1)	2
Giorgi TKESHELASHVILI		A	10	(1)	1

Name	Nat	Pos	Aps	(s)	Gls
Manuchar TSIKARISHVILI		M	2	(1)	
Beka TSISKARAULI		M		(1)	
Nodar TSKVITINIDZE		A	1		

FC MESKHETI AKHALTSIKHE

Coach - Koba Tediashvili

Founded - 1936

2007				
10/8	Mglebi	h	1-0	*Chkhetiani*
18/8	Zestafoni	h	0-2	
24/8	Lokomotivi Tbilisi	a	3-2	*Kaidarashvili 2, Jvania*
2/9	Dila	h	2-0	*Kaidarashvili (p), Inasaridze*
14/9	Olimpi	a	0-0	
23/9	Sioni	h	2-2	*og (Mentesashvili), Apriamashvili*
28/9	Borjomi	a	0-2	
5/10	Merani	h	2-1	*Jvania, Inasaridze*
20/10	Spartaki Tskhinvali	a	2-0	*Inasaridze 2*
27/10	Dinamo Tbilisi	h	0-2	
24/11	Ameri	h	1-2	*Sudadze*
1/12	WIT	a	0-3	
5/12	Batumi	a	2-1	*Gongadze M., Chkhetiani*
2008				
1/3	Zestafoni	a	1-4	*Samadashvili*
8/3	Lokomotivi Tbilisi	h	0-0	
11/3	Mglebi	a	0-1	
16/3	Dila	a	1-0	*Takadze M.*
22/3	Olimpi	h	0-0	
30/3	Sioni	a	0-1	
5/4	Borjomi	h	2-0	*Inasaridze 2*
12/4	Merani	a	4-0	*Inasaridze 2 (1p), Kiknadze, Mushkudiani*
18/4	Spartaki Tskhinvali	h	0-0	
23/4	Dinamo Tbilisi	a	1-5	*Mushkudiani*
2/5	Batumi	h	3-2	*Koshkadze 2, Samadashvili*
11/5	Ameri	a	0-0	
20/5	WIT	h	2-0	*Inasaridze (p), Samadashvili*

Name	Nat	Pos	Aps	(s)	Gls
Vakhtang AKOPIAN		D	8		
Temur APRIAMASHVILI		M	3	(3)	1
Zviad CHKHEYIANI		M	13		2
Zurab DZAMSASHVILI		D	9		
Gela DZAMUNASHVILI		G	2	(1)	
Mamuka GONGADZE		A	3	(6)	1
Teimuraz GONGADZE		D	10	(1)	
Paata GVIRJISHVILI		M	24	(2)	
Hayk HAKOBYAN	ARM	M	1	(2)	
David INASARIDZE		A	18	(8)	9
Giga JVANIA		D	9	(1)	2
Aleksandre KAIDARASHVILI		A	9		3
Giorgi KEVLISHVILI		D		(6)	
Koba KHANISHVILI		M	11	(1)	
Irakli KIKNADZE		M	5	(4)	1
Zaza KOBESASHVILI		D	14	(5)	
Giorgi KOCHORISHVILI		D	1		
Aleksandre KOSHKADZE		M	12		2
Dimitri LEKISHVILI		D	24		
Levan MEREBASHVILI		D	12		
Zurab MUSHKUDIANI		A	6	(4)	2
Giorgi NADIRASHVILI		D	17		
Temur RAKVIASHVILI		D	11	(1)	
Mamuka RUSIA		A	1	(1)	
Guram SAMADASHVILI		M	2	(8)	3
Giorgi SOMKHISHVILI		G	24		
Gela SUDADZE		M	3	(12)	1
Ivane TAKADZE		M		(1)	
Mikheil TAKADZE		M	18	(5)	1
Aleksandre TELIASHVILI		M	3	(1)	
Irakli TSNOBILADZE		M		(1)	
Giorgi TURMANIDZE		M	13		

FC MGLEBI ZUGDIDI

Coach - Besik Sherozia

Founded - 2005

2007				
10/8	Meskheti	a	0-1	
17/8	Merani	h	1-0	*Chedia*
25/8	Zestafoni	a	0-2	
1/9	Spartaki Tskhinvali	h	2-0	*Gabedava, Bakarand*
14/9	Lokomotivi Tbilisi	a	1-0	*Kiria D.*
22/9	Dinamo Tbilisi	h	1-2	*Kiria D.*
28/9	Dila	a	3-1	*Chedia 2, Krasovski (p*
6/10	Batumi	h	1-0	*Chedia*
21/10	Olimpi	a	1-2	*Chedia*
27/10	Ameri	h	0-1	
24/11	WIT	h	0-3	
2/12	Borjomi	a	3-4	*Chedia, Kutalia D. 2*
6/12	Sioni	a	1-3	*Bakarandze*
2008				
2/3	Merani	a	1-0	*Kiria D.*
8/3	Zestafoni	h	0-0	
11/3	Meskheti	h	1-0	*Krasovski*
15/3	Spartaki Tskhinvali	a	0-0	
22/3	Lokomotivi Tbilisi	h	0-0	
30/3	Dinamo Tbilisi	a	0-1	
5/4	Dila	h	5-0	*Jvania, Chkadua, Janashia, Ekonia Z., Kakabadze*
12/4	Batumi	a	0-2	
19/4	Olimpi	h	0-2	
25/4	Ameri	a	0-5	
2/5	Sioni	h	1-0	*Janashia*
11/5	WIT	a	1-2	*Kiria G.*
20/5	Borjomi	h	4-2	*Kutalia D. 2, Chkadua, Janashia*

Name	Nat	Pos	Aps	(s)	Gls
Paata BAKARANDZE		A	5	(6)	2
Giorgi CHEDIA		A	9		6
Nikoloz CHITANAVA		G	1	(1)	
Mamuka CHKADUA		M	9	(6)	2
Akaki DEVADZE		G	1		
Giorgi EKONIA		M	2	(7)	
Zurab EKONIA		D	21		1
Giorgi GABEDAVA		M	4	(8)	1
Manuchar IVARDAVA		G	21	(1)	
Zamir JANASHIA		A	10	(4)	3
Vladimer JOJUA		M	10		
Ilia JISHKARIANI		M		(3)	
Giga JVANIA		D	12		1
Murtaz KAKABADZE		D	22		1
Varlam KALDANI		G	3		
David KIRIA		M	23	(1)	3
Giorgi KIRIA		M	4	(2)	1
Leri KHOKHONISHVILI		D	8		
Gela KHUBUA		M	11		
Nika KHUKHIA		M	6	(3)	
Giorgi KRASOVSKI		M	20		2
Papuna KOMETIANI		D	4	(8)	
Aleksandre KUCHUKHIDZE		M		(2)	
David KUTALIA		A	5	(4)	4
Levan KUTALIA		M	4	(3)	
Vladimer LIPARTIA		M		(6)	
Nodar MACHAVARIANI		D	24		
David NARSIA		D	3	(1)	

imuraz PARULAVA		D	8		
van TSURTSUMIA		M	15	(5)	
van VARTAGAVA		M	21		

FC OLIMPI RUSTAVI

Coach - Varlam Kilasonia; (11/8/07) (Anatoliy Piskovets (UKR)); (16/3/08) Khvicha Kasrashvili

Founded - 1991

MAJOR HONOURS: Georgian League - (1) 2007.

007				
/8	Dinamo Tbilisi	h	0-2	
/8	Batumi	a	1-0	*Koshkadze*
/8	Ameri	h	1-0	*Jikia*
9	WIT	a	1-2	*Jikia*
/9	Meskheti	h	0-0	
/9	Zestafoni	a	1-2	*Koshkadze*
/9	Lokomotivi Tbilisi	h	1-0	*Jikia*
10	Dila	a	1-1	*Jikia*
/10	Mglebi	h	2-1	*Dvalishvili, Jikia*
/10	Sioni	h	1-0	*og (Sturua)*
/11	Merani	h	2-0	*Devdariani, Kakhelishvili*
12	Spartaki Tskhinvali	a	2-0	*Orbeladze, Jikia*
12	Borjomi	a	0-0	
008				
/2	Dinamo Tbilisi	a	2-1	*Devdariani, Omelianov*
3	Batumi	h	1-0	*Devdariani*
3	Ameri	a	1-2	*Omelianov*
/3	WIT	h	0-1	
/3	Meskheti	a	0-0	
/3	Zestafoni	h	0-3	
4	Lokomotivi Tbilisi	a	1-0	*og (Parulava)*
/4	Dila	h	1-0	*Makhviladze (p)*
/4	Mglebi	a	2-0	*Mgeladze, Devdariani*
/4	Sioni	a	2-1	*Getsadze, Kakhelishvili*
5	Borjomi	h	1-0	*Makhviladze (p)*
/5	Merani	a	1-0	*Gabedava*
/5	Spartaki Tskhinvali	h	1-0	*Imedadze*

ame	Nat	Pos	Aps	(s)	Gls
nest AKOUASSAGA	GAB	D	9	(1)	
ikheil ALAVIDZE		G	4		
imuraz APRIAMASHVILI		M		(1)	
avid CHICHVEISHVILI		D	2		
orgi CHIVADZE		M	1	(1)	
avid DEVDARIANI		A	18	(2)	4
ba DVALI		A		(2)	
adimer DVALISHVILI		A	10	(2)	1
orgi GABEDAVA		M	7	(3)	1
vaz GETSADZE		M	20		1
orgi IASHVILI		D		(2)	
igol IMEDADZE		A	1	(6)	1
zo JIKIA		A	13		6
adimer JOJUA		M	9	(4)	
orgi KAKHELISHVILI		A	19	(3)	2
sha KEBADZE		M	9	(3)	
ela KHUBUA		M	10	(1)	
ikheil KORSANTIA		M	1	(2)	
nton KOVALEVSKIY	UKR	M	3	(1)	
eksandre KOSHKADZE		M	2	(10)	2
koloz KRUASHVILI		D	1		
orgi LOMAIA		G	5	(1)	
ikheil MAKHVILADZE		D	24		2
haudry Gildas MASSOUANGA	CGO	D	4	(2)	
irza MERLANI		G	10		
ikheil MESKHI		M		(2)	
viad METREVELI		M		(1)	
ika MGELADZE		M	10	(5)	1
a MODEBADZE		M		(2)	
iorgi NAVALOVSKI		D	13		
Olexandr OMELIANOV	UKR	M	12	(1)	2
Sergo ORBELADZE		D	24	(1)	1
Giorgi REKHVIASHVILI		M	4	(2)	
Archil SEBISKVERADZE		M	6	(3)	
Beka SHEKRILADZE		G	7		
Levan SILAGADZE		D	21	(1)	
Nika STEPANISHVILI		M	4	(4)	
Vladan ZIVKOVIĆ	SRB	M	3	(4)	

FC SIONI BOLNISI

Coach - Nodar Akobia; (11/8/07) Giorgi Kipshidze

Founded - 1936

MAJOR HONOURS: Georgian League - (1) 2006.

2007				
11/8	Spartaki Tskhinvali	h	1-1	*Kardava*
18/8	Dinamo Tbilisi	a	0-3	
24/8	Batumi	h	1-0	*Tchassem*
2/9	Ameri	a	0-2	
14/9	WIT	h	3-1	*Sanikidze (p), Rakviashvili, Tchassem*
23/9	Meskheti	a	2-2	*Kardava 2*
28/9	Zestafoni	h	0-2	
7/10	Lokomotivi Tbilisi	a	0-1	
19/10	Dila	h	5-1	*Tchassem, Bajelidze, Kardava, Kutateladze 2*
28/10	Olimpi	a	0-1	
24/11	Borjomi	h	0-1	
2/12	Merani	a	1-1	*Tchassem*
6/12	Mglebi	h	3-1	*Tchassem, Kardava, og (Khukhia)*
2008				
26/2	Spartaki Tskhinvali	a	2-0	*Boyomo, Kvitaishvili*
1/3	Dinamo Tbilisi	h	1-2	*Tchassem*
7/3	Batumi	a	1-1	*Tchassem*
16/3	Ameri	h	0-0	
21/3	WIT	a	0-4	
30/3	Meskheti	h	1-0	*Avaliani*
4/4	Zestafoni	a	1-3	*Bajelidze*
12/4	Lokomotivi Tbilisi	h	0-3	
18/4	Dila	a	1-0	*Jikia*
25/4	Olimpi	h	1-2	*Avaliani*
2/5	Mglebi	a	0-1	
11/5	Borjomi	a	5-2	*Avaliani, Svanidze, Shavgulidze, Jikia, og (Lomidze)*
20/5	Merani	h	5-0	*Tchassem, Sanikidze 2 (1p), Jikia, Avaliani*

Name	Nat	Pos	Aps	(s)	Gls
Zurab AVALIANI		M	7	(4)	4
Levan BAJELIDZE		M	22	(2)	2
Mindia BOBGIASHVILI		G	11		
Fridolin BOYOMO	CMR	D	20	(2)	1
Giorgi CHELIDZE		M	3	(5)	
Zaza CHELIDZE		M	4	(5)	
Valierian GAGUA		M	2	(3)	
Giga IASHVILI		G	8		
Shota JIKIA		A	8	(3)	3
Besik KARDAVA		A	7	(6)	5
Giorgi KETASHVILI		D		(2)	
Mikheil KOBAURI		D	10		
Mikheil KOSTAVA		M		(1)	
Murman KURASPEDIANI		D	20	(2)	
Zviad KUTATELADZE		M	1	(6)	2
Giorgi KUTSURUA		M	5	(3)	
Giorgi KVITAISHVILI		M	11	(7)	1
Manuchar KVITSIANI		M		(4)	
Mamuka MENTESASHVILI		D	2	(3)	
Nika NADIRADZE		M	11	(1)	
David NAKANI		M	1	(1)	

Name	Nat	Pos	Aps	(s)	Gls
Otar NAKOPIA		M		(1)	
Archil NOZADZE		M	1		
Beka NOZADZE		M	10		
Giorgi OKROPIRIDZE		M	19	(2)	
Temur RAKVIASHVILI		D	10	(1)	1
Levan SANIKIDZE		A	23		3
Levan SHAVGULIDZE		M	11	(1)	1
Zviad STURUA		G	7		
David SVANIDZE		D	19		1
Giorgi TAVBERIDZE		D	3		
Eric Romeo TCHASSEM	CMR	A	22	(1)	8
Giorgi TUKHASHVILI		M		(1)	
Lasha VASHAKIDZE		M	8	(5)	

FC SPARTAKI TSKHINVALI

Coach - Koba Jorjikashvili

Founded - 2007

Date	Opponent		Score	Scorers
2007				
11/8	Sioni	a	1-1	*Tarkhnishvili*
17/8	Borjomi	h	0-0	
24/8	Merani	a	1-0	*Medoev (p)*
1/9	Mglebi	a	0-2	
15/9	Dinamo Tbilisi	h	0-3	
22/9	Batumi	a	1-0	*Janelidze*
29/9	Ameri	h	0-1	
7/10	WIT	a	0-1	
20/10	Meskheti	h	0-2	
27/10	Zestafoni	a	0-2	
24/11	Dila	a	0-0	
1/12	Olimpi	h	0-2	
5/12	Lokomotivi Tbilisi	h	2-0	*Chirikashvili (p), Janelidze*
2008				
26/2	Sioni	h	0-2	
1/3	Borjomi	a	1-2	*Dzaria*
7/3	Merani	h	1-0	*Tkeshelashvili*
15/3	Mglebi	h	0-0	
22/3	Dinamo Tbilisi	a	1-2	*Gongadze*
30/3	Batumi	h	0-1	
4/4	Ameri	a	0-2	
12/4	WIT	h	0-0	
18/4	Meskheti	a	0-0	
26/4	Zestafoni	h	2-2	*Khidasheli 2*
2/5	Lokomotivi Tbilisi	a	2-2	*Khidasheli, Dzaria*
11/5	Dila	h	3-0	*(w/o; match abandoned after 45 minutes at 1-0 Kvaratskhelia)*
20/5	Olimpi	a	0-1	

Name	Nat	Pos	Aps	(s)	Gls
Konstantine AVALIANI		M	4	(3)	
Avtandil BAGASHVILI		M	1		
Zurab BAKHTURIDZE		D	18	(3)	
Irakli CHIRIKASHVILI		M	11		1
Lado DATUNASHVILI		M	6	(2)	
Giorgi DARBAIDZE		M	4	(6)	
Irakli DZARIA		A	21	(1)	2
Nukri GOGOKHIA		M	20	(1)	
David GOGOLADZE		A	1	(2)	
Mamuka GONGADZE		A	8	(3)	1
Giorgi IVANASHVILI		M	2	(4)	
David JANELIDZE		A	8	(4)	2
Nikoloz KAVTARADZE		M		(2)	
Revaz KEMOKLIDZE		D	22		
Giorgi KETASHVILI		D	3	(1)	
Besik KHACHIPERADZE		D	22		
Giorgi KHIDESHELI		A	23		3
Zurab KHIZANISHVILI		M	1	(2)	
Besarion KODALAEV		G	14		
Vaja KORIDZE		D	5		
Akaki KUPREISHVILI		D	12	(5)	
Vakhtang KVARATSKHELIA		A	5	(7)	1
Maksime KVILITAIA		G	12		
Lasha MAMUKASHVILI		D	25		
Zaza MEDOEV		A	1	(11)	1
Dimitri PARAMONOV		M	5		
Alan TADTAEV		M		(4)	
Tornike TARKHNISHVILI		D	21		1
Giorgi TEKTUMANIDZE		M	1	(7)	
Giorgi TKESHELASHVILI		A	8	(3)	1
Kakhaber TSKVITAIA		D	1	(1)	
Kakhaber ZAMTARADZE		M	1	(1)	

FC WIT GEORGIA

Coach - Nestor Mumladze

Founded - 1968

MAJOR HONOURS: Georgian League - (1) 2004.

Date	Opponent		Score	Scorers
2007				
10/8	Zestafoni	a	1-1	*Sakhokia*
18/8	Lokomotivi Tbilisi	h	1-0	*Klimiashvili*
24/8	Dila	a	1-0	*Lomaia*
1/9	Olimpi	h	2-1	*Gelashvili, Sakhokia*
14/9	Sioni	a	1-3	*Gelashvili*
23/9	Borjomi	h	1-2	*Gelashvili*
28/9	Merani	a	3-0	*Melkadze, Datunashvi G., Gelashvili*
7/10	Spartaki Tskhinvali	h	1-0	*Razmadze (p)*
19/10	Dinamo Tbilisi	a	1-0	*Razmadze (p)*
28/10	Batumi	h	4-1	*Gelashvili, Sakhokia, Klimiashvili, Datunashvili G.*
24/11	Mglebi	a	3-0	*Gelashvili 2, Melkadze*
1/12	Meskheti	h	3-0	*Datunashvili G., Gelashvili, Guchashvili*
5/12	Ameri	a	3-0	*(w/o; match abandoned after 55 minutes at 1-0 Melkadze (p))*
2008				
24/2	Zestafoni	h	2-1	*Bechvaia, Melkadze*
1/3	Lokomotivi Tbilisi	a	1-0	*Razmadze*
7/3	Dila	h	2-0	*Datunaishvili G., Lipartia*
16/3	Olimpi	a	1-0	*Datunaishvili P.*
21/3	Sioni	h	4-0	*Klimiashvili, Sakhokia 2, Melkadze*
29/3	Borjomi	a	2-1	*Datunaishvili G., Beriashvili*
5/4	Merani	h	3-0	*Bechvaia, Datunaishvili P., Lipartia*
12/4	Spartaki Tskhinvali	a	0-0	
18/4	Dinamo Tbilisi	h	0-0	
25/4	Batumi	a	3-0	*Bechvaia 2, Kvelashvili*
3/5	Ameri	h	0-1	
11/5	Mglebi	h	2-1	*Lipartia, Sakhokia*
20/5	Meskheti	a	0-2	

Name	Nat	Pos	Aps	(s)	Gls
Guram ADAMADZE		D	1		
Giga BECHVAIA		D	19	(2)	4
Grigol BEDIASHVILI		G	25		
Giorgi BERIASHVILI		A	3	(16)	1
Giorgi DATUNAISHVILI		M	24	(1)	5
Pavle DATUNAISHVILI		M	21	(2)	2
Nikoloz GELASHVILI		A	13		8
Vasil GUCHASHVILI		A	11	(12)	1
Revaz INJGIA		M	3	(8)	
Giorgi JANELIDZE		M		(1)	
Lahsa JAPARIDZE		D	17	(1)	
Aleksi KAISHAURI		D	6	(1)	

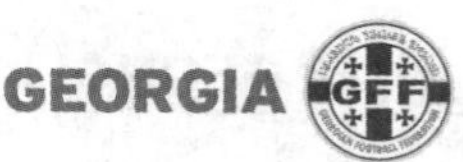

akli KLIMIASHVILI		M	22	(2)	3
iorgi KVAGINADZE		M	1	(3)	
leksandre KVAKHADZE		D	24		
miran KVELASHVILI		M	3	(3)	1
ba LIPARTIA		M	2	(11)	3
avid LOMAIA		D	23		1
avid MAISASHVILI		M	1	(1)	
iorgi MELKADZE		M	19	(5)	5
rdalion MIKABERIDZE		G	1	(1)	
iorgi PIRVELI		D	1		
uka RAZMADZE		M	23		3
aza SAKHOKIA		A	23	(2)	6
achana TSKHADADZE		A		(2)	

FC ZESTAFONI

Coach - Temur Makharadze

Founded - 1936

MAJOR HONOURS: Georgian Cup - (1) 2008.

007				
0/8	WIT	h	1-1	*Vieira*
3/8	Meskheti	a	2-0	*Vieira, Pipia*
5/8	Mglebi	h	2-0	*Ionanidze 2*
1/8	Lokomotivi Tbilisi	h	5-0	*Chelidze G. Nod., Gotsiridze, Ionanidze, Oniani, Vieira*
4/9	Dila	a	2-1	*Chelidze G. Nod. 2*
1/9	Olimpi	h	2-1	*Pipia 2*
3/9	Sioni	a	2-0	*Sajaia (p), Chelidze G. Nod.*
'10	Borjomi	h	1-0	*Chelidze G. Nod*
1/10	Merani	a	1-0	*Ionanidze*
3/10	Spartaki Tskhinvali	h	2-0	*Chelidze G. Nod, Oniani*
4/11	Batumi	h	4-0	*Chelidze G. Nod, Jônatas, Pipia, Ionanidze*
'12	Ameri	a	2-1	*Chelidze G. Nod. (p), Jônatas*
'12	Dinamo Tbilisi	a	0-2	
008				
4/2	WIT	a	1-2	*Bito'o*
'3	Meskheti	h	4-1	*Bito'o, Ionanidze 3*
'3	Mglebi	a	0-0	
6/3	Lokomotivi Tbilisi	a	1-1	*Vieira*
1/3	Dila	h	5-0	*Vieira 3, Kvaskhvadze N. 2*
0/3	Olimpi	a	3-0	*Vieira 2, Gotsiridze*
'4	Sioni	h	3-1	*Vieira (p), Bito'o, Ionanidze*
3/4	Borjomi	a	2-0	*Kvaskhvadze N., Kessany*
8/4	Merani	h	6-1	*Kvaskhvadze N., Gotsiridze 3, Kessany, Vieira*
6/4	Spartaki Tskhinvali	a	2-2	*Kessany, Gelashvili*
'5	Dinamo Tbilisi	h	0-1	
1/5	Batumi	a	0-0	
0/5	Ameri	h	3-1	*Vieira, Gelashvili, Kvaskhvadze N.*

ame	Nat	Pos	Aps	(s)	Gls
rnest AKOUASSAGA	GAB	D	6		
leksi BENASHVILI		M	2	(5)	
tienne BITO'O	GAB	A	10	(9)	3
rigol CHANTURIA		G	18		
iorgi Nod. CHELIDZE		A	10	(1)	8
iorgi Nug. CHELIDZE		M	3	(1)	
aga CHKHETIANI		A	3		
akha CHKHETIANI		M	12		
urtaz DAUSHVILI		M	7	(3)	
DSON Oliveira dos Santos	BRA	D	1	(1)	
oris GELACHEISHVILI		M		(1)	
Nikoloz GELASHVILI		A	3	(3)	2
Shalva GONGADZE		D	8	(6)	
Beka GOTSIRIDZE		A	18	(2)	5
Zurab IONANIDZE		A	1	19	9
David JANELIDZE		M		(1)	
JÔNATAS de Oliveira Torres	BRA	M	12	(2)	2
Paul Ulrich KESSANY	GAB	M	21		3
Giorgi KHIDESHELI		D	7	(8)	
Giorgi KHUMARASHVILI		M		(1)	
Nikoloz KVASKHVADZE		M	15	(2)	5
Roin KVASKHVADZE		G	8	(1)	
Ucha LOBJANIDZE		D	20		
Roin ONIANI		M	25		2
Gogi PIPIA		A	9	(3)	4
Edik SAJAIA		D	22		1
Lasha SATSERADZE		M		(2)	
Sevasti TODUA		D	25	(1)	
Gilvan Gomes VIEIRA	BRA	M	20	(1)	12

PROMOTED CLUB

FC GAGRA

Coach – Giorgi Chiabrishvili

Founded - 2004

SECOND LEVEL FINAL TABLES 2007/08

East		Pld	W	D	L	F	A	Pts
1	FC Gagra	27	16	6	5	59	36	54
2	FC Dinamo-2 Tbilisi	27	14	7	6	41	24	49
3	FC WIT Georgia-2	27	14	6	7	41	21	48
4	FC Meshakre Agara	27	13	9	5	34	22	48
5	FC Chikhura Sachkhere	27	12	7	8	40	37	43
6	FC Olimpi-2 Rustavi	27	9	8	10	35	41	35
7	FC Kakheti	27	10	4	13	38	41	34
8	FC Ameri-2 Tbilisi	27	9	2	16	42	44	29
9	FC Olimpiki Tbilisi	27	7	4	16	38	52	25
10	FC ND-Merani-2 Tbilisi	27	1	7	19	20	70	10

West		Pld	W	D	L	F	A	Pts
1	FC Magaroeli Chiatura	27	21	4	2	56	17	67
2	FC Meshakhte Tkibuli	27	14	2	11	39	41	44
3	FC Merani Martvili	27	13	5	9	36	25	44
4	FC Zestafoni-2	27	12	4	11	39	28	40
5	FC Kolkheti Poti	27	11	7	9	36	33	40
6	FC Torpedo Kutaisi	27	11	6	10	37	31	39
7	FC Kolkheti Khobi	27	10	8	9	35	27	38
8	FC Samtredia	27	9	5	13	35	50	32
9	FC Universiteti Kutaisi	27	9	3	15	24	29	30
10	FC Fazisi Racha	27	2	2	23	17	73	8

PROMOTION/RELEGATION PLAY-OFF

(18/5/08)

Gagra 2, Magaroeli 2 (aet; 1-4 on pens)

(24/5/08)

Spartaki 1, Gagra 0

N.B. FC Magaroeli Chiatura did not meet licensing requirements for Umaglesi Liga; FC Gagra promoted instead.

GEORGIA

DOMESTIC CUP 2007/08

SAKARTVELOS TASI

FIRST ROUND

(4/8/07 & 27/8/07)
WIT v Agara 1-0; 2-1 *(3-1)*
Sioni v Magaroeli 0-1; 2-5 *(2-6)*
Dila v Zooveti 4-0; 1-0 *(5-0)*
Lokomotivi Tbilisi v Olimpiki 1-0; 2-1 *(3-1)*
Meskheti v Skuri 10-0; 0-0 *(10-0)*

(4/8/07 & 29/8/07)
Samtredia v Mglebi 0-2; 0-3 *(0-5)*

(5/8/07 & 27/8/07)
Merani Tbilisi v Chikhura 1-0; 2-0 *(3-0)*
Spartaki Tskhinvali v Gagra 0-2; 2-0 *aet (4-2 on pens)*
Borjomi v Merani Martvili 4-0; 2-2 *(6-2)*
Batumi v Universiteti Kutaisi 3-0; 0-1 *(3-1)*

(5/8/07 & 29/8/07)
Kakheti v Dusheti 3-2; 0-0 *(3-2)*

(29/8/07 & 5/9/07)
Torpedo Kutaisi v Kolkheti Poti 0-0; 2-1 *(2-1)*

SECOND ROUND

GROUP 1

(18/9/07 & 1/11/07)
Ameri v Torpedo Kutaisi 6-1; 3-0
Meskheti v Spartaki Tskhinvali 1-0; 0-1

(2/10/07 & 5/11/07)
Ameri v Meskheti 4-0; 2-1

(3/10/07 & 5/11/07)
Torpedo Kutaisi v Spartaki Tskhinvali 0-2; 0-4

(23/10/07 & 27/11/07)
Spartaki Tskhinvali v Ameri 2-1; 0-2

(24/10/07 & 27/11/07)
Meskheti v Torpedo Kutaisi 4-0; 1-0

1. Ameri 15pts; 2. Spartaki Tskhinvali 12pts; 3. Meskheti 9pts; 4. Torpedo Kutaisi 0pts.

GROUP 2

(18/9/07 & 1/11/07)
WIT v Lokomotivi Tbilisi 3-0; 4-0

(26/9/07 & 1/11/07)
Dinamo Tbilisi v Magaroeli 2-0; 0-0

(2/10/07 & 5/11/07)
Dinamo Tbilisi v WIT 3-2; 2-3

(3/10/07 & 5/11/07)
Lokomotivi Tbilisi v Magaroeli 0-1; 0-3

(24/10/07 & 27/11/07)
WIT v Magaroeli 0-1; 1-1
Lokomotivi Tbilisi v Dinamo Tbilisi 1-2; 2-7

1. Dinamo Tbilisi 13pts; 2. Magaroeli 11pts; 3. WIT 10pts; 4. Lokomotivi Tbilisi 0pts.

GROUP 3

(18/9/07 & 1/11/07)
Olimpi v Merani Tbilisi 2-0; 0-0

(18/9/07 & 17/11/07)
Borjomi v Batumi 2-0; 1-2

(2/10/07 & 5/11/07)
Merani Tbilisi v Batumi 0-1; 0-0
Olimpi v Borjomi 3-1; 1-2

(24/10/07 & 27/11/07)
Borjomi v Merani Tbilisi 1-0; 2-1
Batumi v Olimpi 0-1; 0-1

1. Borjomi 12pts; 2. Olimpi 10pts; 3. Batumi 7pts; 4. Merani 5pts.

GROUP 4

(18/9/07 & 31/10/07)
Mglebi v Dila 1-1; 0-1

(18/9/07 & 1/11/07)
Zestafoni v Kakheti 4-0; 2-0

(2/10/07 & 4/11/07)
Kakheti v Dila 1-3; 0-4

(2/10/07 & 5/11/07)
Zestafoni v Mglebi 6-3; 0-2

(24/10/07 & 27/11/07)
Dila v Zestafoni 1-1; 0-3

(25/10/07 & 27/11/07)
Mglebi v Kakheti 3-1; 2-1

1. Zestafoni 13pts; 2. Dila 11pts; 3. Mglebi 10pts; 4. Kakheti 0pts.

QUARTER-FINALS

(17/2/08 & 11/3/08)
Dila 3 *(Tsinamdzgvrishvili 23, Baliashvili 38, Shatakishvili 85)*, Borjomi [illegible] *(Tediashvili 83, Chirikashvili 90)*
Borjomi 3 *(Dering 5, Peikrishvili 56, Chirikashvili 62)*, Dila 1 *(Sadagashvili 39,*
(Borjomi 5-4)

(17/2/08 & 12/3/08)
Olimpi 0, Zestafoni 1 (Gotsiridze 85)
Zestafoni 1 (Ionanidze 57p), Olimpi 0
(Zestafoni 2-0)

(18/2/08 & 11/3/08)
Spartaki Tskhinvali 0, Dinamo Tbilisi 0
Dinamo Tbilisi 2 *(Krško 59, Khmaladze 76)*, Spartaki Tskhinvali 1 *(Gongadze 29)*
(Dinamo Tbilisi 2-1)

(19/2/08 & 12/3/08)
Magaroeli 1 *(Mdivnishvili 82)*, Ameri 2 *(Dobrovolski 65, Dekanosidze 81)*
Ameri 4 *(Davitashvili 57, Shalamberidze 63, Gotsiridze 73, Kakashvili 89)*, Magaroeli 0
(Ameri 6-1)

SEMI-FINALS

(8/4/08 & 7/5/08)
Dinamo Tbilisi 1 *(Vatsadze 65)*, Zestafoni 1 *(Gotsiridze 51)*
Zestafoni 1 *(Oniani 62)*, Dinamo Tbilisi 0
(Zestafoni 2-1)

(9/4/08 & 7/5/08)
Ameri 4 *(Chikviladze 13, Gotsiridze 52, Memarnishvili 73, Elbakidze 90)*, Borjomi 1 *(Chkhetiani 83)*
Borjomi 1 *(Megreladze 13)*, Ameri 1 *(Dolidze 7)*
(Ameri 5-2)

FINAL

(16/5/08)
Boris Paichadze National Stadium, Tbilisi
FC ZESTAFONI 2 *(Oniani 57, Gotsiridze 62)*
FC AMERI TBILISI 1 *(Tatanashvili 90)*
Referee – *Paniashvili*
ZESTAFONI – *Kvaskhvadze R., Akouassaga, Lobjanidze, Khidesheli, Todua, Kessany, Sajaia, Kvaskhvadze N. (Daushvili 72), Oniani, Gotsiridze (Gongadze 81), Vieira (Ionanidze 85).*
AMERI – *Nadirashvili, Memarnishvili, Elbakidze (Tatanashvili 65), Chikviladze, Davitnidze, Dolidze (Chimakadze 83), Dobrovolski, Didava, Shalamberidze (Alavidze 61), Dekanosidze, Gotsiridze.*

Favourites give it their best shot

ermany went into UEFA EURO 2008™ as the tournament favourites. It was a burden they were happy to bear. They were by no means the lassiest team on view, but they did what so many ierman teams of the past had managed, and muscled heir way through to the final. Spain would prove too trong for them in Vienna, but Joachim Löw's side efused to concede defeat to superior opponents, and : was a credit to their gallantry and endeavour that hey kept the destiny of the Henri Delaunay trophy indecided right up to the final whistle.

lready beaten 2-1 by Croatia in the group stage, iermany could have no complaints about finishing unners-up. Indeed, they had been second best for nuch of their semi-final against a depleted Turkey – n encounter many observers had predicted Germany vould win with ease. As it turned out, they had to rely n a last-minute goal – a superb effort by full-back hilipp Lahm – to book their place in the ournament's showpiece at the Ernst-Happel-Stadion.

Ruthless finishing

lthough they drew a blank against Spain, it was the eam's ability to put away their chances that took hem into a sixth UEFA European Championship final. hey had 24 shots on target in their six games – a elatively meagre tally – but from that they produced en goals, an extraordinary conversion rate that ingled them out as the most ruthless finishers at the ournament.

laving finished third, on home soil, at the 2006 FIFA Vorld Cup, it would not be unreasonable to suggest hat coming second at UEFA EURO 2008™ represented a positive step forward – and a feather in the cap of coach Löw, promoted to the role after previously vorking as assistant to Jürgen Klinsmann. If there was one technical area in which Löw deserved particular credit, it was for his work on the team's set-pieces. Free-kicks produced three of Germany's goals, and several others were sourced from wide areas, especially the left flank, where full-back Lahm and three-goal striker-turned-midfielder Lukas Podolski were especially productive.

Germany's defensive shortcomings were exposed by Croatia, Portugal and Turkey, each of whom put two goals past them, but the central unit of veteran goalkeeper Jens Lehmann and defensive pillars Per Mertesacker and Christoph Metzelder did well to stem the Spanish tide and concede just one goal in the final. With two goals apiece, Miroslav Klose, Bastian Schweinsteiger and captain Michael Ballack could also claim to have made notable contributions to the tournament.

Ballack, in particular, proved once again that he is one of the world's great 'tournament players'. Having also lost in the final of the UEFA Champions League a few weeks earlier, the desolation on his face after the

Michael Ballack re-affirmed his major tournament credentials at UEFA EURO 2008™

defeat to Spain, for which he had been an injury doubt until just before kick-off, was wholly understandable. He would not have received much solace from being selected for the official Team of the Tournament – alongside two other Germans, Lahm and Podolski – but his excellent form throughout the month was an impressive retort to those who had written off the 31-year-old as a has-been after a season and a half of struggle at Chelsea FC.

Having failed so miserably at the previous two UEFA European Championships – the opening 2-0 win over Poland in Klagenfurt was the Nationalmannschaft's first victory at the event since the Euro '96 final – Germany are now able to go into a World Cup qualifying campaign on the front foot for the first time in over a decade. It is hardly tempting fate to suggest that a country which has never failed to qualify for a major tournament will be present in South Africa in 2010, but with a vibrant Russia in their qualifying group, Löw and his players can afford no complacency. Most of those who featured at UEFA EURO 2008™ will still be along for the World Cup ride, although it remains to be seen how long Lehmann, aged 38, can keep going, especially with uncapped young pretenders such as René Adler and Manuel Neuer straining at the leash.

Crowd-pulling Bundesliga

The German Bundesliga may be lacking in glamour and pulling power these days compared to the mighty Premier League in England, La Liga in Spain and Serie A in Italy, but it is still as good as any for entertainment and excitement, which is why it tops the attendance figure tables. With average gates in 2007/08 of 39,444, the Bundesliga was not only the best supported football league in Europe but also the third best of any worldwide professional sports league – behind America's National Football League (NFL) and the Australian Rules Football League (AFL). Ten of its 18 clubs attracted over 40,000 spectators per game.

BV Borussia Dortmund, as usual, topped the rankings with 72,510, but it was FC Bayern München, second with 69,000, who filled their stadium without fail every other weekend – no surprise considering the quality of the team's football during a season in which they won the League and Cup double for the fourth time in seven years.

Bayern responded to the humiliation of finishing

New signings Luca Toni (left) and Fr
Ribéry raised the bar for Ba

fourth in 2006/07, and thus failing to qualify for the UEFA Champions League for the first time in 12 seasons, by splashing the cash on three high-profile new signings – French wing wizard Franck Ribéry, Italian centre-forward Luca Toni and German striker Klose. All three would justify the outlay, especially Ribéry and Toni, who each enjoyed stunning debut campaigns in Germany. The Frenchman's skill and invention, not to mention his quirky looks and character, made him the league's great entertainer, while the big Italian simply carried on where he had left off at ACF Fiorentina, scoring goals galore. He ended the season as the Bundesliga's top marksman, with 24, added another ten in the UEFA Cup, and was also on target twice in the German Cup final as Bayern overcame Dortmund 2-1 after extra time in Berlin.

League Cup winners also (they beat FC Schalke 04 1-0 in the final of the pre-season event), Bayern missed out on only one prize – the UEFA Cup. Highly fancied to win it for the second time, they came extremely close, but after a miraculous late comeback in extra time away to Getafe CF in the quarter-final, they were shot down in flames in the semi-final by a masterful performance from FC Zenit St. Petersburg, going down 4-0 in Russia after a 1-1 draw at home in the Allianz Arena.

: was unusual for Bayern to be absent from the UEFA :hampions League, but their UEFA Cup run eclipsed nything that Germany's three representatives could nanage in the main event. Reigning Bundesliga hampions VfB Stuttgart lost five of their six matches nd finished bottom of their group. Werder Bremen ould only finish third in their section and lasted two ounds of the UEFA Cup. Schalke fared best, reaching he quarter-finals after a Neuer-inspired penalty hoot-out win over FC Porto, but their inability to core in seven of their ten matches took much of the loss off their achievement. Aside from Bayern and remen, there were three other German teams nvolved in post-Christmas UEFA Cup combat, and hey all fell by the wayside one after the other – 1.FC lürnberg in the round of 32, Hamburger SV in the ound of 16, and Bayer 04 Leverkusen (Hamburg's onquerors) in the quarter-finals, where, like Bayern a ew weeks later, they succumbed to the brilliance of ussian champions Zenit.

:motional farewells

3remen and Schalke re-qualified for another shot at he UEFA Champions League after finishing second nd third, respectively, in the Bundesliga. However, hey were both a long way distant of champions 3ayern, who led the table from first kick to last, won at oth the Weserstadion and the Veltins-Arena, emained unbeaten at home, and lost only twice – at Stuttgart in the autumn and, remarkably, at FC Energie Cottbus in the spring. The title was secured with a rather downbeat goalless draw at VfL Wolfsburg, but Bayern rounded off the season in style a fortnight later with a 4-1 home win over Hertha BSC 3erlin, with Toni scoring a hat-trick and two of the club's giants of the modern era – goalkeeper/captain Oliver Kahn and coach Ottmar Hitzfeld – both making emotional farewells. While Kahn closed his career – after 557 games for the club – the tearful Hitzfeld ended his brief second spell in charge by leaving to take on a fresh challenge as the new coach of Switzerland. With Bayern he had won five Bundesliga titles, three German Cups and, the jewel in the crown, the 2001 UEFA Champions League – a competition he had also won previously with Dortmund.

The task for Bayern's new coach, Klinsmann, will be to emulate Hitzfeld by taking Bayern to the top of the European tree. The former Germany boss was signed up, out of the blue, in January, thus returning to the club he graced in the mid-1990s as a player. One suspects there will be plenty of renewed media references to 'FC Hollywood' if things go awry for the man who has spent most of his years since retirement warming down in the sunshine of California.

Thomas Schaaf does not share Klinsmann's charisma, but the longest-serving coach in the Bundesliga will celebrate a decade as Bremen boss in May 2009. He has led the club into the UEFA Champions League every season since winning the Bundesliga/DFB-Pokal double in 2004, and although there was a sense of underachievement in Europe for his team in 2007/08, the Green and Whites delivered the goods again in the Bundesliga. A 4-0 home defeat to Bayern was not the best of starts, but despite the absence through injury of key midfielder Torsten Frings, they almost caught up their conquerors at Christmas, and by the end of the season, despite a shaky spring, Schaaf's all-out-attacking unit had outscored the champions by 75 goals to 68. Diego was their star attraction, the brilliant Brazilian No10 scoring 13 goals himself and assisting in the construction of many others. Markus

Diego pulled the strings all season long for Werder Bremen

GERMANY

Deutscher Fussball-Bund (DFB)

Otto-Fleck-Schneise 6
Postfach 710265
D-60492 Frankfurt am Main
tel - +49 69 67880
fax - +49 69 6788266
website - www.dfb.de
email - info@dfb.de
Year of Formation – 1900
President – Theo Zwanziger
General Secretary - Wolfgang Niersbach
Press Officer – Harald Stenger

*INTERNATIONAL HONOURS**
FIFA World Cup - (3) 1954, 1974, 1990.
UEFA European Championship - (3) 1972, 1980, 1996.

*INTERNATIONAL TOURNAMENT APPEARANCES**
FIFA World Cup - (16) 1934 (3rd), 1938, 1954 (Winners), 1958 (4th), 1962 (qtr-finals), 1966 (runners-up), 1970 (3rd), 1974 (Winners), 1978 (2nd phase), 1982 (runners-up), 1986 (runners-up), 1990 (Winners), 1994 (qtr-finals), 1998 (qtr-finals), 2002 (runners-up), 2006 (3rd place).
UEFA European Championship - (10) 1972 (Winners), 1976 (runners-up), 1980 (Winners), 1984, 1988 (semi-finals), 1992 (runners-up), 1996 (Winners), 2000, 2004, 2008 (runners-up).

TOP FIVE ALL-TIME CAPS
Lothar Matthäus (150); Jürgen Klinsmann (108); Jürgen Kohler (105); Franz Beckenbauer (103); Thomas Hässler (101)

TOP FIVE ALL-TIME GOALS
Gerd Müller (68); Jürgen Klinsmann & Rudi Völler (47); Karl-Heinz Rummenigge (45); Uwe Seeler (43)

(before 1992 as West Germany)*

NATIONAL TEAM RESULTS 2007/08

22/8/07	England	A	Wembley	2-1	*Kuranyi (26), Pander (40)*
8/9/07	Wales (ECQ)	A	Cardiff	2-0	*Klose (6, 60)*
12/9/07	Romania	H	Cologne	3-1	*Schneider (45), Odonkor (65), Podolski (82)*
13/10/07	Republic of Ireland (ECQ)	A	Dublin	0-0	
17/10/07	Czech Republic (ECQ)	H	Munich	0-3	
17/11/07	Cyprus (ECQ)	H	Hanover	4-0	*Fritz (2), Klose (20), Podolski (53), Hitzlsperger (82)*
21/11/07	Wales (ECQ)	H	Frankfurt	0-0	
6/2/08	Austria	A	Vienna	3-0	*Hitzlsperger (53), Klose (63), Gómez (80)*
26/3/08	Switzerland	A	Basle	4-0	*Klose (23), Gómez (61, 67), Podolski (89)*
27/5/08	Belarus	H	Kaiserslautern	2-2	*Klose (10), Korytko (20og)*
31/5/08	Serbia	H	Gelsenkirchen	2-1	*Neuville (74), Ballack (82)*
8/6/08	Poland (ECF)	N	Klagenfurt (AUT)	2-0	*Podolski (20, 72)*
12/6/08	Croatia (ECF)	N	Klagenfurt (AUT)	1-2	*Podolski (79)*
16/6/08	Austria (ECF)	A	Vienna	1-0	*Ballack (49)*
19/6/08	Portugal (ECF)	N	Basel (SUI)	3-2	*Schweinsteiger (22), Klose (26), Ballack (61)*
25/6/08	Turkey (ECF)	N	Basel (SUI)	3-2	*Schweinsteiger (26), Klose (79), Lahm (90)*
29/6/08	Spain (ECF)	N	Vienna (AUT)	0-1	

ATIONAL TEAM APPEARANCES 2007/08

:h – Joachim LÖW	3/2/60		Eng	WAL	Rou	IRL	CZE	CYP	WAL	Aut	Sui	Blr	Srb	POL	CRO	AUT	POR	TUR	ESP	Caps	Goals
LEHMANN	10/11/69	Arsenal (ENG)	G	G		G		G	G	G	G	G	G	G	G	G	G	G	G	62	-
FRIEDRICH	29/5/79	Hertha	D	D	s46	D	D	D			s72		s46			D	D	D	D	61	-
MERTESACKER	29/9/84	Bremen	D	D		D	D46	D	D	D	D	D	D46	D	D	D	D	D	D	49	1
toph METZELDER	5/11/80	Real Madrid (ESP)	D	D	D46	D	D	D	D			D	D	D	D	D	D	D	D	47	-
tian PANDER	28/8/83	Schalke	D	D46																2	1
pp LAHM	11/11/83	Bayern	M					D	D	D	D87	D	D46	D	D	D	D	D	D46	47	3
d ODONKOR	21/2/84	Betis (ESP)	M54		s60		M					M79	s79		s46					16	1
TROCHOWSKI	22/3/84	Hamburg	M72	s46	M	M90	M46	M66			s87	s67								12	-
d SCHNEIDER	17/11/73	Leverkusen	M90		M60					M59										81	4
nas HITZLSPERGER	5/4/82	Stuttgart	M	M	M46			M	M46	M82	M	D		s75		s60	M73	M	M58	38	5
n KURANYI	2/3/82	Schalke	A	A72		A	A			A59	s75		A70	s91	s82				s58	50	19
erto HILBERT	16/10/84	Stuttgart	s54	M	D			s77	s56	s74										8	-
n ROLFES	21/1/82	Leverkusen	s72		s46	s18	s46		s46	s87	s79		s70				M	M46		12	-
zalo CASTRO	11/6/87	Leverkusen	s90		s46	s90			D56											5	-
an SCHWEINSTEIGER	1/8/84	Bayern		M	M	M18	M65			M	M	M46	M79	s56	s66		M83	M	M	56	15
cell JANSEN	4/11/85	Bayern		M	D46	D	D				D79		D84	D	D46		s89	s92	s46	27	1
slav KLOSE	9/6/78	Bayern		A87				A	A	A	A58	A54		A91	A	A	A89	A92	A79	81	41
s PODOLSKI	4/6/85	Bayern		s72	A	s64	A	M	M	s59	s58	A54	s46	M	M	M83	M	M	M	54	28
ck HELMES	1/3/84	Köln		s87	A							s54								5	-
HILDEBRAND	5/4/79	Valencia (ESP)			G		G													7	-
uel FRIEDRICH	13/9/79	Leverkusen			D					D74										9	1
en FRINGS	22/11/76	Bremen				M	M					M67	M70	M	M	M		s46	M	77	10
nens FRITZ	7/12/80	Bremen				M	s46	M77	M		M72	s79	M	M56	M82	M93	s83			18	2
o GÓMEZ	10/7/85	Stuttgart				A64	s65	A73	A71	s59	A75		A	A75	A66	A60			s79	14	6
BOROWSKI	2/5/80	Bremen						s66	M							s93	s73			33	2
HANKE	5/11/83	Hannover						s73												12	1
er NEUVILLE	1/5/73	Mönchengladbach							s71			s54	s70			s83				69	10
o WESTERMANN	14/8/83	Schalke								D	D		s84							3	-
ael BALLACK	26/9/76	Chelsea (ENG)								M87	M	M46	M	M	M	M	M	M	M	87	38
aine JONES	3/11/81	Schalke								s82		s46								2	-
ko MARIN	30/3/89	Mönchengladbach										s46								1	-

Rosenberg and Hugo Almeida also chipped in with some important goals. So too, in the latter half of the campaign, did Ivan Klasnić, who made a remarkable recovery from a kidney transplant.

Schalke's run to the quarter-finals of the UEFA Champions League and third place in the Bundesliga were not enough to keep coach Mirko Slomka in a job. He was shown the door in April after a 5-1 hammering at Bremen came hard on the heels of the team's European elimination by FC Barcelona, where their struggles in front of goal came to a head in alarming fashion.

There was a frantic finish to the scrap for UEFA Cup places. Dortmund, though sub-standard again in the

GERMANY

Bundesliga – despite those massive crowds – secured their ticket as runners-up to Bayern in the Cup, but the other two spots remained up for grabs right through to the final afternoon. Hamburg, who endured a poor second half to the campaign, suddenly came to life with a 7-0 drubbing of Karlsruher SC that earned fourth place on goal difference ahead of VfL Wolfsburg, giving Dutch coach Huub Stevens the perfect send-off ahead of his move back home to PSV Eindhoven.

Ambitious Wolfsburg, led by ex-Hamburg legend Felix Magath, were outstanding in the spring and secured the other UEFA Cup berth with an impressive 4-2 victory in Dortmund, though just as important was their 4-0 home win seven days earlier over Stuttgart, who, as a consequence, dropped into sixth position, which carried only a UEFA Intertoto Cup berth – a considerable fall from grace for Armin Veh's reigning champions, despite Mario Gómez's 19 goals, although not unusual as the club had also failed to qualify for Europe the season after their title-winning campaigns of 1983/84 and 1991/92. Leverkusen were the big losers of the final day, missing out on European football altogether after a 1-0 home defeat by Bremen – a disappointing end to a generally lacklustre season, the last under coach Michael Skibbe.

At the bottom of the league Cottbus and DSC Arminia Bielefeld surprisingly escaped the drop while Nürnberg the Cup winners in 2007, were ensnared along with the more predictable pair of FC Hansa Rostock and MSV Duisburg, the latter finishing on the bottom of the hea after losing 11 of their 17 matches at home.

Village club going places

Two traditional giants from the west won promotion, with VfL Borussia Mönchengladbach, backed by average crowds of 40,427, winning the Zweite Bundesliga, and 1.FC Köln, boasting even larger suppo (43,747), finishing third. Each of the two clubs revealed exciting young talents who came close to making Germany's UEFA EURO 2008™ squad – Marko Marin (Mönchengladbach) and Patrick Helmes (Köln) -but the biggest story from the second division was provided b TSG 1899 Hoffenheim, the village club bankrolled by computer software tycoon Dietmar Hopp – the 'Germa Bill Gates'. Thanks to heavy investment and some stylis football under their progressive coach Ralf Rangnick, Hoffenheim won a second successive promotion to reach the Bundesliga, where, from January 2009, they will stage their home games in the brand new 30,000-capacity Rhein-Neckar-Arena.

DOMESTIC LEAGUE 2007/08

BUNDESLIGA FINAL TABLE

			Home					Away					Total					
		Pld	W	D	L	F	A	W	D	L	F	A	W	D	L	F	A	Pts
1	FC Bayern München	34	12	5	0	41	8	10	5	2	27	13	22	10	2	68	21	76
2	Werder Bremen	34	13	0	4	48	19	7	6	4	27	26	20	6	8	75	45	66
3	FC Schalke 04	34	10	4	3	29	13	8	6	3	26	19	18	10	6	55	32	64
4	Hamburger SV	34	9	5	3	30	11	5	7	5	17	15	14	12	8	47	26	54
5	VfL Wolfsburg	34	7	6	4	28	17	8	3	6	30	29	15	9	10	58	46	54
6	VfB Stuttgart	34	12	2	3	39	19	4	2	11	18	38	16	4	14	57	57	52
7	Bayer 04 Leverkusen	34	9	4	4	32	13	6	2	9	25	27	15	6	13	57	40	51
8	Hannover 96	34	8	5	4	32	27	5	5	7	22	29	13	10	11	54	56	49
9	Eintracht Frankfurt	34	8	4	5	24	24	4	6	7	19	26	12	10	12	43	50	46
10	Hertha BSC Berlin	34	9	3	5	21	18	3	5	9	18	26	12	8	14	39	44	44
11	Karlsruher SC	34	6	6	5	23	22	5	4	8	15	31	11	10	13	38	53	43
12	VfL Bochum	34	5	9	3	32	28	5	2	10	16	26	10	11	13	48	54	41
13	BV Borussia Dortmund	34	7	5	5	29	24	3	5	9	21	38	10	10	14	50	62	40
14	FC Energie Cottbus	34	8	2	7	25	20	1	7	9	10	36	9	9	16	35	56	36
15	DSC Arminia Bielefeld	34	7	4	6	21	18	1	6	10	14	42	8	10	16	35	60	34
16	1. FC Nürnberg	34	5	7	5	21	18	2	3	12	14	33	7	10	17	35	51	31
17	FC Hansa Rostock	34	5	4	8	17	21	3	2	12	13	31	8	6	20	30	52	30
18	MSV Duisburg	34	3	3	11	19	29	5	2	10	17	26	8	5	21	36	55	29

TOP GOALSCORERS

24 Luca TONI (Bayern)
19 Mario GÓMEZ (Stuttgart)
15 Kevin KURANYI (Schalke)
14 Ivica OLIĆ (Hamburg)
Markus ROSENBERG (Bremen)
13 Marko PANTELIĆ (Hertha)
Mladen PETRIĆ (Dortmund)
DIEGO (Bremen)
Stanislav ŠESTÁK (Bochum)
12 Rafael VAN DER VAART (Hambur

CLUB-BY-CLUB

DSC ARMINIA BIELEFELD

Coach – Ernst Middendorp; (10/12/07) (Detlev Dammeier); (1/1/08) Michael Frontzeck

Founded - 1905

007				
1/8	Wolfsburg	a	3-1	*Wichniarek, Eigler, Kirch*
3/8	Eintracht	h	2-2	*Kučera, Wichniarek*
5/8	Hertha	h	2-0	*Masmanidis, Wichniarek*
'9	Duisburg	a	0-3	
5/9	Hansa	h	4-2	*Böhme, Eigler 2, Wichniarek*
2/9	Schalke	a	0-3	
5/9	Hannover	h	0-2	
9/9	Bremen	a	1-8	*Wichniarek*
'10	Hamburg	h	0-1	
1/10	Karlsruhe	a	0-0	
7/10	Energie	h	1-1	*Kamper*
'11	Leverkusen	a	0-4	
1/11	Nürnberg	h	3-1	*Kauf, Wichniarek, Zuma*
4/11	Bochum	a	0-3	
'12	Bayern	h	0-1	
'12	Dortmund	a	1-6	*Kirch*
5/12	Stuttgart	h	2-0	*Kamper, Wichniarek*
008				
'2	Wolfsburg	h	0-1	
'2	Eintracht	a	1-2	*Wichniarek*
5/2	Hertha	a	0-1	
3/2	Duisburg	h	0-2	
'3	Hansa	a	1-1	*Eigler*
'3	Schalke	h	0-2	
5/3	Hannover	a	2-2	*Mijatović, Eigler*
3/3	Bremen	h	1-1	*Kirch*
9/3	Hamburg	a	1-1	*Bollmann*
'4	Karlsruhe	h	1-0	*Kampantais*
2/4	Energie	a	0-1	
6/4	Leverkusen	h	1-0	*Mijatović*
6/4	Nürnberg	a	2-2	*Wichniarek, Bollmann*
'5	Bochum	h	2-0	*Mijatović, Kamper*
'5	Bayern	a	0-2	
0/5	Dortmund	h	2-2	*Marx (p), Wichniarek*
7/5	Stuttgart	a	2-2	*Tesche, Eigler*

o	Name	Nat	Pos	Aps	(s)	Gls
0	Jörg BÖHME		M	17	(5)	1
	Markus BOLLMANN		D	15	(6)	2
	Christian EIGLER		A	22	(7)	6
3	Rowen FERNANDEZ	RSA	G	14	(1)	
0	Nils FISCHER		M		(2)	
	Petr GABRIEL	CZE	D	10	(2)	
	Mathias HAIN		G	20		
4	Daniel HALFAR		A	10	(6)	
0	Dirk HEINEN		G		(1)	
7	Leonidas KAMPANTAIS	GRE	D	1	(7)	1
4	Jonas KAMPER	DEN	A	9	(22)	3
	Rüdiger KAUF		M	28	(1)	1
3	Oliver KIRCH		D	22	(3)	3
1	David KOBYLÍK	CZE	M		(2)	
9	Bernd KORYNIETZ		D	10	(5)	
1	Radim KUČERA	CZE	D	31		1
1	Matthias LANGKAMP		D	13		
	Thorben MARX		M	23	(1)	1
0	Ioannis MASMANIDIS		M	4	(4)	1
6	Andre MIJATOVIĆ	CRO	D	24		3
5	Siyabonga NKOSI	RSA	M	6	(2)	
	Tobias RAU		D	8	(2)	
2	Markus SCHULER		D	28	(1)	
32	Robert TESCHE		M	13	(2)	1
36	Thilo VERSICK		M		(1)	
18	Artur WICHNIAREK	POL	M	33		10
22	Sibusiso ZUMA	RSA	A	13	(7)	1

BAYER 04 LEVERKUSEN

Coach – Michael Skibbe

Founded - 1904

MAJOR HONOURS: UEFA Cup - (1) 1988; German Cup - (1) 1993.

2007				
11/8	Energie	h	0-0	
19/8	Hamburg	a	0-1	
25/8	Karlsruhe	h	3-0	*og (Franz), Friedrich, Gekas*
31/8	Schalke	a	1-1	*Gekas*
15/9	Bochum	h	2-0	*Haggui, Friedrich*
23/9	Hannover	a	3-0	*Kießling, Vidal, Gekas (p)*
26/9	Nürnberg	a	2-1	*Kießling, Barnetta*
29/9	Bayern	h	0-1	
7/10	Eintracht	a	1-2	*og (Russ)*
20/10	Dortmund	h	2-2	*Gekas, Kießling*
27/10	Stuttgart	a	0-1	
3/11	Arminia	h	4-0	*Barbarez 2, Gekas 2*
11/11	Wolfsburg	a	2-1	*Barnetta, Kießling*
24/11	Duisburg	h	4-1	*Barbarez, Rolfes, Freier (p), Gekas*
1/12	Hertha	a	3-0	*Ramelow, Barnetta, Barbarez*
9/12	Hansa	h	3-0	*Rolfes, Freier (p), Gekas*
15/12	Bremen	a	2-5	*Barnetta, Kießling*
2008				
2/2	Energie	a	3-2	*Rolfes 2 (1p), Bulykin*
9/2	Hamburg	h	1-1	*Friedrich*
16/2	Karlsruhe	a	2-2	*Rolfes, Kießling*
23/2	Schalke	h	1-0	*Friedrich*
2/3	Bochum	a	0-2	
9/3	Hannover	h	2-0	*Gekas, Barnetta*
16/3	Nürnberg	h	4-1	*Haggui, og (Gláuber), Gekas, Kießling*
22/3	Bayern	a	1-2	*Bulykin*
29/3	Eintracht	h	0-2	
6/4	Dortmund	a	1-2	*Kießling*
13/4	Stuttgart	h	3-0	*Rolfes 2, Kießling*
16/4	Arminia	a	0-1	
27/4	Wolfsburg	h	2-2	*Gekas, og (Ricardo Costa)*
4/5	Duisburg	a	2-3	*Sinkiewicz, Barnetta*
7/5	Hertha	h	1-2	*Sinkiewicz*
10/5	Hansa	a	2-1	*Rolfes (p), Castro (p)*
17/5	Bremen	h	0-1	

No	Name	Nat	Pos	Aps	(s)	Gls
1	René ADLER		G	33		
36	Sergej BARBAREZ	BIH	A	26	(3)	4
7	Tranquillo BARNETTA	SUI	M	31	(1)	6
13	Dmitriy BULYKIN	RUS	A	6	(8)	2
29	Jan-Ingwer CALLSEN-BRAKER		D	6	(4)	
27	Gonzalo CASTRO		D	33		1
14	Sascha DUM		M	1	(16)	
4	Ricardo FATY	FRA	M		(2)	
22	Benedikt FERNANDEZ		G	1		
8	Paul FREIER		M	7	(12)	2
5	Manuel FRIEDRICH		D	32		4
10	Theofanis GEKAS	GRE	A	19	(10)	11

No	Name	Nat	Pos	Aps	(s)	Gls
17	Vratislav GREŠKO	SVK	D	15	(6)	
2	Karim HAGGUI	TUN	D	24		2
45	Jens HEGELER		M		(1)	
11	Stefan KIESSLING		A	31		9
26	Michal PAPADOPULOS	CZE	A	1	(6)	
28	Carsten RAMELOW		M	3	(1)	1
19	Marcel RISSE		M	1	(2)	
6	Simon ROLFES		M	34		8
15	Hans SARPEI		M	22	(5)	
25	Bernd SCHNEIDER		M	13	(2)	
16	Pirmin SCHWEGLER	SUI	M	6	(5)	
20	Lukas SINKIEWICZ		D	12	(7)	2
23	Arturo VIDAL	CHI	D	17	(7)	1

FC BAYERN MÜNCHEN

Coach – Ottmar Hitzfeld

Founded - 1903

MAJOR HONOURS: European Champion Clubs' Cup/UEFA Champions League - (4) 1974, 1975, 1976, 2001; UEFA Cup - (1) 1996; World Club Cup - (2) 1976, 2001; German League - (21) 1932, 1969, 1972, 1973, 1974, 1980, 1981, 1985, 1986, 1987, 1989, 1990, 1994, 1997, 1999, 2000, 2001, 2003, 2005, 2006, 2008; German Cup - (14) 1957, 1966, 1967, 1969, 1971, 1982, 1984, 1986, 1998, 2000, 2003, 2005, 2006, 2008.

2007				
11/8	Hansa	h	3-0	*Toni, Klose 2*
18/8	Bremen	a	4-0	*Ribéry (p), Toni, Altıntop, Ottl*
25/8	Hannover	h	3-0	*Toni, Van Bommel, Altıntop*
2/9	Hamburg	a	1-1	*Klose*
15/9	Schalke	h	1-1	*Klose*
23/9	Karlsruhe	a	4-1	*Toni, Klose, Altıntop, Zé Roberto*
26/9	Energie	h	5-0	*Klose 3, Demichelis, Toni*
29/9	Leverkusen	a	1-0	*Toni*
7/10	Nürnberg	h	3-0	*Toni 2, Zé Roberto*
20/10	Bochum	a	2-1	*Ribéry, Schweinsteiger*
28/10	Dortmund	a	0-0	
3/11	Eintracht	h	0-0	
10/11	Stuttgart	a	1-3	*Toni*
24/11	Wolfsburg	h	2-1	*Klose, Ribéry*
2/12	Arminia	a	1-0	*Ribéry*
8/12	Duisburg	h	0-0	
15/12	Hertha	a	0-0	
2008				
1/2	Hansa	a	2-1	*Ribéry, Toni*
10/2	Bremen	h	1-1	*Zé Roberto*
17/2	Hannover	a	3-0	*Toni 3*
24/2	Hamburg	h	1-1	*Zé Roberto*
1/3	Schalke	a	1-0	*Klose*
8/3	Karlsruhe	h	2-0	*Toni, Ribéry*
15/3	Energie	a	0-2	
22/3	Leverkusen	h	2-1	*Toni 2*
29/3	Nürnberg	a	1-1	*Podolski*
6/4	Bochum	h	3-1	*Lúcio, Ribéry (p), Lell*
13/4	Dortmund	h	5-0	*Podolski, Zé Roberto, Toni 2, Ottl*
16/4	Eintracht	a	3-1	*Van Buyten, Toni 2*
27/4	Stuttgart	h	4-1	*Toni, Van Bommel, Ribéry 2*
4/5	Wolfsburg	a	0-0	
7/5	Arminia	h	2-0	*Ribéry, Podolski*
10/5	Duisburg	a	3-2	*Ottl, Podolski 2*
17/5	Hertha	h	4-1	*Toni 3, Ribéry*

No	Name	Nat	Pos	Aps	(s)	Gls
8	Hamit ALTINTOP	TUR	M	17	(6)	3
35	BRENO Vinícius Rodrigues Borges	BRA	D		(1)	
6	Martín DEMICHELIS	ARG	D	28		1
23	Marcell JANSEN		D	16	(1)	
1	Oliver KAHN		G	26		
18	Miroslav KLOSE		A	24	(3)	10
39	Toni KROOS		M	3	(9)	
21	Philipp LAHM		D	21	(1)	
30	Christian LELL		D	26	(3)	1
3	Lucimar Ferreira da Silva "LÚCIO"	BRA	D	24		1
16	Andreas OTTL		M	8	(11)	3
11	Lukas PODOLSKI		A	8	(17)	5
22	Michael RENSING		G	8	(2)	
7	Franck RIBÉRY	FRA	M	26	(2)	11
2	Willy SAGNOL	FRA	D	8	(1)	
19	Jan SCHLAUDRAFF		A	1	(7)	
31	Bastian SCHWEINSTEIGER		M	21	(9)	1
20	José Ernesto SOSA	ARG	M	7	(8)	
9	Luca TONI	ITA	A	31		24
17	Mark VAN BOMMEL	NED	M	26	(1)	2
5	Daniel VAN BUYTEN	BEL	D	18	(1)	1
34	Sandro WAGNER		M		(4)	
15	José ZÉ ROBERTO da Silva Júnior	BRA	M	27	(3)	5

VFL BOCHUM 1848

Coach – Marcel Koller (SUI)

Founded - 1848

2007				
11/8	Bremen	h	2-2	*Šesták, Bechmann*
19/8	Energie	a	2-1	*Bechmann 2*
24/8	Hamburg	h	2-1	*Šesták, Imhof*
1/9	Hannover	a	2-3	*Bechmann, Maltritz (p*
15/9	Leverkusen	a	0-2	
21/9	Eintracht	h	0-0	
26/9	Stuttgart	a	0-1	
29/9	Nürnberg	h	3-3	*Mięciel, Šesták 2*
5/10	Dortmund	a	1-2	*Mięciel*
20/10	Bayern	h	1-2	*Grote*
27/10	Hertha	a	0-2	
4/11	Wolfsburg	h	5-3	*Šesták 2, Maltritz (p), Fuchs, Epalle*
9/11	Duisburg	a	2-0	*Imhof, Bechmann*
24/11	Arminia	h	3-0	*Mięciel 2, Dabrowski*
1/12	Schalke	a	0-1	
8/12	Karlsruhe	h	2-2	*Šesták 2*
16/12	Hansa	a	0-2	
2008				
3/2	Bremen	a	2-1	*Auer, Yahia*
9/2	Energie	h	3-3	*og (Ispa), Šesták, Auer*
17/2	Hamburg	a	0-3	
22/2	Hannover	h	2-1	*og (Cherundolo), Auer*
2/3	Leverkusen	h	2-0	*Zdebel, Dabrowski*
8/3	Eintracht	a	1-1	*Azaouagh*
15/3	Stuttgart	h	1-1	*Dabrowski*
22/3	Nürnberg	a	1-1	*Šesták*
29/3	Dortmund	h	3-3	*Dabrowski, Auer 2*
6/4	Bayern	a	1-3	*Azaouagh*
12/4	Hertha	h	1-1	*Yahia*
15/4	Wolfsburg	a	1-0	*Šesták*
26/4	Duisburg	h	1-1	*Šesták*
3/5	Arminia	a	0-2	
6/5	Schalke	h	0-3	
10/5	Karlsruhe	a	3-1	*Azaouagh, Dabrowski, Šesták*
17/5	Hansa	h	1-2	*Mavraj*

No	Name	Nat	Pos	Aps	(s)	Gls
14	Benjamin AUER		A	15	(2)	5
22	Mimoun AZAOUAGH		M	11	(3)	3
7	Tommy BECHMANN	DEN	A	9	(11)	5
24	Philipp BÖNIG		D	24	(1)	
17	Olexiy BYELIK	UKR	A	1	(3)	
2	Matias CONCHA	SWE	D	16	(2)	

No	Name	Nat	Pos	Aps	(s)	Gls
	Christoph DABROWSKI		M	28		5
	Pavel DRSEK	CZE	D	2	(10)	
	Joël EPALLE	CMR	A	20	(6)	1
	Danny FUCHS		M	11	(6)	1
	Dennis GROTE		A	7	(11)	1
	Ivo ILIČEVIĆ	CRO	M	3	(3)	
	Daniel IMHOF	SUI	M	18	(6)	2
	Jan LAŠTŮVKA	CZE	G	25		
	Marcel MALTRITZ		D	31		2
	Mergim MAVRAJ		D	1	(1)	1
	Martin MEICHELBECK		D	3	(2)	
	Marcin MIĘCIEL	POL	A	11	(14)	4
	Shinji ONO	JPN	M	5	(7)	
	Marc PFERTZEL	FRA	M	28		
	René RENNO		G	9	(1)	
	Oliver SCHRÖDER		D	6	(9)	
	Stanislav ŠESTÁK	SVK	A	32	(1)	13
	Antar YAHIA	ALG	D	33		2
	Tomasz ZDEBEL	POL	M	25	(1)	1

BV BORUSSIA DORTMUND

Coach – Thomas Doll

Founded - 1909

MAJOR HONOURS: UEFA Champions League - (1) 1997; UEFA Cup Winners' Cup - (1) 1966; World Club Cup - (1) 1997; German League - (6) 1956, 1957, 1963, 1995, 1996, 2002; German Cup - (2) 1965, 1989.

007				
2/8	Duisburg	h	1-3	*Kringe*
8/8	Schalke	a	1-4	*Valdez*
5/8	Energie	h	3-0	*Kringe, Klimowicz 2*
/9	Hansa	a	1-0	*Federico*
4/9	Bremen	h	3-0	*Petrić 2, Klimowicz*
2/9	Hertha	a	2-3	*Petrić 2*
5/9	Hamburg	h	0-3	
9/9	Karlsruhe	a	1-3	*Wörns*
/10	Bochum	h	2-1	*Tinga, Federico*
0/10	Leverkusen	a	2-2	*Petrić 2*
8/10	Bayern	h	0-0	
/11	Hannover	a	1-2	*Kringe*
0/11	Eintracht	h	1-1	*Kringe*
5/11	Nürnberg	a	0-2	
/12	Stuttgart	a	2-1	*og (Delpierre), Petrić*
/12	Arminia	h	6-1	*Tinga, og (Schuler), Petrić, Valdez (p), Kringe, Federico*
5/12	Wolfsburg	a	0-4	
008				
2/2	Duisburg	a	3-3	*Kehl, Klimowicz 2*
0/2	Schalke	h	2-3	*Federico, Petrić*
6/2	Energie	a	2-0	*Petrić 2*
3/2	Hansa	h	1-0	*Klimowicz*
/3	Bremen	a	0-2	
/3	Hertha	h	1-1	*Kehl*
5/3	Hamburg	a	0-1	
22/3	Karlsruhe	h	1-1	*Petrić*
29/3	Bochum	a	3-3	*Kehl, Petrić, Tinga*
5/4	Leverkusen	h	2-1	*Frei, Dedé*
13/4	Bayern	a	0-5	
17/4	Hannover	h	1-3	*Frei*
25/4	Eintracht	a	1-1	*Błaszczykowski*
2/5	Nürnberg	h	0-0	
5/5	Stuttgart	h	3-2	*Tinga, Frei 2*
10/5	Arminia	a	2-2	*Buckley, og (Fernandez)*
17/5	Wolfsburg	h	2-4	*Frei 2*

No	Name	Nat	Pos	Aps	(s)	Gls
25	Mehmet AKGÜN		A	1		
2	Martin AMEDICK		D	11	(5)	
41	Alexander BADE		G		(1)	
16	Jakub BŁASZCZYKOWSKI	POL	M	22	(2)	1
3	Markus BRZENSKA		D	11	(1)	
26	Delron BUCKLEY	RSA	A	11	(20)	1
17	Leonardo de Déus Santos "DEDÉ"	BRA	D	30		1
23	Philipp DEGEN	SUI	D	10		
34	Christian EGGERT		M		(1)	
8	Giovanni FEDERICO	ITA	M	25	(5)	4
13	Alexander FREI	SUI	A	9	(4)	6
24	Daniel GORDON		M		(3)	
38	Nico HILLENBRAND		D		(1)	
30	Marcel HÖTTECKE		G	5		
15	Mats HUMMELS		D	10	(3)	
5	Sebastian KEHL		M	14		3
19	Diego Fernando KLIMOWICZ	ARG	A	13	(15)	6
21	Robert KOVAČ	CRO	D	20	(2)	
6	Florian KRINGE		M	25	(2)	5
22	Marc-André KRUSKA		M	13	(10)	
32	Franck Patrick NJAMBE	CMR	M	1	(1)	
31	Christopher NÖTHE		A	1	(2)	
10	Mladen PETRIĆ	CRO	M	28	(1)	13
14	Antonio RUKAVINA	SRB	D	14		
39	Shar SENESIE		A		(3)	
14	Euzebiusz SMOLAREK	POL	A	1	(1)	
7	Paulo César Fonseca "TINGA"	BRA	M	33		4
28	Sebastian TYRALA		M		(1)	
9	Nelson Haedo VALDEZ	PAR	A	18	(9)	2
1	Roman WEIDENFELLER		G	14		
4	Christian WÖRNS		D	19	(1)	1
20	Marc ZIEGLER		G	15		

MSV DUISBURG

Coach – Rudi Bommer

Founded - 1902

2007				
12/8	Dortmund	a	3-1	*Ishiaku 2, Tararache (p)*
18/8	Wolfsburg	h	1-3	*Lavrić*
25/8	Stuttgart	a	0-1	
1/9	Arminia	h	3-0	*Maicon, Ishiaku 2*
16/9	Hertha	h	1-2	*Lavrić*
22/9	Hansa	a	0-2	
25/9	Schalke	h	0-2	
30/9	Hannover	a	1-2	*Ishiaku*
6/10	Bremen	h	1-3	*Ailton*
19/10	Energie	a	2-1	*Schlicke, Grlić*
28/10	Hamburg	h	0-1	
4/11	Karlsruhe	a	0-1	
9/11	Bochum	h	0-2	
24/11	Leverkusen	a	1-4	*Mokhtari*
2/12	Nürnberg	h	1-0	*Grlić*
8/12	Bayern	a	0-0	
16/12	Eintracht	h	0-1	
2008				
2/2	Dortmund	h	3-3	*Filipescu, Willi, Tararache (p)*
9/2	Wolfsburg	a	1-2	*Niculescu*
16/2	Stuttgart	h	2-3	*Niculescu, Ishiaku*
23/2	Arminia	a	2-0	*Schröter, Ishiaku*
29/2	Hertha	a	0-2	
8/3	Hansa	h	1-1	*Grlić*
14/3	Schalke	a	1-2	*Georgiev*
22/3	Hannover	h	1-1	*Lamey*
29/3	Bremen	a	2-1	*Grlić, Ishiaku*
4/4	Energie	h	0-1	
12/4	Hamburg	a	1-0	*Grlić*
16/4	Karlsruhe	h	0-1	
26/4	Bochum	a	1-1	*Niculescu*
4/5	Leverkusen	h	3-2	*Ishiaku 2, Georgiev*
7/5	Nürnberg	a	0-2	
10/5	Bayern	h	2-3	*Tararache, Daun*
17/5	Eintracht	a	2-4	*Niculescu, Daun*

No	Name	Nat	Pos	Aps	(s)	Gls
34	AÍLTON Gonçalves da Silva	BRA	A	4	(4)	1
41	Fernando Horacio ÁVALOS	ARG	D	9	(1)	
1	Sven BEUCKERT		G	3		
13	Adam BODZEK		D	6	(1)	
22	Pablo CÁCERES	URU	D	16	(2)	
17	Markus DAUN		A	3	(16)	2
6	FERNANDO	BRA	D	9	(5)	
3	Iulian FILIPESCU	ROU	D	18	(2)	1
7	Blagoy GEORGIEV	BUL	M	27	(4)	2
20	Ivica GRLIĆ	BIH	M	28		5
10	Mohamadou IDRISSOU	CMR	A	11	(1)	
19	Manasseh ISHIAKU	NGA	A	23	(2)	10
15	Michael LAMEY	NED	D	21	(4)	1
9	Klemen LAVRIČ	SVN	A	8	(10)	2
30	MAICON Thiago Pereira de Souza	BRA	M	14	(6)	1
16	Youssef MOKHTARI	MAR	M	5	(2)	1
25	Sascha MÖLDERS		A	2	(9)	
32	Georges NDOUM	CMR	D	1	(1)	
21	Markus NEUMEYR		M		(3)	
10	Claudiu NICULESCU	ROU	A	16	(1)	4
18	José Vítor ROQUE JÚNIOR	BRA	D	4		
4	Björn SCHLICKE		D	27		1
16	Silvio SCHRÖTER		A	2	(1)	1
27	Tom STARKE		G	31		
8	Mihai TARARACHE	ROU	M	31		3
11	Christian TIFFERT		M	21	(4)	
28	Olivier VEIGNEAU	FRA	D	4	(3)	
40	Bojan VRUČINA	CRO	A	1	(7)	
2	Christian WEBER		D	8	(3)	
29	Tobias WILLI		M	21	(4)	1

EINTRACHT FRANKFURT

Coach – Friedhelm Funkel

Founded - 1899

MAJOR HONOURS: UEFA Cup - (1) 1980; German League - (1) 1959; German Cup - (4) 1974, 1975, 1981, 1988.

2007				
11/8	Hertha	h	1-0	*Amanatidis*
18/8	Arminia	a	2-2	*Meier, Russ*
26/8	Hansa	h	1-0	*Meier*
1/9	Bremen	a	1-2	*Thurk*
15/9	Hamburg	h	2-1	*Meier 2*
21/9	Bochum	a	0-0	
26/9	Karlsruhe	h	0-1	
30/9	Energie	a	2-2	*Amanatidis 2 (1p)*
7/10	Leverkusen	h	2-1	*Kyrgiakos 2*
20/10	Nürnberg	a	1-5	*Takahara*
26/10	Hannover	h	0-0	
3/11	Bayern	a	0-0	
10/11	Dortmund	a	1-1	*Amanatidis*
24/11	Stuttgart	h	1-4	*Köhler*
1/12	Wolfsburg	a	2-2	*Chris, Fink*
8/12	Schalke	h	2-2	*Toski, Amanatidis*
16/12	Duisburg	a	1-0	*Amanatidis*
2008				
2/2	Hertha	a	3-0	*Fenin 3*
8/2	Arminia	h	2-1	*Amanatidis, Fenin*
16/2	Hansa	a	0-1	
23/2	Bremen	h	1-0	*Amanatidis*
2/3	Hamburg	a	1-4	*Kyrgiakos*
8/3	Bochum	h	1-1	*Toski*
15/3	Karlsruhe	a	1-0	*Fink*
20/3	Energie	h	2-1	*Caio, Russ*
29/3	Leverkusen	a	2-0	*og (Kießling), Mantzios*
5/4	Nürnberg	h	1-3	*Fink*
12/4	Hannover	a	1-2	*Russ*
16/4	Bayern	h	1-3	*Köhler*
25/4	Dortmund	h	1-1	*Köhler*
3/5	Stuttgart	a	1-4	*Amanatidis*
7/5	Wolfsburg	h	2-3	*Amanatidis (p), Weissenberger*
10/5	Schalke	a	0-1	
17/5	Duisburg	h	4-2	*Amanatidis, Fenin 2, Heller*

No	Name	Nat	Pos	Aps	(s)	Gls
18	Ioannis AMANATIDIS	GRE	A	31	(1)	11
30	CAIO César Alves dos Santos	BRA	M	1	(9)	1
31	Mounir CHAFTAR		D		(6)	
29	Christian Maicon Hening "CHRIS"	BRA	D	9	(1)	1
17	Martin FENIN	CZE	A	16	(1)	6
6	Michael FINK		M	31	(1)	3
3	Aaron GALINDO	MEX	D	21	(1)	
9	Marcel HELLER		A		(4)	1
24	Martin HESS		A		(1)	
20	Junichi INAMOTO	JPN	M	21	(3)	
7	Benjamin KÖHLER		A	25	(4)	3
27	Sotiris KYRGIAKOS	GRE	D	24		3
22	Kreso LJUBIČIC	CRO	M		(1)	
15	Mehdi MAHDAVIKIA	IRN	M	12	(8)	
8	Evangelos MANTZIOS	GRE	A	2	(8)	1
14	Alexander MEIER		M	11		4
1	Oka NIKOLOV	MKD	G	11	(1)	
2	Patrick OCHS		D	29		
4	Christoph PREUSS		M	3	(4)	
21	Markus PRÖLL		G	23		
23	Marco RUSS		D	26	(3)	3
16	Christoph SPYCHER	SUI	D	30		
8	Albert STREIT		M	11		
19	Naohiro TAKAHARA	JPN	A	4	(4)	1
11	Michael THURK		A	6	(6)	1
32	Faton TOSKI		M	8	(4)	2
5	Aleksandar VASOSKI	MKD	D	3	(2)	
10	Markus WEISSENBERGER	AUT	M	16	(6)	1

FC ENERGIE COTTBUS

Coach – Petrik Sander; (23/9/07) (Heiko Weber); (28/9/07) Bojan Prašnikar (SVN)

Founded - 1966

2007				
11/8	Leverkusen	a	0-0	
19/8	Bochum	h	1-2	*Skela*
25/8	Dortmund	a	0-3	
11/9	Nürnberg	h	1-1	*Sørensen*
15/9	Stuttgart	a	0-3	
22/9	Wolfsburg	h	1-2	*Sørensen*
26/9	Bayern	a	0-5	
30/9	Eintracht	h	2-2	*Rangelov 2*
6/10	Hertha	a	0-0	
19/10	Duisburg	h	1-2	*Rost*
27/10	Arminia	a	1-1	*Sørensen*
2/11	Schalke	h	1-0	*Bassila*
10/11	Hansa	a	2-3	*Da Silva, Skela*
24/11	Bremen	h	0-2	
1/12	Karlsruhe	h	2-0	*Angelov, Rangelov*
8/12	Hamburg	a	0-0	
14/12	Hannover	h	5-1	*Bassila, Sørensen, Rangelov 2, Ziebig*
2008				
2/2	Leverkusen	h	2-3	*Papadopulos, Bassila*
9/2	Bochum	a	3-3	*Papadopulos, Skela, Jelić*
16/2	Dortmund	h	0-2	
24/2	Nürnberg	a	1-1	*Sørensen*
8/3	Wolfsburg	a	0-3	
11/3	Stuttgart	h	0-1	
15/3	Bayern	h	2-0	*Jelić 2*
20/3	Eintracht	a	1-2	*Rost*
30/3	Hertha	h	2-1	*Skela 2 (1p)*

4	Duisburg	a	1-0	*Skela*
/4	Arminia	h	1-0	*Skela (p)*
/4	Schalke	a	0-5	
/4	Hansa	h	2-1	*Rost, Rangelov*
5	Bremen	a	0-2	
5	Karlsruhe	a	1-1	*Rivić*
/5	Hamburg	h	2-0	*Rivić, Sørensen*
/5	Hannover	a	0-4	

o	Name	Nat	Pos	Aps	(s)	Gls
	Efstathios ALONEFTIS	CYP	M	3	(9)	
	Stanislav ANGELOV	BUL	D	31		1
	Christian BASSILA	FRA	M	21	(2)	3
	Steffen BAUMGART		A	2	(6)	
	Mario CVITANOVIĆ	CRO	D	31		
	Vragel DA SILVA	BRA	D	20	(1)	1
	Kristian IPSA	CRO	D	2	(2)	
	Branko JELIĆ	SRB	A	8	(7)	3
	Francis KIOYO	CMR	A	6	(5)	
	Mariusz KUKIELKA	POL	M	14		
	Igor MITRESKI	MKD	D	32		
	Christian MÜLLER		M		(1)	
	Michal PAPADOPULOS	CZE	A	7	(7)	2
	Tomislav PIPLICA	BIH	G	10		
	Ivan RADELJIĆ	BIH	D	9	(7)	
	Dimitar RANGELOV	BUL	A	16	(6)	6
	Stiven RIVIĆ	CRO	A	17	(11)	2
	Timo ROST		M	33		3
	SHAO Jiayi	CHN	M	1	(13)	
	Ervin SKELA	ALB	M	34		7
	Dennis SØRENSEN	DEN	A	31	(2)	6
	Zoltán SZELESI	HUN	D	1		
	Gerhard TREMMEL		G	24		
	Przemysław TRYTKO	POL	A		(1)	
	Dušan VASILJEVIĆ	SRB	M	2	(10)	
	Daniel ZIEBIG		D	19	(6)	1

HAMBURGER SV

Coach – Huub Stevens (NED)

Founded - 1919

MAJOR HONOURS: UEFA Cup Winners' Cup - (1) 1983; EFA European Cup-Winners' Cup - (1) 1977; German League - (6) 1923, 1928, 1960, 1979, 1982, 1983; German Cup - (3) 1963, 1976, 1987.

007				
1/8	Hannover	a	1-0	*Benjamin*
9/8	Leverkusen	h	1-0	*Van der Vaart (p)*
4/8	Bochum	a	1-2	*Van der Vaart (p)*
/9	Bayern	h	1-1	*Zidan*
5/9	Eintracht	a	1-2	*Van der Vaart (p)*
2/9	Nürnberg	h	1-0	*Van der Vaart*
5/9	Dortmund	a	3-0	*Guerrero, Van der Vaart, Olić*
9/9	Wolfsburg	h	2-2	*Reinhardt, Van der Vaart*
/10	Arminia	a	1-0	*Van der Vaart*
0/10	Stuttgart	h	4-1	*Olić 3, Mathijsen*
8/10	Duisburg	a	1-0	*Kompany*
/11	Hertha	h	2-1	*Guerrero, Reinhardt*
0/11	Schalke	a	1-1	*Olić*
5/11	Hansa	h	2-0	*Van der Vaart, Olić*
/12	Bremen	a	1-2	*Van der Vaart*
/12	Energie	h	0-0	
5/12	Karlsruhe	a	1-1	*Olić*
008				
/2	Hannover	h	1-1	*Olić*
/2	Leverkusen	a	1-1	*Van der Vaart*
7/2	Bochum	h	3-0	*Olić, Jarolím 2*
4/2	Bayern	a	1-1	*Olić*
/3	Eintracht	h	4-1	*Guerrero 2, De Jong, Zidan*
9/3	Nürnberg	a	0-0	
15/3	Dortmund	h	1-0	*Guerrero*
22/3	Wolfsburg	a	1-1	*Reinhardt*
29/3	Arminia	h	1-1	*Guerrero*
5/4	Stuttgart	a	0-1	
12/4	Duisburg	h	0-1	
15/4	Hertha	a	0-0	
26/4	Schalke	h	0-1	
3/5	Hansa	a	3-1	*Olić 2, Van der Vaart*
7/5	Bremen	h	0-1	
10/5	Energie	a	0-2	
17/5	Karlsruhe	h	7-0	*Van der Vaart (p), Guerrero 3, Trochowski, Olić 2*

No	Name	Nat	Pos	Aps	(s)	Gls
28	Otto ADDO	GHA	M		(4)	
3	Thimothée ATOUBA	CMR	D	18	(4)	
32	Änis BEN-HATIRA		M		(3)	
30	Collin BENJAMIN	NAM	D	12	(5)	1
19	Jérôme BOATENG		D	26	(1)	
24	Miso BREČKO	SVN	M	5	(9)	
18	Romeo CASTELEN	NED	M	7	(6)	
22	Eric Maxim CHOUPO-MOTING		A	1	(12)	
8	Nigel DE JONG	NED	M	28	(1)	1
20	Guy DEMEL	CIV	M	24	(2)	
13	Mario FILLINGER		M		(1)	
9	José Paolo GUERRERO	PER	A	24	(5)	9
12	Wolfgang HESL		M		(1)	
14	David JAROLÍM	CZE	M	28		2
10	Vincent KOMPANY	BEL	D	18	(4)	1
5	Joris MATHIJSEN	NED	D	31		1
6	Vadis ODJIDJA-OFOE	BEL	M		(2)	
11	Ivica OLIĆ	CRO	A	28	(4)	14
16	Anton PUTSILO	BLR	M		(3)	
4	Bastian REINHARDT		D	29	(3)	3
1	Frank ROST		G	34		
34	Sidney SAM		A		(4)	
2	Juan Pablo SORÍN	ARG	M	1	(4)	
15	Piotr TROCHOWSKI		M	25	(7)	1
23	Rafael VAN DER VAART	NED	M	28	(1)	12
7	Mohamed ZIDAN	EGY	A	7	(13)	2

HANNOVER 96

Coach – Dieter Hecking

Founded - 1896

MAJOR HONOURS: German League - (2) 1938, 1954; German Cup - (1) 1992.

2007				
11/8	Hamburg	h	0-1	
17/8	Karlsruhe	a	2-1	*Hanke, Balitsch*
25/8	Bayern	a	0-3	
1/9	Bochum	h	3-2	*Hanke, Rosenthal, Hashemian*
15/9	Nürnberg	a	2-2	*Hanke 2*
23/9	Leverkusen	h	0-3	
26/9	Arminia	a	2-0	*Huszti (p), Pinto*
30/9	Duisburg	h	2-1	*Schulz C. 2*
6/10	Stuttgart	a	2-0	*Huszti 2 (1p)*
21/10	Wolfsburg	h	2-2	*Pinto, Tarnat*
26/10	Eintracht	a	0-0	
3/11	Dortmund	h	2-1	*Huszti (p), Schulz C.*
10/11	Hertha	a	0-1	
24/11	Schalke	h	2-3	*Huszti 2 (1p)*
30/11	Hansa	a	3-0	*Fahrenhorst, Hanke, Štajner*
8/12	Bremen	h	4-3	*Hanke 3, og (Baumann)*
14/12	Energie	a	1-5	*Kleine*
2008				
2/2	Hamburg	a	1-1	*Huszti*

9/2	Karlsruhe	h	2-2	*Balitsch, Rosenthal*
17/2	Bayern	h	0-3	
22/2	Bochum	a	1-2	*Hanke*
1/3	Nürnberg	h	2-1	*Bruggink, Huszti*
9/3	Leverkusen	a	0-2	
15/3	Arminia	h	2-2	*Bruggink, Štajner*
22/3	Duisburg	a	1-1	*Štajner*
30/3	Stuttgart	h	0-0	
5/4	Wolfsburg	a	2-3	*Bruggink, Štajner*
12/4	Eintracht	h	2-1	*Pinto, Schulz C.*
17/4	Dortmund	a	3-1	*Bruggink, Fahrenhorst, Huszti*
26/4	Hertha	h	2-2	*Hanke, Štajner*
3/5	Schalke	a	1-1	*Bruggink*
6/5	Hansa	h	3-0	*Balitsch, Rosenthal 2*
10/5	Bremen	a	1-6	*Huszti*
17/5	Energie	h	4-0	*Bruggink, Štajner, Vinicius, Balitsch*

No	Name	Nat	Pos	Aps	(s)	Gls
14	Hanno BALITSCH		M	28	(1)	4
33	Ferhat BIKMAZ	TUR	M		(1)	
10	Arnold BRUGGINK	NED	M	18	(8)	6
6	Steven CHERUNDOLO	USA	D	33		
1	Robert ENKE		G	34		
22	Frank FAHRENHORST		D	20	(3)	2
35	Sören HALFAR		D	2		
9	Mike HANKE		A	31		10
16	Vahid HASHEMIAN	IRN	A	1	(19)	1
11	Szabolcs HUSZTI	HUN	M	32	(1)	10
4	Valérien ISMAËL	FRA	D	14		
5	Thomas KLEINE		D	8	(1)	1
17	Gaëtan KREBS	FRA	M	4	(6)	
8	Altin LALA	ALB	M	23	(4)	
21	Benjamin LAUTH		A	5	(16)	
7	Sérgio PINTO	POR	M	16	(4)	3
34	Konstantin RAUSCH		M	1	(1)	
26	Jan ROSENTHAL		M	15	(8)	4
35	Bastian SCHULZ		M		(2)	
19	Christian SCHULZ		D	26	(3)	4
24	Jiří ŠTAJNER	CZE	A	16	(10)	6
18	Michael TARNAT		D	16		1
2	VINÍCIUS Bergantin	BRA	D	27	(1)	1
23	Chavdar YANKOV	BUL	M	2	(6)	
15	Salvatore ZIZZO	USA	M		(2)	
3	Dariusz ŻURAW	POL	D	2	(3)	

FC HANSA ROSTOCK

Coach – Frank Pagelsdorf

Founded – 1965

MAJOR HONOURS: GDR League – (1) 1991; GDR Cup – (1) 1991.

2007				
11/8	Bayern	a	0-3	
18/8	Nürnberg	h	1-2	*Orestes*
26/8	Eintracht	a	0-1	
1/9	Dortmund	h	0-1	
15/9	Arminia	a	2-4	*Kern, Bülow*
22/9	Duisburg	h	2-0	*Hähnge, Kern (p)*
25/9	Hertha	a	3-1	*Rahn, Hähnge, Dorn*
29/9	Stuttgart	h	2-1	*Rathgeb, Orestes*
6/10	Wolfsburg	a	0-1	
20/10	Schalke	h	1-1	*Stein*
27/10	Karlsruhe	h	0-0	
3/11	Bremen	a	0-1	
10/11	Energie	h	3-2	*Kern 3*
25/11	Hamburg	a	0-2	
30/11	Hannover	h	0-3	
9/12	Leverkusen	a	0-3	
16/12	Bochum	h	2-0	*Bülow, Hähnge*
2008				
1/2	Bayern	h	1-2	*Kern*
9/2	Nürnberg	a	1-1	*Rahn*
16/2	Eintracht	h	1-0	*Rahn*
23/2	Dortmund	a	0-1	
1/3	Arminia	h	1-1	*Bartels*
8/3	Duisburg	a	1-1	*Agali*
15/3	Hertha	h	0-0	
22/3	Stuttgart	a	1-4	*Orestes*
28/3	Wolfsburg	h	0-1	
5/4	Schalke	a	0-1	
12/4	Karlsruhe	a	2-1	*Bartels 2*
15/4	Bremen	h	1-2	*Hähnge*
26/4	Energie	a	1-2	*Ćetković*
3/5	Hamburg	h	1-3	*og (Mathijsen)*
6/5	Hannover	a	0-3	
10/5	Leverkusen	h	1-2	*Menga*
17/5	Bochum	a	2-1	*Kern, Bartels*

No	Name	Nat	Pos	Aps	(s)	Gls
28	Victor AGALI	NGA	A	20	(3)	1
27	Fin BARTELS		M	15	(4)	4
22	Stefan BEINLICH		M	7	(2)	
31	Kai BÜLOW		M	27	(2)	2
8	Đorđije ĆETKOVIĆ	MNE	M	8	(5)	1
23	DIEGO MORAIS Pacheco	BRA	D	2	(5)	
20	Régis DORN	FRA	D	2	(13)	1
33	GLEDSON da Silva Menezes	BRA	D	10		
21	Jörg HAHNEL		G	6		
11	Sebastian HÄHNGE		A	10	(8)	4
9	Enrico KERN		A	32		7
2	Dexter LANGEN		D	23	(2)	
5	Benjamin LENSE		D	4	(3)	
16	Assani LUKIMYA	COD	D	2	(5)	
26	Addy-Waku MENGA	COD	A	3	(9)	1
4	ORESTES Júnior Alves	BRA	D	31	(1)	3
3	Heath PEARCE	USA	D	7	(12)	
15	Christian RAHN		M	28		3
17	Tobias RATHGEB		M	30		1
7	René RYDLEWICZ		M	2	(3)	
24	Marcel SCHIED		A	1	(1)	
13	Tim SEBASTIAN		D	31		
18	Amir SHAPOURZADEH	IRN	A	6	(9)	
12	Marc STEIN		D	28	(1)	1
25	Simon TÜTING		M		(1)	
1	Stefan WÄCHTER		G	28		
10	Zafer YELEN	TUR	M	11	(9)	

HERTHA BSC BERLIN

Coach – Lucien Favre (SUI)

Founded - 1892

MAJOR HONOURS: German League - (2) 1930, 1931.

2007				
11/8	Eintracht	a	0-1	
18/8	Stuttgart	h	3-1	*Chahed (p), Fathi, Okoronkwo*
25/8	Arminia	a	0-2	
1/9	Wolfsburg	h	2-1	*Pantelić, Okoronkwo*
16/9	Duisburg	a	2-1	*Pantelić 2*
22/9	Dortmund	h	3-2	*Pantelić, Lúcio, Okoronkwo*
25/9	Hansa	h	1-3	*Pantelić*
27/9	Schalke	a	0-1	
6/10	Energie	h	0-0	
20/10	Bremen	a	2-3	*Gilberto, Okoronkwo*
27/10	Bochum	h	2-0	*og (Maltritz), Pantelić*
3/11	Hamburg	a	1-2	*Ebert*
10/11	Hannover	h	1-0	*André Lima*
23/11	Karlsruhe	a	1-2	*Pantelić*
1/12	Leverkusen	h	0-3	

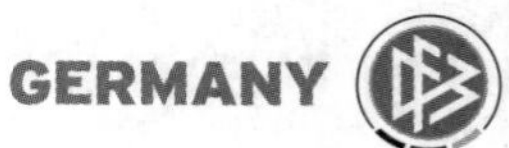

2	Nürnberg	a	1-2	*Lustenberger*
'12	Bayern	h	0-0	
08				
	Eintracht	h	0-3	
	Stuttgart	a	3-1	*Pantelić 2, Raffael*
'2	Arminia	h	1-0	*Raffael*
'2	Wolfsburg	a	0-0	
'2	Duisburg	h	2-0	*Raffael, Pantelić*
	Dortmund	a	1-1	*Pantelić*
'3	Hansa	a	0-0	
'3	Schalke	h	1-2	*Chahed (p)*
'3	Energie	a	1-2	*Mineiro*
	Bremen	h	1-2	*André Lima*
'4	Bochum	a	1-1	*Skácel*
'4	Hamburg	h	0-0	
'4	Hannover	a	2-2	*Chahed (p), Piszczek*
	Karlsruhe	h	3-1	*Kaćar, Pantelić, Skácel*
	Leverkusen	a	2-1	*Pantelić, Chahed (p)*
'5	Nürnberg	h	1-0	*Raffael*
'5	Bayern	a	1-4	*Domovchiyski*

Name	Nat	Pos	Aps	(s)	Gls
ANDRÉ Barreto Silva LIMA	BRA	A	10	(5)	2
Bryan ARGUEZ	USA	M		(1)	
Pascal BIELER		D	1	(5)	
Sofian CHAHED		M	31	(2)	4
Pál DÁRDAI	HUN	M	13	(10)	
Valeri DOMOVCHIYSKI	BUL	A		(4)	1
Jaroslav DROBNÝ	CZE	G	34		
Patrick EBERT		M	25	(2)	1
Chinedu EDE		A	1	(3)	
Malik FATHI		D	22		1
Arne FRIEDRICH		D	30		
GILBERTO da Silva Melo	BRA	M	14	(1)	1
Tobias GRAHN	SWE	M	6	(7)	
Gojko KAĆAR	SRB	M	17		1
Srđan LAKIĆ	CRO	A		(1)	
LÚCIO Carlos Cajueiro Souza	BRA	M	7	(1)	1
Fabian LUSTENBERGER	SUI	M	18	(6)	1
Carlos Luciano da Silva "MINEIRO"	BRA	M	17	(9)	1
Christian MÜLLER		M	1		
Solomon OKORONKWO	NGA	A	3	(19)	4
Marko PANTELIĆ	SRB	A	27	(1)	13
Łukasz PISZCZEK	POL	A	12	(12)	1
RAFFAEL de Araújo	BRA	A	15		4
Andreas SCHMIDT		M	5	(1)	
Josip ŠIMUNIĆ	CRO	D	29		
Rudolf SKÁCEL	CZE	M	15	(1)	2
Ibrahima TRAORÉ	FRA	M		(1)	
Steve VON BERGEN	SUI	D	21	(4)	

KARLSRUHER SC

Coach – Edmund Becker

Founded - 1894

MAJOR HONOURS: German League - (1) 1909; German Cup - (2) 1955, 1956.

07				
/8	Nürnberg	a	2-0	*Hajnal 2*
/8	Hannover	h	1-2	Franz
/8	Leverkusen	a	0-3	
)	Stuttgart	h	1-0	*Hajnal*
/9	Wolfsburg	a	2-1	*Eggimann, Eichner*
'9	Bayern	h	1-4	*Porcello*
/9	Eintracht	a	1-0	*Franz*
/9	Dortmund	h	3-1	*Porcello, Eggimann, Freis*
10	Schalke	a	2-0	*Timm 2*
/10	Arminia	h	0-0	
/10	Hansa	a	0-0	
4/11	Duisburg	h	1-0	*Eggimann*
10/11	Bremen	a	0-4	
23/11	Hertha	h	2-1	*Hajnal, Freis*
1/12	Energie	a	0-2	
8/12	Bochum	a	2-2	*Hajnal, Freis*
15/12	Hamburg	h	1-1	*Timm*
2008				
2/2	Nürnberg	h	2-0	*Eichner, Kennedy*
9/2	Hannover	a	2-2	*Kennedy, Hajnal*
16/2	Leverkusen	h	2-2	*Freis, Kennedy*
23/2	Stuttgart	a	1-3	*Hajnal*
1/3	Wolfsburg	h	3-1	*Eggimann, Kennedy, og (Ricardo Costa)*
8/3	Bayern	a	0-2	
15/3	Eintracht	h	0-1	
22/3	Dortmund	a	1-1	*Freis*
29/3	Schalke	h	0-0	
5/4	Arminia	a	0-1	
12/4	Hansa	h	1-2	*Freis*
16/4	Duisburg	a	1-0	*Hajnal*
26/4	Bremen	h	3-3	*Freis 2, Kapllani*
3/5	Hertha	a	1-3	*Kapllani*
6/5	Energie	h	1-1	*Buck*
10/5	Bochum	h	1-3	*Eggimann*
17/5	Hamburg	a	0-7	

No	Name	Nat	Pos	Aps	(s)	Gls
4	Godfried ADUOBE	GHA	M	18	(6)	
19	Stefan BUCK		D	5	(8)	1
6	Bradley CARNELL	RSA	M	13	(4)	
23	Florian DICK		D	1	(2)	
5	Mario EGGIMANN	SUI	D	33		5
21	Christian EICHNER		D	33		2
3	Maik FRANZ		D	29		2
18	Sebastian FREIS		A	23	(8)	8
77	Andreas GÖRLITZ		D	31		
30	Tamás HAJNAL	HUN	M	32		8
20	Aleksandre IASHVILI	GEO	A	19	(9)	
9	Edmond KAPLLANI	ALB	A	14	(14)	2
17	Joshua KENNEDY	AUS	A	10		4
14	Jean-Francois KORNETZKY	FRA	G	6		
1	Markus MILLER		G	28		
13	Michael MUTZEL		M	28	(1)	
11	Sanibal ORAHOVAC	MNE	A		(4)	
10	Massimilian PORCELLO		M	18	(7)	2
8	Timo STAFFELDT		M	3	(13)	
28	Lars STINDL		M		(2)	
16	Martin STOLL		D	6	(2)	
7	Christian TIMM		A	24	(6)	3

1. FC NÜRNBERG

Coach – Hans Meyer; (11/2/08) Thomas von Heesen

Founded - 1900

MAJOR HONOURS: German League - (9) 1920, 1921, 1924, 1925, 1927, 1936, 1948, 1961, 1968; German Cup - (4) 1935, 1939, 1962, 2007.

2007				
12/8	Karlsruhe	h	0-2	
18/8	Hansa	a	2-1	*Galásek, Kluge*
25/8	Bremen	h	0-1	
1/9	Energie	a	1-1	*Wolf*
15/9	Hannover	h	2-2	*Misimović, Mintál*
22/9	Hamburg	a	0-1	
26/9	Leverkusen	h	1-2	*Mintál (p)*
29/9	Bochum	a	3-3	*Kluge 2, Misimović*
7/10	Bayern	a	0-3	
20/10	Eintracht	h	5-1	*Charisteas, Mintál 2, Misimović (p), Kennedy*
27/10	Wolfsburg	a	1-3	*Misimović (p)*
3/11	Stuttgart	h	0-1	
11/11	Arminia	a	1-3	*Wolf*

25/11	Dortmund	h	2-0	*Galásek, Charisteas*
2/12	Duisburg	a	0-1	
9/12	Hertha	h	2-1	*Charisteas, Misimović*
15/12	Schalke	a	1-2	*Charisteas*
2008				
2/2	Karlsruhe	a	0-2	
9/2	Hansa	h	1-1	*Koller*
16/2	Bremen	a	0-2	
24/2	Energie	h	1-1	*Engelhardt*
1/3	Hannover	a	1-2	*Misimović*
9/3	Hamburg	h	0-0	
16/3	Leverkusen	a	1-4	*Misimović*
22/3	Bochum	h	1-1	*Misimović*
29/3	Bayern	h	1-1	*Misimović*
5/4	Eintracht	a	3-1	*Charisteas, Vittek, Misimović*
16/4	Stuttgart	a	0-3	
20/4	Wolfsburg	h	1-0	*Koller*
26/4	Arminia	h	2-2	*Mintál, Saenko*
2/5	Dortmund	a	0-0	
7/5	Duisburg	h	2-0	*Charisteas, Pinola*
10/5	Hertha	a	0-1	
17/5	Schalke	h	0-2	

No	Name	Nat	Pos	Aps	(s)	Gls
27	Jacques ABARDONADO	FRA	D	9	(1)	
17	Nicky ADLER		M	5	(8)	
3	Michael BEAUCHAMP	AUS	D	10	(2)	
32	Leon BENKO	CRO	A		(3)	
29	Jaromír BLAŽEK	CZE	G	25		
9	Angelos CHARISTEAS	GRE	A	20	(4)	6
22	Marco ENGELHARDT		M	16	(6)	1
6	Tomáš GALÁSEK	CZE	M	30	(1)	2
4	Leandro Honorato GLÁUBER	BRA	D	15	(4)	
2	Lars JACOBSEN	DEN	D	6	(1)	
20	Joshua KENNEDY	AUS	A	3	(9)	1
18	Daniel KLEWER		G	9	(1)	
24	Peer KLUGE		M	22		3
19	Jan KOLLER	CZE	A	14		2
15	Jan KRISTIANSEN	DEN	M	15	(4)	
11	Marek MINTÁL	SVK	M	23	(8)	5
10	Zvjezdan MISIMOVIĆ	BIH	M	23	(5)	10
36	Jawhar MNARI	TUN	M	14	(7)	
35	Chhunly PAGENBURG		A		(1)	
25	Horacio Javier PINOLA	ARG	D	19		1
28	Dominik REINHARDT		D	24	(1)	
13	Ivan SAENKO	RUS	A	20	(6)	1
16	Ralf SCHMIDT		D	3	(5)	
23	Matthew SPIRANOVIC	AUS	D	6	(1)	
21	Dario VIDOSIC	AUS	M		(4)	
33	Róbert VITTEK	SVK	A	13	(4)	1
5	Andreas WOLF		D	30		2

FC SCHALKE 04

Coach – Mirko Slomka; (13/4/08) Mike Büskens & Youri Mulder (NED)

Founded - 1904

MAJOR HONOURS: UEFA Cup - (1) 1997; German League - (7) 1934, 1935, 1937, 1939, 1940, 1942, 1958; German Cup - (4) 1937, 1972, 2001, 2002.

2007				
10/8	Stuttgart	a	2-2	*Kobiashvili, Rakitić*
18/8	Dortmund	h	4-1	*Bordon, Pander, Asamoah, Kuranyi*
26/8	Wolfsburg	a	1-1	*Altıntop*
31/8	Leverkusen	h	1-1	*Kuranyi*
15/9	Bayern	a	1-1	*Rakitić*
22/9	Arminia	h	3-0	*Kuranyi, Asamoah, Rafinha (p)*
25/9	Duisburg	a	2-0	*Altıntop, Kuranyi*
28/9	Hertha	h	1-0	*Rafinha (p)*
6/10	Karlsruhe	h	0-2	
20/10	Hansa	a	1-1	*Asamoah*
27/10	Bremen	h	1-1	*Grossmüller*
2/11	Energie	a	0-1	
10/11	Hamburg	h	1-1	*Krstajić*
24/11	Hannover	a	3-2	*Kuranyi 2, Altıntop*
1/12	Bochum	h	1-0	*Bordon*
8/12	Eintracht	a	2-2	*Westermann 2*
15/12	Nürnberg	h	2-1	*Asamoah, og (Engelhardt)*
2008				
2/2	Stuttgart	h	4-1	*Kuranyi 2, Westerma Zé Roberto*
10/2	Dortmund	a	3-2	*Asamoah, og (Amedick), Ernst*
15/2	Wolfsburg	h	1-2	*Sánchez*
23/2	Leverkusen	a	0-1	
1/3	Bayern	h	0-1	
8/3	Arminia	a	2-0	*Varela, Altıntop*
14/3	Duisburg	h	2-1	*Kuranyi, Westermann*
23/3	Hertha	a	2-1	*Asamoah, Jones*
29/3	Karlsruhe	a	0-0	
5/4	Hansa	h	1-0	*Altıntop*
12/4	Bremen	a	1-5	*Kuranyi*
15/4	Energie	h	5-0	*og (Da Silva), Kuranyi*
26/4	Hamburg	a	1-0	*Kuranyi*
3/5	Hannover	h	1-1	*Altıntop*
6/5	Bochum	a	3-0	*Asamoah, Rakitić, Bordon*
10/5	Eintracht	h	1-0	*Krstajić*
17/5	Nürnberg	a	2-0	*Bordon 2*

No	Name	Nat	Pos	Aps	(s)	Gls
19	Halil ALTINTOP	TUR	A	17	(8)	6
14	Gerald ASAMOAH		A	23	(7)	7
26	Mimoun AZAOUAGH		M		(5)	
25	Zlatan BAJRAMOVIĆ	BIH	M	9	(3)	
5	Marcelo José BORDON	BRA	D	31		5
8	Fabian ERNST		M	32	(1)	1
21	Carlos Javier GROSSMÜLLER	URU	M	5	(6)	1
23	Benedikt HÖWEDES		D	3	(3)	
13	Jermaine JONES		M	29	(1)	1
3	Levan KOBIASHVILI	GEO	M	8	(5)	1
20	Mladen KRSTAJIĆ	SRB	D	23		2
22	Kevin KURANYI		A	31	(1)	15
9	Søren LARSEN	DEN	A	2	(8)	
11	Peter LØVENKRANDS	DEN	A	6	(14)	
1	Manuel NEUER		G	34		
17	Mesut ÖZIL		M	6	(5)	
24	Christian PANDER		D	17		1
18	Márcio Rafael "RAFINHA"	BRA	D	31	(1)	2
10	Ivan RAKITIĆ	CRO	M	23	(6)	3
16	Darío Octavio RODRÍGUEZ	URU	D	1	(2)	
27	Vicente SÁNCHEZ	URU	A	5	(9)	1
6	Albert STREIT		M	5	(5)	
7	Gustavo Antonio VARELA	URU	M	2		1
2	Heiko WESTERMANN		D	31	(1)	4
15	José ZÉ ROBERTO de Oliveira	BRA	M		(3)	1

VFB STUTTGART

Coach – Armin Veh

Founded - 1893

MAJOR HONOURS: German League - (5) 1950, 1952, 1984, 1992, 2007; German Cup - (3), 1954, 1958, 1997.

2007				
10/8	Schalke	h	2-2	*Khedira, Pardo (p)*
18/8	Hertha	a	1-3	*Hitzlsperger*
25/8	Duisburg	h	1-0	*Gómez*
2/9	Karlsruhe	a	0-1	

9	Energie	h	3-0	*Cacau, Ewerthon, Gómez*
9	Bremen	a	1-4	*Gómez*
9	Bochum	h	1-0	*Hilbert*
9	Hansa	a	1-2	*Gómez*
0	Hannover	h	0-2	
10	Hamburg	a	1-4	*Tasci*
10	Leverkusen	h	1-0	*Beck*
1	Nürnberg	a	1-0	*Gómez*
11	Bayern	h	3-1	*Gómez 2, Baştürk*
11	Eintracht	a	4-1	*Hilbert, Marica, Hitzlsperger, Cacau*
2	Dortmund	h	1-2	*Fernando Meira*
2	Wolfsburg	h	3-1	*Marica, Cacau, Hitzlsperger*
12	Arminia	a	0-2	

)8

	Schalke	a	1-4	*Da Silva*
	Hertha	h	1-3	*Gómez*
2	Duisburg	a	3-2	*Gómez 2, Hitzlsperger*
2	Karlsruhe	h	3-1	*Gómez, Hilbert, Cacau*
	Bremen	h	6-3	*Gómez 3, Cacau 2, og (Mertesacker)*
3	Energie	a	1-0	*Fernando Meira*
3	Bochum	a	1-1	*Hitzlsperger*
3	Hansa	h	4-1	*Pardo (p), Cacau, Gómez, Bastürk*
3	Hannover	a	0-0	
	Hamburg	h	1-0	*Hilbert*
4	Leverkusen	a	0-3	
4	Nürnberg	h	3-0	*Cacau, Da Silva, Fernando Meira*
4	Bayern	a	1-4	*Da Silva*
	Eintracht	h	4-1	*Bastürk 2, Gómez, Cacau*
	Dortmund	a	2-3	*Gómez 2*
5	Wolfsburg	a	0-4	
5	Arminia	h	2-2	*Gómez (p), Fischer*

Name	Nat	Pos	Aps	(s)	Gls
Yildiray BAŞTÜRK	TUR	M	24	(2)	4
Andreas BECK		D	12	(6)	1
Arthur BOKA	CIV	D	11	(6)	
Jeronimo de Silva "CACAU"	BRA	A	24	(3)	9
Antônio DA SILVA	BRA	M	10	(10)	3
Mathieu DELPIERRE	FRA	D	22		
EWERTHON Henrique de Souza	BRA	A	3	(8)	1
Alexander FARNERUD	SWE	M	3	(8)	
FERNANDO MEIRA	POR	D	27	(1)	3
Manuel FISCHER		A		(2)	1
Mario GÓMEZ		A	23	(2)	19
Roberto HILBERT		M	30	(2)	4
Thomas HITZLSPERGER		M	23	(2)	5
Sami KHEDIRA		M	19	(5)	1
Ludovic MAGNIN	SUI	D	21	(6)	
Ciprian MARICA	ROU	A	15	(13)	2
Silvio MEISSNER		M		(8)	
Ricardo OSORIO	MEX	D	20	(2)	
Pavel PARDO	MEX	M	29		2
Peter PERCHTOLD		M		(2)	
Marco PISCHORN		D	1	(3)	
David PISOT		D	1		
Sergiu Marian RADU	ROU	A	1	(1)	
Raphael SCHÄFER		G	23		
Julian SCHUSTER		M		(2)	
Serdar TASCI		D	20	(1)	1
Christian TRÄSCH		M	1		
Sven ULREICH		G	11		

WERDER BREMEN

Coach – Thomas Schaaf

Founded - 1899

MAJOR HONOURS: UEFA Cup Winners' Cup - (1) 1992; German League - (4) 1965, 1988, 1993, 2004; German Cup - (5) 1961, 1991, 1994, 1999, 2004.

2007

11/8	Bochum	a	2-2	*Diego (p), Sanogo*
18/8	Bayern	h	0-4	
25/8	Nürnberg	a	1-0	*Harnik*
1/9	Eintracht	h	2-1	*Sanogo, Pasanen*
14/9	Dortmund	a	0-3	
22/9	Stuttgart	h	4-1	*Hugo Almeida 2, Sanogo, Diego*
25/9	Wolfsburg	a	1-1	*Diego*
29/9	Arminia	h	8-1	*Niemeyer, Hugo Almeida 2, Sanogo 2, Mertesacker, Rosenberg, Diego*
6/10	Duisburg	a	3-1	*Jensen, Sanogo, Andreasen*
20/10	Hertha	h	3-2	*Hugo Almeida, Rosenberg, Andreasen*
27/10	Schalke	a	1-1	*Naldo*
3/11	Hansa	h	1-0	*Hugo Almeida*
10/11	Karlsruhe	h	4-0	*Diego 2, Hugo Almeida, Naldo*
24/11	Energie	a	2-0	*Diego (p), Mosquera*
1/12	Hamburg	h	2-1	*Sanogo, Pasanen*
8/12	Hannover	a	3-4	*Rosenberg 2, Diego (p)*
15/12	Leverkusen	h	5-2	*Klasnić 2, Diego, Fritz, Rosenberg*

2008

3/2	Bochum	h	1-2	*Jensen*
10/2	Bayern	a	1-1	*Diego*
16/2	Nürnberg	h	2-0	*Rosenberg, Klasnić*
23/2	Eintracht	a	0-1	
1/3	Dortmund	h	2-0	*Rosenberg 2*
8/3	Stuttgart	a	3-6	*Hugo Almeida, Boenisch, Rosenberg*
16/3	Wolfsburg	h	0-1	
23/3	Arminia	a	1-1	*Diego (p)*
29/3	Duisburg	h	1-2	*Diego*
5/4	Hertha	a	2-1	*Rosenberg, Borowski*
12/4	Schalke	h	5-1	*Baumann, Sanogo, Rosenberg, Klasnić 2*
15/4	Hansa	a	2-1	*Frings, Klasnić*
26/4	Karlsruhe	a	3-3	*Diego, Özil, Sanogo*
3/5	Energie	h	2-0	*Rosenberg, Hugo Almeida*
7/5	Hamburg	a	1-0	*Hugo Almeida*
10/5	Hannover	h	6-1	*Hugo Almeida, Naldo, Borowski, Klasnić, Rosenberg, Hunt*
17/5	Leverkusen	a	1-0	*Rosenberg*

No	Name	Nat	Pos	Aps	(s)	Gls
16	Leon ANDREASEN	DEN	M	3	(7)	2
6	Frank BAUMANN		M	21	(2)	1
2	Sebastian BOENISCH		D	6	(3)	1
24	Tim BOROWSKI		M	20	(1)	2
19	CARLOS ALBERTO Gomes de Jesus	BRA	M		(2)	
10	DIEGO Ribas de Cunha	BRA	M	30		13
22	Torsten FRINGS		M	11		1
8	Clemens FRITZ		D	18	(5)	1
34	Martin HARNIK	AUT	A	3	(6)	1
23	HUGO ALMEIDA	POR	A	18	(4)	11
14	Aaron HUNT		A	6	(8)	1
20	Daniel JENSEN	DEN	M	27		2

17	Ivan KLASNIĆ	CRO	A	9	(7)	7
36	Max KRUSE		M		(1)	
29	Per MERTESACKER		D	32		1
27	John Jairo MOSQUERA	COL	A		(3)	1
4	Ronaldo Aparecido "NALDO"	BRA	D	32		3
25	Peter NIEMEYER		M	1	(2)	1
15	Patrick OWOMOYELA		D	4	(5)	
11	Mesut ÖZIL		M	6	(6)	1
3	Petri PASANEN	FIN	D	27	(1)	2
9	Markus ROSENBERG	SWE	A	21	(9)	14
18	Boubacar SANOGO	CIV	A	17	(4)	9
28	Kevin SCHINDLER		A		(4)	
27	Christian SCHULZ		D	3		
13	Duško TOŠIĆ	SRB	D	12		
33	Christian VANDER		G	3		
7	Jurica VRANJEŠ	CRO	M	13	(9)	
1	Tim WIESE		G	31		

VFL WOLFSBURG

Coach – Felix Magath

Founded - 1945

2007				
11/8	Arminia	h	1-3	*Radu*
18/8	Duisburg	a	3-1	*Marcelinho, Madlung, Radu*
26/8	Schalke	h	1-1	*Krzynówek*
1/9	Hertha	a	1-2	*Dejagah*
16/9	Karlsruhe	h	1-2	*Krzynówek*
22/9	Energie	a	2-1	*Džeko, Krzynówek*
25/9	Bremen	h	1-1	*Josué*
29/9	Hamburg	a	2-2	*Grafite (p), Dejagah*
6/10	Hansa	h	1-0	*Džeko*
21/10	Hannover	a	2-2	*Marcelinho, Dejagah*
27/10	Nürnberg	h	3-1	*og (Charisteas), Grafite, Dejagah*
4/11	Bochum	a	3-5	*Schäfer, Grafite 2*
11/11	Leverkusen	h	1-2	*og (Friedrich)*
24/11	Bayern	a	1-2	*Dejagah*
1/12	Eintracht	h	2-2	*Gentner, Džeko*
8/12	Stuttgart	a	1-3	*Džeko*
15/12	Dortmund	h	4-0	*Schäfer, Ricardo Costa, Gentner, Džeko*
2008				
2/2	Arminia	a	1-0	*Grafite*
9/2	Duisburg	h	2-1	*Schäfer, Grafite*
15/2	Schalke	a	2-1	*Grafite 2 (1p)*
23/2	Hertha	h	0-0	
1/3	Karlsruhe	a	1-3	*Schäfer*
8/3	Energie	h	3-0	*Gentner, Marcelinho 2*
16/3	Bremen	a	1-0	*Grafite*
22/3	Hamburg	h	1-1	*Ljuboja*
28/3	Hansa	a	1-0	*Krzynówek*
5/4	Hannover	h	3-2	*Dejagah 2, Marcelinho*
15/4	Bochum	h	0-1	
20/4	Nürnberg	a	0-1	
27/4	Leverkusen	a	2-2	*Džeko, Hasebe*
4/5	Bayern	h	0-0	
7/5	Eintracht	a	3-2	*Grafite, Schäfer, Džeko*
10/5	Stuttgart	h	4-0	*Marcelinho, Džeko, Ricardo Costa, Dejagah*
17/5	Dortmund	a	4-2	*Riether, Marcelinho, Schäfer, Grafite*

No	Name	Nat	Pos	Aps	(s)	Gls
8	Daniel BAIER		M	9	(6)	
16	Diego BENAGLIO	SUI	G	17		
13	Isaac BOAKYE	GHA	A	1	(1)	
24	Ashkan DEJAGAH		M	19	(12)	8
9	Edin DŽEKO	BIH	A	17	(11)	8
25	Christian GENTNER		M	26	(5)	3
23	Edinaldo Batista Libanio "GRAFITE"	BRA	A	22	(2)	11
13	Makoto HASEBE	JPN	M	13	(3)	1
1	Simon JENTZSCH		G	15		
7	JOSUÉ Anunciado de Oliveira	BRA	M	28	(2)	1
37	Sergej KARIMOV		D	3	(1)	
10	Jacek KRZYNÓWEK	POL	M	11	(8)	4
11	Alexander LAAS		M		(4)	
12	André LENZ		G	2	(1)	
40	Danijel LJUBOJA	SRB	A	4	(4)	1
17	Alexander MADLUNG		D	23	(4)	1
32	MARCELINHO dos Santos	BRA	M	33		7
16	Uwe MÖHLRE		D	1		
19	Vlad MUNTEANU	ROU	M	4	(6)	
36	Mame Cheikh NIANG	SEN	A		(4)	
2	Facundo Hernán QUIROGA	ARG	D	10	(2)	
29	Sergiu Marian RADU	ROU	A	4	(7)	2
5	RICARDO Miguel Moreira da COSTA	POR	D	19	(1)	2
20	Sascha RIETHER		M	25	(2)	1
14	Jonathan SANTANA	PAR	M	7	(3)	
4	Marcel SCHÄFER		M	28	(1)	6
6	Jan ŠIMŮNEK	CZE	D	26	(4)	
28	Pablo THIAM	GUI	M	6	(4)	
3	Peter VAN DER HEYDEN	BEL	D	1		

PROMOTED CLUBS

VFL BORUSSIA MÖNCHENGLADBAC

Coach – Jos Luhukay (NED)

Founded - 1900

MAJOR HONOURS: UEFA Cup - (2) 1975, 1979; German League - (5) 1971, 1975, 1976, 1977; German Cup - (3) 1960, 1973, 1995..

TSG 1899 HOFFENHEIM

Coach – Ralf Rangnick

Founded – 1899

1. FC KÖLN

Coach – Christoph Daum

Founded - 1948

MAJOR HONOURS: German League - (3) 1962, 1964, 1978; German Cup - (4) 1968, 1977, 1978, 1983.

SECOND LEVEL FINAL TABLE 2007/

		Pld	W	D	L	F	A
1	VfL Borussia Mönchengladbach	34	18	12	4	71	38
2	TSG 1899 Hoffenheim	34	17	9	8	60	40
3	1. FC Köln	34	17	9	8	62	44
4	FSV Mainz 05	34	16	10	8	62	36
5	SC Freiburg	34	15	10	9	49	44
6	SpVgg Greuther Fürth	34	14	10	10	53	47
7	Alemannia Aachen	34	14	9	11	49	44
8	SV Wehen Wiesbaden	34	11	11	12	47	53
9	FC St. Pauli Hamburg	34	11	9	14	47	53
10	TuS Koblenz	34	12	11	11	46	47
11	TSV 1860 München	34	9	14	11	42	45
12	VfL Osnabrück	34	10	10	14	43	54
13	1. FC Kaiserslautern	34	9	12	13	37	37
14	FC Augsburg	34	10	8	16	39	51
15	Kickers Offenbach	34	9	11	14	38	60
16	FC Erzgebirge Aue	34	7	11	16	49	57
17	SC 07 Paderborn	34	6	13	15	33	54
18	FC Carl Zeiss Jena	34	6	11	17	45	68

N.B. TuS Koblenz – 6 pts deducted

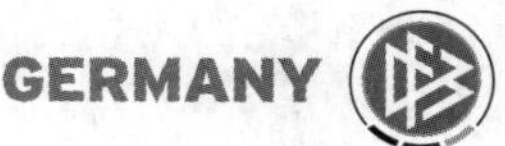

DOMESTIC CUP 2007/08

DFB-POKAL

ST ROUND

3/07)
ffenheim 4, Augsburg 2 *(aet)*

4/07)
dhausen 0, Offenbach 4
abrück 0, Mönchengladbach 1
l 0, 1860 München 3
Pauli 1, Leverkusen 0
gdeburg 1, Dortmund 4
erhaching 0, Hertha 3
unschweig 0, Bremen 1
en 1, Hannover 3
en 2, Energie 2 *(aet; 6-5 on pens)*
helmshaven 0, Kaiserslautern 4
born 0, Hansa 8
hen Wiesbaden 1, Stuttgart 2

3/07)
a 0, Jena 3
ppertal 1, Aue 1 *(aet; 4-3 on pens)*
ngen 1, Freiburg 3
toria Hamburg 0, Nürnberg 6
l 0, Hamburger SV 5
men II 4, Köln 2 (aet)
on Berlin 1, Frankfurt 4
elsberg 0, Duisburg 4
erkusen II 0, Paderborn 1
ünd 0, Aachen 3
ustrelitz 0, Karlsruhe 2 *(aet)*
velse 0, Koblenz 3
sden 0, Bochum 1
genporten 0, Arminia 2
rzburg 0, Wolfsburg 4
r 0, Schalke 9
rms 1, Mainz 6
rmstadt 1, Greuther Fürth 3

3/07)
ghausen 1, Bayern 1 *(aet; 3-4 on pens)*

COND ROUND

/10/07)
men II 2, St. Pauli 2 *(aet; 4-2 on pens)*
ppertal 2, Hertha 0
chen 3, Bochum 2
nsa 6, Offenbach 0
60 München 2, Mainz 1
lsruhe 0, Wolfsburg 1
ffenheim 2, Greuther Fürth 1
alke 2, Hannover 0 *(aet)*

/10/07)
en 2, Kaiserslautern 1
ttgart 3, Paderborn 2 *(aet)*
mburger SV 3, Freiburg 1
men 4, Duisburg 0
rtmund 2, Frankfurt 1
olenz 1, Arminia 2 *(aet)*
a 2, Nürnberg 2 *(aet; 5-4 on pens)*
yern 3, Mönchengladbach 1

THIRD ROUND

(29/1/08)
Hoffenheim 2, Rostock 1
Aachen 2, 1860 München 3
Wuppertal 2, Bayern 5
Dortmund 2, Bremen 1

(30/1/08)
Jena 2, Arminia 1 *(aet)*
Essen 0, Hamburger SV 3
Bremen II 2, Stuttgart 3
Wolfsburg 1, Schalke 1 *(aet; 5-3 on pens)*

QUARTER-FINALS

(26/2/08)
Dortmund 3 *(Frederico 20, Tinga 23, Petrić 54)*, Hoffenheim 1 *(Copado 38p)*
Stuttgart 2 *(Gómez 81, 94)*, Jena 2 *(Werner 32, Müller 120)* *(aet; 4-5 on pens)*

(27/2/08)
Wolfsburg 2 *(Grafite 17, Marcelinho 109)*, Hamburger SV 1 *(Van der Vaart 70) (aet)*
Bayern 1 *(Ribéry 120p)*, 1860 München 0 *(aet)*

SEMI-FINALS

(18/3/08)
Dortmund 3 *(Tinga 13, Klimowicz 70, Petrić 87)*, Jena 0

(19/3/08)
Bayern 2 *(Ribéry 60, Klose 66)*, Wolfsburg 0

FINAL

(19/4/08)
Olympiastadion, Berlin
FC BAYERN MÜNCHEN 2 *(Toni 11, 103)*
BV BORUSSIA DORTMUND 1 *(Petrić 90)*
(aet)
Referee – *Kircher*
BAYERN – *Kahn, Lell, Lúcio, Demichelis, Lahm, Van Bommel, Zé Roberto (Ottl 113), Schweinsteiger (Sagnol 84), Ribéry, Klose (Podolski 69), Toni.*
DORTMUND – *Ziegler; Rukavina (Buckley 79), Wörns, Kovač, Dedé, Kehl (Valdez 86), Błaszczykowski, Tinga, Kringe, Petrić, Frei (Klimowicz 71).*
Sent off: *Błaszczykowski (108)*

Holders go home with nothing

UEFA EURO 2004™ gave Greek football fans the memory of a lifetime, but it was a very different story for coach Otto Rehhagel and his players in 2008.

Even with the core of the title-winning squad from Portugal still in place, the defence of the Henri Delaunay trophy always looked an extremely tall order, and after three defeats in Salzburg against Sweden (0-2), Russia (0-1) and Spain (1-2), Greece not only went home empty-handed but with the worst record of all 16 competing teams. Having seen their team qualify for the finals in such style, amassing more points, 31, than any other UEFA EURO 2008™ participant, Greek fans were entitled to feel badly let down.

The team's misadventure began against Sweden, with Rehhagel adopting an extremely cautious approach. The holders' chief priority was evidently to keep things tight in defence and get a draw, but once they went behind, they were unable to chase the game. Greece faced Russia knowing that a second defeat would eliminate them, but while their general play improved, their attack again looked unimaginative, and after veteran goalkeeper Antonis Nikopolidis had gifted Russia the lead, once again they could not respond.

The final match, against Spain, was a dead rubber, and although Rehhagel's team lost, they did at least score a goal – headed home from a free-kick in vintage summer-of-2004 style by Angelos Charisteas. The Gree No9 deserved his goal for perseverance alone, but the were few other plus points, and the overriding feeling was that UEFA EURO 2004™ had simply been a gloriou one-off, a remarkable flash in the pan.

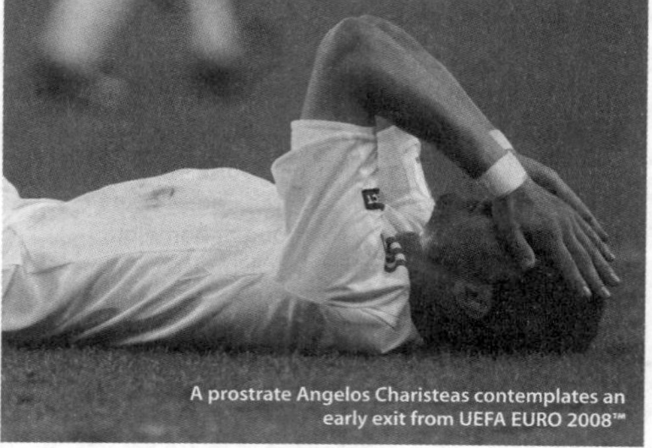

A prostrate Angelos Charisteas contemplates an early exit from UEFA EURO 2008™

Creative void

It was understandable that Rehhagel sought to go wit the same safety-first strategy that had served him so well in Portugal. The problem was that the team posed no goal threat other than from set-pieces. A shortage c pace and, especially, a lack of creativity rendered them almost helpless when they were obliged to attack in open play. Greece could have done with the craft and ingenuity of Olympiacos CFP schemer Ieroklis Stoltidis. By popular demand the 33-year-old left-footer had finally been called up by Rehhagel in February, but disappointingly he declined the invitation, citing his ag and heavy workload at club level.

After the tournament, while the Hellenic Football Federation confirmed that Rehhagel, 69, would be stayir on for the 2010 FIFA World Cup qualifying campaign, in which Greece have a very favourable draw, Nikopolidis announced that he had played his last international, the 37-year-old goalkeeper bowing out on 90 caps.

To some extent 2007/08 was a better season for Greek clubs than for the national team. Five Superleague representatives –more than from any other country - reached the UEFA Cup group phase, and while only AE Athens FC and Panathinaikos FC progressed further, Greece had a third team playing post-Christmas European football thanks to Olympiacos's qualification for the first knockout round of the UEFA Champions League. The Piraeus giants made it through a tough group and in so doing shed their burden of never having won an away fixture in the competition. A 3-1 win at Bremen finally ended a 31-match barren run and not untypically, once the rot had stopped, they went and won in Rome too, overcoming Lazio 2-1.

e goalkeeper
ıis Nikopolidis
d his
ational career
FA EURO 2008™

mpiacos's European breakthrough was
sterminded by coach Takis Lemonis, but after
mination by Chelsea FC in the early spring, he was
missed and replaced by his assistant, Spaniard Josep
gura. It seemed a harsh move, but a general
illusionment with the team's style had set in and
hough Olympiacos were still battling on both
mestic fronts, Petros Kokkalis, son of Sokratis and the
b's new president, chose to act.

lamarias controversy

e worst performance during Lemonis's last few weeks
me in the Superleague fixture away to lowly Apollon
amarias FC. The home side had not won for two
onths but they posted a sensational 1-0 victory over
e defending champions – or so they thought. It later
erged that Roman Wallner, Kalamarias's newly
cruited Austrian striker, was ineligible under FIFA rules
he had already played for two clubs – Falkirk FC and
milton Academical FC – during the season. Thus, the
ult was overturned to a 3-0 win for Olympiacos. It was
ecision that would have a significant bearing on the
tcome of the Superleague title.

ympiacos's bid for an eleventh championship win in
years was severely tested by both AEK and
nathinaikos. It was a fascinating three-way tussle, with
any twists and turns, highs and lows. AEK made the best start, winning their first six matches without conceding a goal, but the other two also had their surges and spells at the top. It was all down to which team could keep their nerve, and ultimately, yet again, that team was Olympiacos. A 4-0 thrashing from AEK left them with no room for manoeuvre, but they safely negotiated their last three matches – and survived an appeal from Kalamarias to have the walkover win overturned – to become champions for the 36th time. Four weeks later they added a 23rd Greek Cup win to their roll of honour after a 2-0 triumph in the final against an Aris Thessaloniki FC side led by former Olympiacos coach Dušan Bajević.

It was another Serb, striker Darko Kovačević, who opened the scoring in the Cup final. He was Olympiacos's top marksman in the league, scoring 17 goals, his tally being compiled in a curious fashion, with at least one in every home game before the turn of year but only away goals thereafter. His compatriot, skipper Predrag Đorđević, enjoyed another excellent campaign as he celebrated a record eleventh title with the club, while the Greek influence was headed by Stoltidis, Nikopolidis and youngster Konstantinos Mitroglou, whose goals in the run-in, like those of the captain, were priceless.

Play-off struggle

AEK, uncrowned since 1994, were bitter runners-up. Inspired intermittently by Brazilian superstar Rivaldo and consistently by Argentine striker Ismael Blanco (with 19 goals the Superleague's top scorer), they finished strongly but were ultimately undone by the back-to-back defeats in early February against Panionios GSS and Larissa FC that cost coach Lorenzo Serra Ferrer his job. His replacement, Nikos Kostenoglou, did well until the end-of-season play-offs – newly introduced to decide European qualification – in which AEK won only two of their six games and surrendered second place, and a UEFA Champions League qualifying berth, to Panathinaikos. Kostenoglou was replaced by former player Georgios Donis for 2008/09.

Panathinaikos were glad to finish second rather than third, but as their centenary year target had been first they, like AEK, changed coach, with José Peseiro making way for Dutchman Henk ten Cate. Under Peseiro, the Greens were very strong at home but fragile away – as a 4-0 pasting by Olympiacos in the Cup plainly demonstrated. They were also over-reliant for goals on Dimitris Salpingidis, who scored 15 in the regular league campaign while the next best any other player managed was three.

GREECE

Ellinikos Podosfairikis Omospondias (EPO)

Syngrou Avenue 137
GR-17121 Athens
tel - +30 210 9306000
fax - +30 210 9359666
website - www.epo.gr
email - epo@epo.gr
Year of Formation – 1926
President - Vassilis Gagatsis
General Secretary - Ioannis Economides
Press Officer – Michalis Tsapidis
Stadium – OACA Spyro Louis (Olympic), Athens (72,080)

INTERNATIONAL HONOURS
UEFA European Championship - (1) 2004.

INTERNATIONAL TOURNAMENT APPEARANCES
FIFA World Cup - (1) 1994.
UEFA European Championship - (3) 1980, 2004 (Winners), 2008.

TOP FIVE ALL-TIME CAPS
Theodoros Zagorakis (120); Efstratios Apostolakis (96); Angelos Basinas (91); Antonis Nikopolidis (90); Anastasios Mitropoulos & Dimitrios Saravakos (7

TOP FIVE ALL-TIME GOALS
Nikolaos Anastopoulos (29); Dimitrios Saravakos (22); Dimitrios "Mimis" Papaioannou (20); Angelos Charistea (19); Nikolaos Machlas (18)

NATIONAL TEAM RESULTS 2007/08

22/8/07	Spain	H	Thessaloniki	2-3	*Gekas (19), Katsouranis (44)*
12/9/07	Norway (ECQ)	A	Oslo	2-2	*Kyrgiakos (7, 30)*
13/10/07	Bosnia-Herzegovina (ECQ)	H	Athens	3-2	*Charisteas (10), Gekas (58), Liberopoulos (73)*
17/10/07	Turkey (ECQ)	A	Istanbul	1-0	*Amanatidis (79)*
17/11/07	Malta (ECQ)	H	Athens	5-0	*Gekas (32, 72, 74), Basinas (54), Amanatidis (61)*
21/11/07	Hungary (ECQ)	A	Budapest	2-1	*Vanczák (22og), Basinas (59p)*
5/2/08	Czech Republic B	N	Nicosia (CYP)	1-0	*Salpingidis (80)*
6/2/08	Finland	N	Nicosia (CYP)	2-1	*Charisteas (67), Katsouranis (72)*
26/3/08	Portugal	N	Dusseldorf (GER)	2-1	*Karagounis (33, 60)*
19/5/08	Cyprus	H	Patras	2-0	*Ninis (5), Katsouranis (59p)*
24/5/08	Hungary	A	Budapest	2-3	*Amanatidis (44), Liberopoulos (90)*
1/6/08	Armenia	N	Offenbach (GER)	0-0	
10/6/08	Sweden (ECF)	N	Salzburg (AUT)	0-2	
14/6/08	Russia (ECF)	N	Salzburg (AUT)	0-1	
18/6/08	Spain (ECF)	N	Salzburg (AUT)	1-2	*Charisteas (42)*

Aris and Panionios, both hyper-dependent on foreign imports, were also involved in the play-offs, but with Aris reaching the Cup final and claiming the second UEFA Cup spot via that route, they were only there for show. Panionios, coached by German Ewald Lienen, earned their UEFA Intertoto Cup berth with a strong showing in the spring, while great credit was also due to Asteras Tripolis FC, who beat each of the Big Three at home – an astonishing feat for a club making their Super League debut.

On the negative side, PAOK FC suffered boardroom upheaval and lost half of their matches while Atron FC and GAS Veria dropped out of the top flight alongside bottom club Kalamarias, who never fully recovered from the trauma of the victory that neve against Olympiacos.

TIONAL TEAM APPEARANCES 2007/08

n – Otto REHHAGEL (GER)	9/8/38		Esp	NOR	BIH	TUR	MLT	HUN	Cze	Fin	Por	Cyp	Hun	Arm	SWE	RUS	ESP	Caps	Goals
ris NIKOPOLIDIS	4/1/71	Olympiacos	G46		G		G	s46		G46	G		G22	G	G	G	G	90	-
kas SEITARIDIS	4/6/81	Atlético (ESP)	D46	D64		D					s46		D67	D	D	D40		58	1
s TOROSIDIS	10/6/85	Olympiacos	D46	D	D	D	D48			D	D46		D	s46	D	D		15	-
os DELLAS	31/1/76	AEK	D46	D	D	D	D					D63	D67	D46	D70	D	D	45	1
lis KAPSIS	18/10/73	APOEL (CYP)	D					D										36	1
os BASINAS	3/1/76	Mallorca (ESP)	M78	M76	M	M	M	M		M	M		M78	M	M	M	M	91	7
doros ZAGORAKIS	27/10/71	PAOK	M17															120	3
s KATSOURANIS	21/6/79	Benfica (POR)	M64	M	M		M	M		M	M	M	M	M	M	M	M	52	6
gios KARAGOUNIS	6/3/77	Panathinaikos	M	M	M	M	M70	M		M69	M77	M79		M46	M	s40	M74	76	6
GEKAS	23/5/80	Leverkusen (GER)	A	A	A81	A56	A	A82		A78	A46	A	A46	s46	A46	s61		29	6
ris SALPINGIDIS	18/8/81	Panathinaikos	A	A46				A	s46	s46	s68	A46		A46			A86	21	1
is GOUMAS	24/5/75	Panathinaikos	s17						D		s46	s63						45	-
s CHALKIAS	30/5/74	Aris	s46	G		G		G46	G46			G	s22					15	-
os TZOGLOU	19/3/79	Olympiacos	s46	M	D		D	D		D46	D46		s67	s46		M		30	1
s VINTRA	5/2/81	Panathinaikos	s46					D	D46		s46	D71	s67				D	19	-
kevas ANTZAS	18/8/76	Olympiacos	s46	s64	s81	M				D	D46		M	s46	D		s62	26	-
ris OOPOULOS	20/10/81	Panathinaikos	s64															20	2
ndros TZIOLIS	13/2/85	Panathinaikos	s78				s70	M46	M		s77	s46					s74	9	-
s KYRGIAKOS	23/7/79	Eintracht (GER)		D	D	D	D	D		D71	D		D	D	D	D	D62	41	4
LIBEROPOULOS	4/8/75	AEK		s46	s69	s56	s46		A	s78		s46	s78			A61		60	13
gios SAMARAS	21/2/85	Man. City (ENG) /Celtic (SCO)		s76		s59		s46	A63		s46		s46	s46	s46			19	3
los CHARISTEAS	9/2/80	Nürnberg (GER)			A69	A59				A	A68		A	A	A	A	A	68	19
is AMANATIDIS	3/12/81	Eintracht (GER)			A70	A	A	s82		A46	A46		A46	A46	s70	A80	A	29	3
s NAKOPOULOS	12/7/74	Bolton (ENG)			s70		M46		M46		s46	M63	s46			s80	s86	77	12
aos SPIROPOULOS	10/10/83	Panionios /Panathinaikos					s48		D	s69		D		D46			D	6	-
tis STATHOPOULOS	9/6/88	AEK							D46	s71		D						3	-
lis KAFES	24/6/78	AEK							M									31	3
ris MAKOS	18/1/87	Panionios							M46			s79						2	-
nos KOTSOLIS	6/5/79	Larissa							s46									4	-
giotis LAGOS	18/7/85	AEK							s46	s46								8	-
m DOPOULOS	3/5/84	Aris							s46									1	-
os MELISSIS	1/12/82	PAOK							s46			s71						2	-
os TODOULOPOULOS	19/12/86	PAOK							s63			s63						2	-
ostomos ILIDIS	15/1/75	Atromitos								s46								1	-
os NINIS	3/4/90	Panathinaikos										M46						1	1

GREECE

DOMESTIC LEAGUE 2007/08

SUPERLEAGUE FINAL TABLE

	Pld	Home W	D	L	F	A	Away W	D	L	F	A	Total W	D	L	F	A	Pts
1 Olympiacos CFP	30	13	2	0	32	9	8	5	2	26	14	21	7	2	58	23	70
2 AEK Athens FC	30	11	2	2	38	9	11	0	4	27	8	22	2	6	65	17	68
3 Panathinaikos FC	30	12	3	0	21	4	8	3	4	23	14	20	6	4	44	18	66
4 Aris Thessaloniki FC	30	8	5	2	21	9	6	3	6	12	11	14	8	8	33	20	50
5 Panionios GSS	30	8	3	4	23	23	5	3	7	16	19	13	6	11	39	42	45
6 Larissa FC	30	9	6	0	27	14	2	6	7	8	16	11	12	7	35	30	45
7 Asteras Tripolis FC	30	7	6	2	14	7	4	5	6	14	17	11	11	8	28	24	44
8 Skoda Xanthi FC	30	8	1	6	23	18	2	5	8	10	21	10	6	14	33	39	36
9 PAOK FC	30	9	2	4	22	12	1	3	11	7	23	10	5	15	29	35	35
10 Iraklis FC	30	5	5	5	14	13	3	6	6	14	21	8	11	11	28	34	35
11 Levadiakos FC	30	8	2	5	20	20	2	1	12	11	31	10	3	17	31	51	33
12 OFI Crete FC	30	7	1	7	23	18	2	4	9	16	31	9	5	16	39	49	32
13 Ergotelis FC	30	5	6	4	17	19	2	3	10	11	23	7	9	14	28	42	30
14 Atromitos FC	30	5	2	8	15	18	3	3	9	8	18	8	5	17	23	36	29
15 GAS Veria	30	5	5	5	13	14	0	3	12	8	30	5	8	17	21	44	23
16 Apollon Kalamarias FC	30	4	5	6	12	19	1	3	11	15	38	5	8	17	27	57	22

N.B. Apollon Kalamarias FC – 1 pt deducted.

TOP GOALSCORERS

19 Ismael BLANCO (AEK)
17 Darko KOVAČEVIĆ (Olympiacos
15 Dimitrios SALPINGIDIS (Panathinaikos)
14 Rafik DJEBBOUR (Panionios)
Tomasz RADZINSKI (Xanthi)
11 Nikolaos LIBEROPOULOS (AEK)
10 Lambros CHOUTOS (Panionios)
Predrag ĐORĐEVIĆ (Olympiaco
9 Lucio Alejo FILOMENO (Tripolis
8 Eduardo Ariel BUSTOS MONTO (Levadiakos)
Danijel CESAREC (Tripolis)
Sergio Contreras KOKE (Aris)
LUCIANO de Souza (Atromitos)
Emanuel PERRONE (Kalamarias/Atromitos)
RIVALDO Vitor Borba Ferreira (A
Stilianos SFAKIANAKIS (OFI)

PLAY-OFFS

UEFA Champions League qualification

(23/4/08)
Aris 1 *(Koke 74)*, Panathinaikos 1 *(Papadopoulos 87p)*
AEK 5 *(Edinho 28, Rivaldo 39, 77, Blanco 74, Kallon 90)*, Panionios 0

(30/4/08)
Panionios 1 *(Yao Kumordzi 80)*, Aris 0
Panathinaikos 4 *(Papadopoulos 8, Marcelo Mattos 27, Ivanschitz 32, 44)*, AEK 1 *(Rivaldo 71)*

(4/5/08)
AEK 1 *(Liberopoulos 54)*, Aris 0
Panionios 1 *(Djebbour 74)*, Panathinaikos 2 *(Manucho 16, 82)*

(7/5/08)
Aris 4 *(Nebegleras 6, Javito 39, 48, Koke 56)*, AEK 0
Panathinaikos 3 *(Karagounis 21, 41, Manucho 64)*, Panionios 0

(11/5/08)
Panathinaikos 3 *(Karagounis 56, 63, N'Doye 62)*, Aris 1 *(Thiago Genti*
Panionios 2 *(Fernández 21, Skoufalis 89)*, AEK 2 *(Rivaldo 25p, Liberopoulo*

(14/5/08)
Aris 3 *(Toni Calvo 6, Ivić 48, Amoroso 75p)*, Panionios 3 *(Sialmas 8, 82 Kapetanos 39)*
AEK 1 *(Nsaliwa 51)*, Panathinaikos 1 *(Marcelo Mattos 26)*

	Pld	Home W	D	L	F	A	Away W	D	L	F	A	Total W	D	L	F	A	Pts
2 Panathinaikos FC	6	3	0	0	10	2	1	2	0	4	3	4	2	0	14	5	21
3 AEK Athens FC	6	2	1	0	7	1	0	1	2	3	10	2	2	2	10	11	16
4 Aris Thessaloniki FC	6	1	2	0	8	4	0	0	3	1	5	1	2	3	9	9	7
5 Panionios GSS	6	1	1	1	4	4	0	1	2	3	11	1	2	3	7	15	5

N.B. Points carried forward from regular league: AEK 8 pts, Panathinaikos 7 pts, Aris 2 pts, Panionios 0 pts.

CLUB-BY-CLUB

AEK ATHENS FC

Coach – Lorenzo Serra Ferrer (ESP); (12/2/08) Nikolaos Kostenoglou

Founded – 1924

MAJOR HONOURS: Greek League – (11) 1939, 1940, 1963, 1968, 1971, 1978, 1979, 1989, 1992, 1993, 1994; Greek Cup – (13) 1932, 1939, 1949, 1950, 1956, 1964, 1966, 1978, 1983, 1996, 1997, 2000, 2002.

2007

23/9	Atromitos	h	2-0	*Blanco 2*
26/9	Veria	a	1-0	*Blanco*
30/9	Levadiakos	a	4-0	*Tözsér, Blanco, Edson, Kor*
7/10	Panionios	a	3-0	*Liberopoulos, Rivaldo (p), Júlio César*
20/10	Larissa	h	1-0	*Manduca*
28/10	Xanthi	a	1-0	*Blanco*
4/11	Iraklis	h	1-2	*Liberopoulos*
11/11	Panathinaikos	a	1-2	*Liberopoulos*
25/11	OFI	h	4-0	*Rivaldo, Manduca, Blanco, Pappas*

2	Aris	a	1-0	*Dellas*
2	Kalamarias	h	4-0	*Liberopoulos 2, Rivaldo (p), Blanco*
'12	Olympiacos	a	0-1	
'12	Ergotelis	a	4-1	*Dellas, Manduca, Liberopoulos 2*
'12	PAOK	h	2-0	*Blanco, Júlio César*
08				
	Tripolis	a	1-2	*Blanco,*
'1	Veria	h	5-1	*Rivaldo, Kafes, Blanco 2 (1p), Pavlis*
'1	Atromitos	a	1-0	*Liberopoulos*
'1	Levadiakos	h	3-0	*Rivaldo, og (Emeran), Blanco*
	Panionios	h	2-3	*Kallon, Blanco*
	Larissa	a	0-1	
'2	Iraklis	a	1-0	*Liberopoulos*
	Panathinaikos	h	1-1	*Rivaldo (p)*
	Xanthi	h	3-0	*Blanco, Júlio César, Edinho*
	OFI	a	4-1	*Blanco, og (Pitsos), og (Bărcăuan), Edinho*
'3	Aris	h	1-1	*Edinho*
'3	Kalamaria	a	1-0	*Edinho*
'3	Olympiacos	h	4-0	*Blanco, Edinho, Liberopoulos, Kafes,*
	Ergotelis	h	3-1	*Rivaldo (p), Kafes, Blanco*
'4	PAOK	a	4-0	*Papastathopoulos, Blanco, Liberopoulos, Kallon*
'4	Tripolis	h	2-0	*Rivaldo, Blanco*

Name	Nat	Pos	Aps	(s)	Gls
Rodolfo ARRUABARRENA	ARG	D	16		
Ismael BLANCO	ARG	A	24	(4)	19
Christos BOURBOS		M	11		
Traianos DELLAS		D	21	(1)	2
EDINHO Arnaldo	POR	A	9	(1)	5
EDSON Ramos	BRA	D	20	(4)	1
Nikolaos GEORGEAS		D	4	(2)	
GERALDO Washington ALVES	POR	D	18	(3)	
JÚLIO CÉSAR da Silva Sousa	BRA	A	6	(11)	3
Pantelis KAFES		M	18	(2)	3
Mohamed KALLON	SLE	A	4	(5)	2
Pantelis KAPETANOS		A	1	(1)	
Panagiotis KONE		M	1	(10)	1
Panagiotis LAGOS		M	8	(3)	
Nikolaos LIBEROPOULOS		A	23	(1)	11
Jürgen MACHO	AUT	G	17		
Gustavo MANDUCA	BRA	M	18	(2)	3
Emanuel Evaristo "MANÚ"	POR	A	2	(11)	
Marcello MORETTO de Souza	BRA	G	13	(2)	
Tamandani NSALIWA	CAN	M	12	(6)	
Sokratis PAPASTATHOPOULOS		D	22	(2)	1
Charilaos PAPPAS		A	2	(6)	1
Mihail PAVLIS		A		(5)	1
Vasilios PLIATSIKAS		M	5	(3)	
RIVALDO Vítor Borba Ferreira	BRA	M	28	(1)	8
Panagiotis TAHTSIDIS		M		(1)	
Daniel TŐZSÉR	HUN	M	7	(5)	1
Vasilios ZIKOS		M	20		

APOLLON KALAMARIAS FC

Coach – Thomas Katsavakis

Founded – 1926

07				
	OFI	a	2-3	*Wellington, Spiridakis*
/9	Aris	h	0-0	
/9	Panionios	h	0-2	
10	Olympiacos	a	0-1	
/10	Ergotelis	h	2-1	*Karaliopoulos, Bushi*
/10	PAOK	a	1-4	*Perrone*
4/11	Tripolis	h	2-2	*Favalli, Amponsah*
11/11	Veria	a	2-0	*Bushi, Perrone*
25/11	Atromitos	h	0-2	
2/12	Levadiakos	h	2-0	*Karaliopoulos, Brito*
9/12	AEK	a	0-4	
16/12	Larissa	h	1-1	*Brito*
22/12	Xanthi	a	1-6	*Perrone*
30/12	Iraklis	h	1-1	*Favalli*
2008				
6/1	Panathinaikos	a	0-1	
13/1	OFI	h	1-1	*Perrone*
19/1	Aris	a	2-2	*Brito, Bushi*
27/1	Panionios	a	1-2	*Karaliopoulos*
3/2	Olympiacos	h	0-3	*(w/o; original result 1-0 Barkoglou)*
10/2	Ergotelis	a	2-2	*Brito, Barkoglou*
17/2	PAOK	h	0-2	
23/2	Tripolis	a	1-1	*Hetemaj*
2/3	Veria	h	1-0	*Barkoglou*
9/3	Atromitos	a	0-3	
16/3	Levadiakos	a	0-2	
23/3	AEK	h	0-1	
30/3	Larissa	a	1-2	*Bushi (p)*
6/4	Xanthi	h	1-0	*Barkoglou*
13/4	Iraklis	a	2-5	*Barkoglou, Wellington*
20/4	Panathinaikos	h	1-3	*Barkoglou*

No	Name	Nat	Pos	Aps	(s)	Gls
25	Kofi AMPONSAH	GHA	D	14	(2)	1
21	Georgios BARKOGLOU		M	11	(1)	6
24	Eduardo BRITO	BRA	M	22	(4)	4
20	Alban BUSHI	ALB	A	11	(6)	4
10	Lucas Gabriel FAVALLI	ARG	M	23	(2)	2
2	Aristidis GALANOPOULOS		D	27		
23	Apostolos GIANNOU		A		(8)	
13	Vasilios HATZIVASILIADIS		A		(1)	
56	Perparim HETEMAJ	FIN	M	7	(4)	1
18	Merkourios KARALIOPOULOS		M	19	(5)	3
7	Dimitrios KARAMANLIS		M	2	(6)	
15	Christos KELPEKIS		G	4		
5	Georgios KOLTSIS		D	25		
6	Dimitrios KONTODIMOS		M	1	(5)	
30	Pavol KOVÁČ	SVK	G	26		
17	Konstantinos LAZARIDIS		A		(1)	
3	Maciej MURAWSKI	POL	M	12		
8	Nikolaos PAPADOPOULOS		D	21	(2)	
31	Emmanuel PERRONE	ARG	A	11	(3)	4
26	Stergios PSIANOS		M	2	(2)	
4	Nikolaos SAMOUILIDIS		M	7	(3)	
19	Ahilleas SARAKATSANOS		M	23		
14	Vanče ŠIKOV	MKD	D	18	(4)	
22	Emmanouil SPIRIDAKIS		M	3	(5)	1
16	Ioannis STATHIS		D	4	(1)	
27	Giuseppe VELA JÚNIOR	BRA	M	9	(4)	
9	Roman WALLNER	AUT	A	1		
11	WELLINGTON Gonçalves	BRA	A	16	(12)	2
33	Ioannis ZAPROPOULOS		D	11	(8)	

ARIS THESSALONIKI FC

Coach – Juan Oliva (ESP); (7/9/07) Dušan Bajević (SRB)

Founded – 1914

MAJOR HONOURS: Greek League – (3) 1928, 1932, 1946; Greek Cup - (1) 1970.

2007				
1/9	Panionios	h	0-0	
23/9	Kalamarias	a	0-0	
29/9	Olympiacos	h	1-1	*Marco Aurélio*
7/10	Ergotelis	a	1-0	*Ronaldo*
21/10	PAOK	h	3-1	*Koke 2, Nacho García*
27/10	Tripolis	a	0-0	
4/11	Veria	h	1-0	*Ronaldo*
11/11	Atromitos	a	2-1	*Nacho García, Siston*

24/11	Levadiakos	a	0-2	
2/12	AEK	h	0-1	
9/12	Larissa	a	0-1	
15/12	Xanthi	h	2-0	*Nacho García, Felipe*
23/12	Iraklis	a	2-0	*Felipe, Javito*
30/12	Panathinaikos	h	0-1	
2008				
6/1	OFI	a	1-0	*Ivić*
12/1	Panionios	a	3-0	*Toni Calvo (p), Koke 2*
19/1	Kalamarias	h	2-2	*Ivić 2*
27/1	Olympiacos	a	0-1	
3/2	Ergotelis	h	2-0	*Papadopoulos (p), Felipe*
10/2	PAOK	a	0-3	
17/2	Tripolis	h	2-0	*Koke, Marco Aurélio*
23/2	Veria	a	0-1	
2/3	Atromitos	h	2-0	*Koke, Amoroso*
8/3	Levadiakos	h	1-0	*Ivić*
16/3	AEK	a	1-1	*Thiago Gentil*
23/3	Larissa	h	1-1	*Toni Calvo*
30/3	Xanthi	a	2-0	*Siston, Nacho García*
6/4	Iraklis	h	2-2	*Toni Calvo (p), Koke*
13/4	Panathinaikos	a	0-1	
20/4	OFI	h	2-0	*Javito, Koke*

No	Name	Nat	Pos	Aps	(s)	Gls
30	Márcio AMOROSO	BRA	A	8	(1)	1
9	ANDERSON COSTA	BRA	A		(3)	
1	Konstantinos CHALKIAS		G	22		
14	FELIPE Sanchón	ESP	A	20	(6)	3
29	Georgios GOUGOULIAS		A		(2)	
18	Vladimir IVIĆ	SRB	M	19	(5)	4
26	Sanel JAHIĆ	BIH	M	14	(2)	
20	Francisco Javier "JAVITO"	ESP	A	12	(14)	2
16	JONAN GARCÍA	ESP	M		(1)	
15	Nikolaos KARABELAS		M	5	(4)	
12	Marian KELEMEN	SVK	G	8		
7	Anastasios KIRIAKOS		M		(3)	
27	Sergio Contreras "KOKE"	ESP	A	26	(1)	8
23	Georgios KOLTSIDAS		D		(1)	
11	Efthimios KOULOUHERIS		D	4	(3)	
22	MARCO AURÉLIO Ribeiro	BRA	D	21	(1)	2
8	Ronald NACHO GARCÍA	BOL	M	19	(2)	4
6	Konstantinos NEBEGLERAS		M	25		
2	Darcy NETO	BRA	D	24		
4	Avraam PAPADOPOULOS		D	27		1
19	Athanasios PAPAZOGLOU		A	1	(6)	
28	Athanasios PRITTAS		M	7	(11)	
5	RONALDO Guiaro	BRA	D	24	(1)	2
11	Diogo Rodrigues SISTON	BRA	M	16	(8)	2
24	THIAGO GENTIL	BRA	A	3	(8)	1
7	Antonio TONI CALVO	ESP	M	14	(7)	3
32	Kristi VANGJELI	ALB	D	11	(3)	

ASTERAS TRIPOLIS FC

Coach – Paulo Luiz Campos (BRA);
(25/2/08) Panagiotis Tzanavaras

Founded – 1931

2007				
2/9	Larissa	h	0-1	
22/9	Xanthi	a	0-2	
30/9	Iraklis	h	0-0	
7/10	Panathinaikos	h	1-0	*Rogério (p)*
21/10	OFI	a	3-0	*Cesarec 2, Panteliadis*
27/10	Aris	h	0-0	
4/11	Kalamarias	a	2-2	*Filomeno 2*
10/11	Olympiacos	h	1-0	*Filomeno*
25/11	Ergotelis	a	3-0	*Filomeno, Cesarec, Rogério (p)*
2/12	PAOK	h	2-0	*Filomeno, Cesarec*
9/12	Panionios	h	1-0	*Filomeno*
16/12	Veria	a	0-1	
23/12	Atromitos	h	1-0	*Zoundi*
30/12	Levadiakos	a	0-0	
2008				
6/1	AEK	h	2-1	*Filomeno, Jean Carlo*
13/1	Larissa	a	1-1	*Cesarec*
20/1	Xanthi	h	0-0	
27/1	Iraklis	a	0-0	
3/2	Panathinaikos	a	0-2	
10/2	OFI	h	1-1	*Filomeno*
17/2	Aris	a	0-2	
23/2	Kalamarias	h	1-1	*Filomeno*
1/3	Olympiacos	a	1-1	*Cardozo*
9/3	Ergotelis	h	1-1	*Kanakoudis*
15/3	PAOK	a	1-0	*Milano*
23/3	Panionios	a	1-4	*Milano*
30/3	Veria	h	2-0	*Cesarec 2*
6/4	Atromitos	a	2-0	*Cesarec, Damonte*
13/4	Levadiakos	h	1-2	*Machado*
20/4	AEK	a	0-2	

No	Name	Nat	Pos	Aps	(s)	Gls
40	Georgios ABARIS		G	27		
79	Nikolaos ANASTASOPOULOS		G	1		
8	Horacio Ramón CARDOZO	ARG	M	26		1
9	Danijel CESAREC	CRO	A	18	(6)	8
24	Israel Alejandro DAMONTE	ARG	M	10		1
31	Lucio Alejo FILOMENO	ARG	A	27		9
55	Sokratis FITANIDIS		D	12	(1)	
15	FLÁVIO Pinto de Souza	BRA	D	9	(1)	
4	Nikolaos HATZOPOULOS		D		(2)	
44	Elias IOANNOU		A	4	(8)	
11	JEAN CARLOS Dondé	BRA	D	13	(2)	1
80	Martin KAMBUROV	BUL	A	1	(3)	
2	Cyril KALI	FRA	D	2	(2)	
6	Petros KANAKOUDIS		M	11	(10)	1
77	Anastasios KIRIAKOS		M	6	(1)	
99	Nikolaos KOUSKOUNAS		A		(1)	
84	Antonios LADAKIS		M	14	(7)	
20	Nikolaos LAZARIDIS		M	29		
3	Fernando MACHADO	URU	D	24		1
21	Gastón Enrique MARTINA	ARG	M		(1)	
27	Carlos Alberto MASARA	ARG	D	20	(1)	
7	Mauro Ramiro MILANO	ARG	M	1	(4)	2
26	Xenofon MOSHOGIANNIS		D	1	(1)	
18	Sokratis OFRIDOPOULOS		D	11	(3)	
10	Savvas PANTELIADIS		M		(3)	1
10	Matías Nicolás PAVONI	ARG	M	5	(3)	
77	Nikolaos POURTOULIDIS		M		(2)	
5	Emmanouil PSOMAS		D	19	(1)	
25	ROGÉRIO Martins	BRA	M	17	(3)	2
30	Ioannis SIMEONIDIS		G	2		
22	Nikolaos-Georgios STRATAKIS		M	3	(7)	
16	Nikolaos TROIRIS		M		(1)	
17	Jaouad ZAIRI	MAR	A	15	(2)	
14	Patrick ZOUNDI	BFA	A	2	(11)	1

ATROMITOS FC

Coach – Guillermo Hoyos (ARG);
(27/3/08) Paulo Luiz Campos (BRA)

Founded – 1923

2007				
2/9	Levadiakos	h	2-1	*og (Theodosiadis), Korakakis*
23/9	AEK	a	0-2	
29/9	Larissa	h	2-0	*Marcelo Oliveira, Luciano*
7/10	Xanthi	a	1-0	*Geladaris*
21/10	Iraklis	h	1-1	*Luciano*
28/10	Panathinaikos	a	0-2	
4/11	OFI	h	1-0	*Luciano*
11/11	Aris	h	1-2	*Luciano*
25/11	Kalamarias	a	2-0	*Castro, Cirio*

12	Olympiacos	h	1-3	*Korakakis*
12	Ergotelis	a	0-0	
/12	PAOK	h	0-0	
/12	Tripolis	a	0-1	
/12	Veria	h	1-0	*Luciano*
08				
1	Panionios	h	0-2	
/1	Levadiakos	a	1-2	*Luciano*
/1	AEK	h	0-1	
/1	Larissa	a	0-2	
2	Xanthi	h	2-3	*Tsigas 2*
2	Iraklis	a	1-1	*Luciano*
/2	OFI	a	1-0	*Perrone*
3	Aris	a	0-2	
3	Panathinaikos	h	0-1	
3	Kalamarias	h	3-0	*Perrone, Kripintiris, Luciano*
/3	Olympiacos	a	0-2	
/3	Ergotelis	h	1-2	*Perrone*
/3	PAOK	a	0-1	
4	Tripolis	h	0-2	
/4	Veria	a	1-1	*Rovas*
/4	Panionios	a	1-2	*Perrone*

	Name	Nat	Pos	Aps	(s)	Gls
	Georgios ANATOLAKIS		D	23	(1)	
	Vasilios APOSTOLOPOULOS		D	2	(1)	
	César CASTRO	VEN	D	8	(2)	1
	Sergio CIRIO	ESP	A	17	(8)	1
	Dimitrios GELADARIS		D	24	(1)	1
	Georgios GEORGIOU		D	8	(4)	
	Ángel Bochy HOYOS	ARG	M		(3)	
	Dimitrios IOANNOU		M	20	(1)	
	JOSÉ LUIS Reyes	ESP	A	13		
	Petros KAMINIOTIS		M		(1)	
	Ioannis KARALIS		M		(2)	
	Ioannis KATEMIS		M	17	(3)	
	Georgios KORAKAKIS		M	26		2
	Christos KOUTSOSPIROS		A	6	(4)	
	Michail KRIPINDIRIS		M	5	(7)	1
	Ioannis LAZANAS		A	4	(1)	
	Leandro Franco «LÊ»	BRA	M	5	(3)	
	LUCIANO de Sousa	BRA	M	24	(1)	8
	MARCELO OLIVEIRA	BRA	D	23		1
	Stergios MARINOS		A	13	(3)	
	Roberto MERINO	PER	M	4	(7)	
	David Derlis Colli MEZA	PAR	M		(2)	
	Chrisostomos MIHAILIDIS		G	30		
	Nikolaos NIKOLOPOULOS		A	3	(3)	
	Konstantinos PAGONIS		M		(1)	
	Emmanuel PERRONE	ARG	A	7	(1)	4
	Vasilios ROVAS		M	12	(7)	1
	Roberto SÁNCHEZ	PAR	A	1	(10)	
	Ioannis SKOPELITIS		M	12		
	Lucas TREJO	ARG	D	14	(2)	
	Athanasios TSIGAS		A	9	(1)	2

ERGOTELIS FC

Coach – Nikolaos Karageorgiou

Founded – 1929

007				
/9	Iraklis	a	1-0	*Melissas*
3/9	Panathinaikos	h	0-3	
0/9	OFI	a	1-4	*Júnior (p)*
/10	Aris	h	0-1	
1/10	Kalamarias	a	1-2	*Júnior (p)*
8/10	Olympiacos	h	3-3	*Júnior 2 (1p), Theodoridis*
/11	Panionios	h	1-1	*Kordonouris*
1/11	PAOK	a	0-1	
5/11	Tripolis	h	0-3	
/12	Veria	a	1-1	*Melissas*
/12	Atromitos	h	0-0	
16/12	Levadiakos	a	0-0	
23/12	AEK	h	1-4	*Ognjenović*
29/12	Larissa	h	0-0	
2008				
6/1	Xanthi	a	0-1	
13/1	Iraklis	h	1-0	*Načevski*
20/1	Panathinaikos	a	0-1	
26/1	OFI	h	1-1	*og (Issa)*
3/2	Aris	a	0-2	
10/2	Kalamarias	h	2-2	*Vakouftsis, Mathis*
16/2	Olympiacos	a	0-1	
24/2	Panionios	a	1-2	*Ogunsoto*
1/3	PAOK	h	2-0	*Júnior, Grammozis*
9/3	Tripolis	a	1-1	*Ogunsoto*
15/3	Veria	h	2-0	*Kiliaras D., Ogunsoto*
22/3	Atromitos	a	2-1	*Budimir, Ogunsoto*
30/3	Levadiakos	h	2-1	*Ogunsoto, Kiliaras D.*
6/4	AEK	a	1-3	*Kordonouris*
13/4	Larissa	a	2-3	*Júnior, Ogunsoto*
20/4	Xanthi	h	2-0	*Júnior (p), Vakouftsis*

No	Name	Nat	Pos	Aps	(s)	Gls
24	Venizelos ANIFANTAKIS		D	5		
84	Grigorios ATHANASIOU		G	1	(1)	
25	Mario BUDIMIR	CRO	A	7	(17)	1
1	Iosif DASKALAKIS		G	22		
31	Michail FRAGOULAKIS		M	9	(13)	
27	Eleftherios GIALOUSIS		D	10		
11	Dimitrios GRAMMOZIS		M	23		1
20	Altin HAXHI	ALB	M	9		
5	Mario HIEBLINGER	AUT	D	28		
15	JÚNIOR Manuel Silva	BRA	M	26	(1)	7
29	Nikolaos KARELIS		A		(1)	
4	Labros KEFALOUKOS		A	9	(4)	
18	Daniel KENEDY	POR	D	13		
10	Dimitrios KILIARAS		M	17	(7)	2
12	Ioannis KILIARAS		M		(2)	
6	Panagiotis KORDONOURIS		D	29		2
13	Vasilios KOUTSIANIKOULIS		M	2	(10)	
44	Clint MATHIS	USA	A		(8)	1
33	Charidimos MATHHEAKIS		D	4	(1)	
8	Paschalis MELISSAS		M	20	(1)	2
17	Darko MILADIN	CRO	D	17		
14	Dragan NAČEVSKI	MKD	A	1	(11)	1
23	Perica OGNJENOVIĆ	SRB	A	14		1
40	Patrick Babatunde OGUNSOTO	NGA	A	12		6
30	Zsolt POSZA	HUN	G	7		
26	Ivan TASIĆ	SRB	M	15	(5)	
7	Georgios THEODORIDIS		M	18	(6)	1
70	Georgios VAKOUFTSIS		A	12	(1)	2

IRAKLIS FC

Coach – Evangelos Vlahos; (17/8/07) Ivan Jovanović (SRB); (17/12/07) (Ioannis Tzifopoulos); (24/12/07) Ángel Pedraza (ESP)

Founded – 1908

MAJOR HONOURS: Greek Cup – (1) 1976.

2007				
2/9	Ergotelis	h	0-1	
22/9	PAOK	a	0-3	
30/9	Tripolis	a	0-0	
7/10	Veria	h	1-1	*Malagueño*
21/10	Atromitos	a	1-1	*og (Georgiou)*
27/10	Levadiakos	h	1-0	*Nikolopoulos*
4/11	AEK	a	2-1	*Emerson, Rodrigo*
11/11	Larissa	h	1-1	*Emerson (p)*
25/11	Xanthi	a	3-0	*Papadopoulos, Hloros 2*
2/12	Panionios	a	1-1	*Nikolopoulos*
9/12	Panathinaikos	h	0-1	
16/12	OFI	a	0-2	
23/12	Aris	h	0-2	
30/12	Kalamarias	a	1-1	*Malagueño*

2008				
5/1	Olympiacos	h	1-2	*Katsabis*
13/1	Ergotelis	a	0-1	
20/1	PAOK	h	1-0	*Giantsis*
27/1	Tripolis	h	0-0	
3/2	Veria	a	2-1	*Giantsis, Luciano Fonseca*
9/2	Atromitos	h	1-1	*Luciano Fonseca*
20/2	Levadiakos	a	0-3	
24/2	AEK	h	0-1	
2/3	Larissa	a	0-1	
9/3	Xanthi	h	1-1	*Malagueño*
16/3	Panionios	h	1-0	*Aarón (p)*
22/3	Panathinaikos	a	1-1	*Luciano Fonseca*
30/3	OFI	h	1-0	*García*
6/4	Aris	a	2-2	*Giantsis, Komvolidis*
13/4	Kalamarias	h	5-2	*Marqués, Komvolidis, Aarón 2, Giantsis*
20/4	Olympiacos	a	1-3	*Malagueño*

No	Name	Nat	Pos	Aps	(s)	Gls
31	AARÓN Ñiguez	ESP	A	10	(2)	3
13	Dimitrios ASLANIDIS		M		(1)	
1	Georgios BANDIS		G	1		
22	Jože BENKO	SVN	A	1	(4)	
83	George BINHO	BRA	M	5	(2)	
37	BRUNO Garcia LEITE	BRA	D	6	(2)	
8	Juraj CZINEGE	SVK	M	4	(4)	
55	Erikkos-Sideris DRABIS		A	1		
50	EDINHO	BRA	D	5		
10	EMERSON de Andrade Santos	BRA	M	12	(2)	2
90	FLÁVIO Dias Ribeiro	BRA	A	7	(1)	
27	Sebastián Miguel GARCÍA	ARG	M	16	(4)	1
18	Konstantinos GIANNOULIS		M	12		
19	Dimitrios GIANTSIS		A	13	(7)	4
7	Ioannis HLOROS		A	10	(4)	2
16	Georgios IOANNIDIS		M	7	(4)	
4	Anastasios KATSABIS		D	29		1
9	Angelos KOMVOLIDIS		A	3	(3)	2
20	LUCIANO Perazzolo FONSECA	BRA	A	6	(2)	3
15	Javier Hernán MALAGUEÑO	ARG	D	27	(1)	4
21	Nebojša MARINKOVIĆ	SRB	M	4	(3)	
7	José MARQUÉS	ESP	A	13	(1)	1
14	Dimitrios MAVROGENIDIS		D	18	(3)	
11	Nikolaos NIKOLOPOULOS		A	9	(6)	2
33	Ioannis PAPADOPOULOS		M	11	(10)	1
17	Emmanouil PAPASTERIANOS		M	10	(3)	
2	Grigorios PAPAZAHARIAS		D	7	(3)	
23	Haralambos PERPERIDIS		M	3		
6	Elias POURSANIDIS		M	17	(8)	
26	Alain RAGUEL	FRA	D	12	(1)	
30	RODRIGO Tosi Neto	BRA	M	7	(2)	1
78	URKO Rafael Pardo	ESP	G	29		
66	Javier XAVI MORO	ESP	M	5	(2)	
5	Martin ZBONČÁK	CZE	D	10	(1)	

LARISSA FC

Coach – Georgios Donis

Founded – 1964

MAJOR HONOURS: Greek League – (1) 1988; Greek Cup – (2) 1985, 2007.

2007				
2/9	Tripolis	a	1-0	*Alexandrou*
23/9	Veria	h	1-1	*Bakayoko*
29/9	Atromitos	a	0-2	
7/10	Levadiakos	h	3-3	*og (Dia), Parra, Galitsios*
20/10	AEK	a	0-1	
28/10	Panionios	a	1-3	*Bakayoko*
4/11	Xanthi	h	0-0	
11/11	Iraklis	a	1-1	*Cleiton (p)*
25/11	Panathinaikos	h	2-2	*Cleiton, Galitsios*
2/12	OFI	a	0-0	
9/12	Aris	h	1-0	*Parra*
16/12	Kalamarias	a	1-1	*Cleiton*
23/12	Olympiacos	h	0-0	
29/12	Ergotelis	a	0-0	
2008				
6/1	PAOK	a	0-1	
13/1	Tripolis	h	1-1	*Cleiton*
20/1	Veria	a	0-1	
27/1	Atromitos	h	2-0	*Kožlej, Cleiton (p)*
2/2	Levadiakos	a	1-0	*Alexandrou*
9/2	AEK	h	1-0	*Żurawski*
16/2	Panionios	h	1-0	*Tümer*
24/2	Xanthi	a	1-1	*Kiriakidis*
2/3	Iraklis	h	1-0	*Żurawski (p)*
9/3	Panathinaikos	a	0-2	
16/3	OFI	h	5-1	*Cleiton, Żurawski, Tümer, Fotakis 2*
23/3	Aris	a	1-1	*Parra*
30/3	Kalamarias	h	2-1	*Cleiton, Żurawski*
6/4	Olympiacos	a	1-2	*Tümer*
13/4	Ergotelis	h	3-2	*Tümer, Parra 2*
20/4	PAOK	h	4-3	*Kotsios, Tümer, Żurawski 2 (2p)*

No	Name	Nat	Pos	Aps	(s)	Gls
19	Nektarios ALEXANDROU	CYP	A	14	(2)	2
33	Panagiotis BAHRAMIS		M	4	(7)	
29	Ibrahima BAKAYOKO	CIV	A	19	(4)	2
31	Mihail BOUKOUVALAS		M	1	(3)	
10	CLEITON Silva	BRA	A	27	(1)	7
4	Nikolaos DABIZAS		D	20		
20	Marko FÖRSTER	GER	D	14	(2)	
18	Georgios FOTAKIS		M	26		2
7	Georgios GALITSIOS		D	27		2
6	Dimitrios GIKAS		M	2	(4)	
42	Matías Walter IGLESIAS	ARG	M	13	(2)	
21	Christos KALANTZIS		A	6	(9)	
77	Panagiotis KATSIAROS		D	12	(5)	
1	Fotios KIPOUROS		G	13		
5	Elias KIRIAKIDIS		M	19	(5)	1
2	Elias KOTSIOS		D	22		1
26	Stefanos KOTSOLIS		G	17		
99	Jozef KOŽLEJ	SVK	A	3	(11)	1
13	Andreas LAMBROPOULOS		A	1	(6)	
9	Facundo Manuel Carlos PARRA	ARG	A	7	(16)	5
17	Marcelo SARMIENTO	ARG	M	26	(2)	
14	TÜMER Metin	TUR	M	7	(2)	5
3	Stilianos VENETIDIS		D	19		
24	Anastasios VENETIS		D	1	(4)	
22	Alexandros VERGONIS		M	1	(1)	
8	Maciej ŻURAWSKI	POL	A	9	(2)	6

LEVADIAKOS FC

Coach – Georgi Vasilev (BUL); (5/3/08) Haralambos Tennes

Founded – 1961

2007				
2/9	Atromitos	a	1-2	*Dimbala*
23/9	Panionios	a	0-2	
30/9	AEK	h	0-4	
7/10	Larissa	a	3-3	*Dimbala 2, Touré*
21/10	Xanthi	h	2-1	*Sisić, Anderson do Ó*
27/10	Iraklis	a	0-1	
4/11	Panathinaikos	h	0-4	
11/11	OFI	a	2-1	*Šišić, Zisopoulos*
24/11	Aris	h	2-0	*Bustos Montoya 2*
2/12	Kalamarias	a	0-2	
8/12	Olympiacos	a	0-4	
16/12	Ergotelis	h	0-0	
22/12	PAOK	a	0-1	
30/12	Tripolis	h	0-0	

08				
	Veria	a	1-3	*Bustos Montoya*
'1	Atromitos	h	2-1	*Bustos Montoya 2*
'1	Panionios	h	1-0	*Bustos Montoya*
'1	AEK	a	0-3	
	Larissa	h	0-1	
'2	Xanthi	a	1-4	*Anderson do Ó*
'2	Iraklis	h	3-0	*Leonardo (p), Bustos Montoya 2*
'2	Panathinaikos	a	0-1	
	OFI	h	0-3	
	Aris	a	0-1	
'3	Kalamarias	h	2-0	*Leonardo (p), José Luis*
'3	Olympiacos	h	1-3	*Dimbala*
'3	Ergotelis	a	1-2	*Leonardo*
	PAOK	h	2-0	*Leonardo (p), Andralas*
'4	Tripolis	a	2-1	*Paraskevaidis, Dimbala*
'4	Veria	h	5-3	*Andralas 2, Leonardo 2 (1p), Dimbala*

Name	Nat	Pos	Aps	(s)	Gls
ANDERSON DO Ó Oliveira	BRA	D	26	(2)	2
Paraskevas ANDRALAS		M	18	(6)	3
Srđan BLAZIĆ	MNE	G	24		
Eduardo BUSTOS MONTOYA	ARG	A	23	(2)	8
Yero DIA	FRA	D	4	(1)	
Dimitrios DIAMANTIS		M	9	(4)	
Patrick DIMBALA	BEL	A	26	(4)	6
Fritz EMERAN	RWA	D	22		
Ioannis FIRINIDIS		G	2		
JOSÉ LUIS Reyes	ESP	A	4	(7)	1
Nikolaos KARAKOSTAS		G	4	(2)	
Élie KROUPI	CIV	A	2	(6)	
Zsolt LACZKO	HUN	M		(7)	
LEONARDO Pereira	BRA	M	17	(10)	6
Konstantinos LOUBOUTIS		D	9		
Christos MITSIS		D	3		
Athanasios MOULOPOULOS		D	6		
Georgios PARASKEVAIDIS		D	17	(3)	1
Anastasios PASTOS		D	6	(1)	
Jacques PAVIOT	FRA	D	5	(2)	
Samuel PIETRE	FRA	M	4	(8)	
Goran POPOV	MKD	D	17	(3)	
Ivan RUSEV	BUL	M	10	(5)	
Sebastian SCHINDZIELORZ	GER	M	22		
Mirnes ŠIŠIČ	SVN	M	9		2
Theodosios THEODOSIADIS		D	13	(2)	
Bassala TOURÉ	MLI	M	9	(5)	1
Georgios ZISOPOULOS		M	19	(8)	1

OFI CRETE FC

Coach – Reiner Maurer (GER); (16/11/07) Georgios Parashos

Founded – 1925

MAJOR HONOURS: Greek Cup – (1) 1987.

007				
9	Kalamarias	h	3-2	*Issa, Bărcăuan, Nwafor*
/9	Olympiacos	a	2-6	*Sfakianakis, og (Torosidis)*
/9	Ergotelis	h	4-1	*Leozinho 2, Popović, Šimić*
10	PAOK	a	2-2	*Leozinho, Kounenakis*
/10	Tripolis	h	0-3	
/10	Veria	a	1-2	*Popović*
'11	Atromitos	a	0-1	
/11	Levadiakos	h	1-2	*Sfakianakis*
/11	AEK	a	0-4	
'12	Larissa	h	0-0	
'12	Xanthi	a	0-1	
/12	Iraklis	h	2-0	*Nwafor, Šimić*
/12	Panathinaikos	a	1-3	*Nwafor*
/12	Panionios	a	3-1	*Taralidis 2, Nwafor*

2008				
6/1	Aris	h	0-1	
13/1	Kalamarias	a	1-1	*Taralidis*
20/1	Olympiacos	h	0-1	
26/1	Ergotelis	a	1-1	*Leozinho (p)*
3/2	PAOK	h	2-0	*Kounenakis, Nwafor*
10/2	Tripolis	a	1-1	*Sfakianakis*
17/2	Veria	h	3-0	*Sfakianakis 2, Petropoulos*
24/2	Atromitos	h	0-1	
2/3	Levadiakos	a	3-0	*Sfakianakis, Petropoulos, Šimić*
9/3	AEK	h	1-4	*Sfakianakis*
16/3	Larissa	a	1-5	*Petropoulos*
23/3	Xanthi	h	2-0	*Petropoulos, Taralidis*
30/3	Iraklis	a	0-1	
6/4	Panathinaikos	h	4-1	*Drulić (p), Šimić, Sfakianakis, Popović*
13/4	Panionios	h	1-2	*Popović*
20/4	Aris	a	0-2	

No	Name	Nat	Pos	Aps	(s)	Gls
5	Dimitrios ARVANITIS		D	14	(3)	
4	Cosmin BĂRCĂUAN	ROU	D	23		1
10	Goran DRULIĆ	SRB	A	11	(6)	1
18	Vladimir GADZHEV	BUL	M	12	(7)	
14	Siniša GAGULA	SRB	D	4		
33	Fabian GERBER	GER	M	17	(6)	
13	Pierre ISSA	RSA	D	23		1
21	Konstantinos KOKKINAKIS		D		(2)	
32	Nikolaos KOUNENAKIS		D	23	(1)	2
23	Maxim LAROQUE	FRA	A	1	(2)	
77	LEOZINHO Sales	BRA	M	8	(8)	4
31	Emmanouil MONIAKIS		D	3	(10)	
11	Joseph NWAFOR	NGA	A	14	(10)	5
1	Tristan PEERSMAN	BEL	G	6		
29	Antonios PETROPOULOS		A	9	(1)	4
8	Minas PITSOS		D	25		
27	Dimitrios PLIAGAS		A	1	(3)	
28	Vasilios PLOUSIS		D		(4)	
9	Zdravko POPOVIĆ	CRO	A	19	(8)	4
17	Emmanouil ROUMBAKIS		M	19	(6)	
19	Stilianos SFAKIANAKIS		M	18	(5)	8
7	Aleksandar ŠIMIĆ	SRB	M	24	(2)	4
3	Konstantinos STAVRAKAKIS		M	9	(4)	
17	Ioannis TARALIDIS		M	23	(1)	4
30	Alexandros TZORVAS		G	24		

OLYMPIACOS CFP

Coach –Panagiotis Lemonis; (11/3/08) José "Pep" Segura (ESP)

Founded – 1925

MAJOR HONOURS: Greek League – (36) 1931, 1933, 1934, 1936, 1937, 1938, 1947, 1948, 1951, 1954, 1955, 1956, 1957, 1958, 1959, 1966, 1967, 1973, 1974, 1975, 1980, 1981, 1982, 1983, 1987, 1997, 1998, 1999, 2000, 2001, 2002, 2003, 2005, 2006, 2007, 2008; Greek Cup – (23) 1947, 1951, 1952, 1953, 1954, 1957, 1958, 1959, 1960, 1961, 1963, 1965, 1968, 1971, 1973, 1975, 1981, 1990, 1992, 1999, 2005, 2006, 2008.

2007				
2/9	Panathinaikos	a	0-0	
23/9	OFI	h	6-2	*Júlio César, Lua-Lua 2, Kovačević 2, Đorđević*
29/9	Aris	a	1-1	*Galletti*
6/10	Kalamarias	h	1-0	*Kovačević*
20/10	Panionios	h	4-1	*Lua-Lua, Kovačević, Stoltidis, Galletti (p)*
28/10	Ergotelis	a	3-3	*Júlio César, Kovačević, Đorđević (p)*
3/11	PAOK	h	2-1	*Torosidis, Kovačević*
10/11	Tripolis	a	0-1	
24/11	Veria	h	1-0	*Kovačević*
2/12	Atromitos	a	3-1	*Stoltidis, Lua-Lua,*

				Kovačević
8/12	Levadiakos	h	4-0	*Stoltidis, Kovačević, Đorđević (p), Mitroglou*
16/12	AEK	h	1-0	*Kovačević*
23/12	Larissa	a	0-0	
29/12	Xanthi	h	2-1	*Lua-Lua, Kovačević*
2008				
5/1	Iraklis	a	2-1	*Kovačević 2*
13/1	Panathinaikos	h	1-1	*Antzas*
20/1	OFI	a	1-0	*Núñez*
27/1	Aris	h	1-0	*Đorđević (p)*
3/2	Kalamarias	a	3-0	*(w/o; original result 0-1)*
10/2	Panionios	a	4-0	*Kovačević 2, Đorđević (p), Núñez*
16/2	Ergotelis	h	1-0	*Đorđević*
23/2	PAOK	a	1-1	*Kovačević*
1/3	Tripolis	h	1-1	*Júlio César*
9/3	Veria	a	1-0	*Patsatzoglou*
15/3	Atromitos	h	2-0	*Sisić, Júlio César*
23/3	Levadiakos	a	3-1	*Galletti, Belluschi, Kovačević*
30/3	AEK	a	0-4	
6/4	Larissa	h	2-1	*Sisić, Mitroglou*
13/4	Xanthi	a	4-1	*Zewłakow, Đorđević 3*
20/4	Iraklis	h	3-1	*Mitroglou 2, Đorđević*

No	Name	Nat	Pos	Aps	(s)	Gls
18	Paraskevas ANTZAS		D	22		1
8	Rodrigo Javier ARCHUBI	ARG	M	2	(2)	
25	Fernando Daniel BELLUSCHI	ARG	M	8	(3)	1
11	Predrag ĐORĐEVIĆ	SRB	M	28		10
3	Didier DOMI	FRA	D	2		
7	Luciano Martín GALLETTI	ARG	M	23	(1)	3
55	JÚLIO CÉSAR Santos	BRA	D	18	(1)	4
24	Georgios KATSIKOGIANNIS		M	1	(3)	
23	Michalis KONSTANTINOU	CYP	A	1	(9)	
9	Darko KOVAČEVIĆ	SRB	A	27	(1)	17
28	Cristian Raúl LEDESMA	ARG	M	16	(2)	
4	Jesus Geraldo LEONARDO	BRA	D	10	(1)	
32	Lomana Trésor LUA LUA	COD	A	20	(1)	5
20	Eleftherios MATSOUKAS		A		(1)	
19	Konstantinos MENDRINOS		M	6	(8)	
22	Konstantinos MITROGLOU		A	2	(10)	4
16	Marco NÉ	CIV	M		(3)	
71	Antonios NIKOPOLIDIS		G	29		
10	Leonel Jorge NÚÑEZ	ARG	A	4	(15)	2
30	Anastasios PANTOS		D	16	(3)	
92	Kiriakos PAPADOPOULOS		D		(3)	
2	Chistos PATSATZOGLOU		D	17	(3)	1
15	RAÚL BRAVO Sanfelix	ESP	D	6	(1)	
87	Michail M. SIFAKIS		G	1	(1)	
77	Mirnes ŠIŠIČ	SVN	M	3	(9)	2
6	Ieroklis STOLTIDIS		M	25	(2)	3
35	Vasilios TOROSIDIS		M	23	(3)	1
14	Michał ŻEWŁAKOW	POL	D	20	(1)	1

PANATHINAIKOS FC

Coach – José Peseiro (POR)

Founded – 1908

MAJOR HONOURS: Greek League – (19) 1930, 1949, 1953, 1960, 1961, 1962, 1964, 1965, 1969, 1970, 1972, 1977, 1984, 1986, 1990, 1991, 1995, 1996, 2004; Greek Cup - (16) 1940, 1948, 1955, 1967, 1969, 1977, 1982, 1984, 1986, 1988, 1989, 1991, 1993, 1994, 1995, 2004.

2007				
2/9	Olympiacos	h	0-0	
23/9	Ergotelis	a	3-0	*Romero 2, Salpingidis*
29/9	PAOK	h	2-0	*Karagounis (p), Salpingidis*
7/10	Tripolis	a	0-1	
21/10	Veria	a	2-0	*Ivanschitz, Salpingidis*
28/10	Atromitos	h	2-0	*Papadopoulos, Salpingidis*
4/11	Levadiakos	a	4-0	*Salpingidis, Ivanschit. Tziolis, Mantzios*
11/11	AEK	h	2-1	*Salpingidis, Mantzios*
25/11	Larissa	a	2-2	*Tziolis, Marcelo Matto*
1/12	Xanthi	h	0-0	
9/12	Iraklis	a	1-0	*og (Katsabis)*
15/12	Panionios	a	0-1	
23/12	OFI	h	3-1	*Mantzios, og (Issa), Salpingidis*
30/12	Aris	a	1-0	*og (Papadopoulos)*
2008				
6/1	Kalamarias	h	1-0	*Salpingidis (p)*
13/1	Olympiacos	a	1-1	*N'Doye*
20/1	Ergotelis	h	1-0	*Salpingidis*
27/1	PAOK	a	1-0	*Salpingidis*
3/2	Tripolis	h	2-0	*N'Doye, Salpingidis*
9/2	Veria	h	1-0	*Ivanschitz*
24/2	Levadiakos	h	1-0	*Goumas*
2/3	AEK	a	1-1	*Hélder Postiga*
5/3	Atromitos	a	1-0	*Sarriegi*
9/3	Larissa	h	2-0	*Manucho, Salpingidis*
16/3	Xanthi	a	2-3	*Hélder Postiga, Salpingidis*
22/3	Iraklis	h	1-1	*Goumas*
30/3	Panionios	h	2-1	*Papadopoulos (p), Salpingidis (p)*
6/4	OFI	a	1-4	*Salpingidis*
13/4	Aris	h	1-0	*Karagounis*
20/4	Kalamarias	a	3-1	*og (Galanopoulos) 2, Papadopoulos*

No	Name	Nat	Pos	Aps	(s)	Gls
6	Filippos DARLAS		D		(2)	
17	Elini DIMOUTSOS		M	8	(5)	
2	Joseph ENAKARHIRE	NGA	D	2		
15	Panagiotis FYSSAS		D	2		
1	Mario GALINOVIĆ	CRO	G	19		
10	Ezequiel GONZÁLEZ	ARG	M	8	(3)	
8	Ioannis GOUMAS		D	18		2
12	HÉLDER Manuel POSTIGA	POR	A	5	(6)	2
27	Andreas IVANSCHITZ	AUT	M	16	(8)	3
21	Georgios KARAGOUNIS		M	25	(2)	2
20	Sotirios LEONDIOU		M	1		
18	Arkadiusz MALARZ	POL	G	11		
26	Evangelo MANTZIOS		A	6	(3)	3
36	Mateus MANUCHO	ANG	A	2	(2)	1
4	MARCELO Mendonca MATTOS	BRA	M	23	(4)	1
23	Simão MATE JÚNIOR	MOZ	M	8	(8)	
5	Nasief MORRIS	RSA	D	21		
25	Dame N'DOYE	SEN	M	10	(9)	2
29	Mikael NILSSON	SWE	M	22	(1)	
7	Sotirios NINIS		M	1	(3)	
11	Dimitrios PAPADOPOULOS		A	15	(11)	3
9	Sebastián ROMERO	ARG	M	7	(5)	2
14	Dimitrios SALPINGIDIS		A	23	(6)	15
3	Josu SARRIEGUI Zumárraga	ESP	D	18	(2)	1
19	Anthony ŠERIĆ	CRO	D	11	(1)	
31	Nikolaos SPIROPOULOS		D	8		
22	Alexandros TZIOLIS		M	24	(3)	2
24	Loukas VINTRA		D	16	(3)	

PANIONIOS GSS

Coach – Ewald Lienen (GER)

Founded – 1890

MAJOR HONOURS: Greek Cup – (2) 1979, 1998.

2007				
1/9	Aris	a	0-0	
23/9	Levadiakos	h	2-0	*Djebbour 2*
30/9	Kalamarias	a	2-0	*Pletsch, Djebbour (p)*
7/10	AEK	h	0-3	

/10	Olympiacos	a	1-4	*Djebbour (p)*
/10	Larissa	h	3-1	*Djebbour 2, Sialmas*
1	Ergotelis	a	1-1	*Nicolaou*
/11	Xanthi	h	3-2	*Pletsch, Djebbour, Goundoulakis*
/11	PAOK	a	1-3	*Pletsch*
2	Iraklis	h	1-1	*Djebbour*
2	Tripolis	a	0-1	
/12	Panathinaikos	h	1-0	*Djebbour*
/12	Veria	a	1-1	*Aravidis*
/12	OFI	h	1-3	*Aravidis*
08				
	Atromitos	a	2-0	*Sialmas, Majstorović*
/1	Aris	h	0-3	
/1	Levadiakos	a	0-1	
/1	Kalamarias	h	2-1	*Fernández, Djebbour*
2	AEK	a	3-2	*Djebbour, Choutos 2*
/2	Olympiacos	h	0-4	
/2	Larissa	a	0-1	
/2	Ergotelis	h	2-1	*Djebbour, Choutos*
3	Xanthi	a	2-1	*Choutos 2*
3	PAOK	h	0-0	
/3	Iraklis	a	0-1	
/3	Tripolis	h	4-1	*Yao Kumordzi, Djebbour (p), Choutos 2*
/3	Panathinaikos	a	1-2	*Djebbour (p)*
4	Veria	h	2-2	*Yao Kumordzi, Goundoulakis*
/4	OFI	a	2-1	*Choutos, Fernández*
/4	Atromitos	h	2-1	*Choutos 2 (1p)*

No	Name	Nat	Pos	Aps	(s)	Gls
	Christos ARAVIDIS		A	5	(12)	2
	Sékou BERTHÉ	MLI	D	15	(1)	
	Lambros CHOUTOS		A	14		10
	Fousseni DIAWARA	MLI	D	11		
	Rafik DJEBBOUR	ALG	A	24		14
	Darío FERNÁNDEZ	ARG	M	22	(2)	2
	Jozef GÁSPÁR	SVK	D	1	(2)	
	Kleopas GIANNOU		G	3		
	Fanourios GOUNDOULAKIS		M	20	(7)	2
	Efthimios GOUSOULIS		M		(2)	
	Mehmet HETEMAJ	FIN	D	3	(2)	
	Konstantinos KAPETANOS		M	2	(13)	
	Alban KONDI	ALB	A	6	(2)	
	Miroslav KÖNIG	SVK	G	5	(1)	
	Ioannis KONTOES		D	1		
	Evangelos KOUTSOPOULOS		D	15	(2)	
	Dario KREŠIĆ	CRO	G	20		
	Luís LOURENÇO da Silva	POR	A		(1)	
	Ivica MAJSTOROVIĆ	CRO	M	25	(1)	1
	Grigorios MAKOS		D	26	(1)	
	Ioannis MANIATIS		D	24	(1)	
3	Marios NICOLAOU	CYP	A	20	(6)	1
	Pavel PLASKONNYI	BLR	D		(4)	
	Marcelo PLETSCH	BRA	D	17		3
	Dimitrios SIALMAS		A	2	(8)	2
	Emmanouil SKOUFALIS		M	10	(11)	
	Nikolaos SPIROPOULOS		D	17		
2	Haralambos TAMBASIS		G	2		
5	WAGNER Ribeiro	BRA	M	5	(5)	
5	Bernard YAO KUMORDZI	GHA	M	15	(2)	2

PAOK FC

Coach –Georgios Parashos; (3/9/07) Manuel Fernando Santos (POR)

Founded – 1926

MAJOR HONOURS: Greek League – (2) 1976, 1985; Greek Cup – (4) 1972, 1974, 2001, 2003.

007				
/9	Xanthi	a	0-1	
22/9	Iraklis	h	3-0	*Melissis, Vangelis, Lakis*
29/9	Panathinaikos	a	0-2	
6/10	OFI	h	2-2	*Vangelis, Konstantinidis*
21/10	Aris	a	1-3	*Balafas*
28/10	Kalamarias	h	4-1	*Melissis, Hristodoulopoulos, Salmon, Konstantinidis*
3/11	Olympiacos	a	1-2	*Konstantinidis*
11/11	Ergotelis	h	1-0	*Salmon*
25/11	Panionios	h	3-1	*Georgiadis, Konstantinidis, Malezas*
2/12	Tripolis	a	0-2	
8/12	Veria	h	2-0	*Toni, Salmon*
15/12	Atromitos	a	0-0	
22/12	Levadiakos	h	1-0	*Lakis*
30/12	AEK	a	0-2	
2008				
6/1	Larissa	h	1-0	*Hristodoulopoulos*
13/1	Xanthi	h	0-1	
20/1	Iraklis	a	0-1	
27/1	Panathinaikos	h	0-1	
3/2	OFI	a	0-2	
10/2	Aris	h	3-0	*Hristodoulopoulos, Balafas, Salmon*
17/2	Kalamarias	a	2-0	*Lakis, Iliev*
23/2	Olympiacos	h	1-1	*Toni*
1/3	Ergotelis	a	0-2	
8/3	Panionios	a	0-0	
15/3	Tripolis	h	0-1	
22/3	Veria	a	0-0	
30/3	Atromitos	h	1-0	*Georgiadis (p)*
6/4	Levadiakos	a	0-2	
13/4	AEK	h	0-4	
20/4	Larissa	a	3-4	*Athanasiadis 2, Balafas*

No	Name	Nat	Pos	Aps	(s)	Gls
28	Stefanos ATHANASIADIS		A	1	(3)	2
21	Agenaldo BAIANO	BRA	D	19	(1)	
25	Sotirios BALAFAS		M	22	(2)	3
4	Ilias CHARALAMBOUS	CYP	M	19	(1)	
1	Daniel Fernandes "DANI"	POR	G	30		
9	Viorel FRUNZĂ	MDA	A	1	(3)	
30	Goran GAVRANČIĆ	SRB	D	7		
11	Georgios GEORGIADIS		A	17	(8)	2
34	Evangelos GEORGIOU		D	2		
10	Lazaros HRISTODOULOPOULOS		M	18	(7)	3
8	Stilanos ILIADIS		M	13	(4)	
14	Ivica ILIEV	SRB	A	6	(11)	1
44	Ruud KNOL	NED	D	23		
3	Pantelis KONSTANTINIDIS		M	18	(6)	4
23	Vasilios LAKIS		M	15	(7)	3
13	Stilianos MALEZAS		D	9	(2)	1
5	Christos MELISSIS		D	24		2
46	Huseyin MUMIN		M	4	(2)	
16	Dimitrios ORFANOS		A	1	(4)	
88	Ioannis PEHLIVANIS		M	1		
29	Glen SALMON	RSA	A	22	(2)	4
7	SÉRGIO Paulo CONCEIÇÃO	POR	M	4	(3)	
27	Mirosław SZNAUCNER	POL	D	19		
10	Antonio González "TONI"	ESP	M	9	(7)	2
18	Lambros VAGGELIS		M	13	(3)	2
22	Ricardo Matias VERÓN	ARG	M	10	(1)	
15	Zisis VRYZAS		A	3	(10)	

GAS VERIA

Coach – Dimitrios Kalaitzidis; (15/10/07) Ratko Dostanić (SRB); (12/12/07) Ioannis Matzourakis; (12/3/08) Panagiotis Tsalouhidis; (23/3/08) Leonidas Ifantidis

Founded – 1960

2007				
23/9	Larissa	a	1-1	*Krivokapić*
26/9	AEK	h	0-1	

30/9	Xanthi	h	1-1	*Samaras*
7/10	Iraklis	a	1-1	*Seedorf*
21/10	Panathinaikos	h	0-2	
28/10	OFI	h	2-1	*Alexiou, Herrera*
4/11	Aris	a	0-1	
11/11	Kalamarias	h	0-2	
24/11	Olympiacos	a	0-1	
2/12	Ergotelis	h	1-1	*Koltzos*
8/12	PAOK	a	0-2	
16/12	Tripolis	h	1-0	*Samaras*
23/12	Panionios	h	1-1	*Bykowski*
30/12	Atromitos	a	0-1	
2008				
6/1	Levadiakos	h	3-1	*Alexiou, Krivokapić, De Lange*
12/1	AEK	a	1-5	*Bykowski*
20/1	Larissa	h	1-0	*Ndaw*
26/1	Xanthi	a	0-2	
3/2	Iraklis	h	1-2	*Ndaw*
9/2	Panathinaikos	a	0-1	
17/2	OFI	a	0-3	
23/2	Aris	h	1-0	*Bykowski*
2/3	Kalamarias	a	0-1	
9/3	Olympiacos	h	0-1	
15/3	Ergotelis	a	0-2	
22/3	PAOK	h	0-0	
30/3	Tripolis	a	0-2	
6/4	Panionios	a	2-2	*Seedorf, Gélson*
13/4	Atromitos	h	1-1	*Gélson*
20/4	Levadiakos	a	3-5	*Ndaw, og (Diamantis), Herrera*

No	Name	Nat	Pos	Aps	(s)	Gls
4	Ioannis ALEXIOU		D	19	(2)	2
1	Loukas APOSTOLIDIS		G	9		
81	Dimitrios BALAFAS		D	3	(2)	
9	Maciej BYKOWSKI	POL	A	16	(7)	3
6	Paul DE LANGE	NED	M	14	(1)	1
3	Marcos Vinícius FALEIRO	BRA	M		(1)	
28	Razvan FRITEA	ROU	M		(3)	
12	Geraldo dos Santos Júnior "GÉLSON"	BRA	A	3	(4)	2
22	Carlos GILVAN	BRA	M	5	(6)	
16	Luis GUADALUPE	PER	D	3	(2)	
40	Esteban HERRERA	ARG	A	18	(5)	2
10	Júlio César Fereira "JULINHO"	BRA	M	10		
38	Nikolaos KALTSAS		M	1		
17	Miha KLINE	SVN	D	5	(2)	
13	Georgios KOLTZOS		D	26		1
30	Dimitrios KOTTARIDIS		G	4		
14	Radovan KRIVOKAPIĆ	SRB	M	24	(1)	2
39	MÁRCIO Fabiano GIOVANINI	BRA	D	8	(2)	
24	Georgios MELABIANAKIS		M	5	(1)	
25	José Adolfo Zambrano MENDOZA	PER	M	7	(3)	
32	Lucien METTOMO	CMR	D	6		
27	Karim MOUZAOUI	MAR	A		(5)	
15	Mustapha Kamal NDAW	GAM	A	11	(3)	3
26	Ricardo David Gómez PÁEZ	VEN	M	4	(13)	
20	Triantafillos PARMAXIDIS		M	9	(6)	
21	Dimitrios PETKAKIS		D	20		
34	Juan Martin PIETRAVALLO	ARG	M	3	(1)	
18	Saša RANIČ	SVN	M	6	(3)	
29	RICARDO Mion COSTA	BRA	A		(3)	
5	Dimitrios SAMARAS		D	25	(1)	2
7	Stefano SEEDORF	NED	M	9	(7)	2
19	Efstathios STEFANIDIS		A	14	(2)	
23	Joost TEROL	NED	G	17		
11	Nikolaos TSIMBLIDIS		A	21	(3)	
36	Theodoros VASILAKAKIS		D	5	(1)	

SKODA XANTHI FC

Coach – Emilio Ferrera (BEL); (22/10/07) Nikolaos Kehagias

Founded – 1967

2007				
1/9	PAOK	h	1-0	*Poy*
22/9	Tripolis	h	2-0	*Poy, Labriakos*
30/9	Veria	a	1-1	*Barkoglou*
7/10	Atromitos	h	0-1	
21/10	Levadiakos	a	1-2	*Radzinski*
28/10	AEK	h	0-1	
4/11	Larissa	a	0-0	
11/11	Panionios	a	2-3	*Radzinski 2*
25/11	Iraklis	h	0-3	
1/12	Panathinaikos	a	0-0	
9/12	OFI	h	1-0	*Zuela*
15/12	Aris	a	0-2	
22/12	Kalamarias	h	6-1	*Poy 2, Radzinski 3, Barkoglou*
29/12	Olympiacos	a	1-2	*Radzinski*
2008				
6/1	Ergotelis	h	1-0	*og (Miladin)*
13/1	PAOK	a	1-0	*Radzinski*
20/1	Tripolis	a	0-0	
26/1	Veria	h	2-0	*Radzinski, Labriakos*
2/2	Atromitos	a	3-2	*Labriakos, Grzelak 2*
10/2	Levadiakos	h	4-1	*Tziortziopoulos, Radzinski, Grzelak, Pen*
24/2	Larissa	h	1-1	*Grzelak*
2/3	Panionios	h	1-2	*Labriakos*
5/3	AEK	a	0-3	
9/3	Iraklis	a	1-1	*Grzelak*
16/3	Panathinaikos	h	3-2	*Radzinski 3*
23/3	OFI	a	0-2	
30/3	Aris	h	0-2	
6/4	Kalamarias	a	0-1	
13/4	Olympiacos	h	1-4	*Labriakos*
20/4	Ergotelis	a	0-2	

No	Name	Nat	Pos	Aps	(s)	Gls
77	Piero Fernando Niezen ALVA	PER	A	4	(10)	
11	Georgios BARKOGLOU		M	4	(4)	2
46	Emmanouil BERTOS		M	2		
38	CHIQUINHO Delgado	POR	A		(3)	
6	Angelos DIGOZIS		M	22	(1)	
29	Athanasios DINAS		A	1		
78	Gastón Rubén ESMERADO	ARG	M	2	(3)	
21	Konstantinos FLISKAS		D	5	(11)	
30	Gamadiel GARCÍA	CHI	A	3	(4)	
19	Rafał GRZELAK	POL	M	12	(1)	5
24	Michael GSPURNING	AUT	G	14		
96	Dimitrios HASOMERIS		A	1	(2)	
34	Vlasios KAZAKIS		A	3	(1)	1
7	Dimitrios KONTODIMOS		M	9		
28	Athanasios KOSTOULAS		D	29		
13	Stavros LABRIAKOS		A	21	(5)	5
33	Sotirios LIBEROPOULOS		G	8	(1)	
99	Marius MITU	ROU	M		(1)	
4	Patrice NOUKEU	CMR	M		(2)	
5	Ioannis PAPADIMITRIOU		D	23		
15	Sebastián Ariel PENCO	ARG	A	3	(6)	1
10	Mauro POY	ARG	A	16	(1)	4
9	Diego QUINTANA	ARG	M	23	(3)	
27	Tomasz RADZINSKI	CAN	A	23	(2)	13
17	Antonios RIKKA		M	23		
14	Pantelis RIZOGIANNIS		M	10	(1)	
18	Stavros STATHAKIS		D	1	(3)	
8	Ante TOMIĆ	CRO	M	10	(12)	
1	Ivan TURINA	CRO	G	8		
31	Stavros TZIORTZIOPOULOS		D	11	(1)	1
25	Spiridon VALLAS		D	8	(7)	
18	Mikael YOURASSOWSKI	BEL	D	5		
32	Francisco ZUELA	ANG	D	26	(1)	

PROMOTED CLUBS

PANSERRAIKOS FC
Coach – Giannis Papakostas
Founded - 1964

THRASIVOULOS FILIS FC
Coach – Athanasios Tsiolis
Founded - 1938

PANTHRAKIKOS FC
Coach – Kostas Vasilakakis
Founded - 1963

ECOND LEVEL FINAL TABLE 2007/08

	Pld	W	D	L	F	A	Pts
Panserraikos FC	34	19	10	5	48	20	67
Thrasivoulos Filis FC	34	18	7	9	44	27	61
Panthrakikos FC	34	17	10	7	44	31	60
PAS Giannina	34	16	9	9	54	38	57
Ionikos FC	34	15	9	10	37	28	54
Kallithea FC	34	15	7	12	40	35	52
Kerkyra FC	34	13	11	10	39	33	50
Agrotikos Asteras FC	34	14	5	15	44	47	47
Ethnikos Piraeus FC	34	11	12	11	32	36	45
Ilisiakos FC	34	13	4	17	31	38	43
Kalamata FC	34	11	9	14	30	33	42
Ethnikos Asteras FC	34	10	11	13	32	37	41
Pierikos FC	34	10	14	10	28	33	41
Kastoria FC	34	10	9	15	26	41	39
Ethnikos Olympiakos Volou FC	34	9	12	13	33	38	39
Egaleo FC	34	10	9	15	28	34	39
Chaidari FC	34	8	14	12	30	31	38
Agios Dimitrios FC	34	2	8	24	22	62	14

N.B. Panthrakikos 1 pt deducted. Pierikos 3 pts deducted.

OMESTIC CUP 2007/08

KYPELLO ELLADOS

H ROUND

07)
ea 1, Kalamarias 2

/07)
o 1, Xanthi 2
kos Katerinis 1, Levadiakos 0
piakos Volos 1, Atromitos 1 *(aet; 5-6 on pens)*
za 3, Veria 0 (w/o)
voulos 4, PAOK 2

)/07)
Dimitrios 0, Aris 1 *(aet)*
ikos Asteras 1, Ergotelis 0
olis 0, Larissa 4
niakos 0, Tripolis 2

)/07)
piakos/Ethnikos Volos 0, Iraklis 1

(31/10/07)
Ethnikos Asteras 1, Panathinaikos 3
Kastoria 2, Panionios 3

(1/11/07)
Ethnikos Piraeus 1, OFI 2 *(aet)*
Fostiras 0, AEK 2

(5/12/07)
Diagoras 1, Olympiacos 2

FIFTH ROUND

(9/1/08)
Agrotikos Asteras 1, OFI 1
Ethnikos Katerinis 0, Aris 3
Xanthi 2, AEK 0
Thrasivoulos 3, Preveza 0

(10/1/08)
Kalamarias 1, Larissa 2

(16/1/08)
Tripolis 0, Atromitos 1
Olympiacos 4, Panathinaikos 0

(17/1/08)
Iraklis 1, Panionios 0

Replay

(13/2/08)
OFI 5, Agrotikos Asteras 0

QUARTER-FINALS

(27/2/08 & 19/3/08)
Olympiacos 2 *(Mendrinos 5, 9)*, Iraklis 0
Iraklis 2 *(Aarón 42, Flávio 87)*, Olympiacos 2 *(Núñez 10, Mitroglou 23)*
(Olympiacos 4-2)

(27/2/08 & 20/3/08)
Xanthi 0, Aris 0
Aris 1 *(Jahić 72)*, Xanthi 0
(Aris 1-0)

(28/2/08 & 19/3/08)
Atromitos 3 *(Perrone 68, Tsigas 76, Geladaris 84)*, OFI 1 *(Sfakianakis 24)*
OFI 2 *(Simić 66, Taralidis 72)*, Atromitos 1 *(Luciano 88)*
(Atromitos 4-3)

(5/3/08 & 19/3/08)
Thrasivoulos 1 (Haralambakis 33), Larissa 0
Larissa 1 *(Tümer 69)*, Thrasivoulos 3 *(Barrientos 49, 74, 89)*
(Thrasivoulos 4-1)

SEMI-FINALS

(2/4/08 & 16/4/08)
Aris 1 *(Toni Calvo 90p)*, Atromitos 0
Atromitos 1 *(Nikolopoulos 90)*, Aris 2 *(Koke 78, Ivić 82)*
(Aris 3-1)
Thrasivoulos 2 *(Anastasakos 30, Bris 35)*, Olympiacos 3 *(Mendrinos 18, Núñez 29, Kovačević 89)*
Olympiacos 3 *(Kovačević 14, Konstantinou 15, Núñez 21)*, Thrasivoulos 1 *(Manikas 33)*
(Olympiacos 6-3)

FINAL

(17/5/08)
Kaftanzoglio stadium, Thessaloniki
OLYMPIACOS CFP 2 *(Kovačević 34, Zewłakow 53)*
ARIS THESSALONIKI FC 0
Referee – *Kasnaferis*
OLYMPIACOS – *Nikopolidis, Torosidis, Raúl Bravo, Antzas, Zewłakow, Patsatzoglou, Stoltidis, Galletti (Šišić 85), Đorđević, Kovačević (Konstantinou 89), Mitroglou (Pantos 80).*
ARIS – *Kelemen, Neto, Karabelas (Felipe 61), Papadopoulos, Ronaldo (Thiago Gentil 80), Nebegleras, Jahić, Siston, Ivić, Koke, Javito (Toni Calvo 63).*

MTK youngsters return title to Budapest

The three-year reign of provincial club Debreceni VSC came to an end in 2007/08 as MTK Budapest, the youngest team in the division, reclaimed the NB I title for the capital.

Led by experienced coach József Garami, MTK reaped the dividends of the youth academy they had set up in an old castle in the town of Agard, 50 kilometres from Budapest, at the beginning of the decade. The Sándor Károly Akadémia, named after the club's famous right-winger, and launched by club owner Gábor Várszegi, was an ambitious and expensive project, but its first generation of graduates were the cornerstone of MTK's first championship win for five years, with no fewer than 17 members of Garami's triumphant squad having come through the club's youth development programme, including up-and-coming Hungarian internationals József Kanta, László Zsidai and Zoltán Pollák. The only players over 30 in the team were veteran goalkeeper/captain Zoltán Végh and giant Serbian defender Mladen Lambulić – the team's sole foreigner.

László Zsidai (left) – one of the prominent young academy graduates in MTK's championship-winning side

MTK had finished runners-up to Debrecen in 2006/07 after allowing a halfway lead to slip. This time, with a year of extra experience, the young guns managed t keep their noses in front after going into the winter break with a four-point advantage. Defeated just onc in the autumn, by early-season pace-setters Budapes Honvéd FC, MTK lost three times in the spring. Crucially, though, they won the head-to-head clash away to Debrecen, 2-0, and then held their nerve in the closing weeks with the defending champions in hot pursuit.

The Blue and Whites' 23rd national title was secured i the penultimate round when they won 3-0 at Rákospalotai EAC, with Lambulić scoring two of the goals and the club's leading marksman, 23-year-old Gábor Urbán, bagging the other. Although MTK's lead over Debrecen was just two points with one game remaining, the title was safely under lock and key as the final fixture of their campaign was at home to Sopron FC, a club that had withdrawn from the leagu in mid-season due to financial problems and forfeited all their remaining matches with a 3-0 defeat.

Perfect pick-me-up

Debrecen's bid for a fourth successive title was thus thwarted, but they had been the best team in the NB during the spring, registering 35 points (to MTK's 32), and two days after surrendering the championship they provided their fans with the perfect pick-me-up, thrashing Honvéd 7-0 away from home in the first leg of the Hungarian Cup final. 'Loki' had been denied the double by the same opponents the previous season when Honvéd beat them on penalties in the Cup final but now, with the fixture restored to a two-legged affair, Debrecen had got their revenge and rendered the return game meaningless. They went on to win it 2-1, thus recording the biggest margin of victory in the Hungarian Cup final for 75 years.

Debrecen's season had started badly with elimination from the second qualifying round of the UEFA

ıampions League by IF Elfsborg. The team's Czech ›ach Miroslav Beránek worked under a cloud of sappointment thereafter and when the team ended e autumn campaign with three successive draws, lling five points behind MTK, he resigned. With the am's shining light, young Hungarian international ft-winger Balázs Dzsudzsák, leaving in the winter to in PSV Eindhoven, new coach András Herczeg erának's assistant) appeared to have his work cut ıt, but he kept the team on the right track and was most rewarded with the double.

urprise packages

ɔart from MTK the only team to beat Debrecen in the ring were Győri ETO FC, who, to general tonishment, finished third – their first 'podium' finish ıce 1985/86. A mere sixth at Christmas, they made ıch a strong start to the spring campaign that for a hile they were in genuine contention for the title. :perienced coach Sándor Egervári, who led MTK to the ıampionship in 1998/99, demonstrated his pedigree, did captain Péter Stark, a former Hungarian ternational defender whose father had played in the 985/86 Győr team. The other overachievers were FC hérvár. Close to following Sopron out of the league ıring the winter, they were rescued by wealthy ısinessman István Garancsi, who took control of the ub, settled their financial concerns, brought in a new ɔach, László Disztl, and a new technical director, yörgy Mezey, then beamed in satisfaction as the team n up seven successive victories to finish fifth.

With Sopron departed and FC Tatabánya stranded, the issue of relegation was resolved early. The greater intrigue lay in whether Ferencvárosi TC, the country's most decorated and popular club, could win promotion back to the elite. The answer was no, although 'Fradi' did safeguard their future after a buy-out from an English consortium headed by Sheffield United FC chairman Kevin McCabe. Kecskeméti TE proved too strong for the fallen Budapest giants in the Eastern section of the second division, while Szombathelyi Haladás FC won promotion from the Western pool.

Koeman takes charge

Having sunk to new depths in the UEFA EURO 2008™ qualifying campaign, finishing sixth in Group 3, Hungary decided to wipe the slate clean and remove Péter Várhidi from the position of national coach, handing it instead to Dutchman Erwin Koeman. MLSZ president István Kisteleki was known to be a long-standing admirer of Dutch football, so to some degree the appointment of Koeman – the older brother of Ronald and also a member of the Netherlands' victorious Euro '88 team – was no surprise. He made a bright start, too, with his charges defeating Greece 3-2 and holding Croatia 1-1. Not that Hungary needed rousing for friendlies, having already beaten another two UEFA EURO 2008™ participants, Italy and Poland, earlier in the season. The 3-2 win over the Azzurri was particularly noteworthy as it was the first time Hungary had ever treated the Budapest public to a victory over reigning world champions.

Magyar Labdrúgó Szövetség (MLSZ)

Kőérberek-Tóváros
Kánai út 314/24 hrsz.
H-1112 Budapest
tel - +36 1 5779500
fax - +36 1 5779503
website - www.mlsz.hu
email - mlsz@mlsz.hu
Year of Formation – 1901
President – István Kisteleki
Press Officer – Péter Serényi
Stadium – Ferenc Puskás, Budapest (35,817)

INTERNATIONAL TOURNAMENT APPEARANCES
FIFA World Cup - (9) 1934 (2nd round), 1938 (runners-up), 1954 (runners-up), 1958, 1962 (qtr-finals), 1966 (qtr finals), 1978, 1982, 1986.
UEFA European Championship - (2) 1964 (3rd), 1972 (4th).

TOP FIVE ALL-TIME CAPS
József Bozsik (101); László Fazekas (92); Gyula Grosics (86); Ferenc Puskás (85); Imre Garaba (82)

TOP FIVE ALL-TIME GOALS
Ferenc Puskás (84); Sándor Kocsis (75); Imre Schlosser (59); Lajos Tichy (51), György Sárosi (42)

HUNGARY

NATIONAL TEAM RESULTS 2007/08

22/8/07	Italy	H	Budapest	3-2	*Juhász (62), Gera (65p), Feczesin (75)*
8/9/07	Bosnia-Herzegovina (ECQ)	H	Szekesfehervar	1-0	*Gera (39p)*
12/9/07	Turkey (ECQ)	A	Istanbul	0-3	
13/10/07	Malta (ECQ)	H	Budapest	2-0	*Feczesin (34), Tőzsér (78)*
17/10/07	Poland	A	Lodz	1-0	*Hajnal (80p)*
17/11/07	Moldova (ECQ)	A	Chisinau	0-3	
21/11/07	Greece (ECQ)	H	Budapest	1-2	*Buzsáky (7)*
6/2/08	Slovakia	N	Limassol (CYP)	1-1	*Gera (54)*
26/3/08	Slovenia	H	Zalaegerszeg	0-1	
24/5/08	Greece	H	Budapest	3-2	*Dzsudzsák (46), Juhász (59), Vadócz (63)*
31/5/08	Croatia	H	Budapest	1-1	*Kovač N. (45og)*

NATIONAL TEAM APPEARANCES 2007/08

Coach - Péter VÁRHIDI 8/5/58 /(1/5/08) Erwin KOEMAN (NED) 20/9/61			Ita	BIH	TUR	MLT	Pol	MDA	GRE	Svk	Svn	Gre	Cro	Caps	Go
Márton FÜLÖP	3/5/83	Leicester (ENG) /Sunderland (ENG)	G	G	G71	G	G	G	G	G	G	G	G	15	-
Zoltán SZÉLESI	22/11/81	Energie (GER) /Strasbourg (FRA)	D	D	D	D		D	D	M	D	D	s89	15	-
Roland JUHÁSZ	1/7/83	Anderlecht (BEL)	D	D	D	D	D		D	D	D	D	D	36	3
Tamás VASKÓ	20/2/84	Bristol City (ENG)	D	D	D	D	D	D	D				D	11	-
Vilmos VANCZÁK	20/6/83	Sion (SUI)	D73	D	M		D	D	D	D	D	D		31	-
Ádám VASS	9/9/88	Brescia (ITA)	M	M	M	M	M		M	M83	M80			10	-
Dániel TŐZSÉR	12/5/85	AEK (GRE)	M59	M		M	M77	M38	M85	s83	M74			15	1
Tamás HAJNAL	15/3/81	Karlsruhe (GER)	M59	M72	M		M90	M	M76	M46		M83	M	23	1
Zoltán GERA	22/4/79	West Brom (ENG)	A90	M	M	M	M78	M		A		M89	M	53	1[illegible]
Tamás PRISKIN	27/9/96	Watford (ENG) /Preston (ENG)	A73		A66		s46	A	A	s75	A63			17	6
Balázs DZSUDZSÁK	23/12/86	Debrecen /PSV (NED)	A82	A93	M82	M88	A46	A71		s46		M	M64	10	1
LEANDRO de Almeida	19/3/82	Debrecen	s59			s88	s77		s85					10	-
Attila FILKOR	12/7/88	Internazionale (ITA)	s59	s89		M75	s90		s76					6	-
Csaba CSIZMADIA	30/5/85	Mattersburg (AUT)	s73	s72	D		D	D		D	s80			12	-
Róbert FECZESIN	22/6/86	Brescia (ITA)	s73	A89		A83	A46	s71	s81					8	3
Péter HALMOSI	25/9/79	Plymouth (ENG)	s82	s93	s82		s46		M81	s57				18	-
Ákos BUZSÁKY	7/5/82	Plymouth (ENG) /QPR (ENG)	s90			s75	s78	s38	M	M75	M46			11	1
Balázs TÓTH	24/9/81	Genk (BEL)			s66									23	-
János BALOGH	29/11/82	Debrecen			s71									1	-
Béla BALOGH	20/12/84	Colchester (ENG)				D		s39						9	-
Péter RAJCZI	3/4/81	Pisa (ITA)				s83								11	3
Krisztián VADÓCZ	30/5/85	NEC (NED)						M39			s74	M	M	12	2
Zsolt LŐW	29/4/79	Hoffenheim (GER)								D		D		24	1
Szabolcs HUSZTI	18/4/83	Hannover (GER)								A57	M	A	A	30	6
Krisztián TÍMÁR	4/10/79	Plymouth (ENG)									D			1	-
László ZSIDAI	16/7/86	MTK									M39			2	-
Tibor TISZA	10/11/84	Újpest									s39			5	-
István FERENCZI	14/9/77	Barnsley (ENG)									s46			9	2
Péter OROSZ	19/8/81	Wacker (AUT)									s63	s83	s64	3	-

...TIONAL TEAM APPEARANCES 2007/08 (contd.)

			Ita	BIH	TUR	MLT	Pol	MDA	GRE	Svk	Svn	Gre	Cro	Caps	Goals
...ÁRDAI	16/3/76	Hertha (GER)										M	M89	51	5
...s KOLTAI	30/4/87	Győr										s89		1	-
...ó BODNÁR	25/2/79	Salzburg (AUT)											D	33	-
...zsár BODOR	27/4/82	Roda (NED)											D	13	-

DOMESTIC LEAGUE 2007/08

...MZETI BAJNOKSÁG I FINAL TABLE

		Home					Away					Total					
	Pld	W	D	L	F	A	W	D	L	F	A	W	D	L	F	A	Pts
...TK Budapest	30	9	4	2	33	14	11	2	2	34	9	20	6	4	67	23	66
...ebreceni VSC	30	13	1	1	40	10	6	6	3	27	19	19	7	4	67	29	64
...yőri ETO FC	30	11	4	0	42	18	5	6	4	22	17	16	10	4	64	35	58
...jpest FC	30	7	5	3	27	18	9	2	4	31	22	16	7	7	58	40	55
...C Fehérvár	30	11	3	1	31	8	6	0	9	17	24	17	3	10	48	32	54
...aposvári Rákóczi FC	30	7	5	3	22	20	7	4	4	26	18	14	9	7	48	38	51
...alaegerszegi TE	30	8	4	3	33	18	5	3	7	22	21	13	7	10	55	39	46
...udapest Honvéd FC	30	6	4	5	24	18	6	3	6	21	18	12	7	11	45	36	43
...asas SC	30	6	3	6	17	19	6	2	7	24	26	12	5	13	41	45	41
...yíregyháza	30	9	1	5	25	13	2	6	7	9	24	11	7	12	34	37	40
...aksi SE	30	7	4	4	28	20	2	6	7	23	31	9	10	11	51	51	37
...ákospalotai EAC	30	5	5	5	26	30	2	4	9	16	30	7	9	14	42	60	30
...iósgyőri VTK	30	3	6	6	24	29	2	7	6	19	34	5	13	12	43	63	28
...iófoki BFC	30	5	4	6	20	17	1	5	9	13	29	6	9	15	33	46	27
...C Tatabánya	30	1	3	11	19	38	1	1	13	15	55	2	4	24	34	93	10
...C Sopron	30	1	3	11	5	34	1	2	12	5	39	2	5	23	10	73	0

...FC Sopron withdrew after 15 rounds,their remaining games being awarded as 0-3 defeats; ...opron - 11 pts deducted.

TOP GOALSCORERS

18 Róbert WALTNER (ZTE)
17 Gábor URBÁN (MTK)
16 Lóránt OLÁH (Kaposvár)
15 Tibor TISZA (Újpest)
Attila TÖKÖLI (Paks)
14 Dorge Rostand KOUEMAHA (Debrecen)
Attila SIMON (Diósgyőr)
13 Péter BAJZÁT (Győr)
12 József KANTA (MTK)
Norbert NÉMETH (Vasas)

CLUB-BY-CLUB

BUDAPEST HONVÉD FC

Coach – Attila Supka; (20/3/08) (László Vass); (28/3/08) István Borgulya

Founded - 1909

MAJOR HONOURS: Hungarian League – (13) 1950, 1950 (autumn), 1952, 1954, 1955, 1980, 1984, 1985, 1986, 1988, 1989, 1991, 1993; Hungarian Cup – (6) 1926, 1964, 1985, 1989, 1996, 2007.

...007

...2/7	REAC	a	3-0	*Bárányos, Abraham, Pomper*
...9/7	Sopron	a	1-0	*Benjamin*
.../8	Fehérvár	h	5-1	*Dobos (p), Palásthy, Diego, Bárányos, Hercegfalvi*
...1/8	Paks	a	3-0	*Hercegfalvi, Abraham 2*
...9/8	Újpest	h	1-4	*Bárányos (p)*
...4/8	Diósgyőr	a	2-2	*Hercegfalvi 2*
.../9	Debrecen	h	3-1	*Hercegfalvi, Tóth B., Bárányos*
...5/9	Siófok	a	2-1	*Palásthy, Abass*
...1/9	ZTE	h	2-1	*Abraham, Bárányos*
.../10	MTK	a	2-1	*Abraham, Abass*
6/10	Kaposvár	h	0-1	
20/10	Győr	h	2-2	*Hercegfalvi, Vincze Z.*
2/11	Vasas	a	2-0	*Abraham, Hercegfalvi*
10/11	Nyíregyháza	h	0-0	
24/11	Tatabánya	a	3-4	*og (Filó), Abraham, Hercegfalvi*

2008

23/2	REAC	h	1-1	*Filó*
3/3	Sopron	h	3-0	*(w/o)*
7/3	Fehérvár	a	0-0	
15/3	Paks	h	2-1	*Zsolnai, og (Éger)*
21/3	Újpest	a	0-1	
28/3	Diósgyőr	h	0-1	
5/4	Debrecen	a	0-1	
12/4	Siófok	h	1-1	*Abass*
21/4	ZTE	a	1-2	*Abass*
27/4	MTK	h	0-2	
5/5	Kaposvár	a	0-1	
10/5	Győr	a	2-2	*Diego, Dobos*
19/5	Vasas	h	0-1	
25/5	Nyíregyháza	a	0-3	
1/6	Tatabánya	h	4-1	*Abraham 2, Bárányos 2*

No	Name	Nat	Pos	Aps	(s)	Gls
13	Dieng Cheikh ABASS	SEN	A	9	(13)	4
18	Guie Gneki ABRAHAM	CIV	A	23	(2)	9
4	Yusuf ADEWUNMI	NGA	D	5	(3)	
22	Zsolt BÁRÁNYOS		M	23	(1)	7
5	Angouna BENJAMIN	CIV	D	21	(1)	1
31	Balázs BERDÓ		M	7	(4)	
8	Pascal BOREL	GER	G	7	(1)	
19	DIEGO Riganato Rodrigues	BRA	M	11	(8)	2
9	Attila DOBOS		M	15		2
28	Veledar ESAD	GER	M	1	(2)	
66	Tamás FILÓ		D	7	(1)	1
25	Attila FRITZ		M		(2)	
71	George GEBRO	LBR	M	2		
79	Eugénio Bila GENITO	MOZ	M	27		
21	Zoltán HERCEGFALVI		A	23	(2)	8
17	László HORVÁTH		M		(1)	
7	Gellért IVANCSICS		M	17	(8)	
27	Gábor KOÓS		A		(11)	
25	József MAGASFÖLDI		A	5	(5)	
2	József MOGYORÓSI		D	3		
8	Edouard NDJODO	CMR	A		(1)	
55	Norbert PALÁSTHY		A	2	(4)	2
6	Tibor POMPER		D	7	(2)	1
36	Szabolcs SCHINDLER		D	12		
20	Mico SMILJANIĆ	SRB	D	25		
29	Ákos TAKÁCS		D	10		
3	Balázs TÓTH		D	7	(2)	1
1	Iván TÓTH		G	22		
29	Mihály TÓTH		A	2	(2)	
14	Gábor VINCZE		M	4		
23	Zoltán VINCZE		D	20	(4)	1
11	Róbert ZSOLNAI		A	2	(5)	1

DEBRECENI VSC

Coach – Miroslav Beránek (CZE); (29/11/07) András Herczeg

Founded - 1902

MAJOR HONOURS: Hungarian League – (3) 2005, 2006, 2007; Hungarian Cup – (3) 1999, 2001, 2008.

2007

22/7	Diósgyőr	a	2-1	*Kouemaha 2*
27/7	Győr	h	2-0	*Dzsudzsák, Demjén*
3/8	Siófok	a	1-1	*Rudolf*
11/8	ZTE	h	3-2	*Dzsudzsák 2, Demjén*
17/8	MTK	a	2-3	*Rudolf, Kouemaha (p)*
25/8	Kaposvár	h	4-0	*Kerekes, Kouemaha, Sándor, Leandro*
2/9	Honvéd	a	1-3	*Leandro*
14/9	Vasas	h	2-0	*Komlósi, Kerekes*
22/9	Nyíregyháza	a	1-1	*Kerekes*
29/9	Tatabánya	h	4-1	*Kerekes, Dzsudzsák, Sándor, Stojkov (p)*
6/10	REAC	a	4-0	*Kiss, Kouemaha, Sándor, Dzsudzsák*
20/10	Sopron	h	4-2	*Kouemaha 4*
5/11	Fehérvár	a	0-0	
10/11	Paks	h	1-1	*Kouemaha*
23/11	Újpest	a	1-1	*Leandro*

2008

22/2	Diósgyőr	h	3-0	*Kerekes 2, Kiss*
1/3	Győr	a	1-3	*Czvitkovics*
10/3	Siófok	h	2-0	*Kouemaha, Czvitkovics,*
15/3	ZTE	a	2-1	*Dombi, Czvitkovics*
22/3	MTK	h	0-2	
30/3	Kaposvár	a	2-2	*Leandro, Bíró*
5/4	Honvéd	h	1-0	*Kerekes*
11/4	Vasas	a	3-0	*Kouemaha 2, Czvitkovics*
19/4	Nyíregyháza	h	4-1	*Huszák, Takács, og (Bagoly), Leandro (p)*
26/4	Tatabánya	a	2-1	*Takács, Kerekes*
3/5	REAC	h	4-0	*Czvitkovics, Kerekes 2, Leandro*
10/5	Sopron	a	3-0	*(w/o)*
17/5	Fehérvár	h	3-0	*Huszák, Czvitkovics, Kouemaha*
23/5	Paks	a	2-2	*Leandro, Bogdanović*
31/5	Újpest	h	3-1	*Bogdanović 2, Kerekes*

No	Name	Nat	Pos	Aps	(s)	Gls
12	János BALOGH		G	13		
22	Csaba BERNÁTH		D	14	(3)	
13	Péter BÍRÓ		D	8	(1)	1
10	Igor BOGDANOVIĆ	SRB	A	4	(3)	3
26	Daniel CHIGOU	CMR	A		(1)	
24	Norbert CSERNYÁNSZKY		G	4		
77	Péter CZVITKOVICS		M	16	(4)	6
27	Gábor DEMJÉN		M	4	(5)	2
7	Tibor DOMBI		M	13	(9)	1
19	Balázs DZSUDZSÁK		M	12	(1)	5
88	Tamás HUSZÁK		M	5	(2)	2
21	Thierry ISSIÉMOU	GAB	M	1		
8	Zsombor KEREKES		A	12	(14)	11
30	Zoltán KISS		M	25	(1)	2
16	Ádám KOMLÓSI		D	20	(2)	1
40	Dorge Rostand KOUEMAHA	CMR	A	23	(4)	14
4	LEANDRO de Almeida		M	26	(1)	7
18	Péter MÁTÉ		D	6	(1)	
17	Norbert MÉSZÁROS		D	25		
20	Róbert NAGY		M	1		
28	Zoltán NAGY		D	1		
1	Vukašin POLEKSIĆ	MNE	G	12		
15	László REZES		A		(1)	
14	Gergely RUDOLF		A	6	(7)	2
9	Tamás SÁNDOR		M	13	(6)	3
26	Ibrahima SIDIBE	SEN	A	10	(4)	
29	István SPITZMÜLER		M		(1)	
32	Aco STOJKOV	MKD	A	4	(6)	1
55	Péter SZAKÁLY		M	1	(5)	
3	Csaba SZATMÁRI		D	3		
23	Péter SZILÁGYI		A		(1)	
2	István SZŰCS		D	6	(1)	
6	Zoltán TAKÁCS		D	14		2
5	Dragan VUKMIR	SRB	M	15	(2)	
18	Róbert ZSOLNAI		A	2		

DIÓSGYŐRI VTK

Coach – János Pajkos; (29/9/07) Attila Vágó

Founded - 1910

MAJOR HONOURS: Hungarian Cup – (2) 1977, 1980.

2007

22/7	Debrecen	h	1-2	*Katona*
28/7	Siófok	h	0-3	
3/8	ZTE	a	1-4	*Douva*
10/8	MTK	h	2-2	*Carr, Elek*
18/8	Kaposvár	a	1-1	*Simon*
24/8	Honvéd	h	2-2	*Sipeki, Simon (p)*
31/8	Vasas	a	0-0	
15/9	Nyíregyháza	h	0-0	
21/9	Tatabánya	a	2-2	*Simon, Douva*
29/9	REAC	h	0-1	
6/10	Sopron	a	1-0	*Simon*
19/10	Fehérvár	h	2-0	*Sipeki, Simon*
3/11	Paks	a	2-2	*Simon, Sipeki*
9/11	Újpest	h	1-4	*Bessong*
24/11	Győr	a	1-5	*Ebala*

2008

22/2	Debrecen	a	0-3	
1/3	Siófok	a	0-4	
8/3	ZTE	h	1-1	*Sebők*

'/3	MTK	a	1-1	*Homma*
'/3	Kaposvár	h	2-1	*Sebők, Cardozo*
/3	Honvéd	a	1-0	*Homma*
4	Vasas	h	4-5	*Homma, Simon, Lipusz, Elek*
:/4	Nyíregyháza	a	1-2	*Homma*
/4	Tatabánya	h	2-2	*Simon 2 (1p)*
/4	REAC	a	5-5	*Simon 2, Homma 2, Kamber*
5	Sopron	h	3-0	*(w/o)*
/5	Fehérvár	a	1-3	*Pintér*
'/5	Paks	h	3-3	*Simon 3 (1p)*
/5	Újpest	a	2-2	*Homma, Virágh*
/5	Győr	h	1-3	*Kamber*

Name	Nat	Pos	Aps	(s)	Gls
Arouna BABA PELÉ	CMR	A		(1)	
Steve BESSONG Leo	CMR	A	5	(2)	1
Gonzalo CARDOZO	PAR	A	2	(5)	1
Victor Pony CARR	LBR	A	2	(3)	1
Abdou Halidou DOUVA	CMR	A	12	(3)	2
Christian Bodiong EBALA	CMR	M	8	(1)	1
Norbert ELEK		D	28		2
Norbert FARKAS		D	7	(1)	
Marcell FODOR		D	4	(2)	
Kassim GUYAZOU	TOG	M	2		
Gyula HEGEDŰS		D	27		
Kazuo HOMMA	JPN	A	10	(3)	7
Tamás HUSZÁK		M		(5)	
Norbert KÁLLAI		D	9	(6)	
Đorđe KAMBER	SRB	M	12		2
Joseph KANGA	CMR	A		(1)	
Attila KATONA		D	12	(1)	1
Gábor KERÉNYI		D	2		
Dávid KLEIBER		A		(2)	
László KÖTELES		G	27		
István KÖVESFALVI		G	1	(1)	
Béla LAKATOS		M	13	(3)	
Norbert LIPUSZ		M	11	(9)	1
Gergő MENYHÉRT		M		(2)	
József MOGYORÓSI		D	12		
Tamás NAGY		A		(5)	
Matías NAVARRETE	ARG	M	1	(2)	
Peguy NGAM	CMR	M	1	(4)	
Florin Ioan PELECACI	ROU	M	6	(4)	
Zoltán PINTÉR		M	12		1
Abass RASSOU	CMR	A	4		
Szilárd REBECSÁK		M	1	(2)	
Vilmos SEBŐK		D	11		2
Attila SIMON		A	27	(1)	14
István SIPEKI		M	14		3
Pál SZALMA		G	1		
Tamás SZÉLPÁL		M	6	(6)	
Dane TRBOVIĆ	SRB	D	2	(2)	
Csaba VÁMOSI		D	4	(1)	
Gergely VIDA		D		(1)	
Aladár VIRÁGH		D	9	(1)	1
Zoltán VITELKI		M	14	(6)	

FC FEHÉRVÁR

Coach – Marijan Vlak (CRO); (4/1/08) László Disztl

Founded - 1941

MAJOR HONOURS: Hungarian Cup – (1) 2006.

007

3/7	MTK	a	0-2	
0/7	Kaposvár	h	1-1	*Božić*
/8	Honvéd	a	1-5	*Božić*
1/8	Vasas	h	5-2	*Sitku 2 (1p), Dajić, Farkas, Božić*
8/8	Nyíregyháza	a	1-0	*Farkas*
25/8	Tatabánya	h	7-0	*Vayer, Farkas, Simek, Dajić, Dvéri, Sitku, og (Pastva)*
1/9	REAC	a	2-0	*Simek 2*
15/9	Sopron	h	2-0	*Csobánki, Sitku (p)*
22/9	Győr	a	1-4	*Sitku (p)*
29/9	Paks	a	1-2	*og (Éger)*
5/10	Újpest	h	1-2	*Dajić*
19/10	Diósgyőr	a	0-2	
5/11	Debrecen	h	0-0	
10/11	Siófok	a	0-1	
24/11	ZTE	h	2-0	*Dvéri, Farkas*
2008				
25/2	MTK	h	1-0	*Sitku*
1/3	Kaposvár	a	0-1	
7/3	Honvéd	h	0-0	
15/3	Vasas	a	2-1	*Sitku (p), Koller*
22/3	Nyíregyháza	h	2-1	*Dvéri, Simek*
30/3	Tatabánya	a	3-1	*Koller, og (Herbert), Dajić*
5/4	REAC	h	2-1	*Polonkai, Sitku*
12/4	Sopron	a	3-0	*(w/o)*
19/4	Győr	h	1-0	*Dajić*
26/4	Paks	h	3-0	*Dvéri, Nagy, Koller*
2/5	Újpest	a	0-1	
10/5	Diósgyőr	h	3-1	*og (Elek), Dvéri, Nagy*
17/5	Debrecen	a	0-3	
25/5	Siófok	h	1-0	*Nagy*
2/6	ZTE	a	3-1	*Horváth, Nagy, Sitku*

No	Name	Nat	Pos	Aps	(s)	Gls
19	Tibor BARANYAI		D	5	(1)	
20	Mario BOŽIĆ	BIH	M	12	(3)	3
18	Ádám CSOBÁNKI		M	6	(15)	1
11	Jusuf DAJIĆ	BIH	A	21	(6)	5
2	Mihajlo DENISOV	UKR	D	2	(1)	
4	Dávid DISZTL		A	1	(1)	
27	Pavol ĎURICA	SVK	M		(2)	
10	Zsolt DVÉRI		M	13	(12)	5
14	Balázs FARKAS		M	27		4
23	Zsolt FEHÉR		D	7	(4)	
24	András FEJES		D		(1)	
24	Ádám HORVÁTH		D		(1)	
3	Gábor HORVÁTH		D	23	(1)	1
13	Gábor KOCSIS		M	9	(2)	
5	Ákos KOLLER		D	25		3
16	Norbert LATTENSTEIN		M	1	(6)	
20	Pál LÁZÁR		D	11		
19	Péter LELKES		A		(1)	
27	Balázs MAGYAR		M		(1)	
4	Dávid MOHL		D	28		
15	Dániel NAGY		M	15	(8)	4
12	Viktor NÉMETH		G	4	(1)	
15	Milán PÁLFI		M		(1)	
8	Attila POLONKAI		M	12	(1)	1
1	Zsolt SEBŐK		G	25		
6	Tamás SIFTER		M	13		
7	Péter SIMEK		M	27		4
9	Illés SITKU		A	25		9
25	Viktor VADÁSZ		D	1	(2)	
11	Gábor VAYER		M	6	(3)	1

GYŐRI ETO FC

Coach – Sándor Egervári

Founded - 1904

MAJOR HONOURS: Hungarian League – (3) 1963 (autumn), 1982, 1983; Hungarian Cup – (4) 1965, 1966, 1967, 1979.

2007

27/7	Debrecen	a	0-2	
4/8	Tatabánya	h	2-1	*Bogdanović, og (Farkas V.)*
11/8	Siófok	a	1-0	*Stark*

18/8	REAC	h	2-1	*Bajzát, Bogdanović*
25/8	ZTE	a	0-0	
29/8	Nyíregyháza	a	0-1	
1/9	Sopron	h	1-1	*og (Fehér Z.)*
17/9	MTK	a	2-2	*Nikolov, Brnović*
22/9	Fehérvár	h	4-1	*Brnović, Bajzát, Bogdanović, Bank*
29/9	Kaposvár	a	1-1	*Jäkl*
6/10	Paks	h	3-3	*Nikolov, Völgyi, Bogdanović*
20/10	Honvéd	a	2-2	*Bajzát 2*
3/11	Újpest	h	4-2	*Völgyi, Bajzát 2, Tokody*
10/11	Vasas	a	1-1	*Koltai*
24/11	Diósgyőr	h	5-1	*Józsi, Bajzát 2, Bogdanović, Kovács*
2008				
23/2	Nyíregyháza	h	5-0	*Tokody 2, Völgyi, Dudás, Brnović*
1/3	Debrecen	h	3-1	*Stark (p), Völgyi, Böőr*
8/3	Tatabánya	a	3-1	*Brnović, Böőr 2*
15/3	Siófok	h	4-1	*Völgyi, Dudás, Koltai, Brnović*
24/3	REAC	a	2-2	*Brnović, Böőr*
29/3	ZTE	h	3-2	*Pákolicz, Brnović 2*
5/4	Sopron	a	3-0	*(w/o)*
12/4	MTK	h	1-0	*Nikolov*
19/4	Fehérvár	a	0-1	
26/4	Kaposvár	h	1-1	*Brnović*
3/5	Paks	a	1-2	*Tokody*
10/5	Honvéd	h	2-2	*Bajzát, Varga L.*
16/5	Újpest	a	3-1	*Bajzát 2, og (Juhár)*
25/5	Vasas	h	2-1	*Bajzát, Józsi*
31/5	Diósgyőr	a	3-1	*Böőr, Brnović, Bajzát*

No	Name	Nat	Pos	Aps	(s)	Gls
19	Péter BAJZÁT		A	14	(4)	13
5	István BANK		M	18		1
10	Igor BOGDANOVIĆ	SRB	A	13	(1)	5
18	Zoltán BÖŐR		M	6	(9)	5
11	Bojan BRNOVIĆ	MNE	A	19	(6)	10
33	Arsène COPA	GAB	M		(1)	
16	Imre CSERMELYI		M		(3)	
21	Ádám DUDÁS		M	5	(4)	2
28	Eugène FOMUMBOD	CMR	D	6	(4)	
16	Balázs GRANÁT		A	1	(2)	
8	György JÓZSI		M	27	(2)	2
7	Antal JÄKL		D	18	(6)	1
16	Máté KISS		M		(2)	
29	Tamás KOLTAI		M	12	(6)	2
3	Zoltán KOVÁCS		D	4	(6)	1
9	Zsolt MÜLLER		M	6	(3)	
25	Balázs NIKOLOV		D	26		3
20	Tibor NYÁRI		M		(1)	
13	Dávid PÁKOLICZ		M	11	(3)	1
32	Péter STARK		D	29		2
26	Zoran SUPIĆ	SRB	D	27		
1	Saša STEVANOVIĆ	SRB	G	29		
23	Tibor TOKODY		A	16	(7)	4
17	Rudolf URBAN	SVK	M	1	(1)	
12	László VARGA		M	1	(3)	1
6	Róbert VARGA		D	6	(7)	
55	Zoltán VARGA		G		(1)	
14	Dániel VÖLGYI		M	24	(2)	5

KAPOSVÁRI RÁKÓCZI FC

Coach – László Prukner

Founded - 1923

2007				
21/7	Sopron	h	1-1	*Szakály P.*
30/7	Fehérvár	a	1-1	*Zahorecz (p)*
4/8	Paks	h	2-1	*Alves, Zahorecz (p)*
13/8	Újpest	a	2-0	*Oláh, Vasiljević*
18/8	Diósgyőr	h	1-1	*Oláh*
25/8	Debrecen	a	0-4	
1/9	Siófok	h	4-3	*Alves 2 (1p), Oláh, Vasiljević*
15/9	ZTE	a	1-2	*Zahorecz (p)*
22/9	MTK	h	0-3	
29/9	Győr	h	1-1	*Oláh*
6/10	Honvéd	a	1-0	*Oláh*
20/10	Vasas	h	1-0	*Oláh*
3/11	Nyíregyháza	a	2-0	*Alves 2*
10/11	Tatabánya	h	4-2	*Grúz, Alves 2, Leandro*
24/11	REAC	a	1-1	*Leandro*
2008				
23/2	Sopron	a	3-0	*(w/o)*
1/3	Fehérvár	h	1-0	*Nikolić*
8/3	Paks	a	1-1	*Alves*
14/3	Újpest	h	0-3	
22/3	Diósgyőr	a	1-2	*Leandro*
30/3	Debrecen	h	2-2	*Szakály D., Oláh*
5/4	Siófok	a	2-0	*Oláh, Grúz*
14/4	ZTE	h	0-2	
18/4	MTK	a	2-3	*Obrić, Nikolić*
26/4	Győr	a	1-1	*Oláh*
5/5	Honvéd	h	1-0	*Oláh*
10/5	Vasas	a	2-1	*Alves (p), Oláh*
17/5	Nyíregyháza	h	1-1	*Alves*
25/5	Tatabánya	a	6-2	*Alves, Oláh 3, Leandro, Nikolić*
1/6	REAC	h	3-0	*Oláh 2, Nikolić*

No	Name	Nat	Pos	Aps	(s)	Gls
9	André ALVES	BRA	A	29		11
18	László BALOGH		M		(1)	
11	Bojan BOŽOVIĆ	MNE	A		(10)	
20	Zoltán FARKAS		M	1	(1)	
21	Károly GRASZL		M	15	(2)	
7	Norbert GRASZL		M		(4)	
26	Tamás GRÚZ		M	27	(1)	2
27	László HORVÁTH		G		(1)	
6	Róbert KOVÁCSEVICS		D	4	(8)	
10	LEANDRO da Silva	BRA	M	19	(3)	4
25	Béla MARÓTI		M	26		
13	Tamás MEZŐ		D	3	(4)	
1	Árpád MILINTE		G	29		
13	Nemanja NIKOLIĆ	SRB	A	4	(8)	4
5	Nemanja OBRIĆ	SRB	M	2	(8)	1
14	Lóránt OLÁH		A	29		16
19	Krisztián PEST		M	16	(5)	
17	Viktor PETRÓK		D	14		
3	Attila PINTÉR		D	28		
8	István RIBI		D	3	(6)	
15	Admir SULJIČ	SVN	D	2	(4)	
24	Dénes SZAKÁLY		M	15	(6)	1
5	Péter SZAKÁLY		M	14		1
22	Dušan VASILJEVIĆ	SRB	M	14		2
28	Krisztián ZAHORECZ		D	25		3

MTK BUDAPEST

Coach – József Garami

Founded - 1888

MAJOR HONOURS: Hungarian League – (23) 1904, 1908, 1914, 1917, 1918, 1919, 1920, 1921, 1922, 1923, 1924, 1925, 1929, 1936, 1937, 1951, 1953, 1958, 1987, 1997, 1999, 2003, 2008; Hungarian Cup – (12) 1910, 1911, 1912, 1914, 1923, 1925, 1932, 1952, 1968, 1997, 1998, 2000.

2007				
23/7	Fehérvár	h	2-0	*Bori, Urbán*
28/7	Paks	a	4-1	*Pátkai, Kanta, Zsidai, Hrepka*
6/8	Újpest	h	0-0	

/8	Diósgyőr	a	2-2	*Urbán 2*
/8	Debrecen	h	3-2	*Kanta (p), Urbán, Kulcsár*
/8	Siófok	a	1-1	*Kanta*
9	ZTE	h	4-1	*Urbán, Bori, Kanta, Szabó*
'/9	Győr	h	2-2	*Lambulić, Szabó*
:/9	Kaposvár	a	3-0	*Urbán, Kanta, Pátkai*
10	Honvéd	h	1-2	*Bori*
10	Vasas	a	3-0	*Kulcsár 2, Pátkai*
:/10	Nyíregyháza	h	2-0	*Bori, Szabó*
11	Tatabánya	a	3-1	*Pátkai, Pintér, Urbán*
'/11	REAC	h	3-0	*Pátkai, Pál, Bori*
/11	Sopron	a	5-1	*Urbán 4, og (Sifter)*
08				
/2	Fehérvár	a	0-1	
3	Paks	h	1-1	*Kanta*
3	Újpest	a	3-1	*Lambulić, Kanta 2 (2p)*
'/3	Diósgyőr	h	1-1	*Kanta*
:/3	Debrecen	a	2-0	*Pál, Pollák*
/3	Siófok	h	3-0	*Urbán 2, Lambulić*
4	ZTE	a	1-0	*Hrepka*
'/4	Győr	a	0-1	
;/4	Kaposvár	h	3-2	*Urbán, Lambulić, Szabó*
'/4	Honvéd	a	2-0	*Pátkai, Szabó*
5	Vasas	h	0-2	
5	Nyíregyháza	a	2-0	*Kanta, Urbán*
'/5	Tatabánya	h	5-1	*Pollák, Pintér, Kanta 2, Urbán*
/5	REAC	a	3-0	*Lambulić 2, Urbán*
/5	Sopron	h	3-0	*(w/o)*

o	Name	Nat	Pos	Aps	(s)	Gls
	Endre BAJÚSZ		D	2	(1)	
	Péter BONIFERT		M	1		
	Gábor BORI		M	8	(3)	5
	Levente HORVÁTH		D	24		
	Ádám HREPKA		A	14	(1)	2
	József KANTA		M	25	(1)	12
	Tamás KECSKÉS		M		(21)	
	Tamás KULCSÁR		A	23	(6)	3
	István LADÓCZKI		M	1	(5)	
	Mladen LAMBULIĆ	SRB	D	28		6
	László LENCSE		A	1	(2)	
	Marcell MOLNÁR		M	1	(3)	
	András PÁL		A	9	(8)	2
	Máté PÁTKAI		M	26	(2)	6
	Ádám PINTÉR		D	26		2
	Zoltán POLLÁK		D	26		2
	István RODENBÜCHER		D	7	(3)	
	Attila SIMON		A	1		
	Ádám SZABÓ		M	14	(13)	5
	Zoltán SZATMÁRI		G		(1)	
	Adrián SZEKERES		D	2	(3)	
	Gábor URBÁN		A	25		17
	Dániel VADNAI		D	3		
	András VÁGI		M		(1)	
	Zoltán VÉGH		G	29		
	László ZSIDAI		M	23	(2)	1

NYÍREGYHÁZA FC

Coach – Attila Révész

Founded - 1959

)07				
3/7	Tatabánya	a	1-0	*Montvai (p)*
'8	REAC	h	2-0	*Lippai, Bagoly*
1/8	Sopron	a	1-1	*Miskolczi*
3/8	Fehérvár	h	0-1	
5/8	Paks	a	0-3	
9/8	Győr	h	1-0	*Hegedűs*
1/9	Újpest	h	1-2	*Zaleh*
15/9	Diósgyőr	a	0-0	
22/9	Debrecen	h	1-1	*Menougong*
29/9	Siófok	a	1-0	*Szilágyi*
6/10	ZTE	h	2-1	*Cornaci, Vukadinović*
22/10	MTK	a	0-2	
3/11	Kaposvár	h	0-2	
10/11	Honvéd	a	0-0	
24/11	Vasas	h	2-1	*Szilágyi, Montvai*
2008				
23/2	Győr	a	0-5	
1/3	Tatabánya	h	5-0	*Granát, Szilágyi, Bagoly, Lippai, Dosso*
8/3	REAC	a	2-2	*Kovács, Dosso*
15/3	Sopron	h	3-0	*(w/o)*
22/3	Fehérvár	a	1-2	*Cornaci*
29/3	Paks	h	1-2	*Szilágyi*
7/4	Újpest	a	0-1	
12/4	Diósgyőr	h	2-1	*Granát, Miskolczi*
19/4	Debrecen	a	1-4	*Bagoly (p)*
26/4	Siófok	h	2-0	*Dosso, og (Miklósvári)*
3/5	ZTE	a	0-0	
9/5	MTK	h	0-2	
17/5	Kaposvár	a	1-1	*Miskolczi*
25/5	Honvéd	h	3-0	*og (Filo), Lippai, Ramos*
30/5	Vasas	a	1-3	*Lippai (p)*

No	Name	Nat	Pos	Aps	(s)	Gls
6	Árpád AMBRUSZ		D	19		
26	Gábor BAGOLY		D	20	(2)	3
3	Claudiu CORNACI	ROU	D	19	(1)	2
23	György CSÉKE		D	8	(1)	
28	Sindou DOSSO	CIV	A	12	(2)	3
11	Balázs GRANÁT		A	9	(2)	2
17	Tibor HEGEDŰS		M	23	(1)	1
1	Dániel ILLYÉS		G	7		
8	Béla KOVÁCS		M	3		1
11	Balázs KRAJNC		A		(1)	
33	Filip LĂZĂREANU	ROU	G	20		
10	Ákos LIPPAI		M	23	(1)	4
1	Gábor MÁTHÉ		G	1		
18	Yves MBOUSSI	CMR	M	11		
21	George MENOUGONG	CMR	A	13	(9)	1
20	Tibor MINCZÉR		M	7	(14)	
12	László MISKOLCZI		M	19	(5)	3
8	Tibor MOLDOVAN		A	6	(1)	
7	Tibor MONTVAI		A	7	(6)	2
	Dávid NAGY		M		(1)	
24	Szabolcs PERÉNYI		D	11	(2)	
17	Luis RAMOS	HON	M	11		1
28	Claudio ROJAS	ARG	M		(2)	
18	Marius SAVA	ROU	A	4	(1)	
4	Tamás SIPOS		D	1	(4)	
25	Norbert SZILÁGYI		A	7	(9)	4
55	Tamás TAKÁCS		G	1		
9	Dejan VUKADINOVIĆ	SRB	M	11	(14)	1
30	WELTON Carlos Silva	BRA	A	3		
5	Attila ZABOS		M	18	(3)	
19	Iván ZALEH	ARG	D	25	(1)	1

PAKSI SE

Coach – Ferenc Lengyel; (25/9/07) Imre Gellei

Founded - 1952

2007				
20/7	ZTE	a	1-3	*Márkus*
28/7	MTK	h	1-4	*Márkus*
4/8	Kaposvár	a	1-2	*Márkus*
11/8	Honvéd	h	0-3	
20/8	Vasas	a	2-3	*Heffler, Horváth F.*
25/8	Nyíregyháza	h	3-0	*Hanák, Horváth F.,*

				Márkus
1/9	Tatabánya	a	4-2	*Heffler 2, Molnár, Horváth F.*
15/9	REAC	h	0-2	
22/9	Sopron	a	1-1	*Éger*
29/9	Fehérvár	h	2-1	*Buzás (p), Tököli*
6/10	Győr	a	3-3	*Tököli, Balaskó (p), Márkus*
20/10	Újpest	a	1-3	*Kiss*
3/11	Diósgyőr	h	2-2	*Tököli, Kiss*
10/11	Debrecen	a	1-1	*Éger*
24/11	Siófok	h	1-1	*Tököli*
2008				
23/2	ZTE	h	0-3	
1/3	MTK	a	1-1	*Báló*
8/3	Kaposvár	h	1-1	*Tököli*
15/3	Honvéd	a	1-2	*Éger*
22/3	Vasas	h	3-0	*Böde, Zováth, Tököli (p)*
29/3	Nyíregyháza	a	2-1	*Weitner, Tököli (p)*
5/4	Tatabánya	h	6-0	*Kiss, Éger, Kriston, Tököli 3*
12/4	REAC	a	1-2	*Kiss*
19/4	Sopron	h	3-0	*(w/o)*
26/4	Fehérvár	a	0-3	
3/5	Győr	h	2-1	*Tököli 2*
12/5	Újpest	h	2-0	*Tököli, Heffler*
17/5	Diósgyőr	a	3-3	*Böde, Tököli 2 (1p)*
23/5	Debrecen	h	2-2	*Báló, Belényesi*
1/6	Siófok	a	1-1	*Tamási*

No	Name	Nat	Pos	Aps	(s)	Gls
18	Iván BALASKÓ		M	3	(11)	1
7	Tamás BÁLÓ		M	15	(5)	2
83	Miklós BELÉNYESI		A	5	(4)	1
13	Dániel BÖDE		M	10	(10)	2
20	Attila BUZÁS		M	8	(5)	1
9	Tamás CSEHI		D	10	(7)	
73	László ÉGER		D	27		4
14	Viktor HANÁK		D	22	(1)	1
16	Tibor HEFFLER		M	20	(3)	4
99	Ferenc HORVÁTH		A	5	(2)	3
49	Sándor HORVÁTH		D	14	(3)	
10	Tamás KISS		M	22	(5)	4
1	Attila KOVÁCS		G	29		
27	Attila KRISTON		M	12	(1)	1
8	Tibor MÁRKUS		A	18	(3)	5
19	István MÉSZÁROS		M		(1)	
2	Zoltán MOLNÁR		D	16	(2)	1
3	Miklós SALAMON		D	27		
26	Gábor TAMÁSI		M	11	(7)	1
21	Attila TÖKÖLI		A	21	(1)	15
8	László VARGA		A		(1)	
87	Barnabás VÁRI		A	2	(5)	
24	Ádám WEITNER		M		(8)	1
6	János ZOVÁTH		M	22		1

RÁKOSPALOTAI EAC

Coach – Zoltán Aczél

Founded - 1912

2007				
22/7	Honvéd	h	0-3	
30/7	Vasas	h	2-0	*Madar, Kőhalmi*
4/8	Nyíregyháza	a	0-2	
11/8	Tatabánya	h	3-2	*Nyerges 2, Torma*
18/8	Győr	a	1-2	*Kapcsos*
25/8	Sopron	a	1-2	*Torma*
1/9	Fehérvár	h	0-2	
15/9	Paks	a	2-0	*Torma, Nyerges*
22/9	Újpest	h	1-1	*Polonkai*
29/9	Diósgyőr	a	1-0	*Nyerges*
6/10	Debrecen	h	0-4	
20/10	Siófok	a	0-1	
3/11	ZTE	h	1-2	*Pusztai*
12/11	MTK	a	0-3	
24/11	Kaposvár	h	1-1	*Torma*
2008				
23/2	Honvéd	a	1-1	*Torma*
3/3	Vasas	a	1-2	*Torma*
8/3	Nyíregyháza	h	2-2	*Nyerges, Torma*
15/3	Tatabánya	a	1-1	*Varga Z.*
24/3	Győr	h	2-2	*Somorjai, Torma*
29/3	Sopron	h	3-0	*(w/o)*
5/4	Fehérvár	a	1-2	*Nyerges*
12/4	Paks	h	2-1	*Varga, Somorjai*
19/4	Újpest	a	4-4	*Nyerges 2, Horváth, Varga*
26/4	Diósgyőr	h	5-5	*Dancs 2, Varga, Somorjai 2 (2p)*
3/5	Debrecen	a	0-4	
10/5	Siófok	h	4-2	*Somorjai, Torma 3*
17/5	ZTE	a	3-3	*Somorjai 2, Kovács*
26/5	MTK	h	0-3	
1/6	Kaposvár	a	0-3	

No	Name	Nat	Pos	Aps	(s)	Gls
7	Gergő CSERI		D	27		
15	Roland DANCS			13	(1)	2
2	Balázs DINKA		D	10	(11)	
20	Károly ERŐS		M	26		
1	Mátyás ESTERHÁZY		G	1		
1	Balázs FARKAS		G	7		
26	Tamás GASPARIK		D		(2)	
17	Gábor HORVÁTH		D	25	(1)	1
8	Vince KAPCSOS		M	26		1
13	Tamás KISS		M		(5)	
14	Balázs KOVÁCS		M	1	(8)	1
6	András KŐHALMI		M	20	(2)	1
21	Csaba MADAR		M	9	(4)	1
19	Frank MATONDO	CGO	M		(1)	
4	Tamás NAGY		A	3	(7)	
11	Krisztián NYERGES		A	23	(1)	8
22	Attila POLONKAI		M	14		1
20	Olivér PUSZTAI		D	2	(3)	1
23	Gergő RÁSA		M	5	(9)	
5	Balázs SALLAI		M	28		
21	András SELEI		M	1	(5)	
22	Tamás SOMORJAI		M	13		7
12	Levente SZÁNTAI		G	21		
10	Gábor TORMA		A	24	(2)	11
9	Zoltán VARGA		M	13	(6)	4
3	Aladár VIRÁGH		D	6	(5)	
24	Norbert ZANA		M	1	(5)	

BFC SIÓFOK

Coach – Antal Botos; (15/10/07) Barnabás Tornyi; (15/1/08) Ald Dolcetti (ITA)

Founded - 1921

MAJOR HONOURS: Hungarian Cup – (1) 1984.

2007				
21/7	Újpest	h	2-4	*Tusori, Homonyik*
28/7	Diósgyőr	a	3-0	*Kuttor, Fülöp 2*
3/8	Debrecen	h	1-1	*Melczer*
11/8	Győr	h	0-1	
18/8	ZTE	a	0-2	
25/8	MTK	h	1-1	*Fülöp*
1/9	Kaposvár	a	3-4	*Kuttor, Fülöp 2 (1p)*
15/9	Honvéd	h	1-2	*Kanta*
24/9	Vasas	a	0-0	
29/9	Nyíregyháza	h	0-1	

10	Tatabánya	a	2-2	*Lakić, Fülöp*
/10	REAC	h	1-0	*Kanta*
11	Sopron	a	0-0	
/11	Fehérvár	h	1-0	*Gajda*
/11	Paks	a	1-1	*Kanta*
008				
/2	Újpest	a	0-3	
3	Diósgyőr	h	4-0	*Magasföldi 2, Bonifert, Melczer*
/3	Debrecen	a	0-2	
/3	Győr	a	1-4	*Csopkai*
/3	ZTE	h	1-1	*Magasföldi*
/3	MTK	a	0-3	
/4	Kaposvár	h	0-2	
/4	Honvéd	a	1-1	*Miklósvári*
/4	Vasas	h	1-3	*Gajda*
/4	Nyíregyháza	a	0-2	
/5	Tatabánya	h	3-0	*Bonifert, Magasföldi 2 (1p)*
/5	REAC	a	2-4	*Melczer, Magasföldi*
7/5	Sopron	h	3-0	*(w/o)*
/5	Fehérvár	a	0-1	
/6	Paks	h	1-1	*Melczer*

o	Name	Nat	Pos	Aps	(s)	Gls
	Sándor AMBRUS		D	13	(3)	
3	Marko BASARA	SRB	M	5	(2)	
3	Péter BONIFERT		A	8	(4)	2
1	Zsolt CSÓKA		D	4		
2	István CSOPAKI		M	6	(5)	1
	Milán DISZTL		M		(1)	
3	Eugène FOMUMBOD	CMR	D	11		
	András FORGÁCS		D	28		
5	Zoltán FÜLÖP		A	12	(3)	6
0	István GAJDA		A	12	(14)	2
4	Adrian GAMAN	ROU	D	3		
	Lajos HEGEDŰS		G	28		
	Gábriel HOMONYIK		M	15	(10)	1
4	Attila HORVÁTH		M	1	(1)	
6	Bence HORVÁTH		A	1	(3)	
1	Szabolcs KANTA		M	15	(1)	3
8	Ákos KOZMOR		A	7	(7)	
9	Dániel KÖNTÖS		D	2	(5)	
	Attila KUTTOR		D	14		2
4	Ognjen LAKIĆ	SRB	A		(1)	1
	András LÁSZLÓ		D	22		
21	Roland LIPCSEI		M	2	(3)	
	József MAGASFÖLDI		A	11	(2)	6
	Dávid MÁRTON		M		(1)	
17	Vilmos MELCZER		M	21	(4)	4
20	János MIKLÓSVÁRI		D	16	(1)	1
3	Lajos NAGY		M	24	(1)	
21	Igor POPOVIĆ	CRO	D	5	(1)	
22	András SÁNTA		G	1		
14	András SELEI		M		(4)	
5	László SÜTŐ		D	10	(3)	
6	Richárd TUSORI		D	22	(2)	1

FC SOPRON

Coach – Lajos Détári; (1/10/07) Vincenzo Cosco (ITA)

Founded - 1945

MAJOR HONOURS: Hungarian Cup – (1) 2005.

2007				
21/7	Kaposvár	a	1-1	*Sira*
29/7	Honvéd	h	0-1	
4/8	Vasas	a	0-2	
11/8	Nyíregyháza	h	1-1	*Tchana*
18/8	Tatabánya	a	1-0	*Tchana*
25/8	REAC	h	2-1	*Belić 2*
1/9	Győr	a	1-1	*Hullám*
15/9	Fehérvár	a	0-2	
22/9	Paks	h	1-1	*Sira*
29/9	Újpest	a	0-4	
6/10	Diósgyőr	h	0-1	
20/10	Debrecen	a	2-4	*Zana, Belić*
3/11	Siófok	h	0-0	
10/11	ZTE	a	0-4	
29/11	MTK	h	1-5	*Tchana*

No	Name	Nat	Pos	Aps	(s)	Gls
14	Orlando AQUINO	ITA	A	3	(4)	
9	Danilo BELIĆ	SRB	A	10		3
23	Botond BIRTALAN		A	1	(6)	
29	Sándor CSIKÓS		M	4	(1)	
17	Zoltán CSONTOS		M	7	(2)	
91	Roland DANCS		M	13	(2)	
5	Fabrice DEFFO	CMR	M	2		
24	András DLUSZTUS		D	5	(2)	
34	Attila FARKAS		D	14		
19	Zoltán FEHÉR		M	13		
79	Gábor FREUD		M		(7)	
3	Cristian GALLIANO	ITA	D	2		
30	Cosmin GIURA	ROU	D	4	(1)	
21	Gábor GYÖMBÉR		D	6	(2)	
10	Tamás GYÖRÖK		M	6		
	Tamás HORVÁTH		M		(1)	
22	Attila HULLÁM		M	2	(4)	1
7	Sándor KÁROLYI		M	4	(1)	
85	Csaba KÖDÖBÖCZ		M	6	(3)	
	László LEGOZA		M		(1)	
66	Zoltán PINTÉR		M	11	(1)	
15	Predrag POCUCA	SRB	D	2		
8	László REINHARDT		M	4	(3)	
33	Tamás SIFTER		M	14		
6	István SIRA		A	5	(2)	2
1	Tamás TAKÁCS		G	5		
26	Jimmy Jones TCHANA	FRA	A	7		3
55	Zoltán VARGA		G	10		
11	Norbert ZANA		A	5	(2)	1

FC TATABÁNYA

Coach – Ferenc Mészáros; (19/8/07) László Borbély (SVK); (11/12/07) Ottavio Zambrano (ECU)

Founded - 1910

2007				
20/7	Vasas	a	1-3	*Kriston*
28/7	Nyíregyháza	h	0-1	
4/8	Győr	a	1-2	*Filó*
11/8	REAC	a	2-3	*Filó, Nógrádi*
18/8	Sopron	h	0-1	
25/8	Fehérvár	a	0-7	
1/9	Paks	h	2-4	*Filó, og (Salamon)*
15/9	Újpest	a	0-3	
21/9	Diósgyőr	h	2-2	*Takács, Hajdú*
29/9	Debrecen	a	1-4	*Takács*
6/10	Siófok	h	2-2	*Hajdú, Sándor*
20/10	ZTE	a	1-4	*Hajdú*
3/11	MTK	h	1-3	*Caugherty*
10/11	Kaposvár	a	2-4	*Megyesi, Takács*
24/11	Honvéd	h	4-3	*Béres, Weisz 2, Pastva*
2008				
23/2	Vasas	h	0-2	
1/3	Nyíregyháza	a	0-5	
8/3	Győr	h	1-3	*Béres*
15/3	REAC	h	1-1	*Béres*
22/3	Sopron	a	3-0	*(w/o)*
30/3	Fehérvár	h	1-3	*Béres*
5/4	Paks	a	0-6	

12/4	Újpest	h	2-3	*Vámosi, Megyesi*
19/4	Diósgyőr	a	2-2	*Pérez, Megyesi*
26/4	Debrecen	h	1-2	*Vámosi (p)*
3/5	Siófok	a	0-3	
10/5	ZTE	h	0-2	
175	MTK	a	1-5	*Lázár*
25/5	Kaposvár	h	2-6	*Németh, Ferenczi*
1/6	Honvéd	a	1-4	*Kovács*

No	Name	Nat	Pos	Aps	(s)	Gls
2	László ALMÁSI		M	11	(1)	
84	Dániel ASZTALOS		M	4		
14	Balázs BALOGH		D	15	(3)	
3	Zoltán BALOGH		M	21	(2)	
7	Attila BATICS		A		(2)	
18	Norbert BAZSIKA		A		(3)	
9	Tamás Ferenc BÉRES		A	11	(3)	4
4	Ryan CAUGHERTY	USA	M	4	(3)	1
21	András DIENES		D	20	(1)	
22	Viktor DOMBAI		A	2	(1)	
66	Viktor FARKAS		D	22	(2)	
17	Gábor FERENCZI		M	6	(13)	1
6	Tamás FILÓ		D	11	(1)	3
5	Jesús FLORES	MEX	M	6	(1)	
5	Norbert HAJDU		M	15		3
1	Roland HERBERT		G	8		
84	Péter HORVÁTH		A	4	(2)	
15	István KOVÁCS		M	5	(6)	1
12	Miroslav KOZAK		A	3	(2)	
27	Attila KRISTON		M	13	(1)	1
31	Péter KURUCZ		G	8	(1)	
4	Zsolt LÁZÁR		M	6	(2)	1
79	László MEGYESI		M	22	(1)	3
88	Richard NAGY		A		(2)	
25	Attila NÉMETH		M	13	(4)	1
9	Árpád NÓGRÁDI		A	1	(1)	1
28	Barna PAPUCSEK		A		(1)	
2	Milan PASTVA	SVK	D	8	(1)	1
10	Juan PÉREZ	MEX	M	18	(4)	1
18	Vukašin POLEKSIĆ	MNE	G	13		
99	István SÁNDOR		M	7	(5)	1
16	Gábor SZILÁGYI		A	5	(1)	
11	Marcell TAKÁCS		A	7	(3)	3
11	Bence TARCSA		D	2	(2)	
7	Márk UGHY		M	4	(1)	
13	Csaba VÁMOSI		D	13		2
30	Tamás WEISZ		M	11		2

ÚJPEST FC

Coach – István Urbányi; (21/4/08) Lázár Szentes

Founded - 1885

MAJOR HONOURS: Hungarian League – (20) 1930, 1931, 1933, 1935, 1939, 1945, 1946, 1947, 1960, 1969, 1970, 1971, 1972, 1973, 1974, 1975, 1978, 1979, 1990, 1998; Hungarian Cup – (8) 1969, 1970, 1975, 1982, 1983, 1987, 1992, 2002.

2007

21/7	Siófok	a	4-2	*Foxi, Nagy, Rajczi 2*
27/7	ZTE	h	1-1	*Foxi*
6/8	MTK	a	0-0	
13/8	Kaposvár	h	0-2	
19/8	Honvéd	a	4-1	*Korcsmár, Sándor, Foxi, Sadjo (p)*
27/8	Vasas	h	1-1	*Kovács*
1/9	Nyíregyháza	a	2-1	*Radulovic, Roiha*
15/9	Tatabánya	h	3-0	*Tisza, Kovács, Dourandi*
22/9	REAC	a	1-1	*Lee*
29/9	Sopron	h	4-0	*Tisza 2, Dourandi, Foxi*
5/10	Fehérvár	a	2-1	*Kovács, Tisza*
20/10	Paks	h	3-1	*Dourandi, Kovács, Sándor*
3/11	Győr	a	2-4	*Sándor, Kovács*
9/11	Diósgyőr	a	4-1	*Kovács, Tisza (p), Sadjo (p), Foxi (p)*
23/11	Debrecen	h	1-1	*Korcsmár*

2008

23/2	Siófok	h	3-0	*Dourandi 2, Moldovan*
29/2	ZTE	a	1-4	*Tisza*
8/3	MTK	h	1-3	*Ebala*
14/3	Kaposvár	a	3-0	*Tisza 2, Hajdú*
21/3	Honvéd	h	1-0	*Tisza (p)*
31/3	Vasas	a	1-0	*Tisza*
7/4	Nyíregyháza	h	1-0	*Dourandi*
12/4	Tatabánya	a	3-2	*Tisza 2, Korcsmár*
19/4	REAC	h	4-4	*Dudić, Tisza 2 (2p), Foxi*
26/4	Sopron	a	3-0	*(w/o)*
2/5	Fehérvár	h	1-0	*Sándor*
12/5	Paks	a	0-2	
16/5	Győr	h	1-3	*Tisza*
25/5	Diósgyőr	h	2-2	*Foxi, Sándor*
31/5	Debrecen	a	1-3	*Regedei*

No	Name	Nat	Pos	Aps	(s)	Gls
1	Szabolcs BALAJCZA		G	29		
29	BISOYE Ismaila	NGA	M	1		
24	Attila BÖJTE		D	27	(2)	
5	Mario BOŽIĆ	BIH	M	13		
11	Dennis DOURANDI	CMR	A	11	(7)	6
2	Ivan DUDIĆ	SRB	D	7	(1)	1
19	Christian Bodiong EBALA	CMR	M	3	(1)	1
20	FOXI Kethevoama	CTA	M	24	(2)	7
14	Ákos FÜZI		D	2		
18	Tamás GYÖRÖK		M	1	(5)	
9	Ronald HABI		M	19	(3)	
8	Norbert HAJDÚ		M	11	(3)	1
30	Imre HIBÓ		M		(1)	
6	Attila HULLÁM		M	2		
15	Tamás JUHÁR		D	4	(2)	
15	Zoltán KISS		M	1	(1)	
21	Zsolt KORCSMÁR		M	21	(1)	3
10	Zoltán KOVÁCS		A	17	(11)	6
2	LEE Do-kwon	KOR	M	1	(6)	1
14	Tibor MOLDOVAN	ROU	A	1	(4)	1
31	Olivér NAGY		M	1	(4)	1
	Kingsley OGBODO	NGA	M		(1)	
6	Tamás PETŐ		M	3	(1)	
7	Sasa RADULOVIC	AUS	M	16	(3)	1
8	Péter RAJCZI		A	5		2
16	Csaba REGEDEI		D	12	(7)	1
17	Paulus ROIHA	FIN	M	3	(3)	1
3	Haman SADJO	CMR	D	23		2
4	György SÁNDOR		M	19	(1)	5
	Attila SZÉKI		M		(1)	
22	Marcell TAKÁCS		A		(3)	
4	Densill THEOBALD	TRI	M	2	(5)	
28	Tibor TISZA		A	19	(3)	15
19	Tamás VASKÓ		D	1		
25	Krisztián VERMES		D	20	(1)	

VASAS SC

Coach – Géza Mészöly

Founded - 1911

MAJOR HONOURS: Hungarian League – (6) 1957 (spring), 1961, 1962, 1965, 1966, 1977; Hungarian Cup – (4) 1955, 1973, 1981, 1986.

2007

20/7	Tatabánya	h	3-1	*Németh N., Kenesei, Odrobéna*
30/7	REAC	a	0-2	

'8	Sopron	h	2-0	*Lázok, Somorjai*
/8	Fehérvár	a	2-5	*Rebryk, Lázok (p)*
)/8	Paks	h	3-2	*Németh N., Lázok, Tandari*
7/8	Újpest	a	1-1	*Tandari*
1/8	Diósgyőr	h	0-0	
4/9	Debrecen	a	0-2	
4/9	Siófok	h	0-0	
8/9	ZTE	a	3-3	*Tóth A. 2, Sowunmi*
/10	MTK	h	0-3	
0/10	Kaposvár	a	0-1	
'11	Honvéd	h	0-2	
0/11	Győr	h	1-1	*Németh N. (p)*
4/11	Nyíregyháza	a	1-2	*Németh N.*
008				
3/2	Tatabánya	a	2-0	*Németh N., Lázok*
/3	REAC	h	2-1	*Piller, Divić*
/3	Sopron	a	3-0	*(w/o)*
5/3	Fehérvár	h	1-2	*Németh N. (p)*
2/3	Paks	a	0-3	
1/3	Újpest	h	0-1	
/4	Diósgyőr	a	5-4	*Kincses, Pavičević, Sowunmi, Németh N. 2 (1p)*
1/4	Debrecen	h	0-3	
9/4	Siófok	a	3-1	*Németh N. 2 (1p), Lázok (p)*
5/4	ZTE	h	1-0	*Kincses*
/5	MTK	a	2-0	*Pavičević, Divić*
0/5	Kaposvár	h	1-2	*Lázok*
9/5	Honvéd	a	1-0	*Pandur*
5/5	Győr	a	1-2	*Németh N.*
30/5	Nyíregyháza	h	3-1	*Lázok, Pandur, Németh N.*

No	Name	Nat	Pos	Aps	(s)	Gls
38	Jean ADDO Sagna	SEN	M		(7)	
9	Balázs B. TÓTH		M	15	(11)	
27	Zsolt BALOG		D	27	(1)	
17	Martin BIELÍK	SVK	M		(4)	
26	Csaba BORSZÉKI		G	2	(1)	
20	Zoltán BÜKSZEGI		A		(3)	
19	Petar DIVIĆ	SRB	A	5	(4)	2
18	Ákos FÜZI dr.		D	3		
20	Thierry ISSIÉMOU	GAB	M		(2)	
37	Róbert JOVÁNCZAI		A		(3)	
20	Krisztián KENESEI		A	1		1
23	Péter KINCSES		M	25	(3)	2
7	Károly KISS		M	5	(4)	
4	Márton KISS		D		(1)	
25	Gábor KOVÁCS		D	5		
11	János LÁZOK		M	25	(1)	7
31	Roland MUNDI		M	5	(3)	
33	Gábor NÉMETH		G	27		
8	Norbert NÉMETH		M	26	(1)	12
6	Nenad NIKOLIĆ	SRB	D	2		
17	Péter ODROBÉNA		M	2	(3)	1
5	Péter PANDUR		D	20	(2)	2
10	Čedomir PAVIČEVIĆ	SRB	M	23		2
32	József PILLER		M	11	(9)	1
22	Denis REBRYK	UKR	A	6	(6)	1
13	Tamás SKITA		A		(2)	
6	Tamás SOMORJAI		M	9	(3)	1
30	Thomas SOWUNMI		A	16	(1)	2
14	Tamás TANDARI		A	5	(4)	2
21	András TÓTH		D	20		2
25	Balázs TÓTH		D	8	(4)	
28	Mariusz UNIERZYSKI	POL	D	26		

ZALAEGERSZEGI TE

Coach – Slavko Petrović (SRB); (30/4/08) Mihály Nagy

Founded - 1920

MAJOR HONOURS: Hungarian League – (1) 2002.

2007				
20/7	Paks	h	3-1	*Tóth Z., Waltner 2 (1p)*
27/7	Újpest	a	1-1	*Tóth N.*
3/8	Diósgyőr	h	4-1	*Pekič, Waltner 2 (1p), Vulin*
11/8	Debrecen	a	2-3	*Koplárovics, Pekič*
18/8	Siófok	h	2-0	*Waltner 2*
25/8	Győr	h	0-0	
3/9	MTK	a	1-4	*Pekič*
15/9	Kaposvár	h	2-1	*Waltner 2*
21/9	Honvéd	a	1-2	*Tóth Z.*
28/9	Vasas	h	3-3	*Meyé 2 (1p), Tóth N. (p)*
6/10	Nyíregyháza	a	1-2	*Koplárovics*
20/10	Tatabánya	h	4-1	*Pekič, Meyé (p), Koplárovics, Mijatovič*
3/11	REAC	a	2-1	*Tóth Z., Meyé (p)*
10/11	Sopron	h	4-0	*Meyé 2 (1p), Kádár, Koplárovics*
24/11	Fehérvár	a	0-2	
2008				
23/2	Paks	a	3-0	*Meyé 2, Balázs*
29/2	Újpest	h	4-1	*Zatara 2, Waltner, Meyé*
8/3	Diósgyőr	a	1-1	*Waltner*
15/3	Debrecen	h	1-2	*Botiş*
22/3	Siófok	a	1-1	*Waltner*
29/3	Győr	a	2-3	*Waltner 2*
4/4	MTK	h	0-1	
14/4	Kaposvár	a	2-0	*Meyé, Waltner (p)*
21/4	Honvéd	h	2-1	*Waltner 2*
25/4	Vasas	a	0-1	
3/5	Nyíregyháza	h	0-0	
10/5	Tatabánya	a	2-0	*Waltner, Mijatovič*
17/5	REAC	h	3-3	*Zatara, og (Kapcsos), Waltner*
24/5	Sopron	a	3-0	*(w/o)*
2/6	Fehérvár	h	1-3	*Pekič*

No	Name	Nat	Pos	Aps	(s)	Gls
1	Đorđe BABALJ	SRB	G	15		
17	Zsolt BALÁZS		A	1	(17)	1
6	Sorin BOTIŞ	ROU	D	17	(1)	1
10	Milan DAVIDOV	SRB	M	26	(2)	
15	Mahamadou DIAWARA	FRA	A	3	(5)	
2	Ivan DUDIĆ	SRB	D	12		
	Csaba FERKÓ		M	1		
41	Tibor FÜLÖP		M		(1)	
32	András HORVÁTH		M		(1)	
3	Tamás KÁDÁR		D	7	(2)	1
2	Gergely KOCSÁRDI		D	7	(3)	
19	Béla KOPLÁROVICS		M	19	(8)	4
51	Gergő KOVÁCS		A	1		
13	Tihamér LUKÁCS		M	2	(6)	
14	Árpád MAJOROS		M		(2)	
16	Péter MÁTÉ		M	26		
21	Roguy MEYÉ	GAB	A	17	(4)	10
22	Matej MILJATOVIČ	SVN	M	24		2
7	Balázs MOLNÁR		M	22	(1)	
11	Damir PEKIČ	SVN	A	14	(8)	5
12	Krisztián POGACSICS		G	1	(2)	
5	Péter POLGÁR	SVK	D	18	(2)	
8	Zoltán TÓTH		M	14	(6)	3
20	Norbert TÓTH		M	9	(5)	2
1	Géza VLASZÁK		G	13		
4	Lovre VULIN	CRO	D	21		1
9	Róbert WALTNER		A	21		18
20	Imad ZATARA	SWE	M	8	(4)	3

HUNGARY

PROMOTED CLUBS

SZOMBATHELYI HALADÁS FC

Coach – Aurél Csertői
Founded – 1919

KECSKEMÉTI TE

Coach – Tomislav Sivić (SRB)
Founded – 1911

SECOND LEVEL FINAL TABLES 2007/08

WEST		Pld	W	D	L	F	A	Pts
1	Szombathelyi Haladás FC	30	21	8	1	68	19	71
2	FC Felcsút	30	20	6	4	61	25	66
3	Gyírmót SE	30	17	7	6	66	38	58
4	Lombard Pápa FC	30	15	11	4	40	26	56
5	Integrál-DAC	30	15	4	11	56	43	49
6	Pécsi MFC	30	14	6	10	46	34	48
7	Kozármisleny SE	30	8	16	6	31	29	40
8	Budaörsi SC	30	9	12	9	47	44	39
9	Dunaújváros FC	30	11	5	14	39	47	38
10	Barcsi SC	30	10	7	13	38	43	37
11	Kaposvölgye VSC	30	8	10	12	45	44	34
12	FC Ajka	30	8	9	13	52	52	33
13	ESMTK	30	8	5	17	36	60	29
14	Komlói Bányász SK	30	6	8	16	28	64	26
15	Soroksár SC	30	3	8	19	22	50	16
16	Mosonmagyaróvári TE 1904	30	3	6	21	18	75	13

N.B. Mosonmagyaróvár - 2 pts deducted; Soroksár - 1 pt deducted.

EAST		Pld	W	D	L	F	A	P
1	Kecskeméti TE	30	24	3	3	74	23	7
2	Szolnok MÁV FC	30	20	3	7	52	29	6
3	Ferencvárosi TC	30	18	8	4	63	35	6
4	Makói FC	30	13	11	6	52	34	5
5	Vác-Újbuda LTC	30	13	6	11	57	45	4
6	Vecsési FC	30	12	9	9	43	42	4
7	Kazincbarcika SC	30	11	11	8	43	41	4
8	Bőcs KSC	30	11	9	10	47	42	4
9	Jászberényi SE-VASAS	30	9	9	12	28	36	3
10	Ceglédi VSE	30	10	5	15	33	53	3
11	Baktalórántháza VSE	30	8	10	12	31	43	3
12	Tököl KSK	30	9	5	16	28	52	3
13	BKV Előre SC	30	8	5	17	43	49	2
14	Orosháza FC	30	7	8	15	41	56	2
15	Tuzsér SE	30	6	5	19	29	59	2
16	Mezőkövesdi SE	30	4	7	19	26	51	1

DOMESTIC CUP 2007/08

MAGYAR KUPA

THIRD ROUND

(28/8/07)
Eger 0, Diósgyőr 3
Ferencváros 0, Paks 0

(29/8/07)
Andráshida 1, Barcs 0
Ásotthalom 0, Tisza Volán 5
BKV Előre 0, Fehérvár 5
Bonyhád 0, ZTE 10
Budaörs 1, Soroksár 0 *(aet)*
Celldömölk 0, Sopron 3
Demecser 0, Cigánd 1
Felcsút 3, Újpest 1
Gyirmót 1, Haladás 1 *(aet; 4-2 on pens)*
Kaposvölgye 3, Pécs 2 *(aet)*
Kemecse 0, Kazincbarcika 1
Komló 1, Kaposvár 3
Letenye 2, Balatonlelle 2
Martfű 1, Békéscsaba 8
Mór 4, Budafok 0
Mosonmagyaróvár 2, Tatabánya 3
Nagyecsed 0, Mezőkövesd 2
Pénzügyőr 2, Vác-Újbuda 2
Putnok 2, Baktalórántháza 0
Sárosd 2, REAC 8
Szekszárd 2, Siófok 2
Velence 4, Zsámbék 0
Veszprém 0, Integrál DAC 3

(5/9/07)
Bőcs 0 Nyíregyháza 2
Hatvan 0, Vasas 10
Jánosháza 0, Győr 7
Orosháza 1, Kecskemét 2

FOURTH ROUND

(25/9/07)
Kazincbarcika 2, REAC 1

(26/9/07)
Andráshida 0, Győr 3
Békéscsaba 2, Nyíregyháza 5
Budaörs 1, Kaposvölgye 1 *(aet; 3-4 on pens)*
Cigánd 0, Vasas 5
Felcsút 0, Ferencváros 1
Gyimőt 2, Tatabánya 2
Integrál-DAC 2, ZTE 1
Kecskemét 2, Debrecen 4
Mezőkövesd 1, Diósgyőr 3
Mór 1, Sopron 2
Pénzügyőr 1, Kaposvár 7
Putnok 0, MTK 0
Szekszárd 7, Letenye 0
Tisza Volán 1, Honvéd 4
Velence 0, Fehérvár 12
N.B. In third and fourth rounds, lower-division clubs qualify after drawn matches.

FIFTH ROUND

(23/10/07 & 7/11/07)
Szekszárd v Integrál-DAC 0-4; 0-7 *(0-11)*

(24/10/07 & 6/11/07)
Kazincbarcika v Diósgyőr 3-1; 1-1 *(4-2)*

(24/10/07 & 7/11/07)
Gyírmót v Nyíregyháza 2-0; 0-1 *(2-1)*
Putnok v Vasas 1-3; 1-3 *(2-6)*
Ferencváros v Kaposvár 2-2; 1-2 *(3-4)*
Győr v Fehérvár 1-1; 2-3 *(3-4)*
Kaposvölgye v Debrecen 2-5; 2-6 *(4-11)*
Honvéd v Sopron 2-1; 3-0 *(5-1)*

QUARTER-FINALS

(18/3/08 & 25/3/08)
Kazincbarcika 2 *(Stevica 10, Binder 15p)*, Honvéd 2 *(Zsolnai 24, Dobos 57p)*
Honvéd 4 *(Abass 13, 77, Hercegfalvi 74, 90p)*, Kazincbarcika 2 *(Kovács 7, Stevica 38)*
(Honvéd 6-4)

(19/3/08 & 25/3/08)
Integrál-DAC 0, Vasas 1 *(Németh N. 8)*
Vasas 1 *(Sowunmi 63)*, Integrál-DAC 2 *(Ludánszki 22p, Laki 76)*
(2-2; Integrál-DAC on away goals)

Gyirmót 2 *(Varga 7, Oross 15)*, Kaposvár 4 *(Pintér 42, Grúz 53, Oláh 64, Nikolić 71)*
Kaposvár 3 *(Szakály D. 44, Zahorecz 48, Alves 55)*, Gyirmót 0
(Kaposvár 7-2)

(19/3/08 & 27/3/08)
Fehérvár 2 *(Farkas 8, Sitku 67)*, Debrecen 1 *(Leandro 59)*
Debrecen 3 *(Bogdanović 31, Kerekes 56, Ďurica 87og)*, Fehérvár 1 *(Koller 84)*
(Debrecen 4-3)

SEMI-FINALS

(1/4/08 & 9/4/08)
Honvéd 4 *(Dobos 19p, Hercegfalvi 54, 89, Kovács Z. 96og)*, Kaposvár 0
Kaposvár 1 *(Pomper 83og)*, Honvéd 2 *(Smiljanić 35, Genito 44)*
(Honvéd 6-1)

(2/4/08 & 8/4/08)
Integrál-DAC 1 *(Laki 24)*, Debrecen 4 *(Rudolf 16, 48, Kouemaha 67, Demjén 76p)*
Debrecen 6 *(Bogdanović 36, 74p, 87, 90, Czvitkovics 71, Huszák 85)*, Integrál-DAC 0
(Debrecen 10-1)

FINAL

(28/5/08)
József Bozsik stadium, Budapest
BUDAPEST HONVÉD FC 0
DEBRECENI VSC 7 *(Leandro 9, Rudolf 17, Czvitkovics 29, 82, Kouemaha 58, 78, 89)*
Referee – *Kassai*
HONVÉD – *Tóth, Adewunmi, Smiljanić, Filó (Abraham 46), Vincze Z., Dobos, Genito, Pomper, Ivancsics, Hercegfalvi (Berdó 65), Bárányos (Diego 55).*
DEBRECEN – *Poleksić, Bernáth, Komlósi (Szatmári 14), Szűcs, Takács, Huszák (Dombi 59), Kiss, Leandro (Bogdanović 78), Czvitkovics, Rudolf, Kouemaha.*
Sent off: *Adewunmi 57, Dobos 73*

(4/6/08)
Oláh Gábor Út stadium, Debrecen
DEBRECENI VSC 2 *(Czvitkovics 74., Leandro 76)*
BUDAPEST HONVÉD FC 1 *(Filó 39)*
Referee – *Vad II*
DEBRECEN – *Balogh, Bernáth, Szatmári, Bíró, Takács, Dombi (Huszák 46), Leandro, Kiss, Czvitkovics, Kerekes, Bogdanović (Rudolf, 65).*
HONVÉD – *Borel, Vincze Z., Filó, Smiljanić, Bojtor, Koós (Abass 54), Pomper, Bárányos, Diego, Abraham, Hercegfalvi (Zsolnai 70).*
(DEBRECENI VSC 9-1)

Valur bring end to FH reign

he 2007 season in Iceland was lively and exciting. Valur Reykjavík broke FH Hafnarfjördur's three-year monopoly of the championship to finish as Iceland's ›p team for the first time in 20 years, winning their 20th tle in the process. KR Reykjavík confounded expert pinion by spending almost the entire season at the ottom of the league. Furthermore, the Icelandic ummer was especially warm, helping to break the ague's attendance record with a new all-time-high verage figure of 1,329.

was the last season with ten teams in the country's top ivision, the Úrvalsdeild. With expansion to 12 clubs in 008, only the bottom club was relegated while three ame up from the second division. Still, the relegation crap, just like the title race, went thrillingly to the wire.

ate drama

H seemed set for their fourth successive title as they ed for the first 16 rounds. In the penultimate fixture hey faced Valur at home. With a two-point lead, they new that victory would clinch the title. But Valur had ther plans and deservedly won 2-0 with goals from aldur Adalsteinsson and experienced international triker Helgi Sigurdsson. That precious win put Valur in he driving seat with a game to go. FH did what they ould to retrieve the situation by coming from a goal ehind to beat Vikingur Reykjavík 3-1 and send their pponents down, but Valur also won, 1-0 at ewcomers HK Kópavogur, thanks to an early goal rom centre-back Atli Sveinn Thórarinsson. The Valur upporters' hearts skipped a beat in the final minute when the ball struck the hand of one of their defenders nside the penalty area. Fortunately, the referee was unconvinced, blew for the end of the game seconds ater, and Valur's fans could finally enjoy success after he longest barren period in the club's history.

FH partly made up for their disappointment a week later by winning the Icelandic Cup for the first time, beating Fjölnir Reykjavík 2-1 in the final at Laugardalsvöllur. Fjölnir had just been promoted to the top flight for the first time and they gave the favourites a tough contest, but two goals from Matthías Gudmundsson, the winner halfway through extra time, ensured that FH had something to celebrate.

A poor finish to the UEFA EURO 2008™ qualifiers signalled the end of Eyjólfur Sverrisson's two-year reign as Iceland's national coach. The team looked in fine fettle in September when they drew 1-1 at home to Spain (having led for most of the match courtesy of a brilliant header by Emil Hallfredsson) and then beat Northern Ireland 2-1. But October was grim indeed. First the team crumbled at home to Latvia, losing 4-2 – a result that overshadowed Eidur Gudjohnsen's feat of becoming his country's record goalscorer - then they were humiliatingly defeated 3-0 by minnows Liechtenstein in Vaduz.

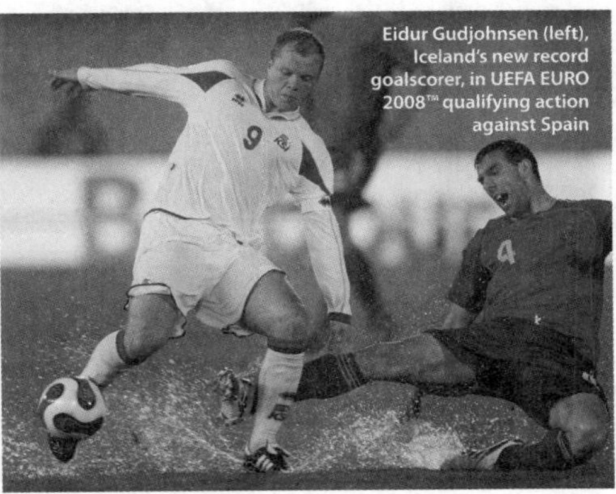
Eidur Gudjohnsen (left), Iceland's new record goalscorer, in UEFA EURO 2008™ qualifying action against Spain

Jóhannesson takes over

Ten days later, the Icelandic FA decided that Sverrisson's contract would not be renewed and hired Ólafur Jóhannesson to guide the team through the 2010 FIFA World Cup qualifiers. Jóhannesson had just left FH after five succesful years, and his first assignment was away to Denmark in the final qualifier. His team lost 3-0, but good results in early 2008, including three successive wins, suggested that Jóhannesson was on the right track.

ICELAND

Knattspyrnusamband Íslands (KSÍ)

Laugardalur
IS-104 Reykjavík
tel - +354 5 102900
fax - +354 5 689793
website - www.ksi.is
email - ksi@ksi.is
Year of Formation – 1947
President - Geir Thorsteinsson
General Secretary – Thórir Hákonarson
Press Officer – Ómar Smárason
Stadium - Laugardalsvöllur, Reykjavík (9,800)

TOP FIVE ALL-TIME CAPS
Rúnar Kristinsson (104); Gudni Bergsson (80); Hermann Hreidarsson (76); Birkir Kristinsso (74); Arnór Gudjohnsen (73)

TOP FIVE ALL-TIME GOALS
Eidur Smári Gudjohnsen (20); Ríkhardur Jónsson (17); Ríkhardu Dadason & Arnór Gudjohnsen (14); Thórdur Gudjónsson (13)

NATIONAL TEAM RESULTS 2007/08

22/8/07	Canada	H	Reykjavik	1-1	*Thorvaldsson (65)*
8/9/07	Spain (ECQ)	H	Reykjavik	1-1	*Hallfredsson (40)*
12/9/07	Northern Ireland (ECQ)	H	Reykjavik	2-1	*Björnsson (6), Gillespie (90+1og)*
13/10/07	Latvia (ECQ)	H	Reykjavik	2-4	*Gudjohnsen (4, 52)*
17/10/07	Liechtenstein (ECQ)	A	Vaduz	0-3	
21/11/07	Denmark (ECQ)	A	Copenhagen	0-3	
2/2/08	Belarus	N	Ta' Qali (MLT)	0-2	
4/2/08	Malta	A	Ta' Qali	0-1	
6/2/08	Armenia	N	Ta' Qali (MLT)	2-0	*Gudmundsson (45), Thorvaldsson (72)*
16/3/08	Faroe Islands	H	Kopavogur	3-0	*Sævarsson J. (45), Benjaminsen (72og), Gudmundsson (80)*
26/3/08	Slovakia	A	Zlate Moravce	2-1	*Thorvaldsson (71), Gudjohnsen (82)*
28/5/08	Wales	H	Reykjavik	0-1	

NATIONAL TEAM APPEARANCES 2007/08

Coach – Eyjólfur SVERRISSON 3/8/68 /(29/10/07) Ólafur JÓHANNESSON 30/6/57			Can	ESP	NIR	LVA	LIE	DEN	Blr	Mlt	Arm	Fro	Svk	Wal	Caps	Goa
Dadi LÁRUSSON	19/6/73	FH	G46												3	-
Grétar Rafn STEINSSON	9/1/82	AZ (NED) /Bolton (ENG)	D	M	M	M25		D					D66		25	3
Ívar INGIMARSSON	20/8/77	Reading (ENG)	D84	D	D	D	D								30	-
Ragnar SIGURDSSON	19/6/86	Göteborg (SWE)	D	D	D	D	D	D		D46	D		D		9	-
Hermann HREIDARSSON	11/7/74	Portsmouth (ENG)	D63	D	D		D	D			D73				76	5
Kári ÁRNASON	13/10/82	AGF (DEN)	M	M	M88	s25									16	1
Brynjar Björn GUNNARSSON	16/10/75	Reading (ENG)	M68			M	M85	M							65	4
Jóhannes Karl GUDJÓNSSON	25/5/80	Burnley (ENG)	M	M79		M	M58								34	1
Baldur Ingimar ADALSTEINSSON	12/2/80	Valur	A	s79					s46	M46	s73	M73			8	-
Gunnar Heidar THORVALDSSON	1/4/82	Hannover (GER) /Vålerenga (NOR)	A79	A88	A79	A65	A71	A	s77	A72	A73		s63	M80	20	5
Emil HALLFREDSSON	29/6/84	Reggina (ITA)	A84	M	M	M	A	M73					M90	M69	15	1

TIONAL TEAM APPEARANCES 2007/08 (contd.)

			Can	ESP	NIR	LVA	LIE	DEN	Blr	Mlt	Arm	Fro	Svk	Wal	Caps	Goals
THORGEIRSSON	18/1/77	Fylkir	s46							G				s46	4	-
ar JÓNSSON	29/7/80	Göteborg (SWE)	s63			D				D	s83				18	-
SIGURDSSON	17/9/74	Valur	s68			s65	s71		A77	s46		A58			62	10
Thór VIDARSSON	24/4/84	FH	s79						s80	M	s83	M73			5	-
n Örn SIGURDSSON	7/10/80	Brann (NOR)	s84	D	D	D88	D	D7					D	D	30	2
r Páll GUNNARSSON	21/3/80	Stabæk (NOR)	s84					M84					s89		20	2
Gautur ARASON	7/5/75	Vålerenga (NOR)		G	G	G	G	G							64	-
Thór VIDARSSON	15/3/78	De Graafschap (NED)		M69	M		M								52	2
r Ingi SKÚLASON	1/4/83	Helsingborg (SWE)		s69	s79								M		6	-
nn Smári BJÖRNSSON	7/1/81	Brann (NOR)		s88	A53	s88	s58								5	1
Smári GUDJOHNSEN	15/9/78	Barcelona (ESP)			s53	M	A						A89		50	20
r Gunnar ÁSGEIRSSON	30/6/80	FH			s88		s85	s84							3	-
dór Elmar BJARNASON	4/3/87	Celtic (SCO) /Lyn (NOR)						M	M46				M63	s69	6	-
n GÍSLASON	15/3/80	Brøndby (DEN)						M	M62	s46	M		M		22	-
r GARDARSSON	15/9/84	FH						s7							1	-
rt Gunnthór JÓNSSON	18/8/88	Hearts (SCO)						s73						M59	2	-
n Logi MAGNÚSSON	5/9/80	KR							G						1	-
Már SÆVARSSON	11/11/84	Valur							D	D	D	D		D	7	-
i Eggerts GUDJÓNSSON	26/2/79	ÍA							D	M	M83				20	1
veinn THÓRARINSSON	24/1/80	Valur							D	D	D	D	s66	D	8	-
i Ólafur EIRÍKSSON	28/3/82	Valur							D		s73	D82	D		6	-
Einar GUNNARSSON	22/4/89	AZ (NED)							M80			M	M	M75	4	-
i Thór VIDARSSON	5/3/88	Twente (NED)							M80						1	-
gvi GUDMUNDSSON	30/7/74	FH							M66	s63	M83	M84	s90		42	12
s Gudni SÆVARSSON	28/11/83	KR							s62	s72	M	M		s75	5	1
fur HÉDINSSON	1/1/85	GAIS (SWE)							s66	M63	M65				3	-
i Rafn PÁLMASON	9/11/84	Valur							s80	M	s65	s73		M	5	-
an STURLUSON	27/12/75	Valur									G	G	G	G46	5	-
ir EINARSSON	20/4/87	ÍA										D84			1	-
l Jóhann BALDVINSSON	18/12/80	Breidablik										s58			16	-
grímur JÓNASSON	4/5/86	Keflavík										s73			1	-
tur Logi VALGARDSSON	27/9/88	FH										s82			1	-
mann THÓRISSON	30/1/87	Breidablik										s84			1	-
mundur Reynir INARSSON	21/1/89	KR										s84			1	-
di SIGURDSSON	12/10/81	Lyn (NOR)												D	38	1
n Thór THÓRDARSON	27/3/75	ÍA												A59	6	1
i Valur DANÍELSSON	13/7/81	Elfsborg (SWE)												s59	7	-
nes SIGURDSSON	10/4/83	Sundsvall (SWE)												s59	13	1
ór SMÁRASON	7/9/88	Heerenveen (NED)												s80	1	-

ICELAND

DOMESTIC LEAGUE 2007

ÚRVALSDEILD FINAL LEAGUE TABLE 2007

		Pld	Home W	D	L	F	A	Away W	D	L	F	A	Total W	D	L	F	A	Pts
1	Valur Reykjavík	18	4	4	1	19	14	7	1	1	22	6	11	5	2	41	20	38
2	FH Hafnarfjördur	18	5	3	1	22	11	6	1	2	20	15	11	4	3	42	26	37
3	ÍA Akranes	18	6	1	2	18	12	2	5	2	16	15	8	6	4	34	27	30
4	Fylkir	18	3	3	3	11	10	5	2	2	12	8	8	5	5	23	18	29
5	Breidablik	18	3	5	1	16	10	2	4	3	13	10	5	9	4	29	20	24
6	Keflavík	18	3	3	3	12	13	2	3	4	14	19	5	6	7	26	32	21
7	Fram Reykjavík	18	3	2	4	12	14	0	5	4	13	17	3	7	8	25	31	16
8	KR Reykjavík	18	2	3	4	10	15	1	4	4	7	15	3	7	8	17	30	16
9	HK Kópavogur	18	4	3	2	14	13	0	1	8	3	22	4	4	10	17	35	16
10	Víkingur Reykjavík	18	1	2	6	6	17	2	3	4	9	13	3	5	10	15	30	14

N.B. Only one team relegated as the league was expanded to 12 teams for the 2008 season.

TOP GOALSCORERS

14 Jónas Grani GARDARSSON (Fra
12 Helgi SIGURDSSON (Valur)
8 Tryggvi GUDMUNDSSON (FH)
Siniša Valdimar KEKIĆ (Víkingur
7 Vjekoslav SVADUMOVIĆ (ÍA)
Hjálmar THÓRARINSSON (Fram)
Magnús Páll GUNNARSSON (Breidablik)
Bjarni GUDJÓNSSON (ÍA)
6 Arnar GUNNLAUGSSON (FH)
Símun SAMUELSEN (Keflavík)
Prince RAJCOMAR (Breidablik)
Matthías VILHJÁLMSSON (FH)
Matthías GUDMUNDSSON (FH)

CLUB-BY-CLUB

BREIDABLIK

Coach – Ólafur H. Kristjánsson

Founded - 1950

2007				
13/5	Fylkir	h	0-1	
20/5	KR	a	1-1	*Gunnarsson M.*
24/5	Keflavík	h	2-2	Sigurdsson, Gunnarsson M.
28/5	Valur	h	0-0	
8/6	Víkingur	a	1-1	*Gunnarsson M.*
14/6	ÍA	h	3-0	*Gunnarsson M., Sigurdsson, Zivanović*
20/6	FH	a	1-2	*Petrović*
26/6	HK	h	3-0	*Sigurdsson, Rajcomar, Sigurgeirsson*
3/7	Fram	a	0-1	
16/7	Fylkir	a	3-0	*Steindórsson 2, Jónsson G.*
25/7	KR	h	1-1	*Zivanović*
9/8	Keflavík	a	3-0	*Zivanović, Rajcomar, Thorsteinsson*
16/8	Valur	a	2-2	*Rajcomar 2*
26/8	Víkingur	h	1-1	*Steindórsson*
30/8	ÍA	a	1-2	*Rajcomar*
16/9	FH	h	4-3	*Zivanović, Rajcomar, Gunnarsson M., og (Helgason)*
23/9	HK	a	1-1	*og (Albertsson)*
29/9	Fram	h	2-2	*Gunnarsson M. 2 (1p)*

No	Name	Nat	Pos	Aps	(s)	Gls
4	Arnór ADALSTEINSSON		D	17		
6	Kári ÁRSÆLSSON		D	1		
5	Srđan GASIĆ	SRB	D	18		
8	Arnar GRÉTARSSON		M	17		
2	Árni K. GUNNARSSON		D	17		
10	Magnús Páll GUNNARSSON		A	11	(6)	7
1	Hjörvar HAFLIDASON		G	4		
22	Ellert HREINSSON		A	1	(2)	
24	Casper JACOBSEN	DEN	G	14		
23	Gunnar Örn JÓNSSON		M	9	(7)	1
19	Kristinn JÓNSSON		D	2	(2)	
16	Gudmundur KRISTJÁNSSON		M	2	(2)	
14	Gudjón LÝDSSON		M		(1)	
25	Nenad PETROVIĆ	SRB	M	14		1
9	Prince RAJCOMAR	NED	A	16		6
7	Kristján Óli SIGURDSSON		M	7	(6)	3
11	Olgeir SIGURGEIRSSON		M	12	(4)	1
30	Kristinn STEINDÓRSSON		A	6	(5)	3
15	Gudmann THÓRISSON		D	16		
13	Steinthór THORSTEINSSON		M	1	(9)	1
21	Nenad ZIVANOVIĆ	SRB	A	13	(5)	4

FH HAFNARFJÖRDUR

Coach – Ólafur Jóhannesson

Founded - 1929

MAJOR HONOURS: Icelandic League - (3) 2004, 2005, 2006; Icelandic Cup - (1) 2007.

2007				
12/5	ÍA	a	3-2	*Gudmundsson T. (p), Gunnlaugsson A., Gudmundsson M.*
20/5	Keflavík	a	2-1	*Gunnlaugsson A., Gudmundsson M.*
24/5	HK	h	4-0	*Gudmundsson T. 2, Gudmundsson M., Gunnlaugsson A.*
29/5	Fram	a	2-0	*Gudmundsson M., Gudmundsson T. (p)*
10/6	Fylkir	h	0-0	
14/6	KR	a	2-0	*Ásgeirsson, Saevarsson*
20/6	Breidablik	h	2-1	*Gudmundsson T., Gunnlaugsson A.*
27/6	Valur	a	1-4	*Vilhjálmsson*
3/7	Víkingur	h	4-1	*Vilhjálmsson, Gudmundsson M., Saevarsson, Gudnason*
14/7	ÍA	h	1-1	*Gudmundsson T. (p)*
28/7	Keflavík	h	3-2	*Ólafsson, Vilhjálmsson, Bjarnason*
13/8	Fram	h	3-3	*Vidarsson, Ásgeirsson, Saevarsson*

/8	HK	a	2-2	*Gudmundsson T. 2*
/8	Fylkir	a	2-1	*Vilhjálmsson 2*
/8	KR	h	5-1	*Ásgeirsson 3, Nielsen, Ólafsson*
/9	Breidablik	a	3-4	*Helgason, Gunnlaugsson A., Vilhjálmsson*
/9	Valur	h	0-2	
/9	Víkingur	a	3-1	*Siim, Gudmundsson M., Gunnlaugsson A.*

No	Name	Nat	Pos	Aps	(s)	Gls
	Ásgeir G. ÁSGEIRSSON		M	14	(3)	5
	Freyr BJARNASON		D	14		1
	Allan DYRING	DEN	A		(4)	
	Sverrir GARDARSSON		D	17		
5	Matthías GUDMUNDSSON		A	18		6
	Tryggvi GUDMUNDSSON		A	17		8
	Atli GUDNASON		A	1	(13)	1
	Arnar GUNNLAUGSSON		A	8	(5)	6
	Bjarki GUNNLAUGSSON		M	6	(2)	
	Audun HELGASON		D	2	(1)	1
	Dadi LÁRUSSON		G	18		
	Tommy NIELSEN	DEN	D	16	(1)	1
	Sigurvin ÓLAFSSON		M	6	(2)	2
4	Gudmundur SAEVARSSON		D	18		3
	Dennis M. SIIM	DEN	M	11	(3)	1
9	Ólafur Páll SNORRASON		M		(2)	
7	Hjörtur Logi VALGARDSSON		D	4	(3)	
	Davíd Thór VIDARSSON		M	17	(1)	1
3	Matthías VILHJÁLMSSON		A	11	(6)	6

FRAM REYKJAVÍK

Coach – Ólafur Thórdarson

Founded - 1908

MAJOR HONOURS: Icelandic League - (18) 1913, 1914, 1915, 1916, 1917, 1918, 1921, 1922, 1923, 1925, 1939, 1946, 1947, 1962, 1972, 1986, 1988, 1990; Icelandic Cup - (7) 1970, 1973, 1979, 1980, 1985, 1987, 1989.

2007				
3/5	Valur	a	1-1	*Árnason*
0/5	Víkingur	h	0-2	
4/5	ÍA	a	2-2	*Gardarsson, Björnsson*
9/5	FH	h	0-2	
0/6	HK	a	1-2	*Gardarsson*
4/6	Keflavík	a	1-2	*Thórarinsson*
8/6	Fylkir	h	3-1	*Thórarinsson 2 (1p), Gardarsson*
8/6	KR	a	1-2	*Thórarinsson*
/7	Breidablik	h	1-0	*Gardarsson*
6/7	Valur	h	0-2	
5/7	Víkingur	a	1-2	*Gardarsson*
/8	ÍA	h	2-4	*Gardarsson 2*
6/8	FH	a	3-3	*Gardarsson 2, Thórarinsson*
6/8	HK	h	3-0	*Steen, Óskarsson, Thórarinsson*
0/8	Keflavík	h	2-2	*Thórarinsson, Gardarsson*
6/9	Fylkir	a	1-1	*Gardarsson*
3/9	KR	h	1-1	*Björnsson*
9/9	Breidablik	a	2-2	*Gardarsson 2 (1p)*

No	Name	Nat	Pos	Aps	(s)	Gls
2	Ódinn ÁRNASON		D	15	(2)	1
22	Ívar BJÖRNSSON		A	8	(9)	2
13	Henrik EGGERTS	DEN	M	7		
29	Jón Gudni FJÓLUSON		D	1	(2)	
9	Jónas Grani GARDARSSON		A	17	(1)	13
17	Grímur Björn GRÍMSSON		A	1	(2)	
4	Vidar GUDJÓNSSON		M		(2)	
7	Dadi GUDMUNDSSON		D	14	(3)	
1	Hannes HALLDÓRSSON		G	18		
28	Kristinn Ingi HALLDÓRSSON		M		(3)	
27	Kristján HAUKSSON		D	12	(1)	
19	Andri L. KARVELSSON		D	6	(1)	
6	Reynir LEÓSSON		D	17		
25	Guðmundur MAGNÚSSON		A		(2)	
15	Hans MATHIESEN	DEN	M	11	(1)	
14	Henry NWOSU	GER	A	1		
26	Jón Orri ÓLAFSSON		D		(1)	
3	Ingvar ÓLASON		M	15	(2)	
8	Theódór ÓSKARSSON		M	7	(4)	1
21	Igor PESIĆ	SRB	M	9		
11	Patrik REDO	SWE	M	5	(6)	
16	Alexander STEEN	SWE	M	15	(3)	1
5	Eggert STEFÁNSSON		D	5		
10	Hjálmar THÓRARINSSON		A	14	(3)	7

FYLKIR

Coach – Leifur Gardarsson

Founded - 1967

MAJOR HONOURS: Icelandic Cup - (2) 2001, 2002.

2007				
13/5	Breidablik	a	1-0	*Christiansen*
20/5	Valur	h	1-2	*Hilmisson*
24/5	Víkingur	a	1-0	*Gíslason*
28/5	ÍA	h	2-2	*Gíslason, Christiansen*
10/6	FH	a	0-0	
14/6	HK	h	1-0	*Adalgeirsson*
18/6	Fram	a	1-3	*Gíslason*
27/6	Keflavík	a	0-1	
4/7	KR	h	0-0	
16/7	Breidablik	h	0-3	
24/7	Valur	a	4-2	*Gravesen (p), Gíslason, Hilmisson, Ingason*
9/8	Víkingur	h	1-0	*Christiansen*
16/8	ÍA	a	2-0	*Hilmisson 2*
26/8	FH	h	1-2	*Einarsson (p)*
30/8	HK	a	2-1	*Gravesen 2*
16/9	Fram	h	1-1	*Christiansen*
23/9	Keflavík	h	4-0	*Ingason 3, Gravesen (p)*
29/9	KR	a	1-1	*Gravesen (p)*

No	Name	Nat	Pos	Aps	(s)	Gls
10	Hermann ADALGEIRSSON		M	3	(6)	1
31	Kjartan Andri BALDVINSSON		A		(2)	
17	Mads BEIERHOLM	DEN	M	6	(5)	
11	Kjartan Ágúst BREIDDAL		M		(1)	
23	Christian CHRISTIANSEN	DEN	A	15	(1)	4
8	Páll EINARSSON		M	4	(12)	1
26	Pape Mamadou FAYE		A		(1)	
28	Valur Fannar GÍSLASON		M	15		4
6	Peter GRAVESEN	DEN	M	15	(1)	5
19	Freyr GUDLAUGSSON		D		(1)	
14	Haukur Ingi GUDNASON		A	9	(4)	
21	David HANNAH	SCO	D	18		
3	Gudni Rúnar HELGASON		D	10	(2)	
29	Björn Orri HERMANNSSON		D		(1)	
22	Halldór A. HILMISSON		A	16	(2)	4
24	Albert B. INGASON		A	8	(5)	4
16	Andrés JÓHANNESSON		D	13	(3)	
15	Vídir LEIFSSON		D	17		
5	Ólafur STÍGSSON		M	13	(2)	
18	Fjalar THORGEIRSSON		G	18		
20	Arnar ÚLFARSSON		D		(3)	
2	Kristján VALDIMARSSON		D	18		

HK KÓPAVOGUR

Coach – Gunnar Gudmundsson

Founded - 1970.

2007

13/5	Víkingur	a	0-0	
21/5	ÍA	h	1-0	*Stefánsson*
24/5	FH	a	0-4	
28/5	Keflavík	a	0-3	
10/6	Fram	h	2-1	*Stefánsson, Sigmundsson*
14/6	Fylkir	a	0-1	
20/6	KR	h	2-0	*Stefánsson, Jäger*
26/6	Breidablik	a	0-3	
4/7	Valur	h	1-4	*og (Einarsson)*
16/7	Víkingur	h	2-2	*Júlíusson, Llorens*
26/7	ÍA	a	1-4	*Ólafsson*
16/8	Keflavík	h	2-1	*Jäger, Stefánsson*
19/8	FH	h	2-2	*Bett, Birgisson*
26/8	Fram	a	0-3	
30/8	Fylkir	h	1-2	*Thórsson*
16/9	KR	a	2-3	*Magnússon H.M., Stefánsson*
23/9	Breidablik	h	1-1	*Birgisson (p)*
29/9	Valur	a	0-1	

No	Name	Nat	Pos	Aps	(s)	Gls
5	Ásgrímur ALBERTSSON		D	18		
28	Calum Thór BETT		M	8	(6)	1
9	Thórdur BIRGISSON		A	11	(6)	2
4	Jóhann BJÖRNSSON		D	3		
29	Almir COSIĆ	BIH	M	3	(8)	
8	Stefán Jóhann EGGERTSSON		D	18		
24	Hólmar Örn EYJÓLFSSON		M	12		
15	Eythór GUDNASON		A	2	(3)	
1	Gunnleifur GUNNLEIFSSON		G	18		
18	Kristján Ari HALLDÓRSSON		M	4	(6)	
2	Thorlákur HILMARSSON		M		(1)	
27	Oliver JÄGER	SUI	A	11	(3)	2
7	Ólafur V. JÚLÍUSSON		M	3	(7)	1
21	Finnbogi LLORENS		D	17		1
6	Davíd MAGNÚSSON		D	9	(2)	
11	Hördur Már MAGNÚSSON		M	4	(2)	1
3	Finnur ÓLAFSSON		M	10	(2)	1
26	Aaron PALOMARES		M	6		
13	Rúnar Páll SIGMUNDSSON		M	13		1
17	Bjarki Már SIGVALDASON		M		(2)	
10	Jón Thorgrímur STEFÁNSSON		M	16	(2)	5
19	Hermann Geir THÓRSSON		D	9	(2)	1
14	Brynjar VÍDISSON		M	3		

ÍA AKRANES

Coach – Gudjón Thórdarson

Founded - 1946

MAJOR HONOURS: Icelandic League - (18) 1951, 1953, 1954, 1957, 1958, 1960, 1970, 1974, 1975, 1977, 1983, 1984, 1992, 1993, 1994, 1995, 1996, 2001; Icelandic Cup - (9) 1978, 1982, 1983, 1984, 1986, 1993, 1996, 2000, 2003.

2007

12/5	FH	h	2-3	*Gudjónsson B. (p), Gudjónsson T.*
21/5	HK	a	0-1	
24/5	Fram	h	2-2	*Gudmundsson, Brynjarsson*
28/5	Fylkir	a	2-2	*Ákason, Svadumović*
10/6	KR	h	3-1	*Gudjónsson B., Magnússon, Reynisson*
14/6	Breidablik	a	0-3	
19/6	Valur	h	2-1	*Cingel, Gudjónsson B. (p)*
26/6	Víkingur	a	3-0	*Svadumović 2, Ákaso*
4/7	Keflavík	h	2-1	*Gudjónsson B. 2 (1p)*
14/7	FH	a	1-1	*Björnsson*
26/7	HK	h	4-1	*Gudjónsson T. 2, Svadumović, Júlíusso*
9/8	Fram	a	4-2	*Gudjónsson B., Ákaso Gudjónsson T., Gudjónsson A.*
16/8	Fylkir	h	0-2	
26/8	KR	a	1-1	*Svadumović*
30/8	Breidablik	h	2-1	*Svadumović, Cingel*
17/9	Valur	a	2-2	*Sigurdarson 2*
23/9	Víkingur	h	1-0	*Júlíusson*
29/9	Keflavík	a	3-3	*Svadumović, Gudjónsson B., Ákaso*

No	Name	Nat	Pos	Aps	(s)	Gls
14	Jón Vilhelm ÁKASON		M	17	(1)	4
8	Ellert Jón BJÖRNSSON		D	11		1
26	Gísli Freyr BRYNJARSSON		M		(6)	1
18	Dario CINGEL	CRO	D	15		2
5	Heimir EINARSSON		D	18		
15	Arnar Már GUDJÓNSSON		M	1	(2)	1
4	Bjarni GUDJÓNSSON		M	17		7
17	Gudmundur B. GUDJÓNSSON		D	2	(2)	
10	Thórdur GUDJÓNSSON		M	9	(2)	4
2	Árni Thór GUDMUNDSSON		D	17		1
1	Páll Gísli JÓNSSON		G	18		
9	Andri JÚLÍUSSON		A	7	(9)	2
22	Ragnar LEÓSSON		A		(2)	
6	Helgi Pétur MAGNÚSSON		M	17		1
7	Dean MARTIN	ENG	M	4	(1)	
11	Kári Steinn REYNISSON		M	7	(8)	1
30	Trausti SIGURBJÖRNSSON		G		(1)	
16	Björn B. SIGURDARSON		A	9	(2)	2
19	Vjekoslav SVADUMOVIĆ	CRO	A	15		7
3	Gudjón H. SVEINSSON		D	14	(2)	

KEFLAVÍK

Coach – Kristján Gudmundsson

Founded - 1929

MAJOR HONOURS: Icelandic League - (4) 1964, 1969, 1971, 1973; Icelandic Cup - (4) 1975, 1997, 2004, 2006.

2007

14/5	KR	a	2-1	*Steinarsson (p), Samuelsen*
20/5	FH	h	1-2	*Samuelsen*
24/5	Breidablik	a	2-2	*Kotilainen, Antoníussc*
28/5	HK	h	3-0	*Kristjánsson T., Samuelsen, Steinarssc*
9/6	Valur	a	2-2	*Kristjánsson T., Sigurdsson*
14/6	Fram	h	2-1	*Kristjánsson T., Sigurdsson*
20/6	Víkingur	a	2-1	*Kristjánsson T., Steinarsson (p)*
27/6	Fylkir	h	1-0	*Samuelsen*
4/7	ÍA	a	1-2	*Jónasson*
15/7	KR	h	1-1	*Samuelsen*
28/7	FH	a	2-3	*Sigurdsson, Kotilainen (p)*
9/8	Breidablik	h	0-3	
16/8	HK	a	1-2	*Steinarsson (p)*
26/8	Valur	h	1-3	*Samuelsen*
30/8	Fram	a	2-2	*Steinarsson, Kristjánsson T.*
16/9	Víkingur	h	0-0	
23/9	Fylkir	a	0-4	
29/9	ÍA	h	3-3	*Jónasson 2, Antoníusson*

Name	Nat	Pos	Aps	(s)	Gls
Gudjón Á. ANTONÍUSSON		D	18		2
Stefán Örn ARNARSON		A		(4)	
Einar Orri EINARSSON		M	3	(3)	
Einar Örn EINARSSON		A	1	(1)	
Sigurbergur ELÍSSON		M		(1)	
Thorsteinn A. GEORGSSON		D	1	(1)	
Bjarki F. GUDMUNDSSON		G	6	(1)	
Ingvi Rafn GUDMUNDSSON		M		(3)	
Kenneth GUSTAFSSON	SWE	D	10		
Sigurbjörn HAFTHÓRSSON		M	1		
Högni HELGASON		D		(6)	
Ómar JÓHANNSSON		G	12		
Hallgrímur JÓNASSON		D	16	(1)	3
Nicolai JØRGENSEN	DEN	D	11	(2)	
Marco KOTILAINEN	SWE	M	16	(2)	2
Pétur H. KRISTJÁNSSON		A	1	(5)	
Thórarinn KRISTJÁNSSON		A	12	(2)	5
Magnús MATTHÍASSON		A		(2)	
Gudmundur Vidar METE		D	11	(2)	
Branislav MILIĆEVIĆ	SRB	D	15		
Jónas Gudni SAEVARSSON		M	16		
Símun SAMUELSEN	FRO	M	14		6
Baldur SIGURDSSON		M	15		3
Gudmundur STEINARSSON		A	15	(2)	5
Miloš TANASIĆ	SRB	A		(1)	
Magnús S. THORSTEINSSON		A	4	(5)	

KR REYKJAVÍK

Coach – Teitur Thórdarson; (29/7/07) Logi Ólafsson

Founded – 1899

MAJOR HONOURS: Icelandic League – (24) 1912, 1919, 1926, 1927, 28, 1929, 1931, 1932, 1934, 1941, 1948, 1949, 1950, 1952, 1955, 1959, 961, 1963, 1965, 1968, 1999, 2000, 2002, 2003; Icelandic Cup – (10) 1960, 1961, 1962, 1963, 1964, 1966, 1967, 1994, 1995, 1999.

07

/5	Keflavík	h	1-2	*Takefusa*
/5	Breidablik	h	1-1	*Kristjánsson*
/5	Valur	a	1-2	*Gunnarsson*
/5	Víkingur	h	1-2	*Jónasson*
/6	ÍA	a	1-3	*Takefusa*
/6	FH	h	0-2	
/6	HK	a	0-2	
/6	Fram	h	2-1	*Thórhallsson, Pétursson*
	Fylkir	a	0-0	
/7	Keflavík	a	1-1	*Takefusa*
/7	Breidablik	a	1-1	*Magnússon K.*
3	Valur	h	0-3	
/8	Víkingur	a	1-0	*Jónsson*
/8	ÍA	h	1-1	*Pétursson*
/8	FH	a	1-5	*Lárusson*
/9	HK	h	3-2	*Hjartarson, Kristjánsson, Takefusa*
/9	Fram	a	1-1	*Hauksson*
/9	Fylkir	h	1-1	*Hauksson*

Name	Nat	Pos	Aps	(s)	Gls
Tryggvi BJARNASON		D	5		
Eggert Rafn EINARSSON		D	6	(1)	
Kristján FINNBOGASON		G	7		
Skúli Jón FRIDGEIRSSON		D	12	(2)	
Gudmundur R. GUNNARSSON		D	12	(2)	1
Ágúst Thór GYLFASON		D	7	(2)	
Óskar Örn HAUKSSON		M	6	(8)	2
Grétar Ó. HJARTARSON		A	15	(3)	1
Atli JÓHANNSSON		M	6	(3)	
Henning JÓNASSON		D	1	(4)	1
Gunnlaugur JÓNSSON		D	18		1
Vigfús A. JÓSEPSSON		D	1		
Sigthór JÚLÍUSSON		D	6		
12 Rúnar KRISTINSSON		M	12	(2)	
14 Sigmundur KRISTJÁNSSON		M	14	(1)	2
6 Bjarnólfur LÁRUSSON		M	10	(1)	1
5 Kristinn J. MAGNÚSSON		M	12	(1)	1
22 Stefán Logi MAGNÚSSON		G	11		
13 Pétur H. MARTEINSSON		D	15		
29 Ásgeir Örn ÓLAFSSON		M	3	(1)	
27 Ingimundur ÓSKARSSON		A		(2)	
24 Gudmundur PÉTURSSON		A	3	(4)	2
10 Björgólfur TAKEFUSA		A	10	(8)	4
9 Jóhann THÓRHALLSSON		A	6	(8)	1

VALUR REYKJAVÍK

Coach – Willum Thór Thórsson

Founded - 1911

MAJOR HONOURS: Icelandic League – (20) 1930, 1933, 1935, 1936, 1937, 1938, 1940, 1942, 1943, 1944, 1945, 1956, 1966, 1967, 1976, 1978, 1980, 1985, 1987, 2007; Icelandic Cup - (9) 1965, 1974, 1976, 1977, 1988, 1990, 1991, 1992, 2005.

2007

13/5	Fram	h	1-1	*Sigurdsson*
20/5	Fylkir	a	2-1	*Mortensen, Carlsen*
24/5	KR	h	2-1	*Sigurdsson 2*
28/5	Breidablik	a	0-0	
9/6	Keflavík	h	2-2	*Vilhjálmsson, Hjaltason*
13/6	Víkingur	h	3-1	*Sigurdsson 2 (1p), Pálmason*
19/6	ÍA	a	1-2	*Mortensen*
27/6	FH	h	4-1	*Benediktsson 2, Sigurdsson, og (Nielsen)*
4/7	HK	a	4-1	*Saevarsson, Sigurdsson, Pálmason, Vilhjálmsson*
16/7	Fram	a	2-0	*Benediktsson, Haflidason*
24/7	Fylkir	h	2-4	*Hjaltason, Sigurdsson*
8/8	KR	a	3-0	*Adalsteinsson 2, Sigurdsson*
16/8	Breidablik	h	2-2	*Sigurdsson 2*
26/8	Keflavík	a	3-1	*og (Milićević), Benediktsson, Bett*
2/9	Víkingur	a	5-1	*Einarsson, Benediktsson, Adalsteinsson, Mortensen, Pálmason*
17/9	ÍA	h	2-2	*Thórarinsson, Pálmason*
23/9	FH	a	2-0	*Adalsteinsson, Sigurdsson*
29/9	HK	h	1-0	*Thórarinsson*

No	Name	Nat	Pos	Aps	(s)	Gls
16	Baldur I. ADALSTEINSSON		M	17		4
23	Gudmundur BENEDIKTSSON		A	15	(3)	5
8	Baldur BETT		M	13		1
20	René CARLSEN	DEN	D	14		1
4	Gunnar EINARSSON		D	6	(2)	1
21	Bjarni Ólafur EIRÍKSSON		M	7	(2)	
14	Kristinn HAFLIDASON		M		(3)	1
17	Gudmundur HAFSTEINSSON		A		(1)	
30	Daníel HJALTASON		M	2	(10)	2
7	Sigurbjörn HREIDARSSON		M	10	(4)	
15	Dennis Bo MORTENSEN	DEN	A	3	(13)	3
11	Pálmi Rafn PÁLMASON		M	18		4
6	Birkir Már SAEVARSSON		D	17		1
10	Helgi SIGURDSSON		A	18		12
2	Barry SMITH	SCO	D	17		
1	Kjartan STURLUSON		G	18		
5	Atli S. THÓRARINSSON		D	18		2
9	Hafthór VILHJÁLMSSON		M	5	(10)	2

ICELAND

VÍKINGUR REYKJAVÍK

Coach – Magnús Gylfason

Founded - 1908

MAJOR HONOURS: Icelandic League - (5) 1920, 1924, 1981, 1982, 1991; Icelandic Cup – (1) 1971.

2007				
13/5	HK	h	0-0	
20/5	Fram	a	2-0	*Atlason, Kekić*
24/5	Fylkir	h	0-1	
28/5	KR	a	2-1	*Sveinbjörnsson, Kekić*
8/6	Breidablik	h	1-1	*Úlfarsson V.*
13/6	Valur	a	1-3	*Kekić (p)*
20/6	Keflavík	h	1-2	*Kekić (p)*
26/6	ÍA	h	0-3	
3/7	FH	a	1-4	*og (Lárusson)*
16/7	HK	a	2-2	*Kekić (p), Gudjónsson*
25/7	Fram	h	2-1	*Kekić 2 (1p)*
9/8	Fylkir	a	0-1	
16/8	KR	h	0-1	
26/8	Breidablik	a	1-1	*Kristjánsson*
2/9	Valur	h	1-5	*Atlason*
16/9	Keflavík	a	0-0	
23/9	ÍA	a	0-1	
29/9	FH	h	1-3	*Kekić*

No	Name	Nat	Pos	Aps	(s)	Gls
16	Hermann ALBERTSSON		D	6	(5)	
23	Egill ATLASON		A	11	(6)	2
7	Björn Vidar ÁSBJÖRNSSON		A	2	(5)	
25	Hördur S. BJARNASON		D	13	(1)	
30	Höskuldur EIRÍKSSON		D	7		
10	Jökull I. ELÍSABETARSON		M	11	(1)	
20	Dragan GALIĆ	SRB	A		(5)	
5	Miloš GLOGOVAC	SRB	D	9		
4	Jón GUDBRANDSSON		D	3	(1)	
2	Vidar GUDJÓNSSON		M	5	(3)	1
18	Bjarni HALLDÓRSSON		G	10		
28	Jón B. HERMANNSSON		M	14	(1)	
24	Arnar JÓNSSON		M		(1)	
1	Ingvar Thór KALE		G	7		
9	Siniša Valdimar KEKIĆ		A	17		8
8	Gunnar KRISTJÁNSSON		M	17	(1)	1
22	Magnús Thór MAGNÚSSON		G	1	(1)	
11	Grétar S. SIGURDARSON		D	18		
3	Arnar Jón SIGURGEIRSSON		M	9	(4)	
14	Pétur Örn SVANSSON		M		(5)	
17	Stefán K. SVEINBJÖRNSSON		M	11	(4)	1
21	Thorvaldur S. SVEINSSON		D	15	(3)	
6	Haukur A. ÚLFARSSON		M	2	(1)	
13	Valur A. ÚLFARSSON		D	10	(4)	1

PROMOTED CLUBS

GRINDAVÍK

Coach – Milan Stefán Janković

Founded - 1935

THRÓTTUR REYKJAVÍK

Coach – Gunnar Oddsson

Founded - 1949

FJÖLNIR REYKJAVÍK

Coach – Ásmundur Arnarsson

Founded – 1988

SECOND LEVEL FINAL TABLE 2007

		Pld	W	D	L	F	A	Pts
1	Grindavík	22	15	2	5	47	21	47
2	Thróttur Reykjavík	22	15	2	5	47	24	47
3	Fjölnir Reykjavík	22	14	3	5	61	29	45
4	ÍBV Vestmannaeyjar	22	13	5	4	42	23	44
5	Fjardabyggd	22	11	4	7	23	17	37
6	Leiknir Reykjavík	22	6	7	9	22	27	25
7	Thór Akureyri	22	6	6	10	33	40	24
8	Njardvík	22	5	8	9	25	32	23
9	Stjarnan	22	5	5	12	39	44	20
10	Víkingur Ólafsvík	22	5	5	12	22	33	20
11	KA Akureyri	22	5	4	13	14	45	19
12	Reynir Sandgerdi	22	3	7	12	22	62	16

N.B. As the Icelandic premier league was expanded to 12 teams, three teams were promoted and only one relegated.

DOMESTIC CUP 2007

VISA-BIKAR

FIFTH ROUND

(10/7/07)
Fjardabyggd 3, Fjölnir 4
KR 1, Valur 1 *(aet; 0-3 on pens)*
ÍA 2, Víkingur R. 1 *(aet)*
ÍBV 0, FH 3
Haukar 2, Fram 2 *(aet; 4-3 on pens)*

(11/7/07)
Thróttur R. 0, Keflavík 1
Thór 1, Fylkir 4
Breidablik 3, HK 1 *(aet)*

QUARTER-FINALS

(12/8/07)
Fylkir 3 *(Sveinsson 3og , Hilmisson 98, 116)*,
ÍA 1 *(Sigurdarson 41) (aet)*
Breidablik 3 *(Gunnarsson 62, Rajcomar 74, Sigurdsson 84og)*, Keflaví
(Kristjánsson P. 85)

(13/8/07)
Fjölnir 4 *(Gudmundsson G. 53, 61, Markan 65, Leifsson 80)*, Haukar 3
(Ingólfsson 31, Johnson 67og, Eidsson 85)
Valur 0, FH 1 *(Ásgeirsson 90+1)*

SEMI-FINALS

(2/9/07)
FH 3 *(Ásgeirsson 52, Gudmundsson T. 100, Gudnason 120)*, Breidablik
(Rajcomar 65) (aet)

(3/9/07)
Fjölnir 2 *(Gudmundsson G. 56p, Björnsson 113)*, Fylkir 1 *(Ingason 43)*

FINAL

(6/10/07)
Laugardalsvöllur, Reykjavík
FH HAFNARFJÖRDUR 2 *(Gudmundsson M. 17, 105)*
FJÖLNIR REYKJAVÍK 1 *(Gudmundsson G. 86p)*
(aet)
Referee - *Markússon*
FH – *Lárusson, Saevarsson, Gardarsson, Nielsen, Bjarnason, Ásgeirsso Vidarsson, Gunnlaugsson B. (Ólafsson 68), Gudmundsson M. (Gudnas 112), Gunnlaugsson A. (Vilhjálmsson 87), Gudmundsson T.*
FJÖLNIR – *Ingason, Einarsson, Gunnarsson R., Ásgeirsson, Gunnarsso Leifsson (Ástthórsson 82), Gunnarsson I., Rúnarsson (Johnson 90), Gudmundsson G., Hákonarson (Ásgrímsson 96), Markan.*

Historic double for Beitar Jerusalem

season when all of their principal rivals appeared be taking a year's sabbatical, Beitar Jerusalem FC nfirmed themselves as the top dogs in Israel's Ligat 'Al, successfully defending the championship with om to spare. They also added a first State Cup tory for 19 years to complete the first double in e club's history.

e season did not start well, with immediate mination from Europe by Danish club FC København the second qualifying round of the UEFA Champions ague. Club owner Arkady Gaydamak had made no cret of his desire and ambition to see Beitar dining at rope's top table, and to this end he had sacked 06/07 title-winning coach Yossi Mizrahi and replaced n with the more experienced European campaigner hak Shum. But Shum's first two competitive games re the 1-0 defeat in Copenhagen and the second-leg draw in Jerusalem that put an end to the European eam for another season.

ff to a flier

th nothing else to distract them, Beitar set about conquering domestic terrain. New Brazilian striker mulo proved an instant hit. Recruited too late to face benhavn, he fired Beitar to a succession of wins in e league. With prospective challengers Maccabi Haifa , Maccabi Tel-Aviv FC and Hapoel Tel-Aviv FC all aking horrendous starts, Beitar's opening burst of six ns and a draw in the opening seven games set them for a trouble-free run to the title. Their first defeat d not arrive until mid-January, and such was their erwhelming superiority over the rest that they were ised to wrap things up as early as round 28 (of 33) th victory in a home fixture against relegation-reatened Maccabi Herzliya FC.

at, however, was when Beitar's fans decided to spoil the fun. They had been warned by the police not to vade the pitch at the Teddi stadium to celebrate the le triumph, but with Beitar leading 1-0 and four inutes still to play, that is exactly what they did. Worse still, once on the playing surface they refused to budge, forcing the referee to abandon the game. Gaydamak, among others, was furious and launched a scathing attack on the club's unruly followers. The ball was now in the court of the Israeli FA's disciplinary committee. Their initial decision was to award the match to Herzliya, but the other relegation contenders complained that this was giving their rivals an unfair advantage and after further appeals and counter-appeals, which forced the postponement of the entire 29th round of games, it was finally decided that the fixture would be replayed - over a month after its original date.

By then, as far as Beitar were concerned, the match was irrelevant, because three days earlier, on Saturday 17 May, they clinched the league title by defeating second-placed Maccabi Netanya FC 3-0. Having lost their three previous games, the win was met with

Double winners Beitar Jerusalem (stripes) in State Cup action against Bnei Sakhnin

ISRAEL

Israel Football Association (IFA)

Ramat Gan Stadium
299 Aba Hilell Street
IL-52134 Ramat Gan
tel - +972 3 617 15 03
fax - +972 3 570 20 44
website – www.football.org.il
email - info@football.org.il
Year of Formation - 1928
President – Abraham Luzon
Press Officer – Gil Levanoni
Stadium – Ramat Gan, Tel-Aviv (40,000)

INTERNATIONAL TOURNAMENT APPEARANCES
FIFA World Cup - (1) 1970.

TOP FIVE ALL-TIME CAPS
Arik Benado (94); Alon Harazi (88); Amir Schelach (85); Mordechay Spiegler (84); Nir Klinger (83)

TOP FIVE ALL-TIME GOALS
Mordechay Spiegler (32); Yehushua Feigenboim (24); Ronen Harazi (23); Nahum Stelmach (22); Gideon Damti (2C

NATIONAL TEAM RESULTS 2007/08

22/8/07	Belarus	A	Minsk	1-2	*Gershon (29p)*
8/9/07	England (ECQ)	A	Wembley	0-3	
13/10/07	Croatia (ECQ)	A	Zagreb	0-1	
17/10/07	Belarus	H	Tel-Aviv	2-1	*Baruchyan (38), Alberman (72)*
17/11/07	Russia (ECQ)	H	Tel-Aviv	2-1	*Barda (10), Golan (90+2)*
21/11/07	FYR Macedonia (ECQ)	H	Tel-Aviv	1-0	*Barda (35)*
6/2/08	Romania	H	Tel-Aviv	1-0	*Golan (25)*
26/3/08	Chile	H	Tel-Aviv	1-0	*Benayoun (30)*

some relief by the Beitar faithful and there was no damaging pitch invasion to ruin the festivities on a famous day for the Gaydamak family, with Arkady's son Aleksandr, the owner of Portsmouth FC, having overseen his club's FA Cup triumph at Wembley earlier in the day.

Penalty revenge

The championship-clinching victory over Netanya came four days after Beitar had achieved the first leg of the double by defeating Hapoel Tel-Aviv in the State Cup final at the Ramat Gan stadium. Having lost on penalties to the same opponents in the finals of 1999 and 2000, there was sweet vengeance for the team from the Holy City as they made it third time lucky by claiming victory by the same method, winning 5-4 on spot-kicks after a 0-0 draw. Season's stalwarts Gal Alberman, Michael Zandberg, Idan Tal, Toto Tamuz and, lastly, ex-Hapoel Tel-Aviv skipper Shimon Gershon all converted for Beitar before goalkeeper Tvrtko Kale made the decisive save from Reuven Oved to give his club the trophy for the sixth time and deny the opposition a State Cup hat-trick.

The confirmation of Beitar's league triumph the following weekend enabled Hapoel Tel-Aviv to seal a place in the 2008/09 UEFA Cup, but there would be no European participation for city rivals Maccabi Tel-Aviv, whose league campaign was so off-beam that they only just avoided relegation. It was particularly bad at the start, which was not surprising as the team's confidence had been shattered by early European embarrassments against FC Santa Coloma from Andorra and Turkish second division club Kayseri Erciyesspor. Maccabi Haifa's fortunes were not dissimilar, and long-serving coach Roni Levi's post-season departure was not unexpected after the Green

TIONAL TEAM APPEARANCES 2007/08

– Dror KASHTAN	1/10/44		Blr	ENG	CRO	Blr	RUS	MKD	Rou	Chi	Caps	Goals
AWAT	17/10/77	Deportivo (ESP)	G46	G			G	G	G46	G46	34	-
SHPUNGIN	3/4/87	M. Tel-Aviv	D	D			D	D			8	-
N HAIM	31/3/82	Chelsea (ENG)	D	D	D	D46	D	D	D46		40	-
n GERSHON	6/10/77	Beitar Jerusalem	D65	D	D	D87			s46	D	50	4
IV	16/3/81	Beitar Jerusalem	D46	D			D	D	D	D	14	-
BADIR	12/3/74	H. Tel-Aviv	M	M							74	12
AL	13/9/75	Beitar Jerusalem	M80	M							69	6
BERMAN	17/4/83	Beitar Jerusalem	M		M	M	M			M	18	1
BENAYOUN	5/5/80	Liverpool (ENG)	M	M	M				M	M78	63	15
ITZHAKI	25/9/84	Beitar Jerusalem /Genk (BEL)	A46	A46			A62	A72	A46	A46	8	1
to COLAUTTI	24/5/82	Mönchengladbach (GER)	A69					A55			9	6
VIDOVICH	17/12/76	M. Haifa	s46		G	G46			s46	s46	46	-
BEN DAYAN	27/11/78	M. Netanya	s46						D		13	-
TOAMA	9/8/79	Standard (BEL)	s46								6	-
RUL	18/9/80	M. Netanya	s65			s46			D67	D	5	-
AMUZ	1/4/88	Beitar Jerusalem	s69	s46	s67	s69					10	2
EFAELOV	26/4/86	M. Haifa	s80								1	-
ENADO	5/12/73	Beitar Jerusalem		M57							94	-
KATAN	27/1/81	M. Haifa		A73							31	5
GOLAN	4/10/82	M. Petach-Tikva /Lokeren (BEL)		s57	s58	A77	s69		A60	A46	24	3
el ZANDBERG	16/4/80	Beitar Jerusalem		s73							19	4
IESHUMAR	10/8/83	M. Haifa			D	D					2	-
NTEBI	1/8/74	H. Tel-Aviv			D	D					11	-
COHEN	4/3/84	M. Netanya /Bolton (ENG)			M	M	M	M	M	M	6	-
n BARUCHYAN	20/3/85	Beitar Jerusalem			M58	M63		s72	s60	s46	5	1
v BARDA	15/12/81	Genk (BEL)			A76	A	A	A	A	A75	7	2
ALILI	18/6/79	Sivasspor (TUR)			A67	s77					29	7
e OHAYON	24/5/83	Winterthur (SUI) /Ashdod			s76	s63	s64	M	M67	s75	6	-
AHAR	10/8/89	QPR (ENG)				A69	A69	s55			7	2
STRAUBER	20/8/74	M. Netanya				s46					7	-
HAIMOVICH	7/4/83	Bnei Yehuda				s87					1	-
KEINAN	15/9/84	M. Haifa					D	D			3	-
BUZAGLO	14/1/88	Bnei Sakhnin					M64	M46			2	-
BEN SHUSHAN	23/5/85	Beitar Jerusalem					s62	s46	s46	s46	12	2
SABAN	17/2/80	M. Netanya							s67	D	13	-
GAZAL	9/6/82	M. Tel-Aviv							s67		9	-
SULIN	9/4/91	Barcelona B (ESP)								s78	1	-

ended up in fifth place 20 points off the summit.

The bigger clubs' misfortunes inevitably meant happy times for some of the smaller fry. Perhaps the most heartening story was the third-place finish – and UEFA Cup qualification – of newly promoted Hapoel Kiryat Shmona FC, the team from the northern town that was heavily bombarded by the Hezbollah during the Lebanese border conflict of summer 2006. Young coach Ran Ben Shimon made such an impact that he was signed up by Maccabi Tel-Aviv.

Another team from the north, Arab club Bnei Sakhnin FC, also surpassed themselves by finishing fourth to qualify for the UEFA Intertoto Cup. Their main claim to fame was a pair of victories from each of their two visits to Jerusalem, with young star of the season, 20-year-old striker Maor Buzaglo, finding the net in both matches, the first a stunning last-minute winner to end Beitar's unbeaten run. He linked up superbly with Armenian forward Ilya Jevruyan, scoring nine goals and adding 12 assists in his (maximum) 33 appearances. Both Buzaglo and Javruyan left to work under Ben Shimon at Maccabi Tel-Aviv in 2008/09.

Perhaps the club with most to celebrate was Bnei Yehuda Tel-Aviv FC, who staged an astonishing comeback from the dead to rescue themselves from relegation. After 24 matches the club were bottom of the league, eleven points from safety and without a coach following the resignation of Eli Cohen. But in stepped goalkeeping coach Yacob Assiag to launch the most remarkable fightback, steering the club to eight victories in those last nine matches. They need all of them, too, eventually finishing one point above the drop zone, which was filled by Herzliya and the unfortunate Hapoel Kfar-Saba FC who, despite boasting the league's top scorer, 15-goal Ghanaian striker Samuel Yeboah, were relegated instead of Maccabi Petach-Tikva FC on goal difference.

World Cup optimism

Israel's national team did not qualify for UEFA EURO 2008™, but Dror Kashtan's team put up a magnifice fight. Back-to-back defeats in England (0-3) and Croatia (0-1) ended their hopes but they recovered well – despite losing captain Yossi Benayoun to inju - and even offered England a massive helping hand by defeating Russia 2-1 with a last-minute Omer Golan strike at Ramat Gan in their penultimate fixture. But after Steve McClaren's team lost to Croatia, thus spurning Israel's olive branch, and Kashtan's men beat FYR Macedonia, Israel were abl to claim proudly that they had accumulated the same number of points as England over the 12-match programme. Faced with a much easier 2010 FIFA World Cup group, in which UEFA EURO 2008™ flops Greece and Switzerland are their principal adversaries, there is genuine and justifiable optimis that Israel can end 40 years of hurt and qualify for the finals in South Africa.

DOMESTIC LEAGUE 2007/08

LIGAT HA'AL FINAL TABLE

	Pld	Home					Away					Total					
		W	D	L	F	A	W	D	L	F	A	W	D	L	F	A	Pts
1 Beitar Jerusalem FC	33	12	2	3	36	9	8	5	3	25	14	20	7	6	61	23	67
2 Maccabi Netanya FC	33	7	5	5	19	14	9	5	2	21	10	16	10	7	40	24	58
3 Hapoel Ironi Kiryat Shmona FC	33	10	5	2	26	16	5	6	5	17	18	15	11	7	43	34	56
4 Bnei Sakhnin FC	33	6	7	4	18	16	9	3	4	17	13	15	10	8	35	29	55
5 Maccabi Haifa FC	33	8	4	5	21	13	5	4	7	17	14	13	8	12	38	27	47
6 Maccabi Tel-Aviv FC	33	7	5	4	20	17	4	3	10	23	26	11	8	14	43	43	41
7 Hapoel Tel-Aviv FC	33	7	1	8	16	16	5	4	8	19	24	12	5	16	35	40	41
8 FC Ashdod	33	8	3	5	23	20	3	3	11	13	32	11	6	16	36	52	39
9 Bnei Yehuda Tel-Aviv FC	33	6	2	8	19	23	5	3	9	12	20	11	5	17	31	43	38
10 Maccabi Petach-Tikva FC	33	6	4	7	16	20	4	3	9	12	19	10	7	16	28	39	37
11 Hapoel Kfar-Saba FC	33	2	6	8	17	30	7	4	6	20	24	9	10	14	37	54	37
12 Maccabi Herzliya FC	33	2	4	10	11	23	5	5	7	21	28	7	9	17	32	51	30

TOP GOALSCORER

15 Samuel YEBOAH (H. Kfar-Saba

12 Dimitar Ivanov MAKRIEV (Ashc
RÔMULO Marcos (Beitar Jerus
Yannick KAMANAN (M. Tel-Avi
Moshe BIRON (Bnei Yehuda)

10 Yero BELLO (H. Ironi Kiryat)
Ilya JEVRUYAN (Bnei Sakhnin)

9 Yossi SHIVHON (M. Tel-Aviv)
Maor BUZAGLO (Bnei Sakhnin
Yuval AVIDOR (H. Ironi Kiryat)

CLUB-BY-CLUB

FC ASHDOD

Coach – Alon Hazan; (19/4/08) (Haim Revivo); (14/5/08) Yossi Mizrahi

Founded - 1999

07				
/8	M. Tel-Aviv	a	1-1	*Shriki*
'8	M. Haifa	h	1-0	*Holtzman*
/9	H. Ironi Kiryat	a	1-2	*Gosso*
/9	M. Netanya	h	1-6	*Nachum*
10	Beitar Jerusalem	a	0-5	
/10	Bnei Yehuda	h	3-0	*Nachum, Suffo, Shriki*
/10	H. Tel-Aviv	a	2-0	*Shriki, Offir*
11	M. Herzliya	h	0-1	
/11	Bnei Sakhnin	a	0-3	
/11	H. Kfar Saba	a	1-3	*Shriki*
12	M. Petach-Tikva	h	1-3	*Masudi*
12	M. Tel-Aviv	h	0-0	
/12	M. Haifa	a	0-3	
08				
1	H. Ironi Kiryat	h	0-0	
/1	M. Netanya	a	0-3	
/1	Beitar Jerusalem	h	1-2	*Revivo*
/1	Bnei Yehuda	a	2-3	*Makriev, Shriki*
2	H. Tel-Aviv	h	1-1	*Makriev*
2	M. Herzliya	a	1-1	*Shriki*
/2	Bnei Sakhnin	h	3-1	*Ohayon, Makriev, og (Colma)*
/2	H. Kfar Saba	h	2-4	*Makriev, Shriki*
3	M. Petach-Tikva	a	0-0	
3	M. Petach-Tikva	a	3-0	*og (Hadar), Makriev, Shriki*
/3	H. Kfar Saba	h	3-1	*Makriev 2, Ohayon*
/3	M. Tel-Aviv	a	0-2	
/3	H. Tel-Aviv	h	2-1	*Makriev 2*
4	M. Herzliya	a	0-2	
/4	Bnei Yehuda	a	0-2	
5	Beitar Jerusalem	h	1-0	*Checkul*
/5	M. Netanya	a	0-1	
/5	H. Ironi Kiryat	h	2-0	*Makriev 2*
/5	Bnei Sakhnin	a	2-1	*Ohayon 2*
/5	M. Haifa	h	2-0	*Makriev, Revivo (p)*

No	Name	Nat	Pos	Aps	(s)	Gls
	Sammy ADJEI	GHA	G	28		
	Andrés AIMAR	ARG	M		(3)	
	Eyal ALMOCHNINO		D	6		
	ANDRÉ LUIZ de Moura	BRA	D		(2)	
	Micki ATTIA		D	10	(1)	
	Moshe BEN LULU		A		(7)	
	Rahamim CHECKUL		M	14	(10)	1
	Kobi DAJANI		M	12	(12)	
	Orel EDRY		M		(1)	
5	Cristian GONZÁLEZ	URU	D	20		
7	Jean-Jacques GOSSO	CIV	M	23	(4)	1
	Shay HOLTZMAN		A	11	(10)	1
	Vedran JEŠE	CRO	D	28		
3	Ahmed KASUM		M	7	(4)	
2	Amir LAVIE		M		(5)	
	Dimitar Ivanov MAKRIEV	BUL	A	18		12
	Idan MALIHI		M	7	(1)	
0	Alain MASUDI	COD	M	11	(3)	1
4	Nir NACHUM		A	8	(12)	2
8	Yossi OFFIR		M	22	(6)	1
	Moshe OHAYON		M	15		4
0	Lior REUVEN		D	15		
0	David REVIVO		M	28	(1)	2
27	Idan SADE		A		(2)	
1	Yossi SHEKEL		G	5		
14	Idan SHRIKI		A	29	(1)	8
11	Patrick SUFFO	CMR	A	4		1
6	Tomer TAYAR		M		(3)	
16	Adir TOBUL		D	31		
3	Idan TZION		D		(1)	
20	Maor ZOHAR		D	11	(4)	

BEITAR JERUSALEM FC

Coach – Itzhak Shum

Founded - 1939

MAJOR HONOURS: Israeli League - (6) 1987, 1993, 1997, 1998, 2007, 2008; Israeli Cup - (6) 1976, 1979, 1985, 1986, 1989, 2008.

2007				
19/8	Bnei Yehuda	h	3-0	*Tamuz, Zandberg, Álvarez*
26/8	H. Tel-Aviv	a	2-1	*Rômulo, Itzhaki*
15/9	M. Herzliya	h	4-2	*Rômulo 2, Baruchyan 2*
30/9	Bnei Sakhnin	a	2-2	*Rômulo, Itzhaki*
7/10	Ashdod	h	5-0	*Rômulo 2, Baruchyan, Zandberg, Tal*
20/10	M. Petach-Tikva	a	2-1	*Ben Shushan 2*
28/10	M. Tel-Aviv	h	2-0	*Itzhaki, Boateng*
4/11	M. Haifa	a	0-0	
10/11	H. Ironi Kiryat	h	0-0	
25/11	M. Netanya	a	1-0	*Rômulo*
1/12	H. Kfar Saba	h	4-0	*Tal, Rômulo, Tamuz, Alberman*
9/12	Bnei Yehuda	a	3-0	*Tal (p), Alberman 2*
16/12	H. Tel-Aviv	h	1-0	*Álvarez*
2008				
5/1	M. Herzliya	a	1-1	*Tal*
12/1	Bnei Sakhnin	h	0-1	
20/1	Ashdod	a	2-1	*Rômulo, Baruchyan*
26/1	M. Petach-Tikva	h	2-1	*Ben Shushan, Baruchyan*
3/2	M. Tel-Aviv	a	0-0	
16/2	H. Ironi Kiryat	a	3-0	*Rômulo, Alberman, Ben Shushan*
19/2	M. Haifa	h	1-0	*Ben Shushan*
24/2	M. Netanya	h	2-0	*Tal, Alberman*
2/3	H. Kfar Saba	a	1-1	*Rômulo*
8/3	M. Haifa	a	1-0	*Boateng*
15/3	M. Petach-Tikva	h	4-0	*Ben Shushan, Baruchyan, Tal, Rômulo (p)*
22/3	H. Kfar Saba	a	4-0	*Boateng, Ziv, Alberman, Tal*
30/3	M. Tel-Aviv	h	1-1	*Boateng*
6/4	H. Tel Aviv	a	1-3	*Zandberg*
5/5	Ashdod	a	0-1	
10/5	Bnei Yehuda	h	0-1	
17/5	M. Netanya	h	3-0	*Baruchyan (p), Zandberg, Tamuz*
20/5	M. Herzliya	h	3-1	*Viza, Baruchyan, Alberman*
24/5	H. Ironi Kiryat	a	2-3	*Tamuz 2*
30/5	Bnei Sakhnin	h	1-2	*Tamuz*

No	Name	Nat	Pos	Aps	(s)	Gls
18	Gal ALBERMAN		M	25	(3)	7
2	Cristian ÁLVAREZ	CHI	D	25	(1)	2
3	David AMSALEM		D	5	(6)	
26	Hen AZRIEL		A	3	(15)	
8	Aviram BARUCHYAN		M	20	(12)	8

No	Name	Nat	Pos	Aps	(s)	Gls
7	Amit BEN SHUSHAN		A	18	(8)	6
6	Tomer BEN-YOSEF		D	10	(2)	
4	Arik BENADO		D	29		
20	Derek BOATENG	GHA	M	31		4
23	Tal ELMISHALI		A		(1)	
5	Shimon GERSHON		D	27	(1)	
29	Shay HADAD		D		(1)	
9	Barak ITZHAKI		A	9		3
1	Tvrtko KALE	CRO	G	32		
12	Shemoel KOZOKIN		D	4	(1)	
23	Milovan MIROSEVIC	CHI	M	1	(8)	
28	RÔMULO Marques Antoneli	BRA	A	24	(5)	12
22	Sagie SHTRAUS		G	1		
11	Idan TAL		M	26	(4)	7
10	Toto TAMUZ		A	10	(17)	6
21	Idan VERED		M	1	(1)	
17	César Junior VIZA	PER	M	7	(8)	1
15	Michael ZANDBERG		M	24	(3)	4
14	Yoav ZIV		D	31		1

BNEI SAKHNIN FC

Coach – Elisha Levi

Founded - 1993

2007				
18/8	M. Haifa	a	1-0	*Ganaym H.*
25/8	H. Ironi Kiryat	h	0-0	
15/9	M. Netanya	a	2-1	*Yeye, Buzaglo*
30/9	Beitar Jerusalem	h	2-2	*Jevruyan, Buzaglo*
6/10	Bnei Yehuda	a	0-3	
20/10	H. Tel-Aviv	h	1-0	*Buzaglo*
27/10	M. Herzliya	a	1-0	*Jevruyan*
3/11	H. Kfar Saba	a	0-0	
10/11	Ashdod	h	3-0	*Ganaym H., Jevruyan, Buzaglo*
24/11	M. Petach-Tikva	a	0-2	
2/12	M. Tel-Aviv	h	3-2	*Ganaym H., Jevruyan, Buzaglo*
8/12	M. Haifa	h	1-1	*Ganaym H.*
15/12	H. Ironi Kiryat	a	0-0	
2008				
5/1	M. Netanya	h	0-0	
12/1	Beitar Jerusalem	a	1-0	*Buzaglo*
19/1	Bnei Yehuda	h	0-0	
26/1	H. Tel-Aviv	a	1-0	*Apostu*
2/2	M. Herzliya	h	0-3	
9/2	H. Kfar Saba	h	1-1	*Colma*
16/2	Ashdod	a	1-3	*Apostu*
23/2	M. Petach-Tikva	h	1-0	*Apostu*
1/3	M. Tel-Aviv	a	0-0	
8/3	M. Netanya	h	1-1	*Ganaym B.*
15/3	H. Ironi Kiryat	a	1-0	*Jevruyan*
22/3	Bnei Yehuda	h	1-3	*Buzaglo*
29/3	M. Haifa	h	1-0	*Jevruyan*
5/4	M. Petach-Tikva	a	4-0	*Apostu, Jevruyan 2, Abu Ria*
12/4	H. Kfar Saba	h	2-0	*Buzaglo, Jevruyan*
3/5	M. Tel-Aviv	a	1-3	*Abu Ria*
10/5	H. Tel-Aviv	h	0-1	
17/5	M. Herzliya	a	2-0	*Jevruyan, Ganaym H.*
24/5	Ashdod	h	1-2	*Yeye*
30/5	Beitar Jerusalem	a	2-1	*Buzaglo, Apostu*

No	Name	Nat	Pos	Aps	(s)	Gls
13	Mohamad ABU RIA		M	2	(14)	2
8	Ala'a ABU SALACH		M	4	(11)	
26	Radu Bogdan APOSTU	ROU	A	16	(4)	5
14	Haim BANON		M	4	(11)	
24	Geva BARKAY		D	1	(5)	
11	Maor BUZAGLO		A	33		9
28	Islam CNA'AN		D	2	(6)	
1	Meir COHEN		G	33		
20	John Jairo COLMA	COL	M	26		1
12	Bassem GANAYM		D	31		1
17	Hamed GANAYM		M	26	(5)	5
16	Haled HALAULA		M	29	(2)	
10	Ilya JEVRUYAN	ARM	A	30	(1)	10
25	Leonid KRUPNIK	UKR	D	31		
19	LIANDRO Vilas Boas Simioni	BRA	A		(3)	
18	Ali OTMAN		D	1	(16)	
7	Aabed RABACH		D	33		
21	Musa SHA'ABAN		A		(5)	
5	Łukasz SURMA	POL	M	30		
9	Liron VILNER		A	1	(7)	
6	Lemkebe YEYE	CIV	D	30		2

BNEI YEHUDA TEL-AVIV FC

Coach – Nitzan Shirazi; (2/12/07) (Yacob Assiag); (15/12/07) E Cohen; (18/3/08) Yacob Assiag

Founded - 1935

MAJOR HONOURS: Israeli League - (1) 1990; Israeli Cup - (2) 1968, 198

2007				
19/8	Beitar Jerusalem	a	0-3	
25/8	H. Kfar Saba	a	0-0	
15/9	H. Tel-Aviv	h	1-1	*Biton M.*
29/9	M. Herzliya	a	2-0	*Biton M., og (Azaria)*
6/10	Bnei Sakhnin	h	3-0	*Biton M., Baldut (p), Duarte*
20/10	Ashdod	a	0-3	
27/10	M. Petach-Tikva	h	0-1	
3/11	M. Tel-Aviv	a	1-3	*Rozen*
10/11	M. Haifa	h	0-3	
24/11	H. Ironi Kiryat	a	1-2	*Rozen*
1/12	M. Netanya	h	1-2	*Lukman*
8/12	Beitar Jerusalem	h	0-3	
15/12	H. Kfar Saba	h	0-2	
2008				
5/1	H. Tel-Aviv	a	0-1	
12/1	M. Herzliya	h	0-1	
19/1	Bnei Sakhnin	a	0-0	
26/1	Ashdod	h	3-2	*Bardon 2, Biton M.*
2/2	M. Petach-Tikva	a	0-1	
9/2	M. Tel-Aviv	h	0-4	
16/2	M. Haifa	a	0-1	
23/2	H. Ironi Kiryat	h	1-1	*Atar*
1/3	M. Netanya	a	0-0	
8/3	H. Ironi Kiryat	a	0-2	
15/3	H. Tel-Aviv	h	2-3	*Bardon, Atar*
22/3	Bnei Sakhnin	a	3-1	*Atar 2, Cahlon*
29/3	M. Herzliya	h	2-0	*Baldut, Biton M.*
5/4	M. Haifa	a	1-0	*Biton M.*
12/4	Ashdod	h	2-0	*Cahlon, Biton M.*
3/5	M. Petach-Tikva	a	1-0	*og (Pesser)*
10/5	Beitar Jerusalem	a	1-0	*Biton M.*
17/5	H. Kfar Saba	h	3-0	*Biton M. 2, Kovačević*
24/5	M. Netanya	a	2-3	*Baldut, Biton M*
31/5	M. Tel-Aviv	h	1-0	*Biton M*

No	Name	Nat	Pos	Aps	(s)	Gls
10	Eli ABARBANEL		M	19	(6)	
33	Nil ABARBANEL		G	5	(2)	
3	Salem ABU SIAM		D	16	(2)	
1	Bamidele AIYENUGBA	NGA	G	28		
19	Eliran ASAO		A	1	(3)	
11	Eliran ATAR		A	11	(9)	4
15	Yair AZULAY		D	9	(8)	
17	Itzhak AZOZ		D	19	(4)	

Name	Nat	Pos	Aps	(s)	Gls
Assi BALDUT		M	29		3
Cédric BARDON	FRA	A	17		3
Eli BITON		M	6	(16)	
Moshe BITON		A	29	(2)	12
Tamir CAHLON		M	6	(12)	2
José DUARTE	BRA	A	12	(2)	1
Ze'ev HAIMOVICH		D	33		
Mohamad HATARI		A		(1)	
Selver HODŽIĆ	BIH	D	10	(2)	
Hrvoje KOVAČEVIĆ	CRO	D	28	(3)	1
Imoro LUKMAN	GHA	D	23	(5)	1
Idan MALIHI		M	4	(1)	
Milan MARTINOVIĆ	SRB	D	15		
Oz RALLY		M	23	(8)	
Yossi ROZEN		M	8	(5)	2
Liron ZAIRI		M	12	(3)	

HAPOEL IRONI KIRYAT SHMONA FC

Coach – Ran Ben Shimon

Founded - 1894

07				
/8	M. Herzliya	h	3-0	*Bello, Lavie, Hasarma*
/8	Bnei Sakhnin	a	0-0	
/9	Ashdod	h	2-1	*Amungwa, Hasarma*
/9	M. Petach-Tikva	a	1-3	*Bello*
10	M. Tel-Aviv	h	1-0	*Avidor*
/10	M. Haifa	a	0-1	
/10	H. Kfar Saba	h	2-2	*Bello, Avidor*
11	M. Netanya	h	0-0	
/11	Beitar Jerusalem	a	0-0	
/11	Bnei Yehuda	h	2-1	*Amasha, Suan*
12	H. Tel-Aviv	a	1-0	*Avidor*
12	M. Herzliya	a	3-1	*Bello 3*
/12	Bnei Sakhnin	h	0-0	
08				
1	Ashdod	a	0-0	
/1	M. Petach-Tikva	h	2-1	*Suan, Hasarma*
/1	M. Tel-Aviv	a	2-2	*Avidor 2*
/1	M. Haifa	h	1-1	*Amungwa*
2	H. Kfar Saba	a	3-2	*Avidor, Lavie, Tzarfati (p)*
2	M. Netanya	a	0-0	
/2	Beitar Jerusalem	h	0-3	
/2	Bnei Yehuda	a	1-1	*Avidor*
3	H. Tel-Aviv	h	2-1	*Ofori-Quaye, Guel*
3	Bnei Yehuda	h	2-0	*Tzarfati, Bello*
/3	Bnei Sakhnin	h	0-1	
/3	M. Haifa	a	1-2	*Bello*
/3	M. Petach-Tikva	h	1-0	*Avidor*
4	H. Kfar Saba	a	3-1	*Guel, Lavie, Suan*
/4	M. Tel-Aviv	h	3-1	*Bello 2, Tzarfati (p)*
5	H. Tel-Aviv	a	0-2	
/5	M. Herzliya	h	2-2	*Biton, Ofori-Quaye*
/5	Ashdod	a	0-2	
/5	Beitar Jerusalem	h	3-2	*Ofori-Quaye, Kojok, Avidor*
6	M. Netanya	a	2-1	*Hasarma, Ofori-Quaye*

No	Name	Nat	Pos	Aps	(s)	Gls
4	Wiam AMASHA		M	13	(16)	1
2	Daniel AMOS		G	8		
5	Emmanuel AMUNGWA	CMR	A	25	(7)	2
1	Yuval AVIDOR		A	27	(4)	9
	Barak BACHAR		D	32		
	Yero BELLO	NGA	A	20	(7)	10
0	Beni BEN ZAKEN		M		(9)	
3	Yossi BITTON		D	2	(2)	1
1	Yossi DORA		M	4	(19)	
	Shavit ELIMELECH		G	25		
2	Tchiressoua GUEL	CIV	M	33		2
17	Salah HASARMA		D	33		4
4	Ran KOJOK		D	3	(4)	1
5	Yaniv LAVIE		D	31		3
15	Nsimba MUKANU	COD	M	1	(2)	
6	Amir NUSBAUM		D	31		
24	Peter OFORI-QUAYE	GHA	A	16	(9)	4
16	Maor PERETZ		D	1		
20	Adrian ROCHET		M		(8)	
27	Abbas SUAN		M	29		3
15	Tommer SWISSA		A		(6)	
8	Guy TZARFATI		M	29		3

HAPOEL KFAR-SABA FC

Coach – Eli Ohana

Founded - 1936

MAJOR HONOURS: Israeli League - (1) 1982; Israeli Cup - (3) 1975, 1980, 1990.

2007				
18/8	M. Petach-Tikva	a	1-0	*Luz*
25/8	Bnei Yehuda	h	0-0	
17/9	M. Tel-Aviv	a	1-0	*Yeboah*
29/9	H. Tel-Aviv	h	1-1	*Yeboah*
6/10	M. Haifa	a	1-2	*Agbor*
20/10	M. Herzliya	h	2-3	*Luz, Yeboah*
27/10	H. Ironi Kiryat	a	2-2	*Lira, Israilevich*
3/11	Bnei Sakhnin	h	0-0	
10/11	M. Netanya	a	3-2	*Yeboah 2, Yadin*
24/11	Ashdod	h	3-1	*Yeboah 2, Yadin*
1/12	Beitar Jerusalem	a	0-4	
8/12	M. Petach-Tikva	h	0-0	
15/12	Bnei Yehuda	a	2-0	*Zarko, Yeboah*
2008				
5/1	M. Tel-Aviv	h	0-3	
12/1	H. Tel-Aviv	a	2-1	*Luz 2 (1p)*
19/1	M. Haifa	h	0-3	
26/1	M. Herzliya	a	0-0	
2/2	H. Ironi Kiryat	h	2-3	*Uzan, Israilevich*
9/2	Bnei Sakhnin	a	1-1	*Douglas*
16/2	M. Netanya	h	1-2	*González*
23/2	Ashdod	a	4-2	*Yeboah 3, Douglas*
2/3	Beitar Jerusalem	h	1-1	*Dayan*
8/3	M. Herzliya	h	3-3	*Luz (p), Israilevich, Yeboah*
15/3	Ashdod	a	1-3	*Yeboah*
22/3	Beitar Jerusalem	h	0-4	
29/3	M. Netanya	a	1-1	*Douglas*
5/4	H. Ironi Kiryat	h	1-3	*Knafo*
12/4	Bnei Sakhnin	a	0-2	
3/5	M. Haifa	h	1-0	*og (Crosa)*
10/5	M. Petach-Tikva	a	0-1	
17/5	Bnei Yehuda	a	0-3	
24/5	M. Tel-Aviv	h	2-3	*Israilevich, Yeboah*
31/5	H. Tel-Aviv	a	1-0	*Yeboah*

No	Name	Nat	Pos	Aps	(s)	Gls
17	Yahuza ABUBAKARI	GHA	M	23	(6)	
28	Julius AGBOR	CMR	A	1	(2)	1
15	Avi AVINU		A	1	(13)	
8	Guy DAYAN		A	1	(7)	1
5	DOUGLAS da Silva	BRA	D	31		3
11	Kfir EDRI		M	2		
23	Bill GONZÁLEZ	CRC	A	8	(9)	1
22	Guy HAIMOV		G	2		
10	Guillermo ISRAILEVICH	ARG	M	30	(1)	5
16	Gil KAIN		D	6	(4)	
99	Avi KNAFO		A	19	(11)	1
1	Ohad LEVITTE		G	31		
6	Lirodiou Goncalves "LIRA"	BRA	D	25		1
9	Benzion LUZ		M	26	(2)	5

No	Name	Nat	Pos	Aps	(s)	Gls
19	Maor MELICSOHN		M	10	(5)	
21	Kobi MOYAL		M	11	(8)	
15	Eyal SHEN		M		(1)	
7	Idan SHUM		D	9	(4)	
14	Eliran SIMON		D	12	(5)	
4	Offer TALKER		D	6	(8)	
77	Uri UZAN		D	32		1
26	Avihai YADIN		M	19		1
20	Samuel YEBOAH	GHA	A	33		15
18	Liron ZARKO		M	25	(4)	1

HAPOEL TEL-AVIV FC

Coach – Guy Luzon; (26/11/07) (Yossi Abuksis); (4/12/07) Eli Guttman

Founded - 1928

MAJOR HONOURS: Israeli League - (11) 1934, 1935, 1940, 1943, 1957, 1966, 1969, 1981, 1986, 1988, 2000; Israeli Cup - (11) 1928, 1934, 1937, 1938, 1940, 1960, 1972, 1999, 2000, 2006, 2007.

2007				
20/8	M. Netanya	a	0-0	
26/8	Beitar Jerusalem	h	1-2	*Fábio Júnior*
15/9	Bnei Yehuda	a	1-1	*Dos Santos*
29/9	H. Kfar Saba	a	1-1	*Oved*
8/10	M. Herzliya	h	0-2	
20/10	Bnei Sakhnin	a	0-1	
29/10	Ashdod	h	0-2	
3/11	M. Petach-Tikva	a	1-2	*Badir*
11/11	M. Tel-Aviv	h	1-0	*Fábio Júnior*
24/11	M. Haifa	a	0-2	
3/12	H. Ironi Kiryat	h	0-1	
8/12	M. Netanya	h	0-1	
15/12	Beitar Jerusalem	a	0-1	
2008				
5/1	Bnei Yehuda	h	1-0	*Fábio Júnior*
12/1	H. Kfar Saba	h	1-2	*og (González)*
19/1	M. Herzliya	a	3-2	*Dego 2 (1p), Telkiyski*
26/1	Bnei Sakhnin	h	0-1	
2/2	Ashdod	a	1-1	*Arbeitman*
9/2	M. Petach-Tikva	h	2-1	*Telkiyski, Natcho*
17/2	M. Tel-Aviv	a	3-1	*Telkiyski, Fábio Júnior 2*
23/2	M. Haifa	h	2-0	*Natcho, Arbeitman*
1/3	H. Ironi Kiryat	a	1-2	*Dego*
9/3	M. Tel-Aviv	a	1-2	*Chen*
15/3	Bnei Yehuda	a	3-2	*og (Haimovich), Arbeitman, Topuzakov*
22/3	M. Herzliya	h	2-1	*Abutbul (p), Natcho*
29/3	Ashdod	a	1-2	*Natcho*
6/4	Beitar Jerusalem	h	3-1	*Dego (p), Fábio Júnior, Telkiyski*
12/4	M. Netanya	a	0-3	
3/5	H. Ironi Kiryat	h	2-0	*Dego (p), Arbeitman*
10/5	Bnei Sakhnin	a	1-0	*Duani*
18/5	M. Haifa	h	1-1	*Dego*
24/5	M. Petach-Tikva	a	2-1	*Telkiyski, Badir*
31/5	H. Kfar Saba	h	0-1	

No	Name	Nat	Pos	Aps	(s)	Gls
26	ABEDI Robson Vicente Gonçalves	BRA	M	8	(1)	
18	Shay ABUTBUL		M	20	(2)	1
20	Ygal ANTEBI		D	29		
28	Shlomi ARBEITMAN		A	14	(3)	4
22	Lior ASULIN		A	8	(2)	
10	Walid BADIR		M	30	(1)	2
16	Lior BACHSHI		D	1		
21	Dani BONDAREV		D	11		
23	Omri CANADA		D	16		
3	Tal CHEN		D	11	(8)	1
26	Roee DAYAN		A	2	(10)	
9	Barukh DEGO		M	25	(3)	6
29	Rami DUANI		D	9	(8)	1
28	Itay ELKASLASI		M	1		
1	Vincent ENYEAMA	NGA	G	24		
27	FÁBIO JÚNIOR	BRA	A	22	(10)	6
4	GABRIEL dos Santos	BRA	D	13		1
14	Yakir LOSKY		M		(3)	
30	Amar MANTZUR		D	5	(3)	
24	Mazuwa N'SUMBU	COD	M	28		
6	Bebars NATCHO		M	19	(7)	4
12	Reuven OVED		M	8	(17)	1
16	Adi SABAG		A	2	(7)	
22	Galil BEN SENAN		G	9		
25	Gal SHISH		D	4	(2)	
7	Idan SROR		M	9	(8)	
31	Dimitar TELKIYSKI	BUL	M	18	(1)	5
5	Elin TOPUZAKOV	BUL	D	17	(1)	1
87	UMIT Güzelses	TUR	D		(2)	

MACCABI HAIFA FC

Coach – Roni Levi

Founded – 1913

MAJOR HONOURS: Israeli League - (10) 1984, 1985, 1989, 1991, 1994, 2001, 2002, 2004, 2005, 2006; Israeli Cup - (5) 1962, 1991, 1993, 1995, 199

2007				
18/8	Bnei Sakhnin	h	0-1	
25/8	Ashdod	a	0-1	
16/9	M. Petach-Tikva	h	0-1	
29/9	M. Tel-Aviv	a	3-0	*Paulinho, Katan 2*
6/10	H. Kfar Saba	h	2-1	*Renato, Rosso*
20/10	H. Ironi Kiryat	h	1-0	*Afek*
27/10	M. Netanya	a	1-2	*Boccoli*
4/11	Beitar Jerusalem	h	0-0	
10/11	Bnei Yehuda	a	3-0	*Renato, Keinan, Afek*
24/11	H. Tel-Aviv	h	2-0	*Keinan, Renato*
1/12	M. Herzliya	a	1-0	*Renato*
8/12	Bnei Sakhnin	a	1-1	*Katan (p)*
15/12	Ashdod	h	3-0	*Renato, og (Jese), Masile*
2008				
5/1	M. Petach-Tikva	a	1-1	*Katan*
12/1	M. Tel-Aviv	h	3-1	*Rosso, Afek, Gita*
19/1	H. Kfar Saba	a	3-0	*Rafaelov, og (Lira), og (Kair*
26/1	H. Ironi Kiryat	a	1-1	*Rosso*
2/2	M. Netanya	h	0-2	
16/2	Bnei Yehuda	h	1-0	*Boccoli*
19/2	Beitar Jerusalem	a	0-1	
23/2	H. Tel-Aviv	a	0-2	
1/3	M. Herzliya	h	1-1	*Katan*
8/3	Beitar Jerusalem	h	0-1	
16/3	M. Netanya	a	2-0	*Fanteni 2*
22/3	H. Ironi Kiryat	h	2-1	*Renato, Fanteni (p)*
29/3	Bnei Sakhnin	a	0-1	
5/4	Bnei Yehuda	h	0-1	
12/4	M. Petach-Tikva	h	0-0	
3/5	H. Kfar Saba	a	0-1	
11/5	M. Tel Aviv	h	3-3	*Fanteni 3*
18/5	H. Tel-Aviv	a	1-1	*Rafaelov*
24/5	M. Herzliya	h	3-0	*Rafaelov, Kiyal, Gita (p)*
31/5	Ashdod	a	0-2	

No	Name	Nat	Pos	Aps	(s)	Gls
9	Omri AFEK		M	14	(9)	3
28	Shlomi ARBEITMAN		A	2	(5)	
7	Gustavo BOCCOLI	BRA	M	25	(1)	2
4	Diego CROSA	ARG	D	29		
19	Mor DAHAN		D	2	(3)	
25	Eliran DANIN		D	8	(3)	
1	Nir DAVIDOVITCH		G	30		

Name	Nat	Pos	Aps	(s)	Gls
Guy FILOSOF		D		(1)	
Thembinkosi FANTENI	RSA	A	13	(1)	6
Muhamad GDIR		A	1		
Oshri GITA		A	3	(18)	2
Alon HARAZI		D	18	(2)	
Tommer HEMED		A	3	(4)	
Yaniv KATAN		A	26	(3)	5
Lohab KIEL		D		(1)	
Dekel KEINAN		D	23	(1)	2
Adoram KEISE		D	3		
Biram KIYAL		M	25	(4)	1
René LIMA	ARG	M	7	(2)	
Shai MAIMON		D	11	(6)	
Tshepo MASILELA	RSA	D	23	(1)	1
Maor MELICSOHN		M	2	(4)	
Eyal MESHUMAR		D	17	(6)	
PAULINHO Jau	BRA	M	9	(3)	1
Lior REFAELOV		M	14	(10)	3
RENATO Eduardo	BRA	M	24	(2)	6
Giovanni ROSSO	CRO	M	26	(2)	3
Łukasz SURMA	POL	M	1		
Yahav YULZARI		G	3		
Israel ZAGURI		M	1	(2)	

MACCABI HERZLIYA FC

Coach – Fredi David

Founded - 1926

07				
/8	H. Ironi Kiryat	a	0-3	
/8	M. Netanya	h	1-2	*Radi*
/9	Beitar Jerusalem	a	2-4	*Malka, Boxenboim*
/9	Bnei Yehuda	h	0-2	
10	H. Tel-Aviv	a	2-0	*Makasi 2*
/10	H. Kfar Saba	a	3-2	*Menashe, Radi, Boxenboim*
/10	Bnei Sakhnin	h	0-1	
11	Ashdod	a	1-0	*Radi*
/11	M. Petach-Tikva	h	1-1	*Edree*
/11	M. Tel-Aviv	a	0-2	
12	M. Haifa	h	0-1	
12	H. Ironi Kiryat	h	1-3	*Makasi*
/12	M. Netanya	a	0-0	
08				
1	Beitar Jerusalem	h	1-1	*Menashe*
/1	Bnei Yehuda	a	1-0	*N'Toya-Zoa*
/1	H. Tel-Aviv	h	2-3	*Mashiach, Menashe*
/1	H. Kfar Saba	h	0-0	
2	Bnei Sakhnin	a	3-0	*N'Toya-Zoa, Radi, Vukomanović*
2	Ashdod	h	1-1	*Vukmanović*
/2	M. Petach-Tikva	a	1-1	*og (Pesser)*
/2	M. Tel-Aviv	h	1-3	*Boxenboim*
3	M. Haifa	a	1-1	*Boxenboim*
3	H. Kfar Saba	a	3-3	*Hemed 3*
/3	M. Tel-Aviv	h	1-0	*Menashe*
/3	H. Tel-Aviv	a	1-2	*Boxenboim (p)*
/3	Bnei Yehuda	a	0-2	
4	Ashdod	h	2-0	*Jaiyeoba 2*
5	M. Netanya	h	0-2	
/5	H. Ironi Kiryat	a	2-2	*og (Nusbaum), Rikan*
/5	Bnei Sakhnin	h	0-2	
/5	Beitar Jerusalem	a	1-3	*Rikan*
/5	M. Haifa	a	0-3	
/5	M. Petach-Tikva	h	0-1	

No	Name	Nat	Pos	Aps	(s)	Gls
	Oshri ALFASI		M	6	(5)	
	Eitan AZARIA		D	19	(3)	
9	Shay BANAY		M	1	(1)	
18	Shay BITON		M	2	(12)	
20	Omer BOXENBOIM		M	31	(1)	5
17	Dayo DAVIES	NGA	M	27		
22	Amir EDREE		G	4		
12	Kfir EDREE		M	25	(2)	1
21	Rahamim HALIS		D	4	(3)	
19	Tommer HEMED		A	8	(8)	3
13	Ekundayo JAYEOBA	NGA	A	3	(8)	2
25	Josh KENNET	ENG	M	7	(5)	
16	Assaf KRISSPIS		A	16	(6)	
2	Barak LAVIE		D	2		
14	Said MAKASI	RWA	A	14	(1)	3
5	Haim MALKA		D	23	(2)	1
12	Asi MASHIACH		M	17		1
7	Shalev MENASHE		A	21	(7)	4
1	Pieter MERLIER	BEL	G	3		
3	MÁRCIO Giovanini	BRA	D	12		
6	Mitja MÖREC	SVN	D	26	(3)	
24	Tcham N'TOYA-ZOA	COD	A	17	(4)	2
23	Itamar NITZAN		G	26		
9	Maharan RADI		M	30	(2)	4
27	Avi RIKAN		M	3	(5)	2
10	Elnatan SALMI		A	5	(7)	
15	Adi SOFER		M	1	(1)	
3	Ivan VUKOMANOVIĆ	SRB	M	10	(2)	2

MACCABI NETANYA FC

Coach – Reuven Atar

Founded - 1942

MAJOR HONOURS: Israeli League - (5) 1971, 1974, 1978, 1980, 1983; Israeli Cup - (1) 1978.

2007				
20/8	H. Tel-Aviv	h	0-0	
25/8	M. Herzliya	a	2-1	*Shechter, og (Malka)*
15/9	Bnei Sakhnin	h	1-2	*Ben Dayan*
29/9	Ashdod	a	6-1	*Taga, Shechter 2, Cohen T., Yampolsky, Ba*
6/10	M. Petach-Tikva	h	1-0	*og (Amar)*
21/10	M. Tel-Aviv	a	2-0	*Ba, og (Martinović)*
27/10	M. Haifa	h	2-1	*Ben Dayan, Rozental (p)*
3/11	H. Ironi Kiryat	a	0-0	
10/11	H. Kfar Saba	h	2-3	*Awudu 2*
25/11	Beitar Jerusalem	h	0-1	
1/12	Bnei Yehuda	a	2-1	*Tsegay, Ma'abi*
8/12	H. Tel-Aviv	a	1-0	*Awudu*
15/12	M. Herzliya	h	0-0	
2008				
5/1	Bnei Sakhnin	a	0-0	
12/1	Ashdod	h	3-0	*Tsegay, Yampolsky, Ben Dayan*
19/1	M. Petach-Tikva	a	0-0	
27/1	M. Tel-Aviv	h	1-0	*Awudu*
2/2	M. Haifa	a	2-0	*Awudu, Kioyo*
9/2	H. Ironi Kiryat	h	0-0	
16/2	H. Kfar Saba	a	2-1	*Tsegay, Kioyo*
24/2	Beitar Jerusalem	a	0-2	
1/3	Bnei Yehuda	h	0-0	
8/3	Bnei Sakhnin	a	1-1	*Shechter*
16/3	M. Haifa	h	0-2	
22/3	M. Petach-Tikva	a	1-0	*Tazameta*
29/3	H. Kfar Saba	h	1-1	*Awudu*
5/4	M. Tel-Aviv	a	0-0	
12/4	H. Tel-Aviv	h	3-0	*Shechter 2, Yampolsky*
3/5	M. Herzliya	a	2-0	*Shechter, Tsegay*
10/5	Ashdod	h	1-0	*Kioyo*
17/5	Beitar Jerusalem	a	0-3	
24/5	Bnei Yehuda	h	3-2	*Ben Dayan, Kioyo, Tazameta*
1/6	H. Ironi Kiryat	h	1-2	*Tazamata*

No	Name	Nat	Pos	Aps	(s)	Gls
11	Stanislav ANGELOVIČ	SVK	D	6	(4)	
10	Samadu AWUDU	GHA	A	27	(3)	6
24	Georges BA	CIV	A	7	(1)	2
19	Dedi BEN DAYAN		D	28		4
29	Asael BEN SHABAT		D		(1)	
20	Marius BUNDEA	ROU	M	8	(1)	
16	Jorge López CABALLERO	COL	M	5	(4)	
29	Almog COHEN		M	24	(4)	
21	Tamir COHEN		M	13		1
26	Chen EZRA		M		(4)	
30	Snir GOATA		M	9	(9)	
25	Golan HERMON		D	10	(5)	
4	Francis KIOYO	CMR	A	11	(1)	4
21	Tal MAABI		D	18	(3)	1
3	Luis MARÍN	CRC	D	32		
12	Omer PERETZ		A		(1)	
22	Sebastián ROZENTAL	CHI	M	4	(10)	1
14	Klimi SABAN		D	30	(1)	
9	Itay SHECHTER		A	20	(5)	7
1	Liran SHTRAUBER		G	33		
5	Avi STRUL		D	24	(1)	
15	Amir TEGA		M	6	(10)	1
2	Thierry TAZAMETA	CMR	A	13	(2)	3
7	Yehiel TSEGAY		M	14	(14)	4
28	Adam VAYER		M		(1)	
18	Alon WEISSBERG		A		(1)	
11	Dele YAMPOLSKY		A	21	(10)	3

MACCABI PETACH-TIKVA FC

Coach – Yossi Mizrahi; (13/11/07) Ofer Fabian; (27/1/08) Guy Luzon

Founded – 1912

MAJOR HONOURS: Israeli Cup – (2) 1935, 1952.

Date	Opponent		Score	Scorers
2007				
18/8	H. Kfar Saba	h	0-1	
25/8	M. Tel-Aviv	h	3-2	*og (Shitrit), Tzemach, Savić*
16/9	M. Haifa	a	1-0	*Golan*
29/9	H. Ironi Kiryat	h	3-1	*Golan, Tzemach, Sarsor*
6/10	M. Netanya	a	0-1	
20/10	Beitar Jerusalem	h	1-2	*Golan*
27/10	Bnei Yehuda	a	1-0	*Ogbuke*
3/11	H. Tel-Aviv	h	2-1	*Amar, Preda*
10/11	M. Herzliya	a	1-1	*Kadusi*
24/11	Bnei Sakhnin	h	2-0	*Kadusi, Golan*
2/12	Ashdod	a	3-1	*Golan, Kaku, Kadusi*
8/12	H. Kfar Saba	a	0-0	
15/12	M. Tel-Aviv	a	1-2	*Kadusi*
2008				
5/1	M. Haifa	h	1-1	*Tzemach*
12/1	H. Ironi Kiryat	a	1-2	*Kadusi*
19/1	M. Netanya	h	0-0	
26/1	Beitar Jerusalem	a	1-2	*Damari O.*
2/2	Bnei Yehuda	h	1-0	*Cohen L.*
9/2	H. Tel-Aviv	a	1-2	*Damari N.*
16/2	M. Herzliya	h	1-1	*og (Edree)*
23/2	Bnei Sakhnin	a	0-1	
1/3	Ashdod	h	0-0	
8/3	Ashdod	h	0-3	
15/3	Beitar Jerusalem	a	0-4	
22/3	M. Netanya	h	0-1	
29/3	H. Ironi Kiryat	a	0-1	
5/4	Bnei Sakhnin	h	0-4	
12/4	M. Haifa	a	0-0	
3/5	Bnei Yehuda	h	0-1	
10/5	H. Kfar Saba	h	1-0	*Sarsor*
17/5	M. Tel-Aviv	a	1-2	*Tzemach*
24/5	H. Tel-Aviv	h	1-2	*Ben Haim*
31/5	M. Herzliya	a	1-0	*Damari O.*

No	Name	Nat	Pos	Aps	(s)	Gls
3	Ismaeel AMAR		D	25	(1)	1
18	Roee BEKEL		M	6	(3)	
16	Tal BEN HAIM		A	5		1
20	Liran COHEN		M	27	(4)	1
22	Ohad COHEN		G	33		
5	Nitzan DAMARI		D	20	(1)	1
9	Omer DAMARI		A	14	(9)	2
23	Xavier DIRCEU	BRA	M	27	(2)	
11	Dovev GABAY		A	6	(5)	
12	Kobi GANON		D	27	(1)	
30	Oded GAVISH		D		(1)	
33	Irakli GEPERIDZE	GEO	A	3	(9)	
15	Omer GOLAN		A	12	(1)	5
21	Omer HADAR		D	6	(2)	
10	Ohad KADUSI		A	20	(9)	5
14	Blessing KAKU	NGA	M	24	(3)	1
17	Uri LUZON		M		(1)	
4	Merad MEGAMADOV		D	26		
9	Felix OGBUKE	NGA	A	8	(9)	1
6	Naor PESSER		D	23	(5)	
15	Dani PREDA		M	2	(15)	1
27	Robil SARSSOR		A	11	(10)	2
7	Nenad SAVIĆ	SUI	M	9	(4)	1
26	Soli TZEMACH		M	29	(1)	4

MACCABI TEL-AVIV FC

Coach – Eli Cohen; (27/8/07) (Victor Peretz); (5/9/07) Nir Levin

Founded - 1906

MAJOR HONOURS: Israeli League - (18) 1937, 1939, 1941, 1947, 1950, 195 1952, 1954, 1956, 1968, 1970, 1972, 1977, 1979, 1992, 1995, 1996, 2003; Israeli Cup - (22) 1929, 1930, 1933, 1941, 1946, 1947, 1954, 1955, 1958, 19 1964, 1965, 1967, 1970, 1977, 1987, 1988, 1994, 1996, 2001, 2002, 2005.

Date	Opponent		Score	Scorers
2007				
18/8	Ashdod	h	1-1	*Nimni*
25/8	M. Petach-Tikva	a	2-3	*Kamanan, Nimni*
16/9	H. Kfar Saba	h	0-1	
29/9	M. Haifa	h	0-3	
6/10	H. Ironi Kiryat	a	0-1	
21/10	M. Netanya	h	0-2	
28/10	Beitar Jerusalem	a	0-2	
3/11	Bnei Yehuda	h	3-1	*Shivhon, Kamanan 2*
11/11	H. Tel-Aviv	a	0-1	
24/11	M. Herzliya	h	2-0	*Azran, Shivhon*
2/12	Bnei Sakhnin	a	2-3	*Shivhon, Ron*
8/12	Ashdod	a	0-0	
15/12	M. Petach-Tikva	h	2-1	*Shivhon 2*
2008				
5/1	H. Kfar Saba	a	3-0	*og (Douglas), Kamanan, Mishaelov*
13/1	M. Haifa	a	1-3	*Shivhon*
19/1	H. Ironi Kiryat	h	2-2	*Kamanan, Gan*
27/1	M. Netanya	a	0-1	
3/2	Beitar Jerusalem	h	0-0	
9/2	Bnei Yehuda	a	4-0	*Bizera, Masudi, Kamanan*
17/2	H. Tel-Aviv	h	1-3	*Mesika*
23/2	M. Herzliya	a	3-1	*Kamanan, Bizera, Masu*
1/3	Bnei Sakhnin	h	0-0	
9/3	H. Tel-Aviv	h	2-1	*Kamanan, Shivhon*
15/3	M. Herzliya	a	0-1	
23/3	Ashdod	h	2-0	*Shivhon, Assous*
30/3	Beitar Jerusalem	a	1-1	*Shivhon*
5/4	M. Netanya	h	0-0	
12/4	H. Ironi Kiryat	a	1-3	*Haddad*
3/5	Bnei Sakhnin	h	3-1	*Gan, Masudi, Kamana*

'5	M.Haifa	a	3-3	*Masudi 2, Malul*
'5	M. Petach-Tikva	h	2-1	*Gan, Kamanan*
'5	H. Kfar Saba	a	3-2	*Masudi, Kamanan, Gan*
'5	Bnei Yehuda	a	0-1	

Name	Nat	Pos	Aps	(s)	Gls
Jonathan ASSOUS	FRA	D	16		1
Yaniv AZRAN		A	14	(4)	1
Dudu BITON		A	1	(9)	
Joe BIZERA	URU	D	16		2
Liron DIAMANT		D		(1)	
Orel EDRI		M		(1)	
Lior GAN		D	23	(1)	4
Ravid GAZAL		M	17	(7)	
Rudy HADDAD	FRA	M	24	(8)	1
Oz IFRAH		D	4		
Dragoslav JEVRIĆ	SRB	G	33		
Yannick KAMANAN	FRA	A	31		12
Nisso KAPILOTO		D	5		
Dor MALUL		D	6	(12)	1
Milan MARTINOVIĆ	SRB	D	12		
Alain MASUDI	COD	M	14		6
Erez MESIKA		D	19	(8)	1
Moshe MISHAELOV		D	16	(4)	1
Avi NIMNI		M	4	(2)	2
Omer PERETZ		A	2	(9)	
José RAMALHO	BRA	M	8		
Dan ROMAN		M	17	(3)	
Omri RON		A		(10)	1
Uri SHITRIT		D	23	(3)	
Yossi SHIVHON		M	21	(3)	9
Yuval SHPUNGIN		D	29		
Avi YEHIEL		D	2	(3)	
Shiran YEINI		M	6	(9)	

PROMOTED CLUBS

HAKOAH AMIDAR RAMAT GAN FC

Coach – Dudu Dahan

Founded - 1961

MAJOR HONOURS: Israeli League – (2) 1965, 1973; Israeli Cup – (2) 1969, 1971.

HAPOEL PETACH TIKVA FC

Coach – Uri Malmilian; (15/1/08) Eli Mahpud

Founded – 1935

MAJOR HONOURS: Israeli League – (6) 1955, 1959, 1960, 1961, 1962, 1963; Israeli Cup – (2) 1957, 1992.

SECOND LEVEL FINAL TABLE 2007/08

		Pld	W	D	L	F	A	Pts
1	Hakoah Amidar Ramat Gan FC	33	16	9	8	41	30	57
2	Hapoel Petach Tikva FC	33	16	6	11	40	27	54
3	Hapoel Haifa FC	33	15	7	11	36	29	52
4	Hapoel Be'er Sheva FC	33	14	9	10	31	18	51
5	Hapoel Bnei Lod FC	33	14	7	12	41	42	49
6	Hapoel Ramat Gan FC	33	13	9	11	33	38	48
7	Hapoel Ra'anana FC	33	11	13	9	34	31	46
8	Ironi Ramat HaSharon FC	33	11	10	12	33	37	43
9	Maccabi Ahi Nazareth FC	33	10	11	12	37	39	41
10	Hapoel Acre FC	33	9	10	14	29	32	37
11	Hapoel Ironi Rishon LeZion FC	33	7	16	10	31	38	37
12	Hapoel Nazareth Illit FC	33	5	7	21	28	53	22

DOMESTIC CUP 2007/08

STATE CUP

HIRD ROUND

26/2/08)
amat HaSharon 3, H. Ra'anana 1
I. Kiryar Ata 1, Bnei Lod 0
I. Ramat-Gan 1, H. Asi Gilboa 0
nei Yehuda 2, M. Kfar-Kana 0
ishon LeZion 1, H. Akko 1
I. Petach-Tikva 4, M. Herzliya 3
I. Ironi Bat Yam 0, Hakoah M. Amidar 2
I. Hadera 0, M. Ahi Nazareth 4
I. Be'er Sheva 1, H. Marmorek 1 *(aet; 4-1 on pens)*
eitar Shimshon Tel-Aviv 1, M. Tel-Aviv 0
I. Haifa 1, H. Kfar-Saba 2
shdod 0, H. Ironi Kiryat Shmona 2
I. Tel-Aviv 4, H. Nazareth Ilit 2
I. Petach-Tikva 0, M. Haifa 2

27/2/08)
I. Netanya 3, H. Um El Fahem 3 *(aet; 3-1 on pens)*
Bnei Sakhnin 1, Beitar Jerusalem 1 *(aet; 1-3 on pens)*

FOURTH ROUND

(11/3/08)
Beitar Shimshon Tel-Aviv 2, H. Petach-Tikva 0
Hakoah M. Amidar 0, H. Ramat-Gan 0 *(aet; 5-3 on pens)*
Bnei Yehuda 1, Ramat HaSharon 0
Rishon LeZion 4, H. Kfar-Saba 4 *(aet; 4-5 on pens)*
Ahi Nazareth 0, Beitar Jerusalem 3

(12/3/08)
H. Ironi Kiryat Shmona 2, M. Kiryar Ata 1
H. Be'er Sheva 0, H. Tel-Aviv 1
M. Netanya 1, M. Haifa 0

QUARTER-FINALS

(2/4/08)
Hakoah M. Amidar 1 *(Badash 54p)*, M. Netanya 1 *(Tazameta 20) (aet; 0-3 on pens)*
H. Tel-Aviv 2 *(Fábio Júnior 43, Telkiyski 76)*, Bnei Yehuda 0

(3/4/08)
H. Ironi Kiryat Shmona 1 *(Avidor 24)*, Beitar Shimshon Tel-Aviv 2 *(Exbard 65, 88)*
Beitar Jerusalem 3 *(Ben Shushan 1, 26, Ziv 85)*, H. Kfar -Saba 2 *(González 73, Talker 76)*

SEMI-FINALS

(16/4/08)
Beitar Jerusalem 1 *(Ziv 102)*, M. Netanya 0 *(aet)*
H. Tel-Aviv 1 *(Dego 66)*, Beitar Shimshon Tel-Aviv 1 *(Alian 82) (aet; 9-8 on pens)*

FINAL

(13/5/08)
Ramat Gan stadium, Ramat Gan
BEITAR JERUSALEM FC 0
HAPOEL TEL-AVIV FC 0
(aet; 5-4 on pens)
Referee – *Levi*
BEITAR JERUSALEM – *Kale, Ziv, Gershon, Benado, Álvarez, Boateng, Alberman, Tal, Baruchyan (Azriel 105), Ben Shushan (Zandberg 46), Rômulo (Tamuz 75).*
H. TEL-AVIV – *Enyeama, Canada, Topuzakov, Badir, Antebi, N'Sumbu (Natcho 100), Abutbul, Dego, Telkiyski (Sror 111), Arbeitman (Oved 53), Fábio Júnior.*

World champions fail EURO test

Italy were unable to add the European crown to the world title they won two years earlier in Germany. Although it took a penalty shoot-out defeat by the eventual champions to eliminate them from UEFA EURO 2008™, the tournament was not a positive experience for the Azzurri, particularly not for head coach Roberto Donadoni, who was sacked on his return to Italy and replaced by Marcello Lippi, the man who led the country to victory at the 2006 FIFA World Cup.

Donadoni insisted he was proud of his players for their efforts in Switzerland and Austria, but the harsh reality was that the world champions played four matches and won only one – against a France team that lost their best player to injury early on and were down to ten men not long afterwards. Furthermore, Italy scored only three goals, two of them in that victory over Les Bleus – a penalty and a deflected free-kick. The other, from defender Christian Panucci against Romania, came from about a metre out. It was hardly the stuff of world champions.

While the loss of World Cup-winning captain Fabio Cannavaro to injury on the eve of the tournament was a cruel blow, it was not, paradoxically, in defence where Italy struggled. Granted, their opening 3-0 defeat against the Netherlands was a cause for considerable concern, but Donadoni acted swiftly, removing both Andrea Barzagli and Marco Materazzi and remodelling the entire back four. In the next three games the new-look defence, with Panucci and Giorgio Chiellini working well in tandem, conceded one goal.

Misfiring forward line

It was the lack of pace and creativity in the final third that proved Italy's biggest handicap. Luca Toni has tremendous physical presence, but at times it appeared that the Azzurri's default modus operandi in attack was to launch high balls towards his forehead. Various options were used by Donadoni to provide Toni with attacking support, but none of Alessandro Del Piero, Antonio Cassano or Antonio Di Natale foun[d] any consistent form when it mattered, and not one Italy forward scored. Discipline was also a problem. Italy's count of nine yellow cards included two apiece for key midfielders Andrea Pirlo and Gennaro Gattuso, the AC Milan duo thus having to sit out the quarter-final against Spain and leaving Donadoni, once again with the task of restructuring a constantly changing, unsettled side.

If certain Azzurri players, such as Toni, Materazzi, Gattuso and Di Natale, will want to forget UEFA EURO 2008™ in a hurry, others will feel that the tournament served either to uphold or improve their reputations. Gianluigi Buffon, as expected, was excellent in goal, making a crucial penalty save from Romania's Adrian Mutu and an even better one from Karim Benzema

Alessandro Del Pi[ero] struggles to take i[t in] as Italy lose [on] penalties to Sp[ain]

gainst France. Chiellini was immense against Spain, uggesting that the former left-back's natural position in the centre of defence, where he could be the ng-term replacement for Cannavaro. Pirlo's creative romptings were conspicuous by their absence in e quarter-final, where Italy's midfield was clogged o with defensively-minded workhorses, the best of em being Daniele De Rossi, man of the match gainst France.

ppi, great coach though he is, may discover that inning the World Cup a second time is far more fficult than it was at his first attempt – and not only ecause the finals will be staged outside Europe. As e holders are no longer exempt, his first task will be steer a safe course through a qualifying group that romises no easy away fixtures and will also bring him p against another former Juventus coaching legend and ex-Azzurri boss), Giovanni Trapattoni, the new an in charge of the Republic of Ireland.

leither Lippi nor Trapattoni has worked in Serie A for nany years, but they will both surely have empathised vith the plight of one of the younger members of heir profession, Roberto Mancini, as he was dismissed s the coach of FC Internazionale Milano not long fter he had just led the team to a record third uccessive Italian championship title.

urthermore, the 2007/08 triumph was the most ubstantial of the three. The first scudetto had been won only by default after Juventus were stripped of he title due to the Calciopoli fraud scandal. The econd was won with Juve in Serie B and most of the other potential challengers handicapped by point deductions. Only the third was achieved on an even playing field.

Inter in top gear

Nevertheless, Inter began the campaign as strong favourites. They started at full throttle, and before long they had created daylight at the top of the table between themselves and the rest, hitting the heights with a brilliant 4-1 win at AS Roma. It was almost a repeat of the previous season as they reached Christmas undefeated, their international all-star squad rotating with smooth efficiency around consistent core contributors like goalkeeper Júlio César, captain Javier Zanetti, all-purpose midfielder Esteban Cambiasso and the impressive, productive strike pairing of Zlatan Ibrahimović and Julio Cruz, the latter keeping out the likes of Adriano, Hernán Crespo

Esteban Cambiasso – a core contributor to Internazionale's scudetto triumph

and new signing David Suazo with a succession of important goals.

By the turn of the year Inter were in a commanding position, with 43 points on the board from 17 games and a seven-point lead over second-placed Roma. The team were also sitting pretty in Europe, having recovered from an opening defeat by Fenerbahçe SK to win their UEFA Champions League group with five successive victories, the irrepressible Ibrahimović making his mark in that competition also with five goals.

With the Nerazzurri carrying on where they left off in Serie A after Christmas, albeit with a couple of generous penalties helping them to successive home wins against Parma FC and Empoli FC, Mancini's side were being hailed as the best team in Europe. That was all very well, but they had to prove it, and in the first knockout round of the UEFA Champions League they faced five-time winners Liverpool FC. It would prove to be a humbling experience, with Inter having a defender sent off early in both matches, going down 2-0 at Anfield and, three weeks later, 1-0 in Milan. In the wake of elimination Mancini announced his intention to quit the club, then retracted it. It was a strange episode, and it raised the suspicion that not all was well within the Inter camp.

In between the two Liverpool defeats, Inter's form started to desert them in Serie A. They rescued themselves from a home defeat against Roma with a fortunate late equaliser from Zanetti (after a brilliant Francesco Totti strike for the visitors), but their unbeaten record would last just four days longer, mid-table SSC Napoli halting their run with a shock 1-0 win in Naples. Now their lead over Roma was down to six points (it had at one stage climbed to eleven) and, with confidence ebbing away, Inter suddenly had a fight on their hands. As the pressure of the run-in intensified with every passing week, Inter got nervous. After dropping seven points out of nine in late March – including a home defeat to Juventus – they held things together well with four straight wins – thanks largely to the brilliance of 17-year-old Mario Balotelli, a replacement for the injured Ibrahimović. So despite losing 2-1 in the derby to Milan, they still required only a victory at home to AC Siena in the penultimate round to clinch the title.

But as 55,000 fans in the San Siro prepared for a party, Siena refused to play ball, coming twice from behind to draw 2-2. With Roma simultaneously beating Atalanta BC 2-1, Inter's lead was down to a solitary point - with one game remaining. The fixture calendar could not have served up a better climax because Inter and Roma were both away from home against teams battling against relegation, Parma FC and Catania Calcio, respectively. Furthermore, in order to maintain security, following the tragic deaths of two football supporters at motorway service stations, an Italian government ban was placed on travelling Inter and Roma fans.

Ibrahimović strikes

For much of the afternoon Luciano Spalletti's Roma side were poised to pip Inter at the post. An early goal from Montenegrin striker Mirko Vučinić put the Giallorossi in front in Sicily, and with Inter toiling away without a breakthrough in heavy rain at Parma, Roma were a point in front. But cometh the hour, cometh the man, and Ibrahimović, who had not played for almost two months, came off the bench in the second half to score two goals – the first a brilliant low strike from distance – and win the game. With news that Inter were back in control, Roma eased off and Catania came back to equalise, the 1-1 draw ensuring their safety while Parma, after 18 years in the top flight, and unlucky Empoli, the victims of Catania's late strike, went down alongside already relegated AS Livorno Calcio.

Inter striker Zlatan Ibrahimović fires in the first of his two title-clinching goals against Parma

Ibrahimović's heroic intervention had rescued Inter from ignominy, but the intense anxiety of the closing weeks was too much for club president Massimo Moratti, who decided that enough was enough and that Mancini had to go. It was not long before the identity of his replacement was revealed – the charismatic, eccentric former FC Porto and Chelsea FC manager José Mourinho.

Roma, who could reflect on their 1-1 draw at the San Siro and a last-minute derby defeat against S.S. Lazio (2-3) as the moments the scudetto had slipped through their grasp, would find some consolation for their narrow championship defeat by beating Inter in the Coppa Italia final six days later. It was the fourth year in a row that the two teams had met in the final, but, unusually, the 2008 showpiece was played over one leg – in Roma's Stadio Olimpico. Although they were still without Totti, who had missed the last four league matches through injury, Spalletti's men triumphed 2-1, the winning goal coming from Italian international Simone Perrotta, who had also scored in each of the two legs of the 2007 final. It was Roma's ninth win the competition, putting them level on top with Juventus in the all-time roll of honour.

/ finishing second in the league and winning the ɹp, Roma's 2007/08 campaign was a repeat of the revious one – albeit that they finished only three oints behind Inter rather than 22. There was more éjà vu in Europe where, for the second successive eason, the Giallorossi were knocked out of the UEFA hampions League quarter-finals by Manchester nited FC. It was not quite the trouncing of a year arlier, but the 3-0 aggregate scoreline was still onclusive enough to suggest that Roma are still, like ter, short of the special qualities required to scale urope's highest peak. They did, however, have to do ithout the injured Totti for both legs, the skipper aving played a lead role in the team's impressive imination of Real Madrid CF in the preceding round.

oma were the last Italian team standing in the UEFA hampions League. Their local rivals Lazio, who nished a lowly 12th in Serie A despite 14 goals apiece om strike pair Tommaso Rocchi and Goran Pandev, nished bottom of their group, while Milan, the olders, became the first of the three Serie A giants elled by English opposition when they were brilliantly rushed aside by Arsenal FC at the San Siro in the first nockout round.

Ailan miss out

:arlo Ancelotti's side won the UEFA Super Cup – 3-1 gainst Sevilla FC in Monaco - and the FIFA Club World :up – 4-2 in the final against CA Boca Juniors in 'okohama – to swell their list of international titles to world-record 18, but otherwise they suffered a ugely disappointing season. Unaccustomed to leparting the UEFA Champions League so early, they vould have to go without top-level European football or another 18 months after their defeat by Arsenal, ecause in Serie A they could finish no higher than ifth. The trip to Japan for the Club World Cup caused a ieavy backlog of fixtures, and after failing to record a ome win in Serie A until January, when precocious Brazilian teenager Pato arrived on the scene, Milan vere always playing catch-up. The best they could ever hope for was fourth place, but just as they achieved that objective with their derby win against nter in round 36, they lost away to Napoli and were overtaken by an ecstatic ACF Fiorentina.

UEFA Champions League qualification was a welcome consolation prize for the Viola after they had been knocked out of the UEFA Cup by a resilient Rangers FC on penalties. Having twice used that method of advancement themselves – against FC Groningen and Everton FC – Claudio Prandelli and his players could scarcely complain, but they deserved better after an impressive campaign in which, unlike many other Italian participants, they gave the UEFA Cup due recognition and fielded full-strength teams.

Juventus, back in Serie A after their enforced demotion, finished six points ahead of Fiorentina. With ex-Chelsea manager Claudio Ranieri having replaced Didier Deschamps as coach, Juve's renaissance began in earnest, and while there were initially reservations about the team's prospects of challenging for a UEFA Champions League place, those were soon allayed. Thanks chiefly to the prolific goalscoring of old hands Del Piero and David Trezeguet, the league's top two marksmen with 21 and 20 goals respectively, Juve spent virtually the entire season lodged in third place – always too far behind Inter and Roma to challenge for the scudetto but never seriously threatened from below.

Alexandre Pato, Milan's new Brazilian boy wonder, in UEFA Champions League action against Arsenal

ITALY

Federazione Italiana Giuoco Calcio (FIGC)

Via Gregorio Allegri 14
CP 2450
IT-00198 Roma
tel - +39 06 84911
fax - +39 06 84912526
website - www.figc.it
email - figc.segreteria@figc.it
Year of Formation – 1898
President – Giancarlo Abete
General Secretary – Antonio Di Sebastiano
Press Officer – Antonello Valentini
Stadium – Stadio Olimpico, Rome (81,193)

INTERNATIONAL HONOURS
FIFA World Cup - (4) 1934, 1938, 1982, 2006.
UEFA European Championship - (1) 1968.

INTERNATIONAL TOURNAMENT APPEARANCES
FIFA World Cup - (16) 1934 (Winners), 1938 (Winners), 1950, 1958, 1962, 1966, 1970 (runners-up), 1974, 1978 (4th), 1982 (Winners), 1986 (2nd round), 1990 (3rd), 1994 (runners-up), 1998 (qtr-finals), 2002 (2nd round), 2006 (Winners).
UEFA European Championship - (7) 1968 (Winners), 1980 (4th), 1988 (semi-finals), 1996, 2000 (runners-up), 2004, 2008 (qtr-finals).

TOP FIVE ALL-TIME CAPS
Paolo Maldini (126); Fabio Cannavaro (116); Dino Zoff (112); Giacinto Facchetti (94); Alessandro Del Piero (89)

TOP FIVE ALL-TIME GOALS
Luigi Riva (35); Giuseppe Meazza (33); Silvio Piola (30); Roberto Baggio & Alessandro Del Piero (27)

NATIONAL TEAM RESULTS 2007/08

Date	Opponent		Venue	Score	Scorers
22/8/07	Hungary	A	Budapest	1-3	*Di Natale (49)*
8/9/07	France (ECQ)	H	Milan	0-0	
12/9/07	Ukraine (ECQ)	A	Kiev	2-1	*Di Natale (41, 77)*
13/10/07	Georgia (ECQ)	H	Genoa	2-0	*Pirlo (44), Grosso (84)*
17/10/07	South Africa	H	Siena	2-0	*Lucarelli (82, 90)*
17/11/07	Scotland (ECQ)	A	Glasgow	2-1	*Toni (2), Panucci (90+1)*
21/11/07	Faroe Islands (ECQ)	H	Modena	3-1	*Benjaminsen (11og), Toni (36), Chiellini (41)*
6/2/08	Portugal	N	Zurich (SUI)	3-1	*Toni (45), Pirlo (50), Quagliarella (78)*
26/3/08	Spain	A	Elche	0-1	
30/5/08	Belgium	H	Florence	3-1	*Di Natale (9, 41), Camoranesi (49)*
9/6/08	Netherlands (ECF)	N	Berne (SUI)	0-3	
13/6/08	Romania (ECF)	N	Zurich (SUI)	1-1	*Panucci (56)*
17/6/08	France (ECF)	N	Zurich (SUI)	2-0	*Pirlo (25p), De Rossi (62)*
22/6/08	Spain (ECF)	N	Vienna (AUT)	0-0	*(aet; 2-4 on pens)*

UC Sampdoria, inspired by the magic of on-loan forward Cassano, and Udinese Calcio, with an in-form Italian international striker of their own in 17-goal Di Natale, joined Milan in the UEFA Cup, while Napoli, whose top scorer was Slovakian boy wonder Marek Hamšík, capped an impressive return to Serie A by qualifying for the UEFA Intertoto Cup. Hoping to make similar post-promotion progress in 2008/09 were Serie B champions AC Chievo Verona, runners-up Bologna FC and play-off winners US Lecce.

ATIONAL TEAM APPEARANCES 2007/08

:h – Roberto DONADONI 9/9/63			Hun	FRA	UKR	GEO	Rsa	SCO	FRO	Por	Esp	Bel	NED	ROU	FRA	ESP	Caps	Goals
luigi BUFFON	28/1/78	Juventus	G	G	G	G		G			G	G	G	G	G	G	86	-
simo ODDO	14/6/76	Milan	D46	D	s78	D			D	D80							34	1
o CANNAVARO	13/9/73	Real Madrid (ESP)	D	D	D			D	D53	D	D	D46					116	1
o MATERAZZI	19/8/78	Internazionale	D46								D46		D54				41	2
luca ZAMBROTTA	19/2/77	Barcelona (ESP)	D	D	D			D		D29	s69	D	D	D	D	D	75	2
simo AMBROSINI	29/5/77	Milan	M		M	M88		M	M58	M		s75	M	s85	s55	M	35	-
ea PIRLO	19/5/79	Milan	M	M	M	M		M		M	M46	M	M	M	M55		49	8
rto AQUILANI	7/7/84	Roma	M66		s68						s60	M75			s82	M108	7	-
sandro DEL PIERO	9/11/74	Juventus	M46	M83								s46	s64	M77		s108	89	27
o QUAGLIARELLA	31/10/83	Udinese	M		s85	A72			s58	s77				s77			9	3
TONI	20/5/77	Bayern (GER)	A46			A		A	A74	A70	A46	A75	A	A	A	A	38	15
ea BARZAGLI	8/5/81	Palermo	s46	D	D	D		D		D52	s46	D	D				23	-
po INZAGHI	9/8/73	Milan	s46	A65													57	25
nio DI NATALE	13/10/77	Udinese	s46	s83	M	A		A68		M	M75	A46	A64			s75	20	7
o GROSSO	28/11/77	Lyon (FRA)	s46			D			D	s29	D	s46	s54	D	D	D	35	3
elo PALOMBO	25/9/81	Sampdoria	s66				s59										4	-
iele DE ROSSI	24/7/83	Roma		M			M59	s87	M	M52	M			M	M	M	36	5
ro CAMORANESI	4/10/76	Juventus		M58	M78			A83			M	A61	A75	M85	s64	s58	39	4
naro GATTUSO	9/1/78	Milan		M		M		M87			s46	M	M		M82		60	1
one PERROTTA	17/9/77	Roma		s58	M68				M	s52	M60			M57	M64	M58	44	2
iano LUCARELLI	4/10/75	Shakhtar (UKR)		s65			A										6	3
stian PANUCCI	12/4/73	Roma			D	D		D			D69	D46	D	D	D	D	57	4
enzo IAQUINTA	21/11/79	Juventus			A85			s68	M		s75						23	1
quale FOGGIA	3/6/83	Cagliari				s72	M59										2	-
ano MAURI	8/1/80	Lazio				s88	M										6	-
co AMELIA	2/4/82	Livorno					G		G	G							6	-
tian ZACCARDO	21/12/81	Palermo					D										17	1
sandro GAMBERINI	27/8/81	Fiorentina					D62			s52							2	-
iele BONERA	31/5/81	Milan					D81		s53								13	-
rgio CHIELLINI	14/8/84	Juventus					D	s83	D			s46		D	D	D	13	1
ardo MONTOLIVO	18/1/85	Fiorentina					M73										1	-
sandro ROSINA	31/1/84	Torino					M86										1	-
erto GILARDINO	5/7/82	Milan					s59		s74								25	9
drea DOSSENA	11/9/81	Udinese					s62										1	-
onio NOCERINO	9/4/85	Juventus					s73										1	-
ndomenico MESTO	25/5/82	Udinese					s81										3	-
nco SEMIOLI	20/6/80	Fiorentina					s86										3	-
faele PALLADINO	17/4/84	Juventus							M	M77							2	-
rco BORRIELLO	16/6/82	Genoa								s70	s46	s75					3	-
rco CASSETTI	29/5/77	Roma								s80							3	-
tonio CASSANO	12/7/82	Sampdoria										s61	s75	s57	A	A75	15	3

ITALY

DOMESTIC LEAGUE 2007/08

SERIE A FINAL TABLE

		Pld	Home					Away					Total					Pts
			W	D	L	F	A	W	D	L	F	A	W	D	L	F	A	
1	FC Internazionale Milano	38	15	3	1	41	14	10	7	2	28	12	25	10	3	69	26	85
2	AS Roma	38	15	3	1	43	20	9	7	3	29	17	24	10	4	72	37	82
3	Juventus	38	12	5	2	39	12	8	7	4	33	25	20	12	6	72	37	72
4	ACF Fiorentina	38	12	4	3	35	18	7	5	7	20	21	19	9	10	55	39	66
5	AC Milan	38	8	7	4	31	18	10	3	6	35	20	18	10	10	66	38	64
6	UC Sampdoria	38	10	7	2	35	18	7	2	10	21	28	17	9	12	56	46	60
7	Udinese Calcio	38	9	4	6	30	29	7	5	7	18	24	16	9	13	48	53	57
8	SSC Napoli	38	11	4	4	27	16	3	4	12	23	37	14	8	16	50	53	50
9	Atalanta BC	38	8	7	4	36	28	4	5	10	16	28	12	12	14	52	56	48
10	Genoa CFC	38	8	4	7	23	22	5	5	9	21	30	13	9	16	44	52	48
11	US Città di Palermo	38	8	7	4	25	21	4	4	11	22	36	12	11	15	47	57	47
12	S.S. Lazio	38	9	4	6	28	23	2	9	8	19	28	11	13	14	47	51	46
13	AC Siena	38	6	9	4	24	17	3	8	8	16	28	9	17	12	40	45	44
14	Cagliari Calcio	38	8	5	6	22	20	3	4	12	18	36	11	9	18	40	56	42
15	Torino FC	38	5	7	7	19	19	3	9	7	17	30	8	16	14	36	49	40
16	Reggina Calcio	38	8	5	6	24	19	1	8	10	13	37	9	13	16	37	56	40
17	Calcio Catania	38	8	6	5	21	14	0	7	12	12	31	8	13	17	33	45	37
18	Empoli FC	38	5	7	7	18	21	4	2	13	11	31	9	9	20	29	52	36
19	Parma FC	38	7	6	6	28	26	0	7	12	14	36	7	13	18	42	62	34
20	AS Livorno Calcio	38	3	8	8	18	28	3	4	12	17	32	6	12	20	35	60	30

TOP GOALSCORERS

21 Alessandro DEL PIERO (Juventu

20 David TREZEGUET (Juventus)

19 Marco BORRIELLO (Genoa)

17 Antonio DI NATALE (Udinese)
Zlatan IBRAHIMOVIĆ (Internazionale)
Adrian MUTU (Fiorentina)

15 AMAURI (Palermo)
KAKÁ (Milan)

14 Goran PANDEV (Lazio)
Tommaso ROCCHI (Lazio)
Francesco TOTTI (Roma)

CLUB-BY-CLUB

ATALANTA BC

Coach - Luigi Del Neri

Founded – 1907

MAJOR HONOURS: Italian Cup – (1) 1963.

2007

26/8	Reggina	a	1-1	*Doni (p)*
2/9	Parma	h	2-0	*Zampagna, Carrozzieri*
16/9	Fiorentina	a	2-2	*Doni, Zampagna*
23/9	Lazio	h	2-1	*Langella, Zampagna*
26/9	Siena	a	1-1	*Doni (p)*
30/9	Sampdoria	a	0-3	
6/10	Udinese	h	0-0	
21/10	Torino	h	2-2	*Ferreira Pinto, Doni (p)*
28/10	Empoli	a	1-0	*Doni*
31/10	Cagliari	h	2-2	*Capelli, Doni*
4/11	Catania	a	2-1	*Langella 2*
24/11	Internazionale	a	1-2	*Floccari*
2/12	Napoli	h	5-1	*Floccari, Langella, Doni, Carozzieri, Ferreira Pinto*
9/12	Juventus	a	0-1	
16/12	Palermo	h	1-3	*Tissone*
23/12	Livorno	a	1-1	*Tissone*

2008

13/1	Roma	h	1-2	*Ferreira Pinto*
19/1	Genoa	a	1-2	*Doni (p)*
23/1	Milan	h	2-1	*Langella, Tissone*
27/1	Reggina	h	2-2	*Rivalta, Langella*
3/2	Parma	a	3-2	*Pellegrino, Bellini, Floccari*
9/2	Fiorentina	h	2-2	*Muslimovic 2*
17/2	Lazio	a	0-3	
24/2	Siena	h	2-2	*Floccari 2*
27/2	Sampdoria	h	4-1	*Doni 2, Floccari, Capell*
2/3	Udinese	a	0-2	
9/3	Torino	a	0-1	
16/3	Empoli	h	4-1	*Langella, Doni, Padoin*
19/3	Cagliari	a	0-1	
22/3	Catania	h	0-0	
30/3	Milan	a	2-1	*Floccari, Langella*
6/4	Internazionale	h	0-2	
13/4	Napoli	a	0-2	
20/4	Juventus	h	0-4	
27/4	Palermo	a	0-0	
4/5	Livorno	h	3-2	*Doni, Ferreira Pinto, Padoin*
11/5	Roma	a	1-2	*Bellini*
18/5	Genoa	h	2-0	*Floccari, Marconi*

No	Name	Nat	Pos	Aps	(s)	Gls
3	Manuel BELLERI		D	13	(7)	
6	Gianpaolo BELLINI		D	23		2
8	Antonino BERNARDINI		M	2	(4)	
9	Giocomo BONAVENTURA		M		(1)	
27	Daniele CAPELLI		D	20	(3)	2
80	Moris CARROZZIERI		D	20		2

No	Name	Nat	Pos	Aps	(s)	Gls
0	Ferdinando COPPOLA		G	38		
	Francisco José COSTINHA	POR	M	1		
5	Diego DE ASCENTIS		M	21	(10)	
	Marino DEFENDI		A		(6)	
2	Cristiano DONI		M	29	(1)	12
9	Adriano FERREIRA PINTO	BRA	M	38		4
2	Riccardo FISSORE		D	1	(1)	
3	Sergio FLOCCARI		A	29	(5)	8
7	Tiberio GUARENTE		M	23	(4)	
0	Simone INZAGHI		A	1	(18)	
3	Antonio LANGELLA		A	25	(2)	8
	Thomas MANFREDINI		D	15	(2)	
1	Michele MARCONI		A		(4)	1
1	Zlatan MUSLIMOVIĆ	BIH	A	4	(6)	2
2	Simone PADOIN		M	15	(16)	3
	Michele PAOLUCCI		A	2	(7)	
6	Michele PELLEGRINO	ARG	D	22	(4)	1
6	Claudio RIVALTA		D	29	(1)	1
	Leonardo José TALAMONTI	ARG	D	8	(1)	
1	Fernando Damián TISSONE	ARG	M	29	(6)	3
	Riccardo ZAMPAGNA		A	10		3

CAGLIARI CALCIO

Coach - Marco Giampaolo; (13/11/07) Nedo Sonetti; (27/12/07) Davide Ballardini

Founded – 1920

MAJOR HONOURS: Italian League - (1) 1970.

2007

26/8	Napoli	a	2-0	*Matri, Foggia (p)*
2/9	Juventus	h	2-3	*Foggia 2 (2p)*
16/9	Parma	a	1-1	*Matri*
23/9	Palermo	h	0-1	
26/9	Lazio	a	1-3	*Acquafresca*
30/9	Siena	h	1-0	*Foggia (p)*
7/10	Genoa	a	0-2	
21/10	Catania	h	1-1	*Matri*
27/10	Torino	a	0-2	
31/10	Atalanta	a	2-2	*Fini (p), Matri*
4/11	Sampdoria	h	0-3	
25/11	Milan	h	1-2	*Acquafresca*
2/12	Livorno	h	0-0	
5/12	Roma	a	0-2	
9/12	Empoli	a	1-4	*Conti*
16/12	Internazionale	h	0-2	
23/12	Fiorentina	a	1-5	*Fini*

2008

13/1	Udinese	h	0-1	
20/1	Reggina	a	0-2	
27/1	Napoli	h	2-1	*Matri, Conti*
3/2	Juventus	a	1-1	*Bianco*
10/2	Parma	h	1-1	*Jeda*
17/2	Palermo	a	1-2	*og (Cavani)*
24/2	Lazio	h	1-0	*Matri*
27/2	Siena	a	0-1	
2/3	Genoa	h	2-1	*Acquafresca, og (Rubinho)*
9/3	Catania	a	1-2	*Conti*
16/3	Torino	h	3-0	*Jeda, Acquafresca 2 (1p)*
19/3	Atalanta	h	1-0	*Acquafresca (p)*
22/3	Sampdoria	a	1-1	*Foggia*
29/3	Roma	h	1-1	*og (Ferrari)*
5/4	Milan	a	1-3	*Conti*
13/4	Livorno	a	2-1	*Acquafresca 2*
20/4	Empoli	h	2-0	*Acquafresca, Fini*
27/4	Internazionale	a	1-2	*Biondini*
4/5	Fiorentina	h	2-1	*Jeda, Conti*
11/5	Udinese	a	2-0	*Acquafresca, Cossu*
18/5	Reggina	h	2-2	*Larrivey, Bianco*

No	Name	Nat	Pos	Aps	(s)	Gls
9	Robert ACQUAFRESCA		A	20	(12)	10
31	Alessandro AGOSTINI		D	27	(1)	
20	Paolo BIANCO		D	30		2
8	Davide BIONDINI		M	21	(6)	1
22	Joe Emerson BIZERA	URU	D	7	(2)	
4	Alessandro BUDEL		M	5	(4)	
21	Michele CANINI		D	17	(1)	
4	Luca CAPECCHI		G	1		
5	Daniele CONTI		M	32		5
7	Andrea COSSU		A	13	(3)	1
33	Enrico COTZA		M	1	(3)	
7	Antonino D´AGOSTINO		M	4	(7)	
3	Cristiano DEL GROSSO		D	13	(4)	
29	Michele FERRI		D	22	(5)	
23	Michele FINI		M	22	(9)	3
10	Pasquale FOGGIA		M	24	(9)	5
16	Marco FORTIN		G	12		
27	Jedaias Capucho Neves "JEDA"	BRA	A	18	(2)	3
19	Joaquín LARRIVEY	ARG	A	11	(16)	1
6	Diego Luis LÓPEZ	URU	D	25	(1)	
28	Daniele MAGLIOCCHETTI		D	2		
26	Marco MANCOSU		M	3	(7)	
2	Davide MARCHINI		M		(1)	
1	Vincenzo MARRUOCCO		G	5		
32	Alessandro MATRI		A	20	(14)	6
18	Andrea PAROLA		M	29	(4)	
14	Francesco PISANO		D	14	(3)	
13	Marco STORARI		G	20		

CALCIO CATANIA

Coach - Silvio Baldini; (1/4/08) Walter Zenga

Founded - 1946

2007

26/8	Parma	a	2-2	*Morimoto, Baiocco*
2/9	Genoa	h	0-0	
16/9	Internazionale	a	0-2	
23/9	Fiorentina	h	0-1	
26/9	Empoli	h	1-0	*Martínez*
30/9	Milan	a	1-1	*Martínez*
7/10	Livorno	h	1-0	*Sardo*
21/10	Cagliari	a	1-1	*Terlizzi*
28/10	Sampdoria	h	2-0	*Mascara, Martínez*
31/10	Siena	a	1-1	*Vargas*
4/11	Atalanta	h	1-2	*Spinesi*
11/11	Torino	a	1-1	*Martínez*
25/11	Napoli	a	0-2	
2/12	Palermo	h	3-1	*Mascara, Spinesi (p), Martínez*
8/12	Lazio	a	0-2	
15/12	Udinese	h	2-0	*Mascara 2*
23/12	Reggina	a	1-3	*Vargas*

2008

12/1	Juventus	h	1-1	*Spinesi*
20/1	Roma	a	0-2	
27/1	Parma	h	0-0	
3/2	Genoa	a	1-2	*og (Bovo)*
10/2	Internazionale	h	0-2	
17/2	Fiorentina	a	1-2	*Vargas*
24/2	Empoli	a	0-2	
27/2	Milan	h	1-1	*Spinesi*
2/3	Livorno	a	0-1	
9/3	Cagliari	h	2-1	*Silvestri, og (Canini)*
16/3	Sampdoria	a	1-3	*Stovini*
19/3	Siena	h	0-0	
22/3	Atalanta	a	0-0	
30/3	Torino	h	1-2	*Spinesi*
6/4	Napoli	h	3-0	*Colucci, Spinesi, Vargas*
12/4	Palermo	a	0-1	

20/4	Lazio	h	1-0	*Spinesi (p)*
27/4	Udinese	a	1-2	*Vargas*
4/5	Reggina	h	1-2	*Martínez*
11/5	Juventus	a	1-1	*Martínez*
18/5	Roma	h	1-1	*Martínez*

No	Name	Nat	Pos	Aps	(s)	Gls
22	Pablo Sebastián ÁLVAREZ	ARG	D	2	(4)	
14	Anderson de Oliveira "BABÚ"	BRA	A		(2)	
17	Davide BAIOCCO		M	30	(3)	1
27	Marco BIAGIANTI		M	16	(2)	
1	Albano BIZZARRI	ARG	G	7		
26	Fabio CASERTA		M		(1)	
9	Giuseppe COLUCCI		M	19	(6)	1
8	Mark EDUSEI	GHA	M	23	(4)	
20	Marcello GAZZOLA		M	2	(1)	
13	Mariano Julio IZCO	ARG	M	22	(10)	
22	Ezequiel Cristián LLAMA	ARG	M		(1)	
25	Jorge Andrés MARTÍNEZ	URU	A	22	(9)	8
10	Giuseppe MASCARA		A	32	(3)	4
15	Takayuki MORIMOTO	JPN	A	2	(12)	1
32	Riccardo NARDINI		D		(1)	
11	Inácio João Batista "PIÁ"	BRA	A	3	(5)	
16	Ciro POLITO		G	31		
3	Rocco SABATO		D	12	(7)	
2	Gennaro SARDO		D	21	(1)	1
5	Matías Agustín SILVESTRE	ARG	D	9	(2)	
21	Cristian SILVESTRI		D	18	(3)	1
4	Andrea SOTTIL		D	5	(2)	
24	Gionatha SPINESI		A	28	(4)	7
6	Lorenzo STOVINI		D	36		1
19	Giacomo TEDESCO		M	21	(8)	
23	Christian TERLIZZI		D	23	(2)	1
7	Juan Manuel VARGAS	PER	D	34	(2)	5

EMPOLI FC

Coach - Luigi Cagni; (26/11/07) Alberto Malesani; (31/3/08) Luigi Cagni

Founded - 1921

2007				
26/8	Fiorentina	a	1-3	*Saudati*
1/9	Internazionale	h	0-2	
15/9	Lazio	a	0-0	
23/9	Napoli	h	0-0	
26/9	Catania	a	0-1	
30/9	Palermo	h	3-1	*Pozzi, Giovinco, Vannucchi (p)*
7/10	Siena	a	0-3	
21/10	Milan	a	1-0	*Saudati*
28/10	Atalanta	h	0-1	
31/10	Juventus	a	0-3	
4/11	Roma	h	2-2	*Vannucchi, Giovinco*
10/11	Sampdoria	a	0-3	
25/11	Torino	h	0-0	
2/12	Parma	a	0-1	
9/12	Cagliari	h	4-1	*Pozzi 4*
16/12	Genoa	h	1-1	*Giovinco*
23/12	Udinese	a	2-2	*Raggi, Marzoratti*
2008				
12/1	Reggina	h	1-1	*Saudati (p)*
20/1	Livorno	a	0-1	
27/1	Fiorentina	h	0-2	
3/2	Internazionale	a	0-1	
10/2	Lazio	h	1-0	*Vannucchi*
17/2	Napoli	a	3-1	*Pozzi 2, Budel*
24/2	Catania	h	2-0	*Giovinco, Budel*
27/2	Palermo	a	0-2	
2/3	Siena	h	0-2	
9/3	Milan	h	1-3	*Buscé*
16/3	Atalanta	a	1-4	*Vannucchi*
19/3	Juventus	h	0-0	
22/3	Roma	a	1-2	*Giovinco*
30/3	Sampdoria	h	0-2	
6/4	Torino	a	1-0	*Vannucchi*
13/4	Parma	h	1-1	*Giovinco*
20/4	Cagliari	a	0-2	
27/4	Genoa	a	1-0	*Abate*
4/5	Udinese	h	0-1	
11/5	Reggina	a	0-2	
18/5	Livorno	h	2-1	*Buscé, Saudati*

No	Name	Nat	Pos	Aps	(s)	Gls
6	Ignazio ABATE		M	9	(15)	1
14	Daniele ADANI		D	6		
77	Luca ANTONINI		M	28	(4)	
3	Nicola ASCOLI		D		(1)	
23	Daniele BALLI		G	21		
1	Davide BASSI		G	17		
32	Alessandro BUDEL		M	17	(2)	2
24	Antonio BUSCÉ		M	29	(1)	2
18	Guillermo GIACOMAZZI	URU	M	11	(9)	
21	Sebastian GIOVINCO		M	20	(15)	6
19	Claudio MARCHISIO		M	22	(4)	
8	Francesco MARIANINI		M	16	(9)	
16	Lino MARZORATTI		D	30	(2)	1
5	Davide MORO		M	24	(8)	
17	Gianluca MUSACCI		M	1	(1)	
2	Felice PICCOLO		D	18	(2)	
9	Nicola POZZI		A	12	(5)	7
50	Francesco PRATALI		D	14	(1)	
46	Andrea RAGGI		D	32	(1)	1
11	Luca SAUDATI		A	24	(6)	4
7	Vittorio TOSTO		D	26	(6)	
15	Richard VANIGLI		D	8	(5)	
10	Ighli VANNUCCHI		M	31	(3)	5
27	Rey VOLPATO		A	2	(11)	

ACF FIORENTINA

Coach - Cesare Prandelli

Founded – 1926

MAJOR HONOURS: UEFA Cup Winners' Cup - (1) 1961; Italian League - (2) 1956, 1969; Italian Cup - (6) 1940, 1961, 1966, 1975, 1996, 2001.

2007				
26/8	Empoli	h	3-1	*Pazzini, Mutu, Montolivo*
3/9	Milan	a	1-1	*Mutu*
16/9	Atalanta	h	2-2	*og (Rivalta), Vieri*
23/9	Catania	a	1-0	*Mutu*
26/9	Roma	h	2-2	*Gamberini, Mutu (p)*
29/9	Livorno	a	3-0	*Osvaldo 2, Santana*
7/10	Juventus	h	1-1	*Mutu (p)*
21/10	Siena	h	3-0	*Pazzini, Mutu, Vieri*
28/10	Genoa	a	0-0	
31/10	Napoli	h	1-0	*Vieri*
3/11	Lazio	a	1-0	*Pazzini*
11/11	Udinese	h	1-2	*Pazzini*
25/11	Reggina	a	0-0	
2/12	Internazionale	h	0-2	
8/12	Palermo	a	0-2	
16/12	Sampdoria	a	2-2	*Mutu, Donadel*
23/12	Cagliari	h	5-1	*Montolivo, Mutu 2 (1p), Santana 2*
2008				
13/1	Parma	a	2-1	*Mutu 2 (1p)*
19/1	Torino	h	2-1	*Vieri (p), Mutu (p)*
27/1	Empoli	a	2-0	*Mutu, Pazzini*
3/2	Milan	h	0-1	

2	Atalanta	a	2-2	*Pazzini, Semioli*
'/2	Catania	h	2-1	*Kuzmanović, Mutu*
/2	Roma	a	0-1	
'/2	Livorno	h	1-0	*Papa Waigo*
3	Juventus	a	3-2	*Gobbi, Papa Waigo, Osvaldo*
3	Siena	a	0-1	
/3	Genoa	h	3-1	*Santana, Mutu, Pazzini*
/3	Napoli	a	0-2	
/3	Lazio	h	1-0	*Pazzini*
/3	Udinese	a	1-3	*Vieri*
'4	Reggina	h	2-0	*Pazzini, Mutu*
/4	Internazionale	a	0-2	
/4	Palermo	h	1-0	*Donadel*
'/4	Sampdoria	h	2-2	*Vieri, Mutu (p)*
'5	Cagliari	a	1-2	*Santana*
1/5	Parma	h	3-1	*Santana, Semioli, Osvaldo*
3/5	Torino	a	1-0	*Osvaldo*

o	Name	Nat	Pos	Aps	(s)	Gls
5	Vlada AVRAMOV	SRB	G	1	(1)	
7	Federico BALZARETTI		D	4	(2)	
9	Daniele CACIA		A		(3)	
	Dario DAINELLI		D	18	(3)	
	Marco DONADEL		M	27	(4)	2
	Sébastien FREY	FRA	G	35		
	Alessandro GAMBERINI		D	31		1
9	Massimo GOBBI		M	15	(8)	1
0	Martin JØRGENSEN	DEN	M	14	(12)	
	Per KRØLDRUP	DEN	D	18		
2	Zdravko KUZMANOVIĆ	SRB	M	25	(9)	1
1	Fabio LIVERANI		M	22	(6)	
2	Cristiano LUPATELLI		G	2		
8	Riccardo MONTOLIVO		M	31	(3)	2
0	Adrian MUTU	ROU	A	28	(1)	17
	Pablo Daniel OSVALDO		A	7	(6)	5
7	PAPA WAIGO Ndiaye	GHA	A	2	(5)	2
23	Manuel PASQUAL		D	25	(4)	
3	Michele PAZIENZA		M	3	(5)	
29	Gianpaolo PAZZINI		A	29	(2)	9
5	Alessandro POTENZA		D	11	(4)	
24	Mario Alberto SANTANA	ARG	M	22	(4)	6
7	Franco SEMIOLI		M	13	(8)	2
21	Tomáš UJFALUŠI	CZE	D	28		
13	Anthony VANDEN BORRE	BEL	D		(2)	
32	Christian VIERI		A	7	(19)	6

GENOA CFC

Coach - Gian Piero Gasperini

Founded – 1893

MAJOR HONOURS: Italian League – (9) 1898, 1899, 1900, 1902, 1903, 1904, 1915, 1923, 1924; Italian Cup – (1) 1937.

2007				
26/8	Milan	h	0-3	
2/9	Catania	a	0-0	
16/9	Livorno	h	1-1	*Borriello*
23/9	Sampdoria	a	0-0	
26/9	Udinese	h	3-2	*Borriello 3 (1p)*
30/9	Napoli	a	2-1	*og (Cannavaro), Sculli*
7/10	Cagliari	h	2-0	*Borriello, Di Vaio*
21/10	Juventus	a	0-1	
28/10	Fiorentina	h	0-0	
31/10	Internazionale	a	1-4	*Konko*
4/11	Palermo	h	3-3	*Leon 2, Borriello*
11/11	Reggina	a	0-2	
24/11	Roma	h	0-1	
2/12	Torino	a	1-1	*Borriello*
9/12	Siena	h	1-3	*Figueroa*
16/12	Empoli	a	1-1	*Masiello*
22/12	Parma	h	1-0	*Borriello (p)*
2008				
13/1	Lazio	a	2-1	*Borriello 2 (1p)*
19/1	Atalanta	h	2-1	*Borriello, Figueroa*
27/1	Milan	a	0-2	
3/2	Catania	h	2-1	*Danilo, Borriello (p)*
10/2	Livorno	a	1-1	*Di Vaio*
17/2	Sampdoria	h	0-1	
24/2	Udinese	a	5-3	*Leon, Sculli, Borriello 3*
27/2	Napoli	h	2-0	*Sculli, Borriello (p)*
2/3	Cagliari	a	1-2	*Lucerelli*
9/3	Juventus	h	0-2	
16/3	Fiorentina	a	1-3	*Masiero*
19/3	Internazionale	h	1-1	*Borriello*
22/3	Palermo	a	3-2	*Figueroa, Milanetto, Konko*
30/3	Reggina	h	2-0	*Borriello, Rossi*
5/4	Roma	a	2-3	*Rossi, Leon*
13/4	Torino	h	3-0	*Di Vaio, Borriello, Sculli*
20/4	Siena	a	1-0	*Konko*
27/4	Empoli	h	0-1	
4/5	Parma	a	0-1	
11/5	Lazio	h	0-2	
18/5	Atalanta	a	0-2	

No	Name	Nat	Pos	Aps	(s)	Gls
4	Francesco BEGA		D	8	(2)	
22	Marco BORRIELLO		A	32	(3)	19
3	Cesare BOVO		D	26	(1)	
5	Manuel COPPOLA		M	1	(2)	
18	Domenico CRISCITO		D	16		
8	Sacramento Valério DANILO	BRA	M	19	(3)	1
25	Gaetano DE ROSA		D	14	(2)	
21	Marco DI VAIO		A	9	(13)	3
29	Lima Rodrigues FABIANO	BRA	D	22	(6)	
9	Luciano Gabriel FIGUEROA	ARG	A	5	(16)	3
30	Mirco GASPARETTO		A	1		
23	Tommaso GHINASSI		D		(1)	
28	Ivan JURIĆ	CRO	M	31	(3)	
24	Abdoulay KONKO		M	36	(1)	3
11	Julio Cesar LEÓN	HON	A	22	(7)	4
16	Alessandro LUCARELLI		D	23	(6)	1
34	Andrea MASIELLO		D	2	(2)	1
10	Matias Nicolás MASIERO	URU	M		(2)	1
77	Omar MILANETTO		M	26	(3)	1
20	PAPA WAIGO Ndiaye	GHA	A	3	(6)	
19	Matteo PARO		M	16	(4)	
15	Silvano RAGGIO GARIBALDI		M		(2)	
7	Marco ROSSI		M	29	(4)	2
83	Rubens Fernando Moedim "RUBINHO"	BRA	G	29		
33	Gleison Pinto SANTOS	BRA	D	11	(5)	
73	Alessio SCARPI		G	9	(5)	
14	Giuseppe SCULLI		A	27	(7)	4
68	Anthony VANDEN BORRE	BEL	D		(6)	
38	Rodrigues Fonseca WILSON	BRA	M	1	(2)	

FC INTERNAZIONALE MILANO

Coach - Roberto Mancini

Founded – 1908

MAJOR HONOURS: European Champion Clubs' Cup - (2) 1964, 1965; UEFA Cup - (3) 1991, 1994, 1998; World Club Cup - (2) 1964, 1965; Italian League - (16) 1910, 1920, 1930, 1938, 1940, 1953, 1954, 1963, 1965, 1966, 1971, 1980, 1989, 2006, 2007, 2008; Italian Cup - (5) 1939, 1978, 1982, 2005, 2006.

2007				
26/8	Udinese	h	1-1	*Stanković*
1/9	Empoli	a	2-0	*Ibrahimović 2*
16/9	Catania	h	2-0	*Crespo, César*
23/9	Livorno	a	2-2	*Ibrahimović 2 (1p)*

26/9	Sampdoria	h	3-0	*Ibrahimović 2, Figo*
29/9	Roma	a	4-1	*Ibrahimović (p), Crespo, Cruz, Córdoba*
6/10	Napoli	h	2-1	*Cruz 2*
20/10	Reggina	a	1-0	*Adriano*
28/10	Palermo	a	0-0	
31/10	Genoa	h	4-1	*Córdoba, Cambiasso, Suazo, Cruz (p)*
4/11	Juventus	a	1-1	*Cruz*
24/11	Atalanta	h	2-1	*Suazo, Cruz*
2/12	Fiorentina	a	2-0	*Jiménez, Cruz*
5/12	Lazio	h	3-0	*Ibrahimović (p), Maicon, Suazo*
9/12	Torino	h	4-0	*Ibrahimović (p), Cruz, Jiménez, Córdoba*
16/12	Cagliari	a	2-0	*Cruz, Suazo*
23/12	Milan	h	2-1	*Cruz, Cambiasso*
2008				
13/1	Siena	a	3-2	*Ibrahimović 2 (1p), Cambiasso*
20/1	Parma	h	3-2	*Cambiasso, Ibrahimović 2 (1p)*
27/1	Udinese	a	0-0	
3/2	Empoli	h	1-0	*Ibrahimović (p)*
10/2	Catania	a	2-0	*Cambiasso, Suazo*
16/2	Livorno	h	2-0	*Suazo 2*
24/2	Sampdoria	a	1-1	*Crespo*
27/2	Roma	h	1-1	*Zanetti*
2/3	Napoli	a	0-1	
8/3	Reggina	h	2-0	*Ibrahimović (p), Burdisso*
16/3	Palermo	h	2-1	*Vieira, Jiménez*
19/3	Genoa	a	1-1	*Suazo*
22/3	Juventus	h	1-2	*Maniche*
29/3	Lazio	a	1-1	*Crespo*
6/4	Atalanta	a	2-0	*Vieira, Balotelli*
13/4	Fiorentina	h	2-0	*Cambiasso, Balotelli*
20/4	Torino	a	1-0	*Cruz*
27/4	Cagliari	h	2-1	*Cruz, Materazzi*
4/5	Milan	a	1-2	*Cruz*
11/5	Siena	h	2-2	*Vieira, Balotelli*
18/5	Parma	a	2-0	*Ibrahimović 2*

No	Name	Nat	Pos	Aps	(s)	Gls
10	ADRIANO Leite Ribeiro	BRA	A	3	(1)	1
45	Mario Barwuah BALOTELLI		A	7	(4)	3
16	Nicolás Andrés BURDISSO	ARG	D	20	(4)	1
19	Esteban Matías CAMBIASSO	ARG	M	33		6
31	CÉSAR Aparecido Rodrigues	BRA	M	13	(4)	1
26	Cristian Eugen CHIVU	ROU	D	23	(3)	
2	Iván Ramiro CÓRDOBA	COL	D	20		3
18	Hernán Jorge CRESPO	ARG	A	12	(7)	4
9	Julio Ricardo CRUZ	ARG	A	22	(6)	13
15	Olivier DACOURT	FRA	M	6	(3)	
7	Luís Filipe FIGO	POR	M	10	(7)	1
8	Zlatan IBRAHIMOVIĆ	SWE	A	22	(4)	17
11	Luis Antonio JIMÉNEZ	CHI	M	11	(4)	3
12	JÚLIO CÉSAR Soares Espindola	BRA	G	35		
13	MAICON Douglas Sisenando	BRA	D	31		1
28	Nuno Ribeiro "MANICHE"	POR	M	4	(4)	1
23	Marco MATERAZZI		D	16	(7)	1
6	MAXWELL Scherrer Cabelino Andrade	BRA	D	27	(5)	
22	Paolo ORLANDONI		G	1	(1)	
30	Vítor Hugo Gomes Passos "PELÉ"	POR	M	4	(11)	
24	Nélson Enrique RIVAS	COL	D	6	(5)	
25	Walter Adrián SAMUEL	ARG	D	12		
21	Santiago SOLARI	ARG	M	2	(3)	
5	Dejan STANKOVIĆ	SRB	M	19	(2)	1
29	David Óscar SUAZO	HON	A	9	(18)	8
1	Francesco TOLDO		G	2	(1)	
14	Patrick VIEIRA	FRA	M	13	(3)	3
4	Javier ZANETTI	ARG	M	35	(3)	1

JUVENTUS

Coach - Claudio Ranieri

Founded – 1897

MAJOR HONOURS: European Champion Clubs' Cup/UEFA Champion League - (2) 1985, 1996; UEFA Cup Winners' Cup - (1) 1984; UEFA Cup (3) 1977, 1990, 1993; UEFA Super Cup - (2) 1984, 1997; World Club Cup - (2) 1985, 1996; Italian League - (27) 1905, 1926, 193 1932, 1933, 1934, 1935, 1950, 1952, 1958, 1960, 1961, 1967, 1972, 197 1975, 1977, 1978, 1981, 1982, 1984, 1986, 1995, 1997, 1998, 2002, 200 Italian Cup - (9) 1938, 1942, 1959, 1960, 1965, 1979, 1983, 1990, 1995.

2007				
25/8	Livorno	h	5-1	*Trezeguet 3, Iaquinta 2 (1p)*
2/9	Cagliari	a	3-2	*Trezeguet, Del Piero, Chiellini*
16/9	Udinese	h	0-1	
23/9	Roma	a	2-2	*Trezeguet, Iaquinta*
26/9	Reggina	h	4-0	*Legrottaglie, Salihamidžić, Trezeguet, Palladino*
30/9	Torino	a	1-0	*Trezeguet*
7/10	Fiorentina	a	1-1	*Iaquinta*
21/10	Genoa	h	1-0	*Del Piero*
27/10	Napoli	a	1-3	*Del Piero*
31/10	Empoli	h	3-0	*Trezeguet 3 (1p)*
4/11	Internazionale	h	1-1	*Camoranesi*
11/11	Parma	a	2-2	*Legrottaglie, Iaquinta*
25/11	Palermo	h	5-0	*Trezeguet, Iaquinta, Del Piero 2 (1p), Marchionni*
1/12	Milan	a	0-0	
9/12	Atalanta	h	1-0	*Nedvěd*
15/12	Lazio	a	3-2	*Trezeguet, Del Piero 2*
23/12	Siena	h	2-0	*Salihamidžić, Trezeguet*
2008				
12/1	Catania	a	1-1	*Del Piero (p)*
20/1	Sampdoria	h	0-0	
27/1	Livorno	a	3-1	*Trezeguet 2, Del Piero*
3/2	Cagliari	h	1-1	*Nedvěd*
10/2	Udinese	a	2-1	*Camoranesi, Iaquinta*
16/2	Roma	h	1-0	*Del Piero*
23/2	Reggina	a	1-2	*Del Piero*
26/2	Torino	h	0-0	
2/3	Fiorentina	h	2-3	*Sissoko, Camoranesi*
9/3	Genoa	a	2-0	*Grygera, Trezeguet*
16/3	Napoli	h	1-0	*Iaquinta*
19/3	Empoli	a	0-0	
22/3	Internazionale	a	2-1	*Camoranesi, Trezeguet*
6/4	Palermo	a	2-3	*Del Piero 2*
12/4	Milan	h	3-2	*Del Piero, Salihamidžić 2*
16/4	Parma	h	3-0	*Trezeguet, Palladino, og (Morrone)*
20/4	Atalanta	a	4-0	*Stendardo, Del Piero 3*
27/4	Lazio	h	5-2	*Chiellini 2, Camoranesi, Del Piero, Trezeguet*
4/5	Siena	a	0-1	
11/5	Catania	h	1-1	*Del Piero*
17/5	Sampdoria	a	3-3	*Del Piero 2 (1p), Trezeguet (p)*

No	Name	Nat	Pos	Aps	(s)	Gls
4	Sergio Bernardo ALMIRÓN	ARG	M	5	(4)	
12	Emanuele BELARDI		G	4	(1)	
2	Alessandro BIRINDELLI		D	4	(3)	
1	Gianluigi BUFFON		G	34		
8	Mauro German CAMORANESI		M	18	(4)	5

Name	Nat	Pos	Aps	(s)	Gls
Luca CASTIGLIA		M		(2)	
Giorgio CHIELLINI		D	30		3
Domenico CRISCITO		D	8		
Alessandro DEL PIERO		A	32	(5)	21
Zdeněk GRYGERA	CZE	D	22	(2)	1
Vincenzo IAQUINTA		A	9	(15)	8
JORGE Manuel ANDRADE	POR	D	4		
Nicola LEGROTTAGLIE		D	31	(2)	2
Marco MARCHIONNI		M	1	(10)	1
Cristian MOLINARO		D	30	(1)	
Pavel NEDVĚD	CZE	M	28	(3)	2
Antonio NOCERINO		M	23	(9)	
Rubén OLIVERA	URU	M		(1)	
Raffaele PALLADINO		A	14	(12)	2
Cristian PASQUATO		A		(1)	
Hasan SALIHAMIDŽIĆ	BIH	M	21	(5)	4
Mohamed Lamine SISSOKO	MLI	M	12	(3)	1
Guglielmo STENDARDO		D	3	(2)	1
TIAGO Cardoso Mendes	POR	M	10	(10)	
David TREZEGUET	FRA	A	35	(1)	20
Cristiano ZANETTI		M	26		
Jonathan ZEBINA	FRA	D	14	(2)	

S.S. LAZIO

Coach - Delio Rossi

Founded – 1900

MAJOR HONOURS: UEFA Cup Winners' Cup - (1) 1999; UEFA Super Cup - (1) 1999; Italian League - (2) 1974, 2000; Italian Cup - (4) 1958, 1998, 2000, 2004.

2007

Date	Opponent		Score	Scorers
25/8	Torino	h	2-2	*Pandev, Rocchi*
2/9	Sampdoria	a	0-0	
15/9	Empoli	h	0-0	
23/9	Atalanta	a	1-2	*Mutarelli*
26/9	Cagliari	h	3-1	*Rocchi 2, Pandev*
30/9	Reggina	a	1-1	*Kolarov*
7/10	Milan	h	1-5	*Mauri*
21/10	Livorno	a	1-0	*Pandev*
28/10	Udinese	h	0-1	
31/10	Roma	a	2-3	*Rocchi, Ledesma*
3/11	Fiorentina	h	0-1	
25/11	Parma	h	1-0	*Firmani*
2/12	Siena	a	1-1	*Pandev*
5/12	Internazionale	a	0-3	
8/12	Catania	h	2-0	*Rocchi, Pandev*
15/12	Juventus	h	2-3	*Pandev 2*
23/12	Palermo	a	2-2	*Firmani, Tare*

2008

Date	Opponent		Score	Scorers
13/1	Genoa	h	1-2	*Mauri*
20/1	Napoli	a	2-2	*Ledesma, Pandev*
27/1	Torino	a	0-0	
3/2	Sampdoria	h	2-1	*Mauri, Rocchi*
10/2	Empoli	a	0-1	
17/2	Atalanta	h	3-0	*Rocchi 2 (2p), Pandev*
24/2	Cagliari	a	0-1	
27/2	Reggina	h	1-0	*Bianchi (p)*
1/3	Milan	a	1-1	*Bianchi*
9/3	Livorno	h	2-0	*Rocchi, Pandev*
15/3	Udinese	a	2-2	*Rocchi, Ledesma*
19/3	Roma	h	3-2	*Pandev, Rocchi (p), Behrami*
22/3	Fiorentina	a	0-1	
29/3	Internazionale	h	1-1	*Rocchi*
6/4	Parma	a	2-2	*Pandev, Bianchi*
13/4	Siena	h	1-1	*Mutarelli*
20/4	Catania	a	0-1	
27/4	Juventus	a	2-5	*Bianchi, Siviglia*
4/5	Palermo	h	1-2	*Pandev (p)*
11/5	Genoa	a	2-0	*Pandev, Rocchi*
18/5	Napoli	h	2-1	*Rocchi, Firmani*

No	Name	Nat	Pos	Aps	(s)	Gls
22	Ivan ARTIPOLI		D	1		
32	Marco BALLOTTA		G	29		
10	Roberto BARONIO		M	6	(2)	
85	Valon BEHRAMI	SUI	M	21	(1)	1
9	Rolando BIANCHI		A	9	(6)	4
25	CRIBARI Emilson Sanchez	BRA	D	29	(2)	
6	Ousmane DABO	FRA	M	10	(3)	
29	Lorenzo DE SILVESTRI		D	17	(7)	
81	Simone DEL NERO		M	2	(3)	
15	Modibo DIAKITÉ	FRA	D	1		
4	Fabio FIRMANI		M	5	(2)	3
3	Aleksandar KOLAROV	SRB	D	17	(7)	1
24	Cristián Daniel LEDESMA	ARG	M	31	(1)	3
20	Ayodele Stephen MAKINWA	NGA	A	6	(8)	
68	Christian José MANFREDINI		M	15	(8)	
11	Stefano MAURI		M	18	(6)	3
23	Mourad MEGHNI	FRA	M	7	(12)	
26	Gaby MUDINGAYI	BEL	M	21	(6)	
1	Néstor MUSLERA	URU	G	9		
5	Massimo MUTARELLI		M	22	(2)	2
19	Goran PANDEV	MKD	A	30	(2)	14
2	Ştefan Andrei RADU	ROU	D	11		
18	Tommaso ROCCHI		A	31	(5)	14
7	David ROZEHNAL	CZE	D	7	(3)	
6	Lionel Sebastian SCALONI	ARG	M	7	(5)	
13	Sebastiano SIVIGLIA		D	19		1
2	Guglielmo STENDARDO		D	13		
17	Igli TARE	ALB	A	4	(14)	1
21	Fabio VIGNAROLI		A	3	(6)	
8	Luciano ZAURI		D	17	(1)	

AS LIVORNO CALCIO

Coach - Fernando Orsi; (10/10/07) Giancarlo Camolese; (28/4/08) Fernando Orsi

Founded - 1915

2007

Date	Opponent		Score	Scorers
25/8	Juventus	a	1-5	*Loviso*
2/9	Palermo	h	2-4	*Rossini, Grandoni*
16/9	Genoa	a	1-1	*Tavano (p)*
23/9	Internazionale	h	2-2	*De Vezze, Loviso (p)*
26/9	Napoli	a	0-1	
29/9	Fiorentina	h	0-3	
7/10	Catania	a	0-1	
21/10	Lazio	h	0-1	
28/10	Parma	a	2-3	*Tavano 2 (1p)*
31/10	Reggina	a	3-1	*Pulzetti, og (Valdez), Rossini*
4/11	Udinese	h	0-0	
11/11	Siena	a	3-2	*Tavano, Bergvold, Knežević*
25/11	Sampdoria	h	3-1	*Knežević, Tavano 2*
2/12	Cagliari	a	0-0	
9/12	Roma	h	1-1	*Diego Tristán*
23/12	Atalanta	h	1-1	*Grandoni*

2008

Date	Opponent		Score	Scorers
13/1	Torino	a	2-1	*Tavano 2*
20/1	Empoli	h	1-0	*Tavano (p)*
27/1	Juventus	h	1-3	*Bogdani*
2/2	Palermo	a	0-1	
10/2	Genoa	h	1-1	*Tavano*
13/2	Milan	a	1-1	*Pulzetti*
16/2	Internazionale	a	0-2	
24/2	Napoli	h	1-2	*Diamanti*
27/2	Fiorentina	a	0-1	
2/3	Catania	h	1-0	*Diamanti*
9/3	Lazio	a	0-2	
16/3	Parma	h	1-1	*Vidigal*
19/3	Reggina	h	1-1	*Bogdani*

22/3	Udinese	a 0-2	
30/3	Siena	h 0-0	
6/4	Sampdoria	a 0-2	
13/4	Cagliari	h 1-2	*Galante*
19/4	Roma	a 1-1	*Diamanti*
27/4	Milan	h 1-4	*Knežević*
4/5	Atalanta	a 2-3	*Rossini, Pavan*
11/5	Torino	h 0-1	
18/5	Empoli	a 1-2	*Diamanti*

No	Name	Nat	Pos	Aps	(s)	Gls
17	Edgar ÁLVAREZ	HON	M	3	(5)	
1	Marco AMELIA		G	33		
69	David BALLERI		D	25	(3)	
9	Martin BERGVOLD	DEN	M	12	(1)	1
81	Erjon BOGDANI	ALB	A	13	(15)	2
14	Alfonso DE LUCIA		G	5	(1)	
11	Daniele DE VEZZE		M	23	(4)	1
23	Alessandro DIAMANTI		A	14	(12)	4
22	DIEGO TRISTÁN	ESP	A	17	(4)	1
3	Antonio FILIPPINI		M	21	(4)	
4	Emanuele FILIPPINI		M	10	(10)	
6	Fabio GALANTE		D	33	(1)	1
16	Giuliano GIANNICHEDDA		M	5	(3)	
77	Alessandro GRANDONI		D	33	(1)	2
24	Filip KRSTIĆ	GER	M		(1)	
15	Dario KNEŽEVIĆ	CRO	D	35		3
21	Massimo LOVISO		M	16	(3)	2
79	Matteo MELARA		D	4		
26	Giovanni PASQUALE		D	35		
32	Simone PAVAN		D	8	(8)	1
7	Nico PULZETTI		M	23	(3)	2
18	Rahman REZAEI	IRN	D	1	(4)	
20	Fausto ROSSINI		A	5	(15)	3
33	Feitosa Dos Santos "SIDNY"	BRA	M	1	(1)	
10	Francesco TAVANO		A	28	(2)	10
86	Tommaso VAILATTI		M	1	(3)	
8	José Luís VIDIGAL	POR	M	14	(3)	1
78	Francesco VOLPE		A		(2)	

AC MILAN

Coach - Carlo Ancelotti

Founded – 1899

MAJOR HONOURS: European Champion Clubs' Cup/UEFA Champions League - (7) 1963, 1969, 1989, 1990, 1994, 2003, 2007; UEFA Cup Winners' Cup - (2) 1968, 1973; UEFA Super Cup - (5) 1989, 1990, 1995, 2003, 2007; World Club Cup - (4) 1969, 1989, 1990, 2007; Italian League - (17) 1901, 1906, 1907, 1951, 1955, 1957, 1959, 1962, 1968, 1979, 1988, 1992, 1993, 1994, 1996, 1999, 2004; Italian Cup - (5) 1967, 1972, 1973, 1977, 2003.

2007			
26/8	Genoa	a 3-0	*Ambrosini, Kaká 2 (1p)*
3/9	Fiorentina	h 1-1	*Kaká (p)*
15/9	Siena	a 1-1	*Nesta*
22/9	Parma	h 1-1	*Seedorf*
26/9	Palermo	a 1-2	*Seedorf*
30/9	Catania	h 1-1	*Kaká (p)*
7/10	Lazio	a 5-1	*Ambrosini, Kaká 2 (1p), Gilardino 2*
21/10	Empoli	h 0-1	
28/10	Roma	h 0-1	
31/10	Sampdoria	a 5-0	*Kaká, Gilardino 2, Gourcuff, Seedorf*
3/11	Torino	h 0-0	
25/11	Cagliari	a 2-1	*Gilardino, Pirlo*
1/12	Juventus	h 0-0	
23/12	Internazionale	a 1-2	*Pirlo*
2008			
13/1	Napoli	h 5-2	*Ronaldo 2, Seedorf, Kaká, Pato*
20/1	Udinese	a 1-0	*Gilardino*
23/1	Atalanta	a 1-2	*Gattuso*
27/1	Genoa	h 2-0	*Pato 2*
30/1	Reggina	a 1-0	*Gilardino*
3/2	Fiorentina	a 1-0	*Pato*
10/2	Siena	h 1-0	*Paloschi*
13/2	Livorno	h 1-1	*Pirlo (p)*
16/2	Parma	a 0-0	
24/2	Palermo	h 2-1	*Ambrosini, Inzaghi*
27/2	Catania	a 1-1	*Pato*
1/3	Lazio	h 1-1	*Oddo (p)*
9/3	Empoli	a 3-1	*Pato, Ambrosini, Kaká*
15/3	Roma	a 1-2	*Kaká*
19/3	Sampdoria	h 1-2	*Paloschi*
22/3	Torino	a 1-0	*Pato*
30/3	Atalanta	h 1-2	*Maldini*
5/4	Cagliari	h 3-1	*Kaká, Inzaghi 2*
12/4	Juventus	a 2-3	*Inzaghi 2*
20/4	Reggina	h 5-1	*Kaká 3 (2p), Inzaghi, Pato*
27/4	Livorno	a 4-1	*Inzaghi 3, Seedorf*
4/5	Internazionale	h 2-1	*Inzaghi, Kaká*
11/5	Napoli	a 1-3	*Seedorf*
18/5	Udinese	h 4-1	*Pato, Inzaghi, Cafu, Seedorf*

No	Name	Nat	Pos	Aps	(s)	Gls
23	Massimo AMBROSINI		M	31	(2)	4
25	Daniele BONERA		D	17	(4)	
32	Christian BROCCHI		M	10	(14)	
2	Marcos Evangelista de Moraes "CAFU"	BRA	D	8	(7)	1
1	Nélson de Jesus Silva "DIDA"	BRA	G	13		
31	Rodrigo Izecson Santos Leite "DIGÃO"	BRA	D		(1)	
5	EMERSON Ferreira Da Rosa	BRA	M	6	(9)	
19	Giuseppe FAVALLI		D	19	(7)	
8	Gennaro Ivan GATTUSO		M	30	(1)	1
11	Alberto GILARDINO		A	20	(10)	7
20	Yoann GOURCUFF	FRA	M	4	(11)	1
9	Filippo INZAGHI		A	14	(7)	11
18	Marek JANKULOVSKI	CZE	D	10	(4)	
16	Željko KALAC	AUS	G	25		
4	Kakhaber KALADZE	GEO	D	30	(2)	
22	Ricardo Izecson Santos Leite "KAKÁ"	BRA	M	30		15
3	Paolo MALDINI		D	15	(2)	1
13	Alessandro NESTA		D	28	(1)	1
44	Massimo ODDO		D	21	(4)	1
43	Alberto PALOSCHI		A	1	(6)	2
7	Alexandre Rodrigues da Silva "PATO"	BRA	A	13	(5)	9
21	Andrea PIRLO		M	32	(1)	3
99	RONALDO Luiz Nazário de Lima	BRA	A	4	(2)	2
10	Clarence SEEDORF	NED	M	31	(1)	7
27	Cláudio dos Santos Sérgio "SERGINHO"	BRA	D	5	(6)	
17	Dario ŠIMIĆ	CRO	D	1	(3)	

SSC NAPOLI

Coach - Edoardo Reja

Founded – 1921

MAJOR HONOURS: UEFA Cup – (1) 1989 ; Italian League – (2) 1987, 1990; Italian Cup – (3) 1962, 1976, 1987.

2007			
26/8	Catania	h 0-2	
2/9	Udinese	a 5-0	*Zalayeta 2, Domizzi, Lavezzi, Sosa*

/9	Sampdoria	h	2-0	*Zalayeta, Hamšík*
/9	Empoli	a	0-0	
/9	Livorno	h	1-0	*Sosa*
/9	Genoa	h	1-2	*Domizzi (p)*
10	Internazionale	a	1-2	*Sosa*
/10	Roma	a	4-4	*Lavezzi, Hamšík, Gargano, Zalayeta*
/10	Juventus	h	3-1	*Gargano, Domizzi 2 (2p)*
/10	Fiorentina	a	0-1	
11	Reggina	h	1-1	*Lavezzi*
/11	Palermo	a	1-2	*Bogliacino*
/11	Catania	h	2-0	*Zalayeta 2*
12	Atalanta	a	1-5	*Sosa*
12	Parma	h	1-0	*Zalayeta*
/12	Siena	a	1-1	*Bogliacino*
/12	Torino	h	1-1	*Hamšík*
)08				
/1	Milan	a	2-5	*Sosa, Domizzi (p)*
)/1	Lazio	h	2-2	*Hamšík 2*
/1	Catania	a	1-2	*Hamšík*
2	Udinese	h	3-1	*og (Zapata), Lavezzi 2*
)/2	Sampdoria	a	0-2	
/2	Empoli	h	1-3	*Mannini*
/2	Livorno	a	2-1	*Calaio 2*
7/2	Genoa	a	0-2	
3	Internazionale	h	1-0	*Zalayeta*
3	Roma	h	0-2	
5/3	Juventus	a	0-1	
)/3	Fiorentina	h	2-0	*Lavezzi 2*
2/3	Reggina	a	1-1	*Sosa*
)/3	Palermo	h	1-0	*Hamšík*
/4	Catania	a	0-3	
3/4	Atalanta	h	2-0	*Hamšík, Lavezzi*
)/4	Parma	a	2-1	*Domizzi (p), Bogliacino*
7/4	Siena	h	0-0	
/5	Torino	a	1-2	*Contini*
1/5	Milan	h	3-1	*Hamšík, Domizzi (p), Garics*
8/5	Lazio	a	1-2	*Domizzi*

o	Name	Nat	Pos	Aps	(s)	Gls
	Manuele BLASI		M	27		
8	Mariano Adrián BOGLIACINO	URU	M	16	(19)	3
1	Emanuele CALAIÒ		A	7	(19)	2
8	Paolo CANNAVARO		D	34		
7	Marco CAPPARELLA		M		(2)	
6	Matteo CONTINI		D	22	(6)	1
6	Andrea CUPI		D	16		
4	Samuele DALLA BONA		M		(2)	
0	Roberto DE ZERBI		M	1	(2)	
1	Maurizio DOMIZZI		D	29		8
3	Walter Alejandro GARGANO	URU	M	34		2
4	György GARICS	AUT	D	17	(9)	1
2	Matteo GIANELLO		G	16		
	Gianluca GRAVA		D	13	(6)	
7	Marek HAMŠÍK	SVK	M	34	(3)	9
	Gennaro IEZZO		G	19		
	Ezequiel Iván LAVEZZI	ARG	A	34	(1)	8
	Rubén Darío MALDONADO	PAR	D	1	(1)	
1	Daniele MANNINI		M	15		1
	Francesco MONTERVINO		M	1	(8)	
0	Nicolás Gaston NAVARRO	ARG	G	3		
	Michele PAZIENZA		M	8	(5)	
	Erminio RULLO		D	2	(2)	
3	Fabiano SANTACROCE		D	11	(2)	
9	Mirko SAVINI		D	29		
	Roberto Carlos SOSA	ARG	A	8	(22)	6
25	Marcelo ZALAYETA	URU	A	21	(1)	8

US CITTÀ DI PALERMO

Coach - Stefano Colantuono; (26/11/07) Francesco Guidolin; (24/3/08) Stefano Colantuono

Founded - 1900

2007				
26/8	Roma	h	0-2	
2/9	Livorno	a	4-2	*Rinaudo, Miccoli 2, Amauri*
16/9	Torino	h	1-1	*Simplício*
23/9	Cagliari	a	1-0	*Zaccardo*
26/9	Milan	h	2-1	*Diana, Miccoli*
30/9	Empoli	a	1-3	*Cavani*
7/10	Reggina	h	1-1	*Amauri*
21/10	Udinese	a	1-1	*Amauri*
28/10	Internazionale	h	0-0	
31/10	Parma	h	1-1	*Amauri (p)*
4/11	Genoa	a	3-3	*Cavani, Brienza, Amauri*
10/11	Napoli	h	2-1	*Tedesco 2*
25/11	Juventus	a	0-5	
2/12	Catania	a	1-3	*Caserta*
8/12	Fiorentina	h	2-0	*Miccoli, Simplício*
16/12	Atalanta	a	3-1	*Cavani, og (Langella), Amauri*
23/12	Lazio	h	2-2	*Simplício, Amauri*
2008				
13/1	Sampdoria	a	0-3	
20/1	Siena	h	2-3	*Amauri, Miccoli (p)*
26/1	Roma	a	0-1	
2/2	Livorno	h	1-0	*Miccoli*
10/2	Torino	a	1-3	*Amauri*
17/2	Cagliari	h	2-1	*Cavani, Janković*
24/2	Milan	a	1-2	*Bresciano*
27/2	Empoli	h	2-0	*Simplício, Rinaudo*
2/3	Reggina	a	0-0	
8/3	Udinese	h	1-1	*Simplício*
16/3	Internazionale	a	1-2	*og (Materazzi)*
19/3	Parma	a	1-2	*Cavani*
22/3	Genoa	h	2-3	*Amauri 2 (1p)*
30/3	Napoli	a	0-1	
6/4	Juventus	h	3-2	*Amauri 2, Cassani*
12/4	Catania	h	1-0	*Miccoli*
19/4	Fiorentina	a	0-1	
27/4	Atalanta	h	0-0	
4/5	Lazio	a	2-1	*Amauri 2*
11/5	Sampdoria	h	0-2	
18/5	Siena	a	2-2	*Janković, Miccoli*

No	Name	Nat	Pos	Aps	(s)	Gls
1	Federico AGLIARDI		G	8	(2)	
11	AMAURI Carvalho de Oliveira	BRA	A	34		15
42	Federico BALZARETTI		D	16		
43	Andrea BARZAGLI		D	33	(1)	
21	Giuseppe BIAVA		D	23	(1)	
23	Marco BRESCIANO	AUS	M	12	(14)	1
19	Franco BRIENZA		A	3	(5)	1
9	Edgar CANI	ALB	A		(1)	
3	Ciro CAPUANO		D	11	(1)	
18	Paolo CARBONARO		A		(1)	
20	Fabio CASERTA		M	24	(3)	1
16	Mattia CASSANI		D	18	(8)	1
7	Edinson CAVANI	URU	A	17	(16)	5
53	Alberto COSSENTINO		D		(1)	
22	Luca DI MATTEO		M		(2)	
32	Aimo Stefano DIANA		M	12	(3)	1
12	Alberto FONTANA		G	30		
14	Roberto GUANA		M	27	(5)	
17	Boško JANKOVIĆ	SRB	M	14	(12)	2
10	Fabrizio MICCOLI		A	19	(3)	8
8	Giulio MIGLIACCIO		M	26	(5)	

No	Name	Nat	Pos	Aps	(s)	Gls
26	Marco PISANO		D	3	(3)	
77	Leandro RINAUDO		D	20	(2)	2
30	Fábio Henrique SIMPLÍCIO	BRA	M	29	(3)	5
4	Giovanni TEDESCO		M	7	(10)	2
2	Cristian ZACCARDO		D	32	(3)	1

PARMA FC

Coach - Domenico Di Carlo; (11/3/08) Héctor Cúper (ARG); (12/5/08) Andrea Manzo

Founded – 1913

MAJOR HONOURS: UEFA Cup Winners' Cup - (1) 1993; UEFA Cup - (2) 1995, 1999; UEFA Super Cup - (1) 1994; Italian Cup - (3) 1992, 1999, 2002.

2007				
26/8	Catania	h	2-2	*Pisanu, Rossi*
2/9	Atalanta	a	0-2	
16/9	Cagliari	h	1-1	*Corradi*
22/9	Milan	a	1-1	*Pisanu*
26/9	Torino	h	2-0	*Reginaldo, Corradi*
30/9	Udinese	a	1-2	*Corradi*
7/10	Roma	h	0-3	
21/10	Sampdoria	a	0-3	
28/10	Livorno	h	3-2	*Morrone, Paci, Morfeo*
31/10	Palermo	a	1-1	*Morrone*
4/11	Siena	h	2-2	*Corradi, Matteini*
11/11	Juventus	h	2-2	*Gasbarroni (p), Pisanu*
25/11	Lazio	a	0-1	
2/12	Empoli	h	1-0	*Paci*
9/12	Napoli	a	0-1	
16/12	Reggina	h	3-0	*Corradi, Pisanu, Paci*
22/12	Genoa	a	0-1	
2008				
13/1	Fiorentina	h	1-2	*Coly*
20/1	Internazionale	a	2-3	*Cigarini, Gasbarroni*
27/1	Catania	a	0-0	
3/2	Atalanta	h	2-3	*Lucarelli, Gasbarroni (p)*
10/2	Cagliari	a	1-1	*Reginaldo*
16/2	Milan	h	0-0	
23/2	Torino	a	4-4	*Gasbarroni 2, Morrone, Budan*
27/2	Udinese	h	2-0	*Lucarelli, Cigarini (p)*
1/3	Roma	a	0-4	
9/3	Sampdoria	h	1-2	*Budan*
16/3	Livorno	a	1-1	*Reginaldo*
19/3	Palermo	h	2-1	*Budan 2 (1p)*
22/3	Siena	a	0-2	
6/4	Lazio	h	2-2	*Budan, Paci*
13/4	Empoli	a	1-1	*Lucarelli*
16/4	Juventus	a	0-3	
20/4	Napoli	h	1-2	*Budan (p)*
27/4	Reggina	a	1-2	*Cigarini (p)*
4/5	Genoa	h	1-0	*Lucarelli*
11/5	Fiorentina	a	1-3	*Budan*
18/5	Internazionale	h	0-2	

No	Name	Nat	Pos	Aps	(s)	Gls
29	Cristian ANELLI		D		(1)	
6	Luca ANTONELLI		D	2	(6)	
5	Luca BUCCI		G	30	(1)	
20	Igor BUDAN	CRO	A	10	(5)	7
7	Paolo CASTELLINI		D	34		
21	Luca CIGARINI		M	27	(5)	3
33	Ferdinand COLY	SEN	D	20	(1)	1
32	Bernardo CORRADI		A	21	(6)	5
23	Daniele DESSENA		M	17	(11)	
19	Giulio FALCONE		D	28		
24	FERNANDO COUTO	POR	D	15	(2)	
18	Andrea GASBARRONI		M	19	(7)	5
30	Pietro LORENZINI		A		(1)	
9	Cristiano LUCARELLI		A	12	(4)	4
17	McDonald MARIGA	KEN	M	11	(7)	
15	Leandro Antonio MARTÍNEZ	ARG	M		(1)	
8	Davide MATTEINI		A	1	(11)	1
22	Federico MORETTI		M		(1)	
10	Domenico MORFEO		M		(11)	1
4	Stefano MORRONE		M	36		3
28	Massimo PACI		D	21	(1)	4
9	Daniele PAPONI		A	1	(6)	
55	Francesco PARRAVICINI		M	10	(6)	
99	Nicola PAVARINI		G	8	(1)	
11	Andrea PISANU		M	25	(1)	4
24	Aleksandar PRIJOVIĆ	SRB	A		(1)	
83	REGINALDO Ferreira da Silva	BRA	A	31	(4)	3
13	Marco ROSSI		D	13	(2)	1
16	Alessio TOMBESI		D		(2)	
2	Damiano ZENONI		M	26	(5)	

REGGINA CALCIO

Coach - Massimo Ficcadenti; (1/11/07) Renzo Ulivieri; (3/3/08) Nevio Orlandi

Founded - 1914

2007				
26/8	Atalanta	h	1-1	*Amoruso*
2/9	Torino	a	2-2	*Amoruso, Cozza*
16/9	Roma	h	0-2	
22/9	Udinese	a	0-2	
26/9	Juventus	a	0-4	
30/9	Lazio	h	1-1	*Cozza*
7/10	Palermo	a	1-1	*Amoruso*
20/10	Internazionale	h	0-1	
28/10	Siena	a	0-0	
31/10	Livorno	h	1-3	*Amoruso*
4/11	Napoli	a	1-1	*Vigiani*
11/11	Genoa	h	2-0	*Amoruso, Joelson*
25/11	Fiorentina	h	0-0	
1/12	Sampdoria	a	0-3	
16/12	Parma	a	0-3	
23/12	Catania	h	3-1	*Vigiani 3*
2008				
12/1	Empoli	a	1-1	*Ceravolo*
20/1	Cagliari	h	2-0	*Brienza, Cozza*
27/1	Atalanta	a	2-2	*Vigiani, Barreto*
30/1	Milan	h	0-1	
3/2	Torino	h	1-3	*Amoruso*
9/2	Roma	a	0-2	
17/2	Udinese	h	1-3	*Modesto*
23/2	Juventus	h	2-1	*Brienza, Amoruso (p)*
27/2	Lazio	a	0-1	
2/3	Palermo	h	0-0	
8/3	Internazionale	a	0-2	
16/3	Siena	h	4-0	*Brienza 2, Cozza, Missiroli*
19/3	Livorno	a	1-1	*Brienza*
22/3	Napoli	h	1-1	*Brienza*
30/3	Genoa	a	0-2	
6/4	Fiorentina	a	0-2	
13/4	Sampdoria	h	1-0	*Brienza*
20/4	Milan	a	1-5	*Barreto*
27/4	Parma	h	2-1	*Cozza 2*
4/5	Catania	a	2-1	*Amoruso 2 (1p)*
11/5	Empoli	h	2-0	*Barreto, Amoruso*
18/5	Cagliari	a	2-2	*Amoruso 2 (1p)*

No	Name	Nat	Pos	Aps	(s)	Gls
20	Pablo Menendez ÁLVAREZ	URU	M	5	(7)	
17	Nicola AMORUSO		A	30	(3)	12
6	Salvatore ARONICA		D	35		
8	Edgar Osvaldo BARRETO	PAR	M	31	(5)	3

Name	Nat	Pos	Aps	(s)	Gls
Franco BRIENZA		M	18	(2)	7
Andrea CAMPAGNOLO		G	35		
Emmanuel CASCIONE		M	25	(5)	
Giovanni CERAVOLO		A	12	(9)	1
Nicolò CHERUBIN		D	4	(2)	
Bruno CIRILLO		D	18		
Andrea COSTA		D	4	(6)	
Francesco COZZA		M	17	(10)	6
Emil HALLFREDSSON	ISL	M	16	(5)	
Inácio José JOELSON	BRA	A	4	(9)	1
Maurizio LANZARO		D	33		
Ayodele Stephen MAKINWA	NGA	A	5	(4)	
Simone MISSIROLI		M	14	(10)	1
Francesco MODESTO		D	31	(1)	1
José Núñez MONTIEL	PAR	M		(5)	
Nenad NOVAKOVIĆ	SRB	G	3		
Kris STADSGAARD	DEN	D	2	(3)	
Christian Ricardo STUANI	URU	A	1	(11)	
Luca TOGNOZZI		M	13	(9)	
Mike TULLBERG	DEN	A	3	(2)	
Carlos Adrián VALDEZ	URU	D	32	(1)	
Luca VIGIANI		M	27	(2)	5

AS ROMA

Coach - Luciano Spalletti

Founded – 1927

MAJOR HONOURS: Inter Cities Fairs Cup - (1) 1961; Italian League - (3) 1942, 1983, 2001; Italian Cup - (9) 1964, 1969, 1980, 1981, 1984, 1986, 1991, 2007, 2008.

007

6/8	Palermo	a	2-0	*Mexès, Aquilani*
/9	Siena	h	3-0	*Aquilani, Giuly, Totti*
6/9	Reggina	a	2-0	*Juan, Totti*
3/9	Juventus	h	2-2	*Totti 2*
6/9	Fiorentina	a	2-2	*Mancini, Giuly*
9/9	Internazionale	h	1-4	*Perrotta*
/10	Parma	a	3-0	*Totti 2, Mancini*
0/10	Napoli	h	4-4	*Totti (p), Perrotta, De Rossi, Pizarro*
8/10	Milan	a	1-0	*Vučinić*
1/10	Lazio	h	3-2	*Vučinić, Mancini, Perrotta*
/11	Empoli	a	2-2	*Giuly, Brighi*
4/11	Genoa	a	1-0	*Panucci*
/12	Udinese	h	2-1	*Juan, Taddei*
/12	Cagliari	h	2-0	*Taddei 2*
/12	Livorno	a	1-1	*De Rossi*
6/12	Torino	a	0-0	
2/12	Sampdoria	h	2-0	*Totti 2 (1p)*

008

3/1	Atalanta	a	2-1	*Totti, Mancini*
0/1	Catania	h	2-0	*Giuly, De Rossi (p)*
6/1	Palermo	h	1-0	*Mancini*
/2	Siena	a	0-3	
/2	Reggina	h	2-0	*Panucci, Mancini*
6/2	Juventus	a	0-1	
4/2	Fiorentina	h	1-0	*Cicinho*
7/2	Internazionale	a	1-1	*Totti*
/3	Parma	h	4-0	*Aquilani, og (Falcone), Totti, Vučinić*
/3	Napoli	a	2-0	*Perrotta, Totti (p)*
15/3	Milan	h	2-1	*Giuly, Vučinić*
19/3	Lazio	a	2-3	*Taddei, Perrotta*
22/3	Empoli	h	2-1	*Tonetto, Panucci*
29/3	Cagliari	a	1-1	*Totti*
5/4	Genoa	h	3-2	*Taddei, Vučinić, De Rossi (p)*
13/4	Udinese	a	3-1	*Vučinić, Taddei, Giuly*
19/4	Livorno	h	1-1	*Vučinić*
27/4	Torino	h	4-1	*Pizarro (p), Vučinić, Mancini 2*
4/5	Sampdoria	a	3-0	*Panucci, Pizarro, Cicinho*
11/5	Atalanta	h	2-1	*Panucci, De Rossi*
18/5	Catania	a	1-1	*Vučinić*

No	Name	Nat	Pos	Aps	(s)	Gls
17	Edgar ÁLVAREZ	HON	M		(1)	
15	Vitorino Gabriel ANTUNES	POR	D		(5)	
8	Alberto AQUILANI		M	11	(10)	3
29	Ahmed Amipah BARUSSO	GHA	M		(3)	
33	Matteo BRIGHI		M	6	(18)	1
77	Marco CASSETTI		D	21	(6)	
3	Cicero João de Cezare "CICINHO"	BRA	D	18	(12)	2
1	Gianluca CURCI		G	1	(1)	
16	Daniele DE ROSSI		M	34		5
32	Alexander DONI	BRA	G	37		
18	Mauro ESPOSITO		A		(8)	
21	Matteo FERRARI		D	16		
14	Ludovic GIULY	FRA	A	17	(15)	6
4	Silveira dos Santos "JUAN"	BRA	D	19	(3)	2
30	Alessandro MANCINI	BRA	M	28	(3)	8
5	Philippe MEXÈS	FRA	D	30	(1)	1
2	Christian PANUCCI		D	21	(6)	5
20	Simone PERROTTA		M	25	(4)	5
7	David PIZARRO	CHI	M	28	(3)	3
11	Rodrigo TADDEI		M	25	(1)	6
22	Max TONETTO		D	33	(2)	1
10	Francesco TOTTI		A	25		14
9	Mirko VUČINIĆ	MNE	A	23	(10)	9

UC SAMPDORIA

Coach - Walter Mazzarri

Founded – 1946

MAJOR HONOURS: UEFA Cup Winners' Cup - (1) 1990; Italian League - (1) 1991; Italian Cup - (4) 1985, 1988, 1989, 1994.

2007

26/8	Siena	a	2-1	*Bellucci, Montella*
2/9	Lazio	h	0-0	
16/9	Napoli	a	0-2	
23/9	Genoa	h	0-0	
26/9	Internazionale	a	0-3	
30/9	Atalanta	h	3-0	*Bellucci, Sammarco, Cassano*
7/10	Torino	a	0-1	
21/10	Parma	h	3-0	*Montella, Bellucci 2*
28/10	Catania	a	0-2	
31/10	Milan	h	0-5	
4/11	Cagliari	a	3-0	*Volpi, Caracciolo, Maggio*
10/11	Empoli	h	3-0	*og (Giacomazzi), Montella, Sammarco*
25/11	Livorno	a	1-3	*Bellucci*
1/12	Reggina	h	3-0	*Bellucci 2, Sammarco*
9/12	Udinese	a	2-3	*Bellucci (p), Maggio*
16/12	Fiorentina	h	2-2	*Gastaldello, Cassano*
22/12	Roma	a	0-2	

2008

13/1	Palermo	h	3-0	*Bellucci, Sammarco, Cassano*
20/1	Juventus	a	0-0	
26/1	Siena	h	1-0	*Cassano*
3/2	Lazio	a	1-2	*Cassano*
10/2	Napoli	h	2-0	*Delvecchio, Franceschini*
17/2	Genoa	a	1-0	*Maggio*
24/2	Internazionale	h	1-1	*Cassano*
27/2	Atalanta	a	1-4	*Volpi*

2/3	Torino	h	2-2	*Sala, Cassano*
9/3	Parma	a	2-1	*Maggio, Bonazzoli*
16/3	Catania	h	3-1	*Palombo, Accardi, Bellucci*
19/3	Milan	a	2-1	*Maggio, Delvecchio*
22/3	Cagliari	h	1-1	*Franceschini*
30/3	Empoli	a	2-0	*Sammarco, og (Marzoratti)*
6/4	Livorno	h	2-0	*Maggio, Bonazzoli*
13/4	Reggina	a	0-1	
20/4	Udinese	h	3-0	*Cassano, Bellucci 2 (1p)*
27/4	Fiorentina	a	2-2	*Maggio, Gastaldello*
4/5	Roma	h	0-3	
11/5	Palermo	a	2-0	*Cassano, Maggio*
17/5	Juventus	h	3-3	*Cassano, Maggio, Montella*

No	Name	Nat	Pos	Aps	(s)	Gls
5	Pietro ACCARDI		D	18	(4)	1
33	Alessandro BASTRINI		D	1	(2)	
11	Claudio BELLUCCI		A	27	(5)	12
13	Emiliano BONAZZOLI		A	10	(20)	2
16	Hugo Armando CAMPAGNARO	ARG	D	22		
29	Andrea CARACCIOLO		A	6	(6)	1
99	Antonio CASSANO		A	18	(4)	10
1	Luca CASTELLAZZI		G	26		
40	Gennaro DELVECCHIO		M	18	(8)	2
90	Vincenzo FIORILLO		G		(1)	
19	Daniele FRANCESCHINI		M	25	(5)	2
28	Daniele GASTALDELLO		D	28	(1)	2
22	Ikechukwu KALU	NGA	A		(5)	
6	Stefano LUCCHINI		D	23	(3)	
7	Christian MAGGIO		D	28	(1)	9
32	Leonardo Martín MIGLIÓNICO	URU	D		(4)	
83	Antonio MIRANTE		G	12	(1)	
9	Vincenzo MONTELLA		A	8	(5)	4
17	Angelo PALOMBO		M	33		1
46	Mirko PIERI		D	29	(3)	
8	Andrea POLI		M		(1)	
14	Luigi SALA		D	22	(4)	1
21	Paolo SAMMARCO		M	24	(6)	5
4	Sergio VOLPI		M	20	(8)	2
77	Cristian ZENONI		M	12	(4)	
3	Reto ZIEGLER	SUI	M	8	(12)	

AC SIENA

Coach - Andrea Mandorlini; (12/11/07) Mario Beretta

Founded - 1904

2007				
26/8	Sampdoria	h	1-2	*Corvia*
2/9	Roma	a	0-3	
15/9	Milan	h	1-1	*Maccarone*
23/9	Torino	a	1-1	*Maccarone*
26/9	Atalanta	h	1-1	*Loria*
30/9	Cagliari	a	0-1	
7/10	Empoli	h	3-0	*Maccarone (p), Locatelli, Galloppa*
21/10	Fiorentina	a	0-3	
28/10	Reggina	h	0-0	
31/10	Catania	h	1-1	*De Ceglie*
4/11	Parma	a	2-2	*De Ceglie, Galloppa*
11/11	Livorno	h	2-3	*Maccarone, Loria*
25/11	Udinese	a	0-2	
2/12	Lazio	h	1-1	*Maccarone*
9/12	Genoa	a	3-1	*Frick 2, Loria*
16/12	Napoli	h	1-1	*Frick*
23/12	Juventus	a	0-2	
2008				
13/1	Internazionale	h	2-3	*og (Córdoba), Forestieri*
20/1	Palermo	a	3-2	*Locatelli, Maccarone, Loria*
26/1	Sampdoria	a	0-1	
3/2	Roma	h	3-0	*Vergassola, og (Tonetto), Frick*
10/2	Milan	a	0-1	
17/2	Torino	h	0-0	
24/2	Atalanta	a	2-2	*Bertotto, Locatelli*
27/2	Cagliari	h	1-0	*Maccarone*
2/3	Empoli	a	2-0	*Portanova, Riganò*
9/3	Fiorentina	h	1-0	*Maccarone*
16/3	Reggina	a	0-4	
19/3	Catania	a	0-0	
22/3	Parma	h	2-0	*Maccarone 2 (1p)*
30/3	Livorno	a	0-0	
6/4	Udinese	h	1-1	*Kharja*
13/4	Lazio	a	1-1	*Loria*
20/4	Genoa	h	0-1	
27/4	Napoli	a	0-0	
4/5	Juventus	h	1-0	*Kharja*
11/5	Internazionale	a	2-2	*Maccarone, Kharja*
18/5	Palermo	h	2-2	*Maccarone 2*

No	Name	Nat	Pos	Aps	(s)	Gls
22	ALBERTO do Carmo Nieto	BRA	M	2	(13)	
73	Valerio BERTOTTO		D	16		1
29	Cristian BUCCHI		A	6	(4)	
70	Calil Prosperi CAETANO	BRA	A		(2)	
10	Enrico CHIESA		A	1	(1)	
5	Paul Constantin CODREA	ROU	M	25	(4)	
55	Manuel COPPOLA		M	10	(2)	
9	Daniele CORVIA		A	1	(13)	1
11	Paolo DE CEGLIE		M	24	(5)	2
31	Demetrios ELEFTHEROPOULOS	GRE	G	12		
33	Daniele FICAGNA		D	5	(2)	
30	Fernando Martin FORESTIERI	ARG	A	4	(13)	1
7	Mario FRICK	LIE	A	20	(7)	4
14	Daniele GALLOPPA		M	26	(4)	2
18	Leandro GRIMI	ARG	D	13		
28	Mirko GUADALUPI		M		(1)	
23	Lukáš JAROLÍM	CZE	M	19	(5)	
50	Anssi JAAKKOLA	FIN	G		(1)	
6	Houssine KHARJA	MAR	M	12	(3)	3
20	Tomas LOCATELLI		A	23	(7)	3
15	Simone LORIA		D	36		5
32	Massimo MACCARONE		A	35		13
1	Alexander MANNINGER	AUT	G	26		
99	Richard Anibal PORTA	URU	A		(1)	
90	Daniele PORTANOVA		D	37		1
9	Christian RIGANÒ		A	6	(11)	1
13	Luca ROSSETTINI		D	20	(5)	
21	Andrea ROSSI		D	10	(5)	
8	Simone VERGASSOLA		M	29	(2)	1

TORINO FC

Coach - Walter Novellino; (16/4/08) Gianni De Biasi

Founded – 1906

MAJOR HONOURS: Italian League – (7) 1928, 1943, 1946, 1947, 1948, 1949, 1976; Italian Cup – (5) 1936, 1943, 1968, 1971, 1993.

2007				
25/8	Lazio	a	2-2	*Rosina, Vailatti*
2/9	Reggina	h	2-2	*Rosina, Ventola*
16/9	Palermo	a	1-1	*Recoba*
23/9	Siena	h	1-1	*Dellafiore*
26/9	Parma	a	0-2	
30/9	Juventus	h	0-1	
7/10	Sampdoria	h	1-0	*Corini*
21/10	Atalanta	a	2-2	*Ventola, Motta*
27/10	Cagliari	h	2-0	*Rosina, og (Ferri)*

/10	Udinese	a	1-2	*Ventola*
11	Milan	a	0-0	
/11	Catania	h	1-1	*Malonga*
/11	Empoli	a	0-0	
12	Genoa	h	1-1	*Lanna*
12	Internazionale	a	0-4	
/12	Roma	h	0-0	
/12	Napoli	a	1-1	*Rosina (p)*

08

/1	Livorno	h	1-2	*Bottone*
/1	Fiorentina	a	1-2	*Grella*
/1	Lazio	h	0-0	
2	Reggina	a	3-1	*Rosina 2 (2p), Stellone*
/2	Palermo	h	3-1	*Diana, Di Michele 2*
/2	Siena	a	0-0	
/2	Parma	h	4-4	*Stellone 2, Natali, Di Michele*
/2	Juventus	a	0-0	
3	Sampdoria	a	2-2	*Comotto, Di Michele (p)*
3	Atalanta	h	1-0	*Barone*
/3	Cagliari	a	0-3	
/3	Udinese	h	0-1	
/3	Milan	h	0-1	
/3	Catania	a	2-1	*Diana, Di Michele*
/4	Empoli	h	0-1	
/4	Genoa	a	0-3	
/4	Internazionale	h	0-1	
/4	Roma	a	1-4	*Ventola*
/5	Napoli	h	2-1	*Rosina (p), Di Michele*
1/5	Livorno	a	1-0	*Rosina*
8/5	Fiorentina	h	0-1	

o	Name	Nat	Pos	Aps	(s)	Gls
	Simone BARONE		M	22		1
0	Saša BJELANOVIĆ	CRO	A	10	(9)	
9	Davide BOTTONE		M	2	(7)	1
	Gianluca COMOTTO		D	22	(1)	1
	Eugenio CORINI		M	27	(5)	1
5	Hernán Paolo DELLAFIORE		D	25	(3)	1
2	Marco DI LORETO		D	28	(1)	
7	David DI MICHELE		A	18	(7)	6
9	Aimo Stefano DIANA		M	17		2
1	Alberto FONTANA		G	6	(2)	
1	Ivan FRANCESCHINI		D		(1)	
3	Vincenzo GRELLA	AUS	M	23	(5)	1
3	Salvatore LANNA		D	27	(2)	1
1	Nikola LAZETIĆ	SRB	M	10	(5)	
2	Dominque MALONGA	FRA	A		(9)	1
	Marco MOTTA		D	14	(10)	1
4	Cesare NATALI		D	24		1
6	Masashi OGURO	JPN	A		(3)	
	Marco PISANO		D	14		
	Álvaro RECOBA	URU	A	12	(10)	1
0	Alessandro ROSINA		M	31	(4)	8
3	Matteo RUBIN		D	2	(4)	
	Matteo SERENI		G	32		
7	Roberto STELLONE		A	18	(3)	3
28	Tommaso VAILATTI		M	3	(4)	1
	Nicola VENTOLA		A	11	(10)	4
27	Paolo ZANETTI		M	20	(4)	

UDINESE CALCIO

Coach - Pasquale Marino

Founded - 1896

2007

26/8	Internazionale	a	1-1	*og (Córdoba)*
2/9	Napoli	h	0-5	
16/9	Juventus	a	1-0	*Di Natale*
23/9	Reggina	h	2-0	*Di Natale 2*
26/9	Genoa	a	2-3	*Asamoah, Mesto*
30/9	Parma	h	2-1	*Quagliarella, Zapata*
6/10	Atalanta	a	0-0	
21/10	Palermo	h	1-1	*Asamoah*
28/10	Lazio	a	1-0	*Asamoah*
31/10	Torino	h	2-1	*Floro Flores, Inler*
4/11	Livorno	a	0-0	
24/11	Fiorentina	a	2-1	*Quagliarella, Di Natale*
2/12	Siena	h	2-0	*Quagliarella, Di Natale*
5/12	Roma	a	1-2	*Quagliarella*
9/12	Sampdoria	h	3-2	*Di Natale, Quagliarella 2*
16/12	Catania	a	0-2	
23/12	Empoli	h	2-2	*Dossena, Di Natale*

2008

13/1	Cagliari	a	1-0	*Quagliarella*
19/1	Milan	h	0-1	
27/1	Internazionale	h	0-0	
3/2	Napoli	a	1-3	*Pepe*
9/2	Juventus	h	1-2	*Dossena*
17/2	Reggina	a	3-1	*Pepe, Di Natale 2*
24/2	Genoa	h	3-5	*Di Natale 2 (2p), Floro Flores*
27/2	Parma	a	0-2	
2/3	Atalanta	h	2-0	*Quagliarella, Di Natale*
8/3	Palermo	a	1-1	*Felipe*
15/3	Lazio	h	2-2	*Ferronetti, Di Natale*
19/3	Torino	a	1-0	*Pepe*
22/3	Livorno	h	2-0	*Quagliarella, Di Natale*
30/3	Fiorentina	h	3-1	*Inler, Quagliarella, Di Natale*
6/4	Siena	a	1-1	*Floro Flores*
13/4	Roma	h	1-3	*Di Natale*
20/4	Sampdoria	a	0-3	
27/4	Catania	h	2-1	*Di Natale, Quagliarella*
4/5	Empoli	a	1-0	*Quagliarella*
11/5	Cagliari	h	0-2	
18/5	Milan	a	1-4	*Mesto*

No	Name	Nat	Pos	Aps	(s)	Gls
18	Gyan ASAMOAH	GHA	A	9	(4)	3
28	Viktor BOUDIANSKI	RUS	M	1		
14	Antonio CANDREVA		M		(3)	
25	Antonio CHIMENTI		G	3		
6	Andrea CODA		D	16	(4)	
17	Riccardo COLOMBO		D		(4)	
4	Gaetano D'AGOSTINO		M	34	(1)	
10	Antonio DI NATALE		A	35	(1)	17
8	Andrea DOSSENA		D	35		2
23	Roman EREMENKO	FIN	M	3	(4)	
19	FELIPE da Silva Dalbelo Dias	BRA	D	22		1
32	Damiano FERRONETTI		D	11	(5)	1
83	Antonio FLORO FLORES		A	12	(25)	3
22	Samir HANDANOVIČ	SVN	G	35		
88	Gökhan INLER	SUI	M	37		2
15	Mauricio ISLA	CHI	M	2	(8)	
24	Aleksandar LUKOVIĆ	SRB	D	29	(3)	
20	Giandomenico MESTO		D	26	(2)	2
5	Christian OBODO	NGA	M		(1)	
9	Michele PAOLUCCI		A		(2)	
7	Simone PEPE		A	23	(10)	3
11	Giampiero PINZI		M	1	(12)	
27	Fabio QUAGLIARELLA		A	35	(2)	12
86	Guilherme SIQUEIRA	BRA	D	2	(2)	
66	Tomáš SIVOK	CZE	M	1	(1)	
2	Cristián Valencia ZAPATA	COL	D	26	(1)	1
21	Tomáš ZÁPOTOČNÝ	CZE	D	20	(1)	

PROMOTED CLUBS

AC CHIEVO VERONA

Coach – Giuseppe Iachini
Founded - 1929

BOLOGNA FC

Coach – Daniele Arrigoni
Founded – 1909
MAJOR HONOURS: Italian League - (7) 1925, 1929, 1936, 1937, 1939, 1941, 1964; Italian Cup - (2) 1970, 1974.

US LECCE

Coach – Giuseppe Papadopulo
Founded - 1908

SECOND LEVEL FINAL TABLE 2007/08

		Pld	W	D	L	F	A	Pts
1	AC Chievo Verona	42	24	13	5	77	43	85
2	Bologna FC	42	24	12	6	58	29	84
3	US Lecce	42	23	14	5	70	29	83
4	UC AlbinoLeffe	42	23	9	10	67	48	78
5	Brescia Calcio	42	20	12	10	59	40	72
6	Pisa Calcio	42	19	14	9	61	44	71
7	Rimini Calcio FC	42	20	9	13	68	46	69
8	Ascoli Calcio	42	16	14	12	64	49	62
9	AC Mantova	42	16	12	14	56	49	60
10	Frosinone Calcio	42	15	11	16	63	67	56
11	AS Bari	42	13	16	13	50	55	55
12	US Triestina Calcio	42	13	12	17	55	67	51
13	US Grosseto FC	42	10	19	13	47	54	49
14	FC Messina Peloro	42	13	10	19	38	62	49
15	Piacenza Calcio	42	13	8	21	43	59	47
16	Modena FC	42	10	16	16	57	65	46
17	Treviso FBC	42	11	12	19	41	52	45
18	Vicenza Calcio	42	10	15	17	43	60	45
19	US Avellino	42	8	12	22	42	64	36
20	Ravenna Calcio	42	8	11	23	48	75	35
21	Spezia Calcio	42	6	16	20	45	66	33
22	AC Cesena	42	5	17	20	37	66	32

PROMOTION PLAY-OFFS

(4/6/08 & 8/6/08)
Pisa 0, Lecce 1
Lecce 2, Pisa 1
(Lecce 3-1)

Brescia 1, AlbinoLeffe 0
AlbinoLeffe 2, Brescia 1
(2-2; AlbinoLeffe on higher position in regular season)

(11/6/08 & 15/6/08)
AlbinoLeffe 0, Lecce 1
Lecce 1, AlbinoLeffe 1
(Lecce 2-1)

DOMESTIC CUP 2007/08

COPPA ITALIA

SECOND ROUND

(18/8/07)
Ascoli 3, Genoa 2 *(aet)*
Bari 2, Vicenza 0
Bologna 1, Triestina 1 *(aet; 3-4 on pens)*
Napoli 3, Pisa 1 *(aet)*
Ravenna 1, Piacenza 2
Rimini 3, Treviso 1

THIRD ROUND

(29/8/07)
Ascoli 2, Atalanta 1 *(aet)*
Cagliari 2, Siena 1
Napoli 1, Livorno 1 *(aet; 4-3 on pens)*
Parma 1, Juventus 3
Reggina 3, Piacenza 2
Torino 3, Rimini 2 *(aet)*
Triestina 0, Catania 0 *(aet; 2-4 on pens)*
Udinese 3, Bari 0

FOURTH ROUND

(6/12/07 & 15/1/08)
Empoli v Juventus 2-1; 3-5 *(5-6)*
(11/12/07 & 16/1/08)
Ascoli v Fiorentina 1-1; 0-2 *(1-3)*
(12/12/07 & 16/1/08)
Cagliari v Sampdoria 1-0; 0-4 *(1-4)*
(19/12/07 & 16/1/08)
Torino v Roma 3-1; 0-4 *(3-5)*
Udinese v Palermo 0-0; 1-0 *(1-0)*
(19/12/07 & 17/1/08)
Lazio v Napoli 2-1; 1-1 *(3-2)*
Reggina v Internazionale 1-4, 0-3 *(1-7)*
(20/12/07 & 16/1/08)
Milan v Catania 1-2; 1-1 *(2-3)*

QUARTER-FINALS

(23/1/08 & 29/1/08)
Sampdoria 1 *(Ziegler 63)*, Roma 1 *(Vučinić 70)*
Roma 1 *(Mancini 62)*, Sampdoria 0
(Roma 2-1)

(23/1/08 & 30/1/08)
Internazionale 2 *(Cruz 54, 75)*, Juventus 2 *(Del Piero 80, Boumsong 86,*
Juventus 2 *(Del Piero 14, Iaquinta 31)*, Internazionale 3 *(Balotelli 10,55*
Cruz 39p)
(Internazionale 5-4)

Udinese 3 *(Ferronetti 9, Pepe 72p, Felipe 77)*, Catania 2 *(Izco 12, Martíne*
Catania 2 *(Spinesi 44p, Morimoto 90)*, Udinese 1 *(Pepe 1)*
(4-4; Catania on away goals)

(24/1/08 & 30/1/08)
Lazio 2 *(Kolarov 21, Behrami 22)*, Fiorentina 1 *(Pazzini 40)*
Fiorentina 1 *(Semioli 16)*, Lazio 2 *(Kolarov 34, Rocchi 62)*
(Lazio 4-2)

SEMI-FINALS

(16/4/08 & 7/5/08)
Internazionale 0, Lazio 0
Lazio 0, Internazionale 2 *(Pelé 53, Cruz 87)*
(Internazionale 2-0)

(16/4/08 & 8/5/08)
Roma 1 *(Totti 47)*, Catania 0
Catania 1 *(Silvestri 29)*, Roma 1 *(Aquilani 26p)*
(Roma 2-1)

FINAL

(24/5/08)
Stadio Olimpico, Roma
AS ROMA 2 *(Mexès 36, Perrotta 55)*
FC INTERNAZIONALE MILANO 1 *(Pelé 62)*
Referee – *Morganti*
ROMA – *Doni, Cassetti, Juan, Mexès, Tonetto, De Rossi, Pizarro, Giuly (Cicinho 68), Aquilani (Panucci 90), Perrotta (Brighi 74), Vučinić.*
INTERNAZIONALE – *Toldo, Maicon, Burdisso, Chivu, Maxwell, Zanetti (Crespo 90), Balotelli, Vieira, Stanković (Pelé 47), César (Jiménez 63), Sua:*

Aktobe's title, Tobol's Cup

Appropriately enough, the two most consistently impressive teams in Kazakhstan over the 2007 season were each rewarded with a major prize. K Aktobe, champions in 2005 and runners-up in 2006, regained the Superleague title, finishing eight points nead of second-placed FC Tobol Kostanay, who made mends by winning the Kazakhstan Cup, eliminating ktobe en route to a handsome victory in the final over C Ordabasy Shymkent.

ktobe, coached by Russian Vladimir Mukhanov, were vorthy champions. Their 30-match campaign ontained only two defeats and they dropped only two oints at home. While their attack, spearheaded by 16-oal Moldovan international Serghey Rogaciov, was uietly efficient, their defence was exceptional, onceding just 12 goals over the entire campaign, nree in the last 12 matches and none in the last six.

erial winner Smakov

ktobe wrapped up the title with a 2-0 victory at home o FC Alma-Ata in their penultimate fixture. Leading he celebrations was team captain Samat Smakov, oon to be voted Kazakhstan Player of the Year for the econd time. The international defender, who joined he club at the beginning of the season from FC Kairat Almaty and started all 30 matches, was accustomed to he sensation of winning the title having done so three imes previously – with FC Yelimai Semipalatinsk, C Irtysh Pavlodar and Kairat.

Tobol were entitled to claim exhaustion at the end of a ear in which their relatively small squad played 44 matches – 30 in the league, six in the Cup and eight in Europe. While Aktobe's European ambitions ended early, Tobol made sensational progress in the UEFA ntertoto Cup, becoming one of eleven 'winners' after successfully seeing off FC Zestafoni of Georgia, FC Slovan Liberec of the Czech Republic and OFI Crete FC of Greece. Their summer odyssey finally came to an end in the second qualifying round of the UEFA Cup at the hands of Polish club Groclin Grodzisk Wielkopolski.

A resilient Tobol side, coached by Dmitriy Ogai and featuring Kazakhstan international midfielders Ruslan Baltiyev and Nurbol Zhumaskaliev, were much too good in the Cup final for Ordabasy, winning at a canter. A couple of set-piece goals from Baltiyev saw them on their way to a resounding 3-0 win, bringing the club their first domestic trophy.

Litvinenko honoured

The Cup final was preceded by a minute's silence in honour of former Kazakhstan international striker Oleg Litvinenko, who had been discovered dead at his home a fortnight earlier. Litvinenko, 33, was the country's all-time domestic top scorer with 149 league goals and won the last of his 28 caps in February 2006.

Kazakhstan ended a difficult debut UEFA European Championship qualifying campaign with striker Dmitriy Byakov scoring in four successive matches. Head coach Arno Pijpers was handed a new two-year contract to lead the team into 2010 FIFA World Cup combat, but the team's confidence took a double battering in May when they were heavily beaten twice in four days, going down 6-0 to Russia and 3-0 to Montenegro.

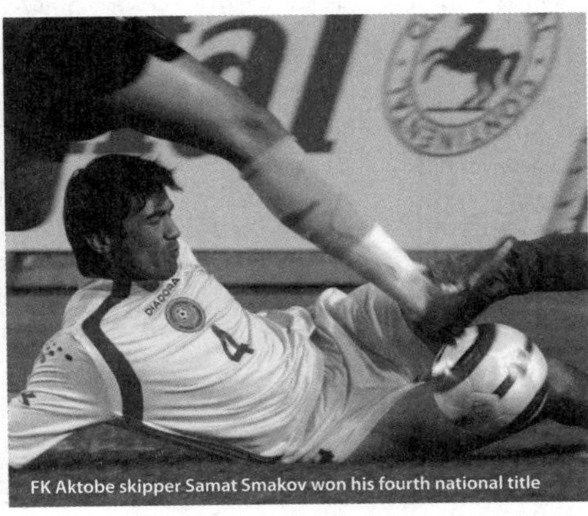

FK Aktobe skipper Samat Smakov won his fourth national title

Kazakstanning Futbol Federatsiyasi (KFF

Satpayev Street 29/3
KZ-480072 Almaty
tel - +7 727 292 4492
fax - +7 727 292 1885
website – www.kff.kz
email - kfo@mail.online.kz
Year of Formation – 1914
President - Adilbek Dzhaksybekov
General Secretary - Aliya Duissekeyeva
Press Officer – Aleksandr Keplin
Stadium – Almaty Centralny, Almaty (25,057)

TOP FIVE ALL-TIME CAPS
Ruslan Baltiyev (64); Samat Smakov (52); Nurbol Zhumaskaliev (44); Aleksandr Familtsev (35); Andrei Karpovich (35)

TOP FIVE ALL-TIME GOALS
Viktor Zubarev (12); Ruslan Baltiyev (10); Dmitry Byakov (8); Oleg Litvinenko & Igor Avdeev (6)

NATIONAL TEAM RESULTS 2007/08

22/8/07	Finland (ECQ)	A	Tampere	1-2	*Byakov (23)*
8/9/07	Tajikistan	H	Almaty	1-1	*Nurdauletov (54)*
12/9/07	Belgium (ECQ)	H	Almaty	2-2	*Byakov (39), Smakov (77p)*
13/10/07	Poland (ECQ)	A	Warsaw	1-3	*Byakov (20)*
17/10/07	Portugal (ECQ)	H	Almaty	1-2	*Byakov (90+3)*
21/11/07	Armenia (ECQ)	A	Yerevan	1-0	*Ostapenko (64)*
24/11/07	Serbia (ECQ)	A	Belgrade	0-1	
3/2/08	Azerbaijan	N	Antalya (TUR)	0-0	
6/2/08	Moldova	N	Antalya (TUR)	0-1	
26/3/08	Armenia	N	Rotterdam (NED)	0-1	
23/5/08	Russia	A	Moscow	0-6	
27/5/08	Montenegro	A	Podgorica	0-3	

NATIONAL TEAM APPEARANCES 2007/08

Coach - Arno PIJPERS (NED)	21/4/59		FIN	Tjk	BEL	POL	POR	ARM	SRB	Aze	Mda	Arm	Rus	Mne	Caps	Goa
David LORIA	31/10/81	Shakhtyor Karagandy /Halmstad (SWE)	G	G	G	G	G	G	G			G	G	G	31	
Egor AZOVSKI	10/1/85	Ordabasy /Astana	D	D	D66					D		D		D	20	-
Aleksandr KUCHMA	9/12/80	Astana	D	D	D	D	D	D		D	D	D	D	D	33	2
Samat SMAKOV	8/12/78	Aktobe	D		D	D	D		D	D	D	D	D	s33	52	1
Farhadbek IRISMETOV	10/8/81	Tobol	D	D69	D		D	D	D				D	D	26	-
Sergey SKORYKH	25/5/84	Tobol	M69	M51	M	M81	M	M	M			M	M	M76	16	-
Ruslan BALTIYEV	16/9/78	Tobol	M	s51		M		M	M86	M	M	M		M	64	10
Sergei LARIN	22/7/86	Alma-Ata	M78	M57	M73	M73	M37	M61		s82	s65				25	-
Nurbol ZHUMASKALIEV	11/5/81	Tobol	M	M63	M	M	M	M	s73	M	M	M	M	M	44	5
Dmitry BYAKOV	9/4/78	Alma-Ata /Astana	A	A82	A	A85	A	A	A	A74	A	A89			31	8
Sergei OSTAPENKO	23/2/86	Tobol /Antwerp (BEL)	A70	A66	A	A	A	A	s73	A85	s60	A	s46	A74	13	1
Anton CHICHULIN	27/10/84	Astana	s69	M52											21	1
Murat SUYUMAGAMBETOV	14/10/83	Astana /Shakhtyor Karagandy	s70	s66	s73	s73			A73	s85	A60	s78	A46	s74	19	3

...TIONAL TEAM APPEARANCES 2007/08 (contd.)

			FIN	Tjk	BEL	POL	POR	ARM	SRB	Aze	Mda	Arm	Rus	Mne	Caps	Goals
ASHIRBEKOV	21/10/82	Aktobe /Shakhtyor Karagandy	s78			s85			s86	s74			M78	M33	15	2
NURDAULETOV	6/11/82	Tobol		D		D	s89	D	D		D	s89	D		12	1
...i KARPOVICH	18/1/81	Dinamo Moskva (RUS)		s52	M	s81	M89		M		M79		M58	s76	35	2
...i LYAPKIN	16/9/76	Khimki (RUS)		s57	s66	D	s37	s61	D73						15	-
...n AZOVSKI	4/6/86	Alma-Ata		s63											11	-
KUMISBEKOV	9/2/79	Astana		s69											9	-
...n ZHALMAGAMBETOV	11/7/83	Astana /Antwerp (BEL)		s82			D	D	D	D	D	D		D	28	-
...andr MOKIN	19/6/81	Astana								G	G				4	-
...bek ASANBAEV	13/9/79	Aktobe								M82	M65	M78			4	-
...RODIONOV	26/7/85	Alma-Ata								M68	s79				12	1
...ei TRAVIN	27/4/79	Alma-Ata								s68					18	-
...LIEV	27/10/80	Kayserispor (TUR)											D44		2	-
LOGVINENKO	22/7/88	Aktobe											s44 /80		1	-
...a KHOKHLOV	27/10/83	Aktobe											s58	s62	17	-
...nbyl KUKEEV	20/9/88	Alma-Ata											s78	M62	11	-
...rkhan IBRAEV	22/3/88	Tobol											s80		1	-

DOMESTIC LEAGUE 2007

...PERLEAGUE FINAL TABLE

		Home					Away					Total					
	Pld	W	D	L	F	A	W	D	L	F	A	W	D	L	F	A	Pts
...K Aktobe	30	14	1	0	31	4	8	5	2	24	8	22	6	2	55	12	72
...C Tobol Kostanay	30	13	2	0	41	5	6	5	4	19	15	19	7	4	60	20	64
...C Shakhtyor ...aragandy	30	11	4	0	29	9	6	3	6	16	14	17	7	6	45	23	58
...C Irtysh Pavlodar	30	12	2	1	23	8	4	2	9	11	19	16	4	10	34	27	52
...C Zhetysu ...aldykorgan	30	8	4	3	20	14	5	3	7	13	18	13	7	10	33	32	46
...C Alma-Ata	30	9	4	2	24	9	4	1	10	11	23	13	5	12	35	32	44
...C Vostok	30	8	2	5	17	14	4	3	8	13	24	12	5	13	30	38	41
...C Astana	30	9	4	2	26	7	2	4	9	8	18	11	8	11	34	25	41
...C Ordabasy ...hymkent	30	8	4	3	18	7	1	7	7	10	22	9	11	10	28	29	38
...C Kaisar Kyzylorda	30	8	5	2	19	13	2	2	11	8	24	10	7	13	27	37	37
...C Yesil Bogatyr ...etropavlovsk	30	6	7	2	12	6	2	6	7	12	22	8	13	9	24	28	37
...C Ekibastuzets	30	8	4	3	17	10	0	4	11	11	28	8	8	14	28	38	32
...C Kairat Almaty	30	7	1	7	17	20	2	2	11	6	23	9	3	18	23	43	30
...K Atyrau	30	7	3	5	23	19	1	3	11	6	20	8	6	16	29	39	30
...C Okzhetpes ...okshetau	30	5	3	7	15	21	3	2	10	11	35	8	5	17	26	56	29
...C Taraz	30	3	4	8	13	18	0	2	13	5	32	3	6	21	18	50	15

FC Ekibastuzets excluded at end of season; FC Okzhetpes Kokshetau remain in Superleague.

TOP GOALSCORERS

17 Zhafar IRISMETOV (Alma-Ata)

16 Serghey ROGACIOV (Aktobe)

10 Sergei OSTAPENKO (Tobol)
Murat SUYUMAGAMBETOV (Astana)

9 Nurbol ZHUMASKALIEV (Tobol)
Ulugbek BAKAEV (Tobol)
Aleksandr MITROFANOV (Aktobe)
Yuriy AKSENYOV (Vostok)

8 Levan MELKADZE (Shakhtyor Karagandy)
Sergey STRUKOV (Irtysh)
Mihails MIHOLAPS (Shakhtyor Karagandy)

CLUB-BY-CLUB

FK AKTOBE

Coach – Vladimir Mukhanov (RUS)

Founded – 1967

MAJOR HONOURS: Kazakhstan League - (2) 2005, 2007.

2007				
31/3	Kaisar	a	0-0	
4/4	Kairat	a	2-0	*Golovskoy (p), Khayrullin*
8/4	Shakhtyor Karagandy	h	0-0	
14/4	Alma-Ata	a	1-0	*Nikolaev*
22/4	Zhetysu	a	3-0	*Nikolaev, Ashirbekov, Mitrofanov*
25/4	Yesil Bogatyr	h	2-1	*Rogaciov, Mitrofanov*
29/4	Taraz	h	5-0	*Mitrofanov, Rogaciov 3, Ashirbekov*
5/5	Ordabasy	a	0-0	
12/5	Atyrau	h	1-0	*Rogaciov (p)*
16/5	Vostok	h	1-0	*Badlo*
20/5	Tobol	a	0-0	
25/5	Okzhetpes	h	2-1	*Buleshev, Mitrofanov*
11/6	Irtysh	a	1-2	*Rogaciov*
16/6	Astana	h	2-0	*Rogaciov, Mitrofanov*
23/6	Vostok	a	1-2	*Rogaciov (p)*
30/6	Ekibastuzets	h	3-1	*Mitrofanov, Rogaciov 2*
8/7	Yesil Bogatyr	a	1-1	*Rogaciov*
28/7	Ekibastuzets	a	3-1	*Rogaciov, Khayrullin, Kiselev*
26/8	Irtysh	h	1-0	*Mitrofanov*
31/8	Okzhetpes	a	6-0	*Khayrullin 2, Bogomolov, Logvinenko 2, Kosolapov*
17/9	Tobol	h	1-0	*Khayrullin*
22/9	Atyrau	a	2-1	*Smakov (p), Rogaciov*
30/9	Ordabasy	h	2-1	*Rogaciov, Kosolapov*
3/10	Astana	a	2-1	*Smakov (p), Rogaciov*
6/10	Taraz	a	2-0	*Kosolapov, Rogaciov*
20/10	Zhetysu	h	2-0	*Smakov (p), Badlo*
26/10	Shakhtyor Karagandy	a	0-0	
1/11	Kairat	h	2-0	*Bogomolov, Asanbaev*
4/11	Alma-Ata	h	2-0	*Pushkarev, Mitrofanov (p)*
10/11	Kaisar	h	5-0	*Khayrullin, Golovskoy, Badlo, Bogomolov, Mitrofanov*

No	Name	Nat	Pos	Aps	(s)	Gls
20	Igor ABDUSHEEV		M	2	(1)	
22	Ulugbek ASANBAEV		M	10	(13)	1
18	Kairat ASHIRBEKOV		M	7	(14)	2
5	Pyotr BADLO		D	28		3
77	Andrei BOGOMOLOV		M	12	(6)	3
81	Alibek BULESHEV		A	2	(14)	1
17	Konstantin GOLOVSKOY		M	19	(4)	2
34	Zhasulan DEKHANOV		G	14		
15	Maxim FOKIN		D	7	(11)	
11	Vladislav KISELEV		M	2	(1)	1
10	Marat KHAYRULLIN	RUS	M	27	(3)	6
7	Alexei KOSOLAPOV		D	17		3
23	Yuri LOGVINENKO		M	13	(3)	2
9	Aleksandr MITROFANOV		M	29	(1)	9
1	Andrei MOREV		G	16		
24	Alexei NIKOLAEV	UZB	D	19	(1)	2
28	Zhandos ORAZALIEV		M		(2)	
21	Andrei PUSHKAREV		A	21	(4)	1
27	Serghey ROGACIOV	MDA	A	25	(3)	16
6	Aleksandr SAVIN		A	2	(3)	
12	Andrei SHKURIN		D	13		
8	Samat SMAKOV		D	30		3
14	Alisher TAZHIBAI ULU		M	15	(5)	

FC ALMA-ATA

Coach – Antonius Joor (NED); (10/6/07) Arno Pijpers (NED)

Founded – 2000

MAJOR HONOURS: Kazakhstan Cup – (1) 2006.

2007				
31/3	Yesil Bogatyr	h	1-0	*Borovskoy*
3/4	Kaisar	a	0-1	
8/4	Kairat	h	2-0	*Byakov, Shakhmetov*
14/4	Aktobe	h	0-1	
22/4	Shakhtyor Karagandy	a	1-1	*Byakov*
25/4	Astana	h	0-0	
29/4	Zhetysu	h	1-3	*Irismetov*
5/5	Taraz	a	2-1	*Irismetov 2*
12/5	Ordabasy	h	1-1	*Irismetov*
16/5	Ekibastuzets	h	0-0	
20/5	Atyrau	a	0-1	
26/5	Tobol	h	2-1	*Rodionov, Irismetov (*
11/6	Okzhetpes	a	0-1	
17/6	Irtysh	h	3-1	*Irismetov 3 (1p)*
23/6	Astana	a	1-0	*Kenzhekhanov (p)*
1/7	Vostok	h	2-1	*Larin 2*
8/7	Ekibastuzets	a	0-1	
27/8	Okzhetpes	h	4-0	*Azovski, Larin, Kovale Irismetov*
15/9	Atyrau	h	1-0	*Kirov*
19/9	Irtysh	a	0-1	
22/9	Ordabasy	a	0-4	
30/9	Taraz	h	4-0	*Irismetov 3 (1p), Azovski*
3/10	Vostok	a	2-1	*Irismetov, Kenzhekhanov*
6/10	Zhetysu	a	2-1	*Rodionov, Irismetov*
23/10	Tobol	a	2-4	*Irismetov, Kenzhekhanov*
26/10	Kairat	a	1-3	*Larin*
1/11	Kaisar	h	2-0	*Irismetov 2*
4/11	Aktobe	a	0-2	
7/11	Shakhtyor Karagandy	h	1-1	*Kovalev*
10/11	Yesil Bogatyr	a	0-1	

No	Name	Nat	Pos	Aps	(s)	Gls
28	Maxim AZOVSKI		A	13		2
20	Viktor BERCO	MDA	M	14	(2)	
33	Andriyan BOGDAN	RUS	G	13		
2	Arman BOLATBEK		D	5	(1)	
20	Vadim BOROVSKOY		M	13	(7)	1
9	Dmitry BYAKOV		M	15	(4)	2
11	Zhafar IRISMETOV	UZB	A	28	(2)	17
19	Vladimir IVANOV		M		(9)	
10	Daniyar KENZHEKHANOV		A	11	(9)	3
14	Aleksandr KIROV		D	26		1
4	Yevgeniy KLIMOV		D	16	(1)	
23	Yevgeny KOSTRUB		M	5	(16)	
24	Viktor KOVALEV		D	29		2
7	Sergei LARIN		M	19	(2)	4
33	Pavel LEUSAS	LTU	G	9		
17	Valeriy LIKHOBABENKO		M	4	(4)	
18	Dias ORAZBAEV		D	3	(3)	
22	Denis RODIONOV		M	22	(2)	2
1	Andrei SHABANOV		G	8	(1)	

Name	Nat	Pos	Aps	(s)	Gls
Marat SHAKHMETOV		M	25	(1)	1
Kirill SHESTAKOV		M	3	(6)	
Andrei TRAVIN		M	4	(1)	
Kayrat UTABAEV		D	15		
Andrei VOLODIN		D	5	(4)	
Ilya VOROTNIKOV		D	25	(1)	

FC ASTANA

Coach – Ivan Azovski; (1/7/07) Aleksandr Irkhin (RUS)

Founded – 1964

MAJOR HONOURS: Kazakhstan League – (3) 2000, 2001, 2006; Kazakhstan Cup – (3) 2000, 2002, 2005.

07				
'3	Zhetysu	a	0-2	
	Ordabasy	a	0-0	
	Atyrau	h	1-0	*Suyumagambetov*
'4	Taraz	h	2-0	*Chichulin, Suchkov*
'4	Tobol	a	0-2	
'4	Alma-Ata	a	0-0	
'4	Okzhetpes	h	2-0	*Kochkaev, Chichulin*
;	Irtysh	a	0-1	
'5	Kaisar	h	1-0	*Kenzhesariev*
'5	Shakhtyor Karagandy	a	1-2	*Suchkov*
'5	Vostok	h	1-1	*Zhalmagambetov*
'5	Ekibastuzets	a	0-0	
'6	Yesil Bogatyr	h	1-1	*Zhalmagambetov*
/6	Aktobe	a	0-2	
/6	Alma-Ata	h	0-1	
/6	Kairat	a	2-0	*Kenzhesariev, Kumisbekov*
	Shakhtyor Karagandy	h	3-0	*Abdualiev, Suchkov, Kenzhesariev*
/7	Kairat	h	5-0	*Suyumagambetov 3, Suchkov 2*
/8	Yesil Bogatyr	a	0-2	
)	Ekibastuzets	h	3-0	*Svach, Kenzhesariev 2*
/9	Vostok	a	0-2	
/9	Kaisar	a	1-2	*Suyumagambetov*
/9	Irtysh	h	0-0	
10	Aktobe	h	1-2	*Suyumagambetov*
10	Okzhetpes	a	0-0	
/10	Tobol	h	4-1	*Suyumagambetov 3, Zhalmagambetov*
/10	Atyrau	a	2-3	*Chichulin, Suymagambetov*
11	Ordabasy	h	1-0	*Kenzhesariev*
11	Taraz	a	2-0	*Suchkov, Kochkaev*
/11	Zhetysu	h	1-1	*Kuchma*

No	Name	Nat	Pos	Aps	(s)	Gls
	Kuanysch ABDUALIEV		M	7	(6)	1
	Igor AKSYONOV	RUS	M	17	(4)	
	Piraly ALIYEV		M	15		
	Maxim AZOVSKI		A	9	(2)	
	Beket BAIMBETOV		M	2	(3)	
	Sergei BOYCHENKO		G	30		
	Viktor BULATOV	RUS	M	10	(1)	
	Anton CHICHULIN		D	25	(1)	3
5	Dean GENCHEV	BUL	M	3	(7)	
)	Maxim KAZNACHEEV		D	1	(2)	
	Emil KENZHESARIEV		D	29		6
3	Tugan KHAMKHOEV		A		(4)	
)	Kirill KOCHKAEV		A	17	(6)	2
	Aleksandr KUCHMA		D	27		1
4	Zhambyl KUKEEV		M	22	(4)	
	Aidar KUMISBEKOV		D	22	(3)	1
4	Yevgeny SEMIN		M		(2)	
	Eduard SERGIENKO		M	9	(8)	
3	Mikhail SHISHKIN		D	5	(1)	
15	Aleksandr SUCHKOV		M	26	(2)	6
19	Mikhail SUKHOV		M	1	(3)	
9	Murat SUYUMAGAMBETOV		A	21		10
34	Jaroslav SVACH	CZE	D	8		1
27	Arsen TLEKHUGOV		A		(6)	
4	Maxim ZHALMAGAMBETOV		D	24	(3)	3

FK ATYRAU

Coach – Vyatseslav Yeremeev; (15/7/07) Bakhtiyar Bayseitov

Founded – 1980

2007				
31/3	Tobol	h	0-4	
4/4	Irtysh	h	1-2	*Boshnyak*
8/4	Astana	a	0-1	
14/4	Okzhetpes	a	2-1	*Boshnyak, Tatishev (p)*
22/4	Vostok	h	2-0	*Zaitsev, Sobkovich*
28/4	Ekibastuzets	a	0-1	
5/5	Yesil Bogatyr	h	0-2	
12/5	Aktobe	a	0-1	
20/5	Alma-Ata	h	1-0	*Guzenko*
9/6	Shakhtyor Karagandy	h	0-5	
16/6	Zhetysu	a	1-2	*Kravchenko*
23/6	Taraz	h	3-0	*Erokhin, Boshnyak, Tatishev*
30/6	Ordabasy	a	0-3	
3/7	Kairat	a	1-3	*Chureev*
8/7	Kaisar	a	1-1	*Tatishev*
21/7	Kaisar	h	4-0	*Sofroni 2, Tatishev 2*
28/7	Ordabasy	h	0-0	
4/8	Taraz	a	0-0	
11/8	Zhetysu	h	1-1	*Erokhin (p)*
27/8	Shakhtyor Karagandy	a	1-2	*Strelbin*
1/9	Kairat	h	3-0	*Sofroni, Boichenko, Boshnyak*
15/9	Alma-Ata	a	0-1	
22/9	Aktobe	h	1-2	*Boichenko*
30/9	Yesil Bogatyr	a	0-0	
6/10	Ekibastuzets	h	1-1	*Erokhin (p)*
20/10	Vostok	a	0-1	
26/10	Astana	h	3-2	*Sobkovich 2, Kravchenko*
1/11	Irtysh	a	0-2	
4/11	Okzhetpes	h	3-0	*Sofroni, Erokhin (p), Boichenko*
10/11	Tobol	a	0-1	

No	Name	Nat	Pos	Aps	(s)	Gls
24	Radik AITZHANOV		D	10	(4)	
5	Omar BERDYEV	TKM	D	12		
20	Evgheniy BOICHENKO	MDA	M	8	(2)	3
39	Zhakhar BOSHNYAK	UKR	A	13	(10)	4
39	Zhakhar BOSHNYAK	UKR	G	1		
8	Valentin CHUREEV		A	27		1
25	Ernar DYSENOV		M	2		
29	Andrei EROKHIN		D	27		4
11	Oleh GOLOVAN	UKR	M	13		
15	Yuriy GURA		M	7		
14	Andrei GUZENKO		M	22	(1)	1
18	Samat KARASHBAEV		A	5	(3)	
27	Dauren KENZHEBEK		M		(1)	
25	Roman KISMETOV		M	10		
10	Viktor KOZHUSHKO		M	14	(9)	
16	Anton KOZOREZ		G	1		
1	Georgiy KRASOVSKIY	UKR	G	17	(2)	
3	Viktor KRAVCHENKO		D	21	(3)	2
23	Vasily LOBASHOV		M	1		
11	Oleg MOCHULYAK		A	7		
17	Spartak MURTAZAEV		D	1	(1)	
20	Yevgeny NESTEROV		A		(5)	

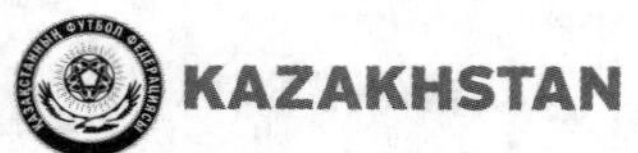

KAZAKHSTAN

No	Name	Nat	Pos	Aps	(s)	Gls
31	Rustam SHAYMARDANOV		D	7		
12	Sakenzhan SHOMAEV		M	1	(2)	
28	Mikhail SCHISHKIN		D	13		
7	Aleksandr SOBKOVICH		D	18	(5)	3
28	Vyacheslav SOFRONI	MDA	A	12	(1)	4
15	Aleksandr STAKHIV		A	6	(6)	
21	Igor STRELBIN		D	9		1
9	Beybit TATISHEV		A	12	(14)	5
4	Andrei TETUSHKIN		D	8	(3)	
5	Darkhan TLEULIEV		M	8	(3)	
4	Sergei ZAITSEV		D	6	(1)	1
6	Malik ZHANTLEYOV		M		(4)	
16	Andrei ZVETKOV		G	11		
13	Dmitry SHOMKO		D	2	(1)	
25	Eduard STOLBOVOY		G	27		
15	Yevgeny SVESHNIKOV		D	18	(3)	1
26	Dajanchklych URAZOV	TKM	A	4	(8)	1
3	Vitaliy USHAKOV		M	23	(1)	2
18	Igor VOINOV		A	4	(10)	
17	Yuriy ZVONARENKO		A	1	(5)	

FC EKIBASTUZETS

Coach – Vitaly Sparyshev

Founded – 1979

2007

1/4	Kairat	a	0-1	
4/4	Zhetysu	a	2-3	*Aubakirov A., Ivanov*
8/4	Taraz	h	2-0	*Lunev, Sveshnikov*
14/4	Shakhtyor Karagandy	h	0-0	
22/4	Ordabasy	a	0-1	
28/4	Atyrau	h	1-0	*Lunev*
5/5	Tobol	a	0-2	
12/5	Okzhetpes	h	2-0	*Aubakirov A., Anisim*
16/5	Alma-Ata	a	0-0	
20/5	Irtysh	h	1-0	*Ivanov*
25/5	Astana	h	0-0	
9/6	Vostok	a	2-3	*Ivanov, Gefel*
16/6	Kaisar	a	2-3	*Aubakirov T., Lunev*
23/6	Yesil Bogatyr	h	1-1	*Galenko*
30/6	Aktobe	a	1-3	*Galenko*
8/7	Alma-Ata	h	1-0	*Ushakov (p)*
28/7	Aktobe	h	1-3	*Burtsev*
4/8	Yesil Bogatyr	a	1-1	*og (Keker)*
12/8	Kaisar	h	1-0	*Burtsev*
26/8	Vostok	h	3-1	*Ushakov, Bulgakov, Baimbetov*
1/9	Astana	a	0-3	
15/9	Irtysh	a	1-1	*Lunev*
22/9	Okzhetpes	a	0-1	
30/9	Tobol	h	0-1	
6/10	Atyrau	a	1-1	*Urazov*
20/10	Ordabasy	h	1-1	*Aubakirov A.*
27/10	Taraz	a	1-3	*Bralin*
4/11	Shakhtyor Karagandy	a	0-2	
7/11	Zhetysu	h	2-0	*Baimbetov, Lunev*
10/11	Kairat	h	1-3	*Aubakirov A.*

No	Name	Nat	Pos	Aps	(s)	Gls
4	Pyotr ANISIM		D	23	(1)	1
5	Zurab ARCHVADZE	GEO	D	24		
19	Azamat AUBAKIROV		A	21	(4)	4
23	Tlektes AUBAKIROV		M	9	(12)	1
8	Gani BAIMBETOV		M	13		2
7	Andrei BARSUKOV		M	4	(2)	
12	Aydyn BRALIN		M	1	(3)	1
10	Aleksandr BULGAKOV		M	24	(1)	1
28	Andrei BURTSEV		M	10	(6)	2
8	Erkin EDIGENOV		D		(1)	
6	Yevgeny GALENKO		M	14	(7)	2
20	Andrei GEFEL	RUS	M	13	(11)	1
11	Sergei IVANOV		A	24		3
9	Yevgeny LUNEV		M	20	(2)	5
21	Ruslan MIKLOSHEVICH	UKR	D	28		
16	Ruslan NARYMBAEV		G	1		
1	Viktor RASKULOV		G	2		
2	Nail SHABAEV		D	20	(2)	

FC IRTYSH PAVLODAR

Coach – Sergei Volgin

Founded – 1965

MAJOR HONOURS: Kazakhstan League – (5) 1993, 1997, 1999, 200 2003; Kazakhstan Cup – (1) 1997.

2007

31/3	Taraz	a	1-0	*Prosekov*
4/4	Atyrau	a	2-1	*Strukov, Turenko*
8/4	Tobol	h	1-1	*Turenko*
14/4	Ordabasy	h	1-0	*Ibraev*
22/4	Okzhetpes	a	2-1	*Kostenski, Chernyshc*
28/4	Kaisar	h	1-0	*Kolomyts*
5/5	Astana	h	1-0	*Noskov*
12/5	Vostok	a	0-1	
20/5	Ekibastuzets	a	0-1	
26/5	Yesil Bogatyr	a	0-0	
11/6	Aktobe	h	2-1	*Strukov 2*
17/6	Alma-Ata	a	1-3	*Turenko*
23/6	Kairat	a	2-0	*Strukov, Prosenko*
30/6	Shakhtyor Karagandy	a	1-2	*Bolshakov*
8/7	Zhetysu	h	3-2	*Noskov, Turenko (p), Zarechni*
21/7	Zhetysu	a	0-3	
28/7	Shakhtyor Karagandy	h	2-0	*Maltsev, Noskov*
26/8	Aktobe	a	0-1	
1/9	Yesil Bogatyr	h	2-0	*Noskov, Veretennikov*
15/9	Ekibastuzets	h	1-1	*Strukov*
19/9	Alma-Ata	h	1-0	*Ovchinov*
22/9	Vostok	h	3-1	*Strukov 2, Nesterenko*
30/9	Astana	a	0-0	
6/10	Kaisar	a	1-3	*Bolshakov*
11/10	Kairat	h	1-0	*Strukov*
20/10	Okzhetpes	h	0-1	
26/10	Tobol	a	0-1	
1/11	Atyrau	h	2-0	*Noskov, Zarechni*
4/11	Ordabasy	a	1-2	*Noskov*
10/11	Taraz	h	2-1	*Veretennikov, Bolshakov*

No	Name	Nat	Pos	Aps	(s)	Gls
11	Aleksandr ANDREEV		A	1	(4)	
24	Dmitry BOLSHAKOV		M	16	(10)	3
3	Vladislav CHERNYSHOV		D	13		1
16	Dmitry DRALOV		G	2		
	Azamat ERSALIMOV		M	3	(3)	
19	Sabyrkhan IBRAEV		M	15	(2)	1
25	Erdos KAZYBEKOV		D	14		
4	Yuriy KOLOMYTS	RUS	D	27		1
6	Slavi KOSTENSKI	BUL	D	11		1
7	Gleb MALTSEV		M	4	(5)	1
22	Nikolai NESTERENKO		M	28		1
8	Vladimir NOSKOV		A	19	(3)	6
17	Yevgeniy OVCHINOV		D	26		1
23	Maxim PRIMAK		M	9	(2)	
14	Vasily PROSEKOV		A	7	(11)	2
1	Daniil RIKHARD		G	28		
18	Baurzhan SAGYNDYK		D		(3)	
18	Pavel SHABALIN		A		(9)	
20	Alexei SHAKIN		M	10	(9)	
9	Sergey STRUKOV	RUS	A	28	(1)	8
5	Dmitry TURENKO		D	24		4

	Name	Nat	Pos	Aps	(s)	Gls
	Oleg VERETENNIKOV	RUS	M	12	(1)	2
	Konstantin ZARECHNI		M	16	(7)	2
	Konstantin ZOTOV		M	17	(4)	

FC KAIRAT ALMATY

Coach – Sergei Klimov; (23/6/07) Vakhid Masudov

Founded – 1954

AJOR HONOURS: Kazakhstan League – (2) 1992, 2004; Kazakhstan Cup – (5) 1992, 1996, 1999, 2001, 2003.

07				
4	Ekibastuzets	h	1-0	*Sakhalbaev*
4	Aktobe	h	0-2	
4	Alma-Ata	a	0-2	
/4	Yesil Bogatyr	a	0-2	
/4	Kaisar	a	1-2	*Gavrilenko*
/4	Shakhtyor Karagandy	h	0-2	
5	Zhetysu	a	0-0	
/5	Taraz	h	0-0	
/5	Ordabasy	a	1-2	*Abdulin*
6	Tobol	a	0-1	
/6	Okzhetpes	h	2-4	*Orazaliyev, Eszhanov*
/6	Irtysh	h	0-2	
/6	Astana	h	0-2	
7	Atyrau	h	3-1	*og (Erokhin), Gavrilenko, Kolbaev*
7	Vostok	a	0-1	
/7	Vostok	h	0-2	
/7	Astana	a	0-5	
8	Okzhetpes	a	1-0	*Buleshev*
/8	Tobol	h	0-2	
9	Atyrau	a	0-3	
/9	Ordabasy	h	3-0	*Aleynikov, Buleshev, Gavrilenko*
/9	Taraz	a	0-0	
'10	Zhetysu	h	1-0	*Begović*
'10	Shakhtyor Karagandy	a	0-1	
/10	Irtysh	a	0-1	
/10	Kaisar	h	2-1	*Avdeev, Birkurmanov*
/10	Alma-Ata	h	3-1	*og (Vorotnikov), Birkurmanov, Aleynikov*
'11	Aktobe	a	0-2	
'11	Yesil Bogatyr	h	2-1	*Sakhalbaev, Buleshev*
)/11	Ekibastuzets	a	3-1	*Birkurmanov, Buleshev, Abdulin*

o	Name	Nat	Pos	Aps	(s)	Gls
5	Renat ABDULIN		D	29		2
0	Konstantin ALEYNIKOV		M	17	(4)	2
	Aydar ARGIMBAYEV		A		(9)	
	Vitaliy ARTEMOV		D	26	(1)	
0	Igor AVDEEV		D	14		1
2	Nenad BEGOVIĆ	SRB	M	12		1
	Erlen BEKMUKHAEV		M	22	(5)	
	Arman BIRKURMANOV		D	11	(1)	3
0	Alibek BULESHEV		A	13	(2)	4
4	Vlado DANILOV	MKD	M	5	(1)	
1	Almas ESZHANOV		M	12	(11)	1
6	Artem GAVRILENKO		A	16	(9)	3
9	Rustem KALIEV		A		(5)	
5	Sergey KAPUTIN		D	10		
0	Maksat KOLBAEV		M	8		1
0	Dauren KUSAINOV		A	13	(2)	
1	Yevgeny MALININ	KGZ	M	12	(1)	
3	Timur MOLDAGALIEV		D	6	(1)	
7	Raim MUSAEV		M	1	(3)	
3	Yevgeny NOKHRIN		D	5	(6)	
2	Vyacheslav NURMAGAMBETOV		A	10	(2)	
	Zhandos ORAZALIYEV		M	14		1
	Yuriy OSIPENKO		M	8	(1)	
	Valery PASTUKHOV		A	1	(3)	
23	Vladimir RIBIĆ	SRB	A	11	(1)	
7	Ruslan SAKHALBAEV		M	20	(6)	2
18	Denis SOLOVYEV	RUS	G	9		
25	Oleg TARASOV		A	3	(8)	
31	Erlan TLEVKULOV		G		(1)	
18	Andrei TSVETKOV		G	10	(1)	
24	Vladimir VELIZHANIN		D	1		
1	Ilya YUROV		G	11		

FC KAISAR KYZYLORDA

Coach – Sergei Gorohovodatsky

Founded – 1968

2007				
31/3	Aktobe	h	0-0	
3/4	Alma-Ata	h	1-0	*Fomenko*
8/4	Okzhetpes	h	0-0	
14/4	Tobol	a	0-1	
22/4	Kairat	h	2-1	*Tazhimbetov, Fomenko*
28/4	Irtysh	a	0-1	
5/5	Shakhtyor Karagandy	h	1-0	*og (Kornienko)*
12/5	Astana	a	0-1	
20/5	Zhetysu	h	0-1	
26/5	Vostok	a	1-0	*Fomenko*
9/6	Taraz	h	2-0	*Fomenko, Baltaev*
16/6	Ekibastuzets	h	3-2	*Syzdykov, Tazhimbetov 2*
23/6	Ordabasy	h	3-1	*Gogiashvili, Baltaev, Tazhimbetov*
30/6	Yesil Bogatyr	a	0-1	
8/7	Atyrau	h	1-1	*Gogiashvili*
21/7	Atyrau	a	0-4	
28/7	Yesil Bogatyr	h	0-0	
4/8	Ordabasy	a	0-1	
12/8	Ekibastuzets	a	0-1	
26/8	Taraz	a	3-0	*Tsygalko 2, Bayzhanov*
1/9	Vostok	h	0-4	
15/9	Zhetysu	a	1-1	*Shoytymov*
22/9	Astana	h	2-1	*Baltaev 2*
30/9	Shakhtyor Karagandy	a	0-2	
6/10	Irtysh	h	3-1	*Tsygalko 2, Baltaev*
21/10	Kairat	a	1-2	*Tsygalko*
26/10	Okzhetpes	a	2-2	*Tazhimbetov, Tsygalko*
1/11	Alma-Ata	a	0-2	
4/11	Tobol	h	1-1	*Bayzhanov (p)*
10/11	Aktobe	a	0-5	

No	Name	Nat	Pos	Aps	(s)	Gls
33	Akhmet ALAYDAROV		G	3	(1)	
22	Aziz ANARMETOV		M	25	(1)	
3	Aldan BALTAEV		D	24		5
20	Aidos BAYTENOV		M	3	(2)	
77	Maksat BAYZHANOV		M	29		2
12	Anatoly BERDYGIN		A	1	(8)	
21	Darkhan BEKISHEV		D		(1)	
23	Abumuslim BOGATYREV	RUS	M	4	(5)	
14	Aschat BORANTAEV		D	29		
7	Medet DUZBAEV		M		(1)	
21	Bakhytzhan IBRAGIMOV		M	2	(1)	
8	Arturas FOMENKO	LTU	A	14	(1)	4
23	Giorgi GOGIASHVILI	GEO	M	11	(6)	2
27	Vladimir KASHTANOV		M	18	(11)	
15	Maxim KAZNACHEEV		D	1	(4)	
4	Vladimir KOZLENKO	UKR	D	12	(4)	
13	Yerlan MAKHAMBEDYEV		D	3	(1)	
17	Zhasulan MOLDAKARAEV		A	4	(13)	
5	Aleksandr MOSKALENKO		D	25		
15	Samat NAURYZBAEV		D	1	(3)	
1	Roman NESTERENKO		G	27		
9	Marat SARSENOV		D	1		

No	Name	Nat	Pos	Aps	(s)	Gls
2	Yerlan SHOYTYMOV		D	24	(1)	1
10	Talgat SYZDYKOV		M	24	(1)	1
18	Daurenbek TAZHIMBETOV		A	27	(1)	5
8	Maxim TSYGALKO	BLR	A	11	(1)	6
11	Islam ZHUNUSBEKOV		M	7	(18)	

FC OKZHETPES KOKSHETAU

Coach – Vladimir Glevich; (10/7/07) Kayrat Aymanov; (08/10/07) Vladimir Glevich

Founded – 1968

2007				
31/3	Ordabasy	a	1-0	*Pastukhov*
4/4	Tobol	h	0-0	
8/4	Kaisar	a	0-0	
14/4	Atyrau	h	1-2	*Pastukhov*
22/4	Irtysh	h	1-2	*Dosmanbetov*
29/4	Astana	a	0-2	
5/5	Vostok	h	0-1	
12/5	Ekibastuzets	a	0-2	
20/5	Yesil Bogatyr	h	2-1	*Pastukhov, Aliyev*
25/5	Aktobe	a	1-2	*Kiselev*
11/6	Alma-Ata	h	1-0	*Ivanov*
16/6	Kairat	a	4-2	*og (Abdulin), Shapovalov, Kiselev, Dosmanbetov*
23/6	Shakhtyor Karagandy	h	1-2	*Pastukhov*
30/6	Zhetysu	a	1-2	*Ivanov*
6/7	Taraz	h	3-2	*Kalyubin (p), Dosmanbetov, Shapovalov*
21/7	Taraz	a	0-3	
28/7	Zhetysu	h	0-1	
1/8	Kairat	h	0-1	
4/8	Shakhtyor Karagandy	a	1-3	*Aliyev*
27/8	Alma-Ata	a	0-4	
31/8	Aktobe	h	0-6	
15/9	Yesil Bogatyr	a	1-1	*Dosmanbetov*
22/9	Ekibastuzets	h	1-0	*Zakharchenko*
30/9	Vostok	a	0-1	
6/10	Astana	h	0-0	
20/10	Irtysh	a	1-0	*Chonkayev*
26/10	Kaisar	h	2-2	*Chonkayev 2 (2p)*
1/11	Tobol	a	1-10	*Chonkayev*
4/11	Atyrau	a	0-3	
10/11	Ordabasy	h	3-1	*Chonkayev (p), Kalyubin, Dosmanbetov*

No	Name	Nat	Pos	Aps	(s)	Gls
14	Akhmed ALABERGENOV		M	16	(3)	
13	Artem ALEKHIN		D	7	(2)	
17	Kanat ALIYEV		M	25	(1)	2
87	Yaroslav BAGINSKY		G	9	(1)	
24	Vyachesav BOGATYREV		M	2	(1)	
20	Gakharman CHONKAYEV	TKM	A	12	(3)	5
2	Valery DENISOV		D	1	(1)	
10	Serik DOSMANBETOV		A	25		5
5	Yuriy DYAK		M	10	(6)	
7	Sergey IVANOV		M	18	(5)	2
4	Oleg FISTICAN	MDA	D	28		
21	Rasim GUSEYNOV		M	1	(5)	
23	Yerzhan KABYLBEKOV		M		(2)	
16	Sergey KALYUBIN		M	20	(4)	2
9	Vladislav KISELEV		M	13		2
27	Alik KHAIDAROV	TKM	D	11	(5)	
18	Oleg KHAN		M	7	(9)	
8	Samat KUSHERBAEV		M	5		
6	Sergey LABODOVSKY		A	6	(3)	
22	Denis LEDENEV		A	5	(3)	
9	Yuriy MOKROUSOV		M	2	(2)	
1	Andrei NENASHEV		G	17	(1)	
15	Yermek NURGALIEV		M	2	(8)	
6	Valery PASTUKHOV		A	15	(1)	4
77	Arslan SATYBALDIN		G	4		
3	Valeriy SHAPOVALOV	UKR	D	25		2
25	Roman SKRYPNYK		D	19	(2)	
24	Zhadyger TISHTYBAEV		M	1	(1)	
19	Yevgeniy ZAKHARCHENKO		M	24	(1)	1

FC ORDABASY SHYMKENT

Coach – Marco Bragonja (NED)

Founded – 1998

2007				
31/3	Okzhetpes	h	0-1	
3/4	Astana	h	0-0	
8/4	Vostok	a	2-1	*Đurđević, Nesteruk*
14/4	Irtysh	a	0-1	
22/4	Ekibastuzets	h	1-0	*Nesteruk*
29/4	Yesil Bogatyr	a	0-0	
5/5	Aktobe	h	0-0	
12/5	Alma-Ata	a	1-1	*Pischulin*
20/5	Kairat	h	2-1	*Tleshev (p), Volodin*
25/5	Shakhtyor Karagandy	a	0-0	
9/6	Zhetysu	h	3-0	*Kamelov, Zhumakhanov, Pischulin*
16/6	Taraz	a	2-2	*Đurđević, Tleshev*
23/6	Kaisar	a	1-3	*Sabirov*
30/6	Atyrau	h	3-0	*Tleshev, Đurđević, Karakulov (p)*
28/7	Atyrau	a	0-0	
1/8	Taraz	h	2-1	*Zhumakhanov, Đurđević*
4/8	Kaisar	h	1-0	*Karakulov (p)*
8/8	Tobol	a	0-3	
26/8	Zhetysu	a	1-1	*Đurđević*
1/9	Shakhtyor Karagandy	h	0-2	
16/9	Kairat	a	0-3	
22/9	Alma-Ata	h	4-0	*Tleshev 2, Đurđević 2*
30/9	Aktobe	a	1-2	*Kusainov*
6/10	Yesil Bogatyr	h	0-1	
20/10	Ekibastuzets	a	1-1	*Nesteruk*
26/10	Vostok	h	0-0	
29/10	Tobol	h	0-0	
1/11	Astana	a	0-1	
4/11	Irtysh	h	2-1	*Tleshev, Maymakov*
10/11	Okzhetpes	a	1-3	*Zhumakhanov*

No	Name	Nat	Pos	Aps	(s)	Gls
3	Yegor AZOVSKI		D	29		
9	Zhandos AMETOV		M	11	(2)	
6	Bekzat BEYSENOV		M	3	(3)	
11	Dragan ĐURĐEVIĆ	SRB	A	12	(12)	7
12	Dias KAMELOV		M	14	(2)	1
7	Kuanysh KARAKULOV		M	28		2
	Aydos KENZHEBAEV		D	1		
2	Segey KOZYLIN		D	24	(2)	
20	Dauren KUSAINOV		A	5	(4)	1
15	Sergei MAKSIMOV		M	16	(2)	
23	Nurbolat MAYMAKOV		A	3	(10)	1
1	Aleksandr MOKIN		G	28		
16	Murat MUKASHEV		G	2		
4	Mukhtar MUKHTAROV		D	1	(2)	
8	Andriy NESTERUK	UKR	A	14	(6)	3
17	Tanat NUSERBAYEV		A	9	(15)	
22	Pavel PISCHULIN		D	10	(10)	2
	Timur PRIMZHANOV		D	1		
5	Dmitry PROTORCHIN		D	27		

Name	Nat	Pos	Aps	(s)	Gls
Oleg SABIROV		D	26		1
Murat TLESHEV		A	14	(6)	6
Darkhan TLEULIEV		M		(1)	
VEBERSON Andrade dos Santos	BRA	A	3	(3)	
Denis VOLODIN		M	25	(1)	1
Sanat ZHUMAKHANOV		D	24	(3)	3

FC SHAKHTYOR KARAGANDY

Coach – Juha Malinen (FIN); (10/8/07) Revaz Dzodzhuashvili (GEO)

Founded – 1958

)7				
3	Vostok	h	1-1	*Finonchenko (p)*
	Yesil Bogatyr	h	5-1	*Miholaps, Lovtchev, Kostyuk, Khasenov, Melkadze*
	Aktobe	a	0-0	
4	Ekibastuzets	a	0-0	
'4	Alma-Ata	h	1-1	*Finonchenko*
'4	Kairat	a	2-0	*Finonchenko 2*
	Kaisar	a	0-1	
'5	Zhetysu	h	3-1	*Miholaps (p), Kenetaev, Ederekho*
'5	Astana	h	2-1	*Glushko 2*
'5	Taraz	a	1-0	*Glushko*
'5	Ordabasy	h	0-0	
	Atyrau	a	5-0	*Rusnac 2, Kostyuk, Lovtchev, Miholaps*
'6	Tobol	h	3-1	*Miholaps 2, Kornienko*
'6	Okzhetpes	a	2-1	*Ederekho, og (Satybaldin)*
'6	Irtysh	h	2-1	*Miholaps, Kenetaev*
	Astana	a	0-3	
'7	Irtysh	a	0-2	
	Okzhetpes	h	3-1	*Kratochvil, Brezný, Khasenov*
/8	Tobol	a	2-4	*Khomenko, Finonchenko*
/8	Atyrau	h	2-1	*Melkadze, Rusnac*
	Ordabasy	a	2-0	*Nozadze, Finoncnenko (p)*
/9	Taraz	h	2-0	*Melkadze, Kornienko (p)*
/9	Zhetysu	a	0-1	
/9	Kaisar	h	2-0	*Miholaps, Melkadze*
10	Kairat	h	1-0	*Melkadze*
/10	Aktobe	h	0-0	
1	Yesil Bogatyr	a	1-0	*Miholaps*
1	Ekibastuzets	h	2-0	*Melkadze 2*
1	Alma-Ata	a	1-1	*Melkadze*
/11	Vostok	a	0-1	

No	Name	Nat	Pos	Aps	(s)	Gls
	Konstantin BERNATSKY		M		(1)	
	Daniel BREZNÝ	CZE	M	8	(2)	1
	Rafael EDEREKHO	NGR	A	2	(13)	2
	Andrei FINONCHENKO		A	23	(3)	6
	Andrey FOSHIY		D	1	(1)	
	Giorgi GABIDAURI	GEO	A	6	(6)	
	Mikhail GLUSHKO		A	4	(7)	3
	Aleksandr GRIGORENKO		G	11		
	Ruslan KENETAEV		M	16	(9)	2
	Aleksandr KISLITSIN		D	25	(1)	
	Rinat KHASENOV		M	16	(9)	2
	Dmitriy KHOMENKO		A	1	(3)	1
	Oleg KORNIENKO		D	25		2
	Sergey KOSTYUK		M	15	(9)	2
	Karel KRATOCHVIL	CZE	D	4	(2)	1
	David LORIA		G	18		
28	Yevgeny LOVTCHEV		M	28		2
18	Levan MELKADZE	GEO	A	16	(5)	8
11	Mihails MIHOLAPS	LVA	A	23	(3)	8
10	Marlan MUZHIKOV		M	1	(1)	
	Yevgeniy NESTEROV		A	1	(2)	
7	Lasha NOZADZE	GEO	A	12	(2)	1
4	Veaceslav RUSNAC	MDA	M	26	(2)	3
9	Maxim SAMCHENKO		D	23	(4)	
16	Sergey SARANA		G	1		
3	Igor SOLOSHENKO		D	23		
21	Pavel VELEBA	CZE	A	1	(2)	

FC TARAZ

Coach – Sergei Tagiev; (20/5/07) Askar Kushekbaev

Founded – 1961

MAJOR HONOURS: Kazakhstan League – (1) 1996; Kazakhstan Cup – (1) 2004

2007				
31/3	Irtysh	h	0-1	
3/4	Vostok	h	3-0	*Kotov, Shapurin, Mazbaev*
8/4	Ekibastuzets	a	0-2	
14/4	Astana	a	0-2	
22/4	Yesil Bogatyr	h	0-0	
29/4	Aktobe	a	0-5	
5/5	Alma-Ata	h	1-2	*Shapurin*
13/5	Kairat	a	0-0	
16/5	Tobol	h	1-3	*Yakovlev*
20/5	Shakhtyor Karagandy	h	0-1	
26/5	Zhetysu	a	0-1	
9/6	Kaisar	a	0-2	
16/6	Ordabasy	h	2-2	*Ostrushko, Yakovlev*
23/6	Atyrau	a	0-3	
6/7	Okzhetpes	a	2-3	*Alimbaev, Dzhatkanbaev*
21/7	Okzhetpes	h	3-0	*Yevstigneev V., Yakovlev, Litvinenko*
1/8	Ordabasy	a	1-2	*Shapurin*
4/8	Atyrau	h	0-0	
26/8	Kaisar	h	0-3	
1/9	Zhetysu	h	0-1	
16/9	Shakhtyor Karagandy	a	0-2	
22/9	Kairat	h	0-0	
30/9	Alma-Ata	a	0-4	
3/10	Tobol	a	0-2	
6/10	Aktobe	h	0-2	
20/10	Yesil Bogatyr	a	1-2	*og (Shvydko)*
27/10	Ekibastuzets	h	3-1	*Shapurin, Mazbaev 2*
1/11	Vostok	a	0-0	
4/11	Astana	h	0-2	
10/11	Irtysh	a	1-2	*Dzhatkanbaev*

No	Name	Nat	Pos	Aps	(s)	Gls
16	Aleksandr ALIYEV		G	1	(1)	
3	Galymzhan ALIMBAEV		M	3	(15)	1
21	Eldar BAIMESHOV		D	2	(3)	
	Aziz BAYSHAKOV		M	2		
2	Arman BIRKURMANOV		D	11		
22	Erzhan DZHATKANBAEV		M	4	(5)	2
14	Almat DOSMAGAMBETOV		M	1		
12	Ruslan ESATOV		M	6	(3)	
24	Egor GLADKOV		M	16	(1)	
8	Konstantin KOTOV		M	7		1
5	Nurtaz KURGULIN		D	17	(1)	
8	Oleg LITVINENKO		A	2	(2)	1
10	Nurken MAZBAEV		A	13	(11)	3
21	Denis MAMONOV		D	1		
1	Igor MIKHAILOV	UZB	G	18		
	Nurmat MIRZABAEV		M	1	(2)	

No	Name	Nat	Pos	Aps	(s)	Gls
2	Samat NAURYZBAEV		D	14		
11	Oleg NEDASHKOVSKI		A	15	(4)	
7	Azamat NIYAZYMBETOV		M	12	(7)	
20	Vladimir OSTRUSHKO	UKR	D	12	(1)	1
25	Vladimir PLOTNIKOV		G	11		
9	Alexei SHAPURIN		A	22	(2)	4
4	Yermek SHOKANOV		D	6	(2)	
6	Vyacheslav SOBOLEV		M	26		
23	Kairat SULEY		A	20	(6)	
17	Vladimir YAKOVLEV		A	24	(1)	3
15	Erlan YELEUSINOV		D	14	(1)	
19	Dmitry YEVSTIGNEEV		M	24		
18	Vitaliy YEVSTIGNEEV		M	18	(1)	1
20	Sergey ZHUNENKO	RUS	D	7	(1)	

FC TOBOL KOSTANAY

Coach – Dmitriy Ogai

Founded – 1967

MAJOR HONOURS: Kazakhstan Cup – (1) 2007

2007				
31/3	Atyrau	a	4-0	*Ostapenko, og (Erokhin), Urazov 2*
4/4	Okzhetpes	a	0-0	
8/4	Irtysh	a	1-1	*Baltiyev*
14/4	Kaisar	h	1-0	*Baltiyev (p)*
22/4	Astana	h	2-0	*Zhumaskaliev, Ostapenko*
25/4	Zhetysu	h	0-0	
29/4	Vostok	a	2-1	*Ostapenko, Bakaev*
5/5	Ekibastuzets	h	2-0	*Yurin, Sabalakov*
12/5	Yesil Bogatyr	a	0-0	
16/5	Taraz	a	3-1	*Zhumaskaliev, Nurgaliev, Ostapenko*
20/5	Aktobe	h	0-0	
26/5	Alma-Ata	a	1-2	*Urazov*
9/6	Kairat	h	1-0	*Sabalakov*
16/6	Shakhtyor Karagandy	a	1-3	*Yurin*
4/8	Zhetysu	a	2-1	*Ostapenko, Baltiyev (p)*
8/8	Ordabasy	h	3-0	*Skorykh, Bakaev 2 (1p)*
11/8	Shakhtyor Karagandy	h	4-2	*Baltiyev 2 (1p), Bakaev 2*
26/8	Kairat	a	2-0	*Baltiyev, Zhumaskaliev*
17/9	Aktobe	a	0-1	
22/9	Yesil Bogatyr	h	3-0	*Ostapenko 2, Zhumaskaliev*
30/9	Ekibastuzets	a	1-0	*Zhumaskaliev*
3/10	Taraz	h	2-0	*Zhumaskaliev 2*
6/10	Vostok	h	7-0	*Zhumaskaliev, Bakaev 3, og (Seytbekov), Sabalakov, Baltiyev*
20/10	Astana	a	1-4	*Zhumaskaliev*
23/10	Alma-Ata	h	4-2	*Urazov, Bakaev, Meshkov, Sabalakov*
26/10	Irtysh	h	1-0	*Dimitrov*
29/10	Ordabasy	a	0-0	
1/11	Okzhetpes	h	10-1	*Yurin 2, Ostapenko 3, Urazov, Nurdauletov, Nurgaliev, Nurmagambetov 2*
4/11	Kaisar	a	1-1	*Lotov*
10/11	Atyrau	h	1-0	*Yurin*

No	Name	Nat	Pos	Aps	(s)	Gls
20	Chingiz ABUGALIEV		M	8	(3)	
10	Ulugbek BAKAEV	UZB	A	14	(9)	9
25	Ruslan BALTIYEV		M	21	(2)	7
3	Stanimir DIMITROV	BUL	D	25		1
14	Valeriy GARKUSHA		A		(1)	
2	Farhadbek IRISMETOV		D	25	(1)	
13	Andrei KHARABARA		M	17	(7)	
15	Oleg LOTOV		D	9	(1)	1
6	Yevgeny MESHKOV		M	9	(8)	1
18	Daniyar MUKANOV		D	25		
5	Kayrat NURDAULETOV		M	29	(1)	1
7	Azat NURGALIEV		M	22	(6)	2
19	Vyacheslav NURMAGAMBETOV		A		(3)	2
23	Sergei OSTAPENKO		A	16	(10)	10
35	Aleksandr PETUKHOV		G	27		
1	Kirill PRYADKIN		G	3	(1)	
17	Talgat SABALAKOV		M	1	(18)	4
22	Sergey SKORYKH		M	26	(1)	1
11	Didarkych URAZOV	TKM	A	9	(8)	5
9	Nurbol ZHUMASKALIEV		M	26	(1)	9
24	Igor YURIN		M	18	(3)	5

FC VOSTOK

Coach – Pavel Evteev; (1/6/07) Aleksandr Golokolosov

Founded – 1963

MAJOR HONOURS: Kazakhstan Cup – (1) 1994.

2007				
31/3	Shakhtyor Karagandy	a	1-1	*Kolpakov*
3/4	Taraz	a	0-3	
8/4	Ordabasy	h	1-2	*Aksenyov (p)*
14/4	Zhetysu	h	0-2	
22/4	Atyrau	a	0-2	
29/4	Tobol	h	1-2	*Udalov*
5/5	Okzhetpes	a	1-0	*Udalov*
12/5	Irtysh	h	1-0	*Gurtuev (p)*
16/5	Aktobe	a	0-1	
20/5	Astana	a	1-1	*Tolok*
26/5	Kaisar	h	0-1	
9/6	Ekibastuzets	h	3-2	*Aksenyov 2, Yusupov*
16/6	Yesil Bogatyr	a	1-0	*og (Kischenko)*
23/6	Aktobe	h	2-1	*Aksenyov, Gurtuev*
1/7	Alma-Ata	a	1-2	*Malkov*
8/7	Kairat	h	1-0	*Ditkovsky*
21/7	Kairat	a	2-0	*Aksenyov, Tsgura*
12/8	Yesil Bogatyr	h	2-2	*Gurtuev 2*
26/8	Ekibastuzets	a	1-3	*Gurtuev*
1/9	Kaisar	a	4-0	*Gurtuev, og (Anarmetov), Tsgura 2*
16/9	Astana	h	2-0	*Udalov, Aksenyov*
22/9	Irtysh	a	1-3	*Aksenyov (p)*
30/9	Okzhetpes	h	1-0	*Tsgura*
3/10	Alma-Ata	h	1-2	*Aksenyov*
6/10	Tobol	a	0-7	
20/10	Atyrau	h	1-0	*Aksenyov*
26/10	Ordabasy	a	0-0	
1/11	Taraz	h	0-0	
4/11	Zhetysu	a	0-1	
10/11	Shakhtyor Karagandy	h	1-0	*Gurtuev*

No	Name	Nat	Pos	Aps	(s)	Gls
34	Yuriy AKSENYOV		D	29		9
2	Anatoly BOGDANOV		A	28		
23	Sergei DITKOVSKY		A	14	(13)	1
4	Vyacheslav ERBES		M	2	(9)	
9	Yuriy GURA		M	6	(1)	
12	Vladimir GURTUEV		A	23	(6)	7
3	Zviad JELADZE	GEO	D	29		
12	Giga JVANIA	GEO	D	3	(7)	
20	Giorgiy KOLPAKOV		D	25	(1)	1
15	Anatoly MALKOV		M	26	(4)	1
8	Anton MOLTUSINOV		M	1	(9)	
6	Daulet NURASYLOV		A	3	(12)	
22	Igor OSIPCHUK		G	29		
9	Hennadiy SHCHEKOTILIN	UKR	A	1		
13	Azamat SEYTBEKOV		M	18	(4)	

Name	Nat	Pos	Aps	(s)	Gls
Ivan SIVOZHELEZOV		G	1		
Yevgeniy S.TARASOV		D	27		
Oleg TOLOK	RUS	D	9	(4)	1
Serhiy TSGURA	UKR	M	14	(4)	4
Pavel UDALOV		A	18	(10)	3
Darkhan YUSUPOV		M	11	(2)	1
Maxim ZUEV		D	13	(3)	

FC YESIL BOGATYR PETROPAVLOVSK

Coach – Yevgeny Yarovenko (UKR)
Founded – 1968

07				
/3	Alma-Ata	a	0-1	
4	Shakhtyor Karagandy	a	1-5	*Urazbakhtin (p)*
4	Zhetysu	a	1-1	*Shvydko*
/4	Kairat	h	2-0	*Danaev, Urazbakhtin*
/4	Taraz	a	0-0	
/4	Aktobe	a	1-2	*Shevchenko*
/4	Ordabasy	h	0-0	
5	Atyrau	a	2-0	*Grigoryan, Averchenko*
/5	Tobol	h	0-0	
/5	Okzhetpes	a	1-2	*Urazbakhtin (p)*
/5	Irtysh	h	0-0	
/6	Astana	a	1-1	*Karguzhinov*
/6	Vostok	h	0-1	
3/6	Ekibastuzets	a	1-1	*Urazbakhtin*
/6	Kaisar	h	1-0	*Voskanyan*
7	Aktobe	h	1-1	*Keker*
3/7	Kaisar	a	0-0	
8	Ekibastuzets	h	1-1	*Solomin*
2/8	Vostok	a	2-2	*Averchenko, Voskanyan*
5/8	Astana	h	2-0	*Shvydko, Averchenko*
/9	Irtysh	a	0-2	
5/9	Okzhetpes	h	1-1	*Averchenko*
2/9	Tobol	a	0-3	
/9	Atyrau	h	0-0	
/10	Ordabasy	a	1-0	*Voskanyan*
/10	Taraz	h	2-1	*Voskanyan, Averchenko*
6/10	Zhetysu	h	1-0	*Oganesov*
/11	Shakhtyor Karagandy	h	0-1	
/11	Kairat	a	1-2	*Voskanyan*
0/11	Alma-Ata	h	1-0	*Shvydko*

o	Name	Nat	Pos	Aps	(s)	Gls
	Akhmet AKHMETZHANOV		M	13	(9)	
0	Yevgeniy AVERCHENKO		D	27	(2)	5
8	Yuriy CHUKHLEBA		M	29		
3	Alexei DANAEV		D	11	(2)	1
	David GRIGORYAN	ARM	M	17		1
9	Zhanat KARGUZHINOV		M	14	(4)	1
7	Kirill KEKER		D	30	(1)	1
5	Dmitry KISCHENKO		D	21	(2)	
2	Vladimir LOGINOVSKY		G	29		
	Andriy LOSNIKOV	UKR	M	23	(1)	
2	Vladimir NIKLEVICH		G	1		
5	Anton OGANESOV		A	7	(3)	1
	Sergei OSADCHI		D	13	(2)	
	Alikhan SHADIYEV		M	3		
1	Maxim SHEVCHENKO		M	9	(13)	1
7	Kuat SHINIKULOV		M	3	(1)	
2	Stanislav SHULYAK		M	2	(5)	
	Igor SHVYDKO		D	26		3
4	Nikolay SOLOMIN		A	8	(15)	1
4	Aleksandr STAKHIV		A		(7)	
9	Rafael URAZBAKHTIN		A	22	(1)	4
0	Aleksandr YAROVENKO		M		(7)	
	Sergei YUREVICH		A	1	(10)	
3	Dmitry YURKOV		M		(1)	
0	Aram VOSKANYAN	ARM	A	21	(3)	5

FC ZHETYSU TALDYKORGAN

Coach – Vladimir Linchevsky
Founded – 1981

2007				
31/3	Astana	h	2-0	*Kadyrkulov, Munteanu*
4/4	Ekibastuzets	h	3-2	*Kutsov, Kenbaev, Kitsak*
8/4	Yesil Bogatyr	h	1-1	*Kutsov*
14/4	Vostok	a	2-0	*Usmanov 2*
22/4	Aktobe	h	0-3	
25/4	Tobol	a	0-0	
29/4	Alma-Ata	a	3-1	*Krokhmal 2, Zabelin (p)*
5/5	Kairat	h	0-0	
12/5	Shakhtyor Karagandy	a	1-3	*Kenbaev*
20/5	Kaisar	a	1-0	*Krutskevich*
26/5	Taraz	h	1-0	*Kenbaev*
9/6	Ordabasy	a	0-3	
16/6	Atyrau	h	2-1	*Usmanov, Krutskevich*
30/6	Okzhetpes	h	2-1	*Usmanov, Krokhmal*
8/7	Irtysh	a	2-3	*Kenbaev 2*
21/7	Irtysh	h	3-0	*Zheylitbaev, Munteanu (p), Krutskevich*
28/7	Okzhetpes	a	1-0	*Sorokin*
4/8	Tobol	h	1-2	*Karakenov*
11/8	Atyrau	a	1-1	*Munteanu*
26/8	Ordabasy	h	1-1	*Zheylitbaev*
1/9	Taraz	a	1-0	*Mamonov*
15/9	Kaisar	h	1-1	*Mamonov*
22/9	Shakhtyor Karagandy	h	1-0	*Munteanu (p)*
1/10	Kairat	a	0-1	
6/10	Alma-Ata	h	1-2	*Mikhaylov*
20/10	Aktobe	a	0-2	
26/10	Yesil Bogatyr	a	0-1	
4/11	Vostok	h	1-0	*Mamonov*
7/11	Ekibastuzets	a	0-2	
10/11	Astana	a	1-1	*Kutsov*

No	Name	Nat	Pos	Aps	(s)	Gls
9	Zhandos AKHMETOV		D	5		
19	Ruslan BARZUKAYEV		M		(5)	
16	Igor GLUSHKO		G	5		
2	Ruslan GUMAR		D	7	(6)	
5	Murat ISKAKOV		D	14	(1)	
14	Askhat KADYRKULOV		M	9	(2)	1
17	Galym KARAKENOV		M	14	(6)	1
24	Erzat KENBAEV		A	19	(6)	5
	Dias KHAMZIN		M		(2)	
6	Vitaly KITSAK		M	23	(4)	1
23	Aleksandr KROKHMAL		A	15	(7)	3
22	Aleksandr KRUTSKEVICH		D	17	(8)	3
20	Sergei KUTSOV		D	6	(4)	3
9	Sergei LABODOVSKY		A	1	(4)	
18	Dmitry MAMONOV		M	18	(6)	3
11	Georgy MEGRELADZE		A	6	(2)	
15	Ruslan MIKHAYLOV		A	3	(3)	1
25	Constantin MUNTEANU	ROU	D	24	(1)	4
1	Yuriy NOVIKOV		G	24		
4	Kostyantyn PANIN	UKR	M	15	(8)	
44	Boris POLYAKOV		D	20	(1)	
11	Timur PRIMZHANOV		M	1	(1)	
21	Arslan SATYBALDIN		G	1		
12	Alexei SOROKIN		D	21	(2)	1
10	Rustam USMANOV		A	12	(8)	4
3	Maxim ZABELIN		D	23	(1)	1
7	Serik ZHEYLITBAEV		M	27	(2)	2

PROMOTED CLUBS

FC MEGASPORT ALMATY
Coach – Vladimir Gulyamkhaidarov
Founded – 2006

FC ENERGETIK PAVLODAR
Coach – Valeriy Zhuravlev
Founded - 2003

SECOND LEVEL FINAL TABLES 2007

	Conference North-East	Pld	W	D	L	F	A	Pts
1	FC Energetik Pavlodar	26	24	0	2	62	10	72
2	FC Kazakhmys Satpaev	26	22	3	1	67	14	69
3	FC Aksu Stepnogorsk	26	18	4	4	65	25	58
4	FC Avangard Petropavlovsk	26	13	5	8	35	34	44
5	FC Karasay Sarbazdari Kaskelen	26	12	3	11	47	39	39
6	FC Irtysh-2 Pavlodar	26	12	2	12	50	42	38
7	FC Asbest Zhitikara	26	10	5	11	34	42	35
8	FC Bolat Temirtau	26	9	5	12	30	33	32
9	FK Semey	26	7	8	11	29	49	29
10	FC Shakhtyor-Yunost Karagandy	26	6	6	14	25	38	24
11	FC Tobol-2 Kostanay	26	5	8	13	32	49	23
12	FC Vostok-2 Ust-Kamenogorsk	26	5	5	16	25	61	20
13	FC Rakhat Astana	26	4	6	16	25	56	18
14	FC Batyr Ekibastus	26	0	10	16	8	42	10

	Conference South-West	Pld	W	D	L	F	A	Pts
1	FC Megasport Almaty	22	21	1	0	89	10	64
2	FC Akzhayuk Uralsk	22	18	2	2	57	14	56
3	FC Kaspiy Aktau	22	13	4	5	46	23	43
4	FK Aktobe-Jas	22	11	4	7	38	32	37
5	FC Zhetysu-2 Taldykorgan	22	8	5	9	32	46	29
6	FC Gornyak Hromtau	22	7	6	9	31	39	27
7	FC Ordabasy-2 Shymkent	22	7	2	13	38	58	23
8	FC Kaisar-Zhas Kyzylorda	22	6	5	11	25	38	23
9	FC Cesna Almaty	22	6	5	11	33	30	23
10	FC Zhambyl Taraz	22	4	6	12	22	38	18
11	FC Zhastar Uralsk	22	5	1	16	21	70	16
12	FC Munayly Atyrau	22	4	3	15	27	61	15

PROMOTION PLAY-OFF FINAL TABLE

		Pld	W	D	L	F	A	Pts
1	FC Megasport Almaty	3	1	2	0	4	1	5
2	FC Kazakhmys Satpaev	3	1	2	0	4	1	5
3	FC Energetik Pavlodar	3	0	3	0	3	3	3
4	FC Akzhayuk Uralsk	3	0	1	2	1	7	1

N.B. FC Kazakhmys Satpaev declined promotion; FC Energetik Pavlodar promoted instead.

DOMESTIC CUP 2007

KUBOK KAZAKHSTANA

FIRST ROUND

(16/4/07)
Semey 0, Ekibastuzets 2 *(aet)*

(17/4/07)
Batyr 0, Taraz 2 *(aet)*

(18/4/07)
Akzhayuk 0, Aktobe 4
Kaspiy 1, Kaisar 2
Ordabasy-2 2, Zhetysu 5
Cesna 2, Astana 3
Kazakhmys 0, Tobol 2 *(aet)*
Avangard 1, Kairat 2
Rakhat 2, Okzhetpes 3
Energetik 1, Shakhtyor Karag
(aet; 4-5 on pens)
Megasport 2, Alma-Ata 1
Karasay Sarbazdari 0, Yesil Bogatyr 5
Aktobe-Jas 1, Atyrau 2
Zhambyl 0, Ordabasy 4
Asbest 0, Irtysh 3

(19/4/07)
Munayly 0, Vostok 3

SECOND ROUND

(8/5/07)
Aktobe 4, Zhetysu 0
Taraz 1, Tobol 4
Shakhtyor Karagandy 3, Atyrau 2
Kaisar 2, Yesil Bogatyr 1
Astana 2, Ekibastuzets 2 *(aet; 3-5 on pens)*
Megasport 1, Irtysh 0 (aet)
Ordabasy 2, Vostok 0

(9/5/2007)
Kairat 2, Okzhetpes 0

QUARTER-FINALS

(3/9/07 & 26/9/07)
Tobol 3 *(Smakov 2og, Kharabara 15, Baltiyev 75)*, Aktobe 1 *(Rogaciov*
Aktobe 0, Tobol 0
(Tobol 3-1)

(4/9/07 & 26/9/07)
Kaisar 0, Shakhtyor Karagandy 0
Shakhtyor Karagandy 1 *(Finonchenko 52)*, Kaisar 1 *(Bayzhanov 47)*
(1-1; Kaisar on away goal)

Kairat 0, Ordabasy 1 *(Đurđević 67)*
Ordabasy 0, Kairat 0
(Ordabasy 1-0)

(5/9/07 & 26/9/07)
Ekibastuzets 0, Megasport 0
Megasport 1 *(Mataganov 75p)*, Ekibastuzets 2 *(Burtsev 17, Baimbetov*
(Ekibastuzets 2-1)

SEMI-FINALS

(23/10/07)
Ekibastuzets 1 *(Aubakirov A. 85)*, Ordabasy 1 *(Tleshev 90p) (aet; 3-5 on*

(7/11/07)
Kaisar 1 *(Bayzhanov 72p)*, Tobol 2 *(Bakaev 5, Urazov 52)*

FINAL

(29/11/07)
Tsentralny, Taraz
FC TOBOL KOSTANAY 3 *(Baltiyev 28, 62p, Yurin 70)*
FC ORDABASY SHYMKENT 0
Referee – *Slambekov*
TOBOL – *Petukhov, Irismetov, Dimitrov, Mukanov, Nurdauletov, Skorykh, Yurin (Lotov 80), Baltiyev, Zhumaskaliev, Nurgaliev (Sabalakov 66), Baka (Kharabara 76).*
ORDABASY – *Mokin, Azovski, Protorchin, Karakulov, Ametov, Zhumakhanov, Kamelov (Nesteruk 76), Maksimov, Sabirov, Pischulin, Tleshev (Nuserbayev 64).*

Ventspils storm back to retain title

eemingly out of contention midway through the season, FK Ventspils staged an incredible comeback in the second half of the campaign to ertake fellow title challengers SK Liepājas Metalurgs, Skonto and FK Rīga and claim the Virslīga title for e second year in a row.

even points off the pace in mid-summer, Ventspils, d still by their title-winning coach of the previous ason, Roman Grigorchuk, were faced with the ospect of having to produce a flawless run of form in e autumn to give themselves a chance of clawing ack the deficit and retaining their crown. Remarkably, ey did just that, reeling off eleven straight wins and curing top spot in their penultimate match. As in 006, the man who scored the title-clinching goal was ors Sļesarčuks, who struck in the 27th minute as entspils overcame former champions Skonto 1-0 in a scheduled midweek fixture in Riga.

op scorer Rimkus

the midst of their series of Virslīga victories, which cluded two over early-season pace-setters etalurgs, Ventspils also kept enough in reserve to in the Latvian Cup for the fourth time in five years. ey defeated Skonto on penalties in the semi-final efore predictably seeing off the Virslīga's bottom club K Olimps with ease in the final, winning 3-0. The man ho opened the scoring – from the penalty spot – in e final, veteran Latvian international striker Vīts imkus, would also go on to claim the league's top-corer prize, hitting 20 goals in all, including crucial inners against both Rīga and Metalurgs in the run-in.

entspils were not so fortunate in Europe, where they ere put in their place by FC Salzburg in the second ualifying round of the UEFA Champions League, oing down 7-0 on aggregate, or in the inaugural altic League, with Metalurgs pulverising them 8-2 on ggregate in the final. And there would be isappointment also in the 2008 Latvian Cup final, rought forward from September to June, when, after again overcoming Skonto in the semis (and Metalurgs in the quarter-final), they were defeated on penalties, after a 1-1 draw, by underdogs FC Daugava.

While Daugava were delighted to collect their first major trophy, there was no added bonus of European qualification. Because of the calendar change of the Latvian Cup the UEFA Cup place reserved for that competition had already been attributed to 2007 runners-up Olimps, a team that could feel fortunate on two counts given that an expansion of the Virslīga from eight to ten clubs in 2008 rescued them from otherwise certain relegation (they lost 24 of their 28 matches and failed to win once at home).

Latvia's most-capped international Vitālijs Astafjevs (left) rises above Spain's Xavi Hernández

Metalurgs arguably had most to regret from the 2007 campaign. The Baltic League title was scant consolation after they had let slip such a big lead in the Virslīga, and at the end of the season their Lithuanian coach Benjaminas Zelkevičius, who had led the club to the title in 2005, decided to pack his bags and leave. His place was taken by former Latvia head coach Jurijs Andrejevs.

Skonto out of Europe

While Metalurgs, as league runners-up, joined Olimps in the 2008/09 UEFA Cup, Rīga, the season's surprise package, finished two points above Skonto to take third place and qualify for the UEFA Intertoto Cup. While Rīga, coached by Sergejs Semjonovs, celebrated a first-ever top-three placing – and it could have been more than that but for successive away defeats to all three title rivals in September and October - it was the first time that Skonto, champions 14 seasons running from 1991 to 2004, had failed to represent Latvia in Europe. There was, however, one consolation prize for the club, coached by Englishman Paul Ashworth, as veteran skipper Vitālijs Astafjevs was rewarded with the title of 2007 Latvian Footballer of the Year.

Astafjevs not only delivered the goods for his club but, at 37, continued to perform with distinction for the Latvian national side. He started all eleven internationals played by his country in 2007/08 – and, despite his age, finished all but one of them – to increase his record total of caps to 144. Seven of those matches resulted in victory, three of them coming in UEFA EURO 2008™ qualification as Latvia ended the campaign much better under restored former head coach Aleksandrs Starkovs than they had started it under Andrejevs.

Although those three wins – against Northern Ireland (1-0 home), Iceland (4-2 away) and Liechtenstein (4-1 home) - alternated with predictable defeats away to Spain, Denmark and Sweden, there was some satisfaction in accumulating 12 points and finishing ahead of Iceland in the final Group F table. Indeed, renewed confidence seemed to flood through the players as they registered four wins in a row in the first half of 2008, including one apiece against local rivals Estonia and Lithuania to earn victory in the annual tri-nation Baltic Cup.

Verpakovskis closes in

Maris Verpakovskis, the diminutive striker who starred for Latvia at UEFA EURO 2004™, was absent for the Baltic Cup games, which meant that he was unable to score the goal he needed to become Latvia's joint-all-time leading marksman. The five goals he struck in UEFA EURO 2008™ qualification raised his cumulative total to 23, one short of the figure set in the pre-World War II era by Ēriks Pētersons.

Verpakovskis spent 2007/08 playing his club football in Croatia for HNK Hajduk Split, but there was a return to Latvia for his long-time national team strike-partner Marians Pahars, a former English Premier League star with Southampton FC, who rejoined Skonto for the 2008 season – after announcing his international retirement, at 31, with 75 caps and 15 goals to his name.

Latvijas Futbola Federācija (LFF)

Augsiela 1
LV-1009 Rīga
tel - +371 6729 2988
fax - +371 6731 5604
website - www.lff.lv
email - futbols@lff.lv
Year of Formation – 1921
President - Guntis Indriksons
General Secretary - Janis Mežeckis
Press Officer – Martins Hartmanis
Stadium - Skonto, Riga (8,887)

INTERNATIONAL TOURNAMENT APPEARANCES
UEFA European Championship - (1) 2004.

TOP FIVE ALL-TIME CAPS
Vitalijs Astafjevs (144); Imants Bleidelis (106); Mihails Zemļinskis (105); Igors N. Stepanovs (96); Andrejs Rubins (93)

TOP FIVE ALL-TIME GOALS
Ēriks Pētersons (24); Maris Verpakovskis (23); Marians Pahars & Jurijs Laizāns (15); Vitalijs Astafjevs & Alberts Šeibelis (14)

ATIONAL TEAM RESULTS 2007/08

'07	Moldova	H	Riga	1-2	*Astafjevs (31)*
7	Northern Ireland (ECQ)	H	Riga	1-0	*Baird (69og)*
'07	Spain (ECQ)	A	Oviedo	0-2	
)/07	Iceland (ECQ)	A	Reykjavik	4-2	*Kļava (27), Laizāns (31), Verpakovskis (37, 46)*
)/07	Denmark (ECQ)	A	Copenhagen	1-3	*Gorkšs (80)*
/07	Liechtenstein (ECQ)	H	Riga	4-1	*Karlsons (14), Verpakovskis (30), Laizāns (63), Višņakovs (87)*
/07	Sweden (ECQ)	A	Stockholm	1-2	*Laizāns (26).*
)8	Georgia	A	Tbilisi	3-1	*Karlsons (6), Stepanovs (16), Astafjevs (34)*
/08	Andorra	A	Andorra la Vella	3-0	*Ivanovs (11), Pereplotkins (24), Rimkus (41)*
/08	Estonia	H	Riga	1-0	*Laizāns (48p)*
)8	Lithuania	H	Riga	2-1	*Pereplotkins (56), Alunderis (77og)*

ATIONAL TEAM APPEARANCES 2007/08

ch - Aleksandrs STARKOVS 26/6/55			Mda	NIR	ESP	ISL	DEN	LIE	SWE	Geo	And	Est	Ltu	Caps	Goals
sandrs KOĻINKO	18/6/75	Rubin (RUS)	G						G	s46	s46			80	-
tars ZIRNIS	25/4/77	Liepājas Metalurgs	D	D	D	D	D	D	D	s90	s58		D	56	-
rs KĻAVA	8/8/83	Liepājas Metalurgs	D67	D	D	D	D	D		D90	D46	D		23	1
ss IVANOVS	11/1/84	Liepājas Metalurgs	D	D	D	D	D	D	D	D	D	D	D	19	1
ss KAČANOVS	27/11/79	Ventspils	D				s91			s90	s46	D	D	12	-
sejs VIŠŅAKOVS	3/2/84	Skonto	M64		s74	M92	M78	s82	s43	M46	M58	M78		29	4
ijs ASTAFJEVS	3/4/71	Skonto	M	M	M	M	M	M	M49	M	M	M	M	144	14
nts BLEIDELIS	16/8/75	Liepājas Metalurgs	M59	M	M74			M82	M43					106	10
rejs RUBINS	26/11/78	Liepājas Metalurgs	M59	M	M			M	M	s46	s58			93	8
s LAIZĀNS	6/1/79	Kuban (RUS) /Shinnik (RUS)	M87	M	M	M	M	M	M		M	M	M	92	15
s KARLSONS	7/6/81	Liepājas Metalurgs /De Graafschap (NED)	A	A71	A63	A59		A71	A62	A78		A	A	27	6
RIMKUS	21/6/73	Ventspils	s59	s71		s59	A63	s77		s78	A66	A58		73	11
ksandrs CAUŅA	19/1/88	Skonto	s59							M46		s76	M72	6	-
rejs PEREPĻOTKINS	27/12/84	Skonto	s64							s84	A66	s58	A82	7	2
pars GORKŠS	6/11/81	Blackpool (ENG)	s67	D	D	D	D	D	D	D	D58	D	D	17	1
adijs SOLOŅICINS	3/1/80	Liepājas Metalurgs	s87			M	M		s49	M90	M58	M76	s72	26	1
dris VAŅINS	30/4/80	Ventspils		G	G	G	G	G		G46	G46	G	G	14	-
ris VERPAKOVSKIS	15/10/79	Hajduk (CRO)		A90	A88	A78		A77	A	A84	s66			70	23
taps BLANKS	30/1/86	Skonto		s90	s88									17	-
rians PAHARS	5/8/76	Anorthosis (CYP)			s63	s78	A91	s71	s62					75	15
ijs ŽIGAJEVS	14/11/85	Rīga				s92	s78			s46	s58		M	5	-
drejs BUTRIKS	20/12/82	Ventspils					s63				s66		s82	3	-
rs N. STEPANOVS	21/1/76	EfB (DEN) /Shinnik (RUS)							D	D	D			96	4
dimirs KOLESNIČENKO	4/5/80	Ventspils										s78		32	4

LATVIA

DOMESTIC LEAGUE 2007

VIRSLĪGA FINAL LEAGUE TABLE 2007

		Home					Away					Total					
	Pld	W	D	L	F	A	W	D	L	F	A	W	D	L	F	A	Pts
1 FK Ventspils	28	12	1	1	40	6	6	5	3	19	10	18	6	4	59	16	60
2 SK Liepājas Metalurgs	28	9	2	3	20	8	9	2	3	22	13	18	4	6	42	21	58
3 FK Rīga	28	12	2	0	30	9	5	4	5	18	19	17	6	5	48	28	57
4 Skonto FC	28	8	4	2	28	13	8	3	3	26	14	16	7	5	54	27	55
5 FC Daugava	28	5	4	5	18	16	4	2	8	15	22	9	6	13	33	38	33
6 FK Jūrmala	28	5	2	7	20	15	2	3	9	8	36	7	5	16	28	51	26
7 FC Dinaburg	28	3	2	9	12	24	3	0	11	11	34	6	2	20	23	58	20
8 JFK Olimps	28	0	2	12	9	34	2	0	12	6	29	2	2	24	15	63	8

N.B. No relegation; Virslīga extended to ten clubs for 2008 season.

TOP GOALSCORERS

20 Vīts RIMKUS (Ventspils)
15 Andrei NIKOLAYEV (Rīga)
12 Girts KARLSONS (Liepājas Metalurgs)
11 Nikolai RYNDYUK (Daugava)
7 Vitālijs ASTAFJEVS (Skonto)
Kristaps BLANKS (Skonto)
Marián DIRNBACH (Skonto)
Artjoms RUDŅEVS (Daugava)
Aleksejs VIŠŅAKOVS (Skonto)
6 Andrejs BUTRIKS (Ventspils)
Mindaugas KALONAS (Liepājas Metalurgs)
Aleksandr KATASONOV (Jūrmal
Igors SĻESARČUKS (Ventspils)
Jurijs ŽIGAJEVS (Rīga)

CLUB-BY-CLUB

FC DAUGAVA

Coach – Sergei Petrenko (RUS); (20/5/07) Igor Gamula (RUS)
Founded - 2001
MAJOR HONOURS: Latvian Cup - (1) 2008.

2007				
7/4	Liepājas Metalurgs	a	1-3	*Ryndyuk*
13/4	Rīga	h	1-3	*Douglas*
20/4	Skonto	a	1-3	*Kučys*
29/4	Dinaburg	a	1-2	*Afanasjevs*
4/5	Olimps	h	2-0	*Douglas, Krasņakovs*
8/5	Ventspils	a	1-3	*Ryndyuk*
12/5	Liepājas Metalurgs	h	1-2	*Ryndyuk*
20/5	Rīga	a	2-3	*Baga 2*
24/5	Skonto	h	1-3	*Ryndyuk*
10/6	Jūrmala	a	2-1	*Ryndyuk 2*
13/6	Dinaburg	h	1-3	*Kučys*
26/6	Olimps	a	1-1	*Ryndyuk*
30/6	Ventspils	h	1-1	*Afanasjevs*
8/7	Liepājas Metalurgs	h	0-1	
13/7	Rīga	h	2-2	*Rudņevs 2*
24/7	Jūrmala	h	1-0	*Kučys*
28/7	Skonto	a	1-3	*Ryndyuk (p)*
8/8	Jūrmala	h	5-0	*Tiberkanine 2, Rudņevs, og (Valkov), Ryndyuk*
12/8	Dinaburg	a	2-0	*Tiberkanine, Rudņevs*
26/8	Olimps	h	1-0	*Ryndyuk*
16/9	Ventspils	a	0-1	
22/9	Liepājas Metalurgs	a	0-0	
27/9	Rīga	a	1-2	*Rudņevs*
4/10	Skonto	h	1-1	*Danilin*
7/10	Jūrmala	a	1-0	*Rudņevs*
21/10	Dinaburg	h	1-0	*Ryndyuk*
27/10	Olimps	a	1-0	*Rudņevs*
4/11	Ventspils	h	0-0	

Name	Nat	Pos	Aps	(s)	Gls
Valērijs AFANASJEVS		M	27		2
Andrey AKOPYANTS	UZB	M	4	(6)	
Aleksei BAGA	BLR	M	9	(5)	2
Nauris BULVITIS		D	5	(2)	
Vyacheslav DANILIN	RUS	M	18	(3)	1
Viktors DOBRECOVS		A	3	(4)	
DOUGLAS Wilson Barros da Silva	BRA	A	9	(10)	2
Vadims FJODOROVS		G	14		
Jean GONÇALVES da Silva	BRA	M	1	(6)	
Stanimir GOSPODINOV	BUL	D	10	(1)	
Aleksandrs ISAKOVS		D	22	(1)	
Aleksandrs IVANOVS		D	7		
Andrejs KOVAĻOVS		M		(2)	
Jurijs KRASŅAKOVS		D	4	(3)	1
Aurimas KUČYS	LTU	D	19	(2)	3
Aleksejs KUPLOVS-OGINSKIS		M	13	(3)	
Pyotr MARSHINSKY	RUS	M	4	(2)	
Ruslans MIHALČUKS		M	18	(2)	
Pavel NAGLIS		G	9	(1)	
Erik Matos OLIVEIRA	BRA	M	5	(4)	
Nikolajs POĻAKOVS		D	5		
Yevgeniy POSTNIKOV	RUS	D	19		
Jan RADEVIČS		M		(2)	
Artjoms RUDŅEVS		M	12	(7)	7
Nikolai RYNDYUK	BLR	A	23	(5)	11
Jevgenijs SAZONOVS		G	5		
Jurijs SOKOLOVS		M	10		
Rashid TIBERKANINE	MAR	A	11	(3)	3
Oļegs TIMOFEJEVS		M	4		
Igors TOLKAČS		A	1		
Dilaver ZRNANOVIĆ	BIH	D	8	(1)	
Vadims ŽUĻOVS		M	9	(6)	

FC DINABURG

Coach – Sergei Popkov (RUS); (10/5/07) Tamaz Pertia (GEO)
Founded - 1996

2007				
7/4	Jūrmala	a	0-1	
15/4	Liepājas Metalurgs	a	1-2	*Trinitatsky*
20/4	Olimps	h	1-0	*Sokolovs*
25/4	Ventspils	a	0-4	
29/4	Daugava	h	2-1	*Kuleshov, Sokolovs*
4/5	Rīga	a	0-2	
8/5	Skonto	h	2-2	*Koļcovs 2*
12/5	Jūrmala	h	0-0	
16/5	Skonto	h	0-3	
20/5	Liepājas Metalurgs	h	1-2	*Rodin (p)*
24/5	Olimps	a	2-0	*Krjauklis, Yashkin*
9/6	Ventspils	h	2-4	*Sokolovs 2 (1p)*
13/6	Daugava	a	3-1	*Vaļuškins, Krjauklis, Kostenko*

/7	Liepājas Metalurgs	a	1-4	*Krjauklis*
/7	Olimps	h	1-2	*Kaziyev*
8	Jūrmala	a	0-3	
/8	Daugava	h	0-2	
/8	Ventspils	a	0-6	
/8	Rīga	a	1-3	*Žuromskis*
/8	Rīga	h	0-2	
/9	Skonto	h	0-4	
/9	Jūrmala	h	3-0	*Rodin (p), Kaziyev 2*
/9	Liepājas Metalurgs	h	0-1	
10	Olimps	a	3-2	*Koļcovs, Kaziyev 2*
10	Ventspils	h	0-3	
/10	Daugava	a	0-1	
/10	Rīga	h	0-1	
11	Skonto	a	0-2	

ame	Nat	Pos	Aps	(s)	Gls
eksei ABRAMOV	RUS	M	10	(9)	
'eksejs BORUNS		M	8	(3)	
mitrijs ČEBOTARJEVS		M		(15)	
mitrijs ČUGUNOVS		D	3		
aksims DAŅILOVS		A	6		
aksims DEŅISEVIČS		M		(6)	
ekar GIORGADZE	GEO	M		(1)	
aris ELTERMANIS		G	11		
adims FJODOROVS		G	3		
aur KAZIYEV	RUS	A	13		5
avels KOĻCOVS		A	22	(1)	3
evan KORGALIDZE	GEO	M	11	(2)	
uslans KOROĻOVS		M	1	(10)	
leksei KOSTENKO	RUS	A	11	(1)	1
itus KRJAUKLIS		D	26	(1)	3
ladimir KULESHOV	RUS	M	18	(6)	1
ergejs LABECKIS		M		(3)	
evgenijs LAIZĀNS		G	14		
adims LOGINS		D	21		
ndrei MARKOV	RUS	M	6		
likhail POPOV	RUS	D	10	(3)	
avel RYZHEVSKY	BLR	A	7	(3)	
an RODIN	RUS	M	18	(4)	2
evgenijs SIMONOVS		D	9	(2)	
ānis SKVORCOVS		D	4	(1)	
urijs SOKOLOVS		M	14		4
leksei TRINITATSKY	RUS	M	10	(1)	1
mitriy ULYANOV	RUS	M	5	(2)	
ergejs VAĻUŠKINS		M	12	(6)	1
ladimirs VOLKOVS		A	7		
rtyom YASHKIN	RUS	A	6	(2)	1
lareks ZUNTNERS		A	1	(1)	
ndrejs ŽUROMSKIS		D	21	(1)	1

FK JŪRMALA

Coach – Oleg Stogov (RUS); (1/7/07) Gatis Ērglis

Founded - 2003

007				
7/4	Dinaburg	h	1-0	*Katasonov*
4/4	Olimps	a	2-0	*Katasonov 2*
20/4	Ventspils	h	3-1	*Dzyuba, Katasonov, Bleidelis (p)*
29/4	Rīga	h	0-0	
4/5	Skonto	a	2-2	*Bleidelis, Katasonov*
3/5	Liepājas Metalurgs	h	3-4	*Bleidelis, Dzyuba, Katasonov*
12/5	Dinaburg	a	0-0	
16/5	Ventspils	h	0-1	
20/5	Olimps	h	5-0	*Kalns 2, Smirnovs, Kaplan, Nezhelev*
24/5	Ventspils	a	1-1	*Nezhelev*
10/6	Daugava	h	1-2	*Bleidelis (p)*
26/6	Skonto	h	1-2	*Dzyuba*
30/6	Liepājas Metalurgs	a	0-2	
12/7	Olimps	a	2-1	*Kalns, Daņilovs*
19/7	Rīga	a	0-2	
24/7	Daugava	a	0-1	
4/8	Dinaburg	h	3-0	*Aldev, Malašenoks, Paplavskis*
8/8	Daugava	a	0-5	
12/8	Rīga	h	2-0	*Malašenok 2*
26/8	Skonto	a	0-4	
16/9	Liepājas Metalurgs	h	1-1	*Halvitovs*
22/9	Dinaburg	a	0-3	
26/9	Olimps	h	0-2	
4/10	Ventspils	a	0-10	
7/10	Daugava	h	0-1	
21/10	Rīga	a	1-2	*Freimanis*
27/10	Skonto	h	0-1	
4/11	Liepājas Metalurgs	a	0-3	

Name	Nat	Pos	Aps	(s)	Gls
Ventzislav ALDEV	BUL	A	14	(1)	1
Igors AVANESOVS		M		(1)	
Romans BEZZUBOVS		A	18	(7)	
Imants BLEIDELIS		M	14	(1)	4
Dmitriy CHIGAZOV	RUS	G	4		
Edijs DAŅILOVS		M	12	(2)	1
Konstantin DZYUBA	RUS	A	14	(1)	3
Gints FREIMANIS		M	12	(1)	1
Otar GOGBERASHVILI	GEO	M		(1)	
Maxim GRIGORYEV	RUS	D	3	(5)	
Aleksandrs GUBINS		M	1	(5)	
Dmitrijs HALVITOVS		D	8	(2)	1
Jurgis KALNS		A	22	(6)	3
Ilya KAPLAN	RUS	A	9	(2)	1
Aleksandr KATASONOV	RUS	A	15	(1)	6
Jurijs KSENZOVS		M	17	(6)	
Artjoms KUZŅECOVS		M	13		
Vaļentins LOBAŅOVS		D	4	(1)	
Oļegs MALAŠENOKS		A	8	(6)	3
Anatoliy NEZHELEV	RUS	M	13		2
Dmitrijs PAPLAVSKIS		M		(13)	1
Nikolajs POĻAKOVS		D	13		
Vadims SIŅICINS		D	23	(3)	
Maris SMIRNOVS		D	15		1
Pavels ŠTEINBORS		G	24		
Ivan TODOROV	BUL	D	3	(10)	
Stanimir VALKOV	BUL	M	13		
Oļegs ŽATKINS		M	3	(5)	
Vladimirs ŽAVORONKOVS		D	13		

SK LIEPĀJAS METALURGS

Coach– Benjaminas Zelkevičius (LTU)

Founded – 1996

MAJOR HONOURS: Latvian League – (1) 2005; Latvian Cup – (1) 2006.

2007				
7/4	Daugava	h	3-1	*Karlsons, Miceika, Kalonas*
15/4	Dinaburg	h	2-1	*Kalonas 2*
19/4	Rīga	a	0-3	
25/4	Olimps	h	1-0	*Kets*
29/4	Skonto	a	4-0	*Tamošauskas, Soloņicins, Kalonas, Torres*
4/5	Ventspils	h	2-0	*Soloņicins, Karlsons*
8/5	Jūrmala	a	4-3	*Karlsons 2, Miceika, Ivanovs*
12/5	Daugava	a	2-1	*Kruglyak (p), Karlsons*
20/5	Dinaburg	a	2-1	*Karlsons, Kalonas (p)*
24/5	Rīga	h	0-0	
10/6	Olimps	a	2-1	*Karlsons 2*
21/6	Skonto	h	0-2	
26/6	Ventspils	a	2-0	*Kļava, Karlsons*
30/6	Jūrmala	h	2-0	*Kets, Karlsons*
8/7	Daugava	a	1-0	*Ferreira*
13/7	Dinaburg	h	4-1	*Kamešs, Kruglyak, Ivanovs, Kalonas*
28/7	Rīga	a	0-2	
6/8	Olimps	h	1-0	*Rubins*
11/8	Skonto	a	0-0	
26/8	Ventspils	h	0-2	
16/9	Jūrmala	a	1-1	*Karlsons*

22/9	Daugava	h	0-0	
30/9	Dinaburg	a	1-0	*Bleidelis*
4/10	Rīga	h	2-0	*Torres, Karlsons*
8/10	Olimps	a	3-0	*Miceika, Tamošauskas, Soloņicins*
22/10	Skonto	h	0-1	
27/10	Ventspils	a	0-1	
4/11	Jūrmala	h	3-0	*Soloņicins 2, Kļava*

Name	Nat	Pos	Aps	(s)	Gls
Imants BLEIDELIS		M	11		1
Antonio FERREIRA de Oliveira	BRA	D	26		1
Deniss IVANOVS		D	28		2
Antons JEMEĻINS		D		(2)	
Mindaugas KALONAS	LTU	M	17		6
Vladimirs KAMEŠS		M	2	(1)	1
Girts KARLSONS		A	26	(1)	12
Yevgeniy KETS	RUS	M	5	(5)	2
Oskars KĻAVA		D	20	(5)	2
Andriy KRUGLYAK	UKR	A	10	(12)	2
Aleksandr LAKTIONOV	RUS	A	1	(4)	
Darius MICEIKA	LTU	A	15	(3)	3
Dmitrijs MIHAILOVS		M		(1)	
Igor PETKOVIĆ	SRB	A	5	(6)	
Vadim PETRENKO	LTU	M	1		
Andrejs RUBINS		M	7	(1)	1
Genadijs SOLOŅICINS		M	28		5
Viktors SPOLE		G	28		
Pavels SURŅINS		D	18	(8)	
Tomas TAMOŠAUSKAS	LTU	M	25		2
Cristián TORRES	ARG	A	9	(9)	2
Dzintars ZIRNIS		D	24	(2)	
Andrejs ŽURAVĻOVS		D	2	(8)	

FK OLIMPS

Coach - Mihails Konevs

Founded - 2005

2007				
7/4	Skonto	a	0-1	
14/4	Jūrmala	h	0-2	
20/4	Dinaburg	a	0-1	
25/4	Liepājas Metalurgs	a	0-1	
29/4	Ventspils	h	1-1	*Ziļs*
4/5	Daugava	a	0-2	
8/5	Rīga	h	2-3	*Zolotarjovs, Sputajs*
12/5	Skonto	h	1-4	*Sputajs*
20/5	Jūrmala	a	0-5	
24/5	Dinaburg	h	0-2	
10/6	Liepājas Metalurgs	h	1-2	*Kazura*
21/6	Ventspils	a	0-2	
26/6	Daugava	h	1-1	*Solovjovs*
30/6	Rīga	a	2-3	*og (Zakreševskis), Sputajs*
7/7	Skonto	a	0-3	
12/7	Jūrmala	h	1-2	*Kostjuks (p)*
28/7	Dinaburg	a	2-1	*Solovjovs, Turkovs*
6/8	Liepājas Metalurgs	a	0-1	
13/8	Ventspils	h	0-5	
26/8	Daugava	a	0-1	
16/9	Rīga	h	0-2	
22/9	Skonto	h	0-3	
26/9	Jūrmala	a	2-0	*Lukjanovs (p), Solovjovs*
4/10	Dinaburg	h	2-3	*Kostjuks, Lukjanovs*
8/10	Liepājas Metalurgs	h	0-3	
22/10	Ventspils	a	0-4	
27/10	Daugava	h	0-1	
4/11	Rīga	a	0-4	

Name	Nat	Pos	Aps	(s)	Gls
Vadims GAIĻUS		D	12		
Aleksandrs FERTOVS		A	13		
Kaspars IKSTENS		G	1		
Edijs IVAŠKO		D	23	(2)	
Tomass JEVDOKIMOVS		M	1	(3)	
Kirils JEĻKINS		M	8	(2)	
Ilic KANDOV	GER	D	13	(4)	
Jevgenijs KAZURA		D	26		1
Andrejs KOSTJUKS		M	17	(8)	2
Igors KOZLOVS		M	15		
Ivans LUKJANOVS		A	10		2
Arturs MAGEJENKOVS		M		(7)	
Hermanis MAĻIŅŠ		G	27		
Armands PETERSONS		M		(1)	
Deniss PETRENKO		D	15	(1)	
Viktors ŠEKOVS		D	1	(2)	
Dmitrijs ŠIĻUKS		D	12	(3)	
Alans SIŅEĻŅIKOVS		D		(2)	
Aleksandrs SOLOVJOVS		A	19	(5)	3
Ivans SPUTAJS		M	20	(7)	3
Andrejs ŠTOLCERS		A	7	(1)	
Igors TARASOVS		M	25	(2)	
Daniils TURKOVS		M	21	(5)	1
Dmitrijs VALEGŽANINS		M		(5)	
Maksims ZABOROVS		M		(6)	
Vitālijs ZIĻS		A	9	(7)	1
Dmitrijs ZOLOTARJOVS		M	13	(6)	1

FK RĪGA

Coach – Sergejs Semjonovs

Founded – 1999

MAJOR HONOURS: Latvian Cup - (1) 1999.

2007				
7/4	Ventspils	h	1-0	*Dorosh (p)*
13/4	Daugava	a	3-1	*Landyrev, Žigajevs, Mihadjuks*
19/4	Liepājas Metalurgs	h	3-0	*Skoblyakov, Nikolayev (1p)*
25/4	Skonto	h	1-0	*Agafonov*
29/4	Jūrmala	a	0-0	
4/5	Dinaburg	h	2-0	*Žigajevs, Yakovenko*
8/5	Olimps	a	3-2	*Koļesņikovs, Agafonov, Nikolayev*
12/5	Ventspils	a	0-1	
20/5	Daugava	h	3-2	*Mihadjuks, Nikolayev (p), Volos*
24/5	Liepājas Metalurgs	a	0-0	
10/6	Skonto	a	4-4	*Mežeckis, Nikolayev (p), Žigajevs 2*
30/6	Olimps	h	3-2	*Mihadjuks, Karalius, Landyrev*
8/7	Ventspils	h	0-0	
13/7	Daugava	a	2-2	*Nikolayev (p), Žavoronkovs*
19/7	Jūrmala	h	2-0	*Landyrev, Nikolayev (p)*
28/7	Liepājas Metalurgs	h	2-0	*Nikolayev (p), Landyrev*
7/8	Skonto	h	2-2	*Mežeckis, Žigajevs*
12/8	Jūrmala	a	0-2	
26/8	Dinaburg	h	3-1	*Nikolayev 2, Mihadjuks*
30/8	Dinaburg	a	2-0	*Landyrev, Rafaļskis*
16/9	Olimps	a	2-0	*Agafonov, Nikolayev (p)*
21/9	Ventspils	a	1-2	*Nikolayev (p)*
27/9	Daugava	h	2-1	*Nikolayev 2 (2p)*
4/10	Liepājas Metalurgs	a	0-2	
8/10	Skonto	a	0-3	
21/10	Jūrmala	h	2-1	*Zakreševskis, Skoblyakov*
27/10	Dinaburg	a	1-0	*Skoblyakov*
4/11	Olimps	h	4-0	*Žigajevs, Mihadjuks, Koļesņikovs, Nikolayev*

Name	Nat	Pos	Aps	(s)	Gls
Andrei AGAFONOV	RUS	M	19	(4)	3
Orest DOROSH	UKR	M	12	(5)	1
Martinas KARALIUS	LTU	A	2	(3)	1
Ivan KARAMANOV	BUL	M	1	(4)	
Aleksejs KOĻESŅIKOVS		M	9	(8)	2
Igors KORABĻOVS		D	22		
Yevgeniy LANDYREV	RUS	A	13	(5)	5
Roberts MEŽECKIS		D	13	(3)	2
Pavels MIHADJUKS		D	24	(2)	5

Name	Nat	Pos	Aps	(s)	Gls
ıitry NAĻIVAIKO		D	11	(1)	
drei NIKOLAYEV	RUS	A	26		15
ʋgeni NOVIKOV	EST	M	9	(2)	
das PAPEČKYS	LTU	D	9		
drejs PAVLOVS		G	28		
nislavs PIHOCKIS		M	2	(2)	
nitrijs PLUKAITIS		M		(1)	
aksims RAFAĻSKIS		M	8	(8)	1
nis RINKUS		M	4		
egs SEMJONOVS		A	1		
nitriy SKOBLYAKOV	RUS	M	28		3
rgei SOKOLOV	RUS	M	1		
riy VOLOS	UKR	A	3	(8)	1
rhiy YAKOVENKO	UKR	A	8	(15)	1
turs ZAKREŠEVSKIS		D	17		1
adimir ŽAVORONKOV		D	12		1
rijs ŽIGAJEVS		A	26	(1)	6

SKONTO FC

Coach – Paul Ashworth (ENG)

Founded – 1991

AJOR HONOURS: Latvian League - (14) 1991, 1992, 1993, 1994, 1995, 996, 1997, 1998, 1999, 2000, 2001, 2002, 2003, 2004; Latvian Cup - (7) 1992, 1995, 1997, 1998, 2000, 2001, 2002.

07				
4	Olimps	h	1-0	*Kalniņš*
/4	Ventspils	a	0-2	
/4	Daugava	h	3-1	*Kalniņš 2, Laizāns (p)*
/4	Rīga	a	0-1	
/4	Liepājas Metalurgs	h	0-4	
5	Jūrmala	h	2-2	*Cauņa, Višņakovs*
5	Dinaburg	a	2-2	*Astafjevs, Višņakovs*
/5	Olimps	a	4-1	*Astafjevs 2 (2p), Piaček, Blanks*
/5	Dinaburg	h	3-0	*Piaček, Laizāns, Astafjevs*
/5	Ventspils	h	0-0	
/5	Daugava	a	3-1	*Blanks, Astafjevs (p), Laizāns*
)/6	Rīga	h	4-4	*Cauņa, Blanks, Perepļotkins, Dirnbach*
/6	Liepājas Metalurgs	a	2-0	*Dirnbach, Kalniņš*
5/6	Jūrmala	a	2-1	*Astafjevs, Dirnbach*
'7	Olimps	h	3-0	*Blanks, Višņakovs (p), Gamezardashvili*
2/7	Ventspils	a	1-3	*Sluka*
3/7	Daugava	h	3-1	*Dirnbach, Kožans, Piaček*
'8	Rīga	a	2-2	*Blanks, Kožans*
1/8	Liepājas Metalurgs	h	0-0	
5/8	Jūrmala	h	4-0	*Cauņa, Blanks, Piaček, Dirnbach (p)*
5/9	Dinaburg	a	4-0	*Sluka, Dirnbach (p), Višņakovs, Morozs*
2/9	Olimps	a	3-0	*Morozs 2, Višņakovs*
'10	Daugava	a	1-1	*Perepļotkins*
/10	Rīga	h	3-0	*Astafjevs, Perepļotkins, Višņakovs*
2/10	Liepājas Metalurgs	a	1-0	*Cauņa*
7/10	Jūrmala	a	1-0	*Dirnbach*
1/10	Ventspils	h	0-1	
/11	Dinaburg	h	2-0	*Višņakovs (p), Blanks*

ame	Nat	Pos	Aps	(s)	Gls
ʼitālijs ASTAFJEVS		M	23	(1)	7
ristaps BLANKS		A	19	(4)	7
leksandrs CAUŅA		M	19	(5)	4
Marián DIRNBACH	SVK	A	15	(5)	7
avels DOROŠEVS		G	15		
aal ELIAVA	GEO	D	11	(2)	
adims GAIĻUS		D	6		
avid GAMEZARDASHVILI	GEO	D	24	(1)	1
ergejs GOLUBEVS		D	8	(1)	
aivas HŠČANOVIČS		D	3	(1)	
atis KALNIŅŠ		A	12	(10)	4
Igors KOZLOVS		D		(4)	
Sergejs KOŽANS		D	19	(1)	2
Oļegs LAIZĀNS		M	4	(12)	3
Ivans LUKJANOVS		A		(2)	
Viktors MOROZS		M	25	(2)	3
Andrejs PEREPĻOTKINS		M	19	(5)	3
Jozef PIAČEK	SVK	D	23		4
Andrejs PIEDELS		G	13		
Igors SEMJONOVS		M	2	(5)	
Marian SLUKA	SVK	M	17	(4)	2
Vitālijs SMIRNOVS		D		(4)	
Andrejs ŠTOLCERS		M		(1)	
Maxim USANOV	RUS	D	8	(1)	
Aleksejs VIŠŅAKOVS		M	23	(5)	7

FK VENTSPILS

Coach – Roman Grigorchuk (UKR)

Founded – 1997

MAJOR HONOURS: Latvian League – (2) 2006, 2007; Latvian Cup - (4) 2003, 2004, 2005, 2007.

2007				
7/4	Rīga	a	0-1	
14/4	Skonto	h	2-0	*Ndeki, Ziziļevs*
20/4	Jūrmala	a	1-3	*Rimkus (p)*
25/4	Dinaburg	h	4-0	*og (Sokolovs), Rimkus, Ndeki, og (Krjauklis).*
29/4	Olimps	a	1-1	*Ndeki*
4/5	Liepājas Metalurgs	a	0-2	
8/5	Daugava	h	3-1	*Kačanovs, Zangareyev, Sernetsky*
12/5	Rīga	h	1-0	*Sernetsky*
16/5	Jūrmala	a	1-0	*Sernetsky*
20/5	Skonto	a	0-0	
24/5	Jūrmala	h	1-1	*Rimkus*
9/6	Dinaburg	a	4-2	*Rimkus 3, Zangareyev*
21/6	Olimps	h	2-0	*Dubenskiy, Rimkus*
26/6	Liepājas Metalurgs	h	0-2	
30/6	Daugava	a	1-1	*Sernetsky*
8/7	Rīga	a	0-0	
12/7	Skonto	h	3-1	*Sernetsky, Ziziļevs, Menteshashvili*
13/8	Olimps	a	5-0	*Cilinšek, Rimkus (p), Sļesarčuks, Koļesnicenko, Ziziļevs*
18/8	Dinaburg	h	6-0	*Sļesarčuks, Ziziļevs, Rimkus 3, Butriks*
26/8	Liepājas Metalurgs	a	2-0	*Tigirlas, Kosmačovs*
16/9	Daugava	h	1-0	*Rimkus*
21/9	Rīga	h	2-1	*Zangareyev, Rimkus*
4/10	Jūrmala	h	10-0	*Butriks 5, Rimkus 3, Sļesarčuks, Ndeki*
8/10	Dinaburg	a	3-0	*Tigirlas, Rimkus 2*
22/10	Olimps	h	4-0	*Sļesarčuks 2, Zangareyev, Rimkus*
27/10	Liepājas Metalurgs	h	1-0	*Rimkus*
31/10	Skonto	a	1-0	*Sļesarčuks*
4/11	Daugava	a	0-0	

Name	Nat	Pos	Aps	(s)	Gls
Vladimirs BESPALOVS		M	1		
Andrejs BUTRIKS		A	12	(5)	6
Pavels DAVIDOVS		G	16	(1)	
Zakhar DUBENSKIY	RUS	M	24	(1)	1
Saša CILINŠEK	SRB	D	10		1
Alexandru DEDOV	MDA	A		(1)	
Artjoms GONČARS		M	4	(4)	
Kristaps GREBIS		A	1	(10)	
Pavels HOHLOVS		M		(1)	
Visvaldis IGNATĀNS		M		(1)	
David IMEDASHVILI	GEO	M		(1)	
Deniss KAČANOVS		D	26		1
Vladimirs KOĻESNIČENKO		M	16	(8)	1
Jevgenijs KOSMAČOVS		M	8	(6)	1
Rolands KRJAUKLIS		M		(1)	

LATVIA

Artis LAZDIŅŠ		A	2	(1)	
Zurab MENTESHASHVILI	GEO	M	19	(3)	1
Aleksandr MYSIKOV	RUS	M	5	(13)	
Jean-Paul NDEKI	CMR	D	19	(1)	4
Igor POKARYNIN	RUS	M	2	(3)	
Vīts RIMKUS		A	26	(1)	20
Mihails RJUMŠINS		M	1		
Igors SAVČENKOVS		D	10		
Serhiy SERNETSKIY	UKR	A	8	(5)	5
Igors SĻESARČUKS		A	17	(5)	6
Deniss SOKOĻSKIS		D	6	(2)	
Aleksejs SOĻEIČUKS		D	12	(2)	
Igor TIGIRLAS	MDA	M	7	(2)	2
Andris VAŅINS		G	12		
Sergei ZANGAREYEV	RUS	M	16	(2)	4
Mihails ZIZIĻEVS		M	27		4
Arturs ZJUZINS		D	1		

PROMOTED CLUBS

FK VINDAVA VENTSPILS

Coach – Andrejs Lapsa

Founded - 2007

SK BLĀZMA RĒZEKNE

Coach – Nikolai Yuzhanin (RUS)

Founded - 2007

SECOND LEVEL FINAL TABLE 2007

		Pld	W	D	L	F	A	Pts
1	FK Vindava Ventspils	30	26	2	2	116	11	80
2	SK Blāzma Rēzekne	30	25	4	1	111	11	79
3	FK Auda Rīga	30	20	5	5	104	31	65
4	FS Metta/Latvijas Universitāte Rīga	30	18	7	5	67	23	61
5	FK Jelgava	30	16	6	8	70	43	54
6	Jaunība-Parex Rīga	30	16	3	11	71	51	51
7	JFC Kauguri-PBLC Jūrmala	30	14	4	12	67	55	46
8	RFS Flaminko Rīga	30	14	2	14	60	62	44
9	Zibens/Zemessardze Ilūkste	30	13	3	14	79	68	42
10	FK Valmiera	30	12	4	14	63	59	40
11	FSK Daugava-90 Rīga	30	11	6	13	51	72	39
12	FK Tukums-2000	30	11	3	16	61	75	36
13	Multibanka Rīga	30	6	1	23	40	99	19
14	Tranzīts Ventspils	30	4	4	22	29	103	16
15	Abuls Smiltene	30	3	2	25	22	163	11
-	FK Ilūkste/BJSS	30	2	2	26	8	93	8

NB: FK Ilūkste/BJSS withdrew after round 18; all remaining matches forfeited 3-0.

DOMESTIC CUP 2007

LATVIJAS KAUSS

FOURTH ROUND

(27/5/07)

Metta-LU Rīga 2, Olimps 3
Blāzma Rēzekne 1, Ventspils 3
Vindava Ventspils 0, Metalurgs 1
Jaunība-Parex Rīga 0, Skonto 7
Varavīksne VOVA Liepāja 0, Jūrmala 5
Auda 1, Daugava 6
Daugava-90 Rīga 1, Dinaburg 3
Dinamo-Rīnuži LASD Rīga 0, Rīga 2 *(aet)*

QUARTER-FINALS

(17/6/07)

Ventspils 3 *(Sļesarčuks 6, Sernetsky 27, Zangareyev 34)*, Metalurgs 0
Rīga 1 *(Nikolayev 87)*, Skonto 3 *(Dirnbach 3, Blanks 49, Cauņa 72)*
Jūrmala 0, Daugava 1 *(Kuplovs-Oginskis 45+1)*
Olimps 1 *(Kazura 89)*, Dinaburg 1 *(Krjauklis 12) (aet; 5-4 on pens)*

SEMI-FINALS

(3/9/07)

Daugava 1 *(Ryndyuk 5p)*, Olimps 2 *(Solovjovs 48, Turkovs 90+3)*
Skonto 0, Ventspils 0 *(aet; 3-4 on pens)*

FINAL

(30/9/07)

Skonto stadium, Riga
FK VENTSPILS 3 *(Rimkus 39p, Butriks 58, 70)*
JFK OLIMPS 0
Referee – *Sipailo*
VENTSPILS – *Vaņins, Kačanovs, Ndeki (Soļeičuks 74), Cilinšek, Dubens Zangareyev (Tigirlas 80), Menteshashvili, Ziziļevs, Sļesarčuks (Mysikov Rimkus, Butriks.*
OLIMPS – *Maļinš, Kazura, Šiļuks, Ivaško, Kandov, Zolotarjovs (Sputajs Štolcers, Kostjuks, Turkovs, Solovjovs (Ziļs 62), Tarasovs.*

DOMESTIC CUP 2008

LATVIJAS KAUSS

FOURTH ROUND

(30/4/08)

Nikars 0, Rīga 9
Spartaks 0, Skonto 4
Olimps 0, Daugava 1
Blāzma Rēzekne 0, Dinaburg 0 *(aet; 10-9 on pens)*
Jēkabpils 0, Vindava 3
Viesulis 0, Metalurgs 13
Jelgava 0, Ventspils 2
Metta-LU Rīga 1, Jūrmala 3

QUARTER-FINALS

(7/5/08)

Ventspils 3 *(Tigirlas 31, Rimkus 51, Koļesņičenko 55)*, Metalurgs 1 *(Beniušis 40)*
Skonto 2 *(Pahars 9, Dvalishvili 72)*, Rīga 0
Jūrmala 3 *(Ivaško 7, Gospodars 72, Malašenoks 90p)*, Blāzma Rēzekne 0
Daugava 2 *(Sokolovs 15, Ryndyuk 84p)*, Vindava 1 *(Bespalovs 45)*

SEMI-FINALS

(21/5/08)

Ventspils 2 *(Tigirlas 53, Zangareyev 81)*, Skonto 1 *(Laizāns 69)*
Jūrmala 1 *(Gospodars 37p)*, Daugava 2 *(Ryndyuk 8p, Danilin 49)*

FINAL

(15/6/08)

Skonto stadium, Riga
FC DAUGAVA 1 *(Šimič 79)*
FK VENTSPILS 1 *(Savčenkovs 43)*
(aet; 3-0 on pens)
Referee – *Direktorenko*
DAUGAVA – *Davidovs, Timofejevs, Logins, Trkulja (Gospodinov 90), Gab Sokolovs (Afanasjevs 109), Tiberkanine (Šimič 70), Danilin, Akopyants, Ryndyuk, Rudņevs.*
VENTSPILS – *Vaņins, Kačanovs, Cilinšek, Savčenkovs, Dubenskiy, Koļesņičenko, Zangareyev (Tigirlas 70), Menteshashvili, Ziziļevs, Rimkus (Kalns 56). Butriks (Dedov 82).*

Historic double for FC Vaduz

C Vaduz, coached by Switzerland's most-capped international, Heinz Hermann, made history in 2007/08 by becoming the first club from Liechtenstein) earn promotion into the Swiss top division.

he principality's flagship club made up for play-off eartbreaks in 2004 and 2005 by winning the Challenge eague, Switzerland's second division, with a game to pare. It was a stunning achievement, but one condition f Vaduz's accession is that should they win the Super eague, they will not, as outsiders, be able to proclaim hemselves Swiss champions. Furthermore, they cannot epresent Switzerland in European competition.

nother Cup stroll

lot that the second of those vetoes is a concern as 'aduz are virtually guaranteed an annual UEFA Cup erth via Liechtenstein's domestic knockout ompetition, the FL 1 Cup. They won the trophy for the leventh consecutive year in 2008 – and the 37th time in ll – and, as usual, it was a stroll. Their three matches ielded 18 goals for and none against, with FC Balzers eing slain 4-0 in the final. Two of those goals were cored by Brazilian striker Gaspar, who was also the :hallenge League's top scorer with 31 goals. He, like oach Hermann, was rewarded with a contract extension fter a brilliant debut campaign.

The Liechtenstein national side, coached by Hans-Peter Zaugg, went from the sublime to the ridiculous, thrilling their supporters with a 3-0 win over Iceland in their final home UEFA EURO 2008™ qualifier – to lift their final points haul to seven - then falling to a ghastly 7-1 defeat against fellow flyweights Malta. Serie A star Mario Frick, the country's all-time leading scorer, overtook Daniel Hasler to become Liechtenstein's most-capped player as well in the subsequent 3-0 defeat by Switzerland.

Mario Frick – more caps and goals than any other Liechtenstein international

Liechtensteiner Fussballverband (FLV)

Postfach 165
FL-9490 Vaduz
tel – +423 2374747
fax – +423 2374748
website – www.lfv.li
email – info@lfv.li
Year of Formation – 1934
President – Reinhard Walser
General Secretary – Roland Ospelt
Press Officer – Judith Frommelt
Stadium – Rheinpark, Vaduz (4,548)

TOP FIVE ALL-TIME CAPS
Mario Frick (79); Daniel Hasler (78); Martin Stocklasa (75); Martin Telser (74); Peter Jehle (65)

TOP FIVE ALL-TIME GOALS
Mario Frick (13); Franz Burgmeier (7); Thomas Beck & Martin Stocklasa (5); Manfred Moser, Fabio D'Elia & Benjamin Fischer (2)

LIECHTENSTEIN

NATIONAL TEAM RESULTS 2007/08

22/8/07	Northern Ireland (ECQ)	A	Belfast	1-3	*Frick M. (89)*
12/9/07	Denmark (ECQ)	A	Aarhus	0-4	
13/10/07	Sweden (ECQ)	H	Vaduz	0-3	
17/10/07	Iceland (ECQ)	H	Vaduz	3-0	*Frick M. (28), Beck T. (80, 82)*
17/11/07	Latvia (ECQ)	A	Riga	1-4	*Zirnis (13og)*
26/3/08	Malta	A	Ta' Qali	1-7	*Burgmeier (51)*
30/5/08	Switzerland	A	St.Gallen	0-3	

NATIONAL TEAM APPEARANCES 2007/08

Coach – Hans-Peter ZAUGG (SUI) 2/12/82			NIR	DEN	SWE	ISL	LVA	Mlt	Sui	Caps	Go
Peter JEHLE	22/1/82	Boavista (POR)	G	G	G	G	G	G	G	65	-
Michael STOCKLASA	2/12/80	Eschen-Mauren	D38							52	1
Martin STOCKLASA	29/5/79	Dynamo Dresden (GER)	D	D		D	D	D	D	75	5
Martin TELSER	16/10/78	Balzers	D	D	D	D	D			74	1
Fabio D'ELIA	19/1/83	Eschen-Mauren	D	M		s91		D		40	2
Michele POLVERINO	26/9/84	Vaduz	M	M				M	M	6	-
Ronny BÜCHEL	19/3/82	Eschen-Mauren	M	M	M	M	M80	M	s83	56	-
Daniel FRICK	19/6/78	Balzers	M	s46	M60		s72			28	-
Christoph BIEDERMANN	30/1/87	Eschen-Mauren	M62					s72		2	-
Raphael ROHRER	31/5/85	Vaduz	M74	M	M	M68	M72	M28	M65	32	1
Mario FRICK	7/9/74	Siena (ITA)	A	A84	A74	A91	A	A	A83	79	1
Yves OEHRI	15/3/87	Winterthur (SUI)	s38	D46	D	D			D83	8	-
Stefan BÜCHEL	30/6/86	Eschen-Mauren	s62							4	-
Roger BECK	3/8/83	BW Feldkirch (AUT)	s74	s84	s74	s68	s71		s65	34	1
Marco RITZBERGER	27/12/86	Vaduz		D46			D		M	15	-
Franz BURGMEIER	7/4/82	Basel (SUI) /Thun (SUI)		M	D	M	M	M	D	45	7
Thomas BECK	21/2/81	BW Feldkirch (AUT)		s46	M	s62			s65	62	5
Daniel HASLER	18/5/74	Vaduz			D	D	D			78	1
Martin BÜCHEL	19/2/87	Zürich (SUI)			M61		s80		M	19	-
Benjamin FISCHER	19/10/80	Vaduz			s60	M62	M71		A65	15	2
Andreas GERSTER	24/11/82	Eschen-Mauren			s61	M	M	s28	D	31	-
Franz-Josef VOGT	30/10/85	Balzers						D64		13	-
Martin WILLE	29/5/86	Balzers						D		1	-
David HASLER	4/5/90	Basel (SUI)						A72	s83	2	-
Martin RECHSTEINER	15/2/89	Balzers						s64		1	-

DOMESTIC CUP 2007/08

FL1 CUP

FIRST ROUND

(11/8/07)
Ruggell II 0, Balzers III 1
Trisenberg II 0, Schaan II 6

(12/8/07)
Vaduz III 1, Triesen 5

(22/8/07)
Triesen 0, Vaduz II 2

SECOND ROUND

(18/9/07)
Balzers II 2, Triesenberg 1
Triesen 0, Schaan 4

(19/9/07)
Balzers III 0, Schaan II 6
Vaduz II 0, Balzers 10

QUARTER-FINALS

(23/10/07)
Schaan II 0, Vaduz 5

(30/10/07)
Ruggell 1, Balzers II 0

(31/10/07)
Schaan 1, Eschen-Mauren 4

(7/12/07)
Eschen-Mauren II 0, Balzers 8

SEMI-FINALS

(1/4/08)
Ruggell 0, Vaduz 9

(2/4/08)
Eschen-Mauren 1, Balzers 3

FINAL

(1/5/08)
Rheinparkstadion, Vaduz
FC VADUZ 4 *(Grossklaus 29, Gaspar 37, 59, Alexandre 81)*
FC BALZERS 0
Referee – *Johann*
VADUZ – *Wüthrich, Reinmann, Harnwell (Džombić 46), Aquaro, Cerrone (Fischer 46), Polverino (Ritzberger 57), Rohrer, Alexandre, Sturm, Grossklaus, Gaspar.*
BALZERS – *Vogt R., Telser, Ioanna (Krajina 51), Ritter, Vogt F-J., Christen, Söldi, Rechtsteiner, Tinner (Abdi 74), Wille (Hermann 66), Frick D.*

Record eighth title for FBK Kaunas

or the second season running FBK Kaunas won Lithuania's A Lyga at a canter. In securing their eighth championship title (in nine years), they became the ountry's record champions. The comprehensive, ıncontested nature of their 2007 triumph would suggest hat an end to their dominance is not imminent.

(aunas might have allowed intrigue to linger early on but ›nce they engaged top gear they were in a class of their ›wn and eventually finished 15 points ahead of runners-ıp FK Sūduva. The consistency of their results was ›articularly impressive given the disruption off the field. On four occasions Kaunas changed coach, and even the nan who had two spells in charge and eventually saw :hem home, ex-USSR international Andrei Zygmantovich, vas not officially sanctioned in the role because he lacked :he necessary coaching qualifications.

Artful Rafael

There were also personnel changes in the playing squad, the link-up with Scottish club Heart of Midlothian FC costing Kaunas the services of two key players – Ričardas Beniušis and Audrius Kšanavičius – halfway through the season. Beniušis struggled in Scotland but was on fire for Kaunas in the early weeks, scoring ten goals in the first seven matches and eventually leaving with a league-best tally of 17. Only two players – 26-goal Povilas Lukšys, of third-placed FK Ekranas, and his Kaunas team-mate Mindaugas Grigalevičius, on 18 – would better that tally, although it was another Kaunas man on double figures, 13-goal Rafael Ledesma, who was voted A Lyga Player of the Year. The creative Brazilian playmaker was widely recognised as the driving force of Kaunas's triumph and he also made a major contribution to the team's 2008 Cup win (their fourth), scoring a hat-trick in the semi-final against Ekranas and a late winner in the final to defeat FK Vėtra.

ıdrius Kšanavičius ft Lithuanian ıampions FBK Kaunas idway through the ›ason for Scottish ub Hearts

Another classy Brazilian was Willer Oliveira, whose goals and skills helped Sūduva claim second place. Eighteen-year-old Linas Klimavičius, the younger brother of Lithuanian international Arūnas, also made an impressive contribution in defence after his mid-season transfer from Ekranas and was voted Rookie of the Year. But the biggest asset at Sūduva was their charismatic coach Algimantas Gabrys.

There was chaos at two A Lyga clubs, with FC Vilnius falling into disrepair due to sponsorship withdrawal after a blistering start to the campaign and FK Interas, the club promoted from seventh place in the I Lyga, making a mockery of their presence by fielding 60 players and suffering a succession of crushing defeats. They bade farewell to the top flight by fielding only nine players in the final game against Ekranas, a total reduced to six during the match, forcing the referee to abandon it early in the second half.

Danilevičius honoured

By contrast, the Lithuanian national side signed off from their UEFA EURO 2008™ qualifying campaign with a bang, registering 2-0 wins over both Ukraine (at home) and Georgia (away). In scoring against Ukraine, captain Tomas Danilevičius became his country's all-time top scorer. Despite struggling to get a game in Italy for Bologna FC, he was also voted Lithuania's Footballer of the Year for the second year in a row.

Lietuvos Futbolo Federacija (LFF)

Seimyniskiu 15
LT-2005 Vilnius
tel - +370 5 2638741
fax - +370 5 2638740
website - www.lff.lt
email – info@futbolas.lt
Year of Formation – 1922
President - Liutauras Varanavičius
General Secretary - Julius Kvedaras
Press Officer – Vaiva Zizaite
Stadium – S. Darius ir S. Girėnas, Kaunas (7,262)

TOP FIVE ALL-TIME CAPS
Andrius Skerla (66); Aurelijus Skarbalius (65); Gintaras Staučė (61); Andrejus Tereškinas (56); Deividas Šemberas (55)

TOP FIVE ALL-TIME GOALS
Tomas Danilevičius (13); Antanas Lingis (12); Edgaras Jankauskas (10); Virginijus Baltušnikas (9); Jaroslavas Citavičius, Valdas Ivanauskas, Darius Maciulevičius & Robertas Poškus (8)

NATIONAL TEAM RESULTS 2007/08

Date	Opponent		Venue	Score	Scorers
22/8/07	Turkmenistan	H	Kaunas	2-1	*Danilevičius (42, 47)*
8/9/07	Scotland (ECQ)	A	Glasgow	1-3	*Danilevičius (61p)*
12/9/07	Faroe Islands (ECQ)	H	Kaunas	2-1	*Jankauskas (8), Danilevičius (53)*
17/10/07	France (ECQ)	A	Nantes	0-2	
17/11/07	Ukraine (ECQ)	H	Kaunas	2-0	*Savėnas (41), Danilevičius (67)*
21/11/07	Georgia (ECQ)	A	Tbilisi	2-0	*Kšanavičius (52, 90+6)*
26/3/08	Azerbaijan	H	Vilnius	1-0	*Klimavičius (38)*
27/5/08	Czech Republic	A	Prague	0-2	
31/5/08	Estonia	N	Jurmala (LVA)	1-0	*Mižigurskis (87)*
1/6/08	Latvia	A	Riga	1-2	*Beniušis (81)*
4/6/08	Russia	N	Burghausen (GER)	1-4	*Savėnas (24)*

NATIONAL TEAM APPEARANCES 2007/08

Coach – Algimantas LIUBINSKAS 24/11/51

Player	DoB	Club	Tkm	SCO	FRO	FRA	UKR	GEO	Aze	Cze	Est	Lva	Rus	Caps	Goal
Žydrūnas KARČEMARSKAS	24/5/83	Dinamo Moskva (RUS)	G	G	G	G	G	G	G	G		G	G	33	-
Marius STANKEVIČIUS	15/7/81	Brescia (ITA)	D76	D56			M	M	M	M69				38	1
Andrius SKERLA	29/4/77	Vėtra /Korona (POL)	D	D	D	D	D	D	D	D		D	D	66	1
Vidas ALUNDERIS	27/3/79	Zagłębie Lubin (POL)	D71		D			D		D	s46	D	s84	13	-
Arūnas KLIMAVIČIUS	5/10/82	Dinamo Moskva (RUS)	D	D	D	D	D		D	D				14	1
Deividas ČESNAUSKIS	30/6/81	Hearts (SCO)	M46	M	M31					M75		M	M69	30	4
Kęstutis IVAŠKEVIČIUS	17/4/85	Hearts (SCO)	M46		M									2	-
Deividas ŠEMBERAS	2/8/78	CSKA Moskva (RUS)	M	M	D				M	M59		M	D48	55	-
Audrius KŠANAVIČIUS	28/1/77	Hearts (SCO)	M46	s46	M	M77		M	M46	s46 /77				15	2
Tomas DANILEVIČIUS	18/7/78	Bologna (ITA) /Grosseto (ITA)	A	A	A	A	A82		A87	A		A	A	47	13
Andrius VELIČKA	5/4/79	Hearts (SCO) /Viking (NOR)	A64	A46	s32	s84	s82	s52	s46					16	1
Mindaugas KALONAS	28/2/84	unattached /Kuban (RUS) /Rīga (LVA)	s46	M	s31	M63	s90	s67		s77	M	s46	s61	21	-
Igoris MORINAS	21/2/75	Žalgiris	s46	M46		M	s17	s76						51	7

ATIONAL TEAM APPEARANCES 2007/08 (contd.)

			Tkm	SCO	FRO	FRA	UKR	GEO	Aze	Cze	Est	Lva	Rus	Caps	Goals
ius MIKOLIŪNAS	2/5/84	Hearts (SCO)	s46	s46	M32			M76	M83			M68	M76	26	1
as RADZINEVIČIUS	5/6/81	České Budějovice (CZE) /Liberec (CZE)	s64						s87					21	1
antas ZELMIKAS	3/1/80	Tavriya (UKR)	s71											6	-
mas KUČYS	22/2/81	Daugava (LVA) /Naftovyk-Ukrnafta (UKR)	s76		s86	M84			s80	M46	M53			16	-
as ŽVIRGŽDAUSKAS	18/3/75	Halmstad (SWE)		D		D	D	D		s59	D46	D46	D	54	-
aras JANKAUSKAS	12/3/75	AEK (CYP) /Belenenses (POR) /unattached		s56	A86	A	A90	A52	A46	s75		A76		54	10
as DEDURA	1/8/78	Spartak Moskva (RUS)				D	M	M	D	D			M	33	1
ntas SAVĖNAS	27/8/82	Ekranas /Nosta (RUS)				s63	M	M67	s46 /80			M61	M61	24	3
as LABUKAS	10/1/84	Oțelul (ROU)				s77					A66		s48	8	-
diminas PAULAUSKAS	27/10/82	Ekranas					D	D						19	-
as PAPEČKYS	28/9/78	Górnik Zabrze (POL)					M17		D	s60		D	D84	7	-
drius JOKŠAS	12/1/79	Tavriya (UKR)							s83	s69	M50			17	-
bertas POŠKUS	5/5/79	Zenit (RUS)								A60		s61	A76	40	8
lius GRYBAUSKAS	2/6/84	Oțelul (ROU)									G			4	-
edas SKROBLAS	11/3/84	Ekranas									D		s69	2	-
dijus MAJUS	5/1/84	Vėtra									D			2	-
is JANKAUSKAS	27/9/82	Vėtra									D			1	-
nas TAMOŠAUSKAS	22/5/83	Liepājas Metalurgs (LVA)									M82	s68		14	1
ardas BENIUŠIS	23/4/80	Liepājas Metalurgs (LVA)									A89	s76	s76	21	2
rvydas ŠERNAS	22/7/84	Vėtra									s50		s76	2	-
rius MICEIKA	22/2/83	Liepājas Metalurgs (LVA)									s53			7	1
ndaugas GRIGALEVIČIUS	3/12/81	Kaunas									s66			2	-
erijus MIŽIGURSKUS	22/4/83	Vindava (LVA)									s82			1	1
as PILIBAITIS	5/4/85	Kaunas									s89			4	-

DOMESTIC LEAGUE 2007

FF A LYGA FINAL LEAGUE TABLE

		Home					Away					Total					
	Pld	W	D	L	F	A	W	D	L	F	A	W	D	L	F	A	Pts
FBK Kaunas	36	12	4	2	45	11	13	4	1	46	15	25	8	3	91	26	83
FK Sūduva	36	12	4	2	35	13	8	4	6	31	21	20	8	8	66	34	68
FK Ekranas	36	11	5	2	50	15	8	4	6	33	21	19	9	8	83	36	66
FK Žalgiris	36	12	2	4	37	18	6	8	4	27	16	18	10	8	64	34	64
FK Vėtra	36	11	3	4	31	13	7	4	7	24	17	18	7	11	55	30	61
FK Atlantas	36	6	4	8	21	18	7	2	9	33	27	13	6	17	54	45	45
FC Vilnius	36	7	4	7	33	28	6	2	10	21	35	13	6	17	54	63	45
KFK Šiauliai	36	7	3	8	20	24	6	3	9	27	26	13	6	17	47	50	45
FK Šilutė	36	5	3	10	21	36	1	1	16	7	50	6	4	26	28	86	22
FK Interas	36	1	1	16	10	79	1	1	16	6	75	2	2	32	16	154	8

B. FC Vilnius refused licence for A Lyga season 2008; FK Šilute spared relegation play-off as no I Lyga teams ught promotion.

TOP GOALSCORERS

26 Povilas LUKŠYS (Ekranas)

18 Mindaugas GRIGALEVIČIUS (Kaunas)

17 Ričardas BENIUŠIS (Kaunas)

16 Luka ANČIĆ (Atlantas)

13 RAFAEL Ledesma (Kaunas)
José NEGREIROS (Sūduva)
Viktor RASKOV (Šiauliai)

12 WILLER Souza Oliveira (Sūduva)
Valerijus MIŽIGURSKIS (Žalgiris)
Vitalijus KAVALIAUSKAS (Ekranas)

LITHUANIA

CLUB-BY-CLUB

FK ATLANTAS

Coach – Vacys Lekevičius

Founded - 1960

MAJOR HONOURS: Lithuanian Cup - (2) 2001, 2003 (spring).

2007				
7/4	Žalgiris	h	1-2	*Ančić*
11/4	Vėtra	a	1-2	*Ančić*
15/4	Ekranas	h	1-1	*Ančić (p)*
18/4	Kaunas	a	0-4	
22/4	Interas	h	0-0	
25/4	Šiauliai	a	3-1	*Navikas, Silić, Petreikis*
29/4	Vilnius	h	1-2	*Silić*
5/5	Šilutė	h	0-2	
8/5	Sūduva	a	0-1	
12/5	Žalgiris	a	1-1	*Ančić*
19/5	Vėtra	h	3-1	*Gnedojus, Nesterenko, Ančić*
26/5	Ekranas	a	2-1	*Daunoravičius, Ančić*
9/6	Kaunas	h	1-2	*Ančić*
17/6	Vilnius	a	0-1	
20/6	Šiauliai	h	0-0	
24/6	Šilutė	a	1-1	*Ančić*
8/7	Sūduva	h	0-1	
12/7	Žalgiris	h	1-3	*Daunoravičius*
28/7	Ekranas	h	5-0	*Petreikis, Nesterenko, Jonathan, Navikas, Žvingilas*
5/8	Šiauliai	a	2-0	*Petreikis 2*
12/8	Interas	h	3-0	*Jonathan, Navikas, Begić*
19/8	Kaunas	a	1-2	*Petreikis*
25/8	Vilnius	h	1-0	*Gudelj*
1/9	Šilutė	h	2-0	*Ančić, Žvingilas*
15/9	Sūduva	a	0-1	
18/9	Žalgiris	a	0-3	
22/9	Vėtra	h	1-2	*Gnedojus*
26/9	Interas	a	6-0	*Jonathan, Ančić 4 (1p), Gudelj*
30/9	Ekranas	a	1-3	*Gudelj*
6/10	Kaunas	h	0-2	
9/10	Interas	a	7-0	*Petreikis 2, Jonathan 2, Navikas, Gudelj 2*
24/10	Vėtra	a	1-3	*Ančić (p)*
27/10	Šiauliai	h	0-0	
30/10	Vilnius	a	4-1	*Nesterenko, Ančić (p), og (Stempkovski), Gudelj*
4/11	Šilutė	a	3-2	*Jonathan, Delić, Petreikis*
10/11	Sūduva	h	1-0	*Ančić (p)*

No	Name	Nat	Pos	Aps	(s)	Gls
28	Luka ANČIĆ	CRO	A	24	(2)	16
29	Karolis ATUTIS		D		(1)	
18	Ivo BEGIĆ	CRO	D	17	(1)	1
21	Evaldas BIELSKIS		D		(1)	
17	Zigmantas BUTKUS		D	20	(2)	
4	CARLOS HENRIQUE	BRA	D	8	(3)	
22	Mindaugas DAUNORAVIČIUS		A	13	(5)	2
14	Jure DELIĆ	CRO	A	14		1
9	Israel DOUGLAS	NGA	A	3	(3)	
20	Kazimieras GNEDOJUS		D	33		2
25	Mantas GRIGAITIS		M		(1)	
27	Hrvatin GUDELJ	CRO	M	19		6
15	JONATHAN Torres	BRA	A	17		6
26	Deividas KARMONAS		M		(2)	
1	Arnas LEKEVIČIUS		G	35		
2	Romualdas MACIULEVIČIUS		D	4	(4)	
13	Donatas NAVIKAS		M	33		4
3	Bogdans NESTERENKO	LVA	D	21	(1)	3
5	Justas NOREIKA		M	4	(8)	
7	Andrius PANCEROVAS		M		(3)	
11	Andrius PETREIKIS		M	34		8
31	Paulius POCIUS		G	1	(4)	
30	Jelen POKORN	SVN	M	13		
19	Darius RAMONAS		D	17	(1)	
6	Povilas ŠARŪNAS		D	32		
8	Mateo SILIĆ	CRO	M	21	(1)	2
16	Donatas SURBLYS		M	4	(12)	
24	Evaldas UŽKURAITIS		D	1	(10)	
10	Rimantas ŽVINGILAS		A	8	(19)	2

FK EKRANAS

Coach – Saulius Širmelis; (3/7/07) Darius Butkus

Founded - 1964

MAJOR HONOURS: Lithuanian League - (2) 1993, 2005; Lithuanian Cup - (2) 1998, 2000.

2007				
7/4	Šiauliai	h	2-0	*Kavaliauskas, Tomkevičius*
11/4	Vilnius	h	0-0	
15/4	Atlantas	a	1-1	*Klimavičius*
18/4	Sūduva	h	1-1	*Kavaliauskas*
22/4	Žalgiris	a	0-1	
25/4	Vėtra	h	0-0	
29/4	Šilutė	a	5-0	*Bička 2, og (Vičius), Kavaliauskas 2*
5/5	Kaunas	a	1-1	*Savėnas*
8/5	Interas	h	6-1	*Savėnas 3 (1p), Lukšys, Gleveckas, Kavaliauskas*
12/5	Šiauliai	h	2-1	*Lukšys 2*
15/5	Sūduva	h	0-0	
19/5	Vilnius	a	2-1	*Pogreban, Lukšys*
26/5	Atlantas	h	1-2	*Lukšys*
9/6	Sūduva	a	1-1	*Pogreban*
17/6	Šilutė	h	6-1	*Bička, Lukšys, Pogreban, Savėnas, og (Vaikasas), Gleveckas*
20/6	Vėtra	a	0-1	
24/6	Kaunas	h	2-2	*Pogreban, Savėnas*
30/6	Žalgiris	h	4-1	*Savėnas (p), Bička 2, Kavaliauskas*
8/7	Interas	a	4-0	*Kavaliauskas, Lukšys 3 (1p)*
12/7	Šiauliai	a	1-0	*Lukšys*
24/7	Vilnius	h	3-1	*Lukšys 3 (1p)*
28/7	Atlantas	a	0-5	
7/8	Vėtra	h	2-1	*Rähn, Varnas*
11/8	Žalgiris	a	1-4	*og (Choruži)*
25/8	Šilutė	a	3-0	*Bička (p), Lukšys, Varnas*
2/9	Kaunas	a	1-2	*Varnas*
15/9	Interas	h	10-0	*Lukšys 6 (1p), Bička, Varnas 2, Šidlauskas*
22/9	Vilnius	a	2-1	*Lukšys, Savėnas*
30/9	Atlantas	h	3-1	*Lukšys, Kavaliauskas 2*
3/10	Šiauliai	a	3-0	*Savėnas (p), Pogreban, Tomkevičius*
6/10	Sūduva	a	1-2	*Skroblas*
21/10	Žalgiris	h	2-0	*Varnas, Kavaliauskas*
27/10	Vėtra	a	1-1	*Savėnas*
30/10	Šilutė	h	5-0	*Varnas 2, Lukšys 2, Gardzijauskas*
4/11	Kaunas	h	1-3	*Pogreban*
10/11	Interas	a	6-0	*Lukšys 2, Kavaliauskas 2, Savėnas, Bička (abandoned after 47 minutes; result stood)*

Name	Nat	Pos	Aps	(s)	Gls
Andrius ARLAUSKAS		M		(1)	
Žilvinas BANYS		M		(4)	
Deimantas BIČKA		M	35		8
Dominykas GALKEVIČIUS		M	12	(14)	
Mindaugas GARDZIJAUSKAS		M	18	(1)	1
Dainius GLEVECKAS		D	11	(1)	2
Tadas KAUNECKAS		G	1		
Vitalijus KAVALIAUSKAS		A	32	(1)	12
Linas KLIMAVIČIUS		D	15		1
Povilas LUKŠYS		A	29	(5)	26
Deividas PADAIGIS		D	6	(2)	
Gediminas PAULAUSKAS		D	31		
Serghei POGREBAN	MDA	M	34	(2)	6
Taavi RÄHN	EST	D	21	(2)	1
Laurynas RIMAVIČIUS		D	18	(4)	
Dainius SAULĖNAS		A		(19)	
Mantas SAVĖNAS		M	25	(2)	11
Andrius ŠIDLAUSKAS		M	6	(18)	1
Alfredas SKROBLAS		D	28		1
Arvydas SKRUPSKIS		G	3		
Bogdan STEFANOVIĆ	SRB	G	32	(1)	
Tautvydas ŠVELNA		A		(1)	
Giedrius TOMKEVIČIUS		M	23	(2)	2
Egidijus VARNAS		A	16	(12)	8

FK INTERAS

Coach – Ivan Švabovič

Founded - 1979

2007

7/4	Kaunas	h	2-3	*Jeršovas 2*
11/4	Šilutė	h	1-1	*Naumov*
15/4	Šiauliai	a	1-4	*Naumov*
18/4	Vilnius	h	0-3	
22/4	Atlantas	a	0-0	
25/4	Sūduva	h	0-7	
29/4	Žalgiris	a	2-3	*Gordej, Krasnovskis*
/5	Vėtra	h	0-2	
/5	Ekranas	a	1-6	*Krasnovskis*
12/5	Kaunas	a	0-8	
15/5	Vėtra	a	0-3	
19/5	Šilutė	h	3-0	*Rinaldo, Astrauskas 2*
26/5	Šiauliai	h	1-4	*Astrauskas*
10/6	Vilnius	a	0-4	
17/6	Žalgiris	h	0-2	
30/6	Sūduva	a	0-2	
/7	Ekranas	h	0-4	
11/7	Kaunas	h	1-6	*Slepakovas*
22/7	Šilutė	a	0-3	
28/7	Šiauliai	a	2-0	*Matulevičius, Naumov*
/8	Sūduva	h	2-3	*Kakabadze, Papšys*
12/8	Atlantas	a	0-3	
18/8	Vilnius	h	0-5	
25/8	Žalgiris	a	0-7	
/9	Vėtra	h	0-7	
5/9	Ekranas	a	0-10	
8/9	Kaunas	a	0-3	*(w/o)*
22/9	Šilutė	a	0-2	
26/9	Atlantas	h	0-6	
30/9	Šiauliai	h	0-7	
6/10	Vilnius	a	0-9	
9/10	Atlantas	h	0-7	
30/10	Žalgiris	h	0-6	
4/11	Vėtra	a	0-3	
7/11	Sūduva	a	0-5	
10/11	Ekranas	h	0-6	*(abandoned after 47 minutes; result stood)*

No	Name	Nat	Pos	Aps	(s)	Gls
7	Viktor AFANASENKO	BLR	M	12	(1)	
	Michail ANENKOV		M	2	(1)	
	Pavel ANTONIAN			1		
	Dmitrij AREFJEV		D	4		
31	Nerijus ASTRAUSKAS		A	4	(3)	3
11	Arsenij BUINICKIJ		A	15	(2)	
6	Besik CHIGLADZE	GEO	M	6		
	Aleksandr CHITUN		M	4		
24	Gvidas ČIURSINAS		D	3	(2)	
33	Vladimir DERENDIAJEV		M	3		
1	Audrius DILYS		G	12	(1)	
12	Piotr DUBROVSKIJ		G	15		
	Gytis GALKAUSKAS		A		(1)	
23	Denis GORDEJ		D	19	(1)	1
5	Mantas GRIBAUSKAS		D	8		
29	Oleg GURIN		A		(2)	
17	Ivan JERIOMENKO		A	3		
25	Valentin JERIOMENKO		M	13	(1)	
13	Artūras JERŠOVAS		A	17	(2)	2
1	Šarūnas JUREVIČIUS		G	1		
2	Suliko KAKABADZE	GEO	A	6	(1)	1
89	Povilas KRASNOVSKIS		A	11	(5)	2
	Anton KURACHTIN		M	1		
6	Jurij KUZNECOV		D	3		
28	Denis LAVRINOVIČ		G	1		
28	Denis LAVRINOVIČ		M	2		
	Jevgenij LOVSKIS				(1)	
4	Valdas MACIANSKIS		D	16	(1)	
9	Deividas MATULEVIČIUS		A	7	(8)	1
30	Nikolaj MIŠČENKO		D	2	(1)	
30	Nikolaj MIŠČENKO		G	1		
10	Jevgenij MOROZ		D	15	(4)	
39	Anton NAUMOV		M	11	(2)	3
20	Arvydas NOVIKOVAS		A	6	(6)	
19	Paulius OLIŠAUSKAS		M	9	(2)	
	Oleg ORLOV		D		(1)	
32	Aleksandr OSIPOVICH	BLR	A	4		
	Dmitrij OSTROVSKIJ		M		(1)	
14	Marius PAPŠYS		M	6	(10)	1
17	Viktor PAŠIN		M	11	(2)	
1	Maksim PEREPEČIN		G	2		
15	Giorgi PURTSELADZE	GEO	M	2	(1)	
15	Marius RIMAS		D	1		
8	RINALDO Jordão de Paulo Neto	BRA	M	11	(1)	1
16	Marius ŠALKAUSKAS		G	2		
18	Vitalijus SAVICKAS		D	16	(2)	
22	Gintas ŠIRMELIS		M	10	(2)	
	Denis SIZ				(1)	
2	Rolandas SLEPAKOVAS		D	12	(3)	1
	Konstantin SOLOVJEV		G	1		
26	Marius STANAITIS		D	22	(1)	
27	Aleksandr ŠUKŠTUL		M	8	(1)	
	Aleksej TICHANOVSKIJ		M	1	(2)	
3	Eduard TUČINSKIJ		D	12	(3)	
	Denis VASILKOV		A	1	(1)	
24	Konstantinas VELIKOVAS		M	8	(2)	
	Jurijus VOLKOVSKIS		D	1		
28	Jan VOLODZKO		M	12	(1)	
	Vladimir VOLOSATOV		A	4		
34	Oleksandr ZABARA	UKR	M	3		

N.B. Only nine players fielded in final fixture against FK Ekranas.

FBK KAUNAS

Coach – Vladimir Kurnev (BLR); (18/4/07) Angel Chervenkov (BUL); (30/6/07) Andrei Zygmantovich (BLR); (30/8/07) (Antonius Joor (NED)); (1/10/07) Andrei Zygmantovich (BLR)

Founded - 1960

MAJOR HONOURS: Lithuanian League - (8) 1999 (autumn), 2000, 2001, 2002, 2003, 2004, 2006, 2007; Lithuanian Cup - (4) 2002, 2004, 2005, 2008.

2007

7/4	Interas	a	3-2	*Beniušis, Kšanavičius, Bagužis*
11/4	Šiauliai	h	2-1	*Beniušis, Kvartskhelia*

15/4	Vilnius	a	2-2	*Beniušis 2*
18/4	Atlantas	h	4-0	*Beniušis 3, Rafael*
22/4	Sūduva	a	1-1	*Beniušis*
25/4	Žalgiris	h	1-1	*Beniušis*
29/4	Vėtra	a	1-0	*Beniušis*
5/5	Ekranas	h	1-1	*Činikas*
9/5	Šilutė	h	4-0	*Bagužis, Rafael (p), Fridrikas, Mendy*
12/5	Interas	h	8-0	*Beniušis 3, Rafael, Mendy (p), Rimkevičius, Strakhanovich, Pehlić*
15/5	Šiauliai	h	4-0	*Rafael, Beniušis, Rimkevičius, Grigalevičius*
19/5	Šiauliai	a	0-0	
26/5	Vilnius	h	1-0	*Grigalevičius*
9/6	Atlantas	a	2-1	*Bagužis, Kšanavičius*
17/6	Vėtra	h	1-2	*Grigalevičius*
20/6	Žalgiris	a	0-1	
24/6	Ekranas	a	2-2	*Rafael, Beniušis*
30/6	Sūduva	h	1-1	*Beniušis*
8/7	Šilutė	h	2-0	*Rimkevičius 2*
11/7	Interas	a	6-1	*Kvartskhelia, Rafael, Beniušis, Rimkevičius, Radžius, Grigalevičius*
29/7	Vilnius	a	2-0	*Grigalevičius 2*
5/8	Žalgiris	h	1-1	*Rafael*
11/8	Sūduva	a	4-0	*Pehlić, Grigalevičius, Kvartskhelia, Činikas*
19/8	Atlantas	h	2-1	*Rafael, Manchkhava*
25/8	Vėtra	a	1-0	*Rafael*
2/9	Ekranas	h	2-1	*Grigalevičius, Radžius*
15/9	Šilutė	a	5-2	*Rimkevičius 3, Rafael 2*
18/9	Interas	h	3-0	*(w/o)*
22/9	Šiauliai	a	3-1	*Grigalevičius, Kvartskhelia 2*
30/9	Vilnius	h	6-0	*Pehlić, Rimkevičius 2, Grigalevičius 3*
6/10	Atlantas	a	2-0	*Grigalevičius, Rafael*
21/10	Sūduva	h	2-1	*Rafael, Rimkevičius*
27/10	Žalgiris	a	5-0	*Grigalevičius 3, Laurišas, Mendy*
30/10	Vėtra	h	0-1	
4/11	Ekranas	a	3-1	*Grigalevičius 2, Radžius*
10/11	Šilutė	a	4-1	*Khubutia, Barevičius, Valkanov, Birkštys*

No	Name	Nat	Pos	Aps	(s)	Gls
3	Vytautas ANDRIUŠKEVIČIUS		D	1		
16	Mohamed Larbi AROURI	TUN	M	1	(2)	
18	Mindaugas BAGUŽIS		D	29	(1)	3
17	Muharem BAJRAMI	MKD	M		(1)	
9	Giedrius BAREVIČIUS		M	11	(2)	1
19	Andrius BARTKUS		M	7	(2)	
28	Donatas BENDINSKAS		M	1		
8	Ričardas BENIUŠIS		A	18		17
15	Vytautas BIRKŠTYS		M	1	(1)	1
26	Marius ČINIKAS		M	16	(9)	2
12	Esteban Javier DREER	ARG	G	3		
25	Mantas FRIDRIKAS		D	7	(1)	1
10	Mindaugas GRIGALEVIČIUS		A	17	(7)	18
18	Jaunius JUOZAITIS		M		(1)	
1	Marián KELLO	SVK	G	11		
8	Akaki KHUBUTIA	GEO	D	4		1
16	Audrius KŠANAVIČIUS		M	8	(10)	2
23	Dainius KUNEVIČIUS		D	22	(5)	
20	Givi KVARTSKHELIA	GEO	M	24	(2)	5
19	Aivaras LAURIŠAS		A	4	(4)	1
1	Mindaugas MALINAUSKAS		G	14		
6	Nukri MANCHKHAVA	GEO	M	18	(2)	1
4	Pascal MENDY	SEN	D	14	(7)	3
3	Adrian MROWIEC	POL	D	19	(1)	
27	Edin PEHLIĆ	BIH	M	15	(8)	3
2	Nerijus RADŽIUS		D	30	(2)	3
11	RAFAEL Ledesma	BRA	A	29	(3)	13
7	Artūras RIMKEVIČIUS		A	16	(12)	11
5	Darius SANAJEVAS		M	8	(2)	
24	Fernando SCREPIS	ARG	M	11	(1)	
22	Modestas STONYS		G	7		
13	Oleg STRAKHANOVICH	BLR	M	10	(7)	1
24	Mindaugas STRAUKA		M		(1)	
17	Yanko VALKANOV	BUL	D	5	(5)	1
21	Tomas VYŠNIAUSKAS		M	2	(1)	
14	Vygantas ZUBAVIČIUS		M	2	(2)	

KFK ŠIAULIAI

Coach – Darius Magdišauskas; (9/6/07) Rytis Tavoras

Founded - 1995

2007

7/4	Ekranas	a	0-2	
11/4	Kaunas	a	1-2	*Viktoravičius*
15/4	Interas	h	4-1	*Raskov 3, Viktoravičius*
18/4	Šilutė	h	1-0	*Tsyganenko*
22/4	Vilnius	a	1-2	*Raskov*
25/4	Atlantas	h	1-3	*Raskov*
29/4	Sūduva	a	2-0	*Lukoševičius, Raskov*
5/5	Žalgiris	h	0-1	
8/5	Vėtra	a	1-2	*Zabara*
12/5	Ekranas	a	1-2	*Kirhners*
15/5	Kaunas	a	0-4	
19/5	Kaunas	h	0-0	
26/5	Interas	a	4-1	*Raskov 2, Šilėnas, Kukly*
9/6	Šilutė	a	1-2	*Butavičius*
17/6	Sūduva	h	1-3	*Pšelenskis*
20/6	Atlantas	a	0-0	
24/6	Žalgiris	a	1-1	*Viktoravičius*
1/7	Vilnius	h	3-0	*(w/o)*
12/7	Ekranas	h	0-1	
28/7	Interas	h	0-2	
2/8	Vėtra	h	2-1	*Garuckas, Lukoševičius*
5/8	Atlantas	h	0-2	
12/8	Vilnius	a	4-2	*Kirhners 2 (p), Raskov 2*
18/8	Šilutė	h	2-1	*Kirhners 2 (1p)*
24/8	Sūduva	a	0-3	
1/9	Žalgiris	h	0-0	
15/9	Vėtra	a	0-1	
22/9	Kaunas	h	1-3	*Butavičius*
30/9	Interas	a	7-0	*Lukoševičius, Kirhners 3 (2p), Šilėnas, Kuklys, Viktoravičius*
3/10	Ekranas	h	0-3	
6/10	Šilutė	a	2-1	*Timinskas, Kirhners (p)*
21/10	Vilnius	h	1-1	*Raskov*
27/10	Atlantas	a	0-0	
30/10	Sūduva	h	2-1	*Lunskis, Kuklys*
4/11	Žalgiris	a	2-1	*Šilėnas 2*
10/11	Vėtra	h	2-1	*Raskov 2*

No	Name	Nat	Pos	Aps	(s)	Gls
27	Davidas ARLAUSKIS		D	22	(1)	
13	Giedrius ARLAUSKIS		G	19		
	Saimonas BURKŠAITIS		D	2	(3)	
21	Gediminas BUTAVIČIUS		M	22	(3)	2
77	Aurimas GARUCKAS		M	11	(4)	1
19	Edvinas JASAITIS		M		(5)	
9	Gintaras JUODEIKIS		D	31		
1	Šarūnas JUREVIČIUS		G	1		
14	Intars KIRHNERS	LVA	D	32		9
18	Justinas KRIŠTOPAITIS		M		(1)	
8	Mantas KUKLYS		M	21	(6)	3
83	Vilius LAPEIKIS		D	17	(5)	
7	Mindaugas LUKOŠEVIČIUS		M	25	(3)	3

)	Ingus LUKOVIČS	LVA	G	15	(1)	
5	Deivydas LUNSKIS		D	32		1
6	Armando dos Santos MANDINHO	BRA	M	4	(2)	
3	Paulius OLIŠAUSKAS		M	1	(5)	
	Andrej ORIOL		D	7		
	Ernestas PILYPAS				(1)	
	Edvardas PŠELENSKIS		M	7	(8)	1
9	Viktor RASKOV	UKR	A	26	(5)	13
3	Paulius ŠIDLAUSKAS		M		(3)	
)	Vaidas ŠILĖNAS		M	31	(1)	4
2	Tadas ŠPUKAS		A	1	(1)	
	Donatas STROCKIS		D	3	(7)	
	Gediminas TIMINSKAS		M	8	(4)	1
5	Valeriy TSYGANENKO	BLR	A	20	(9)	1
	Rokas URBELIS		M		(3)	
1	Vaidas VIKTORAVIČIUS		A	7	(17)	4
0	Oleksandr ZABARA	UKR	M	10	(5)	1
	Egidijus ŽUKAUSKAS		D	10		

FK ŠILUTĖ

Coach – Darius Gvildys; (9/5/07) Eugenijus Riabovas

Founded - 2002

007				
/4	Sūduva	a	1-4	*Straleckas*
1/4	Interas	a	1-1	*Bezykornovas*
5/4	Žalgiris	h	0-0	
8/4	Šiauliai	a	0-1	
2/4	Vėtra	h	0-3	
5/4	Vilnius	a	0-4	
9/4	Ekranas	h	0-5	
/5	Atlantas	a	2-0	*Bezykornovas, Straleckas*
/5	Kaunas	a	0-4	
2/5	Sūduva	h	1-3	*Straleckas*
9/5	Interas	a	0-3	
6/5	Žalgiris	a	0-2	
/6	Šiauliai	h	2-1	*Vičius, Bezykornovas (p)*
7/6	Ekranas	a	1-6	*Straleckas*
0/6	Vilnius	h	0-2	
4/6	Atlantas	h	1-1	*Vičius*
/7	Kaunas	a	0-2	
2/7	Sūduva	a	0-3	
7/7	Vėtra	a	0-3	
2/7	Interas	h	3-0	*Bezykornovas (p), Podelis, Petkevičius*
8/7	Žalgiris	h	0-0	
/8	Vilnius	a	0-2	
2/8	Vėtra	h	3-0	*(w/o; original result 1-3 Bezykornovas)*
8/8	Šiauliai	a	1-2	*Karalius*
5/8	Ekranas	h	0-3	
/9	Atlantas	a	0-2	
5/9	Kaunas	h	2-5	*Bezykornovas, Vičius*
8/9	Sūduva	h	2-4	*Brezina, Bezykornovas*
2/9	Interas	h	2-0	*Vičius 2*
0/9	Žalgiris	a	0-3	
/10	Šiauliai	h	1-2	*Vičius*
21/10	Vėtra	a	1-3	*Marozas*
27/10	Vilnius	h	1-0	*Bezykornovas*
30/10	Ekranas	a	0-5	
4/11	Atlantas	h	2-3	*Marozas, Šulkevičius*
10/11	Kaunas	h	1-4	*Podelis*

No	Name	Nat	Pos	Aps	(s)	Gls
10	Marius BEZYKORNOVAS		M	33		8
5	Ivan BREZINA	SVK	D	28	(5)	1
23	Ilia ERLIKH	BLR	M		(3)	
32	Aidas FABIJONAS		G	2	(1)	
6	Ilgiz FATTAKHOV	RUS	M	2	(7)	
22	Edvardas GAURILOVAS		D	15	(1)	
1	Mihael HERTELENDI	SVN	G	17	(1)	
29	Marius JUDICKAS		M	1	(1)	
21	Audrius JUOZAITIS		D	11	(6)	
6	Martynas KARALIUS		D	6		1
3	Akaki KHUBUTIA	GEO	D	17	(2)	
8	Tadas KIJANSKAS		D	11	(1)	
30	Šarūnas KILIJONAS		G	4	(1)	
7	Pavel KOVACHEV	BUL	M	18	(8)	
14	Eimantas MAROZAS		A	8	(4)	2
26	Manfredas MASIULIS		M	2	(1)	
25	Martynas NORMANTAS		A	6	(7)	
16	Linas OSTREIKA		M	14	(3)	
24	Vladas PETKEVIČIUS		A	2	(8)	1
8	Vadim PETRENKO		M	9	(4)	
20	Gintas PODELIS		A	17	(7)	2
12	Darius REGELSKIS		D	20		
4	Andrius SANAJEVAS		D	16		
13	Petru STINGA	MDA	A	7	(10)	
11	Tadas STRALECKAS		A	5	(4)	4
9	Valentinas ŠULKEVIČIUS		M	17	(2)	1
2	Paulius VAIKASAS		D	23	(2)	
15	Mindaugas VALANČIUS		D	9	(6)	
18	Nerijus VALSKIS		M	16	(6)	
31	Laurynas VERTELIS		G	13	(1)	
17	Gediminas VIČIUS		M	32		6
14	Vygantas ZUBAVIČIUS		M	15		

FK SŪDUVA

Coach – Algimantas Gabrys

Founded - 2002

MAJOR HONOURS: Lithuanian Cup - (1) 2006.

2007				
7/4	Šilutė	h	4-1	*Sobol, Willer, Kozyuberda, Juška*
10/4	Žalgiris	a	0-1	
15/4	Vėtra	h	1-0	*Maciulevičius*
18/4	Ekranas	a	1-1	*Kozyuberda*
22/4	Kaunas	h	1-1	*Willer*
25/4	Interas	a	7-0	*Willer 2 (1p), Mačiulis 2, Juška, Kerys, Kozyuberda*
29/4	Šiauliai	h	0-2	
5/5	Vilnius	a	1-3	*Miklinevičius*
8/5	Atlantas	h	1-0	*Willer*
12/5	Šilutė	a	3-1	*Willer, Klevinskas G., Juška*
15/5	Ekranas	a	0-0	
19/5	Žalgiris	h	1-1	*Urbšys*
26/5	Vėtra	a	0-0	
9/6	Ekranas	h	1-1	*Miklinevičius*
17/6	Šiauliai	a	3-1	*Kozyuberda, Juška, Willer*
20/6	Interas	h	2-0	*Mačiulis, Kerys*
24/6	Vilnius	h	1-0	*Willer*
30/6	Kaunas	a	1-1	*Urbšys*
8/7	Atlantas	a	1-0	*Klevinskas G.*
12/7	Šilutė	h	3-0	*Urbšys, og (Regelskis), Willer*
24/7	Žalgiris	a	1-4	*Negreiros*
7/8	Interas	a	3-2	*Negreiros 2, Urbšys*
11/8	Kaunas	h	0-4	
24/8	Šiauliai	h	3-0	*Negreiros 2, Urbšys*
2/9	Vilnius	a	3-0	*Mikuckis, Negreiros, Willer*
15/9	Atlantas	h	1-0	*Maciulevičius (p)*
18/9	Šilutė	a	4-2	*Willer, Braga, Negreiros, Maciulevičius*
22/9	Žalgiris	h	1-0	*og (Vilėniškis)*
26/9	Vėtra	h	1-1	*Willer*
30/9	Vėtra	a	1-0	*Maciulevičius*

6/10	Ekranas	h	2-1	*Negreiros, Maciulevičius (p)*
21/10	Kaunas	a	1-2	*Jasaitis*
30/10	Šiauliai	a	1-2	*Braga*
4/11	Vilnius	h	7-1	*Klevinskas G., Negreiros 3, Mikuckis, Maciulevičius, Miklinevičius (p)*
7/11	Interas	h	5-0	*Miklinevičius (p), Klevinskas G., Negreiros 2, Kozyuberda*
10/11	Atlantas	a	0-1	

No	Name	Nat	Pos	Aps	(s)	Gls
11	Otávio BRAGA	BRA	A	11	(4)	2
2	Gvidas GRIGAS		D	10	(6)	
29	Karolis JASAITIS		M	14	(8)	1
10	Gvidas JUŠKA		A	17	(12)	4
16	Artūras KERYS		M	1	(8)	2
4	Giedrius KLEVINSKAS		D	10	(3)	4
55	Saulius KLEVINSKAS		G	27		
13	Linas KLIMAVIČIUS		D	11		
8	Serhiy KOZYUBERDA	UKR	M	23	(1)	5
12	Povilas LEIMONAS		D	8	(3)	
14	Šarūnas LITVINAS		M		(3)	
15	Darius MACIULEVIČIUS		M	27	(6)	6
21	Nerijus MAČIULIS		M	9	(7)	3
26	MAIKEL Feldmann	BRA	A		(3)	
7	Tomas MIKLINEVIČIUS		M	31		4
5	Tomas MIKUCKIS		D	33	(1)	2
6	Andrei MILEVSKIY	BLR	D	3	(1)	
99	José Edicaros Lima NEGREIROS	BRA	A	12	(5)	13
20	Gytis PADIMANSKAS		G	1	(1)	
23	Serhiy POTAPOV	UKR	M	2	(2)	
24	Vitaliy SHUGANOV	BLR	A	8	(2)	
3	Marius SKINDERIS		D	30		
9	Giedrius SLAVICKAS		M	14	(12)	
19	Vaidas SLAVICKAS		D	19	(2)	
25	Aleksandr SOBOL	BLR	D	23		1
22	Dovydas URBA		G	8		
17	Andrius URBŠYS		M	17	(7)	5
18	WILLER Souza Oliveira	BRA	M	27	(6)	12

FK VĖTRA

Coach – Aleksandr Tarkhanov (RUS); (15/6/07) Donatas Vencevičius

Founded - 1996

2007

7/4	Vilnius	a	0-0	
11/4	Atlantas	h	2-1	*Stankevičius 2 (1p)*
15/4	Sūduva	a	0-1	
18/4	Žalgiris	h	1-1	*Severino*
22/4	Šilutė	a	3-0	*og (Sanajevas), Severino, Jankauskas*
25/4	Ekranas	a	0-0	
29/4	Kaunas	h	0-1	
5/5	Interas	a	2-0	*Butrimavičius, Stankevičius*
8/5	Šiauliai	h	2-1	*Juška, Karčemarskas*
12/5	Vilnius	h	1-2	*Pedro Botelho*
15/5	Interas	h	3-0	*Severino 2, Raliukonis*
19/5	Atlantas	a	1-3	*Tselyuk*
26/5	Sūduva	h	0-0	
9/6	Žalgiris	a	0-1	
17/6	Kaunas	a	2-1	*Juška, Stankevičius*
20/6	Ekranas	h	1-0	*Panka*
12/7	Vilnius	a	0-0	
17/7	Šilutė	h	3-0	*Butrimavičius, Budimir, Stankevičius*
2/8	Šiauliai	a	1-2	*Šernas*
7/8	Ekranas	a	1-2	*Karčemarskas*
12/8	Šilutė	a	0-3	*(w/o; original result 3- Juška, Karčemarskas, Kvartskhelia)*
18/8	Žalgiris	h	2-1	*Šernas, Miloševski*
25/8	Kaunas	h	0-1	
1/9	Interas	a	7-0	*Malinin, Božinovski, Grigaitis 2, og (Miščenko), Karčemarskas 2*
15/9	Šiauliai	h	1-0	*Karčemarskas*
18/9	Vilnius	h	5-1	*Miloševski 2, Šernas, Karčemarskas, Grigaiti*
22/9	Atlantas	a	2-1	*Miloševski 2 (1p)*
26/9	Sūduva	a	1-1	*Kvartskhelia*
30/9	Sūduva	h	0-1	
6/10	Žalgiris	a	2-0	*Božinovski, Šernas*
21/10	Šilutė	h	3-1	*Stankevičius (p), Butrimavičius, Juška*
24/10	Atlantas	h	3-1	*Šernas, Butrimavičius, Miloševski*
27/10	Ekranas	h	1-1	*Šernas*
30/10	Kaunas	a	1-0	*Butrimavičius*
4/11	Interas	h	3-0	*Vėževičius, Božinovski, Kvartskhelia*
10/11	Šiauliai	a	1-2	*Miloševski*

No	Name	Nat	Pos	Aps	(s)	Gls
9	Maksut AZIZI	SVN	A	2	(9)	
15	Marius BIRŠKYS		M	1		
8	Bobi BOŽINOVSKI	MKD	M	21	(1)	3
6	Marijan BUDIMIR	CRO	D	25		1
23	Gediminas BUTRIMAVIČIUS		M	30	(1)	5
24	Gjoko CVETANOVSKI	MKD	A	14		
14	Evaldas GRIGAITIS		A	1	(14)	3
5	Algis JANKAUSKAS		D	23		1
77	Egidijus JUŠKA		A	29	(4)	4
26	Rolandas KARČEMARSKAS		A	8	(18)	7
21	Tadas KIJANSKAS		D	13	(2)	
12	Stanislav KOZYREV	RUS	G	16		
18	Vakhtang KVARTSKHELIA	GEO	A	5	(7)	3
20	Denis MALININ	RUS	A	9	(5)	1
7	Dejan MILOŠESKI	MKD	M	18	(3)	7
17	Mindaugas PANKA		M	19		1
99	PEDRO Henrique BOTELHO	BRA	D	22		1
	Andrius PLIKAITIS				(1)	
4	Julius RALIUKONIS		D	12		1
33	Nerijus SASNAUSKAS		D	9	(2)	
10	Darvydas ŠERNAS		M	20	(1)	6
70	SEVERINO Lima de Moura	BRA	A	18	(1)	4
55	Andrius SKERLA		D	22		
11	Vitalis STANKEVIČIUS		A	21	(9)	6
27	Almir SULEJMANOVIČ	SVN	D	3	(2)	
18	Yuriy TARKHANOV	RUS	M		(3)	
16	Denis TSELYUK	RUS	A		(6)	1
22	Andrei USACHOV	RUS	D	13		
12	Povilas VALINČIUS		G		(1)	
19	Robertas VĖŽEVIČIUS		M	2	(15)	1
1	Vaidas ŽUTAUTAS		G	20		

FC VILNIUS

Coach – Antanas Vingilys

Founded - 2003

2007

7/4	Vėtra	h	0-0	
11/4	Ekranas	a	0-0	
15/4	Kaunas	h	2-2	*Kleyr 2*
18/4	Interas	a	3-0	*Andreson, Muller, Adilson*
22/4	Šiauliai	h	2-1	*Rodolfo, Rodnei*
25/4	Šilutė	h	4-0	*Muller, og (Kijanskas), Kleyr 2*

9/4	Atlantas	a	2-1	*Kleyr, Muller*
/5	Sūduva	h	3-1	*Kleyr, Muller, Rodnei*
/5	Žalgiris	a	2-1	*Kleyr, Muller*
2/5	Vėtra	a	2-1	*Muller, Lukša*
9/5	Ekranas	h	1-2	*Kleyr*
6/5	Kaunas	a	0-1	
0/6	Interas	h	4-0	*Kleyr, Rodolfo, Marcio, Everton*
7/6	Atlantas	h	1-0	*Laurišas*
0/6	Šilutė	a	2-0	*Rodolfo, Paulinho*
4/6	Sūduva	a	0-1	
/7	Šiauliai	a	0-3	*(w/o)*
/7	Žalgiris	h	1-1	*Paulinho*
2/7	Vėtra	h	0-0	
4/7	Ekranas	a	1-3	*Kleyr*
9/7	Kaunas	h	0-2	
/8	Šilutė	h	2-0	*og (Šulkevičius), Paulinho*
2/8	Šiauliai	h	2-4	*Kleyr, Binho*
8/8	Interas	a	5-0	*Ivanov A., Viršilo, Lukša, Zagurskas (p), Matulevičius*
25/8	Atlantas	a	0-1	
/9	Sūduva	h	0-3	
5/9	Žalgiris	a	1-3	*Matulevičius*
8/9	Vėtra	a	1-5	*Eliošius*
22/9	Ekranas	h	1-2	*Eliošius*
30/9	Kaunas	a	0-6	
6/10	Interas	h	9-0	*Papšys 3, Savickas, og (Solovjev), Stempkovski, Freidgeimas 2, Zagurskas*
21/10	Šiauliai	a	1-1	*Ivanov A.*
27/10	Šilutė	a	0-1	
30/10	Atlantas	h	1-4	*Eliošius*
4/11	Sūduva	a	1-7	*Stempkovski*
10/11	Žalgiris	h	0-6	

No	Name	Nat	Pos	Aps	(s)	Gls
11	ADILSON Tibes Granemann	BRA	A	2	(7)	1
21	Wasiu AKANNI	NGA	A	2	(8)	
8	ANDRESON Dourado Ribas	BRA	M	19	(1)	1
15	Darius ARTIOMOVAS		D	13	(1)	
62	Nerijus ASTRAUSKAS		A	2	(1)	
89	Valentin BARANOVSKIJ		M	2	(4)	
20	BINHO Erasmo Santos Silva	BRA	D	22		1
63	Brunas BISKYS		A	1	(1)	
22	Ernestas BISKYS		M	4	(3)	
19	Algirdas BREIKŠTAS		M	14		
86	Jevgenij DOVKŠA		A	1	(4)	
42	Tadas ELIOŠIUS		A	6	(2)	3
22	EVERTON Antônio Pereira	BRA	M	3	(4)	1
3	Georgas FREIDGEIMAS		D	27		2
27	Tadas GRAŽIŪNAS		D	5		
24	Aleksandr IVANOV		A	8	(2)	2
65	Vikentij IVANOV		D	12		
17	Igoris JAKOVLEVAS		G	1		
9	KLEYR Vieira dos Santos	BRA	A	19		11
61	Povilas KRASNOVSKIS		A		(1)	
99	Gediminas KRUŠA		M		(1)	
77	Aivaras LAURIŠAS		A	2	(2)	1
44	Pavel LEUS		G	9	(1)	
5	Vytautas LUKŠA		M	21	(2)	2
6	MÁRCIO da Rosa Loyola	BRA	D	5	(7)	1
88	Deividas MATULEVIČIUS		M	9	(1)	2
10	MULLER Santos da Silva	BRA	A	14	(3)	6
67	Dmitrij OVSEJUK		D	6	(1)	
10	Marius PAPŠYS		M	3	(2)	3
9	Viktor PAŠIN		M	4		
7	José Paulo Maciel Júnior PAULINHO	BRA	M	21		3
68	Vladas POCEVIČIUS		M	12	(1)	
13	Ramūnas RADAVIČIUS		M	21	(1)	
16	RODNEI Francisco de Lima	BRA	D	21		2
18	RODOLFO Kumbrevicius Adorno	BRA	A	6	(4)	3
16	Marius ŠALKAUSKAS		G	2		
69	Vitalijus SAVICKAS		D	1		1
41	Gediminas SKROCKAS		M	5	(5)	
4	Andrejus SOKOLOVAS		D	8		
46	Pavel STEMPKOVSKI		D	9	(2)	2
44	Mantas TAMULIONIS		G	8		
12	Liudvikas VALIUS		G	15		
66	Vitalijus VIRŠILO		D	12		1
35	Eivinas ZAGURSKAS		M	7	(4)	2
55	Artūras ŽULPA		M	1	(3)	

FK ŽALGIRIS

Coach – Arminas Narbekovas

Founded - 1947

MAJOR HONOURS: Lithuanian League - (3) 1991, 1992, 1999; Lithuanian Cup - (5) 1991, 1993, 1994, 1997, 2003 (autumn).

2007				
7/4	Atlantas	a	2-1	*Morinas, Lukoševičius*
10/4	Sūduva	h	1-0	*Misiuk*
15/4	Šilutė	a	0-0	
18/4	Vėtra	a	1-1	*Lukoševičius*
22/4	Ekranas	h	1-0	*Lukoševičius*
25/4	Kaunas	a	1-1	*Mižigurskis*
29/4	Interas	h	3-2	*Morinas 2 (1p), Misiuk*
5/5	Šiauliai	a	1-0	*Misiuk*
8/5	Vilnius	h	1-2	*Mižigurskis*
12/5	Atlantas	h	1-1	*og (Nesterenko)*
19/5	Sūduva	a	1-1	*Morinas*
26/5	Šilutė	h	2-0	*Poderis (p), Morinas*
9/6	Vėtra	h	1-0	*Bursuc*
17/6	Interas	a	2-0	*Mižigurskis, Poderis*
20/6	Kaunas	h	1-0	*Morinas*
24/6	Šiauliai	h	1-1	*Morinas*
30/6	Ekranas	a	1-4	*Mižigurskis*
8/7	Vilnius	a	1-1	*Mižigurskis*
12/7	Atlantas	a	3-1	*Choruži, Morinas, Steško A.*
24/7	Sūduva	h	4-1	*Mižigurskis 2, Lemežis, Dubina*
28/7	Šilutė	a	0-0	
5/8	Kaunas	a	1-1	*Bursuc*
11/8	Ekranas	h	4-1	*Ostap, Morinas, Čurlinov, Lemežis*
18/8	Vėtra	a	1-2	*Ostap*
25/8	Interas	h	7-0	*Kožiak, Čurlinov 4, Mižigurskis 2*
1/9	Šiauliai	a	0-0	
15/9	Vilnius	h	3-1	*Ostap, Mižigurskis, Kožiak*
18/9	Atlantas	h	3-0	*Lemežis, Bursuc, Morinas*
22/9	Sūduva	a	0-1	
30/9	Šilutė	h	3-0	*Čurlinov, Radavičius, Mižigurskis*
6/10	Vėtra	h	0-2	
21/10	Ekranas	a	0-2	
27/10	Kaunas	h	0-5	
30/10	Interas	a	6-0	*Aleksa 2, Lemežis, Mižigurskis, Choruži, Radavičius*
4/11	Šiauliai	h	1-2	*Čurlinov*
10/11	Vilnius	a	6-0	*Čurlinov 3, Bursuc,*

No	Name	Nat	Pos	Aps	(s)	Gls
5	Gerdas ALEKSA		D	9	(2)	2
28	Iulian BURSUC	MDA	M	30	(1)	4
9	Marijan CHORUŽI		M	28	(4)	2
18	Cvetan ČURLINOV	MKD	A	10	(5)	10

2	Aleksei DUBINA	BLR	D	16	(3)	1
8	Ján KOŽIAK	SVK	A	4	(6)	2
15	Virmantas LEMEŽIS		M	23	(7)	6
20	Andrius LIPSKIS		M		(1)	
32	Edvinas LUKOŠEVIČIUS		D	30		3
3	Andrius MILIŠKEVIČIUS		M	4	(8)	
22	Nikolaj MISIUK		A	7	(11)	3
10	Valerijus MIŽIGURSKIS		A	23	(9)	12
14	Igoris MORINAS		M	36		10
4	Bertrand NGAPOUNOU	CMR	D	17		
27	Anatoly OSTAP	MDA	M	25	(2)	3
33	Eimantas PODERIS		M	23	(6)	2
16	Andrius PUOTKALIS		A		(2)	
25	Ramūnas RADAVIČIUS		M	9		2
21	Marius RAPALIS		G	21		
6	Donatas REMĖZA		M		(1)	
11	Aleksandras ROMAŠOVAS		A	1	(4)	
1	Ernestas ŠETKUS		G	15		
30	Artūras STEŠKO		M	2	(13)	1
29	Igoris STEŠKO		D	34		
31	Algirdas SURGAUTAS		G		(1)	
7	Arvydas VEIKUTIS		M	1	(3)	
17	Raimondas VILĖNIŠKIS		M	28	(1)	

PROMOTED CLUBS

SECOND LEVEL FINAL TABLES 2007

		Pld	W	D	L	F	A	Pts
1	FK Alytis Alytus	27	18	6	3	68	15	60
2	FK Rodiklis Kaunas	27	17	6	4	82	25	57
3	FK Nevėžis Kėdainiai	27	15	7	5	48	21	52
4	FK Kruoja Pakruojis	27	14	4	9	48	31	46
5	FK Lietava Jonava	27	12	6	9	45	30	42
6	FK Banga Gargždai	27	10	10	7	44	15	40
7	LKKA ir Teledema Kaunas	27	15	3	9	101	36	48
8	FK Kauno Jėgeriai	27	11	6	10	51	37	39
9	FK Glestum Klaipėda	27	6	6	15	31	68	24
10	FK Vilkmergė Ukmergė	27	6	3	18	34	74	21
11	FK Tauras ERRA Tauragė	27	4	3	20	24	144	15
12	FSK Anykščiai	27	2	4	21	18	98	10

N.B. Alytis Alytus and Rodiklis Kaunas both declined promotion.

First Phase		Pld	W	D	L	F	A	Pts
1	FK Rodiklis Kaunas	22	16	3	3	76	20	51
2	FK Alytis Alytus	22	14	5	3	61	14	47
3	FK Nevėžis Kėdainiai	22	13	6	3	44	17	45
4	FK Kruoja Pakruojis	22	13	4	5	45	23	43
5	FK Lietava Jonava	22	11	4	7	41	25	37
6	FK Banga Gargždai	22	9	7	6	42	12	34
7	LKKA ir Teledema Kaunas	22	10	3	9	76	34	33
8	FK Kauno Jėgeriai	22	7	6	9	34	30	27
9	FK Vilkmergė Ukmergė	22	5	3	14	31	60	18
10	FK Glestum Klaipėda	22	4	6	12	23	59	18
11	FK Tauras ERRA Tauragė	22	3	2	17	17	126	11
12	FSK Anykščiai	22	1	3	18	14	84	6

N.B. After 22 games league split into top and bottom halves of six teams each.

DOMESTIC CUP 2007/0

LFF TAURĖ

FOURTH ROUND

(15/8/07)
Atlantas 1, Banga 0
Lietava 2, Interas 5
Nevėžis 2, Alytis 0
Rodiklis 3, Sakuona 1
Šiauliai 1, Kruoja 0 *(aet)*
Šilutė 1, Vilnius 1 *(aet; 2-4 on pens)*

(19/8/07)
Gariūnai 1, Sūduva 7
Švyturys Marijampolė 0, Kauno Jėgeriai 0 *(aet; 3-4 on pens)*

FIFTH ROUND

(28/8/07)
Atlantas 5, Nevėžis 2
Šiauliai 5, Interas 1
Vilnius 3, Kauno Jėgeriai 0

(3/10/07)
Rodiklis Kaunas 1, Sūduva 2

QUARTER-FINALS

(3/10/07)
Kaunas 4 *(Rimkevičius 20, Rafael 75, Screpis 80, Činikas 90)*, Žalgiris 2 *(Poderis 47, Bursuc 69)*
Vėtra 3 *(Cvetanovski 23, Karčemarskas 33, Gražiūnas 47og)*, Vilnius 2 *(Eliošius 11, Zagurskas 83p)*

(24/10/07)
Ekranas 1 *(Lukšys 15)*, Sūduva 1 *(Klevinskas G. 78) (aet; 4-3 on pens)*

(24/11/07)
Šiauliai 3 *(Šilėnas 49, Lapeikis 98, Viktoravičius 104)*, Atlantas 2 *(Ramonas 70, Delić 109) (aet)*

SEMI-FINALS

(16/4/08 & 30/4/08)
Šiauliai 0, Vėtra 1 *(Šernas 40)*
Vėtra 3 *(Šernas 23, Milošeski 27, Stankevičius 70)*, Šiauliai 0
(Vėtra 4-0)

Kaunas 1 *(Rafael 66)*, Ekranas 0
Ekranas 1 *(Varnas 13)*, Kaunas 5 *(Rafael 31, 43, 54, Grigalevičius 75, Pehlić 88p)*
(Kaunas 6-1)

FINAL

(17/5/08)
Žalgirio stadionas, Vilnius
FBK KAUNAS 2 *(Radžius 49, Rafael 89)*
FK VĖTRA 1 *(Šernas 25)*
Referee - *Kancleris*
KAUNAS – *Kello, Radžius, Kančelskis, Činikas, Manchkhava, Pehlić, ukša (Zubavičius 85), Mendy, Pilibaitis, Rafael, Grigalevičius (Mrowiec 89).*
VĖTRA – *Smishko, Jankauskas, Kijanskas, Majus, Borovskij, Ostap (Razulis 89), Butavičius (Lemežis 55), Milošeski, Šernas, Butrimavičius, Sofroni (Blažys 89).*

Leweck's late winner ends drought

he Centralnyi stadium in the Belarussian town of Gomel may in time become a shrine to Luxembourg football fans for it was there, on the evening of 13 ctober 2007, that Luxembourg finally won a competitive ternational match for the first time in 12 years.

ating Belarus in that UEFA EURO 2008™ tie was an lded bonus. Having lost 55 consecutive qualifying ties, ıxembourg would have been delighted simply to get a aw. In fact, there were many in the camp beseeching idfielder Daniel Da Mota to run down the clock when, ith the score at 0-0, he took possession five minutes into oppage time. Instead he swung the ball into the penalty ea, where his fellow substitute Alphonse 'Fons' Leweck elped himself to a little slice of sporting history by eading it into the net.

ıxembourg's last competitive win had come at home to alta in September 1995 – a month before their last mpetitive point, in a goalless draw at home …Belarus. Now, the drought over, Luxembourg could reathe again, and they almost caused another upset the llowing month when they restricted the Netherlands to 1-0 win in Rotterdam, almost grabbing an equaliser ght at the death. Not surprisingly, Luxembourg's nproved form earned head coach Guy Hellers a four-year ‹tension to his contract.

ne captain of the national side, Sébastien Remy, also njoyed himself in club colours as he skippered F91 udelange to their fourth successive National Division tle. He was one of few indigenous players in a team ominated by French imports and led by a French coach, lichel Lefloachman. The best of the cross-border gionnaires was newcomer Emmanuel Coquelet, who ot only topped the league's scoring charts with 20 goals ut also scooped the Player of the Year prize.

)ominant Dudelange

udelange were once again far too strong for the pposition. Indeed, their superiority was more marked nan ever – as the final figures showed. They played 26 matches, won 23 of them – including all 15 before Christmas – and were defeated just once. Their title triumph was sewn up as early as 17 March, making them the first 2007/08 domestic champions in the whole of Europe. Their final winning margin was a massive 21 points over runners-up Racing FC Union Lëtzebuerg.

Racing, the merger club from the capital, qualified for the UEFA Cup for the first time and were joined in that competition by CS Grevenmacher, who won the Luxembourg Cup, beating FC Victoria Rosport 4-1 in the final. Grevenmacher had thumped the same opponents 6-0 in the league six days earlier, thus ending their six-year stay in the top flight. Also relegated automatically were CS Pétange, the sensational Cup conquerors of champions Dudelange. FC Wiltz '71 also went down after a play-off defeat by FC Sporting Steinfort, who were promoted alongside US Rumelange and CS Fola Esch.

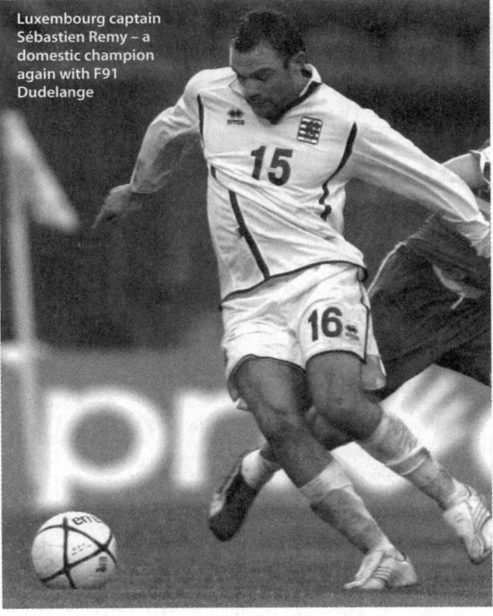
Luxembourg captain Sébastien Remy – a domestic champion again with F91 Dudelange

Fédération Luxembourgeoise de Football (FLF)

BP5
Rue de Limpach
LU-3901 Mondercange
tel - +352 488 665 1
fax - +352 488 665 82
website - www.football.lu
email - flf@football.lu
Year of Formation – 1908
President - Paul Philipp
General Secretary - Joël Wolff
Press Officer – Marc Diedrich
Stadium - Josy Barthel, Luxembourg (8,000)

TOP FIVE ALL-TIME CAPS
Carlo Weis (88); Jeff Strasser (83); Francois Konter (77); Roby Langers (73); Manuel Cardoni (68)

TOP FIVE ALL-TIME GOALS
Leon Mart (16); Gusty Kemp (15); Camille Libar (14); Nicolas Kettel (13); François Müller (12)

NATIONAL TEAM RESULTS 2007/08

22/8/07	Georgia	H	Luxembourg	0-0	
8/9/07	Slovenia (ECQ)	H	Luxembourg	0-3	
12/9/07	Bulgaria (ECQ)	A	Sofia	0-3	
13/10/07	Belarus (ECQ)	A	Gomel	1-0	*Leweck (90+5)*
17/10/07	Romania (ECQ)	H	Luxembourg	0-2	
17/11/07	Netherlands (ECQ)	A	Rotterdam	0-1	
30/1/08	Saudi Arabia	A	Riyadh	1-2	*Peters (88p)*
26/3/08	Wales	H	Luxembourg	0-2	
27/5/08	Cape Verde Islands	H	Luxembourg	1-1	*Leweck (77)*

NATIONAL TEAM APPEARANCES 2007/08

Coach - Guy HELLERS	**10/10/64**		**Geo**	**SVN**	**BUL**	**BLR**	**ROU**	**NED**	**Ksa**	**Wal**	**Cpv**	**Caps**	**Go**
Jonathan JOUBERT	12/9/79	Dudelange	G	G	G	G	G	G	G	G	G	20	-
Mario MUTSCH	3/9/84	Aarau (SUI)	D	M	M	D	D	D		D	D	25	-
Eric HOFFMANN	21/6/84	Etzella	D	D	D		D	D	D	D	D	49	-
Kim KINTZIGER	2/4/87	Differdange	D		D	D	D	D	D	D	D	20	-
Jérôme BIGARD	16/2/85	Dudelange	D	D	D							8	-
Ben PAYAL	8/9/88	Dudelange	M46	s46	s46	M79	M68	M			M62	15	-
René PETERS	15/6/81	Hesperange	M	M	M	M	M	M	M	s46	M	57	2
Gilles BETTMER	31/3/89	Freiburg (GER)	M	M	M83	M	M49	M66			M	17	-
Claudio LOMBARDELLI	4/10/87	Jeunesse Esch	M70	M46		M45			M58			16	-
Dan COLLETTE	2/4/85	Jeunesse Esch	A61		s46				s26 /90			19	-

ATIONAL TEAM APPEARANCES 2007/08 (contd.)

			Geo	SVN	BUL	BLR	ROU	NED	Ksa	Wal	Cpv	Caps	Goals
KITENGE	12/11/87	Emmendingen (GER)	A54	s63		A61	A57	A50					
		/Lienden (NED)							A75	s53	A70	10	-
s FERREIRA	24/8/80	Etzella	s46	M		s79	s49		M		s62	18	-
el HUSS	4/10/79	Grevenmacher	s54	A63	A46							46	2
el DA MOTA	11/9/85	Etzella	s61	s52	s83	s61	s57	s85	A26	s66	s70	11	-
on DE SOUSA	24/2/88	Jeunesse Esch	s70								s90	6	-
STRASSER	5/10/74	Metz (FRA)		D	M			D		M		83	5
nie PEIFFER	7/4/80	Differdange		D52	D46							2	-
stien REMY	19/4/74	Dudelange			M	M	M	M		M	M90	51	-
oît LANG	19/12/83	Fola Esch				D	D		D	D46		7	-
WAGNER	3/12/69	Differdange				D	D	D	D	D		5	-
onse LEWECK	12/12/81	Etzella				s45	s68	s66	s58	M66	s54	40	3
lien JOACHIM	10/8/86	Jamoigne (BEL)						s50 /85					
		/Differdange								A53	A54	15	1
rd GEISBUSCH	4/5/88	Fola Esch							D90			1	-
o LUKIC	22/5/83	Dudelange							s75	s90		2	-
than PROIETTI	17/7/82	Hamm							s90			1	-
y TWIMUMU	25/8/90	Jeunesse Arlonaise (BEL)							s90			1	-
GERSON	5/2/90	Kongsvinger (NOR)								M90		1	-
simo MARTINO	18/9/90	Racing									D	1	

DOMESTIC LEAGUE 2007/08

ATIONAL DIVISION FINAL TABLE

		Home					Away					Total					
	Pld	W	D	L	F	A	W	D	L	F	A	W	D	L	F	A	Pts
F91 Dudelange	26	12	1	0	33	5	11	1	1	41	7	23	2	1	74	12	71
Racing FC Union Lëtzebuerg	26	9	2	2	31	14	5	6	2	19	14	14	8	4	50	28	50
AS Jeunesse Esch	26	8	4	1	29	11	5	2	6	22	28	13	6	7	51	39	45
FC Etzella Ettelbruck	26	7	2	4	29	26	6	3	4	25	22	13	5	8	54	48	44
FC Avenir Beggen	26	5	2	6	17	17	6	2	5	24	21	11	4	11	41	38	37
CS Grevenmacher	26	6	4	3	25	15	4	2	7	20	21	10	6	10	45	36	36
FC Differdange 03	26	8	0	5	31	21	3	2	8	12	22	11	2	13	43	43	35
FC RM Hamm Benfica	26	5	2	6	19	23	4	3	6	13	25	9	5	12	32	48	32
FC Swift Hesperange	26	3	5	5	13	21	5	2	6	23	23	8	7	11	36	44	31
UN Käerjéng 97	26	3	5	5	16	22	5	1	7	14	18	8	6	12	30	40	30
FC Progrès Niedercorn	26	4	4	5	16	22	3	3	7	15	24	7	7	12	31	46	28
FC Wiltz 71	26	5	2	6	16	19	1	5	7	17	29	6	7	13	33	48	25
FC Victoria Rosport	26	5	2	6	19	25	1	4	8	10	31	6	6	14	29	56	24
CS Pétange	26	3	4	6	17	24	1	3	9	10	26	4	7	15	27	50	19

TOP GOALSCORERS

20 Emmanuel COQUELET (Dudelange)

18 Aoued AOUAÏCHIA (Hamm)
Daniel DA MOTA (Etzella)

16 Daniel HUSS (Grevenmacher)

15 Didier CHAILLOU (Progrès)

14 Aderito Vaz DOS REIS (Avenir)

12 Thomas GRUSZCZYNSKI (Dudelange)
Sergio PUPOVAC (Racing)

11 Stéphane MARTINE (Racing)

10 Pierre PISKOR (Differdange)
Loïc CANTONNET (Jeunesse Esch)
Soriba CAMARA (Racing)

CLUB-BY-CLUB

FC AVENIR BEGGEN

Coach – Fernando Gutiérrez (ARG)

Founded - 1915

MAJOR HONOURS: Luxembourg League - (6) 1969, 1982, 1984, 1986, 1993, 1994; Luxembourg Cup - (7) 1983, 1984, 1987, 1992, 1993, 1994, 2002.

2007

5/8	Jeunesse Esch	h	1-2	*Reisinho*
12/8	Differdange	a	3-2	*Dos Reis, Lazaar, Gomes*
19/8	Käerjéng	h	2-1	*Gomes, Dos Reis*
26/8	Dudelange	a	0-1	
2/9	Hesperange	h	1-3	*Dos Reis*
16/9	Rosport	a	3-1	*Dos Reis 2, Reisinho*
23/9	Hamm	a	3-1	*Poirot, Gomes, Dos Reis*
30/9	Progrès	h	1-2	*Gomes*
7/10	Pétange	a	2-1	*Nzita, Vieira*
21/10	Grevenmacher	h	1-2	*Alomerović Assim*
28/10	Racing	a	4-1	*og (Babačić), Dos Reis 2, Vieira*
4/11	Wiltz	h	1-2	*Lazaar*
11/11	Etzella	a	2-2	*Nzita, Lazaar*
25/11	Differdange	h	1-0	*Gomes*
2/12	Käerjéng	a	3-3	*Dos Reis, Alomerović Assim, Gomes*

2008

17/2	Hesperange	a	1-2	*Oliveira M.*
24/2	Dudelange	h	1-0	*Dos Reis*
2/3	Rosport	h	4-1	*Alomerović Asmir, Dos Reis 2, Stojadinovic*
9/3	Hamm	h	3-1	*Stojadinovic, Toyisson, Dos Reis*
16/3	Progrès	a	1-2	*Nzita*
30/3	Pétange	h	1-1	*Reisinho (p)*
6/4	Grevenmacher	a	0-2	
20/4	Racing	h	0-0	
27/4	Wiltz	a	2-0	*Olavo, Dos Reis*
4/5	Etzella	h	0-2	
18/5	Jeunesse Esch	a	0-3	

Name	Nat	Pos	Aps	(s)	Gls
Asmir ALOMEROVIĆ	BIH	M	7	(2)	1
Assim ALOMEROVIĆ	BIH	M	24		2
Daniele BEI		M	10		
Philippe CHRISMOUSSE	FRA	G	26		
Abdu DIAGNÉ	FRA	M		(4)	
Mato DURIC		A	2	(7)	
José GOMES	CPV	A	19		6
Mourad LAZAAR	MAR	M	7	(10)	3
Bobby MENDES	POR	M	15	(5)	
Patrick MINAS	POR	M	14	(4)	
Geoffrey MONIVAS	FRA	D	14	(3)	
Randy NZITA	COD	M	16	(5)	3
Spencer OLAVO	CPV	M	22	(1)	1
Miguel OLIVEIRA	POR	M	1		1
Jérôme POIROT	FRA	D	8	(9)	1
Miguel REISINHO	POR	M	19	(2)	3
Laurent ROCHETTE	BEL	D	11		
Igor STOJADINOVIC		M	11	(3)	2
João TAVARES	CPV	M	1	(4)	
Basile TOYISSON	TOG	D	13	(2)	1
Aderito Vaz DOS REIS	CPV	A	22		14
Gabriel VIEIRA	POR	M	24		2
Aldo ZAMPA	ITA	D		(1)	

FC DIFFERDANGE 03

Coach – Maurice Spitoni

Founded – 2003

2007

4/8	Hesperange	a	2-1	*Ribeiro B., Piskor*
12/8	Avenir	h	2-3	*Wagner 2*
18/8	Hamm	a	3-2	*Wagner, Christophe, Piskor (p)*
26/8	Progrès	h	1-2	*Piskor*
1/9	Pétange	a	1-0	*Ribeiro B.*
19/9	Grevenmacher	h	0-3	
23/9	Racing	a	0-0	
30/9	Wiltz	h	4-1	*Lebresne, Ribeiro P., Piskor 2*
7/10	Etzella	a	0-2	
21/10	Jeunesse Esch	h	3-0	*Piskor, Kintziger, Christophe*
4/11	Käerjéng	a	2-2	*Christophe, Piskor*
11/11	Dudelange	h	2-4	*Christophe, Piskor (p)*
25/11	Avenir	a	0-1	
28/11	Rosport	h	2-1	*Peiffer, Ribeiro P.*
16/12	Hamm	h	2-3	*og (Lopez), Albanese*

2008

17/2	Pétange	h	2-1	*Piskor, Joachim*
24/2	Progrès	a	0-1	
9/3	Racing	h	3-1	*Schauls, Joachim, Albanese*
12/3	Grevenmacher	a	2-3	*Joachim, Wagner*
16/3	Wiltz	a	0-3	
30/3	Etzella	h	3-1	*Joachim 2, Amodio*
5/4	Jeunesse Esch	a	0-2	
20/4	Rosport	a	2-3	*Piskor (p), Schauls*
27/4	Käerjéng	h	5-0	*Wagner, Joachim, Bukvic, Christophe, Carème*
4/5	Dudelange	a	0-2	
18/5	Hesperange	h	2-1	*Christophe, Schauls*

Name	Nat	Pos	Aps	(s)	Gls
Mirko ALBANESE		A	1	(14)	2
Paolo AMODIO		A	4	(3)	1
Ante BUKVIC		D	21		1
Laurent CARÈME	FRA	M	8	(11)	1
David CHALMANDRIER		M		(1)	
Marcel CHRISTOPHE		A	20	(2)	6
Miguel DA COSTA	POR	G	1		
Ibrahim DIOP	FRA	M	1	(1)	
Adel GARA		A		(1)	
Karim GROUNE	FRA	D	7		
Aurélien JOACHIM		A	9	(2)	6
Michel KETTENMEYER		M	10	(5)	
Kim KINTZIGER		D	25		1
Max KRIPPLER		M	4	(6)	
Philippe LEBRESNE	FRA	M	23	(1)	1
Andy MAY		M	1	(5)	
Jérémie PEIFFER		D	17	(1)	1
Igor PEREIRA	POR	A		(1)	
Pierre PISKOR	FRA	A	20		10
Bruno RIBEIRO	POR	M	10	(4)	2
Pedro RIBEIRO	POR	A	8	(11)	2
André RODRIGUES	POR	D	11	(3)	
Manou SCHAULS		D	14	(2)	3
Yannick SCHLENTZ		G	25		
Darío SORAIRE	ARG	M	21	(1)	
Jean WAGNER		D	25		5

F91 DUDELANGE

Coach – Michel Leflochmoan (FRA)

Founded - 1991

MAJOR HONOURS: Luxembourg League - (7) 2000, 2001, 2002, 2005, 2006, 2007, 2008; Luxembourg Cup - (3) 2004, 2006, 2007.

2007

5/8	Käerjéng	h	1-0	*Coquelet*
12/8	Rosport	a	7-0	*Di Gregorio 2 (1p),*

				Guthleber, Hug, Gruszczynski, Bigard, og (Habte)
/8	Hesperange	a	2-0	Lukic, Gruszczynski (p)
/8	Avenir	h	1-0	Bigard
)	Hamm	a	5-1	Bellini, Coquelet 2, Guthleber, Lukic
'9	Progrès	h	4-1	Louadj, Gruszczynski 2, Bellini
/9	Pétange	a	4-0	Coquelet 3, Souto
/9	Grevenmacher	h	1-0	Gruszczynski
0	Racing	a	2-0	Louadj, Bellini
/10	Wiltz	h	1-0	Souto
'10	Etzella	a	3-1	Louadj 2, Guthleber
1	Jeunesse Esch	h	6-2	Remy 2, Gruszczynski (p), Coquelet, Nascimento, Biver
/11	Differdange	a	4-2	Gruszczynski, Coquelet 2, Souto
/11	Rosport	h	3-0	Gruszczynski, Louadj (p), Coqulelet (p)
2	Hesperange	h	2-0	Guthleber, Louadj

08

/2	Hamm	h	3-0	Di Gregorio 2, Lukic
'2	Avenir	a	0-1	
3	Progrès	a	5-1	Coquelet 3, og (Palazzo), Zeghdane
3	Pétange	h	1-0	Coquelet
/3	Grevenmacher	a	2-0	Hug, Di Gregorio
/3	Racing	h	1-1	Gruszczynski
4	Wiltz	a	2-0	Coquelet, Nascimento
'4	Etzella	h	7-1	Coquelet 2, Zeghdane, Franceschi, Gruszczynski 3
/4	Jeunesse Esch	a	1-1	Bellini
5	Differdange	h	2-0	Bellini, Remy
/5	Käerjéng	a	4-0	Coquelet 3 (1p), Lukic

ame	Nat	Pos	Aps	(s)	Gls
han BELLINI	FRA	M	20	(1)	5
rôme BIGARD		D	16	(2)	2
c BIVER		A	1	(13)	1
ristophe BORBICONI	FRA	D	5	(1)	
nmanuel COQUELET	FRA	A	22	(1)	20
ris DI GREGORIO	FRA	A	8	(2)	5
exandre FRANCESCHI	FRA	D	24		1
omas GRUSZCZYNSKI	FRA	A	15	(3)	12
urent GUTHLEBER	FRA	D	23		4
reddine HAMMANI	TUN	M	2		
ël HUG	FRA	M	23		2
ierry JOLY	FRA	M	1		
nathan JOUBERT		G	26		
mir LOUADJ	FRA	M	14	(1)	6
rko LUKIC		A	6	(16)	4
milton NASCIMENTO	CPV	M	5	(11)	2
ïc MOUNY	FRA	D	25		
n PAYAL		M	1	(7)	
n POLIDORI		A		(2)	
bastien REMY		M	14	(8)	3
nny SOUTO	CPV	M	25		3
hit ZEGHDANE	FRA	M	10	(5)	2

FC ETZELLA ETTELBRUCK

Coach – Luc Holtz; (10/5/07) Fränz Novak

Founded - 1917

MAJOR HONOURS: Luxembourg Cup - (1) 2001.

)07

8	Hamm	a	1-2	Leweck C.
2/8	Progrès	h	4-2	Da Luz, Mannon, Févry, Da Mota Daniel
3/8	Pétange	a	1-1	Da Mota Daniel
5/8	Grevenmacher	h	1-5	Bernard
'9	Racing	a	2-3	Mannon, Rocha
19/9	Wiltz	h	3-1	Lopes 2, Da Mota Daniel
23/9	Rosport	h	1-2	Leweck A.
30/9	Jeunesse Esch	a	2-2	Lopes, Da Luz
7/10	Differdange	h	2-0	Hoffmann (p), Lopes
21/10	Käerjéng	a	0-0	
28/10	Dudelange	h	1-3	Da Mota Daniel
4/11	Hesperange	a	5-1	Hoffmann, Leweck A. 2, Da Mota Daniel, Leweck C.
11/11	Avenir	h	2-2	Leweck C., Rocha
25/11	Progrès	a	3-0	Leweck A., Da Mota Daniel, Rocha
2/12	Pétange	h	3-1	Hoffmann, Da Mota Daniel 2 (1p)

2008

17/2	Racing	h	2-2	Da Luz, Da Mota Daniel
24/2	Grevenmacher	a	1-0	Rocha
2/3	Wiltz	a	3-1	Leweck C., Holtz, Da Mota Daniel
9/3	Rosport	a	3-2	Da Mota David, Da Mota Daniel, Leweck A. (p)
16/3	Jeunesse Esch	h	5-4	Da Luz 2, Da Mota Daniel 2, Leweck C. (p)
30/3	Differdange	a	1-3	Da Mota Daniel
6/4	Käerjéng	h	0-3	
23/4	Dudelange	a	1-7	Da Mota Daniel
27/4	Hesperange	h	2-1	Da Mota Daniel, Da Luz
4/5	Avenir	a	2-0	Da Mota Daniel, Da Mota David
18/5	Hamm	h	3-0	Da Luz, Da Mota Daniel, Fernandes

Name	Nat	Pos	Aps	(s)	Gls
Nilton ALVES Tavares	CPV	M		(1)	
Daniel BERNARD		M	5	(4)	1
Marc BINSFELD		D	12	(2)	
Gabriel BOMBÉLÉ	BEL	A		(1)	
Claudio DA LUZ		A	24		7
Daniel DA MOTA		A	22	(1)	18
David DA MOTA	POR	D	13	(2)	2
Luca DAMMICO	ITA	A	1	(1)	
DELGADO	POR	M		(1)	
Christophe DIEDERICH		G	12		
Sidney DO ROSARIO	CPV	M		(5)	
Gilles ENGELDINGER		D	18	(3)	
Ben FEDERSPIEL		D	4	(3)	
Jorge FERNANDES		M	21	(1)	1
Carlos FERREIRA		M	22	(3)	
Fabian FÉVRY	BEL	A	4	(2)	1
Joé FLICK		G	14		
Eric HOFFMANN		D	24		3
Luc HOLTZ		M		(13)	1
Alphonse LEWECK		M	19	(2)	5
Charles LEWECK		M	25		5
Carlos LISBOA	POR	A	2	(5)	
Cleudir LOPES	CPV	A	5		4
Paul MANNON		M	7	(1)	2
Jacques PLEIN		D	10	(2)	
Claude REITER		D	10	(7)	
Nilton ROCHA	CPV	A	12	(5)	4
Jonathan ZINELLI		M		(1)	

CS GREVENMACHER

Coach – Claude Osweiler

Founded - 1909

MAJOR HONOURS: Luxembourg League - (1) 2003; Luxembourg Cup - (4) 1995, 1998, 2003, 2008.

2007

5/8	Rosport	a	0-3	
12/8	Racing	a	2-4	Huss 2 (1p)
18/8	Wiltz	h	2-2	Huss, Thimmesch

26/8	Etzella	a	5-1	*Heinz, Sözen 2, Fleck 2*
2/9	Jeunesse Esch	h	4-2	*Sözen, Huss 2, Fleck*
19/9	Differdange	a	3-0	*Huss, Munoz, Di Domenico (p)*
23/9	Käerjéng	h	1-0	*Fleck*
30/9	Dudelange	a	0-1	
7/10	Hesperange	h	1-2	*Munoz*
21/10	Avenir	a	2-1	*Huss, Sözen*
4/11	Progrès	a	3-1	*Huss 2 (1p), Sözen*
11/11	Pétange	h	3-1	*Lörig, Fleck, Huss*
25/11	Racing	h	1-1	*Di Domenico (p)*
2/12	Wiltz	a	1-1	*Wolff*
5/12	Hamm	h	0-0	
2008				
17/2	Jeunesse Esch	a	1-2	*Munoz*
24/2	Etzella	h	0-1	
9/3	Käerjéng	a	1-2	*Schmitt V.*
12/3	Differdange	h	3-2	*Huss, Siebenaler, Lörig*
16/3	Dudelange	h	0-2	
30/3	Hesperange	a	1-1	*Huss*
6/4	Avenir	h	2-0	*Fleck, Huss*
20/4	Hamm	a	0-2	
27/4	Progrès	h	2-2	*Huss 2 (1p)*
4/5	Pétange	a	1-2	*Munoz*
18/5	Rosport	h	6-0	*Munoz 3, Huss, Sözen, Thimmesch*

Name	Nat	Pos	Aps	(s)	Gls
Christian ALBRECHT	GER	D	20	(1)	
Nouar BENLARIBI	FRA	D	8	(1)	
Anton BOZIC		M	5	(6)	
Christian BRAUN		M	1		
Sven DI DOMENICO		M	23		2
Paul ENGEL		D	5	(4)	
Michael FLECK	GER	A	15	(6)	6
Tim HEINZ		D	15		1
Nino HELBIG	GER	M	11	(6)	
Jérôme HENROT	FRA	D		(2)	
Daniel HUSS		A	25		16
Mathias JÄNISCH		M	11	(5)	
Tobias LÖRIG	GER	D	24		2
Tom MUNOZ		A	11	(12)	7
Marc OBERWEIS		G	24		
Marc PLEIMLING	GER	G	2	(1)	
Michael SCHMITT	GER	M	5	(1)	
Volker SCHMITT	GER	D	13	(2)	1
Tom SIEBENALER		M	6		1
Fatih SÖZEN	GER	A	12	(5)	6
Thierry STEIMETZ	FRA	M	10	(1)	
Luc THIMMESCH		M	14	(7)	2
Julien TURNAU	FRA	D	8	(2)	
Stefan WAGNER	GER	A	1	(6)	
Eric WOLFF	GER	M	17	(5)	1

FC RM HAMM BENFICA

Coach – Augusto Dias Martins (POR); (22/10/07) Reinaldo Gomes (POR); (6/12/07) Michael Lofy (GER)

Founded – 2004

2007				
5/8	Etzella	h	2-1	*Huberty, Aouaïchia*
13/8	Jeunesse Esch	a	1-1	*Aouaïchia*
18/8	Differdange	h	2-3	*Huberty, Aouaïchia*
26/8	Käerjéng	a	2-1	*Huberty, Molinero*
2/9	Dudelange	h	1-5	*Kehal*
19/9	Hesperange	a	0-2	
23/9	Avenir	h	1-3	*Huberty*
30/9	Rosport	a	1-0	*Aouaïchia*
7/10	Progrès	a	0-3	
21/10	Pétange	h	0-2	
4/11	Racing	h	0-3	
11/11	Wiltz	a	3-3	*Aouaïchia 3*
25/11	Jeunesse Esch	h	0-1	
5/12	Grevenmacher	a	0-0	
16/12	Differdange	a	3-2	*Kehal 2, Aouaïchia*
2008				
17/2	Dudelange	a	0-3	
24/2	Käerjéng	h	2-0	*Kehal, Calado*
2/3	Hesperange	h	3-1	*Aouaïchia 3*
9/3	Avenir	a	1-3	*Kehal*
16/3	Rosport	h	2-2	*Aouaïchia, Kehal*
30/3	Progrès	h	3-1	*Hergott, Aouaïchia 2*
6/4	Pétange	a	2-1	*Aouaïchia 2*
20/4	Grevenmacher	h	2-0	*Cicchirillo, Aouaïchia*
27/4	Racing	a	0-3	
4/5	Wiltz	h	1-1	*Aouaïchia*
18/5	Etzella	a	0-3	

Name	Nat	Pos	Aps	(s)	Gls
Norbert ALMEIDA	POR	M	2	(2)	
Pasquale ANTONICELLI	ITA	M	4	(13)	
Aoued AOUAÏCHIA	FRA	A	23	(1)	18
José BARETTO	POR	D	7		
Abdellah BETTAHAR	FRA	D	12		
Andrea BORELLI		D	8	(9)	
Denis CABRILLON		D	11	(5)	
Angelo CALADO Ventura	POR	M	9	(1)	1
Frédéric CICCHIRILLO	FRA	A	4	(7)	1
Yannick COSTA POVOA	POR	M		(5)	
Patrick Figueiredo LADEIRA	POR	M		(1)	
Stéphane HERGOTT	FRA	D	22		1
Fabian HUBERTY	BEL	A	12	(1)	4
Evariste KABONGO	COD	M	24		
Djilali KEHAL	FRA	M	25		6
José LIMA	POR	M	11		
David LOPEZ	FRA	D	25		
Kevin MOLINERO	FRA	M	19		1
Ernes MUHOVIĆ	BIH	M	2	(5)	
Jonathan PROIETTI		M	17	(1)	
Ricardo RAMIRES	POR	M	9		
Abderahmane SALLANI	MAR	D	14	(2)	
Pit THEIS		G	20	(1)	
Jérome WINCKEL		G	6		

AS JEUNESSE ESCH

Coach – Jacques Muller

Founded - 1907

MAJOR HONOURS: Luxembourg League - (27) 1921, 1937, 1951, 1954 1958, 1959, 1960, 1963, 1967, 1968, 1970, 1973, 1974, 1975, 1976, 197 1980, 1983, 1985, 1987, 1988, 1995, 1996, 1997, 1998, 1999, 2004; Luxembourg Cup - (12) 1935, 1937, 1946, 1954, 1973, 1974, 1976, 198 1988, 1997, 1999, 2000.

2007				
5/8	Avenir	a	2-1	*Sabotic, Martin*
13/8	Hamm	h	1-1	*Rougeaux*
18/8	Progrès	a	2-3	*Cantonnnet, Sagramola*
26/8	Pétange	h	4-1	*Stoklosa 2, Baudry (p), Collette*
2/9	Grevenmacher	a	2-4	*Cantonnet, Deidda*
19/9	Racing	h	2-0	*Cantonnet 2*
23/9	Wiltz	a	4-0	*Marchal 3, Baudry*
30/9	Etzella	h	2-2	*Marchal, Deidda*
7/10	Rosport	h	2-0	*Rougeaux, Cantonnet*
21/10	Differdange	a	0-3	
4/11	Dudelange	a	2-6	*Marchal, Piron*
11/11	Hesperange	h	4-1	*Marchal 3, Martin*
25/11	Hamm	a	1-0	*Cantonnet*
28/11	Käerjéng	h	2-3	*Piron, Baudry*
2/12	Progrès	h	0-0	
2008				
17/2	Grevenmacher	h	2-1	*Piron, Rougeaux*
24/2	Pétange	a	2-2	*Piron, Martin*
2/3	Racing	a	0-3	
9/3	Wiltz	h	4-1	*Cantonnet, Rougeaux, Martin, Marchal (p)*
16/3	Etzella	a	4-5	*Stoklosa, Baudry,*

				Martin, Cantonnet
'/3	Rosport	a	1-0	*Cantonnet (p)*
	Differdange	h	2-0	*Piron 2*
'/4	Käerjéng	a	1-0	*Rougeaux*
'/4	Dudelange	h	1-1	*Rougeaux*
	Hesperange	a	1-1	*Piron*
'/5	Avenir	h	3-0	*Rougeaux, Piron, Cantonnet*

me	Nat	Pos	Aps	(s)	Gls
nnick AFOUN		D		(1)	
vier BAUDRY	FRA	D	17	(3)	4
c CANTONNET	FRA	A	22	(3)	10
rc CHAUVEHEID	BEL	M	10		
dric CLERC	FRA	M	8	(3)	
n COLLETTE		M	16	(1)	1
yton DE SOUSA		D	5	(4)	
io DEIDDA	ITA	A		(18)	2
phane GILLET		G	18		
n LEHNEN		D	21	(2)	
udio LOMBARDELLI		M	7	(4)	
dy MARCHAL	FRA	A	13	(3)	9
vin MARTIN	FRA	M	26		5
urent PELLEGRINO	FRA	D	24		
phane PIRON	BEL	A	17	(3)	8
ris RAMDEDOVIĆ	SRB	D	1	(4)	
vy ROUGEAUX	FRA	M	20	(4)	7
ad SABOTIC		M	24	(2)	1
ris SAGRAMOLA		A	4	(10)	1
bastien SCHERER	FRA	G	8		
mian STOKLOSA	GER	D	21	(3)	3
ki WAGNER	GER	M	4	(3)	
lain WEITE TCHUMOU		M		(1)	

UN KÄERJÉNG 97

Coach – Angelo Fiorucci

Founded – 1997

07				
	Dudelange	a	0-1	
'8	Hesperange	h	1-5	*Thill*
'8	Avenir	a	1-2	*Marinelli*
'8	Hamm	h	1-2	*Pace*
	Progrès	a	3-1	*Pace, Matos, Kivunghe*
'9	Pétange	h	3-0	*Mukenge, Boulahfari 2*
'9	Grevenmacher	a	0-1	
'9	Racing	h	0-1	
0	Wiltz	a	1-0	*Fassbender*
'10	Etzella	h	0-0	
1	Differdange	h	2-2	*Martins, Bianchini*
'11	Rosport	h	1-1	*Scholer*
'11	Hesperange	a	2-0	*Fassbender, Kivunghe*
'11	Jeunesse Esch	a	3-2	*Mukenge 2, Bianchini*
2	Avenir	h	3-3	*Ramdedović (p), Boulahfari, Rolandi*
08				
'2	Progrès	h	1-1	*Fassbender*
'2	Hamm	a	0-2	
2	Pétange	a	0-0	
	Grevenmacher	h	2-1	*Mukenge, Bianchini*
'3	Racing	a	0-2	
'3	Wiltz	h	2-1	*Fassbender 2*
	Etzella	a	3-0	*Mukenge 3*
'4	Jeunesse Esch	h	0-1	
'4	Differdange	a	0-5	
	Rosport	a	1-2	*Bianchini*
'5	Dudelange	h	0-4	

me	Nat	Pos	Aps	(s)	Gls
ik AKSOY	FRA	M	3	(1)	
nnick BIANCHINI		A	10	(9)	4
chid BOULAHFARI	FRA	M	20	(4)	3
ny CUNHA	POR	D		(1)	
ilo DA COSTA	POR	D	20		
Luc DEMEYER		A		(1)	
Steve DUNKEL		G	2	(1)	
Jean-Philippe FACQUES	FRA	D	14	(2)	
Frédéric FASSBENDER	FRA	A	7	(6)	5
Alessandro FIORANI		M	1	(3)	
Mutamba KIVUNGHE	BEL	M	17	(2)	2
Kevin LEITE		D	22	(3)	
Franco LUISI		M	1	(1)	
Jérôme MARCOLINO		D		(2)	
Vito MARINELLI		M	18	(5)	1
Gil MARTINS	POR	M	8	(1)	1
Florian MATEOS	FRA	A	7	(7)	
Telmo MATOS	POR	D	13	(7)	1
Remy MUKENGE	FRA	A	16	(6)	7
Elmedin MUSLIĆ	CRO	M	1		
Carlo PACE		A	10	(1)	2
Henid RAMDEDOVIĆ	MNE	D	25	(1)	1
Julien ROLANDI	FRA	M	24		1
Cleyton SANTOS PIRES	CPV	M	2		
Frank SCHAMMEL		M		(1)	
Christophe SCHOLER		D	16	(5)	1
Sergio SILVA COSTA	POR	G	24		
Xavier THILL	FRA	A	1	(5)	1
Karim ZAMOUM	FRA	D	4	(1)	

CS PÉTANGE

Coach – Bernard Mladinović (SRB); (23/9/07) Florim Alijaj (BIH)

Founded - 1909

MAJOR HONOURS: Luxembourg Cup – (1) 2005.

2007				
5/8	Racing	h	2-2	*Morocutti 2*
12/8	Wiltz	a	0-1	
18/8	Etzella	h	1-1	*Cangini*
26/8	Jeunesse Esch	a	1-4	*Peinado*
1/9	Differdange	h	0-1	
19/9	Käerjéng	a	0-3	
23/9	Dudelange	h	0-4	
28/9	Hesperange	a	2-2	*Dervisević 2 (2p)*
7/10	Avenir	h	1-2	*Zoglia*
21/10	Hamm	a	2-0	*Derra, Zoglia*
28/10	Progrès	h	1-2	*Morocutti*
4/11	Rosport	a	1-2	*Dervisević*
11/11	Grevenmacher	a	1-3	*Dervisević (p)*
25/11	Wiltz	h	3-2	*Dervisević, Derra, Morocutti*
2/12	Etzella	a	1-3	*Morocutti*
2008				
17/2	Differdange	a	1-2	*Derra*
24/2	Jeunesse Esch	h	2-2	*Steger, Morocutti*
29/2	Käerjéng	h	0-0	
9/3	Dudelange	a	0-1	
16/3	Hesperange	h	1-3	*Steger*
30/3	Avenir Beggen	a	1-1	*Steger*
6/4	Hamm	h	1-2	*Morocutti*
20/4	Progrès	a	0-0	
27/4	Rosport	h	3-2	*Fiorentino 2, Morocutti*
4/5	Grevenmacher	h	2-1	*Steger 2*
18/5	Racing	a	0-4	

Name	Nat	Pos	Aps	(s)	Gls
Alen ALOMEROVIĆ	BIH	M	5	(3)	
Abdellah BENCHAMMA	ALG	A	1	(9)	
Rachid BENMERIENNE	ALG	A	2	(7)	
Alija BESIC		G	24		
Mourad BOUKELLAL	ALG	M	21	(2)	
David CANGINI	FRA	M	17		1
Tun DEFAY		D	4	(2)	
Ousmane DERRA	BFA	M	17	(5)	3
Jasmin DERVISEVIĆ	SRB	M	16		5
Hervé FELLER		G	2		
Mimo FIORENTINO	ITA	A	9	(10)	2
Tony GASPAR	POR	M		(1)	
Jasmin HODŽIĆ	BIH	D	3	(4)	

Grégory LUJIEN	FRA	D	11		
Virgil MAGRI	BEL	M	2		
Dario MARIC		D	20	(1)	
Didier MATUSZYK	FRA	D	18	(2)	
Manuel MOROCUTTI		M	21	(5)	8
Damir MUHOVIC		M	18	(2)	
Stefano NONNIS	FRA	D	10		
Junior NOUBISSI	CIV	D	1	(1)	
Douglas PEINADO	BRA	D	18		1
Enver SABOTIĆ	BIH	D	5	(4)	
Ericson SANTOS	POR	M	6	(8)	
André STEGER	GER	A	9		5
David TEXEIRA	POR	M	6	(5)	
Namandian TRAORÉ	GUI	A	8	(1)	
Aurélien ZOGLIA	FRA	A	12		2

FC PROGRÈS NIEDERCORN

Coach – Serge Thill; (14/11/07) Jean-Paul Defrang; (5/2/08) Alex Wilhelm

Founded – 1919

MAJOR HONOURS: Luxembourg League – (3) 1953, 1978, 1981; Luxembourg Cup – (4) 1933, 1945, 1977, 1978.

2007				
5/8	Wiltz	h	2-2	*Chaillou 2 (2p)*
12/8	Etzella	a	2-4	*Cabral, Colleatte*
18/8	Jeunesse Esch	h	3-2	*Kabran, Muller, Gilgemann*
26/8	Differdange	a	2-1	*Pinto, Colleatte*
3/9	Käerjéng	h	1-3	*Chaillou (p)*
19/9	Dudelange	a	1-4	*Chaillou*
23/9	Hesperange	h	2-2	*Chaillou, Ghin*
30/9	Avenir	a	2-1	*Chaillou, Rigo*
7/10	Hamm	h	3-0	*Chaillou 2, Pinto*
21/10	Rosport	a	1-2	*Colleatte*
28/10	Pétange	a	2-1	*Chaillou, Pinto*
4/11	Grevenmacher	h	1-3	*Chaillou*
11/11	Racing	a	1-3	*Chaillou (p)*
25/11	Etzella	h	0-3	
2/12	Jeunesse Esch	a	0-0	
2008				
17/2	Käerjéng	a	1-1	*Chaillou*
24/2	Differdange	h	1-0	*Chaillou*
2/3	Dudelange	h	1-5	*Chaillou*
9/3	Hesperange	a	0-1	
16/3	Avenir	h	2-1	*Pinto, Ghin*
30/3	Hamm	a	1-3	*Chaillou (p)*
6/4	Rosport	h	0-0	
20/4	Pétange	h	0-0	
27/4	Grevenmacher	a	2-2	*Kabran 2*
4/5	Racing	h	0-1	
18/5	Wiltz	a	0-1	

Name	**Nat**	**Pos**	**Aps**	**(s)**	**Gls**
Norbert ALMEIDA	POR	M	5	(1)	
Nélson CABRAL	CPV	M	6	(6)	1
David CASTELLANI		G	2		
Didier CHAILLOU	FRA	M	21		15
Marc CHAUSSY		D	18	(2)	
François COLLEATTE	FRA	A	25		3
Amer DAUTBASIĆ	BIH	A	2	(5)	
Philippe FELGEN		G	23		
Enzo GHIN	FRA	D	22		2
Thomas GILGEMANN	FRA	D	26		1
Sven GORZA		M		(3)	
Lambert KABRAN	FRA	A	13	(9)	3
Christophe KAUFMANN	FRA	M	23		
Maurizio MASI		M	23		
Sammy MULLER		A	2	(12)	1
Rocco PALAZZO	ITA	D	2		
Thomas PANEL	FRA	D	1	(1)	
Paulo PINTO	POR	M	18	(7)	4
Jonathan RIGO	FRA	D	26		1
David SOARES MARQUES	POR	D	8	(6)	
Serge THILL		M		(2)	
Xavier THILL	FRA	A	8	(2)	
Daniel VIEIRA	POR	M		(1)	
Christophe WILWERT		G	1		
Nico ZHAN		D	11	(2)	

RACING FC UNION LËTZEBUERG

Coach – Álvaro Cruz (POR)

Founded - 2005

2007				
5/8	Pétange	a	2-2	*Camara 2*
12/8	Grevenmacher	h	4-2	*Pupovac 2, Martine, Belli*
18/8	Rosport	h	4-1	*Schnell, Martine 2, Pupovac*
25/8	Wiltz	a	2-1	*Camara, Feller*
2/9	Etzella	a	3-2	*Pupovac 3*
19/9	Jeunesse Esch	a	0-2	
23/9	Differdange	h	0-0	
30/9	Käerjéng	a	1-0	*Schnell (p)*
7/10	Dudelange	h	0-2	
21/10	Hesperange	a	4-1	*Belabed 2, Feller, Pupovac*
28/10	Avenir	h	1-4	*Schnell (p)*
4/11	Hamm	a	3-0	*Camara, Pupovac 2*
11/11	Progrès	h	3-1	*Pupovac, Schnell, Martine*
25/11	Grevenmacher	a	1-1	*Schnell (p)*
2/12	Rosport	a	1-1	*Schnell (p)*
2008				
17/2	Etzella	h	2-2	*Martine, Belabed*
24/2	Wiltz	h	3-1	*Belabed, Schnell, Martine*
2/3	Jeunesse Esch	h	3-0	*Martine, Pupovac, Camara*
9/3	Differdange	a	1-3	*De Cae*
16/3	Käerjéng	h	2-0	*Belabed (p), Martine*
29/3	Dudelange	a	1-1	*Martine*
6/4	Hesperange	h	1-1	*Camara*
20/4	Avenir	a	0-0	
27/4	Hamm	h	3-0	*Camara 2, Martine*
4/5	Progrès	a	1-0	*Belabed*
18/5	Pétange	h	4-0	*Pupovac, Camara 2, Martine*

Name	**Nat**	**Pos**	**Aps**	**(s)**	**Gl**
Almin BABAČIĆ	BIH	D	10	(8)	
Rachid BELABED	BEL	M	24	(1)	6
Anouar BELLI	BEL	M	5	(2)	1
Soriba CAMARA	GUI	A	21	(1)	10
Michael CARVALHO	POR	A	3	(4)	
Ricardo CENTRONE		M	15	(10)	
Matthew DE CAE	WAL	M	20	(3)	1
Kris D`EXCELLE		M		(5)	
Ramos DOS SANTOS	POR	M		(6)	
Jeff FELLER		D	21	(1)	2
Samuel FORTES	POR	M		(2)	
Stéphane MARTINE	FRA	M	23	(1)	11
Massimo MARTINO		D	6	(3)	
Adis OMEROVIĆ	BIH	M	11	(3)	
Jeff OSTER		G	4	(1)	
Sergio PUPOVAC	FRA	A	18		12
Marc RAUS		D	8	(10)	
Marc REUTER		G	22		
Tom SCHNELL		D	19	(1)	7
Marco SIMÕES	POR	M	20	(2)	
Héctor VARELA	CPV	M		(5)	
Vinh Long WILLESMIN	FRA	D	22		
Saber ZENNANE	FRA	D	14		

FC SWIFT HESPERANGE

Coach – Luc Muller (BEL); (6/3/08) Jean-Marie Nurenberg & Daniel Andreosso

Founded - 1916

MAJOR HONOURS: Luxembourg Cup - (1) 1990.

007

'8	Differdange	h	1-2	*Mendes*
2/8	Käerjéng	a	5-1	*Medina 2, Mendes, Tavares, Roncen*
8/8	Dudelange	h	0-2	
6/8	Rosport	a	2-1	*Schiltz, Schmidt*
/9	Avenir	a	3-1	*Diakhaté, Medina 2*
9/9	Hamm	h	2-0	*Mendes, Schmidt*
3/9	Progrès	a	2-2	*Benachour 2*
8/9	Pétange	h	2-2	*Diakhaté, Ambali*
/10	Grevenmacher	a	2-1	*Mendes, Diakhaté*
1/10	Racing	h	1-4	*Medina*
8/10	Wiltz	a	1-2	*Peters*
'11	Etzella	h	1-5	*Medina*
1/11	Jeunesse Esch	a	1-4	*og (Lehnen)*
5/11	Käerjéng	h	0-2	
/12	Dudelange	a	0-2	

008

7/2	Avenir	h	2-1	*Diakhaté, Calvaruso*
4/2	Rosport	h	0-0	
/3	Hamm	a	1-3	*Benachour*
/3	Progrès	h	1-0	*Schiltz*
6/3	Pétange	a	3-1	*Mendes, Diakhaté, Schiltz*
0/3	Grevenmacher	h	1-1	*Schiltz*
/4	Racing	a	1-1	*Peters (p)*
0/4	Wiltz	h	1-1	*Peters (p)*
7/4	Etzella	a	1-2	*Mendes*
/5	Jeunesse Esch	h	1-1	*Diakhaté*
8/5	Differdange	a	1-2	*Oliveira*

ame	Nat	Pos	Aps	(s)	Gls
aheed AMBALI	NGA	A	6	(13)	1
idi BABA	FRA	M	11	(1)	
lalik BENACHOUR	FRA	M	20	(1)	3
lex BOUKHETAIA	FRA	G	25		
hristophe CALVARUSO	FRA	M	6	(3)	1
onathan DE CAE	WAL	M		(1)	
lohamed DIAKHATÉ	FRA	D	24		6
lugo DIAS	POR	D	5	(6)	
van FAUSTINO	POR	D	6	(6)	
aphael KURAJA	COD	D	13		
elso MALHEIRO GONCALVES	POR	G	1		
bdelatif MANSOURI	FRA	A	1	(2)	
ldino MEDINA	CPV	A	13	(8)	6
lain MENDES	FRA	A	23		6
régory MOLITOR		M	16	(4)	
teve OLIVEIRA	POR	M	10	(3)	1
ndy PERL		A		(3)	
ené PETERS		M	26		3
hristophe QUIRING		M		(1)	
aphaël RONCEN	FRA	A	4	(5)	1
nibal SANTOS	CPV	D	16	(2)	
aurent SCHILTZ		A	21	(1)	4
avid SCHMIDT		A	6	(1)	2
rmando TAVARES	CPV	D	23		1
lvaro VAZ PORTAL	POR	M	5	(3)	
cott WILTGEN		D	5	(2)	
ucas ZATON	ESP	M		(1)	

FC VICTORIA ROSPORT

Coach – Reiner Brinsa (GER)

Founded - 1928

2007

5/8	Grevenmacher	h	3-0	*Görres, Wagner, Boussi*
12/8	Dudelange	h	0-7	
18/8	Racing	a	1-4	*Güntepe*
26/8	Hesperange	h	1-2	*Güntepe*
2/9	Wiltz	a	0-3	
16/9	Avenir	h	1-3	*Zöllner*
23/9	Etzella	a	2-1	*Weber, Boussi*
30/9	Hamm	h	0-1	
7/10	Jeunesse Esch	a	0-2	
21/10	Progrès	h	2-1	*Habte, Wagner*
4/11	Pétange	h	2-1	*Gaspar F., Boussi*
11/11	Käerjéng	a	1-1	*Halimović*
25/11	Dudelange	a	0-3	
28/11	Differdange	a	1-2	*Gaspar G.*
2/12	Racing	h	1-1	*Wagner*

2008

17/2	Wiltz	h	2-2	*Zöllner (p), Wagner*
24/2	Hesperange	a	0-0	
2/3	Avenir	a	1-4	*Wagner*
9/3	Etzella	h	2-3	*Wagner, Berens*
16/3	Hamm	a	2-2	*Berens, Wagner*
30/3	Jeunesse Esch	h	0-1	
6/4	Progrès	a	0-0	
20/4	Differdange	h	3-2	*Boussi, Zöllner (p), Pott*
27/4	Pétange	a	2-3	*Halimović 2*
4/5	Käerjéng	h	2-1	*Wagner, Halimović*
18/5	Grevenmacher	a	0-6	

Name	Nat	Pos	Aps	(s)	Gls
Pedro AZEVEDO	POR	D	4	(10)	
Thomas BERENS	GER	M	11		2
Achmed BOUSSI	GER	A	25		4
Frank BUSCHMANN	GER	D	20		
Achim EBERHARD	GER	M	15	(6)	
Fábio GASPAR	POR	M	20	(4)	1
Gabriel GASPAR	POR	M	19	(2)	1
Denis GIESE	GER	D	16	(3)	
Marc GÖRRES	GER	M	5	(7)	1
Ercemil GÜNTEPE	GER	M	9	(4)	2
Sammy HABTE	GER	D	24		1
Dejvid HALIMOVIĆ	BIH	A		(10)	4
Olivier LICKES		D	16	(2)	
Pol MICHELS		M		(1)	
Laurent MOND		G	26		
Alex PAULOS		D	12	(7)	
Alex POTT		A	6	(12)	1
Frank WAGNER	GER	A	20		8
Mike WEBER		D	17		1
Patrick ZÖLLNER	GER	M	21	(1)	3

FC WILTZ 71

Coach – Joël Crahay (BEL); (24/4/08) Marc Glod

Founded - 1971

2007

5/8	Progrès	a	2-2	*Massart, Florkin (p)*
12/8	Pétange	h	1-0	*Florkin (p)*
18/8	Grevenmacher	a	2-2	*Florkin 2 (2p)*
25/8	Racing	h	1-2	*Mujkić S.*
2/9	Rosport	h	3-0	*Caprasse, Kopecky, Grommen*
19/9	Etzella	a	1-3	*Grommen*
23/9	Jeunesse Esch	h	0-4	
30/9	Differdange	a	1-4	*Ngoma-Muanda*
6/10	Käerjéng	h	0-1	
21/10	Dudelange	a	0-1	
28/10	Hesperange	h	2-1	*Libambu, Alves*
4/11	Avenir	a	2-1	*Alves, Florkin*
11/11	Hamm	h	3-3	*Rosamilia 2, Florkin*
25/11	Pétange	a	2-3	*Grommen 2*
2/12	Grevenmacher	h	1-1	*Kopecky*

2008

17/2	Rosport	a	2-2	*Rosamilia 2*
24/2	Racing	a	1-3	*Remacle*
2/3	Etzella	h	1-3	*Rosamilia*
9/3	Jeunesse Esch	a	1-4	*Remacle*
16/3	Differdange	h	3-0	*Rosamilia, Kalabić 2*

30/3	Käerjéng	a	1-2	*Caprasse*
6/4	Dudelange	h	0-2	
20/4	Hesperange	a	1-1	*Remacle*
27/4	Avenir	h	0-2	
4/5	Hamm	a	1-1	*Kalabić*
18/5	Progrès	h	1-0	*Libambu*FC

Name	Nat	Pos	Aps	(s)	Gls
Anis ADROVIĆ	BIH	M	1	(3)	
Bruno ALVES	POR	A	12	(3)	2
Moussa BAH	GUI	D	8	(6)	
Fernando BARBOSA	POR	A		(1)	
Gianni BUTAZZONI	ITA	D	1	(1)	
Kevin CAPRASSE	BEL	M	19	(3)	2
Steve COLBACH		G	11	(1)	
Anel COSIĆ	BIH	M		(4)	
Manuel DOS SANTOS	POR	M	9	(4)	
Vedad DURAKU	BIH	D		(10)	
Philippe FLORKIN	BEL	M	25	(1)	6
Arnaud FRANSQUET	BEL	G	9		
Johan GROMMEN	BEL	A	9	(1)	4
Emko KALABIĆ	SRB	A	7	(7)	3
Tom KOPECKY		D	23		2
Guy LIBAMBU	BEL	D	25		2
Jiresse MAKENGO	COD	M		(5)	
Gaëtan MASSART	BEL	A	7		1
Mehmet MUJKIĆ	BIH	M	2	(4)	
Sevad MUJKIĆ	BIH	D	22		1
Ngabo MWIZERWA	BEL	M	5	(4)	
Blaise NGOMA-MUANDA	COD	M	15	(2)	1
Christian PAULY		G	6		
Gauthier REMACLE	BEL	M	24	(1)	3
Fabrizio ROSAMILIA	BEL	A	6	(5)	6
Steve SCHAACK		D	22		
Dimitri WAVREILLE	BEL	D	18	(1)	

PROMOTED CLUBS

US RUMELANGE

Coach – Marc Thomé

Founded - 1908

MAJOR HONOURS: Luxembourg Cup - (2) 1968, 1975.

CS FOLA ESCH

Coach – Michael Lofy

Founded – 1906

MAJOR HONOURS: Luxembourg League - (5) 1918, 1920, 1922, 1924, 1930; Luxembourg Cup - (3) 1923, 1924, 1955.

FC SPORTING STEINFORT

Coach – Waldemar Korycki (POL)

Founded - 2007.

SECOND LEVEL FINAL TABLE 2007/08

		Pld	W	D	L	F	A	Pts
1	US Rumelange	26	21	1	4	62	22	64
2	CS Fola Esch	26	18	4	4	72	25	58
3	FC Sporting Steinfort	26	17	5	4	53	23	56
4	FC Mondercange	26	15	5	6	76	41	50
5	FC Minerva Lintgen	26	13	4	9	48	43	43
6	Union Mertert/Wasserbillig	26	11	5	10	55	37	38
7	FC Jeunesse Canach	26	9	7	10	30	40	34
8	FC Erpeldange 72	26	8	9	9	42	44	33
9	FC Sporting Mertzig	26	8	5	13	34	50	29
10	FC Atert Bissen	26	8	4	14	50	46	28
11	FC Cebra 01	26	8	4	14	41	54	28
12	FC Mamer 32	26	6	8	12	37	45	26
13	FC Blue Boys Muhlenbach	26	6	3	17	31	60	21
14	CS Oberkorn	26	1	2	23	16	117	5

PROMOTION/RELEGATION PLAY-OFF

(31/5/08)

FC Wiltz 0, Sporting Steinfort 2

DOMESTIC CUP 2007/08

COUPE DE LUXEMBOURG

1/16 FINALS

(5/3/08)

Mertzig 2, Wiltz 0
Jeunesse Canach 2, Jeunesse Esch 3
Steinfort 2, Avenir 0
Erpeldange 1, Hamm 1 *(aet; 3-5 on pens)*
Mondercange 0, Pétange 5
Fola 1, Käerjéng 1 *(aet; 5-4 on pens)*
Lorentzweiler 0, Racing 4
Oberkorn 0, Etzella 5
Hostert 1, Rosport 3
Diekirch 1, Grevenmacher 3
Mertert/Wasserbillig 0, Progrès 0 *(aet; 6-5 on pens)*
Bertrange 2, Differdange 1
Muhlenbach 3, Hesperange 2
Mamer 6, Bastendorf 1
Bous 0, Sandweiler 4

(6/3/08)

Rumelange 2, Dudelange 4

1/8 FINALS

(21/3/08)

Jeunesse Esch 5, Racing 1
Bertrange 0, Grevenmacher 6

(22/3/08)

Sandweiler 0, Dudelange 8
Steinfort 1, Etzella 3 *(aet)*
Fola 0, Rosport 4
Mertert/Wasserbillig 1, Pétange 1 *(aet; 1-3 on pens)*
Mamer 0, Hamm 3
Muhlenbach 1, Mertzig 1 *(aet; 5-6 on pens)*

QUARTER-FINALS

(12/4/08)

Grevenmacher 3 *(Fleck 72, Bozic 80, Sözen 90)*, Jeunesse Esch 0
Dudelange 0, Pétange 1 *(Steger 56)*

(13/4/08)

Hamm 6 *(Kehal 12, 34, 41, Aouaïchia 26, 68, 83)*, Etzella 0
Mertzig 0, Rosport 4 *(Zöllner 44, 49p, Wagner 53, Pott 70)*

SEMI-FINALS

(10/5/08)

Hamm 0, Grevenmacher 1 *(Di Domenico 41)*
Rosport 1 *(Zöllner 51)*, Pétange 1 *(Morocutti 38) (aet ; 5-4 on pens)*

FINAL

(24/5/08)

Stade Josy Barthel, Luxembourg
CS GREVENMACHER 4 *(Munoz 11, Huss 24, Di Domenico 68, Thimmesch*
FC VICTORIA ROSPORT 1 *(Wagner 81)*
Referee – *Pinto Da Costa*
GREVENMACHER – *Oberweis, Turnau, Helbig, Albrecht, Lörig, Jänisch (Er 74), Steimetz, Di Domenico, Bozic (Thimmesch 71), Huss, Munoz (Sözen 6*
ROSPORT – *Mond, Paulos, Buschmann (Gaspar G. 74), Habte, Giese (Pott 53), Eberhard, Berens, Zöllner, Gaspar F. (Halimović 64), Boussi, Wagner.*

FYR MACEDONIA

)ouble with a price or Rabotnički

Rabotnički made amends for the concession of eir Prva Liga crown to FK Pobeda in 2006/07 by inning not only the league title but also the nal Cup to become the first double winners in FYR donia for eight years.

/hile there was much for the Rabotnički fans to rate during a season in which they were virtually allenged domestically and also reached the first d of the UEFA Cup, where they lost narrowly to sh Premier League club Bolton Wanderers FC, they forced to swallow a bitter pill at the close of the aign when it was announced that the club's n and sponsor for the previous decade, Kometal, witching its allegiance to Skopje rivals FK Vardar. mmediate consequence of this was the transfer of of Rabotnički's top players to Vardar and a likely ge in the pecking order of the two clubs from the al in 2008/09.

regnable lead

otnički's reign of power – three titles in four years s about to end, they certainly went out with a . Mindful of how they had let the title slip through fingers in 2006/07 with a faulty finish, they erased ossibility of a repeat by taking command right the start and building up an impregnable lead. ng opened up with a 0-0 draw at defending pions Pobeda, they notched eleven victories in next 12 games and were still unbeaten at the er break, by which time they were ten points clear e top of the table.

e spring Rabotnički had to do without the services eir leading goalscorer, 20-year-old striker Ivan ovski, who, after finding the net nine times during utumn, was sold to Serbian giants FK Crvena da. Curiously he would remain the club's leading sman by the end of the campaign, with no other r reaching double figures. But if scoring goals was abotnički's forte, keeping them out at the other certainly was. They conceded only eleven goals all season – an average of one every three games – and recorded 24 clean sheets. Furthermore, Dragoljub Bekvalac's team kept their goal intact in six out of eight Cup games, including the final, in which they defeated FK Milano 2-0 with a brace of goals from one of their most consistent performers, attacking midfielder Nderim Nedžipi.

Milano goal-machine

Runners-up in the Cup, Milano also finished second in the league – albeit a distant 13 points adrift of the champions. In many ways the newly promoted provincials from Kumanovo were the team of the season. It was their first campaign in the Prva Liga and, unlike Rabotnički, they scored goals at will, racking up 74 of them in their 33 matches (compared with the champions'

FYR Macedonia's top footballer – Goran Pandev of Lazio

FYR MACEDONIA

Fudbalska Federatsija na Makedonija (FFM)

8-ma Udarna Brigada 31a
MK-1000 Skopje
tel - +389 2 3229042
fax - +389 2 3165448
email - fsm@fsm.org.mk
website – www.ffm.com.mk
President - Haralampie Hadzi-Risteski
General Secretary - Nikola Kostov
Press Officer – Zoran Nikolovski
Stadium - Gradski, Skopje (17,828)

TOP FIVE ALL-TIME CAPS
Goce Sedloski (84); Artim Šakiri (73); Petar Miloševski (53); Georgi Hristov (48); Veliče Šumulikoski (48)

TOP FIVE ALL-TIME GOALS
Georgi Hristov (16); Artim Šakiri (15); Goran Pandev (11); Goran Maznov (10); Saša Ciric (8)

NATIONAL TEAM RESULTS 2007/08

22/8/07	Nigeria	H	Skopje	0-0	
8/9/07	Russia (ECQ)	A	Moscow	0-3	
12/9/07	Estonia (ECQ)	H	Skopje	1-1	*Maznov (30)*
17/10/07	Andorra (ECQ)	H	Skopje	3-0	*Naumoski (30), Sedloski (44), Pandev (59)*
17/11/07	Croatia (ECQ)	H	Skopje	2-0	*Maznov (71), Naumoski (83)*
21/11/07	Israel (ECQ)	A	Tel-Aviv	0-1	
6/2/08	Serbia	H	Skopje	1-1	*Noveski (59)*
26/3/08	Bosnia-Herzegovina	A	Zenica	2-2	*Maznov (40, 45)*
26/5/08	Poland	N	Reutlingen (GER)	1-1	*Maznov (45)*

meagre tally of 51) and providing the league's top two scorers in 15-goal Ivica Gligorovski and 14-goal Saša Stojanović. Milano's big problem was their inability to score against, and beat, Rabotnički. In fact, as well as losing the Cup final, they were beaten by the champions in all three league encounters (2-1, 1-0, 3-1). Still, they qualified for the UEFA Cup twice over, with FK Pelister joining them after finishing in a comfortable third place.

Milano were also responsible for inflicting on Vardar their heaviest ever defeat, 9-1. There was a reason for this, however, with the esteemed club from the capital fielding a youth team due to a boycott of its regular first-teamers over unpaid wages. This defeat was one of five with which Vardar ended the season, and although they finished fourth, they were 32 points behind Rabotnički and just six away from the promotion/relegation play-off mark. FK Sileks and FK Bashkimi, the two teams that filled the play-off spots, both survived, which left just the bottom two, FK Shkendija 79 and FK Cementarnica 55, making the descent into the second tier.

Katanec stays on

The national team of FYR Macedonia did nothing mo than tread water in 2007/08, although they did finally their home hoodoo by winning in Skopje after an 11- barren run, beating Andorra and Croatia back-to-back UEFA EURO 2008™ qualifiers. The team's Slovenian coa Srečko Katanec was offered a new two-year contract, which, after some deliberation and with certain condi he accepted. The countdown to the 2010 FIFA World C qualifying programme began with three successive d – and three more goals for striker Goran Maznov, whic brought his cumulative international total to ten. One ahead of him was Goran Pandev, who, while relatively quiet for his country, reaffirmed his emergence as a genuine European star with another terrific season for Lazio – both in Serie A and the UEFA Champions Leag

TIONAL TEAM APPEARANCES 2007/08

- Srečko KATANEC (SVN) 16/7/63			Nga	RUS	EST	AND	CRO	ISR	Srb	Bih	Pol	Caps	Goals
ILOŠEVSKI	6/12/73	Paralimni (CYP)	G	G	G		G	G	G46	s46	G	53	-
ıdar VASOSKI	21/11/79	Eintracht (GER)	D46	D88	D						s46	34	2
EDLOSKI	10/4/74	Mattersburg (AUT)	D77	D	D	D	D88	D	D60	D	D	84	7
TRESKI	19/2/79	Energie (GER)	D	D		D	D	D	D	D	D	45	1
AZAREVSKI	9/6/83	Groclin (POL)	M60	M	M	M	M	M	M				
		/Metalist (UKR)								M	M46	23	-
POPOV	24/1/84	Levadiakos (GRE)	M	M		M	M	M	M	M	M58	17	1
ŠUMULIKOSKI	24/4/81	Bursaspor (TUR)	M	M	M	M	M	M					
		/Ipswich (ENG)							M70	M		48	1
TASEVSKI	20/5/84	Levski (BUL)	M	M	M	M84	M	M46	M60	M	M46	22	-
GROZDANOSKI	30/1/83	Omonia (CYP)	M46		M		M	M66					
		/Vojvodina (SRB)							s46	s61	M	36	3
MAZNOV	22/4/81	Tom (RUS)	A46	s46	A	A62	A	A60	A	A66	A46	35	10
OJKOV	29/4/83	Debrecen (HUN)	A70	A46	A81			A	s64	s66	s58	27	4
GRNČAROV	12/8/82	Gent (BEL)	s46				s88		s60			10	-
TRAJANOV	9/8/78	Chernomorets (BUL)	s46	s46	M46	s84				s72	M69	30	2
BALDOVALIEV	4/3/83	Lokomotiv Sofia (BUL)	s46									4	1
POLOŽANI	25/6/82	Koblenz (GER)	s60		s46	s75	s84	s46					
		/Dinamo Tirana (ALB)							s60	s46 /61	s46	10	-
SAVIĆ	1/10/85	Vardar	s70									1	-
ŠIKOV	19/7/85	Apollon (GRE)	s77									1	-
ndar MITRESKI	5/8/80	Köln (GER)		M46								33	-
PANDEV	27/7/83	Lazio (ITA)		A		M			A64	M72	A58	37	11
TOLESKI	5/9/77	Most (CZE)		s88	s81							18	1
e NOVESKI	28/4/79	Mainz (GER)			D	D	D	D	D	D46	D46	22	2
PAČOVSKI	28/6/82	Rabotnički				G			s46	G46		5	-
AUMOSKI	29/7/83	Mattersburg (AUT)				A75	A84			A46	s46	23	4
a RISTIĆ	23/5/82	Jeonbuk (KOR)				s62		s60			s69	5	1
GEORGIEVSKI	14/6/79	Slavia Sofia (BUL)						s66	M46				
		/Zhejiang (CHN)									s46	4	-
ANČEVSKI	16/9/74	Paralimni (CYP)							s70			28	-
av VAJS	27/7/79	Rabotnički								s46		8	-
t PETROV	2/6/78	CSKA Sofia (BUL)									s58	23	-

FYR MACEDONIA

DOMESTIC LEAGUE 2007/08

PRVA LIGA FINAL TABLE

		Home					Away					Total					
	Pld	W	D	L	F	A	W	D	L	F	A	W	D	L	F	A	Pts
1 FK Rabotnički	33	15	2	0	32	4	9	5	2	19	7	24	7	2	51	11	79
2 FK Milano	33	16	0	1	56	9	5	3	8	18	27	21	3	9	74	36	66
3 FK Pelister	33	12	4	1	28	10	5	3	8	14	17	17	7	9	42	27	58
4 FK Vardar	33	10	4	3	31	13	2	7	7	14	27	12	11	10	45	40	47
5 FK Renova	33	9	5	3	21	11	4	3	9	13	23	13	8	12	34	34	47
6 FK Pobeda	33	9	6	2	28	14	3	3	10	20	34	12	9	12	48	48	45
7 FK Makedonija GP Skopje	33	11	4	1	25	7	2	1	14	9	35	13	5	15	34	42	44
8 FK Napredok	33	11	4	1	30	17	0	5	12	8	32	11	9	13	38	49	42
9 FK Sileks	33	7	6	3	21	13	3	5	9	12	23	10	11	12	33	36	41
10 FK Bashkimi	33	7	4	5	25	24	1	2	14	15	39	8	6	19	40	63	30
11 FK Shkendija 79	33	7	1	8	17	23	0	4	13	9	34	7	5	21	26	57	26
12 FK Cementarnica 55	33	4	5	7	13	17	1	4	12	11	29	5	9	19	24	46	24

N.B. FK Bashkimi withdrew before 2008/09 season.

TOP GOALSCORER

15 Ivica GLIGOROVSKI (Milano)
13 Saša STOJANOVIĆ (Milano)
12 Besrat IBRAIMI (Napredok)
Boško STUPIĆ (Sileks)
11 Argjend BEKIRI (Renova/Shke
10 Jovan KOSTOVSKI (Vardar)
Predrag ŽIVADINOVIĆ (Bashki
Ersen SALI (Milano/Bashkimi)
9 Ivan TRIČKOVSKI (Rabotnički)
8 Goran NAUMOVSKI (Napredo
Blagojče GLAVEVSKI (Pelister)
Kemal ALOMEROVIĆ (Milano)
Armend ALIMI (Bashkimi/Mila
Nderim NEDZIPI (Rabotnički)

CLUB-BY-CLUB

FK BASHKIMI

Coach – Erkan Jusuf; (16/12/07) Nedžat Šabani

Founded - 1947

MAJOR HONOURS: Macedonian Cup - (1) 2005.

2007				
5/8	Makedonija	a	0-3	
12/8	Sileks	h	0-2	
19/8	Pobeda	a	1-2	*Alimi (p)*
26/8	Napredok	h	4-1	*Živadinović 3, Stojanović*
2/9	Renova	a	1-1	*Živadinović*
16/9	Shkendija	h	1-0	*Šabani B.*
23/9	Cementarnica	a	0-3	
30/9	Milano	h	2-2	*Živadinović, Aziri*
7/10	Vardar	a	1-6	*Antonievič*
10/10	Rabotnički	h	0-4	
21/10	Pelister	a	0-1	
28/10	Makedonija	h	5-4	*Živadinović, Alimi (p), Boškovski Z., Antonievič, Biševac*
4/11	Sileks	a	3-4	*Antonievič., Biševac, Boškovski Z.*
11/11	Pobeda	h	3-4	*Alimi 2 (1p), Živadinović*
25/11	Napredok	a	0-2	
2/12	Renova	h	1-3	*Ramadani*
9/12	Shkendija	a	0-1	
16/12	Cementarnica	h	0-2	
2008				
1/3	Milano	a	2-4	*Sali, Kerimi*
9/3	Vardar	h	1-1	*Konjanovski*
16/3	Rabotnički	a	0-1	
23/3	Pelister	h	0-0	
30/3	Renova	a	0-0	
2/4	Pobeda	h	2-0	*Stojanović, Kalaba*
6/4	Pelister	a	3-1	*Sali 3*
13/4	Vardar	h	2-0	*Sali, Stojanović*
19/4	Milano	a	1-2	*Živadinović*
23/4	Rabotnički	h	1-0	*Sali*
26/4	Napredok	a	0-1	
4/5	Sileks	h	2-0	*Živadinović, Sali*
11/5	Shkendija	a	3-4	*Stojanović, Živadino Trajčev*
18/5	Cementarnica	h	1-1	*Ismaili*
31/5	Makedonija	a	0-3	

Name	Nat	Pos	Aps	(s)	Gl
Ferid AGUSI		M	9	(3)	
Hajdin AJDINI		M		(1)	
Burhan ALIJI		M		(7)	
Armend ALIMI		M	16	(4)	4
Džerald ANDRIU		M		(1)	
Dalibor ANTONIEVIĆ		D	16	(8)	3
Avni AZIRI		M	15	(6)	1
Asan BILALI		M		(2)	
Omer BIŠEVAC		D	26	(2)	2
Zlatko BOŠKOVSKI		M	19	(3)	2
Tomislav BOŠKOVSKI		D	16	(2)	
Ferdi FAZLIU		M			
Goran GANČEV		D	2	(5)	
Marko GJOROVIĆ		D	10	(2)	
Durim HIDA		M		(1)	
Skender ISMAILI		M	22	(5)	1
Abdulrazak JAKUBU		M		(2)	
Leonard KALABA		M	5	(5)	1
Mladen KARLIČIĆ		G	20	(2)	
Jeton KERIMI		D	14	(1)	1
Aleksandar KONJANOVSKI		D	12		1
Zoran MARKOVSKI		G	13		
Bekim RAMADANI		M	10	(1)	1
Ersen SALI		A	15		7
Bunjamin ŠABANI		A	6	(2)	1
Samir ŠABANI		M	19	(8)	
Haki SPAHIU		M		(2)	
Vladimir STOJANOVIĆ		M	23	(4)	4
Dalibor STOJKOVIĆ		M	9	(1)	

če TODOROVSKI	D	10	(3)	
an TRAJKOVSKI	A	11	(1)	
an TRENEVSKI	D	11	(2)	
ca TRAJČEV	D	11		1
rag ŽIVADINOVIĆ	A	23	(7)	10

FK CEMENTARNICA 55

Coach – Dragi Stefanovski

Founded - 1955

MAJOR HONOURS: Macedonian Cup - (1) 2003.

7

	Shkendija	h	1-1	*Tiago (p)*
	Milano	a	1-5	*Spasovski*
	Rabotnički	h	0-1	
	Makedonija	a	0-1	
	Pobeda	h	0-2	
	Renova	a	0-2	
	Bashkimi	h	3-0	*Spasovski, Filho, Angelovski*
	Vardar	h	2-2	*Filho 2*
	Pelister	a	1-2	*Tiago*
10	Sileks	h	1-1	*Angelovski*
10	Napredok	a	1-2	*Filho*
10	Shkendija	a	0-1	
1	Milano	h	1-2	*Tiago*
11	Rabotnički	a	0-0	
11	Makedonija	h	0-1	
2	Pobeda	a	3-4	*Jakovlevski, Belčev, Mihajlov*
2	Renova	h	1-0	*Tiago*
12	Bashkimi	a	2-0	*Mihajlov, Ristovski*

08

	Vardar	a	0-1	
	Pelister	h	0-1	
3	Sileks	a	0-2	
3	Napredok	h	0-0	
3	Pobeda	a	1-1	*Vasiljević*
	Pelister	h	0-1	
	Vardar	a	1-1	*Filho*
4	Milano	h	2-1	*Dimitrovski, og (Ristov)*
4	Rabotnički	a	0-2	
4	Napredok	h	1-0	*Tiago*
4	Sileks	a	0-2	
	Shkendija	h	1-1	*Tiago*
5	Makedonija	a	0-2	
5	Bashkimi	a	1-1	*Belčev*
5	Renova	h	0-3	

me	Nat	Pos	Aps	(s)	Gls
r ANGELOVSKI		M	15	(4)	2
vo ARSOVSKI		M		(3)	
rjan BELČEV		D	11	(7)	2
jan BLAŽEVSKI		M	4	(3)	
rtin BOGATINOV		G	12		
agan BRNJARČEVSKI		M	18	(2)	
židar DIMITROVSKI		D	28	(1)	1
sé Carlos Filho	BRA	A	25	(2)	5
ran GROŠEV		G	19	(1)	
ran HRISTOVSKI		M	21	(2)	
ne IVANOVSKI		D	29	(1)	
agan JAKOVLEVSKI		A	15	(6)	1
rica KONESKI		A	1	(2)	
rko KOSTADINOVSKI		D	1	(4)	
orgji MANEVSKI		M	1	(3)	
adimir MEDIĆ		D	11	(6)	
tar MIHAJLOV		M	21	(2)	2
agoja MILEVSKI		D	30	(4)	
arko NEDELKOVSKI		D	3	(2)	
Edin NUREDINOSKI		G	2		
Vane PANDEV		D	2	(3)	
Bojan PETROVSKI		M	4	(2)	
Darko RANGOTOV		A	5	(1)	
Milan RISTOVSKI		A	8	(3)	1
Vladimir SPASOVSKI		A	21	(3)	2
Ilija STEFANOVSKI		A		(1)	
Dimitar STOJANOVSKI		M	4	(2)	
TIAGO Galdino Rodrigues	BRA	A	29	(1)	6
Dimče TODOROVSKI		D	7	(5)	
Igor TRIPUNOV		M	1	(2)	
Vladimir TUNESKI		M	14	(4)	
Milos VASILJEVIĆ		D	1	(5)	1

FK MAKEDONIJA GP SKOPJE

Coach – Radmilo Ivančević (SRB); (26/8/07) Robert Stojanovski; (11/11/07) Ilčo Georgievski

Founded - 1932

MAJOR HONOURS: Macedonian Cup - (1) 2006.

2007

5/8	Bashkimi	h	3-0	*og (Stojković), Stojanovski, Stankovski*
12/8	Pobeda	h	2-1	*Milošević (p), Mojsov*
19/8	Renova	a	1-2	*Mitrev*
26/8	Cementarnica	h	1-0	*Stojanovski*
2/9	Vardar	a	1-4	*Despotovski*
16/9	Pelister	h	0-2	
23/9	Sileks	a	0-1	
30/9	Napredok	h	1-0	*Despotovski*
7/10	Shkendija	a	0-0	
10/10	Milano	h	3-0	*Milošević 2 (1p), Brnjarčevski*
21/10	Rabotnički	a	0-3	
28/10	Bashkimi	a	4-5	*Fazli 2, Milošević, Iliev*
4/11	Pobeda	a	1-4	*Stojanovski*
11/11	Renova	h	2-1	*Simovski, Fazli*
25/11	Cementarnica	a	1-0	*Milošević*
2/12	Vardar	h	1-1	*Despotovski*
9/12	Pelister	a	0-1	
16/12	Sileks	h	1-1	*Brnjarčevski*

2008

2/3	Napredok	a	0-1	
9/3	Shkendija	h	4-1	*Mojsov, Brnjarcevski, Džonbalaj 2*
16/3	Milano	a	0-5	
23/3	Rabotnički	h	0-0	
29/3	Rabotnički	a	0-1	
2/4	Renova	a	0-2	
5/4	Napredok	h	1-0	*Milevski*
13/4	Pobeda	a	0-2	
20/4	Sileks	h	0-0	
23/4	Pelister	a	0-2	
26/4	Shkendija	h	1-0	*Brnjarčevski (p)*
4/5	Vardar	a	1-0	*Stojanovski*
11/5	Cementarnica	h	2-0	*Milevski, Kolekevski*
18/5	Milano	a	0-2	
30/5	Bashkimi	h	3-0	*Brnjarčevski, Džonbalaj, Kolekevski*

Name	Nat	Pos	Aps	(s)	Gls
Vangel ALTIPARMAKOVSKI		M		(6)	
Elfat BAJRAMI		D		(4)	
Aleksandar BOŠKOVSKI		M	3	(4)	
Dragan BRNJARČEVSKI		M	12	(3)	
Toni BRNJARČEVSKI		M	26	(2)	5
Vladimir DESPOTOVSKI		D	25	(3)	3
Goran DIMOVSKI		D	21	(1)	
Malsor DŽONBALAJ		A	21	(2)	3

Samir FAZLI		M	26	(2)	3
Lazar ILIEV		D	4	(5)	1
Ivica ILIEVSKI		M		(4)	
Čedomir ILIEVSKI		M		(3)	
Nikola JAKIMOVSKI		D	1	(4)	
Daniel JOVANOVSKI		D	24		
Filip KOLEKESKI		A	2	(4)	2
Milan KRIVOKAPIĆ	SRB	M	1		
Blagojče LJAMČEVSKI		D	20		
Marjan MADŽAROVSKI		G	2		
Bobi MILEVSKI		D	8		2
Vladan MILOSAVLJEVIĆ	SRB	M	14		
Miroslav MILOŠEVIĆ	SRB	M	15	(4)	5
Vasko MITREV		M	25	(1)	1
Daniel MOJSOV		D	27	(1)	2
Šaban REDŽEP		D		(5)	
Goran SILJANOVSKI		D		(4)	
Goran SIMOV		G	31		
Dušan SIMOVSKI		M	25	(2)	1
Goran STANKOVSKI		A	2	(2)	1
Aleksandar STOJANOVSKI		A	25	(4)	4
Flamur TAIRI		M	3	(7)	

FK MILANO

Coach – Bilbil Sokoli; (10/10/07) Gjore Jovanovski

Founded - 1990

2007				
5/8	Renova	a	2-1	*Sali, Ljimani*
12/8	Cementarnica	h	5-1	*Gligorovski, Ljimani, Miserdovski, Alomerović 2*
19/8	Vardar	a	0-0	
26/8	Pelister	h	3-0	*Alomerović, Brando, Gligorovski*
2/9	Sileks	a	0-0	
16/9	Napredok	h	3-1	*Brando 2, Sali*
23/9	Shkendija	a	3-1	*Miserdovski, Sali, Isufi*
30/9	Bashkimi	a	2-2	*Miserdovski, Alomerović*
7/10	Rabotnički	h	1-2	*Gligorovski (p)*
10/10	Makedonija	a	0-3	
21/10	Pobeda	h	4-0	*Gligorovski 2, Ilievski, Stojanović*
28/10	Renova	h	3-0	*Stojanović 2, Miserdovski*
4/11	Cementarnica	a	2-1	*og (Dimitrovski), Stojanović*
11/11	Vardar	h	1-0	*Miserdovski*
25/11	Pelister	a	0-3	
2/12	Sileks	h	4-0	*Gligorovski 2, Alomerović, Ilievski*
9/12	Napredok	a	1-2	*Miserdovski*
16/12	Shkendija	h	1-0	*Lazarevski*
2008				
1/3	Bashkimi	h	4-2	*Gligorovski 2, Krstev, Manevski*
8/3	Rabotnički	a	0-1	
16/3	Makedonija	h	5-0	*Gligorovski 2, Manevski 2, Alomerović*
23/3	Pobeda	a	1-4	*Jovanovski*
30/3	Napredok	h	3-0	*Gligorovski 2, Alimi*
2/4	Sileks	a	1-0	*Ilievski*
5/4	Shkendija	h	4-0	Brando, Manevski 2, Alimi
13/4	Cementarnica	a	1-2	*Stojanović (p)*
19/4	Bashkimi	h	2-1	*Stojanović 2*
23/4	Renova	a	2-1	*Alomerović, Stojanović*
26/4	Pobeda	h	2-1	*Stojanović, Ristov*
4/5	Pelister	a	2-3	*Stojanović, Ilievski*
11/5	Vardar	h	9-1	*Gaši 2, Gligorovski [illegible] (1p), Stojanović 2, Alomerović, Brando, Manevski*
18/5	Makedonija	h	2-0	*Stojanović, Alimi*
31/5	Rabotnički	a	1-3	*Alimi*

Name	**Nat**	**Pos**	**Aps**	**(s)**	**G[illegible]**
Burhan ALIJI		D		(5)	
Armend ALIMI		M		(6)	4
Kemal ALOMEROVIĆ		M	26	(5)	8
Erdogan BRANDO		M	25	(3)	5
Fisnik GAŠI		M	25	(1)	2
Ivica GLIGOROVSKI		A	27	(1)	[illegible]
Boško GJUROVIĆ		M		(5)	
Ali ILBER		A	25	(2)	
Milan ILIEVSKI		D	26	(2)	4
Orhan ISUFI		M	18	(1)	1
Zoran JOVANOVSKI		D	29		1
Jeton KERIMI		D	2	(2)	
Ljupčo KMETOVSKI		G	17		
Aleksandar KONJANOVSKI		M	2	(2)	
Saško KRSTEV		A		(4)	1
Liridon KUKAJ		D	1	(2)	
Sašo LAZAREVSKI		D	25	(1)	1
Mensur LJIMANI		M	18	(2)	2
Filip MADZOVSKI		G	5		
Borce MANEVSKI		M	4	(5)	6
Zoran MARKOVSKI		G	2		
Zoran MISERDOVSKI		A	2	(6)	6
Edin NUREDINOSKI		G	9		
Saško RISTOV		M	19		1
Ersen SALI		A	4	(5)	3
Faruk STATOVCI		D	26	(1)	
Saša STOJANOVIĆ		M	24	(5)	[illegible]
Dragan TRAJKOVSKI		A	2	(7)	

FK NAPREDOK

Coach – Dragan Bočeski

Founded - 1928

2007				
5/8	Vardar	a	1-5	*Ibraimi*
12/8	Pelister	h	1-1	*Ibraimi*
19/8	Sileks	a	1-1	*Ibraimi*
26/8	Bashkimi	a	1-4	*Ibraimi*
2/9	Shkendija	h	2-0	*Ničeski 2 (2p)*
16/9	Milano	a	1-3	*Naumovski*
23/9	Rabotnički	h	0-2	
30/9	Makedonija	a	0-1	
7/10	Pobeda	h	1-1	*Ničeski (p)*
10/10	Renova	a	1-2	*Ničeski (p)*
21/10	Cementarnica	h	2-1	*Ibraimi, Naumovski*
28/10	Vardar	h	0-0	
4/11	Pelister	a	1-1	*Levkov*
11/11	Sileks	h	2-1	*Nastov, Ničeski*
25/11	Bashkimi	h	2-0	*Levkov, Ibraimi*
2/12	Shkendija	a	1-2	*Ibraimi*
9/12	Milano	h	2-1	*Naumovski 2*
16/12	Rabotnički	a	0-3	
2008				
2/3	Makedonija	h	1-0	*Naumovski*
9/3	Pobeda	a	1-4	*Pop Panev*
16/3	Renova	h	3-1	*og (Stanković), Angelevski, Ibraimi*
23/3	Cementarnica	a	0-0	
29/3	Milano	a	0-3	
2/4	Rabotnički	h	0-0	

	Makedonija	a	0-1	
	Sileks	a	0-0	
	Shkendija	h	4-3	*Naumovski 2, Ibraimi, Levkov*
	Cementarnica	a	0-1	
	Bashkimi	h	1-0	*Ibraimi*
	Renova	a	0-0	
	Pobeda	h	4-3	*Levkov 2, Ibraimi 2 (1p)*
	Pelister	a	0-1	
	Vardar	h	5-3	*Arslani, Simjanovski, Ničeski 2, Naumovski*

e	Nat	Pos	Aps	(s)	Gls
ANGELESKI		M	25	(1)	1
bin ARSLANI		D	21	(2)	1
ASKOV		M	19	(2)	
CVETANOVSKI		D		(5)	
DAMJANOSKI		D		(6)	
DŽANGAROVSKI		M	24		
t IBRAIMI		M	24	(1)	12
ILIEV		D		(3)	
LIEV		M	20	(1)	
KORUNOVSKI		G	20		
KULESKI		A		(6)	
KUZMANOV		D		(7)	
oj LEVKOV		M	23	(2)	5
slav MICKOVSKI		D	22	(1)	
NASTOV		M	22		1
n NAUMOVSKI		A	22	(2)	8
nio NIČESKI		M	27	(2)	7
n POP PANEV		D	20	(1)	1
o SIMJANOVSKI		D	22		1
sandar STOJANOVSKI		M		(4)	
o STOJKOSKI		M		(3)	
sandar TOLESKI		A	2	(4)	
la TRIPUNOVSKI		M	18	(2)	
TRPENOSKI		A	19	(1)	
an UGRENOVIĆ		G	5		
el VELJANOVSKI		D		(4)	
ZAFIROSKI		M		(7)	
la ZERDESKI		G	8		

FK PELISTER

Coach – Nedžat Husein

Founded - 1945

MAJOR HONOURS: Macedonian Cup - (1) 2001.

7				
	Sileks	h	1-0	*Blaževski*
	Napredok	a	1-1	*Rutevski (p)*
	Shkendija	h	3-0	*Júnior 2, Jovanov*
	Milano	a	0-3	
	Rabotnički	h	0-0	
	Makedonija	a	2-0	*Momirovski, Todorovski*
	Pobeda	h	1-1	*Júnior*
	Renova	a	0-1	
	Cementarnica	h	2-1	*Glavevski, Rutevski (p)*
0	Vardar	a	0-1	
0	Bashkimi	h	1-0	*Glavevski*
0	Sileks	a	3-2	*og (Marković), Blaževski 2*
	Napredok	h	1-1	*Rutevski (p)*
1	Shkendija	a	0-1	
1	Milano	h	3-0	*Stepanovski, Rutevski, Glavevski*
2	Rabotnički	a	0-1	
2	Makedonija	h	1-0	*Momirovski*
12	Pobeda	a	1-2	*Glavevski*

2008				
2/3	Renova	h	1-1	*Simonovski*
9/3	Cementarnica	a	1-0	*Glavevski*
16/3	Vardar	h	2-1	*Todorovski, Elmazovski*
23/3	Bashkimi	a	0-0	
30/3	Shkendija	h	1-0	*Momirovski (p)*
2/4	Cementarnica	a	1-0	*Glavevski*
6/4	Bashkimi	h	1-3	*Momirovski*
12/4	Renova	a	1-2	*Júnior*
20/4	Pobeda	h	4-0	*Blaževski, Miranda, Glavevski, Todorovski*
23/4	Makedonija	h	2-0	*Blaževski, Elmazovski*
26/4	Vardar	a	3-1	*Miranda 3*
4/5	Milano	h	3-2	*Todorovski, Momirovski 2*
11/5	Rabotnički	a	0-0	
18/5	Napredok	h	1-0	*Glavevski*
31/5	Sileks	a	1-2	*Blaževski*

Name	Nat	Pos	Aps	(s)	Gls
Dejan BLAŽEVSKI		M	26	(1)	6
Mile DIMOV		M	25	(2)	
Ilir ELMAZOVSKI		D	25	(1)	2
Blagojče GLAVEVSKI		A	27	(4)	8
Mirko IVANOVSKI		M	1	(7)	
Tomi JOVANOV		D	2	(8)	1
JÚNIOR Souza Machado	BRA	A	27	(3)	4
Ljupčo MICEVSKI		M	21		
Adriano MIRANDA	BRA	A	16	(5)	4
Igor MOMIROVSKI		M	25	(2)	6
Trajče NIKOV		G	2		
Goran PAŠOVSKI		G	31		
Mile PETKOVSKI		M	16		
Nikola PETKOVSKI		M	21		
Toni PITOŠKA		M		(4)	
Bruno PRESILSKI		M	22	(3)	
Blagojče RUTEVSKI		M	18	(5)	4
Zoran SIMONOVSKI		D		(4)	1
Stefan SPIROVSKI		D		(3)	
Goran STAVREVSKI		D	2	(5)	
Metodija STEPANOVSKI		D	27	(1)	1
Zoran STERJOVSKI		M		(2)	
Nikola STOJANOVSKI		M		(6)	
Goce TODOROVSI		M	26	(1)	4
Ive TRIFUNOVSKI		A	1	(6)	
Toni VELJANOVSKI		M	2	(6)	

FK POBEDA

Coach – Nikolče Zdravevski

Founded - 1941

MAJOR HONOURS: Macedonian League - (2) 2004, 2007; Macedonian Cup - (1) 2002.

2007				
5/8	Rabotnički	h	0-0	
12/8	Makedonija	a	1-2	*Nacev*
19/8	Bashkimi	h	2-1	*Obradović, Nastoski*
26/8	Renova	h	0-0	
2/9	Cementarnica	a	2-0	*Nacev, Kapinkovski*
16/9	Vardar	h	0-0	
23/9	Pelister	a	1-1	*Nacev*
30/9	Sileks	h	1-0	*Gešovski*
7/10	Napredok	a	1-1	*Gjorović*
10/10	Shkendija	h	1-1	*Gjorović*
21/10	Milano	a	0-4	
28/10	Rabotnički	a	2-4	*Almeida, Gjorović*
4/11	Makedonija	h	4-1	*Meglenski (p), Gjorović 2, Itua*
11/11	Bashkimi	a	4-3	*Manevski 2 , og (Šabani S.), Gešovski*

FYR MACEDONIA

25/11	Renova	a	0-2	
2/12	Cementarnica	h	4-3	*Gešovski 2, Almeida, Itua*
9/12	Vardar	a	0-0	
16/12	Pelister	h	2-1	*Gjorović 2*
2008				
2/3	Sileks	a	0-1	
9/3	Napredok	h	4-1	*Kapinkovski, Nastoski, Aceski, Tripunovski*
16/3	Shkendija	a	0-3	*(w/o)*
23/3	Milano	h	4-1	*Jovanović, Gešovski, Obradović, Nestorovski*
30/3	Cementarnica	h	1-1	*Gešovski*
2/4	Bashkimi	a	0-2	
6/4	Renova	h	0-1	
13/4	Makedonija	h	2-0	*Gešovski, Dameski*
20/4	Pelister	a	0-4	
23/4	Vardar	h	0-2	
26/4	Milano	a	1-2	*Cuculi*
4/5	Rabotnički	h	2-0	*Dameski, Altiparmakovski*
11/5	Napredok	a	3-4	*Nestorovski 3*
18/5	Sileks	h	1-1	*Kapinkovski*
31/5	Shkendija	a	5-1	*Nestorovski 2, Zojčevski, Altiparmakovski 2*

Name	Nat	Pos	Aps	(s)	Gls
Nove ACESKI		M	14	(1)	1
Rodrigo ALMEIDA		A	22	(1)	2
Vangel ALTIPARMAKOVSKI		A	6	(6)	3
Robert BOŠKOVSKI		M	2	(1)	
Ardian CUCULI		D		(5)	1
Blagojče DAMESKI		M	22	(3)	2
Blagoja GEŠOVSKI		A	20	(3)	7
Marko GJOROVIĆ		D	14	(2)	7
N' Dinga Rok ITUA	CGO	D	21	(5)	2
Miodrag JOVANOVIĆ	SRB	M	24	(1)	1
Jesus da Silva "JILSON"	BRA	M	18	(3)	
Dimitar KAPINKOVSKI		M	25	(4)	3
Slagjan KRALJEVSKI		G			
Aleksandar KRSTESKI		D	20	(4)	
Borče MANEVSKI		M	11		2
Toni MEGLENSKI		M	21	(3)	1
Filip MIRČESKI		M		(4)	
Marjan NACEV		D	25	(3)	3
Kliment NASTOSKI		M	19	(2)	2
Ilija NESTOROVSKI		M	7	(4)	6
Jovica OBRADOVIĆ	SRB	D	22	(2)	2
Nebojša STOJKOVIĆ	SRB	M	2	(6)	
Martin ŠIŠKOV		D	2	(4)	
Igor TALEVSKI		M	2	(4)	
Nikola TRIPUNOVSKI		M		(3)	1
Darko TOFILOSKI		G	29	(4)	
Sašo VELJANOVSKI		A	1		
Aleksandar VRTESKI		G	3	(4)	
Ivan ZOJČEVSKI		M		(2)	1

FK RABOTNIČKI

Coach – Dragoljub Bekvalac (SRB)

Founded - 1937

MAJOR HONOURS: Macedonian League - (3) 2005, 2006, 2008; Macedonian Cup - (1) 2008.

2007				
5/8	Pobeda	a	0-0	
12/8	Renova	h	3-0	*Tričkovski 2 (1p), Nedžipi*
19/8	Cementarnica	a	1-0	*Velkovski*
26/8	Vardar	h	1-0	*Pejčić*
2/9	Pelister	a	0-0	
16/9	Sileks	h	4-1	*Nedžipi 2, Tričkovs*
23/9	Napredok	a	2-0	*Tričkovski, Pejčić*
30/9	Shkendija	h	2-0	*Osmani, Milisavlje*
7/10	Milano	a	2-1	*Milisavljević, Gligo*
10/10	Bashkimi	a	4-0	*Velkovski 2, Nedži*
21/10	Makedonija	h	3-0	*Tričkovski 2, Velko*
28/10	Pobeda	h	4-2	*Vajs, Milisavljević, Tričkovski, Nedžipi*
4/11	Renova	a	1-0	*Stanišić*
11/11	Cementarnica	h	0-0	
25/11	Vardar	a	0-0	
2/12	Pelister	h	1-0	*Kirovski*
9/12	Sileks	a	2-1	*Lukmon 2*
16/12	Napredok	h	3-0	*Kirovski, Tričkovski, Gligorov*
2008				
2/3	Shkendija	a	2-1	*Stanišić, Milisavlje*
8/3	Milano	h	1-0	*Nedžipi*
16/3	Bashkimi	h	1-0	*Jančevski*
23/3	Makedonija	a	0-0	
29/3	Makedonija	h	1-0	*Nedžipi*
2/4	Napredok	a	0-0	
5/4	Sileks	h	1-0	*Gjosevski*
13/4	Shkendija	a	3-0	*(w/o)*
19/4	Cementarnica	h	2-0	*Vajs, Osmani*
23/4	Bashkimi	a	0-1	
26/4	Renova	h	2-0	*Jovanović, Aksenti*
4/5	Pobeda	a	0-2	
11/5	Pelister	h	0-0	
18/5	Vardar	a	2-1	*Jovanović 2*
31/5	Milano	h	3-1	*Pejčić, Jovanović, Velkovski*

Name	Nat	Pos	Aps	(s)	G
Eftim AKSENTIEV		D	3		
Vasko BOŽINOVSKI		D	20	(2)	
Ertan DEMIRI		M	25	(1)	
Sašo GJORESKI		D		(6)	
Nikola GJOŠEVSKI		D	4		
Nikola GLIGOROV		A	25	(2)	
Mensur IDRIZI		M		(7)	
Stojan IGNJATOV		M	2		
Blaže ILIJOSKI		A	2	(4)	
Boban JANČEVSKI		A	5	(5)	
Ivan JOVANOVIĆ	SRB	D	10		
Hristijan KIROVSKI		A	4	(2)	
Ljupčo KMETOVSKI		G	4		
Željko KOVAČEVIĆ	SRB	D	10	(6)	
Dimitrija LAZAREVSKI		D	15	(6)	
Adekunle Lukmon	NGA	D	22		[illegible]
Dančo MASEV		A	11	(5)	
Filip MADŽOVSKI		G	6		
Bojan MIHAJLOVIĆ	SRB	M	8	(4)	
Nemanja MILISAVLJEVIĆ	SRB	D	21	(4)	4
Nderim NEDŽIPI		M	28		8
Minas OSMANI		M	17	(5)	2
Tome PAČOVSKI		G	22		
Ivan PEJČIĆ	SRB	A	12	(4)	3
Ismet SELIM		D	1	(3)	
Lazar STANIŠIĆ	SRB	D	22		2
Nikola STOJANOVSKI		M			
Ivan TRIČKOVSKI		A	15		9
Miroslav VAJS		D	24	(1)	2
Krste VELKOVSKI		A	14	(5)	5

FK RENOVA

Coach – Vlatko Kostov; (15/11/07) Bilbil Sokoli

Founded - 2003

Date	Opponent		Result	Scorers
2007				
5/8	Milano	h	1-2	*Stojanov I.*
12/8	Rabotnički	a	0-3	
19/8	Makedonija	h	2-1	*Ljivoreka, Savevski I. (p)*
26/8	Pobeda	a	0-0	
2/9	Bashkimi	h	1-1	*Stojanov I.*
16/9	Cementarnica	h	2-0	*Bekiri Ar. (p), Gjurčevski*
23/9	Vardar	a	0-1	
30/9	Pelister	h	1-0	*Bekiri Ar. (p)*
7/10	Sileks	a	0-0	
10/10	Napredok	h	2-1	*Savevski I., Nuhiu*
21/10	Shkendija	a	2-0	*Bekiri Ar., Ismaili*
28/10	Milano	a	0-3	
4/11	Rabotnički	h	0-1	
11/11	Makedonija	a	1-2	*Nuhiu*
25/11	Pobeda	h	2-0	*Nuhiu 2*
2/12	Bashkimi	a	3-1	*Bekiri Ar. 2 (2p), Memedi*
9/12	Cementarnica	a	0-1	
16/12	Vardar	h	1-1	*Iseni*
2008				
2/3	Pelister	a	1-1	*Iseni*
9/3	Sileks	h	1-1	*Andonov*
16/3	Napredok	a	1-2	*Andonov*
23/3	Shkendija	h	1-0	*Aliu*
30/3	Bashkimi	h	0-0	
2/4	Makedonija	h	2-0	*Iseni 2*
6/4	Pobeda	a	1-0	*Andonov*
12/4	Pelister	h	2-1	*Miserdovski, Aliu*
20/4	Vardar	a	1-3	*Memedi*
23/4	Milano	h	1-2	*Trajčov*
26/4	Rabotnički	a	0-2	
4/5	Napredok	h	0-0	
11/5	Sileks	a	0-3	
18/5	Shkendija	h	2-0	*Iseni, Nuhiu*
31/5	Cementarnica	a	3-0	*Emini, Despotovski, Gafuri*

Name	Nat	Pos	Aps	(s)	Gls
Ferat ABDULI		G	1		
Ilber ALIU		M	4	(6)	2
Marjan ANDONOV		M	5	(5)	3
Argjend BEKIRI		A	21	(3)	5
Agron BEKIRI		M	1	(4)	
Zoran DESPOTOVSKI		A	2	(5)	1
Armend ELEZI		G	7		
Asani ELMEDIN		A		(4)	
Vulnet EMINI		M	26	(5)	1
Armend GAFURI		M	2	(6)	1
Blagoja GJURČEVSKI		M	16	(1)	1
Darko IGNJATOVSKI		M	4	(7)	
Artan ILJAZI		D			
Genc ISENI		A	24	(2)	5
Ismail ISMAILI		A	25	(2)	1
Ljubo KOVAČEVIĆ		G	25	(1)	
Perparim LJIVOREKA		M	11	(6)	1
Agron MEMEDI		M	26	(3)	2
Zoran MISERDOVSKI		A	5	(2)	1
Fisnik NUHIU		M	21	(4)	5
Šaćir REDŽEPI		M	22	(6)	
Igor SAVEVSKI		M	2		2
Darko SAVEVSKI		M	22	(3)	
Zvonimir STANKOVIĆ		D	21	(4)	
Panče STOJANOV		M	22	(3)	
Igorče STOJANOV		D	25	(3)	2
Vanče TRAJČOV		M	23	(1)	1

FK SHKENDIJA 79

Coach – Katip Osmani; (28/10/07) Zoran Smileski; (21/3/08) Borče Hristov; (2/5/08) Ejup Sulejmani

Founded - 1979

Date	Opponent		Result	Scorers
2007				
5/8	Cementarnica	a	1-1	*Ramadani*
12/8	Vardar	h	0-1	
19/8	Pelister	a	0-3	
26/8	Sileks	h	0-1	
2/9	Napredok	a	0-2	
16/9	Bashkimi	a	0-1	
23/9	Milano	h	1-3	*Mustafi*
30/9	Rabotnički	a	0-2	
7/10	Makedonija	h	0-0	
10/10	Pobeda	a	1-1	*Delioski*
21/10	Renova	h	0-2	
28/10	Cementarnica	h	1-0	*Ferati*
4/11	Vardar	a	1-4	*Delioski*
11/11	Pelister	h	1-0	*Emurlahu*
25/11	Sileks	a	1-1	*Saliu*
2/12	Napredok	h	2-1	*Selimi, Zeadini*
9/12	Bashkimi	h	1-0	*Delioski*
16/12	Milano	a	0-1	
2008				
2/3	Rabotnički	h	1-2	*Huseini*
9/3	Makedonija	a	1-4	*Rutevski*
16/3	Pobeda	h	3-0	*(w/o)*
23/3	Renova	a	0-1	
30/3	Pelister	a	0-1	
2/4	Vardar	h	1-0	*Bekiri*
5/4	Milano	a	0-4	
13/4	Rabotnički	h	0-3	*(w/o)*
20/4	Napredok	a	3-4	*Milošević, Bekiri, Idrizi*
23/4	Sileks	h	1-2	*Bekiri*
26/4	Makedonija	a	0-1	
4/5	Cementarnica	a	1-1	*Stojanović*
11/5	Bashkimi	h	4-3	*Bekiri 3 (1p), Hadžibulić*
18/5	Renova	a	0-2	
31/5	Pobeda	h	1-5	*Huseini*

Name	Nat	Pos	Aps	(s)	Gls
Festim ADEMI		A	12	(4)	
Vebi ALIEVSKI		G	15		
Agon ALILI		M			
Baškim ARIFI		D	14	(4)	
Elfat BAJRAMI		M	12	(3)	
Petar BASNARKOV		G	15		
Argjend BEKIRI		A	9		6
Ardijan CUCULI		D	18	(3)	
Cvete DELIOSKI		M	18	(4)	3
Dejan DIMITROVSKI		D	7	(2)	
Mohammadou Moustapha DIOP	SEN	A	6	(2)	
Buletin DURMIŠI		A	5		
Burhan EMURLAHU		A	5	(1)	1
Hišam EMRULI		M	3		
Papa Birane FALL	SEN	D	15	(6)	
Blerim FERATI		M	21	(3)	1
Mensur IDRIZI		M	4	(2)	1
Semir HADŽIBULIĆ	BIH	M	4	(5)	1
Muhamed HUSEINI		M	22	(2)	2
Nuriman ISMAILJI		M	27	(5)	
Armend JUSUFI		G	1	(1)	
Jusuf KASAMI		D	5	(4)	
Ivica LAZAREV		A	4	(1)	
Buramedin MUSAI		A	6	(6)	
Suhejb MUSTAFI		M	15	(2)	1
Ilija MILOŠEVIĆ		A	4	(1)	1
Argjend RAMADANI		M	7	(1)	1

Blagojče RUTEVSKI		M	10	(5)	1
Mumin SALIU		M	8		1
Erhan SELIMI		M	19	(5)	1
Artim ŠAKIRI		A	5	(1)	
Jusuf Papa SOW	SEN	D	7	(1)	
Dimitar SPASOVSKI		A	3		
Zoran STOJANOVIĆ		M			1
Aleksandar TENEKIDŽIEV		A	8	(1)	
Nikola TONEV		D	3		
Driton ZEADINI		M	2		1
Valmir ZIBERI		M	2	(1)	

FK SILEKS

Coach – Marjan Sekulovski

Founded - 1965

MAJOR HONOURS: Macedonian League - (3) 1996, 1997, 1998; Macedonian Cup - (2) 1994, 1997.

2007

5/8	Pelister	a	0-1	
12/8	Bashkimi	a	2-0	*Gligorov, Stupić*
19/8	Napredok	h	1-1	*Stupić*
26/8	Shkendija	a	1-0	*Aksentiev*
2/9	Milano	h	0-0	
16/9	Rabotnički	a	1-4	*Aksentiev*
23/9	Makedonija	h	1-0	*Natkov*
30/9	Pobeda	a	0-1	
7/10	Renova	h	0-0	
10/10	Cementarnica	a	1-1	*Gligorov*
21/10	Vardar	h	1-1	*Stupić*
28/10	Pelister	h	2-3	*Natkov, Šalevski*
4/11	Bashkimi	h	4-3	*Stupić 2, Aksentiev, Gligorov*
11/11	Napredok	a	1-2	*Gligorov (p)*
25/11	Shkendija	h	1-1	*Tančevski*
2/12	Milano	a	0-4	
9/12	Rabotnički	h	1-2	*Mickov*
16/12	Makedonija	a	1-1	*Natkov (p)*

2008

2/3	Pobeda	h	1-0	*Zarevski*
9/3	Renova	a	1-1	*Stupić*
16/3	Cementarnica	h	2-0	*Natkov (p), Divjak*
23/3	Vardar	a	0-1	
30/3	Vardar	a	1-2	*Ali*
2/4	Milano	h	0-1	
5/4	Rabotnički	a	0-1	
13/4	Napredok	h	0-0	
20/4	Makedonija	a	0-0	
23/4	Shkendija	a	2-1	*Stupić, Marković*
26/4	Cementarnica	h	2-0	*Stupić 2*
4/5	Bashkimi	a	0-2	
11/5	Renova	h	3-0	*Gligorov, Natkov, Stupić*
18/5	Pobeda	a	1-1	*Ristić*
31/5	Pelister	h	2-1	*Stupić 2*

Name	Nat	Pos	Aps	(s)	Gls
Eftim AKSENTIEV		A	17	(1)	3
Musa ALI	NGA	A		(7)	1
Duško ANDONOV	SRB	D	12	(4)	
Aleksandar ANGELOVSKI		A	25	(3)	
Antonio BOGATINOV		M	3	(4)	
Daniel BOŽINOVSKI		G	1		
Igor DIMOV		G	23		
Ivan DISIĆ	SRB	G	9		
Marko DIVJAK		M	14	(3)	1
Mihail DONEV		M	16	(4)	
Gligor GLIGOROV		D	25	(1)	5
Branislav JANEVSKI		M	22	(3)	
Dejan LESKAROSKI		D	15	(1)	
Milan MARKOVIĆ	SRB	D	22	(3)	1
Marjan MICKOV		D	24	(3)	1
Mirče NATKOV		M	27	(2)	5
Dejan PEŠIĆ		A		(4)	
Mladen RISTIĆ	SRB	A	5	(4)	1
Zoran ŠALEVSKI		M	18	(4)	1
Boško STUPIĆ	BIH	M	26	(3)	12
Goran STOJANOVSKI		M		(5)	
Nikolče TANČEVSKI		A	21	(2)	1
Blaže TODOROVSKI		A	6	(1)	
Darko TRAJČEV		M	7	(2)	
Aleksandar VASILEV		M	22	(1)	
Slavčo VELKOVSKI		M	1	(2)	
Gjorgji ZAREVSKI		D	2	(4)	1

FK VARDAR

Coach – Dragan Kanatlarovski; (10/8/07) Zoran Stratev; (5/4/08) Kiril Dojčinovski

Founded - 1947

MAJOR HONOURS: Macedonian League - (5) 1993, 1994, 1995, 2002, 2003; Yugoslav Cup - (1) 1961; Macedonian Cup - (5) 1993, 1995, 1998, 1999, 2007.

2007

5/8	Napredok	h	5-1	*Kostovski 3, Stanković, Savić*
12/8	Shkendija	a	1-0	*Savić*
19/8	Milano	h	0-0	
26/8	Rabotnički	a	0-1	
2/9	Makedonija	h	4-1	*Sekulovski, Ristevski, Kostovski, Emurlahu*
16/9	Pobeda	a	0-0	
23/9	Renova	h	1-0	*Savić*
30/9	Cementarnica	a	2-2	*Braga, Kostovski*
7/10	Bashkimi	h	6-1	*Kostovski 2, Emurlahu, Milisavljev, og (Stojković), Peev*
10/10	Pelister	h	1-0	*Milisavljev*
21/10	Sileks	a	1-1	*Kostovski*
28/10	Napredok	a	0-0	
4/11	Shkendija	h	4-1	*Stjepanović (p), Milosavljev, Kostovski 2*
11/11	Milano	a	0-1	
25/11	Rabotnički	h	0-0	
2/12	Makedonija	a	1-1	*Peev*
9/12	Pobeda	h	0-0	
16/12	Renova	a	1-1	*Stjepanović*

2008

2/3	Cementarnica	h	1-0	*Ristevski*
9/3	Bashkimi	a	1-1	*Savić*
16/3	Pelister	a	1-2	*Bajevski*
23/3	Sileks	h	1-0	*Emurlahu*
30/3	Sileks	h	2-1	*Ejupi, Lepović*
2/4	Shkendija	a	0-1	
6/4	Cementarnica	h	1-1	*Bajevski (p)*
13/4	Bashkimi	a	0-2	
20/4	Renova	h	3-1	*Ejupi, Mojsov, Peev*
23/4	Pobeda	a	2-0	*Petrov, og (Cuculi)*
26/4	Pelister	h	1-3	*Peev*
4/5	Makedonija	h	0-1	
11/5	Milano	a	1-9	*Bajevski (p)*
18/5	Rabotnički	h	1-2	*Bajevski (p)*
31/5	Napredok	a	3-5	*Ejupi, Serafimovski 2*

Name	Nat	Pos	Aps	(s)	Gls
Aleksandar BAJEVSKI		A	9	(2)	4
Martin BOGATINOV		G	2		
Radenko BOJOVIĆ	SRB	D	19	(5)	
Aguinaldo de Jesus BRAGA	BRA	M	19	(2)	1
Filip DESPOTOVSKI		D	19	(7)	
Muzafer EJUPI		A	10	(2)	3

ırhan EMURLAI		M	17		3
RANKA Irapuan Júnior	BRA	M	4	(1)	
ırdan GEORGIEVSKI		G	24	(3)	
ıce KORUNOVSKI		G	7		
ıran KOSTENCOVSKI		D	4		
ıvan KOSTOVSKI		M	18	(2)	10
an KOVACEVSKI		D	4	(1)	
iloš LEPOVIĆ		A	8	(2)	1
adan MILOSAVLJEV	SRB	M	14	(2)	3
orgji MOJSOV		D	15	(7)	1
iver PEEV		M	22	(3)	4
ilan PERENDIJA	SRB	D	21	(5)	
lip PETROV		M	12	(7)	1
ːo POCEV		A	14	(1)	
eksandar RADOVIĆ	SRB	M			
imče RISTEVSKI		M	7	(3)	2
atko RISTOV		M	4	(2)	
orče RISTOVSKI		A	4	(1)	
ušan SAVIĆ		A	16	(5)	4
adimir SEKULOVSKI		D	20	(7)	1
enad SERAFIMOVSKI		M	5	(1)	2
lip SPASESKI		D	11	(7)	
aven STANKOVIĆ	SRB	M	14	(1)	1
stoja STJEPANOVIĆ		M	12	(2)	2
arko STOJANOV		M	2		
ikola TONEV		D	4	(7)	
ragan TRAJKOVIĆ		M	2	(1)	

PROMOTED CLUBS

FK TURNOVO
Coach – Vlatko Kostov
Founded - 1950

FK METALURG SKOPJE
Coach – Baže Lazarevski
Founded - 1964

ECOND LEVEL FINAL TABLE 2007/08

	Pld	W	D	L	F	A	Pts
FK Turnovo	32	22	5	5	58	23	71
FK Metalurg Skopje	32	20	7	5	47	24	67
FK Miravci	32	20	5	7	60	22	65
FK Belasica	32	16	7	9	49	37	55
FK Skopje	32	16	6	10	52	44	54
FK Drita	32	13	8	11	47	30	47
FK Teteks	32	14	5	13	32	30	47
FK Sloga Jugomagnat	32	13	5	14	36	34	44
FK Ohrid 2004	32	12	5	15	43	52	41
FK Madžari Solidarnost	32	12	4	16	33	39	40
FK Nov Milenium	32	10	9	13	41	36	39
FK Alumina	32	10	9	13	28	37	39
FK Vardar Negotino	32	11	6	15	42	58	39
FK Lokomotiva Skopje	32	12	2	18	40	47	38
FK Bregalnica	32	9	10	13	36	43	37
FK Karaorman	32	8	2	22	23	57	26
FK Vlazrimi	32	4	5	23	28	82	17

. FK Ilinden disqualified after Round 18; all previous results annulled.

PROMOTION/RELEGATION PLAY-OFFS
(8/6/08)
Bashkimi 4, Miravci 1
Sileks 2, Belasica 0

DOMESTIC CUP 2007/08

KUP NA MAKEDONIJA

FIRST ROUND

(19/9/07)
Ilinden 0, Pobeda Prilep 0 *(5-4 on pens)*
Gostivar 3, Vardar Skopje 6
Metalurg 0, Sileks 4
Novaci 0, Teteks 0 *(3-4 on pens)*
Drita 0, Skopje 1
Prevalec 0, Pelister 6
Arsimi 0, Makedonija GP 4
Vlaznimi 2, Renova 4
Maleš 1, Milano 8
Fortuna 0, Shkendija 1
Nov Milenium 1, Turnovo 1 *(5-3 on pens)*
Filip Vtori 0, Napredok 0 (4-5 on pens)
Vardar Negotino 10, Vlazrimi 3
Pobeda Vinica 0, Bregalnica 1
Kadino 0, Rabotnički 13
Bratstvo 0, Baškimi 3 *(w/o)*

SECOND ROUND

(24/10/07 & 7/11/07)
Baškimi v Makedonija GP 3-4; 0-2 *(3-6)*
Ilinden v Shkendija 0-1; 2-0 *(2-1)*
Milano v Bregalnica 3-0; 2-0 *(5-0)*
Vardar Negotino v Nov Milenium 2-3; 1-4 *(3-7)*
Renova v Napredok 5-1; 1-1 *(6-2)*
Sileks v Skopje 0-1; 1-1 *(1-2)*
Teteks v Vardar Skopje 0-3; 0-1 *(0-4)*
Pelister v Rabotnički 0-0; 0-4 *(0-4)*

QUARTER-FINALS

(28/11/07 & 12/12/07)
Makedonija GP 2 *(Brnjarčevski 2, Stojanovski 83)*, Skopje 1 *(Popovski 84)*
Skopje 0, Makedonija GP 0
(Makedonija GP 2-1)

Rabotnički 2 *(Braga 62og, Pejčić 68)*, Vardar 0
Vardar 1 *(Savić 68)*, Rabotnički 0
(Rabotnički 2-1)

Nov Milenium 3, Ilinden 0 *(w/o)*
Ilinden v Nov Milenium *(not played)*
(Nov Milenium 3-0)

Milano 2 *(Ristov 10, Stojanović 22)*, Renova 0
Renova 2 *(Bekiri Ar. 48, Stojanov P. 71)*, Milano 2 *(Stojanović 21, 59)*
(Milano 4-2)

SEMI-FINALS

(9/4/08 & 7/5/08)
Rabotnički 0, Makedonija GP 0
Makedonija GP 1 *(Jovanovski 88)*, Rabotnički 1 *(Jančevski 53)*
(Rabotnički 1-1 on away goal)

Milano 4 *(Krstev 43, Alimi 75, Brando 84, Stojanović 90)*, Nov Milenium 0
Nov Milenium 1 *(Mitrov 48)*, Milano 2 *(Lazarevski 55, Isufi 65)*
(Milano 6-1)

FINAL

(24/5/08)
Gradski stadion, Skopje
FK RABOTNIČKI 2 *(Nedžipi 24, 42)*
FK MILANO 0
Referee – *Petkovski*
RABOTNIČKI – *Pačovski, Mihajlović, Demiri, Lazarevski, Lukmon, Kovačević, Stanišić, Nedžipi (Milisavljević 61), Jančevski (Velkovski 75), Masev (Gligorov 89), Pejčić.*
MILANO – *Nuredinoski, Ilievski, Lazarevski, Ristov, Jovanovski, Gaši, Statovci, Alomerović (Manevski 46), Alimi (Isufi 83), Gligorovski (Aliji 46), Stojanović.*

Valletta scratch seven-year itch

After an interminable seven-year wait, Valletta FC finally got their hands on the Maltese Premier League trophy again, winning it in style thanks to a 20-match unbeaten run that lasted from mid-October right through to the first weekend of May when their triumph was confirmed.

Valletta would lose their last two matches and still finish five points clear, but it was not plain sailing for the Lilywhites. They started modestly and it was only after they hammered defending champions Marsaxlokk FC 7-0 on 1 December, with top-scoring Argentine striker Sebastián Monesterolo bagging four goals, that they built up the necessary momentum to mount a serious challenge.

Leaders by a point after the 18-match cut-off, Valletta found their best form in the play-offs, beating the other five teams one after the other and clinching the title on the evening of 3 May when Marsaxlokk lost 2-0 to Birkirkara FC. Twenty-four hours later they celebrated with a 2-0 win over early-season pacesetters Floriana FC. No one was prouder of Valletta's 19th title than club chairman Victor Scriha, who had joined after presiding over Marsaxlokk's shock triumph in 2006/07.

Birkirkara denied Valletta the double by beating them 4-2 in a thrilling FA Trophy semi-final. They also won the final, captain Michael Galea's second goal of the game, in the 90th minute, bringing the Stripes their fourth Trophy in seven years.

Mighty Mifsud

Malta registered a record five points in their UEFA EURO 2008™ qualifying campaign, the fifth coming in an impressive 2-2 draw at home to Turkey. Although he did not score in that game, the talk of the team was star striker Michael Mifsud, who notched five goals in a 7-1 win over Liechtenstein – Malta's record victory – and ended the season with an all-time tally of 20. Mifsud also made waves in England, notably by scoring two goals for Coventry City FC at Old Trafford to knock mighty Manchester United FC out of the League Cup.

Michael Mifsud – goals galore for both Malta and his English club Coventry City

Malta Football Association (MFA)

Millennium Stand (Floor 2)
National Stadium
MT-Ta' Qali ATD 4000
tel - +356 21 222697
fax - +356 21 245136
website - www.mfa.com.mt
email – info@mfa.com.mt
Year of Formation – 1900
President - Joseph Mifsud
General Secretary - Joseph Gauci
Press Officer – Alex Vella
Stadium - National, Ta' Qali (17,797)

TOP FIVE ALL-TIME CAPS
David Carabott (121); Carmel Busuttil (111); Gilbert Agius (108); Joe Brincat (103); John Buttigieg (95)

TOP FIVE ALL-TIME GOALS
Carmel Busuttil (23); Michael Mifsud (20); David Carabott (12); Gilbert Agius & Hubert Suda (8)

ATIONAL TEAM RESULTS 2007/08

/07	Albania	A	Tirana	0-3	
07	Turkey (ECQ)	H	Ta' Qali	2-2	*Said (41), Schembri (76)*
/07	Armenia	H	Ta' Qali	0-1	
0/07	Hungary (ECQ)	A	Budapest	0-2	
0/07	Moldova (ECQ)	H	Ta' Qali	2-3	*Scerri (71), Mifsud M. (84p)*
1/07	Greece (ECQ)	A	Athens	0-5	
1/07	Norway (ECQ)	H	Ta' Qali	1-4	*Mifsud M. (53)*
08	Armenia	H	Ta' Qali	0-1	
08	Iceland	H	Ta' Qali	1-0	*Frendo (18)*
08	Belarus	H	Ta' Qali	0-1	
/08	Liechtenstein	H	Ta' Qali	7-1	*Mifsud M. (2p, 17, 21p, 59, 69), Pace (35), Said (90+4)*
/08	Austria	A	Graz	1-5	*Mifsud M. (41)*

ATIONAL TEAM APPEARANCES 2007/08

ch – Dušan FITZEL (CZE)	**15/4/63**		**Alb**	**TUR**	**Arm**	**HUN**	**MDA**	**GRE**	**NOR**	**Arm**	**Isl**	**Blr**	**Lie**	**Aut**	**Caps**	**Goals**
io MUSCAT	18/8/76	Hibernians	G46		G					G					65	-
eph MIFSUD	7/9/84	Valletta	D77		D			D			D		D72		5	-
n SAID	15/5/73	Sliema	D	D		D	D	D		D		D66	s72	D	82	5
erick BRIFFA	24/8/81	Sliema	D	M88	D	M	D	D	D	D	s73	D85	D66	M	30	-
AZZOPARDI	12/8/82	Sliema	D46	D	s46	D	D91	D	D		s46	D		s71	34	-
ie PACE	1/1/77	Marsaxlokk	M	M			M	M	M		M	s65	M	M85	21	2
rge MALLIA	10/10/78	Birkirkara	M46	s83		M	M			M46	s84	M	s79	s85	61	5
ert AGIUS	21/2/74	Valletta	M	M	M82					M73		M65	M46	M	108	8
nne BARBARA	10/6/82	Sliema	M46						s83	A73	s20 /84		A46	s64	21	3
ence SCERRI	3/4/84	Hibernians	A91	s91	s46	s83	s46	s68	s87						11	1
dre SCHEMBRI	27/5/86	Braunschweig (GER)	A90	A91	A46	A83	A46	A68	A					A71	18	3
tin HABER	9/6/81	Haidari (GRE)	s46	G		G	G	G	G			G		s46	27	-
avon FRENDO	1/7/85	Marsaxlokk	s46		M					s46	M89	s46		s46	7	1
phen WELLMAN	31/8/82	Marsaxlokk	s46		D46				D	s73	D				21	1
drew COHEN	13/5/81	Hibernians	s46		s64		s46	s61	s86	s46	A		s46		24	-
on XUEREB	3/10/79	Hibernians	s77		s76					D		s66			4	-
derick BAJADA	4/1/83	Sliema	s90			s91				M86	s89				10	-
neth SCICLUNA	15/6/79	Valletta	s91	D	s82	D	M46			s86	M	s85	s66		19	-
e DIMECH	11/1/77	Macclesfield (ENG)		D	D76	D	D		D		D46	D	D	D	57	1
n WOODS	31/12/76	Sliema		M83	A	M91	M		M83	A46	A20	M46	s46		36	1
chael MIFSUD	17/4/81	Coventry (ENG)		A		A	A	M78	A87			A	A	A64	57	20
vin SAMMUT	26/5/81	Marsaxlokk		s88	M64	M66		M61			M73	s81	M46		24	-
er PULLICINO	17/6/76	Marsaxlokk			M			M	M	s73	M46				22	-
o NWOKO	15/10/84	Leixões (POR)				s66	s91	A	M86			A81	M79	M46	7	-

MALTA

NATIONAL TEAM APPEARANCES 2007/08 (contd.)

			Alb	TUR	Arm	HUN	MDA	GRE	NOR	Arm	Isl	Blr	Lie	Aut	Caps	Goa
Gareth SCIBERRAS	29/3/83	Marsaxlokk						s78		s60	s46	M			13	-
Shaun BAJADA	19/10/83	Birkirkara								M			D	D	3	-
Ryan FENECH	20/4/86	Hamrun								M60			s46	s46	3	-
Andrew HOGG	2/3/85	Valletta									G		G	G46	5	-
Jonathan CARUANA	24/7/86	Hibernians												D46	1	-

DOMESTIC LEAGUE 2007/08

PREMIER LEAGUE FINAL TABLES

SECOND PHASE

Championship Pool	Pld	W	D	L	F	A	Pts
1 Valletta FC	28	17	7	4	58	27	40
2 Marsaxlokk FC	28	16	3	9	56	40	35
3 Birikirkara FC	28	13	8	7	46	26	34
4 Sliema Wanderers FC	28	15	5	8	47	33	34
5 Floriana FC	28	10	6	12	40	42	22
6 Hamrun Spartans FC	28	7	7	14	42	60	15

Relegation Pool	Pld	W	D	L	F	A	Pts
7 Hibernians FC	24	10	8	6	35	27	26
8 Msida St Joseph FC	24	10	4	10	41	46	24
9 Pietà Hotspurs FC	24	6	0	18	27	53	11
10 Mqabba FC	24	3	2	19	24	62	8

FIRST PHASE

	Pld	W	D	L	F	A	Pts
1 Valletta FC	18	10	6	2	40	16	36 (18)
2 Marsaxlokk FC	18	10	3	5	35	26	33 (17)
3 Sliema Wanderers FC	18	9	5	4	31	18	32 (16)
4 Floriana FC	18	8	4	6	33	28	28 (14)
5 Birkirkara FC	18	7	6	5	27	18	27 (14)
6 Hamrun Spartans FC	18	7	6	5	30	29	27 (14)
7 Hibernians FC	18	6	7	5	22	19	25 (13)
8 Msida St Joseph FC	18	6	3	9	25	35	21 (11)
9 Pietà Hotspurs FC	18	5	0	13	21	40	15 (8)
10 Mqabba FC	18	2	0	16	15	50	6 (3)

N.B Figures in brackets indicate points carried forward to the Second Phase.

TOP GOALSCORERS

19 Sebastián MONESTEROLO (Valletta)

14 Marcelo PEREIRA (Mqabba)

12 Julio ALCORSÉ (Hibernians/Marsaxlokk)

11 Terence SCERRI (Hibernians)
Jean Pierre MIFSUD TRIGANZA (Birkirkara)
Njongo Lobe PRISO DODING (Msida)

10 Aleksander MADZAR (Sliema/Marsaxlokk)
Frank TEMILE (Valletta)
Ryan DARMANIN (Floriana)
Alfred EFFIONG (Hamrun)
Ivan WOODS (Sliema)

CLUB-BY-CLUB

BIRKIRKARA FC

Coach – John Buttigieg

Founded - 1950

MAJOR HONOURS: Maltese League - (2) 2000, 2006; Maltese Cup - (4) 2002, 2003, 2005, 2008.

2007			
26/8	Hibernians	1-1	*Hartvig*
29/8	Mqabba	1-0	*Galea M.*
15/9	Sliema	2-0	*Galea M., Hartvig*
23/9	Marsaxlokk	2-0	*Tabone, Hartvig*
27/9	Pietà	1-2	*Galea M.*
1/10	Msida	1-1	*Tamboulas*
5/10	Hamrun	2-2	*Bajada, Yanchev*
24/11	Valletta	0-1	
1/12	Floriana	3-2	*Bajada, Mifsud Triganza, Paris T.*
8/12	Hibernians	0-2	
19/12	Mqabba	4-1	*Fenech, Mifsud Triganza, Anastasi, Tabone (p)*
30/12	Sliema	1-1	*Mifsud Triganza*
2008			
5/1	Marsaxlokk	1-3	*Bajada*
13/1	Pietà	2-0	*Sylla, Hartvig*
26/1	Msida	0-0	
9/2	Hamrun	5-0	*Sylla 2, Tabone 2, Galea M.*
18/2	Valletta	1-2	*Mifsud Triganza (p)*
22/2	Floriana	0-0	
13/3	Sliema	3-1	*Sylla 2, Mifsud Triganza*
17/3	Valletta	1-1	*Bajada*
23/3	Marsaxlokk	2-1	*Tabone, Mifsud Triganza*
30/3	Floriana	2-0	*Mifsud Triganza 2*
5/4	Hamrun	4-0	*Mifsud Triganza 3 (1p), Galea M.*
19/4	Sliema	1-2	*Sylla*
28/4	Valletta	1-2	*Sylla*
3/5	Marsaxlokk	2-0	*Zerafa, Galea M.*
8/5	Floriana	1-1	*Sylla*
13/5	Hamrun	2-0	*Hartvig, Yanchev*

No	Name	Nat	Pos	Aps	(s)	Gls
13	Martin ANASTASI		M	11	(8)	1
2	Shaun BAJADA		M	27	(2)	4
22	Omar BORG		G	19		
18	Adrian CIANTAR		M	5	(3)	
6	Pawlu FENECH		M	27		1
3	Angelo GALEA		D	3		

Name	Nat	Pos	Aps	(s)	Gls
Lino GALEA		M	17		
Michael GALEA		A	11	(8)	6
Ronald HARTVIG	DEN	D	26		5
Lee LOMBARDI		D	6	(6)	
George MALLIA		M	25	(1)	
Jean Pierre MIFSUD TRIGANZA		A	15	(9)	11
Bernard PARIS		G	9		
Tomas PARIS		D	12	(10)	1
Roderick SAMMUT		D	12	(5)	
Boris SANDJO	CTA	A	1		
Luke SCIBERRAS		D		(1)	
Kenneth SPITERI		D	1	(2)	
Ahmed Davy SYLLA	CIV	A	13	(2)	8
Alan TABONE		M	24	(2)	5
Marceline TAMBOULAS	CTA	M	5		1
Antoine ZAHRA		M		(8)	
Clint ZAMMIT		M		(1)	
Joseph ZERAFA		M	12	(7)	1
Emil YANCHEV	BUL	D	27		2

FLORIANA FC

Coach – Danilo Dončić (SRB)

Founded - 1894

MAJOR HONOURS: Maltese League - (25) 1910, 1912, 1913, 1921, 1922, 1925, 1927, 1928, 1929, 1931, 1935, 1937, 1950, 1951, 1952, 1953, 1955, 1958, 1962, 1968, 1970, 1973, 1975, 1977, 1993; Maltese Cup - (18) 1938, 1945, 1947, 1949, 1950, 1953, 1954, 1955, 1957, 1958, 1961, 1966, 1967, 1972, 1976, 1981, 1993, 1994.

007			
7/8	Valletta	3-2	*Caruana C. 2, Mifsud*
1/8	Hibernians	1-0	*Caruana C.*
5/9	Mqabba	3-1	*Mifsud, Caruana C., Brincat M.*
1/9	Sliema	2-2	*Darmanin 2*
7/9	Marsaxlokk	2-3	*Sevasta, Micallef M.*
/10	Pietà	4-0	*Krsteski, Mifsud, Bolasie, Micallef M.*
5/10	Msida	2-0	*Brincat M., Krsteski*
24/11	Hamrun	1-1	*Darmanin*
1/12	Birkirkara	2-3	*Krsteski, Cassar*
8/12	Valletta	0-4	
15/12	Hibernians	1-1	*Cilia*
27/12	Mqabba	4-1	*Micallef M. 2, Darmanin, Cilia*
2008			
5/1	Sliema	1-0	*Darmanin*
12/1	Marsaxlokk	1-4	*Darmanin*
20/1	Pietà	3-1	*Cassar, Darmanin, Bolasie*
10/2	Msida	2-3	*Darmanin, Levnajić*
18/2	Hamrun	1-2	*Bolasie*
22/2	Birkirkara	0-0	
12/3	Marsaxlokk	1-2	*Cilia*
17/3	Hamrun	1-1	*Krsteski*
23/3	Valletta	0-1	
30/3	Birkirkara	0-2	
5/4	Sliema	2-0	*Darmanin, og (Chetcuti)*
21/4	Marsaxlokk	0-2	
26/4	Hamrun	2-1	*Bolasie, Micallef M. (p)*
4/5	Valletta	0-2	
8/5	Birkirkara	1-1	*Darmanin*
15/5	Sliema	0-2	

No	Name	Nat	Pos	Aps	(s)	Gls
1	Simon AGIUS		G	25		
11	Yala BOLASIE	ENG	M	20	(3)	4
19	Joseph BORG		M	6	(2)	
4	Julian BRIFFA		D	19	(2)	
21	Jermain BRINCAT		D		(5)	
22	Mauro BRINCAT		M	22	(4)	2
14	Owen BUGEJA		D	5	(4)	
6	Matthew CAMILLERI		D	1		
10	Christian CARUANA		M	14	(4)	4
2	Mario CARUANA		D	1	(2)	
8	Christian CASSAR		M	24		2
13	Clifton CIANTAR		D	18	(7)	
7	Trevor CILIA		M	21	(2)	3
18	Ryan DARMANIN		A	18	(6)	10
15	Sunday EBOH	NGA	D	11	(1)	
20	Mark Gauci		M	2	(10)	
12	Partick GRECH		M		(1)	
5	Darko KRSTESKI	MKD	D	17		4
24	Zoran LEVNAJIĆ	CRO	M	24		1
29	Jurgen MICALLEF		G	3		
9	Manolito MICALLEF		M	25	(2)	5
13	Adrian MIFSUD		A	8	(3)	3
16	Duncan PISANI		D	14	(7)	
3	Emanuel SEVASTA		D	10	(3)	1

HAMRUN SPARTANS FC

Coach – Marco Gerada

Founded - 1907

MAJOR HONOURS: Maltese League - (7) 1914, 1918, 1947, 1983, 1987, 1988, 1991; Maltese Cup - (6) 1983, 1984, 1987, 1988, 1989, 1992.

2007			
26/8	Mqabba	2-1	*Briffa, Sultana*
31/8	Sliema	0-3	
16/9	Marsaxlokk	1-0	*Spiteri*
22/9	Pietà	2-3	*Mangion, Spiteri*
26/9	Msida	1-0	*Spiteri*
5/10	Birkirkara	2-2	*Spiteri, Fenech Ry.*
20/10	Valletta	0-0	
24/11	Floriana	1-1	*Effiong*
2/12	Hibernians	2-2	*Effiong, Sultana*
9/12	Mqabba	3-0	*Sultana, Fenech Ry., Effiong*
26/12	Sliema	1-1	*Spiteri*
30/12	Marsaxlokk	7-3	*Spiteri, Mangion, Effiong 2, Sultana, Fenech Ry., Cucciardi*
2008			
6/1	Pietà	3-0	*Spiteri 2, Sultana (p)*
13/1	Msida	1-2	*Sultana*
19/1	Valletta	1-4	*og (Scicluna)*
9/2	Birkirkara	0-5	
18/2	Floriana	2-1	*Effiong, Fenech Ry.*
25/2	Hibernians	1-1	*Timotić*
13/3	Valletta	1-4	*Effiong*
17/3	Floriana	1-1	*Effiong*
22/3	Sliema	0-2	
29/3	Marsaxlokk	1-3	*Cucciardi*
5/4	Birkirkara	0-4	
19/4	Valletta	2-4	*Spiteri, Effiong*
26/4	Floriana	1-2	*Agius*
4/5	Sliema	3-5	*Meilak, Effiong, Sultana (p)*
9/5	Marsaxlokk	3-4	*Meilak, Sultana, Timotić*
13/5	Birkirkara	0-2	

No	Name	Nat	Pos	Aps	(s)	Gls
18	Lee James AGUIS		A	3	(5)	1
5	Aaron ATTARD		D	10	(3)	
2	Mark Anthony BONNICI		D	15	(2)	
7	Kevin BORG		M	12	(9)	
6	Evano BRIFFA		M	12	(2)	1
30	Mauro BUSUTTIL		A	1	(2)	
20	Christian CACCIOTOLO		M		(7)	
3	Diego Armando CUCCIARDI		A	8	(11)	2
33	Dalton CARUANA		M		(1)	
13	John DEBATTISTA		D	9	(10)	
22	Alfred EFFIONG	NGA	A	24	(2)	10
1						

	Michael FALZON		G	15		
8	Roderick FENECH		D	24		
10	Ryan FENECH		M	24		4
17	Neville GALEA		M	12	(2)	
14	Rupert MANGION		M	24		2
9	Steve MEILAK		A	18	(6)	2
4	Precious MONYE	NGA	D	21	(1)	
21	Gejtanu SPITERI		A	24	(1)	9
12	Sean SULLIVAN		G	13		
11	Stefan SULTANA		A	15	(6)	8
19	Brano TIMOTIĆ	SRB	D	24		2

HIBERNIANS FC

Coach – Robert Gatt

Founded - 1922

MAJOR HONOURS: Maltese League - (9) 1961, 1967, 1969, 1979, 1981, 1982, 1994, 1995, 2002; Maltese Cup - (8) 1962, 1970, 1971, 1980, 1982, 1998, 2006, 2007.

2007

26/8	Birkirkara	1-1	*Scerri T.*
31/8	Floriana	0-1	
17/9	Valletta	1-1	*Cohen*
21/9	Mqabba	2-0	*Scerri T. Doffo*
25/9	Sliema	1-2	*Alcorsé*
30/9	Marsaxlokk	1-1	*Scerri T.*
6/10	Pietà	2-0	*Alcorsé, Scerri T.*
21/10	Msida	4-0	*Scerri T., Cohen 2 (1p), Agius*
2/12	Hamrun	2-2	*Cohen, Uzeh*
8/12	Birkirkara	2-0	*Chukunyere, Scerri T.*
15/12	Floriana	1-1	*Failla*
26/12	Valletta	0-0	

2008

3/1	Mqabba	1-0	*Mifsud*
12/1	Sliema	1-2	*Agius*
19/1	Marsaxlokk	0-5	
27/1	Pietà	2-0	*Aguis, Cohen*
16/2	Msida	0-2	
25/2	Hamrun	1-1	*Mifsud*
16/3	Msida	3-0	*Doffo, Camilleri B., Scerri T.*
30/3	Pietà	2-1	*Cohen, Scerri T.*
6/4	Mqabba	4-2	*Xuereb 2 (1p), Scerri T. 2 (1p)*
28/4	Msida	1-3	*Failla*
9/5	Pietà	2-1	*Doffo, Scerri T.*
13/5	Mqabba	1-1	*Doffo*

No	Name	Nat	Pos	Aps	(s)	Gls
17	Edmond AGIUS		M	23		3
11	Julio ALCORSÉ	ARG	A	8	(5)	2
6	Daniel BALZAN		G	2	(1)	
3	Roderick BRIFFA		D		(1)	
13	Bronwen BUGEJA		D		(1)	
12	Alex CAMILLERI		G	3		
16	Ben CAMILLERI		M	8	(6)	1
14	Triston CARUANA		M	2	(1)	
18	Kevin CASSAR		D	8	(1)	
21	Jonathan CARUANA		D	21	(1)	
20	Ndubisi CHUKENYERE	NGA	A	9	(7)	1
10	Andrew COHEN		A	21	(2)	6
8	Pablo DOFFO	ARG	M	22		4
7	Clayton FAILLA		M	21	(1)	2
19	Abade Narcisse FISH	CMR	M	3	(2)	
2	Timothy FLERI SOLER		D	6		
22	Kurt FORMOSA		D		(3)	
28	Gary INGUANEZ		M		(2)	
25	Adrian MIFSUD		A	3	(3)	2
27	Ryan MINTOFF		D	10	(2)	
1	Mario MUSCAT		G	19		
15	Jonathan PEARSON		M	4	(7)	
4	Adrian PULIS		D	13	(3)	
9	Terence SCERRI		A	21	(3)	11
24	Jonathan SCERRI		M	3	(5)	
26	Edafe UZEH	NGA	M	15	(1)	1
23	Julian VELLA		M	1	(3)	
5	Aaron XUEREB		D	18	(3)	2

MARSAXLOKK FC

Coach – Brian Talbot (ENG)

Founded - 1949

MAJOR HONOURS: Maltese League - (1) 2007.

2007

29/8	Pietà	3-1	*Gomes, Sammut, Frendo*
1/9	Msida	3-1	*Frendo, Pullicino, Da Sil*
16/9	Hamrun	0-1	
23/9	Birkirkara	0-2	
27/9	Floriana	3-2	*Licari, Gomes, Templeman*
30/9	Hibernians	1-1	*Camenzuli*
5/10	Mqabba	1-0	*Barbara*
21/10	Sliema	0-1	
1/12	Valletta	0-7	
9/12	Pietà	1-0	*Sammut (p)*
19/12	Msida	5-0	*Pace, Pullicino, Barbar 2, Licari*
30/12	Hamrun	3-7	*Barbara, Licari 2 (1p)*

2008

5/1	Birkirkara	3-1	*Licari, Frendo 2*
12/1	Floriana	4-1	*Alcorsé, Barbara, Licar Sciberras G.*
19/1	Hibernians	5-0	*Sammut, Alcorsé, Barbara, Pace, Licari (p*
27/1	Mqabba	2-0	*Alcorsé 2*
9/2	Sliema	0-0	
22/2	Valletta	1-1	*Sammut*
12/3	Floriana	2-1	*Madzar 2*
16/3	Sliema	4-2	*Madzar 2, Alcorsé 2*
23/3	Birkirkara	1-2	*Frendo*
29/3	Hamrun	3-1	*Alcorsé 2 (1p), Camenzuli*
6/4	Valletta	1-2	*Pullicino*
21/4	Floriana	2-0	*Sammut, Mamo*
26/4	Sliema	0-1	
3/5	Birkirkara	0-2	
9/5	Hamrun	4-3	*Sammut, Alcorsé 2, Madzar*
17/5	Valletta	4-0	*Pace, Wellmann 2, Madzar*

No	Name	Nat	Pos	Aps	(s)	Gls
9	Julio ALCORSÉ	ARG	A	12	(2)	10
15	Mark BARBARA		A	11	(9)	6
11	William CAMENZULI		D	18		2
5	Renato CONCEIÇÃO	BRA	D	24	(1)	
12	André Rocha DA SILVA	BRA	M	3	(7)	1
74	Reuben DEBONO		G	24		
26	Cleaven FRENDO		A	16	(3)	5
1	Reuben GAUCI		G	4		
13	Wendell GOMES	BRA	A	9	(2)	2
2	Malcolm LICARI		D	18	(4)	7
10	Aleksander MADZAR	MNE	A	10	(2)	6
14	Charlo MAGRO		D	21	(1)	
3	Carlo MAMO		D	17	(2)	1
18	Jamie PACE		M	26	(2)	3
8	Peter PULLICINO		M	23	(2)	3
7	Kevin SAMMUT		M	27		6
19	Dylan SCIBERRAS		D		(1)	
4	Gareth SCIBERRAS		M	10	(5)	1
16	Steve SCICLUNA		M		(1)	
27	Shawn TELLUS		D	3	(6)	

17	Trevor TEMPLEMAN	M	17	(6)	1
6	Stephen WELLMAN	D	15	(5)	2

MQABBA FC

Coach – Joe Falzon; (13/2/08) Borislav Giorev (BUL)

Founded - 1957

2007

26/8	Hamrun	1-2	*Baldacchino*
29/8	Birkirkara	0-1	
15/9	Floriana	1-3	*Silva (p)*
21/9	Hibernians	0-2	
26/9	Valletta	1-3	*Pereira*
30/9	Sliema	3-2	*Pereira 3*
5/10	Marsaxlokk	0-1	
20/10	Pietà	1-6	*Pereira (p)*
25/11	Msida	3-4	*Calleja C., Pereira, Nogueira*
9/12	Hamrun	0-3	
19/12	Birkirkara	1-4	*Zarb*
27/12	Floriana	1-4	*Silva (p)*

2008

3/1	Hibernians	0-1	
6/1	Valletta	1-2	*Zarb*
20/1	Sliema	0-4	
27/1	Marsaxlokk	0-2	
10/2	Pietà	0-5	
25/2	Msida	2-1	*Bonnici, Pereira*
12/3	Pietà	2-0	*Pereira 2 (1p)*
22/3	Msida	2-4	*Pereira 2 (1p)*
6/4	Hibernians	2-4	*Pereira, Briffa M.*
3/5	Pietà	0-1	
8/5	Msida	2-2	*Pereira 2 (1p)*
13/5	Hibernians	1-1	*Briffa M.*

No	Name	Nat	Pos	Aps	(s)	Gls
21	Clifford Gatt BALDACCHINO		D	21	(1)	1
2	Mauro BONNICI		D	18	(3)	1
18	Edric BORG		M	1	(5)	
7	Marlon BRIFFA		M	22	(1)	2
3	Roderick BRIFFA		D	6	(4)	
4	Albert BUSUTTIL		M	16	(6)	
10	Claudio CALLEJA		M	17		1
1	Kris CALLEJA		G	21		
13	Matthew COCKS		M	15	(4)	
19	Joseph FENECH		D		(5)	
16	Lee GALEA		D	13	(4)	
17	John MINTOFF		A	9	(12)	
11	John Paul MUSCAT		A	7	(7)	
14	Elliot NAVARRO		M	2	(3)	
5	Italo NOGUEIRA	BRA	D	20	(1)	1
12	Morgan ONYORAH	NGA	A		(2)	
9	Marcelo PEREIRA	BRA	A	23		14
15	Mark PSAILA		D	18	(2)	
6	Paul PSAILA		G	2	(1)	
8	Fábio SILVA	BRA	M	15	(4)	2
20	Dylan ZARB		A	18	(2)	2

MSIDA ST JOSEPH FC

Coach – Patrick Curmi

Founded - 1906

2007

27/8	Sliema	0-3	
1/9	Marsaxlokk	1-3	*Baldacchino*
16/9	Pietà	1-0	*Ogbonna*
22/9	Valletta	1-1	*Magri*
26/9	Hamrun	0-1	
1/10	Birkirkara	1-1	*Priso Doding (p)*
6/10	Floriana	0-2	
21/10	Hibernians	0-4	
25/11	Mqabba	4-3	*Priso Doding, Borg, Calcado 2*
2/12	Sliema	1-4	*Borg*
19/12	Marsaxlokk	0-5	
27/12	Pietà	7-0	*Calcado, Priso Doding 4, Farrugia A. 2*

2008

3/1	Valletta	1-3	*Calcado*
13/1	Hamrun	2-1	*Farrugia T. Calcado*
26/1	Birkirkara	0-0	
10/2	Floriana	3-2	*Farrugia T., Farrugia A., Priso Doding*
16/2	Hibernians	2-0	*Priso Doding, Dos Santos (p)*
25/2	Mqabba	1-2	*Farrugia A.*
16/3	Hibernians	0-3	
22/3	Mqabba	4-2	*Farrugia T. 2, Calcado 2*
21/4	Pietà	3-1	*Dos Santos, Priso Doding, Calcado*
28/4	Hibernians	3-1	*Calcado, Priso Doding, Dos Santos*
8/5	Mqabba	2-2	*Camilleri G., Farrugia T.*
15/5	Pietà	4-2	*Farrugia A., Farrugia T. 2, Priso Doding*

No	Name	Nat	Pos	Aps	(s)	Gls
11	Roderick BALDACCHINO		M	15	(5)	1
52	Manuel BARTOLO		G	16		
4	Patrick BORG		D	9	(9)	2
16	Clive BRINCAT		D	19		
18	Dino CACHIA		M	23		
12	Pedro dos Santos CALCADO	BRA	A	14	(1)	9
9	Gilbert CAMILLERI		A	4	(4)	1
1	Matthew CAMILLERI		G	4	(1)	
30	Gilberto DOS SANTOS	BRA	M	10	(3)	3
20	Karl EBEJER		M	4	(2)	
7	Adrian FARRUGIA		M	21		5
22	Tyrone FARRUGIA		M	22		7
13	Andre FORMOSA		M	3	(1)	
15	Kurth GRECH		D		(2)	
24	Stefano GRIMA		D	21		
6	Glenn MAGRI		M		(6)	1
17	Lydon MICALLEF		M	3	(3)	
31	Gallen MIFSUD		G			
10	Lawrence MIZZI		A	3	(7)	
14	George OGBONNA	NGA	M	5		1
28	Yacine OUAHCHIA	ALG	A	5	(1)	
25	Njongo Lobe PRISO DODING	CMR	A	19	(1)	11
21	Pio SCIRIHA		D	18		
19	Adam SPITERI		M	3	(3)	
8	Andrew SPITERI		M	8	(4)	
3	Clive SPITERI		D	1	(7)	
2	Kenneth SPITERI		D	9		
18	Jonathan VELLA		G	4	(2)	
5	Stacy VELLA		D	1	(4)	

PIETÀ HOTSPURS FC

Coach – Carmel Busuttil

Founded - 1968

2006

29/8	Marsaxlokk	1-3	*Herrera*
1/9	Valletta	1-3	*Galabov*
16/9	Msida	0-1	
22/9	Hamrun	3-2	*Herrera 2, Kondev (p)*
27/9	Birkirkara	2-1	*Goodlip, Refalo Q.*
1/10	Floriana	0-4	
6/10	Hibernians	0-2	
20/10	Mqabba	6-1	*Deliminkov, Deanov 3, Herrera, Kondev (p)*
25/11	Sliema	1-0	*Deliminkov*
9/12	Marsaxlokk	0-1	
15/12	Valletta	0-3	
27/12	Msida	0-7	

MALTA

2008

6/1	Hamrun	0-3	
13/1	Birkirkara	0-2	
20/1	Floriana	1-3	*Herrera*
27/1	Hibernians	0-2	
10/2	Mqabba	5-0	*Deanov 2, Kondev 2 (1p), Refalo Q.*
16/2	Sliema	1-2	*Pulo*
12/3	Mqabba	0-2	
30/3	Hibernians	1-2	*Kondev (p)*
21/4	Msida	1-3	*Deanov*
3/5	Mqabba	1-0	*Deanov*
9/5	Hibernians	1-2	*Sulas*
15/5	Msida	2-4	*Kondev (p), Pulo*

No	Name	Nat	Pos	Aps	(s)	Gls
2	Pierre AQUILINA		D	5	(1)	
6	Gary BUSUTTIL		M	1	(1)	
15	David CAMENZULI		D	4	(1)	
20	Ryan CAMILLERI		D	11	(2)	
8	Silvan CASCALDI		M	7	(5)	
24	Cleavon CASSAR		D	13	(3)	
29	Kyle DARMANIN		D	2	(1)	
7	Martin DEANOV	BUL	M	19		7
3	Peycho DELIMINIKOV	BUL	D	12		2
25	Clint FARRUGIA		D		(2)	
11	Daniel GATT		D	4	(3)	
30	Clifford GAUCI		M		(1)	
22	Rumen Angelov GALABOV	BUL	D	16	(1)	1
32	Dean GERA		M	5	(2)	
17	Glanville GOODLIP		A	9	(1)	1
31	Ismael GRECH		D	1	(2)	
23	Sheldon GRECH		M	8	(5)	
33	Ruben GRIPPA		M	4	(1)	
19	Edward HERRERA		D	20	(1)	5
16	Svetlan KONDEV	BUL	M	20		6
21	Dylan KOKAVESSIS		A	2	(2)	
26	Christ MCKAY		M	2		
4	Shaun MICALLEF		D		(3)	
18	Dominic MIFSUD		M	15	(3)	
1	Miguel MONTFORT		G	17		
10	Carl PULO		M	13	(4)	2
9	Quilin REFALO		A	13	(3)	2
14	Rendal REFALO		M	2	(2)	
13	Carl SAMMUT		D	17	(2)	
5	Bernard SCIBERRAS		D	9	(1)	
27	Francesco SULAS		M	4	(5)	1
12	Mark VELLA		G	5		
23	Melchior VELLA		D	2	(6)	
28	Kersten VELLA		G	2		
34	Ben ZAMMIT		M		(1)	

SLIEMA WANDERERS FC

Coach – Ray Farrugia; (26/11/07) Stephen Azzopardi

Founded - 1909

MAJOR HONOURS: Maltese League - (26) 1920, 1923, 1924, 1926, 1930, 1933, 1934, 1936, 1938, 1939, 1940, 1949, 1954, 1956, 1957, 1964, 1965, 1966, 1971, 1972, 1976, 1989, 1996, 2003, 2004, 2005; Maltese Cup - (19) 1935, 1936, 1937, 1940, 1946, 1948, 1951, 1952, 1956, 1959, 1963, 1965, 1968, 1969, 1974, 1979, 1990, 2000, 2004.

2007			
27/8	Msida	3-0	*Barbara 2, Madzar*
31/8	Hamrun	3-0	*Milovanović, Barbara 2 (1p)*
15/9	Birkirkara	0-2	
21/9	Floriana	2-2	*Madzar, Briffa*
25/9	Hibernians	2-1	*Bajada, Woods*
30/9	Mqabba	2-3	*Barbara, Muscat*
4/10	Valletta	2-1	*Said, Madzar*
21/10	Marsaxlokk	1-0	*Said*
25/11	Pietà	0-1	
2/12	Msida	4-1	*Madzar, Anonam, Bartolo, Briffa*
26/12	Hamrun	1-1	*Woods (p)*
30/12	Birkirkara	1-1	*Woods*
2008			
5/1	Floriana	0-1	
12/1	Hibernians	2-1	*Da Silva, Said*
20/1	Mqabba	4-0	*Woods, og (Bonnici), Barbara, Turner*
26/1	Valletta	2-2	*Woods 2 (1p)*
9/2	Marsaxlokk	0-0	
16/2	Pietà	2-1	*og (Sciberras), Anonam*
13/3	Birkirkara	1-3	*Woods*
16/3	Marsaxlokk	2-4	*Muscat, Woods*
22/3	Hamrun	2-0	*Bartolo, Bajada*
29/3	Valletta	0-2	
5/4	Floriana	0-2	
19/4	Birkirkara	2-1	*Barbara 2*
26/4	Marsaxlokk	1-0	*Woods*
4/5	Hamrun	5-3	*Woods, Bartolo 2, Bajada 2*
10/5	Valletta	1-0	*Nisević*
15/5	Floriana	2-0	*Briffa, Anonam*

No	Name	Nat	Pos	Aps	(s)	Gls
18	Orosco ANONAM		A	8	(15)	3
22	Murphy AKANJI	NGA	G	21		
20	Ian AZZOPARDI		D	19	(2)	
10	Roderick BAJADA		M	23	(4)	4
46	Etienne BARBARA		A	21	(2)	8
11	Matthew BARTOLO		M	17	(8)	4
1	Henry BONELLO		G	7	(1)	
24	Roderick BRIFFA		M	21	(3)	3
13	Jeffrey CHETCUTI		D	17	(2)	
3	Ian CIANTAR		D	8	(6)	
21	Miguel CIANTAR		A	1	(2)	
9	André Rocha DA SILVA	BRA	M	9	(3)	1
5	Claude MATTOCKS		M		(1)	
6	Aleksander MADZAR	MNE	A	12	(2)	4
12	Nesko MILOVANOVIĆ	SRB	M	8	(2)	1
2	Alex MUSCAT		D	21	(1)	2
5	Branko NISEVIĆ	SRB	D	10	(2)	1
15	Chucks NWOKO		M		(1)	
25	Sharlon PACE		D	12	(3)	
4	Brian SAID		D	25		3
8	Mark SCERRI		M	15	(3)	
7	Noel TURNER		M	7	(6)	1
13	Julian VELLA		M	3	(3)	
16	Carlos Eduardo VENTURA		D	2	(4)	
14	Ivan WOODS		A	21	(1)	10

VALLETTA FC

Coach – Paul Zammit

Founded - 1943

MAJOR HONOURS: Maltese League - (19) 1915, 1932, 1945, 1946, 1948, 1959, 1960, 1963, 1974, 1978, 1980, 1984, 1990, 1992, 1997, 1998, 1999, 2001, 2008; Maltese Cup - (11) 1960, 1964, 1975, 1977, 1978, 1991, 1995, 1996, 1997, 1999, 2001.

2007			
27/8	Floriana	2-3	*Zammit 2*
1/9	Pietà	3-1	*Zammit, Monesterolo, Agius G.*
17/9	Hibernians	1-1	*Giglio (p)*
22/9	Msida	1-1	*Mattocks*
26/9	Mqabba	3-1	*Zammit, Monesterolo, Bondin*
4/10	Sliema	1-2	*Monesterolo*

20/10	Hamrun	0-0	
24/11	Birkirkara	1-0	*Mifsud*
1/12	Marsaxlokk	7-0	*Monesterolo 4, Backhaus, Zammit, Temile*
8/12	Floriana	4-0	*Zammit, Monesterolo, Scicluna, Temile*
15/12	Pietà	3-0	*Backhaus, Temile, Agius G.*
26/12	Hibernians	0-0	
2008			
3/1	Msida	3-1	*Monesterolo 2 (2p), Zammit*
6/1	Mqabba	2-1	*Scicluna, Zammit*
19/1	Hamrun	4-1	*Camilleri, Monesterolo 3*
26/1	Sliema	2-2	*Giglio 2*
18/2	Birkirkara	2-1	*Backhaus, Monesterolo*
22/2	Marsaxlokk	1-1	*Camilleri*
13/3	Hamrun	4-1	*Temile 2, Monesterolo, Mifsud*
17/2	Birkirkara	1-1	*Monesterolo*
23/3	Floriana	1-0	*Temile*
29/3	Sliema	2-0	*Temile 2*
6/4	Marsaxlokk	2-1	*Giglio, Monesterolo*
19/4	Hamrun	4-2	*Monesterolo, Grioli, Temile, Falzon*
28/4	Birkirkara	2-1	*Grioli, Monesterolo*
4/5	Floriana	2-0	*Temile, Agius G.*
10/5	Sliema	0-1	
17/5	Marsaxlokk	0-4	

No	Name	Nat	Pos	Aps	(s)	Gls
11	Bryan AGIUS		D	3	(7)	
7	Gilbert AGIUS		D	18	(3)	3
22	Heiner BACKHAUS	GER	M	26	(1)	3
13	Steve BEZZINA		D	23		
4	Jonathan BONDIN		D	5	(10)	1
10	David CAMILLERI		M	23	(2)	2
1	Saviour DARMANIN		G	6	(2)	
20	Dyson FALZON		A	14	(12)	1
12	Keith FENECH		M	2	(4)	
18	Renie FORACE		D	6	(2)	
26	Stefan GIGLIO		M	18	(4)	4
6	Massimo GRIMA		D	3		
2	Justin GRIOLI		M	20	(4)	2
24	Andrew HOGG		G	22		
16	Kurt MAGRO		M		(8)	
8	Claude MATTOCKS		M	5	(7)	1
5	Josef MIFSUD		D	25		2
21	Sebastián MONESTEROLO	ARG	A	25	(2)	19
17	Kenneth SCICLUNA		D	24	(1)	2
14	Frank TEMILE	NGA	A	20		10
9	Ian ZAMMIT		A	20	(6)	8

PROMOTED CLUBS

TARXIEN RAINBOWS FC

Coach – John Vella

Founded - 1944

QORMI FC

Coach – Jesmond Zerafa

Founded - 1961

SECOND LEVEL FINAL TABLE 2007/08

		Pld	W	D	L	F	A	Pts
	Tarxien Rainbows FC	18	12	3	3	32	17	39
	Mosta FC	18	11	4	3	34	18	37
	Qormi FC	18	11	4	3	37	22	37
	Senglea Athletics FC	18	10	1	7	32	23	31
	Dingli Swallows FC	18	8	3	7	34	27	27
	Vittoriosa Stars FC	18	8	1	9	33	29	25
	St George's FC	18	6	3	9	27	33	21
	St Patrick FC	18	4	4	10	21	27	16
	Mellieha FC	18	3	4	11	21	43	13
10	Marsa FC	18	3	1	14	23	55	10

PROMOTION PLAY-OFFS

(23/05/08)

Mosta 0, Qormi 0 *(aet; 3-4 on pens)*

(Qormi 4-3)

DOMESTIC CUP 2007/08

FA TROPHY

FIRST ROUND

(3/11/07)

Valletta 4, St Patricks 0

St George's 2, Pietà 3

(4/11/07)

Mqabba 3, Vittoriosa 2

Mosta 0, Hamrun 2

(11/11/07)

Floriana 7, Mellieha 1

Senglea 4, Msida 3 *(aet)*

(10/11/07)

Qormi 1, Tarxien 5

Marsa 0, Dingli 7

SECOND ROUND

(2/3/08)

Mqabba 0, Dingli 1

Floriana 3, Senglea 2 *(aet)*

(1/3/08)

Hamrun 1, Pietà 0

Valletta 5, Tarxien 0

QUARTER-FINALS

(12/4/08)

Hibernians 1 *(Scerri T. 67)*, Valletta 2 *(Temile 46, Agius G. 87)*

Hamrun 3 *(Spiteri 30, 53, 93)*, Dingli 1 *(Agius 19)*

(13/4/08)

Floriana 2 *(Darmanin 61, Micallef M. 65)*, Sliema 1 *(Barbara 51)*

Marsaxlokk 1 *(Mamo 1)*, Birkirkara 2 *(Sylla 52, Mifsud Triganza 70)*

SEMI-FINALS

(19/5/08)

Hamrun 4 *(Meilak 25, Effiong 29, Spiteri 33, Fenech Ry. 75)*, Floriana 2 *(Brincat M. 45, Darmanin 64)*

Birkirkara 4 *(Sylla 42, 51, Tabone 61, Mallia 68)*, Valletta 2 *(Monesterolo 19, Mifsud 73)*

FINAL

(24/5/08)

Ta'Qali

BIRKIRKARA FC 2 *(Galea M. 59, 90)*

HAMRUN SPARTANS FC 1 *(Fenech Ry. 65)*

Referee – *Zammit*

BIRKIRKARA – *Paris B., Paris T., (Galea L. 67), Fenech, Galea M., Tabone, Lombardi, Bajada, Zerafa, Sylla (Mifsud Triganza 90), Mallia, Yanchev.*

HAMRUN – *Sullivan, Monye, Attard, Fenech Ro., Meilak, Fenech Ry., Mangion, Galea (Sultana 90), Timotic, Spiteri, Effiong.*

Dobrovolski turns the tide

Moldova ended their UEFA EURO 2008™ qualifying campaign as one of the competition's in-form teams. Inspired by their new coach, ex-USSR international and Olympic gold medallist Igor Dobrovolski, they claimed ten points from their final four games. The previous eight fixtures had yielded just two.

A splendid 1-0 win away to Bosnia-Herzegovina preceded a 1-1 home draw with Turkey and a 3-2 victory in Malta. Dobrovolski's young charges saved their best till last by beating Hungary 3-0 in Chisinau, enabling them to end the campaign above the Hungarians in fifth place – an inconceivable prospect with two thirds of their programme complete.

Dobrovolski was rewarded with a new two-year contract. He was also voted Moldova's Coach of the Year. The Player of the Year prize went to young defender Alexandr Epureanu, elected just ahead of his veteran FK Moskva team-mate Radu Rebeja, who ended the international season with a record-equalling 69 caps, the same total as Moldova's all-time leading scorer Serghei Clescenco, who, a year after ending his international career, quit the game altogether. Another departure from the international scene was that of the country's second highest scorer, Serghey Rogaciov, who bowed out aged 30. The fine form of Viorel Frunza and Igor Bugaiov, who scored three goals each in those last four qualifiers (despite being paired up front only once) clearly influenced Rogaciov's decision.

Alexandr Epureanu, the 2007 Moldovan Player of the Year

Sheriff still in charge

The domestic scene was again dominated by FC Sheriff. Their record-equalling eighth Divizia Națională title – all of them consecutive - was achieved with the same degree of ease and authority as most of the previous seven. Unlike in 2006/07 they did actually lose a game – at home to FC Zimbru Chişinău just after the winter break – but with 26 wins in 30 matches, their supremacy was never threatened.

The Kuchuk father-and-son combination of coach Leonid and striker Aleksei remained pivotal, although the latter was rivalled in the goalscoring department during the spring by youngster Serghey Alexeev. It was Sheriff's defensive figures that stood out – just eight goals conceded in the league and none at all in the six matches they played in the Moldovan Cup. They completed their fourth double by overcoming FC Nistru Otaci 1-0 in the final with a headed goal from newly recruited veteran Moldovan international Ivan Testimitanu. It was Nistru's seventh defeat in eight Cup finals.

FC Dacia Chişinău joined Nistru in the UEFA Cup by finishing league runners-up under their impressive young coach Emil Caras. Dacia had begun the season by going three rounds of the UEFA Intertoto Cup, forcing them to delay their league start by a month. That was not the only disruption to the Divizia Națională. What started out as an expanded 12-team league became an eleven-club affair at halfway when FC Rapid Ghidighici withdrew. Their results were subsequently annulled, and further confusion followed at the end of the season when Rapid returned to the top flight after a merger with CSCA-Steaua Chişinău and FC Politehnica Chişinău withdrew on the eve of the 2008/09 campaign. With one club, FC Academia UTM Chişinău, promoted, it left the top league sporting an unwieldy eleven clubs for the second season running.

Federaţia Moldovenească de Fotbal (FMF)

Str. Tricolorului 39
MD-2012 Chişinău
tel - +373 22 210410
fax - +373 22 210432
website - www.fmf.md
email - fmf@fmf.md
Year of Formation – 1990
President - Pavel Cebanu
General Secretary - Nicolae Cebotari
Press Officer – Vasile Vatamanu
Stadium - Zimbru, Chisinau (10,796)

TOP FIVE ALL-TIME CAPS
Serghey Clescenco & Radu Rebeja (69); Ivan Testimitanu (56); Serghey Rogaciov (52); Valery Catînsus (51)

TOP FIVE ALL-TIME GOALS
Serghey Clescenco (11); Serghey Rogaciov (9); Iurie Miterev (8); Serghey Dadu (7); Viorel Frunza (6)

ATIONAL TEAM RESULTS 2007/08

/8/07	Latvia	A	Riga	2-1	*Frunza (23), Bordian (53)*
9/07	Norway (ECQ)	H	Chisinau	0-1	
/9/07	Bosnia-Herzegovina (ECQ)	A	Sarajevo	1-0	*Bugaiov (22)*
/10/07	Turkey (ECQ)	H	Chisinau	1-1	*Frunza (11)*
/10/07	Malta (ECQ)	H	Ta' Qali	3-2	*Bugaiov (24p), Frunza (31, 35)*
/11/07	Hungary (ECQ)	H	Chisinau	3-0	*Bugaiov (12), Josan (23), Alexeev (86)*
2/08	Kazakhstan	N	Antalya (TUR)	1-0	*Bugaiov (13)*
/5/08	Croatia	A	Rijeka	0-1	
/5/08	Armenia	H	Tiraspol	2-2	*Arakelyan (42og), Alexeev (74)*

ATIONAL TEAM APPEARANCES 2007/08

ach – Igor DOBROVOLSKI	27/8/67		Lva	NOR	BIH	TUR	MLT	HUN	Kaz	Cro	Arm	Caps	Goals
rghey PASCENCO	18/12/82	Sheriff	G46	G			G					12	-
exandr EPUREANU	27/9/86	Moskva (RUS)	D	D	D	D		D	D	D	D	15	1
du REBEJA	8/6/73	Moskva (RUS)	D	D	M			D		D	M	69	2
henady OLEXICI	23/8/78	Amkar (RUS)	D	D78		s89		s93				42	-
talie BORDIAN	11/8/84	Metalist Kharkiv (UKR)	D70	M	D	D	D	D				12	1
exandr GATCAN	27/3/84	Rubin (RUS)	M57	M	M85	M89	M77		M82	M79	s74	16	1
rghey NAMASCO	19/6/84	Tiraspol	M		s63	s67	s69	M	M	M		13	2
ctor COMLEONOC	23/2/79	SKA Rostov (RUS)	M	M	M63	M	M69		M64	M85	M66	15	-
enis ZMEU	8/5/85	Vaslui (ROU)	M62	M65		M67	s77	M93	s46	M68	s90	13	-
rghey ROGACIOV	20/5/77	Aktobe (KAZ)	A46	s78	s73							52	9
orel FRUNZA	6/12/79	Ceahlăul (ROU) /PAOK (GRE)	A	A		A86	A83		s46	A79	A	22	6
icolae CALANCEA	29/8/86	Zimbru	s46		G	G			G46			6	-
or BUGAIOV	26/6/84	Chornomorets (UKR) /Ceahlăul (ROU)	s46	A	A		A	A	A73	A59	A72	13	5

MOLDOVA

NATIONAL TEAM APPEARANCES 2007/08 (contd.)

			Lva	NOR	BIH	TUR	MLT	HUN	Kaz	Cro	Arm	Caps	Goal
Andrey CORNEENCOV	1/4/82	Sheriff	s57		M	M	M					15	-
Igor TIGIRLAS	24/2//84	Ventspils (LVA)	s62 /66									3	-
Semion BULGARU	26/5/85	Sheriff	s66					s50				5	-
Anatol DOROS	21/3/83	Standard (AZE)	s70		A73		s83					3	
Serghey LASCENCOV	24/3/80	Karpaty (UKR)		D	D		D	D	D	D	D	24	-
Alexandr SUVOROV	2/2/87	Sheriff /Tiraspol		s65						s85	M90	6	-
Victor GOLOVATENCO	28/4/84	Khimki (RUS)			D	D	D		D	D	D	14	-
Nicolai JOSAN	18/9/83	Iskra-Stal /KamAZ (RUS)			s85	M	M	M	M			9	1
Alexei SAVINOV	19/4/79	Zimbru				D						18	-
Denis CALINCOV	15/9/85	unattached				s86		A64	s73			9	-
Serghey STROENCO	22/2/67	Tiligul					D					46	-
Stanislav NAMASCO	10/11/86	Tiraspol /Sheriff						G	s46	G	G	5	-
Evgheny CEBOTARI	16/10/84	Ceahlăul (ROU)						M50		s68	M74	3	-
Serghey ALEXEEV	31/5/86	Sheriff						s64	A46	s79	s68	10	3
Valery ANDRONIC	21/12/82	Inter Gaz (ROU)							M46	s79	s66	11	-
Ivan TESTIMITANU	27/4/74	unattached							s64			56	5
Denis ILESCU	20/1/87	Anzhi (RUS)							s82			1	-
Georgy OVSIANNICOV	12/10/85	Olimpia Bălţi								s59	s72	2	-
Igor ARMAS	14/7/87	Zimbru									D68	1	-

DOMESTIC LEAGUE 2007/08

DIVIZIA NAŢIONALĂ FINAL TABLE

		Home					Away					Total					
	Pld	W	D	L	F	A	W	D	L	F	A	W	D	L	F	A	Pts
1 FC Sheriff	30	13	1	1	40	5	13	2	0	28	3	26	3	1	68	8	81
2 FC Dacia Chişinău	30	11	2	2	32	12	8	3	4	28	16	19	5	6	60	28	62
3 FC Nistru Otaci	30	9	4	2	17	5	8	4	3	17	12	17	8	5	34	17	59
4 FC Tiraspol	30	9	2	4	18	12	7	5	3	18	9	16	7	7	36	21	55
5 FC Zimbru Chişinău	30	5	9	1	23	10	8	4	3	20	11	13	13	4	43	21	52
6 FC Iskra-Stali	30	6	5	4	14	12	3	3	9	9	22	9	8	13	23	34	35
7 FC Tiligul Tiraspol	30	5	5	5	10	13	2	3	10	6	23	7	8	15	16	36	29
8 FC Olimpia Bălţi	30	5	3	7	16	20	2	3	10	8	26	7	6	17	24	46	27
9 FC Dinamo Bender	30	4	2	9	18	28	3	3	9	12	29	7	5	18	30	57	26
10 CSCA-Steaua Chişinău	30	3	1	11	11	24	2	2	11	10	31	5	3	22	21	55	18
11 FC Politehnica Chişinău	30	1	2	12	1	21	2	4	9	6	18	3	6	21	7	39	15

TOP GOALSCORERS

14 Igor PICUSCIAC (Tiraspol/Sheriff)
13 Collins NGAHA (Nistru)
Aleksei KUCHUK (Sheriff)
Jaba DVALI (Dacia Chişinău)
12 Aleksei ZHDANOV (Zimbru)
10 Serghey ALEXEEV (Sheriff)
9 Ghenadie ORBU (Dacia Chişinău)
Dumitru GUSILA (Dacia Chişinău)
Eric SACKEY (Olimpia Bălţi)
7 Andrei PORFIREANU (Tiraspol)
Maxim FRANTUZ (Zimbru)

N.B. No relegation as FC Rapid Ghidighici withdrew after round 16 (with all results annulled) and FC Politehnica Chişinău withdrew before 2008/09 season. FC Rapid Ghidighici and CSCA-Steaua Chişinău merged into CSCA-Rapid Ghidighici for 2008/09 season.

CLUB-BY-CLUB

CSCA-STEAUA CHIŞINĂU

Coach - Ivan Madricenco; (21/3/08) Pavel Irichuk (UKR)

Founded - 1992

2007				
4/7	Tiraspol	h	0-1	
8/7	Dinamo Bender	h	3-0	*Cigoreanu 2, Negara*
14/7	Rapid	a	0-2	*(match annulled)*
22/7	Tiligul	h	0-1	
28/7	Zimbru	a	1-3	*Vdovicenco*
11/8	Olimpia Bălţi	a	1-4	*Rascu*
17/8	Nistru	h	0-1	
25/8	Iskra-Stali	a	1-1	*Paladi*
29/8	Poli Chişinău	h	0-1	
3/9	Dacia Chişinău	a	0-1	
15/9	Tiraspol	a	0-1	
23/9	Dinamo Bender	a	2-1	*Paladi, Martun*
29/9	Rapid	h	0-3	*(match annulled)*
21/10	Tiligul	a	0-1	
29/10	Zimbru	h	0-3	
3/11	Sheriff	a	0-3	
11/11	Olimpia Bălţi	h	0-1	
15/11	Sheriff	h	1-4	*Vicolas*
2008				
3/3	Nistru	a	0-3	
7/3	Iskra-Stali	h	0-2	
12/3	Poli Chişinău	a	2-0	*Istrati S. 2*
16/3	Dacia Chişinău	h	0-3	
20/3	Nistru	a	1-2	*Luca*
30/3	Zimbru	h	1-3	*Darii*
3/4	Tiraspol	a	0-2	
8/4	Iskra-Stali	h	2-3	*Potlog, Luca (p)*
12/4	Tiligul	a	0-0	
20/4	Olimpia Bălţi	h	1-1	*og (Orlovschi)*
25/4	Dinamo Bender	a	1-2	*Cigoreanu*
30/4	Dacia Chişinău	h	2-0	*Cigoreanu, Luca*
11/5	Poli Chişinău	h	1-0	*Istrati S.*
16/5	Sheriff	a	1-7	*Cigoreanu*

No	Name	Nat	Pos	Aps	(s)	Gls
16	Manuel AMARANDEI	ROU	D	9	(1)	
15	Ivan ARABADJI		D	7		
	Anatol BOESTEAN		D	12		
	Maxim BUGACIUC		D	7	(4)	
4	Vitaly BUDIGAI		D	10	(2)	
8	Evgheny BUZA		M	2	(2)	
	Stefan CARAULAN		M	6	(2)	
19	Artiom CARP		D	7		
10	Boris CEBOTARI		D	7		
	Serghey CEBOTARI		D	5		
	Alexandr CHIRILOV		G	2		
5	Andrei CHIRSHUL		D	13	(1)	
17	Leonid CIGOREANU		A	17	(5)	5
12	Mihail CIOBANU		G	4	(2)	
	Evgheny CIOBU		M	9	(2)	
14	Marcel CIORTAN		M	10		
11	Ndadi DANIEL	NGA	A	5	(1)	
	Serghei DARII		M	6	(4)	1
	Iulian ERHAN		D	6		
6	Serghey FONDOS		D	15	(1)	
10	Valentin FURDUI		M	15	(6)	
16	Serghey GRADINARI		A	2	(2)	
	Victor GONDEA		M		(1)	
	Radu GROSU		M		(1)	
	Roman GUSAN		M	7		
7	Serghei ISTRATI		M	7	(4)	3
	Vadim ISTRATI		G		(1)	
9	Evgheny LAVRINOVICI		M	4	(2)	
2	Stanislav LUCA		A	10	(2)	3
	Victor MARIAN		M	1	(1)	
14	Vitalie MANALIU		A	3	(3)	
9	Igor MARTUN		A	2	(4)	1
11	Igor MORARI		M	21	(1)	
2	Vitaly MOSTOVOI		D	7	(3)	
15	Andrei NEGARA		M	3	(7)	1
5	Victor NINICU		D	2		
13	Adrian PALADI		M	4	(11)	2
1	Adrian PATRAS		G	24		
4	Vladimir POTLOG		M	9	(2)	1
3	Ruslan RASCU		D	12	(1)	1
14	Serghey SECU		D	11		
	Veaceslav SOFRONI		A	2		
18	Alexandr STADIICIUC		D	14	(1)	
8	Andrei TURCU		M	5	(5)	
	Alexandr VDOVICENCO		D	3	(1)	1
2	Andrian VICOLAS		M	3	(9)	1

FC DACIA CHIŞINĂU

Coach – Emil Caras; (3/5/08) Vasily Coselev

Founded - 2000

2007				
5/8	Olimpia Bălţi	h	3-0	*Martin, Lopes, Negrescu*
11/8	Nistru	a	1-0	*Orbu*
16/8	Iskra-Stali	h	2-1	*Bologhan, Martin*
21/8	Dinamo Bender	a	7-3	*Gusila, Osipenco 2, Soimu 2, Calin, Lopes*
25/8	Poli Chişinău	a	2-0	*Pusca, Orbu*
29/8	Tiraspol	a	1-1	*Gusila (p)*
3/9	CSCA Chişinău	h	1-0	*Mincev*
9/9	Tiligul	a	0-0	
16/9	Dinamo Bender	h	5-1	*Martin (p), Dvali, Daraselia, Bologhan (p), Orbu*
20/9	Zimbru	h	1-5	*og (Kriuchikhin)*
24/9	Rapid	a	1-2	*Orbu (match annulled)*
28/9	Tiligul	h	2-1	*Lopes, Orbu*
3/10	Sheriff	a	0-2	
21/10	Zimbru	a	1-0	*Daraselia*
29/10	Sheriff	h	0-1	
3/11	Olimpia Bălţi	a	4-1	*Dvali 2, Osipenco, Orbu*
11/11	Nistru	h	2-0	*Gusila, Orbu*
2008				
3/3	Iskra-Stali	a	3-1	*Gusila (p), Martin 2*
7/3	FC Politecnica	h	3-1	*Gusila, Dvali, Orbu*
11/3	Tiraspol	h	4-0	*Korgalidze, Dvali, Soimu, Orbu*
16/3	CSCA Chişinău	a	3-0	*Dvali, Soimu, Orbu*
20/3	Poli Chişinău	h	2-0	*Gusila 2*
30/3	Sheriff	a	1-2	*Gusila*
8/4	Nistru	h	2-2	*Dvali 2*
12/4	Zimbru	a	2-3	*og (Andronic I.), Onica*
21/4	Tiraspol	h	0-0	
25/4	Iskra-Stali	a	0-0	
30/4	CSCA Chişinău	a	0-2	
3/5	Tiligul	h	3-0	*Dvali 2, Pusca*
11/5	Olimpia Bălţi	a	3-1	*Dvali 2, Gusila*
16/5	Dinamo Bender	h	2-0	*Onica, Dvali*

No	Name	Nat	Pos	Aps	(s)	Gls
5	Maxim ANDRONIC		M	28		
16	Dimitar BELCHEV	BUL	D	1	(5)	
19	Vadim BOLOGHAN		D	27		2
6	Marius CALIN	ROU	M	10	(10)	1
25	Ustin CERGA		G		(1)	
1	Alexandru CHIRILOV		G	2		
22	Levan KORGALIDZE	GEO	A	13		1
15	Adrian CUCOVEI		D	7	(3)	

No	Name	Nat	Pos	Aps	(s)	Gls
21	Vitali DARASELIA	GEO	M	5	(3)	2
17	Jaba DVALI	GEO	A	17	(7)	13
10	Dumitru GUSILA		A	17	(5)	9
20	Serghei JAPALAU		M	4	9	
11	Miguel LOPES	POR	M	3	(14)	3
2	Vitalie MARDARI		D	13	(1)	
7	Andrei MARTIN		M	23	(5)	5
3	Nicolae MINCEV		D	30		1
12	Mihail MORARU		G	28		
13	Igor NEGRESCU		D	6	(4)	1
18	Alexandru ONICA		M	7	(8)	2
8	Valery ONILA		M	7	(11)	
9	Ghenadie ORBU		M	18	(11)	9
20	Yuri OSIPENCO		M	15		3
4	Ghenadie PUSCA		M	21	(2)	2
14	Iurie SOIMU		M	23	(7)	4
3	Alexei SAVINOV		D	5		

FC DINAMO BENDER

Coach – Iuri Hodichin

Founded - 1950

2007

8/7	CSCA Chişinău	a	0-3	
14/7	Tiraspol	h	0-3	
22/7	Rapid	h	0-2	*(match annulled)*
28/7	Tiligul	a	1-3	*Mihaliov S.*
6/8	Zimbru	h	1-2	*Namasco (p)*
12/8	Sheriff	a	0-5	
17/8	Olimpia Bălţi	h	1-3	*Namasco*
21/8	Dacia Chişinău	h	3-7	*Mihaliov S., Elchin, Dizov*
25/8	Nistru	a	1-3	*Mihalev M.*
29/8	Iskra-Stali	h	0-0	
2/9	Poli Chişinău	a	2-0	*Agafonov, Namasco*
16/9	Dacia Chişinău	a	1-5	*Casian*
23/9	CSCA Chişinău	h	1-2	*Costrov*
28/9	Tiraspol	a	1-2	*Mihaliov M.*
21/10	Rapid	a	1-1	*Namasco (p) (match annulled)*
3/11	Zimbru	a	0-0	
11/11	Sheriff	h	1-2	*Tivirenco*
15/11	Tiligul	h	3-0	*Tivirenco 2, Namasco*

2008

2/3	Olimpia Bălţi	a	0-1	
7/3	Nistru	h	2-2	*Mihaliov M., Mihalev S.*
13/3	Iskra-Stali	a	1-0	*Agafonov*
16/3	Poli Chişinău	h	2-0	*Titucenco, Namasco*
20/3	Zimbru	a	3-3	*Costrov 2, Mihaliov M.*
30/3	Tiraspol	h	0-2	
3/4	Iskra-Stali	a	1-1	*Cemirtan*
8/4	Tiligul	h	1-0	*Casian*
12/4	Olimpia Bălţi	a	0-1	
25/4	CSCA Chişinău	h	2-1	*Tofan, Mihaliov M.*
30/4	Nistru	h	1-2	*Titucenco*
3/5	Poli Chişinău	a	1-0	*Mihaliov M.*
11/5	Sheriff	h	0-2	
16/5	Dacia Chişinău	a	0-2	

No	Name	Nat	Pos	Aps	(s)	Gls
14	Veaceslav AGAFONOV		M	22	(3)	2
3	Igor BARDUC		D	18		
13	Dmitry BAILEVICI		M	1	(7)	
17	Alexandr BICOV		M	4	(7)	
7	Alexei BOBU		M	8	(8)	
4	Alexei CASIAN		M	26	(2)	2
16	Vadim CEMIRTAN		A	3	(10)	1
77	Pavel CHALININ		G	20		
15	Denis CHIRILIUC		A	2	(1)	
16	Igor COSTROV		M	22	(1)	3
16	Alexei DIZOV		M	1	(9)	1
5	Vladimir DRAGAN		D	16	(1)	
8	Oleg ELCHIN		M	7	(1)	1
5	Alexandr HODICHIN		D	8	(3)	
	Dmitry LISICO		M	4	(3)	
10	Maxim MIHALIOV		A	25		6
9	Serghei MIHALIOV		A	17	(8)	3
1	Alexandr NASONOV		G	2	(1)	
6	Alexandr NAMASCO		D	24	(2)	5
1	Mihail PAIUS		G	8	(2)	
2	Alexandr SVET		D	27	(1)	
7	Artur SPINU		M	1	(8)	
13	Roman STRATULAT		M	3	(4)	
4	Nicolai TITUCENCO		D	20	(2)	2
11	Evgheny TIVERENCO		A	12	(9)	3
18	Leonid TOFAN		D	29		1

FC ISKRA-STALI

Coach – Vladimir Barisev; (1/12/07) Vlad Goian

Founded - 2002

2007

4/7	Tiligul	a	0-0	
8/7	Zimbru	h	0-0	
12/7	Sheriff	a	0-3	
22/7	Olimpia Bălţi	h	2-0	*Soimu, Romaniuc*
28/7	Nistru	a	0-1	
5/8	Tiraspol	a	1-0	*Gritiuc*
11/8	Poli Chişinău	h	1-0	*Romaniuc*
16/8	Dacia Chişinău	a	1-2	*Soimu*
25/8	CSCA Chişinău	h	1-1	*Cheban*
29/8	Dinamo Bender	a	0-0	
2/9	Rapid	h	1-1	*Donici (match annulled)*
16/9	Tiligul	h	1-0	*Melnicenco (p)*
24/9	Zimbru	a	0-1	
28/9	Sheriff	h	0-3	
21/10	Olimpia Bălţi	a	0-1	
29/10	Nistru	h	1-2	*Josan*
3/11	Tiraspol	h	1-0	*Soimu*
11/11	Poli Chişinău	a	0-0	

2008

3/3	Dacia Chişinău	h	1-3	*Tofan*
7/3	CSCA Chişinău	a	2-0	*Grosu, Druta*
12/3	Dinamo Bender	h	0-1	
20/3	Tiligul	h	2-1	*Ionita, Burcovschi*
30/3	Olimpia Bălţi	a	2-3	*Skorohod, Ionita*
3/4	Dinamo Bender	h	1-1	*Ionita (p)*
8/4	CSCA Chişinău	a	3-2	*Grosu, Romaniuc, Bogdan*
13/4	Poli Chişinău	h	3-0	*Bogdan, Bugneac, Druta*
21/4	Sheriff	a	0-6	
25/4	Dacia Chişinău	h	0-0	
3/5	Nistru	a	0-1	
11/5	Zimbru	h	0-0	
15/5	Tiraspol	a	0-2	

No	Name	Nat	Pos	Aps	(s)	Gls
13	Vasile ARLET		D	5		
	Mihail ARSENI		M		(1)	
6	Victor BARISEV		M	9	(1)	
13	Dmitry BERBINSCHI		D	9	(1)	
15	Dmitry BOGDAN		D	12		2
16	Andrei BUGNEAC		A	8	(3)	1
21	Andrei BURCOVSCHI		M	27		1
11	Serhiy CHEBAN	UKR	A	9	(10)	1
23	Igor CERNOMOR	UKR	M	8	(1)	
33	Sergiu DIACONU		G	2		
5	Andrei DONICI		M	17		
10	Aurel DRUTA		M	12	(2)	2
12	Alexandr DUMIC		G	7		
17	Dmytro EFIMOV	UKR	M	6		
1	Artyom GAIDUCHEVICI		G	12		
2	Sergiu GAFINA		D	18	(2)	
	GASAN		M		(3)	
7	Maxim GHERIN		M	5	(8)	
19	Serghey GRITIUC		A	9	(3)	1
20	Alexandr GROSU		D	12	(2)	2
10	Nicolai JOSAN		M	11		1

Name	Nat	Pos	Aps	(s)	Gls
Oleh JURCA	UKR	D	10	(1)	
Artur IONITA		M	14		3
Anatol LEU		G	10		
Ghenady LOSCAN		A		(8)	
Vladimir MELNICENCO		A	14		1
Vitaliy PLAMADEALA		M	2	(7)	
Denis RASSULOV		A	3	(1)	
Marcel RESITCA		A	1		
Iury ROMANIUC		M	21	(1)	3
Yuriy SKOROHOD	UKR	A	9	(4)	1
Maxym SYCHEV	UKR	D	21	(3)	
Oleg SOIMU		M	10	(6)	3
Igor TAMPEI		A	1	(9)	
Alexandr TOFAN		M	6	(7)	1
Victor VERBETSCHI		D	9	(3)	
Sergiu ZACON		M	1	(2)	

FC NISTRU OTACI

Coach – Valeriy Zazdravnykh (RUS); (18/9/07) Nicolae Bunea

Founded - 1953

MAJOR HONOURS: Moldovan Cup – (1) 2005.

07

	Zimbru	a	1-1	*Taranu*
	Sheriff	h	0-0	
/7	Olimpia Bălţi	a	1-0	*Dolgov*
/7	Tiraspol	a	2-1	*Studzinskiy 2*
7	Iskra-Stali	h	1-0	*Muhovikov*
	Poli Chişinău	a	2-0	*Taranu, Marinchuk*
/8	Dacia Chişinău	h	0-1	
/8	CSCA Chişinău	a	1-0	*Ngaha*
/8	Dinamo Bender	h	3-1	*Groshev, Ngaha 2*
/8	Rapid	a	2-2	*Ngaha 2 (match annulled)*
	Tiligul	h	0-0	
/9	Zimbru	h	1-0	*Malitskiy*
/9	Sheriff	a	0-1	
/9	Olimpia Bălţi	h	0-0	
/10	Tiraspol	h	2-1	*Ngaha, Mekang*
/10	Iskra-Stali	a	2-1	*Ngaha, Mekang*
1	Poli Chişinău	h	0-0	
/11	Dacia Chişinău	a	0-2	

08

	CSCA Chişinău	h	3-0	*Ngaha 2, og (Boestean)*
	Dinamo Bender	a	2-2	*Ngaha, Malitskiy*
/3	Tiligul	a	1-0	*Stepanchuk*
/3	CSCA Chişinău	h	2-1	*Ngaha 2*
/3	Poli Chişinău	a	1-0	*Iepureanu (p)*
	Sheriff	h	0-1	
	Dacia Chişinău	a	2-2	*Tcaciuc An. 2*
/4	Zimbru	h	2-0	*Ngaha, Tcaciuc An.*
/4	Tiraspol	a	0-1	
/4	Dinamo Bender	a	2-1	*Iepureanu, Ngaha*
	Iskra-Stali	h	1-0	*Savchenko*
/5	Tiligul	a	0-0	
/5	Olimpia Bălţi	h	2-0	*Malitskiy, Ngaha*

No	Name	Nat	Pos	Aps	(s)	Gls
	Mihal ARSENII		M		(10)	
	Serghey BUTELSCHI		M	11	(1)	
	Vladimir CACICAN		M	12	(5)	
	Oleg COLTUNOVSCI		A	4	(8)	
	Dmitry DOLGOV		D	17		1
	Georgy EREMIA		D	1	(5)	
	Denis ERSOV		G	30		
	Iury GREAPCA		D	4	(3)	
	Iury GROSHEV		M	29		1
	Serghey IEPUREANU		M	8		2
	Evgheny LIVITSCHI		D		(1)	
	Anton LISIUK	UKR	A	1	(3)	
	Valentin LUPASCU		D	23	(3)	
	Olexandr MALITSKIY	UKR	M	19	(3)	3
	Denis MARINCHUK	UKR	D	4	(8)	1
23	Andrei MATIURA		M	4	(1)	
3	Habib Gock MEKANG	CMR	D	29		2
24	Olexandr MAXIMOV	UKR	A		(2)	
13	Anton MUHOVIKOV	UKR	A	12	(3)	1
15	Collins NGAHA	CMR	A	21	(8)	13
	Pavel NOVIKOV	UKR	M		(1)	
	Roman POLIANSKIY	UKR	M	1		
4	Mamady SANGARE	CMR	D	13		
17	Vyacheslav SAVCHUK	UKR	M	3	(3)	
16	Vyacheslav SAVCHENKO	UKR	M	9		1
11	Evgeny SICIOV		M	2	(9)	
6	Igor SOLTANICI		D	12	(2)	
17	Serhiy STEPANCHUK	UKR	M	3	(1)	1
11	Aleksandr STUDZINSKIY	RUS	A	6	(3)	2
4	Vladimir SURUCEANU		M	4	(8)	
9	Vladimir TARANU		A	12	(4)	2
19	Alexandr TCACIUC		M	15	(9)	
8	Andrei TCACIUC		A	21	(5)	3

FC OLIMPIA BĂLŢI

Coach – Lilian Popescu; (6/2/08) Valery Pogorelov

Founded - 1984

2007

4/7	Sheriff	a	0-2	
8/7	Tiraspol	a	1-2	*Sackey*
13/7	Nistru	h	0-1	
22/7	Iskra-Stali	a	0-2	
28/7	Poli Chişinău	h	0-1	
5/8	Dacia Chişinău	a	0-3	
11/8	CSCA Chişinău	h	4-1	*Cernih 2, Litvinchuk, Ribak*
17/8	Dinamo Bender	a	3-1	*Seydou, Sackey*
25/8	Rapid	h	1-0	*Sackey (match annulled)*
30/8	Tiligul-Tiras	a	1-2	*Sackey*
3/9	Zimbru	h	0-1	
16/9	Sheriff	h	0-1	
23/9	Tiraspol	h	0-2	
28/9	Nistru	a	0-0	
21/10	Iskra-Stali	h	1-0	*Lilyk*
29/10	Poli Chişinău	a	0-0	
3/11	Dacia Chişinău	h	1-4	*Sackey*
11/11	CSCA Chişinău	a	1-0	*Gritcan*

2008

3/3	Dinamo Bender	h	1-0	*Sackey*
11/3	Tiligul	h	1-1	*Gritcan*
16/3	Zimbru	a	0-7	
20/3	Tiraspol	a	0-1	
30/3	Iskra-Stali	h	3-2	*Ovsiannikov 2, Sackey*
3/4	Tiligul	a	1-2	*Orlovschi*
12/4	Dinamo Bender	h	1-0	*Ovsiannikov*
20/4	CSCA Chişinău	a	1-1	*Ovsiannikov*
25/4	Poli Chişinău	h	2-2	*Cernih, Andries*
30/4	Zimbru	h	1-1	*Sackey*
3/5	Sheriff	a	0-1	
11/5	Dacia Chişinău	h	1-3	*Sackey*
16/5	Nistru	a	0-2	

No	Name	Nat	Pos	Aps	(s)	Gls
25	Vitaly ANDRIES		M	9	(10)	1
	Lado AKHALAIA	GEO	M	1	(1)	
12	Yevhen BAHURINSKIY	UKR	G	13		
24	Georgy BOGHIU		A	9		
20	Serhiy BRONNIKOV	UKR	D	17		
10	Iury CERNIH		M	16	(11)	3
12	Evgheny CHEPTENE		G	9		
17	Vladimir CHEPTENARI		D		(2)	
1	Denis CRISTOFOVICI		G	4		
16	Roman ESANU		A	6	(8)	
14	Alexandr FURTUNA		M		(1)	
19	Alexei GONCEAROV		D	25		
18	Dmitry GRITCAN		A	17	(6)	2
32	Leonid GROZA		G	4	(2)	

No	Name	Nat	Pos	Aps	(s)	Gls
24	Maxim HOVANSCHI		M		(2)	
22	Dmytro KUZNETOV	UKR	D	16		
23	Edem KWAME	GHA	M	3	(5)	
7	Vitaliy LILYK	UKR	M	29		1
5	Serhiy LITVINCHUK	UKR	D	23	(3)	1
21	Evgheny OGORODNIC		D	4	(1)	
8	Serghey ORLOV		M	7	(5)	
2	Nicolai ORLOVSCHI		D	14	1	1
9	Georgy OVSIANNIKOV		D	10	(3)	4
10	Alexandr PATROMAN		M	7	(3)	
22	Maxim REPINETSCHI		A	11	(5)	
13	Vasiliy RIBAK	UKR	A	12	(1)	1
15	Yevgeniy ROGIZNIY	UKR	M	6	(5)	
4	Eric SACKEY	GHA	A	27	(1)	9
14	Murtaila SEYDOU	GHA	M	8	(6)	1
23	Leonid SHARF	USA	D	12	(3)	
6	Serghey TANURCOV		M	4	(7)	
15	Oleh TURSCHI	UKR	M	7	(6)	

FC POLITEHNICA CHIŞINĂU

Coach – Ion Caras

Founded - 1964

2007

4/7	Rapid	a	1-0	*Cojusea (match annulled)*
8/7	Tiligul	h	0-1	
13/7	Zimbru	a	0-0	
28/7	Olimpia Bălţi	a	1-0	*Galearschi*
6/8	Nistru	h	0-2	
11/8	Iskra-Stali	a	0-1	
17/8	Tiraspol	a	1-2	*Marian*
25/8	Dacia Chişinău	h	0-2	
29/8	CSCA Chişinău	a	1-0	*Soltan*
2/9	Dinamo Bender	h	0-2	
15/9	Rapid	h	0-0	*(match annulled)*
20/9	Sheriff	h	0-1	
24/9	Tiligul	a	0-1	
28/9	Zimbru	h	0-1	
21/10	Sheriff	a	0-1	
29/10	Olimpia Bălţi	h	0-0	
3/11	Nistru	a	0-0	
11/11	Iskra-Stali	h	0-0	

2008

2/3	Tiraspol	h	0-2	
7/3	Dacia Chişinău	a	1-3	*Krimov*
12/3	CSCA Chişinău	h	0-2	
16/3	Dinamo Bender	a	0-2	
20/3	Dacia Chişinău	a	0-2	
30/3	Nistru	h	0-1	
3/4	Zimbru	a	0-0	
8/4	Tiraspol	h	0-3	
13/4	Iskra-Stali	a	0-3	
20/4	Tiligul	h	1-0	*Galearschi*
25/4	Olimpia Bălţi	a	2-2	*Galearschi, Ustinov (p)*
30/4	Sheriff	h	0-3	
3/5	Dinamo Bender	h	0-1	
11/5	CSCA Chişinău	a	0-1	

No	Name	Nat	Pos	Aps	(s)	Gls
3	Oleg BELAN		M	5	(4)	
	Vitaliy BIKOV	RUS	M	3	(4)	
13	Aleksei BONDAREV	RUS	M	12		
24	Evgheny BULMAGA		D	1	(1)	
11	Mihail COJUSEA		A	9	(4)	
28	Evgheny COLIEV		A		(3)	
17	Vladimir DRAGOVOZOV		A	10	(3)	
6	Aurel DRUTA		M	14	(1)	
18	Maxim GAICIUC		D	12		
16	Dionisie GALEARSCHI		A	18	(7)	3
4	Evgheny GILCA		D	11	(1)	
7	Lilian GOLBAN		M	3	(5)	
12	Anton IVANOV	RUS	G	16		
1	Veaceslav JIGAILOV		G	14		
27	Evgheniy KAPLIN	RUS	M	6	(1)	
29	Serghey KAPUSTIN		D		(3)	
3	Aleksandr KRIMOV	RUS	D	13		1
21	Aurel MARDARI		M	10	(5)	
9	Victor MARIAN		M	13	(3)	1
15	Anton MATVEEV		A	3		
24	Dmitriy MINIAEV	RUS	M	15	(5)	
22	Alexandr MORARU		D	2	(3)	
18	Vadim NASHKO	RUS	A	10		
2	Ghenadie OCHINCA		D	7	(7)	
5	Denis ORBU		M	9	(2)	
14	Vladimir PETCOV		D	29		
5	Vyacheslav SHAMRAEV	RUS	D	11	2	
15	Veaseslav SOLTAN		M	12	(2)	1
8	Iliya SOSHNIN	RUS	M	12		
20	Evgheny SUROV	RUS	D	7		
19	Ignat TIAN	UZB	M	7	(2)	
	Ion TABIRTA		D	1	(1)	
10	Eduard TOMASCOV		M	13		
10	Maxim USTINOV	RUS	M	12		1
	Serghey VEVERITA		M		(1)	
2	Ion VRABIE		D	10		

FC RAPID GHIDIGHICI

Coach – Vlad Goian

Founded - 2005

2007

4/7	Poli Chişinău	h	0-1	
14/7	CSCA Chişinău	h	2-0	*Tanurcov (p), Bugneac*
22/7	Dinamo Bender	a	3-0	*Maxim 2, Grosu*
28/7	Tiraspol	h	2-1	*Luca, Tanurcov*
5/8	Tiligul	h	3-1	*Maxim, Tanurcov (p), Bugneac*
11/8	Zimbru	a	0-2	
17/8	Sheriff	h	0-2	
25/8	Olimpia Bălţi	a	0-1	
29/8	Nistru	h	2-2	*Grosu, Maxim*
2/9	Iskra-Stali	a	1-1	*Bugneac*
15/9	Poli Chişinău	a	0-0	
24/9	Dacia Chişinău	h	2-1	*Kaladzhiev, Maxim*
29/9	CSCA Chişinău	a	3-0	*Bereghici, Maxim 2*
21/10	Dinamo Bender	h	1-1	*Tanurcov (p)*
3/11	Tiligul	a	0-1	
11/11	Zimbru	h	0-1	

No	Name	Nat	Pos	Aps	(s)	Gls
22	Lado AKHALAIA	GEO	D		(2)	
19	Manuel AMARANDEI	ROU	D	15		
6	Ivan ARABADJI		D	3	(1)	
23	Andrei BEREGHICI		M	4	(11)	1
7	Anatol BOESTEAN		D	7	(3)	
2	Dmitry BOGDAN		D	8		
25	Andrei BUGNEAC		A	12	(2)	3
3	Ion CARAMAN		D	8		
9	Serghey DARIE		A		(7)	
33	Serghey DIACONU		G	10		
4	Ion DONICA		D	16		
26	Marius DRULE	ROU	D	6		
	DRUTA		A	1		
13	Alexandr GROSU-jr		M	11	(5)	2
20	Serghey ISTRATI		M	6	(9)	
17	Georgi KALADZHIEV	BUL	M	5	(8)	1
27	Stanislav LUCA		A	12	(3)	1
11	Alexandr MAXIM		A	14	(2)	7
	Alexandr MAXIMOV		M		(1)	
1	Ghenadie MOSNEAGA		G	6		
8	Victor PLAMADEALA		M	16		
21	Vladimir TANURCOV		M	14		4
18	Alexandr TOFAN		M		(2)	
10	Andrei TURCU		M	2	(3)	

N.B. Rapid withdrew after 16 games. All matches annulled. Above statistics therefore unofficial and for information only.

FC SHERIFF

Coach – Leonid Kuchuk (BLR)

Founded - 1997

AJOR HONOURS: Moldovan League - (8) 2001, 2002, 2003, 2004, 2005, 2006, 2007, 2008; Moldovan Cup - (5) 1999, 2001, 2002, 2006, 2008.

007				
7	Olimpia Bălţi	h	2-0	*Gnanou, Kuchuk*
7	Nistru	a	0-0	
/7	Iskra-Stali	h	3-0	*Bulgaru, Gorodetschi, Nadson*
/8	Dinamo Bender	h	5-0	*Tarkhnishvili (p), Gorodetschi 2, Balima, Tiago*
/8	Rapid	a	2-0	*Tiago, Suvorov (match annulled)*
/8	Tiligul	h	3-0	*Tarkhnishvili (p), Wallace, Negrut*
)/8	Zimbru	a	1-1	*Corneencov*
/9	Tiraspol	h	0-0	
5/9	Olimpia Bălţi	a	1-0	*Kuchuk*
)/9	Poli Chişinău	a	1-0	*Gnanou*
4/9	Nistru	h	1-0	*Gnanou*
3/9	Iskra-Stali	a	3-0	*Wallace, Kuchuk, Nadson*
/10	Dacia Chişinău	h	2-0	*Kuchuk 2*
1/10	Poli Chişinău	h	1-0	*Tarkhnishvili (p)*
9/10	Dacia Chişinău	a	1-0	*Tiago*
/11	CSCA Chişinău	h	3-0	*Arbănaş, Kuchuk, Wallace*
1/11	Dinamo Bender	a	2-1	*Gnanou, Tarkhnishvili*
5/11	CSCA Chişinău	a	4-1	*Alexeev 2, Kajkut, Gorodetschi*
008				
/3	Tiligul	a	1-0	*Picusciac*
2/3	Zimbru	h	0-1	
6/3	Tiraspol	a	2-0	*Tiago, Rouamba*
0/3	Dacia Chişinău	h	2-1	*Picusciac, Balima*
/4	Nistru	a	1-0	*Kuchuk*
/4	Zimbru	h	4-2	*Mamah, Tiago, Rodríguez, Alexeev*
2/4	Tiraspol	a	2-0	*Alexeev, Balima*
1/4	Iskra-Stali	h	6-0	*Erokhin, Balima, Alexeev, Kuchuk 2, Gorodetschi*
5/4	Tiligul	a	4-0	*Kuchuk 2, Erokhin, Alexeev*
0/4	Poli Chişinău	a	3-0	*Alexeev 2, Kuchuk*
/5	Olimpia Bălţi	h	1-0	*Corneencov*
1/5	Dinamo Bender	a	2-0	*Kajkut 2*
6/5	CSCA Chişinău	h	7-1	*Kuchuk (p), Negrut 2, Alexeev 2, Rouamba, Picusciac*

No	Name	Nat	Pos	Aps	(s)	Gls
26	Serghey ALEXEEV		A	10	(11)	10
18	Cristian ARBĂNAŞ	ROU	D	18	(6)	1
4	Wilfred Benjamin BALIMA	BFA	M	21	(6)	4
22	Semion BULGARU		D	7		1
3	Kennedy CHINWO	NGA	D	9	(2)	
7	Andrey CORNEENCOV		M	15	(3)	2
21	Nicolás DEMALDE	ARG	D	1	(5)	
27	Ştefan ENESCU	ROU	M	4	(2)	
15	Kwami ENINFUL	TOG	D	9		
16	Aleksandr EROKHIN	RUS	M	7		2
23	Nelson FRED	BRA	M	3	(2)	
2	Ibrahim GNANOU	BFA	M	10	(1)	4
8	Evgheny GORODETSCHI		M	9	(11)	5
19	Saša KAJKUT	BIH	A	10	(5)	3
9	Aleksei KUCHUK	BLR	A	16	(5)	13
24	Abdul Gafar MAMAH	TOG	D	23	(2)	1
25	Alexandr MELENCIUC		G	16		
1	Stanislav NAMASCO		G	9		
28	José NADSON	BRA	D	15	(3)	2
20	George NEGRUT	ROU	M	10	(8)	3
1	Serghey PASCENCO		G	5		
11	Igor PICUSCIAC		A	10	(2)	3
	Andrei RADIOLA		D	2		
21	Ionuţ RADU	ROU	A	1	(2)	
22	Luis RODRÍGUEZ	ARG	M	7	(1)	1
6	Florent ROUAMBA	BFA	M	17	(8)	2
16	Paul SANDA	ROU	A	1	(4)	
11	Alexandr SUVOROV		A	2	(3)	
5	Vazha TARKHNISHVILI	GEO	D	29		4
4	Ivan TESTIMITANU		D	3	(4)	
20	Alberto TIAGO	BRA	A	16	(5)	4
4	Fernando WALLACE	BRA	M	15	(1)	3

FC TILIGUL TIRASPOL

Coach – Octavio Zambrano (ECU); (1/12/07) Valery Vasiliev

Founded - 1961

MAJOR HONOURS: Moldovan Cup - (3) 1993, 1994, 1995.

2007				
4/7	Iskra-Stalii	h	0-0	
8/7	Poli Chişinău	a	1-0	*Soko*
22/7	CSCA Chişinău	a	1-0	*Soko*
28/7	Dinamo Bender	h	3-1	*Dindikov, Mosquera 2*
5/8	Rapid	a	1-3	*Cuznetov (match annulled)*
10/8	Tiraspol	h	0-2	
17/8	Zimbru	h	0-1	
26/8	Sheriff	a	0-3	
30/8	Olimpia Bălţi	h	2-1	*Cuznetov, Keita*
3/9	Nistru	a	0-0	
9/9	Dacia Chişinău	h	0-0	
16/9	Iskra-Stali	a	0-1	
24/9	Poli Chişinău	h	1-0	*Bulat*
28/9	Dacia Chişinău	a	1-2	*Keita*
21/10	CSCA Chişinău	h	1-0	*Bulat*
3/11	Rapid	h	1-0	*Bulat (match annulled)*
11/11	Tiraspol	a	1-3	*Popovici*
15/11	Dinamo Bender	a	0-3	
2008				
2/3	Zimbru	a	0-0	
7/3	Sheriff	h	0-1	
11/3	Olimpia Bălţi	a	1-1	*Camara*
16/3	Nistru	h	0-1	
20/3	Iskra-Stali	a	1-2	*Grosu*
3/4	Olimpia Bălţi	h	2-1	*Bulat (p), Camara*
8/4	Dinamo Bender	a	0-1	
12/4	CSCA Chişinău	h	0-0	
20/4	Poli Chişinău	a	0-1	
25/4	Sheriff	h	0-4	
30/4	Tiraspol	h	1-1	*Bacal*
3/5	Dacia Chişinău	a	0-3	
11/5	Nistru	h	0-0	
16/5	Zimbru	a	0-3	

No	Name	Nat	Pos	Aps	(s)	Gls
11	Dumitru BACAL		A	15	(6)	1
9	Facinet BANGOURA	GUI	M	4	(1)	
7	Andrei BEREGHICI		D	8	(5)	
13	Victor BULAT		M	25	(2)	3
10	Mohamed CAMARA	GUI	D	21	(2)	2
3	Ivan CARAMAN		D	13		
8	Alexandru CHELTUIALA		D	23		
21	Dinu CARP		M	10	(1)	
18	Yury CERNOV		M	2	(3)	
2	Serghey CUZNETOV		D	15		1
16	Victor DIDENCO		A		(9)	
16	Olexandr DINDIKOV	UKR	M	7	(4)	1
16	Ivan DONICA		M	9	(2)	
9	Ibrahim DIOP	SEN	A	3	(1)	
	Mauricio DORIGON	BRA	A		(1)	
9	Serghey GRITIUC		A	7	(2)	
11	Alexandr GROSU		M	9	(1)	1
16	Serghey GUSACOV		D	20	(2)	
5	Stanislav IASCHIN		D	3	(2)	

3	Omar KEITA	GUI	M	4	(4)	2
1	Evgheny MATIUGHIN		G	16		
17	Angelo MACHUKA	PAR	M	10		
10	Jackson MOSQUERA	ECU	A	10	(4)	2
1	Ghenady MOSNEAGA		G	5		
8	Denis NACONECHNII		M		(3)	
14	Dmitry POPOVICI		M	15	(9)	1
14	Jackson PRECIADO	ECU	M	1	(2)	
8	Mihail PASECNIUC		M	2	(6)	
17	Alexandr PETROV		M	1	(2)	
8	Denis PROCOPISIN		A	1		
7	Jerome ROBENS	HAI	M	6	(6)	
13	Dmitry SMERECINSCHI		M		(7)	
9	Seykou SOKO	SEN	A	8	(2)	2
6	Serghey STROENCO		D	24	(1)	
15	Mohamed THIAM	GUI	M	14	(1)	
18	Andrei TONTICI		A	10	(4)	
12	Alexandr ZVIAGINTEV		G	9		

FC TIRASPOL

Coach – Vladimir Reva (UKR)

Founded - 1993

MAJOR HONOURS: (as FC Constructorul Chişinău) Moldovan League - (1) 1997; Moldovan Cup - (2) 1996, 2000.

2007				
4/7	CSCA Chişinău	a	1-0	*Rudac*
8/7	Olimpia Bălţi	h	2-1	*Porfireanu, Rudac*
14/7	Dinamo Bender	a	3-0	*Picusciac 3 (1p)*
22/7	Nistru	h	1-2	*Zislis*
28/7	Rapid	a	1-2	*Picusciac (match annulled)*
5/8	Iskra-Stali	h	0-1	
10/8	Tiligul	a	2-0	*Porfireanu, Picusciac*
17/8	Poli Chişinău	h	2-1	*Picusciac 2*
26/8	Zimbru	a	1-1	*Picusciac*
29/8	Dacia Chişinău	h	1-1	*Zislis*
3/9	Sheriff	a	0-0	
15/9	CSCA Chişinău	h	1-0	*Porfireanu*
23/9	Olimpia Bălţi	a	2-0	*Picusciac, Porfireanu*
28/9	Dinamo Bender	h	2-1	*Sidorenco, Picusciac*
21/10	Nistru	a	1-2	*Porfireanu*
3/11	Iskra-Stali	a	0-1	
11/11	Tiligul	h	3-1	*Picusciac 2, Namasco Se.*
2008				
2/3	Poli Chişinău	a	2-0	*Suvorov, Zislis*
6/3	Zimbru	h	0-0	
11/3	Dacia Chişinău	a	0-4	
16/3	Sheriff	h	0-2	
20/3	Olimpia Bălţi	h	1-0	*Novicov*
30/3	Dinamo Bender	a	2-0	*Porfireanu, Zislis*
3/4	CSCA Chişinău	h	2-0	*Cheptine, Bondarciuc*
8/4	Poli Chişinău	a	3-0	*Namasco Se., Cheptine, Sidorenco*
12/4	Sheriff	h	0-2	
21/4	Dacia Chişinău	a	0-0	
25/4	Nistru	h	1-0	*Bondarciuc*
30/4	Tiligul	a	1-1	*Zislis*
3/5	Zimbru	a	0-0	
15/5	Iskra-Stali	h	2-0	Novicov, Porfireanu

No	Name	Nat	Pos	Aps	(s)	Gls
11	Olexandr BYCHKOV	UKR	M	15	(1)	
19	Iury BONDARCIUC		A	10	(14)	2
22	Anatol CHEPTINE		M	4	(8)	2
14	Mihail DODUL		D	27		
21	Dmitry GLIGA		M	13	(10)	
23	Victor GOLOVATENCO		D	3		
12	Seghey JURIC		G	14		
24	Igor KARPOVICH	BLR	D	10		
6	Andrei MUTULESCU	ROU	M	9	(3)	
22	Serghey NAMASCO		M	24	(1)	2
1	Stanislav NAMASCO		G	15		
22	Evgheny NICHITIN		M	1	(4)	
18	Victor NOSENCO		D	16	(2)	
3	Andrei NOVICOV		D	16	(1)	2
16	Alexandr PASCENCO		M	4	(12)	
8	Igor PICUSCIAC		A	15	(1)	11
20	Andrei PORFIREANU		M	28		7
5	Serhiy REVA	UKR	M	7	(12)	
13	Nicolai RUDAC		M	13	(12)	2
7	Andrei SECRIERU		M	26	(3)	
19	Kiril SIDORENKO	UKR	D	29		2
16	Alexandr SUVOROV		A	3	(2)	1
15	Stanislav SOLODEAC		D	3	(2)	
12	Oleg TUGULEA		G	1		
21	Răzvan TUDOR	ROU	M		(6)	
2	Andrei VERBETSCHI		D	8	(12)	
17	Alexandr ZISLIS		A	16	(6)	5

FC ZIMBRU CHIŞINĂU

Coach – Aleksandr Sevidov

Founded - 1947

MAJOR HONOURS: Moldovan League - (8) 1992, 1993, 1994, 1995, 199 1998, 1999, 2000; Moldovan Cup - (5) 1997, 1998, 2003, 2004, 2007.

2007				
4/7	Nistru	h	1-1	*Frantuz*
8/7	Iskra-Stali	a	0-0	
13/7	Poli Chişinău	h	0-0	
28/7	CSCA Chişinău	h	3-1	*Frantuz 2, Cojocari A.*
6/8	Dinamo Bender	a	2-1	*Nikulin, Ionita*
11/8	Rapid	h	2-0	*Zhdanov, Berbinschi (match annulled)*
17/8	Tiligul	a	1-0	*Frantuz*
26/8	Tiraspol	h	1-1	*Catan*
30/8	Sheriff	h	1-1	*Zhdanov*
3/9	Olimpia Bălţi	a	1-0	*Cojocari A.*
16/9	Nistru	a	0-1	
20/9	Dacia Chişinău	a	5-1	*Zhdanov 2, Nikulin 2, Kovalchuk*
24/9	Iskra-Stali	h	1-0	*Zhdanov*
28/9	Poli Chişinău	a	1-0	*Zhdanov*
21/10	Dacia Chişinău	h	0-1	
29/10	CSCA Chişinău	a	3-0	*Zhdanov 2 (1p), Petrosyan*
3/11	Dinamo Bender	h	0-0	
11/11	Rapid	a	1-0	*Zhdanov (match annulled)*
2008				
2/3	Tiligul	h	0-0	
6/3	Tiraspol	a	0-0	
12/3	Sheriff	a	1-0	*Cojocari A. (p)*
16/3	Olimpia Bălţi	h	7-0	*Hakobyan 2, Levandovschi, Zhdanov 2 (1p), Andronic O. (p), Antoniuc A.*
20/3	Dinamo Bender	h	3-3	*Lomidze, Zhdanov 2*
30/3	CSCA Chişinău	a	3-1	*Catan, Šimić, Antoniuc A.*
3/4	Poli Chişinău	h	0-0	
8/4	Sheriff	a	2-4	*Zhdanov (p), Olexici*
12/4	Dacia Chişinău	h	3-2	*Levandovschi 2, Sidorenco*
21/4	Nistru	a	0-2	
30/4	Olimpia Bălţi	a	1-1	*Frantuz*
3/5	Tiraspol	h	0-0	
11/5	Iskra-Stali	a	0-0	
16/5	Tiligul	h	3-0	*Levandovschi, Frantuz 2 (1p)*

No	Name	Nat	Pos	Aps	(s)	Gls
10	Karen ALEKSANYAN	ARM	M	3		
6	Igor ANDRONIC		D	22	(3)	
10	Oleg ANDRONIC		A	3	(4)	1
16	Alexandr ANTONIUC		A	7	(9)	2
25	Maxim ANTONIUC		A		(3)	
2	Igor ARMAS		M	6	(1)	
4	Alexandr BELIUGA		D	10		
4	Dumitru BERBINSCHI		D	11		
18	Serhiy BOIKO	UKR	M	5	(2)	

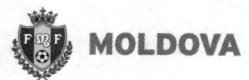

Ion BOJII		D		(1)	
Nicolae CALANCEA		G	16		
Radu CATAN		M	17	(9)	2
Artem CARP		M		(2)	
Oleg CLONIN		M	6	(1)	
Andrei COJOCARI		M	23	(2)	3
Serghei COJOCARI		M		(2)	
Ivan DEMERJI		M		(2)	
Iulian ERHAN		D	11	(3)	
Maxim FRANTUZ		M	15	(3)	7
Mykola GIBALIUK	UKR	D	4	(1)	
Ara HAKOBYAN	ARM	A	16	(2)	2
Artur IONITA		A		(2)	1
Kiril KOVALCHUK	UKR	M	6	(7)	1
Sergei KRIUCHIKHIN	RUS	D	8		
Iurie LEVANDOVSCHI		A	13	(12)	4
Mamuka LOMIDZE	GEO	D	22		1
Andrian NEGAI		G	9	(1)	
Aleksandr NIKULIN	RUS	A	5	(7)	3
Ghenady OLEXICI		D	7	(1)	1
Galust PETROSYAN	ARM	A		(4)	1
Filip POPESCU	ROU	M	1	(1)	
Ion POPUSOI		M		(3)	
Alexei SAVINOV		M	12		
Evgheny SIDORENCO		A	2	(5)	1
Bojan ŠIMIĆ	SRB	D	19		1
Valentin STAN	ROU	M	14	(1)	
Maxim VILCOV		M		(3)	
Anatoliy VORONA	UKR	M	12		
Mykola VORONYUK	UKR	G	5		
Aleksei ZHDANOV	RUS	A	20	(4)	12

PROMOTED CLUBS

FC ACADEMIA UTM CHIŞINĂU

Coach – Vitalie Culibaba

Founded - 2006

ECOND LEVEL FINAL TABLE 2007/08

	Pld	W	D	L	F	A	Pts
FC Sheriff-2	32	24	3	5	79	19	75
FC Beşiktaş Chişinău	32	21	5	6	73	32	68
FC Academia UTM Chişinău	32	18	10	4	73	23	64
FC Petrocub Sarata Galbena	32	19	6	7	51	27	63
FC Floreni Anenii Noi	32	15	8	9	63	45	53
FC Locomotiva Bălţi	32	14	8	10	61	57	50
FC Viitorul Step Soci	32	15	4	13	61	45	49
FC Cahul 2005	32	14	5	13	44	43	47
USC Gagauziya Comrat	32	13	8	11	43	54	47
FC Zimbru-2 Chişinău	32	13	5	14	52	39	44
FC Dinamo-2 Bender	32	10	7	15	46	56	37
FC Eikomena Serata Galbena	32	9	7	16	29	57	34
FC Intersport -Aroma Cobusca Nouă	32	8	9	15	32	59	33
FC Dacia-2 Chişinău	32	7	10	15	36	50	31
FC Olimpia-2 Bălţi	32	7	4	21	25	61	25
FC Moldova-03 Ungheni	32	7	4	21	24	81	25
FC Izvoras-67 Ratuş	32	5	3	24	28	72	18

FC Sheriff-2 ineligible for promotion. FC Beşiktaş Chişinău did not in licence for first level; FC Academia UTM Chişinău promoted instead. apid-2 Ghidighici withdrew after round 16 - all results annulled.

DOMESTIC CUP 2007/08

CUPA MOLDOVA

SECOND ROUND

(6/9/07)
Locomotiva 2, Floreni 3
Podiş 2, Ungheni 0
Cricova 2, Flacăra 0
Cantemir 1, Gagauziya 3
Sinteza 1, Beşiktaş 8
Petrocub 1, Academia 2
CSCA Chişinău 1, Iskra-Stali 0
Rapid 0, Dinamo Bender 2

1/8 FINALS

(7/10/07)
Dinamo Bender 1, Zimbru 2
Academia 1, Poli Chişinău 3
Beşiktaş 0, Nistru 1
Tiligul 4, Gagauzia 1
Cricova 0, Tiraspol 2
Dacia Chişinău 5, Podiş 0
CSCA Chişinău 0, Sheriff 3
Floreni 0, Olimpia Bălţi 0 *(aet; 7-8 on pens)*

QUARTER-FINALS

(25/10/07 & 7/11/07)
Tiraspol 1 *(Gliga 6)*, Dacia Chişinău 0
Dacia Chişinău 0, Tiraspol 1 *(Zislis 90)*
(Tiraspol 2-0)

Zimbru 1 *(Zhdanov 24)*, Poli Chişinău 0
Poli Chişinău 1 *(Dragovozov 90)*, Zimbru 2 *(Vorona 20, Zhdanov 85)*
(Zimbru 3-1)

Nistru 1 *(Muhovikov 45p)*, Tiligul 0
Tiligul 0, Nistru 2 *(Tcaciuc An. 20, Ngaha 21)*
(Nistru 3-0)

Olimpia Bălţi 0, Sheriff 2 *(Alexeev 71, Gnanou 77)*
Sheriff 3 *(Corneencov 10p, 17, Kuchuk 17)*, Olimpia Bălţi 0
(Sheriff 5-0)

SEMI-FINALS

(16/4/08 & 7/5/08)
Nistru 2 *(Groshev 3, Coltunovsci 90+2)*, Zimbru 1 *(Levandovschi 55)*
Zimbru 2 *(Antoniuc A. 2, Clonin 69)*, Nistru 3 *(Savchenko 37, Iepureanu 96, 109) (aet)*
(Nistru 5-3)

(16/4/08 & 7/5/08)
Tiraspol 0, Sheriff 0
Sheriff 1 *(Kuchuk 86)*, Tiraspol 0
(Sheriff 1-0)

FINAL

(20/5/08)
Zimbru stadium, Chisinau
FC SHERIFF 1 *(Testimitanu 49)*
FC NISTRU OTACI 0
Referee – *Satchi*
SHERIFF – *Melenciuc, Chinwo, Testimitanu (Negrut 86), Tarkhnishvili, Balima (Picusciac 69), Eninful, Rouamba, Tiago (Alexeev 64), Mamah, Erokhin (Arbănaş 64), Kuchuk.*
NISTRU – *Ersov, Lupasco (Coltunovsci 86), Mekang, Soltanici, Cacican, Tcaciuc An., Malitskiy (Iepureanu 46), Ngaha, Savchenko (Eremia 76), Groshev, Tcaciuc Al.*

World Cup excitemen builds

As the only one of the 53 UEFA member associations not involved in UEFA EURO 2008™, Montenegro is understandably gripped with excitement at the onset of the qualifying campaign for the 2010 FIFA World Cup.

While it is universally accepted that qualification for the finals in South Africa is beyond the scope of coach Zoran Filipović and his players, the thrill of competing on the international stage as an independent nation for the first time should guarantee in itself a memorable campaign. Montenegro have been drawn in a highly competitive section that features reigning world champions Italy. The home game with the Azzurri in March 2009 is sure to generate huge interest irrespective of how the team have fared in their opening two matches in Podgorica against Bulgaria and the Republic of Ireland.

Positive preparation

In preparation for the big kick-off Montenegro played six friendlies in 2007/08, and although they finished on a low with a 4-0 defeat by Romania, the overall balance was positive, with three wins and a draw countering two losses. The highlight of the season came in March when Norway were beaten 3-1 in Podgorica.

Like all national teams from the Balkan region, Montenegro are heavily reliant on their foreign-based players, and there were some stellar performances from the exiles in 2007/08, with AS Roma striker Mirko Vučinić, the scourge of Real Madrid CF in the UEFA Champions League, leading the way. Simon Vukčević had a fine season with Sporting Clube de Portugal, reaching the UEFA Cup quarter-finals and winning the Portuguese Cup, while Branko Bošković was a prominent member of the SK Rapid Wien side that won the Austrian championship. A number of others helped FK Partizan to win the double in neighbouring Serbia, while classy young midfielder Nikola Drinčić, who played for Serbia at the 2007 UEFA European Under-21 Championship before switching his allegiance to Montenegro, helped FC Amkar Perm to the final of the Russian Cup and opened the scoring against PFC CSKA Moskva.

The summer of 2007 saw Montenegrin clubs enter UEF competition for the first time, and the best that could b said about their collective endeavours is that there is room for improvement. Of the four teams involved, onl one managed to win their opening tie – champions FK Zeta, who overcame FBK Kaunas of Lithuania in dramat fashion (5-4 on aggregate with a late winning goal) to reach the second qualifying round of the UEFA Champions League, where, not unexpectedly, they lost to Scottish heavyweights Rangers FC.

Budućnost pip Zeta

Zeta were unable to claim a return ticket to the most prestigious European club competition but they could not have come much closer to retaining their league title. They ended the season tied on 66 points (from 33 matches) with two other clubs, FK Budućnost Podgoric and FK Mogren, losing out to Budućnost only on the head-to-head rule.

In truth, although Zeta had led the race for several weeks, it wasn't quite as close as it looked because Budućnost, coached by Branko Babić, actually sealed their victory with a match to spare. With better individu records in their three encounters with both Zeta and Mogren (in each case they had won one game and

Mirko Vučinić of Roma – a key member of the Montenegro national

awn the other two), they became champions after otecting their three-point lead with a 4-0 home win er FK Dečić in the penultimate round. Their last-day feat against lowly FK Bokelj – which ended a glorious n of 21 matches unbeaten – was purely academic.

dućnost's title triumph was more than adequate mpensation for their heartbreaking Cup final defeat Mogren ten days earlier when they conceded a late ualiser and lost 6-5 on penalties. Not that Mogren were less than deserving winners. Their consistent performances in both competitions took many by surprise. A mere fifth in the inaugural Prva Liga, their sudden transformation into genuine challengers to the big two of Zeta and Budućnost constituted the success story of the season - although it was no coincidence that the man who carried Mogren to new heights, Dejan Vukičević, was Zeta's 2006/07 title-winning coach. Curiously, Zeta were led in 2007/08 by Vukičević's older brother Mladen.

Fudbalski savez Crne Gore (FSCG)

Ulica 19. decembar 13
ME-81000 Podgorica
tel - +382 20 445600
fax - +382 20 445660
website – www.fscg.cg.yu
email - fscgmontenegro@cg.yu
Year of Formation - 2006
President – Dejan Savićević
General Secretary – Momir Đurđevac
Stadium – Podgorica Gradski, Podgorica (12,000)

TOP FIVE ALL-TIME CAPS
Vladimir Božović (9); Savo Pavićević, Milan Jovanović & Luka Pejović (8); Vukašin Poleksić, Jovan Tanasijević, Milan Purović & Risto Lakić (7)

TOP FIVE ALL-TIME GOALS
Mirko Vučinić (4); Radomir Đalović (3); Igor Burzanović (2); Branko Bošković & Nikola Drinčić (1)

ATIONAL TEAM RESULTS 2007/08

07	Slovenia	H	Podgorica	1-1	*Vučinić (28p)*
07	Sweden	H	Podgorica	1-2	*Vučinić (16)*
/07	Estonia	A	Tallinn	1-0	*Vučinić (41)*
08	Norway	H	Podgorica	3-1	*Burzanović (8), Bošković (37), Đalović (60)*
08	Kazakhstan	H	Podgorica	3-0	*Đalović (15, 45+2), Drinčić (21)*
08	Romania	A	Bucharest	0-4	

ATIONAL TEAM APPEARANCES 2007/08

– Zoran FILIPOVIĆ 6/2/53			Svn	Swe	Est	Nor	Kaz	Rou	Caps	Goals
šin POLEKSIĆ	30/8/82	Tatabánya (HUN) /Debrecen (HUN)	G	G46	G46	G			7	-
PAVIĆEVIĆ	11/12/80	Hajduk Kula (SRB) /Vojvodina (SRB)	D86	D77	D46	D	D	D	8	-
slav BATAK	15/8/77	Ankaraspor (TUR)	D	D	D				6	-
TANASIJEVIĆ	20/1/78	Dinamo Moskva (RUS)	D		D	D	D70	D58	7	-
JOVANOVIĆ	21/7/83	Univ Cluj (ROU)	D64	D85		D	D74	D65	8	-
TUMBASEVIĆ	14/1/85	Zeta	M						4	-
o BOŠKOVIĆ	21/6/80	Rapid Wien (AUT)	M78	M77		M67	M46	M58	6	1
n VUKČEVIĆ	29/1/86	Sporting (POR)	M		M30	M30	M		5	-
mir BOŽOVIĆ	13/11/81	Rapid Bucureşti (ROU)	M	s77	M	M	M60	M	9	-
VUČINIĆ	1/10/83	Roma (ITA)	A	A	A		s77	A74	6	4
PUROVIĆ	7/5/85	Sporting (POR)	A74	s72			s74	s74	7	-

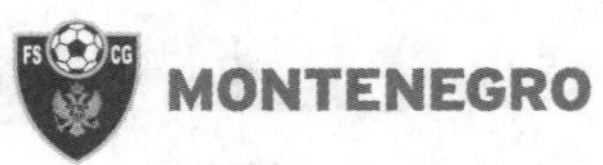

MONTENEGRO

NATIONAL TEAM APPEARANCES 2007/08

			Svn	Swe	Est	Nor	Kaz	Rou	Caps	G
Luka PEJOVIĆ	30/7/85	Grbalj /Mogren	s64	s85	D	D58	D	s58	8	
Srđan RADONJIĆ	8/5/81	OB (DEN)	s74						3	
Nedeljko VLAHOVIĆ	15/1/84	Budućnost Podgorica	s78						1	
Risto LAKIĆ	3/7/83	Budućnost Podgorica /Partizan (SRB)	s86	s77	s46	s85			7	
Vlado JEKNIĆ	14/8/83	Wehen (GER)		D	s85				5	
Milorad PEKOVIĆ	5/8/77	Mainz (GER)		M	M85		s46	M63	4	
Nikola DRINČIĆ	7/9/84	Amkar (RUS)		M	M	M	M	M	5	
Igor BURZANOVIĆ	25/8/85	Crvena Zvezda (SRB)		M80		M73		M46	6	
Dragan BOGAVAC	7/4/80	Koblenz (GER) /Paderborn (GER)		A72	A72	s30	A	A46	5	
Darko BOŽOVIĆ	9/8/78	Partizan (SRB)		s46	s46				2	
Mitar NOVAKOVIĆ	27/9/81	OFK (SRB)		s80	s72	s67		s63	4	
Radomir ĐALOVIĆ	29/11/82	Rijeka (CRO)			s30 /82	A85	A77	s58	4	
Nikola NIKEZIĆ	13/6/81	Le Havre (FRA)			s82				1	
Dejan OGNJANOVIĆ	21/6/78	Estoril (POR)				s58	s70	s65	3	
Nikola VUJOVIĆ	23/6/81	Budućnost Podgorica				s73			3	
Mladen BOŽOVIĆ	1/8/84	Partizan (SRB)					G67	G	3	
Elsad ZVEROTIĆ	31/10/86	Wil (SUI)					s60	s46	2	
Ivan JANJUŠEVIĆ	11/7/86	Mogren					s67		1	
Stevan JOVETIĆ	2/11/89	Partizan (SRB)						s46	2	

DOMESTIC LEAGUE 2007/08

PRVA LIGA FINAL TABLE

		Home					Away					Total					
	Pld	W	D	L	F	A	W	D	L	F	A	W	D	L	F	A	Pts
1 FK Budućnost Podgorica	33	12	4	1	30	6	6	8	2	13	7	18	12	3	43	13	66
2 FK Zeta	33	11	4	2	30	12	8	5	3	26	16	19	9	5	56	28	66
3 FK Mogren	33	11	4	2	28	11	8	5	3	18	10	19	9	5	46	21	66
4 OFK Grbalj	33	8	7	2	21	11	6	6	4	19	14	14	13	6	40	25	55
5 FK Rudar Pljevlja	33	9	4	4	24	12	5	6	5	14	14	14	10	9	38	26	52
6 FK Lovćen	33	7	6	3	17	11	4	4	9	11	19	11	10	12	28	30	43
7 FK Dečić	33	6	5	5	14	13	4	3	10	12	24	10	8	15	26	37	38
8 OFK Petrovac	33	4	6	6	19	22	4	6	7	17	24	8	12	13	36	46	36
9 FK Kom	33	7	4	6	18	22	2	5	9	11	27	9	9	15	29	49	36
10 FK Bokelj	33	5	2	9	13	17	3	6	8	11	21	8	8	17	24	38	32
11 FK Sutjeska	33	3	8	5	12	17	2	3	12	7	27	5	11	17	19	44	23
12 FK Mladost Podgorica	33	2	5	9	5	16	2	2	13	11	28	4	7	22	16	44	19

TOP GOALSCORERS

13 Miloš ĐALAC (Grbalj/Zeta)

11 Božo MILIĆ (Grbalj)

10 Ivan JABLAN (Lovćen)
Mirza LJUMIĆ (Kom)
Miodrag ZEC (Mogren)

9 Fatos BEĆIRAJ (Budućnost Podgorica)
Ivan KNEŽEVIĆ (Zeta)
Minja LJUMOVIĆ (Dečić)
Bogdan MILIĆ (Budućnost Podgorica)
Blazo PERUTOVIĆ (Lovćen)
Nikola VUJOVIĆ (Mogren)

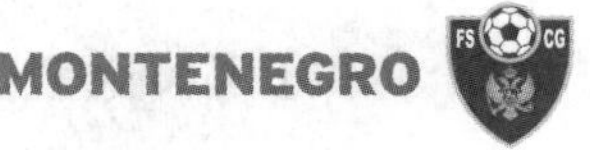

CLUB-BY-CLUB

FK BOKELJ

Coach - Aleksandar Miljenović; (26/11/07) Ivo Donković

Founded – 1930

07				
/8	Rudar	a	0-0	
/8	Dečić	h	1-0	*Vemić*
/8	Grbalj	a	0-1	
/8	Sutjeska	h	0-1	
9	Budućnost Podgorica	a	0-1	
/9	Zeta	h	0-1	
/9	Mogren	a	0-1	
/9	Kom	a	0-2	
10	Petrovac	h	0-2	
/10	Mladost Podgorica	a	1-0	*Vujović*
/10	Lovćen	h	1-1	*Vujović*
11	Rudar	h	0-2	
/11	Dečić	a	1-3	*Vemić*
/11	Grbalj	h	0-1	
12	Sutjeska	a	0-0	
12	Budućnost Podgorica	h	0-1	
/12	Zeta	a	1-0	*Vujović*
08				
/2	Mogren	h	0-2	
3	Kom	h	1-2	*Delić*
3	Petrovac	a	4-2	*Lasić 2, Borović 2*
/3	Mladost Podgorica	h	2-0	*Delić, Borović*
/3	Lovćen	a	0-0	
/3	Mogren	a	0-0	
4	Rudar	h	0-1	
/4	Grbalj	a	0-1	
/4	Kom	h	2-2	*Babača, Borović*
/4	Petrovac	a	0-0	
/4	Lovćen	h	1-0	*Usanović*
5	Dečić	a	1-1	*Babača*
/5	Mladost Podgorica	a	0-1	
/5	Sutjeska	h	4-1	*Vujović 2, Usanović, Radusinović*
/5	Zeta	a	3-8	*Međedović, Jovanović 2*
/5	Budućnost Podgorica	h	1-0	*Babača*

ame	Nat	Pos	Aps	(s)	Gls
ead BABAČA		M	29	(1)	3
iodrag BOGDANOVIĆ		M	15		
aven BOROVIĆ		M	20	(8)	4
dis CINDRAK		M	11	(2)	
iloš DELIĆ		M	11	(1)	2
ebojša ĐORĐEVIĆ		M	8		
orko ĐUKOVIĆ		D	11	(5)	
enis FETAHOVIĆ		D	13		
iloš JOVANOVIĆ		M	29	(2)	2
enad KAŠĆELAN		A		(1)	
amir LASIĆ		A	12	(2)	2
oran LENAC		G	12		
ražen MEĐEDOVIĆ		M	9	(3)	1
leksandar MIKIJELJ		D	13	(2)	
ozo PEJOVIĆ		D	16	(4)	
or RADUSINOVIĆ		D	31		1
iodrag STANOJEVIĆ		D	30		
ejan ŠUŠKAVČEVIĆ		G	16		
iodrag TODOROVIĆ		G	5		
iloš TOMOVIĆ		A	12	(1)	
ojan USANOVIĆ		M	13	(9)	2
roš VEMIĆ	SRB	A	8	(2)	2
arko VUJOVIĆ		A	30	(3)	5
etar VUKOTIĆ		A	9	(7)	

FK BUDUĆNOST PODGORICA

Coach - Saša Petrović; (28/10/07) Mojaš Radonjić; (21/11/07) Branko Babić

Founded – 1925

MAJOR HONOURS: Montenegrin League - (1) 2008.

2007				
10/8	Sutjeska	a	1-1	*Đurišić*
18/8	Kom	a	0-1	
25/8	Zeta	h	2-1	*Scepanović, Milić B.*
29/8	Mogren	a	1-1	*Vuković N.*
1/9	Bokelj	h	1-0	*Vlahović*
15/9	Petrovac	a	1-1	*Šofranac*
22/9	Mladost Podgorica	h	1-0	*Đurišić*
29/9	Lovćen	a	1-0	*Vukčević P.*
6/10	Rudar	h	1-1	*Carapić*
20/10	Dečić	a	1-0	*Mugoša*
27/10	Grbalj	h	2-3	*Mugoša, Sekulić*
4/11	Sutjeska	h	2-0	*Milić B., Mugoša*
10/11	Kom	h	0-0	
25/11	Zeta	a	0-0	
1/12	Mogren	h	1-1	*Sekulić*
8/12	Bokelj	a	1-0	*Perišić*
15/12	Petrovac	h	1-0	*Sekulić*
2008				
23/2	Mladost Podgorica	a	1-0	*Bećiraj*
1/3	Lovćen	h	1-0	*Vukčević P. (p)*
9/3	Rudar	a	1-0	*Bećiraj*
15/3	Dečić	h	2-0	*Vukčević P. (p), Bećiraj*
19/3	Grbalj	a	1-1	*Bećiraj*
29/3	Sutjeska	h	4-0	*Bećiraj, Milić 2, Vukčević P.*
5/4	Zeta	a	0-0	
12/4	Mladost Podgorica	h	2-0	*Delić, Vuković N.*
20/4	Mogren	h	3-0	*Vukčević P. 2, Bećiraj*
26/4	Rudar	a	0-0	
30/4	Grbalj	h	0-0	
3/5	Kom	a	4-1	*Bećiraj 2, Vujadinović (p), Milić*
10/5	Petrovac	h	3-0	*Čarapić, Milić 2*
14/5	Lovćen	a	0-0	
17/5	Dečić	h	4-0	*Vukčević P., Milić 2, Bećiraj*
24/5	Bokelj	a	0-1	

Name	Nat	Pos	Aps	(s)	Gls
Fatos BEĆIRAJ		A	15		9
Balša BOŽOVIĆ		M	1	(4)	
Draško BOŽOVIĆ		M	5	(3)	
Mladen BOŽOVIĆ		G	14		
Ivan ČARAPIĆ		D	18	(2)	2
Ivan DELIĆ		M	19	(5)	1
Milan ĐURIŠIĆ		M	20	(7)	2
Diego HAIME	ARG	M	5	(8)	
Risto LAKIĆ		D	17		
Gustavo LÓPEZ	ARG	M	15		
Bogdan MILIĆ		A	14	(12)	9
Dražen MILIĆ		A	2		
Marko MUGOŠA		M	4	(6)	3
Goran PERIŠIĆ		D	18	(5)	1
Aleksandar RADOVIĆ		D	4		
Mirko RAIČEVIĆ		M	31		
Blažo RAJOVIĆ		D	15	(3)	
Marko ŠĆEPANOVIĆ		M	15	(8)	1
Radislav SEKULIĆ		A	13	(9)	3
Nenad ŠOFRANAC		M	5	(7)	1
Darjan TODOROVIĆ		M		(4)	
Marko VIDOVIĆ		M	6	(4)	
Nedeljko VLAHOVIĆ		M	8	(3)	1

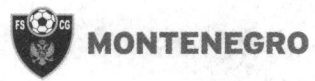

Name	Nat	Pos	Aps	(s)	Gls
Krenar VOKŠI		M	2	(1)	
Miroslav VUJADINOVIĆ		G	19		1
Nikola VUKČEVIĆ		D	25	(2)	
Petar VUKČEVIĆ		M	29	(2)	7
Ivan VUKOVIĆ		A	6	(10)	
Nemanja VUKOVIĆ		D	18	(1)	2

FK DEČIĆ

Coach - Bozo Vuković

Founded - 1926

2007				
11/8	Mogren	h	1-1	*Lekić E.*
18/8	Bokelj	a	0-1	
25/8	Petrovac	h	2-1	*Camaj A. 2*
29/8	Mladost Podgorica	a	3-0	*Kajosević, Camaj A., Ljumović*
1/9	Lovćen	h	1-0	*Ljumović*
15/9	Rudar	a	1-2	*Jovanović*
22/9	Kom	h	2-0	*Ljumović 2*
29/9	Grbalj	h	0-0	
6/10	Sutjeska	a	0-2	
20/10	Budućnost Podgorica	h	0-1	
27/10	Zeta	a	1-2	*Ljumović*
3/11	Mogren	a	0-2	
10/11	Bokelj	h	3-1	*Lekić E. 2, Kajosević*
24/11	Petrovac	a	1-1	*Kajosević*
1/12	Mladost Podgorica	h	0-0	
9/12	Lovćen	a	2-0	*Ljumović 2*
15/12	Rudar	h	0-1	
2008				
23/2	Kom	a	1-0	*Tuzović*
1/3	Grbalj	a	1-3	*Tuzović*
8/3	Sutjeska	h	1-0	*Ljumović*
15/3	Budućnost Podgorica	a	0-2	
19/3	Zeta	h	0-1	
29/3	Rudar	a	0-2	
5/4	Grbalj	h	1-0	*Ljumović*
12/4	Kom	a	0-2	
19/4	Petrovac	h	1-1	*Camaj A.*
26/4	Lovćen	a	0-0	
30/4	Mladost Podgorica	a	1-0	*Kajosević*
3/5	Bokelj	h	1-1	*Gutić*
10/5	Sutjeska	a	1-1	*Lekić E.*
14/5	Zeta	h	1-4	*Camaj A.*
17/5	Budućnost Podgorica	a	0-4	
24/5	Mogren	h	0-1	

Name	Nat	Pos	Aps	(s)	Gls
John ALLEN	USA	M	1	(3)	
Boban ČABARKAPA		D	15		
Albino CAMAJ		A	20		5
Valento CAMAJ		M	27		
Idriz ĐOKOVIĆ		D	3	(2)	
Edin ĐOKOVIĆ		M	10	(4)	
Hasim ĐOKOVIĆ		M	32		
Vedad DREŠEVIĆ		G	33		
Hilmo GUTIĆ		D	32		1
Ervin HADŽIBURIĆ		D	10	(4)	
Damir HAVERIĆ		D	2	(3)	
Marko JOVANOVIĆ	SRB	A	28	(3)	1
Damir KAJOŠEVIĆ		A	30	(1)	4
Amir KOLJENOVIĆ		D	3	(6)	
Buto KRKANOVIĆ		M	1		
Igor KUČ		D	2		
Muhamed LEKIĆ		M	1	(1)	
Edin LEKIĆ		A	27		4
Minja LJUMOVIĆ		M	27	(4)	9
Denis ORAHOVAC		A	2	(2)	
Nijazim PADOVIĆ		M	7	(9)	
Stanko PELEVIĆ		A	4	(6)	

Name	Nat	Pos	Aps	(s)	Gls
Miladin RADOVIĆ		M	27	(1)	
Amilcar RAMIREZ	USA	M	5	(5)	
Enes ŠABANADŽOVIĆ		A	3	(10)	
Denis TUZOVIĆ		M	11		2

OFK GRBALJ

Coach - Dragan Aničić; (22/10/07) Nebojša Vignjević

Founded - 1970

2007				
11/8	Zeta	h	1-2	*Đalac*
17/8	Mogren	a	3-0	*(w/o)*
25/8	Bokelj	h	1-0	*Đalac*
29/8	Petrovac	a	2-4	*Đalac, Milić*
1/9	Mladost Podgorica	h	2-1	*Grujić, Ajković*
15/9	Lovćen	a	2-3	*Ajković, Milić*
22/9	Rudar	h	1-1	*Milić*
29/9	Dečić	a	0-0	
6/10	Kom	h	0-0	
31/10	Sutjeska	h	1-1	*Bošković*
27/10	Budućnost Podgorica	a	3-2	*Ajković, Grujić, Nedov*
3/11	Zeta	a	0-1	
10/11	Mogren	h	0-2	
24/11	Bokelj	a	1-0	*Đalac*
1/12	Petrovac	h	1-1	*Pavićević*
8/12	Mladost Podgorica	a	2-1	*Milić 2*
15/12	Lovćen	h	2-0	*Milić, Bošković*
2008				
23/2	Rudar	a	0-0	
1/3	Dečić	h	3-1	*Bošković, Pavićević 2*
8/3	Kom	a	0-0	
15/3	Sutjeska	a	0-0	
19/3	Budućnost Podgorica	h	1-1	*Milić (p)*
29/3	Lovćen	h	2-0	*Kasalića 2*
5/4	Dečić	a	0-1	
12/4	Bokelj	h	1-0	*Bošković*
19/4	Sutjeska	a	1-1	*Ajković*
26/4	Zeta	h	0-0	
30/4	Budućnost Podgorica	a	0-0	
3/5	Mogren	h	0-0	
10/5	Rudar	a	3-1	*og (Vuković), Franciśković, Milić*
14/5	Mladost Podgorica	h	2-0	*Pavićević, Bošković*
17/5	Kom	h	3-1	*Milić 2, Nikolić (p)*
24/5	Petrovac	a	2-0	*Milić, Kasalića*

Name	Nat	Pos	Aps	(s)	Gls
Drazen AJKOVIĆ		M	30	(1)	4
Dragan BOŠKOVIĆ		A	27	(4)	5
Miloš ĐALAC		A	15	(3)	4
Igor DRAGIĆEVIĆ		D	16		
Ivica FRANCIŠKOVIĆ	SRB	M	16		1
Goran GRUJIĆ	SRB	M	29	(2)	2
Milan IVANOVIĆ		D	9		
Marko KASALICA		A	3	(10)	3
Srđan KLJAJEVIĆ		G	31		
Marko KNEŽEVIĆ		G	1		
Milan KNEŽEVIĆ		M	1		
Mihailo KRAČKOVIĆ		M		(1)	
Bojan MAGAZIN		M	2	(6)	
Slobodan MAZIĆ	SRB	D	26	(5)	
Božo MILIĆ		A	27	(3)	11
Aleksandar NEDOVIĆ		M	14		1
Nemanja NIKOLIĆ		M	25	(1)	1
Milivoje NOVOVIĆ		D	5	(2)	
Darko PAVIĆEVIĆ		A	12	(15)	4
Luka PEJOVIĆ		D	3		
Gavrilo PETROVIĆ		D	16		
Saša POPOVIĆ	SRB	D	12		
Željko POPOVIĆ		D	12	(1)	
Saša RADENOVIĆ		M	12	(6)	

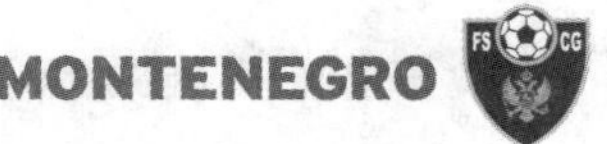

Name	Nat	Pos	Aps	(s)	Gls
vića RADOJIČIĆ		A	3	(4)	
šan SADŽAKOV	SRB	D		(4)	
ris SAVIĆ		D	5	(1)	

FK KOM

Coach - Goran Đurović

Founded - 1958

07				
/8	Mladost Podgorica	a	2-0	*Ljumić, Tomić D.*
/8	Budućnost Podgorica	h	1-0	*Ljumić (p)*
/8	Lovćen	a	0-0	
/8	Zeta	h	2-1	*Ljumić 2*
9	Rudar	a	0-3	
/9	Mogren	h	1-3	*Ljumić (p)*
/9	Dečić	a	0-2	
/9	Bokelj	h	2-0	*Jovanović, Dragićević I.*
10	Grbalj	a	0-0	
/10	Sutjeska	a	0-1	
11	Mladost Podgorica	h	0-0	
/11	Budućnost Podgorica	a	0-0	
/11	Lovćen	h	0-4	
/11	Petrovac	h	1-0	*Brnović*
12	Zeta	a	0-2	
12	Rudar	h	2-1	*Popović V., Tomić D.*
/12	Mogren	a	1-3	*Rogošić (p)*
08				
/2	Dečić	h	0-1	
3	Bokelj	a	2-1	*Dragićević R. (p), Rogošić*
3	Grbalj	h	0-0	
/3	Petrovac	a	1-1	*Brnović*
/3	Sutjeska	h	2-1	*Vojvodić, Ljumić (p)*
/3	Petrovac	h	1-3	*Brnović*
4	Lovćen	a	0-1	
/4	Dečić	h	2-0	*Ljumić 2*
/4	Bokelj	a	2-2	*Ljumić, Vojvodić*
/4	Sutjeska	h	1-1	*Brnović*
/4	Zeta	a	1-4	*Milić L.*
5	Budućnost Podgorica	h	1-4	*Ljumić*
/5	Mogren	a	1-4	*Vlahović*
/5	Rudar	h	0-0	
/5	Grbalj	a	1-3	*Vlahović (p)*
/5	Mladost Podgorica	h	2-3	*Jovanović, Milić L.*

ame	Nat	Pos	Aps	(s)	Gls
edrag BRNOVIĆ		M	32		4
đan ĐURASOVIĆ		A	2	(5)	
or DRAGIĆEVIĆ		M	16		1
adislav DRAGIĆEVIĆ		D	32		1
an GOLUBOVIĆ	SRB	M	32		
iroje JOVANOVIĆ		M	25		2
elimir KALUĐEROVIĆ		M	3	(3)	
laden KAPOR		D	12	(2)	
emanja KLJAJEVIĆ		D	26		
irza LJUMIĆ		A	26	(3)	10
arko LUBARDA		G	33		
edrag MILAČIĆ		M		(6)	
an MILIĆ		M	2	(8)	
ka MILIĆ		M	3	(5)	2
arko MILONJIĆ		A	4	(5)	
avrilo PETROVIĆ		D	6		
ihailo PETROVIĆ		D		(4)	
avor POPOVIĆ		D	5	(9)	
iloš POPOVIĆ		M	3	(9)	
ado POPOVIĆ		M	26	(2)	1
ikola ROGOŠIĆ		D	13	(2)	2
anilo TOMIĆ		M	15	(9)	2
eljko TOMIĆ		A	8	(5)	
edeljko VLAHOVIĆ		M	10		2
emanja VOJVODIĆ		D	15	(2)	2

Name	Nat	Pos	Aps	(s)	Gls
Relja VUČINIĆ		A	1	(5)	
Miloš VUKČEVIĆ		D	2	(2)	
Dalibor ZONJIĆ		D	11		

FK LOVĆEN

Coach - Nikola Rakojević

Founded - 1913

2007				
11/8	Petrovac	h	2-2	*Jablan, Ćetković*
18/8	Mladost Podgorica	a	1-0	*Jablan*
25/8	Kom	h	0-0	
29/8	Rudar	h	1-0	*Jablan (p)*
1/9	Dečić	a	0-1	
15/9	Grbalj	h	3-2	*Mester, Perutović, Nikolić*
22/9	Sutjeska	a	1-1	*og (Nerić)*
29/9	Budućnost Podgorica	h	0-1	
6/10	Zeta	a	0-1	
20/10	Mogren	h	1-0	*Perutović*
27/10	Bokelj	a	1-1	*Jablan*
3/11	Petrovac	a	1-1	*Jablan*
10/11	Mladost Podgorica	h	2-0	*Jablan, Djurović*
24/11	Kom	a	4-0	*Mester, Perutović, Jablan 2*
1/12	Rudar	a	0-2	
9/12	Dečić	h	0-2	
15/12	Grbalj	a	0-2	
2008				
23/2	Sutjeska	h	4-1	*Perutović 2, Jablan, Nikolić*
1/3	Budućnost Podgorica	a	0-1	
8/3	Zeta	h	1-1	*Perutović*
15/3	Mogren	a	0-1	
19/3	Bokelj	h	0-0	
29/3	Grbalj	a	0-2	
5/4	Kom	h	1-0	*Perutović*
12/4	Petrovac	a	1-0	*Đurović*
19/4	Mladost Podgorica	a	1-0	*Jablan (p)*
26/4	Dečić	h	0-0	
30/4	Bokelj	a	0-1	
3/5	Sutjeska	h	0-1	
10/5	Zeta	a	1-1	*Mester*
14/5	Budućnost Podgorica	h	0-0	
17/5	Mogren	a	0-4	
24/5	Rudar	h	2-1	*Perutović 2*

Name	Nat	Pos	Aps	(s)	Gls
Vladan ADŽIĆ		D	25		
Dusan BORILOVIĆ		D	11	(6)	
Nenad ĆETKOVIĆ		D	4		
Sasa ĆETKOVIĆ		D	28		1
Marko ĐUROVIĆ		A	7	(4)	2
Dragan DRAŠKOVIĆ		G	22		
Ivan JABLAN		A	29		10
Janoš KATO		G	11		
Jovan KRIVOKAPIĆ		M	1		
Miloš LALIČIĆ		A	5	(2)	
Nenad LIPOVINA		D	2	(3)	
Srđa LOPIČIĆ		M	9	(4)	
Radivoje MARIĆ		A	2	(4)	
Milan MEŠTER		M	29		3
Dusan MILOŠEVIĆ		D	10	(5)	
Andrija MIRKOVIĆ		D	17		
Ivan MIRKOVIĆ		M	11	(4)	
Baćo NIKOLIĆ		M	17	(4)	2
Andrija PEJAKOVIĆ		M	2	(4)	
Blazo PERUTOVIĆ		A	30		9
Bracan POPOVIĆ		D	26		
Dušan SADŽAKOV	SRB	D	18	(4)	
Vladan TATAR		M	25	(7)	
Marko VUJOVIĆ		M	1	(1)	
Darko VUKAŠINOVIĆ		D	21	(4)	

MONTENEGRO

FK MLADOST PODGORICA

Coach - Dimitrije Mitrović; (30/8/07) Vojislav Pejović; (7/1/08) Slobodan Šćepanović

Founded - 1950

2007

11/8	Kom	h	0-2	
18/8	Lovćen	h	0-1	
25/8	Rudar	a	1-3	*Ljumović*
29/8	Dečić	h	0-3	
1/9	Grbalj	a	1-2	*Ljumović (p)*
15/9	Sutjeska	h	0-0	
22/9	Budućnost Podgorica	a	0-1	
29/9	Zeta	h	1-1	*Martinović*
6/10	Mogren	a	1-2	*Bukilić Ig.*
20/10	Bokelj	h	0-1	
27/10	Petrovac	a	1-2	*Đukić*
3/11	Kom	a	0-0	
10/11	Lovćen	a	0-2	
24/11	Rudar	h	0-0	
1/12	Dečić	a	0-0	
8/12	Grbalj	h	1-2	*Grbović*
15/12	Sutjeska	a	1-2	*Grbović*

2008

23/2	Budućnost Podgorica	h	0-1	
1/3	Zeta	a	0-1	
8/3	Mogren	h	0-2	
15/3	Bokelj	a	0-2	
19/3	Petrovac	h	0-0	
29/3	Zeta	a	1-2	*Grbić*
5/4	Petrovac	h	1-1	*Ljumović (p)*
12/4	Budućnost Podgorica	a	0-2	
19/4	Lovćen	h	0-1	
26/4	Mogren	a	0-2	
30/4	Dečić	h	0-1	
3/5	Rudar	a	2-1	*Ljumović (p), Krstović*
10/5	Bokelj	h	1-0	*Krstović*
14/5	Grbalj	a	0-2	
17/5	Sutjeska	h	1-0	*Đukić*
24/5	Kom	a	3-2	*Krstović, Raičević, Vučinić*

Name	Nat	Pos	Aps	(s)	Gls
Damir ALKOVIĆ		A	1	(3)	
Igor BUKILIĆ		A	7	(1)	1
Ivan BUKILIĆ		A	11	(2)	
Aleksandar ČAĐENOVIĆ		M	5		
Predrag ĐUKIĆ	SRB	M	25	(1)	2
Danilo ĐUROVIĆ		M		(1)	
Slobodan DROBNJAK		M	10	(4)	
Petar GRBIĆ		A	9	(3)	1
Boris GRBOVIĆ		D	30		2
Ranko KALEZIĆ		M	1	(1)	
Predrag KALUĐEROVIĆ		M	5	(4)	
Dejan KARAN	SRB	D	26		
Andrija KOVAČEVIĆ		D	7	(1)	
Kristijan KRSTOVIĆ		M	15	(8)	3
Nenad LAKOVIĆ		M	5	(2)	
Marko LJUMOVIĆ		D	28	(2)	4
Nikola MARKUŠ		D	9	(1)	
Lazar MARTINOVIĆ		M	17	(6)	
Vuk MARTINOVIĆ		D	28		1
Ilija MUGOŠA		M	5	(3)	
Peter OLADOTUN	NGA	A	1		
Stevan PAVIĆEVIĆ		A	2	(1)	
Boris PAVLOVIĆ		A	3	(2)	
Igor RADOVIĆ		D	32		
Lazar RADULOVIĆ		M	4		
Mileta RADULOVIĆ		G	33		
Marko RAIČEVIĆ		M	9	(4)	1
Slobodan ROVČANIN		M	15	(2)	
Vladan SERATLIĆ		A	7	(2)	

Mirko TAMINDŽIJA		A	1	(5)	
Relja VUČINIĆ		A	2		1
Predrag VUJIŠIČ		M	5	(2)	
Miodrag VUKIĆEVIĆ		D	5	(1)	

FK MOGREN

Coach - Miodrag Bajović; (26/8/07) Dejan Vukičević

Founded – 1920

MAJOR HONOURS: Montenegrin Cup - (1) 2008.

2007

12/8	Dečić	a	1-1	*Zec R.*
17/8	Grbalj	h	0-3	*(w/o)*
25/8	Sutjeska	a	0-0	
29/8	Budućnost Podgorica	h	1-1	*Bojić*
2/9	Zeta	a	0-1	
15/9	Kom	a	3-1	*Milić (p), Zec M., Tiodorović*
22/9	Bokelj	h	1-0	*Milić*
29/9	Petrovac	a	2-0	*Zec R., Zec M.*
6/10	Mladost Podgorica	h	2-1	*Zec R., Zec M.*
20/10	Lovćen	a	0-1	
27/10	Rudar	h	1-1	*Zec M.*
3/11	Dečić	h	2-0	*Zec M., Pejović*
10/11	Grbalj	a	2-0	*Vujović N., Milić*
24/11	Sutjeska	h	1-0	*Zec R.*
1/12	Budućnost Podgorica	a	1-1	*Gluščević*
8/12	Zeta	h	2-2	*Vujović N., Gluščević*
15/12	Kom	h	3-1	*Vujović N. 2, Gluščevi*

2008

23/2	Bokelj	a	2-0	*Gluščević, Vujović N.*
2/3	Petrovac	h	0-1	
8/3	Mladost Podgorica	a	2-0	*Vujović N., Zec M.*
15/3	Lovćen	h	1-0	*Božović*
19/3	Rudar	a	0-0	
29/3	Bokelj	h	0-0	
5/4	Sutjeska	a	2-1	*Božović, Gluščević*
12/4	Zeta	h	2-0	*Gluščević (p), Zec M.*
20/4	Budućnost Podgorica	a	0-3	
26/4	Mladost Podgorica	h	2-0	*Radulović 2*
30/4	Rudar	h	2-0	*Vujović N., Milić*
3/5	Grbalj	a	0-0	
10/5	Kom	h	4-1	*Vujović N., Nerić 2, Mi*
14/5	Petrovac	a	2-1	*Božović, Gluščević*
17/5	Lovćen	h	4-0	*Jovanović, Zec M. 3*
24/5	Dečić	a	1-0	*Vujović N.*

Name	Nat	Pos	Aps	(s)	Gls
Bojan BEGOVIĆ		M	8	(1)	
Žarko BELADA		D	19	(1)	
Veselin BOJIĆ		D	24		1
Balša BOŽOVIĆ		M	7	(5)	3
Damir ČAKAR		M	13	(1)	
Srđan DAMJANOVIĆ		D	21	(3)	
Vukajlo ĐUKIĆ		D	3	(2)	
Novak DRAKULOVIĆ		D	8	(2)	
Vladimir GLUŠČEVIĆ		A	25	(1)	7
Ivan JANJUŠEVIĆ		G	24		
Goran JOVANOVIĆ	SRB	M	20	(6)	1
Bojan KALEZIĆ		A	5	(8)	
Goran MATOVIĆ		M	5	(1)	
Drazen MEĐEDOVIĆ		M	5	(3)	
Saša MIKIJELJ		D	6	(4)	
Drazen MILIĆ		A	10	(10)	5
Milenko NERIĆ		A	4	(8)	2
Luka PEJOVIĆ		D	22		1
Miljan RADOVIĆ		M	8	(1)	
Milan RADULOVIĆ		D	20		2
Dejan ŠUŠKAVČEVIĆ		G	8		
Luka TIODOROVIĆ		M	13	(4)	1
Nikola VUJOVIĆ		A	25	(2)	9

ıdimir VUJOVIĆ	M	11	(1)	
manja VUKAŠINOVIĆ	A	4	(7)	
tko ZEC	M	11	(12)	4
odrag ZEC	A	23	(4)	10

OFK PETROVAC

Coach - Milorad Malovrazić; (21/3/08) Obren Sarić

Founded - 1969

ı07				
/8	Lovćen	a	2-2	*Burzanović 2*
/8	Rudar	h	1-0	*Nikezić*
/8	Dečić	a	1-2	*Radulović*
ı/08	Grbalj	h	4-2	*Zvićer, Marčić, Stanisić, Lakić*
9	Sutjeska	a	1-0	*Dragićević*
/9	Budućnost Podgorica	h	1-1	*Nenezić*
:/9	Zeta	a	1-4	*Zvićer*
ı/9	Mogren	h	0-2	
10	Bokelj	a	2-0	*Burzanović, Mihailović*
'/10	Mladost Podgorica	h	2-1	*Burzanović, Zvićer*
11	Lovćen	h	1-1	*Stanisić*
ı/11	Rudar	a	0-1	
ı/11	Dečić	h	1-1	*Stanisić*
ı/11	Kom	a	0-1	
12	Grbalj	a	1-1	*Nikezić*
'12	Sutjeska	h	2-0	*Stanisić, Zvićer*
ı/12	Budućnost Podgorica	a	0-1	
ı08				
ı/2	Zeta	h	1-1	*Burzanović*
'3	Mogren	a	1-0	*Burzanović*
'3	Bokelj	h	2-4	*Zvićer, Mihailović*
ı/3	Kom	h	1-1	*Lakić*
ı/3	Mladost Podgorica	a	0-0	
ı/3	Kom	a	3-1	*Dragićević, Divanović, Nenezić*
'4	Mladost Podgorica	a	1-1	*Dragićević*
2/4	Lovćen	h	0-1	
ı/4	Dečić	a	1-1	*Marković*
ı/4	Bokelj	h	0-0	
ı/4	Sutjeska	a	1-1	*Vuković*
'5	Zeta	h	2-3	*Dragićević, Forgić*
ı/5	Budućnost Podgorica	a	0-3	
4/5	Mogren	h	1-2	*Dragićević*
7/5	Rudar	a	2-5	*Šofranac, Radulović*
4/5	Grbalj	h	0-2	

ıame	**Nat**	**Pos**	**Aps**	**(s)**	**Gls**
oran BURZANOVIĆ		M	22	(2)	6
ıehmed DIVANOVIĆ		M	19	(11)	1
ıdravko DRAGIĆEVIĆ		A	26	(3)	5
ıarko DŽEVERDANOVIĆ		M	4	(1)	
ıoran FORGIĆ	SRB	A	3	(7)	1
ıniša GRAOVAC		D	16		
ıiloš LAKIĆ		D	29		2
udolf MARČIĆ		M	11		1
ıarko MARKOVIĆ		M	2	(2)	1
ıikola MIHAILOVIĆ		D	28	(1)	2
ıiladin NELEVIĆ		D	15	(7)	
ıarko NENEZIĆ		D	26	(2)	2
ıiloš NIKEZIĆ		A	11	(9)	2
ıoban OBRADOVIĆ	BIH	M	12	(1)	
ıanja PEJOVIĆ		G	2		
ıarko RADULOVIĆ		D	26		2
ıbren SARIĆ		M	15	(6)	
ıikola ŠEVALJEVIĆ		G	31		
ıenad ŠOFRANAC		M	16		1
ıija ŠOLJAGA		A	2		
ıetar STANIŠIĆ	SRB	M	15		4
ıiomir VUKOVIĆ		A	5	(2)	1
ırsto ZVICER		A	27	(1)	5

FK RUDAR PLJEVLJA

Coach - Mirko Marić; (4/5/08) Branislav Milačić

Founded - 1914

MAJOR HONOURS: Montenegrin Cup - (1) 2007.

2007				
11/8	Bokelj	h	0-0	
18/8	Petrovac	a	0-1	
25/8	Mladost Podgorica	h	3-1	*Vraneš, Sekulić, Minić*
29/8	Lovćen	a	0-1	
1/9	Kom	h	3-0	*Karadžić 2, Minić*
15/9	Dečić	h	2-1	*Vuković, Nestorović*
22/9	Grbalj	a	1-1	*Sekulić*
29/9	Sutjeska	h	1-0	*Nestorović*
6/10	Budućnost Podgorica	a	1-1	*Basić*
21/10	Zeta	h	1-2	*Bojović*
27/10	Mogren	a	1-1	*Jovanović*
3/11	Bokelj	a	2-0	*Ivanisević, Bojović*
10/11	Petrovac	h	1-0	*Ivanisević*
24/11	Mladost Podgorica	a	0-0	
1/12	Lovćen	h	2-0	*Reljić, Jovanović*
8/12	Kom	a	1-2	*Karadžić (p)*
15/12	Dečić	a	1-0	*Nestorović*
2008				
23/2	Grbalj	h	0-0	
1/3	Sutjeska	a	2-1	*Ivanisević, Nedović*
9/3	Budućnost Podgorica	h	0-1	
16/3	Zeta	a	1-0	*Alex*
19/3	Mogren	h	0-0	
29/3	Dečić	h	2-0	*Milenković 2*
5/4	Bokelj	a	1-0	*Sekulić*
12/4	Sutjeska	h	2-0	*Ivanisević, Alex*
19/4	Zeta	a	2-2	*Alex 2*
26/4	Budućnost Podgorica	h	0-0	
30/4	Mogren	a	0-2	
3/5	Mladost Podgorica	h	1-2	*Sekulić*
10/5	Grbalj	h	1-3	*Alex*
14/5	Kom	a	0-0	
17/5	Petrovac	h	5-2	*Alex, Sekulić, Milenković 2, Ivanisević*
24/5	Lovćen	a	1-2	*Vraneš*

Name	**Nat**	**Pos**	**Aps**	**(s)**	**Gls**
ALEX de Sousa	BRA	A	13	(2)	6
Fadil BAŠIĆ		D	28		1
Mijuško BOJOVIĆ		D	31		2
Borko BRAŠANAC		G	1	(1)	
Radosav BULIĆ		M	12	(6)	
Marko ČELEBIĆ		A	4		
Dejan DAMJANOVIĆ		D	16	(7)	
Marko ĐURETIĆ		M		(2)	
Branimir IVANISEVIĆ		M	27		5
Ivica JOVANOVIĆ	SRB	A	5	(2)	2
Ivica JOVIĆ		D		(5)	
Miodrag KARADŽIĆ		M	7	(3)	3
Slobodan KRIVOKAPIĆ		D	10	(2)	
Zijad LUJINOVIĆ		A	2	(3)	
Ramiz LUKOVAC		A	2	(1)	
Milan MIJATOVIĆ		G	16		
Vladimir MILENKOVIĆ	SRB	A	9	(5)	4
Aleksandar MINIĆ		A	18	(2)	2
Aleksandar NEDOVIĆ		M	13	(2)	1
Dušan NESTOROVIĆ	SRB	D	17	(4)	3
Nikola PETROVIĆ	SRB	M	1	(7)	
Miloš RADANOVIĆ		G	16		
Demir RAMOVIĆ		M		(2)	
Stevan RELJIĆ		M	14	(1)	1
Nikola SEKULIĆ		M	27	(1)	5
Nikola TOMIĆ	SRB	M	25	(2)	
Miloš VRANEŠ		M	19	(3)	2
Zoran VUKOVIĆ		D	30		1

FK SUTJESKA

Coach - Pero Giljen; (15/4/08) Brajan Nenezić

Founded – 1927

2007				
10/8	Budućnost Podgorica	h	1-1	*Kasalića*
18/8	Zeta	a	0-1	
25/8	Mogren	h	0-0	
29/8	Bokelj	a	1-0	*Đikanović*
1/9	Petrovac	h	0-1	
15/9	Mladost Podgorica	a	0-0	
22/9	Lovćen	h	1-1	*Nerić*
29/9	Rudar	a	0-1	
6/10	Dečić	h	2-0	*Kasalića, Radović*
31/10	Grbalj	a	1-1	*Radović*
27/10	Kom	h	1-0	*Đikanović*
4/11	Budućnost Podgorica	a	0-2	
10/11	Zeta	h	0-3	*(w/o)*
24/11	Mogren	a	0-1	
1/12	Bokelj	h	0-0	
8/12	Petrovac	a	0-2	
15/12	Mladost Podgorica	h	2-1	*Adrović A., Perošević*
2008				
23/2	Lovćen	a	1-4	*Adrović A.*
1/3	Rudar	h	1-2	*Adrović A.*
8/3	Dečić	a	0-1	
15/3	Grbalj	h	0-0	
19/3	Kom	a	1-2	*Peričić*
29/3	Budućnost Podgorica	a	0-4	
5/4	Mogren	h	1-2	*Marković*
12/4	Rudar	a	0-2	
19/4	Grbalj	h	1-1	*Kaluđerović*
26/4	Kom	a	1-1	*Haverić*
30/4	Petrovac	h	1-1	*Adrović A.*
3/5	Lovćen	a	1-0	*Adrović A.*
10/5	Dečić	h	1-1	*Peričić*
14/5	Bokelj	a	1-4	*Peričić*
17/5	Mladost Podgorica	a	0-1	
24/5	Zeta	h	0-3	

Name	Nat	Pos	Aps	(s)	Gls
Admir ADROVIĆ		M	28	(4)	5
Zijad ADROVIĆ		M	15		
Boris BOŽOVIĆ		A	4	(11)	
Nenad BUBANJA		D	11		
Boris BULAJIĆ		M	28	(4)	
Darko BULATOVIĆ		D	31		
Tomislav ĆIRAKOVIĆ		M	4	(1)	
Ivan ČOLAKOVIĆ		A	17	(8)	
Ivan ĆUZOVIĆ		A	12		
Đorđije ĐIKANOVIĆ		D	17		2
Aleksandar DUBLJEVIĆ		D	30	(1)	
Mirko DURUTOVIĆ		D	16	(3)	
Vladan GILJEN		G	27		
Damir HAVERIĆ		M	2	(5)	1
Ivan JANJUŠEVIĆ		G	3		
Vasilije JOVOVIĆ		M		(1)	
Bojan KALEZIĆ		M	4		
Jovan KALUĐEROVIĆ		A	2	(9)	1
Marko KASALICA		A	11		2
Boris LAKIĆEVIĆ		G	1		
Miladin MARKOVIĆ		M	7	(5)	1
Milenko NERIĆ		A	2	(3)	1
Mirko NIKOLIĆ		M		(3)	
Ervin PERIČIĆ		A	11	(2)	3
Petar PEROŠEVIĆ		M	18	(3)	1
Ilija RADOVIĆ		D	17		2
Mihailo RADULOVIĆ		G	1	(1)	
Miroslav TODOROVIĆ		A	15		
Ivan VUJAČIĆ		M	11	(6)	
Danijel VUKOVIĆ	BIH	M	7	(8)	

FK ZETA

Coach - Slobodan Halilović; (30/8/07) Mladen Vukičević

Founded – 1927

MAJOR HONOURS: Montenegrin League - (1) 2007.

2007				
11/8	Grbalj	a	2-1	*Ivanović B., Colaković*
18/8	Sutjeska	h	1-0	*Stjepanović*
25/8	Budućnost Podgorica	a	1-2	*Tumbasević*
29/8	Kom	a	1-2	*Knežević*
2/9	Mogren	h	1-0	*Boljević*
15/9	Bokelj	a	1-0	*Ivanović B.*
22/9	Petrovac	h	4-1	*Cadu, Marinković, Knežević, Ivanović B.*
29/9	Mladost Podgorica	a	1-1	*Marković*
6/10	Lovćen	h	1-0	*Marković*
21/10	Rudar	a	2-1	*Sávio 2*
27/10	Dečić	h	2-1	*Ivanović B., Sávio*
3/11	Grbalj	h	1-0	*Cadu*
10/11	Sutjeska	a	3-0	*(w/o)*
25/11	Budućnost Podgorica	h	0-0	
1/12	Kom	h	2-0	*Kaluđerović M., Peličić*
8/12	Mogren	a	2-2	*Marinković, Boljević (p*
15/12	Bokelj	h	0-1	
2008				
23/2	Petrovac	a	1-1	*Lucas*
1/3	Mladost Podgorica	h	1-0	*Đalac*
8/3	Lovćen	a	1-1	*Đalac*
16/3	Rudar	h	0-1	
19/3	Dečić	a	1-0	*Cadu*
29/3	Mladost Podgorica	h	2-1	*Đalac 2*
5/4	Budućnost Podgorica	h	0-0	
12/4	Mogren	a	0-2	
19/4	Rudar	h	2-2	*Peličić Z., Cadu*
26/4	Grbalj	a	0-0	
30/4	Kom	h	4-1	*Kaluđerović M., Knežević 3*
3/5	Petrovac	a	3-2	*Cadu, Đalac, Ivanović*
10/5	Lovćen	h	1-1	*Đalac (p)*
14/5	Dečić	a	4-1	*Ćulafić, Knežević 2, Sáv*
17/5	Bokelj	h	8-3	*Cadu 3, Đalac 2, Knežević 2, Ivanović B.*
24/5	Sutjeska	a	3-0	*og (Dževerdanović), Ćulafić, Đalac*

Name	Nat	Pos	Aps	(s)	Gls
Marcelo ALBUQUERQUE Baiano	BRA	D	11	(7)	
Vladimir BOLJEVIĆ		M	12	(8)	2
Carlos Mendes CADU	BRA	M	25		8
Marko ĆETKOVIĆ		M	3		
Marko ČOLAKOVIĆ		M	22	(4)	1
Danilo ĆULAFIĆ		M	10	(5)	2
Miloš ĐALAC		A	13		9
DANILO dos Santos	BRA	M	1	(2)	
Vuk ĐURIĆ		M	11	(4)	
Nenad ĐUROVIĆ		M	8		
Blažo IGUMANOVIĆ		D	20	(5)	
Saša IVANOVIĆ		G	29		
Bojan IVANOVIĆ		M	28	(2)	6
Aleksandar JOVIĆ	SRB	G	3	(1)	
Aleksandar KALUĐEROVIĆ		D	22	(2)	
Miroslav KALUĐEROVIĆ		D	31		2
Ivan KNEŽEVIĆ		A	14	(8)	9
Žarko KORAĆ		A	3	(1)	
Miloš KRKOTIĆ		M	1	(8)	
LUCAS Precheski	BRA	A	5	(9)	1
Mirko MARINKOVIĆ	SRB	A	9	(2)	2
Darko MARKOVIĆ		M	17		2
Ivan NOVOVIĆ		M	3	(14)	
Vladan PELIČIĆ		D	2	(2)	
Zarija PELIČIĆ		M	7	(9)	2

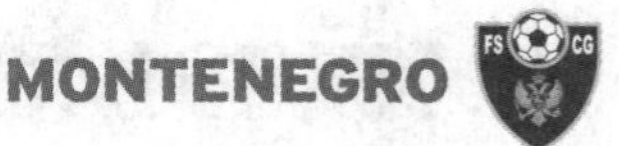

ilan RADULOVIĆ		D	3		
VIO Oliveira do Valle	BRA	M	24	(1)	4
aven STJEPANOVIĆ		A	4		1
nko TUMBASEVIĆ		M	2		1
ilan VUČKOVIĆ		D	9	(2)	

PROMOTED CLUBS

FK JEZERO
Coach – Zoran Madzevski
Founded - 1948

FK JEDINSTVO BIJELO POLJE
Coach – Sava Kovačević
Founded - 1922

ECOND LEVEL FINAL TABLE 2007/08

	Pld	W	D	L	F	A	Pts
FK Jezero	33	19	7	7	41	20	64
FK Čelik Nikšić	33	18	6	9	48	27	60
FK Jedinstvo Bijelo Polje	33	17	8	8	47	22	59
FK Berane	33	15	10	8	40	21	55
FK Ibar	33	15	5	13	41	36	49
FK Zabjelo	33	12	12	9	40	45	48
FK Bratstvo	33	12	4	17	44	48	40
FK Crvena Stijena	33	10	10	13	23	30	39
FK Arsenal Tivat	33	9	11	13	28	30	38
FK Otrant	33	9	9	15	39	52	36
FK Gusinje	33	7	10	16	23	45	30
FK Tekstilac	33	6	6	21	20	58	24

FK Crvena Stijena, FK Ibar & FK Gusinje - 1 pt deducted.

PROMOTION/RELEGATION PLAY-OFFS

(28/5/08 & 1/6/08)
Sutjeska 1, Čelik 0
Čelik 0, Sutjeska 0
(Sutjeska 1-0)

Bokelj 0, Jedinstvo 0
nstvo 3, Bokelj 0 *(w/o; original game abandoned at 1-0 after 80 mins)*
(Jedinstvo 3-0)

OMESTIC CUP 2007/08

KUPA CRNE GORE

ROUND

'07)
ar 0, Budućnost Podgorica 2

'07)
3, Bratstvo 0
lo 0, Lovćen 0 *(2-4 on pens)*
ja 97 0, Mogren 3
ar 0, Mladost Podgorica 1
vac 3, Gusinje 0
Zeta 3, Tekstilac 1
Grbalj 4, Čelik 0
Bokelj 1, Berane 1 *(3-5 on pens)*
Prvjenac 0, Kom 3
Arsenal Tivat 0, Jedinstvo 0 *(4-1 on pens)*
Ribnica 1, Bar 1 *(5-6 on pens)*
Ibar 1, Crvena Stijena 0
Otrant 1, Jezero 1 *(5-3 on pens)*
Byes - Sutjeska & Rudar Pljevlja

SECOND ROUND

(24/10/07 & 7/11/07)
Grbalj v Bar 7-0; 2-0 *(9-0)*
Dečić v Rudar Pljevlja 0-1, 0-2 *(0-3)*
Budućnost Podgorica v Kom 3-0, 3-0 *(6-0)*
Zeta v Mladost Podgorica 1-0, 0-0 *(1-0)*
Otrant v Arsenal Tivat 0-2, 2-0 *(2-3 on pens)*
Berane v Ibar 1-0, 3-2 *(4-2)*
Petrovac v Lovćen 2-0, 1-3 *(Petrovac on away goal)*

(24/10/07 & 28/11/07)
Mogren v Sutjeska 1-1, 1-0 *(2-1)*

QUARTER-FINALS

(5/12/07 & 12/12/07)
Zeta 0, Budućnost Podgorica 0
Budućnost Podgorica 2 *(Vukčević N. 61, Lakić 70)*, Zeta 1 *(Cadu 77)*
(Budućnost Podgorica 2-1)

Rudar Pljevlja 0, Grbalj 0
Grbalj 0, Rudar Pljevlja 2 *(Minić 28, Vraneš 58)*
(Rudar Pljevlja 2-0)

Berane 1 *(Bajović 52)*, Arsenal Tivat 1 *(Fatić 82)*
Arsenal Tivat 1 *(Kašćelan 52)*, Berane 1 *(Lalević 65)*
(2-2; Berane 4-3 on pens)

Mogren 0, Petrovac 0
Petrovac 0, Mogren 1 *(Drakulović 49)*
(Mogren 1-0)

SEMI-FINALS

(2/4/08 & 16/4/08)
Berane 0, Budućnost Podgorica 0
Budućnost Podgorica 4 *(López 10, Milić B. 19, Bećiraj 33 , Vukčević P. 37p)*, Berane 0
(Budućnost Podgorica 4-0)

Rudar Pljevlja 0, Mogren 0
Mogren 1 *(Jovanović 80)*, Rudar Pljevlja 0
(Mogren 1-0)

FINAL

(7/5/08)
Gradski stadium, Podgorica
FK MOGREN 1 *(Zec R. 84)*
FK BUDUĆNOST PODGORICA 1 *(Vukčević P. 53)*
(aet; 6-5 on pens)
Referee - *Kaluđerović*
MOGREN: *Janjušević, Begović, Pejović, Radulović, Papović (Bulatović 74), Jovanović, Čakar (Nerić 55), Božović, Zec M. (Zec R. 81), Vujović, Gluščević.*
BUDUĆNOST PODGORICA - *Vujadinović, Perišić (Sekulić 90+3), Rajović, Čarapić, Vuković N., Raičević, López, Vidović (Vuković I. 71), Delić (Đurišić 46), Vukčević P., Bećiraj.*

Brilliant Oranje peak too soon

Backed by thousands upon thousands of travelling fans, the Netherlands lit up the early stages of UEFA EURO 2008™. Marco van Basten's team were the star attraction of the group stage, destroying the two finalists of the 2006 FIFA World Cup, Italy and France, with a combination of clinical counterattacking and fabulous finishing. They even managed to make light work of Romania with a reserve XI. But then, in the quarter-final against Russia, it all went wrong.

Such was the superiority of the Russians in Basel that it was an achievement in itself for the Oranje to take them to extra time. But Andrei Arshavin and co finished them off with the kind of ruthlessness that had been the Netherlands' own trademark during their first three games in Berne. In the aftermath of defeat all manner of theories circulated about why the Dutch challenge had petered out so suddenly. Many of these focused on psychological factors such as the devastating news that defender Khalid Boulahrouz's prematurely born baby had died, or that complacency had sunk in, with training less intense, after the ease with which the team had swept aside the Italians and the French and won their group. Then there was the change of venue, an increase in temperature, and reports of loud noise outside the team hotel throughout the previous night. Perhaps the real reason was that Van Basten, the apprentice, was simply outwitted by Guus Hiddink, the sorcerer, and that the Dutch were beaten at their own game by a team still pumped full of adrenalin following their brilliant win against Sweden, whereas most of the Dutch players had had eight days off.

Wesley Sneijder embraces Netherlands coach Marco van Basten after a vintage display against Italy

So the Netherlands did not win UEFA EURO 2008™, or even come close, but they certainly provided plenty of entertainment, scoring ten goals in four games – the best average at the tournament. Many of them were straight from the top drawer, such as Wesley Sneijder's counterattacking classic against Italy and Arjen Robben's violent shot from an 'impossible' angle against France.

Special Sneijder

Sneijder, who also scored a beauty against Les Bleus and was voted Man of the Match in the first two games, had an especially fine tournament, but many other Dutchmen rose magnificently to the challenge, such as Edwin van der Sar, who bowed out of international football as the Netherlands' most-capped player with a series of outstanding displays in goal; Ruud van Nistelrooy, who re-affirmed his reputation as a world-class centre-forward; Rafael van der Vaart, who finally did justice to his elaborate talent on the big stage; and the unsung duo of Nigel de Jong and Orlando Engelaar, feisty as well as economical in their holding midfield roles. Giovanni van Bronckhorst, André Ooijer, Dirk Kuyt and Robin van Persie all enjoyed moments of great satisfaction, too.

Conjuring up this modern-day version of Total Football – a strategy that, unusually for the Netherlands, eschewed the use of conventional wingers - was Van Basten. Seeking to become the first man to win the UEFA European Championship as player and coach, he did enough in Switzerland to further his iconic reputation. He had already announced that he would be ending his four-year spell as Bondscoach and returning to his former club AFC Ajax. Also decided well in advance of UEFA EURO

008™ was the identity of his replacement – 56-year-old ert van Marwijk. With such a vibrant young squad at his sposal, the ex-Feyenoord boss, and former UEFA Cup inner, must be licking his lips. A 2010 FIFA World Cup ualifying group including Iceland, FYR Macedonia, orway and Scotland should, on the face of it, pose little ıreat to the Netherlands' participation in South Africa.

EFA EURO 2008™ was an eventful and exciting end to hat had been a fairly drab domestic season in the etherlands. There was precious little success in Europe or the Eredivisie elite, with only one club maintaining n interest after Christmas – and that in the 'wrong' ompetition as PSV Eindhoven dropped from the UEFA Champions League into the UEFA Cup. They were eaten by ACF Fiorentina in the quarter-finals of that vent, but they did win the Eredivise for a record-equalling fourth season in a row.

Pragmatic PSV

t was arguably the least glamorous of the four titles. Attacking play was largely sacrificed in favour of ollecting points, and that was only possible thanks to he consistent brilliance of Brazilian goalkeeper Heurelho Gomes. Oddly for a title-winning team, PSV used three coaches – with a fourth booked in for 2008/09. On the last day of October, Ronald Koeman quit PSV for Valencia CF. He was replaced, temporarily, by his assistant Jan Wouters, under whom the club endured a bleak spell, and then, from the turn of the year, by Sef Vergoossen, a good friend of PSV general director Jan Reker but who had never coached a top club. Under Vergoossen, PSV efficiently picked up the points, but with the exception of new signing Balázs Dzsudzsák, an ebullient Hungarian left-winger, it was with functional rather than fantasy football. Nevertheless, one of Vergoossen's first matches brought a 2-0 win away to Ajax – in a match postponed from its original date due to a police strike - and that proved decisive, with Eindhoven's finest taking the title by three points from the Amsterdammers. Vergoossen, his job done, would make way for Hamburger SV's Huub Stevens at the end of the campaign.

Ajax had a thoroughly forgettable season. One European calamity followed another as, for the second successive year, they unexpectedly lost their UEFA Champions League qualifier – to SK Slavia Praha – and then fell in the first round of the UEFA Cup – beaten by NK Dinamo Zagreb. With the club eliminated from Europe before October for the first time in 18 years, few tears were shed by the club's fans when coach Henk ten

Heurelho Gomes – the main man in PSV Eindhoven's Eredivisie title triumph

Cate fled to become Avram Grant's assistant at Chelsea FC. He was replaced by youth academy chief Adrie Koster, who, although he kept Ajax in the hunt for the league, was only ever there to keep the bench warm for Van Basten.

Twente topple Ajax

Klaas Jan Huntelaar was Ajax's best player, scoring 33 goals to top the Eredivisie charts by a street. But he was unable to maintain that form in the end-of-season play-offs, where Ajax's misery continued as they lost out on a UEFA Champions League place to the underdogs of FC Twente. Superbly coached by Fred Rutten (who would leave for FC Schalke 04 and be replaced by ex-England manager Steve McClaren), Twente crowned a magnificent season by overcoming Ajax 2-1 on aggregate in the play-off final, both goals coming from Swiss international striker Blaise Nkufo, who also struck 22 times in the regular league campaign.

While Feyenoord, despite the return of Van Marwijk from BV Borussia Dortmund and a raft of new high-profile signings, again struggled in the league, finishing sixth, they did mark their Centenary by winning the Dutch Cup. With PSV disqualified for fielding an ineligible player and Ajax ousted in the fourth round, the Rotterdammers had a relatively easy run to the final – staged, as usual, in their own De Kuip stadium, where they overcame Roda JC 2-0 to regain the trophy after a 13-year wait.

While Louis van Gaal's AZ Alkmaar, the nearly men of 2006/07, suffered a catastrophic fall from grace, 2007/08 proved a memorable season for NAC Breda, who, in addition to knocking Ajax out of the Dutch Cup, won 12 of their 17 league games after Christmas to finish third in the Eredivisie – their highest ever placing. NEC Nijmegen, coached by ex-Feyenoord midfielder Mario Been, caused an even bigger surprise, recovering from a shaky start to post a sensational sequence of results in the spring that extended into the play-offs, where they won all six matches, including a 6-0 thrashing of NAC, to qualify for the UEFA Cup. There was jubilation also for promoted FC Volendam and ADO Den Haag, the latter earning their place via the play-offs at the expense of VVV-Venlo, who followed SC Excelsior into the Eerste Divisie.

Koninklijke Nederlandse Voetbalbond (KNVB)

Woudenbergseweg 56-58
Postbus 515
NL-3700 AM Zeist
tel - +31 3434 99211
fax - +31 3434 99189
website - www.knvb. nl
Email – concern@knvb.nl
Year of Formation – 1889
General Secretary - Harry Been
Press Officer – Kees Jansma

INTERNATIONAL HONOURS
UEFA European Championship - (1) 1988.

INTERNATIONAL TOURNAMENT APPEARANCES
FIFA World Cup - (8) 1934, 1938, 1974 (runners-up), 1978 (runners-up), 1990 (2nd round), 1994 (qtr-finals), 1998 (4th), 2006 (2nd round).
UEFA European Championship - (8) 1976 (3rd), 1980, 1988 (Winners), 1992 (semi-finals), 1996 (qtr-finals), 2000 (semi-finals), 2004 (semi-finals), 2008 (qtr-finals).

TOP FIVE ALL-TIME CAPS
Edwin van der Sar (128); Frank de Boer (112); Phillip Cocu (101); Clarence Seedorf (87); Marc Overmars (86)

TOP FIVE ALL-TIME GOALS
Patrick Kluivert (40); Dennis Bergkamp (37), Faas Wilkes (35); Abe Lenstra, Johan Cruijff & Ruud van Nistelrooy (33)

NATIONAL TEAM RESULTS 2007/08

22/8/07	Switzerland	A	Geneva	1-2	*Kuyt (52)*
8/9/07	Bulgaria (ECQ)	H	Amsterdam	2-0	*Sneijder (22), Van Nistelrooy (58)*
12/9/07	Albania (ECQ)	A	Tirana	1-0	*Van Nistelrooy (90+1)*
13/10/07	Romania (ECQ)	A	Constanta	0-1	
17/10/07	Slovenia (ECQ)	H	Eindhoven	2-0	*Sneijder (14), Huntelaar (86)*
17/11/07	Luxembourg (ECQ)	H	Rotterdam	1-0	*Koevermans (43)*
21/11/07	Belarus (ECQ)	A	Minsk	1-2	*Van der Vaart (89)*
6/2/08	Croatia	A	Split	3-0	*Heitinga (9), Huntelaar (36), Vennegoor of Hesselink (89)*
26/3/08	Austria	A	Vienna	4-3	*Huntelaar (37, 86), Heitinga (67), Vennegoor of Hesselink (82)*
24/5/08	Ukraine	H	Rotterdam	3-0	*Kuyt (23), Huntelaar (38), Babel (64)*
29/5/08	Denmark	H	Eindhoven	1-1	*Van Nistelrooy (29)*
1/6/08	Wales	H	Rotterdam	2-0	*Robben (35), Sneijder (54)*
9/6/08	Italy (ECF)	N	Berne (SUI)	3-0	*Van Nistelrooy (26), Sneijder (31), Van Bronckhorst (79)*
13/6/08	France (ECF)	N	Berne (SUI)	4-1	*Kuyt (9), Van Persie (59), Robben (72), Sneijder (90+2)*
17/6/08	Romania (ECF)	N	Berne (SUI)	2-0	*Huntelaar (54), Van Persie (87)*
21/6/08	Russia (ECF)	N	Basel (SUI)	1-3	*Van Nistelrooy (86)*

ATIONAL TEAM APPEARANCES 2007/08

ch – Marco VAN BASTEN 31/10/64			Sui	BUL	ALB	ROU	SVN	LUX	BLR	Cro	Aut	Ukr	Den	Wal	ITA	FRA	ROU	RUS	Caps	Goals
rten KELENBURG	22/9/82	Ajax	G			G	G		G			G					G		12	-
JALIENS	15/9/78	AZ	D46			s68	D												10	-
HEITINGA	15/11/83	Ajax	D	D		D68	D			D	D	D62	D	D46	s77		D	s54	39	5
ed BOUMA	15/6/78	Aston Villa (ENG)	D	D	D63	D	D	D	D		s46	D73				s78	D		35	2
EMANUELSON	16/6/86	Ajax	D		s63		D	s77		s75									11	-
y DE ZEEUW	26/5/83	AZ	M	M81	M	M	M	D	M69	M	M46	M73	M	M46			M		16	-
ley SNEIJDER	9/6/84	Real Madrid (ESP)	M46	M73	M		M	M	M46	M	A90		A82	M	M	M		M	48	11
anni BRONCKHORST	5/2/75	Feyenoord	M	M	M	M		M	M66	M	M	D62	D	D46	D	D		D	81	5
el DER VAART	11/2/83	Hamburg (GER)	A46		s46	A	A29	M	A	M84	M	M79	M65	M67	M	M78		M	58	12
d NISTELROOY	1/7/76	Real Madrid (ESP)	A46	A	A	A		A46					A65	A	A70	A		A	64	33
in VAN PERSIE	6/8/83	Arsenal (ENG)	A	A	A46		A59				A69				s70	s55	M	s46	28	9
id BOULAHROUZ	28/12/81	Sevilla (ESP)	s46	s66								s62			D77	D	D58	D54	26	-
ence SEEDORF	1/4/76	Milan (ITA)	s46	s73		M	M	M77			s46								87	11
KUYT	22/7/80	Liverpool (ENG)	s46		s75			s46	s46			M	s65	s46	M81	M55	s61	M46	42	8
BABEL	19/12/86	Liverpool (ENG)	s46	A	A75	s78	s62	s84	A	A55	s69	s62	s77						25	5
in VAN DER SAR	29/10/70	Man.United (ENG)		G	G			G		G			G	G	G	G		G	128	-
io MELCHIOT	4/11/76	Wigan (ENG)		D66	D			D	D	D71				s46			s58		22	-
MATHIJSEN	5/4/80	Hamburg (GER)		D	D	D		D	D	D	D46	s73	D	D80	D	D		D	35	2
el DE JONG	30/11/84	Hamburg (GER)		s81					s69	s71		s73	s46	s46	M	M		M	26	-
ré OOIJER	11/7/74	Blackburn (ENG)			D	D84	s59		D		D	D	D46	D	D	D		D	40	2
n ROBBEN	23/1/84	Real Madrid (ESP)				A78	s29 /62						A77	M		s46	M61		35	10
ny KOEVERMANS	1/11/78	PSV				s84		A84	A										4	1
s Jan HUNTELAAR	12/8/83	Ajax					A			A75	A	A					A83		13	8
ndo ENGELAAR	24/8/79	Twente							s66			M	M65	M46	M	M46	M	M62	10	-
DE CLER	8/11/78	Feyenoord								D	D80	s62	s65	s46			D		16	-
him AFELLAY	2/4/86	PSV								s55		M62	s82	s67	s81		M	s62	8	-
VENNEGOOR OF SSELINK	7/11/78	Celtic (SCO)								s84	s80		s65	s80			s83		17	3
k TIMMER	3/12/71	Feyenoord									G								5	-
ny LANDZAAT	6/5/76	Feyenoord									s90	s79							38	1

DOMESTIC LEAGUE 2007/08

EREDIVISIE FINAL TABLE

	Pld	Home W	D	L	F	A	Away W	D	L	F	A	Total W	D	L	F	A	Pts
1 PSV Eindhoven	34	12	4	1	41	12	9	5	3	24	12	21	9	4	65	24	72
2 AFC Ajax	34	12	3	2	57	20	8	6	3	37	25	20	9	5	94	45	69
3 NAC Breda	34	8	3	6	24	22	11	3	3	24	18	19	6	9	48	40	63
4 FC Twente	34	11	4	2	29	14	6	7	4	23	18	17	11	6	52	32	62
5 SC Heerenveen	34	9	3	5	56	26	9	3	5	32	22	18	6	10	88	48	60
6 Feyenoord	34	12	3	2	40	12	6	3	8	24	29	18	6	10	64	41	60
7 FC Groningen	34	9	2	6	23	19	6	4	7	30	35	15	6	13	53	54	51
8 NEC Nijmegen	34	8	5	4	30	17	6	2	9	19	33	14	7	13	49	50	49
9 Roda JC	34	8	5	4	31	24	4	6	7	24	31	12	11	11	55	55	47
10 FC Utrecht	34	8	3	6	35	27	5	4	8	24	28	13	7	14	59	55	46
11 AZ Alkmaar	34	8	4	5	25	14	3	6	8	23	39	11	10	13	48	53	43
12 BV Vitesse	34	7	5	5	24	19	5	2	10	22	36	12	7	15	46	55	43
13 Sparta Rotterdam	34	7	5	5	33	26	2	2	13	19	50	9	7	18	52	76	34
14 Heracles Almelo	34	6	5	6	19	20	2	3	12	15	44	8	8	18	34	64	32
15 Willem II	34	7	2	8	33	24	1	5	11	7	25	8	7	19	40	49	31
16 De Graafschap	34	3	6	8	17	30	4	3	10	16	34	7	9	18	33	64	30
17 VVV-Venlo	34	4	4	9	24	36	3	4	10	20	40	7	8	19	44	76	29
18 SC Excelsior	34	5	4	8	21	32	2	2	13	11	43	7	6	21	32	75	27

TOP GOALSCORERS

33 Klaas Jan HUNTELAAR (Ajax)
22 Blaise NKUFO (Twente)
17 Luis SUÁREZ (Ajax)
16 Robin NELISSE (Utrecht)
15 Markus BERG (Groningen)
Michael BRADLEY (Heerenveen)
Kenneth PEREZ (PSV/Ajax)
14 Danny KOEVERMANS (PSV)
Miralem SULEJMANI (Heerenvee
13 Roy MAKAAY (Feyenoord)
Gerald SIBON (Heerenveen)

PLAY-OFFS

UEFA CHAMPIONS LEAGUE QUALIFICATION

(1/5/08 & 5/5/08)
SC Heerenveen 1 *(Sibon 71)*, AFC Ajax 2 *(Suárez 61, Heitinga 76)*
AFC Ajax 3 *(Perez 45+4p, 55, Rommedahl 48)*, SC Heerenveen 1 *(Pranjić 63)*
(Ajax 5-2)

(29/4/08 & 3/5/08)
FC Twente 3 *(Wielaert 32, Denneboom 80, Huysegems 90+1)*, NAC Breda 0
NAC Breda 1 *(Fehér 54)*, FC Twente 5 *(Huysegems 52, 77, Nkufo 56, Hersi 66, Braafheid 90p)*
(Twente 8-1)

(10/5/08 & 18/5/08)
FC Twente 2 *(Nkufo 66p, 76)*, AFC Ajax 1 *(Suárez 44)*
AFC Ajax 0, FC Twente 0
(Twente 2-1)

UEFA CUP QUALIFICATION

(1/5/08 & 4/5/08)
FC Utrecht 2 *(Schaken 24, Nelisse 27)*, FC Groningen 2 *(Lovre 52, Levchenko 90+1)*
FC Groningen 3 *(Berg 54, 75, Švejdík 73)*, FC Utrecht 1 *(Vandenbergh 68)*
(Groningen 5-3)

(1/5/08 & 4/5/08)
Roda JC 0, NEC Nijmegen 1 *(Holman 6)*
NEC Nijmegen 2 *(Van Beukering 40, Kivuvu 84)*, Roda JC 0
(NEC 3-0)

(8/5/08 & 11/5/08)
NEC Nijmegen 1 *(Lens 71)*, FC Groningen 0
FC Groningen 1 *(Berg 60)*, NEC Nijmegen 3 *(Holman 5, Vadócz 45+1, Davids 72)*
(NEC 4-1)

(8/5/08 & 12/5/08)
SC Heerenveen 2 *(Paulo Henrique 75, 83)*, NAC Breda 0
NAC Breda 2 *(Idabdelhay 28, Veenstra 84)*, SC Heerenveen 2 *(Sibon 42, 74)*
(Heerenveen 4-2)

(15/5/08 & 18/5/08)
NEC Nijmegen 6 *(Olsson 14, 2? Holman 50, Lens 63, 67, El Akchaoui 71p)*, NAC Breda 0
NAC Breda 0, NEC Nijmegen 1 *(Lens 61)*
(NEC 7-0)

CLUB-BY-CLUB

AFC AJAX

Coach - Henk ten Cate; (9/10/07) Adrie Koster

Founded - 1900

MAJOR HONOURS: European Champion Clubs' Cup/ UEFA Champions League - (4) 1971, 1972, 1973, 1995; UEFA Cup Winners' Cup - (1) 1987; UEFA Cup - (1) 1992; UEFA Super Cup - (3) 1972, 1973, 1995; World Club Cup - (2) 1972, 1995; Dutch League - (29) 1918, 1919, 1931, 1932, 1934, 1937, 1939, 1947, 1957, 1960, 1966, 1967, 1968, 1970, 1972, 1973, 1977, 1979, 1980, 1982, 1983, 1985, 1990, 1994, 1995, 1996, 1998, 2002, 2004; Dutch Cup - (17) 1917, 1943, 1961, 1967, 1970, 1971, 1972, 1979, 1983, 1986, 1987, 1993, 1998, 1999, 2002, 2006, 2007.

2007

19/8	De Graafschap	a	8-1	*Huntelaar 4 (1p), Suárez, Maduro 2, Bakircioglü*
26/8	Heerenveen	h	4-1	*Suárez 2, Vermaelen, Schilder*
2/9	Groningen	h	2-2	*Suárez, Huntelaar*
15/9	Heracles	a	1-0	*Huntelaar*
23/9	AZ	a	3-2	*Huntelaar, Suárez 2*
30/9	VVV	h	6-1	*Luque 2, Maduro, Rommedahl, Delorge, Huntelaar*
7/10	Sparta	a	2-2	*Huntelaar, De Jong*
20/10	NEC	h	0-0	
28/10	Utrecht	a	1-0	*Huntelaar*
4/11	Roda	h	4-2	*Huntelaar, Suárez, Luque, Rommedahl*

1/11	Feyenoord	a	2-2	*Rommedahl, De Jong*
25/11	Vitesse	h	4-1	*Suárez, Gabri, Luque (p), Huntelaar*
2/12	NAC	h	1-3	*Huntelaar*
/12	Willem II	a	3-2	*Bakircioglü, Suárez, Vertonghen*
23/12	Excelsior	a	1-2	*Maduro*
27/12	Twente	h	2-2	*Huntelaar, og (Breinburg)*
30/12	VVV	a	2-2	*Suárez, Huntelaar*
2008				
13/1	AZ	h	6-1	*Vertonghen, Perez (p), Huntelaar 2, Bakircioglü, Leonardo*
20/1	NEC	a	1-1	*Huntelaar*
23/1	Utrecht	h	2-0	*Huntelaar, Heitinga*
27/1	Vitesse	a	2-2	*Emanuelson, Suárez*
30/1	PSV	h	0-2	
3/2	Feyenoord	h	3-0	*Heitinga, Huntelaar 2*
10/2	Roda	a	1-2	*Huntelaar*
15/2	Sparta	h	6-2	*Heitinga 2, Huntelaar, Lindgren, Perez 2*
24/2	NAC	a	3-2	*Huntelaar, Emanuelson, Heitinga*
2/3	Excelsior	h	4-0	*Huntelaar 2, Emanuelson, Leonardo*
16/3	Willem II	h	4-1	*Huntelaar, Suárez 3*
19/3	PSV	a	0-0	
23/3	Twente	a	1-2	*og (Douglas)*
29/3	Heerenveen	a	4-2	*Suárez, Perez (p), Huntelaar 2*
6/4	De Graafschap	h	4-1	*Huntelaar 3, Perez*
16/4	Groningen	a	2-1	*Lindgren, Suárez*
20/4	Heracles	h	5-1	*Suárez, Perez 2, Huntelaar, Heitinga*

No	Name	Nat	Pos	Aps	(s)	Gls
7	Kennedy BAKIRCIOGLÜ	SWE	A	12	(6)	3
31	Jürgen COLIN		D	6	(6)	
13	Edgar DAVIDS		M	14		
15	Laurent DELORGE	BEL	M	2	(2)	1
24	Mitchell DONALD		A		(3)	
5	Urby EMANUELSON		D	28	(3)	3
18	GABRIel García de la Torre	ESP	M	26		1
30	Dennis GENTENAAR		G	3	(2)	
2	John HEITINGA		D	33		6
37	Jan-Arie VAN DER HEIJDEN		M		(2)	
9	Klaas Jan HUNTELAAR		A	34		33
38	Siem DE JONG		M	13	(9)	2
28	Michael KROHN-DEHLI	DEN	M		(1)	
6	Samuel Osei KUFFOUR	GHA	D		(2)	
11	LEONARDO Vítor Santiago	BRA	A	1	(7)	2
23	Rasmus LINDGREN	SWE	M	9	(2)	2
10	Albert LUQUE Martos	ESP	M	9	(7)	4
6	Hedwiges MADURO		M	12	(3)	4
20	George OGĂRARU	ROU	D	15	(1)	
29	Kenneth PEREZ	DEN	M	13	(3)	7
19	Dennis ROMMEDAHL	DEN	A	14	(16)	3
26	Jeffrey SARPONG		M		(1)	
22	Robbert SCHILDER		M	3	(5)	1
3	Bruno SILVA	URU	D	12		
3	Jaap STAM		D	6		
1	Maarten STEKELENBURG		G	31		
16	Luis SUÁREZ	URU	A	29	(4)	17
8	Ismael URZAIZ	ESP	A		(3)	
4	Thomas VERMAELEN	BEL	D	17	(2)	1
17	Jan VERTONGHEN	BEL	D	28	(3)	2
25	Gregory VAN DER WIEL		D	4	(2)	

AZ ALKMAAR

Coach - Louis van Gaal

Founded - 1967

MAJOR HONOURS: Dutch League - (1) 1981; Dutch Cup - (3) 1978, 1981, 1982.

2007				
18/8	VVV	h	4-0	*Agustien, Ari 2 (1p), Međunjanin*
25/8	Vitesse	a	0-1	
31/8	Excelsior	h	3-0	*Agustien, Steinsson, De Zeeuw*
16/9	Sparta	a	2-2	*Jenner, El Hamdaoui*
23/9	Ajax	h	2-3	*De Zeeuw, Dembélé*
30/9	Heracles	a	1-2	*Dembélé*
7/10	Groningen	h	2-2	*Ari, De Zeeuw*
21/10	Heerenveen	h	0-1	
28/10	NAC	a	3-2	*Opdam, Ari, Jenner*
3/11	NEC	h	4-0	*Cziommer, Jaliens, Ari, De Zeeuw*
11/11	PSV	a	1-1	*Ari*
24/11	Willem II	h	2-0	*Ari, Dembélé*
2/12	Twente	a	1-2	*Pellè*
9/12	Utrecht	h	2-1	*Pocognoli, De Zeeuw*
23/12	Roda	h	1-1	*Pellè*
30/12	Heracles	h	1-0	*Steinsson*
2008				
13/1	Ajax	a	1-6	*Ari*
16/1	De Graafschap	a	2-1	*Mendes da Silva, Dembélé*
19/1	Heerenveen	a	0-4	
22/1	NAC	h	1-2	*Pocognoli*
25/1	Willem II	a	0-3	
30/1	Feyenoord	a	2-2	*Pellè, El Hamdaoui*
2/2	PSV	h	0-2	
10/2	NEC	a	2-5	*Mendes da Silva, El Hamdaoui*
17/2	Groningen	a	1-2	*Jaliens*
23/2	Twente	h	0-0	
1/3	Roda	a	1-1	*Cziommer*
12/3	Feyenoord	h	0-1	
16/3	Utrecht	a	2-2	*De Zeeuw, El Hamdaoui*
22/3	De Graafschap	h	0-0	
30/3	Vitesse	h	2-1	*Moreno, Jenner*
6/4	VVV	a	3-2	*Ari, El Hamdaoui 2*
13/4	Excelsior	a	1-1	*Donk*
20/4	Sparta	h	1-0	*El Hamdaoui*

No	Name	Nat	Pos	Aps	(s)	Gls
17	Kemy AGUSTIEN		M	19	(6)	2
9	Ariclenes da Silva Ferreira "ARI"	BRA	A	22	(7)	9
10	Simon CZIOMMER	GER	M	15	(5)	2
18	Moussa DEMBÉLÉ	BEL	A	33		4
14	Ryan DONK		D	19	(5)	1
24	Mounir EL HAMDAOUI		A	11	(12)	7
27	Aron Einar GUNNARSSON	ISL	M		(1)	
2	Kew JALIENS		D	30		2
7	Julian JENNER		A	5	(16)	3
12	Milano KOENDERS		D	8	(5)	
11	Maarten MARTENS	BEL	M	7		
22	Haris MEĐUNJANIN		M	5	(7)	1
6	David MENDES DA SILVA		D	26	(2)	2
30	Héctor MORENO	MEX	D	8		1
15	Kiki MUSAMPA		M	1	(4)	
4	Barry OPDAM		D	32		1
29	Graziano PELLÈ	ITA	A	16	(11)	3
5	Sebastien POCOGNOLI	BEL	D	20	(8)	2
15	Simon Busk POULSEN	DEN	M	3	(5)	
16	Sergio ROMERO	ARG	G	12		
23	Grétar Rafn STEINSSON	ISL	D	15	(1)	2
25	Ruud VORMER		M	14	(2)	
21	Boy WATERMAN		G	22		
20	Demy DE ZEEUW		M	31		6

SC EXCELSIOR

Coach - Ton Lokhoff
Founded - 1902

2007

18/8	Twente	h	0-2	
25/8	VVV	a	1-3	*Den Ouden*
31/8	AZ	a	0-3	
15/9	Heerenveen	h	2-5	*Den Ouden 2*
23/9	Groningen	h	1-3	*Den Ouden*
29/9	Roda	a	3-3	*Den Ouden (p), Voskamp 2*
6/10	NEC	h	2-0	*Steur, Voskamp*
20/10	Feyenoord	a	0-1	
27/10	Heracles	h	1-1	*Korf*
3/11	Sparta	h	4-3	*Den Ouden 2 (1p), Voskamp, Luyckx*
10/11	De Graafschap	a	1-1	*Van Guldener*
24/11	PSV	h	1-4	*Pardo*
1/12	Willem II	a	0-6	
8/12	NAC	h	0-3	
16/12	Vitesse	a	0-3	
23/12	Ajax	h	2-1	*Pique, Den Ouden*
27/12	Utrecht	a	1-4	*Van Guldener*
30/12	Roda	h	1-2	*Voskamp*

2008

12/1	Groningen	a	2-3	*Den Ouden, Guijo-Velasco*
18/1	Feyenoord	h	2-1	*Van Guldener, Den Ouden*
22/1	Heracles	a	0-2	
26/1	PSV	a	1-2	*Den Ouden*
2/2	De Graafschap	h	1-1	*Luyckx*
10/2	Sparta	a	1-0	*Van Steensel*
16/2	NEC	a	1-0	*Den Ouden*
23/2	Willem II	h	0-0	
2/3	Ajax	a	0-4	
8/3	Vitesse	h	1-2	*Voskamp (p)*
15/3	NAC	a	0-2	
22/3	Utrecht	h	0-2	
29/3	VVV	h	2-1	*Van Steensel, Braber*
5/4	Twente	a	0-1	
13/4	AZ	h	1-1	*Luijckx*
20/4	Heerenveen	a	0-5	

Name	Nat	Pos	Aps	(s)	Gls
Adnan ALISIC		M	10	(1)	
Jeffrey ALTHEER		D	18	(2)	
Sigourney BANDJAR		D	30		
Daan BOVENBERG		D	1	(1)	
Robert BRABER		A	20	(3)	1
Aykut DEMIR	TUR	D	14	(1)	
René VAN DIEREN		M	8		
Ronald GRAAFLAND		G	30		
Michel VAN GULDENER		A	8	(16)	3
Daniel GUIJO-VELASCO	BEL	M	7	(3)	1
Ryan KOOLWIJK		D	7		
Tjeerd KORF		A	13	(16)	1
Kees LUYCKX		M	32		3
Jörg VAN NIEUWENHUIJZEN		G	4	(1)	
Jos VAN NIEUWSTADT		D	32		
Geert DEN OUDEN		A	31	(3)	12
Sebastián PARDO	CHI	M	17	(1)	1
Ard VAN PEPPEN		D	6	(2)	
Mitchell PIQUE		D	26	(2)	1
Eldridge ROJER		A	4		
Jarda SIMR	CZE	M		(3)	
Koen STAM		D	7		
Leen VAN STEENSEL		D	20	(4)	2
Sebastiaan STEUR		A	10	(9)	1
Johan VOSKAMP		A	11	(17)	6
Sieme ZIJM		D	8	(5)	

FEYENOORD

Coach - Bert van Marwijk
Founded - 1908

MAJOR HONOURS: European Champion Clubs' Cup/UEFA Champions League - (1) 1970; UEFA Cup - (2) 1974, 2002; World Club Cup - (1) 1970; Dutch League - (14) 1924, 1928, 1936, 1938, 1940, 1961, 1962, 1965, 1969, 1971, 1974, 1984, 1993, 1999; Dutch Cup - (11) 1930, 1935, 1965, 1969, 1980, 1984, 1991, 1992, 1994, 1995, 2008.

2007

19/8	Utrecht	a	3-0	*Bruins, Hofs, Makaay*
26/8	NAC	h	5-0	*Makaay (p), Vlaar, Nuri 2, De Guzman*
1/9	Willem II	h	2-0	*Bruins, Makaay*
16/9	Roda	a	3-1	*Makaay (p), De Guzman 2*
23/9	PSV	a	0-4	
29/9	Heerenveen	h	2-0	*Makaay, Hofs*
7/10	Vitesse	a	1-0	*Hofs*
20/10	Excelsior	h	1-0	*Van Bronckhorst*
27/10	Twente	a	0-2	
4/11	De Graafschap	h	2-0	*De Guzman, Makaay (p)*
11/11	Ajax	h	2-2	*Van Bronckhorst, De Guzman*
25/11	Groningen	a	2-3	*Makaay, Nuri*
2/12	Heracles	h	6-0	*Makaay 2, Hofland, Slory, Van Bronckhorst, Wijnaldum*
9/12	VVV	a	0-0	
23/12	NEC	a	2-0	*De Guzman 2*
26/12	Sparta	h	2-0	*Makaay 2*
30/12	Heerenveen	a	1-1	*Slory*

2008

12/1	PSV	h	0-1	
18/1	Excelsior	a	1-2	*Buijs*
24/1	Twente	h	3-1	*Bruins, Makaay, De Cler*
27/1	Groningen	h	1-1	*og (Fledderus)*
30/1	AZ	h	2-2	*Van Bronckhorst, Bahia*
3/2	Ajax	a	0-3	
9/2	De Graafschap	a	3-1	*Makaay, Hofs 2*
17/2	Vitesse	h	1-0	*De Guzman*
23/2	Heracles	a	3-3	*Bahia, Landzaat, Hofs*
2/3	NEC	h	1-3	*Van Bronckhorst*
12/3	AZ	a	1-0	*De Guzman*
15/3	VVV	h	4-1	*Bruins, Van Bronckhorst, Mols, Nuri*
23/3	Sparta	a	2-3	*Lucius, Van Bronckhorst*
30/3	NAC	a	1-3	*Fer*
6/4	Utrecht	h	3-1	*Bruins, Landzaat, Nuri*
13/4	Willem II	a	1-3	*Bahia*
20/4	Roda	h	3-0	*Bruins, Nuri, Mols*

No	Name	Nat	Pos	Aps	(s)	Gls
4	André BAHIA	BRA	D	27	(2)	3
27	Diego BISESWAR		A		(1)	
8	Giovanni VAN BRONCKHORST		M	32		7
22	Luigi BRUINS		M	26	(1)	6
7	Danny BUIJS		M	6	(17)	1
5	Tim DE CLER		D	32		1
32	Sherif EKRAMY	EGY	G	1		
28	Leroy FER		D	7	(6)	1
18	Serginho GREENE		D	13	(9)	
33	Jonathan DE GUZMAN		M	33		9
3	Kevin HOFLAND		D	27		1
10	Nicky HOFS		M	14	(9)	6
19	Denny LANDZAAT		M	11		2
16	LEE Chun-soo	KOR	A	4	(8)	
6	Theo LUCIUS		M	28	(1)	1
9	Roy MAKAAY		A	28		13
14	Michael MOLS		A	7	(15)	2
37	Erwin MULDER		G	1		

	Name	Nat	Pos	Aps	(s)	Gls
17	NURI Sahin	TUR	M	28	(1)	6
11	Andwélé SLORY		A	10	(7)	2
31	Henk TIMMER		G	32		
20	Ron VLAAR		D	4		1
25	Georginio WIJNALDUM		M	3	(7)	1

DE GRAAFSCHAP

Coach - Jan De Jonge

Founded - 1954

Date	Opponent		Score	Scorers
2007				
19/8	Ajax	h	1-8	*De Groot*
26/8	Groningen	a	2-0	*De Groot, Powel*
2/9	Utrecht	a	2-2	*De Groot 2*
15/9	VVV	h	3-2	*De Groot, Fung A Wing, Keller*
22/9	Vitesse	a	2-0	*Fränkel, Powel*
30/9	Twente	h	0-0	
6/10	NAC	a	0-1	
19/10	Sparta	h	4-0	*Schöne, Powel, Hese, De Groot*
27/10	Roda	a	0-1	
4/11	Feyenoord	a	0-2	
10/11	Excelsior	h	1-1	*Fung-A-Wing*
24/11	Heerenveen	a	3-2	*De Groot, Schöne, Powel*
1/12	PSV	h	0-1	
8/12	Heracles	a	0-2	
15/12	NEC	h	1-1	*Schöne*
21/12	Willem II	a	2-1	*Powel, De Groot*
30/12	Twente	a	0-2	
2008				
13/1	Vitesse	h	0-3	
16/1	AZ	h	1-2	*Schöne*
20/1	Sparta	a	1-6	*Vidarsson*
23/1	Roda	h	2-1	*Schöne (p), Powel*
26/1	Heerenveen	h	0-3	
2/2	Excelsior	a	1-1	*Tarvajärvi*
9/2	Feyenoord	h	1-3	*Schöne*
17/2	NAC	h	0-1	
24/2	PSV	a	1-4	*Schöne*
1/3	Willem II	h	1-2	*Tarvajärvi*
8/3	NEC	a	1-3	*Tarvajärvi*
15/3	Heracles	h	0-0	
22/3	AZ	a	0-0	
28/3	Groningen	h	1-1	*Johnson*
6/4	Ajax	a	1-4	*Tarvajärvi*
13/4	Utrecht	h	1-1	*Johnson*
20/4	VVV	a	0-3	

Name	Nat	Pos	Aps	(s)	Gls
Diego BISESWAR		A	5	(6)	
René BOT		D	4	(6)	
Jordy BUIJS		D	6		
Jim VAN FESSEM		G	34		
Purrel FRÄNKEL		D	21	(3)	1
Cerezo FUNG-A-WING		D	32		2
Donny De GROOT		A	21	(7)	8
Leon HESE		D	25	(4)	1
Michael JANSEN		D	4	(1)	
Will JOHNSON	CAN	A	8	(18)	2
Girts KARLSONS	LVA	A	2	(3)	
Stephan KELLER	SUI	D	31		1
Rogier MEIJER		M	25	(1)	
Joep VAN DEN OUWELAND		M	2	(10)	
Ard VAN PEPPEN		D	1	(1)	
Berry POWEL		A	22		6
Reinier ROBBEMOND		M	9	(14)	
Lasse SCHÖNE	DEN	M	33	(1)	7
Resit SCHUURMAN		D	34		
Rik SEBENS		M		(1)	
Kevin SISSING		A		(2)	
Niklas TARVAJÄRVI	FIN	A	12	(16)	4
Arnar Thór VIDARSSON	ISL	M	32		1
Joost VOLMER		D	11	(1)	

FC GRONINGEN

Coach - Ron Jans

Founded - 1926

Date	Opponent		Score	Scorers
2007				
18/8	NAC	a	3-0	*Lovre, Nevland, Fledderus*
26/8	De Graafschap	h	0-2	
2/9	Ajax	a	2-2	*Berg 2*
14/9	Utrecht	h	0-2	
23/9	Excelsior	a	3-1	*Nevland, Berg, Levchenko (p)*
29/9	Sparta	h	1-0	*Lovre*
7/10	AZ	a	2-2	*Berg, Švejdík*
21/10	Twente	h	1-0	*Meerdink*
28/10	NEC	a	1-5	*Van de Laak (p)*
4/11	Vitesse	h	0-0	
11/11	Roda	a	1-5	*Nevland*
25/11	Feyenoord	h	3-2	*Berg 2, Nevland*
1/12	VVV	h	1-0	*Berg*
9/12	Heerenveen	a	2-4	*Nevland 2*
16/12	Willem II	h	1-0	*Silva*
22/12	Heracles	a	2-1	*Nijland, Van der Laak*
26/12	PSV	h	2-1	*Lindgren, Berg*
29/12	Sparta	a	3-1	*Nijland 2, Lovre*
2008				
12/1	Excelsior	h	3-2	*Lovre 2, Berg*
20/1	Twente	a	1-3	*Lovre*
23/1	NEC	h	5-1	*Fledderus 2 (1p), Berg, Lovre, Hiariej*
27/1	Feyenoord	a	1-1	*Berg*
3/2	Roda	h	1-1	*Powel*
9/2	Vitesse	a	1-2	*Meerdink*
17/2	AZ	h	2-1	*Berg 2 (1p)*
24/2	VVV	a	5-2	*Lovre, Berg 2, Powel, Nijland*
2/3	Heracles	h	1-2	*Powel*
8/3	Willem II	a	2-1	*og (Bælum), De Roover*
14/3	Heerenveen	h	0-1	
22/3	PSV	a	0-3	
28/3	De Graafschap	a	1-1	*Powel*
6/4	NAC	h	1-2	*Lovre*
16/4	Ajax	h	1-2	*Cahais*
20/4	Utrecht	a	0-1	

Name	Nat	Pos	Aps	(s)	Gls
Marcus BERG	SWE	A	21	(4)	15
Matias CAHAIS	ARG	D	4	(6)	1
Mark-Jan FLEDDERUS		M	18	(11)	3
Tom HIARIEJ		D	18	(3)	1
Danny HOLLA		M	5	(1)	
Marnix KOLDER		A	4	(2)	
Rogier KROHNE		A		(1)	
Arnold KRUISWIJK		D	30		
Koen VAN DE LAAK		A	13	(5)	2
Martijn VAN DER LAAN		D		(1)	
Yevgeniy LEVCHENKO	RUS	M	11	(4)	1
Rasmus LINDGREN	SWE	M	20		1
Brian VAN LOO		G	34		
Goran LOVRE	SRB	M	33		9
Tim MATAVŽ	SVN	A	1	(14)	
Paul MATTHIJS		M	3		
Martijn MEERDINK		M	18	(4)	2
Shkodran METAJ		M	15	(6)	

Name	Nat	Pos	Aps	(s)	Gls
Erik NEVLAND	NOR	A	13	(2)	6
Stefan NIJLAND		A	12	(11)	4
Serdar ÖZTURK	TUR	A		(1)	
Berry POWEL		A	12		4
Sepp DE ROOVER	BEL	D	8	(3)	1
Sander ROZEMA		M		(1)	
Gibril SANKOH	SLE	D	31		
Bruno SILVA	URU	D	17		1
Fredrik STENMAN	SWE	D	28		
Ondrej ŠVEJDÍK	CZE	D	5	(4)	1
Jeroen VELDMATE		D		(4)	

SC HEERENVEEN

Coach - Gertjan Verbeek

Founded - 1920

Date	Opponent		Score	Scorers
2007				
17/8	Willem II	h	0-0	
26/8	Ajax	a	1-4	*Sulejmani*
1/9	Sparta	h	3-3	*Sibon, Pranjić, og (Roberts)*
15/9	Excelsior	a	5-2	*Sulejmani, Sibon 2, Zuiverloon, Bradley*
23/9	Utrecht	h	2-3	*Bradley, Sulejmani*
29/9	Feyenoord	a	0-2	
7/10	Heracles	h	9-0	*Afonso Alves 7, Sibon 2*
21/10	AZ	a	1-0	*Afonso Alves*
27/10	VVV	a	4-0	*Bak-Nielsen, Afonso Alves 2, Matusiak*
3/11	PSV	h	2-1	*Bak-Nielsen, og (Kromkamp)*
11/11	Vitesse	a	1-0	*Bradley*
24/11	De Graafschap	h	2-3	*Dingsdag, Pranjić (p)*
2/12	NEC	a	1-0	*Poulsen*
9/12	Groningen	h	4-2	*og (Lovre), Bradley 3*
15/12	NAC	a	5-1	*Sibon 2, Sulejmani, Paulo Henrique 2*
22/12	Twente	h	1-2	*Afonso Alves*
27/12	Roda	a	0-1	
30/12	Feyenoord	h	1-1	*Sibon*
2008				
13/1	Utrecht	a	2-2	*Pranjić, Bradley*
19/1	AZ	h	4-0	*Pranjić (p), Poulsen, Sulejmani, Bradley*
23/1	VVV	h	5-1	*Bradley, Sulejmani, Poulsen, Sibon, Pranjić*
26/1	De Graafschap	a	3-0	*Bradley 2, Sulejmani*
2/2	Vitesse	h	7-0	*Sulejmani, Pranjić, Bradley, Zuiverloon, Beerens 2, Prager*
9/2	PSV	a	1-1	*Bradley*
16/2	Heracles	a	2-2	*Beerens, Sulejmani*
24/2	NEC	h	2-3	*Beerens, Roorda*
1/3	Twente	a	0-1	
8/3	NAC	h	3-0	*og (Mtiliga), Sulejmani 2*
14/3	Groningen	a	1-0	*Sulejmani*
22/3	Roda	h	4-3	*Bradley 2, Paulo Henrique, Beerens*
29/3	Ajax	h	2-4	*Sulejmani, Pranjić*
5/4	Willem II	a	3-2	*Pranjić (p), Beerens, Sibon*
13/4	Sparta	a	2-4	*Pranjić, Sibon*
20/4	Excelsior	h	5-0	*Sibon 2, Sulejmani, og (Bandjar), Roorda*

No	Name	Nat	Pos	Aps	(s)	Gls
10	AFONSO ALVES	BRA	A	7	(1)	11
3	Kristian BAK NIELSEN	DEN	D	15		2
8	Roy BEERENS		M	16	(12)	6
6	Michael BRADLEY	USA	M	33		15
4	Michel BREUER		D	31		
5	Michael DINGSDAG		D	32		1
22	Henrico DROST		D	12	(3)	
24	Rob VAN DIJK		G	14	(1)	
17	Gonzalo GARCÍA-GARCÍA	URU	M	1	(4)	
17	Christian GRINDHEIM	NOR	M	7	(2)	
36	Timmi JOHANSEN	DEN	D	4	(3)	
16	Calvin JONG-A-PIN		D	13	(6)	
18	Niek LOOHUIS		M	1		
9	Radosław MATUSIAK	POL	A	2	(8)	1
12	PAULO HENRIQUE Tarneiro	BRA	A		(13)	3
7	Jakob POULSEN	DEN	M	19	(11)	3
14	Thomas PRAGER	AUT	M	5	(10)	1
23	Danijel PRANJIĆ	CRO	M	33		9
33	Geert Arend ROORDA		M	17	(5)	2
35	Gerald SIBON		A	33	(1)	13
31	Arnór SMÁRASON	ISL	A		(2)	
21	Miralem SULEJMANI	SRB	A	26	(8)	14
15	Michal ŠVEC	CZE	M	3	(2)	
25	Brian VANDENBUSSCHE	BEL	G	20		
2	Gianni ZUIVERLOON		D	30		2

HERACLES ALMELO

Coach - Ruud Brood; (24/12/07) Hendrie Kruzen; (2/1/08) Gert Heerkes

Founded - 1903

Date	Opponent		Score	Scorers
2007				
19/8	PSV	h	0-2	
24/8	Roda	a	1-2	*Klavan*
1/9	NAC	a	1-4	*Everton*
15/9	Ajax	h	0-1	
22/9	Sparta	a	1-1	*Everton*
30/9	AZ	h	2-1	*Everton, Maas (p)*
7/10	Heerenveen	a	0-9	
20/10	Vitesse	h	2-2	*Everton, Maas (p)*
27/10	Excelsior	a	1-1	*Gluščević*
4/11	Twente	h	0-3	
9/11	NEC	a	0-3	
24/11	VVV	h	0-0	
2/12	Feyenoord	a	0-6	
8/12	De Graafschap	h	2-0	*Gluščević, Quansah*
16/12	Utrecht	a	1-3	*Bosnar*
22/12	Groningen	h	1-2	*Quansah*
27/12	Willem II	h	1-0	*Quansah*
30/12	AZ	a	0-1	
2008				
13/1	Sparta	h	2-0	*Quansah, Van den Bergh*
19/1	Vitesse	a	0-2	
22/1	Excelsior	h	2-0	*Lakić, Everton*
271	VVV	a	5-0	*Looms, García-García, Lakić 2, Gluščević*
2/2	NEC	h	0-2	
8/2	Twente	a	1-2	*García-García*
16/2	Heerenveen	h	2-2	*García-García, Schilder*
23/2	Feyenoord	h	3-3	*Everton, Lakić 2 (1p)*
2/3	Groningen	a	2-1	*Everton, Lakić*
7/3	Utrecht	h	2-1	*Everton, Lakić*
15/3	De Graafschap	a	0-0	
23/3	Willem II	a	1-2	*Schilder*
29/3	Roda	h	0-0	
6/4	PSV	a	0-2	
13/4	NAC	h	0-1	
20/4	Ajax	a	1-5	*Klavan*

No	Name	Nat	Pos	Aps	(s)	Gls
10	Ricky VAN DEN BERGH		M	16	(8)	1
30	Nino BEUKERT		A		(3)	
2	Emmanuel BOAKYE	GHA	D	23	(2)	

No	Name	Nat	Pos	Aps	(s)	Gls
2	Eddy BOSNAR	AUS	D	13	(1)	1
5	Tim BREUKERS		M	3	(3)	
8	Karim BRIDJI		A	11	(3)	
5	Martin CHRISTENSEN	DEN	M	6	(5)	
1	Björn DAELEMANS	BEL	D	4	(5)	
1	EVERTON Ramos da Silva	BRA	A	24	(9)	8
9	Gonzalo GARCÍA-GARCÍA	URU	M	16		3
	Igor GLUŠČEVIĆ	SRB	A	11	(15)	3
3	Nick DE GRAAF		A		(1)	
5	Ragnar KLAVAN	EST	D	23	(6)	2
	Srđan LAKIĆ	CRO	A	19	(9)	7
	Mark LOOMS		D	29	(1)	1
	Rob MAAS		M	26		2
20	Kai MICHALKE	GER	M	15	(6)	
	Rahim OUÉDRAOGO	BFA	M	19		
	Martin PIECKENHAGEN	GER	G	34		
7	Kwame QUANSAH	GHA	A	27	(3)	4
23	Robbert SCHILDER		M	8	(3)	2
4	Marnix SMIT		D	5	(5)	
7	Remon DE VRIES		M	12	(2)	
4	Jan WUYTENS	BEL	D	30		

NAC BREDA

Coach - Ernie Brandts

Founded - 1912

MAJOR HONOURS: Dutch League - (1) 1921; Dutch Cup - (1) 1973.

2007				
18/8	Groningen	h	0-3	
26/8	Feyenoord	a	0-5	
1/9	Heracles	h	4-1	*Kolkka, Fehér, Amoah 2*
16/9	NEC	a	1-0	*De Graaf*
21/9	VVV	a	3-1	*Lurling, Zwaanswijk, De Graaf (p)*
29/9	PSV	h	1-1	*Amoah*
6/10	De Graafschap	h	1-0	*Sikora*
21/10	Willem II	a	0-0	
28/10	AZ	h	2-3	*Lurling 2 (1p)*
4/11	Utrecht	a	1-0	*Amoah*
10/11	Twente	a	1-1	*Amoah*
23/11	Roda	h	0-0	
2/12	Ajax	a	3-1	*og (Vertonghen), Amoah, Ammi*
8/12	Excelsior	a	3-0	*Zwaanswijk, Amoah, Elshot*
15/12	Heerenveen	h	1-5	*Tamerus*
27/12	Vitesse	h	1-2	*De Graaf*
30/12	PSV	a	0-2	
2008				
12/1	VVV	h	0-0	
19/1	Willem II	h	1-0	*og (Bælum)*
22/1	AZ	a	2-1	*Idabdelhay 2*
26/1	Roda	a	2-0	*Sikora, Idabdelhay*
1/2	Twente	h	1-0	*Zwaanswijk (p)*
6/2	Sparta	a	1-0	*Idabdelhay*
9/2	Utrecht	h	1-0	*Penders*
17/2	De Graafschap	a	1-0	*Molhoek*
24/2	Ajax	h	2-3	*Amoah, Penders*
1/3	Sparta	h	3-0	*Fehér, Lurling 2*
8/3	Heerenveen	a	0-3	
15/3	Excelsior	h	2-0	*Idabdelhay, Kolkka*
21/3	Vitesse	a	3-3	*Idabdelhay, og (Van der Schaaf), Molhoek*
30/3	Feyenoord	h	3-1	*Elshot, Molhoek, Amoah*
6/4	Groningen	a	2-1	*Ammi, Amoah*
13/4	Heracles	a	1-0	*De Graaf*
20/4	NEC	h	1-3	*Amoah*

No	Name	Nat	Pos	Aps	(s)	Gls
22	Ahmed AMMI	MAR	D	15	(9)	2
14	Matthew AMOAH	GHA	A	20	(5)	11
2	Kurt ELSHOT		D	31		2
26	Csaba FEHÉR	HUN	M	27	(3)	2
27	Sander FISCHER		D		(1)	
5	Sander VAN GESSEL		M	3	(12)	
6	Tim GILISSEN		M	10	(11)	
24	Donny GORTER		M	1		
7	Edwin DE GRAAF		M	11	(1)	4
20	Fouad IDABDELHAY	MAR	A	5	(12)	6
25	Johan JANSEN		G	1		
11	Joonas KOLKKA	FIN	A	29	(3)	2
28	Tyrone LORAN		D	10	(4)	
10	Anthony LURLING		A	29		5
8	Rogier MOLHOEK		M	25	(1)	3
19	Patrick MTILIGA	DEN	D	30		
3	Rob PENDERS		D	27		2
12	Victor SIKORA		A	10	(11)	2
23	Ronnie STAM		D	26	(3)	
9	Gert Jan TAMERUS		A	1	(9)	1
16	Jelle TEN ROUWELAAR		G	32		
15	Rogier VEENSTRA		A		(5)	
1	Edwin ZOETEBIER		G	1		
4	Patrick ZWAANSWIJK		D	30		3

NEC NIJMEGEN

Coach - Mario Been

Founded - 1900

2007				
18/8	Roda	h	1-1	*Van Beukering*
25/8	PSV	a	0-5	
2/9	Vitesse	a	0-1	
16/9	NAC	h	0-1	
23/9	Twente	a	0-3	
30/9	Willem II	h	1-0	*Worm (p)*
6/10	Excelsior	a	0-2	
20/10	Ajax	a	0-0	
28/10	Groningen	h	5-1	*El-Akchaoui (p), Davids, Van Beukering 2, Olsson*
3/11	AZ	a	0-4	
9/11	Heracles	h	3-0	*Van Beukering, Lens, Nalbantoglu*
25/11	Utrecht	a	2-3	*Olsson, Davids*
2/12	Heerenveen	h	0-1	
9/12	Sparta	a	0-1	
15/12	De Graafschap	a	1-1	*El-Akchaoui*
23/12	Feyenoord	h	0-2	
26/12	VVV	h	2-2	*Janssen 2*
30/12	Willem II	a	0-3	
2008				
11/1	Twente	h	2-2	*El-Akchaoui (p), Van Beukering*
20/1	Ajax	h	1-1	*Lens*
23/1	Groningen	a	1-5	*Van Beukering*
27/1	Utrecht	h	2-0	*Van Beukering, Holman*
2/2	Heracles	a	2-0	*Lens, og (Ouédraogo)*
10/2	AZ	h	5-2	*Bobson, Holman, Van Beukering (p), Wisgerhof, Drost*
16/2	Excelsior	h	0-1	
24/2	Heerenveen	a	3-2	*Lens, Holman, El-Akchaoui*
2/3	Feyenoord	a	3-1	*Holman, Olsson, Lens*
8/3	De Graafschap	h	3-1	*Holman 2, Vadócz*
16/3	Sparta	h	4-2	*Bobson, Pothuizen 2, El-Akchaoui*
23/3	VVV	a	2-1	*Van Beukering, Sibum*

29/3	PSV	h	0-0	
4/4	Roda	a	2-0	*Van Beukering, Lens*
13/4	Vitesse	h	1-0	*Vadócz*
20/4	NAC	a	3-1	*Lens 2, Van Beukering*

No	Name	Nat	Pos	Aps	(s)	Gls
24	Naim AARAB	BEL	D	1	(5)	
1	Gábor BABOS	HUN	G	34		
9	Jhon VAN BEUKERING		A	23	(5)	11
11	Kevin BOBSON		A	14		2
22	Bart VAN BRAKEL		M	1	(3)	
8	Lorenzo DAVIDS		M	22	(7)	2
21	Jeroen DROST		D	2	(3)	1
5	Youssef EL-AKCHAOUI		D	34		5
20	Abdelkarim FACHTALI		A		(4)	
18	Daníel FERNÁNDEZ Artola	ESP	D	1	(3)	
10	Brett HOLMAN	AUS	M	26	(1)	6
16	Ádám HREPKA	HUN	A	1	(6)	
19	Tim JANSSEN		A	11	(4)	2
4	Dominique KIVUVU		M	17	(5)	
17	Jeremain LENS		A	29	(2)	8
14	Muslu NALBANTOGLU	TUR	D	29	(3)	1
26	Saidi NTIBAZONKIZA	BDI	A	3	(3)	
2	Jonas OLSSON	SWE	D	26	(1)	3
6	Patrick POTHUIZEN		D	9	(4)	2
21	Alexander PRENT		A	3	(10)	
16	Bas SIBUM		M	14		1
11	Ferne SNOYL		M	3	(1)	
23	Krisztián VADÓCZ	HUN	M	26	(1)	2
29	Bob VERWEIJ		D		(1)	
3	Peter WISGERHOF		D	32		1
7	Rutger WORM		A	13	(11)	1

PSV EINDHOVEN

Coach - Ronald Koeman; (31/10/07) Jan Wouters; (1/1/08) Sef Vergoossen

Founded - 1913

MAJOR HONOURS: European Champion Clubs' Cup/UEFA Champions League - (1) 1988; UEFA Cup - (1) 1978; Dutch League - (21) 1929, 1935, 1951, 1963, 1975, 1976, 1978, 1986, 1987, 1988, 1989, 1991, 1992, 1997, 2000, 2001, 2003, 2005, 2006, 2007, 2008; Dutch Cup - (8) 1950, 1974, 1976, 1988, 1989, 1990, 1996, 2005.

2007

19/8	Heracles	a	2-0	*Afellay, Zonneveld*
25/8	NEC	h	5-0	*Lazović 2, Addo, Fagner, Bakkal*
1/9	Twente	a	0-0	
15/9	Vitesse	h	1-0	*Koevermans*
23/9	Feyenoord	h	4-0	*Perez 2, Méndez, Koevermans*
29/9	NAC	a	1-1	*Perez*
6/10	Willem II	h	3-0	*Koevermans 2, Farfán*
20/10	VVV	h	3-1	*Bakkal, Koevermans 2*
28/10	Sparta	a	4-1	*Lazović, Zonneveld, Farfán, Perez*
3/11	Heerenveen	a	1-2	*Lazović*
11/11	AZ	h	1-1	*Farfán*
24/11	Excelsior	a	4-1	*Bakkal, Koevermans, Lazović, Perez (p)*
1/12	De Graafschap	a	1-0	*Farfán*
7/12	Roda	h	2-4	*Koevermans 2*
22/12	Utrecht	h	4-1	*Perez 2, Lazović, Koevermans*
26/12	Groningen	a	1-2	*Alcides*
30/12	NAC	h	2-0	*Koevermans, Perez*

2008

12/1	Feyenoord	a	1-0	*Bakkal*
20/1	VVV	a	1-1	*Dzsudzsák*
23/1	Sparta	h	3-1	*Lazović, Kromkamp, Čulina*
26/1	Excelsior	h	2-1	*Dzsudzsák, Koevermans*
30/1	Ajax	a	2-0	*Dzsudzsák, Bakkal*
2/2	AZ	a	2-0	*Lazović, Afellay*
9/2	Heerenveen	h	1-1	*Bakkal*
16/2	Willem II	a	1-0	*Simons (p)*
24/2	De Graafschap	h	4-1	*Lazović 2, Bakkal, Simons (p)*
2/3	Utrecht	a	1-3	*Simons (p)*
16/3	Roda	a	1-1	*Farfán*
19/3	Ajax	h	0-0	
22/3	Groningen	h	3-0	*Koevermans 2, Bakkal*
29/3	NEC	a	0-0	
6/4	Heracles	h	2-0	*Simons, Farfán*
13/4	Twente	h	1-1	*Farfán*
20/4	Vitesse	a	1-0	*Lazović*

No	Name	Nat	Pos	Aps	(s)	Gls
18	Eric ADDO	GHA	D	12		1
20	Ibrahim AFELLAY		M	23	(1)	2
16	Ismail AISSATI		M	5	(11)	
13	ALCIDES Araújo Alves	BRA	D	19	(2)	1
28	Otman BAKKAL		M	23	(8)	8
15	Jason ČULINA	AUS	M	9	(9)	1
4	Manuel DA COSTA Trindade	POR	D		(1)	
22	Balázs DZSUDZSÁK	HUN	A	17		3
23	FAGNER Conserva Lemos	BRA	D		(3)	1
17	Jefferson FARFÁN	PER	A	27	(2)	7
1	Heurelho da Silva "GOMES"	BRA	G	34		
10	Danny KOEVERMANS		A	14	(15)	14
10	Arouna KONÉ	CIV	A	1		
2	Jan KROMKAMP		D	26		1
9	Danko LAZOVIĆ	SRB	A	26	(5)	11
26	Tom VAN DER LEEGTE		M		(2)	
24	Dirk MARCELLIS		D	24	(2)	
8	Edison Vicente MÉNDEZ	ECU	M	10	(10)	1
11	Kenneth PEREZ	DEN	A	14		8
14	Slobodan RAJKOVIĆ	SRB	D	5	(8)	
19	Jonathan REIS	BRA	A		(3)	
3	Carlos Arnoldo SALCIDO	MEX	D	33		
6	Timmy SIMONS	BEL	M	33		4
7	Mika VÄYRYNEN	FIN	M		(1)	
29	Génaro ZEEFUIK		A		(2)	
5	Mike ZONNEVELD		D	19	(2)	2

RODA JC

Coach - Raymond Atteveld

Founded - 1962

MAJOR HONOURS: Dutch Cup - (2) 1997, 2000.

2007

18/8	NEC	a	1-1	*Lamah*
24/8	Heracles	h	2-1	*Lamah, Kah*
2/9	VVV	a	5-3	*Oper 2, Yulu Matondo 2, Van Tornhout*
16/9	Feyenoord	h	1-3	*Tioté*
22/9	Willem II	a	0-1	
29/9	Excelsior	h	3-3	*Janssen, Lamah, Saeijs*
7/10	Twente	a	1-0	*De Fauw*
21/10	Utrecht	h	1-1	*Bodor*
27/10	De Graafschap	h	1-0	*Meeuwis (p)*
4/11	Ajax	a	2-4	*Lamah, Hadouir*
11/11	Groningen	h	5-1	*Hadouir, Lamah, Oper 2, Cissé*
23/11	NAC	a	0-0	
1/12	Vitesse	h	3-2	*Lamah 2, Saeijs*
7/12	PSV	a	4-2	*De Fauw, Meeuwis, Oper, Hadouir*
14/12	Sparta	h	2-3	*og (Schenkel), Meeuwis (p)*

BV VITESSE

Coach - Aad de Mos

Founded - 1892

Date	Opponent		Score	Scorers
2007				
19/8	Sparta	a	2-1	*Van Der Schaaf, Swerts*
25/8	AZ	h	1-0	*Kolk*
2/9	NEC	h	1-0	*Gommans*
15/9	PSV	a	0-1	
22/9	De Graafschap	h	0-2	
30/9	Utrecht	a	4-2	*Swerts, Sprockel, Junker, Megrelishvili*
7/10	Feyenoord	h	0-1	
20/10	Heracles	a	2-2	*Due, Sprockel*
26/10	Willem II	h	1-0	*Kolk*
4/11	Groningen	a	0-0	
11/11	Heerenveen	h	0-1	
25/11	Ajax	a	1-4	*Junker*
1/12	Roda	a	2-3	*Sansoni, Gommans*
8/12	Twente	h	2-2	*Junker 2*
16/12	Excelsior	h	3-0	*Kolk 2, Gommans (p)*
23/12	VVV	a	0-2	
27/12	NAC	a	2-1	*Kolk, Gommans*
30/12	Utrecht	h	2-2	*Gommans, Junker*
2008				
13/1	De Graafschap	a	3-0	*Kolk 2, Takak*
19/1	Heracles	h	2-0	*Van der Schaaf, Kolk*
22/1	Willem II	a	0-4	
27/1	Ajax	h	2-2	*Junker, Gommans*
2/2	Heerenveen	a	0-7	
9/2	Groningen	h	2-1	*Gommans, Van der Schaaf*
17/2	Feyenoord	a	0-1	
23/2	Roda	h	1-1	*Janssen*
29/2	VVV	h	1-3	*Kolk*
8/3	Excelsior	a	2-1	*Pryor, Lorca*
15/3	Twente	a	3-4	*Lorca, Kolk, Claudemir*
21/3	NAC	h	3-3	*Claudemir, Kolk 2*
30/3	AZ	a	1-2	*Swerts*
5/4	Sparta	h	3-0	*Junker, Janssen, Claudemir*
13/4	NEC	a	0-1	
20/4	PSV	h	0-1	

No	Name	Nat	Pos	Aps	(s)	Gls
19	Fred BENSON	GHA	A	1		
24	Jaime BRUINIER		M		(1)	
23	Alexander BÜTTNER		A		(1)	
8	CLAUDEMIR Domingues de Souza	BRA	A	6	(3)	3
25	Kevin VAN DIERMEN		D	1	(5)	
8	Anders DUE	DEN	M	6	(2)	1
17	Giovanny ESPINOZA	ECU	D	17		
9	Harrie GOMMANS		A	16	(11)	7
14	Theo JANSSEN		M	16	(3)	2
10	Mads JUNKER	DEN	A	20	(8)	7
18	Onur KAYA	BEL	M	2	(9)	
21	Cees KEIZER		M	1	(1)	
7	Santi KOLK		A	30	(2)	12
11	Juan LORCA	CHI	A	13	(14)	2
5	Haim MEGRELISHVILI	ISR	D	20	(4)	1
30	Anduele PRYOR		A	8	(7)	1
22	Balázs RABÓCZKI	HUN	G		(2)	
3	Sébastien SANSONI	FRA	D	26	(1)	1
6	Remco VAN DER SCHAAF		M	29		3
4	Civard SPROCKEL		D	32		2
28	Gill SWERTS	BEL	D	32	(2)	3
16	Jasar TAKAK		M	17	(6)	1
33	Stephan VEENBOER		G	1		
1	Piet VELTHUIZEN		G	33		
2	Paul VERHAEGH		D	33		
29	Ricky VAN WOLFSWINKEL		A		(1)	
31	Abubakari YAKUBU	GHA	M	12	(5)	
68	YU Hai	CHN	A	2	(6)	

VVV-VENLO

Coach - André Wetzel

Founded - 1903

Date	Opponent		Score	Scorers
2007				
18/8	AZ	a	0-4	
25/8	Excelsior	h	3-1	*Blondelle, Amrabat, El Gaaouiri*
2/9	Roda	h	3-5	*Kantelberg, Linssen, Amrabat*
15/9	De Graafschap	a	2-3	*Leemans, Kantelberg*
21/9	NAC	h	1-3	*Linssen*
30/9	Ajax	a	1-6	*Soltani*
5/10	Utrecht	h	1-2	*Leemans*
20/10	PSV	a	1-3	*El Gaaouiri*
27/10	Heerenveen	h	0-4	
2/11	Willem II	a	2-1	*Auassar, Kahya*
10/11	Sparta	h	2-0	*Oost, Amrabat*
24/11	Heracles	a	0-0	
1/12	Groningen	a	0-1	
9/12	Feyenoord	h	0-0	
15/12	Twente	a	1-1	*Amrabat*
23/12	Vitesse	h	2-0	*Amrabat 2*
26/12	NEC	a	2-2	*Kantelberg, Calabro*
30/12	Ajax	h	2-2	*Ofrany, Calabro*
2008				
12/1	NAC	a	0-0	
20/1	PSV	h	1-1	*Ofrany*
23/1	Heerenveen	a	1-5	*Calabro*
27/1	Heracles	h	0-5	
3/2	Sparta	a	0-2	
10/2	Willem II	h	1-1	*Reekers*
17/2	Utrecht	a	4-1	*Calabro 2 (1p), Oost 2*
24/2	Groningen	h	2-5	*Leemans, Oost*
29/2	Vitesse	a	3-1	*Oost (p), Amrabat 2*
11/3	Twente	h	0-2	
15/3	Feyenoord	a	1-4	*Honda*
23/3	NEC	h	1-2	*Honda*
29/3	Excelsior	a	1-2	*Soltani*
6/4	AZ	h	2-3	*Oost, Amrabat (p)*
13/4	Roda	a	1-4	*Soltani*
20/4	De Graafschap	h	3-0	*og (Volmer), Amrabat, Ofrany*

No	Name	Nat	Pos	Aps	(s)	Gls
24	Nordin AMRABAT		A	31	(2)	10
3	Adil AUASSAR		M	16	(5)	1
1	Kevin BEGOIS	BEL	G	13		
26	Siebe BLONDELLE	BEL	D	9	(7)	1
14	Sandro CALABRO		A	4	(8)	5
22	Raymond VAN DRIEL		G	1		
21	Samir EL GAAOUIRI		A	7	(15)	2
5	Niels FLEUREN		D	33		
29	Keisuke HONDA	JPN	M	12	(2)	2
9	Paul JANS		A	7	(3)	
19	Peter JUNGSCHLÄGER		M	6	(1)	
20	Ekrem KAHYA		M	22	(2)	1
10	Leon KANTELBERG		M	8	(8)	3
6	Ken LEEMANS	BEL	M	14	(5)	3
8	Edwin LINSSEN		M	30		2
2	Mike MAMPUYA	BEL	D	32	(1)	
11	Rachid OFRANY		A	15	(11)	3
31	Jason OOST		A	24	(7)	6
15	Peter REEKERS		D	25		1
27	Ferry DE REGT		D	1	(1)	
7	Karim SOLTANI	FRA	A	15	(13)	3

12	Michael TIMISELA		D	1	(2)	
4	Sjors VERDELLEN		D	28		
16	Danny WINTJENS		G	20		

WILLEM II

Coach - Dennis van Wijk; (5/11/07) Andries Jonker

Founded - 1896

MAJOR HONOURS: Dutch League - (3) 1916, 1952, 1955; Dutch Cup - (2) 1944, 1963.

2007				
17/8	Heerenveen	a	0-0	
25/8	Sparta	h	2-2	*Hadouir, Boutahar*
1/9	Feyenoord	a	0-2	
16/9	Twente	h	1-3	*Messoudi (p)*
22/9	Roda	h	1-0	*Kargbo*
30/9	NEC	a	0-1	
6/10	PSV	a	0-3	
21/10	NAC	h	0-0	
26/10	Vitesse	a	0-1	
2/11	VVV	h	1-2	*Kargbo*
10/11	Utrecht	h	1-4	*Poepon*
24/11	AZ	a	0-2	
1/12	Excelsior	h	6-0	*Poepon 2, Demouge 2, Boutahar, Van der Struijk (p)*
8/12	Ajax	h	2-3	*Bobson, Swinkels*
16/12	Groningen	a	0-1	
21/12	De Graafschap	h	1-2	*Van der Struijk (p)*
27/12	Heracles	a	0-1	
30/12	NEC	h	3-0	*Poepon 3*
2008				
12/1	Roda	a	1-1	*Poepon*
19/1	NAC	a	0-1	
22/1	Vitesse	h	4-0	*Swinkels, Poepon, Boutahar, Douglas*
25/1	AZ	h	3-0	*Messoudi, Boutahar, Van der Struijk (p)*
3/2	Utrecht	a	0-2	
10/2	VVV	a	1-1	*Cristiano*
16/2	PSV	h	0-1	
23/2	Excelsior	a	0-0	
1/3	De Graafschap	a	2-1	*Poepon, Demouge*
8/3	Groningen	h	1-2	*Van der Struijk (p)*
16/3	Ajax	a	1-4	*Demouge*
23/3	Heracles	h	2-1	*Mourad, Demouge*
30/3	Sparta	a	2-2	*Messoudi, Demouge*
5/4	Heerenveen	h	2-3	*Boutahar, Poepon*
13/4	Feyenoord	h	3-1	*Demouge 2, Boutahar*
20/4	Twente	a	0-2	

No	Name	Nat	Pos	Aps	(s)	Gls
1	Maikel AERTS		G	19		
17	Mehmet AKGÜN	GER	A	5	(1)	
3	Thomas BÆLUM	DEN	D	29	(1)	
11	Kevin BOBSON		A	13	(2)	1
8	Said BOUTAHAR	MAR	M	30	(1)	6
10	CRISTIANO dos Santos Rodrigues	BRA	A	4	(9)	1
9	Frank DEMOUGE		A	17	(6)	8
33	Daan VAN DINTHER		D	1		
7	Darl DOUGLAS		A	7	(9)	1
10	Mounir EL HAMDAOUI		A	2		
8	Christophe GRÉGOIRE	BEL	M	14		
7	Anouar HADOUIR	MAR	A	1	(1)	1
30	Delano HILL		D	13	(8)	
12	Jens JANSE		D	32		
22	Ibrahim KARGBO	SLE	D	28		2
18	Danny MATHIJSSEN		M	18	(5)	
14	Mohamed MESSOUDI	BEL	M	22	(4)	3
28	George MOURAD	SWE	A	8	(7)	1
23	Steef NIEUWENDAAL		M	3	(8)	
19	Rydell POEPON		A	25	(7)	10
4	Frank VAN DER STRUIJK		D	33		4
15	Arjan SWINKELS		D	27	(4)	2
16	Kenneth VERMEER		G	15	(1)	
20	Niels VORTHOREN		M	3	(16)	
2	Nuelson WAU		D	3	(4)	
17	Jonathan WILMET	BEL	A		(2)	
6	Sergio ZIJLER		A	2	(3)	

PROMOTED CLUBS

FC VOLENDAM

Coach – Stanley Menzo

Founded - 1920

ADO DEN HAAG

Coach – Wiljan Vloet

Founded – 1971

MAJOR HONOURS: Dutch Cup - (1) 1975.

SECOND LEVEL FINAL TABLE 2007/0

		Pld	W	D	L	F	A	P
1	FC Volendam (*4,*6)	38	22	11	5	90	46	[illegible]
2	RKC Waalwijk (*2)	38	22	11	5	84	44	[illegible]
3	FC Den Bosch (*1)	38	21	7	10	61	37	[illegible]
4	FC Zwolle (*5)	38	18	13	7	70	42	[illegible]
5	MVV Maastricht	38	16	12	10	66	50	[illegible]
6	ADO Den Haag	38	16	10	12	58	50	[illegible]
7	Helmond Sport	38	17	7	14	53	52	[illegible]
8	TOP Oss	38	15	10	13	58	61	[illegible]
9	FC Emmen	38	14	11	13	61	74	[illegible]
10	Go Ahead Eagles (*3)	38	16	3	19	60	64	[illegible]
11	RBC Roosendaal	38	13	10	15	46	49	[illegible]
12	FC Dordrecht	38	12	11	15	59	52	[illegible]
13	FC Omniworld	38	11	14	13	56	55	[illegible]
14	Stormvogels Telstar	38	14	4	20	41	51	[illegible]
15	BV Veendam	38	11	14	13	57	67	[illegible]
16	Fortuna Sittard	38	10	10	18	48	69	[illegible]
17	SC Cambuur Leeuwarden	38	10	9	19	50	68	[illegible]
18	AGOVV Apeldoorn	38	12	5	21	66	98	[illegible]
19	FC Eindhoven	38	8	8	22	49	83	[illegible]
20	HFC Haarlem	38	5	14	19	39	60	[illegible]

N.B. (*) period champions

PROMOTION/RELEGATION PLAY-OFFS

FIRST ROUND

(22/4/08 & 26/4/08)

Go Ahead Eagles 1, ADO Den Haag 1
ADO Den Haag 3, Go Ahead Eagles 0
(ADO Den Haag 4-1)

(22/4/08 & 26/4/08)

TOP Oss 2, Helmond Sport 2
Helmond Sport 3, TOP Oss 0
(Helmond Sport 5-2)

SECOND ROUND (BEST OF THREE)

(1/5/08, 4/5/08 & 7/5/08)

ADO Den Haag 1, VVV-Venlo 0
VVV-Venlo 1, ADO Den Haag 0

ADO Den Haag 2, VVV-Venlo 0
(ADO Den Haag)

(1/5/08, 4/5/08 & 7/5/08)
MVV Maastricht 1, RKC Waalwijk 0
RKC Waalwijk 2, MVV Maastricht 0
RKC Waalwijk 4, MVV Maastricht 0
(RKC Waalwijk)

(1/5/08, 4/5/08 & 7/5/08)
FC Zwolle 0, FC Den Bosch 1
FC Den Bosch 1, FC Zwolle 2
FC Zwolle 1, FC Den Bosch 0
(FC Zwolle)

(1/5/08 & 4/5/08)
Helmond Sport 2, De Graafschap 3
De Graafschap 3, Helmond Sport 1
(De Graafschap)

THIRD ROUND (BEST OF THREE)

(11/5/08, 15/5/08 & 18/5/08)
ADO Den Haag 1, RKC Waalwijk 1
RKC Waalwijk 2, ADO Den Haag 2
ADO Den Haag 2, RKC Waalwijk 1
(ADO Den Haag)

(11/5/08 & 15/5/08)
FC Zwolle 1, De Graafschap 3
De Graafschap 0, FC Zwolle 0
(De Graafschap)

OMESTIC CUP 2007/08

KNVB-BEKER

ND ROUND

07)
ick 1887 1, Omniworld 8
, MVV 3
oven 4, Vitesse 2
ıa Sittard 3, Emmen 1
ond Sport 0, Go Ahead Eagles 1
4, AGOVV 4 *(aet; 4-5 on pens)*
, RBC 3
nburg 0, Roda JC 2
ss 1, Veendam 2
0, Dordrecht 2
em 1, Willem II 1 *(aet; 4-3 on pens)*
dam 4, Sparta 4 *(aet; 2-4 on pens)*

07)
e Ster 1, DOTO 0
nveen (second team) 0, PSV 3
vere axed from the cup-competiton for fielding the suspended Da Costa)
meervogels 1, Groningen 8
ken Boys 1, Ajax 2 *(aet)*
0, SC Heerenveen 3
Hardenberg 5, VVSB 2 *(aet)*
ineek 2, Zwolle 2 *(aet; 3-4 on pens)*
ick '28 0, Den Haag 0 *(aet; 3-4 on pens)*
ior 3, VVV 2
r (second team) 1, NAC 2
ndaal 1, Quick Boys 3
, Bennekom 0
effers/Kegro 2, ASWH 0
oord 3, Utrecht 0

07)
vijk 1, De Graafschap 5

AFC 0, Den Bosch 4
Cambuur 1, AZ 0
Telstar 1, Heracles 2
Deurne 3, Meerssen 0
Twente 1, NEC 2 *(aet)*

THIRD ROUND

(30/10/07)
Heracles Almelo 3, Omniworld 0
MVV 1, FC Dordrecht 3
Fortuna Sittard 1, Den Bosch 3
Zwolle 1, Go Ahead Eagles 0
Cambuur Leeuwarden 1, Excelsior 2
Eindhoven 1, Haarlem 3 *(aet)*
Hardenberg 0, AGOVV 1
Roda 3, De Graafschap 2 *(aet)*

(31/10/07)
Ajax 3, Heerenveen 1
Groene Ster 1, Quick Boys 2
Sparta 2, NAC 3
RKC 4, Veendam 0
De Treffers/Kegro 1, NEC 5
Deurne 2, UNA 0

(1/11/08)
Den Haag 1, Heerenveen (second team) 3
Feyenoord 3, FC Groningen 1

FOURTH ROUND

(15/1/08)
Deurne 0, Feyenoord 4
RKC 1, Haarlem 1 *(aet; 3-5 on pens)*
Dordrecht 4, AGOVV 3 *(aet)*
Roda 3, Excelsior 0
NEC 0, Zwolle 2

(16/1/08)
NAC 4, Ajax 2
Heracles Almelo 1, Den Bosch 0
Quick Boys 1, Heerenveen (second team) 1 *(aet; 3-1 on pens)*

QUARTER-FINALS

(26/2/08)
Haarlem 1 *(Berkleef 6)*, Heracles 5 *(Schilder 9, Everton 17, 43, 69, Lakić 23)*
Dordrecht 1 *(Muhamadu 60)*, Roda 3 *(Lamah 28, De Jong 51, Hadouir 82)*

(27/2/08)
Quick Boys 0, NAC 3 *(Amoah 11, Penders 39, Lurling 84)*

(28/2/08)
Feyenoord 2 *(Makaay 8, Mols 83)*, Zwolle 1 *(Toze 43)*

SEMI-FINALS

(18/3/08)
Feyenoord 2 *(Mols 54, Landzaat 75)*, NAC 0

(19/3/08)
Heracles 2 *(García-García 17, Van Den Bergh 80)*, Roda 2 *(Meeuwis 18, Janssen 55) (aet; 3-5 on pens)*

FINAL

(27/4/08)
De Kuip, Rotterdam
FEYENOORD 2 *(Landzaat 8, De Guzman 36)*
RODA JC 0
Referee – *Van Hulten*
FEYENOORD – *Timmer, Lucius, Bahia, Hofland (Greene 46), De Cler, Landzaat, Van Bronckhorst, De Guzman, Nuri (Fer 72), Bruins, Mols (Makaay 67).*
RODA – *Castro, Sonkaya (Cissé 46), De Fauw, Saeijs, Bodor, Tioté (Van Tornhout 83), Meeuwis, Janssen, Hadouir (Van Kouwen 46), Oper, Lamah.*

Linfield tighten their grip

Linfield FC's stranglehold on Northern Irish football remained as tight as ever in 2007/08 as the Belfast Blues won the League and Cup double for the third successive season. Even for a club as festooned with titles as Linfield, that was a special feat. The last time they – or anyone else – had completed a hat-trick of doubles was way back in 1893. And just to cap a truly unforgettable season for manager David Jeffrey and his players, they also won the League Cup, after a 3-2 victory over Crusaders FC in the final.

The key to Linfield's success was the phenomenal consistency of the team's twin strikers, Peter Thompson and Glenn Ferguson, who between them scored 71 of the team's 118 goals in all competitions. Thompson's personal haul of 44, which included a top-scoring 29 in the Premier League and both goals in the Irish Cup final – a 2-1 win over Coleraine FC - earned him a recall to the international arena, and he marked the occasion by grabbing his first goal for Northern Ireland in a 4-1 friendly victory over Georgia at Windsor Park in March.

Prolific Linfield striker Peter Thompson (left) celebrates his first goal for Northern Ireland with team-mate Warren Feeney

Linfield's main challengers for the Premier League title were local. Firstly, there was the old enemy, Glentoran FC. Newly led by former Queens Park Rangers FC and Northern Ireland defender Alan McDonald, the Glens maintained consistent pressure throughout the season, and won the traditional Boxing Day fixture against the Blues 1-0, but they were unable to extend a long winning run in the reverse fixture at Windsor Park three rounds from the end, the 0-0 draw effectively scuppering their hopes of dislodging Linfield from their perch. Eddie Patterson's Cliftonville FC, another club from the capital, were a threat for much of the campaign, remaining unbeaten in their first 20 matches, but the wheels came off spectacularly in the final sprint and they dropped to a distant third.

New league set up

Promotion and relegation took a back seat as the Irish Football Association (IFA) moved forward with their plans for a 12-team invitational league to be introduced for the 2008/09 season. Controversy arose when Portadown FC, one of the leading clubs in the province over the past two decades, and fifth in 2007/08, failed to get their application for the new league into the governing body by the 31 March deadline. A desperate appeal for clemency by the Mid-Ulster club fell on deaf ears, and they were forced to start afresh in the newly formed Intermediate Premier League. Also failing to make it into the top twelve were Armagh City FC, Larne FC, Limavady United FC and Donegal Celtic FC, who all fell short of the criteria laid down by the IFA. On the other hand, First Division Bangor FC ticked all the boxes and thus returned to the top flight after a 12-year absence.

On the international front, Northern Ireland's brave and determined bid to reach the final tournament of UEFA EURO 2008™ ended in failure – largely as a result of two devastating back-to-back defeats in Latvia and Iceland.

Following the inopportune departure of Lawrie Sanchez to Fulham FC in the summer, former international player Nigel Worthington, who won 66 caps for Northern

David Healy receives a plaque from UEFA president Michel Platini in recognition of his UEFA European Championship qualifying goalscoring record

reland, was installed as manager until the end of the ualifying campaign. His first match ended in a 3-1 home vin over group minnows Liechtenstein thanks to another wo goals from the ever-prolific David Healy and one from ew scoring sensation Kyle Lafferty. But then came the ill-ated trips to Riga and Reyjkavik, a Chris Baird own-goal iving Latvia a surprise 1-0 win and, four days later, nother own goal, this time from Keith Gillespie, in the ast minute, handing a deserved 2-1 victory to Iceland.

Healy strikes again

Those two reverses more or less ended Northern Ireland's chances, though faint hope was rekindled the following month when Lafferty's majestic strike earned a prized point away to Sweden. The dream was then kept alive until the final fixture when, at a rain-soaked Windsor Park, Northern Ireland beat Denmark 2-1, the winner coming from a sublime chip by David Healy, his 13th goal of the qualifying series. Alas, Sweden's victory over Latvia rendered a 1-0 defeat against Spain irrelevant and consigned Northern Ireland to third place.

It had been a magnificent campaign, the best for over 20 years, and there was some tangible reward for it in the form of a trophy presented to Healy by UEFA President Michel Platini to comemmorate his final tally of 13 goals – a new record for the UEFA European Championship qualifying competition, beating the old mark of 12 set by Croatian striker Davor Šuker on the road to UEFA EURO '96. The accolades did not stop there, as the 28-year-old Fulham FC striker was awarded with the MBE in the Queen's Birthday Honours in June.

Stadium controversy

The controversy over where the proposed new national stadium should be built came no closer to a conclusion. A suggestion that it be constructed on the site of the old Maze Prison, on the outskirts of Belfast, was rejected. Fresh proposals for a new stadium in the heart of the capital were subsequently submitted, but the fear in the province is that if, in the meantime, the money is not found to bring Windsor Park up to the required UEFA standard, Northern Ireland might find themselves obliged to play their home internationals somewhere on the British mainland.

Irish Football Association (IFA)

20 Windsor Avenue
GB-Belfast BT9 6EE
tel - +44 2890 669458
fax - +44 2890 667620
website - www.irishfa.com
email - enquiries@irishfa.com
Year of Formation – 1880
President – Raymond Kennedy
General Secretary - Howard Wells
Press Officer – Sueann Harrisonn
Stadium - Windsor Park, Belfast (20,332)

INTERNATIONAL TOURNAMENT APPEARANCES
FIFA World Cup - (3) 1958 (qtr-finals), 1982 (2nd phase), 1986.

TOP FIVE ALL-TIME CAPS
Pat Jennings (119); Mal Donaghy (91); Sammy McIlroy (88); Keith Gillespie (81); Jimmy Nicholl (73)

TOP FIVE ALL-TIME GOALS
David Healy (34); Colin Clarke & Billy Gillespie (13); Gerry Armstrong, Joe Bambrick, Ian Dowie & Jimmy Quinn (12)

NORTHERN IRELAND

NATIONAL TEAM RESULTS 2007/08

22/8/07	Liechtenstein (ECQ)	H	Belfast	3-1	*Healy (5, 35), Lafferty (56)*
8/9/07	Latvia (ECQ)	A	Riga	0-1	
12/9/07	Iceland (ECQ)	A	Reykjavik	1-2	*Healy (72p)*
17/10/07	Sweden (ECQ)	A	Solna	1-1	*Lafferty (72)*
17/11/07	Denmark (ECQ)	H	Belfast	2-1	*Feeney (62), Healy (80)*
21/11/07	Spain (ECQ)	A	Las Palmas	0-1	
6/2/08	Bulgaria	H	Belfast	0-1	
26/3/08	Georgia	H	Belfast	4-1	*Lafferty (25, 36), Healy (33), Thompson (87)*

NATIONAL TEAM APPEARANCES 2007/08

Coach – Nigel WORTHINGTON	4/11/61		LIE	LVA	ISL	SWE	DEN	ESP	Bul	Geo	Caps	Goa
Maik TAYLOR	4/9/71	Birmingham (ENG)	G	G	G	G	G	G	G83	G80	68	-
Michael DUFF	11/1/78	Burnley (ENG)	D	D	D						20	-
George McCARTNEY	29/4/81	West Ham (ENG)	D	D	D	D87			D46		25	1
Chris BAIRD	25/2/82	Fulham (ENG)	D	D	D		s85	D	s46	D	32	-
Stephen CRAIGAN	29/10/76	Motherwell (SCO)	D			D	D	D	s46	D59	35	-
Sammy CLINGAN	13/1/84	Nottingham Forest (ENG)	M	M	M	M	M	M	M		15	-
Keith GILLESPIE	18/2/75	Sheffield United (ENG)	M85	M	M		M74		M78	M	81	2
Steve DAVIS	1/1/85	Fulham (ENG)	M	M	M79	M	M	M				
		/Rangers (SCO)							s46	M70	28	1
Chris BRUNT	14/12/84	West Brom (ENG)	M62	s66	M83	M	M	M59	M		17	-
David HEALY	5/8/79	Fulham (ENG)	A	A	A	A	A	A	A	A70	64	34
Kyle LAFFERTY	16/9/87	Burnley (ENG)	A75	A71		A		s59	A60	A46	16	5
Stuart ELLIOTT	23/7/78	Hull (ENG)	s62	M66								
		/Doncaster (ENG)								M	39	4
Warren FEENEY	17/1/81	Cardiff (WAL)	s75							s46	24	3
		/Swansea (WAL)		s71	A		A85	A72				
Steve JONES	25/10/76	Burnley (ENG)	s85		s83						29	1
Jonny EVANS	3/1/88	Man. United (ENG)		D	D		D					
		/Sunderland (ENG)							D46	D	10	-
Grant McCANN	15/4/80	Barnsley (ENG)			s79						16	1
Aaron HUGHES	8/11/79	Fulham (ENG)				D	D	D	D	D	59	-
Gareth McAULEY	5/12/79	Leicester (ENG)				D	D	D	D	s59	10	-
Ivan SPROULE	18/2/81	Bristol City (ENG)				M	s74	M46			11	1
Tony CAPALDI	12/8/81	Cardiff (WAL)				s87					22	-
Steve ROBINSON	10/12/74	Luton (ENG)						s46			7	-
Martin PATERSON	10/5/87	Scunthorpe (ENG)						s72	s60		2	-
Damien JOHNSON	18/11/78	Birmingham (ENG)							M46	M46	48	-
Peter THOMPSON	2/5/84	Linfield							s78	s70	7	1
Alan MANNUS	19/5/82	Linfield							s83	s80	3	-
Michael O'CONNOR	6/10/87	Crewe (ENG)								s46	1	-
Michael GAULT	15/4/83	Linfield								s70	1	-

DOMESTIC LEAGUE 2007/08

EMIER LEAGUE FINAL TABLE

		Home					Away					Total					
	Pld	W	D	L	F	A	W	D	L	F	A	W	D	L	F	A	Pts
infield FC	30	13	2	0	34	5	10	3	2	37	13	23	5	2	71	18	74
lentoran FC	30	12	2	1	35	12	10	3	2	34	12	22	5	3	69	24	71
liftonville FC	30	9	4	2	35	20	9	2	4	20	12	18	6	6	55	32	60
isburn Distillery FC	30	7	4	4	16	8	10	3	2	34	20	17	7	6	50	28	58
ortadown FC	30	8	0	7	23	24	7	2	6	21	15	15	2	13	44	39	47
allymena United FC	30	7	5	3	20	17	5	3	7	22	24	12	8	10	42	41	44
rusaders FC	30	8	2	5	25	20	4	5	6	20	27	12	7	11	45	47	43
lewry City FC	30	7	4	4	23	21	6	0	9	22	31	13	4	13	45	52	43
oleraine FC	30	5	4	6	22	28	6	3	6	19	22	11	7	12	41	50	40
ungannon Swifts FC	30	6	3	6	23	23	3	6	6	15	21	9	9	12	38	44	36
onegal Celtic FC	30	6	3	6	26	21	3	5	7	13	26	9	8	13	39	47	35
lenavon FC	30	4	0	11	17	27	5	3	7	20	24	9	3	18	37	51	30
arne FC	30	3	2	10	23	35	4	2	9	21	36	7	4	19	44	71	25
stitute FC	30	2	5	8	12	19	3	3	9	11	22	5	8	17	23	41	23
imavady United FC	30	4	3	8	16	25	2	2	11	10	32	6	5	19	26	57	23
rmagh City FC	30	3	4	8	17	26	2	2	11	12	30	5	6	19	29	56	21

lo promotion or relegation. A new 12-team Invitational League to begin in 2008/09.

TOP GOALSCORERS

29 Peter THOMPSON (Linfield)
20 Paul McVEIGH (Donegal Celtic)
19 Gary HAMILTON (Glentoran)
15 Kevin KELBIE (Ballymena)
14 Glenn FERGUSON (Linfield)
13 Gary BROWNE (Lisburn)
11 David RAINEY (Crusaders)
10 Stephen CARSON (Coleraine)
Gary McCUTCHEON (Portadown)
Ryan McILMOYLE (Limavady)

CLUB-BY-CLUB

ARMAGH CITY FC

Manager – Gary McKinstry

Founded - 1964

007

2/9	Glentoran	a	0-1	
9/9	Crusaders	h	2-2	*og (Hunter), Forker*
'10	Cliftonville	a	1-2	*Hyndes*
3/10	Linfield	h	1-3	*Hawthorne*
0/10	Portadown	a	1-2	*Hawthorne*
7/10	Limavady	h	1-0	*Forker*
'11	Ballymena	h	1-2	*McSorley (p)*
0/11	Dungannon	a	1-5	*Hawthorne*
4/11	Lisburn	h	4-1	*McBirney, Coney, McCann 2*
'12	Larne	a	2-0	*Fitzpatrick G., Coney*
'12	Donegal Celtic	h	1-1	*McCann*
5/12	Institute	a	1-1	*Cullen*
2/12	Coleraine	h	0-1	
5/12	Newry	a	0-3	
9/12	Glenavon	h	2-0	*Forker, Hawthorne*
008				
'1	Crusaders	a	1-1	*Forker*
'1	Glentoran	h	0-5	
9/1	Cliftonville	h	0-1	
5/1	Linfield	a	1-2	*Coney*
'2	Limavady	a	3-0	*Coney, McCann (p), Mackay*
5/2	Portadown	h	1-1	*Coney*
3/2	Lisburn	a	0-1	
'3	Dungannon	h	0-1	
5/3	Ballymena	a	1-2	*Fitzpatrick G.*
2/3	Larne	h	2-5	*Forker, McCann*
5/3	Donegal Celtic	a	0-3	
'4	Institute	h	1-1	*McCann*
12/4	Newry	h	1-2	*McCann (p)*
19/4	Coleraine	a	0-2	
26/4	Glenavon	a	0-5	

Name	Nat	Pos	Aps	(s)	Gls
Stuart ADDIS		G	29		
Tony CLARKE		D		(1)	
Sean CLEARY		D	14		
Paul COLGAN		G	1		
Shane CONEY		A	24	(3)	5
Kevin CONNOLLY		D		(1)	
Liam CULLEN		M	23	(4)	1
Chris FAY		A		(2)	
Gary FITZPATRICK		D	21		2
Terry FITZPATRICK		M	14		
Conor FORKER		A	10	(13)	5
Ciaran FRIEL		D	6		
Mark GRACEY		D	25		
David HAWTHORNE		M	28	(1)	4
John HOOKS		D	1		
Stephen HYNDES		M	14	(1)	1
Michael KERR		D	2		
Iain LATIMER		D	16	(5)	
Cian MACKEY	IRL	A	6		1
Colin MAGILL		A	3		
Philip McBIRNEY		D	17		1
Austin McCANN	IRL	M	19	(8)	7
Will McDONAGH	IRL	M	5		
Shane McGEOWN		D	4	(3)	
Shea McGERRIGAN		M	6	(2)	
Ciaran McMULLAN		A	1	(5)	
Pete McNEILL		A	4	(2)	
Johnny McSORLEY		M	4	(13)	1
Keith PERCY		M		(1)	
James SLATER		A	11	(10)	

NORTHERN IRELAND

Name	Nat	Pos	Aps	(s)	Gls
Mark TURKINGTON		D	18		
Chris WALKER		D	4		

BALLYMENA UNITED FC

Manager – Tommy Wright

Founded - 1928

MAJOR HONOURS: Irish Cup – (6) 1929, 1940, 1958, 1981, 1984, 1989.

2007				
22/9	Glenavon	a	2-1	*Kelbie, Walsh (p)*
29/9	Glentoran	h	0-4	
6/10	Crusaders	a	0-3	
13/10	Cliftonville	h	0-1	
20/10	Linfield	a	0-1	
27/10	Portadown	h	2-1	*Kelbie, Walsh*
3/11	Armagh	a	2-1	*Walsh (p), Lowry*
10/11	Limavady	h	3-0	*Walsh, Lowry, Kelbie*
24/11	Dungannon	h	0-0	
7/12	Larne	h	3-0	*Kelbie, Fitzgerald, Cushley*
15/12	Donegal Celtic	a	2-0	*Watson Al., Scates*
18/12	Lisburn	a	2-0	*Kelbie, Cushley*
22/12	Institute	h	2-1	*Kelbie 2*
26/12	Coleraine	a	1-1	*Lowry*
29/12	Newry	h	2-1	*Kelbie 2*
2008				
1/1	Glentoran	a	4-2	*Scates, Haveron, Melaugh, Kelbie*
5/1	Glenavon	h	0-0	
19/1	Crusaders	h	2-2	*Melaugh, Walsh*
26/1	Cliftonville	a	2-3	*Kelbie, Wray*
1/2	Portadown	a	1-2	*Kelbie*
16/2	Linfield	h	0-4	
23/2	Dungannon	a	1-2	*Melaugh*
15/3	Armagh	h	2-1	*King, Kelbie*
22/3	Lisburn	h	2-2	*Kelly, Watson Al.*
25/3	Larne	a	1-2	*Kelbie*
28/3	Limavady	a	1-3	*Melaugh*
5/4	Donegal Celtic	h	0-0	
12/4	Coleraine	h	2-0	*Wray 2*
19/4	Institute	a	1-1	*King*
26/4	Newry	a	2-2	*Kelbie, McNeill*

Name	Nat	Pos	Aps	(s)	Gls
Gary BAIRD		M	1	(1)	
Nigel BOYD		D	2		
Aaron CALLAGHAN		D	7	(1)	
Lee COLLIGAN		M		(2)	
David CUSHLEY		A	7	(4)	2
Darrin FITZGERALD		A	3	(6)	1
Johnny FLYNN		D	12	(1)	
Gary HAVERON		D	22	(1)	1
Kevin KELBIE	SCO	A	29		15
Simon KELLY	IRL	D	19		1
Stuart KING		M	18	(4)	2
Stephen LOWRY		M	16	(5)	3
Craig McLEAN		D	26		
Paul McNEILL		A	1	(4)	1
Gavin MELAUGH		M	27		4
Paul MURPHY	IRL	G	30		
Lee PATRICK		M	5	(16)	
Mark PICKING		M	7	(13)	
Dean POOLEY	IRL	D	2		
Randal REID		A	1	(5)	
Garth SCATES		M	26	(3)	2
Davitt WALSH	IRL	A	11	(8)	5
Michael WARD		A	8	(2)	
Aiden WATSON		M	5	(1)	
Albert WATSON		D	28		2
Thomas WRAY		D	17		3

CLIFTONVILLE FC

Manager – Eddie Patterson

Founded – 1879

MAJOR HONOURS: Irish League - (3) 1906, 1910, 1998; Irish Cup (8) 1883, 1888, 1897, 1900, 1901, 1907, 1909, 1979.

2007				
24/9	Linfield	h	2-2	*McAlinden, O'Neill*
29/9	Portadown	a	2-0	*Holland M., Scannell C*
6/10	Armagh	h	2-1	*McAlinden, Scannell R*
13/10	Ballymena	a	1-0	*Holland B.*
20/10	Dungannon	h	2-1	*Murphy, O'Connor*
27/10	Lisburn	a	2-1	*O'Neill, Holland M.*
3/11	Larne	h	1-1	*O'Connor*
10/11	Donegal Celtic	a	2-0	*Murphy, O'Connor*
24/11	Institute	h	2-0	*Murphy (p), McMullan*
1/12	Coleraine	a	3-0	*Murphy 2 (1p), McMullan*
4/12	Newry	h	2-0	*Scannell C., McMullan*
15/12	Glenavon	a	2-1	*O'Connor, McMullan*
22/12	Glentoran	h	4-2	*Scannell C. 2, Holland M., McMullan*
26/12	Crusaders	a	1-1	*Holland B.*
2008				
7/1	Linfield	a	0-0	
19/1	Armagh	a	1-0	*McAlinden (p)*
26/1	Ballymena	h	3-2	*O'Hara, Holland M., Murphy*
29/1	Portadown	h	2-1	*Scannell C. 2*
1/2	Lisburn	h	2-2	*Scannell R., Murphy (p*
5/2	Limavady	h	4-1	*Scannell C., Smyth 2, O'Neill*
16/2	Dungannon	a	0-1	
23/2	Institute	a	2-1	*Johnston, O'Neill*
8/3	Donegal Celtic	h	5-1	*Martin 2, McMullan, Holland M., Holland B.*
15/3	Larne	a	2-1	*Holland M. 2*
22/3	Coleraine	h	1-2	*Johnston*
25/3	Newry	a	0-1	
5/4	Glenavon	h	3-3	*O'Hara, Scannell C., McMullan*
18/4	Glentoran	a	1-2	*O'Connor*
22/4	Crusaders	h	0-1	
26/4	Limavady	a	1-3	*Scannell C.*

Name	Nat	Pos	Aps	(s)	Gls
Ciaran BOYD		A		(3)	
Shea CAMPBELL		A	5	(4)	
Ryan CATNEY		M	9	(6)	
Sean CLEARY		D	5	(1)	
John CONNOLLY	IRL	G	30		
Niall DEVINE		M		(1)	
Liam FLEMING		D	13	(5)	
Barry HOLLAND		M	20	(2)	3
Mark HOLLAND		A	24	(1)	7
Barry JOHNSTON		M	26		2
Daniel LYONS		A	1	(3)	
John MARTIN		A	10	(8)	2
David McALINDEN		D	15	(2)	3
George McMULLAN		M	24	(5)	7
Francis MURPHY		M	26		7
Kieran O'CONNOR		A	21	(3)	5
Declan O'HARA		D	24		2
Stephen O'NEILL		A	2	(17)	4
Patrick PEARSE		D		(1)	
Chris SCANNELL		A	29		9
Ronan SCANNELL		D	29		2
Aaron SMYTH		D	17	(3)	2

COLERAINE FC

Manager – Marty Quinn

Founded – 1927

MAJOR HONOURS: Irish League – (1) 1974; Irish Cup – (5) 1965, 1972, 1975, 1977, 2003.

2007				
22/9	Lisburn	h	1-4	*Hutchinson*
29/9	Larne	a	2-1	*Gaston, Boyce*
6/10	Donegal Celtic	h	3-2	*Hutchinson, Tolan, Carson*
13/10	Institute	a	0-0	
20/10	Limavady	a	0-0	

'/10	Newry	h	0-1	
'11	Glenavon	a	0-1	
)/11	Glentoran	h	1-4	*Boyce*
4/11	Crusaders	a	4-3	*Neill, Cassidy 2, Boyce*
'/11	Linfield	a	0-4	
'12	Cliftonville	h	0-3	
;/12	Portadown	h	1-1	*Anderson*
2/12	Armagh	a	1-0	*Boyce*
;/12	Ballymena	h	1-1	*Patton D.*
)/12	Dungannon	a	1-4	*McCallion*
)08				
'1	Larne	h	4-1	*Patton G., Patton D. 2, Carson*
)/1	Donegal Celtic	a	1-1	*og (McClean)*
;/1	Institute	h	2-1	*Cassidy, Whitehead*
)/1	Lisburn	a	0-2	
'2	Newry	a	2-0	*Carson, Hunter*
;/2	Limavady	h	1-0	*Carson*
3/2	Crusaders	h	3-3	*Carson 3*
'3	Glentoran	a	1-2	*McVey (p)*
;/3	Glenavon	h	0-1	
2/3	Cliftonville	a	2-1	*Carson, Watt*
;/3	Linfield	h	1-4	*Hunter*
'4	Portadown	a	5-1	*McCallion, Dooley, Carson, Patton D., Hunter*
2/4	Ballymena	a	0-2	
)/4	Armagh	h	2-0	*Carson, Whitehead*
;/4	Dungannon	h	2-2	*Hutchinson, McVey*

ame	Nat	Pos	Aps	(s)	Gls
oel ANDERSON		M	10	(3)	1
oward BEVERLAND		D	14		
arren BOYCE		M	12	(3)	4
ephen CARSON		M	23	(2)	10
arren CASSIDY		D	15	(4)	3
ewart CLANACHAN		D	13		
atthew CROSSAN	IRL	D	11		
ephen DOOLEY		A	4	(3)	1
an EWART		D	1	(2)	
aul GASTON		D	9		1
ean HENEGHAN		M	5	(6)	
artin HUNTER		M	11	(2)	3
evor HUTCHINSON		M	7	(8)	3
ommy McCALLION		M	28		2
dam McCART		D	1	(1)	
aurence McCORMICK		G	12		
addy McLAUGHLIN		D	10		
yan McLAUGHLIN		D	6	(1)	
yle McVEY		D	25	(1)	2
ohn NEILL		D	24	(4)	1
avid O'HARE		G	18		
avid PATTON		A	23	(5)	4
ordon PATTON		A	2	(6)	1
ody TOLAN		A	15	(5)	1
ohn WATT		M	22	(4)	1
amien WHITEHEAD	ENG	A	9	(9)	2

CRUSADERS FC

Manager – Stephen Baxter

Founded – 1898

MAJOR HONOURS: Irish League – (4) 1973, 1976, 1995, 1997; Irish Cup (2) 1967, 1968.

007				
2/9	Portadown	h	0-2	
)/9	Armagh	a	2-2	*Doherty, Lockhart*
'10	Ballymena	h	3-0	*Coulter 2, Morrow*
3/10	Dungannon	a	1-1	*Rainey*
)/10	Lisburn	h	1-3	*og (Matthews)*
'/10	Larne	a	3-0	*Morrow, Rainey, McAllister*
'11	Donegal Celtic	h	2-0	*Rainey, Morrow*
)/11	Institute	a	1-3	*Coates*
4/11	Coleraine	h	3-4	*Smyth, Doherty, Lockhart*
'12	Newry	a	1-1	*Spence (p)*
11/12	Glenavon	h	2-1	*Spence (p), Coulter*
15/12	Glentoran	a	0-3	
22/12	Limavady	a	2-1	*Rainey 2*
26/12	Cliftonville	h	1-1	*Tumilty*
29/12	Linfield	a	0-5	
2008				
1/1	Armagh	h	1-1	*Rainey*
5/1	Portadown	a	0-2	
19/1	Ballymena	a	2-2	*Coates, Coulter*
26/1	Dungannon	h	1-0	*Rainey*
16/2	Lisburn	a	0-1	
23/2	Coleraine	a	3-3	*Hyndes, Coulter, Brown*
1/3	Larne	h	4-1	*Owens, Coulter, Spence (p), Brown*
8/3	Institute	h	1-0	*Coates*
15/3	Donegal Celtic	a	0-3	
22/3	Newry	h	4-1	*Lockhart (p), Rainey, Owens, Morrow*
25/3	Glenavon	a	4-0	*Lockhart, Rainey, Owens 2*
5/4	Glentoran	h	0-2	
19/4	Limavady	h	2-1	*Rainey 2*
22/4	Cliftonville	a	1-0	*Lockhart*
26/4	Linfield	h	0-3	

Name	Nat	Pos	Aps	(s)	Gls
Seamus BROWN		A	5	(3)	2
Declan CADDELL		A	1	(6)	
Colin COATES		D	19	(1)	3
Stephen COULTER		A	25	(1)	6
Anto CRAWFORD		A		(4)	
Eamon DOHERTY		M	24	(1)	2
Alain EMERSON		M	8	(2)	
Tony GORMAN	IRL	M	4	(2)	
Aaron HOGG		G	4		
Andy HUNTER		D	2	(1)	
Stephen HYNDES		M	7	(4)	1
Aaron KERR		G	21		
Lee LENAGHAN		M		(2)	
Darren LOCKHART		M	20	(2)	5
Wayne LORRIMER		D	1		
David MAGOWAN		D	25	(1)	
Eamon McALLISTER		M	14	(13)	1
Stephen McBRIDE		D	28	(1)	
Mark McQUILLAN		A		(1)	
Aaron MONTGOMERY		D	3		
Chris MORROW		M	28		4
Jordan OWENS		A	4	(7)	4
David RAINEY		A	30		11
Martin REILLY	IRL	A	6	(8)	
Gregg SHANNON		G	5		
Gary SMYTH		D	26		1
Barry SPENCE		D	16	(2)	3
Ryan TUMILTY		M	4	(8)	1
Gareth WALSH		M		(1)	

DONEGAL CELTIC FC

Manager – Paddy Kelly

Founded – 1970

2007				
22/9	Limavady	a	1-0	*McVeigh*
29/9	Institute	h	0-1	
6/10	Coleraine	a	2-3	*McDonald, Bradley L.*
13/10	Newry	h	2-3	*White, Donaghy*
20/10	Glenavon	a	1-0	*McVeigh*
27/10	Glentoran	h	3-3	*McDonald, Gargin, Donaghy*
3/11	Crusaders	a	0-2	
10/11	Cliftonville	h	0-2	
24/11	Linfield	a	0-2	
1/12	Portadown	h	0-1	
7/12	Armagh	a	1-1	*Munster*
15/12	Ballymena	h	0-2	
26/12	Lisburn	h	1-2	*Gargin*

31/12	Institute	a	1-1	*McDonald*
2008				
19/1	Coleraine	h	1-1	*McClean*
22/1	Larne	a	2-4	*McVeigh, Bradley L.*
26/1	Newry	a	1-1	*McVeigh*
29/1	Limavady	h	3-1	*Kearney 2, McVeigh*
1/2	Glentoran	a	1-5	*McVeigh*
5/2	Dungannon	a	0-0	
16/2	Glenavon	h	2-0	*McVeigh 2*
23/2	Linfield	h	1-1	*Kearney*
8/3	Cliftonville	a	1-5	*Donaghy*
15/3	Crusaders	h	3-0	*Hamill, Kearney, McVeigh (p)*
22/3	Portadown	a	1-2	*McVeigh*
25/3	Armagh	h	3-0	*McVeigh 3 (1p)*
5/4	Ballymena	a	0-0	
12/4	Lisburn	a	1-0	*McVeigh (p)*
19/4	Dungannon	h	3-1	*Hamill, McVeigh 2 (1p)*
26/4	Larne	h	4-3	*McVeigh 4 (1p)*

Name	**Nat**	**Pos**	**Aps**	**(s)**	**Gls**
Sean ARMSTRNG		A	16	(11)	
Andrew BONNER		D	13	(2)	
Liam BRADLEY		M	24	(2)	2
Paul BRADLEY		D	17	(2)	
Declan BROWN		G	21		
Ciaran CALDWELL		D	1	(1)	
Noel CARDWELL		M	7	(12)	
Anto CRAWFORD		A	3	(7)	
Ciaran DONAGHY		D	24	(3)	3
Kevin DUFF		D	3	(4)	
Ciaran GARGIN		M	22	(6)	2
Rory HAMILL		A	12		2
Daniel HANNA		A	1	(3)	
Stephen HARBINSON		G	9		
Tony HEAGNEY		D	17	(2)	
Colm KEARNEY		A	8	(3)	4
James LAVERY		A	7	(6)	
Stephen McALORUM		M	26	(1)	
Gerard McCABE		D	6	(2)	
Michael McCLEAN		D	19	(1)	1
Paul McDONALD		M	16	(4)	3
Paul McVEIGH		A	28		20
David MUNSTER		D	28		1
Alan MURRAY		M		(1)	
Robbie WHITE		A	2	(4)	1

DUNGANNON SWIFTS FC

Manager – Harry Fay

Founded – 1949

2007				
22/9	Newry	a	0-3	
28/9	Glenavon	h	1-4	*Baron*
6/10	Glentoran	a	1-1	*og (Leeman)*
13/10	Crusaders	h	1-1	*McAllister*
20/10	Cliftonville	a	1-2	*McGinn*
27/10	Linfield	h	4-0	*McGinn, og (Murphy), Campbell, McCabe*
3/11	Portadown	a	1-0	*McAllister*
10/11	Armagh	h	5-1	*McAree (p), Campbell 2, McAllister, McCabe*
24/11	Ballymena	a	0-0	
1/12	Limavady	h	0-2	
7/12	Lisburn	h	0-3	
15/12	Larne	a	3-3	*Baron, McGinn, Gallagher (p)*
26/12	Institute	a	0-1	
29/12	Coleraine	h	4-1	*Hegarty, McAree (p), Campbell, McGinn*
2008				
1/1	Glenavon	a	2-1	*McMinn, Friel*
4/1	Newry	h	4-6	*Friel 2, McAree (p), McAllister*
19/1	Glentoran	h	0-0	
26/1	Crusaders	a	0-1	
5/2	Donegal Celtic	h	0-0	
16/2	Cliftonville	h	1-0	*Hegarty*
20/2	Linfield	a	1-2	*Friel*
23/2	Ballymena	h	2-1	*McAllister 2*
8/3	Armagh	a	1-0	*Hegarty*
15/3	Portadown	h	0-3	
22/3	Limavady	a	1-1	*McAllister*
25/3	Lisburn	a	1-1	*McCarron*
5/4	Larne	h	1-0	*McAllister*
12/4	Institute	h	0-1	
19/4	Donegal Celtic	a	1-3	*Friel*
26/4	Coleraine	a	2-2	*Tomelty, Friel*

Name	**Nat**	**Pos**	**Aps**	**(s)**	**Gls**
Paul BARON		A	4	(8)	2
Shea CAMPBELL		A	16	(1)	4
Stephen CUNNINGHAM		D		(1)	
John CURRAN		D	26	(1)	
Sean FERRY		A	1	(6)	
Terry FITZPATRICK		M	12		
Paul FORKER		A	2	(3)	
Austin FRIEL		A	14	(4)	6
John GALLAGHER		D	26	(1)	1
Michael HEGARTY		M	22	(3)	3
Barry KELLY		A		(1)	
Mark MAGENNIS		M	1	(5)	
Fergal McALISKEY		D	1		
Mark McALLISTER		A	20	(3)	8
Rodney McAREE		M	10	(2)	3
Shane McCABE		M	10		2
Adrian McCAFFREY		M	3	(5)	
Aiden McCARRON		A	6	(1)	1
Ryan McCLUSKEY		M	9	(1)	
Mark McCONKEY		M	9	(9)	
Aaron McELWEE		D	1	(1)	
Shea McGERRIGAN		A	6	(5)	
Niall McGINN		M	18		4
Duwayne McMANUS		A		(1)	
Adam McMINN		D	24	(1)	1
Johnny MONTGOMERY		D	24		
Darren MURPHY		D	13	(1)	
Dwayne NELSON		G	29		
Ormond OKUNAIYA		M	4	(6)	
Jamie TOMELTY		M	13		1
Matt WALTON	USA	M	5		
James WARDEL		M		(2)	
David WELLS		G	1		

GLENAVON FC

Manager – Colin Malone; (12/1/08) Terry Cochrane

Founded – 1889

MAJOR HONOURS: Irish League – (3) 1952, 1957, 1960; Irish Cup – (5) 1957, 1959, 1961, 1992, 1997.

2007				
22/9	Ballymena	h	1-2	*Gibson*
28/9	Dungannon	a	4-1	*Gibson, Murray, Carville, Kearney*
6/10	Lisburn	h	2-3	*Cowan, Gawley*
13/10	Larne	a	4-3	*Kearney 2, Gawley, Hamlin*
20/10	Donegal Celtic	h	0-1	
27/10	Institute	a	3-2	*Hamlin (p), Kearney 2*
3/11	Coleraine	h	1-0	*Walsh C.*
10/11	Newry	a	1-2	*Walsh C.*
24/11	Limavady	a	0-1	
1/12	Glentoran	h	1-2	*Meehan*
11/12	Crusaders	a	1-2	*Murray*
15/12	Cliftonville	h	1-2	*Harper*
22/12	Linfield	a	2-3	*Cowan, Bracken (p)*
26/12	Portadown	h	0-3	
29/12	Armagh	a	0-2	
2008				
1/1	Dungannon	h	1-2	*Bracken*

	Ballymena	a	0-0	
'1	Lisburn	a	0-0	
'1	Larne	h	2-3	*McMahon, Molloy*
:	Institute	h	2-0	*Murray, Jameson*
'2	Donegal Celtic	a	0-2	
'2	Limavady	h	0-3	
;	Newry	h	1-0	*Harper*
'3	Coleraine	a	1-0	*Morris*
'3	Glentoran	a	0-3	
'3	Crusaders	h	0-4	
	Cliftonville	a	3-3	*Molloy 2, Stewart*
'4	Portadown	a	1-0	*McCain*
'4	Linfield	h	0-2	
'4	Armagh	h	5-0	*McMahon 2, Walsh C., og (Gracey), Molloy*

me	Nat	Pos	Aps	(s)	Gls
vid BRACKEN	IRL	A	6	(1)	2
ıl CAIRNDUFF		G	3		
ıl CARVILLE		D	14	(6)	1
ıathan COWAN		D	17		2
gh DICKSON		D	11		
ran DONNELLY	ENG	M	4	(3)	
ın DOUGLAS		M	5	(3)	
al GAWLEY		M	15		2
hard GIBSON		A	2		2
drew HAGEMAN	IRL	M	2	(1)	
vis HAMLIN	ENG	M	12	(1)	2
rian HARPER	ENG	A	23	(1)	2
rk HAUGHEY		D	2		
rty HAVERON		A		(2)	
than JAMESON	ENG	A	3		1
m KEARNEY		A	6	(4)	5
:k KEOGH	IRL	M		(1)	
phen MAGENNIS		A	9	(1)	
; McADAM		D	9	(1)	
ven McCAIN		M	2	(5)	1
vin McDONNELL	IRL	D	25	(1)	
ran McGUIGAN		D	2	(1)	
:hael McKERR		D	10	(1)	
rard McMAHON		M	19	(3)	3
ry MEEHAN		M	12	(2)	1
vor MOLLOY	IRL	A	14		4
vid MORRIS		A	5		1
de MURPHY	CAY	G	25		
non MURRAY		M	12	(7)	3
ris O'HARE	ENG	A		(2)	
nond OKUNAIYA		M	8	(8)	
ıl RICE		G	2		
nmy STEWART		M	9	(6)	1
rk TURKINGTON		D	12		
nor WALSH		M	24	(1)	3
ıl WALSH		A	6	(3)	

GLENTORAN FC

Manager – Alan McDonald

Founded – 1882

AJOR HONOURS: Irish League – (22) 1894, 1897, 1905, 1912, 1913, 21, 1925, 1931, 1951, 1953, 1964, 1967, 1968, 1970, 1972, 1977, 1981, 988, 1992, 1999, 2003, 2005; Irish Cup – (20) 1914, 1917, 1921, 1932, 33, 1935, 1951, 1966, 1973, 1983, 1985, 1986, 1987, 1988, 1990, 1996, 1998, 2000, 2001, 2004.

07				
'9	Armagh	h	1-0	*Fordyce*
'9	Ballymena	a	4-0	*Hamill, Hamilton 2, Halliday*
0	Dungannon	h	1-1	*Hamilton*
'10	Lisburn	a	2-1	*Leeman, og (Ferguson)*
'10	Larne	h	1-0	*Hamill*
'10	Donegal Celtic	a	3-3	*Scullion 3*
1	Institute	h	4-0	*Hamilton, McCann, Nixon, Morgan*
'11	Coleraine	a	4-1	*Hamilton, McCann, Nixon (p), Neill*
24/11	Newry	h	2-1	*Fordyce, Hill*
1/12	Glenavon	a	2-1	*Neill, Nixon (p)*
7/12	Limavady	a	0-1	
15/12	Crusaders	h	3-0	*Fordyce, Halliday, Hamilton*
22/12	Cliftonville	a	2-4	*Hamilton 2*
26/12	Linfield	h	1-0	*Halliday*
29/12	Portadown	a	2-0	*Hill, Hamilton*
2008				
1/1	Ballymena	h	2-4	*Hamilton, Neill*
5/1	Armagh	a	5-0	*Hamilton 3, Halliday, Hill (p)*
19/1	Dungannon	a	0-0	
26/1	Lisburn	h	2-2	*Neill 2*
1/2	Donegal Celtic	h	5-1	*Scullion, Boyce, Halliday, Neill, Fordyce*
16/2	Larne	a	3-0	*Hamilton 3*
23/2	Newry	a	3-0	*Scullion, Fordyce 2*
7/3	Coleraine	h	2-1	*Scullion, Hamilton*
15/3	Institute	a	2-1	*Nixon (p), Fordyce*
22/3	Glenavon	h	3-0	*Nixon (p), Scullion, Boyce*
25/3	Limavady	h	3-0	*Boyce 2, McCabe*
5/4	Crusaders	a	2-0	*Fitzgerald 2*
12/4	Linfield	a	0-0	
18/4	Cliftonville	h	2-1	*Hamilton, Halliday*
26/4	Portadown	h	3-1	*Halliday, Hamilton, Fordyce*

Name	Nat	Pos	Aps	(s)	Gls
Ryan BERRY		M	3	(9)	
Darren BOYCE		M	4	(7)	4
Philip CARSON		M	7	(2)	
Michael DOUGHERTY		G	10	(3)	
Dean FITZGERALD		M	11	(6)	2
Daryl FORDYCE		M	25	(1)	8
Mark GLENDINNING		D		(2)	
Michael HALLIDAY		A	27	(2)	7
Rory HAMILL		A	3	(11)	2
Gary HAMILTON		A	28		19
Jason HILL		D	25	(1)	3
Chris KEENAN		G	1		
Paul LEEMAN		D	29		1
Shane McCABE		M	14		1
Tim McCANN		M	4	(1)	2
Will McDONAGH	IRL	M		(1)	
Jamie McGOVERN		D	8	(7)	
Brendan McMENAMIN		D		(3)	
Chris MORGAN		A	3	(4)	1
Elliott MORRIS		G	19		
Kyle NEILL		D	20	(3)	6
Colin NIXON		D	29		5
David SCULLION		M	28		7
Philip SIMPSON		M	1		
Peter STEELE		A		(3)	
Michael WARD		A	5	(8)	
Sean WARD		D	26		

INSTITUTE FC

Manager – Liam Beckett; (17/3/08) John Gregg

Founded – 1905

2007				
22/9	Larne	h	0-1	
29/9	Donegal Celtic	a	1-0	*Ogilby (p)*
6/10	Limavady	a	2-2	*Ogilby (p), Campbell R.*
13/10	Coleraine	h	0-0	
20/10	Newry	a	1-2	*Ogilby (p)*
27/10	Glenavon	h	2-3	*McKenna, Scoltock*
3/11	Glentoran	a	0-4	
10/11	Crusaders	h	3-1	*Lowry, Ogilby, Campbell R.*
24/11	Cliftonville	a	0-2	
1/12	Linfield	h	0-1	
7/12	Portadown	a	1-2	*Lowry*
15/12	Armagh	h	1-1	*Semple*

22/12	Ballymena	a	1-2	*og (Watson Al.)*
26/12	Dungannon	h	1-0	*Crawford*
29/12	Lisburn	a	0-0	
31/12	Donegal Celtic	h	1-1	*McCreadie*
2008				
5/1	Larne	a	2-1	*Ogilby, McCreadie*
19/1	Limavady	h	0-0	
26/1	Coleraine	a	1-2	*Semple*
1/2	Glenavon	a	0-2	
16/2	Newry	h	0-2	
23/2	Cliftonville	h	1-2	*Divin*
8/3	Crusaders	a	0-1	
15/3	Glentoran	h	1-2	*Boyle*
22/3	Linfield	a	0-1	
25/3	Portadown	h	1-2	*Campbell S.*
5/4	Armagh	a	1-1	*Moran*
12/4	Dungannon	a	1-0	*McCreadie*
19/4	Ballymena	h	1-1	*McCreadie*
26/4	Lisburn	h	0-2	

Name	Nat	Pos	Aps	(s)	Gls
Ruairi BOYLE		D	22	(1)	1
Ryan CAMPBELL		A	12	(4)	2
Stephen CAMBELL		M	12	(8)	1
Andrew CRAWFORD		A	6	(18)	1
Martin CUTMORE		D	23	(3)	
Iarfhlaith DAVOREN	IRL	A	7		
Conor DEANE		D		(1)	
Declan DIVIN		M	9	(2)	1
Michael DOHERTY		G	20		
Ciaran FERRY		A	2	(11)	
David KEE		M	19	(2)	
Neil LARMOUR		D		(1)	
Philip LOWRY		M	29		2
Emmett MAPP		G	1		
Ruairi McCLEAN		M	11	(4)	
Ryan McCREADIE		A	19	(7)	4
Ryan McGARVEY		D		(1)	
Liam McKENNA	IRL	D	5		1
Kyle MORAN		A	2	(6)	1
John O'LOUGHLIN		M	9	(5)	
David OGILBY		D	29		5
Graeme PHILSON		D	7		
Alan RYAN		G	9	(2)	
Mark SCOLTOCK		D	21	(2)	1
Ryan SEMPLE		M	28		2
Eamon SEYDAK		D	25	(1)	

LARNE FC

Manager – Paul Curran; (18/12/07) Tommy Leeman; (8/1/08) Graeme McConnell

Founded – 1890

2007				
22/9	Institute	a	1-0	*Rafferty*
29/9	Coleraine	h	1-2	*Hunter*
6/10	Newry	a	2-2	*Black R., Black A.*
13/10	Glenavon	h	3-4	*Black A. (p), McLaughlin D. 2*
20/10	Glentoran	a	0-1	
27/10	Crusaders	h	0-3	
3/11	Cliftonville	a	1-1	*Lagan*
10/11	Linfield	h	1-5	*Hunter*
24/11	Portadown	a	1-5	*Verner*
1/12	Armagh	h	0-2	
7/12	Ballymena	a	0-3	
15/12	Dungannon	h	3-3	*Fulton, Lagan 2*
22/12	Lisburn	a	0-2	
26/12	Limavady	h	2-2	*Black A., Moran*
2008				
1/1	Coleraine	a	1-4	*Hamilton*
5/1	Institute	h	1-2	*Hunter*
19/1	Newry	h	3-0	*Black R., Hand, Anderson*
22/1	Donegal Celtic	h	4-2	*Fulton, og (McAlorum), Black R., Hamilton*
26/1	Glenavon	a	3-2	*Anderson, Black A. (p Hand*
16/2	Glentoran	h	0-3	
23/2	Portadown	h	1-2	*Black A. (p)*
1/3	Crusaders	a	1-4	*Anderson*
8/3	Linfield	a	0-3	
15/3	Cliftonville	h	1-2	*Black A.*
22/3	Armagh	a	5-2	*Black R., Black A. 2, Miskimmon, Fulton*
25/3	Ballymena	h	2-1	*Fulton, Hamilton*
5/4	Dungannon	a	0-1	
12/4	Limavady	a	3-2	*McLaughlin D. 2, Lag*
19/4	Lisburn	h	1-2	*Miskimmon*
26/4	Donegal Celtic	a	3-4	*Miskimmon, Lagan 2 (*

Name	Nat	Pos	Aps	(s)	Gl
Noel ANDERSON		M	13	(1)	3
Aaron BLACK		D	21		8
Ross BLACK		D	28	(1)	4
Andrew CLEARY		D	28		
Noel CORRIGAN		M	24	(4)	
Jonathan COWAN		D	6	(1)	
Jamie DICKENSON		M		(2)	
Andrew DICKSON		M	13	(6)	
Ryan DOHERTY		D		(1)	
Bertie FULTON		A	27	(1)	4
Pardraig GOLLOGLEY	IRL	D	2		
Paul HAMILTON		D	23		3
Glenn HAND		M	12	(2)	2
Craig HARRIS		D	6	(1)	
Liam HOGAN		D	6	(3)	
Marty HUNTER		M	13	(2)	3
Chris KEENAN		G	22		
Daryl KERNOHAN		D		(4)	
Anthony LAGAN		A	22	(2)	6
Johnny LYNCH		M	1	(4)	
Damien McLAUGHLIN		A	10	(7)	4
Ryan McLOUGHLIN		M	1	(5)	
Mark MISKIMMON		A	6	(5)	3
Kyle MORAN		A	13	(5)	1
Gary RAFFERTY		A	2	(13)	1
Aaron ROBINSON		D	16		
Alex SPACKMAN		G	7		
Marty VERNER		A	7	(1)	1
David WILTON		G	1		

LIMAVADY UNITED FC

Manager – Ollie Mullan

Founded – 1876

2007				
22/9	Donegal Celtic	h	0-1	
29/9	Linfield	a	0-3	
6/10	Institute	h	2-2	*McIlmoyle 2 (2p)*
13/10	Portadown	a	0-2	
20/10	Coleraine	h	0-0	
27/10	Armagh	a	0-1	
2/11	Newry	h	1-3	*Boyd*
10/11	Ballymena	a	0-3	
24/11	Glenavon	h	1-0	*Ferry*
1/12	Dungannon	a	2-0	*McIlmoyle, Boyd*
7/12	Glentoran	h	1-0	*McIlmoyle*
15/12	Lisburn	a	0-5	
22/12	Crusaders	h	1-2	*Tommins*
26/12	Larne	a	2-2	*Curran, McIlmoyle (p*
2008				
1/1	Linfield	h	0-4	
19/1	Institute	a	0-0	
26/1	Portadown	h	0-2	
29/1	Donegal Celtic	a	1-3	*Brown*
1/2	Armagh	h	0-3	
5/2	Cliftonville	a	1-4	*Brown*
16/2	Coleraine	a	0-1	
23/2	Glenavon	a	3-0	*Brown, McIlmoyle, Bo*
14/3	Newry	a	0-3	

?/3	Dungannon	h	1-1	*McIlmoyle*
?/3	Glentoran	a	0-3	
?/3	Ballymena	h	3-1	*Tommins 2, McClean*
?4	Lisburn	h	1-2	*McIlmoyle*
?/4	Larne	h	2-3	*Brown, McIlmoyle*
?/4	Crusaders	a	1-2	*Brown*
?/4	Cliftonville	h	3-1	*McKeever, McIlmoyle, Brown*

ame	Nat	Pos	Aps	(s)	Gls
avid BELL		D	5	(2)	
lan BLAIR		D	1		
att BOYD		A	16	(5)	3
aul BROWN		A	15		6
ary CROSSAN	IRL	M	3	(2)	
atthew CROSSAN	IRL	D	15		
arry CURRAN	IRL	M	15	(2)	1
atthew FERRIS		M		(2)	
artin FERRY		D	24	(1)	1
ugh FRAME	NZL	A	5	(4)	
aul GASTON		D	6	(3)	
e GRAY		M	12	(1)	
ony GRAY		D	1	(1)	
am KEARNEY		M	18	(2)	
oghan KELLY		D	11	(2)	
ephen KELLY		D	1	(1)	
avid KING		M	26		
aul KING		D	2		
onor LYNCH		M	22	(1)	
yan McILMOYLE		M	28		10
eclan McKEEVER		A	6	(4)	1
ian McLEAN		M	4	(1)	1
evor McLERNON		M	12	(2)	
ian McNULTY		D		(1)	
avin McQUEEN		A		(2)	
lenn MILLAR		G	30		
aine MORRISON		M		(1)	
yan MULLAN		D	24		
ephen O'DONNELL	IRL	M	1	(1)	
yan STEWART		A	3	(3)	
areth TOMMINS		A	23	(2)	3
yan TOSH		M	1		

LINFIELD FC

Manager – David Jeffrey

Founded – 1886

MAJOR HONOURS: Irish League – (48) 1891, 1892, 1893, 1895, 1898, 1902, 1904, 1907, 1908, 1909, 1911, 1914, 1922, 1923, 1930, 1932, 1934, 1935, 1949, 1950, 1954, 1955, 1956, 1959, 1961, 1962, 1966, 1969, 1971, 1975, 1978, 1979, 1980, 1982, 1983, 1984, 1985, 1986, 1987, 1989, 1993, 1994, 2000, 2001, 2004, 2006, 2007, 2008; Irish Cup – (39) 1891, 1892, 1893, 1895, 1898, 1899, 1902, 1904, 1912, 1913, 1915, 1916, 1919, 1922, 1923, 1930, 1931, 1934, 1936, 1939, 1942, 1945, 1946, 1948, 1950, 1953, 1960, 1962, 1963, 1970, 1978, 1980, 1982, 1994, 1995, 2002, 2006, 2007, 2008.

2007				
?4/9	Cliftonville	a	2-2	*Ferguson, Stewart*
?9/9	Limavady	h	3-0	*Ferguson 2, O'Kane*
?/10	Portadown	h	1-0	*Thompson*
?3/10	Armagh	a	3-1	*Mouncey 2, Thompson*
?0/10	Ballymena	h	1-0	*Thompson*
?7/10	Dungannon	a	0-4	
?/11	Lisburn	h	2-1	*Dickson, Thompson*
?0/11	Larne	a	5-1	*Thompson 3, Ferguson, Stewart*
?4/11	Donegal Celtic	h	2-0	*Thompson, Bailie*
?7/11	Coleraine	h	4-0	*Ferguson 3 (1p), McAreavey*
?/12	Institute	a	1-0	*Ferguson*
?5/12	Newry	a	3-0	*Murphy, Ferguson (p), Thompson*
?2/12	Glenavon	h	3-2	*Thompson, Ferguson (p), Mulgrew*
?6/12	Glentoran	a	0-1	
?9/12	Crusaders	h	5-0	*Gault, Murphy, Thompson 3*
2008				
1/1	Limavady	a	4-0	*Thompson 4*
7/1	Cliftonville	h	0-0	
19/1	Portadown	a	5-2	*Gault, Thompson 3, Stewart*
26/1	Armagh	h	2-1	*Thompson (p), Murphy*
16/2	Ballymena	a	4-0	*Kearney 2, Mouncey, Thompson*
20/2	Dungannon	h	2-1	*Kearney, Thompson*
23/2	Donegal Celtic	a	1-1	*Ferguson*
8/3	Larne	h	3-0	*Stewart 2, Thompson*
15/3	Lisburn	a	0-0	
22/3	Institute	h	1-0	*Mulgrew*
25/3	Coleraine	a	4-1	*Stewart, Curran, Thompson 2*
5/4	Newry	h	5-0	*Stewart, Ferguson (p), Thompson 2, Dickson*
12/4	Glentoran	h	0-0	
19/4	Glenavon	a	2-0	*Kearney, Thompson*
26/4	Crusaders	a	3-0	*Ferguson 2, Dickson*

Name	Nat	Pos	Aps	(s)	Gls
Noel BAILIE		D	25	(1)	1
Damien CURRAN		M	13	(6)	1
Mark DICKSON		A	8	(13)	3
Stephen DOUGLAS		D	15	(2)	
Conor DOWNEY		M	3	(5)	
Jim ERVIN		D	15	(1)	
Glenn FERGUSON		A	27	(2)	14
Michael GAULT		M	29		2
Oran KEARNEY		M	9	(8)	4
Kris LINDSAY		D	7	(3)	
Alan MANNUS		G	30		
Paul McAREAVEY		M	16	(3)	1
Timothy McCANN		D	1	(1)	
Pat McSHANE		D	16		
Tim MOUNCEY		M	7	(6)	3
Jamie MULGREW		M	18	(2)	2
William MURPHY		D	28	(1)	3
Aiden O'KANE		D	23	(4)	1
Thomas STEWART		A	11	(10)	7
Peter THOMPSON		A	29		29

LISBURN DISTILLERY FC

Manager – Paul Kirk

Founded – 1879

MAJOR HONOURS: Irish League – (6) 1896, 1899, 1901, 1903, 1906, 1963; Irish Cup – (12) 1884, 1885, 1886, 1889, 1894, 1896, 1903, 1905, 1910, 1925, 1956, 1971.

2007				
22/9	Coleraine	a	4-1	*Waterworth 2, Browne 2 (1p)*
29/9	Newry	h	1-0	*Muir*
6/10	Glenavon	a	3-2	*Waterworth, Browne, Ward*
13/10	Glentoran	h	1-2	*Waterworth (p)*
20/10	Crusaders	a	3-1	*Cooling, Armour, Allen*
27/10	Cliftonville	h	1-2	*Browne (p)*
3/11	Linfield	a	1-2	*McCann P.*
10/11	Portadown	h	1-0	*McCann P.*
24/11	Armagh	a	1-4	*McConnell*
7/12	Dungannon	a	3-0	*Browne 3 (1p)*
15/12	Limavady	h	5-0	*Browne, Waterworth, Muir, Buchanan, Shaw*
18/12	Ballymena	h	0-2	
22/12	Larne	h	2-0	*Browne 2*
26/12	Donegal Celtic	a	2-1	*Browne, Waterworth*
29/12	Institute	h	0-0	
2008				
1/1	Newry	a	4-1	*Waterworth 2, McConnell, Cooling*
19/1	Glenavon	h	0-0	
26/12	Glentoran	a	2-2	*Waterworth, Kingsberry*
29/1	Coleraine	h	2-0	*Armour, McCann R.*

1/2	Cliftonville	a	2-2	*McConnell, McCann R.*
16/2	Crusaders	h	1-0	*McConnell*
23/2	Armagh	h	1-0	*McCann R.*
8/3	Portadown	a	1-0	*Muir*
15/3	Linfield	h	0-0	
22/3	Ballymena	a	2-2	*Armour (p), McConnell*
25/3	Dungannon	h	1-1	*Armour*
5/4	Limavady	a	2-1	*Buchanan, Browne*
12/4	Donegal Celtic	h	0-1	
19/4	Larne	a	2-1	*Kilmartin, Browne*
26/4	Institute	a	2-0	*Allen 2*

Name	Nat	Pos	Aps	(s)	Gls
Curtis ALLEN		A	1	(6)	3
Darrne ARMOUR		A	13	(7)	4
Ryan BLAYNEY		D		(1)	
Gary BROWNE		A	20	(2)	13
Wayne BUCHANAN		D	23	(5)	2
Mark COOLING		M	9	(6)	2
Greg DIXON		M		(1)	
Michael FERGUSON		D	10	(2)	
Neil GAWLEY		M	8	(3)	
Aaron JOHNSTON		A		(2)	
Andrew KILMARTIN		M	23	(2)	1
Chris KINGSBERRY		M	14		1
Jonathan MAGEE		D	13	(2)	
Philip MATTHEWS		G	28		
Peter McCANN		D	27		2
Ryan McCANN		M	27		3
Chris McCLUSKEY		G	1		
Nathan McCONNELL		A	12	(11)	5
Jim McMENAMIN		D	5	(4)	
Paul MUIR		D	30		3
Stephen SHAW		A	10	(6)	1
Stuart THOMPSON		D	24	(1)	
Julian WARD	ENG	M	9	(9)	1
Andrew WATERWORTH		A	17		9
Dvaid WILTON		G	1		
James WRIGHT		M	2	(2)	
Dean YOULE		M	3	(9)	

NEWRY CITY FC

Manager – Gerry Flynn

Founded – 1923

2007				
22/9	Dungannon	h	3-0	*Friars S. 2, Willis*
29/9	Lisburn	a	0-1	
6/10	Larne	h	2-2	*Garrett, Feeney L.*
13/10	Donegal Celtic	a	3-2	*Clarke 2, Feeney C.*
20/10	Institute	h	2-1	*Garrett, Anderson*
27/10	Coleraine	a	1-0	*Friars E.*
2/11	Limavady	a	3-1	*Friars E., Friars S., Garrett*
10/11	Glenavon	h	2-1	*Garrett, Friars S.*
24/11	Glentoran	a	1-2	*Garrett*
1/12	Crusaders	h	1-1	*Friars E.*
4/12	Cliftonville	a	0-2	
15/12	Linfield	h	0-3	
22/12	Portadown	a	2-3	*Prigent, Clarke*
26/12	Armagh	h	3-0	*Clarke, Friars S,, Friars E.*
29/12	Ballymena	a	1-2	*Clarke*
2008				
1/1	Lisburn	h	1-4	*Collins*
4/1	Dungannon	a	6-4	*Keegan, Friars E. 2, Hudson, Collins, Clarke*
19/1	Larne	a	0-3	
26/1	Donegal Celtic	h	1-1	*Feeney C.*
4/2	Coleraine	h	0-2	
16/2	Institute	a	2-0	*Friars E., Clarke (p)*
23/2	Glentoran	h	0-3	
8/3	Glenavon	a	0-1	
14/3	Limavady	h	3-0	*Morgan 2, Clarke*
22/3	Crusaders	a	1-4	*McLaughlin*
25/3	Cliftonville	h	1-0	*McLaughlin*
5/4	Linfield	a	0-5	
12/4	Armagh	a	2-1	*Collins, Morgan*
19/4	Portadown	h	2-1	*Garrett, Morgan*
26/4	Ballymena	h	2-2	*McLaughlin, Clarke (p*

Name	Nat	Pos	Aps	(s)	Gls
Tony ANDERSON		A	11	(10)	1
Wayne BROWN		A	2	(8)	
Richard CLARKE		M	29		9
Andrew COLEMAN		G	3		
Michale COLLINS		M	10		3
Ian CURRAN		D	11	(5)	
Paul DONEGAN		D	12	(6)	
Cullen FEENEY		D	22	(1)	2
Lee FEENEY		A	6	(12)	1
Stephen FERGUYSON		M	14	(1)	
Emmett FRIARS		D	28		7
Sean FRIARS		M	18	(4)	5
Stephen GARRETT		A	15	(4)	6
Niall HUDSON	IRL	D	15	(3)	1
Kenny KEARNS		D		(3)	
Kevin KEEGAN		M	15	(5)	1
Darren KING		M	21	(2)	
Cormac McARDLE	IRL	M		(1)	
Joe McDONNELL		M	22	(1)	
Paddy McLAUGHLIN		D	24		3
Chris MORGAN		A	14	(1)	4
Paul PRIGENT		M	7	(7)	1
Robert ROBINSON		G	27		
Tony SMITH		A		(2)	
James WILLIS		A	4	(3)	1

PORTADOWN FC

Manager – Ronnie McFall

Founded - 1924

MAJOR HONOURS: Irish League – (4) 1990, 1991, 1996, 2002; Irish Cup - (3) 1991, 1999, 2005.

2007				
22/9	Crusaders	a	2-0	*Hagan, McCutcheon*
29/9	Cliftonville	h	0-2	
6/10	Linfield	a	0-1	
13/10	Limavady	h	2-0	*Convery, McCann*
20/10	Armagh	h	2-1	*McCutcheon, Smith*
27/10	Ballymena	a	1-2	*McCutcheon*
3/11	Dungannon	h	0-1	
10/11	Lisburn	a	0-1	
24/11	Larne	h	5-1	*Convery, McCutcheon, Topley 2, Smith*
1/12	Donegal Celtic	a	1-0	*McCutcheon*
7/12	Institute	h	2-1	*McCutcheon (p), Smith*
15/12	Coleraine	a	1-1	*McCutcheon*
22/12	Newry	h	3-2	*Braniff, Haire, Smith*
26/12	Glenavon	a	3-0	*McKeown, Smith 2*
29/12	Glentoran	h	0-2	
2008				
5/1	Crusaders	h	2-0	*Topley, McCutcheon*
19/1	Linfield	h	2-5	*Braniff, McCutcheon (p*
26/1	Limavady	a	2-0	*McCutcheon, Boyle*
29/1	Cliftonville	a	1-2	*Liggett*
1/2	Ballymena	h	2-1	*Boyle, og (Haveron)*
16/2	Armagh	a	1-1	*Koudou*
23/2	Larne	a	2-1	*Koudou (p), Liggett*
8/3	Lisburn	h	0-1	
15/3	Dungannon	a	3-0	*Topley, Boyle, Braniff*
22/3	Donegal Celtic	h	2-1	*Liggett 2*
25/3	Institute	a	2-1	*Smith, Topley*
5/4	Coleraine	h	1-5	*McCann*
12/4	Glenavon	h	0-1	
19/4	Newry	a	1-2	*Smith*
26/4	Glentoran	a	1-3	*Smith*

me	Nat	Pos	Aps	(s)	Gls
il ARMSTRONG		G	4	(1)	
rdan BAKER		A		(2)	
esley BOYLE		M	15	(2)	3
vin BRANIFF		A	27		3
chard CLARKE		M	8	(4)	
ris COLEMAN		D	2		
chael COLLINS		M	4		
nn CONVERY		D	25		2
ilip CRAIG		D	24	(1)	
all DERRY		M	1	(9)	
nor HAGAN		M	6		1
ron HAIRE		A		(4)	1
ter KENNEDY		D	15	(2)	
né KOUDOU	CIV	A	6	(1)	2
ry LIGGETT		A	5	(6)	4
nie MARKS		M		(1)	
rc McCANN		M	12	(7)	2
vid McCULLOUGH		M	4	(2)	
ry McCUTCHEON	SCO	A	19	(1)	10
reth McKEOWN		D	23	(2)	1
vid MISKELLY		G	26	(1)	
ith O'HARA		D	24	(1)	
nit PASA	TUR	M	6	(2)	
ss REDMAN		D	28		
dy SMITH		A	16		9
an TEGGART		M	9	(2)	
nny TOPLEY		M	21	(4)	5

PROMOTED CLUBS

BANGOR FC

Manager – Paul Millar

Founded – 1918

MAJOR HONOURS: Irish Cup – (1) 1993.

ECOND LEVEL FINAL TABLE 2007/08

	Pld	W	D	L	F	A	Pts
oughgall FC	22	15	4	3	42	21	49
Dundela FC	22	12	3	7	38	28	39
angor FC	22	10	7	5	43	33	37
allyclare Comrades FC	22	10	6	6	28	17	36
obermore United FC	22	10	5	7	41	32	35
Carrick Rangers FC	22	10	3	9	34	30	33
anbridge Town FC	22	10	2	10	38	38	32
rds FC	22	8	3	11	32	28	27
Coagh United FC	22	7	6	9	27	35	27
larland & Wolff Velders FC	22	6	8	8	19	27	26
urgan Celtic FC	22	5	3	14	22	44	18
ortstewart FC	22	1	6	15	19	50	9

lo automatic promotion or relegation. Bangor admitted into new am Invitational League in 2008/09.

OMESTIC CUP 2007/08

IRISH CUP

FTH ROUND

2/1/08)

ds 1, Brantwood 1
magh 1, Crusaders 5
llyclare 0, Ballymoney 0
nbridge 2, Abbey Villa 3
leraine 1, Tobermore 0
Donegal Celtic 3, Carrick Rangers 0
Dundela 4, Portstewart 0
Glenavon 1, Bangor 2
Glentoran 0, Lisburn 0
Institute 6, Dunmurry 0
Killyleagh 0, Downpatrick 1
Larne 2, Cliftonville 3
Limavady 1, Dungannon 1
Loughgall 0, Linfield 3
Newry 2, Ballymena 2
Portadown 1, Newington 0

Replays

(15/1/08)
Ards 0, Brantwood 1
(16/1/08)
Lisburn 1, Glentoran 3
(22/1/08)
Ballymena 0, Newry 0 *(aet; 4-2 on pens)*
(23/1/08)
Dungannon 2, Limavady 1
(29/1/08)
Ballyclare 1, Ballymoney 0

SIXTH ROUND

(9/2/08)
Ballyclare 2, Institute 2
Cliftonville 1, Crusaders 0
Coleraine 5, Brantwood 1
Donegal Celtic 1, Abbey Villa 0
Dungannon 0, Glentoran 2
Linfield 3, Bangor 0
Newry 1, Dundela 1
Portadown 2, Downpatrick 1

Replays

(12/2/08)
Institute 2, Ballyclare 0
Newry 1, Dundela 0

QUARTER-FINALS

(1/3/08)
Cliftonville 4 *(Martin 51, Scannell C. 58, Murphy 73, Redman 80og)*, Portadown 3 *(Boyle 8, Braniff 49, Convery 87)*
Glentoran 1 *(Hamilton 12)*, Donegal Celtic 2 *(Hamill 7, 23)*
Institute 0, Coleraine 0
Newry 1 *(Willis 16)*, Linfield 1 *(Ferguson 8)*

Replays

(4/3/08)
Coleraine 5 *(Neill 13, Carson 21, McVey 52p, Cassidy 65, Tolan 72)*, Institute 1 *(Philson 4)*
Linfield 4 *(Kearney 2, Ferguson 8, 78p, Thompson 82)*, Newry 0

SEMI-FINALS

(29/3/08)
Cliftonville 1 *(O'Connor 57)*, Linfield 2 *(Mulgrew 28, Thompson 33)*
Coleraine 1 *(Dooley 84)*, Donegal Celtic 1 *(McClean 64)*

Replay

(1/4/08)
Coleraine 2 *(Hunter 14, Patton D. 120)*, Donegal Celtic 1 *(Armstrong 60) (aet)*

FINAL

(3/5/08)
Windsor Park, Belfast
LINFIELD FC 2 *(Thomspon 49, 52)*
COLERAINE FC 1 *(McLaughlin P. 19)*
Referee – *Malcolm*
LINFIELD – *Mannus, Lindsay, O'Kane, Gault, Murphy, McAreavey (Dickson 46), Mulgrew, Kearney (Curran 87), Ferguson, Thompson, Bailie.*
COLERAINE – *O'Hare, Neill, Clanachan, McLaughlin P., McVey, Hunter, Watt (Dooley 75), Patton D., Tolan, McCallion, Carson.*

Brann back in the big time

Norway's second city of Bergen finally had a footballing feat to celebrate in 2007 as local club SK Brann, one of the country's best supported teams, ended a 44-year wait to become national champions for the third time.

It was a thoroughly deserved victory. Brann sustained a high performance level from start to finish and played attractive football. They were especially strong at home, the rebuilt Brann stadium, invariably filled to its 17,824 capacity, proving to be a veritable fortress. Brann dropped only four points there all season, winning eleven of their home matches and drawing the other two. They were in contention from the start, holding their own in the spring and summer and making a confident dart for the line during a

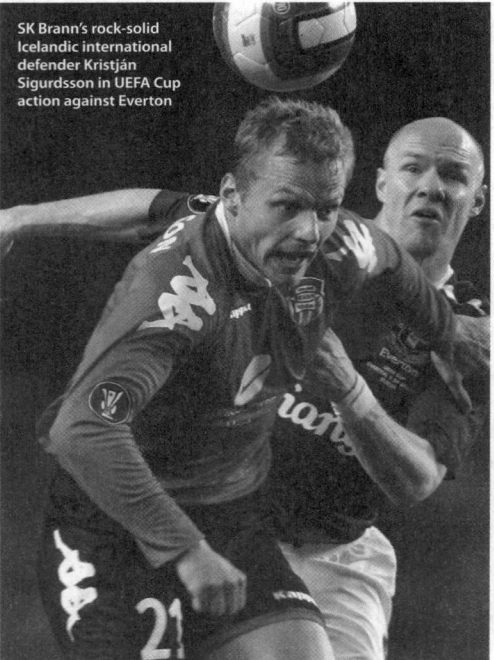

SK Brann's rock-solid Icelandic international defender Kristján Sigurdsson in UEFA Cup action against Everton

magnificent month of September, during which they also eliminated Belgian giants Club Brugge KV from the UEFA Cup. A stunning 5-1 away win over title riva Lillestrøm SK practically put them out of reach, and although a surprise 2-1 defeat at Aalesunds FK delayed the party until the penultimate weekend, th town was painted red in earnest when Brann trounce Viking FK 5-2 in their final home game, with leading marksman Thorstein Helstad consolidating his place the head of the Tippeligaen score charts by supplyin four of the goals.

Brann's head coach Mons Ivar Mjelde, a local man, wa living proof of the virtue of patience. Having been appointed with little coaching experience in January 2003, at a time when Brann had a team that appeare to be going nowhere, he was expected to be jettisoned, like many Brann coaches before him, afte only a short spell at the helm. But the club held their nerve and were rewarded at the end of his fifth seas in charge with the ultimate prize. At the time of the club's triumph, Mjelde was the longest-serving coach in the Tippeligaen.

Inspirational skipper

Brann's on-field inspiration was captain Martin Andresen. The Norwegian international midfielder, who left to become player-coach at Vålerenga Fotbal at the end of the season, was the heart and soul of th side. Alongside him there were also excellent midfiel performances from Petter Vaagan Moen and new signing (from Rosenborg BK) Jan Gunnar Solli. Goalkeeper Håkon Opdal did enough to establish himself as Norway's No1 while in defence the Iceland duo of Ólafur Bjarnason and Kristján Sigurdsson were rock solid. As for the attack, that was led brilliantly by Helstad, who scored as many goals as his shirt numb – 22 – and enjoyed, at 30, the best season of a chequered career.

In addition to their 26 Tippeligaen games, Brann were in action ten times in Europe in 2007, and were still ir

e UEFA Cup at the turn of the year. Indeed, the draw r the round of 16 set up the enticing prospect of an '-Norwegian clash with Rosenborg. Unfortunately, oth clubs went out a round earlier, Brann suffering eavily at the hands of Everton FC while Rosenborg ere eliminated by ACF Fiorentina.

osenborg reached that stage after finishing third in eir UEFA Champions League group, where they erformed very creditably, drawing at Chelsea FC (and fectively getting manager José Mourinho the sack) nd doing a remarkable double over Valencia CF. heir European exploits came at the end of a poor ear domestically, in which they finished fifth in the ppeligaen. Although strong at home, where they gistered a Norwegian-record average gate of 9,903, they suffered repeatedly on their travels. Head oach Knut Tørum, who had received high praise for inning the league title in 2006, was heavily criticised nd lost his job in late October, with assistant Trond enriksen taking over temporarily until Erik Hamrén, e Swedish coach of Danish club Aalborg BK, took ver in June 2008.

tabæk Fotball finished higher than ever before in the ippeligaen, taking the runners-up spot behind Brann. Vith an average attendance at their outdated adderud stadium of just 5,570 – the lowest in the ivision – they overachieved in grand style. Top of the able at the mid-season break, they came unstuck at e restart but recovered well and in their little-and-rge midfield combination of Alanzinho, a tricky razilian, and Somen A. Tchoyi, a giant Cameroonian, ossessed two of the league's outstanding imports. heir Icelandic/Swedish strike partnership was another npressive double act, with Veigar Páll Gunnarsson nd Daniel Nannskog scoring 34 of the team's 53 goals etween them (only slightly down on their 2006 ratio f 37/53).

Canaries' Cup

Viking FK and Lillestrøm SK, who swapped coaches at he start of the season (Uwe Rösler joining Viking and om Nordlie moving to Lillestrøm), finished third and ourth, respectively, but it was Lillestrøm who had the ast laugh by winning the Norwegian Cup for the first ime since 1985. Beaten finalists three times since, the Canaries sang again after winning the final 2-0 against FK Haugesund – the first non-Tippeligaen team to play n the Ullevaal showpiece for a decade. Canadian orward Olivier Occean was the star of the show, scoring both goals.

Thorstein Helstad – the Tippeligaen's top scorer in 2007

Haugesund never came close to winning promotion from the Adeccoligaen. That prize went to Molde FK and HamKam Fotball, who made a direct return a year after relegation, and to FK Bodø/Glimt, the first team for seven years to win promotion via the play-offs. Their victims were Odd Grenland, relegated together with Sandefjord Fotball and – two years after they almost won the league – IK Start.

Disastrous defeat

Norway came close to qualifying for UEFA EURO 2008™ but missed out on a first major tournament for eight years after a calamitous 2-1 home defeat by rivals Turkey in their penultimate fixture. A win in Oslo would have confirmed qualification, and even a draw would have keep them two points ahead of the Turks with just one game remaining. But it was not to be. On a misty night in the Norwegian capital, with the Ullevaal

NORWAY

Norges Fotballforbund (NFF)

Servicebok 1
Ullevaal stadion
NO-0840 Oslo
tel - +47 210 29300
fax - +47 210 29301
website - www.fotball.no
email - nff@fotball.no
Year of Formation – 1902
President - Sondre Kåfjord
General Secretary - Karen Espelund
Press Officer – Jon Jamessen
Stadium - Ullevaal, Oslo (25,300)

INTERNATIONAL TOURNAMENT APPEARANCES
FIFA World Cup - (3) 1938, 1994, 1998 (2nd round).
UEFA European Championship - (1) 2000.

TOP FIVE ALL-TIME CAPS
Thorbjørn Svenssen (103); Henning Berg (100); Erik Thorstvedt (97); Øyvind Leonhardsen (86); Kjetil Rekdal (83)

TOP FIVE ALL-TIME GOALS
Jørgen Juve (33); Einar Gundersen (26); Harald Hennum (25); Tore André Flo & Ole Gunnar Solskjær (23)

NATIONAL TEAM RESULTS 2007/08

22/8/07	Argentina	H	Oslo	2-1	*Carew (11p, 58)*
8/9/07	Moldova (ECQ)	A	Chisinau	1-0	*Iversen (48)*
12/9/07	Greece (ECQ)	H	Oslo	2-2	*Carew (15), Riise J.A. (39)*
17/10/07	Bosnia-Herzegovina (ECQ)	A	Sarajevo	2-0	*Hagen (5), Riise B.H. (74)*
17/11/07	Turkey (ECQ)	H	Oslo	1-2	*Hagen (12)*
21/11/07	Malta (ECQ)	A	Ta' Qali	4-1	*Iversen (25, 27p, 45), Gamst Pedersen (75)*
6/2/08	Wales	A	Wrexham	0-3	
26/3/08	Montenegro	A	Podgorica	1-3	*Carew (72)*
28/5/08	Uruguay	H	Oslo	2-2	*Elyounoussi (50), Riise J.A. (85)*

packed to the rafters, Åge Hareide's team could not deliver. They got off to a great start when centre-back Erik Hagen put them in front with a superb overhead kick, but a goalkeeping error (one of many suffered during the campaign) gifted Turkey an equaliser, and Nihat Kahveci won the game for the visitors with an outstanding individual goal in the second half.

There was still a glimmer of hope for Norway, who knew that they would qualify if they won in Malta and Turkey failed to do likewise at home to Bosnia-Herzegovina. But it proved forlorn. While Steffen Iversen fired a hat-trick to help Norway to a 4-1 victory on the Mediterranean island, Nihat reinforced his role as Norway's nemesis with the only goal in Istanbul.

Despite the disappointment, Hareide, who was appointed in January 2004, kept hold of his job, signing a new two-year contract. His next task is to negotiate a 2010 FIFA World Cup qualifying programme that sees the Scandinavians placed in the only five-team group – alongside the Netherlands, FYR Macedonia, Iceland and Scotland. Clearly it will be tough for Norway to top that section and take the sole automatic qualifying place, but a play-off place is within the team's grasp and Hareide will expect big performances on the road to South Africa from key players such as John Carew, Morten Gamst Pedersen, John Arne Riise and Brede Hangeland, all of whom spent the 2007/08 season living the high life in the English Premier League.

ATIONAL TEAM APPEARANCES 2007/08

ch – Åge HAREIDE	23/9/53		Arg	MDA	GRE	BIH	TUR	MLT	Wal	Mne	Uru	Caps	Goals
on André OPDAL	11/6/82	Brann	G46	G	G	G	G	G	G46	G		12	-
André STORBÆK	21/9/78	Vålerenga	D	D	D	D	D88	D	D	D46	s79	17	-
ny JOHNSEN	10/6/69	Vålerenga	D									62	3
e HANGELAND	20/6/81	København (DEN)	D	D	D	D	D	D					
		/Fulham (ENG)							D61	D	D	44	-
Arne RIISE	24/9/80	Liverpool (ENG)	D	D	D	D	D	D	D	D	D	71	8
n Helge RIISE	21/6/83	Lillestrøm	M73	M	M93	M92	M	M75				9	1
tin ANDRESEN	2/2/77	Brann	M	M	M	M							
		/Vålerenga							M	M46	M83	39	3
tofer HÆSTAD	9/12/83	Start	M				M68	s75					
		/Vålerenga							s46	s77		24	1
iel Omoya BRAATEN	25/5/82	Bolton (ENG)	A90			s76			A			16	2
CAREW	5/9/79	Aston Villa (ENG)	A83	A	A		A	A68	A46	A	A	71	21
ten GAMST PEDERSEN	8/9/81	Blackburn (ENG)	A73	A	A	M	A	A	A	M46	A70	40	8
e Almenning JARSTEIN	29/9/84	Odd Grenland	s46										
		/Rosenborg							s46		G	3	-
kander TETTEY	4/4/86	Rosenborg	s73				M					2	-
Iver STRAND	7/5/83	Tromsø	s73									4	-
Gunnar SOLLI	19/4/81	Brann	s83		M70	M				M77	A76	34	1
n Anders BJØRKØY	8/1/79	Fredrikstad	s90			s92			s77			4	-
il WÆHLER	16/3/76	Vålerenga		D66								3	-
stian GRINDHEIM	17/7/83	Vålerenga		M		M58							
		/Heerenveen (NED)							s46		M46	17	-
fen IVERSEN	10/11/76	Rosenborg		A68	A80		A84	A84		s46		73	19
ar RISETH	21/4/72	Rosenborg		s66	s80			M				52	4
rstein HELSTAD	28/4/77	Brann		s68	s70	A76	s84	s68				29	9
HAGEN	20/7/75	Zenit (RUS)			D	D	D	D				28	3
de KIPPE	17/1/78	Lillestrøm			s93				s61			8	-
urd RUSHFELDT	11/12/72	Tromsø				s58	s88	s84				38	7
Ciljan SKJELBRED	16/6/87	Rosenborg					s68	M		M	M46	5	-
Modou KAH	30/7/80	Roda (NED)							D			10	1
drik STRØMSTAD	20/1/82	Start							M46	M77	s46	15	2
NEVLAND	10/11/77	Fulham (ENG)							M77	s77	s70	6	-
e REGINIUSSEN	10/6/86	Tromsø								D	D	2	-
Inge HØILAND	20/9/77	Stabæk								s46	D79	15	-
k BAKKE	13/9/77	Brann								s46		27	-
k ELYOUNOUSSI	23/2/88	Fredrikstad									s46	1	1
lim DEMIDOV	10/10/86	Rosenborg									s76	1	-
ar KARADAS	9/8/81	Brann									s83	10	1

NORWAY

DOMESTIC LEAGUE 2007

TIPPELIGAEN FINAL LEAGUE TABLE

	Pld	Home W	D	L	F	A	Away W	D	L	F	A	Total W	D	L	F	A	Pts
1 SK Brann	26	11	2	0	37	14	6	1	6	22	25	17	3	6	59	39	54
2 Stabæk Fotball	26	8	3	2	27	16	6	3	4	26	19	14	6	6	53	35	48
3 Viking FK	26	9	4	0	28	11	5	1	7	22	29	14	5	7	50	40	47
4 Lillestrøm SK	26	7	3	3	28	15	5	5	3	19	13	12	8	6	47	28	44
5 Rosenborg BK	26	9	3	1	34	13	3	2	8	19	26	12	5	9	53	39	41
6 Tromsø IL	26	8	2	3	23	16	4	2	7	22	28	12	4	10	45	44	40
7 Vålerenga Fotball	26	6	5	2	19	14	4	1	8	15	20	10	6	10	34	34	36
8 Fredrikstad FK	26	8	3	2	22	14	1	6	6	15	26	9	9	8	37	40	36
9 FC Lyn Oslo	26	9	2	2	31	16	1	2	10	12	30	10	4	12	43	46	34
10 Strømsgodset IF	26	4	3	6	19	26	4	3	6	15	21	8	6	12	34	47	30
11 Aalesunds FK	26	6	1	6	25	27	3	2	8	15	29	9	3	14	40	56	30
12 Odd Grenland	26	5	0	8	17	19	3	3	7	16	24	8	3	15	33	43	27
13 IK Start	26	4	5	4	17	15	2	3	8	17	29	6	8	12	34	44	26
14 Sandefjord Fotball	26	4	1	8	21	24	0	3	10	5	29	4	4	18	26	53	16

TOP GOALSCORERS

22 Thorstein HELSTAD (Brann)
19 Daniel NANNSKOG (Stabæk)
18 Peter IJEH (Viking)
15 Veigar Páll GUNNARSSON (Stabæk)
13 Steffen IVERSEN (Rosenborg)
12 Olivier OCCEAN (Lillestrøm)
Morten MOLDSKRED (Tromsø)
10 Arild SUNDGOT (Lillestrøm)
9 Tarik ELYOUNOUSSI (Fredrikstad)
Yssouf KONÉ (Rosenborg)
Morten BERRE (Vålerenga)

CLUB-BY-CLUB

AALESUNDS FK

Coach – Per Joar Hansen

Founded – 1914

2007

9/4	Start	h	2-4	*Austnes, Skiri*
15/4	Sandefjord	a	0-3	
22/4	Fredrikstad	h	3-3	*Ørsal 2, Kihlberg*
29/4	Odd Grenland	a	0-3	
7/5	Lillestrøm	h	1-3	*Kihlberg*
13/5	Lyn	a	0-0	
16/5	Strømsgodset	a	4-0	*Aarøy, Kihlberg, Fredriksen, Austnes*
28/5	Viking	h	0-2	
10/6	Tromsø	a	2-0	*Olsen, Aarøy*
17/6	Stabæk	h	1-4	*Olsen*
20/6	Brann	a	1-2	*Fjørtoft*
23/6	Vålerenga	h	1-0	*Aarøy*
2/7	Rosenborg	a	2-2	*Aubynn, Brown*
22/7	Start	a	2-1	*Aarøy 2*
29/7	Sandefjord	h	4-1	*Parr, Olsen, Gudmundsson, Bahoken (p)*
5/8	Fredrikstad	a	1-2	*Silva*
12/8	Odd Grenland	h	2-1	*Silva 2*
26/8	Lillestrøm	a	0-7	
2/9	Lyn	h	3-1	*Austnes, Aubynn, Skiri*
17/9	Strømsgodset	h	3-2	*Silva (p), Kibebe, Aubynn*
22/9	Viking	a	0-3	
30/9	Tromsø	h	2-3	*Aubynn 2 (1p)*
7/10	Stabæk	a	2-4	*Skiri, Austnes*
20/10	Brann	h	2-1	*Skiri, Aarøy*
28/10	Vålerenga	a	1-2	*Austnes*
3/11	Rosenborg	h	1-2	*og (Koppinen)*

No	Name	Nat	Pos	Aps	(s)	Gls
8	Tor Hogne AARØY		A	19	(1)	6
13	Joakim ALEXANDERSSON	SWE	D	2	(3)	
23	Jeffrey AUBYNN	SWE	A	11		5
10	Joakim Rune AUSTNES		M	24		5
15	Gustave BAHOKEN	CMR	D	19		1
24	Adin BROWN	USA	G	21		1
18	Karl Oskar FJØRTOFT		M	19	(5)	1
7	Trond FREDRIKSEN		M	14	(10)	1
3	Haraldur GUDMUNDSSON	ISL	D	22		1
5	Erlend HOLM		M	5	(5)	
16	Enar JÄÄGER	EST	D	17	(2)	
4	Benjamin KIBEBE	SWE	D	26		1
77	Magnus KIHLBERG	SWE	M	16	(1)	3
19	Peter Orry LARSEN		M		(2)	
12	Andreas LIE		G	5		
20	Mattias NYLUND	SWE	D	6	(3)	
17	Lasse OLSEN		A	11	(8)	3
14	Jonathan PARR		M	5	(14)	1
21	Thomas PEDERSEN		M		(3)	
11	Håvard SAKARIASSEN		A	7	(1)	
22	Denis SELIMOVIČ	SVN	M		(4)	
25	Diego SILVA	BRA	A	9	(5)	4
2	Amund SKIRI		D	23	(2)	4
6	Peter WERNI		D		(1)	
11	Dag Roar ØRSAL		M	5	(2)	2

SK BRANN

Coach – Mons Ivar Mjelde

Founded – 1908

MAJOR HONOURS: Norwegian League – (3) 1962, 1963, 2007; Norwegian Cup – (6) 1923, 1925, 1972, 1976, 1982, 2004.

2007

10/4	Stabæk	a	1-0	*Helstad*
16/4	Strømsgodset	h	3-1	*Helstad 2, Winters*
22/4	Vålerenga	h	4-1	*Sæternes 4*
29/4	Rosenborg	a	0-3	
5/5	Start	h	2-2	*Andresen, Vaagan Moen*
12/5	Sandefjord	a	3-2	*Helstad, Winters, Sigurdsson*
16/5	Fredrikstad	h	2-2	*Corrales, Helstad*
28/5	Odd Grenland	a	2-0	*Sigurdsson, Winters*
10/6	Lillestrøm	h	3-1	*Andresen (p), Helstad 2*
16/6	Lyn	a	0-6	
20/6	Aalesund	h	2-1	*Vaagan Moen, Sæternes*
24/6	Viking	a	1-3	*Andresen (p)*

7	Tromsø	h	2-1	*Vaagan Moen, Andresen (p)*
/7	Stabæk	h	3-0	*Helstad 3*
/7	Strømsgodset	a	4-2	*Sigurdsson, Helstad 3*
8	Vålerenga	a	0-2	
/8	Rosenborg	h	3-2	*Winters 2, Bakke*
/8	Start	a	1-1	*Björnsson*
9	Sandefjord	h	1-0	*Sigurdsson*
/9	Fredrikstad	a	4-0	*El Fakiri, Karadas, Helstad 2*
/9	Odd Grenland	h	4-0	*Andresen (p), Huseklepp, Vaagan Moen, Helstad*
)/9	Lillestrøm	a	5-1	*Vaagan Moen, Björnsson, Andresen (p), Helstad, Solli*
10	Lyn	h	3-1	*Helstad, Karadas 2*
)/10	Aalesund	a	1-2	*Solli*
/10	Viking	h	5-2	*Karadas, Helstad 4 (1p)*
11	Tromsø	a	0-3	

o	Name	Nat	Pos	Aps	(s)	Gls
	Martin ANDRESEN		M	23		6
7	Eirik BAKKE		M	6	(4)	1
3	Ólafur Örn BJARNASON	ISL	D	23	(1)	
3	Armann Smári BJÖRNSSON	ISL	A	7	(8)	2
	Ramiro CORRALES	USA	D	8	(3)	1
	Bjørn DAHL		D	13	(2)	
	Hassan EL FAKIRI		M	5	(4)	1
	Ardian GASHI		M	9	(2)	
	Cato GUNTVEIT		D	16		
5	Erlend HANSTVEIT		D	18	(1)	
	Helge HAUGEN		M	1	(3)	
2	Thorstein HELSTAD		A	23	(1)	22
3	Erik HUSEKLEPP		M	4	(18)	1
4	Tijan JAITEH	GAM	M	7	(4)	
	Azar KARADAS		A	2	(6)	4
0	Trond Fredrik LUDVIGSEN		M		(1)	
2	Håkon André OPDAL		G	25		
1	Kristján Örn SIGURDSSON	ISL	D	24	(1)	4
6	Joakim SJÖHAGE	SWE	A	1	(2)	
	Jan Gunnar SOLLI		M	25		2
0	Bengt SÆTERNES		A	8	(2)	5
	Johan THORBJØRNSEN		G	1	(2)	
1	Petter VAAGAN MOEN		M	24	(1)	5
6	Knut WALDE		D	1	(2)	
7	Robbie WINTERS	SCO	A	12	(7)	5

FREDRIKSTAD FK

Coach – Anders Grönhagen (SWE)

Founded – 1903

MAJOR HONOURS: Norwegian League – (9) 1938, 1939, 1949, 1951, 1952, 1954, 1957, 1960, 1961; Norwegian Cup – (11) 1932, 1935, 1936, 1938, 1940, 1950, 1957, 1961, 1966, 1984, 2006.

007				
/4	Lillestrøm	a	0-3	
4/4	Lyn	h	3-1	*Hoås, Elyounoussi, West*
2/4	Aalesund	a	3-3	*Bjørkøy 2 (1p), Elyounoussi*
9/4	Viking	h	2-0	*Elyounoussi, Prytz*
/5	Tromsø	a	1-4	*Bjørkøy*
3/5	Stabæk	h	1-2	*Bjørkøy*
6/5	Brann	a	2-2	*Piiroja 2*
6/5	Vålerenga	h	1-0	*Jóhansson*
0/6	Rosenborg	a	1-1	*Elyounoussi*
7/6	Start	h	3-0	*Fofana, Elyounoussi, Jóhansson*
0/6	Sandefjord	a	2-2	*Kvisvik, Jóhansson*
4/6	Strømsgodset	a	1-2	*Piiroja*
/7	Odd Grenland	h	1-1	*Bjørkøy (p)*
2/7	Lillestrøm	h	0-0	
0/7	Lyn	a	0-0	
/8	Aalesund	h	2-1	*Gashi, Bjørkøy*
12/8	Viking	a	2-2	*Gashi, Kvisvik*
26/8	Tromsø	h	2-1	*Gashi, Elyounoussi*
3/9	Stabæk	a	2-0	*Bjørkøy (p), Tegström*
16/9	Brann	h	0-4	
24/9	Vålerenga	a	0-2	
30/9	Rosenborg	h	4-3	*Gashi 2, Elyounoussi, Jóhansson*
6/10	Start	a	1-3	*Jóhansson*
21/10	Sandefjord	h	2-0	*Elyounoussi 2*
28/10	Strømsgodset	h	1-1	*Tegström*
3/11	Odd Grenland	a	0-2	

No	Name	Nat	Pos	Aps	(s)	Gls
18	Christian BERG		M		(4)	
23	John Anders BJØRKØY		M	25		7
25	Erik BRÅTHEN		G		(1)	
2	Pål André CZWARTEK		D	22	(1)	
13	Tarik ELYOUNOUSSI		A	25		9
20	Ismael Beko FOFANA	CIV	A	15	(8)	1
21	Ardian GASHI		M	11		5
3	Patrik GERRBRAND	SWE	D	25		
10	Øyvind HOÅS		A	2	(6)	1
27	Gardar JÓHANSSON	ISL	A	14	(4)	5
26	Serge Konan KOUADIO	CIV	A	3	(5)	
14	Raymond KVISVIK		M	15	(5)	2
17	Vidar MARTINSEN		D	6		
7	Ciaran MARTYN	IRL	M	5	(3)	
24	Miikka MULTAHARJO	FIN	M	11	(4)	
9	Raio PIIROJA	EST	D	21	(1)	3
15	Anders PRYTZ	SWE	D	11		1
6	Hans Erik RAMBERG		M	13	(7)	
1	Rami SHAABAN	SWE	G	23		
5	Agim SHABANI		D	2	(5)	
22	Johan SJÖBERG	SWE	D	11		
19	Anders STADHEIM		M	2	(4)	
12	Lasse STAW		G	3	(1)	
19	Andreas TEGSTRÖM	SWE	A	5	(1)	2
21	Mihály TÓTH	HUN	A	1		
22	Hermanni VUORINEN	FIN	A		(1)	
7	Kasey WEHRMAN	AUS	M	11		
11	Brian WEST	USA	A	4	(9)	1

LILLESTRØM SK

Coach – Tom Nordlie

Founded – 1917

MAJOR HONOURS: Norwegian League (5) 1959, 1976, 1977, 1986, 1989; Norwegian Cup – (5) 1977, 1978, 1981, 1985, 2007.

2007				
9/4	Fredrikstad	h	3-0	*Occean, Sundgot, Riise*
15/4	Odd Grenland	a	1-0	*Occean*
23/4	Strømsgodset	a	1-1	*Occean*
30/4	Lyn	h	3-1	*Myklebust, Wehrman, Sundgot*
7/5	Aalesund	a	3-1	*Sundgot, og (Kibebe), Myklebust*
13/5	Viking	h	4-1	*Myklebust 2, Riise, Occean*
16/5	Tromsø	a	1-2	*Sundgot (p)*
28/5	Stabæk	h	1-1	*Brenne*
10/6	Brann	a	1-3	*Occean*
17/6	Vålerenga	h	0-1	
21/6	Rosenborg	a	1-1	*Occean*
24/6	Start	h	1-0	*Occean*
1/7	Sandefjord	a	2-0	*Søgård, Brenne*
22/7	Fredrikstad	a	0-0	
28/7	Odd Grenland	h	1-1	*Søgård*
6/8	Strømsgodset	h	2-0	*Myklebust, Sundgot*
12/8	Lyn	a	4-0	*Occean 2, Mouelhi 2 (1p)*
26/8	Aalesund	h	7-0	*Sundgot 3, Stefanutto, Occean 2, og (Skiri)*
2/9	Viking	a	1-1	*Riise*
16/9	Tromsø	h	0-3	

NORWAY

23/9	Stabæk	a	1-3	*Sundgot*
30/9	Brann	h	1-5	*Myklebust*
7/10	Vålerenga	a	3-1	*Occean, Sundgot, Brenne*
21/10	Rosenborg	h	4-1	*Andresen, Søgård, Brenne, Myklebust*
28/10	Start	a	0-0	
3/11	Sandefjord	h	1-1	*Mouelhi (p)*

No	Name	Nat	Pos	Aps	(s)	Gls
23	Pål Steffen ANDRESEN		D	23		1
4	Eirik BERTHEUSSEN		D		(1)	
14	Simen BRENNE		M	21	(2)	4
21	Karim ESSEDIRI	TUN	A		(8)	
26	Otto FREDRIKSON	FIN	G	13		
12	Tore Andreas GUNDERSEN		A		(3)	
8	Martin HUSÁR	SVK	M		(1)	
5	Dan Anton JOHANSEN	DEN	D	5	(5)	
15	Marius JOHNSEN		D	7	(2)	
20	Markus KIESENEBNER	AUT	M		(1)	
13	Frode KIPPE		D	18		
25	Khaled MOUELHI	TUN	M	18	(2)	3
1	Heinz MÜLLER	GER	G	13		
11	Magnus MYKLEBUST		A	22	(3)	7
30	Olivier OCCEAN	CAN	A	25		12
2	Anders RAMBEKK		D	26		
10	Bjørn Helge RIISE		A	24		3
3	Shane STEFANUTTO	AUS	D	23	(3)	1
6	Pål STRAND		A	2	(8)	
18	Arild SUNDGOT		A	17	(9)	10
7	Espen SØGÅRD		M	20	(6)	3
17	Kasey WEHRMAN	AUS	M	9	(3)	1

FC LYN OSLO

Coach – Henning Berg

Founded – 1896

MAJOR HONOURS: Norwegian League – (2) 1964, 1968; Norwegian Cup – (8) 1908, 1909, 1910, 1911, 1945, 1946, 1967, 1968.

2007				
9/4	Sandefjord	h	3-0	*Powell, Tessem (p), Larsen*
14/4	Fredrikstad	a	1-3	*Bala*
22/4	Odd Grenland	h	3-1	*Sokolowski, Holmen 2*
30/4	Lillestrøm	a	1-3	*Gíslason*
6/5	Strømsgodset	a	1-1	*Hoff*
13/5	Aalesund	h	0-0	
16/5	Viking	a	2-4	*Stensaas, Ogbuke*
28/5	Tromsø	h	4-3	*Hoff, Powell, Ogbuke, Knudtzon*
10/6	Stabæk	a	2-3	*Stensaas, Knudtzon*
16/6	Brann	h	6-0	*Powell, Ogbuke, Gíslason 3 (2p), Knudtzon*
20/6	Vålerenga	a	0-0	
25/6	Rosenborg	h	2-1	*Ogbuke 2*
1/7	Start	a	1-0	*Knudsen*
21/7	Sandefjord	a	1-3	*Tessem*
30/7	Fredrikstad	h	0-0	
5/8	Odd Grenland	a	0-2	
12/8	Lillestrøm	h	0-4	
26/8	Strømsgodset	h	1-0	*Hoff*
2/9	Aalesund	a	1-3	*Holmen*
16/9	Viking	h	2-3	*Hoff, Ighalo*
23/9	Tromsø	a	1-2	*Hoff*
30/9	Stabæk	h	3-2	*Berntsen, Hoff, Knudsen*
8/10	Brann	a	1-3	*Brink*
21/10	Vålerenga	h	3-1	*Simonsen, Ighalo, Holmen*
28/10	Rosenborg	a	0-3	
3/11	Start	h	4-1	*Ighalo, Knudsen, Sokolowski 2*

No	Name	Nat	Pos	Aps	(s)	Gls
25	Matias Jesus ALMEYDA	ARG	M		(2)	
11	Ezekiel BALA	NGA	A	1	(6)	1
	Jo Inge BERGET		A		(3)	
22	Tommy BERNTSEN		D	10	(2)	1
6	Christian BRINK		D	20	(3)	1
24	Johan DAHLIN	SWE	G	3	(1)	
29	Mads DAHM		D	1	(8)	
2	Rasmus DAUGAARD	DEN	D	2	(1)	
23	Lars-Kristian ERIKSEN		D	15		
8	Stefán GÍSLASON	ISL	M	12		4
1	Eddie GUSTAFSSON	SWE	G	23		
8	Emil HALLFREDSSON	ISL	M		(1)	
16	Espen HOFF		M	22	(1)	6
14	Kim Kristian HOLMEN		A	9	(12)	4
20	Odion Jude IGHALO	NGA	A	6	(1)	3
18	Bjarne K. INGEBRETSEN		A		(4)	
26	Endre Fotland KNUDSEN		M	6	(2)	3
15	Erling KNUDTZON		M	17	(3)	3
13	Kevin LARSEN		D	3	(6)	1
19	Dylan MACALLISTER	AUS	A	4	(1)	
17	Kim André MADSEN		D	7	(4)	
25	Paul OBIEFULE	NGA	M	6		
20	Chinedu Obasi OGBUKE	NGA	A	11		5
9	Enrique ORTIZ	ARG	D	7		
10	Magnus POWELL	SWE	A	14	(4)	3
4	Indridi SIGURDSSON	ISL	D	20		
27	Magne SIMONSEN		M	6	(1)	1
7	Tomasz SOKOLOWSKI		M	19	(2)	3
5	Ståle STENSAAS		D	20		2
21	Jo TESSEM		A	22	(2)	2

ODD GRENLAND

Coach – Arne Sandstø & Gaute Larsen; (28/9/07) Ove Flindt Bjerg (DEN)

Founded – 1894

MAJOR HONOURS: Norwegian Cup – (12) 1903, 1904, 1905, 1906, 191 1915, 1919, 1922, 1924, 1926, 1931, 2000.

2007				
9/4	Strømsgodset	a	1-2	*De Ornelas*
15/4	Lillestrøm	h	0-1	
22/4	Lyn	a	1-3	*Gulsvik*
29/4	Aalesund	h	3-0	*Ruud (p), Gulsvik, Pospě*
6/5	Viking	a	1-2	*Borchers*
13/5	Tromsø	h	0-1	
16/5	Stabæk	a	0-1	
28/5	Brann	h	0-2	
10/6	Vålerenga	a	1-1	*Gulsvik*
18/6	Rosenborg	h	1-2	*Nilsson (p)*
21/6	Start	a	2-1	*Pospěch, Ruud*
24/6	Sandefjord	h	4-0	*Sørensen 2, og (Adrianc Dale*
1/7	Fredrikstad	a	1-1	*Ruud*
22/7	Strømsgodset	h	0-1	
28/7	Lillestrøm	a	1-1	*Ruud*
5/8	Lyn	h	2-0	*Pospěch, Bärlin*
12/8	Aalesund	a	1-2	*Akabueze*
26/8	Viking	h	1-3	*Akabueze*
2/9	Tromsø	a	4-2	*Ruud, Bärlin 2, Sørense*
16/9	Stabæk	h	1-5	*Ruud (p)*
23/9	Brann	a	0-4	
30/9	Vålerenga	h	1-4	*Ruud*
7/10	Rosenborg	a	1-4	*Pospěch*
21/10	Start	h	2-0	*Fevang, Bärlin*
28/10	Sandefjord	a	2-0	*Bärlin 2*
3/11	Fredrikstad	h	2-0	*Ruud, Bärlin*

No	Name	Nat	Pos	Aps	(s)	Gls
26	Chukwuma AKABUEZE	NGA	A	1	(8)	2
16	Jan Tore AMUNDSEN		M	13	(6)	
13	Stefan BÄRLIN	SWE	A	10	(2)	7
8	Nat BORCHERS	USA	D	19		1
20	Tarjei DALE		A	2	(5)	1
2	Fernando DE ORNELAS	VEN	A	12	(4)	1
25	Marius ENGER		A		(1)	

	Morten FEVANG		M	11		1
3	Fredrik GULSVIK		A	7	(14)	3
1	Steffen HAGEN		D	15	(2)	
5	Torjus HANSÉN		D	17	(1)	
1	Petter Bruer HANSSEN		M	16	(4)	
	Olof HVIDÉN-WATSON	SWE	A	1	(5)	
2	Espen ISAKSEN		G	1	(2)	
2	Rune Almenning JARSTEIN		G	25		
4	Christopher JOYCE	ENG	A		(2)	
	Tuomo KÖNÖNEN	FIN	D	24		
0	Magnus LEKVEN		M	2	(5)	
4	André MURI		D	13		
	Per NILSSON	SWE	D	12		1
2	Zbyněk POSPĚCH	CZE	A	17	(2)	4
8	Espen RUUD		M	23		8
7	Sven Fredrik STRAY		D	1		
	Tommy SVINDAL LARSEN		M	19		
9	Jacob SØRENSEN	DEN	M	21	(4)	3
	Trond Viggo TORESEN		M	4	(6)	

ROSENBORG BK

Coach – Knut Tørum; (25/10/07) Trond Henriksen

Founded – 1917

MAJOR HONOURS: Norwegian League – (20) 1967, 1969, 1971, 1985, 988, 1990, 1992, 1993, 1994, 1995, 1996, 1997, 1998, 1999, 2000, 2001, 2002, 2003, 2004, 2006; Norwegian Cup – (9) 1960, 1964, 1971, 1988, 1990, 1992, 1995, 1999, 2003.

007				
/4	Viking	a	1-1	*Sapara*
5/4	Tromsø	h	4-3	*Skjelbred, Iversen 2, Tettey*
1/4	Stabæk	a	1-2	*Koppinen*
9/4	Brann	h	3-0	*Sapara 2, Koppinen*
/5	Vålerenga	a	1-2	*Iversen (p)*
3/5	Strømsgodset	h	1-2	*Iversen (p)*
6/5	Start	h	4-1	*Ya 2, Braaten, Iversen*
7/5	Sandefjord	a	2-1	*Ya, Iversen*
0/6	Fredrikstad	h	1-1	*Koppinen*
8/6	Odd Grenland	a	2-1	*Skjelbred, Ya*
1/6	Lillestrøm	h	1-1	*Storflor*
5/6	Lyn	a	1-2	*Sapara*
/7	Aalesund	h	2-2	*Iversen, Braaten*
2/7	Viking	h	4-2	*Ya 2, Iversen 2*
8/7	Tromsø	a	1-2	*Tettey*
/8	Stabæk	h	3-0	*Iversen (p), Koppinen, Koné*
1/8	Brann	a	2-3	*Traoré, Riseth*
5/8	Vålerenga	h	2-0	*Tettey, Koné*
/9	Strømsgodset	a	1-1	*Koné*
5/9	Start	a	1-2	*Dorsin*
3/9	Sandefjord	h	2-0	*Strand, Koné*
0/9	Fredrikstad	a	3-4	*Iversen 3 (1p)*
/10	Odd Grenland	h	4-1	*Koné 2 (1p), Tettey, Sapara (p)*
1/10	Lillestrøm	a	1-4	*Koné (p)*
8/10	Lyn	h	3-0	*Koné, Strand, Sapara*
/11	Aalesund	a	2-1	*Koné, Sapara*

lo	Name	Nat	Pos	Aps	(s)	Gls
1	Jo Sondre AAS		A		(3)	
	Ole Christer BASMA		D	16	(2)	
5	Daniel Omoya BRAATEN		A	12	(3)	2
3	Mikael DORSIN	SWE	D	23		1
3	Lars HIRSCHFELD	CAN	G	26		
4	Steffen IVERSEN		A	20	(3)	13
3	Michael JAMTFALL		A	1	(4)	
	Yssouf KONÉ	BFA	A	12	(7)	9
	Miika KOPPINEN	FIN	D	19		4
6	Bjørn Tore KVARME		D	8	(4)	
8	Alejandro LAGO	URU	D	3	(1)	
2	Andreas NORDVIK		D	1	(3)	
0	Vidar RISETH		D	11	(3)	1
27	Marek SAPARA	SVK	M	26		7
15	Per Ciljan SKJELBRED		M	17	(8)	2
4	Fredrik STOOR	SWE	D	14	(7)	
17	Øyvind STORFLOR		A	6	(8)	1
6	Roar STRAND		M	20		2
19	Alexander TETTEY		M	22	(1)	4
20	Abdou Razack TRAORÉ	CIV	A	15	(3)	1
8	Didier Konán YA	CIV	A	14	(6)	6

SANDEFJORD FOTBALL

Coach – Tor Thodesen

Founded – 1998

2007				
9/4	Lyn	a	0-3	
15/4	Aalesund	h	3-0	*Thorsen, Isaksen, Knarvik*
22/4	Viking	a	0-0	
29/4	Tromsø	h	2-1	*Madsen, Tegström*
6/5	Stabæk	a	1-1	*Arkivuo*
12/5	Brann	h	2-3	*Adriano, og (Sigurdsson)*
16/5	Vålerenga	a	0-2	
27/5	Rosenborg	h	1-2	*Knarvik (p)*
11/6	Start	a	1-3	*Isaksen*
17/6	Strømsgodset	h	0-1	
20/6	Fredrikstad	h	2-2	*Adriano 2*
24/6	Odd Grenland	a	0-4	
1/7	Lillestrøm	h	0-2	
21/7	Lyn	h	3-1	*Arkivuo 2, Knarvik*
29/7	Aalesund	a	1-4	*Adriano*
5/8	Viking	h	4-1	*Jensen, Zanetti, og (Gaarde), Knarvik*
12/8	Tromsø	a	1-2	*Sobotzik (p)*
27/8	Stabæk	h	2-3	*Nhleko, Jensen*
2/9	Brann	a	0-1	
16/9	Vålerenga	h	1-3	*Madsen*
23/9	Rosenborg	a	0-2	
1/10	Start	h	1-3	*Madsen*
7/10	Strømsgodset	a	0-4	
21/10	Fredrikstad	a	0-2	
28/10	Odd Grenland	h	0-2	
3/11	Lillestrøm	a	1-1	*Adriano*

No	Name	Nat	Pos	Aps	(s)	Gls
10	ADRIANO Munoz	BRA	A	18	(5)	5
6	Mikael ANDERSSON	SWE	M	1	(3)	
19	Kari ARKIVUO	FIN	M	24		3
12	Espen BUGGE PETTERSEN		G	22		
2	Thomas EFTEDAL		M	1	(1)	
2	Alexander GABRIELSEN		D	6		
14	Tuomas HAAPALA	FIN	M	2	(4)	
16	Samuel ISAKSEN		M	23		2
3	Martin JENSEN	DEN	D	21	(1)	2
21	Olav Tuelo JOHANNESEN		A		(6)	
24	Fredrik KJØLNER		D	26		
7	Tommy KNARVIK		M	24		4
22	Sampo KOSKINEN	FIN	D	4	(4)	
21	Albert KRUEZIU		A		(4)	
5	Birger MADSEN		D	23		3
18	Erik MJELDE		M	9	(4)	
23	Nkosinathi NHLEKO	RSA	A	6	(1)	1
4	Jan Frode NORNES		D	4	(6)	
14	Gudmundur PÉTURSSON	ISL	A		(6)	
27	Jon André RØYRANE		M	1	(7)	
13	Ørjan RØYRANE		M		(3)	
1	Peter SKOV-JENSEN	DEN	G	4		
8	Thomas SOBOTZIK	GER	M	11	(1)	1
15	Ebrima SOHNA	GAM	M	13	(3)	
11	Andreas TEGSTRÖM	SWE	A	14	(3)	1
9	Fredrik THORSEN		A	11	(3)	1
17	Olav ZANETTI		D	18	(3)	1

STABÆK FOTBALL

Coach – Jan Jönsson (SWE)

Founded – 1912

MAJOR HONOURS: Norwegian Cup – (1) 1998.

2007				
10/4	Brann	h	0-1	
15/4	Vålerenga	a	1-1	*Nannskog*
21/4	Rosenborg	h	2-1	*Gunnarsson 2 (1p)*
29/4	Start	a	1-1	*Nannskog*
6/5	Sandefjord	h	1-1	*Nannskog*
13/5	Fredrikstad	a	2-1	*Alanzinho, Gunnarsson*
16/5	Odd Grenland	h	1-0	*Gunnarsson*
28/5	Lillestrøm	a	1-1	*Tchoyi*
10/6	Lyn	h	3-2	*Segerström, Tchoyi, Nannskog*
17/6	Aalesund	a	4-1	*Tchoyi, Nannskog, Alanzinho, Hauger*
20/6	Viking	h	2-1	*Nannskog 2*
24/6	Tromsø	a	1-0	*Alanzinho*
1/7	Strømsgodset	h	3-2	*Nannskog, Gunnarsson, Keller*
22/7	Brann	a	0-3	
29/7	Vålerenga	h	2-2	*Hauger, Nannskog*
4/8	Rosenborg	a	0-3	
13/8	Start	h	1-1	*Nannskog*
27/8	Sandefjord	a	3-2	*Alanzinho, Gunnarsson, Nannskog*
3/9	Fredrikstad	h	0-2	
16/9	Odd Grenland	a	5-1	*Gunnarsson 3 (1p), Nannskog, Stenvoll*
23/9	Lillestrøm	h	3-1	*Kjølø, Keller, Gunnarsson*
30/9	Lyn	a	2-3	*Nannskog, og (Sigurdsson)*
7/10	Aalesund	h	4-2	*Alanzinho, Nannskog, Gunnarsson 2*
22/10	Viking	a	1-2	*Tchoyi*
28/10	Tromsø	h	5-0	*Gunnarsson, Nannskog 4 (1p)*
3/11	Strømsgodset	a	5-0	*Gunnarsson 2 (1p), Nannskog, Hauger, Høiland*

No	Name	Nat	Pos	Aps	(s)	Gls
25	ALANZINHO	BRA	M	26		5
8	Petter FURUSETH-OLSEN		A	3	(1)	
10	Veigar Páll GUNNARSSON	ISL	A	25		15
7	Henning HAUGER		M	21	(5)	3
26	Bjørnar HOLMVIK		D	10	(11)	
3	Jon Inge HØILAND		D	3		1
9	Christian KELLER	DEN	M	22	(3)	2
4	Mike KJØLØ		D	16	(1)	1
1	Jon KNUDSEN		G	26		
27	Eirik MARKEGÅRD		A	1	(3)	
11	Daniel NANNSKOG	SWE	A	26		19
24	Espen NYSTUEN		M	1	(8)	
17	Espen OLSEN		A		(6)	
20	Inge Andrè OLSEN		D	5	(2)	
19	Branimir POLJAC		M		(4)	
18	Thomas ROGNE		D		(3)	
5	Pontus SEGERSTRÖM	SWE	D	22	(1)	1
15	Morten Morisbak SKJØNSBERG		D	26		
21	Tommy STENERSEN		M	5	(7)	
6	Tom STENVOLL		M	22	(1)	1
28	Jens Waltorp SØRENSEN	DEN	G		(1)	
13	Somen A. TCHOYI	CMR	M	26		4

IK START

Coach – Stig Inge Bjørnebye; (5/9/07) (Bård Wiggen); (10/9/07) Benny Lennartsson (SWE)

Founded – 1905

MAJOR HONOURS: Norwegian League – (2) 1978, 1980.

2007				
9/4	Aalesund	a	4-2	*Børufsen, Bärlin, Hæstad M., Hæstad K.*
15/4	Viking	h	1-1	*Ygor*
22/4	Tromsø	a	1-1	*Pedersen*
29/4	Stabæk	h	1-1	*Nielsen*
5/5	Brann	a	2-2	*Børufsen 2*
10/5	Vålerenga	h	1-0	*Fevang*
16/5	Rosenborg	a	1-4	*Lie*
25/5	Strømsgodset	h	2-3	*Valencia, Børufsen*
11/6	Sandefjord	h	3-1	*Paulsen, Pedersen, Hæstad M.*
17/6	Fredrikstad	a	0-3	
21/6	Odd Grenland	h	1-2	*Nielsen*
24/6	Lillestrøm	a	0-1	
1/7	Lyn	h	0-1	
22/7	Aalesund	h	1-2	*Børufsen*
29/7	Viking	a	0-2	
5/8	Tromsø	h	1-1	*og (Reginiussen)*
13/8	Stabæk	a	1-1	*Årst*
26/8	Brann	h	1-1	*Hæstad K.*
2/9	Vålerenga	a	2-3	*Borre, Årst (p)*
15/9	Rosenborg	h	2-1	*Hulsker, Årst*
23/9	Strømsgodset	a	2-3	*Årst 2*
1/10	Sandefjord	a	3-1	*Hulsker, Borre, Lie*
6/10	Fredrikstad	h	3-1	*Strømstad, Hulsker, Borre*
21/10	Odd Grenland	a	0-2	
28/10	Lillestrøm	h	0-0	
3/11	Lyn	a	1-4	*Årst*

No	Name	Nat	Pos	Aps	(s)	Gls
28	Bjarte Lunde AARSHEIM		M	3	(4)	
21	Anthonay ANNAN	GHA	M	6	(5)	
16	Stefan BÄRLIN	SWE	A	7	(4)	1
20	Bård BORGERSEN		D		(2)	
15	Martin BORRE	DEN	A	11	(2)	3
31	BRUNO Rato Silva	BRA	A	1	(8)	
14	Espen BØRUFSEN		A	14	(7)	5
17	Lars Martin ENGEDAL		D	7	(5)	
11	Geir Ludvig FEVANG		A	5	(2)	1
6	Jóhannes HARDARSON	ISL	M	4	(4)	
16	Bernt HULSKER		A	7	(2)	3
24	Kenneth HØIE		G	13		
23	Kristofer HÆSTAD		M	21	(1)	2
27	Morten HÆSTAD		A	11	(3)	2
10	Atle Roar HÅLAND		D	23		
8	Aram KHALILI		A		(1)	
30	Christer KLEIVEN		M	3	(5)	
18	Jon Midttun LIE		A	15	(2)	2
26	Jesper MATHISEN		A		(2)	
66	David NIELSEN	DEN	A	5	(3)	2
1	Rune NILSSEN		G	11	(1)	
9	Inge André OLSEN		D	7	(1)	
2	Kristoffer PAULSEN		D	25		1
4	Steinar PEDERSEN		D	22		2
13	Tommy RUNAR		G	2		
7	Fredrik STRØMSTAD		M	21		1
8	Alex VALENCIA		A	6	(2)	1
9	Ben WRIGHT	ENG	A	1	(1)	
19	YGOR Maciel Santiago	BRA	M	23	(3)	1
25	Ole Martin ÅRST		A	12		6

STRØMSGODSET IF

Coach – Dag Eilev Fagermo

Founded – 1907

MAJOR HONOURS: Norwegian League – (1) 1970; Norwegian Cup – (4) 1969, 1970, 1973, 1991.

2007				
9/4	Odd Grenland	h	2-1	*Andersson, Kovács*
16/4	Brann	a	1-3	*George*
23/4	Lillestrøm	h	1-1	*Bergdølmo (p)*
28/4	Vålerenga	a	0-0	
6/5	Lyn	h	1-1	*Deila (p)*

3/5	Rosenborg	a	2-1	*Ohr, Deila*
6/5	Aalesund	h	0-4	
5/5	Start	a	3-2	*Kovács 3*
/6	Viking	h	1-2	*og (Ross)*
7/6	Sandefjord	a	1-0	*Nyan*
0/6	Tromsø	h	1-2	*George*
4/6	Fredrikstad	h	2-1	*Sørum, Aas*
/7	Stabæk	a	2-3	*Sørum, Bergdølmo (p)*
2/7	Odd Grenland	a	1-0	*Sørum*
9/7	Brann	h	2-4	*Finstad 2*
/8	Lillestrøm	a	0-2	
12/8	Vålerenga	h	1-2	*Aas*
26/8	Lyn	a	0-1	
1/9	Rosenborg	h	1-1	*Bergdølmo*
17/9	Aalesund	a	2-3	*Kovács, Leonhardsen*
23/9	Start	h	3-2	*og (Pedersen), George, Bergdølmo (p)*
29/9	Viking	a	0-3	
7/10	Sandefjord	h	4-0	*Bergdølmo (p), George, Nyan, Ohr*
21/10	Tromsø	a	2-2	*Bergdølmo (p), Winsnes*
28/10	Fredrikstad	a	1-1	*Andersen*
3/11	Stabæk	h	0-5	

No	Name	Nat	Pos	Aps	(s)	Gls
6	Alexander AAS		D	25		2
2	Glenn ANDERSEN		D	16	(6)	1
20	Mattias ANDERSSON	SWE	A	6		1
3	André BERGDØLMO		D	25		6
4	Ronny DEILA		D	17		2
25	Kenneth DOKKEN		M	1	(11)	
5	Samir FAZLAGIC		D	17	(3)	
9	Thomas FINSTAD		A	2	(7)	2
13	Christer GEORGE		A	19	(2)	4
17	Keijo HUUSKO	FIN	M	15	(3)	
1	Espen JOHNSEN		G	22		
22	Einar KALSÆG		A	6	(3)	
39	Péter KOVÁCS	HUN	A	16	(7)	5
12	Adam LARSEN		G	4		
7	Øyvind LEONHARDSEN		M	9	(3)	1
30	Trond Fredrik LUDVIGSEN		A	3	(3)	
14	Fredrik NORDKVELLE		M	5	(4)	
8	Ousman NYAN		M	21		2
22	Steffen NYSTRØM		A	2	(5)	
10	Stian OHR		A	24	(1)	2
18	Kristian SØRLI		D	4	(8)	
16	Thomas SØRUM		A	10	(6)	3
21	Fredrik WINSNES		M	14		1
11	Trygve ÅSE LUNDE		A	3	(3)	

TROMSØ IL

Coach – Steinar Nilsen

Founded – 1920

MAJOR HONOURS: Norwegian Cup – (2) 1986, 1996.

2007				
9/4	Vålerenga	h	1-0	*Sequeira*
15/4	Rosenborg	a	3-4	*Bernier 2, Årst (p)*
22/4	Start	h	1-1	*Rushfeldt*
29/4	Sandefjord	a	1-2	*Rushfeldt*
6/5	Fredrikstad	h	4-1	*Sequeira, Strand, Årst, Steen*
13/5	Odd Grenland	a	1-0	*Strand*
16/5	Lillestrøm	h	2-1	*Rushfeldt, og (Stefanutto)*
28/5	Lyn	a	3-4	*Reginiussen, Rushfeldt, og (Tessem)*
10/6	Aalesund	h	0-2	
17/6	Viking	a	1-3	*Håkonsen*
20/6	Strømsgodset	a	2-1	*Rushfeldt, Moldskred*
24/6	Stabæk	h	0-1	
1/7	Brann	a	1-2	*Håkonsen*
22/7	Vålerenga	a	2-2	*Moldskred, Sequeira*
28/7	Rosenborg	h	2-1	*Moldskred 2*
5/8	Start	a	1-1	*Sequeira*
12/8	Sandefjord	h	2-1	*Lindpere, Moldskred*
26/8	Fredrikstad	a	1-2	*Karim*
2/9	Odd Grenland	h	2-4	*Rushfeldt, Moldskred*
16/9	Lillestrøm	a	3-0	*Strand, Lindpere, Reginiussen*
23/9	Lyn	h	2-1	*Moldskred, Yndestad*
30/9	Aalesunds FK	a	3-2	*Moldskred, Strand, Rushfeldt*
7/10	Viking	h	2-1	*Lindpere, og (Soma)*
21/10	Strømsgodset	h	2-2	*Moldskred, Rushfeldt*
28/10	Stabæk	a	0-5	
3/11	Brann	h	3-0	*Moldskred 3*

No	Name	Nat	Pos	Aps	(s)	Gls
14	Stephen ADEMOLU	CAN	A	2	(4)	
9	Patrice BERNIER	CAN	M	6	(3)	2
1	Knut BORCH		G	2		
17	Vegard BRAATEN		A		(1)	
8	Thomas HAFSTAD		D	8	(1)	
6	Helge HAUGEN		M	13		
26	Tom HØGLI		M	12	(2)	
15	Yngvar HÅKONSEN		D	14	(3)	2
20	Bovar KARIM	SWE	M		(6)	1
19	Martin KNUDSEN		M	17	(1)	
22	Joel LINDPERE	EST	M	23	(1)	3
4	Morten MOLDSKRED		A	17	(5)	12
21	Hans NORDBY		D		(1)	
24	Henrik NORDNES		D	2	(4)	
12	Sead RAMOVIĆ	BIH	G	21		
3	Tore REGINIUSSEN		D	24		2
14	Roger RISHOLT		M	1	(5)	
10	Sigurd RUSHFELDT		A	20	(1)	8
27	Douglas SEQUEIRA	CRC	M	20	(4)	4
13	Kenny STAMATOPOLOUS	CAN	G	3	(1)	
5	Christian STEEN		D	25		1
18	Lars Iver STRAND		M	23		4
25	Hördur SVEINSSON	ISL	A		(2)	
7	Joachim WALLTIN		M		(6)	
16	Hans Åge YNDESTAD		D	21	(2)	1
11	Ruben YTTERGÅRD JENSSEN		M		(15)	
25	Ole Martin ÅRST		A	12	(1)	2

VIKING FK

Coach – Uwe Rösler (GER)

Founded – 1899

MAJOR HONOURS: Norwegian League – (8) 1958, 1972, 1973, 1974, 1975, 1979, 1982, 1991; Norwegian Cup – (5) 1953, 1959, 1979, 1989, 2001.

2007				
9/4	Rosenborg	h	1-1	*Ijeh*
15/4	Start	a	1-1	*Berg*
22/4	Sandefjord	h	0-0	
29/4	Fredrikstad	a	0-2	
6/5	Odd Grenland	h	2-1	*Ijeh 2*
13/5	Lillestrøm	a	1-4	*Ijeh*
16/5	Lyn	h	4-2	*Ødegaard, Stokholm (p), Pimpong, Berg*
28/5	Aalesund	a	2-0	*Soma, Pimpong*
9/6	Strømsgodset	a	2-1	*Ijeh, Sigurdsson*
17/6	Tromsø	h	3-1	*Stokholm, Ijeh 2*
20/6	Stabæk	a	1-2	*Gaarde*
24/6	Brann	h	3-1	*Ijeh, Gaarde, Berg*
30/6	Vålerenga	a	3-1	*Gaarde 2, Ijeh*
22/7	Rosenborg	a	2-4	*Sigurdsson 2*
29/7	Start	h	2-0	*Ijeh, Stokholm (p)*
5/8	Sandefjord	a	1-4	*Sigurdsson*
12/8	Fredrikstad	h	2-2	*Ijeh, Stokholm (p)*
26/8	Odd Grenland	a	3-1	*Steenslid, Ijeh, Samuelsen*
2/9	Lillestrøm	h	1-1	*Gaarde*
16/9	Lyn	a	3-2	*Ijeh, Ødegaard, Berg*
22/9	Aalesund	h	3-0	*Ødegaard, Ijeh, Gaarde*
29/9	Strømsgodset	h	3-0	*Steenslid, Ødegaard 2*

NORWAY

7/10	Tromsø	a	1-2	*Stokholm (p)*
22/10	Stabæk	h	2-1	*Ijeh 2*
28/10	Brann	a	2-5	*Berg, Nisja*
3/11	Vålerenga	h	2-1	*Ijeh 2*

No	Name	Nat	Pos	Aps	(s)	Gls
4	Peter ABELSSON	SWE	D	6	(9)	
18	Andreas Ulland ANDERSEN		M		(1)	
22	Iven AUSTBØ		G	17		
11	Søren BERG	DEN	A	22	(2)	5
28	Birkir BJARNASON	ISL	M	1	(5)	
14	André DANIELSEN		M	18	(7)	
6	Allan GAARDE	DEN	M	17	(3)	6
9	Peter IJEH	NGA	A	23		18
23	René KLINGBEIL	GER	D	6	(1)	
1	Thomas MYHRE		G	9		
8	Vidar NISJA		M		(1)	1
19	Trygve NYGAARD		M		(2)	
5	Thomas PEREIRA		D	21	(1)	
20	Razak PIMPONG	GHA	A	8	(7)	2
17	Maurice ROSS	SCO	D	17		
99	Jone SAMUELSEN		M	20	(2)	1
21	Hannes SIGURDSSON	ISL	A	11	(14)	4
15	Ragnvald SOMA		D	26		1
3	Børre STEENSLID		D	22	(1)	2
7	Nikolai STOKHOLM	DEN	M	24		5
8	Øyvind SVENNING		D	4	(1)	
16	Jørgen TENGESDAL		D	2	(5)	
10	Alexander ØDEGAARD		A	12	(9)	5

VÅLERENGA FOTBALL

Coach – Petter Myhre; (27/7/07) (Harald Aabrekk); (14/8/07) Harald Aabrekk

Founded – 1913

MAJOR HONOURS: Norwegian League – (5) 1965, 1981, 1983, 1984, 2005; Norwegian Cup – (3) 1980, 1997, 2002.

2007				
9/4	Tromsø	a	0-1	
15/4	Stabæk	h	1-1	*Fredheim Holm*
22/4	Brann	a	1-4	*Storbæk*
28/4	Strømsgodset	h	0-0	
6/5	Rosenborg	h	2-1	*Berre, Wæhler*
10/5	Start	a	0-1	
16/5	Sandefjord	h	2-0	*Berre, Lange*
26/5	Fredrikstad	a	0-1	
10/6	Odd Grenland	h	1-1	*Lange*
17/6	Lillestrøm	a	1-0	*Berre*
20/6	Lyn	h	0-0	
23/6	Aalesund	a	0-1	
30/6	Viking	h	1-3	*og (Steenslid)*
22/7	Tromsø	h	2-2	*Jalland 2*
29/7	Stabæk	a	2-2	*Johnsen, Storbæk (p)*
5/8	Brann	h	2-0	*Berre 2*
12/8	Strømsgodset	a	2-1	*Johnsen, Berre*
25/8	Rosenborg	a	0-2	
2/9	Start	h	3-2	*Jalland, Fredheim Holm 2 (1p)*
16/9	Sandefjord	a	3-1	*Grindheim, Berre 2*
24/9	Fredrikstad	h	2-0	*Thomassen, Thorvaldsson*
30/9	Odd Grenland	a	4-1	*og (Muri), Zajić, Berre, Jalland*
7/10	Lillestrøm	h	1-3	*Thorvaldsson*
21/10	Lyn	a	1-3	*Grindheim*
28/10	Aalesund	h	2-1	*Grindheim, Fredheim Holm*
3/11	Viking	a	1-2	*Storbæk*

No	Name	Nat	Pos	Aps	(s)	Gls
1	Arni Gautur ARASON	ISL	G	26		
11	Morten BERRE		M	24	(1)	9
31	Kristian BRIX		M	3	(1)	
6	Freddy DOS SANTOS		M	22	(3)	
17	Mohammed FELLAH		M	2	(5)	
7	Daniel FREDHEIM HOLM		A	23		4
23	Arnar FØRSUND		D	1	(2)	
19	Christian GRINDHEIM		M	21	(1)	3
4	Thomas HOLM		M	4	(3)	
20	Jørgen HORN		D	6	(3)	
9	Jørgen JALLAND		M	15	(6)	4
3	Allan Kierstein JEPSEN	DEN	D	25	(1)	
22	Ronny JOHNSEN		D	16	(1)	2
18	Rune LANGE		A	4	(7)	2
21	Alexander MATHISEN		A	1	(5)	
8	Sebastian MILA	POL	M	8	(6)	
5	André MURI		D	6	(2)	
27	Glenn ROBERTS		A	2	(4)	
13	Jarl-André STORBÆK		D	26		3
25	Steinar STRØMNES		M		(1)	
10	Jan Derek SØRENSEN		A	8	(13)	
16	Dan THOMASSEN	DEN	D	12		1
34	Gunnar Heidar THORVALDSSON	ISL	A	6	(1)	2
24	Kjetil WÆHLER		D	20	(1)	1
26	Bojan ZAJIĆ	SRB	M	5	(2)	1

PROMOTED CLUBS

MOLDE FK

Coach – Kjell Jonevret (SWE)

Founded - 1911

MAJOR HONOURS: Norwegian Cup - (2) 1994, 2005.

HAMKAM FOTBALL

Coach – Arne Erlandsen

Founded - 1918

FK BODØ/GLIMT

Coach – Kåre Ingebrigtsen

Founded - 1916

MAJOR HONOURS: Norwegian Cup - (2) 1975, 1993.

SECOND LEVEL FINAL TABLE 2007

		Pld	W	D	L	F	A	Pt
1	Molde FK	30	22	3	5	62	28	69
2	HamKam Fotball	30	21	5	4	82	36	68
3	FK Bodø/Glimt	30	17	4	9	66	39	55
4	Kongsvinger IL	30	16	5	9	56	42	53
5	Moss FK	30	15	8	7	46	37	53
6	Bryne FK	30	14	7	9	57	38	49
7	Sogndal Fotball	30	13	5	12	48	44	44
8	FK Haugesund	30	10	9	11	49	52	39
9	Notodden FK	30	11	3	16	49	54	36
10	Hønefoss BK	30	8	11	11	34	52	35
11	Raufoss IL	30	10	5	15	37	61	35
12	Løv-Ham Fotball	30	9	6	15	39	44	33
13	FK Sparta Sarpsborg	30	8	8	14	50	52	32
14	Tromsdalen UIL	30	7	8	15	37	56	29
15	Skeid Fotball	30	4	8	18	32	60	20
16	FK Mandalskameratene	30	4	7	19	43	92	19

N.B. The Norwegian FA refused Raufoss Fotball a licence for the 20[illegible] Adeccoligaen. They were replaced by FK Sparta Sarpsborg, who thu[illegible] avoided relegation.

PROMOTION/RELEGATION PLAY-OFFS

(8/11/07)

Odd Grenland 0, Bodø/Glimt 1

(12/11/07)

Bodø/Glimt 3, Odd Grenland 2

(Bodø/Glimt 4-2)

DOMESTIC CUP 2007

NORGESMESTERSKAP

FIRST ROUND

(19/5/07)
Byåsen 4, Levanger 0
Gjøvik-Lyn 0, Raufoss 3
Kvik Halden 2, Sparta Sarpsborg 1
Lisleby 0, Fredrikstad 5
Lofoten 3, Mjølner 2
Manglerud Star 5, Kjelsås 2
Pors 2, Asker 0
Randaberg 3, Sandnes Ulf 2 *(aet)*
Skarp 1, Mo 2
Tollnes 1, Arendal 4
Træff 0, Kristiansund 5
Åsane 3, Fana 1

(20/5/07)
Askøy 4, Loddefjord 2 *(aet)*
Bossekop 1, Tromsdalen 3
Brumunddal 0, HamKam 3
Bærum 2, Lørenskog 0
Djerv 1919 1, Haugesund 6
Egersund 0, Viking 6
Eik-Tønsberg 1, FK Tønsberg 9
Fagerborg 1, Drøbak/Frogn 3
Fet 1, Lyn 10
Fjellhamar 2, Nybergsund 5
Fjøra 3, Hødd 1
Flisa 3, Lillestrøm 6
Follo 3, Ullensaker/Kisa 1
Greåker 0, Moss 1
Hammerfest 0, Bodø/Glimt 4
Herkules 0, Notodden 3
Innstranden 1, Alta 3
KIL/Hemne 3, Molde 1
Kolstad 0, Ranheim 5
Kopervik 2, Stavanger IF 0
Korsvoll 3, Ringsaker 1 (aet)
Lillehammer 1, Hønefoss 4
Namsos 1, Rosenborg 5
Nordstrand 1, Groruddalen 5
Norheimsund 0, Løv-Ham 4
NTNUI 3, Strindheim 5
Orkla 3, Nardo 0
Os 1, Baune 0
Rommen 1, Eidsvold Turn 0
Sandar 0, Sandefjord 5
Senja 0, Tromsø 3
Skjetten 1, Skeid 2
Sprint/Jeløy 0, Sarpsborg 3
Stjørdals/Blink 2, Harstad 1
Stryn 1, Sogndal 0
Strømmen 1, Kongsvinger 2
Svarstad 0, Odd Grenland 5
Sykkylven 0, Aalesund 7
Tiller 1, Steinkjer 3
Toten 0, Vålerenga 3
Trio 0, Brann 5
Vardeneset 0, Bryne 4
Vigør 1, Fløy 5
Vindbhart 2, Start 6
Volda 2, Averøykameratene 0
Vollen 0, Mjøndalen 5
Øygard 2, Fyllingen 0
Åkra 2, Vard Haugesund 3
Ålgård 1, Mandalskameratene 4
Åmot 0, KFUM Oslo 4
Åskollen 2, Strømsgodset 6
Åssiden 1, Stabæk 9

SECOND ROUND

(13/6/07)
Alta 1, Steinkjer 0
Arendal 1, Odd Grenland 3
Askøy 0, Bryne 5
Bærum 2, HamKam 0
Fjøra 0, Stabæk 4
Fløy 0, Haugesund 1 *(aet)*
Follo 1, Korsvoll 1 *(aet; 2-4 on pens)*
Groruddalen 0, Notodden 1 *(aet)*
Hønefoss 3, Os 0
KFUM Oslo 2, Skeid 3 (aet)
Kongsvinger 5, Pors Grenland 0
Kopervik 3, Mandalskameratene 1
Kristiansund 0, Manglerud Star 0 *(aet; 5-6 on pens)*
Kvik Halden 0, Lyn 5
Lofoten 1, Bodø/Glimt 3 *(aet)*
Løv-Ham 3, Åsane 1
Mjøndalen 2, Vålerenga 3
Mo 3, Ranheim 2
Nybergsund 4, Strindheim 1
Orkla 0, Lillestrøm 5
Randaberg 0, Viking 6
Raufoss 0, Drøbak/Frogn 2 *(aet)*
Rommen 0, Moss 7
Sarpsborg 0, Fredrikstad 4
Stjørdals-Blink 0, Tromsø 6
Stryn 2, Strømsgodset 9
Tromsdalen 3, Byåsen 2
Volda 1, Aalesund 3 *(aet)*
Øygard 0, Brann 5

(14/6/07)
KIL/Hemne 3, Rosenborg 4 *(aet)*
Tønsberg 2, Sandefjord 0
Vard Haugesund 0, Start 5

THIRD ROUND

(26/6/07)
Vålerenga 4, Mo 1

(27/6/07)
Aalesund 2, Alta 0
Bodø/Glimt 1, Hønefoss 0
Drøbak/Frogn 0, Viking 2
Fredrikstad 1, Nybergsund 2
Haugesund 4, Løv-Ham 0
Kopervik 0, Brann 5
Korsvoll 2, Stabæk 5 *(aet)*
Manglerud Star 0, Start 1
Moss 0, Strømsgodset 3
Notodden 2, Kongsvinger 1 *(aet)*
Odd Grenland 4, FK Tønsberg 1
Tromsø 4, Tromsdalen 1 *(aet)*

(28/7/07)
Bryne FK 1, Lyn 2
Lillestrøm 4, Bærum 0
Skeid 0, Rosenborg 2 *(aet)*

FOURTH ROUND

(25/7/07)
Lillestrøm 1, Aalesund 0
Lyn 1, Bodø/Glimt 0
Rosenborg 1, Odd Grenland 2
Start 0, Haugesund 1
Strømsgodset 4, Notodden 1
Viking 2, Brann 0

(26/7/07)
Nybergsund 3, Vålerenga 1

(8/8/07)
Stabæk 3, Tromsø 0

QUARTER-FINALS

(18/8/07)
Haugesund 6 *(Weaver 13p, 40, 48, Johansen 16, Larsen 76, Antoine-Curier 84p)*, Nybergsund 1 *(Bredvold 78)*
Odd Grenland 2 *(Fevang 42, 65)*, Viking 1 *(Stokholm 32p)*

(19/8/07)
Strømsgodset IF 2 *(Bergdølmo 58, Ohr 73)*, Stabæk 4 *(Gunnarsson 24, 30p, Nannskog 94, Tchoyi 109) (aet)*
Lyn 0, Lillestrøm 1 *(Kippe 65)*

SEMI-FINALS

(26/9/07)
Haugesund 1 *(Rodrigues 11)*, Odd Grenland 0
Lillestrøm 2 *(Brenne 10, Sundgot 39)*, Stabæk 0

FINAL

(11/11/07)
Ullevaal stadion, Oslo
LILLESTRØM SK 2 *(Occean 57, 90)*
FK HAUGESUND 0
Referee – *Staberg*
LILLESTRØM – *Fredrikson, Rambekk, Andresen, Kippe, Johnsen (Stefanutto 68), Mouelhi, Brenne, Søgård, Riise, Occean, Myklebust (Sundgot 58).*
HAUGESUND – *Kristiansen, Strøm, Storm, Horneland, Castro (Johansen 86), Ørsal, Rodrigues, Brandshaug (Andreassen 65), Eike (Larsen 65), Weaver, Johnsen.*

POLAND

Confident qualifiers struggle at higher level

Poland reached the UEFA European Championship finals for the first time thanks to an impressive qualifying campaign in which they topped their group ahead of Portugal. But if that feat won the team's veteran Dutch coach Leo Beenhakker widespread acclaim, and official state recognition, there was nothing much for him, his players or the legions of visiting Polish fans to celebrate at the final tournament in Austria.

Brazilian-born Rog Guerreiro celebrates aft scoring Poland's only go at UEFA EURO 2008

Poland finished bottom of Group B with one point and one goal. Defeated by two goals from 'one of their own', Polish-born Lukas Podolski, in the opening game against Germany, the defensive mistakes they made in Klagenfurt were repeated in the opening stages of the second match, against Austria in Vienna, four days later, but fortunately the outstanding goalkeeping of Artur Boruc kept them in the game and they took a fortunate lead when, against the run of play and from an offside position, the team's recently naturalised Brazilian-born playmaker, Roger Guerreiro, stabbed the ball home from close range. A last-minute equalising penalty awarded to, and converted by, Austria enraged Beenhakker, and although there were flaws in his argument, it was not difficult to understand why he was so upset. With that decision, and goal, Poland's chances of qualification had gone from reasonable to virtually non-existent.

They would lose their final game to an understrength Croatia in any case, but even if they had won, it would have served no purpose with Germany simultaneously beating Austria. So, as in the FIFA World Cups of 2002 and 2006, Poland's tournament was over after the first round, the emerging theme being that while the current crop of Polish players are good enough to qualify for the big tournaments, they are unable to cope with the extra step-up in quality required at the finals.

Lack of sharpness

An injury sustained in the opening game by captain Maciej Żurawski that ruled him out of the tournament did not help matters; nor did the sharp decline in form of Euzebiusz Smolarek, the man whose nine qualifying goals had been so instrumental in taking Poland to the finals. He was not the only member of the squad who underperformed, but it was the lack of sharpness up front that contributed most to the team's downfall. The two Polish players who emerged in credit were Boruc, who continually came to the rescue of a disorganised defence, and Roger, who did much more than score the team's only goal, his deft left foot providing touches of real quality amidst the mediocrity.

Poland have another UEFA European Championship to look forward to, on home soil, in four years' time, but their first objective will be to complete a hat-trick of World Cup qualifications. Beenhakker will take the team into battle again and, despite the disappointment of the summer, should feel confident of earning at least a play-off spot in a group containing the Czech Republic, Northern Ireland, San Marino, Slovakia and Slovenia.

Like many Poland coaches before him, Beenhakker has not been afraid to hand out international caps liberally to players plying in their trade in the Ekstraklasa, the Polish domestic league. Nine 'locals' made it into the UEFA EURO 2008™ squad, including three from Wisła Kraków, the runaway 2007/08 Polish champions, and two from Legia Warszawa, who denied Wisła the double by defeating them on penalties (after a goalless draw) in the final of the Polish Cup.

Wisła shine again

It was Legia also who prevented Wisła from going through the whole of the Ekstraklasa campaign undefeated when they beat Maciej Skorża's newly crowned team 2-1 in Warsaw four rounds from the end. Having surrendered the league title in both 2005/06 and 2006/07, Poland's team of the decade reasserted their supremacy in ruthless fashion. With their reborn 23-goal hitman Paweł Brożek, twin of team-mate Piotr, leading the way in attack – he never went more than three games without scoring – and a backline featuring Arkadiusz Głowacki and Marcin Baszczyński keeping things tight in defence, the White Star shone as brightly as in any of the club's four other title wins since 2000. Having finished a miserable eighth and failed to qualify for Europe the previous season, it was quite a comeback under newly appointed Skorża, a 36-year-old who had worked as assistant to former Polish national coach Paweł Janas and led Groclin Grodzisk Wielkopolski to Polish Cup victory in 2006/07.

Legia also had a season without European football after they were banned following serious crowd misbehaviour at a UEFA Intertoto Cup game in neighbouring Lithuania. Jan Urban, a former Polish international midfielder, came in as coach and not only brought Legia the Cup for the first time in 11 years but also took them to second place in the Ekstraklasa. Although Roger and Zimbabwean striker Takesure Cinyawa provided exotic skills and goals, Legia's strength was their defence, which conceded just 17 goals in the league and only one in seven Polish Cup games.

Enforced relegation

The feats of Wisła and Legia were rather overshadowed, however, by the continuing fall-out from a long-standing and all-encompassing corruption investigation that eventually led to the enforced relegation of four clubs. Two of them – GKS Zagłębie Sosnowiec and RTS Widzew Łódź – finished in the bottom two places anyway so were obliged to drop down to the third level, whereas Koronia Kielce and 2006/07 champions Zagłębie Lubin were removed from the top flight after finishing sixth and fifth, respectively. KS Polonia Bytom were also sent down but earned readmission after a successful appeal.

These issues led to confusion over which teams would come up from the second division, but finally, several weeks after the conclusion of the campaign, it was decided that the top four teams would all be allowed up. Ironically the team in fourth place, Arka Gdynia, had been relegated for their involvement in the corruption affair a year earlier. There was further post-season disruption when Groclin, who had finished third in the Ekstraklasa, merged with Polonia Warszawa, seventh in the second division, and re-located from their small-town base in western Poland to the capital city, losing their name also in the process.

Polski Związek Piłki Nożnej (PZPN)

Miodowa 1
PL-00-080 Warszawa
tel - +48 22 5512200
fax - +48 22 5512240
website - www.pzpn.pl
email - pzpn@pzpn.pl
Year of Formation – 1919
President - Michał Listkiewicz
General Secretary - Zdzisław Kręcina
Press Officer - Michał Kocięba
Stadium – Sląski-Narodowy, Chorzów (47,202)

INTERNATIONAL TOURNAMENT APPEARANCES
FIFA World Cup - (7) 1938, 1974 (3rd), 1978 (2nd phase), 1982 (3rd), 1986 (2nd round), 2002, 2006.
UEFA European Championship – (1) 2008.

TOP FIVE ALL-TIME CAPS
Grzegorz Lato (100); Kazimierz Deyna (97); Jacek Bąk (96); Władysław Żmuda (91); Antoni Szymanowski (82)

TOP FIVE ALL-TIME GOALS
Włodzimierz Lubański (48); Grzegorz Lato (45); Kazimierz Deyna (41); Ernest Pol (39); Andrzej Szarmach (32)

POLAND

NATIONAL TEAM RESULTS 2007/08

22/8/07	Russia	A	Moscow	2-2	*Krzynówek (73), Błaszczykowski (77)*
8/9/07	Portugal (ECQ)	A	Lisbon	2-2	*Lewandowski (44), Krzynówek (88)*
12/9/07	Finland (ECQ)	A	Helsinki	0-0	
13/10/07	Kazakhstan (ECQ)	H	Warsaw	3-1	*Smolarek (56, 65, 66)*
17/10/07	Hungary	H	Lodz	0-1	
17/11/07	Belgium (ECQ)	H	Chorzow	2-0	*Smolarek (45, 49)*
21/11/07	Serbia (ECQ)	H	Belgrade	2-2	*Murawski (28), Matusiak (46)*
15/12/07	Bosnia-Herzegovina B	N	Antalya (TUR)	1-0	*Goliński (42)*
2/2/08	Finland B	N	Paphos (CYP)	1-0	*Kokoszka (42)*
6/2/08	Czech Republic	N	Larnaca (CYP)	2-0	*Łobodziński (6), Lewandowski (29)*
27/2/08	Estonia	H	Wronki	1-0	*Matusiak (38), Zahorski (72)*
26/3/08	United States	H	Krakow	0-3	
26/5/08	FYR Macedonia	N	Reutlingen (GER)	1-1	*Matusiak (84)*
27/5/08	Albania	N	Reutlingen (GER)	1-0	*Żurawski (3)*
31/5/08	Denmark	H	Chorzow	1-1	*Krzynówek (43)*
8/6/08	Germany (ECF)	N	Klagenfurt (AUT)	0-2	
12/6/08	Austria (ECF)	N	Vienna (AUT)	1-1	*Roger (30)*
16/6/08	Croatia (ECF)	N	Klagenfurt (AUT)	0-1	

NATIONAL TEAM APPEARANCES 2007/08

Coach – Leo BEENHAKKER (NED)	2/8/42		Rus	POR	FIN	KAZ	Hun	BEL	SRB	Bih	Fin	Cze	Est	Usa	Mkd	Alb	Den	GER	AUT	CRO	Caps	Goa
Artur BORUC	20/2/80	Celtic (SCO)	G46	G	G	G		G				G46		G			G	G	G	G	37	-
Paweł GOLAŃSKI	12/10/82	Steaua (ROU)	D46	s55	D										D		s46	D75	s46		12	1
Jacek BĄK	24/3/73	Austria Wien (AUT)	D46			D		D	D77			D46		D		D	D	D	D		96	3
Dariusz DUDKA	9/12/83	Wisła Kraków	D	M	D	M	D					M		M	s46	M81	M	M	M	D	29	2
Grzegorz BRONOWICKI	4/8/80	Crvena Zvezda (SRB)	D	D55		D		D	D			D77		D	D46						14	-
Jakub BŁASZCZYKOWSKI	14/12/85	Dortmund (GER)	M	M	M			s46													13	1
Mariusz LEWANDOWSKI	18/5/79	Shakhtar (UKR)	M	M	M	M	M46	M	M			M		M	M46	M	M	M	M	M46	50	3
Maciej IWAŃSKI	7/5/81	Zagłębie Lubin	M67																		3	1
Radosław SOBOLEWSKI	13/12/76	Wisła Kraków	M67		M		M	M													32	1
Jacek KRZYNÓWEK	15/5/76	Wolfsburg (GER)	M	M	M	M		M				M		M46		M81	M78	M	M	M	82	15
Radosław MATUSIAK	1/1/82	Palermo (ITA) /Heerenveen (NED) /Wisła Kraków	A76	s56			A46		s46				A	s46	A						15	7
Tomasz KUSZCZAK	20/3/82	Man. United (ENG)	s46												G						6	-
Marcin WASILEWSKI	9/6/80	Anderlecht (BEL)	s46	D		s46	D83	D	D			D		D		D	D	D	D	D	30	1
Michał ŻEWŁAKOW	22/4/76	Olympiacos (GRE)	s46	D	D	D46		D	s77			D				D9		D	D	D	79	2
Wojciech ŁOBODZIŃSKI	20/10/82	Zagłębie Lubin /Wisła Kraków	s67	s73		M80		M46	M		M46	M83		s46		M80	s46	M65	s83	M55	19	2
Mariusz JOP	3/8/78	Moskva (RUS)	s67	D	D	D	D		D			s46			D		D		D46		25	-
Łukasz PISZCZEK	3/6/85	Hertha (GER)	s76											M46				s65			4	-

ATIONAL TEAM APPEARANCES 2007/08

			Rus	POR	FIN	KAZ	Hun	BEL	SRB	Bih	Fin	Cze	Est	Usa	Mkd	Alb	Den	GER	AUT	CRO	Caps	Goals
ebiusz SMOLAREK	9/1/81	Racing (ESP)		A73	A80	A		M85				A66		s46		s46	M77	A	A	s55	34	13
ciej ŻURAWSKI	12/9/76	Celtic (SCO) /Larissa (GRE)		A56	s80	s46		A82				s46		A46		A61	A46	A46			72	17
egorz RASIAK	12/1/79	Southampton (ENG)			A65				A46												37	8
rek SAGANOWSKI	31/10/78	Southampton (ENG)			s65	A46									s59	s80	s77	s75	A83	A69	26	3
nil KOSOWSKI	3/8/77	Wisła Kraków				s80	M	s85	M19												50	4
asz FABIAŃSKI	18/4/85	Arsenal (ENG)					G		G			s46				G					8	-
nasz KIELBOWICZ	21/2/76	Legia					D82														9	-
nrad GOLOS	15/9/82	Górnik Zabrze					M46						s63								3	-
asz GARGUŁA	25/2/81	Bełchatów					M46				M46		M63	s46	M87		s78				12	1
emysław KAŹMIERCZAK	5/5/82	Porto (POR)					s46														9	1
rek ZIENCZUK	24/9/78	Wisła Kraków					s46				M80		M64								9	-
nasz ZAHORSKI	22/11/84	Górnik Zabrze					s46		s19	A	s46	s66	s64		A	s61	A46			s69	10	1
weł BROŻEK	21/4/83	Wisła Kraków					s46			A69	A73			A46							11	1
ub WAWRZYNIAK	7/7/83	Legia					s82		M	D82	D	s77	D		s46	D	D46			D	12	-
egorz BARTCZAK	21/6/85	Zagłębie Lubin					s83			D46											2	-
ał MURAWSKI	9/10/81	Lech						s82	M		s46	s83			M	s81			s85	M	11	1
riusz PAWEŁEK	17/3/81	Wisła Kraków								G											3	-
am KOKOSZKA	6/10/86	Wisła Kraków								D	D		D		D	s9				s46	8	2
nasz LISOWSKI	4/4/85	Widzew								D	D46		D								3	-
mon PAWŁOWSKI	4/11/86	Zagłębie Lubin								M46											1	-
rcin KUS	2/9/81	Korona								M	D										7	-
chał PAZDAN	21/9/87	Górnik Zabrze								M69	M72		M		s87	s81					5	-
chał GOLINSKI	17/3/81	Zagłębie Lubin								M69	M		M	s63							5	1
riusz PAWELEC	14/4/86	Górnik Zabrze								s46			D63								2	-
ał BOGUSKI	9/6/84	Wisła Kraków								s46											1	-
tr KUKLIS	14/1/86	Widzew								s69			s63								2	-
dosław MAJEWSKI	15/12/86	Groclin								s69	s72		s63		M59						4	-
tłomiej GRZELAK	9/8/81	Legia Warszawa								s69											4	2
tr MADEJSKI	2/8/83	Górnik Zabrze								s82											1	-
bastian PRZYROWSKI	30/11/81	Groclin									G		G								4	-
tr BROŻEK	21/4/83	Wisła Kraków									s46										1	-
wid NOWAK	30/11/84	Bełchatów									s73										1	-
mil GROSICKI	8/6/88	Legia /Sion (SUI)									s80		M63								2	-
tur WICHNIAREK	28/2/77	Arminia (GER)										A46									17	4
kadiusz RADOMSKI	27/6/77	Austria Wien (AUT)												D63							30	-
GER Guerreiro	25/5/82	Legia														M46	s46	s46	M85	M	5	1

POLAND

DOMESTIC LEAGUE 2007/08

EKSTRAKLASA FINAL TABLE

		Home					Away					Total					
	Pld	W	D	L	F	A	W	D	L	F	A	W	D	L	F	A	Pts
1 Wisła Kraków	30	14	1	0	42	6	10	4	1	26	12	24	5	1	68	18	77
2 Legia Warszawa	30	12	1	2	30	7	8	2	5	18	10	20	3	7	48	17	63
3 Groclin Grodzisk Wielkopolski	30	10	4	1	28	6	8	2	5	24	18	18	6	6	52	24	60
4 KKS Lech Poznań	30	11	2	2	34	13	6	4	5	21	19	17	6	7	55	32	57
5 Zaglębie Lubin	30	9	3	3	24	14	6	4	5	19	16	15	7	8	43	30	52
6 Korona Kielce	30	9	4	2	24	13	6	2	7	14	19	15	6	9	38	32	51
7 MKS Cracovia Kraków	30	8	3	4	21	13	3	3	9	9	19	11	6	13	30	32	39
8 Górnik Zabrze	30	7	3	5	19	15	4	3	8	15	24	11	6	13	34	39	39
9 GKS Bełchatów	30	7	4	4	18	16	2	7	6	8	16	9	11	10	26	32	38
10 KS Ruch Chorzów	30	6	5	4	21	17	2	5	8	14	24	8	10	12	35	41	34
11 ŁKS Łódź	30	4	4	7	12	11	3	5	7	13	20	7	9	14	25	31	30
12 MKS Odra Wodzisław Śląski	30	4	3	8	15	23	4	2	9	13	24	8	5	17	28	47	29
13 KS Polonia Bytom	30	4	4	7	10	15	3	3	9	12	30	7	7	16	22	45	28
14 Jagiellonia Białystok	30	5	4	6	18	20	2	2	11	9	37	7	6	17	27	57	27
15 RTS Widzew Łódź	30	5	5	5	18	19	0	6	9	9	23	5	11	14	27	42	26
16 GKS Zagłębie Sosnowiec	30	3	4	8	12	23	1	0	14	7	35	4	4	22	19	58	16

N.B. Zagłębie Lubin and Korona Kielce also relegated for disciplinary reasons; Groclin Grodzisk Wielkopolski merged into KSP Polonia Warszawa for 2008/09 season.

TOP GOALSCORERS

23 Paweł BROŻEK (Wisła Kraków)

16 Adrian SIKORA (Groclin)
Marek ZIEŃCZUK (Wisła Kraków)

15 Takesure CHINYAMA (Legia)

12 Hernan Edson RENGIFO (Lech)

11 Dawid JARKA (Górnik Zabrze)

10 Edi ANDRADINA (Korona)
Maciej IWAŃSKI (Zagłębie Lubin)
Marcin ROBAK (Korona)
Tomasz ZAHORSKI (Górnik Zabrze)
Marcin ZAJĄC (Lech)

CLUB-BY-CLUB

GKS BEŁCHATÓW

Coach – Orest Lenczyk; (21/3/08) Jan Złomańczuk

Founded – 1977

2007				
28/7	Korona	h	2-0	*Costly, Popek*
5/8	Widzew	a	0-0	
11/8	Zagłębie Lubin	h	0-1	
19/8	Groclin	a	0-0	
25/8	Wisła Kraków	h	0-0	
2/9	Odra	h	3-1	*Nowak, Dziedzic, Jarzębowski*
16/9	Lech	a	1-1	*Dziedzic*
22/9	Jagiellonia	h	2-0	*Popek, Costly*
28/9	Legia	a	1-4	*Popek*
6/10	Bytom	h	0-3	
19/10	Ruch	a	1-1	*Jarzębowski*
26/10	Łódź	h	1-0	*Wróbel*
2/11	Górnik Zabrze	a	0-2	
10/11	Zagłębie Sosnowiec	h	2-0	*Garguła, Rachwał*
24/11	Cracovia	a	2-0	*Garguła, Wróbel*
1/12	Korona	a	2-2	*Costly, Pietrasiak (p)*
8/12	Widzew	h	3-1	*Stolarczyk (p), Costly, Nowak*
2008				
23/2	Zagłębie Lubin	a	0-1	
1/3	Groclin	h	0-4	
9/3	Wisła Kraków	a	0-2	
14/3	Odra	a	0-1	
20/3	Lech	h	0-3	
29/3	Jagiellonia	a	1-0	*Garguła*
6/4	Legia	h	2-2	*Jarzębowski, Dziedzic*
12/4	Bytom	a	0-0	
19/4	Ruch	h	2-0	*Costly, Jarzębowski*
26/4	Łódź	a	0-2	
3/5	Górnik Zabrze	h	0-0	
7/5	Zagłębie Sosnowiec	a	0-0	
10/5	Cracovia	h	1-1	*Dziedzic*

No	Name	Nat	Pos	Aps	(s)	Gls
6	Edward CECOT		D	18	(5)	
53	Mateusz CETNARSKI		M	3	(6)	
9	Carlos Yair COSTLY Molina	HON	A	15	(11)	5
14	Maciej DĄBROWSKI		D	1		
80	Janusz DZIEDZIC		A	10	(7)	4
10	Łukasz GARGUŁA		M	26		3
3	Rafał GRODZICKI		D	4	(6)	
18	Jhoel HERRERA ZEGARRA	PER	D	3	(1)	
11	Krzysztof JANUS		M	3	(6)	
8	Tomasz JARZĘBOWSKI		M	28	(1)	4
40	Dominik KISIEL		G	2		
57	Michał KORENIK		A		(1)	
16	Marcin KOWALCZYK		D	13		
27	Krzysztof Damian KOZIK		G	3		
60	Grzegorz KUŚWIK		A		(2)	
1	Piotr LECH		G	4		
33	Paweł MAGDOŃ		D	6	(1)	
28	Artur MARCINIAK		D	3	(3)	
55	Krzysztof MICHALAK		M	1	(1)	
17	Dawid NOWAK		A	10	(7)	2
15	Dariusz PIETRASIAK		D	24		1
4	Jacek POPEK		D	25	(2)	3
20	Patryk RACHWAŁ		M	23	(2)	1
12	Łukasz SAPELA		G	21		
11	Alexander SÁNCHEZ REYES	PER	M		(5)	
7	Maciej STOLARCZYK		D	23	(1)	1
5	Paweł STRĄK		M	23		
24	Jakub TOSIK		M	2	(4)	
25	Mariusz UJEK		A	15	(7)	
23	Tomasz WRÓBEL		M	21	(4)	2
29	Mariusz ZAWODZIŃSKI		A		(1)	

MKS CRACOVIA KRAKÓW

Coach – Stefan Majewski

Founded - 1906

MAJOR HONOURS: Polish League – (5) 1921, 1930, 1932, 1937, 1948.

2007

29/7	Legia	a	0-1	
4/8	Ruch	h	1-0	*Pawlusiński*
11/8	Bytom	a	0-1	
18/8	Jagiellonia	h	2-0	*Kłus, Moskała*
25/8	Łódź	h	0-0	
1/9	Górnik Zabrze	a	0-1	
15/9	Groclin	h	3-1	*Witkowski, Moskała 2*
22/9	Widzew	a	0-2	
29/9	Zagłębie Sosnowiec	h	1-0	*Witkowski*
6/10	Korona	a	0-2	
20/10	Wisła Kraków	h	1-2	*Dudzic*
26/10	Lech	a	1-3	*og (Kucharski)*
3/11	Zagłębie Lubin	h	1-2	*Szczoczarz*
10/11	Odra	a	1-0	*Moskała*
24/11	Bełchatów	h	0-2	
30/11	Legia	h	0-2	
7/12	Ruch	a	0-2	

2008

23/2	Bytom	h	1-1	*og (Owczarek)*
1/3	Jagiellonia	a	2-0	*Witkowski, Pawlusiński (p)*
8/3	Łódź	a	0-0	
15/3	Górnik Zabrze	h	3-0	*Dudzic, Pawlusiński (p), Kulig*
22/3	Groclin	a	0-0	
29/3	Widzew	h	1-0	*Pawlusiński*
5/4	Zagłębie Sosnowiec	a	2-1	*og (Marek), Pawlusiński*
12/4	Korona	h	1-1	*Polczak*
20/4	Wisła Kraków	a	1-2	*Kulig*
26/4	Lech	h	3-2	*Witkowski 3*
3/5	Zagłębie Lubin	a	1-3	*Tupalski*
7/5	Odra	h	3-0	*Dudzic, Nowak, Kulig*
10/5	Bełchatów	a	1-1	*Polczak*

No	Name	Nat	Pos	Aps	(s)	Gls
26	Tomasz BALIGA		D		(1)	
8	Arkadiusz BARAN		M	27		
21	Marcin BOJARSKI		M	5	(9)	
33	Marcin CABAJ		G	27		
37	Bartłomiej DUDZIC		A	17	(12)	3
40	Karol GREGOREK		A		(3)	
13	Michał KARWAN		D	1	(3)	
10	Dariusz KŁUS		M	27		1
34	Karol KOSTRUBAŁA		M	5	(9)	
4	Przemysław KULIG		D	27		3
20	Árpád MAJOROS	HUN	M	3	(7)	
18	Tomasz MOSKAŁA		A	21	(5)	4
19	Paweł NOWAK		M	29		1
30	Sławomir OLSZEWSKI		G	3	(1)	
9	Dariusz PAWLUSIŃSKI		M	26	(3)	5
16	Piotr POLCZAK		D	13		2
6	Krzysztof RADWAŃSKI		D	30		
15	Łukasz SKRZYŃSKI		D	15		
23	Łukasz SZCZOCZARZ		A	4	(6)	1
32	Paweł SZWAJDYCH		M	4	(4)	
14	Kacper TATARA		A		(1)	
17	Łukasz TUPALSKI		D	10		1
25	Mateusz URBAŃSKI		D	5	(2)	
5	Tomasz WACEK		D	3	(7)	
3	Jacek WIŚNIEWSKI		D	4	(8)	
11	Kamil WITKOWSKI		A	19	(4)	6
27	Paweł WOJCIECHOWSKI		D	5	(2)	

GÓRNIK ZABRZE

Coach – Ryszard Wieczorek

Founded - 1948

MAJOR HONOURS: Polish League – (14) 1957, 1959, 1961, 1963, 1964, 1965, 1966, 1967, 1971, 1972, 1985, 1986, 1987, 1988; Polish Cup – (6) 1965, 1968, 1969, 1970, 1971, 1972.

2007

5/8	Legia	h	0-3	
11/8	Lech	a	1-4	*Jarka*
14/8	Wisła Kraków	a	0-2	
17/8	Ruch	h	1-0	*Hajto (p)*
25/8	Jagiellonia	a	1-1	*Gierczak*
1/9	Cracovia	h	1-0	*Jarka*
14/9	Bytom	h	4-0	*Jarka 3, Gierczak*
19/9	Odra	h	1-0	*Jarka*
29/9	Groclin	a	1-3	*Gołoś*
6/10	Zagłębie Sosnowiec	h	4-2	*Jarka 4*
20/10	Łódź	a	1-0	*Zahorski*
27/10	Korona	a	2-3	*Zahorski, og (Kuś)*
2/11	Bełchatów	h	2-0	*Zahorski 2*
10/11	Zagłębie Lubin	a	1-1	*Brzęczek*
23/11	Widzew	h	1-1	*Smirnovs*
2/12	Wisła Kraków	h	1-3	*Brzęczek*
8/12	Legia	a	0-2	

2008

24/2	Lech	h	0-1	
2/3	Ruch	a	2-3	*Brzęczek, Zahorski*
8/3	Jagiellonia	h	3-0	*Madejski, Zahorski, Jarka*
15/3	Cracovia	a	0-3	
22/3	Bytom	a	1-0	*Hajto*
30/3	Odra	a	2-0	*Zahorski 2*
4/4	Groclin	h	0-0	
11/4	Zagłębie Sosnowiec	a	2-0	*Zahorski, Brzęczek*
20/4	Łódź	h	1-1	*Zahorski*
26/4	Korona	h	0-3	
3/5	Bełchatów	a	0-0	
7/5	Zagłębie Lubin	h	0-1	
10/5	Widzew	a	1-2	*Madejski*

No	Name	Nat	Pos	Aps	(s)	Gls
25	Marko BAJIĆ	SRB	M	9	(3)	
10	Jerzy BRZĘCZEK		M	26		4
26	Adam DANCH		M	16	(8)	
15	Piotr GIERCZAK		A	19	(5)	2
5	Konrad GOŁOŚ		M	22	(2)	1
7	Tomasz HAJTO		D	25		2
20	Sławomir JARCZYK		D	11	(2)	
11	Dawid JARKA		A	22	(7)	11
27	Marius KIŽYS	LTU	M	7	(6)	
12	Tomasz LASKOWSKI		G	1		
8	Piotr MADEJSKI		M	21	(7)	2
21	Mariusz MAGIERA		D	12		
4	Piotr MALINOWSKI		M	5	(14)	
16	Adam MARCINIAK		D		(1)	
9	Tomasz MOSKAL		A	6	(14)	
82	Sebastian NOWAK		G	3		
6	Tadas PAPEČKYS	LTU	D	15	(1)	
3	Patrik PAVLENDA	SVK	D	9		
19	Mariusz PAWELEC		D	15		
2	Michał PAZDAN		D	17	(2)	
28	Boris PESKOVIČ	SVK	G	24		
13	Piotr RUSZKUL		A		(3)	
1	Mateusz SŁAWIK		G	2	(1)	
31	Maris SMIRNOVS	LVA	D	15	(1)	1
23	Dariusz STACHOWIAK		M		(7)	
24	Marcin WODECKI		A		(2)	
22	Tomasz ZAHORSKI		A	28	(2)	10

GROCLIN GRODZISK WIELKOPOLSKI

Coach – Jacek Zieliński I

Founded - 1922

MAJOR HONOURS: Polish Cup – (2) 2005, 2007.

2007

27/7	Ruch	h	1-4	*Sikora (p)*

5/8	Jagiellonia	a	3-1	*Piechniak, Lato, Babnič*
12/8	Legia	a	0-1	
19/8	Bełchatów	h	0-0	
25/8	Bytom	a	2-0	*Ivanovski, Rocki*
2/9	Łódź	h	2-0	*Sikora, Majewski*
15/9	Cracovia	a	1-3	*Piechniak*
23/9	Zagłębie Sosnowiec	a	3-1	*Lato, Ivanovski, og (Hosic)*
29/9	Górnik Zabrze	h	3-1	*Piechniak, Mynář (p), Majewski*
7/10	Zagłębie Lubin	a	2-1	*Lato, Ivanovski*
19/10	Lech	h	1-0	*Lato*
27/10	Widzew	a	0-1	
3/11	Korona	h	4-0	*Mynář (p), Sikora 3*
10/11	Wisła Kraków	a	0-3	
24/11	Odra	h	0-0	
30/11	Ruch	a	2-1	*Sikora 2*
8/12	Jagiellonia	h	3-1	*Kozioł, Piechniak, Sikora*
2008				
23/2	Legia	h	1-0	*Rocki*
1/3	Bełchatów	a	4-0	*Sikora 2, Świerczewski, Piechniak*
8/3	Bytom	h	5-0	*Sikora 3, Lato, Telichowski*
15/3	Łódź	a	2-1	*Ivanovski, Sikora*
22/3	Cracovia	h	0-0	
29/3	Zagłębie Sosnowiec	h	3-0	*Ivanovski, Muszalik, Piechniak*
4/4	Górnik Zabrze	a	0-0	
13/4	Zagłębie Lubin	h	2-0	*Sikora, Kumbev*
19/4	Lech	a	1-2	*Muszalik*
26/4	Widzew	h	3-0	*Lato, og (Ukah), Majewski*
4/5	Korona	a	1-1	*Sikora*
7/5	Wisła Kraków	h	0-0	
10/5	Odra	a	3-2	*Majewski, Sokołowski 2*

No	Name	Nat	Pos	Aps	(s)	Gls
27	Peter BABNIČ	SVK	M	4	(6)	1
25	Sergio BATATA		M	1	(4)	
27	Michał CIARKOWSKI		M		(2)	
8	Filip IVANOVSKI	MKD	A	16	(9)	5
6	Tomasz JODŁOWIEC		M	25	(1)	
16	Szymon KAŹMIEROWSKI		A	2	(2)	
10	Amadeusz KŁODAWSKI		M		(4)	
18	Igor KOZIOŁ		D	10	(2)	1
26	Pance KUMBEV	MKD	D	21	(1)	1
20	Jarosław LATO		M	30		6
4	Vlade LAZAREVSKI	MKD	D	12	(3)	
23	Radosław MAJEWSKI		M	22	(6)	4
21	Mariusz MUSZALIK		M	12	(11)	2
2	Radek MYNÁŘ	CZE	D	25		2
19	Radosław NOLKA		M		(1)	
5	Bartosz OLEJNICZAK		D	1	(1)	
7	Piotr PIECHNIAK		M	23	(3)	6
12	Sebastian PRZYROWSKI		G	30		
22	Piotr ROCKI		A	10	(15)	2
9	Adrian SIKORA		A	27		16
11	Marek SOKOŁOWSKI		M	26	(2)	2
14	Bartosz ŚLUSARSKI		A	4		
77	Piotr ŚWIERCZEWSKI		M	9	(2)	1
15	Błażej TELICHOWSKI		D	10	(9)	1
17	Łukasz TUPALSKI		D	2	(1)	
33	Saşa YUNISOĞLU	AZE	D	8		

JAGIELLONIA BIAŁYSTOK

Coach – Artur Płatek; (27/4/08) Józef Antoniak

Founded - 1932

2007				
28/7	Bytom	h	2-1	*Sobociński, Jarecki*
5/8	Groclin	h	1-3	*Wincel (p)*
11/8	Łódź	h	1-0	*Truszkowski*
18/8	Cracovia	a	0-2	
25/8	Górnik Zabrze	h	1-1	*Kwiek*
31/8	Zagłębie Sosnowiec	a	1-3	*Everton*
15/9	Korona	h	0-0	
22/9	Bełchatów	a	0-2	
29/9	Widzew	h	2-1	*Wasiluk, Sotirović*
6/10	Wisła Kraków	a	0-5	
19/10	Zagłębie Lubin	h	0-0	
27/10	Odra	a	3-1	*Sotirović 2, Sobociński*
3/11	Lech	h	4-2	*Markiewicz, Sotirović, og (Kikut), Dzienis*
9/11	Legia	a	0-0	
24/11	Ruch	h	1-1	*Sobociński*
1/12	Bytom	a	1-0	*Sobociński*
8/12	Groclin	a	1-3	*Sotirović*
2008				
22/2	Łódź	a	0-0	
1/3	Cracovia	h	0-2	
8/3	Górnik Zabrze	a	0-3	
15/3	Zagłębie Sosnowiec	h	2-1	*Kwiek, Sobociński*
22/3	Korona	a	0-1	
29/3	Bełchatów	h	0-1	
5/4	Widzew	a	0-2	
12/4	Wisła Kraków	h	1-2	*Tumicz*
19/4	Zagłębie Lubin	a	2-5	*Sotirović, Jarecki*
26/4	Odra	h	2-3	*Sotirović, Tumicz*
2/5	Lech	a	1-6	*Sotirović*
7/5	Legia	h	1-2	*Sobociński*
10/5	Ruch	a	0-4	

No	Name	Nat	Pos	Aps	(s)	Gls
11	Rafał BAŁECKI		A	1		
99	Jacek BANASZYŃSKI		G	25		
10	BRUNO Coutinho Martins	BRA	M	3	(2)	
22	Jacek CHAŃKO		D		(4)	
23	Mateusz CIELUCH		A		(1)	
13	Mariusz DZIENIS		M	20	(2)	1
26	EVERTON António Pereira	BRA	M	9	(1)	1
21	Jacek FALKOWSKI		M	9	(8)	
3	Vahan GEVORGYAN		M	6	(2)	
4	Karol JANIK		A		(2)	
27	Dariusz JARECKI		M	27	(1)	2
33	Radosław KAŁUŻNY		D	19	(3)	
30	Ernest KONON		A	1	(2)	
1	Maciej KUDRYCKI		G		(1)	
15	Aleksander KWIEK		M	22	(3)	2
9	Dariusz ŁATKA		M	22		
8	Mariusz MARCZAK		M	4	(7)	
28	Jacek MARKIEWICZ		M	25		1
20	Adrian NAPIERAŁA		D	6		
32	Łukasz NAWOTCZYŃSKI		D	26		
16	Bartłomiej NIEDZIELA		M	2	(18)	
17	Alexis NORAMBUENA RUZ	CHI	D	8		
6	Michał RENUSZ		M	7	(2)	
29	RODNEI Francisco de Lima	BRA	D	11		
12	Grzegorz SANDOMIERSKI		G	5		
7	Remigiusz SOBOCIŃSKI		A	24	(3)	6
38	Tomasz SOKOŁOWSKI I		M	4	(4)	
18	Dawid SOŁDECKI		M	1		
69	Vuk SOTIROVIĆ	SRB	A	16	(9)	8
24	Marcin TRUSZKOWSKI		A	4	(4)	1
31	Łukasz TUMICZ		A		(6)	2
14	Marek WASILUK		D	22	(3)	1
6	Marcin WINCEL		D	1	(1)	1

KORONA KIELCE

Coach – Jacek Zieliński II

Founded - 1973

2007				
28/7	Bełchatów	a	0-2	

/8	Lech	h	1-0	*Andradina*
0/8	Wisła Kraków	a	0-4	
8/8	Odra	h	2-0	*Robak 2*
6/8	Ruch	a	2-1	*Robak, Andradina (p)*
/9	Bytom	h	4-0	*Robak 2, Sasin, Kuś*
5/9	Jagiellonia	a	0-0	
1/9	Legia	h	1-0	*Bonin*
9/9	Łódź	a	1-0	*Andradina*
/10	Cracovia	h	2-0	*Andradina, Hermes*
9/10	Zagłębie Sosnowiec	a	3-2	*Robak, Bonin, Gajtkowski*
7/10	Górnik Zabrze	h	3-2	*Robak, Zganiacz, Andradina*
'11	Groclin	a	0-4	
1/11	Widzew	a	2-0	*Kaczmarek, Zabłocki*
4/11	Zagłębie Lubin	h	1-4	*Andradina*
/12	Bełchatów	h	2-2	*Robak, Skerla*
/12	Lech	a	0-1	
008				
2/2	Wisła Kraków	h	1-1	*Sobolewski*
/3	Odra	a	0-1	
/3	Ruch	h	0-2	
4/3	Bytom	a	2-0	*Andradina, Zabłocki*
2/3	Jagiellonia	h	1-0	*Skerla*
0/3	Legia	a	0-2	
/4	Łódź	h	2-0	*Gajtkowski, Andradina*
2/4	Cracovia	a	1-1	*Andradina*
9/4	Zagłębie Sosnowiec	h	2-0	*Zganiacz, Robak*
6/4	Górnik Zabrze	a	3-0	*Robak, Sobolewski, Gajtkowski*
/5	Groclin	h	1-1	*Sobolewski*
/5	Widzew	h	1-1	*Andradina*
0/5	Zagłębie Lubin	a	0-1	

lo	Name	Nat	Pos	Aps	(s)	Gls
6	Edi ANDRADINA	BRA	A	27	(1)	10
9	Robert BEDNAREK		D	27		
5	Grzegorz BONIN		M	16	(7)	2
	Tomasz BRZYSKI		D	1		
	Piotr CELEBAN		D	11	(2)	
.0	Marcin DRZYMONT		D	26		
8	Krzysztof GAJTKOWSKI		A	4	(9)	3
7	HERMES Neves Soares	BRA	M	19	(1)	1
	HERNÂNI José da Rosa	BRA	D	13	(2)	
	Marcin KACZMAREK		M	14	(8)	1
5	Maciej KOWALCZYK		A	3	(8)	
0	Wojciech KOWALEWSKI		G	10		
3	Paweł KRÓL		M		(1)	
3	Marcin KUŚ		D	21		1
	Maciej MIELCARZ		G	20		
1	Tomasz NOWAK		M	5	(19)	
1	Marcin ROBAK		A	25	(3)	10
4	Sławomir RUTKA		D	3		
	Paweł SASIN		M	16	(3)	1
	Andrius SKERLA	LTU	D	18	(3)	2
9	Paweł SOBOLEWSKI		M	12	(1)	3
	Piotr ŚWIERCZEWSKI		M	5	(4)	
8	Cezary WILK		M	11	(3)	
4	Jakub ZABŁOCKI		A	2	(7)	2
0	Mariusz ZGANIACZ		M	21	(3)	2

KKS LECH POZNAŃ

Coach – Franciszek Smuda

Founded - 1922

MAJOR HONOURS: Polish League – (5) 1983, 1984, 1990, 1992, 1993; Polish Cup – (4) 1982, 1984, 1988, 2004.

2007				
28/7	Zagłębie Sosnowiec	h	4-2	*Murawski, Zając 2, Reiss*
3/8	Korona	a	0-1	
11/8	Górnik Zabrze	h	4-1	*Reiss, Wilk, Rengifo, Zając*
18/8	Zagłębie Lubin	a	1-1	*Wilk*
24/8	Widzew	h	1-0	*Rengifo*
1/9	Wisła Kraków	a	2-4	*Wilk, og (Cléber)*
16/9	Bełchatów	h	1-1	*Zając*
22/9	Ruch	h	6-2	*Zając 2, Reiss, Kucharski, Rengifo, Quinteros (p)*
29/9	Odra	a	2-1	*Quinteros, Zając*
6/10	Legia	h	1-0	*Rengifo*
19/10	Groclin	a	0-1	
26/10	Cracovia	h	3-1	*Rengifo 2, Injac*
3/11	Jagiellonia	a	2-4	*og (Dzienis), Rengifo*
10/11	Bytom	h	1-0	*Reiss*
24/11	Łódź	a	2-1	*Rengifo, Zając*
1/12	Zagłębie Sosnowiec	a	0-0	
7/12	Korona	h	1-0	*Reiss*
2008				
24/2	Górnik Zabrze	a	1-0	*Quinteros*
29/2	Zagłębie Lubin	h	0-0	
7/3	Widzew	a	1-1	*Rengifo*
15/3	Wisła Kraków	h	1-2	*og (Brożek Pi.)*
20/3	Bełchatów	a	3-0	*Bosacki, Rengifo, Injac*
29/3	Ruch	a	2-0	*Quinteros, og (Grodzicki)*
5/4	Odra	h	2-0	*Wojtkowiak, Pitry*
12/4	Legia	a	1-0	*Pitry*
19/4	Groclin	h	2-1	*Murawski, Bandrowski*
26/4	Cracovia	a	2-3	*Zając, Quinteros*
2/5	Jagiellonia	h	6-1	*Cueto 2, Zając, Quinteros, Pitry 2*
7/5	Bytom	a	2-2	*Rengifo, Pitry*
10/5	Łódź	h	1-2	*Rengifo*

No	Name	Nat	Pos	Aps	(s)	Gls
24	Tomasz BANDROWSKI		M	12	(1)	1
19	Bartosz BOSACKI		D	13		1
20	Anderson Denyro CUETO Sánchez	PER	P	4	(5)	2
3	Ivan ĐURĐEVIĆ	SRB	D	21	(1)	
77	Emilian DOLHA	ROU	G	10		
6	Marcin DYMKOWSKI		D	7		
17	Dawid FLORIAN		A		(8)	
25	Luis Alfonso HENRIQUEZ	PAN	M	9	(3)	
21	Dimitrije INJAC	SRB	M	12	(11)	2
23	Marcin KIKUT		D	28		
26	Maciej KONONOWICZ		A		(2)	
27	Krzysztof KOTOROWSKI		G	20	(1)	
4	Dawid KUCHARSKI		D	21		1
14	Ilian MITSANSKI	BUL	A	1	(1)	
29	Tomasz MIDZIERSKI		D	1		
16	Rafał MURAWSKI		M	29		2
8	Przemysław PITRY		A	4	(22)	5
15	Henry Edson QUINTEROS	PER	M	25		6
9	Piotr REISS		A	20	(4)	5
11	Hernan Trigoso RENGIFO	PER	A	22	(6)	12
13	Maciej SCHERFCHEN		M	6		
28	Mariusz SZYSZKA		M		(2)	
18	Zlatko TANEVSKI	MKD	D	12		
5	Jakub WILK		M	13	(10)	3
22	Grzegorz WOJTKOWIAK		D	11		1
7	Marcin ZAJĄC		M	29	(1)	10

LEGIA WARSZAWA

Coach – Jan Urban

Founded - 1916

MAJOR HONOURS: Polish League – (8) 1955, 1956, 1969, 1970, 1994, 1995, 2002, 2006; Polish Cup – (13) 1955, 1956, 1964, 1966, 1973, 1980, 1981, 1989, 1990, 1994, 1995, 1997, 2008.

2007				
29/7	Cracovia	h	1-0	*Chinyama*
5/8	Górnik Zabrze	a	3-0	*Radović, Roger (p),*

				Edson
12/8	Groclin	h	1-0	*Grzelak*
17/8	Łódź	a	1-0	*Grzelak*
25/8	Zagłębie Sosnowiec	h	5-0	*Astiz, Giza, Grosicki, Roger, Chinyama*
31/8	Zagłębie Lubin	a	2-0	*og (Tiago Gomes), Korzym*
14/9	Widzew	h	3-1	*Vuković, Chinyama, Edson*
21/9	Korona	a	0-1	
28/9	Bełchatów	h	4-1	*Giza, Chinyama 2, Radović*
6/10	Lech	a	0-1	
19/10	Odra	h	0-1	
28/10	Wisła Kraków	a	0-1	
4/11	Ruch	h	2-0	*Edson, Chinyama*
9/11	Jagiellonia	h	0-0	
24/11	Bytom	a	2-1	*Roger, Chinyama*
30/11	Cracovia	a	2-0	*Chinyama 2*
8/12	Górnik Zabrze	h	2-0	*Chinyama, Rybus*
2008				
23/2	Groclin	a	0-1	
1/3	Łódź	h	2-1	*Chinyama 2*
7/3	Zagłębie Sosnowiec	a	1-2	*Chinyama*
16/3	Zagłębie Lubin	h	3-0	*Radović, Burchardt, Ekwueme*
22/3	Widzew	a	1-0	*Giza*
30/3	Korona	h	2-0	*Chinyama, Roger*
6/4	Bełchatów	a	2-2	*Roger, Rybus*
12/4	Lech	h	0-1	
19/4	Odra	a	2-0	*Borysiuk, Vuković*
27/4	Wisła Kraków	h	2-1	*Rybus 2*
3/5	Ruch	a	0-0	
7/5	Jagiellonia	a	2-1	*Grzelak, Roger (p)*
10/5	Bytom	h	3-1	*Chinyama, Smoliński 2*

No	Name	Nat	Pos	Aps	(s)	Gls
26	Iñaki ASTIZ Ventura	ESP	D	23		1
5	Błażej AUGUSTYN		D	2	(2)	
21	Ariel BORYSIUK		M	4	(4)	1
23	Piotr BRONOWICKI		D	7	(2)	
9	Marcin BURKHARDT		M	2	(8)	1
19	Takesure CHINYAMA	ZIM	A	24	(4)	15
4	Dickson CHOTO	ZIM	D	12		
27	EDSON Luiz da Silva	BRA	M	19		3
30	Martins EKWUEME	NGA	M	4	(9)	1
7	Piotr GIZA		M	22	(2)	3
8	Kamil GROSICKI		M	5	(6)	1
18	Bartłomiej GRZELAK		A	12	(8)	3
11	Tomasz KIEŁBOWICZ		D	19	(4)	
13	Maciej KORZYM		A		(9)	1
33	Kamil MAJKOWSKI		A	2	(4)	
82	Ján MUCHA	SVK	G	29		
6	ROGER Guerreiro		M	27	(1)	6
32	Miroslav RADOVIĆ	SRB	M	22	(5)	3
31	Maciej RYBUS		M	3	(7)	4
25	Jakub RZEŹNICZAK		D	20	(1)	
1	Wojciech SKABA		G	1		
28	Marcin SMOLIŃSKI		M	6	(5)	2
3	Wojciech SZALA		D	21	(1)	
20	Sebastian SZAŁACHOWSKI		M		(3)	
37	Wojciech TROCHIM		A		(1)	
14	Aleksandar VUKOVIĆ	SRB	M	25	(2)	2
24	Jakub WAWRZYNIAK		D	17		
17	Przemysław WYSOCKI		D	2	(2)	

ŁKS ŁÓDŹ

Coach – Wojciech Borecki; (1/10/07) Mirosław Jabłoński; (17/3/08) Marek Chojnacki

Founded - 1908

MAJOR HONOURS: Polish League – (2) 1958, 1998; Polish Cup – (1) 1957.

2007				
28/7	Odra	a	2-2	*Madej, Szczot*
4/8	Bytom	h	0-0	
11/8	Jagiellonia	a	0-1	
17/8	Legia	h	0-1	
25/8	Cracovia	a	0-0	
2/9	Groclin	a	0-2	
15/9	Zagłębie Sosnowiec	h	3-0	*Arifović, Madej, Komorowski*
22/9	Zagłębie Lubin	a	1-2	*Arifović*
29/9	Korona	h	0-1	
5/10	Widzew	a	0-0	
20/10	Górnik Zabrze	h	0-1	
26/10	Bełchatów	a	0-1	
3/11	Wisła Kraków	h	0-1	
10/11	Ruch	a	0-0	
24/11	Lech	h	1-2	*Madej (p)*
30/11	Odra	h	0-1	
8/12	Bytom	a	1-0	*Madej (p)*
2008				
22/2	Jagiellonia	h	0-0	
1/3	Legia	a	1-2	*Adamski*
8/3	Cracovia	h	0-0	
15/3	Groclin	h	1-2	*Kujawa*
20/3	Zagłębie Sosnowiec	a	3-1	*Arifović 2, Madej (p)*
29/3	Zagłębie Lubin	h	2-1	*Szczot, Madej*
5/4	Korona	a	0-2	
11/4	Widzew	h	2-0	*Adamski, Kłos*
20/4	Górnik Zabrze	a	1-1	*Arifović*
26/4	Bełchatów	h	2-0	*Madej (p), Szczot (p)*
4/5	Wisła Kraków	a	2-5	*Jovino, Arifović*
7/5	Ruch	h	1-1	*Szczot*
10/5	Lech	a	2-1	*Jovino, Vayer*

No	Name	Nat	Pos	Aps	(s)	Gls
5	Marcin ADAMSKI		D	13		2
18	ANDRESON Dourado Ribas	BRA	M	7	(1)	
16	Ensar ARIFOVIĆ	BIH	A	23	(4)	6
26	Paweł BUDNIAK		A		(2)	
4	Tarik CERIĆ	BIH	D	9		
22	Adam CIEŚLIŃSKI		A		(1)	
15	Jacek DĄBROWSKI		M	7	(3)	
7	Labinot HALITI	ALB	M	3		
26	JOVINO Juca Viana	BRA	M	12		2
17	Mladen KAŠĆELAN	MNE	M	14		
11	Marcin KLATT		A	6	(6)	
15	KLEYR Vieira dos Santos	BRA	A	1	(3)	
2	Tomasz KŁOS		D	27		1
31	Maecin KOMOROWSKI		D	8	(4)	1
21	Rafał KUJAWA		N	1	(8)	1
28	Zdzisław LESZCZYŃSKI		D	7	(2)	
23	Robert ŁAKOMY		D	22		
27	Michał ŁOCHOWSKI		D		(1)	
12	Kostyantyn MAKHNOVSKIY	UKR	G	2		
10	Łukasz MADEJ		M	29		7
9	Sebastian MILA		M	11	(1)	
6	Arkadiusz MYSONA		D	14	(3)	
9	Miroslav OPSENICA	SRB	M	6	(1)	
1	Marcin PAJĄK		G	1	(1)	
27	PAULINHO Bezerra Maciel Júnior	BRA	M	13	(4)	
19	Stefan POTOCKI		A		(3)	
3	Sebastian PRZYBYSZEWSKI		D	2	(6)	
25	Mieczysław SIKORA		A	11	(10)	
14	Robert SZCZOT		M	24	(3)	4
15	Adrian ŚWIĄTEK		A		(6)	
5	Łukasz TRAŁKA		M	6	(2)	
29	Ivan UDAREVIĆ	CRO	D		(1)	
8	Gábor VAYER	HUN	M	4	(4)	1
20	Adrian WOŹNICZKA		D	20	(3)	
30	Bogusław WYPARŁO		G	27		

MKS ODRA WODZISŁAW ŚLĄSKI

Coach – Mariusz Kuras; (1/10/07) Janusz Białek; (8/4/08) Paweł Sibik; (8/5/08) Janusz Białek

Founded - 1922

2007				
28/7	Łódź	h	2-2	*Iwan, Socha*
4/8	Zagłębie Sosnowiec	h	1-0	*Biskup*
11/8	Widzew	h	1-1	*Nowacki*
18/8	Korona	a	0-2	
25/8	Zagłębie Lubin	h	1-3	*Świerzyński*
2/9	Bełchatów	a	1-3	*Grzegorzewski (p)*
15/9	Wisła Kraków	h	2-2	*Grzegorzewski (p), Malinowski*
22/9	Górnik Zabrze	a	0-1	
29/9	Lech	h	1-2	*Grzegorzewski*
5/10	Ruch	h	2-0	*Seweryn, Socha*
19/10	Legia	a	1-0	*Szary*
27/10	Jagiellonia	h	1-3	*Nowacki (p)*
3/11	Bytom	a	0-1	
10/11	Cracovia	h	0-1	
24/11	Groclin	a	0-0	
30/11	Łódź	a	1-0	*Nowacki*
8/12	Zagłębie Sosnowiec	a	2-0	*Woś, Seweryn*
2008				
23/2	Widzew	a	3-4	*Mitsanski 2, Woś*
1/3	Korona	h	1-0	*Mitsanski*
8/3	Zagłębie Lubin	a	0-3	
14/3	Bełchatów	h	1-0	*Socha*
22/3	Wisła Kraków	a	0-0	
30/3	Górnik Zabrze	h	0-2	
5/4	Lech	a	0-2	
13/4	Ruch	a	2-3	*Mitsanski 2*
19/4	Legia	h	0-2	
26/4	Jagiellonia	a	3-2	*Woś 2, Socha*
3/5	Bytom	h	0-2	
7/5	Cracovia	a	0-3	
10/5	Groclin	h	2-3	*Aleksander, Kowalczyk*

No	Name	Nat	Pos	Aps	(s)	Gls
24	Arkadiusz ALEKSANDER		A	3	(14)	1
20	Jakub BISKUP		M	15	(9)	1
6	Artur BŁAŻEJEWSKI		M	1	(2)	
2	Witold CICHY		D	16	(1)	
33	Dariusz DUDEK		D	16	(5)	
18	Jakub GRZEGORZEWSKI		A	11		3
23	Bartosz HINC		M	19	(4)	
8	Bartosz IWAN		M	4	(6)	1
13	Grzegorz JAKOSZ		D	7	(9)	
15	Marcin KOKOSZKA		M	22		
16	Jacek KOWALCZYK		D	23	(1)	1
5	Jacek KURANTY		M	17	(5)	
1	Paweł LINKA		G	1		
9	Marcin MALINOWSKI		M	19		1
8	Ilian MITSANSKI	BUL	A	13		5
6	Marcin NOWACKI		M	15	(1)	3
29	Krzysztof PILARZ		G	16		
18	Błażej RADLER		D	3	(2)	
22	Daniel RYGEL	CZE	M	4	(5)	
11	Damian SEWERYN		M	20	(8)	2
10	Bartłomiej SOCHA		A	10	(12)	4
12	Adam STACHOWIAK		G	13		
21	Sławomir SZARY		D	28		1
4	Piotr SZYMICZEK		D	4	(4)	
19	Tomasz ŚWIERZYŃSKI		A	1	(2)	1
7	Jan WOŚ		M	29		4

KS POLONIA BYTOM

Coach – Dariusz Fornalak; (17/12/07) Michał Probierz

Founded - 1945

MAJOR HONOURS: Polish League – (2) 1954, 1962.

2007				
28/7	Jagiellonia	a	1-2	*Podstawek (p)*
4/8	Łódź	a	0-0	
11/8	Cracovia	h	1-0	*Zieliński*
18/8	Zagłębie Sosnowiec	a	0-1	
25/8	Groclin	h	0-2	
1/9	Korona	a	0-4	
14/9	Górnik Zabrze	a	0-4	
23/9	Wisła Kraków	a	0-5	
28/9	Zagłębie Lubin	h	1-0	*Podstawek*
6/10	Bełchatów	a	3-0	*Zieliński 2, Radzewicz*
20/10	Widzew	h	1-1	*Podstawek (p)*
27/10	Ruch	a	0-2	
3/11	Odra	h	1-0	*Podstawek*
10/11	Lech	a	0-1	
24/11	Legia	h	1-2	*Wolański*
1/12	Jagiellonia	h	0-1	
8/12	Łódź	h	0-1	
2008				
23/2	Cracovia	a	1-1	*Wolański*
29/2	Zagłębie Sosnowiec	h	1-0	*Trzeciak*
8/3	Groclin	a	0-5	
14/3	Korona	h	0-2	
22/3	Górnik Zabrze	h	0-1	
28/3	Wisła Kraków	h	1-2	*Bažík*
5/4	Zagłębie Lubin	a	0-0	
12/4	Bełchatów	h	0-0	
18/4	Widzew	a	4-2	*Radzewicz, Dziółka, Podstawek, Trzeciak*
25/4	Ruch	h	1-1	*Solecki*
3/5	Odra	a	2-0	*Wolański 2*
7/5	Lech	h	2-2	*Podstawek, Staňo*
10/5	Legia	a	1-3	*Zieliński*

No	Name	Nat	Pos	Aps	(s)	Gls
19	Marek BAŽÍK	SVK	M	9	(1)	1
31	Adrian CHOMIUK		D	5	(2)	
22	Jakub DZIÓŁKA		D	17	(2)	1
24	Rafał GRZYB		M	29		
16	Rafał JABŁOŃSKI		M		(1)	
3	Grzegorz JURCZYK		D	14		
17	Mateusz KAMIŃSKI		D	1	(1)	
87	Seweryn KIEŁPIN		G	2		
81	Radoslav KRAL	SVK	D	6	(4)	
18	Ireneusz MARCINKOWSKI		D	15	(2)	
11	Mariusz MĘŻYK		A	6	(10)	
23	Wojciech MRÓZ		M	2	(7)	
5	Tomasz OWCZAREK		D	18	(5)	
33	Michal PESKOVIČ	SVK	G	10		
4	Piotr PLEWNIA		M	3	(2)	
10	Grzegorz PODSTAWEK		A	24	(3)	6
20	Mariusz PRZYBYLSKI		M	11		
9	Marcin RADZEWICZ		M	18	(6)	2
21	Hubert ROBASZEK		M	9	(6)	
15	Artur ROZMUS		A	3	(3)	
2	Arkadiusz SOJKA		D	9	(2)	
4	Valeriy SOKOLENKO	UKR	D	13		
15	Mariusz SOLECKI		A	1	(5)	1
20	Tomasz SOSNA		D	5		
3	Pavol STAŇO	SVK	D	15	(2)	1
1	Marcin SUCHAŃSKI		G	10		
6	Jacek TRZECIAK		M	20	(6)	2
14	Paweł WOJCIECHOWSKI		D	9	(1)	
7	Janusz WOLAŃSKI		M	23	(4)	4
25	Michał ZIELIŃSKI		A	15	(14)	4
12	Grzegorz ŻMIJA		G	8		

KS RUCH CHORZÓW

Coach – Dušan Radolský (SVK)

Founded - 1920

MAJOR HONOURS: Polish League – (14) 1933, 1934, 1935, 1936, 1938, 1951, 1952, 1953, 1960, 1968, 1974, 1975, 1979, 1989; Polish Cup – (3) 1951, 1974, 1996.

POLAND

2007				
27/7	Groclin	a	4-1	*Fabus, Balaz, Jezierski, Grzyb (p)*
4/8	Cracovia	a	0-1	
10/8	Zagłębie Sosnowiec	h	1-0	*Sokołowski*
17/8	Górnik Zabrze	a	0-1	
26/8	Korona	h	1-2	*Mikulėnas*
9/1	Widzew	a	2-2	*Grzyb (p), Jezierski*
15/9	Zagłębie Lubin	h	2-2	*Fabus, Jezierski*
22/9	Lech	a	2-6	*Grzyb, Jezierski*
30/9	Wisła Kraków	h	0-3	
5/10	Odra	a	0-2	
19/10	Bełchatów	h	1-1	*Grzyb (p)*
27/10	Bytom	h	2-0	*Grzyb, Fabus*
4/11	Legia	a	0-2	
10/11	Łódź	h	0-0	
24/11	Jagiellonia	a	1-1	*Grzyb*
30/11	Groclin	h	1-2	*Balaz*
7/12	Cracovia	h	2-0	*og (Wacek), Grzyb*
2008				
23/2	Zagłębie Sosnowiec	a	0-0	
2/3	Górnik Zabrze	h	3-2	*Ćwielong, Baran, Nowacki*
8/3	Korona	a	2-0	*Ćwielong (p), Balaz*
15/3	Widzew	h	1-1	*Fabus*
22/3	Zagłębie Lubin	a	1-2	*og (Bartczak G.)*
29/3	Lech	h	0-2	
5/4	Wisła Kraków	a	0-2	
13/4	Odra	h	3-2	*Pulkowski, Fabus 2*
19/4	Bełchatów	a	0-2	
25/4	Bytom	a	1-1	*Balaz*
3/5	Legia	h	0-0	
7/5	Łódź	a	1-1	*Ćwielong*
10/5	Jagiellonia	h	4-0	*Janoszka, Feruga, Pulkowski, Ćwielong*

No	Name	Nat	Pos	Aps	(s)	Gls
4	Ireneusz ADAMSKI		D	23	(2)	
20	Pavol BALAZ	SVK	M	21	(3)	4
3	Grzegorz BARAN		D	29		1
16	Grzegorz BONK		M	8	(4)	
22	Tomasz BRZYSKI		D	13		
7	Piotr ĆWIELONG		A	8	(3)	4
9	Grzegorz DOMŻALSKI		M	2	(9)	
5	Toni GOLEM	CRO	D	8	(2)	
15	Rafał GRODZICKI		D	7	(2)	
6	Wojciech GRZYB		M	26	(2)	7
24	Martin FABUŠ	SVK	A	28	(1)	6
27	Daniel FERUGA		M	1	(3)	1
29	Ariel JAKUBOWSKI		D	19	(3)	
14	Łukasz JANOSZKA		A	9	(16)	1
76	Remigiusz JEZIERSKI		A	12	(2)	4
15	Marcin KLACZKA		D	3	(2)	
7	Murilo Rufino Barbosa LILO	BRA	M		(3)	
13	Przemysław ŁUDZIŃSKI		A		(1)	
18	Gražvydas MIKULĖNAS	LTU	A	2	(2)	1
96	Robert MIODUSZEWSKI		G	18		
2	Jovan NINKOVIĆ	SRB	D	2	(2)	
11	Marcin NOWACKI		M	12	(1)	1
1	Sebastian NOWAK		G	7		
8	Krzysztof NYKIEL		D	19	(2)	
23	Michał OSIŃSKI		D	8	(2)	
30	Matko PERDIJIĆ	CRO	G	1	(1)	
80	Krzysztof PILARZ		G	4		
17	Michał PULKOWSKI		M	28		2
21	Maciej SADLOK		M	2	(6)	
18	Marcin SOBCZAK		A		(3)	
22	Tomasz SOKOŁOWSKI I		M	3	(8)	1
28	Gabor STRAKA	SVK	M	7	(1)	

RTS WIDZEW ŁÓDŹ

Coach – Michał Probierz; (6/9/07) Marek Zub; (21/4/08) Janusz Wójcik

Founded - 1910

MAJOR HONOURS: Polish League – (4) 1981, 1982, 1996, 1997; Polish Cup – (1) 1985.

2007				
27/7	Zagłębie Lubin	a	1-2	*Napoleoni*
5/8	Bełchatów	h	0-0	
11/8	Odra	a	1-1	*Kuklis*
18/8	Wisła Kraków	h	1-3	Napoleoni
24/8	Lech	a	0-1	
1/9	Ruch	h	2-2	*Kuklis, Bogunović*
14/9	Legia	a	1-3	*Kuklis*
22/9	Cracovia	h	2-0	*Bogunović, Budka*
29/9	Jagiellonia	a	1-2	*og (Rodnei)*
5/10	Łódź	h	0-0	
20/10	Bytom	a	1-1	*Budka*
27/10	Groclin	h	1-0	*Napoleoni*
3/11	Zagłębie Sosnowiec	a	0-0	
11/11	Korona	h	0-2	
23/11	Górnik Zabrze	a	1-1	*Oshadogan*
1/12	Zagłębie Lubin	h	1-1	*Masłowski*
8/12	Bełchatów	a	1-3	*Mierzejewski*
2008				
23/2	Odra	h	4-3	*Kowalczyk M. (p), Panka, Lisowski, Kuklis*
1/3	Wisła Kraków	a	0-1	
7/3	Lech	h	1-1	*Szymanek*
15/3	Ruch	a	1-1	*Napoleoni*
22/3	Legia	h	0-1	
29/3	Cracovia	a	0-1	
5/4	Jagiellonia	h	2-0	*Napoleoni 2*
11/4	Łódź	a	0-2	
18/4	Bytom	h	2-4	*Budka, Napoleoni*
26/4	Groclin	a	0-3	
2/5	Zagłębie Sosnowiec	h	0-1	
7/5	Korona	a	1-1	*Budka*
10/5	Górnik Zabrze	h	2-1	*Oziębała 2*

No	Name	Nat	Pos	Aps	(s)	Gls
24	Saša BOGUNOVIĆ	SRB	A	7	(3)	2
20	Alain Elvis BONO Mack Mboune	CMR	M	3	(2)	
28	Łukasz BROŹ		D	17	(4)	
11	Mateusz BROŹ		M	1	(3)	
16	Adrian BUDKA		M	26	1	4
33	DOUGLAS Freitas Cardozo	BRA	A	1	(3)	
21	Bartosz FABINIAK		G	27		
26	Piotr GRZELCZAK		A	1	(12)	
15	GUSTAVO	BRA	A		(1)	
1	Jakub HŁADOWCZAK		G	3		
6	Wojciech JARMUŻ		D	4	(2)	
8	Łukasz JUSZKIEWICZ		M	23		
23	Bartosz KANIECKI		G		(1)	
5	Robert KŁOS		D	23		
27	Maciej KOWALCZYK		A	8	(1)	1
34	Robert KOWALCZYK		M		(3)	
25	Piotr KUKLIS		M	22	(5)	4
30	Radosław KURSA		D	3		
17	Tomasz LISOWSKI		D	19	(3)	1
14	Łukasz MASŁOWSKI		M	18	(3)	1
9	Łukasz MIERZEJEWSKI		M	18	(6)	1
10	Stefano NAPOLEONI	ITA	M	21	(6)	7
2	Joseph Dayo OSHADOGAN	ITA	D	12		1
20	Przemysław OZIĘBAŁA		A	2	(3)	2
18	Mindaugas PANKA	LTU	M	11	(6)	1
31	Grzegorz PIECHNA		A	5	(2)	
13	Krzysztof SOKALSKI		A	2	(5)	
19	Piotr STAWARCZYK		D	12	(5)	
7	Sławomir SZELIGA		D	12	(9)	
29	Wojciech SZYMANEK		D	5		1
4	Ugochukwu UKAH	NGA	D	24		

WISŁA KRAKÓW

Coach – Maciej Skorża

Founded - 1906

MAJOR HONOURS: Polish League – (11) 1927, 1928, 1949, 1950, 1978, 1999, 2001, 2003, 2004, 2005, 2008; Polish Cup – (4) 1926, 1967, 2002, 2003.

007				
8	Zagłębie Lubin	a	1-0	*Brożek Pa.*
/8	Korona	h	4-0	*Brożek Pa. 2, Cléber (p), Niedzielan*
/8	Górnik Zabrze	h	2-0	*Cléber (p), Brożek Pa.*
/8	Widzew	a	3-1	*Zieńczuk, Cléber (p), Brożek Pa.*
/8	Bełchatów	a	0-0	
9	Lech	h	4-2	*Brożek Pa. 2, Jean Paulista 2*
/9	Odra	a	2-2	*Zieńczuk 2*
/9	Bytom	h	5-0	*Zieńczuk, Kosowski, Boguski, Brożek Pi., Dudu*
/9	Ruch	a	3-0	*Zieńczuk, Sobolewski, Cantoro*
10	Jagiellonia	h	5-0	*Zieńczuk 2, Brożek Pa., Jean Paulista, Brożek Pi.*
/10	Cracovia	a	2-1	*Zieńczuk, Boguski*
/10	Legia	h	1-0	*Zieńczuk*
11	Łódź	a	1-0	*Dudka*
/11	Groclin	h	3-0	*Zieńczuk, Brożek Pa., og (Kumbev)*
/11	Zagłębie Sosnowiec	a	3-1	*Boguski, Brożek Pa. 2*
12	Górnik Zabrze	a	3-1	*Jean Paulista, Sobolewski, Zieńczuk*
12	Zagłębie Lubin	h	2-1	*Brożek Pa., Zieńczuk*
008				
/2	Korona	a	1-1	*Kokoszka*
3	Widzew	h	1-0	*Brożek Pa.*
3	Bełchatów	h	2-0	*Zieńczuk, Brożek Pa.*
/3	Lech	a	2-1	*Zieńczuk, Brożek Pa.*
/3	Odra	h	0-0	
/3	Bytom	a	2-1	*Baszczyński, Łobodziński*
4	Ruch	h	2-0	*Brożek Pa., Jirsák*
/4	Jagiellonia	a	2-1	*Matusiak, Zieńczuk*
/4	Cracovia	h	2-1	*Brożek Pa. 2*
/4	Legia	a	1-2	*Brożek Pa.*
5	Łódź	h	5-2	*Díaz, Zieńczuk, Brożek Pa. 2, Jean Paulista*
5	Groclin	a	0-0	
/5	Zagłębie Sosnowiec	h	4-0	*Cléber (p), Brożek Pa. 2, Jirsák*

o	Name	Nat	Pos	Aps	(s)	Gls
	Marcin BASZCZYŃSKI		D	26	(1)	1
	Rafał BOGUSKI		M	22	(5)	3
3	Paweł BROŻEK		A	25	(3)	23
	Piotr BROŻEK		M	17	(9)	2
	Ilie CEBANU	MDA	G	1		
5	CLÉBER Guedes de Lima	BRA	D	26		4
)	Roberto Mauro CANTORO	ARG	M	27	(1)	1
	Piotr ĆWIELONG		A	1	(5)	
5	Junior Enrique DÍAZ Campbell	CRC	D	3	(4)	1
4	Dariusz DUDKA		M	17	(3)	1
)	MacPherlin DUDU Omagbemi	NGA	A	2	(7)	1
	Arkadiusz GŁOWACKI		D	25	(1)	
)	JEAN PAULISTA	BRA	A	11	(12)	5
5	Tomáš JIRSÁK	CZE	M	4	(16)	2
2	Marcin JUSZCZYK		G	3		
	Grzegorz KMIECIK		A		(1)	
3	Adam KOKOSZKA		D	9	(1)	1
	Kamil KOSOWSKI		M	12	(1)	1
	Wojciech ŁOBODZIŃSKI		M	11		1
9	Patryk MAŁECKI		A		(7)	
1	Radosław MATUSIAK		A	4	(4)	1
29	Krzysztof MĄCZYŃSKI		M	1	(1)	
18	Andrzej NIEDZIELAN		A	4	(4)	1
81	Mariusz PAWEŁEK		G	26		
7	Radosław SOBOLEWSKI		M	25		2
14	Przemysław SZABAT		D		(1)	
2	Michael THWAITE	AUS	D		(1)	
17	Marek ZIEŃCZUK		M	28		16

ZAGŁĘBIE LUBIN

Coach – Czesław Michniewicz; (22/10/07) Rafał Ulatowski

Founded - 1945

MAJOR HONOURS: Polish League – (2) 1991, 2007

2007				
27/7	Widzew	h	2-1	*André Nunes, Iwański*
4/8	Wisła Kraków	h	0-1	
11/8	Bełchatów	a	1-0	*Iwański*
18/8	Lech	h	1-1	*Arboleda*
25/8	Odra	a	3-1	*Arboleda, André Nunes, Chałbiński*
31/8	Legia	h	0-2	
15/9	Ruch	a	2-2	*Iwański, Chałbiński*
22/9	Łódź	h	2-1	*Iwański, Arboleda*
28/9	Bytom	a	0-1	
7/10	Groclin	h	1-2	*Arboleda*
19/10	Jagiellonia	a	0-0	
27/10	Zagłębie Sosnowiec	h	2-1	*Goliński, Stasiak*
3/11	Cracovia	a	2-1	*Włodarczyk, Pawłowski*
10/11	Górnik Zabrze	h	1-1	*Rui Miguel*
24/11	Korona	a	4-1	*Pawłowski, Iwański, Plizga 2*
1/12	Widzew	a	1-1	*Rui Miguel*
9/12	Wisła Kraków	a	1-2	*Arboleda*
2008				
23/2	Bełchatów	h	1-0	*Kolendowicz*
29/2	Lech	a	0-0	
8/3	Odra	h	3-0	*Stasiak, Włodarczyk, Iwański*
16/3	Legia	a	0-3	
22/3	Ruch	h	2-1	*Stasiak, Rui Miguel*
29/3	Łódź	a	1-2	*Bartczak M.*
5/4	Bytom	h	0-0	
13/4	Groclin	a	0-2	
19/4	Jagiellonia	h	5-2	*Alunderis, Rui Miguel, Chałbiński 3*
26/4	Zagłębie Sosnowiec	a	3-0	*Włodarczyk, Iwański (p), Plizga*
3/5	Cracovia	h	3-1	*Iwański 2 (2p), Pawłowski*
7/5	Górnik Zabrze	a	1-0	*Goliński*
10/5	Korona	h	1-0	*Iwański*

No	Name	Nat	Pos	Aps	(s)	Gls
27	Vidas ALUNDERIS	LTU	D	8	(1)	1
99	ANDRÉ Luís Correia NUNES	BRA	A	6	(4)	2
5	Manuel Santos ARBOLEDA	COL	D	14	(1)	5
19	Grzegorz BARTCZAK		D	28	(1)	
8	Mateusz BARTCZAK		M	14	(1)	1
11	Michał CHAŁBIŃSKI		A	16	(7)	5
77	Michał GOLIŃSKI		M	21	(3)	2
25	Łukasz HANZEL		M		(1)	
7	Maciej IWAŃSKI		M	27	(1)	10
14	Dariusz JACKIEWICZ		M	12	(3)	
84	Radosław JANUKIEWICZ		G	1	(1)	
15	Przemysław KOCOT		D	3	(2)	
20	Robert KOLENDOWICZ		M	14	(5)	1
18	Mate LAČIĆ	CRO	D	9		
9	Wojciech ŁOBODZIŃSKI		M	12	(3)	
22	Łukasz MIERZEJEWSKI		M		(1)	
23	Szymon PAWŁOWSKI		A	16	(10)	3
24	Marcin PIETROŃ		M	1	(3)	
16	Damian PIOTROWSKI		M	1	(1)	
21	Dawid PLIZGA		A	6	(8)	3

No	Name	Nat	Pos	Aps	(s)	Gls
30	Aleksander PTAK		G	20		
17	RUI MIGUEL Melo Rodrigues	POR	M	17	(4)	4
6	Andrzej SZCZYPKOWSKI		M	2	(2)	
13	Sreten SRETENOVIĆ	SRB	D	18	(1)	
4	Michał STASIAK		D	29		3
3	TIAGO Henrique Damil GOMES	POR	D	14	(4)	
1	Michal VÁCLAVÍK	CZE	G	9		
33	Piotr WŁODARCZYK		A	12	(10)	3
9	Michał ZAPAŚNIK		A		(1)	

GKS ZAGŁĘBIE SOSNOWIEC

Coach – Jerzy Kowalik; (23/10/07) Andrzej Orzeszek; (31/10/07) Romuald Szukiełowicz; (18/12/07) Andrzej Orzeszek; (24/3/08) Piotr Pierścionek

Founded - 1918

MAJOR HONOURS: Polish Cup – (4) 1962, 1963, 1977, 1978.

2007				
28/7	Lech	a	2-4	*Kmiecik, Berensztajn (p)*
4/8	Odra	a	0-1	
10/8	Ruch	a	0-1	
18/8	Bytom	h	1-0	*Folc*
25/8	Legia	a	0-5	
31/8	Jagiellonia	h	3-1	*Folc 2, Gawęcki*
15/9	Łódź	a	0-3	
23/9	Groclin	h	1-3	*Bagnicki*
29/9	Cracovia	a	0-1	
6/10	Górnik Zabrze	a	2-4	*Folc, Bednár*
19/10	Korona	h	2-3	*og (Drzymont), Pach*
27/10	Zagłębie Lubin	a	1-2	*Folc*
3/11	Widzew	h	0-0	
10/11	Bełchatów	a	0-2	
25/11	Wisła Kraków	h	1-3	*Bednár*
1/12	Lech	h	0-0	
8/12	Odra	h	0-2	
2008				
23/2	Ruch	h	0-0	
29/2	Bytom	a	0-1	
7/3	Legia	h	2-1	*Bałecki, Folc*
15/3	Jagiellonia	a	1-2	*Komorowski*
20/3	Łódź	h	1-3	*Małecki*
29/3	Groclin	a	0-3	
5/4	Cracovia	h	1-2	*Małecki (p)*
11/4	Górnik Zabrze	h	0-2	
19/4	Korona	a	0-2	
26/4	Zagłębie Lubin	h	0-3	
2/5	Widzew	a	1-0	*Marek*
7/5	Bełchatów	h	0-0	
10/5	Wisła Kraków	a	0-4	

No	Name	Nat	Pos	Aps	(s)	Gls
3	Admir ADŽEM	BIH	D	6	(1)	
27	Piotr BAGNICKI		A	5	(5)	1
27	Rafał BAŁECKI		A	1	(3)	1
21	Vladimír BEDNÁR	SVK	M	12	(3)	2
12	Adam BENSZ		G	17	(1)	
14	Jacek BERENSZTAJN		M	13	(2)	1
5	Rafał BERLIŃSKI		M	22	(1)	
20	Jarosław BIAŁEK		M	3	(1)	
20	Wojciech BIAŁEK		D	4		
6	Krzysztof BODZIONY		M	4	(1)	
14	Bartłomiej CHWALIBOGOWSKI		M	5	(3)	
24	Tomasz CIESIELSKI		D	5	(5)	
11	Paweł CYGNAR		M	11	(7)	
8	Yevhen DEMYDENKO	UKR	M		(2)	
13	Marcin FOLC		A	17	(7)	6
22	Dariusz GAWĘCKI		M	5		1
25	Szymon GĄSIŃSKI		G	8	(1)	
17	Dženan HOSIĆ	BIH	D	24		
4	Grzegorz KALICIAK		D	12	(1)	
10	Arkadiusz KŁODA		D	20		
31	Grzegorz KMIECIK		A	6	(4)	1
7	Dariusz KOHUT		M		(1)	
22	Marcin KOMOROWSKI		D	11		1
77	Yevhen KOPYL	UKR	G	4		
26	Dariusz KOZUBEK		M	10	(1)	
77	Grzegorz KURDZIEL		G	1		
9	Tomasz ŁUCZYWEK		M	10		
30	Patryk MAŁECKI		A	19	(1)	2
19	Adrian MAREK		D	17	(1)	1
23	Sebastian OLSZAR		A	5	(3)	
8	Przemysław OZIĘBAŁA		A	4	(4)	
18	Sławomir PACH		M	14	(5)	1
23	Jacek PACZKOWSKI		M	1	(1)	
15	Jarosław PIĄTKOWSKI		M	4	(5)	
28	Rafał PIETRZAK		A		(1)	
30	Krystian PRYMULA	GER	M	1	(1)	
4	Dawid RYNDAK		M		(1)	
35	Michał SKÓRSKI		D	9	(4)	
7	Dawid SKRZYPEK		M	12	(4)	
88	Marcin SMARZYŃSKI		A		(1)	
16	Tomasz SZATAN		M	5	(3)	
29	Wojciech SZWED		M		(2)	
26	Arkadiusz ŚWIDER		D	2	(2)	
2	Konrad TOMSIA		D	1		
2	David TOPOLSKI		D		(1)	

PROMOTED CLUBS

KS LECHIA GDAŃSK

Coach – Dariusz Kubicki

Founded - 1945

MAJOR HONOURS: Polish Cup - (1) 1983.

WKS ŚLĄSK WROCŁAW

Coach – Ryszard Tarasiewicz

Founded – 1947

MAJOR HONOURS: Polish League - (1) 1977; Polish Cup - (2) 1976, 1

KS PIAST GLIWICE

Coach – Piotr Mandrysz

Founded - 1945

ARKA GDYNIA

Coach – Wojciech Stawowy; (16/4/08) Robert Jończyk

Founded – 1929

MAJOR HONOURS: Polish Cup - (1) 1979.

SECOND LEVEL FINAL TABLE 2007/0

		Pld	W	D	L	F	A
1	KS Lechia Gdańsk	34	21	6	7	55	34
2	WKS Śląsk Wrocław	34	18	10	6	55	30
3	KS Piast Gliwice	34	17	11	6	45	23
4	Arka Gdynia	34	19	10	5	61	30
5	Znicz Pruszków	34	18	8	8	54	28
6	TS Podbeskidzie Bielsko-Biała	34	19	7	8	53	27
7	KSP Polonia Warszawa	34	14	8	12	45	36
8	Wisła Płock	34	14	8	12	52	51
9	GKS Jastrzębie	34	12	9	13	43	51
10	GKS Katowice	34	11	10	13	38	39
11	ZKS Stal Stalowa Wola	34	11	7	16	30	48
12	LKP Motor Lublin	34	10	5	19	33	55
13	OKS Odra Opole	34	8	11	15	28	39
14	KS Warta Poznań	34	7	11	16	29	45
15	Kmita Zabierzów	34	6	13	15	28	40
16	MKS Tur Turek	34	7	10	17	23	46
17	ŁKS Łomża	34	8	6	20	32	59
18	KS Pelikan Łowicz	34	6	10	18	37	60

DOMESTIC CUP 2007/08

PUCHAR POLSKI

;T ROUND

8/07)
ı Wysokie Mazowieckie 1, Jagiellonia 2
cimski Brzesko 0, Zagłębie Sosnowiec 2

8/07)
orak Iława 3, Łomża 1
z Pruszków 1, Piast Gliwice 0
decja II Nowy Sącz 0, Podbeskidzie Bielsko-Biała 0 *(aet; 3-2 on*
s)
szłość Rogów 1, Unia Janikowo 2
oń Oleśnica 3, Górnik Polkowice 0
kniarz Konstantynów Łódzki 0, Stal Stalowa Wola 0 *(aet; 1-3 in*
s)
t Otwock 2, Bytom 1 *(aet)*
oria Koronowo 1, Ostrowiec Świętokrzyski 0
ta Jarocin 1, Lechia Gdańsk 4
ıy 3, Kmita Zabierzów 0
ovia II Bytów 0, Polonia Warszawa 1
dź Legnica 2, Śląsk Wrocław 3 *(aet)*

/07)
nik Gracze 2, Odra Opole 3 *(aet)*
isza Bydgoszcz 0, Ruch 3 *(w/o)*

'OND ROUND

9/07)
ellonia 2, Widzew 4
oń Oleśnica 0, Wisła Płock 3
oria Koronowo 0, Zagłębie Lubin 3
onia Warszawa 3, Lech 2
a Opole 1, Bełchatów 0
decja II Nowy Sącz 0, Legia 4

'9/07)
k Wrocław 2, Wisła Kraków 2 *(aet; 4-5 on pens)*
ıy 0, Odra Wodzisław Śląski 0 *(aet; 4-2 on pens)*
hia 2, Górnik Zabrze 2 *(aet; 5-4 on pens)*
z Pruszków 2, Cracovia 5
h 2, Górnik Łęczna 0
orak Iława 1, Groclin 2
a Janikowo 1, Arka 2 *(aet)*
t Otwock 0, Łódź 1

'10/07)
ona 2, Zagłębie Sosnowiec 0
Stalowa Wola 3, Pogoń Szczecin 0 *(w/o)*

FINALS

'10/07)
h 1, Widzew 0
a Opole 0, Zagłębie Lubin 2
onia Warszawa 3, Korona 1
Stalowa Wola 1, Groclin 3

'10/07)
covia 0, Arka 1
hy 1, Wisła Kraków 3
gia 1, Łódź 0

'11/07)
hia 5, Wisła Płock 1

QUARTER-FINALS

(1/4/08 & 8/4/08)
Groclin 1 *(Ivanovski 26)*, Ruch 0
Ruch 1 *(Fabuš 18)*, Groclin 1 *(Batata 90)*
(Groclin 2-1)

(1/4/08 & 9/4/08)
Arka 0, Wisła Kraków 0
Wisła Kraków 2 *(Zieńczuk 45, Cantoro 67)*, Arka 1 *(Przytuła 90)*
(Wisła Kraków 2-1)

(2/4/08 & 9/4/08)
Zagłębie Lubin 5 *(Iwański 18, Rui Miguel 27, 55, Chałbiński 38, 75)*,
Polonia Warszawa 0
Polonia Warszawa 2 *(Piechna 5, 87)*, Zagłębie Lubin 3 *(Włodarczyk 27, Plizga 59, 68)*
(Zagłębie Lubin 8-2)

Legia 1 *(Wawrzyniak 64)*, Lechia 0
Lechia 0, Legia 1 *(Roger 86)*
(Legia 2-0)

SEMI-FINALS

(22/4/08 & 30/4/08)
Legia 0, Zagłębie Lubin 0
Zagłębie Lubin 1 *(Pawłowski 29)*, Legia 1 *(Chinyama 58)*
(1-1; Legia on away goal)

(23/4/08 & 30/4/08)
Wisła Kraków 0, Groclin 0
Groclin 0, Wisła Kraków 1 *(Brożek Pa. 65)*
(Wisła Kraków 1-0)

FINAL

(13/5/08)
Stadion BOT GKS, Belchatow
LEGIA WARSZAWA 0
WISŁA KRAKÓW 0
(aet; 3-2 on pens)
Referee – *Gilewski*
LEGIA – *Mucha, Szala, Iñaki Astiz, Choto, Wawrzyniak, Radović, Vuković, Roger, Rybus (Majkowski 89), Grzelak (Borysiuk 90), Chinyama (Smoliński 112).*
WISŁA KRAKÓW – *Pawełek, Baszczyński, Głowacki, Cléber, Brożek Pi., Łobodziński (Jirsák 59), Cantoro, Sobolewski, Zieńczuk, Boguski (Díaz 97), Matusiak (Jean Paulista 46).*

Promise unfulfilled as Scolari bows out

It was a tournament that started promisingly for Portugal, but ultimately UEFA EURO 2008™ proved an unfulfilling experience as Luiz Felipe Scolari's highly-fancied team, featuring the man tagged as the world's No1 player, dropped out at the quarter-final stage, beaten 3-2 by Germany.

Cristiano Ronaldo and co were impressive for only half of their stay in Switzerland. They clinched first place in Group A after putting Turkey and the Czech Republic to the sword in Geneva, but, as Croatia and the Netherlands also discovered to their cost, the policy of resting an entire team for the final group fixture checked Portugal's momentum, and when Scolari's first XI re-appeared after a week of inactivity to take on Germany in Basel, the early spark had gone.

Although Portugal's second string lost 2-0 to Switzerland, that in itself was no disaster. A greater threat to the harmony and confidence within the cam it seemed, was posed by a couple of side-issues - the inopportune revelation that Scolari had been appoin as the new manager of Chelsea FC, and the ongoing soap opera surrounding Ronaldo's purported move fr Manchester United FC to Real Madrid CF.

Deco was back to his best for Portugal at UEFA EURO 2008™

Only two Portuguese players made it into UEFA's All-Star squad, right-back José Bosingwa and centre-bac Pepe – defenders both, which rather contradicted th team's reputation for thrilling attacking play. In truth, was defensive vulnerability, and in particular a failure deal with set-pieces, that proved Portugal's downfall against Germany.

Scolari in credit

One disappointing defeat, however damaging, could not mask the overall success of Scolari's lengthy tenu which included second place at UEFA EURO 2004™, a semi-final spot at the 2006 FIFA World Cup and a quarter-final berth at UEFA EURO 2008™. The chronol may suggest a team in decline, but that would be unf on the Brazilian. Portugal were the only team to reach the last eight in all three of those tournaments, and while some players remained central figures througho his reign, he had to replace several highly influential stalwarts, such as Rui Costa, Luís Figo and Pauleta.

Ronaldo, the latest Portuguese superstar, blew hot an cold at UEFA EURO 2008™, which of course was never going to be enough to please an expectant public aft his stupendous season with Manchester United, but t revelation afterwards that he was hampered by a foot injury was clearly a mitigating factor in his modest performance. The colossal Pepe aside, Portugal's most impressive player was the wonderfully inventive Deco with the similarly-styled João Moutinho, small and clever, not far behind.

As Scolari went to Chelsea, Carlos Queiroz, Sir Alex Ferguson's assistant at Manchester United, left Old Trafford to become Portugal's new coach. It is his seco

: in the job, and the man who launched his coaching ·er by leading Portugal's embryonic 'golden eration' to back-to-back FIFA World Youth Cup wins 989 and 1991 will believe that, with the quality of ·ers at his disposal, his own prodigy Ronaldo at the front, happy days should lie ahead. As a former ch of the South African national team, Queiroz will e the advantage of being on familiar territory at the 0 World Cup.

rto's title hat-trick

'orto became the champions of Portugal for the d season in a row – and the 23rd time in all – in 7/08. Despite the sale of Pepe, to Real Madrid CF, Brazilian midfielder Anderson, to Manchester ted, the Dragões wiped the floor with the osition, sealing the title weeks in advance and shing the campaign with a 14-point margin of ory that would have been greater but for a six-point ishment inflicted on them for their part in a major ·uption scandal dating from 2003/04 that came to t during the course of the season.

to initially faced the prospect of being excluded from 2008/09 UEFA Champions League but they were ored on appeal. For the players, and coach Jesualdo ·eira, who took the club to new heights of domestic remacy, the affair was an annoyance but little more. ocent parties all, they rattled off the victories with ıless efficiency, winning 24 of their 30 matches, uding all of the first eight, and never giving the htest flicker of hope to SL Benfica and Sporting be de Portugal that they might be unsettled by the hering storm clouds.

entine striker Lisandro López had a particularly morable campaign, topping the Primeira Liga score rts by a landslide with 24 goals. Superbly supported his fellow countryman Lucho González and mesmeric ger Ricardo Quaresma, the 25-year-old scored at the of almost a goal a game. He also registered three es in the UEFA Champions League, including the nner' at home to FC Schalke 04 in the last-16 tie that to lost on penalties. They had earlier won their group, ich included Liverpool FC, Olympique de Marseille l Beşiktaş JK.

nfica, by contrast, suffered a shaky UEFA Champions gue campaign, but two goals in Donetsk from their werful new Paraguayan forward Óscar Cardozo abled them to pursue their European interests in the FA Cup, where, shortly after the departure of their

Sporting skipper João Moutinho lifts the Portuguese Cup after his team's victory over champions FC Porto in Lisbon

Spanish coach, José Antonio Camacho, they fell in the round of 16 to Spanish opposition, Getafe CF. Sporting also switched from the UEFA Champions League to the UEFA Cup. It might have been a different story but for an unlucky late own-goal conceded at home to AS Roma after resident Brazilian hitman Liedson had scored three goals in two games against the Italians to take his cumulative club total into three figures. Sporting progressed to the UEFA Cup quarter-finals, where they were beaten at home, and eliminated, by Rangers FC.

Sporting retain Cup

Domestically, with Porto uncatchable in the league, the only prize on offer was the Portuguese Cup. The two Lisbon giants met in the semi-final and produced a thriller, with Sporting eventually prevailing 5-3 after they had been two goals down. Standing between Sporting coach Paulo Bento and a second successive Taça de Portugal was Jesualdo Ferreira and his double-chasing Porto side. A cagey contest was to produce an unlikely hero when Sporting's young Brazilian striker Rodrigo Tiuí came off the bench in extra time and scored twice late on to win the Cup. It was the first time Sporting had won the trophy back-to-back since 1974.

Federação Portuguesa de Futebol (FPF)

Rua Alexandre Herculano 58
CP 24013
PT-1251-977 Lisboa
tel - +351 21 3252700
fax - +351 21 3252780
website - www.fpf.pt
email - info@fpf.pt
Year of Formation – 1914
President - Gilberto Madaíl
Press Officer – Onofre Costa
Stadium – Estádio Nacional, Lisbon (48,000)

INTERNATIONAL TOURNAMENT APPEARANCES
FIFA World Cup - (4) 1966 (3rd), 1986, 2002, 2006 (4th).
UEFA European Championship - (5) 1984 (semi-finals), 1996 (qtr-finals), 2000 (semi-finals), 2004 (runners-up), 2008 (qtr-finals).

TOP FIVE ALL-TIME CAPS
Luís Figo (127); Fernando Couto (110); Rui Costa (94); Pedro Resendes "Paule[ta]" (88); João Vieira Pinto (81)

TOP FIVE ALL-TIME GOALS
Pedro Resendes "Pauleta" (47); Eusébi[o] Ferreira Silva (41); Luís Figo (32); Nuno Gomes (29); Rui Costa (26)

NATIONAL TEAM RESULTS 2007/08

Date	Opponent		Venue	Score	Scorers
22/8/07	Armenia (ECQ)	A	Yerevan	1-1	*Cristiano Ronaldo (37)*
8/9/07	Poland (ECQ)	H	Lisbon	2-2	*Maniche (50), Cristiano Ronaldo (73)*
12/9/07	Serbia (ECQ)	H	Lisbon	1-1	*Simão (11)*
13/10/07	Azerbaijan (ECQ)	A	Baku	2-0	*Bruno Alves (12), Hugo Almeida (45)*
17/10/07	Kazakhstan (ECQ)	A	Almaty	2-1	*Makukula (84), Cristiano Ronaldo (90+1)*
17/11/07	Armenia (ECQ)	H	Leiria	1-0	*Hugo Almeida (42)*
21/11/07	Finland (ECQ)	H	Porto	0-0	
6/2/08	Italy	N	Zurich (SUI)	1-3	*Ricardo Quaresma (77)*
26/3/08	Greece	N	Dusseldorf (GER)	1-2	*Nuno Gomes (75)*
31/5/08	Georgia	H	Viseu	2-0	*João Moutinho (19), Simão (44p)*
7/6/08	Turkey (ECF)	N	Geneva (SUI)	2-0	*Pepe (61), Raul Meireles (90+3)*
11/6/08	Czech Republic (ECF)	N	Geneva (SUI)	3-1	*Deco (8), Cristiano Ronaldo (63), Ricardo Quaresma (90+1)*
15/6/08	Switzerland (ECF)	A	Basel (SUI)	0-2	
19/6/08	Germany (ECF)	N	Basel (SUI)	2-3	*Nuno Gomes (40), Hélder Postiga (87)*

That victory capped a fine end to the season for the Lisbon Lions, who, with seven wins in their last eight league games, took the UEFA Champions League spot guaranteed to the runners-up. Benfica, however, ended an ignominious campaign on a low, with unfancied Vitória SC, from Guimaraes, recovering from a 5-0 home defeat by Porto to pip them to the all-important third place. CS Marítimo, from Madeira, and Vitória FC, from Setubal, joined Benfica in the UEFA Cup, while SC Brag[a] finished seventh to qualify for the UEFA Intertoto Cup. UD Leiria, Portugal's Intertoto representatives in 2007, were relegated after finishing bottom of the Primeira Liga. FC Paços de Ferreira would normally have accompanied them down, but they gained a reprieve when Boavista FC were punished for their part in the corruption scandal and forcibly relegated instead.

TIONAL TEAM APPEARANCES 2007/08

– Luiz Felipe SCOLARI (BRA) 9/11/48			ARM	POL	SRB	AZE	KAZ	ARM	FIN	Ita	Gre	Geo	TUR	CZE	SUI	GER	Caps	Goals
)O Pereira	11/2/76	Betis (ESP)	G	G	G	G	G	G	G	G	G	G46	G	G	G	G	79	-
FERREIRA	18/1/79	Chelsea (ENG)	D		D	D	D			s46	D	D	D	D	D41	D	51	-
L Monteiro	4/1/80	Valencia (ESP)	D	s12		D75	D				s46	s63			D		48	1
ANDRADE	9/4/78	Juventus (ITA)	D76														51	3
NDO MEIRA	5/6/78	Stuttgart (GER)	D	D	D			D	M	s46	M46	s63	s92	s75	M	s31	53	2
MEIRELES	17/3/83	Porto	M		s83				s73	s62	s69	s46	s83		M		11	1
Mendes	2/5/81	Juventus (ITA)	M														38	1
son Souza "DECO"	27/8/77	Barcelona (ESP)	M	M	M77	M	M			M46		M46	M92	M		M	56	4
ANO RONALDO	5/2/85	Man. United (ENG)	A	A	A	A	A	A	A	A		A46	A	A		A	58	21
Sabrosa	31/10/79	Atlético (ESP)	A63	A81	A			M77			M18	A46	A83	A80		A	64	15
R POSTIGA	2/8/82	Porto /Panathinaikos(GRE)	A61									s63			A74	s73	34	11
GOMES	5/7/76	Benfica	s61	A69	A65				A77		A	A63	A69	A79		A67	72	29
DO QUARESMA	26/9/83	Porto	s63	s69	s65	A70	A85	A60	A84	A	M69	s46		s80	A		23	3
) ALVES	27/11/81	Porto	s76	D	D	D	D	D	D	D	s46	s46			D		12	1
O CANEIRA	9/2/79	Valencia (ESP)		D12				D	D	D46	D46						25	-
OSINGWA	24/8/82	Porto		D	D			D	D	D69		D63	D	D		D	11	-
ndo Teixeira "PETIT"	25/9/76	Benfica		M	M					M46		M46	M	M		M73	57	4
Ribeiro "MANICHE"	11/11/77	Atlético (ESP) /Internazionale (ITA)		M	M83	M	M59	M	M73	M62							47	7
MOUTINHO	8/9/86	Sporting		s81	s77		s85				s18	M73	M	M75	s71	M31	17	1
DO CARVALHO	18/5/78	Chelsea (ENG)				D	D			D	D	D46	D	D		D	46	4
EL VELOSO	11/5/86	Sporting				M	M	M	M		M69	s46			M71		7	-
) ALMEIDA	23/5/84	Bremen (GER)				A	A63	A68		s57	s46	s73		s79	s74		11	2
unha "NANI"	17/11/86	Man. United (ENG)				s70	s59	s77	s84	s46		s46	s69		A	s67	16	2
E RIBEIRO	9/11/81	Boavista				s75				s69	s69				s41		9	-
MAKUKULA	4/3/81	Marítimo /Benfica					s63	s68	s77	A57							4	1
JEL FERNANDES	5/2/86	Valencia (ESP)						s60									3	1
r Ferreira "PEPE"	26/2/83	Real Madrid (ESP)							D		D46	D63	D	D	D	D	7	1
OS MARTINS	29/4/82	Recreativo (ESP)									M						3	-
uim Silva "QUIM"	13/11/75	Benfica										s46					26	-

PORTUGAL

DOMESTIC LEAGUE 2007/08

PRIMEIRA LIGA FINAL TABLE

	Pld	Home W	Home D	Home L	Home F	Home A	Away W	Away D	Away L	Away F	Away A	Total W	Total D	Total L	Total F	Total A	Pts
1 FC Porto	30	13	1	1	33	4	11	2	2	27	9	24	3	3	60	13	69
2 Sporting Clube de Portugal	30	12	3	0	34	10	4	4	7	12	18	16	7	7	46	28	55
3 Vitória SC	30	11	2	2	20	12	4	6	5	15	19	15	8	7	35	31	53
4 SL Benfica	30	7	6	2	26	10	6	7	2	19	11	13	13	4	45	21	52
5 CS Marítimo	30	8	3	4	21	12	6	1	8	18	16	14	4	12	39	28	46
6 Vitória FC	30	8	4	3	23	12	3	8	4	14	21	11	12	7	37	33	45
7 SC Braga	30	7	5	3	19	11	3	6	6	13	23	10	11	9	32	34	41
8 CF Os Belenenses	30	5	5	5	17	17	6	5	4	18	16	11	10	9	35	33	40
9 Boavista FC	30	7	6	2	22	16	1	6	8	10	25	8	12	10	32	41	36
10 CD Nacional	30	6	3	6	11	13	3	5	7	12	15	9	8	13	23	28	35
11 A. Naval 1º Maio	30	4	5	6	12	22	5	2	8	14	23	9	7	14	26	45	34
12 A. Académica de Coimbra	30	3	10	2	15	15	3	4	8	16	23	6	14	10	31	38	32
13 CF Estrela da Amadora	30	6	5	4	21	15	0	8	7	8	26	6	13	11	29	41	31
14 Leixões SC	30	3	8	4	18	17	1	6	8	9	20	4	14	12	27	37	26
15 FC Paços de Ferreira	30	5	5	5	19	20	1	2	12	12	29	6	7	17	31	49	25
16 UD Leiria	30	2	4	9	13	23	1	3	11	12	30	3	7	20	25	53	13

N.B. CF Os Belenenses – 3 pts deducted; UD Leiria – 3 pts deducted; FC Porto - 6 pts deducted; Boavista FC relegated instead of FC Paços de Ferreira.

TOP GOALSCORER

24 LISANDRO LÓPEZ (Porto)
13 Óscar CARDOZO (Benfica)
12 WELDON Andrade (Belenense
11 WESLEY Silva (Paços de Ferrei
Roland LINZ (Braga)
LIEDSON Muniz (Sporting)
9 Marcelo Silva "MARCELINHO" (Naval 1º Maio)
Cláudio Aguiar "LITO" (Acadé
8 JOÃO PAULO Ribeiro (Leiria)
JORGE RIBEIRO (Boavista)
JOSÉ PEDRO Salazar (Belenen
RICARDO QUARESMA (Porto)

CLUB-BY-CLUB

A. ACADÉMICA DE COIMBRA

Coach - Manuel Machado; (16/9/07) Domingos Paciência

Founded - 1887

MAJOR HONOURS: Portuguese Cup - (1) 1939.

2007

17/8	Sporting	a	1-4	*Gyánó*
26/8	Leiria	h	1-1	*Joeano (p)*
2/9	Marítimo	a	0-2	
16/9	Paços de Ferreira	h	1-0	*Hélder Barbosa*
24/9	Boavista	a	0-0	
1/10	Leixões	h	1-1	*Lito*
7/10	Porto	h	0-1	
27/10	Belenenses	a	0-0	
4/11	Amadora	h	3-3	*Lito 3*
11/11	Setúbal	a	1-3	*N'Doye*
24/11	Benfica	h	1-3	*Lito*
3/12	Guimarães	a	1-2	*Pavlović*
16/12	Nacional	h	1-0	*Cris*
22/12	Naval 1º Maio	a	1-0	*Cris*
2008				
4/1	Braga	h	3-3	*Hélder Barbosa, Tiero, Joeano*
13/1	Sporting	h	1-1	*Pavlović*
27/1	Leiria	a	1-3	*Edgar*
3/2	Marítimo	h	1-0	*Edgar*
17/2	Paços de Ferreira	a	1-1	*Lito*
25/2	Boavista	h	1-1	*Kaká*
1/3	Leixões	a	2-2	*Joeano 2*
9/3	Porto	a	0-1	
15/3	Belenenses	h	0-0	
29/3	Amadora	a	1-3	*Lito*
5/4	Setúbal	h	0-0	
11/4	Benfica	a	3-0	*Miguel Pedro, Berger, Luís Aguiar*
18/4	Guimarães	h	0-0	
27/4	Nacional	a	3-0	*og (Edson), Cris, Edga*
4/5	Naval 1º Maio	h	1-1	*Lito*
10/5	Braga	a	1-2	*Lito*

No	Name	Nat	Pos	Aps	(s)	Gls
5	Markus BERGER	AUT	D	7	(2)	1
82	CLÉBER Manttui	BRA	D	2	(1)	
17	Bruno Silva "CRIS"	BRA	M	22	(2)	3
38	CRISTIANO Araújo		M		(1)	
26	EDGAR Silva	BRA	A	5	(6)	3
22	FILIPE SARMENTO		A	2		
3	Gaoussou FOFANA	CIV	A	3	(5)	
29	Szabolcs GYÁNÓ	HUN	A	1	(3)	1
7	HÉLDER BARBOSA		M	7	(9)	2
6	IRINEU Couto	BRA	D	1		
25	IVANILDO Cassama		A	9	(13)	
2	JOEANO Chaves	BRA	A	11	(11)	4
4	Carlos Ferrari "KAKÁ"	BRA	D	30		1
11	Cláudio Aguiar "LITO"	CPV	M	24	(3)	9
21	Carlos Magalhães "LITOS"		D	5		
85	LUÍS AGUIAR	URU	M	11	(1)	1
10	MIGUEL António PEDRO		M	14	(8)	1
78	Dame N'DOYE	SEN	M	8	(2)	1

No	Name	Nat	Pos	Aps	(s)	Gls
	NUNO PILOTO		M	22		
	Rui ORLANDO		D	26		
	PAULO SÉRGIO Gomes		M	14	(7)	
	Milorad PAVLOVIĆ	SRB	M	15	(1)	2
	Pedro Rocha "PEDRINHO"		D	10	(1)	
	PEDRO Miguel COSTA		D	18	(1)	
	PEDRO ROMA		G	28		
	Walter PERALTA	URU	A		(1)	
	RICARDO Nunes		G	1		
	RUI NEREU		G	1		
	William TIERO	GHA	M	14	(11)	1
	VÍTOR VINHA		D	15		
	Djilli VOUHO	CIV	A	4	(1)	

CF OS BELENENSES

Coach - Jorge Jesus

Founded - 1919

AJOR HONOURS: Portuguese League - (1) 1946; Portuguese Cup - (6) 1927, 1929, 1933, 1942, 1960, 1989.

07

8	Naval 1º Maio	a	1-1	*Fernando*
8	Braga	h	0-2	
	Sporting	a	0-1	
9	Leiria	h	2-1	*Evandro Paulista, Hugo Alcântara*
9	Marítimo	a	0-2	
9	Paços de Ferreira	h	1-0	*Evandro Roncatto*
0	Boavista	a	4-2	*José Pedro 2 (1p), Silas, Gómez*
'10	Académica	h	0-0	
1	Porto	a	1-1	*José Pedro*
1	Leixões	h	1-1	*José Pedro*
'11	Amadora	h	0-0	
'11	Setúbal	a	1-1	*Weldon*
'12	Benfica	h	1-0	*Weldon*
'12	Guimarães	a	0-1	

08

	Nacional	h	1-1	*Evandro Roncatto*
'1	Naval 1º Maio	h	0-3	*(w/o; original result 2-1 Evandro Roncatto, Meyong (p))*
'1	Braga	a	1-1	*Rolando*
	Sporting	h	1-0	*José Pedro*
/2	Leiria	a	2-1	*Weldon 2*
/2	Marítimo	h	1-3	*Weldon*
	Paços de Ferreira	a	2-1	*José Pedro (p), og (Peçanha)*
/3	Boavista	h	2-3	*Silas, Weldon*
/3	Académica	a	0-0	
/3	Porto	h	1-2	*Weldon*
	Leixões	a	2-1	*Weldon 2*
/4	Amadora	a	2-0	*Rolando, José Pedro*
/4	Setúbal	h	5-0	*Weldon 2, José Pedro, João Paulo 2*
/4	Benfica	a	0-2	
5	Guimarães	h	1-1	*Weldon*
/5	Nacional	a	2-1	*og (Cardozo), João Paulo*

No	Name	Nat	Pos	Aps	(s)	Gls
	Anderson Conrado "AMARAL"	BRA	D	11	(3)	
	Miguel AREIAS		D	3	(2)	
	CÂNDIDO COSTA		D	16	(8)	
	Paulo COSTINHA		G	14		
	Vukašin DEVIĆ	BIH	D	5	(4)	
	EDSON Silva	BRA	M	2		
	EVANDRO Nascimento "PAULISTA"	BRA	M		(5)	1
	EVANDRO RONCATTO	BRA	A	24	(4)	3
	FERNANDO Moura		M	3	(12)	1
6	Gabriel GÓMEZ	PAN	M	20	(5)	1
28	GONÇALO BRANDÃO		M		(2)	
16	HUGO ALCANTARA	BRA	D	25		1
20	HUGO LEAL		M	7	(1)	
99	Julio César JACOBI	BRA	G	10	(1)	
75	Edagaras JANKAUSKAS	LTU	A		(5)	
9	JOÃO PAULO Oliveira	BRA	A	4	(16)	3
11	JOSÉ PEDRO Salazar		M	30		8
14	Luís Mendes "MANO"		M	1	(1)	
8	MARCO FERREIRA		M	1	(5)	
1	MARCO GONÇALVES		G	6	(1)	
14	António MENDONÇA	ANG	M	2	(3)	
19	Albert MEYONG	CMR	A		(1)	1
22	RAFAEL BASTOS	BRA	M	5	(7)	
4	RODRIGO Alvim		D	27	(1)	
13	ROLANDO Fonseca		D	30		2
5	RUBEN AMORIM		M	28	(1)	
10	Jorge Fernandes "SILAS"		M	29		2
7	WELDON Andrade	BRA	A	27		12

SL BENFICA

Coach - Fernando Santos; (25/8/07) José António Camacho (ESP); (12/3/08) Fernando Chalana

Founded - 1904

MAJOR HONOURS: European Champion Clubs' Cup - (2) 1961, 1962; Portuguese League - (31) 1936, 1937, 1938, 1942, 1943, 1945, 1950, 1955, 1957, 1960, 1961, 1963, 1964, 1965, 1967, 1968, 1969, 1971, 1972, 1973, 1975, 1976, 1977, 1981, 1983, 1984, 1987, 1989, 1991, 1994, 2005; Portuguese Cup - (27) 1930, 1931, 1935, 1940, 1943, 1944, 1949, 1951, 1952, 1953, 1955, 1957, 1959, 1962, 1964, 1969, 1970, 1972, 1980, 1981, 1983, 1985, 1986, 1987, 1993, 1996, 2004.

2007

18/8	Leixões	a	1-1	*Petit*
25/8	Guimarães	h	0-0	
2/9	Nacional	a	3-0	*Cardozo 2 (1p), Rui Costa*
15/9	Naval 1º Maio	h	3-0	*Rodríguez, Rui Costa, Nuno Gomes*
23/9	Braga	a	0-0	
29/9	Sporting	h	0-0	
7/10	Leiria	a	2-1	*Nuno Gomes 2*
28/10	Marítimo	h	2-1	*Cardozo (p), Adu*
3/11	Paços de Ferreira	a	2-1	*Rodríguez, Katsouranis*
11/11	Boavista	h	6-1	*Cardozo, Maxi Pereira, Rodríguez, og (Ricardo Silva), Nuno Gomes 2 (1p)*
24/11	Académica	a	3-1	*Rui Costa, Luisão, Adu*
1/12	Porto	h	0-1	
15/12	Belenenses	a	0-1	
20/12	Amadora	h	3-0	*Rodríguez, Cardozo (p), Nuno Gomes*

2008

5/1	Setúbal	a	1-1	*Mantorras*
12/1	Leixões	h	0-0	
26/1	Guimarães	a	3-1	*Cardozo 2, Maxi Pereira*
2/2	Nacional	h	0-0	
17/2	Naval 1º Maio	a	2-0	*Rodríguez, Nuno Assis*
24/2	Braga	h	1-1	*Luisão*
2/3	Sporting	a	1-1	*Cardozo*
9/3	Leiria	h	2-2	*Zoro, Cardozo*
16/3	Marítimo	a	1-1	*Cardozo*
30/3	Paços de Ferreira	h	4-1	*Rodríguez, Cardozo, Rui Costa 2*
6/4	Boavista	a	0-0	
11/4	Académica	h	0-3	
20/4	Porto	a	0-2	
26/4	Belenenses	h	2-0	*Luisão, Cardozo*
4/5	Amadora	a	0-0	
11/5	Setúbal	h	3-0	*Katsouranis, Cardozo, Nuno Gomes*

No	Name	Nat	Pos	Aps	(s)	Gls
30	Freddy ADU	USA	A		(11)	2
19	Gonzalo BERGESSIO	ARG	M		(3)	
18	Gilles BINYA	CMR	M	14	(2)	
24	Hans-Jörg BUTT	GER	G		(1)	
7	Óscar CARDOZO	PAR	A	24	(5)	13
16	Fábio COENTRÃO		M	1	(2)	
23	DAVID LUIZ	BRA	D	8		
20	Ángel DI MARIA	ARG	M	13	(13)	
15	Andrés DÍAZ	ARG	M		(1)	
3	EDCARLOS Santos	BRA	D	15	(1)	
8	Konstantinos KATSOURANIS	GRE	D	27		2
5	Leonardo Bastos "LÉO"	BRA	D	26	(1)	
2	LUÍS FILIPE		D	14	(5)	
4	Anderson Luís "LUISÃO"	BRA	D	19		3
38	Ariza MAKUKULA		A	1	(2)	
9	Pedro MANTORRAS	ANG	A		(9)	1
14	Maximiliano Pereira "MAXI PEREIRA"	URU	M	21	(2)	2
28	MIGUEL Vítor		D	2		
22	NÉLSON Marcos		D	19		
25	NUNO ASSIS		M	8	(9)	1
21	Nuno Ribeiro "NUNO GOMES"		A	20	(5)	7
6	Armando Teixeira "PETIT"		M	16	(1)	1
24	Joaquim Silva "QUIM"		G	30		
26	Cristian RODRÍGUEZ	URU	M	22	(2)	6
32	ROMEU Ribeiro		M		(5)	
10	RUI COSTA		M	27	(2)	5
33	László SEPSI	ROU	D	2	(5)	
17	Marco ZORO	CIV	D	1	(1)	1

BOAVISTA FC

Coach - Jaime Pacheco

Founded - 1903

MAJOR HONOURS: Portuguese League - (1) 2001; Portuguese Cup - (5) 1975, 1976, 1979, 1992, 1997.

2007				
19/8	Leiria	a	0-0	
26/8	Marítimo	h	0-2	
1/9	Paços de Ferreira	a	1-1	*Bangoura*
15/9	Leixões	h	0-0	
24/9	Académica	h	0-0	
29/9	Porto	a	0-2	
8/10	Belenenses	h	2-4	*Marcelão 2*
28/10	Amadora	a	0-0	
4/11	Setúbal	h	3-3	*Fleurival, Jorge Ribeiro, Marcelão*
11/11	Benfica	a	1-6	*Jorge Ribeiro*
26/11	Guimarães	h	3-2	*Fary, og (Radanović), Ricardo Silva*
2/12	Nacional	a	0-2	
16/12	Naval 1º Maio	h	2-0	*Fary, Grzelak*
23/12	Braga	a	0-0	
2008				
5/1	Sporting	h	2-0	*Marcelão, Jorge Ribeiro*
13/1	Leiria	h	3-1	*Marcelão, Jorge Ribeiro, Fary*
28/1	Marítimo	a	0-2	
3/2	Paços de Ferreira	h	4-3	*Laionel 3, Jorge Ribeiro*
16/2	Leixões	a	2-2	*Obi, Marcelão*
25/2	Académica	a	1-1	*Mateus*
1/3	Porto	h	0-0	
10/3	Belenenses	a	3-2	*Jorge Ribeiro, Luis Loureiro, og (Candido Costa)*
16/3	Amadora	h	2-1	*Mateus, Jorge Ribeiro*
31/3	Setúbal	a	1-3	*Jorge Ribeiro*
6/4	Benfica	h	0-0	
12/4	Guimarães	a	0-1	
20/4	Nacional	h	1-0	*Diakité*
27/4	Naval 1º Maio	a	0-1	
4/5	Braga	h	0-0	
11/5	Sporting	a	1-2	*Ivan*

No	Name	Nat	Pos	Aps	(s)	G
26	Brayan ANGULO	COL	M	13		
44	Rodrigo ARAÚJO	BRA	D	1		
99	Sambegou BANGOURA	GUI	A	6	(7)	1
21	Milorad BOSANČIĆ	SRB	M	1		
73	BRUNO Pinheiro		M	12	(4)	
13	CARLOS Alberto FERNANDES		G	9		
15	Mourtala DIAKITÉ	MLI	D	21	(2)	1
20	EDGAR Pacheco		A	3	(4)	
25	Guy ESSAME	CMR	M	1		
9	FARY Faye	SEN	A	11	(6)	3
6	David FLEURIVAL	FRA	M	27	(1)	1
22	Milan GAJIĆ	SRB	M	2	(1)	
37	GILBERTO Silva		D	16	(7)	
11	Rafał GRZELAK	POL	M	8	(1)	1
34	HUGO MONTEIRO		M		(5)	
10	Yasser HUSSAIN	QAT	M	2	(9)	
77	IVAN Santos		M	1	(8)	1
82	Peter JEHLE	LIE	G	21		
16	JORGE RIBEIRO		D	26		8
14	LAIONEL Ramalho	BRA	A	13	(6)	3
12	LUÍS LOUREIRO		M	7	(6)	1
33	Anderson Silva "MARCELÃO"	BRA	D	26		6
30	MÁRIO SILVA		D	9		
18	MATEUS Costa	ANG	A	23	(2)	2
8	MOISÉS Pinheiro	BRA	D	13	(2)	
88	Charles OBI	NGA	A	2	(1)	1
5	Oladapu OLUFEMI	NGA	M	2	(2)	
24	PEDRO MOREIRA		D	1	(5)	
3	RICARDO SILVA		D	18		1
7	Luciano RISSUT	BRA	D	18	(2)	
19	Paulo Nsimba "ZÉ KALANGA"	ANG	A	17	(5)	

SC BRAGA

Coach - Jorge Costa; (3/11/07) (António Caldas); (23/11/07) Manuel Machado; (18/4/08) António Caldas

Founded - 1921

MAJOR HONOURS: Portuguese Cup - (2) 1966, 1992.

2007				
18/8	Porto	h	1-2	*João Pinto*
25/8	Belenenses	a	2-0	*César Peixoto (p), Vandinho*
1/9	Amadora	h	2-1	*Rodríguez, Linz*
14/9	Setúbal	a	1-3	*César Peixoto (p)*
23/9	Benfica	h	0-0	
30/9	Guimarães	a	0-1	
8/10	Nacional	h	1-0	*Linz (p)*
29/10	Naval 1º Maio	a	1-1	*Linz (p)*
3/11	Leixões	a	0-3	
11/11	Sporting	h	3-0	*Frechaut, Linz, Jorgin*
23/11	Leiria	a	0-0	
2/12	Marítimo	h	2-1	*Wender, Linz*
14/12	Paços de Ferreira	a	2-0	*Linz, Vandinho*
23/12	Boavista	h	0-0	
2008				
4/1	Académica	a	3-3	*Linz 2, Jorginho*
12/1	Porto	a	0-4	
25/1	Belenenses	h	1-1	*Linz*
1/2	Amadora	a	1-1	*Jorginho*
17/2	Setúbal	h	2-3	*Linz, Jailson*
24/2	Benfica	a	1-1	*Zé Manel*
29/2	Guimarães	h	0-0	
8/3	Nacional	a	1-0	*Zé Manel*
16/3	Naval 1º Maio	h	3-0	*og (Lopes), Wender, Jailsc*

3	Leixões	h	0-0	
	Sporting	a	0-2	
4	Leiria	h	0-1	
4	Marítimo	a	1-4	*César Peixoto (p)*
4	Paços de Ferreira	h	2-1	*Linz, Frechaut*
	Boavista	a	0-0	
5	Académica	h	2-1	*Matheus, João Tomás*

Name	Nat	Pos	Aps	(s)	Gls
BRENO SILVA	BRA	D	2	(1)	
CARLOS FERNANDES		D	16		
Vítor CASTANHEIRA		M	2	(6)	
CÉSAR PEIXOTO		A	15	(4)	3
Pablo CONTRERAS	CHI	D	13		
Daniel Castro "DANI MALLO"	ESP	G	7		
Nuno FRECHAUT		M	17	(5)	2
Yasser HUSSAIN	QAT	M	6	(2)	
JAILSON Santos	BRA	A	10	(17)	2
JOÃO TOMÁS		A	3	(7)	1
JOÃO PEREIRA		D	27		
JOÃO Vieira PINTO		A	7	(2)	1
Jorge Sousa "JORGINHO"	BRA	M	14	(2)	3
Anilton JÚNIOR	BRA	D	2	(2)	
Pawel KIESZEK	POL	G	11		
LENNY FELISBINO	BRA	A		(1)	
Roland LINZ	AUT	A	21	(6)	11
Andrés MADRID	ARG	M	10	(1)	
MATHEUS Nascimento	BRA	A	6	(4)	1
José Aguiar "MIGUELITO"		D	7	(3)	
PAULO JORGE Gomes		D	27		
PAULO SANTOS		G	12		
Halleson Honorato "PHILCO"	BRA	A		(3)	
ROBERTO BRUM	BRA	M	18	(2)	
Alberto RODRÍGUEZ	URU	M	17		1
STÉLVIO Cruz		M	4	(5)	
Vanderson Almeida "VANDINHO"	BRA	M	21	(2)	2
Wenderson Said "WENDER"	BRA	A	23	(3)	2
ZÉ MANEL Fernandes		M	12	(7)	2

CF ESTRELA DA AMADORA

Coach - Daúto Faquirá

Founded – 1932

MAJOR HONOURS: Portuguese Cup - (1) 1990.

07				
/8	Nacional	a	0-0	
/8	Naval 1º Maio	h	3-1	*Carlos, Wagnão, Mateus*
9	Braga	a	1-2	*N´Diaye*
/9	Sporting	h	0-2	
/9	Leiria	a	0-0	
/9	Marítimo	h	1-1	*Tiago Gomes*
10	Paços de Ferreira	a	1-2	*Anselmo*
/10	Boavista	h	0-0	
11	Académica	a	3-3	*Maurício, Anselmo, Wagnão*
/11	Porto	h	2-2	*Maurício, Mateus (p)*
/11	Belenenses	a	0-0	
12	Leixões	h	2-0	*Mateus 2*
/12	Setúbal	h	0-1	
/12	Benfica	a	0-3	
008				
1	Guimarães	h	4-1	*Nuno Viveiros, og (Geromel), Hélder Cabral, Pedro Pereira*
3/1	Nacional	h	0-1	
7/1	Naval 1º Maio	a	1-1	*Vítor Moreno*
/2	Braga	h	1-1	*Fernando (p)*
7/2	Sporting	a	0-2	
3/2	Leiria	h	4-2	*Mendonça, Anselmo 2, og (Éder)*
2/3	Marítimo	a	1-1	*Maurício*
8/3	Paços de Ferreira	h	1-0	*Anselmo*
16/3	Boavista	a	1-2	*Giancarlo*
29/3	Académica	h	3-1	*Anselmo, Maurício, Vítor Moreno*
5/4	Porto	a	0-6	
12/4	Belenenses	h	0-2	
20/4	Leixões	a	0-0	
28/4	Setúbal	h	0-0	
4/5	Benfica	a	0-0	
11/5	Guimarães	a	0-4	

No	Name	Nat	Pos	Aps	(s)	Gls
18	Jeremiah ANI	NGA	A	1	(3)	
9	ANSELMO Cardoso		A	17	(7)	6
17	Adul BALDÉ	GUI	A		(3)	
4	CARLOS Cardoso	BRA	D	8		1
26	CELESTINO Soares		M	8	(5)	
8	DANIEL Anjos	BRA	M	2	(2)	
33	ELSON Silva	BRA	M			
11	Fábio FERNANDES		M		(1)	
16	FERNANDO Reges	BRA	M	26		1
33	GIANCARLO Moro	BRA	A	2	(6)	1
55	HÉLDER CABRAL		D	19		1
3	HUGO CARREIRA		M	9	(9)	
85	LUÍS AGUIAR	BRA	A	3	(4)	
28	Marcelo Alves "MARCELO GOIANIRA"	BRA	M	8	(1)	
35	MARCELO Resende	BRA	M	1		
14	MARCO PAULO		M	8	(8)	
10	MATEUS Borges	BRA	M	27	(2)	4
15	MAURÍCIO Fernandes	BRA	D	28		4
23	António MENDONÇA	ANG	A	9		1
99	João Gomes "MOSSORÓ"	BRA	A	2	(1)	
5	Deme N´DIAYE	SEN	M	14	(3)	1
1	NÉLSON Pereira		G	26		
13	NUNO VIVEIROS		A	4	(9)	1
25	PEDRO ALVES		G	4	(1)	
7	PEDRO PEREIRA		M	6	(14)	1
2	RUI DUARTE		D	29		
19	RUI PEDRO Ramalho		M	1	(3)	
79	Moses SAKHI	GHA	A	5	(2)	
30	TIAGO GOMES		M	21		1
32	VÍTOR MORENO	CPV	M	10	(4)	2
34	Wagner Santos "WAGNÃO"	BRA	D	25	(2)	2
24	Yonathan Auyanet "YONI"	ESP	M	7		

LEIXÕES SC

Coach - Carlos Brito; (15/3/08) António Pinto

Founded – 1907

MAJOR HONOURS: Portuguese Cup - (1) 1961.

2007				
18/8	Benfica	h	1-1	*Nwoko*
26/8	Paços de Ferreira	a	1-1	*Cadete*
31/8	Guimarães	h	2-2	*Paulo Machado, Vieirinha*
15/9	Boavista	a	0-0	
23/9	Nacional	h	1-1	*Nuno Diogo*
1/10	Académica	a	1-1	*Hugo Morais*
7/10	Naval 1º Maio	h	0-1	
29/10	Porto	a	0-3	
3/11	Braga	h	3-0	*Roberto, China, Jorge Gonçalves*
9/11	Belenenses	a	1-1	*Nwoko*
24/11	Sporting	h	1-1	*og (Abel)*
2/12	Amadora	a	0-2	
16/12	Leiria	h	2-1	*Roberto, Diogo Valente*
23/12	Setúbal	h	1-1	*Jorge Gonçalves*

2008				
6/1	Marítimo	a	1-2	*og (Ricardo Esteves)*
12/1	Benfica	a	0-0	
27/1	Paços de Ferreira	h	1-0	*Roberto*
3/2	Guimarães	a	1-2	*Jorge Gonçalves*
16/2	Boavista	h	2-2	*Jorge Gonçalves 2*
24/2	Nacional	a	0-1	
1/3	Académica	h	2-2	*Roberto (p), Jorge Gonçalves (p)*
9/3	Naval 1º Maio	a	1-2	*Roberto*
15/3	Porto	h	1-2	*Roberto*
30/3	Braga	a	0-0	
7/4	Belenenses	h	1-2	*Paulo Machado*
13/4	Sporting	a	0-2	
20/4	Amadora	h	0-0	
27/4	Leiria	a	3-1	*Jorge Gonçalves, Hugo Morais, Castanheira*
4/5	Setúbal	a	0-2	
11/5	Marítimo	h	0-1	

No	Name	Nat	Pos	Aps	(s)	Gls
21	ANTÓNIO Livramento		M		(6)	
1	António Pimparel "BETO"		G	26		
20	Marco CADETE		D	7	(1)	1
22	Vítor CASTANHEIRA		M	7		1
14	Bruno Silva "CHINA"		M	29		1
11	DIOGO VALENTE		A	9	(8)	1
4	ÉLVIS Pereira	BRA	D	24		
3	EZEQUIAS Melo	BRA	D	25		
23	FILIPE OLIVEIRA		M	23	(1)	
29	HUGO MORAIS		M	23	(6)	2
29	JAIME Aquino	BRA	M	2	(3)	
15	JOÃO MOREIRA		A		(6)	
13	JOEL Ricardo		D	9	(1)	
77	JORGE BAPTISTA		G	4		
25	JORGE DUARTE		M	6	(3)	
19	JORGE GONÇALVES		A	28	(1)	7
26	NUNO AMARO		M	5		
5	NUNO DIOGO		D	14	(2)	1
27	NUNO SILVA		D	19		
18	Udochukwo NWOKO	NGA	A	2	(11)	2
6	PAULO MACHADO		M	20	(5)	2
8	PEDRO CERVANTES		M	10	(11)	
9	ROBERTO Ballesteros	BRA	A	27		6
2	RUBEN Ribeiro		M		(1)	
28	TALES Schutz	BRA	A	2	(8)	
17	Adelino Freitas "VIEIRINHA"		A	9	(13)	1
16	Paulo VINÍCIUS	BRA	M		(2)	

CS MARÍTIMO

Coach - Sebastião Lazaroni (BRA)

Founded – 1910

MAJOR HONOURS: Portuguese Cup – (1) 1926.

2007				
18/8	Paços de Ferreira	h	3-1	*Makukula 2, Ediglê*
26/8	Boavista	a	2-0	*Kanu 2*
2/9	Académica	h	2-0	*Makukula, Bruno*
15/9	Porto	a	0-1	
23/9	Belenenses	h	2-0	*Kanu, Makukula*
30/9	Amadora	a	1-1	*Fernando Silva*
7/10	Setúbal	h	0-0	
28/10	Benfica	a	1-2	*Kanu*
5/11	Guimarães	h	0-1	
12/11	Nacional	a	2-0	*Makukula, Wénio*
25/11	Naval 1º Maio	h	0-1	
2/12	Braga	a	1-2	*Makukula*
16/12	Sporting	h	1-2	*Bruno Fogaça*
23/12	Leiria	a	2-1	*Bruno Fogaça, Djalma*

2008				
6/1	Leixões	h	2-1	*Bruno Fogaça, Arno*
11/1	Paços de Ferreira	a	1-3	*Márcio Mossoró*
28/1	Boavista	h	2-0	*Makukula, Djalma*
3/2	Académica	a	0-1	
15/2	Porto	h	0-3	
23/2	Belenenses	a	3-1	*Bruno (p), Marcinho, Márcio Mossoró*
2/3	Amadora	h	1-1	*Bruno (p)*
7/3	Setúbal	a	0-1	
16/3	Benfica	h	1-1	*Ytalo*
28/3	Guimarães	a	0-1	
6/4	Nacional	h	1-0	*Bruno Fogaça*
13/4	Naval 1º Maio	a	3-0	*Márcio Mossoró 2, Anderson*
19/4	Braga	h	4-1	*Marcinho, João Luiz, Márcio Mossoró 2*
27/4	Sporting	a	1-2	*Bruno Fogaça*
4/5	Leiria	h	2-0	*Bruno (p), Edigle*
11/5	Leixões	a	1-0	*Márcio Mossoró*

No	Name	Nat	Pos	Aps	(s)	Gls
11	ADRIANO Silvestre	BRA	M		(1)	
19	ANDERSON Gomes	BRA	A	1	(4)	1
25	ANDRÉ PINTO	BRA	A	1	(3)	
17	Grégory ARNOLIN	FRA	D	11	(4)	1
35	Papa Babacar "BABA"	SEN	M	1	(3)	
21	Nuno Sousa "BRIGUEL"		D	5	(4)	
10	BRUNO Fernandes		M	24		4
16	BRUNO FOGAÇA	BRA	A	11	(7)	5
48	DJALMA Campos	BRA	A	7	(8)	2
5	EDDER PÉREZ	VEN	D	1	(2)	
3	EDIGLÊ Farias	BRA	D	24	(1)	2
81	Edvaldo FABIANO	BRA	D	29		
18	FÁBIO FELÍCIO		M	19	(2)	
18	FERNANDO SILVA		D	3	(2)	1
40	GONÇALO Abreu		M		(1)	
44	JOÃO GUILHERME		D	1	(2)	
20	JOÃO LUIZ Vieira	BRA	M	11	(2)	1
7	Elias Rosa "KANU"	BRA	A	15	(7)	4
18	LUÍS OLIM		A	3	(8)	
9	Aziza MAKUKULA		A	13		7
26	Márcio Silva "MARCINHO"	BRA	M	20	(7)	2
8	José Costa "MÁRCIO MOSSORÓ"	BRA	A	23	(7)	7
26	MARCOS Oliveira	BRA	G	30		
13	OLBERDAM Serra	BRA	M	21		
22	RICARDO ESTEVES		D	25		
32	TITO Andrade		A	1	(2)	
4	Antoine VAN DER LINDEN	NED	D	22	(1)	
15	WÊNIO Pio	BRA	M	8	(2)	1
59	YTALO Santos	BRA	A		(2)	1

CD NACIONAL

Coach - Predrag Jokanović (SRB)

Founded – 1910

2007				
18/8	Amadora	h	0-0	
27/8	Setúbal	a	1-1	*Lipatin*
2/9	Benfica	h	0-3	
17/9	Guimarães	a	0-1	
23/9	Leixões	a	1-1	*Lipatin*
30/9	Naval 1º Maio	h	2-0	*Fellype Gabriel, Cássio*
8/10	Braga	a	0-1	
27/10	Sporting	h	0-0	
4/11	Leiria	a	3-1	*Juliano, Juninho, Fellype Gabriel*
12/11	Marítimo	h	0-2	
25/11	Paços de Ferreira	a	0-1	
2/12	Boavista	h	2-0	*Zé Vítor, Lipatin*

12	Académica	a	0-1	
12	Porto	h	1-0	*Lipatin*
)8				
	Belenenses	a	1-1	*Lipatin*
1	Amadora	a	1-0	*Alonso*
1	Setúbal	h	0-0	
	Benfica	a	0-0	
2	Guimarães	h	1-0	*Fabiano*
2	Leixões	h	1-0	*Juliano*
	Naval 1º Maio	a	1-1	*Juliano (p)*
	Braga	h	0-1	
3	Sporting	a	1-4	*Lipatin*
3	Leiria	h	2-0	*Juliano (p), Fábio Coentrão*
	Marítimo	a	0-1	
'4	Paços de Ferreira	h	1-2	*Cardozo*
'4	Boavista	a	0-1	
'4	Académica	h	0-3	
	Porto	a	3-0	*Fábio Coentrão 2, Juninho*
'5	Belenenses	h	1-2	*Fábio Coentrão*

	Name	Nat	Pos	Aps	(s)	Gls
	ADRIANO Rodrigues	BRA	A	5	(12)	
	ALONSO Matos	BRA	D	24		1
	Fernando ÁVALOS	ARG	D	12	(1)	
	Diego BENAGLIO	SUI	G	16		
	Rafael Whiby "BRACALLI"	BRA	G	14		
	BRUNO AMARO		D	8	(3)	
	BRUNO BASTO		D	3		
	Fernando CARDOZO	BRA	D	23		1
	CÁSSIO Barbosa	BRA	M	2	(7)	1
	CLÉBER Monteiro	BRA	D	25		
	EDSON Sitta	BRA	M	14		
	Eduardo "EDU SALES"	BRA	A	4	(5)	
	FABIANO OLIVEIRA	BRA	A	3		1
	FÁBIO COENTRÃO		A	11	(4)	4
	FELIPE Lopes	BRA	D	6	(1)	
	FELLYPE GABRIEL	BRA	M	14		2
	Rafik HALLICHE	ALG	D	2	(1)	
	IGOR PITA		D	2		
	JOÃO COIMBRA		M	5	(3)	
	JOÃO MOREIRA		A	1	(7)	
	JULIANO Spadacio	BRA	M	29		4
	Júnior Arcanjo "JUNINHO"	BRA	M	14	(8)	2
	Marcelo LIPATIN	URU	A	16	(10)	6
	Bruno PATACAS		D	28		
	PEDRO PITA		M		(1)	
	REINALDO SILVA Zacarias	BRA	M		(1)	
	RICARDO FERNANDES		D	27		
	RICARDO PATEIRO		M	2	(8)	
	RODRIGO Silva	BRA	A	14	(8)	
	José Vieira "ZÉ VÍTOR"		M	6	(5)	1

A. NAVAL 1º MAIO

Coach - Francisco Chaló; (21/9/07) (Fernando Mira); (7/10/07) Ulisses Morais

Founded – 1893

)07				
)/8	Belenenses	h	1-1	*Paulão*
5/8	Amadora	a	1-3	*Marcelinho*
/9	Setúbal	h	0-0	
5/9	Benfica	a	0-3	
/9	Guimarães	h	1-4	*Paulão*
)/9	Nacional	a	0-2	
/10	Leixões	a	1-0	*Marcelinho (p)*
9/10	Braga	h	1-1	*Saulo*
'11	Sporting	a	1-4	*Diego Angelo*
1/11	Leiria	h	1-0	*Marcelinho*
5/11	Marítimo	a	1-0	*og (Van der Linden)*
2/12	Paços de Ferreira	h	2-1	*Elivelton, João Ribeiro*
16/12	Boavista	a	0-2	
22/12	Académica	h	0-1	
2008				
6/1	Porto	a	0-1	
13/1	Belenenses	a	3-0	*(w/o; original result 1-2 Marcelinho)*
27/1	Amadora	h	1-1	*Marcelinho*
4/2	Setúbal	a	2-1	*Marcelinho, Marinho*
17/2	Benfica	h	0-2	
22/2	Guimarães	a	0-1	
2/3	Nacional	h	1-1	*Marcelinho*
9/3	Leixões	h	2-1	*Saulo, Marcelinho*
16/3	Braga	a	0-3	
30/3	Sporting	h	1-4	*Marcelinho*
6/4	Leiria	a	2-0	*Paulão, Marinho*
13/4	Marítimo	h	0-3	
20/4	Paços de Ferreira	a	2-2	*Marcelinho, Diego Angelo*
27/4	Boavista	h	1-0	*Delfim*
4/5	Académica	a	1-1	*Diego Angelo*
10/5	Porto	h	0-2	

No	Name	Nat	Pos	Aps	(s)	Gls
50	Felipe AMARAL	BRA	M		(1)	
5	BRUNO LAZARONI	BRA	M	5	(3)	
7	Carlos Rodrigues "CARLITOS"		A		(3)	
6	João Gonçalves "CHINA"		M	28		
14	DELFIM Teixeira		M	20	(3)	1
23	Davide DIAS		M	26	(2)	
66	DIEGO ANGELO	BRA	M	22		3
22	Carlos Silva "DUDU"	BRA	M	11	(13)	
11	EANES Santana	BRA	M		(3)	
9	ELIVELTON Gregory	BRA	A	5	(14)	1
33	Marcio Trombetta "GAÚCHO"	BRA	A	6	(2)	
8	GILMAR Rocha	BRA	M	19	(5)	
25	Nicolas GODEMECHE	FRA	M	17	(7)	
22	HUGO SANTOS		M	4	(7)	
13	IGOR Rocha		M	3	(1)	
17	JOÃO RIBEIRO		A	22	(6)	1
4	Fabrício LOPES	BRA	M	4	(7)	
20	Marcelo Silva "MARCELINHO"	BRA	A	25	(1)	10
77	Mario Tomás "MARINHO"		A	10	(4)	2
28	MÁRIO SÉRGIO		D	28		
3	Paulo Afonso "PAULÃO"	BRA	D	27		3
21	RODRIGO Marques "CAFÉ"	BRA	G		(1)	
27	SAULO Santos	BRA	A	17	(5)	2
1	Pedro TABORDA	BRA	G	15	(1)	
15	WANDEIR Oliveira	BRA	A	1		
25	WILSON Júnior	BRA	G	15	(1)	

FC PAÇOS DE FERREIRA

Coach - José Mota

Founded – 1950

2007				
18/8	Marítimo	a	1-3	*Dedé*
26/8	Leixões	h	1-1	*Edson*
1/9	Boavista	h	1-1	*Cristiano*
16/9	Académica	a	0-1	
23/9	Porto	h	0-2	
30/9	Belenenses	a	0-1	
8/10	Amadora	h	2-1	*Furtado, Renato Queirós*
27/10	Setúbal	a	1-3	*Luiz Carlos (p)*
3/11	Benfica	h	1-2	*Tiago Valente*
10/11	Guimarães	a	0-0	
25/11	Nacional	h	1-0	*Wesley*
2/12	Naval 1º Maio	a	1-2	*Renato Queirós*
14/12	Braga	h	0-2	
22/12	Sporting	a	1-2	*Edson*

PORTUGAL

2008

6/1	Leiria	h	2-1	*Wesley 2*
11/1	Marítimo	h	3-1	*Edson, Wesley 2*
27/1	Leixões	a	0-1	
3/2	Boavista	a	3-4	*Ricardinho, Wesley, Cristiano*
17/2	Académica	h	1-1	*Wesley*
23/2	Porto	a	0-3	
3/3	Belenenses	h	1-2	*William*
8/3	Amadora	a	0-1	
16/3	Setúbal	h	2-1	*Edson 2*
30/3	Benfica	a	1-4	*Wesley (p)*
4/4	Guimarães	h	2-2	*William, Wesley*
13/4	Nacional	a	2-1	*Chico Silva, Wesley*
20/4	Naval 1º Maio	h	2-2	*William, Wesley*
25/4	Braga	a	1-2	*William*
4/5	Sporting	h	0-1	
11/5	Leiria	a	1-1	*William*

No	Name	Nat	Pos	Aps	(s)	Gls
30	ANTONIELTON Ferreira	BRA	D	16	(2)	
5	Vitorino ANTUNES		D	2		
74	CARLOS CARNEIRO		A		(6)	
3	Francisco Silva "CHICO SILVA"		D	20		1
12	Júlio COELHO		G	4		
10	CRISTIANO Moraes	BRA	M	24	(3)	2
77	Adérito Carvalho "DEDÉ"	ANG	M	19	(6)	1
11	Edson Almeida "EDSON DI"	BRA	A	2	(5)	
7	EDSON Nobre	ANG	A	22	(3)	5
88	FÁBIO PAIM		A		(7)	
17	FERNANDO PILAR	BRA	M	7	(7)	
96	FILIPE ANUNCIAÇÃO		M	19	(5)	
20	José FURTADO		A	8	(10)	1
16	Josualdo Oliveira "KIKO"	BRA	D	16		
14	LUIZ CARLOS	BRA	D	11	(1)	1
18	Ricardo Duarte "MANGUALDE"		D	18		
9	Márcio Gesteira "MÁRCIO CARIOCA"	BRA	A	5	(3)	
6	PAULO GOMES		M	2		
66	PAULO SOUSA		M	12	(1)	
24	Peterson PEÇANHA	BRA	G	26		
8	Pedro Monteiro "PEDRINHA"		M	19	(4)	
1	PEDRO Correia		G		(1)	
13	RENATO QUEIRÓS		A	2	(10)	2
15	Cicero Sousa "RICARDINHO"	BRA	A	9	(10)	1
4	ROVÉRSIO Barros	BRA	D	21	(1)	
55	TIAGO VALENTE		D	12		1
23	Hugo VALDIR		D	4	(1)	
80	WESLEY Silva	BRA	A	20	(2)	11
90	WILLIAM Modibo	CMR	M	10	(1)	5

FC PORTO

Coach - Jesualdo Ferreira

Founded – 1893

MAJOR HONOURS: European Champion Clubs' Cup/UEFA Champions League - (2) 1987, 2004; UEFA Cup - (1) 2003; UEFA Super Cup - (1) 1987; World Club Cup - (1) 1987; Portuguese League - (23) 1935, 1939, 1940, 1956, 1959, 1978, 1979, 1985, 1986, 1988, 1990, 1992, 1993, 1995, 1996, 1997, 1998, 1999, 2003, 2004, 2006, 2007, 2008; Portuguese Cup - (17) 1922, 1925, 1932, 1937, 1956, 1958, 1968, 1977, 1984, 1988, 1991, 1994, 1998, 2000, 2001, 2003, 2006

2007

18/8	Braga	a	2-1	*Ricardo Quaresma 2*
26/8	Sporting	h	1-0	*Raul Meireles*
2/9	Leiria	a	3-0	*Sektioui, Lisandro López, João Paulo*
15/9	Marítimo	h	1-0	*Lisandro López*
23/9	Paços de Ferreira	a	2-0	*Lisandro López 2*
29/9	Boavista	h	2-0	*Lisandro López 2*
7/10	Académica	a	1-0	*Lucho González (p)*
29/10	Leixões	h	3-0	*Lisandro López 2, Sektioui*
2/11	Belenenses	h	1-1	*Hélder Postiga*
11/11	Amadora	a	2-2	*Lisandro López, Rau Meireles*
25/11	Setúbal	h	2-0	*Lisandro López, Rica Quaresma*
1/12	Benfica	a	1-0	*Ricardo Quaresma*
15/12	Guimarães	h	2-0	*Sektioui, Lisandro López*
21/12	Nacional	a	0-1	

2008

6/1	Naval 1º Maio	h	1-0	*Raul Meireles*
12/1	Braga	h	4-0	*Lisandro López 2, Ra Meireles, Farías*
27/1	Sporting	a	0-2	
2/2	Leiria	h	4-0	*Bosingwa, Farías 2, Lisandro López*
15/2	Marítimo	a	3-0	*Lisandro López 2, Sektioui*
23/2	Paços de Ferreira	h	3-0	*Lisandro López 2, Mariano González*
1/3	Boavista	a	0-0	
9/3	Académica	h	1-0	*Ricardo Quaresma*
15/3	Leixões	a	2-1	*Lisandro López, Sektioui*
30/3	Belenenses	a	2-1	*Lisandro López, Luch González (p)*
5/4	Amadora	h	6-0	*Lucho Gonzalez 2, Sektioui, Ricardo Quaresma, Bruno Alv Lisandro López*
12/4	Setúbal	a	2-1	*Lisandro López, Mariano González*
20/4	Benfica	h	2-0	*Lisandro López 2*
27/4	Guimarães	a	5-0	*Bruno Alves, Ricardo Quaresma 2, Farías, Adriano*
3/5	Nacional	h	0-3	
10/5	Naval 1º Maio	a	2-0	*Farías 2*

No	Name	Nat	Pos	Aps	(s)	Gls
28	ADRIANO Louzada	BRA	A	4	(12)	1
18	Mario BOLATTI	ARG	M	4	(11)	
12	José BOSINGWA		D	22	(1)	1
2	BRUNO ALVES		D	27		2
35	André CASTRO		M		(2)	
5	Marek ČECH	SVK	D	14	(2)	
29	EDGAR Silva	BRA	A	1	(1)	
19	Ernesto FARÍAS	ARG	A	7	(9)	6
13	Jorge FUCILE	URU	D	21		
21	HÉLDER BARBOSA		A		(4)	
23	HÉLDER POSTIGA		A	2	(4)	1
1	HELTON Arruda	BRA	G	25		
26	JOÃO PAULO Andrade		D	7	(1)	1
25	Przemysław KAŹMIERCZAK	POL	M	3	(8)	
20	LEANDRO LIMA	BRA	A		(8)	
15	Dorvalino Maciel "LINO"	BRA	D	4	(2)	
9	LISANDRO LÓPEZ	ARG	A	27		24
8	Luis "LUCHO" GONZÁLEZ	ARG	M	28		4
11	MARIANO GONZÁLEZ	ARG	M	6	(15)	2
33	NUNO Herlander Espírito Santo		G	4		
6	PAULO ASSUNÇÃO	BRA	M	26		
3	PEDRO EMANUEL		D	18	(1)	
16	RAUL MEIRELES		M	27	(1)	4
7	RICARDO QUARESMA		A	26	(1)	8
17	Tarik SEKTIOUI	MAR	A	17	(6)	6
4	Milan STEPANOV	SRB	D	9		
24	Hugo VENTURA Guedes		G	1		

SPORTING CLUBE DE PORTUGAL

Coach - Paulo Bento

Founded - 1906

MAJOR HONOURS: UEFA Cup Winners' Cup - (1) 1964; Portuguese eague - (18) 1941, 1944, 1947, 1948, 1949, 1951, 1952, 1953, 1954, 8, 1962, 1966, 1970, 1974, 1980, 1982, 2000, 2002; Portuguese Cup -) 1923, 1934, 1936, 1938, 1941, 1945, 1946, 1948, 1954, 1963, 1971, 1973, 1974, 1978, 1982, 1995, 2002, 2007, 2008.

7

8	Académica	h	4-1	*Derlei, Liedson, Tonel, João Moutinho (p)*
8	Porto	a	0-1	
	Belenenses	h	1-0	*Liedson*
9	Amadora	a	2-0	*Liedson, Vukčević*
9	Setúbal	h	2-2	*João Moutinho (p), Purović*
9	Benfica	a	0-0	
0	Guimarães	h	3-0	*Izmailov 2, Tonel*
10	Nacional	a	0-0	
1	Naval 1º Maio	h	4-1	*João Moutinho, Liedson, Vukčević, Gladstone*
11	Braga	a	0-3	
11	Leixões	a	1-1	*Purović*
2	Leiria	h	1-1	*Izmailov*
12	Marítimo	a	2-1	*Vukčević 2*
12	Paços de Ferreira	h	2-1	*Vukčević, Romagnoli (p)*

08

	Boavista	a	0-2	
1	Académica	a	1-1	*Tonel*
1	Porto	h	2-0	*Vukčević, Izmailov*
	Belenenses	a	0-1	
2	Amadora	h	2-0	*João Moutinho, Liedson*
2	Setúbal	a	0-1	
	Benfica	h	1-1	*Vukčević*
	Guimarães	a	0-2	
3	Nacional	h	4-1	*Liedson 2, João Moutinho, Yannick Djaló*
3	Naval 1º Maio	a	4-1	*Miguel Veloso, Liedson 2, Yannick Djaló*
	Braga	h	2-0	*Yannick Djaló 2*
4	Leixões	h	2-0	*Tonel, Liedson*
4	Leiria	a	1-4	*Liedson*
4	Marítimo	h	2-1	*Romagnoli 2*
5	Paços de Ferreira	a	1-0	*Yannick Djaló*
5	Boavista	h	2-1	*Romagnoli (p), Rodrigo Tiuí*

	Name	Nat	Pos	Aps	(s)	Gls
	ABEL Ferreira		D	27	(1)	
	ADRIEN SILVA		M	3	(4)	
	ANDERSON POLGA	BRA	D	25		
	BRUNO PEREIRINHA		M	6	(17)	
	Celso Honorato "CELSINHO"	BRA	M	1	(6)	
	Wanderlei Silva "DERLEI"	BRA	A	3	(1)	1
	Pontus FARNERUD	SWE	M	4	(11)	
	GLADSTONE Valentina	BRA	D	7	(6)	1
	Leandro GRIMI	ARG	D	9		
	Marián HAD	SVK	D	2	(3)	
	Marat IZMAILOV	RUS	A	19	(4)	4
	JOÃO MOUTINHO		M	30		5
	LIEDSON Muniz	BRA	A	26		11
	MIGUEL VELOSO		M	28	(1)	1
	Carlos PAREDES	PAR	M			
	Luis PÁEZ	PAR	A		(2)	
	PEDRO SILVA	BRA	D	1	(2)	
	Milan PUROVIĆ	MNE	A	9	(6)	2
22	Rodrigo Rocha "RODRIGO TIUÍ"	BRA	A	5	(4)	1
30	Leandro ROMAGNOLI	ARG	M	22	(4)	4
8	RONNY Araújo	BRA	D	19	(1)	
1	RUI PATRÍCIO		G	20		
34	Vladimir STOJKOVIĆ	SRB	G	9		
16	TIAGO Ferreira		G	1		
13	António Sousa "TONEL"		D	27		4
10	Simon VUKČEVIĆ	MNE	A	18	(8)	7
20	YANNICK DJALÓ		A	9	(7)	5

UD LEIRIA

Coach - Paulo Duarte; (11/11/07) Vítor Oliveira

Founded – 1966

2007

19/8	Boavista	h	0-0	
26/8	Académica	a	1-1	*João Paulo*
2/9	Porto	h	0-3	
16/9	Belenenses	a	1-2	*João Paulo*
23/9	Amadora	h	0-0	
30/9	Setúbal	a	0-2	
7/10	Benfica	h	1-2	*Cadu Siva*
26/10	Guimarães	a	1-2	*João Paulo*
4/11	Nacional	h	1-3	*Paulo César*
11/11	Naval 1º Maio	a	0-1	
23/11	Braga	h	0-0	
2/12	Sporting	a	1-1	*Toñito*
16/12	Leixões	a	1-2	*João Paulo*
23/12	Marítimo	h	1-2	*Sougou*

2008

6/1	Paços de Ferreira	a	1-2	*João Paulo*
13/1	Boavista	a	1-3	*João Paulo*
27/1	Académica	h	3-1	*João Paulo 2, Laranjeiro (p)*
2/2	Porto	a	0-4	
18/2	Belenenses	h	1-2	*Harison*
23/2	Amadora	a	2-4	*Paulo César, Ferreira*
1/3	Setúbal	h	0-2	
9/3	Benfica	a	2-2	*Paulo César, N´Gal*
14/3	Guimarães	h	0-1	
30/3	Nacional	a	0-2	
6/4	Naval 1º Maio	h	0-2	
14/4	Braga	a	1-0	*N'Gal*
20/4	Sporting	h	4-1	*Paulo César 2, N'Gal, Cadu Siva*
27/4	Leixões	h	1-3	*Éder (p)*
4/5	Marítimo	a	0-2	
11/5	Paços de Ferreira	h	1-1	*Éder Gaúcho*

No	Name	Nat	Pos	Aps	(s)	Gls
14	Luís Joaquim "ALHANDRA"		M	9	(7)	
23	BRUNO MIGUEL		D	15	(1)	
11	Carlos Silva "CADU SILVA"	BRA	A	19	(4)	2
22	Danielson Monteiro "DANI"	BRA	A		(1)	
5	ÉDER Bonfim	BRA	D	27	(1)	1
55	Éder Silveira "ÉDER GAUCHO"	BRA	D	21		1
15	Hugo FARIA		M	18	(7)	
1	FERNANDO Prass	BRA	G	30		
13	Josiesley FERREIRA	BRA	A	2	(3)	1
77	Nery HARISON	BRA	M	11		1
4	HUGO COSTA		D	12		
32	JESSUI Nascimento	BRA	A		(4)	
30	JOÃO PAULO Ribeiro		A	13	(4)	8
25	Nuno LARANJEIRO		D	15	(1)	1
50	Patrick LOPES	BRA	M	12	(1)	
3	Antoni ŁUKASIEWICZ	POL	M	7	(6)	
19	MACIEL Cunha	BRA	A	6	(2)	
99	Marcelo Quarterole "MARCELINHO"	BRA	A	1	(2)	
20	MARCO Soares		M		(1)	

35	André MARQUES		D	2		
26	NÉLSON Sousa		M	2	(1)	
7	Serge N´GAL	CMR	A	12	(8)	3
9	PAULO CÉSAR Rosa	BRA	A	25	(4)	5
17	RENATO ASSUNÇÃO		D	4		
27	Arvid SMIT	NED	M	12		
18	Papa Mamadou SOUGOU	SEN	A	19	(4)	1
66	TIAGO Pereira		M	25		
21	Antonio González "TOÑITO"	ESP	M	10	(13)	1
28	Ousseni ZONGO	BFA	M	1	(1)	

VITÓRIA FC

Coach - Carlos Carvalhal

Founded - 1910

MAJOR HONOURS: Portuguese Cup - (3) 1965, 1967, 2005.

2007				
19/8	Guimarães	a	1-1	*Matheus*
27/8	Nacional	h	1-1	*Paulinho*
2/9	Naval 1º Maio	a	0-0	
14/9	Braga	h	3-1	*Matheus, Elías, Edinho*
23/9	Sporting	a	2-2	*Elías, Matheus*
30/9	Leiria	h	2-0	*Mateus, Edinho*
7/10	Marítimo	a	0-0	
27/10	Paços de Ferreira	h	3-1	*Auri, Edinho, Bruno Gama*
4/11	Boavista	a	3-3	*Cláudio Pitbull, Auri, Edinho*
11/11	Académica	h	3-1	*Matheus, Elías, Cláudio Pitbull*
25/11	Porto	a	0-2	
30/11	Belenenses	h	1-1	*og (Ruben Amorim)*
16/12	Amadora	a	1-0	*Edinho*
23/12	Leixões	a	1-1	*Filipe Gonçalves*
2008				
5/1	Benfica	h	1-1	*Edinho*
14/1	Guimarães	h	0-1	
27/1	Nacional	a	0-0	
4/2	Naval 1º Maio	h	1-2	*Bruno Severino*
17/2	Braga	a	3-2	*Robson, Ricardo Chaves, Elías*
24/2	Sporting	h	1-0	*Bruno Ribeiro*
1/3	Leiria	a	2-0	*Cláudio Pitbull, Bruno Gama*
7/3	Marítimo	h	1-0	*Cláudio Pitbull (p)*
16/3	Paços de Ferreira	a	1-2	*Ricardo Chaves*
31/3	Boavista	h	3-1	*Bruno Gama, Cláudio Pitbull 2 (1p)*
5/4	Académica	a	0-0	
12/4	Porto	h	1-2	*Hugo*
21/4	Belenenses	a	0-5	
28/4	Amadora	h	0-0	
4/5	Leixões	h	2-0	*Cláudio Pitbull, Bruno Gama*
11/5	Benfica	a	0-3	

No	Name	Nat	Pos	Aps	(s)	Gls
13	ADALTO Silva	BRA	D	17	(3)	
15	AURI Faustino	BRA	D	29		2
7	BRUNO GAMA		M	12	(12)	4
11	BRUNO RIBEIRO		M	5	(8)	1
29	BRUNO SEVERINO		A		(9)	1
87	Cláudio Mejolaro "CLÁUDIO PITBULL"	BRA	A	23	(2)	7
9	Arnaldo Lopes "EDINHO"	BRA	A	4	(11)	6
77	EDUARDO Reis		G	30		
8	ELIAS Silva	BRA	M	30		4
10	FILIPE GONÇALVES		A	9	(16)	1
3	HUGO Vieira		D	5	(1)	1
14	JANÍCIO Martins	CPV	D	28		
17	Jorge Galufo "JORGINHO"		D	13	(1)	
30	KIM Byung-Suk	KOR	A	2	(3)	
19	LEANDRO Branco	BRA	A	13	(7)	
50	Leonardo Bonifácio "LÉO BONFIM"	BRA	D	1		
20	Leonardo Coelho "LÉO MACAE"	BRA	M		(1)	
99	MATHEUS Nascimento	BRA	A	15		5
18	Paulo Sobrinho "PAULINHO"	BRA	M	14	(10)	1
16	RICARDO CHAVES		M	27	(2)	2
4	Severino ROBSON	BRA	D	27	(1)	1
6	SANDRO Mendes	CPV	M	26	(1)	

VÍTORIA SC

Coach - Manuel Cajuda

Founded - 1922

2007				
19/8	Setúbal	h	1-1	*Fajardo*
25/8	Benfica	a	0-0	
31/8	Leixões	a	2-2	*Fajardo 2*
17/9	Nacional	h	1-0	*Tiago Targino*
21/9	Naval 1º Maio	a	4-1	*Flávio Meireles, Fajar Mrdaković, Ghilas*
30/9	Braga	h	1-0	*Geromel*
6/10	Sporting	a	0-3	
26/10	Leiria	h	2-1	*Mrdaković, Rabiola*
5/11	Marítimo	a	1-0	*Ghilas*
10/11	Paços de Ferreira	h	0-0	
26/11	Boavista	a	2-3	*Felipe, Tiago Targino*
3/12	Académica	h	2-1	*Ghilas, Mrdaković*
15/12	Porto	a	0-2	
22/12	Belenenses	h	1-0	*Ghilas*
2008				
6/1	Amadora	a	1-4	*Mrdaković*
14/1	Setúbal	a	1-0	*Mrdaković*
26/1	Benfica	h	1-3	*Ghilas*
3/2	Leixões	h	2-1	*Marquinho, Roberto*
17/2	Nacional	a	0-1	
22/2	Naval 1º Maio	h	1-0	*Desmarets*
29/2	Braga	a	0-0	
9/3	Sporting	h	2-0	*Sereno, Fajardo*
14/3	Leiria	a	1-0	*Ghilas*
28/3	Marítimo	h	1-0	*Roberto*
4/4	Paços de Ferreira	a	2-2	*Desmarets 2*
12/4	Boavista	h	1-0	*Mrdaković*
18/4	Académica	a	0-0	
27/4	Porto	h	0-5	
4/5	Belenenses	a	1-1	*Flávio Meireles*
11/5	Amadora	h	4-0	*Flávio Meireles, Alan, Andrézinho, Desmaret*

No	Name	Nat	Pos	Aps	(s)	Gls
27	ALAN Silva	BRA	A	29		1
25	André Soares "ANDRÉZINHO"	BRA	D	28	(1)	1
8	Carlos Cunha "CARLITOS"		A	11	(11)	
16	DANILO Ferraro	BRA	D	2		
20	Yves DESMARETS	FRA	M	26	(4)	4
17	João Paulo FAJARDO		M	13	(14)	5
11	FILIPE CONCEIÇÃO	BRA	A		(4)	1
26	FLÁVIO MEIRELES		M	29		3
19	Pedro GEROMEL	BRA	D	29		1
5	Kamel GHILAS	ALG	A	21	(9)	6
80	JOÃO ALVES		M	29		
3	LUCIANO AMARAL	BRA	D	12		
6	MÁRCIO MARTINS	BRA	M	1	(1)	
39	Marco Aurélio "MARQUINHO"	BRA	A		(2)	1
29	Jacques MOMHA	CMR	D	9	(2)	
18	João Teixeira "MORENO"		M	3	(11)	
9	Miljan MRDAKOVIĆ	SRB	A	25	(2)	6
1	NILSON Junior	BRA	G	30		
27	NUNO SANTOS		G		(1)	

Tiago Lopes "RABIOLA"		A	1	(3)	1
Siniša RADANOVIĆ	SRB	D	4		
ROBERTO Felix	BRA	A	1	(13)	2
Henrique SERENO		D	27		1
Tiago Silva "TIAGO TARGINO"		A		(10)	2

PROMOTED CLUBS

CD TROFENSE
Coach – António Conceição "Toni"
Founded - 1930

RIO AVE FC
Coach – João Eusébio
Founded - 1939

COND LEVEL FINAL TABLE 2007/08

	Pld	W	D	L	F	A	Pts
D Trofense	30	13	13	4	35	22	52
o Ave FC	30	13	12	5	38	26	51
C Vizela	30	13	11	6	40	22	50
il Vicente FC	30	13	11	6	43	34	50
C Olhanense	30	12	9	9	33	33	45
C Beira-Mar	30	10	12	8	30	32	42
D Estoril-Praia	30	11	8	11	41	38	41
D Aves	30	10	9	11	43	39	39
C Varzim	30	9	11	10	29	27	38
D Santa Clara	30	10	7	13	31	50	37
ortimonense SC	30	8	13	9	26	30	37
ondomar SC	30	8	11	11	37	37	35
C Freamunde	30	9	8	13	42	49	35
D Feirense	30	8	9	13	25	27	33
C Penafiel	30	7	8	15	28	39	29
D Fatima	30	5	10	15	25	41	25

OMESTIC CUP 2007/08

TAÇA DE PORTUGAL

ROUND

7)
0, Porto 2

7)
nses 2, Paços de Ferreira 2 *(aet; 4-5 on pens)*
4, Torreense 0
al 5, Cova Piedade 0
g 4, Louletano 0

7)
es 0, Monsanto 0 *(aet; 6-5 on pens)*
ra 4, Fátima 2 *(aet)*
1, Freamunde 0
o 0, Guimarães 1
o Valdevez 3, Tocha 1
Mar 1, Torre de Moncorvo 1 *(aet; 3-2 on pens)*
a 3, Académica 1
ha 2, Braga 3
ado 1, Olhanense 2
se 4, Lusitania 1
1, Juventude Évora 2

Lagoa 3, Santa Clara 2
Leiria 2, Nelas 0
Messinense 0, Gil Vicente 2 *(aet)*
Moreirense 4, Machico 0
Oliveirense 4, Mondinense 0
Operário 0, Setúbal 1
Penafiel 2, Vizela 1
Real Massamá 0, Aves 1
Rio Ave 6, Rebordosa 1
Sertanense 2, Portimonense 1
Serzedelo 0, Naval 1° Maio 3
Byes – Boavista, Marítimo

FIFTH ROUND

(19/1/08)
Beira Mar 0, Moreirense 1
Benfica 1, Feirense 0
Porto 2, Aves 0
Setúbal 1, Leiria 0
Sporting 4, Lagoa 0
(20/1/08)
Amadora 1, Braga 0
Gil Vicente 3, Juventude Évora 0
Guimarães 1,Nacional 0
Leixões 1, Anadia 0
Naval 1° Maio 4, Boavista 1
Oliveirense 0, Marítimo 1
Paços de Ferreira 4, Abrantes 0
Penafiel 1, Sertanense 1 *(aet; 4-5 on pens)*
Rio Ave 3, Olhanense 3 *(aet; 2-1 on pens)*
Bye - Atlético Valdevez

SIXTH ROUND

(9/2/08)
Sporting 2, Marítimo 1
(10/2/08)
Atlético Valdevez 0, Moreirense
Benfica 4, Paços de Ferreira 1
Gil Vicente 1, Leixões 0 *(aet)*
Naval 1° Maio 3, Rio Ave 1 *(aet)*
Sertanense 0, Porto 4
Setúbal 1, Guimarães 1 *(aet; 4-1 on pens)*
Bye - Amadora

QUARTER-FINALS

(27/2/08)
Benfica 2 *(Rui Costa 70, Makukula 87)*, Moreirense 0
Naval 1° Maio 1 *(Paulão 65)*, Setúbal 2 *(Leandro 60, Robson 69)*
Porto 1 *(Sektioui 17)*, Gil Vicente 0
Sporting 1 *(Purović 90)*, Amadora 0

SEMI-FINALS

(16/4/08)
Setúbal 0, Porto 3 *(Jorginho 39og, Lucho González 51, 60)*
Sporting 5 *(Yannick Djaló 66, 84, Liedson 75, Derlei 79, Vukčević 90)*, Benfica 3 *(Rui Costa 18, Nuno Gomes 30, Rodríguez 81)*

FINAL

(18/5/08)
Estádio Nacional, Lisbon
SPORTING CLUBE DE PORTUGAL 2 *(Rodrigo Tiuí 110,118)*
FC PORTO 0
(aet)
Referee – *Olegário Benquerença*
SPORTING - *Rui Patrício, Abel (Rodrigo Tiuí 91), Tonel, Anderson Polga, Grimi, Miguel Veloso, João Moutinho, Izmailov (Bruno Pereirinha 76), Romagnoli, Yannick Djaló, Derlei (Gladstone 116).*
PORTO - *Nuno, João Paulo, Pedro Emanuel, Bruno Alves, Fucile, Paulo Assunção (Sektioui 111), Raul Meireles (Kaźmierczak 104), Lucho González, Mariano González (Lino 78), Ricardo Quaresma, Lisandro Lopez.*

Debut title for Drogheda United

There was a chaotic start to the 2007 League of Ireland season when the Premier Division licence of 2006 champions Shelbourne FC was revoked due to financial irregularities in their application. An official investigation into the club's affairs dragged on until mid-February, by which time the Dublin club had almost folded. When the investigation was finally concluded, a fortnight before the start of the new season, Shelbourne were granted a First Division licence, with their place in the 12-team Premier Division going to relegated Waterford United FC.

Drogheda United's Declan O'Brien holds aloft the League of Ireland Premier Division trophy

Change of guard

With Shelbourne's demise, it was time for a change o guard, and the next few months witnessed the emergence of a new force in Irish football, Drogheda United FC. Although Saint Patrick's Athletic FC got of to a flier, winning seven of their first eight games, on Drogheda got into their stride there was only going be one champion. The Drogs picked up points consistently, losing just one away game, and three in all, as they cruised to the title with a seven-point leac over St Pat's.

Although they had been successful in the 2005 FAI Cup and other knockout competitions, it was the County Louth side's first ever league title – a success that finally enabled them to emerge from the shadov of their regional rivals, nine-time champions Dundalk FC. Manager Paul Doolin's expensively constructed side were deserved winners, although it was the goa of low-key signing Guy Bates, an Englishman recruite from Belgian second division side KV Oostende, that gave the side the boost they needed to push on and clinch the title with a couple of games to spare. Drogheda also retained the cross-border Setanta Cup by beating Irish League champions Linfield FC on penalties in the final.

Longford lose out

At the other end of the table, despite the heroics of striker David Mooney who topped the Premier Divisio scoring charts with 19 goals, a six-point deduction for financial irregularities proved too much of a handicap for Longford Town FC. They ended up bottom of the table and were relegated; without the points-deduction they would have been in the clear. Waterford, despite their late entry, performed adequately with what was essentially a First Division squad. They survived automatic relegation but were unable to avoid a sixth successive defeat in the promotion/relegation play-offs.

The First Division title race went to the wire. Having led for the first two thirds of the season, Dundalk fell away as both Finn Harps FC and Cobh Ramblers FC strung together lengthy unbeaten runs. Cobh topped the table, returning to the top flight for the first time since 1995. A new two-tiered play-off system saw third-placed Dundalk travel to second-placed Finn Harps for the right to play Waterford for a place in the 2008 Premier Division. In-form Finn Harps proved too strong for both opponents and secured promotion via the play-offs for the first time - at the sixth attempt.

The FAI Cup provided Cork City FC with some much appreciated relief after a tough season on and off the pitch. Denis Behan scored the only goal of a windswept final at the RDS showgrounds in Dublin as Longford, Cup winners in 2003 and 2004, for once failed to live up to their 'cup specialists' reputation, ending a thoroughly miserable campaign by adding Cup final defeat to relegation. To add insult to injury, they also then lost long-serving manager Alan Mathews to Cork. The League Cup went to Derry City FC, 1-0 victors over Bohemian FC, for an unprecedented third successive season.

Derry dumped

The recent improvement of Irish clubs' performances in European competitions was not maintained in 2007. After Shelbourne did the honourable thing and withdrew from the UEFA Champions League, their place was taken by runners-up Derry, but with former Scotland international John Robertson newly appointed as manager, they unexpectedly crashed out in the first round to Armenian champions FC Pyunik after a 2-0 defeat in the scorching heat of Yerevan. UEFA Cup results were not much better. Drogheda eased through the first qualifying round with a 4-1 aggregate win over San Marino's SP Libertas before succumbing to a Henrik Larsson-inspired Helsingsborgs IF by the same margin. St Pat's' UEFA Cup campaign was short-lived. After a decent scoreless draw at home to Odense BK, they were soundly beaten 5-0 in Denmark.

It was a season of underachievement and upheaval for the Republic of Ireland national team. Any hopes of qualifying for UEFA EURO 2008™ fell by the wayside in September as back-to-back internationals in Slovakia and the Czech Republic yielded a solitary point. Ireland played well in Bratislava but conceded a late equaliser to surrender two valuable points, whereas in Prague a strong Czech Republic side were good value for their 1-0 win even without the helping hand provided by Stephen Hunt's sending-off early in the second half. With only pride now to play for, the pressure mounted on manager Stephen Staunton. A creditable 0-0 draw at Croke Park against Germany provided some breathing space, but a dismal 1-1 draw four days later at the same venue against Cyprus, rescued only with a last-minute equaliser, induced howls of derision from the stands and left Staunton's position untenable. After just 17 games in charge he was duly dismissed, and Under-21s boss Don Givens oversaw the 2-2 draw in Wales that enabled Ireland to finish third in the group – an achievement of sorts considering that they went into the campaign as fourth seeds.

Ireland's new head coach – Giovanni Trapattoni

Trapattoni takes charge

And so began the long search for a new manager. Countless names were put forward, from former international players and TV pundits with no managerial experience to established managers of English Premier League clubs and other international teams. It was almost worth the wait when legendary Italian coach Giovanni Trapattoni was finally unveiled as the new man in charge. The appointment was not without its controversy. It was revealed at a press conference that half of Trapattoni's considerable salary would be paid by businessman Denis O'Brien. Whatever the motivation behind that generous contribution, it raised the FAI's ambition and bargaining power to unprecedented heights. Qualification for the 2010 FIFA World Cup will not be easy – particularly with holders Italy to contend with – but the appointment of 'Il Trap', and a draw and win in his first two matches, has certainly fuelled the Irish fans with a new sense of optimism.

Football Association of Ireland (FAI)

National Sports Campus
Abbotstown
IE-Dublin 15
Tel - +353 1 8999500
Fax - +353 1 8999501
website - www.fai.ie
email - info@fai.ie
Year of Formation – 1921
Chairman – David J. Blood
General Secretary – John Delaney
Press Officer – Gerry McDermott
Stadium – Croke Park, Dublin (82,500)

INTERNATIONAL TOURNAMENT APPEARANCES
FIFA World Cup - (3) 1990 (qtr-finals), 1994 (2nd round), 2002 (2nd round).
UEFA European Championship - (1) 1988.

TOP FIVE ALL-TIME CAPS
Stephen Staunton (102); Niall Quinn (91); Tony Cascarino (88); Kevin Kilbane (87); Shay Given (86)

TOP FIVE ALL-TIME GOALS
Robbie Keane (33); Niall Quinn (21); Frank Stapleton (20); John Aldridge, Tony Cascarino & Don Givens (19)

NATIONAL TEAM RESULTS 2007/08

22/8/07	Denmark	A	Aarhus	4-0	*Keane (29, 40), Long (54, 66)*
8/9/07	Slovakia (ECQ)	A	Bratislava	2-2	*Ireland (7), Doyle (57)*
12/9/07	Czech Republic (ECQ)	A	Prague	0-1	
13/10/07	Germany (ECQ)	H	Dublin	0-0	
17/10/07	Cyprus (ECQ)	H	Dublin	1-1	*Finnan (90+2)*
17/11/07	Wales (ECQ)	A	Cardiff	2-2	*Keane (31), Doyle (60)*
6/2/08	Brazil	H	Dublin	0-1	
24/5/08	Serbia	H	Dublin	1-1	*Keogh (90)*
29/5/08	Colombia	N	London (ENG)	1-0	*Keane (3)*

NATIONAL TEAM APPEARANCES 2007/08

Coach – Stephen STAUNTON 19/1/69 /(24/10/07) Don GIVENS 9/8/49 /(13/2/08) Giovanni TRAPATTONI (ITA) 17/3/39			Den	SVK	CZE	GER	CYP	WAL	Bra	Srb	Col	Caps	Goals
Wayne HENDERSON	16/9/83	Preston (ENG)	G									6	-
Stephen CARR	29/8/76	Newcastle (ENG)	D									44	-
Steve FINNAN	24/4/76	Liverpool (ENG)	D62			D	D	D				50	2
John O'SHEA	30/4/81	Man. United (ENG)	D	D	D38		M	D	D		D	45	1
Richard DUNNE	21/9/79	Man. City (ENG)	D	D	D	D			D	D	D	42	5
Aiden McGEADY	4/4/86	Celtic (SCO)	M	M61	M62	s80	s63	M	M		M	18	-
Darren POTTER	21/12/84	Wolves (ENG)	M66					s87	s46			5	-
Andy REID	29/7/82	Charlton (ENG)	M46		M	M	M	M87				27	4

ATIONAL TEAM APPEARANCES 2007/08 (contd.)

			Den	SVK	CZE	GER	CYP	WAL	Bra	Srb	Col	Caps	Goals
phen HUNT	1/8/81	Reading (ENG)	M46		s38		M74	s60	s72	M81		11	-
vin DOYLE	18/9/83	Reading (ENG)	A46	A89	A	A70	A	A	A72	A86	A	18	5
obie KEANE	8/7/80	Tottenham (ENG)	A56	A	A	A	A	A	A	A70	A85	81	33
rron GIBSON	25/10/87	Man. United (ENG)	s46	s61								2	-
dy KEOGH	16/5/86	Wolves (ENG)	s46		s82	M80	M63			s81	M90	7	1
ane LONG	22/1/87	Reading (ENG)	s46		s62	s70				s86		8	3
ryl MURPHY	15/3/83	Sunderland (ENG)	s56	s89						s70	s85	6	-
vin KILBANE	1/2/77	Wigan (ENG)	s62	M	M	M	D	D	D			87	7
phen KELLY	6/9/83	Birmingham (ENG)	s66	D	D	D			D	D		11	-
ay GIVEN	20/4/76	Newcastle (ENG)		G	G	G	G	G	G			86	-
ul McSHANE	6/1/86	Sunderland (ENG)		D	D		D	D		D	D	11	-
e CARSLEY	28/2/74	Everton (ENG)		M	M82	M		M	M			39	-
phen IRELAND	22/8/86	Man. City (ENG)		M76								6	4
nathan DOUGLAS	22/11/81	Leeds (ENG)		s76			s74					9	-
ey O'BRIEN	17/2/86	Bolton (ENG)				D	D46					3	-
m MILLER	13/2/81	Sunderland (ENG)					s46	M60	M46	M	M	18	1
mien DUFF	2/3/79	Newcastle (ENG)							M	M		68	7
an KIELY	10/10/70	West Brom (ENG)								G	G	10	-
mien DELANEY	20/7/81	QPR (ENG)								D	D	2	-
nn WHELAN	13/1/84	Stoke (ENG)								M	M	2	-
sley HOOLAHAN	20/5/82	Blackpool (ENG)									s90	1	-

DOMESTIC LEAGUE 2007

EAGUE OF IRELAND PREMIER DIVISION FINAL TABLE

		Home					Away					Total					
	Pld	W	D	L	F	A	W	D	L	F	A	W	D	L	F	A	Pts
Drogheda United FC	33	10	4	2	28	14	9	7	1	20	10	19	11	3	48	24	68
Saint Patrick's Ath FC	33	10	4	2	34	14	8	3	6	20	15	18	7	8	54	29	61
Bohemians FC	33	10	6	1	24	6	6	4	6	11	11	16	10	7	35	17	58
Cork City FC	33	7	6	3	19	11	8	4	5	25	21	15	10	8	44	32	55
Shamrock Rovers FC	33	8	5	3	17	6	6	4	7	19	20	14	9	10	36	26	51
Sligo Rovers FC	33	7	3	6	21	20	5	2	10	13	25	12	5	16	34	45	41
Derry City FC	33	6	5	6	18	15	2	8	6	12	16	8	13	12	30	31	37
Galway United FC	33	4	5	8	15	19	3	9	4	13	16	7	14	12	28	35	35
Bray Wanderers AFC	33	6	5	5	18	18	2	5	10	12	30	8	10	15	30	48	34
UCD FC	33	4	6	7	19	23	3	4	9	12	21	7	10	16	31	44	31
Waterford United FC	33	5	5	7	13	19	2	4	10	10	28	7	9	17	23	47	30
Longford Town FC	33	6	4	7	17	19	3	4	9	17	30	9	8	16	34	49	29

3. Longford Town FC – 6 pts deducted

TOP GOALSCORERS

19 David MOONEY (Longford)
15 Mark QUIGLEY (St Patrick's)
14 Roy O'DONOVAN (Cork)
12 Tadhg PURCELL (Shamrock Rovers)
11 Eamon ZAYED (Drogheda)
10 Andy MYLER (Shamrock Rovers)
Fahrudin KUDOZOVIĆ (Sligo)
9 Matthew JUDGE (Sligo)
8 Denis BEHAN (Cork)
Glen CROWE (Bohemians)
Derek GLYNN (Galway)
Kevin McHUGH (Derry)
Gary O'NEILL (St Patrick's)
Shane ROBINSON (Drogheda)

CLUB-BY-CLUB

BOHEMIAN FC

Manager – Seán Connor

Founded – 1890

MAJOR HONOURS: League of Ireland – (9) 1924, 1928, 1930, 1934, 1936, 1975, 1978, 2001, 2003 (interim); FAI Cup – (6) 1928, 1935, 1970, 1976, 1992, 2001; Irish Cup – (1) 1908.

2007				
9/3	Drogheda	h	0-0	
16/3	Bray	a	0-1	
30/3	Waterford	a	1-0	*Crowe*
3/4	Shamrock Rovers	h	2-1	*Crowe, McGuinness*
6/4	Sligo	h	1-0	*Kelly*
13/4	St Patrick's	a	0-0	
20/4	Galway	h	1-1	*Heary O.*
27/4	Derry	a	0-0	
4/5	UCD	h	0-0	
11/5	Longford	h	5-0	*Crowe 3, Kelly, Rice*
18/5	Cork	a	1-2	*McGuinness*
25/5	Galway	a	1-0	*Crowe*
28/5	St Patrick's	h	2-0	*Rice, Rossiter (p)*
2/6	Sligo	a	1-2	*Rossiter (p)*
25/6	Waterford	h	1-0	*Mansaram*
29/6	Shamrock Rovers	a	0-0	
9/7	Bray	h	2-0	*Hunt, Rice*
13/7	Drogheda	a	0-1	
21/7	Derry	h	0-0	
27/7	UCD	a	0-1	
4/8	Longford	a	0-3	
10/8	Cork	h	2-1	*Hunt, Mansaram*
24/8	Drogheda	h	1-1	*McCann*
31/8	Bray	a	3-0	*Rossiter, McCann, Crowe*
14/9	Waterford	a	0-0	
17/9	Shamrock Rovers	h	0-2	
28/9	Sligo	h	3-0	*O'Donnell, Mansaram, Rossiter*
5/10	St Patrick's	a	1-0	*Mansaram*
12/10	Galway	h	2-0	*Turner, Crowe*
19/10	Derry	a	2-1	*Pooley, McGinley*
22/10	UCD	h	2-0	*McGinley, Mansaram*
2/11	Longford	h	0-0	
9/11	Cork	a	1-0	*og (Kelly)*

No	Name	Nat	Pos	Aps	(s)	Gls
30	Alan BLAYNEY	NIR	G	3		
5	Liam BURNS	NIR	D	25	(1)	
3	Des BYRNE		D	19	(3)	
9	Glen CROWE		A	32		8
8	Neale FENN		A	14	(9)	
25	Keith GALLAGHER		G		(1)	
7	Fergal HARKIN		M	7	(10)	
2	Owen HEARY		D	29		1
6	Thomas HEARY		D	13	(4)	
4	Kevin HUNT	ENG	M	21	(4)	2
10	John Paul KELLY		A	18	(7)	2
14	Chris KINGSBERRY	NIR	M	11	(1)	
12	Darren MANSARAM	ENG	A	18	(10)	5
	Gary MATTHEWS		G	1		
23	Ryan McCANN	SCO	M	9	(1)	2
17	Mike McGINLAY	ENG	A	5	(1)	2
15	Jason McGUINNESS		D	22	(2)	2
23	Mick MOONEY		M		(2)	
1	Brian MURPHY		G	29		
24	Stephen O'DONNELL		M	11	(1)	1
20	Dean POOLEY	ENG	D	16	(3)	1
18	Conor POWELL		D	21	(2)	
21	Stephen RICE		M	17	(4)	3
22	Dean RICHARDSON	SCO	D	3	(2)	
19	Mark ROSSITER		D	8	(10)	4
11	Harpal SINGH	ENG	M	4	(4)	
16	Chris TURNER	NIR	M	7	(3)	1

BRAY WANDERERS AFC

Manager –Eddie Gormley

Founded - 1942

MAJOR HONOURS: FAI Cup – (2) 1990, 1999.

2007				
9/3	Derry	a	0-1	
16/3	Bohemians	h	1-0	*Dunphy*
23/3	Waterford	a	2-1	*Tresson, Fox*
30/3	St Patrick's	a	1-3	*Cawley*
6/4	Shamrock Rovers	h	0-2	
12/4	UCD	a	0-2	
20/4	Cork	h	1-1	*Caffrey (p)*
27/4	Galway	h	0-1	
5/5	Longford	a	1-1	*Georgescu*
18/5	Sligo	h	2-0	*Delaney, Georgescu*
29/5	UCD	h	2-1	*Delaney, McCabe*
1/6	Shamrock Rovers	a	0-1	
22/6	St Patrick's	h	0-0	
26/6	Drogheda	a	1-4	*Cawley*
1/7	Waterford	h	2-1	*Fox, Georgescu*
9/7	Bohemians	a	0-2	
20/7	Galway	a	1-0	*Cawley*
27/7	Longford	h	1-3	*Mulroy*
6/8	Drogheda	h	1-2	*Duggan*
11/8	Sligo	a	0-3	
24/8	Derry	a	0-3	
27/8	Cork	a	2-2	*Georgescu, Kavanagh*
31/8	Bohemians	h	0-3	
7/9	Waterford	a	0-0	
14/9	St Patrick's	a	2-4	*Kavanagh, Dunphy*
2/10	Shamrock Rovers	h	3-0	*Cawley, Delaney, O'Shea*
5/10	UCD	a	1-1	*Onwubiko*
12/10	Cork	h	1-1	*Kavanagh*
15/10	Derry	h	1-1	*Dunphy*
19/10	Galway	h	1-1	*Cawley (p)*
22/10	Longford	a	0-1	
2/11	Drogheda	a	1-1	*Cawley (p)*
9/11	Sligo	h	2-1	*Cawley, O'Shea*

No	Name	Nat	Pos	Aps	(s)	Gls
23	John BRODERICK		A		(6)	
10	Paul CAFFREY		M	12	(5)	1
8	Alan CAWLEY		M	28	(2)	7
14	Andrew COUSINS		M	1		
3	Gary CRONIN		M	32		
16	Chris DEANS		D	23	(2)	
5	Clive DELANEY		D	29		3
20	Mark DUGGAN		M	22	(4)	1
22	Paul DUNPHY		A	12	(10)	3
6	Stephen FOX		M	31		2
9	Andrei GEORGESCU	ROU	A	14	(7)	4
7	Stephen GOUGH		D	8	(6)	
26	Stephen HURLEY		M	10	(7)	
12	Ronan IVORY		D	13		
11	Patrick KAVANAGH		M	17	(1)	3
24	Ray KENNY		D	15	(3)	
17	Stephen LAWLESS		M		(1)	
18	Gary McCABE		A	14	(8)	1
14	John MULROY		A		(1)	1
1	Chris O'CONNOR	AUS	G	6		
19	Emeka ONWUBIKO		A	4	(6)	1
15	James O'SHEA		M	17	(8)	2

	Colm TRESSON		D	18	(1)	1
1	David TYRELL		M	5	(5)	
	Derek TYRELL			D	5	(3)
25	Steve WILLIAMS	WAL	G	27		

CORK CITY FC

Manager – Damien Richardson

Founded - 1984

MAJOR HONOURS: League of Ireland – (2) 1993, 2005; FAI Cup – (2) 1998, 2007.

2007				
9/3	Waterford	a	0-1	
16/3	Galway	h	0-0	
23/3	UCD	a	1-0	*O'Donovan*
30/3	Longford	h	2-0	*O'Donovan 2*
9/4	Derry	a	4-1	*O'Donovan, Softić, Murray, Behan*
13/4	Shamrock Rovers	h	0-0	
20/4	Bray	a	1-1	*Horgan*
27/4	Drogheda	a	2-2	*O'Donovan 2 (1p)*
3/5	St Patrick's	h	1-0	*O'Donovan (p)*
12/5	Sligo	a	1-4	*Murphy*
18/5	Bohemians	h	2-1	*O'Flynn, O'Donovan*
29/5	Shamrock Rovers	a	0-2	
1/6	Derry	h	1-1	*O'Flynn*
26/6	Longford	a	2-1	*O'Donovan 2*
10/7	Galway	a	2-1	*O'Donovan 2*
17/7	Waterford	h	2-0	*O'Donovan, McSweeney*
22/7	Drogheda	h	0-0	
27/7	St Patrick's	a	1-1	*Behan*
3/8	Sligo	h	1-2	*O'Donovan*
10/8	Bohemians	a	1-2	*Farrelly*
24/8	Waterford	a	3-0	*Farrelly, Murray, Gamble*
27/8	Bray	h	2-2	*O'Flynn, McSweeney*
31/8	Galway	h	0-0	
10/9	UCD	h	4-1	*O'Flynn, Murray, McSweeney 2*
14/9	Longford	h	3-2	*Behan 2, McSweeney*
28/9	Derry	a	2-1	*Behan, O'Flynn*
5/10	Shamrock Rovers	h	1-0	*Behan*
8/10	UCD	a	2-1	*O'Brien, Behan*
12/10	Bray	a	1-1	*Behan*
19/10	Drogheda	a	1-2	*og (Gavin)*
22/10	St Patrick's	h	0-1	
3/11	Sligo	a	1-0	*Kelly*
9/11	Bohemians	h	0-1	

No	Name	Nat	Pos	Aps	(s)	Gls
21	Denis BEHAN		A	16	(14)	8
17	Colm CARROLL		A		(1)	
1	Michael DEVINE		G	26	(1)	
4	Gareth FARRELLY		M	17		2
8	Joe GAMBLE		M	27		1
15	Colin HEALY		M	18		
2	Neal HORGAN		D	32		1
30	Liam KEARNEY		M	28	(2)	
24	Sean KELLY		D	18	(2)	1
26	Cathal LORDAN		M	1	(1)	
14	Cillian LORDAN		D	15	(6)	
16	Mark McNULTY		G	7		
20	Leon McSWEENEY		M	14	(4)	5
19	Darren MURPHY		M	2	(7)	1
6	Dan MURRAY	ENG	D	32		3
7	Colin O'BRIEN		M	9	(7)	1
5	Brian O'CALLAGHAN		D	14	(2)	
10	Roy O'DONOVAN		A	17	(1)	14
9	John O'FLYNN		A	22	(3)	5
	Gary PHILPOTT		G		(1)	
3	Darragh RYAN		D	16	(2)	
18	Admir SOFTIĆ	BIH	M	13	(5)	1
11	Billy WOODS		M	19	(8)	

DERRY CITY FC

Manager – Pat Fenlon; (22/5/07) (Peter Hutton (NIR)); (2/7/07) John Robertson (SCO)

Founded - 1928

MAJOR HONOURS: League of Ireland – (2) 1989, 1997; FAI Cup – (4) 1989, 1995, 2002 (interim), 2006; Irish League – (1) 1965; Irish Cup – (3) 1949, 1954, 1964.

2007				
9/3	Bray	h	1-0	*McHugh*
17/3	Sligo	a	2-0	*Molloy, McHugh*
23/3	St Patrick's	h	0-1	
30/3	Drogheda	a	1-2	*og (Gavin)*
9/4	Cork	h	1-4	*Hutton*
13/4	Waterford	a	1-0	*Hutton*
20/4	UCD	h	0-1	
27/4	Bohemians	h	0-0	
4/5	Galway	a	1-1	*Farren*
14/5	Shamrock Rovers	h	1-0	*McCourt*
19/5	Longford	a	0-0	
25/5	UCD	a	1-1	*McHugh*
29/5	Waterford	h	1-1	*Hynes*
1/6	Cork	a	1-1	*Farren*
22/6	Drogheda	h	0-1	
29/6	St Patrick's	a	1-2	*McGlynn*
6/7	Sligo	h	4-1	*Farren 2, McGlynn, Martyn*
21/7	Bohemians	a	0-0	
29/7	Galway	h	0-0	
4/8	Shamrock Rovers	a	1-1	*Morrow*
10/8	Longford	h	3-1	*Morrow, McHugh, Martyn*
24/8	Bray	h	3-0	*Hutton, McHugh, Morrow*
1/9	Sligo	a	0-0	
7/9	St Patrick's	h	1-0	*og (Gibson)*
14/9	Drogheda	a	0-1	
28/9	Cork	h	1-2	*Brennan*
5/10	Waterford	a	1-2	*McCourt (p)*
12/10	UCD	h	0-0	
15/10	Bray	a	1-1	*McGlynn*
19/10	Bohemians	h	1-2	*McHugh*
26/10	Galway	a	0-1	
2/11	Shamrock Rovers	h	1-1	*McHugh*
9/11	Longford	a	1-3	*McHugh*

No	Name	Nat	Pos	Aps	(s)	Gls
9	Gary BECKETT	NIR	A	4	(2)	
11	Killian BRENNAN		M	22	(4)	1
15	Kevin DEERY	NIR	M	19	(4)	
18	Mark FARREN	NIR	A	20	(10)	4
3	Sean HARGAN	NIR	D	15	(3)	
	Gareth HARKIN		A		(2)	
7	Ruaidhri HIGGINS	NIR	M	22	(6)	
4	Peter HUTTON	NIR	D	24		3
24	Peter HYNES		A	6	(7)	1
16	Pat JENNINGS	ENG	G	31		
6	Darren KELLY	NIR	D	14		
8	Ciaran MARTYN		M	16	(1)	2
20	Neil McCAFFERTY	NIR	M	3	(6)	
2	Eddie McCALLION	NIR	D	27		
5	Mark McCHRYSTAL	NIR	D	2	(1)	
23	Patrick McCOURT	NIR	M	16	(1)	2
21	David McDAID		A	1	(3)	
27	David McEWAN	SCO	G	1		
14	Gareth McGLYNN		M	23	(5)	3
10	Kevin McHUGH		A	23	(8)	8
17	Barry MOLLOY	NIR	M	26	(1)	1
25	Alan MOORE		M		(4)	
28	Sammy MORROW	NIR	A	6	(2)	3
22	Greg O'HALLORAN		D	4	(2)	
12	Ken OMAN		D	25		

5	Dave ROGERS	ENG	D	12		
6	Seamus SHARKEY		D		(1)	
1	Ola TIDMAN	SWE	G	1		

DROGHEDA UNITED FC

Manager – Paul Doolin

Founded - 1919

MAJOR HONOURS: League of Ireland – (1) 2007; FAI Cup – (1) 2005.

2007				
9/3	Bohemians	a	0-0	
16/3	UCD	h	3-2	*O'Brien, Fitzpatrick, Zayed*
23/3	Galway	a	3-2	*Fitzpatrick, O'Brien, Zayed*
30/3	Derry	h	2-1	*O'Brien, Cahill*
6/4	Longford	a	1-0	*Robinson*
13/4	Sligo	h	3-0	*Zayed 2, O'Brien*
20/4	Shamrock Rovers	a	2-1	*Robinson 2*
27/4	Cork	h	2-2	*Robinson (p), Ristilä*
4/5	Waterford	a	1-1	*O'Brien*
21/5	St Patrick's	a	0-1	
25/5	Shamrock Rovers	h	0-2	
29/5	Sligo	a	2-0	*Shelley, Robinson (p)*
1/6	Longford	h	1-1	*Byrne*
22/6	Derry	a	1-0	*Ristilä*
26/6	Bray	h	4-1	*Keddy, Gartland, Whelan, Ristilä*
6/7	UCD	a	1-0	*O'Keefe*
13/7	Bohemians	h	1-0	*Grant*
22/7	Cork	a	0-0	
27/7	Waterford	h	3-0	*Zayed, Keddy, O'Keefe*
6/8	Bray	a	2-1	*Baker, Robinson*
10/8	St Patrick's	h	2-0	*Robinson, Zayed*
20/8	Galway	h	2-2	*Keddy, Zayed*
24/8	Bohemians	a	1-1	*og (Heary O.)*
3/9	UCD	h	0-1	
7/9	Galway	a	1-1	*Bates*
14/9	Derry	h	1-0	*Bates*
29/9	Longford	a	2-1	*Bates, Keegan*
5/10	Sligo	h	1-0	*Gavin*
12/10	Shamrock Rovers	a	2-0	*Zayed 2*
19/10	Cork	h	2-1	*Zayed, Bates*
26/10	Waterford	a	1-1	*Robinson*
2/11	Bray	h	1-1	*Zayed*
9/11	St Patrick's	a	0-0	

No	Name	Nat	Pos	Aps	(s)	Gls
27	Richie BAKER		M	6	(2)	1
25	Guy BATES	ENG	A	9	(1)	4
15	Stephen BRADLEY		M	9	(2)	
16	Stuart BYRNE		M	28	(1)	1
26	Ollie CAHILL		M	22	(2)	1
1	Daniel CONNOR		G	22		
10	Glen FITZPATRICK		A	8	(1)	2
6	Graham GARTLAND		M	25		1
5	Jason GAVIN		D	14		1
12	Tony GRANT		A	7	(14)	1
4	Stephen GRAY		D	11	(4)	
11	James KEDDY		M	12	(5)	3
18	Paul KEEGAN		M	19	(11)	1
2	Damien LYNCH		D	12	(1)	
9	Declan O'BRIEN		A	7		5
22	Aidan O'KEEFE		A	1	(14)	2
19	Sami RISTILÄ	FIN	M	7	(5)	3
7	Shane ROBINSON		M	32		8
14	Brian SHELLEY		D	31		1
28	John TAMBOURAS	AUS	D	7	(2)	
23	Mikko VILMUNEN	FIN	G	11	(1)	
3	Simon WEBB		D	27		
8	Gavin WHELAN		M	9	(7)	1
17	Eamon ZAYED		A	27	(4)	11

GALWAY UNITED FC

Manager – Tony Cousins

Founded - 1937

MAJOR HONOURS: FAI Cup – (1) 1991.

2007				
9/3	Sligo	h	0-2	
16/3	Cork	a	0-0	
23/3	Drogheda	h	2-3	*O'Flynn, Murphy*
30/3	Shamrock Rovers	a	0-1	
6/4	St Patrick's	h	0-1	
13/4	Longford	h	1-1	*O'Flynn*
20/4	Bohemians	a	1-1	*Murphy*
27/4	Bray	a	1-0	*Murphy*
4/5	Derry	h	1-1	*O'Flynn (p)*
11/5	Waterford	a	0-1	
18/5	UCD	h	0-0	
25/5	Bohemians	h	0-1	
29/5	Longford	a	3-0	*O'Flynn (p), Glynn 2*
1/6	St Patrick's	a	2-1	*Glynn 2*
22/6	Shamrock Rovers	h	1-1	*Glynn*
10/7	Cork	h	1-2	*O'Brien*
14/7	Sligo	a	1-1	*Glynn*
20/7	Bray	h	0-1	
29/7	Derry	a	0-0	
3/8	Waterford	h	1-2	*og (Hedderman)*
10/8	UCD	a	2-2	*Glynn, O'Flynn*
20/8	Drogheda	a	2-2	*Murphy, O'Brien*
24/8	Sligo	h	2-0	*Charles, Cooke*
31/8	Cork	a	0-0	
7/9	Drogheda	h	1-1	*Lester*
14/9	Shamrock Rovers	a	0-4	
28/9	St Patrick's	h	0-1	
5/10	Longford	h	2-1	*Keane A. (p), Charles*
12/10	Bohemians	a	0-2	
19/10	Bray	a	1-1	*O'Flynn (p)*
26/10	Derry	h	1-0	*Charles*
2/11	Waterford	a	0-0	
9/11	UCD	h	2-1	*Keane A. (p), Glynn*

Name	Nat	Pos	Aps	(s)	Gls
Chris ARMSTRONG	ENG	A	3	(1)	
Dimitris BRINIAS	AUS	G	1		
Wesley CHARLES	VIN	D	29	(2)	3
Billy CLEARY		D		(1)	
David COOKE		M	8	(9)	1
Iarfhlaith DAVOREN		A	2	(1)	
Shaun FAGAN	SCO	M	6	(3)	
Vinny FAHERTY		A	5	(10)	
Cathal FAHY		A		(1)	
John FITZGERALD		D	13		
Ciaran FOLEY		M	20	(6)	
Derek GLYNN		A	19	(10)	8
Alan GOUGH		G	1		
Colm JAMES		M	14	(2)	
Alan KEANE		D	15		2
Johnathan KEANE		M		(1)	
John LESTER		M	28	(3)	1
Liam McKENNA		D	1	(3)	
Michael Yeboah MENSAH	NED	A	1		
Jason MOLLOY		M		(1)	
Barry MORAN		A	15	(5)	
Alan MURPHY		A	28	(3)	4
Regillio NOOITMEER	NED	D	28		
Derek O'BRIEN		M	32		2
Stephen O'FLYNN		A	20	(3)	6
Greg O'HALLORAN		D	10	(2)	
Phillip REILLY		D	9	(1)	
Daryl ROBSON	ENG	M	5	(4)	
Gary ROGERS		G	31		
John RUSSELL		A	11	(10)	
Shane TRACEY		M	8	(5)	

LONGFORD TOWN FC

Manager – Alan Mathews

Founded - 1924

MAJOR HONOURS: FAI Cup – (2) 2003, 2004.

2007				
0/3	St Patrick's	h	1-2	*Mooney*
6/3	Shamrock Rovers	a	0-2	
3/3	Sligo	h	0-1	
0/3	Cork	a	0-2	
/4	Drogheda	h	0-1	
3/4	Galway	a	1-1	*Mooney*
0/4	Waterford	h	1-0	*Mooney*
7/4	UCD	a	2-2	*Martin R., Reilly*
/5	Bray	h	1-1	*Freeman*
1/5	Bohemians	a	0-5	
9/5	Derry	h	0-0	
5/5	Waterford	a	1-2	*Mooney (p)*
9/5	Galway	h	0-3	
/6	Drogheda	a	1-1	*Mooney (p)*
6/6	Cork	h	1-2	*Deegan*
0/6	Sligo	a	1-2	*Wexler*
/7	Shamrock Rovers	h	0-3	
5/7	St Patrick's	a	2-4	*Mooney, Sullivan*
1/7	UCD	h	1-0	*Deegan*
7/7	Bray	a	3-1	*Mooney 2, Baker*
/8	Bohemians	h	3-0	*Mooney 2, Duffy*
0/8	Derry	a	1-3	*Mooney (p)*
5/8	St Patrick's	h	2-1	*Mooney (p), Brennan*
1/8	Shamrock Rovers	a	1-0	*Mooney*
/9	Sligo	h	1-1	*Mooney*
4/9	Cork	a	2-3	*James, Prunty*
9/9	Drogheda	h	1-2	*Ryan*
/10	Galway	a	1-2	*Mooney*
5/10	Waterford	h	1-1	*Sullivan*
9/10	UCD	a	1-0	*Baker*
2/10	Bray	h	1-0	*Mooney (p)*
/11	Bohemians	a	0-0	
/11	Derry	h	3-1	*Mooney 3 (1p)*

Name	Nat	Pos	Aps	(s)	Gls
essie BAKER		A	16	(4)	2
amien BRENNAN		D	29		1
ary DEEGAN		M	30		2
lichael DEMPSEY		G	6		
evin DOHERTY		D	22	(1)	
aire DOYLE		M	19	(2)	
amie DUFFY	USA	M	10	(3)	1
avid FREEMAN		A	24	(1)	1
olm JAMES		M	8	(5)	1
ean KELLY		D	1		
hay KELLY		G	27	(1)	
avid LEE		A		(3)	
ohn MARTIN		M	11		
obbie MARTIN		M	18	(4)	1
avid MOONEY		A	32		19
lan O'RIORDAN		M	2	(3)	
ean PRUNTY		M	31		1
ohn REILLY		M	12	(8)	1
lark RUTHERFORD	ENG	M	23	(2)	
n RYAN		D	6	(4)	1
atrick SULLIVAN		D	28		2
n WEXLER	USA	A	8	(9)	1

SAINT PATRICK'S ATHLETIC FC

Manager – John McDonnell

Founded - 1929

MAJOR HONOURS: League of Ireland – (7) 1952, 1955, 1956, 1990, 1996, 1998, 1999; FAI Cup – (2) 1959, 1961.

2007				
0/3	Longford	a	2-1	*Quigley M. 2*
6/3	Waterford	h	3-0	*Ndo, Murphy A. 2*
23/3	Derry	a	1-0	*Murphy A.*
30/3	Bray	h	3-1	*Quigley M. 3*
6/4	Galway	a	1-0	*Quigley M.*
13/4	Bohemians	h	0-0	
21/4	Sligo	a	4-0	*O'Neill (p), og (McKenzie), og (Kelly), Mulcahy*
27/4	Shamrock Rovers	h	2-1	*Murphy A., Maguire*
3/5	Cork	a	0-1	
11/5	UCD	a	2-2	*Quigley M., O'Neill*
21/5	Drogheda	h	1-0	*Foley*
25/5	Sligo	h	3-1	*O'Neill, Quigley M., O'Connor*
28/5	Bohemians	a	0-2	
1/6	Galway	h	1-2	*Quigley M.*
22/6	Bray	a	0-0	
29/6	Derry	h	2-1	*Quigley M. 2*
6/7	Waterford	a	1-2	*Mulcahy*
15/7	Longford	h	4-2	*Keane, Murphy A., Guy, Kirby*
23/7	Shamrock Rovers	a	0-0	
27/7	Cork	h	1-1	*Guy*
6/8	UCD	h	1-1	*Kirby*
10/8	Drogheda	a	0-2	
25/8	Longford	a	1-2	*Quigley M.*
31/8	Waterford	h	4-1	*Fahey, Quigley M., Barker 2*
7/9	Derry	a	0-1	
14/9	Bray	h	4-2	*O'Neill (p), Barker, Gibson, Keane*
28/9	Galway	a	1-0	*Guy*
5/10	Bohemians	h	0-1	
12/10	Sligo	a	3-2	*Quigley M., O'Neill, Murphy A.*
19/10	Shamrock Rovers	h	5-0	*Kirby 2, Gibson 2, O'Neill*
22/10	Cork	a	1-0	*O'Neill*
2/11	UCD	a	3-0	*O'Neill, Paisley, Quigley M.*
9/11	Drogheda	h	0-0	

No	Name	Nat	Pos	Aps	(s)	Gls
	Keith BARKER		A	3	(4)	3
2	Stephen BRENNAN		D	31		
20	Brendan CLARKE		G	3	(1)	
19	Kevin CORNWALL		A	1	(2)	
8	Keith FAHEY		M	31	(1)	1
	Glen FITZPATRICK		A	5	(7)	
6	Colm FOLEY		D	11	(2)	1
14	Michael FOLEY-SHERIDAN		M	3	(6)	
3	John FROST		D	16	(7)	
17	Billy GIBSON	SCO	M	15	(1)	3
23	Ryan GUY	USA	A	5	(14)	3
	Robbie HORGAN		G	1		
10	Michael KEANE		M	13	(1)	2
7	Alan KIRBY		M	26	(1)	4
12	Eamonn LYNCH		A		(2)	
25	Michal MAČEK	CZE	M		(1)	
5	Darragh MAGUIRE		D	23	(4)	1
4	David MULCAHY		D	11	(3)	2
15	Anto MURPHY		M	21	(2)	6
28	Paul MURPHY		M		(1)	
18	Joseph NDO	CMR	M	14	(2)	1
21	Sean O'CONNOR		M	4	(13)	1
9	Gary O'NEILL		A	24	(3)	8
24	Stephen PAISLEY		D	24		1
11	Mark QUIGLEY		A	31	(1)	15
16	Stephen QUIGLEY		D	2	(2)	
4	Dave ROGERS	ENG	D	16		
10	Mark ROONEY		A		(7)	
1	Barry RYAN		G	29		

SHAMROCK ROVERS FC

Manager – Pat Scully

Founded - 1901

MAJOR HONOURS: League of Ireland – (15) 1923, 1925, 1927, 1932, 1938, 1939, 1954, 1957, 1959, 1964, 1984, 1985, 1986, 1987, 1994; FAI Cup – (24) 1925, 1929, 1930, 1931, 1932, 1933, 1936, 1940, 1944, 1945, 1948, 1955, 1956, 1962, 1964, 1965, 1966, 1967, 1968, 1969, 1978, 1985, 1986, 1987.

2007

9/3	UCD	a	0-0	
16/3	Longford	h	2-0	*Kelleher 2*
30/3	Galway	h	1-0	*Rowe*
3/4	Bohemians	a	1-2	*Purcell*
6/4	Bray	a	2-0	*Purcell 2*
13/4	Cork	a	0-0	
20/4	Drogheda	h	1-2	*Cassidy*
27/4	St Patrick's	a	1-2	*Purcell*
4/5	Sligo	h	1-0	Rowe
14/5	Derry	a	0-1	
25/5	Drogheda	a	2-0	*Purcell 2*
29/5	Cork	h	2-0	*Ferguson, Rowe*
1/6	Bray	h	1-0	*Purcell*
22/6	Galway	a	1-1	*Purcell*
29/6	Bohemians	h	0-0	
6/7	Longford	a	3-0	*Tyrell, Rowe, Myler*
10/7	Waterford	h	2-0	*Rowe, Purcell (p)*
16/7	UCD	h	2-0	*Rowe, Purcell*
23/7	St Patrick's	h	0-0	
27/7	Sligo	a	0-2	
4/8	Derry	h	1-1	*Myler*
10/8	Waterford	a	2-0	*Myler 2*
24/8	UCD	a	4-2	*Purcell, Myler 3 (1p)*
31/8	Longford	h	0-1	
14/9	Galway	h	4-0	*Myler 3, Amond*
17/9	Bohemians	a	2-0	*O'Connor Dan., Purcell*
2/10	Bray	a	0-3	
5/10	Cork	a	0-1	
12/10	Drogheda	h	0-2	
19/10	St Patrick's	a	0-5	
27/10	Sligo	h	0-0	
2/11	Derry	a	1-1	*Cassidy*
9/11	Waterford	h	0-0	

Name	Nat	Pos	Aps	(s)	Gls
Padraig AMOND		A	2	(4)	1
Tommy BARRETT		M	7	(3)	
David CASSIDY		M	25	(5)	2
Robbie CLARKE		M	21	(3)	
Wayne COLBERT		M	1	(3)	
Robbie CREEVY		M	2	(1)	
Owen DOYLE		A	5	(5)	
Jamie DUFFY	USA	M	5	(3)	
Barry FERGUSON		D	29		1
Robbie KELLEHER		M	2	(1)	2
Ciarán KILDUFF		A		(3)	
Mark LANGTRY		D	1	(1)	
Dean LAWRENCE		D	12	(1)	
Stephen MAHER		M	1		
John MARTIN		M	8	(1)	
David McGILL		M	9	(4)	
Eric McGILL		M	12	(2)	
John McGUINNESS		G		(3)	
Chris MULHALL		M	3	(3)	
Barry MURPHY		G	28		
Andy MYLER		A	18	(11)	10
Ger O'BRIEN		D	29	(1)	
Stephen O'BRIEN		G	5		
Danny O'CONNOR		D	25	(1)	1
David O'CONNOR		M	10	(5)	
Derek PENDER		D	17		
Aidan PRICE		D	9		
Tadhg PURCELL		A	22	(7)	12
Alan REYNOLDS		M	6	(1)	
Ger ROWE		A	21	(8)	6
Ian RYAN		D	9	(4)	
Paul SHIELS		M	7	(3)	
David TYRELL		M	11	(1)	1
David VICKERY		A	1	(1)	
Glen WALSH		D		(1)	

SLIGO ROVERS FC

Manager – (Dessie Cawley & Leo Tierney); (27/4/07) Paul Cook (ENG)

Founded - 1928

MAJOR HONOURS: League of Ireland – (2) 1937, 1977; FAI Cup – (2) 1983, 1994.

2007

9/3	Galway	a	2-0	*Curran, McCartney*
17/3	Derry	h	0-2	
23/3	Longford	a	1-0	*Kuduzović*
1/4	UCD	h	1-0	*Kuduzović*
6/4	Bohemians	a	0-1	
13/4	Drogheda	a	0-3	
21/4	St Patrick's	h	0-4	
28/4	Waterford	h	1-1	*Kuduzović*
4/5	Shamrock Rovers	a	0-1	
12/5	Cork	h	4-1	*Judge 2, Turner 2 (1p)*
18/5	Bray	a	0-2	
25/5	St Patrick's	a	1-3	*Turner*
29/5	Drogheda	h	0-2	
2/6	Bohemians	h	2-1	*Judge, Kuduzović (p)*
22/6	UCD	a	2-0	*Hughes, Judge*
30/6	Longford	h	2-1	*Kuduzović (p), Cretaro*
6/7	Derry	a	1-4	*Judge*
14/7	Galway	h	1-1	*Judge*
20/7	Waterford	a	2-1	*Kuduzović 2*
27/7	Shamrock Rovers	h	2-0	*Hughes, Judge*
3/8	Cork	a	2-1	*Hughes, Kuduzović*
11/8	Bray	h	3-0	*Judge, Kuduzović (p), Manson*
24/8	Galway	a	0-2	
1/9	Derry	h	0-0	
8/9	Longford	a	1-1	*Hughes*
15/9	UCD	h	2-1	*Hughes, Foy (p)*
28/9	Bohemians	a	0-3	
5/10	Drogheda	a	0-1	
12/10	St Patrick's	h	2-3	*Judge, Kuduzović*
20/10	Waterford	h	1-2	*Turner*
27/10	Shamrock Rovers	a	0-0	
3/11	Cork	h	0-1	
9/11	Bray	a	1-2	*Kelly*

Name	Nat	Pos	Aps	(s)	Gls
Choice AISIEN	NGA	A	3	(4)	
Tomislav ARCABA	AUS	G	7		
Piotr BAJDZIAK	POL	M	3	(4)	
Mark BOYD	ENG	M	11	(3)	
Richard BRUSH	ENG	G	26		
Brian CASH		A	10	(7)	
Seamus COLEMAN		D	25	(1)	
Mikey CREANE		M		(2)	
Raffael CRETARO		M	27	(3)	1
Gary CURRAN		M	6	(9)	1
Sean FLANNERY		A		(2)	
Keith FOY		D	19	(8)	1
Matt GORDON	AUS	M	5	(4)	
Adam HUGHES	AUS	M	25	(1)	5
Mark HUTCHISON	SCO	D		(1)	
Matthew JUDGE	ENG	A	24	(2)	9
Kevin JULIAN		D		(1)	
Sean KELLY		D	5	(4)	1
Fahrudin KUDUZOVIĆ	BIH	M	32		10
Stephen MANSON	SCO	M	14	(9)	1
Jason McCARTNEY		A	7	(3)	1
Glen McCORMACK		D	1		
Jamie McKENZIE	SCO	D	30	(2)	
Ross McLOUGHLIN		A	1	(1)	
Brian McMORROW		M	1	(2)	
Gary MELLY		M	1		

James MEREDITH	ENG	D	4		
Gino O'BOYLE		A		(3)	
Conor O'GRADY		M	27	(1)	
Gavin PEERS		D	23		
Levi TIERNEY		A		(1)	
Chris TURNER	NIR	M	10	(2)	4
Zoltán VASAS	HUN	D	5	(1)	
Danny VENTRE	ENG	D	11		

UNIVERSITY COLLEGE DUBLIN FC

Manager – Pete Mahon

Founded - 1895

MAJOR HONOURS: FAI Cup – (1) 1984.

2007				
9/3	Shamrock Rovers	h	0-0	
16/3	Drogheda	a	2-3	*Doyle T., Oprea*
23/3	Cork	h	0-1	
1/4	Sligo	a	0-1	
6/4	Waterford	h	3-0	*Byrne C., Byrne P. 2*
12/4	Bray	h	2-0	*Doyle T., Sammon*
20/4	Derry	a	1-0	*Purcell*
27/4	Longford	h	2-2	*Byrne P., Sammon*
4/5	Bohemians	a	0-0	
11/5	St Patrick's	h	2-2	*Purcell, Byrne P.*
18/5	Galway	a	0-0	
25/5	Derry	h	1-1	*McNally*
29/5	Bray	a	1-2	*Doyle T.*
1/6	Waterford	a	3-1	*Byrne P. 2 (1p), Byrne C.*
22/6	Sligo	h	0-2	
6/7	Drogheda	h	0-1	
16/7	Shamrock Rovers	a	0-2	
21/7	Longford	a	0-1	
27/7	Bohemians	h	1-0	*Sammon (p)*
6/8	St Patrick's	a	1-1	*Doyle T.*
10/8	Galway	h	2-2	*Doyle T., Fitzgerald*
24/8	Shamrock Rovers	h	2-4	*Sammon, Fitzgerald*
3/9	Drogheda	a	1-0	*Bermingham*
10/9	Cork	a	1-4	*McFaul*
15/9	Sligo	a	1-2	*Murphy*
28/9	Waterford	h	2-1	*Sammon (p), Byrne C.*
5/10	Bray	h	1-1	*Sammon*
8/10	Cork	h	1-2	*McWalter*
12/10	Derry	a	0-0	
19/10	Longford	h	0-1	
22/10	Bohemians	a	0-2	
2/11	St Patrick's	h	0-3	
9/11	Galway	a	1-2	*Byrne P.*

Name	Nat	Pos	Aps	(s)	Gls
Ian BERMINGHAM		D	22	(1)	1
Greg BOLGER		D	1	(4)	
Conan BYRNE		M	28	(2)	3
Paul BYRNE		A	16	(4)	7
Paul CROWLEY		M	13	(6)	
Derek DOYLE		M		(2)	
Tony DOYLE		M	19	(4)	5
Ronan FINN		M	17	(6)	
Shane FITZGERALD		M	5	(2)	2
Darren FORSYTH		A	1	(3)	
Killian GALLAGHER		D	2	(3)	
Matt GREGG	ENG	G	15		
Peter HYNES		A	4	(4)	
Conor KENNA		D	32	(1)	
Bryan KING		M	11	(5)	
Alan MAHON		D	29		
Tony McDONNELL		M	12	(7)	
Shane McFAUL		M	24		1
Evan McMILLAN		D	6	(3)	
Alan McNALLY		D	28	(1)	1
Patrick McWALTER		M	12	(1)	1
Francis MORAN		A	1	(1)	
Paul MURPHY		M		(2)	1
Bogdan OPREA	ROU	A	2	(3)	1
James O'SULLIVAN		M		(1)	
Timmy PURCELL		M	6	(16)	2
Darren QUIGLEY		G	18		
Conor SAMMON		A	30	(1)	6
Brian SHORTALL		D	9	(3)	

WATERFORD UNITED FC

Manager – Gareth Cronin

Founded - 1930

MAJOR HONOURS: League of Ireland – (6) 1966, 1968, 1969, 1970, 1972, 1973; FAI Cup – (2) 1937, 1980.

2007				
9/3	Cork	h	1-0	*Cooling*
16/3	St Patrick's	a	0-3	
23/3	Bray	h	1-2	*Brosnan*
30/3	Bohemians	h	0-1	
6/4	UCD	a	0-3	
13/4	Derry	h	0-1	
20/4	Longford	a	0-1	
28/4	Sligo	a	1-1	*og (McKenzie)*
4/5	Drogheda	h	1-1	*Kavanagh*
11/5	Galway	h	1-0	*Sullivan*
25/5	Longford	h	2-1	*Breen, Sullivan*
29/5	Derry	a	1-1	*Brosnan*
1/6	UCD	h	1-3	*McCarthy*
25/6	Bohemians	a	0-1	
1/7	Bray	a	1-2	*Sullivan*
6/7	St Patrick's	h	2-1	*McCarthy, Sullivan*
10/7	Shamrock Rovers	a	0-2	
17/7	Cork	a	0-2	
20/7	Sligo	h	1-2	*Bermingham*
27/7	Drogheda	a	0-3	
3/8	Galway	a	2-1	*Breen, Sullivan*
10/8	Shamrock Rovers	h	0-2	
24/8	Cork	h	0-3	
31/8	St Patrick's	a	1-4	*Hedderman*
7/9	Bray	h	0-0	
14/9	Bohemians	h	0-0	
28/9	UCD	a	1-2	*McCarthy*
5/10	Derry	h	2-1	*Sullivan, Kiely*
15/10	Longford	a	1-1	*Kiely*
20/10	Sligo	a	2-1	*Sullivan, Mulcahy A.*
26/10	Drogheda	h	1-1	*Warren*
2/11	Galway	h	0-0	
9/11	Shamrock Rovers	a	0-0	

Name	Nat	Pos	Aps	(s)	Gls
Karl BERMINGHAM		M	10	(2)	1
David BREEN		D	30		2
Robert BROSNAN		A	16	(9)	2
Kenny BROWNE		D	15	(3)	
Willie BRUTON		A		(2)	
Stephen COOLING		M	5	(1)	1
Dean DELANEY		G	30		
Gary DUNPHY		A		(1)	
Patrick FLYNN		D	29		
David GRINCELL		A		(4)	
Shane HARTE		M	11	(3)	
John HAYES		D	14	(4)	
Robbie HEDDERMAN		D	26	(1)	1
Packie HOLDEN		G	3		
Daryl KAVANAGH		M	12	(10)	1
Alan KEARNEY		M	4	(5)	
Alan KEELY		D	7	(3)	
Willie John KIELY		A	11	(6)	2
Cathal LORDAN		M	4	(6)	
Paul McCARTHY		M	32		3
Conor McDONALD		A		(3)	
Alan MULCAHY		M	9	(10)	1
David MULCAHY		D	6	(1)	
Alan REYNOLDS		M	3	(2)	
Ray SCULLY		M	23	(2)	
Vinny SULLIVAN		A	32		7
Dave WARREN		M	31	(1)	1
Declan WOODGATE		A		(1)	

DOMESTIC CUP 2007

FAI CUP

SECOND ROUND

(14/6/07)
Dundalk 3, Athlone 0

(15/6/07)
Derry 2, Monaghan 0
Drogheda 0, Bohemians 1
Galway 2, Finn Harps 2
Limerick 1, Wexford 1
Malahide United 2, Cherry Orchard 1
Phoenix 0, St Patrick's 4
Shelbourne 0, Cork 1
Tolka Rovers 2, Waterford 2

(16/6/07)
Douglas Hall 4, Cobh 0
Kildare 0, Kilkenny 1
Longford 1, Celbridge Town 0
Salthill Devon 0, UCD 4
Shamrock Rovers 2, Sligo 3

(17/6/07)
Bray 7, St Mochta's 0
Fanad United 1, St John Bosco 0

Replays

(18/6/07)
Finn Harps 0, Galway 0 *(aet; 4-2 on pens)*

(19/6/07)
Waterford 4, Tolka Rovers 1
Wexford 0, Limerick 1

THIRD ROUND

(16/8/07)
Dundalk 1, UCD 2

(17/8/07)
Limerick 1, Douglas Hall 1
Cork 5, Kilkenny 1
Bray 1, St Patrick's 2
Waterford 1, Sligo 1

(18/8/07)
Longford 2, Fanad United 0
Finn Harps 0, Derry 1

(19/8/07)
Malahide United 0, Bohemians 1

Replays

(21/8/07)
Sligo 2, Waterford 2 *(aet; 3-4 on pens)*

(22/8/07)
Douglas Hall 0, Limerick 1

QUARTER-FINALS

(21/9/07)
Derry 0, UCD 1 *(Sammon 60)*

(22/9/07)
Longford 3 *(Baker 72, Mooney 81, Duffy 90)*, Limerick 1 *(Tierney 85p)*
Waterford 1 *(Warren 10)*, Cork 1 *(Behan 49)*

(24/9/07)
St Patrick's 1 *(Fahey 56)*, Bohemians 2 *(Mansaram 25, 65)*

Replay

(25/9/07)
Cork 4 *(Behan 11, 35, 84, Kearney 61)*, Waterford 0

SEMI-FINALS

(26/10/07)
Bohemians 0, Cork 2 *(Kearney 24, 77)*

(28/10/07)
UCD 0, Longford 1 *(Martin R. 39)*

FINAL

(2/12/07)
RDS (Royal Dublin Society), Dublin
CORK CITY FC 1 *(Behan 60)*
LONGFORD TOWN FC 0
Referee - *McKeon*
CORK - *Devine, Lordan Ci., O'Callaghan, Murray, Woods (O'Brien 67), McSweeney, Gamble, Healy, Kearney (Farrelly 85), Behan, O'Flynn.*
LONGFORD – *Kelly Sh., Sullivan, Brennan, Doherty, Prunty, Duffy (Reilly 78), Doyle, Rutherford, Martin R., Mooney, Baker (Wexler 55).*
Sent off: Sullivan (89).

PROMOTED CLUBS

COBH RAMBLERS FC

Manager – Stephen Henderson
Founded – 1922

FINN HARPS FC

Manager – Paul Hegarty
Founded – 1954
MAJOR HONOURS: FAI Cup - (1) 1974.

SECOND LEVEL FINAL TABLE 2007

		Pld	W	D	L	F	A	Pts
1	Cobh Ramblers FC	36	22	11	3	57	17	77
2	Finn Harps FC	36	23	7	6	61	20	76
3	Dundalk FC	36	19	9	8	56	30	66
4	Limerick 37 FC	36	14	11	11	46	41	53
5	Shelbourne FC	36	11	10	15	46	46	43
6	Athlone Town AFC	36	11	8	17	40	55	41
7	Kildare County FC	36	9	12	15	48	62	39
8	Monaghan United FC	36	9	11	16	38	52	38
9	Wexford Youths FC	36	7	10	19	32	55	31
10	Kilkenny City AFC	36	5	11	20	33	79	26

N.B. – Kilkenny City AFC resigned from the league prior to the start of the 2008 season. Their place was taken by the newly formed club Sporting Fingal FC from Dublin.

PROMOTION/RELEGATION PLAY-OFFS

SEMI FINAL
(16/11/07)
Finn Harps 2, Dundalk 0

FINAL
(20/11/07)
Finn Harps 3, Waterford 0
(23/11/07)
Waterford 3, Finn Harps 3
(Finn Harps 6-3)

Missed penalty gives cause for regret

Romania were given little hope of reaching the UEFA EURO 2008™ quarter-finals when the draw unkindly threw them into a first-round group ontaining France, Italy and the Netherlands. But, in ne event, Victor Piţurcă's team were not far short of chieving their objective.

lad Adrian Mutu converted a late penalty against aly, Romania would probably have gone into their nal fixture against the Dutch with four points rather nan two. But Gianluigi Buffon, Mutu's former Juventus eam-mate, made the save and Romania's dream ffectively died. Granted, qualification was still in the ricolorii's hands as they travelled to Berne to take on a nuch-changed, already qualified Oranje side. But the onviction, it seemed, had gone, and with the xception of Mutu, who gave everything in an attempt o atone for his error, Romania were clearly second est to the Dutch 'second XI' and seldom looked like aining the victory required to guarantee their xtended stay in the competition.

ouches of class

n the whole, despite the inevitable disappointment f a winless first-round exit, Romania had no reason to eproach themselves. Their first major tournament ppearance since EURO 2000™ was no calamity. They nowed discipline, organisation and the odd touch of ass – mainly from Mutu, captain Cristian Chivu, left-ack Răzvan Raţ and goalkeeper Bogdan Lobonţ – to old both 2006 FIFA World Cup finalists to draws. But aving got the better of the Netherlands in their ualifying group, beating them for the first time, 1-0 in onstanta, to top the section, they were unable – espite the favourable circumstances – to repeat the ick in the Swiss capital.

ţurcă emerged from the tournament with credit, his ctical acumen plain for all to see. His next mission is ensure a Romanian presence at the 2010 World Cup a tough but far from impossible task given that a ding France are likely to be their principal challengers. However, if Romania are to be successful, they will probably need to find a complementary strike-partner for Mutu and, especially, someone prepared to show a bit of original thinking in central midfield.

Although a sizeable proportion of Romania's UEFA EURO 2008™ squad – eleven players out of 23 - was drafted from the Romanian domestic league, it could be argued that Seria I was hijacked by foreigners in 2007/08. For the first time in 17 years the championship title went to a club from outside Bucharest. It was won by a CFR 1907 Cluj team stuffed to the brim with imports, the majority of them from Portugal, Brazil and Argentina. Indeed, on 30 March 2008 history was made when CFR took to the field in a crucial away fixture against defending champions FC Dinamo 1948 Bucureşti with not one Romanian in their ranks.

In fairness CFR had a Romanian coach, Ioan Andone, and it was to his enormous credit that he constructed a successful team so quickly. The former Dinamo and Romania defender was, in common with many of his players, new to the club, but within no time CFR were

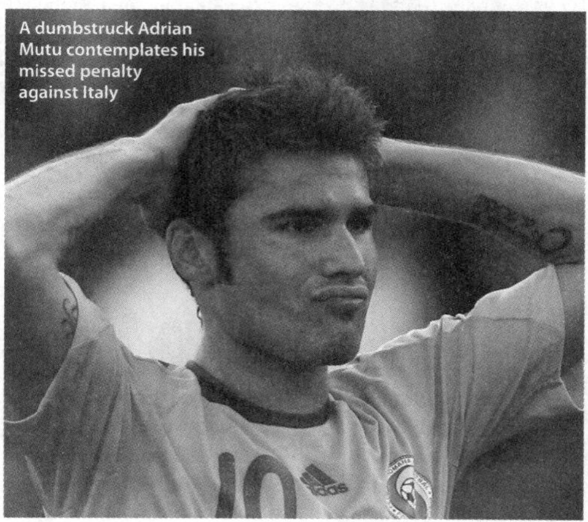
A dumbstruck Adrian Mutu contemplates his missed penalty against Italy

Federatia Română de Fotbal (FRF

Casa Fotbalului
Str. Serg. Serbanica Vasile 12
22186 Bucureşti
tel - +40 21 3250678
fax - +40 21 3250679
website - www.frf.ro
email - frf@frf.ro
Year of Formation – 1909
President - Mircea Sandu
General Secretary - Adalbert Kassai
Press Officer – Paul-Daniel Zaharia
Stadium - Lia Manoliu, Bucureşti (53,926)

INTERNATIONAL TOURNAMENT APPEARANCES
FIFA World Cup - (7) 1930, 1934, 1938, 1970, 1990 (2nd round), 1994 (qtr-finals), 1998 (2nd round).
UEFA European Championship - (4) 1984, 1996, 2000 (qtr-finals), 2008.

TOP FIVE ALL-TIME CAPS
Dorinel Munteanu (134); Gheorghe Hagi (124); Gheorghe Popescu (115); Laszlo Bölöni (102); Dan Petrescu (95)

TOP FIVE ALL-TIME GOALS
Gheorghe Hagi (35); Iuliu Bodola (30); Adrian Mutu (29); Viorel Moldovan (25); Laszlo Bölöni (23)

NATIONAL TEAM RESULTS 2007/08

22/8/07	Turkey	H	Bucharest	2-0	*Dică (61), Mutu (70)*
8/9/07	Belarus (ECQ)	A	Minsk	3-1	*Mutu (16, 77p), Dică (42)*
12/9/07	Germany	A	Cologne	1-3	*Goian (3)*
13/10/07	Netherlands (ECQ)	H	Constanta	1-0	*Goian (71)*
17/10/07	Luxembourg (ECQ)	A	Luxembourg	2-0	*Petre F. (42), Marica (61)*
17/11/07	Bulgaria (ECQ)	A	Sofia	0-1	
21/11/07	Albania (ECQ)	H	Bucharest	6-1	*Dică (22, 71p), Tamaş (53), Niculae D. (62, 65), Marica (69p)*
6/2/08	Israel	A	Tel-Aviv	0-1	
26/3/08	Russia	H	Bucharest	3-0	*Marica (45), Niculae D. (60), Niculae M. (75)*
31/5/08	Montenegro	H	Bucharest	4-0	*Mutu (15), Ghionea (49), Dică (55, 69)*
9/6/08	France (ECF)	N	Zurich (SUI)	0-0	
13/6/08	Italy (ECF)	N	Zurich (SUI)	1-1	*Mutu (55)*
17/6/08	Netherlands (ECF)	N	Berne (SUI)	0-2	

not only challenging the traditional powerhouses of the capital, Dinamo, FC Steaua Bucureşti and FC Rapid Bucureşti, but stealing a march on them all and heading the Seria I table.

Steaua surge

At the winter break, the club's centenary year at an end, CFR held a five-point lead over Rapid, with Steaua a further three points back. But after a controversial 3-1 defeat at Steaua in their first away fixture after the spring resumption, the team's confidence began to drain away and they dropped points unexpectedly. Steaua, on the other hand, free from European obligations after finishing bottom of their UEFA Champions League group in the autumn - during which coach Gheorghe Hagi had quit over claims of interference by club owner Gigi Becali - and reinvigorated by another club icon, Marius Lăcătuş, as well as a new intake of foreigners, used the victory ove CFR as a springboard for a ten-match winning run. Tha included a 3-0 walkover against Rapid when the refe

ATIONAL TEAM APPEARANCES 2007/08

ch - Victor PIŢURCĂ	8/5/56		Tur	BLR	Ger	NED	LUX	BUL	ALB	Isr	Rus	Mne	FRA	ITA	NED	Caps	Goals
dan Ionuţ LOBONŢ	18/1/78	Dinamo Bucureşti	G	G		G	G	G	G	G		G46	G	G	G	66	-
e MARIN	8/9/73	Steaua	D	D	D											9	-
n Nicolae GOIAN	12/12/80	Steaua	D	D	D70	D	D	D58	D	D	D		D	D		21	3
ian CHIVU	26/10/80	Internazionale (ITA)	D62	D	M24	M	M87	M		M	M46	M46	M	M	M	62	3
van RAŢ	26/5/81	Shakhtar (UKR)	D	D	D76	D	D	D	D		D87	D46	D	D	D	51	1
Constantin CODREA	4/4/81	Siena (ITA)	M66	M90	M62	M		M82				s46	s64	M	M72	36	1
l Matei RĂDOI	22/3/81	Steaua	M46								M	M46	M93	M25		45	1
entin PETRE	15/1/76	CSKA Sofia (BUL)	M46	s56			M		M65	s46 /83	M62	M58		M60	s82	52	5
lae Constantin DICĂ	9/5/80	Steaua	M79	M67	M85		M68		M	s46	s46	s46	s93	s25	s72	28	8
an MUTU	8/1/79	Fiorentina (ITA)	A	A	A	A				A	A46	A46	A78	A88	A	64	29
an Andrei MARICA	2/10/85	Stuttgart (GER)	A81		A72	A70	A	s65	A73	A46	A46	A46				24	8
nel Ionel MUNTEANU	25/6/68	Vaslui	s46	s67	s62											134	16
el NICOLIŢĂ	7/1/85	Steaua	s46	M	M	M		M		M46	s62	s58	M	s60	M82	23	1
an RADU	22/10/86	Dinamo Bucureşti /Lazio (ITA)	s62		s76					D90		D				8	-
in LAZĂR	24/4/81	Rapid Bucureşti	s66													3	-
an CRISTEA	30/11/83	Dinamo Bucureşti	s79		s85		s68					s46				6	-
diu Iulian NICULESCU	23/6/76	Dinamo Bucureşti	s81													8	-
diu PETRE	22/3/82	Steaua		M	s24	M	s87	M		M	s35					22	1
iu Marian RADU	10/8/77	Wolfsburg (GER)		M56												1	-
en TRICĂ	5/8/76	CFR		s90				s82								4	-
uţ COMAN	28/3/79	Rapid Bucureşti			G											9	-
riel Sebastian TAMAŞ	9/11/83	Auxerre (FRA)			D	D	D	D	D78	D90	D35	D46	D	D	D	35	2
us Marcel CONSTANTIN	25/10/84	Rapid Bucureşti			s70				s78							3	-
orghe BUCUR	8/4/80	Poli Timişoara			s72				s65	s83						8	2
rge Cristian OGĂRARU	3/2/80	Ajax (NED)				D	D	D	D	s87	s71					7	-
iel George NICULAE	6/10/82	Auxerre (FRA)				s70	A76	A	A		s46	s46	A	A	s59	25	5
rei Silviu RGĂRITESCU	1/1/80	Dinamo Bucureşti					D		M							3	-
n Daniel BRATU	2/1/80	Dinamo Bucureşti					s76									10	2
ţ Costinel MAZILU	9/2/82	Rapid Bucureşti						A65	s73							10	2
van COCIŞ	19/2/83	Lokomotiv Moskva (RUS)						s58	M	M	M85	M46	M64	s88	M	24	1
nin CONTRA	15/12/75	Getafe (ESP)								D87	D71	D58	D	D	D	66	7
nin Iosif MOŢI	3/12/84	Dinamo Bucureşti								s90		s46				2	-
ai Mircea NEŞU	19/2/83	Steaua								s90						4	-
us Cornel POPA	12/4/76	Poli Timişoara									G89	s46 /79				2	-
us Constantin NICULAE	16/5/81	Inverness (SCO)									s46	s46	s78		A59	32	13
an ALIUŢĂ	4/2/78	Poli Timişoara									s85					4	-
lo SEPSI	7/6/86	Benfica (POR)									s87					1	-
van Marian STANCA	18/1/80	Dacia Mioveni									s89					1	-
n GHIONEA	11/5/79	Steaua										s46			D	11	1
ţ Cristian SĂPUNARU	5/4/84	Rapid Bucureşti										s58				1	-
rd Cornel STĂNCIOIU	3/3/81	CFR										s79				1	-

abandoned the match (at 1-0 to Rapid) after being struck by a projectile thrown from the crowd.

Steaua eventually overtook CFR and looked poised to claim their 24th title, but there was to be a major twist in the plot in the penultimate round as they went down 2-1 away to arch-rivals Dinamo while CFR scraped a nervy 1-0 win at home to CF Gloria 1922 Bistriţa. Now CFR were back in the driving seat, with a one-point lead and a final match away to already relegated local rivals FC Universitatea Cluj. It looked a straightforward task for Andone's men but it proved to be anything but, and they were immensely relieved to win the game with a penalty from Portuguese defender Cadu – especially as their opponents, down to ten men, squandered a golden opportunity to equalise in the last minute.

Joy unconfined

CFR's first title tasted doubly sweet as, thanks to Romania's improved UEFA coefficient, it guaranteed the club a place in the group phase of the 2008/09 UEFA Champions League. Three days after their league triumph there was yet more joy as they defeated AFC Unirea Valahorum Urziceni 2-1 in the final of the Romanian Cup – a competition without semi-final representation from Bucharest for the very first time - to complete an extraordinary double.

CFR 1907 Cluj celebrate the Romanian Cup win that completed their domestic double triumph

DOMESTIC LEAGUE 2007/08

LIGA I FINAL TABLE

			Home					Away					Total					
		Pld	W	D	L	F	A	W	D	L	F	A	W	D	L	F	A	Pts
1	CFR 1907 Cluj	34	13	3	1	29	10	10	4	3	23	12	23	7	4	52	22	76
2	FC Steaua Bucureşti	34	14	3	0	31	5	9	3	5	20	14	23	6	5	51	19	75
3	FC Rapid Bucureşti	34	8	3	6	30	20	10	4	3	22	11	18	7	9	52	31	61
4	FC Dinamo 1948 Bucureşti	34	7	5	5	28	22	10	5	2	27	14	17	10	7	55	36	61
5	AFC Unirea Valahorum Urziceni	34	10	5	2	22	9	6	8	3	20	15	16	13	5	42	24	61
6	FC Politehnica 1921 Ştiinţa Timişoara	34	12	3	2	35	15	4	6	7	22	29	16	9	9	57	44	57
7	FC Vaslui	34	8	5	4	25	14	4	6	7	19	20	12	11	11	44	34	47
8	FC Oţelul Galaţi	34	10	1	6	28	19	4	3	10	19	31	14	4	16	47	50	46
9	FC Universitatea Craiova	34	8	5	4	25	18	4	2	11	17	30	12	7	15	42	48	43
10	CF Gloria 1922 Bistriţa	34	8	5	4	23	17	3	4	10	11	23	11	9	14	34	40	42
11	FC Politehnica Iaşi	34	11	2	4	29	18	0	6	11	8	23	11	8	15	37	41	41
12	CS Pandurii Lignitul Târgu Jiu	34	7	3	7	18	18	4	4	9	18	25	11	7	16	36	43	40
13	FC Farul Constanţa	34	5	6	6	13	14	5	4	8	12	24	10	10	14	25	38	40
14	FC Gloria Buzău	34	8	4	5	20	19	2	3	12	10	37	10	7	17	30	56	37
15	FC Ceahlăul Piatra Neamţ	34	7	5	5	18	12	3	1	13	15	34	10	6	18	33	46	36
16	CS Dacia Mioveni	34	4	6	7	17	22	3	4	10	9	21	7	10	17	26	43	31
17	FCM UTA Arad	34	3	5	9	14	23	3	3	11	16	29	6	8	20	30	52	26
18	FC Universitatea Cluj	34	3	6	8	20	25	1	5	11	12	33	4	11	19	32	58	23

TOP GOALSCORERS

21 Ionel Daniel DĂNCIULESCU (Dinamo Bucureşti)

17 Gabriel Emil JULA (Oţelul)

16 Gheorghe BUCUR (Poli Timişoar
Marko LJUBINKOVIĆ (Vaslui)

15 Florin Constantin COSTEA (Univ Craiova)

14 Florin Daniel BRATU (Dinamo Bucureşti)

13 Eugen TRICĂ (CFR)

11 Cristian Ambrozie COROIAN (Gloria Bistriţa)
Cristian Gastón FABBIANI (CFR)

9 Cristian Costin DĂNĂLACHE (Unirea)
Nicolae Constantin DICĂ (Steaua
Ionuţ Costinel MAZILU (Rapid Bucureşti)

CLUB-BY-CLUB

FC CEAHLĂUL PIATRA NEAMŢ

Coach – Viorel Hizo

Founded - 1919

007				
7/7	Steaua	a	1-2	*Vranjković (p)*
/8	Gloria Buzău	h	4-0	*Cebotaru, Rusmir, Frunză, Ayza*
0/8	Dinamo Bucureşti	h	0-3	
9/8	Farul	a	0-2	
4/8	Poli Iaşi	h	1-0	*Golban*
/9	CFR	a	1-2	*Golban*
6/9	Pandurii	h	2-1	*Forminte, Frunză*
2/9	Unirea	a	0-2	
/10	UTA	a	1-0	*Oprea*
1/10	Vaslui	h	1-1	*Ayza*
8/10	Dacia Mioveni	a	1-2	*Frunză*
1/10	Gloria Bistriţa	h	2-0	*Oprea, Doicaru*
/11	Univ Cluj	a	1-1	*Frunză*
1/11	Oţelul	h	0-1	
5/11	Poli Timişoara	a	2-3	*Răducan, Viţelaru*
/12	Univ Craiova	h	1-0	*Rusmir*
/12	Steaua	h	0-1	
4/12	Gloria Buzău	a	1-4	*Doicaru*
9/12	Rapid Bucureşti	h	0-1	
008				
2/2	Dinamo Bucureşti	a	1-2	*Forminte*
9/2	Farul	h	0-1	
/3	Poli Iaşi	a	0-1	
5/3	CFR	h	0-0	
9/3	Pandurii	a	0-1	
3/3	Unirea	h	0-0	
9/3	Rapid Bucureşti	a	1-5	*Doicaru*
/4	UTA	h	1-1	*Rusmir*
/4	Vaslui	a	1-0	*Černoch*
2/4	Dacia Mioveni	h	1-1	*Guemamdia (p)*
8/4	Gloria Bistriţa	a	1-0	*Rusmir (p)*
3/4	Univ Cluj	h	3-0	*Guemamdia 2, Doicaru*
6/4	Oţelul	a	1-4	*Forminte*
/5	Poli Timişoara	h	2-1	*Doicaru, Rusmir*
/5	Univ Craiova	a	2-3	*Rusmir 2*

o	Name	Nat	Pos	Aps	(s)	Gls
6	Roberto AYZA Berca	BRA	A	10	(6)	2
3	Vasile Valentin AVĂDANEI		D	4		
9	Daniel Ionuţ BARNA		M	18		
5	Ionuţ BĂDESCU		D	7		
9	Marian Alexandru BĂNUŢĂ		M		(1)	
6	Igor BUGAEV	MDA	A	7	(2)	
5	Eugeniu CEBOTARU	MDA	M	17	(10)	1
0	Marius Marian CROITORU		M	11	(3)	
6	Vasilică CRISTOCEA		M	14		
7	Martin ČERNOCH	CZE	A	6	(3)	1
	Radu DOICARU		A	11	(18)	5
	Bruno João Fernandes Borges NANDINGA	POR	D	20		
	Hugo Miguel Magalhaes ÉVORA	CPV	D	2	(1)	
9	Vinícius de Oliveira FABRON	BRA	A		(1)	
4	Liviu Mihai FLORICEL		M	2	(3)	
4	Alexandru Gheorghe FORMINTE		D	21	(2)	3
4	Viorel FRUNZĂ	MDA	A	13	(2)	4
1	Haykel GUEMAMDIA	TUN	A	5	(2)	3
3	Lucian GOIAN		D	1	(1)	
5	Alexandru GOLBAN	MDA	A	11	(3)	2
	Mohammed HAMZA	GHA	M	18	(1)	
	Marius Sandu IORDACHE		D	5	(3)	
	Muhamed Lamine Jabula Sano "MALA"	GNB	M	7	(2)	
12	Florin MATACHE		G	3		
8	Ionuţ MATEI		M	1	(3)	
1	Cătălin Emanuel MULŢESCU		G	21		
4	Florin Gheorghe NOHAI		D	21	(1)	
10	Peter OMODUEMUKE	NGA	M	11	(1)	
11	Mircea Vasile OPREA		A	21	(10)	2
23	Ivan PECHA	SVK	D	7	(3)	
7	Narcis Claudiu RĂDUCAN		M	3	(2)	1
25	Dejan RUSMIR	SRB	M	22	(4)	7
22	George SAVU		G	10		
8	Constantin SCHUMACHER		M	14		
6	Rareş SOPORAN		A	1		
2	Andrei VIŢELARU		D	23	(3)	1
10	Vojislav VRANJKOVIĆ	SRB	M	6	(9)	1

CFR 1907 CLUJ

Coach – Ioan Andone

Founded – 1907

MAJOR HONOURS: Romanian League – (1) 2008; Romanian Cup - (1) 2008.

2007				
1/8	Oţelul	a	1-0	*Trică (p)*
5/8	Poli Timişoara	h	2-2	*Semedo, Trică*
12/8	Univ Craiova	a	3-1	*Trică, Didy 2*
19/8	Steaua	h	0-0	
25/8	Gloria Buzău	a	2-1	*Trică, Fabbiani*
2/9	Ceahlăul	h	2-1	*Panin, Cadu (p)*
16/9	Farul	a	2-0	*Fabbiani 2*
23/9	Poli Iaşi	h	2-1	*Semedo, Didy*
30/9	Dinamo Bucureşti	h	1-1	*Didy*
6/10	Pandurii	a	1-0	*Didy*
21/10	Unirea	h	2-0	*Sandberg, Didy*
28/10	Rapid Bucureşti	a	2-1	*Trică, Fabbiani*
1/11	UTA	h	2-0	*Fabbiani, Semedo*
4/11	Vaslui	a	2-0	*Trică, Culio*
11/11	Dacia Mioveni	h	1-0	*Trică*
24/11	Gloria Bistriţa	a	2-2	*Fabbiani, Cadu (p)*
2/12	Univ Cluj	h	2-0	*Fabbiani, Trică*
9/12	Oţelul	h	3-1	*Didy, Tony, Fabbiani*
16/12	Poli Timişoara	a	0-1	
2008				
23/2	Univ Craiova	h	4-1	*Semedo, Fabbiani 2, Trică*
2/3	Steaua	a	1-3	*Trică*
7/3	Gloria Buzău	h	2-0	*Trică, Dubarbier*
15/3	Ceahlăul	a	0-0	
19/3	Farul	h	2-1	*Dorsin, Trică*
22/3	Poli Iaşi	a	0-1	
30/3	Dinamo Bucureşti	a	2-1	*Semedo 2*
6/4	Pandurii	h	1-2	*Trică*
10/4	Unirea	a	1-1	*Dani*
13/4	Rapid Bucureşti	h	1-0	*Ruiz*
19/4	UTA	a	3-0	*Cadu (p) Dubarbier, Fabbiani*
23/4	Vaslui	h	1-0	*Ruiz*
26/4	Dacia Mioveni	a	0-0	
3/5	Gloria Bistriţa	h	1-0	*Dubarbier*
7/5	Univ Cluj	a	1-0	*Cadu (p)*

No	Name	Nat	Pos	Aps	(s)	Gls
9	Adrian Gheorghe ANCA		A		(5)	
22	Euripedes Daniel Adão" AMOREIRINHA"	POR	D	1	(1)	
20	"CADÚ" Ricardo Manuel Sousa	POR	D	29		4
33	Nicolas CANALES	CHI	A		(1)	
1	NUNO CLARO Simões Coimbra	POR	G	15		
19	Emmanuel Juan CULIO	ARG	M	29	(3)	1

No	Name	Nat	Pos	Aps	(s)	Gls
31	"DANI" Daniel Ricardo da Silva	POR	M	27	(2)	1
17	Ciprian Ioan DEAC		A		(10)	
29	Cleidimar Magalhaes Silva "DIDY"	BRA	A	17	(1)	7
33	Mikael DORSIN	SWE	D	7	(1)	1
7	Sebastián DUBARBIER	ARG	M	11	(4)	3
23	Cristián Gastón FABBIANI	ARG	A	21	(7)	11
21	Tavares Martins Frederico Manuel "FREDY"	POR	D		(1)	
13	Lars HIRSCHFELD	CAN	G	5		
25	André Filipe Ribeiro LEÃO	POR	M	11	(4)	
5	MANUEL JOSÉ Azevdo Vieira	POR	M	3	(17)	
14	Alin Ilie MINTEUAN		M	8	(10)	
6	Gabriel MUREŞAN		D	12	(10)	
11	Ibazito OGBONNA	NGA	A		(2)	
8	Pedro Miguel de OLIVEIRA	POR	M		(1)	
4	Cristian Călin PANIN		D	28		1
8	Sixto Raimundo PERALTA Salso		M	3	(5)	
99	Diego Alejandro RUIZ	ARG	A	6	(7)	2
3	Niklas SANDBERG	SWE	D	9	(1)	1
16	António Sanchez SEMEDO	POR	A	30	(3)	6
27	André Felipe Galiassi de SOUSA	BRA	D	27	(1)	
44	Eduard Cornel STĂNCIOIU		G	14	(1)	
2	Anthony da Silva "TONY"	POR	D	32		1
10	Eugen TRICĂ		M	29	(1)	13

CS DACIA MIOVENI

Coach – Florin Marin; (10/10/07) Sorin Cârţu

Founded - 2000

2007				
28/7	Rapid Bucureşti	h	1-2	*Costescu*
4/8	UTA	a	0-1	
10/8	Vaslui	h	2-2	*Baicu, Lupaşcu*
18/8	Dinamo Bucureşti	a	1-1	*Daouda*
26/8	Gloria Bistriţa	a	0-1	
2/9	Univ Cluj	h	1-0	*og (Jovanović M.)*
15/9	Oţelul	a	1-3	*Vrăjitoarea*
22/9	Poli Timişoara	h	2-2	*Olteanu, Balauru*
30/9	Univ Craiova	a	0-1	
7/10	Steaua	h	1-2	*og (Rada)*
20/10	Gloria Buzău	a	1-0	*Daouda*
28/10	Ceahlăul	h	2-1	*Bratu 2*
1/11	Farul	a	1-1	*Balauru*
4/11	Poli Iaşi	h	2-1	*Neagoe R., Trofin*
11/11	CFR	a	0-1	
25/11	Pandurii	h	1-1	*Neagoe R.*
1/12	Unirea	a	2-0	*Bratu, Costescu*
9/12	Rapid Bucureşti	a	0-3	
16/12	UTA	h	0-1	
2008				
23/2	Vaslui	a	0-3	
1/3	Dinamo Bucureşti	h	1-2	*Savu*
7/3	Gloria Bistriţa	h	0-0	
16/3	Univ Cluj	a	0-0	
19/3	Oţelul Galaţi	h	1-0	*Bratu*
23/3	Poli Timişoara	a	2-1	*Frăsineanu, Savu*
30/3	Univ Craiova	h	1-2	*Frăsineanu*
6/4	Steaua Bucureşti	a	0-2	
9/4	Gloria Buzău	h	0-0	
12/4	Ceahlăul	a	1-1	*Neagoe R.*
20/4	Farul	h	2-3	*Neagoe R., Bratu*
23/4	Poli Iaşi	a	0-1	
26/4	CFR	h	0-0	
4/5	Pandurii	a	0-1	
7/5	Unirea	h	0-3	

No	Name	Nat	Pos	Aps	(s)	Gls
3	Ilie Nico BAICU		D	26	(3)	1
23	Nicolae Dan BALAURU		M	17	(5)	2
13	Cristian Nicolae BRATU		A	27	(3)	5
19	Hristu CHIACU		M	5	(5)	
25	Octavian CHIHAIA		A	4	(7)	
17	Ionuţ CHIRCIU		M	6	(2)	
16	Daniel Ştefan COSTESCU		A	7	(5)	2
6	Mariko DAOUDA	CIV	D	31		2
5	Ciprian Virgil DIANU		D	1		
21	Cornel DOBRE		D	13	(1)	
21	Cornel FRĂSINEANU		M	9		2
5	Robert Daniel GHINDEANU		D	13	(1)	
2	Liviu HAPAINĂ		D	5	(1)	
1	Iulian Mihai ILIE		G	5		
15	Claudiu IONESCU		A	1	(7)	
33	Vasile JULA		D	9	(4)	
11	Daniel Ştefan LUPAŞCU		A	7	(5)	1
16	Vasile Casian MICLĂUŞ		D	5	(1)	
7	Mădălin MURGAN		M	22	(1)	
20	Andrei NEAGOE		M	8	(4)	
18	Robert Gabriel NEAGOE		M	25	(5)	4
24	Giani Liviu NEGOIŢĂ		M	8	(8)	
22	Mircea Teodor OLTEAN		G	1		
4	Mihai OLTEANU		D	28	(2)	1
11	Ionuţ SAVU		A	11	(2)	2
30	Horaţiu SĂTMAR		M		(2)	
2	Emil Adrian SCARLATACHE		D	10		
17	Martín SEBASTIÁN Paul	ARG	A	1	(5)	
12	Răzvan Marian STANCA		G	28		
8	Ionel Sorin TROFIN		M	13	(7)	1
10	Iulian VLADU		M	13	(4)	
14	Irinel Constantin VOICU		D	11	(1)	
9	Bogdan VRĂJITOAREA		A	4	(7)	1

FC DINAMO 1948 BUCUREŞTI

Coach – Mircea Rednic; (20/9/07) Walter Zenga (ITA); (28/11/07) Cornel Ţălnar; (4/3/08) Gheorghe Mulţescu; (31/3/08) Cornel Ţălnar

Founded - 1948

MAJOR HONOURS: Romanian League - (18) 1955, 1962, 1963, 1964, 1965, 1971, 1973, 1975, 1977, 1982, 1983, 1984, 1990, 1992, 2000, 2002, 2004, 2007; Romanian Cup - (12) 1959, 1964, 1968, 1982, 1984, 1986, 1990, 2000, 2001, 2003, 2004, 2005.

2007				
29/7	Gloria Buzău	a	2-1	*Cristea, Niculescu*
4/8	Vaslui	h	0-2	
10/8	Ceahlăul	a	3-0	*Niculescu, Dănciulescu, Cristea*
18/8	Dacia Mioveni	h	1-1	*Dănciulescu*
1/9	Gloria Bistriţa	h	0-1	
15/9	Poli Iaşi	a	5-2	*Cristea, Goian, Dănciulescu 3*
23/9	Univ Cluj	h	2-1	*Mărgăritescu, Cristea*
30/9	CFR	a	1-1	*Cristea*
7/10	Oţelul	h	6-1	*Moţi, Bratu 2, Dănciulescu 3 (1p)*
21/10	Pandurii	a	1-0	*Mărgăritescu*
24/10	Farul	a	1-0	*Cristea*
27/10	Poli Timişoara	h	1-1	*Cristea*
31/10	Unirea	a	0-0	
3/11	Univ Craiova	a	1-1	*Dănciulescu*
11/11	Rapid Bucureşti	h	0-2	
25/11	Steaua	a	0-1	
1/12	UTA	h	3-1	*Cristea, Bratu 2*
8/12	Gloria Buzău	h	2-0	*Bratu, Dănciulescu*
16/12	Vaslui	a	1-2	*Bratu*
2008				
22/2	Ceahlăul	h	2-1	*Bratu, Dănciulescu*
1/3	Dacia Mioveni	a	2-1	*Bratu, Zicu*
9/3	Farul	h	0-0	
14/3	Gloria Bistriţa	a	1-1	*Bratu (p)*
19/3	Poli Iaşi	h	2-1	*Dănciulescu, Miranda*
22/3	Univ Cluj	a	2-1	*Dănciulescu (p), Zicu*
30/3	CFR	h	1-2	*Dănciulescu*
5/4	Oţelul Galaţi	a	1-0	*Dănciulescu*
9/4	Pandurii	h	1-2	*Miranda*

2/4	Poli Timişoara	a	1-1	*Dănciulescu (p)*
)/4	Unirea	h	1-1	*Torje*
3/4	Univ Craiova	h	4-4	*Dănciulescu 2, Bratu 2*
5/4	Rapid Bucureşti	a	2-1	*Bratu 2*
/5	Steaua Bucureşti	h	2-1	*Bratu (p), Dănciulescu*
/5	UTA	a	3-1	*Dănciulescu 2, Munteanu*

o	Name	Nat	Pos	Aps	(s)	Gls
5	George BLAY	GHA	D	17	(1)	
5	Florin Daniel BRATU		A	23	(5)	14
	Gabriel BOŞTINĂ		M	9	(11)	
2	Hristu CHIACU		M	1	(9)	
)	Adrian CRISTEA		M	30	(2)	8
)	Ionel Daniel DĂNCIULESCU		A	29	(3)	21
5	Zie DIABATÉ	CIV	D		(1)	
	Gabriel DUMITRESCU		M		(1)	
	Fabrice FERNANDES	FRA	M	2		
4	Mariano Antonio FERNANDES	ARG	D		(2)	
)	John Christian GALLIQUIO Castro	PER	D	8		
9	Liviu GANEA		A		(5)	
3	Lucian GOIAN		D	11	(7)	1
2	Ivan GVOZDENOVIĆ	SRB	M	1	(1)	
3	Silviu IZVORANU		D	15	(6)	
	Bogdan Ionuţ LOBONŢ		G	32		
	Silviu Andrei MĂRGĂRITESCU		M	26		2
	Osvaldo Noé MIRANDA	ARG	A	7	(4)	2
	Cosmin Iosif MOŢI		D	23		1
	Cătălin Constantin MUNTEANU		M	22	(8)	1
	Nicolae MUŞAT		D	2		
3	Valentin Vasile NĂSTASE		D	2		
	Claudiu Iulian NICULESCU		A	12	(4)	2
1	Daniel Ionel OPRIŢA		A	1	(4)	
5	Georgian PĂUN		A		(2)	
4	Nino PEKARIĆ	SRB	D	2	(1)	
	Cristian Corneliu PULHAC		D	28	(1)	
5	Ştefan Daniel RADU		D	19		
3	Deniss ROMANOVS	LVA	G	2		
5	Adrian ROPOTAN		M	26	(4)	
4	Emil Adrian SCARLATACHE		D		(1)	
	Flavius Vladimir STOICAN		D	7		
7	Blagoja TODOROVSKI	MKD	D	2		
2	Gabriel TORJE		M	6	(9)	1
2	Vojislav VRANJKOVIĆ	SRB	M	4	(2)	
3	Ianis Alin ZICU		M	5	(7)	2

FC FARUL CONSTANŢA

Coach – Constantin Gache; (27/11/07) Marin Ion

Founded – 1949

007				
3/7	Univ Craiova	a	0-4	
/8	Steaua	h	0-1	
2/8	Gloria Buzău	a	0-1	
9/8	Ceahlăul	h	2-0	*Ciobanu, Florea D.*
/9	Poli Iaşi	a	1-1	*Chigou*
5/9	CFR	h	0-2	
1/9	Pandurii	a	1-0	*Maxim*
9/9	Unirea	h	0-1	
/10	Rapid Bucureşti	a	0-2	
1/10	UTA	h	1-0	*Nanu*
4/10	Dinamo Bucureşti	h	0-1	
8/10	Vaslui	a	1-1	*Băcilă*
/11	Dacia Mioveni	h	1-1	*Chigou*
/10	Gloria Bistriţa	a	0-1	
0/11	Univ Cluj	h	0-0	
5/11	Oţelul	a	0-2	
/12	Poli Timişoara	h	1-1	*Nanu*
/12	Univ Craiova	h	3-1	*Maxim (p), Gerlem, Florea D.*
6/12	Steaua	a	0-3	
008				
2/2	Gloria Buzău	h	0-0	
29/2	Ceahlăul	a	1-0	*Şchiopu (p)*
9/3	Dinamo Bucureşti	a	0-0	
14/3	Poli Iaşi	h	1-1	*Chico*
19/3	CFR	a	1-2	*Todoran*
23/3	Pandurii	h	1-2	*Nae*
29/3	Unirea	a	0-0	
5/4	Rapid Bucureşti	h	0-0	
10/4	UTA	a	1-0	*og (Amoreirinha)*
13/4	Vaslui	h	2-1	*Nae, Gerlem*
20/4	Dacia Mioveni	a	3-2	*Nae, Gosic, Gerlem*
24/4	Gloria Bistriţa	h	1-0	*Şchiopu (p)*
26/4	Univ Cluj	a	2-1	*Nae, Băcilă*
4/5	Oţelul Galaţi	h	0-2	
7/5	Poli Timişoara	a	1-4	*Todoran*

No	Name	Nat	Pos	Aps	(s)	Gls
3	Ion BARBU		D	20	(1)	
21	Cosmin Nicolae BĂCILĂ		M	26	(6)	2
22	Francisco José Castro Fernandes "CHICO"	POR	A	11	(3)	1
9	Daniel CHIGOU	CMR	A	7	(4)	2
8	Ştefan CIOBANU		A	2	(2)	1
1	George CURCĂ		G	25		
2	Ştefănel Răzvan FARMACHE		D	26	(1)	
24	Kehinde Abdul FATAI Feyi	NGA	A		(5)	
20	Laurenţiu FLOREA		D	4	(3)	
11	Daniel Constantin FLOREA		A	1	(7)	2
21	William Jesus Almeida GERLEM	BRA	A	21	(1)	3
6	Decebal GHEARĂ		D	11	(3)	
28	Dragan GOSIĆ	SRB	A	8	(4)	1
34	Mihai GURIŢĂ		A	7	(5)	
17	Ionuţ LARIE		M	1	(3)	
16	Muhamed Lamine Jabula Sano "MALA"	GNB	M	10	(2)	
27	Florin Sandu MAXIM		D	29	(1)	2
22	Gaston MENDY	SEN	M	10	(9)	
13	Liviu MIHAI II		M	1	(1)	
25	Marius NAE		M	10	(14)	4
15	Emil NANU		A	12	(9)	2
18	Florin Ioan NEAGA		A		(1)	
4	Marcel Laurenţiu OTVOŞ		M		(2)	
16	Vasile PĂCURARU		D	2	(3)	
23	Florin PĂTRAŞCU		D	24	(1)	
8	Marius Adrian SOARE		M		(1)	
5	Cristian ŞCHIOPU		D	30		2
19	Ben TEEKLOH	LBR	D	11	(1)	
7	Dinu Marius TODORAN		M	28		2
30	Adrian VLAS		G	9		
14	Claudiu VOICULEŢ		M	28	(2)	

CF GLORIA 1922 BISTRIŢA

Coach – Ioan Ovidiu Sabău

Founded - 1922

MAJOR HONOURS: Romanian Cup - (1) 1994.

2007				
2/8	Unirea	h	2-2	*Dumitra, Frăsinescu*
5/8	Rapid Bucureşti	a	2-2	*Tilincă, Coroian*
11/8	UTA	h	2-1	*Frăsinescu, Coroian*
18/8	Vaslui	a	0-2	
26/8	Dacia Mioveni	h	1-0	*Tilincă*
1/9	Dinamo Bucureşti	a	1-0	*Hadzibulić*
15/9	Univ Cluj	a	2-2	*Coroian 2*
22/9	Oţelul	h	2-1	*Goroian, Pârvu*
29/9	Poli Timişoara	a	1-3	*Coroian (p)*
5/10	Univ Craiova	h	0-1	
27/10	Gloria Buzău	h	3-2	*Tilincă 2, Rus*
31/10	Ceahlăul	a	0-2	
4/10	Farul	h	1-0	*Dobre*
9/11	Poli Iaşi	a	0-2	
24/11	CFR	h	2-2	*Abrudan, Dobre*
30/11	Pandurii	a	3-1	*Târnăvean 2, Tilincă*

3/12	Steaua	a	0-1	
9/12	Unirea	a	0-2	
15/12	Rapid Bucureşti	h	1-2	*og (Bozović)*
2008				
24/2	UTA	a	1-0	*Coroian*
1/3	Vaslui	h	0-0	
7/3	Dacia Mioveni	a	0-0	
14/3	Dinamo Bucureşti	h	1-1	*Coroian*
19/3	Univ Cluj	h	2-0	*Tilincă, Dobre*
23/3	Oţelul Galaţi	a	0-2	
29/3	Poli Timişoara	h	0-0	
5/4	Univ Craiova	a	1-1	*Dobre*
10/4	Steaua Bucureşti	h	1-3	*Toma*
14/4	Gloria Buzău	a	0-1	
18/4	Ceahlăul	h	0-1	
23/4	Farul	a	0-1	
26/4	Poli Iaşi	h	2-0	*Coroian 2 (1p)*
3/5	CFR	a	0-1	
7/5	Pandurii	h	3-1	*Coroian (p), Trtovać, Moldovan*

No	Name	Nat	Pos	Aps	(s)	Gls
19	Octavian ABRUDAN		D	16	(1)	1
14	Sebastian Zoltan ACHIM		M	7	(2)	
22	Septimiu Călin ALBUŢ		G	9	(2)	
8	Iulian ARHIRE		M	6	(2)	
26	Andrei BOZEŞAN		M	1		
17	Flavius Lucian BĂD		A		(15)	
5	Enache CÂJU		A	8	(5)	
10	Simão Ayres CERQUEIRA	BRA	A		(1)	
4	Claudiu CODOBAN		M	1	(3)	
7	Cristian Ambrozie COROIAN		M	22	(2)	11
15	Sergiu Vasile COSTEA		M	1		
4	Marius CURTUIUŞ		M	2	(2)	
14	Răzvan DAMIAN		M		(1)	
14	Ciprian DANCIU		M	5	(1)	
6,16	Răzvan Gabriel DOBRE		A	22	(6)	4
23	Octavian DRĂGAN		A	1	(1)	
26	Ion DUMITRA		M	16	(4)	1
18	Cosmin Vali FRĂSINESCU		D	22		2
26	Răzvan Daniel FRITEA		M		(1)	
15	Florin GANEA		M	8	(2)	
11	Sead HADZIBULIĆ	SRB	A	10	(9)	1
24	Dan Marius MATEI		D	28		
4	Flavius MOLDOVAN		D	1	(1)	1
17	Andrei Iosif MUREŞAN		M	5	(2)	
21	Adrian NALAŢI		M	22	(9)	
19	Sandu NEGREAN		A	10	(1)	
15	Lucian PÂRVU		M	4	(2)	1
3	Mădălin Marius POPA		D	6		
29	Marin PRIBAĆ		A	3	(1)	
23, 28	Kenan RAGIPOVIĆ	SRB	A	16	(3)	
2	Vasile Mircea RUS		D	11	(1)	1
8	László SEPSI½		D	19		
4	George ŞOLTUZ		D	4		
12	Ciprian Anton TĂTĂRUŞANU		G	25		
29	Călin TÂRNĂVEAN		A	3	(3)	2
9	Cosmin TILINCĂ		A	22	(8)	6
3	Dorin TOMA		D	19	(2)	1
4	Jasmin TRTOVAĆ	SRB	D	4		1
30	Lucian TURCU		M	15	(6)	

FC GLORIA BUZĂU

Coach – Ilie Stan; (16/8/07) Ştefan Stoica

Founded - 1971

2007				
29/07	Dinamo Bucureşti	h	1-2	*Ioviţă*
3/8	Ceahlăul	a	0-4	
12/8	Farul	h	1-0	*Ionescu*
17/8	Poli Iaşi	a	0-3	
25/8	CFR	h	1-2	*Ionescu*
31/8	Pandurii	a	0-3	
14/9	Unirea	h	0-0	
23/9	Rapid Bucureşti	a	0-0	
29/9	UTA	h	1-0	*Ioviţă*
7/10	Vaslui	a	1-4	*Liţu*
20/10	Dacia Mioveni	h	0-1	
27/10	Gloria Bistriţa	a	2-3	*Paleacu 2 (2p)*
30/10	Univ Cluj	h	3-2	*Nejneru, Kleyr, og (Par*
3/11	Oţelul	a	3-2	*Vlaicu, Simion, Ionescu*
10/11	Poli Timişoara	h	2-1	*Jozić, Vlaicu*
23/11	Univ Craiova	a	1-3	*Paleacu*
30/11	Steaua	h	1-1	*Bunică*
8/12	Dinamo Bucureşti	a	0-2	
14/12	Ceahlăul	h	4-1	*Liţu, Eze, Ionescu 2*
2008				
22/2	Farul	a	0-0	
2/3	Poli Iaşi	h	1-1	*Liţu*
7/3	CFR	a	0-2	
16/3	Pandurii	h	1-3	*Ionescu (p)*
20/3	Unirea	a	0-2	
23/3	Rapid Bucureşti	h	1-0	*Liţu*
30/3	UTA	a	1-2	*Ionescu*
6/4	Vaslui	h	1-1	*Ioviţă*
9/4	Dacia Mioveni	a	0-0	
14/4	Gloria Bistriţa	h	1-0	*Ionescu*
20/4	Univ Cluj	a	2-1	*Ioviţă, Bicfalvi*
23/4	Oţelul Galaţi	h	0-4	
26/4	Poli Timişoara	a	0-1	
3/5	Univ Craiova	h	1-0	*Nunes*
7/5	Steaua Bucureşti	a	0-5	

No	Name	Nat	Pos	Aps	(s)	Gls
71	Mihai BARBU		G	8		
14	Erik BICFALVI		M	6	(8)	1
14	Romică BUNICĂ		A	2	(13)	1
5	Constantin DOICARU		M	14	(7)	
26	Dino EZE	NGA	M	28	(5)	1
21	Alexandru FILIP		D	11	(3)	
23	Mihăiţă GHEORGHE		M	1	(1)	
13	Cosmin Octavian GHEORGHIŢĂ		D	16	(3)	
17	Stere Alexandru GUDA		A	3	(5)	
17	Mihai GURIŢĂ		A	4		
31	Alexandru IACOB		D		(2)	
7	Viorel ION		A		(2)	
20	Claudiu IONESCU		M	28	(2)	8
9	Valentin IOVIŢĂ		M	19	(10)	4
17	Salih JABER	IRQ	A		(1)	
4	Nikola JOZIĆ	SRB	D	17	(2)	1
99	Vieira dos Santos "KLEYR"	BRA	A	7	(1)	1
9	Alin Constantin LIŢU		A	18	(6)	4
32	Mihai MINCĂ		G	25		
18	Marian NEJNERU		M	19	(6)	1
23	Emil Ducu NINU		D	14		
42	André Luís Correia Diogo NUNES	BRA	A	6	(2)	1
3	Ghenadie OCHINCĂ	MDA	D	1		
30	Răzvan Iulian OCHIROŞII		M	2	(1)	
8	Alin Vasile PALEACU		M	21	(4)	3
3	Costel PETRE		D	6	(2)	
2	Dorin POPA		M		(2)	
11	Andreas POPESCU		M	1		
21	Valentin SIMION		A	24	(1)	1
11	Alexandru STOICA		M	2		
1	Cristian STOICESCU		G	1		
10	Eduard ŞOTROCAN		A	1	(1)	
25	Marius ŞULEAP		A	9	(3)	
6	Alexandru TUDOSE		D	28		
15	Cătălin VLAICU		D	31		2
29	Alin Ştefan VIGARIU		M	1	(1)	

FC OŢELUL GALAŢI

Coach – Petre Grigoraş

Founded - 1964

007

8	CFR	h	0-1	
8	Pandurii	a	0-1	
/8	Unirea	h	3-2	*Gado, Zhelev, Szekely*
3/8	Rapid Bucureşti	a	2-4	*Jula (p), Szekely*
5/8	UTA	h	2-1	*og (Roszel), Jula (p)*
9	Vaslui	a	0-2	
5/9	Dacia Mioveni	h	3-1	*Jula 2 (1p), Szekely*
2/9	Gloria Bistriţa	a	1-2	*Costin*
9/9	Univ Cluj	h	2-1	*Paraschiv, Nogo*
10	Dinamo Bucureşti	a	1-6	*Zhelev*
0/10	Poli Timişoara	a	1-4	*Stan*
7/10	Univ Craiova	h	2-1	*Paraschiv, Zhelev*
/10	Steaua	a	1-3	*Szekely*
11	Gloria Buzău	h	2-3	*Jula 2 (1p)*
/11	Ceahlăul	a	1-0	*Ilie*
5/11	Farul	h	2-0	*Jula, Stan (p)*
12	Poli Iaşi	a	2-2	*Szekely, Stan*
12	CFR	a	1-3	*Jula*
5/12	Pandurii	h	3-1	*Jula 2 (1p), Paraschiv*
008				
3/2	Unirea	a	0-0	
3	Rapid Bucureşti	h	0-1	
3	UTA	a	1-0	*Jula (p)*
5/3	Vaslui	h	0-3	*(w/o; original result 1-1 Deac)*
9/3	Dacia Mioveni	a	0-1	
3/3	Gloria Bistriţa	h	2-0	*Szekely, Stan*
9/3	Univ Cluj	a	1-2	*Zhelev*
4	Dinamo Bucureşti	h	0-1	
4	Poli Timişoara	h	3-1	*Viglianti, Deac, Stan*
2/4	Univ Craiova	a	1-1	*Paraschiv*
9/4	Steaua Bucureşti	h	0-1	
3/4	Gloria Buzău	a	4-0	*Jula 3, Viglianti*
5/4	Ceahlăul	h	4-1	*Jula 2 (1p), Viglianti, Paraschiv*
5	Farul	a	2-0	*Jula, Zhelev*
5	Poli Iaşi	h	0-0	

o	Name	Nat	Pos	Aps	(s)	Gls
4	Alexandru Viorel AVRAM		M		(1)	
5	Pavel BEGANSKI	BLR	A		(3)	
7	Gheorghe BOGHIU	MDA	A	1	(1)	
2	Valentin BORŞ		G	3	(1)	
0	Sergiu BRUJAN		M	7	(4)	
	Marian CÂRJĂ		D	1	(2)	
	Samuel COJOC		M	4	(3)	
8	Sergiu Ioan Viorel COSTIN		M	25	(1)	1
3	Ciprian Ioan DEAC		A	15		2
	Robert ELEK		A		(21)	
1	Ramses GADO		A	14	(2)	1
9	Gabriel Nicu GIURGIU		M	13	(1)	
	Paulius GRYBAUSKAS	LTU	G	8	(2)	
4	Silviu ILIE		M	19	(8)	1
	Adrian Mădălin IONESCU		M	3	(5)	
	Laurenţiu Cătălin IORGA		M	10	(8)	
7	Gabriel Emil JULA		A	33		17
5	KIM Gil-Sik	KOR	A	5	(1)	
2	Stoyan KOLEV	BUL	G	15		
9	Ismail KOUHA	MAR	G	8		
	Tadas LABUKAS	LTU	A	5	(17)	
1	Bertrand NGAPOUNOU	CMR	D	2		
	Salif NOGO	BFA	D	19		1
0	Gabriel Ioan PARASCHIV		M	30		5
0	Eduard RATNIKOV	EST	M	1	(2)	
5	Adrian SĂLĂGEAN		M	7	(4)	
6	Cristian SÂRGHI		M	15	(2)	
5	Dorin Constantin SEMEGHIN		D	16	(1)	
9	Daniel Dorin STAN		A	26	(1)	5
8	Janos Joszef SZEKELY		M	26		6
	Gabriel Alejandro VIGLIANTI	ARG	M	11	(4)	3
1	Zhivko ZHELEV	BUL	D	32		5

CS PANDURII LIGNITUL TÂRGU JIU

Coach – Eugen Neagoe; (12/12/07) (Gabriel Zahiu); (1/2/08) Joaquim Teixeira (POR); (5/3/08) Eugen Neagoe

Founded – 1974

2007

29/07	Univ Cluj	a	1-1	*Djakpa*
5/8	Oţelul	h	1-0	*Mihai*
11/8	Poli Timişoara	a	1-3	*Iordache (p)*
18/8	Univ Craiova	h	2-0	*Păcurar, Stromajer*
31/8	Gloria Buzău	h	3-0	*Rus, Vasilache, Păcurar*
16/9	Ceahlăul	a	1-2	*Mihai*
21/9	Farul	h	0-1	
30/9	Poli Iaşi	a	0-1	
6/10	CFR	h	0-1	
21/10	Dinamo Bucureşti	h	0-1	
28/10	Unirea	a	0-1	
1/11	Rapid Bucureşti	h	1-3	*Stângă*
4/11	UTA	a	3-3	*Stângă, Iordache 2 (1p)*
9/11	Vaslui	h	1-1	*Orac*
12/11	Steaua	a	0-0	
25/11	Dacia Mioveni	a	1-1	*Mihai*
30/11	Gloria Bistriţa	h	1-3	*Rusu*
9/12	Univ Cluj	h	2-2	*Iordache, og (Bilica)*
15/12	Oţelul	a	1-3	*Djapka (p)*
2008				
24/2	Poli Timişoara	h	1-3	*Piţurcă*
2/3	Univ Craiova	a	0-1	
8/3	Steaua	h	0-1	
16/3	Gloria Buzău	a	3-1	*Vasilache, Orac, Păcurar (p)*
19/3	Ceahlăul	h	1-0	*Păcurar*
23/3	Farul	a	2-1	*Piţurcă, Iordache (p)*
30/3	Poli Iaşi	h	1-0	*Arrieta*
6/4	CFR	a	2-1	*og (Sousa), Iordache*
9/4	Dinamo Bucureşti	a	2-1	*Piţurcă, Arrieta*
13/4	Unirea	h	1-1	*Păcurar*
19/4	Rapid Bucureşti	a	0-1	
22/4	UTA	h	2-1	*Arrieta, Popete*
26/4	Vaslui	a	0-1	
4/5	Dacia Mioveni	h	1-0	*Piţurcă*
7/5	Gloria Bistriţa	a	1-3	*Wandeir*

No	Name	Nat	Pos	Aps	(s)	Gls
19	José ANILTON Júnior	BRA	D	2		
9	Ibón Pérez ARRIETA	ESP	A	3	(6)	3
12	Robert BĂLĂŢ		G	3		
6	Carlos Alexandre CARDOSO	BRA	D	6	(2)	
4	Alin Nicu CHIBULCUTEAN		D	31		
8	Alexandru Mugurel DEDU		M	2	(2)	
25	Constant DJAPKA	CIV	M	27	(1)	2
22	Ibrahim DOSSEY	GHA	G	9		
7	Ionuţ Daniel DRAGOMIR		D	1		
24	Constantin GRECU		D	1	(2)	
1	Adnan GUŠO	BIH	G	7		
30	Ilie IORDACHE		M	29	(2)	6
32	JESSUI Silva do Nascimento	BRA	A	1		
23	Jackson José LUCAS	BRA	A	4	(1)	
2	Sergiu Sebastian MÂNDREAN		D	9	(4)	
20	Liviu MIHAI I		A	15	(1)	3
80	João Pedro MINGOTE Ribeiro	POR	G	15		
8	Fábio NUNES Fernandes	BRA	M		(3)	
11	Daniel ORAC		A	21	(5)	2
5	Alexandru PĂCURAR		M	5	10	5
15	Carlos Pedro Carvalho de Sousa "PINTASSILGO"	POR	M	1	(1)	
28	Alexandru PIŢURCĂ		A	23	(4)	4
14	Laurenţiu Florin POPETE		M	20	(4)	1
9	Adrian POPESCU		M	2	(4)	
3	Alin Valer RUS		M	22		1
16	Adrian RUSU		D	15	(9)	1

No	Name	Nat	Pos	Aps	(s)	Gls
60	Marco Paulo Silva SOARES	POR	M	1		
21	Florin Cornel STÂNGĂ		A	30	(3)	2
18	Jaka ŠTROMAJER	SVN	A	15	(13)	1
17	Robert Dumitru VANCEA		M	23		
10	Ciprian VASILACHE		D	19	(1)	2
6	Marin VĂTAVU		M	7	(3)	
19	Sorin VINTILESCU		A		(9)	
16, 24	Mircea VOICU		M	3	(8)	
7	WANDEIR Oliveira dos Santos	BRA	A	2	(1)	1

FC POLITEHNICA IAŞI

Coach – Ionuţ Popa

Founded - 1945

2007				
29/7	Poli Timişoara	a	1-3	*Sfârlea*
4/8	Univ Craiova	h	2-1	*Mijin, Bâlbă*
11/8	Steaua	a	0-1	
17/8	Gloria Buzău	h	3-0	*Černoch, Ciobanu, Silvăşan*
24/8	Ceahlăul	a	0-1	
1/9	Farul	h	1-1	*Bâlbă*
15/9	Dinamo Bucureşti	h	2-5	*Bâlbă, Naidin (p)*
23/9	CFR	a	1-2	*Naidin*
30/9	Pandurii	h	1-0	*Miclea*
7/10	Unirea	a	0-1	
20/10	Rapid Bucureşti	h	0-2	
26/10	UTA	a	0-0	
30/10	Vaslui	h	0-1	
4/11	Dacia Mioveni	a	1-2	*Tincu1*
9/11	Gloria Bistriţa	h	2-0	*Bâlbă, Miclea*
24/11	Univ Cluj	a	1-1	*Miclea*
2/12	Oţelul	h	2-2	*Milea, Černoch*
9/12	Poli Timişoara	h	2-1	*Bâlbă, Kalai*
15/12	Univ Craiova	a	1-2	*Černoch*
2008				
24/2	Steaua	h	2-1	*og (Nicoliţă), Onuţ*
2/3	Gloria Buzău	a	1-1	*Sfârlea*
9/3	Ceahlăul	h	1-0	*Bâlbă*
14/3	Farul	a	1-1	*Cristea (p)*
19/3	Dinamo Bucureşti	a	1-2	*Cristea*
22/3	CFR	h	1-0	*Cristea (p)*
30/3	Pandurii	a	0-1	
4/4	Unirea	h	2-3	*Cristea, Paruolo*
9/4	Rapid Bucureşti	a	0-3	
13/4	UTA	h	4-1	*Cristea 2 (1p), Bâlbă 2*
19/4	Vaslui	a	0-0	
23/4	Dacia Mioveni	h	1-0	*Pălimaru*
26/4	Gloria Bistriţa	a	0-2	
2/5	Univ Cluj	h	3-0	*Bersnjak, Buta, Miclea*
7/5	Oţelul Galaţi	a	0-0	

No	Name	Nat	Pos	Aps	(s)	Gls
5	Branko BAKOVIĆ	SRB	M	4	(3)	
9	Mihai Ionuţ BÂLBĂ		A	22	(3)	8
1	Cristian Gigi BRĂNŢ		G	34		
7	Dominik BERŠNJAK	SVK	A	14		1
77	Cornel BUTA		D	12	(14)	1
30	Radu Eduard CIOBANU		D	14	(3)	1
10	Andrei CRISTEA		A	13		6
27	Martin ČERNOCH	CZE	A	4	(6)	3
19	Sergiu HOMEI		D	27	(1)	
23	Adrian ILIE		D	17	(4)	
22	Iosif KALAI		D	10	(4)	1
17	Alexandru Dan LEUCUŢĂ		A		(1)	
18	Romulus Daniel MICLEA		M	12	(11)	4
11	Svetozar MIJIN	SRB	M	14	(5)	1
25	Ciprian MILEA		M	19	(6)	1
28	Cristian Lucian MUNTEANU		M	32		
21	Leonard Toni NAIDIN		M	30		2
3	Bogdan Mihai ONUŢ		D	25	(2)	1
8	Gustavo PARUOLO	ARG	M	13	(7)	1
29	Clement PĂLIMARU		A	6	(10)	1
5	Andrej PEČNIK	SVN	D	13		
14	Sebastian SFÂRLEA		M	24	(6)	2
10	Cristian Radu SILVĂŞAN		A	12	(1)	1
24	Bogdan STRATON		M	1	(2)	
20	Paul Cătălin TINCU		M	1	(8)	1
2	Adrian TOMA		D	1	(1)	

FC POLITEHNICA 1921 ŞTIINŢA TIMIŞOARA

Coach – Dušan Uhrin jr (CZE)

Founded – 2002

2007				
29/7	Poli Iaşi	h	3-1	*Pleşan, Bucur 2*
5/8	CFR	a	2-2	*Pleşan 2*
11/8	Pandurii	h	3-1	*Bucur 2, Ganea*
17/8	Unirea	a	1-4	*Alexa (p)*
26/8	Rapid Bucureşti	h	1-1	*Bucur*
1/9	UTA	a	3-2	*Bucur 3*
14/9	Vaslui	h	2-1	*Rusič 2*
22/9	Dacia Mioveni	a	2-2	*Bucur, Torje*
29/9	Gloria Bistriţa	h	3-1	*Cânu 2, Agunbiade*
6/10	Univ Cluj	a	2-1	*Rădoi, Bucur*
20/10	Oţelul	h	4-1	*og (Borş), McKain, Karamyan Art. 2*
27/10	Dinamo Bucureşti	a	1-1	*Cânu*
1/11	Univ Craiova	a	1-2	*Bucur*
4/11	Steaua	h	2-0	*Rusič, Gueye*
10/11	Gloria Buzău	a	1-2	*Karamyan Art.*
25/11	Ceahlăul	h	3-2	*Bucur 2, Cânu*
2/12	Farul	a	1-1	*Karamyan Art.*
9/12	Poli Iaşi	a	1-2	*Rusič*
16/12	CFR	h	1-0	*Aliuţă*
2008				
24/2	Pandurii	a	3-1	*Bucur, Agunbiade, Borbely*
3/3	Unirea	h	0-0	
9/3	Rapid Bucureşti	a	1-0	*Karamyan Arm.*
15/3	UTA	h	2-0	*Karamyan Arm., Agunbiade*
19/3	SC Vaslui	a	0-3	
23/3	Dacia Mioveni	h	1-2	*Rusič*
29/3	Gloria Bistriţa	a	0-0	
5/4	Univ Cluj	h	3-0	*Karamyan Arm., Karamyan Art., Ganea*
9/4	Oţelul Galaţi	a	1-3	*Karamyan Arm.*
12/4	Dinamo Bucureşti	h	1-1	*Rusič*
18/4	Univ Craiova	h	1-3	*og (Dina)*
21/4	Steaua Bucureşti	a	1-1	*Bucur*
26/4	Gloria Buzău	h	1-0	*Bucur*
4/5	Ceahlăul	a	1-2	*Martínez*
7/5	Farul	h	4-1	*Bădoi, Luchin, Ganea, Martínez*

No	Name	Nat	Pos	Aps	(s)	Gls
31	Abiodun AGUNBIADE	NGA	M	26	(5)	3
5	Dan ALEXA		M	16	(1)	1
7	Marian ALIUŢĂ		M	19	(5)	1
15	Mircea AXENTE		A		(4)	
30	Valentin BĂDOI		M	15		1
27	Tiberiu Gabriel BĂLAN		M	1	(5)	
17	Balázs BORBÉLY	SVK	D	9		1
4	Miloš BREZINSKÝ	SVK	D	13		
18	Gheorghe BUCUR		A	26	(2)	16
23	Gabriel CÂNU		D	21		4
15	Andrei CRISTEA		A	1	(6)	
2	Cristian Ioan DANCIA		D	13	(1)	
9	Ioan Viorel GANEA		A	17	(1)	3
24	Mansour GUEYE	SEN	A	3	(10)	1
11	Arman KARAMYAN	ARM	D	10	(8)	4
77	Artavazd KARAMYAN	ARM	M	31		5
27	Jasmin LATOVLEVICI		D	6	(1)	
16	Srdjan LUCHIN		D	14	(1)	1
8	Elvio Raul MARTÍNEZ	ARG	M	4	(4)	2

Name	Nat	Pos	Aps	(s)	Gls
Jonathan David McKAIN	AUS	D	13		1
Carlos Alberto					
Leurenço MILHAZES	POR	M	15		
Costel Fane PANTILMON		G	4	(1)	
Mihăiţă Păunel PLEŞAN		M	2		3
Marius Cornel POPA		G	30		
Adrian Alexandru POPOVICI		A		(1)	
Alin Robert RAŢIU		D	6	(3)	
Sorin Nicuşor RĂDOI		D	4	(3)	1
Dejan RUSIČ	SVN	A	14	(6)	6
George SCUTARU		M	1		
John Wayne SRHOJ	AUS	M	9	(11)	
Stelian STANCU		D	16	(3)	
Gabriel TORJE		M	9	(8)	1
Dare VRŠIČ	SVN	M	6	(5)	

FC RAPID BUCUREŞTI

Coach – Cristiano Bergodi (ITA); (22/10/07) Mircea Rednic; (25/3/08) Marian Rada

Founded - 1923

MAJOR HONOURS: Romanian League - (3) 1967, 1999, 2003; omanian Cup - (13) 1935, 1937, 1938, 1939, 1940, 1941, 1942, 1972, 1975, 1998, 2002, 2006, 2007.

07				
/7	Dacia Mioveni	a	2-1	*Mazilu 2*
	Gloria Bistriţa	h	2-2	*Buga, Mazilu*
/8	Univ Cluj	a	2-1	*Grigorie, og (Cordoş)*
/8	Oţelul	h	4-2	*Mazilu, Maftei, Burdujan, Dică (p)*
/8	Poli Timişoara	a	1-1	*Burdujan*
	Univ Craiova	h	2-0	*Césinha, Dobroiu*
/9	Steaua	a	0-0	
/9	Gloria Buzău	h	0-0	
0	Farul	h	2-0	*Dică (p), Mazilu*
/10	Poli Iaşi	a	2-0	*Săpunaru, Buga*
/10	CFR	h	1-2	*Burdujan*
1	Pandurii	a	3-1	*Burdujan, Mazilu 2*
1	Unirea	h	1-1	*Maftei*
/11	Dinamo Bucureşti	a	2-0	*Césinha, Mazilu*
/11	UTA	a	0-1	
2	Vaslui	h	2-1	*Césinha, Mazilu*
2	Dacia Mioveni	h	3-0	*Burdujan, Grigorie, Césinha*
/12	Gloria Bistriţa	a	2-1	*Buga, Dică (p)*
/12	Ceahlăul	a	1-0	*Burdujan*
)8				
/2	Univ Cluj	h	1-2	*Pancu*
	Oţelul	a	1-0	*Boya*
	Poli Timişoara	h	0-1	
/3	Univ Craiova	a	1-1	*Boya*
/3	Steaua Bucureşti	h	0-3	*(w/o; match abandoned after 72nd min at 1-0 Săpunaru)*
/3	Gloria Buzău	a	0-1	
/3	Ceahlăul	h	5-1	*Césinha, Boya 2, Lazăr 2*
	Farul	a	0-0	
	Poli Iaşi	h	3-0	*Grigore, Pancu, Buga*
/4	CFR	a	0-1	
/4	Pandurii	h	1-0	*Lazăr*
/4	Unirea	a	1-0	*Despotović*
/4	Dinamo Bucureşti	h	1-2	*Boya*
	UTA	h	2-3	*Boya 2*
	Vaslui	a	4-2	*Despotović 3, Lazăr*

	Name	Nat	Pos	Aps	(s)	Gls
	Elinton Snchotene ANDRADE	BRA	G	9	(2)	
	Pierre BOYA	CMR	A	14	(7)	7
	Vladimir BOŽOVIĆ	MNE	M	26		
	Mugurel Mihai BUGA		M	14	(9)	4
	Lucian BURDUJAN		A	18	(5)	6
	Carlos César dos Santos "CÉSINHA"	BRA	A	31	(1)	5
1	Dănuţ Dumitru COMAN		G	25		
23	Marius Marcel CONSTANTIN		D	30		
9	Ranko DESPOTOVIĆ	SRB	A	6	(2)	4
10	Emil Cosmin DICĂ		M	21	(8)	3
27	Ionuţ Alexandru DOBROIU		A	2	(2)	1
18	Nicolae GRIGORE		M	17	(8)	1
8	Ştefan Costel GRIGORIE		M	13	(7)	2
16	Nicolae Ovidiu HEREA		M	12	(14)	
30	JOÃO PAULO Pinto Ribeiro	POR	A	3	(7)	
15	Costin LAZĂR		M	23	(1)	4
4	Philippe LÉONARD	BEL	D	8	(2)	
24	Vasile MAFTEI		D	33		2
6	Vasco Miguel Lopes de MATOS	POR	M	2	(2)	
9	Ionuţ Costinel MAZILU		A	15		9
17	Marius Constantin MĂLDĂRĂŞANU		M	7	(7)	
19	Daniel Gabriel PANCU		M	5	(3)	2
14	Dănuţ PERJĂ		D	4	(4)	
21	Ionuţ Cristian SĂPUNARU		D	32		1
5	Ionuţ Cristian STANCU		M	1	(1)	
25	Romeo Constantin STANCU		M		(3)	
2	Marcos Roberto Nascimento TAMANDARÉ	BRA	D	3	(4)	

FC STEAUA BUCUREŞTI

Coach – Gheorghe Hagi; (18/9/07) (Massimo Pedrazzini (ITA)); (28/10/07) Marius Lăcătuş

Founded - 1947

MAJOR HONOURS: European Champion Clubs' Cup - (1) 1986; UEFA Super Cup - (1) 1986; Romanian League - (23) 1951, 1952, 1953, 1956, 1960, 1961, 1968, 1976, 1978, 1985, 1986, 1987, 1988, 1989, 1993, 1994, 1995, 1996, 1997, 1998, 2001, 2005, 2006; Romanian Cup - (21) 1949, 1950, 1951, 1952, 1955, 1962, 1966, 1967, 1969, 1970, 1971, 1976, 1979, 1985, 1987, 1988, 1989, 1992, 1996, 1997, 1999.

2007				
27/7	Ceahlăul	h	2-1	*Dică 2 (1p)*
3/8	Farul	a	1-0	*Dică*
11/8	Poli Iaşi	h	1-0	*Bicfalvi*
19/8	CFR	a	0-0	
2/9	Unirea	a	0-1	
16/9	Rapid Bucureşti	h	0-0	
22/9	UTA	a	1-1	*Nicoliţă*
29/9	Vaslui	h	1-0	*Rada*
7/10	Dacia Mioveni	a	2-1	*Iacob 2*
28/10	Univ Cluj	a	1-2	*Nicoliţă*
31/10	Oţelul	h	3-1	*Dică 2 (1p), og (Semeghin)*
4/11	Poli Timişoara	a	0-2	
10/11	Univ Craiova	h	1-0	*Nicoliţă*
12/11	Pandurii	h	0-0	
25/11	Dinamo Bucureşti	h	1-0	*Neaga*
30/11	Gloria Buzău	a	1-1	*Dică*
3/12	Gloria Bistriţa	h	1-0	*og (Toma)*
9/12	Ceahlăul	a	1-0	*Badea*
16/12	Farul	h	3-0	*Zaharia, Dică, og (Şchiopu)*
2008				
24/2	Poli Iaşi	a	1-2	*Mendoza*
2/3	CFR	h	3-1	*og (Hirschfeld), Moreno D., Petre*
8/3	Pandurii	a	1-0	*Petre*
16/3	Unirea	h	1-0	*Habibou*
20/3	Rapid Bucureşti	a	3-0	*(w/o; match abandoned after 72nd min at 0-1)*
23/3	UTA	h	2-1	*Moreno P., Badea*
30/3	Vaslui	a	1-0	*Moreno P.*
6/4	Dacia Mioveni	h	2-0	*Goian, Moreno P.*
10/4	Gloria Bistriţa	a	3-1	*Dică 2, og (Hadzibulić)*
14/4	Univ Cluj	h	4-0	*Pleşan, Golański, Neaga, Moreno D.*
19/4	Oţelul Galaţi	a	1-0	*Pleşan*
21/4	Poli Timişoara	h	1-1	*Goian*

26/4	Univ Craiova	a	2-1	*Moreno P., Moreno D.*
4/5	Dinamo Bucureşti	a	1-2	*Ghionea*
7/5	Gloria Buzău	h	5-0	*Moreno P., Moreno D. 2, Neaga, Mendoza*

No	Name	Nat	Pos	Aps	(s)	Gls
17	Eugen Cătălin BACIU		D	9	(5)	
9	Valentin Vasile BADEA		A	7	(9)	2
29	Valentin Emanoil BĂDOI		M	5	(5)	
7	Eric BICFALVI		M	1	(8)	1
11	Gabriel BOŞTINĂ		M	1		
12	Cornel CERNEA		G	1		
14	Vasilică CRISTOCEA		M	4	(4)	
26	Marius Marian CROITORU		M	5	(7)	
10	Nicolae Constantin DICĂ		A	29	(1)	9
13	Ifeanyi EMEGHARA	NGA	D	12		
24	Sorin GHIONEA		D	11	(1)	1
3	Nicolae Dorin GOIAN		D	23		2
4	Paweł GOLAŃSKI	POL	D	18	(3)	1
11	Mahamadou HABIBOU	FRA	A		(8)	1
19	Victoraş Constantin IACOB		A	5	(2)	2
20	Florin LOVIN		M	20	(4)	
18	Petre MARIN		D	16	(2)	
29	Andrés Augusto MENDOZA	PER	A	14	(1)	2
27	Dayro Mauricio MORENO Galindo	COL	A	5	(6)	5
22	José Alcides "Pepe" MORENO	COL	A	15		5
25	Adrian Constantin NEAGA		A	16	(10)	3
15	Mihai Mircea NEŞU		D	18	(3)	
16	Bănel NICOLIŢĂ		M	24	(3)	3
8	Ovidiu PETRE		M	25	(1)	2
23	Mihăiţă Păunel PLEŞAN		M	11	(3)	2
5	Ionuţ Alin RADA		D	17	(1)	1
6	Mirel Matei RĂDOI		M	16		
84	Romeo Constantin SURDU		A	5	(7)	
30	Dorel ZAHARIA		A	8	(6)	1
1	Róbinson ZAPATA	COL	G	33		

AFC UNIREA VALAHORUM URZICENI

Coach – Dan Vasile Petrescu

Founded - 1954

2007

2/8	Gloria Bistriţa	a	2-2	*Mara, Dănălache*
5/8	Univ Cluj	h	3-2	*Dănălache 2, Stancu*
11/8	Oţelul	a	2-3	*Dănălache, Bilaşco*
17/8	Poli Timişoara	h	4-1	*Stancu 2, Pădureţu, Onofraş*
24/8	Univ Craiova	a	1-0	*Stancu (p)*
2/9	Steaua	h	1-0	*Galamaz*
14/9	Gloria Buzău	a	0-0	
22/9	Ceahlăul	h	2-0	*Bilaşco, Stancu*
29/9	Farul	a	1-0	*Apostol*
7/10	Poli Iaşi	h	1-0	*Onofraş*
21/10	CFR	a	0-2	
28/10	Pandurii	h	1-0	*Bilaşco*
31/10	Dinamo Bucureşti	h	0-0	
4/11	Rapid Bucureşti	a	1-1	*Mara*
10/11	UTA	h	1-0	*Dănălache*
25/11	Vaslui	a	1-1	*Bilaşco*
1/12	Dacia Mioveni	h	0-2	
9/12	Gloria Bistriţa	h	2-0	*og (Danciu), Onofraş*
16/12	Univ Cluj	a	2-0	*Bilaşco, Galamaz*

2008

23/2	Oţelul	h	0-0	
3/3	Poli Timişoara	a	0-0	
8/3	Univ Craiova	h	2-2	*Mara, Onofraş*
16/3	Steaua Bucureşti	a	0-1	
20/3	Gloria Buzău	h	2-0	*Galamaz, Petre*
23/3	Ceahlăul	a	0-0	
29/3	Farul	h	0-0	
4/4	Poli Iaşi	a	3-2	*Mara 2, Onofraş*
10/4	CFR	h	1-1	*Dănălache*
13/4	Pandurii	a	1-1	*Bilaşco*
20/4	Dinamo Bucureşti	a	1-1	*Stancu (p)*
23/4	Rapid Bucureşti	h	0-1	
26/4	UTA	a	2-1	*Brandán, Mara (p)*
3/5	Vaslui	h	2-0	*Balint, Onofraş*
7/5	Dacia Mioveni	a	3-0	*Dănălache 3*

No	Name	Nat	Pos	Aps	(s)	Gls
20	Bogdan Aurelian ALDEA		A		(2)	
32	Iulian Cătălin APOSTOL		M	11	(8)	1
1	Giedrius ARLAUSKIS	LTU	G	4		
24	György László BALINT		D	16	(3)	1
7	Marius Ioan BILAŞCO		A	19	(9)	6
19	Pablo Daniel BRANDÁN	ARG	D	9	(4)	1
23	Valeriu Ionuţ BORDEANU		D	26	(2)	
17	Jacob Geoffrey BURNS	AUS	M	9		
8	Cristian CONSTANTIN		M	7	(11)	
15	Cristian Costin DĂNĂLACHE		A	16	(11)	9
9,6	George Daniel GALAMAZ		D	32		3
77	Cătălin GRIGORE		G	1		
10	Bogdan Ion MARA		A	28	(3)	6
22	Cosmin Nicolae MĂRGINEAN		M		(1)	
4	Ersin MEHMEDOVIĆ	SRB	D	21	(2)	
29	Daniel George MUNTEANU		D	12		
9	Valentin NEGRU		M	13	(3)	
16	Epaminonda NICU		D	16	(3)	
11	Marius Daniel ONOFRAŞ		A	15	(15)	6
25	Răzvan PĂDUREŢU		M	22	(7)	1
2	Ciprian Cătălin PETRE		M	20	(7)	1
3	RICARDO Vilana Gomes	BRA	M	23	(2)	
5	Gheorghe ROHAT		D	3		
5	Liviu RUSU		D	2		
14	Bogdan STANCU		A	20	(9)	6
12	Bogdan STELEA		G	28		
13	Srđan ŽAKULA	SRB	G	1		

FC UNIVERSITATEA CLUJ

Coach – Adrian Falub; (10/10/07) Gheorghe Mulţescu; (8/1/08) Alpar Meszaros

Founded - 1919

MAJOR HONOURS: Romanian Cup - (1) 1965.

2007

29/7	Pandurii	h	1-1	*Goga*
5/8	Unirea	a	2-3	*Olah, Goga*
12/8	Rapid Bucureşti	h	1-2	*Jovanović N.*
19/8	UTA	a	1-1	*Park*
25/8	Vaslui	h	2-3	*Sabo (p), Süller*
2/9	Dacia Mioveni	a	0-1	
15/9	Gloria Bistriţa	h	2-2	*Park, Jovanović N.*
23/9	Dinamo Bucureşti	a	1-2	*Sabo*
29/9	Oţelul	a	1-2	*Süller*
6/10	Poli Timişoara	h	1-2	*Jovanović N.*
19/10	Univ Craiova	a	1-1	*Savu*
28/10	Steaua	h	2-1	*Jovanović N., Goga*
30/10	Gloria Buzău	a	2-3	*Jovanović M., Savu*
3/11	Ceahlăul	h	1-1	*Jovanović N.*
10/11	Farul	a	0-0	
24/11	Poli Iaşi	h	1-1	*Astorga*
2/12	CFR	a	0-2	
9/12	Pandurii	a	2-2	*Astorga, Goga*
16/12	Unirea	h	0-2	

2008

23/2	Rapid Bucureşti	a	2-1	*Bundea, Goga*
1/3	UTA	h	2-2	*Silvăşan 2*
9/3	Vaslui	a	0-0	
16/3	Dacia Mioveni	h	0-0	
19/3	Gloria Bistriţa	a	0-2	
22/3	Dinamo Bucureşti	h	1-2	*Băd*
29/3	Oţelul Galaţi	h	2-1	*Goga, Silvăşan (p)*
5/4	Poli Timişoara	a	0-3	
9/4	Univ Craiova	h	2-0	*Goga, Băd*

/4	Steaua Bucureşti	a	0-4	
/4	Gloria Buzău	h	1-2	*Jovanović N.*
/4	Ceahlăul	a	0-3	
/4	Farul	h	1-2	*Goga*
5	Poli Iaşi	a	0-3	
5	CFR	h	0-1	

Name	Nat	Pos	Aps	(s)	Gls
André Izepon ASTORGA	BRA	D	9	(3)	2
Marius Achim BACIU		D	9		
Erison da Silva Santos Carnieta "BAIANO"	BRA	M	9	(2)	
Flavius BĂD		A	5	(8)	2
Fábio BILICA	BRA	D	17		
Mugur Cristian BOLOHAN		D	8	(1)	
Fabien BOUDARÈNE	FRA	M	7	(1)	
Petre BUDEAN		A	3	(3)	
Zeno Marius BUNDEA		M	12	(1)	1
Laurenţiu BUŞ		M	1	(4)	
Gigel COMAN		D	21	(4)	
Andrei CORDOŞ		D	9	(2)	
Sergiu Vasile COSTEA		M		(3)	
Cristian DANCIA		D	10		
Bogdan Alexandru DOLHA		M	4	(5)	
EDVAN Correira do Nascimento	BRA	D	7	(1)	
Vasile GHINDARU		M	6	(3)	
Dorin GOGA		A	31		8
Sorin IODI		D	6	(2)	
Milan JOVANOVIĆ	MNE	D	15	(1)	1
Nemanja JOVANOVIĆ	SRB	A	28	(1)	6
Romik KHACHATRYAN	ARM	M	12		
Pieter MERLIER	BEL	G	14		
Călin MOLDOVAN		G	5		
Andrei MUREŞAN		M	3	(2)	
Sandu NEGREAN		A	2	(11)	
Adrian OLAH		M	17		1
PARK Jae-Hong	KOR	D	14		2
Sorin Nicuşor RĂDOI		D	9		
Claudiu Nicu RĂDUCANU		A	2	(7)	
Radu SABO		M	7	(9)	2
Alin Mircea SAVU		M	14	(9)	2
Cristian Radu SILVĂŞAN		A	9		3
Ciprian SUCIU		A		(5)	
Marius Robert SÜLLER		D	7	(3)	2
Emil Attila SZOLOMAJER		G	5		
George ŞOLTUZ		D	8	(1)	
Martin TUDOR		G	10		
Bogdan UNGURUŞAN		D	18		
Mamadou ZONGO	BFA	A	1	(1)	

FC UNIVERSITATEA CRAIOVA

Coach – Florin Cioroianu; (26/8/07) Ovidiu Stângă; (17/9/07) Daniel Mogoşanu; (9/10/07) Nicolò Napoli (ITA)

Founded - 1948

MAJOR HONOURS: Romanian League - (4) 1977, 1980, 1981, 1991; Romanian Cup - (6) 1977, 1978, 1981, 1983, 1991, 1993.

07

/7	Farul	h	4-0	*Costea F., Tănasă 3*
3	Poli Iaşi	a	1-2	*Ciucă*
/8	CFR	h	1-3	*Stoica*
/8	Pandurii	a	0-2	
/8	Unirea	h	0-1	
9	Rapid Bucureşti	a	0-2	
/9	UTA	h	0-1	
/9	Vaslui	a	0-2	
/9	Dacia Mioveni	h	1-0	*Luţu*
10	Gloria Bistriţa	a	1-0	*Woobay*
/10	Univ Cluj	h	1-1	*og (Park)*
/10	Oţelul	a	1-2	*Woobay*
11	Poli Timişoara	h	2-1	*Costea F., Baird*
11	Dinamo Bucureşti	h	1-1	*Tănasă*
10/11	Steaua	a	0-1	
23/11	Gloria Buzău	h	3-1	*Costea F. 2, Woobay*
2/12	Ceahlăul	a	0-1	
8/12	Farul	a	1-3	*Costea F.*
15/12	Poli Iaşi	h	2-1	*Mitchell, Rose*
2008				
23/2	CFR	a	1-4	*Costea F.*
2/3	Pandurii	h	1-0	*Costea F.*
8/3	Unirea	a	2-2	*Baird, Woobay*
16/3	Rapid Bucureşti	h	1-1	*Costea F.*
20/3	UTA	a	1-0	*Costea F.*
23/3	Vaslui	h	2-1	*Costea F. 2*
30/3	Dacia Mioveni	a	2-1	*Luţu, Dina*
5/4	Gloria Bistriţa	h	1-1	*Dina*
9/4	Univ Cluj	a	0-2	
12/4	Oţelul Galaţi	h	1-1	*Dina*
18/4	Poli Timişoara	a	3-1	*Costea F. 2, Dina*
23/4	Dinamo Bucureşti	a	4-4	*Dina, Costea F. 2, Gângioveanu*
26/4	Steaua Bucureşti	h	1-2	*Prepeliţă*
3/5	Gloria Buzău	a	0-1	
7/5	Ceahlăul	h	3-2	*Dina 2, og (Pecha)*

No	Name	Nat	Pos	Aps	(s)	Gls
17	Michael BAIRD	AUS	A	12	(4)	2
3	Marius Radu BARBU		M	2	(1)	
5	Marian Sorin BUŞU		D	1		
22	Nicuşor Dragoş BĂNICĂ		G	3		
2	Ştefan Nicolae BĂRBOIANU		M	8	(10)	
23	Mircea Alexandru BORNESCU		G	29		
7	Mădălin Marius CIUCĂ		D	12		1
10	Florin Constantin COSTEA		A	30		15
9	Mihai Alexandru COSTEA		A		(4)	
19	Cătălin CRĂCIUN		A		(2)	
24	Paul CURTEANU		D	1		
18	Ovidiu Liviu DĂNĂNAE		M	30		
13	Spase DILEVSKI	AUS	M	15	(1)	
20	Mihai DINA		M	15	(7)	7
3	Marius Valerică GĂMAN		D	4	(3)	
15	Valerian Zaharia GÂRLĂ		M		(2)	
28	Constantin GÂNGIOVEANU		M	7	(1)	1
29	Constantin Viorel GĂRGĂLIE		D	10	(3)	
33	Andrei IONESCU		M	15	(5)	
1	Silviu LUNG jr.		G	2		
32	Ionuţ Ion LUŢU		M		(17)	2
4	Josh MITCHELL	AUS	D	29		1
16	Lucian PÂRVU		M	1		
30	Andrei PREPELIŢĂ		M	30		1
27	Joshua ROSE	AUS	M	33		1
8	Robert SĂCEANU		M	10	(7)	
6	Dorel STOICA		D	30		1
3,9	Ovidiu STOIANOF		A	1	(8)	
11	Ciprian Ion TĂNASĂ		A	15	(6)	4
19	Cristian Gabriel VELCOVICI		D	7	(5)	
77	Julius Gibrilla WOOBAY	SLE	A	22	(10)	4

FCM UTA ARAD

Coach – Marius Lăcătuş; (1/10/07) (Roland Nagy); (15/10/07) Marin Barbu; (18/3/08) Gabriel Stan; (14/4/08) (Roland Nagy); (20/4/08) Ionuţ Chirilă

Founded - 1945

MAJOR HONOURS: Romanian League - (6) 1947, 1948, 1950, 1954, 1969, 1970; Romanian Cup - (2) 1948, 1953.

2007

27/7	Vaslui	a	2-2	*Varga, Radovanović*
4/8	Dacia Mioveni	h	1-0	*Bălţoi*
11/8	Gloria Bistriţa	a	1-2	*Edson*
19/8	Univ Cluj	h	1-1	*Varga*
25/8	Oţelul	a	1-2	*Edson*
1/9	Poli Timişoara	h	2-3	*Todea, Bălţoi*
15/9	Univ Craiova	a	1-0	*og (Prepeliţă)*

22/9	Steaua	h	1-1	*Edson (p)*
29/9	Gloria Buzău	a	0-1	
6/10	Ceahlăul	h	0-1	
21/10	Farul	a	0-1	
26/10	Poli Iaşi	h	0-0	
1/11	CFR	a	0-2	
4/11	Pandurii	h	3-3	*og (Stângă), Ilie 2 (1p)*
10/11	Unirea	a	0-1	
25/11	Rapid Bucureşti	h	1-0	*Bălţoi*
1/12	Dinamo Bucureşti	a	1-3	*Drida*
8/12	Vaslui	h	1-1	*Bălţoi*
16/12	Dacia Mioveni	a	1-0	*Todea*
2008				
24/2	Gloria Bistriţa	h	0-1	
1/3	Univ Cluj	a	2-2	*Bălţoi, Amoreirinha*
8/3	Oţelul	h	0-1	
15/3	Poli Timişoara	a	0-2	
20/3	Univ Craiova	h	0-1	
23/3	Steaua Bucureşti	a	1-2	*Mihuţ*
30/3	Gloria Buzău	h	2-1	*Marincău, Edson*
6/4	Ceahlăul	a	1-1	*Dan*
10/4	Farul	h	0-1	
13/4	Poli Iaşi	a	1-4	*Roszel*
19/4	CFR	h	0-3	
22/4	Pandurii	a	1-2	*Hidişan*
26/4	Unirea	h	1-2	*Hidişan*
2/5	Rapid Bucureşti	a	3-2	*Todea, Hora, Ibeh*
7/5	Dinamo Bucureşti	h	1-3	*Bălţoi*

No	Name	Nat	Pos	Aps	(s)	Gls
2	Euripedes Daniel Adão "AMOREIRINHA"	POR	D	8		1
25	Ionuţ BĂLAN		D	27	(1)	
9	Alexandru BĂLŢOI		A	27		6
4	Doru Claudiu BUICAN		D	9	(1)	
28	Constantin BUMBAC		D	3	(3)	
6	Daniel CHIRIŢĂ		D	14	(2)	
16	Alin Florin CHIŢĂ		D	28	(2)	
21	Corneliu Ioan CODREANU		D		(1)	
5	Florin Cristian DAN		M	16	(5)	1
21	Ivan ĐOKOVIĆ	SRB	M	2	(1)	
19	Ioan Adrian DRIDA		A	3	(5)	1
8	EDSON Rolando Silva Sousa	POR	A	7	(11)	4
7	Dănuţ Cornel FRĂSINEANU		M	7	(1)	
10	Florin HIDIŞAN		M	21	(8)	2
15	Adrian Ioan HORA		M	20	(3)	1
40	Sebastian Dumitru HUŢAN		G	8		
24	Robert Mihai IACOB		M		(9)	
14	Jackie Yke IBEH	NGA	M	5		1
11	Mircea ILIE		A	13	(7)	2
21	Raul Paul MARINCĂU		D	6	(1)	1
16	Radu Leon MĂRGINEAN		M	11		
12	Marius Ioan MÂRNE		G	7	(2)	
14	Daniel Cristian MELINTE		F	2	(2)	
17	Dorin Adrian MIHUŢ		F	10	(1)	1
21	Iulian Ilie MIU		F	2		
7	Pedro Miguel de OLIVEIRA	POR	M	3	(5)	
24	Daniel Ionel OPRIŢA		A	3	(3)	
29	Cosmin Mihai PAŞCOVICI		M	6	(1)	
33	Branko RADOVANOVIĆ	SRB	A	3	(1)	1
22	Robert ROSZEL		M	4	(11)	1
20	Bruno Martins SIMÃO	POR	M	22	(1)	
80	Iulian Teodor Ştefan		M		(2)	
18	Cristian TODEA		M	25		3
30	Daniel Ovidiu TUDOR		G	19		
23	Norbert VARGA		D	9	(2)	2
3	Nikola Miodrag VASILIJEVIĆ	SRB	D	11	(3)	
24	Cosmin Marian VĂSÂIE		D	3		
27	Dorel ZAHARIA		A	10		

FC VASLUI

Coach – Dorinel Ionel Munteanu; (1/4/08) Emil Săndoi

Founded - 2002

2007				
27/7	UTA	h	2-2	*Ljubinković, Temwanjera*
4/8	Dinamo Bucureşti	a	2-0	*Bălace, Gheorghiu*
10/8	Dacia Mioveni	a	2-2	*Ljubinković 2*
18/8	Gloria Bistriţa	h	2-0	*Ljubinković (p), Gheorghiu*
25/8	Univ Cluj	a	3-2	*Sabou, Ljubinković, Jovanović*
2/9	Oţelul	h	2-0	*Ljubinković, Jovanovi*
14/9	Poli Timişoara	a	1-2	*Ljubinković (p)*
23/9	Univ Craiova	h	2-0	*Ljubinković, Sabou*
29/9	Steaua	a	0-1	
7/10	Gloria Buzău	h	4-1	*Ljubinković 3, Bukvić*
21/10	Ceahlăul	a	1-1	*Ljubinković*
28/10	Farul	h	1-1	*Frunză*
30/10	Poli Iaşi	a	1-0	*Temwanjera*
4/11	CFR	h	0-2	
9/11	Pandurii	a	1-1	*Bukvić*
25/11	Unirea	h	1-1	*Bukvić*
1/12	Rapid Bucureşti	a	1-2	*Matei*
8/12	UTA	a	1-1	*Buhăescu*
16/12	Dinamo Bucureşti	h	2-1	*Frunză 2*
2008				
23/2	Dacia Mioveni	h	3-0	*Ljubinković, og (Jula), Temwanjera*
1/3	Gloria Bistriţa	a	0-0	
9/3	Univ Cluj	h	0-0	
16/3	Oţelul Galaţi	a	3-0	*(w/o; original result 1- N'Doye)*
19/3	Poli Timişoara	h	3-0	*Andronic, Zmeu, Ljubinković (p)*
23/3	Univ Craiova	a	1-2	*Frunză*
30/3	Steaua Bucureşti	h	0-1	
6/4	Gloria Buzău	a	1-1	*Matei*
9/4	Ceahlăul	h	0-1	
13/4	Farul	a	1-2	*Ljubinković (p)*
19/4	Poli Iaşi	h	0-0	
23/4	CFR	a	0-1	
26/4	Pandurii	h	1-0	*Ljubinković*
3/5	Unirea	a	0-2	
7/5	Rapid Bucureşti	h	2-4	*Temwanjera 2*

No	Name	Nat	Pos	Aps	(s)	Gls
3	Dorian ANDRONIC		D	13	(3)	1
24	Ştefan APOSTOL		D	21		
17	Silviu Constantin BĂLACE		D	26	(2)	1
15	Bogdan Constantin BUHUŞ		D	26	(1)	
18	Vasile BUHĂESCU		A	7	(8)	1
26	Milorad BUKVIĆ	SRB	A	4	(15)	3
21	Bogdan Viorel COTOLAN		D		(1)	
2	Mihai Marius DOBOŞ		M	1	(4)	
10	Sorin FRUNZĂ		M	24	(6)	4
11	Adrian GHEORGHIU		M	23	(3)	2
81	Cristian HĂISAN		G	34		
6	Laurenţiu Marin IVAN		D	8	(8)	
30	Petar JOVANOVIĆ	SRB	D	13	(10)	2
20	Marko LJUBINKOVIĆ	SRB	M	30		16
27	Hugo Duarte de Sousa LUZ	POR	D	9		
5	Ştefan Adrian MARDARE		D	28		
23	Marius MATEI		A	14	(6)	2
25	Şerban MORARU		M	7		
7	Dorinel Ionel MUNTEANU		M	16		
21	Ousmane N'DOYE	SEN	M	13		1
9	Răzvan NEAGU		A		(9)	
14	Veljko NIKITOVIĆ	SRB	M	1		
4	Bogdan Vasile PANAIT		D	4	(8)	
16	Daniel SABOU		M	20		2
19	Mike TEMWANJERA	ZIM	A	23	(3)	5
8	Denis ZMEU	MDA	M	9	(8)	1

PROMOTED CLUBS

FC BRAŞOV
Coach – Răzvan Lucescu
Founded – 1937

CS OTOPENI
Coach – Liviu Ciobotariu
Founded – 2001

FC ARGEŞ PITEŞTI
h – Ionuţ Badea; (10/3/08) Dragoş Radu; (7/4/08) Ionuţ Badea
Founded – 1953
MAJOR HONOURS: Romanian League - (2) 1972, 1979.

CS GAZ METAN MEDIAŞ
Coach – Cristian Pusztai
Founded – 1945

COND LEVEL FINAL TABLES 2007/08

I	Pld	W	D	L	F	A	Pts
‑C Braşov	34	24	6	4	81	23	78
‑S Otopeni	34	21	6	7	74	43	69
‑C Petrolul Ploieşti	34	19	7	8	61	31	64
‑C Prefab 05 Modelu	34	17	7	10	54	36	58
‑S Concordia Chiajna	34	17	6	11	52	45	57
‑C Forex Braşov	34	15	6	13	36	24	51
‑CM Dunărea Giurgiu	34	13	10	11	37	43	49
‑C Delta Tulcea	34	14	6	14	37	37	48
‑C Botoşani	34	13	8	13	34	41	47
‑C Dinamo 1948 Bucureşti II	34	12	9	13	59	73	45
‑C Progresul Bucureşti	34	12	9	13	38	35	44
‑C Sportul Studenţesc Bucureşti	34	10	12	12	37	46	42
‑CM Câmpina	34	10	8	16	31	48	38
‑CM Bacău	34	8	14	12	33	37	38
‑S Inter Gaz Bucureşti	34	9	7	18	44	52	34
‑SM Focşani	34	8	10	16	39	51	34
‑CM Dunărea Galaţi	34	7	7	20	26	66	28
‑C Săcele	34	2	12	20	13	55	18

rogresul Bucureşti - 1 pt deducted.

II	Pld	W	D	L	F	A	Pts
‑C Argeş Piteşti	34	25	5	4	77	22	79
‑S Gaz Metan Mediaş	34	24	1	9	77	43	73
‑SM Râmnicu Vâlcea	34	18	7	9	56	39	61
‑C Unirea Alba Iulia	34	18	6	10	56	36	60
‑C Drobeta Turnu Severin	34	17	7	10	46	33	58
‑S Jiul Petroşani	34	18	8	8	53	29	57
‑S Mureşul Deva	34	14	8	12	39	40	50
FC Bihor Oradea	34	13	8	13	31	34	47
CF Liberty Oradea	34	13	8	13	36	33	47
FCM Târgovişte	34	12	11	11	45	40	47
CS Industria Sârmei Câmpei Turzii	34	11	8	15	29	38	41
CS Minerul Lupeni	34	10	11	13	41	45	41
CFR Timişoara	34	11	6	17	34	45	39
FC Arieşul Turda	34	10	8	16	35	49	38
FCM Reşiţa	34	9	6	19	38	65	33
FC Politehnica 1921 Ştiinţa Timişoara II	34	9	6	19	27	56	33
FC Caracal	34	6	7	21	32	56	25
FC Corvinul Hunedoara	34	4	7	23	21	70	19

FC Argeş Piteşti - 1 pt deducted; Jiul Petroşani - 5 pts deducted.

DOMESTIC CUP 2007/08

CUPA ROMÂNIEI

1/16 FINALS

(25/9/07)
FC Prefab 05 Modelu 0, Poli Timişoara 3

(26/9/07)
ACU Arad 0, Dacia Mioveni 2
Bacău 0, Steaua 4
Baia Mare 1, Unirea 4
Braşov 1, Gloria Bistriţa 0
Tricolorul Breaza 0, Gloria Buzău 1
Concordia Chiajna 0, Oţelul 6
Sănătatea Cluj 1, UTA 0
Univ Cluj 3, Vaslui 0
Mureşul Deva 2, Poli Iaşi 3
Drobeta Turnu Severin 1, Ceahlăul 3
Jiul 3, Farul 2
Săcele 0, CFR 3

(27/9/07)
Bacău II 0, Rapid Bucureşti 3
Progresul Bucureşti 0, Dinamo Bucureşti 2
Pandurii 1, Univ Craiova 0 *(aet)*

1/8 FINALS

(5/12/07)
Gloria Buzău 2, Poli Timişoara 2 *(aet; 5-3 on pens)*
Sănătatea Cluj 0, Dinamo Bucureşti 4
Univ Cluj 0, Pandurii 2
Poli Iaşi 0, Rapid Bucureşti 3
Dacia Mioveni 3, Ceahlăul 0
Jiul 0, CFR 1

(6/12/07)
Braşov 2, Oţelul 2 *(aet; 5-4 on pens)*
Unirea 2, Steaua 0

QUARTER-FINALS

(27/2/08)
Dacia Mioveni 1 *(Neagoe R. 57p)*, Dinamo Bucureşti 0
Unirea 1 *(Mara 71)*, Rapid Bucureşti 0

(28/2/08)
CFR 1 *(Ruiz 94)*, Braşov 0 *(aet)*
Pandurii 0, Gloria Buzău 0 *(aet; 2-3 on pens)*

SEMI-FINALS

(16/4/08)
Gloria Buzău 0, Unirea 1 *(Pădureţu 88)*
CFR 3 *(Ruiz 1, 81, Dani 78)*, Dacia Mioveni 0

FINAL

(10/5/08)
Ceahlăul stadium, Piatra Neamt
CFR 1907 CLUJ 2 *(Ruiz 49, Semedo 64)*
AFC UNIREA VALAHORUM URZICENI 1 *(Dănălache 58)*
Referee – *Bogaciu*
CFR – *Stăncioiu, Tony, Cadu, Sousa, Panin, Manuel José (Trică 71), Dani, Peralta (Mureşan 80), Culio, Semedo, Ruiz (Fabbiani 76).*
UNIREA – *Stelea, Balint, Galamaz, Munteanu, Bordeanu, Mara (Bilaşco 72), Ricardo, Brandán, Pădureţu (Negru 66), Dănălache, Stancu (Onofraş 32).*

Hiddink's young guns provide a breath of fresh air

Having qualified for UEFA EURO 2008™ by the back door – thanks to England's largesse - little was expected of Russia in Austria and Switzerland. But the youngest squad at the tournament, brilliantly commanded by veteran Dutch coach Guus Hiddink, did the nation proud, not only reaching the semi-finals but doing so with a brand of football that was thrilling to watch.

Two heavy defeats by Spain may have book-ended the team's campaign in disappointing fashion, but what came in between was sufficient to make the summer of 2008 a very special one for Russian football. An unexpected place in the last four was achieved with a commitment to inventive, attacking, one-touch football that made Hiddink's team - and particularly star forwar Andrei Arshavin – compulsive viewing. The aesthetic manner in which they dismantled Greece, Sweden and, above all, the Netherlands, knocking each of their opponents out of the tournament, will live long in the memory.

Guus Hiddink led an exciting young Russia team to the UEFA EURO 2008™ semi-finals

Majestic strike

Russia's first instinct in each game they played was to attack, and to do so with a style of play that was not ju pleasing on the eye but very difficult for their opponen to withstand. Even before Arshavin returned from the two-match suspension he had incurred for his red card in the final qualifying game in Andorra, there was a distinctive method and purpose to Russia's play. Poor defending cost the team dear in the opening game against Spain, but even in falling to a 4-1 defeat, the signs were there that Russia had not travelled south simply to make up the numbers.

With Greece defeated 1-0, Russia had to beat Sweden t accede to the quarter-finals. They did so in majestic style, the reintroduction of Arshavin bringing a new, exciting dimension to the attack. Had Russia been able to finish off all the wonderful moves they knitted together, they would have scored a hatful. It was a similar story against the Netherlands in Basel, with Hiddink getting one over his compatriots as Arshavin and co led the Dutch a merry dance for much of the game only to be taken to extra time as a result of a chronic inability to take their chances. Fortunately, justice was done as the little schemer set up one goal and scored another to round off a brilliant 3-1 win.

The semi-final appeared to be a game too far for Hiddink's braves. Spain, as in the opening game, had th measure of the Russians and won convincingly in the end with three unanswered second-half goals. Russia

Igor Denisov opens the scoring for Zenit St. Petersburg in the UEFA Cup final

ɔuldn't get into any sort of rhythm, with the service to ʳshavin and centre-forward Roman Pavlyuchenko eing cleverly stifled at source by the hard-working ɔanish midfield.

leroes galore

ıevitably, as with any eliminated team, Russia departed ıe tournament with regret, wondering what might ave been. But, if truth be told, a semi-final place was far ıore than had been expected of them – after all, Russia ad never progressed beyond the group stage in any of ıeir four previous major tournaments - and that was orne out by the enthusiastic reception that greeted the quad on their return to Moscow. If Hiddink and rshavin were the principal heroes, there were many thers who significantly raised their profile. avlyuchenko, though occasionally profligate, scored ıree goals and led the line with energy and nthusiasm. Yuriy Zhirkov, on the left, and Aleksandr nyukov, on the right, were excellent attacking full-acks. Igor Akinfeev confirmed his reputation as one of urope's best young goalkeepers, his quick throw-outs launching many a Russian counterattack. Sergei Semak made a triumphant return to the team after a lengthy absence, filling the dual role of captain and midfield anchorman with commendable composure, while Konstantin Zyryanov and Igor Semshov were the key components, along with Arshavin, of the team's intricate pass-and-move game.

That all but one of the 23 players in Hiddink's UEFA EURO 2008™ squad were affiliated to Russian Premier-Liga clubs speaks volumes about the growing strength of the Russian domestic game. Evidently, after the showcasing of their talents in Austria and Switzerland, there will now be stringent attempts by the big western European clubs to lure Russia's finest away from home with contract offers they cannot refuse. That is the harsh reality of free-market football. But in a country of Russia's magnitude there will always be plenty of hidden gems, and with many foreign players now seeing the Russian Premier-Liga as an attractive financial proposition, standards should remain high.

UEFA Cup triumph

FC Zenit St. Petersburg's 2007/08 UEFA Cup victory was the perfect advertisement for Russian club football. Like the national team, Zenit were coached by a Dutchman, Dick Advocaat, and they also played in a manner to please the purist, with the artful Arshavin as the key attacking component alongside big, blond striker Pavel Pogrebnyak who, cursed by bad luck, not only missed the UEFA Cup final against Rangers FC through suspension but also suffered an injury while playing for Russia on the eve of UEFA EURO 2008™ that prevented him from playing any part in the tournament.

Pogrebnyak's contribution to Zenit's UEFA Cup triumph was eleven goals, including two in the momentous 4-0 win at home to competition favourites FC Bayern München in the second leg of the semi-final, a match for which Arshavin was suspended. Zenit had begun the competition in the second qualifying round and, after eliminating future Belgian champions R. Standard de Liège, finished only third in their group. They also required the away-goals rule to eliminate Villarreal CF and Olympique de Marseille, but against German opposition in the quarter-finals and semi-finals they let rip, hammering Bayer 04 Leverkusen 4-1 away with an unforgettable counterattacking display before crushing the hopes of Bayern in St. Petersburg. In the final, with Arshavin, Zyryanov, captain Anatoliy Tymoshchuk and another impressive midfielder, Igor Denisov, weaving their magic, Rangers were swept away, the 2-0 victory in

Rossiyskiy Futbolny Soyuz (RFS

7 Narodnaya Street
RU-115172 Moskva
tel - +7 495 5401300
fax - +7 495 5401305
website - www.rfs.ru
email - rsf@roc.ru
Year of Formation – 1912
President – Vitaliy Mutko
General Secretary - Aleksei Sorokin
Press Officer – Artem Vagin
Stadium - Luzhniki, Moskva (79,530)

*INTERNATIONAL HONOURS**
UEFA European Championship - (1) 1960.

*INTERNATIONAL TOURNAMENT APPEARANCES**
FIFA World Cup - (9) 1958 (qtr-finals), 1962 (qtr-finals), 1966 (4th), 1970 (qtr-finals), 1982 (2nd phase), 1986 (2nd round), 1990, 1994, 2002.
UEFA European Championship - (9) 196 (Winners), 1964 (runners-up), 1968 (4th 1972 (runners-up), 1988 (runners-up), 1992, 1996, 2004, 2008 (semi-finals).
(before 1992 as USSR; 1992 as CIS)*

TOP FIVE ALL-TIME CAPS (including USSR/CIS)
Viktor Onopko (113); Oleh Blokhin (112 Rinat Dasaev (91); Albert Shesternyov (90); Anatoliy Demyanenko (80)

TOP FIVE ALL-TIME GOALS (including USSR/CIS)
Oleh Blokhin (42); Oleh Protasov (29); Vladimir Beschastnykh (26); Valentin Ivanov (26); Eduard Streltsov (25)

the City of Manchester Stadium justly rewarding Zenit for the quality of their play and giving Russia a second winner of the competition three years after PFC CSKA Moskva's against-the-odds triumph in 2005.

The next step for Russian football is to make headway in the UEFA Champions League. With the 2008 final taking place in Moscow, there were high hopes that either CSKA or FC Spartak Moskva could both rise to the challenge. But it was not to be. Spartak were eliminated in the third qualifying round, losing on penalties to Celtic FC, while CSKA collected just one point from a group containing FC Internazionale Milano, Fenerbahçe SK and PSV Eindhoven.

Champions Zenit

Perhaps Zenit can point the way forward in 2008/09 as they compete in the UEFA Champions League for the first time, a guaranteed place in the group stage their reward for winning the Russian Premier-Liga title in 2007.

The club's first national title since 1984, when they triumphed in the old Soviet Supreme League, was achieved with more or less the same group of players that would go on to lift the UEFA Cup six months later, with Arshavin, Pogrebnyak, Tymoshchuk and 2007 Russian Player of the Year Zyryanov very much to the fore. Challenged strongly by Spartak and for a spell by defending champions CSKA, Zenit had to keep their momentum going right through to the finish and secure the title only on the final day after a 1-0 win away to FC Saturn Moskovskaya Oblast enabled them to protect a two-point cushion over a Spartak side that had won both of the head-to-head duels earlier in the season.

Zenit's title-winning goal against Saturn was scored, with the aid of a deflection, by Czech midfielder Radek Širl – his first, and last, of the season – 14 minutes into the game. With victory imperative, there were plenty of hairy moments before the final whistle brought joy and relief for Advocaat and his players. For Spartak, coached by former goalkeeper Stanislav Cherchesov, a mid-season replacement for Vladimir Fedotov, the frustratio of coming second was a familiar feeling after they had also finished runners-up in 2005 and 2006. Despite the consistent goalscoring of Pavlyuchenko, the excellent goalkeeping of Croatian international Stipe Pletikosa and the evergreen midfield promptings of skipper Yego Titov, that cherished tenth Russian title, which Spartak have been pursuing since 2001, remained elusive.

CSKA finished the campaign strongly and, in Russian internationals Akinfeev, Sergei Ignashevich and the Berezutskiy twins, Vasiliy and Aleksei, continued to have the best defence in the land. But their title was effectively surrendered during a barren run in June and July when, hit by international commitments involving their colourful Brazilian forward pairing of Jô and Vágne Love - absent, respectively, for the FIFA Under-20 World

ATIONAL TEAM RESULTS 2007/08

3/07	Poland	H	Moscow	2-2	*Sychev (21), Pavlyuchenko (34)*
'07	FYR Macedonia (ECQ)	H	Moscow	3-0	*Berezutskiy V. (6), Arshavin (83), Kerzhakov (86)*
9/07	England (ECQ)	A	Wembley	0-3	
10/07	England (ECQ)	H	Moscow	2-1	*Pavlyuchenko (69p, 73)*
11/07	Israel (ECQ)	A	Tel-Aviv	1-2	*Bilyaletdinov (61)*
11/07	Andorra (ECQ)	A	Andorra la Vella	1-0	*Sychev (38)*
3/08	Romania	A	Bucharest	0-3	
5/08	Kazakhstan	H	Moscow	6-0	*Pogrebnyak (26p), Bystrov (45), Zyryanov (59), Bilyaletdinov (85p), Torbinskiy (89), Sychev (90)*
5/08	Serbia	N	Burghausen (GER)	2-1	*Pogrebnyak (12), Pavlyuchenko (48)*
'08	Lithuania	N	Burghausen (GER)	4-1	*Zyryanov (33), Arshavin (52), Pavlyuchenko (64), Bystrov (80)*
6/08	Spain (ECF)	N	Innsbruck (AUT)	1-4	*Pavlyuchenko (86)*
6/08	Greece (ECF)	N	Salzburg (AUT)	1-0	*Zyryanov (33)*
6/08	Sweden (ECF)	N	Innsbruck (AUT)	2-0	*Pavlyuchenko (24), Arshavin (50)*
6/08	Netherlands (ECF)	N	Basel (SUI)	3-1	*Pavlyuchenko (56), Torbinskiy (112), Arshavin (116) (aet)*
6/08	Spain (ECF)	N	Vienna (AUT)	0-3	

ATIONAL TEAM APPEARANCES 2007/08

ch – Guus HIDDINK (NED)	**8/1/46**		**Pol**	**MKD**	**ENG**	**ENG**	**ISR**	**AND**	**Rou**	**Kaz**	**Srb**	**Ltu**	**ESP**	**GRE**	**SWE**	**NED**	**ESP**	**Caps**	**Goals**
dimir GABULOV	19/10/83	Kuban	G46	G		G	G	G										5	-
liy BEREZUTSKIY	20/6/82	CSKA Moskva	D46	D	D	D46	D68	D38	D65	s56	s46	D		s87			D	31	1
is KOLODIN	11/1/82	Dinamo Moskva	D			s90		D		D56	D	D46	D	D	D	D		17	-
ksei BEREZUTSKIY	20/6/82	CSKA Moskva	D58	D	D	D	D	D	D			D14						32	-
SEMSHOV	6/4/78	Dinamo Moskva	M	M	M40	M	M30		M	M46	M82	s46	M58	M	M	M69	M56	32	-
iyar BILYALETDINOV	27/2/85	Lokomotiv Moskva	M	M	M	M	M	M	M61	M	M71	s46	M	M70	M66	s69	s56	28	2
y ZHIRKOV	20/8/83	CSKA Moskva	M46		M	M	M	M	M	D	D80		D	D87	D	D	D	24	-
SAENKO	17/10/83	Nürnberg (GER)	M							s46	s82			s70	s66	M81	M57	11	-
drei ARSHAVIN	29/5/81	Zenit	A	A	A	A90	A	A				A			A	A	A	37	13
nan PAVLYUCHENKO	15/12/81	Spartak Moskva	A46	A66	s63	s58	A52		s60	s46	s15	s46	A	A	A90	A115	A	22	9
itriy SYCHEV	26/10/83	Lokomotiv Moskva	A	A70	A63		s52	A	s65	s46	A66	A55	A46			s115	s57	44	15
on SHUNIN	27/1/87	Dinamo Moskva	s46															1	-
ksandr ANYUKOV	28/9/82	Zenit	s46 /86	s89	D80	D	D	D	D	D46	D46		D	D	D	D	D	37	1
stantin ZYRYANOV	5/10/77	Zenit	s46	M	M	M	M	M		M	M	M46	M	M	M	M	M	17	3
el POGREBNYAK	8/11/83	Zenit	s46				s68			A46	A15							9	4
itriy TORBINSKIY	28/4/84	Spartak Moskva	s58			s46	s30	s38											
		/Lokomotiv Moskva							s61	s46	s71	M	s58	M		s81		14	2
nan VOROBYOV	24/3/84	Khimki	s86															1	-
gei IGNASHEVICH	14/7/79	CSKA Moskva		D	D	D	D		D	s62		D		D	D	D	D	41	3
dimir BYSTROV	31/1/84	Spartak Moskva		M89	s40				M	M46	s66	s55	s46 /70		s90			22	4
ksandr KERZHAKOV	27/11/82	Sevilla (ESP)		s66	s80	A58		A										44	13
cheslav MALAFEYEV	4/3/79	Zenit		s70	G							G						16	-
r AKINFEEV	8/4/86	CSKA Moskva							G	G	G		G	G	G	G	G	25	-
nan SHIROKOV	6/7/81	Zenit							M	D62	D	s46	D					5	-
nan ADAMOV	21/6/82	Moskva							A60			A46	s70					3	-
gei SEMAK	27/2/76	Rubin								M	M	M46	M	M	M	M	M	51	4
nat YANBAYEV	7/4/84	Lokomotiv Moskva									s80	s14						2	-

Cup and the Copa América - they went five games without a goal. Even so, there were 13 goals apiece over the season from the pair – just one behind the Premier-Liga's joint-leading hot shots, Pavlyuchenko and Roman Adamov of fourth-placed FC Moskva.

CSKA's Cup

Although 2007 ended trophyless for CSKA, the double winners of 2005 and 2006 made a bright start to 2008 by regaining the Russian Cup. Two goals down in the final at the Lokomotiv stadium to in-form FC Amkar Perm, Valeriy Gazzayev's team were rescued by a goal apiece from Vágner Love and Jô, who had both earlier struck the woodwork, and went on to take the trophy 4-1 on penalties. As a consequence Amkar missed out not only on a first major trophy but also on a debut visit to the UEFA Cup. CSKA's win maintained the status quo as far as 2008/09 European qualification was concerned, with Zenit and Spartak in the UEFA Champions League, CSKA and Moskva, newly coached by Ukrainian legend Oleh Blokhin, in the UEFA Cup, and Saturn in the UEFA Intertoto Cup.

Relegation ensnared FC Rostov and FC Kuban Krasnodar, the latter returning whence they had come a year earlier only because they recorded fewer victories than FC Krylya Sovetov Samara and FC Luch-Energia Vladivostok who both finished on the same number of points. FC Shinnik Yaroslavl, on the other hand, made an immediate return to the Premier-Liga under ex-Russian international striker Sergei Yuran and were escorted up to the top flight by FC Terek Grozny, the exiled Chechnyan club securing promotion after just two seasons away.

CSKA Moskva's Brazilian duo Vágner Love (left) and Dudu celebrate their 2008 Russian Cup win over Amkar Perm

DOMESTIC LEAGUE 2007

PREMIER-LIGA FINAL TABLE

			Home					Away					Total					
		Pld	W	D	L	F	A	W	D	L	F	A	W	D	L	F	A	Pts
1	FC Zenit St. Petersburg	30	10	4	1	28	14	8	3	4	26	18	18	7	5	54	32	61
2	FC Spartak Moskva	30	11	3	1	31	12	6	5	4	19	18	17	8	5	50	30	59
3	PFC CSKA Moskva	30	10	4	1	28	6	4	7	4	15	18	14	11	5	43	24	53
4	FC Moskva	30	12	0	3	28	15	3	7	5	12	17	15	7	8	40	32	52
5	FC Saturn Moskovskaya Oblast	30	6	7	2	14	8	5	5	5	20	20	11	12	7	34	28	45
6	FC Dinamo Moskva	30	8	5	2	21	10	3	3	9	16	25	11	8	11	37	35	41
7	FC Lokomotiv Moskva	30	7	4	4	25	19	4	4	7	14	23	11	8	11	39	42	41
8	FC Amkar Perm	30	7	7	1	25	14	3	4	8	5	13	10	11	9	30	27	41
9	FC Khimki	30	8	5	2	21	10	1	5	9	11	23	9	10	11	32	33	37
10	FC Rubin Kazan	30	8	3	4	22	16	2	2	11	9	3	10	5	15	31	39	35
11	FC Tom Tomsk	30	7	3	5	22	14	1	8	6	15	21	8	11	11	37	35	35
12	FC Spartak Nalchik	30	6	5	4	14	12	2	4	9	15	26	8	9	13	29	38	33
13	FC Krylya Sovetov Samara	30	7	2	6	20	16	1	6	8	15	30	8	8	14	35	46	32
14	FC Luch-Energia Vladivostok	30	6	6	3	18	9	2	2	11	8	30	8	8	14	26	39	32
15	FC Kuban Krasnodar	30	4	7	4	17	18	3	4	8	10	20	7	11	12	27	38	32
16	FC Rostov	30	1	8	6	14	21	1	4	10	4	23	2	12	16	18	44	18

TOP GOALSCORERS

14 Roman ADAMOV (Moskva)
Roman PAVLYUCHENKO (Sparta
Moskva)

13 João "JÔ" Alves de Assis Silva (CSKA Moskva)
VÁGNER "LOVE" Silva de Sousa (CSKA Moskva)

11 Pavel POGREBNYAK (Zenit)
Dmitriy SYCHEV (Lokomotiv Moskva)

10 Andrei ARSHAVIN (Zenit)
Andrei KARYAKA (Saturn)
Martin KUSHEV (Amkar)

9 Dmitriy KIRICHENKO (Saturn)
Denis KOLODIN (Dinamo Moskv
Goran MAZNOV (Tom)
David MUJIRI (Krylya Sovetov)
Konstantin ZYRYANOV (Zenit)

CLUB-BY-CLUB

FC AMKAR PERM

Coach – Rashid Rakhimov

Founded – 1993

007				
1/3	Rostov	h	3-1	*Belorukov, Kobenko, Dujmović*
8/3	Spartak Moskva	a	0-0	
1/3	Dinamo Moskva	h	1-1	*Belorukov*
/4	Zenit	h	1-1	*Kushev*
4/4	Luch-Energia	a	0-1	
1/4	Tom	h	3-3	*Kobenko, Popov, Savin*
9/4	Krylya Sovetov	a	0-1	
/5	Kuban	h	0-0	
3/5	Rubin	a	0-1	
0/5	CSKA Moskva	h	1-1	*Drinčić*
/6	Khimki	h	3-1	*Kushev, Savin, Dujmović*
6/6	Spartak Nalchik	a	1-0	*Belorukov*
0/6	Lokomotiv Moskva	a	1-0	*Savin*
4/6	Moskva	h	1-1	*Kushev*
0/6	Saturn	a	0-2	
4/7	Spartak Moskva	h	0-1	
0/7	Dinamo Moskva	a	0-0	
8/7	Zenit	a	0-0	
/8	Luch-Energia	h	1-0	*Kushev (p)*
2/8	Tom	a	1-0	*Grishvin*
8/8	Krylya Sovetov	h	4-1	*Lavrik, Kushev 2, Peev*
6/8	Kuban	a	1-1	*Kushev*
/9	Rubin	h	2-1	*Kushev 2 (1p)*
3/9	CSKA Moskva	a	0-1	
9/9	Lokomotiv Moskva	h	1-0	*Grishvin*
/10	Khimki	a	0-1	
1/10	Spartak Nalchik	h	1-1	*Kushev (p)*
7/10	Moskva	a	1-3	*Cherenchikov*
/11	Saturn	h	3-1	*Belorukov, Popov, Peev*
1/11	Rostov	a	0-2	

o	Name	Nat	Pos	Aps	(s)	Gls
7	Ildar AKHMETZYANOV		D		(4)	
1	Dmitriy BELORUKOV		D	28		4
3	Ivan CHERENCHIKOV		M	9		1
8	Nikola DRINČIĆ	SRB	M	22	(3)	1
2	Tomislav DUJMOVIĆ	CRO	M	27	(1)	2
5	Miklós GAÁL	HUN	D	26		
	Vitaliy GRISHVIN		M	8	(17)	2
0	Andrei KOBENKO		M	23	(4)	2
9	Martin KUSHEV	BUL	A	21	(5)	10
	Andrei LAVRIK	BLR	M	10	(1)	1
0	Ivan LEVENETS		G	30		
	Marko MILOVANOVIĆ	SRB	D		(1)	
	Konstantin PARAMONOV		A	2	(2)	
	Georgi Ivanov PEEV	BUL	M	29		2
4	Aleksei POPOV		D	29		2
1	Yevgeniy SAVIN		A	18	(11)	3
7	Yevgeniy SHCHERBAKOV		M		(1)	
6	Predrag SIKIMIĆ	SRB	A	1	(3)	
4	Zahari SIRAKOV	BUL	D	28		
3	Antonio SOLDEVILLA	ESP	M	2	(3)	
	Sergei VOLKOV		A	17	(7)	

PFC CSKA MOSKVA

Coach – Valeriy Gazzayev

Founded – 1911

MAJOR HONOURS: UEFA Cup – (1) 2005; USSR League - (7) 1946, 1947, 1948, 1950, 1951, 1970, 1991; Russian League - (3) 2003, 2005, 2006; USSR Cup - (5) 1945, 1948, 1951, 1955, 1991; Russian Cup - (4) 2002, 2005, 2006, 2008.

2007				
11/3	Rubin	h	3-1	*Aldonin, Ignashevich (p), Jô*
18/3	Dinamo Moskva	a	1-1	*Vágner Love*
31/3	Lokomotiv Moskva	h	2-0	*Ramón, Vágner Love*
8/4	Khimki	a	1-1	*Krasić*
15/4	Spartak Nalchik	h	2-0	*Jô, Krasić*
22/4	Moskva	a	1-2	*Vágner Love*
29/4	Saturn	h	3-1	*Berezutskiy V., Zhirkov, Vágner Love*
6/5	Rostov	a	1-1	*Jô*
12/5	Spartak Moskva	h	1-1	*Krasić*
20/5	Amkar	a	1-1	*Vágner Love*
26/5	Zenit	h	2-0	*Jô 2*
10/6	Luch-Energia	a	0-4	
16/6	Tom	h	0-0	
24/6	Krylya Sovetov	a	0-1	
1/7	Kuban	h	0-0	
14/7	Dinamo Moskva	h	0-1	
22/7	Lokomotiv Moskva	a	2-1	*Vágner Love 2*
29/7	Khimki	h	0-0	
5/8	Spartak Nalchik	a	1-1	*Jô*
12/8	Moskva	h	2-0	*Ignashevich, Vágner Love*
18/8	Saturn	a	2-2	*Vágner Love 2 (1p)*
26/8	Rostov	h	4-0	*Jô 2, Vágner Love, Krasić*
2/9	Spartak Moskva	a	1-1	*Janczyk*
23/9	Amkar	h	1-0	*Jô*
29/9	Zenit	a	1-2	*Vágner Love*
7/10	Luch-Energia	h	4-0	*Jô 2, Vágner Love (p), Dudu Cearense*
20/10	Tom	a	1-0	*og (Maznov)*
28/10	Krylya Sovetov	h	4-2	*Eduardo Ratinho, Jô 2 (1p), Zhirkov*
3/11	Kuban	a	1-0	*Aldonin*
11/11	Rubin	a	1-0	*Ignashevich*

No	Name	Nat	Pos	Aps	(s)	Gls
35	Igor AKINFEEV		G	10		
22	Yevgeniy ALDONIN		M	22	(5)	2
6	Aleksei BEREZUTSKIY		D	26		
24	Vasiliy BEREZUTSKIY		D	25	(1)	1
44	Nikita BURMISTROV		A	2	(4)	
88	CANER Erkin	TUR	M	2	(6)	
7	DANIEL da Silva CARVALHO	BRA	A	3	(1)	
20	"DUDU CEARENSE" Alessandro Silva de Sousa	BRA	A	11	(4)	1
21	EDUARDO "RATINHO" Correia Piller Filho	BRA	M	2	(4)	1
57	Sergei GORELOV		M		(2)	
50	Anton GRIGORYEV		D	7	(3)	
8	Rolan GUSEV		M	5	(11)	
4	Sergei IGNASHEVICH		D	25	(1)	3
19	Dawid JANCZYK	POL	A	1	(9)	1
10	João "JÔ" Alves de Assis Silva	BRA	A	26	(1)	13
17	Miloš KRASIĆ	SRB	M	22		4
11	Pavel MAMAYEV		M	2	(2)	
1	Veniamin MANDRYKIN		G	19	(1)	

No	Name	Nat	Pos	Aps	(s)	Gls
15	Chidi ODIAH	NGA	D	1	(3)	
33	Yevgeniy POMAZAN		G	1		
25	Elvir RAHIMIĆ	BIH	M	26	(1)	
5	RAMÓN Osni Moreira Lage	BRA	A	12	(6)	1
2	Deividas ŠEMBERAS	LTU	D	24		
39	Ivan TARANOV		M	2	(11)	
42	Dmitriy TIKHONOV		A	2		
9	VÁGNER "LOVE" Silva de Sousa	BRA	A	23		13
18	Yuriy ZHIRKOV		M	29		2

FC DINAMO MOSKVA

Coach – Andrei Kobelev

Founded - 1923

MAJOR HONOURS: USSR League - (11) 1936, 1937, 1940, 1945, 1949, 1954, 1955, 1957, 1959, 1963, 1976 (spring); USSR Cup - (6) 1937, 1953, 1967, 1970, 1977, 1984; Russian Cup - (1) 1995.

2007				
11/3	Spartak Moskva	h	0-1	
18/3	CSKA Moskva	h	1-1	*Pimenov*
31/3	Amkar	a	1-1	*Kolodin (p)*
7/4	Lokomotiv Moskva	h	2-1	*Kombarov D., Semshov*
14/4	Zenit	a	0-3	
21/4	Khimki	h	2-1	*Kolodin (p), og (Trivunović)*
28/4	Luch-Energia	a	1-0	*Danny*
5/5	Spartak Nalchik	h	2-0	*Khokhlov, Kombarov K.*
12/5	Tom	a	0-1	
20/5	Moskva	h	0-0	
26/5	Krylya Sovetov	a	2-3	*Kolodin 2 (2p)*
10/6	Saturn	h	1-1	*Khokhlov*
17/6	Kuban	a	4-0	*Khokhlov 2, Danny, Kombarov D.*
23/6	Rostov	h	3-0	*Kolodin (p), Danny 2*
1/7	Rubin	a	1-2	*Kolodin (p)*
14/7	CSKA Moskva	a	1-0	*Pimenov*
20/7	Amkar	h	0-0	
28/7	Lokomotiv Moskva	a	2-2	*Pimenov 2*
4/8	Zenit	h	4-2	*Kolodin 2 (1p), Danny, Pimenov*
11/8	Khimki	a	0-1	
18/8	Luch-Energia	h	1-0	*Kombarov K.*
26/8	Spartak Nalchik	a	1-4	*Klimavičius*
31/8	Tom	h	3-1	*Semshov 2, Kombarov K.*
22/9	Moskva	a	1-4	*Kombarov K.*
30/9	Krylya Sovetov	h	1-1	*Kolodin*
6/10	Saturn	a	1-2	*Semshov*
21/10	Kuban	h	1-0	*Semshov*
27/10	Rostov	a	0-0	
3/11	Rubin	h	0-1	
11/11	Spartak Moskva	a	1-2	*Danny*

No	Name	Nat	Pos	Aps	(s)	Gls
19	CÍCERO Sances Semedo Sacimiro	POR	A	9	(7)	
26	Dias de Castro "CUSTÓDIO"	POR	M	3	(5)	
10	DANNY Miguel Alves Gomes	POR	M	28		6
15	Aleksandr DIMIDKO		D	1	(2)	
6	Leandro Sebastián FERNÁNDEZ	ARG	D	23	(2)	
16	Tsvetan GENKOV	BUL	A	3	(6)	
13	Vladimir GRANAT		D	27		
21	Žydrunas KARČEMARSKAS	LTU	G	7		
2	Andrei KARPOVICH	KAZ	M	7	(4)	
8	Dmitriy KHOKHLOV		M	29		4
24	Arunas KLIMAVIČIUS	LTU	D	12	(2)	1
25	Denis KOLODIN		D	27		9
9	Dmitriy KOMBAROV		M	28	(1)	2
7	Kirill KOMBAROV		M	25	(4)	4
17	Aleksandr LOBKOV		D	1		
11	Ruslan PIMENOV		A	16	(7)	5
4	Jovan TANASIJEVIĆ	MNE	D	24	(2)	
5	Igor SEMSHOV		M	28		5
1	Anton SHUNIN		G	23		
40	Fyodor SMOLOV		A		(3)	
3	Aleksandr TOCHILIN		D	9	(5)	
27	Aleksandr ZAIKIN		M		(1)	

FC KHIMKI

Coach – Vladimir Kazachyonok; (7/9/07) Slavoljub Muslin (SRB)

Founded - 1997

2007				
10/3	Krylya Sovetov	a	0-1	
17/3	Kuban	h	1-0	*Tikhonov*
31/3	Rubin	a	1-2	*Antipenko*
8/4	CSKA Moskva	h	1-1	*Vorobyov*
14/4	Lokomotiv Moskva	a	0-1	
21/4	Dinamo Moskva	a	1-2	*Tikhonov*
28/4	Spartak Nalchik	h	1-0	*Trivunović*
5/5	Moskva	a	2-0	*Čeh (p), Arkhipov*
13/5	Saturn	h	0-0	
19/5	Rostov	a	1-1	*Arkhipov*
25/5	Spartak Moskva	h	3-0	*Shirokov, Arkhipov, Jovanović*
9/6	Amkar	a	1-3	*Yevstafyev*
16/6	Zenit	h	2-2	*Arkhipov, Shirokov*
23/6	Luch-Energia	a	1-1	*Shirokov*
1/7	Tom	h	1-1	*Čeh*
14/7	Kuban	a	1-1	*Shirokov*
18/7	Lokomotiv Moskva	h	1-2	*Antipenko*
29/7	CSKA Moskva	a	0-0	
1/8	Rubin	h	0-0	
11/8	Dinamo Moskva	h	1-0	*Blatnjak*
18/8	Spartak Nalchik	a	1-1	*Blatnjak*
26/8	Moskva	h	1-3	*Antipenko*
1/9	Saturn	a	0-1	
21/9	Rostov	h	1-0	*Antipenko*
29/9	Spartak Moskva	a	0-2	
6/10	Amkar	h	1-0	*Shirokov*
21/10	Zenit	a	1-4	*Tikhonov (p)*
27/10	Luch-Energia	h	3-0	*Tikhonov, Mrđa 2*
3/11	Tom	a	1-3	*Yevstafyev*
11/11	Krylya Sovetov	h	4-1	*Shirokov 2, Antipenko, Yevstafyev*

No	Name	Nat	Pos	Aps	(s)	Gls
20	Aleksandr ANTIPENKO		A	17	(7)	5
9	Anton ARKHIPOV		A	12	(4)	4
21	Roman BEREZOVSKIY	ARM	G	28		
33	Vladimir BESCHASTNYKH		A	1	(1)	
19	Dragan BLATNJAK	BIH	A	28		2
30	Andrei CHICHKIN		G	2		
10	Nastja ČEH	SVN	M	16	(8)	2
3	Yuriy DROZDOV		M	5	(3)	
4	Viktor GOLOVATENKO		D	3		
23	Dmitriy GOLYSHEV		M		(1)	
34	Konstantin LOZBINEV		M		(1)	
18	Miodrag JOVANOVIĆ	SRB	D	23		1
2	Dmitriy LYAPKIN		D	10	(3)	
8	Ajdin MAKSUMIĆ	BIH	M	4	(5)	
33	Dragan MRĐA	SRB	A	4	(2)	2
38	Kirill ORLOV		D	26	(1)	
24	Matas SAMUSIOVAS	LTU	D	3	(8)	
7	Dmitriy PARFYONOV		D	5	(4)	
9	Aleksei SEMYONOV		M		(2)	
32	Marko ŠIMIĆ	CRO	A		(1)	
37	Roman SHIROKOV		M	27		7
14	Andrei STEPANOV	EST	D	22	(1)	
11	Andrei TIKHONOV		M	26	(2)	4
6	Vule TRIVUNOVIĆ	BIH	D	29		1

No	Name	Nat	Pos	Aps	(s)	Gls
28	Roman VOROBYOV		M	26	(1)	1
7	Aleksandr YEVSTAFYEV		A	11	(7)	3
77	Robert ZEBELYAN	ARM	A	2	(8)	
5	Aleksei ZHITNIKOV		M		(4)	

FC KRYLYA SOVETOV SAMARA

Coach – Sergei Oborin; (17/08/07) Aleksandr Tarkhanov

Founded – 1942

2007				
10/3	Khimki	h	1-0	*Shevchenko*
17/3	Spartak Nalchik	a	0-0	
31/3	Moskva	h	0-0	
7/4	Saturn	a	1-1	*Mujiri*
14/4	Rostov	h	0-1	
22/4	Spartak Moskva	a	0-1	
29/4	Amkar	h	1-0	*Branco*
6/5	Zenit	a	1-1	*Branco*
12/5	Luch-Energia	h	3-0	*Medvedev, Mujiri, Shvetsov*
20/5	Tom	a	2-1	*Topić, Skvernyuk*
26/5	Dinamo Moskva	h	3-2	*Medvedev, Topić, Booth*
9/6	Kuban	h	2-3	*Topić, Mujiri (p)*
16/6	Rubin	a	0-1	
24/6	CSKA Moskva	h	1-0	*Mujiri*
30/6	Lokomotiv Moskva	a	2-5	*Branco, Medvedev*
15/7	Spartak Nalchik	h	1-2	*Bober*
21/7	Moskva	a	1-3	*Trifonov*
29/7	Saturn	h	0-1	
4/8	Rostov	a	1-1	*Bober (p)*
11/8	Spartak Moskva	h	0-2	
18/8	Amkar	a	1-4	*Bober (p)*
25/8	Zenit	h	1-3	*Bober*
1/9	Luch-Energia	a	0-0	
23/9	Tom	h	1-1	*Mujiri*
30/9	Dinamo Moskva	a	1-1	*Mujiri (p)*
6/10	Kuban	a	2-3	*Topić, Medvedev*
21/10	Rubin	h	3-0	*Topić, Booth, Quintero*
28/10	CSKA Moskva	a	2-4	*Mujiri, Łagiewka*
3/11	Lokomotiv Moskva	h	3-1	*Topić 2, Mujiri*
11/11	Khimki	a	1-4	*Mujiri (p)*

No	Name	Nat	Pos	Aps	(s)	Gls
50	Benoît Christian ANGBWA	NGA	D	22	(1)	
5	Timur BITOKOV		D	1		
7	Anton BOBER		M	26	(2)	4
22	Matthew Paul BOOTH	RSA	D	28		2
14	Serge BRANCO	CMR	D	27		3
2	Maxim BUDNIKOV		D	2	(3)	
6	Juan Carlos ESCOBAR Rodríguez	COL	M	10	(1)	
25	Suad FILEKOVIČ	SVN	M	3	(3)	
10	Mahach GADJIYEV		M	5	(4)	
23	Yevgeniy KALESHIN		M	10		
9	Denis KOVBA		M	25	(3)	
24	Sergei KUZNETSOV		M	9		
4	Krzysztof ŁAGIEWKA	POL	D	28		1
3	LEÍLTON Silva dos Santos	BRA	D	1	(12)	
31	Eduardo Eugenio LOBOS Landuetta	CHI	G	15		
21	Alexandr MAKAROV		G	15		
13	Aleksei MEDVEDEV		A	22	(7)	4
20	David MUJIRI	GEO	M	21	(5)	9
16	PEDRO Henrique Botelho	BRA	D	1		
11	Darwin Carlos QUINTERO Villalba	COL	A	3	(8)	1
18	Igor SHEVCHENKO		A	5	(9)	1
33	Ivan SHPAKOV		A		(6)	
26	Aleksandr SHVETSOV		M	7	(8)	1
19	Aleksei SKVERNYUK	BLR	M	18	(3)	1
75	Marko TOPIĆ	BIH	A	22	(4)	7

No	Name	Nat	Pos	Aps	(s)	Gls
8	Oleg TRIFONOV		M	4	(4)	1
17	Dmitriy Vyacheslavovich VASILYEV		A		(5)	

FC KUBAN KRASNODAR

Coach –Pavlo Yakovenko (UKR); (19/4/07) Leonid Nazarenko; (7/8/07) Soferbiy Yeshugov

Founded - 1928

2007				
11/3	Lokomotiv Moskva	h	0-0	
17/3	Khimki	a	0-1	
1/4	Spartak Nalchik	h	2-2	*Orekhov, Yanbaev*
7/4	Moskva	a	0-1	
13/4	Saturn	h	2-2	*Danishevskiy, Ricardo Baiano*
21/4	Rostov	a	1-0	*Laizāns*
29/4	Spartak Moskva	h	0-0	
5/5	Amkar	a	0-0	
13/5	Zenit	h	1-1	*Laizāns*
19/5	Luch-Energia	a	1-1	*Laizāns*
26/5	Tom	h	2-1	*Tlisov, Ivanov*
9/6	Krylya Sovetov	a	3-2	*Ivanov 2 (1p), Ricardo Baiano*
17/6	Dinamo Moskva	h	0-4	
23/6	Rubin	h	0-1	
1/7	CSKA Moskva	a	0-0	
14/7	Khimki	h	1-1	*Ivanov*
22/7	Spartak Nalchik	a	0-1	
29/7	Moskva	h	4-1	*Kuzmichyov 2, Ricardo Baiano, Tlisov*
3/8	Saturn	a	0-2	
12/8	Rostov	h	1-0	*Kuzmichyov*
19/8	Spartak Moskva	a	0-4	
26/8	Amkar	h	1-1	*Kirilenko*
2/9	Zenit	a	0-1	
22/9	Luch-Energia	h	0-1	
30/9	Tom	a	0-2	
6/10	Krylya Sovetov	h	3-2	*Tlisov, Kuzmichyov, Petkov*
21/10	Dinamo Moskva	a	0-1	
27/10	Rubin	a	2-2	*Laizāns, Okoduwa*
3/11	CSKA Moskva	h	0-1	
11/11	Lokomotiv Moskva	a	3-2	*Petkov, Ushenin 2*

No	Name	Nat	Pos	Aps	(s)	Gls
33	Shamil ASILDAROV		A	6	(7)	
55	Džemal BERBEROVIĆ	BIH	D	5		
7	Leonid BOYEV		A	2	(1)	
55	Vitaliy COCHIEV		M	1	(2)	
11	Aleksandr DANISHEVSKIY		A	4	(1)	1
31	Andrei DIKAN		G	1		
1	Vladimir GABULOV		G	29		
10	Spartak GOGNIEV		A	9	(3)	
6	JEFTHON Ferreira de Sena	BRA	D	25	(3)	
30	Nebojša JELENKOVIĆ	SRB	M	2		
3	Georgiy JIOEV		D		(1)	
99	Oleg IVANOV		M	11	(7)	4
21	Vitaliy KALESHIN		M	29		
33	Mindaugas KALONAS	LTU	M		(1)	
4	Denis KIRILENKO		M	2	(12)	1
28	Vladimir KUZMICHYOV		A	9	(5)	4
5	Jurijs LAIZĀNS	LVA	M	19	(5)	4
85	Aleksandr LEBEDEV	BLR	A	2	(2)	
29	Roman LENGYEL	CZE	D	29		
86	Emmanuel Osei OKODUWA	NGA	A	8		1
19	Valentin OKOROCHKOV		M		(1)	
2	Aleksandr OREKHOV		D	25		1
16	Ivailo PETKOV	BUL	D	13	(1)	2
9	RICARDO Lago Santos "BAIANO"	BRA	M	13	(10)	3
27	Akeksandr SEMIZYAN		A		(2)	

No	Name	Nat	Pos	Aps	(s)	Gls
28	Igor STRELKOV		A	4	(3)	
8	Artur TLISOV		M	27	(2)	3
11	Andrei TOPCHU		M	4	(5)	
17	Andrei USHENIN		D	21	(1)	2
77	Renat YANBAEV		M	10	(2)	1
3	Nikolai ZAITSEV		D	1		
22	Aslan ZASEYEV		D	5	(2)	
7	Robert ZEBELYAN	ARM	A		(2)	
18	Konstantin ZUYEV		M	14	(2)	

FC LOKOMOTIV MOSKVA

Coach – Anatoliy Byshovets (UKR)

Founded - 1923

MAJOR HONOURS: Russian League - (2) 2002, 2004; USSR Cup - (2) 1936, 1957; Russian Cup - (5) 1996, 1997, 2000, 2001, 2007.

2007				
11/3	Kuban	a	0-0	
17/3	Rubin	h	2-1	*Rodolfo, Cociş*
31/3	CSKA Moskva	a	0-2	
7/4	Dinamo Moskva	a	1-2	*Cociş*
14/4	Khimki	h	1-0	*Bilyaletdinov*
22/4	Spartak Nalchik	a	0-0	
28/4	Moskva	h	1-1	*Ivanović*
5/5	Saturn	a	1-1	*Rodolfo*
13/5	Rostov	h	2-0	*Gurenko, Sychev*
19/5	Spartak Moskva	a	2-1	*Bilyaletdinov, Sychev*
11/6	Zenit	a	1-1	*Sychev*
16/6	Luch-Energia	a	0-3	
20/6	Amkar	h	0-1	
24/6	Tom	a	2-4	*Sychev, Traoré*
30/6	Krylya Sovetov	h	5-2	*Ivanović, Sychev (p), Bilyaletdinov, Traoré, Samedov*
18/7	Khimki	a	2-1	*Traoré, Rodolfo*
22/7	CSKA Moskva	h	1-2	*Ivanović*
25/7	Rubin	a	0-3	
28/7	Dinamo Moskva	h	2-2	*Sychev, Odemwingie*
11/8	Spartak Nalchik	h	3-1	*Spahić (p), Samedov 2*
19/8	Moskva	a	2-1	*Traoré, Sychev*
25/8	Saturn	h	0-2	
2/9	Rostov	a	2-0	*Odemwingie, Sychev*
23/9	Spartak Moskva	h	4-3	*Odemwingie 2, Sychev, Asatiani*
29/9	Amkar	a	0-1	
7/10	Zenit	h	1-0	*Spahić (p)*
20/10	Luch-Energia	h	1-1	*Sychev*
28/10	Tom	h	0-0	
3/11	Krylya Sovetov	a	1-3	*Spahić*
11/11	Kuban	h	2-3	*Sychev (p), Traoré*

No	Name	Nat	Pos	Aps	(s)	Gls
30	Malkhaz ASATIANI	GEO	M	12	(2)	1
63	Diniyar BILYALETDINOV		M	28		3
25	Răzvan COCIŞ	ROU	A	9	(5)	2
27	Haminu DRAMANI	GHA	M	1	(2)	
15	"FININHO" Vinícius Aparecido	BRA	D	6	(8)	
41	Sergei GURENKO	BLR	D	29		1
26	Marián HAD	SVK	D	3		
6	Branislav IVANOVIĆ	SRB	D	26		3
7	Marat IZMAILOV		M	1	(3)	
22	Eldin JAKUPOVIĆ	BIH	G	15		
44	Ruslan KAMBOLOV		D		(1)	
20	Roman KONTSEDALOV		M	7	(5)	
23	Eric KORCHAGIN		A	1	(5)	
10	Dmitriy LOSKOV		M	13		
8	Vladimir MAMINOV		M	6	(3)	
9	Garry O'CONNOR	SCO	A	3	(6)	
9	Peter ODEMWINGIE	NGA	A	13	(1)	4
14	Oleg PASHININ		D	1	(2)	
33	Ivan PELIZZOLI	ITA	G	12		
21	Aleksei POLYAKOV		G	3		
4	RODOLFO Dantes Bispo	BRA	D	17		3
40	Alexandr SAMEDOV		M	20	(3)	3
17	Dmitriy SENNIKOV		D	10		
5	Emir SPAHIĆ	BIH	D	23		3
11	Dmitriy SYCHEV		A	27	(2)	11
19	Dramane TRAORÉ	MLI	A	12	(9)	5
55	Renat YANBAYEV		M	10	(2)	
69	Sergei YEFIMOV		D	21	(3)	
24	Chaker ZOUAGHI	TUN	M	1		

FC LUCH-ENERGIA VLADIVOSTOK

Coach – Sergei Pavlov

Founded - 1957

2007				
10/3	Moskva	h	0-1	
18/3	Saturn	a	1-0	*Adjindjal B. (p)*
1/4	Rostov	h	1-1	*Adjindjal B. (p)*
8/4	Spartak Moskva	a	1-2	*Ivanov*
14/4	Amkar	h	1-0	*Bazayev*
22/4	Zenit	h	0-1	
28/4	Dinamo Moskva	h	0-1	
5/5	Tom	h	0-0	
12/5	Krylya Sovetov	a	0-3	
19/5	Kuban	h	1-1	*Bazayev*
26/5	Rubin	a	0-3	
10/6	CSKA Moskva	h	4-0	*Tikhonovetskiy, Ivanov, Bazayev 2*
16/6	Lokomotiv Moskva	h	3-0	*Ivanov 2, Sheshukov*
23/6	Khimki	h	1-1	*Tikhonovetskiy*
30/6	Spartak Nalchik	a	0-2	
14/7	Saturn	h	2-1	*Tikhonovetskiy (p), Sheshukov*
21/7	Rostov	a	1-1	*Tikhonovetskiy*
28/7	Spartak Moskva	h	1-1	*Smirnov D.N.*
4/8	Amkar	a	0-1	
11/8	Zenit	a	1-3	*Strelkov*
18/8	Dinamo Moskva	a	0-1	
25/8	Tom	a	1-3	*og (Klimov)*
1/9	Krylya Sovetov	h	0-0	
22/9	Kuban	a	1-0	*Strelkov*
29/9	Rubin	h	2-0	*Semochko, Strelkov*
7/10	CSKA Moskva	a	0-4	
20/10	Lokomotiv Moskva	a	1-1	*Gvazava*
27/10	Khimki	a	0-3	
3/11	Spartak Nalchik	h	2-1	*Strelkov 2*
11/11	Moskva	a	1-3	*Astafyev*

No	Name	Nat	Pos	Aps	(s)	Gls
15	Beslan ADJINDJAL		M	28	(1)	2
21	Ruslan ADJINDJAL		M	27		
29	Aleksei ARKHIPOV		M	1	(2)	
11	Maksim ASTAFYEV		A	7	(9)	1
27	Georgiy BAZAYEV		M	18	(7)	4
33	Denis BOLSHAKOV		M		(2)	
23	Marek ČECH	CZE	G	25		
1	Aleksandr CHIKHRADZE		G	5		
22	Levani GVAZAVA	GEO	M	5	(4)	1
8	Aleksei IVANOV		M	18		4
5	Igor KRALEVSKI	MKD	D	15	(3)	
7	Yevgeniy KUZNETSOV		M	1	(4)	
9	Vitaliy LANKO	BLR	A	9	(2)	
2	Konstantin LOBOV		D	4	(5)	
14	Semyon MELNIKOV		A	1	(7)	
12	Rade NOVKOVIĆ	SRB	D	11	(2)	
20	Andrei OSPESHINSKIY		A	1	(6)	
6	Marián PALÁT	CZE	D	4		
3	Dmytro SEMOCHKO	UKR	D	25		1

17	Aleksandr SHESHUKOV		M	25	(1)	2
33	Sergei SHTANYUK	BLR	D	27		
25	Anatoliy SKVORTSOV		D	6	(1)	
24	Dmitriy A. SMIRNOV		M	23	(1)	
30	Dmitriy N. SMIRNOV		D	13	(2)	1
28	Nenad STOJANOVIĆ	SRB	A	7	(5)	
12	Igor STRELKOV		A	9	(4)	5
10	Aleksandr TIKHONOVETSKIY		A	14	(7)	4
77	Roman VOIDEL		M	1		

FC MOSKVA

Coach –Loeonid Slutskiy

Founded – 1977

2007				
10/3	Luch-Energia	a	1-0	*Bracamonte*
17/3	Tom	h	2-0	*Adamov 2*
31/3	Krylya Sovetov	a	0-0	
7/4	Kuban	h	1-0	*Bystrov (p)*
14/4	Rubin	a	1-1	*Semak*
22/4	CSKA Moskva	h	2-1	*Barrientos, Semak*
28/4	Lokomotiv Moskva	a	1-1	*Bracamonte*
5/5	Khimki	h	0-2	
12/5	Spartak Nalchik	a	0-1	
20/5	Dinamo Moskva	a	0-0	
10/6	Rostov	a	1-1	*Adamov*
17/6	Spartak Moskva	h	2-0	*Semak, Adamov*
24/6	Amkar	a	1-1	*Golyshev*
1/7	Zenit	h	0-3	*(w/o; original result 1-2 Adamov)*
15/7	Tom	a	2-1	*Barrientos, Bystrov*
21/7	Krylya Sovetov	h	3-1	*Adamov 2 (1p), Barrientos*
25/7	Saturn	h	3-2	*Semak, Barrientos, Ivanov*
29/7	Kuban	a	1-4	*Čížek*
5/8	Rubin	h	2-1	*Bystrov, Semak*
12/8	CSKA Moskva	a	0-2	
19/8	Lokomotiv Moskva	h	1-2	*Adamov*
26/8	Khimki	a	3-1	*Adamov 3 (2p)*
31/8	Spartak Nalchik	h	1-0	*Maxi López*
22/9	Dinamo Moskva	h	4-1	*Adamov, Čížek, Bystrov, Ivanov*
30/9	Saturn	a	0-0	
6/10	Rostov	h	1-0	*Maxi López*
20/10	Spartak Moskva	a	1-3	*Maxi López*
27/10	Amkar	h	3-1	*Maxi López 3*
3/11	Zenit	a	0-1	
11/11	Luch-Energia	h	3-1	*Adamov 2, Krunić*

No	Name	Nat	Pos	Aps	(s)	Gls
21	Roman ADAMOV		A	27	(1)	14
16	Anton AMELCHENKO	BLR	G	3	(1)	
3	Pablo BARRIENTOS	ARG	M	22		4
19	Héctor BRACAMONTE	ARG	A	9	(8)	2
6	Pyotr BYSTROV		M	23	(2)	4
11	Tomáš ČÍŽEK	CZE	M	7	(16)	2
15	Alexandru EPUREANU	MDA	D	15	(8)	
2	Dmitriy GODUNOK		D	21	(1)	
35	Dmitriy GOLUBOV		A	3	(4)	
17	Pavel GOLYSHEV		M	8	(4)	1
7	Damian GORAWSKI	POL	M	2	(4)	
4	Roman HUBNIK	CZE	D	5		
77	Stanislav IVANOV	MDA	M	21	(3)	2
25	Mariusz JOP	POL	D	9		
12	Sergei KOZKO		G	1		
28	Branislav KRUNIĆ	BIH	A	7	(14)	1
22	Oleg KUZMIN		D	24	(1)	
18	Maximiliano "MAXI" Gaston LÓPEZ	ARG	A	6	(3)	6
10	Maximiliano Nicolás MORALEZ	ARG	A	4	(2)	
14	Kirill NABABKIN		D	6	(2)	
23	Isaac OKORONKWO	NGA	D	13		
5	Radu REBEJA	MDA	M	13	(7)	
9	Sergei SEMAK		M	28	(1)	5
8	Pompiliu STOICA	ROU	D	26	(1)	
18	Andrei TOCHU		D	1		
30	Yuriy ZHEVNOV	BLR	G	26		

FC ROSTOV

Coach – Sergei Balakhnin; (17/7/07) (Pavlo Yakovenko (UKR)); (21/7/07) Oleg Dolmatov

Founded – 1930

2007				
11/3	Amkar	a	1-3	*Pjanović*
18/3	Zenit	h	2-3	*Pjanović, Kanyenda*
1/4	Luch-Energia	a	1-1	*Dantsev*
8/4	Tom	h	2-2	*Kalachev, Vinogradov*
14/4	Krylya Sovetov	a	1-0	*Kanyenda*
21/4	Kuban	h	0-1	
29/4	Rubin	a	0-0	
6/5	CSKA Moskva	h	1-1	*Pjanović*
13/5	Lokomotiv Moskva	a	0-2	
19/5	Khimki	h	1-1	*Osinov (p)*
26/5	Spartak Nalchik	a	0-0	
10/6	Moskva	h	1-1	*Kanyenda*
16/6	Saturn	a	0-1	
23/6	Dinamo Moskva	a	0-3	
1/7	Spartak Moskva	h	1-3	*Kanyenda*
15/7	Zenit	a	0-2	
21/7	Luch-Energia	h	1-1	*Kalachev*
29/7	Tom	a	1-1	*Osinov*
4/8	Krylya Sovetov	h	1-1	*Buznikin*
12/8	Kuban	a	0-1	
19/8	Rubin	h	1-1	*Osinov*
26/8	CSKA Moskva	a	0-4	
2/9	Lokomotiv Moskva	h	0-2	
21/9	Khimki	a	0-1	
30/9	Spartak Nalchik	h	0-1	
6/10	Moskva	a	0-1	
21/10	Saturn	h	1-3	*Stavpets*
27/10	Dinamo Moskva	h	0-0	
3/11	Spartak Moskva	a	0-3	
11/11	Amkar	h	2-0	*Starkov, Osinov*

No	Name	Nat	Pos	Aps	(s)	Gls
23	Sergei BENDZ		D	18	(2)	
16	Ilya BLIZNYUK	UKR	G	7		
8	Andrei BOCHKOV		M	25	(3)	
17	Maksim BURCHENKO		M	12	(9)	
70	Maksim BUZNIKIN		A	13	(8)	1
28	Aleksandr DANISHEVSKIY		A	4	(1)	
6	Aleksandr DANTSEV		M	13	(10)	1
19	Konstantin GARBUZ		A		(1)	
1	Roman GERUS		G	23	(2)	
18	Gia GRIGOLAVA		D		(1)	
2	Martin HORÁK	CZE	D	11	(1)	
27	Georgiy JIOYEV		D	3		
15	Timofei KALACHEV	BLR	M	27		2
7	Ilia KALASHNIKOV		M	1	(2)	
14	Essau Boxer KANYENDA	MWI	A	21	(4)	4
3	Miloš KRUŠČIĆ	SRB	D	24	(1)	
37	Vladimir HOZIN		M		(1)	
24	Pavel MOGILEVSKIY		D	23		
74	Albert NAGY		M	7		
22	Sergei OMELYANCHUK	BLR	D	18	(4)	
30	Mikhail OSINOV		M	28	(1)	4
21	Robertas POŠKUS	LTU	A	2	(3)	
10	Mihajlo PJANOVIĆ	SRB	A	9	(2)	3

No	Name	Nat	Pos	Aps	(s)	Gls
4	Anton ROGOCHIY		D	1		
69	Sergei SHUDROV		M	2		
86	Ivan STARKOV		M	4		1
35	Aleksandr STAVPETS		M	4	(1)	1
26	Maksym TRUSEVYCH	UKR	M	2	(3)	
9	Sergei VINOGRADOV		M	2	(9)	1
5	Milan VJEŠTICA	SRB	D	26		

FC RUBIN KAZAN

Coach – Kurban Berdyev (TKM)

Founded – 1958

2007

11/3	CSKA Moskva	a	1-3	*Gabriel*
17/3	Lokomotiv Moskva	a	1-2	*Gilmullin*
31/3	Khimki	h	2-1	*Jean Narde, Gatcan*
8/4	Spartak Nalchik	a	0-1	
14/4	Moskva	h	1-1	*Ryazantsev*
21/4	Saturn	a	0-1	
29/4	Rostov	h	0-0	
6/5	Spartak Moskva	a	1-2	*Budylin (p)*
13/5	Amkar	h	1-0	*Gabriel*
20/5	Zenit	a	1-2	*Gabriel*
26/5	Luch-Energia	h	3-0	*Gabriel, Bairamov 2*
9/6	Tom	a	0-2	
16/6	Krylya Sovetov	h	1-0	*Ryazantsev*
23/6	Kuban	a	1-0	*Ryazantsev*
1/7	Dinamo Moskva	h	2-1	*Ryazantsev, Bairamov*
25/7	Lokomotiv Moskva	h	3-0	*Ryazantsev, Budylin (p), Yarkin*
1/8	Khimki	a	0-0	
5/8	Moskva	a	1-2	*Budylin (p)*
12/8	Saturn	h	0-1	
19/8	Rostov	a	1-1	*Bairamov*
25/8	Spartak Moskva	h	3-1	*Paunović, Noboa, Hasan*
1/9	Amkar	a	1-2	*Jean Narde*
23/9	Zenit	h	1-4	*Petrović*
26/9	Spartak Nalchik	h	2-1	*Salukvadze, Hasan*
29/9	Luch-Energia	a	0-2	
7/10	Tom	h	1-3	*Volkov*
21/10	Krylya Sovetov	a	0-3	
27/10	Kuban	h	2-2	*Hasan, Dyadyun*
3/11	Dinamo Moskva	a	1-0	*Hasan*
11/11	CSKA Moskva	h	0-1	

No	Name	Nat	Pos	Aps	(s)	Gls
77	Ansar AYUPOV		M	8	(6)	
32	Vladimir BAIRAMOV		A	15	(8)	4
18	Jambulat BAZAYEV		M		(3)	
81	Slim BENACHOUR	TUN	M	6	(4)	
22	Sergei BUDYLIN		M	24		3
3	Orlando CALISTO de Sousa	BRA	D	1	(2)	
54	Vladimir DYADYUN		A	2	(3)	1
20	"FÁBIO" Alexandre Felício Duarte	POR	M	2	(4)	
5	Andrei FYODOROV		D	9	(2)	
31	GABRIEL Fernando Atz	BRA	D	20		4
26	Alexandru GATCAN	MDA	M	18	(1)	1
17	Lenar GILMULLIN		D	11		1
8	Pyotr GITSELOV		M	5	(4)	
53	Sergei GOLYATKIN		D	6		
20	Gabriel Nicu GIURGIU	ROU	M	2	(2)	
7	JAILSON Alexandre Alves	BRA	A	2	(5)	
4	JEAN Ferreira NARDE	BRA	D	15	(4)	2
79	Pavel HARCIK	TKM	G	1		
99	HASAN Kabze	TUR	A	11		4
41	Andrei KIREYEV		M	2	(1)	
1	Aleksandrs KOLINKO	LVA	G	27		
16	Cristián Fernando NOBOA Tello	ECU	M	9	(5)	1
27	Veljko PAUNOVIĆ	SRB	A	12	(4)	1
18	Branimir PETROVIĆ	SRB	M	1	(5)	1
10	Damani RALPH	JAM	A		(1)	
29	Nukri REVISHVILI	GEO	G	2		
15	Aleksandr RYAZANTSEV		M	17	(1)	5
9	Lasha SALUKVADZE	GEO	D	15		1
6	MacBeth-Mao SIBAYA	RSA	M	22	(2)	
21	Mikhail SINYOV		D	19		
2	Stjepan TOMAŠ	CRO	D	11		
98	Dmitriy Vladimirovich VASILYEV		D	16		
11	Vitaliy VOLKOV		M	19	(3)	1
46	Aleksandr YARKIN		A		(4)	1

FC SATURN MOSKOVSKAYA OBLAST

Coach – Vladimír Weiss (SVK); (1/6/07) Gadzhi Gadzhiyev

Founded - 1946

2007

11/3	Zenit	a	1-1	*Karyaka (p)*
18/3	Luch-Energia	h	0-1	
31/3	Tom	a	1-1	*Vukčević*
7/4	Krylya Sovetov	h	1-1	*Kirichenko*
13/4	Kuban	a	2-2	*Česnauskis, Lebedenko*
21/4	Rubin	h	1-0	*Česnauskis*
29/4	CSKA Moskva	a	1-3	*Lebedenko*
5/5	Lokomotiv Moskva	h	1-1	*Gyan*
13/5	Khimki	a	0-0	
19/5	Spartak Nalchik	h	1-1	*Kirichenko*
10/6	Dinamo Moskva	a	1-1	*og (Tanasijević)*
16/6	Rostov	h	1-0	*Kirichenko*
22/6	Spartak Moskva	a	0-2	
30/6	Amkar	h	2-0	*Kirichenko, Karyaka*
14/7	Luch-Energia	a	1-2	*Karyaka*
21/7	Tom	h	0-0	
25/7	Moskva	a	2-3	*Česnauskis, Karyaka*
29/7	Krylya Sovetov	a	1-0	*Shilla*
3/8	Kuban	h	2-0	*Karyaka, Kirichenko*
12/8	Rubin	a	1-0	*Kirichenko*
18/8	CSKA Moskva	h	2-2	*Karyaka 2*
25/8	Lokomotiv Moskva	a	2-0	*Kirichenko (p), Loskov (p)*
1/9	Khimki	h	1-0	*Ivanov*
22/9	Spartak Nalchik	a	3-1	*Yevseyev, Česnauskis, Ivanov*
30/9	Moskva	h	0-0	
6/10	Dinamo Moskva	h	2-1	*Eremenko (p), Karyaka*
21/10	Rostov	a	3-1	*Kirichenko 2 (1p), Karyaka*
28/10	Spartak Moskva	h	0-0	
3/11	Amkar	a	1-3	*Karyaka*
11/11	Zenit	h	0-1	

No	Name	Nat	Pos	Aps	(s)	Gls
16	Aleksei BOTVINYEV		G	2		
18	Edgaras ČESNAUSKIS	LTU	M	21	(1)	4
6	Ján ĎURICA	SVK	D	25		
3	Rolandas DŽIAUKŠTAS	LTU	D		(1)	
11	Aleksei EREMENKO	FIN	A	14	(8)	1
20	Mahach GADJIYEV		M		(1)	
9	Baffour GYAN	GHA	A	9	(14)	1
77	Gogita GOGUA	GEO	M	8	(7)	
5	Aleksei IGONIN		D	29		
88	Aleksei IVANOV		M	11		2
26	Martin JAKUBKO	SVK	A	2	(2)	
21	Andrei KARYAKA		M	28		10
1	Antonin KINSKÝ	CZE	G	28		
14	Dmitriy KIRICHENKO		A	22	(5)	9
22	Igor LEBEDENKO		A	18	(8)	2
10	Dmitriy LOSKOV		M	14	(1)	1
15	Ruslan NAKHUSHEV		M	18	(2)	
8	Pyotr NEMOV		M	10	(17)	

24	Artyom PERSHIN		M	5	(2)	
13	Dušan PETKOVIĆ	SRB	D	1		
4	Peter PETRÁŠ	SVK	D	21	(2)	
25	Dmitriy POLOVINCHUK		D	7		
19	Illiasu SHILLA	GHA	D	24		1
29	Pavel SOLOMIN		A		(2)	
35	Ivan TEMNIKOV		M		(2)	
7	Oleg VLASOV		M	1	(7)	
10	Simon VUKČEVIĆ	MNE	M	3	(1)	1
17	Sergei YASHIN		A		(2)	
33	Valeriy YESIPOV		A	1	(1)	
2	Vadim YEVSEYEV		D	8		1

FC SPARTAK MOSKVA

Coach – Vladimir Fedotov; (21/6/07) Stanislav Cherchesov

Founded - 1922

MAJOR HONOURS: USSR League - (12) 1936, 1938, 1939, 1952, 1953, 1956, 1958, 1962, 1969, 1979, 1987, 1989; Russian League - (9) 1992, 1993, 1994, 1996, 1997, 1998, 1999, 2000, 2001; USSR Cup - (10) 1938, 1939, 1946, 1947, 1950, 1958, 1963, 1965, 1971, 1992; Russian Cup - (3) 1994, 1998, 2003.

2007				
11/3	Dinamo Moskva	a	1-0	*Titov*
18/3	Amkar	h	0-0	
31/3	Zenit	a	3-1	*Titov, Stranzl, Bystrov (p)*
8/4	Luch-Energia	h	2-1	*Titov, Prudnikov*
15/4	Tom	a	1-1	*Dzyuba*
22/4	Krylya Sovetov	h	1-0	*Torbinskiy*
29/4	Kuban	a	0-0	
6/5	Rubin	h	2-1	*Titov, Boyarintsev*
12/5	CSKA Moskva	a	1-1	*Bystrov*
19/5	Lokomotiv Moskva	h	1-2	*Pavlyuchenko*
25/5	Khimki	a	0-3	
10/6	Spartak Nalchik	h	2-2	*Titov, Pavlyuchenko*
17/6	Moskva	a	0-2	
22/6	Saturn	h	2-0	*Stranzl, Pavlyuchenko*
1/7	Rostov	a	3-1	*Kováč, Torbinskiy, Bazhenov*
14/7	Amkar	a	1-0	*Titov*
21/7	Zenit	h	3-1	*Pavlyuchenko 2 (1p), Bazhenov*
28/7	Luch-Energia	a	1-1	*Prudnikov*
5/8	Tom	h	3-2	*Torbinskiy, Pavlyuchenko, Boyarintsev*
11/8	Krylya Sovetov	a	2-0	*Bazhenov, Pavlyuchenko*
19/8	Kuban	h	4-0	*Pavlyuchenko 3, Bystrov*
25/8	Rubin	a	1-3	*Welliton*
2/9	CSKA Moskva	h	1-1	*Mozart (p)*
23/9	Lokomotiv Moskva	a	3-4	*Pavlyuchenko 3 (1p)*
29/9	Khimki	h	2-0	*Bazhenov, Titov*
8/10	Spartak Nalchik	a	2-1	*Kalynychenko 2*
20/10	Moskva	h	3-1	*Dedura, Géder, Welliton*
28/10	Saturn	a	0-0	
3/11	Rostov	h	3-0	*Kalynychenko, Welliton, Boyarintsev*
11/11	Dinamo Moskva	h	2-1	*Pavlyuchenko, Welliton*

No	Name	Nat	Pos	Aps	(s)	Gls
32	Nikita BAZHENOV		A	13	(3)	4
7	Denis BOYARINTSEV		M	7	(17)	3
23	Vladimir BYSTROV		M	16	(2)	3
27	Serghey COVALCIUC	MDA	M	1	(1)	
70	Ignas DEDURA	LTU	D	6		1
55	Oleg DINEYEV		M	1		
40	Artyom DZYUBA		A	7	(9)	1
2	Malta Camilo Antônio "GÉDER"	BRA	D	13	(1)	1
59	Andrei IVANOV		D	7		
13	Martin JIRÁNEK	CZE	D	11		
25	Maksym KALYNYCHENKO	UKR	M	13	(9)	3
1	Dmitriy KHOMICH		G	1		
15	Radoslav KOVÁČ	CZE	M	22	(4)	1
36	Fyodor KUDRYASHOV		D	6	(1)	
24	MOZART Santos Batista	BRA	M	18		1
31	Sergei PARSHIVLYUK		M		(2)	
10	Roman PAVLYUCHENKO		A	21	(1)	14
22	Stipe PLETIKOSA	CRO	G	29		
18	Aleksandr PRUDNIKOV		A	3	(9)	2
21	Quincy OWUSU-ABEYIE	GHA	A	4	(2)	
20	Aleksei REBKO		M	3		
34	Renat SABITOV		D	12	(3)	
49	Roman SHISHKIN		D	25	(1)	
6	Costin Florin ŞOAVĂ	ROU	D	17	(1)	
3	Martin STRANZL	AUT	D	18	(1)	2
9	Yegor TITOV		M	27		7
14	Dmitriy TORBINSKIY		M	19	(5)	3
11	WELLITON Soares de Morais	BRA	A	10	(2)	4

FC SPARTAK NALCHIK

Coach – Yuriy Krasnozhan

Founded – 1935

2007				
10/3	Tom	a	0-2	
17/3	Krylya Sovetov	h	0-0	
1/4	Kuban	a	2-2	*Ricardo Jesus 2*
8/4	Rubin	h	1-0	*Shumeiko*
15/4	CSKA Moskva	a	0-2	
22/4	Lokomotiv Moskva	h	0-0	
28/4	Khimki	a	0-1	
5/5	Dinamo Moskva	a	0-2	
12/5	Moskva	h	1-0	*og (Hubnik)*
19/5	Saturn	a	1-1	*Ricardo Jesus*
26/5	Rostov	h	0-0	
10/6	Spartak Moskva	a	2-2	*Ricardo Jesus 2*
16/6	Amkar	h	0-1	
24/6	Zenit	a	3-4	*Amisulashvili, Pylypchuk, Uzdenov*
30/6	Luch-Energia	h	2-0	*Đudović, Pylypchuk*
15/7	Krylya Sovetov	a	2-1	*Đudović, Amisulashvili*
22/7	Kuban	h	1-0	*Dzahmishev*
5/8	CSKA Moskva	h	1-1	*Faizulin*
11/8	Lokomotiv Moskva	a	1-3	*Rodenkov*
18/8	Khimki	h	1-1	*Ricardo Jesus*
26/8	Dinamo Moskva	h	4-1	*Faizulin, Pylypchuk, Samsonov, Kazharov*
31/8	Moskva	a	0-1	
22/9	Saturn	h	1-3	*Shumeiko*
26/9	Rubin	a	1-2	*Amisulashvili*
30/9	Rostov	a	1-0	*Rodenkov*
8/10	Spartak Moskva	h	1-2	*Pylypchuk*
21/10	Amkar	a	1-1	*Faizulin*
28/10	Zenit	h	0-3	
3/11	Luch-Energia	a	1-2	*Ricardo Jesus*
11/11	Tom	h	1-0	*Kazharov*

No	Name	Nat	Pos	Aps	(s)	Gls
28	Aleksandre AMISULASHVILI	GEO	D	29		3
19	Marat DZAHMISHEV		A	1	(12)	1
20	Miodrag ĐUDOVIĆ	SRB	D	17	(2)	2
10	Viktor FAIZULIN		M	28		3
17	Valentin FILATOV		D	26		
33	Kazbek GETERIYEV		M	2	(3)	
7	Levani GVAZAVA	GEO	D	7	(7)	
13	Kaplan HUAKO		D	1		
5	Nazir KAZHAROV		A	8	(5)	2

No	Name	Nat	Pos	Aps	(s)	Gls
23	Aleksei KOSTENKO		M	1		
18	Vladimir KISENKOV		D	3	(2)	
35	Sergei KRASHCHENKO		G	4		
5	Vitaliy LANKO	BLR	M	11	(5)	
15	Aslan MASHUKOV		M	26	(1)	
29	Aleksei MARTYNOV		A	1	(1)	
34	Darijan MATIČ	SVN	M	4	(11)	
32	Denis POPOV		A	2	(2)	
9	Serhiy PYLYPCHUK	UKR	M	25	(4)	4
30	Dejan RADIĆ	SRB	G	23		
21	RICARDO JESUS da Silva	BRA	A	29	(1)	7
14	Yuriy RODENKOV		A	9	(16)	2
8	Oleg SAMSONOV		M	21	(2)	1
6	Vitaliy SHUMEIKO	UKR	D	10	(3)	2
27	Andrei SIDELNIKOV		G	3		
4	Maxim USANOV		D	1	(1)	
11	Roman UZDENOV		A	5	(9)	1
46	Viktor VASIN		D	1		
3	Dmitriy YATCHENKO		A	18		
4	Denis YEVSIKOV		D	14		

FC TOM TOMSK

Coach – Valeriy Petrakov

Founded – 1957

2007				
10/3	Spartak Nalchik	h	2-0	*Klimov, Mladenov*
17/3	Moskva	a	0-2	
31/3	Saturn	h	1-1	*Vejić*
8/4	Rostov	a	2-2	*Kiselyov 2*
15/4	Spartak Moskva	h	1-1	*Kiselyov*
21/4	Amkar	a	3-3	*Skoblyakov, Serdyukov, og (Popov)*
28/4	Zenit	h	0-1	
5/5	Luch-Energia	a	0-0	
12/5	Dinamo Moskva	h	1-0	*Bulyga*
20/5	Krylya Sovetov	h	1-2	*Skoblyakov*
26/5	Kuban	a	1-2	*Klimov*
6/6	Rubin	h	2-0	*Klimov, Kiselyov*
16/6	CSKA Moskva	a	0-0	
24/6	Lokomotiv Moskva	h	4-2	*Tarasov, Shirko 2, Michkov (p)*
1/7	Khimki	a	1-1	*Michkov (p)*
15/7	Moskva	h	1-2	*Kiselyov*
21/7	Saturn	a	0-0	
29/7	Rostov	h	1-1	*Klimov*
5/8	Spartak Moskva	a	2-3	*Michkov (p), Bulyga*
12/8	Amkar	h	0-1	
19/8	Zenit	a	1-2	*Catînsus*
25/8	Luch-Energia	h	3-1	*Radosavljević, Skoblyakov, Kulchiy*
31/8	Dinamo Moskva	a	1-3	*Skoblyakov*
23/9	Krylya Sovetov	a	1-1	*Maznov*
30/9	Kuban	h	2-0	*Maznov 2 (1p)*
7/10	Rubin	a	3-1	*Maznov 3*
20/10	CSKA Moskva	h	0-1	
28/10	Lokomotiv Moskva	a	0-0	
3/11	Khimki	h	3-1	*Maznov 3*
11/11	Spartak Nalchik	a	0-1	

No	Name	Nat	Pos	Aps	(s)	Gls
99	Anton ARKHIPOV		A	7	(1)	
12	Aleksei BUGAYEV		D	16	(1)	
10	Vitaliy BULYGA	BLR	A	12	(11)	2
21	Valeriu CATÎNSUS	MDA	M	30		1
11	Yevgeniy KALESHIN		M	4	(1)	
33	Vasiliy KHOMUTOVSKIY	BLR	G	12		
8	Denis KISELYOV		A	11	(3)	5
3	Valeriy KLIMOV		M	29		4
7	Aleksandr KULCHIY	BLR	M	21	(1)	1
14	Sergei LEBEDKOV		M		(1)	
11	Goran MAZNOV	MKD	A	6	(1)	9
6	Dmitriy MICHKOV		M	28		3
17	Aleksandar MLADENOV	BUL	M	6	(10)	1
2	Ruslan MOSTOVOI		D	19	(3)	
18	Igor NOVAKOVIĆ	CRO	M		(1)	
25	Sergei PAREIKO	EST	G	13	(1)	
40	Andrei PROSHIN	UKR	D	2		
23	Aleksander RADOSAVLJEVIČ	SVN	D	8	(4)	1
55	Sergei RYZHIKOV		G	5		
9	Serdyukov SERDYUKOV		A	15	(10)	1
22	Aleksandr SHIRKO		A	4	(9)	2
5	Sergei SKOBLYAKOV		M	28	(2)	4
15	Viktor STROYEV		D	2	(7)	
20	Dmitriy TARASOV		M	11	(13)	1
84	Hrvoje VEJIĆ	CRO	D	21		1
4	Vasiliy YANOTOVSKIY		M	10	(2)	
19	Denis YEVSIKOV		D	10	(2)	

FC ZENIT ST. PETERSBURG

Coach –Dick Advocaat (NED)

Founded - 1925

MAJOR HONOURS: UEFA Cup – (1) 2008; USSR League - (1) 1984; Russian League – (1) 2007; USSR Cup - (1) 1944; Russian Cup - (1) 1999.

2007				
11/3	Saturn	h	1-1	*Fatih*
18/3	Rostov	a	3-2	*Zyryanov, Tymoshchuk, Arshavin*
31/3	Spartak Moskva	h	1-3	*Pogrebnyak*
8/4	Amkar	a	1-1	*Zyryanov*
14/4	Dinamo Moskva	h	3-0	*Domínguez, Pogrebnyak, Denisov*
22/4	Luch-Energia	a	1-0	*Zyryanov*
28/4	Tom	a	1-0	*Pogrebnyak*
6/5	Krylya Sovetov	h	1-1	*Pogrebnyak (p)*
13/5	Kuban	a	1-1	*Pogrebnyak*
20/5	Rubin	h	2-1	*Škrteľ, Arshavin*
26/5	CSKA Moskva	a	0-2	
11/6	Lokomotiv Moskva	h	1-1	*Anyukov*
16/6	Khimki	a	2-2	*Tymoshchuk (p), Arshavin*
24/6	Spartak Nalchik	h	4-3	*Pogrebnyak (p), Arshavin, Radimov, Anyukov*
1/7	Moskva	a	3-0	*(w/o; original result 2-1 Arshavin, Tymoshchuk)*
15/7	Rostov	h	2-0	*Domínguez, Arshavin*
21/7	Spartak Moskva	a	1-3	*Arshavin*
28/7	Amkar	h	0-0	
4/8	Dinamo Moskva	a	2-4	*Tymoshchuk (p), Fatih*
11/8	Luch-Energia	h	3-1	*Zyryanov 2, Arshavin*
19/8	Tom	h	2-1	*Kim 2*
25/8	Krylya Sovetov	a	3-1	*Zyryanov, Arshavin, Pogrebnyak*
2/9	Kuban	h	1-0	*Zyryanov*
23/9	Rubin	a	4-1	*Pogrebnyak 2, Zyryanov, Denisov*
29/9	CSKA Moskva	h	2-1	*Pogrebnyak, Denisov*
7/10	Lokomotiv Moskva	a	0-1	
21/10	Khimki	h	4-1	*Pogrebnyak, Zyryanov, Lombaerts, Fatih*
28/10	Spartak Nalchik	a	3-0	*Lombaerts, Domínguez, Fatih*
3/11	Moskva	h	1-0	*Arshavin*
11/11	Saturn	a	1-0	*Šírl*

No	Name	Nat	Pos	Aps	(s)	Gls
22	Aleksandr ANYUKOV		D	21	(1)	2
10	Andrei ARSHAVIN		M	30		10

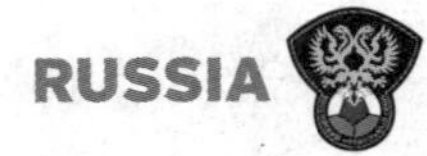

1	Kamil ČONTOFALSKÝ	SVK	G	11	(2)	
27	Igor DENISOV		M	14	(9)	3
7	Alejandro Damián DOMÍNGUEZ	ARG	A	17	(7)	3
9	FATİH Tekke	TUR	A	11	(5)	4
14	Erik HAGEN	NOR	D	13	(2)	
88	Oleksandr HORSHKOV	UKR	M	9	(2)	
5	KIM Dong-jin	KOR	D	24		2
4	Ivica KRIŽANAC	CRO	D	11	(4)	
75	Yuriy LEBEDEV		M	1		
6	Nicolas LOMBAERTS	BEL	D	13		2
16	Vyacheslav MALAFEYEV		G	19		
87	Ilia MAXIMOV		M		(6)	
8	Pavel POGREBNYAK		A	17	(7)	11
2	Vladislav RADIMOV		M	12	(5)	1
25	Fernando RICKSEN	NED	D	12	(2)	
11	Radek ŠÍRL	CZE	M	19	(3)	1
3	Martin ŠKRTEĽ	SVK	D	23		1
44	Anatoliy TYMOSHCHUK	UKR	M	29		4
18	Konstantin ZYRYANOV		M	24	(3)	9

PROMOTED CLUBS

FC SHINNIK YAROSLAVL

Coach – Sergei Yuran

Founded - 1957

FC TEREK GROZNY

Coach – Voit Talgayev

Founded – 1946

MAJOR HONOURS: Russian Cup - (1) 2004

SECOND LEVEL FINAL TABLE 2007

	Pld	W	D	L	F	A	Pts
FC Shinnik Yaroslavl	42	28	8	6	68	30	92
FC Terek Grozny	42	28	6	8	69	27	90
FC Sibir Novosibirsk	42	25	11	6	80	39	86
FC KamAZ Naberezhnye Chelny	42	23	8	11	67	34	77
FC Ural Yekaterinburg	42	21	14	7	70	33	77
FC Torpedo Moskva	42	21	6	15	75	59	69
FC Nosta Novotroitsk	42	16	16	10	63	40	64
FC Dinamo Bryansk	42	16	11	15	49	52	59
FC Salyut-Energia Belgorod	42	17	6	19	44	45	57
FC Anzhi Makhachkala	42	16	9	17	41	44	57
FC Zvezda Irkutsk	42	16	8	18	60	47	56
FC Alania Vladikavkaz	42	15	11	16	56	56	56
FC SKA-Energia Khabarovsk	42	14	14	14	50	48	56
FC Mashuk-KMV Pyatigorsk	42	14	13	15	53	55	55
FC Baltika Kaliningrad	42	14	12	16	53	49	54
FC Metallurg-Kuzbass Novokuznetsk	42	15	8	19	53	70	53
FC SKA Rostov-na Donu	42	14	11	17	50	60	53
FC Avangard Kursk	42	15	6	21	50	55	51
FC Mordovia Saransk	42	13	4	25	44	88	43
FC Tekstilschik-Telekom Ivanovo	42	10	8	24	38	68	38
FC Sodovik Srerlitamak	42	8	10	24	32	65	34
FC Spartak-MZHK Ryazan	42	1	4	37	21	122	7

N.B. FC Spartak-MZHK Ryazan withdrew after round 22. Remaining matches awarded as 0-3 defeats.

DOMESTIC CUP 2007/08

KUBOK ROSSII

1/16 FINALS

(27/6/07)
Baltika 0, CSKA Moskva 1
Torpedo 1, Khimki 2
Lukhovitsy 1, Rubin 2
Shinnik 1, Spartak Nalchik 2 *(aet)*
Dinamo Bryansk 1, Zenit 4
Avangard 0, Dinamo Moskva 3
Salyut-Energia 0, Tom 0 *(aet; 2-3 on pens)*
Rostov-na-Donu 0, Rostov 3
Terek 1, Spartak Moskva 1 *(aet; 4-3 on pens)*
Rotor 1, Amkar 2
NoSta 0, Moskva 0 *(aet; 2-4 on pens)*
KamAZ 1, Krylya Sovetov 0
Ural 1, Lokomotiv Moskva 0
Metallurg-Kuzbass 1, Kuban 2
Metallurg Krasnoyarsk 1 Luch-Energia 0
SKA-Energia 1, Saturn 2

1/8 FINALS

(8/8/07)
CSKA Moskva 2, Khimki 0
Spartak Nalchik 3, Rubin 2 *(aet)*
Zenit 9, Dinamo Moskva 3
Rostov 0, Tom 1
Amkar 3, Terek 1
KamAZ 0, Moskva 1
Kuban 2, Ural 3 *(aet)*
Saturn 2, Metallurg Krasnoyarsk 1

QUARTER- FINALS

(16/9/07)
Amkar 2 *(Kobenko 10, Kushev 29)*, Moskva 1 *(Semak 12)*
Ural 2 *(Kozhanov 14, 35)*, Saturn 1 *(Karyaka 21)*

(31/10/07)
CSKA Moskva 2 *(Jô 55, Daniel Carvalho 73)*, Spartak Nalchik 1 *(Kazharov 4)*
Zenit 0, Tom 0 *(aet; 3-4 on pens)*

SEMI-FINALS

(16/4/08)
CSKA Moskva 2 *(Krasić 14, Ignashevich 51)*, Tom 1 *(Klimov 27)*
Amkar 1*(Dujmović 53)*, Ural 0

FINAL

(17/5/08)
Lokomotiv stadium, Moscow
PFC CSKA MOSKVA 2 *(Vágner Love 66, Jô 74)*
FC AMKAR PERM 2 *(Drinčić 57, Dujmović 64)*
(aet; 4-1 on pens)
Referee – *Sukhina*
CSKA MOSKVA – *Akinfeev, Berezutskiy V., Ignashevich (Rahimić 67), Berezutskiy A., Krasić, Šemberas, Aldonin (Dzagoev 61),Dudu (Janczyk 87), Zhirkov, Jô, Vágner Love.*
AMKAR – *Gabulov, Sirakov (Cherenchikov 70), Popov, Belorukov, Gaál, Peev (Afanasyev 90), Drinčić, Dujmović, Starkov, Sikimić (Inijaz 77), Kushev.*

'Double double' for Murata

S.S. Murata reinforced their position as the dominant club in San Marino, winning the League and Cup double for the second successive season.

It was a personal triumph for 44-year-old player-coach Massimo Agostini, once a Serie A star with AS Roma and SSC Napoli. He was handed the coaching reins at the start of the season, although not before his predecessor Gianluigi Pasquali had enjoyed the farewell gift of leading a club from San Marino into the UEFA Champions League for the first time when Murata took on – and lost to – Finnish champions Tampere United in the first qualifying round.

Among the Murata players involved in the first leg was a specially invited guest, Agostini's former Roma team-mate Aldair, but it was club regular Cristian Protti who registered San Marino's first goal in the competition, and he would be the man of the moment again nine-and-a-half months later as he struck the only goal in the final of the Coppa Titano.

A month later, with AC Juvenes/Dogana again providing the opposition, Murata clinched a second double – and a return to the UEFA Champions League – with victory in the league play-off final. Agostini's team prevailed 1-0 again, although this time they had to wait until seven minutes from time for their goal, Protti turning provider for Carlo Valentini to strike the decisive blow.

San Marino's bid for a first ever UEFA European Championship qualifying point ended in vain. They have now lost all 46 matches played in the competition, scoring just six goals and conceding precisely 200. Andy Selva found the net in the creditable 2-1 home defeat by Wales to lift his all-time international tally to seven goals – six more than any other San Marino player.

Federazione Sammarinese Giuoco Calcio (FSGC)

Via Campo dei Giudei 14
SM-47899 San Marino
tel - +378 054 999 0515
fax - +378 054 999 2348
website – www.fsgc.sm
email – fsgc@omniway.sm
Year of Formation – 1931
President – Giorgio Crescentini
General Secretary – Luciano Casadei
Press Officer – Elisa Felici

TOP FIVE ALL-TIME CAPS
Mirco Gennari (48); Ivan Matteoni & Damiano Vannucci (44); Federico Gasperoni & Luca Gobbi (41)

TOP FIVE ALL-TIME GOALS
Andy Selva (7)

N.B. No other player has scored more than one goal.

NATIONAL TEAM RESULTS 2007/08

22/8/07	Cyprus (ECQ)	H	Serravalle	0-1	
8/9/07	Czech Republic (ECQ)	H	Serravalle	0-3	
12/9/07	Cyprus (ECQ)	A	Nicosia	0-3	
13/10/07	Slovakia (ECQ)	A	Dubnica	0-7	
17/10/07	Wales (ECQ)	H	Serravalle	1-2	*Selva (73)*
21/11/07	Slovakia (ECQ)	H	Serravalle	0-5	

IATIONAL TEAM APPEARANCES 2007/08

ach – Giampaolo MAZZA (ITA) 26/2/56			CYP	CZE	CYP	SVK	WAL	SVK	Caps	Goals
lo SIMONCINI	30/8/86	San Marino (ITA)	G	G			G		8	-
rlo VALENTINI	15/3/82	NovaValmarecchia (ITA)	D	D	D	M	D	D	29	-
nluca BOLLINI	24/3/80	NovaValmarecchia (ITA)	D77	D85		D57		D61	4	-
ssandro DELLA VALLE	8/6/82	Scot Due Emme (ITA)	D	D		D	D	D	21	-
cola ALBANI	15/4/81	Secchiano (ITA) /Saludecio (ITA)	D		D81	D	D		31	1
miano VANNUCCI	30/7/77	Libertas /Perticara (ITA)	D	D	D	M	D76	M	44	-
tteo BUGLI	10/3/83	Secchiano (ITA)	M	M67	M	M68	s76		10	-
bio BOLLINI	19/9/83	Murata	M63	M58	M				3	-
vanni BONINI	5/9/86	Real Misano (ITA)	M84	M	M73		s62		9	-
dy SELVA	23/5/76	Sassuolo (ITA)	A	A	A		A	A50	40	7
nuel MARANI	7/6/84	Morciano (ITA)	A	A	A87	A85		A	13	1
tteo ANDREINI	10/10/81	Tre Fiori	s63	s58	D	D	M	s84	16	-
cola CIACCI	7/7/82	Lunano (ITA)	s77						11	1
derico NANNI	3/6/84	Sant´Ermete (ITA)	s84		s87	M			6	-
vide SIMONCINI	30/8/86	Torcona (ITA) /Santa Giustina (ITA)		D			D	D	8	-
bio VITAIOLI	5/4/84	Secchiano (ITA)		s67	D	D	s80		5	-
olo MARIOTTI	5/11/79	Pennarossa		s85	s73				4	-
derico VALENTINI	22/1/82	NovaValmarecchia (ITA)			G	G		G	5	-
como BENEDETTINI	7/10/82	Tre Fiori			s81	s57			2	-
ca BONIFAZI	12/11/82	Tre Fiori				s68	M62		3	-
rco DE LUIGI	21/3/78	Santa Giustina (ITA) /Virtus				s85	A80	s50	18	-
cardo MUCCIOLI	27/8/74	Savarna (ITA)					M	M	27	-
uro MARANI	9/3/75	Pennarossa						D84	16	-
chele MARANI	16/11/82	Cattolica (ITA)						M	25	-
icol BERRETTI	1/5/89	Santarcangiolese (ITA)						s61	1	-

DOMESTIC LEAGUE 2007/08

AMPIONATO SAMMARINESE FINAL TABLES

RST PHASE

oup A	Pld	W	D	L	F	A	Pts
SP Tre Penne	21	13	5	3	51	22	44
SP Tre Fiori	21	10	6	5	35	26	36
AC Juvenes/Dogana	21	10	6	5	31	18	36
SP Cailungo	21	10	6	5	37	24	36
S.S. Pennarossa	21	7	4	10	33	42	25
S.S. Folgore/Falciano	21	6	4	11	21	37	22
Domagnano FC	21	4	5	12	36	54	17
S.S. Fiorentino	21	1	1	19	17	60	4

Group B	Pld	W	D	L	F	A	Pts
1 S.S. Murata	20	12	7	1	46	15	43
2 SP La Fiorita	20	12	6	2	39	24	42
3 SC Faetano	20	11	4	5	45	18	37
4 S.S. Virtus	20	9	7	4	34	23	34
5 S.S. Cosmos	20	6	5	9	21	33	23
6 SP Libertas	20	5	6	9	27	36	21
7 S.S. San Giovanni	20	1	2	17	15	56	5

TOP GOALSCORERS

16 Marco FANTINI (Juvenes/Dogana)
14 Stefano BULLINI (Tre Penne)
13 Alessandro GIUNTA (Tre Fiori)
11 Marco CASADEI (Tre Penne)
Alberto CELLI (Domagnano)
10 Simone AMADORI (Tre Penne)
Alessandro PANCOTTI (Pennarossa)
9 Francesco ROSSI (Cailungo)
8 Lorenzo BOSCHI (Cailungo)
Fabio FELICI (Domagnano)
Giacomo GAMBERINI (Juvenes/Dogana)
Steven VENERUCCI (Fiorentino)

SAN MARINO

CHAMPIONSHIP PLAY-OFFS

FIRST ROUND
(7/5/08)
Tre Fiori 1 *(Aruta 60)*, Faetano 0
La Fiorita 0, Juvenes/Dogana 0 *(aet; 3-4 on pens)*

SECOND ROUND
(12/5/08)
Tre Penne 1 *(Protti 14)*, Juvenes/Dogana 5 *(Gamberini 11, 57, 75, Ceci 29, Santini 73)*
Murata 2 *(Marani 60p, Di Giuli 79)*, Tre Fiori 2 *(Andreini 33, Aruta 58) (aet; 4-1 on pens)*

THIRD ROUND
(16/5/08)
Tre Penne 1 *(Protti 57p)*, Faetano 2 *(Olivieri 51, Moroni 88)*
Tre Fiori 1 *(Aruta 71)*, La Fiorita 0
(Tre Penne and La Fiorita eliminated)

FOURTH ROUND
(19/5/08)
Juvenes/Dogana 0, Murata 2 *(Protti 40, Di Giuli 90)*

FIFTH ROUND
(22/5/08)
Faetano 2 *(Valentini 33, Folli 42)*, Tre Fiori 1 *(Amici 39)*
(Tre Fiori eliminated)

SEMI-FINAL
(27/5/08)
Juvenes/Dogana 1 *(Santini 98)*, Faetano 0 *(aet)*
(Faetano eliminated)

FINAL
(3/6/08)
Stadio Olimpico, Serravalle
S.S. MURATA 1 *(Valentini 83)*
AC JUVENES/DOGANA 0
Referee – *Zanotti*
MURATA – *Donati D., Fretta, D'Orsi, Albani N., Vitaioli (Raschi 84), Valentini, Teodorani (Donati F. 88), Vannoni, Marani, Di Giuli (Bollini 71), Protti.*
JUVENES/DOGANA – *Montanari, Selva, Renzi (Babboni 81), Santini (Ercolani 88), Ceci, Vagnetti (Zonzini C. 46), Rossi, Galli, Marzocchi, Fantini, Gamberini.*

DOMESTIC CUP 2007/08

COPPA TITANO

FIRST PHASE
(Played in Groups)

GROUP A
(14/9/07)
Juvenes/Dogana 2, San Giovanni 1
Cosmos 4, Fiorentino 3
(18/9/07)
Fiorentino 1, Juvenes/Dogana 1
San Giovanni 1, Faetano 0
(21/9/07)
Faetano 1, Juvenes/Dogana 3
Cosmos 5, San Giovanni 0
(24/10/07)
San Giovanni 1, Fiorentino 2
Faetano 1, Cosmos 3
(7/11/07)
Juvenes/Dogana 0, Cosmos 0
Fiorentino 1, Faetano 3
(20/1/08)
Fiorentino 0, Cosmos 1
San Giovanni 0, Juvenes/Dogana 2
(26/1/08)
Faetano 2, San Giovanni 0
Juvenes/Dogana 5, Fiorentino 0
(12/3/08)
San Giovanni 3, Cosmos 2
Juvenes/Dogana 0, Faetano 0
(18/3/08)
Cosmos 0, Faetano 1
(19/3/08)
Fiorentino 2, San Giovanni 3
(1/4/08)
Faetano 5, Fiorentino 2
(2/4/08)
Cosmos 0, Juvenes/Dogana 0

Final Standings
1 Juvenes/Dogana 16 pts;
2 Cosmos 14 pts;
3 Faetano 13 pts *(qualified)*
4 San Giovanni 9 pts;
5 Fiorentino 4 pts *(eliminated)*

GROUP B
(14/9/07)
Cailungo 1, Folgore/Falciano 1
(15/9/07)
Libertas 1, Tre Penne 2
(18/9/07)
Folgore/Falciano 1, La Fiorita 1
(19/9/07)
Tre Penne 0, Cailungo 1
(20/9/07)
Libertas 2, Folgore/Falciano 0
(21/9/07)
La Fiorita 2, Cailungo 2
(23/10/07)
Folgore/Falciano 1, Tre Penne 7
(24/10/07)
La Fiorita 2, Libertas 2
(6/11/07)
Cailungo 1, Libertas 0
Tre Penne 1, La Fiorita 0
(19/1/08)
Tre Penne 0, Libertas 1
(20/1/08)
Folgore/Falciano 0, Cailungo 2
(26/1/08)
Cailungo 2, Tre Penne 2
(27/1/08)
La Fiorita 2, Folgore/Falciano 0
(11/3/08)
Folgore/Falciano 0, Libertas 4
Cailungo 1, La Fiorita 2
(18/3/08)
Tre Penne 4, Folgore/Falciano 1
Libertas 4, La Fiorita 3
(1/4/08)
Libertas 0, Cailungo 1
(2/4/08)
La Fiorita 4, Tre Penne 2

Final Standings
1 Cailungo 15 pts;
2 Tre Penne 13 pts;
3 Libertas 13 pts *(qualified)*
4 La Fiorita 12 pts;
5 Folgore/Falciano 2 pts *(eliminated)*

GROUP C
(15/9/07)
Tre Fiori 1, Virtus 1
Murata 3, Pennarossa 1
(19/9/07)
Virtus 5, Domagnano 3
Pennarossa 0, Tre Fiori 5
(20/9/07)
Murata 1,Virtus 2
Domagnano 0, Tre Fiori 1
(23/10/07)
Domagnano 1, Murata 1
Virtus 2, Pennarossa 4
(6/11/07)
Tre Fiori 2, Murata 1
(7/11/07)
Pennarossa 2, Domagnano 2
(19/1/08)
Pennarossa 2, Murata 3
Virtus 0, Tre Fiori 1
(27/1/08)
Tre Fiori 2, Pennarossa 1
Domagnano 0, Virtus 0
(11/3/08)
Virtus 2, Murata 3
(12/3/08)
Tre Fiori 4, Domagnano 0
(19/3/08)
Murata 0, Domagnano 1
Pennarossa 5, Virtus 3
(1/4/08)
Domagnano 3, Pennarossa 2
(2/4/08)
Murata 2, Tre Fiori 0

Final Standings
1 Tre Fiori 19 pts;
2 Murata 13 pts *(qualified)*
3 Domagnano 9 pts;
4 Virtus 8 pts;
5 Pennarossa 7 pts *(eliminated)*

QUARTER-FINALS
(24/4/08)
Juvenes/Dogana 2 *(Gamberini 63, 83)*, Libertas 1 *(Algeri 77)*
Tre Fiori 4 *(Canarezza 83, Andreini 96, 109, Aruta 119)*, Tre Penne 2 *(Valentini 55, Bullini 68) (aet)*
Cailungo 1 *(Boschi 61)*, Faetano 2 *(Olivieri 18, Moretti 39)*
Murata 3 *(Di Giuli 73, Valentini 80, Protti 90)*, Cosmos 0

SEMI-FINALS
(28/4/08)
Juvenes/Dogana 1 *(Santini 49)*, Tre Fiori 1 *(Lisi 17) (aet; 6-5 on pens)*
Faetano 0, Murata 2 *(Protti 16, 80)*

FINAL
(2/5/08)
Stadio Olimpico, Serravalle
S.S. MURATA 1 *(Protti 20)*
AC JUVENES/DOGANA 0
Referee – *Rossi*
MURATA – *Scalabrelli, Raschi (Vitaioli 59), Albani N., D'Orsi, Fretta, Valentini, Teodorani, Bollini (Marani 66), Vannoni, Protti, Di Giuli (Gasperoni 83).*
JUVENES/DOGANA – *Montanari, Selva, Renzi, Marzocchi, Zonzini D., Rossini (Zonzini C. 57), Ceci (Vagnetti 83), Galli, Rossi, Fantini, Gamberini.*

A shortage of happy endings

The 2007/08 season was one of frustrating near-misses for Scottish teams – both at club and international level. Despite an encouraging level of collective progress in European competition and a series of famous victories against top-class foreign opponents, total satisfaction was lacking in most quarters.

Ultimately the fans with most to smile about were those of Celtic FC, who sealed a third straight Scottish Premier League title win under embattled manager Gordon Strachan. The Bhoys left it late, coming from behind to pip an overburdened and exhausted Rangers FC on the final day thanks chiefly to a couple of narrow Old Firm wins at Parkhead. Celtic's success at home followed another Jekyll and Hyde UEFA Champions League campaign, where, having qualified for the group stage with a penalty shoot-out win over FC Spartak Moskva, they continued to prove formidable adversaries at home and easy meat on their travels.

Meanwhile, the Scotland national team capped their historic win over France in Glasgow with an even more momentous 1-0 victory in Paris, yet still found themselves edged out of the UEFA EURO 2008™ qualification race by Les Bleus and world champions Italy.

Rangers, in their first full season back under the command of legendary manager Walter Smith, won both domestic knockout competitions and reached a European final for the first time in 36 years. But their 2-0 defeat in Manchester to FC Zenit St. Petersburg, coupled with the surrender of the SPL title to Celtic, left their huge support sharing in the disappointment of many other fan-bases up and down the land.

O'Donnell tragedy

Despite all the drama, the season was overshadowed by tragedy. On the afternoon of 29 December, Phil O'Donnell, the captain of Motherwell FC, collapsed and lost consciousness during a match against Dundee United FC. Despite efforts to revive him, both on the pitch and in hospital, the former Scotland international passed away a few hours later. He left behind a wife and four children, and his untimely death sent shockwaves through Scottish football.

Football inevitably took a back seat for a few days afterwards, with several games, including the Old Firm derby, being postponed, but as play resumed it began to look as if Celtic, O'Donnell's former club, would struggle to hold on to their SPL crown. Given their utter dominance of the previous two campaigns, not to mention a safe passage through to the first knockout round of the UEFA Champions League (while Rangers, calamitously, dropped into the UEFA Cup after a home defeat by Olympique Lyonnais), Strachan's team, starring Australian striker Scott McDonald, Irish winger Aiden McGeady and Polish goalkeeper Artur Boruc, were hot favourites to retain the title. They topped the table at

The late Motherwell captain, Phil O'Donnell

Scottish Football Association (SFA)

Hampden Park
GB-Glasgow G42 9AY
tel - +44 141 6166000
fax - +44 141 6166001
website - www.scottishfa.co.uk
email - info@scottishfa.co.uk
Year of Formation – 1873
President – George Peat
Chief Executive – Gordon Smith
Press Officer – Rob Shorthouse
Stadium - Hampden Park, Glasgow (52,054)

INTERNATIONAL TOURNAMENT APPEARANCES
FIFA World Cup - (8) 1954, 1958, 1974, 1978, 1982, 1986, 1990, 1998.
UEFA European Championship - (2) 1992, 1996.

TOP FIVE ALL-TIME CAPS
Kenny Dalglish (102); Jim Leighton (91); Alex McLeish (77); Paul McStay (76); Tommy Boyd (72)

TOP FIVE ALL-TIME GOALS
Kenny Dalglish & Denis Law (30); Hughie Gallacher (24); Lawrie Reilly (22), Ally McCoist (19)

NATIONAL TEAM RESULTS 2007/08

22/8/07	South Africa	H	Aberdeen	1-0	*Boyd (71)*
8/9/07	Lithuania (ECQ)	H	Glasgow	3-1	*Boyd (31), McManus (77), McFadden (83)*
12/9/07	France (ECQ)	A	Paris	1-0	*McFadden (64)*
13/10/07	Ukraine (ECQ)	H	Glasgow	3-1	*Miller (4), McCulloch (10), McFadden (68)*
17/10/07	Georgia (ECQ)	A	Tbilisi	0-2	
17/11/07	Italy (ECQ)	H	Glasgow	1-2	*Ferguson (65)*
26/3/08	Croatia	H	Glasgow	1-1	*Miller (30)*
30/5/08	Czech Republic	A	Prague	1-3	*Clarkson (85)*

New Year, but their Glaswegian arch-rivals swiftly overtook them and led for fully four months. By the time of the SPL split, Rangers were five points ahead.

UEFA Cup run

The Gers spent most of the season battling strongly on four fronts. They claimed the first part of what they hoped would be an unprecedented 'quadruple' when they defeated Dundee United on penalties in the League Cup final. Thereafter Europe took centre stage as Smith's resilient troops, marshalled at the back by towering Spanish defender Carlos Cuéllar and from the centre of the park by captain Barry Ferguson, staged a series of backs-to-the-wall UEFA Cup performances in various illustrious continental outposts, seeing off Panathinaikos FC, Werder Bremen, Sporting Clube de Portugal and, in a breathless, if goalless, semi-final penalty contest, ACF Fiorentina to book themselves a mid-May date in Manchester. The occasion would be marred by fan trouble in the city centre, where legions of ticketless fans had gathered, but the greater despair came inside the City of Manchester Stadium where Rangers, still banking heavily on their defence, were generally outplayed by Zenit and conceded twice in the second half to lose 2-0.

With the SPL title escaping their clutches a few days later, Rangers missed out on the two trophies that really mattered, and would find scant consolation in defeating rank outsiders Queen of the South FC 3-2 in the Scottish Cup final. The UEFA Cup run had been great fun while it lasted, but it led to dreadful fixture congestion, and the obligation to play so many matches over a short period – and with an injury-hit squad – effectively handed the domestic crown back to Celtic on a plate. Not that Celtic supporters saw it that way. Indeed, while Strachan's manner and methods continued to divide opinion among the Parkhead faithful, there was no questioning

ATIONAL TEAM APPEARANCES 2007/08

ch – Alex McLEISH	21/1/59		Rsa	LTU	FRA	UKR	GEO	ITA				
'1/08) George BURLEY	3/6/56								Cro	Cze	Caps	Goals
ȷ GORDON	31/12/82	Sunderland (ENG)	G	G	G	G	G	G	G	G	31	-
HUTTON	30/11/84	Rangers	D	D	D	D		D				
		/Tottenham (ENG)							D		7	-
hen McMANUS	10/9/82	Celtic	D	D	D	D	D	D	D	D58	13	1
ell ANDERSON	25/10/78	Sunderland (ENG)	D									
		/Plymouth (ENG)							s70		11	-
IcEVELEY	2/11/85	Derby (ENG)	D	D					s62		3	-
CALDWELL	12/4/82	Celtic	M57						D70	D	27	2
en FLETCHER	1/2/84	Man. United (ENG)	M	M	M26		M	M	M90	M	36	4
t BROWN	25/6/85	Celtic	M72	M	M	M76		M74	M66		9	-
es McFADDEN	14/4/83	Everton (ENG)	M46	s69	A76	A80	A	A			37	13
y O'CONNOR	7/5/83	Birmingham (ENG)	A68	A76	s76	s80					14	4
ny MILLER	23/12/79	Celtic	A68									
		/Derby (ENG)				A	A66	s74	A	A	37	11
hen PEARSON	2/10/82	Derby (ENG)	s46		s26	M	M66				10	-
/ ROBSON	7/11/78	Dundee United	s57									
		/Celtic								M83	2	-
ȷ BEATTIE	16/1/84	West Brom (ENG)	s68	s76			s66				7	1
3OYD	18/8/83	Rangers	s68	A			s66	s92	s72		14	7
TEALE	21/7/78	Derby (ENG)	s72	M69								
		/Plymouth (ENG)							s66		11	-
d WEIR	10/5/70	Rangers		D	D	D	D	D			60	1
McCULLOCH	14/5/78	Rangers		M76	M	M60		M92			15	1
ın MALONEY	24/1/83	Aston Villa (ENG)		s76		s76	M		M72	s68	11	1
am ALEXANDER	10/10/71	Burnley (ENG)			D		D		s90		32	-
/ FERGUSON	2/2/78	Rangers			M	M	M	M			43	3
HARTLEY	19/10/76	Celtic			M			M	M	M	19	1
NAYSMITH	16/11/78	Sheffield United (ENG)				D		D	D62	D	40	1
stian DAILLY	21/10/73	Southampton (ENG)				s60						
		/Rangers								s58	66	5
me MURTY	13/11/74	Reading (ENG)					D				4	-
en FLETCHER	26/3/87	Hibernian							A46		1	-
n RAE	28/11/77	Cardiff (WAL)							s46	M72	13	-
McNAUGHTON	28/8/82	Cardiff (WAL)								D90	4	-
es MORRISON	25/5/86	West Brom (ENG)								A68	1	-
d CLARKSON	10/9/85	Motherwell								s72	1	1
McCORMACK	18/8/86	Motherwell								s83	1	-
stophe BERRA	31/1/85	Hearts								s90	1	-

his team's remarkable tenacity and resolve. Even when the league seemed lost, Celtic refused to roll over, and they were ultimately rewarded with not only another championship triumph but also the club's first title hat-trick for 34 years.

In Europe, the first knockout round of the UEFA Champions League was Celtic's terminus for the second successive year. They added to their collection of famous home wins with last-gasp victories over AC Milan and FC Shakhtar Donetsk in the group stage, but the Bhoys were overwhelmed as a Lionel Messi-inspired FC Barcelona came calling in the early spring, falling to their first home loss in European competition since Barça's previous visit in 2004. Defeats without scoring in all four away fixtures confirmed Celtic's reputation as the weakest of all UEFA Champions League travellers.

Tartan Army torture

Rangers could maybe teach Celtic a thing or two about winning on foreign soil. Likewise Scotland after their extraordinary win in the Parc des Princes that completed a UEFA EURO 2008™ qualifying double over France. Unfortunately, however, it was not enough to end the country's long spell in the international wilderness. Although James McFadden's wonder goal in Paris was followed by a 3-1 win over Ukraine at Hampden, when push came to shove, Scotland – as so often in the past - were found wanting. A torrid 2-0 loss in Tbilisi set the stage for a must-win encounter with Italy at Hampden, but a late sucker-punch of a goal damned the Scots to glorious failure yet again.

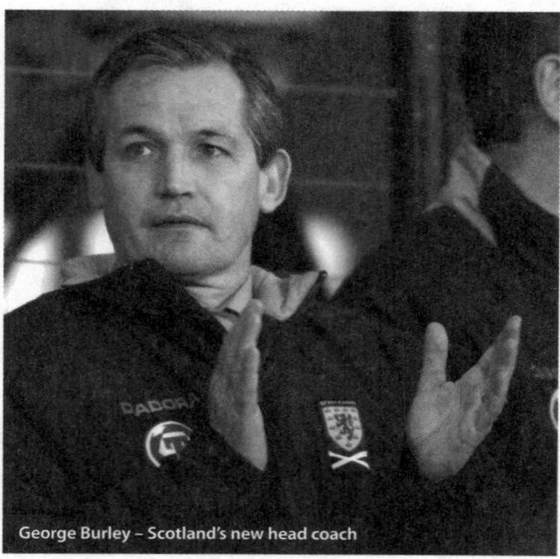

George Burley – Scotland's new head coach

Just as Walter Smith had abandoned the Tartan Army for club football, so too did Alex McLeish, who, with the qualification dream turned to dust, departed to take the reins at Birmingham City FC (with whom he would suffer relegation from the English Premier League). In to replace him, after a lengthy period of reflection, came former Heart of Midlothian FC manager George Burley. His tenure began with a decent 1-1 draw at home to Croatia but was followed by a 3-1 defeat in the Czech Republic.

Gretna grounded

The battle to avoid relegation from the SPL proved to be no such thing. Gretna FC, who had fought their way up from the Third Division under the auspices of multi-millionaire Brooks Mileson, were cast into severe difficulty when the benefactor mysteriously withdrew his financial support after a period of illness. Player after player left the debt-stricken, point-deducted club until a ramshackled but dedicated bunch of loan signings, youth-squad members and the odd dedicated pro saw them lurch towards the inevitable drop. Modest Lanarkshire outfit Hamilton Academical FC's impressive youth policy paid off as they won the race to replace Gretna, who subsequently withdrew from the league entirely.

Motherwell secured a welcome return to European football, their third-place finish a fitting tribute to their dearly departed captain and reward for the talent and dedication shown by manager Mark McGhee and his squad. McGhee's former club Aberdeen FC fell just short of European qualification after enjoying a memorable UEFA Cup campaign. The Dons squeezed through the group stage before going out to FC Bayern München, giving their fans a teasing reminder of a time when they were once a force in the European game.

Dundee United also missed out on Europe as Hibernian FC opted to take up Scotland's fifth continental spot in the UEFA Intertoto Cup. Slot number four, in the UEFA Cup, went for the third season running to losing Scottish Cup finalists from outside the top flight, on this occasion Queen of the South. Having eliminated Celtic's conquerors Aberdeen 4-3 in an epic semi-final, the underdogs from Dumfries provided a real scare for Rangers in the Hampden showpiece, coming back from the dead with two goals in quick succession before eventually losing to a second goal of the afternoon from the Gers' underused goal-machine Kris Boyd, who had also scored both of his team's goals, and the decisive penalty, in the League Cup final two months earlier.

DOMESTIC LEAGUE 2007/08

OTTISH PREMIER LEAGUE FINAL TABLE

		Home					Away					Total					
	Pld	W	D	L	F	A	W	D	L	F	A	W	D	L	F	A	Pts
eltic FC	38	14	4	1	42	7	14	1	4	42	19	28	5	5	84	26	89
angers FC	38	18	0	1	50	10	9	5	5	34	23	27	5	6	84	33	86
lotherwell FC	38	9	4	6	30	26	9	2	8	20	20	18	6	14	50	46	60
berdeen FC	38	11	5	4	33	21	4	3	11	17	37	15	8	15	50	58	53
undee United FC	38	9	6	4	26	14	5	4	10	27	33	14	10	14	53	47	52
ibernian FC	38	10	5	4	34	22	4	5	10	15	23	14	10	14	49	45	52
alkirk FC	38	8	6	5	21	16	5	4	10	24	33	13	10	15	45	49	49
eart of Midlothian FC	38	8	4	7	27	26	5	5	9	20	29	13	9	16	47	55	48
verness Caledonian histle FC	38	9	2	8	32	28	4	2	13	19	34	13	4	21	51	62	43
aint Mirren FC	38	7	4	8	17	27	3	7	9	9	27	10	11	17	26	54	41
ilmarnock FC	38	7	5	7	26	23	3	5	11	13	29	10	10	18	39	52	40
retna FC	38	4	3	11	18	34	1	5	14	14	49	5	8	25	32	83	13

Gretna – 10 pts deducted.
ue splits into top and bottom halves after the 33rd game, with each team playing five further matches sively against clubs from its half of the table.

TOP GOALSCORERS

25 Scott McDONALD (Celtic)

15 Jan VENNEGOOR OF HESSELINK (Celtic)

14 Kris BOYD (Rangers)
Christopher PORTER (Motherwell)

13 Steven FLETCHER (Hibernian)
Noel HUNT (Dundee United)
Barry ROBSON (Dundee United/Celtic)

12 David CLARKSON (Motherwell)
Jean-Claude DARCHEVILLE (Rangers)
Lee MILLER (Aberdeen)

CLUB-BY-CLUB

ABERDEEN FC

Manager - Jimmy Calderwood

Founded - 1903

MAJOR HONOURS: UEFA Cup Winners' Cup - (1) 1983; EFA Super Cup - (1) 1983; Scottish League - (4) 1955, 1980, 1984, 1985; Scottish Cup - (7) 1947, 1970, 1982, 1983, 1984, 1986, 1990; Scottish League Cup - (5) 1956, 1977, 1986, 1990, 1996.

)07

8	Dundee United	a	0-1	
/8	Hearts	h	1-1	*Nicholson*
/8	Celtic	h	1-3	*Brewster*
/8	Hibernian	a	3-3	*Brewster 2, Smith Ja.*
9	Kilmarnock	a	1-0	*Miller*
/9	Motherwell	h	1-2	*Smith Ja.*
/9	Rangers	a	0-3	
/9	Gretna	h	2-0	*Diamond, Smith Ja.*
10	St Mirren	h	4-0	*Severin 2 (2p), Miller 2*
/10	Inverness	a	2-1	*Young, og (Tokely)*
/10	Falkirk	h	1-1	*Severin (p)*
11	Dundee United	h	2-0	*Aluko, Miller*
/11	Hearts	a	1-4	*De Visscher*
/11	Celtic	a	0-3	
12	Hibernian	h	3-1	*Miller, Clark, Young*
12	Kilmarnock	h	2-1	*Nicholson (p), Miller*
/12	Motherwell	a	0-3	
/12	Rangers	h	1-1	*Miller*
/12	Gretna	a	1-1	*Lovell*
/12	St Mirren	a	1-0	*Lovell*

)08

1	Inverness	h	1-0	*Nicholson (p)*
1	Falkirk	a	0-0	
/1	Dundee United	a	0-3	
/1	Hearts	h	0-1	
/2	Celtic	h	1-5	*Miller*
/2	Hibernian	a	1-3	*Diamond*
24/2	Kilmarnock	a	1-3	*og (Combe)*
27/2	Motherwell	h	1-1	*Diamond*
1/3	Rangers	a	1-3	*Lovell*
15/3	Gretna	h	3-0	*Maguire, Miller (p), Nicholson*
22/3	St Mirren	h	1-1	*Mair*
29/3	Inverness	a	4-3	*Aluko, Nicholson, Miller, Maguire*
7/4	Falkirk	h	2-1	*Maguire 2*
19/4	Celtic	a	0-1	
26/4	Hibernian	h	2-1	*Mackie, Miller (p)*
3/5	Dundee United	h	2-1	*Foster, Touzani*
10/5	Motherwell	a	1-2	*Aluko*
22/5	Rangers	h	2-0	*Miller, Mackie*

No	Name	Nat	Pos	Aps	(s)	Gls
26	Sone ALUKO	ENG	A	10	(10)	3
23	Craig BREWSTER		A	2	(1)	3
23	David BUS	NED	D	3	(3)	
3	Richard BYRNE	IRL	D	11	(2)	
38	Gary CARROLL		A			
11	Chris CLARK		M	17	(1)	1
21	Andrew CONSIDINE		D	21	(1)	
36	Jonathan CRAWFORD		D			
24	Jeffrey DE VISSCHER	NED	M	13	(9)	1
5	Alexander DIAMOND		D	26	(0)	3
11	Stuart DUFF		M	6	(4)	
14	Richard FOSTER		M	27	(6)	1
2	Michael HART		D	18	(0)	
44	Ryan JACK		M			
30	Greg KELLY		G			
1	Jamie LANGFIELD		G	25		
9	Steven LOVELL	ENG	A	7	(15)	3
10	Darren MACKIE		A	13	(6)	2
22	Christopher MAGUIRE		A	14	(14)	4
18	Lee MAIR		D	15	(3)	1

28	Alan MAYBURY	IRL	D	13		
4	Jackie McNAMARA		D	12	(5)	
29	Neil McVITIE		D			
16	Lee MILLER		A	32	(4)	12
8	Barry NICHOLSON		M	38		5
39	Peter PAWLETT		M			
42	Scott ROSS		D			
6	Scott SEVERIN		M	33	(2)	3
17	Daniel SMITH	ENG	D	1	(2)	
7	Jamie SMITH		M	16	(1)	3
25	Jonathan SMITH	ENG	A		(1)	
33	Stuart SMITH		M			
20	Derek SOUTAR		G	13		
15	Karim TOUZANI	NED	D	8	(6)	1
27	Josh WALKER	ENG	M	3	5	
19	Derek YOUNG		M	21	(3)	2

CELTIC FC

Manager - Gordon Strachan

Founded - 1888

MAJOR HONOURS: European Champion Clubs' Cup - (1) 1967; Scottish League - (42) 1893, 1894, 1896, 1898, 1905, 1906, 1907, 1908, 1909, 1910, 1914, 1915, 1916, 1917, 1919, 1922, 1925, 1936, 1938, 1954, 1966, 1967, 1968, 1969, 1970, 1971, 1972, 1973, 1974, 1977, 1979, 1981, 1982, 1986, 1988, 1998, 2001, 2002, 2004, 2006, 2007, 2008; Scottish Cup - (34) 1892, 1899, 1900, 1904, 1907, 1908, 1911, 1912, 1914, 1923, 1925, 1927, 1931, 1933, 1937, 1951, 1954, 1965, 1967, 1969, 1971, 1972, 1974, 1975, 1977, 1980, 1985, 1988, 1989, 1995, 2001, 2004, 2005, 2007; Scottish League Cup - (13) 1957, 1958, 1966, 1967, 1968, 1969, 1970, 1975, 1983, 1998, 2000, 2001, 2006.

2007

5/8	Kilmarnock	h	0-0	
11/8	Falkirk	a	4-1	*og (Milne), Miller, Nakamura, Vennegoor of Hesselink*
19/8	Aberdeen	a	3-1	*Donati, Miller 2*
25/8	Hearts	h	5-0	*og (Berra), Donati, Brown, Vennegoor of Hesselink (p), Nakamura*
2/9	St Mirren	a	5-1	*Brown, McDonald, Vennegoor of Hesselink, og (Miranda), McManus*
15/9	Inverness	h	5-0	*Vennegoor of Hesselink 2, Donati, Nakamura, og (McGuire)*
23/9	Hibernian	a	2-3	*McGeady, Caldwell*
26/9	Dundee United	h	3-0	*McDonald 3*
7/10	Gretna	a	2-1	*Killen, McDonald*
20/10	Rangers	a	0-3	
27/10	Motherwell	h	3-0	*McDonald 3 (1p)*
3/11	Kilmarnock	a	2-1	*McDonald 2*
24/11	Aberdeen	h	3-0	*Vennegoor of Hesselink, McGeady, McDonald*
1/12	Hearts	a	1-1	*McDonald*
8/12	St Mirren	h	1-1	*Riordan*
11/12	Falkirk	h	4-0	*McDonald (p), McGeady 3*
16/12	Inverness	a	2-3	*Vennegoor of Hesselink 2*
22/12	Hibernian	h	1-1	*Jarošík*
26/12	Dundee United	a	2-0	*Vennegoor of Hesselink, McManus*
29/12	Gretna	h	3-0	*McDonald, Brown, McGeady*

2008

19/1	Kilmarnock	h	1-0	*og (Corrigan)*
27/1	Falkirk	a	1-0	*McDonald*
10/2	Aberdeen	a	5-1	*Nakamura, McGeady, McDonald 2, Robson*
16/2	Hearts	h	3-0	*Vennegoor of Hesselir McDonald, Hinkel*
24/2	St Mirren	a	1-0	*Nakamura*
27/2	Inverness	h	2-1	*McDonald, Samaras*
1/3	Hibernian	a	2-0	*Naylor, Samaras*
12/3	Dundee United	h	0-0	
23/3	Gretna	a	3-0	*McDonald, Vennegoo of Hesselink, Samaras*
29/3	Rangers	a	0-1	
5/4	Motherwell	h	0-1	
13/4	Motherwell	a	4-1	*McManus, McDonald, Vennegoor of Hesselink*
16/4	Rangers	h	2-1	*Nakamura, Vennegoo of Hesselink*
19/4	Aberdeen	h	1-0	*Samaras*
27/4	Rangers	h	3-2	*McDonald 2, Robson (*
3/5	Motherwell	a	2-1	*McDonald, Samaras*
11/5	Hibernian	h	2-0	*McManus, McDonald*
22/5	Dundee United	a	1-0	*Vennegoor of Hesselin*

No	Name	Nat	Pos	Aps	(s)	Gls
6	Bobo BALDÉ	GUI	D	4		
1	Artur BORUC	POL	G	30		
21	Mark BROWN		G	8		
8	Scott BROWN		M	31	(3)	3
52	Paul CADDIS		D		(2)	
5	Gary CALDWELL		D	35		1
54	Ryan CONROY		M	2		
18	Massimo DONATI	ITA	M	22	(3)	3
11	Paul HARTLEY		M	23	(4)	
2	Andreas HINKEL	GER	D	16		1
23	Ben HUTCHINSON	ENG	A		(2)	
20	Jiří JAROŠÍK	CZE	M	6	(2)	1
41	John KENNEDY		D	5	(2)	
33	Christopher KILLEN	NZL	A	2	(18)	1
27	Scott McDONALD	AUS	A	35	(1)	25
46	Aiden McGEADY	IRL	M	35	(1)	7
55	Paul McGOWAN		A		(1)	
44	Stephen McMANUS		D	37		4
9	Kenny MILLER		A	1	(1)	3
25	Shunsuke NAKAMURA	JPN	M	24	(2)	6
3	Lee NAYLOR	ENG	D	33		1
45	James O'BRIEN	IRL	M		(1)	
48	Darren O'DEA	IRL	D	3	(3)	
24	Jean-Joël PERRIER-DOUMBÉ	CMR	D	2		
17	Steven PRESSLEY		D	5		
14	Derek RIORDAN		A	2	(6)	1
19	Barry ROBSON		M	9	(6)	2
9	Giorgos SAMARAS	GRE	A	5	(11)	5
26	Cillian SHERIDAN	IRL	A		(1)	
15	Evander SNO	NED	M	3	(9)	
10	Jan VENNEGOOR OF HESSELINK	NED	A	31	(1)	15
12	Mark WILSON		D	8	(3)	
7	Maciej ŻURAWSKI	POL	A	1	(4)	

DUNDEE UNITED FC

Manager - Craig Levein

Founded - 1909

MAJOR HONOURS: Scottish League - (1) 1983; Scottish Cup - (1) 1994; Scottish League Cup - (2) 1980, 1981.

2007

4/8	Aberdeen	h	1-0	*Robertson D.*
13/8	Kilmarnock	a	1-2	*Hunt*
18/8	Hibernian	h	0-0	
25/8	Inverness	a	3-0	*Dillon, Robson 2 (2p)*
1/9	Falkirk	h	2-0	*Hunt, Robson*
16/9	St Mirren	h	2-0	*Hunt, Robertson J.*
22/9	Gretna	a	2-3	*Buaben, Wilkie*

/9	Celtic	a	0-3	
10	Motherwell	h	1-0	*Dods*
/10	Hearts	a	3-1	*Robertson J. 2, Robson (p)*
/10	Rangers	h	2-1	*Wilkie, Robson (p)*
11	Aberdeen	a	0-2	
/11	Kilmarnock	h	2-0	*Hunt, Bauben*
/11	Hibernian	a	2-2	*Robertson D. 2*
12	Inverness	h	0-1	
12	Falkirk	a	0-3	
/12	St Mirren	a	3-0	*Robertson D., Hunt, Flood*
/12	Gretna	h	1-2	*Hunt*
/12	Celtic	h	0-2	
/12	Motherwell	a	3-5	*Robertson D., Hunt 2*
08				
1	Hearts	h	4-1	*Robson 3 (2p), Hunt*
1	Rangers	a	0-2	
/1	Aberdeen	h	3-0	*Hunt, Robson 2*
/1	Kilmarnock	a	2-1	*Robson, Conway*
2	Hibernian	h	1-1	*Hunt (p)*
/2	Inverness	a	1-1	*Buaben*
/2	Falkirk	h	0-0	
/2	St Mirren	h	1-1	*Dillon*
3	Gretna	a	3-0	*Kenneth, Gomis, Robertson D.*
/3	Celtic	a	0-0	
/3	Motherwell	h	2-0	*Swanson, De Vries*
/3	Hearts	a	0-1	
4	Rangers	h	3-3	*Kalvenes, Hunt, og (Cuéllar)*
/4	Hibernian	h	1-1	*Hunt (p)*
/4	Motherwell	a	2-2	*og (Craigan), Wilkie*
5	Aberdeen	a	1-2	*Swanson*
/5	Rangers	a	1-3	*De Vries*
/5	Celtic	h	0-1	

Name	Nat	Pos	Aps	(s)	Gls
Prince BUABEN	GHA	M	20	(4)	3
Greg CAMERON		M	1	(2)	
Craig CONWAY		M	7	(8)	1
Jonathan DALY	IRL	A	3	(6)	
Mark DE VRIES	NED	A	11	(3)	2
Sean DILLON	IRL	D	33		2
Darren DODS		D	33		1
Stuart DUFF		M	4	5	
Willo FLOOD	IRL	M	33	(3)	1
Morgaro GOMIS	FRA	M	36		1
David GOODWILLIE		A		(2)	
Daniel GRAINGER	ENG	D	12	(2)	
Noel HUNT	IRL	A	34	(2)	13
Christian KALVENES	NOR	D	18	(1)	1
Gary KENNETH		D	14	(5)	1
Mark KERR		M	24	(6)	
Mihael KOVAČEVIĆ	SUI	D	4		
Euan McLEAN		G	5	(1)	
Fraser MILLIGAN		M		(1)	
James O'BRIEN	IRL	M	5	(5)	
Eric ODHIAMBO	ENG	A	1	(3)	
Steven ROBB		M	3	(9)	
David ROBERTSON		M	16	(4)	6
Jordan ROBERTSON	ENG	A	12	(2)	3
Barry ROBSON		M	21		11
Johhny RUSSELL		A		(2)	
Daniel SWANSON		M	4	(8)	2
Grzegorz SZAMOTULSKI	POL	G	18		
Lee WILKIE		D	31		3
Łukasz ZAŁUSKA	POL	G	15		

FALKIRK FC

Manager - John Hughes

Founded - 1876

MAJOR HONOURS: Scottish Cup - (2) 1913, 1957

2007				
4/8	Gretna	a	4-0	*Higdon 2, Moutinho, Latapy*
11/8	Celtic	h	1-4	*Higdon*
18/8	Rangers	a	2-7	*Riera, Barrett*
25/8	St Mirren	h	0-1	
1/9	Dundee United	a	0-2	
15/9	Hibernian	h	1-1	*Moutinho*
22/9	Motherwell	h	1-0	*Latapy*
29/9	Inverness	a	2-4	*Milne, Arfield*
6/10	Hearts	a	2-4	*Barrett, Moutinho*
20/10	Kilmarnock	h	1-1	*Finnigan*
28/10	Aberdeen	a	1-1	*Cregg*
3/11	Gretna	h	2-0	*Barr, Barrett*
24/11	Rangers	h	1-3	*Moutinho*
1/12	St Mirren	a	5-1	*Moutinho 2, Thomson, Barrett, Finnigan*
8/12	Dundee United	h	3-0	*Moutinho, Barrett, Higdon*
11/12	Celtic	a	0-4	
15/12	Hibernian	a	1-1	*Barrett*
22/12	Motherwell	a	3-0	*Higdon 2, Cregg*
26/12	Inverness	h	1-0	*Aafjes*
29/12	Hearts	h	2-1	*Finnigan, Higdon*
2008				
2/1	Kilmarnock	a	1-0	*Finnigan*
5/1	Aberdeen	h	0-0	
19/1	Gretna	a	0-2	
27/1	Celtic	h	0-1	
9/2	Rangers	a	0-2	
16/2	St Mirren	h	4-0	*Arfield 2, Cregg 2*
23/2	Dundee United	a	0-0	
27/2	Hibernian	h	0-2	
1/3	Motherwell	h	0-0	
15/3	Inverness	a	1-0	*Clarke*
22/3	Hearts	a	0-0	
29/3	Kilmarnock	h	0-0	
7/4	Aberdeen	a	1-2	*Finnigan*
19/4	Gretna	h	0-0	
26/4	St Mirren	a	0-1	
5/5	Hearts	h	2-1	*Scobbie, Finnigan*
10/5	Inverness	h	2-1	*Higdon, Finnigan*
17/5	Kilmarnock	a	1-2	*Moutinho*

No	Name	Nat	Pos	Aps	(s)	Gls
14	Gerard AAFJES	NED	D	23	(3)	1
18	Brian ALLISON		D	1	(2)	
16	Scott ARFIELD		M	31	(4)	3
20	Darren BARR		D	33		1
9	Graham BARRETT	IRL	A	26	(7)	6
12	Stephen BRADLEY	IRL	M	1	(2)	
8	Billy CLARKE	IRL	A	1	(7)	1
26	Liam CRAIG		M		(6)	
4	Patrick CREGG	IRL	M	36		4
21	Carl FINNIGAN	ENG	A	19	(12)	7
11	Michael HIGDON	ENG	A	24	(4)	8
3	Dean HOLDEN	NIR	D	20		
1	Timothy KRUL	NED	G	22		
10	Russell LATAPY	TRI	M	12	(20)	2
6	Kevin McBRIDE		M	15		
15	Kenneth MILNE		D	24	(4)	1
22	Christopher MITCHELL		D	3	(2)	
23	Kevin MOFFAT		A		(2)	
7	Pedro MOUTINHO	POR	A	29	(8)	8
17	Robert OLEJNIK	AUT	G	12	(1)	
19	Arnau RIERA	ESP	M	13	(6)	1

SCOTLAND

27	Dayne ROBERTSON		A		(1)	
5	Jack ROSS		D	23		
33	Thomas SCOBBIE		D	29	(4)	1
24	Mark STEWART		A		(3)	
40	Shane SUPPLE	IRL	G	4		
8	Steven THOMSON		M	17	(1)	1
25	Roman WALLNER	AUT	A		(2)	

GRETNA FC

Manager - Rowan Alexander; (6/11/07) David Irons; (19/2/08) Mick Wadsworth (ENG)

Founded - 1946

2007				
4/8	Falkirk	h	0-4	
11/8	Hibernian	a	2-4	*Yantorno, McMenamin*
18/8	Hearts	a	1-1	*Barr*
25/8	Motherwell	h	1-2	*Osman*
1/9	Rangers	a	0-4	
15/9	Kilmarnock	h	1-2	*Skelton*
22/9	Dundee United	h	3-2	*Cowan 2, Jenkins*
29/9	Aberdeen	a	0-2	
7/10	Celtic	h	1-2	*Yantorno*
20/10	St Mirren	a	0-1	
27/10	Inverness	h	0-4	
3/11	Falkirk	a	0-2	
10/11	Hibernian	h	0-1	
25/11	Hearts	h	1-1	*og (Kingston)*
1/12	Motherwell	a	0-3	
15/12	Kilmarnock	a	3-3	*Skelton, Grainger (p), Horwood*
22/12	Dundee United	a	2-1	*Deuchar, Deverdics*
26/12	Aberdeen	h	1-1	*Jenkins*
29/12	Celtic	a	0-3	
2008				
5/1	Inverness	a	0-3	
16/1	Rangers	h	1-2	*Deuchar*
19/1	Falkirk	h	2-0	*Deuchar, Murray*
9/2	Hearts	a	0-2	
13/2	Hibernian	a	2-4	*Skelton, Deuchar*
16/2	Motherwell	h	1-3	*McGill*
24/2	Rangers	a	2-4	*Deuchar 2*
27/2	Kilmarnock	h	4-2	*Deverdics, Meynell, Barr, Buscher*
6/3	Dundee United	h	0-3	
15/3	Aberdeen	a	0-3	
23/3	Celtic	h	0-3	
29/3	St Mirren	a	0-2	
5/4	Inverness	h	1-2	*Barr*
9/4	St Mirren	h	0-0	
19/4	Falkirk	a	0-0	
26/4	Kilmarnock	a	1-1	*Barr*
3/5	Inverness	a	1-6	*Hogg*
10/5	St Mirren	a	0-0	
13/5	Hearts	h	1-0	*Skelton*

No	Name	Nat	Pos	Aps	(s)	Gls
7	Ryan BALDACCHINO	ENG	M	4	(4)	
2	Craig BARR		D	22	(4)	4
30	Mickaël BUSCHER	FRA	A	8	(9)	1
33	Anthony CAIG	ENG	G	7		
5	Martin CANNING		D		(1)	
29	Aurélien COLLIN	FRA	D	18	(1)	
4	David COWAN	ENG	D	10	(1)	2
14	Kenneth DEUCHAR		A	11	(4)	6
20	Nicky DEVERDICS	ENG	M	20	(5)	2
45	Nathan FISHER	ENG	D		(1)	
24	Greg FLEMING		G	28		
8	James GRAFY			6	(2)	
10	David GRAHAM		A	2	(8)	
3	Daniel GRAINGER	ENG	D	9	(1)	1
42	Rostyn GRIFFITHS	AUS	M	9	(3)	
36	Daniel HALL	ENG	D	14	(1)	
17	Steven HOGG	ENG	M	4	(7)	1
31	Evan HORWOOD	ENG	D	15		1
21	Christopher INNES		D	21		
15	Allan JENKINS		M	16	(4)	2
38	John Paul KISSOCK	ENG	M	10	(1)	
40	Artur KRYSIAK	POL	G	3	(1)	
35	Henry MAKINWA	NGA	A	7	(6)	
12	Brendan McGILL	IRL	M	15	(5)	1
16	Ryan McGUFFIE		M	5	(4)	
19	Fraser McLAREN		A		(3)	
9	Colin McMENAMIN		A	7	(5)	1
41	Rhys MEYNELL	ENG	D	14	(2)	1
26	Paul MURRAY	ENG	M	31	(1)	1
37	Kyle NAUGHTON	ENG	D	18		
27	Abdul OSMAN	ENG	M	16	(2)	1
18	Erik PAARTALU	AUS	M	3	(6)	
43	Erik SCHULTZ-EKLUND	SWE	M		(1)	
11	Gavin SKELTON	ENG	M	37	(1)	4
46	Nathan TAYLOR	ENG	A		(6)	
39	Ben WILKINSON	ENG	M	7	(6)	
28	Fabián YANTORNO	URU	A	21		2

HEART OF MIDLOTHIAN FC

Manager - Anatoly Korobochka (UKR) & Stephen Frail; (1/1/08) Stephen Frail

Founded - 1874

MAJOR HONOURS: Scottish League - (4) 1895, 1897, 1958, 1960; Scottish Cup - (7) 1891, 1896, 1901, 1906, 1956, 1998, 2006; Scottish League Cup - (4) 1955, 1959, 1960, 1963.

2007				
6/8	Hibernian	h	0-1	
12/8	Aberdeen	a	1-1	*Stewart*
18/8	Gretna	h	1-1	*Driver*
25/8	Celtic	a	0-5	
3/9	Motherwell	a	2-0	*Kingston, Velička*
15/9	Rangers	h	4-2	*Driver, Tall, Stewart (p), Ivaškevičius*
22/9	Inverness	a	1-2	*og (Black)*
30/9	St Mirren	a	3-1	*Driver, Stewart (p), Velička*
6/10	Falkirk	h	4-2	*Ksanavičius, Žaliūkas, Velička, Nadé*
20/10	Dundee United	h	1-3	*Kingston*
27/10	Kilmarnock	a	1-3	*Tall*
4/11	Hibernian	a	1-1	*Nadé*
11/11	Aberdeen	h	4-1	*Driver, Velička, Tall, Nadé*
25/11	Gretna	a	1-1	*Kingston*
1/12	Celtic	h	1-1	*Velička (p)*
8/12	Motherwell	h	1-2	*Driver*
15/12	Rangers	a	1-2	*Velička*
22/12	Inverness	h	2-3	*Berra, Velička (p)*
26/12	St Mirren	h	0-1	
29/12	Falkirk	a	1-2	*Palazuelos*
2008				
2/1	Dundee United	a	1-4	*Berra*
5/1	Kilmarnock	h	1-1	*Velička*
19/1	Hibernian	h	1-0	*Velička*
26/1	Aberdeen	a	1-0	*Nadé*
9/2	Gretna	h	2-0	*Velička 2 (1p)*
16/2	Celtic	a	0-3	
23/2	Motherwell	a	1-0	*og (Craigan)*
27/2	Rangers	h	0-4	
1/3	Inverness	a	3-0	*Karapidis, Elliott 2*
15/3	St Mirren	a	1-1	*Mikoliūnas*
22/3	Falkirk	h	0-0	
29/3	Dundee United	h	1-0	*Kingston*

4	Kilmarnock	a	0-0	
/4	St Mirren	h	3-2	*Jónsson, Glen, Kingston*
/4	Inverness	h	1-0	*Glen*
5	Falkirk	a	1-2	*Česnauskis*
/5	Kilmarnock	h	0-2	
/5	Gretna	a	0-1	

Name	Nat	Pos	Aps	(s)	Gls
Steven BANKS	ENG	G	28		
Anthony BASSO	FRA	G	7		
Ričardas BENIUŠIS	LTU	A	1	(7)	
Christophe BERRA		D	35		2
Deividas ČESNAUSKIS	LTU	M	10	(3)	1
Andrew DRIVER	ENG	M	23	(2)	5
Calum ELLIOTT		A	14	(10)	2
Gary GLEN		A	5	(1)	2
José GONÇALVES	POR	D	23		
Kęstutis IVAŠKEVIČIUS	LTU	M	8	(9)	1
Eggert JÓNSSON	ISL	M	25	(3)	1
Tomas KANČELSKIS	LTU	D	1		
Hristos KARAPIDIS	GRE	D	15	(1)	1
Laryea KINGSTON	GHA	M	16	(2)	5
Audrius KSANAVIČIUS	LTU	M	17	(5)	1
Eduardas KURSKIS	LTU	G	3		
Juho MÄKELÄ	FIN	A	1	(4)	
Neil McCANN		M		(3)	
Ryan McGOWAN	AUS	D		(1)	
Saulius MIKOLIŪNAS	LTU	M	14	(11)	1
Jamie MOLE	ENG	A	2	(3)	
Christian NADÉ	FRA	A	17	(7)	4
Robbie NEILSON		D	33		
Rubén PALAZUELOS	ESP	M	24	(5)	1
Mauricio PINILLA	CHI	A		(2)	
Michal POSPÍŠIL	CZE	A		(8)	
Scott ROBINSON		A		(1)	
Fernando SCREPIS	ARG	M	3	(2)	
Michael STEWART		M	23	(5)	3
Ibrahim TALL	SEN	D	12		3
Jason THOMSON		D	5		
Andrius VELIČKA	LTU	A	16	(4)	11
Lee WALLACE		M	16	(5)	
Marius ŽALIŪKAS	LTU	M	21	(5)	1

HIBERNIAN FC

Manager - John Collins; (20/12/07) (Tommy Craig); (10/1/08) Mixu Paatelainen (FIN)

Founded - 1875

AJOR HONOURS: Scottish League - (4) 1903, 1948, 1951, 1952; Scottish Cup - (2) 1887, 1902; Scottish League Cup - (3) 1973, 1992, 2007.

)07				
8	Hearts	a	1-0	*Kerr*
/8	Gretna	h	4-2	*Zemmama 2, Fletcher, McCann*
/8	Dundee United	a	0-0	
/8	Aberdeen	h	3-3	*Zemmama, Fletcher, Shiels*
9	Inverness	h	1-0	*Fletcher (p)*
/9	Falkirk	a	1-1	*Donaldson (p)*
/9	Celtic	h	3-2	*Fletcher, Gathuessi, Shiels*
/9	Kilmarnock	h	4-1	*Donaldson 3 (2p), Antoine-Curier*
'10	Rangers	a	1-0	*Murphy*
)/10	Motherwell	a	1-2	*Fletcher (p)*
'/10	St Mirren	h	0-1	
'11	Hearts	h	1-1	*og (Berra)*
)/11	Gretna	a	1-0	*Fletcher*
/11	Dundee United	h	2-2	*Benjelloun, Antoine-Curier (p)*
2/12	Aberdeen	a	1-3	*Fletcher*
8/12	Inverness	a	0-2	
15/12	Falkirk	h	1-1	*Donaldson (p)*
22/12	Celtic	a	1-1	*Murphy*
26/12	Kilmarnock	a	1-2	*Shiels (p)*
29/12	Rangers	h	1-2	*Zemmama*
2008				
5/1	St Mirren	a	1-2	*Antoine-Curier*
19/1	Hearts	a	0-1	
9/2	Dundee United	a	1-1	*Rankin*
13/2	Gretna	h	4-2	*Nish, Fletcher 3 (1p)*
17/2	Aberdeen	h	3-1	*Zemmama, Shiels, Fletcher*
23/2	Inverness	h	2-0	*Nish, Fletcher*
27/2	Falkirk	a	2-0	*og (Ross), Rankin*
1/3	Celtic	h	0-2	
12/3	Motherwell	h	1-0	*Nish*
15/3	Kilmarnock	h	2-0	*Morais, Fletcher*
22/3	Rangers	a	1-2	*Shiels*
29/3	Motherwell	a	0-1	
5/4	St Mirren	h	2-0	*Nish, Zemmama*
20/4	Dundee United	a	1-1	*Shiels*
26/4	Aberdeen	a	1-2	*Shiels*
4/5	Rangers	h	0-0	
11/5	Celtic	a	0-2	
22/5	Motherwell	h	0-2	

No	Name	Nat	Pos	Aps	(s)	Gls
27	Mickaël ANTOINE-CURIER	FRA	A	8	(5)	3
10	Abdessalam BENJELLOUN	MAR	A	5	(10)	1
14	Guillaume BEUZELIN	FRA	M	25	2	
28	Ross CAMPBELL		A	2	(3)	
24	Martin CANNING		D	11		
23	Ross CHISHOLM		M	13	(5)	
8	Clayton DONALDSON	ENG	A	11	(7)	5
9	Steven FLETCHER		A	29	(3)	13
19	Thierry GATHUESSI	CMR	D	18	(5)	1
29	Damon GRAY	ENG	A		(2)	
33	Paul HANLON		D	5	(2)	
4	Chris HOGG	ENG	D	34		
24	Torben JONELEIT	GER	D		(2)	
5	Robert JONES	ENG	D	30		
6	Brian KERR		M	23	(2)	1
50	Yves Makubu MA-KALAMBAY	BEL	G	29		
2	Kevin McCANN		D	19		1
25	Darren McCORMACK		D	2	(2)	
21	Andrew McNEIL		G	9	(1)	
12	Filipe MORAIS	POR	M	19	(9)	1
3	David MURPHY	ENG	D	17		2
26	Ian MURRAY		M	14	(1)	
24	Colin NISH		A	13	(2)	4
15	Patrick NOUBISSIE	FRA	M	4		
11	Alan O'BRIEN	IRL	M	6	(17)	
20	John RANKIN		M	15	(2)	2
22	Dean SHIELS	NIR	M	14	(8)	7
16	Lewis STEVENSON		M	18	(3)	
3	Abderraouf ZARABI	ALG	D	7		
7	Merouane ZEMMAMA	MAR	M	18	(10)	6

INVERNESS CALEDONIAN THISTLE FC

Manager - Charlie Christie; (20/8/07) (Donald Park); (27/8/07) Craig Brewster

Founded - 1994

2007				
4/8	Rangers	h	0-3	
11/8	Motherwell	a	1-2	*Tokely*
18/8	St Mirren	a	1-2	*Cowie*
25/8	Dundee United	h	0-3	
1/9	Hibernian	a	0-1	

15/9	Celtic	a	0-5	
22/9	Hearts	h	2-1	*Wyness, Brewster*
29/9	Falkirk	h	4-2	*Wyness 2, Duncan, Black*
6/10	Kilmarnock	a	2-2	*og (Ford), Cowie*
21/10	Aberdeen	h	1-2	*Wyness*
27/10	Gretna	a	4-0	*Wyness (p), Cowie, Wilson, McBain*
3/11	Rangers	a	0-2	
10/11	Motherwell	h	0-3	
24/11	St Mirren	h	1-0	*Cowie*
1/12	Dundee United	a	1-0	*Black*
8/12	Hibernian	h	2-0	*Niculae 2*
16/12	Celtic	h	3-2	*Rankin (p), Proctor, Cowie*
22/12	Hearts	a	3-2	*Duncan, Rankin (p), Bayne*
26/12	Falkirk	a	0-1	
29/12	Kilmarnock	h	3-1	*Niculae 2, Cowie*
2008				
2/1	Aberdeen	a	0-1	
5/1	Gretna	h	3-0	*Niculae 2, Rankin (p)*
20/1	Rangers	h	0-1	
9/2	St Mirren	a	1-1	*Munro*
16/2	Dundee United	h	1-1	*Paatelainen*
20/2	Motherwell	a	1-3	*Cowie*
23/2	Hibernian	a	0-2	
27/2	Celtic	a	1-2	*Niculae*
1/3	Hearts	h	0-3	
15/3	Falkirk	h	0-1	
22/3	Kilmarnock	a	1-4	*Black (p)*
29/3	Aberdeen	h	3-4	*og (Bus), Duncan, McBain*
5/4	Gretna	a	2-1	*McBain, Cowie*
19/4	Kilmarnock	h	3-0	*Imrie, og (Lilley), Niculae*
26/4	Hearts	a	0-1	
3/5	Gretna	h	6-1	*Imrie, McAllister, Wilson, Cowie, Tokely, Vigurs*
10/5	Falkirk	a	1-2	*Wilson (p)*
17/5	St Mirren	h	0-0	

No	Name	Nat	Pos	Aps	(s)	Gls
9	Graham BAYNE		A	9	(17)	1
8	Ian BLACK		M	31	(2)	3
28	Craig BREWSTER		A	1	(1)	1
15	Don COWIE		M	35	(2)	9
12	Russell DUNCAN		M	33	(1)	3
1	Michael FRASER		G	36		
10	Richard HART		M		(7)	
16	Richard HASTINGS	CAN	D	31	(2)	
11	Douglas IMRIE		M	12	(3)	2
26	Guy KERR		D		(1)	
30	Zbigniew MAŁKOWSKI	POL	G	2		
13	Rory McALLISTER		A	3	(7)	1
6	Roy McBAIN		M	31	(2)	3
5	Stuart McCAFFREY		D	7		
21	Dean McDONALD	ENG	A		(5)	
3	Philip McGUIRE		D	23	(1)	
11	Alan MORGAN		M		(3)	
14	Grant MUNRO		D	33		1
18	Marius NICULAE	ROU	A	33	(2)	8
20	Markus PAATELAINEN	FIN	M	4	(7)	1
29	David PROCTOR		D	16	(5)	1
24	John RANKIN		M	11	(4)	3
2	Ross TOKELY		D	34	(1)	2
27	Iain VIGURS		M	1	(3)	1
7	Barry WILSON		M	13	(12)	3
19	Dennis WYNESS		A	19	(5)	5

KILMARNOCK FC

Manager - Jim Jeffries

Founded - 1869

MAJOR HONOURS: Scottish League - (1) 1965; Scottish Cup - (3) 1920, 1929, 1997.

2007				
5/8	Celtic	a	0-0	
13/8	Dundee United	h	2-1	*Gibson, Nish*
18/8	Motherwell	a	2-1	*Lilley, Dodds*
25/8	Rangers	h	1-2	*Invincibile*
1/9	Aberdeen	h	0-1	
15/9	Gretna	a	2-1	*Gibson, Jarvis*
22/9	St Mirren	h	0-0	
29/9	Hibernian	a	1-4	*Nish*
6/10	Inverness	h	2-2	*Koudou, Nish*
20/10	Falkirk	a	1-1	*Wright F.*
27/10	Hearts	h	3-1	*Wales, Nish (p), Gibson*
3/11	Celtic	h	1-2	*Wright F.*
10/11	Dundee United	a	0-2	
24/11	Motherwell	h	0-1	
1/12	Rangers	a	0-2	
8/12	Aberdeen	a	1-2	*Fernández*
15/12	Gretna	h	3-3	*Invincibile, Fernández, Nish*
22/12	St Mirren	a	0-0	
26/12	Hibernian	h	2-1	*Nish, Taouil*
29/12	Inverness	a	1-3	*Nish (p)*
2008				
2/1	Falkirk	h	0-1	
5/1	Hearts	a	1-1	*Di Giacomo*
19/1	Celtic	a	0-1	
26/1	Dundee United	h	1-2	*Wales*
9/2	Motherwell	a	0-1	
17/2	Rangers	h	0-2	
24/2	Aberdeen	h	3-1	*Bryson 2, Wright F.*
27/2	Gretna	a	2-4	*Ford, Gibson*
1/3	St Mirren	h	1-0	*Invincibile*
15/3	Hibernian	a	0-2	
22/3	Inverness	h	4-1	*Wright F., Bryson 2, Flannigan*
29/3	Falkirk	a	0-0	
5/4	Hearts	h	0-0	
19/4	Inverness	a	0-3	
26/4	Gretna	h	1-1	*Fernández*
3/5	St Mirren	a	0-1	
10/5	Hearts	a	2-0	*Murray, Di Giacomo*
17/5	Falkirk	h	2-1	*Taouil, Di Giacomo*

No	Name	Nat	Pos	Aps	(s)	Gls
24	Craig BRYSON		M	16	(3)	4
27	Timothy CLANCY	IRL	D	10	(1)	
1	Alan COMBE		G	37		
30	Martyn CORRIGAN		D	7		
40	David COX		A		(2)	
19	Paul DALGLISH		A	3	(3)	
18	Paul DI GIACOMO		A	4	(6)	3
16	Rhian DODDS	CAN	M	6	(3)	1
20	David FERNÁNDEZ	ESP	A	16	(13)	3
29	Iain FLANNIGAN		M	7	(1)	1
6	Simon FORD	ENG	D	28		1
2	James FOWLER		M	34		
17	William GIBSON		M	9	(14)	4
23	Jamie HAMILL		M	29	(3)	
13	Chad HARPUR	RSA	G	1		
3	Garry HAY		D	26		
11	Daniel INVINCIBILE	AUS	M	27		3
33	Ryan JARVIS	ENG	A	4	(5)	1
12	Allan JOHNSTON		M	14	(8)	
22	Aimé KOUDOU	CIV	A	2	(4)	1
4	David LILLEY		D	23	(1)	1

Name	Nat	Pos	Aps	(s)	Gls
Gary LOCKE		M	7	(10)	
Alan MORGAN		M		(3)	
Grant MURRAY		D	8	(3)	1
Steven NAISMITH		A	4		
Colin NISH		A	20	(2)	7
Ryan O'LEARY		D	16	(3)	
Eric SKORA	FRA	M		(1)	
Mehdi TAOUIL	MAR	M	19	(3)	2
Gary WALES		A	16	(8)	2
Kyle WRIGHT		D	10		
Frazer WRIGHT		D	15		4

MOTHERWELL FC

Manager - Mark McGhee

Founded - 1886

OR HONOURS: Scottish League - (1) 1932; Scottish Cup - (2) 1952, 1991; Scottish League Cup - (1) 1951.

7

	St Mirren	a	1-0	*McGarry*
	Inverness	h	2-1	*O'Donnell, McCormack (p)*
	Kilmarnock	h	1-2	*Clarkson*
	Gretna	a	2-1	*Lasley, Porter*
	Hearts	h	0-2	
	Aberdeen	a	2-1	*Quinn, Porter*
	Falkirk	a	0-1	
	Rangers	h	1-1	*Porter*
	Dundee United	a	0-1	
0	Hibernian	h	2-1	*McCormack 2*
0	Celtic	a	0-3	
	St Mirren	h	1-1	*Porter*
1	Inverness	a	3-0	*Clarkson 2, Smith D.*
1	Kilmarnock	a	1-0	*O'Donnell*
	Gretna	h	3-0	*Clarkson 2, Porter*
	Hearts	a	2-1	*Porter, og (Žaliūkas)*
2	Aberdeen	h	3-0	*McCormack 2 (1p), McGarry*
2	Falkirk	h	0-3	
2	Rangers	a	1-3	*Quinn*
2	Dundee United	h	5-3	*Hughes, Porter, McCormack, Clarkson 2*

8

	St Mirren	a	1-3	*Clarkson*
	Kilmarnock	h	1-0	*Clarkson*
	Gretna	a	3-1	*Porter, McCormack 2*
	Inverness	h	3-1	*Clarkson 2, Porter*
	Hearts	h	0-1	
	Aberdeen	a	1-1	*Smith D.*
	Falkirk	a	0-0	
	Hibernian	a	0-1	
	Dundee United	a	0-2	
	Hibernian	h	1-0	*Clarkson*
	Celtic	a	1-0	*Lappin*
	Celtic	h	1-4	*og (McManus)*
	Dundee United	h	2-2	*Porter 2*
	Celtic	h	1-2	*Porter*
	Rangers	a	0-1	
	Aberdeen	h	2-1	*Smith D., Porter*
	Rangers	h	1-1	*Porter*
	Hibernian	a	2-0	*Lappin, Murphy (p)*

No	Name	Nat	Pos	Aps	(s)	Gls
	David CLARKSON		A	34	(1)	12
	Steven CRAIGAN	NIR	D	38		
	Luke DANIELS	ENG	G	2		
	Marc FITZPATRICK		M	19	(11)	
	Lewis GRABBAN	ENG	M		(5)	
	Martin GREHAN		A		(1)	
	Steven HAMMELL		D	15		
	Stephen HUGHES		M	29	(2)	1
	William KINNIBURGH		D		(1)	
8	Simon LAPPIN		M	7	(7)	2
14	Keith LASLEY		M	25	(7)	1
27	Stephen MAGUIRE		M		(1)	
17	Robert MALCOLM		M	8		
11	Ross McCORMACK		A	30	(6)	8
18	Steven McGARRY		M	27	(3)	2
6	Brian McLEAN		D	6	(3)	
44	Robert McHUGH		A		(1)	
8	Simon MENSING	GER	M		(2)	
21	Daniel MURPHY	IRL	D		(2)	
32	Jamie MURPHY		A		(16)	1
10	Phil O'DONNELL		M	15	(3)	2
3	James PATERSON		M	20		
9	Christopher PORTER	ENG	A	34	(3)	14
22	Paul QUINN		D	31		2
4	Mark REYNOLDS		D	38		
23	Darren SMITH		M	4	(19)	3
1	Graeme SMITH		G	36		

RANGERS FC

Manager - Walter Smith

Founded - 1873

MAJOR HONOURS: UEFA Cup Winners' Cup - (1) 1972; Scottish League - (51) 1891, 1899, 1900, 1901, 1902, 1911, 1912, 1913, 1918, 1920, 1921, 1923, 1924, 1925, 1927, 1928, 1929, 1930, 1931, 1933, 1934, 1935, 1937, 1939, 1947, 1949, 1950, 1953, 1956, 1957, 1959, 1961, 1963, 1964, 1975, 1976, 1978, 1987, 1989, 1990, 1991, 1992, 1993, 1994, 1995, 1996, 1997, 1999, 2000, 2003, 2005; Scottish Cup - (32) 1894, 1897, 1898, 1903, 1928, 1930, 1932, 1934, 1935, 1936, 1948, 1949, 1950, 1953, 1960, 1962, 1963, 1964, 1966, 1973, 1976, 1978, 1979, 1981, 1992, 1993, 1996, 1999, 2000, 2002, 2003, 2008; Scottish League Cup - (25) 1947, 1949, 1961, 1962, 1964, 1965, 1971, 1976, 1978, 1979, 1982, 1984, 1985, 1987, 1988, 1989, 1991, 1993, 1994, 1997, 1999, 2002, 2003, 2005, 2008.

2007

4/8	Inverness	a	3-0	*Ferguson 2, Novo*
11/8	St Mirren	h	2-0	*Ferguson, Cousin*
18/8	Falkirk	h	7-2	*Cousin 2, Whittaker, Boyd, Darcheville 2, Broadfoot*
25/8	Kilmarnock	a	2-1	*Beasley, Darcheville*
1/9	Gretna	h	4-0	*Boyd, Webster, Cuéllar, og (Collin)*
15/9	Hearts	a	2-4	*Cousin (p), Beasley*
23/9	Aberdeen	h	3-0	*McCulloch, Naismith, Boyd*
29/9	Motherwell	a	1-1	*Boyd (p)*
6/10	Hibernian	h	0-1	
20/10	Celtic	h	3-0	*Novo 2 (1p), Ferguson*
28/10	Dundee United	a	1-2	*Cousin (p)*
3/11	Inverness	h	2-0	*Cuéllar, Boyd*
24/11	Falkirk	a	3-1	*Cuéllar, Darcheville, Boyd*
1/12	Kilmarnock	h	2-0	*Darcheville, Whittaker*
15/12	Hearts	h	2-1	*McCulloch 2*
23/12	Aberdeen	a	1-1	*Adam*
26/12	Motherwell	h	3-1	*Cousin, og (Porter), Boyd*
29/12	Hibernian	a	2-1	*Naismith, Cousin*

2008

5/1	Dundee United	h	2-0	*Naismith, Ferguson*
16/1	Gretna	a	2-1	*Ferguson, Cousin*
20/1	Inverness	a	1-0	*Darcheville*
26/1	St Mirren	h	4-0	*Burke, Boyd, Whittaker 2*
9/2	Falkirk	h	2-0	*Boyd, Naismith*
17/2	Kilmarnock	a	2-0	*Cuéllar, Boyd*
24/2	Gretna	h	4-2	*Cousin, Naismith, Burke, Boyd*
27/2	Hearts	a	4-0	*Darcheville 2, Novo 2*
1/3	Aberdeen	h	3-1	*Dailly, Adam, Boyd*
22/3	Hibernian	h	2-1	*Darcheville, Novo*
29/3	Celtic	h	1-0	*Thomson*

SCOTLAND

6/4	Dundee United	a	3-3	*Weir, Novo, Boyd*
16/4	Celtic	a	1-2	*Novo*
27/4	Celtic	a	2-3	*Weir, Cousin*
4/5	Hibernian	a	0-0	
7/5	Motherwell	h	1-0	*Ferguson*
10/5	Dundee United	h	3-1	*Novo 2, Darcheville*
17/5	Motherwell	a	1-1	*Dailly*
19/5	St Mirren	a	3-0	*Boyd, Darcheville 2*
22/5	Aberdeen	a	0-2	

No	Name	Nat	Pos	Aps	(s)	Gls
11	Charlie ADAM		M	12	(4)	2
25	Neil ALEXANDER		G	7	(1)	
20	DaMarcus BEASLEY	USA	M	8	(3)	2
9	Kris BOYD		A	17	(11)	14
21	Kirk BROADFOOT		D	14	(1)	1
4	Thomas BUFFEL	BEL	A		(1)	
17	Chris BURKE		M	10	(1)	2
29	Daniel COUSIN	GAB	A	20	(6)	10
24	Carlos CUÉLLAR	ESP	D	36		4
23	Christian DAILLY		M	12		2
19	Jean-Claude DARCHEVILLE	FRA	A	14	(16)	12
12	Steven DAVIS	NIR	M	11	(1)	
14	Amdy FAYE	SEN	M	2	(2)	
6	Barry FERGUSON		M	37	(1)	7
43	John FLECK		M		(1)	
36	Dean FURMAN	RSA	M		(1)	
7	Brahim HEMDANI	ALG	D	12		
2	Alan HUTTON		D	20		
27	Lee McCULLOCH		M	19	(3)	3
1	Alan McGREGOR		G	31		
18	Steven NAISMITH		A	12	(9)	5
10	Nacho NOVO	ESP	A	10	(18)	10
5	Saša PAPAC	BIH	D	22		
8	Kevin THOMSON		M	25	(1)	1
22	Andrew WEBSTER		D	1		1
3	David WEIR		D	37		2
28	Steven WHITTAKER		M	29	(1)	4

SAINT MIRREN FC

Manager - Gus McPherson

Founded - 1877

MAJOR HONOURS: Scottish Cup - (3) 1926, 1959, 1987.

2007

4/8	Motherwell	h	0-1	
11/8	Rangers	a	0-2	
18/8	Inverness	h	2-1	*Miranda, Corcoran*
25/8	Falkirk	a	1-0	*Mehmet*
2/9	Celtic	h	1-5	*Miranda*
16/9	Dundee United	a	0-2	
22/9	Kilmarnock	a	0-0	
30/9	Hearts	h	1-3	*Corcoran*
7/10	Aberdeen	a	0-4	
20/10	Gretna	h	1-0	*Mehmet*
27/10	Hibernian	a	1-0	*Mehmet*
3/11	Motherwell	a	1-1	*Kean*
24/11	Inverness	a	0-1	
1/12	Falkirk	h	1-5	*Mehmet*
8/12	Celtic	a	1-1	*McGinn*
15/12	Dundee United	h	0-3	
22/12	Kilmarnock	h	0-0	
26/12	Hearts	a	1-0	*McGinn*
29/12	Aberdeen	h	0-1	

2008

5/1	Hibernian	h	2-1	*Maxwell, Mason*
19/1	Motherwell	h	3-1	*Corcoran, Maxwell 2*
26/1	Rangers	a	0-4	
9/2	Inverness	h	1-1	*Mehmet*
16/2	Falkirk	a	0-4	
24/2	Celtic	h	0-1	
27/2	Dundee United	a	1-1	*Dorman*
1/3	Kilmarnock	a	0-1	
15/3	Hearts	h	1-1	*Hamilton*
22/3	Aberdeen	a	1-1	*Dorman*
29/3	Gretna	h	2-0	*Dargo, Mehmet*
5/4	Hibernian	a	0-2	
9/4	Gretna	a	0-0	
19/4	Hearts	a	2-3	*McCay, Mason*
26/4	Falkirk	h	1-0	*Dorman*
3/5	Kilmarnock	h	1-0	*Haining*
10/5	Gretna	h	0-0	
17/5	Inverness	a	0-0	
19/5	Rangers	h	0-3	

No	Name	Nat	Pos	Aps	(s)	G
25	David BARRON		D	18		
46	Christopher BIRCHALL	TRI	M	5	(4)	
14	Garry BRADY		M	16	(2)	
12	Richard BRITTAIN		M	2	(4)	
11	Alexander BURKE		A	7	(3)	
15	Mark CORCORAN		M	18	(8)	3
17	Craig DARGO		A	15	(1)	1
24	Mark DOCHERTY		M		(1)	
8	Andrew DORMAN	ENG	M	18		3
5	William HAINING		D	29		1
z	James HAMILTON		A	7	(8)	1
21	Mark HOWARD	ENG	G	10		
10	Stewart KEAN		A	15	(17)	1
4	Gary MASON		M	31		2
16	Ian MAXWELL		D	17		3
27	Mark McAUSLAND		D		(1)	
23	Ryan McCAY		M	10	(2)	1
26	Stephen McGINN		M	10	(15)	2
9	Billy MEHMET	IRL	A	32	(5)	6
28	Andrew MILLEN		D	8	(1)	
19	Franco MIRANDA	ARG	D	20	(4)	2
20	Craig MOLLOY		M		(5)	
7	Hugh MURRAY		M	27	(2)	
22	Stephen O'DONNELL		M	5	(5)	
6	John POTTER		D	31		
3	Alain REID		D	10	(2)	
1	Christopher SMITH		G	28		
2	David VAN ZANTEN	IRL	D	29		

PROMOTED CLUBS

HAMILTON ACADEMICAL FC

Coach – Billy Reid

Founded - 1874

SECOND LEVEL FINAL TABLE 2007/

		Pld	W	D	L	F	A
1	Hamilton Academical FC	36	23	7	6	62	27
2	Dundee FC	36	20	9	7	58	30
3	Saint Johnstone FC	36	15	13	8	60	45
4	Queen of the South FC	36	14	10	12	47	43
5	Dunfermline Athletic FC	36	13	12	11	36	41
6	Partick Thistle FC	36	11	12	13	40	39
7	Livingston FC	36	10	9	17	55	66
8	Greenock Morton FC	36	9	10	17	40	58
9	Clyde FC	36	9	10	17	40	59
10	Stirling Albion FC	36	4	12	20	41	71

DOMESTIC CUPS 2007/8

SCOTTISH CUP

RTH ROUND

/08)
c 3, Stirling Albion 0
rk 2, Aberdeen 2
nock Morton 2, Gretna 2
ilton Academical 0, Brechin City 0
rnian 3, Inverness 0
ts 2, Motherwell 2
irren 3, Dumbarton 0
en of the South 4, Linlithgow Rose 0

/08)
tly 1, Dundee 3
gston 2, Cowdenbeath 0
hnstone 3, Raith Rovers 1

/08)
e 0, Dundee United 1

/08)
ck Thistle 2, Dunfermline Athletic 1

/08)
Rangers 2, Ross County 4
gers 6, East Stirlingshire 0

/08)
rie United 0, Kilmarnock 2

ays

/08)
deen 3, Falkirk 1
herwell 1, Hearts 0
na 0, Greenock Morton 3

H ROUND

'08)
rdeen 1, Hamilton Academical 0
nock Morton 0, Queen of the South 2
arnock 1, Celtic 5
gston 0, Partick Thistle 0
irren 0, Dundee United 0

'08)
rnian 0, Rangers 0

2/08)
herwell 1, Dundee 2

2/08)
County 0, St Johnstone 1

ays

2/08)
ck Thistle 1, Livingston 1 *(aet; 5-4 on pens)*

2/08)
dee United 0, St Mirren 1

'08)
gers 1, Hibernian 1

ARTER-FINALS

'08)
en of the South 2 *(Dobbie 52, McCann 90)*, Dundee 0
hnstone 1 *(Craig 32p)*, St Mirren 1 *(Dorman 73)*
rdeen *1 (De Visscher 78)*, Celtic 1 *(Vennegoor of Hesselink 90)*

(19/3/08)
Rangers 1 *(Boyd 69)*, Partick Thistle 1 *(Gray 67)*

Replays

(18/3/08)
St Mirren 1 *(Mehmet 70p)*, St Johnstone 3 *(Quinn 13, Jackson 20, MacDonald 28)*
Celtic 0, Aberdeen 1 *(Mackie 69)*

(14/4/08)
Partick Thistle 0, Rangers 2 *(Novo 27, Burke 40)*

SEMI-FINALS

(12/4/08)
Queen of the South 4 *(Tosh 22, Burns 49, O'Connor 56, Stewart 60)*, Aberdeen 3 *(Considine 36, 59, Nicholson 53)*

(20/4/08)
St Johnstone 1 *(McBreen 93)*, Rangers *1 (Novo 102p) (aet; 3-4 on pens)*

FINAL

(24/5/08)
Hampden Park, Glasgow
RANGERS FC 3 *(Boyd 33, 72, Beasley 43)*
QUEEN OF THE SOUTH FC 2 *(Tosh 50, Thomson 53)*
Referee – *Dougal*
RANGERS – *Alexander, Whittaker, Cuéllar, Weir, Papac, McCulloch, Ferguson, Thomson, Beasley (Davis 76), Boyd, Darcheville (Fleck 86).*
QUEEN OF THE SOUTH – *MacDonald, McCann (Robertson 86), Thomson, Aitken, Harris, McQuilken (Stewart 76), MacFarlane, Tosh, Burns, Dobbie (O'Neill 82), O'Connor.*

SCOTTISH LEAGUE CUP

QUARTER-FINALS

(31/10/07)
Aberdeen 4 *(Nicholson 10p, 22, 78p, Miller 45)*, Inverness 1 *(Bayne 68)*
Celtic 0, Hearts 2 *(Velička 77, 86)*
Dundee United 3 *(Hunt 10, 77, 85)*, Hamilton 1 *(Offiong 79p)*
Motherwell 1 *(Quinn 90)*, Rangers 2 *(Novo 22, Boyd 53)*

SEMI-FINALS

(30/1/08)
Rangers 2 *(Ferguson 50, Darcheville 69)*, Hearts 0

(5/2/08)
Aberdeen 1 *(Considine 18)*, Dundee United 4 *(Dods 22, Kalvenes 59, Conway 65, Gomis 77)*

FINAL

(16/3/08)
Hampden Park, Glasgow
RANGERS FC 2 *(Boyd 85, 113)*
DUNDEE UNITED FC 2 *(Hunt 34, De Vries 95)*
(aet; 3-2 on pens)
Referee - *Clark*
RANGERS - *McGregor, Broadfoot, Cuéllar, Weir, Papac (Boyd 60), Burke (Whittaker 116), Hemdani (Darcheville 46), Ferguson, Dailly, Davis, McCulloch.*
DUNDEE UNITED - *Załuska, Kovačević, Kenneth, Wilie, Kalvenes, Buaben (Robertson D. 95), Flood, Kerr, Gomis, Hunt (Conway 78), De Vries.*

Partizan atone for European exclusion

Banned from competing in Europe after spectator disorder in a UEFA Cup first qualifying round tie in Bosnia-Herzegovina, FK Partizan switched their attention instead to domestic matters and successfully held off the eternal threat of Belgrade rivals FK Crvena Zvezda to win the Serbian League and Cup double.

UEFA's disciplinary committee threw Partizan out of the UEFA Cup after repeated violence among their travelling support forced the referee to call a temporary halt to play in the game against HŠK Zrinjski in Mostar. Partizan won the match 6-1, with the help of a hat-trick from their new Senegalese striker Lamine Diarra (against his old club), and also beat their hapless opponents 5-0 in Belgrade, but then came the exclusion order and suddenly the club's European adventure was over almost before it had begun.

Fan violence is, alas, nothing new in Serbia. Another major incident occurred a few months later, when followers of Crvena Zvezda viciously assaulted a police officer. The outcome was a three-match home

Senegalese striker Lamine Diarra scored goals galore in his debut season with double-winners Partizan

spectator ban for 'Red Star', the first of those being t big derby match against Partizan. It was the 132nd meeting between the Belgrade giants but the first t be played in an empty stadium.

Staged on 1 March, on the first day back after the winter break, the fixture had added curiosity in that both teams went into it with new coaches. Partizan, the leaders by six points at the shutdown, had lost t services of Miroslav Đukić to the Serbian national si and appointed ex-player – but rookie coach – Slaviš Jokanović in his place. Crvena Zvezda, meanwhile, h dismissed Milorad Kosanović after a heavy UEFA Cu defeat in Greece in November and handed the job t the relatively untried Aleksandar Janković, a former Crvena Zvezda player and long-time assistant to much-travelled veteran coach Slavoljub Muslin.

Inauspicious start

Despite the empty stands and terraces Crvena Zvez made home advantage count and won the game 4- It was Partizan's first defeat of the campaign, and ar inauspicious start for Jokanović, but there would be no lasting damage. The Black and Whites won each their next four matches without conceding a goal, and although they were then held up by three successive draws – including one at home to Crven Zvezda (1-1) – they rediscovered their form in the ru in, winning their last eight games to finish five poin ahead of their arch-rivals and claim their 20th championship crown.

Jokanović's coaching career got off to the perfect st because Partizan also won the Serbian Cup. The only Superliga club they encountered en route to victory was Crvena Zvezda, whom they memorably defeate 3-2 in the semi-finals, Diarra sending Partizan on the way with two first-half goals. The 24-year-old West African would be the man of the match in the final also, scoring all three goals as Partizan comfortably disposed of second-level strugglers FK Zemun 3-0. Diarra was not finished yet. He subsequently found t

Partizan winger Zoran Tošić was one of the central figures in the club's League and Cup double triumph

: in each of Partizan's final three Superliga fixtures, luding the winning goal on the final day away to FK oredak that wrapped up the title.

rra's success, added to that of team-mates Juca m Brazil) and Moreira (from Portugal), justified tizan's pre-season policy of buying in players from oad. Crvena Zvezda followed a similar line in ruitment, but with less favourable results. Their st successful import, Segundo Castillo from ador, had already starred in the club's 2006/07 uble triumph. The new intake for 2007/08, which luded purchases from countries as diverse as Chad, ombia and Poland, proved less productive, and one them, Portuguese midfielder Lucas, even had to quit game due to a heart defect which had not been ked up on his medical.

hough Crvena Zvezda were unable to win a third cessive league title, they did go through the entire match campaign unbeaten. Evidently it was the ponderance of draws – 12 in total – that proved ir downfall, and that would cost Janković his job, h the illustrious Czech coach Zdeněk Zeman being ed in the summer to take his place.

FK Vojvodina finished 13 points behind runners-up Crvena Zvezda in third place but 16 points ahead of fourth-placed FK Borac to qualify for the UEFA Cup with ease – despite losing their best player, attacking midfielder Gojko Kačar, to Hertha BSC Berlin during the winter break. Kačar scored ten goals, including a hat-trick in a 3-3 draw with Partizan, in the autumn and would surely have taken the Superliga top-scorer prize had he stayed. Instead it went to Crvena Zvezda's former RSC Anderlecht striker Nenad Jestrović, with just 13 goals. Another mid-season departure to Germany was that of Partizan's Serbian international full-back Antonio Rukavina to BV Borussia Dortmund, but Partizan did manage to hold on to their other prize asset, winger Zoran Tošić, and he proved to be the leading local attraction in the Superliga during the spring.

Kačar and Tošić were two of the younger members of the Serbian squad that reached the final of the 2007 UEFA European Under-21 Championship, and they were both duly introduced to the full national team in 2007/08. With Miroslav Đukić, the U21s' coach in the Netherlands, having taken over the senior side, it can be anticipated that several more youngsters will be thrown into the fray during the 2010 FIFA World Cup qualifying campaign.

End for Clemente

Failure to qualify for UEFA EURO 2008™ proved fatal to Javier Clemente. A 3-2 defeat in Brussels followed by three successive draws - one of which, in Lisbon, saw defender Ivica Dragutinović bizarrely come to blows with Portugal coach Luiz Felipe Scolari – ended Serbian interest, and the final two home games, against Poland and Azerbaijan (the latter postponed a week because of snow) were played out in virtually empty stadiums.

Đukić did not get his new reign off to the best of starts, failing to win any of his first five friendlies, but his case was not helped by the turmoil at the Serbian FA, with recently appointed Director of Football Dragan Džajić, one of the country's all-time great players, being taken into custody on charges of embezzlement in February and federation president Zvezdan Terzić fleeing to the United States to avoid arrest for alleged similar offences. Serbia's hopes of a successful World Cup run will hinge both on stability off the field and the form on it of key players such as Nemanja Vidić, Dejan Stanković and highly talented young ACF Fiorentina midfielder Zdravko Kuzmanović.

SERBIA

Fudbalski savez Srbije (FSS)

Terazije 35
CP 263
RS-11000 Beograd
tel - +381 11 3233447
fax - +381 11 3233433
website - www.fss.org.yu
email - office@fss.org.yu
Year of Formation – 1919
President – Tomislav Karadžić
General Secretary – Zoran Laković
Press Officer – Aleksandar Bošković
Stadium – FK Crvena Zvezda, Beograd (51,398)

*INTERNATIONAL TOURNAMENT APPEARANCES**
FIFA World Cup - (10) 1930 (semi-finals), 1950, 1954 (qtr-finals), 1958 (qtr-finals), 1962 (4th), 1974 (2nd phase), 1982, 1990 (qtr-finals), 1998 (2nd round), 2006.
UEFA European Championship - (5) 19 (runners-up), 1968 (runners-up), 1976 (4th), 1984, 2000 (qtr-finals).

(before 2006 as Yugoslavia; 2006 as Serbia & Montenegro)*

TOP FIVE ALL-TIME CAPS
Savo Milošević (101); Dragan Džajić (8 Dragan Stojković (84); Predrag Mijatov & Dejan Stanković (73)

TOP FIVE ALL-TIME GOALS
Stjepan Bobek (38); Milan Galić (37); Blagoje Marjanović (36); Savo Miloševi (35); Rajko Mitić (32)

NATIONAL TEAM RESULTS 2007/08

22/8/07	Belgium (ECQ)	A	Brussels	2-3	*Kuzmanović (73, 90+1)*
8/9/07	Finland (ECQ)	H	Belgrade	0-0	
12/9/07	Portugal (ECQ)	A	Lisbon	1-1	*Ivanović (88)*
13/10/07	Armenia (ECQ)	A	Yerevan	0-0	
17/10/07	Azerbaijan (ECQ)	A	Baku	6-1	*Tošić D. (4), Žigić (17, 42), Janković (41), Smiljanić (75), Lazović (*
21/11/07	Poland (ECQ)	H	Belgrade	2-2	*Žigić (68), Lazović (70)*
24/11/07	Kazakhstan (ECQ)	H	Belgrade	1-0	*Ostapenko (79og)*
6/2/08	FYR Macedonia	A	Skopje	1-1	*Lazović (43)*
26/3/08	Ukraine	A	Odessa	0-2	
24/5/08	Republic of Ireland	A	Dublin	1-1	*Pantelić (75)*
28/5/08	Russia	N	Burghausen (GER)	1-2	*Pantelić (40)*
31/5/08	Germany	A	Gelsenkirchen	1-2	*Janković (19)*

NATIONAL TEAM APPEARANCES 2007/08

Coach – Javier CLEMENTE (ESP) 12/3/50 /(25/12/07) Miroslav ĐUKIĆ 19/2/66			BEL	FIN	POR	ARM	AZE	POL	KAZ	Mkd	Ukr	Irl	Rus	Ger	Caps	G
Vladimir STOJKOVIĆ	28/7/83	Sporting (POR)	G	G	G	G	G				G	G		G	17	
Antonio RUKAVINA	26/1/84	Partizan /Dortmund (GER)	D	D	D	D	D	D		D89	D	D	s69	D	12	
Ivica DRAGUTINOVIĆ	13/11/75	Sevilla (ESP)	D	D	D			D		D70		D		D	40	
Mladen KRSTAJIĆ	4/3/74	Schalke (GER)	D					D64							57	
Nemanja VIDIĆ	21/10/81	Man. United (ENG)	D		D					D70	D75		D46	D	31	

TIONAL TEAM APPEARANCES 2007/08 (contd.)

			BEL	FIN	POR	ARM	AZE	POL	KAZ	Mkd	Ukr	Irl	Rus	Ger	Caps	Goals
n KOROMAN	19/9/78	Crvena Zvezda	M56												36	1
KOVAČEVIĆ	11/11/80	Lens (FRA)	M	M	M	M	M65	M		s59	s82	s90	M		26	-
JANKOVIĆ	1/3/84	Palermo (ITA)	M	M54		s73	M68	s76	s24	s46	s75	M	s46	M82	15	4
o KUZMANOVIĆ	22/9/87	Fiorentina (ITA)	M	M	M71	M61	M	M		M59	M	M	s59	M	12	2
LAZOVIĆ	17/5/83	PSV (NED)	A70	A62		s62	s68	s46		A59	A46	A70		s46	22	6
PANTELIĆ	15/9/78	Hertha (GER)	A56		s61	A62	s73					s70	A46	A46	18	3
KRASIĆ	1/11/84	CSKA Moskva (RUS)	s56	M	M61	M73		M76	M24	s59					11	-
JOVANOVIĆ	18/4/81	Standard (BEL)	s56	s54	A			A	A63	s59	s46				8	1
SMILJANIC	19/11/86	Espanyol (ESP)	s70				s65			M	M82	M90		M	6	1
av IVANOVIĆ	22/4/84	Lokomotiv Moskva (RUS) /Chelsea (ENG)		D	D	D	D	D	D		D	D	s46	D	13	1
TOŠIĆ	19/1/85	Bremen (GER)		D53		D	D	s64		s70					8	1
STANKOVIĆ	11/9/78	Internazionale (ITA)		M	M	M					M75				73	13
TOŠIĆ	28/4/87	Partizan		s53	M61	s61	M			M59	s82		M	s82	8	-
ŽIGIĆ	25/9/80	Valencia (ESP)		s62	s61	A	A73	A	A70	A70	A69		s46		29	11
JLJAJ	29/10/79	Shakhtar (UKR)			s71		M	M46	M						52	2
STEPANOV	2/4/83	Porto (POR)				D									6	-
BIŠEVAC	31/8/83	Lens (FRA)					D								3	-
AVRAMOV	5/4/79	Fiorentina (ITA)						G	G						2	-
TEVANOVIĆ	24/6/83	OFK Beograd							D						1	-
TUTORIĆ	5/3/83	Crvena Zvezda							D						1	-
ANĐELKOVIĆ	15/6/82	Crvena Zvezda							D						1	-
KAČAR	26/1/87	Vojvodina /Hertha (GER)							M	s70		s86	M59		4	-
DESPOTOVIĆ	21/1/83	Vojvodina /Rapid Bucureşti (ROU)							A				A46		2	-
BABOVIĆ	7/1/87	OFK Beograd /Nantes (FRA)							s63	s70		M81		M	4	-
nir FEJSA	14/8/88	Hajduk Kula							s70						1	-
ILIĆ	20/9/77	OFK Beograd								G46					1	-
nja RNIĆ	30/9/84	Partizan								D	s75				3	-
m SULEJMANI	5/12/88	Heerenveen (NED)								M46	M82				2	-
KAHRIMAN	19/11/84	Konyaspor (TUR)								s46					1	-
NINKOV	20/4/85	Crvena Zvezda								s89			D69		2	-
ndar LUKOVIĆ	23/10/82	Udinese (ITA)									D				8	-
IĆ	30/12/77	Salzburg (AUT)									s69	M86	s76	M73	40	6
dan RAJKOVIĆ	3/2/89	PSV (NED)										D	D		2	-
n MARKOVIĆ	28/9/81	Dynamo Kyiv (UKR)										s81			16	-
nir DIŠLJENKOVIĆ	2/7/81	Metalurh Donetsk (UKR)											G		2	-
ndar KOLAROV	10/11/85	Lazio (ITA)											D		1	-
MILOVANOVIĆ	21/1/84	Crvena Zvezda											M76	s73	2	-

SERBIA

DOMESTIC LEAGUE 2007/08

SUPERLIGA FINAL TABLE

		Home					Away					Total					
	Pld	W	D	L	F	A	W	D	L	F	A	W	D	L	F	A	Pts
1 FK Partizan	33	11	6	0	37	15	13	2	1	26	8	24	8	1	63	23	80
2 FK Crvena Zvezda	33	12	5	0	40	11	9	7	0	25	11	21	12	0	65	22	75
3 FK Vojvodina	33	11	4	2	33	13	7	4	5	20	20	18	8	7	53	33	62
4 FK Borac	33	8	5	4	20	13	4	5	7	9	20	12	10	11	29	33	46
5 FK Napredak	33	8	1	7	12	11	3	7	7	13	22	11	8	14	25	33	41
6 FK Čukarički	33	6	4	7	15	17	4	6	6	16	15	10	10	13	31	32	40
7 FK Mladost Lučani	33	7	6	4	23	17	1	8	7	9	24	8	14	11	32	41	38
8 FK Hajduk Kula	33	5	8	3	15	11	3	5	9	10	20	8	13	12	25	31	37
9 OFK Beograd	33	5	5	6	16	19	4	4	9	15	26	9	9	15	31	45	36
10 FK Smederevo	33	5	5	6	12	15	5	1	11	21	29	10	6	17	33	44	36
11 FK Banat	33	3	4	9	17	28	3	6	8	17	29	6	10	17	34	57	28
12 FK Bežanija	33	4	3	9	20	22	1	1	15	11	36	5	4	24	31	58	19

TOP GOALSCORER

13 Nenad JESTROVIĆ (Crvena Z

12 Lamine DIARRA (Partizan)
Stevan JOVETIĆ (Partizan)
Predrag RANĐELOVIĆ (Bežan

10 Gojko KAČAR (Vojvodina)
Nenad MILIJAŠ (Crvena Zvez

9 Dejan MILOVANOVIĆ (Crvena Zvezda)

8 Igor BURZANOVIĆ (Crvena Z
Segundo CASTILLO (Crvena
Predrag PAVLOVIĆ (Napreda
Nebojša PRTENJAK (Mladost
Zoran TOŠIĆ (Partizan)

CLUB-BY-CLUB

FK BANAT

Coach - Petar Kurćubić; (31/10/07) Žarko Soldo; (2/4/08) Ljubinko Drulović

Founded - 2006

2007				
19/8	Vojvodina	h	1-1	*Stojaković (p)*
26/8	Partizan	a	2-4	*Markovski M., Milošević*
1/9	Čukarički	a	1-2	*Mikić*
9/9	Borac	a	0-0	
15/9	OFK Beograd	h	2-1	*Mikić 2*
22/9	Napredak	a	2-0	*Branković, Mikić*
29/9	Mladost Lučani	h	0-0	
7/10	Crvena Zvezda	a	0-2	
20/10	Smederevo	h	2-3	*Trnavac, Mikić*
27/10	Hajduk Kula	a	0-0	
31/10	Bežanija	h	2-1	*Milošević, og (Vanić)*
3/11	Borac	h	2-1	*Mikić (p), Vujović*
10/11	Vojvodina	a	0-1	
1/12	Partizan	h	0-2	
8/12	Čukarički	h	1-3	*Stojaković*
12/12	OFK Beograd	a	2-0	*Stojaković, Mikić*
15/12	Napredak	h	0-1	
2008				
2/3	Mladost Lučani	a	1-1	*Osmanović*
8/3	Crvena Zvezda	h	2-2	*Milošević, Vujović*
15/3	Smederevo	a	1-0	*Baljak*
22/3	Hajduk Kula	h	1-2	*Vujović*
29/3	Bežanija	a	2-6	*Baljak, Vujović (p)*
2/4	Čukarički	a	0-2	
5/4	Mladost Lučani	h	2-2	*Milošević, Urumov*
12/4	Smederevo	a	1-1	*Osmanović*
19/4	Bežanija	a	3-3	*Vujović, Markovski A., Baljak*
26/4	OFK Beograd	h	1-2	*Urumov*
30/4	Hajduk Kula	a	0-0	
3/5	Napredak	h	0-4	
10/5	Partizan	a	1-3	*Urumov (p)*
14/5	Crvena Zvezda	h	1-2	*Vujović*
17/5	Vojvodina	a	1-4	*Vujović*
25/5	Borac	h	0-1	

No	Name	Nat	Pos	Aps	(s)	G
16	Rašo BABIĆ		D	8		
29	Darko BALJAK		D	13	(5)	
27	Slobodan BOKIĆ		A	1	(2)	
25	Siniša BRANKOVIĆ		M	13	(1)	
23	Davor ČAVRIĆ		M	4		
1	Nenad FILIPOVIĆ		G	8		
26	Nemanja GAVRANIĆ		M		(1)	
23	Darko JOVANDIĆ		D	5	(4)	
8	Marko JOVANOVIĆ		A	8	(4)	
25	Ivan KOSTIĆ		M		(1)	
15	Ilija LALEVIĆ	MNE	M		(2)	
30	Nenad MARINKOVIĆ		M	2	(3)	
17	Aleksandar MARKOVSKI		M	19	(7)	
15	Marko MARKOVSKI		A	6		
11	Igor MATIĆ		M	9	(2)	
19	Dragan MIČIĆ		A		(5)	
8	Borislav MIKIĆ		M	15		
5	Željko MILOSEVIĆ		D	25		
24	Marin MIOK		M	6	(7)	
14	Nenad MIŠKOVIĆ		D	7	(4)	
4	Marko MITROVIĆ		M	15		
2	Milko NOVAKOVIĆ	MNE	D	2		
19	Dejan OSMANOVIĆ		A		(4)	
9	Marinko PETKOVIĆ		A	9	(13)	
22	Danilo PUSTINJAKOVIĆ		G	25		
12	Srðan RADOSAVLJEV		M	14	(1)	
12	Branko SAVIĆ		D	16		
16	Ljubomir STEVANOVIĆ		M	9	(3)	
20	Igor STOJAKOVIĆ		M	15	(1)	
7	Milan STUPAR		M	21	(2)	
21	Milutin TRNAVAC		D	28	(2)	
6	Zoran URUMOV		D	16		
10	Dejan VASIĆ		M	1	(7)	
13	Vladimir VESELINOV		M	6	(6)	
18	Goran VUJOVIĆ	MNE	A	24	(5)	
4	Marko ZORIĆ		D	13		

FK BEŽANIJA

Coach - Miloljub Ostojić; (1/9/07) Ratko Dostanić; (6/10/07) Ljubiša Stamenković

Founded - 1921

007

1/8	OFK Beograd	h	1-2	*Vukajlović (p)*
3/8	Napredak	a	0-1	
5/8	Mladost Lučani	h	0-0	
/9	Crvena Zvezda	a	0-2	
5/9	Smederevo	h	2-0	*Ranđelović 2*
3/9	Hajduk Kula	a	0-1	
9/9	Čukarički	h	1-2	*Barać*
/10	Borac	h	1-2	*Ranđelović (p)*
1/10	Vojvodina	a	1-3	*Isidorović*
7/10	Partizan	h	0-2	
1/10	Banat	a	1-2	*Lazić*
/11	OFK Beograd	a	0-1	
0/11	Napredak	h	2-1	*Ranđelović (p), Vanić*
/12	Mladost Lučani	a	0-3	*(w/o)*
/12	Crvena Zvezda	h	0-1	
2/12	Smederevo	a	1-2	*Mihajlović*
5/12	Hajduk Kula	h	1-0	*Vukajlović*

008

/3	Čukarički	a	2-0	*Ranđelović, Somé Salombo*
/3	Borac	a	1-4	*Pajović*
5/3	Vojvodina	h	0-1	
2/3	Partizan	a	0-2	
9/3	Banat	h	6-2	*Somé Salombo 2, Ranđelović 2, Kolaković, Putinčanin*
/4	Partizan	a	2-2	*Kolaković, Somé Salombo*
4	Smederevo	h	1-2	*Ranđelović*
2/4	Crvena Zvezda	a	1-4	*Ranđelović*
9/4	Banat	h	3-3	*Hong, Ranđelović 2 (1p)*
5/4	Vojvodina	a	2-3	*Mihajlović 2*
0/4	OFK Beograd	h	2-2	*Putinčanin, Ranđelović*
5	Borac	a	0-2	
0/5	Hajduk Kula	h	0-1	
4/5	Čukarički	a	0-1	
7/5	Napredak	h	0-1	
5/5	Mladost Lučani	a	0-3	

o	Name	Nat	Pos	Aps	(s)	Gls
	Vladimir BARAĆ		M	8	7	1
	Ljuba BARANIN		D	14	(2)	
	Marko BUNA		A		(2)	
	Marko ĐALOVIĆ		M	11	(1)	
	HONG Yong-Jo	PRK	A	7		1
	Marko ILIĆ		M		(2)	
	Nemanja ILIĆ		D	17	(3)	
	Darko ISIDOROVIĆ		A	11	(10)	1
	Srđan IVANOVIĆ		M	1	(5)	
	Slobodan JANKOVIĆ		G	8		
	Dragoljub JEREMIĆ		D	3	(3)	
	Goran JOVIĆ		M		(1)	
	Miloš KOLAKOVIĆ		A	11	(2)	2
	Nikica KOŠUTIĆ		M	4	(3)	
	Nikola LEKOVIĆ		D	1	(1)	
	Predrag LAZIĆ		M	10	(3)	1
	Darko LOVRIĆ		D	11		
	Dušan MIHAJLOVIĆ		M	25		3
	Zoran MIJANOVIĆ		G	12		
	Marko MILIĆ	CRO	M		(3)	
	Danilo NIKOLIĆ		D	13	(3)	
	Marko NIKOLIĆ		M	1	(5)	
	Nebojša OBRADOVIĆ		M	1	(2)	
	Dejan OSMANOVIĆ		A		(1)	
	Srđan OSTOJIĆ		G	2	(1)	
21	Tomislav PAJOVIĆ		D	18	(2)	1
12	Bojan PAVLOVIĆ	MNE	G	8	(1)	
5	Vladan PAVLOVIĆ		M	8	(2)	
24	Vasilije PRODANOVIĆ		M	18		
17	Marko PUTINČANIN		M	16	(2)	2
9	Predrag RANĐELOVIĆ		A	23	(2)	12
15	Bojan ŠARANOV		G	2		
19	Ibrahim SOMÉ SALOMBO	COD	A	11		4
2	Perica STANČESKI		D	19	(3)	
16	Milan STOJANOVIĆ		M	9	(4)	
35	Stefan TRMČIĆ		A		(1)	
23	Kristijan TUCAKOVIĆ		D	12	(1)	
4	Nenad VANIĆ		D	17		1
6	Aleksandar VASILJEVIĆ		D	9		
19	Vladimir VUKAJLOVIĆ		M	11	(1)	2
18	Rade VUKOTIĆ		A		(1)	

FK BORAC

Coach - Miodrag Božović (MNE); (1/3/08) Milovan Rajevac

Founded - 1926

2007

17/8	OFK Beograd	a	0-2	
26/8	Napredak	h	1-0	*Injac*
1/9	Mladost Lučani	a	0-1	
9/9	Banat	h	0-0	
15/9	Crvena Zvezda	h	0-0	
22/9	Smederevo	a	1-0	*Dmitrović (p)*
29/9	Hajduk Kula	h	2-0	*Petrović, Simić*
6/10	Bežanija	a	2-1	*Injac, Pavlović*
20/10	Čukarički	h	1-1	*Bošković*
28/10	Vojvodina	h	2-4	*Pavlović, Injac*
31/10	Partizan	a	0-0	
3/11	Banat	a	1-2	*Pavlović*
10/11	OFK Beograd	h	2-0	*Injac, Dmitrović*
1/12	Napredak	a	0-0	
8/12	Mladost Lučani	h	2-0	*Simić, Kocić*
12/12	Crvena Zvezda	a	0-4	
15/12	Smederevo	h	0-2	

2008

2/3	Hajduk Kula	a	0-0	
8/3	Bežanija	h	4-1	
15/3	Čukarički	a	0-0	*Jevtić 2, Spasojević, Milunović*
22/3	Vojvodina	a	2-1	*Antić, Lazović*
30/3	Partizan	h	0-1	
2/4	OFK Beograd	h	0-0	
5/4	Hajduk Kula	a	1-1	*Jevtić*
12/4	Napredak	h	1-1	*Lazović*
20/4	Partizan	a	0-1	
26/4	Crvena Zvezda	h	0-2	
30/4	Vojvodina	a	0-5	
3/5	Bežanija	h	2-0	*Dmitrović (p), Lazović*
10/5	Čukarički	h	2-1	*Pavlović, Stojanović*
14/5	Mladost Lučani	a	1-2	*Đoković*
17/5	Smederevo	h	1-0	*Stojanović*
25/5	Banat	a	1-0	*Rendulić*

No	Name	Nat	Pos	Aps	(s)	Gls
13	Zoran ANTIĆ		D	28		1
9	Ivan BOSKOVIĆ	MNE	A	5	(11)	1
24	Nemanja BRAJOVIĆ		M	1	(2)	
6	Boban DMITROVIĆ		D	29		3
7	Ivan ĐOKOVIĆ		M	5	(6)	1
4	Dragan DRAGUTINOVIĆ		D	26		
1	Nenad ERIĆ		G	17		
12	Branko GRAHOVAC	MNE	G	1		
7	Nenad INJAC		A	11	(5)	4
16	Aleksandar JEVTIĆ		A	15		3
20	Saša KOCIĆ		M	17	(5)	1

No	Name	Nat	Pos	Aps	(s)	Gls
11	Vladimir KRNJINAC		M	30		
17	Nenad LAZAREVSKI		D	4	(12)	
22	Darko LAZOVIĆ		M	5	(10)	3
19	Dragan MILOVANOVIĆ		A	4	(4)	
21	Nemanja MILUNOVIĆ		D		(2)	1
14	Marko MUGOŠA	MNE	M	9	(2)	
18	Bojan PAVLOVIĆ		M	14	(3)	4
3	Dragiša PEJOVIĆ		D	15	(5)	
8	Rade PETROVIĆ	MNE	M	17		1
16	Stojan PILIPOVIĆ		M	4	(4)	
27	Mirko POLEDICA		D	12		
1	Saša RADIVOJEVIĆ		G	15		
5	Zoran RENDULIĆ		D	19	(3)	1
22	Nikola SIMIĆ		M	15	(2)	2
28	Vladan SPASOJEVIĆ		M	11	(11)	1
10	Boban STOJANOVIĆ		A	13	(2)	2
2	Miloš ŽIVKOVIĆ		D	8	(1)	
10	Irfan VUSLJANIN		M	13		

FK CRVENA ZVEZDA

Coach - Milorad Kosanović; (11/11/07) Aleksandar Janković

Founded - 1945

MAJOR HONOURS: European Champion Clubs' Cup - (1) 1991; World Club Cup - (1) 1991; Yugoslav/Serbian League - (25) 1951, 1953, 1956, 1957, 1959, 1960, 1964, 1968, 1969, 1970, 1973, 1977, 1980, 1981, 1984, 1988, 1990, 1991, 1992, 1995, 2000, 2001, 2004, 2006, 2007; Yugoslav/Serbian Cup - (22) 1948, 1949, 1950, 1958, 1959, 1964, 1968, 1970, 1971, 1982, 1985, 1990, 1993, 1995, 1996, 1997, 1999, 2000, 2002, 2004, 2006, 2007.

2007				
11/8	Čukarički	h	0-0	
18/8	Smederevo	h	1-0	*Koroman*
1/9	Bežanija	h	2-0	*Koroman, Castillo*
15/9	Borac	a	0-0	
23/9	Vojvodina	h	1-1	*Milijaš*
29/9	Partizan	a	2-2	*Koroman 2*
7/10	Banat	h	2-0	*Barcos 2*
21/10	OFK Beograd	a	2-0	*Burzanović, Milijaš*
28/10	Napredak	h	1-1	*Molina*
31/10	Mladost Lučani	a	1-1	*Castillo*
3/11	Čukarički	a	1-0	*Milijaš*
11/11	Smederevo	a	5-2	*Jestrović 3 (1p), Milovanović, Molina*
28/11	Hajduk Kula	a	2-0	*Milovanović, Jestrović (p)*
2/12	Hajduk Kula	h	1-1	*Burzanović (p)*
9/12	Bežanija	a	1-0	*Misdongarde*
12/12	Borac	h	4-0	*Basta, Milovanović 2, Lucas*
15/12	Vojvodina	a	1-1	*Koroman*
2008				
1/3	Partizan	h	4-1	*Milovanović, Castillo 2, Milijaš (p)*
8/3	Banat	a	2-2	*Rašković, Jestrović*
15/3	OFK Beograd	h	2-0	*Castillo, Jestrović*
22/3	Napredak	a	1-0	*Jestrović*
29/3	Mladost Lučani	h	2-2	*Milovanović, Burzanović*
2/4	Napredak	h	5-0	*Misdongarde 3, Castillo, Milovanović*
5/4	Partizan	a	1-1	*Burzanović*
12/4	Bežanija	h	4-1	*Milijaš 3, Milovanović*
19/4	Vojvodina	h	5-1	*Burzanović 2, Jestrović, Milijaš 2 (1p)*
26/4	Borac	a	2-0	*Jestrović, Castillo*
30/4	Čukarički	h	1-0	*Jestrović*
3/5	Mladost Lučani	a	1-0	*Castillo*
10/5	Smederevo	h	4-3	*Koroman, Burzanović, Milijaš, Milovanović*
14/5	Banat	a	2-1	*Jestrović 2*
17/5	OFK Beograd	h	1-0	*Jestrović*
25/5	Hajduk Kula	a	1-1	*Burzanović*

No	Name	Nat	Pos	Aps	(s)	Gls
3	Dušan ANĐELKOVIĆ		D	27	(1)	
19	Miloš BAJALICA		D	7	(2)	
33	Boban BAJKOVIĆ	MNE	G	4		
22	Zoran BANOVIĆ	MNE	G	3	(1)	
9	Hernán BARCOS	ARG	A	4	(5)	2
30	Dušan BASTA		M	16	(4)	1
25	Marko BLAŽIĆ		M	1	(2)	
17	Vladimir BOGDANOVIĆ		M	4	(8)	
18	Grzegorz BRONOWICKI	POL	D	12	(1)	
10	Igor BURZANOVIĆ	MNE	M	18	(7)	8
35	Segundo Alejandro CASTILLO	ECU	M	26		8
33	Filip ĐORĐEVIĆ		A	2	(5)	
6	Vladimir ĐORĐEVIĆ		D	1	(1)	
21	Ibrahima Knouma GUEYE	SEN	D	23		
88	Nenad JESTROVIĆ		A	19	(3)	13
8	Ognjen KOROMAN		M	29	(1)	6
20	João Nuno Silva Cardoso "LUCAS"	POR	M	12	(1)	1
7	Nenad MILIJAŠ		M	28	(1)	10
32	Dejan MILOVANOVIĆ		M	24	(2)	9
15	Betoligar MISDONGARDE	CHA	A	7	(8)	4
23	Mauricio Alejandro MOLINA Uribe	COL	M	8	(3)	2
24	Pavle NINKOV		D	13		
31	Saša RADIVOJEVIĆ		G	1		
1	Ivan RANĐELOVIĆ		G	25		
27	Milanko RAŠKOVIĆ		A	6	(7)	1
25	Franclin SALAS	ECU	A	1	(3)	
14	Nenad TOMOVIĆ		D	11	(1)	
5	Nikola TRAJKOVIĆ		M		(10)	
11	Ivan TRIČKOVSKI	MKD	A	3	(8)	
14	Aleksandar TRIŠOVIĆ		M	3	(1)	
13	Đorđe TUTORIĆ		D	25	(4)	

FK ČUKARIČKI

Coach - Vladan Milojević; (25/8/07) Dragoslav Stepanović

Founded - 1926

2007				
11/8	Crvena Zvezda	a	0-0	
18/8	Partizan	h	0-3	
25/8	Smederevo	a	0-1	
1/9	Banat	h	2-1	*Popović L., Bojović*
15/9	Hajduk Kula	a	1-1	*Ćulum*
22/9	OFK Beograd	h	0-2	
29/9	Bežanija	a	2-1	*Petković M., Blažić*
6/10	Napredak	h	0-0	
20/10	Borac	a	1-1	*Ćulum*
27/10	Mladost Lučani	h	2-0	*Ninkov, Blažić*
31/10	Vojvodina	a	0-0	
3/11	Crvena Zvezda	h	0-1	
10/11	Partizan	a	1-1	*Janković*
1/12	Smederevo	h	2-2	*Tubić (p), Blažić*
8/12	Banat	a	3-1	*Vilotić, Petković M., Bojović*
12/12	Hajduk Kula	h	1-1	*Blažić (p)*
15/12	OFK Beograd	a	3-0	*Bojović, Popović L., Marjanović*
2008				
2/3	Bežanija	h	0-2	
8/3	Napredak	a	2-0	*Aganović, Marković G.*
15/3	Borac	h	0-0	
22/3	Mladost Lučani	a	1-2	*Popović L. (p)*
29/3	Vojvodina	h	1-0	*Popović L.*
2/4	Banat	h	2-0	*Popović L., Petković M.*
5/4	OFK Beograd	a	1-1	*og (Markoski)*
12/4	Hajduk Kula	h	0-1	
19/4	Napredak	a	0-2	

6/4	Partizan	h	0-1	
0/4	Crvena Zvezda	a	0-1	
/5	Vojvodina	h	1-3	*Bojović*
0/5	Borac	a	1-2	*Bojović*
4/5	Bežanija	h	1-0	*Stjepanović*
7/5	Mladost Lučani	h	3-0	*Bojović, Aganović, Popović L.*
5/5	Smederevo	a	0-1	

No	Name	Nat	Pos	Aps	(s)	Gls
5	Admir AGANOVIĆ	BIH	A	12	(2)	2
8	Rudolph BESTER	NAM	A	10	(2)	
5	Marko BLAŽIĆ		M	16		4
	Milan BOJOVIĆ		A	11	(16)	6
1	Milan ĆULUM		M	13	(4)	2
	Mihajlo DOBRAŠINOVIĆ		M	10	(8)	
7	Jovan DŽIKNIĆ		A		(1)	
	Bojan ISAILOVIĆ		G	30		
6	Goran JANKOVIĆ		M	20	(6)	1
5	Ivan KALIČANIN		M	4	(2)	
2	Milan LUKAČ		G	3		
9	Saša MARJANOVIĆ		M	15	(2)	1
4	Goran MARKOVIĆ		M	13	(4)	1
0	Marko MAROVIĆ		D	9	(1)	
3	Albert NAĐ		M	9		
4	Pavle NINKOV		D	15		1
3	Drazen OKUKA		D	11	(1)	
	Mitar PEKOVIĆ	MNE	D	26	(3)	
7	Dejan PERIĆ		M	9	(12)	
3	Igor PETKOVIĆ		M	9	(4)	
2	Miša PETKOVIĆ		A	15	(5)	3
0	Miroslav PETRONIJEVIĆ		M		(1)	
	Mirko POLEDICA		D	11	(1)	
	Lazar POPOVIĆ		A	19	(6)	6
3	Minja POPOVIĆ		D	1	(5)	
	Nebojša SAVIĆ		D	13	(4)	
	Darko STANOJEVIĆ		D	2		
4	Ostoja STJEPANOVIĆ	MKD	M	6	(2)	1
0	Stanko SVITLICA		A	9		
	Nemanja TUBIĆ		D	12	(1)	1
	Milan VILOTIĆ		D	16	(2)	1
	Nenad VISNJIĆ		D	14	(3)	
3	Dejan VUKOJEVIĆ		A		(1)	

FK HAJDUK KULA

Coach - Žarko Soldo; (6/10/07) Mihajlo Bošnjak; (21/10/07) (Radmilo Jovanović); (3/11/07) Miroslav Vukašinović

Founded - 1925

007				
1/8	Napredak	h	2-0	*Kozoš, Radivojević*
8/8	Mladost Lučani	a	0-0	
/9	Smederevo	a	0-1	
5/9	Čukarički	h	1-1	*Kozoš*
3/9	Bežanija	h	1-0	*Vasiljević*
9/9	Borac	a	0-2	
/10	Vojvodina	h	1-2	*Komazec*
1/10	Partizan	a	1-2	*Habenšus*
7/10	Banat	h	0-0	
1/10	OFK Beograd	a	1-3	*Perić*
/11	Napredak	a	0-1	
0/11	Mladost Lučani	h	2-2	*Fejsa L., og (Milošević I.)*
3/11	Crvena Zvezda	h	0-2	
/12	Crvena Zvezda	a	1-1	*Radivojević*
/12	Smederevo	h	3-1	*Perić 2, Vasiljević*
2/12	Čukarički	a	1-1	*Perić*
5/12	Bežanija	a	0-1	
008				
/3	Borac	h	0-0	
/3	Vojvodina	a	0-1	
15/3	Partizan	h	0-1	
22/3	Banat	a	2-1	*Mrđanin, Radivojević*
29/3	OFK Beograd	h	1-0	*Radivojević*
2/4	Vojvodina	a	1-4	*Todorović*
5/4	Borac	h	1-1	*Perić*
12/4	Čukarički	a	1-0	*Perić*
19/4	Mladost Lučani	h	0-0	
26/4	Smederevo	a	0-0	
30/4	Banat	h	0-0	
4/5	OFK Beograd	a	1-1	*Dojkić*
10/5	Bežanija	a	1-0	*Komazec*
14/5	Napredak	h	2-0	*Komazec, Jovanović*
17/5	Partizan	a	0-1	
25/5	Crvena Zvezda	h	1-1	*Komazec*

No	Name	Nat	Pos	Aps	(s)	Gls
12	Ljubo ANDRIJAŠEVIĆ		G		(1)	
8	Nikola BOGIĆ		M	31		
6	Radoš BULATOVIĆ		D	5	(7)	
5	Ivan ĆIRKA		D	12	(1)	
6	Đorđe ČOTRA		D	2		
11	Aleksandar DAVIDOV		M	5	(1)	
15	Bojan DOJKIĆ		D	5	(4)	1
13	Srđan ĐUKANOVIĆ	MNE	M	1	(4)	
2	Duško DUKIĆ		D	4	(1)	
1	Anđelko ĐURIČIĆ		G	33		
3	Darko FEJSA		D	24	(1)	
10	Ljubomir FEJSA		M	32		1
16	Goran HABENŠUS		D	22	(3)	1
22	Aleksandar JOVANOVIĆ		M	6	(13)	1
25	Filip KASALICA	MNE	A	2	(4)	
21	Nikola KOMAZEC		A	11	(16)	4
17	Igor KOZOŠ		D	31		2
14	Blažo LALEVIĆ	MNE	D	1	(1)	
23	Vladan MILOSAVLJEV		M	2	(3)	
27	Milan MILUTINOVIĆ		M		(1)	
26	Đorđe MRĐANIN		D	12	(1)	1
2	Savo PAVIĆEVIĆ	MNE	D	13		
18	Milan PERIĆ		A	25	(3)	6
7	Jovan RADIVOJEVIĆ		M	23	(3)	4
20	Aleksandar SIMČEVIĆ		D		(2)	
23	Nebojša ŠODIĆ		D	3	(9)	
13	Srđan STANIĆ	MNE	M	26		
14	Nenad TODOROVIĆ		D	3		1
5	Damir TOPČAGIĆ		D	2	(2)	
19	Branislav TRAJKOVIĆ		D	9	(4)	
9	Miodrag VASILJEVIĆ		A	18	(7)	2
24	Dušan ZELIĆ		M		(2)	

FK MLADOST LUČANI

Coach - Nenad Milovanović

Founded - 1952

2007				
11/8	Smederevo	a	0-0	
18/8	Hajduk Kula	h	0-0	
25/8	Bežanija	a	0-0	
1/9	Borac	h	1-0	*Aganović*
15/9	Vojvodina	a	1-2	*Jeremić S.*
22/9	Partizan	h	1-4	*Jevđović*
29/9	Banat	a	0-0	
6/10	OFK Beograd	h	2-2	*Useni, Žunić*
20/10	Napredak	a	1-0	*Mijajlović*
27/10	Čukarički	a	0-2	
31/10	Crvena Zvezda	h	1-1	*Useni*
3/11	Smederevo	h	3-2	*Prtenjak, Milošević I., Žunić*
10/11	Hajduk Kula	a	2-2	*Avramović, Jevđović*
1/12	Bežanija	h	3-0	*(w/o)*
8/12	Borac	a	0-2	

12/12	Vojvodina	h	0-1	
15/12	Partizan	a	0-4	
2008				
2/3	Banat	h	1-1	*Žunić*
8/3	OFK Beograd	a	1-1	*Grkajac*
15/3	Napredak	h	1-1	*Žunić*
22/3	Čukarički	h	2-1	*Grkajac 2*
29/3	Crvena Zvezda	a	2-2	*Prtenjak 2 (1p)*
2/4	Smederevo	h	0-1	
5/4	Banat	a	2-2	*Prtenjak, Grkajac*
12/4	OFK Beograd	h	3-1	*Milošević I., Prtenjak 2*
19/4	Hajduk Kula	a	0-0	
26/4	Napredak	h	0-0	
30/4	Partizan	a	0-2	
3/5	Crvena Zvezda	h	0-1	
10/5	Vojvodina	a	0-2	
14/5	Borac	h	2-1	*Prtenjak (p), Jeremić S.*
17/5	Čukarički	a	0-3	
25/5	Bežanija	h	3-0	*Jeremić S., Useni, Prtenjak*

No	Name	Nat	Pos	Aps	(s)	Gls
23	Admir AGANOVIĆ		A	8	(3)	1
9	Nemanja ARSENIJEVIĆ		A	4	(4)	
22	Marko AVRAMOVIĆ		M	12	(8)	1
13	Igor DIMITRIJEVIĆ		G	10		
18	Darko ĐURĐEVIĆ		M	3	(2)	
32	Igor GRKAJAC		A	12	(4)	4
33	Sinisa JEREMIĆ		M	1	(1)	
3	Slaviša JEREMIĆ		D	23		3
9	Radivoje JEVĐOVIĆ		A	3	(13)	2
12	Marjan JUGOVIĆ		A		(8)	
8	Goran LUKOVIĆ		M	18	(2)	
14	Slavko MARIĆ		D	27		
27	Neven MARKOVIĆ		D	8	(2)	
10	Milan MIJAJLOVIĆ		A	11	(10)	1
23	Milovan MIJATOVIĆ		D	4	(2)	
28	Bogdan MILOSEVIĆ		D		(1)	
4	Ivan MILOSEVIĆ		D	24		2
1	Bojan MIŠIĆ		G	22	(1)	
16	Aleksandar PETROVIĆ		M	16	(5)	
19	Srđan PJEVAČ		M	22	(2)	
21	Nebojša PRTENJAK		M	18	(5)	8
7	Đorđe RAJKOVIĆ		M	4	(2)	
11	Uros SINĐIĆ		M	21	(5)	
20	Nermin USENI		M	23	(2)	3
18	Nenad VASIĆ		A	5	(10)	
17	Radojica VASIĆ		M	27		
5	Dragiša ŽUNIĆ		D	26		4

FK NAPREDAK

Coach - Mladen Dodić; (29/9/07) (Zvonko Petrović); (20/10/07) Saša Nikolić

Founded - 1946

2007				
11/8	Hajduk Kula	a	0-2	
18/8	Bežanija	h	1-0	*Pavlović P.*
26/8	Borac	a	0-1	
2/9	Vojvodina	h	0-1	
16/9	Partizan	a	1-3	*Pavlović P.*
22/9	Banat	h	0-2	
29/9	OFK Beograd	a	1-1	*Stamenković B.*
6/10	Čukarički	a	0-0	
20/10	Mladost Lučani	h	0-1	
28/10	Crvena Zvezda	a	1-1	*Pavlović P.*
31/10	Smederevo	h	3-1	*Milovanović, Pavlović P. 2*
3/11	Hajduk Kula	h	1-0	*Pavlović P.*
10/11	Bežanija	a	1-2	*og (Vanić)*
1/12	Borac	h	0-0	
8/12	Vojvodina	a	0-2	
12/12	Partizan	h	0-2	
15/12	Banat	a	1-0	*Vujović*
2008				
2/3	OFK Beograd	h	2-0	*Gajić (p), Petronijević*
8/3	Čukarički	h	0-2	
15/3	Mladost Lučani	a	1-1	*Babić*
22/3	Crvena Zvezda	h	0-1	
29/3	Smederevo	a	1-1	*Đorđević*
2/4	Crvena Zvezda	a	0-5	
5/4	Vojvodina	h	1-0	*Petronijević*
12/4	Borac	a	1-1	*Branković*
19/4	Čukarički	h	2-0	*Gajić 2 (2p)*
26/4	Mladost Lučani	a	0-0	
30/4	Smederevo	h	1-0	*Punoševac*
3/5	Banat	a	4-0	*Pavlović P. 2, Punoševac, Vujović*
10/5	OFK Beograd	h	1-0	*Vujović*
14/5	Hajduk Kula	a	0-2	
17/5	Bežanija	a	1-0	*Petronijević*
25/5	Partizan	h	0-1	

No	Name	Nat	Pos	Aps	(s)	Gls
4	Ivan BABIĆ		D	11		1
11	Vladan BINIĆ	CZE	M	1	(10)	
27	Vladimir BRANKOVIĆ		D	15		1
4	Fabio Carleandro DA SILVA	BRA	D	8	(1)	
2	Marko ĐORĐEVIĆ		D	27	(1)	1
21	Dušan DUNJIĆ		D	21	(2)	
10	Milan GAJIĆ		A	15		3
14	Danijel GAŠIĆ		D	1	(3)	
5	Goran GOGIĆ		M	27		
27	Nikola IGNJATIJEVIĆ		D	7	(1)	
11	Predrag ILIĆ		A	3	(5)	
22	Predrag JEREMIĆ		M		(2)	
19	Radivoje JEVĐOVIĆ		A	8	(2)	
6	Aleksandar MIJATOVIĆ		D	28		
10	Dragan MILOVANOVIĆ		A	5	(4)	1
16	Srđan NOVKOVIĆ		M	14	(1)	
7	Predrag PAVLOVIĆ		M	31		8
3	Radmilo PAVLOVIĆ		M	8	(6)	
31	Dušan PETRONIJEVIĆ		M	21	(5)	3
15	Igor PETROVIĆ		M		(1)	
23	Josip PROJIĆ		D	9	(6)	
30	Bratislav PUNOŠEVAC		A	10	(6)	2
25	Dalibor RADOVANOVIĆ		G		(1)	
8	Nenad ŠLJIVIĆ		M	27		
18	Nenad SREČKOVIĆ		A	2	(4)	
9	Bojan STAMENKOVIĆ		M	5	(13)	1
1	Saša STAMENKOVIĆ		G	33		
20	Goran STOJKOVIĆ		D	5	(4)	
17	Dragan TADIĆ		A	8	(3)	
22	Vladimir TINTOR		M		(6)	
24	Predrag VUJOVIĆ		M	13	(11)	3

OFK BEOGRAD

Coach - Branko Vukašinović; (20/3/08) Ljupko Petrović; (23/4/08) Mihajlo Ivanović

Founded - 1911

MAJOR HONOURS: Yugoslav League - (5) 1931, 1933, 1935, 1936, 1939; Yugoslav Cup - (4) 1953, 1955, 1962, 1966.

2007				
11/8	Bežanija	a	2-1	*Novaković, Kaluđerović*
17/8	Borac	h	2-0	*Kaluđerović, Krstičić*
26/8	Vojvodina	a	1-1	*Arsenijević*
2/9	Partizan	h	0-1	
15/9	Banat	a	1-2	*Novaković*
22/9	Čukarički	a	2-0	*Novaković, Veselinović*
29/9	Napredak	h	1-1	*Nuhi*
6/10	Mladost Lučani	a	2-2	*Kaluđerović, Beljić*
21/10	Crvena Zvezda	h	0-2	
27/10	Smederevo	a	1-0	*Marjanović*

31/10	Hajduk Kula	h	3-1	*Babović, Kaluđerović 2*
3/11	Bežanija	h	1-0	*Babović*
10/11	Borac	a	0-2	
2/12	Vojvodina	h	0-0	
8/12	Partizan	a	1-5	*Babović*
12/12	Banat	h	0-2	
15/12	Čukarički	h	0-3	
2008				
2/3	Napredak	a	0-2	
8/3	Mladost Lučani	h	1-1	*De Oliveira*
15/3	Crvena Zvezda	a	0-2	
23/3	Smederevo	h	1-2	*Kaluđerović*
29/3	Hajduk Kula	a	0-1	
2/4	Borac	a	0-0	
5/4	Čukarički	h	1-1	*Stevanović*
12/4	Mladost Lučani	a	1-3	*Krstičić*
19/4	Smederevo	h	2-1	*Bosančić (p), De Oliveira*
26/4	Banat	a	2-1	*Novaković, Lazić*
30/4	Bežanija	a	2-2	*Marjanović, Bosančić (p)*
4/5	Hajduk Kula	h	1-1	*Kaluđerović*
10/5	Napredak	a	0-1	
14/5	Partizan	h	1-3	*Markoski*
17/5	Crvena Zvezda	a	0-1	
25/5	Vojvodina	h	2-0	*Novaković, Beljić*

No	Name	Nat	Pos	Aps	(s)	Gls
16	Miloš ADAMOVIĆ		M	9	(2)	
20	Nemanja ARSENIJEVIĆ		A	3	(1)	1
10	Stefan BABOVIĆ		M	15		3
35	Saša BALIĆ		D	1		
25	Nikola BELJIĆ		D	10	(11)	2
10	Miloš BOSANCIĆ		M	11	(1)	2
21	Ivan ĆIRKA		D	7		
20	William Arthur DE OLIVEIRA	BRA	M	8	(4)	2
15	Milan ILIĆ		D	1		
1	Radiša ILIĆ		G	33		
8	Đorđe IVELJA		M	21	(2)	
9	Petar JELIĆ	BIH	A	4	(6)	
11	Andrija KALUĐEROVIĆ		A	17	(11)	7
30	Nenad KRSTIČIĆ		M	16	(9)	2
5	Branko LAZAREVIĆ		D	25		
18	Predrag LAZIĆ		M	12	(2)	1
22	Emir LOTINAC		D	6	(3)	
14	Rodoljub MARJANOVIĆ		A	9	(8)	2
6	Bojan MARKOSKI	MKD	D	21		1
33	Vlado MARKOVIĆ	MKD	D	12	(2)	
26	Novak MARTINOVIĆ		D	5		
17	Zoran MILOVAC		M	1	(4)	
27	Milovan MILOVIĆ		D	5	(1)	
34	Igor MIŠAN		M		(1)	
13	Mitar NOVAKOVIĆ	MNE	M	30	(1)	5
19	Ajazdin NUHI		M	21	(5)	1
9	Đorđe RAKIĆ		A	1		
32	Stefan ŠĆEPOVIĆ	MNE	A	2	(2)	
20	Aleksandar SIMČEVIĆ		D	3	(3)	
4	Nebojša SKOPLJAK		D	11	(4)	
2	Ivan STEVANOVIĆ		D	30		1
14	Nenad TODOROVIĆ		D	5		
23	Dalibor VESELINOVIĆ		A	8	(14)	1
7	Irfan VUSLJANIN		M		(1)	

FK PARTIZAN

Coach - Miroslav Đukić; (25/12/07) Slaviša Jokanović

Founded - 1945

MAJOR HONOURS: Yugoslav/Serbian League - (20) 1947, 1949, 1961, 1962, 1963, 1965, 1976, 1978, 1983, 1986, 1987, 1993, 1994, 1996, 1997, 1999, 2002, 2003, 2005, 2008; Yugoslav/Serbian Cup (10) 1947, 1952, 1954, 1957, 1989, 1992, 1994, 1998, 2001, 2008.

2007				
11/8	Vojvodina	a	1-0	*Jovetić*
18/8	Čukarički	a	3-0	*Moreira, Jovetić, Lazetić*
26/8	Banat	h	4-2	*Diarra, Jovetić, Lazić., Moreira*
2/9	OFK Beograd	a	1-0	*Jovetić*
16/9	Napredak	h	3-1	*Tošić, Diarra, Lazić*
22/9	Mladost Lučani	a	4-1	*Diarra 2, Lazevski, Stjepanović*
29/9	Crvena Zvezda	h	2-2	*Jovetić, Moreira*
6/10	Smederevo	a	1-1	*Jovetić (p)*
21/10	Hajduk Kula	h	2-1	*Jovetić, Lazić*
27/10	Bežanija	a	2-0	*Lazić, Juca*
31/10	Borac	h	0-0	
4/11	Vojvodina	h	3-3	*Diarra, Jovetić, Tošić*
10/11	Čukarički	h	1-1	*Juca (p)*
1/12	Banat	a	2-0	*Tošić, Lazevski*
8/12	OFK Beograd	h	5-1	*Diarra, Moreira, Jovetić (p), Rukavina, Lazić*
12/12	Napredak	a	2-0	*Moreira, Jovetić*
15/12	Mladost Lučani	h	4-0	*Juca, Diarra, Tošić, Jovetić*
2008				
1/3	Crvena Zvezda	a	1-4	*Lazić*
8/3	Smederevo	h	1-0	*Đorđević*
15/3	Hajduk Kula	a	1-0	*Đorđević*
22/3	Bežanija	h	2-0	*Čadikovski 2*
30/3	Borac	a	1-0	*Đorđević*
2/4	Bežanija	h	2-2	*Đorđević (p), Moreira*
5/4	Crvena Zvezda	h	1-1	*Juca*
12/4	Vojvodina	a	1-1	*Đorđević (p)*
20/4	Borac	h	1-0	*Diarra*
26/4	Čukarički	a	1-0	*Tošić*
30/4	Mladost Lučani	h	2-0	*Diarra, Jovetić*
3/5	Smederevo	a	1-0	*Tošić*
10/5	Banat	h	3-1	*Tošić 2, Juca*
14/5	OFK Beograd	a	3-1	*Moreira, Đorđević (p), Diarra*
17/5	Hajduk Kula	h	1-0	*Diarra*
25/5	Napredak	a	1-0	*Diarra*

No	Name	Nat	Pos	Aps	(s)	Gls
1	Darko BOŽOVIĆ	MNE	G	24		
27	Mladen BOŽOVIĆ	MNE	G	9	(1)	
88	Dragan ČADIKOVSKI	MKD	A	4	(3)	2
82	Marko ĆETKOVIĆ	MNE	M		(6)	
26	Lamine DIARRA	SEN	A	30	(1)	12
44	Nenad ĐORĐEVIĆ		D	14		6
20	Pedro Rocha Andrade "EDNILSON"	POR	M	11	(3)	
13	Marko JOVANOVIĆ		D	3	(6)	
35	Stevan JOVETIĆ	MNE	A	26	(1)	12
8	Juliano Roberto Antonello "JUCA"	BRA	M	25		5
24	Srđan KNEZEVIĆ		D	6	(4)	
16	Risto LAKIĆ	MNE	D	1	(1)	
11	Žarko LAZETIĆ		A	3	(12)	1
18	Aleksandar LAZEVSKI	MKD	D	13	(3)	2
14	Đorđe LAZIĆ		M	28	(2)	6
33	Darko MALETIĆ	BIH	M	13	(15)	
21	Miloš MIHAJLOV		D	15		
31	Nikola MITROVIĆ		M	5	(10)	
10	Almani Samori MOREIRA da Silva	POR	M	28		7
37	Ivan OBRADOVIĆ		D	19		
4	Nemanja RNIĆ		D	24	(1)	
3	Antonio RUKAVINA		D	17		1
5	Milovan SIKIMIĆ		D	5		
34	Branislav STANIĆ		M		(1)	
99	Slaven STJEPANOVIĆ		A	1	(6)	1
17	Zoran TOŠIĆ		M	30	(2)	8
9	Borko VESELINOVIĆ		A		(3)	
39	VICTOR HUGO de Manique Jesus	BRA	A		(2)	
6	Milan VJEŠTICA		D	9		
25	Živko ŽIVKOVIĆ		G		(1)	

FK SMEDEREVO

Coach - Goran Milojević; (11/11/07) Radmilo Ivančević

Founded - 1924

MAJOR HONOURS: Yugoslav Cup - (1) 2003.

Date	Opponent		Score	Scorers
2007				
11/8	Mladost Lučani	h	0-0	
18/8	Crvena Zvezda	a	0-1	
25/8	Čukarički	h	1-0	*Osmanović*
1/9	Hajduk Kula	h	1-0	*Čukić*
15/9	Bežanija	a	0-2	
22/9	Borac	h	0-1	
29/9	Vojvodina	a	1-2	*Andrić*
6/10	Partizan	h	1-1	*Zečević*
20/10	Banat	a	3-2	*Mudrinić, Zafirović, Radosavljević*
27/10	OFK Beograd	h	0-1	
31/10	Napredak	a	1-3	*Zečević*
3/11	Mladost Lučani	a	2-3	*Osmanović, Nikolić*
11/11	Crvena Zvezda	h	2-5	*Popović, Mudrinić (p)*
1/12	Čukarički	a	2-2	*Čukić, Mirosavljević*
8/12	Hajduk Kula	a	1-3	*Mirosavljević (p)*
12/12	Bežanija	h	2-1	*Kasom, Popović*
15/12	Borac	a	2-0	*Mirosavljević 2*
2008				
1/3	Vojvodina	h	1-0	*Mladenović*
8/3	Partizan	a	0-1	
15/3	Banat	h	0-1	
23/3	OFK Beograd	a	2-1	*Gegić, Mladenović*
29/3	Napredak	h	1-1	*Mudrinić*
2/4	Mladost Lučani	a	1-0	*Mladenović*
5/4	Bežanija	a	2-1	*Mudrinić, Mladenović*
12/4	Banat	h	1-1	*Martinović*
19/4	OFK Beograd	a	1-2	*Ćeran (p)*
26/4	Hajduk Kula	h	0-0	
30/4	Napredak	a	0-1	
3/5	Partizan	h	0-1	
10/5	Crvena Zvezda	a	3-4	*Čukić, Mladenović, Atanacković*
14/5	Vojvodina	h	1-2	*Mudrinić*
17/5	Borac	a	0-1	
25/5	Čukarički	h	1-0	*Atanacković*

No	Name	Nat	Pos	Aps	(s)	Gls
16	Mirko ANDRIĆ		D	11	(1)	1
20	Branislav ATANACKOVIĆ		M	5	(5)	2
30	Dragan ĆERAN		A	3	(11)	1
5	Vladan ČUKIĆ		M	26	(1)	3
27	Zoran ĐURAŠKOVIĆ		A	1	(15)	
16	Nemanja ĐUROVIĆ		A	3	(3)	
1	Srđan DUŠIĆ		G	4	(2)	
2	Miroslav GEGIĆ		D	11	(4)	1
21	Petar KASOM		A	19	(5)	1
17	Novak MARTINOVIĆ		D	7	(1)	1
14	Aleksandar MILJKOVIĆ		M		(1)	
77	Nenad MIROSAVLJEVIĆ		A	10	(2)	4
8	Nenad MLADENOVIĆ		A	16		5
10	Vladimir MUDRINIĆ		M	28		5
17	Zvonko NEDELJKOVIĆ		M	3	(3)	
7	Milan NIKOLIĆ		M	6	(5)	1
8	Zoran NOVAKOVIĆ		A	4	(5)	
29	Dejan OSMANOVIĆ		A	9	(5)	2
24	Aleksandar PETROVIĆ		M	26	(1)	
13	Ivan POPOVIĆ		D	26	(1)	2
22	Miloš RADANOVIĆ	MNE	G	15		
11	Dragan RADOSAVLJEVIĆ		M	25	(1)	1
4	Ivan RADOVANOVIĆ		D	10	(3)	
12	Dejan RANKOVIĆ		G	14	(1)	
3	Marko SOČANAC		D	22	(1)	
22	Predrag STAMENKOVIĆ		D	11		
26	Đorđe ZAFIROVIĆ		M	6	(7)	1
18	Bojan ZAVIŠIĆ		D	7	(3)	
9	Milorad ZEČEVIĆ		A	25	(1)	2
19	Dejan ŽIVKOVIĆ		M	10	(5)	

FK VOJVODINA

Coach - Milovan Rajevac; (23/9/07) Ivan Brzić

Founded - 1914

MAJOR HONOURS: Yugoslav League - (2) 1966, 1989.

Date	Opponent		Score	Scorers
2007				
11/8	Partizan	h	0-1	
19/8	Banat	a	1-1	*Despotović*
26/8	OFK Beograd	h	1-1	*Drakulić*
2/9	Napredak	a	1-0	*Pekarić*
15/9	Mladost Lučani	h	2-1	*Kačar, Drakulić*
23/9	Crvena Zvezda	a	1-1	*Kačar*
29/9	Smederevo	h	2-1	*Kačar, Despotović (p)*
6/10	Hajduk Kula	a	2-1	*Kačar, Drakulić*
21/10	Bežanija	h	3-1	*Kačar 2, Despotović*
28/10	Borac	a	4-2	*Kačar, Buač, Despotović, Tumbasović*
31/10	Čukarički	h	0-0	
4/11	Partizan	a	3-3	*Kačar 3*
10/11	Banat	h	1-0	*Buač*
2/12	OFK Beograd	a	0-0	
8/12	Napredak	h	2-0	*Stošić, Drakulić*
12/12	Mladost Lučani	a	1-0	*Pekarić*
15/12	Crvena Zvezda	h	1-1	*Popović*
2008				
1/3	Smederevo	a	0-1	
9/3	Hajduk Kula	h	1-0	*Buač (p)*
15/3	Bežanija	a	1-0	*Tumbasović*
22/3	Borac	h	1-2	*Popović*
29/3	Čukarički	a	0-1	
2/4	Hajduk Kula	h	4-1	*Tadić 2, Buač (p), Aleksić*
5/4	Napredak	a	0-1	
12/4	Partizan	h	1-1	*Buač*
19/4	Crvena Zvezda	a	1-5	*Grozdanovski*
26/4	Bežanija	h	3-2	*Tadić, og (Lovrić), Aleksić*
30/4	Borac	h	5-0	*Grozdanovski 2, Vukajlović, Radović, Tadić*
3/5	Čukarički	a	3-1	*Grozdanovski, Vukajlović, Tadić*
10/5	Mladost Lučani	h	2-0	*Buač, Tadić*
14/5	Smederevo	a	2-1	*Grozdanovski, Buač*
17/5	Banat	h	4-1	*Đurovski, Sepuya 2, Tadić*
25/5	OFK Beograd	a	0-2	

No	Name	Nat	Pos	Aps	(s)	Gls
33	Danijel ALEKSIĆ		A	4	(8)	2
1	Đorđe BABALJ		G	8		
30	Željko BRKIĆ		G	14		
10	Vladimir BUAČ		A	30	(1)	7
18	Marko ĐALOVIĆ		M	2		
21	Ranko DESPOTOVIĆ		A	16		4
9	Saša DRAKULIĆ		A	2	(10)	4
24	Igor ĐURIĆ		D	26		
20	Mario ĐUROVSKI		M	8	(5)	1
21	Vlatko GROZDANOVSKI	MKD	A	11	(2)	5
4	Gojko KAČAR		M	15	(2)	10
1	Damir KAHRIMAN		G	11		
2	Joseph Nestroy KIZITO	UGA	M	22	(1)	
19	Žarko KORAĆ	MNE	A		(4)	
23	Leo LERINC		M	1	(1)	
3	Slobodan MARKOVIĆ		M	1	(1)	
8	Milan MILUTINOVIĆ		M		(4)	
26	Miroslav MILUTINOVIĆ		D	15	(4)	
18	Nenad NASTIĆ		D	2		
22	Miodrag PANTELIĆ		A	7	(6)	

6	Savo PAVIĆEVIĆ	MNE	D	11		
6	Nino PEKARIĆ		D	13		2
13	Aleksandar POPOVIĆ		M	24	(2)	2
11	Srđan RADOSAVLJEV		M	2	(1)	
23	Ilija RADOVIĆ	MNE	D	6	(4)	1
7	Dragan ŠARAC		D	10	(1)	
9	Eugene SEPUYA	UGA	A	3	(10)	2
32	Goran SMILJANIĆ		M		(2)	
5	Miloš STOJČEV		M	1	(7)	
16	Miodrag STOŠIĆ		D	26		1
31	Dušan TADIĆ		M	24	(4)	7
27	Veseljko TRIVUNOVIĆ		M	24	(2)	
14	Janko TUMBASOVIĆ	MNE	M	11	(10)	2
8	Vladimir VUKAJLOVIĆ		M	11	(2)	2
11	Ljubiša VUKELJA		A	2	(2)	
7	Dragomir VUKOBRATOVIĆ		M		(1)	

PROMOTED CLUBS

FK JAVOR
Coach – Radovan Ćurčić
Founded - 1912

FK JAGODINA
Coach – Miljojko Gošić
Founded - 1918

FK RAD
Coach – Aleksandar Janjić
Founded - 1958

SECOND LEVEL FINAL TABLE 2007/08

		Pld	W	D	L	F	A	Pts
	FK Javor	34	18	16	0	38	12	70
	FK Jagodina	34	15	13	6	37	19	58
	FK BSK Borča	34	17	7	10	38	21	58
	FK Rad	34	16	9	9	50	34	57
	FK Voždovac	34	16	9	9	39	27	57
	FK Metalac	34	13	10	11	33	26	49
	FK Srem	34	14	5	15	43	41	47
	FK Mladost Apatin	34	13	8	13	30	31	47
	FK ČSK Pivara	34	11	13	10	34	29	46
0	FK Novi Sad	34	12	10	12	31	30	46
1	FK Sevojno	34	11	12	11	34	34	45
2	FK Novi Pazar	34	12	9	13	29	39	45
3	FK Hajduk Beograd	34	12	8	14	28	33	44
4	FK Radnički Niš	34	11	10	13	29	31	43
5	FK Zemun	34	10	12	12	28	40	42
6	FK Vlasina	34	9	10	15	35	47	37
7	OFK Mladenovac	34	7	9	18	28	51	30
8	FK Radnički Pirot	34	1	6	27	16	55	9

PROMOTION PLAY-OFFS

(28/5/08)
BSK Borča 0, Metalac 0 *(5-4 on pens)*
Rad 1, Voždovac 1 *(3-1 on pens)*
(1/6/08)
BSK Borča 0, Rad 0 *(2-4 on pens)*
(7/6/08)
Rad 3, Smederevo 1
(11/6/08)
Smederevo 2, Rad 1 *(Rad 4-3)*

DOMESTIC CUP 2007/08

KUPA SRBIJE

FIRST ROUND

(25/9/07)
Sinđelić Niš 1, BSK Borča 0

(26/9/07)
Banat 2, Sevojno 2 *(5-4 on pens)*
Bežanija 3, ČSK Pivara 1
Big Bull 2, Čukarički 4
Hajduk Kula 4, Radnički Pirot 1
Inđija 3, Vojvodina 2
Javor 3, Mladost Lučani 0
Mladost Apatin 1, Srem 2
Mokra Gora 1, Zemun 1 *(3-4 on pens)*
Napredak 4, BASK 0
Novi Pazar 0, Smederevo 3
OFK Beograd 2, Mladenovac 0
Partizan 4, Rad 1
Radnički Niš 2, Borac 0
Teleoptik 1, Crvena Zvezda 2
Vlasina 2, Voždovac 1

SECOND ROUND

(23/10/07)
Radnički Niš 0, Banat 1

(24/10/07)
Hajduk 0, Javor 1
Sinđelić Niš 2, Bežanija 0
Srem 0, Partizan 3
Inđija 0, OFK Beograd 2
Smederevo 1, Čukarički 1 *(3-5 on pens)*
Zemun 1, Vlasina 1 *(6-5 on pens)*

(23/2/08)
Crvena Zvezda 3, Napredak 1

QUARTER-FINALS

(19/3/08)
Čukarički 1 *(Ćulum 90)*, Crvena Zvezda 1 *(Milijaš 89) (0-3 on pens)*
Partizan 5 *(Čadikovski 23, 37, Juca 54, Lazić 61, Lazetić 74)*, Sinđelić Niš 1 *(Lazarević 47)*
OFK Beograd 1 *(Kaluđerović 21)*, Javor 1 *(Cvetković 42p) (5-4 on pens)*
Zemun 1 *(Mijailović 59)*, Banat 0

SEMI-FINALS

(14/4/08)
Crvena Zvezda 2 (Burzanović 54, Jestrović 67), Partizan 3 (Diarra 13, 22, Jovetić 79)
Zemun 1 (Vujošević 5), OFK Beograd 1 (Veselinović 51) (5-4 on pens)

FINAL

(7/5/08)
Stadion FK Partizan, Belgrade
FK PARTIZAN 3 *(Diarra 12, 41, 90)*
FK ZEMUN 0
Referee – *Krstić*
PARTIZAN – *Božović M., Rnić, Đorđević, Obradović, Maletić, Juca (Mitrović 58), Moreira (Stjepanović 74), Lazić, Tošić, Diarra, Jovetić (Čadikovski 88).*
ZEMUN – *Jovšić, Cvejić (Milčić 74), Ivanović (Lekić 57), Jovanović, Mitrović, Jandrić, Mijailović (Vranić 57), Todorov, Živanović, Srećo, Zlatković.*

Weiss return revives Artmedia

It is a commonly asserted footballing truism that players or coaches who return to a former club seldom achieve as much second time around. So when Vladimír Weiss, the man who coached FC Artmedia Petržalka to the 2004/05 Slovakian title and into the group stage of the UEFA Champions League, returned from Russia to resume command at the club in the summer of 2007, many locals were sceptical about what might happen. As it turned out, Weiss proved to be just as successful as before – perhaps even more so – as he led Artmedia to the Slovakian League and Cup double.

It was a command performance from Weiss and his players, especially in the Super Liga, where they dethroned defending champions and hot favourites MŠK Žilina with a scintillating run in the second half of the season, going 20 matches unbeaten and claiming the title with two matches to spare after a remarkable match in Senec, which Artmedia won 5-4 thanks to an 89th-minute penalty from their best player and captain, Ján Kozák.

One-nil specialists

Žilina, led still by their 2007/08 title-winning coach Pavel Vrba, were the better of the two title challengers in the autumn, winning both of the head-to-head encounters with Artmedia, but the balance of power swung completely in the spring. Not only did Artmedia win the third direct encounter in the league, in early April, to take over at the top (and stay there), they also beat their league rivals twice in the two-legged semi-final of the Sloavkian Cup. All three victories were by a 1-0 margin, and that was Artmedia's favoured result in the Cup final, too, as an injury-time goal from Czech striker Zděnek Pospěch brought victory over an FC Spartak Trnava side seeking their first silverware for a decade.

After steering Artmedia to the domestic double, Vladimír Weiss (right) was appointed as Slovakia's national team coach

Trnava's reward for reaching the Cup final was a place in the UEFA Cup. Newly promoted FC ViOn Zlaté Moravce, who had claimed that prize the previous season by actually winning the trophy, went into their first Super Liga campaign with high hopes, but they found life in the upper echelon tougher than expected and struggled badly, especially away from home where they failed to win. Fortunately for them, there was one team who fared even worse, AS Trenčín, and they dropped out of the division with just three wins, to be replaced by runaway second division champions 1. FC Tatran Prešov.

The standard of football in Slovakia is not high enough to expect the clubs to make much progress in European competition, but hopes remain reasonably high for the national team, so there was considerable dissatisfaction with fourth place in their UEFA EURO 2008™ qualifying group - especially after they had reached the play-offs for the 2006 FIFA World Cup.

Kocian dismissed

Ján Kocian, who replaced Dušan Galis as Slovakia's head coach in November 2006, was unable to get the best out of a decent bunch of footballers performing successfully with high-grade foreign clubs, such as Martin Škrteľ (Liverpool FC), Marek Sapara (Rosenborg BK), Matej Krajčík (SK Slavia Praha) and young Serie A sensation Marek Hamšík (SSC Napoli). Thus, in June, after a run of three successive friendly defeats, he was relieved of his duties and replaced – to the displeasure of Artmedia fans but the great joy of most other Slovakians – by Vladimír Weiss.

Slovenský Futbalový zväz (SFZ)

Junácka 6
SK-83280 Bratislava
tel - +421 2 49249150
fax - +421 2 49249554
website - www.futbalsfz.sk
Email – office@futbalsfz.sk
Year of Formation – 1938
President - František Laurinec
General Secretary – Miloš Tomáš
Press Officer – Ivan Čeredejev
Stadium - Tehelné pole, Bratislava (29,935)

TOP FIVE ALL-TIME CAPS
Miroslav Karhan (84); Szilárd Németh (58); Stanislav Varga (54); Róbert Tomaschek (52); Róbert Vittek (51)

TOP FIVE ALL-TIME GOALS
Szilárd Németh (22); Róbert Vittek (15); Marek Mintál (14); Peter Dubovský & Miroslav Karhan (12)

NATIONAL TEAM RESULTS 2007/08

22/8/07	France	H	Trnava	0-1	
8/9/07	Republic of Ireland (ECQ)	H	Bratislava	2-2	*Klimpl (37), Čech (90+1)*
12/9/07	Wales (ECQ)	H	Trnava	2-5	*Mintál (12, 57)*
13/10/07	San Marino (ECQ)	H	Dubnica	7-0	*Hamšík (24), Šesták (32, 57), Sapara (37), Škrteľ (51), Hološko (54), Ďurica (76p)*
17/10/07	Croatia	A	Rijeka	0-3	
17/11/07	Czech Republic (ECQ)	A	Prague	1-3	*Kadlec (79og)*
21/11/07	San Marino (ECQ)	A	Serravalle	5-0	*Michalík (42), Hološko (51), Hamšík (53), Čech (57, 83)*
6/2/08	Hungary	N	Limassol (CYP)	1-1	*Šesták (64)*
26/3/08	Iceland	H	Zlate Moravce	1-2	*Mintál (87)*
20/5/08	Turkey	N	Bielefeld (GER)	0-1	
24/5/08	Switzerland	A	Lugano	0-2	

NATIONAL TEAM APPEARANCES 2007/08

Coach – Ján KOCIAN	**13/3/58**		**Fra**	**IRL**	**WAL**	**SMR**	**Cro**	**CZE**	**SMR**	**Hun**	**Isl**	**Tur**	**Sui**	**Caps**	**Goals**
Stefan SENECKÝ	6/1/80	Nitra /Ankaraspor (TUR)	G	G	G				G	G46		G		6	-
Matej KRAJČÍK	19/3/78	Slavia (CZE)	D85	D		D		D	D63	s46	s79	D		16	-
Maroš KLIMPL	4/7/80	Midtjylland (DEN)	D	D	D									19	1
Jan ĎURICA	10/12/81	Saturn (RUS)	D	D	D	D	s75			D67	s64			24	1
Marián HAD	16/9/82	Sporting (POR)	D67											14	-
Stanislav ŠESTÁK	16/12/82	Bochum (GER)	M46	M65	M46	M60		s67	M75	M	M	M85		19	3
Marek HAMŠÍK	27/7/87	Napoli (ITA)	M85	M	M	M	M	M58	M	M59	M	M	M90	13	2
Marek SAPARA	31/7/82	Rosenborg (NOR)	M72	M71	M	M79		M		s59	M46			14	2
Marek ČECH	26/1/83	Porto (POR)	M	D	M	M	M46	D	D	M	D	M68	D84	27	3
Marek MINTÁL	2/9/77	Nürnberg (GER)	A46	A	A			A67		A	s46	M67	s71	41	14

NATIONAL TEAM APPEARANCES 2007/08 (contd.)

Coach – Ján KOCIAN	13/3/58		Fra	IRL	WAL	SMR	Cro	CZE	SMR	Hun	Isl	Tur	Sui	Caps	Goals
Róbert VITTEK	1/4/82	Nürnberg (GER)	A								s46	A78	M	51	15
Filip HOLOŠKO	17/1/84	Manisaspor (TUR) /Beşiktaş (TUR)	s46	A	A	A71	A62	s58	A	A77	M46	s78	s46	28	4
Samuel SLOVÁK	17/10/75	Slovan	s46											20	-
Igor ŽOFČÁK	10/4/83	Sparta (CZE) /Jablonec (CZE)	s67		s64							s68		12	-
Ján KOZÁK	22/4/80	Artmedia	s72			M		M	M					9	-
Miloš BREZINSKÝ	2/4/84	Sparta (CZE) /Poli Timişoara (ROU)	s85				D75						D	3	-
Zdeno ŠTRBA	9/7/76	Žilina	s85				M	M		M59	s64			9	-
Vratislav GREŠKO	24/4/77	Leverkusen (GER)		M	D64									34	2
Branislav OBŽERA	29/8/81	Artmedia		s65	s46								M76	3	-
Filip ŠEBO	24/2/84	Valenciennes (FRA)		s71		s71	s62							7	5
Peter PETRÁŠ	7/5/79	Saturn (RUS)			D		D		s63					7	-
Kamil ČONTOFALSKÝ	3/6/78	Zenit (RUS)				G		G						34	-
Martin ŠKRTEĽ	15/12/84	Zenit (RUS) /Liverpool (ENG)				D	D	D		D	D	D		25	4
Otto SZABÓ	1/3/81	Slovan				D	s84		s46					3	-
Blažej VAŠČÁK	21/11/83	Cesena (ITA)				s60	M68			s67			s76	4	-
Andrej HESEK	12/6/81	Nitra				s79	A							2	-
Luboš HAJDÚCH	6/3/80	Ružomberok					G46							5	-
Peter ŠINGLÁR	24/7/79	Liberec (CZE)					D84							5	-
Dušan KUCIAK	21/5/85	Žilina					s46							2	-
Peter GRAJCIAR	17/9/83	Nitra					s46							1	-
Robert JEŽ	10/7/81	Žilina					s68				s46			2	-
Ľubomír MICHALÍK	13/8/83	Bolton (ENG)						D	D					4	2
Karol KISEL	15/3/77	Sparta (CZE)						M88	M46					25	1
Juraj HALENÁR	28/6/83	Artmedia						s88	s75	s77				3	-
Tomáš HUBOČAN	17/9/85	Žilina /Zenit (RUS)							D	D	D64	D		5	-
Balász BORBÉLY	2/10/79	Artmedia /Poli Timişoara (ROU)							M	s59	M64			12	-
Marián ČIŠOVSKÝ	2/11/79	Artmedia								D46	D79			7	-
Ján MUCHA	12/5/82	Legia (POL)								s46	G		G	3	-
Martin JAKUBKO	26/2/79	Saturn (RUS)									A46	s67	A71	14	2
Radoslav ZABAVNÍK	16/9/80	Terek (RUS)										D	M	29	1
Martin PETRÁŠ	2/11/79	Triestina (ITA)										M90	D	28	1
Jaroslav KOLBAS	10/1/85	Košice										s85	M46	2	-
Ján NOVÁK	6/3/85	Košice										s90		1	-
Peter PEKARÍK	30/10/86	Žilina											D	2	-
Kornel SALÁTA	24/1/85	Artmedia											s84	1	-
Peter DOLEŽAJ	5/4/81	Spartak Trnava											s90	2	-

DOMESTIC LEAGUE 2007/08

SUPER LIGA FINAL TABLE

		Pld	Home					Away					Total					Pts
			W	D	L	F	A	W	D	L	F	A	W	D	L	F	A	
1	FC Artmedia Petržalka	33	15	1	1	41	14	12	2	2	36	16	27	3	3	77	30	84
2	MŠK Žilina	33	14	2	1	46	8	8	5	3	29	22	22	7	4	75	30	73
3	FC Nitra	33	13	2	2	24	7	4	4	8	16	19	17	6	10	40	26	57
4	FC Spartak Trnava	33	10	4	2	32	12	5	3	9	20	28	15	7	11	52	40	52
5	ŠK Slovan Bratislava	33	10	3	4	34	19	5	3	8	12	18	15	6	12	46	37	51
6	MFK Košice	33	10	4	3	35	15	3	2	11	10	29	13	6	14	45	44	45
7	MFK Ružomberok	33	6	8	3	29	19	4	6	6	17	24	10	14	9	46	43	44
8	Dukla Banská Bystrica	33	6	6	4	19	14	4	3	10	22	23	10	9	14	41	37	39
9	FK ŽTS Dubnica	33	6	4	6	16	17	1	8	8	18	36	7	12	14	34	53	33
10	FC Senec	33	6	5	5	26	22	0	5	12	4	29	6	10	17	30	51	28
11	FC ViOn Zlaté Moravce	33	6	3	7	15	24	0	4	13	7	42	6	7	20	22	66	25
12	AS Trenčín	33	3	5	8	18	28	0	2	15	8	49	3	7	23	26	77	16

N.B. FC Senec merged into FK DAC 1904 Dunajská Streda for 2008/09 season.

TOP GOALSCORERS

17 Ján NOVÁK (Košice)
16 Juraj HALENÁR (Artmedia)
15 Peter ŠTYVAR (Žilina)
13 Mário BREŠKA (Žilina)
Mouhamadou SEYE (Dubnica)
11 Ján KOZÁK (Artmedia)
10 Ivan LIETAVA (Banská Bystrica)
Marek BAKOŠ (Ružomberok)
Admir VLADAVIĆ (Žilina)
Jaroslav KOLBAS (Košice)

CLUB-BY-CLUB

FC ARTMEDIA PETRŽALKA

Coach - Vladimír Weiss

Founded - 1898

MAJOR HONOURS: Slovakian League – (2) 2005, 2008; Slovakian Cup - (2) 2004, 2008.

2007

15/7	Zlaté Moravce	h	5-0	*Oravec, Halenár 2, Guédé, Ďurica M. (p)*
22/7	Žilina	a	0-1	
29/7	Trenčín	h	3-2	*Fodrek, Halenár, Guédé*
5/8	Slovan	h	2-1	*Obžera, Ďurica M.*
11/8	Ružomberok	a	3-0	*Obžera 2, Piroška*
19/8	Košice	h	0-0	
26/8	Nitra	a	0-1	
2/9	Banská Bystrica	h	6-3	*Fodrek 2, Halenár, Piroška 2,Guédé*
15/9	Senec	a	3-2	*Obžera, Halenár, Ďurica M.*
23/9	Spartak Trnava	h	3-1	*Halenár 2, Fodrek*
28/9	Dubnica	a	3-1	*Kozák 2, (1p), Halenár*
6/10	Zlaté Moravce	a	3-1	*og (Ondrejka), Halenár 2*
21/10	Žilina	h	2-3	*Halenár, Fodrek*
27/10	Trenčín	a	4-1	*Čišovský 2, Kozák, Halenár*
5/11	Slovan	a	2-1	*Fodrek, Čišovský*
11/11	Ružomberok	h	3-0	*Guédé, Čišovský, Ďurica P.*
24/11	Košice	a	1-0	*Čišovský*
2/12	Nitra	h	1-0	*Piroška*

2008

1/3	Banská Bystrica	a	2-2	*Oravec 2*
9/3	Senec	h	3-1	*Oravec, Kozák (p), Čišovský*
15/3	Spartak Trnava	a	2-0	*Kozák (p), Pospěch*
23/3	Dubnica	h	1-0	*Oravec*
30/3	Zlaté Moravce	h	4-0	*Kozák (p), Saláta, Kléber, Halenár*
5/4	Žilina	a	1-0	*Halenár*
13/4	Trenčín	h	1-0	*Kozák*
20/4	Slovan	h	2-1	*Halenár 2*
26/4	Ružomberok	a	2-2	*Fodrek, Saláta*
4/5	Košice	h	1-0	*Čišovský*
10/5	Nitra	a	3-0	*Obžera, Pospěch, Urbánek*
17/5	Banská Bystrica	h	2-1	*Kozák (p), Piroška*
20/5	Senec	a	5-4	*Pospěch 3, Guédé, Kozák (p)*
27/5	Spartak Trnava	h	2-1	*Obžera, Kozák*
31/5	Dubnica	a	2-0	*Kléber, Kozák*

Name	Nat	Pos	Aps	(s)	Gls
Yusuf-Muri ADEWUNMI	NGA	D	1	(1)	
Balázs BORBÉLY		D	13		
Peter BURÁK		D	22	(1)	
Juraj CZINEGE		M	3	(2)	
Marian ČIŠOVSKÝ		D	28		7
Juraj ČOBEJ		G		(1)	
Peter ČVIRIK		D	9	(1)	
Radek DOSOUDIL	CZE	D	32		
Martin ĎURICA		D	6	(5)	3
Pavol ĎURICA		A	5	(8)	1
Pavol FARKAŠ		D	13	(4)	
Branislav FODREK		M	15	(11)	7
Vratislav GAJDOŠ		M	2	(9)	
Karim GUÉDÉ	TOG	M	30	(1)	5
Juraj HALENÁR		A	22	(2)	16
Miroslav HÝLL		G	8	(1)	
Ľuboš KAMENÁR		G	25		
KLÉBER Silva do Nascimento	BRA	M	13		2
Ján KOZÁK		M	31		11
Martin MIKULIČ		A	1	(1)	
Patrik MRÁZ		D	10	(8)	
Branislav OBŽERA		M	19	(4)	6
Tomáš ORAVEC		A	11	(6)	5
Juraj PIROŠKA		A	9	(17)	5
Zbyněk POSPĚCH	CZE	A	5	(5)	5

Name	Nat	Pos	Aps	(s)	Gls
Ľubomír REITER		A		(1)	
Kornel SALÁTA		D	13		2
Dušan SNINSKÝ		D	1		
Tomáš UHLÍK		A		(1)	
Aleš URBÁNEK	CZE	D	16	(6)	1

FK ŽTS DUBNICA

Coach - Anton Dragúň; (10/8/07) Juraj Bútora

Founded – 1926

2007				
18/7	Slovan	a	1-4	*Kuzma*
21/7	Ružomberok	h	0-0	
28/7	Košice	a	0-0	
4/8	Nitra	h	0-2	
12/8	Banská Bystrica	a	1-0	*Zápotoka T.*
18/8	Senec	h	1-1	*Seye*
25/8	Spartak Trnava	a	1-1	*Seye*
1/9	Trenčín	a	2-2	*Seye, Kiška*
15/9	Zlaté Moravce	h	4-1	*Zápotoka J., Seye 2, Filo*
22/9	Žilina	a	1-4	*Zápotoka J.*
28/9	Artmedia	h	1-3	*Filo*
6/10	Slovan	h	2-1	*Kuzma, Filo*
20/10	Ružomberok	a	2-2	*Seye 2*
27/10	Košice	h	0-1	
3/11	Nitra	a	1-1	*Zápotoka J.*
10/11	Banská Bystrica	h	1-0	*Bruško*
23/11	Senec	a	1-2	*Seye*
3/12	Spartak Trnava	h	0-1	
2008				
1/3	Trenčín	h	2-1	*Seye 2*
9/3	Zlaté Moravce	a	0-0	
15/3	Žilina	h	0-2	
23/3	Artmedia	a	0-1	
29/3	Slovan	a	2-3	*Kiška 2*
6/4	Ružomberok	h	1-1	*Bruško*
12/4	Košice	a	2-6	*Kuzma, Seye*
19/4	Nitra	h	2-1	*Seye, Kuzma*
26/4	Banská Bystrica	a	2-3	*Bruško (p), Zápotoka T.*
3/5	Senec	h	0-0	
10/5	Spartak Trnava	a	1-1	*Zápotoka T.*
17/5	Trenčín	a	1-1	*Ľupták*
13/5	Zlaté Moravce	h	2-0	*Bruško, Seye*
27/5	Žilina	a	0-5	
31/5	Artmedia	h	0-2	

Name	Nat	Pos	Aps	(s)	Gls
Jozef ADÁMIK		D	31		
Branislav BAJZA		D	1		
Tomáš BRUŠKO		M	15	(3)	4
Igor DRŽÍK		M	29	(1)	
Miroslav DUGA		D	4	(1)	
Michal FILO		A	3	(6)	3
Matej GORELKA		A		(1)	
Erik GRENDEL		M	4	(1)	
Milan HARVILKO		M		(1)	
Ľuboš CHMELÍK		M	7	(3)	
Marek IGAZ		G	1		
Peter JÁNOŠÍK		D	1	(4)	
Peter KIŠKA		A	19	(10)	3
Dušan KOLMOKOV		G	1		
Miroslav KOPČAN		G	1		
Marek KUZMA		A	17	(4)	4
Matej LENDVAY		M	1	(7)	
Erik ĽUPTÁK		A	3	(7)	1
Róbert MATEJOV		A		(3)	
Milan MUJKOŠ		D	1		
Martin NOSEK		D	26	(2)	
Jozef OBERT		M	24	(6)	
Marcel ONDRÁŠ		D	24	(1)	
Dušan PERNIŠ		G	30		
Dalibor PLEVA		D	23	(1)	
Mouhamadou SEYE	SEN	A	26	(2)	13
Ján SOKOL		A		(2)	
Cyril ŠPENDLA		D	11		
Ľubomír URGELA		A	1	(1)	
Ján ZÁPOTOKA		M	17	(3)	3
Lukáš ZÁPOTOKA		M	7	(10)	
Tomáš ZÁPOTOKA		M	19	(11)	3
Marián ZIMEN		D	16	(2)	

DUKLA BANSKÁ BYSTRICA

Coach - Rudolf Rehák; (18/9/07) Pavol Michálik & Peter Dzúrik; (27/9/07) Štefan Horný

Founded - 1965

MAJOR HONOURS: Slovakian Cup – (1) 2005.

2007				
14/7	Nitra	a	0-1	
21/7	Trenčín	a	3-0	*Semeník, Palic, Hučko*
28/7	Senec	h	2-0	*Vuković, Seman (p)*
4/8	Spartak Trnava	a	0-1	
12/8	Dubnica	h	0-1	
19/8	Zlaté Moravce	a	2-3	*Kulík, Tomaček*
25/8	Žilina	h	1-3	*Semeník*
2/9	Artmedia	a	3-6	*Ďuriš, Saláta, Seman*
15/9	Slovan	h	0-0	
22/9	Ružomberok	a	2-2	*Kotrys, Saláta*
29/9	Košice	h	1-2	*Saláta*
6/10	Nitra	h	1-0	*Saláta*
20/10	Trenčín	h	1-1	*Ďuriš*
28/10	Senec	a	1-1	*Semeník*
3/11	Spartak Trnava	h	0-0	
10/11	Dubnica	a	0-1	
24/11	Zlaté Moravce	h	1-0	*Debnár*
1/12	Žilina	a	0-1	
2008				
1/3	Artmedia	h	2-2	*Filo, Debnár*
8/3	Slovan	a	0-1	
15/3	Ružomberok	h	1-1	*Hučko*
22/3	Košice	a	3-1	*Ďuriš, Gajdoš, Šulek*
29/3	Nitra	a	0-1	
5/4	Trenčín	a	3-1	*Velický, Ďuriš, Filo*
12/4	Senec	h	2-0	*Kotrys, Hučko*
19/4	Spartak Trnava	a	0-1	
26/4	Dubnica	h	3-2	*Kulík, Ďuriš (p), Uškovič*
3/5	Zlaté Moravce	a	4-0	*Gajdoš, Uškovič, Ďuriš, Pečovský*
10/5	Žilina	h	1-1	*Poljovka*
17/5	Artmedia	a	1-2	*Poljovka*
20/5	Slovan	h	0-1	
27/5	Ružomberok	a	0-0	
31/5	Košice	h	3-0	*Uškovič 2, Hučko*

Name	Nat	Pos	Aps	(s)	Gls
Peter BOROŠ		G	25		
Ondrej DEBNÁR		D	21	(2)	2
Peter ĎURICA		M	3	(3)	
Michal ĎURIŠ		M	23	(3)	6
Michal FILO		A	5	(2)	2
Aboubatare FOFANA	GUI	A	3	(3)	
Vratislav GAJDOŠ		M	13		2
Filip HERDA	CZE	M	17	(1)	
Tomáš HUČKO		M	26	(4)	4
Peter JÁNOŠÍK		D	1		
Marián JARABICA		D		(2)	
Zdenko KAMAS		M	1	(2)	
David KOTRYS	CZE	D	24	(3)	2

Name	Nat	Pos	Aps	(s)	Gls
Radovan KULÍK		M	14	(11)	2
Tomáš LIBIČ		M		(1)	
Ivan LIETAVA		A	1		
Tomáš MEDVEĎ		A	3	(6)	
Marcel PALIC		M	6	(3)	1
Michal PANČÍK		M	26	(2)	
Tomáš PANČÍK		D	5	(9)	
Viktor PEČOVSKÝ		M	30		1
Martin POLJOVKA		D	14		2
Kornel SALÁTA		D	17		4
Marek SEMAN		D	14	(1)	2
Róbert SEMENÍK		A	7	(8)	3
Tomáš STRNÁD	CZE	M	12	(3)	
Ján ŠTUBER		D	1		
Peter ŠULEK		M	2	(7)	1
Ladislav TOMAČEK		A	4	(4)	1
Dušan UŠKOVIČ		M	7	(4)	4
Stanislav VELICKÝ		M	12	(2)	1
Ján VICIAN		A		(1)	
Milan VUKOVIĆ	SRB	A	7	(4)	1
Ľubomír VYSKOČ		M	11	(4)	
Richard ZAJAC		G	8		

MFK KOŠICE

Coach - Ján Kozák

Founded – 2005

Date	Opponent		Score	Scorers
2007				
14/7	Senec	h	0-0	
21/7	Spartak Trnava	a	1-5	*Piatka*
28/7	Dubnica	h	0-0	
7/8	Zlaté Moravce	a	1-2	*Bjedov*
11/8	Žilina	h	2-0	*Jurčo, Kolbas*
19/8	Artmedia	a	0-0	
25/8	Slovan	h	3-0	*Novák, Kolbas, Bjedov*
1/9	Ružomberok	a	0-1	
15/9	Trenčín	h	4-0	*Majerník, Majoroš, Piatka, Kolbas (p)*
22/9	Nitra	h	2-1	*Cicman, Kolbas*
29/9	Banská Bystrica	a	2-1	*Novák, Piatka*
5/10	Senec	a	1-1	*Kolbas (p)*
20/10	Spartak Trnava	h	3-2	*Kolbas, Novák, Majoroš*
27/10	Dubnica	a	1-0	*Novák*
3/11	Zlaté Moravce	h	3-0	*Bašista, Jurčo, Kolbas (p)*
10/11	Žilina	a	0-4	
24/11	Artmedia	h	0-1	
1/12	Slovan	a	1-2	*Novák*
2008				
1/3	Ružomberok	h	1-0	*Jurčo*
8/3	Trenčín	a	2-1	*Novák 2*
15/3	Nitra	a	0-1	
22/3	Banská Bystrica	h	1-3	*Kolbas*
29/3	Senec	h	4-0	*Novák 4*
5/4	Spartak Trnava	a	0-2	
12/4	Dubnica	h	6-2	*Šimko, Novák 4, Kolbas (p)*
19/4	Zlaté Moravce	a	1-2	*Škutka*
28/4	Žilina	h	2-2	*Bicák, Kolbas*
4/5	Artmedia	a	0-1	
10/5	Slovan	h	1-1	*Novák*
17/5	Ružomberok	a	0-3	
20/5	Trenčín	h	2-1	*Milinković, Matić*
27/5	Nitra	h	1-2	*Novák (p)*
31/5	Banská Bystrica	a	0-3	

Name	Nat	Pos	Aps	(s)	Gls
Peter BAŠISTA		D	21		1
Mário BICÁK		M	24	(2)	1
Košja BJEDOV	SRB	A	6	(3)	2
Róbert CICMAN		D	28	(3)	1
Lukáš DŽOGAN		D	8	(5)	
Lukáš JANIČ		A		(2)	
Martin JUHÁR		M	3	(2)	
Pavol JURČO		A	18	(5)	3
Patrik KAMINSKÝ		D	18	(1)	
Stanislav KIŠŠ		D	16		
Jaroslav KOLBAS		M	31	(1)	10
Kamil KUZMA		M	1	(2)	
Tomáš LABUN		M	2	(4)	
Ivan LIŠIVKA		D		(2)	
Pavol MAJERNÍK		M	32		1
Jozef MAJOROŠ		M	16	(8)	2
Nemanja MATIĆ	SRB	M	21	(5)	1
Marko MILINKOVIĆ	SRB	M	7	(14)	1
Ján NOVÁK		A	18	(4)	17
Pavol PIATKA		A	2	(9)	3
Gejza PULEN		G	3		
Matúš PUTNOCKÝ		G	30		
Filip SERENČIN		A		(2)	
Stanislav SMREK		D	1		
Roman ŠIMKO		D	21	(5)	1
Radoslav ŠKOLNÍK		D	29	(1)	
Dávid ŠKUTKA		A	1	(3)	1
Mikuláš TÓTH		D		(1)	
Miroslav VIAZANKO		A	6	(5)	

FC NITRA

Coach - Pavel Hapal (CZE)

Founded – 1919

Date	Opponent		Score	Scorers
2007				
14/7	Banská Bystrica	h	1-0	*Jakubjak*
20/7	Senec	a	1-0	*Áč*
29/7	Spartak Trnava	h	3-2	*Gruber, Farkaš M., Hesek*
4/8	Dubnica	a	2-0	*Čeman, Gruber (p)*
11/8	Zlaté Moravce	h	2-0	*Čurgali, Hesek (p)*
18/8	Žilina	a	0-0	
26/8	Artmedia	h	1-0	*Janíček*
1/9	Slovan	a	1-2	*Šimončič*
15/9	Ružomberok	h	3-0	*Karlík, Grajciar, Hesek*
22/9	Košice	a	1-2	*Babic*
29/9	Trenčín	h	2-0	*Štajer, Hesek*
6/10	Banská Bystrica	a	0-1	
22-10	Senec	h	2-0	*Štajer 2*
29/10	Spartak Trnava	a	1-2	*Hesek*
3/11	Dubnica	h	1-1	*Štajer*
11/11	Zlaté Moravce	a	0-0	
26/11	Žilina	h	0-1	
2/12	Artmedia	a	0-1	
2008				
1/3	Slovan	h	1-0	*Vrána*
8/3	Ružomberok	a	2-2	*Gruber (p), Semeník*
15/3	Košice	h	1-0	*Semeník*
22/3	Trenčín	a	2-1	*Farkaš M., Bača*
29/3	Banská Bystrica	h	1-0	*Bača*
4/4	Senec	a	0-1	
12/4	Spartak Trnava	h	0-0	
19/4	Dubnica	a	1-2	*Semeník*
26/4	Zlaté Moravce	h	2-0	*Kolár 2*
3/5	Žilina	a	1-1	*Gruber*
10/5	Artmedia	h	0-3	
17/5	Slovan	a	2-3	*Karlík, Gruber*
20/5	Ružomberok	h	1-0	*Semeník*
27/5	Košice	a	2-1	*Sloboda, Bača*
31/5	Trenčín	h	3-0	*Grajciar 2, Semeník*

SLOVAKIA

Name	Nat	Pos	Aps	(s)	Gls
Michal ÁČ		A	3	(2)	1
Martin BABIC		M	9	(15)	1
Martin BAČA	CZE	A	11		3
Adrian ČEMAN		D	13	(6)	1
Ondrej ČURGALI		A	5	(11)	1
Marián ĎATKO		D	33		
Michal FARKAŠ		M	14	(8)	2
Pavol FARKAŠ		D	3		
Róbert GLENDA		M		(1)	
Peter GRAJCIAR		M	30	(1)	3
Jan GRUBER	CZE	M	30		5
Matej GUZMICKY		M	1		
Andrej HESEK		A	17		5
Lukáš HNILICA		M		(1)	
Erik HRNČÁR		D	10	(1)	
Lukáš HROŠŠO		G	22		
Michal JAKUBJAK		M	1	(1)	1
Tomáš JANÍČEK	CZE	D	27	(1)	1
Karol KARLÍK		D	15	(5)	2
Ľuboš KOLÁR		A	3	(1)	2
Marek KOSTOLÁNI		M	14	(10)	
Marek KOŠÚT		A		(1)	
Ján LEŠKO		D		(3)	
Irakli LILUASHVILI	GEO	A		(6)	
Jaroslav MACHOVEC		M	3	(2)	
Róbert SEMENÍK		A	13	(1)	5
Štefan SENECKÝ		G	8		
Roman SLOBODA		M	5	(6)	1
Miloš ŠIMONČIČ		M	17		1
Arnold ŠIMONEK		A	1		
Ján ŠTAJER		M	15	(2)	4
Martin TÓTH		D	31		
Tomáš TUJVEL		G	3		
Pavel VRÁNA	CZE	A	6	(10)	1

MFK RUŽOMBEROK

Coach - Přemysl Bičovský; (25/3/08) Ladislav Jurkemik

Founded - 1906

MAJOR HONOURS: Slovakian League – (1) 2006; Slovakian Cup – (1) 2006.

2007				
15/7	Spartak Trnava	h	2-0	*Bakoš M., Kukoľ*
21/7	Dubnica	a	0-0	
28/7	Zlaté Moravce	h	3-0	*Božok, Novotný, Zošák*
4/8	Žilina	a	1-3	*Zošák*
11/8	Artmedia	h	0-3	
19/8	Slovan	a	1-0	*Balaško*
25/8	Trenčín	h	4-1	*Siva, Bakoš M., Pilár, Maslo P.*
1/9	Košice	h	1-0	*Jurč*
15/9	Nitra	a	0-3	
22/9	Banská Bystrica	h	2-2	*Bakoš M. 2*
28/9	Senec	a	3-2	*Siva, Števko 2 (1p)*
6/10	Spartak Trnava	a	2-2	*Kukoľ, Zošák (p)*
20/10	Dubnica	h	2-2	*Kucka, Pilár*
28/10	Zlaté Moravce	a	2-1	*Bakoš M., Zošák*
3/11	Žilina	h	1-2	*Kucka*
11/11	Artmedia	a	0-3	
24/11	Slovan	h	0-2	
1/12	Trenčín	a	3-0	*Bakoš M., Kucka, Maslo J.*
2008				
1/3	Košice	a	0-1	
8/3	Nitra	h	2-2	*Števko, Novotný*
15/3	Banská Bystrica	a	1-1	*Ďubek*
23/3	Senec	h	1-1	*Sivčević*
29/3	Spartak Trnava	h	4-0	*Maslo J., Kucka, Sivčević 2*
6/4	Dubnica	a	1-1	*Zošák*
12/4	Zlaté Moravce	h	2-2	*Bakoš M., Kucka*
19/4	Žilina	a	1-4	*Pilár*
26/4	Artmedia	h	2-2	*Sivčević, Zošák*
3/5	Slovan	a	0-0	
11/5	Trenčín	h	0-0	
17/5	Košice	h	3-0	*Bakoš M., Števko, Maslo J.*
20/5	Nitra	a	0-1	
27/5	Banská Bystrica	h	0-0	
31/5	Senec	a	2-2	*Bakoš M. 2 (1p)*

Name	Nat	Pos	Aps	(s)	Gls
Lukáš BAKOŠ		D		(1)	
Marek BAKOŠ		A	21	(1)	10
Roman BALAŠKO		D	10		1
Miroslav BOŽOK		M	24	(3)	1
Michal DEMETER		D	14	(1)	
Juraj DOVIČOVIČ		M		(4)	
Tomáš ĎUBEK		M	10	(2)	1
Michal GALLO		D	7		
Ľuboš HAJDÚCH		G	29		
Daniel JURČ		D	19	(4)	1
Miroslav KASAJ		M		(1)	
Jan KRÁLIK	CZE	M		(1)	
Juraj KUCKA		M	22	(2)	5
Vladimír KÚKOĽ		A	9	(7)	2
Miloš LAČNÝ		M	1	(3)	
Martin LAURINC		D	14	(3)	
Andrej LOVÁS		M		(2)	
Michal MACEK	CZE	M		(3)	
Viliam MACKO		M	16	(6)	
Ján MASLO		D	27		3
Peter MASLO		M	8	(14)	1
Jiří NOVOTNÝ	CZE	D	30		2
Pavol PILÁR		A	24	(6)	3
Matej SIVA		D	20	(3)	2
Milomir SIVČEVIĆ	SRB	M	15	(7)	4
Roman SMIEŠKA		G	4		
Matej ŠAVOL		G		(1)	
Roland ŠTEVKO		A	9	(10)	4
Róbert TOMKO		A		(3)	
Štefan ZOŠÁK		M	29		6
Igor ŽOFČÁK		M	1		

FC SENEC

Coach - Ivan Galád; (30/10/07) Branislav Kriška & Jozef Valovič

Founded – 1991

2007				
14/7	Košice	a	0-0	
20/7	Nitra	h	0-1	
28/7	Banská Bystrica	a	0-2	
4/8	Trenčín	a	1-2	*Kozár*
10/8	Spartak Trnava	h	1-3	*Lukáč*
18/8	Dubnica	a	1-1	*Ujlaky*
24/8	Zlaté Moravce	h	1-1	*Kováč*
1/9	Žilina	a	0-2	
15/9	Artmedia	h	2-3	*Pecha, Ujlaky*
22/9	Slovan	a	0-3	
28/9	Ružomberok	h	2-3	*Pinte, Najman*
5/10	Košice	h	1-1	*Kozár*
22/10	Nitra	a	0-2	
28/10	Banská Bystrica	h	1-1	*Kozár*
2/11	Trenčín	h	3-0	*Kuráň 2, Papaj*
10/11	Spartak Trnava	a	0-1	
23/11	Dubnica	h	2-1	*Pinte (p), Ujlaky*
2/12	Zlaté Moravce	a	0-1	
2008				
29/2	Žilina	h	0-0	
9/3	Artmedia	a	1-3	*Medveď*

14/3	Slovan	h	1-0	*Kuráň*
23/3	Ružomberok	a	1-1	*Gaucho*
29/3	Košice	a	0-4	
4/4	Nitra	h	1-0	*Gaucho*
12/4	Banská Bystrica	a	0-2	
21/4	Trenčín	a	0-0	
25/4	Spartak Trnava	h	4-1	*Gaucho 3 (1p), Hoferica*
3/5	Dubnica	a	0-0	
9/5	Zlaté Moravce	h	1-0	*Marcin*
17/5	Žilina	a	0-1	
20/5	Artmedia	h	4-5	*Gaucho 2, Medveď, Sľuka*
27/5	Slovan	a	0-4	
31/5	Ružomberok	h	2-2	*Gaucho, og (Jurč)*

Name	Nat	Pos	Aps	(s)	Gls
Stanislav ANGELOVIČ		D	3		
Radoslav AUGUSTÍN		M	6	(10)	
Peter BABNIČ		M		(1)	
Jozef BOZSIK		A		(1)	
Marek BUBENKO		M	11	(1)	
Michal DRAHNO		D	29		
Tomáš EKHARDT		D	2		
Samuel FüZIK		M	8	(7)	
Csaba GÁBRIŠ		D	10	(2)	
Rogerio Marcio GAÚCHO	BRA	A	15		8
Ľuboš HANZEL		D	11		
Michal HLADKÝ		M		(2)	
Peter HOFERICA		M	6	(8)	1
Jan JELÍNEK	CZE	D	5		
Peter KITAŠ		M	6	(5)	
Lubor KNAPP	CZE	M	14		
Martin KOIŠ		D	6		
Roman KONEČNÝ		D	5		
Matej KOVÁČ		M	28	(2)	1
Tomáš KOZÁR		A	11	(9)	3
Juraj KURÁŇ		M	12	(8)	3
Milan LUKÁČ		D	15	(4)	1
Ján MARCIN		D	24		1
Tomáš MEDVEĎ		A	6	(6)	2
Ján NAJMAN		A	6		1
Ján NOVOTA		G	18		
Ján NEMČEK		M	10	(3)	
Ján PAPAJ		M	15		1
Ivan PECHA		D	14		1
Atila PINTE		M	20		2
Branislav RZSESZOTO		G	1		
Ján SLOVENČIAK		G	14		
Marián SĽUKA		M	6	(5)	1
Peter ŠKRABÁK		M	1	(1)	
Ján ŠLAHOR		A	2	(7)	
Marek UJLAKY		M	13		3
Ján VALÁŠEK		A		(1)	
Patrik VOLF		D	10		

ŠK SLOVAN BRATISLAVA

Coach - Boris Kitka; (31/3/08) Ladislav Pecko

Founded - 1919

MAJOR HONOURS: UEFA Cup Winners' Cup - (1) 1969; Czechoslovakian League - (8) 1949, 1950, 1951, 1955, 1970, 1974, 1975, 1992; Slovakian League - (7) 1940, 1941, 1942, 1944, 1994, 1995, 1996; Czechoslovakian Cup - (5) 1962, 1963, 1968, 1974, 1982; Slovakian Cup - (9) 1970, 1972, 1974, 1976, 1982, 1983, 1989, 1994, 1997.

2007				
18/7	Dubnica	h	4-1	*Hanek, Meszároš, og (Bajza), Masaryk*
22/7	Zlaté Moravce	a	0-1	
28/7	Žilina	h	2-3	*Struhár, Slovák*
5/8	Artmedia	a	1-2	*Szabó*
11/8	Trenčín	h	2-1	*Hanek, Ibragimov*
19/8	Ružomberok	h	0-1	
25/8	Košice	a	0-3	
1/9	Nitra	h	2-1	*Ibragimov (p), Meszároš*
15/9	Banská Bystrica	a	0-0	
22/9	Senec	h	3-0	*Meszároš, P. Sedlák, Sylvestr*
30/9	Spartak Trnava	a	1-1	*Meszároš*
6/10	Dubnica	a	1-2	*Mojský*
20/10	Zlaté Moravce	h	2-2	*Sylvestr, P. Sedlák*
27/10	Žilina	a	0-3	
5/11	Artmedia	h	1-2	*Hanek*
12/11	Trenčín	a	2-1	*Švestka, Szabó*
24/11	Ružomberok	a	2-0	*Sylvestr, Ibragimov (p)*
1/12	Košice	h	2-1	*Sylvestr, Meszároš*
2008				
1/3	Nitra	a	0-1	
8/3	Banská Bystrica	h	1-0	*Sylvestr*
14/3	Senec	a	0-1	
22/3	Spartak Trnava	h	2-3	*Dobrotka, Slovák*
29/3	Dubnica	h	3-2	*Masaryk, Slovák, Sylvestr*
5/4	Zlaté Moravce	a	1-0	*Dobrotka*
14/4	Žilina	h	0-0	
20/4	Artmedia	a	1-2	*Slovák*
26/4	Trenčín	h	3-0	*Masyryk, Ižvold, Meszároš*
3/5	Ružomberok	h	0-0	
10/5	Košice	a	1-1	*Hanek*
17/5	Nitra	h	3-2	*Szabó, og.(Tóth), Masaryk*
20/5	Banská Bystrica	a	1-0	*Szabó*
27/5	Senec	h	4-0	*Slovák (p), Masaryk 2, Breznaník*
31/5	Spartak Trnava	a	1-0	*Slovák*

Name	Nat	Pos	Aps	(s)	Gls
Michal BREZNANÍK		M	12	(9)	1
Marek ČEMBA		A		(1)	
Peter ČERNÁK		M	15		
Martin DOBROTKA		D	27		2
Michal HANEK		D	28		4
Jaroslav CHLEBEK		M	15	(1)	
Aziz IBRAGIMOV	UZB	A	6	(11)	3
Matej IŽVOLT		M	16	(4)	1
Ivan JANEK		D	12	(1)	
Daniel KISS		G	10		
Kristián KOLČÁK		M		(2)	
Daniel KOSMEĽ		D	21	(4)	
Michal KUBALA		M	1	(2)	
Pavol MASARYK		A	17	(5)	6
Ľubomír MESZÁROŠ		A	17	(10)	6
Peter MELEK		M		(4)	
Tomáš MOJSKÝ		D	9	(3)	1
Ján MUCHA		G	21		
Miroslav POLIAČEK		M	11	(4)	
Dominik RODINGER	CZE	G	2		
Pavol SEDLÁK		M	14	(11)	2
Julio César SERRANO	ARG	M	15		
Roland SCHLEIFER		M		(1)	
Samuel SLOVÁK		M	24	(1)	6
Peter STRUHÁR		D	13	(6)	1
Otto SZABÓ		D	24		4
Jakub SYLVESTR		A	24	(7)	6
Peter ŠTEPANOVSKÝ		M		(3)	
Martin ŠVESTKA	CZE	D	9	(1)	1

FC SPARTAK TRNAVA

Coach - Josef Mazura (CZE); (6/5/08) Jozef Adamec

Founded - 1923

MAJOR HONOURS: Czechoslovakian League - (5) 1968, 1969, 1971, 1972, 1973; Czechoslovakian Cup - (4) 1967, 1971, 1975, 1986; Slovakian Cup - (5) 1971, 1975, 1986, 1991, 1998.

2007

15/7	Ružomberok	a	0-2	
21/7	Košice	h	5-1	*Ďuriš 2, Bernáth, Barčík (p), Filipović*
29/7	Nitra	a	2-3	*Kožuch, Bernáth*
4/8	Banská Bystrica	h	1-0	*Kožuch*
10/8	Senec	a	3-1	*Kopačka, Bernáth, Tomčák*
18/8	Trenčín	a	2-0	*Barčík, Tomčák*
25/8	Dubnica	h	1-1	*Ďuriš*
2/9	Zlaté Moravce	a	0-0	
15/9	Žilina	h	4-1	*Hruška, Kopúnek, Tomčák, Kožuch*
23/9	Artmedia	a	1-3	*Tomčák*
30/9	Slovan	h	1-1	*Kožuch*
6/10	Ružomberok	h	2-2	*Filipović, Tomčák*
20/10	Košice	a	2-3	*Bernáth, og (Kaminský)*
29/10	Nitra	h	2-1	*Michalík, Doležaj*
3/11	Banská Bystrica	a	0-0	
10/11	Senec	h	1-0	*Barčík*
24/11	Trenčín	h	6-0	*Doležaj, Filipović, Barčík, Bernáth 2, Pončák*
3/12	Dubnica	a	1-0	*Tomčák*

2008

1/3	Zlaté Moravce	h	2-0	*Filipović, Bernáth*
8/3	Žilina	a	1-2	*Doležaj (p)*
15/3	Artmedia	h	0-2	
22/3	Slovan	a	3-2	*Vaculík, Barčík, Kožuch*
29/3	Ružomberok	a	0-4	
5/4	Košice	h	2-0	*Hruška, Bernáth*
12/4	Nitra	a	0-0	
19/4	Banská Bystrica	h	1-0	*Hruška*
25/4	Senec	a	1-4	*Bernáth*
5/5	Trenčín	a	1-2	*Michalík*
10/5	Dubnica	h	1-1	*Guldán*
17/5	Zlaté Moravce	a	2-0	*Guldán, Hruška*
20/5	Žilina	h	3-1	*Hruška, Kožuch, Doležaj*
27/5	Artmedia	a	1-2	*Kožuch*
31/5	Slovan	h	0-1	

Name	Nat	Pos	Aps	(s)	Gls
Miroslav BARČÍK		M	30	(1)	5
Ľuboš BERNÁTH		A	23	(5)	9
Marek BOHÁČEK		M		(1)	
Ivan CÍFERSKÝ		D	10	(3)	
Nenad DJUROVIČ		M		(3)	
Peter DOLEŽAJ		D	27		4
Peter ĎURIŠ		M	27	(3)	3
Andrej FILIP		D		(1)	
Borivoje FILIPOVIĆ	SRB	A	8	(16)	4
Cheileh Amdy GUEYE	SEN	M		(1)	
Martin GULDÁN		A	4	(4)	2
Ľuboš HANZEL		D	4	(2)	
Tomáš HANZEL		D	12	(1)	
Lukáš HLAVATOVIČ		D	2	(3)	
Miroslav HRDINA		G	2		
Martin HRUŠKA	CZE	M	26	(1)	5
Peter JAKUBIČKA		D	16	(1)	
Pavol KAMESCH		G	13		
Pavol KOPAČKA		M	21	(4)	1
Kamil KOPÚNEK		M	27		1
Vladimír KOŽUCH		A	23	(5)	7
Martin MIHÁLIK		D		(1)	
Rastislav MICHALÍK		M	10	(9)	2
Babacar NIANG	SEN	D	8		
Martin POLJOVKA		D	17		
Vladimír PONČÁK		D	23	(1)	1
Roman PROCHÁZKA		M		(1)	
Ladislav RYBÁNSKY		G	13		
El Hadji SAMBA Kebe	SEN	A		(2)	
Igor SÚKENNÍK		M		(1)	
Marián TOMČÁK		A	9	(17)	6
Lukáš VACULÍK	CZE	D	3	(3)	1
Lukáš VIDO		M		(3)	
Jan VOJÁČEK	CZE	G	5		

AS TRENČÍN

Coach - Rob McDonald (ENG); (1/1/08) Martin Stano

Founded – 1992

2007

14/7	Žilina	a	1-7	*Doubek*
21/7	Banská Bystrica	h	0-3	
29/7	Artmedia	a	2-3	*Doubek, Jašurek*
4/8	Senec	h	2-1	*Mičenec (p), Hlohovský*
11/8	Slovan	a	1-2	*Kamenský*
18/8	Spartak Trnava	h	0-2	
25/8	Ružomberok	a	1-4	*Hlohovský*
1/9	Dubnica	h	2-2	*Godál, Mičenec (p)*
15/9	Košice	a	0-4	
22/9	Zlaté Moravce	h	4-0	*Horváth, Križko 3*
29/9	Nitra	a	0-2	
6/10	Žilina	h	2-2	*Minarčík (p), Horváth*
20/10	Banská Bystrica	a	1-1	*Hlohovský*
27/10	Artmedia	h	1-4	*Kamenský*
2/11	Senec	a	0-3	
12/11	Slovan	h	1-2	*Godál*
24/11	Spartak Trnava	a	0-6	
1/12	Ružomberok	h	0-3	

2008

1/3	Dubnica	a	1-2	*og (Adámik)*
8/3	Košice	h	1-2	*Sluijter*
16/3	Zlaté Moravce	a	0-2	
22/3	Nitra	h	1-2	*Depetris*
29/3	Žilina	a	0-4	
5/4	Banská Bystrica	h	1-3	*Depetris*
13/4	Artmedia	a	0-1	
21/4	Senec	h	0-0	
26/10	Slovan	a	0-3	
5/5	Spartak Trnava	h	2-1	*Jašurek, Depetris*
11/5	Ružomberok	a	0-0	
17/5	Dubnica	h	1-1	*Depetris*
20/5	Košice	a	1-2	*Horváth*
27/5	Zlaté Moravce	h	0-0	
31/5	Nitra	a	0-3	

Name	Nat	Pos	Aps	(s)	Gls
Prince ADDAI	GHA	A	6	(1)	
Aldo BÁEZ	ARG	M	8	(2)	
Peter ČÖGLEY		D	21	(2)	
Martin DOUBEK	CZE	A	10	(3)	2
David DEPETRIS	ARG	M	11	(2)	4
Lukáš GÁLIK		D	7		
Roman GERGEL		M	19	(9)	
Boris GODÁL		M	15	(2)	2
Roman HODÁL		G	15		
Csaba HORVÁTH		D	31		3
Filip HLOHOVSKÝ		A	26	(5)	3
Angelos CHANTI	GRE	A	5	(6)	

Name	Nat	Pos	Aps	(s)	Gls
Miloš JAKÚBEK		D	11	(6)	
Bronislav JAŠUREK	CZE	M	24	(7)	2
Jaroslav KAMENSKÝ		A	11	(3)	2
Martin KASÁLEK	CZE	M	16		
Peter KLEŠČÍK		M	29	(1)	
Juraj KRIŽKO		A	9	(11)	3
Michal LESÁK	CZE	M	11		
Tomáš MARČEK		M	16	(3)	
Milan MIČENEC		D	10	(1)	2
Martin MINARČÍK		D	13	(3)	1
Dalibor ROŽNÍK		G	5		
Matej ROŽNÍK		M	1	(2)	
Thijs SLUIJTER	NED	M	13		1
Igor SZKUKÁLEK		D		(2)	
Lukáš ŠEBEK		A	4	(4)	
Danny VAN DER REE	NED	D	3	(1)	
Miloš VOLEŠÁK		G	13		
Martin ZUBO		A		(3)	

MŠK ŽILINA

Coach - Pavel Vrba (CZE)

Founded - 1908

MAJOR HONOURS: Slovakian League - (4) 2002, 2003, 2004, 2007.

2007				
14/7	Trenčín	h	7-1	*Breška 2, Vladavić 2, Nemec, Porázik, Štyvar*
22/7	Artmedia	h	1-0	*Štyvar*
28/7	Slovan	a	3-2	*Jež, Štyvar, Porázik*
4/8	Ružomberok	h	3-1	*Jež 2, Lietava*
11/8	Košice	a	0-2	
18/8	Nitra	h	0-0	
25/8	Banská Bystrica	a	3-1	*Lietava 2, Breška*
1/9	Senec	h	2-0	*Štyvar 2*
15/9	Spartak Trnava	a	1-4	*Devátý*
22/9	Dubnica	h	4-1	*Porázik 3, Jež*
30/9	Zlaté Moravce	a	2-1	*Štyvar, Lietava*
6/10	Trenčín	a	2-2	*og (Kasálek), Štyvar*
21/10	Artmedia	a	3-2	*Štyvar, Jež, Devátý*
27/10	Slovan	h	3-0	*Vladavić (p), Štyvar, Lietava*
3/11	Ružomberok	a	2-1	*Štyvar, Porázik*
10/11	Košice	h	4-0	*Breška 3, og (Školník)*
26/11	Nitra	a	1-0	*Jež*
1/12	Banská Bystrica	h	1-0	*Breška*
2008				
29/2	Senec	a	0-0	
8/3	Spartak Trnava	h	2-1	*Vladavić 2*
15/3	Dubnica	a	2-0	*Breška, Lietava*
22/3	Zlaté Moravce	h	4-1	*Devátý, Lietava 2, Breška*
29/3	Trenčín	h	4-0	*Lietava 2, Breška 2*
5/4	Artmedia	h	0-1	
14/4	Slovan	a	0-0	
19/4	Ružomberok	h	4-1	*Jež (p), Breška 2 (1p), Štyvar*
28/4	Košice	a	2-2	*Štyvar, Vladavić (p)*
3/5	Nitra	h	1-1	*Štyvar*
10/5	Banská Bystrica	a	1-1	*Jež*
17/5	Senec	h	1-0	*Adauto*
20/5	Spartak Trnava	a	1-3	*Adauto*
27/5	Dubnica	h	5-0	*Ďurica, Adauto, Štyvar 2, Vladavić (p)*
31/5	Zlaté Moravce	a	6-1	*Adauto 3, Vladavić 3*

Name	Nat	Pos	Aps	(s)	Gls
Evandro ADAUTO da Silva	BRA	A	4	(6)	6
Juraj ANČIC		M		(8)	
Ivan BELÁK		M	8	(10)	
Bello BABATOUNDE	BEN	D		(1)	
Mário BREŠKA		A	24	(3)	13
Pavel DEVÁTÝ	CZE	M	24	(3)	
Martin ĎURICA		M	4	(5)	1
Eldar HASANOVIĆ	BIH	M	1	(1)	
Tomáš HUBOČAN		D	9		
Juraj CHUPÁČ		D	2	(1)	
Róbert JEŽ		M	31		8
František KORISTEK		A		(2)	
Dušan KUCIAK		G	33		
Vladimír LEITNER		D	28		
Ivan LIETAVA		A	18	(10)	10
Adam NEMEC		A	1	(1)	1
Mário PEČÁLKA		D	16	(5)	
Peter PEKARÍK		D	31		
Martin POLEŤ		D		(3)	
Andrej PORÁZIK		A	10	(8)	6
Csaba SZÓRÁD		D	2	(5)	
Zdeno ŠTRBA		M	32		3
Peter ŠTYVAR		A	20	(9)	15
Lukáš TESÁK		M	7	(10)	
Velimir VIDIĆ	BIH	D	8		
Admir VLADAVIĆ	BIH	M	22	(6)	10
Benjamin VOMÁČKA	CZE	D	28	(1)	

FC VION ZLATÉ MORAVCE

Coach - Ján Rosinský

Founded - 1995

MAJOR HONOURS: Slovakian Cup – (1) 2007.

2007				
15/7	Artmedia	a	0-5	
22/7	Slovan	h	1-0	*Černák*
28/7	Ružomberok	a	0-3	
7/8	Košice	h	2-1	*Juska, Klabal*
11/8	Nitra	a	0-2	
19/8	Banská Bystrica	h	3-2	*og (Herda), Gibala, Farkaš*
24/8	Senec	a	1-1	*Gibala*
2/9	Spartak Trnava	h	0-0	
15/9	Dubnica	a	1-4	*Kuračka*
22/9	Trenčín	a	0-4	
30/9	Žilina	h	1-2	*Tóth*
6/10	Artmedia	h	1-3	*Černák (p)*
20/10	Slovan	a	2-2	*Hözl, Černák*
28/10	Ružomberok	h	1-2	*Hözl*
3/11	Košice	a	0-3	
11/11	Nitra	h	0-0	
24/11	Banská Bystrica	a	0-1	
2/12	Senec	h	1-0	*Černák*
2008				
1/3	Spartak Trnava	a	0-2	
9/3	Dubnica	h	0-0	
16/3	Trenčín	h	2-0	*Ujlaky, Choma*
22/3	Žilina	a	1-4	*Greguška*
30/3	Artmedia	a	0-4	
5/4	Slovan	h	0-1	
12/4	Ružomberok	a	2-2	*Minarčík, Tóth*
19/4	Košice	h	2-1	*Greguška, Juska*
26/4	Nitra	a	0-2	
3/5	Banská Bystrica	h	0-4	
9/5	Senec	a	0-1	
17/5	Spartak Trnava	h	0-2	
13/5	Dubnica	a	0-2	
27/5	Trenčín	a	0-0	
31/5	Žilina	h	1-6	Hözl

SLOVAKIA

Name	Nat	Pos	Aps	(s)	Gls
Vladimír BALÁT		M	1	(6)	
Ivan BARTOŠ		A	3	(6)	
Martin BEDNÁŘ	CZE	D	9	(2)	
Patrik BREZINA		G	17		
Peter ČERNÁK		M	15		4
Ondrej ČÍŽ		D	19	(5)	
Peter FARKAŠ		D	14	(11)	1
Miloš GIBALA		A	7	(9)	2
Roman GREGUŠKA		M	26	(3)	2
Ján HÖZL		M	28	(1)	3
Maroš CHOMA		D	14	(9)	1
Martin CHREN		A	10	(14)	
Ján JUSKA		M	29	(3)	2
Jiří KLABAL	CZE	D	26	(1)	1
Peter KURAČKA		M	18		1
Cyril MARON		M	5	(4)	
Pavol MACKOVČIN		D	3	(3)	
Martin MINARČÍK		D	13		1
Martin ONDREJKA		M	23		
Peter PAHÚLYI		G	1		
Patrik PAVLENDA		D	18		
Lukáš PELEGRÍNI		M	9	(9)	
Michal PEŠKOVIČ		G	13		
Jindřich SKÁCEL	CZE	G	2		
Karol ŠLAVKA		D	4		
Miroslav TÓTH		A	18	(2)	2
Marek UJLAKY		M	12		1
Ladislav ŽÁK		A		(1)	
Roman ŽEMBERA		D	6	(2)	

PROMOTED CLUB

1. FC TATRAN PREŠOV

Coach - Roman Pivarník

Founded - 1891

MAJOR HONOURS: Slovakian Cup - (1) 1992.

SECOND LEVEL FINAL TABLE 2007/08

		Pld	W	D	L	F	A	Pts
1	1. FC Tatran Prešov	33	23	8	2	64	14	77
2	ŽP ŠPORT Podbrezová	33	15	10	8	49	34	55
3	Inter Bratislava	33	15	8	10	49	40	53
4	FK LAFC Lučenec	33	15	6	12	53	45	51
5	FC Rimavská Sobota	33	13	11	9	40	32	50
6	HFK Prievidza	33	11	10	12	46	56	43
7	FK Slovan Duslo Šaľa	33	11	8	14	40	46	41
8	MFK Košice B	33	10	7	16	41	47	37
9	MFK Zemplín Michalovce	33	11	4	18	33	42	37
10	HFC Humenné	33	8	12	13	30	37	36
11	FK Slavoj Trebišov	33	9	7	17	31	60	34
12	MFK Stará Ľubovňa	33	7	9	17	35	58	30

DOMESTIC CUP 2007/08

SLOVENSKÝ POHÁR

SECOND ROUND

(3/9/07)

Dunajská Streda 2, Nové Mesto nad Váhom 0
MFK Topoľčany 1, Inter Bratislava 3
Dolná Ždaňa 0, ZŤS Dubnica 2
Dolný Kubín 2, Žiar nad Hronom 3
MFK Košice 1, AFC Lučenec 0
MFK Ružomberok 2, Dukla Banská Bystrica 0
Spartak Vráble 0, Slovan Bratislava 3
Spišská Nová Ves 1, Tesla Stropkov 0
FC Senec 1, FC Nitra 3
AS Trenčín 1, Duslo Šaľa 0
SFM Senec 0, Spartak Trnava 2
Odeva Lipany 2, 1.HFC Humenné 4
FK Rakytovce 0, Tatran Prešov 3

THIRD ROUND

(22/10/07)

AS Trenčín 0, MFK Košice 2
Žiar nad Hronom 1, FC Nitra 5
ZŤS Dubnica 0, Inter Bratislava 2
Zlaté Moravce 0, Slovan Bratislava 1
Tatran Prešov 2, Spišská Nová Ves 0
MŠK Žilina 3, MFK Ružomberok 0
Dunajská Streda 0, Artmedia Petržalka 0 *(2-4 on pens)*
HFC Humenné 0, Spartak Trnava 1

QUARTER FINALS

(2/4/08)

MFK Košice 2 *(Novák 50, Jurčo 80)*, Slovan Bratislava 0
Slovan Bratislava 0, MFK Košice 0
(MFK Košice 2-0)

Inter Bratislava 0, Artmedia Petržalka 4 *(Mráz 3, Fodrek 33, Halenár 53, Piroška 78)*
Artmedia Petržalka 2 *(Piroška 59, Fodrek 77)*, Inter Bratislava 1 *(Petrán*
(Artmedia Petržalka 6-1)

MŠK Žilina 2 *(Tesák 4, Jež 42)*, FC Nitra 2 *(Gruber 57, Babic 90)*
FC Nitra 2 *(Hesek 85, Gruber 90)*, MFK Žilina 2 *(Belák 71, Jež 77p)*
(4-4; Žilina 4-3 on pens)

Tatran Prešov 0, Spartak Trnava 1 *(Ďuriš 38)*
Spartak Trnava 0, Tatran Prešov 0
(Spartak Trnava 1-0)

SEMI-FINALS

(16/4/08 & 23/4/08)
MŠK Žilina 0, Artmedia Petržalka 1 *(Čišovský 10)*
Artmedia Petržalka 1 *(Kozák 84p)*, MŠK Žilina 0
(Artmedia Petržalka 2-0)

MFK Košice 0, Spartak Trnava 0
Spartak Trnava 3 *(Ďuriš 32, Kožuch 34, Doležaj 87p)*, *MFK Košice 1 (Nová*
(Spartak Trnava 3-1)

FINAL

(1/5/08)
Stadion Pod Dubňom, Žilina
FC ARTMEDIA PETRŽALKA 1 *(Pospěch 90)*
FC SPARTAK TRNAVA 0
Referee - *Micheľ*
ARTMEDIA – *Kamenár, Čišovský, Dosoudil, Saláta, Burák, Obžera (Pospě 55), Kozák, Czinege (Cleber 67), Fodrek, Piroška (Oravec 90), Halenár.*
SPARTAK TRNAVA – *Rybanský, Jakubička, Hanzel T., Doležaj, Pončák, Kopúnek, Hruška (Vaculík 73), Bernáth, Barčík, Ďuriš (Tomčák 90), Kožuc (Filipović 61).*

Repeat performance from Domžale

Having won the Slovenian championship for the first time in 2006/07, NK Domžale repeated the trick in 2007/08. Once again, Slaviša Stojanović's side were able to freewheel to victory after powering into a virtually unassailable lead in the first half of the season. Although they stuttered in the spring, they came on strong in the closing weeks to end up a full 12 points clear of closest challengers FC Koper.

The personnel may have altered slightly, with veteran Slovenian international goalgetters Sebastjan Cimerotič and Ermin Rakovič notably having flown the nest, but Domžale remained a consistent winning-machine. New arrival Dario Zahora, a former Croatian champion with NK Dinamo Zagreb who had scored ten goals in the first half of the previous season for Koper, proved a major asset. He formed a productive strike partnership with Zlatan Ljubijankič in the autumn – before the latter's mid-season sale to Belgian club KAA Gent – and finished the season with all guns blazing, scoring eight goals in his last four games to take the Prva Liga's top scorer prize with a final tally of 22.

Slovenian international Andraž Kirm enjoyed an excellent season with champions Domžale

Consistent Kirm

Thanks mainly to Zahora, Domžale ended up with the best 'goals for' figure in the final table – one more than Koper – to go with the best 'goals against' record – a distinction that was never going to escape them thanks to the consistently resilient defensive work of stalwart performers like goalkeeper Dejan Nemec and centre-back Luka Elsner. The team's most consistent all-rounder was 23-year-old Slovenian national team regular Andraž Kirm, a player reportedly observed with interest by various Italian clubs but who decided to stay with the club for the summer UEFA Champions League qualifying campaign. If that was good news for the Domžale fans, the bad was the close-season departure of both Zahora and coach Stojanovič, the latter deciding that after two championship wins with the club he needed a fresh challenge so left to join NK Celje instead.

Koper, the Slovenian Cup winners of the two previous seasons, had a worthy league campaign under coach Vlado Badžim, finishing a clear second. Although they were incapable of beating Domžale, they did manage to hold them in three of their four league encounters. When the two clubs were split in the draw for the Slovenian Cup semi-finals, the likelihood was that they would meet in the final. But neither made it, Domžale losing out to NK Maribor while Koper's bid for a Cup hat-trick bit the dust after defeats in both legs against NK IB Ljubljana.

Rakovič double

IB Ljubljana, the only top-flight club from the capital and the private plaything of Slovenia's wealthiest man, gaming-machine tycoon Jože Pečečnik, were to take the Cup, beating Maribor, the country's record champions, 2-1 in Celje. Rakovič, a summer recruit from Domžale and also a former Maribor player, was

Nogometna Zveza Slovenije (NZS)

Cerinova 4
PP 3986
SI-1001 Ljubljana
tel - +386 1 530 0400
fax - +386 1 530 0410
website - www.nzs.si
email - nzs@nzs.si
Year of Formation – 1920
President - Rudolf Zavrl
General Secretary – Dane Jošt
Press Officer – Uroš Stanič
Stadium –Arena Petrol, Celje (10,085)

INTERNATIONAL TOURNAMENT APPEARANCES
FIFA World Cup - (1) 2002.
UEFA European Championship - (1) 2000.

TOP FIVE ALL-TIME CAPS
Zlatko Zahovič (80); Milenko Ačimovič & Aleš Čeh (74); Džoni Novak (71); Marinko Galič (66)

TOP FIVE ALL-TIME GOALS
Zlatko Zahovič (35); Sašo Udovič (16); Ermin Šilja (14); Milenko Ačimovič (13); Primož Gliha (10)

NATIONAL TEAM RESULTS 2007/08

22/8/07	Montenegro	A	Podgorica	1-1	*Vršič (42)*
8/9/07	Luxembourg (ECQ)	A	Luxembourg	3-0	*Lavrič (7, 47), Novakovič (37)*
12/9/07	Belarus (ECQ)	H	Celje	1-0	*Lavrič (3p)*
13/10/07	Albania (ECQ)	H	Celje	0-0	
17/10/07	Netherlands (ECQ)	A	Eindhoven	0-2	
21/11/07	Bulgaria (ECQ)	H	Celje	0-2	
6/2/08	Denmark	H	Nova Gorica	1-2	*Novakovič (38)*
26/3/08	Hungary	A	Zalaegerszeg	1-0	*Šišič (59)*
26/5/08	Sweden	A	Gothenburg	0-1	

the star of the show, scoring both Interblock goals, the second of them deciding the outcome 19 minutes from time.

With neither of the two Cup finalists in a position to qualify for Europe via the league, the match was a straight fight for a UEFA Cup place. IB Ljubljana's delight in seizing their first trophy was more than matched by the prospect of entering Europe for the first time. Pečečnik's ambitions for the club are far-reaching, the keystone for development being regular participation on the continental stage.

Maribor, the only Slovenian club to have taken part in the group phase of the UEFA Champions League, have now gone four years without a trophy – and five without a league win since their seven-in-a-row surge that straddled the turn of the century. Slovenia's greatest ever player, UEFA EURO 2000™ star Zlatko Zahovič, was appointed as the club's general manager at the start of the season, and while there was never a dull moment while he was around, his decision to install his friend Milko Đurovski as coach did not meet with the approval of the Maribor fans. The best thing by far that happened to the club during his first, eventful, year in charge was the unveiling of the club's renovated Ljudski vrt stadium – a modern, pristine 10,000-seat facility that is the envy of the other clubs in the league. There was also more positive news at the end of the season when Zahovič recruited his former national team captain, Darko Milanič, from third-placed NK Gorica, as Maribor's new coach.

While newly promoted NK Livar found life in the top league much too hot to handle and occupied bottom place all season, the battle to avoid the relegation play-off place was fiercely contested. In the end only eight points separated fourth and ninth position. NK Drava, who used no fewer than five coaches over the course of the season, had the misfortune of facing champions Domžale on the final day, and a 6-0 defeat plunged them into the play-offs. However, they held

ATIONAL TEAM APPEARANCES 2007/08

ach - Matjaž KEK	9/9/61		Mne	LUX	BLR	ALB	NED	BUL	Den	Hun	Swe	Caps	Goals
nir HANDANOVIČ	14/7/84	Udinese (ITA)	G	G	G	G	G	G	G	G	G	23	-
nko ILIČ	6/2/83	Betis (ESP)	D54		D82	s77	D	s48	D85	s70	D	28	-
ja MÖREC	21/3/83	M. Herzliya (ISR)	D	D	D	D	D	D	D	D	D	10	-
ijan CIPOT	25/8/76	Luzern (SUI)	D83	s82	D	D						26	-
an JOKIČ	17/5/86	Sochaux (FRA)	D65		D	D77	s81	D		D	D88	19	-
on ŽLOGAR	24/11/77	Anorthosis (CYP)	M	D82		M	M	M	M77	M	M	32	1
Iraž KIRM	6/9/84	Domžale	M	M64	M	M	M81	M	M	M89	M	9	-
ibor STEVANOVIČ	27/9/84	Real Sociedad (ESP) /Alavés (ESP)	M80	M	M75			M56	 s55	 M	 M60	 9	 -
e VRŠIČ	26/9/84	Poli Timişoara (ROU)	M80	M78	s67							5	2
er BIRSA	7/8/86	Sochaux (FRA)	A54		A67	A82	A67	A48	A85	A53		19	-
nen LAVRIČ	12/6/81	Duisburg (GER)	A	A	A	A	A	A65	s85			25	6
ut SEMLER	25/2/85	Varteks (CRO)	s54									7	-
o BREČKO	1/5/84	Hamburg (GER)	s54	D	s82	D	D	D	D	D70	M83	14	-
KOKOT	23/10/79	Wehen (GER)	s65	D					s85			10	-
an ŠUKALO	24/8/81	Koblenz (GER)	s80									32	2
LAZIČ	30/10/79	IB Ljubljana	s80									2	-
e MIHELIČ	5/7/88	Maribor	s83	s78		s82						3	-
ert KOREN	20/9/80	West Brom (ENG)		M	M	M	M	M				30	1
voje NOVAKOVIČ	18/5/79	Köln (GER)		A	A	A61	s67	s65	A	A77	A83	20	6
Irej KOMAC	4/12/79	Djurgården (SWE)		s64			M85	s56				30	-
a ŽINKO	23/3/83	Domžale			s75				s77			3	-
an RUSIČ	5/12/82	Poli Timişoara (ROU)				s61			s75			4	-
tjan CESAR	9/7/82	West Brom (ENG)					D	D	D56			27	2
an LJUBIJANKIČ	15/12/83	Domžale /AA Gent (BEL)					s85				 s83	 5	 1
nes ŠIŠIČ	8/8/81	Olympiacos (GRE)							M75	M	M71	3	1
er JUKAN	28/11/78	Koper							M55	s53		2	-
ej MAVRIČ	29/1/79	Koblenz (GER)							s56			28	1
ko ŠULER	9/3/83	AA Gent (BEL)								D	D	2	-
ko DEDIČ	5/10/84	Piacenza (ITA)								s77		7	-
jan MATIČ	28/5/83	IB Ljubljana								s89	s60	3	-
an BURGIČ	25/9/84	AIK (SWE)									s71	3	-
an ZELJKOVIĆ	9/5/80	IB Ljubljana									s83	1	-
a ELSNER	2/8/82	Domžale									s88	1	-

on to their status by prevailing 2-1 over two legs against SC Bonifika, runners-up in the second division to automatically promoted champions NK Rudar Velenje. It was an unfortunate case of déjà vu for Bonifika, who had lost the same fixture a year earlier, 3-2 to Interblock.

The Slovenian national team struggled through their UEFA EURO 2008™ qualifying group from beginning to end. Led for the last nine matches of the campaign by ex-Maribor title-winning coach Matjaž Kek, they finished an embarrassing sixth in Group G with just three wins and only Luxembourg beneath them. A very youthful team, they will hope to have learnt from the experience and to give a better account of themselves in the 2010 FIFA World Cup qualifying campaign.

Class shortage

On paper at least, Slovenia would appear to have landed in one of the more favourable groups, with the Czech Republic, Northern Ireland, Poland, San Marino and Slovakia for company, but it would be a miraculous achievement if they could emulate Zahovič's 'golden generation' and reach the finals. There are no truly international-class individuals at Kek's disposal, although Klemen Lavrič is emerging as a useful captain and Samir Handanovič, the first choice at Italian Serie A club Udinese Calcio, as a fine goalkeeper. Much-travelled 29-year-old striker Milivoje Novakovič had arguably the most impressive season of all Slovenia's international exiles in 2007/08, helping 1.FC Köln back into the Bundesliga with a league-best tally of 20 goals in the German second division.

DOMESTIC LEAGUE 2007/08

PRVA LIGA FINAL TABLE

			Home					Away					Total					
		Pld	W	D	L	F	A	W	D	L	F	A	W	D	L	F	A	Pts
1	NK Domžale	36	11	5	2	38	16	11	5	2	31	12	22	10	4	69	28	76
2	FC Koper	36	11	5	2	38	22	7	5	6	30	28	18	10	8	68	50	64
3	NK Gorica	36	8	6	4	33	24	8	3	7	28	26	16	9	11	61	50	57
4	NK Maribor	36	6	6	6	29	29	8	4	6	26	17	14	10	12	55	46	52
5	NK IB Ljubljana	36	7	4	7	26	20	7	4	7	23	22	14	8	14	49	42	50
6	NK Primorje	36	10	3	5	29	15	4	3	11	23	26	14	6	16	52	41	48
7	NK Nafta	36	9	5	4	23	20	3	6	9	20	36	12	11	13	43	56	47
8	NK Celje	36	7	1	10	21	22	6	5	7	21	29	13	6	17	42	51	45
9	NK Drava	36	8	2	8	22	30	5	3	10	23	34	13	5	18	45	64	44
10	NK Livar	36	2	3	13	19	47	2	2	14	20	48	4	5	27	39	95	17

TOP GOALSCORERS

22 Dario ZAHORA (Domžale)
17 David BUNDERLA (Primorje)
14 Abdulrazak EKPOKI (Gorica)
Andrej PEČNIK (Celje)
13 Enes DEMIROVIĆ (Gorica)
10 Marko KMETEC (Drava)
Dimitar Ivanov MAKRIEV (Maribo
Milan OSTERC (Gorica)
Ermin RAKOVIČ (Interblock)
9 Doris KELENC (Drava)
Andraž KIRM (Domžale)
Janez PERME (Livar)

CLUB-BY-CLUB

NK CELJE

Coach – Pavel Pinni

Founded – 1946

MAJOR HONOURS: Slovenian League - (1) 1964; Slovenian Cup - (2) 1964, 2005.

2007				
21/7	Primorje	h	2-1	*Pečnik, og (Mlakar)*
28/7	IB Ljubljana	a	1-1	*Pečnik*
4/8	Nafta	h	0-0	
11/8	Drava	h	6-0	*Beršnjak, Marlon, Sešlar, Rusič, Gorinšek, og (Šterbal)*
18/8	Gorica	a	0-0	
25/8	Koper	h	0-1	
1/9	Livar	a	2-1	*Biščan 2*
15/9	Domžale	h	2-0	*Pečnik, Beršnjak (p)*
22/9	Maribor	a	1-0	*Pečnik*
16/9	Primorje	a	2-0	*Pečnik, Puc*
29/9	IB Ljubljana	h	1-2	*Pečnik*
2/10	Nafta	a	0-2	
6/10	Drava	a	2-0	*Biščan, Puc*
10/10	Gorica	h	0-2	
27/10	Koper	a	2-4	*Beršnjak, Pečnik*
31/10	Livar	h	1-2	*Beršnjak (p)*
3/11	Domžale	a	1-2	*Beršnjak*
10/11	Maribor	h	0-2	
24/11	Primorje	h	0-2	
1/12	IB Ljubljana	a	1-1	*Halilovič*
2008				
1/3	Nafta	h	2-0	*Jovandić, Dvorančič*
8/3	Drava	h	0-2	
15/3	Gorica	a	0-0	
22/3	Koper	h	0-2	
29/3	Livar	a	5-1	*Pečnik 3 (1p), Dvorančič 2*
5/4	Domžale	h	0-1	
9/4	Maribor	a	2-5	*Puc, Pečnik (p)*
12/4	Primorje	a	0-5	

19/4	IB Ljubljana	h	2-1	*Pečnik, Puc*
26/4	Nafta	a	0-0	
3/5	Drava	a	2-1	*Petričević, Halilovič*
7/5	Gorica	h	4-2	*Pečnik 2, Sešlar, Petričević*
10/5	Koper	a	0-2	
17/5	Livar	h	1-0	*Korun*
24/5	Domžale	a	0-4	
31/5	Maribor	h	0-2	

No	Name	Nat	Pos	Aps	(s)	Gls
13	Saša BAKARIČ		A	1	(4)	
11	Dragan BENIĆ	BIH	M	1	(13)	
17	Dominik BERŠNJAK		M	17	(1)	5
20	Darijo BIŠČAN		A	8	(19)	3
10	Engster Linck Inácio DALTRO	BRA	M		(6)	
8	Slaviša DVORANČI		A	5	(7)	3
4	Sebastjan GOBEC		D	19		
16	Gorazd GORINŠEK		M	29	(4)	1
27	Damir HADŽIČ		D	18	(1)	
5	Denis HALILOVIČ		M	21	(1)	2
9	Darko JOVANDIĆ	SRB	A	5		1
15	Dejan KELHAR		D	12	(1)	
17	Uroš KORUN		D	9	(6)	1
4	Marko KRIŽNIK		D	22	(1)	
25	Ognjen LEKIĆ	FRA	M	10	(10)	
30	Rogério Schwantes MARLON	BRA	A	19		1
1	Amel MUJČINOVIČ		G	18		
7	Andrej PEČNIK		M	35		14
24	Frane PETRIČEVIĆ	CRO	M	8	(2)	2
26	Blaž PUC		A	17	(8)	4
23	Miroslav RADULOVIĆ	CRO	D	17		
9	Dejan RUSIČ		A	6		1
19	Simon SEŠLAR		M	30		2
31	Aleksander ŠELIGA		G	18		
18	Rok ŠTRAUS		M	2	(6)	
29	Jure TRAVNER		D	28		
11	Dejan URBANČ		M	21	(4)	

NK DOMŽALE

Coach – Slaviša Stojanovič

Founded – 1948

MAJOR HONOURS: Slovenian League - (2) 2007, 2008.

2007

21/7	Gorica	a	1-1	*og (Komel)*
28/7	Koper	h	0-0	
4/8	Nafta	a	6-0	*Kirm 2, Zahora 2 (1p), Ljubijankič, Dvorančič*
11/8	Livar	a	1-0	*Kirm*
18/8	Maribor	h	4-0	*Žinko 2 (1p), Žeželj, Kirm*
25/8	Primorje	a	2-0	*Zahora 2 (1p)*
1/9	IB Ljubljana	h	2-1	*Žeželj, Žinko*
15/9	Celje	a	0-2	
22/9	Drava	h	4-1	*Zahora 3, Žeželj*
16/9	Gorica	h	2-3	*Zahora (p), Ljubijankič*
29/9	Koper	a	3-2	*Aljančič 2, Ljubijankič*
2/10	Livar	h	2-1	*Janković, Zahora*
6/10	Nafta	h	5-0	*Zahora 2 (1p), Ljubijankič 2 (1p), Brezič*
10/10	Maribor	a	1-0	*Zahora*
27/10	Primorje	h	2-1	*Janković, Aljančič*
31/10	IB Ljubljana	a	2-0	*Brezič, Žinko*
3/11	Celje	h	2-1	*Ljubijankič 2*
10/11	Drava	a	0-0	
24/11	Gorica	a	0-2	
1/12	Koper	h	1-1	*Žinko*

2008

1/3	Livar	a	2-1	*Kirm 2*
8/3	Nafta	a	0-0	
15/3	Maribor	h	0-0	
22/3	Primorje	a	0-0	
29/3	IB Ljubljana	h	1-2	*og (Jelečevič)*
5/4	Celje	a	1-0	*Knezović*
9/4	Drava	h	2-1	*Zahora 2*
12/4	Gorica	h	1-1	*Kirm*
19/4	Koper	a	2-2	*Benko 2*
26/4	Livar	h	1-1	*Kirm*
3/5	Nafta	h	2-0	*Benko, Knezović*
7/5	Maribor	a	1-0	*Benko*
10/5	Primorje	h	3-2	*Zahora, Juninho, Aljančič*
17/5	IB Ljubljana	a	3-2	*Zahora 2, Benko*
24/5	Celje	h	4-0	*Zahora 3, og (Halilovič)*
31/5	Drava	a	6-0	*Zahora 2, Kirm, Jusufi, Žinko (p), Benko*

No	Name	Nat	Pos	Aps	(s)	Gls
3	Janez ALJANČIČ		D	33	(1)	4
87	Tadej APATIČ		M	14	(1)	
8	Jože BENKO		A	9	(2)	6
76	Danijel BREZIČ		M	28		2
32	Daro BRLJAK		G		(1)	
16	Džengis ČAVUŠEVIČ		A		(6)	
11	Alen ČORALIČ		M	4	(7)	
9	Slaviša DVORANČIČ		A		(6)	1
29	Luka ELSNER		D	34		
	Dejan GRABIČ		M	4	(9)	
5	Rok HANŽIČ		D	19		
7	Siniša JANKOVIĆ	SRB	M	17	(4)	2
10	Júnior Wilson "JUNINHO"	BRA	M	12	(2)	1
99	Plumb JUSUFI	CRO	M	1	(7)	1
30	Andraž KIRM		M	31	(1)	9
25	Ivan KNEZOVIĆ	CRO	D	24		2
11	Tim LODUCA		A		(4)	
20	Zlatan LJUBIJANKIČ		A	18		7
77	Dejan NEMEC		G	35		
15	Jaroslav PEŠKAR	CZE	M	5	(12)	
26	Jalen POKORN		M	12	(2)	
9	Borut SEMLER		A	4	(6)	
17	Dalibor STOJANOVIČ		M		(2)	
18	Darko TOPIČ		M		(2)	
12	Andrej TROHA		G	1		
22	Dalibor VARGA		D	6	(1)	
33	Haris VUČKIČ		M		(1)	
19	Dario ZAHORA	CRO	A	33	(1)	22
2	Darko ZEC		M	10	(10)	
14	Dražen ŽEŽELJ		A	19	(6)	3
23	Luka ŽINKO		M	23	(1)	6

NK DRAVA

Coach – Dražen Besek (CRO); (18/8/07) Primož Gliha; (15/9/07) Franci Fridl; (22/9/07) Milan Djuričić (CRO); (17/5/08) Robert Pevnik

Founded - 1933

2007

21/7	Maribor	h	1-3	*Emeršič*
28/7	Primorje	a	1-2	*Kmetec*
4/8	IB Ljubljana	h	2-0	*Ogu, Prejac*
11/8	Celje	a	0-6	
18/8	Nafta	h	2-2	*Kelenc, Zilić*
25/8	Gorica	h	1-0	*Grbec*
1/9	Koper	a	1-2	*Bošnjak*
15/9	Livar	h	1-3	*Kronaveter*
22/9	Domžale	a	1-4	*Kmetec*
16/9	Maribor	a	3-1	*Drevenšek (p), Kmetec, Kelenc*

29/9	Primorje	h	3-2	*Bošnjak, Kmetec, Zilić*
2/10	IB Ljubljana	a	1-4	*Tisnikar*
6/10	Celje	h	0-2	
10/10	Nafta	a	1-1	*Zilić*
27/10	Gorica	a	1-1	*Zilić*
31/10	Koper	h	1-0	*Kelenc*
3/11	Livar	a	2-4	*Sahiti 2*
10/11	Domžale	h	0-0	
24/11	Maribor	h	1-2	*Kelenc*
1/12	Primorje	a	1-1	*Grbec*
2008				
1/3	IB Ljubljana	h	0-2	
8/3	Celje	a	2-0	*Kelenc 2*
15/3	Nafta	h	2-1	*Kmetec 2*
22/3	Gorica	h	1-3	*Kelenc*
29/3	Koper	a	3-2	*Kmetec 2, Horvat*
5/4	Livar	h	3-1	*Emeršič, Zilić, Grbec*
9/4	Domžale	a	1-2	*Kmetec*
12/4	Maribor	a	0-1	
19/4	Primorje	h	1-0	*Radetić*
26/4	IB Ljubljana	a	2-1	*Bošnjak, Drevenšek*
3/5	Celje	h	1-2	*Kmetec*
7/5	Nafta	a	0-1	
10/5	Gorica	a	0-1	
17/5	Koper	h	2-1	*Bošnjak, Grbec*
24/5	Livar	a	3-0	*Kelenc 2, Ogu*
31/5	Domžale	h	0-6	

No	Name	Nat	Pos	Aps	(s)	Gls
11	Miljenko BOŠNJAK	BIH	M	27	(2)	4
28	Daniel Marcelo CALAMANTE	ARG	M	12	(3)	
22	Mladen DABANOVIČ		G	5		
21	Nenad ĐAKOVIĆ	SRB	M		(4)	
20	Marko DREVENŠEK		M	29	(5)	2
2	Mitja EMERŠIČ		D	34		2
3	Ivan FILIPOVIČ		M	3		
1	Dejan GERMIČ		G	7		
10	Javier Antonio GRBEC		A	2	(20)	4
18	Marko GRIŽONIČ		M	32	(2)	
25	Lucas Mario HORVAT		A	33		1
70	Doris KELENC		M	32	(3)	9
9	Marko KMETEC		A	27	(3)	10
15	Rok KRONAVETER		M	6	(5)	1
29	Tomaž MURKO		G	24		
19	Dejan NOVAK		A		(1)	
8	Eugene OBI Ohunta	NGA	M	5	(2)	
29	John Ogouchukwu OGU	NGA	M	7	(20)	2
13	Andrej PREJAC		D	35		1
24	Igor RADETIĆ	CRO	D	13		1
12	Orhan SAHITI		A	5	(1)	2
16	Mariusz Adam SOSKA	POL	A	6	(4)	
5	Emil ŠTERBAL		D	13	(2)	
7	Jan ŠTRUKELJ		M		(4)	
6	Borut TISNIKAR		D	17	(5)	1
77	Sead ZILIĆ	BIH	A	20	(9)	5
27	Herman Alexander ZUPAN		M	2	(5)	

NK GORICA

Coach – Darko Milanič

Founded – 1938

MAJOR HONOURS : Slovenian League - (4) 1996, 2004, 2005, 2006; Slovenian Cup - (2) 2001, 2002.

2007				
21/7	Domžale	h	1-1	*Demirović*
28/7	Maribor	a	1-2	*Osterc*
4/8	Primorje	h	1-0	*Rexhaj*
11/8	IB Ljubljana	a	1-0	*Šuler*
18/8	Celje	h	0-0	
25/8	Drava	a	0-1	
1/9	Nafta	h	3-4	*Šuler, Krstič, og (Matijašec)*
15/9	Koper	h	2-3	*Velikonja, Šuler*
22/9	Livar	a	1-0	*Osterc*
16/9	Domžale	a	3-2	*Osterc 2, Demirović*
29/9	Maribor	h	3-2	*Nikolič, Osterc, Ekpoki*
2/10	Primorje	a	2-1	*Demirović, Nikolič*
6/10	IB Ljubljana	h	1-0	*Demirović (p)*
10/10	Celje	a	2-0	*Demirović, Velikonja*
27/10	Drava	h	1-1	*Osterc*
31/10	Nafta	a	1-1	*Šuler*
3/11	Koper	a	0-1	
10/11	Livar	h	1-1	*Osterc*
24/11	Domžale	h	2-0	*Šuler, Osterc*
1/12	Maribor	a	3-0	*Ekpoki 2, Osterc*
2008				
1/3	Primorje	h	1-3	*Demirović*
8/3	IB Ljubljana	a	0-3	
15/3	Celje	h	0-0	
22/3	Drava	a	3-1	*Komel 2, Demirović*
29/3	Nafta	h	4-1	*Ekpoki 2, Osterc, Krstič*
5/4	Koper	h	2-4	*Demirović 2*
9/4	Livar	a	3-3	*Ekpoki 3*
12/4	Domžale	a	1-1	*Živec*
19/4	Maribor	h	2-1	*Demirović, Komel*
26/4	Primorje	a	0-1	
3/5	IB Ljubljana	h	2-2	*Ekpoki 2*
7/5	Celje	a	2-4	*Ekpoki, Cvijanovič*
10/5	Drava	h	1-0	*Ekpoki*
17/5	Nafta	a	2-1	*Velikonja, Demirović (p)*
24/5	Koper	a	3-4	*Demirović, Komel, Ekpoki (p)*
31/5	Livar	h	6-1	*Velikonja 2, Demirović, Ekpoki, Nikolić, Đukić B.*

No	Name	Nat	Pos	Aps	(s)	Gls
9	Gregor BALAŽIČ		M	7	(2)	
25	Damir ČEHIČ		D		(1)	
27	Goran CVIJANOVIČ		D	19	(5)	1
21	Rusmin DEDIČ		D	21		
24	Enes DEMIROVIĆ	BIH	M	34		13
29	Bojan ĐUKIĆ	CRO	M	9	(3)	1
7	Darko ĐUKIČ		A	7	(7)	
33	Abdulrazak EKPOKI	NGA	A	17	(5)	14
13	Domen FRATINA		D	10	(1)	
35	Goran GALEŠIĆ	BIH	M	2	(4)	
16	Alen JOGAN		M	24	(1)	
21	Marko KOCIČ		D		(1)	
19	Sebastjan KOMEL		M	30	(1)	4
15	Mladen KOVAČEVIČ		A		(6)	
8	Nebojsa KOVAČEVIČ		M	33		
10	Admir KRŠIČ		M	13	(9)	2
4	Peter LERANT	SVK	D	16		
	Tim MATAVŽ		A	1	(2)	
2	Dragoljub NIKOLIČ		M	20		3
32	Milan OSTERC		A	26		10
22	Mitja PIRIH		G	19		
31	Danijel RAKUŠČEK		M	5	(12)	
26	Gzim REXHAJ		M	3	(5)	1
77	César ROMERO dos Santos	BRA	A	2	(5)	
12	Vasja SIMČIČ		G	17		
5	Marko ŠULER		D	19		5
11	Etien VELIKONJA		M	19	(12)	5
23	Simon ŽIVEC		M	23	(1)	1

NK IB LJUBLJANA

Coach – Dragan Skočić (CRO)

Founded – 1985

MAJOR HONOURS: Slovenian Cup - (1) 2008.

07				
/7	Nafta	h	1-0	*Rakovič (p)*
/7	Celje	h	1-1	*Rakovič*
3	Drava	a	0-2	
/8	Gorica	h	0-1	
'8	Koper	a	1-1	*Akoto*
/8	Livar	h	5-1	*Rakovič 2, Jolić 2, Rodič*
)	Domžale	a	1-2	*Elsner*
/9	Maribor	h	0-1	
'9	Primorje	a	0-2	
/9	Nafta	a	3-1	*Rakovič, Jolić, Gerić*
/9	Celje	a	2-1	*Pregelj, Rodič*
0	Drava	h	4-1	*Zeljkovič, Rodič, Čoralič, Rakovič*
0	Gorica	a	0-1	
/10	Koper	h	2-2	*Čoralič 2*
/10	Livar	a	2-1	*Rodič, Zeljkovič*
'10	Domžale	h	0-2	
1	Maribor	a	1-0	*Rakovič*
'11	Primorje	h	1-0	*Rendulić*
/11	Nafta	h	1-1	*Rakovič*
2	Celje	h	1-1	*Rendulić*
08				
3	Drava	a	2-0	*Elsner, Zeljkovič*
3	Gorica	h	3-0	*Pregelj 2, Matič*
/3	Koper	a	1-2	*Matič*
/3	Livar	h	1-0	*Jelečevič*
'3	Domžale	a	2-1	*Jolić, Pregelj*
	Maribor	h	1-0	*Jolić*
	Primorje	a	2-0	*Jolić, Zavrl*
/4	Nafta	a	0-1	
'4	Celje	a	1-2	*Grabus*
/4	Drava	h	1-2	*Jolić*
5	Gorica	a	2-2	*Rakovič, Zeljkovič*
5	Koper	h	1-2	*Jolić*
'5	Livar	a	2-2	*Zeljkovič, Pregelj*
'5	Domžale	h	2-3	*Gerič, Matič*
/5	Maribor	a	1-1	*Rakovič*
/5	Primorje	h	1-2	*Gerič*

Name	Nat	Pos	Aps	(s)	Gls
Eldin ADILOVIĆ	BIH	A		(2)	
Eric Jean Marie AKOTO	TOG	D	30		1
Alen ČORALIČ		M	2	(13)	3
Rok ELSNER		D	28	(2)	2
Dejan GERIČ		M	16	(17)	3
Dejan GRABIČ		M	15		
Suvad GRABUS	BIH	M	20	(3)	1
Boštjan JELEČEVIČ		D	13	(5)	1
Ivan JOLIĆ	BIH	A	26	(8)	8
Igor LAZIČ		D	24		
Luka MAJCEN		M	1	(8)	
Rok MARINIČ		D	11		
Darijan MATIČ		M	14		3
Žan OSREDKAR		M		(1)	
Zoran PAVLOVIČ		M	1	(1)	
Martin PREGELJ		M	24	(2)	5
Ermin RAKOVIČ		A	27	(2)	10
Krunoslav RENDULIĆ	CRO	M	21	(1)	2
Aleksandar RODIČ		A	16	(3)	
Matjaž ROZMAN		G	27		
Enes RUJOVIČ		M	5	(12)	
Erik SALKIČ		A	27	(6)	
Janez STRAJNAR		G	9		
Janez ZAVRL		M	14	(6)	1
Zoran ZELJKOVIČ		M	25	(2)	5

FC KOPER

Coach – Vlado Badžim

Founded – 1950

MAJOR HONOURS: Slovenian League - (2) 1985, 1988; Slovenian Cup - (3) 1991, 2006, 2007.

2007				
21/7	Livar	h	2-0	*Galun 2*
28/7	Domžale	a	0-0	
4/8	Maribor	h	2-1	*Volaš, Jukan (p)*
11/8	Primorje	a	0-2	
18/8	IB Ljubljana	h	1-1	*Rajčevič*
25/8	Celje	a	1-0	*og (Gorinšek)*
1/9	Drava	h	2-1	*Volaš 2*
15/9	Gorica	a	3-2	*Jukan, Božičić, og (Dedić)*
22/9	Nafta	h	1-1	*Plut*
16/9	Livar	a	6-1	*Mejač, Jukan (p), Volaš, Plut, Ibeji, Vidovič*
29/9	Domžale	h	2-3	*Rajčevič, Jukan*
2/10	Maribor	a	3-3	*Jukan (p), Volaš, Plut*
6/10	Primorje	h	1-1	*Galun*
10/10	IB Ljubljana	a	2-2	*Volaš, Rajčevič*
27/10	Celje	h	4-2	*Jukan, Viler, Plut, Ibeji*
31/10	Drava	a	0-1	
3/11	Gorica	h	1-0	*Volaš*
10/11	Nafta	a	0-2	
24/11	Livar	h	4-0	*Volaš, Vidovič 2, Elshani*
1/12	Domžale	a	1-1	*Mejač*
2008				
1/3	Maribor	h	1-1	*Plut*
9/3	Primorje	a	0-4	
15/3	IB Ljubljana	h	2-1	*Ibeji, Rastovac*
22/3	Celje	a	2-0	*Đukič 2*
29/3	Drava	h	2-3	*Đukič 2*
5/4	Gorica	a	4-2	*Đukič, Plut, Amusan, Božič R.*
9/4	Nafta	h	3-1	*Jukan 2 (1p), Đukič*
12/4	Livar	a	2-1	*Božičič, Viler*
19/4	Domžale	h	2-2	*Plut, Amusan*
26/4	Maribor	a	3-3	*Đukič, Rastovac, Amusan*
3/5	Primorje	h	2-1	*Amusan, og (Panikvar)*
7/5	IB Ljubljana	a	2-1	*Đukič, Rajčevič*
10/5	Celje	h	2-0	*Mejač, Ibeji*
17/5	Drava	a	1-2	*Amusan*
24/5	Gorica	h	4-3	*Amusan 2, Rastovac, Rajčevič*
31/5	Nafta	a	0-1	

No	Name	Nat	Pos	Aps	(s)	Gls
39	Sunday AMUSAN	NGA	A	6	(9)	7
11	Josip BARIŠIĆ	CRO	D	6	(1)	
9	Patrik BORDON		D	2	(2)	
8	Marko BOŽIČ		M	5		
20	Rok BOŽIČ		M	8	(3)	1
33	Saša BOŽIČIČ		M	29	(4)	2
9	Darko DJUKIČ		A	14		8
11	Arlind ELSHANI		A	1	(6)	1
8	Emanuel GALUN		M	5	(13)	3
6	Enes HANDANAGIČ		D	23	(4)	
1	Ermin HASIČ		G	34		
10	Sunday Chibuke IBEJI	NGA	A	25	(5)	4
18	Amer JUKAN		M	26	(1)	8
24	Mihael KOVAČEVIČ		M	1		
21	Aleš MEJAČ		D	29	(1)	3
35	Tochukwu NWANKWO	NGA	A	1	(2)	
5	Jan PAHOR		D	6		
3	Sandi PAVLOVIČ		A	1	(9)	
7	Vito PLUT		A	22	(10)	7
26	Aleksander RAJČEVIČ		A	34	(1)	5

No	Name	Nat	Pos	Aps	(s)	Gls
9	Milan RAKIČ		M	2	(9)	
27	Andrej RASTOVAC		D	25		3
99	Andraž STRUNA		M		(1)	
23	Miloš SUČEVIČ		M		(2)	
30	Admir SUHONJIČ		G	2		
4	Elvis ŠAHINOVIČ		M	12	(6)	
22	Edin ŠEČIČ		M	19	(7)	
29	Damir VIDOVIČ		M	2	(3)	3
15	Juan Sebastián Cruz VITAGLIANO	ARG	M	15		
28	Mitja VILER		M	22	(4)	2
9	Dalibor VOLAŠ		M	19	(1)	8

NK LIVAR

Coach – Boris Vrščaj; (22/9/07) Tomaž Kavčič

Founded - 1973

2007				
21/7	Koper	a	0-2	
28/7	Nafta	a	1-3	*Božičič*
4/8	Maribor	a	2-3	*Kremenovič 2*
11/8	Domžale	h	0-1	
18/8	Primorje	h	0-5	
25/8	IB Ljubljana	a	1-5	*Prudič*
1/9	Celje	h	1-2	*Bogdanovič*
15/9	Drava	a	3-1	*Perme 2, Božičič*
22/9	Gorica	h	0-1	
16/9	Koper	h	1-6	*Kremenovič (p)*
29/9	Nafta	h	1-1	*Perme*
2/10	Domžale	a	1-2	*Perme*
6/10	Maribor	h	0-6	
10/10	Primorje	a	2-4	*Adilovič E., Kremenovič*
27/10	IB Ljubljana	h	1-2	*Brezovački*
31/10	Celje	a	2-1	*Agič, og (Křižnik)*
3/11	Drava	h	4-2	*Kremenovič 2, Božičič, og (Prejac)*
10/11	Gorica	a	1-1	*Stranjak*
24/11	Koper	a	0-4	
1/12	Nafta	a	2-4	*Adilovič E. 2*
2008				
1/3	Domžale	h	1-2	*Perme*
8/3	Maribor	a	2-3	*og (Džinič), Bečiri*
15/3	Primorje	h	3-0	*LoDuca, Bečiri, Barbič*
22/3	IB Ljubljana	a	0-1	
29/3	Celje	h	1-5	*Božičič*
5/4	Drava	a	1-3	*Perme*
9/4	Gorica	h	3-3	*LoDuca 2, Perme*
12/4	Koper	h	1-2	*LoDuca*
19/4	Nafta	h	0-1	
26/4	Domžale	a	1-1	*Kastelič*
3/5	Maribor	h	0-3	
7/5	Primorje	a	0-3	
10/5	IB Ljubljana	h	2-2	*Brezovački (p), Perme*
17/5	Celje	a	0-1	
24/5	Drava	h	0-3	
31/5	Gorica	a	1-6	*Perme*

No	Name	Nat	Pos	Aps	(s)	Gls
1	Adi ADILOVIĆ	BIH	G	1		
9	Eldin ADILOVIĆ	BIH	A	4	(3)	3
8	Amir AGIČ		M	24	(1)	1
26	Maksut AZIZI		M	3	(6)	
20	Patrik BARBIČ		A	4		1
4	Erdžan BEČIRI		D	7	(2)	2
16	Dušan BOGDANOVIČ		M	16	(6)	1
28	Dejan BOŽIČIČ		M	18	(9)	4
26	Rok BREZARIČ		D	6	(2)	
33	Blaž BREZOVAČKI		M	20		2
27	Fuad GAZIBEGOVIČ		M	28	(1)	
30	Darko KARAPETROVIČ		M	18		
10	David KASTELIČ		D	14	(3)	1
33	Adrian Rusell KEKEC		M		(1)	
29	Samir KERIČ		D	3	(5)	
7	Saša KOSTIČ		A	2	(4)	
7	Darko KREMENOVIČ		A	14	(2)	6
21	Duško KUZMANOVIČ		A		(1)	
1	Ljubiša LJUBOJEVIČ		G		(1)	
18	Tim LoDUCA		A	12	(1)	4
5	Armin LULIČ		M	24	(1)	
20	Marko LUNDER		D	3	(5)	
26	Milan MARIČ		M		(2)	
18	Denis MEŠANOVIČ		D	9	(2)	
4	Gregor MOHAR		M	15	(2)	
2	Adi MUMINOVIČ		M	24	(4)	
11	Janez PERME		A	23	(3)	9
9	Simon PRUDIČ		M	14	(5)	1
3	Aleksander RAILIČ		D	7		
19	Milan SAMARDŽIČ		M	6		
14	Boban SAVIĆ	SRB	G	29		
23	Robert STRANJAK		M	10	(9)	1
15	Sebastjan ŠINKOVEC		M		(8)	
6	Alen ŠUTEJ		M	18	(4)	
3	Darko TOPIČ		M	14	(2)	
12	Klemen ZALETEL		G	6	(1)	

NK MARIBOR

Coach – Marjan Pušnik; (25/8/07) Milko Đurovski (MKD); (10/11/07) Branko Horjak

Founded – 1958

MAJOR HONOURS: Slovenian League - (12) 1961, 1976, 1982, 1984, 1986, 1997, 1998, 1999, 2000, 2001, 2002, 2003; Slovenian Cup - (18, 1965, 1966, 1968, 1973, 1974, 1978, 1980, 1982, 1984, 1986, 1987, 198 1990, 1992, 1994, 1997, 1999, 2004.

2007				
21/7	Drava	a	3-1	*Makriev 2, Mezga*
28/7	Gorica	h	2-1	*Mihelič, Makriev (p)*
4/8	Koper	a	1-2	*Makriev (p)*
11/8	Livar	h	3-2	*Mihelič 2 (1p), Brulc*
18/8	Domžale	a	0-4	
25/8	Nafta	a	1-1	*Makriev*
1/9	Primorje	h	0-0	
15/9	IB Ljubljana	a	1-0	*Popović*
22/9	Celje	h	0-1	
16/9	Drava	h	1-3	*Čadikovski*
29/9	Gorica	a	2-3	*Makriev, Džinič*
2/10	Koper	h	3-3	*Čadikovski, Mihelič, Džinič*
6/10	Livar	a	6-0	*Makriev 3 (1p), Čadikovski, Brulc, Jelič*
10/10	Domžale	h	0-1	
27/10	Nafta	h	3-3	*Jelič, Zajc, Popović*
31/10	Primorje	a	0-0	
3/11	IB Ljubljana	h	0-1	
10/11	Celje	a	2-0	*Mihelič (p), Mujakovič*
24/11	Drava	a	2-1	*Bačinovič, Makriev*
1/12	Gorica	h	0-3	
2008				
1/3	Koper	a	1-1	*Džinič*
8/3	Livar	h	3-2	*Mezga, Filekovič, Jelič*
15/3	Domžale	a	0-0	
22/3	Nafta	a	1-0	*og (Caban)*
29/3	Primorje	h	1-1	*Mezga*
5/4	IB Ljubljana	a	0-1	
9/4	Celje	h	5-2	*Jelič 2, Mezga, Zajc, Pavlovič (p)*
12/4	Drava	h	1-0	*Volaš*
19/4	Gorica	a	1-2	*Bačinovič*
26/4	Koper	h	3-3	*Tavares, Mezga, Pavlovič*
3/5	Livar	a	3-0	*Tavares 2, Volaš*

5	Domžale	h	0-1	
/5	Nafta	h	3-1	*Pavlovič, Nilton, Tavares*
/5	Primorje	a	0-1	
/5	IB Ljubljana	h	1-1	*Pavlovič*
/5	Celje	a	2-0	*Jelič 2*

Name	Nat	Pos	Aps	(s)	Gls
Armin BAČINOVIČ		D	13	(8)	2
Mitja BRULC		A	10	(7)	2
Dragan ČADIKOVSKI	MKD	A	9	(3)	3
Abdoulaye DIARRA	CIV	A		(1)	
Timotej DODLEK		M		(7)	
Elvedin DŽINIČ		D	18	(7)	2
Suad FILEKOVIČ		D	10	(1)	1
Willy FONDJA	FRA	D	5		
Aljaž GRAŠIČ		M		(1)	
Dragan JELIČ		M	15	(17)	7
Marko KOKOL		A		(3)	
Markko KOLSI	FIN	M	2	(4)	
Lubomír KUBICA	CZE	M	32		
Vladislav LUNGU	MDA	M	11		
Dimitar Ivanov MAKRIEV	BUL	A	19		10
Aleš MAJER		M	2	(1)	
Dejan MEZGA	CRO	M	27	(5)	5
Rene MIHELIČ		M	28		5
Amel MUJAKOVIČ		M	5	(3)	1
NILTON Cardoso Fernandes Rogeiro	CPV	D	14		1
Leon PANIKVAR		A	5	(3)	
Zoran PAVLOVIČ		M	14	(1)	4
Andrej PEČNIK		D	6	(3)	
Marko POPOVIĆ	SRB	M	34		2
Marko PRIDIGAR		G	31		
Marko RANILOVIČ		G	5		
Miral SAMARDŽIČ		M	20		
Zdravko ŠARABA	BIH	D	9		
Dejan ŠKOLNIK		M	9	(4)	
Marcos Magno Morales TAVARES	BRA	M	11	(1)	4
David TOMAŽIČ ŠERUGA		M	18		
Dalibor VOLAŠ		A	12	(2)	2
Gorazd ZAJC		A	2	(16)	2

NK NAFTA

Coach – Milko Đurovski (MKD); (18/8/07) Štefan Škaper; 5/9/07) Nebojša Vučičević (SRB); (1/3/08) Nenad Graćan (CRO); (15/3/08) Damir Rob

Founded - 1945

07				
/7	IB Ljubljana	a	0-1	
/7	Livar	h	3-1	*Trenevski 3 (2p)*
3	Celje	a	0-0	
/8	Domžale	h	0-6	
/8	Drava	a	2-2	*Eterović, Sebők*
/8	Maribor	h	1-1	*Sebők*
9	Gorica	a	4-3	*Eterović, Sebők, Repina, Bukovec*
/9	Primorje	h	2-1	*Gerenčar, Čeh*
/9	Koper	a	1-1	*Eterović*
/9	IB Ljubljana	h	1-3	*Lunder*
/9	Livar	a	1-1	*Repina*
10	Celje	h	2-0	*Repina (p), og (Berđnjak)*
10	Domžale	a	0-5	
/10	Drava	h	1-1	*Ortiz*
/10	Maribor	a	3-3	*Ošlaj, Kocsardi, Repina*
/10	Gorica	h	1-1	*Eterović*
11	Primorje	a	2-1	*Eterović 2*
/11	Koper	h	2-0	*Repina, Eterović (p)*
/11	IB Ljubljana	a	1-1	*Bukovec*
12	Livar	h	4-2	*Sebők 3, Gerenčar*

2008				
1/3	Celje	a	0-2	
8/3	Domžale	h	0-0	
15/3	Drava	a	1-2	*Vasiljev*
22/3	Maribor	h	0-1	
29/3	Gorica	a	1-4	*Trenevski*
5/4	Primorje	h	2-1	*og (Kreft), Sebők*
9/4	Koper	a	1-3	*Trenevski*
12/4	IB Ljubljana	h	1-0	*Čeh*
19/4	Livar	a	1-0	*Ošlaj*
26/4	Celje	h	0-0	
3/5	Domžale	a	0-2	
7/5	Drava	h	1-0	*Repina*
10/5	Maribor	a	1-3	*Vaš*
17/5	Gorica	h	1-2	*Ošlaj*
24/5	Primorje	a	1-2	*Trenevski*
31/5	Koper	h	1-0	*Eterović (p)*

No	Name	Nat	Pos	Aps	(s)	Gls
4	Mihael BUKOVEC		D	18		2
11	Gregor BUNC		A	34		
23	Stjepan CABAN	CRO	M	10	(1)	
21	Aljaž ČAVNIK		D	1	(8)	
24	Aleš ČEH		M	32	(1)	2
30	Mate ETEROVIĆ	CRO	A	22	(7)	8
15	Borut GERENČAR		M	21	(8)	2
31	Robert KOCET		M		(1)	
5	Gergely KOCSÁRDI	HUN	M	18		1
32	Stanislav KUZMA		G	30		
12	Aleš LUK		G	6	(3)	
18	Matjaž LUNDER		D	25	(5)	1
3	Bojan MATJAŠEC		M	27	(4)	
11	Amel MUJAKOVIČ		M	10	(3)	
6	Levin OPERANOVIČ		D		(3)	
7	José Luis ORTÍZ	BOL	A	19	(3)	1
29	Damjan OŠLAJ		D	31		3
19	Andrej REPINA		A	14	(15)	6
9	József SEBŐK	HUN	A	25	(1)	7
28	Igor ŠOŠTARIČ		M	2	(11)	
10	Viktor TRENEVSKI	MKD	A	14	(2)	6
14	Konstantin VASSILJEV	EST	M	13	(2)	1
25	Arpad VAŠ		D	5	(3)	1
27	Sandro VINKO		M		(4)	
33	Vedran VINKO		D	2	(1)	
2	Boštjan ZEMLJIC		D	17	(5)	

NK PRIMORJE

Coach – Bojan Prašnikar; (29/9/07) Ljubo Modrijan; (2/10/07) Borivoje Lučić (BIH)

Founded – 1924

MAJOR HONOURS : Slovenian Cup - (1) 1976.

2007				
21/7	Celje	a	1-2	*Zatkovič*
28/7	Drava	h	2-1	*Andrusko (p), Kalin*
4/8	Gorica	a	0-1	
11/8	Koper	h	2-0	*Bunderla 2*
18/8	Livar	a	5-0	*Bunderla 3, Teinović 2*
25/8	Domžale	h	0-2	
1/9	Maribor	a	0-0	
15/9	Nafta	a	1-2	*Bunderla (p)*
22/9	IB Ljubljana	h	2-0	*Bunderla 2 (1p)*
16/9	Celje	h	0-2	
29/9	Drava	a	2-3	*Zatkovič (p), Kosmač*
2/10	Gorica	h	1-2	*Tahirović*
6/10	Koper	a	1-1	*Andrusko (p)*
10/10	Livar	h	4-2	*Zatkovič 2, Kalin, Bunderla*
27/10	Domžale	a	1-2	*Bunderla*
31/10	Maribor	h	0-0	

SLOVENIA

3/11	Nafta	h	1-2	*Bunderla*
10/11	IB Ljubljana	a	0-1	
24/11	Celje	a	2-0	*Bunderla (p), Zatkovič*
1/12	Drava	h	1-1	*Kreft*
2008				
1/3	Gorica	a	3-1	*Šaranović 3*
9/3	Koper	h	4-0	*Bunderla 2, Cvijanovič, Džuzdanovič*
15/3	Livar	a	0-3	
22/3	Domžale	h	0-0	
29/3	Maribor	a	1-1	*Kreft*
5/4	Nafta	a	1-2	*Bunderla (p)*
9/4	IB Ljubljana	h	0-2	
12/4	Celje	h	5-0	*Šaranović 2 (1p), Džuzdanovič 2, Zatkovič*
19/4	Drava	a	0-1	
26/4	Gorica	h	1-0	*Bunderla*
3/5	Koper	a	1-2	*Šaranović*
7/5	Livar	h	3-0	*Bunderla, Kalin, Kosmač*
10/5	Domžale	a	2-3	*Škerjanc, Zatkovič*
17/5	Maribor	h	1-0	*Teinović*
24/5	Nafta	h	2-1	*Džuzdanovič, Mlakar*
31/5	IB Ljubljana	a	2-1	*Serdarevič, Džuzdanovič*

No	Name	Nat	Pos	Aps	(s)	Gls
11	Attila ANDRUSKÓ	HUN	D	15	(5)	2
22	Denis BALOH		G	5	(1)	
12	Branko BUČAR		G		(1)	
6	David BUNDERLA		A	31	(3)	17
5	Miroslav CVIJANOVIČ		M	31		1
3	Alen DŽUZDANOVIČ		A	17	(3)	5
20	Ivica GUBERAC		D	1	(9)	
7	Peter KALIN		M	4	(15)	3
24	Nace KOSMAČ		M	25	(6)	2
17	Boštjan KREFT		D	11	(14)	2
16	Igor KRSTIČ		M	22	(3)	
27	Zsolt László MAKRA	HUN	M	2	(5)	
2	Emir MEHANOVIČ		D		(1)	
23	Matej MLAKAR		M	33		1
1	Igor NENEZIČ		G	31		
4	Vladimir OSTOJIČ		M	34		
13	Leon PANIKVAR		M	10	(2)	
18	Luka PRAŠNIKAR		A		(3)	
10	Nedžad SERDAREVIČ		M	6	(4)	1
9	Edin ŠARANOVIĆ	BIH	A	11	(1)	6
15	Davor ŠKERJANC		M	25	(10)	1
10	Denis TAHIROVIĆ	CRO	D	3	(7)	1
8	Dalibor TEINOVIĆ	CRO	D	31	(2)	3
21	Tadej TOMAŽIČ		M		(3)	
26	Jan VIDIČ		M	18	(2)	
19	Mitja ZATKOVIČ		A	30		7

PROMOTED CLUB

NK RUDAR VELENJE

Coach – Marjan Pušnik

Founded – 1948

SECOND LEVEL FINAL TABLE 2007/08

		Pld	W	D	L	F	A	Pts
1	NK Rudar Velenje	27	15	5	7	70	31	50
2	SC Bonifika	27	12	7	8	44	29	43
3	NK Bela Krajina	27	12	7	8	40	30	43
4	NK Aluminij	27	12	5	10	39	30	41
5	NK Mura 05	27	10	7	10	31	42	37
6	NK Krško	27	9	9	9	33	42	36
7	NK Zavrč	27	10	6	11	36	35	36
8	NK Zagorje	27	9	8	10	43	45	35
9	NK Triglav Gorenjska	27	10	5	12	36	40	35
10	NK Krka	27	4	5	18	23	71	17

PROMOTION/RELEGATION PLAY-OFFS

(4/6/08)
Drava 2, Bonifika 0

(8/6/08)
Bonifika 1, Drava 0
(Drava 2-1)

DOMESTIC CUP 2007/0

POKAL HERVIS

THIRD ROUND

(19/9/07)
Drava 0, Olimpija Bežigrad 1
IB Ljubljana 2, Primorje 2 *(aet; 7-6 on pens)*
Livar 1, Koper 4
Krško 1, Nafta 3 *(aet)*
Bela Krajina 3, Gorica 1
Maribor 4, Dravinja 1
Celje 6, Izola 1
Domžale 7, Malečnik 1

QUARTER-FINALS

(24/10/07)
Maribor 3 *(Popović 19, Makriev 44, 81)*, Olimpija Bežigrad 1 *(Pavlin 3*
IB Ljubljana 3 *(Jolić 64, Zeljković 70, Čoralič 83)*, Nafta 1 *(Eterović 45)*
Bela Krajina 0, Koper 1 *(Volaš 36)*
Domžale 3 *(Ljubijankič 9, 80, Zahora 20)*, Celje 1 *(Sešlar 37)*

SEMI-FINALS

(16/4/08 & 30/4/08)
Maribor 1 *(Jelič 57)*, Domžale 0
Domžale 1 *(Čavuševič 85)*, Maribor 1 *(Volaš 19)*
(Maribor 2-1)

IB Ljubljana 2 *(Zeljkovič 45, 90p)*, Koper 1 *(Ibeji 70)*
Koper 2 *(Božičič 29, Amusan 87)*, IB Ljubljana 3 *(Gerič 25, Rakovič 45, Rujovič 90)*
(IB Ljubljana 5-3)

FINAL

(13/5/08)
Petrol Arena, Celje
NK IB LJUBLJANA 2 *(Rakovič 31, 71)*
NK MARIBOR 1 *(Rozman 52og)*
Referee - *Skomina*
IB LJUBLJANA – *Rozman, Grabus, Gerič, Elsner, Grabič, Salkič, Prege (Rujovič 65), Zeljkovič, Matič, Rakovič (Rodič 76), Jolić (Zavrl 90).*
MARIBOR – *Pridigar, Mezga, Školnik, Filekovič (Bačinovič 47), Kubica, Popović, Pavlovič, Mihelič (Jelič 75), Nilton, Tavares, Volaš.*

SPAIN

Comprehensive winners and worthy champions

pain did not just win UEFA EURO 2008™, they won it convincingly. They were the best team in the tournament and fully deserved their victory. In ach of their six matches they were the superior team. ney won five of them in regulation time and revailed in the other – against world champions Italy in a penalty shoot-out. The quality of their football as routinely high, and they boasted several of the ompetition's outstanding individuals. All in all, it was pretty comprehensive victory.

ehind every successful team, of course, there is a ood coach. Luis Aragonés used all his years of xperience to create a team that was not just efficient nd harmonious but also fluent and attractive. At 69 ears of age, the doyen of the Spanish coaching aternity knew what he wanted and did it his way. ome people may not have liked it – and the omission f record goalscorer Raúl González was a big issue ith many – but all is always well that ends well, and ragonés, who proved his class with his tactical exibility and clever man-management, was entitled o bask in the glory for all it was worth. Not that he id. Instead, he just packed his things, quit the job and oved on to a new challenge in Turkey with enerbahçe SK.

)ominant team

ven before they overcame Germany 1-0 in the final to nd 44 years without a major international trophy, pain were the tournament's top team. In overcoming oachim Löw's side, Spain added the scalp of Germany o those of Russia (twice), Sweden, Greece and Italy. It as an impressive casualty list. Furthermore, in none f those victories could Spain be accused of enjoying xcessive good fortune. They won fair and square very time, not once benefiting from the award of a enalty and always playing eleven against eleven. ven in the goalless draw against Italy, they were the ominant team, having twice as many shots on target. y winning that encounter, Spain became the only roup winners to progress into the semi-final. They also hurdled a psychological barrier by ending a long-standing quarter-final curse.

Picking out star individuals from Aragonés's team was not easy – indeed UEFA's Technical Study Group must have deliberated long and hard before giving the Player of the Tournament award to FC Barcelona schemer Xavi Hernández - because Spain were supremely well served in every department. Captain Iker Casillas lived up to his reputation as one of the world's foremost goalkeepers. That he was seldom called into emergency action was chiefly down to the excellence of the players in front of him. Sergio Ramos, Carles Puyol, Carlos Marchena and Joan Capdevila proved a doughty and disciplined back four, brilliantly screened by Brazilian-born holding midfielder Marcos Senna.

The Spain midfield was very productive, their slick "tiqui-taca" passing game a prominent, and aesthetic, feature of the team's play. In addition to Senna, the first-choice triumvirate of Andrés Iniesta, Xavi and

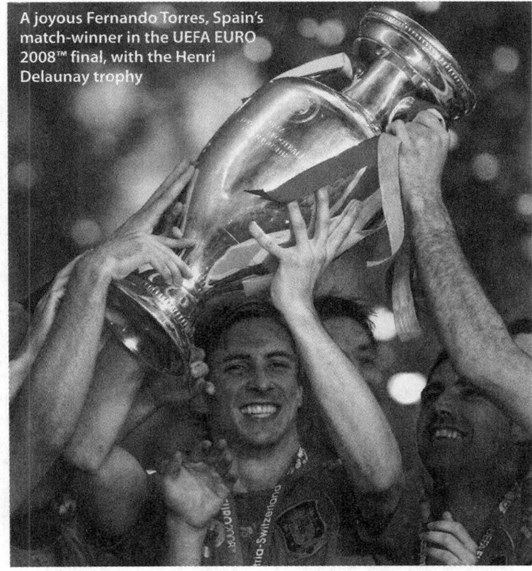
A joyous Fernando Torres, Spain's match-winner in the UEFA EURO 2008™ final, with the Henri Delaunay trophy

David Silva could all look back on the tournament with pride. A perfect blend of craft and graft, they were supplemented for the final and most of the semi-final by pass-master Cesc Fàbregas, the 21-year-old demonstrating the full range of his extraordinary talent with a virtuoso display against Russia in Vienna.

David Villa held on to his top scorer crown despite registering all four of his goals in the opening two games and missing the final with a calf injury. He was a constant source of danger up front, and took his chances brilliantly. Fernando Torres might have felt disappointed going into the final with just one goal to his credit, but his fabulous match-winning strike, and all-round performance, against Germany changed all that.

Having waited so many years for a big title, the afterglow of victory is bound to stay with Spain for a long time. But the team have no time to rest on their laurels with the 2010 FIFA World Cup campaign up and running just 69 days after their night of glory in the Ernst-Happel-Stadion. Aragonés has been replaced by another hardy veteran, ex-Real Madrid CF coach Vicente Del Bosque, and with all the participants at UEFA EURO 2008™ young enough, and keen enough, to carry on for the next two years, it can safely be assumed that the same group of players will still be serving their country in South Africa. A qualifying group that contains Armenia, Belgium, Bosnia-Herzegovina, Estonia and Turkey should hold little fear for the reigning European champions.

It is unusual in Spain for the national team to take precedence over the country's two big clubs, Barcelona and Real Madrid. For the three-strong Barça contingent in the UEFA EURO 2008™ squad – Iniesta, Puyol and Xavi - victory in Vienna made up for a disappointing season that ended, like the one before, without a trophy. Conversely, for the two representatives from Real – Casillas and Sergio Ramos – the triumph with Spain added to the satisfaction of a successful season in La Liga, the club from the capital having won their second Spanish title in a row, and the 31st in their history.

Schuster success

2007/08 was by no means a vintage campaign for the club, and there were times when it seemed that new coach Bernd Schuster, who had come in for Fabio Capello with a brief to liven up the team's style of play, might go the way of the Italian – not least when Real were eliminated from the UEFA Champions League by

Bernd Schuster – a Spanish title-winner in his first season as Real Madrid coach

AS Roma, their fourth last-16 exit in as many years. But a strong, confident finish to La Liga, crystallised by a memorable 4-1 thumping of arch-rivals Barcelona at the Estadio Bernabéu three days after they had sealed the title with a 2-1 win at CA Osasuna, ensured that the season ended on a memorable high.

Real led for most of the season. A magnificent 5-0 victory at Villarreal CF in their opening away game got Schuster's reign off to a bright start. The German, recruited from Getafe CF and a former Real (and Barça) player, had brought in a whole host of new players, including Brazilian/Portuguese defender Pepe, German centre-back Christoph Metzelder and the Dutch trio of Wesley Sneijder, Arjen Robben and Royston Drenthe. Making way for them were Roberto Carlos, David Beckham, Emerson, Iván Helguera and Antonio Cassano. The general consensus was that the squad had been considerably strengthened, thus creating great expectations that Schuster and his players were not always able to fill. Although Real performed peerlessly at the Bernabéu, winning their first eleven home games, their away form often flattered to deceive. They did, however, give their fans the perfect Christmas present with a 1-0 victory over Barcelona at Camp Nou – only their second league win in the enemy's lair in 23 years – to go into the festive break with a seven-point lead.

ɔur wins out of four in January stretched Real's dvantage to nine points, but the early spring, during hich Real crashed out of Europe, also proved atastrophic in La Liga as they lost five games out of ght. It was crisis time at the Bernabéu, but with the pposition either failing to take advantage or too far drift to challenge, Real were able to weather the orm and hold their position. The final nine matches elded the team's most consistent form of the season, nd on the first weekend of May, thanks to two ramatic late goals that turned defeat into victory at sasuna, the championship was theirs.

lthough celebrations in Madrid lasted long into the ight, some Real fans would have gladly delayed the arty by another three days. For that was the date of eir return clash with Barcelona at the Bernabéu. As it anspired, the Catalonian visitors had to go through e painful process of forming a guard of honour for e newly crowned champions, who then proceeded rub Barça's noses in it with a rampant display that rought a comprehensive 4-1 win.

ttingly, the man who opened the scoring was Raúl. It as the Real skipper's 18th goal of an exceptional eason, his best for years. He would finish up as the ub's top scorer – just ahead of Ruud van Nistelrooy, ho had missed a large chunk of the spring campaign rough injury. Casillas was, as usual, a haven of ustained excellence in goal, winning the prestigious amora prize for the first time, while Pepe, when he layed, brought strength and presence to the centre f defence, and Sneijder added quality to the midfield. he Dutchman started the season especially well and ediscovered his top form in the run-in, when other oungsters like Fernando Gago, Gonzalo Higuaín and larcelo came to the fore. Robinho, on the other hand, as brilliant in the autumn – both in La Liga and the EFA Champions League - but faded away alarmingly the spring.

arça in disarray

or Barcelona, who had lost the previous title by the arrowest of margins on the final day, the vast 18-oint gap that separated them from Real in the final able was a source of extreme embarrassment. They aved in long before the end. Torn apart by injuries, isputes and precious egos, with the problematic and ut-of-form Ronaldinho a constant concern, they ould not even finish second. The beginning of the nd for coach Frank Rijkaard was the club's exit from he UEFA Champions League. Paradoxically, the team played some of their best football in the second leg of the semi-final against Manchester United FC at Old Trafford, with the magical Lionel Messi showing all of his sublime skills, but a lack of ruthlessness in front of goal resulted in defeat, elimination and another season without silverware.

Local favourites like Puyol, Xavi and goalkeeper Víctor Valdés tried to pull the team together but with so many mutinous elements to withstand, they generally fought a losing battle. Of the new signings, Gabriel Milito and Yaya Touré did reasonably well, but Thierry Henry was a big disappointment, and his French colleague Éric Abidal was unable to consolidate a good start. Samuel Eto'o and Deco were injured for much of the campaign, whereas Ronaldinho, for mysterious reasons, just stopped playing. Most of the positives were provided by the brilliant Messi (also injured in the spring) and teenage striker Bojan Krkić, whose natural ability was matched by a fierce will to win – something many of his senior colleagues did not appear to share.

Rijkaard, who had produced some wonderfully entertaining teams during his time at Camp Nou – and

Barcelona's Lionel Messi – a shaft of light in the gloom at Camp Nou

Real Federación Española de Fútbol (RFEF

Ramón y Cajal s/n
Apartado de Correos 385
ES-28230 Las Rozas (Madrid)
tel - +34 91 4959800
fax - +34 91 4959801
website - www.rfef.es
email - rfef@tsai.es
Year of Formation – 1909
President - Ángel María Villar Llona
General Secretary – Jorge Pérez Arias
Press Officer – Paloma Antolanz

INTERNATIONAL HONOURS
UEFA European Championship - (2) 1964, 2008.

INTERNATIONAL TOURNAMENT APPEARANCES
FIFA World Cup - (12) 1934, 1950 (4th), 1962, 1966, 1978, 1982 (2nd phase), 1986 (qtr-finals), 1990 (2nd round), 1994 (qtr-finals), 1998, 2002 (qtr-finals), 2006 (2nd round).
UEFA European Championship - (8) 1964 (Winners), 1980, 1984 (runners-up), 1988, 1996 (qtr-finals), 2000 (qtr-finals), 2004, 2008 (Winners).

TOP FIVE ALL-TIME CAPS
Andoni Zubizarreta (126); Raúl González (102); Fernando Ruiz Hierro (89); Iker Casilla (82); José Antonio Camacho (81)

TOP FIVE ALL-TIME GOALS
Raúl González (44); Fernando Ruiz Hierro (29); Fernando Morientes (27); Emilio Butragueño (26); Alfredo Di Stéfano (23)

NATIONAL TEAM RESULTS 2007/08

22/8/07	Greece	A	Thessaloniki	3-2	*Marchena (37), Silva (66, 90+3)*
8/9/07	Iceland (ECQ)	A	Reykjavik	1-1	*Iniesta (86)*
12/9/07	Latvia (ECQ)	H	Oviedo	2-0	*Xavi (13), Fernando Torres (85)*
13/10/07	Denmark (ECQ)	A	Aarhus	3-1	*Tamudo (14), Sergio Ramos (40), Riera (89)*
17/10/07	Finland	A	Helsinki	0-0	
17/11/07	Sweden (ECQ)	H	Madrid	3-0	*Capdevila (14), Iniesta (39), Sergio Ramos (65)*
21/11/07	Northern Ireland (ECQ)	H	Las Palmas	1-0	*Xavi (52)*
6/2/08	France	H	Malaga	1-0	*Capdevila (79)*
26/3/08	Italy	H	Elche	1-0	*David Villa (78)*
31/5/08	Peru	H	Huelva	2-1	*David Villa (38), Capdevila (90+2)*
4/6/08	United States	H	Santander	1-0	*Xavi (79)*
10/6/08	Russia (ECF)	N	Innsbruck (AUT)	4-1	*David Villa (20, 44, 75), Fàbregas (90+1)*
14/6/08	Sweden (ECF)	N	Innsbruck (AUT)	2-1	*Fernando Torres (15), David Villa (90+2)*
18/6/08	Greece (ECF)	N	Salzburg (AUT)	2-1	*De la Red (61), Güiza (88)*
22/6/08	Italy (ECF)	N	Vienna (AUT)	0-0	*(aet; 4-2 on pens)*
26/6/08	Russia (ECF)	N	Vienna (AUT)	3-0	*Xavi (50), Güiza (73), Silva (82)*
29/6/08	Germany (ECF)	N	Vienna (AUT)	1-0	*Fernando Torres (33)*

of course had won the UEFA Champions League - was replaced by local hero Josep 'Pep' Guardiola, who had impressed club president Joan Laporta with his work at B-team level. Although lacking senior coaching experience, Guardiola, as a club icon, can be sure of popular support, but he will have his work cut out to prevent a Real title hat-trick in 2008/09.

Barcelona's fall from grace enabled Villarreal to surprise everyone by nipping in and taking the runners-up spot

ATIONAL TEAM APPEARANCES 2007/08

ach – Luis ARAGONÉS 28/7/38			Gre	ISL	LVA	DEN	Fin	SWE	NIR	Fra	Ita	Per	Usa	RUS	SWE	GRE	ITA	RUS	GER	Caps	Goals
sé Manuel REINA	31/8/82	Liverpool (ENG)	G				G		G							G				10	-
IGEL David López	10/3/81	Celta /Villarreal	D							s46 /75										5	-
rlos MARCHENA	31/7/79	Valencia	D	D	D	D	s46	D		D46	D	D	D	D	D		D	D	D	47	2
ANITO Gutiérrez	23/7/76	Betis	D	D	D					s75						D				24	2
ariano PERNÍA	4/5/77	Atlético	D	D26	D		D		D											11	1
AQUÍN Sánchez	21/7/81	Valencia	M82	M69	M77	M69	s55	s52	s47											51	4
vid ALBELDA	1/9/77	Valencia	M66	s26	M	M64	M	M		M62										51	-
VI Hernández	25/1/80	Barcelona	M70	M	M	M	s46	M	M67	M	M	M46	M	M	M59		M60	M69	M	63	8
vid SILVA	8/1/86	Valencia	M	M	M69		A55	M66	M		M58	M84	M57	M77	M		M	M	M66	19	3
RNANDO TORRES	20/3/84	Liverpool (ENG)	A46	A57	A					A23	A46	A46	A46	A54	A		A85	A69	A78	54	17
VID VILLA	3/12/81	Valencia	A76	A	A48			A52	s67	s46	s46	A66		A	A		A	A34		35	18
ndrés INIESTA	11/5/84	Barcelona	s46	s57	s48	M	M46	M52	M	M	M	M61		M63	M59	M58	M59	M	M	29	4
BI ALONSO	25/11/81	Liverpool (ENG)	s66	M						s62	s58	M46	M46	s77		M		s69	s63	47	1
IS GARCÍA rnández	6/2/81	Espanyol	s70	s69		s78	A73				s67									7	-
iguel Ángel NGULO	23/6/77	Valencia	s76		s77		M55													11	-
sc FÀBREGAS	4/5/87	Arsenal (ENG)	s82		s69	M78	s73	M	M47	M	M67	s46	M84	s54	s59	M	s60	s34	M63	32	1
er CASILLAS	20/5/81	Real Madrid		G	G	G		G		G	G	G	G	G	G		G	G	G	82	-
RGIO RAMOS	30/3/86	Real Madrid		D	D	D	D	D	D	D46	D75	D	D	D	D		D	D	D	39	4
úl ALBIOL	4/9/85	Valencia				D			D	D	s17				s24	D				6	-
an CAPDEVILA	3/2/76	Villarreal				D		D		D	D	D	D53	D	D		D	D	D	23	3
úl TAMUDO	19/10/77	Espanyol				A	s55	s52	s57											13	5
BLO Ibáñez	3/8/81	Atlético				s64	D		D	s46										23	-
bert RIERA	15/4/82	Espanyol				s69	M	s66		M46	s58									5	1
rles PUYOL	13/4/78	Barcelona					D46	D			D17	D	D	D	D24		D	D	D	66	1
arcos SENNA	17/7/76	Villarreal							M		M58	s46	s46	M	M		M	M	M	16	-
aniel GÜIZA	17/8/80	Mallorca							A57	s23		s46	s46			A	s85	s69	s78	8	2
varo ARBELOA	17/1/83	Liverpool (ENG)									s75		s84			D				3	-
ntiago CAZORLA	13/12/84	Villarreal										s61	M	s63	s59	s58	s59		s66	7	-
ubén DE LA RED	5/6/85	Getafe										s66	s57			M				3	1
RGIO GARCÍA	9/6/83	Zaragoza										s84				M				2	-
RNANDO AVARRO	25/6/82	Mallorca											s53			D				2	-

– the small-town club's highest ever placing. The 2006 UEFA Champions League semi-finalists' guaranteed return to that competition was made possible by a late surge of six successive wins – all without conceding a goal. Spain hero Senna was the pivotal figure in a nicely balanced team that seemed strengthened, rather than weakened, by the loss of unwanted former playmaker-in-chief Juan Ramón Riquelme. Coach Manuel Pellegrini made the best of a small squad in which Turkish international Nihat Kahveci rediscovered his best goalscoring form, dynamic young Italian striker Giuseppe Rossi came of age, Capdevila and Santi Cazorla proved irrepressible touchline raiders, veteran French winger Robert Pires successfully reinvented himself in central midfield, and South American duo Gonzalo Rodríguez and Diego Godín emerged as a towering partnership in central defence.

Villarreal's local rivals Valencia CF won the Copa del Rey, convincingly beating Getafe in the final, but while their Cup form throughout was excellent, it was totally at odds with an otherwise troubled campaign in which Quique Sánchez Flores was ousted as coach by public demand and his replacement, Ronald Koeman, proved even more unpopular, expelling three club stalwarts – David Albelda, Santiago Cañizares and Miguel Ángel Angulo – for disciplinary reasons and struggling to put any kind of decent run together in La Liga. Relegation was a serious concern, and Koeman was dismissed five days after the Cup win when the team went down 5-1 in Bilbao. With the Dutchman gone, however, Valencia had a strong finish and, remarkably, ended up tenth.

Sevilla striker Luís Fabiano had plenty of goals to celebrate in 2007/08

Sevilla FC's season was shaped by two dramatic events – the tragic death of their popular young midfielder Antonio Puerta, who collapsed of heart failure in the opening game of the season in August, and the departure of their trophy-collecting coach Juande Ramos to Tottenham Hotspur FC in October. Manuel Jiménez did a decent job as Ramos's replacement, but while Brazilian striker Luís Fabiano enjoyed an excellent goal-strewn season and winger Diego Capel emerged as a genuine – if at times over-theatrical - talent, the consistency of old was lacking, and after going out of the UEFA Champions League on penalties to Fenerbahçe SK, they were unable to return to that competition in 2008/09, missing out on the head-to-head rule to Club Atlético de Madrid.

Pichichi pinched

Atlético claimed fourth place thanks to the class and efficiency of their South American strike-force of Sergio 'Kun' Agüero and Diego Forlán, who made up for a generally feeble defence. Supported well from the flanks by fit-again Maxi Rodríguez and new signing Simão, the pair scored 35 goals between them. Real Racing Club Santander were the opposite to Atlético – excellent at the back but shot-shy up front – but they qualified for Europe for the first time, joining Valencia and Sevilla in the UEFA Cup. Seventh-placed RCD Mallorca had La Liga's best individual marksman in Daniel Güiza, who pinched the Pichichi prize from Luís Fabiano with a glut of goals in the closing weeks, lifting his final tally to 27.

Fourth-equal in the Pichichi listing was 18-goal Ricardo Oliveira of Real Zaragoza, but the Brazilian striker could not prevent his team from suffering an unlikely relegation. Despite an impressive-looking squad that also featured Argentine internationals Roberto Ayala, Pablo Aimar and 15-goal Diego Milito, Zaragoza could not handle the pressure and lost 3-2 at Mallorca on the final day to slip into the drop zone, enabling Osasuna, Real Valladolid CF and RC Recreativo de Huelva to scramble to safety at the end of an intense battle. Real Murcia CF and Levante UD also went down, the latter with huge financial problems, while the promotion places went to CD Numancia de Soria, Málaga CF and Real Sporting de Gijón, with the Basques of Real Sociedad de Fútbol just missing out.

DOMESTIC LEAGUE 2007/08

PRIMERA DIVISIÓN FINAL TABLE

	Pld	Home					Away					Total					
		W	D	L	F	A	W	D	L	F	A	W	D	L	F	A	Pts
1 Real Madrid CF	38	17	0	2	53	18	10	4	5	31	18	27	4	7	84	36	85
2 Villarreal CF	38	12	5	2	33	15	12	0	7	30	25	24	5	9	63	40	77
3 FC Barcelona	38	14	2	3	46	12	5	8	6	30	31	19	10	9	76	43	67
4 Club Atlético de Madrid	38	12	2	5	45	26	7	5	7	21	21	19	7	12	66	47	64
5 Sevilla FC	38	13	1	5	46	20	7	3	9	29	29	20	4	14	75	49	64
6 Real Racing Club Santander	38	11	3	5	24	18	6	6	7	18	23	17	9	12	42	41	60
7 RCD Mallorca	38	9	6	4	35	22	6	8	5	34	32	15	14	9	69	54	59
8 UD Almería	38	9	5	5	18	14	5	5	9	24	31	14	10	14	42	45	52
9 RC Deportivo La Coruña	38	9	3	7	24	23	6	4	9	22	24	15	7	16	46	47	52
10 Valencia CF	38	7	3	9	24	31	8	3	8	24	31	15	6	17	48	62	51
11 Athletic Club Bilbao	38	7	8	4	22	14	6	3	10	18	29	13	11	14	40	43	50
12 RCD Espanyol	38	8	3	8	21	23	5	6	8	22	30	13	9	16	43	53	48
13 Real Betis Balompié	38	7	4	8	27	26	5	7	7	18	25	12	11	15	45	51	47
14 Getafe CF	38	7	7	5	24	22	5	4	10	20	26	12	11	15	44	48	47
15 Real Valladolid CF	38	6	9	4	19	18	5	3	11	23	39	11	12	15	42	57	45
16 RC Recreativo de Huelva	38	6	7	6	24	25	5	4	10	16	35	11	11	16	40	60	44
17 CA Osasuna	38	8	4	7	25	21	4	3	12	12	23	12	7	19	37	44	43
18 Real Zaragoza	38	9	7	3	36	24	1	5	13	14	37	10	12	16	50	61	42
19 Real Murcia CF	38	6	4	9	21	26	1	5	13	15	39	7	9	22	36	65	30
20 Levante UD	38	5	4	10	22	34	2	1	16	11	41	7	5	26	33	75	26

TOP GOALSCORERS

27 Daniel González GÜIZA (Mallorca)

24 LUÍS FABIANO Clemente (Sevilla)

19 Sergio Leonel AGÜERO (Atlético)

18 DAVID VILLA Sánchez (Valencia)
Ricardo OLIVEIRA (Zaragoza)
RAÚL González Blanco (Real Madrid)

17 NIHAT Kahveci (Villarreal)

16 Samuel ETO'O Fils (Barcelona)
Diego Martín FORLÁN Corazo (Atlético)
Frédéric KANOUTÉ (Sevilla)
Ruud VAN NISTELROOY (Real Madrid)

CLUB-BY-CLUB

UD ALMERÍA

Coach – Unai Emery

Founded - 1989

2007				
26/8	Deportivo	a	3-0	*Negredo, Soriano, Crusat*
2/9	Valencia	h	1-2	*Negredo*
15/9	Real Madrid	a	1-3	*Uche*
23/9	Mallorca	h	1-1	*Mané*
26/9	Murcia	a	1-0	*Felipe Melo*
30/9	Racing	h	0-1	
7/10	Athletic	a	1-1	*Felipe Melo*
21/10	Osasuna	h	2-0	*Felipe Melo (p), Negredo*
28/10	Barcelona	a	0-2	
31/10	Zaragoza	h	0-1	
4/11	Levante	a	0-3	
11/11	Atlético	h	0-0	
25/11	Villarreal	a	1-1	*Negredo*
1/12	Sevilla	h	1-0	*Acasiete*
9/12	Valladolid	h	1-0	*Negredo*
16/12	Betis	a	1-3	*Negredo (p)*
22/12	Getafe	h	0-2	
2008				
6/1	Recreativo	a	1-1	*Mané*
13/1	Espanyol	h	1-0	*Uche*
20/1	Deportivo	h	1-0	*Pulido*
27/1	Valencia	a	1-0	*Felipe Melo*
2/2	Real Madrid	h	2-0	*Juanito, Negredo (p)*
10/2	Mallorca	a	0-0	
17/2	Murcia	h	1-0	*Negredo*
24/2	Racing	a	0-1	
2/3	Athletic	h	1-1	*Negredo (p)*
9/3	Osasuna	a	1-2	*Corona*
16/3	Barcelona	h	2-2	*Pulido, Uche*
23/3	Zaragoza	a	1-1	*Negredo*
30/3	Levante	h	2-1	*Soriano, Felipe Melo*
6/4	Atlético	a	3-6	*Felipe Melo, Juanma Ortiz, Negredo*
13/4	Villarreal	h	1-0	*Acasiete*
19/4	Sevilla	a	4-1	*og (Dani Alves), Negredo 2, Juanma Ortiz*
27/4	Valladolid	a	0-1	
4/5	Betis	h	1-1	*Pulido*
7/5	Getafe	a	2-4	*Crusat, Paunović*
11/5	Recreativo	h	0-2	
18/5	Espanyol	a	3-1	*Felipe Melo, Crusat, Paunović*

No	Name	Nat	Pos	Aps	(s)	Gls
18	Santiago ACASIETE Aradiela	PER	D	17	(3)	2
2	BRUNO Saltor Grau		D	34		
6	José Luis CABRERA Cava		M	1	(2)	
21	CARLOS GARCÍA Badías		D	35		
11	Domingo CISMA González		D	9	(2)	
13	David COBEÑO Iglesias		G	17		

15	Miguel Ángel García "CORONA"		M	21	(11)	1
8	Albert CRUSAT Domene		A	31	(3)	3
28	DIEGO ALVES Carreira	BRA	G	21	(1)	
4	FELIPE MELO de Carvalho	BRA	M	30	(4)	7
25	GUILHERME Oliveira Santos	BRA	D		(2)	
12	IRINEY Santos da Silva	BRA	M	2	(6)	
10	JOSÉ ORTIZ Bernal		A	5	(19)	
24	JUANITO Gutiérrez Robles		D	28	(3)	1
17	JUANMA ORTIZ Palazón		A	30	(3)	2
3	Aitor LÓPEZ REKARTE		D	4	(6)	
22	MANÉ Jiménez Ortiz		D	36		2
19	NATALIO Lorenzo Poquet		A	2	(11)	
9	Álvaro NEGREDO Sánchez		A	34	(2)	13
7	Veljko PAUNOVIĆ	SRB	A	1	(6)	2
14	Rubén Martín PULIDO		D	24	(2)	3
23	Fernando SORIANO Marcos		M	26	(8)	2
5	Kalu UCHE	NGA	A	10	(20)	3

ATHLETIC CLUB BILBAO

Coach – Joaquín Caparrós

Founded – 1898

MAJOR HONOURS: Spanish League - (8) 1930, 1931, 1934, 1936, 1943, 1956, 1983, 1984; Spanish Cup – (23) 1903, 1904, 1910, 1911, 1914, 1915, 1916, 1921, 1923, 1930, 1931, 1932, 1933, 1943, 1944, 1945, 1950, 1955, 1956, 1958, 1969, 1973, 1984.

2007

26/8	Osasuna	h	0-0	
2/9	Barcelona	a	1-3	*Susaeta*
15/9	Zaragoza	h	1-1	*Susaeta*
23/9	Levante	a	2-1	*Aduriz 2*
26/9	Atlético	h	0-2	
30/9	Villarreal	a	0-1	
7/10	Almería	h	1-1	*Etxeberria*
21/10	Valladolid	a	2-1	*Aduriz 2*
27/10	Betis	h	0-0	
31/10	Getafe	a	0-2	
4/11	Recreativo	h	2-0	*Etxeberria 2*
11/11	Espanyol	a	1-2	*Gabilondo*
25/11	Deportivo	h	2-2	*og (Barragán), David López*
2/12	Valencia	a	3-0	*Yeste, Llorente 2*
8/12	Real Madrid	h	0-1	
16/12	Mallorca	a	0-0	
23/12	Murcia	h	1-1	*Koikili*

2008

6/1	Racing	a	0-1	
12/1	Sevilla	h	2-0	*Yeste, Susaeta*
20/1	Osasuna	a	0-2	
27/1	Barcelona	h	1-1	*og (Thuram)*
3/2	Zaragoza	a	0-1	
10/2	Levante	h	1-0	*Aduriz*
17/2	Atlético	a	2-1	*Susaeta, Llorente*
24/2	Villarreal	h	1-2	*Llorente*
2/3	Almería	a	1-1	*Llorente*
9/3	Valladolid	h	2-0	*Gabilondo 2*
15/3	Betis	a	2-1	*Yeste, David López (p)*
23/3	Getafe	h	1-0	*Etxeberria*
30/3	Recreativo	a	1-1	*Aduriz*
6/4	Espanyol	h	1-0	*Garmendia*
13/4	Deportivo	a	0-3	
20/4	Valencia	h	5-1	*Javi Martínez, Llorente 2, Iraola, Aduriz*
27/4	Real Madrid	a	0-3	
4/5	Mallorca	h	1-2	*Llorente*
7/5	Murcia	a	2-1	*Llorente, Gabilondo*
11/5	Racing	h	0-0	
18/5	Sevilla	a	1-4	*Aduriz (p)*

No	Name	Nat	Pos	Aps	(s)	Gls
23	Aritz ADURIZ Zubeldia		A	20	(13)	8
20	AITOR OCIO Carrión		D	27		
5	Fernando AMOREBIETA Mardaras		D	34		
13	Daniel ARANZUBIA Aguado		G	9	(1)	
1	ARMANDO Riveiro de Aguilar		G	16		
43	Urko ARROYO Arribas		M	1		
21	David CUÉLLAR Tainta		M	1	(6)	
25	DAVID LÓPEZ Moreno		M	20	(11)	2
3	Asier DEL HORNO Cosgaya		D	13	(3)	
17	Joseba ETXEBERRIA Lizardi		A	20	(5)	4
2	Unai EXPÓSITO Medina		D	2	(1)	
11	Igor GABILONDO del Campo		M	21	(5)	4
8	Joseba GARMENDIA Elorriaga		M	8	(10)	1
18	Carlos GURPEGUI Nausia		M	5		
1	Gorka IRAIZOZ Moreno		G	13		
15	Andoni IRAOLA Sagama		D	35	(1)	1
24	JAVI MARTÍNEZ Aginaga		M	33	(1)	1
12	KOIKILI Lertxundi del Campo		D	25	(2)	1
9	Fernando LLORENTE Torres		A	25	(10)	9
22	Iñaki MUÑOZ Oroz		M	3	(10)	
19	Ander MURILLO García		D	1	(5)	
16	Pablo ORBAIZ Lesaca		M	20	(3)	
14	Luis PRIETO Zalbidegoitia		D	1	(2)	
45	Aitor RAMOS Leniz		A	2	(3)	
27	Markel SUSAETA Lasjurain		M	23	(6)	4
7	Roberto Martínez Rípodas "TIKO"		M	2		
4	USTARITZ Aldekoaotalora Astarloa		D	14	(6)	
28	Ion VÉLEZ Martínez		A	2	(7)	
10	Francisco Javier YESTE Navarro		M	21	(3)	3
6	Ibán ZUBIAURRE Urrutia		D	1		

CLUB ATLÉTICO DE MADRID

Coach – Javier Aguirre (MEX)

Founded – 1903

MAJOR HONOURS: UEFA Cup Winners' Cup – (1) 1962; World Club Cup – (1) 1974; Spanish League – (9) 1940. 1941, 1950, 1951, 1966, 1970, 1973, 1977, 1996; Spanish Cup – (9) 1960, 1961, 1965, 1972, 1976, 1985, 1991, 1992, 1996.

2007

25/8	Real Madrid	a	1-2	*Agüero*
2/9	Mallorca	h	1-1	*Pernía*
16/9	Murcia	a	1-1	*Agüero*
23/9	Racing	h	4-0	*Raúl García, Agüero, Forlán, Simão*
26/9	Athletic	a	2-0	*Agüero, Forlán*
30/9	Osasuna	h	2-0	*Raúl García, Agüero*
7/10	Barcelona	a	0-3	
21/10	Zaragoza	h	4-0	*Luis García, Forlán, Maxi 2 (1p)*
28/10	Levante	a	1-0	*Forlán*
31/10	Sevilla	h	4-3	*Maniche, Agüero, Maxi, Jurado*
4/11	Villarreal	h	3-4	*Pablo, Simão, Agüero*
11/11	Almería	a	0-0	
25/11	Valladolid	h	4-3	*Maniche, Maxi 2, og (Pedro López)*
2/12	Betis	a	2-0	*Forlán, Raul García*
9/12	Getafe	h	1-0	*Forlán*
16/12	Recreativo	a	0-0	
23/12	Espanyol	h	1-2	*Simão*

2008

6/1	Deportivo	a	3-0	*Forlán, Agüero, Jurado*
13/1	Valencia	h	1-0	*Agüero*
20/1	Real Madrid	h	0-2	
27/1	Mallorca	a	0-1	
3/2	Murcia	h	1-1	*Luis García*
10/2	Racing	a	2-0	*Forlán 2*
17/2	Athletic	h	1-2	*Antonio López*
24/2	Osasuna	a	1-3	*Forlán*

/3	Barcelona	h	4-2	*Agüero 2, Maxi, Forlán (p)*
/3	Zaragoza	a	1-2	*Simão*
6/3	Levante	h	3-0	*Simão, Forlán 2*
2/3	Sevilla	a	2-1	*Maxi, Agüero*
9/3	Villarreal	a	0-3	
/4	Almería	h	6-3	*Antonio López, Forlán (p), Simão 2, Agüero 2*
3/4	Valladolid	a	1-1	*Maxi*
9/4	Betis	h	1-3	*Agüero*
7/4	Getafe	a	1-1	*Agüero*
/5	Recreativo	h	3-0	*Camacho 2, Agüero*
/5	Espanyol	a	2-0	*Agüero, Forlán*
1/5	Deportivo	h	1-0	*Forlán*
8/5	Valencia	a	1-3	*Agüero*

lo	Name	Nat	Pos	Aps	(s)	Gls
3	Christian ABBIATI	ITA	G	20	(1)	
0	Sergio Leonel AGÜERO	ARG	A	35	(2)	19
	ANTONIO LÓPEZ Guerrero		D	23	(1)	2
9	Ignacio CAMACHO Barnola		M	9	(1)	2
	CLÉBER SANTANA Loureiro	BRA	M	11	(12)	
9	Miguel Ángel DE LAS CUEVAS		M	1	(12)	
2	Fabiano ELLER dos Santos	BRA	D	14	(4)	
	Diego Martín FORLÁN Corazo	URU	A	35	(1)	16
4	JOSHUA Zapata González		M		(1)	
5	José Manuel JURADO Marín		M	3	(13)	2
25	LEO Neoren FRANCO	ARG	G	18		
	LUIS Javier GARCÍA Sanz		A	12	(18)	2
8	Nuno Ricardo Ribeiro "MANICHE"	POR	M	15		2
1	MAXI Rubén Rodríguez	ARG	M	32	(3)	8
20	Miguel A. Ferrer Martínez "MISTA"		A	2	(4)	
5	Thiago MOTTA	BRA	M	3	(3)	
22	PABLO Ibáñez Tébar		D	34		1
21	Luis Armando PEREA	COL	D	30		
4	Mariano Andrés PERNIA		D	28	(1)	1
3	RAÚL GARCÍA Escudero		M	35		3
17	José Antonio REYES Calderón		M	10	(16)	
2	Giourkas SEITARIDIS	GRE	D	12	(2)	
24	SIMÃO Pedro Fonseca Sabrosa	POR	A	25	(5)	7
23	Juan VALERA Espín		M	5	(3)	
14	ZÉ Eduardo Rosa Vale de CASTRO	POR	D	6	(2)	

FC BARCELONA

Coach – Frank Rijkaard (NED)

Founded – 1899

MAJOR HONOURS: European Champion Clubs' Cup/UEFA Champions League – (2) 1992, 2006; UEFA Cup Winners' Cup - (4) 1979, 1982, 1989, 1997; Inter Cities Fairs Cup - (3) 1958, 1960, 1966; UEFA Super Cup (2) – 1992, 1997; Spanish League – (18) 1929, 1945, 1948, 1949, 1952, 1953, 1959, 1960, 1974, 1985, 1991, 1992, 1993, 1994, 1998, 1999, 2005, 2006; Spanish Cup – (24) 1910, 1912, 1913, 1920, 1922, 1925, 1926, 1928, 1942, 1951, 1952, 1953, 1957, 1959, 1963, 1968, 1971, 1978, 1981, 1983, 1988, 1990, 1997, 1998.

2007				
26/8	Racing	a	0-0	
2/9	Athletic	h	3-1	*Ronaldinho 2 (1p), Touré*
16/9	Osasuna	a	0-0	
22/9	Sevilla	h	2-1	*Messi 2 (1p)*
26/9	Zaragoza	h	4-1	*Messi 2, Iniesta, Márquez*
29/9	Levante	a	4-1	*Henry 3, Messi*
7/10	Atlético	h	3-0	*Deco, Messi, Xavi*
20/10	Villarreal	a	1-3	*Bojan*
28/10	Almería	h	2-0	*Henry, Messi (p)*
1/11	Valladolid	a	1-1	*Ronaldinho*
4/11	Betis	h	3-0	*Henry, Ronaldinho 2*
10/11	Getafe	a	0-2	
24/11	Recreativo	h	3-0	*Milito, Bojan, Messi (p)*
1/12	Espanyol	a	1-1	*Iniesta*
9/12	Deportivo	h	2-1	*Ronaldinho (p), Xavi*
15/12	Valencia	a	3-0	*Eto'o 2, Gudjohnsen*
23/12	Real Madrid	h	0-1	
2008				
5/1	Mallorca	a	2-0	*Márquez, Eto'o*
12/1	Murcia	h	4-0	*Gudjohnsen, Bojan, Eto'o 2*
20/1	Racing	h	1-0	*Henry*
27/1	Athletic	a	1-1	*Bojan*
3/2	Osasuna	h	1-0	*Xavi*
9/2	Sevilla	a	1-1	*Xavi*
16/2	Zaragoza	a	2-1	*Henry, Ronaldinho (p)*
24/2	Levante	h	5-1	*Xavi, Messi, Eto'o 3*
1/3	Atlético	a	2-4	*Ronaldinho, Eto'o*
9/3	Villarreal	h	1-2	*Xavi*
16/3	Almería	a	2-2	*Bojan, Eto'o*
23/3	Valladolid	h	4-1	*Eto'o, Iniesta, Bojan 2*
29/3	Betis	a	2-3	*Bojan, Eto'o*
6/4	Getafe	h	0-0	
12/4	Recreativo	a	2-2	*Eto'o 2*
19/4	Espanyol	h	0-0	
26/4	Deportivo	a	0-2	
4/5	Valencia	h	6-0	*Messi (p), Xavi, Henry 2, Bojan 2*
7/5	Real Madrid	a	1-4	*Henry*
11/5	Mallorca	h	2-3	*Henry, Eto'o*
17/5	Murcia	a	5-3	*Eto'o, Henry, Giovani*

No	Name	Nat	Pos	Aps	(s)	Gls
22	Éric ABIDAL	FRA	D	28	(2)	
27	BOJAN Krkic Pérez		A	14	(17)	10
20	Anderson Luis de Souza "DECO"	POR	M	14	(4)	1
15	José EDMÍLSON Gomes Moraes	BRA	M	5	(6)	
9	Samuel ETO'O Fils	CMR	A	18		16
18	Santiago EZQUERRO Marín		A	1	(2)	
37	FALI Romero Serrano		D		(1)	
17	GIOVANI dos Santos Ramírez	MEX	A	10	(18)	3
7	Eidur Smári GUDJOHNSEN	ISL	A	12	(11)	2
14	Thierry HENRY	FRA	A	27	(3)	12
8	Andrés INIESTA Luján		M	28	(3)	3
4	Rafael MÁRQUEZ Álvarez	MEX	D	15	(8)	2
19	Lionel Andrés MESSI	ARG	A	23	(5)	10
3	Gabriel Alejandro MILITO	ARG	D	26	(1)	1
23	OLEGUER Presas Renom		D	7	(5)	
33	PEDRITO Rodríguez Ledesma		A		(2)	
13	José Manuel PINTO Colorado		G	3		
5	Carles PUYOL Sofarcada		D	29	(1)	
10	RONALDINHO de Assís Moreira	BRA	A	13	(4)	8
38	José Manuel RUEDA Sampedro		M		(1)	
30	Víctor SÁNCHEZ Mata		M		(1)	
16	SYLVINHO Mendes Campos Júnior	BRA	D	10	(4)	
21	Liliam THURAM	FRA	D	17	(1)	
24	Yaya TOURÉ Gnégnéri	CIV	M	25	(1)	1
36	Víctor VÁZQUEZ Solsona		A		(1)	
1	VÍCTOR VALDÉS Arribas		G	35		
6	XAVI Hernández Creus		M	33	(2)	7
11	Gianluca ZAMBROTTA	ITA	D	25	(4)	

REAL BETIS BALOMPIÉ

Coach – Héctor Cúper (ARG); (3/12/07) Francisco Chaparro

Founded – 1907

MAJOR HONOURS: Spanish League – (1) 1935; Spanish Cup – (2) 1977, 2005.

2007				
26/8	Recreativo	a	1-1	*Nano*
2/9	Espanyol	h	2-2	*Fernando, Sóbis*
16/9	Deportivo	a	0-1	
23/9	Valencia	h	1-2	*Sóbis*

27/9	Real Madrid	a 0-2	
30/9	Mallorca	h 3-0	*Xisco, Sóbis, Edú*
7/10	Murcia	a 0-0	
21/10	Racing	h 1-1	*Xisco*
27/10	Athletic	a 0-0	
31/10	Osasuna	h 0-3	
4/11	Barcelona	a 0-3	
11/11	Zaragoza	h 2-1	*Pavone 2*
25/11	Levante	a 3-4	*Arzu, Edú (p), Pavone*
2/12	Atlético	h 0-2	
9/12	Villarreal	a 1-0	*Capi*
16/12	Almería	h 3-1	*Edú (p), Pavone 2*
23/12	Valladolid	a 0-0	
2008			
6/1	Sevilla	a 0-3	
13/1	Getafe	h 3-2	*Pavone 2, Edú*
20/1	Recreativo	h 1-1	*Edú*
27/1	Espanyol	a 2-1	*Rivera, Edú*
2/2	Deportivo	h 0-1	
10/2	Valencia	a 1-3	*Edú*
16/2	Real Madrid	h 2-1	*Edú, González*
24/2	Mallorca	a 1-1	*Edú*
2/3	Murcia	h 4-0	*og (Arzo), Edú, Pavone, Sóbis (p)*
9/3	Racing	a 0-3	
15/3	Athletic	h 1-2	*González*
23/3	Osasuna	a 1-0	*González*
29/3	Barcelona	h 3-2	*Edú 2, Juanito*
6/4	Zaragoza	a 3-0	*González 2, Pavone*
13/4	Levante	h 0-1	
19/4	Atlético	a 3-1	*Juande, Xisco, Capi*
27/4	Villarreal	h 0-1	
4/5	Almería	a 1-1	*Odonkor*
7/5	Valladolid	h 1-1	*González*
11/5	Sevilla	h 0-2	
18/5	Getafe	a 1-1	*Nano*

No	Name	Nat	Pos	Aps	(s)	Gls
26	ALEX ORTIZ Ramos		D	1		
8	Arturo García Muñoz "ARZU"		M	24	(2)	1
17	Marko BABIĆ	CRO	D	5	(5)	
7	Juan Pablo CAFFA	ARG	M	11	(9)	
14	Jesús Capitán Prado "CAPI"		M	26	(1)	2
13	CASTO Espinosa Barriga		G	9		
12	DAMIÀ Abella Pérez		D	24	(2)	
25	Antonio DOBLAS Santana		G	1		
10	Luís Eduardo Schmidt "EDÚ"	BRA	A	29	(1)	12
9	FERNANDO Miguel Fernández		M	3	(7)	1
11	Mark Dennis GONZÁLEZ Hoffman	CHI	M	18	(6)	6
6	Branko ILIČ	SVN	D	17	(1)	
24	JOSÉ MARI Romero Poyón		A	6	(7)	
27	JUANDE Prados López		M	17	(5)	1
4	JUANITO Gutiérrez Moreno		D	33		1
22	William Lanes de LIMA	BRA	D	6	(3)	
2	Juan A Andreu Alvarado "MELLI"		D	22	(4)	
15	Victoriano Rivas Álvaro "NANO"		D	5	(1)	2
23	David ODONKOR	GER	M	9	(11)	1
16	Hugo Mariano PAVONE	ARG	A	23	(7)	9
1	RICARDO A. Martins Soares	POR	G	28		
5	David RIVAS Rodríguez		D	9	(2)	
18	Alberto RIVERA Pizarro		M	22	(4)	1
21	Rafael SÓBIS do Nascimento	BRA	A	17	(9)	4
20	Leandro Daniel SOMOZA	ARG	M	10	(5)	
32	TONI Sánchez Cabeza		D		(1)	
3	Fernando VEGA Torres		D	29	(2)	
19	XISCO Javier Muñoz Llompart		A	13	(9)	3
29	Alejandro ZAMORA Barbero		D	1		

RC DEPORTIVO LA CORUÑA

Coach – Miguel Ángel Lotina

Founded – 1906

MAJOR HONOURS: Spanish League – (1) 2000; Spanish Cup – (2) 1995, 2002.

2007			
26/8	Almería	h 0-3	
2/9	Valladolid	a 2-2	*Taborda, Riki*
16/9	Betis	h 1-0	*Guardado*
23/9	Getafe	a 0-0	
26/9	Recreativo	h 0-2	
30/9	Espanyol	a 0-1	
7/10	Sevilla	a 1-0	*Riki*
20/10	Valencia	h 2-4	*Xisco, Bodipo*
28/10	Real Madrid	a 1-3	*Xisco*
31/10	Mallorca	h 1-1	*Guardado (p)*
4/11	Murcia	a 2-0	*Xisco, Guardado*
11/11	Racing	h 0-1	
25/11	Athletic	a 2-2	*Riki, Taborda*
2/12	Osasuna	h 1-2	*Rubén*
9/12	Barcelona	a 1-2	*Cristian*
16/12	Zaragoza	h 1-1	*Coloccini*
23/12	Levante	a 1-0	*Sergio (p)*
2008			
6/1	Atlético	h 0-3	
13/1	Villarreal	a 3-4	*Sergio (p), Pablo Amo, Guardado*
20/1	Almería	a 0-1	
27/1	Valladolid	h 3-1	*Lopo, Xisco, Guardado*
2/2	Betis	a 1-0	*Pablo Amo*
9/2	Getafe	h 1-1	*og (Mario)*
17/2	Recreativo	a 2-3	*Verdú (p), Riki*
24/2	Espanyol	h 2-0	*Coloccini, Lafita*
1/3	Sevilla	h 2-1	*Wilhelmsson (p), Lafita*
9/3	Valencia	a 2-2	*Sergio, Lafita*
15/3	Real Madrid	h 1-0	*og (Pepe)*
22/3	Mallorca	a 0-1	
30/3	Murcia	h 3-1	*Xisco 3*
6/4	Racing	a 3-1	*Xisco 2, Coloccini*
13/4	Athletic	h 3-0	*Coloccini, Sergio (p), Filipe Luís*
20/4	Osasuna	a 1-0	*Sergio (p)*
26/4	Barcelona	h 2-0	*Juan Rodríguez, Pablo Amo*
3/5	Zaragoza	a 0-1	
7/5	Levante	h 1-0	*Riki*
11/5	Atlético	a 0-1	
18/5	Villarreal	h 0-2	

No	Name	Nat	Pos	Aps	(s)	Gls
12	ADRIÁN López Álvarez		A	3	(4)	
16	ANTONIO TOMÁS González		M	8	(4)	
1	Dudu AOUATE	ISR	G	28		
25	AYTHAMI Artiles Oliva		M	1		
19	Antonio BARRAGÁN Fernández		D	8	(2)	
7	Rodolfo BODIPO Díaz		A	7	(12)	1
29	David Vázquez González "CHAPI"		A		(1)	
5	Fabricio COLOCCINI	ARG	D	38		4
20	CRISTIAN Hidalgo González		A	7	(7)	1
6	Julián Bobbi DE GUZMÁN	CAN	M	33	(2)	
30	FABRICIO Agosto Ramírez		G	6		
3	FILIPE LUÍS Kasmirski	BRA	D	32	(1)	1
18	José A. GUARDADO Hernández	MEX	M	22	(4)	5
22	JUAN RODRÍGUEZ Villamuela		M	18	(8)	1
17	Ángel LAFITA Castillo		M	18	(6)	3
32	LAURE Sanabria Ruiz		D	1		
4	Alberto LOPO García		D	21		1
2	MANUEL PABLO García Díaz		D	34		
13	Gustavo Adolfo MUNÚA Vera	URU	G	4		
14	PABLO ÁLVAREZ Núñez		M		(1)	

4	PABLO AMO Aguado		D	19		3
8	Adrián López Rodríguez "PISCU"		D	15		
1	Iván Sánchez Rico "RIKI"		A	8	(24)	5
6	Sergio Rodríguez García "RODRI"		D	1		
5	RUBÉN Castro Martín		A	2	(5)	1
	SERGIO González Soriano		M	29	(3)	5
	Sebastián TABORDA	URU	A	3	(13)	2
1	Juan Carlos VALERÓN Santana		M		(5)	
0	Joan VERDÚ Fernández		M	16	(8)	1
4	Christian WILHELMSSON	SWE	M	13	(2)	1
3	XISCO Jiménez Tejada		A	23	(2)	9

RCD ESPANYOL

Coach – Ernesto Valverde

Founded – 1900

MAJOR HONOURS: Spanish Cup – (4) 1929, 1940, 2000, 2006.

007				
6/8	Valladolid	h	0-1	
/9	Betis	a	2-2	*Luis García 2*
6/9	Getafe	h	1-0	*Soriano*
2/9	Recreativo	a	1-2	*Riera*
5/9	Sevilla	a	3-2	*Ángel, Luis García, Tamudo*
0/9	Deportivo	h	1-0	*Tamudo*
/10	Valencia	a	2-1	*Riera, Luis García*
0/10	Real Madrid	h	2-1	*Riera, Tamudo*
7/10	Mallorca	a	2-2	*og (Arango), Tamudo (p)*
/11	Murcia	h	0-0	
/11	Racing	a	1-1	*Tamudo (p)*
1/11	Athletic	h	2-1	*Tamudo, og (Aitor Ocio)*
5/11	Osasuna	a	2-1	*Ángel, Valdo*
/12	Barcelona	h	1-1	*Corominas*
/12	Zaragoza	a	3-3	*Tamudo, Valdo, Zabaleta*
5/12	Levante	h	1-0	*Jarque*
3/12	Atlético	a	2-1	*Tamudo, Luis García*
008				
/1	Villarreal	h	3-0	*Tamudo 2, Valdo*
3/1	Almería	a	0-1	
0/1	Valladolid	a	1-2	*Torrejón*
7/1	Betis	h	1-2	*Luis García*
/2	Getafe	a	1-0	*Soriano*
0/2	Recreativo	h	1-2	*Ewerthon*
6/2	Sevilla	h	2-4	*Luis García, Corominas*
4/2	Deportivo	a	0-2	
/3	Valencia	h	2-0	*Luis García 2 (1p)*
/3	Real Madrid	a	1-2	*Valdo*
6/3	Mallorca	h	2-1	*Luis García 2 (1p)*
3/3	Murcia	a	0-4	
0/3	Racing	h	0-3	
/4	Athletic	a	0-1	
3/4	Osasuna	h	0-1	
9/4	Barcelona	a	0-0	
27/4	Zaragoza	h	1-1	*Riera*
/5	Levante	a	1-1	*Luis García (p)*
/5	Atlético	h	0-2	
11/5	Villarreal	a	0-2	
18/5	Almería	h	1-3	*Luis García (p)*

No	Name	Nat	Pos	Aps	(s)	Gls
14	ÁNGEL Martínez Cervera		M	21	(7)	2
26	Francisco CASILLA Cortés		G	3	(1)	
2	Francisco Javier CHICA Torres		D	12	(5)	
6	CLEMENTE Juan Rodríguez		D	13	(4)	
20	Ferrán COROMINAS Telechea		A	13	(13)	2
3	DAVID GARCÍA de la Cruz		D	17		
9	Iván DE LA PEÑA López		M	7	(5)	
12	EWERTHON Henrique de Souza	BRA	A	5	(3)	1
21	Daniel JARQUE González		D	30	(1)	1
16	JONATAS Domingos	BRA	A	2	(7)	
24	JONATHAN SORIANO Casas		A	8	(16)	2
31	JORDI Gómez García-Penche		M		(3)	
1	Idriss Carlos KAMENI	CMR	G	30		
4	Jesús María LACRUZ Gómez		D	13	(5)	
13	Iñaki LAFUENTE Sancha		G	5		
10	LUIS GARCIA Fernández		A	36	(1)	13
17	Mohammed El Yaagoubi "MOHA"	MAR	M	3	(6)	
22	MOISÉS HURTADO Pérez		M	32	(2)	
11	Albert RIERA Ortega		M	30	(6)	4
18	Francisco Joaquín Pérez RUFETE		M	5	(5)	
27	Albert SERRÁN Polo		D	1		
25	Milan SMILJANIĆ	SRB	M	16	(14)	
23	Raúl TAMUDO Montero		A	22	(3)	10
19	Marc TORREJÓN Moya		D	36		1
7	Valmiro López Rocha "VALDO"		A	27	(4)	4
8	Pablo Javier ZABALETA Girod	ARG	M	31	(1)	1

GETAFE CF

Coach – Michael Laudrup (DEN)

Founded - 1983

2007				
25/8	Sevilla	a	1-4	*Pablo Hernández*
2/9	Recreativo	h	1-1	*Del Moral*
16/9	Espanyol	a	0-1	
23/9	Deportivo	h	0-0	
26/9	Valencia	a	1-2	*Braulio*
30/9	Real Madrid	h	0-1	
7/10	Mallorca	a	2-4	*Sousa 2*
21/10	Murcia	h	2-0	*Kepa, Casquero*
28/10	Racing	a	0-2	
31/10	Athletic	h	2-0	*Casquero, Uche*
4/11	Osasuna	a	2-0	*Pablo Hernández (p), Granero*
10/11	Barcelona	h	2-0	*Del Moral, Albín*
25/11	Zaragoza	a	1-1	*Sousa*
2/12	Levante	h	2-1	*Braulio 2*
9/12	Atlético	a	0-1	
16/12	Villarreal	h	1-3	*Kepa*
22/12	Almería	a	2-0	*Licht, Granero*
2008				
6/1	Valladolid	h	0-3	
13/1	Betis	a	2-3	*De la Red (p), Del Moral*
19/1	Sevilla	h	3-2	*Casquero, Albín, Contra*
27/1	Recreativo	a	3-1	*Albín, Granero, Del Moral*
3/2	Espanyol	h	0-1	
9/2	Deportivo	a	1-1	*Uche*
17/2	Valencia	h	0-0	
24/2	Real Madrid	a	1-0	*Uche*
2/3	Mallorca	h	3-3	*Mario Cotelo, Albín, og (Ramis)*
9/3	Murcia	a	3-0	*Pablo Hernández, Albín, Casquero*
16/3	Racing	h	2-1	*Uche, Gavilán*
23/3	Athletic	a	0-1	
30/3	Osasuna	h	0-2	
6/4	Barcelona	a	0-0	
13/4	Zaragoza	h	0-0	
20/4	Levante	a	1-3	*De la Red (p)*
27/4	Atlético	h	1-1	*Albín*
4/5	Villarreal	a	0-2	
7/5	Almería	h	4-2	*Albín, Del Moral 2, Granero (p)*
11/5	Valladolid	a	0-0	
18/5	Betis	h	1-1	*Del Moral*

No	Name	Nat	Pos	Aps	(s)	Gls
13	Roberto Carlos ABBONDANZIERI	ARG	G	34		
8	ALBERTO Aguilar Leiva		M		(2)	
16	Juan Ángel ALBÍN Leites	URU	M	17	(13)	7
4	David BELENGUER Reverte		D	23	(1)	

9	BRAULIO Nóbrega Rodríguez		A	11	(8)	3
22	Francisco J. CASQUERO Paredes		M	27	(6)	4
3	Daniel Alberto "CATA" DÍAZ	ARG	D	30		
6	Fabio CELESTINI	SUI	M	19	(3)	
2	Cosmin Marius CONTRA	ROU	D	7	(6)	1
21	David CORTÉS Caballero		D	30	(2)	
10	Rubén DE LA RED Gutiérrez		A	29	(2)	2
8	Jaime GAVILÁN Martínez		M	9	(7)	1
25	Esteban GRANERO Molina		M	19	(8)	4
26	JUANFRAN Moreno Fuertes		A		(1)	
17	KEPA Blanco González		A	5	(10)	2
12	Lucas Matías LICHT	ARG	D	33		1
14	Manuel DEL MORAL Fernández		A	25	(9)	7
5	Pedro MARIO Álvarez Abrante		D	11	(4)	
15	NACHO Pérez Santamaría		M	4	(3)	
7	MARIO Gutiérrez COTELO		M	9	(4)	1
24	PABLO HERNÁNDEZ Domínguez		M	23	(5)	3
20	Miguel PALLARDÓ González		M	6	(8)	
19	Franck SIGNORINO	FRA	D	3	(2)	
11	Francisco David SOUSA Franquelo		M	12	(1)	3
23	Manuel TENA López		D	10	(2)	
18	Ikechukwu UCHE	NGA	A	18	(4)	4
1	Óscar Alfredo USTARI	ARG	G	4		

LEVANTE UD

Coach: Abel Resino; (8/10/07) Giovanni De Biasi (ITA); (16/4/08) José Ángel Moreno

Founded – 1939

2007				
26/8	Mallorca	a	0-3	
1/9	Murcia	h	0-0	
16/9	Racing	a	0-1	
23/9	Athletic	h	1-2	*Riganò*
26/9	Osasuna	a	1-4	*Ettien*
29/9	Barcelona	h	1-4	*Viqueira (p)*
7/10	Zaragoza	a	0-3	
20/10	Sevilla	h	0-2	
28/10	Atlético	h	0-1	
31/10	Villarreal	a	0-3	
4/11	Almería	h	3-0	*Riganò 3*
11/11	Valladolid	a	0-1	
25/11	Betis	h	4-3	*Tommasi, Riga 2, Javi Fuego*
2/12	Getafe	a	1-2	*Riga*
9/12	Recreativo	h	0-2	
15/12	Espanyol	a	0-1	
23/12	Deportivo	h	0-1	
2008				
6/1	Valencia	a	0-0	
13/1	Real Madrid	h	0-2	
20/1	Mallorca	h	2-2	*Geijo, Álvaro*
27/1	Murcia	a	3-2	*Álvaro, Riga (p), Pedro León*
3/2	Racing	h	1-1	*Riga*
10/2	Athletic	a	0-1	
17/2	Osasuna	h	2-1	*Álvaro, Geijo*
24/2	Barcelona	a	1-5	*Riga (p)*
2/3	Zaragoza	h	2-1	*Geijo, Riga*
9/3	Sevilla	a	1-2	*Riga*
16/3	Atlético	a	0-3	
23/3	Villarreal	h	1-2	*Miguel Ángel*
30/3	Almería	a	1-2	*Iborra*
6/4	Valladolid	h	0-3	
13/4	Betis	a	1-0	*Pedro León*
20/4	Getafe	h	3-1	*Juanma, Berson, Pedro León*
27/4	Recreativo	a	0-2	
4/5	Espanyol	h	1-1	*Juanma*
7/5	Deportivo	a	0-1	
11/5	Valencia	h	1-5	*Serrano*
18/5	Real Madrid	a	2-5	*Geijo 2*

No	Name	Nat	Pos	Aps	(s)	Gls
4	ÁLVARO Luís Major de Aquino	BRA	D	26	(2)	3
32	ARMANDO Lozano Sánchez		D	7	(5)	
9	Shota ARVELADZE	GEO	A		(4)	
12	Mathieu BERSON	FRA	M	20	(3)	1
5	Bruno CIRILLO	ITA	D	14	(1)	
21	Laurent COURTOIS	FRA	M	22	(4)	
3	DAVID Castedo Escudero		D	18		
23	Iñaki DESCARGA Retegui		D	28	(2)	
7	Felix Dja ETTIEN	CIV	M	3	(10)	1
19	Alexandre GEIJO Pazos		A	22	(10)	5
30	Vicente IBORRA de la Fuente		A	4	(10)	1
6	JAVI FUEGO Martínez		M	17	(7)	1
22	JUANMA Gómez Sánchez		M	34	(1)	2
1	Vladan KUJOVIĆ	SRB	G	13		
2	MANOLO Gaspar Haro		D	11	(3)	
20	Albert MEYONG Zé	CMR	A		(1)	
16	MIGUEL ÁNGEL Lozano Ayala		M	18	(5)	1
14	PEDRO LEÓN ánchez Gil		M	12	(12)	3
28	Manuel REINA Rodríguez		G	8		
10	Mustapha RIGA	GHA	M	28	(5)	8
20	Christian RIGANÒ	ITA	A	11	(2)	4
24	Miguel ROBUSTÉ Colomer		D	3	(1)	
17	Luis Manuel RUBIALES Béjar		D	19	(1)	
26	SAÚL Fernández García		M	5	(15)	
11	SÁVIO Bortolini Pimentel	BRA	A	12		
18	José Manuel SERRANO Arenas		D	29		1
13	Marco STORARI	ITA	G	17		
15	Damiano TOMMASI	ITA	M	15		1
8	Emilio José VIQUEIRA Moure		M	2	(7)	1

RCD MALLORCA

Coach – Gregorio Manzano

Founded – 1916

MAJOR HONOURS: Spanish Cup – (1) 2003.

2007				
26/8	Levante	h	3-0	*Ibagaza 2 (1p), Güiza*
2/9	Atlético	a	1-1	*Güiza*
16/9	Villarreal	h	0-1	
23/9	Almería	a	1-1	*Güiza*
26/9	Valladolid	h	4-2	*Nunes, Arango 2, Víctor*
30/9	Betis	a	0-3	
7/10	Getafe	h	4-2	*Ibagaza (p), Arango 2, Ramis*
21/10	Recreativo	a	2-0	*Güiza, Tuni*
27/10	Espanyol	h	2-2	*Arango, Güiza*
31/10	Deportivo	a	1-1	*Güiza*
3/11	Valencia	h	0-2	
11/11	Real Madrid	a	3-4	*Varela 2, Güiza*
24/11	Sevilla	a	2-1	*Ibagaza, Varela*
2/12	Murcia	h	1-1	*Webo*
9/12	Racing	a	1-3	*Webo*
16/12	Athletic	h	0-0	
23/12	Osasuna	a	1-3	*Güiza*
2008				
5/1	Barcelona	h	0-2	
13/1	Zaragoza	a	2-2	*Varela, Güiza*
20/1	Levante	a	2-2	*Güiza 2*
27/1	Atlético	h	1-0	*Arango*
3/2	Villarreal	a	1-1	*Basinas (p)*
10/2	Almería	h	0-0	
17/2	Valladolid	a	1-1	*Ibagaza (p)*
24/2	Betis	h	1-1	*Varela*
2/3	Getafe	a	3-3	*Güiza, Arango, Ramis*
9/3	Recreativo	h	7-1	*Arango 3, Güiza 2, Borja Valero 2*
16/3	Espanyol	a	1-2	*Güiza*
22/3	Deportivo	h	1-0	*Arango*
30/3	Valencia	a	3-0	*Güiza 2, Ramis*
5/4	Real Madrid	h	1-1	*Borja Valero*

13/4	Sevilla	h	2-3	*Güiza, Webo*
20/4	Murcia	a	4-1	*Güiza 3, Arango*
27/4	Racing	h	3-1	*Nunes, Trejo, Güiza*
4/5	Athletic	a	2-1	*Güiza 2*
7/5	Osasuna	h	2-1	*Güiza, Trejo*
11/5	Barcelona	a	3-2	*Borja Valero, Webo, Güiza*
18/5	Zaragoza	h	3-2	*Güiza, Webo, Castro*

No	Name	Nat	Pos	Aps	(s)	Gls
33	ALBERTO López Arteseros		M		(1)	
18	Juan Fernando ARANGO Sáenz	VEN	M	34	(4)	12
22	Sergio Martínez BALLESTEROS		D	16		
6	Angelos BASINAS	GRE	M	21	(11)	1
8	BORJA VALERO Iglesias		M	17	(18)	4
12	Gonzalo CASTRO Irazábal	URU	M	1	(8)	1
17	DAVID NAVARRO Pedrós		D	15	(3)	
3	FERNANDO NAVARRO Corbacho		D	36		
14	Daniel González GÜIZA		A	36	(1)	27
24	HÉCTOR Berenguel del Pino		D	29		
10	Ariel Miguel IBAGAZA	ARG	M	29	(3)	5
23	JONÁS Manuel Gutiérrez	ARG	M	24	(6)	
25	Germán Darío LUX	ARG	G	9	(1)	
15	Francisco J. MOLINERO Calderón		D	4	(1)	
1	Miguel Ángel MOYÁ Rumbo		G	29		
26	Emilio NSUE López		A		(2)	
16	Juan Carlos de Araújo NUNES	POR	D	35		2
4	Guillermo Ariel PEREYRA	ARG	M	18		
2	Iván RAMIS Barrios		D	11	(3)	3
5	Lionel Sebastián SCALONI	ARG	D	5	(1)	
20	Óscar Guido TREJO	ARG	A	2	(15)	2
11	Antonio L Adrover Colom "TUNI"		A	9	(7)	1
7	Fernando VARELA Ramos		D	28	(5)	5
19	VÍCTOR Casadesús Castaño		A	2	(8)	1
9	Pierre Achille WEBO Kouamo	CMR	A	8	(7)	5

REAL MURCIA CF

Coach – Lucas Alcaraz; (6/3/08) Javier Clemente

Founded - 1908

2007				
25/8	Zaragoza	h	2-1	*Mejía, Baiano*
1/9	Levante	a	0-0	
16/9	Atlético	h	1-1	*Gallardo*
23/9	Villarreal	a	0-2	
26/9	Almería	h	0-1	
30/9	Valladolid	a	4-1	*De Lucas, Baiano, Iván Alonso, Abel*
7/10	Betis	h	0-0	
21/10	Getafe	a	0-2	
28/10	Recreativo	h	1-0	*Regueiro*
1/11	Espanyol	a	0-0	
4/11	Deportivo	h	0-2	
10/11	Valencia	a	0-3	
24/11	Real Madrid	h	1-1	*De Lucas*
2/12	Mallorca	a	1-1	*Iñigo*
9/12	Sevilla	a	1-3	*Baiano*
16/12	Racing	h	2-1	*Goitom, Baiano*
23/12	Athletic	a	1-1	*Baiano (p)*
2008				
6/1	Osasuna	h	2-0	*Goitom, Abel (p)*
12/1	Barcelona	a	0-4	
20/1	Zaragoza	a	1-3	*Iván Alonso*
27/1	Levante	h	2-3	*Iván Alonso, og (Kujović)*
3/2	Atlético	a	1-1	*Jofre (p)*
9/2	Villarreal	h	0-1	
17/2	Almería	a	0-1	
24/2	Valladolid	h	0-1	
2/3	Betis	a	0-4	
9/3	Getafe	h	0-3	
15/3	Recreativo	a	2-4	*De Lucas, Iván Alonso (p)*
23/3	Espanyol	h	4-0	*Iván Alonso 2 (1p), Abel (p), Richi*
30/3	Deportivo	a	1-3	*De Lucas*
6/4	Valencia	h	1-0	*Iván Alonso*
13/4	Real Madrid	a	0-1	
20/4	Mallorca	h	1-4	*Baiano*
26/4	Sevilla	h	0-0	
4/5	Racing	a	2-3	*Aquino, Iván Alonso*
7/5	Athletic	h	1-2	*Iván Alonso*
11/5	Osasuna	a	1-2	*Abel*
17/5	Barcelona	h	3-5	*Ochoa, Iván Alonso (p), Abel*

No	Name	Nat	Pos	Aps	(s)	Gls
10	ABEL Gómez Merino		M	14	(16)	5
30	ALBERTO García Cabrera		G	1		
31	Daniel AQUINO Pintos		A	10	(3)	1
5	César ARZO Amposta		D	27	(1)	
18	Joao Fernando Nelo "BAIANO"	BRA	A	19	(8)	6
6	BRUNO Herrero Arias		M		(2)	
1	Fabián Héctor CARINI	URU	G	10		
21	Iván Javier CUADRADO Alonso		D	9	(2)	
23	CURRO TORRES Ruiz		D	2		
12	David Gutiérrez DE COZ		D	20		
9	Enrique DE LUCAS Martínez		M	28	(2)	4
17	Francisco GALLARDO León		M	4	(6)	1
7	Henok GOITOM	SWE	A	21	(10)	2
22	ÍÑIGO Vélez de Mendizábal		A	9	(14)	1
19	IVÁN Daniel ALONSO Vallejo	URU	A	23	(6)	10
11	JOFRE Mateu González		M	8	(6)	1
6	Abderahman KABOUS	FRA	M	7		
3	Alejandro MARAÑÓN Pérez		D	5		
14	Álvaro MEJÍA Pérez		D	30		1
25	José María MOVILLA Cubero		M	21	(5)	
13	Antonio NOTARIO Caro		G	27		
4	Juan Cruz OCHOA López		D	17	(1)	1
15	PABLO Gabril GARCÍA Pérez	URU	M	21		
16	Francisco PEÑA Romero		D	35		
2	Stéphane Jean PIGNOL	FRA	D	15	(2)	
32	Juan Pedro PINA Martínez		D	2	(1)	
8	Mario Ignacio REGUEIRO Pintos	URU	M	15	(8)	1
20	RICHI Pérez de Zabalza		M	15	(11)	1
24	ROSINEI Adolfo	BRA	M	3	(8)	

CA OSASUNA

Coach – José Ángel Ziganda

Founded – 1920

2007				
26/8	Athletic	a	0-0	
16/9	Barcelona	h	0-0	
23/9	Zaragoza	a	1-2	*Juanfran*
26/9	Levante	h	4-1	*Pandiani 2, Juanfran, Javi García*
30/9	Atlético	a	0-2	
7/10	Villarreal	h	3-2	*og (Javi Venta), Dady, Javi García*
21/10	Almería	a	0-2	
28/10	Valladolid	h	2-2	*Dady 2*
31/10	Betis	a	3-0	*Cruchaga, Dady, Vela*
4/11	Getafe	h	0-2	
11/11	Recreativo	a	0-1	
25/11	Espanyol	h	1-2	*Portillo*
2/12	Deportivo	a	2-1	*Plašil, Dady*
5/12	Sevilla	h	1-1	*Plašil*
8/12	Valencia	h	0-0	
16/12	Real Madrid	a	0-2	
23/12	Mallorca	h	3-1	*Héctor Font, Plašil, Hugo Viana*
2008				
6/1	Murcia	a	0-2	
13/1	Racing	h	0-2	

20/1	Athletic	h	2-0	*Dady, Vela*
26/1	Sevilla	a	1-2	*Sola*
3/2	Barcelona	a	0-1	
10/2	Zaragoza	h	1-0	*Plašil*
17/2	Levante	a	1-2	*Monreal*
24/2	Atlético	h	3-1	*Sola, Vela, Héctor Font*
2/3	Villarreal	a	0-0	
9/3	Almería	h	2-1	*Sola, Cruchaga*
16/3	Valladolid	a	0-0	
23/3	Betis	h	0-1	
30/3	Getafe	a	2-0	*Flaño M., Puñal (p)*
5/4	Recreativo	h	0-1	
13/4	Espanyol	a	1-0	*Astudillo*
20/4	Deportivo	h	0-1	
27/4	Valencia	a	0-3	
4/5	Real Madrid	h	1-2	*Puñal (p)*
7/5	Mallorca	a	1-2	*Portillo*
11/5	Murcia	h	2-1	*Dady, Juanfran*
18/5	Racing	a	0-1	

No	Name	Nat	Pos	Aps	(s)	Gls
24	Mauricio ASTUDILLO Martín	ARG	M	10	(3)	1
40	César AZPILICUETA Tanco		M	28	(1)	
19	Enrique CORRALES Martín		D	11	(1)	
7	César CRUCHAGA Lasa		D	26	(2)	2
18	Eduardo Fernandes Pereira "DADY"	POR	A	19	(11)	7
23	Ludovic DELPORTE	FRA	M	2	(7)	
27	Ion ECHAIDE Sola		D		(1)	
1	Juan ELÍA Vallejo		G	1	(2)	
24	Ion ERICE Domínguez		M	2	(2)	
28	Jokin Arcaya ESPARZA		M	1	(1)	
26	Andrés FERNÁNDEZ Moreno		G		(1)	
17	Javier FLAÑO Bezunartea		D	4		
4	Miguel FLAÑO Bezunartea		D	28		1
8	HÉCTOR FONT Romero		M	15	(17)	2
20	HUGO Miguel Ferreira VIANA	POR	M	1	(8)	1
2	José IZQUIERDO Martínez		D	9		
16	JAVI GARCÍA Fernández		M	21	(4)	2
14	JOSETXO Romero Urtasun		D	21		
12	JUANFRAN Torres Belén		M	31	(3)	3
5	Xavier MARGAIRAZ	SUI	M	11	(2)	
3	Ignacio MONREAL Eraso		D	27		1
25	Javad NEKOUNAM	IRN	M		(2)	
11	Walter Gerardo PANDIANI Urquiza	URU	A	7	(11)	2
6	Jaroslav PLAŠIL	CZE	M	30	(4)	4
9	Javier García PORTILLO		A	9	(9)	2
10	Francisco PUÑAL Martínez		M	34	(1)	2
13	RICARDO López Felipe		G	37		
22	Enrique SOLA Clemente		A	12	(8)	3
21	Carlos Alberto VELA Garrido	MEX	A	21	(12)	3

REAL RACING CLUB SANTANDER

Coach – Marcelino García Toral

Founded - 1913

2007

26/8	Barcelona	h	0-0	
1/9	Zaragoza	a	1-1	*Serrano*
16/9	Levante	h	1-0	*Munitis*
23/9	Atlético	a	0-4	
26/9	Villarreal	h	0-2	
30/9	Almería	a	1-0	*Garay*
7/10	Valladolid	h	2-0	*Smolarek, Tchité*
21/10	Betis	a	1-1	*Jorge López*
28/10	Getafe	h	2-0	*Serrano, Jorge López*
31/10	Recreativo	a	0-0	
4/11	Espanyol	h	1-1	*Tchité*
11/11	Deportivo	a	1-0	*Tchité*
25/11	Valencia	h	1-0	*Jorge López*
1/12	Real Madrid	a	1-3	*Munitis*
9/12	Mallorca	h	3-1	*Jorge López, Duscher, Munitis*
16/12	Murcia	a	1-2	*Smolarek*
22/12	Sevilla	a	1-4	*Garay*

2008

6/1	Athletic	h	1-0	*og (Llorente)*
13/1	Osasuna	a	2-0	*Colsa, Pablo Álvarez*
20/1	Barcelona	a	0-1	
27/1	Zaragoza	h	2-2	*Bolado, Tchité*
3/2	Levante	a	1-1	*Duscher (p)*
10/2	Atlético	h	0-2	
17/2	Villarreal	a	0-0	
24/2	Almería	h	1-0	*Tchité*
2/3	Valladolid	a	1-0	*Duscher*
9/3	Betis	h	3-0	*Duscher, Garay, Tchité*
16/3	Getafe	a	1-2	*Smolarek*
23/3	Recreativo	h	2-0	*Órteman, Smolarek*
30/3	Espanyol	a	3-0	*Serrano, Munitis, Bolado*
6/4	Deportivo	h	1-3	*Jorge López*
12/4	Valencia	a	2-1	*Colsa, Tchité*
20/4	Real Madrid	h	0-2	
27/4	Mallorca	a	1-3	*Duscher (p)*
4/5	Murcia	h	3-2	*Munitis 2, Jorge López*
7/5	Sevilla	h	0-3	
11/5	Athletic	a	0-0	
18/5	Osasuna	h	1-0	*Bolado*

No	Name	Nat	Pos	Aps	(s)	Gls
21	AYOZE Díaz Díaz		D	22	(8)	
32	Iván BOLADO Palacios		A	8	(6)	3
24	CÉSAR González NAVAS		D	17	(1)	
5	CHRISTIAN Fernández Salas		D		(2)	
8	Gonzalo COLSA Albendea		M	35	(3)	2
1	Fabio COLTORTI	SUI	G	6	(1)	
19	Damián I. Saravia "DAMICHON"	PER	M		(1)	
6	Aldo Pedro DUSCHER	ARG	M	33	(1)	5
4	Ezequiel Marcelo GARAY	ARG	D	22		3
23	JONATHAN VALLE Trueba		M	1	(7)	
18	JORDI López Felpeto		M	4	(10)	
7	JORGE LÓPEZ Montaña		M	32	(3)	6
17	LUIS FERNÁNDEZ Gutiérrez		D	17	(2)	
26	LUISMA Villa López		D		(1)	
27	Iván MARCANO Sierra		D	2		
22	José MORATÓN Taeño		D	10	(8)	
10	Pedro MUNITIS Álvarez		A	28	(3)	6
3	ORIOL Lozano Farrán		D	22	(2)	
2	Sergio Daniel ÓRTEMAN	URU	M	3	(2)	1
5	PABLO ÁLVAREZ Núñez		M	10	(8)	1
14	Pablo PINILLOS Caro		D	30	(2)	
2	SAMUEL San José Fernández		M		(1)	
16	SERGIO SÁNCHEZ Ortega		D	13	(6)	
11	Óscar SERRANO Rodríguez		M	29	(5)	3
12	Euzebiusz SMOLAREK	POL	A	23	(11)	4
9	Mohamed TCHITÉ	COD	A	19	(14)	7
13	TOÑO Rodríguez Martínez		G	32		

REAL MADRID CF

Coach – Bernd Schuster (GER)

Founded – 1902

MAJOR HONOURS: European Champion Clubs' Cup/UEFA Champions League – (9) 1956, 1957, 1958, 1959, 1960, 1966, 1998, 2000, 2002; UEFA Cup – (2) 1985, 1986; UEFA Super Cup – (1) 2002; World Club Cup – (3) 1960, 1998, 2002; Spanish League – (31) 1932, 1933, 1954, 1955, 1957, 1958, 1961, 1962, 1963, 1964, 1965, 1967, 1968, 1969, 1972, 1975, 1976, 1978, 1979, 1980, 1986, 1987, 1988, 1989, 1990, 1995, 1997, 2001, 2003, 2007, 2008; Spanish Cup – (17) 1905, 1906, 1907, 1908, 1917, 1934, 1936, 1946, 1947, 1962, 1970, 1974, 1975, 1980, 1982, 1989, 1993.

2007				
25/8	Atlético	h	2-1	*Raúl, Sneijder*
2/9	Villarreal	a	5-0	*Raúl, Sneijder 2, Van Nistelrooy, Guti*
15/9	Almería	h	3-1	*Saviola, Sneijder, Higuaín*
23/9	Valladolid	a	1-1	*Saviola*
27/9	Betis	h	2-0	*Raúl (p), Júlio Baptista*
30/9	Getafe	a	1-0	*Sergio Ramos*
7/10	Recreativo	h	2-0	*Van Nistelrooy, Higuaín*
20/10	Espanyol	a	1-2	*Sergio Ramos*
28/10	Deportivo	h	3-1	*Van Nistelrooy (p), Raúl, Robinho*
31/10	Valencia	a	5-1	*Raúl, Van Nistelrooy 2, Sergio Ramos, Robinho*
3/11	Sevilla	a	0-2	
11/11	Mallorca	h	4-3	*Robinho 2, Raúl, Van Nistelrooy*
24/11	Murcia	a	1-1	*Robinho*
1/12	Racing	h	3-1	*Raúl 2, og (Sergio Sánchez)*
8/12	Athletic	a	1-0	*Van Nistelrooy*
16/12	Osasuna	h	2-0	*Van Nistelrooy, Sneijder*
23/12	Barcelona	a	1-0	*Júlio Baptista*
2008				
6/1	Zaragoza	h	2-0	*Van Nistelrooy, Robinho*
13/1	Levante	a	2-0	*Van Nistelrooy 2*
20/1	Atlético	a	2-0	*Raúl, Van Nistelrooy*
27/1	Villarreal	h	3-2	*Robinho 2, Sneijder*
2/2	Almería	a	0-2	
10/2	Valladolid	h	7-0	*Júlio Baptista, Raúl 2 (1p), Robben, Guti 2, Drenthe*
16/2	Betis	a	1-2	*Drenthe*
24/2	Getafe	h	0-1	
1/3	Recreativo	a	3-2	*Raúl, Robinho 2*
8/3	Espanyol	h	2-1	*Higuaín, Raúl (p)*
15/3	Deportivo	a	0-1	
23/3	Valencia	h	2-3	*Raúl 2*
30/3	Sevilla	h	3-1	*Heinze, Raúl. Higuaín*
5/4	Mallorca	a	1-1	*Sneijder*
13/4	Murcia	h	1-0	*Sneijder*
20/4	Racing	a	2-0	*Raúl, Higuaín*
27/4	Athletic	h	3-0	*Saviola, Robben, Higuaín*
4/5	Osasuna	a	2-1	*Robben, Higuaín*
7/5	Barcelona	h	4-1	*Raúl, Robben, Higuaín, Van Nistelrooy (p)*
11/5	Zaragoza	a	2-2	*Van Nistelrooy, Robinho*
18/5	Levante	h	5-2	*Van Nistelrooy 2, Sergio Ramos 2, Sneijder*

No	Name	Nat	Pos	Aps	(s)	Gls
24	Javier Ángel BALBOA Osa		M		(5)	
5	Fabio CANNAVARO	ITA	D	33		
1	Iker CASILLAS Fernández		G	36		
13	Jordi CODINA Rodríguez		G	1		
6	Mahamadou DIARRA	MLI	M	25	(5)	
15	Royston DRENTHE	NED	D	7	(11)	2
25	Jerzy DUDEK	POL	G	1		
8	Fernando Rubén GAGO	ARG	M	21	(10)	
14	José M. Gutiérrez Hernández "GUTI"		M	27	(5)	3
16	Gabriel Iván HEINZE	ARG	D	17	(3)	1
20	Gonzalo HIGUAÍN	ARG	A	7	(18)	8
19	JÚLIO César BAPTISTA	BRA	M	13	(14)	3
12	MARCELO Vieira da Silva Junior	BRA	D	24		
21	Christoph METZELDER	GER	D	7	(2)	
2	MÍCHEL SALGADO Fernández		D	6	(2)	
3	Képler L. Lima Ferreira "PEPE"	POR	D	17	(2)	
7	RAÚL González Blanco		A	36	(1)	18
11	Arjen ROBBEN	NED	M	13	(9)	4
10	Robson de Souza "ROBINHO"		A	27	(5)	11
18	Javier Pedro SAVIOLA	ARG	A	4	(4)	3
4	SERGIO RAMOS García		D	33		5
23	Wesley SNEIJDER	NED	M	27	(3)	9
9	Roberto SOLDADO Rillo		A	1	(4)	
22	Miguel TORRES Gómez		D	13	(7)	
17	Ruud VAN NISTELROOY	NED	A	22	(2)	16

RC RECREATIVO DE HUELVA

Coach – Víctor Muñoz; (4/2/08) Manuel Zambrano

Founded – 1889

2007				
26/8	Betis	h	1-1	*Sinama-Pongolle*
2/9	Getafe	a	1-1	*Sinama-Pongolle*
16/9	Sevilla	a	1-4	*Aitor*
22/9	Espanyol	h	2-1	*Javi Guerrero 2*
26/9	Deportivo	a	2-0	*Carlos Martins, Javi Guerrero*
30/9	Valencia	h	0-1	
7/10	Real Madrid	a	0-2	
21/10	Mallorca	h	0-2	
28/10	Murcia	a	0-1	
31/10	Racing	h	0-0	
4/11	Athletic	a	0-2	
11/11	Osasuna	h	1-0	*Carlos Martins*
24/11	Barcelona	a	0-3	
2/12	Zaragoza	h	2-1	*Carlos Martins 2*
9/12	Levante	a	2-0	*Camuñas, Jesús Vázquez*
16/12	Atlético	h	0-0	
23/12	Villarreal	a	1-1	*Camuñas*
2008				
6/1	Almería	h	1-1	*Sinama-Pongolle*
13/1	Valladolid	a	1-3	*Camuñas*
20/1	Betis	a	1-1	*Javi Guerrero*
27/1	Getafe	h	1-3	*Camuñas*
3/2	Sevilla	h	1-2	*Beto*
10/2	Espanyol	a	2-1	*Sinama-Pongolle 2*
17/2	Deportivo	h	3-2	*Beto, Sinama-Pongolle, Martín Cáceres*
23/2	Valencia	a	1-1	*Carlos Martins*
1/3	Real Madrid	h	2-3	*Martín Cáceres, Carlos Martins*
9/3	Mallorca	a	1-7	*Marco Rubén*
15/3	Murcia	h	4-2	*Sinama-Pongolle 2, Camuñas, Marquitos*
23/3	Racing	a	0-2	
30/3	Athletic	h	1-1	*og (Amorebieta)*
5/4	Osasuna	a	1-0	*Sinama-Pongolle*
12/4	Barcelona	h	2-2	*Marco Rubén 2*
19/4	Zaragoza	a	0-3	
27/4	Levante	h	2-0	*Ersen, Camuñas*
3/5	Atlético	a	0-3	
7/5	Villarreal	h	0-2	
11/5	Almería	a	2-0	*Jesús Vázquez, Sinama-Pongolle*
18/5	Valladolid	h	1-1	*Javi Guerrero*

No	Name	Nat	Pos	Aps	(s)	Gls
21	AITOR Tornavaca Fernández		M	31	(5)	1
17	Rafael BARBER Rodríguez		M	5	(13)	
22	Roberto Luis Severo "BETO"	POR	D	20	(3)	2
5	Iago BOUZÓN Amoedo		D	25	(2)	
12	CARLOS J. Neto MARTINS	POR	M	31	(1)	6
8	Javier CAMUÑAS Gallego		A	37		6
15	Edwin Arturo CONGO Murillo	COL	A		(6)	
3	DANI BAUTISTA Pina		D	12	(4)	
9	ERSEN Martin	TUR	M	1	(8)	1
6	GERARD López Segú		M	2	(16)	
23	JAVI García GUERRERO		A	15	(11)	5
10	Antonio JESÚS VÁZQUEZ Muñoz		M	33		2

No	Name	Nat	Pos	Aps	(s)	Gls
18	MARCO Gastón RUBÉN Rodríguez	ARG	A	10	(4)	3
7	MARQUITOS García Barreno		M	10	(9)	1
4	José MARTÍN CÁCERES Silva	URU	D	34	(1)	2
2	Eduardo MOYA Castillo		D	15	(1)	
28	Pablo OLIVEIRA Serrano		D	2	(1)	
24	José María "PAMPA" CALVO	ARG	D	13	(1)	
20	POLI Fernández Serrano		D	25	(1)	
16	QUIQUE ÁLVAREZ Sanjuán		D	9	(2)	
11	Laurenţiu Dumitru ROŞU	ROU	A		(4)	
14	Florent SINAMA-PONGOLLE	FRA	A	33	(1)	10
1	Stefano SORRENTINO	ITA	G	38		
19	Silvestre M. Gonçalves VARELA	POR	M	13	(9)	
15	José Ignacio ZAHINOS Sánchez		M	4	(7)	

SEVILLA FC

Coach – Juande Ramos; (26/10/07) Manuel Jiménez

Founded – 1905

MAJOR HONOURS: UEFA Cup – (2) 2006, 2007; UEFA Super Cup – (1) 2006; Spanish League – (1) 1946; Spanish Cup – (4) 1935, 1939, 1948, 2007.

2007				
25/8	Getafe	h	4-1	*Jesús Navas, Luís Fabiano, Kanouté, Kerzhakov*
16/9	Recreativo	h	4-1	*Kerzhakov 2, Kanouté 2*
22/9	Barcelona	a	1-2	*Kanouté*
25/9	Espanyol	h	2-3	*og (Jarque), Koné*
29/9	Zaragoza	a	0-2	
7/10	Deportivo	h	0-1	
20/10	Levante	a	2-0	*Luís Fabiano 2 (1p)*
28/10	Valencia	h	3-0	*Kanouté, Poulsen, Luís Fabiano*
31/10	Atlético	a	3-4	*Luís Fabiano 2, og (Zé Castro)*
3/11	Real Madrid	h	2-0	*Keita, Luís Fabiano*
11/11	Villarreal	a	2-3	*Kanouté, Luís Fabiano*
24/11	Mallorca	h	1-2	*Kanouté*
1/12	Almería	a	0-1	
5/12	Osasuna	a	1-1	*Jesús Navas*
9/12	Murcia	h	3-1	*Luís Fabiano 2, Maresca (p)*
16/12	Valladolid	a	0-0	
22/12	Racing	h	4-1	*Kanouté, Chevantón, Jesús Navas, Adriano*
2008				
6/1	Betis	h	3-0	*Luís Fabiano 2, Dani Alves*
12/1	Athletic	a	0-2	
19/1	Getafe	a	2-3	*Luís Fabiano, Dragutinović*
26/1	Osasuna	h	2-1	*Poulsen, Luís Fabiano (p)*
3/2	Recreativo	a	2-1	*Luís Fabiano 2*
9/2	Barcelona	h	1-1	*Diego Capel*
16/2	Espanyol	a	4-2	*Luís Fabiano, Kanouté, Poulsen, Diego Capel*
23/2	Zaragoza	h	5-0	*Luís Fabiano 2, og (Ayala), og (Diogo), Keita*
1/3	Deportivo	a	1-2	*Kanouté*
9/3	Levante	h	2-1	*Keita, Luís Fabiano*
15/3	Valencia	a	2-1	*Luís Fabiano 2*
22/3	Atlético	h	1-2	*Diego Capel*
30/3	Real Madrid	a	1-3	*Kanouté*
6/4	Villarreal	h	2-0	*Luís Fabiano, Kanouté (p)*
13/4	Mallorca	a	3-2	*Renato, Kanouté, Dani Alves*
19/4	Almería	h	1-4	*Kanouté*
26/4	Murcia	a	0-0	
4/5	Valladolid	h	2-0	*Renato 2*
7/5	Racing	a	3-0	*Fazio 2, og (Moratón)*
11/5	Betis	a	2-0	*Luís Fabiano, Fazio*
18/5	Athletic	h	4-1	*Kanouté 2, Keita, Jesús Navas*

No	Name	Nat	Pos	Aps	(s)	Gls
6	ADRIANO Correia Claro	BRA	M	22	(4)	1
27	Alejandro ALFARO Ligero		M		(2)	
23	Khalid BOULAHROUZ	NED	D	6		
32	José Manuel CASADO Bizcocho		D	1	(1)	
19	Ernesto J CHEVANTÓN Espinosa	URU	A	1	(7)	1
26	José Ángel CRESPO Rincón		D	13		
4	DANI ALVES da Silva	BRA	D	33		2
30	DAVID PRIETO Gálvez		D	8	(1)	
20	Tom DE MUL	BEL	A	3	(3)	
13	Morgan DE SANCTIS	ITA	G	7	(1)	
17	DIEGO CAPEL Trinidad		M	22	(9)	3
3	Ivica DRAGUTINOVIĆ	SRB	D	23		1
5	Sérgio P. Barbosa Valente "DUDA"	POR	M	5	(12)	
14	Julien ESCUDÉ	FRA	D	15	(1)	
28	Federico FAZIO	ARG	D	18	(4)	3
24	Andreas HINKEL	GER	D	2		
7	JESÚS NAVAS González		M	32	(4)	4
35	JUANJO Expósito Ruiz		A		(1)	
12	Frédéric KANOUTÉ	MLI	A	25	(5)	16
21	Seydou KEITA	MLI	M	28	(3)	4
9	Aleksandr KERZHAKOV	RUS	A	6	(5)	3
22	Arouna KONÉ	CIV	A	7	(14)	1
31	LOLO Ortiz Toribio		D	1	(1)	
10	LUÍS FABIANO Clemente	BRA	A	28	(2)	24
25	Enzo MARESCA	ITA	M	12	(9)	1
18	José Luis MARTÍ Soler		M	4	(5)	
15	Aquivaldo MOSQUERA Romaña	COL	D	23	(1)	
1	Andrés PALOP Cervera		G	31		
8	Christian Bager POULSEN	DEN	M	23	(6)	3
16	Antonio PUERTA Pérez		M	1		
11	RENATO Dirnei Florencio Santos	BRA	M	18	(11)	3

VALENCIA CF

Coach – Quique Sánchez Flores (29/10/07) (Óscar Fernández); (4/11/07) Ronald Koeman (NED); (21/4/08) Salvador González "Voro"

Founded – 1919

MAJOR HONOURS: UEFA Cup Winners' Cup – (1) 1980; UEFA Cup – (1) 2004; Inter Cities Fairs Cup – (2) 1962, 1963; UEFA Super Cup – (2) 1980, 2004; Spanish League – (6) 1942, 1944, 1947, 1971, 2002, 2004; Spanish Cup – (7) 1941, 1949, 1954, 1967, 1979, 1999, 2008.

2007				
26/8	Villarreal	h	0-3	
2/9	Almería	a	2-1	*Morientes, Moretti*
15/9	Valladolid	h	2-1	*Morientes, Silva*
23/9	Betis	a	2-1	*Miguel, Joaquín*
26/9	Getafe	h	2-1	*Silva, David Villa*
30/9	Recreativo	a	1-0	*David Villa*
6/10	Espanyol	h	1-2	*Baraja*
20/10	Deportivo	a	4-2	*Joaquín (p), Baraja, Morientes 2*
28/10	Sevilla	a	0-3	
31/10	Real Madrid	h	1-5	*Angulo*
3/11	Mallorca	a	2-0	*Morientes 2*
10/11	Murcia	h	3-0	*Iván Helguera, David Villa 2*
25/11	Racing	a	0-1	
2/12	Athletic	h	0-3	
8/12	Osasuna	a	0-0	
15/12	Barcelona	h	0-3	
22/12	Zaragoza	a	2-2	*Žigić, Silva*
2008				
6/1	Levante	h	0-0	
13/1	Atlético	a	0-1	
19/1	Villarreal	a	0-3	
27/1	Almería	h	0-1	
3/2	Valladolid	a	2-0	*Mata, David Villa*
10/2	Betis	h	3-1	*David Villa 2, Silva*
17/2	Getafe	a	0-0	

23/2	Recreativo	h	1-1	*Mata*
1/3	Espanyol	a	0-2	
9/3	Deportivo	h	2-2	*Mata, David Villa*
15/3	Sevilla	h	1-2	*Albiol*
23/3	Real Madrid	a	3-2	*David Villa 2 (1p), Arizmendi*
30/3	Mallorca	h	0-3	
6/4	Murcia	a	0-1	
12/4	Racing	h	1-2	*David Villa (p)*
20/4	Athletic	a	1-5	*David Villa*
27/4	Osasuna	h	3-0	*David Villa (p), Mata, Joaquín*
4/5	Barcelona	a	0-6	
7/5	Zaragoza	h	1-0	*Silva*
11/5	Levante	a	5-1	*David Villa 3, Mata, Angulo*
18/5	Atlético	h	3-1	*og (Seitaridis), David Villa 2*

No	Name	Nat	Pos	Aps	(s)	Gls
6	David ALBELDA Aliqués		M	11	(4)	
4	Raúl ALBIOL Tortajada		D	32		1
20	ALEXIS Ruano Delgado		D	12	(2)	
10	Miguel Ángel ANGULO Valderrey		A	9	(7)	2
19	Ángel Javier ARIZMENDI de Lucas		A	18	(12)	1
11	Ever Maximiliano BANEGA	ARG	M	7	(5)	
8	Rubén BARAJA Vegas		M	22	(3)	2
12	Marco Antonio Simões CANEIRA	POR	D	19		
1	Santiago CAÑIZARES Ruiz		G	10		
7	DAVID VILLA Sánchez		A	26	(2)	18
22	EDÚ César Daude Gaspar	BRA	M	3	(10)	
3	Manuel H. Tavares FERNANDES	POR	M	5	(2)	
11	Jaime GAVILÁN Martínez		M	2	(1)	
13	Timo HILDEBRAND	GER	G	26		
15	IVÁN HELGUERA Bujía		D	22	(2)	1
17	JOAQUÍN Sánchez Rodríguez		M	26	(8)	3
26	David Rodríguez LOMBÁN		D	1	(2)	
3	Hedwiges MADURO	NED	M	11		
5	Carlos MARCHENA López		D	26	(2)	
16	Juan Manuel MATA García		A	17	(7)	5
23	Luís MIGUEL B. Garcia Monteiro	POR	D	23	(3)	1
34	Ángel MONTORO Sánchez		M	3	(1)	
25	Juan Luis MORA Palacios		G	2		
24	Emiliano MORETTI	ITA	D	28		1
9	Fernando MORIENTES Sánchez		A	11	(11)	6
21	David Jiménez SILVA		M	32	(2)	5
2	Stephen SUNDAY	NGA	M	4	(6)	
14	VICENTE Rodríguez Guillén		M	7	(10)	
18	Nikola ŽIGIĆ	SRB	A	3	(12)	1

REAL VALLADOLID CF

Coach – José Luis Mendilíbar

Founded - 1928

2007				
26/8	Espanyol	a	1-0	*Llorente*
2/9	Deportivo	h	2-2	*García Calvo, Sisi*
15/9	Valencia	a	1-2	*Kome*
23/9	Real Madrid	h	1-1	*Pedro López*
26/9	Mallorca	a	2-4	*Ogbeche, Víctor*
30/9	Murcia	h	1-4	*Llorente*
7/10	Racing	a	0-2	
21/10	Athletic	h	1-2	*Víctor (p)*
28/10	Osasuna	a	2-2	*Álvaro Rubio, Sesma*
1/11	Barcelona	h	1-1	*Llorente*
4/11	Zaragoza	a	3-2	*Víctor 2, Álvaro Rubio*
11/11	Levante	h	1-0	*Sesma*
25/11	Atlético	a	3-4	*Víctor, Sisi, Llorente*
2/12	Villarreal	h	2-0	*Llorente, Víctor*
9/12	Almería	a	0-1	
16/12	Sevilla	h	0-0	
23/12	Betis	h	0-0	
2008				
6/1	Getafe	a	3-0	*Vivar Dorado 2, Álvaro Rubio*
13/1	Recreativo	h	3-1	*Llorente 3*
20/1	Espanyol	h	2-1	*Llorente 2*
27/1	Deportivo	a	1-3	*Víctor*
3/2	Valencia	h	0-2	
10/2	Real Madrid	a	0-7	
17/2	Mallorca	h	1-1	*Llorente*
24/2	Murcia	a	1-0	*Llorente*
2/3	Racing	h	0-1	
9/3	Athletic	a	0-2	
16/3	Osasuna	h	0-0	
23/3	Barcelona	a	1-4	*Sesma (p)*
30/3	Zaragoza	h	2-1	*Víctor (p), Llorente*
6/4	Levante	a	3-0	*Llorente, Víctor, Borja*
13/4	Atlético	h	1-1	*Ogbeche*
20/4	Villarreal	a	0-2	
27/4	Almería	h	1-0	*Sesma*
4/5	Sevilla	a	0-2	
7/5	Betis	a	1-1	*Víctor*
11/5	Getafe	h	0-0	
18/5	Recreativo	a	1-1	*Llorente*

No	Name	Nat	Pos	Aps	(s)	Gls
22	Marcos Sebastián AGUIRRE	ARG	M	3	(5)	
13	ALBERTO López Fernández		G	6	(1)	
4	ALEXIS Suárez Martín		D	6	(5)	
18	ÁLVARO RUBIO Robres		M	35	(2)	3
26	Sergio ASENJO Andrés		G	24		
8	Javier BARAJA Vegas		D	11	(6)	
24	Iñaki BEA Jáuregui		D	6	(1)	
6	BORJA Fernández Fernández		D	16	(15)	1
1	Ludovic BUTELLE	FRA	G	8		
17	Diego CAMACHO Quesada		M	6	(3)	
11	José Luis Sánchez CAPDEVILA		M	9	(6)	
2	Daniel CIFUENTES Alfaro		D	8	(1)	
22	Fabián ESTOYANOFF Poggio	URU	A	1	(3)	
5	José Antonio GARCÍA CALVO		D	33		1
27	KIKE López Delgado		A		(3)	
14	Daniel Armand Ngom KOME	CMR	M	12	(3)	1
9	Joseba LLORENTE Echarri		A	35	(1)	15
23	Vladimir MANCHEV	BUL	A	1	(4)	
3	Alberto MARCOS Rey		D	29	(1)	
12	Bartholomew OGBECHE	NGA	A	3	(16)	2
10	ÓSCAR SÁNCHEZ Fuentes		D	13	(8)	
16	PEDRO LÓPEZ Muñoz		D	28		1
15	RAFA López Gómez		M	21		
19	Jonathan SESMA González		A	24	(8)	4
7	SISI González Martínez		M	31	(5)	2
21	VÍCTOR M Fernández Gutiérrez		A	26	(7)	10
20	Ángel Manuel VIVAR DORADO		M	23	(7)	2

VILLARREAL CF

Coach – Manuel Pellegrini (CHI)

Founded - 1923

2007				
26/8	Valencia	a	3-0	*Tomasson, Rossi (p), Cazorla*
2/9	Real Madrid	h	0-5	
16/9	Mallorca	a	1-0	*Nihat*
23/9	Murcia	h	2-0	*Rossi 2*
26/9	Racing	a	2-0	*Nihat, Rossi*
30/9	Athletic	h	1-0	*Fuentes*
7/10	Osasuna	a	2-3	*Rossi, Godín*
20/10	Barcelona	h	3-1	*Cazorla, Senna 2 (2p)*
28/10	Zaragoza	a	1-4	*Pires*

31/10	Levante	h	3-0	*Guille Franco, Rossi (p), Cygan*
4/11	Atlético	a	4-3	*Rossi, Fuentes, Guille Franco, Nihat*
11/11	Sevilla	h	3-2	*Guille Franco 2, Matías Fernández (p)*
25/11	Almería	h	1-1	*Nihat*
2/12	Valladolid	a	0-2	
9/12	Betis	h	0-1	
16/12	Getafe	a	3-1	*Nihat 2, Cazorla*
23/12	Recreativo	h	1-1	*Nihat*
2008				
5/1	Espanyol	a	0-3	
13/1	Deportivo	h	4-3	*Rossi (p), Nihat 2, Tomasson (p)*
19/1	Valencia	h	3-0	*Pires, Capdevila, Nihat*
27/1	Real Madrid	a	2-3	*Rossi, Capdevila*
3/2	Mallorca	h	1-1	*Rossi (p)*
9/2	Murcia	a	1-0	*Guille Franco*
17/2	Racing	h	0-0	
24/2	Athletic	a	2-1	*Guille Franco, Capdevila*
2/3	Osasuna	h	0-0	
9/3	Barcelona	a	2-1	*Senna (p), Tomasson*
16/3	Zaragoza	h	2-0	*Nihat, Rossi (p)*
23/3	Levante	a	2-1	*Matías Fernández, Guille Franco*
29/3	Atlético	h	3-0	*Cazorla, Nihat 2*
6/4	Sevilla	a	0-2	
13/4	Almería	a	0-1	
20/4	Valladolid	h	2-0	*Nihat, Cazorla*
27/4	Betis	a	1-0	*Senna*
4/5	Getafe	h	2-0	*Nihat 2*
7/5	Recreativo	a	2-0	*Nihat, Guille Franco*
11/5	Espanyol	h	2-0	*Javi Venta, Pires*
18/5	Deportivo	a	2-0	*Matías Fernández, Guille Franco*

No	Name	Nat	Pos	Aps	(s)	Gls
18	ÁNGEL David López Ruano		D	17	(3)	
21	BRUNO Soriano Llidó		M	16	(5)	
10	Rubén Gracia Calmache "CANI"		M	14	(18)	
5	Joan CAPDEVILA Méndez		D	36		3
8	Santiago CAZORLA González		M	28	(8)	5
12	Pascal CYGAN	FRA	D	19	(2)	1
13	DIEGO LÓPEZ Rodríguez		G	20		
23	Sebastián EGUREN Ledesma	URU	M	14	(1)	
20	Fabricio Fabio FUENTES	ARG	D	18		2
4	Diego Roberto GODÍN Leal	URU	D	22	(2)	1
2	GONZALO Javier Rodríguez	ARG	D	17	(1)	
9	GUILLErmo FRANCO Farcuasón	ARG	A	16	(8)	9
17	JAVI Rodríguez VENTA		D	23	(2)	1
3	JOSEMI González Rey		D	1		
6	JOSICO Moreno Verdú		M	10	(3)	
26	JUAN CARLOS Sánchez Martínez		G		(1)	
14	MATÍAS Ariel FERNÁNDEZ	CHI	M	11	(19)	3
24	Antonio Rio MAVUBA	FRA	M	1	(4)	
15	NIHAT Kahveci	TUR	A	25	(9)	17
7	Robert PIRES	FRA	M	27	(5)	3
22	Giuseppe Scurto ROSSI	ITA	A	22	(5)	11
19	Marcos Antonio SENNA		M	34		4
11	Jon Dahl TOMASSON	DEN	A	9	(16)	3
1	Diego VIERA	URU	G	18		

REAL ZARAGOZA

Coach – Víctor Fernández; (14/1/08) (Ander Garitano); (20/1/08) Javier Iruretagoyena; (3/3/08) Manuel Villanova

MAJOR HONOURS: UEFA Cup Winners' Cup – (1) 1995; Inter Cities Fairs Cup – (1) 1964; Spanish Cup – (6) 1964, 1966, 1986, 1994, 2001, 2004.

2007				
25/8	Murcia	a	1-2	*Oliveira*
1/9	Racing	h	1-1	*Oliveira*
15/9	Athletic	a	1-1	*Milito*
23/9	Osasuna	h	2-1	*Matuzalem, Milito (p)*
26/9	Barcelona	a	1-4	*Zapater*
29/9	Sevilla	h	2-0	*D'Alessandro, Sergio García*
7/10	Levante	h	3-0	*Sergio García, Oliveira 2*
21/10	Atlético	a	0-4	
28/10	Villarreal	h	4-1	*Oliveira, Óscar, Milito (p), Sergio García*
31/10	Almería	a	1-0	*Milito (p)*
4/11	Valladolid	h	2-3	*Oliveira, Milito*
11/11	Betis	a	1-2	*D'Alessandro*
25/11	Getafe	h	1-1	*D'Alessandro*
2/12	Recreativo	a	1-2	*Milito*
9/12	Espanyol	h	3-3	*Milito, Oliveira 2*
16/12	Deportivo	a	1-1	*Milito*
22/12	Valencia	h	2-2	*Milito (p), og (Mora)*
2008				
6/1	Real Madrid	a	0-2	
13/1	Mallorca	h	2-2	*Milito 2*
20/1	Murcia	h	3-1	*Oliveira, Milito 2*
27/1	Racing	a	2-2	*Milito, Celades*
3/2	Athletic	h	1-0	*Oliveira*
10/2	Osasuna	a	0-1	
16/2	Barcelona	h	1-2	*Oliveira*
23/2	Sevilla	a	0-5	
2/3	Levante	a	1-2	*Óscar*
8/3	Atlético	h	2-1	*og (Pablo), Milito (p)*
16/3	Villarreal	a	0-2	
23/3	Almería	h	1-1	*Oliveira*
30/3	Valladolid	a	1-2	*Zapater*
6/4	Betis	h	0-3	
13/4	Getafe	a	0-0	
19/4	Recreativo	h	3-0	*Sergio García, Oliveira 2*
27/4	Espanyol	a	1-1	*Oliveira (p)*
3/5	Deportivo	h	1-0	*Ayala*
7/5	Valencia	a	0-1	
11/5	Real Madrid	h	2-2	*Oliveira, Sergio Fernández*
18/5	Mallorca	a	2-3	*Oliveira 2*

No	Name	Nat	Pos	Aps	(s)	Gls
8	Pablo César AIMAR	ARG	M	16	(6)	
6	Roberto Fabián AYALA	ARG	D	33		1
16	Albert CELADES López		M	13	(11)	1
1	CÉSAR SÁNCHEZ Domínguez		G	37		
24	CHUS HERRERO Gómez		D	5	(5)	
4	Luis Carlos CUARTERO Laforga		D	2		
10	Andrés Nicolás D'ALESSANDRO	ARG	M	4	(10)	3
2	Carlos Andrés DIOGO Enseñat	URU	D	29		
14	GABI Fernández Arenas		M	22	(10)	
19	David GENERELO Miranda		M		(4)	
26	Raúl GONI Bayo		D	1	(1)	
11	JUANFRAN García García		D	25	(3)	
25	Javier LÓPEZ VALLEJO		G	1	(1)	
7	Peter LUCCIN	FRA	M	28	(2)	
20	Francisco da Silva "MATUZALEM"	BRA	D	12	(2)	1
22	Diego Alberto MILITO	ARG	A	33	(2)	15
34	Alberto MONTEJO Gañán		M		(1)	
12	Ricardo OLIVEIRA	BRA	A	31	(6)	18
5	ÓSCAR Javier González Marcos		M	16	(16)	2
3	Javier PAREDES Arango		D	17	(6)	
15	Francisco PAVÓN Barahona		D	6	(2)	
23	SERGIO FERNÁNDEZ González		D	25		1
9	SERGIO GARCÍA de la Fuente		A	30	(8)	4
28	Óscar VALERO Navarro		D	2	(2)	
35	VICENTE Pascual Collado		M		(1)	
21	Alberto ZAPATER Arjol		M	30	(6)	2

PROMOTION CLUBS

CD NUMANCIA DE SORIA
Coach – Gonzalo Arconada
Founded - 1945

MÁLAGA CF
Coach – Juan López Muñiz
Founded - 1994

REAL SPORTING DE GIJÓN
Coach – Manuel Preciado
Founded - 1905

SECOND LEVEL FINAL TABLE 2007/08

	Pld	W	D	L	F	A	Pts
CD Numancia de Soria	42	22	11	9	59	38	77
Málaga CF	42	20	12	10	58	42	72
Real Sporting de Gijón	42	20	12	10	61	40	72
Real Sociedad de Fútbol	42	18	14	10	55	39	68
CD Castellón	42	16	13	13	42	37	61
Hércules CF	42	14	16	12	66	55	58
UD Salamanca	42	13	18	11	52	44	57
UD Las Palmas	42	15	12	15	51	55	57
Sevilla Atlético	42	14	14	14	43	48	56
Elche CF	42	14	12	16	44	50	54
CD Tenerife	42	12	17	13	51	57	53
Albacete Balompié	42	13	13	16	37	40	52
SD Éibar	42	14	10	18	42	51	52
Club Gimnàstic de Tarragona	42	12	16	14	49	51	52
Xerez CD	42	12	16	14	47	56	52
RC Celta de Vigo	42	13	13	16	56	55	52
Deportivo Alavés	42	12	15	15	41	47	51
Córdoba CF	42	11	17	14	50	56	50
Racing Club Ferrol	42	12	14	16	46	51	50
Cádiz CF	42	12	13	17	40	47	49
Club Granada 74	42	10	15	17	45	59	45
CP Ejido	42	11	11	20	37	54	44

DOMESTIC CUP 2007/08

COPA DEL REY

URTH ROUND

/11/07 & 2/1/08)
oyano v Barcelona 0-3; 2-2 *(2-5)*
ıia v Sevilla 1-1; 3-4 *(4-5)*
rcules v Athletic 2-2; 0-2 *(2-4)*

/11/07 & 2/1/08)
Palmas v Villarreal 2-4; 1-2 *(3-6)*
laga v Racing 0-0; 0-2 *(0-2)*
ladolid v Murcia 1-1; 3-2 *(4-3)*
ez v Recreativo 0-1; 1-1 *(1-2)*

/11/07 & 3/1/08)
ante v Almería 2-1; 1-1 *(3-2)*

Pontevedra v Zaragoza 1-0; 1-3 *(2-3)*

(12/12/07 & 2/1/08)
Burgos v Getafe 0-1; 1-4 *(1-5)*
Elche v Betis 1-1; 0-3 *(1-4)*
Granada 74 v Atlético 1-2; 1-1 *(2-3)*
Osasuna v Mallorca 2-0; 0-4 *(2-4)*

(19/12/07 & 2/1/08)
Alicante v Real Madrid 1-1; 1-2 *(2-3)*
Espanyol v Deportivo 1-1; 2-1*aet (3-2)*
Real Unión v Valencia 1-2; 0-3 *(1-5)*

FIFTH ROUND

(9/1/08 & 15/1/08)
Sevilla v Barcelona 0-0; 1-1 *(1-1; Barcelona on away goal)*

(9/1/08 & 16/1/08)
Athletic v Espanyol 1-1; 1-1 *(aet; 3-4 on pens)*
Betis v Valencia 1-2; 0-2 *(1-4)*
Getafe v Levante 3-0; 1-0 *(4-0)*
Recreativo v Villarreal 1-0; 0-2 *(1-2)*
Zaragoza v Racing 1-1; 2-4 *(3-5)*

(10/1/08 & 16/1/08)
Atlético v Valladolid 0-0; 1-1 *(1-1; Atlético on away goal)*
Mallorca v Real Madrid 2-1; 1-0 *(3-1)*

QUARTER-FINALS

(23/1/08 & 30/1/08)
Getafe 1 *(De la Red 51)*, Mallorca 0
Mallorca 2 *(Ibagaza 5p, Arango 55)*, Getafe 1 *(Granero 81)*
(2-2; Getafe on away goal)

Valencia 1 *(Silva 32)*, Atlético 0
Atlético 3 *(Miguel 10og, Agüero 18, Valera 60)*, Valencia 2 *(Santana 28og, Mata 35)*
(3-3; Valencia on away goals)

(24/1/08 & 31/1/08)
Racing 2 *(Tchité 74, Smolarek 77)*, Athletic 0
Athletic 3 *(Amorebieta 18, Muñoz 24p, Susaeta 56)*, Racing 3 *(Duscher 53, Tchité 77, Serrano 90+1)*
(Racing 5-3)

Villarreal 0, Barcelona 0
Barcelona 1 *(Henry 41)*, Villarreal 0
(Barcelona 1-0)

SEMI-FINALS

(27/2/08 & 20/3/08)
Barcelona 1 *(Xavi 90+2)*, Valencia 1 *(Villa 70)*
Valencia 3 *(Baraja 17, Mata 44, 72)*, Barcelona 2 *(Henry 71, Eto'o 80)*
(Valencia 4-3)

(28/2/08 & 19/3/08)
Getafe 3 *(De la Red 25, Casquero 58, Del Moral 82)*, Racing 1 *(Smolarek 28)*
Racing 1 *(Munitis 6)*, Getafe 1 *(Casquero 79)*
(Getafe 4-2)

FINAL

(16/4/08)
Vicente Calderón, Madrid
VALENCIA CF 3 *(Mata 4, Alexis 11, Morientes 84)*
GETAFE CF 1 *(Granero 45p)*
Referee – *Undiano Mallenco*
VALENCIA – *Hildebrand, Miguel, Albiol (Caneira 57), Alexis, Moretti (Edú 67), Arizmendi, Baraja, Marchena, Mata, Silva, David Villa (Morientes 74).*
GETAFE – *Ustari, Cortés, Tena (Braulio 76), Cata Díaz, Licht, Contra (Pablo Hernández 55), Casquero (Celestini 64), De la Red, Granero, Del Moral, Albín.*
Sent-off: *Celestini (86).*

Early EURO exit signals end of an era

Sweden went to UEFA EURO 2008™ hoping that their experience would prove decisive in carrying them at least as far as the quarter-finals. But with experience comes age, and in their final group game, against Russia, Lars Lagerbäck's side were given the runaround by a team that was much quicker, livelier and, in essence, much younger.

Lagerbäck had packed his squad, and preferred starting XI, with golden oldies, even recalling 36-year-old Henrik Larsson from international retirement – for the second time – to bolster the team's attack. There were only three players under 25 among his chosen 23, and of those only 24-year-old Fredrik Stoor was entrusted with a place in the starting line-up – and even then because the first-choice right-back, another 36-year-old, Niclas Alexandersson, was injured in the opening game. Promising midfielder Sebastian Larsson, at 23 the youngest member of the squad, saw only 11 minutes of action while defender Andreas Granqvist, also 23, was not used at all.

UEFA EURO 2008™ was the fifth successive major tournament for which Sweden had qualified, and most of the players Lagerbäck sent into battle had played in some or all of the previous four. The Sweden coach was banking on that being an asset, but ultimately it became a liability, and for the first time since UEFA EURO 2000™ the Scandinavians failed to reach the knockout stages.

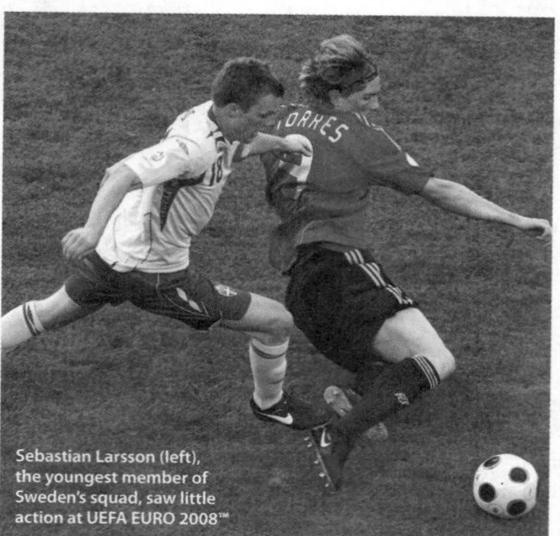

Sebastian Larsson (left), the youngest member of Sweden's squad, saw little action at UEFA EURO 2008™

There were some decent enough individual performances from the men in yellow, but nothing special. Andreas Isaksson had plenty to do, making more saves in the group stage than any other goalkeeper, and emergency left-back Mikael Nilsson, who filled in for the injured Erik Edman, tackled with commitment and gusto. Zlatan Ibrahimović, of whom so much was expected, ended a long international goal drought by finding the net against both Greece and Spain, but he could not produce his very best because of a lingering knee problem. The rest of the Swedish attack was virtually non-existent, although that was partly due to a dearth of creativity in central midfield, where home-based veterans Daniel Andersson and Anders Svensson offered little other than hard work.

Ljungberg quits

Beating Greece 2-0 in their opening game – thanks to Ibrahimović's beautifully struck breakthrough strike and a scrappy second – gave Sweden the perfect start, and although they lost to a last-minute goal against Spain, that was essentially irrelevant as they would still have required a draw against Russia had they kept the score at 1-1. Against the Russians they were simply outclassed – much as they had been against Germany in exiting from the 2006 FIFA World Cup. Alexandersson and veteran striker Marcus Allbäck had already announced that they would be giving up international football prior to the journey to Austria, but there was some surprise when captain Fredrik Ljungberg declared that he would be following suit and even more when Henrik Larsson suggested that he would be happy to play on, if selected, into the 2010 World Cup qualifiers.

Lagerbäck, for one, remains in situ. He signed a new two-year contract at the end of the qualifying campaign, but

Zlatan Ibrahimović ended a long international goal famine at UEFA EURO 2008™

e will be under considerable pressure to rejuvenate his eam on the road to South Africa. One player surprisingly mitted from the UEFA EURO 2008™ party was 21-year-ld striker Marcus Berg. He made his debut against Turkey n February but was not seen again – despite scoring 15 oals in the Dutch Eredivisie, plus another three in the lay-offs, in his debut season for FC Groningen.

efore moving to the Netherlands, Berg was also the star erformer in the 2007 Allsvenskan, scoring 14 goals in ust 17 starts for IFK Göteborg. Although he left midway hrough the season, his total was still good enough to arn him shared ownership of the league's Golden Boot vith Razak Omotoyossi, Henrik Larsson's strike-partner t Helsingborgs IF. Paradoxically, it was after Berg leparted that Göteborg found the consistent form that vould launch them from a mid-table position at halfway p to first place at the finish.

weden's record champions had not won the Allsvenskan title for eleven years, and for much of the season – despite Berg's goals – they appeared too erratic to end that barren sequence. But with former player Stefan Rehn, ably assisted by Jonas Olsson, cleverly rejigging his troops, Gothenburg's finest reeled off an unbeaten 14-match run (the first five with Berg still present) to climb all the way to the summit.

Göteborg wrapped up the title on the final day with a 2-0 victory at home to strugglers Trelleborgs FF that left them a point clear of provincial challengers Kalmar FF. Rehn's men had gone into the game level on points with Stockholm side Djurgårdens IF FF but knew that because of their superior goal difference a win would all but guarantee the title. As it transpired, Djurgården lost 1-0 at home to IF Brommapojkarna, a team virtually relegated. Kalmar had also gone into the season's climax in contention, but with a one-point deficit on the other two. They defeated AIK Solna 2-0, but with Göteborg scoring through Tomas Olsson on seven minutes and Magnus Johansson – a survivor of the club's previous win in 1996 – adding a second after 34, the chances of a late twist to what had been a congested championship race were effectively nullified.

Eighteenth title

Göteborg, Djurgården and Kalmar had all come on strong late in the season, but others such as Halmstads BK, AIK and reigning champions IF Elfsborg had also been heavily in the mix earlier on. It was unusual for the champion club not to break the 50-point barrier, but Göteborg were not too concerned. They were just delighted to claim the 18th national title that had eluded them for so long. The defeat they had suffered a month earlier in the final of the Swedish Cup added to the relief. Bidding to win the national knockout competition for the first time since 1991, they came up against a rampant Kalmar, who, exploiting the advantage of hosting the final in their home stadium, ran out convincing 3-0 winners to claim the Svenska Cupen for the first time in 20 years. The final came in the middle of a purple match for Kalmar, and it was in-form striker César Santin, one of six Brazilians in the squad (but the only one to appear in the final), who proved to be the hero of the day for Nanne Bergstrand's side, scoring two goals.

Kalmar's Cup win ensured their place in the UEFA Cup. With Göteborg and Djurgården also qualifying for continental competition, the Allsvensan's European representation in 2008/09 was wholly different from 2007/08, when Swedish clubs collectively enjoyed their best season in years. With Hammarby making it through

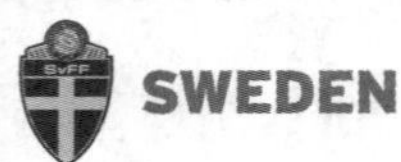

SWEDEN

Svenska Fotbollförbundet (SvFF)

Råsunda Stadion
PO Box 1216
SE-171 23 Solna
tel - +46 8 7350929
fax - +46 8 7350901
website - www.svenskfotboll.se
email - svff@svenskfotboll.se
Year of Formation – 1904
President - Lars-Åke Lagrell
General Secretary - Sune Hellströmer
Press Officer – Jonas Nystedt
Stadium - Råsunda Stadion, Solna (35,972)

INTERNATIONAL TOURNAMENT APPEARANCES
FIFA World Cup - (11) 1934 (2nd round), 1938 (4th), 1950 (3rd), 1958 (runners-up), 1970, 197 (2nd phase), 1978, 1990, 1994 (3rd), 2002 (2nd round), 2006 (2nd round).
UEFA European Championship - (4) 1992 (sem finals), 2000, 2004 (qtr-finals), 2008.

TOP FIVE ALL-TIME CAPS
Thomas Ravelli (143); Roland Nilsson (116); Björn Nordqvist (115); Niclas Alexandersson (109); Henrik Larsson (98)

TOP FIVE ALL-TIME GOALS
Sven Rydell (49); Gunnar Nordahl (43); Henrik Larsson (36); Gunnar Gren (32); Kennet Andersson (31)

NATIONAL TEAM RESULTS 2007/08

22/8/07	United States	H	Gothenburg	1-0	*Källström (56)*
8/9/07	Denmark (ECQ)	H	Solna	0-0	
12/9/07	Montenegro	A	Podgorica	2-1	*Rosenberg (71), Prica (75)*
13/10/07	Liechtenstein (ECQ)	A	Vaduz	3-0	*Ljungberg (19), Wilhelmsson (29), Svensson (56)*
17/10/07	Northern Ireland (ECQ)	H	Solna	1-1	*Mellberg (15)*
17/11/07	Spain (ECQ)	A	Madrid	0-3	
21/11/07	Latvia (ECQ)	H	Solna	2-1	*Allbäck (1), Källström (57)*
13/1/08	Costa Rica	A	San Jose	1-0	*Holmén (49)*
19/1/08	United States	A	Carson	0-2	
6/2/08	Turkey	A	Istanbul	0-0	
26/3/08	Brazil	N	London (ENG)	0-1	
26/5/08	Slovenia	H	Gothenburg	1-0	*Linderoth (41)*
1/6/08	Ukraine	H	Solna	0-1	
10/6/08	Greece (ECF)	N	Salzburg (AUT)	2-0	*Ibrahimović (67), Hansson (72)*
14/6/08	Spain (ECF)	N	Innsbruck (AUT)	1-2	*Ibrahimović (34)*
18/6/08	Russia (ECF)	N	Innsbruck (AUT)	0-2	

NATIONAL TEAM APPEARANCES 2007/08

Coach – Lars LAGERBÄCK		**16/7/48**	Usa	DEN	Mne	LIE	NIR	ESP	LVA	Crc	Usa	Tur	Bra	Svn	Ukr	GRE	ESP	RUS	Caps	Go
Rami SHABAAN	30/6/75	Fredrikstad (NOR) /Hammarby	G		s46						G		s46		s46				16	
Mikael NILSSON	24/6/78	Panathinaikos (GRE)	D46	D	D86		s45	D	D			D83	D46	D78	D	D	D	D79	50	
Petter HANSSON	14/12/76	Rennes (FRA)	D46	D	D46	D	D	D				D			D	D	D	D	35	
Olof MELLBERG	3/9/77	Aston Villa (ENG)	D	D			D	D	D				D	D73	D	D	D	D	85	
Erik EDMAN	11/11/78	Rennes (FRA)	D	D	D	D	D	D	D										55	

ATIONAL TEAM APPEARANCES 2007/08 (contd.)

			Usa	DEN	Mne	LIE	NIR	ESP	LVA	Crc	Usa	Tur	Bra	Svn	Ukr	GRE	ESP	RUS	Caps	Goals
el ANDERSSON	28/8/77	Malmö	M		M	s70		M46		s68	M		s50	M		M	M	M56	65	-
tian ELMSSON	8/12/79	Bolton (ENG) /Deportivo (ESP)	M46	M57		M	M45	M79	M				s57	M	M	M78			52	4
KÄLLSTRÖM	24/8/82	Lyon (FRA)	M	s69	M66	s39	M85	s46	M			M	M		M		s87	s56	57	8
edy RCIOGLÜ	2/11/80	Ajax (NED)	M	s57				s79				M73		A46					14	-
IBRAHIMOVIĆ	3/10/81	Internazionale (ITA)	A66	A89			A	A	A						A56	A71	A46	A	53	20
ELMANDER	27/5/81	Toulouse (FRA)	A76	A		A60	A73					s46	A61	s46	s56 /76	s71	M79	M	38	11
as CONCHA	31/3/80	Bochum (GER)	s46			D	D					s83							8	-
el MAJSTOROVIC	5/4/77	Basel (SUI)	s46		D	D			D			D	D	D					15	1
s ANDERSSON	29/12/71	Göteborg	s46	M	s86					s68	M46		s80	s78	D72	D74			109	7
us ROSENBERG	27/9/82	Bremen (GER)	s66		A	s60		A60				A46	A			s78	s46		23	6
n DJURIC	16/9/84	Halmstad /Zürich (SUI)	s76		M82					A									6	-
eas ISAKSSON	3/10/81	Man. City (ENG)		G	G46	G	G	G	G			G	G46	G	G46	G	G	G	59	-
as LINDEROTH	21/4/79	Galatasaray (TUR)		M	s66	M70	M							M46	M56				75	2
ers SVENSSON	17/7/76	Elfsborg		M69	M66	M	M	M	M	M46	M	M	M50	s46	s56	M	M	M	93	15
PRICA	30/6/80	AaB (DEN)		s89	A					A68	A61								14	2
eas GRANQVIST	16/4/85	Wigan (ENG)			s46									s73					3	-
eas ANSSON	5/7/78	AaB (DEN)			s66		s85				M61								15	-
el DORSIN	6/10/81	Rosenborg (NOR) /CFR (ROU)			s82								s46	s78					12	-
ik LJUNGBERG	16/4/77	West Ham (ENG)				M39		M	M				M57		s46	M	M	M	75	14
us ALLBÄCK	5/7/73	København (DEN)				A	s73	s60	A				s61	A46	s76			s79	74	30
n WILAND	24/1/81	Elfsborg								G									3	-
ik STOOR	28/2/84	Rosenborg (NOR)								D		D62	D	D	s72	s74	D	D	8	-
ias BJÄRSMYR	3/1/86	Göteborg								D	D								2	-
man SLEYMAN	28/12/79	Hammarby								D71									1	-
ang SAFARI	9/2/85	Malmö								D68	s61	s62							3	-
y CHANKO	29/11/79	Hammarby								M68									1	-
n ISHIZAKI	15/5/82	Elfsborg								M68									11	-
uel HOLMÉN	28/6/84	Brøndby (DEN)								M	s61	s73							7	1
eas DAHL	6/6/84	Helsingborg								s46	s78								2	-
r NINGBERG	2/4/86	Helsingborg								s68	D61								2	-
n OREMO	24/10/86	Gefle								s68	s61								2	-
r LARSSON	30/4/84	Halmstad								s71	D								2	-
el LUSTIG	13/12/86	Sundsvall									D								1	-
us NBLOOM	25/6/86	Göteborg									A78								2	-
r ELM	13/11/85	Kalmar									s46								1	-
stian LARSSON	6/6/85	Birmingham (ENG)										M	M80	M78	M46		s79		5	-
cus BERG	17/8/86	Groningen (NED)										A							1	-
ik LARSSON	20/9/71	Helsingborg												s46	A	A	A87	A	98	36

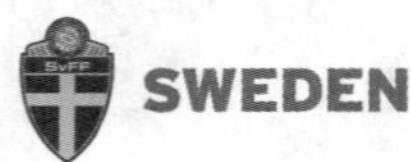

from the UEFA Intertoto Cup and Elfsborg parachuting in from the UEFA Champions League, Sweden had no fewer than five teams in the first round of the UEFA Cup, the others being Helsingborg, AIK and fair play qualifiers BK Häcken. Furthermore, two of them, Elfsborg and Helsingborg, progressed into the group stage, with the latter, inspired by their Omotoyossi-Larsson strike combination, prolonging their adventure into the round of 32, where they finally met their match against PSV Eindhoven.

Helsingborg players celebrate their third goal against Galatasaray in the UEFA

UEFA Cup highlights

With the UEFA Intertoto Cup games included, the Swedish quintet played a total of 46 European matches. Elfsborg's highlights were away wins against the champions of Hungary and Romania, while Helsingborg's amazing 5-1 home win over SC Heerenveen (after a 5-3 defeat in the Netherlands) was later eclipsed by a 3-2 victory at Galatasaray AŞ. Helsingborg ended their European campaign under a new coach, Bo Nilsson, after Englishman Stuart Baxter departed at the end of a domestic campaign in which, despite being the Allsvenskan's top scorers, with 49 goals, they could finish no higher than eighth.

With the top division expanding from 14 clubs to 16 in 2008, Brommapojkarna were the only team to go dowr while three clubs came up. IFK Norrköping, coached by Mats Jingblad, ended five years in the wilderness by winning the second division. The 12-time champions were accompanied up by Ljungskile SK and GIF Sundsvall, the latter finishing a point ahead of UEFA Cu participants Häcken, who had been relegated via the play-offs a year before.

DOMESTIC LEAGUE 2007

ALLSVENSKAN FINAL TABLE

		Home					Away					Total					
	Pld	W	D	L	F	A	W	D	L	F	A	W	D	L	F	A	Pts
1 IFK Göteborg	26	6	5	2	19	10	8	2	3	26	13	14	7	5	45	23	49
2 Kalmar FF	26	8	2	3	20	12	7	1	5	23	20	15	3	8	43	32	48
3 Djurgårdens IF FF	26	9	1	3	22	12	4	6	3	17	12	13	7	6	39	24	46
4 IF Elfsborg	26	5	6	2	23	13	5	4	4	16	17	10	10	6	39	30	40
5 AIK Solna	26	5	4	4	13	8	5	4	4	17	19	10	8	8	30	27	38
6 Hammarby	26	9	0	4	24	10	2	3	8	11	21	11	3	12	35	31	36
7 Halmstads BK	26	6	4	3	21	17	3	5	5	12	24	9	9	8	33	41	36
8 Helsingborgs IF	26	5	4	4	33	18	4	4	5	16	19	9	8	9	49	37	35
9 Malmö FF	26	4	5	4	15	12	5	2	6	14	16	9	7	10	29	28	34
10 Gefle IF	26	7	4	2	16	9	2	3	8	13	21	9	7	10	29	30	34
11 GAIS Göteborg	26	5	4	4	15	17	2	4	7	9	20	7	8	11	24	37	29
12 Örebro SK	26	5	3	5	20	23	1	4	8	8	22	6	7	13	28	45	25
13 Trelleborgs FF	26	3	5	5	15	20	2	3	8	7	18	5	8	13	22	38	23
14 IF Brommapojkarna	26	4	3	6	12	17	1	5	7	9	26	5	8	13	21	43	23

TOP GOALSCORERS

14 Razak OMOTOYOSSI (Helsingbo
Marcus BERG (Göteborg)

12 CÉSAR SANTÍN (Kalmar)

11 Johan OREMO (Gefle)

9 PAULINHO GUARÁ (Hammarby)
Henrik LARSSON (Helsingborg)
Anders SVENSSON (Elfsborg)
JÚNIOR Guimarães (Malmö)

8 THIAGO Quirino (Djurgården)
Sebastián EGUREN (Hammarby)
Stefan ISHIZAKI (Elfsborg)

CLUB-BY-CLUB

AIK SOLNA

Coach – Rikard Norling

Founded - 1891

AJOR HONOURS: Swedish League - (10) 1900, 1901, 1911, 1914, 1916, 1923, 1932, 1937, 1992, 1998; Swedish Cup - (7) 1949, 1950, 1976, 1985, 1996, 1997, 1999.

007				
/4	Kalmar	h	0-1	
7/4	Göteborg	a	2-1	*Burgič, Wilton*
4/4	Hammarby	h	1-0	*Daniel Mendes*
8/4	Malmö	a	0-4	
/5	Helsingborg	h	0-1	
2/5	Brommapojkarna	a	2-0	*Jonsson, Wilton*
1/5	Halmstad	h	1-1	*Jonsson (p)*
8/5	Djurgården	a	1-3	*Daniel Mendes*
0/6	Örebro	h	1-1	*Jonsson (p)*
8/6	Gefle	a	0-0	
5/6	GAIS	a	1-1	*Carlsson*
/7	Trelleborg	h	2-0	*Óbolo, Pavey*
/7	Elfsborg	h	0-1	
2/7	Elfsborg	a	0-2	
3/7	Helsingborg	a	3-2	*Óbolo, Wilton, Valedmarín*
/8	Brommapojkarna	h	3-0	*Johnson, Óbolo, Valdemarín*
2/8	Gefle	h	1-0	*Karlsson*
9/8	Örebro	a	4-1	*Wilton, Óbolo, Stephenson, Tamandi*
6/8	Malmö	h	3-1	*Wilton 2, Pavey*
/9	Hammarby	a	2-1	*Valdemarín 2*
6/9	Halmstad	a	2-2	*Tamandi, Óbolo*
4/9	Djurgården	h	1-1	*Valdemarín*
0/9	GAIS	h	0-0	
/10	Trelleborg	a	0-0	
2/10	Göteborg	h	0-1	
8/10	Kalmar	a	0-2	

lo	Name	Nat	Pos	Aps	(s)	Gls
3	Daniel ARNEFJORD		D	15	(1)	
6	Pierre BENGTSSON		M	2	(4)	
	Miran BURGIČ	SVN	A	4	(2)	1
4	Nicklas CARLSSON		D	15	(2)	1
6	DANIEL MENDES	BRA	A	7	(10)	2
1	Alexander GERNDT		M	2	(3)	
	Kristian HAYNES		A	2	(3)	
1	Bernt HULSKER	NOR	A	3	(3)	
	Nils-Eric JOHANSSON		D	15		
0	Dulee JOHNSON	LBR	M	25		1
8	Markus JONSSON		D	13	(5)	3
	Patrik KARLSSON		D	16	(4)	1
	Pablo MONSALVO	ARG	M	4	(2)	
7	Mauro Iván ÓBOLO	ARG	M	14		5
4	Kenny PAVEY	ENG	M	16	(6)	2
3	Mats RUBARTH		M	6	(4)	
	Per Verner RØNNING	NOR	D	3		
	Niklas SANDBERG		M	8		
0	Khari STEPHENSON	JAM	M	14	(4)	1
7	Jimmy TAMANDI		D	22	(1)	2
	Daniel TJERNSTRÖM		M	21	(2)	
8	Lucas VALDEMARÍN	ARG	A	9	(5)	5
5	Kevin WALKER		M		(2)	
10	WILTON Figueiredo	BRA	A	17	(1)	6
19	Robert ÅHMAN-PERSSON		M	3	(5)	
1	Daniel ÖRLUND		G	26		
29	Gabriel ÖZKAN		M	4	(3)	

IF BROMMAPOJKARNA

Coach – Claes Eriksson

Founded - 1942

2007				
6/4	Djurgården	h	1-0	*Runnemo*
15/4	Kalmar	a	2-2	*Guterstam, Persson*
23/4	Göteborg	h	1-2	*Guterstam*
29/4	Hammarby	a	0-4	
6/5	Trelleborg	a	3-3	*Lagerlöf, Nilsson, Persson (p)*
12/5	AIK	h	0-2	
22/5	Helsingborg	h	1-1	*Talebinejad*
28/5	Halmstad	a	0-1	
11/6	Malmö	h	0-1	
17/6	Örebro	a	0-4	
26/6	Elfsborg	a	0-3	
1/7	GAIS	h	1-0	*Berg*
9/7	Gefle	a	1-1	*Lagerlöf*
16/7	Gefle	h	2-1	*Ekström, Talebinejad*
23/7	Trelleborg	h	0-3	
6/8	AIK	a	0-3	
12/8	Örebro	h	3-1	*Hagernäs, Malmström, Guterstam*
18/8	Malmö	a	0-2	
25/8	Hammarby	h	0-2	
2/9	Göteborg	a	0-0	
16/9	Helsingborg	a	1-1	*Malmström*
22/9	Halmstad	h	1-1	*Haglund*
29/9	Elfsborg	h	1-1	*Ekström*
7/10	GAIS	a	1-2	*Persson (p)*
21/10	Kalmar	h	1-2	*Nilsson*
28/10	Djurgården	a	1-0	*Guterstam*

No	Name	Nat	Pos	Aps	(s)	Gls
12	Michael ALMEBÄCK		D	1	(2)	
16	Pär ASP		D	18	(1)	
29	Mattias ASPER		G	6		
22	Jan-Erik BERG		D	16	(3)	1
20	Kristoffer BJÖRKLUND		G	20		
19	Albin EKDAL		M	9	(6)	
9	Martin EKSTRÖM		M	19	(7)	2
11	Olof GUTERSTAM		A	25		4
7	Joakim HAGERNÄS		M	15	(4)	1
15	Philip HAGLUND		M	6	(9)	1
6	Richard HENRIKSSON		D	24	(2)	
25	Markus KARLSSON		D	13		
14	Thomas LAGERLÖF		M	20	(1)	2
10	Tommy LYCÉN		M	7	(1)	
8	Håkan MALMSTRÖM		D	24		2
23	Mikael NILSSON		A	5	(9)	2
2	Jon PERSSON		D	17	(1)	3
18	Joakim RUNNEMO		A	5	(7)	1
26	Imad SHHADEH	SYR	D	9	(1)	
13	Arash TALEBINEJAD		A	16	(7)	2
21	Christer YOUSSEF		A	9	(6)	
17	Imad ZATARA		M	2	(2)	

DJURGÅRDENS IF FF

Coach – Siggi Jónsson (ISL)

Founded - 1891

MAJOR HONOURS: Swedish League - (11) 1912, 1915, 1917, 1920, 1955, 1959, 1964, 1966, 2002, 2003, 2005; Swedish Cup - (4) 1990, 2002, 2004, 2005.

2007				
6/4	Brommapojkarna	a	0-1	
16/4	Halmstad	h	2-0	*Kusi-Asare, Dahlberg*
21/4	Helsingborg	h	3-1	*Jonson 2, Kusi-Asare*
29/4	Kalmar	a	0-1	
7/5	Elfsborg	a	2-2	*Stoltz, Dahlberg*
14/5	GAIS	h	0-1	
21/5	Trelleborg	a	3-0	*og (Malmqvist), Enrico, Amoah*
28/5	AIK	h	3-1	*Sjölund 2, Enrico*
12/6	Göteborg	h	2-1	*Tauer, Komac*
19/6	Hammarby	a	0-2	
25/6	Örebro	a	0-0	
2/7	Gefle	h	2-1	*Enrico 2*
7/7	Malmö	h	1-0	*Kusi-Asare*
17/7	Malmö	a	1-1	*Davids*
21/7	Elfsborg	h	2-1	*Thiago, Kuivasto*
6/8	GAIS	a	1-1	*Sjölund (p)*
13/8	Hammarby	h	1-0	*Dahlberg*
16/8	Göteborg	a	1-1	*Jonson*
27/8	Kalmar	h	1-3	*Sjölund (p)*
3/9	Helsingborg	a	4-1	*Thiago 2, Sjölund (p), Dahlberg*
17/9	Trelleborg	h	1-1	*Jonson*
24/9	AIK	a	1-1	*Thiago*
29/9	Örebro	h	4-1	*Arneng, Jonson, Kusi-Asare, Thiago*
7/10	Gefle	a	2-0	*Thiago, Enrico*
22/10	Halmstad	a	2-1	*Thiago 2*
28/10	Brommapojkarna	h	0-1	

No	Name	Nat	Pos	Aps	(s)	Gls
20	Patrick AMOAH		A	1	(12)	1
7	Johan ARNENG		M	20	(2)	1
17	Stefan BATAN		M	2	(11)	
14	Kebba CEESAY		D	3	(1)	
2	Matias CONCHA		D	11		
18	Mikael DAHLBERG		A	11	(8)	4
23	Lance DAVIDS	RSA	M	19	(3)	1
10	ENRICO Cardoso	BRA	M	20	(5)	5
26	Kennedy IGBOANANIKE	NGA	A		(2)	
16	Markus JOHANNESSON		M	25		
12	Mattias JONSON		A	15	(1)	5
22	Andrej KOMAC	SVN	M	19	(3)	1
6	Toni KUIVASTO	FIN	D	26		1
9	Jones KUSI-ASARE		A	18	(5)	4
27	Felix MAGRO	ITA	M		(3)	
5	Sölvi OTTESEN	ISL	D	7	(7)	
29	Aki RIIHILAHTI	FIN	M	8	(2)	
11	Daniel SJÖLUND	FIN	A	22	(1)	5
3	Robert STOLTZ		D	5	(2)	1
8	Jan TAUER	GER	D	23		1
19	THIAGO Quirino	BRA	A	5	(8)	8
15	Pa Dembo TOURRAY	GAM	G	26		

IF ELFSBORG

Coach – Magnus Haglund

Founded - 1904

MAJOR HONOURS: Swedish League - (5) 1936, 1939, 1940, 1961, 2006; Swedish Cup - (2) 2001, 2003.

2007				
7/4	Malmö	h	1-1	*Holmén*
17/4	Örebro	a	1-1	*Bajrami*
23/4	Gefle	h	1-1	*Ishizaki*
1/5	Helsingborg	a	1-0	*Augustsson*
7/5	Djurgården	h	2-2	*Jönsson, Svensson A.*
13/5	Kalmar	a	1-2	*Svensson A.*
17/5	Trelleborg	a	2-1	*Svensson M., Svensson A.*
22/5	Göteborg	h	3-1	*Svensson A. 3*
26/5	Hammarby	a	1-0	*Alexandersson*
14/6	GAIS	a	1-2	*Keene*
18/6	Trelleborg	h	2-0	*Keene, Svensson M.*
26/6	Brommapojkarna	h	3-0	*Ishizaki, Keene, Alexandersson*
3/7	Halmstad	a	0-3	
9/7	AIK	a	1-0	*Ishizaki*
12/7	AIK	h	2-0	*Keene, Svensson M.*
21/7	Djurgården	a	1-2	*Berglund*
4/8	Kalmar	h	2-2	*Ishizaki 2*
18/8	GAIS	h	5-1	*Ishizaki, Holmén, Björck, Berglund, Augustsson*
25/8	Helsingborg	h	0-0	
3/9	Gefle	a	2-2	*Svensson A., Svensson M.*
15/9	Göteborg	a	2-2	*Ishizaki 2 (1p)*
24/9	Hammarby	h	1-2	*Svensson M.*
29/9	Brommapojkarna	a	1-1	*Berglund*
8/10	Halmstad	h	1-1	*Svensson A.*
20/10	Örebro	h	0-2	
28/10	Malmö	a	2-1	*Svensson A., Svensson M.*

No	Name	Nat	Pos	Aps	(s)	Gls
6	Daniel ALEXANDERSSON		A	16	(8)	2
5	Martin ANDERSSON		D	15	(1)	
22	Andreas AUGUSTSSON		D	24		2
14	Denni AVDIC		A	6	(13)	
20	Emir BAJRAMI		M	4	(10)	1
18	Fredrik BERGLUND		A	6	(5)	3
19	Fredrik BJÖRCK		D	9		1
2	Mathias FLORÉN		D	8	(2)	
21	Léandre GRIFFIT	FRA	M		(3)	
1	Abbas HASSAN		G	2	(1)	
10	Samuel HOLMÉN		M	18		2
7	Jari ILOLA	FIN	M	18	(1)	
24	Stefan ISHIZAKI		M	24	(1)	8
13	Jon JÖNSSON		M	11		1
4	Johan KARLSSON		M	19	(5)	
17	James KEENE	ENG	A	14	(10)	4
11	Daniel MOBAECK		M	24	(1)	
12	Joakim SJÖHAGE		A	2	(5)	
8	Anders SVENSSON		M	23		9
9	Mathias SVENSSON		A	19	(3)	6
30	Johan WILAND		G	24		

GAIS GÖTEBORG

Coach – Roland Nilsson

Founded - 1894

MAJOR HONOURS: Swedish League - (4) 1919, 1922, 1931, 1954; Swedish Cup - (1) 1942.

2007				
10/4	Hammarby	h	1-1	*Gudmundsson*
16/4	Malmö	a	0-1	
23/4	Örebro	h	1-1	*Östberg*

)/4	Gefle	a	0-1	
'5	Halmstad	h	2-1	*Holmberg 2*
4/5	Djurgården	a	1-0	*Östberg*
1/5	Kalmar	h	0-3	
3/5	Göteborg	a	0-1	
4/6	Elfsborg	h	2-1	*Friberg da Cruz B., Lundgren*
3/6	Helsingborg	a	1-1	*Hédinsson*
5/6	AIK	h	1-1	*Tobiasson*
'7	Brommapojkarna	a	0-1	
'7	Trelleborg	h	3-1	*Friberg da Cruz B. 2, Gustafsson*
4/7	Trelleborg	a	1-0	*Nicklasson*
0/7	Halmstad	a	2-2	*Holmqvist, Ikpe Ekong (p)*
'8	Djurgården	h	1-1	*Lundgren*
2/8	Helsingborg	h	0-3	
3/8	Elfsborg	a	1-5	*Friberg da Cruz B.*
7/8	Gefle	h	1-0	*Lundgren*
'9	Örebro	a	1-2	*Christoforidis*
6/9	Kalmar	a	2-2	*Tobiasson, Christoforidis*
5/9	Göteborg	h	0-1	
0/9	AIK	a	0-0	
'10	Brommapojkarna	h	2-1	*Wánderson, Lundén*
2/10	Malmö	h	1-2	*Christoforidis*
3/10	Hammarby	a	0-4	

o	Name	Nat	Pos	Aps	(s)	Gls
6	Christos CHRISTOFORIDIS	GRE	A	7	(2)	3
8	Henrik DAHL		D		(3)	
	Martin DOHLSTEN		M	3	(11)	
6	David DURMAZ		D	12	(2)	
	Richard EKUNDE	COD	D	19		
	Bobbie FRIBERG DA CRUZ		D	21	(4)	4
2	Johan FRIBERG DA CRUZ		D	3		
1	Jóhann GUDMUNDSSON	ISL	M	15	(3)	1
0	Kenneth GUSTAFSSON		D	25		1
3	Eyjólfur HÉDINSSON	ISL	M	19	(1)	1
1	Anton HOLMBERG		A	7	(7)	2
7	Tobias HOLMQVIST		M	8	(2)	1
	Prince IKPE EKONG	NGA	M	21		1
	Dime JANKULOVSKI		G	26		
	Jonas LUNDÉN		M	16	(1)	1
5	Fredrik LUNDGREN		M	20	(1)	3
	Migen MEMELLI	ALB	A	7	(9)	
4	Daniel NICKLASSON		M	18	(1)	1
0	Anatoli PONOMAREV	AZE	A	2	(3)	
9	Sheriff SUMA	SLE	A	2	(7)	
	Andreas TOBIASSON		D	24	(2)	2
5	WÁNDERSON do Carmo	BRA	M	6	(3)	1
0	Axel WIBRÅN		G		(1)	
	Mattias ÖSTBERG		M	5	(7)	2

GEFLE IF

Coach – Per Olsson

Founded - 1882

007				
'/4	Örebro	h	0-0	
6/4	Helsingborg	a	1-3	*Bapupa*
3/4	Elfsborg	a	1-1	*Ericsson*
0/4	GAIS	h	1-0	*Oremo*
'/5	Kalmar	h	2-1	*Oremo 2*
4/5	Göteborg	a	0-2	
0/5	Hammarby	h	1-0	*Oremo*
7/5	Malmö	a	1-1	*Westlin*
1/6	Trelleborg	a	2-3	*Oremo, Grim*
18/6	AIK	h	0-0	
23/6	Halmstad	h	2-0	*Westlin, Bernhardsson*
2/7	Djurgården	a	1-2	*Makondele*
9/7	Brommapojkarna	h	1-1	*Makondele*
16/7	Brommapojkarna	a	1-2	*Oremo*
30/7	Kalmar	a	1-0	*Lantto*
6/8	Göteborg	h	0-2	
12/8	AIK	a	0-1	
19/8	Trelleborg	h	1-0	*Westlin*
27/8	GAIS	a	0-1	
3/9	Elfsborg	h	2-2	*Oremo, Bernhardsson*
15/9	Hammarby	a	3-4	*Oremo, Westlin 2*
24/9	Malmö	h	2-1	*Oremo, Bapupa*
30/9	Halmstad	a	0-0	
7/10	Djurgården	h	0-2	
21/10	Helsingborg	h	4-0	*Oremo 2, Westlin, Lantto*
28/10	Örebro	a	2-1	*Bernhardsson, Lantto*

No	Name	Nat	Pos	Aps	(s)	Gls
10	Yannick Ngabu BAPUPA	COD	A	12	(3)	2
12	Daniel BERNHARDSSON		M	25		3
11	Johan CLAESSON		M	23	(1)	
18	Andreas DAHLÉN		D	8	(4)	
8	Johannes ERICSSON		M	14	(8)	1
4	André GRIM		D	3	(1)	1
2	Thomas HEDLUND		D	26		
13	Jonatan HELLSTRÖM		D	17	(1)	
1	Mattias HUGOSSON		G	26		
17	Jonas LANTTO		M	6	(16)	3
24	René MAKONDELE	COD	A	17		2
7	Johan OREMO		A	24		11
5	Andreas REVAHL		D	9	(4)	
16	Tomasz STOLPA	POL	A	1	(5)	
20	Daniel WESTLIN		A	21	(2)	6
6	Anders WIKSTRÖM		D	23		
14	Mathias WOXLIN		M	24		
9	Daniel YTTERBOM		A		(6)	
15	Petter ÖSTERBERG		M	7	(9)	

IFK GÖTEBORG

Coach – Stefan Rehn

Founded - 1904

MAJOR HONOURS: UEFA Cup - (2) 1982, 1987; Swedish League - (18) 1908, 1910, 1918, 1935, 1942, 1958, 1969, 1982, 1983, 1984, 1987, 1990, 1991, 1993, 1994, 1995, 1996, 2007; Swedish Cup - (4) 1979, 1982, 1983, 1991.

2007				
6/4	Trelleborg	a	1-1	*Wernbloom*
17/4	AIK	h	1-2	*Berg J.*
23/4	Brommapojkarna	a	2-1	*Berg M., Alexandersson*
30/4	Halmstad	h	1-1	*Wernbloom*
7/5	Örebro	a	4-0	*Berg M., Karisik, Olsson, Vasques*
14/5	Gefle	h	2-0	*Berg M. 2*
22/5	Elfsborg	a	1-3	*Berg M.*
28/5	GAIS	h	1-0	*Berg M. (p)*
12/6	Djurgården	a	1-2	*Berg M.*
17/6	Kalmar	h	3-2	*Wallerstedt 2, Vasques*
27/6	Hammarby	a	1-3	*Johansson M.*
2/7	Malmö	h	1-2	*Berg M. (p)*
10/7	Helsingborg	h	0-0	
15/7	Helsingborg	a	2-2	*Berg M. 2 (1p)*
31/7	Örebro	h	2-0	*Selakovic, Berg M. (p)*
6/8	Gefle	a	2-0	*Berg M. 2*
11/8	Kalmar	a	5-0	*Selakovic, Wernbloom,*

				Berg M., Wallerstedt, Bjärsmyr
16/8	Djurgården	h	1-1	Wallerstedt
28/8	Halmstad	a	3-1	Wernbloom, Wallerstedt, Jónsson
2/9	Brommapojkarna	h	0-0	
15/9	Elfsborg	h	2-2	Svensson, Wallerstedt
25/9	GAIS	a	1-0	Wernbloom
1/10	Hammarby	h	3-0	Alexandersson, og (Johansson D.), Wallerstedt
6/10	Malmö	a	2-0	Selakovic, Hysén
22/10	AIK	a	1-0	Bjärsmyr
28/10	Trelleborg	h	2-0	Olsson, Wernbloom

No	Name	Nat	Pos	Aps	(s)	Gls
10	Niclas ALEXANDERSSON		M	20		2
1	Bengt ANDERSSON		G	26		
24	Jonatan BERG		A	3	(2)	1
21	Marcus BERG		A	17		14
5	Mattias BJÄRSMYR		D	25		2
28	Niklas BÄRKROTH		A	1		
26	Ali GERBA	CAN	A		(1)	
7	Tobias HYSÉN		M	6		1
6	Adam JOHANSSON		D	24		
15	Jakob JOHANSSON		M	4	(5)	
16	Magnus JOHANSSON		D	4	(1)	1
14	Hjálmar JÓNSSON	ISL	D	23		1
20	Eldin KARISIK		M	9	(8)	1
17	George MOURAD		A	2	(11)	
8	Thomas OLSSON		M	18	(1)	2
11	Mathias RANÉGIE		A		(5)	
9	Stefan SELAKOVIC		A	22	(4)	3
22	Ragnar SIGURDSSON	ISL	D	26		
13	Gustav SVENSSON		D	16	(6)	1
18	Jonas WALLERSTEDT		A	12	(13)	7
23	Andrés VASQUES		M	11	(1)	2
19	Pontus WERNBLOOM		M	17	(7)	6

HALMSTADS BK

Coach – Jan Andersson

Founded - 1914

MAJOR HONOURS: Swedish League - (4) 1976, 1979, 1997, 2000; Swedish Cup - (1) 1995.

2007

9/4	Helsingborg	h	2-1	Žvirgždauskas, Tahirovic
16/4	Djurgården	a	0-2	
22/4	Kalmar	h	2-1	Arvidsson 2
30/4	Göteborg	a	1-1	Tahirovic
7/5	GAIS	a	1-2	Djuric
14/5	Trelleborg	h	1-0	Tahirovic
21/5	AIK	a	1-1	Fribrock
28/5	Brommapojkarna	h	1-0	Rosén
11/6	Hammarby	h	2-2	Rosén, Johansson P.
14/6	Malmö	a	2-1	Tahirovic, Rosén
23/6	Gefle	a	0-2	
3/7	Elfsborg	h	3-0	Djuric, Rosén, Mattisson
8/7	Örebro	a	3-0	Westerberg, Jönsson (p), Djuric
16/7	Örebro	h	3-1	Djuric 2, Fribrock
30/7	GAIS	h	2-2	Arvidsson, og (Tobiasson)
5/8	Trelleborg	a	1-1	Djuric
13/8	Malmö	h	1-3	Arvidsson
19/8	Hammarby	a	1-0	Žvirgždauskas
28/8	Göteborg	h	1-3	Arvidsson
2/9	Kalmar	a	0-3	
16/9	AIK	h	2-2	Jönsson (p), Kujovic
22/9	Brommapojkarna	a	1-1	Kujovic
30/9	Gefle	h	0-0	
8/10	Elfsborg	a	1-1	Djuric
22/10	Djurgården	h	1-2	Jönsson
28/10	Helsingborg	a	0-9	

No	Name	Nat	Pos	Aps	(s)	Gls
18	Björn ANKLEV		A		(19)	
10	Magnus ARVIDSSON		A	26		5
20	Magnus BAHNE	FIN	G	19		
14	Dusan DJURIC		M	24		7
7	Martin FRIBROCK		M	16	(4)	2
13	Andreas JOHANSSON		M	21	(4)	
1	Conny JOHANSSON		G		(1)	
11	Joel JOHANSSON		M	1	(1)	
2	Per JOHANSSON		D	10		1
9	Sebastian JOHANSSON		M	6	(3)	
21	Tibor JOZA		D	4	(1)	
4	Tommy JÖNSSON		D	19	(2)	3
8	Ajsel KUJOVIC		A	10	(10)	2
15	Peter LARSSON		D	23		
22	David LORIA	KAZ	G	7		
5	Hans MATTISSON		M	21	(2)	1
24	Anel RASKAJ		M		(3)	
6	Mikael ROSÉN		M	23		4
16	Tim SPARV	FIN	M	5	(7)	
9	Emra TAHIROVIC		A	8	(5)	4
3	Jesper WESTERBERG		D	12	(4)	1
12	Tomas ŽVIRGŽDAUSKAS	LTU	D	25		2
17	Hjalmar ÖHAGEN		M	6	(8)	

HAMMARBY

Coach – Tony Gustavsson

Founded - 1897

MAJOR HONOURS: Swedish League - (1) 2001.

2007

10/4	GAIS	a	1-1	Castro-Tello
14/4	Trelleborg	h	3-0	Paulinho Guará, Zengin, Eguren
24/4	AIK	a	0-1	
29/4	Brommapojkarna	h	4-0	Andersson 2, Traoré, Paulinho Guará
8/5	Malmö	a	1-1	Eguren
13/5	Örebro	h	1-0	Júlíusson
20/5	Gefle	a	0-1	
26/5	Elfsborg	h	0-1	
11/6	Halmstad	a	2-2	Chanko, Paulinho Guará
19/6	Djurgården	h	2-0	Eguren 2
27/6	Göteborg	h	3-1	Eguren, Chanko, Zengin
4/7	Helsingborg	a	2-4	Castro-Tello, Paulinho Guará
11/7	Kalmar	a	0-2	
18/7	Kalmar	h	1-0	Andersson
1/8	Malmö	h	1-0	Paulinho Guará
5/8	Örebro	a	1-3	Paulinho Guará
13/8	Djurgården	a	0-1	
19/8	Halmstad	h	0-1	
25/8	Brommapojkarna	a	2-0	Castro-Tello, Zengin
3/9	AIK	h	1-2	Eguren
15/9	Gefle	h	4-3	Paulinho Guará 3, Andersson
24/9	Elfsborg	a	2-1	Eguren 2 (1p)

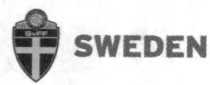

1/10	Göteborg	a	0-3	
8/10	Helsingborg	h	0-2	
21/10	Trelleborg	a	0-1	
28/10	GAIS	h	4-0	*Davies 3, Castro-Tello*

No	Name	Nat	Pos	Aps	(s)	Gls
9	Petter ANDERSSON		M	21	(1)	4
21	Jeffrey AUBYNN		M		(2)	
22	Sebastian CASTRO-TELLO		M	9	(7)	4
6	Louay CHANKO		M	24		2
10	Charlie DAVIES	USA	A	10	(10)	3
8	Sebastián EGUREN	URU	M	22		8
16	Gunnar Thór GUNNARSSON	ISL	D	8	(12)	
26	Simon HELG		M	1		
24	Erland HELLSTRÖM		G	6		
23	Joakim JENSEN		D	2	(9)	
14	Mikkel JENSEN	DEN	M	2		
2	David JOHANSSON		D	21		
5	Emil JOHANSSON		D	8	(2)	
11	Heidar Geir JÚLÍUSSON	ISL	A	1	(10)	1
50	Richard KINGSON	GHA	G	11		
18	Haris LAITINEN		M	19	(5)	
1	Benny LEKSTRÖM		G	6	(1)	
25	Fadi MALKE		D	1	(2)	
3	José MONTEIRO		D	20	(1)	
30	George MOUSSAN		G	3	(1)	
15	Nkosinathi NHLEKO	RSA	A		(2)	
27	Matthias OLSSON		D		(1)	
19	PAULINHO GUARÁ	BRA	A	23	(2)	9
21	Klebér SAARENPÄÄ		D	2	(4)	
7	Suleyman SLEYMAN		D	23		
20	Alagie SOSSEH		A		(3)	
4	Christian TRAORÉ	DEN	D	20	(1)	1
17	Erkan ZENGIN		M	23	(1)	3

HELSINGBORGS IF

Coach – Stuart Baxter (ENG)

Founded - 1907

MAJOR HONOURS; Swedish League - (6) 1929, 1930, 1933, 1934, 1941, 1999; Swedish Cup - (3) 1941, 1998, 2006.

2007

9/4	Halmstad	a	1-2	*Omotoyossi*
16/4	Gefle	h	3-1	*Jakobsson, og (Bernhardsson), Larsson*
21/4	Djurgården	a	1-3	*Jakobsson*
1/5	Elfsborg	h	0-1	
5/5	AIK	a	1-0	*Omotoyossi*
15/5	Malmö	h	0-1	
22/5	Brommapojkarna	a	1-1	*Mariga*
28/5	Örebro	h	4-1	*Karekezi, Larsson, Stefanidis, Omotoyossi*
12/6	Kalmar	a	0-2	
18/6	GAIS	h	1-1	*Stefanidis*
25/6	Trelleborg	a	3-2	*Omotoyossi, Dahl, Jakobsson*
4/7	Hammarby	h	4-2	*Beloufa, Omotoyossi, Larsson, Mariga*
10/7	Göteborg	a	0-0	
15/7	Göteborg	h	2-2	*Omotoyossi 2*
23/7	AIK	h	2-3	*Larsson (p), Jakobsson*
7/8	Malmö	a	1-1	*Omotoyossi*
12/8	GAIS	a	3-0	*Landgren, Omotoyossi, Karekezi*
19/8	Kalmar	h	5-0	*Svanbäck, Dahl, Larsson 2 (1p), Omotoyossi*
25/8	Elfsborg	a	0-0	
3/9	Djurgården	h	1-4	*Makondele*
16/9	Brommapojkarna	h	1-1	*Svanbäck*
24/9	Örebro	a	3-4	*Omotoyossi, Larsson 2*
30/9	Trelleborg	h	1-1	*Dahl*
8/10	Hammarby	a	2-0	*Omotoyossi 2*
21/10	Gefle	a	0-4	
28/10	Halmstad	h	9-0	*Andersson C. 2, Jakobsson, Makondele 2, Omotoyossi, Larsson, Wahlstedt, Landgren*

No	Name	Nat	Pos	Aps	(s)	Gls
21	Christoffer ANDERSSON		D	15		2
1	Daniel ANDERSSON		G	24		
18	Samir BELOUFA	ALG	D	14	(1)	1
22	Oskar BERGLUND		G	2		
24	Fredrik BJÖRCK		D	12		
2	Isaac CHANSA	ZAM	M	1	(1)	
9	Andreas DAHL		M	17	(3)	3
5	Andreas JAKOBSSON		D	24	(2)	5
15	Olivier KAREKEZI	RWA	M	12	(5)	2
6	Imad KHALILI		M		(4)	
19	Martin KOLÁŘ	CZE	M	4	(2)	
4	Andreas LANDGREN		D	4	(6)	2
10	Marcus LANTZ		M	4	(2)	
17	Henrik LARSSON		A	22		9
14	LEANDRO CASTÁN	BRA	D	4		
16	René MAKONDELE	COD	A	4	(1)	3
10	McDonald MARIGA	KEN	M	12	(2)	2
16	Franco MIRANDA	ARG	D	6		
33	Marcus NILSSON		D	1	(1)	
20	Fredrik OLSSON		A		(4)	
11	Razak OMOTOYOSSI	BEN	A	21	(2)	14
25	Oskar RÖNNINGBERG		D	9	(2)	
13	Ólafur SKÚLASON	ISL	M	9	(6)	
19	Babis STEFANIDIS		M	15		2
8	Fredrik SVANBÄCK	FIN	M	18	(5)	2
3	Adama TAMBOURA	MLI	D	11	(2)	
32	Mathias UNKURI		M		(7)	
23	Erik WAHLSTEDT		M	21		1
29	Patrik ÅSTRÖM		A		(2)	

KALMAR FF

Coach – Nanne Bergstrand

Founded - 1910

MAJOR HONOURS: Swedish Cup - (3) 1981, 1987, 2007.

2007

9/4	AIK	a	1-0	*César Santín*
15/4	Brommapojkarna	h	2-2	*Fábio Augusto, César Santín*
22/4	Halmstad	a	1-2	*og (Larsson)*
29/4	Djurgården	h	1-0	*César Santín (p)*
6/5	Gefle	a	1-2	*César Santín*
13/5	Elfsborg	h	2-1	*Ingelsten, Elm V.*
21/5	GAIS	a	3-0	*Rosengren, Johansson, Elm R.*
27/5	Trelleborg	h	0-1	
12/6	Helsingborg	h	2-0	*César Santín 2*
17/6	Göteborg	a	2-3	*Ari, Johansson*
26/6	Malmö	a	2-1	*Sorin, Ari*
2/7	Örebro	h	2-0	*Ari, Ingelsten*
11/7	Hammarby	h	2-0	*Ingelsten, Elm V.*
18/7	Hammarby	a	0-1	
30/7	Gefle	h	0-1	
4/8	Elfsborg	a	2-2	*Elm R., César Santín (p)*

11/8	Göteborg	h	0-5	
19/8	Helsingborg	a	0-5	
27/8	Djurgården	a	3-1	*Ingelsten, Thiago Oliveira, Rydström (p)*
2/9	Halmstad	h	3-0	*Ingelsten, Lantz, Elm V.*
16/9	GAIS	h	2-2	*César Santín, Elm D.*
23/9	Trelleborg	a	3-1	*Elm R., Lantz, César Santín (p)*
1/10	Malmö	h	2-0	*César Santín (p), Ingelsten*
8/10	Örebro	a	3-1	*Larsson 2, Elm V.*
21/10	Brommapojkarna	a	2-1	*Rydström, César Santín*
28/10	AIK	h	2-0	*Ingelsten, César Santín*

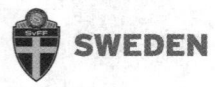

No	Name	Nat	Pos	Aps	(s)	Gls
28	ARI da Silva Ferreira	BRA	A	12		3
22	Milan BARJAKTAREVIC		G	1		
5	Tobias CARLSSON		D	12	(6)	
25	CÉSAR SANTÍN	BRA	A	23		12
29	GIVALDO OLIVEIRA	BRA	A	1	(3)	
6	Mikael EKLUND		D	24		
13	David ELM		A	8	(13)	1
18	Rasmus ELM		M	15	(5)	3
17	Viktor ELM		M	23	(1)	4
11	FÁBIO AUGUSTO	BRA	M	5		1
10	Patrik INGELSTEN		A	26		7
21	Lasse JOHANSSON		M	13	(7)	2
3	Joachim LANTZ		D	5	(4)	2
9	Stefan LARSSON		D	20	(6)	2
7	Daniel PETERSSON		D	1	(5)	
23	Fredrik PETERSSON		M		(3)	
19	RICARDO SANTOS	BRA	A	1	(7)	
14	Patrik ROSENGREN		D	21	(1)	1
8	Henrik RYDSTRÖM		M	25		2
2	Arthur SORIN	FRA	D	25		1
33	THIAGO OLIVEIRA	BRA	A		(2)	1
1	Petter WASTÅ		G	25		

MALMÖ FF

Coach – Sören Åkeby

Founded - 1910

MAJOR HONOURS: Swedish League - (15) 1944, 1949, 1950, 1951, 1953, 1965, 1967, 1970, 1971, 1974, 1975, 1977, 1986, 1988, 2004; Swedish Cup - (14) 1944, 1946, 1947, 1951, 1953, 1967, 1973, 1974, 1975, 1977, 1980, 1984, 1986, 1989.

2007

7/4	Elfsborg	a	1-1	*Johansson*
16/4	GAIS	h	1-0	*Júnior*
22/4	Trelleborg	a	1-2	*Andersson D. (p)*
28/4	AIK	h	4-0	*Júnior 2, Toivonen, Johansson*
8/5	Hammarby	h	1-1	*Andersson D.*
15/5	Helsingborg	a	1-0	*Toivonen*
20/5	Örebro	a	1-1	*Andersson D. (p)*
27/5	Gefle	h	1-1	*Høiland*
11/6	Brommapojkarna	a	1-0	*Skoog*
14/6	Halmstad	h	1-2	*Johansson*
26/6	Kalmar	h	1-2	*Osmanovski*
2/7	Göteborg	a	2-1	*Skoog, Júnior*
7/7	Djurgården	a	0-1	
17/7	Djurgården	h	1-1	*Johansson*
1/8	Hammarby	a	0-1	
7/8	Helsingborg	h	1-1	*Júnior*
13/8	Halmstad	a	3-1	*Johansson, Júnior, Skoog*
18/8	Brommapojkarna	h	2-0	*Andersson D. (p), Júnior*
26/8	AIK	a	1-3	*Toivonen*
1/9	Trelleborg	h	0-0	
17/9	Örebro	h	1-0	*Júnior*
24/9	Gefle	a	1-2	*Skoog*
1/10	Kalmar	a	0-2	
6/10	Göteborg	h	0-2	
22/10	GAIS	a	2-1	*Skoog, Johansson*
28/10	Elfsborg	h	1-2	*Júnior*

No	Name	Nat	Pos	Aps	(s)	Gls
7	Anders ANDERSSON		M	25		
30	Daniel ANDERSSON		M	23		4
19	Johan ANDERSSON		A	2	(3)	
4	Jimmy DIXON	LBR	D	21		
5	GABRIEL de Paulo Limeira	BRA	D	6	(7)	
23	Labinot HARBUZI		A	5	(7)	
14	Jon Inge HØILAND	NOR	D	14		1
31	Jonatan JOHANSSON	FIN	A	17	(3)	6
8	JÚNIOR Guimarães	BRA	A	20	(1)	9
16	Christian JÄRDLER		D	7	(5)	
34	Guillermo MOLINS		A	2	(7)	
17	Joakim NILSSON		M	7	(6)	
18	Edward OFERE	NGA	A	4	(10)	
11	Yksel OSMANOVSKI		M	19	(4)	1
26	Marcus PODE		A	2	(5)	
25	Behrang SAFARI		M	24		
35	Jonas SANDQVIST		G	26		
9	Niklas SKOOG		A	9	(7)	5
13	Babis STEFANIDIS		M	7	(3)	
3	Daniel THEORIN		D		(1)	
20	Ola TOIVONEN		A	21	(3)	3
2	Ulrich VINZENTS	DEN	D	25		

TRELLEBORGS FF

Coach – Conny Karlsson

Founded - 1926

2007

6/4	Göteborg	h	1-1	*Malmqvist*
14/4	Hammarby	a	0-3	
22/4	Malmö	h	2-1	*Augustsson, Mensah*
30/4	Örebro	a	0-2	
6/5	Brommapojkarna	h	3-3	*Senoglu, Thylander 2*
14/5	Halmstad	a	0-1	
17/5	Elfsborg	h	1-2	*Mensah*
21/5	Djurgården	h	0-3	
27/5	Kalmar	a	1-0	*Melander*
11/6	Gefle	h	3-2	*Augustsson, Mensah 2*
18/6	Elfsborg	a	0-2	
25/6	Helsingborg	h	2-3	*Sundin 2*
3/7	AIK	a	0-2	
9/7	GAIS	a	1-3	*Bengtsson R.*
14/7	GAIS	h	0-1	
23/7	Brommapojkarna	a	3-0	*Berg, Westerblad, Senoglu*
5/8	Halmstad	h	1-1	*Bengtsson R.*
19/8	Gefle	a	0-1	
26/8	Örebro	h	0-0	
1/9	Malmö	a	0-0	
17/9	Djurgården	a	1-1	*Sundin*
23/9	Kalmar	h	1-3	*Sundin*
30/9	Helsingborg	a	1-1	*Mensah*
7/10	AIK	h	0-0	
21/10	Hammarby	h	1-0	*Bengtsson R.*
28/10	Göteborg	a	0-2	

No	Name	Nat	Pos	Aps	(s)	Gls
23	Christian AHLSTRÖM		D	2	(1)	
21	Magnus ANDERSSON		A	12	(7)	
22	Jimmie AUGUSTSSON		M	18	(1)	2
26	Jetullah BAHTIRI		A		(5)	
5	Mikael BENGTSSON		D	19	(4)	
25	Rasmus BENGTSSON		A	10	(4)	3
4	Jonatan BERG		A	11		1
27	Jonas BJURSTRÖM		M	8	(1)	
8	Hasan CETINKAYA		M	4	(6)	
20	Yousef FAHKRO		D	4		
30	Christian FEGLER		G	10	(1)	
24	Kristian HAYNES		A	6	(2)	
16	Linus MALMQVIST		D	21	(1)	1
3	Dennis MELANDER		D	20		1
18	Michael MENSAH	GHA	A	20	(2)	5
15	Emil MÅRTENSSON		A	1	(2)	
14	Patrick NILSSON		A	3	(2)	
1	Fredrik PERSSON		G	5		
17	Thommie PERSSON		D	21	(2)	
32	Marcus SAHLMAN		G	11		
11	Olcay SENOGLU	DEN	A	4	(15)	2
2	Jens SLOTH		M	6	(6)	
10	Erik SUNDIN		M	25		4
7	Mattias THYLANDER		D	22	(2)	2
19	Björn WESTERBLAD		A	9	(6)	1
9	Andreas WIHLBORG		D	14		

ÖREBRO SK

Coach – Patrick Walker (IRL); (20/8/07) Urban Hammar

Founded - 1908

2007				
9/4	Gefle	a	0-0	
17/4	Elfsborg	h	1-1	*Halilović*
23/4	GAIS	a	1-1	*Halilović*
30/4	Trelleborg	h	2-0	*Haginge, Larsen (p)*
7/5	Göteborg	h	0-4	
13/5	Hammarby	a	0-1	
20/5	Malmö	h	1-1	*Richardsson*
28/5	Helsingborg	a	1-4	*Nordback*
10/6	AIK	a	1-1	*Rodevåg*
17/6	Brommapojkarna	h	4-0	*Rodevåg, Halilović 2, Walker R.*
25/6	Djurgården	h	0-0	
2/7	Kalmar	a	0-2	
8/7	Halmstad	h	0-3	
16/7	Halmstad	a	1-3	*Henriksson*
31/7	Göteborg	a	0-2	
5/8	Hammarby	h	3-1	*Nordback, Larsen, Anttonen*
12/8	Brommapojkarna	a	1-3	*Walker R.*
19/8	AIK	h	1-4	*Rodevåg*
26/8	Trelleborg	a	0-0	
3/9	GAIS	h	2-1	*Wikström, Barsom*
17/9	Malmö	a	0-1	
24/9	Helsingborg	h	4-3	*Henriksson, Nordback, Anttonen, Rodevåg*
29/9	Djurgården	a	1-4	*og (Johannesson)*
8/10	Kalmar	h	1-3	*Walker R.*
20/10	Elfsborg	a	2-0	*Larsen (p), Anttonen*
28/10	Gefle	h	1-2	*Henriksson*

No	Name	Nat	Pos	Aps	(s)	Gls
9	Patrik ANTTONEN		M	23		3
77	Abgar BARSOM		M	6		1
28	Anton DEDAJ	CRO	M		(1)	
22	James FREMPONG		M	2	(3)	
25	Nordin GERZIĆ	BIH	A		(8)	
19	Patrik HAGINGE		D	25		1
29	Nedim HALILOVIĆ	BIH	A	19	(4)	4
21	Sebastian HENRIKSSON		M	22		3
14	Glenn HOLGERSSON		M	9	(4)	
15	Fredrik JANSSON		D	1		
24	Ian JEFFS	ENG	M		(2)	
5	Lars LARSEN	DEN	M	26		3
10	Jon LUNDBLAD		A	2	(4)	
8	Fredrik NORDBACK	FIN	M	24		3
27	Kristoffer NÄFVER		M	14		
7	Johan PETTERSSON		A	6	(12)	
16	Moses REED		D		(1)	
17	Richard RICHARDSSON		G	2	(1)	1
3	Joel RIDDEZ		M	25		
11	Stefan RODEVÅG		A	20	(6)	4
2	Fredrik SAMUELSSON		D	15	(2)	
23	Kevin WALKER		M	1	(3)	
13	Robert WALKER		M	2	(11)	3
1	Peter WESTMAN		G	24		
4	Magnus WIKSTRÖM		D	18	(1)	1

PROMOTED CLUBS

IFK NORRKÖPING

Coach – Mats Jingblad

Founded - 1897

MAJOR HONOURS: Swedish League – (12) 1943, 1945, 1946, 1947, 1948, 1952, 1956, 1957, 1960, 1962, 1963, 1989. Swedish Cup - (6) 1943, 1945, 1969, 1988, 1991, 1994.

LJUNGSKILE SK

Coach – David Wilson (ENG)

Founded - 1926

GIF SUNDSVALL

Coach – Mika Sankala

Founded - 1903

SECOND LEVEL FINAL TABLE 2007

		Pld	W	D	L	F	A	Pts
1	IFK Norrköping	30	20	3	7	62	29	63
2	Ljungskile SK	30	17	4	9	42	35	55
3	GIF Sundsvall	30	16	6	8	48	32	54
4	BK Häcken	30	17	2	11	51	30	53
5	Bunkeflo IF	30	14	6	10	49	49	48
6	Åtvidabergs FF	30	14	5	11	44	35	47
7	IK Sirius FK	30	13	4	13	53	50	43
8	Degerfors IF	30	10	8	12	34	40	38
9	Mjällby AIF	30	9	9	12	39	40	36
10	Örgryte IS	30	10	6	14	40	52	36
11	Landskrona BoIS	30	9	8	13	39	45	35
12	Enköpings SK FK	30	9	8	13	25	38	35
13	Jönköpings Södra IF	30	9	7	14	35	47	34
14	Falkenbergs FF	30	9	7	14	35	52	34
15	Östers IF	30	8	8	14	28	35	32
16	IF Sylvia	30	6	9	15	36	51	27

DOMESTIC CUP 2007

SVENSKA CUPEN

SECOND ROUND

(19/4/07)
Lärje-Angereds IF 2, Landskrona BoIS 2 *(aet; 4-5 on pens)*
Runtuna IK 0, IFK Norrköping 3
IFK Malmö FK 0, Hammarby 3

(24/4/07)
Carlstad United BK 0, Falkenbergs FF 0 *(aet; 7-6 on pens)*

(25/4/07)
Högaborgs BK 2, Kalmar FF 5
Laholms FK 0, Qviding FIF 2
Enskede IK 0, Trelleborgs FF 2
Melleruds IF 1, IF Brommapojkarna 3
Rydaholms GoIF 0, Assyriska FF 1 *(aet)*
Ersboda SK 1, Degerfors IF 4
Sandvikens IF 0, GIF Sundsvall 2
Rynninge IK 0, Åtvidabergs FF 6
Oskarshamns AIK 0, Bodens BK 1
IFK Timrå 1, Örgryte IS 2
Sirius 2, Mjällby AIF 3
BK Forward 1, Väsby United 3

(26/4/07)
IFK Värnamo 1, Jönköpings Södra IF 0
Gantofta IF 0, Umeå FC 3
Ängelholms FF 2, IFK Göteborg 2 *(aet; 1-4 on pens)*
IFK Falköping FF 0, IF Elfsborg 3
Skövde AIK 2, GAIS 1
Utsiktens BK 1, Ljungskile SK 0
Norrby IF 0, Djurgården 2
Östersunds FK 2, Örebro SK 3
Syrianska IF Kerbura 0, Gefle IF 3
IFK Hässleholm 0, Helsingborgs IF 4
Gamla Upsala SK 0, Halmstads BK 3

(1/5/07)
Stenungsunds IF 0, Malmö FF 11
Enköping 0, AIK 1
Ljungby IF 3, IK Frej 2 *(aet)*

(2/5/07)
Gröndals IK 3, BK Häcken 4
Eskilstuna City FK 0, Östers IF 2

THIRD ROUND

(15/5/07)
Degerfors IF 3, Åtvidabergs FF 2 *(aet)*

(16/5/07)
Väsby United 3, Umeå FC 2 *(aet)*
IFK Värnamo 1, Kalmar FF 5
Carlstad United BK 1, Hammarby 1 *(aet; 3-4 on pens)*
Skövde AIK 2, Assyriska FF 1
Bodens BK 1, Örgryte IS 2 (aet)

(17/5/07)
Halmstads BK 1, IF Brommapojkarna 3
Gefle IF 2, Djurgården 2 *(aet; 5-3 on pens)*
Qviding FIF 1, BK Häcken 2 *(aet)*
Ljungby IF 1, IFK Göteborg 6
Utsiktens BK 0, Helsingborgs IF 4

(23/5/07)
Östers IF 3, Örebro SK 1 *(aet)*

(24/5/07)
IFK Norrköping 1, AIK 0
Landskrona BoIS 2, Malmö FF 1
GIF Sundsvall 1, Trelleborgs FF 0

(6/6/07)
Mjällby AIF 1, IF Elfsborg 1 *(aet; 4-3 on pens)*

FOURTH ROUND

(5/6/07)
IF Brommapojkarna 1, Östers IF 1 *(aet; 4-5 on pens)*

(13/6/07)
Väsby United 2, Degerfors IF 0

(14/6/07)
Hammarby 1, IFK Norrköping 2

(20/6/07)
BK Häcken 0, GIF Sundsvall 2
Örgryte IS 1, Mjällby AIF 1 *(aet; 2-4 on pens)*
Skövde AIK 3, Kalmar FF 3 *(aet; 3-4 on pens)*

(28/6/07)
Helsingborgs IF 1, Landskrona BoIS 2

(5/7/07)
IFK Göteborg 3, Gefle IF 0

QUARTER-FINALS

(26/7/07)
GIF Sundsvall 1 *(Lustig 13)*, Väsby United 2 *(Jagne 47, Catovic 95) (aet)*
Östers IF 0, Kalmar FF 1 *(Ricardo Santos 13)*
IFK Norrköping 2 *(Okkonen 14og, Thordarson 90)*, Landskrona BoIS 3 *(Cederquist 8, 56, Dahlgren 56p)*

(2/8/07)
Mjällby AIF 1 *(Fejzullahu 10)*, IFK Göteborg 2 *(Mourad 90, Jónsson 114) (aet)*

SEMI-FINALS

(8/9/07)
Väsby United 1 *(Jagne 12)*, Kalmar FF 4 *(Elm D. 22, Ingelsten 39, Johansson 81, 90+1)*

(22/9/07)
IFK Göteborg 4 *(Wernbloom 38, 57, 74, Bjärsmyr 62)*, Landskrona BoIS 0

FINAL

(27/9/07)
Fredriksskans, Kalmar
KALMAR FF 3 *(César Santín 22, 88p, Ingelsten 65)*
IFK GÖTEBORG 0
Referee – *Ingvarsson*
KALMAR – *Westå, Sorin, Carlsson, Rosengren, Eklund, Rydström, Elm V., Ingelsten, Elm R., César Santín, Elm D.*
GÖTEBORG – *Andersson, Johansson A. (Mourad 70), Bjärsmyr, Sigurdsson, Jónsson, Alexandersson (Karisik 63), Svensson, Olsson, Hysén (Selakovic 79), Wernbloom, Wallerstedt.*

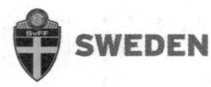

SWITZERLAND

Hard-luck hosts leave the party early

Switzerland spent a long time preparing for UEFA EURO 2008™, but when the action started Jakob "Köbi" Kuhn's team were involved in the tournament competitively for only five days.

The co-hosts of the party were the first to leave. They managed to give the departing Kuhn something of a fanfare send-off with a 2-0 win over Group A winners Portugal, but by then it was too late. Back-to-back defeats by the Czech Republic and Turkey had already consigned them to an early fate.

Cries of rough justice from the locals were not difficult to substantiate. Switzerland were by no means the worst team on view. They played enterprising, attacking football in all three matches, fired in plenty of shots and created several gilt-edged goalscoring opportunities. Unfortunately, most of those chances went begging, which was perhaps understandable given that Alexander Frei, the Swiss captain and all-time leading goalscorer (a milestone he reached on the eve of the tournament), suffered serious knee ligament damage less than halfway through the opening game. With Marco Streller also laid low, the Nati only had one recognised striker, the inexperienced Eren Derdiyok, left standing.

Switzerland captain Alexander Frei is led away in tears, his UEFA EURO 2008™ participation at an end

Hakan Yakin, the 31-year-old midfield playmaker who had enjoyed a brilliant, goal-strewn domestic season in Switzerland with BSC Young Boys, stepped in to offer a helping hand and ended up scoring all three of the team's goals, but even he was left to rue the glorious chance he squandered to put Switzerland 2-0 up in the pivotal second game against Turkey. If the opening defeat by the Czech Republic was hard to take, especially as the home side had dominated and been denied a possible penalty, the loss to Turkey, with virtually the last (deflected) kick of the game, was pure cruelty.

Hitzfeld takes over

Despite the hard-luck story, the harsh reality was that Switzerland had failed. UEFA EURO 2008™ was supposed to see the team at the peak of their powers, two years on from a FIFA World Cup campaign in which they reached the knockout phase and did not concede a goal. The evidence suggested a team in decline, but that need not be the case. One dignified gentleman has been succeeded as the national coach by another, with Ottmar Hitzfeld, the highly-regarded, trophy-collecting German, leaving FC Bayern München to take over the reins from Kuhn.

Hitzfeld will have seen enough at UEFA EURO 2008™ to know that he has at his disposal a collection of players good enough to qualify for the 2010 World Cup. Indeed, a fourth successive major tournament appearance is more probable than possible given the opponents that Switzerland will be up against in what is assuredly the easiest of the eight European qualifying pools - namely Luxembourg, Moldova, Latvia, Israel and Greece. Although Greece are the seeds, they are an ageing team in need of repair, whereas Switzerland can count on a whole host of promising youngsters with time on their side, such as Derdiyok, goalkeeper Fabio Coltorti, right-back Stephan Lichtsteiner, centre-back Philippe Senderos and an entire midfield quartet of Valon Behrami, Gökhan Inler, Gelson Fernandes and Tranquillo Barnetta. With the exception of Barnetta, who was not

Schweizerischer Fussballverband / Association Suisse de Football (SFV/ASF)

Association Suisse de Football
Postfach
CH-3000 Bern 15
tel - +41 31 9508111
fax - +41 31 9508181
website - www.football.ch
email - sfv.asf@football.ch
Year of Formation – 1895
President - Ralph Zloczower
General Secretary - Peter Gilliéron
Press Officer – Pierre Benoit

INTERNATIONAL TOURNAMENT APPEARANCES
FIFA World Cup - (8) 1934, 1938 (qtr-finals), 1950, 1954 (qtr-finals), 1962, 1966, 1994 (2nd round), 2006 (2nd round).
UEFA European Championship - (3) 1996, 2004, 2008.

TOP FIVE ALL-TIME CAPS
Heinz Hermann (117); Alain Geiger (112); Stéphane Chapuisat (103); Johann Vogel (94); Severino Minelli (80)

TOP FIVE ALL-TIME GOALS
Alexander Frei (35); Kubilay Türkyilmaz & Xam Abegglen III (34); André Abegglen II & Jacky Fatton (29)

NATIONAL TEAM RESULTS 2007/08

22/8/07	Netherlands	H	Geneva	2-1	*Barnetta (9p, 51)*
7/9/07	Chile	N	Vienna (AUT)	2-1	*Barnetta (13), Streller (55)*
11/9/07	Japan	N	Klagenfurt (AUT)	3-4	*Magnin (11), Nkufo (13), Djourou (80)*
13/10/07	Austria	H	Zurich	3-1	*Streller (2, 55), Yakin (36)*
17/10/07	USA	H	Basel	0-1	
20/11/07	Nigeria	H	Zurich	0-1	
6/2/08	England	A	Wembley	1-2	*Derdiyok (58)*
26/3/08	Germany	H	Basel	0-4	
24/5/08	Slovakia	H	Lugano	2-0	*Behrami (56), Frei (63)*
30/5/08	Liechtenstein	H	St Gallen	3-0	*Frei (24, 31), Vonlanthen (68)*
7/6/08	Czech Republic (ECF)	H	Basel	0-1	
11/6/08	Turkey (ECF)	H	Basel	1-2	*Yakin (32)*
15/6/08	Portugal (ECF)	H	Basel	2-0	*Yakin (71, 83p)*

fully fit, all of these players performed creditably at UEFA EURO 2008™, and although things did not go to plan, they will surely be richer for the experience.

Basel back on top

If the St. Jakob-Park was the scene of disappointment and despair for fans of Switzerland in June, it had been a place of much raucous celebration a few weeks earlier as local club FC Basel 1893 treated a full house of 38,000 fans to a precious 2-0 victory over Young Boys in the Swiss Super League title decider. Like two years previously, the final match of the season brought together the two title candidates in the country's largest stadium. But, unlike in 2005/06, when Basel lost the title to a last-minute goal from FC Zürich, they rose to the challenge and triumphed second time around. As before, they required only a draw to be champions, but this time there was no need for nail-biting. Two first-half goals, the first from 19-year-old man of the match Valentin Stocker, the second from Switzerland striker Streller, calmed everyone's nerves and allowed the celebration party to get into full swing long before the final whistle.

NATIONAL TEAM APPEARANCES 2007/08

oach – Jakob "Köbi" KUHN 12/10/43			Ned	Chi	Jpn	Aut	Usa	Nga	Eng	Ger	Svk	Lie	CZE	TUR	POR	Caps	Goals
abio COLTORTI	3/12/80	Grasshoppers	G			G										8	-
hilipp DEGEN	15/2/83	Dortmund (GER)	D68	D				D8				s59				30	-
teve VON BERGEN	10/6/83	Hertha (GER)	D		D86		s16			s74						5	-
hilippe SENDEROS	14/2/85	Arsenal (ENG)	D87	D	D	D46			D55	D74	D	D62	D	D	D	31	3
udovic MAGNIN	20/4/79	Stuttgart (GER)	D	D	D46	D85	D	D75			D	D71	D	D	D	53	3
elson FERNANDES	2/9/86	Man. City (ENG)	M66			M81	s46	M	M83	M86	M	M86	M	M76	M	11	-
ökhan INLER	27/6/84	Udinese (ITA)	M	M86	M77	M	M	M	M	M	M	M	M	M	M	20	1
ohan VONLANTHEN	1/2/86	Salzburg (AUT)	M	s46	M71	M17			s46	s79	M68	M	s75	s66	M61	33	6
ranquillo BARNETTA	22/5/85	Leverkusen (GER)	M72	M73	s46	M	M74	M46	M	M79			M	M66	s61	35	6
avier MARGAIRAZ	7/1/84	Osasuna (ESP)	M80	M65	M46	s46	M46		s63							16	1
laise NKUFO	25/5/75	Twente (NED)	A55	A46	A	s76	s46	A	A46	s46						15	2
arco STRELLER	18/6/81	Basel	s55	s46		A76	A46				A64	A59	A			29	11
enjamin HUGGEL	7/7/77	Basel	s66	s86	M67				s83	s86		s86				25	-
tephan LICHTSTEINER	16/1/84	Lille (FRA)	s68		s71	D	D	s8	D46	D	D77	D59	D75	D	D83	15	-
hristoph SPYCHER	30/3/78	Eintracht (GER)	s72	s73	M	s85	s74	s75	D	D		s71				39	-
akan YAKIN	22/2/77	Young Boys	s80	s65	s46	M46	s46	M75	M63	s82	s80	s59	s46	A85	A86	69	18
icardo CABANAS	17/1/79	Grasshoppers	s87								s84			s76	s86	51	4
ascal ZUBERBÜHLER	8/1/71	Xamax		G			G								G	51	-
ohann DJOUROU	18/1/87	Birmingham (ENG) /Arsenal (ENG)		D46	s77	D	D16	D80			s77					17	1
abio CELESTINI	31/10/75	Getafe (ESP)		M	s67	s81	M46									35	2
alon BEHRAMI	19/4/85	Lazio (ITA)		M46	D				s46	M57	M84	M55	M84	M	M	19	2
ario EGGIMANN	24/1/81	Karlsruhe (GER)		s46	s86			D	D	D						5	-
iego BENAGLIO	8/9/83	Nacional (POR) /Wolfsburg (GER)			G			G	G	G	G	G	G	G		14	-
avid DEGEN	15/2/83	Basel				s17	M	s46								9	-
téphane GRICHTING	30/3/79	Auxerre (FRA)				s46	D	s80	s55		s77	s62			s83	19	-
aniel GYGAX	28/8/81	Metz (FRA)						M	M46	s57	s68	s55		s85		35	5
eto ZIEGLER	16/1/86	Sampdoria (ITA)						s75								4	-
ren DERDIYOK	12/6/88	Basel							s46	A46	s64		s84	A	A	6	1
Alexander FREI	15/7/79	Dortmund (GER)								A82	A80	A	A46			60	35
Patrick MÜLLER	17/12/76	Lyon (FRA)									D77	D	D	D	D	81	3

Young Boys, superbly coached by former Swiss international Martin Andermatt and inspired by the goals of Yakin (24) and born-again veteran striker Thomas Häberli (18), had been dogged opponents to the last as they chased their first national title for 20 years, but they did not perform on the day that really mattered, and for that reason could not contest Basel's right to be considered worthy champions.

Cup bonus

There was an extra agenda to the last-day showdown as both clubs were seeking their 12th title and the landmark of becoming the country's third-ranked club in the all-time roll of honour (behind Grasshopper-Club, with 27 titles, and Servette FC, with 17). Not that Basel really needed anything else to celebrate, for theirs had been a season of satisfaction all round. They came unbeaten through the group phase of the UEFA Cup to reach the round of 32, and they also won the other domestic trophy, the Swiss Cup, for the ninth time, beating Challenge League opponents AC Bellinzona 4-1 in the final, conveniently staged on home soil in the St. Jakob-Park, thanks to a stunning burst of three goals in four minutes midway through the second half

The league title was the first under the female presidency of Gigi Oehri, and for Basel coach Christian Gross, the double increased his running total of trophies to eight (four championships, four Cups) in nine seasons at the club. That achievement was matched by Basel captain Ivan Ergić, the Croatian-born, Australian-bred Serbian international midfielder, who first joined the club on loan from Italian giants Juventus in 2000. Ergić was among Basel's most consistent performers in 2007/08 as he took on much of the burden created by an injury to the team's dynamic midfield general Scott Chipperfield. Swedish international defender Daniel Majstorovic was another who shone. Not only was he solid in defence, he also scored ten goals, eight of them from penalties, giving him a 100 per cent spot-kick record. Another impressive all-rounder was Brazilian Eduardo, who played in just about every position other than goalkeeper and was the club's third highest scorer, with eight goals - behind Majstorovic and Streller, who, on his return from the German Bundesliga, would have scored many more than 12 but for persistent injury.

Christian Gross, FC Basel's long-serving and successful coach

Neutrals' favourites

Defending champions Zürich rolled in third in the Super League – two points ahead of local rivals Grasshoppers but 18 adrift of Basel. It was always expecting a lot for the team to maintain the same high level of performance following the departure of their title-winning coach Lucien Favre to Hertha BSC Berlin, not to mention midfield heartbeat Inler to Udinese Calcio and, in mid-season, Brazilian goalgetter Raffael (who joined Favre in Berlin). But although the results were disappointing, the Lions continued to play attractive, polished, purist-friendly football under new coach Bernard Challandes, and as the youngest team in the league, and also the one with invariably the most Swiss players in their starting XI, they had three persuasive reasons to attract neutral support. They also matched Basel by reaching the latter stages of the UEFA Cup, which was some consolation for the disappointment of being eliminated by Beşiktaş JK in the third qualifying round of the UEFA Champions League.

FC Thun, who appeared in the group stage of the UEFA Champions League in 2005/06, lost their place in the top division. Their miserable season on the field was exacerbated by an under-age sex scandal involving several players and ex-players, three of whom were convicted. FC St Gallen, who sacked ex-Switzerland coach Rolf Fringer after a 4-0 home defeat by Thun in October and replaced him with former Bulgarian international Krasimir Balakov, also went down after a play-off defeat to Cup finalists Bellinzona, while history was made as FC Vaduz, from Liechtenstein, won the Challenge League to claim a place in Switzerland's top division for the first time. Curiously, both promoted clubs had European football as well as the Swiss Super League to look forward to in 2008/09.

DOMESTIC LEAGUE 2007/08

UPER LEAGUE FINAL TABLE 2007/08

	Pld	Home W	Home D	Home L	Home F	Home A	Away W	Away D	Away L	Away F	Away A	Total W	Total D	Total L	Total F	Total A	Pts
FC Basel 1893	36	15	2	1	39	12	7	6	5	34	27	22	8	6	73	39	74
BSC Young Boys	36	14	2	2	48	16	7	5	6	34	33	21	7	8	82	49	70
FC Zürich	36	13	3	2	36	13	2	8	8	22	30	15	11	10	58	43	56
Grasshopper-Club	36	9	6	3	33	18	6	3	9	24	31	15	9	12	57	49	54
FC Aarau	36	8	7	3	32	21	3	7	8	15	27	11	14	11	47	48	47
FC Luzern	36	5	9	4	24	23	5	5	8	16	26	10	14	12	40	49	44
FC Sion	36	7	5	6	30	23	4	5	9	18	28	11	10	15	48	51	43
Neuchâtel Xamax FC	36	6	6	6	28	28	4	5	9	20	27	10	11	15	48	55	41
FC St Gallen	36	7	3	8	24	33	2	4	12	15	36	9	7	20	39	69	34
FC Thun	36	3	7	8	14	27	3	2	13	16	43	6	9	21	30	70	27

TOP GOALSCORERS

24 Hakan YAKIN (Young Boys)

18 Raúl Marcelo BOBADILLA (Grasshoppers)
Thomas HÄBERLI (Young Boys)

17 Álvaro Alberto SABORÍO (Sion)

14 Mauro LUSTRINELLI (Luzern)

12 Luiz ROGÉRIO da Silva (Aarau)
RAFFAEL Caetano de Araújo (Zürich)
Marco STRELLER (Basel)

11 Francisco AGUIRRE (St Gallen)

10 António Carlos DOS SANTOS (Grasshoppers)
Cristian Florin IANU (Aarau)
Daniel MAJSTOROVIC (Basel)

CLUB-BY-CLUB

FC AARAU

Coach - Ryszard Komornicki (POL)

Founded - 1902

MAJOR HONOURS: Swiss League - (3) 1912, 1914, 1993; Swiss Cup - (1) 1985.

2007

22/7	Young Boys	h	1-1	*Burki*
25/7	Sion	a	0-3	
28/7	Basel	a	1-1	*Rogério*
5/8	Grasshoppers	h	2-2	*Sermeter (p), Carlinhos*
12/8	Thun	a	5-2	*Sermeter, og (Zahnd), og (Nyman), Ianu, Rogério*
18/8	Luzern	h	0-0	
25/8	Xamax	a	1-2	*Rapisarda*
1/9	Zürich	h	1-1	*Mutsch*
22/9	St Gallen	a	1-1	*Ianu*
26/9	Young Boys	a	1-4	*Sermeter (p)*
30/9	Sion	h	2-0	*Rogério 2*
7/10	Basel	h	0-3	
27/10	Grasshoppers	a	1-1	*Ianu*
1/11	Thun	h	5-0	*Ianu 2, Rogério 2, Bastida*
4/11	Luzern	a	0-0	
11/11	Xamax	h	3-2	*Page, og (Quennoz), Tarone*
2/12	Zürich	a	1-0	*Ianu*
8/12	St Gallen	h	2-2	*Rogério 2*

2008

3/2	St Gallen	h	3-1	*Nushi, Ianu, Rapisarda*
10/2	Luzern	a	0-2	
17/2	Grasshoppers	h	1-2	*Rogério*
24/2	Basel	a	1-2	*Page*
1/3	Young Boys	h	0-2	
9/3	Xamax	a	2-1	*Rogério, Ianu*
16/3	Zürich	h	1-0	*Rapisarda*
19/3	Thun	a	1-1	*Ianu*
22/3	Sion	h	2-0	*Sermeter, Nushi*
30/3	Sion	a	0-1	
4/4	Thun	h	3-0	*Page, Nushi, Ianu*
13/4	Zürich	a	0-0	
17/4	Xamax	h	2-2	*Burki, Rogério*
20/4	Young Boys	a	0-4	
26/4	Basel	h	2-2	*Rogério, Sermeter (p)*
3/5	Grasshoppers	a	0-2	
7/5	Luzern	h	2-1	*Rapisarda, Tarone*
10/5	St Gallen	a	0-0	

No	Name	Nat	Pos	Aps	(s)	Gls
22	Goran ANTIC		A	5	(20)	
13	Sergio José BASTIDA	ARG	M	31	(1)	1
1	Ivan BENITO		G	36		
9	Aymen BOUCHHIOUA	TUN	A		(6)	
6	Sandro BURKI		M	27	(3)	2
8	Carlos Alberto De Almeida CARLINHOS	BRA	M	11	(10)	1
5	Sven CHRIST		D	24	(1)	
15	Jonas ELMER		D	28	(1)	
12	Francisco Gabriel GUERRERO	ARG	A	5	(1)	
16	Cristian Florin IANU	ROU	A	31	(5)	10
7	Paulo MENEZES	BRA	D	34		
20	Djamel MESBAH	FRA	M	24	(7)	
19	Mario MUTSCH	LUX	D	10	(12)	1
11	Kristian NUSHI		M	20	(14)	3
24	Frédéric PAGE		D	26		3
21	Giuseppe RAPISARDA		D	25	(4)	4
10	Luiz ROGÉRIO da Silva	BRA	A	27	(8)	12
17	Gürkan SERMETER		M	29	(3)	5
14	Daniel TARONE		M	3	(10)	2

FC BASEL 1893

Coach - Christian Gross

Founded - 1893

MAJOR HONOURS: Swiss League – (12) 1953, 1967, 1969, 1970, 1972, 1973, 1977, 1980, 2002, 2004, 2005, 2008; Swiss Cup - (9) 1933, 1947, 1963, 1967, 1975, 2002, 2003, 2007, 2008.

2007

22/7	Zürich	h	1-0	*Streller*
25/7	St Gallen	a	3-0	*Chipperfield, Derdiyok 2*
28/7	Aarau	h	1-1	*Chipperfield*
5/8	Young Boys	a	1-5	*Chipperfield*
11/8	Sion	h	3-2	*Majstorovic, Eduardo, Ergić*

SWITZERLAND

19/8	Grasshoppers	a	0-2	
25/8	Luzern	a	4-2	*Majstorovic (p), Streller, Chipperfield 2*
2/9	Thun	h	2-1	*Caicedo, Chipperfield*
23/9	Xamax	a	3-0	*Carlitos, Ergić, Huggel (p)*
26/9	Zürich	a	2-2	*Eduardo, Streller*
30/9	St Gallen	h	3-0	*Streller 2, Caicedo*
7/10	Aarau	a	3-0	*Nakata, Eduardo, Streller*
28/10	Young Boys	h	4-0	*Majstorovic (p), Streller, Chipperfield, Carlitos*
31/10	Sion	a	1-1	*Streller*
3/11	Grasshoppers	h	2-0	*Majstorovic, Caicedo*
11/11	Luzern	h	3-2	*Streller, Caicedo, Degen*
2/12	Thun	a	2-0	*Eduardo, Carlitos*
9/12	Xamax	h	0-1	
2008				
3/2	Young Boys	a	0-2	
9/2	Xamax	h	3-0	*Carlitos, Huggel, Perović*
17/2	Zürich	a	1-1	*Derdiyok*
24/2	Aarau	h	2-1	*Majstorovic (p), Carlitos*
2/3	Thun	a	3-1	*Derdiyok 3*
9/3	St Gallen	h	2-1	*Eduardo, Carlitos*
16/3	Sion	a	2-4	*Eduardo, Stocker*
19/3	Grasshoppers	h	2-1	*Ergić, Eduardo*
22/3	Luzern	h	1-0	*Majstorovic (p)*
29/3	Luzern	a	0-1	
2/4	Grasshoppers	a	1-1	*Derdiyok*
13/4	Sion	h	1-1	*Eduardo*
16/4	St Gallen	a	4-1	*Carlitos, Majstorovic (p), Degen, Perović*
19/4	Thun	h	3-1	*Ergić, Majstorovic (p), Degen*
26/4	Aarau	a	2-2	*Streller, Ergić*
2/5	Zürich	h	4-0	*Streller, Stocker, Majstorovic (p), Huggel*
7/5	Xamax	a	2-2	*Majstorovic (p), Ergić*
10/5	Young Boys	h	2-0	*Stocker, Streller*

No	Name	Nat	Pos	Aps	(s)	Gls
12	Papa Malick BA	SEN	M	10	(6)	
28	Patrik BAUMANN		D		(1)	
15	Franz BURGMEIER	LIE	M		(4)	
24	Adilson Tavares Varela CABRAL		M	2	(6)	
20	Felipe Salvador CAICEDO	ECU	M	12	(6)	4
30	Carlos Alberto Alves CARLITOS	POR	M	27	(5)	7
11	Scott CHIPPERFIELD	AUS	M	10	(6)	7
1	Franco COSTANZO	ITA	G	28		
18	Louis CRAYTON	LBR	G	8		
7	David DEGEN		M	12	(8)	3
31	Eren DERDIYOK		A	14	(13)	7
23	EDUARDO Adelino Da Silva	BRA	A	25	(10)	8
22	Ivan ERGIĆ	SRB	M	31		6
28	Beg FERATI		D	4	(1)	
16	Fabian FREI		M	7	(17)	
3	Ronny HODEL		D	21		
8	Benjamin HUGGEL		M	28	(2)	3
19	Vratislav LOKVENC	CZE	A	2	(4)	
5	Daniel MAJSTOROVIC	SWE	D	32		10
21	François MARQUE	FRA	D	34		
4	Michael MORGANELLA		D		(1)	
6	Koji NAKATA	JPN	D	18		1
9	Marko PEROVIĆ	SRB	M	9	(3)	2
14	Valentin STOCKER		M	8	(3)	3
10	Marco STRELLER		A	20	(3)	12
32	Reto ZANNI		D	34		

GRASSHOPPER-CLUB

Coach - Hanspeter Latour

Founded – 1886

MAJOR HONOURS: Swiss League – (27) 1898, 1900, 1901, 1905, 1921, 1927, 1928, 1931, 1937, 1939, 1942, 1943, 1945, 1952, 1956, 1971, 1978, 1982, 1983, 1984, 1990, 1991, 1995, 1996, 1998, 2001, 2003; Swiss Cup (18) 1926, 1927, 1932, 1934, 1937, 1938, 1940, 1941, 1942, 1943, 1946, 1952, 1956, 1983, 1988, 1989, 1990, 1994.

2007				
18/7	St Gallen	h	2-0	*Renggli, Dos Santos (p)*
25/7	Young Boys	a	2-3	*Cabanas Ri., Salatic*
28/7	Sion	h	0-1	
5/8	Aarau	a	2-2	*Renggli, Bobadilla*
12/8	Luzern	a	3-3	*Bobadilla, Touré 2*
19/8	Basel	h	2-0	*Touré, Dos Santos (p)*
26/8	Thun	a	0-1	
1/9	Xamax	h	1-2	*Bobadilla*
23/9	Zürich	a	0-4	
26/9	St Gallen	a	3-5	*Dos Santos 2, Smiljanic*
29/9	Young Boys	h	3-3	*Zarate, Vallori, Jakupovic*
7/10	Sion	a	1-0	*Bobadilla*
27/10	Aarau	h	1-1	*Dos Santos (p)*
31/10	Luzern	h	1-1	*Bobadilla*
3/11	Basel	a	0-2	
10/11	Thun	h	2-1	*Bobadilla, Dos Santos*
1/12	Xamax	a	1-4	*Renggli*
9/12	Zürich	h	2-1	*Bobadilla, Feltscher F.*
2008				
2/2	Sion	a	2-0	*Zárate, Dos Santos (p)*
10/2	Young Boys	h	3-3	*Bobadilla 3*
17/2	Aarau	a	2-1	*og (Benito), Zárate*
23/2	Xamax	h	2-0	*Rinaldo, Dos Santos*
2/3	Zürich	a	0-1	
8/3	Thun	h	4-0	*Dos Santos, Vallori 2, Bobadilla*
15/3	Luzern	h	2-0	*Bobadilla, Dos Santos*
19/3	Basel	a	1-2	*Cabanas Ri.*
22/3	St Gallen	h	2-3	*Cabanas Ri., Machado*
29/3	St Gallen	a	2-0	*Bobadilla, Salatic*
2/4	Basel	h	1-1	*Bobadilla*
13/4	Luzern	a	0-0	
16/4	Thun	a	2-0	*Bobadilla, Madou*
20/4	Zürich	h	1-1	*Bobadilla*
26/4	Xamax	a	3-1	*Feltscher F., Cabanas Ri., Bobadilla (p)*
3/5	Aarau	h	2-0	*Salatic, Renggli*
7/5	Young Boys	a	0-2	
10/5	Sion	h	2-0	*Bobadilla, Rinaldo*

No	Name	Nat	Pos	Aps	(s)	Gls
31	David BLUMER		A	1	(6)	
25	Raúl Marcelo BOBADILLA	ARG	A	33		18
23	Raul CABANAS	ESP	M		(2)	
15	Ricardo CABANAS		M	19	(4)	4
1	Fabio COLTORTI		G	7		
5	Josip COLINA		D	15	(4)	
24	Fabio DAPRELA		D	9	(2)	
26	Dragan DJUKIC		G	6	(1)	
30	António Carlos DOS SANTOS	BRA	M	25		10
34	Frank FELTSCHER		M	7	(8)	2
29	Rolf FELTSCHER		D	22	(1)	
1	Eldin JAKUPOVIC		G	23		1
28	Fabio KLINGLER		A		(2)	
3	Bruce LALOMBONGO		M		(1)	
20	Luka LAPENDA		A		(1)	
19	Diego LEÓN	ESP	M	1	(4)	
19	Gabriel Teixeira MACHADO	BRA	A	7	(6)	1
22	Franck MADOU	FRA	A		(5)	1
11	Yassin MIKARI	TUN	D	24	(4)	
8	Michel RENGGLI		M	28	(4)	4

6	Paulo RINALDO Cruzado		M	18	(8)	2
35	Veroljub SALATIC		M	30	(3)	3
	Boris SMILJANIC		D	35		1
7	Demba TOURÉ	SEN	A	12	(1)	3
4	Guillermo Juan VALLORI	ESP	D	34		3
27	Kay VOSER		D	21	(2)	
9	Gonzalo Eulogio ZÁRATE	ARG	A	19	(5)	3

FC LUZERN

Coach - Ciriaco Sforza

Founded - 1901

MAJOR HONOURS: Swiss League - (1) 1989; Swiss Cup - (2) 1960, 1992.

2007				
21/7	Xamax	h	1-1	*Cantaluppi (p)*
26/7	Zürich	a	1-4	*og (Tihinen)*
29/7	Young Boys	h	2-2	*Lustrinelli, Chiumiento*
4/8	St Gallen	a	2-1	*Lustrinelli 2*
12/8	Grasshoppers	h	3-3	*Lustrinelli, Cantaluppi 2 (1p)*
18/8	Aarau	a	0-0	
25/8	Basel	h	2-4	*Lustrinelli, Cantaluppi (p)*
3/9	Sion	h	1-1	*Wiss*
22/9	Thun	a	1-0	*Tchouga*
26/9	Xamax	a	3-3	*Lustrinelli, Tchouga, Diethelm*
29/9	Zürich	h	2-2	*Tchouga, Felipe*
6/10	Young Boys	a	1-6	*Tchouga*
27/10	St Gallen	h	1-1	*Bader*
31/10	Grasshoppers	a	1-1	*Felipe*
4/11	Aarau	h	0-0	
11/11	Basel	a	2-3	*Wiss, Tchouga*
1/12	Sion	a	0-0	
8/12	Thun	h	1-2	*Tchouga*
2008				
3/2	Xamax	a	1-0	*Lustrinelli*
10/2	Aarau	h	2-0	*Lustrinelli 2*
16/2	Thun	a	1-0	*Lustrinelli*
24/2	Zürich	h	2-1	*Lustrinelli, Seoane*
1/3	St Gallen	a	1-2	*El Idrissi*
8/3	Sion	h	1-1	*Chiumiento (p)*
15/3	Grasshoppers	a	0-2	
18/3	Young Boys	h	0-3	
22/3	Basel	a	0-1	
29/3	Basel	h	1-0	*Lustrinelli*
13/4	Grasshoppers	h	0-0	
16/4	Sion	a	0-0	
19/4	St Gallen	h	1-0	*Bader*
24/4	Young Boys	a	1-0	*El Idrissi*
27/4	Zürich	a	0-1	
3/5	Thun	h	4-0	*El Idrissi, Schwegler, Lustrinelli, Shi*
7/5	Aarau	a	1-2	*Lustrinelli*
10/5	Xamax	h	0-2	

No	Name	Nat	Pos	Aps	(s)	Gls
3	Pascal BADER		D	12	(11)	2
11	Roland BÄTTIG		M	12	(1)	
17	Mario CANTALUPPI		M	17		4
8	David CHIUMIENTO		M	35		2
14	Fabijan CIPOT	SVN	D	8	(4)	
19	Gerardo CLEMENTE		M	3	(2)	
15	Boubacar DIARRA	FRA	D	14		
21	Michael DIETHELM		D	9	(11)	1
10	Fayçal Mustapha EL IDRISSI	FRA	M	18		3
11	FELIPE Barreto	BRA	A	8	(8)	2
35	Sandro FOSCHINI		M		(5)	
31	Sascha IMHOLZ		M		(1)	
18	Swen KÖNIG		G	3	(1)	
22	Burim KUKELI	SRB	M	9	(1)	
13	Christophe LAMBERT		D	21	(6)	
7	Claudio LUSTENBERGER		D	33		
28	Fabian LUSTENBERGER		M	3		
16	Mauro LUSTRINELLI		A	29		14
27	Rafael Alexandrino Dos Santos MAKANAKI	BRA	M	2		
34	Hervé MAKUKA		M	2	(5)	
23	Mijat MARIĆ	SRB	D	9		
28	Janko PACAR		A		(2)	
22	Ayoub RACHANE	MAR	M	2	(1)	
26	Rexhep SAQI	SRB	M	2	(4)	
4	Roland SCHWEGLER		D	33		1
33	Mato SEGO		M		(2)	
6	Gerardo SEOANE		M	23		1
23	Ahmad SHARBINI	CRO	A		(3)	
9	SHI Jun	CHN	A	4	(10)	1
25	Roberto SOUTO	ESP	D		(1)	
20	Jean-Michel TCHOUGA	CMR	A	17		6
17	Dušan VESKOVAC	SRB	D	14		
24	Alain WISS		M	21	(8)	2
1	David ZIBUNG		G	33		

NEUCHÂTEL XAMAX FC

Coach - Gérard Castella; (17/3/08) Néstor Clausen (ARG)

Founded – 1912

MAJOR HONOURS: Swiss League - (3) 1912, 1914, 1993; Swiss Cup - (1) 1985

2007				
21/7	Luzern	a	1-1	*Szlykowicz*
26/7	Thun	h	1-1	*Merenda*
29/7	Zürich	h	1-1	*Everson*
4/8	Sion	a	1-1	*Chihab*
11/8	Young Boys	h	3-1	*Everson, Rossi, Coly*
18/8	St Gallen	a	1-2	*Malenovic*
25/8	Aarau	h	2-1	*Nuzzolo, Besle*
1/9	Grasshoppers	a	2-1	*Everson, Coly*
23/9	Basel	h	0-3	
26/9	Luzern	h	3-3	*Szlykowicz, Merenda, Chihab*
30/9	Thun	a	1-1	*Nuzzolo*
7/10	Zürich	a	0-1	
27/10	Sion	h	1-3	*Quennoz*
1/11	Young Boys	a	2-3	*Everson, Rossi (p)*
4/11	St Gallen	h	1-1	*Chihab*
11/11	Aarau	a	2-3	*Chihab, Merenda*
1/12	Grasshoppers	h	4-1	*Coly 2, Nuzzolo 2*
9/12	Basel	a	1-0	*Rossi (p)*
2008				
3/2	Luzern	h	0-1	
9/2	Basel	a	0-3	
17/2	Young Boys	h	3-1	*Rossi (p), Szlykowicz 2*
23/2	Grasshoppers	a	0-2	
2/3	Sion	a	0-2	
9/3	Aarau	h	1-2	*Merenda*
15/3	Thun	h	0-2	
18/3	St Gallen	a	0-0	
22/3	Zürich	h	3-1	*Lang, João Paulo, Szlykowicz*
30/3	Zürich	a	1-2	*Coly*
4/4	St Gallen	h	1-0	*Joksimović*
12/4	Thun	a	1-2	*Merenda*
17/4	Aarau	a	2-2	*Rossi, Lang*
20/4	Sion	h	1-1	*Quennoz*
26/4	Grasshoppers	h	1-3	*Merenda*
2/5	Young Boys	a	3-1	*Coly 2, Merenda*
7/5	Basel	h	2-2	*Rossi, Coly*
10/5	Luzern	a	2-0	*Aide Brown, Rossi*

No	Name	Nat	Pos	Aps	(s)	Gls
25	Ideye AIDE BROWN	NGA	A	1	(4)	1
17	Thierno BAH		D	20	(5)	

No	Name	Nat	Pos	Aps	(s)	Gls
8	Roland BÄTTIG		M	5	(4)	
4	Stéphane BESLE	FRA	D	28		1
6	Tariq CHIHAB	MAR	M	27	(3)	4
27	Matar COLY	SEN	A	19	(15)	8
20	Mounir EL HAIMOUR	FRA	D	30	(1)	
8	EVERSON Pereira	BRA	M	26		4
18	Guillaume FAIVRE		G	1		
23	Mike GOMES		D	1	(1)	
16	Pascal JENNY		D	18	(7)	
11	JOÃO PAULO Daniel	BRA	A	6	(3)	1
13	Nebojša JOKSIMOVIĆ	SRB	D	13		1
7	Steven LANG		M	9	(15)	2
19	Milos MALENOVIC		A	2	(4)	1
9	Moreno MERENDA		A	18	(13)	7
14	Raphael NUZZOLO		M	30	(4)	4
5	Alexandre QUENNOZ		D	30		2
15	Richmond RAK		M	12	(14)	
29	Julio Hernán ROSSI	ARG	A	31	(2)	7
10	Johnny SZLYKOWICZ	FRA	M	28	(3)	5
24	Maxime VUILLE		M	1		
1	Laurent WALTHERT		G	1		
22	Sébastien WÜTHRICH		M	5	(3)	
28	Pascal ZUBERBÜHLER		G	34		

FC ST GALLEN

Coach - Rolf Fringer; (8/10/07) Krasimir Balakov (BUL)

Founded - 1879

MAJOR HONOURS: Swiss League – (2) 1904, 2000; Swiss Cup - (1) 1969.

Date	Opponent		Score	Scorers
2007				
18/7	Grasshoppers	a	0-2	
25/7	Basel	h	0-3	
31/7	Thun	a	0-1	
4/8	Luzern	h	1-2	*Gjasula (p)*
10/8	Zürich	a	1-3	*Marazzi*
18/8	Xamax	h	2-1	*Marazzi, Gjasula (p)*
26/8	Sion	h	1-0	*Aguirre*
2/9	Young Boys	a	1-3	*Ural*
22/9	Aarau	h	1-1	*Ural*
26/9	Grasshoppers	h	5-3	*Aguirre, Longo, Marazzi, Gjasula 2 (1p),*
30/9	Basel	a	0-3	
6/10	Thun	h	0-4	
27/10	Luzern	a	1-1	*Gjasula (p)*
31/10	Zürich	h	2-3	*Aguirre, Gjasula*
4/11	Xamax	a	1-1	*Aguirre*
10/11	Sion	a	1-5	*Aguirre*
1/12	Young Boys	h	2-7	*Aguirre 2*
8/12	Aarau	a	2-2	*Fernández, Aguirre*
2008				
3/2	Aarau	a	1-3	*Fernández*
9/2	Zürich	h	1-0	*Aguirre (p)*
16/2	Sion	a	2-1	*Koubský, Weller*
23/2	Thun	h	3-0	*Ural, Callà, Koubský*
1/3	Luzern	h	2-1	*Fernández, Aguirre*
9/3	Basel	a	1-2	*Schneider*
14/3	Young Boys	a	0-3	
18/3	Xamax	h	0-0	
22/3	Grasshoppers	a	3-2	*Ural, Zé Vítor 2*
29/3	Grasshoppers	h	0-2	
4/4	Xamax	a	0-1	
12/4	Young Boys	h	2-0	*Zé Vítor, Ciccone*
16/4	Basel	h	1-4	*Aguirre (p)*
19/4	Luzern	a	0-1	
25/4	Thun	a	1-1	*Bratić*
3/5	Sion	h	1-2	*Ciccone*
7/5	Zürich	a	0-1	
10/5	Aarau	h	0-0	

No	Name	Nat	Pos	Aps	(s)	Gls
34	Nico ABEGGLEN		A		(1)	
9	Francisco AGUIRRE	ARG	A	24	(5)	11
30	Kwabena AGOUDA	GHA	A		(3)	
2	Vidak BRATIĆ	SRB	D	3	(1)	1
7	Davide CALLÀ	ITA	M	18	(1)	1
26	Diego CICCONE	ITA	M	14	(17)	2
24	Moreno COSTANZO		A		(7)	
16	Francesco DI JORIO		M	8	(2)	
21	Adrián FERNÁNDEZ	ARG	A	19	(7)	3
3	FERNANDO César de Souza	BRA	D	18	(2)	
22	Guy Armand FEUTCHINE	CMR	M	6	(1)	
6	Juan Pablo GARAT	ITA	D	16	(3)	
8	Marcos Agustin GELABERT	ARG	M	30		
10	Jürgen GJASULA	GER	M	23	(1)	6
4	Bernt HAAS		D	1		
19	Jiří KOUBSKÝ	CZE	D	31		2
14	Serdal KÜL	TUR	D		(1)	
13	Michael LANG		M		(3)	
20	Dominique LONGO		D	4		1
18	Daniel LOPAR		G	17		
28	Alessandro MAIER		D	1	(1)	
23	David MARAZZI		M	17	(4)	3
5	Mijat MARIĆ	SRB	D	2		
33	Jesús MÉNDEZ	ARG	M	9	(4)	
29	Luís Mário MIRANDA	BRA	A		(6)	
15	Philipp MUNTWILER		M	24	(7)	
1	Stefano RAZZETTI	ITA	G	19		
14	Marc SCHNEIDER		D	17		1
27	Labinot SHEHOLLI	SRB	M		(1)	
11	Alexander TACHIE-MENSAH	GHA	A	1	(6)	
25	Murat URAL		A	14	(16)	4
27	Thomas WELLER	GER	D	17	(1)	1
17	Marc ZELLWEGER		D	33	(1)	
29	José Vítor Jardim "ZÉ VITOR"	POR	M	10	(5)	3

FC SION

Coach - Alberto Bigon (ITA); (17/12/07) Charly Rössli & Maurizio Jacobacci; (25/3/08) Alberto Bigon (ITA)

Founded – 1909

MAJOR HONOURS: Swiss League - (2) 1992, 1997; Swiss Cup - (10) 1965, 1974, 1980, 1982, 1986, 1991, 1995, 1996, 1997, 2006.

Date	Opponent		Score	Scorers
2007				
25/7	Aarau	h	3-0	*Saborío 2, Reset*
28/7	Grasshoppers	a	1-0	*Saborío*
4/8	Xamax	h	1-1	*Nwaneri*
7/8	Thun	a	1-0	*Domínguez*
11/8	Basel	a	2-3	*Vanczák, Chedli*
19/8	Zürich	h	0-5	
26/8	St Gallen	a	0-1	
3/9	Luzern	a	1-1	*Zakrzewski*
23/9	Young Boys	h	1-2	*Adeshina*
27/9	Thun	h	2-1	*Domínguez (p), Paito*
30/9	Aarau	a	0-2	
7/10	Grasshoppers	h	0-1	
27/10	Xamax	a	3-1	*Saborío, Obradović 2*
31/10	Basel	h	1-1	*Saborío*
3/11	Zürich	a	1-4	*Reset*
10/11	St Gallen	h	5-1	*Saborío 2, Vanczák, Domínguez (p), Reset*
1/12	Luzern	h	0-0	
9/12	Young Boys	a	0-1	
2008				
2/2	Grasshoppers	h	0-2	
10/2	Thun	a	2-2	*Sarni, Crettenand*
16/2	St Gallen	h	1-2	*Saborío*
24/2	Young Boys	a	1-3	*Adeshina*
2/3	Xamax	h	2-0	*Saborío, M'Futi*
8/3	Luzern	a	1-1	*Paito (p)*
16/3	Basel	h	4-2	*Domínguez 2, Saborío, Reset*
19/3	Zürich	a	1-2	*Saborío*

22/3	Aarau	a	0-2	
30/3	Aarau	h	1-0	*Grosicki*
4/4	Zürich	h	3-3	*Saborío 2, Beto*
13/4	Basel	a	1-1	*Saborío*
16/4	Luzern	h	0-0	
20/4	Xamax	a	1-1	*Obradović*
27/4	Young Boys	h	1-2	*Saborío*
3/5	St Gallen	a	2-1	*Saborío, Adeshina*
7/5	Thun	h	5-0	*Dominguez 2, M'Futi, Saborío, Grosicki*
10/5	Grasshoppers	a	0-2	

No	Name	Nat	Pos	Aps	(s)	Gls
27	Saidu Alade ADESHINA	NGA	A	15	(12)	3
19	Jocelyn AHOUÉYA	BEN	M	18	(3)	
8	Jamal ALIOUI	MAR	D	19	(3)	
10	Gilberto Galindo BETO	POR	M	22	(4)	1
28	Julien BRELLIER	FRA	M	10	(4)	
31	Arnaud BÜHLER		D	17	(5)	
14	Adel CHEDLI	TUN	M	8		1
16	Didier CRETTENAND		M	2	(3)	1
23	Álvaro José DOMÍNGUEZ	COL	M	27	(6)	7
35	Essam Kamal EL HADARY	EGY	G	5		
13	Bastien GEIGER		D	10	(9)	
21	David GONZALEZ		G	10		
26	Kamil GROSICKI	POL	M	4	(4)	2
2	Carlos Manuel Gonçalves KALI	ANG	D	26	(2)	
24	Mobulu M'FUTI	COD	A	7	(8)	2
6	Mirsad MIJADINOSKI	MKD	D	5	(2)	
3	Obinna NWANERI	NGA	D	27		1
22	Goran OBRADOVIĆ	SRB	M	18	(8)	3
12	Mucuana Martinho PAITO	POR	D	31	(1)	2
7	Virgile RESET	FRA	M	20	(10)	4
9	Álvaro Alberto SABORÍO	CRC	A	27	(7)	17
30	Stéphane SARNI		D	11		1
17	Vilmos VANCZÁK	HUN	D	26	(4)	2
18	Germano VAILATI		G	21		
4	Raphaël WICKY		M	5		
11	Zbigniew ZAKRZEWSKI	POL	A	5	(8)	1

FC THUN

Coach - René van Eck (NED)

Founded - 1898

2007				
26/7	Xamax	a	1-1	*Nyman*
31/7	St Gallen	h	1-0	*Gerber*
4/8	Zürich	a	1-3	*Faye*
7/8	Sion	h	0-1	
12/8	Aarau	h	2-5	*Ferreira, Gavatorta*
19/8	Young Boys	a	0-0	
26/8	Grasshoppers	h	1-0	*Ferreira*
2/9	Basel	a	1-2	*Faye*
22/9	Luzern	h	0-1	
27/9	Sion	a	1-2	*Scarione*
30/9	Xamax	h	1-1	*Rama*
6/10	St Gallen	a	4-0	*Andrist, Rama 2, Scarione*
28/10	Zürich	h	1-1	*Glarner*
1/11	Aarau	a	0-5	
4/11	Young Boys	h	0-0	
10/11	Grasshoppers	a	1-2	*Iashvili*
2/12	Basel	h	0-2	
8/12	Luzern	a	2-1	*Rama, Ba*
2008				
2/2	Zürich	a	0-1	
10/2	Sion	h	2-2	*Faye, Rama*
16/2	Luzern	h	0-1	
23/2	St Gallen	a	0-3	
2/3	Basel	h	1-3	*Zakrzewski*
8/3	Grasshoppers	a	0-4	
15/3	Xamax	a	2-0	*Rama, Scarione*
19/3	Aarau	h	1-1	*Ba*
22/3	Young Boys	a	2-4	*Rama, Scarione*
30/3	Young Boys	h	0-4	
4/4	Aarau	a	0-3	
12/4	Xamax	h	2-1	*Ferreira, Rama*
16/4	Grasshoppers	h	0-2	
19/4	Basel	a	1-3	*Scarione (p)*
25/4	St Gallen	h	1-1	*Scarione (p)*
3/5	Luzern	a	0-4	
7/5	Sion	a	0-5	
10/5	Zürich	h	1-1	*Gerber*

No	Name	Nat	Pos	Aps	(s)	Gls
35	Sidimoulayelfadil ALAOUI		A		(1)	
28	Stephan ANDRIST		M	20	(7)	1
23	Ibrahima BA	SEN	M	12	(8)	2
1	Patrick BETTONI		G	31		
17	Julian BÜHLER		A	1	(6)	
19	Franz BURGMEIER	LIE	M	17		
2	Lukáš DOŠEK	CZE	M	20	(5)	
4	Luís Manuel Duarte CALAPES	POR	D	7		
25	João Paulo DI FÁBIO	BRA	D	22		
21	Nélson FERREIRA	POR	M	34		3
6	Roman FRIEDLI		M	4	(4)	
13	Sandro GALLI		D	2		
8	Alejandro GAVATORTA	ITA	M	24	(2)	1
11	Andreas GERBER		D	32		2
31	Stefan GLARNER		D	15		1
7	Ľubomír GULDAN	SVK	D	18	(6)	
15	Pape Omar FAYE	SEN	M	16	(13)	3
14	Marco HÄMMERLI		D	7	(2)	
10	Sandro IASHVILI	GEO	A	5	(16)	1
33	Benjamin LÜTHI		M	2	(3)	
24	Ari NYMAN	FIN	D	31		1
18	Alain PORTMANN		G	1		
9	Milaim RAMA		A	18	(10)	8
20	Ezequiel Óscar SCARIONE	ARG	M	28	(3)	6
16	Mario SCHÖNENBERGER		M	3	(2)	
22	Sascha STULZ		G	4	(2)	
12	Mirson VOLINA	MKD	M		(1)	
34	Yves ZAHND		D	15		
16	Zbigniew ZAKRZEWSKI	POL	A	7	(8)	1

BSC YOUNG BOYS

Coach – Martin Andermatt

Founded - 1898

MAJOR HONOURS: Swiss League – (11) 1903, 1909, 1910, 1911, 1920, 1929, 1957, 1958, 1959, 1960, 1986; Swiss Cup – (6) 1930, 1945, 1953, 1958, 1977, 1987.

2007				
22/7	Aarau	a	1-1	*Zayatte*
25/7	Grasshoppers	h	3-2	*Yakin, Tiago, Häberli*
29/7	Luzern	a	2-2	*Yakin 2*
5/8	Basel	h	5-1	*João Paulo 2, Raimondi, Asamoa-Frimpong 2*
11/8	Xamax	a	1-3	*Mangane*
19/8	Thun	h	0-0	
25/8	Zürich	a	1-5	*Yakin*
2/9	St Gallen	h	3-1	*Tiago (p), Portillo, Asamoa-Frimpong*
23/9	Sion	a	2-1	*Tiago, Schneuwly M.*
26/9	Aarau	h	4-1	*Kallio 2, Hochstrasser, Häberli*
29/9	Grasshoppers	a	3-3	*Häberli, Varela, Yakin*
6/10	Luzern	h	6-1	*Raimondi, Yakin, Häberli 2, João Paulo, Schneuwly M.*
28/10	Basel	a	0-4	

1/11	Xamax	h	3-2	*Yakin, Raimondi, Häberli*
4/11	Thun	a	0-0	
11/11	Zürich	h	1-1	*Yakin*
1/12	St Gallen	a	7-2	*Yakin 4, Häberli 2, Varela*
9/12	Sion	h	1-0	*Yakin (p)*
2008				
3/2	Basel	h	2-0	*Häberli, Yakin (p)*
10/2	Grasshoppers	a	3-3	*Raimondi 2, Häberli (p)*
17/2	Xamax	a	1-3	*Häberli*
24/2	Sion	h	3-1	*Raimondi, Varela, Häberli*
1/3	Aarau	a	2-0	*og (Christ), Häberli*
9/3	Zürich	h	3-0	*Ghezal, Hochstrasser, Häberli*
14/3	St Gallen	h	3-0	*Yakin, Raimondi, Yapi Yapo*
18/3	Luzern	a	3-0	*Yakin, Häberli, Asamoa-Frimpong*
22/3	Thun	h	4-2	*Ghezal 2, Asamoa-Frimpong, Varela*
30/3	Thun	a	4-0	*Yakin 2 (1p), Häberli, Raimondi*
12/4	St Gallen	a	0-2	
17/4	Zürich	a	2-1	*Yakin 2*
20/4	Aarau	h	4-0	*Yakin 2 (1p), Doubai, Häberli (p)*
24/4	Luzern	h	0-1	
27/4	Sion	a	2-1	*Baykal, Regazzoni*
2/5	Xamax	h	1-3	*Yakin*
7/5	Grasshoppers	h	2-0	*Yakin (p), Häberli*
10/5	Basel	a	0-2	

No	Name	Nat	Pos	Aps	(s)	Gls
31	Joetex ASAMOAH FRIMPONG	GHA	A	5	(17)	5
6	BAYKAL Kulaksizoglu		M	6	(7)	1
18	Paolo COLLAVITI		G	4	(1)	
11	Tapé Moussé DOUBAI	CIV	M	19	(4)	1
2	Saif GHEZAL	TUN	D	15		3
15	Thomas HÄBERLI		A	28		18
22	Xavier HOCHSTRASSER		M	28	(1)	2
9	JOÃO PAULO Daniel	BRA	A	9	(6)	3
33	Toni KALLIO	FIN	D	4	(2)	2
20	Erhan KAVAK	TUR	M		(6)	
3	Aron LIECHTI		D	9	(1)	
6	Abdou Kader MANGANE	SEN	M	7		1
27	Franck MADOU	FRA	A	0	(2)	
12	Miguel Alfredo PORTILLO	ARG	D	29	(3)	1
16	Mario RAIMONDI		M	36		8
8	Alberto REGAZZONI		M	11	(13)	1
21	SHI Jun	CHN	A		(4)	
14	Christian SCHNEUWLY		M		(2)	
26	Marco SCHNEUWLY		A	11	(19)	2
13	Christian SCHWEGLER		D	30		
4	TIAGO Calvano	BRA	D	19	(2)	3
19	Carlos VARELA	ESP	M	24	(5)	4
1	Marco WÖLFLI		G	32		
10	Hakan YAKIN		M	31	(1)	24
30	Gilles YAPI YAPO	CIV	M	18	(5)	1
5	Kamil ZAYATTE	GUI	D	21	(2)	1

FC ZÜRICH

Coach - Bernard Challandes

Founded – 1896

MAJOR HONOURS: Swiss League – (11) 1902, 1924, 1963, 1966, 1968, 1974, 1975, 1976, 1981, 2006, 2007; Swiss Cup – (7) 1966, 1970, 1972, 1973, 1976, 2000, 2005.

2007				
22/7	Basel	a	0-1	
26/7	Luzern	h	4-1	*Chikhaoui, Abdi, Rochat, César (p)*
29/7	Xamax	a	1-1	*og (Zuberbühler)*
4/8	Thun	h	3-1	*Alphonse, Raffael, Chikhaoui*
10/8	St Gallen	h	3-1	*Raffael, César (p), Alphonse*
19/8	Sion	a	5-0	*Raffael 2 (1p), Alphonse 2, Hassli*
25/8	Young Boys	h	5-1	*Abdi 2, Chikhaoui 2, Raffael*
1/9	Aarau	a	1-1	*og (Rapisarda)*
23/9	Grasshoppers	h	4-0	*Chikhaoui, Tihinen, Raffael 2*
26/9	Basel	h	2-2	*Chikhaoui, Hassli*
29/9	Luzern	a	2-2	*Chikhaoui, Stahel*
7/10	Xamax	h	1-0	*Eudis*
28/10	Thun	a	1-1	*og (Gerber)*
31/10	St Gallen	a	3-2	*Alphonse, Raffael, Schönbächler*
3/11	Sion	h	4-1	*Alphonse 2, Raffael 2*

PROMOTED CLUBS

FC VADUZ

Coach – Heinz Hermann

Founded - 1932

MAJOR HONOURS: Liechtenstein Cup - (37) 1949, 1952, 1953, 1954, 1956, 1957, 1958, 1959, 1960, 1961, 1962, 1966, 1967, 1968, 1969, 1970, 1971, 1974, 1980, 1985, 1986, 1988, 1990, 1992, 1995, 1996, 1998, 1999, 2000, 2001, 2002, 2003, 2004, 2005, 2006, 2007, 2008.

AC BELLINZONA

Coach – Vladimir Petković (CRO)

Founded - 1904

MAJOR HONOURS: Swiss Championship - (1) 1948.

SECOND LEVEL FINAL TABLE 2007/08

		Pld	W	D	L	F	A	Pts
1	FC Vaduz	34	21	7	6	75	40	70
2	AC Bellinzona	34	21	6	7	74	39	69
3	FC Wil 1900	34	20	8	6	63	35	68
4	FC Wohlen	34	16	8	10	65	46	56
5	FC Winterthur	34	14	9	11	59	56	51
6	FC Schaffhausen	34	13	10	11	53	40	49
7	FC Concordia BS	34	13	10	11	55	54	49
8	Servette FC	34	12	10	12	55	46	46
9	AC Lugano	34	12	10	12	61	63	46
10	Yverdon-Sport FC	34	10	13	11	39	35	43
11	FC Gossau	34	11	10	13	50	54	43
12	FC La Chaux-de-Fonds	34	12	7	15	53	63	43
13	FC Lausanne-Sport	34	11	9	14	46	47	42
14	FC Locarno	34	12	5	17	37	61	41
15	SC Kriens	34	8	14	12	43	54	38
16	SR Delémont	34	10	7	17	42	58	37
17	FC Chiasso	34	8	9	17	43	68	33
18	SC Cham	34	4	4	26	31	85	16

PROMOTION/RELEGATION PLAY-OFFS

(17/5/08)

Bellinzona 3, St Gallen 2

(20/5/08)

St Gallen 0, Bellinzona 2

(Bellinzona 5-2)

11/11	Young Boys	a	1-1	*Raffael (p)*
2/12	Aarau	h	0-1	
9/12	Grasshoppers	a	1-2	*Raffael*
2008				
2/2	Thun	h	1-0	*Abdi*
9/2	St Gallen	a	0-1	
17/2	Basel	h	1-1	*Chikhaoui (p)*
24/2	Luzern	a	1-2	*Djuric*
2/3	Grasshoppers	h	1-0	*Alphonse*
9/3	Young Boys	a	0-3	
16/3	Aarau	a	0-1	
19/3	Sion	h	2-1	*Tahirovic, Abdi (p)*
22/3	Xamax	a	1-3	*Vasquez*
30/3	Xamax	h	2-1	*Okonkwo, Hassli*
4/4	Sion	a	3-3	*Abdi 2, Alphonse*
13/4	Aarau	h	0-0	
17/4	Young Boys	h	1-2	*Tihinen (p)*
20/4	Grasshoppers	a	1-1	*Schönbächler*
27/4	Luzern	h	1-0	*Aegerter*
2/5	Basel	a	0-4	
7/5	St Gallen	h	1-0	*Eudis*
10/5	Thun	a	1-1	*Tahirovic*

No	Name	Nat	Pos	Aps	(s)	Gls
23	Almen ABDI		M	30	(1)	7
7	Silvan AEGERTER		M	24		1
12	Alexandre ALPHONSE	FRA	A	26	(3)	9
21	Heinz BARMETTLER		D	16	(4)	
26	Martin BÜCHEL	LIE	M	1	(1)	
20	Cléderson CÉSAR	BRA	M	5		2
17	Yassine CHIKHAOUI	TUN	M	18		8
14	Dusan Predrag DJURIC	SWE	M	6	(1)	1
16	Eudi Silva EUDIS	BRA	A	3	(11)	2
32	Andrea GUATELLI	ITA	G	2	(1)	
29	Eric HASSLI	FRA	A	11	(17)	3
6	Sebastian KOLLAR		M	5	(7)	
5	Oumar KONDÉ		M	10	(7)	
33	Luca LADNER		M		(1)	
2	Veli LAMPI	FIN	D	19	(5)	
1	Johnny LEONI		G	34		
25	Orhan MUSTAFI	MKD	A		(1)	
28	Adrian NIKCI		M	1	(4)	
10	Onyekachi Donatus OKONKWO	NGA	M	26	(1)	1
14	RAFFAEL Caetano de Araújo	BRA	A	15		12
19	Alain ROCHAT		D	27	(1)	1
24	Marc SCHNEIDER		D	10	(2)	
27	Marco SCHÖNBÄCHLER		A	12	(3)	2
20	SÍLVIO Carlos	BRA	A	7	(5)	
13	Florian STAHEL		D	28	(4)	1
3	Remo STAUBLI		M		(4)	
15	Daniel STUCKI		D	6	(3)	
8	Emra TAHIROVIC	SWE	A	7	(9)	2
30	Hannu TIHINEN	FIN	D	27		2
9	Andres Javier VASQUEZ	SWE	M	7	(5)	1
4	Adan Jonathan VERGARA	CHI	D	8	(1)	
4	Steve VON BERGEN		D	5		

DOMESTIC CUP 2007/08

SCHWEIZER CUP/COUPE DE SUISSE

FIRST ROUND

(14/9/07)
Baulmes 2, Delémont 1
Biel/Bienne 2, Yverdon 2 *(aet; 3-4 on pens)*
Racing Genève 4, La Chaux-de-Fonds 1
Wettingen 93 1, Kriens 3

(15/9/07)
Baden 1, Locarno 2
Bazenheid 0, Bellinzona 7
Bern 1, Langenthal 2
Brühl St Gallen 4, Schaffhausen 6
Düdingen 1, Concordia Basel 3 *(aet)*
Echallens 0, Lausanne-Sport 3 *(aet)*
Flawil 2, Wil 3
Hägendorf 1, Cham 5
Herrliberg 0, Zürich 6
LeMont 0, Xamax 2
Massongex 0, Etoile Carouge 5
Orpund 1, Binningen 2
Red Star Zürich 0, Winterthur 5
Sarnen 1, Aarau 7
Seefeld Zürich 0, Grasshoppers 4
Stade Lausanne-Ouchy 0, Servette 4
Töss Winterthur 0, St Gallen 8
UGS Genève 0, Sion 7
Versoix 0, Nyon 5
Winkeln St Gallen 2, Gossau 6

(16/9/07)
Bavois 1, Young Boys 3
Biasca 1, Luzern 3
Gordola 1, Chiasso 5
Léchelles 0, Basel 9
Lusitanos La Chaux-de-Fonds 0, Colombier 6
Malcantone 0, Wohlen 4
Porrentruy 0, Thun 4
Tuggen 2, Lugano 2 *(aet; 2-4 on pens)*

SECOND ROUND

(20/10/07)
Cham 0, Thun 1
Chiasso 3, Lugano 1
Colombier 1, Yverdon 3
Concordia Basel 1, Zürich 1 *(aet; 5-6 on pens)*
Schaffhausen 3, Wil 1
Gossau 2, St Gallen 0
Langenthal 2, Luzern 5
Locarno 0, Young Boys 2
Nyon 2, Servette 1
Racing Genève 2, Xamax 5 *(aet)*

(21/10/07)
Baulmes 0, Lausanne-Sport 2 *(aet)*
Binningen 1, Basel 6
Etoile Carouge 0, Sion 2
Kriens 1, Aarau 0
Winterthur 2, Grasshoppers 3
Wohlen 0, Bellinzona 0 *(aet; 4-5 on pens)*

THIRD ROUND

(24/11/07)
Lausanne-Sport 0, Gossau 2
Luzern 0, Thun 1
Schaffhausen 0, Xamax 1

(25/11/07)
Bellinzona 2, Sion 1
Chiasso 0, Young Boys 1
Grasshoppers 0, Basel 1
Kriens 0, Zürich 3
Nyon 2, Yverdon 1

QUARTER-FINALS

(15/12/07)
Basel 2 *(Derdiyok 53, 90)*, Nyon 0
Thun 2 *(Ferreira 5, Rama 120)*, Zürich 1 *(Chikhaoui 11) (aet)*

(16/12/07)
Bellinzona 2 *(Taljević 40p, Grabbi 55)*, Gossau 1 *(Knöpfel 53)*
Xamax 3 *(Rossi 45p, Rak 88, Chihab 110)*, Young Boys 2 *(Regazzoni 77, Schneuwly M. 90) (aet)*

SEMI-FINALS

(27/2/08)
Basel 1 *(Lokvenc 12)*, Thun 0
Bellinzona 0, Xamax 0 *(aet; 4-2 on pens)*

FINAL

(6/4/08)
St. Jakob-Park, Basel
FC BASEL 1893 4 *(Derdiyok 31, Majstorovic 62, Streller 63, Huggel 65)*
AC BELLINZONA 1 *(Pouga 58)*
Referee – *Zimmermann*
BASEL – *Costanzo, Zanni, Majstorovic, Marque, Nakata, Ba, Derdiyok (Streller 46), Huggel, Ergić, Carlitos (Degen 55), Eduardo (Perović 76).*
BELLINZONA – *Bucchi, Belotti (Moresi 46), Mangiarratti, Carbone, Miccolis (Raso 69), Rivera (Conti 73), La Rocca, Lulić, Taljević, Neri, Pouga.*

Comeback kings make the semi-finals

Turkey's passage to the semi-finals of UEFA EURO 2008™ - the furthest the country has ever gone in a UEFA European Championship - was an extraordinary triumph of courage and commitment. The tournament's comeback kings recovered from falling behind in three successive matches, and did so on each occasion with a dramatic goal in the last minute, so it was the height of irony that they should exit the tournament after conceding themselves with 90 minutes on the clock in their semi-final against Germany.

When Philipp Lahm gave Fatih Terim's never-say-die team a taste of their own medicine, they suddenly understood the depth of despair they had earlier inflicted on Switzerland, the Czech Republic and Croatia - for Turkey, like their fallen opponents, had lost despite being the better side. Good fortune undoubtedly played a part in Turkey's progress, but nobody could question the team's remarkable character. With the exception of the opening game, a 2-0 defeat by Portugal, they provided wonderful entertainment, and their stubborn refusal to accept defeat was one of the major talking-points of the tournament.

Hamit Altıntop (centre) was Turkey's top performer at UEFA EURO 2008™

Turkey had demonstrated their defiance by coming from behind to beat Norway 2-1 in a pivotal qualifying tie in Oslo, but their remarkable powers of recovery reached new heights in Switzerland and Austria. Midfielder Arda Turan started the ball rolling with his last-gasp winner against Switzerland in Basel. Then it was Nihat Kahveci's turn to snatch victory from the jaws of defeat with two late goals against the Czech Republic in Geneva. In some respects the quarter-final win over Croatia in Vienna was even more miraculous, victory on penalties coming after Semih Şentürk had equalised with the very last kick of extra time.

Turkey's joy was tempered by the realisation that they would be missing four key players through suspension for the semi-final – Arda, Tuncay Şanlı, Emre Aşik and goalkeeper Volkan Demirel. With a lengthy injury list claiming another high-profile victim in Nihat, Turkey were down to the bare bones against Germany in Basel. But, astonishingly, they produced their best performance of the tournament, and although a familiar script appeared to be in the offing when the predatory Semih squeezed in his third goal of the competition four minutes from time to equalise at 2-2, it was Germany who had the last laugh.

Star man Hamit

There were many heroes, not least Terim, who laid further claim to being Turkey's greatest ever coach. Although he intimated after the team's exit that he would be leaving, he changed his mind and put pen to paper on a new two-year contract extension. Reaching the 2010 FIFA World Cup will be a tough task with European champions Spain in the same section, but Turkey will not take the road to South Africa short on confidence. Arda, Nihat, Tuncay, Semih and – in patches – Volkan and giant centre-back Servet Çetin all demonstrated international class at UEFA EURO 2008™ while Hamit Altıntop, the only Turk in the official Team of the Tournament, suggested he has the talent and versatility – not to mention the film-star looks - to become a truly global star.

amit's twin brother Halil was a surprise omission from ne UEFA EURO 2008™ squad, and there was a certain isgruntlement among many that Terim could find no lace in his 23-man party for legendary striker Hakan ükür, who thus ended his international career with 51 oals – a national record that may never be broken. He chieved that feat in 112 matches – six fewer than his ontemporary, goalkeeper Rüştü Reçber, who raised his ecord tally to 118 caps by replacing the suspended olkan for the UEFA EURO 2008™ games against Croatia nd Germany.

akan's long association with Galatasaray AŞ ended on a igh as he scored the opening goal in the last-day 2-0 ictory over Gençlerbirliği OFTAŞ SK that clinched the 007/08 Turkish Süper Lig title for the Istanbul club. alatasaray had gone into the fixture needing only a raw to finish ahead of defending champions enerbahçe SK and join their arch-rivals as the country's l-time record champions with 17 league titles apiece.

erby decider

had been a tight Süper Lig race, with Beşiktaş JK and natolian outsiders Sivasspor also having their say. But the end, the destiny of the championship came down the derby game between Galatasaray and enerbahçe at Ali Sami Yen on Sunday 27 April. The two ams were level on points. With just two more fixtures follow, it was effectively a winner-takes-all encounter. ener had won the previous league fixture in December, -0, but Gala had got their revenge in a dramatic Cup uarter-final, winning the tie with a last-minute goal fter Fener had lost three players to red cards. Gala's razilian midfield playmaker Lincoln had also been sent ff in the Cup game, and his absence from the big ague decider with a knee injury gave the home fans ause for concern, but it was another imported star, habani Nonda, who would prove the unlikely match-inner, emerging from a 12-match barren run to head ne only goal of the game.

alatasaray had begun the season by recalling their rmer coach, 74-year-old Karl-Heinz Feldkamp, from etirement. A strict disciplinarian, he managed to get the am to play fast and fluent football but was not popular mong the players, and after a derby defeat to Beşiktaş nd a hammering by Bayer 04 Leverkusen in the UEFA up, the Galatasaray board decided, in early April, to ismiss him. Leverkusen boss Michael Skibbe would ventually replace his fellow German but not before ala had seen out the season successfully under a oaching conglomerate headed ostensibly by former assistant Cevat Güler but in reality by general manager Adnan Sezgin.

Shabani Nonda – Galatasaray's match-winner in the Turkish Süper Lig title-decider against Fenerbahçe

Fenerbahçe may have lost the title but they enjoyed a memorable run in Europe, reaching the UEFA Champions League quarter-finals. They were irrepressible at home, winning all six matches at the Şükrü Saracoğlu stadium, from the qualifying-round tie against RSC Anderlecht to the quarter-final first leg against Chelsea FC. The Brazilian influence was profound, with new glamour signing Roberto Carlos at left-back, Edu Dracena in central defence, skipper Alex weaving his magic in midfield and striker Deivid scoring five crucial goals. Piecing it all together was another Brazilian, coach Zico, but he was to be replaced at the end of the season as Fenerbahçe welcomed in man of the moment Luis Aragonés, fresh from his triumph with Spain at UEFA EURO 2008™.

Anfield hammering

Beşiktaş, led diligently by ex-player Ertuğrul Saglam, also competed in the group phase of the UEFA Champions League but made history of the wrong kind when they were thrashed 8-0 by Liverpool FC at Anfield – a fortnight after beating them 2-1 in Istanbul. The Black Eagles went top of the Süper Lig table in mid-March only to suffer back-to-back defeats against İstanbul BB SK and Fenerbahçe and drop out of contention.

TURKEY

Türkiye Futbol Federasyönü (TFF)

Konaklar Mahallesi
Ihlamurlu Sokak 9
4 Levent
TR-80620 İstanbul
tel - +90 212 2827010
fax - +90 212 2827016
website - www.tff.org
email - tff@tff.org
Year of Formation – 1923
General Secretary – Metin Kazancıoğlu
Press Officer – Türker Tozar

IINTERNATIONAL TOURNAMENT APPEARANCES
FIFA World Cup - (2) 1954, 2002 (3rd)
UEFA European Championship - (3) 1996, 2000 (qtr-finals), 2008 (semi-finals).

TOP FIVE ALL-TIME CAPS
Rüstu Reçber (118); Hakan Şükür (112); Bülent Korkmaz (102); Tugay Kerimoğlu (94); Alpay Özalan (90)

TOP FIVE ALL-TIME GOALS
Hakan Şükür (51); Lefter Küçükandonyadis (21); Cemil Turan & Metin Oktay (19); Nihat Kahveci (17)

NATIONAL TEAM RESULTS 2007/08

22/8/07	Romania	A	Bucharest	0-2	
8/9/07	Malta (ECQ)	A	Ta' Qali	2-2	*Halil (45), Servet (78)*
12/9/07	Hungary (ECQ)	H	Istanbul	3-0	*Gökhan Ünal (68), Mehmet Aurélio (72), Halil (90+3)*
13/10/07	Moldova (ECQ)	A	Chisinau	1-1	*Ümit (63)*
17/10/07	Greece (ECQ)	H	Istanbul	0-1	
17/11/07	Norway (ECQ)	A	Oslo	2-1	*Emre Belözoğlu (31), Nihat (59)*
21/11/07	Bosnia-Herzegovina (ECQ)	H	Istanbul	1-0	*Nihat (43)*
6/2/08	Sweden	H	Istanbul	0-0	
26/3/08	Belarus	A	Minsk	2-2	*Tuncay (38), Tümer (71)*
20/5/08	Slovakia	N	Bielefeld (GER)	1-0	*Hakan Balta (63)*
25/5/08	Uruguay	N	Bochum (GER)	2-3	*Arda (13), Nihat (51)*
29/5/08	Finland	N	Duisburg (GER)	2-0	*Tuncay (15), Semih (88)*
7/6/08	Portugal (ECF)	N	Geneva (SUI)	0-2	
11/6/08	Switzerland (ECF)	A	Basel	2-1	*Semih (57), Arda (90+2)*
15/6/08	Czech Republic (ECF)	N	Geneva (SUI)	3-2	*Arda (75), Nihat (87, 89)*
20/6/08	Croatia (ECF)	N	Vienna (AUT)	1-1	*Semih (120+2) (aet; 3-1 on pens)*
25/6/08	Germany (ECF)	N	Basel (SUI)	2-3	*Uğur (22), Semih (86)*

NATIONAL TEAM APPEARANCES 2007/08

Coach - FATİH Terim 14/9/53			Rou	MLT	HUN	MDA	GRE	NOR	BIH	Swe	Blr	Svk	Uru	Fin	POR	SUI	CZE	CRO	GER	Caps
SERDAR Kulbilge	7/7/80	Fenerbahçe	G																	1
SABRİ Sarıoğlu	26/7/84	Galatasaray	D82	D52					s61		s22	s46	s46	D	s46		s46	D	D	19
İBRAHİM Toraman	20/11/81	Beşiktaş	D	D																28
GÖKHAN Zan	7/9/81	Beşiktaş	D			D	D			D		D	D86	D	D55			D	D	23
İBRAHİM Üzülmez	10/3/74	Beşiktaş	D69	D	D	D	D													33
MEHMET Topuz	7/9/83	Kayserispor	M74			D				s62										15

ATIONAL TEAM APPEARANCES 2007/08 (contd.)

			Rou	MLT	HUN	MDA	GRE	NOR	BIH	Swe	Blr	Svk	Uru	Fin	POR	SUI	CZE	CRO	GER	Caps	Goals
ЛİT Altıntop	8/12/82	Bayern (GER)	M	M	D		D	M	M	M62	D22		D46	M78	D76	D	D	M	M	47	2
E Belözoğlu	7/9/80	Newcastle (ENG)	M42	M	s46	M	M71	M	M	M78		s46	M64	M89	M					57	4
A Turan	30/1/87	Galatasaray	M46	M30		M69	s71	M87	M76	s46	s61 /66	s73	M60	s67		M	M	M		22	3
CAY Şanlı	16/1/82	Middlesbrough (ENG)	A	M66	M	A	M	s87	s76		M78	M73	s64	M67	M	A	M	M		58	15
HAN Ünal	23/7/82	Kayserispor	A72		A	A	A				A46									11	3
AT Kahveci	23/11/79	Villarreal (ESP)	s42		A46			A	A90	A86	A		A	A82	A	A85	A	A117		59	17
ER Metin	14/10/74	Fenerbahçe /Larissa (GRE)	s46			s69	s46				s66		s60			M46			s92	26	7
KAN Yaman	27/8/82	Galatasaray	s69																	4	-
İL Altıntop	8/12/82	Schalke (GER)	s72	A	s61					A46		s65	s64							21	5
EYİN Çimşir	26/5/79	Trabzonspor	s74																	27	-
DENİZ deniz	11/1/80	Trabzonspor /Rubin (RUS)	s82	s52	M61		M65		s90	s86		s46		s89		M46		s117	s84	50	6
AN Arıkan	17/8/82	Beşiktaş		G	G	G17														4	-
VET Çetin	17/3/81	Galatasaray		D	D	D	D	D	D	D	D			D	D	D	D			32	1
AN Şükür	1/9/71	Galatasaray		A			s65													112	51
AN Akman	23/2/77	Galatasaray		s30	M67								s46	s78					M81	12	-
İZ Barış	2/7/77	Fenerbahçe		s66																21	-
E Aşık	13/12/73	Ankaraspor			D			D	D				D		s55	D	s63	D		31	2
MET Aurélio	15/12/77	Fenerbahçe			M	M	M	M	M	M	M46	M		M87	M	M	M		M	23	1
DAR Özkan	1/1/87	Beşiktaş			s67						M61									1	-
UK İnan	10/2/85	Manisaspor				M46														1	-
KAN Demirel	27/10/81	Fenerbahçe				s17	G	G		G			G	G	G	G	G			24	-
T Karan	1/10/76	Galatasaray				s46	A46													10	3
HİM Kaş	20/9/86	Beşiktaş						D15				D46								2	-
AN Balta	23/3/83	Galatasaray						D	D	D46	D	D78	D	D	D	D	D	D	D	13	1
İH Şentürk	29/4/83	Fenerbahçe						A67	A61			A65		s82	s76	s46	A46	s76	A	9	4
HAN Gönül	4/1/85	Fenerbahçe						s15	D	D	s78									4	-
UF Şimşek	20/7/75	Denizlispor						s67												1	-
TÜ Reçber	10/5/73	Beşiktaş							G			G						G	G	118	-
IRAY Baştürk	24/12/78	Stuttgart (GER)								M46			M64							49	2
R Boral	14/4/82	Fenerbahçe								s46		s78						s61	M84	10	1
MET Yıldız	14/9/81	Sivasspor								s46										2	-
MET Topal	3/3/86	Galatasaray								s78	M	M46	M	s87		s46	M57	M76	D	9	-
GA Zengin	10/10/83	Trabzonspor									G									2	-
HUN Gülselam	25/12/87	Unterhaching (GER)									D									1	-
UK Şahin	31/1/81	Fenerbahçe									s46									16	-
LÜT Erdinç	25/2/87	Sochaux (FRA)									s46	A46	s86	A75	A46				s81	6	-
E Güngör	1/8/84	Galatasaray										D					D63			2	-
IM Kazım	26/8/86	Fenerbahçe										M	M46	s75	M	s85	s57	M61	M92	9	-

Sivasspor, remarkably, led at Christmas before their inevitable decline, which included home defeats against all three Istanbul giants in the spring. Despite finishing level on points with both second-placed Fenerbahçe and third-placed Beşiktaş they were left with only a UEFA Intertoto Cup place for their troubles. Kayserispor qualified for the UEFA Cup by winning a marathon Turkish Cup final penalty-shoot-out 11-10 after a goalless draw against Gençlerbirliği SK. It was the club's first major honour.

DOMESTIC LEAGUE 2007/08

SÜPER LIG FINAL TABLE

	Pld	Home					Away					Total					Pts
		W	D	L	F	A	W	D	L	F	A	W	D	L	F	A	
1 Galatasaray AŞ	34	13	3	1	35	10	11	4	2	29	13	24	7	3	64	23	79
2 Fenerbahçe SK	34	14	2	1	42	18	8	5	4	30	19	22	7	5	72	37	73
3 Beşiktaş JK	34	11	3	3	33	15	12	1	4	25	17	23	4	7	58	32	73
4 Sivasspor	34	13	1	3	33	17	10	3	4	24	12	23	4	7	57	29	73
5 Kayserispor	34	11	3	3	33	13	4	7	6	17	18	15	10	9	50	31	55
6 Trabzonspor	34	10	3	4	28	19	4	4	9	16	20	14	7	13	44	39	49
7 Denizlispor	34	9	2	6	28	20	4	4	9	20	28	13	6	15	48	48	45
8 MKE Ankaragücü	34	7	6	4	19	21	4	4	9	17	23	11	10	13	36	44	43
9 Gaziantepspor	34	8	6	3	21	19	3	4	10	15	26	11	10	13	36	45	43
10 Ankaraspor AŞ	34	6	7	4	17	14	4	4	9	18	24	10	11	13	35	38	41
11 Gençlerbirliği OFTAŞ SK	34	4	6	7	14	18	6	4	7	16	18	10	10	14	30	36	40
12 İstanbul BB SK	34	8	2	7	23	18	2	6	9	21	29	10	8	16	44	47	38
13 Bursaspor	34	6	7	4	16	14	3	4	10	15	26	9	11	14	31	40	38
14 Konyaspor	34	8	4	5	25	23	2	2	13	12	41	10	6	18	37	64	36
15 Gençlerbirliği SK	34	7	1	9	27	25	2	7	8	17	26	9	8	17	44	51	35
16 Vestel Manisaspor	34	5	6	6	21	22	2	2	13	21	40	7	8	19	42	62	29
17 Rizespor	34	5	4	8	19	28	2	4	11	13	36	7	8	19	32	64	29
18 Kasımpaşa	34	4	4	9	14	24	4	1	12	12	32	8	5	21	26	56	29

N.B. Gençlerbirliği OFTAŞ SK renamed Hacettepe SK for 2008/09 season.

TOP GOALSCORERS

17 SEMİH Şentürk (Fenerbahçe)

15 Filip HOLOŠKO (Manisaspor/Beşiktaş)

14 ALEX de Souza (Fenerbahçe)
Antonio DE NIGRIS (Ankaraspor/Gaziantepspor)
MEHMET Yıldız (Sivasspor)
UMUT Bulut (Trabzonspor)

11 DEIVID de Souza (Fenerbahçe)
GÖKDENİZ Karadeniz (Trabzons
GÖKHAN Ünal (Kayserispor)
HAKAN Şükür (Galatasaray)
Mateja KEŽMAN (Fenerbahçe)
NECATI Ates (Ankaraspor/İstanbul BB)
Shabani NONDA (Galatasaray)
ÜMİT Karan (Galatasaray)

CLUB-BY-CLUB

MKE ANKARAGÜCÜ

Coach – Hans-Peter Briegel (GER); (26/10/07) Hakan Kutlu

Founded – 1910

MAJOR HONOURS: Turkish Cup - (2) 1972, 1981.

2007				
11/8	Ankaraspor	a	2-1	*Yasin, Ahmet*
19/8	Denizlispor	h	3-2	*Kiriță (p), Murat* Duruer, *Bebbe*
26/8	Galatasaray	a	0-1	
1/9	Gençlerbirliği	h	2-2	*Murat Duruer, Kiriță*
16/9	Trabzonspor	a	0-0	
21/9	İstanbul BB	h	1-0	*Elyasa*
28/9	Fenerbahçe	a	0-2	
7/10	Sivasspor	h	2-2	*Kiriță, Jaba*
22/10	Gençlerbirliği OFTAŞ	a	1-2	*Jaba*
28/10	Rizespor	h	1-0	*Burak*
4/11	Bursaspor	a	1-2	*Jaba*
10/11	Gaziantepspor	h	1-0	*Murat Erdoğan*
25/11	Manisaspor	h	1-0	*Kiriță (p)*
1/12	Konyaspor	a	0-1	
8/12	Kasımpaşa	h	2-2	*Murat Erdoğan, Jaba*
16/12	Beşiktaş	a	1-3	*Bebbe*
22/12	Kayserispor	h	1-1	*Bebbe*
2008				
13/1	Ankaraspor	h	1-1	*Gökhan*
20/1	Denizlispor	a	1-1	*Diawara (p)*
27/1	Galatasaray	h	0-4	
10/2	Gençlerbirliği	a	0-1	
17/2	Trabzonspor	h	0-2	
24/2	İstanbul BB	a	2-1	*Bebbe, Kiriță*
1/3	Fenerbahçe	h	0-0	
9/3	Sivasspor	a	2-3	*Elyasa, Jaba (p)*
16/3	Gençlerbirliği OFTAŞ	h	2-0	*Murat Erdoğan, Jaba*
23/3	Rizespor	a	0-0	
30/3	Bursaspor	h	2-0	*Diawara, Tevfik*
6/4	Gaziantepspor	a	1-2	*Gökhan*
13/4	Manisaspor	a	2-1	*Jaba, Murat Erdoğan*
19/4	Konyaspor	h	0-3	
26/4	Kasımpaşa	a	2-2	*Jaba, Elyasa*
4/5	Beşiktaş	h	0-2	
10/5	Kayserispor	a	2-0	*Bebbe, Cem*

o	Name	Nat	Pos	Aps	(s)	Gls
3	ABDULKADİR Kayalı		M	1		
5	Augustine AHINFUL	GHA	A	2	(7)	
	AHMET Dursun		A	6	(3)	1
	Gustavo BEBBE	CMR	A	32	(1)	5
8	BURAK Karaduman		M	6	(1)	1
0	CEM Can		M	33		1
	André DA SILVA	BRA	M	17	(2)	
4	Kaba DIAWARA	GUI	A	1	(10)	2
	ELYASA Süme		D	26	(1)	3
	EMRE Güngör		D	12		
7	ENGİN Aktürk		D	2	(4)	
5	GÖKHAN Emreciksin		A	17		2
5	İBRAHİM Ege		M	18	(4)	
9	İLKEM Özkaynak		D	32		
9	JABA De Carvalho	BRA	A	19	(8)	8
	Giani Stelian KIRIŢĂ	ROU	M	23	(1)	5
	Andrés LAMAS	URU	D	13		
0	MATEUS Alonso	BRA	M	1		
0	MERT Erdoğan		M	1	(1)	
3	MURAT Duruer		M	21	(12)	2
3	MURAT Erdoğan		M	22	(8)	4
0	MUSTAFA Özkan		M	4	(6)	
	ONUR Acar		M		(1)	
3	Gediminas PAULAUSKAS	LTU	D	1		
4	Ibrahim SAID	EGY	D	3	(6)	
	SERKAN Kırıntılı		G	31		
5	ŞEVKİ Koç		M		(3)	
7	TEVFİK Altındağ		D		(8)	1
5	TOLGA Doğantez		D	12		
2	YASİN Çelik		M	15	(2)	1
2	ZAFER Özgültekin		G	3	(1)	

ANKARASPOR AŞ

:oach – Aykut Kocaman; (17/10/07) Hikmet Karaman; (6/3/08) Safet Sušić (BIH)

Founded - 1978

07

/8	Ankaragücü	h	1-2	*Tayfun*
/8	Manisaspor	a	1-2	*Ediz*
/8	Konyaspor	h	1-1	*Murat Tosun*
9	Kasımpaşa	a	1-3	*Tevfik (p)*
/9	Beşiktaş	h	0-0	
/9	Kayserispor	a	1-3	*Necati*
/9	Gaziantepspor	a	0-1	
10	Denizlispor	h	0-0	
/10	Galatasaray	a	0-0	
/10	Gençlerbirliği	h	2-0	*Mehmet, Ferdi*
11	Trabzonspor	a	1-2	*og (Hüseyin)*
/11	İstanbul BB	h	1-1	*Tita*
/11	Fenerbahçe	a	2-4	*Mehmet 2*
12	Sivasspor	h	2-0	*Necati, Tita*
12	Gençlerbirliği OFTAŞ	a	0-0	
/12	Rizespor	h	1-2	*Necati*
/12	Bursaspor	a	0-0	

08

/1	Ankaragücü	a	1-1	*Murat Tosun*
/1	Manisaspor	h	1-0	*Adem*
/1	Konyaspor	a	3-1	*De Nigris, Bilal, Tita (p)*
/2	Kasımpaşa	h	2-0	*Emre, Murat Akyüz*
/2	Beşiktaş	a	2-3	*De Nigris 2*
/2	Kayserispor	h	0-3	
3	Gaziantepspor	h	1-1	*Adem*
3	Denizlispor	a	0-1	
/3	Galatasaray	h	0-1	
/3	Gençlerbirliği	a	3-1	*De Nigris 2, Murat Tosun*
/3	Trabzonspor	h	1-0	*Mehmet*
4	İstanbul BB	a	1-0	*Mehmet*
13/4	Fenerbahçe	h	2-2	*Hamilton, Mehmet*
19/4	Sivasspor	a	1-2	*Erhan*
26/4	Gençlerbirliği OFTAŞ	h	1-0	*Mehmet*
3/5	Rizespor	a	1-0	*De Nigris*
10/5	Bursaspor	h	1-1	*Erhan*

No	Name	Nat	Pos	Aps	(s)	Gls
66	ADEM Koçak		M	33	(1)	2
7	ANIL Taşdemir		M	2	(2)	
30	Radoslav BATAK	MNE	D	15		
19	BİLAL Kısa		M	15	(8)	1
23	Antonio DE NIGRIS	MEX	A	16		6
16	EDİZ Bahtiyaroğlu		D	6	(7)	1
21	EMRE Aşık		D	26		1
61	EREN Aydın		D	1	(3)	
3	ERHAN Albayrak		M	27	(1)	2
48	EVREN Özyiğit		G	1		
53	FERDİ Elmas		A		(9)	1
38	FIRAT Akkoyun		D	2	(1)	
32	HAMILTON Calheiros Ferre	BRA	D	14	(1)	1
50	HÜRRİYET Güçer		M	27	(2)	
10	MEHMET Yılmaz		A	26	(5)	7
4	MUHAMMET HANİFİ Yoldaş		D	8	(3)	
11	MURAT Akyüz		D	13	(4)	1
9	MURAT Tosun		A	8	(13)	3
79	Duarte NECA	POR	M	3	(7)	
35	NECATİ Ateş		A	13	(1)	3
6	ORHAN Ak		D	7	(5)	
20	ÖZER Hurmacı		M	19	(8)	
1	RAMAZAN Kurşunlu		G	4		
2	Fredrik RISP	SWE	D	12		
34	Štefan SENECKÝ	SVK	G	29		
33	TAYFUN Türkmen		A	19	(11)	1
18	TEVFİK Köse		A	1	(6)	1
8	TITA dos Santos	BRA	A	27	(1)	3
37	UĞUR Demirkol		D		(1)	

BEŞİKTAŞ JK

Coach – Ertuğrul Sağlam

Founded – 1903

MAJOR HONOURS: Turkish League - (12) 1957, 1958, 1960, 1966, 1967, 1982, 1986, 1990, 1991, 1992, 1995, 2003; Turkish Cup - (7) 1975, 1989, 1990, 1994, 1998, 2006, 2007.

2007

11/8	Konyaspor	h	1-0	*Bobô*
19/8	Kasımpaşa	a	2-1	*İbrahim Toraman, Ricardinho*
25/8	Gaziantepspor	a	1-0	*Batuhan*
1/9	Kayserispor	h	0-0	
15/9	Ankaraspor	a	0-0	
22/9	Denizlispor	h	3-2	*Tello 2, Bobô*
29/9	Galatasaray	a	1-2	*Tello*
7/10	Gençlerbirliği	h	1-0	*Nobre*
20/10	Trabzonspor	a	3-2	*Burak, Delgado (p), Bobô*
28/10	İstanbul BB	h	0-0	
3/11	Fenerbahçe	a	1-2	*Bobô*
10/11	Sivasspor	h	1-2	*Bobô*
24/11	Gençlerbirliği OFTAŞ	a	1-0	*Bobô*
2/12	Rizespor	h	1-1	*Delgado*
7/12	Bursaspor	a	1-0	*Delgado*
16/12	Ankaragücü	h	3-1	*Tello, Serdar Özkan, Delgado*
21/12	Manisaspor	a	2-1	*Bobô 2 (1p)*

2008

12/1	Konyaspor	a	2-1	*İbrahim Toraman, Nobre*
19/1	Kasımpaşa	h	4-2	*Nobre 2, Cissé, Delgado*

26/1	Gaziantepspor	h	3-1	*Cissé, Nobre, Ricardinho*
9/2	Kayserispor	a	0-2	
16/2	Ankaraspor	h	3-2	*Nobre, Hološko, İbrahim Toraman*
22/2	Denizlispor	a	2-1	*Hološko, Nobre*
2/3	Galatasaray	h	1-0	*Nobre*
7/3	Gençlerbirliği	a	2-1	*İbrahim Toraman, Bobô*
16/3	Trabzonspor	h	3-0	*Nobre, Delgado, Aydın*
22/3	İstanbul BB	a	1-2	*Hološko*
29/3	Fenerbahçe	h	1-2	*Serdar Özkan*
6/4	Sivasspor	a	2-1	*Hološko 2*
11/4	Gençlerbirliği OFTAŞ	h	0-1	
20/4	Rizespor	a	2-1	*İbrahim Kaş, Delgado*
26/4	Bursaspor	h	3-0	*Serdar Özkan, Hološko, Bobô*
4/5	Ankaragücü	a	2-0	*Delgado (p), Tello*
10/5	Manisaspor	h	5-1	*Nobre, İbrahim Kaş 2, Ali, Hološko*

No	Name	Nat	Pos	Aps	(s)	Gls
22	ALİ Tandoğan		M	21	(4)	1
20	AYDIN Karabulut		M	6	(7)	1
8	BAKİ Mercimek		D	10	(1)	
99	BATUHAN Karadeniz		A		(11)	1
13	Deivson Rogério da Silva "BOBÔ"	BRA	A	17	(4)	10
7	BURAK Yılmaz		M	5	(4)	1
90	BÜLENT Uzun		D		(1)	
18	Édouard CISSÉ	FRA	M	23	(2)	2
10	Matías DELGADO	ARG	M	25	(4)	8
15	Lamine DIATTA	SEN	D	3	(3)	
39	EMİR Gökçe		A		(2)	
5	GÖKHAN Zan		D	19	(1)	
84	HAKAN Arıkan		G	12	(2)	
9	Federico HIGUAÍN	ARG	A	4	(5)	
23	Filip HOLOŠKO	SVK	A	16		7
55	İBRAHİM Akın		M	1	(5)	
78	İBRAHİM Kaş		D	13	(2)	3
58	İBRAHİM Toraman		D	31		4
19	İBRAHİM Üzülmez		D	31		
41	KORAY Avcı		M	8	(7)	
3	MEHMET Sedef		M	1	(6)	
6	MEHMET Yozgatlı		M	2	(6)	
11	Márcio (Mert) NOBRE	BRA	A	26	(4)	10
17	RICARDINHO Rodrigues	BRA	M	7	(6)	2
1	RÜŞTÜ Reçber		G	22		
24	Gordon SCHILDENFELD	CRO	D	7	(2)	
2	SERDAR Kurtuluş		D	9	(6)	
21	SERDAR Özkan		M	26	(2)	3
14	Rodrigo TELLO	CHI	M	29		5

BURSASPOR

Coach – Bülent Korkmaz; (25/10/07) Samet Aybaba

Founded – 1963

MAJOR HONOURS: Turkish Cup – (1) 1986.

2007				
12/8	Denizlispor	a	0-0	
19/8	Galatasaray	h	0-1	
25/8	Gençlerbirliği	a	3-1	*Sinan 3*
31/8	Trabzonspor	h	1-1	*Yenal*
16/9	İstanbul BB	a	0-1	
23/9	Fenerbahçe	h	1-1	*Tum*
30/9	Sivasspor	a	2-3	*Veli, Cihan*
6/10	Gençlerbirliği OFTAŞ	h	1-1	*Mustafa*
20/10	Rizespor	a	0-2	
27/10	Gaziantepspor	h	1-1	*Šumulikoski*
4/11	Ankaragücü	h	2-1	*Šumulikoski, Tum*
10/11	Manisaspor	a	1-1	*Tum*
25/11	Konyaspor	h	1-0	*Mustafa*
1/12	Kasımpaşa	a	2-0	*Volkan Şen, Sercan*
7/12	Beşiktaş	h	0-1	
16/12	Kayserispor	a	1-4	*Volkan Şen*
23/12	Ankaraspor	h	0-0	
2008				
13/1	Denizlispor	h	1-1	*Eser*
20/1	Galatasaray	a	0-1	
28/1	Gençlerbirliği	h	2-1	*Veli, Tum*
10/2	Trabzonspor	a	1-2	*Tum*
16/2	İstanbul BB	h	2-2	*Mustafa, Zúñiga*
23/2	Fenerbahçe	a	2-0	*Sinan 2 (1p)*
2/3	Sivasspor	h	0-1	
9/3	Gençlerbirliği OFTAŞ	a	2-2	*Egemen, Flores*
15/3	Rizespor	h	2-1	*Ömer Erdoğan, Mustaf*
22/3	Gaziantepspor	a	0-1	
30/3	Ankaragücü	a	0-2	
6/4	Manisaspor	h	1-0	*Eser*
13/4	Konyaspor	a	0-2	
19/4	Kasımpaşa	h	1-0	*Tum*
26/4	Beşiktaş	a	0-3	
4/5	Kayserispor	h	0-1	
10/5	Ankaraspor	a	1-1	*Zúñiga*

No	Name	Nat	Pos	Aps	(s)	Gls
22	CİHAN Haspolatlı		D	20	(6)	1
50	Lamine CISSÉ	GUI	M		(2)	
16	EGEMEN Korkmaz		D	25		1
89	Ghislain EMO	CMR	A		(1)	
17	EREN Albayrak		M		(2)	
24	ESER Yağmur		A	4	(11)	2
27	Ronald FLORES	BOL	A	5	(1)	1
58	İBRAHİM Dağaşan		M		(3)	
3	İSMAİL Güldüren		D	25	(1)	
87	KORAY Öztürk		D	2	(1)	
12	Collins MBESUMA	ZAM	A		(6)	
15	MUSTAFA Sarp		M	29		4
7	ORHAN Alemdar		M		(2)	
6	OZAN Has		M	17	(5)	
2	ÖMER Barış		D	18	(4)	
4	ÖMER Erdoğan		D	31		1
26	ÖZGÜR Göktaş		D	6	(3)	
9	Daniel PANCU	ROU	M	9	(3)	
25	Maxim ROMASHCHENKO	BLR	M	10	(2)	
14	SERCAN Yıldırım		A	4	(4)	1
21	SERKAN Kurtuluş		M	7	(1)	
11	SİNAN Kaloğlu		A	11	(9)	5
18	Velice ŠUMULIKOSKI	MKD	M	17		2
34	Hervé TUM	CMR	A	26	(2)	6
39	ÜMİT Aydın		M	4	(1)	
5	Jason VANDELANNOITE	BEL	D	7	(2)	
23	Renny VEGA	VEN	G	22		
8	VELİ Acar		M	30	(1)	2
47	VOLKAN Bekiroğlu		M	4	(4)	
20	VOLKAN Şen		M	16	(9)	2
1	YAVUZ Eraydın		G	12		
28	YENAL Tuncer		D	8	(7)	1
99	Ysrael ZÚÑIGA	PER	A	5	(5)	2

DENİZLİSPOR

Coach – Güvenç Kurtar; (15/5/08) Tuncay Özbek

Founded - 1966

2007				
12/8	Bursaspor	h	0-0	
19/8	Ankaragücü	a	2-3	*Selahattin, Musa*
26/8	Manisaspor	h	3-2	*Júlio César, Kratochvíl, Yusuf*
1/9	Konyaspor	a	2-2	*Yusuf 2*
15/9	Kasımpaşa	h	0-1	
22/9	Beşiktaş	a	2-3	*Fatih Egedik 2*

)/9	Kayserispor	h	2-0	*Kratochvíl (p), Bülent*
'10	Ankaraspor	a	0-0	
)/10	Gaziantepspor	a	2-1	*Kratochvíl (p), Yusuf*
3/10	Galatasaray	h	1-2	*Kratochvíl (p)*
'11	Gençlerbirliği	a	2-1	*Yusuf (p), Serhat*
'11	Trabzonspor	h	2-0	*Serhat, Yusuf*
4/11	İstanbul BB	a	2-0	*Yusuf, Hasan*
'12	Fenerbahçe	h	0-1	
'12	Sivasspor	a	0-2	
5/12	Gençlerbirliği OFTAŞ	h	2-1	*Caner 2*
3/12	Rizespor	a	0-2	
)08				
3/1	Bursaspor	a	1-1	*Kratochvíl*
)/1	Ankaragücü	h	1-1	*Gökhan*
'/1	Manisaspor	a	2-3	*Kratochvíl, Fatih Yiğen*
'/2	Konyaspor	h	2-1	*Selahattin, Kotchoni*
'/2	Kasımpaşa	a	0-1	
!/2	Beşiktaş	h	1-2	*Serhat*
3	Kayserispor	a	1-1	*Fatih Egedik*
3	Ankaraspor	h	1-0	*Hasan*
5/3	Gaziantepspor	h	2-1	*Carlos Alberto, Serhat*
3/3	Galatasaray	a	1-2	*Hasan*
'/3	Gençlerbirliği	h	3-2	*Serhat, Yusuf, Carlos Alberto*
4	Trabzonspor	a	0-2	
!/4	İstanbul BB	h	2-3	*Yusuf (p), Selahattin*
'/4	Fenerbahçe	a	1-4	*Güray*
/4	Sivasspor	h	1-2	*Yusuf*
5	Gençlerbirliği OFTAŞ	a	2-0	*og (İlhan), Hasan*
'/5	Rizespor	h	5-1	*Engin 2, Güray 2, Fatih Yiğen*

)	Name	Nat	Pos	Aps	(s)	Gls
	Tomáš ABRAHAM	CZE	M	33		
	ALİ Helvacı		A		(1)	
	ALLYSON Araújo	BRA	D	15		
	BULUT Basmaz		G	1		
	BURAK Akyıldız		D	11	(2)	
	BÜLENT Ertuğrul		D	16		1
	CANER Celep		M	7	(15)	2
	CARLOS ALBERTO	BRA	M	13	(6)	2
	ÇAĞLAR Birinci		M	11	(6)	
	ENGİN Memişler		A	3	(15)	2
	FATİH Egedik		M	16	(12)	3
	FATİH Yiğen		M	23	(6)	2
	GÖKHAN Güleç		A	11	(2)	1
	Papa GUEYE	SEN	M		(1)	
	GÜRAY Vural		M	13	(2)	3
	Souleymanou HAMIDOU	CMR	G	24		
	HASAN Yiğit		D	17	(2)	4
	İLKAY Demir		A		(1)	
	JÚLIO CÉSAR	BRA	M	18	(5)	1
	Christian KOTCHONI	BEN	A	6	(3)	1
	Roman KRATOCHVÍL	SVK	D	22		6
	MURAT Karakoç		M	11	(6)	
	MUSA Kuş		M	9	(6)	1
	SELAHATTİN Kınalı		A	18	(3)	3
	SERHAT Gülpınar		M	23	(4)	5
	SÜLEYMAN Görgün		M		(1)	
	SÜLEYMAN Küçük		G	9	(1)	
	YUSUF Şimşek		M	25		10
	ZAFER Demir		M	19		

FENERBAHÇE SK

Coach – Artur Antunes Coimbra "Zico" (BRA)

Founded – 1907

AJOR HONOURS: Turkish League - (17) 1959, 1961, 1964, 1965, 1968, 70, 1974, 1975, 1978, 1983, 1985, 1989, 1996, 2001, 2004, 2005, 2007; Turkish Cup - (4) 1968, 1974, 1979, 1983.

2007				
10/8	İstanbul BB	a	0-2	
18/8	Gaziantepspor	h	2-1	*Kemal, Semih*
25/8	Sivasspor	h	1-0	*Roberto Carlos*
2/9	Gençlerbirliği OFTAŞ	a	1-1	*Alex*
15/9	Rizespor	h	1-1	*Kežman*
23/9	Bursaspor	a	1-1	*Semih*
28/9	Ankaragücü	h	2-0	*Marco Aurélio, Ali*
6/10	Manisaspor	a	1-1	*Marco Aurélio*
20/10	Konyaspor	h	4-1	*Semih, Alex, Wederson, Edu Dracena*
27/10	Kasımpaşa	a	2-1	*Tümer, Deivid*
3/11	Beşiktaş	h	2-1	*Deivid, Semih*
11/11	Kayserispor	a	1-2	*Semih*
24/11	Ankaraspor	h	4-2	*Alex 3, Semih*
1/12	Denizlispor	a	1-0	*Ali*
8/12	Galatasaray	h	2-0	*Semih, Deivid*
16/12	Gençlerbirliği	a	2-1	*Semih 2*
22/12	Trabzonspor	h	3-2	*Deivid, Semih, Alex*
2008				
13/1	İstanbul BB	h	2-2	*Edu Dracena, Deivid*
20/1	Gaziantepspor	a	5-0	*Kemal, Alex, og (Metin), Deivid 2*
27/1	Sivasspor	a	4-1	*Alex, Semih, Kežman 2*
10/2	Gençlerbirliği OFTAŞ	h	3-1	*Alex (p), Kežman, Roberto Carlos*
15/2	Rizespor	a	4-2	*Deivid, Kežman 2, Selçuk*
23/2	Bursaspor	h	0-2	
1/3	Ankaragücü	a	0-0	
9/3	Manisaspor	h	4-1	*Marco Aurélio, Kežman 2, Selçuk*
16/3	Konyaspor	a	4-1	*Semih 2, Kežman 2*
21/3	Kasımpaşa	h	3-0	*Alex, Semih, Deivid*
29/3	Beşiktaş	a	2-1	*Alex 2*
5/4	Kayserispor	h	2-1	*Alex (p), Semih*
13/4	Ankaraspor	a	2-2	*Alex, Wederson*
19/4	Denizlispor	h	4-1	*Kežman, Deivid, og (Murat), Semih*
27/4	Galatasaray	a	0-1	
4/5	Gençlerbirliği	h	3-2	*Edu Dracena, Semih, Deivid*
10/5	Trabzonspor	a	0-2	

No	Name	Nat	Pos	Aps	(s)	Gls
20	ALEX de Souza	BRA	M	27	(1)	14
18	ALİ Bilgin		M	6	(13)	2
4	Stephen APPIAH	GHA	M	2	(4)	
17	CAN Arat		D	3	(2)	
99	DEIVID de Souza	BRA	A	28	(3)	11
24	DENİZ Barış		M	8		
36	EDU de Souza DRACENA	BRA	D	29		3
77	GÖKHAN Gönül		D	23	(1)	
32	GÜRHAN Gürsoy		M		(3)	
38	İLHAN Parlak		A	1	(4)	
8	KAZIM Kazım		M	10	(18)	
7	KEMAL Aslan		M	6	(2)	2
9	Mateja KEŽMAN	SRB	A	17	(5)	11
2	Diego LUGANO	URU	D	23		
33	Claudio MALDONADO	CHI	M	6	(2)	
15	MARCO (Mehmet) AURÉLIO		M	29	(2)	3
19	ÖNDER Turacı		D	12		
3	ROBERTO CARLOS da Silva	BRA	D	22		2
21	SELÇUK Şahin		M	17	(5)	2
23	SEMİH Şentürk		A	17	(10)	17
22	SERDAR Kulbilge		G	10		
11	TÜMER Metin		M	4	(2)	1
25	UĞUR Boral		M	21	(4)	
1	VOLKAN Demirel		G	24	(1)	
6	WEDERSON da Silva	BRA	M	17	(10)	2
5	YASİN Çakmak		D	12	(3)	

GALATASARAY AŞ

Coach – Karl Heinz Feldkamp (GER); (6/4/08) Cevat Güler

Founded – 1905

MAJOR HONOURS: UEFA Cup - (1) 2000; UEFA Super Cup - (1) 2000; Turkish League - (17) 1962, 1963, 1969, 1971, 1972, 1973, 1987, 1988, 1993, 1994, 1997, 1998, 1999, 2000, 2002, 2006, 2008; Turkish Cup - (14) 1963, 1964, 1965, 1966, 1973, 1976, 1982, 1985, 1991, 1993, 1996, 1999, 2000, 2005.

2007				
12/8	Rizespor	h	4-0	*Lincoln, Volkan, Hakan Şükür 2*
19/8	Bursaspor	a	1-0	*Ümit*
26/8	Ankaragücü	h	1-0	*Lincoln*
2/9	Manisaspor	a	2-2	*Ümit (p), Hakan Şükür*
16/9	Konyaspor	h	6-0	*Nonda 2 (1 p), Carrusca, Hakan Şükür, Ümit, Hasan*
23/9	Kasımpaşa	a	1-0	*Ümit*
29/9	Beşiktaş	h	2-1	*Hakan Balta, Nonda (p)*
7/10	Kayserispor	a	1-1	*Ümit*
21/10	Ankaraspor	h	0-0	
28/10	Denizlispor	a	2-1	*Nonda 2 (1 p)*
4/11	Gaziantepspor	a	1-1	*Servet*
11/11	Gençlerbirliği	h	3-2	*Mehmet Topal, Serkan, Lincoln*
25/11	Trabzonspor	a	1-0	*Serkan*
2/12	İstanbul BB	h	2-2	*Hakan Balta, Ümit*
8/12	Fenerbahçe	a	0-2	
14/12	Sivasspor	h	2-0	*Nonda, Barış*
23/12	Gençlerbirliği OFTAŞ	a	0-0	
2008				
12/1	Rizespor	a	5-2	*Nonda 3, Servet, Arda*
20/1	Bursaspor	h	1-0	*Nonda*
27/1	Ankaragücü	a	4-0	*Hakan Şükür, Arda, Ümit, Serkan*
9/2	Manisaspor	h	6-3	*Barış, Arda (p), Hakan Şükür 3, Ümit*
18/2	Konyaspor	a	1-0	*Ümit*
24/2	Kasımpaşa	h	0-1	
2/3	Beşiktaş	a	0-1	
8/3	Kayserispor	h	2-0	*Sabri, Ümit*
15/3	Ankaraspor	a	1-0	*Ümit*
23/3	Denizlispor	h	2-1	*Okan, Servet*
30/3	Gaziantepspor	h	0-0	
6/4	Gençlerbirliği	a	1-0	*Lincoln*
12/4	Trabzonspor	h	1-0	*Arda*
20/4	İstanbul BB	a	3-0	*og (Kerim), Lincoln, Hakan Şükür*
27/4	Fenerbahçe	h	1-0	*Nonda*
4/5	Sivasspor	a	5-3	*Arda 3, Ayhan, Hakan Şükür*
10/5	Gençlerbirliği OFTAŞ	h	2-0	*Hakan Şükür, Hakan Balta*

No	Name	Nat	Pos	Aps	(s)	Gls
66	ARDA Turan		M	29	(1)	7
18	AYHAN Akman		M	13	(4)	1
1	AYKUT Erçetin		G	13		
8	BARIŞ Özbek		M	22	(8)	2
15	Ahmed BARUSSO	GHA	M	1	(1)	
19	Ismael BOUZID	ALG	D	5	(5)	
16	Marcelo CARRUSCA	ARG	M	2	(1)	1
2	EMRE Güngör		D	15	(1)	
22	HAKAN Balta		D	21	(6)	3
9	HAKAN Şükür		A	21	(7)	11
11	HASAN Şaş		M	5	(5)	1
10	Cássio de Souza Soares "LINCOLN"	BRA	M	17	(2)	5
6	Tobias LINDEROTH	SWE	M	7		
87	MEHMET Güven		M	3	(9)	
14	MEHMET Topal		M	22	(4)	1
20	Shabani NONDA	COD	A	16	(8)	11
7	OKAN Buruk		M	3	(1)	1
54	ORKUN Usak		G	21		
55	SABRİ Sarıoğlu		M	18	(4)	1
61	SERKAN Çalık		M	6	(11)	3
76	SERVET Çetin		D	33		3
4	Rigobert SONG	CMR	D	20	(2)	
33	UĞUR Uçar		D	17	(4)	
99	ÜMİT Karan		A	24	(6)	11
74	VOLKAN Yaman		D	20	(7)	1

GAZİANTEPSPOR

Coach – Mesut Bakkal; (3/1/08) Bünyamin Süral; (7/2/08) Nurullah Sağlam

Founded – 1969

2007				
12/8	Kasımpaşa	h	2-0	*Ali, Zurita*
18/8	Fenerbahçe	a	1-2	*De Nigris*
25/8	Beşiktaş	h	0-1	
2/9	Sivasspor	a	0-2	
16/9	Kayserispor	h	4-3	*De Nigris 3, Uğur*
23/9	Gençlerbirliği OFTAŞ	a	2-1	*Uğur (p), De Nigris*
30/9	Ankaraspor	h	1-0	*Uğur (p)*
7/10	Rizespor	a	1-2	*Ali Cansun*
20/10	Denizlispor	h	1-2	*De Nigris*
27/10	Bursaspor	a	1-1	*Erdal Kılıçaslan (p)*
4/11	Galatasaray	h	1-1	*Erdal Kılıçaslan*
10/11	Ankaragücü	a	0-1	
25/11	Gençlerbirliği	h	2-2	*Ali Cansun 2*
2/12	Manisaspor	a	0-1	
9/12	Trabzonspor	a	2-3	*Ekrem, De Nigris*
15/12	Konyaspor	h	2-1	*Murat, Ekrem*
23/12	İstanbul BB	a	2-1	*De Nigris, Murat*
2008				
12/1	Kasımpaşa	a	1-0	*Ekrem*
20/1	Fenerbahçe	h	0-5	
26/1	Beşiktaş	a	1-3	*Zurita*
10/2	Sivasspor	h	0-0	
17/2	Kayserispor	a	1-3	*Beto*
23/2	Gençlerbirliği OFTAŞ	h	1-1	*Beto*
2/3	Ankaraspor	a	1-1	*Ekrem*
9/3	Rizespor	h	1-1	*Beto*
16/3	Denizlispor	a	1-2	*Beto*
22/3	Bursaspor	h	1-0	*Bülent*
30/3	Galatasaray	a	0-0	
6/4	Ankaragücü	h	2-1	*Bülent 2*
12/4	Gençlerbirliği	a	0-2	
19/4	Manisaspor	h	1-0	*Erdal Kılıçaslan*
26/4	Trabzonspor	h	1-1	*Erdal Güneş*
4/5	Konyaspor	a	1-1	*Özgür*
10/5	İstanbul BB	h	1-0	*Beto*

No	Name	Nat	Pos	Aps	(s)	Gls
17	ALİ Bayraktar		A	4	(3)	1
29	ALİ CANSUN Begeçarslan		A	7	(7)	3
45	BARIŞ Durmaz		M	10		
4	BEKİR İrtegün		D	13	(2)	
25	BETO Soares da Silva	BRA	A	13		5
15	BÜLENT Bölükbaşı		M	11	(8)	3
9	Antonio DE NIGRIS	MEX	A	15		8
20	Manuel DÍAZ	CHI	A		(1)	
12	Armand DEUMI	CMR	D	29		
23	EKREM Dağ		M	27	(6)	4
14	ERDAL Güneş		A	4	(6)	1
21	ERDAL Kılıçaslan		A	11	(18)	3
67	ERGÜN Penbe		M	16	(1)	
26	FARUK Bayar		M		(2)	
52	FATİH Şen		M		(5)	
38	HASAN Yurt		M		(1)	

66	İLHAN Özbay		M	13		
2	İSMAİL Köybaşı		D	1		
37	IVAN Saraiva de Souza	BRA	M	6	(2)	
3	MEHMET Çoğum		D	14		
27	MEHMET Polat		D	26	(1)	
11	METİN Tuğlu		M	12	(2)	
5	MURAT Ceylan		D	23	(4)	2
34	MURAT Şahin		G	10		
10	OĞUZ Dağlaroğlu		G	5	(1)	
1	ÖMER Çatkıç		G	19		
61	ÖZCAN Polat		D		(1)	
30	ÖZGÜR Bayer		M	4	(1)	
36	ÖZGÜR Yıldırım		M	27	(3)	1
99	ÖZGÜRCAN Özcan		A	2	(7)	
24	SONER Örnek		M		(1)	
7	UĞUR Yıldırım		M	13	(1)	3
57	VOLKAN Arslan		M	18	(7)	
8	Cristian ZURITA	ARG	M	21	(8)	2

GENÇLERBİRLİĞİ SK

Coach – Fuat Çapa; (22/9/07) Reinhard Stumpf (GER); (1/11/07) Bülent Korkmaz; (31/1/08) Mesut Bakkal

Founded – 1923

MAJOR HONOURS: Turkish Cup - (2) 1987, 2001.

2007

12/8	Gençlerbirliği OFTAŞ	h	1-2	*Mehmet Çakır*
19/8	Rizespor	a	2-0	*Mehmet Çakır, Engin*
25/8	Bursaspor	h	1-3	*Tuna*
1/9	Ankaragücü	a	2-2	*Mehmet Çakır (p), Okan*
16/9	Manisaspor	h	0-2	
22/9	Konyaspor	a	1-1	*Okan*
30/9	Kasımpaşa	h	3-1	*Carle, Okan, Kahé (p)*
7/10	Beşiktaş	a	0-1	
20/10	Kayserispor	h	1-1	*Kahé*
27/10	Ankaraspor	a	0-2	
4/11	Denizlispor	h	1-2	*Promise*
11/11	Galatasaray	a	2-3	*Kerem, Tuna*
25/11	Gaziantepspor	a	2-2	*Mehmet Çakır, Erhan*
30/11	Trabzonspor	h	2-1	*Burhan, Promise*
9/12	İstanbul BB	a	0-0	
16/12	Fenerbahçe	h	1-2	*Burhan*
23/12	Sivasspor	a	0-2	

2008

12/1	Gençlerbirliği OFTAŞ	a	1-1	*Mehmet Çakır*
20/1	Rizespor	h	4-1	*Mehmet Çakır 2, Okan 2 (1p)*
28/1	Bursaspor	a	1-2	*Tuna*
10/2	Ankaragücü	h	1-0	*Promise*
17/2	Manisaspor	a	2-1	*Burhan, Promise*
23/2	Konyaspor	h	6-1	*Mehmet Nas, Okan 2, Engin, Promise, Burhan*
1/3	Kasımpaşa	a	0-0	
7/3	Beşiktaş	h	1-2	*Kerem*
15/3	Kayserispor	a	0-3	
23/3	Ankaraspor	h	1-3	*Mehmet Nas*
29/3	Denizlispor	a	2-3	*Okan, Promise*
6/4	Galatasaray	h	0-1	
12/4	Gaziantepspor	h	2-0	*og (Mehmet Çoğum), Kahé*
19/4	Trabzonspor	a	0-0	
26/4	İstanbul BB	h	2-1	*Kahé, Promise*
4/5	Fenerbahçe	a	2-3	*Kahé, Hakan*
10/5	Sivasspor	h	0-2	

No	Name	Nat	Pos	Aps	(s)	Gls
15	ADAMU Mohammed	GHA	M	1	(1)	
24	Daniel ADDO	GHA	D	3	(4)	
11	BURHAN Eşer		M	20	(7)	4
19	Nick CARLE	AUS	M	12	(2)	1
12	Abdel Zaher EL SAKA	EGY	D	16		
38	ENGİN Baytar		M	19	(8)	2
34	EREN Aydın		D	11	(3)	
3	ERGÜN Teber		D	9	(1)	
44	ERHAN Güven		D	21	(2)	1
6	ERKAN Özbey		D	15	(1)	
17	FERHAT Kiraz		M	3	(4)	
99	GÖKHAN Tokgöz		G	17		
25	HAKAN Aslantaş		M	10	(2)	1
8	KAHÉ de Souza	BRA	A	14	(12)	5
61	KEREM Şeras		M	23	(8)	2
54	MEHMET Akyüz		M		(5)	
10	MEHMET Çakır		A	26	(5)	7
7	MEHMET Nas		M	32	(1)	2
23	MUSTAFA Çiçek		M		(1)	
9	OKAN Öztürk		A	21	(9)	8
26	ONUR Garip		A		(1)	
22	Nicolás PERIC	CHI	G	7		
55	Nikola PETKOVIĆ	SRB	D	5	(1)	
14	Isaac PROMISE	NGA	A	21	(5)	7
1	RECEP Öztürk		G	10		
83	SANDRO Menconca	BRA	M	1	(2)	
20	SEDAT Yeşilkaya		M	6	(5)	
4	TOLGA Doğantez		D	13		
5	Lamine TRAORÉ	BFA	D	17	(1)	
35	TUNA Üzümcü		D	18	(6)	3
2	Marko ZORIĆ	SRB	D	3	(2)	

GENÇLERBİRLİĞİ OFTAŞ SK

Coach – Osman Özdemir

Founded - 2001

2007

12/8	Gençlerbirliği	a	2-1	*Serkan, Kemal*
17/8	Trabzonspor	h	0-2	
25/8	İstanbul BB	a	0-1	
2/9	Fenerbahçe	h	1-1	*Sterjovski*
15/9	Sivasspor	a	0-1	
23/9	Gaziantepspor	h	1-2	*Bülent*
29/9	Rizespor	h	2-0	*Sterjovski 2*
6/10	Bursaspor	a	1-1	*Bülent (p)*
22/10	Ankaragücü	h	2-1	*Savaş, Serkan*
27/10	Manisaspor	a	2-0	*Serkan, İbrahim*
3/11	Konyaspor	h	0-1	
10/11	Kasımpaşa	a	3-1	*Serkan, İbrahim, Bülent*
24/11	Beşiktaş	h	0-1	
2/12	Kayserispor	a	1-1	*İbrahim*
9/12	Ankaraspor	h	0-0	
16/12	Denizlispor	a	1-2	*Serkan*
23/12	Galatasaray	h	0-0	

2008

12/1	Gençlerbirliği	h	1-1	*Bülent*
19/1	Trabzonspor	a	2-1	*Sandro, İbrahim*
26/1	İstanbul BB	h	3-2	*Bülent, Sandro 2*
10/2	Fenerbahçe	a	1-3	*İlhan*
16/2	Sivasspor	h	0-1	
23/2	Gaziantepspor	a	1-1	*og (Ergün)*
2/3	Rizespor	a	0-0	
9/3	Bursaspor	h	2-2	*Sandro, Giray*
16/3	Ankaragücü	a	0-2	
22/3	Manisaspor	h	1-0	*Murat Kalkan*
30/3	Konyaspor	a	1-0	*Serkan*
5/4	Kasımpaşa	h	0-1	
11/4	Beşiktaş	a	1-0	*Kadir*
20/4	Kayserispor	h	1-1	*Serkan*
26/4	Ankaraspor	a	0-1	
3/5	Denizlispor	h	0-2	
10/5	Galatasaray	a	0-2	

No	Name	Nat	Pos	Aps	(s)	Gls
98	ALİ Bayraktar		A	7	(3)	
24	James BOADU	GHA	A	1	(2)	
34	BÜLENT Kocabey		M	6	(17)	5
44	CEVHER Toktaş		D	1	(2)	
7	ÇAĞATAY Tekin		M	1	(2)	
10	EREN Özen		M	1	(6)	
19	EVERTON da Silva	BRA	M	31	(1)	
1	FERHAT Odabaşı		G	5		
4	GİRAY Kaçar		D	30		1
16	HAKAN Aslantaş		M	11	(4)	
26	İBRAHİM Şahin		A	17	(3)	4
5	İLHAN Eker		D	30		1
17	Aleksandar JEVTIĆ	SRB	A		(6)	
20	KADİR Bekmezci		M	27	(3)	1
11	KEMAL Yıldırım		M	4		1
15	KENAN Çamoğlu		M		(1)	
69	MURAT Kalkan		M	23	(6)	1
3	MURAT Selvi		D	2	(4)	
23	OLGAY Coşkun		M	18	(8)	
67	ORHAN Şam		D	34		
55	Nikola PETKOVIĆ	SRB	D	10		
14	RECEP Biler		G	27		
99	SANDRO Menconca	BRA	M	25	(3)	4
8	SAVAŞ Esen		A	9	(12)	1
22	SERKAN Atak		M	32	(2)	7
9	Mile STERJOVSKI	AUS	A	12	(2)	3
77	UFUK Arslan		M	5	(3)	
90	ULAŞ Güler		G	2		
61	ÜMİT Tütünci		A	1		
30	Shaibu YAKUBU	GHA	A	2	(4)	

İSTANBUL BB SK

Coach – Abdullah Avcı

Founded - 1990

2007				
10/8	Fenerbahçe	h	2-0	*Kerim, Murat*
19/8	Sivasspor	a	1-2	*Gökhan*
25/8	Gençlerbirliği OFTAŞ	h	1-0	*İlyas*
1/9	Rizespor	a	1-3	*Uğur*
16/9	Bursaspor	h	1-0	*Vinícius*
21/9	Ankaragücü	a	0-1	
30/9	Manisaspor	h	4-1	*Sertan, Adriano 3*
7/10	Konyaspor	a	2-3	*Efe, Kerim*
20/10	Kasımpaşa	h	2-0	*Adriano,Órteman*
28/10	Beşiktaş	a	0-0	
4/11	Kayserispor	h	1-1	*İlyas*
10/11	Ankaraspor	a	1-1	*Adriano*
24/11	Denizlispor	h	0-2	
2/12	Galatasaray	a	2-2	*Vinícius, Sertan*
9/12	Gençlerbirliği	h	0-0	
15/12	Trabzonspor	a	1-2	*Erman (p)*
23/12	Gaziantepspor	h	1-2	*Vinícius*
2008				
13/1	Fenerbahçe	a	2-2	*İlyas, Gökhan*
19/1	Sivasspor	h	0-2	
26/1	Gençlerbirliği OFTAŞ	a	2-3	*Kerim, İlyas*
9/2	Rizespor	h	2-1	*İbrahim 2*
16/2	Bursaspor	a	2-2	*İbrahim, og (Mustafa)*
24/2	Ankaragücü	h	1-2	*Vinícius*
1/3	Manisaspor	a	1-1	*Necati*
8/3	Konyaspor	h	5-0	*Necati 2, İlyas, Vinícius, İbrahim*
16/3	Kasımpaşa	a	0-1	
22/3	Beşiktaş	h	2-1	*İbrahim, Necati*
30/3	Kayserispor	a	2-1	*Necati 2 (1p)*
6/4	Ankaraspor	h	0-1	
12/4	Denizlispor	a	3-2	*Necati 2, İlhan*
20/4	Galatasaray	h	0-3	
26/4	Gençlerbirliği	a	1-2	*İbrahim*
3/5	Trabzonspor	h	1-2	*Adriano*
10/5	Gaziantepspor	a	0-1	

No	Name	Nat	Pos	Aps	(s)	Gls
19	ADRIANO Nascimento	BRA	A	23	(6)	6
27	AYDIN Yılmaz		M	3	(4)	
6	EFE İnanç		M	27	(2)	1
17	EKREM Ekşioğlu		D	27		
20	ERMAN Kılıç		M	17	(16)	1
2	EROL Durbakan		D		(1)	
9	GÖKHAN Kaba		A	5	(6)	2
34	HALUK Güngör		G	3	(3)	
1	Kenan HASAGIĆ	BIH	G	28		
23	İBRAHİM Akın		M	13	(4)	6
24	İLHAN Şahin		M	5	(9)	1
10	İLYAS Kahraman		M	26	(3)	5
33	KERİM Zengin		M	23	(4)	3
21	MAHMUT Tekdemir		D	4	(1)	
99	MEHMET ALİ Tunç		G	3		
44	MERT Korkmaz		D	14	(2)	
3	METİN Depe		D	9		
4	MURAT Ocak		D	9	(1)	1
18	NECATİ Ateş		A	11	(1)	8
16	Sergio ÓRTEMAN	URU	M	2	(7)	1
53	RIZVAN Şahin		D	14	(6)	
5	SANCAK Kaplan		D	6	(6)	
11	SERTAN Eser		A	18	(4)	2
8	Razundara TJIKUZU	NAM	M	30		
35	UĞUR Işıkal		M	2	(8)	1
74	ÜNAL Alpuğan		M	1	(3)	
25	Marcus Cesário VINÍCIUS	BRA	D	21		5
55	VOLKAN Koçaloğlu		D	27		
88	ZEKİ Korkmaz		A	3	(4)	

KASIMPAŞA SK

Coach – Kadir Özcan; (3/10/07) Mustafa Yokeş; (15/10/07) Werner Lorant (GER); (5/12/07) Mustafa Yokeş; (19/12/07) Uğur Tütüneker

Founded - 1921

2007				
12/8	Gaziantepspor	a	0-2	
19/8	Beşiktaş	h	1-2	*Askou*
26/8	Kayserispor	a	0-2	
2/9	Ankaraspor	h	3-1	*Fransergio, Téhoué 2*
15/9	Denizlispor	a	1-0	*Serdar*
23/9	Galatasaray	h	0-1	
30/9	Gençlerbirliği	a	1-3	*Téhoué*
5/10	Trabzonspor	h	0-0	
20/10	İstanbul BB	a	0-2	
27/10	Fenerbahçe	h	1-2	*Téhoué*
4/11	Sivasspor	a	0-4	
10/11	Gençlerbirliği OFTAŞ	h	1-3	*Moritz*
25/11	Rizespor	a	0-2	
1/12	Bursaspor	h	0-2	
8/12	Ankaragücü	a	2-2	*Merthan, Özgür*
16/12	Manisaspor	h	2-2	*Téhoué 2*
22/12	Konyaspor	a	1-2	*Yekta*
2008				
12/1	Gaziantepspor	h	0-1	
19/1	Beşiktaş	a	2-4	*Özgür, og (Serdar Özkan)*
27/1	Kayserispor	h	0-2	
10/2	Ankaraspor	a	0-2	
17/2	Denizlispor	h	1-0	*Özgür*
24/2	Galatasaray	a	1-0	*Erhan*
1/3	Gençlerbirliği	h	0-0	
9/3	Trabzonspor	a	1-2	*Erhan*
16/3	İstanbul BB	h	1-0	*Mawaye*

21/3	Fenerbahçe	a	0-3	
30/3	Sivasspor	h	0-4	
5/4	Gençlerbirliği OFTAŞ	a	1-0	*Askou*
13/4	Rizespor	h	0-1	
19/4	Bursaspor	a	0-1	
26/4	Ankaragücü	h	2-2	*Moritz (p), Mawaye*
4/5	Manisaspor	a	2-1	*Moritz, Barbaros*
10/5	Konyaspor	h	2-1	*Alpaslan, Moritz*

No	Name	Nat	Pos	Aps	(s)	Gls
88	Edin ADEMOVIĆ	BIH	A	1	(5)	
54	ALPASLAN Kartal		D	27	(1)	1
33	Jens Berthel ASKOU	DEN	D	31	(1)	2
17	AYDIN Tabak		M		(1)	
23	BARBAROS Barut		M	19	(1)	1
4	CİHAT Arslan		D	8	(2)	
11	Ely CISSÉ	SEN	D	3		
3	Mamoutou COULIBALY	MLI	M	6		
83	DENİZ Aydoğdu		A		(2)	
16	ENDER Alkan		M	2		
61	ERHAN Küçük		A	24	(4)	2
53	EVREN Kürkçü		D	4	(4)	
26	FARUK Bayar		M	13	(7)	
14	FATİH Akyel		D	25		
30	FRANSERGIO Bastos	BRA	D	18	(4)	1
5	GÖKHAN Caba		D	9	(1)	
77	GÖKSEL Akıncı		M	10	(7)	
21	Joseph-Desire MAWAYE	CMR	A	12	(1)	2
46	MEHMET ALİ Şirin		A		(2)	
28	MERTHAN Açıl		M	19	(7)	1
10	André MORITZ	BRA	M	9	(11)	4
32	MURAT Akın		A	15		
27	MUSTAFA Marangoz		M	1	(2)	
7	ÖMER Hacısalihoğlu		D	22		
2	ÖZGÜR Öçal		D	24	(3)	3
19	SERDAR Akdoğan		A	5	(7)	1
22	Khalid SINOUH	MAR	G	23		
18	Jonathan TÉHOUÉ	FRA	A	15		6
68	TOLGA Özgen		G	11		
8	ÜNAL Sarı		M	6	(9)	
6	YASİN Sülün		M	6	(3)	
35	YEKTA Kurtuluş		D	6	(10)	1

KAYSERİSPOR

Coach – Tolunay Kafkas

Founded – 1966

MAJOR HONOURS: Turkish Cup - (1) 2008.

2007

12/8	Manisaspor	h	3-1	*Gökhan, Koray, Mehmet*
19/8	Konyaspor	a	1-1	*Gökhan*
26/8	Kasımpaşa	h	2-0	*Iglesias, Gökhan*
1/9	Beşiktaş	a	0-0	
16/9	Gaziantepspor	a	3-4	*Cángele, Mehmet, Iglesias*
22/9	Ankaraspor	h	3-1	*Iglesias, Gökhan, Ivankov (p)*
30/9	Denizlispor	a	0-2	
7/10	Galatasaray	h	1-1	*Gökhan*
20/10	Gençlerbirliği	a	1-1	*Saidou*
26/10	Trabzonspor	h	1-0	*Kemal*
4/11	İstanbul BB	a	1-1	*Mehmet Eren*
11/11	Fenerbahçe	h	2-1	*Mehmet Eren 2*
25/11	Sivasspor	a	0-1	
2/12	Gençlerbirliği OFTAŞ	h	1-1	*Mehmet*
8/12	Rizespor	a	0-0	
16/12	Bursaspor	h	4-1	*Mehmet, Gökhan 2, Cángele*
22/12	Ankaragücü	a	1-1	*Toledo*

2008

13/1	Manisaspor	a	1-0	*Gökhan*
20/1	Konyaspor	h	3-0	*Cángele, Koray, Kemal*
27/1	Kasımpaşa	a	2-0	*Saidou, Gökhan*
9/2	Beşiktaş	h	2-0	*Koray, Gökhan*
17/2	Gaziantepspor	h	3-1	*Aydın, Kamber, Mehmet*
24/2	Ankaraspor	a	3-0	*Gökhan, Ivankov (p), Mehmet*
2/3	Denizlispor	h	1-1	*Aydın*
8/3	Galatasaray	a	0-2	
15/3	Gençlerbirliği	h	3-0	*Iglesias, Ivankov (p), Mehmet*
23/3	Trabzonspor	a	1-2	*Iglesias*
30/3	İstanbul BB	h	1-2	*Cángele*
5/4	Fenerbahçe	a	1-2	*Saidou*
13/4	Sivasspor	h	0-1	
20/4	Gençlerbirliği OFTAŞ	a	1-1	*Mehmet*
26/4	Rizespor	h	3-0	*Mehmet Eren, Iglesias, Mehmet*
4/5	Bursaspor	a	1-0	*Kemal*
10/5	Ankaragücü	h	0-2	

No	Name	Nat	Pos	Aps	(s)	Gls
18	ALİ Çamdalı		M	3	(2)	
5	ALİ Turan		D	26	(5)	
4	Juan Pablo AVENDAÑO	ARG	D	10	(7)	
25	AYDIN Toscalı		D	30	(1)	2
19	Franco CÁNGELE	ARG	M	22	(3)	4
2	DURMUŞ Bayram		D	12		
15	ERDAL Güneş		A	1	(6)	
17	ERSOY Yılmaz		A	2		
81	FATİH Ceylan		M	3	(6)	
9	GÖKHAN Ünal		A	21	(4)	11
1	HASAN Sönmez		G	4	(1)	
7	Leonardo IGLESIAS	ARG	A	13	(13)	6
27	Dimitar IVANKOV	BUL	G	30		3
38	KAMBER Arslan		M	10	(13)	1
11	KEMAL Okyay		M	17	(12)	3
51	KORAY Çölgeçen		D	22		3
66	MEHMET Topuz		M	31	(1)	9
67	MEHMET EREN Boyraz		A	25	(6)	4
26	ORKUN Bal		M	2		
8	RAGIP Başdağ		M	30	(2)	
20	Alioum SAIDOU	CMR	M	24	(1)	3
61	SAVAŞ Yılmaz		M	2	(1)	
88	TAYFUN Yanar		D	2		
12	Delio César TOLEDO	PAR	D	26	(1)	1
22	TURGAY Bahadır		M	6	(14)	

KONYASPOR

Coach – Nurullah Sağlam; (28/9/07) Ünal Karaman; (26/3/08) Raşit Çetiner

Founded - 1981

2007

11/8	Beşiktaş	a	0-1	
19/8	Kayserispor	h	1-1	*Murat*
26/8	Ankaraspor	a	1-1	*Veysel*
1/9	Denizlispor	h	2-2	*Neca (p), Murat*
16/9	Galatasaray	a	0-6	
22/9	Gençlerbirliği	h	1-1	*Neca*
30/9	Trabzonspor	a	0-1	
7/10	İstanbul BB	h	3-2	*Washington 2, Murat*
20/10	Fenerbahçe	a	1-4	*Washington*
28/10	Sivasspor	h	2-1	*Burak, Murat*
3/11	Gençlerbirliği OFTAŞ	a	1-0	*Veysel*
10/11	Rizespor	h	2-1	*Sabin, Veysel*
25/11	Bursaspor	a	0-1	
1/12	Ankaragücü	h	1-0	*Veysel*
9/12	Manisaspor	h	4-2	*Murat 3, Neca*

15/12	Gaziantepspor	a	1-2	*Erman*
22/12	Kasımpaşa	h	2-1	*Veysel, Erkan*
2008				
12/1	Beşiktaş	h	1-2	*Sedat*
20/1	Kayserispor	a	0-3	
27/1	Ankaraspor	h	1-3	*Kauê*
10/2	Denizlispor	a	1-2	*Veysel*
18/2	Galatasaray	h	0-1	
23/2	Gençlerbirliği	a	1-6	*Yusuf*
29/2	Trabzonspor	h	1-0	*Kauê*
8/3	İstanbul BB	a	0-5	
16/3	Fenerbahçe	h	1-4	*Ceyhun*
23/3	Sivasspor	a	0-3	
30/3	Gençlerbirliği OFTAŞ	h	0-1	
6/4	Rizespor	a	2-2	*Veysel 2*
13/4	Bursaspor	h	2-0	*Téhoué 2*
19/4	Ankaragücü	a	3-0	*Sedat 2, Murat*
26/4	Manisaspor	a	0-2	
4/5	Gaziantepspor	h	1-1	*Murat*
10/5	Kasımpaşa	a	1-2	*Murat*

No	Name	Nat	Pos	Aps	(s)	Gls
14	Mohamed ABDULLAH	EGY	M	3	(2)	
7	João BATISTA	BRA	M	21	(4)	
3	BURAK Özsaraç		D	21	(7)	1
77	CEYHUN Eriş		M	9	(2)	1
5	Abdel Zaher EL SAKA	EGY	D	9		
18	EREN Şen		A	3	(1)	
6	ERKAN Sekman		M	29	(2)	1
19	ERMAN Özgür		M	27	(3)	1
39	FATİH Özer		M		(3)	
37	GÖKHAN Çakır		M	1	(3)	
25	Damir KAHRIMAN	SRB	G	5		
11	KAUÊ Caetano da Silva	BRA	A	31		2
35	KORAY İçten		D	3	(2)	
32	Miloš MIHAJLOV	SRB	D	12	(1)	
42	MUHAMMED Akıncı		M		(2)	
10	MURAT Hacıoğlu		A	22	(12)	10
8	MURAT Kaya		M		(1)	
13	MUSTAFA Er		M	31	(2)	
99	Duarte NECA	POR	M	17		3
61	OĞUZHAN Bahadır		G	20		
4	ÖMER Gündostu		D	24	(2)	
1	ÖZDEN Öngün		G	9		
44	Cédric SABIN	FRA	A	6	(12)	1
15	SEDAT Ağçay		M	20	(8)	3
27	Jonathan TÉHOUÉ	FRA	A	5	(7)	2
50	VEYSEL Cihan		A	24	(6)	8
9	WASHINGTON Silva	BRA	A	6	(13)	3
70	YUSUF Kurtuluş		D	10	(2)	1
12	ZÉ GOMES da Silva	POR	D	6	(4)	

RİZESPOR

Coach – Samet Aybaba; (31/8/07) Safet Sušić (BIH); (1/2/08) Erdoğan Arıca

Founded - 1953

2007				
12/8	Galatasaray	a	0-4	
19/8	Gençlerbirliği	h	0-2	
26/8	Trabzonspor	a	1-5	*Ribeiro*
1/9	İstanbul BB	h	3-1	*Anderson, Fahri, Zafer*
15/9	Fenerbahçe	a	1-1	*Leandro*
23/9	Sivasspor	h	0-2	
29/9	Gençlerbirliği OFTAŞ	a	0-2	
7/10	Gaziantepspor	h	2-1	*Serhat, Anderson*
20/10	Bursaspor	h	2-0	*Anderson, Fahri (p)*
28/10	Ankaragücü	a	0-1	
4/11	Manisaspor	h	1-4	*Fahri*
10/11	Konyaspor	a	1-2	*Altan*
25/11	Kasımpaşa	h	2-0	*Kürşat, Victoria (p)*
2/12	Beşiktaş	a	1-1	*Leandro*
8/12	Kayserispor	h	0-0	
15/12	Ankaraspor	a	2-1	*Ribeiro, Leandro*
23/12	Denizlispor	h	2-0	*Cumhur, Gökhan*
2008				
12/1	Galatasaray	h	2-5	*Altan, Zafer*
20/1	Gençlerbirliği	a	1-4	*Zafer*
28/1	Trabzonspor	h	0-4	
9/2	İstanbul BB	a	1-2	*Ribeiro*
15/2	Fenerbahçe	h	2-4	*Altan 2*
24/2	Sivasspor	a	0-0	
2/3	Gençlerbirliği OFTAŞ	h	0-0	
9/3	Gaziantepspor	a	1-1	*Mustafa*
15/3	Bursaspor	a	1-2	*Emrah (p)*
23/3	Ankaragücü	h	0-0	
30/3	Manisaspor	a	1-2	*Mustafa*
6/4	Konyaspor	h	2-2	*Anderson, Fahri*
13/4	Kasımpaşa	a	1-0	*Mehmet*
20/4	Beşiktaş	h	1-2	*Mustafa*
26/4	Kayserispor	a	0-3	
3/5	Ankaraspor	h	0-1	
10/5	Denizlispor	a	1-5	*Mehmet*

No	Name	Nat	Pos	Aps	(s)	Gls
10	ALTAN Aksoy		M	12	(3)	4
99	ANIL Karaer		D	8	(2)	
7	ANDERSON dos Santos	BRA	A	12	(10)	4
44	Marcos BARBOSA	BRA	D	7	(1)	
53	CUMHUR Bozacı		D	25	(3)	1
34	EMRAH Eren		M	28		1
5	EMRE Toraman		M	8		
63	ERGÜN Teber		D	13	(2)	
3	FAHRİ Tatan		M	23	(2)	4
14	FERDİ Elmas		A	2	(1)	
24	Igor GAL	CRO	D	13	(1)	
1	David GONZÁLEZ	COL	G	30		
19	GÖKHAN Kök		D	26	(3)	1
13	GÖRKEM Görk		D	2		
49	KÜRŞAT Duymuş		D	23		1
83	LEANDRO Rodrigues	BRA	M	24	(5)	3
39	MEHMET Şen		A	4	(4)	2
88	MERTGUL Çapoglu		D	1	(2)	
89	MESUT Yılmaz		D	3		
21	METİN Aktaş		G	1		
25	MURAT Uluç		A		(2)	
35	MUSTAFA Çiçek		M	13		3
42	ÖMER Kesici		A		(1)	
41	ÖZDEN Öngün		G	3		
11	Elionar RIBEIRO	BRA	A	23	(8)	3
61	SERHAT Akyüz		D	19	(4)	1
2	SUAT Usta		D	20	(2)	
9	ŞADİ Çolak		A		(5)	
20	TUFAN Arslan		A	2	(4)	
23	TURGAY Gölbaşı		D		(1)	
17	Gustavo VICTORIA	COL	D	13	(8)	1
8	ZAFER Biryol		A	16	(9)	3

SİVASSPOR

Coach – Bülent Uygun

Founded - 1967

2007				
12/8	Trabzonspor	a	3-0	*(w/o; match abandoned after 89 mins at 0-1)*
19/8	İstanbul BB	h	2-1	*Mehmet, Diallo*
25/8	Fenerbahçe	a	0-1	
2/9	Gaziantepspor	h	2-0	*Mehmet, Balili*
15/9	Gençlerbirliği OFTAŞ	h	1-0	*Murat*
23/9	Rizespor	a	2-0	*Balili, Mohamed Ali*

30/9	Bursaspor	h	3-2	*Mohamed Ali 2, Mehmet*
7/10	Ankaragücü	a	2-2	*Mohamed Ali, Mehmet*
22/10	Manisaspor	h	1-0	*Musa*
28/10	Konyaspor	a	1-2	*Mohamed Ali*
4/11	Kasımpaşa	h	4-0	*Musa, Mohamed Ali 2, Mehmet*
10/11	Beşiktaş	a	2-1	*Mohamed Ali, Qurbanov*
25/11	Kayserispor	h	1-0	*Musa*
2/12	Ankaraspor	a	0-2	
9/12	Denizlispor	h	2-0	*Musa, İlhan*
14/12	Galatasaray	a	0-2	
23/12	Gençlerbirliği	h	2-0	*Mehmet 2*
2008				
13/1	Trabzonspor	h	2-0	*Tsvetkov, Mehmet (p)*
19/1	İstanbul BB	a	2-0	*Mehmet, Tsvetkov*
27/1	Fenerbahçe	h	1-4	*Musa*
10/2	Gaziantepspor	a	0-0	
16/2	Gençlerbirliği OFTAŞ	a	1-0	*Mehmet*
24/2	Rizespor	h	0-0	
2/3	Bursaspor	a	1-0	*Abdurrahman*
9/3	Ankaragücü	h	3-2	*Murat, Petkovic, Mohamed Ali*
14/3	Manisaspor	a	1-1	*Sezer*
23/3	Konyaspor	h	3-0	*Tsvetkov, Uğur, Mehmet*
30/3	Kasımpaşa	a	4-0	*Tsvetkov 4*
6/4	Beşiktaş	h	1-2	*Mehmet*
13/4	Kayserispor	a	1-0	*Mehmet*
19/4	Ankaraspor	h	2-1	*Musa, Mohamed Ali*
26/4	Denizlispor	a	2-1	*Sezer, Hayrettin*
4/5	Galatasaray	h	3-5	*og (Song), Mehmet, Sezer*
10/5	Gençlerbirliği	a	2-0	*Sezer, Musa*

No	Name	Nat	Pos	Aps	(s)	Gls
61	ABDURRAHMAN Dereli		D	31	(1)	1
35	AKIN Vardar		G	14	(1)	
23	AYTAÇ Ak		D		(15)	
17	Pini BALILI	ISR	A	12	(2)	2
72	DEVRAN Ayhan		M	24	(3)	
25	Mamadou DIALLO	GUI	D	13	(1)	1
38	EMRE Efe		D	1	(3)	
11	GÖKHAN Bozkaya		M		(1)	
58	HAYRETTİN Yerlikaya		D	29		1
33	İLHAN Ummak		M	19	(14)	1
9	MEHMET Yıldız		A	33		14
20	MOHAMED ALİ Kurtuluş		M	30	(1)	10
5	MURAT Sözgelmez		D	28		2
7	MUSA Aydın		M	32		7
10	Sérgio Pacheco de OLIVEIRA	BRA	M	4	(5)	
18	Ilqar QURBANOV	AZE	A	1	(9)	1
77	ONUR Tuncer		M	3	(11)	
1	Michael PETKOVIC	AUS	G	20		1
21	Karim SAIDI	TUN	D	12	(1)	
3	SEDAT Bayrak		D	15		
26	SEZER Badur		M	13	(9)	4
8	Kanfory SYLLA	GUI	M	17	(3)	
19	Ivan TSVETKOV	BUL	A	13	(16)	7
68	UĞUR Yıldırım		M		(4)	1
42	YASİR Elmacı		M	10		

TRABZONSPOR

Coach – Ziya Doğan; (27/10/07) Ersun Yanal

Founded – 1967

MAJOR HONOURS: Turkish League - (6) 1976, 1977, 1979, 1980, 1981, 1984; Turkish Cup - (7) 1977, 1978, 1984, 1992, 1995, 2003, 2004.

2007				
12/8	Sivasspor	h	0-3	*(w/o; match abandoned after 89 mins at 1-0 Ersen)*
17/8	Gençlerbirliği OFTAŞ	a	2-0	*Umut, Gökdeniz*
26/8	Rizespor	h	5-1	*Umut 2, Ceyhun 2, Gökdeniz*
31/8	Bursaspor	a	1-1	*Gökdeniz (p)*
16/9	Ankaragücü	h	0-0	
21/9	Manisaspor	a	1-1	*Gökdeniz*
30/9	Konyaspor	h	1-0	*Gökdeniz*
5/10	Kasımpaşa	a	0-0	
20/10	Beşiktaş	h	2-3	*Gökdeniz, Yattara*
26/10	Kayserispor	a	0-1	
2/11	Ankaraspor	h	2-1	*Umut, Ceyhun*
9/11	Denizlispor	a	0-2	
25/11	Galatasaray	h	0-1	
30/11	Gençlerbirliği	a	1-2	*Mustafa*
9/12	Gaziantepspor	h	3-2	*Umut, Gökdeniz 2*
15/12	İstanbul BB	h	2-1	*Gökdeniz 2*
22/12	Fenerbahçe	a	2-3	*Ceyhun 2*
2008				
13/1	Sivasspor	a	0-2	
19/1	Gençlerbirliği OFTAŞ	h	1-2	*Umut*
28/1	Rizespor	a	4-0	*Tayfun, Abdelaziz, Umut 2*
10/2	Bursaspor	h	2-1	*Gökdeniz, Yattara*
17/2	Ankaragücü	a	2-0	*Umut, Abdelaziz*
24/2	Manisaspor	h	2-2	*Tayfun 2*
29/2	Konyaspor	a	0-1	
9/3	Kasımpaşa	h	2-1	*Hüseyin, Barış*
16/3	Beşiktaş	a	0-3	
23/3	Kayserispor	h	2-1	*Umut 2*
29/3	Ankaraspor	a	0-1	
4/4	Denizlispor	h	2-0	*Umut, Barış*
12/4	Galatasaray	a	0-1	
19/4	Gençlerbirliği	h	0-0	
26/4	Gaziantepspor	a	1-1	*Ergin*
3/5	İstanbul BB	a	2-1	*Çağdaş, Umut*
10/5	Fenerbahçe	h	2-0	*Umut, Yattara*

No	Name	Nat	Pos	Aps	(s)	Gls
12	Ayman ABDELAZIZ	EGY	M	26	(3)	2
13	ADNAN Güngör		D	4	(12)	
77	AHMET Şahin		G	7	(1)	
90	BARIŞ Memiş		A	9	(6)	2
99	CELALEDDİN Koçak		M	9	(1)	
21	CEM Demir		A		(2)	
20	CEYHUN Eriş		M	14	(2)	5
4	ÇAĞDAŞ Atan		D	19	(2)	1
38	ERDİNÇ Yavuz		D	20		
7	ERGİN Keleş		A	5	(18)	1
28	ERSEN Martin		A		(2)	1
85	FERHAT Çökmüş		M	14	(6)	
61	GÖKDENİZ Karadeniz		M	24		11
6	HASAN Üçüncü		M	4	(6)	
5	HÜSEYİN Çimşir		M	30		1
15	Daouda JABI	GUI	D	9	(1)	
1	JEFFERSON de Oliveira	BRA	G	2	(1)	
69	KADİR Keleş		M		(1)	
14	Sayed MOAWAD	EGY	M	2	(2)	
16	MUSA Büyük		M	3	(1)	
32	MUSTAFA Keçeli		M	25	(3)	1
35	ONUR Kıvrak		G	3		
8	ÖMER RIZA		A	1	(5)	
3	Fredrik RISP	SWE	D		(1)	
30	SERKAN Balcı		M	22	(3)	
18	TAYFUN Cora		D	27	(2)	3
44	TOLGA Seyhan		D	10	(2)	
29	TOLGA Zengin		G	22		

No	Name	Nat	Pos	Aps	(s)	Gls
10	UMUT Bulut		A	33		14
11	Ibrahima YATTARA	GUI	A	30	(2)	3
86	YUSUF Kurtuluş		D		(1)	

VESTEL MANİSASPOR

Coach – Giray Bulak; (18/1/08) Yılmaz Vural; (13/3/08) Levent Eriş

Founded - 1965

2007				
12/8	Kayserispor	a	1-3	*Hakan*
19/8	Ankaraspor	h	2-1	*Metin, Kalabane*
26/8	Denizlispor	a	2-3	*Hakan, Metin*
2/9	Galatasaray	h	2-2	*Hološko, Selçuk*
16/9	Gençlerbirliği	a	2-0	*Uğur, Hološko*
21/9	Trabzonspor	h	1-1	*Hološko*
30/9	İstanbul BB	a	1-4	*Dvorník*
6/10	Fenerbahçe	h	1-1	*Şener*
22/10	Sivasspor	a	0-1	
27/10	Gençlerbirliği OFTAŞ	h	0-2	
4/11	Rizespor	a	4-1	*Selçuk (p), Hološko 2, Şener*
10/11	Bursaspor	h	1-1	*Ümit*
25/11	Ankaragücü	a	0-1	
2/12	Gaziantepspor	h	1-0	*Hološko (p)*
9/12	Konyaspor	a	2-4	*Hološko 2*
16/12	Kasımpaşa	a	2-2	*Borbiconi, Rafael Marques*
21/12	Beşiktaş	h	1-2	*Uğur*
2008				
13/1	Kayserispor	h	0-1	
20/1	Ankaraspor	a	0-1	
27/1	Denizlispor	h	3-2	*Burak 3*
9/2	Galatasaray	a	3-6	*Selçuk 2, Burak*
17/2	Gençlerbirliği	h	1-2	*Rafael Marques*
24/2	Trabzonspor	a	2-2	*Selçuk, Burak*
29/2	İstanbul BB	h	1-1	*Sezer*
9/3	Fenerbahçe	a	1-4	*Burak*
14/3	Sivasspor	h	1-1	*Burak*
22/3	Gençlerbirliği OFTAŞ	a	0-1	
30/3	Rizespor	h	2-1	*Burak (p), Rafael Marques*
6/4	Bursaspor	a	0-1	
13/4	Ankaragücü	h	1-2	*Metin*
19/4	Gaziantepspor	a	0-1	
26/4	Konyaspor	h	2-0	*Güven, Zè António*
4/5	Kasımpaşa	h	1-2	*Burak*
10/5	Beşiktaş	a	1-5	*Rafael Marques*

No	Name	Nat	Pos	Aps	(s)	Gls
38	ALLYSON Araújo	BRA	D	13	(1)	
33	ANIL Karaer		D		(1)	
5	Stéphane BORBICONI	FRA	D	23	(3)	1
37	BURAK Yılmaz		A	16		9
1	BÜLENT Ataman		G	16		
99	CELALEDDİN Koçak		M	10		
55	Thomas DALGAARD	DEN	A		(2)	
2	Josef DVORNÍK	CZE	D	11		1
34	FERHAT Öztorun		D	19	(2)	
11	GÜVEN Varol		M	7	(13)	1
22	HAKAN Balta		D	4		2
90	HİKMET Balioğlu		A	1		
13	Filip HOLOŠKO	SVK	A	16		8
15	Oumar KALABANE	GUI	D	26		1
41	KORAY Avcı		D	5	(1)	
77	Luís MARTÍNEZ	COL	G	2		
19	METİN Akan		A	28	(6)	3
16	NİZAMETTİN Çalışkan		M	11	(8)	
17	OĞUZ Sabankay		M	2	(10)	
20	OKAN Koç		M	6	(7)	
9	RAFAEL Mariano MARQUES	BRA	A	18	(9)	4
18	SELÇUK İnan		M	30		5
8	SEZER Öztürk		M	6	(12)	1
21	SİNAN Özkan		D	1	(4)	
6	ŞENER Aşkaroğlu		M	22	(1)	2
86	TIAGO Da Silva	POR	A	3	(8)	
14	UFUK Ceylan		G	16		
10	UĞUR İnceman		M	28	(1)	2
4	ÜMİT Bozkurt		D	22	(2)	1
24	YALÇIN Ayhan		D		(1)	
3	YİĞİT Gökoğlan		D		(1)	
50	ZÉ ANTÓNIO dos Santos Silva	POR	M	11	(1)	1
7	Lukáš ZELENKA	CZE	M	1	(3)	
89	ZİHNİ Aydın		M		(1)	

PROMOTED CLUBS

KOCAELISPOR

Coach – Fuat Yaman; (1/11/07) Kayhan Çubuklu; (24/4/08) Engin İpekoğlu

Founded - 1966

MAJOR HONOURS: Turkish Cup - (2) 1997, 2002.

ANTALYASPOR

Coach – Raşit Çetiner; (25/12/07) Ümit Turmuş; (31/3/08) Hikm Karaman

Founded - 1966

ESKIŞEHIRSPOR

Coach – Metin Diyadin; (19/3/08) Nejad Biyedić (BIH)

Founded – 1965

MAJOR HONOURS: Turkish Cup - (1) 1971.

SECOND LEVEL FINAL TABLE 2007/08

		Pld	W	D	L	F	A
1	Kocaelispor	34	19	7	8	59	37
2	Antalyaspor	34	15	16	3	56	33
3	Sakaryaspor	34	16	10	8	55	34
4	Eskişehirspor	34	16	9	9	52	35
5	Diyarbakırspor	34	16	9	9	52	36
6	Boluspor	13	14	7	50	46	4
7	Kayseri Erciyesspor	34	14	10	10	54	41
8	Orduspor	34	12	14	8	39	44
9	Karşıyaka SK	34	11	14	9	44	41
10	Altay SK	34	13	8	13	47	47
11	Giresunspor	34	10	13	11	41	44
12	Malatyaspor	34	12	7	15	44	43
13	Kartalspor	34	10	12	12	52	57
14	Gaziantep BB	34	9	12	13	53	51
15	Samsunspor	34	10	8	16	45	61
16	Elazığspor	34	8	10	16	40	54
17	İstanbulspor	34	6	8	20	25	58
18	Mardinspor	34	3	5	26	26	72

PROMOTION PLAY-OFFS

(16/5/08)

Sakaryaspor 2, Boluspor 2 *(1-3 on pens)*

Eskişehirspor 0, Diyarbakırspor 0 *(6-5 on pens)*

(18/5/08)

Eskişehirspor 2 Boluspor 0

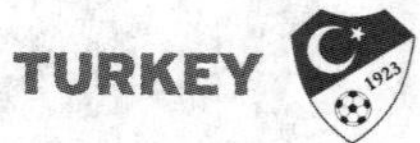

DOMESTIC CUP 2007/08

TÜRKİYE KUPASI

ECOND ROUND

25/9/07)
epecik Belediyespor 1, Ankaragücü 3
ençlerbirliği 4, Akçaabat Sebatspor 1

26/9/07)
ırıkkalespor, 4 Sakaryaspor 2
arıyer 2, Kasımpaşa 0
lanyaspor 1, Sivasspor 0
anlıurfaspor 2, Konyaspor 1
rsinspor 0, Denizlispor 2
nkaraspor 2, Kartalspor 1
stanbul BB 2, DİSKİ 3
dana Demirspor 1, Altay 0
lanisaspor 5, Gaziantep BB 0
aziantepspor 2, Kayseri Erciyesspor 0
ursaspor 1, Boluspor 0
izespor 3, Eskişehirspor 1
ayserispor 3, Diyarbakırspor 1
ençlerbirliği OFTAŞ 4, Uşakspor 0

HIRD ROUND
Played in Groups)

ROUP A

31/10/07)
nkaragücü 3, DİSKİ 1
eşiktaş 1, Rizespor 2

5/1/08)
nkaraspor 2, Ankaragücü 0
ISKİ 0, Beşiktaş 4

8/1/08)
izespor 2, DİSKİ 1
eşiktaş 3, Ankaraspor 1

16/1/08)
nkaraspor 0, Rizespor 0
nkaragücü 1, Beşiktaş 1

23/1/08)
izespor 1, Ankaragücü 0
ISKİ 2, Ankaraspor 3

inal Standings
Rizespor 10 pts; 2 Beşiktaş 7 pts *(qualified)*
Ankaraspor 7 pts; 4 Ankaragücü 4 pts; 5
ISKİ 0 pts *(eliminated)*

ROUP B

30/10/07)
lanisaspor 3, Trabzonspor 0

31/10/07)
ırıkkalespor 1, Adana Demirspor 3

4/1/08)
rabzonspor 5, Kırıkkalespor 0

5/1/08)
ençlerbirliği 3, Manisaspor 0

9/1/08)
ırıkkalespor 0, Gençlerbirliği 4
dana Demirspor 1, Trabzonspor 0

15/1/08)
ençlerbirliği 1, Adana Demirspor 0

(16/1/08)
Manisaspor 2, Kırıkkalespor 1

(24/1/08)
Adana Demirspor 2, Manisaspor 1
Trabzonspor 3, Gençlerbirliği 2

Final Standings
1 Gençlerbirliği 9 pts; 2 Adana Demirspor 9 pts *(qualified)*
3 Trabzonspor 6 pts; 4 Manisaspor 6 pts;
5 Kırıkkalespor 0 pts *(eliminated)*

GROUP C

(30/10/07)
Şanlıurfaspor 3, Alanyaspor 0

(31/10/07)
Fenerbahçe 0, Gaziantepspor 0

(5/1/08)
Gaziantepspor 1, Şanlıurfaspor 1

(6/1/08)
Kayserispor 0, Fenerbahçe 0

(8/1/08)
Alanyaspor 0, Gaziantepspor 3

(9/1/08)
Şanlıurfaspor 1, Kayserispor 1

(16/1/08)
Kayserispor 5, Alanyaspor 0
Fenerbahçe 3, Şanlıurfaspor 2

(23/1/08)
Alanyaspor 3, Fenerbahçe 10
Gaziantepspor 0, Kayserispor 2

Final Standings
1 Fenerbahçe 8 pts; 2 Kayserispor 8 pts *(qualified)*
3 Şanlıurfaspor 5 pts; 4 Gaziantepspor 5 pts;
5 Alanyaspor 0 pts *(eliminated)*

GROUP D

(30/10/07)
Sarıyer 0, Gençlerbirliği OFTAŞ 3

(1/11/07)
Galatasaray 2, Denizlispor 1

(5/1/08)
Bursaspor 2, Galatasaray 2

(6/1/08)
Denizlispor 3, Sarıyer 1

(9/1/08)
Sarıyer 3, Bursaspor 2
Gençlerbirliği OFTAŞ 3, Denizlispor 1

(15/1/08)
Galatasaray 3, Sarıyer 0

(16/1/08)
Bursaspor 1, Gençlerbirliği OFTAŞ 0

(23/1/08)
Gençlerbirliği OFTAŞ 3, Galatasaray 0
Denizlispor 0, Bursaspor 0

Final Standings
1 Gençlerbirliği OFTAŞ 9 pts; 2 Galatasaray 7 pts *(qualified)*
3 Bursaspor 5 pts; 4 Denizlispor 4 pts;
5 Sarıyer 3 pts *(eliminated)*

QUARTER-FINALS

(1/2/08 & 27/2/08)
Gençlerbirliği OFTAŞ 0, Kayserispor 0
Kayserispor 2 *(Toledo 31, Mehmet Topuz 71)*, Gençlerbirliği OFTAŞ 0
(Kayserispor 2-0)

(2/2/08 & 26/2/08)
Adana Demirspor 0, Gençlerbirliği 1 *(Mehmet Çakır 66)*
Gençlerbirliği 2 *(Kahé 57p, Traoré 83)*, Adana Demirspor 2 *(Mehmet 44, Bora 74)*
(Gençlerbirliği 3-2)

(2/2/08 & 27/2/08)
Rizespor 1 *(Anderson 74)*, Beşiktaş 0
Beşiktaş 3 *(Hološko 19, Tello 59, Nobre 74)*, Rizespor 2 *(Suat 26, Ribeiro 65)*
(3-3; Rizespor on away goals)

(3/2/08 & 27/2/08)
Fenerbahçe 0, Galatasaray 0
Galatasaray 2 *(Hakan Şükür 4, Ümit 90)*, Fenerbahçe 1 *(Gökhan 67)*
(Galatasaray 2-1)

SEMI-FINALS

(18/3/08 & 16/4/08)
Rizespor 0, Kayserispor 3 *(Iglesias 22, Cángele 68, Toledo 82)*
Kayserispor 4 *(Toledo 20, Iglesias 55, 76, 89)*, Rizespor 1 *(Leandro 26)*
(Kayserispor 7-1)

(19/3/08& 15/4/08)
Gençlerbirliği 1 *(Burhan 72)*, Galatasaray 0
Galatasaray 1 *(Ümit 89)*, Gençlerbirliği 1 *(Tuna 76)*
(Gençlerbirliği 2-1)

FINAL

(7/5/08)
Atatürk Stadı, Bursa
KAYSERİSPOR 0
GENÇLERBİRLİĞİ SK 0
(aet; 11-10 on pens)
Referee – *Yunus Yıldırım*
KAYSERİSPOR – *Ivankov, Koray, Ali Turan, Aydın, Toledo, Mehmet Eren (Turgay 90), Saidou, Ragıp (Kamber 102), Mehmet Topuz, Iglesias, Cángele (Kemal 105).*
GENÇLERBİRLİĞİ – *Peric, Ergün, Tuna, El Saka, Erkan (Hakan 95), Engin, Kerem, Mehmet Nas, Addo, Promise (Mehmet Çakır 82), Kahé.*

Shakhtar's turn to take the honours

Having missed out on both domestic prizes the previous season, FC Shakhtar Donetsk reclaimed the Ukrainian League and Cup from eternal rivals FC Dynamo Kyiv in 2007/08. The double success justified a lavish pre-season spending spree by the club's wealthy owner Rinat Akhmetov, but there was disappointment for Shakhtar in Europe as they finished bottom of their UEFA Champions League group despite winning their first two matches.

Dynamo suffered their first trophy-less season since Shakhtar's previous double-winning campaign of 2001/02. The country's most prestigious club endured a shocking run of results in the autumn, notably in the UEFA Champions League where they were utterly humiliated, losing all six matches to AS Roma, Sporting Clube de Portugal and Manchester United FC. Coach Anatoliy Demyanenko, who had proved his credentials the previous season by leading Dynamo to a clean sweep of domestic trophies, resigned after the Matchday One 2-0 defeat in Rome under the pretext that he doubted his ability to make the team competitive at the highest European level. Results thereafter bore him out, although his departure, and the instability that followed, was a mitigating factor in the whitewash.

Yuriy Syomin – the new coach at FC Dynamo Kyiv

With Dynamo making their worst ever start to a Ukrainian championship – three draws and a home defeat, to FC Dnipro Dnipropetrovsk, in their first four games – and therefore losing a lot of early ground in the title race to both Shakhtar and Dnipro, whose win in Kiev was one of six out of six in the first few weeks, Demyanenko probably felt that he was on shaky ground anyway. He was replaced internally by the club's vice-president, and former coach (on several occasions), 67-year-old József Szabó. But he lasted only a few weeks before quitting on health grounds and handing the reins over to the considerably younger and fitter Oleh Luzhniy, 39, who stepped in as a caretaker. Before the year was out, however, Dynamo had recruited their fourth coach of the season, the celebrated 60-year-old Russian Yuriy Syomin.

Brutal Cup final

This was a major diversion from the club's traditional policy of appointing ex-Dynamo players, but the early indications were that the introduction of the crafty ex-FC Lokomotiv Moskva legend, who also had a short spell in charge of Russia in 2005, might bring long-term success. Although his first half-season brought no silverware, Dynamo improved sufficiently in the spring to put Shakhtar under considerable pressure. Indeed, by the end of the campaign Syomin had yet to lose a league game. His only defeat came in the final of the Ukrainian Cup against Shakhtar in neutral Kharkiv, a brute of a contest in which referee Viktor Shvetsov felt compelled to brandish five red cards – two to Dynamo and three to Shakhtar, who won the game 2-0 with goals from Olexandr Hladkiy and Olexiy Hai.

That was part one of Shakhtar's double. Part two arrived ten days later, in the final league match of the season, when they beat city rivals FC Metalurh Donetsk 4-1 to finish three points clear at the top of the Vyshcha Liha table. Their lead over Dynamo had been just a single point going into the game, but Syomin's resurgent side were held 2-2 away to third-placed FC Metalist Kharkiv, for whom Serbian striker Marko Dević scored his 19th goal of the season (and eighth in six games) to end up as the championship's top marksman.

Shakhtar's Hladkiy was one of three Ukrainians who finished joint-second on 17 goals. He had topped the chart the previous season, with 13 for FC Kharkiv, but the talented 20-year-old striker could certainly claim to have made big strides forward during his first season

hakhtar Donetsk president Rinat Akhmetov shows off the krainian championship trophy

with the Donetsk club. He outshone expensive new recruit Cristiano Lucarelli, the first Italian to play in Ukraine's top flight, who returned whence he had come after just half a season. Another costly purchase, Mexican international playmaker Nery Castillo, had even greater trouble settling in and was despatched on loan to Manchester City FC in January. The best of Shakhtar's sizeable foreign contingent were long-serving stalwarts like Darijo Srna and Răzvan Raţ - who both went on to star at UEFA EURO 2008™ for Croatia and Romania, respectively - and Brazilian duo Brandão and Fernandinho, who appeared to play with greater freedom and confidence following the sale of their higher-profile compatriots Matuzalem (to Real Zaragoza) and Elano (to Man. City).

Opportunity squandered

Mircea Lucescu ended his fourth season as Shakhtar coach with his third league title (and first Ukrainian Cup), but he was as disappointed as anyone in the way his team squandered a glorious opportunity to reach the knockout phase of the UEFA Champions League for the first time. Having reached the group stage with a dramatic comeback win against FC Salzburg, Shakhtar continued their fine early-season form by beating Celtic FC 2-0 at home and SL Benfica 1-0 away in their opening two ties. Back-to-back defeats by holders AC Milan were not entirely unexpected, but a late goal conceded to Celtic in Glasgow and a wretched 2-1 home defeat by Benfica left them out of Europe altogether.

Metalist and Dnipro, Ukraine's two UEFA Cup participants, both went out in the first round to British opposition, but the two clubs were to enjoy impressive domestic campaigns, enabling them to rejoin the UEFA Cup in 2008/09. At one stage they both aspired for more. At the winter break Dnipro, led by former great Oleh Protasov and inspired by midfield maestro Serhiy Nazarenko, were on top of the table – albeit having played a game more than Shakhtar – but a 4-0 home defeat against Dynamo on their first game back took the wind out of their sails and they hobbled through the spring campaign, never scoring more than one goal in any game. Metalist, with the prolific Dević as their spearhead, finished strongly to overhaul Dnipro and take third spot. They had shown their quality, albeit in defeat, against Everton FC in Europe and received widespread acclaim for the style of their football under experienced coach Myron Markevych.

New national coach

The Ukrainian national side is to be led in the 2010 FIFA World Cup qualifiers by one of the country's most famous former players, ex-UC Sampdoria, Rangers FC and USSR midfielder Olexiy Mykhailychenko. He was appointed after Oleh Blokhin stood down at the end of

Federatsiya Futboly Ukraïny (FFU)

7-A Labotaornyi provulok
PO Box 55
UA-03150 Kyiv
Tel - +380 44 5210535
Fax - +380 44 5228513
website - www.ffu.org.ua
email - info@ffu.org.ua
Year of Formation – 1991
President - Grigoriy Surkis
General Secretary – Olexandr Bandurko
Press Officer – Valeriy Nykonenko
Stadium – NSC Olimpiyskiy, Kiev (83,011)

INTERNATIONAL TOURNAMENT APPEARANCES
FIFA World Cup - (1) 2006 (qtr-finals).

TOP FIVE ALL-TIME CAPS
Olexandr Shovkovskiy (84); Andriy Shevchenko (81); Anatoliy Tymoshchuk (77); Serhiy Rebrov (75); Andriy Gusin (71)

TOP FIVE ALL-TIME GOALS
Andriy Shevchenko (37); Serhiy Rebrov (15); Andriy Gusin & Andriy Vorobei (9); Timerlan Guseinov (8)

NATIONAL TEAM RESULTS 2007/08

22/8/07	Uzbekistan	H	Kiev	2-1	*Hladkiy (30), Rotan (65)*
8/9/07	Georgia (ECQ)	A	Tbilisi	1-1	*Shelayev (7)*
12/9/07	Italy (ECQ)	H	Kiev	1-2	*Shevchenko (71)*
13/10/07	Scotland (ECQ)	A	Glasgow	1-3	*Shevchenko (24)*
17/10/07	Faroe Islands (ECQ)	H	Kiev	5-0	*Kalynychenko (40, 49), Gusev (43, 45), Vorobei (64)*
17/11/07	Lithuania (ECQ)	A	Kaunas	0-2	
21/11/07	France (ECQ)	H	Kiev	2-2	*Voronin (14), Shevchenko (46)*
6/2/08	Cyprus	A	Nicosia	1-1	*Milevskiy (71)*
26/3/08	Serbia	H	Kiev	2-0	*Shevchenko (54), Nazarenko (58)*
24/5/08	Netherlands	A	Rotterdam	0-3	
1/6/08	Sweden	A	Solna	1-0	*Nazarenko (82)*

a disheartening UEFA EURO 2008™ qualifying campaign, his experience as the successful coach of the national Under-21 side – runners-up at the 2006 European finals in Portugal - proving a persuasive factor in his promotion to the top job. He will need some of those youngsters to mature quickly if the 2006 World Cup quarter-finalists are to reappear on the global stage in South Africa. Slaven Bilić's Croatia and Fabio Capello's England pose formidable obstacles, particularly as the talismanic Andriy Shevchenko's best years now appear to be behind him.

Shevchenko's second season at Chelsea FC was even worse than his first, and although he managed to maintain his outstanding international strike-rate with goals against Italy, Scotland and France in the latter stages of the UEFA EURO 2008™ campaign, he is the wrong side of 30 and cannot go on forever. He was well and truly eclipsed as Ukrainian football's most prominent export in 2007/08 by midfielder Anatoliy Tymoshchuk, who captained FC Zenit St. Petersburg to Russian Premier-Liga and UEFA Cup glory. It could be an interesting race between these two to become the first Ukrainian to reach 100 international caps, although 33-year-old goalkeeper Olexandr Shovkovskiy, the current front-runner, may still have a say despite mounting competition for his place from up-and-coming Shakhtar 'keeper Andriy Pyatov, one of the brightest young stars, along with team-mate Hladkiy and Dynamo striker Artem Milevskiy, of a new generation that will hope to peak on home soil at the next UEFA European Championship in 2012.

ATIONAL TEAM APPEARANCES 2007/08

oach - Oleh BLOKHIN 5/11/52 11/1/08) Olexiy MYKHAILYCHENKO 30/3/63			Uzb	GEO	ITA	SCO	FRO	LTU	FRA	Cyp	Srb	Ned	Swe	Caps	Goals
ndriy PYATOV	28/6/84	Shakhtar	G				G	s44	G				G	5	-
ndriy NESMACHNIY	28/2/79	Dynamo Kyiv	D			D	D				D	D		66	-
exandr KUCHER	22/10/82	Shakhtar	D	D	D	D				D			D	9	1
olodymyr YEZERSKIY	15/11/76	Shakhtar	D	D	D	D		D	s81	s75		D46		39	2
ndriy RUSOL	16/1/83	Dnipro	D46	D	D		D			D			D46	41	3
rhiy NAZARENKO	16/2/80	Dnipro	M	M	M69	s62	M	s72		M	M	M74	M	28	5
rhiy DANYLOVSKIY	20/8/81	Metalurh Donetsk	M46											1	-
ras MYKHALYK	28/10/83	Dynamo Kyiv	M46							M88				7	-
axym KALYNYCHENKO	26/1/79	Spartak Moskva (RUS)	M62	s72	M60		M					s46		36	7
exandr HLADKIY	24/8/87	Shakhtar	A46	s88	s69	A	A46			s46	s87		s68	8	1
ndriy SHEVCHENKO	29/9/76	Chelsea (ENG)	A55	A	A	A		A	A		A87	A66		81	37
eh GUSEV	25/4/83	Dynamo Kyiv	s46	M	M88	M46	M62	M	M91	M60	M56			47	6
eh SHELAYEV	5/11/76	Dnipro	s46	M88	M	s73		M72	s85					36	1
exandr HRYTSAI	30/9/77	Dnipro	s46				s69		D					3	-
ndriy VORONIN	21/7/79	Liverpool (ENG)	s46	A72	s60	A	A	A69	A85		A77	A		53	6
ndriy VOROBEI	29/11/78	Dnipro	s55			M62	s62			A46	s88			68	9
uslan ROTAN	29/10/81	Dynamo Kyiv /Dnipro	s62	M80		s46		M	M	M46				33	6
exandr SHOVKOVSKIY	2/1/75	Dynamo Kyiv		G	G	G		G44		G				84	-
natoliy TYMOSHCHUK	30/3/79	Zenit (RUS)		M	M	M73	M69	M	M	M	M	M		77	1
exiy HAI	6/11/82	Shakhtar		s80	M		M	M	M	s60	s56	s46	M	12	-
tem MILEVSKIY	12/1/85	Dynamo Kyiv			s88		s46	s69	s91	s46	s77			13	1
mytro CHYHRYNSKIY	7/11/86	Shakhtar				D	D	D			D	D	s46	10	-
adyslav VASHCHUK	2/1/75	Dynamo Kyiv						D	D					63	1
exandr ROMANCHUK	21/10/84	Arsenal							D81					2	-
rhiy FEDOROV	18/2/75	Dynamo Kyiv							D					29	1
eh DOPILKA	12/3/86	Dynamo Kyiv								D75	D			2	-
acheslav SHEVCHUK	13/5/79	Shakhtar								D75			D	6	-
taliy FEDORIV	21/10/87	Dynamo Kyiv								s75				1	-
taliy MANDZYUK	24/1/86	Dynamo Kyiv								s88	D	D	s46	4	-
acheslav KERNOZENKO	4/6/76	Dnipro									G	G		5	-
enys HOLAIDO	3/6/84	Tavriya									M88	M46		2	-
ryhoriy YARMASH	4/1/85	Vorskla										D	D	2	-
vhen SELEZNEV	20/7/85	Arsenal										s66	M	2	-
erhiy KRAVCHENKO	24/4/83	Vorskla										s74	M	2	-
vhen LEVCHENKO	3/1/78	Groningen (NED)											M46	4	-
olodymyr HOMENYUK	19/7/85	Tavriya											A68	1	-

DOMESTIC LEAGUE 2007/08

VYSHCHA LIHA FINAL TABLE 2007/08

			Home					Away					Total					
		Pld	W	D	L	F	A	W	D	L	F	A	W	D	L	F	A	Pts
1	FC Shakhtar Donetsk	30	12	2	1	40	9	12	0	3	35	15	24	2	4	75	24	74
2	FC Dynamo Kyiv	30	10	2	3	36	18	12	3	0	29	8	22	5	3	65	26	71
3	FC Metalist Kharkiv	30	11	2	2	31	14	8	4	3	20	13	19	6	5	51	27	63
4	FC Dnipro Dnipropetrovsk	30	10	2	3	20	12	8	3	4	20	15	18	5	7	40	27	59
5	SC Tavriya Simferopol	30	9	4	2	28	18	4	4	7	10	22	13	8	9	38	40	47
6	FC Arsenal Kyiv	30	6	4	5	25	17	5	5	5	17	19	11	9	10	42	36	42
7	FC Chornomorets Odesa	30	6	3	6	16	11	5	2	8	11	22	11	5	14	27	33	38
8	FC Vorskla Poltava	30	7	6	2	18	10	2	3	10	10	20	9	9	12	28	30	36
9	FC Metalurh Zaporizhya	30	4	6	5	9	11	5	3	7	15	21	9	9	12	24	32	36
10	FC Karpaty Lviv	30	6	3	6	21	15	3	3	9	8	26	9	6	15	29	41	33
11	FC Zorya Luhansk	30	6	1	8	16	21	3	3	9	8	22	9	4	17	24	43	31
12	FC Metalurh Donetsk	30	5	4	6	16	13	1	9	5	18	26	6	13	11	34	39	31
13	FC Kryvbas Kryvyi Rih	30	3	5	7	13	15	4	4	7	16	24	7	9	14	29	39	30
14	FC Kharkiv	30	3	4	8	8	18	3	5	7	12	14	6	9	15	20	32	27
15	FC Naftovyk-Ukrnafta Okhtyrka	30	3	4	8	11	22	3	4	8	7	16	6	8	16	18	38	26
16	FC Zakarpattya Uzhhorod	30	2	6	7	10	19	1	3	11	7	35	3	9	18	17	54	18

TOP GOALSCORERS

19 Marko DEVIĆ (Metalist)

17 Olexandr HLADKIY (Shakhtar)
Yevhen SELEZNEV (Arsenal)
Olexandr KOSYRIN (Metalurh Donetsk)

15 Ismaël BANGOURA (Dynamo Kyiv)

14 Volodymyr HOMENYUK (Tavriya)

12 BRANDÃO (Shakhtar)

11 FERNANDINHO (Shakhtar)

10 Maksim SHATSKIKH (Dynamo Kyiv

9 Serhiy NAZARENKO (Dnipro)

CLUB-BY-CLUB

FC ARSENAL KYIV

Coach – Olexandr Zavarov

Founded – 2003

Date	Opponent		Score	Scorers
2007				
15/7	Metalurh Donetsk	h	1-3	*Josemar*
22/7	Dynamo Kyiv	a	2-2	*Zakarlyuka, Seleznev*
28/7	Naftovyk-Ukrnafta	h	3-0	*Kuznetsov, Josemar, Essola*
4/8	Zorya	a	1-3	*Symonenko*
11/8	Zakarpattya	h	7-0	*Seleznev 3, Demetradze 2, Bito 2*
17/8	Vorskla	a	1-2	*Seleznev*
26/8	Metalist	h	1-1	*Mizin*
1/9	Shakhtar	a	1-4	*Josemar*
16/9	Tavriya	h	0-1	
23/9	Chornomorets	h	1-2	*Zakarlyuka (p)*
30/9	Dnipro	a	3-1	*Seleznev 2, Zakarlyuka*
6/10	Metalurh Zaporizhya	h	2-1	*Seleznev, Symonenko*
21/10	Karpaty	a	0-0	
27/10	Kryvbas	h	0-0	
3/11	Kharkiv	a	0-2	
10/11	Metalurh Donetsk	a	2-1	*Josemar, Zakarlyuka*
2411	Dynamo Kyiv	h	0-1	
11/12	Naftovyk-Ukrnafta	a	0-1	
2008				
29/2	Zorya	h	1-1	*Seleznev*
8/3	Zakarpattya	a	0-0	
16/3	Vorskla	h	3-2	*Demetradze, Seleznev 2 (1p)*
21/3	Metalist	a	4-2	*Lysenko, Symonenko, Starhorodskiy, Seleznev*
30/3	Shakhtar	h	2-4	*Zakarlyuka, Lysenko*
4/4	Tavriya	a	1-1	*Seleznev*
12/4	Chornomorets	a	1-0	*Seleznev*
18/4	Dnipro	h	2-1	*Seleznev 2 (1p)*
26/4	Metalurh Zaporizhya	a	1-0	*Lysenko*
4/5	Karpaty	h	2-0	*Seleznev, Yevseyev*
11/5	Kryvbas	a	0-0	
17/5	Kharkiv	h	0-0	

No	Name	Nat	Pos	Aps	(s)	Gls
99	ALAN Silva da Souza	BRA	M		(3)	
20	Olexandr BATALSKIY		A		(3)	
5	Yuryi BENIO		D	28		
18	Sendley Sidney BITO	ANT	M	7	(19)	2
77	Aleksandr DANISHEVSKY	RUS	A	2	(7)	
30	Giorgi DEMETRADZE	GEO	A	5	(13)	3
17	Vadym DEONAS VINOKUROV		G	9		
8	Paul ESSOLA Erve Tchamba	CMR	M	27		1
11	JOSEMAR Silva dos Santos	BRA	A	28		4
33	Andriy KHOMYN		D	19	(3)	

6	Sergei KUZNETSOV	BLR	M	23	(5)	1
14	Volodymyr LYSENKO		A	9		3
15	Serhiy LYTOVCHENKO		D	13	(2)	
7	Serhiy MIZIN		M	3	(5)	1
23	Dmytro PARFENOV		D	8		
3	Andriy RASPOPOV		D	22	(1)	
1	Vitaliy REVA		G	21		
2	Olexandr ROMANCHUK		D	16		
34	Vadym RYBALCHENKO		A		(1)	
10	Yevhen SELEZNEV		M	21	(3)	17
39	Artem STARHORODSKIY		M	9	(3)	1
4	Serhiy SYMONENKO		M	24		3
14	Ruslan YAROSH		D		(1)	
16	Yevhen YEVSEYEV		D	9	(1)	1
9	Serhiy ZAKARLYUKA		M	27		5
29	Yaroslav ZAKHAREVYCH		M		(3)	
21	Valeriy ZAVAROV		M		(4)	

FC CHORNOMORETS ODESA

Coach – Vitaliy Shevchenko

Founded – 1958

MAJOR HONOURS: Ukrainian Cup - (2) 1992, 1994.

2007				
18/7	Kharkiv	h	0-1	
25/7	Metalurh Donetsk	a	0-0	
1/8	Dynamo Kyiv	h	0-0	
5/8	Naftovyk-Ukrnafta	a	1-0	*Poltavets (p)*
10/8	Zorya	h	1-0	*Korytko*
18/8	Zakarpattya	a	0-2	
26/8	Vorskla	h	1-0	*Hryshko*
2/9	Metalist	a	0-2	
15/9	Shakhtar	h	1-2	*Venhlynskiy*
23/9	Arsenal	a	2-1	*Korytko 2 (1 p)*
30/9	Tavriya	h	2-0	*Melio, Vázquez*
7/10	Dnipro	h	1-2	*Korytko (p)*
20/10	Metalurh Zaporizhya	a	2-0	*Shyshchenko, Vázquez*
26/10	Karpaty	h	4-0	*Vázquez, Korytko (p), Bugaiov (p), Poltavets*
4/11	Kryvbas	a	0-3	
9/11	Kharkiv	a	1-1	*Korytko (p)*
23/11	Metalurh Donetsk	h	1-0	*Vázquez*
1/12	Dynamo Kyiv	a	2-5	*Haza 2*
2008				
1/3	Naftovyk-Ukrnafta	h	0-1	
8/3	Zorya	a	2-0	*Melio, Biletskyi*
15/3	Zakarpattya	h	3-1	*Melio 2, Korytko (p)*
23/3	Vorskla	a	0-2	
29/3	Metalist	h	0-1	
6/4	Shakhtar	a	1-0	*Korytko (p)*
12/4	Arsenal	h	0-1	
20/4	Tavriya	a	0-3	
25/4	Dnipro	a	0-1	
3/5	Metalurh Zaporizhya	h	1-1	*Melio*
11/5	Karpaty	a	0-2	
17/5	Kryvbas	h	1-1	*Hryshko*

No	Name	Nat	Pos	Aps	(s)	Gls
6	Maxym BILETSKIY		M	28		1
55	Igor BUGAIOV	MDA	M	1	(2)	1
33	Serhiy DANYLOVSKIY		M	1		
33	José Carlos FERNÁNDEZ	PER	A		(2)	
4	Damián Joel GIMÉNEZ	ARG	D	27		
25	Paolo Giancarlo de la HAZA	PER	M	17	(5)	2
37	Dmytro HRYSHKO		D	18		2
10	Oleh HUMENYUK		D	3	(4)	
98	Marko JOVANOVIĆ	SRB	A	3		
23	Pavel KIRILCHIK	BLR	M	1		
77	Andriy KORNEV		M	8	(8)	
7	Vladimir KORYTKO	BLR	A	28		8
8	Andriy KYRLYK		M	4	(1)	
10	Ruslan LEVIHA		A	2	(4)	
33	Ihor LOZO		D		(1)	
79	Álvaro Alejandro MELLO	URU	M	13	(5)	5
2	Gennadiy NIZHEGORODOV	RUS	D	27		
17	Sergei POLITYLO		M		(5)	
3	Valentyn POLTAVETS		M	5	(2)	2
15	Volodymyr PRIYOMOV		A	4	(3)	
1	Vataliy RUDENKO		G	29		
5	Oleh SHANDRUK		D	7	(5)	
12	Yevhen SHIRYAYEV		D	1		
88	Serhiy SHYSHCHENKO		M	13	(4)	1
13	Rinar VALEYEV		A	4	(7)	
39	Denys VASIN		A	1	(2)	
30	Sebastián Rodrigo VÁZQUEZ	URU	M	22		4
10	Oleh VENHLYNSKIY		A	12	(9)	1
14	Edgar VILLAMARÍN	PER	D	8		
24	Kostyantyn YAROSHENKO		M	2	(1)	
18	Olexandr YATSENKO		D	17		
9	Olexandr ZOTOV		M	24		

FC DNIPRO DNIPROPETROVSK

Coach – Oleh Protasov

Founded – 1962

MAJOR HONOURS: USSR League - (2) 1983, 1988; USSR Cup - (1) 1989.

2007				
14/7	Kryvbas	h	2-0	*Samodin, Vorobei*
21/7	Kharkiv	a	2-1	*og (Ribeiro), Nazarenko*
29/7	Metalurh Donetsk	h	4-1	*Vorobei, Shelayev (p), Nazarenko 2 (1 p)*
5/8	Dynamo Kyiv	a	3-1	*Samodin 2, Vorobei*
11/8	Naftovyk-Ukrnafta	h	2-0	*Nazarenko, Kravchenko*
19/8	Zorya	a	1-0	*Samodin*
26/8	Zakarpattya	h	0-0	
2/9	Vorskla	a	1-2	*Nazarenko*
16/9	Metalist	h	3-0	*og (Bordianu), Nazarenko, Liopa*
23/9	Shakhtar	a	1-4	*Vorobei*
30/9	Arsenal	h	1-3	*Kankava*
7/10	Chornomorets	a	2-1	*Vorobei, Samodin*
21/10	Tavriya	h	2-1	*Hrytsai, Shelayev (p)*
28/10	Metalurh Zaporizhya	h	1-0	*Samodin*
2/11	Karpaty	a	1-0	*Liopa*
10/11	Kryvbas	a	2-1	*Samodin, Vorobei*
25/11	Kharkiv	h	1-0	*Kankava*
1/12	Metalurh Donetsk	a	3-0	*Nazarenko, Kankava, Liopa*
2008				
2/3	Dynamo Kyiv	h	0-4	
9/3	Naftovyk-Ukrnafta	a	1-1	*Nazarenko*
16/3	Zorya	h	1-0	*og (Korotetskiy)*
22/3	Zakarpattya	a	1-1	*Holek*
31/3	Vorskla	h	1-0	*Samodin*
6/4	Metalist	a	0-1	
12/4	Shakhtar	h	1-3	*Nazarenko (p)*
18/4	Arsenal	a	1-2	*Vorobei*
25/4	Chornomorets	h	1-0	*Shershun*
4/5	Tavriya	a	1-0	*Mazilu*
11/5	Metalurh Zaporizhya	a	0-0	
17/5	Karpaty	h	0-0	

No	Name	Nat	Pos	Aps	(s)	Gls
22	Denys ANDRIYENKO		M	22	(1)	
9	Kostyantyn BALABANOV		A		(1)	
7	Mladen BARTULOVIĆ	CRO	M	2	(9)	
19	Vitaliy DENISOV	UZB	D	22	(2)	
18	Osmar FERREYRA	ARG	M	3	(4)	
88	Rolan GUSEV	RUS	M	10	(1)	
25	Mario HOLEK	CZE	M	9	(2)	1

No	Name	Nat	Pos	Aps	(s)	Gls
3	Olexandr HRYTSAI		D	19	(2)	1
20	Jaba KANKAVA	GEO	M	13	(9)	3
23	Vyacheslav KERNOZENKO		G	25		
17	Aleksandre KOBAKHIDZE	GEO	M		(1)	
42	Yevhen KONOPLYANKA		A		(2)	
8	Sergei KORNILENKO	BLR	A	3	(6)	
24	Kostyantyn KRAVCHENKO		A	10	(2)	1
77	Artem KUSLIY		G		(1)	
39	Dmytro LIOPA		M	9	(18)	3
21	Olexandr MAXIMOV		M		(3)	
15	Serhiy MATYUKHIN		D	2		
9	Ionuţ Costinel MAZILU	ROU	A	5	(3)	1
28	Serhiy NAZARENKO		M	27		9
29	Ruslan ROTAN		M	4	(4)	
16	Andriy RUSOL		A	28		
10	Sergei SAMODIN	RUS	A	22	(5)	8
30	Yevhen SHAKHOV		M		(5)	
6	Oleh SHELAYEV		M	22		2
4	Bohdan SHERSHUN		D	27		1
1	Maxym STARTSEV		G	5		
5	Vyacheslav SVIDERSKIY		D	6		
11	Andriy VOROBEI		A	26		7
13	Andrei YESCHENKO	RUS	D	9	(5)	

FC DYNAMO KYIV

Coach – Anatoliy Demyanenko; (20/9/07) József Szabó; (3/11/07) Oleh Luzhniy; (1/12/07) Yuriy Syomin (RUS)

Founded – 1927

MAJOR HONOURS: UEFA Cup Winners' Cup - (2) 1975, 1986; UEFA Super Cup - (1) 1975; USSR League - (13) 1961, 1966, 1967, 1968, 1971, 1974, 1975, 1977, 1980, 1981, 1985, 1986, 1990; Ukrainian League - (12) 1993, 1994, 1995, 1996, 1997, 1998, 1999, 2000, 2001, 2003, 2004, 2007; USSR Cup - (9) 1954, 1964, 1966, 1974, 1978, 1982, 1985, 1987, 1990; Ukrainian Cup - (9) 1993, 1996, 1998, 1999, 2000, 2003, 2005, 2006, 2007.

2007

15/7	Shakhtar	a	1-1	*Diogo Rincón*
22/7	Arsenal	h	2-2	*Michael 2*
1/8	Chornomorets	a	0-0	
5/8	Dnipro	h	1-3	*Rebrov*
11/8	Metalurh Zaporizhya	a	1-0	*Marković*
19/8	Karpaty	h	7-3	*Shatskikh, og (Pshenychnykh), Marković, Bangoura 3, Corrêa*
25/8	Kryvbas	a	1-0	*Bangoura*
1/9	Kharkiv	h	2-0	*Bangoura, Michael*
15/9	Metalurh Donetsk	a	2-1	*Shatskikh, Mykhalyk*
22/9	Tavriya	a	4-1	*Milevskiy, Diogo Rincón 2 (1p), Shatskikh*
29/9	Naftovyk-Ukrnafta	h	0-1	
6/10	Zorya	a	2-1	*Shatskikh, Ghioane*
20/10	Zakarpattya	h	1-0	*Diogo Rincón*
27/10	Vorskla	a	1-0	*Bangoura*
3/11	Metalist	h	0-1	
11/11	Shakhtar	h	2-1	*Bangoura 2*
24/11	Arsenal	a	1-0	*Ghioane*
1/12	Chornomorets	h	5-2	*Bangoura (p), Ghioane, Shatskikh, Gusev, Ninković*

2008

2/3	Dnipro	a	4-0	*Corrêa, Bangoura, Gusev, Kravets*
8/3	Metalurh Zaporizhya	h	2-1	*Shatskikh, Ghioane*
15/3	Karpaty	a	2-1	*Shatskikh, Ghioane*
23/3	Kryvbas	h	3-0	*Shatskikh 2, Bangoura*
30/3	Kharkiv	a	1-0	*Ghioane*
5/4	Metalurh Donetsk	h	3-3	*Bangoura, Aliyev, Milevskiy*
12/4	Tavriya	h	3-0	*Aliyev, Kravets, Ghioane*
20/4	Naftovyk-Ukrnafta	a	3-0	*Milevskiy 2, Shatskikh*
26/4	Zorya	h	3-0	*Milevskiy, Aliyev, Kravets*
3/5	Zakarpattya	a	4-1	*Yussuf, Bangoura 3*
11/5	Vorskla	h	2-1	*Ninković, Yarmolenko*
17/5	Metalist	a	2-2	*El Kaddouri, Oliynyk*

No	Name	Nat	Pos	Aps	(s)	Gls
88	Olexandr ALIYEV		M	5	(5)	3
10	Ismaël BANGOURA	GUI	M	14	(6)	15
8	Valentin BELKEVICH	BLR	M	2		
7	Carlos Rodrigo CORRÊA	BRA	M	24	(1)	2
3	Pape DIAKHATÉ	SEN	D	15	(1)	
15	DIOGO Augusto Pacheco da Fontoura "RINCÓN"	BRA	A	11	(2)	4
41	Oleh DOPILKA		D	7		
30	Badr EL KADDOURI	MAR	M	14	(3)	1
18	Balázs FARKAS	HUN	M		(1)	
24	Vitaliy FEDORIV		D	3	(1)	
2	Serhiy FEDOROV		D	3		
32	Goran GAVRANČIĆ	SRB	D	10	(1)	
4	Tiberiu GHIOANE	ROU	D	21	(4)	7
20	Oleh GUSEV		M	18	(2)	2
9	KLÉBER de Souza Freitas	BRA	A	6	(3)	
38	Artem KRAVETS		A	8	(3)	3
21	Taras LUTSENKO		G	4		
19	Volodymyr LYSENKO		A	1	(1)	
29	Vitaliy MANDZYUK		M	5		
81	Marjan MARKOVIĆ	SRB	D	14	(2)	2
11	MICHAEL Pereira da Silva	BRA	M	6	(2)	3
25	Artem MILEVSKIY		A	9	(12)	5
42	Vadym MILKO		M	1		
43	Mykola MOROZYUK		M	1	(3)	
17	Taras MYKHALYK		M	16		1
26	Andriy NESMACHNIY		D	15	(2)	
36	Miloš NINKOVIĆ	SRB	M	10	(7)	2
58	Denys OLIYNYK		A		(1)	1
5	Serhiy REBROV		A	7	(2)	1
44	RODRIGO Baldasso da Costa	BRA	D	5	(1)	
14	Ruslan ROTAN		M	7	(3)	
55	Olexandr RYBKA		G	4		
16	Maksim SHATSKIKH	UZB	A	15	(8)	10
1	Olexandr SHOVKOVSKIY		G	22		
27	Vladyslav VASHCHUK		D	12	(5)	
70	Anatoliy YARMOLENKO		A		(1)	1
37	YUSSUF Atanda Ayila	NGA	D	15		1
49	Roman ZOZULYA		A		(1)	

FC KARPATY LVIV

Coach – Olexandr Ishchenko; (5/9/07) Valeriy Yaremchenko

Founded – 1963

MAJOR HONOURS: USSR Cup – (1) 1969.

2007

13/7	Metalurh Zaporizhya	a	0-1	
20/7	Tavriya	a	1-2	*Kobin*
28/7	Kryvbas	h	3-0	*Batista 2, Khudobyak*
4/8	Kharkiv	a	0-1	
12/8	Metalurh Donetsk	h	0-0	
19/8	Dynamo Kyiv	a	3-7	*Batista, Kovel, Kobin*
25/8	Naftovyk-Ukrnafta	h	1-1	*og (Ptachyk)*
2/9	Zorya	a	1-0	*Batista*
15/9	Zakarpattya	h	2-0	*Kovel, Tkachuk*
22/9	Vorskla	a	0-0	
30/9	Metalist	h	0-2	
7/10	Shakhtar	a	0-3	
21/10	Arsenal	h	0-0	
26/10	Chornomorets	a	0-4	
2/11	Dnipro	h	0-1	
10/11	Metalurh Zaporizhya	h	1-3	*Khudobyak*
24/11	Tavriya	h	4-0	*Kobin, Kovel 3*

2/12	Kryvbas	a 1-0	*Kovel*
2008			
1/3	Kharkiv	h 1-0	*Feshchuk*
7/3	Metalurh Donetsk	a 0-1	
15/3	Dynamo Kyiv	h 1-2	*Oshchypko*
22/3	Naftovyk-Ukrnafta	a 0-0	
17/6	Zorya	h 3-0	*Feshchuk 2, Kirilchik*
5/4	Zakarpattya	a 2-1	*Kirilchik, Khudobyak*
12/4	Vorskla	h 1-2	*Kobin*
19/4	Metalist	a 0-4	
26/4	Shakhtar	h 2-4	*Feshchuk, Khudobyak*
4/5	Arsenal	a 0-2	
11/5	Chornomorets	h 2-0	*Petrivskiy, Feshchuk*
17/5	Dnipro	a 0-0	

No	Name	Nat	Pos	Aps	(s)	Gls
9	William Rocha BATISTA	BRA	A	13		4
2	Volodymyr FEDORIV		D	23	(1)	
10	Maxym FESHCHUK		A	17	(5)	5
7	Samson GODWIN	NGA	M	28		
32	Oleh HOLODYUK		A		(2)	
23	Mykola ISHCHENKO		D	26		
16	Ihor KHUDOBYAK		M	28	(1)	4
33	Pavel KIRILCHIK	BLR	D	16	(7)	2
19	Vasyl KOBIN		M	25	(2)	4
18	Mykhailo KOPOLOVETS		M	4	(21)	
11	Leonid KOVEL	BLR	A	15	(1)	6
9	Denys KOZHANOV		M	4	(6)	
28	Giorgi LOMAIA	GEO	G		(1)	
5	Mykola LAPKO		D	3	(1)	
4	Serghey LASCENCOV	MDA	D	21		
29	Anton LUTSYK		M		(3)	
30	Jaroslav MARTYNYUK		D	1		
37	Yuriy MARTYSHCHUK		G	19	(1)	
1	Maciej Paweł NALEPA	POL	G	11		
13	Olexiy OMELCHENKO		A		(1)	
8	Ihor OSHCHYPKO		M	6	(3)	1
15	Taras PETRIVSKIY		D	7	(6)	1
14	Serhiy PSHENYCHNYKH		M	24	(1)	
6	Oleh SHKRED		D		(1)	
17	Aleksei SUCHKOV	BLR	M	10	(1)	
25	Andriy TKACHUK		M	8	(5)	1
3	Aleksandr YUREVICH	BLR	D	10		
11	Sergei ZENJOV	EST	A	3	(8)	
20	Oleh ZHENYUKH		M	8	(8)	

FC KHARKIV

Coach – Volodymyr Bessonov

Founded – 1998

2007			
18/7	Chornomorets	a 1-0	*Hunchak*
21/7	Dnipro	h 1-2	*Berezovchuk*
28/7	Metalurh Zaporizhya	a 0-0	
4/8	Karpaty	h 1-0	*Hunchak*
12/8	Kryvbas	a 1-1	*Hunchak*
18/8	Tavriya	a 0-1	
24/8	Metalurh Donetsk	h 1-1	*Platon*
1/9	Dynamo Kyiv	a 0-2	
14/9	Naftovyk-Ukrnafta	h 1-0	*Ribeiro*
22/9	Zorya	a 1-2	*Berezovchuk*
29/9	Zakarpattya	h 0-2	
5/10	Vorskla	a 1-1	*Samborskiy*
21/10	Metalist	h 0-2	
28/10	Shakhtar	a 1-2	*Sokolenko*
3/11	Arsenal	h 2-0	*Bilyi 2*
9/11	Chornomorets	h 1-1	*Samborskiy*
25/11	Dnipro	a 0-1	
2/12	Metalurh Zaporizhya	h 0-1	
2008			
1/3	Karpaty	a 0-1	
9/3	Kryvbas	h 0-0	
14/3	Tavriya	h 1-1	*Hunchak*
23/3	Metalurh Donetsk	a 0-0	
26/3	Dynamo Kyiv	h 0-1	
6/4	Naftovyk-Ukrnafta	a 4-1	*Fedetskiy 3, Hunchak*
13/4	Zorya	h 0-1	
20/4	Zakarpattya	a 3-0	*Fedetskiy 2, Batista*
26/4	Vorskla	h 0-3	
2/5	Metalist	a 0-2	
11/5	Shakhtar	h 0-3	
17/5	Arsenal	a 0-0	

No	Name	Nat	Pos	Aps	(s)	Gls
99	Ibrahim ABDOULAYE	TOG	A	5	(7)	
20	Kakhaber ALADASHVILI	GEO	M	8		
10	ANDERSON Mende RIBEIRO	BRA	A	20	(6)	1
9	William Rocha BATISTA	BRA	A	6	(2)	1
7	Andriy BEREZOVCHUK		M	27		2
33	Maxym BILIY		M	15	(12)	2
14	Yevhen CHEBERYACHKO		M	26	(3)	
44	Artem FEDETSKIY		D	22	(2)	5
21	Olexiy GORODOV		M	19		
23	Mykola HRINCHENKO		M	1	(3)	
35	Ruslan HUNCHAK		M	29		5
3	Oleh KARAMUSHKA		D	5		
5	Vitaliy KOMARNYTSKIY		M	16	(4)	
12	Rustam KHUDZHAMOV		G	30		
8	Olexandr MAXIMOV		M		(1)	
34	Vadym MILKO		M	9	(3)	
13	Guvanchmuhamed OVEKOV	TKM	M	8	(4)	
25	Aleksei PANKOVETS	BLR	D	18	(1)	
9	Olexandr PIKHUR		M	4	(11)	
15	Ruslan PLATON		A	10	(3)	1
17, 8	Volodymyr SAMBORSKIY		D	7	(8)	2
11	Andriy SMALKO		M	11	(2)	
4	Andriy SOKOLENKO		D	23	(2)	1
17	Aleksei SUCHKOV	BLR	M	11		

FC KRYVBAS KRYVYI RIH

Coach – Oleh Taran

Founded – 1959

2007			
14/7	Dnipro	a 0-2	
21/7	Metalurh Zaporizhya	h 0-1	
28/7	Karpaty	a 0-3	
4/8	Tavriya	a 3-4	*Kostyshyn, Motuz 2*
12/8	Kharkiv	h 1-1	*Sachko*
18/8	Metalurh Donetsk	a 1-0	*Ivashchenko*
25/8	Dynamo Kyiv	h 0-1	
1/9	Naftovyk-Ukrnafta	a 2-1	*Bylykbashi 2*
16/9	Zorya	h 1-2	*Pashayev*
22/9	Zakarpattya	a 3-2	*Bylykbashi (p), Sachko, Motuz*
29/9	Vorskla	h 3-0	*Sachko, Oprya, Lysytskiy*
7/10	Metalist	a 2-3	*Oprya, Lysytskiy*
20/10	Shakhtar	h 1-0	*Motuz*
27/10	Arsenal	a 0-0	
4/11	Chornomorets	h 3-0	*Oprya, Motuz 2*
10/11	Dnipro	h 1-2	*Kostyshyn*
25/11	Metalurh Zaporizhya	a 1-1	*Melashchenko*
2/12	Karpaty	h 0-1	
2008			
2/3	Tavriya	h 1-1	*Bylykbashi*
9/3	Kharkiv	a 0-0	
15/3	Metalurh Donetsk	h 1-1	*Bylykbashi*
23/3	Dynamo Kyiv	a 0-3	
30/3	Naftovyk-Ukrnafta	h 0-1	
5/4	Zorya	a 2-1	*Bylykbashi, Bartulović*
13/4	Zakarpattya	h 1-1	*Motuz*
19/4	Vorskla	a 1-2	*Bylykbashi (p)*

26/4	Metalist	h	0-3	
3/5	Shakhtar	a	0-1	
11/5	Arsenal	h	0-0	
17/5	Chornomorets	a	1-1	*Melnyk*

No	Name	Nat	Pos	Aps	(s)	Gls
7	Mladen BARTULOVIĆ	CRO	M	6	(4)	1
12	Yevhen BOROVYK		G	11		
18	Ervin BULKU	ALB	M	14	(5)	
17	Dorian BYLYKBASHI	ALB	M	28	(1)	7
4	Olexandr GRANOVSKIY		D	10		
32	Isli HIDI	ALB	G	18		
27	Vasyl HRYTSUK		M	2	(1)	
33	Patrick IBANDA	CMR	D		(3)	
16	Olexandr IVASHCHENKO		A	8	(5)	1
10	Ruslan KOSTYSHYN		M	23	(1)	2
2	Oleh KOTELYUKH		D	13	(6)	
6	Petro KOVALCHUK		D	7	(2)	
22	Vitaliy LYSYTSKIY		M	25	(1)	2
15	Serhiy MATYUKHIN		D	7		
8	Olexandr MELASHCHENKO		A	9	(12)	1
3	Viktor MELNYK		M	22	(5)	1
20	Serhiy MOTUZ		A	7	(19)	7
19	Henri NDREKA	ALB	D	11	(1)	
29	Anatoliy OPRYA		M	25	(3)	3
1	Oleh OSTAPENKO		G	1		
34	Maxym PASHAYEV		M	28	(1)	1
14	Olexandr RADCHENKO		D	15		
21	Igor ROZHKOV	BLR	M	9	(7)	
7	Vasyl SACHKO		A	20	(7)	3
24	Hryhoriy SAKHNYUK		D	1		
5	Aleksandr SHAGOYKO	BLR	D	10	(1)	

FC METALIST KHARKIV

Coach – Myron Markevych

Founded – 1925

MAJOR HONOURS: USSR Cup - (1) 1988.

2007				
14/7	Naftovyk-Ukrnafta	h	2-0	*Dević 2*
21/7	Zorya	a	2-3	*Valyayev, Slyusar*
29/7	Zakarpattya	h	1-0	*Rykun*
4/8	Vorskla	a	1-1	*Nwoga*
12/8	Tavriya	h	3-0	*Fomin, Antonov, Zézé*
19/8	Shakhtar	h	1-3	*Dević*
26/8	Arsenal	a	1-1	*Slyusar*
2/9	Chornomorets	h	2-0	*Dević, Nwoga*
16/9	Dnipro	a	0-3	
23/9	Metalurh Zaporizhya	h	2-1	*Dević (p), Bordianu*
30/9	Karpaty	a	2-0	*Fomin, Valyayev*
7/10	Kryvbas	h	3-2	*Babych, Slyusar, Nwoga*
21/10	Kharkiv	a	2-0	*Obradović (p), Zézé*
27/10	Metalurh Donetsk	h	1-1	*Dević*
3/11	Dynamo Kyiv	a	1-0	*Dević*
11/11	Naftovyk-Ukrnafta	a	2-0	*Slyusar, Antonov*
25/11	Zorya	h	2-1	*Zézé 2*
1/12	Zakarpattya	a	1-0	*Ganczarczyk*
2008				
1/3	Vorskla	h	3-0	*Dević (2p), Fomin*
8/3	Tavriya	a	0-0	
15/3	Shakhtar	a	1-4	*Dević (p)*
21/3	Arsenal	h	2-4	*Edmar, Dević (p)*
29/3	Chornomorets	a	1-0	*Jajá*
6/4	Dnipro	h	1-0	*Slyusar*
13/4	Metalurh Zaporizhya	a	2-0	*Dević 2*
19/4	Karpaty	h	4-0	*Edmar, Jajá, og (Lascencov), Slyusar*
26/4	Kryvbas	a	3-0	*Dević 2, Jajá*
2/5	Kharkiv	h	2-0	*Dević 2 (1p)*
11/5	Metalurh Donetsk	a	1-1	*Devic*
17/4	Dynamo Kyiv	h	2-2	*Dević, Didenko*

No	Name	Nat	Pos	Aps	(s)	Gls
69	Olexiy ANTONOV		A	6	(12)	2
5	Olexandr BABYCH		D	12	(5)	1
19	Serhiy BARYLKO		M		(2)	
37	Vitaly BORDIANU	MDA	D	29	(1)	1
23	Aleksandr DANILOV	BLR	M	6	(3)	
11	Serhiy DAVYDOV		A	2	(2)	
33	Marko DEVIĆ	SRB	M	25	(2)	19
39	Anatoliy DIDENKO		M		(9)	1
8	EDMAR de Lacerda	BRA	A	22		2
24	Ruslan FOMIN		A	6	(2)	3
6	Seweryn GANCARCZYK	POL	D	25	(2)	1
29	Olexandr GORYAINOV		G	24		
14	Lasha JAKOBIA	GEO	M	4		
50	Jackson Avelino Coelho "JAJÁ"	BRA	A	10	(1)	3
51	Serhiy KOSTYUK		M		(1)	
88	Olexiy KURILOV		D		(1)	
4	Vlade LAZAREVSKI	MKD	M	2	(1)	
13	Hicham MAHDOUFI	MAR	D	2	(2)	
10	Onyekachi NWOGA	NGA	M	10	(7)	3
22	Milan OBRADOVIĆ	SRB	D	25		1
30	Papa GUEYE	SEN	M	27	(2)	
20	Anton POSTUPALENKO		M		(1)	
27	Pavlo REBENOK		M	1	(1)	
25	Olexandr RYKUN		M	30		1
9	Valentyn SLYUSAR		M	28		6
1	Andriy TLUMAK		G	6		
10	Aleksandar TRIŠOVIĆ	SRB	M		(7)	
7	Serhiy VAYAYEV		M	26		2
26	Venance ZÉZÉ	CIV	A	2	(26)	4

FC METALURH DONETSK

Coach – Jos Daerden (BEL); (1/12/07) Serhiy Yashchenko; (3/4/08) Nikolai Kostov (BUL)

Founded – 1995

2007				
15/7	Arsenal	a	3-1	*Kosyrin 3*
25/7	Chornomorets	h	0-0	
29/7	Dnipro	a	1-4	*Glad*
3/8	Metalurh Zaporizhya	h	3-0	*Kosyrin 2 (1p), Gómez*
12/8	Karpaty	a	0-0	
18/8	Kryvbas	h	0-1	
24/8	Kharkiv	a	1-1	*Okoduwa*
31/8	Tavriya	a	3-3	*Kosyrin 3*
15/9	Dynamo Kyiv	h	1-2	*Bilozor*
21/9	Naftovyk-Ukrnafta	a	2-2	*Mendoza, Kosyrin*
28/9	Zorya	h	1-0	*Mendoza*
6/10	Zakarpattya	a	1-1	*Kosyrin (p)*
19/10	Vorskla	h	0-0	
27/10	Metalist	a	1-1	*Mendoza*
3/11	Shakhtar	h	0-1	
10/11	Arsenal	h	1-2	*Mitu*
23/11	Chornomorets	a	0-1	
1/12	Dnipro	h	0-3	
2008				
2/3	Metalurh Zaporizhya	a	0-1	
7/3	Karpaty	h	1-0	*Tymchenko*
15/3	Kryvbas	a	1-1	*Gvozdenović*
23/3	Kharkiv	h	0-0	
29/3	Tavriya	h	1-2	*Kosyrin*
5/4	Dynamo Kyiv	a	3-3	*Fernandes, Kosyrin 2*
11/4	Naftovyk-Ukrnafta	h	2-1	*Aílton, Arakelyan*
19/4	Zorya	a	1-1	*og (Skoba)*
26/4	Zakarpattya	h	5-0	*Kosyrin 3 (1p), Tkachenko, Arakelyan*
3/5	Vorskla	a	0-2	
11/5	Metalist	h	1-1	*Checher*
17/5	Shakhtar	a	1-4	*Kosyrin*

No	Name	Nat	Pos	Aps	(s)	Gls
9	AÍLTON Gonçalves da Silva	BRA	A	1	(1)	1
90	ALAN Silva da Souza	BRA	M	3	(10)	
6	Ararat ARAKELYAN	ARM	D	6	(1)	2
15,5	Serhiy BILOZOR		D	21	(1)	1
12	Anis BOUSSAIDI	TUN	M	6	(2)	
17	Erol BULUT	GER	M	18		
15	Vyacheslav CHECHER		D	28		1
8	Jordi CRUIJFF	NED	A	15		
23	Aleksandr DANILOV	BLR	M	7	(1)	
7	Serhiy DANYLOVSKIY		M	22		
66	Vladimir DIŠLJENKOVIĆ	SRB	G	27		
6	Abdoulaye DJIRE	CIV	M	3		
50	Ricardo FERNANDES	POR	D	10		1
21	Daniel Artola FERNÁNDEZ	ESP	D	11	(1)	
27	Rubén Marcelo GÓMEZ	ARG	M	11	(5)	1
2	Andriy GAVRYUSHOV		D	14	(1)	
8	Marko GRUBELIĆ	SRB	M	16		
55	Marcinho Glad GUERREIRO	BRA	M	1	(1)	1
20	Ivan GVOZDENOVIĆ	SRB	M	5	(4)	1
53	Vitaliy HAVRYSH		M	1	(1)	
44	Puis IKEDIA		A	2	(1)	
46	Vitaliy IVANKO		A		(1)	
88	Artem KASYANOV		M	4	(5)	
11, 10	Olexandr KOSYRIN		A	25	(1)	17
25	José LEANDRO de Souza	BRA	M	1	(3)	
55	Samvel MELKONYAN	ARM	M	5	(3)	
10	Andrés Augusto MENDOZA	PER	A	7	(2)	3
22	Bojan NEZIRI	SRB	M	3		
99	Dan Marius MITU	ROU	M	6	(4)	1
9	Vadym MELNYK		M		(5)	
20	Emmanuel Oseyi OKODUWA	NGA	A	6	(1)	1
13	Sérgio Pacheco de OLIVEIRA	BRA	A	8	(2)	
23	Bratislav RISTIĆ	SRB	M		(1)	
42	Volodymyr ROMANENKO		M	7	(4)	
35	Vadym SAPAI		M	4	(5)	
37	Olexandr SYTNYK		A	8	(7)	
11	Serhiy TKACHENKO		M	6		1
30	Ihor TYMCHENKO		A	4	(6)	1
20	Paulo César VOGT	BRA	A	2	(4)	
14	Olexandr VOLOVYK		D	3	(1)	
31	Dmitriy VOROBYOV	RUS	G	3		

FC METALURH ZAPORIZHYA

Coach – Anatoliy Chantsev

Founded – 1949

Date	Opponent		Result	Scorers
2007				
13/7	Karpaty	h	1-0	*Kashevskiy*
21/7	Kryvbas	a	1-0	*Stepanenko*
28/7	Kharkiv	h	0-0	
3/8	Metalurh Donetsk	a	0-3	
11/8	Dynamo Kyiv	h	0-1	
18/8	Naftovyk-Ukrnafta	a	1-0	*Lazarovych*
25/8	Zorya	h	3-0	*Sylyuk 2 (1p), Lazarovych*
1/9	Zakarpattya	a	1-1	*Arzhanov*
15/9	Vorskla	h	1-1	*Vernydub*
23/9	Metalist	a	1-2	*Chelyadinskiy*
29/9	Shakhtar	h	1-3	*Chelyadinskiy*
6/10	Arsenal	a	1-2	*Kvirkvelia*
20/10	Chornomorets	h	0-2	
28/10	Dnipro	a	0-1	
4/11	Tavriya	h	0-0	
10/11	Karpaty	a	3-1	*Kvirkvelia, Chelyadinskiy, Sylyuk*
25/11	Kryvbas	h	1-1	*Vernydub*
2/12	Kharkiv	a	1-0	*Godin*
2008				
2/3	Metalurh Donetsk	h	1-0	*Sylyuk*
8/3	Dynamo Kyiv	a	1-2	*Arzhanov*
16/3	Naftovyk-Ukrnafta	h	1-0	*Kabanov*
22/3	Zorya	a	1-0	*Vernydub*
29/3	Zakarpattya	h	0-0	
6/4	Vorskla	a	1-2	*Kabanov*
13/4	Metalist	h	0-2	
19/4	Shakhtar	a	0-4	
26/4	Arsenal	h	0-1	
3/5	Chornomorets	a	1-1	*og (Hryshko)*
11/5	Dnipro	h	0-0	
17/5	Tavriya	a	2-2	*Lazarovych, Kabanov*

No	Name	Nat	Pos	Aps	(s)	Gls
17	Volodymyr ARZHANOV		M	23	(4)	2
19	Stanislav BOHUSH		G	11		
2	Artem CHELYADINSKIY	BLR	D	28		3
27	Olexiy GODIN		M	19	(6)	1
10	Anton HAI		M	2	(5)	
9	Taras KABANOV		A	13	(2)	3
7	Nikolai KASHEVSKIY	BLR	M	24	(2)	1
38	Serhiy KRIVTSOV		D	4		
23	Maxym KRYVIY		A		(1)	
6	Dato KVIRKVELIA	GEO	M	16	(2)	2
11	Taras LAZAROVYCH		A	12	(13)	3
40	Roman LUTSENKO		D	3		
21	Ruslan LYUBARSKIY		M	18	(2)	
3	Dmytro NEVMYVAKA		D	24	(4)	
6	Dragan PERIŠIČ	SRB	M	2		
31	Yevhen PISOTSKIY		M	8	(7)	
14	Volodymyr POLYOVIY		D	24	(4)	
12	Vitaliy POSTRANSKIY		G	19		
22	Yevhen SANTRAPYNSKYKH		A	2	(3)	
8	Artem SEMENENKO		M		(3)	
30	Denys SMIRNOV		M		(1)	
4	Taras STEPANENKO		D	14	(9)	1
44	Serhiy SYLUYK		D	20	(5)	4
20	Yan TIGOREV	BLR	D	29		
5	Vitaliy VERNYDUB		D	15	(3)	3

FC NAFTOVYK-UKRNAFTA OKHTYRKA

Coach – Serhiy Shevchenko; (11/8/07) Viktor Ishchenko; (25/8/07) Valeriy Gorodov

Founded – 1980

Date	Opponent		Result	Scorers
2007				
14/7	Metalist	a	0-2	
21/7	Shakhtar	h	0-3	
28/7	Arsenal	a	0-3	
5/8	Chornomorets	h	0-1	
11/8	Dnipro	a	0-2	
18/8	Metalurh Zaporizhya	h	0-1	
25/8	Karpaty	a	1-1	*Oliynyk*
1/9	Kryvbas	h	1-2	*Karakevych*
14/9	Kharkiv	a	0-1	
21/9	Metalurh Donetsk	h	2-2	*Dedechko, Ptachyk*
29/9	Dynamo Kyiv	a	1-0	*Sheptytskiy*
6/10	Tavriya	a	0-1	
20/10	Zorya	h	0-0	
27/10	Zakarpattya	a	0-0	
3/11	Vorskla	h	2-0	*Karakevych, Olefir*
11/11	Metalist	h	0-2	
24/11	Shakhtar	a	1-1	*Karakevych (p)*
1/12	Arsenal	h	1-0	*Serdyuk*
2008				
1/3	Chornomorets	a	1-0	*Karakevych*
9/3	Dnipro	h	1-1	*Kotenko*
16/3	Metalurh Zaporizhya	a	0-1	
22/3	Karpaty	h	0-0	
30/3	Kryvbas	a	1-0	*Kučyš (p)*
6/4	Kharkiv	h	1-4	*Zaichuk*
11/4	Metalurh Donetsk	a	1-2	*Karakevych*
20/4	Dynamo Kyiv	h	0-3	

26/4	Tavriya	h	0-1	
4/5	Zorya	a	0-1	
11/5	Zakarpattya	h	3-2	*Karakevych 2 (1p), Ivanov*
17/5	Vorskla	a	1-1	*Karakevych*

No	Name	Nat	Pos	Aps	(s)	Gls
35	Branko BAKOVIĆ	SRB	M	5	(2)	
19	Kostyantyn BALABANOV		A	8	(2)	
24	Yevhen BARYSHNIKOV		D		(1)	
37	Ruslan BIDNENKO		M	4	(2)	
29	Vadim CHIRILOV	MDA	A	3	(2)	
18	Oleh DAVYDOV		D	2	(1)	
22	Denys DEDECHKO		M	9	(1)	1
20	Vasil GIGIADZE	GEO	A	12	(1)	
44	Olexiy IVANOV		M	22		1
21	Roman KARAKEVYCH		A	11	(12)	8
25	Serhiy KARPENKO		D	18	(1)	
7	Vadym KHARCHENKO		M	9	(5)	
16	Andriy KIKOT		M	8	(6)	
28	Ivan KOTENKO		M	13	(9)	1
9	Anatoliy KRETOV		M	15	(7)	
30	Aurimas KUČYS	LTU	D	10		1
5	Andriy KUTSENKO		D	6	(1)	
55	Artem KUSLIY		G	13		
27	Andriy MELNYCHUK		G	6		
46	Anton MONAKHOV		D	22		
45	Valeriy NEFEDOV		D	19		
38	Denys OLIYNYK		M	10	(4)	1
47	Volodymyr OLEFIR		D	4	(3)	1
3	Oleh PTACHYK		D	8		1
6	Andriy PISNYI		M	7		
4	Vyacheslav SERDYUK		D	23		1
16	Oleh SHEPTYTSKIY		A	5	(5)	1
33	Vyacheslav SHARPAR		M	2	(8)	
32	Serhiy SNITKO		M	12	(2)	
15	Vasyl TOVKATSKIY		M		(2)	
77	Eduard VALUŢA	MDA	D	4	(2)	
1	Serhiy VELYCHKO		G	11	(1)	
11	Bohdan YESYP		A	13	(4)	
23	Vladyslav ZAICHUK		D	15	(2)	1
13	Ruslan ZEINALOV		M	1	(1)	

FC SHAKHTAR DONETSK

Coach – Mircea Lucescu (ROU)

Founded – 1936

MAJOR HONOURS: Ukrainian League - (4) 2002, 2005, 2006, 2008; USSR Cup - (4) 1961, 1962, 1980, 1983; Ukrainian Cup - (6) 1995, 1997, 2001, 2002, 2004, 2008.

2007

15/7	Dynamo Kyiv	h	1-1	*Jádson*
21/7	Naftovyk-Ukrnafta	a	3-0	*Lewandowski, Hladkiy 2*
27/7	Zorya	h	3-0	*Jádson, Hladkiy 2*
5/8	Zakarpattya	a	1-0	*Brandão*
11/8	Vorskla	h	2-1	*Fernandinho, Hladkiy*
19/8	Metalist	a	3-1	*Hladkiy, Fernandinho, Ilsinho*
25/8	Tavriya	h	2-0	*Lucarelli 2 (1p)*
1/9	Arsenal	h	4-1	*Brandão 2, Hladkiy, Ilsinho*
15/9	Chornomorets	a	2-1	*Lucarelli (p), Chyhrynskiy*
23/9	Dnipro	h	4-1	*Raţ, Brandão 2 (1p), Hladkiy*
29/9	Metalurh Zaporizhya	a	3-1	*Brandão, Hladkiy 2*
7/10	Karpaty	h	3-0	*Ilsinho, Hladkiy 2*
20/10	Kryvbas	a	0-1	
28/10	Kharkiv	h	2-1	*og (Hunchak), Lucarelli (p)*
3/11	Metalurh Donetsk	a	1-0	*Fernandinho*
11/11	Dynamo Kyiv	a	1-2	*Jádson*
24/11	Naftovyk-Ukrnafta	h	1-1	*Chyhrynskiy*

2008

1/3	Zakarpattya	h	5-0	*Jádson, og (Donets), Hladkiy, Hai, Duljaj*
9/3	Vorskla	a	1-0	*Fernandinho*
15/3	Metalist	h	4-1	*Brandão, Chyhrynskiy, Fernandinho, Luiz Adriano*
23/3	Tavriya	a	2-3	*Brandão, Fernandinho*
30/3	Arsenal	a	4-2	*Jádson, Kravchenko, Brandão, Hai*
6/4	Chornomorets	h	0-1	
12/4	Dnipro	a	3-1	*Brandão, Raţ, Luiz Adriano*
19/4	Metalurh Zaporizhya	h	4-0	*Luiz Adriano, Jádson, Hladkiy (p), Fernandinho*
22/4	Zorya	a	4-1	*Hladkiy 2, Ilsinho, Yezerskiy*
26/4	Karpaty	a	4-2	*Hladkiy, Fernandinho, Brandão 2 (1p)*
3/5	Kryvbas	h	1-0	*Fernandinho*
11/5	Kharkiv	a	3-0	*Kucher, Luiz Adriano, Fernandinho (p)*
17/5	Metalurh Donetsk	h	4-1	*Jádson, Ilsinho, Fernandinho, Kravchenko*

No	Name	Nat	Pos	Aps	(s)	Gls
20	Olexiy BELIK		A	1	(1)	
25	Evaeverson Lemos da Silva "BRANDÃO"	BRA	A	16	(9)	12
9	Nery CASTILLO	MEX	M	5	(3)	
27	Dmytro CHYHRYNSKIY		D	27		3
6	Igor DULJAJ	SRB	D	13	(1)	1
7	Fernando Luís Roza "FERNANDINHO"	BRA	M	29		11
24	Ruslan FOMIN		A		(1)	
19	Olexiy HAI		M	9	(5)	2
21	Olexandr HLADKIY		A	20	(9)	17
3	Tomáš HÜBSCHMAN	CZE	D	18	(1)	
11	Ilson Pereira Dias Júnior "ILSINHO"	BRA	M	17	(3)	5
8	JÁDSON Rodrigues da Silva	BRA	M	22	(5)	7
5	Olexandr KUCHER		D	19	(2)	1
23	Kostyantyn KRAVCHENKO		M		(9)	2
18	Mariusz LEWANDOWSKI	POL	M	11	(7)	1
99	Cristiano LUCARELLI	ITA	A	9	(3)	4
17	LUIZ ADRIANO de Souza	BRA	M	8	(5)	4
29	Ciprian Andrei MARICA	ROU	A		(1)	
15	Volodymyr PRIYOMOV		A		(2)	
28	Olexiy POLYANSKIY		M		(1)	
30	Andriy PYATOV		G	23		
26	Răzvan Dincă RAŢ	ROU	D	18	(1)	2
13	Vyacheslav SHEVCHUK		M	12		
1	Bohdan SHUST		G	5		
12	Dmytro SHUTKOV		G	2		
33	Darijo SRNA	CRO	D	27	(1)	
37	Serhiy TKACHENKO		M		(1)	
10	Zvonimir VUKIĆ	SRB	M	2	(2)	
22	WILLIAN Borges da Silva	BRA	M	5	(14)	
55	Volodymyr YEZERSKIY		D	12	(1)	1

SC TAVRIYA SIMFEROPOL

Coach – Mykhailo Fomenko

Founded – 1958

MAJOR HONOURS: Ukrainian League - (1) 1992.

2007

14/7	Zakarpattya	a	0-1	
20/7	Karpaty	h	2-1	*Idahor 2*
28/7	Vorskla	a	0-0	

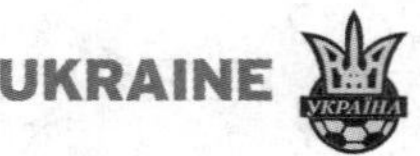

4/8	Kryvbas	h	4-3	*Homenyuk, Edmar 2 (1p), Ilnytskiy*
12/8	Metalist	a	0-3	
18/8	Kharkiv	h	1-0	*Homenyuk*
25/8	Shakhtar	a	0-2	
31/8	Metalurh Donetsk	h	3-3	*Kovpak, Idahor, Homenyuk*
16/9	Arsenal	a	1-0	*Kovpak*
22/9	Dynamo Kyiv	h	1-4	*Homenyuk*
30/9	Chornomorets	a	0-2	
6/10	Naftovyk-Ukrnafta	h	1-0	*Homenyuk*
21/10	Dnipro	a	1-2	*Homenyuk (p)*
28/10	Zorya	h	2-0	*Homenyuk, Jokšas*
4/11	Metalurh Zaporizhya	a	0-0	
10/11	Zakarpattya	h	4-1	*Idahor, Ljubenović, Homenyuk, Kovpak*
24/11	Karpaty	a	0-4	
30/11	Vorskla	h	1-0	*Ljubenović*
2008				
2/3	Kryvbas	a	1-1	*Homenyuk*
8/3	Metalist	h	0-0	
14/3	Kharkiv	a	1-1	*Ljubenović*
23/3	Shakhtar	h	3-2	*Homenyuk 2, Hajduczek*
29/3	Metalurh Donetsk	a	2-1	*Jokšas, Homenyuk*
4/4	Arsenal	h	1-1	*Homenyuk*
12/4	Dynamo Kyiv	a	0-3	
20/4	Chornomorets	h	3-0	*Galyuza, Idahor, Ljubenović*
26/4	Naftovyk-Ukrnafta	a	1-0	*Homenyuk*
4/5	Dnipro	h	0-1	
11/5	Zorya	a	3-2	*Ljubenović, Idahor 2*
17/5	Metalurh Zaporizhya	h	2-2	*Jokšas, Nazarov*

No	Name	Nat	Pos	Aps	(s)	Gls
2	Andriy BOIKO		D	23	(2)	
13, 25	Andriy DIKAN		G	12		
5	Lucian DOBRE	ROU	D	5		
8	EDMAR de Lacerda	BRA	A	5		2
19	Illya GALYUZA		M	26	(1)	1
7	Paweł HAJDUCZEK	POL	D	10	(2)	1
27	Denys HOLAIDO		M	27	(2)	
11	Volodymyr HOMENYUK		A	29	(1)	14
10	Lucky Isi IDAHOR	NGA	A	27	(3)	7
21	Taras ILNYTSKIY		D	16	(3)	1
18	Andrius JOKŠAS	LTU	M	19	(2)	3
9	Olexandr KOVPAK		A	12	(14)	3
20	Kyrylo KOVALCHUK		M	1	(2)	
5	Dmytro KOZACHENKO		G	2		
8	Herman KUTARBA		M		(5)	
14	Yevgeniy LENEV	BLR	D		(2)	
22	Željko LJUBENOVIĆ	SRB	M	27	(1)	5
16	Slobodan MARKOVIĆ	SRB	M	16	(1)	
15	Dmytro NAZAROV		D	10	(1)	1
99	Harrison Orowianor OMOKO	NGA	D	14		
3	Olexandr PERSHIN		D	18		
24	Denys STOYAN		D	5	(7)	
1	Saša TODIĆ	SRB	G	16		
77	Nerijus VASILIAUSKAS	LTU	M	2		
23	Audrius VEIKUTIS	LTU	D		(1)	
13	Andriy ZBOROVSKIY		A	3	(14)	
39	Irmantas ZELMIKAS	LTU	M	5	(2)	

FC VORSKLA POLTAVA

Coach – Anatoliy Momot; (27/12/07) Mykola Pavlov

Founded – 1984

2007				
14/7	Zorya	h	1-1	*Kravchenko*
22/7	Zakarpattya	a	0-0	
28/7	Tavriya	h	0-0	
4/8	Metalist	h	1-1	*Glavina*
11/8	Shakhtar	a	1-2	*Grumić*
17/8	Arsenal	h	2-1	*Grumić, Kravchenko*
26/8	Chornomorets	a	0-1	
2/9	Dnipro	h	2-1	*Glavina, Grumić*
15/9	Metalurh Zaporizhya	a	1-1	*Kravchenko*
22/9	Karpaty	h	0-0	
29/9	Kryvbas	a	0-3	
5/10	Kharkiv	h	1-1	*og (Berezovchuk)*
19/10	Metalurh Donetsk	a	0-0	
27/10	Dynamo Kyiv	h	0-1	
3/11	Naftovyk-Ukrnafta	a	0-2	
11/11	Zorya	a	0-0	*(w/o; awarded to Zorya)*
24/11	Zakarpattya	h	2-0	*Glavina, Markoski*
30/11	Tavriya	a	0-1	
2008				
1/3	Metalist	a	0-3	
9/3	Shakhtar	h	0-1	
16/3	Arsenal	a	2-3	*Chichikov, Curri*
23/3	Chornomorets	h	2-0	*Yesin, og (Yatsenko)*
31/3	Dnipro	a	0-1	
6/4	Metalurh Zaporizhya	h	2-1	*Kravchenko, Curri*
12/4	Karpaty	a	2-1	*Kravchenko, Yanuzi*
19/4	Kryvbas	h	2-1	*Markoski, Curri (p)*
26/4	Kharkiv	a	3-0	*Curri (p), Chichikov, Yesin (p)*
3/5	Metalurh Donetsk	h	2-0	*Chichikov, Curri*
11/5	Dynamo Kyiv	a	1-2	*Yarmash*
17/5	Naftovyk-Ukrnafta	h	1-1	*Curri (p)*

No	Name	Nat	Pos	Aps	(s)	Gls
43	Serhiy ARTYUKH		A		(3)	
48	Volodymyr CHESNAKOV		D	2		
31	Olexiy CHICHIKOV		A	11	(1)	3
36	Olexandr CHIZHOV		M	24		
20	Debatik CURRI	ALB	M	27	(1)	6
38	Armend DALLKU	ALB	D	27		1
3	Filip DESPOTOVSKI	MKD	M	3	(6)	
1	Serhiy DOLHANSKIY		G	28		
15	Serhiy DYACHENKO		M		(1)	
3	Denis GLAVINA	CRO	M	23	(3)	3
10	Miroslav GRUMIĆ	SRB	A	15	(4)	3
32	Saša JURIČIĆ	CRO	D	12		
35	Vasyl KLIMOV		M		(1)	
14	Serhiy KRAVCHENKO		M	26		5
5,8	Denys KULAKOV		M	13	(5)	
11	Ruslan LEVIHA		A	2	(1)	
9	Cătălin LICIU	ROU	A		(2)	
46	Maxym LUBENETS		A		(2)	
7	Jovan MARKOSKI	SRB	M	26		2
25	Hennadiy MEDVEDEV		D	29		
77	Oleh OSTAPENKO		G	1	(1)	
5	Valentyn PLATONOV		M	2	(1)	
12	Adrian PUKANYCH		M	3	(6)	
8	Ihor SHVETS		A	1	(6)	
40	Aleksandar STOJMIROVIĆ	SRB	M		(3)	
19	Eduard TSYKHMEISTRUK		M	2	(4)	
7	Ahmed YANUZI	ALB	A	2	(21)	1
37	Hryhoriy YARMASH		D	28		1
70	Dmytro YESIN		M	12		2

FC ZAKARPATTYA UZHHOROD

Coach – Petro Kushlyk; (26/9/07) Volodymyr Sharan; (20/4/08) Volodymyr Vasyutyk

Founded – 1946

2007				
14/7	Tavriya	h	1-0	*Bundash*
22/7	Vorskla	h	0-0	
29/7	Metalist	a	0-1	

UKRAINE

5/8	Shakhtar	h	0-1	
11/8	Arsenal	a	0-7	
18/8	Chornomorets	h	2-0	*Kozoriz, Martsveladze*
26/8	Dnipro	a	0-0	
1/9	Metalurh Zaporizhya	h	1-1	*og (Perišić)*
15/9	Karpaty	a	0-2	
22/9	Kryvbas	h	2-3	*Kozoriz, Bundash (p)*
29/9	Kharkiv	a	2-0	*Bundash 2*
6/10	Metalurh Donetsk	h	1-1	*Didenko (p)*
20/10	Dynamo Kyiv	a	0-1	
27/10	Naftovyk-Ukrnafta	h	0-0	
4/11	Zorya	a	0-1	
10/11	Tavriya	a	1-4	*Ksionz*
24/11	Vorskla	a	0-2	
1/12	Metalist	h	0-1	
2008				
1/3	Shakhtar	a	0-5	
8/3	Arsenal	h	0-0	
15/3	Chornomorets	a	1-3	*Babych*
22/3	Dnipro	h	1-1	*Donets*
29/3	Metalurh Zaporizhya	a	0-0	
5/4	Karpaty	h	1-2	*Kozoriz*
13/4	Kryvbas	a	1-1	*Platon*
20/4	Kharkiv	h	0-3	
26/4	Metalurh Donetsk	a	0-5	
3/5	Dynamo Kyiv	h	1-4	*Kraja (p)*
11/5	Naftovyk-Ukrnafta	a	2-3	*Kozoriz, Platon*
17/5	Zorya	h	0-2	

No	Name	Nat	Pos	Aps	(s)	Gls
6	Kakhaber ALADASHVILI	GEO	D	10		
33	Dmytro BABENKO		G	26		
6	Kostyantyn BABYCH		A	9		1
18	Volodymyr BRAILA		M	24	(1)	
30	Myroslav BUNDASH		A	13	(10)	4
11	Olexandr BURYI		A	8	(11)	
3	Olexandr CHYZHEVSKIY		D	28		
24	Ihor CHUCHMAN		D	11	(1)	
29	Anatoliy DIDENKO		A	9		1
20	Eddy Lord DOMBRAYE	NGA	M	2	(2)	
4	Andriy DONETS		M	16	(3)	1
22	Ivan KOZORIZ		M	26		4
2	Ervis KRAJA	ALB	D	9		1
7	Olexiy KRYVOSHEYEV		M	14	(2)	
9	Pavlo KSIONZ		A	12	(9)	1
8	Otar MARTSVELADZE	GEO	M	12	(5)	1
23	Vladyslav MYKULYAK		A	20	(7)	
77	Olexandr NAD		G	1		
10	Charles NEWUCHE	NGA	A	1	(6)	
20	Andriy PISNYI		D	4	(4)	
8	Ruslan PLATON		A	9	(2)	2
14	Miloš POPOVIĆ	MNE	M	2		
1	Vsevolod ROMANENKO		G	3	(2)	
5	Ihor SHOPIN		M	14	(9)	
6	Ivan SHUHA		D	3	(1)	
27	Ruslan YAROSH		A	10	(2)	
19	Serhiy YESIN		M	26		
21	Andriy VITOSHYNSKIY		M	1	(6)	
25	Yaroslav VYSHNYAK		D	7	(1)	
27	Serhiy ZELDI		M		(1)	

FC ZORYA LUHANSK

Coach – Olexandr Kosevych; (24/3/08) Anatoliy Volobuyev

Founded – 1923

MAJOR HONOURS: USSR League – (1) 1972.

2007				
14/7	Vorskla	a	1-1	*Tsykhmeistruk*
21/7	Metalist	h	3-2	*Vorobei, Brovkin, Bunjevčević*
27/7	Shakhtar	a	0-3	
4/8	Arsenal	h	3-1	*Bunjevčević (p), Puliz, Brovkin*
10/8	Chornomorets	a	0-1	
19/8	Dnipro	h	0-1	
25/8	Metalurh Zaporizhya	a	0-3	
2/9	Karpaty	h	0-1	
16/9	Kryvbas	a	2-1	*Brovkin 2*
22/9	Kharkiv	h	2-1	*Lutsenko, Konyushenko*
28/9	Metalurh Donetsk	a	0-1	
6/10	Dynamo Kyiv	h	1-2	*og (Milevskiy)*
20/10	Naftovyk-Ukrnafta	a	0-0	
28/10	Tavriya	a	0-2	
4/11	Zakarpattya	h	1-0	*Dunić*
11/11	Vorskla	h	0-0	*(w/o; awarded to Zorya)*
25/11	Metalist	a	1-2	*Shmakov*
2008				
29/2	Arsenal	a	1-1	*Tselykh*
8/3	Chornomorets	h	0-2	
16/3	Dnipro	a	0-1	
22/3	Metalurh Zaporizhya	h	0-1	
29/3	Karpaty	a	0-3	
5/4	Kryvbas	h	1-2	*Lutsenko (p)*
13/4	Kharkiv	a	1-0	*Khramtsov*
19/4	Metalurh Donetsk	h	1-1	*Nwoga*
22/4	Shakhtar	h	1-4	*Vorobei*
26/4	Dynamo Kyiv	a	0-3	
4/5	Naftovyk-Ukrnafta	h	1-0	*Tsimakuridze (p)*
11/5	Tavriya	h	2-3	*Antonov, Skoba (p)*
17/5	Zakarpattya	a	2-0	*Lutsenko, Vorobei*

No	Name	Nat	Pos	Aps	(s)	Gls
26	Olexiy ANTONOV		A	8	(1)	1
2	Shpetim BABAJ	ALB	M	6		
20	Ihor BAZHAN		G	14		
17	Yevhen BREDUN		M	5	(1)	
23	Dmytro BROVKIN		A	11	(6)	4
10	Mirko BUNJEVČEVIĆ	SRB	D	14	(5)	2
88	Vladimer BURDULI	GEO	M	18	(1)	
8	Darko DUNIĆ	SRB	M	22		1
15	Andriy GAVRYUSHOV		D	6		
4	Vladyslav GOLOPYOROV		A		(1)	
17	Dmytro GORBUSHIN		M	1	(7)	
15	Vitaliy KAZANKOV		M		(1)	
24	Dmytro KHOVBOSHA		D	1	(3)	
38	Aleksei KHRAMTSOV	MDA	D	27		1
33	Andriy KOMARNYTSKIY		G	8		
22	Andriy KONYUSHENKO		D	19	(1)	1
5	Ihor KOROTETSKIY		D	8		
51	Vasyl KOSTYUK		A		(2)	
7	Yevhen LUTSENKO		M	12	(5)	3
10	Onyekachi NWOGA	NGA	M	7	(1)	1
55	Igor PETKOVIĆ	SRB	M	1	(3)	
5	Valentyn PLATONOV		M	11	(3)	
6	Olexandr POLOVKOV		D	15	(2)	
11	Alexandru POPOVICI	MDA	A	3	(11)	
3	Jurica PULIZ	CRO	D	8	(2)	1
13	Taufik SALHI	TUN	A	3	(5)	
14	Artem SAVIN		D	14	(1)	
34	Ihor SIKORSKIY		A		(2)	
18	Serhiy SHEVCHUK		M	6	(2)	
21	Yevhen SHMAKOV		M	14	(1)	1
21	Ihor SKOBA		M	5		1
20	Andriy TLUMAK		G	7		
19	Yuriy TSELYKH		A	7	(10)	1
18	Giorgi TSIMAKURIDZE	GEO	D	7	(2)	1
55	Eduard TSYKHMEISTRUK		M	13	(3)	1
9	Dmytro VOROBEI		M	18	(3)	3

PROMOTED CLUBS

FC ILLYCHIVETS MARIUPIL

Coach – Semen Altman; (13/12/07) Olexandr Ishchenko
Founded - 2002

FC LVIV

Coach – Stepan Yurchyshyn
Founded - 2006

SECOND LEVEL FINAL TABLE 2007

		Pld	W	D	L	F	A	Pts
	FC Illychivets Mariupil	38	26	7	5	65	26	85
	FC Lviv	38	23	5	10	58	29	74
	FC Obolon Kyiv	38	22	6	10	67	42	72
	FC Desna Chernihiv	38	20	7	11	61	44	67
	FC Dynamo-2 Kyiv	38	19	6	13	64	52	63
	FC Ihroservis Simferopol	38	18	6	14	50	45	60
	FC Stal Alchevsk	38	15	13	10	52	44	58
	PFC Olexandriya	38	14	15	9	41	32	57
	FC Volyn Lutsk	38	16	8	14	61	55	53
0	MFC Mykolaïv	38	13	13	12	33	27	52
1	FC Krymteplytsia Molodizhne	38	13	11	14	49	43	50
2	FC Dniester Ovidiopol	38	12	13	13	33	39	49
3	FC Enerhetyk Burshtyn	38	13	9	16	39	44	48
4	FC Helios Kharkiv	38	13	8	17	31	41	47
5	PFC Sevastopol	38	12	7	19	38	55	43
6	FC Fenix-Illychivets Kalinin	38	11	8	19	35	56	41
7	FSC Prykarpattya Ivano-Frankivsk	38	11	6	21	37	67	39
8	FC Dnipro Cherkasy	38	8	17	13	43	43	38
9	FC CSCA Kyiv	38	7	6	25	36	74	27
0	FC Stal Dniprodzerzhynsk	38	3	11	24	23	58	20

.B. FC Volyn Lutsk & FC Dnipro Cherkasy – 3pts deducted.

DOMESTIC CUP 2007/08

KUBOK UKRAÏNY

IRD ROUND

/9/07)
iester Ovidiopol 2, Enerhetyk Burshtyn 0

/9/07)
ftovyk-Ukrnafta Okhtyrka 2, Zorya Luhansk 0
exandriya 1, Metalurh Donetsk 2 *(aet)*

/9/07)
mpik Donetsk 1, Desna Chernihiv 2
v 2, Zakarpattya Uzhhorod 1
yazha Shchaslyve 0, Illychivets Mariupil 1
kolaïv 0, Shakhtar Donetsk 1
tan Armyansk 0, Chornomorets Odesa 3
lios Kharkiv 0, Arsenal Kyiv 2
oservis Simferopol 1, Karpaty Lviv 0
va Ternopil 1, Kryvbas Kryvyi Rih 0
vastopol 1, Metalist Kharkiv 3
Yednist Plysky 0, Stal Alchevsk 3
Vorskla Poltava 2, Kharkiv 0
Metalurh Zaporizhya 0, Tavriya Simferopol 1
Dynamo Kyiv 2, Dnipro 0

FOURTH ROUND

(31/10/07)
Dniester Ovidiopol 0, Vorskla Poltava 1
Lviv 1, Illychivets Mariupil 2
Nyva Ternopil 0, Tavriya Simferopol 0 *(aet; 5-6 on pens)*
Ihroservis Simferopol 1, Dynamo Kyiv 4
Stal Alchevsk 1, Desna Chernihiv 2
Chornomorets Odesa 2, Metalist Kharkiv 2 *(aet; 3-1 on pens)*
Desna Chernihiv 1, Naftovyk-Ukrnafta Okhtyrka 1
Shakhtar Donetsk 4, Arsenal Kyiv 1

QUARTER-FINALS

(17/11/07 & 5/12/07)
Naftovyk-Ukrnafta Okhtyrka 2 *(Karakevych 3p, Ivanov 37)*, Metalurh Donetsk 3 *(Kosyrin 38, 73p, Mitu 66)*
Metalurh Donetsk 1 *(Havrysh 22)*, Naftovyk-Ukrnafta Okhtyrka 0
(Metalurh Donetsk 4-2)

(5/12/07 & 8/12/07)
Tavriya Simferopol 2 *(Jokšas 26, Zborovskiy 90+2)*, Dynamo Kyiv 0
Dynamo Kyiv 3 *(Bangoura 2, 48p, Gusev 39)*, Tavriya Simferopol 0
(Dynamo Kyiv 3-2)

(8/12/07 & 12/12/07)
Vorskla Poltava 0, Shakhtar Donetsk 3 *(Chyhrynskiy 55, Raţ 77p, Fernandinho 88)*
Shakhtar Donetsk 1 *(Hai 55)*, Vorskla Poltava 1 *(Curri 64)*
(Shakhtar Donetsk 4-1)

(9/12/07 & 15/12/07)
Illychivets Mariupil 2 *(Lima 43, Krasnoperov 48)*, Chornomorets Odesa 1 *(Vázquez 45+2)*
Chornomorets Odesa 4 *(Biletskiy 46, Korytko 76p, 90, Mello 82)*, Illychivets Mariupil 0
(Chornomorets Odesa 5-2)

SEMI-FINALS

(19/3/08 & 16/4/08)
Chornomorets Odesa 1 *(Korytko 72p)*, Shakhtar Donetsk 2 *(Lewandowski 41, Brandão 64p)*
Shakhtar Donetsk 3 *(Luiz Adriano 4, Kravchenko 72, Duljaj 74)*, Chornomorets Odesa 0
(Shakhtar Donetsk 5-1)
Dynamo Kyiv 2 *(Gusev 43, Aliyev 88)*, Metalurh Donetsk 1 *(Kosyrin 55)*
Metalurh Donetsk 0, Dynamo Kyiv 1 *(Ghioane 68)*
(Dynamo Kyiv 3-1)

FINAL

(7/5/08)
OSK Metalist, Kharkiv
FC SHAKHTAR DONETSK 2 *(Hladkiy 44, Hai 78)*.
FC DYNAMO KYIV 0
Referee - *Shvetsov*
SHAKHTAR - *Pyatov, Srna, Chyhrynskiy, Hübschman, Kucher (Yezerskiy 46), Raţ, Fernandinho, Ilsinho (Willian 86), Duljaj (Hai 75), Brandão, Hladkiy.*
Sent off: *Brandão (64), Yezerskyi (80), Hladkiy (87).*
DYNAMO KYIV - *Shovkovskiy, El Kaddouri, Yussuf, Mandzyuk, Marković (Ninković 46), Diakhaté, Ghioane, Corrêa, Aliyev (Milevskiy 83), Kravets, Bangoura.*
Sent off: *Diakhaté (74), Bangoura (80).*

Young generation offers hope for the future

Half a century has now passed since Wales sent a team to a major international tournament. There have been plenty of near-misses and hard-luck stories during those 50 years, but the attempt to qualify for UEFA EURO 2008™ was not one of them. John Toshack's team not only dropped out of the running early on but also lost their best player, Ryan Giggs, to international retirement in the process.

Wales completed their programme with an erratic collection of results, ranging from the sublime – a 5-2 win away to a Slovakian side that had beaten them 5-1 in Cardiff – to the ridiculous – a 3-1 defeat in Cyprus. Arguably their best result of the 12-match series was the last one – a 0-0 draw against Germany in Frankfurt – although enthusiasm had to be tempered by the knowledge that their opponents, already qualified, were not going flat out for the win. Nevertheless, it was a strong point on which to finish and added to the positive feeling in the Welsh camp generated by the Under-21 team's sensational 4-2 victory over their French equivalents in Cardiff the previous day.

Flynn's flyers

That was the third of a series of five straight wins for Brian Flynn's talented young team, carrying them to the brink of qualification for the 2009 UEFA European Under-21 Championship play-offs – and perhaps a place in the eight-team finals in Sweden, the venue for the senior team's last tournament appearance, at the 1958 FIFA World Cup. Nineteen-year-old striker Ched Evans scored a hat-trick against France and added four further goals in other qualifiers. He was handed his senior debut in May 2008 against Iceland and promptly scored the winning goal three minutes after coming on as a substitute. A star, it seems, could be on the horizon, and with several other talented young guns such as goalkeeper Wayne Hennessey, full-backs Gareth Bale and Chris Gunter, and midfielder Joe Ledley already settled into Toshack's first XI, maybe, just maybe, Wales will be able to develop a new generation of players good enough to end that long, insufferable major tournament hoodoo.

Ledley made headlines for his club, Cardiff City FC, with a spectacular winning goal in the semi-final of the FA Cup against fellow English Championship side Barnsley FC that took the Bluebirds into the final of the world's oldest cup competition for only the third time. Cardiff had been promised one of England's places in the UEFA Cup if they won – a decision that sat uneasily with some – but the issue became irrelevant as Dave Jones' team lost 1-0 at Wembley to Premier League Portsmouth FC. Another 'exiled' club, Swansea City FC, enjoyed a productive season, winning promotion from League One to the Championship, but there were tears in North Wales as Wrexham FC dropped out of the Football League.

South Wales had much to celebrate domestically as Llanelli AFC held off the challenge of defending champions The New Saints FC to win the Welsh Premier League title for the first time. Coached by ex-Wales

Joe Ledley – a young Welshman with a bright international future

international midfielder Peter Nicholas, the team from the famous rugby town won 27 of their 34 matches, losing just three. One of those defeats came on the last day of the season when they were beaten 3-0 by a TNS side under new management following the resignation of their long-serving Englishman Ken McKenna. Losing the match was incidental for Llanelli as they had already claimed the title on the back of a 20-match unbeaten run, but there was some irritation that they could not score a consolation goal, which would have taken their season's tally to 100. Forty of the team's 99 goals were scored by ace marksman Rhys Griffiths, who thus took the WPL's top scorer crown for the third season running.

Llanelli also won the League Cup, beating Rhyl FC 2-0 in the final with first-half goals from Andrew Mumford and Chris Holloway, but the treble eluded them. They reached the final of the Welsh Cup, but there to meet them in Newtown were bogey club Bangor City FC – the only team they had failed to beat in the league. Ashley Stott, the scorer of all three of Bangor's league goals against the champions, also opened the scoring in the final, but Llanelli came back to lead and it looked as if Griffiths' 56th-minute strike would be the winner until Bangor equalised in the last minute. Bangor then added two further goals in extra time to win 4-2 and take the trophy for the sixth time.

The season's surprise package was Neath Athletic FC, who finished seventh in their debut WPL campaign. The other newcomers, Llangefni Town FC, finished bottom and were relegated, their place being taken by Prestatyn Town FC. Caersws FC, who finished 17th, were saved from the drop, however, as there was no team from the southern feeder league with the requisite facilities to replace them.

Football Association of Wales (FAW)

11/12 Neptune Court
Vanguard Way
GB-Cardiff CF24 5PJ
tel - +44 2920 435830
fax - +44 2920 496953
website - www.faw.org.uk
email - dcollins@faw.org.uk
Year of Formation – 1876
President – Peter Rees
General Secretary - David G. Collins
Press Officer – David G. Collins
Stadium - Millennium Stadium, Cardiff (72,500)

INTERNATIONAL TOURNAMENT APPEARANCES
FIFA World Cup - (1) 1958 (qtr-finals).

TOP FIVE ALL-TIME CAPS
Neville Southall (92); Gary Speed (85); Dean Saunders (75); Peter Nicholas & Ian Rush (73)

TOP FIVE ALL-TIME GOALS
Ian Rush (28); Ivor Allchurch & Trevor Ford (23); Dean Saunders (22); Mark Hughes & Cliff Jones (16)

NATIONAL TEAM RESULTS 2007/08

22/8/07	Bulgaria	A	Burgas	1-0	*Eastwood (45)*
8/9/07	Germany (ECQ)	H	Cardiff	0-2	
12/9/07	Slovakia (ECQ)	A	Trnava	5-2	*Eastwood (22), Bellamy (34, 41), Ďurica (78og), Davies S. (90)*
13/10/07	Cyprus (ECQ)	A	Nicosia	1-3	*Collins J. (21)*
17/10/07	San Marino (ECQ)	A	Serravalle	2-0	*Earnshaw (13), Ledley (36)*
17/11/07	Republic of Ireland (ECQ)	H	Cardiff	2-2	*Koumas (23, 89p)*
21/11/07	Germany (ECQ)	A	Frankfurt	0-0	
6/2/08	Norway	H	Wrexham	3-0	*Fletcher (15), Koumas (62, 69)*
26/3/08	Luxembourg	A	Luxembourg	2-0	*Eastwood (38, 47)*
28/5/08	Iceland	A	Reykjavik	1-0	*Evans C. (44)*
1/6/08	Netherlands	A	Rotterdam	0-2	

WALES

NATIONAL TEAM APPEARANCES 2007/08

Coach – John TOSHACK	22/3/49		Bul	GER	SVK	CYP	SMR	IRL	GER	Nor	Lux	Isl	Ned	Caps	Goals
Wayne HENNESSEY	24/1/87	Wolverhampton (ENG)	G	G	G			G	G	G46		G	G	10	-
Sam RICKETTS	11/10/81	Hull (ENG)	D46	D	D	D73	s62		D	D59	D		D77	28	-
Gareth BALE	16/7/89	Tottenham (ENG)	D46	D	D	D	D							11	2
Danny GABBIDON	8/8/79	West Ham (ENG)	D	D	D	D	D	D	D					40	-
Craig MORGAN	18/6/85	Peterborough (ENG)	D46		D	s44				D	D	D	D56	8	-
Lewin NYATANGA	18/8/88	Barnsley (ENG) /Derby (ENG)	D	D		D	D		D	D	D	D	D	21	-
Andrew CROFTS	29/5/84	Gillingham (ENG)	M	s79					s91	s66		s88	s77	12	-
Simon DAVIES	23/10/79	Fulham (ENG)	M60	M79	M	M	M	M	M	M59	M			50	6
David VAUGHAN	18/2/83	Crewe (ENG)	M		s85		M62							13	-
Joe LEDLEY	23/1/87	Cardiff	M46	M46	M85	M	M	M	M	M46		D49	M87	22	1
Freddy EASTWOOD	29/10/83	Wolverhampton (ENG)	A51	A	A73	A58		A60		A59	A	A49	A	9	4
Neal EARDLEY	6/11/88	Oldham (ENG)	s46				D	D81		s59	D65	s49	s87	7	-
Danny COLLINS	6/8/80	Sunderland (ENG)	s46											7	-
Steve EVANS	26/2/79	Wrexham	s46											6	-
Mark JONES	15/8/84	Wrexham	s46											2	-
Robert EARNSHAW	6/4/81	Derby (ENG)	s51	s46		s58	A		A56					39	13
Danny NARDIELLO	22/10/82	QPR (ENG) /Barnsley (ENG)	s60								s84			3	-
James COLLINS	23/8/83	West Ham (ENG)		D	D	D44		D	D					24	1
Jason KOUMAS	25/9/79	Wigan (ENG)		M67				M		M	M84	M88	M73	29	9
Carl ROBINSON	13/10/76	Toronto (CAN)		M	M	M	M	M37		M66			M46	46	1
Carl FLETCHER	7/4/80	Crystal Palace (ENG)		s67	s73			M	M	M	M75	M41		29	1
Craig BELLAMY	13/7/79	West Ham (ENG)			A	A	A					s62	s56	51	15
Danny COYNE	27/8/73	Tranmere (ENG)				G								16	-
Jermaine EASTER	15/1/82	Wycombe (ENG) /Plymouth (ENG)				s73		s60	s56		A46			7	-
Lewis PRICE	19/7/84	Derby (ENG)					G			s46	G46			6	-
Chris GUNTER	21/7/89	Cardiff /Tottenham (ENG)						D	D	D		D	D	6	-
David EDWARDS	3/2/86	Luton (ENG) /Wolverhampton (ENG)						s37	M91	s46		M62	M56	5	-
David COTTERILL	4/12/87	Wigan (ENG)						s81		s59	s75			11	-
Craig DAVIES	9/1/86	Oldham (ENG)								s59				5	-
Ashley WILLIAMS	23/8/84	Stockport (ENG)									D	D	D	3	-
Boaz MYHILL	9/11/82	Hull (ENG)									s46			1	-
Owain TUDUR-JONES	15/10/84	Swansea									s46	s59		2	-
Richard DUFFY	30/8/85	Coventry (ENG)									s65			13	-
Jack COLLISON	2/10/88	West Ham (ENG)										M59	s46	2	-
Chedwyn EVANS	28/12/88	Man. City (ENG)										s41	s56	2	1
Sam VOKES	21/10/89	Bournemouth (ENG)										s49	s73	2	-

DOMESTIC LEAGUE 2007/08

REMIER LEAGUE FINAL TABLE

	Pld	Home W	Home D	Home L	Home F	Home A	Away W	Away D	Away L	Away F	Away A	Total W	Total D	Total L	Total F	Total A	Pts
Llanelli AFC	34	13	2	2	52	13	14	2	1	47	22	27	4	3	99	35	85
The New Saints FC	34	15	1	1	53	11	10	2	5	32	19	25	3	6	85	30	78
Rhyl FC	34	12	2	3	29	12	9	4	4	31	12	21	6	7	60	24	69
Port Talbot Town FC	34	10	5	2	36	18	7	3	7	21	30	17	8	9	57	48	59
Bangor City FC	34	8	7	2	34	16	7	3	7	28	15	15	10	9	62	31	55
Carmarthen Town AFC	34	7	6	4	31	22	8	3	6	28	25	15	9	10	59	47	54
Neath Athletic AFC	34	9	4	4	31	23	6	5	6	26	29	15	9	10	57	52	54
Haverfordwest County AFC	34	9	3	5	36	25	5	2	10	25	34	14	5	15	61	59	47
Aberystwyth Town FC	34	8	3	6	35	23	5	4	8	22	22	13	7	14	57	45	46
Welshpool Town FC	34	6	4	7	23	27	6	6	5	26	25	12	10	12	49	52	46
Airbus UK FC	34	7	4	6	19	18	4	5	8	17	26	11	9	14	36	44	42
NEWI Cefn Druids AFC	34	9	1	7	33	29	3	1	13	12	37	12	2	20	45	66	38
Newtown AFC	34	6	5	6	28	26	3	5	9	19	40	9	10	15	47	66	37
Caernarfon Town FC	34	5	4	8	20	32	5	2	10	22	42	10	6	18	42	74	36
Connah's Quay Nomads FC	34	7	3	7	21	30	2	4	11	21	55	9	7	18	42	85	34
CPD Porthmadog	34	1	4	12	19	38	6	2	9	29	32	7	6	21	48	70	27
Caersws FC	34	2	3	12	20	43	4	5	8	17	29	6	8	20	37	72	26
Llangefni Town FC	34	5	0	12	21	35	2	3	12	18	47	7	3	24	39	82	24

TOP GOALSCORERS

40 Rhys GRIFFITHS (Llanelli)

23 Marc LLOYD-WILLIAMS (Newtown/Rhyl)

19 Martin ROSE (Port Talbot)
Ashley STOTT (Bangor)

18 Danny THOMAS (Carmarthen)

17 Jack CHRISTOPHER (Haverfordwest)

15 Tim HICKS (Carmarthen)
Andy HILL (Neath)

14 Calvin DAVIES (Welshpool)

13 Lee HUNT (Rhyl)
Darren THOMAS (Llangefni)

CLUB-BY-CLUB

ABERYSTWYTH TOWN FC

Manager - Brian Coyne (SCO)

Founded - 1884

MAJOR HONOURS: Welsh Cup – (1) 1900.

2007

18/8	Airbus	a	1-1	*Thomas*
26/8	TNS	h	5-1	*Reed 3, Sherbon, Roberts S.*
1/9	Welshpool	h	2-3	*Cadwallader, Reed*
9/9	Cefn Druids	h	1-0	*Hughes Ga.*
14/9	Llanelli	a	0-1	
18/9	Caersws	a	1-1	*Kellaway*
22/9	Bangor	h	2-1	*Sherbon 2 (1p)*
28/9	Port Talbot	a	1-2	*Thomas*
13/10	Porthmadog	h	2-1	*Reed 2*
20/10	Connah's Quay	a	2-1	*og (Pinch), Sherbon*
26/10	Carmarthen	h	0-2	
10/11	Rhyl	a	0-0	
18/11	Llangefni	h	3-0	*Sherbon 2, Reed*
23/11	Neath	a	2-2	*Passmore, Sherbon*
1/12	Caernarfon	h	4-0	*Reed, Kellaway, Sherbon, Thomas*
15/12	Airbus	h	0-0	
22/12	TNS	a	0-1	
26/12	Haverfordwest	h	2-3	*og (Gilderdale), Kellaway*

2008

1/1	Haverfordwest	a	1-3	Edwards
5/1	Welshpool	a	1-2	Reed
12/1	Cefn Druids	a	2-0	*Evans A. 2*
22/1	Caersws	h	2-1	*Passmore 2*
26/1	Bangor	a	0-1	
8/2	Port Talbot	h	2-4	*Kellaway, Sherbon*
16/2	Porthmadog	a	6-2	*Kellaway 3, Sherbon 2, og (Owen G.)*
23/2	Connah's Quay	h	6-1	*Evans A. 3, Sherbon, Passmore, Roberts S.*
1/3	Newtown	a	2-1	*Cadwallader, Evans A.*
7/3	Carmarthen	a	3-0	*Evans A., Hughes Ga., Passmore*
15/3	Rhyl	h	0-0	
22/3	Llangefni	a	0-3	
25/3	Llanelli	h	1-2	*Da Silva*
5/4	Neath	h	1-2	*Roberts S.*
12/4	Caernarfon	a	0-1	
19/4	Newtown	h	2-2	*Thomas, Evans A.*

Name	Pos	Nat	Aps	(s)	Gls
Steve BOWEN	M			(2)	
Gavin CADWALLADER	M		22		2
Tiago DA SILVA	M	POR	3	(7)	1
Christian EDWARDS	D		34		1
Andy EVANS	A		14	(14)	8
Elian EVANS	D			(3)	

Name	Nat	Pos	Aps	(s)	Gls
Robert EVANS		M	7	(18)	
Lloyd GRIST		D	5	(1)	
Gareth HUGHES		M	21	(3)	2
Glyndwr HUGHES		A	1		
Llewelyn HUGHES		G		(1)	
Sion JAMES		D	31		
Dave JONES		G	20		
Geoff KELLAWAY		M	26	(4)	7
Gari LEWIS		D		(1)	
Bari MORGAN		M	20	(3)	
Richard MORGAN		G	14		
Geraint PASSMORE		M	19	(6)	5
Jamie REED	NIR	A	19	(1)	9
Matthew ROBERTS		D	29		
Stuart ROBERTS		A	21	(8)	3
Luke SHERBON		M	34		12
Aneurin THOMAS		D	34		4

AIRBUS UK FC

Manager - Gareth Owen

Founded - 1946

Date	Opponent		Score	Scorers
2007				
18/8	Aberystwyth	h	1-1	*Owen G. (p)*
25/8	Caersws	a	3-2	*Hallows 2, McIntosh*
31/8	Bangor	h	1-0	*McIntosh*
9/9	Port Talbot	a	0-0	
15/9	Porthmadog	h	2-0	*Owen G., McIntosh*
18/9	Connah's Quay	a	0-1	
22/9	Carmarthen	h	0-1	
28/9	Rhyl	a	1-2	*McIntosh*
13/10	Llangefni	h	1-3	*McIntosh*
20/10	Neath	a	1-2	*Hallows*
27/10	Caernarfon	h	1-2	*Owen G.*
10/11	Newtown	a	1-1	*Hallows*
18/11	Haverfordwest	h	3-1	*Desormeaux 2, McIntosh*
24/11	Llanelli	h	0-1	
1/12	TNS	a	0-0	
7/12	Welshpool	h	1-1	*Hallows*
15/12	Aberystwyth	a	0-0	
22/12	Caersws	h	0-2	
26/12	Cefn Druids	h	3-2	*Allen, Edwards (p), Hallows*
2008				
1/1	Cefn Druids	a	1-4	*Sudlow*
5/1	Bangor	a	0-5	
12/1	Port Talbot	h	1-0	*Hallows*
26/1	Carmarthen	a	1-2	*Owen G. (p)*
8/2	Rhyl	h	0-2	
15/2	Llangefni	a	3-0	*Hughes Dan. 2, Molyneux*
23/2	Neath	h	2-1	*Molyneux, Desormeaux*
1/3	Porthmadog	a	2-2	*Sudlow, Desormeaux*
8/3	Caernarfon	a	3-0	*McIntosh 2, Desormeaux*
15/3	Newtown	h	1-1	*Sudlow*
22/3	Haverfordwest	a	0-4	
1/4	Connah's Quay	h	0-0	
5/4	Llanelli	a	0-1	
11/4	TNS	h	2-0	*McIntosh, Desormeaux*
19/4	Welshpool	a	1-0	*Hallows*

Name	Nat	Pos	Aps	(s)	Gls
Mark ALLEN	ENG	D	33		1
Gareth CAUGHTER		M	14	(4)	
Paul CONNOLLY	ENG	D		(2)	
Ashley CROSSTHWAITE	ENG	G	4		
Rees DARLINGTON		D	10		
John DAVIES		D	26	(1)	
Dan DESORMEAUX	ENG	M	31	(1)	6
Chris DORAN	NIR	G	17		
Ryan EDWARDS		D	34		1
Paul HALLOWS	ENG	A	24	(7)	8
Alan HOOLEY		M	15	(2)	
Steve HOPKINS		D	9		
Andy HUGHES	ENG	G	10		
Danny HUGHES		A		(2)	2
David HUGHES		M	4	(5)	
Adam HUNTER	ENG	M	11	(8)	
James HUSSANEY		A	1	(6)	
Gary LOVELL	ENG	D	9	(1)	
James McINTOSH	ENG	A	29	(4)	9
Larry MILLER	ENG	M		(1)	
Phil MOLYNEUX	ENG	A	16	(10)	2
Charlie OWEN		M	1		
Gareth OWEN		M	28	(1)	4
Andrew STOCKTON	ENG	M		(1)	
Gareth SUDLOW		D	15	(7)	3
Aaron TYRER	ENG	G	3		
Matthew WOODWARD	ENG	D	9		
Darren WRIGHT	ENG	M	21	(3)	

BANGOR CITY FC

Manager - Nev Powell (ENG)

Founded - 1876

MAJOR HONOURS: Welsh League - (2) 1994, 1995; Welsh Cup - (6) 1889, 1896, 1962, 1998, 2000, 2008.

Date	Opponent		Score	Scorers
2007				
18/8	Newtown	a	2-2	*Stott, Davies*
25/8	Haverfordwest	h	2-0	*Hoy, Smyth (p)*
31/8	Airbus	a	0-1	
7/9	TNS	h	1-2	*Smyth*
15/9	Welshpool	a	0-2	
18/9	Cefn Druids	h	5-1	*Smyth 2, Edwards, Davies, Walsh*
22/9	Aberystwyth	a	1-2	*Davies*
29/9	Caersws	h	1-1	*Edwards*
13/10	Llanelli	a	2-0	*Stott 2*
20/10	Port Talbot	a	0-0	
27/10	Porthmadog	h	2-0	*Johnston, Stott*
9/11	Connah's Quay	a	7-0	*Edwards 3 (1p), Webber, Davies, Seargeant, Stott*
18/11	Carmarthen	h	1-1	*Stott*
24/11	Rhyl	a	2-1	*Limbert (p),Seargeant*
30/11	Llangefni	h	2-2	*Stott, Walsh*
15/12	Newtown	h	2-2	*Davies 2*
22/12	Haverfordwest	a	1-0	*Stott*
26/12	Caernarfon	h	5-1	*Walsh 2, Davies, Stott, Beattie*
2008				
1/1	Caernarfon	a	4-0	*Edwards 2, Seargeant, Stott*
5/1	Airbus	h	5-0	*Stott 2, Davies 2, Edwards*
12/1	TNS	a	1-2	*Stott*
19/1	Welshpool	h	1-0	*Webber*
22/1	Cefn Druids	a	6-1	*Stott 4, Seargeant, Davies*
26/1	Aberystwyth	h	1-0	*Seargeant*
9/2	Caersws	a	0-1	
16/2	Llanelli	h	1-1	*Stott*
23/2	Port Talbot	h	0-0	
8/3	Porthmadog	a	0-0	
15/3	Connah's Quay	h	3-2	*Edwards, Stott, Noon*
22/3	Carmarthen	a	1-2	*Limbert*
24/3	Neath	a	0-1	
11/4	Llangefni	a	1-0	*Hoy*

15/4	Rhyl	h 1-2	*Walsh*
19/4	Neath	h 1-1	*Seargeant*

Name	Pos	Nat	Aps	(s)	Gls
Martin BEATTIE	ENG	D	28		1
Les DAVIES		A	32	(1)	10
Sion EDWARDS		M	24	(9)	9
Peter HOY	ENG	D	28	(3)	2
Craig HUTCHINSON	ENG	M	5	(10)	
Caio IWAN		M		(1)	
Mike JOHNSTON	ENG	D	29		1
Kieran KILLACKEY	ENG	M	11	(7)	
Marc LIMBERT		M	33		2
Gary LOVELL	ENG	D	2		
Mel McGINNES		M		(10)	
Alan MORGAN		M		(1)	
Tommy MUTTON		A	1	(2)	
Karl NOON	ENG	A	3	(6)	1
Ben OGILVY		D	1	(4)	
Gareth PARRY		M	2		
Dave ROBERTS		M		(1)	
Christian SEARGEANT	ENG	A	25	(4)	6
Paul SMITH		G	34		
Marc SMYTH	ENG	M	9		4
Ashley STOTT	ENG	A	30	(4)	19
David SWANICK	ENG	D	18	(8)	
Mike WALSH	ENG	M	30	(3)	5
Lee WEBBER	ENG	D	29	(1)	2
Josh WILLIAMS	ENG	M		(2)	

CAERNARFON TOWN FC

Manager - Steve O'Shaughnessy (ENG)

Founded - 1876

2007			
18/8	Port Talbot	h 3-1	*Noone, Glendenning, Rowley*
27/8	Porthmadog	a 3-1	*Noone, og (Roberts P.), Rowley*
1/9	Connah's Quay	h 1-1	*Noone*
9/9	Carmarthen	a 1-1	*Noone*
15/9	Rhyl	h 0-1	
19/9	Llangefni	a 2-1	*Thomas M., Jones B.*
22/9	Neath	h 1-2	*Rowley*
29/9	Llanelli	h 3-4	*Thomas M., Glendenning, Jones B.*
13/10	Newtown	a 1-3	*Jones B.*
20/10	Haverfordwest	h 1-2	*Addo*
27/10	Airbus	a 2-1	*Maxwell (p), og (Doran)*
10/11	TNS	h 1-7	*Thomas M.*
18/11	Welshpool	a 4-2	*Addo 2, Thomas J., Rowley*
24/11	Cefn Druids	h 1-1	*Rowley*
1/12	Aberystwyth	a 0-4	
15/12	Port Talbot	a 1-2	*Thomas J.*
22/12	Porthmadog	h 2-4	*Jones B., Doran Ph.*
26/12	Bangor	a 1-5	*Jones B.*
2008			
1/1	Bangor	h 0-4	
5/1	Connah's Quay	a 0-1	
12/1	Carmarthen	h 2-1	*Addo, Rowley*
19/1	Rhyl	a 1-3	*Rowley*
26/1	Neath	a 2-3	*Addo, Doran Pe.*
5/2	Caersws	h 2-0	*Doran Pe., Jones B.*
9/2	Llanelli	a 1-5	*Jones E.*
15/2	Newtown	h 0-0	
23/2	Haverfordwest	a 1-1	*Rowley*
8/3	Airbus	h 0-3	
15/3	TNS	a 0-4	
22/3	Welshpool	h 1-1	*Clarke*
4/4	Cefn Druids	a 1-5	*Quinn*
12/4	Aberystwyth	h 1-0	*Thomas J.*
16/4	Llangefni	h 1-0	*Buckley*
19/4	Caersws	a 1-0	*Buckley*

Name	Nat	Pos	Aps	(s)	Gls
Paul ADDO	ENG	A	22	(3)	5
Lee BAMBER	ENG	D	29		
Dean BUCKLEY	ENG	A	1	(9)	2
Phil CLARKE	ENG	M	8	(6)	1
Anthony COLE	ENG	M		(4)	
Peter DORAN	ENG	M	12		2
Phil DORAN	ENG	D	31		1
James GLENDENNING	ENG	D	14		2
Mark HARRIS	ENG	D	7	(5)	
Jason HUGHES		G	1		
Mike JAGO	ENG	G	12		
Bobby JONES	ENG	A	20	(9)	6
Eifion JONES		D	29		1
Michael JONES	ENG	D	4	(6)	
David MATHER	ENG	M		(1)	
Layton MAXWELL		M	13	(5)	1
Kevin McGARRY	ENG	D	7	(10)	
Chris NOONE	ENG	A	4		4
David OJAPAH	ENG	M		(3)	
Timothy OJAPAH	ENG	A	27	(3)	
Iwan OWENS		M		(3)	
Gwyn PETERS		M		(1)	
Kieran QUINN	ENG	M	27	(1)	1
Gary ROBERTS		M		(1)	
John ROWLEY		A	26	(6)	8
John ROWLEY		G	2		
Khyle SAMPSON	ENG	A	1	(8)	
James THOMAS	ENG	M	28	(3)	3
Mark THOMAS		M	18		3
Craig VERNON	ENG	G	5		
Dean WALKER	ENG	A		(4)	
Teddy WHELAN	ENG	M	12	(2)	
Vinnie WHELAN	ENG	G	14		

CAERSWS FC

Manager - Mike Barton; (27/2/08) David Taylor

Founded - 1877

2007			
18/8	Haverfordwest	a 0-1	
25/8	Airbus	h 2-3	*Edwards, Evans*
1/9	TNS	a 0-6	
7/9	Welshpool	h 0-3	
14/9	Cefn Druids	a 0-4	
18/9	Aberystwyth	h 1-1	*Meredith*
22/9	Llanelli	a 1-1	*Evans (p)*
29/9	Bangor	a 1-1	*Evans (p)*
13/10	Port Talbot	h 1-4	*Griffiths*
20/10	Porthmadog	a 1-0	*Meredith*
27/10	Connah's Quay	h 3-4	*Evans (p), Edwards, Sawtell*
10/11	Carmarthen	a 3-1	*Griffiths 2, Davies A.*
18/11	Rhyl	h 2-7	*Mitchell, Haynes*
24/11	Llangefni	a 1-0	*Meredith*
1/12	Neath	h 2-2	*og (Morris), Mitchell*
22/12	Airbus	a 2-0	*Evans, Mitchell*
26/12	Newtown	h 1-0	*Mitchell*
2008			
1/1	Newtown	a 2-2	*Haynes, Griffiths*
5/1	TNS	h 1-2	*Evans (p)*
22/1	Aberystwyth	a 1-2	*Evans (p)*
26/1	Llanelli	h 0-5	
5/2	Caernarfon	a 0-2	

9/2	Bangor	h	1-0	*Davies M.*
16/2	Port Talbot	a	1-3	*Evans (p)*
23/2	Porthmadog	h	2-4	*Slater 2*
26/2	Haverfordwest	h	1-2	*Mitchell*
8/3	Connah's Quay	a	0-1	
15/3	Carmarthen	h	1-2	*Evans*
22/3	Rhyl	a	1-2	*Meredith*
25/3	Cefn Druids	h	1-2	*Reynolds*
29/3	Welshpool	a	1-1	*og (Stephens)*
5/4	Llangefni	h	1-1	*Slater*
12/4	Neath	a	2-2	*Slater, Evans*
19/4	Caernarfon	h	0-1	

Name	**Nat**	**Pos**	**Aps**	**(s)**	**Gls**
Name	Nat	Pos	Aps	(s)	Gls
Sean BUTLER		M		(1)	
Andy DAVIES		M	29		1
Jamie DAVIES		M	3	(1)	
Mark DAVIES		D	14		1
Aeron EDWARDS		M	33		2
Graham EVANS		A	32		10
Terry GREEN	ENG	M	3		
Mark GRIFFITHS		A	14	(12)	4
Jamie HAYNES	ENG	M	13	(4)	2
Jonathan JONES	ENG	D	24	(4)	
Darren LEONARD	ENG	D	4		
Gari LEWIS		M	12	(1)	
Sion MEREDITH		M	23	(4)	4
Neil MITCHELL	ENG	A	26	(3)	5
Reuben MOHOUNG	RSA	M	2		
Andy MULLINER		G	34		
Michael PARRY		D	2	(1)	
Ian PROBERT	ENG	M	5		
Nathan PRODGER	ENG	M	1	(16)	
Colin REYNOLDS		D	28		1
Tom REYNOLDS	ENG	M		(4)	
Michael SAWTELL	ENG	D	8	(7)	1
Marcus SHARRARD	ENG	A	1	(1)	
Jon SLATER		M	6	(9)	4
Chris SMOUT	ENG	D	5	(3)	
David TAYLOR		M		(1)	
Andrew THOMAS		D	32		
Steve TOWERS	ENG	D	20	(6)	
Scott WILLIAMS		M		(3)	

CARMARTHEN TOWN AFC

Manager - Deryn Brace

MAJOR HONOURS: Welsh Cup – (1) 2007.

2007				
18/8	Rhyl	a	1-2	*Hicks*
25/8	Llangefni	a	3-0	*Thomas D. 2, Hicks*
31/8	Neath	a	2-1	*Thomas D., Walters*
9/9	Caernarfon	h	1-1	*Thomas D.*
15/9	Newtown	a	1-0	*Cotterall*
18/9	Haverfordwest	h	2-1	*Hicks, Walters*
22/9	Airbus	a	1-0	*Walters*
29/9	TNS	h	0-3	
13/10	Welshpool	a	2-2	*Walters, Thomas D.*
20/10	Cefn Druids	h	4-1	*Hicks 2 Thomas D., Hughes*
26/10	Aberystwyth	a	2-0	*Coombes, Thomas D.*
10/11	Caersws	h	1-3	*Thomas K.*
18/11	Bangor	a	1-1	*Hicks*
23/11	Port Talbot	h	0-0	
1/12	Porthmadog	a	2-1	*Thomas D., Walters*
8/12	Connah's Quay	h	8-0	*Hicks 5, Thomas D. 2, Easter*
15/12	Rhyl	h	0-0	
22/12	Llangefni	h	2-2	*Walters, Hicks*
26/12	Llanelli	h	1-2	*Hicks*
2008				
1/1	Llanelli	a	1-4	*Easter*
5/1	Neath	h	1-1	*Thomas D.*
12/1	Caernarfon	a	1-2	*Thomas D.*
19/1	Newtown	h	2-1	*Coombes, Thomas D.*
22/1	Haverfordwest	a	2-2	*Easter 2*
26/1	Airbus	h	2-1	*Easter, Fowler*
9/2	TNS	a	3-0	*Hicks 2, Fowler*
16/2	Welshpool	h	5-2	*Easter 4 (1p), Thomas D.*
23/2	Cefn Druids	a	1-3	*Thomas D.*
7/3	Aberystwyth	h	0-3	
15/3	Caersws	a	2-1	*Thomas D., Keddle*
22/3	Bangor	h	2-1	*Thomas D. 2*
4/4	Port Talbot	a	0-2	
12/4	Porthmadog	h	0-0	
19/4	Connah's Quay	a	3-4	*Walters 2, Coombes*

Name	**Nat**	**Pos**	**Aps**	**(s)**	**Gls**
Deryn BRACE		D	20	(1)	
Deryn BRACE		G	1		
Phil CATTLIN		D	10	(1)	
Craig COOMBES		M	30	(2)	3
Nathan COTTERRALL		M	30	(2)	1
Mattie DAVIES		A		(2)	
Steffan DAVIES		A		(3)	
Jamal EASTER		M	23	(6)	9
Paul FOWLER		M	34		2
Liam HANCOCK		D	28	(1)	
Tim HICKS		A	31	(2)	15
Jamie HORWOOD		M		(1)	
Richard HUGHES		D	17	(2)	1
Adam JONES		M		(1)	
Paul KEDDLE		D	10	(1)	1
Matthew MAY		M		(1)	
Curtis McDONALD		M		(4)	
Ben MORRIS	ENG	M	1	(11)	
Nicky PALMER		M	5	(4)	
Mark POOLE		G	4		
Neil SMOTHERS		M	20	(3)	
Craig TENNANT		G	1		
Danny THOMAS		M	27	(5)	18
Kris THOMAS		M	32		1
Neil THOMAS		G	28		
Sacha WALTERS		M	21	(11)	8
Gareth WARTON		D	1	(1)	
Ashley WILLIAMS		M		(1)	

CONNAH'S QUAY NOMADS FC

Manager - Jim Hackett (ENG)

Founded - 1946

MAJOR HONOURS: Welsh Cup – (1) 1929

2007				
18/8	Llangefni	a	2-1	*McAllister, Williams (p)*
25/8	Neath	h	2-0	*Dickenson, Williams (p)*
1/9	Caernarfon	a	1-1	*Atherton*
7/9	Newtown	h	1-1	*Baker*
15/9	Haverfordwest	a	2-6	*og (Durham), Melia*
18/9	Airbus	h	1-0	*Williams*
22/9	TNS	a	1-3	*Cadwallader*
28/9	Welshpool	h	3-3	*McAllister, Cook, Williams (p)*
12/10	Cefn Druids	a	2-5	*White, Petrie*
20/10	Aberystwyth	h	1-2	*McAllister*
27/10	Caersws	a	4-3	*McAllister, White, Herbert, Jones C.*

9/11	Bangor	h	0-7	
18/11	Port Talbot	a	1-2	*White*
24/11	Porthmadog	h	1-2	*Melia*
1/12	Llanelli	a	0-4	
8/12	Carmarthen	a	0-8	
15/12	Llangefni	h	2-0	*Melia, Jones C.*
22/12	Neath	a	0-4	
26/12	Rhyl	h	0-5	
2008				
1/1	Rhyl	a	0-1	
5/1	Caernarfon	h	1-0	*Rowlands*
12/1	Newtown	a	1-4	*Baker*
8/2	Welshpool	a	1-1	*og (Harris)*
15/2	Cefn Druids	h	2-1	*Herbert (p), McAllister*
23/2	Aberystwyth	a	1-6	*Herbert (p)*
1/3	Haverfordwest	h	1-1	*Herbert (p)*
8/3	Caersws	h	1-0	*McNutt*
15/3	Bangor	a	2-3	*Herbert, Forde*
22/3	Port Talbot	h	0-1	
1/4	Airbus	a	0-0	
5/4	Porthmadog	a	3-3	*McNutt 2, Jones C.*
12/4	Llanelli	h	0-1	
15/4	TNS	h	1-3	*Courtney*
19/4	Carmarthen	h	4-3	*Courtney, Jones C., McNutt, Williams*

Name	Nat	Pos	Aps	(s)	Gls
Ben ALSTON	ENG	D	29	(1)	
Paul ARMSTRONG	ENG	M	1		
Matt ATHERTON	ENG	A	1	(4)	1
Thomas BAKER	ENG	M	33	(1)	2
Dave BAMFORD		M		(1)	
Adam BEDFORD	ENG	G	1		
Mike BURNS	ENG	D	3		
Mark CADWALLADER	ENG	M	25	(4)	1
Stuart COOK	ENG	M	14	(10)	1
Ged COURTNEY	ENG	A	10	(2)	2
Mike CRONSHAW		M	1	(5)	
Adam DICKINSON	ENG	M	1		1
Danny FORDE	ENG	M	13		1
Paul FORRESTER	ENG	G	1		
Alan GLOVER	ENG	D	17		
Chris HERBERT	ENG	A	14	(14)	5
Adam HITCHEN	ENG	D	5	(3)	
Alan HOOLEY		M	7		
Craig JONES	ENG	M	30	(2)	4
Liam JONES		D	2		
Wes KILGANNON	ENG	M	12	(10)	
Tom LLOYD		M		(2)	
Phil MacDIARMID	ENG	D	5		
John McALLISTER	ENG	A	18	(11)	5
Sam McNUTT	ENG	M	13		4
Chris MELIA	ENG	A	10	(4)	3
Wayne MORGAN	ENG	M	12	(1)	
Jamie PETRIE	ENG	M	5	(7)	1
Gary PINCH	ENG	D	16	(1)	
Tom PRICE	ENG	M	1	(2)	
Paul PRITCHARD		G	32		
Tom ROWLANDS	ENG	M	3		1
Stewart WHITE		A	19	(11)	3
Chris WILLIAMS		D	20		5

HAVERFORDWEST COUNTY AFC

Manager - Derek Brazil (IRL)

Founded - 1899

2007				
18/8	Caersws	h	1-0	*Woodrow*
25/8	Bangor	a	0-2	
31/8	Port Talbot	h	2-1	*Christopher, Hudgell*
9/9	Porthmadog	a	2-0	*Thomas N., Cattlin*
15/9	Connah's Quay	h	6-2	*Woodrow 2, Hudgell 2, Christopher, Thomas N.*
18/9	Carmarthen	a	1-2	*Hudgell*
22/9	Rhyl	h	1-1	*Woodrow*
30/9	Llangefni	a	1-2	*Thomas N.*
12/10	Neath	h	1-2	*Durham*
20/10	Caernarfon	a	2-1	*Woodrow 2*
27/10	Newtown	h	2-3	*Ramasut, Jones (p)*
10/11	Llanelli	h	1-4	*Jones*
18/11	Airbus	a	1-3	*Woodrow*
24/11	TNS	h	0-4	
1/12	Welshpool	a	1-2	*Christopher*
8/12	Cefn Druids	h	3-0	*Christopher 2, George*
22/12	Bangor	h	0-1	
26/12	Aberystwyth	a	3-2	*Ramasut, Coates, Christopher*
2008				
1/1	Aberystwyth	h	3-1	*Christopher 2, Coates*
5/1	Port Talbot	a	2-2	*Christopher, Hudgell*
12/1	Porthmadog	h	3-2	*Christopher 2, Evans*
22/1	Carmarthen	h	2-2	*Bowen, Thomas N.*
26/1	Rhyl	a	0-2	
9/2	Llangefni	h	5-1	*Thomas N. 2, Hartley, Woodrow, Bowen*
15/2	Neath	a	1-2	*Bowen*
23/2	Caernarfon	h	1-1	*Woodrow*
26/2	Caersws	a	2-1	*Hartley, Christopher*
1/3	Connah's Quay	a	1-1	*Christopher*
8/3	Newtown	a	4-1	*Christopher 2, Hartley, Bowen*
14/3	Llanelli	a	2-4	*Ramasut, Thomas N.*
22/3	Airbus	h	4-0	*Thomas 3, Christopher*
5/4	TNS	a	2-6	*Bowen, Christopher*
12/4	Welshpool	h	1-0	*Bowen*
19/4	Cefn Druids	a	0-1	

Name	Nat	Pos	Aps	(s)	Gls
Abdi AHMED	SOM	M	2	(2)	
Asif BASHIR	GER	D	1	(2)	
Luke BOWEN		M	12	(4)	6
Robert BRIERS		D	3	(8)	
Phil CATTLIN		M	11	(3)	1
Jack CHRISTOPHER		A	25	(1)	17
Jonathan COATES		M	23	(9)	2
Ryan DURHAM		D	2	(5)	1
Gareth ELLIOTT		D	29		
Terry EVANS		D	33		1
Craig GEORGE		M	2	(6)	1
Simon GILDERDALE		D	34		
Kyle GRAVES	ENG	D	8		
Mike HARTLEY		D	13	(1)	3
Danny HOOPER		D	3		
Lee HUDGELL		M	28	(2)	5
Lee IDZI		G	34		
Ian JONES		A	6	(3)	2
Wayne JONES		D	12	(1)	
Chris O'SULLIVAN		M	6	(3)	
Tom RAMASUT		M	30		3
Adam RAYMOND		M	2	(11)	
Luke ROBINSON		M		(3)	
Neil THOMAS		M	29		10
Peter THOMAS		D	3	(4)	
Billy VAUGHAN	ENG	M		(1)	
Nicky WOODROW		A	23	(8)	9

WALES

LLANELLI AFC

Manager - Peter Nicholas

Founded - 1892

MAJOR HONOURS: Welsh League – (1) 2008.

2007				
19/8	Welshpool	h	3-0	*Williams C., Mumford, Griffiths*
25/8	Rhyl	a	2-1	*Griffiths, Jones C.*
1/9	Cefn Druids	h	1-0	*Griffiths*
7/9	Llangefni	a	5-1	*Griffiths 2, Mumford 2, Pritchard*
14/9	Aberystwyth	h	1-0	*Pritchard*
19/9	Neath	a	2-0	*Griffiths 2 (1p)*
22/9	Caersws	h	1-1	*Pritchard*
29/9	Caernarfon	a	4-3	*Griffiths 2, Thomas, Follows*
13/10	Bangor	h	0-2	
20/10	Newtown	a	5-3	*Legg, og (Jellicoe), Williams C., Griffiths, Mumford*
26/10	Port Talbot	h	8-0	*Griffiths 3 (1p), Mumford 2, Jones Mark 2, Pritchard*
10/11	Haverfordwest	a	4-1	*Griffiths 2, Williams C., Pritchard*
18/11	Porthmadog	h	1-2	*Jones Mark*
24/11	Airbus	a	1-0	*Griffiths*
1/12	Connah's Quay	h	4-0	*Griffiths 2 (1p), Thomas, Jones Mark*
15/12	Welshpool	a	3-3	*Griffiths 2 (1p), Jones C.*
22/12	Rhyl	h	2-1	*Griffiths 2 (1p)*
26/12	Carmarthen	a	2-1	*Thomas, Jones Mark*
2008				
1/1	Carmarthen	h	4-1	*Griffiths 3, Jones C.*
6/1	Cefn Druids	a	5-2	*Griffiths 3 (1p), Holloway, og (Phillips)*
12/1	Llangefni	h	5-0	*Jones Mark 3, Griffiths 2*
23/1	Neath	h	3-3	*Griffiths, Mumford, Holloway*
26/1	Caersws	a	5-0	*Williams C. 2, Evans 2, Jones Mark*
9/2	Caernarfon	h	5-1	*Phillips, Thomas, Griffiths, Corbisiero, Jones Mark*
16/2	Bangor	a	1-1	*Jones Mark*
4/3	TNS	h	4-0	*Thomas 2, Holloway, Jones C.*
7/3	Port Talbot	a	1-0	*Thomas*
14/3	Haverfordwest	h	4-2	*Griffiths 3, Mumford*
22/3	Porthmadog	a	4-2	*Griffiths 2, Jones C., og (Davies)*
25/3	Aberystwyth	a	2-1	*Pritchard, Corbisiero*
5/4	Airbus	h	1-0	*Mumford (p)*
12/4	Connah's Quay	a	1-0	*Griffiths*
15/4	Newtown	h	5-0	*Griffiths 2, Mumford, Jones C., Lloyd*
19/4	TNS	a	0-3	

Name	**Nat**	**Pos**	**Aps**	**(s)**	**Gls**
Nathan BAILEY		A		(1)	
Antonio CORBISIERO	ENG	M	26	(1)	2
Stephen EVANS		M	2	(5)	2
Jordan FOLLOWS		A		(12)	1
Rhys GRIFFITHS		A	31		40
Ryan HARRISON	ENG	G	26		
Nick HOLLAND		D	12	(8)	
Chris HOLLOWAY		M	20	(6)	3
Craig JONES		M	27	(2)	6
Mark JONES		A	8	(14)	11
Matthew JONES		M	2	(9)	
Stuart JONES		D	21		
Andrew LEGG		M	24	(2)	1
Ryan LEWIS		G	2	(2)	
Gary LLOYD		D	30	(1)	1
Andrew MUMFORD		M	32		10
Lee PHILLIPS		D	22	(1)	1
Mark PRITCHARD		A	24	(9)	6
Duncan ROBERTS	ENG	G	5		
Sam SMALL		A	1	(14)	
Wyn THOMAS		D	33		7
Paul WANLESS	ENG	D	6	(1)	
Craig WILLIAMS		M	19		5
Gareth WILLIAMS		G	1		

LLANGEFNI TOWN FC

Manager - Adie Jones; (29/12/07) Alex Kevan; (29/1/08) Gus Williams

Founded - 1897

2007				
18/8	Connah's Quay	h	1-2	*Lloyd*
25/8	Carmarthen	h	0-3	
1/9	Rhyl	h	0-3	
7/9	Llanelli	h	1-5	*Jones C.*
15/9	Neath	a	0-2	
19/9	Caernarfon	h	1-2	*Lloyd*
22/9	Newtown	a	1-2	*Jones C.*
30/9	Haverfordwest	h	2-1	*Gwynedd 2*
13/10	Airbus	a	3-1	*Gwynedd 2, Thomas*
20/10	TNS	h	0-3	
26/10	Welshpool	a	0-3	
9/11	Cefn Druids	h	2-0	*Owen, Kehoe*
18/11	Aberystwyth	a	0-3	
24/11	Caersws	h	0-1	
30/11	Bangor	a	2-2	*Lloyd, Gwynedd*
15/12	Connah's Quay	a	0-2	
22/12	Carmarthen	a	2-2	*Thomas 2*
26/12	Porthmadog	h	1-4	*Owen (p)*
2008				
1/1	Porthmadog	a	4-2	*Lloyd 2, Thomas, Jones*
5/1	Rhyl	a	1-4	*O'Brien*
12/1	Llanelli	a	0-5	
26/1	Newtown	h	2-3	*Lloyd, Sadler*
9/2	Haverfordwest	a	1-5	*Lloyd*
15/2	Airbus	h	0-3	
23/2	TNS	a	1-7	*Hogg*
1/3	Port Talbot	h	4-1	*Thomas 3, Sadler*
7/3	Welshpool	h	0-1	
14/3	Cefn Druids	a	1-2	*Lloyd*
22/3	Aberystwyth	h	3-0	*Thomas 2, Jones C.*
29/3	Neath	h	4-2	*Thomas 3, Kehoe*
5/4	Caersws	a	1-1	*Thomas*
11/4	Bangor	h	0-1	
16/4	Caernarfon	a	0-1	
19/4	Port Talbot	a	1-3	*Kehoe*

Name	**Nat**	**Pos**	**Aps**	**(s)**	**Gls**
Gareth ALLMAN		M		(1)	
Grahame AUSTIN	ENG	M	28	(3)	
John BOARDMAN	ENG	D	13		
Leigh CRAVEN		A	1	(3)	
Anthony DAVIES	ENG	D	3		
Lee DIXON		D	12	(2)	
Chris EVANS		M	16	(1)	
Ywain GWYNEDD		M	21	(9)	5
Craig HOGG	ENG	D	21		1
Richard HUGHES		M	4	(5)	
Farai JACKSON	ENG	G	29		

Name	Nat	Pos	Aps	(s)	Gls
Adrian V. JONES		M	8	(4)	
Chris JONES		A	27	(3)	4
wan JONES		M		(2)	
Mark JONES		D	10	(5)	
Steven KEHOE		D	30		3
Kevin LLOYD		A	22	(6)	8
Geraint MITCHELL		M	30	(2)	
Chris O'BRIEN	ENG	M	2	(2)	1
Dylan OWEN		M	15	(13)	2
Michael PARRY	ENG	D	3		
Sion PARRY		D	2		
Caerwyn ROBERTS		D	13	(11)	
Danny Glyn ROBERTS		A	10	(5)	
Paul ROBERTS	ENG	D	15		
Tom ROBERTS		M		(1)	
Jason SADLER		M	6	(1)	2
Gerard SMITH	ENG	M	4		
Darren THOMAS		A	24	(6)	13
Simon WILLIAMS	ENG	G	5		

NEATH ATHLETIC AFC

Manager - Andrew Dyer

Founded - 2005

Date	Opponent		Score	Scorers
2007				
18/8	Porthmadog	a	2-0	*Hill 2*
25/8	Connah's Quay	a	0-2	
31/8	Carmarthen	h	1-2	*Hill*
9/9	Rhyl	a	0-1	
15/9	Llangefni	h	2-0	*Shaw, French*
19/9	Llanelli	h	0-2	
22/9	Caernarfon	a	2-1	*Showdery, Hill (p)*
29/9	Newtown	a	0-3	
12/10	Haverfordwest	a	2-1	*D'Auria, Price*
20/10	Airbus	h	2-1	*Hill 2*
27/10	TNS	a	1-3	*Price*
10/11	Welshpool	h	2-5	*French, Hammett*
18/11	Cefn Druids	a	2-0	*Evans, French*
23/11	Aberystwyth	h	2-2	*Shaw, Bevan*
1/12	Caersws	a	2-2	*Hill, Shaw*
15/12	Porthmadog	h	2-1	*French, Shaw*
22/12	Connah's Quay	h	4-0	*Jenkins J., Rees, Bevan, Hill*
26/12	Port Talbot	a	3-3	*French, Shaw, Hill*
2008				
1/1	Port Talbot	h	0-2	
5/1	Carmarthen	a	1-1	*Pockett*
12/1	Rhyl	h	1-1	*French*
23/1	Llanelli	a	3-3	*French, Cronin, Hill*
26/1	Caernarfon	h	3-2	*Pridham 2, Hill*
9/2	Newtown	h	2-0	*French, Hill*
15/2	Haverfordwest	h	2-1	*Rees, Evans*
23/2	Airbus	a	1-2	*Hill (p)*
8/3	TNS	h	2-2	*Price, French*
15/3	Welshpool	a	2-1	*Hill, Pockett*
22/3	Cefn Druids	h	3-0	*Pockett, Hill, Evans*
24/3	Bangor	h	1-0	*Rees*
29/3	Llangefni	a	2-4	*Rees, Cronin*
5/4	Aberystwyth	a	2-1	*Rees 2*
12/4	Caersws	h	2-2	*Rees, Price*
19/4	Bangor	a	1-1	*Bevan*

Name	Nat	Pos	Aps	(s)	Gls
Lee BEVAN		D	31	(1)	3
Clayton BLACKMORE		M	7	(4)	
David BURROWS		D	13		
Sean CRONIN		D	31		2
David D'AURIA		M	8	(2)	1
Simon DYER		A		(1)	
Dale EVANS		M	26	(5)	3
Rob FOLLAND		D	9	(1)	
Richard FRENCH		A	22	(4)	9
Andrew HAMMETT		A		(5)	1
Andy HILL		A	33		15
Carl JENKINS		M	8	(9)	
Jack JENKINS		D	26		1
Gavin JONES		M		(6)	
Nicky JONES		M	1		
Daniel LANCEY		M		(5)	
Craig MORRIS		G	34		
Stephen POCKETT		M	27	(2)	3
Jarrod PRICE		M	26	(6)	4
Chris PRIDHAM		M	25	(1)	2
Matthew REES		M	24	(8)	7
Carl SHAW		A	5	(26)	5
Brian SHOWDERY		D	7		1
Billy TIMOTHY	ENG	D	11	(5)	

NEWI CEFN DRUIDS AFC

Manager - Lee Jones & Wayne Phillips

Founded – 1869

MAJOR HONOURS: Welsh Cup - (8) 1880, 1881, 1882, 1885, 1886, 1898, 1899, 1904.

Date	Opponent		Score	Scorers
2007				
17/8	TNS	h	1-0	*Evans*
24/8	Welshpool	h	0-2	
1/9	Llanelli	a	0-1	
9/9	Aberystwyth	a	0-1	
14/9	Caersws	h	4-0	*Heverin 3, McGinn*
18/9	Bangor	a	1-5	*Lewis*
22/9	Port Talbot	a	1-5	*Holsgrove*
29/9	Porthmadog	a	2-1	*Holsgrove, Heverin*
12/10	Connah's Quay	h	5-2	*Lewis 2, Williams 2, McGinn*
20/10	Carmarthen	a	1-4	*Holsgrove*
26/10	Rhyl	h	1-4	*Lewis*
9/11	Llangefni	a	0-2	
18/11	Neath	h	0-2	
24/11	Caernarfon	a	1-1	*Jones O.*
30/11	Newtown	h	3-0	*Edgar, Williams, Edwards T.*
8/12	Haverfordwest	a	0-3	
14/12	TNS	a	0-3	
21/12	Welshpool	a	1-0	*Phillips*
26/12	Airbus	a	2-3	*Lewis, og (Hunter)*
2008				
1/1	Airbus	h	4-1	*Jones L. 2, og (Allen), Williams*
6/1	Llanelli	h	2-5	*Williams, McGinn*
12/1	Aberystwyth	h	0-2	
22/1	Bangor	h	1-6	*Lewis*
26/1	Port Talbot	h	0-1	
8/2	Porthmadog	h	1-1	*Holsgrove*
15/2	Connah's Quay	a	1-2	*Lewis*
23/2	Carmarthen	h	3-1	*Connolly 2 (1p), McGinn*
7/3	Rhyl	a	0-1	
14/3	Llangefni	h	2-1	*McGinn, Holsgrove*
22/3	Neath	a	0-3	
25/3	Caersws	a	2-1	*Thompson, McGinn*
4/4	Caernarfon	h	5-1	*McGinn 2, Barnett, Connolly, Jones O.*
12/4	Newtown	a	0-1	
19/4	Haverfordwest	h	1-0	*McGinn*

Name	Pos	Nat	Aps	(s)	Gls
Aaron ABY	D		6	(3)	
Daniel BARNETT	D		11		1
Karl CONNOLLY	M	ENG	12		3
Andrew EDGAR	M	ENG	20	(6)	1
Carl EDWARDS	G		12		
Timmy EDWARDS	D		31		1
Ricky EVANS	M		8		1
James FORAN	M	ENG	2		
Khoz HEMATINAFAR	M	IRN	4	(11)	
Mike HEVERIN	A	ENG	8	(6)	4
Kevin HOLSGROVE	M	ENG	20	(9)	5
Andrew JACKSON	D	ENG	3	(1)	
Lee JONES	A		16	(2)	2
Osian JONES	M		8	(9)	2
Geraint LEWIS	M		22	(2)	7
Paul MAZZARELLA	M		13	(5)	
Chris McGINN	M	ENG	24	(6)	9
Chris MULLOCK	G		22		
Waynne PHILLIPS	D		27		1
Mark POWELL	D	ENG	34		
Joey PRICE	M		1	(8)	
Gareth ROBERTS	D		7		
Aled ROWLANDS	D		33		
Josh RUSSELL	A			(1)	
Mike THOMPSON	M	ENG	5	(4)	1
Stuart VERNON	M		3		
Darren WILLIAMS	A		13	(7)	5
Ricky WRIGHT	D		9	(1)	

NEWTOWN AFC

Manager - Darren Ryan

Founded - 1875

MAJOR HONOURS: Welsh Cup - (2) 1879, 1895.

2007				
18/8	Bangor	h	2-2	*Lloyd-Williams, og (Hoy)*
25/8	Port Talbot	a	1-5	*Lloyd Williams*
1/9	Porthmadog	h	4-2	*Lloyd-Williams 2, Scott, Williams-Cooke*
7/9	Connah's Quay	a	1-1	*Moses*
15/9	Carmarthen	h	0-1	
18/9	Rhyl	a	1-2	*Moses*
22/9	Llangefni	h	2-1	*Lloyd-Williams 2*
29/9	Neath	h	3-0	*Lloyd-Williams 2, Jellicoe*
13/10	Caernarfon	h	3-1	*Lloyd-Williams, Mutton, Tolley*
20/10	Llanelli	h	3-5	*Jellicoe, Moses, Lloyd-Williams*
27/10	Haverfordwest	a	3-2	*Lloyd-Williams 2, Mutton*
10/11	Airbus	h	1-1	*Lloyd-Williams*
16/11	TNS	a	0-6	
24/11	Welshpool	h	1-2	*Moses*
30/11	Cefn Druids	a	0-3	
15/12	Bangor	a	2-2	*Lloyd-Williams, Daniels*
22/12	Port Talbot	h	0-0	
26/12	Caersws	a	0-1	
2008				
1/1	Caersws	h	2-2	*Tolley, Williams-Cooke*
5/1	Porthmadog	a	3-2	*Lloyd-Williams 2, Moses*
12/1	Connah's Quay	h	4-1	*Clarke, Tolley, Williams-Cooke, Moses*
19/1	Carmarthen	a	1-2	*Moses*
26/1	Llangefni	a	3-2	*Worton 2, Mutton*
9/2	Neath	a	0-2	
15/2	Caernarfon	a	0-0	
1/3	Aberystwyth	h	1-2	*Mutton*
8/3	Haverfordwest	h	1-4	*Bellis*
15/3	Airbus	a	1-1	*Daniels*
18/3	Rhyl	h	0-2	
22/3	TNS	h	0-0	
4/4	Welshpool	a	1-2	*Seliearts*
12/4	Cefn Druids	h	1-0	*Williams-Cooke*
15/4	Llanelli	a	0-5	
19/4	Aberystwyth	a	2-2	*Seliaerts, Evans C.*

Name	Pos	Nat	Aps	(s)	Gls
Richard ASTLEY	D		3	(6)	
Barry BELLIS	A		6	(10)	1
Hugh CLARKE	D		31		1
Christian COURTNEY	A		1	(3)	
Damien DANIELS	D	NIR	21	(4)	2
Robert DEAN	M	ENG	3	(2)	
Chris EVANS	M		10	(1)	1
Richard EVANS	M			(2)	
Tomos FOULKES	M			(1)	
Daniel GRIFFITHS	M	ENG	4	(4)	
Ian HAVARD	G	ENG	3		
Daniel HOOPER	M		2		
Jack HUGHES	M			(1)	
Robbie JAMES	D		5	(4)	
Daniel JELLICOE	D	ENG	27		2
Dave JONES	G		31		
Graham JONES	M		9		
Matthew LEWIS	M		14	(7)	
Marc LLOYD-WILLIAMS	A		20		16
Colin LOSS	M		14		
Gareth MANSELL	M	ENG	2	(6)	
Craig MOSES	A		22		7
Tommy MUTTON	A		18	(3)	4
Jed RODWAY	M			(1)	
Darren RYAN	A			(2)	
Kevin SCOTT	D		14		1
Karl SELIEARTS	D	ENG	4		2
Shane SUTTON	D	ENG	14	(5)	
Glenn TOLLEY	M	ENG	27		3
Justin WICKHAM	M		2	(5)	
Craig WILLIAMS	D		25	(6)	
Richard WILLIAMS-COOKE	A		17	(5)	4
Adam WORTON	D	ENG	20	(7)	2
Callum WRIGHT	M	ENG	5	(2)	

CPD PORTHMADOG

Manager - Clayton Blackmore; (7/10/07) Viv Williams

Founded - 1884

2007				
18/8	Neath	h	0-2	
27/8	Caernarfon	h	1-3	*Williams*
1/9	Newtown	a	2-4	*Roberts R., Roberts P.*
9/9	Haverfordwest	h	0-2	
15/9	Airbus	a	0-2	
18/9	TNS	h	0-1	
22/9	Welshpool	a	3-0	*Roberts P. 2, Owen C.*
29/9	Cefn Druids	h	1-2	*Roberts P.*
13/10	Aberystwyth	a	1-2	*Orlik*
20/10	Caersws	h	0-1	
27/10	Bangor	a	0-2	
10/11	Port Talbot	h	1-2	*Orlik*
18/11	Llanelli	a	2-1	*og (Thomas), Orlik*
24/11	Connah's Quay	a	2-1	*Parry, Roberts P.*
1/12	Carmarthen	h	1-2	*Beattie*
15/12	Neath	a	1-2	*Owen C.*
22/12	Caernarfon	a	4-2	*Parry 2, Roberts P. 2*
26/12	Llangefni	a	4-1	*Jacobs, Owen C., Roberts P., Smart*

2008

1/1	Llangefni	h	2-4	*Roberts R., Roberts P.*
5/1	Newtown	h	2-3	*Orlik, Jacobs*
12/1	Haverfordwest	a	2-3	*Orlik, Thomas M.*
26/1	Welshpool	h	1-1	*Orlik (p)*
2/2	TNS	a	1-4	*Parry*
8/2	Cefn Druids	a	1-1	*Orlik*
16/2	Aberystwyth	h	2-6	*Owen G., Parry*
23/2	Caersws	a	4-2	*Owen C. 3, Roberts R.*
1/3	Airbus	h	2-2	*Thomas M., Parry*
8/3	Bangor	h	0-0	
15/3	Port Talbot	a	2-4	*Orlik 2 (1p)*
22/3	Llanelli	h	2-4	*Thomas M. (p), og (Phillips)*
24/3	Rhyl	a	0-1	
5/4	Connah's Quay	h	3-3	*Owen C., Roberts R. Roberts P.*
12/4	Carmarthen	a	0-0	
19/4	Rhyl	h	1-0	*Hughes R.*

Name	Pos	Nat	Aps	(s)	Gls
Warren BEATTIE	ENG	M	16		1
Clayton BLACKMORE		M	1	(2)	
Ryan DAVIES		D	11		
Adam DOCKER	ENG	D	2	(1)	
Barry EVANS		D	9	(4)	
Mike FOSTER		D	21	(2)	
Richard HARVEY		G	27		
Danny HUGHES		M	19		
David HUGHES		M	8	(2)	
Matthew HUGHES		A	1		
Richard HUGHES		M	2	(3)	1
Kyle JACOBS	ENG	D	12		2
Carl JONES		M	5	(10)	
Dylan JONES		A		(2)	
John Gwynfor JONES		D	27	(2)	
Karl LUISI	ENG	A	5		
Marcus ORLIK		A	27	(3)	9
Carl OWEN		A	28	(3)	7
Gareth OWEN		D	5		1
Richard OWEN		M	2		
Gareth PARRY		M	28	(1)	6
Paul ROBERTS		A	26	(5)	10
Rhys ROBERTS		D	33		4
Aled ROWLANDS		M	21	(5)	
Jason SADLER		A	8	(2)	
Joe SAGER	ENG	G	7		
Richard SMART	ENG	D	10	(13)	1
Iwan THOMAS		M	2	(4)	
Mark THOMAS		M	10	(2)	3
Iwan WILLIAMS		M	1	(3)	1

PORT TALBOT TOWN FC

Manager - Tony Pennock; (7/11/07) Nicky Tucker

Founded - 1901

2007

18/8	Caernarfon	a	1-3	*Pierce*
25/8	Newtown	h	5-1	*Rose 2, Surman, Blain, Morgan*
31/8	Haverfordwest	a	1-2	*McCreesh*
9/9	Airbus	h	0-0	
15/9	TNS	a	1-2	*Bond*
18/9	Welshpool	h	1-1	*Surman*
22/9	Cefn Druids	h	5-1	*Morgan 3, McCreesh, Rose*
28/9	Aberystwyth	h	2-1	*McCreesh, Morgan*
13/10	Caersws	a	4-1	*Rose 2, John, Bond*
20/10	Bangor	h	0-0	
26/10	Llanelli	a	0-8	
10/11	Porthmadog	a	2-1	*Rose (p) Barrow*
18/11	Connah's Quay	h	2-1	*Rose (p), Baker*
23/11	Carmarthen	a	0-0	
1/12	Rhyl	h	1-2	*Rose (p)*
15/12	Caernarfon	h	2-1	*Barrow, Rose*
22/12	Newtown	a	0-0	
26/12	Neath	h	3-3	*Barrow 2, Bond*

2008

1/1	Neath	a	2-0	*Bond, Barrow*
5/1	Haverfordwest	h	2-2	*Rose (p), McCreesh*
12/1	Airbus	a	0-1	
19/1	TNS	h	1-0	*John*
26/1	Cefn Druids	a	1-0	*Rose*
8/2	Aberystwyth	a	4-2	*Rose, Hanford, John, Blain*
16/2	Caersws	h	3-1	*Blain 2, McCreesh*
23/2	Bangor	a	0-0	
1/3	Llangefni	a	1-4	*Barrow*
7/3	Llanelli	h	0-1	
15/3	Porthmadog	h	4-2	*Rose 2, McCreesh, Barrow*
22/3	Connah's Quay	a	1-0	*Rose (p)*
4/4	Carmarthen	h	2-0	*Rose, McCreesh*
12/4	Rhyl	a	0-5	
15/4	Welshpool	a	3-1	*Rose 2, Blain*
19/4	Llangefni	h	3-1	*Rose, Rees, McCreesh*

Name	Nat	Pos	Aps	(s)	Gls
Sam BAKER		M		(13)	1
Scott BARROW		M	20	(6)	7
Dylan BLAIN		M	21	(7)	5
Chad BOND		A	16	(4)	4
James BURGIN	ENG	M	2		
David BURROWS		D	3	(5)	
Leigh de VULGT		D	31	(2)	
Carl EVANS		M	7	(2)	
Paul EVANS		D	3	(6)	
Stephen EVANS		M	1	(4)	
Craig HANFORD		D	28	(7)	1
Lewis JAMES		M		(1)	
Lee JOHN		M	29		3
Dean JOHNSTON		M	1	(3)	
Daniel LANCEY		M	2	(7)	
Scott McCOUBREY		A		(2)	
Liam McCREESH		M	27	(6)	8
Mark McGIBBON		D	10	(1)	
Kerry MORGAN		A	4	(5)	5
Josh PAYNE		G	3	(1)	
Gareth PHILLIPS		M	25	(1)	
Dyfan PIERCE		D	2		1
Matthew REES		D	30		1
Kristian ROGERS		G	31		
Martin ROSE	ENG	A	32	(1)	19
Kyle SHEPPERD		A	4	(1)	
Lee SURMAN		D	26		2
Matthew THOMPSON		M	16	(6)	

RHYL FC

Manager - John Hulse (ENG)

Founded - 1874

MAJOR HONOURS: Welsh League – (1) 2004; Welsh Cup - (4) 1952, 1953, 2004, 2006.

2007

18/8	Carmarthen	h	2-1	*Kelly, Hunt*
25/8	Llanelli	h	1-2	*Moran (p)*
1/9	Llangefni	a	3-0	*Hunt 2, Roberts*
9/9	Neath	h	1-0	*Moran (p)*

15/9	Caernarfon	a	1-0	*Moran*
18/9	Newtown	h	2-1	*Graves, Jones*
22/9	Haverfordwest	a	1-1	*Moran*
28/9	Airbus	h	2-1	*Moran 2 (1p)*
14/10	TNS	a	0-1	
20/10	Welshpool	h	1-1	*Moran*
26/10	Cefn Druids	a	4-1	*Connolly, O'Neil, Moran, Sharp*
10/11	Aberystwyth	h	0-0	
18/11	Caersws	a	7-2	*Hunt 2, Connolly 2, White, Moran, Jones*
24/11	Bangor	h	1-2	*Hunt*
1/12	Port Talbot	a	2-1	*Jones, Connolly*
15/12	Carmarthen	a	0-0	
22/12	Llanelli	a	1-2	*Hunt*
26/12	Connah's Quay	a	5-0	*Hunt 2, Sharp, Jones, Cameron*
2008				
1/1	Connah's Quay	h	1-0	*Jones*
5/1	Llangefni	h	4-1	*Connolly 2 (1p), Hunt, Horan*
12/1	Neath	a	1-1	*O'Neil*
19/1	Caernarfon	h	3-1	*Jones, Hunt, Connolly*
26/1	Haverfordwest	h	2-0	*Lloyd-Williams, Jones*
8/2	Airbus	a	2-0	*Jones, Lloyd-Williams*
23/2	Welshpool	a	0-1	
7/3	Cefn Druids	h	1-0	*Hunt*
15/3	Aberystwyth	a	0-0	
18/3	Newtown	a	2-0	*Lloyd-Williams, Hunt*
22/3	Caersws	h	2-1	*og (Jones), Sharp*
24/3	Porthmadog	h	1-0	*White*
8/4	TNS	h	0-1	
12/4	Port Talbot	h	5-0	*Sharp 2, Lloyd-Williams 2, Garside*
15/4	Bangor	a	2-1	*Lloyd-Williams 2*
19/4	Porthmadog	a	0-1	

Name	Pos	Nat	Aps	(s)	Gls
Mitchell BOOTH	M			(2)	
James BREWERTON	D			(3)	
Dave CAMERON	A		4	(15)	1
Phil COFFIN	M	ENG		(1)	
Mark CONNOLLY	M	ENG	27	(3)	7
John GANN	G	ENG	3		
Craig GARSIDE	M	ENG	11	(5)	1
Stuart GRAVES	M	ENG	28		1
Matthew HOLT	D		18	(7)	
George HORAN	D	ENG	32		1
Lee HUNT	A	ENG	27		13
Craig JONES	M		31		8
James KELLY	M	ENG	6		1
Lee KENDALL	G		31		
Marc LLOYD-WILLIAMS	A		10	(3)	7
Andy MORAN	A	ENG	19	(1)	9
Paul O'NEIL	D	ENG	29	(1)	2
Gary POWELL	M	ENG		(2)	
Chris ROBERTS	D		23	(2)	1
Carl RUFFER	D	ENG	23		
Chris SHARP	A	SCO	9	(14)	5
Greg STONES	M	ENG	9		
Michael WHITE	A	NZL	11	(11)	2
Gareth WILSON	M		23	(6)	

THE NEW SAINTS FC

Manager - Ken McKenna (ENG); (12/3/08) Dr Andy Cale & Mike Davies (ENG)

Founded - 1959

MAJOR HONOURS: Welsh League - (4) 2000, 2005, 2006, 2007; Welsh Cup – (2) 1996, 2005.

2007				
17/8	Cefn Druids	a	0-1	
26/8	Aberystwyth	a	1-5	*Carter*
1/9	Caersws	h	6-0	*Carter 3, Wilde 2, Holden*
7/9	Bangor	a	2-1	*Carter, Wilde*
15/9	Port Talbot	h	2-1	*Carter, Wilde*
18/9	Porthmadog	a	1-0	*Baker*
22/9	Connah's Quay	h	3-1	*Wilde, Carter, og (Pinch)*
29/9	Carmarthen	a	3-0	*Wilde, Beck, King*
14/10	Rhyl	h	1-0	*Wood*
20/10	Llangefni	a	3-0	*Beck, Holden, Wilde*
27/10	Neath	h	3-1	*Ruscoe 2, Wood*
10/11	Caernarfon	a	7-1	*Wood 2, Beck 2, Holden, Leah (p), Wilde*
16/11	Newtown	h	6-0	*Toner 2, Holden 2, Ruscoe, og (Clarke)*
24/11	Haverfordwest	a	4-0	*Lamb 2, Leah, Toner*
1/12	Airbus	h	0-0	
14/12	Cefn Druids	h	3-0	*Ruscoe 2, Holden*
22/12	Aberystwyth	h	1-0	*Wood*
26/12	Welshpool	a	3-0	*Beck, Ruscoe, Carter*
2008				
1/1	Welshpool	h	2-0	*Ruscoe 2*
5/1	Caersws	a	2-1	*Courtney, Naylor*
12/1	Bangor	h	2-1	*Carter, Lamb*
19/1	Port Talbot	a	0-1	
2/2	Porthmadog	h	4-1	*Townson, Ruscoe, King, Toner*
9/2	Carmarthen	h	0-3	
23/2	Llangefni	h	7-1	*Townson 4, Henry, Wood, og (Mitchell)*
4/3	Llanelli	a	0-4	
8/3	Neath	a	2-2	*Ruscoe, King*
15/3	Caernarfon	h	4-0	*Wood 2, Beck, Wilde*
22/3	Newtown	a	0-0	
5/4	Haverfordwest	h	6-2	*Toner 3, Wilde 2, Wood*
8/4	Rhyl	a	1-0	*Toner*
11/4	Airbus	a	0-2	
15/4	Connah's Quay	a	3-1	*Toner 2, Holmes*
19/4	Llanelli	h	3-0	*Carter 2, Leah*

Name	Pos	Nat	Aps	(s)	Gls
Nikola ANDELIĆ	D	BIH		1	
Phil BAKER	D	ENG	25	(4)	1
Steven BECK	M		20	(4)	6
Gary BRABIN	M	ENG		(2)	
Alfie CARTER	A	ENG	16	(6)	11
Duane COURTNEY	D	ENG	21	(2)	1
Gerard DOHERTY	G	NIR	4		
Paul HARRISON	G	ENG	30		
Paul HENRY	M	ENG	7		1
Barry HOGAN	M	ENG	14	(7)	
Luke HOLDEN	A	ENG	23	(6)	6
Tommy HOLMES	D	ENG	17	(3)	1
Chris KING	M	ENG	30		3
Carl LAMB	A	ENG	5	(13)	3
John LEAH	M	ENG	28	(1)	3
Ryan MARRIOTT	M	ENG	0	(1)	
John McKENNA	M	ENG	1	(4)	
Ronnie MORGAN	A	ENG		(2)	
Martin NAYLOR	D	ENG	7	(8)	1
Scott RUSCOE	M	ENG	33		10
Michael TAYLOR	D	ENG	28		
John TONER	A	CAN	11	(6)	10
Kevin TOWNSON	A	ENG	6	(1)	5
Craig WHITFIELD	M	ENG		(3)	
Michael WILDE	A	ENG	18	(2)	11
Rob WILLIAMS	D	ENG	7	(6)	
Jamie WOOD	M	CAY	22	(7)	9

WELSHPOOL TOWN FC

Manager - Tomi Morgan

Founded - 1878

Date	Opponent		Score	Scorers
2007				
19/8	Llanelli	a	0-3	
24/8	Cefn Druids	a	2-0	*Venables, Davies*
1/9	Aberystwyth	a	3-2	*Davies 2, Venables*
7/9	Caersws	a	3-0	*Venables, Jefferies R., Thompson*
15/9	Bangor	h	2-0	*Jefferies R., Venables*
18/9	Port Talbot	a	1-1	*Jefferies B.*
22/9	Porthmadog	h	0-3	
28/9	Connah's Quay	a	3-3	*Davies 2, Harris*
13/10	Carmarthen	h	2-2	*Shannon 2,*
20/10	Rhyl	a	1-1	*Stephens*
26/10	Llangefni	h	3-0	*Venables 2, Stephens*
10/11	Neath	a	5-2	*Stephens 2, Shannon, Davies, Venables*
18/11	Caernarfon	h	2-4	*Shannon 2*
24/11	Newtown	a	2-1	*Jefferies R., Thomas*
1/12	Haverfordwest	h	2-1	*Davies, Shannon (p)*
7/12	Airbus	a	1-1	*Davies*
15/12	Llanelli	h	3-3	*Davies 3*
21/12	Cefn Druids	h	0-1	
26/12	TNS	h	0-3	
2008				
1/1	TNS	a	0-2	
5/1	Aberystwyth	h	2-1	*Venables, Rogers*
19/1	Bangor	a	0-1	
26/1	Porthmadog	a	1-1	*Shannon (p)*
8/2	Connah's Quay	h	1-1	*Shannon*
16/2	Carmarthen	a	2-5	*Rogers, Davies*
23/2	Rhyl	h	1-0	*Stephens*
7/3	Llangefni	a	1-0	*Davies*
15/3	Neath	h	1-2	*Harris*
22/3	Caernarfon	a	1-1	*Cunnah*
29/3	Caersws	h	1-1	*Davies*
4/4	Newtown	h	2-1	*Stephens, Rogers*
12/4	Haverfordwest	a	0-1	
15/4	Port Talbot	h	1-3	*Stephens*
19/4	Airbus	h	0-1	

Name	Pos	Nat	Aps	(s)	Gls
Daniel BARNETT	D		5	(6)	
Dave CUNNAH	M		14	(11)	1
Calvin DAVIES	A		27	(2)	14
Paul DOWRIDGE	D		34		
Richard HARRIS	M	ENG	31	(1)	2
George HUGHES	M		31	(2)	
Kyle JACOBS	D	ENG	12		
Brett JEFFERIES	D	ENG	19		1
Ross JEFFERIES	D	ENG	22	(4)	3
Danny JONES	G		10		
John KEEGAN	D		15		
Ian MacLEOD	M			(3)	
Gerard McGUIGAN	G		24		
Tomi MORGAN	A			(2)	
Max POWELL	D		1	(3)	
Steve ROGERS	A	ENG	19	(8)	3
Aden SHANNON	A		16	(12)	8
Ross STEPHENS	M		31	(2)	7
Will THOMAS	M		3	(14)	1
Mike THOMPSON	M	ENG	2	(6)	1
Chris VENABLES	M		28	(1)	8
Christian WEBSTER	A			(3)	
Geraint WINDSOR	D		30		

PROMOTED CLUB

PRESTATYN TOWN FC

Manager – Neil Gibson

Founded - 1948

SECOND LEVEL FINAL TABLES 2007/08

NORTH		Pld	W	D	L	F	A	Pts
1	Prestatyn Town FC	32	24	4	4	93	29	76
2	Bala Town FC	32	19	4	9	71	42	61
3	Flint Town United FC	32	16	10	6	62	42	58
4	Llandudno Town FC	32	16	8	8	58	36	56
5	Holyhead Hotspur FC	32	15	9	8	76	53	54
6	Gap Queen's Park FC	32	15	10	7	82	47	52
7	CPD Glantraeth	32	15	6	11	64	55	51
8	Denbigh Town FC	32	13	7	12	52	50	46
9	Guilsfield FC	32	12	5	15	57	62	41
10	Llanfairpwll FC	32	10	10	12	59	71	40
11	Mynydd Isa FC	32	10	9	13	45	51	39
12	Llandyrnog United FC	32	10	8	14	54	69	38
13	Ruthin Town FC	32	10	6	16	41	63	36
14	Buckley Town FC	32	8	9	15	45	80	30
15	CPD Penrhyncoch	32	6	8	18	38	66	26
16	Lex XI FC	32	6	7	19	44	85	22
17	Gresford Athletic FC	32	4	6	22	32	72	18

N.B. CPD Bodedern withdrew; Gap Queen's Park FC, Buckley Town FC & Lex XI FC - 3pts deducted

SOUTH		Pld	W	D	L	F	A	Pts
1	Goytre United FC	34	25	3	6	101	30	78
2	Dinas Powys FC	34	25	1	8	92	34	76
3	Ton Pentre AFC	34	22	7	5	102	33	73
4	ENTO Aberaman Athletic FC	34	21	6	7	75	40	69
5	Bryntirion Athletic FC	34	20	5	9	82	35	65
6	Afan Lido FC	34	17	11	6	58	31	62
7	Newport YMCA AFC	34	19	4	11	88	69	61
8	Caerleon AFC	34	16	7	11	60	42	55
9	Cambrian & Clydach Vale BGFC	34	13	10	11	59	47	49
10	Bridgend Town FC	34	13	6	15	84	68	45
11	Caldicot Town AFC	34	13	3	18	54	65	42
12	Taff's Well AFC	34	11	7	16	53	70	40
13	Pontardawe Town AFC	34	11	6	17	47	55	39
14	Cwmbrân Town AFC	34	10	8	16	56	50	38
15	Croesyceiliog AFC	34	9	5	20	60	80	32
16	Maesteg Park AFC	34	7	6	21	43	83	27
17	Pontypridd Town AFC	34	3	4	27	38	116	13
18	Garw Athletic FC	34	1	1	32	13	217	4

N.B. No club promoted to the Welsh Premier League. Criteria not met by top two clubs.

DOMESTIC CUP 2007/08

WELSH CUP

SECOND ROUND

(6/10/07)

NORTH
Bangor 3, Llandyrnog 0
Brymbo 4, Halkyn 0
Caernarfon 2, Llanfairpwll 1
Caersws 9, Mold 0
Connah's Quay 0, TNS 0 *(aet; 3-2 on pens)*
Corwen 1, Mynydd Isa 3
Guilsfield 3, Airbus 2 *(aet)*
Holyhead 2, Bala 1
Llanberis 1, Newtown 5
Llandudno 1, Cefn Druids 2
Llangefni 5, Hawarden 0
Llanrug 5, Llanrhaedr ym Mochnant 1
Nefyn 2, Chirk 0
Porthmadog 0, Welshpool 2
Queen's Park 3, Penrhyncoch 1
Rhyl 10, Montgomery 0
Tywyn Bryncrug 3, Conwy 2

SOUTH
Aberystwyth 3, Newcastle Emlyn 0
Afan Lido 3, Croesyceiliog 1
Bridgend 1, Bryntirion 2
Caerau Ely 3, Goytre United 2
Caerleon 2, Taff's Well 1
Cardiff Corinthians 2, Ton Pentre 3 *(aet)*
Cwmaman Institute 0, Aberaman Athletic 3
Cwmamman United 0, Dinas Powys 5
Haverfordwest 1, Llantwit Fadre 0
Maesteg Park 2, Briton Ferry 0
Merthyr Saints 1, Carmarthen 2
Neath 6, Llanwern 0
Newport YMCA 4, Cambrian & Clydach Vale 1
Pentwyn Dynamos 3, Llanelli 7
West End 1, Port Talbot 2

THIRD ROUND

(3/11/07)
Aberaman Athletic 3, Caerau Ely 1
Aberystwyth 3, Neath 1
Bryntirion 4, Dinas Powys 2
Caerleon 2, Brymbo 0
Caersws 2, Bangor 3 *(aet)*
Cefn Druids 3, Holyhead 0
Connah's Quay 0, Guilsfield 2
Haverfordwest 3, Ton Pentre 0
Llangefni Town 3, Mynydd Isa 0
Llanrug 3, Llanelli 5
Nefyn 1, Caernarfon 3
Newport YMCA 2, Carmarthen 1
Newtown 2, Maesteg Park 1 *(aet)*
Queen's Park 3, Afan Lido 1
Rhyl 1, Port Talbot 0
Tywyn Bryncrug 1, Welshpool 3 *(aet)*

FOURTH ROUND

(3/2/08)
Aberystwyth 0, Bangor 0 *(aet; 2-3 on pens)*
Bryntirion 1, Welshpool 2
Cefn Druids 0, Aberaman Athletic 0 *(aet; 5-3 on pens)*
Guilsfield 1, Caernarfon 0
Haverfordwest 1, Rhyl 2
Newport YMCA 1, Llangefni 1 *(aet; 4-3 on pens)*
Newtown 1, Llanelli 2
Queen's Park 2, Caerleon 0

QUARTER-FINALS

(1/3/08)
Guilsfield 0, Bangor 6 *(Stott 15, 26, 40, 54, Johnston 22, Noon 45p)*

Newport YMCA 3 *(Heath 67, 85, Sommers 80)*, Welshpool 2 *(Jefferies B. 5, Harris 51)*

Rhyl 3 *(Jones 35, Hunt 57, Sharp 66)*, Queen's Park 2 *(Roberts G. 63 Evans Ricky 90p)*

(2/3/08)
Cefn Druids 3 *(McGinn 16, Connolly 80, 120)*, Llanelli 6 *(Jones S. 50, Edgar 63og, Pritchard 93, Griffiths 105, 112, Follows 115) (aet)*

SEMI-FINALS

(30/3/08)
Rhyl 2 *(Hunt 44, 78)*, Llanelli 5 *(Corbisiero 7, Griffiths 47, 80p, 89, Pritchard 58)*

(5/4/08)
Newport YMCA 1 *(Cueto 87)*, Bangor 3 *(Hoy 42, Stott 51, Edwards 55)*

FINAL

(4/5/08)
Latham Park, Newtown
BANGOR CITY FC 4 *(Stott 20, Seargeant 90, Limberg 97p, Noon 99)*
LLANELLI AFC 2 *(Swanick 48og, Griffiths 56)*
(aet)
Referee – *Southall*
BANGOR – *Smith, Swanick, Hoy, Johnston, Webber (Noon 73), Seargeant, Limbert, Walsh (Killackey 73), Davies, Stott, Edwards (Beattie 57).*
Sent off: *Hoy (4).*
LLANELLI – *Roberts, Phillips, Holloway, Thomas, Mumford, Corbisiero (Evans 46), Jones C. (Jones Ma. 62), Legg, Jones Mat. (Wanless 97), Griffiths, Pritchard.*
Sent off: *Thomas (66); Griffiths (114)*.

THE EUROPEAN FOOTBALL YEARBOOK

TOP 100 PLAYERS OF THE SEASON 2007/08

Overleaf you will find the names of the Top 100 Players of the Season, as selected by myself and the rest of the European Football Yearbook's editorial team. In-depth profiles of these players can be found on the following 50 pages.

The list of nominees was generated as the season progressed, although UEFA EURO 2008™ inevitably had a major bearing on our final selection.

Each profile contains basic and historical statistical data as well as narrative text specific to the 2007/08 season, which, we hope, will clarify and justify the reasons for the player's inclusion.

As with any value judgment, opinions will differ. So, whether you agree or disagree with our choices, please let us have your thoughts. The contact email address is efy@uefa.ch.

Please note that there is no ranking whatsoever within the Top 100. The players are listed alphabetically (by family name – or, in some cases, 'football name') and club histories were up to date on 5 August, 2008.

Enjoy the read.

MIKE HAMMOND
General Editor

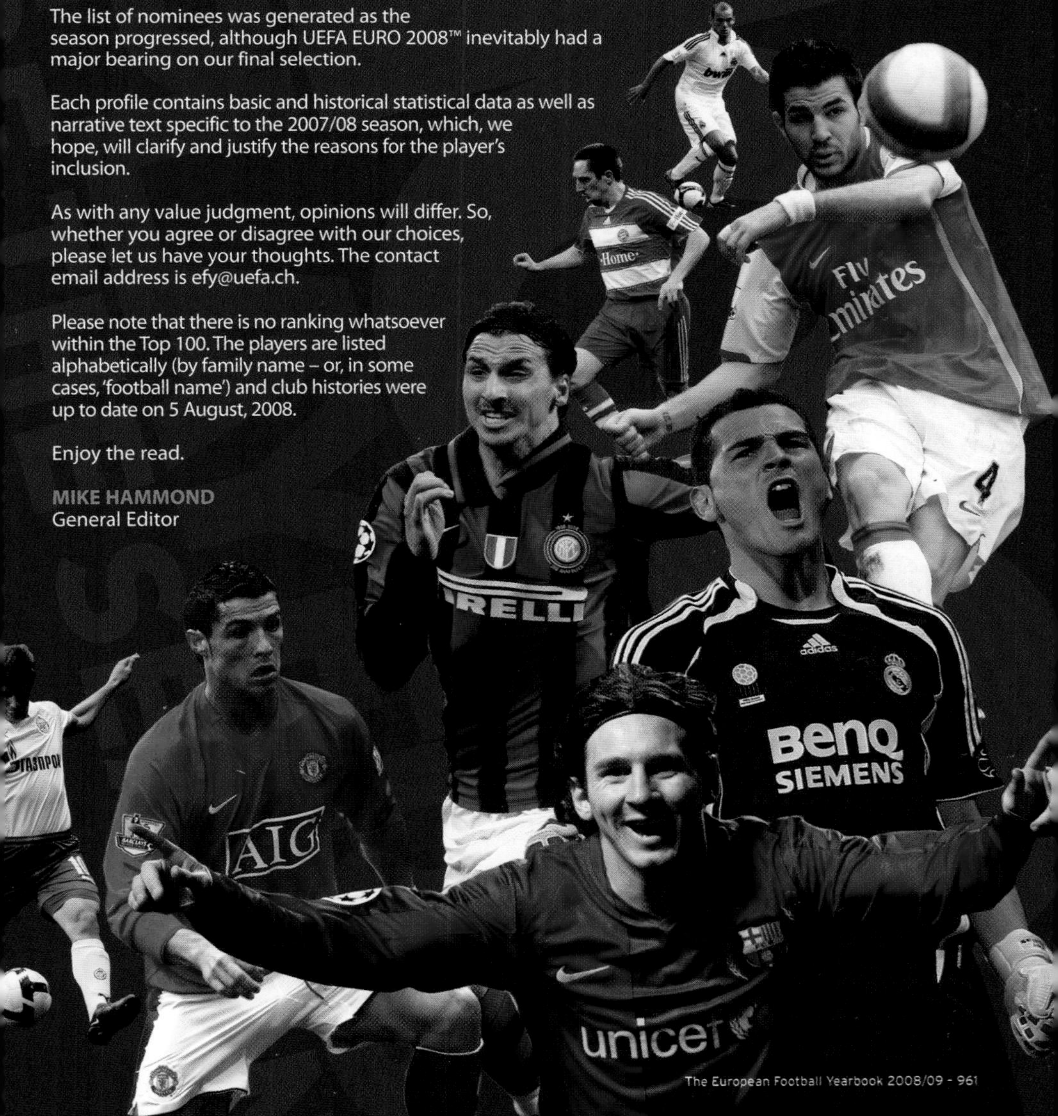

Emmanuel ADEBAYOR (Arsenal FC, Togo)
René ADLER (Bayer 04 Leverkusen, Germany)
Sergio AGÜERO (Club Atlético de Madrid, Argentina)
Aleksandr ANYUKOV (FC Zenit St. Petersburg, Russia)
ARDA Turan (Galatasaray AŞ, Turkey)
Andrei ARSHAVIN (FC Zenit St. Petersburg, Russia)
Gareth BARRY (Aston Villa FC, England)
Karim BENZEMA (Olympique Lyonnais, France)
Dimitar BERBATOV (Tottenham Hotspur FC, Bulgaria)
Marco BORRIELLO (Genoa CFC, Italy)
Joan CAPDEVILA (Villarreal CF, Spain)
Óscar CARDOZO (SL Benfica, Paraguay)
Iker CASILLAS (Real Madrid CF, Spain)
Antonio CASSANO (UC Sampdoria, Italy)
Joe COLE (Chelsea FC, England)
Vedran ĆORLUKA (Manchester City FC, Croatia)
CRISTIANO RONALDO (Manchester United FC, Portugal)
Carlos CUÉLLAR (Rangers FC, Spain)
DAVID VILLA (Valencia CF, Spain)
Steven DEFOUR (R. Standard de Liège, Belgium)
Rubén DE LA RED (Getafe CF, Spain)
Alessandro DEL PIERO (Juventus, Italy)
DIEGO (Werder Bremen, Brazil)
Antonio DI NATALE (Udinese Calcio, Italy)
Didier DROGBA (Chelsea FC, Ivory Coast)
Balázs DZUDSZÁK (PSV Eindhoven, Hungary)
Orlando ENGELAAR (FC Twente, Netherlands)
Patrice EVRA (Manchester United FC, France)
Cesc FÀBREGAS (Arsenal FC, Spain)
Rio FERDINAND (Manchester United FC, England)
FERNANDO TORRES (Liverpool FC, Spain)
Mathieu FLAMINI (Arsenal FC, France)
Sébastien FREY (ACF Fiorentina, France)
Steven GERRARD (Liverpool FC, England)
Heurelho GOMES (PSV Eindhoven, Brazil)
Bafétimbi GOMIS (AS Saint-Étienne, France)
Daniel GÜIZA (RCD Mallorca, Spain)
HAMIT Altıntop (FC Bayern München, Turkey)
John HEITINGA (AFC Ajax, Netherlands)
Thorstein HELSTAD (SK Brann, Norway)
Aleksandr HLEB (Arsenal FC, Belarus)
Steffen HOFMANN (SK Rapid Wien, Germany)
Klaas Jan HUNTELAAR (AFC Ajax, Netherlands)
Alan HUTTON (Rangers FC/Tottenham Hotspur FC, Scotland)
Zlatan IBRAHIMOVIĆ (FC Internazionale Milano, Sweden)
Andrés INIESTA (FC Barcelona, Spain)
Gökhan INLER (Udinese Calcio, Switzerland)
David JAMES (Portsmouth FC, England)
JOÃO MOUTINHO (Sporting Clube de Portugal, Portugal)
Milan JOVANOVIĆ (R. Standard de Liège, Serbia)
Robbie KEANE (Tottenham Hotspur FC, Republic of Ireland)
Ümit KORKMAZ (SK Rapid Wien, Austria)
Martin LAURSEN (Aston Villa FC, Denmark)
Joleon LESCOTT (Everton FC, England)
LISANDRO LÓPEZ (FC Porto, Argentina)
LUCHO GONZÁLEZ (FC Porto, Argentina)
LUÍS FABIANO (Sevilla FC, Brazil)
Javier MASCHERANO (Liverpool FC, Argentina)
Aiden McGEADY (Celtic FC, Republic of Ireland)
Lionel MESSI (FC Barcelona, Argentina)
Luka MODRIĆ (NK Dinamo Zagreb, Croatia)
Adrian MUTU (ACF Fiorentina, Romania)
NIHAT Kahveci (Villarreal CF, Turkey)
Blaise NKUFO (FC Twente, Switzerland)
Ivica OLIĆ (Hamburger SV, Croatia)
Goran PANDEV (S.S. Lazio, FYR Macedonia)
Alexandre PATO (AC Milan, Brazil)
Roman PAVLYUCHENKO (FC Spartak Moskva, Russia)
PEPE (Real Madrid CF, Portugal)
Mladen PETRIĆ (BV Borussia Dortmund, Croatia)
Pavel POGREBNYAK (FC Zenit St. Petersburg, Russia)
RAÚL González (Real Madrid CF, Spain)
Franck RIBÉRY (FC Bayern München, France)
RICARDO QUARESMA (FC Porto, Portugal)
ROGER Guerreiro (Legia Warszawa, Poland)
Roque SANTA CRUZ (Blackburn Rovers FC, Paraguay)
SEMIH Şentürk (Fenerbahçe SK, Turkey)
Marcos SENNA (Villarreal CF, Spain)
SERGIO RAMOS (Real Madrid CF, Spain)
Martin ŠKRTEĽ (FC Zenit St. Petersburg/Liverpool FC, Slovakia)
Wesley SNEIJDER (Real Madrid CF, Netherlands)
Darijo SRNA (FC Shakhtar Donetsk, Croatia)
Ieroklis STOLTIDIS (Olympiacos CFP, Greece)
Václav SVĚRKOŠ (FC Baník Ostrava, Czech Republic)
Carlos TÉVEZ (Manchester United FC, Argentina)
Luca TONI (FC Bayern München, Italy)
Jérémy TOULALAN (Olympique Lyonnais, France)
David TREZEGUET (Juventus, France)
Anatoliy TYMOSHCHUK (FC Zenit St. Petersburg, Ukraine)
Tomáš UJFALUŠI (ACF Fiorentina, Czech Republic)
Edwin VAN DER SAR (Manchester United FC, Netherlands)
Rafael VAN DER VAART (Hamburger SV, Netherlands)
Ivica VASTIC (LASK Linz, Austria)
Nemanja VIDIĆ (Manchester United FC, Serbia)
VOLKAN Demirel (Fenerbahçe SK, Turkey)
XAVI Hernández (FC Barcelona, Spain)
Hakan YAKIN (BSC Young Boys, Switzerland)
Javier ZANETTI (FC Internazionale Milano, Argentina)
Yuriy ZHIRKOV (PFC CSKA Moskva, Russia)
Konstantin ZYRYANOV (FC Zenit St. Petersburg, Russia)

N.B. Clubs indicated are those the players belonged to in the 2007/08 season.

Key to competitions: WCF = FIFA World Cup final tournament; WCQ = FIFA World Cup qualifying round; ECF = UEFA EURO final tournament; ECQ = UEFA EURO qualifying round; CC = FIFA Confederations Cup; CA = Copa América; ANF = African Cup of Nations final tournament; ANQ = African Cup of Nations qualifying round; CGC = Concacaf Gold Cup

Emmanuel ADEBAYOR
Striker
Born 26/2/84, Lome, Togo
Height 190cm, Weight 70kg

As most of the English Premier League's African contingent flew south to Ghana in January 2008 to play in the African Cup of Nations, Emmanuel Adebayor, from non-qualifiers Togo, remained at his club. That was a major fillip for Arsenal FC because the giant centre-forward was in the form of his life. From late December to mid-February he scored nine goals in seven league matches for the Gunners, including at least one in every game. He would end the season as the Premier League's joint-second highest scorer, on 24 goals – an outstanding return for a player who, rather like the man he replaced at the apex of the Arsenal attack, Thierry Henry, was not especially renowned for his goalscoring when he arrived at the north London club. Adebayor's second season at the Emirates Stadium, which included two hat-tricks – both against hapless Derby County FC - totally eclipsed his first (when his league goal tally was eight), and although Arsenal won no trophies, the lanky 24-year-old's skill, movement and finishing ability became a prime asset – so much so that European giants AC Milan and FC Barcelona moved in during the close season with tempting offers to recruit him. In vain, as it proved, with Adebayor committing his future to Arsenal.

International Career

TOGO
Debut – 8/7/00 v Zambia (a, Lusaka, WCQ), lost 0-2
First Goal – 13/10/02 v Mauritania (h, Lome, ANQ), won 1-0
Caps 42; Goals 16
Major Tournaments – African Cup of Nations 2002; African Cup of Nations 2006; FIFA World Cup 2006

Club Career

Clubs: 01-03 FC Metz (FRA); 03-06 AS Monaco FC (FRA); 06- Arsenal FC (ENG)

René ADLER
Goalkeeper
Born 15/1/85,
Leipzig, Germany
Height 191cm,
Weight 85kg

René Adler was widely considered to be the German Bundesliga's outstanding goalkeeper in 2007/08. While Robert Enke, of Hannover 96, and young Manuel Neuer, of FC Schalke 04, both had their supporters, the blond 23-year-old captivated audiences up and down the land with his astonishing reflexes and spectacular saves. It was his first full Bundesliga campaign with Bayer 04 Leverkusen, but nobody would have known it as the former Germany Under-19 captain produced goalkeeping skills worthy of Oliver Kahn in his prime. As the FC Bayern München legend retired from the game at the end of the season, the prospects of Adler becoming his long-term successor in the Nationalmannschaft grew when he was selected ahead of Timo Hildebrand in Joachim Löw's UEFA EURO 2008™ squad. With Jens Lehmann retaining the No1 spot despite a season of inactivity at Arsenal FC, Adler did not get a game. Indeed, he was still uncapped as the tournament came to a close. But with Lehmann now retired from international football, the waiting should not last too much longer..

International Career

GERMANY
Caps 0; Goals 0
Major Tournaments – UEFA EURO 2008™

Club Career

Clubs: 02- Bayer 04 Leverkusen

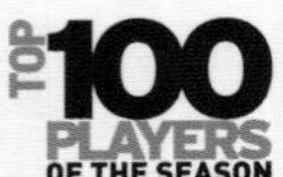

Sergio AGÜERO
Striker
Born 2/6/88, Quilmes, Argentina
Height 172cm, Weight 74kg

Club Atlético de Madrid lost the talismanic Fernando Torres tc Liverpool FC in the summer of 2007. Naturally his departure caused much consternation, but the Atlético fans need not ha worried. They already had the perfect replacement in situ. Ser "Kun" Agüero, the young Argentine striker recruited from CA Independiente in 2006, had played a support role in his debu campaign, but in 2007/08 he was let loose and, with new signing Diego Forlán, a fellow South American, by his side, the 19-year-old took La Liga by storm, scoring 19 goals – level wit Torres's best ever seasonal tally - and playing a key role in the club's fourth-place finish that offered the prospect of UEFA Champions League football at the Vicente Calderón in 2008/0 Agüero was absent when Atlético went out of Europe in 2007 as the team could not cope without him against Bolton Wanderers FC following his red card in the first leg of the rour of-32 tie. Short but strong in the air, he is very fast and extrem difficult to shake off the ball. Brave and committed, too, he ha all the qualities necessary to become a major world star.

International Career

ARGENTINA

Debut – 3/9/06 v Brazil (n, London, friendly), lost 0-3
First Goal – 17/11/07 v Bolivia (h, Buenos Aires, WCQ), won 3-0
Caps 11; Goals 3
Major Tournaments - none

Club Career

Clubs: 02-06 CA Independiente; 06- Club Atlético de Madrid (ESP)

Aleksandr ANYUKOV
Right-Back/Midfielder
Born 28/9/82, Samara, Russia
Height 175cm, Weight 65kg

A feature of Russia's counterattacking excellence at UEFA EUR 2008™ was the ceaseless enthusiasm of their full-backs to bur down the touchline and offer support. Aleksandr Anyukov wa perfect for the right-sided role. The 25-year-old had proved himself on numerous occasions during the qualifying competition, when he cemented his place in Guus Hiddink's f XI, and also while performing a similar role for FC Zenit St. Petersburg. A Russian champion in 2007, he was particularly impressive during the club's triumphant UEFA Cup run, makin 14 appearances (plus two in the qualifying round) and scoring superb goal in the outstanding 4-1 away win at Bayer 04 Leverkusen in the quarter-final. He made a bad start to UEFA EURO 2008™ when a defensive lapse in the opening game enabled Spain to take the lead, but he recovered well and provided a fine assist for Roman Pavlyuchenko, following a typical forward raid, in the 2-0 victory over Sweden.

International Career

RUSSIA

Debut – 25/5/04 v Austria (a, Graz, friendly), drew 0-0
First Goal – 8/6/05 v Germany (a, Monchengladbach, friendly), drew 2-2
Caps 37; Goals 1
Major Tournaments – UEFA EURO 2004™; UEFA EURO 2008™

Club Career

Major Honours – UEFA Cup (2008); Russian Championship (20
Clubs: 00-05 FC Krylya Sovetov Samara; 05- FC Zenit St. Petersburg

ARDA Turan
Attacking Midfielder
Born 31/1/87, Istanbul, Turkey
Height 176cm, Weight 72kg

Turkish footballers invariably struggle when they move abroad, but it can be safely assumed that many top clubs in England, Germany, Italy and Spain would be happy to take a chance on Arda Turan after his lively performances at UEFA EURO 2008™. The versatile youngster, who can play on either side of midfield or in the 'hole' behind the striker(s), went into his first major tournament on a high after winning the Turkish Süper Lig title with Galatasaray AŞ. His brilliant hat-trick in a 5-3 victory over surprise challengers Sivasspor all but sealed the title – his first - for the Istanbul club, and there were more crucial goals to come from him in Switzerland, where he knocked out the co-hosts with a last-minute strike in Basel and began Turkey's extraordinary comeback win against the Czech Republic with the first of their three goals in Geneva. His suspension for the semi-final against Germany was a considerable blow, but, at 21, UEFA EURO 2008™ was assuredly only the beginning for Arda Turan.

International Career

TURKEY
Debut – 16/8/06 v Luxembourg (a, Luxembourg, friendly), won 1-0
First Goal – 25/5/08 v Uruguay (n, Bochum, friendly), lost 2-3
Caps 22; Goals 3
Major Tournaments – UEFA EURO 2008™

Club Career

Major Honours – Turkish Championship (2008)
Clubs: 04- Galatasaray AŞ; 05/06 Vestel Manisaspor (loan)

Andrei ARSHAVIN
Attacking Midfielder/Forward
Born 29/5/81
Height 172cm, Weight 69kg

Andrei Arshavin entered the realms of superstardom at UEFA EURO 2008™ with his two wonderful man-of-the-match displays against Sweden in Innsbruck and the Netherlands in Basel. Unfortunately, he could not repeat the trick against Spain in Vienna, so Russia went no further than the semi-finals, but he had done more than enough in those two games alone to justify his inclusion in Guus Hiddink's squad. Suspended for the opening two matches because of a red card he had collected in the final qualifier against Andorra, Arshavin had made himself an indispensable asset thanks to his inspirational contribution towards FC Zenit St. Petersburg's remarkable Russian Premier-Liga/UEFA Cup double. His ability to skate away from his opponent with a clever touch and burst of acceleration is matched by an innate talent for delivering the perfect pass. He was also the official Man of the Match in the UEFA Cup final against Rangers FC, with losing manager Walter Smith openly admitting that Arshavin's extra class was the game's decisive factor.

International Career

RUSSIA
Debut – 17/5/02 v Belarus (h, Moscow, friendly), drew 1-1
First Goal – 13/2/03 v Romania (n, Limassol, friendly), won 4-2
Caps 37; Goals 13
Major Tournaments - UEFA EURO 2008™

Club Career

Major Honours – UEFA Cup (2008); Russian Championship (2007)
Clubs: 00- FC Zenit St. Petersburg

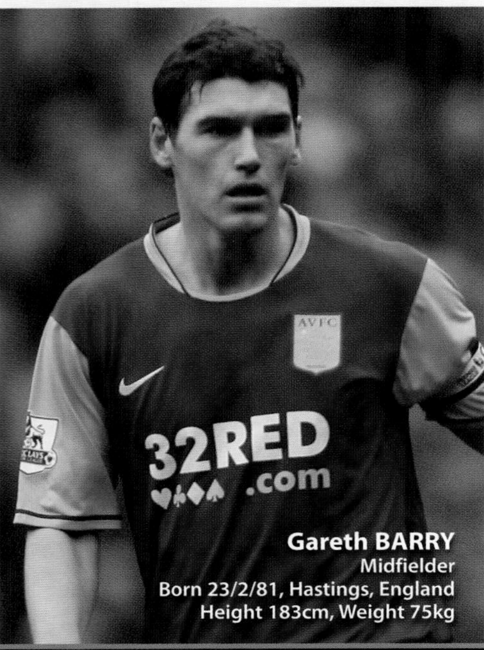

Gareth BARRY
Midfielder
Born 23/2/81, Hastings, England
Height 183cm, Weight 75kg

The reign of Steve McClaren will always be looked back upon a dark period in the history of the England national team. Fail to qualify for UEFA EURO 2008™ turned the ex-Middlesbrough FC boss into something of a national outcast, but at least, unli his predecessor Sven Göran Eriksson, he was prepared to give chance to Gareth Barry. The outstanding player on the field in McClaren's finest hour – the 3-0 home win over Russia at Wembley – and virtually irreplaceable in central midfield thereafter, with new manager Fabio Capello evidently anothe admirer, the Aston Villa FC captain dismissed previously held concerns about his lack of pace with a series of mature, confident displays and he was rewarded with his first international goal – some eight years after his debut – on the end-of-term outing to Trinidad & Tobago. Barry also enjoyed a excellent season with Villa, scoring nine goals in 37 matches, b a desire to join his England midfield partner Steven Gerrard at Liverpool FC led to an uneasy summer as the two clubs engag in a long drawn out tug-o'-war for his services.

International Career

ENGLAND
Debut – 31/5/00 v Ukraine (h, Wembley, friendly), won 2-0
First Goal – 1/6/08 v Trinidad & Tobago (a, Port of Spain, frienc won 3-0
Caps 20; Goals 1
Major Tournaments - UEFA EURO 2000™

Club Career

Clubs: 98- Aston Villa FC

Karim BENZEMA
Striker
Born 17/12/87,
Lyon, France
Height 183cm,
Weight 74kg

Although Karim Benzema has been referred to in certain quarte as the 'new Zinedine Zidane', it is difficult to see any true similari other than that the young striker is French, of Algerian descent a highly talented. A much more accurate analysis of his style of pla would be to compare him with another famous FIFA World Cup winner - and the player Benzema himself cites as a boyhood her Brazilian superstar Ronaldo. There was plenty of opportunity to consider the likeness during a 2007/08 season in which the Olympique Lyonnais youngster ran defences ragged with his dribbling and lacerated them with a succession of brilliant goals. Prolific in Ligue 1, he topped the scoring charts with 20 goals an was the decisive figure in Lyon's seventh successive French title win. He also demonstrated his class in Europe with four goals in seven UEFA Champions League games, including a crucial doub against Rangers FC at Ibrox and a superb strike at home to eventual champions Manchester United FC. UEFA EURO 2008™ not pan out as he, or any other Frenchman, had hoped, but, at 2 he will surely make his mark with Les Bleus in the future.

International Career

FRANCE
Debut – 28/3/07 v Austria (h, Saint-Denis, friendly), won 1-0
First Goal - 28/3/07 v Austria (h, Saint-Denis, friendly), won 1-0
Caps 13; Goals 3
Major Tournaments - UEFA EURO 2008™

Club Career

Major Honours – French Championship (2005, 2006, 2007, 200 French Cup (2008)
Clubs: 04- Olympique Lyonnais

Dimitar BERBATOV
Striker
Born 30/1/81, Blagoevgrad, Bulgaria
Height188cm, Weight 79kg

After a low-key start to the 2007/08 Premier League season, concerns were raised, especially among the supporters of Tottenham Hotspur FC, that Dimitar Berbatov might be a one-season wonder. Not a bit of it. Once the tall, elegant Bulgarian striker had got into his stride, the full repertoire of his talent returned in all its glory. A four-goal salvo against Reading FC sent him into the New Year in a positive frame of mind, and within two months he had his hands on the League Cup – his first major honour for nine years - after helping Spurs to victory over bogey side Chelsea FC in the Wembley final. It was his calmly struck equalising penalty that turned the game, and it would be the most important of all the 23 goals he struck over the season (the same tally as in 2006/07). Four goals for Bulgaria in the autumn UEFA EURO 2008™ qualifiers lifted his international haul to 39, second in the country's all-time rankings, and it is that ability to find the net at all levels, allied to his supreme maverick ball-playing talent, that has had many top clubs, foremost among them European champions Manchester United FC, casting covetous glances towards White Hart Lane.

International Career

BULGARIA
Debut – 17/11/99 v Greece (a, Kozani, friendly), lost 0-1
First Goal – 12/2/00 v Chile (a, Valparaiso, friendly), lost 2-3
Caps 64; Goals 39
Major Tournaments – UEFA EURO 2004™

Club Career

Major Honours – Bulgarian Cup (1999); English League Cup (2008)
Clubs: 92-97 PFC Pirin Blagoevgrad; 97-00 PFC CSKA Sofia; 01-06 Bayer 04 Leverkusen (GER); 06- Tottenham Hotspur FC (ENG)

Marco BORRIELLO
Striker
Born 18/6/82, Naples, Italy
Height 185cm, Weight 79kg

For years Naples-born Marco Borriello was the unwanted child of AC Milan. But now, at last, after a breakthrough season with Genoa CFC in 2007/08, it seems that he is loved after all. After farming him out to others season after season, the Rossoneri have finally fallen for the 26-year-old striker's charms. Frankly, they could not fail to be seduced by the predatory left-footer's brilliant form for Genoa as he scored 19 Serie A goals for the newly promoted club, including two stunning hat-tricks (both, curiously, against Udinese Calcio). He had gone to Genoa in a co-ownership deal, but no sooner had the season ended, with Borriello placed third in the Serie A top-scorer listings and selected for Italy's UEFA EURO 2008™ squad, than Milan recalled him to the San Siro, his objective being to replace veteran Filippo Inzaghi as the club's goal-grabber supreme. An injury picked up in pre-season, however, was expected to delay his return to action with the Rossoneri until a couple of months into the new campaign.

International Career

ITALY
Debut – 6/2/08 v Portugal (n, Zurich, friendly), won 3-1
Caps 3; Goals 0
Major Tournaments - UEFA EURO 2008™

Club Career

Major Honours – UEFA Champions League (2007); UEFA Super Cup (2003); Italian Championship (2004)
Clubs: 00-07 AC Milan; 00/01 Treviso FBC 1993 (loan); 01/02 US Triestina (loan); 03 Empoli FC (loan); 04/05 Reggina Calcio (loan); 05/06 UC Sampdoria (loan); 06 Treviso FBC 1993 (loan); 07/08 Genoa CFC; 08- AC Milan

Joan CAPDEVILA Méndez
Left-Back
Born 2/3/78, Tarrega, Spain
Height 182cm, Weight 72kg

Unused at UEFA EURO 2004™, Joan Capdevila was a prominent member of Spain's title-winning team in 2008. He started all of t five matches that mattered for Luis Aragonés's triumphant side Austria, having cemented his place as the Furia Roja's first-choic left-back with some lively displays in the latter stages of the qualifying competition, during which he also scored his first international goal – in the 3-0 home win over Sweden that clinched Spain's place in the finals. The 30-year-old also enjoyed the finest season of his career at club level, playing 36 league matches for Villarreal CF – more than anyone else – as the 'Yello Submarine' finished runners-up to Real Madrid CF in the Spanis championship, beating the mighty FC Barcelona to the automa UEFA Champions League berth. His performances were all the more impressive as it was his debut season for the club, the mo having come after seven years on the other side of the country RC Deportivo La Coruña. Having played in the UEFA Champions League five years running for Deportivo, his experience could b very useful for Villarreal in 2008/09

International Career

SPAIN

Major Honours – UEFA European Championship (2008)
Debut – 16/10/02 v Paraguay (h, Logrono, friendly), drew 0-0
First Goal – 17/11/07 v Sweden (h, Madrid, ECQ), won 3-0
Caps 23; Goals 3
Major Tournaments – UEFA EURO 2004™; UEFA EURO 2008™

Club Career

Major Honours – Spanish Cup (2002)
Clubs: 97-99 RCD Espanyol; 99-00 Club Atlético de Madrid; 00-
RC Deportivo La Coruña ; 07- Villarreal CF

Óscar CARDOZO
Striker
Born 20/5/83, Juan Eulogio Estigarribia, Paraguay
Height 194cm, Weight 83kg

Strapping Paraguayan striker Óscar Cardozo became SL Benfic second costliest signing of all time (after Simão) when he joine the club from CA Newell's Old Boys in June 2007. Although largely unheard of in Europe – he did not appear for Paraguay the 2006 FIFA World Cup – he quickly got down to business for the Lisbon Eagles, scoring regularly both in the Portuguese Primeira Liga and in the UEFA Champions League. Match-winning goals against Celtic FC and FC Shakhtar Donetsk coulc not keep Benfica in the competition but did earn them extend European involvement in the UEFA Cup, where he scored anot crucial goal to eliminate 1.FC Nürnberg. He rather blotted his copybook by getting sent off early in the round-of-16 tie again Getafe CF (which, without him, Benfica lost), but by the end of the season he had plundered 22 goals in 44 games over four competitions – a handsome return. Tall and physically imposin Cardozo is a handful in the air and, thanks to an explosive left-foot shot, a major threat at free-kicks. He may only use his right foot "for climbing on to the team bus", as the locals joke, and ha an irritating habit of being caught offside, but for a first season Europe the big South American did remarkably well.

International Career

PARAGUAY

Debut – 7/10/06 v Australia (a, Brisbane, friendly), drew 1-1
First Goal – 5/6/07 v Mexico (a, Mexico City, friendly), won 1-0
Caps 16; Goals 2
Major Tournaments – Copa América (2007)

Club Career

Clubs: 05 3 de Febrero; 05-06 Club Nacional; 06-07 CA Newell's Old Boys (ARG); 07- SL Benfica (POR)

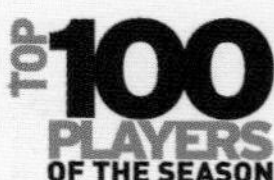

The goalkeeping talents of Iker Casillas have been universally acknowledged for many years – ever since he burst on to the scene as a teenager in 2000 and won the UEFA Champions League with Real Madrid CF – but his global standing moved up several notches in 2007/08. The season ended in glorious fashion when he captained Spain to victory at UEFA EURO 2008™. In truth, he did not have a great deal to do at the tournament, but whenever he was called upon, he was strong and decisive, keeping clean sheets in all three knockout ties and making two heroic penalty saves against Italy in the quarter-final. By coming out on top in that contest ahead of Gianluigi Buffon, Casillas filed a strong claim to be considered as the world's best goalkeeper. Many people in Spain already had him down as the No1. For several seasons, especially through the Galácticos period, he was consistently Real's best player, and it was the same story in 2007/08 as, in addition to winning a fourth La Liga title, he set a personal record of going 572 consecutive minutes unbeaten and also collected the prestigious Zamora trophy for the first time in his career.

Iker CASILLAS Fernández

Goalkeeper
Born 20/5/81, Madrid, Spain
Height 185cm, Weight 79kg

International Career

SPAIN
Major Honours – UEFA European Championship (2008)
Debut – 3/6/00 v Sweden (a, Gothenburg, friendly), drew 1-1
Caps 82; Goals 0
Major Tournaments – UEFA EURO 2000™; FIFA World Cup 2002; UEFA EURO 2004™; FIFA World Cup 2006; UEFA EURO 2008™

Club Career

Major Honours – UEFA Champions League (2000, 2002); UEFA Super Cup (2002); World Club Cup (2002); Spanish Championship (2001, 2003, 2007, 2008)
Clubs: 99- Real Madrid CF
uefa.com team of the year: 2007

Antonio CASSANO

Striker
Born 12/7/82, Bari, Italy
Height 175cm, Weight 75kg

Italy's best player at UEFA 2004™, Antonio Cassano's career suffered a sharp decline over the next few seasons as he struggled with his fitness and a number of disciplinary problems. He was no angel during the 2007/08 season that he spent on loan at UC Sampdoria from Real Madrid CF, incurring a five-match ban for throwing his shirt at the referee after receiving a red card in a Serie A game at home to Torino FC. But with the tantrums came the genius, and after ending the season with ten league goals – most of them of the spectacular variety – the enfant terrible of Italian football was called up by Roberto Donadoni to play in his second UEFA European Championship. In common with all the Azzurri strikers, Cassano was unable to score at UEFA EURO 2008™, but his selection in the starting XI against both France and Spain was confirmation of his renaissance as an international footballer.

International Career

ITALY
Debut – 12/11/03 v Poland (a, Warsaw, friendly), lost 1-3
First Goal - 12/11/03 v Poland (a, Warsaw, friendly), lost 1-3
Caps 15; Goals 3
Major Tournaments - UEFA EURO 2004™; UEFA EURO 2008™

Club Career

Major Honours – Spanish Championship (2007)
Clubs: 99-01 AS Bari; 01-06 AS Roma; 06-08 Real Madrid CF (ESP); 07/08 UC Sampdoria (loan); 08- UC Sampdoria

Joe COLE
Attacking Midfielder
Born 8/11/81, London, England
Height 172cm, Weight 70kg

Although Chelsea FC fought Manchester United FC to the bitter e in both the Premier League and the UEFA Champions League, it w difficult to pinpoint stand-out individuals. The effort was collective, with several members of the club's star-studded squad chipping ir with important contributions. But as the Chelsea fans confirmed when they voted him their Player of the Year, Joe Cole was the tea most consistent performer – a description that might have raised a few eyebrows a couple of seasons earlier when he was often criticised for being too erratic. After missing most of the previous campaign with knee and foot injuries – an absence that also contributed to England's struggles in UEFA EURO 2008™ qualifying the skilful midfielder came back stronger than ever. Avram Grant, unlike José Mourinho, appeared to be seduced by his skills, and by the end of the season Cole had started more games for Chelsea in the Premier League and Europe than anyone else. He was, howeve taken off in extra time of the UEFA Champions League final and substituted by Nicolas Anelka. Perhaps things would have turned out differently if the Englishman, rather than the Frenchman, had been on hand to take that crucial, season-defining penalty…

International Career

ENGLAND
Debut – 25/5/01 v Mexico (h, Derby, friendly), won 4-0
First Goal – 3/6/03 v Serbia & Montenegro (h, Leicester, friendly won 2-1
Caps 50; Goals 7
Major Tournaments – FIFA World Cup 2002; UEFA EURO 2004™ FIFA World Cup 2006

Club Career

Major Honours – English Premier League (2005, 2006); English Cup (2007); English League Cup (2005)
Clubs: 98-03 West Ham United FC; 03- Chelsea FC

Vedran ĆORLUKA
Right-Back/Centre-Back
Born 5/2/86, Doboj, Bosnia-Herzegovina
Height 193cm, Weight 88kg

That Vedran Ćorluka was one of the best right-backs on view at UEFA EURO 2008™ was no surprise. Not only had he been a permanent presence in Slaven Bilić's team for the previous two years, playing from start to finish in all 12 qualifying matches, he also shone consistently for Manchester City FC during his first season in the English Premier League, making 35 appearances, a considerable number of them in the unfamiliar role of central defender. Tall and mobile, Ćorluka was also deployed occasionally by Sven Göran Eriksson, the City manager, in a midfield role, but Bilić, who has called the 22-year-old "the best right-back in the world", is in no doubt as to what his best position is. The youngste combination play on the right flank with Darijo Srna was one of Croatia's main strengths in Austria, both defensively and going forward, and it should continue to serve the team well during the 2010 FIFA World Cup qualifying campaign, in which Ćorluka's present country of residence, England, will be looking for revenge

International Career

CROATIA
Debut – 16/8/06 v Italy (a, Livorno, friendly), won 2-0
Caps 24; Goals 0
Major Tournaments – UEFA EURO 2008™

Club Career

Major Honours – Croatian Championship (2006, 2007); Croatia Cup (2007)
Clubs: 03-07 NK Dinamo Zagreb; 04/05 NK Inter Zaprešić (loan) 07- Manchester City FC (ENG)

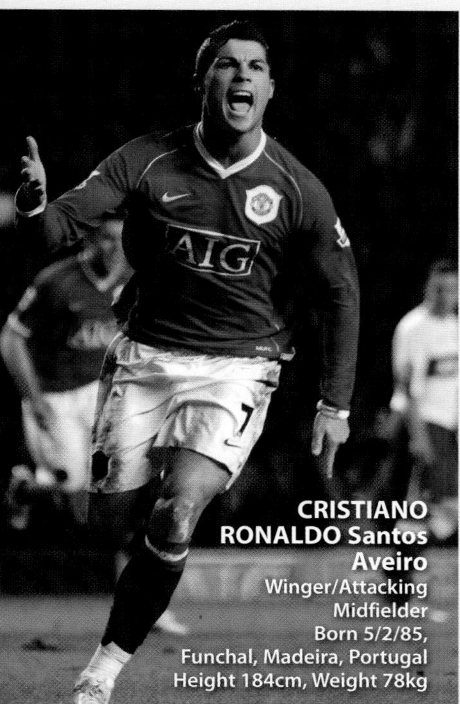

CRISTIANO RONALDO Santos Aveiro
Winger/Attacking Midfielder
Born 5/2/85, Funchal, Madeira, Portugal
Height 184cm, Weight 78kg

Cristiano Ronaldo's contribution towards Manchester United FC's Premier League/UEFA Champions League double has to rank among the greatest ever made by one player to one club in one season. With 31 goals in the former and eight in the latter, he was the leading scorer in both competitions. And that was barely half the story. The 23-year-old magician from Madeira was a show-stopper in just about every game he played, his jinking footwork, flicks and tricks, sumptuous free-kicks, powerful headers and, above all, searing, unstoppable runs driving opposition defences to total distraction. His retention of both Player and Footballer of the Year awards in England was a foregone conclusion. The UEFA Champions League win meant he was forgiven by the United fans for a couple of big penalty misses, but the adulation subsided during the summer when, having failed to take Portugal beyond the UEFA EURO 2008™ quarter-finals – albeit hampered by a foot injury - he was constantly in the news about an alleged 'dream move' to Real Madrid CF.

International Career

PORTUGAL
Debut – 20/8/03 v Kazakhstan (h, Chaves, friendly), won 1-0
First Goal – 12/6/04 v Greece (h, Porto, ECF), lost 1-2
Caps 58; Goals 21
Major Tournaments – UEFA EURO 2004™; FIFA World Cup 2006; UEFA EURO 2008™

Club Career

Major Honours – UEFA Champions League (2008); English Premiership (2007, 2008); English FA Cup (2004); English League Cup (2006)
Clubs: 02-03 Sporting Clube de Portugal; 03- Manchester United FC (ENG)
uefa.com team of the year: 2004, 2007

Carlos Javier CUÉLLAR Jiménez
Centre-Back
Born 23/8/81, Madrid, Spain
Height 190cm, Weight 84kg

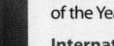

For a player whose arrival in Glasgow was generally greeted with exclamations of "Carlos who?", Rangers FC's €3m signing from CA Osasuna enjoyed a formidable first season in Scotland. The imposing Spanish centre-back, who had made a huge impression on Rangers manager Walter Smith when Osasuna knocked his side out of the 2006/07 UEFA Cup, immediately established himself as a key member of the team, winning the Scottish Premier League Player of the Month award for August and going on to become the defensive linchpin of a Rangers side targeting four trophies. The Spaniard was an instrumental figure in Smith's backs-to-the-wall defensive game-plan - one that, while ultimately unsuccessful in the UEFA Champions League, steered the team all the way to the UEFA Cup final. That they failed to win the trophy was a particular disappointment to Cuéllar as he had come close also the previous season, reaching the semi-finals with Osasuna. An SPL winner's medal also escaped his clutches, but he did win the two domestic Cups and received due acknowledgement for his own excellence when he was voted as both the Scottish Football Writers' Footballer of the Year and the SPL Player of the Year.

International Career

SPAIN
Uncapped

Club Career

Major Honours – Scottish Cup (2008); Scottish League Cup (2008)
Clubs: 01-03 CD Numancia de Soria; 03-07 CA Osasuna; 07- Rangers FC (SCO)

DAVID VILLA Sánchez
Striker
Born 3/12/81, Langreo, Spain
Height 175cm, Weight 69kg

The 2007/08 season ended on a career high for David Villa a he helped Spain to victory at UEFA EURO 2008™. The Valenc CF striker's absence from the final – and most of the semi-fi – with a muscle strain was a source of considerable frustrati but as the tournament's top scorer, with four goals (followir on from seven in the qualifying campaign), he could certair claim to have done his bit as Spain collected their first majo international trophy for 44 years. Those four goals came in Spain's first two group games – a marvellous hat-trick again Russia and a brilliantly taken late winner against Sweden – and he also found the net on his next outing, scoring the al important first penalty in the quarter-final shoot-out agains Italy (a team against whom he had also scored a spectacula late winner in a friendly a few months earlier). Villa travelled Austria full of confidence after ending a difficult season wit Valencia in prime form, winning the Spanish Cup and scorir five goals in his last two league games to lift his seasonal ta to 18. Even before his exploits in Austria, his status as one o the continent's deadliest strikers was beyond dispute.

International Career

SPAIN
Major Honours – UEFA European Championship (2008)
Debut – 9/2/05 v San Marino (h, Almeria, WCQ), won 5-0
First Goal – 16/11/05 v Slovakia (a, Bratislava, WCQ) drew 1-1
Caps 35; Goals 18
Major Tournaments - FIFA World Cup 2006; UEFA EURO 2008

Club Career

Major Honours – Spanish Cup (2004, 2008)
Clubs: 00-03 Real Sporting de Gijón; 03-05 Real Zaragoza; 05- Valencia CF

Steven DEFOUR
Midfielder
Born 15/4/88, Mechelen, Belgium
Height 174cm, Weight 65kg

Belgium's Player of the Year for 2007 by a landslide margin, Steven Defour collected the prestigious Golden Shoe in January. A few months later he had something even bigger and better to celebrate as he captained R. Standard de Liège to their first Belgian League title for a quarter of a century. T diminutive playmaker, handed the captaincy by Standard coach Michel Preud'homme while still only 19, was the toas not only of Liege but also of the whole of Belgium, a countr in desperate need of a young figurehead who might revive the fortunes of a national team that has spent too long in th wilderness. Injuries have limited Defour's impact on the international stage so far, but it goes without saying that he will be a key player for the Diables Rouges in their qualifyin campaign for the 2010 FIFA World Cup. Not dissimilar in appearance and playing style to Andrei Arshavin, Defour ma not pose the same goal threat as the Russian, but he is quic and sprightly and blessed with excellent vision and footwor

International Career

BELGIUM
Debut – 11/5/06 v Saudi Arabia (n, Sittard, friendly), won 2-1
Caps 13; Goals 0
Major Tournaments - none

Club Career

Major Honours – Belgian Championship (2008)
Clubs: 04-06 KRC Genk; 06- R. Standard de Liège

Rubén DE LA RED
Midfielder
Born 5/6/85, Madrid, Spain
Height 186cm, Weight 180kg

Although contracted to Real Madrid CF, Rubén De la Red earned his place in Spain's triumphant UEFA EURO 2008™ squad thanks to his eye-catching performances for Getafe CF, to whom he was despatched on loan for the whole of the 2007/08 season. A clever playmaker with good technical qualities, he is not afraid to help out with the donkey work in midfield. Indeed, he was occasionally used as an emergency defender, and it was while serving as a centre-back that he was red-carded in the epic UEFA Cup quarter-final tie at home to FC Bayern München. Although his European adventure ended on a low, he had done much to take Getafe to that stage of the competition on their European debut, scoring away goals in each of the previous rounds against AEK Athens FC and SL Benfica. Capped for the first time on the eve of UEFA EURO 2008™, he played just one match at the finals but made the most of the opportunity, slamming home a memorable equaliser against Greece.

International Career

SPAIN
Major Honours – UEFA European Championship (2008)
Debut – 31/5/08 v Peru (h, Huelva, friendly), won 2-1
First Goal – 18/6/08 v Greece (n, Salzburg, ECF), won 2-1
Caps 3; Goals 1
Major Tournaments – UEFA EURO 2008™

Club Career

Major Honours – Spanish Championship (2007)
Clubs: 04-07 Real Madrid CF/Castilla CF; 07/08 Getafe CF (loan); 08- Real Madrid CF

Alessandro DEL PIERO
Striker
Born 9/11/74, Conegliano, Italy
Height 175cm, Weight 73kg

With more games and goals for Juventus than any other player in history, Alessandro Del Piero is a living Bianconeri legend. There were few signs of wear and tear evident in the 33-year-old superstar during a 2007/08 season that must rank as one of his very best. In addition to breaking Gaetano Scirea's club record of 552 appearances, the Juve captain followed up his 2006/07 Serie B top-scorer crown by finishing up as the leading marksman in Serie A, with 21 goals, just ahead of his long-time strike partner David Trezeguet. It matched his best-ever Serie A tally, recorded ten years earlier when, at the peak of his powers, he rivalled Brazil's Ronaldo as the No1 footballer in the world. Recalled by popular demand to Italy's UEFA EURO 2008™ squad, his seventh major international tournament, he was used only fleetingly but still managed to conjure up the odd moment of divine skill. A return to the UEFA Champions League in 2008/09 should see him back in the big time with Juventus and striving to add to his competition tally of 36 goals.

International Career

ITALY
Major Honours – FIFA World Cup (2006)
Debut – 25/3/95 v Estonia (h, Salerno, ECQ), won 4-1
First Goal – 15/11/95 v Lithuania (h, Reggio Emilio, ECQ), won 4-0
Caps 89; Goals 27
Major Tournaments – UEFA EURO '96; FIFA World Cup 1998; UEFA EURO 2000™; FIFA World Cup 2002; UEFA EURO 2004™; FIFA World Cup 2006; UEFA EURO 2008™

Club Career

Major Honours – UEFA Champions League (1996); UEFA Super Cup (1996); World Club Cup (1996); Italian Championship (1995, 1997, 1998, 2002, 2003); Italian Cup (1995)
Clubs: 91-93 Calcio Padova; 93- Juventus

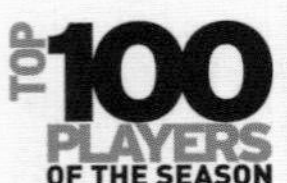

DIEGO Ribas de Cunha
Attacking Midfielder
Born 28/2/85, Ribeirao Preto, Brazil
Height 174cm, Weight 73kg

Considered a luxury player at FC Porto, where he arrived amid much hype from Santos FC in 2004, Diego has been quite the opposite at Werder Bremen, where the club's attack-is-the-bes form-of-defence philosophy has provided the perfect platforn for his exquisite talents, persuading him to extend his contrac until 2011. If his first season in Germany was special, his secon was every bit as good, with almost half of his fellow Bundeslig professionals casting their vote for him in the poll to choose t best player in the first half of the campaign (second-placed Franck Ribéry and third-placed Rafael van der Vaart trailed by some distance in his wake). A classic Brazilian No10, innovativ and unpredictable, he scores as many goals as he creates, and 2007/08 he matched his debut-season total of 13 in the Bundesliga, one of which earned a 1-1 draw away to champio FC Bayern München. Although yet to light up the UEFA Champions League, the humble, even-tempered 23-year-old w have another chance to 'crack Europe' in 2008/09.

International Career

BRAZIL

Major Honours – Copa América (2004, 2007)
Debut – 30/4/03 v Mexico (a, Guadalajara, friendly), drew 0-0
First Goal – 15/7/03 v Honduras (n, Mexico City, CGC), won 2-1
Caps 31; Goals 4
Major Tournaments – Concacaf Gold Cup 2003; Copa América 2004; Copa América 2007

Club Career

Major Honours – World Club Cup (2004); Brazilian Champions (2002, 2004); Portuguese Championship (2006)
Clubs: 01-04 Santos FC; 04-06 FC Porto (POR); 06- Werder Bremen (GER)

Antonio DI NATALE
Striker/Winger
Born 13/10/77, Naples, Italy
Height 177cm, Weight 70kg

Antonio Di Natale's first major tournament was not a memorable one. The dynamic attacker had played a major r in getting Italy to UEFA EURO 2008™ by scoring a brilliant match-winning double for an injury-depleted Azzurri side ir key qualifier against Ukraine in Kiev. But at the finals he was dropped after starting the opening game against the Netherlands, and when he did reappear, as a substitute against Spain, he missed a crucial penalty in the shoot-out. The 30-year-old was in Roberto Donadoni's squad for good reason, however, after a stunning season for Udinese Calcio, the best of his career by some distance, in which he scored Serie A goals, including the winner away to Juventus, to hel the team from north-east Italy finish seventh in Serie A and qualify for the UEFA Cup. Having received no international caps under Marcello Lippi first time around, he has good reason to fear for his international future, but Udinese will b happy to have him on board again in 2008/09.

International Career

ITALY

Debut – 20/11/02 v Turkey (h, Pescara, friendly), drew 1-1
First Goal – 18/2/04 v Czech Republic (h, Palermo, friendly), dr 2-2
Caps 20; Goals 7
Major Tournaments – UEFA EURO 2008™

Club Career

Clubs: 96-04 Empoli FC; 97/98 Iperzola Ponteroncariale (loan); AS Varese 1910 (loan); FCE Viareggio (loan); 04- Udinese Calcio

Didier DROGBA
Striker
Born 11/3/78, Abidjan, Ivory Coast
Height 189cm, Weight 80kg

A brilliant two-goal performance by Didier Drogba in the second leg of the UEFA Champions League semi-final against Liverpool FC took Chelsea FC to the final in Moscow. But if that was the highlight of the season for the big, muscular striker, his low point would come in the showdown at the Luzhniki stadium, when, after slapping Manchester United FC defender Nemanja Vidić in the face three minutes from the end of extra time, he was red-carded - and thus missed a penalty shoot-out in which he was earmarked to take the team's (ultimately fatal) fifth kick. Injuries, operations, international call-ups and the departure of José Mourinho all combined to make 2007/08 a fractious campaign for the 30-year-old, but when he did don the all-blue of Chelsea, he was invariably their most dangerous forward, always imposing his power and physique on the opposition defence and guaranteeing his markers 90 or more uncomfortable, exhausting minutes. Drogba scored six goals in the UEFA Champions League to become Chelsea's all-time leading marksman in Europe and also maintained a 100 per cent strike rate in English domestic Cup finals, albeit this time in defeat.

International Career

IVORY COAST
Debut – 8/9/02 v South Africa (h, Abidjan, ANQ), drew 0-0
First Goal – 11/2/03 v Cameroon (n, Chateauroux, friendly), won 3-0
Caps 50; Goals 33
Major Tournaments – African Cup of Nations 2006; FIFA World Cup 2006; African Cup of Nations 2008

Club Career

Major Honours – English Premier League (2005, 2006); English FA Cup (2007); English League Cup (2005, 2007)
Clubs: 98-02 Le Mans UC 72 (FRA); 02-03 En Avant Guingamp (FRA); 03-04 Olympique de Marseille (FRA); 04- Chelsea FC (ENG)
uefa.com team of the year: 2007

Balázs DZSUDZSÁK
Left Midfielder/ Winger
Born 23/12/86, Nyirlugos, Hungary
Height 179cm, Weight 72kg

Whisper it quietly, but Hungary could be on the verge of bringing through their finest generation of young footballers in years, and 21-year-old Balázs Dzsudzsák is a strong candidate to become the leader of the pack. After winning Hungarian championship titles in each of his first three seasons with Debreceni VSC, he kept his run of success going after leaving 'Loki' for PSV Eindhoven in January 2008 and making a decisive contribution towards the club's Eredivisie title triumph. Debrecen fans were sad to see him go – the club narrowly missed out to MTK Budapest in their bid for a fourth successive title – but PSV's followers took Dzsudzsák immediately to their hearts. They may have struggled to pronounce his name but they certainly appreciated his deft dribbles, pin-point crosses and power-packed left-foot shots. The bonding process was also accelerated by a winning goal away to AFC Ajax.

International Career

HUNGARY
Debut – 2/6/07 v Greece (a, Heraklion, ECQ), lost 0-2
First Goal – 24/5/08 v Greece (h, Budapest, friendly), won 3-2
Caps 10; Goals 1
Major Tournaments - none

Club Career

Major Honours – Hungarian Championship (2005, 2006, 2007); Dutch Championship (2008)
Clubs: 04-08 Debreceni VSC; 08- PSV Eindhoven (NED)

Orlando ENGELAAR
Midfielder
Born 24/8/79, Rotterdam, Netherlands
Height 198cm, Weight 90kg

When Orlando Engelaar was named in the starting XI for the Netherlands' opening match of UEFA EURO 2008™ against Italy, took many Dutch followers by surprise. But the towering 28-yea old's assured performance alongside Nigel de Jong in the Oranj midfield engine room not only justified his selection; it was hail as a Marco van Basten masterstroke. The Netherlands won the game 3-0 and, with Engelaar again outstanding, pulverised Fra 4-1 four days later. It had taken him several years to make the breakthrough at international level, but after an exceptional 2007/08 season with FC Twente, which ended with the Enschec club beating AFC Ajax in a play-off for the right to compete in t UEFA Champions League, Bondscoach Van Basten was convince that he was the man for the job. Twente coach Fred Rutten was another who appreciated Engelaar's talents - to such an extent that when he was appointed as the new coach of leading Germ club FC Schalke 04 in the summer, he decided to take the big midfielder with him.

International Career

NETHERLANDS
Debut – 2/6/07 v South Korea (a, Seoul, friendly), won 2-0
Caps 10; Goals 0
Major Tournaments – UEFA EURO 2008™

Club Career

Clubs: 97-00 Feyenoord; 00-04 NAC Breda; 04-06 KRC Genk (B 06-08 FC Twente; 08- FC Schalke 04 (GER)

Patrice EVRA
Left-Back
Born 15/5/81, Dakar, Senegal
Height 174cm, Weight 67kg

A losing finalist in the UEFA Champions League with AS Mona FC in 2004, Patrice Evra was a winner with Manchester United in 2008. One of United's most lively and consistent performers throughout their triumphant season, he was the team's regula left-back, making ten starts in Europe and 33 in the Premier League. Many questioned whether he would make the grade England following an uncertain start to his Old Trafford career, but under Sir Alex Ferguson's expert tutelage he has develope into a top-quality attacking full-back – nifty, technically gifted and extremely fit. As expected, he went into UEFA EURO 2008 his first major tournament for France, as understudy to Éric Abidal, but with the FC Barcelona player moved into a central position after the opening game, he was selected from the sta for both matches against the Netherlands and Italy. Needless say, Evra will have rather fonder recollections of 2008 in the re of his club than in the blue of his country.

International Career

FRANCE
Debut – 18/8/04 v Bosnia-Herzegovina (h, Rennes, friendly), drew 1-1
Caps 13; Goals 0
Major Tournaments – UEFA EURO 2008™

Club Career

Major Honours – UEFA Champions League (2008); English Premier League (2007, 2008); French League Cup (2003); Engli League Cup (2006)
Clubs: 98-99 SC Marsala (ITA); 99-00 AC Monza (ITA); 00-02 OGC Nice; 02-06 AS Monaco FC; 06- Manchester United FC (ENG)

Francesc "Cesc" FÀBREGAS Soler
Midfielder
Born 4/5/87, Arenys de Mar, Spain
Height 177cm, Weight 69kg

Without a trophy for three years at Arsenal FC, Cesc Fàbregas made up for the shortage of silverware at club level by winning UEFA EURO 2008™ with Spain. Although, curiously, coach Luis Aragonés did not value the young midfield magician highly enough to offer him a regular starting place, Fàbregas took that disappointment in his stride and made vital contributions to Spain's victory – nervelessly converting the winning penalty against Italy, and bossing the semi-final against Russia with some wonderful passing after coming on as a substitute for the injured David Villa. He had also been in rich form for Arsenal for most of the season, especially at the start when he was scoring goals regularly as well as setting them up. His most memorable goal – and performance – came at the San Siro as Arsenal eliminated holders AC Milan from the UEFA Champions League. It was Fàbregas at his very best, the master at work, a truly great footballer at the top of his game, in total control. Even the Milan fans, spellbound by what they had seen, applauded him off at the end.

International Career

SPAIN

Major Honours – UEFA European Championship (2008)
Debut – 1/3/06 v Ivory Coast (h, Valladolid, friendly), won 3-2
First Goal – 10/6/08 v Russia (n, Innsbruck, ECF), won 4-1
Caps 32; Goals 1
Major Tournaments – FIFA World Cup 2006; UEFA EURO 2008™

Club Career

Major Honours – English FA Cup (2005)
Clubs: 03- Arsenal FC (ENG)
uefa.com team of the year: 2006

Rio FERDINAND
Centre-Back
Born 7/11/78, London, England
Height 187 cm, Weight 76 kg

At the age of 29, Rio Ferdinand scaled a career peak in 2007/08. Being appointed (temporary) captain of England by new head coach Fabio Capello was a great honour, but that was a mere by-product of his magnificent form, throughout the season, for Manchester United FC, much of which, because of Gary Neville's injury and Ryan Giggs's reduced game time, he spent as team captain. The remarkable Cristiano Ronaldo apart, Ferdinand was United's most consistent and reliable performer in a season that reached a perfect climax when he and Giggs hoisted aloft the UEFA Champions League trophy in Moscow, having done the same with the Premier League trophy ten days earlier. Oddly, Ferdinand has been to three FIFA World Cups but never played in a UEFA European Championship. Unlike some of his over-rated colleagues in the current England team, he would certainly not have looked out of place at UEFA EURO 2008™.

International Career

ENGLAND

Debut – 15/1/97 v Cameroon (h, Wembley, friendly), won 2-0
First Goal – 15/6/02 v Denmark (n, Niigata, WCF), won 3-0
Caps 68; Goals 2
Major Tournaments – FIFA World Cup 1998; FIFA World Cup 2002; FIFA World Cup 2006

Club Career

Major Honours – UEFA Champions League (2008); English Premier League (2003, 2007, 2008); English League Cup (2006)
Clubs: 95-00 West Ham United FC; 96 AFC Bournemouth (loan); 00-02 Leeds United AFC; 02- Manchester United FC

FERNANDO José TORRES Sanz
Striker
Born 20/3/84, Madrid, Spain
Height 186cm, Weight 78kg

Outshone for much of UEFA EURO 2008™ by his fellow forward David Villa, Fernando Torres waited for the perfect moment to take centre stage. With Villa unavailable for the final, the tall, jet-heeled striker became the star of the show in the Ernst-Happel Stadion, leading the German defence a merry dance with his incisive, dynamic running and, of course, ensuring himself prid place in Spanish football legend for ever more by scoring the game's winning goal. It was the perfect end to an awesomely good season for the 24-year-old and brought him the first majo honour of his career. Transferred from his beloved Club Atlético Madrid to Liverpool FC for a club-record fee in July 2007, he toc to the English game in an instant and went on to score 24 Pren League goals in his debut season, 21 of them at Anfield, where became the new darling of the Kop. The first UEFA Champions League campaign of his career was equally impressive. He scor six goals in ten appearances, including brilliant strikes to knock out Olympique de Marseille, FC Internazionale Milano and Arse FC. He also struck at Chelsea FC – Liverpool's first goal at Stamf Bridge under Rafael Benítez – to take the semi-final into extra time. There would be no final in Moscow for Liverpool, but Torr would more than make up for that disappointment with his Ma of the Match display for Spain in Vienna.

International Career

SPAIN
Major Honours – UEFA European Championship (2008)
Debut – 6/9/03 v Portugal (a, Guimaraes, friendly), won 3-0
First Goal – 28/4/04 v Italy (a, Genoa, friendly), drew 1-1
Caps 54; Goals 17
Major Tournaments – UEFA EURO 2004™; FIFA World Cup 200 UEFA EURO 2008™

Club Career

Clubs: 01-07 Club Atlético de Madrid; 07- Liverpool FC (ENG)

Mathieu FLAMINI
Midfielder
Born 7/3/84, Marseille, France
Height 178cm, Weight 74kg

The 2007/08 season was not even over when Mathieu Flamini signed a four-year contract with AC Milan. It was a big blow fo Arsenal FC and their fans because the Frenchman's fourth and last season at the club had been far and away his best. Grante regular starting place in his favoured central midfield position, Flamini became the perfect foil for playmaker Cesc Fàbregas, h industry, effervescence and economy in possession contributi largely to the team's fluent, controlled passing game. It was no surprise that Milan should come in for his services as he was outstanding in Arsenal's momentous 2-0 victory at San Siro in first knockout round of the UEFA Champions League. Rewarde with his first international cap for France in November 2007, h was included in Raymond Domenech's preliminary squad for UEFA EURO 2008™ but missed out on the final selection - even though skipper Patrick Vieira, the man he was on standby to replace, was not ultimately considered fit enough to play.

International Career

FRANCE
Debut – 16/11/07 v Morocco (h, Saint-Denis, friendly), drew 2
Caps 2; Goals 0
Major Tournaments - none

Club Career

Major Honours – English FA Cup (2005)
Clubs: 03-04 Olympique de Marseille; 04-08 Arsenal FC (ENG); 08- AC Milan (ITA)

Sébastien FREY
Goalkeeper
Born 18/3/80,
Thonon-les-Bains, France
Height 185cm, Weight 90kg

Despite an unconvincing debut for France in their last UEFA EURO 2008™ qualifier against Ukraine in Kiev, Sébastien Frey played so well for his Italian club ACF Fiorentina, both in Serie A and the UEFA Cup, that he was promoted to the position of Les Bleus' No2 goalkeeper at the finals. With Grégory Coupet firmly ensconced at No1, he was unable to add to his two caps in Switzerland, but the message was clear to Frey that he has moved ahead of rival Mickaël Landreau in the pecking order and is now first in the queue to replace Coupet when the 36-year-old calls it a day. Frey's tenth season in Italy was unquestionably his finest, earning him a contract extension with Fiorentina through to 2013. Confident and agile, he particularly distinguished himself with a brilliant performance against Everton FC at Goodison Park in the UEFA Cup, where he made a series of outstanding stops, including one in the penalty shoot-out, to see the Viola into the quarter-finals.

International Career

FRANCE
Debut – 21/11/07 v Ukraine (a, Kiev, ECQ), drew 2-2
Caps 2; Goals 0
Major Tournaments - UEFA EURO 2008™

Club Career

Clubs: 97-98 AS Cannes; 98-01 FC Internazionale Milano (ITA); 99/00 Hellas Verona FC (ITA) (loan); 01-05 Parma FC (ITA); 05- ACF Fiorentina (ITA)

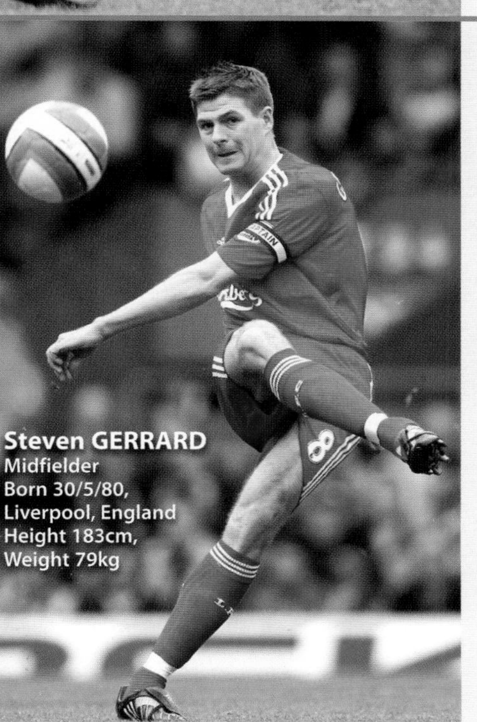

Steven GERRARD
Midfielder
Born 30/5/80,
Liverpool, England
Height 183cm,
Weight 79kg

Steven Gerrard shared in the massive disappointment of England's failure to qualify for UEFA EURO 2008™. Indeed he felt the pain more than anyone as he was the captain for both of the defeats against Russia in Moscow and Croatia at Wembley. But, in the aftermath of elimination and the quest for scapegoats, very few pointed the finger at him. For, as new head coach Fabio Capello confirmed by selecting him from the start in each of his first four matches, Gerrard is quite simply England's best player. For Liverpool FC the all-action midfielder had another magnificent season, forming a particularly fruitful partnership with new signing Fernando Torres. The Spanish goal-machine might have stolen the thunder of a lesser man, but the Liverpool skipper maintained an impressive strike-rate himself, scoring a career-best tally of eleven goals in the Premier League and another half-dozen to add to his copious haul in Europe, including a brilliant late strike in front of the Kop at home to FC Internazionale Milano and a decisive penalty at the same end of the Anfield pitch to decide an epic quarter-final tie against Arsenal FC.

International Career

ENGLAND
Debut – 31/5/00 v Ukraine (h, Wembley, friendly), won 2-0
First Goal – 1/9/01 v Germany (a, Munich, WCQ), won 5-1
Caps 67; Goals 13
Major Tournaments – UEFA EURO 2000™; UEFA EURO 2004™; FIFA World Cup 2006

Club Career

Major Honours – UEFA Champions League (2005); UEFA Cup (2001); UEFA Super Cup (2001, 2005); English FA Cup (2001, 2006); English League Cup (2001, 2003)
Clubs: 98- Liverpool FC
uefa.com team of the year: 2005, 2006, 2007

Heurelho da Silva "GOMES"

Goalkeeper
Born 15/2/81, Joao Pinheiro, Brazil
Height 191cm, Weight 87kg

Once upon a time decent Brazilian goalkeepers were almost as difficult to find as lost Amazonian tribes. Nowadays they are scattered all over the place. Heurelho Gomes may not be a regu in the Brazilian national team but he is undoubtedly one of the classiest of the country's Europe-based contingent. He won his fourth Dutch Eredivisie championship in four seasons at PSV Eindhoven in 2007/08, and it is no exaggeration to claim that th title would not have been won without him. The 27-year-old 'keeper, nicknamed the Octopus for obvious reasons, began the campaign by keeping five successive clean sheets and ended it equally resilient form, unbeaten in five of the last six matches as PSV successfully held off the threat of AFC Ajax. Some of his sav were jaw-droppingly spectacular, and his tremendous presence and agility unnerved many an opponent who seemed favourite score. That was certainly the case when he kept PSV in the UEFA Cup with a brilliant penalty save from Tottenham Hotspur FC midfielder Jermaine Jenas. No wonder Spurs signed him up during the summer, his desire to move away from the Philips stadium having been generated by a fall-out with PSV's general director Jan Reker.

International Career

BRAZIL
Major Honours – FIFA Confederations Cup (2005)
Debut – 13/7/03 v Mexico (a, Mexico City, CGC), lost 0-1
Caps 9; Goals 0
Major Tournaments – Concacaf Gold Cup 2003; FIFA Confederations Cup 2005

Club Career

Major Honours – Brazilian Championship (2003); Dutch Championship (2005, 2006, 2007, 2008); Brazilian Cup (2003); Dutch Cup (2005)
Clubs: 01-04 Cruzeiro EC; 04-08 PSV Eindhoven (NED); 08- Tottenham Hotspur FC (ENG)

Bafétimbi GOMIS

Striker
Born 6/8/85, La Seyne-sur-Mer, France
Height184 cm, Weight 77kg

By scoring two goals on his debut for France – the first player to do so since Zinedine Zidane - in a UEFA EURO 2008™ warm-up match against Ecuador in Grenoble, Bafétimbi Gomis edged out the vastly more experienced Djibril Cissé for a place among Raymond Domenech's chosen 23 for the finals. The pacy dreadlocked striker had propelled himself into international contention with 16 league goals for AS Saint-Étienne in 2007/08 the same number as Cissé managed for Olympique de Marseille and a total that helped Les Verts finish fifth in Ligue 1 and retur to Europe, in the UEFA Cup, after an absence of 26 years. Gomis did not have much of a chance to shine in Switzerland, making only a couple of substitute appearances against Romania and th Netherlands, but the 23-year-old will be the better for the experience and, having chosen France over Senegal, for whom was also eligible, will be determined to press his case for inclusi on the road to the 2010 FIFA World Cup in South Africa.

International Career

FRANCE
Debut – 27/5/08 v Ecuador (h, Grenoble, friendly), won 2-0
First Goal - 27/5/08 v Ecuador (h, Grenoble, friendly), won 2-0
Caps 4; Goals 2
Major Tournaments – UEFA EURO 2008™

Club Career

Clubs: 03- AS Saint-Étienne; 05 ES Troyes AC (loan)

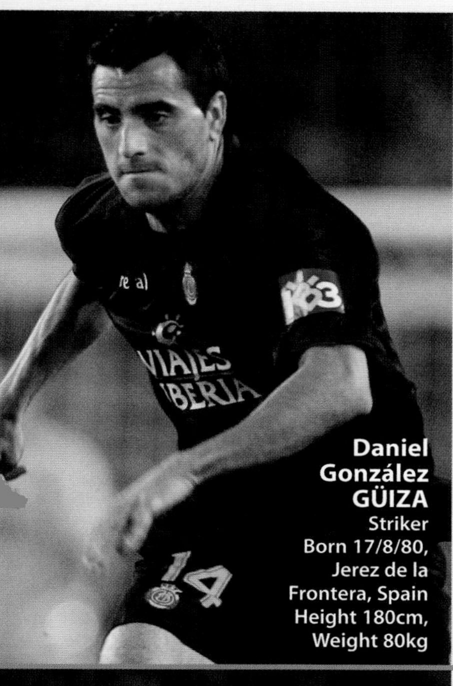

Daniel González GÜIZA
Striker
Born 17/8/80, Jerez de la Frontera, Spain
Height 180cm, Weight 80kg

A flurry of goals for RCD Mallorca in the closing weeks of the 2007/08 season – 16 in his last 13 games, including the winner at FC Barcelona - enabled Daniel Güiza to overtake Sevilla FC's Brazilian striker Luís Fabiano and win the coveted Pichichi prize as La Liga's top scorer. It was an against-the-odds achievement by the previously unsung striker, and was all the more worthy of acclaim for not including a single penalty. He had returned to the holiday island club for a second spell after an impressive 2006/07 season at Getafe CF, but few expected his career to take off as it did. Luis Aragonés, for one, was duly impressed. Having handed him his international debut in Spain's final UEFA EURO 2008™ qualifier at home to Northern Ireland, he took him to the finals, where, despite his understudy status, he scored two goals – against Greece and Russia – and also made a strong impact as a substitute in the final. In fact, Aragonés was so pleased with his contribution that, after quitting the Spain job to take charge at Fenerbahçe SK, he decided to take Güiza with him.

International Career

SPAIN
Major Honours – UEFA European Championship (2008)
Debut – 21/11/07 v Northern Ireland (h, Las Palmas, ECQ), won 1-0
First Goal – 18/6/08 v Greece (n, Salzburg, ECF), won 2-1
Caps 8; Goals 2
Major Tournaments – UEFA EURO 2008™

Club Career

Clubs: 98-99 Xerez CD; 99-02 RCD Mallorca; 99/00 Dos Hermanas CF (loan); 02-03 RC Recreativo de Huelva; 03 FC Barcelona B; 03-05 CF Ciudad de Murcia; 05-07 Getafe CF; 07-08 RCD Mallorca; 08- Fenerbahçe SK (TUR)

HAMIT Altıntop
Right-Back/Midfielder
Born 8/12/82, Gelsenkirchen, Germany
Height 183cm, Weight 82kg

According to some, the best German on the pitch in the first UEFA EURO 2008™ semi-final in Basel was playing for Turkey. Hamit Altıntop, born in Gelsenkirchen, was outstanding not only in that game but also in the team's previous last-gasp victories over Switzerland, the Czech Republic and Croatia. Although deployed initially as a right-back, he later moved into his favoured midfield role and provided all three assists in the dramatic comeback win against the Czechs in Geneva. With his twin brother Halil having been surprisingly axed from the squad, it was almost as if Hamit was playing for two. A mixture of technical poise and warrior spirit, the 25-year-old was bought by FC Bayern München from FC Schalke 04 in summer 2007 (thus leaving his twin behind). Amidst a welter of other, bigger-name signings, the transfer hardly warranted a mention, but he soon proved his worth and was a regular in Ottmar Hitzfeld's side until he broke his toe while playing a friendly international against Belarus in March and therefore missed the climax of Bayern's double-winning season. There was nothing wrong with his fitness, however, in Austria and Switzerland, where he was the sole Turkish player named in UEFA's Team of the Tournament.

International Career

TURKEY
Debut – 18/2/04 v Denmark (h, Adana, friendly), lost 0-1
First Goal – 28/3/07 v Norway (h, Frankfurt-am-Main, ECQ), drew 2-2
Caps 47; Goals 2
Major Tournaments – UEFA EURO 2008™

Club Career

Major Honours – German Championship (2008); German Cup (2008)
Clubs: 00-03 SG Wattenscheid 09 (GER); 03-07 FC Schalke 04 (GER); 07- FC Bayern München (GER)

John HEITINGA
Centre-Back/Right-Back
Born 15/11/83, Alphen aan den Rijn, Netherlands
Height 180cm, Weight 75kg

Crowned the Netherlands' Player of the Year in April 2008, versatile 24-year-old defender John (or Johnny) Heitinga took the prize thanks to an excellent season for both AFC Ajax and the Dutch national team, during which he suddenly added goalscoring to his many talents. He found the net in successive matches for the Oranje in the spring – against Croatia and Austria – but when it came to UEFA EURO 2008™ he was surprisingly omitted from Marco van Basten's first XI and started only the final group game against Romania. Affiliated to AFC Ajax since he was seven years old – after impressing on one of the club's famous talent-spotting open days – Heitinga was to make his best season at the club his last when, in May, he agreed a five-year deal to move to Club Atlético de Madrid. He didn't leave Amsterdam with a trophy but he was certainly sent on his way to Spain with the warmest of wishes from the appreciative, if disappointed, Ajax fans.

International Career

NETHERLANDS
Debut – 18/2/04 v USA (h, Amsterdam, friendly), won 1-0
First Goal – 28/4/04 v Greece (h, Eindhoven, friendly), won 4-0
Caps 39; Goals 5
Major Tournaments - UEFA EURO 2004™; FIFA World Cup 2006; UEFA EURO 2008™

Club Career

Major Honours – Dutch Championship (2002, 2004); Dutch Cup (2002, 2006, 2007)
Clubs: 01-08 AFC Ajax; 08- Club Atlético de Madrid (ESP)

Thorstein HELSTAD
Striker
Born 28/4/77, Hamar, Norway
Height 187cm, Weight 86kg

Thorstein Helstad matched his shirt number by scoring 22 goals for SK Brann in the 2007 Norwegian championship. The experienced, headband-wearing striker, who turned 30 at the start of the season, enjoyed a fabulous campaign, propelling the Bergen club to their first national title in 44 years and topping the Tippeligaen charts for the third time in his career (after doing likewise during his first spell at the club in 2000 and 2001). It was certainly a vast improvement on the 2006 season when he was more often to be seen in Brann's reserve side. Helstad crowned his renaissance with four goals in the 5-2 home win over Viking FK that clinched the title. It lifted his all-time Tippeligaen tally to 97 – second only to Tromsø IL's Sigurd Rushfeldt (129) among players still active. He reached his century with a hat-trick in the first game of the 2008 season and was still in fine goalscoring form when he decided to move abroad in the summer, joining French Ligue 1 club Le Mans UC 72.

International Career

NORWAY
Debut – 16/8/00 v Finland (a, Helsinki, friendly), lost 1-3
First Goal - 16/8/00 v Finland (a, Helsinki, friendly), lost 1-3
Caps 29; Goals 9
Major Tournaments - none

Club Career

Major Honours – Austrian Championship (2003); Norwegian Championship (2004, 2006, 2007); Austrian Cup (2003)
Clubs: 95-97 HamKam Fotball; 98-02 SK Brann; 02-04 FK Austria Wien (AUT); 04-06 Rosenborg BK; 06-08 SK Brann; 08 Le Mans UC 72 (FRA)

Aleksandr HLEB
Attacking Midfielder
Born 1/5/81, Minsk, Belarus
Height 182cm, Weight 72kg

A series of sparkling performances in the Arsenal FC midfield, especially in the first half of the season, lifted Aleksandr Hleb into the 'A-list' category of Premier League foreign imports. His confidence boosted by the last-minute goals he scored for the Gunners in their opening two games of the campaign, against AC Sparta Praha and Fulham FC, the Belarussian international went on to enjoy the best of his three seasons at the north London club, his exceptional skill and acceleration lighting up many games at the Emirates Stadium and elsewhere. His best performance of all came in Arsenal's record UEFA Champions League victory – a 7-0 drubbing of SK Slavia Praha in which he directly contributed to almost every goal. Hleb's form inevitably aroused interest from elsewhere, and in the summer he left Arsenal for FC Barcelona, joining the Catalans on a four-year contract for an €15m fee. His mission at Camp Nou? To replace the departed Ronaldinho.

International Career

BELARUS
Debut – 6/10/01 v Wales (a, Cardiff, WCQ), lost 0-1
First Goal – 17/4/02 v Hungary (a, Debrecen, friendly), won 5-2
Caps 41; Goals 4
Major Tournaments - none

Club Career

Major Honours – Belarussian Championship (1999)
Clubs: 99-00 FC BATE Borisov; 00-05 VfB Stuttgart (GER); 05-08 Arsenal FC (ENG); 08- FC Barcelona (ESP)

Steffen HOFMANN
Midfielder
Born 9/9/80, Würzburg, Germany
Height 170cm, Weight 67kg

Just as in SK Rapid Wien's Austrian title-winning campaign of 2004/05, the key player in their 2007/08 triumph was midfield maestro Steffen Hofmann. Free of the injury problems that had hampered him in 2006/07 – following an ill-starred spell in the German second division with TSV 1860 München – the 27-year-old reasserted himself as Rapid's captain and playmaker-in-chief with a succession of dominant displays. He started all 36 matches, scored ten goals and provided numerous assists as Rapid dethroned defending champions FC Salzburg. The defining performance of his, and Rapid's, season was the incredible 7-0 win away to Salzburg in March that sparked the team's unbeaten surge towards the title. Austria would dearly have liked Hofmann in their ranks for UEFA EURO 2008™ but that hot topic had long since burned out. Although he was entitled to Austrian citizenship through his marriage, he had played for his native Germany in official youth internationals, and because of the length of time that had passed before the application was filed, it meant he was not permitted to make the switch.

International Career

GERMANY
Uncapped

Club Career

Major Honours – Austrian Championship (2005, 2008)
Clubs: 00-02 FC Bayern München; 02-05 SK Rapid Wien (AUT); 06 TSV 1860 München; 06- SK Rapid Wien (AUT)

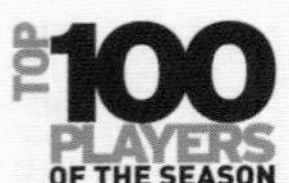

Klaas Jan HUNTELAAR
Striker
Born 12/8/83, Drempt, Netherlands
Height186cm, Weight 80kg

Nobody could have done more than Klaas Jan Huntelaar to try bring AFC Ajax their first Dutch Eredivisie title in four years. The lanky centre-forward confirmed his reputation as the most let finisher in the Netherlands by scoring 33 goals – as many as th three leading scorers of champions PSV Eindhoven combined. Seven of his tally alone came against relegated De Graafschap, including four on the opening day of the season, and he score at least one goal in 24 of his 34 matches. 'The Hunter' was able concentrate solely on domestic prey after Ajax's early exit from Europe but the 25-year-old craves to prove himself on the big stage. Ruud van Nistelrooy has been a barrier to his progress w the Dutch national side, but Huntelaar proved he can be a worthy successor to the now (internationally) retired Real Mad CF striker by scoring in all five internationals he played in durir the 2007/08 season, the last of them against Romania on his major tournament debut at UEFA EURO 2008™. If Huntelaar fel aggrieved by his lack of game time with the Oranje in Switzerland, he was handed a sweetener by Marco van Basten his arrival as the new coach at Ajax when he named him as the club captain for the 2008/09 season.

International Career

NETHERLANDS
Debut – 16/8/06 v Republic of Ireland (a, Dublin, friendly), won
First Goal - 16/8/06 v Republic of Ireland (a, Dublin, friendly), won 4-0
Caps 13, Goals 8
Major Tournaments – UEFA EURO 2008™

Club Career

Major Honours – Dutch Cup (2006, 2007)
Clubs: 02-04 PSV Eindhoven; 03 De Graafschap (loan); 03/04 AGOVV Apeldoorn (loan); 04-06 SC Heerenveen; 06- AFC Ajax

Alan HUTTON
Right-Back
Born 30/11/84, Glasgow, Scotland
Height 185cm, Weight 71kg

Alan Hutton left Rangers FC for Tottenham Hotspur FC in January 2008. Initially the pacy full-back seemed reluctant to He had signed a new five-year contract with the Ibrox club or a few months earlier and did not want to seem disloyal, especially as he had endeared himself to the Rangers fans wit succession of top-grade displays during the first half of the season, starring for the club both in domestic competition an the UEFA Champions League, where he was an ever-present i the group phase. But the power of money – and a bid of €11. – eventually led to his transfer from Glasgow to London, and within a month of his arrival he had won his first trophy in England, playing the full two hours of the League Cup final at Wembley, in which Spurs came from behind to beat favourite Chelsea FC 2-1 after extra time. Born on St. Andrew's Day, Hut also proved his worth for Scotland, establishing himself as the team's right-back with outstanding displays against France at Parc des Princes and Italy at Hampden Park.

International Career

SCOTLAND
Debut – 30/5/07 v Austria (a, Vienna, friendly), won 1-0
Caps 7; Goals 0
Major Tournaments - none

Club Career

Major Honours – Scottish Championship (2003, 2005); English League Cup (2008)
Clubs: 02-08 Rangers FC; 08- Tottenham Hotspur FC (ENG)

Zlatan IBRAHIMOVIĆ
Striker
Born 3/10/81,
Malmo, Sweden
Height 192cm,
Weight 84kg

Even if Zlatan Ibrahimović had not returned from injury to score the two crucial goals on the final day of the season that secured the scudetto for FC Internazionale Milano, he would still have been the team's player of the season. Those two timely strikes in Parma lifted the Swedish international's Serie A tally for the season to 17 goals. They were his first from open play since the home game against the same opposition in January. Hampered by injury throughout the spring, Ibrahimović had been firing on all cylinders in the autumn, also impressing in the UEFA Champions League with five goals, all at the San Siro. It was not a fully fit Zlatan who travelled to UEFA EURO 2008™ with Sweden, but he still made his mark on the tournament by scoring two goals – remarkably, his first for his country since October 2005. The first of them, a vicious rising shot into the top corner against holders Greece, was one of the goals of the tournament.

International Career

SWEDEN
Debut – 31/1/01 v Faroe Islands (h, Vaxjo, friendly), drew 0-0
First Goal – 7/10/01 v Azerbaijan (h, Solna, WCQ), won 3-0
Caps 53; Goals 20
Major Tournaments – FIFA World Cup 2002; UEFA EURO 2004™; FIFA World Cup 2006; UEFA EURO 2008™

Club Career

Major Honours – Dutch Championship (2002, 2004); Italian Championship (2007, 2008); Dutch Cup (2002)
Clubs: 99-01 Malmö FF; 01-04 AFC Ajax (NED); 04-06 Juventus (ITA); 06- FC Internazionale Milano (ITA)
uefa.com team of the year: 2007

Andrés INIESTA Luján
Wide Midfielder
Born 11/5/84,
Fuentealbilla, Spain
Height 170cm,
Weight 65kg

As the only member of Spain's UEFA European Championship-winning squad to start all six matches, Andrés Iniesta can look back on the tournament with supreme satisfaction. The little midfielder's willingness to play anywhere any time has been greatly appreciated for many years at his club, FC Barcelona, but it was only during the qualifying tournament for UEFA EURO 2008™ that his versatile talent was considered indispensable for Spain. He scored three goals en route to the finals, but although he did not add to his tally in Austria, he set up important goals for David Villa and Xavi Hernández in the two games against Russia and was a consistently lively, creative and industrious presence wherever he popped up on the field. Barcelona had a poor season in La Liga but they reached the semi-final of the UEFA Champions League and Iniesta was instrumental in helping them on their way. Midway through the season he was offered, and accepted, a lucrative contract extension that ties him to the club until the summer of 2014. He is not a Catalan by birth, but he is certainly one by association and it would be no surprise if the 24-year-old were to remain at Camp Nou for the remainder of his career

International Career

SPAIN
Major Honours – UEFA European Championship (2008)
Debut – 27/5/06 v Russia (h, Albacete, friendly), drew 0-0
First Goal – 7/2/07 v England (a, Manchester, friendly), won 1-0
Caps 29; Goals 4
Major Tournaments - FIFA World Cup 2006; UEFA EURO 2008™

Club Career

Major Honours – UEFA Champions League (2006); Spanish Championship (2005, 2006)
Clubs: 00- FC Barcelona

Gökhan INLER
Midfielder
Born 27/6/84, Olten, Switzerland
Height 181cm, Weight 80kg

A double Swiss champion with FC Zürich in 2005/06 and 2006/07, Gökhan Inler was never realistically going to comple a domestic league hat-trick when he moved to Italian provinc club Udinese Calcio. But he realised his, and the club's, ambiti for the season by helping the Zebrette qualify for the UEFA Cu Inler was voted as the best foreign newcomer in Serie A durin the first half of the season, and his controlled midfield play would serve Udinese well throughout the campaign. He start 37 of the team's 38 Serie A matches but showed no sign of fatigue at UEFA EURO 2008™, where he was on the field throughout all three of Switzerland's matches – as he had bee for the team's last seven warm-up games. Although the tournament went badly for his team, Inler was impressive individually, having a major influence on Switzerland's farewe 2-0 victory over Portugal. Unless new coach Ottmar Hitzfeld h other ideas, his central midfield partnership with Gelson Fernandes could be around for many years to come.

International Career

SWITZERLAND
Debut – 2/9/06 v Venezuela (h, Basel, friendly), won 1-0
First Goal – 22/3/07 v Jamaica (n, Fort Lauderdale, friendly), won 1
Caps 20; Goals 1
Major Tournaments – UEFA EURO 2008™

Club Career

Major Honours – Swiss Championship (2006, 2007)
Clubs: 02-04 FC Basel 1893; 05-06 FC Aarau; 06-07 FC Zürich; 0 Udinese Calcio (ITA)

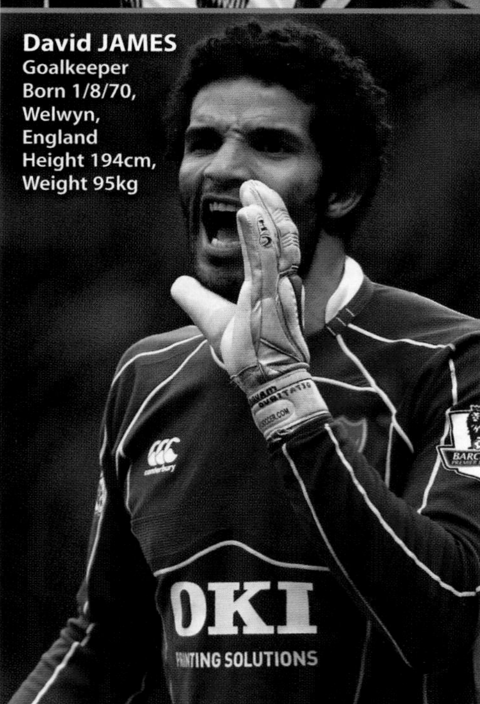

David JAMES
Goalkeeper
Born 1/8/70, Welwyn, England
Height 194cm, Weight 95kg

With Paul Robinson struggling for form and young Scott Carson suffering a nightmare after being thrown into the deep end by Steve McClaren in the crucial UEFA EURO 2008™ qualifier against Croatia, David James, aged 37, was chosen by new England coac Fabio Capello as his No1 goalkeeper and started each of the Italian's first four matches in charge. It may have seemed a retrograde step to some, but it was a decision based on sound logic given that James was far and away the best English goalkeeper in the Premier League during the 2007/08 season. H was also the best in the FA Cup, which he won – after two previc defeats in the final – thanks in no small part to his five clean shee in the competition. The last of those came in the final at Wemble where Portsmouth FC overcame Cardiff City FC 1-0 to claim the famous trophy for the first time in 69 years. James was among th six nominees for the PFA Player of the Year award – the only goalkeeper in the selection and the only player not belonging to one of the 'Big Four'. Whether he remains as England's No1 throu to the 2010 FIFA World Cup finals will doubtless depend on how well he rises to the challenge of the qualifying campaign.

International Career

ENGLAND
Debut – 29/3/97 v Mexico (h, Wembley, friendly), won 2-0
Caps 39; Goals 0
Major Tournaments – FIFA World Cup 2002; UEFA EURO 2004™ FIFA World Cup 2006

Club Career

Major Honours – English FA Cup (2008); English League Cup (199
Clubs: 89-92 Watford FC; 92-99 Liverpool FC; 99-01 Aston Villa FC; 01-04 West Ham United FC; 04-06 Manchester City FC; 06- Portsmouth FC

JOÃO Filipe Iria Santos MOUTINHO
Midfielder
Born 8/9/86, Portimao, Portugal
Height 170cm, Weight 61kg

For his stamina alone in 2007/08, João Moutinho deserved a medal. The young Sporting Clube de Portugal captain played a total of 62 matches for club and country – the largest number ever recorded in one season by a player affiliated to a Portuguese club. That he started and finished the vast majority of those matches, and maintained a high level of form throughout, made his feat even more remarkable. An ever present in the Primeira Liga, the diminutive midfield schemer also figured prominently in the Taça de Portugal, which he lifted for the second successive year after Sporting's extra-time victory over runaway champions FC Porto in the final at the Estádio Nacional in Lisbon. That was not the climax to his marathon campaign, however, as he still had work to do for Portugal at UEFA EURO 2008™. Luiz Felipe Scolari had selected him from the start in only a couple of qualifiers, but in Switzerland, after a superb display – and first international goal – in the last warm-up game against Georgia, he was given a regular berth and enjoyed a fine tournament until he had to withdraw, injured, in the first half of the quarter-final against Germany.

International Career

PORTUGAL
Debut – 17/8/05 v Egypt (h, Ponta Delgada, friendly), won 2-0
First Goal – 31/5/08 v Georgia (h, Viseu, friendly), won 2-0
Caps 17; Goals 1
Major Tournaments – UEFA EURO 2008™

Club Career

Major Honours – Portuguese Cup (2007, 2008)
Clubs: 04- Sporting Clube de Portugal

Milan JOVANOVIĆ
Striker
Born 18/4/81, Cacak, Serbia
Height 188cm, Weight 73kg

Milan Jovanović was crowned Player of the Season in Belgium after a superb campaign with R. Standard de Liège that ended with the club's first championship triumph for 25 years. The 27-year-old striker had done very little of note at his previous clubs FC Shakhtar Donetsk and PFC Lokomotiv Moskva (he made just three substitute appearances when the latter won the 2004 Russian title), but in Belgium he has relaunched his career, earning recognition also at international level with Serbia. He scored 14 league goals in his debut season for Standard and raised that to 16 in 2007/08 – the joint-second best tally in the Eerste Klasse. His most important goals were the two he scored in the 2-1 win away to championship rivals Club Brugge KV in mid-February, the turning point of the season. Les Rouches never looked back after that, and although it was his strike partner Dieumerci Mbokani who stole the headlines with the double that sank RSC Anderlecht and clinched the title, it was Jokanović who was elected by his peers at the end-of-season gathering in Knokke's Casino Kursaal, taking the top award ahead of his Standard team-mate Marouane Fellaini and Anderlecht midfielder Mbark Boussoufa.

International Career

SERBIA
Debut – 2/6/07 v Finland (a, Helsinki, ECQ), won 2-0
First Goal - 2/6/07 v Finland (a, Helsinki, ECQ), won 2-0
Caps 8; Goals 1
Major Tournaments - none

Club Career

Major Honours – Russian Championship (2004); Belgian Championship (2008)
Clubs: 99-03 FK Vojvodina; 03-04 FC Shakhtar Donetsk (UKR); 04-06 FC Lokomotiv Moskva (RUS); 06- R. Standard de Liège (BEL)

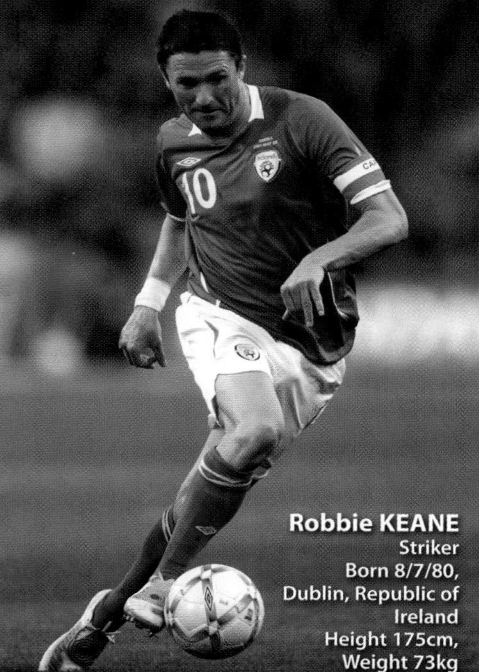

Robbie KEANE
Striker
Born 8/7/80, Dublin, Republic of Ireland
Height 175cm, Weight 73kg

Robbie Keane won the first major trophy of his career when Tottenham Hotspur FC beat Chelsea FC 2-1 after extra time in t 2008 League Cup final at Wembley. And how it showed as the Irishman milked the moment for all it was worth in the post-match celebrations. He was not on target in that game but he score in the brilliant five-goal destruction of arch-rivals Arsenal in the second leg of the semi-final at White Hart Lane. He also found the net 15 times in the Premier League – the same num as his strike partner Dimitar Berbatov – and another four times the UEFA Cup as Spurs reached the round of 16 before losing o penalties to PSV Eindhoven. Keane will be hoping to make a bigger splash in Europe – and to challenge for further domesti honours – following his €25.9m summer transfer to Liverpool F a club, he was at pains to point out on his arrival, that he ferver supported while growing up across the Irish Sea in Dublin. The Republic of Ireland's record scorer raised his running total to 33 goals with the winner against Colombia in May, giving new he coach Giovanni Trapattoni his first victory. Irish fans will be hop for more of the same in the 2010 FIFA World Cup qualifiers.

International Career

REPUBLIC OF IRELAND

Debut – 25/3/98 v Czech Republic (a, Olomouc, friendly), lost 1
First Goal – 14/10/98 v Malta (h, Dublin, ECQ), won 5-0
Caps 81; Goals 33
Major Tournaments – FIFA World Cup 2002

Club Career

Major Honours – English League Cup (2008)
Clubs: 97-99 Wolverhampton Wanderers FC (ENG); 99-00 Coventry City FC (ENG); 00-01 FC Internazionale Milano (ITA); 02 Leeds United AFC (ENG); 02-08 Tottenham Hotspur FC (EN 08- Liverpool FC (ENG)

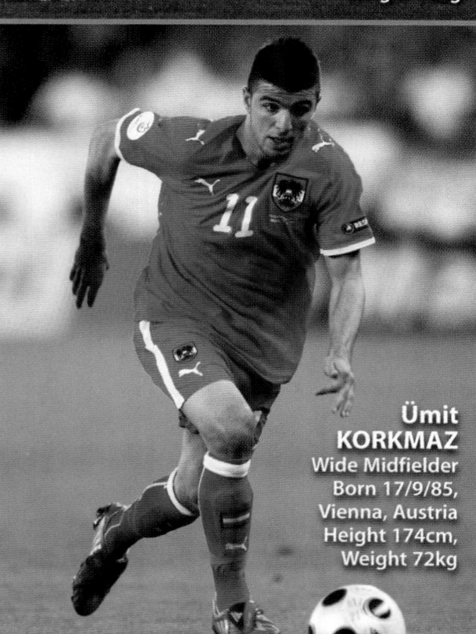

Ümit KORKMAZ
Wide Midfielder
Born 17/9/85, Vienna, Austria
Height 174cm, Weight 72kg

Ümit Korkmaz was Austria's most exciting player at UEFA EURO 2008™. The little crop-haired winger drew a buzz of anticipatior around the Ernst-Happel-Stadion every time he took possessio of the ball. Much of what he attempted did not come off, but h never let it bother him, and his repeated willingness to take on the full-back was a joy to watch. His quick one-twos were anot distinguishing feature, and he also delivered several dangerous crosses. Largely unknown to the international football community before the event – he was, after all, uncapped until the pre-tournament warm-up fixture against Nigeria – Korkma might have become a prime transfer target for some of Europe major clubs after it had he not already agreed a move from SK Rapid Wien to Eintracht Frankfurt. The Rapid fans were upset to see him go, because the 22-year-old had just played a big part i helping the club win the Austrian title. His development in the German Bundesliga will be fascinating to watch, and he is sure feature strongly in Austria's bid to qualify for the 2010 FIFA Worl Cup under new coach Karel Brückner.

International Career

AUSTRIA

Debut – 27/5/08 v Nigeria (h, Graz, friendly), drew 1-1
Caps 5; Goals 0
Major Tournaments – UEFA EURO 2008™

Club Career

Major Honours – Austrian Championship (2008)
Clubs: 05-08 SK Rapid Wien; 08- Eintracht Frankfurt (GER)

Martin LAURSEN

Centre-Back
Born 26/7/77,
Farvang, Denmark
Height 190cm,
Weight 83kg

A career that began at Silkeborg IF back in 1995 and took in several years in Italy reached its zenith for Martin Laursen in 2007/08. For the first time since joining Aston Villa FC, in May 2004, he was able to get through a whole season free of injury. In his first three seasons at the Birmingham club he racked up a mere 27 Premier League games. In the fourth he was an ever present, playing in all 38 matches from the start and being substituted only once – in the opening fixture. He also scored six goals (half of them in memorable 4-4 draws away to Tottenham Hotspur FC and Chelsea FC) and received only one yellow card - quite an achievement for a central defender. Composed on the ball and dominant in the air, Laursen had much to do with Villa's sixth-place finish and qualification for the UEFA Intertoto Cup and was duly voted Player of the Year by the club's supporters. Playing in Europe is nothing new to him as he was a UEFA Champions League and UEFA Super Cup winner with AC Milan in 2003 (albeit as an ununused substitute in both finals). He has also had plenty of international experience and ended the 2007/08 season poised to reach a half-century of caps for Denmark.

International Career

DENMARK
Debut – 29/3/00 v Portugal (a, Leiria, friendly), lost 1-2
First Goal – 10/9/03 v Romania (h, Copenhagen, ECQ), drew 2-2
Caps 49; Goals 2
Major Tournaments – UEFA EURO 2000™; FIFA World Cup 2002; UEFA EURO 2004™

Club Career

Major Honours – UEFA Champions League (2003); UEFA Super Cup (2003); Italian Championship (2004); Italian Cup (2003)
Clubs: 95-98 Silkeborg IF; 98-01 Hellas Verona FC (ITA); 01 Parma FC (ITA); 01-04 AC Milan (ITA); 04- Aston Villa FC (ENG)

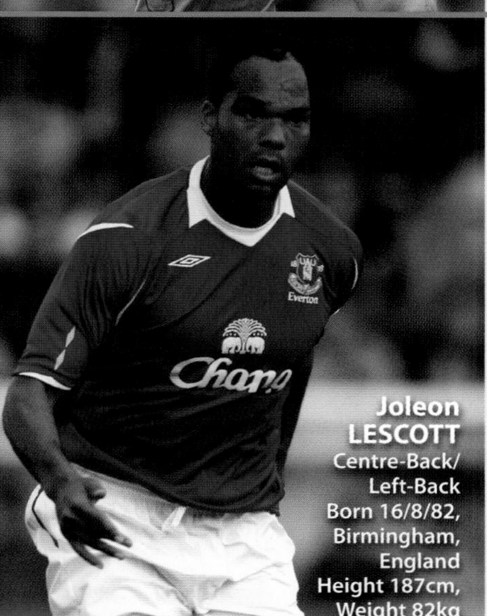

Joleon LESCOTT

Centre-Back/
Left-Back
Born 16/8/82,
Birmingham,
England
Height 187cm,
Weight 82kg

Everton FC finished fifth in the 2007/08 Premier League to qualify for a second successive season in the UEFA Cup. Their most consistent performer over the season was defender Joleon Lescott - quite a feat for a player who was constantly switched back and forth between centre-half and left-back. Excellent in both roles, the issue of which is his best position remains a matter of debate. One thing is for sure - he is as dangerous as any attacker when it comes to set-pieces. He proved that by scoring eight Premier League goals – only Nigerian striker Yakubu scored more for the Merseysiders – plus another two in the first round of the UEFA Cup against FC Metalist Kharkiv. Lescott, who carries facial scar tissue from a near-fatal motor accident when he was aged five, played every minute of Everton's ten-match UEFA Cup run. It was his first experience of European football, and he also made the breakthrough into the international arena when Steve McClaren called him up for the closing stages of England's ill-fated UEFA EURO 2008™ qualifying campaign.

International Career

ENGLAND
Debut – 13/10/07 v Estonia (h, Wembley, ECQ), won 3-0
Caps 5; Goals 0
Major Tournaments - none

Club Career

Clubs: 99-06 Wolverhampton Wanderers FC; 06- Everton FC

LISANDRO LÓPEZ

Striker
Born 2/3/83, Buenos Aires, Argentina
Height 175cm, Weight 74kg

For his first two seasons at FC Porto, Argentine forward Lisand López had been just one of many attacking options. He scored only seven league goals in each of those campaigns and his match ratings were seldom better than run-of-the-mill. Then, i 2007/08, he suddenly burst into life, revealing hitherto hidden talents as a serial goalscorer that would take everyone, Porto coach Jesualdo Ferreira included, by surprise. A flurry of early-season goals cemented his place at the head of the Porto attac and he went on to find the net consistently all season, totallinc 24 in 27 Portuguese Primeira Liga appearances - by some distance the biggest haul in the league – and adding another three in the UEFA Champions League. Physically powerful, he has good aerial technique and a venomous right-foot shot. He also has a knack of being in the right place at the right time in the penalty area. The big question Porto fans are asking themselves is whether, given what went before, Lisandro Lópe astonishing 2007/08 form was simply a one-off. They will soon have their answer.

International Career

ARGENTINA
Debut – 9/3/05 v Mexico (n, Los Angeles, friendly), drew 1-1
Caps 5; Goals 0
Major Tournaments - none

Club Career

Major Honours – Portuguese Championship (2006, 2007, 2008 Portuguese Cup (2006)
Clubs: 02-05 Racing Club; 05- FC Porto (POR)

Luis Óscar "LUCHO" GONZÁLEZ

Midfielder
Born 19/1/81, Buenos Aires, Argentina
Height 185cm, Weight 75kg

Three seasons of continual improvement at FC Porto have left many Portuguese observers curious as to why Lucho González has not been the target of constant transfer interest from the b clubs of England, Spain and Italy. The 27-year-old is the classic 'complete midfielder', committed and industrious in defence a skilful and creative in attack. In 2007/08 the Argentina international was more consistent than ever, rarely letting his performance level drop. He was the cornerstone of Porto's relentless march to the Primeira Liga title – his third in as many seasons at the club he joined from Buenos Aires giants CA Rive Plate in 2005. The club captain and resident penalty taker, he sent Porto on their way to winning their UEFA Champions League group by smashing a spot-kick past Liverpool FC's Pep Reina on Matchday One, and he was the only Porto player to convert his penalty in the round-of-16 shoot-out that they lost to FC Schalke 04.

International Career

ARGENTINA
Debut – 31/1/03 v Honduras (a, San Pedro Sula, friendly), won 3
First Goal - 31/1/03 v Honduras (a, San Pedro Sula, friendly), won 3
Caps 40; Goals 5
Major Tournaments – Copa América 2004; FIFA Confederations Cup 2005; FIFA World Cup 2006; Copa América 2007

Club Career

Major Honours – Argentine Championship (clausura 2004); Portuguese Championship (2006, 2007, 2008); Portuguese Cup (2006)
Clubs: 98-02 CA Huracán; 02-05 CA River Plate; 05- FC Porto (POR)

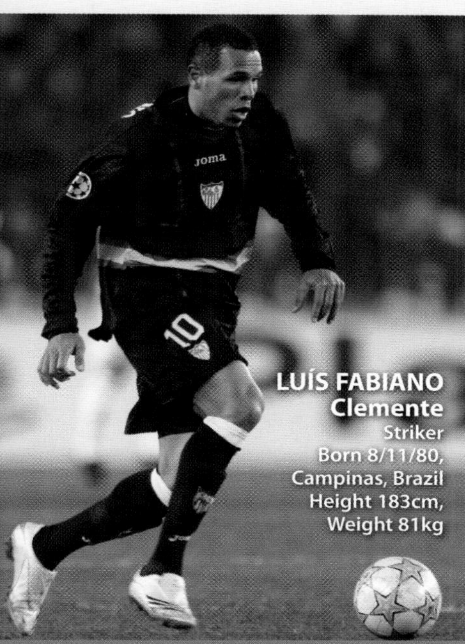

LUÍS FABIANO Clemente
Striker
Born 8/11/80, Campinas, Brazil
Height 183cm, Weight 81kg

The queue of candidates to lead Brazil's attack at the 2010 FIFA World Cup is long and wide, but Luís Fabiano made a purposeful move towards the front with a goal-laden campaign for Sevilla FC in 2007/08. Although he was eventually overtaken for the Pichichi award as La Liga's top scorer by RCD Mallorca's Daniel Güiza after slackening off a bit in the closing weeks, the 27-year-old had every reason to feel proud of his performances, both in domestic competition and in the UEFA Champions League, where he added to three goals in the qualifying round another four in the group stage. The only European home game in which he failed to score was the round-of-16 second leg against Fenerbahçe SK, which Sevilla lost on penalties (after he had been substituted). Strangely, his 24-goal league tally included no hat-tricks – a feat he has yet to achieve after three seasons in La Liga.

International Career

BRAZIL
Major Honours – Copa América (2004)
Debut – 11/6/03 v Nigeria (a, Abuja, friendly), won 3-0
First Goal - 11/6/03 v Nigeria (a, Abuja, friendly), won 3-0
Caps 20; Goals 9
Major Tournaments – FIFA Confederations Cup 2003; Copa América 2004

Club Career

Major Honours – UEFA Cup (2006, 2007); World Club Cup (2004); Spanish Cup (2007)
Clubs: 97-00 UE Ponte Preta; 00-01 Stade Rennais FC (FRA); 01-04 FC São Paulo ; 04-05 FC Porto (POR) ; 05- Sevilla FC (ESP)

Javier MASCHERANO
Midfielder
Born 8/6/84, San Lorenzo, Argentina
Height 170cm, Weight 66kg

Outstanding as Kaká's 'minder' in the 2007 UEFA Champions League final, Javier Mascherano confirmed his talent as one of the world's best defensive midfielders during his first full season with Liverpool FC. He spent most of it as the subject of a complex loan arrangement until, in the early spring, over a year after his arrival on Merseyside, a permanent deal was tied up with the player's owners, Media Sports Investments, at a reported cost of €23.7m. Mascherano's presence in a deep holding role proved precious to the tactical shape of Rafael Benítez's team, enabling captain Steven Gerrard to get forward in support of Fernando Torres. Although Mascherano got himself into hot water with a show of petulance, and red card, in a Premier League game at Manchester United FC, his battling, terrier-like qualities were much in evidence during Liverpool's run to the UEFA Champions League semi-finals. He was especially prominent against FC Internazionale Milano, totally eclipsing his fellow Argentine international midfielder Esteban Cambiasso in both legs.

International Career

ARGENTINA
Debut – 16/7/03 v Uruguay (h, La Plata, friendly), drew 2-2
First Goal – 5/7/07 v Paraguay (n, Barquisimeto, CA), won 1-0
Caps 41; Goals 2
Major Tournaments - Copa América 2004; FIFA Confederations Cup 2005; FIFA World Cup 2006; Copa América 2007

Club Career

Major Honours – Argentine Championship (clausura 2004); Brazilian Championship (2005)
Clubs: 03-05 CA River Plate; 05-06 SC Corinthians (BRA); 06-07 West Ham United FC (ENG); 07- Liverpool FC (ENG)

Aiden McGEADY

Winger/ Attacking Midfielder
Born 4/4/86, Glasgow, Scotland
Height 178cm, Weight72kg

The footballing rat-race is full of young talents who fail to fulfil th initial promise, but Aiden McGeady seems destined not to becor one of them. The Scottish-born Republic of Ireland international received all kinds of rave reviews in his teens, and in 2007/08 he came of age at senior level, enjoying a magnificent season for Celtic FC in the Scottish Premier League, which the club won for the third season running, and also in the UEFA Champions Leagu where he was one of Celtic's key players during a successful grou stage. A crowd-pleasing tricky winger of considerable skill, McGeady was recognised by his fellow professionals when, in Ap he picked up both the SPFA Player of the Year and Young Player the Year awards. All sorts of rumours flew around at the end of th season suggesting a move to England, but the 22-year-old scotched them all when he decided to remain loyal to his boyho heroes and sign a new five-year contract. Should he see out the f term, he will surely become a Hoops legend.

International Career

REPUBLIC OF IRELAND
Debut – 2/6/04 v Jamaica, (n, London, friendly), won 2-1
Caps 18; Goals 0
Major Tournaments - none

Club Career

Major Honours – Scottish Championship (2006, 2007, 2008); Scottish Cup (2005, 2007); Scottish League Cup (2006)
Clubs: 04- Celtic FC (SCO)

Lionel Andrés MESSI

Winger/Striker
Born 24/6/87, Rosario, Argentina
Height 170cm, Weight 65kg

The 'New Maradona' continues to live up to the tag. Lionel Mes had another sensational season for FC Barcelona in 2007/08. From a team perspective, with Barça failing to win a trophy an finishing only third in La Liga, it left a lot to be desired. Individually, however, the young megastar could do little wron The Camp Nou faithful chanted their adoration for Messi while waving their hankies at others. The 21-year-old is by no means perfect – there are times when he takes on the defender simp because he knows he will beat him rather than laying the ball to a better positioned colleague – but those little sins are pardonable for one so young. After all, there is so much to admire – the feints, the bursts of speed, the vicious left-footed shots, the incredible natural skill. In many games during the season Messi was practically unstoppable – by fair means and foul. Two goals against Celtic FC in Glasgow made him the leading scorer in the UEFA Champions League, with six in total and although Cristiano Ronaldo subsequently displaced him, the battle of the 'Best Two Players in the World' in the semi-fina was won by the Argentine hands down. Even though United went through, the Barça winger's dazzling performance in the second leg at Old Trafford took the breath away. If he can stay and sensible and listen to sound advice, there is no limit to hov great a footballer Lionel Messi can become.

International Career

ARGENTINA
Debut – 17/8/05 v Hungary (a, Budapest, friendly), won 2-1
First Goal – 1/3/06 v Croatia (n, Basel, friendly), lost 2-3
Caps 30; Goals 9
Major Tournaments – FIFA World Cup 2006, Copa América 200

Club Career

Major Honours – UEFA Champions League (2006); Spanish Championship (2005, 2006)
Clubs: 04- FC Barcelona (ESP)

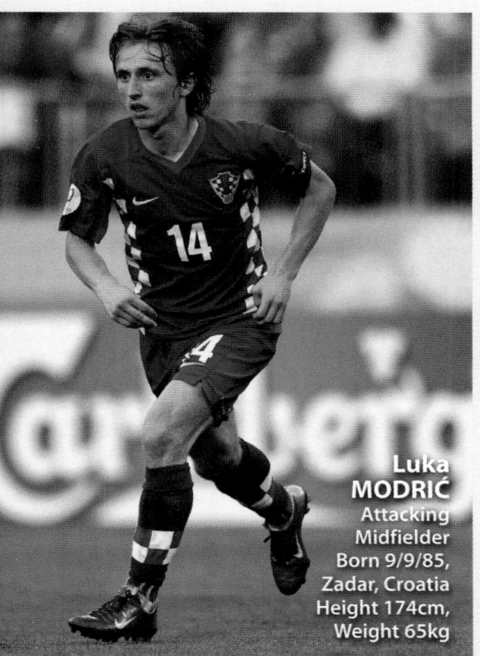

Luka MODRIĆ
Attacking Midfielder
Born 9/9/85, Zadar, Croatia
Height 174cm, Weight 65kg

A new star was born at UEFA EURO 2008™. Luka Modrić was not exactly an unknown when he entered the arena for Croatia's opening match against Austria in Vienna - he had shone repeatedly for Slaven Bilić's side during the qualifying competition, starting every game – but the question was whether the tiny playmaker could deliver on the big stage. The answer was soon apparent. After scoring the winning goal from the penalty spot against Austria, the diminutive No14 ran the show against Germany and did likewise in the quarter-final against Turkey. His missed penalty in the shoot-out against the Turks was unfortunate but could take nothing away from his previous exploits. Modrić had agreed a transfer to Tottenham Hotspur FC before the tournament. He had clearly outgrown the Croatian domestic league, which he won with NK Dinamo Zagreb for the third successive year, contributing 13 goals in 25 appearances. There was a second successive Croatian Cup win, too, against arch-rivals HNK Hajduk Split in the final, to ensure that the so-called 'Croatian Cruijff' left for Tottenham on a high. His progress in England will be monitored with interest.

International Career

CROATIA
Debut – 1/3/06 v Argentina (n, Basel, friendly), won 3-2
First Goal – 16/8/06 v Italy (a, Livorno, friendly), won 2-0
Caps 29; Goals 4
Major Tournaments – FIFA World Cup 2006; UEFA EURO 2008™

Club Career

Major Honours – Croatian Championship (2006, 2007, 2008); Croatian Cup (2007, 2008)
Clubs: 02-08 NK Dinamo Zagreb; 03/04 HŠK Zrinjski (BIH) (loan); 04/05 NK Inter Zaprešić (loan); 08- Tottenham Hotspur FC (ENG)

Adrian MUTU
Striker
Born 8/1/79, Calinesti, Romania
Height 180cm, Weight 74kg

As the No1 attraction in a team embarking on their first major finals for eight years, much was expected of ACF Fiorentina's Adrian Mutu at UEFA EURO 2008™. Unfortunately, the abiding memory of his tournament may well be his penalty miss against Italy, which effectively prevented Romania from reaching the quarter-finals, but that would be to ignore the positive things he did in Switzerland, such as giving Romania the lead earlier in that same game, and doing his level best to repair the damage with a gutsy display in the next match against the Netherlands. In short, Mutu went into the tournament as Romania's top player and came out of it as Romania's top player. Spot-kick misery was a recurring theme for the 29-year-old striker as Fiorentina, seeking a first European title for 47 years, lost on penalties to Rangers FC in the semi-final of the UEFA Cup. Mutu had put them into the last four, scoring all three goals in the quarter-final against PSV Eindhoven, including one extraordinary long-range free-kick. He also scored 17 goals in Serie A to take the Viola into fourth place and pip AC Milan for a place in the UEFA Champions League.

International Career

ROMANIA
Debut – 29/3/00 v Greece (a, Athens, friendly), lost 0-2
First Goal – 26/4/00 v Cyprus (h, Constanta, friendly), won 2-0
Caps 64; Goals 29
Major Tournaments – UEFA EURO 2000™; UEFA EURO 2008™

Club Career

Major Honours – Romanian Championship (2000)
Clubs: 96-99 FC Argeş Piteşti; 99-00 FC Dinamo 1948 Bucureşti; 00-02 FC Internazionale Milano (ITA); 00-02 Hellas Verona FC (ITA) (loan); 02-03 Parma FC (ITA); 03-04 Chelsea FC (ENG); 05-06 Juventus (ITA); 06- ACF Fiorentina (ITA)

NİHAT Kahveci

Striker
Born 23/11/79, Istanbul, Turkey
Height 175cm, Weight 71kg

Nihat's Kahveci's status as a Turkish national hero was proclaimed after he scored winning goals in each of the final two UEFA EURO 2008™ qualifying ties against Norway and Bosnia-Herzegovina. The worship was even greater after he struck his late double in Geneva to give Turkey an astonishing comeback win against the Czech Republic that took them through to the quarter-finals. Unfortunately the tough little striker injured his calf while taking a free-kick in the closing minutes of extra time against Croatia and was not available for the semi-final against Germany. In fact, he was not even there to cheer on his team-mates, having returned to Turkey for treatment. UEFA EURO 2008™ was the climax of a tremendously productive season for the 28-year-old, who top-scored with 17 goals as Villarreal CF surprisingly finished ahead of FC Barcelona to take second place in La Liga and guarantee themselves involvement in the UEFA Champions League. Nihat will be especially keen to do well as he is still awaiting his first goal in the competition after 13 appearances.

International Career

TURKEY

Debut – 7/10/00 v Sweden (a, Gothenburg, WCQ), drew 1-1
First Goal – 6/10/01 v Moldova (a, Chisinau, WCQ), won 3-0
Caps 59; Goals 17
Major Tournaments – FIFA World Cup 2002; FIFA Confederations Cup 2003; UEFA EURO 2008™

Club Career

Major Honours – Turkish Cup (1998)
Clubs: 97-02 Beşiktaş JK; 02-06 Real Sociedad de Fútbol (ESP); 06 Villarreal CF (ESP)

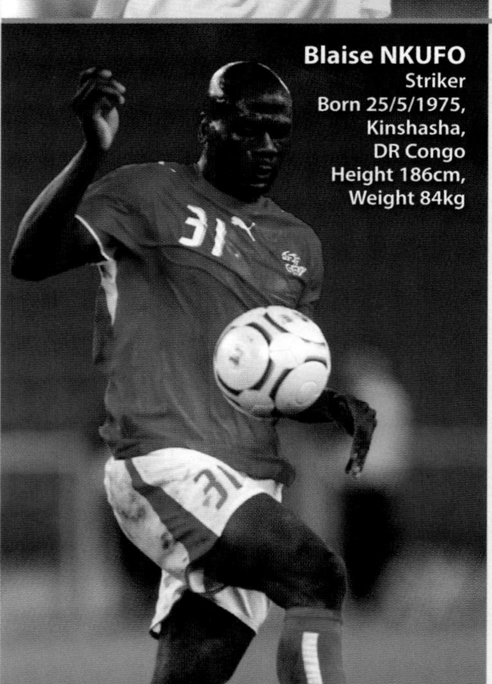

Blaise NKUFO

Striker
Born 25/5/1975, Kinshasha, DR Congo
Height 186cm, Weight 84kg

Born in the Democratic Republic of Congo, where he lost most of his family in civil-war fighting, and subsequently raised by his aunt in the French-speaking part of Switzerland, Blaise Nkufo (or "Kufo" as he would apparently prefer to be known – the 'N' is silent in any case) was set to play for the co-hosts at UEFA EURO 2008™ until he incurred an ankle injury that ruled him out of the tournament. A subsequent injury to Alexander Frei in Switzerland's opening game aggravated the frustration of the striker, who was in prime form having just taken his club, FC Twente, into the qualifying round of the 2008/09 UEFA Champions League at the expense of AFC Ajax in the Dutch play-offs. The burly centre-forward scored two goals in that tie plus another 22 in the regular Eredivisie campaign, which exactly matched his 2006/07 tally. He returned to the Swiss national team set-up in August 2007 after a voluntary five-year absence sparked by a heated row with coach Köbi Kuhn. Although Nkufo is 33, he has agreed a new two-year deal with Twente.

International Career

SWITZERLAND

Debut – 2/9/00 v Russia (h, Zurich, WCQ), lost 0-1
First Goal – 15/5/02 v Canada (h, St Gallen, friendly), lost 1-3
Caps 15; Goals 2
Major Tournaments - none

Club Career

Major Honours – Qatari Championship (1996); Swiss Cup (1998)
Clubs: 93-95 Lausanne-Sports; 95-96 Al-Arabi (QAT); 96-97 Yverdon Sports; 97-98 Lausanne-Sports; 98 Grasshopper-Club; 99 FC Lugano; 00 Grasshopper-Club; 00-01 FC Luzern; 01-02 FSV Mainz 05 (GER); 02-03 Hannover 96 (GER); 03- FC Twente (NED)

Ivica OLIĆ

Winger/Striker
Born 14/9/79, Slavonski Brod, Croatia
Height 182cm, Weight 82kg

A penetrative, scavenging forward with undrainable energy, Ivica Olić was obliged to fill in for the injured Eduardo da Silva – another left-footer – at UEFA EURO 2008™. He worked his socks off and scored the winning goal in the group game against Germany – his tenth at international level – but missed a number of chances against Turkey and was therefore the target of much criticism after Croatia's penalty shoot-out defeat. Although it was argued in his defence that Olić, unlike Eduardo, has never been a natural finisher, he was twice the top scorer – with different clubs – in the Croatian league in the early years of his career, and in 2007/08 he enjoyed a memorable season in front of goal for Hamburger SV, scoring 14 times in the Bundesliga, including a hat-trick against defending champions VfB Stuttgart. He was also named man of the match in Croatia's epic 3-2 victory at Wembley that knocked England out of the competition – an appropriate way in which to celebrate his 50th international appearance.

International Career

CROATIA
Debut – 13/2/02 v Bulgaria (h, Rijeka, friendly), drew 0-0
First Goal – 17/4/02 v Bosnia-Herzegovina (h, Zagreb, friendly), won 2-0
Caps 57; Goals 10
Major Tournaments - FIFA World Cup 2002; UEFA EURO 2004™; FIFA World Cup 2006; UEFA EURO 2008™

Club Career

Major Honours – UEFA Cup (2005); Croatian Championship (2002, 2003); Russian Championship (2003, 2005, 2006); Russian Cup (2005, 2006)
Clubs: 96-98 NK Marsonia; 98-99 Hertha BSC Berlin (GER); 99-02 NK Marsonia; 01/02 NK Zagreb (loan); 02-03 NK Dinamo Zagreb; 03-07 PFC CSKA Moskva (RUS); 07- Hamburger SV (GER)

Goran PANDEV

Striker/Attacking Midfielder
Born 27/7/83, Strumica, FYR Macedonia
Height 184cm, Weight 75kg

If 2007/08 was a season of disappointment for fans of S.S. Lazio, it maintained the onward and upward progress of the team's skilful Macedonian striker Goran Pandev. The technically gifted left-footer scored 14 goals in Serie A – three more than he managed in the previous season and an identical total to that of his strike partner Tommaso Rocchi – but he saved his very best for the UEFA Champions League, and one match in particular, at home to Real Madrid CF, in which he scored two glorious goals, twice cancelling out strikes from Ruud van Nistelrooy. He scored a third goal against Real at the Bernabéu, but that was a mere consolation – and caused him some pain as he collided heavily with the goalpost in doing so. A superstar in his homeland, Pandev will be doing his level best to make FYR Macedonia more competitive in the 2010 FIFA World Cup qualifiers than they were on the road to UEFA EURO 2008™. Coach Srečko Katanec has used him both as an orthodox striker and in the 'hole'. Wherever he plays, he will be striving to score the six goals needed to usurp Georgi Hristov as his country's all-time leading scorer.

International Career

FYR MACEDONIA
Debut – 6/6/01 v Turkey (a, Bursa, WCQ), drew 3-3
First Goal – 21/8/02 v Malta (h, Skopje, friendly), won 5-0
Caps 37; Goals 11
Major Tournaments – none

Club Career

Clubs: 99-01 FK Belasica; 01-04 FC Internazionale Milano (ITA); 02/03 Spezia Calcio 1906 (ITA) (loan); 03/04 AC Ancona (ITA) (loan); 04- S.S. Lazio (ITA)

Alexandre Rodrigues da Silva "PATO"

Striker
Born 2/9/89,
Pato Branco, Brazil
Height 179cm,
Weight 71kg

AC Milan's fascination with Brazilian talent brought Ronaldinho to the club from FC Barcelona during the summer. It remains to be seen whether the former FIFA World Player of the Year still ha it in him to recapture his former glories. One of his battles will b to avoid being overshadowed by his teenage compatriot Pato. The highly talented curly-haired striker – not dissimilar in looks and mannerisms to a young Ole Gunnar Solskjær - was bought from SC Internacional of Porto Alegre in September 2007 but because of Italian age-restriction rules he was unable to make his first-team debut for the Rossoneri until January 2008, which he promptly marked with a goal and a top-class display against SSC Napoli, helping Milan to their first home win of the season Serie A (5-2). Pato ('Duck') scored both goals in a 2-0 win over Genoa CFC in the next home game and ended up with an impressive half-season tally of nine Serie A goals. His UEFA Champions League debut came against Arsenal FC at the Emirates Stadium in London, which a few weeks later was also the venue for his international debut for Brazil, against Sweden. He celebrated it in style by scoring the only goal of the game – a brilliant improvised lob from the right-hand touchline.

International Career

BRAZIL

Debut – 26/3/08 v Sweden (n, London, friendly), won 1-0
First Goal - 26/3/08 v Sweden (n, London, friendly), won 1-0
Caps 3; Goals 1
Major Tournaments - none

Club Career

Major Honours – FIFA Club World Cup (2006); South American Super Cup (2007)
Clubs: 06-08 SC Internacional; 08- AC Milan (ITA)

Roman PAVLYUCHENKO

Striker
Born 15/12/81,
Mostovskoy, Russia
Height 188cm,
Weight 78kg

Having helped to place a couple of nails in England's UEFA EURO 2008™ coffin by coming off the bench to score both goals in the qualifying win in Moscow (2-1), Roman Pavlyuchenko gave a lengthier demonstration of his talent at the finals, earning a place in the official Team of the Tournament with a succession o excellent centre-forward displays. He scored three goals but it could so easily have been more. With the exception of the semi-final against Spain, Russia's football was so fluent going forward that the big blond striker was seldom out of the game. He also helped himself with some outstanding front-running, often leaving his central berth to collect the ball and bring others into play. Had the similarly-styled Pavel Pogrebnyak not been ruled out of the finals through injury, Pavlyuchenko might well have been Guus Hiddink's second choice, but he strengthened his case by finishing joint-top of the 2007 Russian Premier-Liga scoring charts, his 18 goals helping FC Spartak Moskva finish runners-up to Pogrebnyak's FC Zenit St. Petersburg.

International Career

RUSSIA

Debut – 20/8/03 v Israel (h, Moscow, friendly), lost 1-2
First Goal – 8/10/05 v Luxembourg (h, Moscow, WCQ), won 5-1
Caps 22; Goals 9
Major Tournaments – UEFA EURO 2008™

Club Career

Major Honours – Russian Cup (2003)
Clubs: 98-99 FC Dinamo Stavropol; 00-02 SC Rotor Volgograd; 03- FC Spartak Moskva

Képler Laveran Lima Ferreira "PEPE"
Centre-Back
Born 26/2/83, Maceio, Brazil
Height 187cm, Weight 81kg

Twice a Portuguese title winner with FC Porto, in 2005/06 and 2006/07, Pepe completed a personal hat-trick of domestic championship triumphs by helping Real Madrid CF win La Liga in his first season at the club. Although he was unavailable for half of Real's games through injury, he made quite an impact when he played and was the man of the match in Real's all-important 1-0 win at FC Barcelona just before Christmas. Although Brazilian-born, he had played all his professional football in Portugal prior to his €30m move to Madrid and obtained Portuguese citizenship in August 2007. Having been handed his Portugal national team debut in the crucial final UEFA EURO 2008™ qualifier against Finland, the 25-year-old made quite an impression at the finals in Switzerland, defending stoutly and scoring his first international goal in the opening game against Turkey (after having an earlier effort disallowed). He was one of only two Portugal players selected in the UEFA Team of the Tournament.

International Career

PORTUGAL
Debut – 21/11/07 v Finland (h, Porto, ECQ), drew 0-0
First Goal – 7/6/08 v Turkey (n, Geneva, ECF), won 2-0
Caps 7; Goals 1
Major Tournaments – UEFA EURO 2008™

Club Career

Major Honours – World Club Cup (2004); Portuguese Championship (2006, 2007); Spanish Championship (2008); Portuguese Cup (2006)
Clubs: 01-04 CS Marítimo; 04-07 FC Porto; 07- Real Madrid CF (ESP)

Mladen PETRIĆ
Striker
Born 1/1/81, Dubrave, Bosnia-Herzegovina
Height 185cm, Weight 77kg

The UEFA EURO 2008™ qualifying campaign ended on a high for Mladen Petrić with his stunning left-foot drive from distance that restored Croatia's lead against England at Wembley and sent the home side crashing out of the competition. But at the finals there were very different lingering emotions for the shaven-headed striker as his missed penalty in the quarter-final shoot-out against Turkey proved to be Croatia's last kick in the competition. Petrić was not at his best in Austria, which was something of a surprise as he went into the tournament buoyed by an excellent debut season in Germany for BV Borussia Dortmund. Although the Bundesliga's best-supported team struggled in the league, finishing 13th, Petrić ensured there would be no relegation worries by scoring 13 goals. He also found the net in the quarter-final, semi-final and final of the German Cup, his last-minute strike against FC Bayern München in Berlin taking the final into extra time, only for the champions to take the lead again and run out 2-1 winners.

International Career

CROATIA
Debut – 10/11/01 v South Korea (a, Seoul, friendly), lost 0-2
First Goal – 21/8/02 v Wales (h, Varazdin, friendly), drew 1-1
Caps 27; Goals 9
Major Tournaments – UEFA EURO 2008™

Club Career

Major Honours – Swiss Championship (2001, 2003, 2005); Swiss Cup (2007)
Clubs: 98-99 FC Baden (SUI); 99-04 Grasshopper-Club (SUI); 04-07 FC Basel 1893 (SUI); 07- BV Borussia Dortmund (GER)

Pavel POGREBNYAK
Striker
Born 8/11/83, Moscow, Russia
Height 188cm, Weight 81kg

Was there an unluckier man in football than Pavel Pogrebnyak in the early summer of 2008? It is highly doubtful. Having steered FC Zenit St. Petersburg to the final of the UEFA Cup with two superb goals in the 4-0 rout of FC Bayern München, he received a late yellow card that suspended him from the final. Zenit went on to lift the trophy without the man who had scored ten goals (plus another in qualifying), but there would be another stroke of ill fortune for Pogrebnyak just around the corner. Poised to play for Russia at UEFA EURO 2008™, he picked up a knee injury while playing in an eve-of-tournament friendly against Serbia. He had just lashed in one of his unstoppable trademark left-footed free-kicks when he had to leave the field. For several days there was hope that he would make the finals but eventually he had to bow to the inevitable and made his way disconsolately home. Pogrebnyak is young enough, at 24, and certainly talented enough to aspire to such heights again. Having helped Zenit win the Russian title in 2007 – he was the team's top scorer, with 11 goals – he has an immediate opportunity to make up for that double disappointment in the 2008/09 UEFA Champions League.

International Career

RUSSIA
Debut – 16/8/06 v Latvia (h, Moscow, friendly), won 1-0
First Goal - 16/8/06 v Latvia (h, Moscow, friendly), won 1-0
Caps 9; Goals 4
Major Tournaments - none

Club Career

Major Honours – UEFA Cup (2008); Russian Championship (2007)
Clubs: 02-04 FC Spartak Moskva; 03 FC Baltika Kaliningrad (loan); 04 FC Khimki; 05 FC Shinnik Yaroslavl; 06 FC Tom Tomsk; 07- FC Zenit St. Petersburg

RAÚL González
Striker
Born 27/6/77, Madrid, Spain
Height 181cm, Weight 73kg

The non-selection for UEFA EURO 2008™ of national icon Raúl was one of the major pre-tournament topics of debate among the Spanish public. Shunned by Luis Aragonés at a very early stage of the qualifying campaign, following a 3-2 defeat by Northern Ireland in Belfast, the exclusion of the country's all-time record scorer would not have been so controversial had it not been for his brilliant return to form during Real Madrid CF's Spanish title-winning campaign. He played as well as ever in 2007/08, adapting superbly to coach Bernd Schuster's methods, proving more consistent over the season than fellow forwards Robinho and Ruud van Nistelrooy, and scoring 18 La Liga goals plus another five in the UEFA Champions League to raise his record tally in that competition to 61. He may have missed out on his country's finest hour, but the way in which he led by example to skipper Real to their 31st La Liga title proved beyond doubt that there is plenty of life left in the 31-year-old.

International Career

SPAIN
Debut – 9/10/96 v Czech Republic (a, Prague, WCQ), drew 0-0
First Goal – 14/12/96 v Yugoslavia (h, Valencia, WCQ), won 2-0
Caps 102; Goals 44
Major Tournaments - FIFA World Cup 1998; UEFA EURO 2000™; FIFA World Cup 2002; UEFA EURO 2004™; FIFA World Cup 2006

Club Career

Major Honours – UEFA Champions League (1998, 2000, 2002); UEFA Super Cup (2002); World Club Cup (1998, 2002); Spanish Championship (1995, 1997, 2001, 2003, 2007, 2008)
Clubs: 94- Real Madrid CF

Franck RIBÉRY
Attacking Midfielder
Born 1/4/83,
Boulogne-sur-Mer, France
Height 170cm, Weight 62kg

Franck Ribéry was worth every cent of the €26m that FC Bayern München forked out to bring the French international midfielder midfielder from Olympique de Marseille. He was a hit from day one. In fact, he started brilliantly and got even better as the season progressed. His tricks, flicks and slalom runs captivated the sell-out crowds at the Allianz Arena and he thrived on the acclaim. Fellow new signings Luca Toni and Miroslav Klose could not have wished for better service, and the Frenchman was no slouch in front of goal himself, finding the net eleven times in the Bundesliga and scoring winning goals in the quarter-final and semi-final of the German Cup. Bayern won both domestic trophies and reached the semi-finals of the UEFA Cup, in which he also dazzled. His 60-minute virtuoso performance in the group-phase tie at home to Bolton Wanderers FC was out of this world. Ribéry maintained his form at UEFA EURO 2008™ but was let down by his team-mates, and when he left the field on a stretcher after rupturing ankle ligaments early on in the final group game against Italy, there was no way back for Les Bleus.

International Career

FRANCE
Debut – 27/5/06 v Mexico (h, Saint-Denis, friendly), won 1-0
First Goal – 27/6/06 v Spain (n, Hanover, WCF), won 3-1
Caps 30; Goals 4
Major Tournaments – FIFA World Cup 2006; UEFA EURO 2008™

Club Career

Major Honours – German Championship (2008); Turkish Cup (2005); German Cup (2008)
Clubs: 01-02 US Boulogne; 02-03 Olympique Alès; 03-04 Stade Brestois 29; 04-05 FC Metz; 05 Galatasaray AŞ (TUR); 05-07 Olympique de Marseille; 07- FC Bayern München (GER)

RICARDO Andrade QUARESMA Bernardo
Winger
Born 26/9/83, Lisbon, Portugal
Height 175cm, Weight 75kg

Controversially excluded from Portugal's 2006 FIFA World Cup squad, Ricardo Quaresma made it to UEFA EURO 2008™ but, much to the chagrin of the player and his legion of admirers at FC Porto, he barely got a kick - at least not in the games that mattered. He had a full 90-minute run-out with the 'reserves' against Switzerland, but his only other action was ten minutes late on against the Czech Republic – an opportunity he made the most of by scoring Portugal's third goal. Having finished the qualifying campaign as a regular starter in Luiz Felipe Scolari's side, Quaresma was entitled to feel aggrieved. But the coach clearly felt that Simão – a fellow graduate of the celebrated Cantera academy in Lisbon - was a safer bet than the more unpredictable, genial 24-year-old, despite the fact that he had just completed his finest season yet with Porto. The club's third successive title was a foregone conclusion after his winning goal away to SL Benfica in December, and throughout the campaign he thrilled the crowd with his fancy footwork and lethal crosses.

International Career

PORTUGAL
Debut – 10/6/03 v Bolivia (h, Lisbon, friendly), won 4-0
First Goal – 24/3/07 v Belgium (h, Lisbon, ECQ), won 4-0
Caps 23; Goals 3
Major Tournaments – UEFA EURO 2008™

Club Career

Major Honours – World Club Cup (2004); Portuguese Championship (2002, 2006, 2007, 2008); Portuguese Cup (2002, 2006)
Clubs: 00-03 Sporting Clube de Portugal; 03-04 FC Barcelona (ESP); 04- FC Porto

ROGER Guerreiro
Attacking Midfielder
Born 25/5/82, São Paulo, Brazil
Height 186cm, Weight 81kg

Brazilians opting to play international football for European countries are becoming increasingly commonplace. Marcos Senna of Spain, Pepe of Portugal and Marco "Mehmet" Aurélio of Turkey were joined at UEFA EURO 2008™ - in the absence of Croatia's injured Eduardo – by Poland's Roger Guerreiro. Having spent two seasons wooing the Polish public in the colours of Legia Warszawa, first as a Robert Carlos-style overlapping left-back, then as a Rivaldo-esque playmaker, Roger was granted Polish citizenship just in time for the nation's UEFA European Championship debut. Leo Beenhakker was delighted to have him on board, especially as he had just completed an excellent domestic campaign for Legia with a man-of-the-match performance against champions Wisła Kraków in the Polish Cup final. He was left on the bench for the opening game against Germany but made a significant impact as a substitute and was the most impressive player on the field, as well as his team's goalscorer, in the 1-1 draw against Austria four days later.

International Career

POLAND
Debut – 27/5/08 v Albania (n, Reutlingen, friendly), won 1-0
First Goal – 12/6/08 v Austria (a, Vienna, ECF), drew 1-1
Caps 5; Goals 1
Major Tournaments - UEFA EURO 2008™

Club Career

Major Honours – Polish Championship (2006); Polish Cup (2008)
Clubs: 98-02 AD São Caetano (BRA); 02-03 SC Corinthians (BRA); 04 CR Flamengo (BRA); 04 RC Celta de Vigo (ESP); 05 EC Juventude (BRA); 06- Legia Warszawa

Roque SANTA CRUZ
Striker
Born 16/8/81, Asuncion, Paraguay
Height 189cm, Weight 80kg

In 2006/07, it was Benni McCarthy. In 2007/08, Blackburn Rovers FC found a new goalscoring hero in Roque Santa Cruz. The South African scored 18 goals in his Premier League debut season. The big Paraguayan did even better, five goals in the last five games hoisting his tally to 19 (while McCarthy managed just eight). No fewer than 13 of them were scored away from home, including a hat-trick at Lancashire rivals Wigan Athletic FC (which Rovers lost 5-3), helping the club to finish seventh – just outside the European places. It was a tremendous performance from a player who had spent eight largely unsatisfactory seasons in and out of the first team – and the medical room - at FC Bayern München. He had collected plenty of honours at Bayern but never had he displayed such consistency in front of goal. At a cost of €4.5m, Blackburn had got themselves a bargain. With his large frame and aerial dominance, some might say that Santa Cruz is made for English football. But he is no lumbering centre-forward. His technique is refined, his movement clever and his application impeccable.

International Career

PARAGUAY
Debut – 28/4/99 v Mexico (h, Petro Juan Caballero, friendly), won 2-1
First Goal – 17/6/99 v Uruguay (h, Ciudad del Este, friendly), lost 2-3
Caps 61; Goals 20
Major Tournaments – Copa América 1999; FIFA World Cup 2002; FIFA World Cup 2006; Copa América 2007

Club Career

Major Honours – UEFA Champions League (2001); Paraguayan Championship (1997, 1998, 1999); German Championship (2000, 2001, 2003, 2005, 2006); German Cup (2000, 2003, 2005, 2006)
Clubs: 97-99 Club Olimpia; 99-07 FC Bayern München (GER); 07- Blackburn Rovers FC (ENG)

SEMIH Şentürk
Striker
Born 29/4/83, Izmir, Turkey
Height 183cm, Weight 79kg

Semih Şentürk scored Turkey's first and last goals at UEFA EURO 2008™, but the one that carried the heaviest weight was the second of his three - the last-gasp equaliser in the quarter-final against Croatia that preceded the team's successful penalty shoot-out, in which he found the net again with what turned out to be the winning spot-kick. Although Fatih Terim, the Turkey coach, preferred to use the 25-year-old striker as an impact substitute, Semih was very familiar with the role, having filled it for much of the 2007/08 season with his club side Fenerbahçe SK – a season in which his predatory instincts brought him 17 goals, the highest individual total in the Süper Lig. As a reward for his sudden burst of form at club level, Semih was handed his international debut in the crucial UEFA EURO 2008™ qualifier away to Norway. He did well enough to warrant another start in the next big game, at home to Bosnia-Herzegovina, four days later, and then a place in the squad at the finals, before which Fenerbahçe sensibly pre-empted the potential threat of a summer transfer by binding him to a new three-year contract.

International Career

TURKEY
Debut – 17/11/07 v Norway (a, Oslo, ECQ), won 2-1
First Goal – 29/5/08 v Finland (n, Duisburg, friendly), won 2-0
Caps 9; Goals 4
Major Tournaments – UEFA EURO 2008™

Club Career

Major Honours – Turkish Championship (2001, 2004, 2005, 2007)
Clubs: 99- Fenerbahçe SK; 01/02 İzmirspor (loan)

Marcos António SENNA da Silva
Midfielder
Born 17/7/76,
Rio de Janeiro, Brazil
Height 177cm,
Weight70kg

He only appeared once in the qualifying campaign, but at the UEFA EURO 2008™ finals Brazilian-born Marcos Senna gave the impression that he had been holding the fort in Spain's central midfield for years. His peerless contribution to the team's victory was appreciated by the UEFA Technical Committee who included him in their all-star selection. An omission was never likely as his performances were good enough for him to be considered as Player of the Tournament. While the other Spanish midfielders buzzed energetically around him, Senna rarely strayed from his central station, diligently protecting the defence, tackling hard to win possession and distributing the ball with tremendous accuracy and authority. He managed to get forward on occasion and came agonisingly close to scoring his first international goal against both Italy and Germany – though he did find the net emphatically with his penalty in the quarter-final shoot-out against the Azzurri. His form had been equally consistent all season long for Villarreal CF. He played a pivotal role in taking the small-town club to an unexpected runners-up spot in La Liga, dovetailing well with Frenchman Robert Pires.

International Career

SPAIN
Major Honours – UEFA European Championship (2008)
Debut – 1/3/06 v Ivory Coast (h, Valladolid, friendly), won 3-2
Caps 16; Goals 0
Major Tournaments - FIFA World Cup 2006; UEFA EURO 2008™

Club Career

Major Honours – FIFA Club World Cup (2000); Brazilian Championship (1999)
Clubs: 97-98 Rio Branco EC (BRA); 98 América CF (BRA); 99-01 SC Corinthians (BRA); 01 EC Juventude (BRA); 02 AD São Caetano (BRA); 02- Villarreal CF

SERGIO RAMOS García
Right-Back/
Centre-Back
Born 30/3/86,
Seville, Spain
Height 183cm,
Weight 73kg

One of only two Real Madrid CF players in Spain's UEFA EURO 2008™ squad, Sergio Ramos enjoyed an unforgettable season fc both club and country. Restored from the centre of defence to his regular right-back berth by new Real coach Bernd Schuster, the youngster was one of the most consistent performers in the club's second successive Spanish championship, mixing doggec defending with adventurous attacking. He also scored five goals including one apiece in three successive away games during the autumn. A powerful defender with tremendous agility and aeria power, he impressed at the 2006 FIFA World Cup, where he replaced Real team-mate Míchel Salgado as Spain's first-choice right-back, and started eleven of Spain's UEFA EURO 2008™ qualifiers. In Austria he made a hesitant start to the final tournament, at times overdosing on his forward gallops and neglecting his defensive duties, but he had an impressive game against Italy and finished the tournament strongly. At the troph celebrations after the final he sported a t-shirt honouring his former team-mate at Sevilla FC, Antonio Puerta, who died after collapsing on the field of play in the opening game of the Spanish season the previous August.

International Career

SPAIN
Major Honours – UEFA European Championship (2008)
Debut – 26/3/05 v China (h, Salamanca, friendly), won 3-0
First Goal – 13/10/05 v San Marino (a, Serravalle, WCQ), won 6-0
Caps 39; Goals 4
Major Tournaments - FIFA World Cup 2006; UEFA EURO 2008™

Club Career

Major Honours – Spanish Championship (2007, 2008)
Clubs: 02-05 Sevilla FC; 05- Real Madrid CF

Martin ŠKRTEĽ
Centre-Back
Born 15/12/84,
Handlova,
Slovakia
Height 191cm,
Weight 79kg

An aggressive, mean-looking centre-back, Martin Škrteľ was largely unheard of in England when he joined Liverpool FC fror Russian champions FC Zenit St. Petersburg in January 2008. He had a nervous debut at Anfield in an FA Cup tie against non-league side Havant & Waterlooville FC, but before long he was showing the Kop his true colours with a succession of dominant defensive displays, notably in the Merseyside derby against Everton FC and against Arsenal FC in the quarter-finals of the UEFA Champions League. The heir apparent to long-serving Finnish international Sami Hyypiä, Škrteľ was the defensive pilla of Zenit's 2007 Premier-Liga title triumph, his rock-solid displays persuading Liverpool manager Rafael Benítez to part with €8.3n for his services. A regular Slovakian international, the 23-year-ol stopper will doubtless be one of new coach Vladimír Weiss's key players in the 2010 FIFA World Cup qualifying campaign.

International Career

SLOVAKIA
Debut – 9/7/04 v Japan (a, Hiroshima, friendly), lost 1-3
First Goal – 2/9/06 v Cyprus (h, Bratislava, WCQ), won 6-1
Caps 25; Goals 4
Major Tournaments - none

Club Career

Major Honours – Russian Championship (2007)
Clubs: 01-04 AS Trenčín; 04-08 FC Zenit St. Petersburg (RUS); 08- Liverpool FC (ENG)

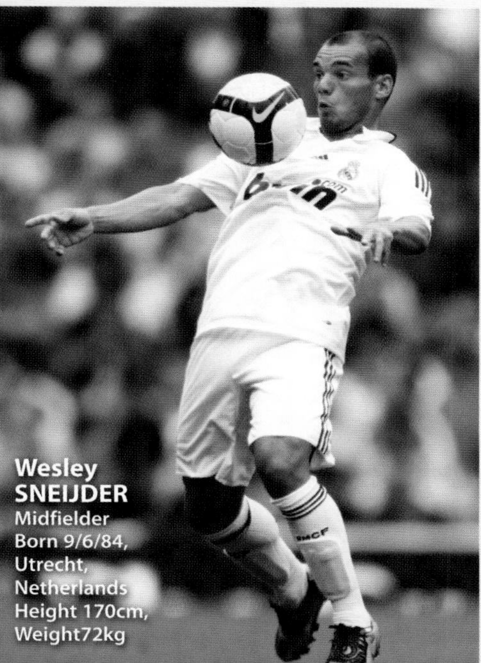

Wesley SNEIJDER
Midfielder
Born 9/6/84,
Utrecht,
Netherlands
Height 170cm,
Weight72kg

Recruited by Real Madrid CF from AFC Ajx for €27m in August 2007, Wesley Sneijder got off to an explosive start in La Liga, scoring four goals in his first three games and producing a master-class display in a 5-0 away win over Villarreal CF. The young Dutchman would go on to play a starring role in Real's Spanish title triumph, ending the campaign almost as well as he had started it, but even those who had admired his two-footed talent week in, week out in La Liga would have been taken back by the astonishing quality of his performances in the Netherlands' first two matches of UEFA EURO 2008™. Sneijder was voted Man of the Match in both of the two stunning victories over Italy (3-0) and France (4-1), capping each of his two supercharged displays with a brilliant goal. Although he was unable to scale such heights again in the quarter-final against Russia, he was one of the Netherlands' best players in the 3-1 defeat. A shoo-in for the Team of the Tournament, he will hope to be one of the Oranje's leading men in South Africa in 2010, but he looked destined to miss the first set of qualifiers – and the early part of the new season for Real – after suffering ligament damage in a pre-season friendly against Arsenal FC in London.

International Career

NETHERLANDS
Debut – 30/4/03 v Portugal (h, Eindhoven, friendly), drew 1-1
First Goal – 11/10/03 v Moldova (h, Eindhoven, ECQ), won 5-0
Caps 48; Goals 11
Major Tournaments – UEFA EURO 2004™; FIFA World Cup 2006; UEFA EURO 2008™

Club Career

Major Honours – Dutch Championship (2004); Spanish Championship (2008); Dutch Cup (2006, 2007)
Clubs: 02-07 AFC Ajax; 07- Real Madrid CF (ESP)

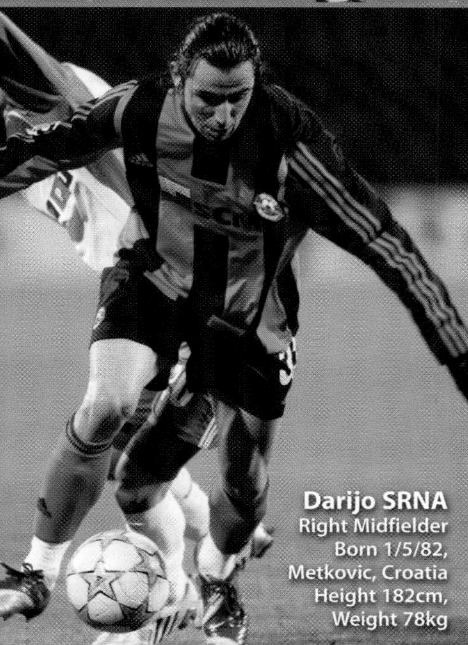

Darijo SRNA
Right Midfielder
Born 1/5/82,
Metkovic, Croatia
Height 182cm,
Weight 78kg

Darijo Srna was inconsolable after Croatia's cruel exit from UEFA EURO 2008™. The only player in Slaven Bilić's team to keep his cool and convert his penalty in the quarter-final shoot-out against Turkey, he had also been one of the team's most effective and exuberant players in regular play throughout the tournament. Pacy and penetrative on the right flank, he had a terrific first game against Austria and followed that up by giving Croatia the lead in their impressive 2-1 win over Germany. It was his 16th international goal, putting him in second place in the country's all-time top-scorer listings – albeit a long way behind 45-goal Davor Šuker. While Srna scores goals and gallops down the touchline at a good pace, it is the quality of his deliveries into the box, both on the run and from set plays, that marks him out as a special player. His dead-ball strikes on goal are also a significant attribute. FC Shakhtar Donetsk have been utilising Srna's talents for the past five years, and in 2007/08 he helped the club to a Ukrainian League and Cup double and into the group phase of the UEFA Champions League.

International Career

CROATIA
Debut – 20/11/02 v Romania (a, Timisoara, friendly), won 1-0
First Goal – 29/3/03 v Belgium (h, Zagreb, ECQ), won 4-0
Caps 58; Goals 16
Major Tournaments - UEFA EURO 2004™; FIFA World Cup 2006; UEFA EURO 2008™

Club Career

Major Honours – Croatian Championship (2001); Ukrainian Championship (2005, 2006, 2008); Croatian Cup (2003); Ukrainian Cup (2004, 2008)
Clubs: 99-03 HNK Hajduk Split; 03- FC Shakhtar Donetsk (UKR)

Ieroklis
STOLTIDIS
Midfielder
Born 2/2/75,
Kozani, Greece
Height 185cm,
Weight 86kg

Greece could have done with a midfielder of Ieroklis Stoltidis's quality at UEFA EURO 2008™, but having been ignored by his country for so long, the Olympiacos CFP playmaker's response to a belated call-up in February 2008 by coach Otto Rehhagel was to politely and graciously decline, using his age (33) and exhaustive workload at club level as the reasons for his decision. Stoltidis also added, with something of a heavy heart, that he would gladly have accepted the invitation had it come earlier in his career. Greece's loss, however, would be Olympiacos's gain as the skilful left-footer enjoyed the best of his five seasons at the club, winning the Greek League and Cup double and also playing a major part in engineering the Piraeus club's long awaited European breakthrough. It was he who scored the first of Olympiacos's three goals in the 3-1 victory at Werder Bremen that finally ended their 31-match run without an away win in the UEFA Champions League, he who provided the defence-splitting pass for team-mate Darko Kovačević to score the winner in their next away game against S.S. Lazio in Rome, and he who scored twice more against Bremen – and provided another assist for Kovačević - in the 3-0 home win that confirmed the Greek champions' qualification for the first knockout round.

International Career

GREECE
Debut – 13/11/99 v Nigeria (h, Kikes, friendly), won 2-0
Caps 6; Goals 0
Major Tournaments - none

Club Career

Major Honours – Greek Championship (2005, 2006, 2007, 2008); Greek Cup (2005, 2006, 2008)
Clubs: 91-92 Pontoi Kozanis FC; 92-03 Iraklis FC; 03- Olympiacos CFP

Václav
SVĚRKOŠ
Striker
Born 1/11/83
Height 183cm,
Weight 72kg

Now you see him, now you don't. Václav Svěrkoš came off the bench to score the winning goal for the Czech Republic in their opening game against Switzerland at UEFA EURO 2008™ - his first at international level – but, despite that heroic invention, was not used again. Whether he meant to slice the ball past Fabio Coltorti or just got lucky with a mishit, it seemed bizarre that Svěrkoš was not called upon against Portugal and Turkey. Perhaps coach Karel Brückner was saving him for the quarter-final that, because of Turkey's stunning late rally in Geneva, never came. Uncapped at the time of Brückner's squad announcement, the 24-year-old striker earned his call-up thanks to an outstanding season with FC Baník Ostrava, for whom he scored 15 goals to top the Czech 1. Liga scoring charts. It was his first season back at Baník, his first professional club, after four seasons of gradually declining fortunes and personal problems while abroad in Germany. Svěrkoš will hope that his goal in Basel is not forgotten by new Czech head coach Petr Rada, who was there in the dug-out to witness it at first hand as Brückner's assistant.

International Career

CZECH REPUBLIC
Debut – 27/5/08 v Lithuania (h, Prague, friendly), won 2-0
First Goal – 7/6/08 v Switzerland (a, Basel, ECF), won 1-0
Caps 3; Goals 1
Major Tournaments – UEFA EURO 2008™

Club Career

Major Honours – Austrian Cup (2007)
Clubs: 01-03 FC Baník Ostrava; 03-07 VfL Borussia Mönchengladbach (GER); 06 Hertha BSC Berlin (GER) (loan); 07 FK Austria Wien (AUT) (loan); 07- FC Baník Ostrava

Carlos Alberto TÉVEZ
Striker
Born 5/2/84, Buenos Aires, Argentina
Height 173cm, Weight 74kg

Having saved West Ham United FC from relegation in 2006/07 with the winning goal away to Manchester United FC on the final day of the season, Carlos Tévez was back at Old Trafford as a United player at the start of the 2007/08 campaign. He would find the place to his liking, scoring eleven league goals there (out of a total of 14) and another three (out of four) in the UEFA Champions League, including a spectacular diving header in the second leg of the quarter-final against AS Roma. The 24-year-old Argentine is not the quickest thing on two legs but his energy levels are outstanding, and his combination of skill, enterprise and tenacity is enough to keep even the smartest defenders on their toes for the full 90 minutes. While Tévez, like everyone else at United in 2007/08, played second fiddle to Cristiano Ronaldo, he outshone fellow striker Wayne Rooney for both consistency of performance and productivity and thoroughly deserved the two winner's medals that came his way in May.

International Career

ARGENTINA
Debut – 30/3/04 v Ecuador (h, Buenos Aires, WCQ), won 1-0
First Goal – 17/7/04 v Peru (a, Chiclayo, CA), won 1-0
Caps 40; Goals 7
Major Tournaments – Copa América 2004; FIFA Confederations Cup 2005; FIFA World Cup 2006; Copa América 2007

Club Career

Major Honours – UEFA Champions League (2008); Copa Libertadores (2005); World Club Cup (2003); Argentinian Championship (apertura 2003); Brazilian Championship (2005); English Premier League (2008)
Clubs: 01-04 CA Boca Juniors (ARG); 05-06 SC Corinthians (BRA); 06-07 West Ham United FC (ENG); 07- Manchester United FC (ENG)

Luca TONI
Striker
Born 26/5/77, Pavullo nel Frignano, Italy
Height 193cm, Weight 88kg

As debut seasons go, Luca Toni's at FC Bayern München was just about perfect. The €11m signing from ACF Fiorentina did everything he was bought to do, and then some. He helped Bayern to a German League and Cup double, and into the semi-finals of the UEFA Cup, by scoring 39 goals in 46 games. The 24 he struck in the Bundesliga earned him the title of Torschützenkönig (goal king), and his tally of ten in eleven games in the UEFA Cup, including two vital last-ditch efforts in the quarter-final at Getafe CF, earned him a joint-share of the top-scorer prize (with FC Zenit St. Petersburg's Pavel Pogrebnyak) in that competition too. The last two of his five German Cup goals came in the final – one in normal time, one in extra time – as Bayern overcame a spirited BV Borussia Dortmund 2-1 in Berlin's Olympiastadion (venue for his, and Italy's, FIFA World Cup triumph two years earlier) to complete their clean sweep of the domestic trophies (they also won the pre-season League Cup). Having given his all for Bayern, it was no surprise that Toni was not at his sharpest at UEFA EURO 2008™.

International Career

ITALY
Major Honours – FIFA World Cup (2006)
Debut – 18/8/04 v Iceland (a, Reykjavik, friendly), lost 0-2
First Goal – 4/9/04 v Norway (h, Palermo, WCQ), won 2-1
Caps 38; Goals 15
Major Tournaments – FIFA World Cup 2006; UEFA EURO 2008™

Club Career

Major Honours – German Championship (2008); German Cup (2008)
Clubs: 94-96 Modena FC; 96-97 Empoli FC; 97-98 US Fiorenzuola 1922; 98-99 AS Cisco Lodigiani; 99-00 Treviso FC; 00-01 Vicenza Calcio; 02-03 Brescia Calcio; 03-05 US Città di Palermo; 05-07 ACF Fiorentina; 07- FC Bayern München (GER)

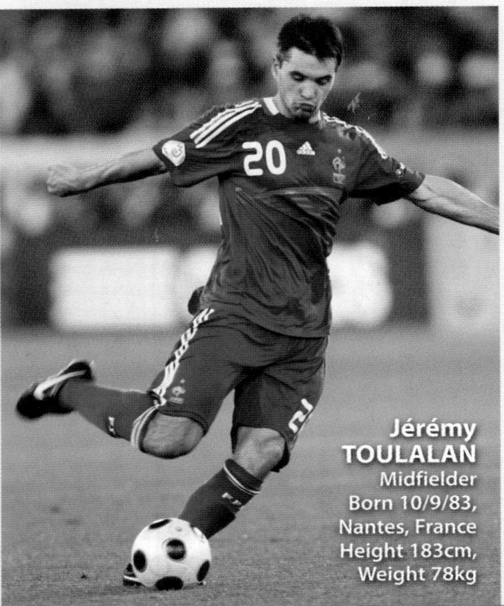

Jérémy TOULALAN
Midfielder
Born 10/9/83, Nantes, France
Height 183cm, Weight 78kg

With captain Patrick Vieira injured, Jérémy Toulalan played alongside Claude Makelele for France at UEFA EURO 2008™. Now, with the latter having taken his leave from the international stage, it could be that the Olympique Lyonnais midfielder will have the anchorman role all to himself during Les Bleus' assault on the 2010 FIFA World Cup in South Africa. Toulalan is one of those indefatigable, hard-working footballe that Éric Cantona might have termed a 'water carrier' – as he infamously described Didier Deschamps. The 25-year-old has long way to go before he can stand comparison with the ma who skippered France to World Cup and UEFA European Championship glory, but the way he conducts himself on the field is not dissimilar. He was one of Lyon's leading lights as they won the Ligue 1/Coupe de France double in 2007/08, appreciated just as much by coach Alain Perrin as he had bee by his predecessor Gérard Houllier. His talents were also recognised by his peers when he was chosen as one of four nominees in the Ligue 1 Player of the Year vote.

International Career

FRANCE
Debut – 11/10/06 v Faroe Islands (h, Montbeliard, ECQ), won 5-
Caps 16; Goals 0
Major Tournaments – UEFA EURO 2008™

Club Career

Major Honours – French Championship (2007, 2008); French C (2008)
Clubs: 01-06 FC Nantes Atlantique; 06- Olympique Lyonnais

David TREZEGUET
Striker
Born 15/10/77, Rouen, France
Height 186 cm, Weight 77kg

It can be safely assumed that David Trezeguet and Raymond Domenech, the head coach of France, do not get on. The Juventus striker scored 20 Serie A goals in 2007/08 – just one behind his team-mate at the top of the Serie A capocannonieri listings, Alessandro Del Piero – and was ready and willing to represent Les Bleus for the sixth time at a major tournament. B Domenech decided that he had enough quality strikers to take with him to UEFA EURO 2008™ and left Trezeguet out of his squad. A poor display in a friendly against England – when he stood in for the injured Karim Benzema - had not helped his case, and that would prove to be the 30-year-old's final appearance for his country. In July, after hearing that Domene had been retained, Trezeguet announced his international retirement. That could be good news for Juve, for whom the Frenchman has a long-term contract until 2011, which, if he se it through, will surely lead to many more club records over and above the one he currently holds as the highest-scoring foreigner ever to play for the Bianconeri, his cumulative tally having risen to 160 in 277 matches, all competitions included, the end of the 2007/08 season.

International Career

FRANCE
Major Honours – FIFA World Cup (1998); UEFA European Championship (2000)
Debut – 28/1/98 v Spain (h, Saint-Denis, friendly), won 1-0
First Goal – 5/6/98 v Finland (a, Helsinki, friendly), won 1-0
Caps 71; Goals 34
Major Tournaments - FIFA World Cup 1998; UEFA EURO 2000™; FIFA World Cup 2002; UEFA EURO 2004™; FIFA World Cup 2006

Club Career

Major Honours – French Championship (1997, 2000); Italian Championship (2002, 2003)
Clubs: 93-95 CA Platense (ARG); 95-00 AS Monaco FC; 00- Juventus (ITA)

Anatoliy TYMOSHCHUK
Midfielder
Born 30/3/79, Lutsk, Ukraine
Height 181cm, Weight 74kg

An impressive performer for Ukraine at the 2006 FIFA World Cup, Anatoliy Tymoshchuk was unable to steer his country to the finals of UEFA EURO 2008™ but he did command international acclaim for his outstanding performances in FC Zenit St. Petersburg's UEFA Cup triumph. A ten-year association with FC Shakhtar Donetsk ended when he joined Zenit for a club-record fee of around €12.7m in January 2007. It was seen as an expensive purchase at the time, but Tymoshchuk proved hugely influential as Zenit went on to win their first domestic title for 23 years. Coach Dick Advocaat saw in the long-haired midfield pivot an ideal captain, and it was the Ukrainian who lifted the UEFA Cup at the City of Manchester Stadium after his team's 2-0 victory over Rangers FC the following May. Nobody deserved it more. The qualifying round aside, he appeared from start to finish in all 15 matches – the only player to do so – and proved an inspirational leader. Disciplined, unfussy and modest, the 29-year-old Ukrainian does not actively seek fame, but with his recent successes for club and country, it is not something he can readily avoid.

International Career

UKRAINE
Debut – 26/4/00 v Bulgaria (a, Sofia, friendly), won 1-0
First Goal – 17/4/02 v Georgia (h, Kiev, friendly), won 2-1
Caps 77; Goals 1
Major Tournaments – FIFA World Cup 2006

Club Career

Major Honours – UEFA Cup (2008); Ukrainian Championship (2002, 2005, 2006); Russian Championship (2007); Ukrainian Cup (2001, 2002, 2004)
Clubs: 95-97 FC Volyn Lutsk; 97-07 FC Shakhtar Donetsk; 07- FC Zenit St. Petersburg (RUS)

Tomáš UJFALUŠI
Centre-Back/ Right-Back
Born 24/3/78, Rymarov, Czech Republic
Height 185cm, Weight 78kg

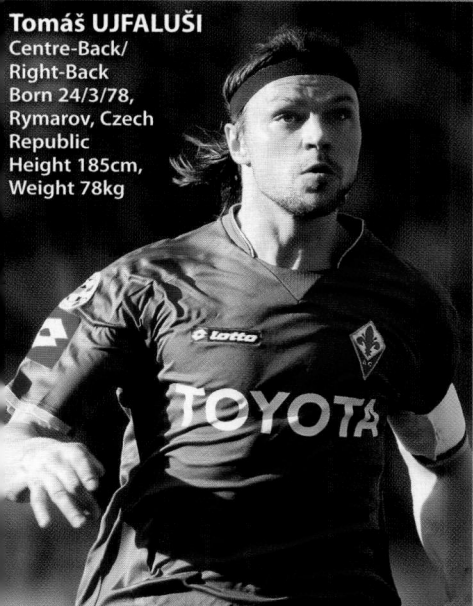

He has been one of European football's most consistent defenders in recent years, but Tomáš Ujfaluši, now 30, has yet to embellish his career with a major trophy. He came close in 2007/08 as ACF Fiorentina reached the semi-finals of the UEFA Cup, only to be eliminated in a penalty shoot-out by Rangers FC. The Czech international did his bit by helping the Viola defence keep clean sheets in both legs, but with the Rangers defence also holding firm, it came down to penalties – and a heartbreaking defeat. There was more suffering to come for Ujfaluši at UEFA EURO 2008™ as the Czech Republic crashed out to Turkey in the first round after looking set for the quarter-finals. The headband-wearing defender was assigned the captaincy following Tomáš Rosický's withdrawal and won the Man of the Match award in the opening game, against Switzerland. He left Italy for Spain in the summer but was still on course for a first appearance in the UEFA Champions League after joining Club Atlético de Madrid, who, like Fiorentina, finished fourth in their domestic league in 2007/08.

International Career

CZECH REPUBLIC
Debut – 28/2/01 v FYR Macedonia (a, Skopje, friendly), drew 1-1
First Goal – 6/9/02 v Yugoslavia (h, Prague, friendly), won 5-0
Caps 71; Goals 2
Major Tournaments - UEFA EURO 2004™; FIFA World Cup 2006; UEFA EURO 2008™

Club Career

Clubs: 96-00 SK Sigma Olomouc; 01-04 Hamburger SV (GER); 04-08 ACF Fiorentina (ITA); 08- Club Atlético de Madrid (ESP)

Edwin VAN DER SAR
Goalkeeper
Born 29/10/70, Voorhout, Netherlands
Height 197cm, Weight 84kg

Thirteen years after winning the UEFA Champions League with AFC Ajax, Edwin van der Sar had his hands on European club football's most coveted piece of silverware for a second time. It w his priceless penalty save from Chelsea FC's Nicolas Anelka that gave Manchester United FC victory over their Premier League riva in the small hours of a Russian Thursday morning in Moscow. The Dutchman was troubled by a groin injury for much of the season but he invariably found his best form when it mattered, concedin only four goals in ten UEFA Champions League matches and non at Old Trafford. Having agreed to remain with United for one mor year, the 37-year-old will be bidding for a Premier League hat-tric in 2008/09. His days as a Dutch international are now over, but he bowed out on a high with some brilliant performances at UEFA EURO 2008™ - his seventh and last major tournament. Even his defiance was unable to stop Russia winning an epic quarter-final, but while he never won a trophy with the Oranje, his final tally of 128 caps is a national record. His 16 appearances at the UEFA European Championship finals is also a tournament record, whic he shares with another post-UEFA EURO 2008™ retiree, Lilian Thuram of France.

International Career

NETHERLANDS
Debut – 7/6/95 v Belarus (a, Minsk, ECQ), lost 0-1
Caps 128; Goals 0
Major Tournaments - FIFA World Cup 1994; UEFA EURO '96; FIF World Cup 1998; UEFA EURO 2000™; UEFA EURO 2004™; FIFA World Cup 2006; UEFA EURO 2008™

Club Career

Major Honours – UEFA Champions League (1995, 2008); UEFA Super Cup (1996); World Club Cup (1995); Dutch Championshi (1994, 1995, 1996, 1998); English Premier League (2007, 2008); Dutch Cup (1993, 1998, 1999); English League Cup (2006)
Clubs: 90-99 AFC Ajax; 99-01 Juventus (ITA); 01-05 Fulham FC (ENG); 05- Manchester United FC (ENG)

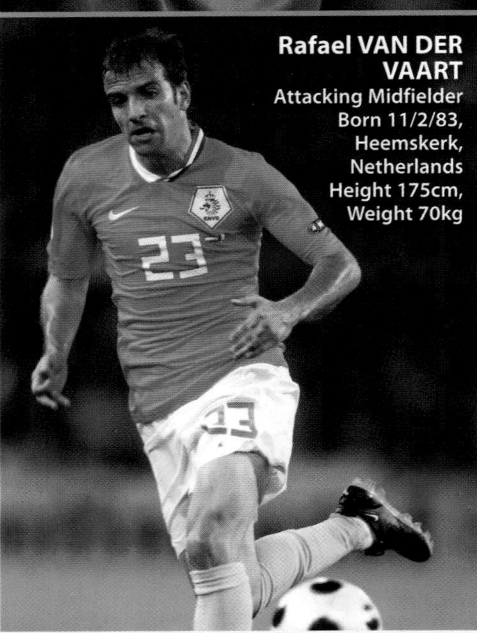

Rafael VAN DER VAART
Attacking Midfielder
Born 11/2/83, Heemskerk, Netherlands
Height 175cm, Weight 70kg

Rafael van der Vaart finally got the move to Spain that many ha been predicting for years when he left Hamburger SV for Real Madrid CF in the summer. He has swelled an already sizeable Dutch contingent at the Bernabéu – Wesley Sneijder, Ruud van Nistelrooy, Royston Drenthe and Arjen Robben - and should fe just as comfortable there as he did at Hamburg, where he had fellow countrymen Joris Mathijsen and Nigel de Jong for company. Van der Vaart's third and last season at Hamburg was just as impressive as the previous two. An enthusiastic captain, he led the team to fourth place in the Bundesliga, scoring 12 goals and providing countless assists. UEFA EURO 2008™ prove to be by far the most memorable of his three major tournaments to date. Like the rest of the Dutch team, he was n at his best against Russia, but he played a major role in the big wins against Italy and France, his sure-footed, penetrative passing contributing to two gala performances by Marco van Basten's team. Van der Vaart should be a star in Spain; his beautiful actress/TV presenter wife Sylvie no doubt too.

International Career

NETHERLANDS
Debut – 6/10/01 v Andorra (h, Arnhem, WCQ), won 4-0
First Goal – 6/9/03 v Austria (h, Rotterdam, ECQ), won 3-1
Caps 58; Goals 12
Major Tournaments - UEFA EURO 2004™; FIFA World Cup 2006; UEFA EURO 2008™

Club Career

Major Honours – Dutch Championship (2002, 2004); Dutch Cu (2002)
Clubs: 00-05 AFC Ajax; 05-08 Hamburger SV (GER); 08- Real Madrid CF (ESP)

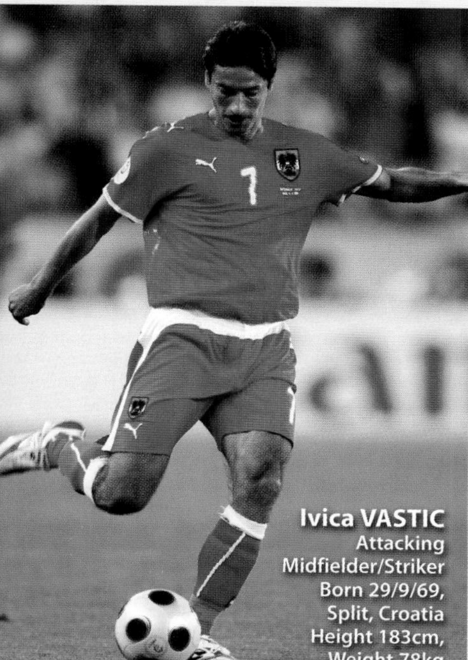

Ivica VASTIC
Attacking Midfielder/Striker
Born 29/9/69, Split, Croatia
Height 183cm, Weight 78kg

Ivica Vastic's return to the Austrian national team, after nearly three years away and at the age of 38, was a major surprise, but the oldest player at UEFA EURO 2008™ did not look out of place at all – or, indeed, his age. He was introduced as a substitute – to the noisy acclaim of the Viennese public – in each of Austria's first two matches, against Croatia and Poland, and had a major impact in both, adding a touch of finesse and composure to the team's attacking play. He even celebrated his 50th international by scoring the last-minute equalising penalty against Poland that kept alive the co-hosts' hopes of reaching the quarter-finals. It proved to be Austria's only goal of the tournament, which rather begged the question why coach Josef Hickersberger chose not to send him on again in the do-or-die final group game against Germany. Vastic's recall was the consequence of a superb season in the Austrian Bundesliga with LASK Linz. He had scored 42 goals for the club in two second division campaigns and maintained his form back in the top flight, scoring 13 times in 32 games – the third highest goal-tally in the league - and captaining the team to a respectable sixth place. It was supposed to be the final season of his career, but he enjoyed it so much that he signed on for another.

International Career

AUSTRIA
Debut – 27/3/96 v Switzerland (h, Vienna, friendly), won 1-0
First Goal – 30/4/97 v Estonia (h, Vienna, WCQ), won 2-0
Caps 50; Goals 14
Major Tournaments - FIFA World Cup 1998; UEFA EURO 2008™

Club Career

Major Honours – Austrian Championship (1998, 1999); Austrian Cup (1996, 1997, 1999)
Clubs: 89-91 RNK Split (CRO); 91-92 First Vienna FC; 92-93 VSE St Pölten; 93-94 FC Admira Wacker; 94 MSV Duisburg (GER); 94-02 SK Sturm Graz; 02-03 Nagoya Grampus 8 (JPN); 03-05 FK Austria Wien; 05- LASK Linz

Nemanja VIDIĆ
Centre-Back
Born 21/10/81, Titovo Uzice, Serbia
Height 188cm, Weight 84kg

Nemanja Vidić is the archetypal no-nonsense defender, but if he is hard, he is also fair, receiving only five yellow cards in 32 Premier League outings in 2007/08. His central-defensive partnership with Rio Ferdinand has developed into the best in England and, by extension – given United's success also in the UEFA Champions League – perhaps the best in Europe, too. The 26-year-old Serbian international was absent through injury for both legs of the UEFA Champions League semi-final against FC Barcelona, but after sitting through that tie as a nervous bystander, he returned for the final and renewed a long-standing feud with Didier Drogba, the outcome of which was a red card late in the game for the Chelsea FC striker after he slapped his adversary in the face. As a proud Serb, Vidić will be keen to make up for recent disappointments at international level by helping Miroslav Đukić's young side steer a course towards the 2010 FIFA World Cup in South Africa – a country he visited for the first time in the summer on a pre-season tour with his club.

International Career

SERBIA
Debut – 12/10/02 v Italy (a, Naples, ECQ), drew 1-1
First Goal – 15/8/05 v Poland (n, Kiev, friendly), lost 2-3
Caps 31; Goals 2
Major Tournaments – FIFA World Cup 2006

Club Career

Major Honours – UEFA Champions League (2008); Serbo-Montenegrin Championship (2004); English Premier League (2007, 2008); Yugoslav Cup (2002); Serbo-Montenegrin Cup (2004); English League Cup (2006)
Clubs: 00-04 FK Crvena Zvezda; 00/01 FK Spartak Subotica (loan); 04-06 FK Spartak Moskva (RUS); 06- Manchester United FC (ENG)

VOLKAN Demirel
Goalkeeper
Born 27/10/81, Istanbul, Turkey
Height 191cm, Weight 92kg

Volkan Demirel's reputation for being brilliant but erratic sprea from Turkey to the rest of Europe during a season in which his profile was raised internationally – firstly by his club Fenerbahç SK's odds-defying run to the quarter-finals of the UEFA Champions League, then by his appearance for Turkey at UEFA EURO 2008™. The 26-year-old goalkeeper finally emerged from the shadow of Rüştü Reçber at Fenerbahçe when the veteran international 'keeper left for Beşiktaş in the summer of 2007. He made the most of the opportunity, especially in Europe, where he played in all ten group and knockout games, taking centre stage in the last-16 elimination of Sevilla FC, when, after gifting couple of early goals to the Spanish side in the second leg, he redeemed himself by saving three penalties. He was Turkey's fi choice, ahead of Rüştü, at UEFA EURO 2008™, but after a brillia display against Switzerland, he foolishly got himself sent off at the end of the next game, just after his team had completed a astonishing comeback against the Czech Republic, and picked up a two-match ban, enabling Rüştü to step in and become th penalty shoot-out hero in the quarter-final against Croatia.

International Career

TURKEY
Debut – 28/4/04 v Belgium (a, Brussels, friendly), won 3-2
Caps 24; Goals 0
Major Tournaments – UEFA EURO 2008™

Club Career

Major Honours – Turkish Championship (2004, 2005, 2007)
Clubs: 00-02 Kartalspor; 02- Fenerbahçe SK

XAVI Hernández
Midfielder
Born 25/1/80, Terrassa, Spain
Height 170cm, Weight 68kg

After a season of disorder and decay at his beloved FC Barcelona, Xavi Hernández revelled in the all-for-one, one-for all atmosphere prevalent in the Spanish camp at UEFA EURO 2008™. He played consistently well throughout the tournament, hunting for the ball, stringing moves together a clocking up vast distances with his perpetual motion. A goalscorer in the semi-final against Russia, he was surprising substituted soon afterwards, but in the final, on Spain's night nights, he had the game of his life, dominating the midfield almost single-handedly, taking responsibility for all of his team's set-pieces, and supplying Fernando Torres with the perfectly weighted angled pass that led to the game's winnir goal. With that brilliant performance fresh in their mind, the UEFA Technical Committee voted Xavi as the official Player of the Tournament. The 28-year-old will still be in his prime for t 2010 FIFA World Cup, but before then he will hope to get Barcelona back on track. With his fellow Catalan Pep Guardio who once played in a similar pivotal midfield role for the club now in charge, Xavi is certain to be a major figure as the club attempt to return to power in Spain and beyond.

International Career

SPAIN
Major Honours – UEFA European Championship (2008)
Debut – 15/11/00 v Netherlands (h, Seville, friendly), lost 1-2
First Goal – 26/3/05 v China (h, Salamanca, friendly), won 3-0
Caps 63; Goals 8
Major Tournaments - FIFA World Cup 2002; UEFA EURO 2004™; FIFA World Cup 2006; UEFA EURO 2008™

Club Career

Major Honours – UEFA Champions League (2006); Spanish Championship (1999, 2005, 2006)
Clubs: 97- FC Barcelona

Hakan YAKIN
Attacking Midfielder
Born 22/2/77, Basel, Switzerland
Height 180cm, Weight 77kg

Switzerland scored three goals at UEFA EURO 2008™. So did their veteran playmaker, Hakan Yakin. The popular 31-year-old put the tournament co-hosts ahead – with the aid of a goalmouth puddle – against the country of his ancestors, Turkey, then notched both goals, one from the penalty spot, en route to a Man of the Match award in the 2-0 win over Portugal that afforded departing coach Köbi Kuhn a winning send-off. Yakin had been given his chance to shine as a result of the injuries sustained by Switzerland's two first-choice strikers, Alexander Frei and Marco Streller. The skilful left-footer was in prime goalscoring form going into the tournament, having topped the Swiss Superleague charts with 24 goals for BSC Young Boys. Renowned more for his individual skill and set-piece expertise than his leadership qualities, he was nevertheless handed the club captaincy at the start of the season by coach Martin Andermatt. It proved an inspired move as Yakin led the Berne team to an unexpected second place behind FC Basel 1893.

International Career

SWITZERLAND
Debut – 19/2/00 v Oman (a, Muscat, friendly), won 4-1
First Goal - 19/2/00 v Oman (a, Muscat, friendly), won 4-1
Caps 69; Goals 18
Major Tournaments - UEFA EURO 2004™; FIFA World Cup 2006; UEFA EURO 2008™

Club Career

Major Honours – Swiss Championship (1998, 2001, 2002, 2004); Swiss Cup (2002, 2003)
Clubs: 93-95 FC Concordia Basel; 95-97 FC Basel 1893; 97 Grasshopper-Club; 98 FC St Gallen; 99-00 Grasshopper-Club; 01-03 FC Basel 1893; 03-04 VfB Stuttgart (GER); 05 Galatasaray AŞ (TUR) (loan); 05-08 BSC Young Boys; 08- Al-Gharafa SC (QAT)

Javier ZANETTI
Right-Back/ Midfielder
Born 10/8/73, Buenos Aires, Argentina
Height178 cm, Weight 73kg

He has been at FC Internazionale Milano for 13 years and captained the club for the last nine. Javier Zanetti is a modern-day Inter legend, of that there is no doubt, and in 2007/08 he skippered the Nerazzurri to their third successive Serie A title. Relocated from full-back to midfield, the little Argentine revelled in the new role, whether on the right flank or through the centre, and was the only Inter player to appear in all 38 league games, all but three of them from the start. Il Capitano epitomised the drive and determination that carried the team to the top of the table and kept them there through to the end. He scored just one goal all season but it was probably Inter's most important – the late equaliser against closest rivals AS Roma in the San Siro at the end of February that earned a 1-1 draw and preserved the club's unbeaten record. Zanetti has played for his country even longer than for his club, and in November 2007 he became Argentina's most-capped international.

International Career

ARGENTINA
Debut – 16/11/94 v Chile (a, Santiago, friendly), won 3-0
First Goal – 22/6/95 v Slovakia (h, Mendoza, friendly), won 6-0
Caps 122; Goals 5
Major Tournaments – Copa América 1995, FIFA World Cup 1998; Copa América 1999; FIFA World Cup 2002; Copa América 2004; FIFA Confederations Cup 2005; Copa América 2007

Club Career

Major Honours – UEFA Cup (1998); Italian Championship (2006, 2007, 2008); Italian Cup (2005, 2006)
Clubs: 92-93 CA Talleres; 93-95 CA Banfield; 95- FC Internazionale Milano (ITA)

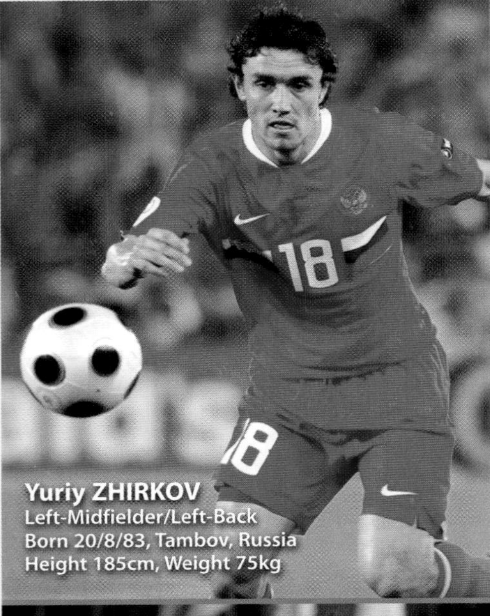

Yuriy ZHIRKOV
Left-Midfielder/Left-Back
Born 20/8/83, Tambov, Russia
Height 185cm, Weight 75kg

A tricky left-winger once dubbed the 'Russian Ronaldinho' by the Moscow press as a tribute to his elaborate ball skills, Yuriy Zhirko played at left-back for Russia at UEFA EURO 2008™ and performed so well in the role that he was included in the official Team of the Tournament. Russia coach Guus Hiddink had always admired the PFC CSKA Moskva player's willingness to play for th team and track back when necessary, so in the final warm-up games before the tournament he switched him into defence. It proved to be an inspired move. With Sergei Semak reintroduced as a holding midfielder, Zhirkov's natural attacking instincts, and those of fellow full-back Aleksandr Anyukov, allowed Russia to play in a more expansive style. The result was thrilling to watch as, against the odds, Hiddink's team of entertainers knocked out Greece, Sweden and the Netherlands and reached the semi-final A UEFA Cup winner in 2005, Zhirkov won his third Russian Cup in four years with CSKA in 2008, stepping up to take the first penal in their shoot-out victory over FC Amkar Perm in the final.

International Career

RUSSIA
Debut – 9/2/05 v Italy (a, Cagliari, friendly), lost 0-2
Caps 24; Goals 0
Major Tournaments – UEFA EURO 2008™

Club Career

Major Honours – UEFA Cup (2005); Russian Championship (2005 2006); Russian Cup (2005, 2006, 2008)
Clubs: 01-03 FC Spartak Tambov; 04- PFC CSKA Moskva

Konstantin ZYRYANOV
Midfielder
Born 5/10/77, Perm, Russia
Height 176cm, Weight 72kg

Konstantin Zyryanov cemented his delayed coming of age as a world-class midfielder at UEFA EURO 2008™. The 30-year-old wa the elegant, unflustered central controller of Russia's imperious one-touch, pass-and-move football that all opponents bar Spai the eventual champions, found impossible to withstand. Under rated and largely undiscovered before he left relegated FC Torpedo Moskva for FC Zenit St. Petersburg at the start of the 2007 season, Zyryanov drew widespread acclaim with a series c outstanding performances, and goals, nine in total, during Zenit's run to the Russian Premier-Liga title. For his sudden rise to prominence, he was duly voted 2007 Russian Footballer of th Year. There would be more to come from him and his club in Europe as Zenit saw off a host of big-name opponents, includin FC Bayern München, to reach the 2008 UEFA Cup final in Manchester, where Zyryanov capped a classy all-round performance with a late second goal in the team's 2-0 win over Rangers FC. He also found the net at UEFA EURO 2008™, scorin the winner against Greece, and joined three other Russians in the official Team of the Tournament. For club and country in 2007/08 Zyryanov lived the impossible dream, giving hope to unheralded thirtysomething footballers everywhere.

International Career

RUSSIA
Debut – 27/5/06 v Spain (a, Albacete, friendly), drew 0-0
First Goal – 23/5/08 v Kazakhstan (h, Moscow, friendly), won 6-0
Caps 17; Goals 3
Major Tournaments – UEFA EURO 2008™

Club Career

Major Honours – UEFA Cup (2008); Russian Championship (200
Clubs: 94-00 FC Amkar Perm; 00-07 FC Torpedo Moskva; 07- FC Zenit St. Petersburg

GRAPHIC GUIDE

UEFA COMPETITION PARTICIPANTS 2008/09

This section contains national federation crests, international kits, club badges for the participants of UEFA competitions and maps for all 53 UEFA member associations.

Key to country pages

◯	UEFA Champions League	©	champions
◯	UEFA Cup	*	domestic Cup winners
◯	UEFA Intertoto Cup	**	(qualified as) domestic Cup runners-up
◯	Clubs in top division	***	(qualified as) domestic League Cup winners
◯	Promoted Clubs	****	Fair Play qualifiers

UEFA MEMBER ASSOCIATIONS

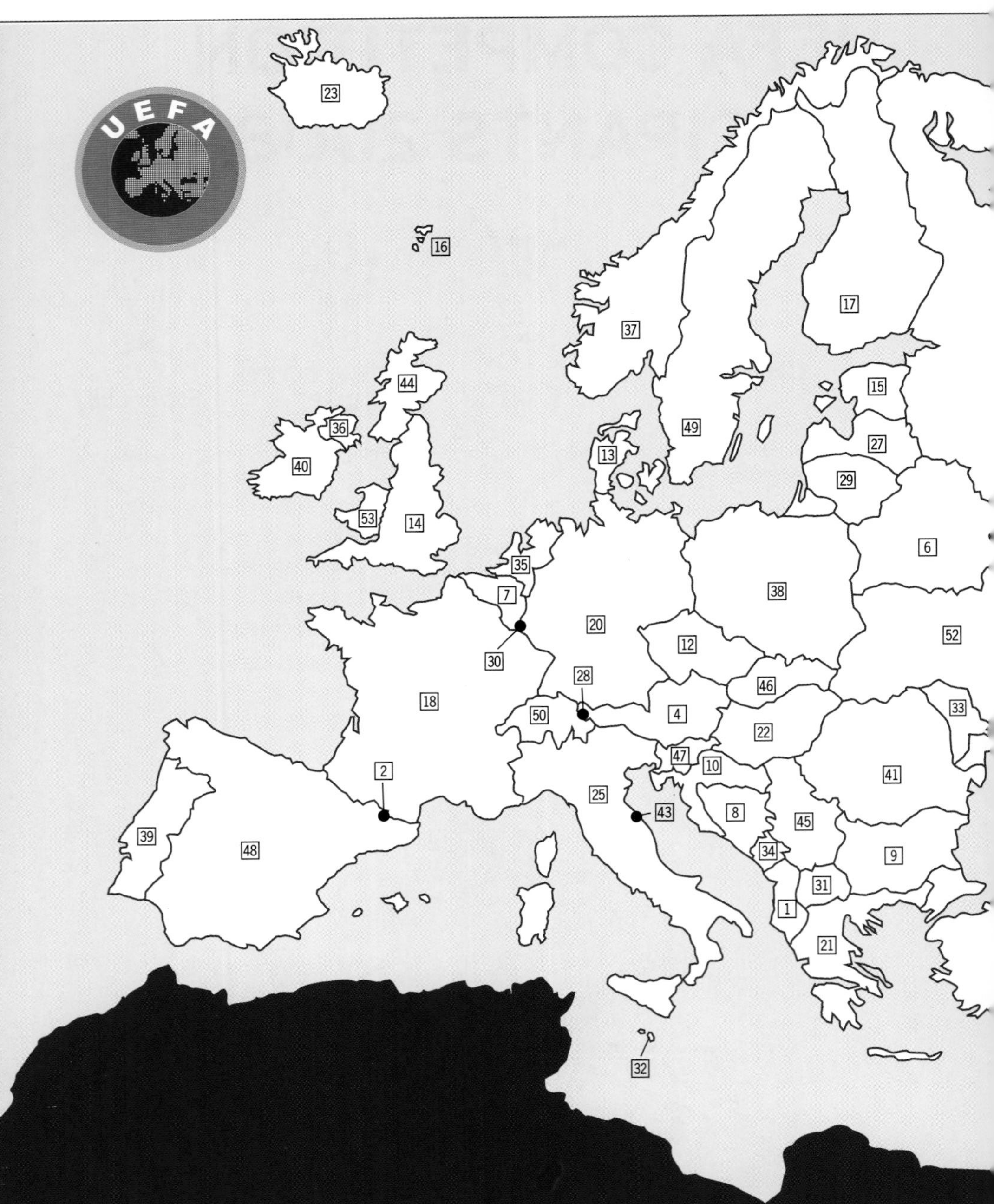

Graphic Guide Index

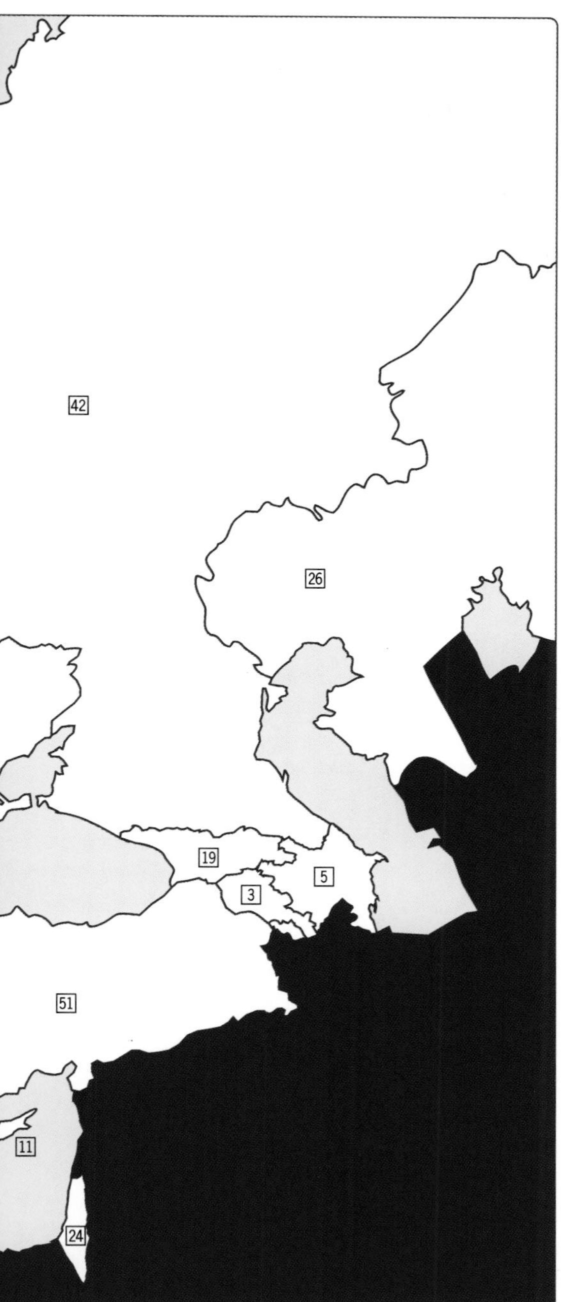

ALBANIA

FEDERATION

HOME INTERNATIONAL KIT

AWAY INTERNATIONAL KIT

K.F. VLLAZNIA 1919

SHKODËR (12)

LEZHË (2)

KRUJË (6)

FOOTBALL CLUB DINAMO 1950

FK PARTIZANI TIRANË 1946

TIRANË (3) (7) (11)
(TIRANA)

(10) DURRËS

(1) KAVAJË

1922 KS BESA

ELBASAN (4)

PEQIN (8)

(14) FIER

LUSHNJË (15)

KORÇË (9)

BALLSH (13)

VLORË (5)

0 — 50 — 100 km

0 — 50 miles

TOP DIVISION CLUBS

1. **KS Besa** *no website* (UEFA Intertoto Cup)
2. **KS Besëlidhja** *no website*
3. **KS Dinamo Tirana** © *no website* (UEFA Champions League)
4. **KS Elbasani** *no website*
5. **KS Flamurtari** *no website*
6. **KS Kastrioti** *no website*
7. **FK Partizani** *partizani.al* (UEFA Cup)
8. **KS Shkumbini** *no website*
9. **KS Skënderbeu** *no website*
10. **KS Teuta** *no website*
11. **KF Tirana** *no website*
12. **KS Vllaznia** * *vllaznia.eu* (UEFA Cup)

PROMOTED CLUBS

13. **KS Bylis** *no website*
14. **KS Apolonia** *no website*
15. **KS Lushnja** *no website*

FEDERATION

HOME INTERNATIONAL KIT

AWAY INTERNATIONAL KIT

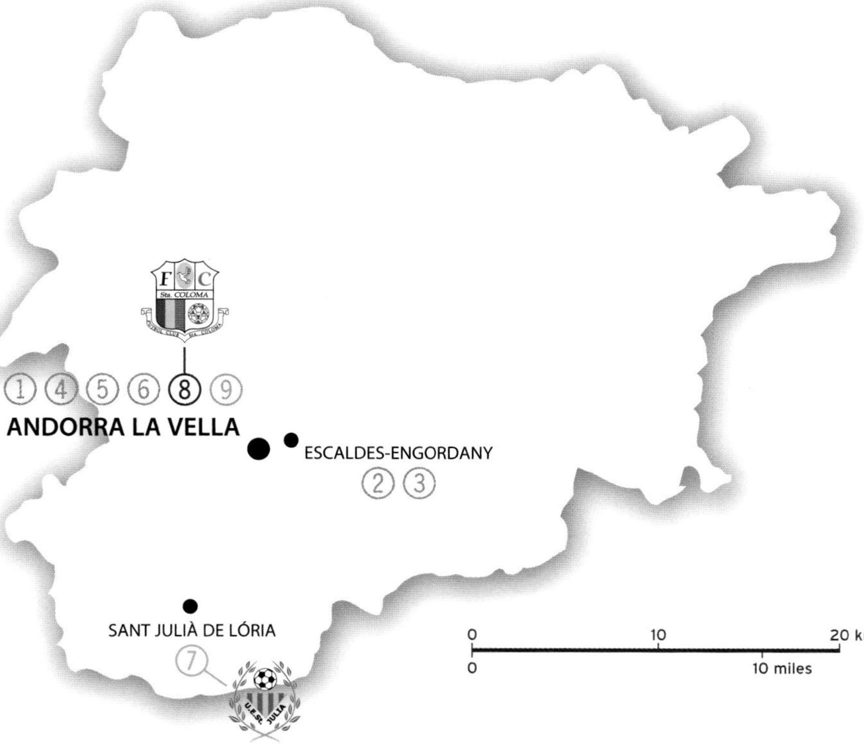

1 4 5 6 8 9

ANDORRA LA VELLA

ESCALDES-ENGORDANY

2 3

SANT JULIÀ DE LÓRIA

7

0 10 20 km

0 10 miles

TOP DIVISION CLUBS

1 **FC Casa Benfica**
no website

2 **UE Engordany**
no website

3 **Inter Club d'Escaldes**
no website

4 **FC Lusitans**
no website

5 **CE Principat**
ceprincipat.com

6 **FC Rànger's**
no website

7 **UE Sant Julià** *
no website

8 **FC Santa Coloma** ©
fcsantacoloma.com

PROMOTED CLUB

9 **UE Santa Coloma**
no website

ARMENIA

FEDERATION

HOME INTERNATIONAL KIT

AWAY INTERNATIONAL KIT

GYUMRI (7)

YEREVAN (1) (2) (4) (5) (6) (8)

(3) KAPAN

0 50 100 km

0 50 miles

TOP DIVISION CLUBS

(1) **FC Ararat Yerevan** * *fcararat.am*	(5) **FC MIKA** *no website*
(2) **FC Banants** *fcbanants.com*	(6) **FC Pyunik** © *fcpyunik.am*
(3) **FC Gandzasar Kapan** *no website*	(7) **FC Shirak** *fcshirak.8m.net*
(4) **FC Kilikia** *no website*	(8) **FC Ulisses Yerevan** *no website*

AUSTRIA

FEDERATION

HOME INTERNATIONAL KIT

AWAY INTERNATIONAL KIT

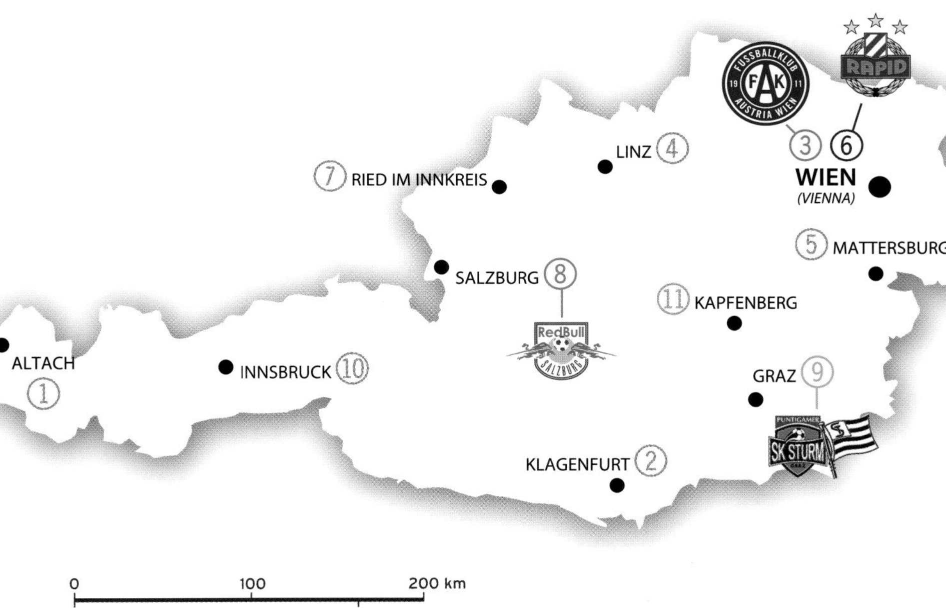

0 100 200 km

0 100 miles

TOP DIVISION CLUBS

1. SCR Altach
   scra.at
2. SK Austria Kärnten
   sk-austriakaernten.at
3. FK Austria Wien
   fk-austria.at
4. LASK Linz
   lask.at
5. SV Mattersburg
   svm.at
6. SK Rapid Wien ©
   skrapid.at
7. SV Ried
   svried.at
8. FC Salzburg
   redbulls.com
9. SK Sturm Graz
   sksturm.at
10. FC Wacker Innsbruck
    fc-wacker-innsbruck.at

PROMOTED CLUB

11. Kapfenberger SV
    ksv-fussball.at

AZERBAIJAN

FEDERATION HOME INTERNATIONAL KIT AWAY INTERNATIONAL KIT

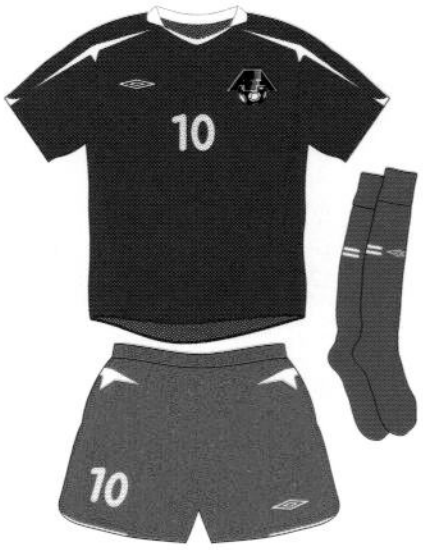

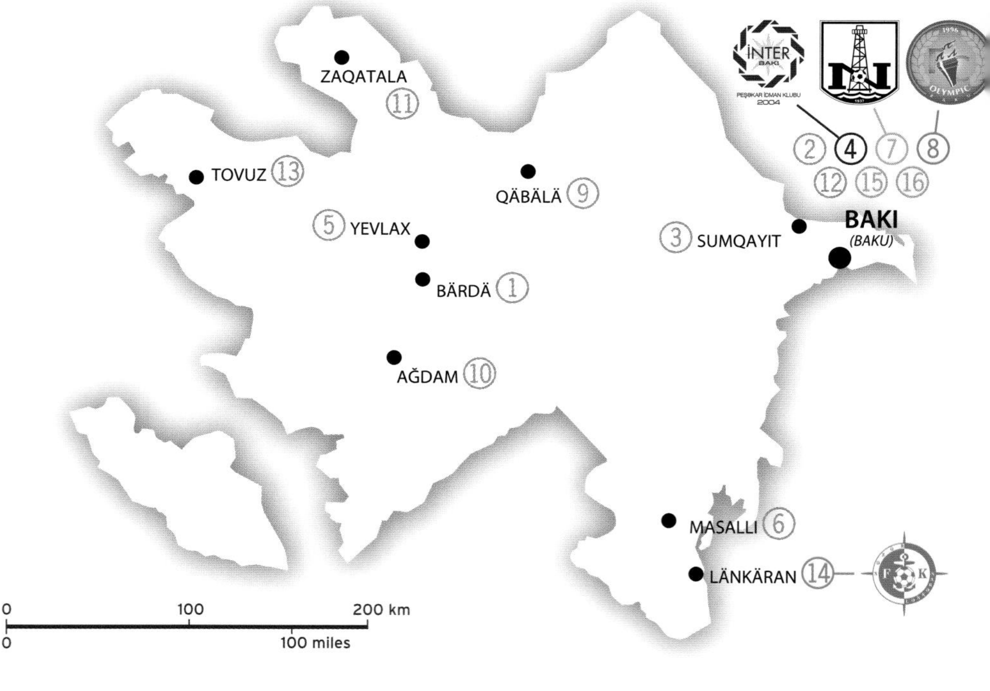

ZAQATALA (11)
TOVUZ (13)
QĀBĀLĀ (9)
(5) YEVLAX
(3) SUMQAYIT
BAKI (BAKU)
BÄRDÄ (1)
AĞDAM (10)
MASALLI (6)
LÄNKÄRAN (14)
(2) (4) (7) (8) (12) (15) (16)

0 100 200 km
0 100 miles

TOP DIVISION CLUBS

1. **FK ABN Bärdä** *no website*
2. **FK Bakı** *bakifc.com*
3. **PFK Gänclärbirliyi** *no website*
4. **PİK İnter Bakı** © *inter.az*
5. **İK Karvan** *karvan.az*
6. **FK Masallı** *no website*
7. **PFK Neftçi** *neftchipfc.com*
8. **FK Olimpik Bakı** *no website*
9. **PFK Qäbälä** *gabalafc.az*
10. **FK Qarabağ** *qarabagh.com*
11. **PFK Simurq** *simurqpfk.com*
12. **FK Standard Bakı** *standard-fc.az*
13. **PFK Turan** *no website*
14. **FK Xäzär Länkäran** * *lankaranfc.com*

PROMOTED CLUBS

15. **PFK Bakılı Bakı** *bakili-fclub.com*
16. **PFK MOİK Bakı** *no website*

FEDERATION HOME INTERNATIONAL KIT AWAY INTERNATIONAL KIT

0 100 200 km
0 100 miles

NOVOPOLOTSK 9
VITEBSK 14
SMORGON 12
1 BORISOV
5 15 MOGILEV
2 ZHDANOVICHI
MINSK
ZHODINO 13
GRODNO 10
4 7 8 17
SOLIGORSK
11
6 GOMEL
BREST 3
16 MIKASHEVICHI

TOP DIVISION CLUBS

1. **FC BATE Borisov** © — *fcbate.by*
2. **FC Darida Zhdanovichi** — *fcdarida.ucoz.ru*
3. **FC Dinamo Brest** — *dynamo.brest.by*
4. **FC Dinamo Minsk** — *dinamo-minsk.com*
5. **FC Dnepr Mogilev** — *no website*
6. **FC Gomel** — *fcgomel.by*
7. **FC Minsk** — *no website*
8. **FC MTZ-RIPO Minsk** * — *mtz-ripo.by*
9. **FC Naftan Novopolotsk** — *fcnaftan.com*
10. **FC Neman Grodno** — *fcneman.com*
11. **FC Shakhtyor Soligorsk** — *fcshakhter.by*
12. **FC Smorgon** — *no website*
13. **FC Torpedo Zhodino** — *tarpeda.zhodzina.info*
14. **FC Vitebsk** — *fc.vitebsk.by*

PROMOTED CLUBS

15. **FC Savit Mogilev** — *no website*
16. **FC Granit Mikashevichi** — *no website*
17. **FC Lokomotiv Minsk** — *no website*

FEDERATION

HOME INTERNATIONAL KIT

AWAY INTERNATIONAL KIT

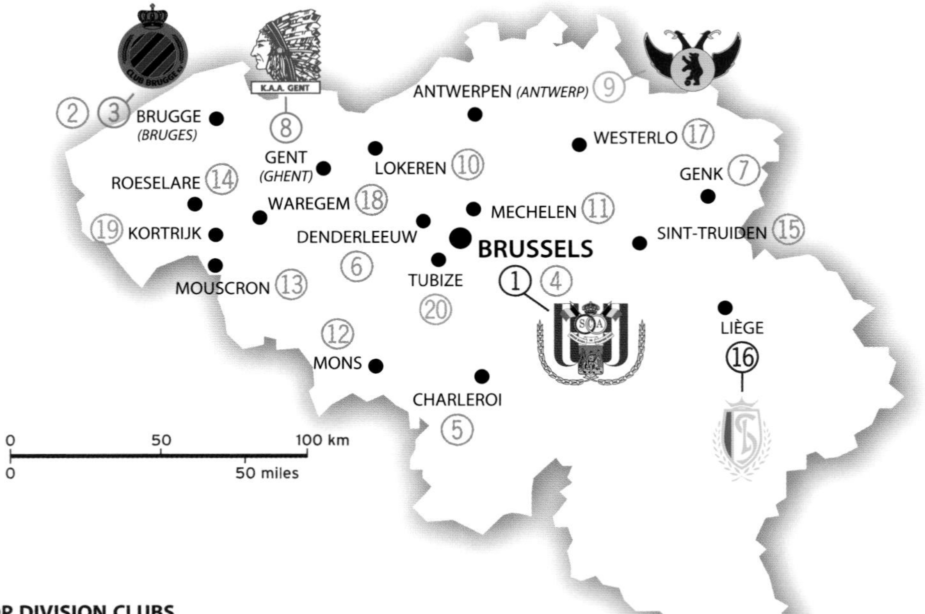

BRUGGE (BRUGES) ② ③
GENT (GHENT) ⑧
ANTWERPEN (ANTWERP) ⑨
WESTERLO ⑰
GENK ⑦
LOKEREN ⑩
ROESELARE ⑭
WAREGEM ⑱
MECHELEN ⑪
KORTRIJK ⑲
DENDERLEEUW ⑥
BRUSSELS ① ④
SINT-TRUIDEN ⑮
TUBIZE ⑳
MOUSCRON ⑬
LIÈGE ⑯
MONS ⑫
CHARLEROI ⑤

0 50 100 km
0 50 miles

TOP DIVISION CLUBS

1. **RSC Anderlecht** * — *rsca.be*
2. **Cercle Brugge KSV** — *cerclebrugge.be*
3. **Club Brugge KV** — *clubbrugge.be*
4. **FC Molenbeek Brussels** — *fc-brussels.be*
5. **R. Charleroi SC** — *sporting-charleroi.be*
6. **FCV Dender EH** — *fcvdendereh.be*
7. **KRC Genk** — *krcgenk.be*
8. **KAA Gent** ** — *kaagent.be*
9. **KFC Germinal Beerschot Antwerpen** — *germinal-beerschot.be*
10. **KSC Lokeren OV** — *sporting.be*
11. **KV Mechelen** — *kvmechelen.be*
12. **RAEC Mons** — *raec-mons.be*
13. **R. Excelsior Mouscron** — *excelsior.be*
14. **KSV Roeselare** — *ksvroeselare.be*
15. **K. Sint-Truidense VV** — *stvv.com*
16. **R. Standard de Liège** © — *standardliege.be*
17. **KVC Westerlo** — *kvcwesterlo.be*
18. **SV Zulte Waregem** — *svzw.be*

PROMOTED CLUBS

19. **KV Kortrijk** — *kvkortrijk.be*
20. **AFC Tubize** — *afctubize.be*

BOSNIA-HERZEGOVINA

FEDERATION

HOME INTERNATIONAL KIT

AWAY INTERNATIONAL KIT

MODRIČA (5)
ORAŠJE (6)
LAKTAŠI (3)
BIHAĆ (2)
GRADAČAC (17)
BANJA LUKA (18)
(15) ŽEPČE
(11) TUZLA
(12) TRAVNIK
ZENICA (1)
SARAJEVO (8) (10) (14)
POSUŠJE (7)
MOSTAR (13) (16)
ŠIROKI BRIJEG (9)
TREBINJE (4)

0 50 100 km
0 50 miles

TOP DIVISION CLUBS

1. **NK Čelik** — *nkcelik.ba*
2. **NK Jedinstvo** — *jedinstvo.org*
3. **FK Laktaši** — *no website*
4. **FK Leotar** — *no website*
5. **FK Modriča** © — *fkmodricamaxima.com*
6. **HNK Orašje** — *no website*
7. **NK Posušje** — *nkposusje.com*
8. **FK Sarajevo** — *fcsarajevo.ba*
9. **NK Široki Brijeg** — *siroki.brijeg.com*
10. **FK Slavija Sarajevo** — *fkslavija.com*
11. **FK Sloboda Tuzla** — *fksloboda.ba*
12. **NK Travnik** — *nktravnik.ba*
13. **FK Velež** — *fkvelez.ba*
14. **FK Željezničar** — *fkzeljeznicar.ba*
15. **NK Žepče** — *no website*
16. **HŠK Zrinjski** * — *hskzrinjski.ba*

PROMOTED CLUBS

17. **NK Zvijezda** — *nkzvijezda.com*
18. **FK Borac** — *no website*

FEDERATION

HOME INTERNATIONAL KIT

AWAY INTERNATIONAL KIT

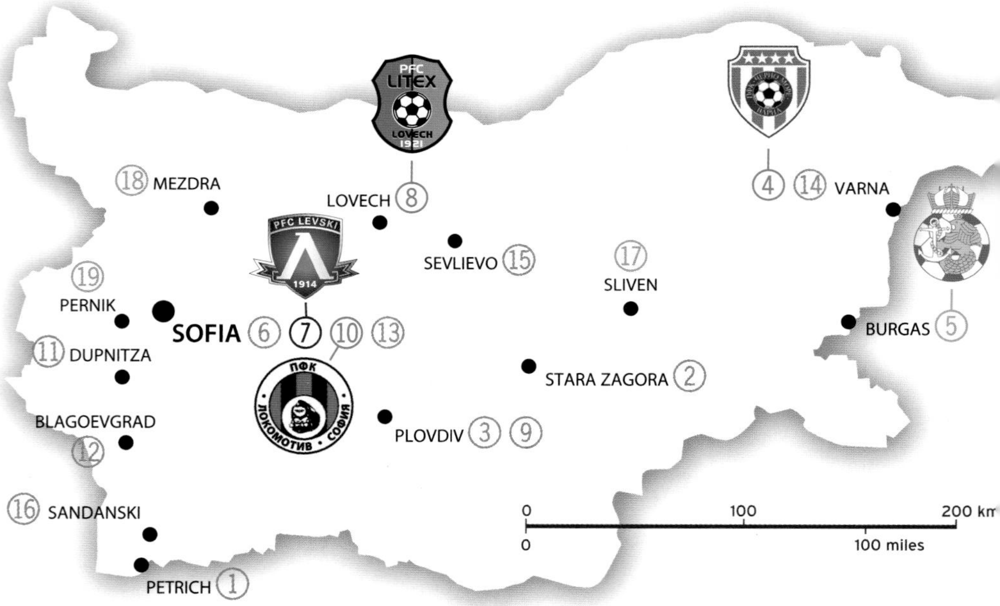

PFC LITEX LOVECH 1921

(18) MEZDRA

LOVECH (8)

(4) (14) VARNA

PFC LEVSKI 1914

SEVLIEVO (15)

(17) SLIVEN

(19) PERNIK

SOFIA (6) (7) (10) (13)

(11) DUPNITZA

ПФК ЛОКОМОТИВ • СОФИЯ

BURGAS (5)

STARA ZAGORA (2)

BLAGOEVGRAD (12)

PLOVDIV (3) (9)

(16) SANDANSKI

PETRICH (1)

0 100 200 km

0 100 miles

TOP DIVISION CLUBS

1. **PFC Belasitsa Petrich**
   rondia-bg.com
2. **PFC Beroe Stara Zagora**
   no website
3. **PFC Botev Plovdiv**
   pfcbotev1912.com
4. **PFC Cherno More Varna**
   chernomorepfc.bg
5. **PFC Chernomorets Burgas**
   chernomoretz-bs.com
6. **PFC CSKA Sofia** ©
   cska.bg
7. **PFC Levski Sofia**
   levski.bg
8. **PFC Litex Lovech** *
   pfclitex.com
9. **PFC Lokomotiv Plovdiv 1936**
   lokomotivpd.com
10. **PFC Lokomotiv Sofia**
    lokomotivsofia.bg
11. **PFC Marek Dupnitza**
    no website
12. **PFC Pirin 1922**
    pirinfc.com
13. **PFC Slavia Sofia**
    pfcslavia.com
14. **PFC Spartak Varna**
    spartak1918.com
15. **PFC Vidima Rakovski**
    no website
16. **PFC Vihren Sandanski**
    fcvihren.com

PROMOTED CLUBS

17. **PFC Sliven 2000**
    no website
18. **PFC Lokomotiv Mezdra**
    lokomotivmezdra.com
19. **PFC Minyor Pernik**
    minyor-pk.com

N.B. CSKA were champions but did not obtain licence to compete in Europe

TOP DIVISION CLUBS

1 **HNK Cibalia**
hnk-cibalia.hr

2 **NK Dinamo Zagreb** ©*
nk-dinamo.hr

3 **HNK Hajduk Split** **
hnkhajduk.hr

4 **NK Inter Zaprešić**
inter.hr

5 **NK Međimurje**
nk-medjimurje.hr

6 **NK Osijek**
nk-osijek.hr

7 **HNK Rijeka**
nk-rijeka.hr

8 **HNK Šibenik**
hnk-sibenik.hr

9 **NK Sjaven Koprivnica**
nk-slaven-belupo.hr

10 **NK Varteks**
nk-varteks.com

11 **NK Zadar**
nk-zadar.hr

12 **NK Zagreb**
nkzagreb.hr

PROMOTED CLUB

13 **NK Croatia Sesvete**
nkcroatiasesvete.hr

FEDERATION HOME INTERNATIONAL KIT AWAY INTERNATIONAL KIT

TOP DIVISION CLUBS

1 **AEK Larnaca FC** *aek.com.cy*

2 **AEL Limassol FC** *ael.eu.com*

3 **Alki Larnaca FC** *alkifc.com*

4 **Anorthosis Famagusta FC** © *anorthosisfc.com* (UEFA Champions League)

5 **APOEL FC** * *apoelfc.com.cy* (UEFA Cup)

6 **Apollon Limassol FC** *apollon.com.cy*

7 **APOP/Kinyras Peyias FC** *apopkinyrasfc.com*

8 **Aris Limassol FC** *no website*

9 **Doxa Katokopia FC** *doxakatokopiasfc.com*

10 **Enosis Neon Paralimni FC** *enpfc.com*

11 **Ethnikos Achnas FC** *achnafc.com* (UEFA Intertoto Cup)

12 **Nea Salamis FC** *neasalamis.com.cy*

13 **Olympiakos Nicosia FC** *no website*

14 **AC Omonia** *omonoia.com.cy* (UEFA Cup)

PROMOTED CLUBS

15 **AEP Paphos FC** *pafosfc.com*

16 **APEP FC** *apepfc.com*

17 **Atromitos Yereskipou FC** *atromitos-geroskipou.com*

CZECH REPUBLIC

FEDERATION

HOME INTERNATIONAL KIT

AWAY INTERNATIONAL KIT

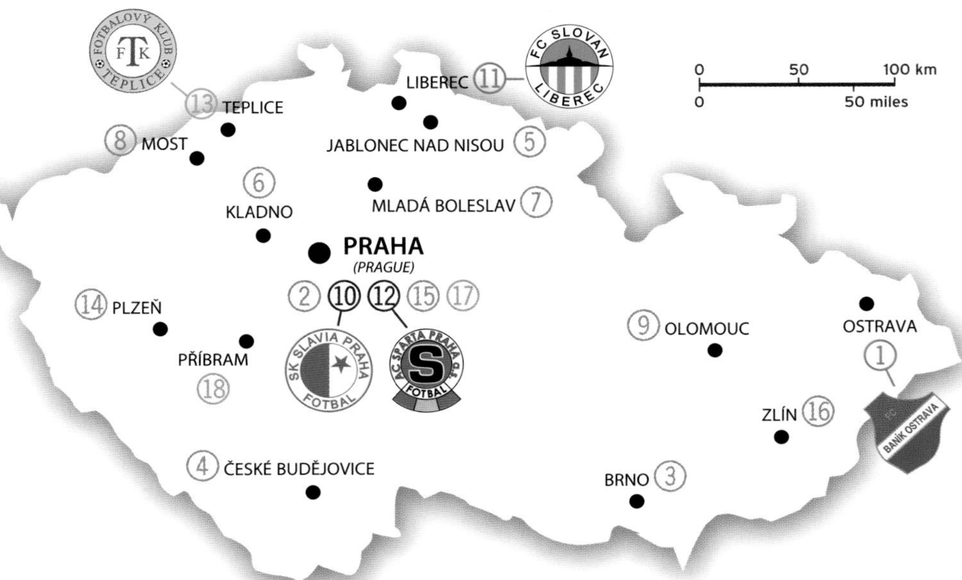

TOP DIVISION CLUBS

1 **FC Baník Ostrava**
fcb.cz

2 **Bohemians 1905**
fc-bohemians.cz

3 **1. FC Brno**
fcdynamo.ru

4 **SK Dynamo České Budějovice**
dynamocb.cz

5 **FK Jablonec 97**
fkjablonec.cz

6 **SK Kladno**
skkladno.cz

7 **FK Mladá Boleslav**
fkmb.cz

8 **FK SIAD Most**
fksiadmost.cz

9 **SK Sigma Olomouc**
sigmafotbal.cz

10 **SK Slavia Praha** ©
slavia.cz

11 **FC Slovan Liberec**
fcslovanliberec.cz

12 **AC Sparta Praha** *
sparta.cz

13 **FK Teplice**
fkteplice.cz

14 **FC Viktoria Plzeň**
fcviktoria.cz

15 **FK Viktoria Žižkov**
fkvz.cz

16 **FC Zlín**
fctescomazlin.cz

PROMOTED CLUBS

17 **Bohemians Praha**
bohemiansfc.cz

18 **FK Marila Příbram**
fkpribram.cz

DENMARK

FEDERATION

HOME INTERNATIONAL KIT

AWAY INTERNATIONAL KIT

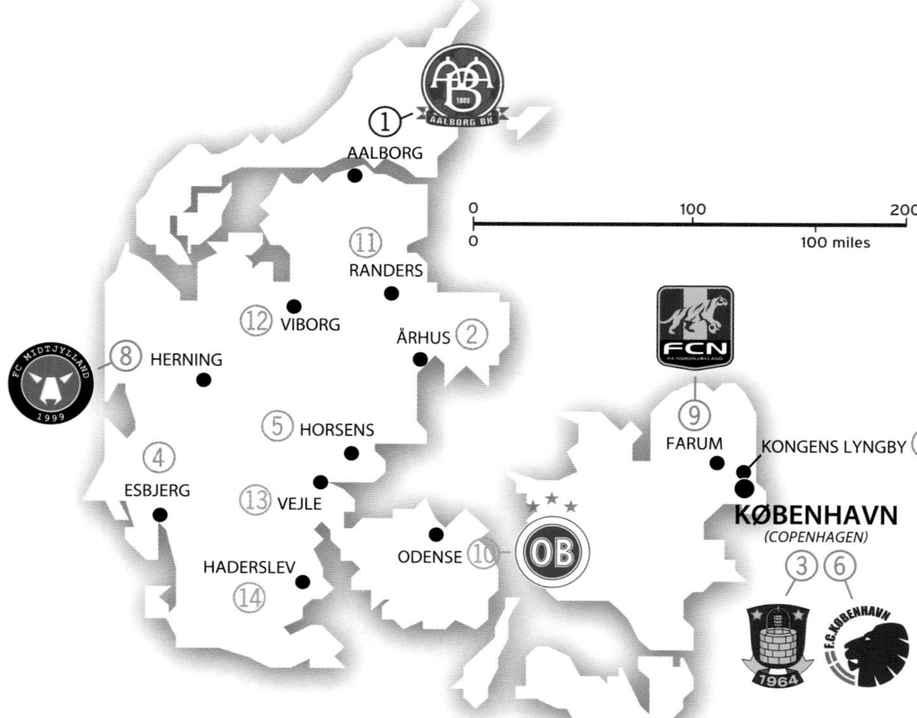

① AALBORG BK
AALBORG
⑪ RANDERS
⑫ VIBORG
ÅRHUS ②
⑧ HERNING
FC MIDTJYLLAND 1999
⑤ HORSENS
④ ESBJERG
⑬ VEJLE
HADERSLEV ⑭
ODENSE ⑩ OB
FCN
⑨ FARUM
KONGENS LYNGBY ⑦
KØBENHAVN
(COPENHAGEN)
③ ⑥
1964
F.C. KØBENHAVN

0 100 200 km
0 100 miles

TOP DIVISION CLUBS

1. **Aalborg BK** © — *aabsport.dk* (Champions League)
2. **AGF Århus** — *agffodbold.dk*
3. **Brøndby IF** * — *brondby.com* (UEFA Cup)
4. **Esbjerg fB** — *efb.dk*
5. **AC Horsens** — *achorsens.dk*
6. **FC København** — *fck.dk* (UEFA Cup)
7. **Lyngby FC** — *lyngby-boldklub.dk*
8. **FC Midtjylland** — *fcm.dk* (UEFA Cup)
9. **FC Nordsjælland** **** — *fcn.dk* (UEFA Cup)
10. **Odense BK** — *ob.dk* (Intertoto Cup)
11. **Randers FC** — *randersfc.dk*
12. **Viborg FF** — *vff.dk*

PROMOTED CLUBS

13. **Vejle BK** — *vejle-boldklub.dk*
14. **SønderjyskE** — *soenderjyske.dk*

FEDERATION

HOME INTERNATIONAL KIT

AWAY INTERNATIONAL KIT

TOP DIVISION CLUBS

1. **Arsenal FC** – *arsenal.com* (Champions League)
2. **Aston Villa FC** – *avfc.co.uk* (Intertoto Cup)
3. **Birmingham City FC** – *bcfc.com*
4. **Blackburn Rovers FC** – *rovers.co.uk*
5. **Bolton Wanderers FC** – *bwfc.co.uk*
6. **Chelsea FC** – *chelseafc.com* (Champions League)
7. **Derby County FC** – *dcfc.co.uk*
8. **Everton FC** – *evertonfc.com* (UEFA Cup)
9. **Fulham FC** – *fulhamfc.com*
10. **Liverpool FC** – *liverpoolfc.tv* (Champions League)
11. **Manchester City FC** **** – *mcfc.co.uk* (UEFA Cup)
12. **Manchester United FC** © – *manutd.com* (Champions League)
13. **Middlesbrough FC** – *mfc.co.uk*
14. **Newcastle United FC** – *nufc.co.uk*
15. **Portsmouth FC** * – *portsmouthfc.co.uk* (UEFA Cup)
16. **Reading FC** – *readingfc.co.uk*
17. **Sunderland AFC** – *safc.com*
18. **Tottenham Hotspur FC** *** – *tottenhamhotspur.com* (UEFA Cup)
19. **West Ham United FC** – *whufc.com*
20. **Wigan Athletic FC** – *wiganlatics.co.uk*

PROMOTED CLUBS

21. **West Bromwich Albion FC** – *wba.co.uk*
22. **Stoke City FC** – *stokecityfc.premiumtv.co.uk*
23. **Hull City AFC** – *hullcityafc.premiumtv.co.uk*

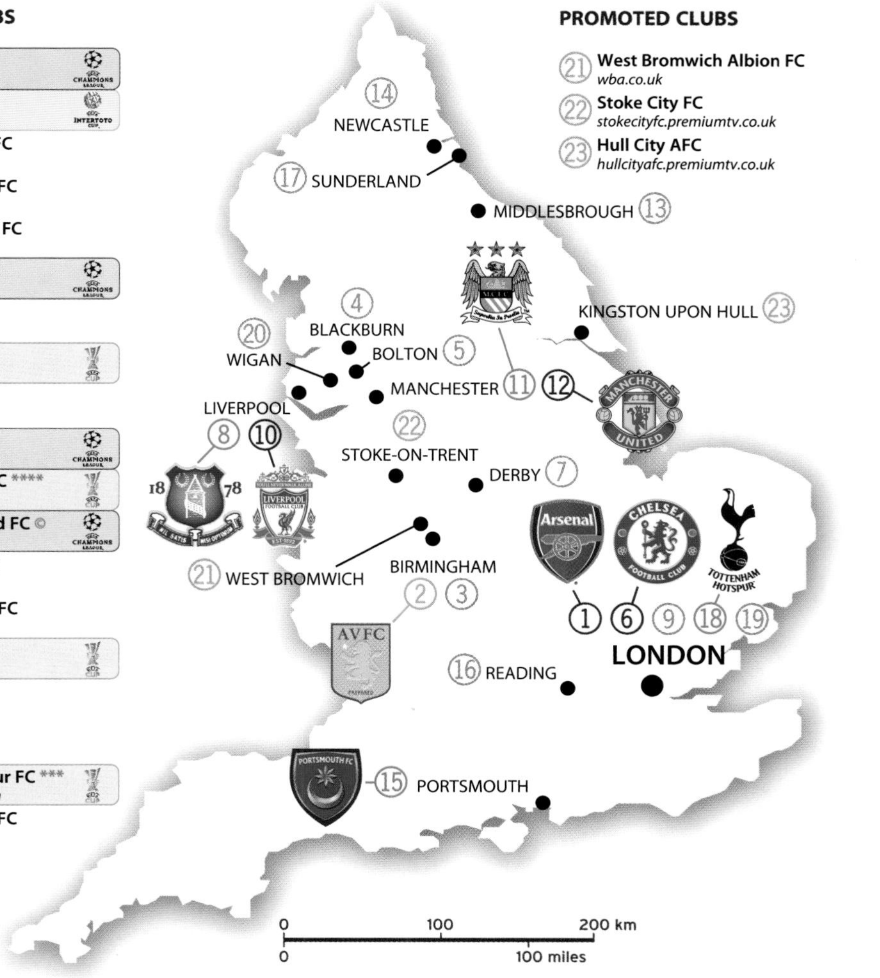

(14) NEWCASTLE
(17) SUNDERLAND
MIDDLESBROUGH (13)
KINGSTON UPON HULL (23)
(4) BLACKBURN
(20) WIGAN
BOLTON (5)
MANCHESTER (11) (12)
LIVERPOOL (8) (10)
(22) STOKE-ON-TRENT
DERBY (7)
(21) WEST BROMWICH
BIRMINGHAM (2) (3)
(1) (6) (9) (18) (19) LONDON
(16) READING
(15) PORTSMOUTH

0 100 200 km
0 100 miles

ESTONIA

FEDERATION

HOME INTERNATIONAL KIT

AWAY INTERNATIONAL KIT

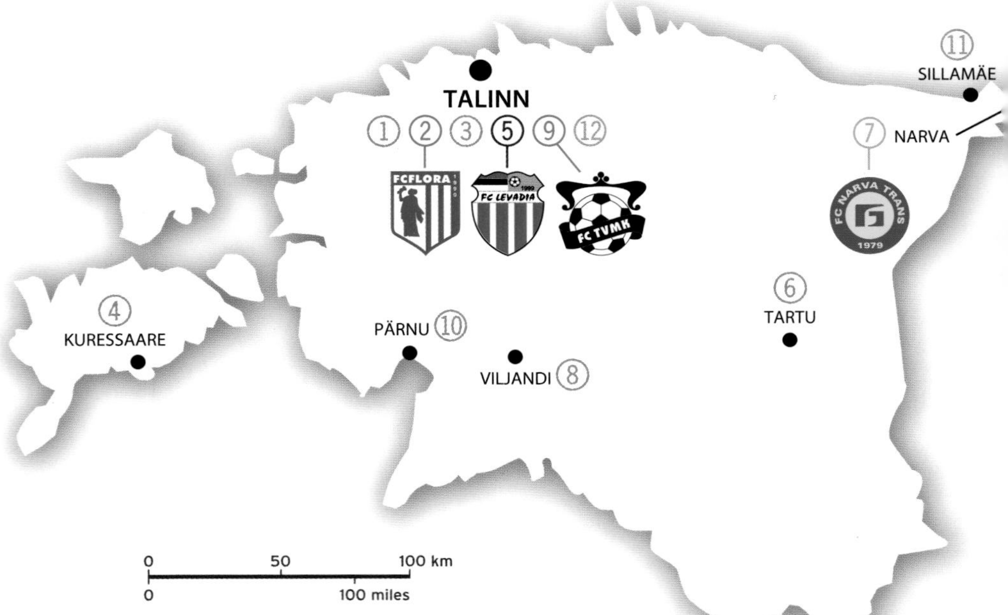

TALINN
(1) (2) (3) (5) (9) (12)

SILLAMÄE (11)

NARVA (7)

(4) KURESSAARE

PÄRNU (10)

VILJANDI (8)

(6) TARTU

0 50 100 km

0 100 miles

TOP DIVISION CLUBS

1. **FC Ajax Lasnamäe** *fcajax.ee*
2. **FC Flora** * *fcflora.ee* (UEFA Cup)
3. **JK Kalev Tallinn** *jkkalev.ee*
4. **FC Kuressaare** *fckuressaare.ee*
5. **FC Levadia Tallinn** © *fclevadia.ee* (UEFA Champions League)
6. **JK Maag Tammeka Tartu** *jkmaagtammeka.net*
7. **JK Trans Narva** *fctrans.ee* (UEFA Intertoto Cup)
8. **JK Tulevik Viljandi** *jktulevik.ee*
9. **FC TVMK Tallinn** *fctvmk.ee* (UEFA Cup)
10. **JK Vaprus Pärnu** *vaprus.ee*

PROMOTED CLUBS

11. **JK Kalev Sillamäe** *kalevsil.ee*
12. **JK Kalju Nõmme** *jkkalju.ee*

FEDERATION

HOME INTERNATIONAL KIT

AWAY INTERNATIONAL KIT

TOP DIVISION CLUBS

1 **AB Argir** *ab.fo*

2 **B36 Tórshavn** *fcb36.org* (UEFA Cup)

3 **B71 Sandur** *b71-sandoy.com*

4 **EB/Streymur** * *eb-streymur.fo* (UEFA Cup)

5 **GÍ Gøta** *no website*

6 **HB Tórshavn** *hb.fo* (Intertoto Cup)

7 **KÍ Klaksvík** *ki-klaksvik.fo*

8 **NSÍ Runavík** © *nsi.fo* (UEFA Champions League)

9 **Skála Ítróttarfelag** *skalaif.fo*

10 **VB/Sumba Vágur** *vb1905.fo*

PROMOTED CLUBS

11 **B68 Toftir** *b68.fo*

12 **ÍF Fuglafjørdur** *if.fo*

NEW MERGER CLUB

13 **Víkingur Gøta** *vikingur.fo*

FEDERATION

HOME INTERNATIONAL KIT

AWAY INTERNATIONAL KIT

TOP DIVISION CLUBS

1. **FC Haka** *fchaka.fi*
2. **HJK Helsinki** *hjk.fi*

3. **FC Honka Espoo** ** *fchonka.fi*
4. **FC International Turku** *fcinter.com*
5. **FF Jaro** *ffjaro.fi*
6. **FC KooTeePee** *fckooteepee.fi*
7. **FC Lahti** *fclahti.fi*
8. **IFK Mariehamn** *ifkmariehamn.com*
9. **Myllykosken Pallo-47** *mypa.fi*
10. **AC Oulu** *acoulu.fi*
11. **Tampere United** ©* *tampereunited.com*
12. **FC TPS Turku** *fc.tps.fi*
13. **FC Viikingit** *fcviikingit.com*
14. **VPS Vaasa** *vps-vaasa.fi*

PROMOTED CLUBS

15. **KuPS Kuopio** *kups.fi*
16. **RoPS Rovaniemi** *rops.fi*

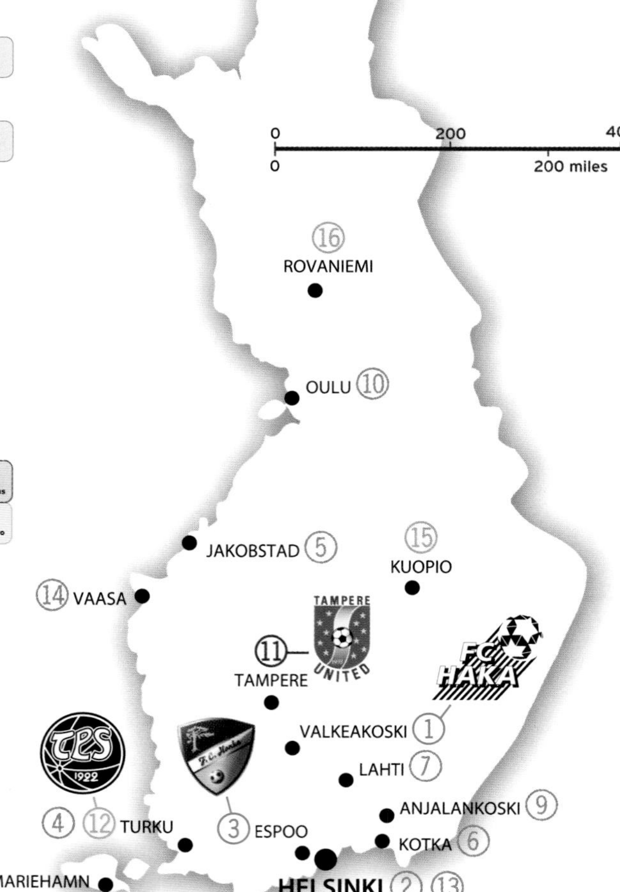

FEDERATION

HOME INTERNATIONAL KIT

AWAY INTERNATIONAL KIT

OP DIVISION CLUBS

1) **AJ Auxerre** *aja.fr*
2) **FC Girondins de Bordeaux** *girondins.com*
3) **SM Caen** *smcaen.fr*
4) **Le Mans UC 72** *muc72.fr*
5) **RC Lens** *rclens.fr*
6) **LOSC Lille Métropole** *losc.fr*
7) **FC Lorient** *Fclweb.fr*
8) **Olympique Lyonnais** ©* *olweb.fr*
9) **Olympique de Marseille** *om.net*
0) **FC Metz** *fcmetz.com*
1) **AS Monaco FC** *asm-fc.com*
2) **AS Nancy-Lorraine** *asnl.net*
3) **OGC Nice** *ogcnice.com*
4) **Paris Saint-Germain FC** *** *psg.fr*
5) **Stade Rennais FC** *staderennais.com*
6) **AS Saint-Étienne** *asse.fr*
7) **FC Sochaux-Montbéliard** *fcsochaux.fr*
8) **RC Strasbourg** *rcstrasbourg.fr*
9) **Toulouse FC** *tfc.info*
0) **Valenciennes FC** *va-fc.com*

PROMOTED CLUBS

21) **Le Havre AC** *hac-foot.com*
22) **FC Nantes** *fcnantes.com*
23) **Grenoble Foot 38** *gf38.fr*

FEDERATION

HOME INTERNATIONAL KIT

AWAY INTERNATIONAL KIT

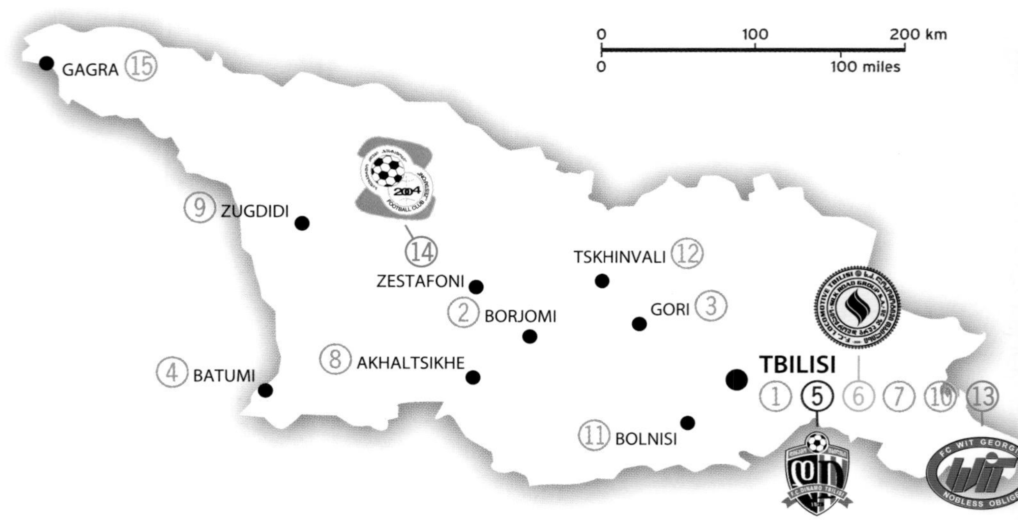

TOP DIVISION CLUBS

1. **FC Ameri Tblisi** *fcameri.ge*
2. **FC Borjomi** *no website*
3. **FC Dila Gori** *no website*
4. **FC Dinamo Batumi** *no website*
5. **FC Dinamo Tbilisi** © *fcdinamo.ge*
6. **FC Lokomotivi Tbilisi** *fcloco.ge*
7. **FC Merani Tbilisi** *no website*
8. **FC Meskheti Akhaltsikhe** *no website*
9. **FC Mglebi Zugdidi** *no website*
10. **FC Olimpi Rustavi** *no website*
11. **FC Sioni Bolnisi** *fcsioni.com*
12. **FC Spartaki Tskhinvali** *no website*
13. **FC WIT Georgia** *witgeorgia.ge*

14. **FC Zestafoni** * *fczestafoni.ge*

PROMOTED CLUB

15. **FC Gagra** *no website*

FEDERATION

HOME INTERNATIONAL KIT

AWAY INTERNATIONAL KIT

TOP DIVISION CLUBS

1 **DSC Arminia Bielefeld** *arminia-bielefeld.de*

2 **Bayer 04 Leverkusen** *bayer04.de*

3 **FC Bayern München** ©* *fcbayern.de*

4 **VfL Bochum 1848** *vfl-bochum.de*

5 **BV Borussia Dortmund** ** *bvb.de*

6 **MSV Duisburg** *msv-duisburg.de*

7 **Eintracht Frankfurt** *eintracht.de*

8 **FC Energie Cottbus** *fcenergie.de*

9 **Hamburger SV** *hsv.de*

10 **Hannover 96** *hannover96.de*

11 **FC Hansa Rostock** *fc-hansa.de*

12 **Hertha BSC Berlin** **** *herthabsc.de*

13 **Karlsruher SC** *ksc.de*

14 **1. FC Nürnberg** *fcn.de*

15 **FC Schalke 04** *schalke04.de*

16 **VfB Stuttgart** *vfb.de*

17 **Werder Bremen** *werder.de*

18 **VfL Wolfsburg** *vfl-wolfsburg.de*

PROMOTED CLUBS

19 **VfL Borussia Mönchengladbach** *borussia.de*

20 **TSG 1899 Hoffenheim** *tsg-hoffenheim.de*

21 **1. FC Köln** *fc-koeln.de*

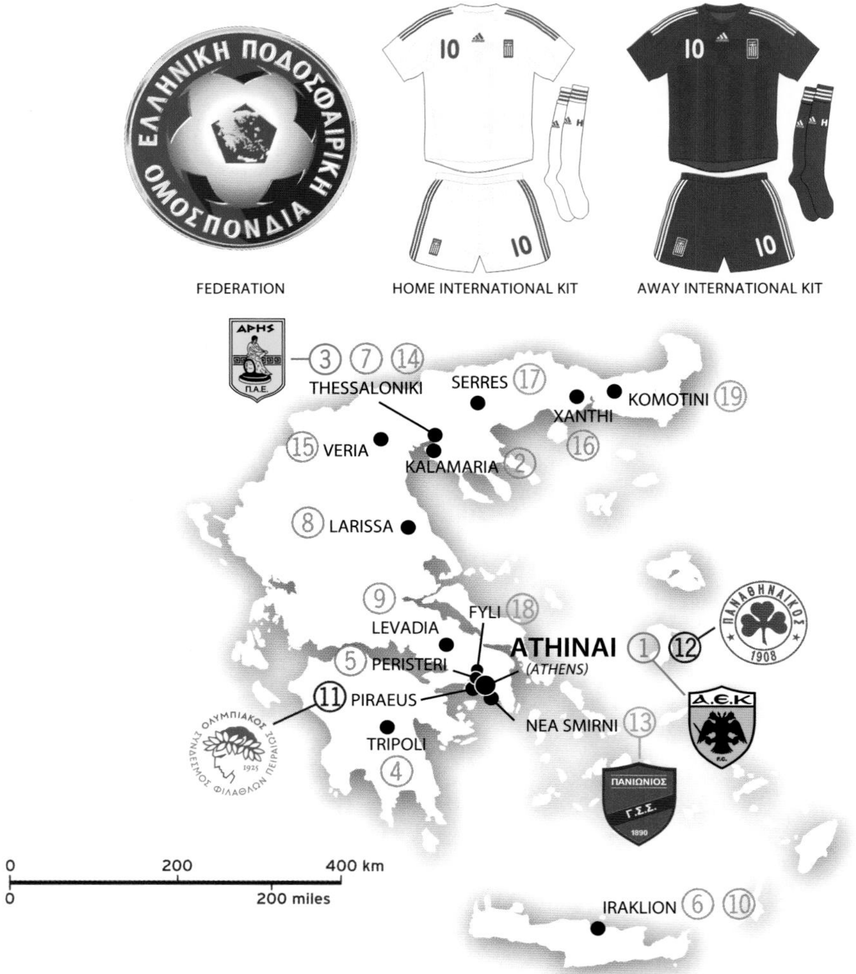

TOP DIVISION CLUBS

1. **AEK Athens FC** *aekfc.gr* (UEFA Cup)
2. **Apollon Kalamarias FC** *apollonkalamariasfc.gr*
3. **Aris Thessaloniki FC **** *arisfc.gr* (UEFA Cup)
4. **Asteras Tripolis FC** *asterastripolis.gr*
5. **Atromitos FC** *atromitosfc.gr*
6. **Ergotelis FC** *ergotelis.gr*
7. **Iraklis FC** *iraklis-fc.gr*
8. **Larissa FC** *ael.gr*
9. **Levadiakos FC** *levadiakos.gr*
10. **OFI Crete FC** *ofi.gr*
11. **Olympiacos CFP ©*** *olympiacos.org* (UEFA Champions League)
12. **Panathinaikos FC** *pao.gr* (UEFA Champions League)
13. **Panionios GSS** *pgss.gr* (UEFA Intertoto Cup)
14. **PAOK FC** *paokfc.gr*
15. **GAS Veria** *veriafc.gr*
16. **Skoda Xanthi FC** *skodaxanthifc.gr*

PROMOTED CLUBS

17. **Panserraikos FC** *panserraikos.gr*
18. **Thrasivoulos Filis FC** *thrasivoulos.gr*
19. **Panthrakikos FC** *panthrakikos.com*

FEDERATION

HOME INTERNATIONAL KIT

AWAY INTERNATIONAL KIT

TOP DIVISION CLUBS

1. **Budapest Honvéd FC** *honvedfc.hu* (INTERTOTO CUP)
2. **Debreceni VSC** * *dvsc.hu* (UEFA CUP)
3. **Diósgyőri VTK** *dvtk.eu*
4. **FC Fehérvár** *fcfehervar.com*
5. **Győri ETO FC** *eto.hu* (UEFA CUP)
6. **Kaposvári Rákóczi FC** *rakoczifc.hu*
7. **MTK Budapest** © *mtkhungaria.hu* (CHAMPIONS LEAGUE)
8. **Nyíregyháza FC** *szpari.hu*
9. **Paksi SE** *paksise.hu*
10. **Rákospalotai EAC** *reacfoci.hu*
11. **BFC Siófok** *bfc-siofok.hu*
12. **FC Sopron** *no website*
13. **FC Tatabánya** *tatabanyafc.hu*
14. **Újpest FC** *ujpestfc.hu*
15. **Vasas SC** *vasasbp.hu*
16. **Zalaegerszegi TE** *ztefc.hu*

PROMOTED CLUBS

17. **Szombathelyi Haladás FC** *haladas.hu*
18. **Kecskeméti TE** *kecskemetite.hu*

FEDERATION | HOME INTERNATIONAL KIT | AWAY INTERNATIONAL KIT

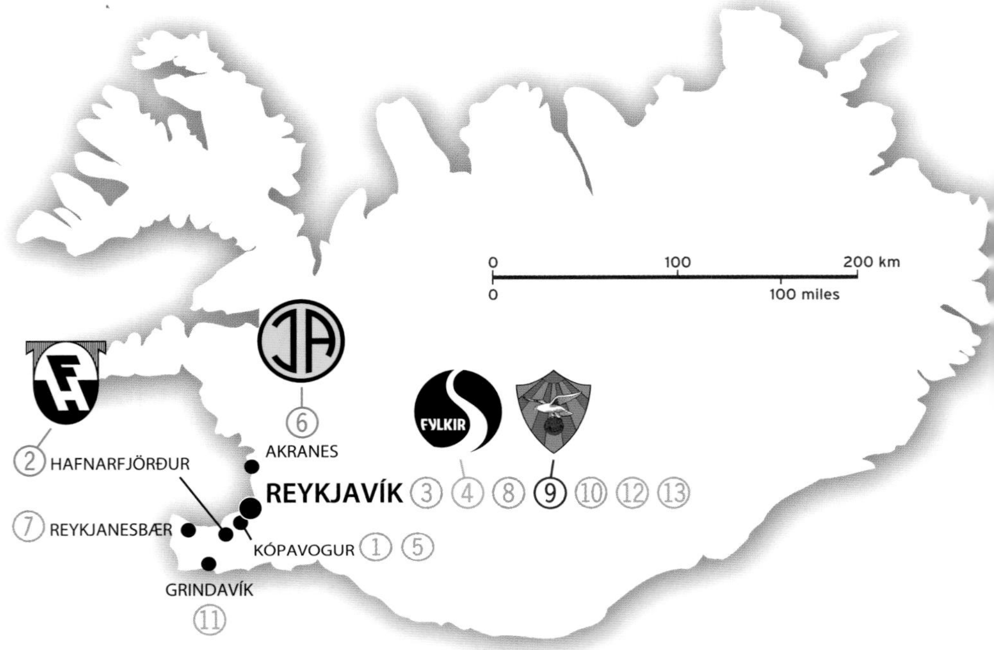

0 100 200 km
0 100 miles

(2) HAFNARFJÖRÐUR
(6) AKRANES
REYKJAVÍK (3) (4) (8) (9) (10) (12) (13)
(7) REYKJANESBÆR
KÓPAVOGUR (1) (5)
GRINDAVÍK (11)

FYLKIR

TOP DIVISION CLUBS

1. **Breidablik** — *breidablik.is*
2. **FH Hafnarfjördur** * — *fhingar.is* (UEFA Cup)
3. **Fram Reykjavík** — *fram.is*
4. **Fylkir** — *fylkir.com* (Intertoto Cup)
5. **HK Kópavogur** — *hk.is*
6. **ÍA Akranes** — *kfia.is* (UEFA Cup)
7. **Keflavík** — *keflavik.is*
8. **KR Reykjavík** — *kr.is*
9. **Valur Reykjavík** © — *valur.is* (UEFA Champions League)
10. **Víkingur Reykjavík** — *vikingur.is*

PROMOTED CLUBS

11. **Grindavík** — *umfg.is*
12. **Thróttur Reykjavík** — *trottur.is*
13. **Fjölnir Reykjavík** — *fjolnir.is*

FEDERATION

HOME INTERNATIONAL KIT

AWAY INTERNATIONAL KIT

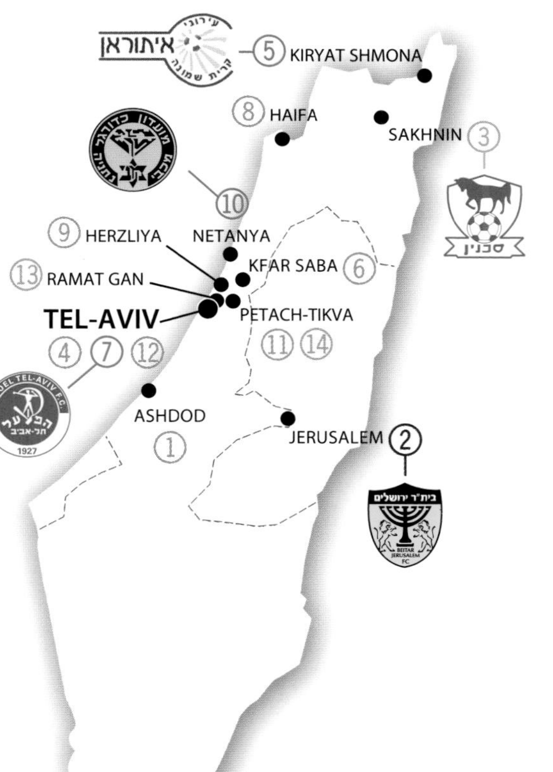

TOP DIVISION CLUBS

1 **FC Ashdod**
fcashdod.com

2 **Beitar Jerusalem FC** ©*
bjerusalem.co.il

3 **Bnei Sakhnin FC**
abna-sakhnin.com

4 **Bnei Yehuda Tel-Aviv FC**
fc-bnei-yehuda.co.il

5 **Hapoel Ironi Kiryat Shmona FC**
iturank8.co.il

6 **Hapoel Kfar-Saba FC**
hapoel-kfs.org

7 **Hapoel Tel-Aviv FC** **
hapoelta-fc.co.il

8 **Maccabi Haifa FC**
maccabi-haifafc.walla.co.il

9 **Maccabi Herzliya FC**
maccabiherzeliya.com

10 **Maccabi Netanya FC**
fcmn.co.il

11 **Maccabi Petach-Tikva FC**
mpt-mib.com

12 **Maccabi Tel-Aviv FC**
maccabi-tlv.co.il

PROMOTED CLUBS

13 **Hakoah Amidar Ramat Gan FC**
hakoach.co.il

14 **Hapoel Petach-Tikva FC**
no website

FEDERATION

HOME INTERNATIONAL KIT

AWAY INTERNATIONAL KIT

TOP DIVISION CLUBS

1. **Atalanta BC**
   atalanta.it
2. **Cagliari Calcio**
   cagliaricalcio.it
3. **Calcio Catania**
   calciocatania.it
4. **Empoli FC**
   empolicalcio.it
5. **ACF Fiorentina** (UEFA Champions League)
   acffiorentina.it
6. **Genoa CFC**
   genoacfc.it
7. **FC Internazionale Milano** © (UEFA Champions League)
   inter.it
8. **Juventus** (UEFA Champions League)
   juventus.com
9. **S.S. Lazio**
   sslazio.it
10. **AS Livorno Calcio**
    livornocalcio.it
11. **AC Milan** (UEFA Cup)
    acmilan.com
12. **SSC Napoli** (Intertoto Cup)
    sscnapoli.it
13. **US Città di Palermo**
    ilpalermocalcio.it
14. **Parma FC**
    fcparma.com
15. **Reggina Calcio**
    regginacalcio.com
16. **AS Roma** * (UEFA Champions League)
    asroma.it
17. **UC Sampdoria** (UEFA Cup)
    sampdoria.it
18. **AC Siena**
    acsiena.it
19. **Torino FC**
    torinofc.it
20. **Udinese Calcio** (UEFA Cup)
    udinese.it

PROMOTED CLUBS

21. **AC Chievo Verona**
    chievoverona.it
22. **Bologna FC**
    bolognafc.it
23. **US Lecce**
    uslecce.it

KAZAKHSTAN

FEDERATION

HOME INTERNATIONAL KIT

AWAY INTERNATIONAL KIT

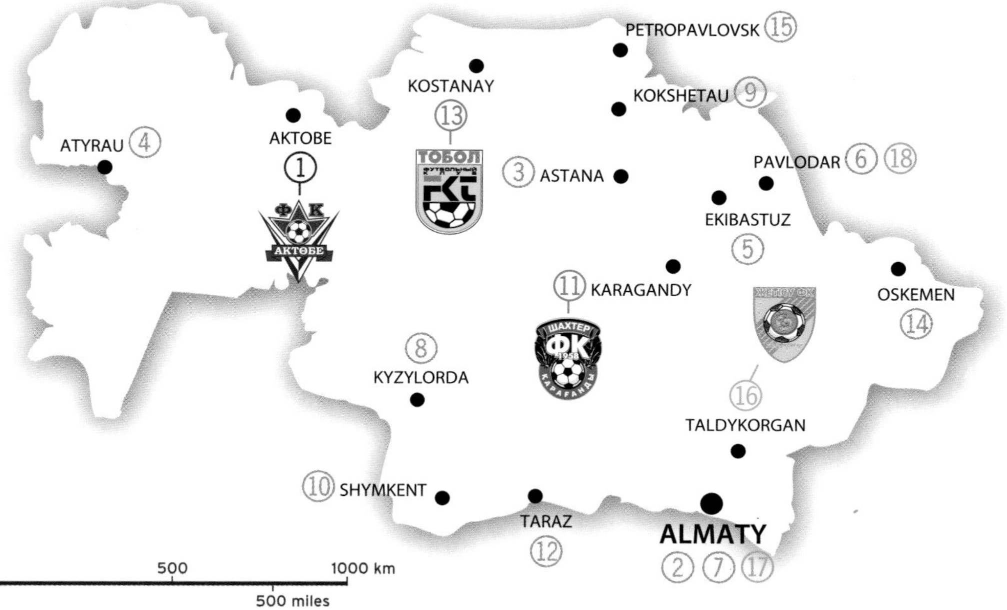

PETROPAVLOVSK (15)
KOSTANAY (13)
KOKSHETAU (9)
ATYRAU (4)
AKTOBE (1)
(3) ASTANA
PAVLODAR (6) (18)
EKIBASTUZ (5)
(11) KARAGANDY
OSKEMEN (14)
(8) KYZYLORDA
(16) TALDYKORGAN
(10) SHYMKENT
TARAZ (12)
ALMATY (2) (7) (17)

500 — 1000 km
500 miles

TOP DIVISION CLUBS

1. **FK Aktobe** ©
fcaktobe.kz
2. **FC Alma-Ata**
fcalma-ata.kz
3. **FC Astana**
fcastana.kz
4. **FK Atyrau**
fcatyrau.kz
5. **FC Ekibastuzets**
no website
6. **FC Irtysh Pavlodar**
fc-irtysh.kz
7. **FC Kairat Almaty**
fc-kairat.kz
8. **FC Kaisar Kyzylorda**
fc-kaysar.kz
9. **FC Okzhetpes Kokshetau**
okzhetpes.kz
10. **FC Ordabasy Shymkent**
fcordabasy.kz
11. **FC Shakhtyor Karagandy**
shahter.kz
12. **FC Taraz**
no website
13. **FC Tobol Kostanay** *
fctobol.kz
14. **FC Vostok**
ukavostok.vpnet.kz
15. **FC Yesil Bogatyr Petropavlovsk**
esil-sko.org
16. **FC Zhetysu Taldykorgan**
fc-zhetisu.kz

PROMOTED CLUBS

17. **FC MegaSport Almaty**
fc-megasport.kz
18. **FC Energetik Pavlodar**
no website

LATVIA

FEDERATION

HOME INTERNATIONAL KIT

AWAY INTERNATIONAL KIT

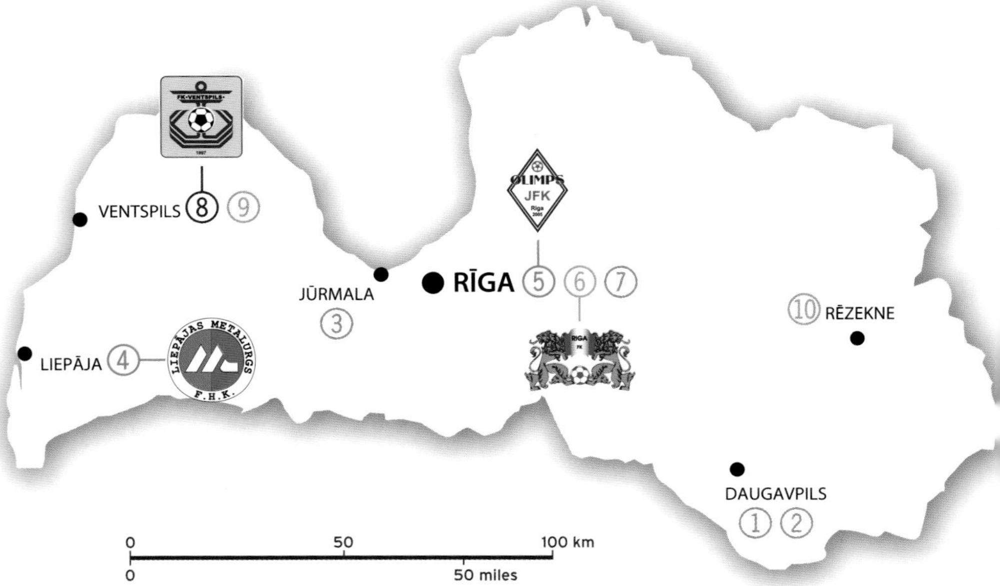

VENTSPILS (8) (9)

JŪRMALA (3)

RĪGA (5) (6) (7)

RĒZEKNE (10)

LIEPĀJA (4)

DAUGAVPILS (1) (2)

0 50 100 km

0 50 miles

TOP DIVISION CLUBS

1. **FC Daugava** *fcdaugava.lv*
2. **FC Dinaburg** *dinaburg.com*
3. **FK Jūrmala** *fcjurmala.lv*
4. **SK Liepājas Metalurgs** *sport.metalurgs.lv*
5. **JFK Olimps** ** *no website*
6. **FK Rīga** *fkriga.lv*
7. **Skonto FC** *skontofc.lv*
8. **FK Ventspils** ©* *fkventspils.lv*

PROMOTED CLUBS

9. **FC Vindava Ventspils** *no website*
10. **SK Blāzma Rēzekne** *no website*

FEDERATION

HOME INTERNATIONAL KIT

AWAY INTERNATIONAL KIT

TOP DIVISION CLUBS

1. **FC Balzers** *fcbalzers.li*
2. **FC USV Eschen-Mauren** *usv.li*
3. **FC Ruggell** *fcruggell.li*
4. **FC Schaan** *fcschaan.li*
5. **FC Triesen** *fctriesen.li*
6. **FC Triesenberg** *fctriesenberg.li*
7. **FC Vaduz** * *fcvaduz.li*

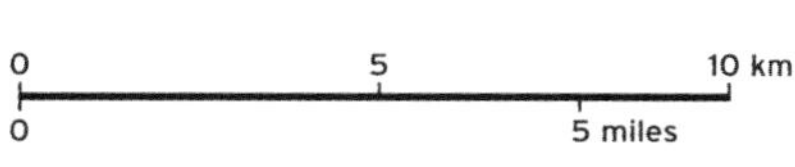

LITHUANIA

FEDERATION

HOME INTERNATIONAL KIT

AWAY INTERNATIONAL KIT

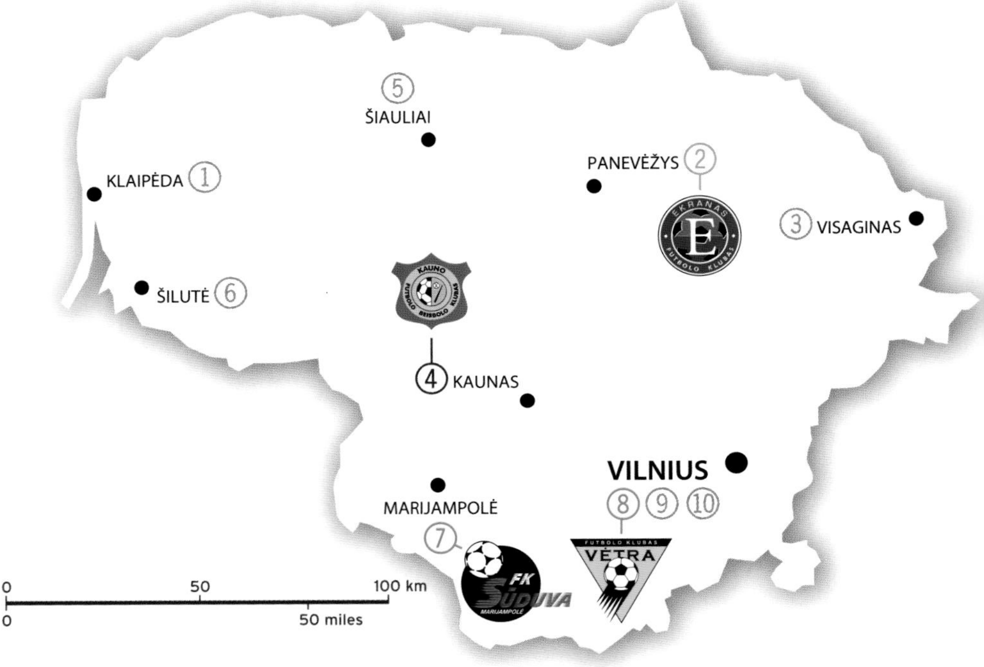

(5) ŠIAULIAI

PANEVĖŽYS (2)

KLAIPĖDA (1)

(3) VISAGINAS

ŠILUTĖ (6)

(4) KAUNAS

VILNIUS (8) (9) (10)

MARIJAMPOLĖ (7)

0 50 100 km

0 50 miles

TOP DIVISION CLUBS

(1) **FK Atlantas**
atlantas.lt

(2) **FK Ekranas**
fkekranas.lt

(3) **FK Interas**
no website

(4) **FBK Kaunas** ©*
fbk.lt

(5) **KFK Šiauliai**
fcsiauliai.lt

(6) **FK Šilutė**
fksilute.lt

(7) **FK Sūduva**
fksuduva.lt

(8) **FK Vėtra** **
fkvetra.lt

(9) **FC Vilnius**
fcvilnius.lt

(10) **FK Žalgiris**
fkzalgiris.lt

LUXEMBOURG

FEDERATION

HOME INTERNATIONAL KIT

AWAY INTERNATIONAL KIT

TOP DIVISION CLUBS

1. **FC Avenir Beggen** *wichtelweb.net*
2. **FC Differdange 03** *fcd03.lu*
3. **F91 Dudelange** © *f91.lu*
4. **FC Etzella Ettelbruck** *fc-etzella.lu*
5. **CS Grevenmacher** * *csg.lu*
6. **FC RM Hamm Benfica** *rmhb.lu*
7. **AS Jeunesse Esch** *jeunesse-esch.lu*
8. **UN Käerjéng 97** *un-kaerjeng.lu*
9. **CS Pétange** *cspetange.lu*
10. **FC Progrès Niedercorn** *progres.lu*
11. **Racing FC Union Lëtzebuerg** *racing-fc.lu*
12. **FC Swift Hesperange** *swifthesper.lu*
13. **FC Victoria Rosport** *fcvictoriarosport.lu*
14. **FC Wiltz 71** *fcwiltz.lu*

PROMOTED CLUBS

15. **US Rumelange** *usrumelange.lu*
16. **CS Fola Esch** *fola.lu*
17. **FC Sporting Steinfort** *scsteinfort.com*

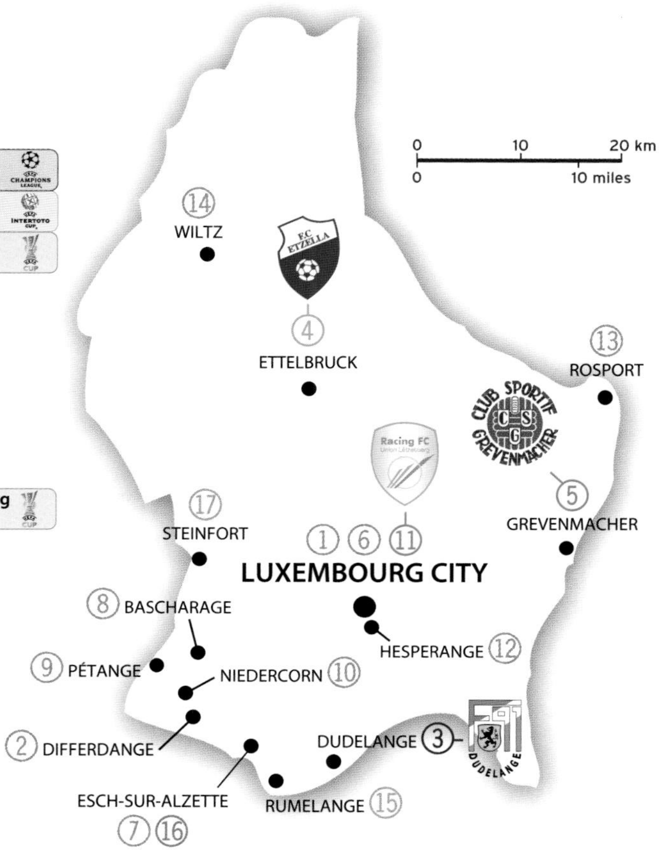

0 10 20 km
0 10 miles

(14) WILTZ
(4) ETTELBRUCK
(13) ROSPORT
(5) GREVENMACHER
(17) STEINFORT
(1) (6) (11) LUXEMBOURG CITY
(8) BASCHARAGE
(12) HESPERANGE
(9) PÉTANGE
NIEDERCORN (10)
(2) DIFFERDANGE
DUDELANGE (3)
ESCH-SUR-ALZETTE (7) (16)
RUMELANGE (15)

FEDERATION

HOME INTERNATIONAL KIT

AWAY INTERNATIONAL KIT

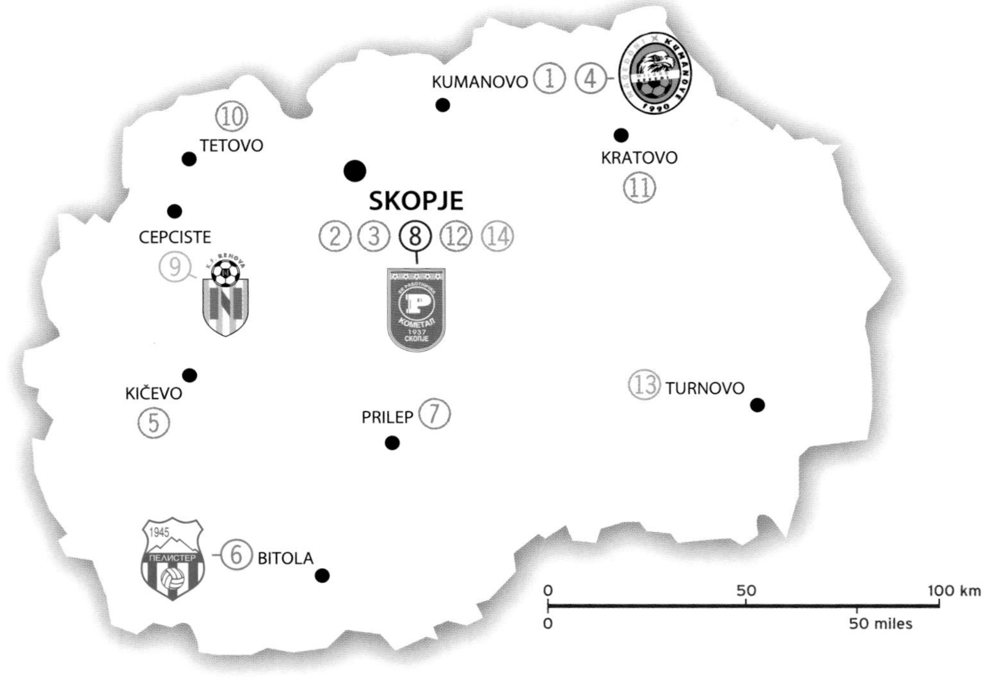

KUMANOVO (1) (4)
(10) TETOVO
KRATOVO (11)
SKOPJE (2) (3) (8) (12) (14)
CEPCISTE (9)
KIČEVO (5)
PRILEP (7)
(13) TURNOVO
(6) BITOLA
0 50 100 km
0 50 miles

TOP DIVISION CLUBS

1. **FK Bashkimi** *kfbashkimi.com.mk*
2. **FK Cementarnica 55** *no website*
3. **FK Makedonija GP Skopje** *fcmakedonija.com.mk*
4. **FK Milano** ** *fcmilano.com.mk*
5. **FK Napredok** *no website*
6. **FK Pelister** *fkpelister.com.mk*
7. **FK Pobeda** *fkpobeda.com.mk*
8. **FK Rabotnički** ©* *fcrabotnicki.com.mk*
9. **FK Renova** *renova.com.mk*
10. **FK Shkendija 79** *kfshkendija79.com.mk*
11. **FK Sileks** *no website*
12. **FK Vardar** *fkvardar.com.mk*

PROMOTED CLUBS

13. **FK Turnovo** *no website*
14. **FK Metalurg Skopje** *no website*

FEDERATION

HOME INTERNATIONAL KIT

AWAY INTERNATIONAL KIT

TOP DIVISION CLUBS

1. **Birkirkara FC** *
birkirkarafc.com
2. **Floriana FC**
florianafc.com
3. **Hamrun Spartans FC**
hamrunspartansfc.com
4. **Hibernians FC**
no website
5. **Marsaxlokk FC**
no website
6. **Mqabba FC**
mqabbafc.com
7. **Msida St Joseph FC**
msidastjoseph.com
8. **Pietà Hotspurs FC**
no website
9. **Sliema Wanderers FC**
no website
10. **Valletta FC** ©
vallettafcofficial.net

PROMOTED CLUBS

11. **Tarxien Rainbows FC**
no website
12. **Qormi FC**
no website

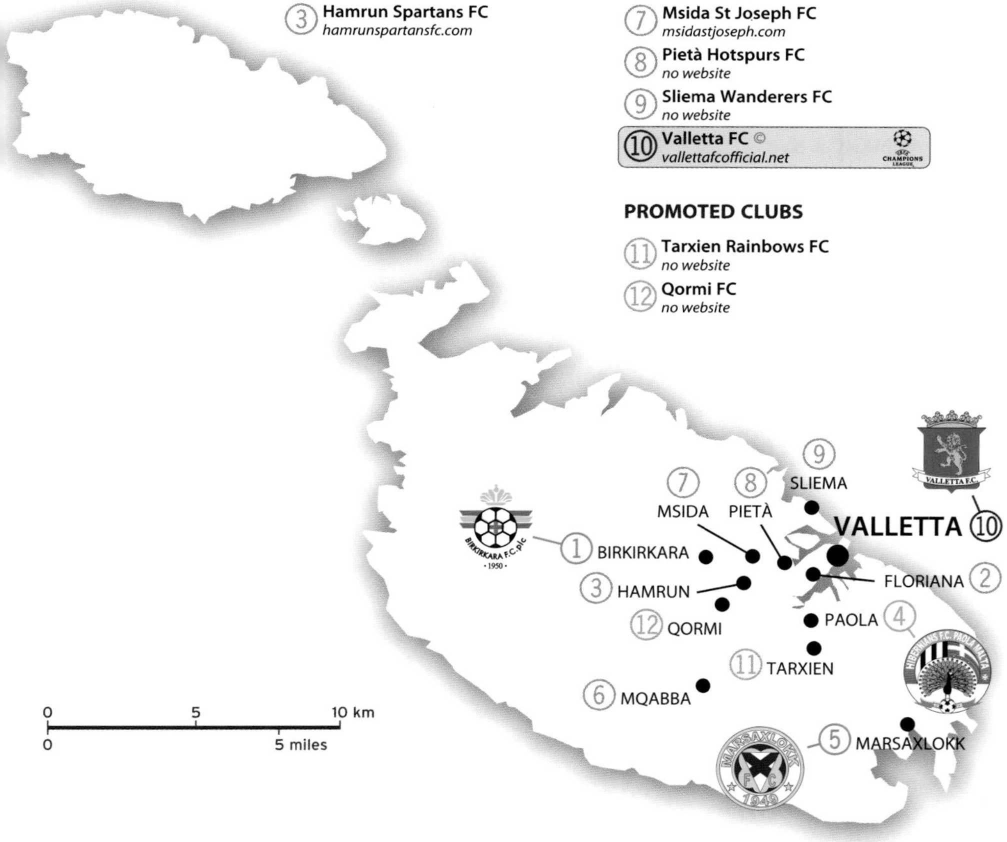

(9) SLIEMA
(7) MSIDA
(8) PIETÀ
VALLETTA (10)
(1) BIRKIRKARA
(3) HAMRUN
FLORIANA (2)
(12) QORMI
PAOLA (4)
(11) TARXIEN
(6) MQABBA
(5) MARSAXLOKK

0 5 10 km
0 5 miles

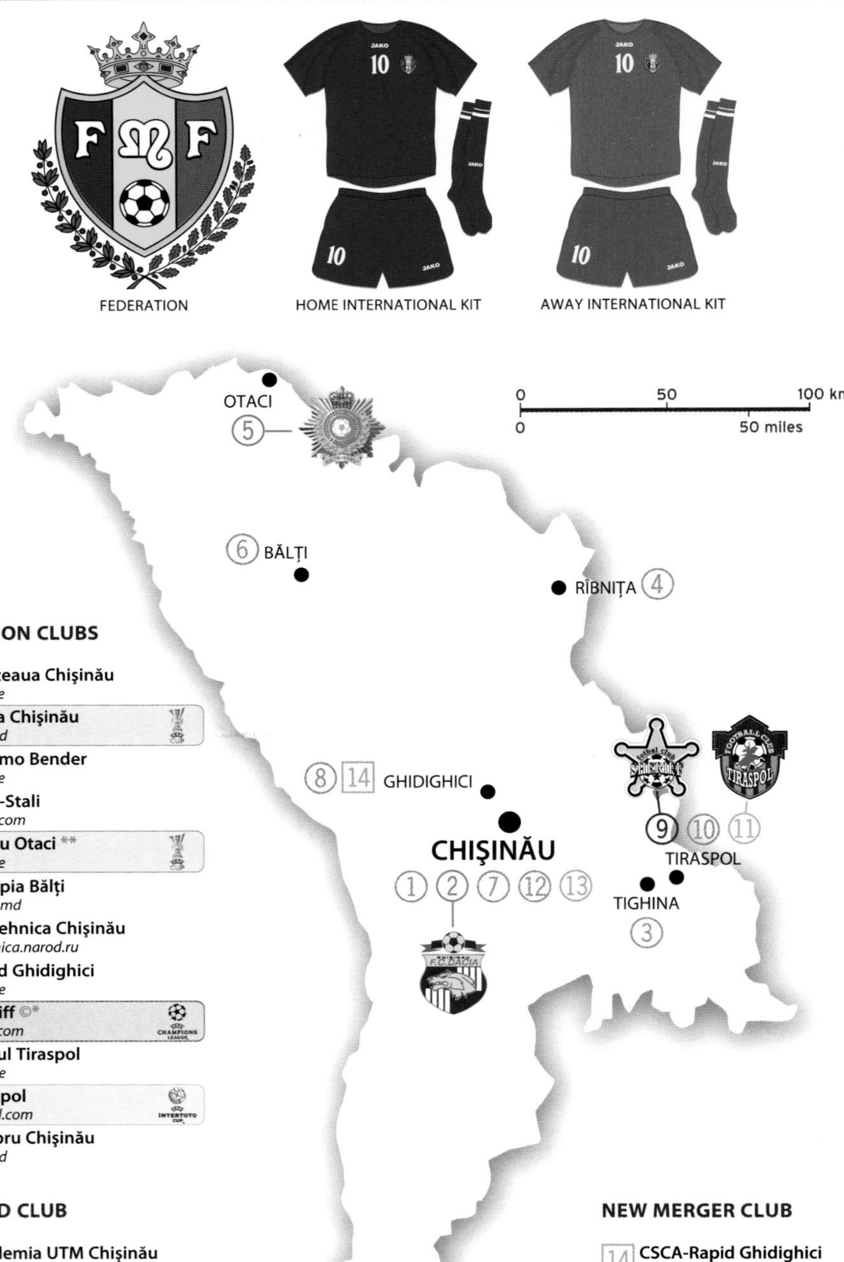

TOP DIVISION CLUBS

1. **CSCA-Steaua Chişinău**
   no website
2. **FC Dacia Chişinău**
   fcdacia.md
3. **FC Dinamo Bender**
   no website
4. **FC Iskra-Stali**
   iskra-stal.com
5. **FC Nistru Otaci** **
   no website
6. **FC Olimpia Bălţi**
   fcolimpia.md
7. **FC Politehnica Chişinău**
   fcpolitehnica.narod.ru
8. **FC Rapid Ghidighici**
   no website
9. **FC Sheriff** ©*
   fc-sheriff.com
10. **FC Tiligul Tiraspol**
    no website
11. **FC Tiraspol**
    fc-tiraspol.com
12. **FC Zimbru Chişinău**
    zimbru.md

PROMOTED CLUB

13. **FC Academia UTM Chişinău**
    no website

NEW MERGER CLUB

14. **CSCA-Rapid Ghidighici**
    no website

MONTENEGRO

FEDERATION

HOME INTERNATIONAL KIT

AWAY INTERNATIONAL KIT

TOP DIVISION CLUBS

1. **FK Bokelj**
   website
2. **FK Budućnost Podgorica** © (UEFA Champions League)
   fkbuducnost.cg.yu
3. **FK Dečić**
   fkdecictuzi.com
4. **OFK Grbalj** (Intertoto Cup)
   no website
5. **FK Kom**
   no website
6. **FK Lovćen**
   fklovcen.cg.yu
7. **FK Mladost Podgorica**
   no website
8. **FK Mogren** * (UEFA Cup)
   fkmogren.com
9. **OFK Petrovac**
   ofkpetrovac.com
10. **FK Rudar Pljevlja**
    fcrudarpljevlja.com
11. **FK Sutjeska**
    no website
12. **FK Zeta** (UEFA Cup)
    fkzeta.com

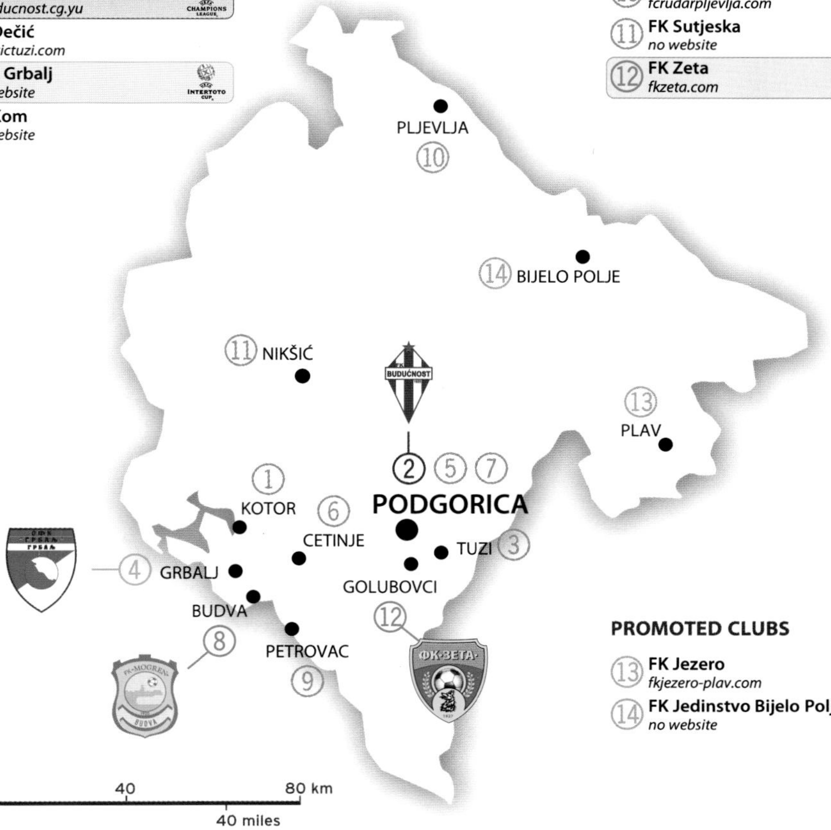

PLJEVLJA (10)
(14) BIJELO POLJE
(11) NIKŠIĆ
(13) PLAV
(2) (5) (7) PODGORICA
(1) KOTOR
(6) CETINJE
TUZI (3)
(4) GRBALJ
GOLUBOVCI
BUDVA (8)
PETROVAC (9)
(12)

PROMOTED CLUBS

13. **FK Jezero**
    fkjezero-plav.com
14. **FK Jedinstvo Bijelo Polje**
    no website

0 40 80 km
0 40 miles

NETHERLANDS

FEDERATION

HOME INTERNATIONAL KIT

AWAY INTERNATIONAL KIT

TOP DIVISION CLUBS

1. **AFC Ajax** *ajax.nl* (UEFA Cup)
2. **AZ Alkmaar** *az.nl*
3. **SC Excelsior** *sbvexcelsior.nl*
4. **Feyenoord** * *feyenoord.com* (UEFA Cup)
5. **De Graafschap** *degraafschap.nl*
6. **FC Groningen** *fcgroningen.nl*
7. **SC Heerenveen** *sc-heerenveen.nl* (UEFA Cup)
8. **Heracles Almelo** *heracles.nl*
9. **NAC Breda** *nac.nl* (UEFA Intertoto Cup)
10. **NEC Nijmegen** *nec-nijmegen.nl* (UEFA Cup)
11. **PSV Eindhoven** © *psv.nl* (UEFA Champions League)
12. **Roda JC** *rodajc.nl*
13. **Sparta Rotterdam** *sparta-rotterdam.nl*
14. **FC Twente** *fctwente.nl* (UEFA Champions League)
15. **FC Utrecht** *fcutrecht.nl*
16. **BV Vitesse** *vitesse.nl*
17. **VVV-Venlo** *vvv-venlo.nl*
18. **Willem II** *willem-ii.nl*

PROMOTED CLUBS

19. **FC Volendam** *fcvolendam.nl*
20. **ADO Den Haag** *adodenhaag.nl*

NORTHERN IRELAND

FEDERATION

HOME INTERNATIONAL KIT

AWAY INTERNATIONAL KIT

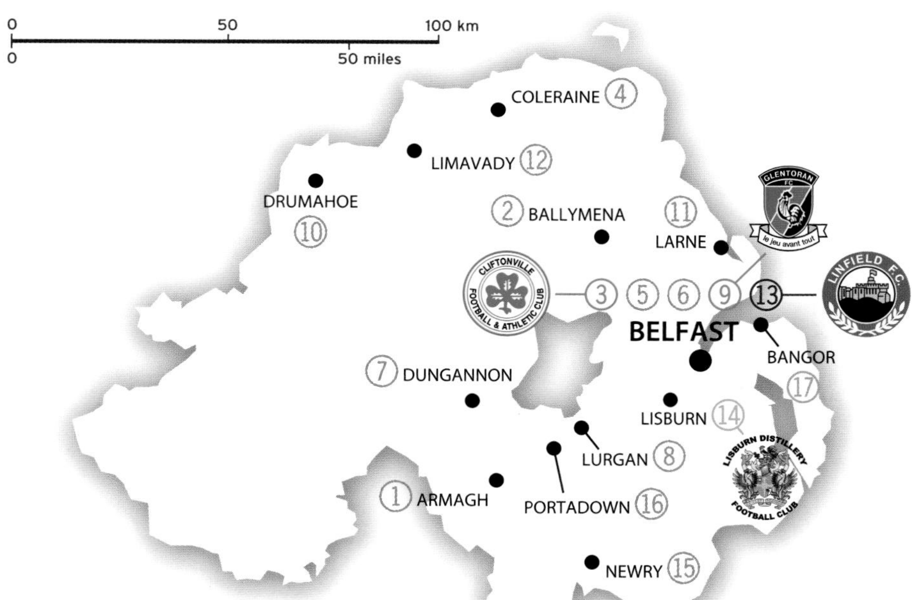

TOP DIVISION CLUBS

1. **Armagh City FC** *armaghcityfc.co.uk*
2. **Ballymena United FC** *ballymenaunitedfc.com*
3. **Cliftonville FC** *cliftonvillefc.net* (UEFA Cup)
4. **Coleraine FC** *colerainefc.com*
5. **Crusaders FC** *crusadersfc.com*
6. **Donegal Celtic FC** *dc-fc.com*
7. **Dungannon Swifts FC** *dungannonswiftsfc.co.uk*
8. **Glenavon FC** *glenavonfc.com*
9. **Glentoran FC** *glentoran.com* (UEFA Cup)
10. **Institute FC** *stutefc.net*
11. **Larne FC** *larnefc.co.uk*
12. **Limavady United FC** *limavadyunited.com*
13. **Linfield FC** ©* *linfieldfc.com* (UEFA Champions League)
14. **Lisburn Distillery FC** *blue.srv2.com/~lisburn* (UEFA Intertoto Cup)
15. **Newry City FC** *newrycityfc.com*
16. **Portadown FC** *portadownfc.co.uk*

PROMOTED CLUB

17. **Bangor FC** *bangorfc.com*

FEDERATION

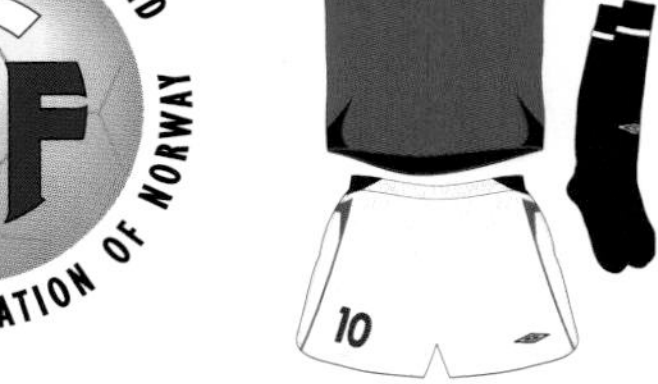

HOME INTERNATIONAL KIT

AWAY INTERNATIONAL KIT

TOP DIVISION CLUBS

1. **Aalesunds FK** *aafk.no*
2. **SK Brann** © *brann.no* (UEFA Champions League)
3. **Fredrikstad FK** *fredrikstadfk.no*
4. **Lillestrøm SK** * *lsk.no* (UEFA Cup)
5. **FC Lyn Oslo** *lyn.no*
6. **Odd Grenland** *oddgrenland.no*
7. **Rosenborg BK** *rbk.no* (UEFA Intertoto Cup)
8. **Sandefjord Fotball** *sandefjordfotball.no*
9. **Stabæk Fotball** *stabak.no* (UEFA Cup)
10. **IK Start** *ikstart.no*
11. **Strømsgodset IF** *godset.no*
12. **Tromsø IL** *til.no*
13. **Viking FK** *viking-fk.no* (UEFA Cup)
14. **Vålerenga Fotball** *vif-fotball.no*

PROMOTED CLUBS

15. **Molde FK** *moldefk.no*
16. **HamKam Fotball** *hamkam.no*
17. **FK Bodø/Glimt** *glimt.no*

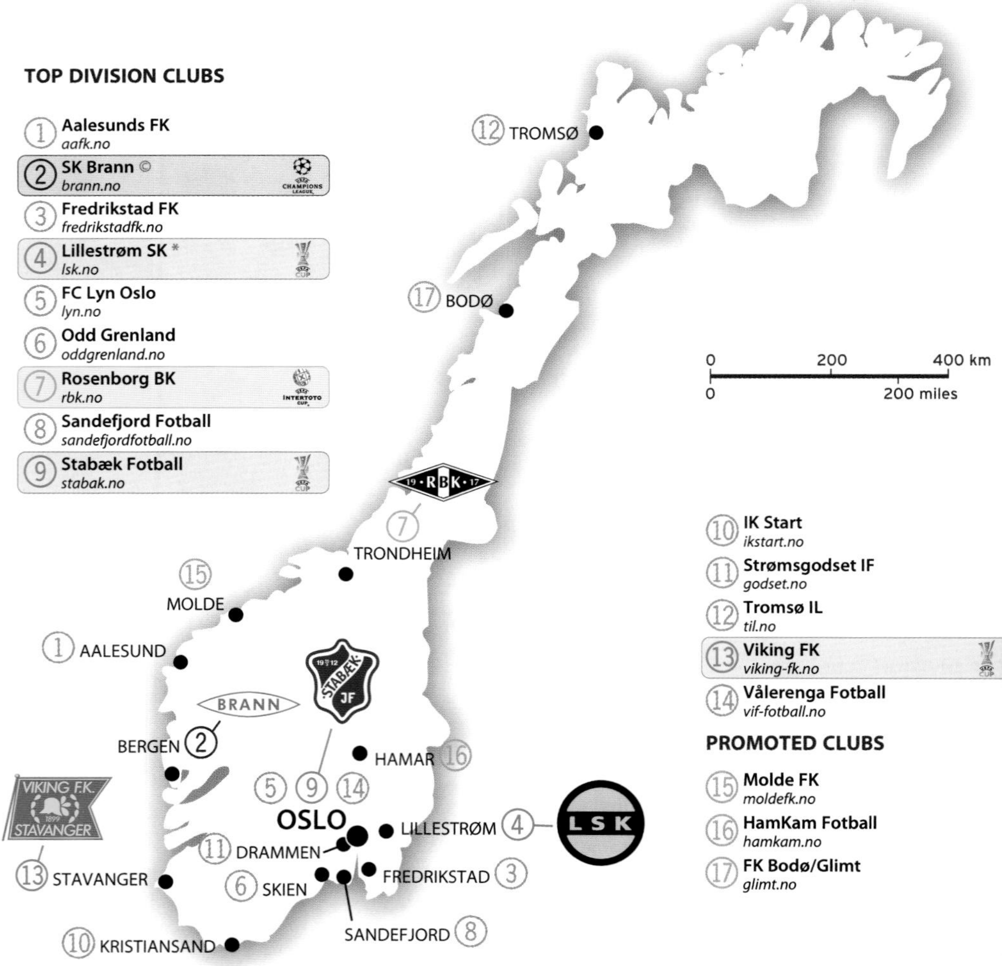

12 TROMSØ
17 BODØ
19 · RBK · 17
7 TRONDHEIM
15 MOLDE
1 AALESUND
BRANN
2 BERGEN
STABÆK 19 12 IF
HAMAR 16
5 9 14 OSLO
LILLESTRØM 4 LSK
11 DRAMMEN
VIKING F.K. 1899 STAVANGER
13 STAVANGER
6 SKIEN
FREDRIKSTAD 3
SANDEFJORD 8
10 KRISTIANSAND

0 200 400 km
0 200 miles

FEDERATION

HOME INTERNATIONAL KIT

AWAY INTERNATIONAL KIT

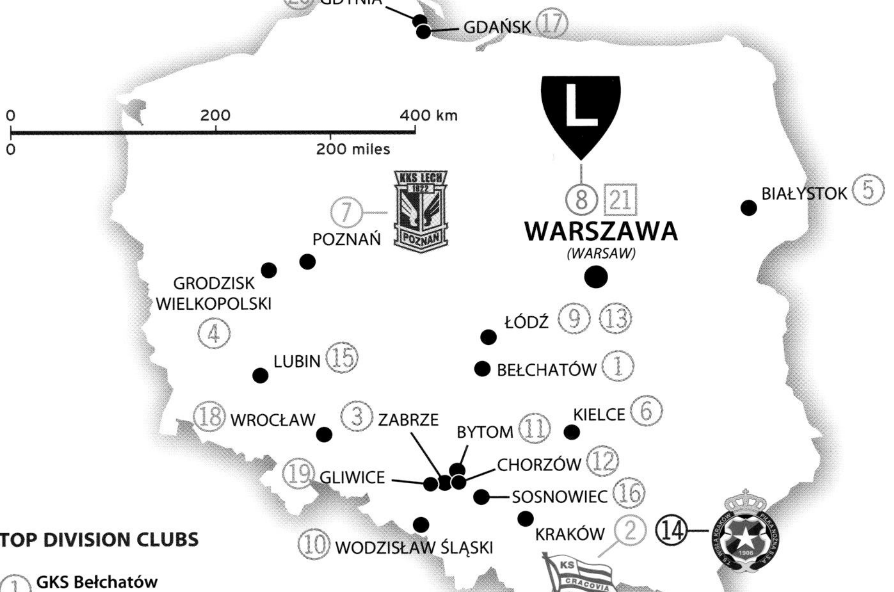

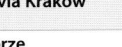

TOP DIVISION CLUBS

1. **GKS Bełchatów**
   gksbelchatow.com
2. **MKS Cracovia Kraków**
   cracovia.pl

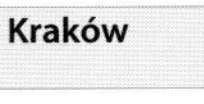

3. **Górnik Zabrze**
   gornikzabrze.pl
4. **Groclin Grodzisk Wielkopolski**
   no website
5. **Jagiellonia Białystok**
   jagiellonia.pl
6. **Korona Kielce**
   korona-kielce.pl
7. **KKS Lech Poznań**
   lech.poznan.pl
8. **Legia Warszawa** *
   legia.pl
9. **ŁKS Łódź**
   lkslodz.com.pl
10. **MKS Odra Wodzisław Śląski**
    odra.wodzislaw.pl
11. **KS Polonia Bytom**
    poloniabytom.com.pl
12. **KS Ruch Chorzów**
    ruchchorzow.com.pl
13. **RTS Widzew Łódź**
    widzew.lodz.pl
14. **Wisła Kraków** ©
    wisla.krakow.pl
15. **Zaglębie Lubin**
    zaglebie-lubin.pl
16. **GKS Zaglębie Sosnowiec**
    zaglebie.sosnowiec.pl

PROMOTED CLUBS

17. **KS Lechia Gdańsk**
    lechia.pl
18. **WKS Śląsk Wrocław**
    slaskwroclaw.pl
19. **KS Piast Gliwice**
    piast.gliwice.pl
20. **Arka Gdynia**
    arka.gdynia

NEW MERGER CLUB

21. **KSP Polonia Warszawa**
    ksppolonia.pl

FEDERATION

HOME INTERNATIONAL KIT

AWAY INTERNATIONAL KIT

TOP DIVISION CLUBS

1. **A. Académica de Coimbra** *academica-oaf.pt*
2. **CF Os Belenenses** *osbelenenses.com*
3. **SL Benfica** *slbenfica.pt* UEFA CUP
4. **Boavista FC** *boavistafc.pt*
5. **SC Braga** *scbraga.pt* UEFA INTERTOTO CUP
6. **CF Estrela da Amadora** *cfeamadora.net*
7. **Leixões SC** *leixoessc.pt*
8. **CS Marítimo** *csmaritimo.pt* UEFA CUP
9. **CD Nacional** *cdnacional.pt*
10. **A. Naval 1° Maio** *naval1demaio.com*
11. **FC Paços de Ferreira** *fcpf.pt*
12. **FC Porto** © *fcporto.pt* UEFA CHAMPIONS LEAGUE
13. **Sporting Clube de Portugal** * *sporting.pt* UEFA CHAMPIONS LEAGUE
14. **UD Leiria** *udl.leirianet.pt*
15. **Vitória FC** *vtfc.pt* UEFA CUP
16. **Vitória SC** *vitoriasc.pt* UEFA CHAMPIONS LEAGUE

5 BRAGA
17 TROFA
18 VILA DO CONDE
GUIMARÃES 16
7 MATOSINHOS
PORTO
PAÇOS DE FERREIRA 11
4 12
10 FIGUEIRA DA FOZ
COIMBRA 1
LEIRIA 14
2 3 13
LISBOA
(LISBON)
AMADORA 6
SETÚBAL
15

0 100 200 km
0 100 miles

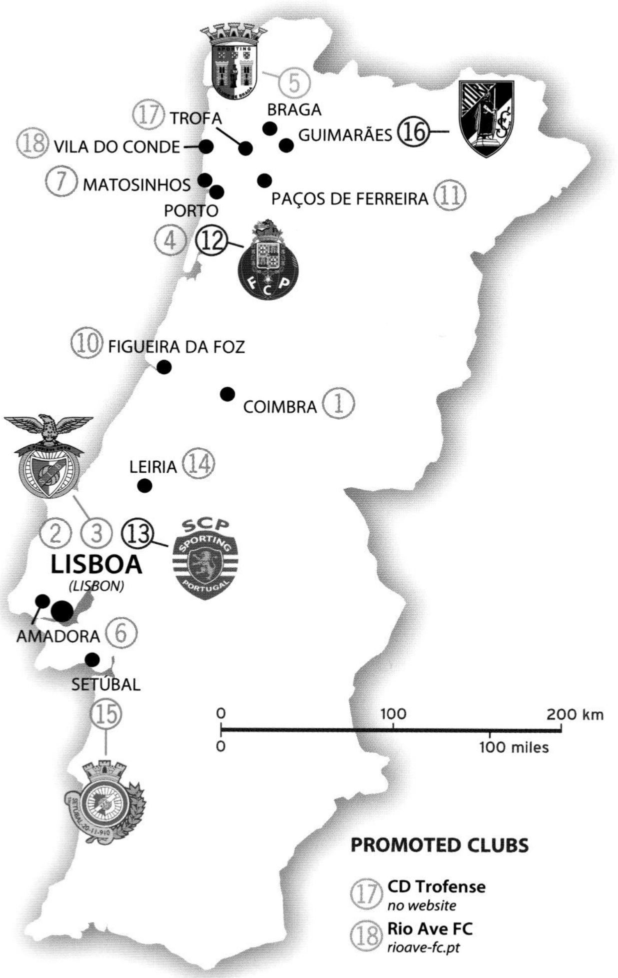

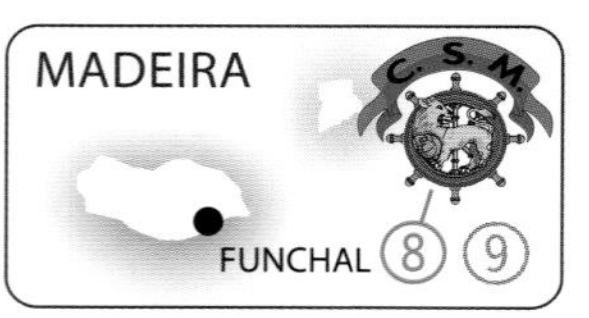

PROMOTED CLUBS

17. **CD Trofense** *no website*
18. **Rio Ave FC** *rioave-fc.pt*

REPUBLIC OF IRELAND

FEDERATION

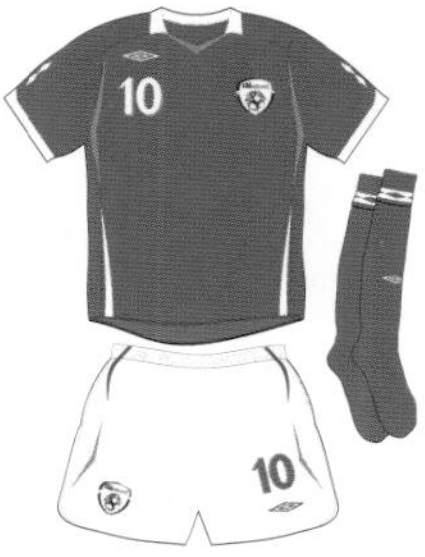

HOME INTERNATIONAL KIT

AWAY INTERNATIONAL KIT

TOP DIVISION CLUBS

1. **Bohemian FC** *bohemians.ie* (Intertoto Cup)
2. **Bray Wanderers AFC** *braywanderers.ie*
3. **Cork City FC** * *corkcityfc.ie* (UEFA Cup)
4. **Derry City FC** *derrycityfc.net*
5. **Drogheda United FC** © *droghedaunited.ie* (Champions League)
6. **Galway United FC** *galwayunitedfc.ie*
7. **Longford Town FC** *ltfc.ie*
8. **Saint Patrick's Athletic FC** *stpatsfc.com* (UEFA Cup)
9. **Shamrock Rovers FC** *shamrockrovers.ie*
10. **Sligo Rovers FC** *sligorovers.com*
11. **University College Dublin FC** *ucdsoccer.com*
12. **Waterford United FC** *waterford-united.ie*

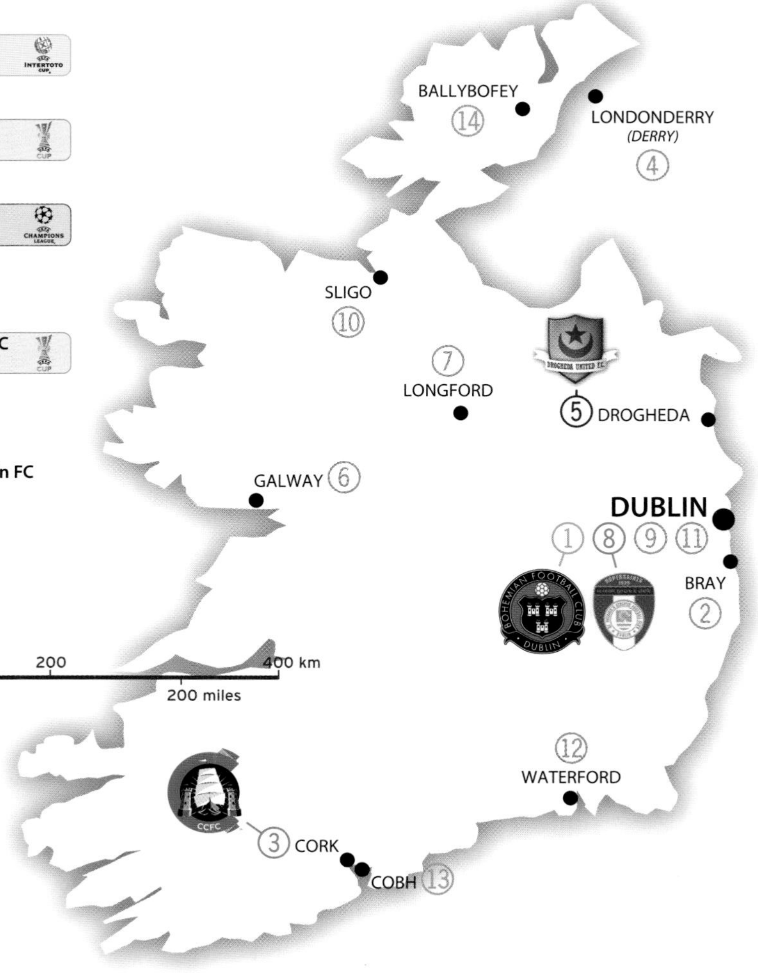

PROMOTED CLUBS

13. **Cobh Ramblers FC** *cobhramblers.ie*
14. **Finn Harps FC** *finnharps.com*

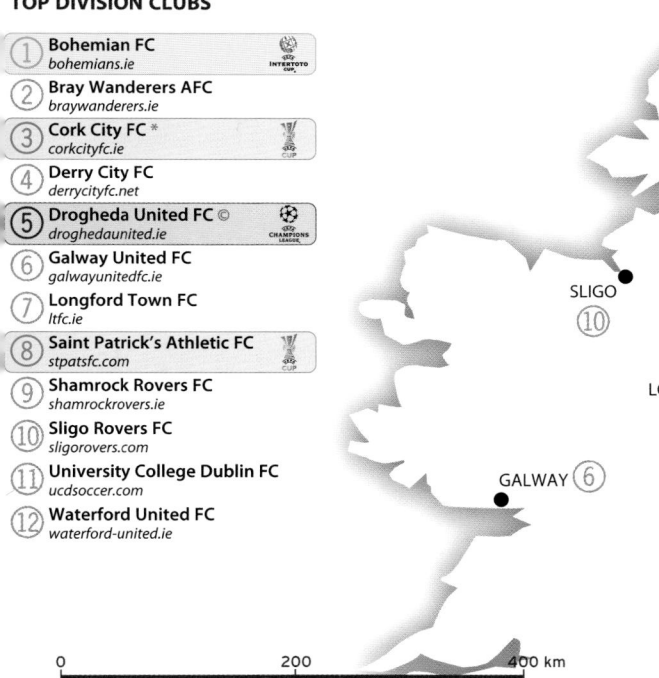

ROMANIA

FEDERATION

HOME INTERNATIONAL KIT

AWAY INTERNATIONAL KIT

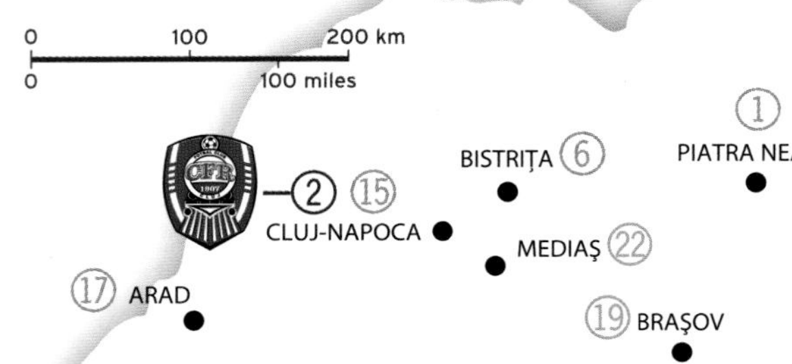

TOP DIVISION CLUBS

1. **FC Ceahlăul Piatra Neamţ** *fcceahlaul.ro*
2. **CFR 1907 Cluj** ©* *cfr1907.ro* (Champions League)
3. **CS Dacia Mioveni** *csdacia-mioveni.ro*
4. **FC Dinamo 1948 Bucureşti** *fcdinamo.ro* (UEFA Cup)
5. **FC Farul Constanţa** *fcfarul.ro*
6. **AFC Gloria 1922 Bistriţa** *cfgloria.ro*
7. **FC Gloria Buzău** *gloriabuzau.ro*
8. **FC Oţelul Galaţi** *otelul-galati.ro*
9. **CS Pandurii Lignitul Târgu Jiu** *pandurii-tg-jiu.ro*
10. **FC Politehnica Iaşi** *politehnicaiasi.ro*
11. **FC Politehnica 1921 Ştiinţa Timişoara** *politimisoara.com* (UEFA Cup)
12. **FC Rapid Bucureşti** *fcrapid.ro* (UEFA Cup)
13. **FC Steaua Bucureşti** *steauafc.ro* (Champions League)
14. **AFC Unirea Valahorum Urziceni** ** *fcunirea.ro* (UEFA Cup)
15. **CFM Universitatea Cluj** *universitateacluj.ro*
16. **FC Universitatea Craiova** *fcuniversitatea.ro*
17. **FC UTA Arad** *uta-arad.ro*
18. **FC Vaslui** *fcvaslui.info* 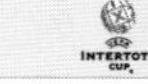 (Intertoto Cup)

PROMOTED CLUBS

19. **FC Braşov** *fcbrasov.ro*
20. **CS Otopeni** *csotopeni.ro*
21. **FC Argeş Piteşti** *argesfc.ro*
22. **CS Gaz Metan Mediaş** *gaz-metan-medias.ro*

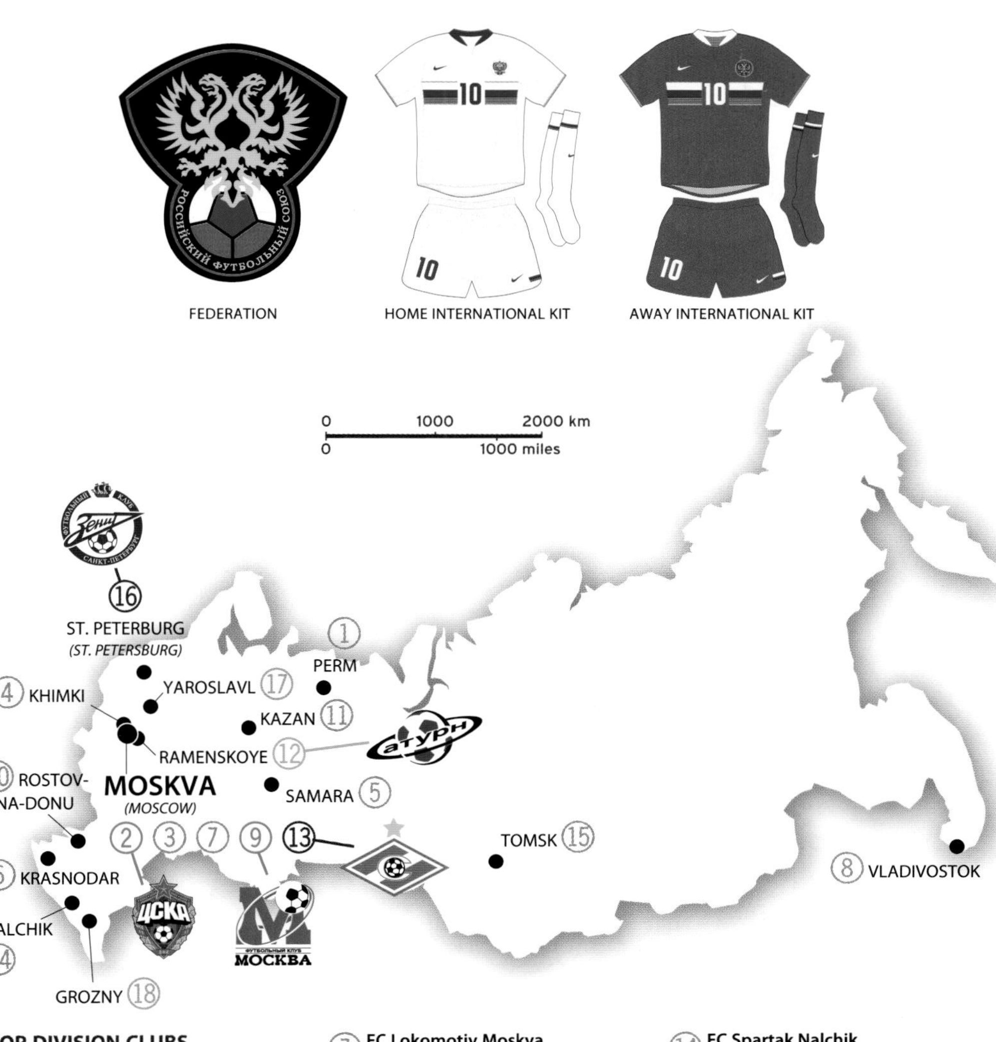

FEDERATION

HOME INTERNATIONAL KIT

AWAY INTERNATIONAL KIT

TOP DIVISION CLUBS

1 **FC Amkar Perm**
amkar.ru

2 **PFC CSKA Moskva** *
pfc-cska.com

3 **FC Dinamo Moskva**
fcdynamo.ru

4 **FC Khimki**
fckhimki.ru

5 **FC Krylya Sovetov Samara**
kc-camapa.ru

6 **FC Kuban Krasnodar**
fckuban.ru

7 **FC Lokomotiv Moskva**
fclm.ru

8 **FC Luch-Energia Vladivostok**
luch-energy.ru

9 **FC Moskva**
fcmoscow.ru

10 **FC Rostov**
fc-rostov.ru

11 **FC Rubin Kazan**
rubin-kazan.ru

12 **FC Saturn Moskovskaya Oblast**
saturn-fc.ru

13 **FC Spartak Moskva**
eng.spartak.com

14 **FC Spartak Nalchik**
spartak-nalchik.ru

15 **FC Tom Tomsk**
football.tomsk.ru

16 **FC Zenit St. Petersburg** ©
fc-zenit.ru

PROMOTED CLUBS

17 **FC Shinnik Yaroslavl**
www.shinnik.yar.ru

18 **FC Terek Grozny**
fc-terek.ru

FEDERATION

HOME INTERNATIONAL KIT

AWAY INTERNATIONAL KIT

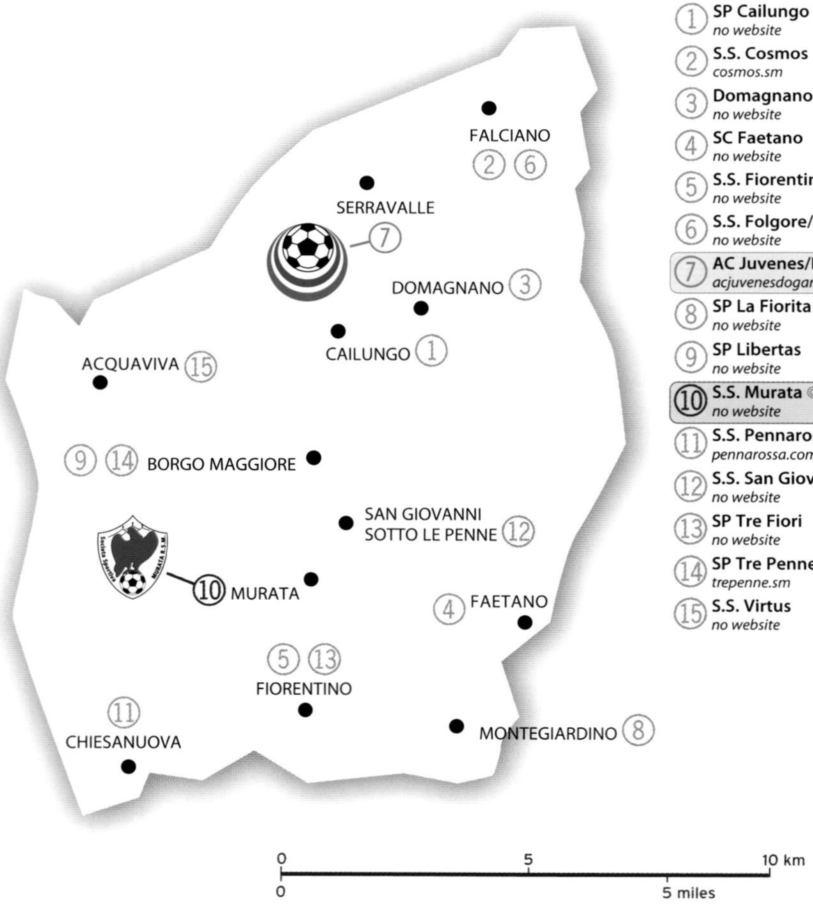

FALCIANO (2) (6)

SERRAVALLE (7)

DOMAGNANO (3)

CAILUNGO (1)

ACQUAVIVA (15)

(9) (14) BORGO MAGGIORE

SAN GIOVANNI SOTTO LE PENNE (12)

(10) MURATA

(4) FAETANO

(5) (13) FIORENTINO

(11) CHIESANUOVA

MONTEGIARDINO (8)

0 5 10 km

0 5 miles

TOP DIVISION CLUBS

1. **SP Cailungo**
   no website
2. **S.S. Cosmos**
   cosmos.sm
3. **Domagnano FC**
   no website
4. **SC Faetano**
   no website
5. **S.S. Fiorentino**
   no website
6. **S.S. Folgore/Falciano**
   no website
7. **AC Juvenes/Dogana** **
   acjuvenesdogana.sm — UEFA CUP
8. **SP La Fiorita**
   no website
9. **SP Libertas**
   no website
10. **S.S. Murata** ©*
    no website — UEFA CHAMPIONS LEAGUE
11. **S.S. Pennarossa**
    pennarossa.com
12. **S.S. San Giovanni**
    no website
13. **SP Tre Fiori**
    no website
14. **SP Tre Penne**
    trepenne.sm
15. **S.S. Virtus**
    no website

FEDERATION

HOME INTERNATIONAL KIT

AWAY INTERNATIONAL KIT

TOP DIVISION CLUBS

1 **Aberdeen FC**
www.afc.premiumtv.co.uk

2 **Celtic FC** ©
celticfc.net
CHAMPIONS LEAGUE

3 **Dundee United FC**
dundeeunitedfc.co.uk

4 **Falkirk FC**
falkirkfc.co.uk

5 **Gretna FC**
no website

6 **Heart of Midlothian FC**
heartsfc.co.uk

7 **Hibernian FC**
hibs.co.uk
INTERTOTO CUP

8 **Inverness Caledonian Thistle FC**
ictfc.premiumtv.co.uk

9 **Kilmarnock FC**
kilmarnockfc.co.uk

10 **Motherwell FC**
www.motherwellfc.co.uk
UEFA CUP

11 **Rangers FC** *
rangers.premiumtv.co.uk
CHAMPIONS LEAGUE

12 **Saint Mirren FC**
stmirren.net

PROMOTED CLUB

13 **Hamilton Academical FC**
acciesfc.co.uk

ADDITIONAL CLUB

14 **Queen of the South FC** **
qosfc.com
UEFA CUP

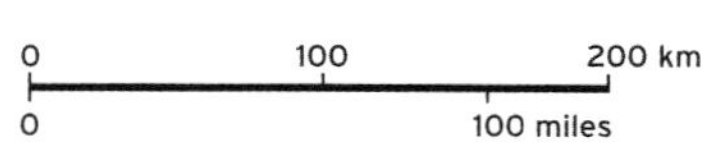

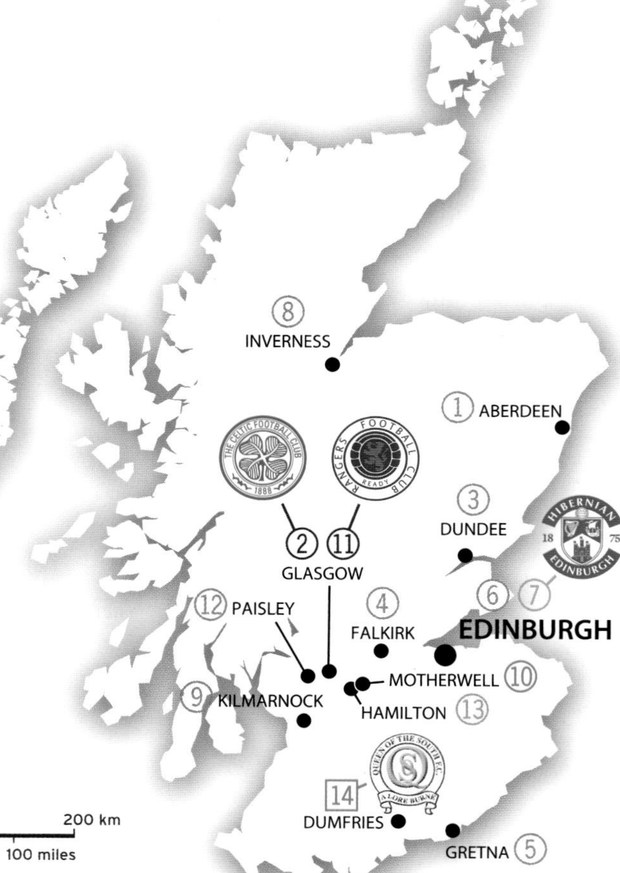

SERBIA

FEDERATION

HOME INTERNATIONAL KIT

AWAY INTERNATIONAL KIT

TOP DIVISION CLUBS

1. **FK Banat** *fcbanat.com*
2. **FK Bežanija** *fcbezanija.com*
3. **FK Borac** *no website*
4. **FK Crvena Zvezda** *crvenazvezdafk.com*
5. **FK Čukarički** *cukarickistankom.com*
6. **FK Hajduk Kula** *fkhajduk.com*
7. **FK Mladost Lučani** *no website*
8. **FK Napredak** *fknapredak.com*
9. **OFK Beograd** *ofkbeograd.co.rs*
10. **FK Partizan** ©* *partizan.rs*
11. **FK Smederevo** *fksmederevo.com*
12. **FK Vojvodina** *fcvojvodina.co.yu*

PROMOTED CLUBS

13. **FK Javor** *no website*
14. **FK Jagodina** *fkjagodina.org.yu*
15. **FK Rad** *fcrad.co.yu*

SLOVAKIA

FEDERATION | HOME INTERNATIONAL KIT | AWAY INTERNATIONAL KIT

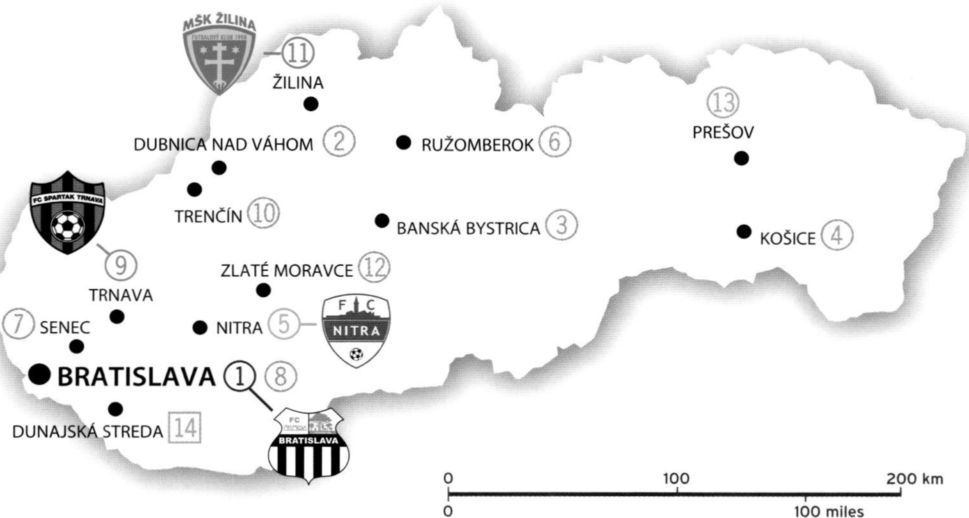

TOP DIVISION CLUBS

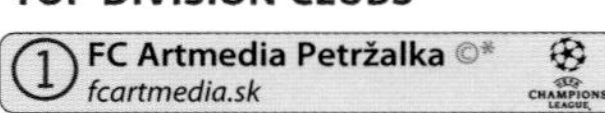

1. FC Artmedia Petržalka ©* — *fcartmedia.sk*
2. FK ŽTS Dubnica — *fkdubnica.sk*
3. Dukla Banská Bystrica — *fkdukla.sk*
4. MFK Košice — *mfkkosice.sk*
5. FC Nitra — *fcnitra.sk*
6. MFK Ružomberok — *futbalruza.sk*
7. FC Senec — *no website*
8. ŠK Slovan Bratislava — *slovanfutbal.com*
9. FC Spartak Trnava ** — *spartak.sk*
10. AS Trenčín — *astn.sk*
11. MŠK Žilina — *mskzilina.sk*
12. FC ViOn Zlaté Moravce — *fcvion.sk*

PROMOTED CLUB

13. 1. FC Tatran Prešov — *1fctatran.sk*

NEW MERGER CLUB

14. FK DAC 1904 Dunajská Streda — *fcdac1904.com*

SLOVENIA

FEDERATION

HOME INTERNATIONAL KIT

AWAY INTERNATIONAL KIT

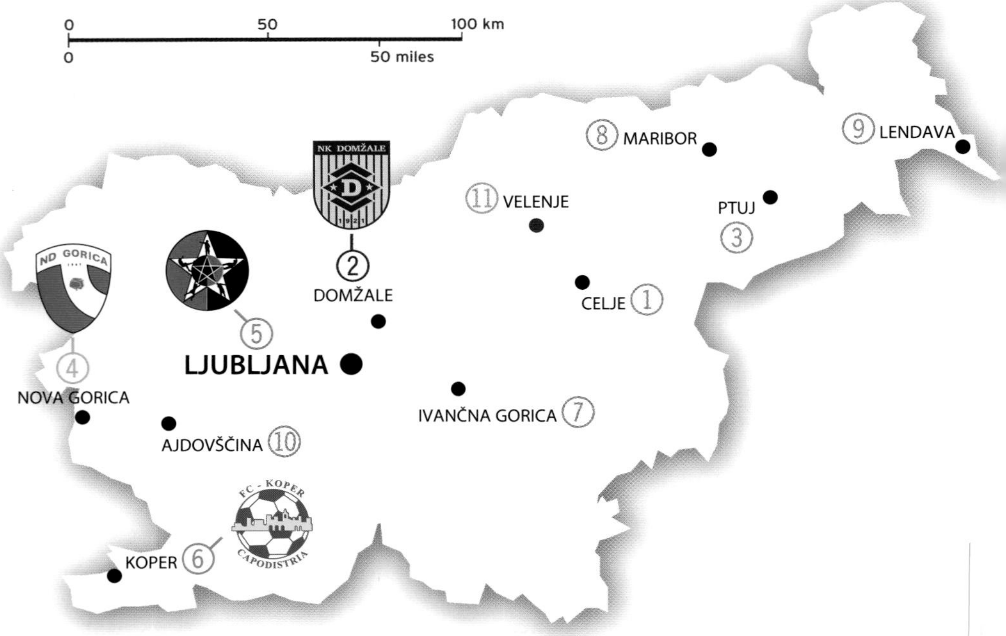

0 50 100 km
0 50 miles

NK DOMŽALE
ND GORICA
FC - KOPER CAPODISTRIA

(8) MARIBOR
(9) LENDAVA
(11) VELENJE
PTUJ (3)
(2) DOMŽALE
CELJE (1)
(5)
(4)
LJUBLJANA
NOVA GORICA
IVANČNA GORICA (7)
AJDOVŠČINA (10)
KOPER (6)

TOP DIVISION CLUBS

(1) **NK Celje**
nk-celje.si

(2) **NK Domžale** ©
nkdomzale.si

(3) **NK Drava**
nkptuj-klub.si

(4) **NK Gorica**
nd-gorica.com

(5) **NK IB Ljubljana** *
nkinterblock.eu

(6) **FC Koper**
fckoper.si

(7) **NK Livar**
no website

(8) **NK Maribor**
nkmaribor.com

(9) **NK Nafta**
nogometniklub-lendava.si

(10) **NK Primorje**
primorje-nklub.si

PROMOTED CLUB

(11) **NK Rudar Velenje**
nkrudar.com

FEDERATION

HOME INTERNATIONAL KIT

AWAY INTERNATIONAL KIT

LA CORUÑA 6
23 GIJÓN
SANTANDER 13
BILBAO 2
PAMPLONA 12
21 SORIA
ZARAGOZA 20
BARCELONA 4 7
VALLADOLID 18
MADRID 3 14
GETAFE 8
VILLARREAL 19
VALENCIA 9 17
PALMA 10
5 16 SEVILLA (SEVILLE)
15 HUELVA
11 MURCIA
22 MÁLAGA
ALMERÍA 1
0 200 400 km
0 200 miles

TOP DIVISION CLUBS

1 **UD Almería**
udalmeriasad.com

2 **Athletic Club Bilbao**
athletic-club.net

3 **Club Atlético de Madrid**
clubatleticodemadrid.com

4 **FC Barcelona**
fcbarcelona.cat

5 **Real Betis Balompié**
realbetisbalompie.es

6 **RC Deportivo de La Coruña**
canaldeportivo.com

7 **RCD Espanyol**
rcdespanyol.cat

8 **Getafe CF**
getafecf.com

9 **Levante UD**
levanteud.com

10 **RCD Mallorca**
rcdmallorca.es

11 **Real Murcia CF**
realmurcia.es

12 **CA Osasuna**
osasuna.es

13 **Real Racing Club Santander**
realracingclub.es

14 **Real Madrid CF** ©
realmadrid.com

15 **RC Recreativo de Huelva**
recreativohuelva.com

16 **Sevilla FC**
sevillafc.es

17 **Valencia CF** *
valenciacf.es

18 **Real Valladolid CF**
realvalladolid.es

19 **Villarreal CF**
villarrealcf.es

20 **Real Zaragoza**
realzaragoza.com

PROMOTED CLUBS

21 **CD Numancia de Soria**
cdnumancia.com

22 **Málaga CF**
malagacf.es

23 **Real Sporting de Gijón**
realsporting.com

SWEDEN

FEDERATION

HOME INTERNATIONAL KIT

AWAY INTERNATIONAL KIT

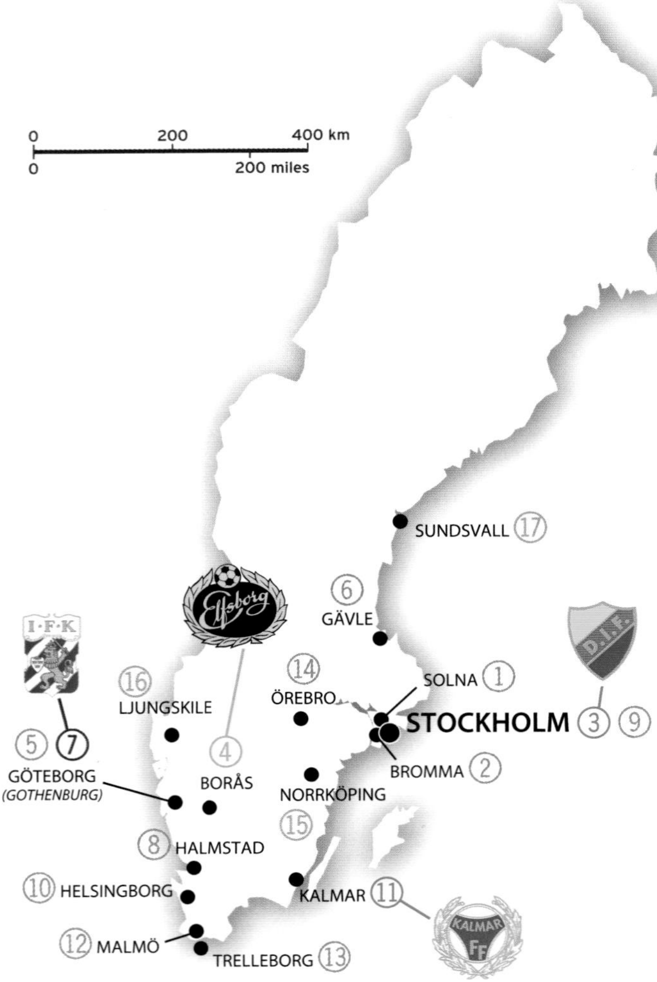

0 200 400 km
0 200 miles

SUNDSVALL (17)
(6) GÄVLE
SOLNA (1)
(14) ÖREBRO
STOCKHOLM (3) (9)
(16) LJUNGSKILE
(5) (7) GÖTEBORG *(GOTHENBURG)*
(4) BORÅS
BROMMA (2)
NORRKÖPING (15)
(8) HALMSTAD
(10) HELSINGBORG
KALMAR (11)
(12) MALMÖ
TRELLEBORG (13)

TOP DIVISION CLUBS

1. **AIK Solna** *aik.se*
2. **IF Brommapojkarna** *brommapojkarna.se*
3. **Djurgårdens IF FF** *dif.se* (UEFA Cup)
4. **IF Elfsborg** *elfsborg.se* (Intertoto Cup)
5. **GAIS Göteborg** *gais.se*
6. **Gefle IF** *gefleiffotboll.se*
7. **IFK Göteborg** © *ifkgoteborg.se* (Champions League)
8. **Halmstads BK** *hbk.se*
9. **Hammarby** *hammarbyfotboll.se*
10. **Helsingborgs IF** *hif.se*
11. **Kalmar FF** * *kalmarff.se* (UEFA Cup)
12. **Malmö FF** *mff.se*
13. **Trelleborgs FF** *trelleborgsff.se*
14. **Örebro SK** *orebro-sk.se*

PROMOTED CLUBS

15. **IFK Norrköping** *ifknorrkoping.se*
16. **Ljungskile SK** *lsk.se*
17. **GIF Sundsvall** *gifsundsvall.se*

SWITZERLAND

FEDERATION

HOME INTERNATIONAL KIT

AWAY INTERNATIONAL KIT

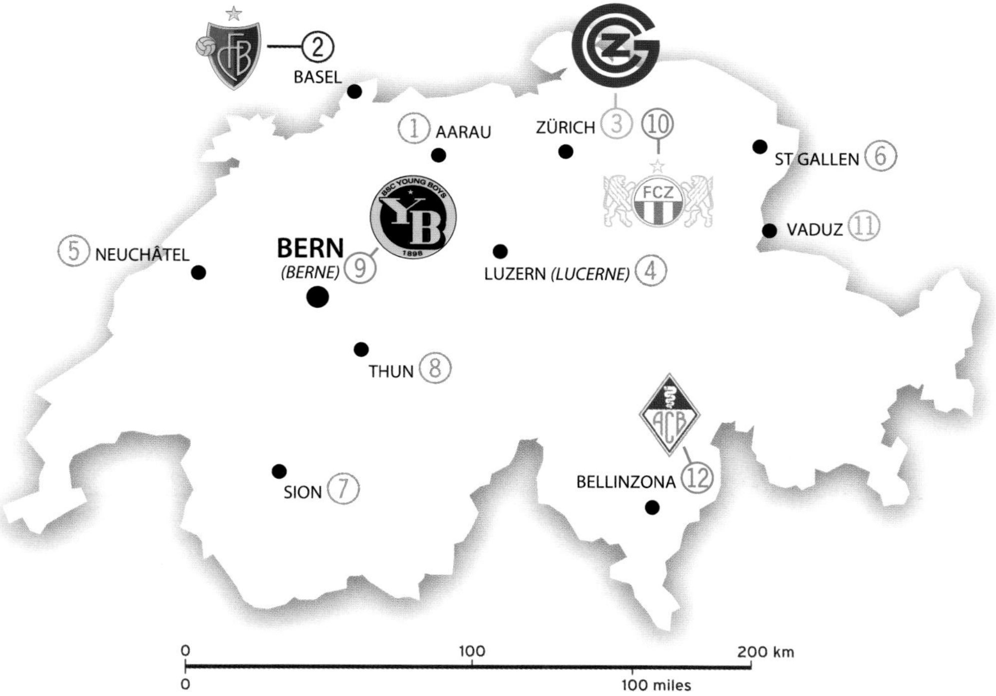

BASEL ②
① AARAU
ZÜRICH ③ ⑩
ST GALLEN ⑥
VADUZ ⑪
⑤ NEUCHÂTEL
BERN (BERNE) ⑨
LUZERN (LUCERNE) ④
THUN ⑧
SION ⑦
BELLINZONA ⑫

0 100 200 km
0 100 miles

TOP DIVISION CLUBS

1. **FC Aarau** *fcaarau.ch*
2. **FC Basel 1893** ©* *fcb.ch* (CHAMPIONS LEAGUE)
3. **Grasshopper-Club** *gcz.ch* (INTERTOTO CUP)
4. **FC Luzern** *fcl.ch*
5. **Neuchâtel Xamax FC** *xamax.ch*
6. **FC St Gallen** *fcsg.ch*
7. **FC Sion** *fc-sion-live.ch*
8. **FC Thun** *fcthun.ch*
9. **BSC Young Boys** *bscyb.ch* (UEFA CUP)
10. **FC Zürich** *fcz.ch* (UEFA CUP)

PROMOTED CLUBS

11. **FC Vaduz** *fcvaduz.li*
12. **AC Bellinzona** ** *acbellinzona.ch* (UEFA CUP)

TURKEY

FEDERATION

HOME INTERNATIONAL KIT

AWAY INTERNATIONAL KIT

TOP DIVISION CLUBS

1. **MKE Ankaragücü** *ankaragucu.org.tr*
2. **Ankaraspor AŞ** *ankaraspor.com.tr*
3. **Beşiktaş JK** *bjk.com.tr* (UEFA Cup)
4. **Bursaspor** *bursaspor.org.tr*
5. **Denizlispor** *denizlispor.org.tr*
6. **Fenerbahçe SK** *fenerbahce.org* (Champions League)
7. **Galatasaray AŞ** © *galatasaray.org* (Champions League)
8. **Gaziantepspor** *gaziantepspor.org.tr*
9. **Gençlerbirliği SK** *genclerbirligi.org.tr*
10. **Gençlerbirliği OFTAŞ SK** *no website*
11. **İstanbul BB SK** *ibbspor.com*
12. **Kasımpaşa SK** *kasimpasaspor.com*
13. **Kayserispor** * *kayserispor.org.tr* (UEFA Cup)
14. **Konyaspor** *konyaspor.org.tr*
15. **Rizespor** *caykurrizespor.org.tr*
16. **Sivasspor** *sivasspor.org.tr* (Intertoto Cup)
17. **Trabzonspor** *trabzonspor.org.tr*
18. **Vestel Manisaspor** *vestelmanisaspor.com*

PROMOTED CLUBS

19. **Kocaelispor** *kocaelispor.org*
20. **Antalyaspor** *antalyaspor.com.tr*
21. **Eskişehirspor** *eskisehirspor.org.tr*

FEDERATION

HOME INTERNATIONAL KIT

AWAY INTERNATIONAL KIT

(1) (4) KYIV (KIEV)
(5) (18) LVIV
(15) UZHHOROD
(11) OKHTYRKA
(14) POLTAVA
KHARKIV (6) (8)
(3) DNIPROPETROVSK
(16) LUHANSK
(7) KRYVYI RIH
ZAPORIZHYA (10)
DONETSK (9) (12)
MARIUPIL (17)
(2) ODESA
SIMFEROPOL (13)

0 200 400 km
0 200 miles

TOP DIVISION CLUBS

1 **FC Arsenal Kyiv** *fcarsenal.com.ua*

2 **FC Chornomorets Odesa** *chernomorets.odessa.ua*

3 **FC Dnipro Dnipropetrovsk** *fcdnipro.dp.ua* (UEFA Cup)

4 **FC Dynamo Kyiv** *fcdynamo.kiev.ua* (Champions League)

5 **FC Karpaty Lviv** *fckarpaty.lviv.ua*

6 **FC Kharkiv** *fckharkov.com.ua*

7 **FC Kryvbas Kryvyi Rih** *fckrivbass.dp.ua*

8 **FC Metalist Kharkiv** *metallist.kharkov.ua* (UEFA Cup)

9 **FC Metalurh Donetsk** *metallurg.donetsk.ua*

10 **FC Metalurh Zaporizhya** *fcmetalurg.com*

11 **FC Naftovyk-Ukrnafta Okhtyrka** *fcnaftovyk.com.ua*

12 **FC Shakhtar Donetsk** ©* *shakhtar.com* (Champions League)

13 **SC Tavriya Simferopol** *sctavriya.com* (Intertoto Cup)

14 **FC Vorskla Poltava** *vorskla.com.ua*

15 **FC Zakarpattya Uzhhorod** *zakarpatie.com.ua*

16 **FC Zorya Luhansk** *zarya-lugansk.com*

PROMOTED CLUBS

17 **FC Illychivets Mariupil** *fcilyich.com.ua*

18 **FC Lviv** *fclviv.com.ua*

FEDERATION

HOME INTERNATIONAL KIT

AWAY INTERNATIONAL KIT

TOP DIVISION CLUBS

1. **Aberystwyth Town FC** *atfc.org.uk*
2. **Airbus UK Broughton FC** *airbusfc.co.uk*
3. **Bangor City FC** * *bangorcityfc.com*
4. **Caernarfon Town FC** *caernarfontown.net*
5. **Caersws FC** *no website*
6. **Carmarthen Town AFC** *carmarthentownafc.net*
7. **Gap Connah's Quay FC** *gap-fc.co.uk*
8. **Haverfordwest County AFC** *haverfordwestcounty.co.uk*
9. **Llanelli AFC** © *llanelliafc.org*
10. **Llangefni Town FC** *llangefnifc.co.uk*
11. **Neath FC** *neathathletic.ik.com*
12. **NEWI Cefn Druids AFC** *cefndruidsafc.co.uk*
13. **Newtown AFC** *newtownafc.co.uk*
14. **CPD Porthmadog** *porthmadogfc.com*
15. **Port Talbot Town FC** *porttalbottown.co.uk*
16. **Rhyl FC** *rhylfc.com*
17. **The New Saints FC** *saints-alive.co.uk*
18. **Welshpool Town FC** *welshpooltownfc.co.uk*

PROMOTED CLUB

19. **Prestatyn Town FC** *prestatyntownfootballclub.co.uk*

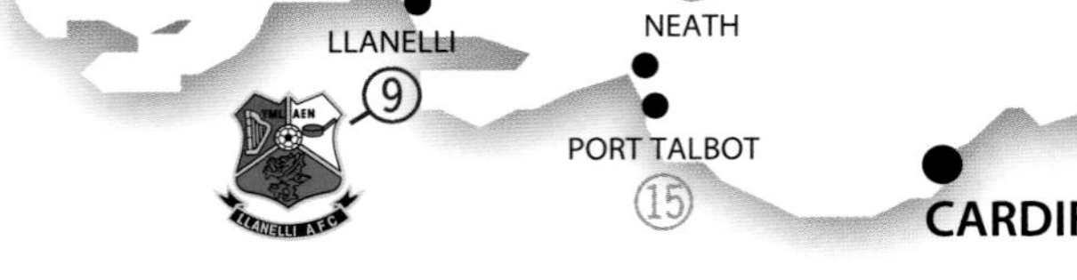

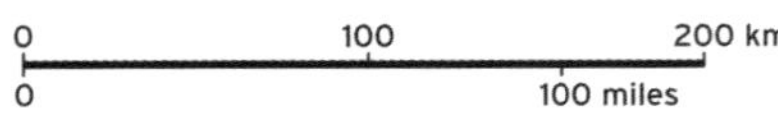

2010 FIFA WORLD CUP
EUROPEAN QUALIFYING FIXTURES

Qualifying procedure

The nine group winners qualify automatically for the final tournament in South Africa. The best eight runners-up will be drawn in four two-legged play-offs, from which the winners will also qualify for the finals, giving Europe 13 places in total.

GROUP 1

(Portugal, Sweden, Denmark, Hungary, Albania, Malta)

6/9/08
Albania-Sweden; Hungary-Denmark; Malta-Portugal

10/9/08
Albania-Malta; Portugal-Denmark; Sweden-Hungary

11/10/08
Denmark-Malta; Hungary-Albania; Sweden-Portugal

15/10/08
Malta-Hungary; Portugal-Albania

11/2/09
Malta-Albania

28/3/09
Albania-Hungary; Malta-Denmark; Portugal-Sweden

1/4/09
Denmark-Albania; Hungary-Malta

6/6/09
Albania-Portugal; Sweden-Denmark

10/6/09
Sweden-Malta

5/9/09
Denmark-Portugal; Hungary-Sweden

9/9/09
Albania-Denmark; Hungary-Portugal; Malta-Sweden

10/10/09
Denmark-Sweden; Portugal-Hungary

14/10/09
Denmark-Hungary; Portugal-Malta; Sweden-Albania

GROUP 2

(Greece, Israel, Switzerland, Moldova, Latvia, Luxembourg)

6/9/08
Israel-Switzerland; Luxembourg-Greece; Moldova-Latvia

10/9/08
Latvia-Greece; Moldova-Israel; Switzerland-Luxembourg

11/10/08
Greece-Moldova; Luxembourg-Israel; Switzerland-Latvia

15/10/08
Greece-Switzerland; Latvia-Israel; Luxembourg-Moldova

28/3/09
Israel-Greece; Luxembourg-Latvia; Moldova-Switzerland

1/4/09
Greece-Israel; Latvia-Luxembourg; Switzerland-Moldova

5/9/09
Israel-Latvia; Moldova-Luxembourg; Switzerland-Greece

9/9/09
Israel-Luxembourg; Latvia-Switzerland; Moldova-Greece

10/10/09
Greece-Latvia; Israel-Moldova; Luxembourg-Switzerland

14/10/09
Greece-Luxembourg; Latvia-Moldova; Switzerland-Israel

GROUP 3

(Czech Republic, Poland, Northern Ireland, Slovakia, Slovenia, San Marino)

6/9/08
Poland-Slovenia; Slovakia-Northern Ireland

10/9/08
Northern Ireland-Czech Republic; San Marino-Poland; Slovenia-Slovakia

11/10/08
Poland-Czech Republic; San Marino-Slovakia; Slovenia-Northern Ireland

15/10/08
Czech Republic-Slovenia; Northern Ireland-San Marino; Slovakia-Poland

19/11/08
San Marino-Czech Republic

11/2/09
San Marino-Northern Ireland

28/3/09
Northern Ireland-Poland; Slovenia-Czech Republic

1/4/09
Czech Republic-Slovakia; Northern Ireland-Slovenia; Poland-San Marino

6/6/09
Slovakia-San Marino

19/8/09
Slovenia-San Marino

5/9/09
Poland-Northern Ireland; Slovakia-Czech Republic

9/9/09
Czech Republic-San Marino; Northern Ireland-Slovakia; Slovenia-Poland

10/10/09
Czech Republic-Poland; Slovakia-Slovenia

14/10/09
Czech Republic-Northern Ireland; Poland-Slovakia; San Marino-Slovenia

GROUP 4

(Germany, Russia, Finland, Wales, Azerbaijan, Liechtenstein)

6/9/08
Liechtenstein-Germany; Wales-Azerbaijan

10/9/08
Azerbaijan-Liechtenstein; Finland-Germany; Russia-Wales

11/10/08
Finland-Azerbaijan; Germany-Russia; Wales-Liechtenstein

15/10/08
Germany-Wales; Russia-Finland

28/3/09
Germany-Liechtenstein; Russia-Azerbaijan; Wales-Finland

1/4/09
Liechtenstein-Russia; Wales-Germany

6/6/09
Azerbaijan-Wales; Finland-Liechtenstein

10/6/09
Finland-Russia

19/8/09
Azerbaijan-Germany

5/9/09
Azerbaijan-Finland; Russia-Liechtenstein

9/9/09
Germany-Azerbaijan; Liechtenstein-Finland; Wales-Russia

10/10/09
Finland-Wales; Liechtenstein-Azerbaijan; Russia-Germany

14/10/09
Azerbaijan-Russia; Germany-Finland; Liechtenstein-Wales

GROUP 5

(Spain, Turkey, Belgium, Bosnia-Herzegovina, Armenia, Estonia)

6/9/08
Armenia-Turkey; Belgium-Estonia; Spain-Bosnia-Herzegovina

10/9/08
Bosnia-Herzegovina-Estonia; Spain-Armenia; Turkey-Belgium

11/10/08
Belgium-Armenia; Estonia-Spain; Turkey-Bosnia-Herzegovina

15/10/08
Belgium-Spain; Bosnia-Herzegovina-Armenia; Estonia-Turkey

28/3/09
Armenia-Estonia; Belgium-Bosnia-Herzegovina; Spain-Turkey

1/4/09
Bosnia-Herzegovina-Belgium; Estonia-Armenia; Turkey-Spain

5/9/09
Armenia-Bosnia-Herzegovina; Spain-Belgium; Turkey-Estonia

9/9/09
Armenia-Belgium; Bosnia-Herzegovina-Turkey; Spain-Estonia

10/10/09
Armenia-Spain; Belgium-Turkey; Estonia-Bosnia-Herzegovina

14/10/09
Bosnia-Herzegovina-Spain; Estonia-Belgium; Turkey-Armenia

GROUP 6

(Croatia, England, Ukraine, Belarus, Kazakhstan, Andorra)

20/8/08
Kazakhstan-Andorra

6/9/08
Andorra-England; Croatia-Kazakhstan; Ukraine-Belarus

10/9/08
Andorra-Belarus; Croatia-England; Kazakhstan-Ukraine

11/10/08
England-Kazakhstan; Ukraine-Croatia

15/10/08
Belarus-England; Croatia-Andorra

1/4/09
Andorra-Croatia; England-Ukraine; Kazakhstan-Belarus

6/6/09
Belarus-Andorra; Croatia-Ukraine; Kazakhstan-England

10/6/09
England-Andorra; Ukraine-Kazakhstan

19/8/09
Belarus-Croatia

5/9/09
Croatia-Belarus; Ukraine-Andorra

9/9/09
Andorra-Kazakhstan; Belarus-Ukraine; England-Croatia

10/10/09
Belarus-Kazakhstan; Ukraine-England

14/10/09
Andorra-Ukraine; England-Belarus; Kazakhstan-Croatia

GROUP 7

(France, Romania, Serbia, Lithuania, Austria, Faroe Islands)

6/9/08
Austria-France; Romania-Lithuania; Serbia-Faroe Islands

10/9/08
Faroe Islands-Romania; France-Serbia; Lithuania-Austria

11/10/08
Faroe Islands-Austria; Romania-France; Serbia-Lithuania

15/10/08
Austria-Serbia; Lithuania-Faroe Islands

28/3/09
Lithuania-France; Romania-Serbia

1/4/09
Austria-Romania; France-Lithuania

6/6/09
Lithuania-Romania; Serbia-Austria

10/6/09
Faroe Islands-Serbia

19/8/09
Faroe Islands-France

5/9/09
Austria-Faroe Islands; France-Romania

9/9/09
Faroe Islands-Lithuania; Romania-Austria; Serbia-France

10/10/09
Austria-Lithuania; France-Faroe Islands; Serbia-Romania

14/10/09
France-Austria; Lithuania-Serbia; Romania-Faroe Islands

GROUP 8

(Italy, Bulgaria, Republic of Ireland, Cyprus, Georgia, Montenegro)

6/9/08
Cyprus-Italy; Georgia-Republic of Ireland; Montenegro-Bulgaria

10/9/08
Italy-Georgia; Montenegro-Republic of Ireland

11/10/08
Bulgaria-Italy; Georgia-Cyprus

15/10/08
Georgia-Bulgaria; Italy-Montenegro; Republic of Ireland-Cyprus

11/2/09
Republic of Ireland-Georgia

28/3/09
Cyprus-Georgia; Montenegro-Italy; Republic of Ireland-Bulgaria

1/4/09
Bulgaria-Cyprus; Georgia-Montenegro; Italy-Republic of Ireland

6/6/09
Bulgaria-Republic of Ireland; Cyprus-Montenegro

5/9/09
Bulgaria-Montenegro; Cyprus-Republic of Ireland; Georgia-Italy

9/9/09
Italy-Bulgaria; Montenegro-Cyprus

10/10/09
Cyprus-Bulgaria; Montenegro-Georgia; Republic of Ireland-Italy

14/10/09
Bulgaria-Georgia; Italy-Cyprus; Republic of Ireland-Montenegro

GROUP 9

(Netherlands, Scotland, Norway, FYR Macedonia, Iceland)

6/9/08
FYR Macedonia-Scotland; Norway-Iceland

10/9/08
Iceland-Scotland; FYR Macedonia-Netherlands

11/10/08
Netherlands-Iceland; Scotland-Norway

15/10/08
Iceland-FYR Macedonia; Norway-Netherlands

28/3/09
Netherlands-Scotland

1/4/09
Netherlands-FYR Macedonia; Scotland-Iceland

6/6/09
Iceland-Netherlands; FYR Macedonia-Norway

10/6/09
Netherlands-Norway; FYR Macedonia-Iceland

19/8/09
Norway-Scotland

5/9/09
Iceland-Norway; Scotland-FYR Macedonia

9/9/09
Norway-FYR Macedonia; Scotland-Netherlands

UEFA Events Calendar 2008/09

NATIONAL TEAM

2009 FIFA CONFEDERATIONS CUP

22/11/08	Final tournament draw
14-29/6/09	Final tournament (South Africa)

2010 FIFA WORLD CUP

20/8/08	Qualification round matches
6/9/08	Qualification round matches
10/9/08	Qualification round matches
11/10/08	Qualification round matches
15/10/08	Qualification round matches
19/11/08	Qualification round matches
11/2/09	Qualification round matches
28/3/09	Qualification round matches
1/4/09	Qualification round matches
6/6/09	Qualification round matches
10/6/09	Qualification round matches
19/8/09	Qualification round matches
5/9/09	Qualification round matches
9/9/09	Qualification round matches
10/10/09	Qualification round matches
14/10/09	Qualification round matches
11/09	Play-off matches
4/12/09	Final tournament draw
11/6-11/7/10	Final tournament (South Africa)

2008-2009 UEFA EUROPEAN UNDER-21 CHAMPIONSHIP

6-7/9/08	Qualifying round matches
9-10/9/08	Qualifying round matches
12/9/08	Play-off draw
11-12/10/08	Play-off matches
14-15/10/08	Play-off matches
20/11/08	Final tournament draw
15-29/6/09	Final tournament (Sweden)

CLUB

2008/09 UEFA CHAMPIONS LEAGUE

28/8/08	Group stage draw
16-17/9/08	Group stage, Matchday 1
30/9-1/10/08	Group stage, Matchday 2
21-22/10/08	Group stage, Matchday 3
4-5/11/08	Group stage, Matchday 4
25-26/11/08	Group stage, Matchday 5
-10/12/08	Group stage, Matchday 6
19/12/08	First knockout round draw
4-25/2/09	First knockout round, first leg
10-11/3/09	First knockout round, second leg
20/3/09	Quarter-finals, semi-finals and final draw
7-8/4/09	Quarter-finals, first leg
14-15/4/09	Quarter-finals, second leg
28-29/4/09	Semi-finals, first leg
5-6/5/09	Semi-finals, second leg
27/5/09	Final (Rome, Italy)

2008/09 UEFA CUP

29/8/08	First round draw
18/9/08	First round, first leg
2/10/08	First round, second leg
7/10/08	Group stage draw
23/10/08	Group stage, Matchday 1
6/11/08	Group stage, Matchday 2
27/11/08	Group stage, Matchday 3
3-4/12/08	Group stage, Matchday 4
17-18/12/08	Group stage, Matchday 5
19/12/08	Round of 32 and Round of 16 draw
18-19/2/09	Round of 32, 1st leg
26/2/09	Round of 32, second leg
12/3/09	Round of 16, first leg
18-19/3/09	Round of 16 second leg
20/3/09	Quarter-finals, semi-finals and final draw
9/4/09	Quarter-finals, first leg
16/4/09	Quarter-finals, second leg
30/4/09	Semi-finals, first leg
7/5/09	Semi-finals, second leg
20/5/09	Final (Istanbul, Turkey)

2008 UEFA SUPER CUP

29/8/08	Final (Monaco)

2008 FIFA CLUB WORLD CUP

12-21/12/08	Final tournament (Japan)

YOUTH & AMATEUR

2008/09 UEFA EUROPEAN UNDER-19 CHAMPIONSHIP

2/10-27/11/08	Qualifying round matches
4/12/08	Elite round draw
1/1-31/5/09	Elite round matches
6/09	Final tournament draw
21/7-2/8/09	Final tournament (Mariupol/Donetsk, Ukraine)

2009/10 UEFA EUROPEAN UNDER-19 CHAMPIONSHIP

3/12/08	Qualifying round draw

2008/09 UEFA EUROPEAN UNDER-17 CHAMPIONSHIP

15/9-28/10/08	Qualifying round matches
4/12/08	Elite round draw
1/1-31/3/09	Elite round matches
3/4/09	Final tournament draw
6-18/5/09	Final tournament (Leipzig/Jena, Germany)

2009/10 UEFA EUROPEAN UNDER-17 CHAMPIONSHIP

3/12/08	Qualifying round draw

2008/09 UEFA REGIONS' CUP

31/8-29/9/08	Preliminary round matches
31/8/08-30/4/09	Intermediary round matches
tbd	Final tournament draw
tbd	Final tournament

WOMEN'S

2009 UEFA EUROPEAN WOMEN'S CHAMPIONSHIP

27/9-2/10/08	Qualification round matches
6/10/08	Play-off draw
25-26/10/08	Play-off matches
29-30/10/08	Play-off matches
18/11/08	Final tournament draw
23/8-10/9/09	Final tournament (Finland)

2008/09 UEFA WOMEN'S CUP

4-9/9/08	First qualifying round matches
9-14/10/08	Second qualifying round matches
5-6/11/08	Quarter-finals, first leg
12-13/11/08	Quarter-finals, second leg
28-29/3/09	Semi-finals, first leg
4-5/4/09	Semi-finals, second leg
16/5/09	Final, first leg (Venue tbd)
23/5/09	Final, second leg (Venue tbd)

2008/09 UEFA EUROPEAN WOMEN'S UNDER-19 CHAMPIONSHIP

24/9-1/10/08	First qualifying round matches
19/11/08	Second qualifying round draw
23-28/4/09	Second qualifying round matches
5/09	Final tournament draw
13-25/7/09	Final tournament (Minsk, Belarus)

2009/10 UEFA EUROPEAN WOMEN'S UNDER-19 CHAMPIONSHIP

18/11/08	First qualifying round draw

2008/09 UEFA EUROPEAN WOMEN'S UNDER-17 CHAMPIONSHIP

13/9-28/10/08	First qualifying round matches
19/11/08	Second qualifying round draw
1/1-mid-April 09	Second qualifying round matches
tbd	Final tournament (Nyon, Switzerland)

2009/10 UEFA EUROPEAN WOMEN'S UNDER-17 CHAMPIONSHIP

18/11/08	First qualifying round draw

2008 FIFA WOMEN'S UNDER-20 WORLD CUP

19/11-7/12/08	Final tournament (Chile)

2008 FIFA WOMEN'S UNDER-17 WORLD CUP

28/10-16/11/08	Final tournament (New Zealand)

FUTSAL

2008/09 UEFA FUTSAL CUP

9-17/8/08	Preliminary round matches
6-14/9/08	Main round matches
19/9/08	Elite round draw
8-16/11/08	Elite round matches
3/09	Final Four draw
23-26/4/09	Final Four (Venue tbd)

2009/10 UEFA EUROPEAN FUTSAL CHAMPIONSHIP

10/9/08	Preliminary round draw
10/9/08	Qualifying round draw
14-22/2/09	Preliminary round matches
19-22/3/09	Qualifying round matches
tbd	Final tournament draw
18-30/1/10	Final tournament (Budapest & Debrecen, Hungary)

2008 UEFA EUROPEAN UNDER-21 FUTSAL TOURNAMENT

17/9/08	Final tournament draw
8-16/12/08	Final tournament (St Petersburg, Russia)

2008 FIFA FUTSAL WORLD CUP

30/9-19/10/08	Final Tournament (Rio de Janeiro & Brasilia Brazil)

tbd = to be decided